# GARDNER'S
# ART
## THROUGH THE
# AGES

### TWELFTH EDITION

# GARDNER'S
# ART
## THROUGH THE
# AGES

## TWELFTH EDITION

FRED S. KLEINER

CHRISTIN J. MAMIYA

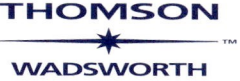

THOMSON
WADSWORTH

AUSTRALIA · CANADA · MEXICO · SINGAPORE · SPAIN
UNITED KINGDOM · UNITED STATES

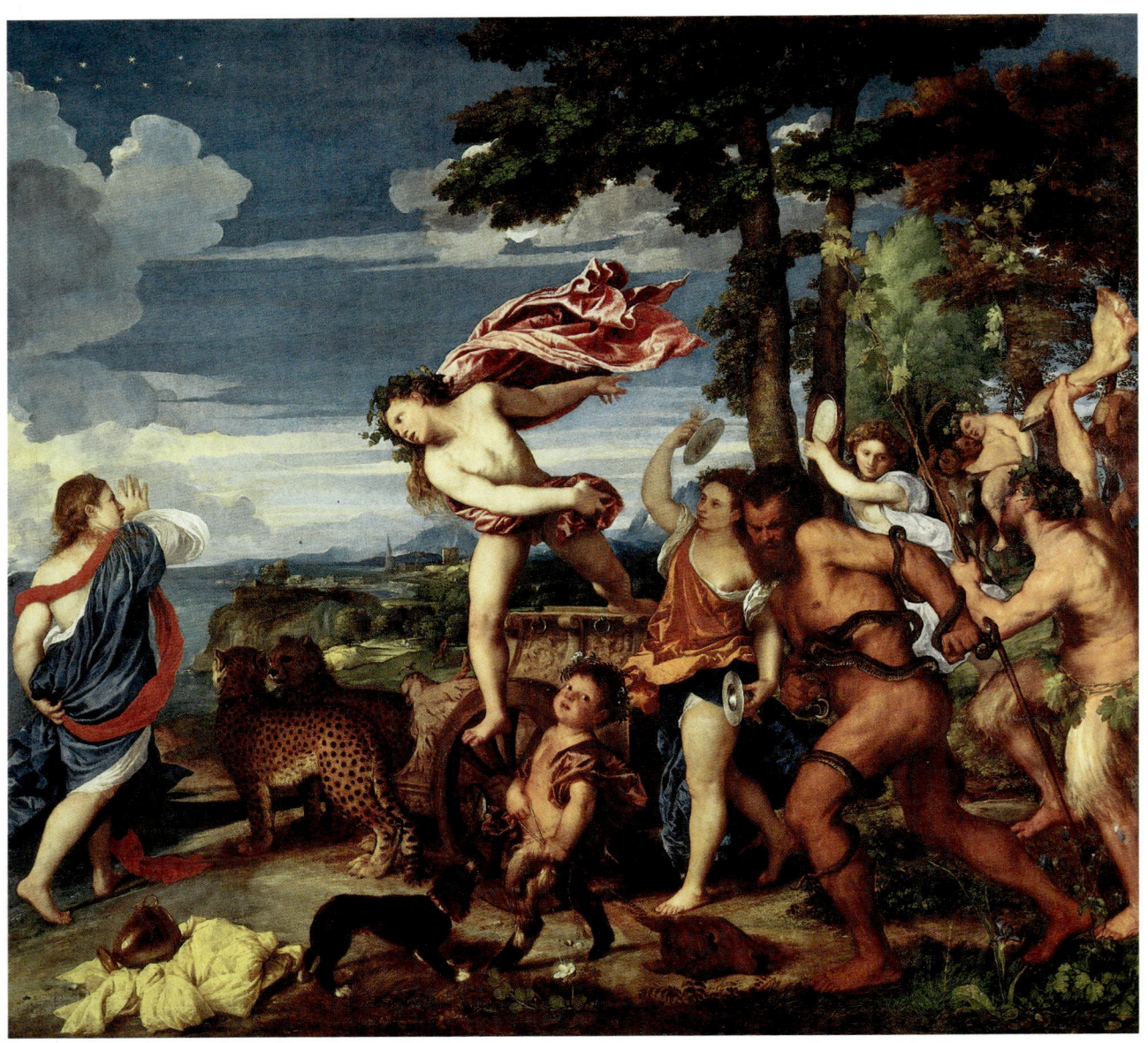

Titian, *Meeting of Bacchus and Ariadne*, 1522–1523. Oil on canvas, 5′ 9″ × 6′ 3″. National Gallery, London.

# About the Cover Art

Titian's *Meeting of Bacchus and Ariadne* (FIG. 22-37) of 1523 presents the viewer with the splendor of 16th-century Venetian painting. Among the most revered of Italian Renaissance artists, Titian, like other Venetian painters, was a master of a sensuous coloristic manner. Here, in *Meeting of Bacchus and Ariadne*, Titian's skills are on full display. The colors are not just rich, but convey a luminosity that matches the soft-colored haze of the light in Venice. *Meeting of Bacchus and Ariadne* was one of three paintings depicting bacchanalian revelry that were commissioned by Alfonso d'Este, duke of Ferrara, for his "pleasure chamber." As the cover illustration of the Twelfth Edition of *Gardner's Art through the Ages,* this impressive work by an artist whose influence continues to the present day serves as a model of artistic vision, coloristic mastery, and painterly authority.

**THOMSON**

**WADSWORTH**

Acquisitions Editor
**JOHN R. SWANSON**

Senior Development Editor
**STACEY SIMS**

Assistant Editor
**AMY MCGAUGHEY**

Editorial Assistant
**BRIANNA BRINKLEY**

Technology Project Manager
**MELINDA NEWFARMER**

Marketing Manager
**MARK ORR**

Marketing Assistant
**ANNABELLE YANG**

Advertising Project Manager
**VICKY WAN**

Project Manager, Editorial Production
**KATHRYN M. STEWART**

Print/Media Buyer
**BARBARA BRITTON**

Permissions Editor
**JOOHEE LEE**

Production Service
**JOAN KEYES, DOVETAIL PUBLISHING SERVICES**

Text Designer
**JOHN WALKER**

Photo Researchers
**CARRIE WARD, LILI WEINER, IMAGE SELECT INTERNATIONAL**

Copy Editors
**MICHELE JONES, GAIL NELSON-BONEBRAKE**

Illustrator
**DARTMOUTH PUBLISHING**

Cover Designer
**BRIAN SALISBURY**

Cover Image
**TITIAN, *MEETING OF BACCHUS AND ARIADNE*, 1522–1523.
OIL ON CANVAS, 5′ 9″ × 6′ 3″. NATIONAL GALLERY, LONDON.
© ERICH LESSING / ART RESOURCE, NEW YORK.**

Cover Printer
**THE LEHIGH PRESS, INC.**

Compositor
**PROGRESSIVE INFORMATION TECHNOLOGIES**

Printer
**R.R. DONNELLEY/WILLARD**

Printed in the United States of America
1 2 3 4 5 6 7 08 07 06 05 04

For more information about our products, contact us at:
Thomson Learning Academic Resource Center
1-800-423-0563

For permission to use material from this text or product, submit a request online at http://www.thomsonrights.com. Any additional questions about permissions can be submitted by e-mail to thomsonrights@thomson.com

**Wadsworth/Thomson Learning**
10 Davis Drive, Belmont, CA 94002-3098
USA

**Asia**
Thomson Learning
5 Shenton Way #01-01, UIC Building
Singapore 068808

**Australia**
Nelson Thomson Learning
102 Dodds Street, South Melbourne, Victoria 3205
Australia

**Canada**
Nelson Thomson Learning
1120 Birchmount Road, Toronto, Ontario M1K 5G4
Canada

**Europe/Middle East/Africa**
Thomson Learning
High Holborn House, 50/51 Bedford Row, London WC1R 4LR
United Kingdom

**Library of Congress Control Number**
2003111627

ISBN 0-15-505090-7

# CONTENTS IN BRIEF

# CONTENTS

# Chapter 3

# Chapter 4

# Chapter 5

# Chapter 6

# Chapter 7

# Chapter 8

# Chapter 9

# Chapter 10

# Chapter 11

# Chapter 12

# Chapter 13

# Chapter 14

# Chapter 15

# Chapter 16

# Chapter 17

# Chapter 18

# Chapter 19

# Chapter 20

# Chapter 21

# Chapter 22

# Chapter 23

# Chapter 24

# Chapter 25

# Chapter 26

# Chapter 27

# Chapter 28

# Chapter 29

# Chapter 30

# Chapter 31

# Chapter 32

# Chapter 33

# Chapter 34

# PREFACE

We take great pleasure in presenting the Twelfth Edition of *Gardner's Art through the Ages*, the most widely read introduction to the history of art in the English language. When Helen Gardner published the first edition of her classic global survey of art and architecture in 1926, she could not have imagined that eight decades later instructors all over the world would still be using her textbook in their classrooms. She would no doubt have been especially proud that the Eleventh Edition of *Art through the Ages* was awarded both the 2001 Texty and McGuffey Book Prizes of the Text and Academic Authors Association as the best college textbook in the humanities and social sciences—the first art history book to win either award and the only title ever to win both prizes in the same year.

The fundamental belief that guided Helen Gardner—that the history of art is essential to a liberal education—is one that we also embrace. The study of art history has as its aim the appreciation and understanding of works of high aesthetic quality and historical significance produced throughout the world and across thousands of years of human history. We think, as she did, that the most effective way to tell the story of art through the ages, especially for those who are studying art history for the first time, is to organize the vast array of artistic monuments according to the civilizations that produced them and to consider each work in roughly chronological order. This approach has not only stood the test of time; it is the most appropriate for narrating the *history* of art. We believe that the enormous variation in the form and meaning of paintings, sculptures, buildings, and other artworks is largely the result of the constantly changing historical, social, economic, religious, and cultural context in which artists and architects worked. A historically based narrative is therefore best suited for a global history of art.

Yet, in other ways, Helen Gardner would not recognize the Twelfth Edition of *Art through the Ages* as her book. Most obvious, perhaps, Pablo Picasso and Arthur B. Davies are no longer treated in a chapter entitled "Contemporary Art in Europe and America." More significantly, however, the discipline of art history has changed markedly in recent decades, and so too has this book. The Twelfth Edition fully reflects the latest art historical research emphases, while maintaining the traditional strengths that have made all the previous editions of *Art through the Ages* so successful. While sustaining attention to style, chronology, iconography, and technique, we pay greater attention than ever before to function and context. We consider artworks with a view toward their purpose and meaning in the society that produced them at the time at which they were produced. We also address the very important role of patronage in the production of art and examine the role of the individuals or groups who paid the artists and influenced the shape the monuments took. We devote more space to the role of women and women artists in societies worldwide over time. Throughout, we have aimed to integrate the historical, political, and social context of art and architecture with the artistic and intellectual aspects. Consequently, we often treat painting, sculpture, architecture, and the so-called minor arts together, highlighting how they all reflect the conventions and aspirations of a common culture, rather than treating them as separate and distinct media. And we feature many works that until recently art historians would not have considered to be "art" at all. In every chapter, we have tried in our choice of artworks and buildings to reflect the increasingly wide range of interests of scholars today, while not rejecting the traditional list of "great" works or the very notion of a "canon." The selection of works encompasses every artistic medium and almost every era and culture.

The changes we have made even with respect to the Eleventh Edition are notable and will be immediately apparent to anyone who examines the Eleventh and Twelfth Editions side by side. Both editions feature more than 1400 photographs, plans, and drawings, but in the new edition nearly every photograph is in color. The only exceptions are works that were created in black-and-white, such as prints or photographs, and a small number of other monuments of which we were unable to obtain a color view that met our very high standards for reproduction.

Every edition of *Art through the Ages* has gone through a rigorous process of review, and the Twelfth Edition is no exception. Each of its 34 chapters has been read by experts in the respective fields. Some chapters were reviewed by as many as six scholars in order to ensure that the text lived up to the Gardner reputation for accuracy as well as readability. Every chapter has been revised. Some have been rewritten almost in their entirety. All feature superb new color illustrations, including a full-page, chapter-opening image reproducing a characteristic work of each period.

The rich illustration program is not, however, confined to the printed page. Every copy of the Twelfth Edition of *Art through the Ages* comes with a complimentary copy of *ArtStudy 2.0*, a CD-ROM that contains hundreds of high-quality digital images of the works discussed in the text. To facilitate the coordinated use of the CD-ROM and the book itself, every monument illustrated on the CD-ROM has an identifying icon appended to the caption of the corresponding figure in the text.

In response to student requests, every chapter of the new edition of *Art through the Ages* now ends with a short Conclusion summarizing the major themes discussed. These summaries face a full-page Chronological Overview of the material presented in the chapter, organized as a vertical timeline, with four "thumb-nail" illustrations of characteristic works in a variety of media, generally including at least one painting, sculpture, and building. Each thumbnail is numbered; the corresponding number appears on the time rule to the left so that the chronological sequence of production is clear.

The most popular features of previous editions of *Art through the Ages* have, of course, been retained. Especially noteworthy are the boxed essays that we introduced in the Eleventh Edition and which were so enthusiastically received by students and instructors alike. As before, these essays are presented in six broad categories.

*Architectural Basics* provide students with a sound foundation for the understanding of architecture. These discussions are concise primers, with drawings and diagrams of the major aspects of design and construction. The information included is essential to an understanding of architectural technology and terminology. The boxes address questions of how and why various forms developed, the problems architects confronted, and the solutions they used to resolve them. Topics discussed include how the Egyptians built the pyramids, the orders of classical architecture, Roman concrete construction, and the design and terminology of mosques, stupas, and Gothic cathedrals.

*Materials and Techniques* essays explain the various media artists employed from prehistoric to modern times. Since materials and techniques often influence the character of works of art, these discussions also contain essential information on why many monuments look the way they do. Hollow-casting bronze statues, fresco painting, Chinese silk, Andean weaving, Islamic tilework, embroidery and tapestry, woodblock prints, and perspective are among the many subjects treated.

*Written Sources* present and discuss key historical documents illuminating important monuments of art and architecture and the careers of some of the world's leading artists, architects, and patrons. The passages we quote permit voices from the past to speak directly to the reader, providing vivid and unique insights into the creation of artworks in all media. Examples include Bernard of Clairvaux's treatise on sculpture in medieval churches, Sinan the Great's commentary on the mosque he built for Selim II, Jean François Marmontel's account of 18th-century salon culture, as well as texts that bring the past to life, such as eyewitness accounts of the volcanic eruption that buried Roman Pompeii and of the fire that destroyed Canterbury Cathedral in medieval England.

*Religion and Mythology* boxes introduce students to the principal elements of the world's great religions, past and present, and to the representation of religious and mythological themes in painting and sculpture of all periods and places. These discussions of belief systems and iconography give readers a richer understanding of some of the greatest artworks ever created. The topics include the gods and goddesses of Egypt, Mesopotamia, Greece, and Rome; the life of Jesus in art; Buddha and Buddhism; Muhammad and Islam; and Aztec religion.

*Art and Society* essays treat the historical, social, political, cultural, and religious context of art and architecture. In some instances, specific monuments are the basis for a discussion of broader themes, as when we use the Hegeso stele to serve as the springboard for an exploration of the role of women in ancient Greek society. In other cases, we discuss how people's evaluation today of artworks can differ from those of the society that produced them, as when we examine the problems created by the contemporary market for undocumented archaeological finds. Other subjects include Egyptian mummification, the art of freed Roman slaves, the Mesoamerican ball game, the shifting fortunes of Vincent van Gogh, Japanese court culture, and Native American artists.

*Art in the News* boxes present accounts of the latest archaeological finds and discussions of current controversies in the history of art. Among the discoveries and issues we highlight are the excavation of the tomb of the sons of the pharaoh Ramses and the restoration of Michelangelo's frescoes in the Sistine Chapel.

As in the past, the Twelfth Edition of *Art through the Ages* is published in a single hardcover version and as two paperbound volumes. Because many students taking the second half of a year-long introductory art history survey course will only have the second volume of the paperbound edition, we have again provided a feature not found in any other textbook currently available: a special set of Volume II boxes on religion, mythology, and architecture entitled *Before 1300*. These discussions immediately follow the Preface to Volume II and provide concise primers on religion and mythology and on architectural terminology and construction methods in the ancient and medieval worlds — information that is essential for understanding the history of art after 1300, both in the West and the East. The subjects of these special boxes are The Gods and Goddesses of Mount Olympus; Buddhism and Hinduism; The Life of Jesus in Art; Greco-Roman Temple Design and the Classical Orders; Arches and Vaults; The Basilican Church; and The Central-Plan Church.

Full-color maps also remain an important element of every chapter of *Art through the Ages*. As in previous editions, we have taken great care to make sure that every site discussed in the text appears on our maps. These maps vary widely in both geographical and chronological scope. Some focus on a small region or even a single city, while others encompass a vast territory and occasionally bridge two or more continents. Several maps plot the art-producing sites of a given area over hundreds, even thousands, of years. In every instance, our aim has been to provide readers with maps that will easily allow them to locate the places where works of art originated or were found and where buildings were erected. To this end we have regularly placed the names of modern nations on maps of the territories of past civilizations. The maps, therefore, are pedagogical tools and do not constitute a historical atlas.

In addition, in order to aid our readers in mastering the vocabulary of art history, we have italicized and defined all art historical terms and other unfamiliar words at their first occurrence in the text — and at later occurrences too, whenever the term has not been used again for several chapters. Definitions of all terms introduced in the text appear once more in the Glossary at the back of the book, which includes pronunciations, a feature introduced in the Eleventh Edition. *Art through the Ages* also has a comprehensive bibliography of books in English, including both general works and a chapter-by-chapter list of more focused studies.

The captions to our more than 1400 illustrations contain a wealth of information, including the name of the artist or architect, if known; the formal title (printed in italics), if assigned, description of the work, or name of the building; the findspot or place of production of the object or location of the building; the date; the material or materials used; the size; and the present location if the work is in a museum or private collection. We urge readers to pay attention to the scales provided on all plans and to all dimensions given in the captions. The objects we illustrate vary enormously in size, from colossal sculptures carved into mountain cliffs and paintings that cover entire walls or ceilings to tiny figurines, coins, and jewelry that one can hold in the hand. Note too the location of the monuments discussed. Although many buildings and museums may be in cities or countries that a reader may never visit, others are likely to be close to home. Nothing can substitute for walking through a building, standing in the presence of a statue, or inspecting the brushwork of a painting close up. Consequently, we have made a special effort to illustrate artworks in geographically wide-ranging public collections.

A work as extensive as a global history of art could not be undertaken or completed without the counsel of experts in all areas of world art. We are especially grateful to Herbert Cole of the University of California, Santa Barbara, for contributing the two chapters on African art, reprising a role he played in the Tenth Edition of *Art through the Ages*. And we remain grateful to Robert L. Brown (University of California, Los Angeles), George Corbin (Lehman College of the City University of New York), Virginia E. Miller (University of Illinois, Chicago), and Quitman Eugene Phillips (University of Wisconsin, Madison) for their contributions to the Eleventh Edition on India and Southeast Asia; Africa and Oceania; the native arts of the Americas; and China, Korea, and Japan, respectively, which laid the foundation for much of the treatment of non-Western art in the Twelfth Edition.

For contributions in the form of extended critiques of the Eleventh Edition or of the penultimate drafts of the Twelfth Edition chapters, as well as other assistance of various sorts, we wish to thank Stanley K. Abe, Duke University; C. Edson Armi, University of California, Santa Barbara; Frederick M. Asher, University of Minnesota; Cynthia Atherton, Middlebury College; Paul G. Bahn, Hull, England; Janis Bergman-Carton, Southern Methodist University; Janet Berlo, University of Rochester; Anne Bertrand, Bard College; Jonathan M. Bloom, Boston College; Kendall H. Brown, California State University, Long Beach; Andrew L. Cohen, University of Central Arkansas; Harry A. Cooper, Fogg Art Museum, Harvard University; Roger J. Crum, University of Dayton; LouAnn Faris Culley, Kansas State University; Thomas E. A. Dale, University of Wisconsin, Madison; Anne D'Alleva, University of Connecticut; Eve D'Ambra, Vassar College; Cindy Bailey Damschroder, University of Cincinnati; Abraham A. Davidson, Temple University; Carolyn Dean, University of California, Santa Cruz; William Diebold, Reed College; Erika Doss, University of Colorado; Daniel Ehnbom, University of Virginia; David Ehrenpreis, James Madison University; Jerome Feldman, Hawaii Pacific University; Peter Fergusson, Wellesley College; Barbara Frank, State University of New York, Stony Brook; Rita E. Freed, Museum of Fine Arts, Boston; Eric G. Garbersen, Virginia Commonwealth University; Clive F. Getty, Miami University; Paula Girshick, Indiana University; Carma R. Gorman, Southern Illinois University, Carbondale; Elizabeth ten Grotenhuis, Boston University; Melinda K. Hartwig, Georgia State University; Marsha Haufler, University of Kansas; Mary Beth Heston, College of Charleston; Hannah Higgins, University of Illinois, Chicago; Charlotte Houghton, The Pennsylvania State University; Aldona Jonaitis, University of Alaska Museum; Adrienne Kaeppler, Smithsonian Institution; Padma Kaimal, Colgate University; Stacy L. Kamehiro, University of Redlands; Thomas DaCosta Kaufmann, Princeton University; Dale Kinney, Bryn Mawr College; Sandy Kita, University of Maryland, College Park; Cecelia F. Klein, University of California, Los Angeles; James Kornwolf, College of William and Mary; Andrew Ladis, University of Georgia, Athens; Ellen Johnston Laing, University of Michigan; Joseph Lamb, Ohio University; Dana Leibsohn, Smith College; Janice Leoshko, University of Texas at Austin; Henry Maguire, Johns Hopkins University; Joan Marter, Rutgers University; Michael Meister, University of Pennsylvania; Samuel C. Morse, Amherst College; Susan E. Nelson, Indiana University; Irene Nero, Southeastern Louisiana University; Esther Pasztory, Columbia University; Jeanette F. Peterson, University of California, Santa Barbara; Elizabeth Piliod, Oregon State University; Martin Powers, University of Michigan; Ingrida Raudzens, Salem State College; Paul Rehak, University of Kansas; Margaret Cool Root, University of Michigan; Lisa Rosenthal, University of Illinois, Urbana-Champaign; Jonathan M. Reynolds, University of Southern California; Conrad Rudolph, University of California, Riverside; Denise Schmandt-Besserat, University of Texas at Austin; Ellen C. Schwartz, Eastern Michigan University; Michael Schwartz, Augusta State University; Raymond A. Silverman, Michigan State University; Jeffrey Chipps Smith, University of Texas at Austin; Anne Rudloff Stanton, University of Missouri, Columbia; Rebecca Stone-Miller, Emory University; Mary C. Sturgeon, University of North Carolina at Chapel Hill; Peter C. Sturman, University of California, Santa Barbara; Melinda Takeuchi, Stanford University; Woodman Taylor, University of Illinois at Chicago; Jehanne Teilhet-Fisk, Florida State University; Dorothy Verkerk, University of North Carolina at Chapel Hill; Monica Blackmun Visonà, Metro State College; Gerald Walker, Clemson University; Martha Ward, University of Chicago; Gregory Warden, Southern Methodist University; Kent R. Weeks, American University in Cairo; Victoria Weston, University of Massachusetts, Boston; Deborah B. Waite, University of Hawaii; Catherine Wilkinson Zerner, Brown University. Innumerable other instructors and students have also sent us helpful reactions, comments, and suggestions for ways to improve the book. We are grateful for their interest and their insights.

Among those at Thomson Wadsworth who worked with us to make the new edition of *Art through the Ages* the best ever are the CEO and president, Susan Badger; senior vice president, editorial, Sean Wakely; vice president and editor-in-chief, Marcus Boggs; publisher, Clark Baxter; executive editor, David Tatom; acquisitions editor, John Swanson; technology project manager, Melinda Newfarmer; our development editors, Helen Triller and Stacey Sims; assistant editor, Amy McGaughey; and editorial assistants, Rebecca Jackson and Brianna Brinkley. This edition of *Art through the Ages* is the most ambitious ever, and the production schedule was the tightest ever. We therefore want to acknowledge the extraordinary efforts of our editorial production manager, Kathryn Stewart, and her team of dedicated professionals: Joan Keyes of Dovetail Publishing Services, our production service; our copy editors, Michele Jones and Gail Nelson-Bonebrake; interior designer, John Walker; cover designer, Brian Salisbury; and photo researchers Carrie Ward, Lili Weiner, and Image Select International. We are also grateful to the marketing staff for their dedication to making this edition a success: senior vice president, marketing, Jonathan Hulbert; director of marketing, Elana Dolberg; executive marketing manager, Diane Wenckebach; executive director of advertising and marketing communications, Margaret Parks; senior channel manager, school, Wadsworth Group, Pat Murphree; marketing manager, Mark Orr; and marketing assistant, Annabelle Yang. Recognition and thanks are also due to our proofreaders, Katherine Hyde and Pete Shanks, and our indexer, Nancy Ball.

We also owe a deep debt of gratitude to our colleagues at Boston University and the University of Nebraska, Lincoln, and to the thousands of students and the scores of teaching fellows in our art history courses over many years in Boston and Lincoln, and at the University of Virginia and Yale University. From them we have learned much that has helped determine the form and content of *Art through the Ages*.

FRED S. KLEINER
CHRISTIN J. MAMIYA

# GARDNER'S
# ART
## through the
# AGES

## TWELFTH EDITION

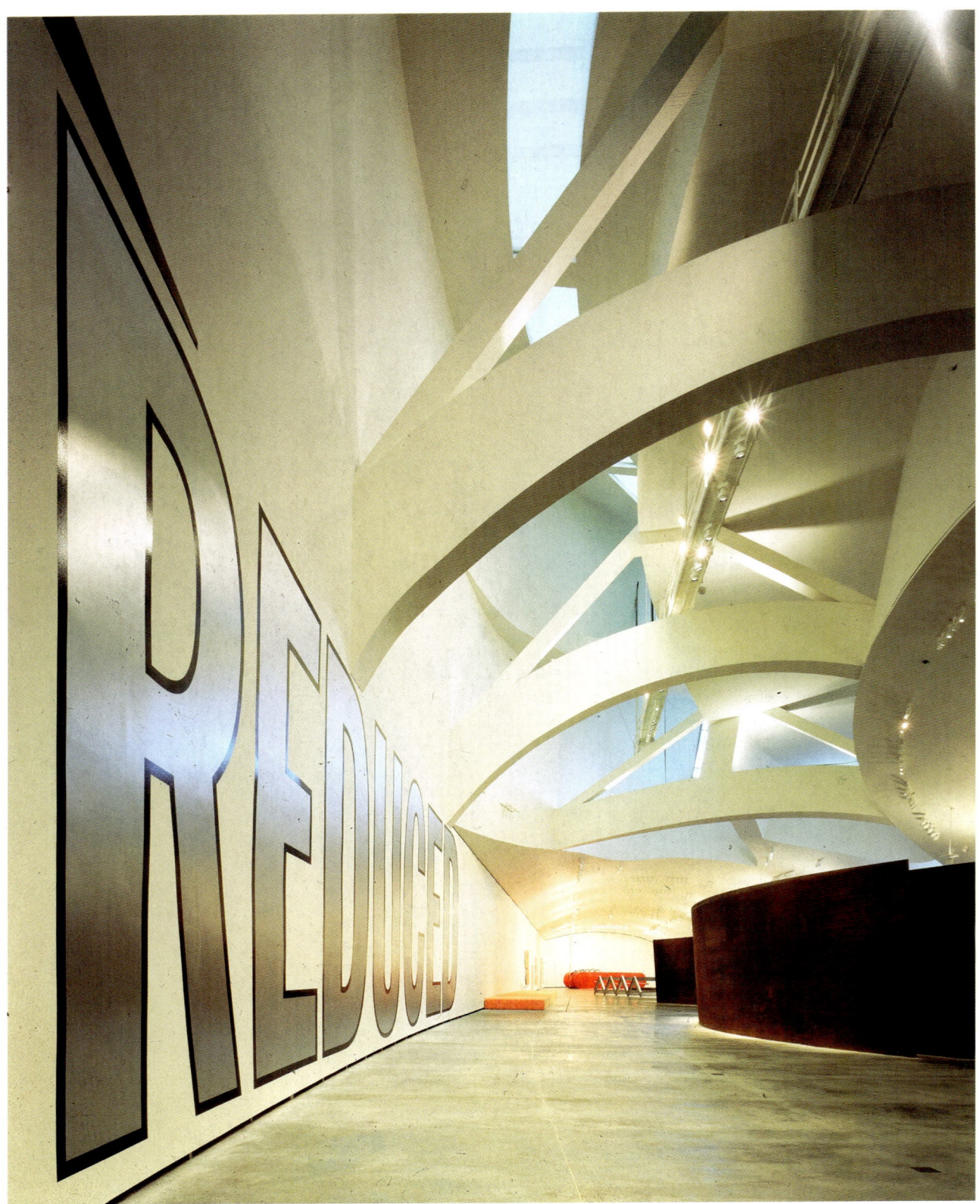

**Intro-1**  Frank Gehry, interior of Guggenheim Museum, Bilbao, Spain, 1997.

# INTRODUCTION

## THE SUBJECTS AND VOCABULARY OF ART HISTORY

People do not often juxtapose the terms *art* and *history.* They tend to think of history as the record and interpretation of past human actions, particularly social and political actions. Most think of art, quite correctly, as part of the present—as something people can see and touch. People cannot, of course, see or touch history's vanished human events. But a visible and tangible artwork is a kind of persisting event. One or more artists made it at a certain time and in a specific place, even if no one now knows just who, when, where, or why. Although created in the past, an artwork continues to exist in the present, long surviving its times. The first painters and sculptors died 30,000 years ago, but their works remain, some of them exhibited in glass cases in museums built only a few years ago.

Modern museum visitors can admire these relics of the remote past and the countless other objects humankind has produced over the millennia without any knowledge of the circumstances that led to the creation of those works. The beauty or sheer size of an object can impress people, the artist's virtuosity in the handling of ordinary or costly materials can dazzle them, or the subject depicted can move them. Viewers can react to what they see, interpret the work in the light of their own experience, and judge it a success or a failure. These are all valid responses to a work of art. But the enjoyment and appreciation of artworks in museum settings (FIG. **Intro-1**) are relatively recent phenomena, as is the creation of artworks solely for museum-going audiences to view.

Today, it is common for artists to work in private studios and to create paintings, sculptures, and other objects commercial art galleries will offer for sale. Usually, someone the artist has never met will purchase the artwork and display it in a setting the artist has never seen. But although this is not a new phenomenon in the history of art—an ancient potter decorating a vase for sale at a village market stall also probably did not know who would buy the pot or where it would be housed—it is not at all typical. In fact, it is exceptional. Throughout history, most artists created the paintings, sculptures, and other objects exhibited in museums today for specific patrons and settings and to fulfill a specific purpose. Often, no one knows the original contexts of those artworks.

Although people may appreciate the visual and tactile qualities of these objects, they cannot understand why they were made or why they look the way they do without knowing the circumstances of their creation. *Art appreciation* does not require knowledge of the historical context of an artwork (or a building). *Art history* does.

Thus, a central aim of art history is to determine the original context of artworks. Art historians seek to achieve a full understanding not only of why these "persisting events" of human history look the way they do but also of why the artistic events happened at all. What unique set of circumstances gave rise to the erection of a particular building or led a specific patron to commission an individual artist to fashion a singular artwork for a certain place? The study of history is therefore vital to art history. And art history is often very important to the study of history. Art objects and buildings are historical documents that can shed light on the peoples who made them and on the times of their creation in a way other historical documents cannot. Furthermore, artists and architects can affect history by reinforcing or challenging cultural values and practices through the objects they create and the structures they build. Thus, the history of art and architecture is inseparable from the study of history, although the two disciplines are not the same. In the following pages, we outline some of the distinctive subjects art historians address and the kinds of questions they ask, and explain some of the basic terminology art historians use when answering their questions. Armed with this arsenal of questions and terms, you will be ready to explore the multifaceted world of art through the ages.

# ART HISTORY IN THE 21ST CENTURY

Art historians study the visual and tangible objects humans make and the structures humans build. Scholars traditionally have classified such works as architecture, sculpture, the pictorial arts (painting, drawing, printmaking, and photography), and the craft arts, or arts of design. The craft arts comprise utilitarian objects, such as ceramics, metalwares, textiles, jewelry, and similar accessories of ordinary living. Artists of every age have blurred the boundaries between these categories, but this is especially true today, when *multimedia* works abound.

From the earliest Greco-Roman art critics on, scholars have studied objects that their makers consciously manufactured as "art" and to which the artists assigned formal titles. But today's art historians also study a vast number of objects that their creators and owners almost certainly did not consider to be "works of art." Few ancient Romans, for example, would have regarded a coin bearing their emperor's portrait as anything but money. Today, an art museum may exhibit that coin in a locked case in a climate-controlled room, and scholars may subject it to the same kind of art historical analysis as a portrait by an acclaimed Renaissance or modern sculptor or painter.

The range of objects art historians study is constantly expanding and now includes, for example, computer-generated images, whereas in the past almost anything produced using a machine would not have been regarded as art. Most people still consider the performing arts—music, drama, and dance—as outside art history's realm because these arts are fleeting, impermanent media. But recently even this distinction between "fine art" and performance art has become blurred. Art historians, however, generally ask the same kinds of questions about what they study, whether they employ a restrictive or expansive definition of art.

## *The Questions Art Historians Ask*

**HOW OLD IS IT?** Before art historians can construct a history of art, they must be sure they know the date of each work they study. Thus, an indispensable subject of art historical inquiry is *chronology,* the dating of art objects and buildings. If researchers cannot determine a monument's age, they cannot place the work in its historical context. Art historians have developed many ways to establish, or at least approximate, the date of an artwork.

*Physical evidence* often reliably indicates an object's age. The material used for a statue or painting—bronze, plastic, or oil-based pigment, to name only a few—may not have been invented before a certain time, indicating the earliest possible date someone could have fashioned the work. Or artists may have ceased using certain materials—such as specific kinds of inks and papers for drawings and prints—at a known time, providing the latest possible dates for objects made of such materials. Sometimes the material (or the manufacturing technique) of an object or a building can establish a very precise date of production or construction. Studying tree rings, for instance, usually can determine within a narrow range the date of a wood statue or a timber roof beam.

*Documentary evidence* also can help pinpoint the date of an object or building when a dated written document mentions the work. For example, official records may note when church officials commissioned a new altarpiece—and how much they paid to which artist.

*Visual evidence,* too, can play a significant role in dating an artwork. A painter might have depicted an identifiable person or a kind of hairstyle, clothing, or furniture fashionable only at a certain time. If so, the art historian can assign a more accurate date to that painting.

*Stylistic evidence* is also very important. The analysis of *style*—an artist's distinctive manner of producing an object, the way a work looks—is the art historian's special sphere. Unfortunately, because it is a subjective assessment, stylistic evidence is by far the most unreliable chronological criterion. Still, art historians sometimes find style a very useful tool for establishing chronology.

**WHAT IS ITS STYLE?** Defining artistic style is one of the key elements of art historical inquiry, although the analysis of artworks solely in terms of style no longer dominates the field the way it once did. Art historians speak of several different kinds of artistic styles.

*Period style* refers to the characteristic artistic manner of a specific time, usually within a distinct culture, such as "Archaic Greek" or "Late Byzantine." But many periods do not display any stylistic unity at all. How would someone define the artistic style of the opening decade of the new millennium in North America? Far too many crosscurrents exist in contemporary art for anyone to describe a period style of the early 21st century—even in a single city such as New York.

*Regional style* is the term art historians use to describe variations in style tied to geography. Like an object's date, its *provenance,* or place of origin, can significantly determine its character. Very often two artworks from the same place made centuries apart are more similar than contemporaneous works from two different regions. To cite one example, usually only an expert can distinguish between an Egyptian statue carved in 2500 BCE and one made in 500 BCE. But no one would mistake an Egyptian statue of 500 BCE for one of the same date made in Greece or Mexico.

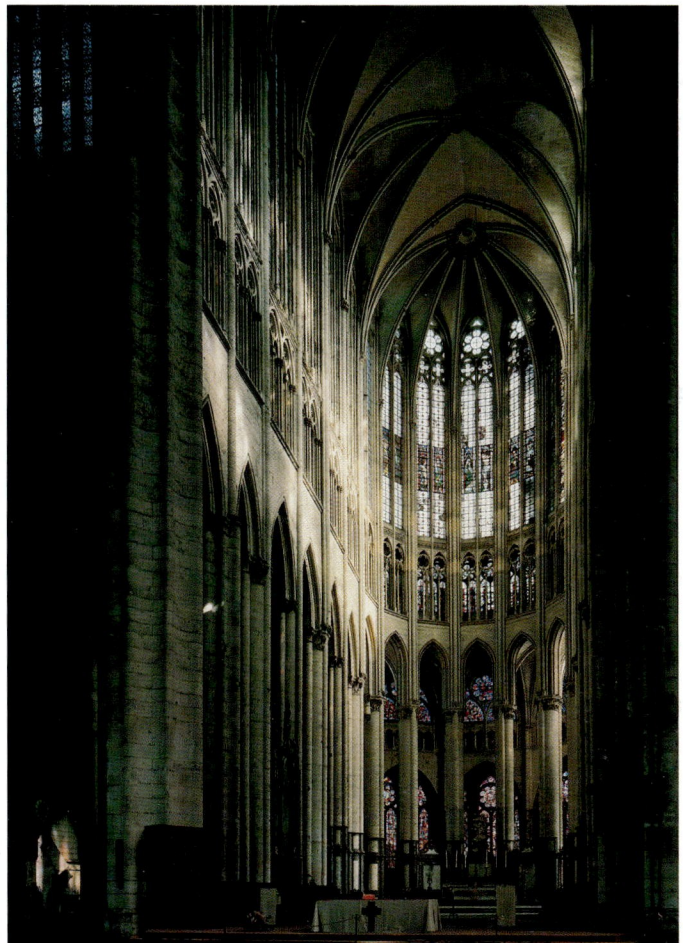

**Intro-2** Choir of Beauvais Cathedral, Beauvais, France, rebuilt after 1284.

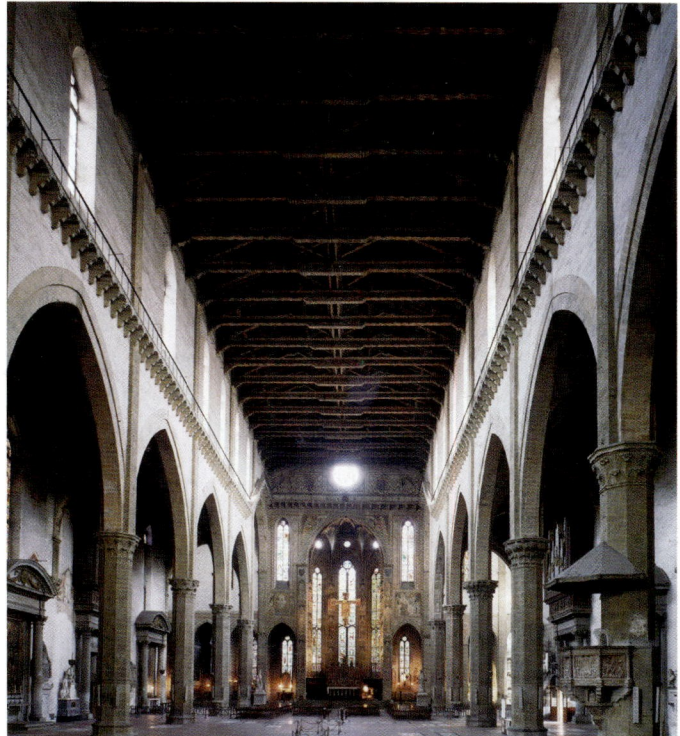

**Intro-3** Interior of Santa Croce, Florence, Italy, begun 1294.

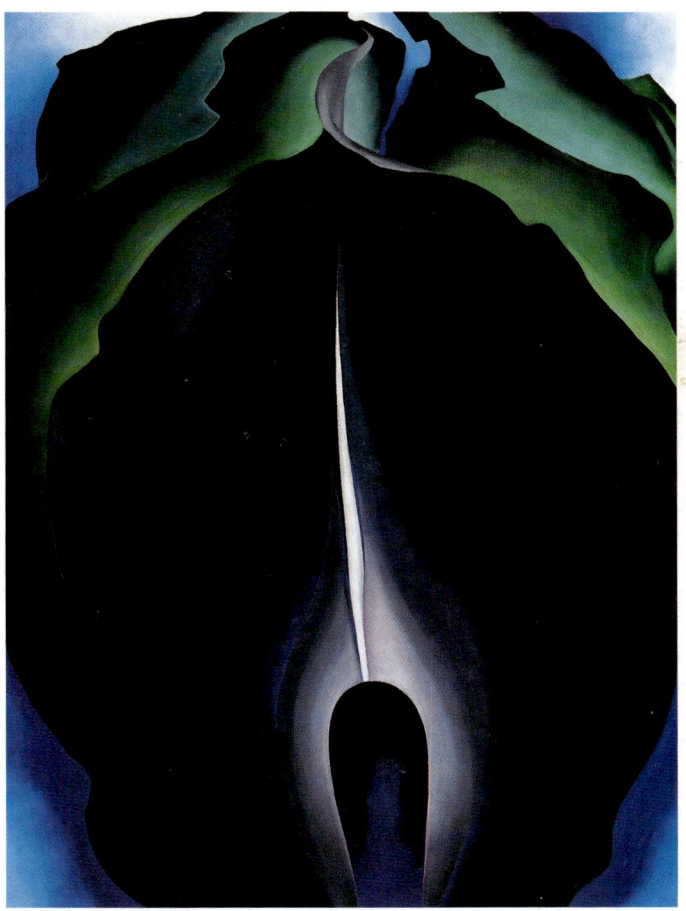

**Intro-4** GEORGIA O'KEEFFE, *Jack-in-the-Pulpit No. 4*, 1930. Oil on canvas, 3′ 4″ × 2′ 6″. National Gallery of Art, Washington (Alfred Stieglitz Collection, bequest of Georgia O'Keeffe).

Considerable variations in a given area's style are possible, however, even during a single historical period. In late medieval Europe during the so-called Gothic age, French architecture differed significantly from Italian architecture. The interiors of Beauvais Cathedral (FIG. **Intro-2**) and Santa Croce in Florence (FIG. **Intro-3**) typify the architectural styles of France and Italy, respectively, at the end of the 13th century. The rebuilding of the choir of Beauvais Cathedral began in 1284. Construction commenced on Santa Croce only 10 years later. Both structures employ the characteristic Gothic pointed arch, yet they contrast strikingly. The French church has towering stone vaults and large expanses of stained-glass windows, whereas the Italian building has a low timber roof and small, widely separated windows. Because the two contemporaneous churches served similar purposes, regional style mainly explains their differing appearance.

*Personal style*, the distinctive manner of individual artists or architects, often decisively explains stylistic discrepancies among monuments of the same time and place. In 1930 the American painter GEORGIA O'KEEFFE produced a series of paintings of flowering plants. One of them was *Jack-in-the-Pulpit No. 4* (FIG. **Intro-4**), a sharply focused close-up view of petals and leaves. O'Keeffe captured the growing plant's slow, controlled motion while converting the plant into a powerful abstract composition of lines, forms, and colors (see the discussion of art historical vocabulary in the next section). Only a year later, another American artist, BEN SHAHN, painted *The Passion of Sacco and Vanzetti*

The different kinds of artistic styles are not mutually exclusive. For example, an artist's personal style may change dramatically during a long career. Art historians then must distinguish among the different period styles of a particular artist, such as the "Blue Period" and the "Cubist Period" of the prolific 20th-century artist Pablo Picasso.

**WHAT IS ITS SUBJECT?** Another major concern of art historians is, of course, subject matter, encompassing the story, or *narrative;* the scene presented; the action's time and place; the persons involved; and the environment and its details. Some artworks, such as modern abstract paintings, have no subject, not even a setting. But when artists represent people, places, or actions, viewers must identify these aspects to achieve complete understanding of the work. Art historians traditionally separate pictorial subjects into various categories, such as religious, historical, mythological, *genre* (daily life), portraiture, *landscape* (a depiction of a place), *still life* (an arrangement of inanimate objects), and their numerous subdivisions and combinations.

*Iconography*—literally, the "writing of images"—refers both to the *content,* or subject of an artwork, and to the study of content in art. By extension, it also includes the study of *symbols,* images that stand for other images or encapsulate ideas. In Christian art, two intersecting lines of unequal length or a simple geometric cross can serve as an emblem of the religion as a whole, symbolizing the cross of Jesus Christ's crucifixion. A symbol also can be a familiar object the artist imbued with greater meaning. A balance or scale, for example, may symbolize justice or the weighing of souls on Judgment Day (FIG. **Intro-6**).

Artists also may depict figures with unique *attributes* identifying them. In Christian art, for example, each of the authors of the New Testament Gospels, the Four Evangelists (FIG. **Intro-7**), has a

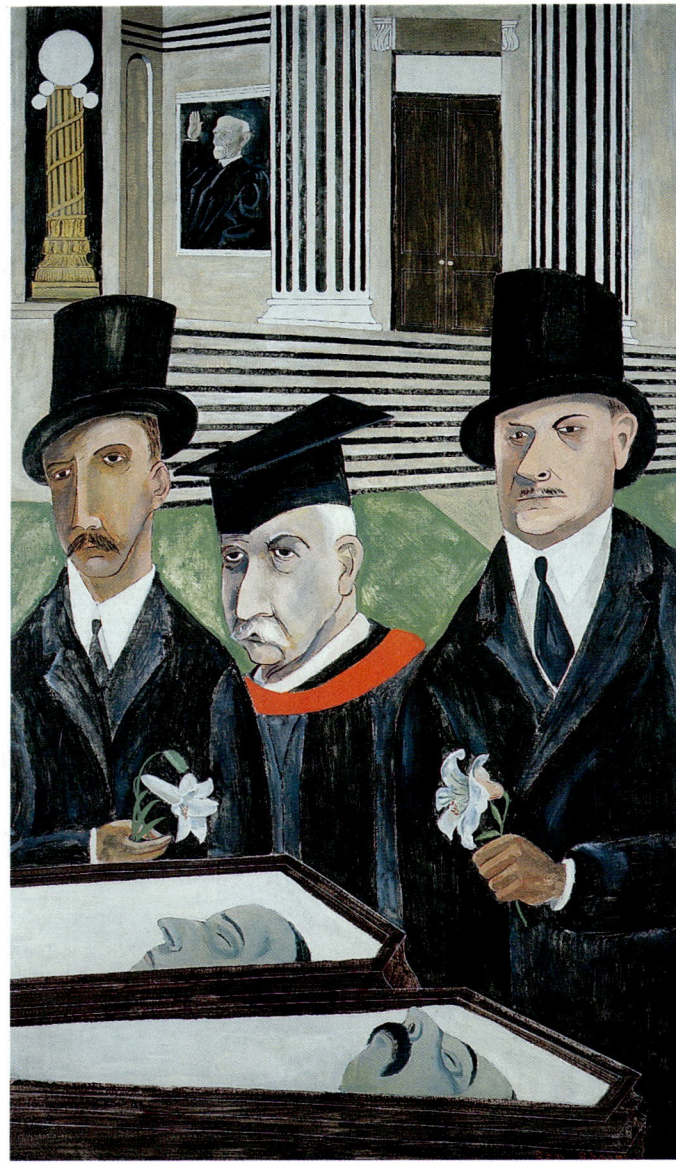

Intro-5 BEN SHAHN, *The Passion of Sacco and Vanzetti,* 1931–1932. Tempera on canvas, 7′ $\frac{1}{2}$″ × 4′. Whitney Museum of American Art, New York (gift of Edith and Milton Lowenthal in memory of Juliana Force).

(FIG. **Intro-5**), a stinging commentary on social injustice inspired by the trial and execution of two Italian anarchists, Nicola Sacco and Bartolomeo Vanzetti. Many people believed Sacco and Vanzetti had been unjustly convicted of killing two men in a holdup in 1920. Shahn's painting compresses time in a symbolic representation of the trial and its aftermath. The two executed men lie in their coffins. Presiding over them are the three members of the commission (headed by a college president wearing academic cap and gown) that declared the original trial fair and cleared the way for the executions. Behind, on the wall of a columned government building, hangs the framed portrait of the judge who pronounced the initial sentence. Personal style, not period or regional style, sets Shahn's canvas apart from O'Keeffe's. The contrast is extreme here because of the very different subjects the artists chose. But even when two artists depict the same subject, the results can vary widely. The *way* O'Keeffe painted flowers and the *way* Shahn painted faces are distinctive and unlike the styles of their contemporaries. (See the "Who Made It?" discussion on page 5.)

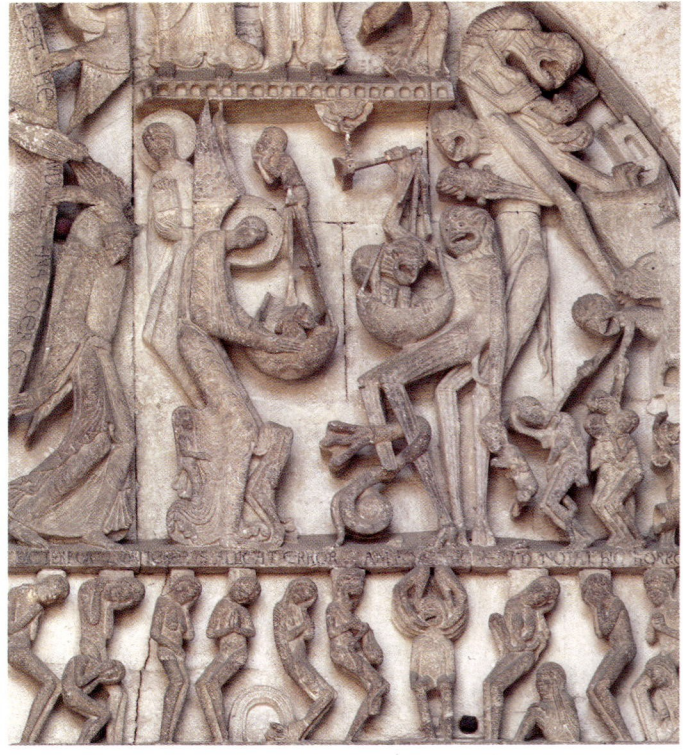

Intro-6 GISLEBERTUS, The weighing of souls, detail of Last Judgment, west tympanum of Saint-Lazare, Autun, France, ca. 1120–1135.

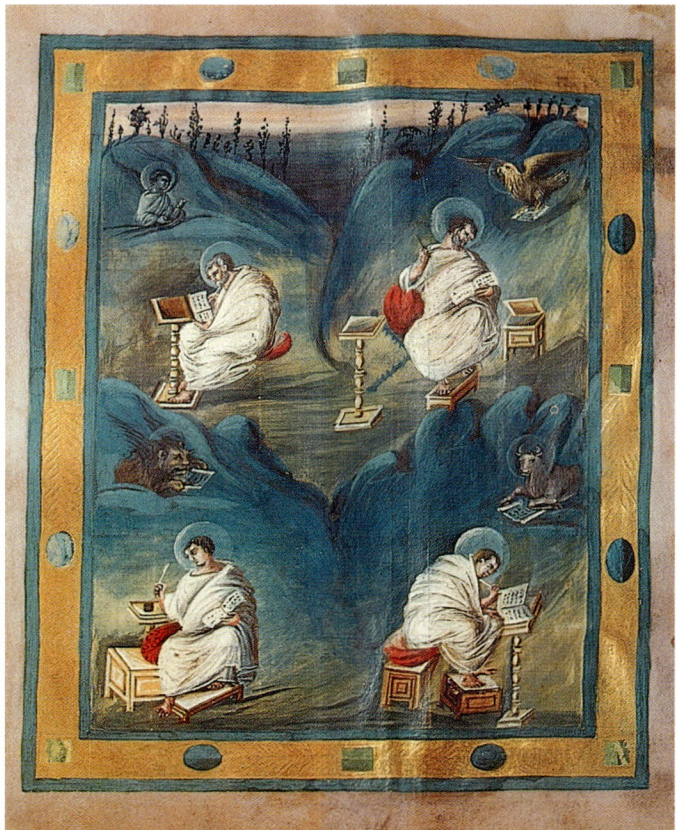

**Intro-7** The Four Evangelists, folio 14 verso of the *Aachen Gospels*, ca. 810. Ink and tempera on vellum, $1' \times 9\frac{1}{2}''$. Cathedral Treasury, Aachen.

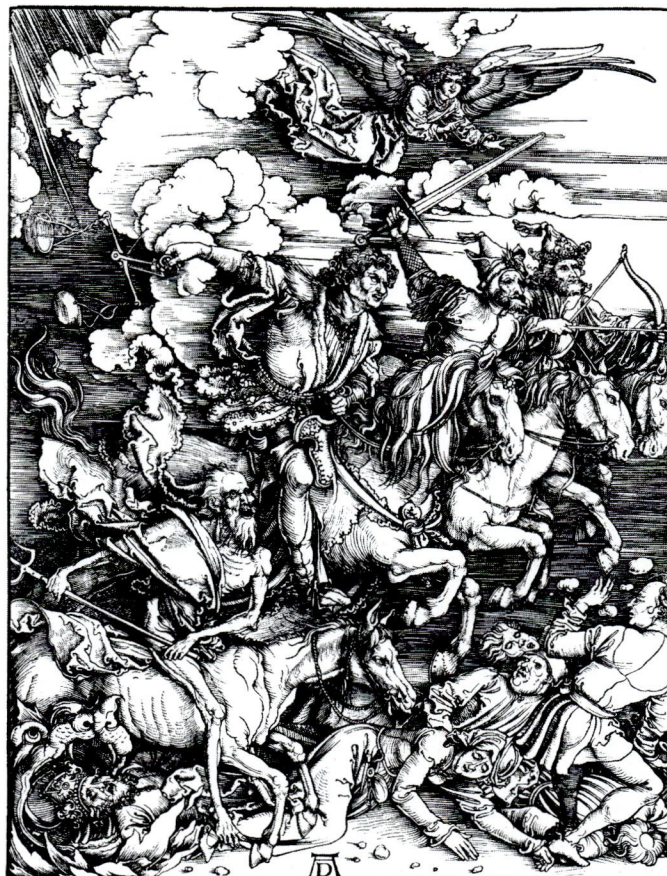

**Intro-8** ALBRECHT DÜRER, *The Four Horsemen of the Apocalypse*, ca. 1498. Woodcut, approx. $1' 3\frac{1}{4}'' \times 11''$. Metropolitan Museum of Art, New York (gift of Junius S. Morgan, 1919).

distinctive attribute. Saint John is known by his eagle, Luke by an ox, Mark by a lion, and Matthew by a winged man.

Throughout the history of art, artists also used *personifications*—abstract ideas codified in bodily form. Worldwide, people visualize Liberty as a robed woman with a torch because of the fame of the colossal statue set up in New York City's harbor in the 19th century. *The Four Horsemen of the Apocalypse* (FIG. **Intro-8**) is a terrifying late-15th-century depiction of the fateful day at the end of time when, according to the Bible's last book, Death, Famine, War, and Pestilence will cut down the human race. The artist, ALBRECHT DÜRER, personified Death as an emaciated old man with a pitchfork. Dürer's Famine swings the scales that will weigh human souls (compare FIG. Intro-6), War wields a sword, and Pestilence draws a bow.

Even without considering style and without knowing a work's maker, informed viewers can determine much about the work's period and provenance by iconographical and subject analysis alone. In *The Passion of Sacco and Vanzetti* (FIG. Intro-5), for example, the two coffins, the trio headed by an academic, and the robed judge in the background are all pictorial clues revealing the painting's subject. The work's date must be after the trial and execution, probably while the event was still newsworthy. And because the two men's deaths caused the greatest outrage in the United States, the painter–social critic was probably American.

**WHO MADE IT?** If Ben Shahn had not signed his painting of Sacco and Vanzetti, an art historian could still assign, or *attribute*,

the work to him based on knowledge of the artist's personal style. Although signing (and dating) works is quite common (but by no means universal) today, in the history of art countless works exist whose artists remain unknown. Because personal style can play a large role in determining the character of an artwork, art historians often try to attribute anonymous works to known artists. Sometimes they attempt to assemble a group of works all thought to be by the same person, even though none of the objects in the group is the known work of an artist with a recorded name. Art historians thus reconstruct the careers of people such as "the Andokides Painter," the anonymous ancient Greek artist who painted the vases produced by the potter Andokides. Scholars base their attributions on internal evidence, such as the distinctive way an artist draws or carves drapery folds, earlobes, or flowers. It requires a keen, highly trained eye and long experience to become a *connoisseur*, an expert in assigning artworks to "the hand" of one artist rather than another. Attribution is, of course, subjective and ever open to doubt. At present, for example, international debate rages over attributions to the famous Dutch painter Rembrandt.

Sometimes a group of artists works in the same style at the same time and place. Art historians designate such a group as a *school*. "School" does not mean an educational institution. The term connotes only chronological, stylistic, and geographic similarity. Art historians speak, for example, of the Dutch school of the 17th century and, within it, of subschools such as those of the cities of Haarlem, Utrecht, and Leyden.

**Intro-9** Augustus wearing the *corona civica* (civic crown), early first century CE. Marble, approx. 1′ 5″ high. Glyptothek, Munich.

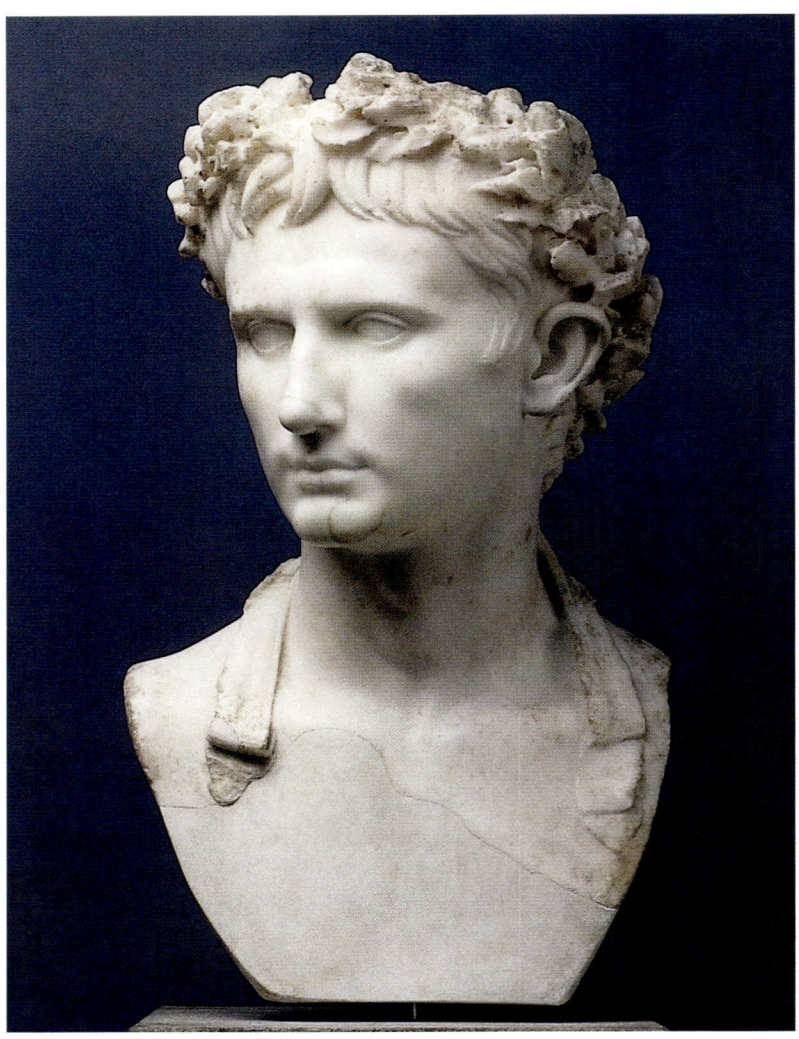

**WHO PAID FOR IT?** The interest many art historians show in attribution reflects their conviction that the identity of an artwork's maker is the major reason the object looks the way it does. For them, personal style is of paramount importance. But in many times and places, artists had little to say about what form their work would take. They toiled in obscurity, doing the bidding of their *patrons,* those who paid them to make individual works or employed them on a continuing basis. The role of patrons in dictating the content and shaping the form of artworks is also an important subject of art historical inquiry.

In the art of portraiture, to name only one category of painting and sculpture, the patron has often played a dominant role in deciding how the artist represented the subject, whether the patron or another person, such as a spouse, son, or mother. Many Egyptian pharaohs and some Roman emperors, for example, insisted that artists depict them with unlined faces and perfect youthful bodies no matter how old they were when portrayed. In these cases, the state employed the sculptors and painters, and the artists had no choice but to depict their patrons in the officially approved manner. This is why Augustus, who lived to age 76, looks so young in his portraits (FIG. **Intro-9**). Although Roman emperor for more than 40 years, Augustus demanded that artists always represent him as a young, godlike head of state.

All modes of artistic production reveal the impact of patronage. Learned monks provided the themes for the sculptural decoration of medieval church portals (FIG. Intro-6). Renaissance princes and popes dictated the subject, size, and materials of artworks destined, sometimes, for buildings constructed according to their specifications. An art historian could make a very long list along these lines, and it would indicate that throughout the history of art, patrons have had diverse tastes and needs and demanded different kinds of art. Whenever a patron contracts an artist or architect to paint, sculpt, or build in a prescribed manner, personal style often becomes a very minor factor in how the painting, statue, or building looks. In such cases, the identity of the patron reveals more to art historians than does the identity of the artist or school. The portrait of Augustus illustrated here (FIG. Intro-9) was the work of a virtuoso sculptor, a master wielder of hammer and chisel. But scores of similar portraits of that emperor exist today. They differ in quality but not in kind from this one. The patron, not the artist, determined the character of such artworks. Augustus's public image never varied.

## The Words Art Historians Use

Like all specialists, art historians have their own specialized vocabulary. That vocabulary consists of hundreds of words, but certain basic terms are indispensable for describing artworks and buildings of any time and place, and we use those terms throughout this book. They make up the essential vocabulary of *formal analysis,* the visual analysis of artistic form. We define the most important of these art historical terms here. For a much longer list, consult the Glossary in this book's end material.

**FORM AND COMPOSITION** *Form* refers to an object's shape and structure, either in two dimensions (for example, a figure painted on a canvas) or in three dimensions (such as a statue carved from a marble block). Two forms may take the same shape but may differ in their color, texture, and other qualities. *Composition* refers to how an artist organizes (composes) forms in an artwork, either by placing shapes on a flat surface or by arranging forms in space.

**MATERIAL AND TECHNIQUE** To create art forms, artists shape materials (pigment, clay, marble, gold, and many more) with tools (pens, brushes, chisels, and so forth). Each of the materials and tools available has its own potentialities and limitations. Part of all artists' creative activity is to select the medium and instrument most suitable to the artists' purpose—or to pioneer the use of new media and tools, such as bronze and concrete in antiquity and cameras and computers in modern times. The processes artists employ, such as applying paint to canvas with a brush, and the distinctive, personal ways they handle materials constitute their *technique.* Form, material, and technique interrelate and are central to analyzing any work of art.

**LINE** *Line* is one of the most important elements defining an artwork's shape or form. A line can be understood as the path of a point moving in space, an invisible line of sight or a visual *axis.* But, more commonly, artists and architects make a line concrete by drawing (or chiseling) it on a *plane,* a flat and two-dimensional surface. A line may be very thin, wirelike, and delicate; it may be thick and heavy; or it may alternate quickly from broad to narrow, the strokes jagged or the outline broken. When a continuous line defines an object's outer shape, art historians call it a *contour line.*

One can observe all of these line qualities in Dürer's *Four Horsemen of the Apocalypse* (FIG. Intro-8). Contour lines define the basic shapes of clouds, human and animal limbs, and weapons. Within the forms, series of short broken lines create shadows and textures. An overall pattern of long parallel strokes suggests the dark sky on the frightening day when the world is about to end.

**COLOR** Light reveals all colors. *Light* in the world of the painter and other artists differs from natural light. Natural light, or sunlight, is whole or *additive* light. As the sum of all the wavelengths composing the visible *spectrum,* it may be disassembled or fragmented into the individual colors of the spectral band. The painter's light in art—the light reflected from pigments and objects—is *subtractive* light. Paint pigments produce their individual colors by reflecting a segment of the spectrum while absorbing all the rest. Green pigment, for example, subtracts or absorbs all the light in the spectrum except that seen as green, which it reflects to the eyes.

*Hue* is the property giving a color its name. Although the spectrum colors merge into each other, artists usually conceive of their hues as distinct from one another. Color has two basic variables—the apparent amount of light reflected and the apparent purity. A change in one must produce a change in the other. Some terms for these variables are *value* or *tonality* (the degree of lightness or darkness) and *intensity* or *saturation* (the purity of a color, its brightness or dullness).

The *color triangle* (FIG. **Intro-10**) JOSEF ALBERS and SEWELL SILLMAN developed clearly shows the relationships among the six main colors. Red, yellow, and blue, the *primary colors,* are the vertexes of the large triangle. Orange, green, and purple, the *sec-*

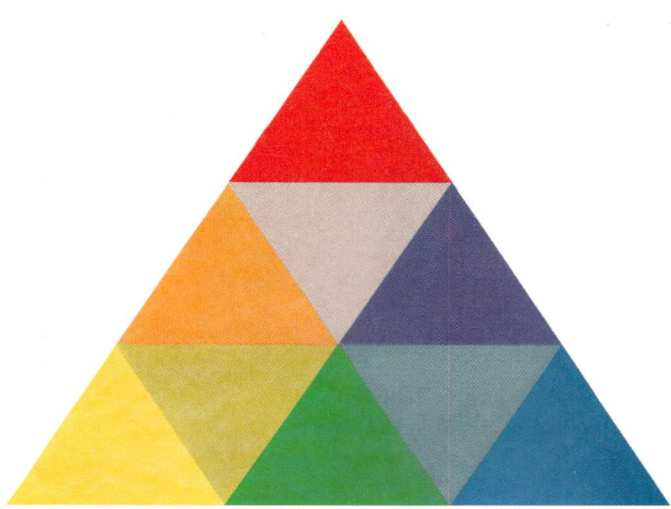

**Intro-10** JOSEF ALBERS and SEWELL SILLMAN, color triangle. Yale University Art Gallery, New Haven.

*ondary colors* resulting from mixing pairs of primaries, lie between them. Colors opposite each other in the spectrum—red and green, purple and yellow, and orange and blue here—are *complementary colors.* They "complement," or complete, each other, one absorbing colors the other reflects. When painters mix complementaries in the right proportions, a neutral tone or gray (theoretically, black) results.

**TEXTURE** *Texture* is the quality of a surface (such as rough or shiny) that light reveals. Art historians distinguish between *actual* texture, or the tactile quality of the surface, and *represented* texture, as when painters depict an object as having a certain texture, even though the pigment is the actual texture. Sometimes artists combine different materials of different textures on a single surface, juxtaposing paint with pieces of wood, newspaper, fabric, and so forth. Art historians refer to this *mixed-media* technique as *collage.* Texture is, of course, a key determinant of any sculpture's character. People's first impulse is usually to handle a piece of sculpture—even though museum signs often warn "Do not touch!" Sculptors plan for this natural human response, using surfaces varying in texture from rugged coarseness to polished smoothness. Textures are often intrinsic to a material, influencing the type of stone, wood, plastic, clay, or metal sculptors select.

**SPACE, MASS, AND VOLUME** *Space* is the bounded or boundless "container" of objects. For art historians, space can be *actual,* the three-dimensional space occupied by a statue or a vase or contained within a room or courtyard. Or it can be *illusionistic,* as when painters depict an image (or illusion) of the three-dimensional spatial world on a two-dimensional surface.

*Mass* and *volume* describe three-dimensional space. In both architecture and sculpture, mass is the bulk, density, and weight of matter in space. Yet the mass need not be solid. It can be the exterior form of enclosed space. "Mass" can apply to a solid Egyptian pyramid or wooden statue, to a church, synagogue, or mosque—architectural shells enclosing sometimes vast spaces—and to a hollow metal statue or baked clay pot. Volume is the space that mass organizes, divides, or encloses. It may be a building's interior spaces, the intervals between a structure's masses, or the amount of space occupied by three-dimensional objects such

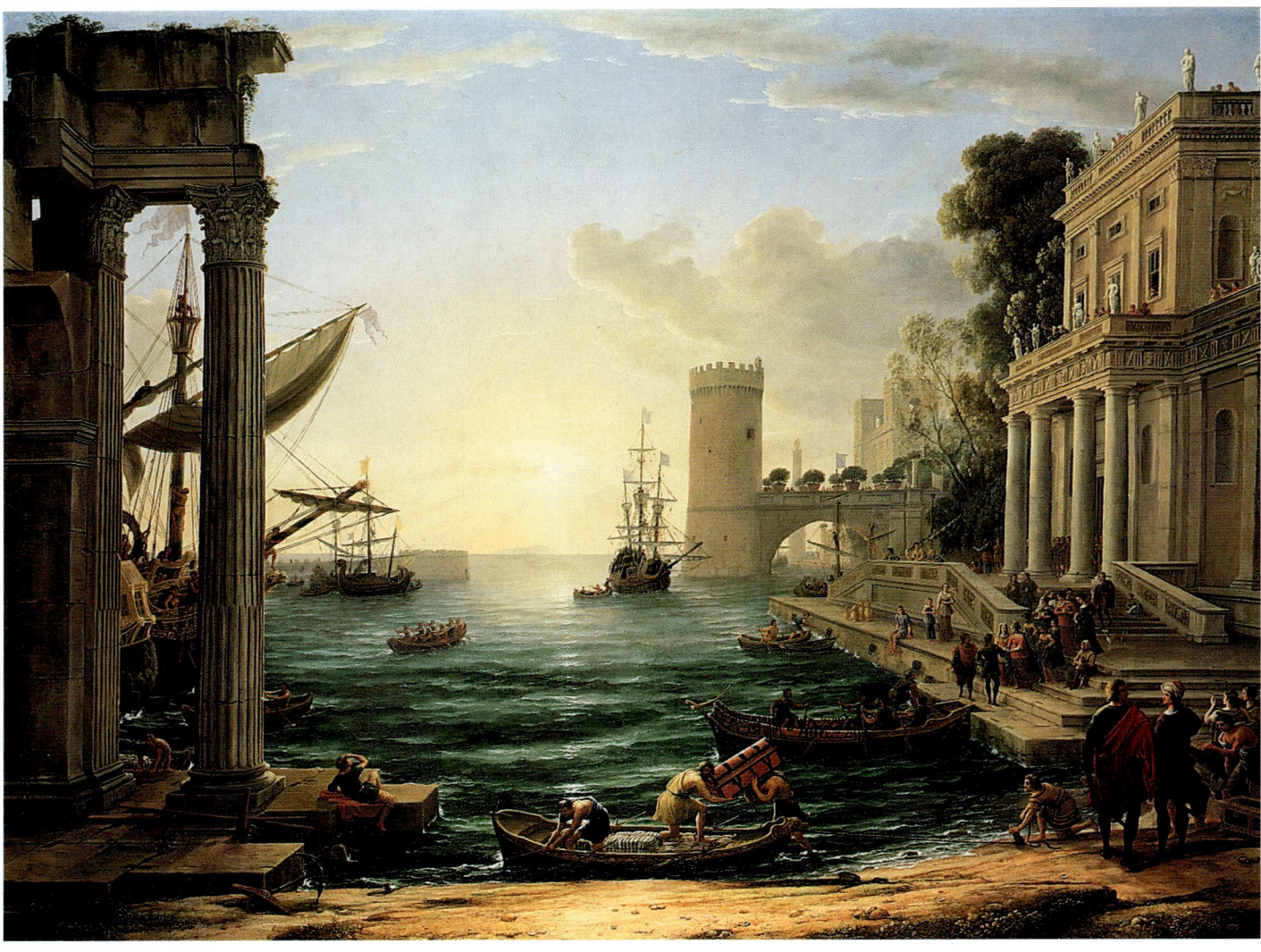

**Intro-11** CLAUDE LORRAIN, *Embarkation of the Queen of Sheba,* 1648. Oil on canvas, approx. 4′ 10″ × 6′ 4″. National Gallery, London.

as sculpture, pottery, or furniture. Volume and mass describe both the exterior and interior forms of a work of art—the forms of the matter of which it is composed and the spaces immediately around the work and interacting with it.

**PERSPECTIVE AND FORESHORTENING** *Perspective* is one of the most important pictorial devices for organizing forms in space. Throughout history, artists have used various types of perspective to create an illusion of depth or space on a two-dimensional surface. The French painter CLAUDE LORRAIN employed several perspectival devices in *Embarkation of the Queen of Sheba* (FIG. **Intro-11**), a painting of a biblical episode set in a 17th-century European harbor with a Roman ruin in the left foreground. For example, the figures and boats on the shoreline are much larger than those in the distance. Decreasing the size of an object makes it appear farther away from viewers. Also, the top and bottom of the port building at the painting's right side are not parallel horizontal lines, as they are in an actual building. Instead, the lines converge beyond the structure, leading viewers' eyes toward the hazy, indistinct sun on the horizon. These perspectival devices—the reduction of figure size, the convergence of diagonal lines, and the blurring of distant forms—have been familiar features of Western art since the ancient Greeks. But it is important to note at the outset that all kinds of perspective

are only pictorial conventions, even when one or more types of perspective may be so common in a given culture that they are accepted as "natural" or as "true" means of representing the natural world.

In *White and Red Plum Blossoms* (FIG. **Intro-12**), a Japanese landscape painting on two folding screens, OGATA KORIN used none of these Western perspective conventions. He showed the two plum trees as seen from a position on the ground, while viewers look down on the stream between them from above. Less concerned with locating the trees and stream in space than with composing shapes on a surface, the painter played the water's gently swelling curves against the jagged contours of the branches and trunks. Neither the French nor the Japanese painting can be said to project "correctly" what viewers "in fact" see. One painting is not a "better" picture of the world than the other. The European and Asian artists simply approached the problem of picture-making differently.

Artists also represent single figures in space in varying ways. When PETER PAUL RUBENS painted *Lion Hunt* (FIG. **Intro-13**) in the early 17th century, he used *foreshortening* for all the hunters and animals—that is, he represented their bodies at angles to the picture plane. When in life one views a figure at an angle, the body appears to contract as it extends back in space. Foreshortening is a kind of perspective. It produces the illusion that one part of the

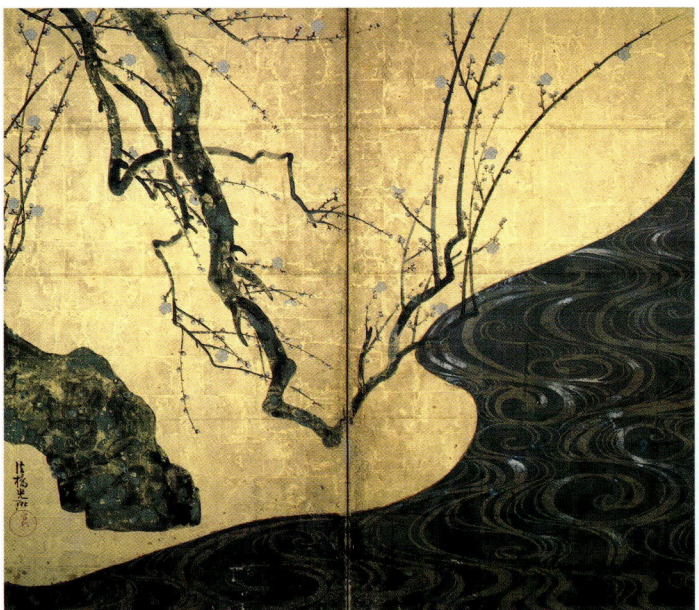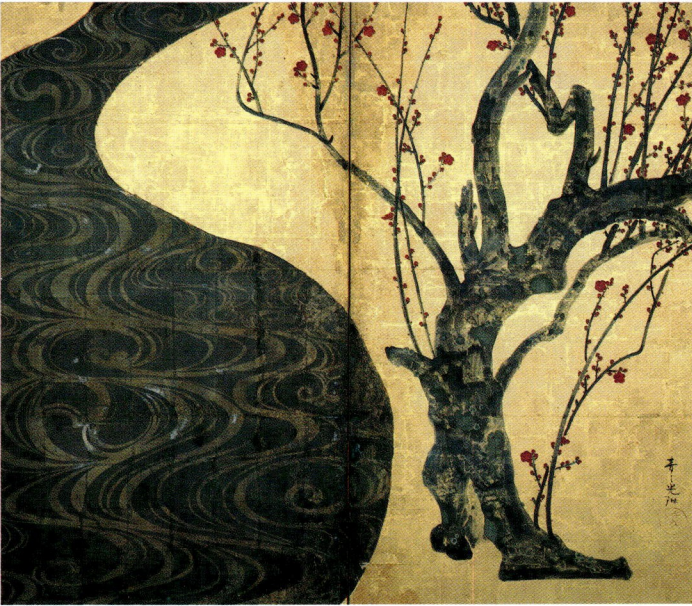

**Intro-12** OGATA KORIN, *White and Red Plum Blossoms,* Edo period, ca. 1710–1716. Pair of twofold screens. Ink, color, and gold leaf on paper, each screen 5′ 1$\frac{5}{8}$″ × 5′ 7$\frac{7}{8}$″. MOA Art Museum, Shizuoka-ken, Japan.

body is farther away than another, even though all the forms are on the same surface. Especially noteworthy in *Lion Hunt* are the gray horse at the left, seen from behind with the bottom of its left rear hoof facing viewers and most of its head hidden by its rider's shield, and the fallen hunter at the painting's lower right corner, whose barely visible legs and feet recede into the distance.

The artist who carved the portrait of the ancient Egyptian official Hesire (FIG. **Intro-14**) did not employ foreshortening. That artist's purpose was to present the various human body parts as clearly as possible, without overlapping. The lower part of Hesire's body is in profile to give the most complete view of the legs, with both the heels and toes of the foot visible. The frontal torso, however, allows viewers to see its full shape, including both shoulders, equal in size, as in nature. (Compare the shoulders of the hunter

on the gray horse or those of the fallen hunter in *Lion Hunt*'s left foreground.) The result, an "unnatural" 90-degree twist at the waist, provides a precise picture of human body parts. Rubens and the Egyptian sculptor used very different means of depicting forms in space. Once again, neither is the "correct" manner.

**PROPORTION AND SCALE** *Proportion* concerns the relationships (in terms of size) of the parts of persons, buildings, or objects. "Correct proportions" may be judged intuitively ("that statue's head seems the right size for the body"). Or proportion may be formalized as a mathematical relationship between the size of one part of an artwork or building and the other parts within the work. Proportion in art implies using a *module,* or basic unit of measure. When an artist or architect uses a formal

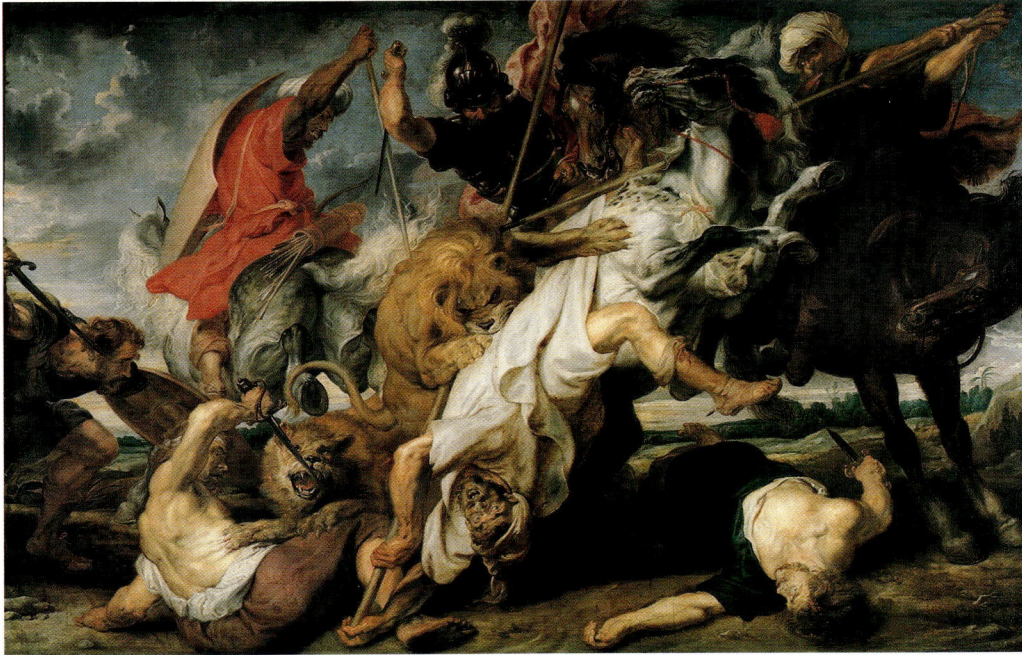

**Intro-13** PETER PAUL RUBENS, *Lion Hunt,* 1617–1618. Oil on canvas, approx. 8′ 2″ × 12′ 5″. Alte Pinakothek, Munich.

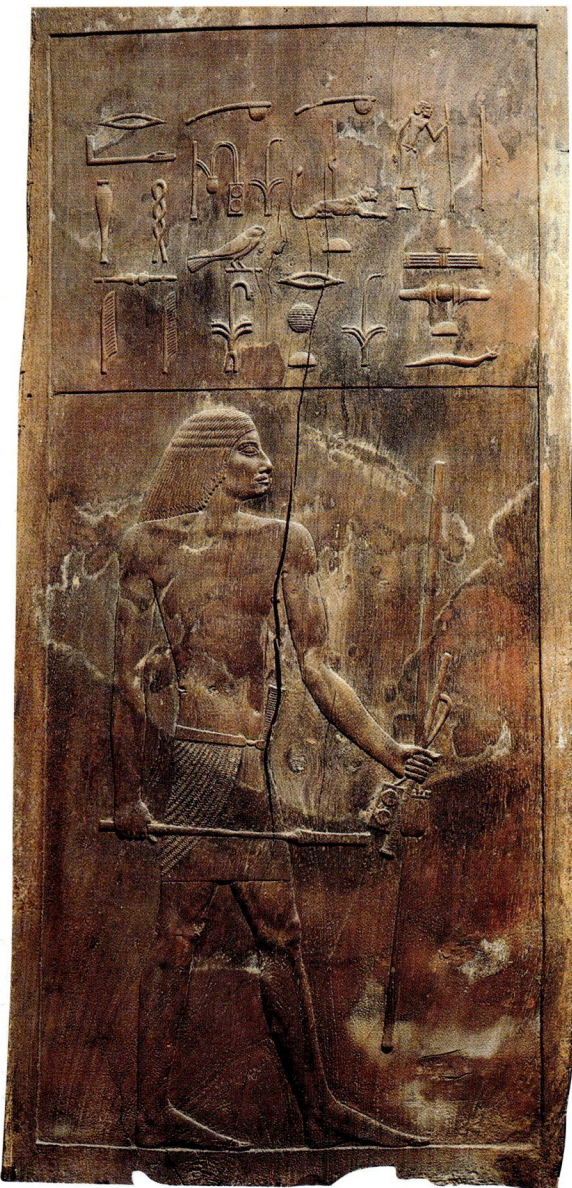

**Intro-14** Hesire, from his tomb at Saqqara, Egypt, Dynasty III, ca. 2650 BCE. Wood, approx. 3′ 9″ high. Egyptian Museum, Cairo.

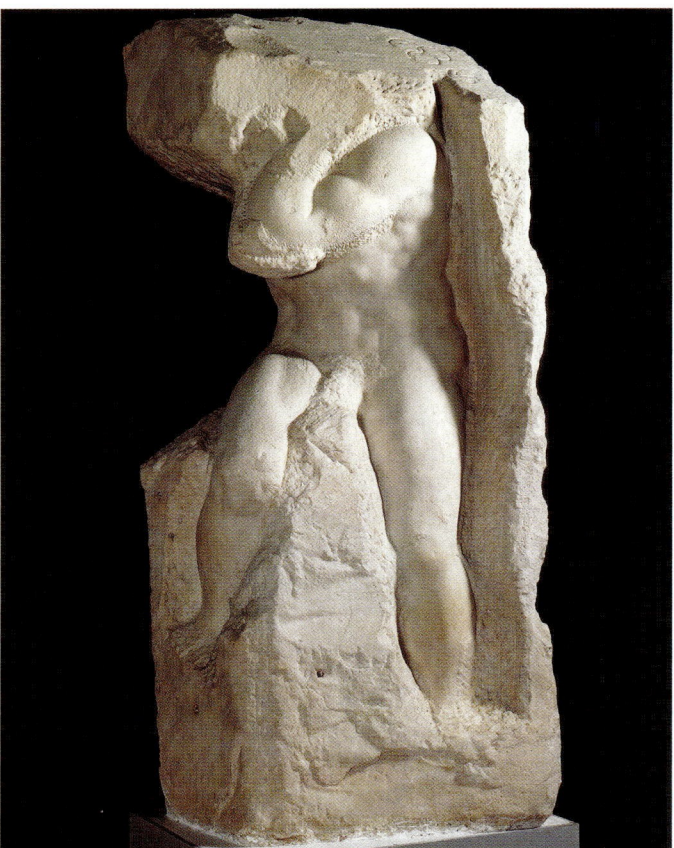

**Intro-15** MICHELANGELO, unfinished captive, 1527–1528. Marble, 8′ 7½″ high. Accademia, Florence.

system of proportions, all parts of a building, body, or other entity will be fractions or multiples of the module. A module might be a column's diameter, the height of a human head, or any other component whose dimensions can be multiplied or divided to determine the size of the work's other parts.

In certain times and places, artists have formulated *canons,* or systems, of "correct" or "ideal" proportions for representing human figures, constituent parts of buildings, and so forth. In ancient Greece, many sculptors formulated canons of proportions so strict and all-encompassing that they calculated the size of every body part in advance, even the fingers and toes, according to mathematical ratios. The ideal of human beauty the Greeks created based on "correct" proportions influenced the work of countless later artists in the Western world (for example, FIG. **Intro-15**) and endures to this day. Proportional systems can differ sharply from period to period, culture to culture, and artist to artist. Part of the task art history students face is to perceive and adjust to these differences.

In fact, many artists have used *disproportion* and distortion deliberately for expressive effect. In the medieval French depiction of the weighing of souls on Judgment Day (FIG. Intro-6), the devilish figure yanking down on the scale has distorted facial features and stretched, lined limbs with animal-like paws for feet. Disproportion and distortion make him appear "inhuman," precisely as the sculptor intended.

In other cases, artists have used disproportion to focus attention on one body part (often the head) or to single out a group member (usually the leader). These intentional "unnatural" discrepancies in proportion constitute what art historians call *hierarchy of scale,* the enlarging of elements considered the most important. On a bronze plaque from Benin, Nigeria (FIG. **Intro-16**), the sculptor enlarged all the heads for emphasis and also varied the size of each figure according to its social status. Central, largest, and therefore most important is the Benin king, mounted on horseback. The horse has been a symbol of power and wealth in many societies from prehistory to the present. That the Benin king is disproportionately larger than his horse, contrary to nature, further aggrandizes him. Two large attendants fan the king. Other figures of smaller size and status at the Benin court stand on the king's left and right and in the plaque's upper corners. One tiny figure next to the horse is almost hidden from view beneath the king's feet.

**CARVING AND CASTING** Sculptural technique falls into two basic categories, *subtractive* and *additive. Carving* is a subtractive technique. The final form is a reduction of the original mass of a

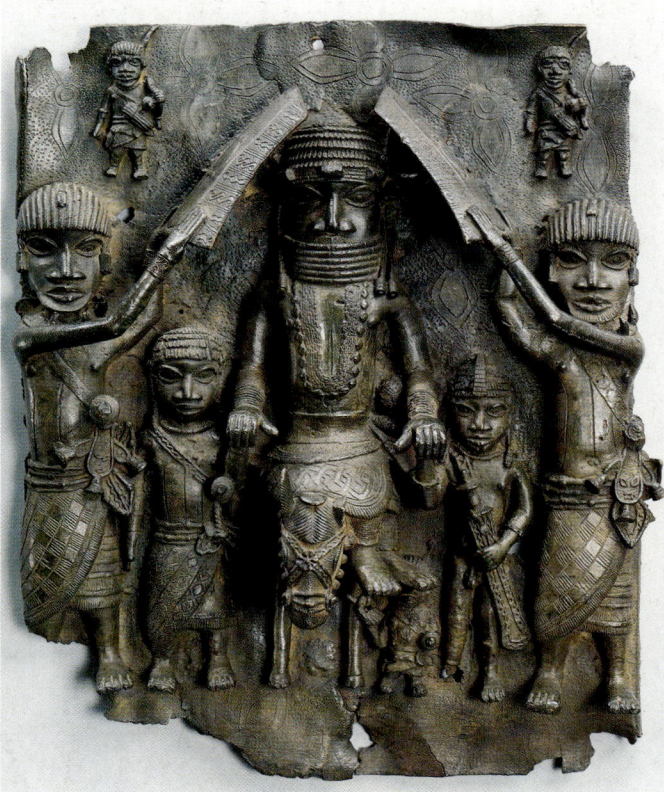

**Intro-16** King on horseback with attendants, from Benin, Nigeria, ca. 1550–1680. Bronze, 1′ 7½″ high. Metropolitan Museum of Art, New York (Michael C. Rockefeller Memorial Collection, gift of Nelson A. Rockefeller).

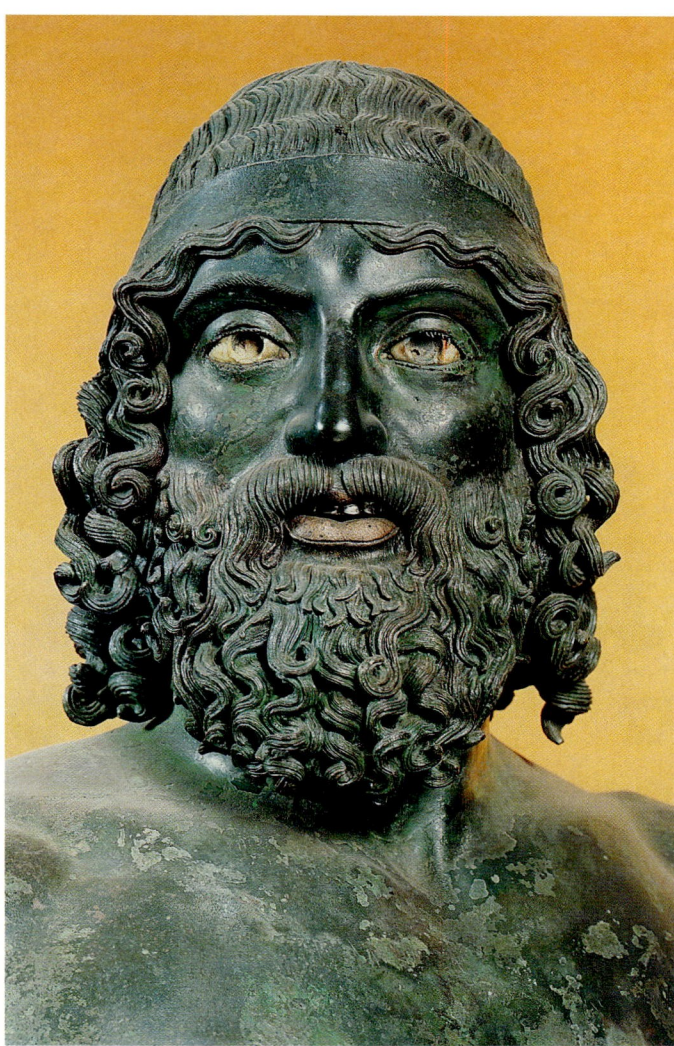

**Intro-17** Head of a warrior, detail of a statue from the sea off Riace, Italy, ca. 460–450 BCE. Bronze, statue approx. 6′ 6″ high. Archaeological Museum, Reggio Calabria.

block of stone, a piece of wood, or another material. Wooden statues were once tree trunks, and stone statues began as blocks pried from mountains. In an unfinished 16th-century marble statue of a bound slave (FIG. Intro-15) by MICHELANGELO, the original shape of the stone block is still visible. Michelangelo thought of sculpture as a process of "liberating" the statue within the block. All sculptors of stone or wood cut away (subtract) "excess material." When they finish, they "leave behind" the statue—in our example, a twisting nude male form whose head Michelangelo never freed from the stone block.

In additive sculpture, the artist builds up the forms, usually in clay around a framework, or *armature.* Or a sculptor may fashion a *mold,* a hollow form for shaping, or *casting,* a fluid substance such as bronze. The ancient Greek sculptor who made the bronze statue of a warrior found in the sea near Riace, Italy, cast the head (FIG. **Intro-17**), limbs, torso, hands, and feet in separate molds and then *welded* them (joined them by heating). Finally, the artist added features, such as the pupils of the eyes (now missing), in other materials. The warrior's teeth are silver, and his lower lip is copper.

RELIEF SCULPTURE Statues or busts that exist independent of any architectural frame or setting and that viewers can walk around are *freestanding* sculptures, or *sculptures in the round,* whether the piece was carved (FIG. Intro-9) or cast (FIG. Intro-17). In *relief sculptures,* the subjects project from the background but remain part of it. In *high relief* sculpture, the images project boldly. In some cases, such as the weighing-of-souls relief at Autun (FIG. Intro-6), the relief is so high that not only do the forms

cast shadows on the background, but some parts are actually in the round. The arms of the scale are fully detached from the background in places—which explains why some pieces broke off centuries ago. In *low relief,* or *bas-relief,* such as the wooden relief of Hesire (FIG. Intro-14), the projection is slight. In a variation of both techniques, *sunken relief,* the sculptor cuts the design into the surface so that the image's highest projecting parts are no higher than the surface itself. Relief sculpture, like sculpture in the round, can be produced either by carving or casting. The plaque from Benin (FIG. Intro-16) is an example of bronze casting in high relief. Artists also can make reliefs by hammering a sheet of metal from behind, pushing the subject out from the background in a technique called *repoussé.*

ARCHITECTURAL DRAWINGS Buildings are groupings of enclosed spaces and enclosing masses. People experience architecture both visually and by moving through and around it, so they perceive architectural space and mass together. These spaces and masses can be represented graphically in several ways, including as plans, sections, elevations, and cutaway drawings.

A *plan,* essentially a map of a floor, shows the placement of a structure's masses and, therefore, the spaces they bound and

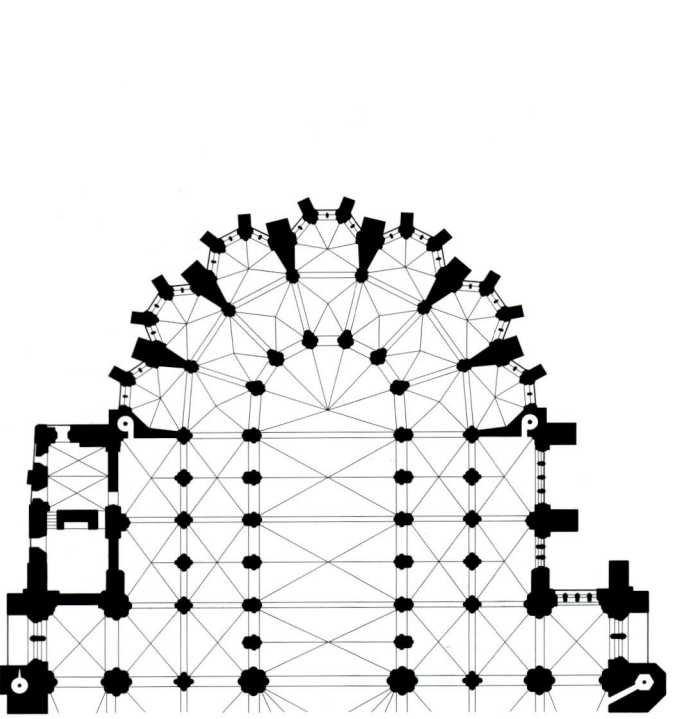
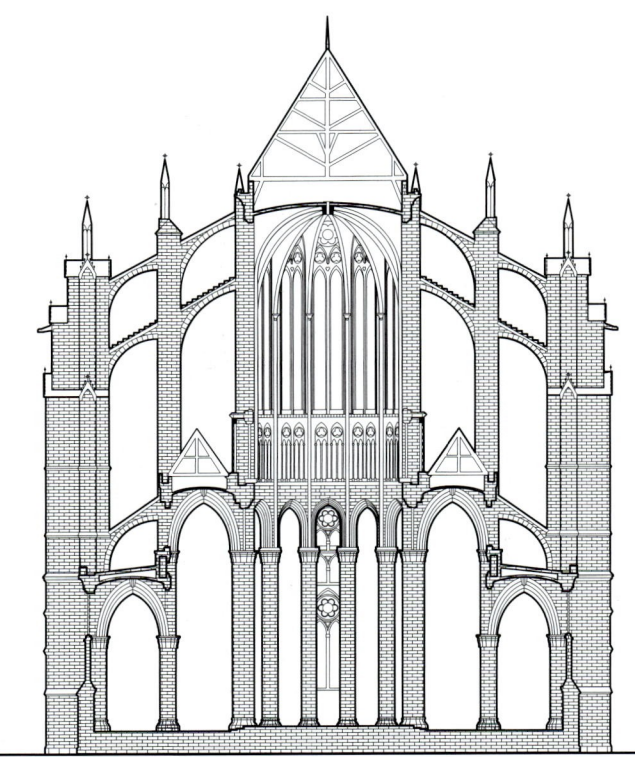

**Intro-18** Plan *(left)* and lateral section *(right)* of Beauvais Cathedral, Beauvais, France, rebuilt after 1284.

enclose. A *section*, like a vertical plan, depicts the placement of the masses as if the building were cut through along a plane. Drawings showing a theoretical slice across a structure's width are *lateral sections*. Those cutting through a building's length are *longitudinal sections*. Illustrated here are the plan and lateral section of Beauvais Cathedral (FIG. **Intro-18**), which may be compared to the photograph of the church's choir (FIG. Intro-2). The plan shows not only the choir's shape and the location of the piers dividing the aisles and supporting the vaults above but also the pattern of the crisscrossing vault *ribs*. The lateral section shows not only the interior of the choir with its vaults and tall stained-glass windows but also the structure of the roof and the form of the exterior *buttresses* that hold the vaults in place.

Other types of architectural drawings appear throughout this book. An *elevation* drawing is a head-on view of an external or internal wall. A *cutaway* combines an exterior view with an interior view of part of a building in a single drawing.

This overview of the art historian's vocabulary is not exhaustive, nor have artists used only painting, drawing, sculpture, and architecture as media over the millennia. Ceramics, jewelry, textiles, photography, and computer art are just some of the numerous other arts. All of them involve highly specialized techniques described in distinct vocabularies. These are considered and defined where they arise in the text.

## Art History and Other Disciplines

By its very nature, the work of art historians intersects with that of others in many fields of knowledge, not only in the humanities but also in the social and natural sciences. To "do their job" well

today, art historians regularly must go beyond the boundaries of what the public and even professional art historians of previous generations traditionally have considered the specialized discipline of art history. Art historical research in the 21st century is frequently *interdisciplinary* in nature. To cite one example, in an effort to unlock the secrets of a particular statue, an art historian might conduct archival research hoping to uncover new documents shedding light on who paid for the work and why, who made it and when, where it originally stood, how its contemporaries viewed it, and a host of other questions. Realizing, however, that the authors of the written documents often were not objective recorders of fact but observers with their own biases and agendas, the art historian may also use methodologies developed in such fields as literary criticism, philosophy, sociology, and gender studies to weigh the evidence the documents provide.

At other times, rather than attempting to master many disciplines at once, art historians band together with other specialists in *multidisciplinary* inquiries. Art historians might call in chemists to date an artwork based on the composition of the materials used or might ask geologists to determine which quarry furnished the stone for a particular statue. X-ray technicians might be enlisted in an attempt to establish whether or not a painting is a forgery. Of course, art historians often contribute their expertise to the solution of problems in other disciplines. A historian, for example, might ask an art historian to determine—based on style, material, iconography, and other criteria—if any of the portraits of a certain king were made after his death. That would help establish the ruler's continuing prestige during the reigns of his successors. (Some portraits of Augustus, FIG. Intro-9, the founder of the Roman Empire, postdate his death by decades, even centuries.)

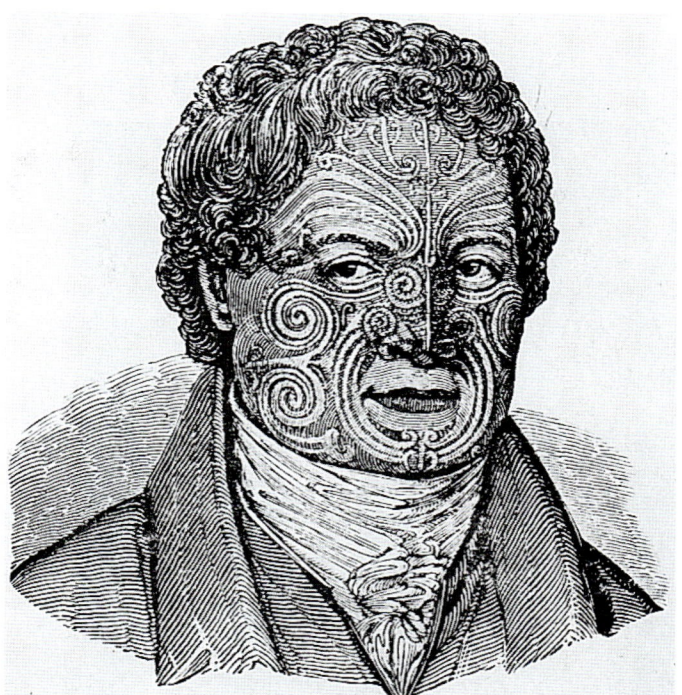
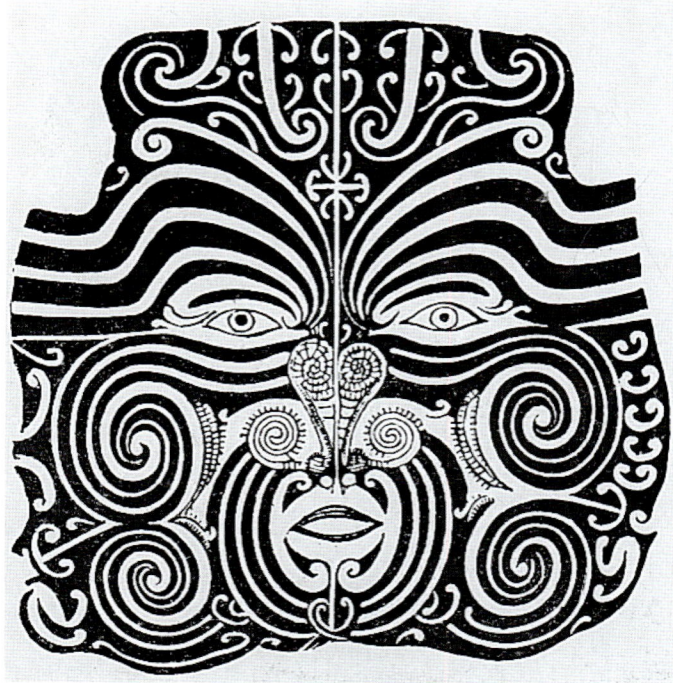

**Intro-19** JOHN SYLVESTER *(left)* and TE PEHI KUPE *(right),* portraits of Maori chief Te Pehi Kupe, 1826. From *The Childhood of Man,* by Leo Frobenius (New York: J. B. Lippincott, 1909).

# DIFFERENT WAYS OF SEEING

The history of art can be a history of artists and their works, of styles and stylistic change, of materials and techniques, of images and themes and their meanings, and of contexts and cultures and patrons. The best art historians analyze artworks from many viewpoints. But no art historian (or scholar in any other field), no matter how broad-minded in approach and no matter how experienced, can be truly objective. Like artists, art historians are members of a society, participants in its culture. How can scholars (and museum visitors and travelers to foreign locales) comprehend cultures unlike their own? They can try to reconstruct the original cultural contexts of artworks, but they are bound to be limited by their distance from the thought patterns of the cultures they study and by the obstructions to understanding — the assumptions, presuppositions, and prejudices peculiar to their own culture — their own thought patterns raise. Art historians may reconstruct a distorted picture of the past because of culture-bound blindness.

A single instance underscores how differently people of diverse cultures view the world and how various ways of seeing can cause sharp differences in how artists depict the world. We illustrate two contemporaneous portraits of a 19th-century Maori chieftain side by side (FIG. **Intro-19**) — one by an Englishman, JOHN SYLVESTER, and the other by the New Zealand chieftain himself, TE PEHI KUPE. Both reproduce the chieftain's facial tattooing. The European artist included the head and shoulders and underplayed the tattooing. The tattoo pattern is one aspect of the likeness among many, no more or less important than the chieftain's dressing like a European. Sylvester also recorded his subject's momentary glance toward the right and the play of light on his hair, fleeting aspects that have nothing to do with the figure's identity.

In contrast, Te Pehi Kupe's self-portrait — made during a trip to Liverpool, England, to obtain European arms to take back to New Zealand — is not a picture of a man situated in space and bathed in light. Rather, it is the chieftain's statement of the supreme importance of the tattoo design that symbolizes his rank among his people. Remarkably, Te Pehi Kupe created the tattoo patterns from memory, without the aid of a mirror. The splendidly composed insignia, presented as a flat design separated from the body and even from the head, is Te Pehi Kupe's image of himself. Only by understanding the cultural context of each portrait can viewers hope to understand why either looks the way it does.

As noted at the outset, the study of the context of artworks and buildings is one of the central aims of art history. Our purpose in writing *Art through the Ages* is to present a history of art and architecture that will help you understand not only the subjects, styles, and techniques of paintings, sculptures, buildings, and other art forms created in all parts of the world for 30 millennia but also their cultural and historical contexts. That story now begins.

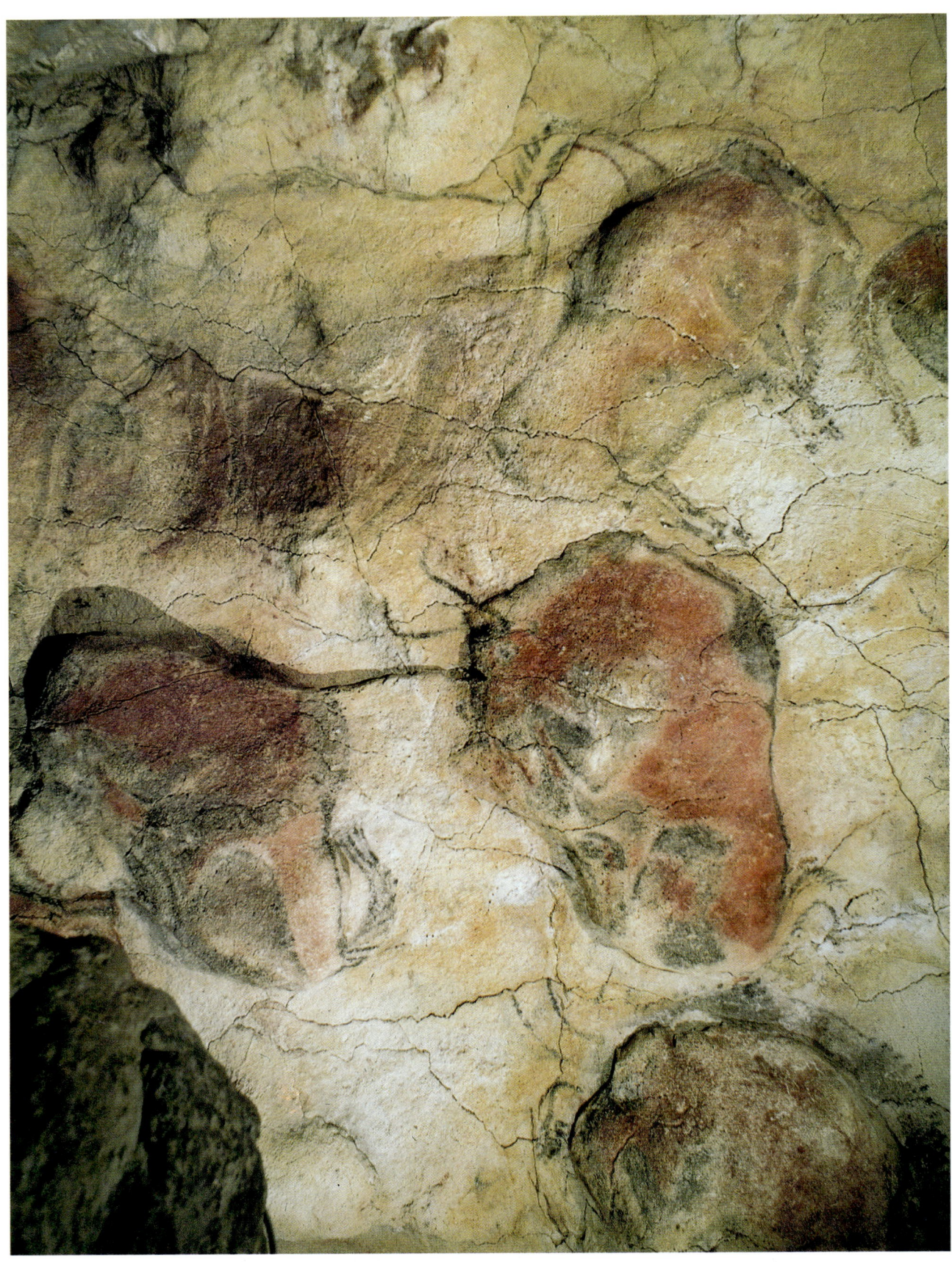

Bison, detail of a painted ceiling in the Altamira cave, Santander, Spain, ca. 12,000–11,000 BCE. Each bison approx. 5′ long.

# 1

# THE BIRTH OF ART

## AFRICA, EUROPE, AND THE NEAR EAST IN THE STONE AGE

Humankind seems to have originated in Africa in the very remote past. From that great continent also comes the earliest evidence of human recognition of abstract images in the natural environment, if not the first examples of what people generally call "art." In 1925, explorers of a cave at Makapansgat in South Africa (see MAP 15-1) discovered bones of *Australopithecus,* a predecessor of modern humans who lived some three million years ago. Associated with the bones was a waterworn reddish brown jasperite pebble (FIG. **1-1**) that bears an uncanny resemblance to a human face. The nearest known source of this variety of ironstone is 20 miles away from the cave. One of the early humans who took refuge in the rock shelter at Makapansgat must have noticed the pebble in a streambed and, awestruck by the "face" on the stone, brought it back for safekeeping.

Is the Makapansgat pebble art? In modern times, many artists have created works people universally consider art by removing objects from their normal contexts, altering them, and then labeling them. In 1917, for example, Marcel Duchamp took a ceramic urinal, set it on its side, called it *Fountain* (see FIG. 33-23), and declared his "ready-made" worthy of exhibition among more conventional artworks. But the artistic environment of the past century cannot be projected into the remote past. For art historians to declare a found object such as the Makapansgat pebble an "artwork," it must have been modified by human intervention beyond mere selection—and it was not. In fact, evidence indicates that, with few exceptions, it was not until three million years later, around 30,000 BCE, that humans *intentionally manufactured* sculptures and paintings. That is when the story of art through the ages really begins.

## PALEOLITHIC ART

The several millennia following 30,000 BCE saw a powerful outburst of creativity. The works produced by the peoples of the Old Stone Age or *Paleolithic* period (from the Greek *paleo,* "old," and *lithos,* "stone") are of an astonishing variety. They range from

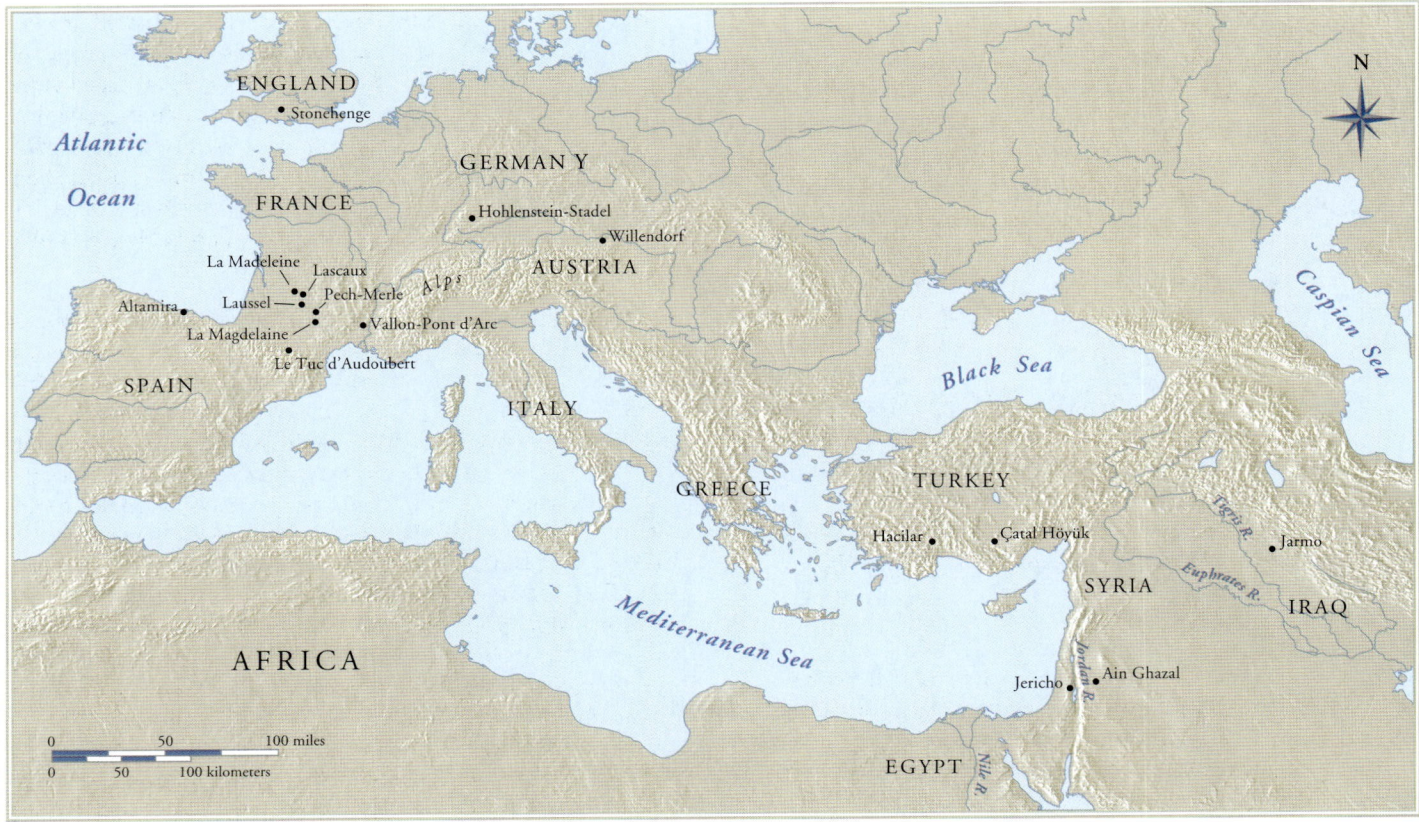

**MAP 1-1** Prehistoric Europe and the Near East.

simple shell necklaces to human and animal forms in ivory, clay, and stone to monumental paintings, engravings, and relief sculptures covering the huge wall surfaces of caves. During the Paleolithic period, humankind went beyond the *recognition* of human and animal forms in the natural environment to the *representation* (literally, the presenting again—in different and substitute form—of something observed) of humans and animals. The immensity of this achievement cannot be exaggerated.

## Africa

**NAMIBIAN ANIMALS** Some of the earliest paintings yet discovered come from Africa, and, like the treasured pebble in the form of a face found at Makapansgat, the oldest African paintings were portable objects. Between 1969 and 1972, scientists working in the Apollo 11 Cave in Namibia (see MAP 15-1) found seven fragments of stone plaques with paint on them, including four or five recognizable images of animals. In most cases, including the example we illustrate (FIG. **1-2**), the species is uncertain, but the forms are always carefully rendered. One plaque depicts a striped beast, possibly a zebra. The charcoal from the archaeological layer in which the Namibian plaques were found has been dated to around 23,000 BCE.

Like every artist in every age in every medium, the painter of the Apollo 11 plaque had to answer two questions before beginning work: *What* shall be my subject? *How* shall I represent it? In Paleolithic art, the almost universal answer to the first question was an animal—bison, mammoth, ibex, and horse were most common. In fact, Paleolithic painters and sculptors depicted humans infrequently and men almost never. In equally stark contrast to today's world, there was also agreement on the best answer to the second question. Virtually every animal in every Paleolithic, *Mesolithic* (Middle Stone Age), and *Neolithic* (New Stone Age) painting was presented in the same manner—in strict profile. The profile is the only view of an animal wherein the head, body, tail, and all four legs can be seen. A frontal view would have concealed most of the body,

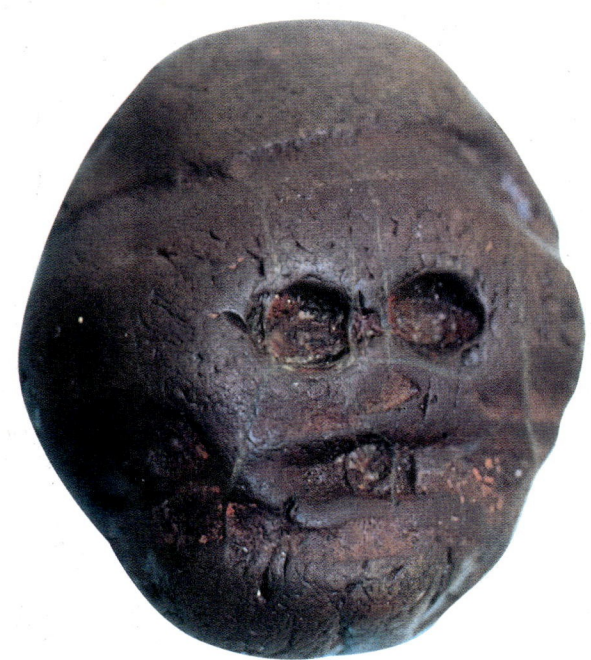

**1-1** Waterworn pebble resembling a human face, from Makapansgat, South Africa, ca. 3,000,000 BCE. Reddish brown jasperite, approx. $2\frac{3}{8}''$ wide.

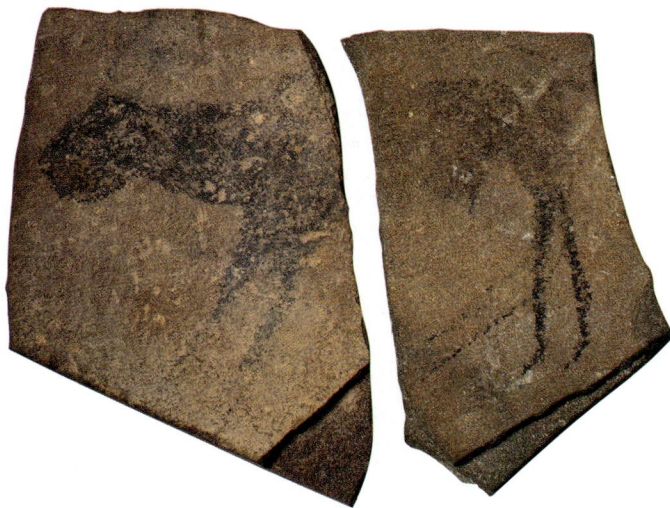

**1-2** Animal facing left, from the Apollo 11 Cave, Namibia, ca. 23,000 BCE. Charcoal on stone, approx. 5″ × 4¼″. State Museum of Namibia, Windhoek.

and a three-quarter view would not have shown either the front or side fully. Only the profile view is completely informative about the animal's shape, and this is why the Stone Age painter always chose it. A very long time passed before artists placed any premium on "variety" or "originality," either in subject choice or in representational manner. These are quite modern notions in the history of art. The aim of the earliest painters was to create a convincing image of the subject, a kind of pictorial definition of the animal capturing its very essence, and only the profile view met their needs.

## Western Europe

**EUROPE'S FIRST SCULPTURES** Even older than the Namibian painted plaques are some of the first sculptures and paintings of western Europe (MAP 1-1), although examples of still greater antiquity may yet be found in Africa, bridging the gap between the Makapansgat pebble and the Apollo 11 painted plaques. One of the earliest sculptures discovered to date is an extraordinary ivory statuette (FIG. 1-3), which may be as old as 30,000 BCE, from a cave at Hohlenstein-Stadel in Germany. Carved out of mammoth ivory and nearly a foot tall—a truly huge image for its era—the statuette represents something that existed only in the vivid imagination of the unknown sculptor who conceived it. It is a human (whether male or female is debated) with a feline head.

Such composite creatures with animal heads and human bodies (and vice versa) were common in the art of the ancient Near East and Egypt (compare, for example, FIGS. 2-10 and 3-39). In those civilizations, surviving texts usually allow historians to name the figures and describe their role in contemporary religion and mythology. But for Stone Age representations, no one knows what their makers had in mind. The animal-headed humans of Paleolithic art sometimes have been called sorcerers and described as magicians wearing masks. Similarly, Paleolithic human-headed animals have been interpreted as humans dressed up as animals. In the absence of any Stone Age written explanations—this is a time before writing, before (or *pre-*) history—researchers can only speculate on the purpose and function of a statuette such as that from Hohlenstein-Stadel.

Art historians are certain, however, that such statuettes were important to those who created them, because manufacturing an ivory figure, especially one a foot tall, was a complicated process. First, a tusk had to be removed from the dead animal by cutting into the ivory where it joined the head. The sculptor then cut the tusk to the desired size and rubbed it into its approximate final shape with sandstone. Finally, a sharp stone blade was used to carve the body, limbs, and head, and a stone *burin* (a pointed engraving tool) to *incise* (scratch) lines into the surfaces, as on the Hohlenstein-Stadel creature's arms. All this probably required at least several days of skilled work.

**WOMEN IN PALEOLITHIC ART** The composite feline-human from Germany is exceptional for the Stone Age. The vast majority of prehistoric sculptures depict either animals or humans. In the earliest art, humankind consists almost exclusively of women as opposed to men, and the painters and sculptors almost invariably showed them nude, although scholars generally assume that in life both women and men wore garments covering parts of their bodies. When archaeologists first discovered Paleolithic statuettes of women, they dubbed them "Venuses," after the Greco-Roman goddess of beauty and love, whom artists usually depicted nude (see FIG. 5-60). The nickname is inappropriate and misleading. Not only does no evidence exist for named gods and goddesses in human form during the Old Stone Age, but also it is doubtful these figurines represented deities of any kind.

One of the oldest and the most famous of the prehistoric female figures is the tiny (only slightly more than four inches tall) limestone figurine of a woman that long has been known as the

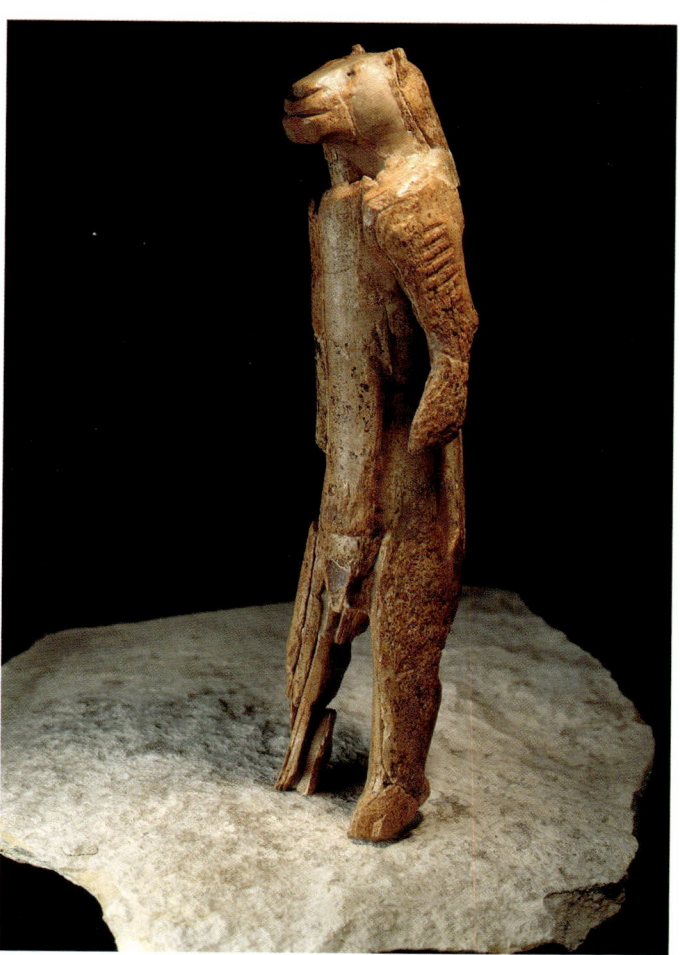

**1-3** Human with feline head, from Hohlenstein-Stadel, Germany, ca. 30,000–28,000 BCE. Mammoth ivory, 11⅝″ high. Ulmer Museum, Ulm.

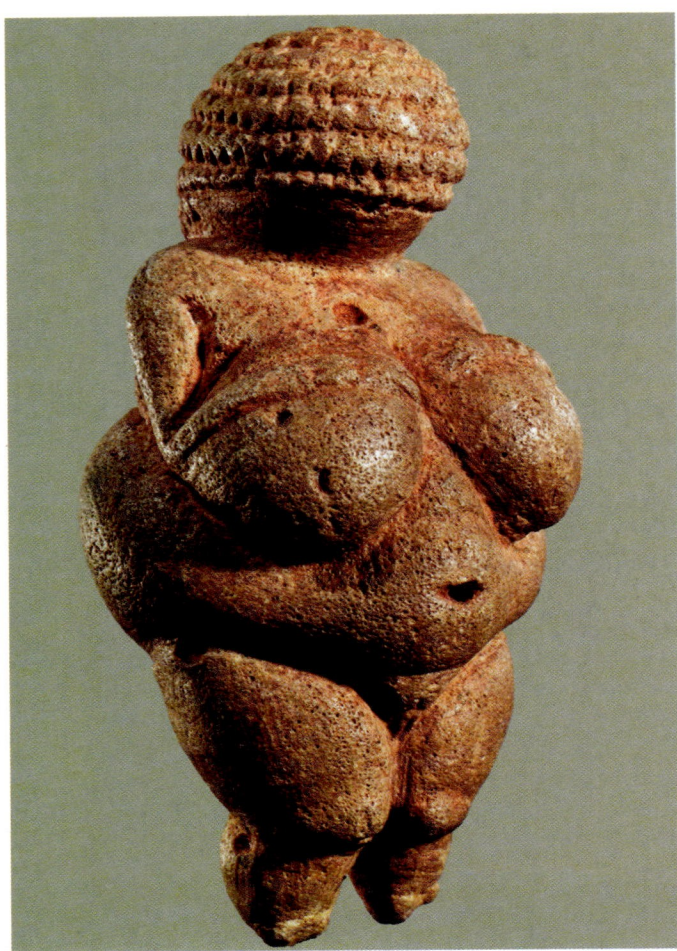

specific than assigning a range of several thousand years to each artifact. But probably later in date than the *Venus of Willendorf* is another female figure (FIG. **1-5**), from Laussel in France. The Willendorf and Hohlenstein-Stadel figures were sculpted in the round (that is, they are freestanding objects). The Laussel woman is one of the earliest relief sculptures known. The sculptor employed a stone chisel to cut into the relatively flat surface of a large rock and create an image that projects from its background.

Today the Laussel relief is exhibited in a museum, divorced from its original context, a detached piece of what once was a much more imposing monument. When the relief was discovered, the Laussel woman (who is about $1\frac{1}{2}$ feet tall, much larger than the Willendorf statuette) was part of a great stone block that measured about 140 cubic feet. The carved block stood in the open air in front of a Paleolithic rock shelter. Such shelters were a common type of dwelling for early humans, along with huts and the mouths of caves. The Laussel relief is one of many examples of open-air art in the Old Stone Age. The popular notions that early humans dwelled exclusively in caves and that all Paleolithic art comes from mysterious dark caverns are false.

After chiseling out the female form and etching the details with a sharp burin, the Laussel sculptor applied red ocher to the body. (The same color is also preserved on parts of the *Venus of Willendorf.*) Contrary to modern misconceptions about ancient art, stone sculptures were frequently painted in antiquity, not only in prehistoric times and in the ancient Near East and Egypt

**1-4** Nude woman *(Venus of Willendorf),* from Willendorf, Austria, ca. 28,000 – 25,000 BCE. Limestone, approx. $4\frac{1}{4}''$ high. Naturhistorisches Museum, Vienna.

*Venus of Willendorf* (FIG. **1-4**) after its findspot in Austria. Its cluster of almost ball-like shapes is unusual, the result in part of the sculptor's response to the natural shape of the stone selected for carving. The anatomical exaggeration has suggested to many that this and similar statuettes served as fertility images. But other Paleolithic stone women of far more slender proportions exist, and the meaning of these images is as elusive as everything else about Paleolithic art. Yet the preponderance of female over male figures in the Old Stone Age seems to indicate a preoccupation with women, whose child-bearing capabilities ensured the survival of the species.

One thing at least is clear. The *Venus of Willendorf* sculptor did not aim for naturalism in shape and proportion. As with most Paleolithic figures, the sculptor did not carve any facial features. Here the carver suggested only a mass of curly hair or, as some researchers have recently argued, a hat woven from plant fibers — evidence for the art of textile manufacture at a very early date. In either case, the emphasis is on female fertility. The breasts of the Willendorf woman are enormous, far larger than the tiny forearms and hands that rest upon them. The carver also took pains to scratch into the stone the outline of the pubic triangle. Sculptors often omitted this detail in other early figurines, leading some scholars to question the nature of these figures as fertility images. Whatever the purpose of such statuettes, the makers' intent seems to have been to represent not a specific woman but the female form.

**THE LAUSSEL SHELTER** Because precision in dating is impossible for the Paleolithic era, art historians usually can be no more

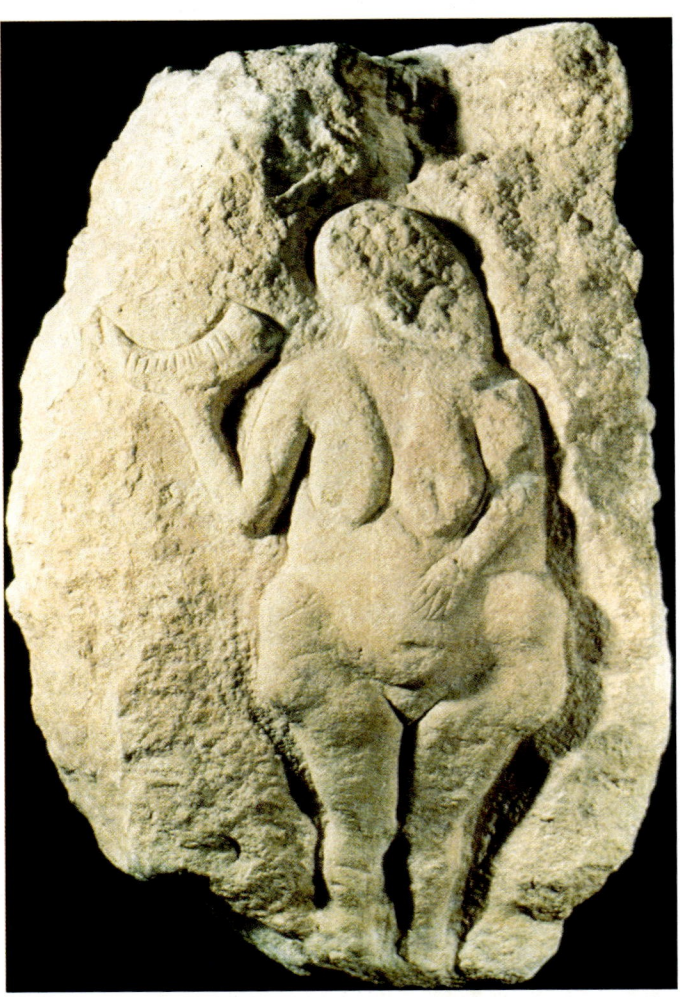

**1-5** Woman holding a bison horn, from Laussel, Dordogne, France, ca. 25,000 – 20,000 BCE. Painted limestone, approx. 1' 6" high. Musée d'Aquitaine, Bordeaux.

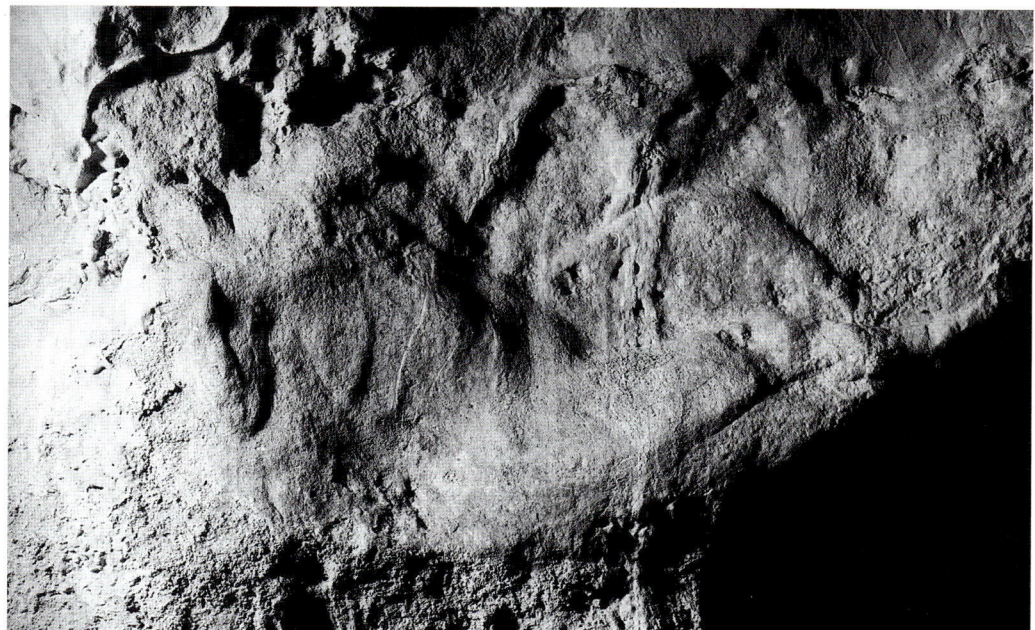

but in the Greco-Roman era as well. The Laussel woman has the same bulbous forms as the earlier Willendorf figurine, with a similar exaggeration of the breasts, abdomen, and hips. The head is once again featureless, but the arms have taken on greater importance. The left arm draws attention to the midsection and pubic area, and the raised right hand holds a bison horn. The meaning of the horn is debated.

**ROCK-CUT WOMEN** At La Magdelaine in France, archaeologists have discovered relief sculptures of nude women on cave walls. The rock-cut reliefs are about half life-size. The example we illustrate (FIG. 1-6) is typical of many Paleolithic reliefs in that the sculptor used the natural contours of the stone wall as the basis for the representation. Old Stone Age painters and sculptors frequently and skillfully used the caves' naturally irregular surfaces—the projections, recessions, fissures, and ridges—to help give the illusion of real presence to their forms. Once

an appropriate rock formation was selected, the sculptor then accentuated the outlines and added internal details to the figure with a stone chisel. The La Magdelaine woman reclines with extended arms and her left leg crossed over her right one. She lacks a head, but the sculptor carefully delineated her large breasts and pubic triangle.

**CLAY BISON** Other Paleolithic sculptors created reliefs by building up forms out of clay rather than by cutting into stone blocks or stone walls. Sometime 12,000 to 17,000 years ago in the low-ceilinged circular space at the end of a succession of cave chambers at Le Tuc d'Audoubert, a master sculptor modeled a pair of bison in clay against a large, irregular freestanding rock (FIG. 1-7). The two bison, like the much older painted animal from the Apollo 11 Cave in Namibia (FIG. 1-2), are in strict profile. Each is about two feet long. They are among the largest Paleolithic sculptures known. The sculptor brought the clay from

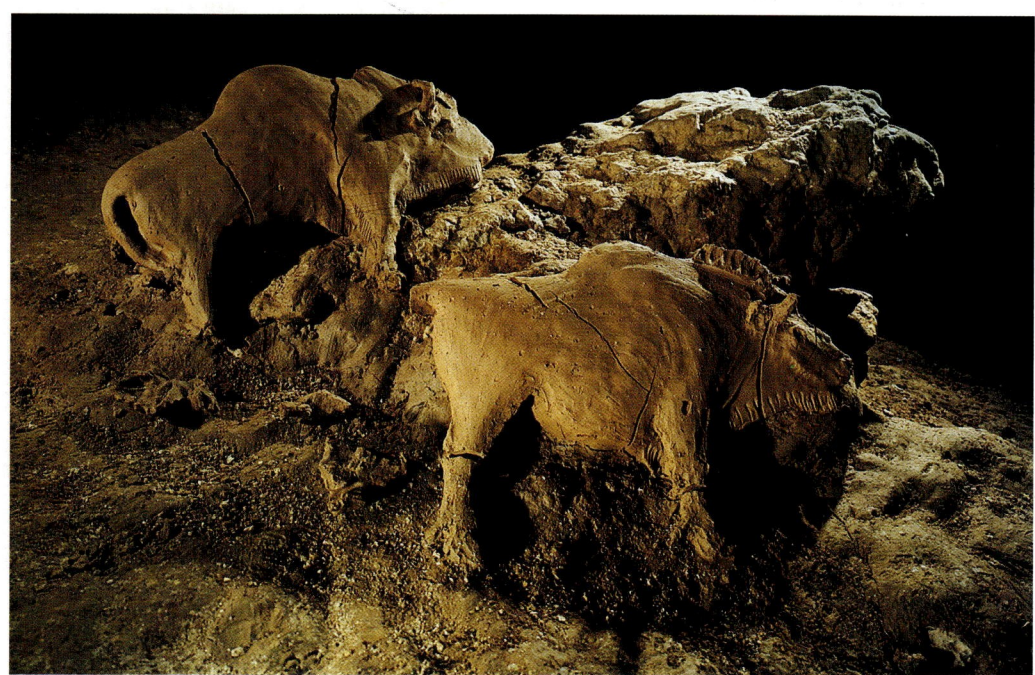

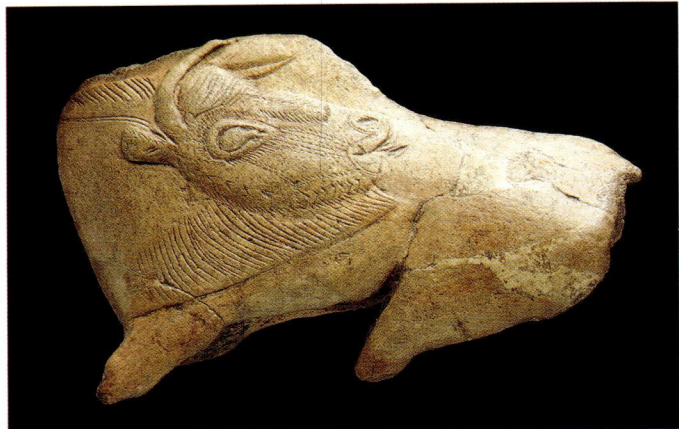

**1-8** Bison with turned head, fragmentary spearthrower, from La Madeleine, Dordogne, France, ca. 12,000 BCE. Reindeer horn, approx. 4″ long. Réunion des Musées Nationaux.

another chamber in the cave complex and modeled it by hand into the overall shape of the animals. The artist then smoothed the surfaces with a spatula-like tool and finally used fingers to shape the eyes, nostrils, mouths, and manes. The cracks in the two animals resulted from the drying process and probably appeared within days of the sculptures' completion.

**ANTLER SCULPTURE** As already noted, sculptors fashioned ivory mammoth tusks into human and animal forms from very early times (FIG. 1-3). Prehistoric carvers also used antlers as a sculptural medium, even though it meant they were forced to work on a very small scale. Our example (FIG. **1-8**), found at La Madeleine in France, is a broken spearthrower in the form of a bison. It is only four inches long and was carved from reindeer antler. The sculptor incised lines into the bison's mane using a sharp burin. Compared to the bison in the cave at Le Tuc d'Audoubert (FIG. 1-7), the engraving is much more detailed and extends to the horns, eye, ear, nostrils, mouth, and the hair on the face. Especially interesting is the engraver's decision to represent the bison with the head turned. The small size of the reindeer horn may have been the motivation for this space-saving device. Whatever the reason, it is noteworthy that the sculptor turned the neck a full 180 degrees to maintain the strict profile Paleolithic sculptors and painters insisted on for the sake of clarity and completeness.

**THE DISCOVERY OF ALTAMIRA** The works examined here thus far, whether portable or fixed to rocky outcroppings or cave walls, are all small. They are dwarfed by the "herds" of painted animals that roam the cave walls of southern France and northern Spain, where some of the most spectacular prehistoric art has been discovered. The first examples of cave paintings were found accidentally by an amateur archaeologist in 1879 at Altamira, Spain. Don Marcelino Sanz de Sautuola was exploring on his estate a cave where he had already found specimens of flint and carved bone. His little daughter Maria was with him when they reached a chamber some 85 feet from the cave's entrance. Because it was dark and the ceiling of the debris-filled cavern was only a few inches above the father's head, the child was the first to discern, from her lower vantage point, the shadowy forms of painted beasts on the cave roof (FIG. **1-9**, a detail of a much larger painting approximately 60 feet long).

Sanz de Sautuola was certain the bison painted on the Altamira ceiling dated back to prehistoric times. Professional

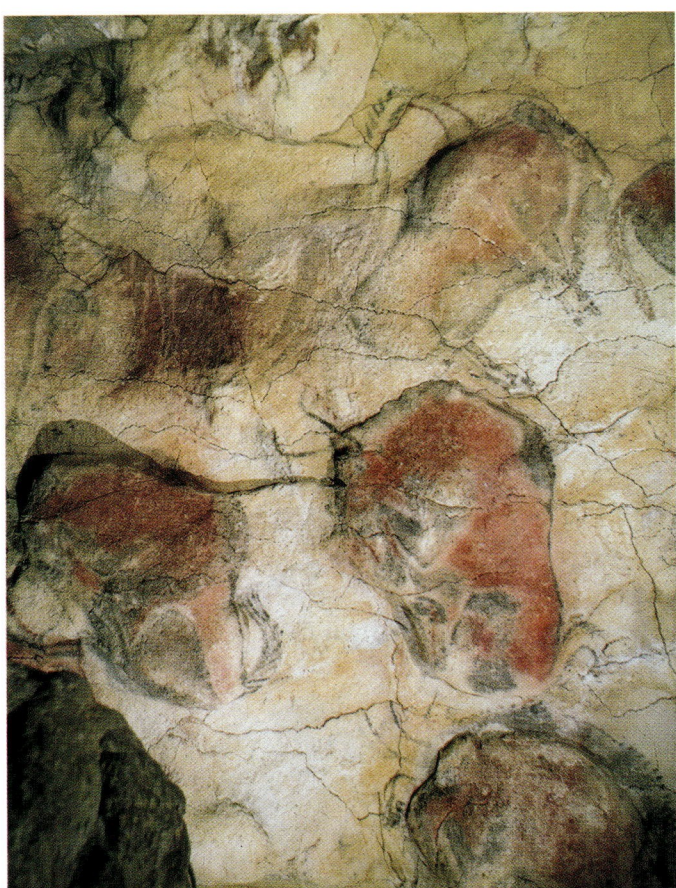

**1-9** Bison, detail of a painted ceiling in the Altamira cave, Santander, Spain, ca. 12,000–11,000 BCE. Each bison approx. 5′ long.

archaeologists, however, doubted the authenticity of these works, and at the Lisbon Congress on Prehistoric Archaeology in 1880, they officially dismissed the paintings as forgeries. But by the close of the century, other caves had been discovered with painted walls partially covered by mineral deposits that would have taken thousands of years to accumulate. Skeptics were finally persuaded that the first paintings were of an age far more remote than they had ever dreamed. Examples of Paleolithic painting now have been found at more than 200 sites (see "Paleolithic Cave Painting," page 21). Prehistorians still regard painted caves as rare occurrences, though, because the images in them, even if they number in the hundreds, were created over a period of some 10,000 to 20,000 years.

**"FLOATING" BISON** The bison at Altamira are 13,000 to 14,000 years old, but the painters of Paleolithic Spain approached the problem of representing an animal in essentially the same way as the painter of the stone plaque from Namibia (FIG. 1-2), who worked in Africa more than 10,000 years earlier. Every one of the Altamira bison is in profile, whether alive and standing or curled up on the ground (probably dead, although this is disputed). To maintain the profile in the latter case, the painter had to adopt a viewpoint above the animal, looking down, rather than the view a person standing on the ground would have.

Modern critics often refer to the Altamira animals as a *group* of bison, but that is very likely a misnomer. The several bison in our illustration do not stand on a common *ground line* (a painted or carved baseline on which figures appear to stand in paintings and reliefs), nor do they share a common orientation. They seem

### Paleolithic Cave Painting

The caves of Altamira (FIG. 1-9), Lascaux (FIGS. 1-11 and 1-13), and other sites in prehistoric Europe had served as underground water channels, a few hundred to several thousand feet long. They are often choked, sometimes almost impassably, by deposits, such as stalactites and stalagmites. Far inside these caverns, well removed from the cave mouths early humans sometimes chose for habitation, painters made pictures on the walls. For light, they used stone lamps filled with marrow or fat, with a wick, perhaps, of moss. For drawing, they used chunks of red and yellow ocher. For painting, they ground these same ochers into powders they mixed with water before applying. Recent analyses of the pigments used show that Paleolithic painters used many different minerals, attesting to a technical sophistication surprising at so early a date.

Large flat stones served as palettes. The painters made brushes from reeds, bristles, or twigs, and may have used a blowpipe of reeds or hollow bones to spray pigments on out-of-reach surfaces. Some caves have natural ledges on the rock walls upon which the painters could have stood in order to reach the upper surfaces of the naturally formed "rooms" and corridors. One Lascaux gallery has holes in one of the walls that once probably anchored a scaffold made of saplings lashed together.

Despite the difficulty of making the tools and pigments, modern attempts at replicating the techniques of Paleolithic painting have demonstrated that skilled workers could cover large surfaces with images in less than a day.

---

almost to float above viewers' heads, like clouds in the sky. And the dead(?) bison are seen in an "aerial view," while the others are seen from a position on the ground. The painting has no setting, no background, no indication of place. The Paleolithic painter was not at all concerned with *where* the animals were or with how they related to one another, if at all. Instead, several *separate* images of a bison adorn the ceiling, perhaps painted at different times, and each is as complete and informative as possible—even if their meaning remains a mystery (see "Art in the Old Stone Age," page 22).

SIGNS AND HANDS That the paintings did have meaning to the Paleolithic peoples who made and observed them cannot, however, be doubted. In fact, signs consisting of checks, dots, squares, or other arrangements of lines often accompany the pictures of animals. Several observers have seen a primitive writing form in these representations of nonliving things. Representations of human hands also are common. At Pech-Merle (FIG. 1-10) in France, painted hands accompany representations of spotted horses. These and the majority of painted hands at other sites are "negative," that is, the painter placed one hand against the wall and then brushed

or blew or spat pigment around it. Occasionally, the painter dipped a hand in the pigment and then pressed it against the wall, leaving a "positive" imprint. These handprints, too, must have had a purpose. Some scholars have considered them "signatures" of cult or community members or, less likely, of individual painters. But like everything else in Paleolithic art, their meaning is unknown.

The *mural* (wall) paintings at Pech-Merle also allow some insight into the reason certain subjects may have been chosen for a specific location. One of the horses (at the right in our illustration) may have been inspired by the rock formation in the wall surface resembling a horse's head and neck. Like the reclining woman at La Magdelaine (FIG. 1-6), the Pech-Merle representations may have been created after someone noticed a resemblance between a chance configuration in nature and an animal or person. The perceived forms were then "finished" by accentuating the outlines with stone tools, as at La Magdelaine, or by the addition of color, as at Pech-Merle. Prehistorians also have observed that nearly all horses and hands are painted on concave surfaces, whereas bison and cattle appear almost exclusively on convex surfaces. What this signifies has yet to be determined.

1-10 Spotted horses and negative hand imprints, wall painting in the cave at Pech-Merle, Lot, France, ca. 22,000 BCE. Approx. 11′ 2″ long.

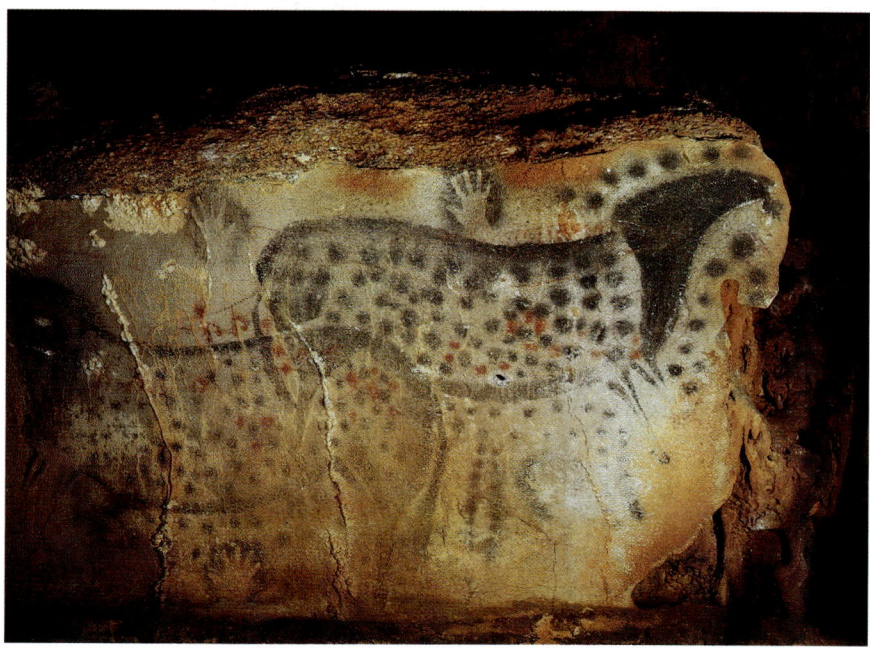

## Art in the Old Stone Age

From the moment in 1879 that cave paintings were discovered at Altamira (FIG. 1-9), scholars have wondered why the hunters of the Old Stone Age decided to cover the walls of dark caverns with animal images. Various theories have been proposed, including that the painted and engraved animals were mere decoration, but this explanation cannot account for the narrow range of subjects or the inaccessibility of many of the representations. In fact, the remoteness and difficulty of access of many of the images, and indications that the caves were used for centuries, are precisely why many scholars have suggested that the prehistoric hunters attributed magical properties to the images they painted and sculpted. According to this argument, by confining animals to the surfaces of their cave walls, the Paleolithic hunters believed they were bringing the beasts under their control. Some have even hypothesized that rituals or dances were performed in front of the images and that these rites served to improve the hunters' luck. Still others have stated that the animal representations may have served as teaching tools to instruct new hunters about the character of the various species they would encounter or even to serve as targets for spears!

In contrast, some scholars have argued that the magical purpose of the paintings and reliefs was not to facilitate the *destruction* of bison and other species. Instead, they believe prehistoric painters and sculptors created animal images to assure the *survival* of the herds on which Paleolithic peoples depended for their food supply and for their clothing.

A central problem for both the hunting-magic and food-creation theories is that the animals that seem to have been diet staples of Old Stone Age peoples are not those most frequently portrayed. At Altamira, for example, faunal remains show that red deer, not bison, were eaten.

Other scholars have sought to reconstruct an elaborate mythology based on the cave paintings and sculptures, suggesting that Paleolithic humans believed they had animal ancestors. Still others have equated certain species with men and others with women and postulated various meanings for the abstract signs that sometimes accompany the images. Almost all of these theories have been discredited over time, and most prehistorians admit that no one knows the intent of these representations. In fact, a single explanation for all Paleolithic animal images, even ones similar in subject, style, and composition (how the motifs are arranged on the surface), is unlikely to apply universally. The works remain an enigma—and always will, because before the invention of writing, no contemporary explanations could be recorded.

**THE BULLS OF LASCAUX** Perhaps the best-known Paleolithic cave is that at Lascaux, near Montignac, France. It is extensively decorated, but most of the paintings are hundreds of feet from any entrance. The most magnificent is a large circular gallery, characteristically far removed from the daylight, called the Hall of the Bulls (FIG. **1-11**). Not all of the painted animals are bulls, despite the modern nickname, and the several species depicted vary in size. Many are represented using colored silhouettes, as in the cave at Altamira (FIG. 1-9) and on the Namibian plaque (FIG. 1-2). Others—such as the great bull at the right in our illustration—were created by outline alone, as were the Pech-Merle horses (FIG. 1-10). On the walls of the Lascaux cave one sees, side by side, the two basic approaches to drawing and painting found repeatedly in the history of art. These differences in style and

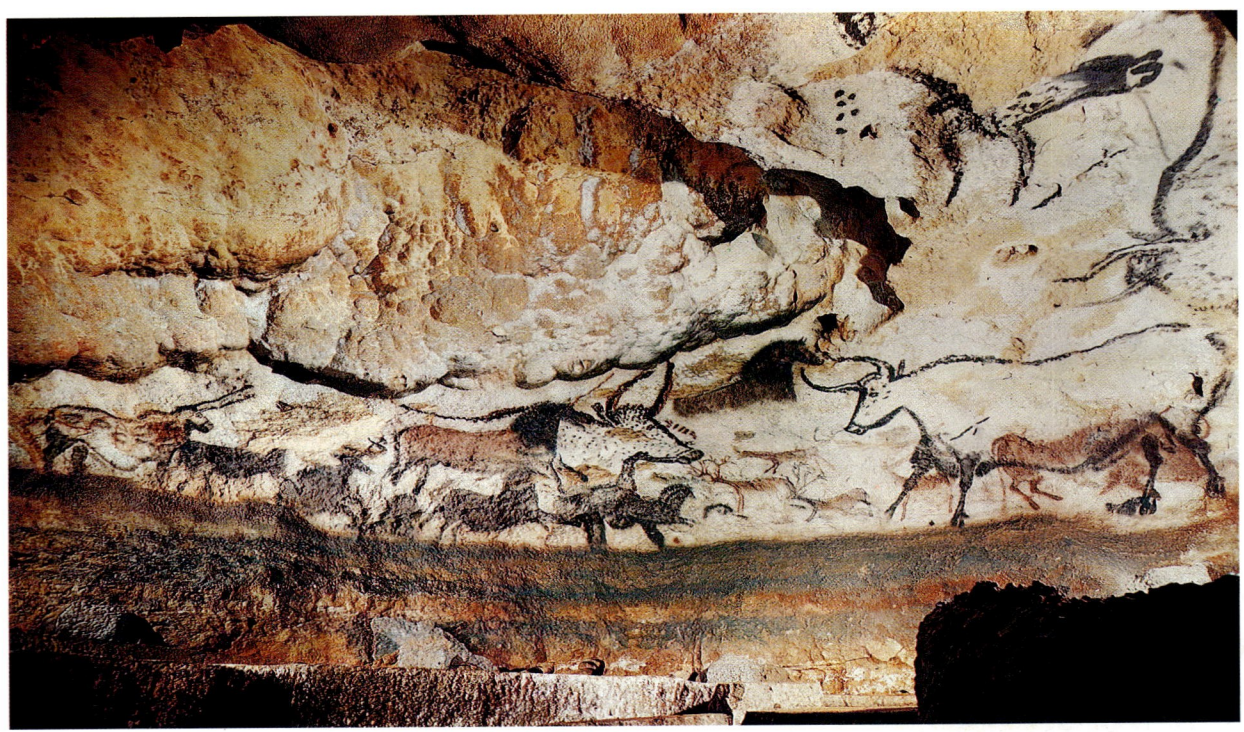

**1-11** Hall of the Bulls (left wall), Lascaux, Dordogne, France, ca. 15,000–13,000 BCE. Largest bull approx. 11′ 6″ long.

### The World's Oldest Paintings?

One of the most spectacular archaeological finds of the past century came to light in December 1994 at Vallon-Pont-d'Arc, France, and was announced at a dramatic press conference in Paris on January 18, 1995. The next day, people around the world were startled when they picked up their morning newspapers or turned on their televisions and saw a sampling of pictures of extraordinary Paleolithic cave paintings. Unlike some other recent "finds" of prehistoric art that proved to be forgeries, the paintings in the Chauvet Cave (named after the leader of the exploration team, Jean-Marie Chauvet) seemed to be authentic. But no one, including Chauvet and his colleagues, guessed at the time of their discovery that *radiocarbon dating* (a measure of the rate of degeneration of carbon 14 in organic materials) of the paintings might establish that the murals in the cave were more than 15,000 years older than those at Altamira (FIG. 1-9). When the scientific tests were completed, the French archaeologists announced that the Chauvet Cave paintings were the oldest yet found anywhere, datable around 30,000–28,000 BCE. Such an early date immediately caused scholars to reevaluate the scheme of "stylistic development" from simple to more complex forms that had been nearly universally accepted for decades.

Many species of animals appear on the Chauvet Cave walls, including several ferocious animals that were never part of the Paleolithic human diet, such as lions and bears. Bears, in fact, hibernated in the cave, and more than 50 bear skulls are still there. When the bears resided in the cave, it was a dangerous place for anyone to venture into.

Several of the paintings discovered by Chauvet's team occupy a special place in the history of art. In the Chauvet Cave, in contrast to Lascaux (FIG. 1-11), the horns of the aurochs (extinct long-horned wild oxen) are shown naturalistically, one behind the other, not in the twisted perspective thought to be universally characteristic of Paleolithic art. Moreover, the two rhinoceroses at the lower right of FIG. 1-12 appear to confront each other, suggesting to some observers that a narrative was intended, another "first" in either painting or sculpture. If the paintings are twice as old as those of Lascaux, Altamira (FIG. 1-9), and Pech-Merle (FIG. 1-10), the assumption that Paleolithic art "evolved" from simple to more sophisticated representations is wrong.

Much research remains to be conducted in the Chauvet Cave, but already the paintings have become the subject of intense controversy. Recently, some archaeologists have contested the early dating of the Chauvet paintings on the grounds that the tested samples were contaminated. The paintings, therefore, may not be revolutionary after all. The dispute exemplifies the frustration— and the excitement—of studying the art of an age so remote that almost nothing remains and almost every new find causes art historians to reevaluate what had previously been taken for granted.

technique alone suggest that the animals in the Hall of the Bulls were painted at different times, and the modern impression of a rapidly moving herd of beasts was probably not the original intent. In any case, the "herd" consists of several different kinds of animals of various sizes moving in different directions.

Another feature of the Lascaux paintings deserves attention. The bulls there show a convention of representing horns that has been called *twisted perspective,* because viewers see the heads in profile but the horns from the front. Thus, the painter's approach is not strictly or consistently *optical* (seen from a fixed viewpoint). Rather, the approach is *descriptive* of the fact that cattle have two horns. Two horns are part of the concept "bull." In strict optical-perspective profile, only one horn would be visible, but to paint the animal in that way would, as it were, amount to an incomplete definition of it. This kind of twisted perspective was the norm in prehistoric painting, but it was not universal. In fact, the recent discovery of Paleolithic paintings in the Chauvet Cave (FIG. **1-12**) at Vallon-Pont-d'Arc in France, where the painters

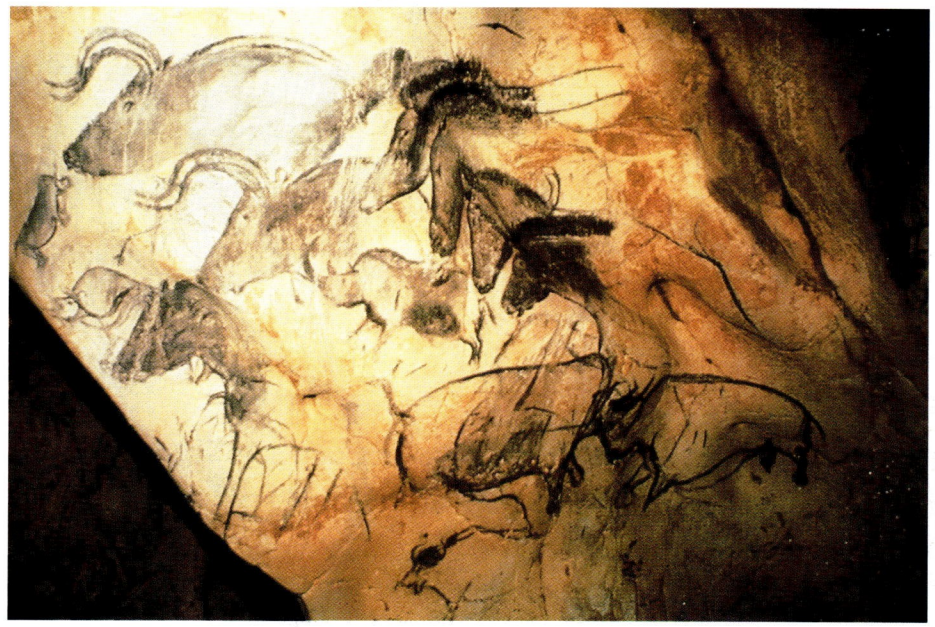

**1-12** Aurochs, horses, and rhinoceroses, wall painting in Chauvet Cave, Vallon-Pont-d'Arc, Ardèche, France, ca. 30,000–28,000 or ca. 15,000–13,000 BCE. Approx. half life-size.

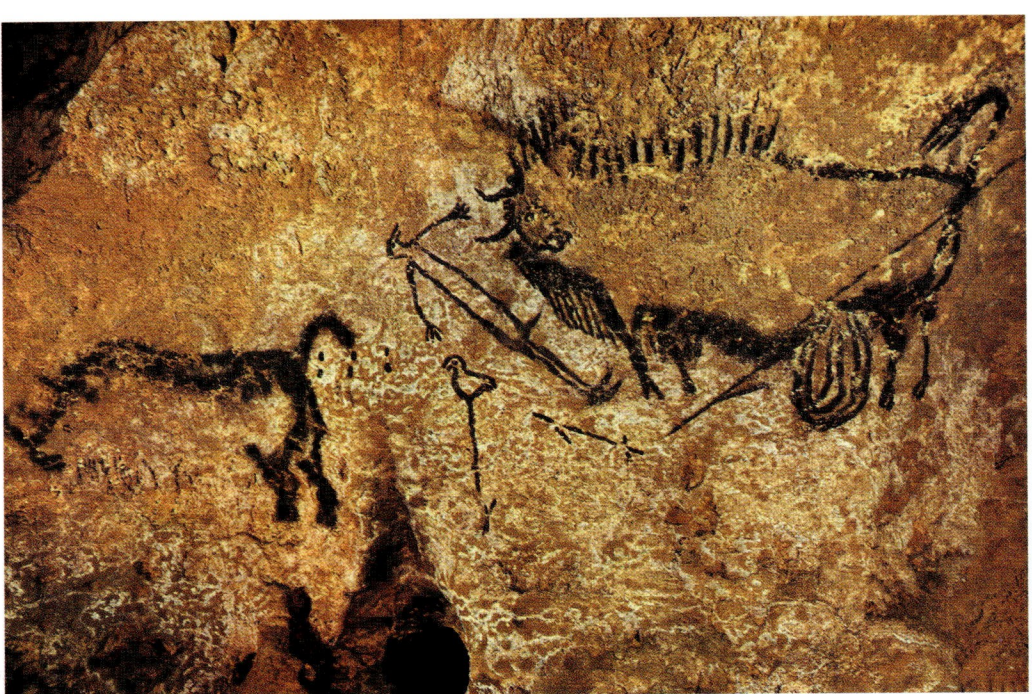

**1-13** Rhinoceros, wounded man, and disemboweled bison, painting in the well, Lascaux, Dordogne, France, ca. 15,000–13,000 BCE. Bison approx. 3′ 8″ long.

represented horns in a more natural way, has caused art historians to rethink many of the assumptions they had made about Paleolithic art (see "The World's Oldest Paintings?" page 23).

**PALEOLITHIC NARRATIVE ART?**  Perhaps the most perplexing painting in all the Paleolithic caves is the one deep in the well shaft at Lascaux (FIG. **1-13**), where man (as opposed to woman) makes one of his earliest appearances in prehistoric painting. At the left is a rhinoceros, rendered with all the skilled attention to animal detail customarily seen in cave art. Beneath its tail are two rows of three dots of uncertain significance. At the right is a bison, more schematically painted, probably by someone else. The second painter nonetheless successfully suggested the bristling rage of the animal, whose bowels are hanging from it in a heavy coil. Between the two beasts is a bird-faced (masked?) man (compare the feline-headed human from Hohlenstein-Stadel, FIG. 1-3) with outstretched arms and hands with only four fingers. The man is depicted with far less care and detail than either animal, but the painter made the hunter's gender explicit by the prominent penis. The position of the man is ambiguous. Is he wounded or dead or merely tilted back and unharmed? Do the staff(?) with the bird on top and the spear belong to him? Is it he or the rhinoceros who has gravely wounded the bison—or neither? Which animal, if either, has knocked the man down, if indeed he is on the ground? Are these three images related at all? Researchers can be sure of nothing, but if the figures were placed beside each other to tell a story, then this is evidence for the creation of complex narrative compositions involving humans and animals at a much earlier date than anyone had imagined only a few generations ago. Yet it is important to remember that even if a story was intended, very few people would have been able to "read" it. The painting, in a deep shaft, is very difficult to reach and could have been viewed only in flickering lamplight. Like all Paleolithic art, the scene in the Lascaux well shaft remains enigmatic.

# NEOLITHIC ART

**THE ICE RECEDES**  Around 9000 BCE, the ice that covered much of northern Europe during the Paleolithic period melted as the climate grew warmer. The reindeer migrated north, and the woolly mammoth and rhinoceros disappeared. The Paleolithic gave way to a transitional period, the Mesolithic, when Europe became climatically, geographically, and biologically much as it is today. Then, for several thousand years at different times in different parts of the globe, a great new age, the Neolithic, dawned. Human beings began to settle in fixed abodes and to domesticate plants and animals. Their food supply assured, many groups changed from hunters to herders, to farmers, and finally to townspeople. Wandering hunters settled down to organized community living in villages surrounded by cultivated fields.

The conventional division of prehistory into the Paleolithic, Mesolithic, and Neolithic periods is based on the development of stone implements. However, a different kind of distinction may be made between an age of food gathering and an age of food production. In this scheme, the Paleolithic period corresponds roughly to the age of food gathering, and the Mesolithic period, the last phase of that age, is marked by intensified food gathering and the taming of the dog. In the Neolithic period, agriculture and stock raising became humankind's major food sources. The transition to the Neolithic occurred first in the ancient Near East (MAP 1-1).

## *Ancient Near East*

**THE BEGINNING OF AGRICULTURE**  The remains of the oldest known settled communities have been found in the grassy uplands bordering the Tigris and Euphrates Rivers in Mesopotamia (parts of modern Syria and Iraq). These regions provided the necessary preconditions for the development of agriculture. Species of native plants, such as wild wheat and barley, were plentiful, as were herds of animals (goats, sheep, and pigs) that could be domesticated. Sufficient rain occurred for the raising of crops. When village farming life was well developed, some settlers, attracted by the greater fertility of the soil and perhaps also by the need to find more land for their rapidly growing populations, moved into the river valleys and deltas of the two rivers.

**NEOLITHIC INNOVATIONS** In addition to systematic agriculture, the new sedentary societies of the Neolithic age originated weaving, metalworking, pottery, and counting and recording with tokens. Soon, these innovations spread from Mesopotamia to northern Syria, Anatolia (Turkey), and Egypt. Village farming communities such as Jarmo in Iraq and Çatal Höyük in southern Anatolia date back to the mid-seventh millennium BCE. The remarkable fortified town of Jericho, before whose walls the biblical Joshua appeared thousands of years later, is even older. Archaeologists are constantly uncovering surprises, and the discovery and exploration of new sites each year is compelling them to revise their views about the emergence of Neolithic society. But three sites known for some time—Jericho, Ain Ghazal, and Çatal Höyük—offer a fascinating picture of the rapid and exciting transformation of human society—and of art—during the Neolithic period.

**JERICHO'S STONE FORTIFICATIONS** By 7000 BCE, agriculture was well established in at least three Near Eastern regions: ancient Palestine, Iran, and Anatolia. Although no remains of domestic cereals have been found that can be dated before 7000 BCE, the advanced state of agriculture at that time presupposes a long development. Indeed, the very existence of a town such as Jericho gives strong support to this assumption. The site of

Jericho—a plateau in the Jordan River valley with an unfailing spring—was occupied by a small village as early as the ninth millennium BCE. This village underwent spectacular development around 8000 BCE, when a new Neolithic town covering about 10 acres was built. Its mud-brick houses sat on round or oval stone foundations and had roofs of branches covered with earth.

As the town's wealth grew and powerful neighbors established themselves, the need for protection resulted in the first known permanent stone fortifications. By approximately 7500 BCE, the town, estimated to have had a population of more than 2,000 people, was surrounded by a wide rock-cut ditch and a 5-foot-thick wall. Into this wall, which has been preserved to a height of almost 13 feet, was built a great circular stone tower (FIG. 1-14), 28 feet high. Almost 33 feet in diameter at the base, the tower has an inner stairway leading to its summit. Not enough of the site has been excavated to determine whether this tower was solitary or one of several similar towers that formed a complete defense system. In either case, a structure such as this, built with only simple stone tools, was a tremendous technological achievement. It constitutes the beginning of the long history of monumental architecture.

**SCULPTURE AT AIN GHAZAL** Near Amman, Jordan, the construction of a highway in 1974 revealed another important Neolithic settlement in ancient Palestine at the site of Ain Ghazal, occupied from the late eighth through the late sixth millennium BCE. The inhabitants built houses of irregularly shaped stones, but carefully plastered and then painted their floors and walls red. The most striking finds at Ain Ghazal, however, are two caches containing three dozen plaster statuettes (FIG. 1-15) and

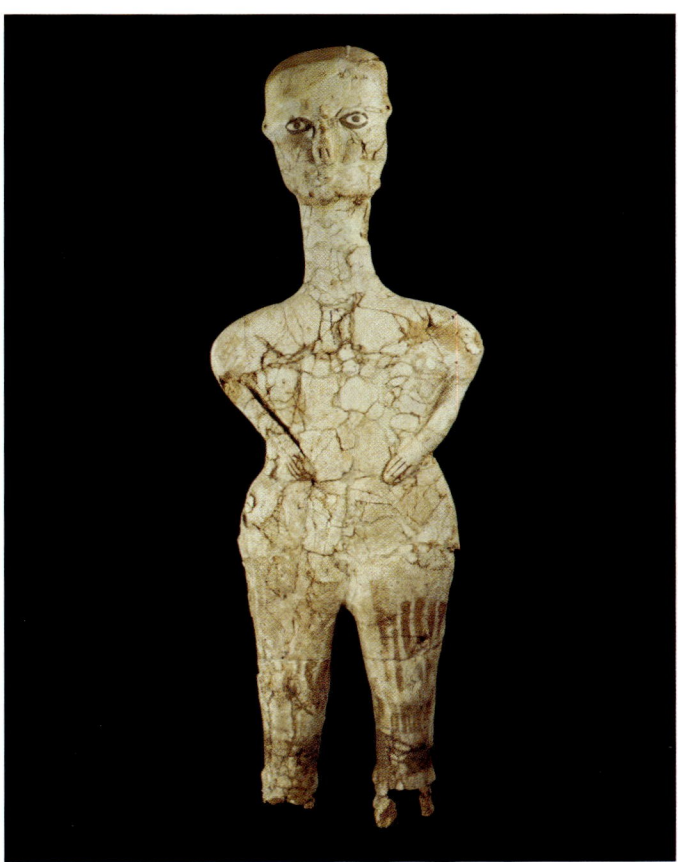

**1-14** Great stone tower built into the settlement wall, Jericho, ca. 8000–7000 BCE.

**1-15** Human figure, from Ain Ghazal, Jordan, ca. 6750–6250 BCE. Plaster, painted and inlaid with cowrie shell and bitumen, 3′ 5¾″ high. Louvre, Paris.

busts, some with two heads, datable to the mid-seventh millennium BCE. The sculptures appear to have been ritually buried. The figures were fashioned of white plaster, which was built up over a core of reeds and twine. Black bitumen, a tarlike substance, was used to delineate the pupils of the eyes, which are inset cowrie shells. Painters added orange and black hair, clothing, and, in some instances, body paint or tattooing. Only rarely did the sculptors indicate the gender of the figures. Whatever their purpose, by their size (as much as three feet tall) and sophisticated technique, the Ain Ghazal statuettes and busts are distinguished from Paleolithic figurines such as the tiny *Venus of Willendorf* (FIG. 1-4) and even the foot-tall ivory statuette from Hohlenstein-Stadel (FIG. 1-3). They mark the beginning of monumental sculpture in the ancient Near East.

**A TOWN WITHOUT STREETS** Remarkable discoveries also have been made in Anatolia. Excavations at Hacilar, Çatal Höyük, and elsewhere have shown that the central Anatolian plateau was the site of a flourishing Neolithic culture between 7000 and 5000 BCE. Twelve successive building levels excavated at Çatal Höyük between 1961 and 1965 have been dated between 6500 and 5700 BCE. On a single site, it is possible to retrace, in an unbroken sequence, the evolution of a Neolithic culture over a period of 800 years. (Only 1 of 32 acres had been explored before the recent resumption of excavations. The new project promises to expand and perhaps revise the current picture of Neolithic life.)

The source of Çatal Höyük's wealth was trade, especially in obsidian, a glasslike volcanic stone Neolithic toolmakers and weapon makers valued highly because it could be chipped into fine cutting edges. Along with Jericho, Çatal Höyük seems to have been one of the first experiments in urban living. The regularity of its plan suggests that the town was built according to some predetermined scheme. A peculiar feature is the settlement's complete lack of streets (FIG. **1-16**). The houses adjoin one another and have no doors. Openings in the roofs provided access to the interiors. The openings also served as chimneys to ventilate the hearth in the combination living room and kitchen that formed the core of the house. Impractical as such an arrangement may

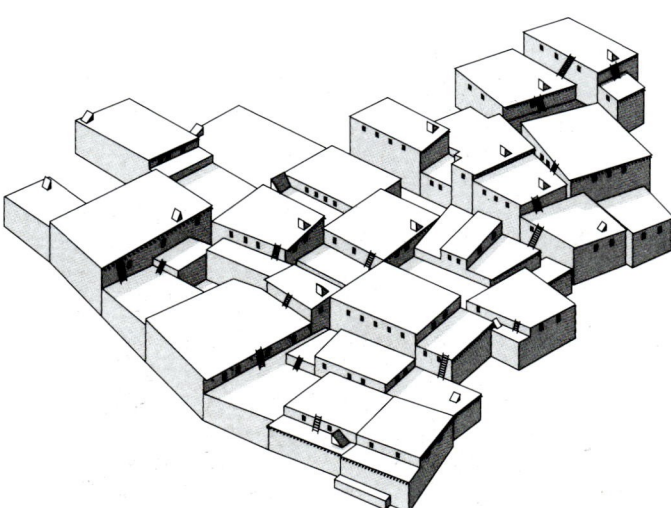

**1-16** Schematic reconstruction drawing of a section of Level VI, Çatal Höyük, Turkey, ca. 6000–5900 BCE (after J. Mellaart).

appear today, it did offer some advantages. The attached buildings were more stable than freestanding structures and, at the limits of the town site, formed a perimeter wall well suited to defense against human or natural forces. Thus, if enemies managed to breach the exterior wall, they would find themselves not inside the town but above the houses with the defenders waiting there on the roof.

The houses, constructed of mud brick strengthened by sturdy timber frames, varied in size but repeated the same basic plan. Walls and floors were plastered and painted, and platforms along walls served as sites for sleeping, working, and eating. The dead were buried beneath the floors. A great number of decorated rooms have been found at Çatal Höyük. The excavators called these rooms shrines, but their function is uncertain. Their number suggests that these rooms played an important role in the life of Çatal Höyük's inhabitants.

The "shrines" are distinguished from the house structures by the greater richness of their interior decoration, which consisted of wall paintings, plaster reliefs, animal heads, and *bucrania* (bovine skulls). Bulls' horns, widely thought to be symbols of masculine potency, are the most common motif in these rooms. In some cases they are displayed next to plaster breasts, symbols of female fertility, projecting from the walls. Many statuettes of stone or *terracotta* (baked clay) also have been found at Çatal Höyük. Most are quite small (2 to 8 inches high) and primarily depict female figures. Only a few reach 12 inches.

**NARRATIVE PAINTING** Although at Çatal Höyük animal husbandry was well established, hunting continued to play an important part in the early Neolithic economy. The importance of hunting as a food source (until about 5700 BCE) is reflected also in wall paintings, where, in the older decorated rooms, hunting scenes predominate. In style and concept, however, the deer hunt mural at Çatal Höyük (FIG. **1-17**) is worlds apart from the wall paintings the hunters of the Paleolithic period produced. Perhaps what is most strikingly new about the Çatal Höyük painting and others like it is the regular appearance of the human figure—not only singly but also in large, coherent groups with a wide variety of poses, subjects, and settings. As noted earlier, humans were unusual in Paleolithic cave paintings, and pictorial narratives have almost never been found. Even the "hunting scene" in the well at Lascaux (FIG. 1-13) is doubtful as a narrative. In Neolithic paintings, human themes and concerns and action scenes with humans dominating animals are central.

In the Çatal Höyük hunt, the group of hunters—and no one doubts it is, indeed, an organized hunting party, not a series of individual figures—shows a tense exaggeration of movement and a rhythmic repetition of basic shapes customary for the period. The painter took care to distinguish important descriptive details—for example, bows, arrows, and garments—and the heads have clearly defined noses, mouths, chins, and hair. The Neolithic painter placed all the heads in profile for the same reason Paleolithic painters universally chose the profile view for representations of animals. Only the side view of the human head shows all its shapes clearly. However, at Çatal Höyük the torsos are presented from the front—again, the most informative viewpoint—while the profile view was chosen for the legs and arms. This *composite view* of the human body is quite artificial because the human body cannot make an abrupt 90-degree shift at the hips. But it is very descriptive

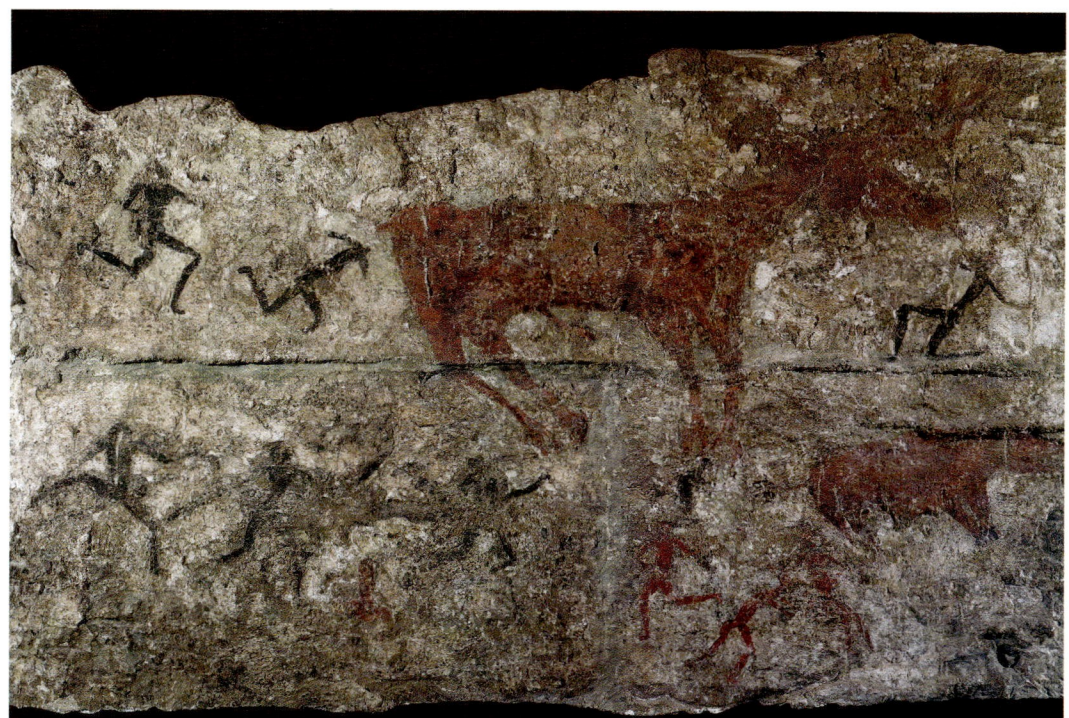

of what a human body is—as opposed to what it looks like from a particular viewpoint. The composite view is another manifestation of the twisted perspective of Paleolithic paintings that combined a frontal view of an animal's two horns with a profile view of the head (FIGS. 1-11 and 1-13). The technique of painting also changed dramatically since Paleolithic times. The pigments were applied with a brush to a white background of dry plaster. The careful preparation of the wall surface is in striking contrast to the direct application of pigment to the rock face.

**THE FIRST LANDSCAPE?** More remarkable still is a painting in one of the older rooms at Çatal Höyük (FIG. **1-18**) that gener-

ally has been acclaimed as the world's first landscape (a picture of a natural setting in its own right, without any narrative content). As such, it remained unique for thousands of years. According to radiocarbon dating, the painting was executed around 6150 BCE. In the foreground is a town, with rectangular houses neatly laid out side by side, probably representing Çatal Höyük itself. Behind the town appears a mountain with two peaks. Many archaeologists think that the dots and lines issuing from the higher of the two cones represent a volcanic eruption, and have suggested that the mountain is the 10,600-foot-high Hasan Dağ. It is located within view of Çatal Höyük and is the only twin-peaked volcano in central Anatolia. The conjectured

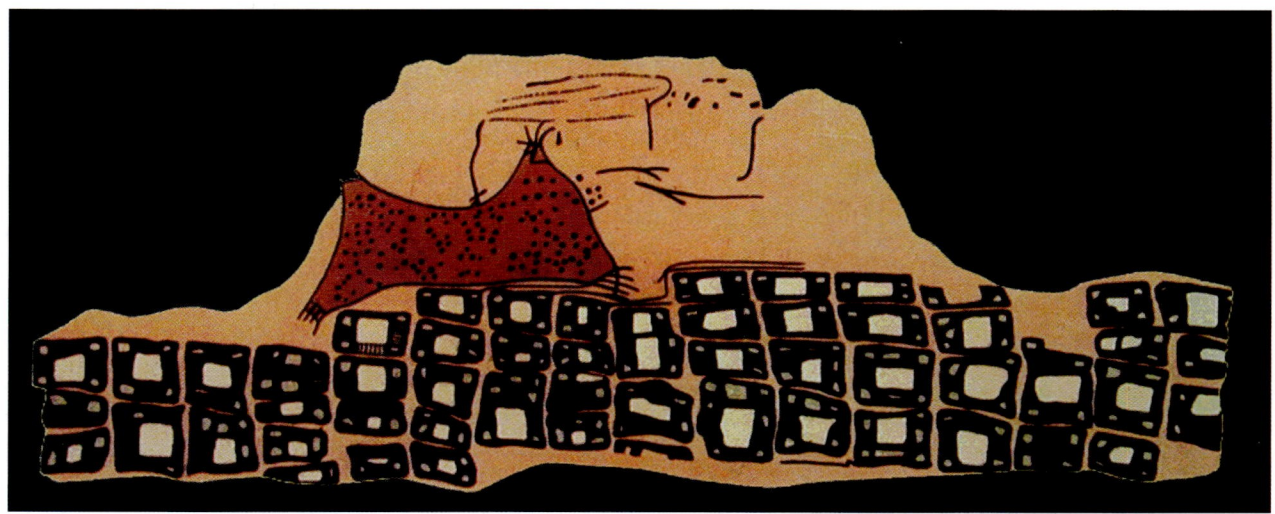

1-18 Landscape with volcanic eruption(?), detail of a watercolor copy of a wall painting from Level VII, Çatal Höyük, Turkey, ca. 6150 BCE.

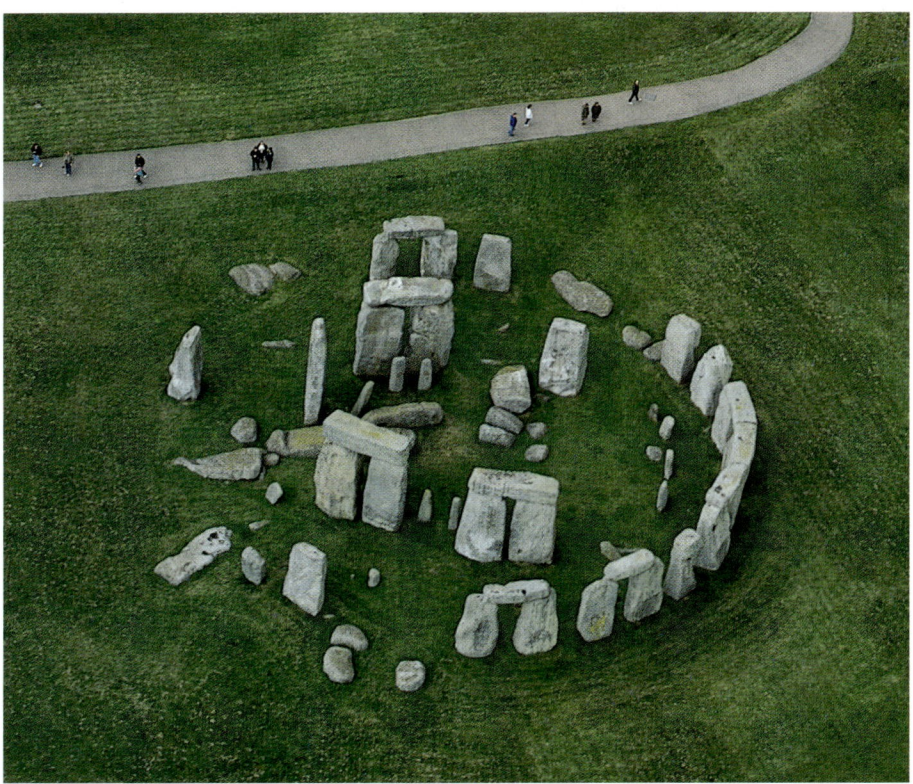

**1-19** Aerial view of Stonehenge, Salisbury Plain, Wiltshire, England, ca. 2550–1600 BCE. Circle is 97′ in diameter; trilithons approx. 24′ high.

volcanic eruption shown in the mural does not necessarily depict a specific historical event. If, however, the Çatal Höyük painting relates a story, even a recurring one, then it cannot be considered a pure landscape. Nonetheless, this mural is the first depiction of a place devoid of both humans and animals.

The rich finds at Çatal Höyük give the impression of a prosperous and well-ordered society that practiced a great variety of arts and crafts. In addition to painting and sculpture, weaving and pottery were well established, and even the technique of smelting copper and lead in small quantities was known before 6000 BCE. The conversion to an agricultural economy appears to have been completed by about 5700.

### Western Europe

**MEGALITHS AND HENGES** In western Europe, where Paleolithic paintings and sculptures abound, no comparably developed towns of the time of Çatal Höyük have been found. However, in succeeding millennia, perhaps as early as 4000 BCE, the local Neolithic populations in several areas developed a monumental architecture employing massive rough-cut stones. The very dimensions of the stones, some as high as 17 feet and weighing as much as 50 tons, have prompted historians to call them *megaliths* (great stones) and to designate the culture that produced them *megalithic*.

Although megalithic monuments are plentiful throughout Europe, the arrangement of huge stones in a circle (called a *cromlech* or *henge*), often surrounded by a ditch, is almost entirely limited to Britain. The most imposing today is Stonehenge (FIG. **1-19**) on the Salisbury Plain in southern England. Stonehenge is a complex of rough-cut sarsen (a form of sandstone) stones and smaller "bluestones" (various volcanic rocks). Outermost is a ring, almost 100 feet in diameter, of large monoliths of sarsen stones capped by

*lintels* (a stone "beam" used to span an opening; see FIG. 4-18). Next is a ring of bluestones, which, in turn, encircle a horseshoe (open end facing east) of *trilithons* (three-stone constructions)— five lintel-topped pairs of the largest sarsens, each weighing 45 to 50 tons. Standing apart and to the east (outside our photograph at the lower right corner) is the "heel-stone," which, for a person looking outward from the center of the complex, would have marked the point where the sun rose at the summer solstice.

Stonehenge probably was built in several phases in the centuries before and after 2000 BCE. It seems to have been a kind of astronomical observatory. The mysterious structures were believed in the Middle Ages to have been the work of the magician Merlin of the King Arthur legend, who spirited them from Ireland. Most archaeologists now consider Stonehenge a remarkably accurate solar calendar. This achievement is testimony to the rapidly developing intellectual powers of Neolithic humans as well as to their capacity for heroic physical effort.

### CONCLUSION

The first sculptures and paintings antedate the invention of writing by tens of thousands of years. No one knows why the first "artists" began to paint and carve images of animals and humans or what role those images played in the lives of Paleolithic hunters. All that is certain is that the statuettes, reliefs, and mural paintings were not created as "art" in the modern sense of the word. But the Paleolithic artists *were* the first to represent the world around them in stone and paint, initiating an intellectual revolution of enormous consequences. They and their Neolithic successors also invented many of the techniques and established many of the conventions that would characterize sculpture and painting for millennia.

30,000 BCE

▮ FIRST PALEOLITHIC PAINTINGS AND SCULPTURES, CA. 30,000–28,000 BCE

1

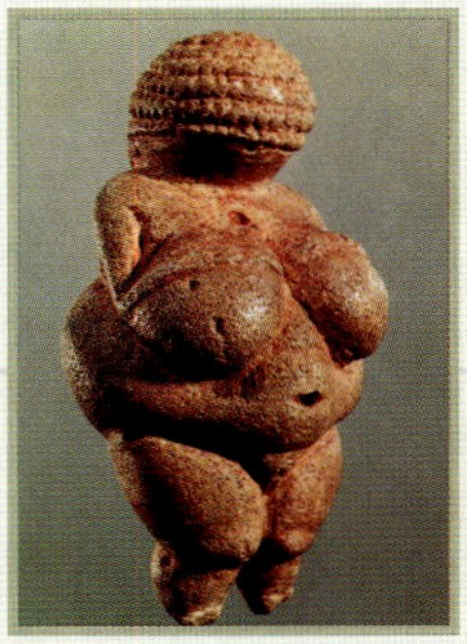

25,000 BCE

1 Nude woman
(*Venus of Willendorf*),
ca. 28,000–25,000 BCE

15,000 BCE

2

12,000 BCE

▮ FINAL RECESSION OF ICE AND ONSET
OF TEMPERATE CLIMATE, CA. 9000 BCE

▮ NEOLITHIC PERIOD BEGINS IN THE NEAR EAST, CA. 8000 BCE

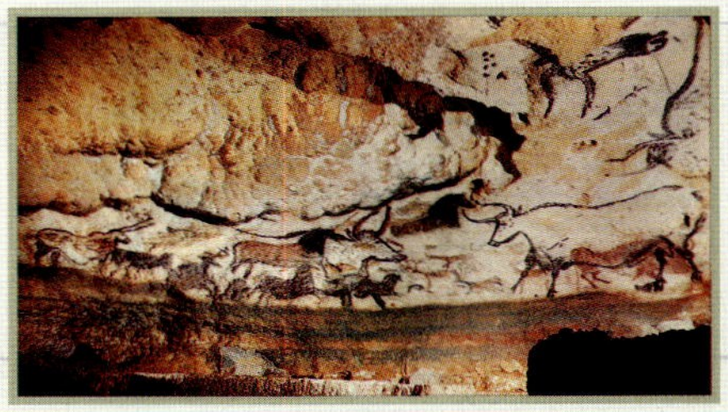

2 Hall of the Bulls, Lascaux, ca. 15,000–13,000 BCE

7500 BCE

▮ EARLIEST FARMING COMMUNITIES, CA. 7000 BCE

3

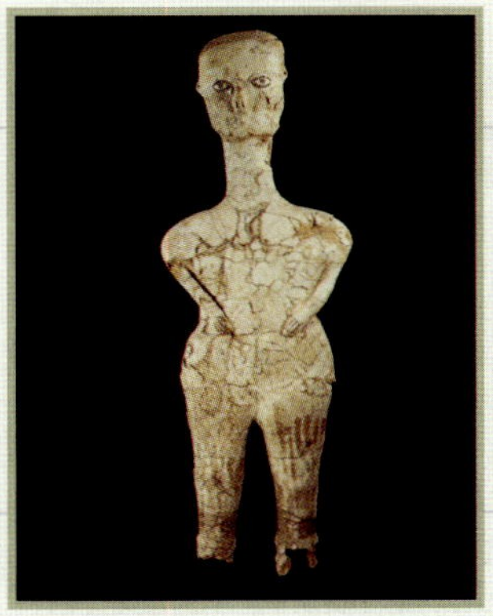

5000 BCE

▮ NEOLITHIC PERIOD BEGINS IN EUROPE, CA. 4000 BCE

3 Plaster figurine from Ain Ghazal,
ca. 6750–6250 BCE

4

2000 BCE

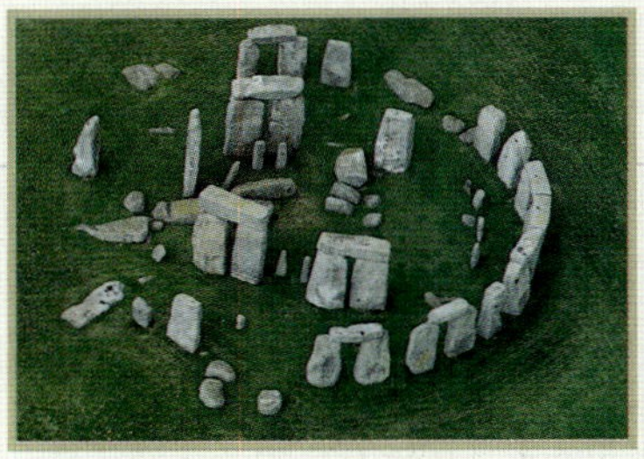

4 Stonehenge, Salisbury Plain,
ca. 2550–1600 BCE

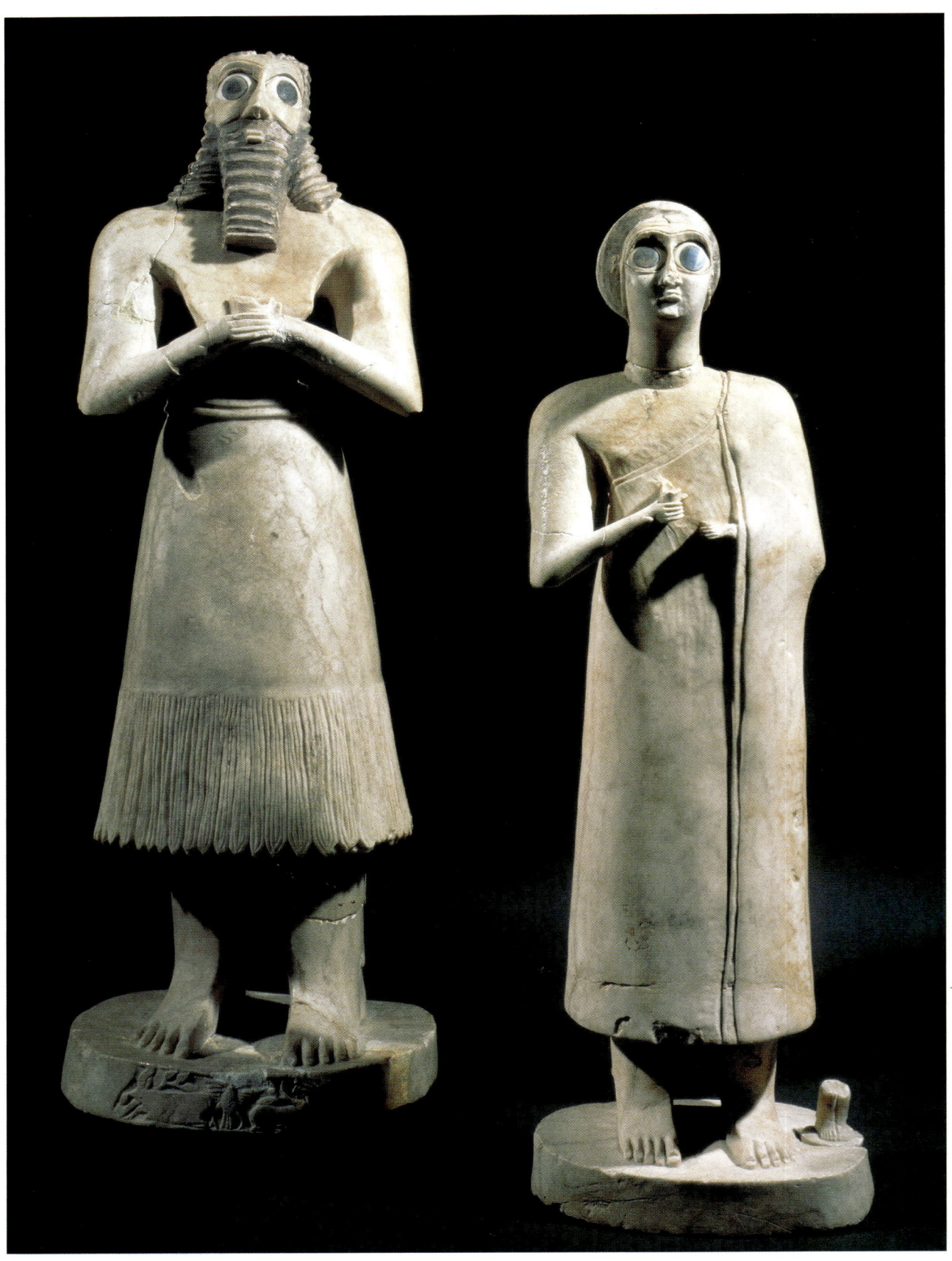

Statuettes of two worshipers, from the Square Temple at Eshnunna (modern Tell Asmar), Iraq, ca. 2700 BCE. Gypsum inlaid with shell and black limestone, male figure approx. 2′ 6″ high. Iraq Museum, Baghdad.

# 2

# THE RISE OF
# CIVILIZATION

## THE ART OF THE ANCIENT NEAR EAST

When humans first gave up the dangerous and uncertain life of the hunter and gatherer for the more predictable and stable life of the farmer and herder, the change in human society was so astounding, so fundamental, that it justly has been called the Neolithic Revolution. This revolutionary change in the nature of daily life first occurred in Mesopotamia—a Greek word that means "the land between the [Tigris and Euphrates] rivers." Mesopotamia is at the core of the region often called the Fertile Crescent, a land mass that forms a huge arc from the mountainous border between Turkey and Syria through Iraq to Iran's Zagros Mountains (MAP 2-1). There, humans first learned how to use the wheel and the plow and how to control floods and construct irrigation canals. The land became a giant oasis, the presumed locale of the biblical Garden of Eden.

As the region that gave birth to three of the world's great modern faiths—Judaism, Christianity, and Islam—the Near East has long been of interest to historians. But not until the 19th century did systematic excavation open the world's eyes to the extraordinary art and architecture of the ancient land between the rivers. After the first discoveries, the great museums of Europe quickly began to acquire Mesopotamian artworks. The instructions the British Museum gave to Austen Henry Layard, one of the pioneers of Near Eastern archaeology, were typical of the treasure-hunting spirit of the era: Obtain as many well-preserved artworks as you can while spending the least possible amount of time and money doing so. Interest heightened with each new find, and soon North American museums also began to collect Near Eastern art.

The most popular 19th-century acquisitions were the stone reliefs depicting warfare and hunting (FIGS. 2-22 and 2-24) and the colossal statues of monstrous human-headed bulls (FIG. 2-21) from the palaces of the Assyrians, rulers of a northern Mesopotamian empire during the ninth to the seventh centuries BCE. But nothing that emerged from the Near Eastern soil attracted as much attention as the treasures Leonard Woolley discovered in the 1920s at the Royal Cemetery at Ur in southern Mesopotamia. The interest in his unearthing of lavish third-millennium Sumerian

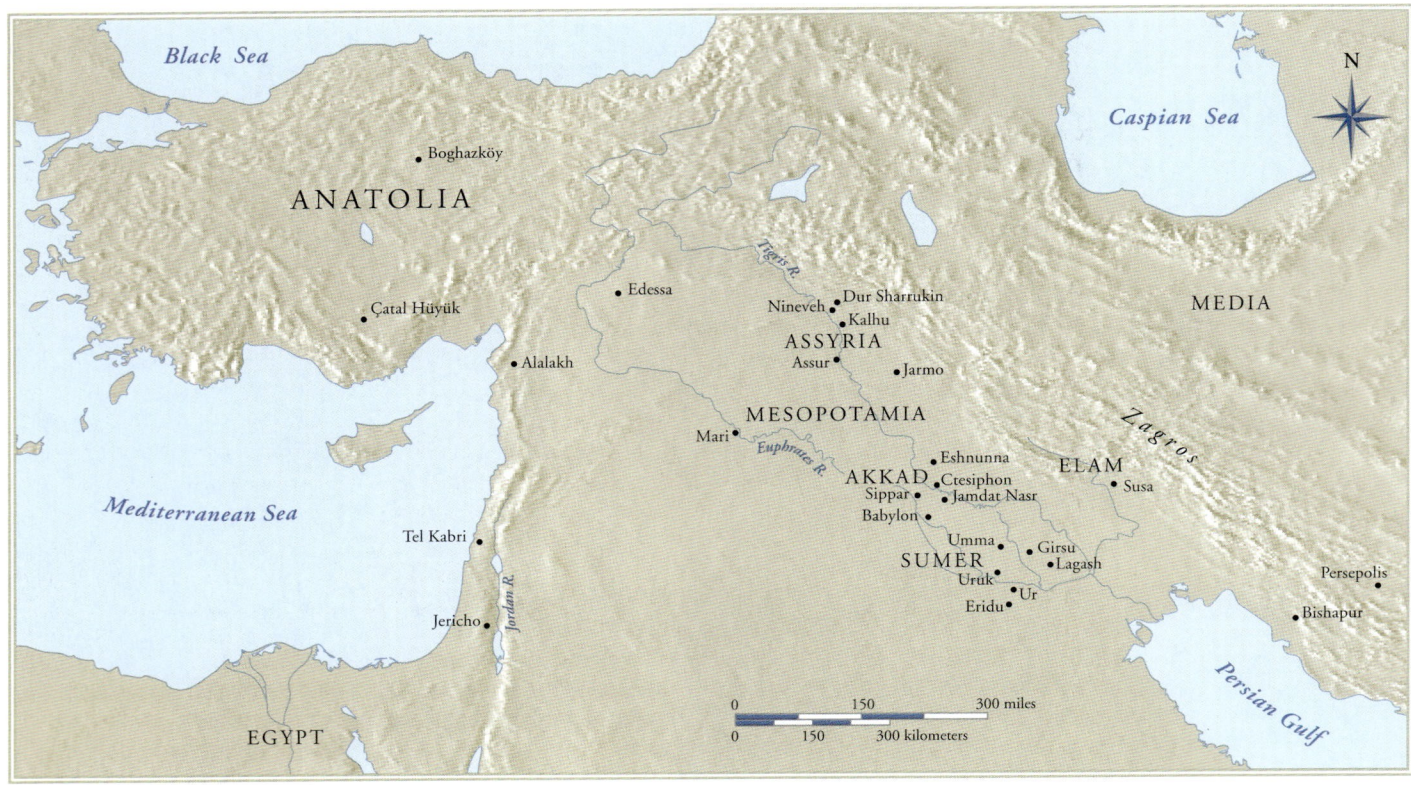

MAP 2-1 The ancient Near East.

burials rivaled the public fascination with the 1922 discovery of the tomb of the Egyptian boy-king Tutankhamen (see FIGS. 3-36 to 3-38). The Ur cemetery yielded gold objects, jewelry, artworks, and musical instruments (FIGS. 2-8 to 2-11) of the highest quality. Europe's royalty and elite frequently visited the site. One of the visitors was the mystery writer Agatha Christie, who later married one of the British archaeologists working at Ur. Her 1936 novel *Murder in Mesopotamia* centers on an excavation in Iraq.

## SUMERIAN ART

The discovery of the treasures of ancient Ur put the Sumerians once again in a prominent position on the world stage. They had been absent for more than 4,000 years. The Sumerians were the people who transformed the vast, flat lower valley between the Tigris and Euphrates into the Fertile Crescent of the ancient world. Sparsely inhabited before the Sumerians, this area is now southern Iraq. In the fourth millennium BCE, the Sumerians established the

2-1 White Temple and ziggurat, Uruk (modern Warka), Iraq, ca. 3200–3000 BCE.

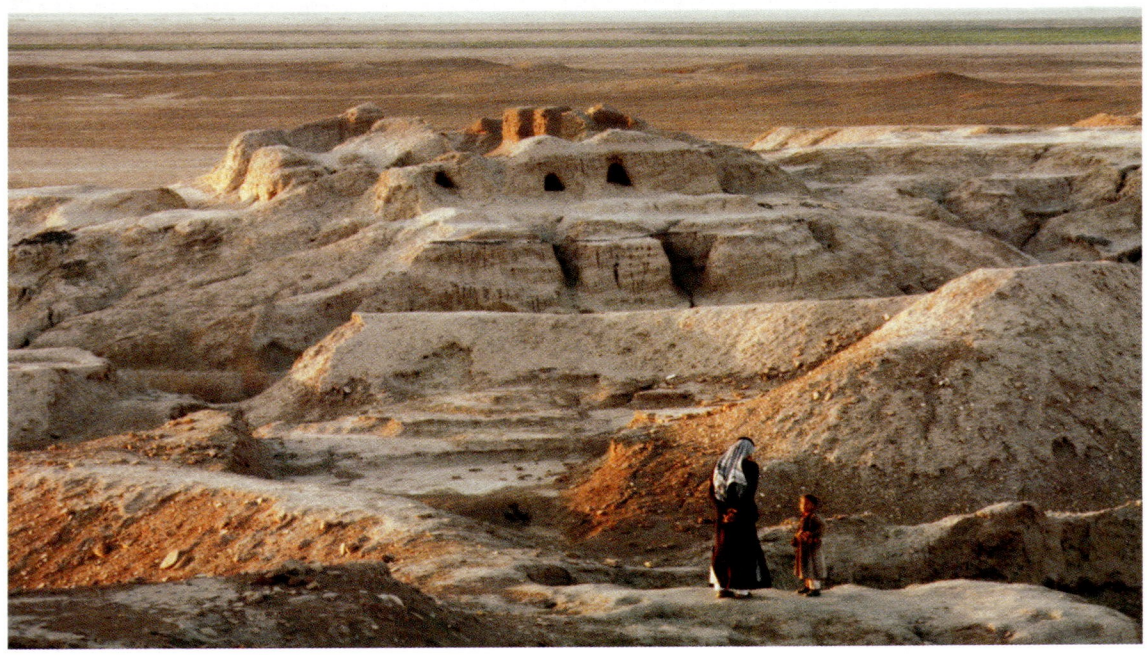

## The Invention of Writing

The oldest written documents are Mesopotamian records of administrative acts and commercial transactions. At first, around 3400–3200 BCE, the Sumerians (in Iraq) and their contemporaries, the Elamites (in Iran), made inventories of cattle, food, and other items by scratching *pictographs* (simplified pictures standing for words) into soft clay with a sharp tool, or *stylus.* The clay plaques hardened into breakable, yet nearly indestructible, tablets. This accounts for the existence today of thousands of documents dating back nearly five millennia. The Sumerians wrote their pictorial signs from the top down and arranged them in boxes they read from right to left. By 3000–2900 BCE, they had further simplified the pictographic signs by reducing them to a group of wedge-shaped *(cuneiform)* signs. The development of cuneiform marked the beginning of writing, as historians strictly define it. By 2600, cuneiform texts were sophisticated enough to express complex grammatical constructions.

The Sumerian and Elamite languages do not belong to any of the major linguistic groups of antiquity and are unrelated to each other, yet historians do not doubt that these early peoples were a major force in the spread of civilization. Thousands of cuneiform tablets, for example, testify to the far-flung network of Sumerian contacts reaching from southern Mesopotamia eastward to the Iranian plateau, northward to Assyria, and westward to Syria. Trade was essential for the Sumerians, because despite their land's fertility, it was poor in such vital natural resources as metal, stone, and wood.

The Sumerians also produced great literature. Their most famous work, known from fragmentary cuneiform texts, is the late-third-millennium *Epic of Gilgamesh,* which antedates Homer's *Iliad* and *Odyssey* by some 1,500 years. It recounts the heroic story of Gilgamesh, legendary king of Uruk and slayer of the monster Huwawa. Translations of the Sumerian epic into several other ancient Near Eastern languages attest to the fame of the original version.

first great urban communities and developed the earliest known writing system (see "The Invention of Writing," above).

**THE FIRST CITY-STATES** Ancient Sumer was not a unified nation; rather, it was made up of a dozen or so independent *city-states.* Each was thought to be under the protection of a different Mesopotamian deity. The Sumerian rulers were the gods' representatives on earth and the stewards of their earthly treasure. The rulers and priests directed all communal activities, including canal construction, crop collection, and food distribution. The development of agriculture to the point where only a portion of the population had to produce food made possible such an organization of the labor force. Some members of the community could thus specialize in other activities, including manufacturing, trade, and administration. Such labor specialization is the hallmark of the first complex urban societies. In the city-states of ancient Sumer, activities that once had been individually initiated became institutionalized for the first time. The community, rather than the family, assumed functions such as defense against enemies and against the caprices of nature. Whether ruled by a single person or a council chosen from among the leading families, these communities gained permanent identities as discrete cities. The city-state was one of the great Sumerian inventions.

**CITY PLANNING AND RELIGION** The Sumerian city plan reflected the central role of the local god in the daily life of the city-state's occupants. The god's temple formed the city's monumental nucleus. It was not only the focus of local religious practice but also an administrative and economic center. It was indeed the domain of the god, whom the Sumerians regarded as a great and rich holder of lands and herds, as well as the protector of the city-state. The vast temple complex, a kind of city within a city, thus had both religious and secular functions. A temple staff of priests and scribes carried on official business, looking after both the god's and the ruler's possessions.

**URUK'S WHITE TEMPLE** The outstanding preserved example of early Sumerian temple architecture is the 5,000-year-old White

Temple (FIG. 2-1) at Uruk, the home of Gilgamesh (see "The Invention of Writing," above). Usually only the foundations of early Mesopotamian temples can still be recognized. The White Temple is a rare exception. Sumerian builders did not have access to stone quarries and instead formed mud bricks for the superstructures of their temples and other buildings. Almost all these structures have eroded over the course of time. The fragile nature of the building materials did not, however, prevent the Sumerians from erecting towering works, such as the Uruk temple, several centuries before the Egyptians built their stone pyramids (see Chapter 3). This says a great deal about the Sumerians' desire to provide monumental settings for the worship of their deities.

Enough of the Uruk complex remains to permit a fairly reliable reconstruction drawing (FIG. 2-2). The temple (whose whitewashed walls lend it its modern nickname) stands on top of a high platform, or *ziggurat,* 40 feet above street level in the city center. A stairway on the far side, not shown, leads to the top but does not end in front of any of the temple doorways, necessitating two or three angular changes in direction. This "bent-axis" approach is the standard arrangement for Sumerian temples, a striking contrast to the linear approach the Egyptians preferred for their temples and tombs (see Chapter 3).

Like other Sumerian temples, the corners of the White Temple are oriented to the cardinal points of the compass. The building, probably dedicated to Anu, the sky god (see "The Gods and Goddesses of Mesopotamia," page 35), is of modest proportions

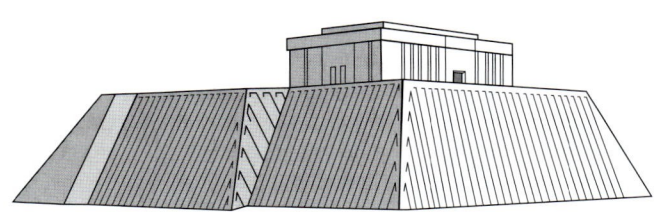

2-2 Reconstruction drawing of the White Temple and ziggurat, Uruk (modern Warka), Iraq, ca. 3200–3000 BCE (after S. E. Piggott).

(61 × 16 feet). By design, it did not accommodate large throngs of worshipers but only a select few, the priests and perhaps the leading community members. The temple has several chambers. The central hall, or *cella,* was set aside for the divinity and housed a stepped altar. The Sumerians referred to their temples as "waiting rooms," a reflection of their belief that the deity would descend from the heavens to appear before the priests in the cella. How or if the Uruk temple was roofed is uncertain.

The Sumerian idea that the gods reside above the world of humans is central to most of the world's religions. Moses ascended Mount Sinai to receive the Ten Commandments from the Hebrew God, and the Greeks placed the home of their gods and goddesses on Mount Olympus. The elevated placement of Mesopotamian temples on giant platforms reaching toward the sky is consistent with this widespread religious concept. Eroded ziggurats still dominate most of the ruined cities of Sumer. The loftiness of the great temple platforms made a profound impression on the peoples of the ancient Near East. The tallest ziggurat of all, at Babylon, was about 270 feet high. Known to the Hebrews as the Tower of Babel, it became the centerpiece of a biblical story about the insolent pride of humans (see "Babylon: City of Wonders," page 49).

**A MARBLE-AND-GOLD INANNA?** The White Temple at Uruk towers over all other vestiges of that ancient city, but a fragmentary white marble female head (FIG. **2-3**) is also an extraordinary achievement at so early a date. The lustrous hard stone had to be imported at great cost. The head is actually only a face with a flat back. It has drilled holes for attachment to a head and body, possibly of wood. Although found in the sacred precinct of the goddess Inanna, the subject is unknown. Many

have suggested that the face is an image of Inanna, but a mortal woman, perhaps a priestess, may be portrayed.

Often the present condition of an artwork can be very misleading, and the Uruk head is a dramatic example. Its original appearance would have been much more vibrant than the pure white fragment archaeologists uncovered. Colored shell or stone filled the deep recesses for the eyebrows and the large eyes. The deep groove at the top of the head anchored a wig, probably made of gold leaf. The hair strands engraved in the metal fell in waves over the forehead and sides of the face. The bright coloration of the eyes, brows, and hair likely overshadowed the soft modeling of the cheeks and mouth. The missing body was probably clothed in expensive fabrics and bedecked with jewels.

**GIFTS FOR A GODDESS** The Sumerians, pioneers in so many areas, also may have been the first to use pictures to tell coherent stories. Sumerian narrative art goes far beyond the Stone Age artists' tentative efforts at storytelling. The so-called *Warka Vase* (FIG. **2-4**) from Uruk (modern Warka) is the first great work of

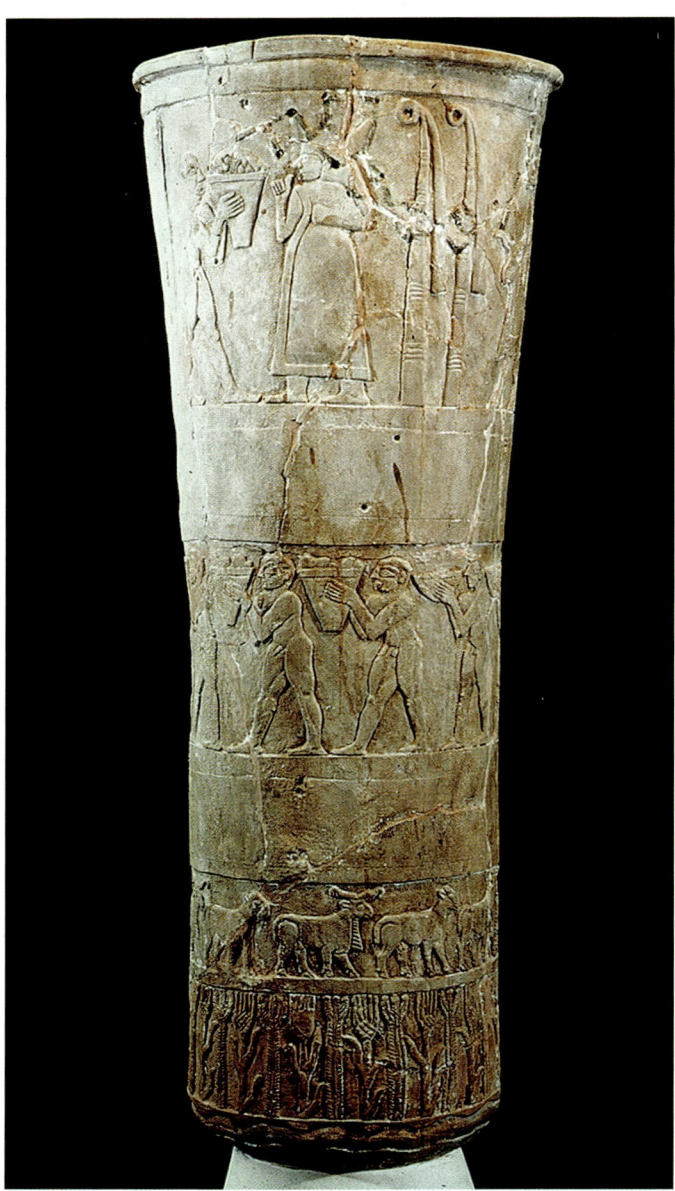

**2-4** Presentation of offerings to Inanna *(Warka Vase),* from Uruk (modern Warka), Iraq, ca. 3200–3000 BCE. Alabaster, 3′ $\frac{1}{4}$″ high. Iraq Museum, Baghdad.

**2-3** Female head (Inanna?), from Uruk (modern Warka), Iraq, ca. 3200–3000 BCE. Marble, approx. 8″ high. Iraq Museum, Baghdad.

### The Gods and Goddesses of Mesopotamia

The Sumerians and their successors in the ancient Near East worshiped numerous deities, mostly nature gods. The Mesopotamian gods and goddesses discussed in this chapter are listed here.

*Anu*, the chief deity of the Sumerians, was the god of the sky and of the city of Uruk. One of the earliest Sumerian temples (FIGS. 2-1 and 2-2) may have been dedicated to his worship.

*Enlil*, Anu's son, was the lord of the winds and the earth. He eventually replaced his father as king of the gods.

*Inanna* was the Sumerian goddess of love and war. Later known as *Ishtar*, she is the most important female deity in all periods of Mesopotamian history. At a very early date, the Sumerians constructed a sanctuary to Inanna at Uruk. Amid the ruins, excavators uncovered fourth-millennium statues and reliefs (FIGS. 2-3 and 2-4) connected with her worship. Whether or not the goddess herself was represented in human form at that time is uncertain. Inanna/Ishtar is unmistakably depicted with her sacred lion in a mural painting in the 18th-century BCE palace of Zimri-Lim at Mari (FIG. 2-17).

*Nanna*, the moon god, also known as *Sin*, was the chief deity of Ur, where his most important shrine was located.

*Utu*, god of the sun, known later as *Shamash*, was especially revered at Sippar. On a Babylonian stele (FIG. 2-16) of ca. 1780 BCE, King Hammurabi presents his law code to Shamash, who is depicted with flames radiating from his shoulders.

*Marduk* was the chief god of the Babylonians. His son *Nabu* was the god of writing and wisdom. *Adad* was the Babylonian god of storms. Nabu's dragon and Adad's sacred bull are depicted on the sixth-century BCE Ishtar Gate at Babylon (FIG. 2-25).

*Ningirsu* was the local god of Lagash and Girsu. His name means "lord of Girsu." Eannatum, one of the early rulers of Lagash, defeated an enemy army with the god's assistance and commemorated Ningirsu's role in the victory on the so-called *Stele of the Vultures* (FIG. 2-7) of ca. 2600–2500 BCE. Gudea (FIG. 2-15), one of Eannatum's Neo-Sumerian successors, built a great temple about 2100 BCE in honor of Ningirsu after the god instructed him to do so in a dream.

*Ashur*, the local deity of Assur, the city that took his name, became the king of the Assyrian gods. He sometimes is identified with Enlil.

---

narrative relief sculpture known. Found within the Inanna temple complex, it depicts a religious festival in honor of the goddess.

The sculptor divided the vase's reliefs into three bands (also called *registers* or *friezes*), and the figures stand on a ground line (the horizontal base of the composition). This new kind of composition marks a significant break with the haphazard figure placement found in earlier art. The register format for telling a story was to have a very long future. In fact, artists still employ registers today in modified form in comic books.

The lowest band on the *Warka Vase* shows ewes and rams—in strict profile, consistent with an approach to representing animals that was then some 20,000 years old—above crops and a wavy line representing water. These and the alternating male and female animals were the staple commodities of the Sumerian economy, but they were also associated with fertility. They underscore that Inanna had blessed Uruk's inhabitants with good crops and increased herds.

A procession of naked men fills the central band. The men carry baskets and jars overflowing with earth's abundance. They will present their bounty to the goddess as a *votive offering* (gift of gratitude to a deity usually made in fulfillment of a vow) and will deposit it in her temple. The spacing of each figure involves no overlapping. The Uruk men, like the prehistoric deer hunters at Çatal Höyük (see FIG. 1-17), are a composite of frontal and profile views, with large staring frontal eyes in profile heads. The artist indicated those human body parts necessary to communicate the human form and avoided positions, attitudes, or views that would conceal the characterizing parts. For example, if the figures were in strict profile, an arm and perhaps a leg would be hidden. The body would appear to have only half its breadth. And the eye would not "read" as an eye at all, because it would not have its distinctive flat oval shape. Art historians call this characteristic early approach to representation *conceptual*, as opposed to

*optical*, because artists who used it did not record the immediate, fleeting aspect of figures. Instead, they rendered the human body's distinguishing and fixed properties. The fundamental forms of figures, not their accidental appearance, dictated the artist's selection of the composite view as the best way to represent the human body.

In the uppermost (and tallest) band is a female figure with a tall horned headdress. Whether she is Inanna or her priestess is not known. A nude male figure brings a large vessel brimming with offerings to be deposited in the goddess's shrine. At the far right and barely visible in our illustration is an only partially preserved clothed man who is usually, if ambiguously, referred to as a "priest-king" because similar figures appear in other Sumerian artworks as leaders in both religious and secular contexts. The greater height of the priest-king and Inanna compared to the offering bearers indicates their greater importance, a convention called hierarchy of scale. Some scholars interpret the scene as a symbolic marriage between the priest-king and the goddess, ensuring her continued goodwill—and reaffirming the leader's exalted position in society.

**ESHNUNNA'S PERPETUAL WORSHIPERS** Further insight into Sumerian religious beliefs and rituals comes from a cache of sculptures reverently buried beneath the floor of a temple at Eshnunna (modern Tell Asmar) when the structure was remodeled. Carved of soft gypsum and inlaid with shell and black limestone, the statuettes range in size from well under a foot to about 30 inches tall. The two largest figures are shown in FIG. 2-5. All of the statuettes represent mortals, rather than deities, with their hands folded in front of their chests in a gesture of prayer, usually holding the small beakers the Sumerians used in religious rites. Hundreds of such goblets have been found in the temple complex at Eshnunna. The men wear belts and fringed

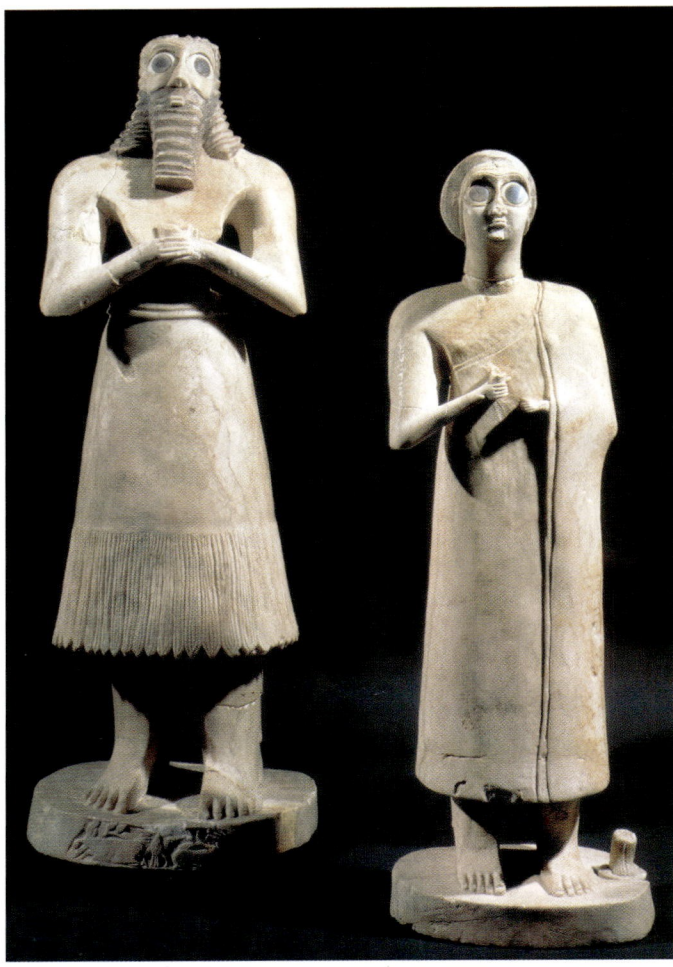

**2-5** Statuettes of two worshipers, from the Square Temple at Eshnunna (modern Tell Asmar), Iraq, ca. 2700 BCE. Gypsum inlaid with shell and black limestone, male figure approx. 2′ 6″ high. Iraq Museum, Baghdad.

skirts. Most have beards and shoulder-length hair. The women wear long robes, with the right shoulder bare. Similar figurines from other sites bear inscriptions giving such information as the name of the donor and the god or even specific prayers to the deity on the owner's behalf. With their heads tilted upward, they wait in the Sumerian "waiting room" for the divinity to appear.

The sculptors of the Eshnunna statuettes employed simple forms, primarily cones and cylinders, for the figures. The statuettes are not portraits in the strict sense of the word, but the sculptors did distinguish physical types. At least one child was portrayed—next to the woman in FIG. 2-5 are the remains of two small legs. Most striking is the disproportionate relationship between the inlaid oversized eyes and the tiny hands. Scholars have explained the exaggeration of the eye size in various ways. But because the purpose of these votive figures was to offer constant prayers to the gods on their donors' behalf, the open-eyed stares most likely symbolize the eternal wakefulness necessary to fulfill their duty.

**THE EUNUCH OF MARI** Another group of Sumerian votive statuettes comes from the Temple of Ishtar at Mari. Of particular interest is the figure of Urnanshe (FIG. 2-6), identified by an inscription. His eyes—inlaid with shell and lapis lazuli (a rich azure-blue stone imported from Afghanistan)—are unwavering in their intense gaze. Like the other figures in the group, Urnanshe

is bare chested, wears a tufted fleece skirt, and holds his arms (now broken) in front of his chest in a gesture of prayer. But he sits on a cushion with legs crossed, and he is beardless, with long straight hair that reaches to the waist, suggesting that he was a eunuch (castrated male). Urnanshe was neither priest nor ruler but the official singer at the Mari court. Another, very fragmentary, statuette portrays Urnanshe with a stringed instrument, that is, in his role as musician and singer at religious ceremonies. His statuettes attest that he stands ever ready to serve the goddess as well as his ruler.

**VICTORY AND VULTURES** The city-states of ancient Sumer were often at war with one another, and warfare is the theme of the so-called *Stele of the Vultures* (FIG. 2-7) from Girsu. A *stele* is a carved stone slab erected to commemorate a historical event or, in some other cultures, to mark a grave (see FIG. 5-55). The Girsu stele presents a labeled historical narrative. (It is not, however, the first historical representation in the history of art. That honor belongs—at the moment—to an Egyptian relief [FIG. 3-2] carved more than three centuries earlier.) Although the *Stele of the Vultures* is fragmentary, cuneiform inscriptions almost everywhere on the monument reveal that it celebrates the victory of Eannatum, the *ensi* (ruler; king?) of Lagash, over the neighboring city-state of Umma. The stele has reliefs on both sides and takes its

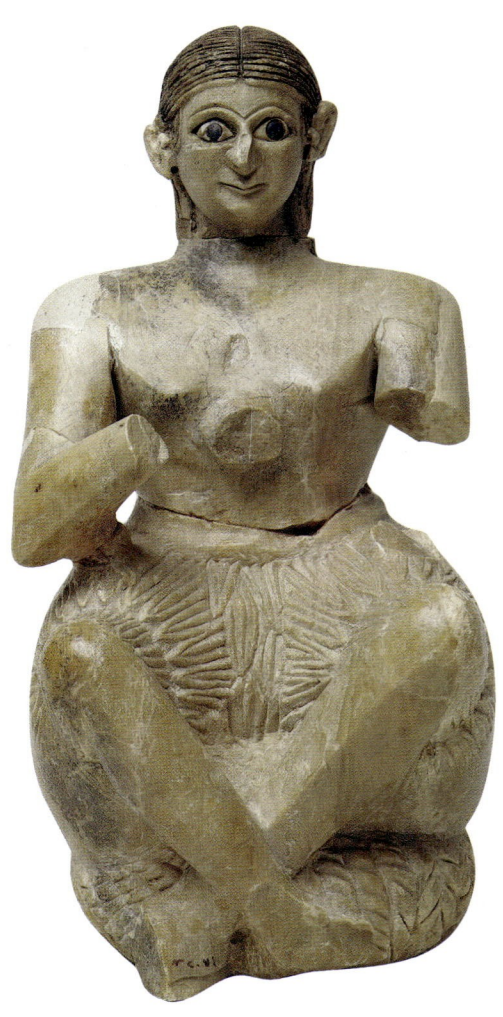

**2-6** Seated statuette of Urnanshe, from the Temple of Ishtar at Mari (modern Tell Hariri), Syria, ca. 2600–2500 BCE. Gypsum inlaid with shell and lapis lazuli, $10\frac{1}{4}$″ high. National Museum, Damascus.

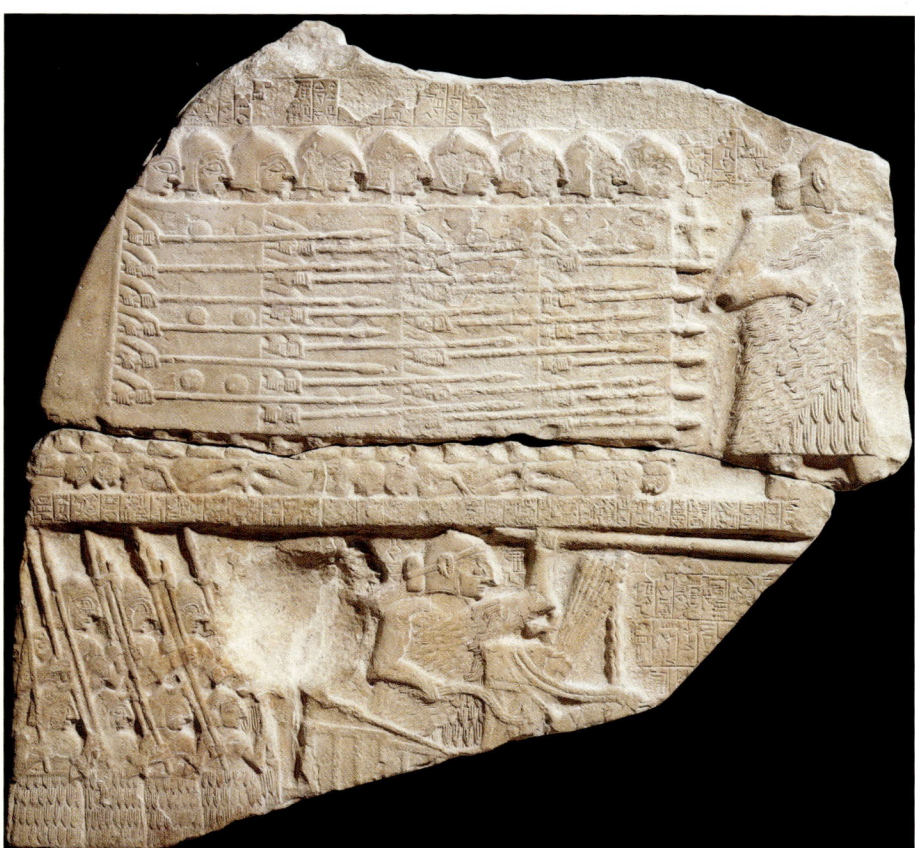

**2-7** Fragment of the victory stele of Eannatum (*Stele of the Vultures*), from Girsu (modern Telloh), Syria, ca. 2600–2500 BCE. Limestone, full stele approx. 5′ 11″ high. Louvre, Paris.

nickname from a fragment with a gruesome scene of vultures carrying off the severed heads and arms of the defeated enemy soldiers. Another fragment shows the giant figure of the local god Ningirsu holding tiny enemies in a net and beating one of them on the head with a mace.

The fragment in FIG. 2-7 depicts Eannatum leading an infantry battalion into battle (above) and attacking from a war chariot (below). The foot soldiers are protected behind a wall of shields and trample naked enemies as they advance. (The fragment that shows vultures devouring corpses belongs just to the right in the same register.) Both on foot and in a chariot, Eannatum is larger than anyone else, except Ningirsu on the other side of the stele. He is shown as the fearless general who paves the way for his army. Lives were lost, however, and Eannatum himself was wounded in the campaign. But the outcome was never in doubt, because Ningirsu fought with the men of Lagash.

Despite its fragmentary state, the *Stele of the Vultures* is an extraordinary document, not only as a very early effort to record historical events in relief but also for the insight it yields about Sumerian society. Through both words and pictures, it provides information about warfare techniques and the special nature of the Sumerian ruler. Eannatum was greater in stature than other men, and Ningirsu watched over him. According to the text, the ensi was born from the god Enlil's semen, which Ningirsu implanted in the womb. When Eannatum was wounded in battle, it says, the god shed tears for him. He was a divinely chosen ruler who presided over all aspects of his city-state, both in war and in peace. This also seems to have been the role of the ensi in the other Sumerian city-states.

**WAR AND PEACE** The spoils of war as well as success in farming and trade brought considerable wealth to some of the city-states of ancient Sumer. Nowhere is this clearer than in the so-called Royal Cemetery at Ur, the city that was home to the biblical Abraham. In the third millennium BCE, the leading families of Ur buried their dead in vaulted chambers beneath the earth. Scholars still debate whether these deceased were true kings and queens or simply aristocrats and priests, but they were laid to rest in regal fashion. Archaeologists exploring the Ur cemetery uncovered gold helmets and daggers with handles of lapis lazuli, golden beakers and bowls, jewelry of gold and lapis, musical instruments, chariots, and other luxurious items. Dozens of bodies were also found in the richest tombs. A retinue of musicians, servants, charioteers, and soldiers was sacrificed in order to accompany the "kings and queens" into the afterlife. Comparable rituals are documented in other societies, for example, in ancient America (see Chapter 14).

Not the costliest object found in the "royal" graves, but probably the most significant from the viewpoint of the history of art, is the so-called *Standard of Ur* (FIG. **2-8**). This rectangular box of uncertain function has sloping sides inlaid with shell, lapis lazuli, and red limestone. The excavator, Leonard Woolley, thought the object was originally mounted on a pole, and he considered it a kind of military standard—hence its nickname. Art historians usually refer to the two long sides of the box as the "war side" and "peace side," but the two sides may represent the first and second parts of a single narrative. The artist divided each into three horizontal bands. The narrative reads from left to right and bottom to top.

On the war side, four ass-drawn four-wheeled war chariots mow down enemies, whose bodies appear on the ground in front of and beneath the animals. The gait of the asses accelerates along the band from left to right. Above, foot soldiers gather up and lead away captured foes. In the uppermost register, soldiers present bound captives (who have been stripped naked to degrade them) to a king-like figure, who has stepped out of his chariot. His central place in

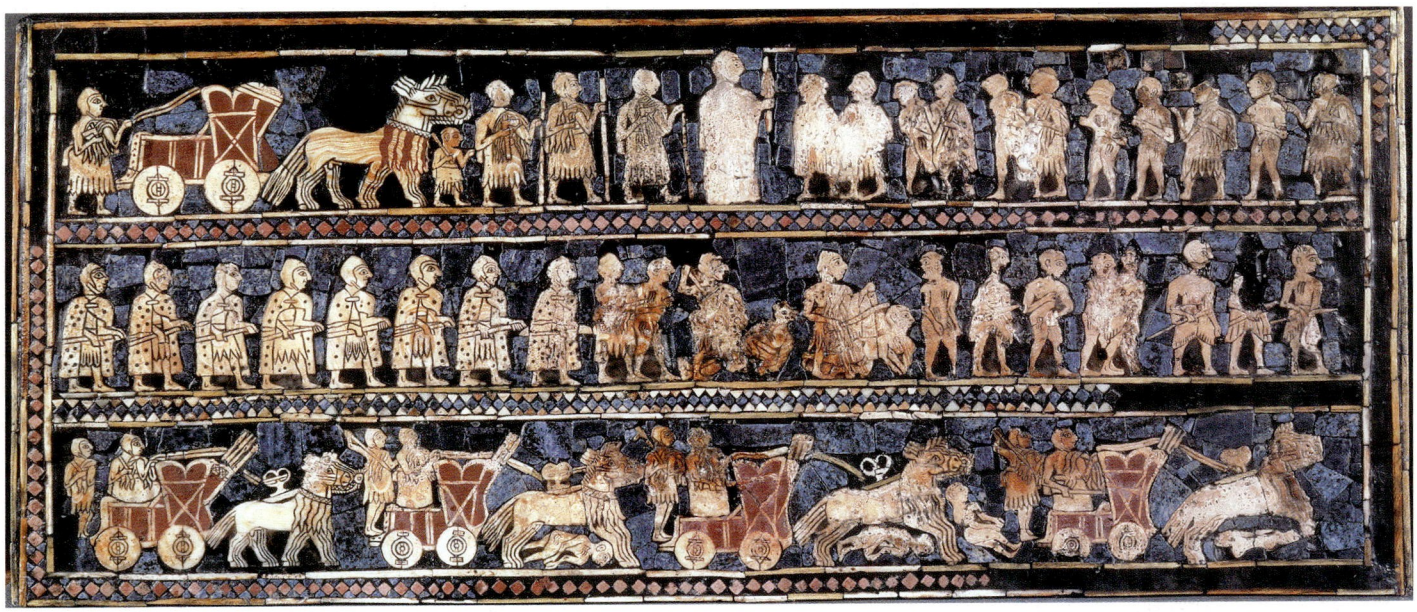

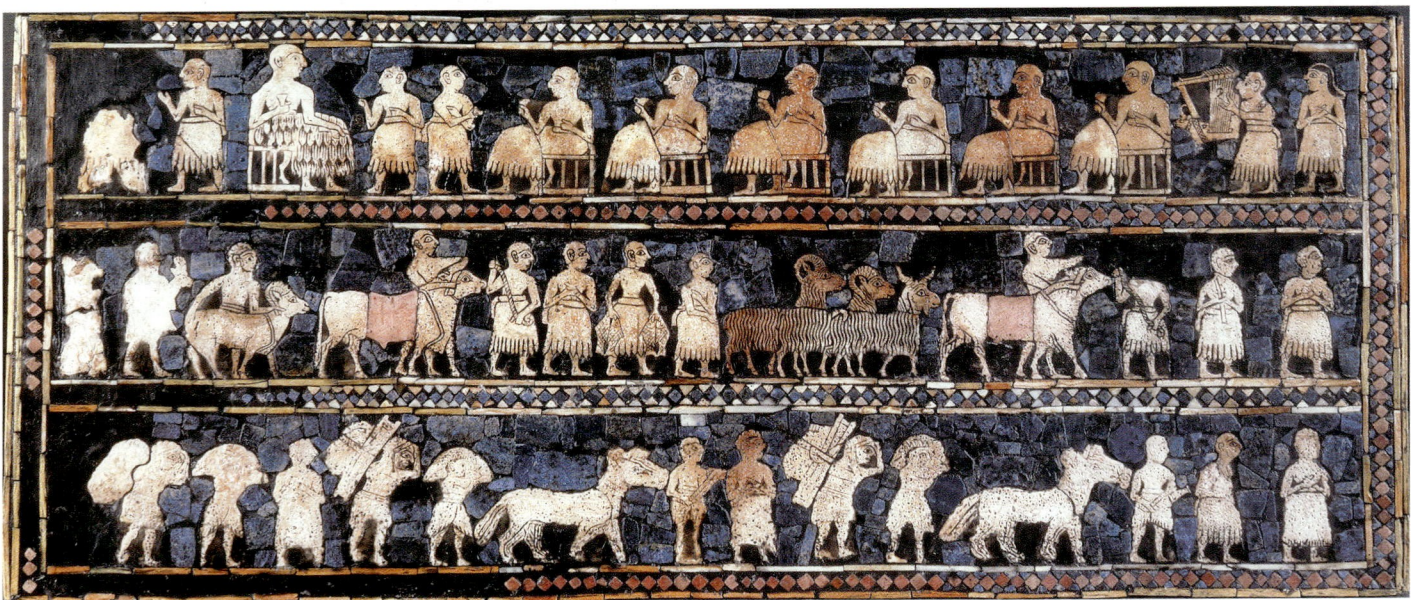

**2-8** War side *(top)* and peace side *(bottom)* of the *Standard of Ur,* from Tomb 779, Royal Cemetery, Ur (modern Tell Muqayyar), Iraq, ca. 2600 BCE. Wood inlaid with shell, lapis lazuli, and red limestone, approx. 8″ × 1′ 7″. British Museum, London.

the composition and his greater stature (his head breaks through the border at the top) set him apart from all the other figures.

In the lowest band on the peace side, men carry provisions, possibly war booty, on their backs. Above, attendants bring animals, perhaps also spoils of war, and fish for the great banquet depicted in the uppermost register. There, seated dignitaries and a larger-than-life "king" (third from the left) feast, while a lyre player and singer (at the far right, with long straight hair—like Urnanshe, FIG. 2-6) entertain the group. Art historians have interpreted the scene both as a victory celebration and as a banquet in connection with cult ritual. The two are not necessarily incompatible. The absence of an inscription prevents connecting the scenes with a specific event or person, but the *Standard of Ur* undoubtedly is another early example of historical narrative.

**ANIMAL ACTORS** From the "King's Grave" at Ur comes a splendid lyre (FIG. 2-9) that, in its restored state, resembles the instrument depicted in the feast scene on the *Standard of Ur.* A magnificent bull's head caps the instrument's sound box. It is fashioned of gold leaf over a wooden core. The hair, beard, and details are of lapis lazuli. The sound box (FIG. 2-10) also features bearded—but here human-headed—bulls in the uppermost of its four inlaid panels. Such imaginary composite creatures are commonplace in the art of the ancient Near East and Egypt. On the Ur lyre, a heroic figure embraces the two man-bulls in a *heraldic composition* (symmetrical on either side of a central figure). His body and that of the scorpion-man in the lowest panel are in composite view. The animals are, equally characteristically, solely in profile: the dog wearing a dagger and carrying a laden

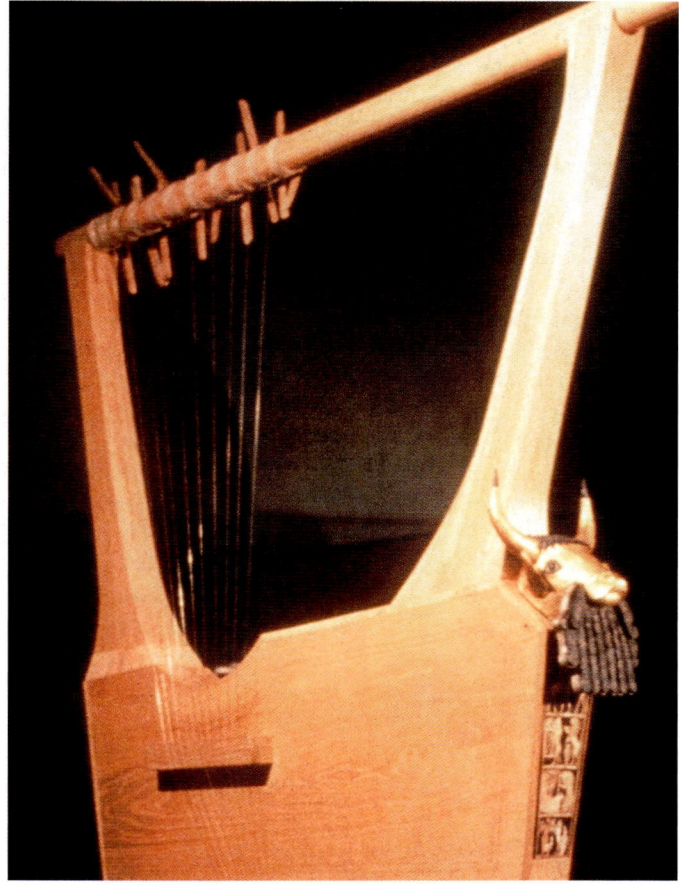

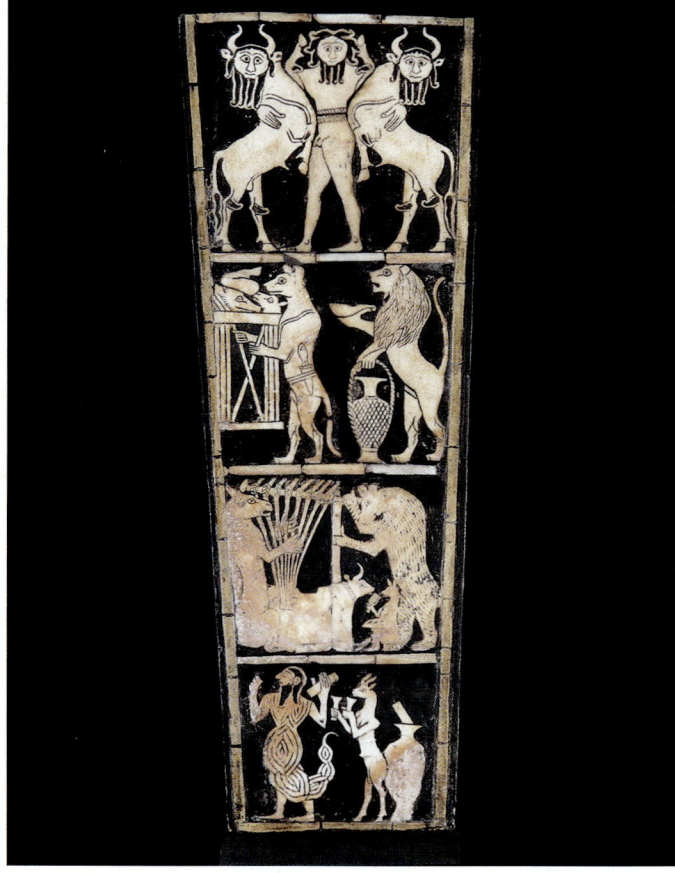

**2-9** Bull-headed lyre (restored) from Tomb 789 ("King's Grave"), Royal Cemetery, Ur (modern Tell Muqayyar), Iraq, ca. 2600 BCE. Gold leaf and lapis lazuli over a wooden core, approx. 5′ 5″ high. University Museum, University of Pennsylvania, Philadelphia.

**2-10** Soundbox of the lyre from Tomb 789 ("King's Grave"), Royal Cemetery, Ur (modern Tell Muqayyar), Iraq, ca. 2600 BCE. Wood with inlaid gold, lapis lazuli, and shell, approx. 1′ 7″ high. University Museum, University of Pennsylvania, Philadelphia.

table, the lion bringing in the beverage service, the ass playing the lyre, the jackal playing the zither, the bear steadying the lyre (or perhaps dancing), and the gazelle bearing goblets. The banquet animals almost seem to be burlesquing the kind of regal feast reproduced on the peace side of the *Standard of Ur*. The meaning of the sound box scenes is unclear. Some scholars have suggested, for example, that the creatures inhabit the land of the dead and that the narrative has a funerary significance. In any event, the sound box is a very early specimen of the recurring theme in both literature and art of animals acting as people. Later examples include Aesop's fables in ancient Greece, medieval bestiaries, and Walt Disney's cartoon animal actors.

**SUMERIAN ART IN MINIATURE** A banquet is also the subject of a *cylinder seal* (FIG. **2-11**) found in the tomb of "Queen" Pu-abi and inscribed with her name. (Many historians prefer to designate her more conservatively and ambiguously as "Lady" Pu-abi.) The seal is typical of the period, consisting of a cylindrical piece of stone engraved to produce a raised impression when rolled over clay (see "Mesopotamian Seals," page 40). In the upper zone, a man and a woman, probably Pu-abi, sit and drink from beakers, attended by servants. Below, male attendants serve two more seated men. Even in miniature and in a medium very different from that of the *Standard of Ur*, the Sumerian artist employed the same figure types and followed the same compositional rules.

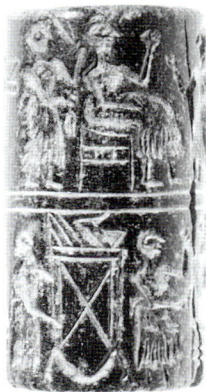 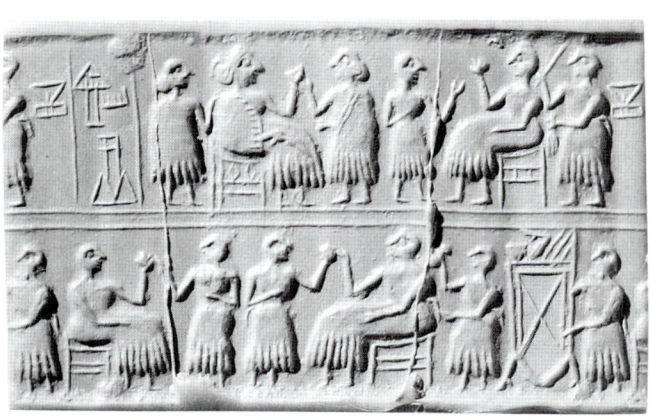

**2-11** Banquet scene, cylinder seal *(left)* and its modern impression *(right)*, from the Tomb of Pu-abi (Tomb 800), Royal Cemetery, Ur (modern Tell Muqayyar), Iraq, ca. 2600 BCE. Lapis lazuli, approx. 2″ high. British Museum, London.

## Mesopotamian Seals

Seals have been unearthed in great numbers at sites throughout Mesopotamia. Generally made of stone—the favorite materials were carnelian, jasper, lapis lazuli, and agate—seals of ivory, glass, and other materials also survive. The seals take two forms: flat *stamp seals* and *cylinder seals.* The latter have a hole drilled lengthwise through the center of the cylinder so that they could be strung and worn around the neck or suspended from the wrist. Cylinder seals were prized possessions, signifying high positions in society, and they frequently were buried with the dead.

The primary function of cylinder seals, however, like the earlier stamp seals, was not to serve as items of adornment. The Sumerians (and other peoples of the Near East) used both stamp and cylinder seals to identify their documents and protect storage jars and doors against unauthorized opening. The oldest seals predate the invention of writing and conveyed their messages with pictographs that ratified ownership. Later seals (FIG. 2-11) often bear long cuneiform inscriptions and record the names and titles of rulers, bureaucrats, and deities. Although sealing is increasingly rare, the tradition lives on today whenever a letter is sealed with a lump of wax and then stamped with a monogram or other identifying mark. Customs officials often still seal packages and sacks with official stamps when goods cross national borders.

In the ancient Near East, artists decorated both stamp and cylinder seals with incised designs, producing a raised pattern when the seal was pressed into soft clay. (Cylinder seals largely displaced stamp seals because they could be rolled over the clay and thus cover a greater area more quickly.) We illustrate a cylinder seal from the Royal Cemetery at Ur and a modern impression made from it (FIG. 2-11). Note how cracks in the stone cylinder become raised lines in the impression and how the engraved figures, chairs, and cuneiform characters appear in relief. Continuous rolling of the seal over a clay strip results in a repeating design, as our illustration also demonstrates at the edges.

The miniature reliefs the seals produce are a priceless source of information about Mesopotamian religion and society. Without them, archaeologists would know much less about how Mesopotamians dressed and dined; what their shrines looked like; how they depicted their gods, rulers, and mythological figures; how they fought wars; and what role women played in ancient Near Eastern society. Clay seal impressions excavated in architectural contexts shed a welcome light on the administration and organization of Mesopotamian city-states. Mesopotamian seals are also an invaluable resource for art historians, providing them with thousands of examples of relief sculpture that span roughly 3,000 years.

---

All the figures are in composite views with large frontal eyes in profile heads, and the seated dignitaries are once again larger in scale to underscore their elevated position in the social hierarchy.

## AKKADIAN, NEO-SUMERIAN, BABYLONIAN, AND HITTITE ART

**THE FIRST NEAR EASTERN KINGS** In 2334 BCE, the loosely linked group of cities known as Sumer came under the domination of a great ruler, Sargon of Akkad. Archaeologists have yet to locate the specific site of the city of Akkad, but it was in the vicinity of Babylon. The Akkadians were Semitic in origin—that is, they were a Near Eastern people who spoke a language related to Hebrew and Arabic. Their language, Akkadian, was entirely different from the language of Sumer, but they used the Sumerians' cuneiform characters for their written documents. Under Sargon (whose name means "true king") and his followers, the Akkadians introduced a new concept of royal power based on unswerving loyalty to the king rather than to the city-state. During the rule of Sargon's grandson, Naram-Sin (r. 2254–2218 BCE), governors of cities were considered mere servants of the king, who, in turn, called himself "King of the Four Quarters"—in effect, ruler of the earth, akin to a god.

**IMPERIAL MAJESTY VANDALIZED** A magnificent copper head of an Akkadian king (FIG. 2-12) found at Nineveh embodies this new concept of absolute monarchy. The head is all that survives of a statue that was knocked over in antiquity, perhaps when the Medes sacked Nineveh in 612 BCE. But the damage to the portrait was not due solely to the statue's toppling. There are also signs of deliberate mutilation. To make a political statement,

the enemy gouged out the eyes (once inlaid with precious or semiprecious stones), broke off the lower part of the beard, and slashed the ears of the royal portrait. Nonetheless, the king's majestic serenity, dignity, and authority are evident. So, too, is the

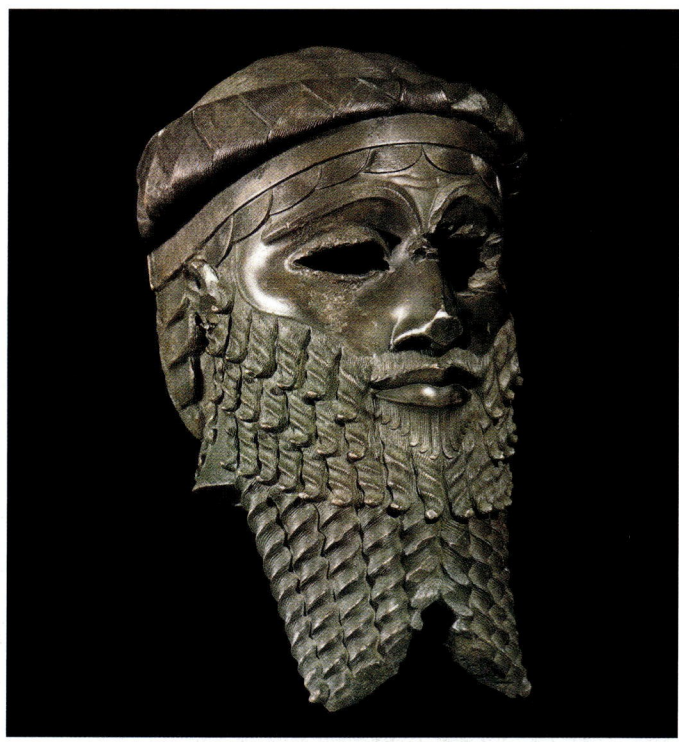

2-12  Head of an Akkadian ruler, from Nineveh (modern Kuyunjik), Iraq, ca. 2250–2200 BCE. Copper, 1' 2$\frac{3}{8}$" high. Iraq Museum, Baghdad.

masterful way the sculptor balanced naturalism and abstract patterning. The artist carefully observed and recorded the man's distinctive features—the profile of the nose and the long, curly beard. The sculptor brilliantly communicated the differing textures of flesh and hair—even the contrasting textures of the mustache, beard, and braided hair on the top of the head. The coiffure's triangles, lozenges, and overlapping disks of hair and the great arching eyebrows that give such character to the portrait reveal that the artist was also sensitive to formal pattern.

No less remarkable is the fact this is a life-size, hollow-cast metal sculpture (see "Hollow-Casting Life-Size Bronze Statues," Chapter 5, page 131), one of the earliest known. The head demonstrates the artisan's sophisticated skill in casting and polishing copper and in engraving the details. The portrait is the earliest known great monumental work of hollow-cast sculpture.

**A GOD-KING CRUSHES AN ENEMY** The godlike sovereignty the kings of Akkad claimed is also evident in the victory stele (FIG. **2-13**) Naram-Sin set up at Sippar. The stele commemorates his defeat of the Lullubi, a people of the Iranian mountains to the east. It is inscribed twice, once in honor of Naram-Sin and once by an Elamite king who had captured Sippar in 1157 BCE and taken the stele as booty back to Susa, where it was found. On the stele, the grandson of Sargon leads his victorious army up the slopes of a wooded mountain. His routed enemies fall, flee, die, or beg for mercy. The king stands alone, far taller than his men, treading on the bodies of two of the fallen Lullubi. He wears the horned helmet signifying divinity—the first time a king appears as a god in Mesopotamian art. At least three favorable stars (the stele is damaged at the top) shine on his triumph.

By storming the mountain, Naram-Sin seems also to be scaling the ladder to the heavens, the same conceit that lies behind the great ziggurat towers of the ancient Near East. His troops march up the mountain behind him in orderly files, suggesting the discipline and organization of the king's forces. The enemy, by contrast, is in disarray, depicted in a great variety of postures—one falls headlong down the mountainside. The sculptor adhered to older conventions in many details, especially by portraying the king and his soldiers in composite views and by placing a frontal two-horned helmet on Naram-Sin's profile head. But in other respects this work shows daring innovation. Here, the sculptor created the first landscape in Near Eastern art since the Çatal Höyük mural (see FIG. 1-18) and set the figures on successive tiers within that landscape. This was a bold rejection of the standard means of telling a story in a series of horizontal registers, the compositional formula that was the rule not only in earlier Mesopotamian art but also in Egyptian art.

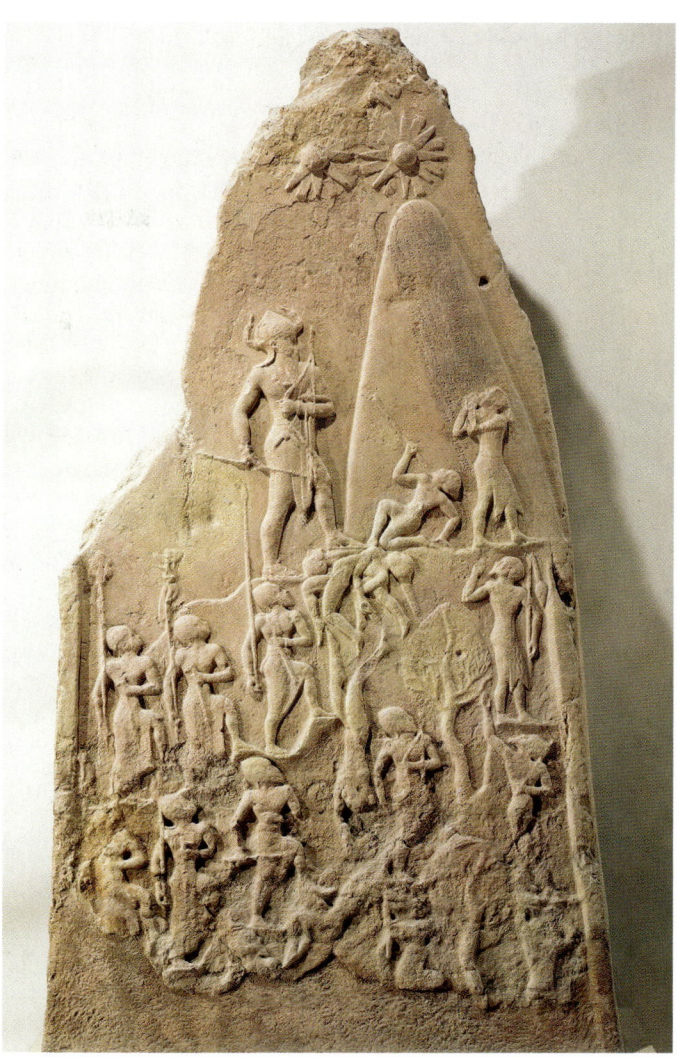

**2-13** Victory stele of Naram-Sin, from Susa, Iran, 2254–2218 BCE. Pink sandstone, approx. 6′ 7″ high. Louvre, Paris.

**THE RESURGENCE OF SUMER** Around 2150 BCE, a mountain people, the Gutians, brought Akkadian power to an end. The cities of Sumer, however, soon united in response to the alien presence, drove the Gutians out of Mesopotamia, and established a Neo-Sumerian state ruled by the kings of Ur. This age, which historians call the Third Dynasty of Ur, saw the construction of the ziggurat at Ur (FIG. 2-14), one of the largest in Mesopotamia.

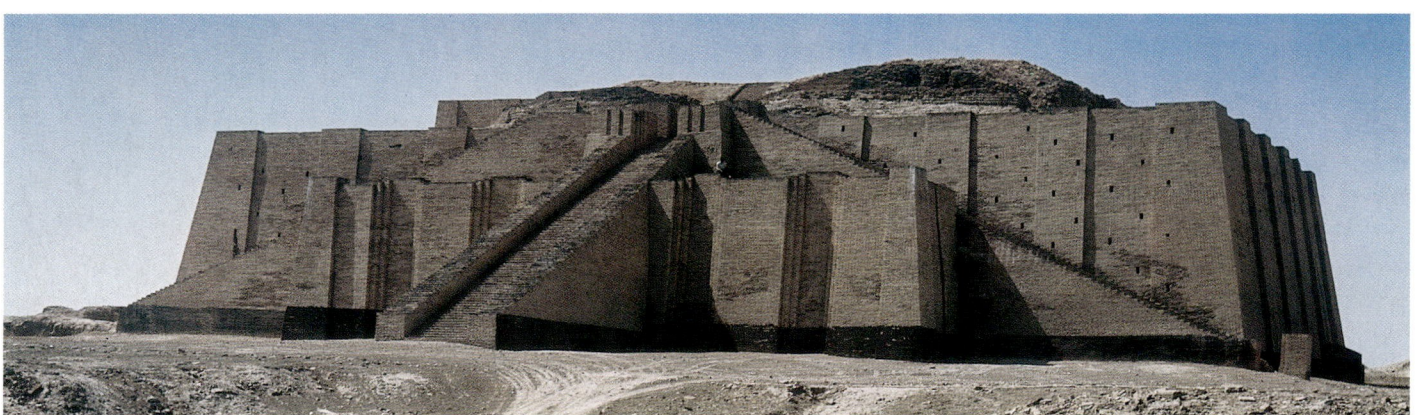

**2-14** Ziggurat (northeastern facade with restored stairs), Ur (modern Tell Muqayyar), Iraq, ca. 2100 BCE.

## The Piety of Gudea

One of the central figures of the Neo-Sumerian age was Gudea, ensi of Lagash ca. 2100 BCE. Nearly two dozen portraits of him survive. All stood in temples where they could render perpetual service to the gods and intercede with the divine powers on his behalf. Although a powerful ruler, Gudea rejected the regal trappings of Sargon of Akkad and his successors in favor of a return to the Sumerian votive tradition of the statuettes from Eshnunna and Mari (FIGS. 2-5 and 2-6). Like the earlier examples, some of Gudea's statues are inscribed with messages to the gods of Sumer. One from Girsu says, "I am the shepherd loved by my king [Ningirsu, the god of Girsu]; may my life be prolonged." Another, also from Girsu, as if in answer to the first, says, "Gudea, the builder of the temple, has been given life."

In fact, Gudea built or rebuilt, at great cost, all the temples where he placed his statues. One characteristic portrait (FIG. 2-15) depicts the pious ruler of Lagash seated with his hands clasped in front of him in a gesture of prayer. The head is unfortunately lost, but the statue is of unique interest because Gudea has a temple plan drawn on a tablet on his lap. The ruler buried accounts of his building enterprises in the temple foundations. The surviving texts describe how the Neo-Sumerians prepared and purified the sites, obtained the materials, and dedicated the completed temples. They also record Gudea's dreams of the gods asking him to erect temples in their honor, promising him prosperity if he fulfilled his duty. In one of these dreams, Ningirsu addresses Gudea:

> When, O faithful shepherd Gudea, thou shalt have started work for me on Erinnu, my royal abode [Ningirsu's new temple], I will call up in heaven a humid wind. It shall bring the abundance from on high. . . . All the great fields will bear for thee; dykes and canals will swell for thee; . . . good weight of wool will be given in thy time.[1]

In our statue, Gudea presents Ningirsu with his plan for the god's new temple. When the structure was completed and his people enjoyed good harvests and plentiful flocks, they knew it was the result of Gudea's piety.

[1] Thorkild Jacobsen, trans., *The Art and Architecture of the Ancient Orient*, by Henri Frankfort, 5th ed. (New Haven: Yale University Press, 1996), 98.

---

The Ur ziggurat was built about a millennium later than that at Uruk (FIGS. 2-1 and 2-2) and is much grander. The base is a solid mass of mud brick 50 feet high. The builders used baked bricks laid in bitumen, an asphaltlike substance, for the facing of the entire monument. Three ramplike stairways of a hundred steps each converge on a tower-flanked gateway. From there another flight of steps probably led to the temple proper, which does not survive.

**GUDEA'S DIORITE PORTRAITS** The most conspicuous preserved sculptural monuments of the Neo-Sumerian age portray Gudea of Lagash (see "The Piety of Gudea," above). His statues show him seated or standing, hands tightly clasped, head shaven, sometimes wearing a woolen brimmed hat, and always dressed in a long garment that leaves one shoulder and arm exposed (FIG. 2-15). Gudea was zealous in granting the gods their due, and the numerous statues he commissioned are an enduring testimony to his piety—and to his wealth and pride. All his portraits are of polished diorite, a rare and costly dark stone that had to be imported. Diorite is also extremely hard and difficult to carve. The prestige of the material—which in turn lent prestige to Gudea's portraits—is evident from an inscription on one of Gudea's statues: "This statue has not been made from silver nor from lapis lazuli, nor from copper nor from lead, nor yet from bronze; it is made of diorite."

**HAMMURABI OF BABYLON** The resurgence of Sumer was short-lived. The last of the kings of the Third Dynasty of Ur fell at the hands of the Elamites, who ruled the territory east of the Tigris River. The following two centuries witnessed the reemergence of the traditional Mesopotamian political pattern of several independent city-states existing side by side. Until Babylon's most powerful king, Hammurabi (r. 1792–1750 BCE), reestablished a centralized government that ruled southern Mesopotamia, Babylon was one of these city-states. Perhaps the most renowned king in Mesopo-

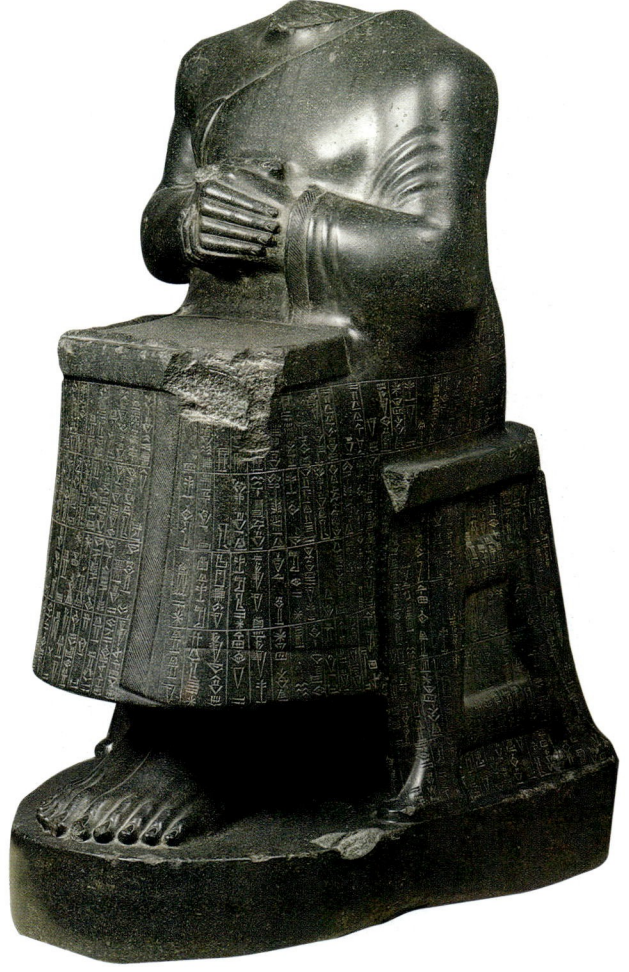

**2-15** Seated statue of Gudea holding temple plan, from Girsu (modern Telloh), Iraq, ca. 2100 BCE. Diorite, approx. 2′ 5″ high. Louvre, Paris.

### Hammurabi's Law Code

In the early 18th century BCE, King Hammurabi of Babylon formulated a comprehensive law code for his people. At the time, parts of Europe were still in the Stone Age (see FIG. 1-19). Even in Greece, it was not until more than 1,000 years later that Draco provided Athens with its first written set of laws. Hammurabi was following the tradition his Sumerian predecessors established. Two similar earlier law codes survive in part, but Hammurabi's laws are the only ones known in great detail, thanks to the chance survival of a tall and narrow stele (FIG. 2-16) depicting the god Shamash extending to Hammurabi the rod and ring that symbolize authority. The symbols derive from builders' tools—measuring rods and coiled rope—and connote the ruler's capacity to build the social order and to measure people's lives, that is, to render judgments. The sculptor thus informed viewers that Hammurabi had the god-given authority to enforce the laws spelled out on the stele. The judicial code, written in Akkadian, was inscribed in 3,500 lines of cuneiform characters. Hammurabi's laws governed all aspects of Babylonian life, from commerce and property to murder and theft to marital fidelity, inheritances, and the treatment of slaves.

We list only a small sample of the infractions described and the penalties imposed (which vary with the person's standing in society).

- If a man puts out the eye of another man, his eye shall be put out.
- If he kills a man's slave, he shall pay one-third of a *mina*.
- If someone steals property from a temple, he will be put to death, as will the person who receives the stolen goods.
- If a man rents a boat and the boat is wrecked, the renter shall replace the boat with another.
- If a married woman dies before bearing any sons, her dowry shall be repaid to her father, but if she gave birth to sons, the dowry shall belong to them.
- If a man's wife is caught in bed with another man, both will be tied up and thrown in the water.

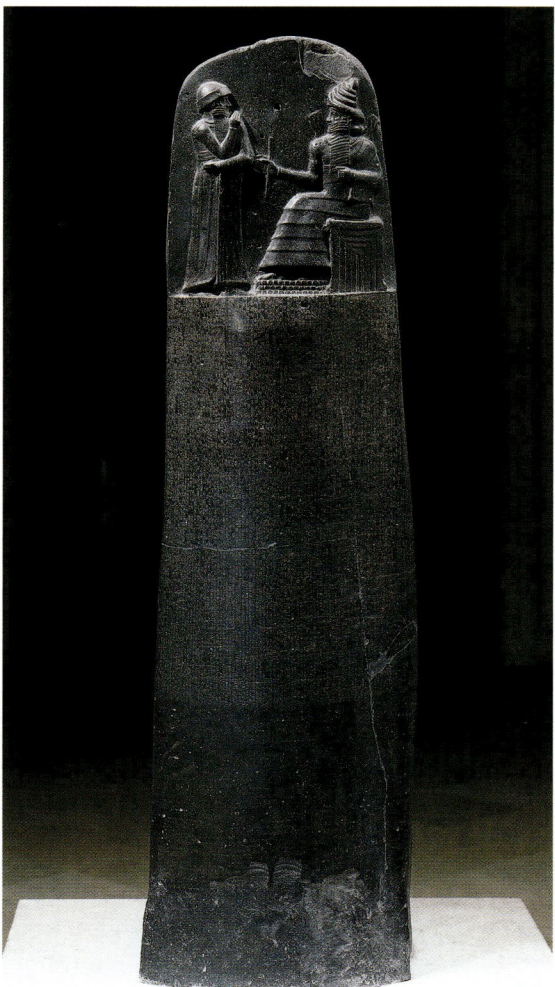

**2-16** Stele with law code of Hammurabi, from Susa, Iran, ca. 1780 BCE. Basalt, approx. 7′ 4″ high. Louvre, Paris.

tamian history, Hammurabi was famous for his conquests. But he is best known today for his law code, which prescribed penalties for everything from adultery and murder to the cutting down of a neighbor's trees (see "Hammurabi's Law Code," above).

The code is inscribed on a tall black-basalt stele (FIG. **2-16**) that was carried off as booty to Susa in 1157 BCE, together with the Naram-Sin stele (FIG. 2-13). At the top is a relief depicting Hammurabi in the presence of the flame-shouldered sun god, Shamash. The king raises his hand in respect. The god bestows on Hammurabi the authority to rule and to enforce the laws.

The sculptor depicted Shamash in the familiar convention of combined front and side views, but with two important exceptions. His great headdress with its four pairs of horns is in true profile so that only four, not all eight, of the horns are visible. And the artist seems to have tentatively explored the notion of foreshortening—a device for suggesting depth by representing a figure or object at an angle, rather than frontally or in profile. The god's beard is a series of diagonal rather than horizontal lines, suggesting its recession from the picture plane.

**ZIMRI-LIM AND ISHTAR** While Hammurabi ruled Babylon, King Zimri-Lim (r. 1779–1757 BCE) controlled the Neo-Sumerian city-state of Mari. Zimri-Lim constructed a huge palace complex at Mari, but in 1757 BCE Hammurabi led an army into the city and destroyed the royal residence. The mud-brick palace walls were adorned with paintings on plaster. Fortunately, despite their extreme fragility, some of the paintings survive. They provide a rare opportunity to study the art of mural painting in Mesopotamia.

The painting we reproduce (FIG. **2-17**) covered one wall of the palace's main courtyard near the entrance to the throne room suite. At the center, the painter represented the *investiture* of Zimri-Lim, the granting of his right to rule, by the goddess Ishtar. The king approaches Ishtar with his right arm raised in greeting and respect, just as Hammurabi appeared before Shamash

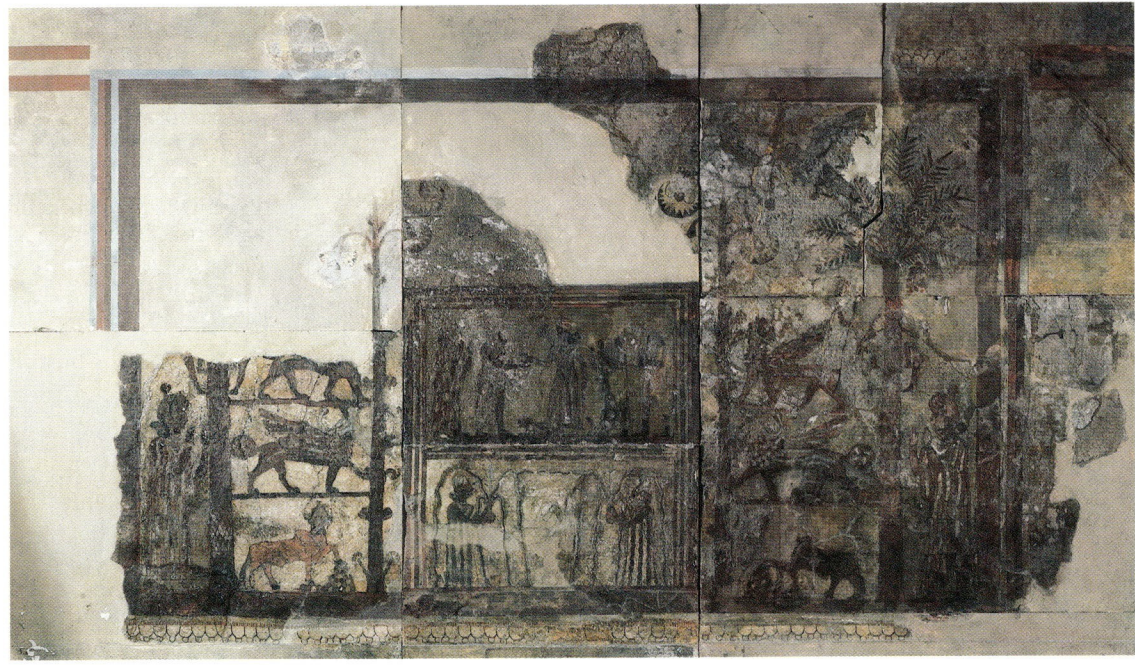

**2-17** Investiture of Zimri-Lim, mural painting from Court 106 of the palace at Mari (modern Tell Hariri), Syria, ca. 1775–1760 BCE. Louvre, Paris.

(FIG. 2-16). The goddess has one foot on her sacred lion and offers Zimri-Lim the emblems of power, the rod and ring. A god and two other goddesses witness the ceremony. Below, two more goddesses display vases from which plants grow and streams of life-giving water flow. Fish swim freely in the current. The general theme is a venerable one. The gods grant royal authority to their chosen kings and prosperity to their people.

As on Hammurabi's stele, the horned crowns the deities wear are in profile, although the painter showed no interest in foreshortening. In fact, such experiments are very uncommon. Innovations in representational modes like this one and the bold abandonment of the register format in favor of a tiered landscape on the Naram-Sin stele (FIG. 2-13) were exceptional in early eras

of the history of art. These occasional departures from the norm testify to the creativity of some ancient Near Eastern artists.

**THE HITTITES' FORTIFIED CAPITAL** The Babylonian Empire toppled in the face of an onslaught by the Hittites, an Anatolian people who conquered and sacked Babylon around 1595 BCE. They then retired to their homeland, leaving Babylon in the hands of the Kassites. Remains of the strongly fortified capital city of the Hittites still may be seen near Boghazköy, Turkey. Constructed of large blocks of heavy stone—a striking contrast to the brick architecture of Mesopotamia—the walls and towers of the Hittites effectively protected them from attack. Symbolically guarding the gateway (FIG. **2-18**) to the Boghazköy

**2-18** Lion Gate, Boghazköy, Turkey, ca. 1400 BCE. Limestone, lions approx. 7′ high. 🔊

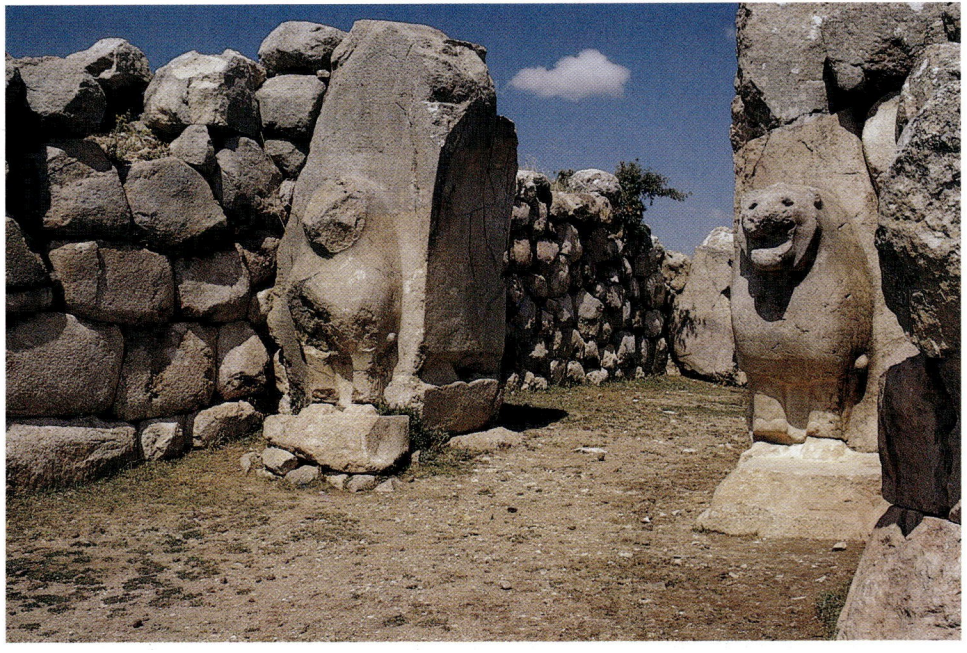

citadel are two huge (seven-foot-high) lions. Their simply carved forequarters project from massive stone blocks on either side of the entrance. These Hittite guardian beasts are early examples of a theme that was to be echoed on many Near Eastern gates. Notable are those of Assyria (FIG. 2-21), one of the greatest empires of the ancient world, and of the reborn Babylon (FIG. 2-25) in the first millennium BCE. But the idea of protecting a city, palace, temple, or tomb from evil by placing wild beasts or fantastic monsters before an entranceway was not unique to the Near Eastern world. Examples abound in Egypt, Greece, Italy, and elsewhere.

# MIDDLE ELAMITE AND ASSYRIAN ART

**ELAM AT ITS HEIGHT** To the east of Sumer, Akkad, and Babylon, the Elamites and their ancestors had occupied southwestern Iran since the fourth millennium BCE. Elam appears in the Bible as early as Genesis 10:22, and Proto-Elamite and Elamite records are among the earliest written documents known (see "The Invention of Writing," page 33). During the second half of the second millennium BCE, Elam reached the height of its political and military power. At this time the Elamites were strong enough to plunder Babylonia and to carry off the stelae of Naram-Sin and Hammurabi (FIGS. 2-13 and 2-16) and reerect them at their capital city, Susa. The Assyrian king Ashurbanipal finally destroyed the empire of Elam in 641 BCE when he sacked Susa. The city would rise again to great importance under the Achaemenid Persian Empire.

**NAPIR-ASU'S IMMOVABLE PORTRAIT** In the ruins of Susa, archaeologists discovered a life-size bronze-and-copper statue of Queen Napir-Asu (FIG. **2-19**), wife of one of the most powerful Elamite kings, Untash-Napirisha. The statue weighs 3,760 pounds even in its fragmentary and mutilated state, because the sculptor, incredibly, cast the statue with a solid bronze core inside a hollow-cast copper shell. The bronze core increased the cost of the statue enormously, but the queen wished her portrait to be a permanent, immovable votive offering in the temple where it was found. In fact, the Elamite inscription on the queen's skirt explicitly asks the gods to protect the statue:

> He who would seize my statue, who would smash it, who would destroy its inscription, who would erase my name, may he be smitten by the curse of [the gods], that his name shall become extinct, that his offspring be barren. . . . This is Napir-Asu's offering.[1]

The statue thus falls within the votive tradition going back to the third millennium BCE and the figurines from Eshnunna and Mari (FIGS. 2-5 and 2-6). In the Elamite statue of Queen Napir-Asu, the Mesopotamian instinct for cylindrical volume is again evident. The portrait's tight silhouette, strict frontality, and firmly crossed hands held close to the body are all enduring characteristics common to the Sumerian statuettes. Yet within these rigid conventions of form and pose, the Elamite artist managed to create refinements that must have come from close observation. The sculptor conveyed the feminine softness of arm and bust, the grace and elegance of the long-fingered hands, the supple and quiet bend of the wrist, the ring and bracelets, and the gown's

patterned fabric. The loss of the head is especially unfortunate. The figure presents a portrait of the ideal queen. The hands crossed over the belly may allude to fertility and the queen's role in assuring peaceful dynastic succession.

**ASSYRIAN FORTRESS-PALACES** During the first half of the first millennium BCE, the fearsome Assyrians vanquished the various warfaring peoples that succeeded the Babylonians and Hittites. The Assyrians took their name from Assur, the city on the Tigris River in northern Iraq named for the god Ashur. At the height of their power, the Assyrians ruled an empire that extended from the Tigris to the Nile Rivers and from the Persian Gulf to Asia Minor. Their palaces have been excavated in large part, yielding not only their plans but also statues, mural paintings, and the most extensive series of narrative reliefs in the ancient Near East.

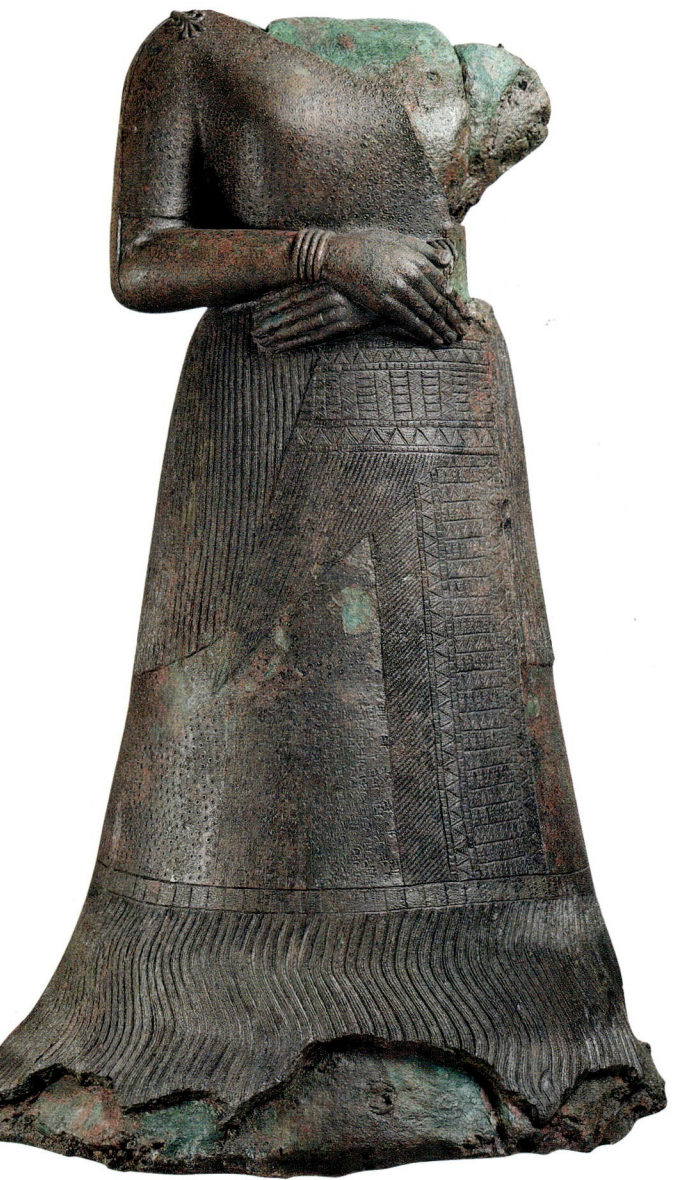

2-19 Statue of Queen Napir-Asu, from Susa, Iran, ca. 1350–1300 BCE. Bronze and copper, 4′ 2¾″ high. Louvre, Paris.

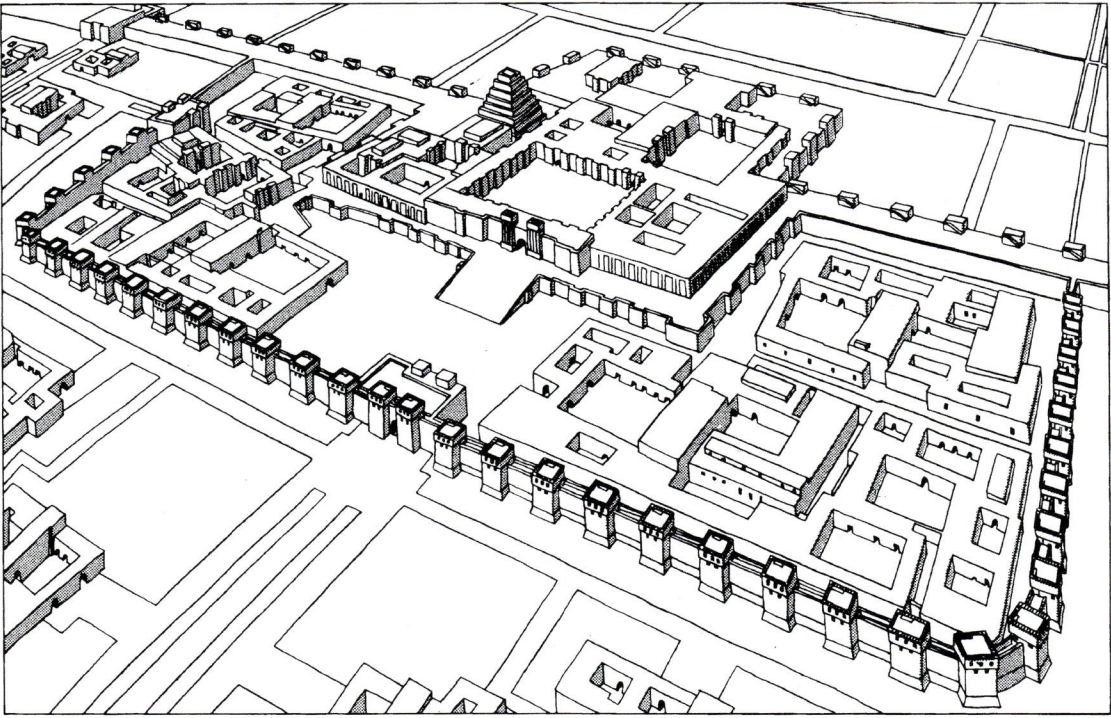

**2-20** Reconstruction drawing of the citadel of Sargon II, Dur Sharrukin (modern Khorsabad), Iraq, ca. 720–705 BCE (after Charles Altman).

The unfinished royal citadel of Sargon II (r. 721–705 BCE) at Dur Sharrukin (FIG. 2-20) reveals in its ambitious layout the confidence of the Assyrian kings in their all-conquering might. Its strong defensive walls also reflect a society ever fearful of attack during a period of almost constant warfare. The city measures about a square mile in area. The palace, elevated on a mound 50 feet high, covered some 25 acres and had more than 200 courtyards and rooms. As our reconstruction drawing shows, although the palace complex layout had a basic symmetry, the plan is rambling. Timber-roofed rectangular rooms and halls are grouped around square and rectangular courts. Behind the main courtyard, whose sides each measured 300 feet, were the residential quarters of the king, who received foreign emissaries in the long, high, brightly painted throne room. All visitors entered from another large courtyard, where giant figures of the king and his courtiers lined the walls.

Sargon II regarded his city and palace as an expression of his grandeur. The Assyrians cultivated an image of themselves as merciless to anyone who dared oppose them, although they were forgiving to those who submitted to their will. Sargon, for example, wrote in an inscription, "I built a city with [the labors of] the peoples subdued by my hand, whom Ashur, Nabu, and Marduk had caused to lay themselves at my feet and bear my yoke." And in another text, he proclaimed, "Sargon, King of the World, has built a city. Dur Sharrukin he has named it. A peerless palace he has built within it."

In addition to the complex of courtyards, throne room, state chambers, service quarters, and guard rooms that made up the palace, the citadel included a great ziggurat and six sanctuaries for six different gods. The ziggurat at Dur Sharrukin may have had as many as seven stories. Four remain, each 18 feet high and painted a different color. A continuous ramp spiraled around the building from its base to the temple at its summit. Here, the legacy of the Sumerian bent-axis approach may be seen more than two millennia after the erection of the White Temple on the ziggurat at Uruk (FIG. 2-1).

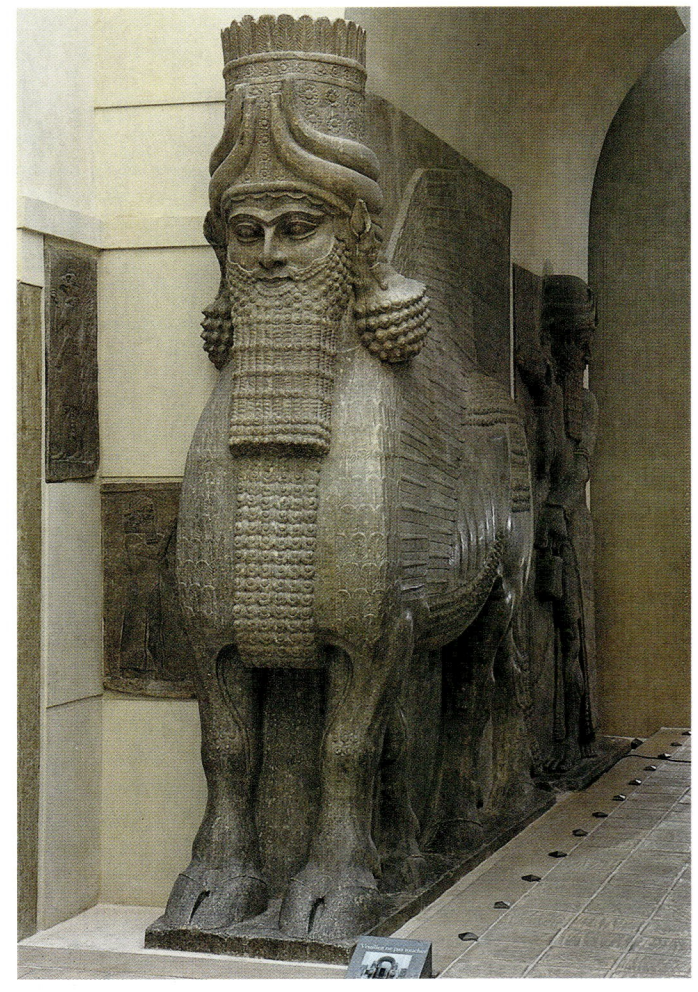

**2-21** Lamassu (winged, human-headed bull), from the citadel of Sargon II, Dur Sharrukin (modern Khorsabad), Iraq, ca. 720–705 BCE. Limestone, approx. 13′ 10″ high. Louvre, Paris.

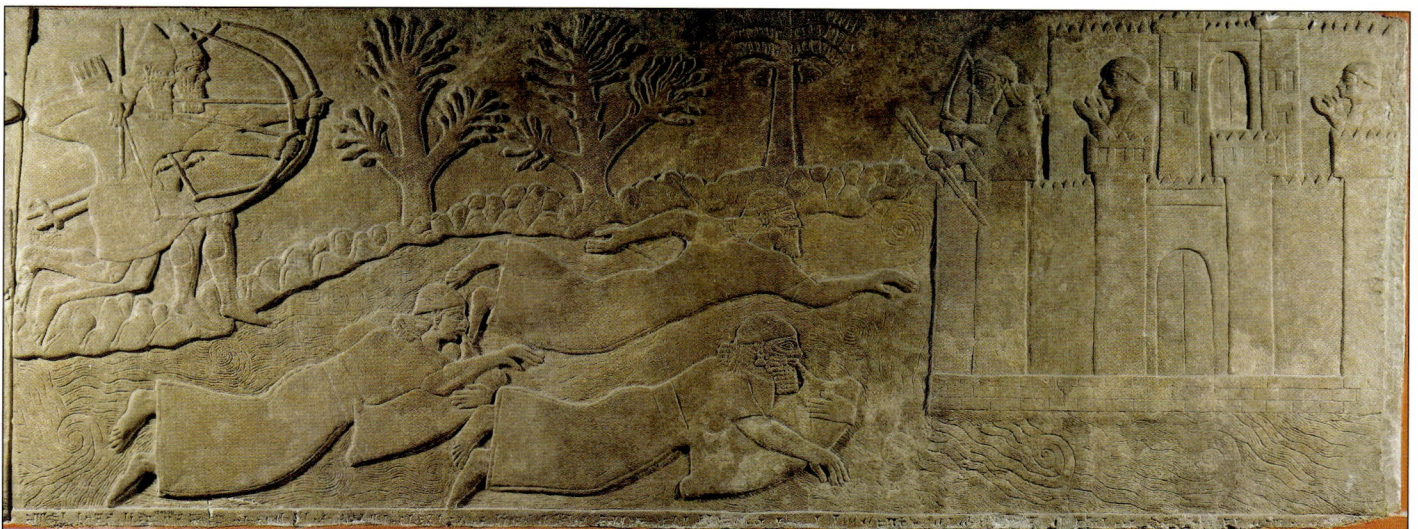

**2-22** Assyrian archers pursuing enemies, relief from the Northwest Palace of Ashurnasirpal II, Kalhu (modern Nimrud), Iraq, ca. 875–860 BCE. Gypsum, 2′ 10$\frac{5}{8}$″ high. British Museum, London.

**MONSTROUS GUARDIANS** Guarding the gate to Sargon's palace were colossal limestone monsters (FIG. **2-21**), which the Assyrians probably called *lamassu*. These winged, man-headed bulls served to ward off the king's enemies. The task of moving and installing such immense stone sculptures was so daunting that several reliefs in the palace of Sargon's successor celebrate the feat, showing scores of men dragging lamassu figures with the aid of ropes and sledges.

The Assyrian lamassu sculptures are partly in the round, but the sculptor nonetheless conceived them as high reliefs on adjacent sides of a corner. They combine the front view of the animal at rest with the side view of it in motion. Seeking to present a complete picture of the lamassu from both the front and the side, the sculptor gave the monster five legs (two seen from the front, four seen from the side). The three-quarter view the modern photographer chose would not have been favored in antiquity. This sculpture, then, is yet another case of early artists' providing a *conceptual picture* of an animal or person and of all its important parts, as opposed to an *optical view* of the lamassu as it actually would stand in space.

**CHRONICLES OF GREAT DEEDS** For their palace walls the Assyrian kings commissioned extensive series of narrative reliefs exalting royal power and piety. The sculptures record not only battlefield victories but also the slaying of wild animals. (The Assyrians, like many other societies before and after, regarded prowess in hunting as a manly virtue on a par with success in warfare.) These narrative reliefs have precedents in Egypt, but in a very different format (see Chapter 3). The degree of documentary detail in the Assyrian reliefs is without parallel in the ancient Near East, even in such narratives as those on the *Stele of the Vultures* (FIG. **2-7**) and the *Standard of Ur* (FIG. **2-8**). Archaeologists have found nothing else comparable made before the Roman Empire (see Chapter 10).

One of the most extensive—and earliest—examples of a cycle of historical narrative reliefs comes from the palace of Ashurnasirpal II (r. 883–859 BCE) at Kalhu. (The Assyrian kings frequently incorporated Ashur's name into their own.) Throughout the palace, painted gypsum reliefs sheathed the lower parts of the mud-brick walls below brightly colored plaster. Rich textiles on the floors contributed to the luxurious ambience. Every relief celebrated the king and bore an inscription naming Ashurnasirpal and describing his accomplishments.

The example we illustrate (FIG. **2-22**) probably depicts an episode that occurred in 878 BCE when Ashurnasirpal drove his enemy's forces into the Euphrates River. In the relief, two Assyrian archers shoot arrows at the fleeing foe. Three enemy soldiers are in the water. One swims with an arrow in his back. The other two attempt to float to safety by inflating animal skins. Their destination is a fort where their compatriots await them. The artist showed the fort as if it were in the middle of the river, but it must, of course, have been on land, perhaps at some distance from where the escapees entered the water. The artist's purpose was to tell the story clearly and economically. In art, distances can be compressed and the human actors enlarged so that they stand out from their environment. (Literally interpreted, the defenders of the fort are too tall to walk through its archway.) The sculptor also combined different viewpoints in the same frame, just as the figures are composites of frontal and profile views. Viewers see the river from above while observing the men, trees, and fort from the side. The artist also made other adjustments for clarity. So as not to hide the archers' faces, the sculptor depicted their bowstrings in front of their bodies but behind their heads. The men will snare their own heads in their bows when they launch their arrows! All these liberties with optical reality result, however, in a vivid and easily legible retelling of a decisive moment in the king's victorious campaign. This was the artist's primary goal.

**ASSYRIAN PAINTING** The Assyrian palace reliefs frequently portrayed the king and his retinue in ceremonial roles or paying homage to the gods. The same subjects occupied the court painters. Unfortunately, Assyrian paintings, because of their fragile nature, are much rarer today than stone reliefs. A fine example of the painter's art is the *glazed brick* (painted and then kiln fired to fuse the color with the baked clay) from

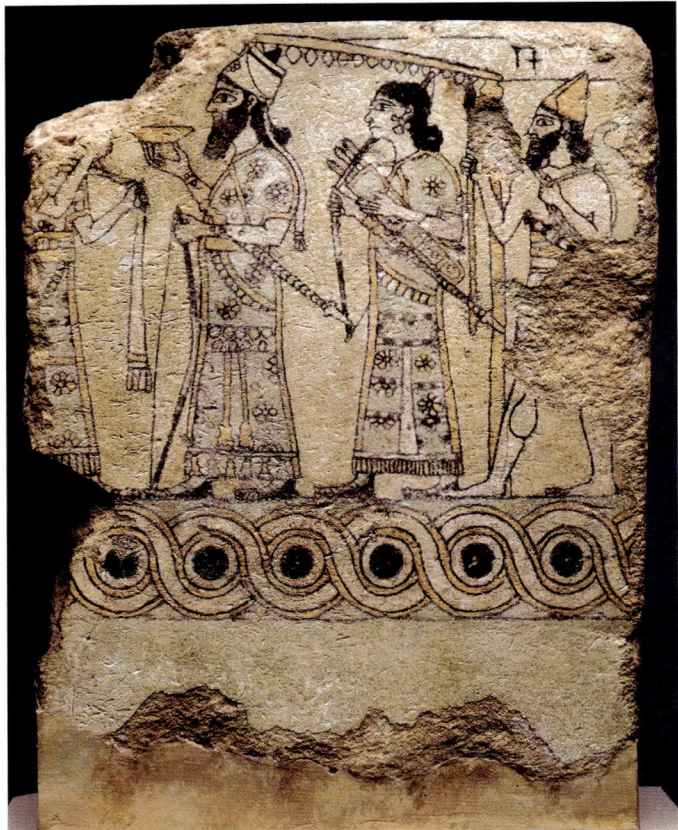

2-23 Ashurnasirpal II with attendants and soldier, from his palace at Kalhu, Iraq, ca. 875–860 BCE. Glazed brick, $11\frac{3}{4}''$ high. British Museum, London.

**NOBLE ANIMAL ADVERSARIES** Two centuries later, sculptors carved hunting reliefs for the Nineveh palace of the conqueror of Elamite Susa, Ashurbanipal (r. 668–627 BCE). The hunt did not take place in the wild but in a controlled environment, ensuring the king's safety and success. In the relief illustrated here (FIG. 2-24), lions released from cages in a large enclosed arena charge the king, who, in his chariot and with his attendants, thrusts a spear into a savage lion. The animal leaps at the king even though it already has two arrows in its body. All around the royal chariot is a pathetic trail of dead and dying animals, pierced by what appear to be far more arrows than needed to kill them. Blood streams from some of the lions, but they refuse to die. The artist brilliantly depicted the straining muscles, the swelling veins, the muzzles' wrinkled skin, and the flattened ears of the powerful and defiant beasts. Modern sympathies make this scene of carnage a kind of heroic tragedy, with the lions as protagonists. It is unlikely, however, that the king's artists had any intention other than to glorify their ruler by showing the king of men pitting himself against and repeatedly conquering the king of beasts. Portraying Ashurbanipal's beastly foes as possessing not merely strength but courage and nobility served to make the king's accomplishments that much grander.

# NEO-BABYLONIAN AND ACHAEMENID PERSIAN ART

The Assyrian Empire was never very secure, and most of its kings had to fight revolts in large sections of the Near East. Assyria's conquest of Elam in the seventh century BCE and frequent rebellions in Babylonia apparently overextended its resources. During the last years of Ashurbanipal's reign, the empire began to disintegrate. Under his successors, it collapsed from the simultaneous onslaught of the Medes from the east and the resurgent Babylonians from the south. Neo-Babylonian kings held sway over the former Assyrian Empire until the Persian conquest.

Ashurnasirpal II's Kalhu palace (FIG. 2-23). It shows the king, taller than everyone else as befits his rank, delicately holding a cup. With it, he will make a *libation* (ritual pouring of liquid) in honor of the protective gods. The artist rendered the figures in outline, lavishing much attention on the patterns of the rich fabrics they wear. The king and the attendant behind him are in consistent profile view, but the rule of showing the eye from the front in a profile head still held. Painted scenes such as this hint at what the Assyrian stone reliefs might have looked like with their original paint intact.

**WONDROUS BABYLON** The most renowned of the Neo-Babylonian kings was Nebuchadnezzar II (r. 604–562 BCE), whose exploits the biblical Book of Daniel recounts. Nebuchadnezzar restored Babylon to its rank as one of the great cities of antiquity. The city's famous hanging gardens were counted among the Seven Wonders of the ancient world, and its enormous ziggurat was

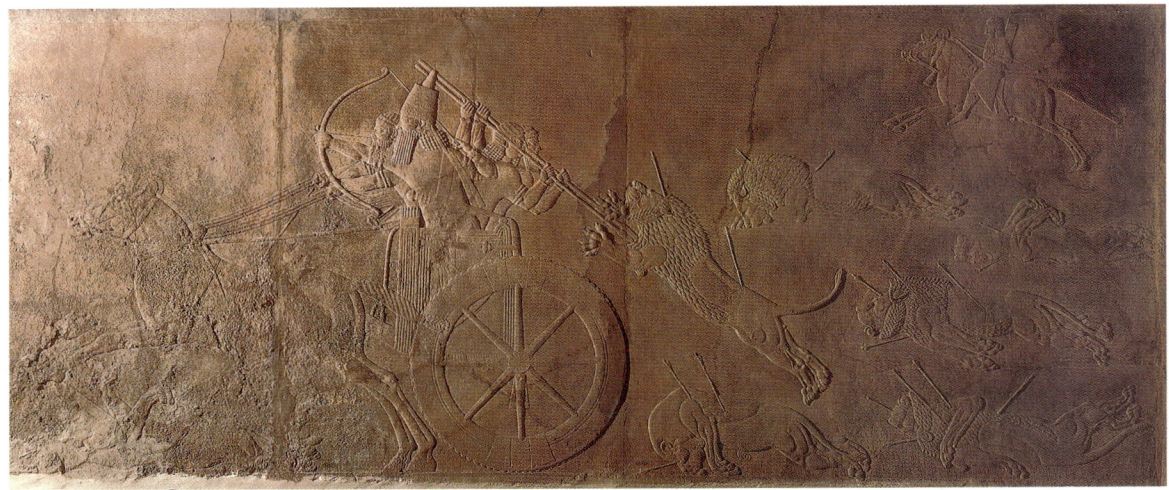

2-24 Ashurbanipal hunting lions, relief from the North Palace of Ashurbanipal, Nineveh (modern Kuyunjik), Iraq, ca. 645–640 BCE. Gypsum, 5′ 4″ high. British Museum, London.

### Babylon: City of Wonders

The uncontested list of the Seven Wonders of the ancient world was not codified until the 16th century. But already in the 2nd century BCE, Antipater of Sidon, a Greek poet, compiled a roster of seven must-see monuments, including six of the seven later Wonders. All of the Wonders were of colossal size and constructed at great expense. Three of them were of great antiquity: the pyramids of Gizeh (see FIG. 3-8), which Antipater described as "man-made mountains," and "the hanging gardens" and "walls of impregnable Babylon."

Babylon was the only site on Antipater's list that could boast two Wonders. Later list makers preferred to distribute the Seven Wonders among seven different cities. Most of these Wonders date to Greek times—the Temple of Artemis at Ephesus, with its 60-foot-tall columns; Phidias's colossal gold-and-ivory statue of Zeus at Olympia; the grandiose tomb of Mausolus (the "Mausoleum") at Halikarnassos; the Colossus of Rhodes, a bronze statue of the sun god 110 feet tall; and the lighthouse at Alexandria, perhaps the tallest building in the ancient world. The pyramids are the oldest and the Babylonian gardens the only Wonder in the category of "landscape architecture."

Several ancient texts describe Babylon's gardens. We quote part of the account Quintus Curtius Rufus wrote in the mid-first century CE:

> On the top of the citadel are the hanging gardens, a wonder celebrated in the tales of the Greeks. . . . Columns of stone were set up to sustain the whole work, and on these was laid a floor of squared blocks, strong enough to hold the earth which is thrown upon it to a great depth, as well as the water with which they irrigate the soil; and the structure supports trees of such great size that the thickness of their trunks equals a measure of eight cubits [about twelve feet].

They tower to a height of fifty feet, and they yield as much fruit as if they were growing in their native soil. . . . To those who look upon [the trees] from a distance, real woods seem to be overhanging their native mountains.[1]

Not qualifying as a Wonder, but in some ways no less impressive, was Babylon's Marduk ziggurat, the biblical Tower of Babel. According to the Bible, humankind's arrogant desire to build a tower to Heaven angered God. The Lord put an end to it by causing the workers to speak different languages, preventing them from communicating with one another. The fifth-century BCE Greek historian Herodotus described the Babylonian temple complex:

> In the middle of the sanctuary [of Marduk] has been built a solid tower . . . which supports another tower, which in turn supports another, and so on: there are eight towers in all. A stairway has been constructed to wind its way up the outside of all the towers; halfway up the stairway there is a shelter with benches to rest on, where people making the ascent can sit and catch their breath. In the last tower there is a huge temple. The temple contains a large couch, which is adorned with fine coverings and has a golden table standing beside it, but there are no statues at all standing there. . . . [The Babylonians] say that the god comes in person to the temple [compare the Sumerian notion of the temple as a "waiting room"] and rests on the couch; I do not believe this story myself.[2]

[1] John C. Rolfe, trans., *Quintus Curtius I* (Cambridge: Harvard University Press, 1971), 337–39.
[2] Robin Waterfield, trans., *Herodotus: The Histories* (New York: Oxford University Press, 1998), 79–80.

---

immortalized in the Bible as the Tower of Babel (see "Babylon: City of Wonders," above).

Nebuchadnezzar's Babylon was a mud-brick city, but dazzling blue-glazed bricks faced the most important monuments. Some of the buildings, such as the Ishtar Gate (FIG. 2-25), with its imposing arched opening flanked by towers, featured glazed bricks with molded reliefs of animals, real and imaginary. Glazed bricks had been used earlier (FIG. 2-23), but the surface of the bricks, even of those with figures, was flat. Each Babylonian brick was molded and glazed separately, then set in proper sequence on the wall. On Ishtar's Gate, profile figures of Marduk's dragon and Adad's bull alternate. Lining the processional way leading up to the gate were reliefs of Ishtar's sacred lion, glazed in yellow, brown, and red against a blue ground.

**THE TRIUMPH OF PERSIA** Although Nebuchadnezzar, "King of Kings" of the biblical Daniel, had boasted that he "caused a mighty wall to circumscribe Babylon . . . so that the enemy who would do evil would not threaten," Cyrus of Persia (r. 559–529 BCE) captured the city in the sixth century. Cyrus, who may have been descended from an Elamite line, was the founder of the Achaemenid dynasty and traced his ancestry back to a mythical King Achaemenes. Babylon was but one of the Persians' conquests. Egypt fell to them in 525 BCE, and by 480 BCE the Persian Empire

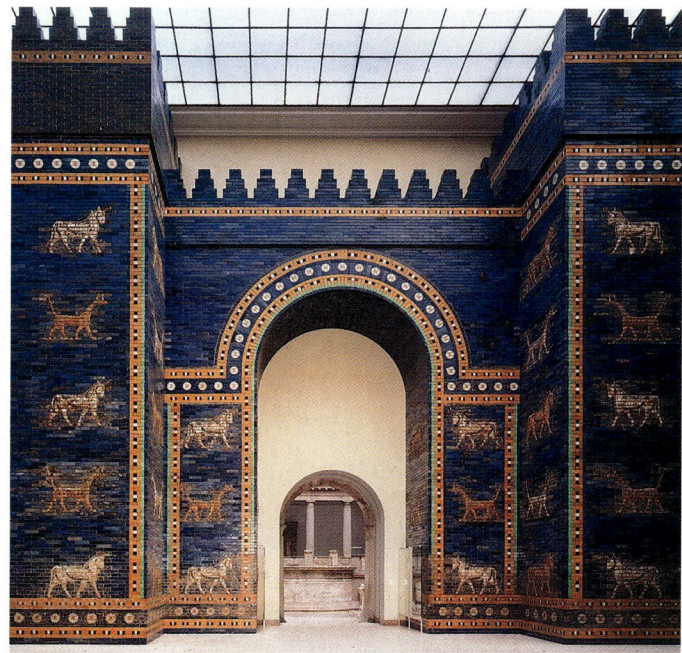

**2-25** Ishtar Gate (restored), Babylon, Iraq, ca. 575 BCE. Glazed brick. Staatliche Museen, Berlin. 🖸

NEO-BABYLONIAN AND ACHAEMENID PERSIAN ART **49**

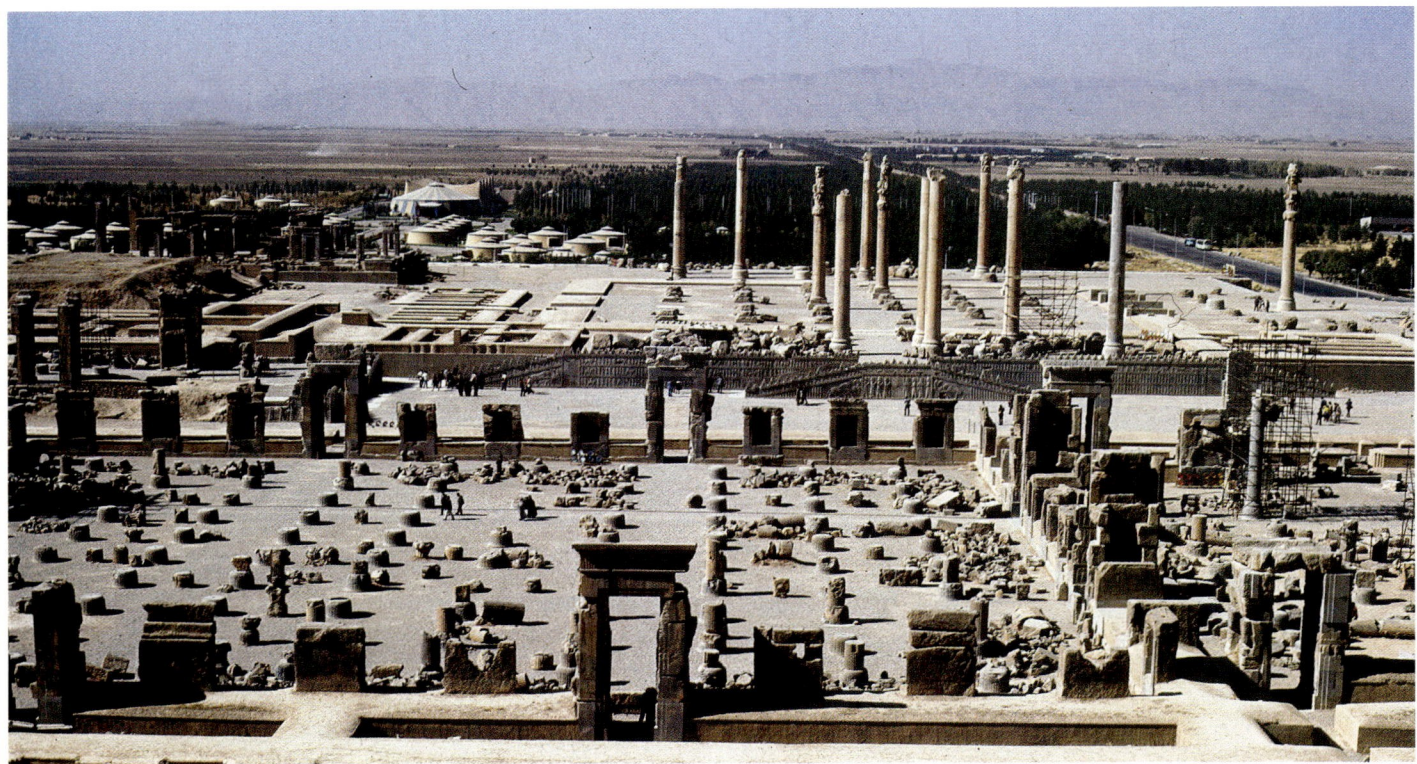

**2-26** Persepolis (royal audience hall in the background), Iran, ca. 521–465 BCE.

was the largest the world had yet known, extending from the Indus River in South Asia to the Danube River in northeastern Europe. Only the successful Greek resistance in the fifth century BCE prevented Persia from embracing southeastern Europe as well (see Chapter 5). The Achaemenid line ended with the death of Darius III in 330 BCE, after his defeat at the hands of Alexander the Great (see FIG. 5-69).

**IMPERIAL PERSEPOLIS** The most important source of knowledge about Persian art and architecture is the ceremonial and administrative complex on the citadel at Persepolis (FIG. **2-26**), which the successors of Cyrus, Darius I (r. 522–486 BCE) and Xerxes (r. 486–465 BCE), built between 521 and 465 BCE. Situated on a high plateau, the heavily fortified complex of royal buildings stood on a wide platform overlooking the plain. Alexander the Great razed the site in a gesture symbolizing the destruction of Persian imperial power. Some said it was an act of revenge for the Persian sack of the Athenian Acropolis in the early fifth century BCE (see Chapter 5). But even in ruins, the Persepolis citadel is impressive.

The approach to the citadel led through a monumental gateway called the Gate of All Lands, a reference to the harmony among the peoples of the vast Persian empire. Assyrian-inspired colossal man-headed winged bulls flanked the great entrance. Broad ceremonial stairways provided access to the platform and the royal audience hall, or *apadana*, a huge hall 60 feet high and 217 feet square, containing 36 colossal columns. An audience of thousands could have stood within the hall.

The reliefs (FIG. **2-27**) decorating the walls of the terrace and staircases leading to the apadana represent processions of royal guards, Persian nobles and dignitaries, and representatives from 23 subject nations bringing the king tribute. Every one of the

emissaries wears his national costume and carries a typical regional gift for the conqueror. The carving of the Persepolis reliefs is technically superb, with subtly modeled surfaces and crisply chiseled details. Traces of color prove that the reliefs were painted, and the original effect must have been even more striking than it is today. Although the Persepolis sculptures may have been inspired by those in Assyrian palaces, they are different in style. The forms are more rounded, and they project more from the background. Some of the details, notably the treatment of drapery folds, echo forms characteristic of Archaic Greek sculpture, and Greek influence seems to be one of the many ingredients of Achaemenid style. Persian art testifies to the active exchange of ideas and artists among all the Mediterranean and Near Eastern civilizations at this date. A building inscription at Susa, for example, names Ionian Greeks, Medes (who occupied the land north of Persia), Egyptians, and Babylonians among those who built and decorated the palace. Under the single-minded direction of its Persian masters, this heterogeneous workforce, with a widely varied cultural and artistic background, created a new and coherent style that perfectly suited the expression of Persian imperial ambitions.

## SASANIAN ART

**THE NEW PERSIAN EMPIRE** Alexander the Great's conquest of Persia in 330 BCE marked the beginning of a long period of first Greek and then Roman rule of large parts of the ancient Near East, beginning with one of Alexander's former generals, Seleucus I (r. 312–281 BCE), founder of the Seleucid dynasty. In the third century CE, however, a new power rose up in Persia that challenged

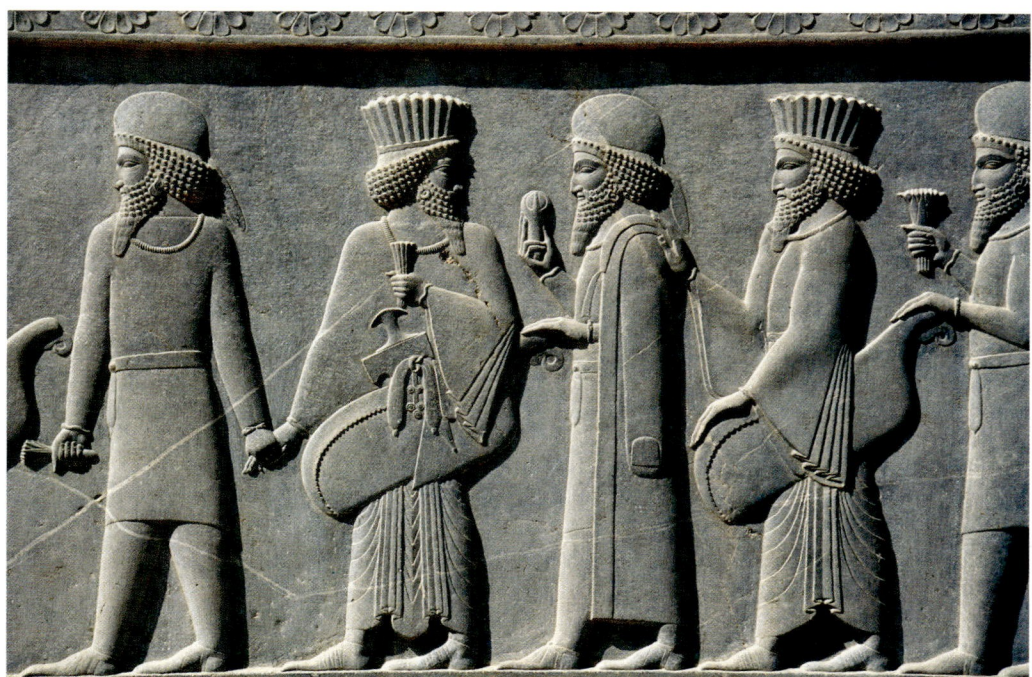

**2-27** Processional frieze (detail) on the terrace of the royal audience hall *(apadana)*, Persepolis, Iran, ca. 521–465 BCE.

the Romans and sought to force them out of Asia. The new rulers called themselves Sasanians. They traced their lineage to a legendary figure named Sasan, said to be a direct descendant of the Achaemenid kings. Their New Persian Empire was founded in 224 CE, when the first Sasanian king, Artaxerxes I (r. 211–241), defeated the Parthians (another of Rome's eastern enemies). It endured more than 400 years, until the Arabs drove the Sasanians out of Mesopotamia in 636, just four years after the death of Muhammad, the prophet and founder of Islam (see Chapter 13).

**SHAPUR AND CTESIPHON** The son and successor of Artaxerxes, Shapur I (r. 241–272), succeeded in further extending Sasanian territory. He also erected a great palace (FIG. **2-28**) at Ctesiphon, the capital his father had established near modern Baghdad in Iraq. The central feature of Shapur's palace was the monumental *iwan*, or brick audience hall, covered by a *barrel vault* (in effect, a deep *arch* over an oblong space) that came almost to a point some 900 feet above the ground. The facade to the left and right of the iwan was divided into a series of horizontal bands made up of *blind arcades*, a series of arches without actual openings, applied as wall decoration. A thousand years later, Islamic architects looked at Shapur's palace and especially its soaring iwan and established it as the standard for judging their own engineering feats (see Chapter 13).

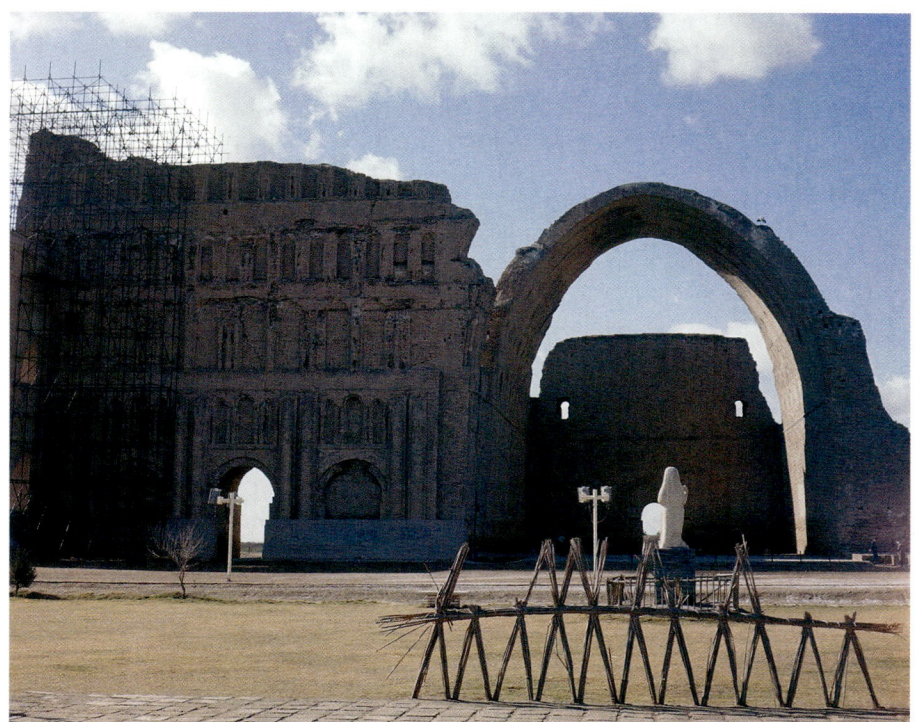

**2-28** Palace of Shapur I, Ctesiphon, Iraq, ca. 250 CE.

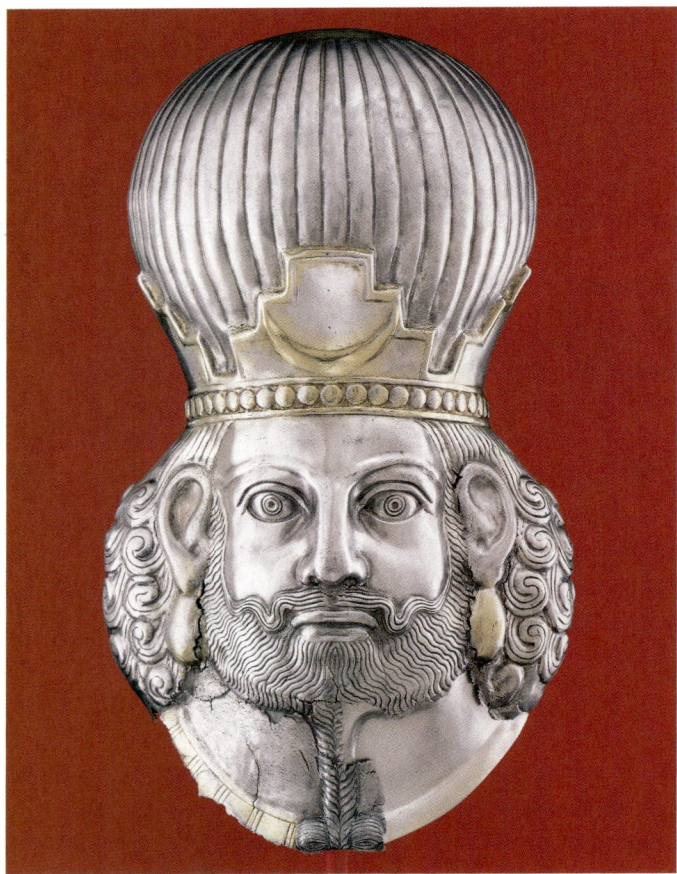

**2-29** Head of a Sasanian king (Shapur II?), ca. 350 CE. Silver with mercury gilding, 1′ 3¾″ high. Metropolitan Museum of Art, New York.

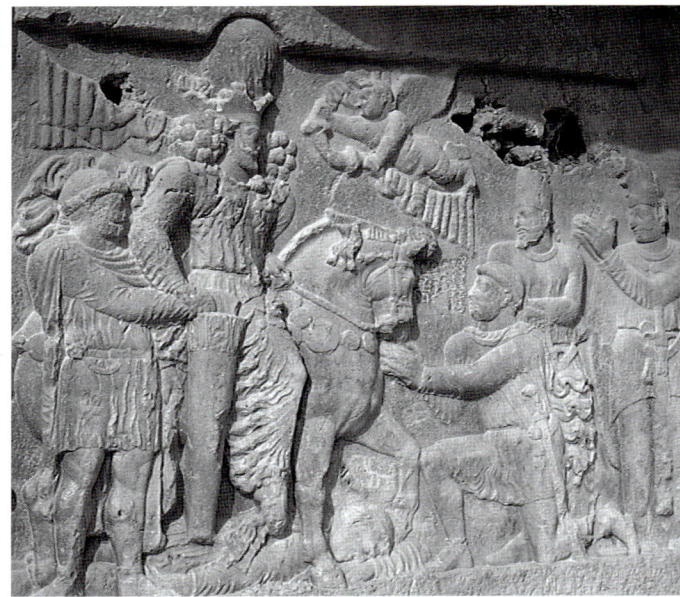

**2-30** Triumph of Shapur I over Valerian, rock-cut relief, Bishapur, Iran, ca. 260 CE.

**SASANIAN SPLENDOR** A silver head (FIG. **2-29**), possibly a portrait of Shapur II (r. 310–379), suggests the splendor of Sasanian court life. It testifies not only to the wealth of the Sasanian dynasty but also to the superb skills of its court artists. The head is slightly under life-size. The sculptor employed the *repoussé* technique, that is, hammered the shape from a single sheet of metal and pushed the features out from behind. The artist then engraved the details into the silver surface to give form and texture to the hair and beard and to lend the eyes an almost hypnotic stare. Selected portions of the portrait have mercury gilding to give the metal an even richer look and to add color. In this work, an unknown sculptor captured the essence of imperial majesty.

**A REVERSAL OF FORTUNES** So powerful was the Sasanian army that in 260 CE Shapur I even succeeded in capturing the Roman emperor Valerian near Edessa (in modern Turkey). His victory over Valerian was so significant an event that Shapur commemorated it in a series of rock-cut reliefs in the cliffs of Bishapur in Iran, far from the site of his triumph. We illustrate a detail (FIG. **2-30**) of one of the Bishapur reliefs. Shapur appears larger than life, riding in from the left and wearing the same distinctive tall Sasanian crown worn by the king in the silver portrait (FIG. **2-29**). The crown breaks through the relief's border

and draws attention to the king. The crumpled body of a Roman soldier lies between the legs of the Sasanian's horse—a time-honored motif (compare the *Standard of Ur,* FIG. 2-8). Here the sculptor probably meant to personify the entire Roman army. At the right, attendants lead in Valerian, who kneels before Shapur and begs for mercy. Above, a *putto*-like (cherub or childlike) figure borrowed from the repertory of Greco-Roman art hovers above the king and brings him a victory garland. Similar scenes of kneeling enemies before triumphant generals are commonplace in Roman art—but at Bishapur the roles are reversed. This appropriation of Roman compositional patterns and motifs in a relief celebrating the Sasanian defeat of the Romans adds another, ironic, level of meaning to the political message in stone.

## CONCLUSION

The birth of civilization—urban life—and the invention of writing both occurred in Mesopotamia in the fourth millennium BCE. There, the Sumerians built the first monumental temples and filled their religious precincts and tombs with statues, reliefs, and objects of gold, lapis lazuli, and other costly materials. Their successors—the Akkadians, Babylonians, Assyrians, Persians, and others—continued the tradition of monumental art and architecture, erecting ruler portraits, stelae recording victories and law codes, and great palaces decorated with painted narrative reliefs. At times challenging both the Greeks and the Romans for supremacy in the Mediterranean, the empires of the ancient Near East finally succumbed to the Arabs in the seventh century CE. Thereafter, the greatest artists and architects of Mesopotamia worked in the service of Islam.

| Period | | | | Timeline | Events | Images |
|---|---|---|---|---|---|---|

URUK

JAMDAT NASR

EARLY DYNASTIC (SUMERIAN)

AKKADIAN DYNASTY

THIRD DYNASTY OF UR (NEO-SUMERIAN)

OLD BABYLONIAN

KASSITES AND MITANNI (MESOPOTAMIA)

HITTITES (ANATOLIA)

MIDDLE ELAMITE PERIOD (IRAN)

ASSYRIAN EMPIRE

NEO-BABYLONIAN AND MEDIAN EMPIRES

ACHAEMENID PERSIAN EMPIRE

SELEUCID, PARTHIAN, AND ROMAN

SASANIAN DYNASTY

3500 BCE

3100 BCE

■ DEVELOPMENT OF WRITING AND THE BEGINNINGS OF RECORDED HISTORY

■ FLOWERING OF INDEPENDENT CITY-STATES

2900 BCE

1 ■ BURIALS IN THE ROYAL CEMETERY, UR

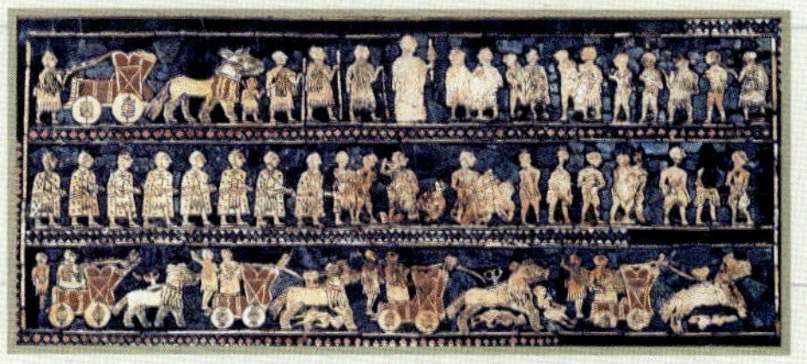

1  Standard of Ur, ca. 2600 BCE

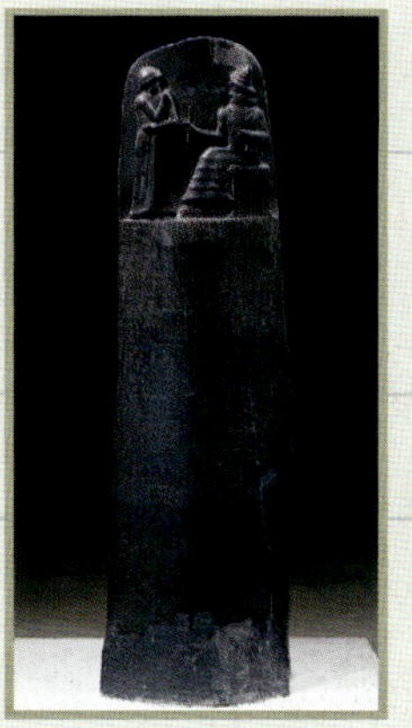

2300 BCE

■ SARGON OF AKKAD, CA. 2300 BCE

■ NARAM-SIN, R. CA. 2254–2218 BCE

2150 BCE

■ GUTIAN INVASION, CA. 2150 BCE

■ GUDEA OF LAGASH, CA. 2100 BCE

2000 BCE

1800 BCE

2 ■ HAMMURABI, R. CA. 1792–1750 BCE

2  Stele of Hammurabi, ca. 1780 BCE

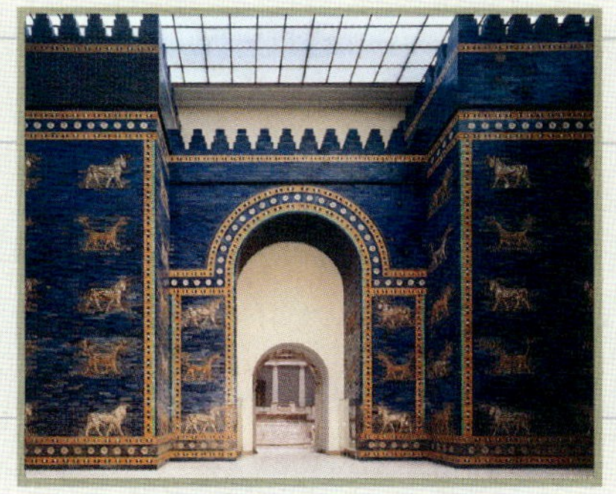

1600 BCE

■ SACK OF BABYLON BY HITTITES, CA. 1595 BCE

1000 BCE

900 BCE

■ ASHURNASIRPAL II, R. 883–859 BCE

■ SARGON II, R. 721–705 BCE

■ ASHURNASIRPAL, R. 668–627 BCE

612 BCE

3 ■ NEBUCHADNEZZAR II, R. 604–562 BCE

3  Ishtar Gate, Babylon, ca. 575 BCE

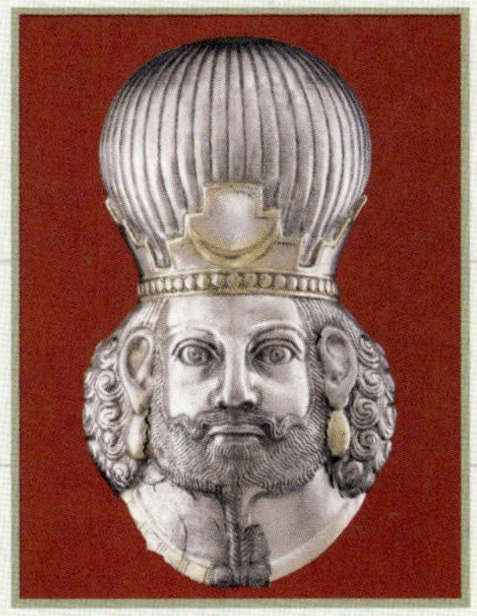

538 BCE

■ DARIUS I, R. 522–486 BCE

■ XERXES, R. 486–465 BCE

■ BATTLE OF ISSUS, 333 BCE

330 BCE

■ DEATH OF ALEXANDER THE GREAT, 323 BCE

■ SELEUCUS I, R. 312–281 BCE

224 CE

■ DEFEAT OF VALERIAN BY SHAPUR I, 260 CE

4 ■ SHAPUR II, R. 310–379 CE

4  Head of Shapur II(?), ca. 350 CE

636 CE

■ FINAL DEFEAT OF PERSIANS BY THE ARABS, 641 CE

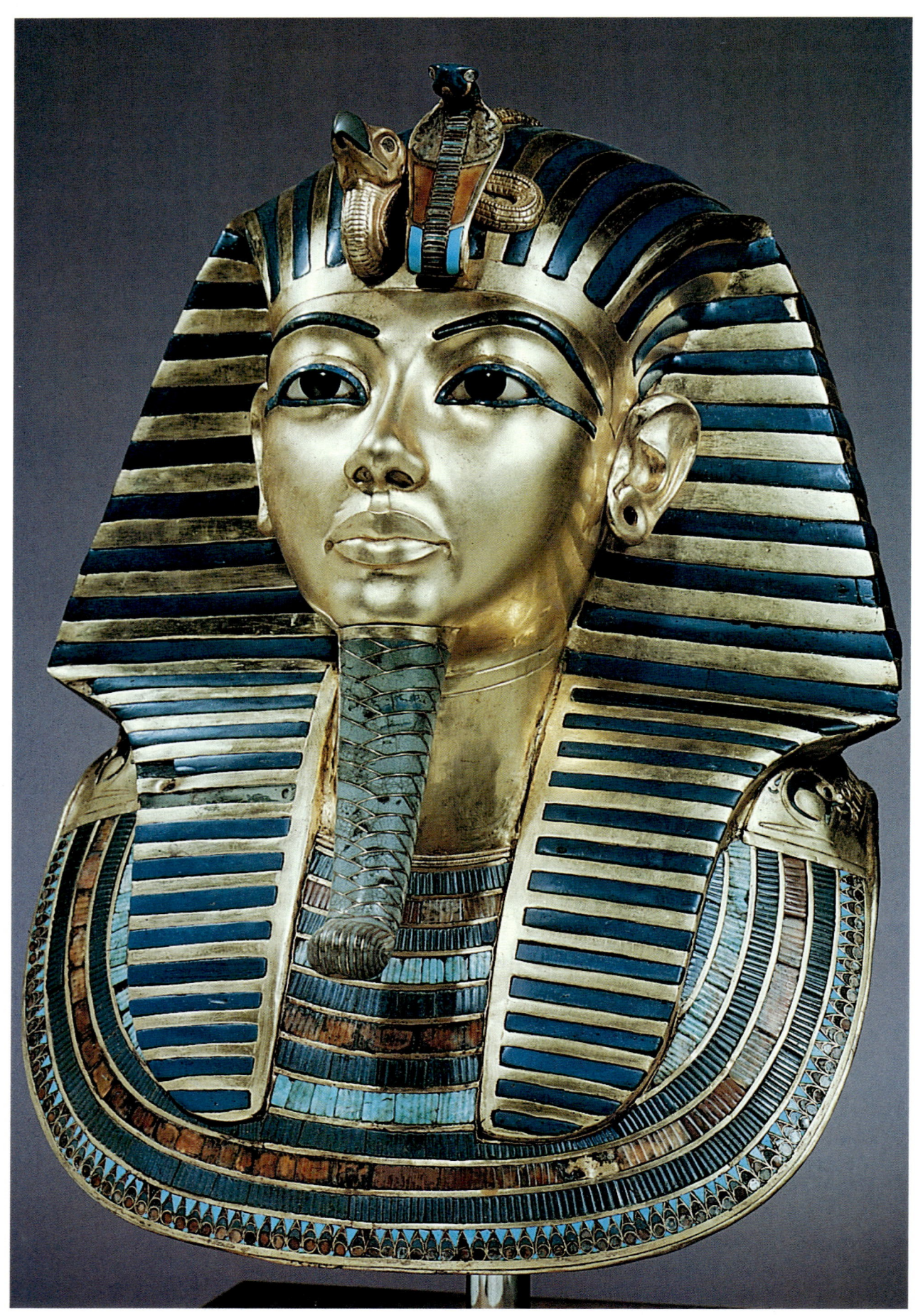

Death mask of Tutankhamen, from the innermost coffin in his tomb at Thebes, Egypt, Dynasty XVIII, ca. 1323 BCE. Gold with inlay of semiprecious stones, 1′ 9¼″ high. Egyptian Museum, Cairo.

# 3

# PHARAOHS AND THE AFTERLIFE

## THE ART OF ANCIENT EGYPT

Nearly 2,500 years ago, the Greek historian Herodotus wrote, "Concerning Egypt itself I shall extend my remarks to a great length, because there is no country that possesses so many wonders, nor any that has such a number of works that defy description."[1] Even today, many would agree with this assessment. The ancient Egyptians left to the world a profusion of spectacular monuments dating across three millennia. From the cliffs of the Libyan and Arabian Deserts they cut giant blocks of stone and erected grand temples to their immortal gods (see "The Gods and Goddesses of Egypt," page 57). From the same imperishable material that symbolized the timelessness of their world, the Egyptians set up countless statues of their equally immortal god-kings and built thousands of tombs to serve as eternal houses of the dead. The solemn and ageless art of the Egyptians expresses the unchanging order that, for them, was divinely established.

The backbone of Egypt was, and still is, the Nile River, whose annual floods supported all life in that ancient land (MAP 3-1). Even more than the Tigris and the Euphrates Rivers of Mesopotamia, the Nile defined the cultures that developed along its banks. Originating deep in Africa, the world's longest river flows through regions that may not receive a single drop of rainfall in a decade. Yet crops thrive from the rich soil that the Nile brings thousands of miles from the African hills. In the time of the *pharaohs,* the ancient Egyptian kings, the land bordering the Nile consisted of marshes dotted with island ridges. Amphibious animals swarmed in the marshes and were hunted through tall forests of *papyrus* and rushes (FIGS. 3-16 and 3-30). Egypt's fertility was famous. When Egypt became a province of the Roman Empire after Queen Cleopatra's death (r. 51–30 BCE), it served as the granary of the Mediterranean world.

**THE BIRTH OF EGYPTOLOGY** Even in the Middle Ages, Egypt's reputation as an ancient land of wonders and mystery lived on. Until the late 18th century, people regarded its undeciphered writing and exotic monuments as treasures of occult wisdom, locked away from any but those initiated in the mystic arts. Scholars knew something of Egypt's history from references in the Old Testament, from Herodotus

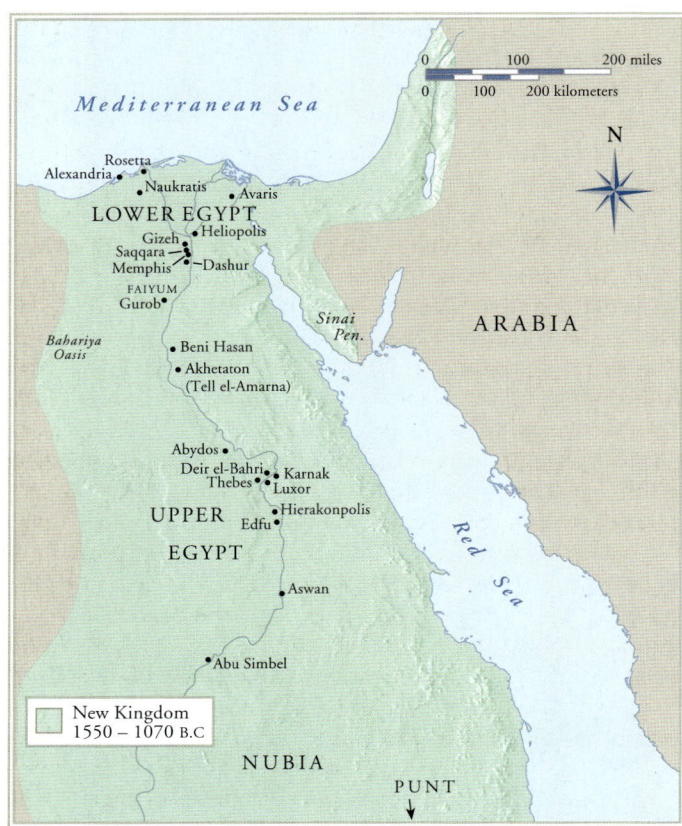

MAP 3-1 Ancient Egypt.

absolute dates of the pharaohs are still debated. The chronologies scholars have proposed for the earliest Egyptian dynasties can vary by as much as two centuries. Exact years cannot be assigned to the reigns of individual pharaohs until 664 BCE (Dynasty XXVI).[2]

At the end of the 18th century, when Europeans rediscovered Egypt, the land of the Nile became the first subject of archaeological exploration. In 1799, Napoleon Bonaparte, on a military expedition to Egypt, took with him a small troop of scholars, linguists, antiquarians, and artists. The chance discovery of the famed *Rosetta Stone,* now in the British Museum, gave the eager scholars a key to deciphering Egyptian *hieroglyphic* writing. The stone bears an inscription in three sections: one in Greek, which was easily read; one in *demotic* (Late Egyptian); and one in formal hieroglyphic. Scholars at once suspected that the text was the same in all three sections and that, using Greek as the key, they could decipher the other two sections. But progress was slow. Eventually, a young linguist, Jean-François Champollion, deduced that the hieroglyphs were not simply pictographs. He proposed that they were the signs of a once-spoken language whose traces survived in Coptic, the later language of Christian Egypt. Champollion's feat established him as a giant in the new field of *Egyptology.*

# THE PREDYNASTIC AND EARLY DYNASTIC PERIODS

## *Painting and Sculpture*

THE OLDEST EGYPTIAN ART The Predynastic, or prehistoric, beginnings of Egyptian civilization are chronologically vague. But tantalizing remains of tombs, paintings, pottery, and other artifacts from around 3500 BCE attest to the existence of a sophisticated culture on the banks of the Nile. A wall painting (FIG. 3-1) from the late Predynastic period, found in a tomb at

and other Greco-Roman authors, and from preserved portions of a history of Egypt written in Greek in the third century BCE by an Egyptian high priest named Manetho. Manetho described the succession of pharaohs, dividing them into the still-useful groups called *dynasties,* but his chronology was inaccurate, and the

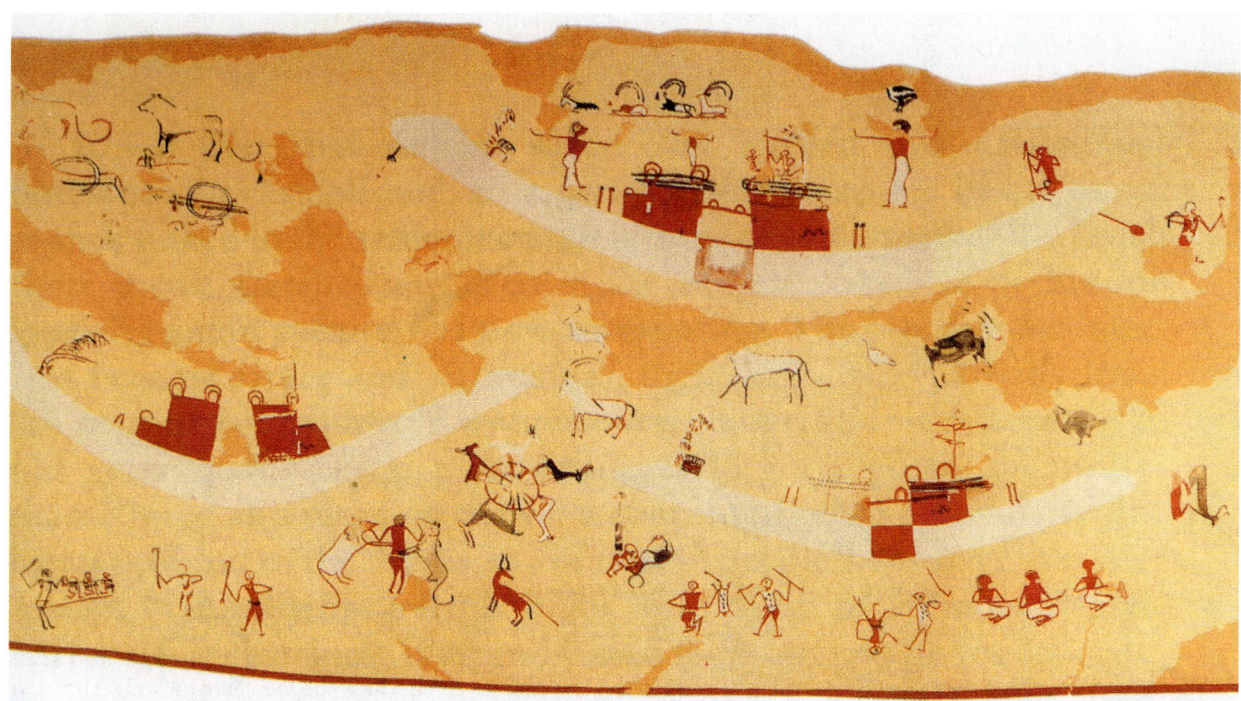

**3-1** People, boats, and animals, detail of a watercolor copy of a wall painting from Tomb 100 at Hierakonpolis, Egypt, Predynastic, ca. 3500–3200 BCE. Paint on plaster, entire painting approx. 16′ 3″ long. Egyptian Museum, Cairo.

### The Gods and Goddesses of Egypt

The worldview of the Egyptians was distinct from those of their neighbors in the ancient Mediterranean and Near Eastern worlds. Egyptians believed that before the beginning of time the primeval waters, called *Nun*, existed alone in the darkness. At the moment of creation, a mound rose out of the limitless waters—just as muddy mounds emerge from the Nile after the annual flood recedes. On this mound the creator god appeared and brought light to the world. In later times, the mound was formalized as a pyramidal stone called the *ben-ben* supporting the supreme god, *Amen,* the god of the sun *(Re).*

The supreme god also created the first of the other gods and goddesses of Egypt. According to one version of the myth, the creator masturbated and produced *Shu* and *Tefnut,* the primary male and female forces in the universe. They coupled to give birth to *Geb* (Earth) and *Nut* (Sky), who bore Osiris, Seth, Isis, and Nephthys. The eldest, *Osiris* (FIG. 3-39), was the god of order and was revered as the king who brought civilization to Egypt. His brother, *Seth,* was his evil opposite, the god of chaos. Seth murdered Osiris and cut him into pieces, which he scattered across Egypt. *Isis* (FIG. 3-39), the sister and consort of Osiris, with the help of *Nephthys* (FIG. 3-39), Seth's wife, succeeded in collecting Osiris's body parts, and with her powerful magic brought him

back to life. The resurrected Osiris fathered a son with Isis—*Horus,* who avenged his father's death and displaced Seth as king of Egypt. Osiris then became the lord of the underworld. Horus is represented in art either as a falcon, considered the noblest bird of the sky, or as a falcon-headed man (FIGS. 3-2, 3-12, 3-28, and 3-39). All Egyptian pharaohs were identified with Horus while alive and with Osiris after they died.

Other Egyptian deities included *Mut,* the consort of the sun god Amen, and *Khonsu,* the moon god, who was their son. *Thoth,* another lunar deity and the god of knowledge and writing, appears in art as an ibis, a baboon, or an ibis-headed man crowned with the crescent moon and the moon disk (FIG. 3-39). When Seth tore out Horus's falcon-eye *(wedjat),* Thoth restored it. He, too, was associated with rebirth and the afterlife. *Hathor,* daughter of Re, was a divine mother of the pharaoh, nourishing him with her milk. She appears in Egyptian art as a cow-headed woman or as a woman with a cow's horns (FIGS. 3-2 and 3-28). *Anubis,* a jackal or jackal-headed deity, was the god of mummification and the weigher of hearts in the underworld (FIG. 3-39). *Maat,* another daughter of Re, was the goddess of truth and justice. Her feather was used to measure the weight of the deceased's heart to determine if the *ka* (life force) would be blessed in the afterlife.

Hierakonpolis, represents what seems to be, at least in part, a funerary scene with people, animals, and large boats. The painting is in the form of a frieze running around three adjacent walls of the tomb. The stick figures and their apparently random arrangement recall the Neolithic painted hunters of Çatal Höyük (see FIG. 1-17). One black and five white boats, symbolic of the journey down the river of life and death, carry cargo of uncertain significance. The figures include a heraldic grouping of two animals flanking a human figure (at the lower left) and a man striking three prisoners with a mace (lower left corner). The heraldic group, a compositional type usually associated with Mesopotamian art (see FIG. 2-10), suggests that influences from Mesopotamia not only had reached Egypt by this time but also already had made the thousand-mile journey up the Nile. The second group, however, is characteristically Egyptian, and the motif was to have a long history in Egyptian painting and sculpture alike.

**THE UNIFICATION OF EGYPT** In Predynastic times, Egypt was divided geographically and politically into Upper Egypt (the southern, upstream part of the Nile Valley), a narrow tract of grassland that encouraged hunting, and Lower (northern) Egypt, where the rich soil of the Nile Delta islands encouraged agriculture and animal husbandry (MAP 3-1). The ancient Egyptians began the history of their kingdom with the unification of the two lands. Until recently, this was thought to have occurred during the rule of the First Dynasty pharaoh Menes, identified by many scholars with King Narmer. Narmer's image and name appear on both sides of a ceremonial *palette* (stone slab with a circular depression) found at Hierakonpolis. The palette (FIG. 3-2) is one of the earliest historical (versus prehistorical) artworks preserved. Although it is no longer regarded as commemorating the

foundation of the first of Egypt's 31 dynasties around 2920 BCE (the last ended in 332 BCE), it does record the unification of Upper and Lower Egypt at the very end of the Predynastic period. Although scholars now believe this unification occurred over several centuries, the *Palette of King Narmer* reflects the ancient Egyptian belief that the creation of the "Kingdom of the Two Lands" was a single great event.

The palette is an elaborate, formalized version of a utilitarian object commonly used in the Predynastic period to prepare eye makeup. (Egyptians used makeup to protect their eyes against irritation and the glare of the sun.) Narmer's palette is important not only as a document marking the transition from the prehistorical to the historical period in ancient Egypt but also as a kind of early blueprint of the formula for figure representation that characterized most Egyptian art for 3,000 years. At the top of each side of the palette are two heads of the goddess Hathor, represented as a cow with a woman's face. Between the Hathor heads is a hieroglyph giving Narmer's name within a frame representing the royal palace, making Narmer's palette the earliest existing labeled work of historical art.

On the back of the palette, the king, wearing the high, white, bowling-pin–shaped crown of Upper Egypt and accompanied by an official who carries his sandals, is shown slaying an enemy. The motif closely resembles the group at the lower left of the Hierakonpolis mural (FIG. 3-1) and became the standard pictorial formula signifying the inevitable triumph of the Egyptian god-kings over their enemies. Above and to the right, the falcon with human arms is Horus, the king's protector. The falcon-god takes captive a man-headed hieroglyph with a papyrus plant growing from it that stands for the land of Lower Egypt. Below the king are two fallen enemies.

On the front of the palette, the elongated necks of two felines form the circular depression that would have held eye makeup in

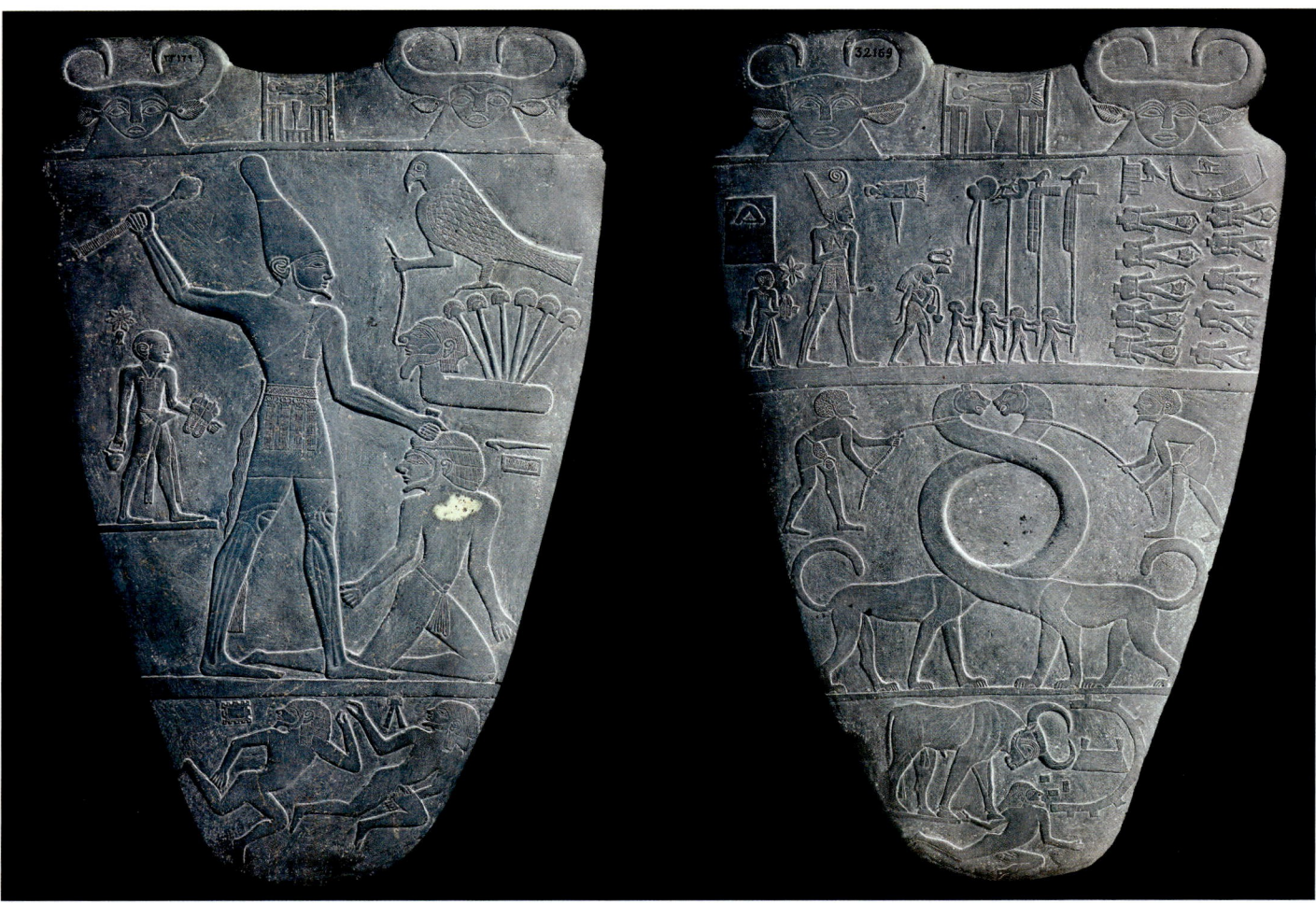

**3-2** *Palette of King Narmer* (*left,* back; *right,* front), from Hierakonpolis, Egypt, Predynastic, ca. 3000–2920 BCE. Slate, approx. 2′ 1″ high. Egyptian Museum, Cairo.

an ordinary palette not made for display. The intertwined necks of the animals may be another pictorial reference to Egypt's unification. In the uppermost register, Narmer, wearing the red crown of Lower Egypt, reviews the beheaded bodies of the enemy. The dead are seen from above, like the bison lying on the ground on the ceiling of the Altamira cave (see FIG. 1-9). The artist depicted each body with its severed head neatly placed between its legs. By virtue of his superior rank, the king, on both sides of the palette, performs his ritual task alone and towers over his own men and the enemy. The king's superhuman strength is symbolized in the lowest band by a great bull knocking down a rebellious city whose fortress walls also are seen in an "aerial view." Specific historical narrative is not the artist's goal in this work. What is important is the characterization of the king as supreme, isolated from and larger than all ordinary men and solely responsible for the triumph over the enemy. Here, at the very beginning of Egyptian history, is evidence of the Egyptian convention of thought, of art, and of state policy that established the pharaoh as a divine ruler.

**PORTRAYING THE HUMAN FIGURE** The artist's portrayal of Narmer on both sides of his palette combines profile views of his head, legs, and arms with front views of his eye and torso. As noted in Chapters 1 and 2, this composite view of the human figure also characterized Mesopotamian art and even some Stone Age paintings. Although the proportions of the human figure changed, the method of its representation became standard. The *Palette of King Narmer* established the basic laws that governed

most Egyptian art for millennia. In the Hierakonpolis painting (FIG. 3-1), the artist scattered the figures across the wall more or less haphazardly. On Narmer's palette, the sculptor subdivided the surface into registers and inserted the pictorial elements into their organized setting in a neat and orderly way. The horizontal lines separating the narratives also define the ground supporting the figures. This was also the preferred mode for narrative art in the ancient Near East (see Chapter 2). Egyptian artists who departed from this compositional scheme did so deliberately, usually to express the absence of order, as in a chaotic battle scene (FIG. 3-38).

## Architecture

**TOMBS AND THE AFTERLIFE** Narmer's palette is exceptional among surviving Egyptian artworks because it is commemorative rather than funerary in nature. Far more typical is the Predynastic mural from Hierakonpolis (FIG. 3-1). In fact, Egyptian tombs provide the principal, if not the exclusive, evidence for the historical reconstruction of Egyptian civilization. The overriding concern in this life was to ensure safety and happiness in the next life. The majority of monuments the Egyptians left behind were dedicated to this preoccupation (see "Mummification and the Afterlife," page 59).

The standard tomb type in early Egypt was the *mastaba* (FIG. **3-3**). The mastaba (Arabic for "bench") was a rectangular brick or stone structure with sloping sides erected over an

## Mummification and the Afterlife

The Egyptians did not make the sharp distinction between body and soul that is basic to many religions. Rather, they believed that from birth a person was accompanied by a kind of other self, the *ka* or life force, which, on the death of the body, could inhabit the corpse and live on. For the ka to live securely, however, the body had to remain as nearly intact as possible. To ensure that it did, the Egyptians developed the technique of embalming (*mummification*) to a high art. Although the Egyptians believed that the god Anubis invented embalming to preserve the body of the murdered Osiris (see "The Gods and Goddesses of Egypt," page 57), they did not practice mummification systematically until the Fourth Dynasty.

The first step in the 10-week process was the surgical removal of the lungs, liver, stomach, and intestines through an incision in the left flank. The Egyptians thought these organs were most subject to decay. The organs were individually wrapped and placed in four containers known as *canopic jars* for eventual deposit in the burial chamber with the corpse. (The jars take their name from the Egyptian port of Canopus, where human-headed jars were worshiped as personifications of Osiris. These jars were not, however, used in embalming.) The brain was extracted through the nostrils and discarded. The Egyptians did not attach any special significance to the brain. But they left in place the heart, necessary for life and regarded as the seat of intelligence.

Next, the body was treated for 40 days with *natron*, a naturally occurring salt compound that dehydrated the body. Then the corpse was filled with resin-soaked linens, and the embalming incision was closed and covered with a representation of the wedjat eye of Horus, a powerful *amulet* (a device to ward off evil and promote rebirth). Finally, the body was treated with lotions and resins and then wrapped tightly with hundreds of yards of linen bandages to maintain its shape. The Egyptians often placed other amulets within the bandages or on the corpse. The most important were heart *scarabs* (gems in the shape of beetles). Spells written on them ensured that the heart would be returned to its owner if it were ever lost. A scroll copy of the *Book of the Dead* (FIG. 3-39) frequently was placed between the legs of the deceased. It contained some 200 spells intended to protect the mummy and the ka in the afterlife. The mummies of the wealthy had their faces covered with funerary masks (FIG. 3-37).

The Egyptian practice of mummification endured for thousands of years, even when Egypt was ruled by Greek kings and later by Roman emperors. Roman mummies with painted portraits (see FIG. 10-63) have long been known. Their number has recently been greatly expanded by the discovery in 1996 of a cemetery at Bahariya Oasis in the desert southwest of Cairo. The site—at least four square miles in size—has come to be called the Valley of the Golden Mummies. The largest tomb found to date contained 32 mummies, but another held 43—some stacked on top of others because the tomb was used for generations and space ran out.

The care with which the dead were laid to rest in the Bahariya cemetery varied markedly with the social position and wealth of the deceased. The bodies of the poorer members of the community were carelessly wrapped in linen and have almost completely decayed. The 60 most elaborate mummies, probably those of successful merchants and their families, have gilded stucco masks. Some also have gilded chest plates with reliefs depicting Egyptian deities, including Thoth holding Maat's feather (compare the weighing scene in FIG. 3-39). Others have painted decoration, and some have eyes of white marble with black obsidian irises and copper eyelashes. The excavators believe the cemetery was still in use as late as the fourth or fifth century CE.

Preserving the deceased's body by mummification was only the first requirement for immortality in ancient Egypt. Food and drink also had to be provided, as did clothing, utensils, and furniture. Nothing that had been enjoyed on earth was to be lacking. Statuettes called *ushabtis* (answerers) also were placed in the tomb. These figurines performed any labor required of the deceased in the afterlife, answering whenever his or her name was called.

Beginning in the Old Kingdom, images of the dead, sculpted in the round and placed in shallow recesses, were also set up in the tomb. They were meant to guarantee the permanence of the person's identity by providing substitute dwelling places for the ka in case the mummy disintegrated. Wall paintings and reliefs recorded the recurring round of human activities. The Egyptians hoped and expected that the images and inventory of life, collected and set up within the protective stone walls of the tomb, would ensure immortality.

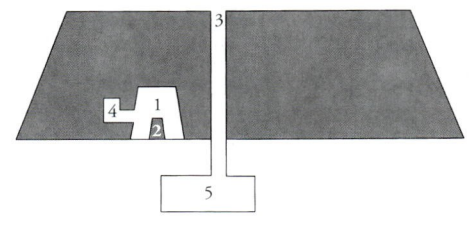 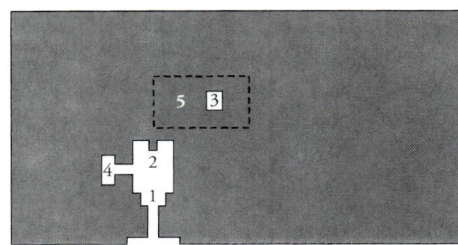 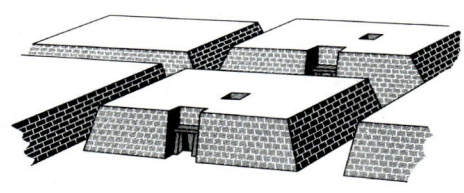

1. Chapel   2. False door   3. Shaft into burial chamber   4. Serdab (chamber for statue of deceased)   5. Burial chamber

**3-3** Section *(left)*, plan *(center)*, and restored view *(right)* of typical Egyptian mastaba tombs.

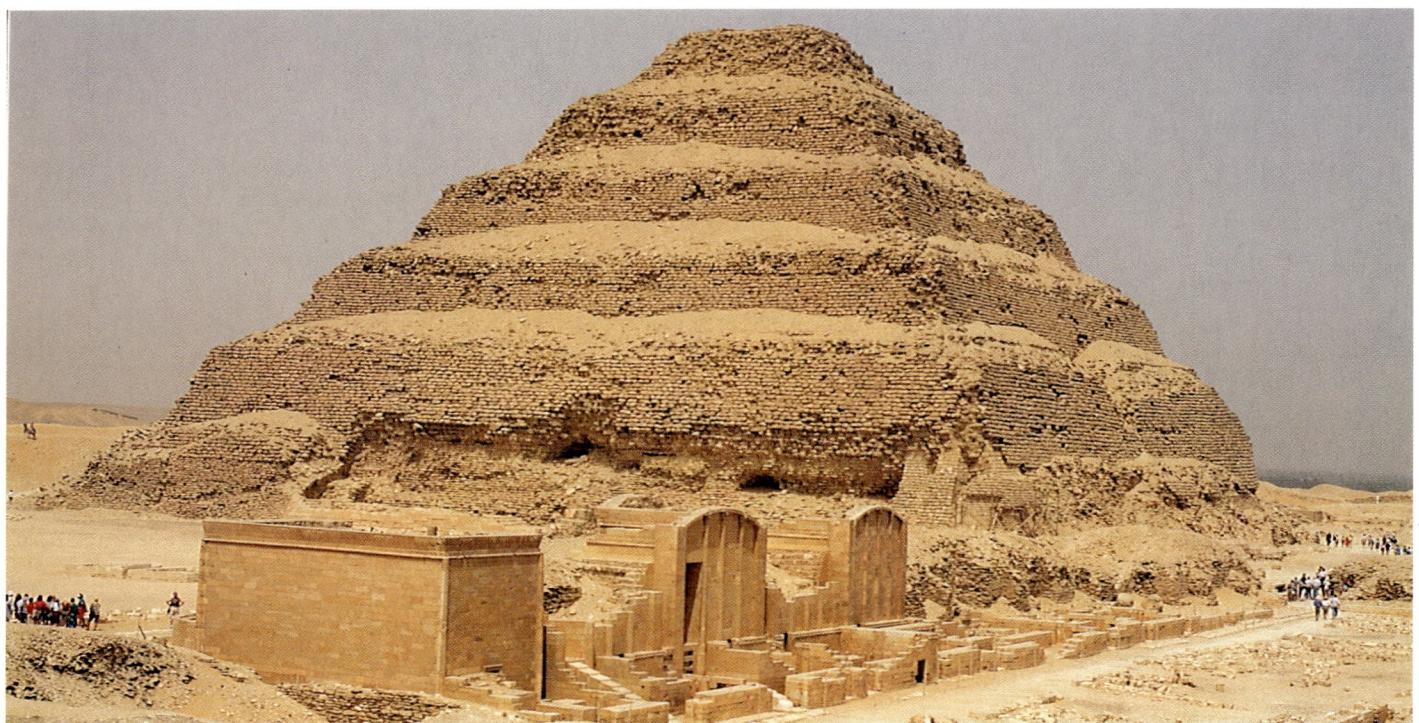

**3-4** Imhotep, Stepped Pyramid and mortuary precinct of Djoser, Saqqara, Egypt, Dynasty III, ca. 2630–2611 bce.

underground burial chamber. A shaft connected this chamber with the outside, providing the ka with access to the tomb. The form probably was developed from earth or stone mounds that had covered even earlier tombs. Although mastabas originally housed single burials, as in our example, during the latter part of the Old Kingdom they were used for multiple family burials and became increasingly complex. The central underground chamber was surrounded by storage rooms and compartments whose number and size increased with time until the area covered far surpassed that of the tomb chamber. Built into the superstructure, or sometimes attached to the outside, was a chapel housing a statue of the deceased in a small concealed chamber called the *serdab*. The chapel's interior walls and the ancillary rooms were decorated with colored relief carvings and paintings of scenes from daily life intended magically to provide the deceased with food and entertainment.

**THE FIRST PYRAMID** One of the most renowned figures in Egyptian history is Imhotep, the royal builder for King Djoser (r. 2630–2611 bce) of the Third Dynasty. Imhotep was a man of legendary talent who served also as the pharaoh's chancellor and high priest of the sun god. After his death, the Egyptians revered Imhotep as a god and in time may have inflated the list of his achievements. Nonetheless, his is the first known name of an artist in recorded history.

The historian Manetho states that Imhotep designed the Stepped Pyramid (FIG. **3-4**) of Djoser at Saqqara, the ancient *necropolis* (Greek for "city of the dead") for Memphis, Egypt's capital at the time. Built before 2600 bce, the pyramid is one of the oldest stone structures in Egypt and, in its final form, the first truly grandiose royal tomb. Begun as a large mastaba with each of its faces oriented toward one of the cardinal points of the compass, the tomb was enlarged at least twice before taking on its

ultimate shape. About 200 feet high, the Stepped Pyramid seems to be composed of a series of mastabas of diminishing size, stacked one on top of another to form a structure that resembles the great ziggurats of Mesopotamia (see FIG. 2-14). Unlike the ziggurats, however, Djoser's pyramid is a tomb, not a temple platform, and its dual function was to protect the mummified king and his possessions and to symbolize, by its gigantic presence, his absolute and godlike power. Beneath the pyramid was a network of underground galleries resembling a palace. It was to be Djoser's new home in the afterlife.

Befitting the god-king's majesty, Djoser's pyramid stands near the center of an immense (37-acre) rectangular enclosure (FIG. **3-5**) surrounded by a monumental (34-foot-high and 5,400-foot-long) wall of white limestone. The huge precinct, with its protective walls and tightly regulated access, stands in sharp contrast to the roughly contemporary Sumerian Royal Cemetery at Ur, where no barriers kept people away from the burial area. Nor did the Mesopotamian cemetery have a temple for the worship of the deified dead. At Saqqara, a funerary temple stands against the northern face of Djoser's pyramid (no. 2 on the plan). Priests performed daily rituals at the temple in celebration of the divine pharaoh.

**FROM PLANT TO STONE** Djoser's funerary temple was but one of many buildings arranged around several courts. Most of the others were dummy structures (no. 6 on the plan) with stone walls enclosing fills of rubble, sand, or gravel. The buildings imitated in stone masonry various types of temporary structures made of plant stems and mats erected in Upper and Lower Egypt to celebrate the Jubilee Festival. This event perpetually reaffirmed the royal existence in the hereafter.

The translation into stone of structural forms previously made out of plants may be seen in the long entrance corridor

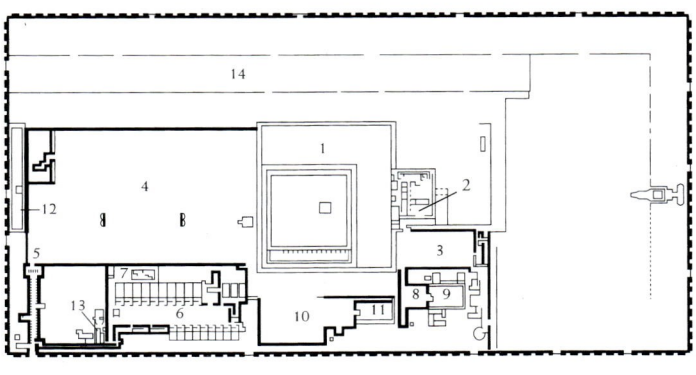

1. Stepped pyramid derived from square-plan mastaba
2. Funerary temple of Djoser
3. Court with serdab
4. Large court with altar and two B-shaped stones
5. Entrance portico
6. Heb-Sed court flanked by sham chapels
7. Small temple
8. Court before North Palace
9. North Palace
10. Court before South Palace
11. South Palace
12. South tomb
13. Royal Pavilion
14. Magazines

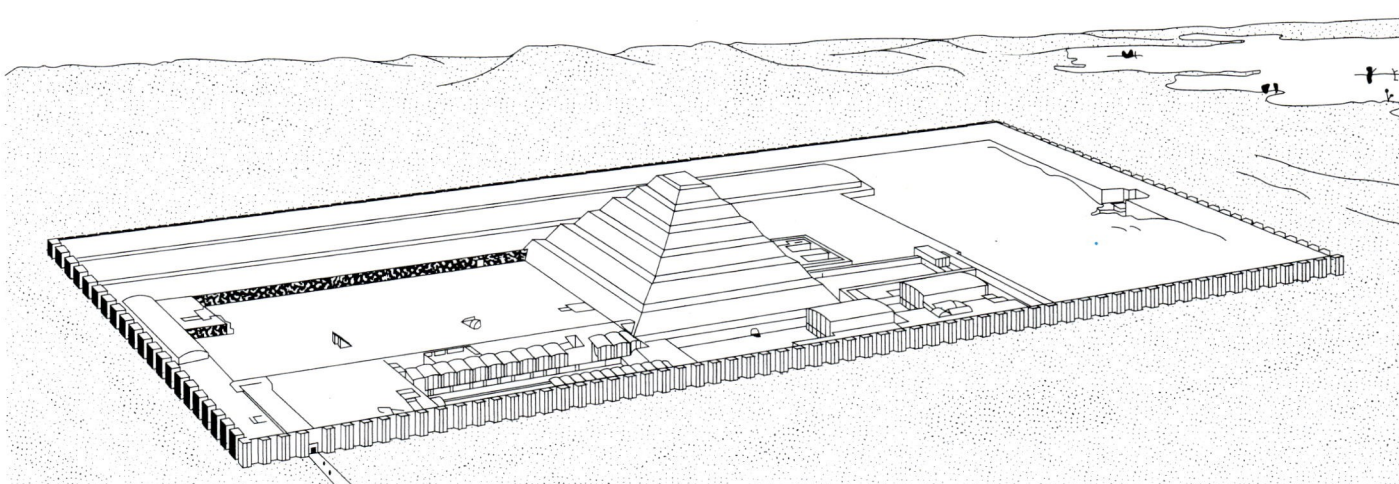

**3-5** Plan *(top)* and restored view *(bottom)* of the mortuary precinct of Djoser, Saqqara, Egypt, Dynasty III, ca. 2630–2611 BCE.

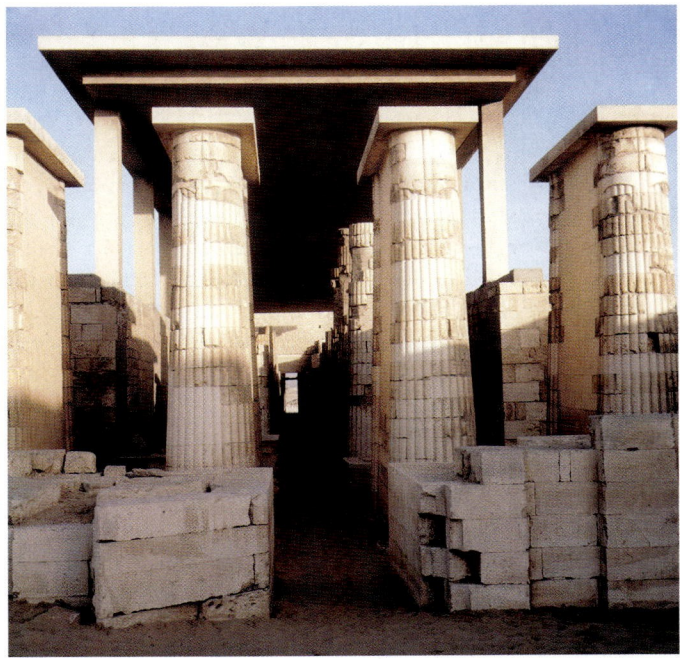

**3-6** Columnar entrance corridor to the mortuary precinct of Djoser, Saqqara, Egypt, Dynasty III, ca. 2630–2611 BCE.

(FIG. **3-6**) to Djoser's funerary precinct. There, *columns* that resemble bundles of reeds project from short spur walls on either side of the once-roofed and dark passageway. A person walking through it would have emerged suddenly into a large courtyard and the brilliant light of the Egyptian sun. To the right, the visitor would have seen the gleaming focus of the entire complex, Djoser's pyramid.

The columns flanking the pathway into Djoser's precinct resemble later Greek columns. Architectural historians have little doubt today that the buildings of ancient Egypt had a profound impact on the designers of the first Greek stone columnar temples (see Chapter 5). The upper parts of the Saqqara entrance portico columns are not preserved, but those of Djoser's North Palace (FIG. **3-7**; no. 9 in FIG. 3-5) still stand. They end in *capitals* ("heads") that take the form of the papyrus blossoms of Lower Egypt. The column shafts resemble papyrus stalks. The later Greek columns also terminate in capitals, although the Greek capitals differ markedly in form. Greek column shafts are also generally freestanding, whereas all the columns in the Saqqara complex are *engaged* (attached) to walls. Still, this is the first appearance of stone columns in the history of architecture.

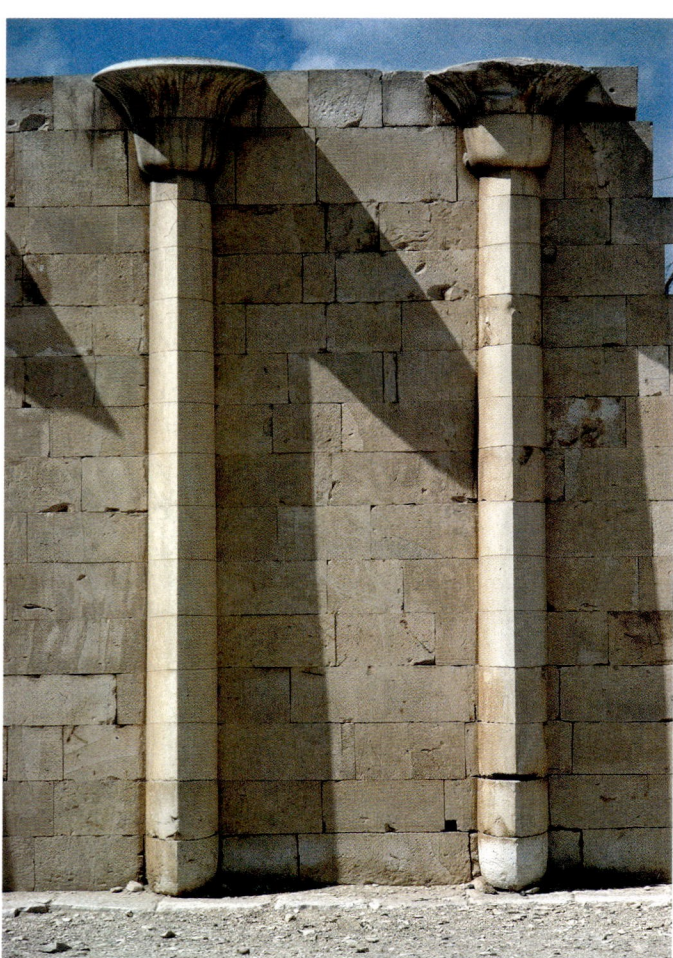

**3-7** Facade of the North Palace of the mortuary precinct of Djoser, Saqqara, Egypt, Dynasty III, ca. 2630–2611 BCE.

# THE OLD KINGDOM

The Old Kingdom is the first of the three great periods of Egyptian history, called the Old, Middle, and New Kingdoms, respectively. Many Egyptologists now begin the Old Kingdom with the first pharaoh of the Fourth Dynasty, Sneferu (r. 2575–2551 BCE), although the traditional division of Kingdoms places Djoser and the Third Dynasty in the Old Kingdom. It ended with the demise of the Eighth Dynasty around 2134 BCE.

## *Architecture*

**PYRAMIDS AND THE SUN GOD** At Gizeh, across the Nile from modern Cairo, stand the three Great Pyramids (FIG. **3-8;** see "Building the Great Pyramids," page 63), the oldest of the Seven Wonders of the ancient world (see "Babylon: City of Wonders," Chapter 2, page 49). The prerequisites for membership in this elite club were colossal size and enormous cost, and the Gizeh pyramids testify to the wealth and pretensions of the Fourth Dynasty pharaohs Khufu (r. 2551–2528 BCE), Khafre (r. 2520–2494 BCE), and Menkaure (r. 2490–2472 BCE).

The three pyramids, built in the course of about 75 years, represent the culmination of an architectural evolution that began with the mastaba. The pyramid form did not evolve out of necessity, and the Egyptian kings could have gone on indefinitely stacking mastabas to make their weighty tombs. The new tomb shape probably reflects the influence of Heliopolis, the seat of the powerful cult of Re, whose emblem was a pyramidal stone, the *ben-ben* (see "The Gods and Goddesses of Egypt," page 57). The Great Pyramids are symbols of the sun. The Pyramid Texts, inscribed on the burial chamber walls of many royal tombs beginning with the Fifth Dynasty Pyramid of Unas (r. 2356–2323 BCE), refer to the sun's rays as the ramp the pharaoh uses to ascend to the heavens.

**3-8** Great Pyramids, Gizeh, Egypt, Dynasty IV. *From left:* Pyramids of Menkaure, ca. 2490–2472 BCE; Khafre, ca. 2520–2494 BCE; and Khufu, ca. 2551–2528 BCE.

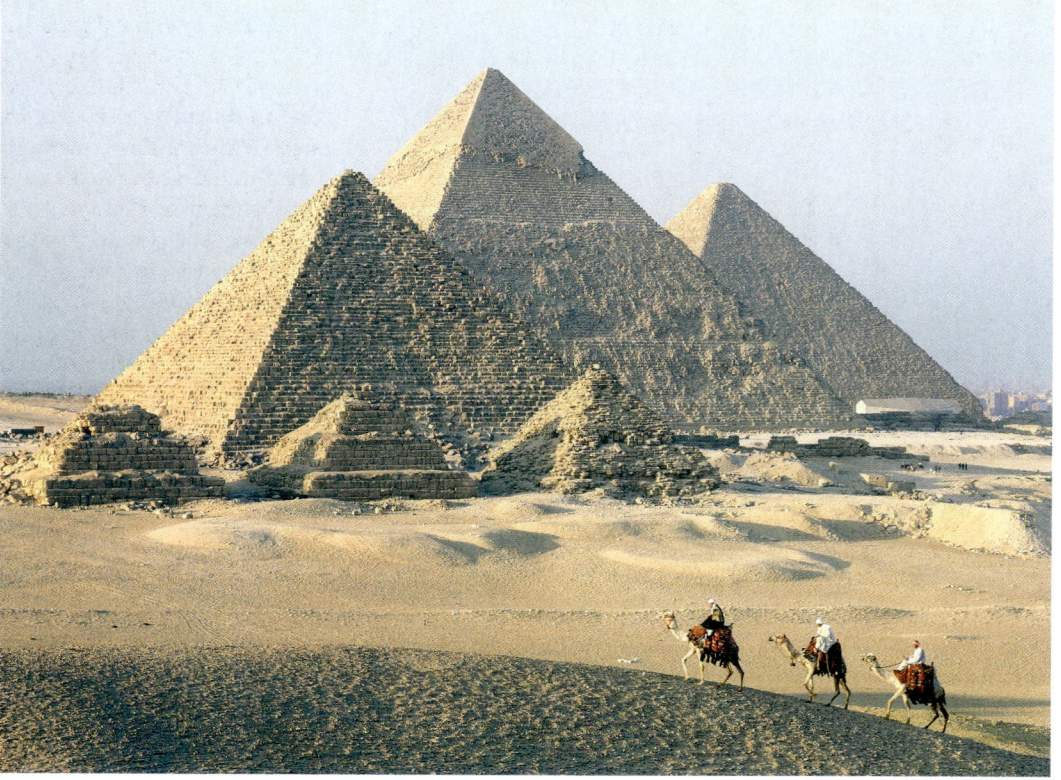

## Building the Great Pyramids

The three Great Pyramids of Khufu, Khafre, and Menkaure at Gizeh (FIG. 3-8) attest to Egyptian builders' mastery of stone masonry and to their ability to mobilize, direct, house, and feed a huge workforce engaged in one of the most labor-intensive enterprises ever undertaken. Like all building projects of this type, the process of erecting the pyramids began with the quarrying of stone, in this case primarily the limestone of the Gizeh plateau itself. Teams of skilled workers had to cut into the rock and remove large blocks of roughly equal size using stone or copper chisels and wooden mallets and wedges. Often, the artisans had to cut deep tunnels to find high-quality stone free of cracks and other flaws. To remove a block, the workers cut channels on all sides and partly underneath. Then they pried the stones free from the bedrock with wooden levers.

After workers liberated the stones, the rough blocks had to be transported to the building site and *dressed* (shaped to the exact dimensions required, with smooth faces for a perfect fit). Small blocks could be carried on a man's shoulders or on the back of a donkey, but the massive blocks used to construct the Great Pyramids were moved using wooden rollers and sleds. The artisans dressed the blocks by chiseling and pounding the surfaces and, in the last stage, by rubbing and grinding the surfaces with fine polishing stones. This kind of construction, in which carefully cut and regularly shaped blocks of stone are piled in successive rows, or *courses,* is called *ashlar masonry.*

To set the ashlar blocks in place, workers erected great rubble ramps against the core of the pyramid. Their size and slope were adjusted as work progressed and the tomb grew in height. Scholars still debate whether the Egyptians used simple linear ramps inclined at a right angle to one face of the pyramid or zigzag or spiral ramps akin to staircases. Linear ramps would have had the advantage of simplicity and would have left three sides of the pyramid unobstructed. But zigzag ramps placed against one side of the structure or spiral ramps winding around the pyramid would have greatly reduced the slope of the incline and would have made the dragging of the blocks easier. Some scholars also have suggested a combination of straight and spiral ramps.

Ropes, pulleys, and levers were used both to lift and to lower the stones, guiding each block into its designated place. Finally, the pyramid was surfaced with a casing of white limestone, cut so precisely that the eye could scarcely detect the joints. A few casing stones still can be seen in the cap that covers the Pyramid of Khafre (FIGS. 3-8, *center,* and 3-11, *left*). They are all that remain after many centuries of stripping the pyramids to supply limestone for the Islamic builders of Cairo.

---

Djoser's Stepped Pyramid (FIG. 3-4) may also have been conceived as a giant stairway. The pyramids were where Egyptian kings were reborn in the afterlife, just as the sun is reborn each day at dawn.

Of the three Fourth Dynasty pyramids at Gizeh, the tomb of Khufu (FIG. 3-9) is the oldest and largest. Except for the galleries and burial chamber, it is an almost solid mass of limestone masonry—a stone mountain built on the same principle as the earlier Stepped Pyramid at Saqqara. When its original stone facing (no. 1 in FIG. 3-9) was intact, the sunlight it reflected would have been dazzling, underscoring the pyramid's role as a solar symbol.

The immensity of the Gizeh pyramids and that of Khufu in particular is indicated by some dimensions. At the base, the length of one side of Khufu's tomb is approximately 775 feet, and its area is some 13 acres. Its present height is about 450 feet (originally 480 feet). The structure contains roughly 2.3 million blocks of stone, each weighing an average of 2.5 tons. Napoleon's scholars calculated that the blocks in the three Great Pyramids were sufficient to build a wall 1 foot wide and 10 feet high around France.

As with Djoser's Stepped Pyramid, the four sides of each of the Great Pyramids are oriented to the cardinal points of the compass. But the funerary temples associated with the three Gizeh pyramids are not placed on the north side, facing the stars of the northern sky, as was Djoser's temple. The temples sit on the east side, facing the rising sun and underscoring their connection with Re.

**KHAFRE AND THE SPHINX** From the remains surrounding the Pyramid of Khafre at Gizeh, archaeologists have been able to reconstruct an entire funerary complex (FIG. 3-10). The complex included the pyramid itself with the pharaoh's burial chamber; the *mortuary temple* adjoining the pyramid on the east side, where offerings were made to the dead king, ceremonies performed, and cloth, food, and ceremonial vessels stored; the covered *causeway,* or raised corridor, whose walls were decorated with painted reliefs; and the *valley temple* at the edge of the floodplain. According to one theory, the complex served not only as the king's tomb and temple but also as his palace in the afterlife.

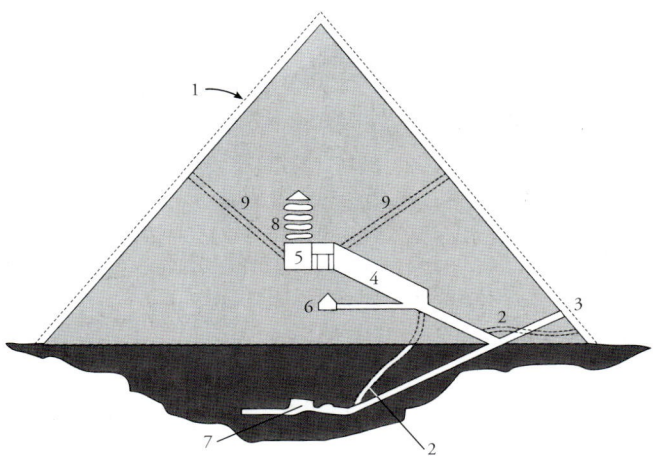

1. Silhouette with original facing stone
2. Thieves' tunnels
3. Entrance
4. Grand gallery
5. King's chamber
6. So-called Queen's chamber
7. False tomb chamber
8. Relieving blocks
9. Airshafts(?)

**3-9** Section of the Pyramid of Khufu, Gizeh, Egypt.

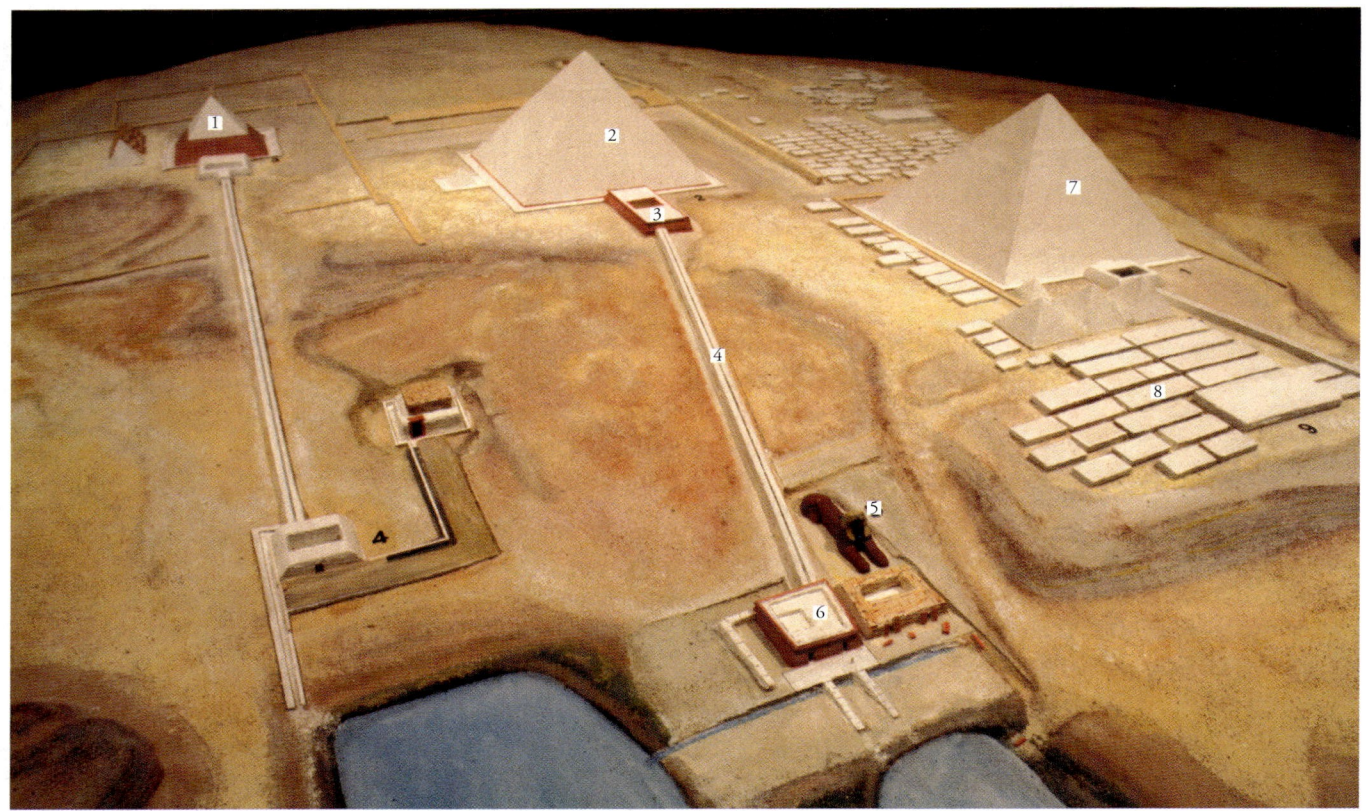

**3-10** Model of the pyramid complex, Gizeh, Egypt. Cambridge, Massachusetts, Harvard University Semitic Museum. 1) Pyramid of Menkaure, 2) Pyramid of Khafre, 3) Mortuary temple of Khafre, 4) Causeway, 5) Great Sphinx, 6) Valley temple of Khafre, 7) Pyramid of Khufu, 8) Pyramids of the royal family and mastabas of nobles

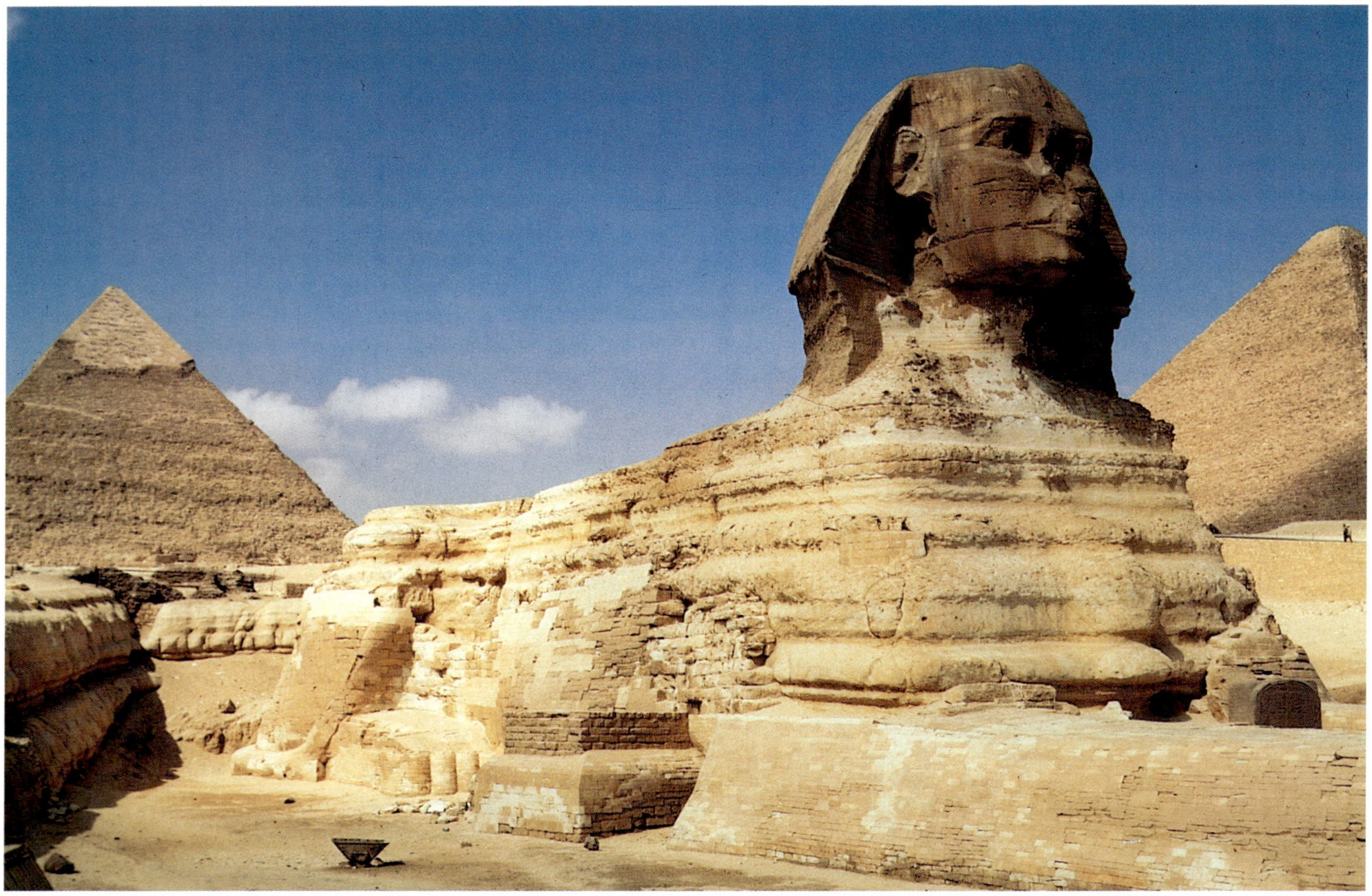

**3-11** Great Sphinx (with Pyramid of Khafre in the background at left), Gizeh, Egypt, Dynasty IV, ca. 2520–2494 BCE. Sandstone, approx. 65′ high, 240′ long.

Beside the causeway and dominating the valley temple of Khafre rises the Great Sphinx (FIG. 3-11). Carved from a spur of rock in an ancient quarry, the colossal statue—the largest in the ancient Near East—is probably an image of Khafre, although some scholars believe it portrays Khufu and was carved before construction of Khafre's complex began. Whoever it portrays, the *sphinx*— a lion with a human head—was associated with the sun god and therefore an appropriate image for a pharaoh. The composite form suggests that the pharaoh combines human intelligence with the awesome strength and authority of the king of beasts.

## Sculpture

**STATUES FOR ETERNITY** As already noted, statues fulfilled an important function in Egyptian tombs. Sculptors created images of the deceased to serve as abodes for the ka should the mummies be destroyed. Although wood, clay, and other materials were used, mostly for images of those not of the royal or noble classes, the primary material for funerary statuary was stone.

The seated statue of Khafre (FIG. 3-12) is one of a series of similar statues carved for the pharaoh's valley temple (FIG. 3-10, no. 6) near the Great Sphinx. The stone is diorite, an exceptionally hard dark stone brought some 400 miles down the Nile from royal quarries in the south. (The Neo-Sumerian ruler Gudea [see FIG. 2-15] so admired diorite that he imported it to faraway Girsu.) Khafre wears a simple kilt and sits rigidly upright on a throne formed of two stylized lions' bodies. Intertwined lotus and papyrus plants—symbol of the united Egypt—are carved between the throne's legs. The falcon-god Horus extends his protective wings to shelter the pharaoh's head. Khafre has the royal false beard fastened to his chin and wears the royal linen *nemes* headdress with the *uraeus* cobra of kingship on the front. The headdress covers his forehead and falls in pleated folds over his shoulders. (The head of the Great Sphinx is similarly attired.) As befitting a divine ruler, Khafre is shown with a well-developed, flawless body and a perfect face, regardless of his actual age and appearance. The Egyptians considered ideal proportions appropriate for representing imposing majesty, and artists used them quite independently of reality. This and all other generalized representations of the pharaohs are not true portraits and were not intended to be. Their purpose was not to record individual features or the distinctive shapes of bodies, but rather to proclaim the godlike nature of Egyptian kingship.

The seated king radiates serenity. The sculptor created this effect, common to Egyptian royal statues, in part by giving the figure great compactness and solidity, with few projecting, breakable parts. The form manifests the purpose: to last for eternity. Khafre's body is attached to the unarticulated slab that forms the back of the king's throne. His arms are held close to the torso and thighs, and his legs are close together and connected to the chair by the stone the artist chose not to remove. The pose is frontal, rigid, and *bilaterally symmetrical* (the same on either side of an axis, in this case the vertical axis). The sculptor suppressed all movement and with it the notion of time, creating an eternal stillness.

To produce the statue, the artist first drew the front, back, and two profile views of the pharaoh on the four vertical faces of the stone block. Next, apprentices chiseled away the excess stone on each side, working inward until the planes met at right angles. Finally, the master sculpted the parts of Khafre's body, the falcon, and so forth. The finishing was done by *abrasion* (rubbing or grinding the surface). This subtractive method of creating the

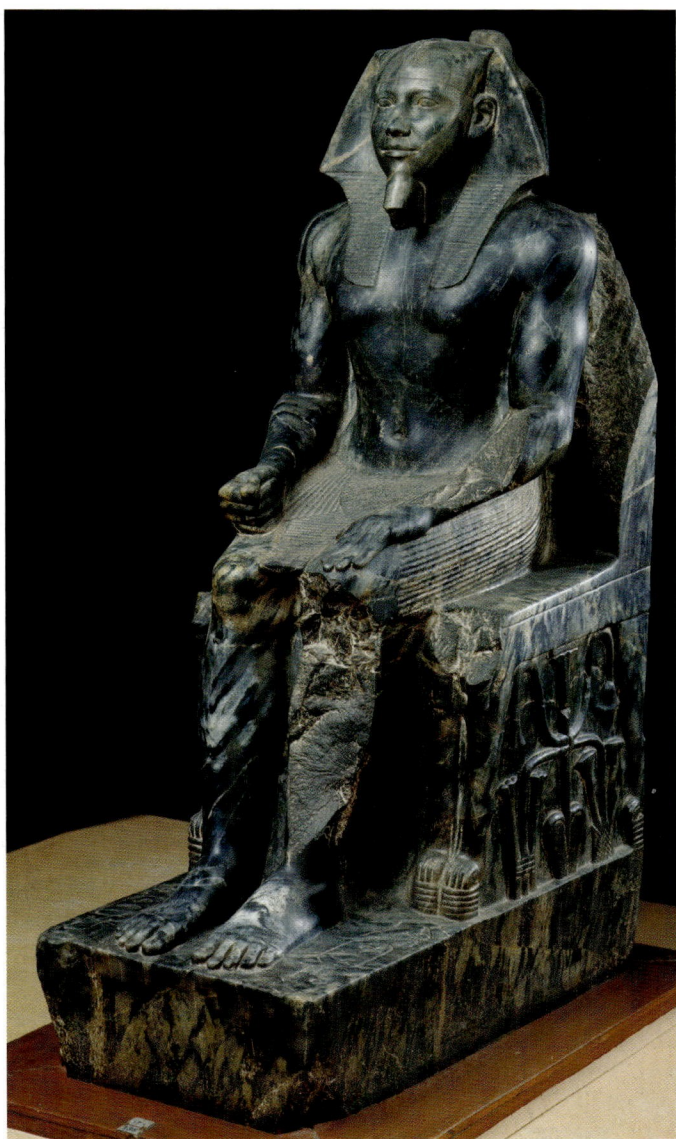

3-12 Khafre, from Gizeh, Egypt, Dynasty IV, ca. 2520–2494 BCE. Diorite, approx. 5′ 6″ high. Egyptian Museum, Cairo.

pharaoh's portrait accounts in large part for the blocklike look of the standard Egyptian statue. Nevertheless, other sculptors, both ancient and modern, with different aims, have transformed stone blocks into dynamic, twisting human forms (see, for example, FIG. 5-85).

**AN EMOTIONLESS EMBRACE** The seated statue is one of only a small number of basic formulaic types the sculptors of the Old Kingdom employed to represent the human figure. Another is the image of a person or deity standing, either alone or in a group. Superb examples of the standing type are the joined portrait statues of Menkaure and one of his wives, probably the queen Khamerernebty (FIG. 3-13). The statue once stood in the valley temple of Menkaure's pyramid complex at Gizeh. Here, too, the figures remain wedded to the stone block from which they were carved, and the sculptor used conventional postures to suggest the timeless nature of these eternal substitute homes for the ka. Menkaure's pose, which is duplicated in countless other Egyptian statues, is rigidly frontal with the arms hanging straight down and close to his well-built body. His hands are clenched into

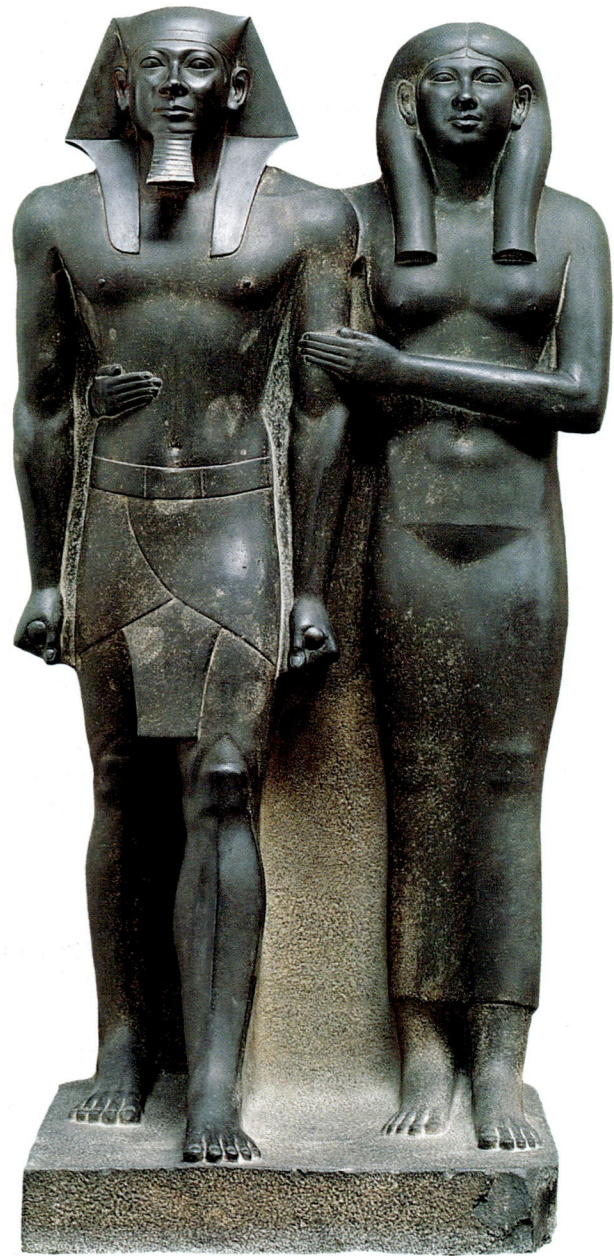

**3-13** Menkaure and Khamerernebty(?), from Gizeh, Egypt, Dynasty IV, ca. 2490–2472 BCE. Graywacke, approx. 4′ 6½″ high. Museum of Fine Arts, Boston.

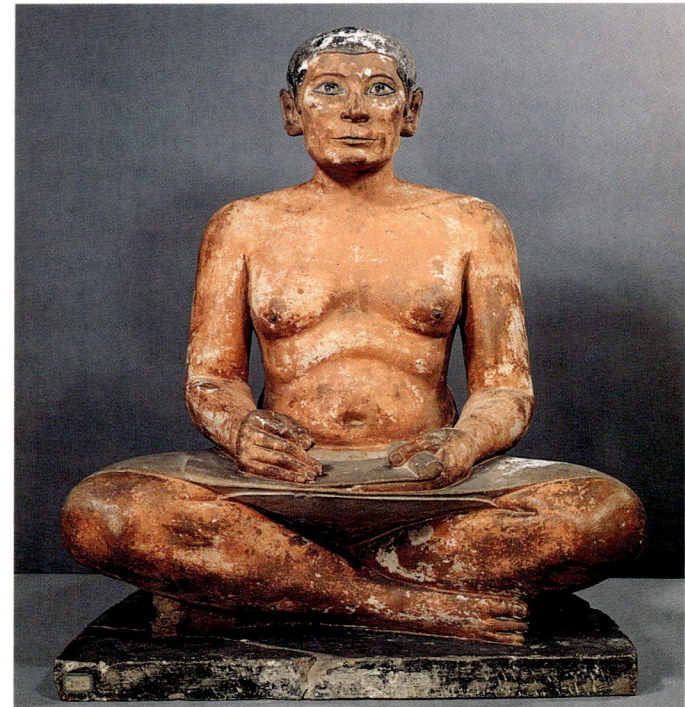

**3-14** Seated scribe (Kay?), from his mastaba at Saqqara, Egypt, Dynasty V, ca. 2450–2350 BCE. Painted limestone, approx. 1′ 9″ high. Louvre, Paris.

fists with the thumbs forward. His left leg is slightly advanced, but no shift occurs in the angle of the hips to correspond to the uneven distribution of weight. Khamerernebty stands in a similar position. Her right arm, however, circles around the king's waist, and her left hand gently rests on his left arm. This frozen stereotypical gesture indicates their marital status. The husband and wife show no other sign of affection or emotion and look not at each other but out into space.

**EGYPTIAN REALISM** Traces of paint remain on the portraits of Menkaure and Khamerernebty. Most Egyptian statues were painted, although sometimes the stone was left its natural color, enhancing the sense of abstraction and timelessness. A striking example of painted statuary is the portrait of a Fifth Dynasty seated scribe sometimes identified as Kay (FIG. **3-14**). Despite the stiff

upright posture and the frontality of head and body, the color lends a lifelike quality to the statue. The head displays an extraordinary sensitivity. The sculptor conveyed the personality of a sharply intelligent and alert individual with a penetration and sympathy seldom achieved at such an early date. The scribe sits directly on the ground, not on a throne nor even on a chair. Although he occupied a position of honor in a largely illiterate society, the scribe was a much lower figure in the Egyptian hierarchy than the pharaoh, whose divinity made him superhuman. In the history of art, especially portraiture, it is almost a rule that as a human subject's importance decreases, formality is relaxed and realism is increased. It is telling that the scribe is shown with sagging chest muscles and a protruding belly. Such signs of age would have been disrespectful and wholly inappropriate in a depiction of an Egyptian god-king. But the statue of the scribe is not a true portrait either. Rather, it is a composite of conventional types. In fact, the scribe's sunken cheeks are difficult to reconcile with his flabby body.

**A PORTRAIT IN WOOD** A second portrait illustrating this rule of relaxed formality and increased realism is the Fifth Dynasty wooden statue of an official named Ka-Aper (FIG. **3-15**). Like the statue of the seated scribe, Ka-Aper's portrait comes from the deceased's simple brick mastaba at Saqqara. Ka-Aper's face is also startlingly alive, even though the paint does not survive. The eyes of rock crystal are intact, however, and heighten the effect. The figure stands erect in the conventional frontal pose used for pharaonic portraits, with the left leg advanced. He is shown with the badges of his rank—a tall walking stick in his left hand and a baton (missing) in his right. Ka-Aper's paunchy physique contrasts even more sharply than the scribe's with the idealized proportions used to portray Khafre and Menkaure. Obesity

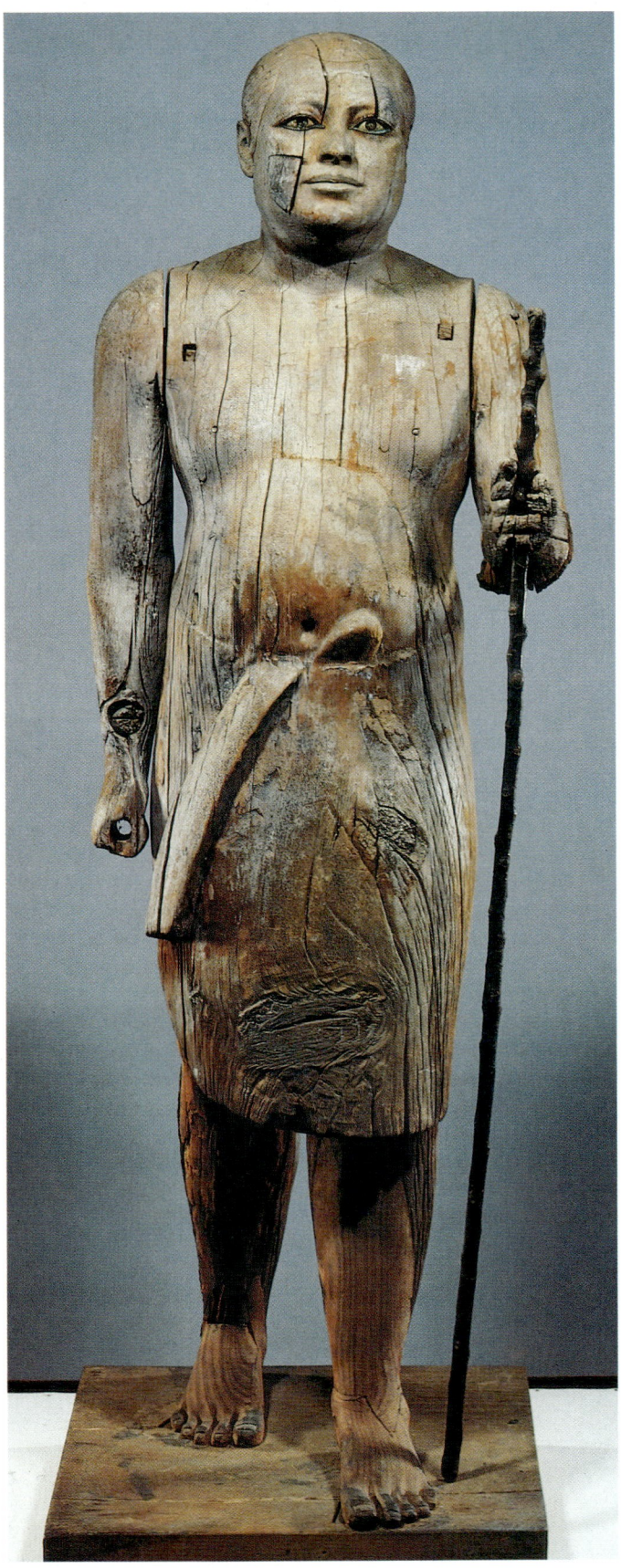

characterizes many nonroyal Old Kingdom portraits, perhaps because it attested to the comfortable life of the person represented and his relatively high position in society. Ka-Aper's statue somewhat retains the shape of the tree trunk from which the sculptor fashioned it (the arms were carved separately and pegged onto the body). Because the statue has no back slab, it seems to stand more freely than the stone images of Menkaure and Khamerernebty. The artist, however, had no more interest in portraying motion than had the sculptor of those royal images in stone.

HUNTING IN THE AFTERLIFE  In Egyptian tombs, the deceased were not represented exclusively in freestanding statuary. Artists also depicted many individuals in relief sculpture and in mural painting, sometimes alone—as on the wooden panel of Hesire discussed in the Introduction (FIG. Intro-14)—and sometimes in a narrative context. The scenes in painted limestone relief that decorate the walls of the mastaba of Ti at Saqqara typify the subjects Old Kingdom patrons favored for the adornment of their final resting places. Ti was an official of the Fifth Dynasty. Depictions of agriculture and hunting fill his tomb. These activities were associated with the provisioning of the ka in the hereafter, but they also had powerful symbolic overtones. In ancient Egypt, success in the hunt, for example, was a metaphor for triumph over the forces of evil.

On one wall (FIG. 3-16), Ti, his men, and his boats move slowly through the marshes, hunting hippopotami and birds in a dense growth of towering papyrus. The reedy stems of the plants are

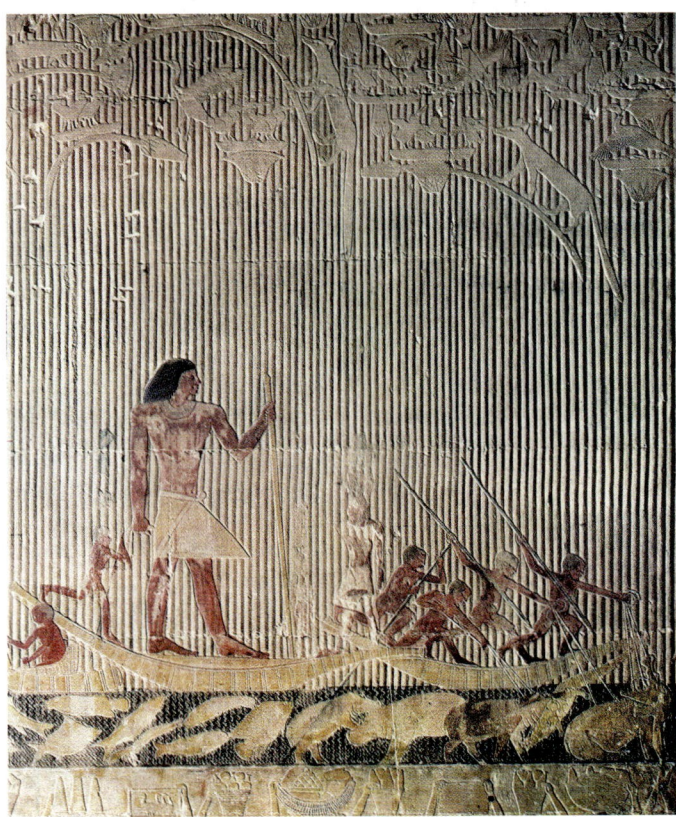

**3-15**  Ka-Aper, from his mastaba at Saqqara, Egypt, Dynasty V, ca. 2450–2350 BCE. Wood, approx. 3′ 7″ high. Egyptian Museum, Cairo.

**3-16**  Ti watching a hippopotamus hunt, relief in the mastaba of Ti, Saqqara, Egypt, Dynasty V, ca. 2450–2350 BCE. Painted limestone, hunting scene approx. 4′ high.

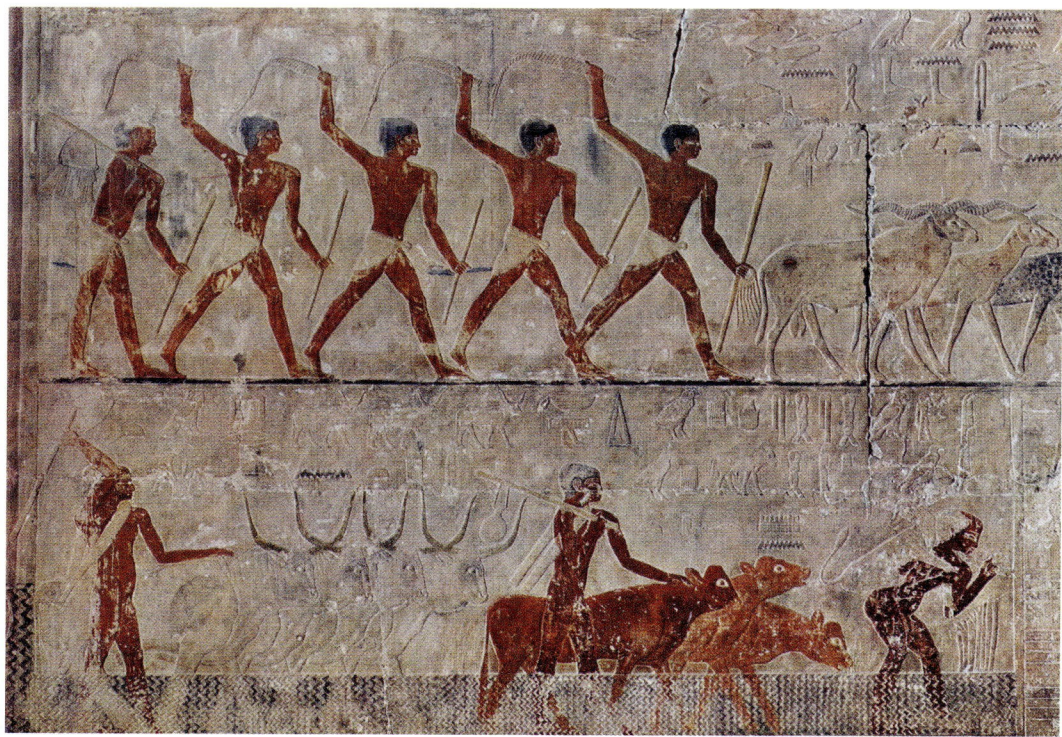

**3-17** Goats treading seed and cattle fording a canal, reliefs in the mastaba of Ti, Saqqara, Egypt, Dynasty V, ca. 2450–2350 BCE. Painted limestone.

delineated with repeated fine grooves that fan out gracefully at the top into a commotion of frightened birds and stalking foxes. The water beneath the boats, signified by a pattern of wavy lines, is crowded with hippopotami and fish. Ti's men seem frantically busy with their spears, while Ti, depicted twice their size, stands aloof. The basic conventions of Egyptian figure representation used half a millennium earlier in the *Palette of King Narmer* (FIG. 3-2) are seen again here. As on the Predynastic palette and the portrait relief of Hesire (see FIG. Intro-14), the artist used the *conceptual* rather than the *optical* approach, representing what was known to be true of the subject, instead of a random view of it, and showing its most characteristic parts at right angles to the line of vision. This conceptual approach expressed a feeling for the constant and changeless aspect of things and was well suited for Egyptian funerary art. Ti's outsize proportions bespeak his rank. His conventional pose contrasts with the realistically rendered activities of his tiny servants and with the naturalistically carved and painted birds and animals among the papyrus buds. Ti's immobility suggests that he is not an actor in the hunt. He does not *do* anything. He simply *is*, a figure apart from time and an impassive observer of life, like his ka.

**THE EGYPTIAN CANON** The idealized and stiff image of Ti is typical of Egyptian relief sculpture. Egyptian artists regularly ignored the endless variations in body types of real human beings. Painters and sculptors did not sketch their subjects from life but applied a strict *canon*, or system of proportions, to the human figure. They first drew a grid on the wall. Then they placed various human body parts at specific points on the network of squares. The height of a figure, for example, was a fixed number of squares, and the head, shoulders, waist, knees, and other parts of the body also had a predetermined size and place within the scheme. This approach to design lasted for thousands of years. Specific proportions might vary from workshop to workshop and change over time, but the principle of the canon persisted.

**FORDING THE NILE** On another wall of Ti's mastaba, the artist represented goats treading in seeds and cattle fording a canal

in the Nile in two registers (FIG. **3-17**). Ti is absent, and all the men and animals participate in the narrative. Despite the sculptor's repeated use of similar poses for most of the human and animal figures, the reliefs are full of anecdotal details. Especially charming is the group at the lower right of our illustration. A youth, depicted in a complex unconventional posture, carries a calf on his back. The animal, not a little afraid, turns its head back a full 180 degrees (compare the Paleolithic bison in FIG. 1-8) to seek reassurance from its mother, who returns the calf's gaze. Scenes such as this demonstrate that Egyptian artists could be close observers of daily life. The absence of the anecdotal (that is, of the time-bound) from their representations of the deceased both in relief and in the round was a deliberate choice. Their primary purpose was to suggest the deceased's eternal existence in the afterlife, not to portray nature. Once again, the scenes may be interpreted on a symbolic, as well as a literal, level. The fording of the Nile was a metaphor for the deceased's passage from life to the hereafter.

## THE MIDDLE KINGDOM

About 2150 BCE, the Egyptians challenged the pharaohs' power, and for more than a century the land was in a state of civil unrest and near anarchy. But in 2040 BCE, the pharaoh of Upper Egypt, Mentuhotep II (r. 2050–1998 BCE), managed to unite Egypt again under the rule of a single king and established the so-called Middle Kingdom (Dynasties XI–XIV).

### Sculpture

**A BROODING PHARAOH** One of Mentuhotep II's successors was Senusret III (r. 1878–1859 BCE), who fought four brutal military campaigns in Nubia. Although Egyptian armies devastated the land and poisoned the wells, Senusret III never fully achieved secure control over the Nubians. In Egypt itself, he attempted, with greater success, to establish a more powerful central government.

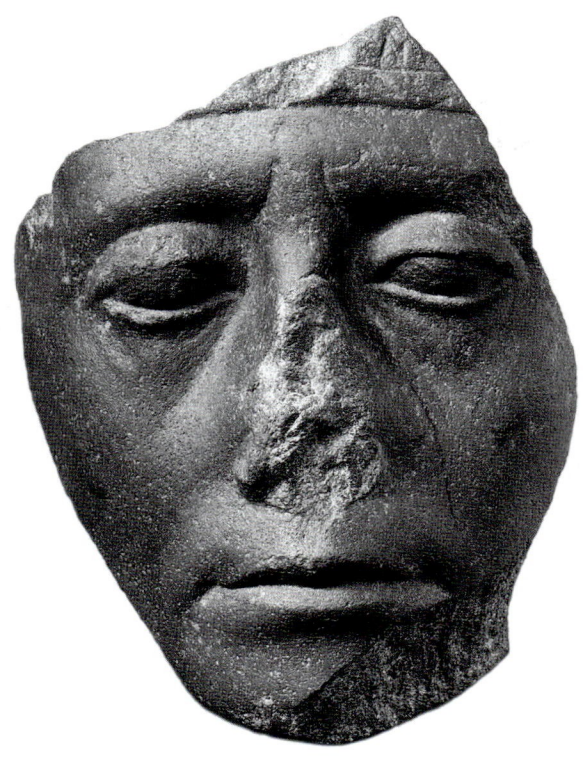

His portraits are of special interest because they represent a sharp break from Old Kingdom practice. Although the king's preserved statues have idealized bodies, the sculptors brought a stunning and unprecedented realism to the rendition of Senusret III's features (FIG. **3-18**). His pessimistic expression reflects the dominant mood of the time and is echoed in Middle Kingdom literature. The strong mouth, the drooping lines about the nose and eyes, and the shadowy brows show a determined ruler who had also shared in the cares of the world, sunk in brooding meditation. The portrait is different in kind from the typically impassive faces of the Old Kingdom. It is personal, almost intimate, in its revelation of the mark of anxiety that a troubled age might leave on the soul of a king.

## Architecture

**MOUNTAIN TOMBS** Senusret III's tomb, at Dashur, is a mudbrick pyramid, but the most characteristic burials of the Middle Kingdom are rock-cut tombs, like those at Beni Hasan (FIG. **3-19**). Such tombs also existed during the Old Kingdom, but the best preserved date to the later period. One of those is the 12th Dynasty tomb of Khnumhotep, who boasted in an inscription of its elaborateness, saying that its doors were of cedar 7 cubits (about 12 feet) high. Expressing the characteristic Egyptian attitude toward the last resting place, he added:

> My chief nobility was I executed a cliff-tomb, for a man should imitate that which his father does. My father made for himself a house of the ka in the town of Menofret, of good stone of Ayan, in order to perpetuate his name forever and establish it eternally.

**3-18** Fragmentary head of Senusret III, Dynasty XII, ca. 1860 BCE. Red quartzite, approx. $6\frac{1}{2}''$ high. Metropolitan Museum of Art, New York.

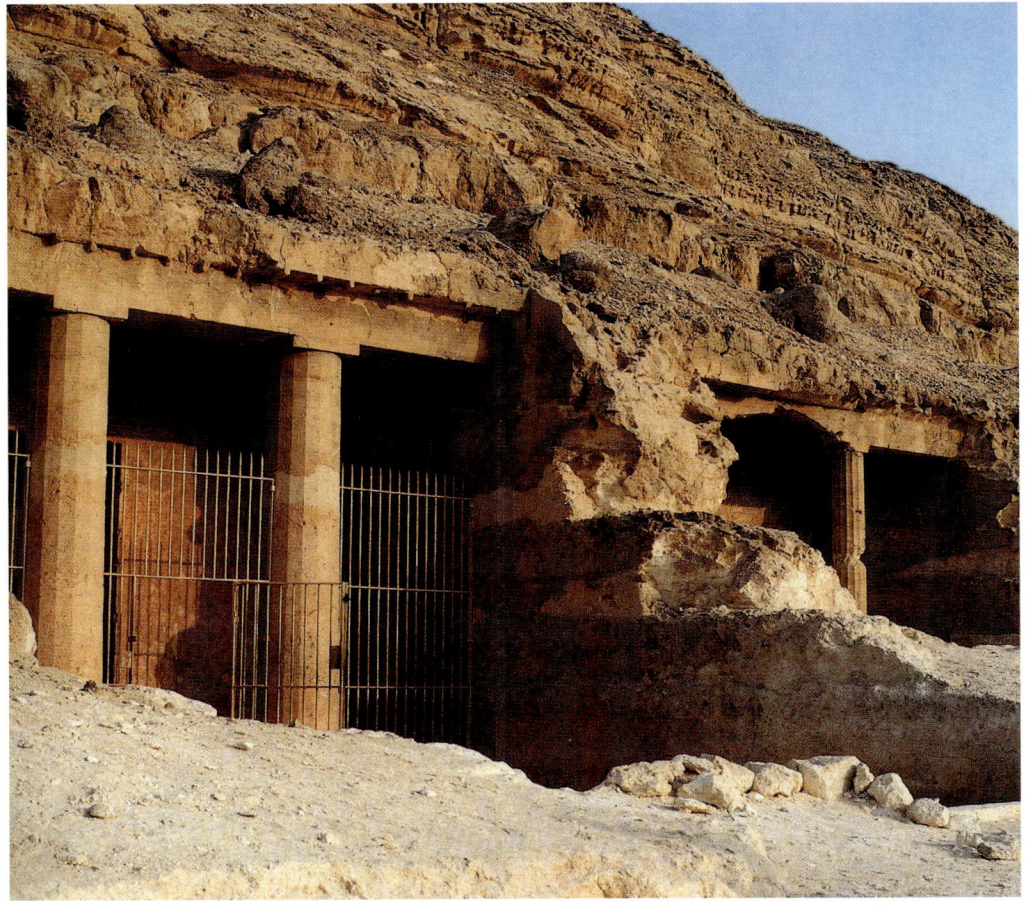

**3-19** Rock-cut tombs BH 3–5, Beni Hasan, Egypt, Dynasty XII, ca. 1950–1900 BCE.

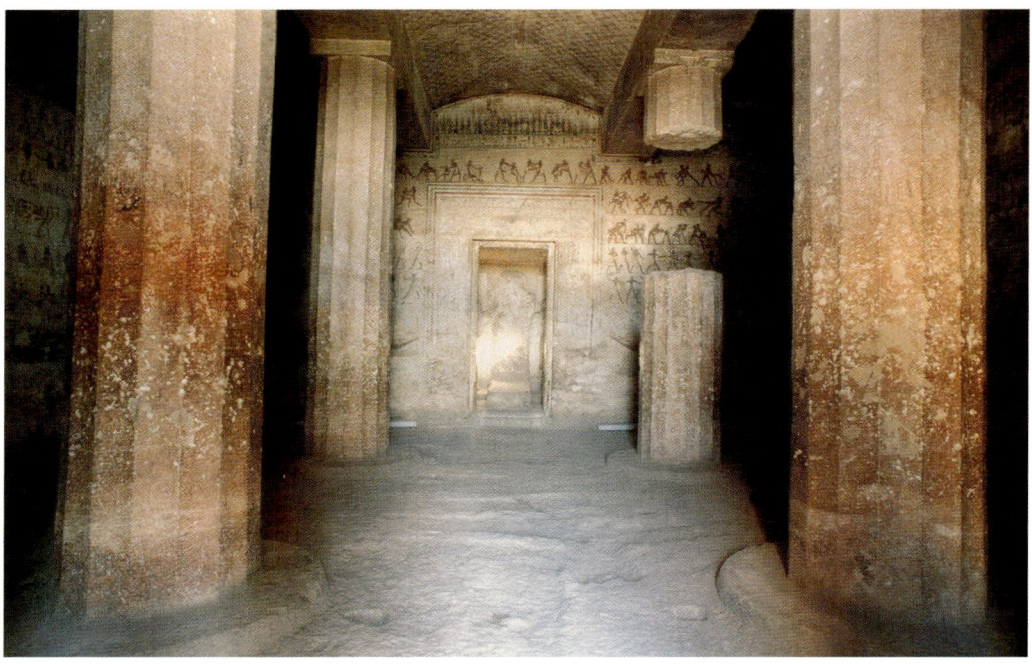

**3-20** Interior hall of the rock-cut tomb of Amenemhet (BH 2), Beni Hasan, Egypt, Dynasty XII, ca. 1950–1900 BCE.

The rock-cut tombs of the Middle Kingdom largely replaced the Old Kingdom mastabas. Hollowed out of the cliffs, these tombs often were fronted by a shallow columnar vestibule (porch), which led into a columned hall and then into a burial chamber. In the hall of the 12th Dynasty tomb of Amenemhet (FIG. **3-20**), the columns serve no supporting function because, like the porch columns, they are continuous parts of the rock fabric. (Note the broken column in the rear suspended from the ceiling like a stalactite.) The column shafts are *fluted* with vertical channels in a manner similar to later Greek columns. Archaeologists believe fluting derived from the dressing of softwood trunks with the rounded cutting edge of the adze. Fluted stone columns are yet another case of Egyptian builders' translating perishable natural forms into permanent architecture. Artists decorated the tomb walls with paintings and painted reliefs, as in former times, and placed statues of the deceased in niches. The statue in Amenemhet's tomb depicts him, his wife, and his mother.

# THE NEW KINGDOM

**EGYPT AT ITS HEIGHT** Like its predecessor, the Middle Kingdom disintegrated, and power passed to the Hyksos, or shepherd kings, who descended on Egypt from the Syrian and Mesopotamian uplands. They brought with them a new and influential culture and that practical animal, the horse. Their innovations in weaponry and war techniques ironically contributed to their own overthrow by native Egyptian kings of the 17th Dynasty around 1600–1550 BCE. Ahmose I (r. 1550–1525 BCE), final conqueror of the Hyksos and first king of the 18th Dynasty, ushered in the New Kingdom, the most brilliant period in Egypt's long history.

At this time, Egypt extended its borders by conquest from the Euphrates River in the east deep into Nubia (the Sudan) to the south (MAP 3-1). A new capital—Thebes, in Upper Egypt, south of the Predynastic royal cemetery at Abydos—became a great and luxurious metropolis with magnificent palaces, tombs, and temples along both banks of the Nile. Visiting embassies and new

and profitable trade with Asia and the Aegean Islands widened foreign contact (see "Minoan Paintings Discovered in Egypt," Chapter 4, page 91).

## Architecture

**HATSHEPSUT'S TEMPLE** If the most impressive monuments of the Old Kingdom are its pyramids, those of the New Kingdom are its grandiose temples, often built to honor pharaohs and queens, as well as gods. Great pharaonic mortuary temples arose along the Nile near Thebes. These shrines provided the rulers with a place for worshiping their patron gods during their lifetimes and then served as temples in their own honor after their death. The temples were elaborate and luxuriously decorated, befitting both the pharaohs and the gods.

The most majestic of these royal mortuary temples, at Deir el-Bahri (FIG. **3-21**), was constructed for the female pharaoh Hatshepsut, one of the most remarkable women of the ancient world (see "Hatshepsut: The Woman Who Would Be King," page 71). Some have attributed the temple to SENMUT, Hatshepsut's chancellor and possible lover, who is described in two inscriptions as royal architect. His association with this project is uncertain, however. Modeled in part on the neighboring Middle Kingdom temple of Mentuhotep II (at the far left in FIG. 3-21), Hatshepsut's temple rises from the valley floor in three colonnaded terraces connected by ramps. It is remarkable how visually well suited the structure is to its natural setting. The long horizontals and verticals of the *colonnades* and their rhythm of light and dark repeat the pattern of the limestone cliffs above. The colonnade *pillars,* which are either simply rectangular or *chamfered* (beveled, or flattened at the edges) into 16 sides, are well proportioned and rhythmically spaced.

In Hatshepsut's day, the terraces were not the barren places they are now but gardens with frankincense trees and rare plants the pharaoh brought from the faraway "land of Punt" on the Red Sea. Her expedition to Punt figures prominently in the poorly preserved but once brightly painted low reliefs that cover many walls of the complex. In addition to representing great deeds, the

### Hatshepsut: The Woman Who Would Be King

In 1479 BCE, Thutmose II, the fourth pharaoh of the 18th Dynasty (r. 1492–1479 BCE), died. His principal wife (and half sister), Queen Hatshepsut (r. 1473–1458 BCE), had not given birth to any sons who survived, so the title of king went to the 12-year-old Thutmose III, son of Thutmose II by a minor wife. (Egyptian pharaohs had extensive harems.) Hatshepsut was named regent for the boy king. Within a few years, however, the queen proclaimed herself pharaoh and insisted that her father Thutmose I had actually chosen her as his successor during his lifetime. Underscoring her claim, one of the reliefs decorating Hatshepsut's enormous funerary complex (FIG. 3-21) depicts Thutmose I crowning his daughter as king in the presence of the Egyptian gods.

Hatshepsut is the first great female monarch whose name has been recorded. (In the 12th Dynasty, Sobekneferu was crowned king of Egypt, but she reigned as pharaoh for only a few years.)

Hatshepsut boasted of having made the "Two Lands to labor with bowed back" for her, and for two decades she ruled what was then the most powerful and prosperous empire in the world.

Hatshepsut commissioned numerous building projects, and sculptors produced portraits of the female pharaoh in great numbers for display in those complexes. Many of Hatshepsut's portraits were destroyed after her death at the order of the resentful Thutmose III (r. 1458–1425 BCE), whose elevation to sole kingship was delayed for two decades when his stepmother declared herself pharaoh. In her surviving portraits, Hatshepsut uniformly wears the costume of the male pharaohs, with royal headdress and kilt, and in some cases even a false ceremonial beard (FIG. 3-22). Many inscriptions refer to Hatshepsut as "*His* Majesty"! In other statues, however, Hatshepsut has delicate features, a slender frame, and breasts, leaving no doubt that artists also represented her as a woman.

---

reliefs also show Hatshepsut's coronation and divine birth. She was said to be the daughter of the god Amen-Re, whose sanctuary was situated on the temple's uppermost level. The painted reliefs of Hatshepsut's mortuary temple constituted the first great tribute to a woman's achievements in the history of art. Their deface-

ment after her death by the jealous and resentful Thutmose III is therefore especially unfortunate.

**A WOMAN PORTRAYED AS A MAN** As many as 200 statues in the round depicting Hatshepsut in various guises complemented

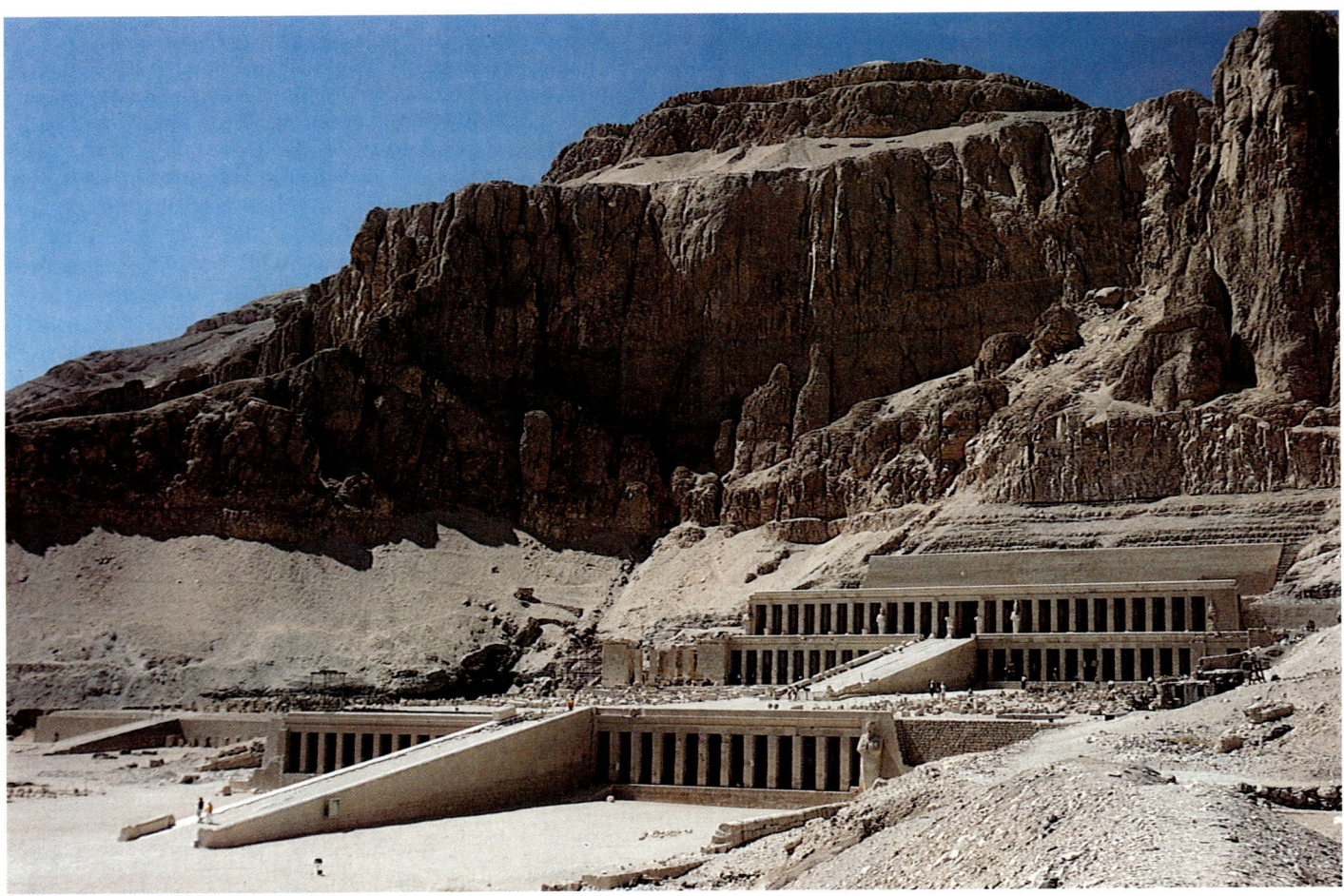

**3-21** Mortuary temple of Hatshepsut (with the Middle Kingdom mortuary temple of Mentuhotep II at left), Deir el-Bahri, Egypt, Dynasty XVIII, ca. 1473–1458 BCE.

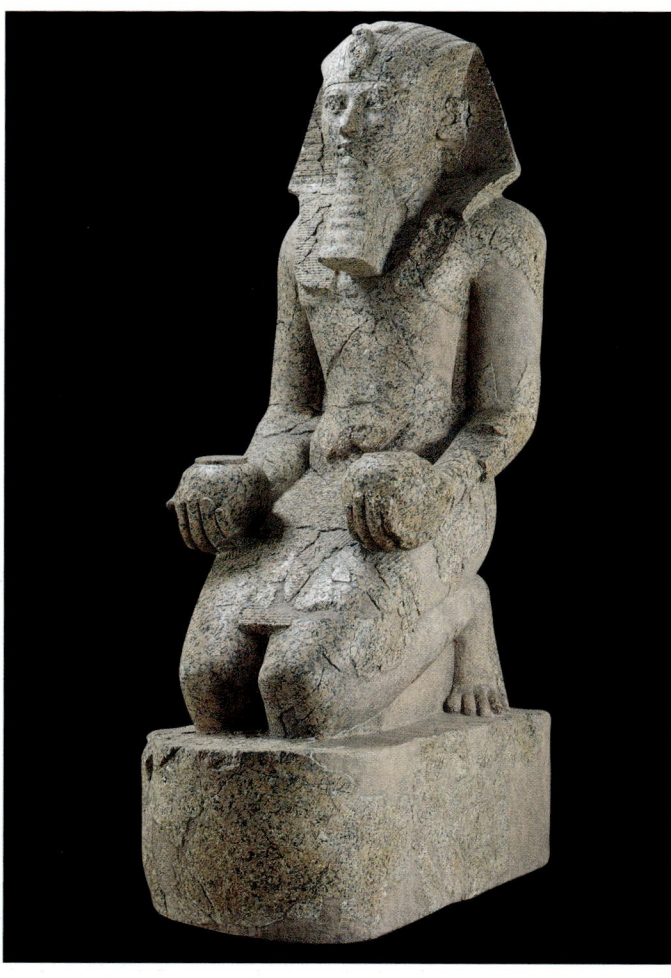

the extensive relief program. Thutmose III removed or shattered them when he became pharaoh. On the lowest terrace, to either side of the processional way, Hatshepsut was repeatedly portrayed as a sphinx. On the uppermost level, the female pharaoh was represented standing, seated, and in the form of a mummy. At least eight colossal kneeling statues in red granite lined the way to the entrance of the Amen-Re sanctuary.

Our example (FIG. 3-22) suffered the same fate as most of Hatshepsut's portraits. After it was smashed, the pieces were thrown in a dump. The statue has been skillfully reassembled from the recovered fragments. Hatshepsut holds a globular offering jar in each hand as she takes part in a ritual in honor of the sun god. (A king kneeled only before a god, never a mortal.) She wears the royal male nemes headdress (compare FIGS. 3-11 to 3-13) and the pharaoh's ceremonial beard. The agents of Thutmose III hacked off the uraeus cobra that once adorned the front of the headdress. The figure is also anatomically male, although other surviving portraits of Hatshepsut represent her with a woman's breasts. The male imagery is, however, consistent with the queen's formal assumption of the title of king and with the many inscriptions that address her as a man.

**COLOSSI IN A CLIFF** Hatshepsut's mortuary temple never fails to impress visitors by its sheer size, and this is no less true of the immense rock-cut temple of Ramses II (r. 1290–1224 BCE) at Abu Simbel (FIG. 3-23). In 1968 the temple was moved nearly 700 feet—an impressive feat in its own right—to its present location to save it from submersion in the Aswan High Dam reservoir. Ramses was Egypt's last great warrior pharaoh, and he ruled for two-thirds of a century, an extraordinary accomplishment in an era when life expectancy was far less than it is today. The pharaoh, proud of his many campaigns to restore the empire, proclaimed his greatness by placing four colossal images of himself on the temple *facade.* The portraits are almost eight times as large as Hatshepsut's kneeling statues and almost a dozen times

**3-22** Hatshepsut with offering jars, from the upper court of her mortuary temple, Deir el-Bahri, Egypt, Dynasty XVIII, ca. 1473–1458 BCE. Red granite, approx. 8′ 6″ high. Metropolitan Museum of Art, New York.

**3-23** Temple of Ramses II, Abu Simbel, Egypt, Dynasty XIX, ca. 1290–1224 BCE. Sandstone, colossi approx. 65′ high.

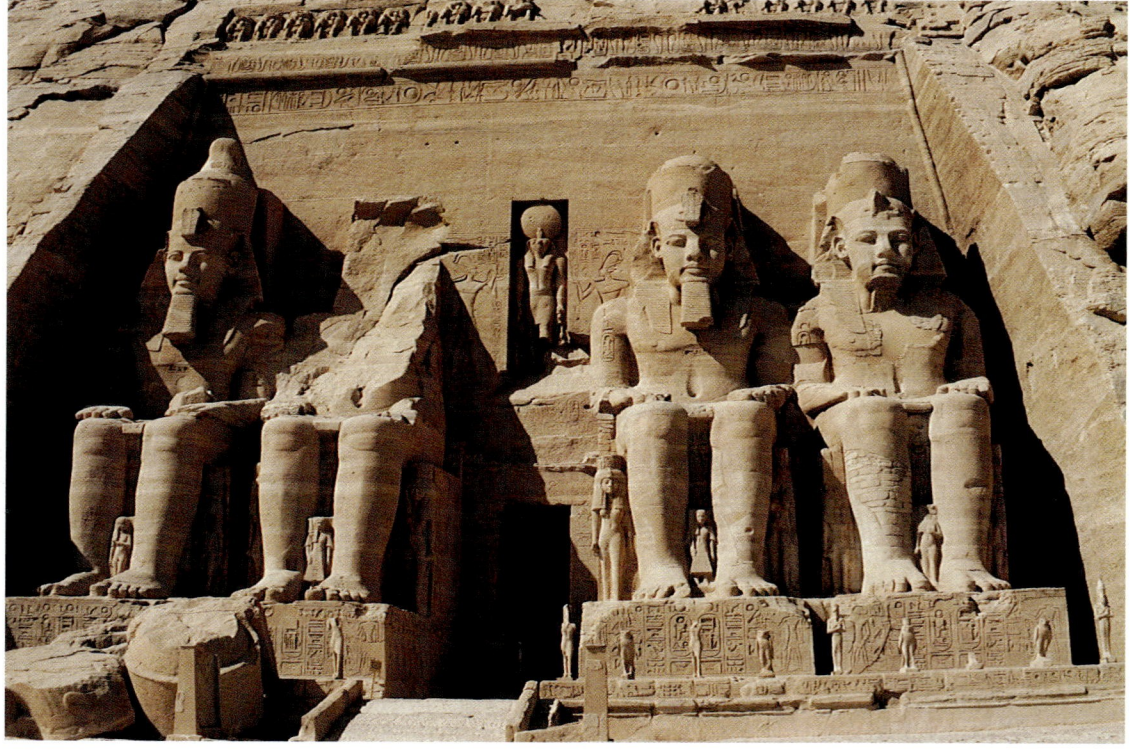

### The Tomb of the Sons of Ramses II

In 1825, James Burton, a British explorer, uncovered the entrance and a few chambers of a royal tomb in the Valley of the Kings at Thebes. (The narrow valley across the Nile from Karnak and Luxor was so named because the tombs of numerous New Kingdom pharaohs are located there.) In an age when archaeological excavation was little more than treasure hunting, archaeologists never fully investigated the tomb (KV5) because no precious objects were found when it was opened. Almost a century later, in 1902, Howard Carter, who later discovered Tutankhamen's tomb, made a probe into KV5, but he, too, concluded that the site was unpromising, and abandoned work there. Later archaeologists ignored the tomb, and its location was forgotten until 1987, when an American team led by Kent R. Weeks found KV5 anew. It wasn't until 1995, however, that the tomb's immense size and unique character were revealed.

KV5 is the largest tomb ever found in the Valley of the Kings and may have been the largest in Egypt. No other Theban tomb has more than 30 chambers—a half dozen is typical—but this tomb has scores of rooms, and it is still only partially excavated. The chambers open onto several long corridors leading out of a central hall, 50 meters square, filled with 16 stone pillars. Inscriptions inside the tomb leave no doubt that this was the burial place of the sons of the great 19th Dynasty pharaoh Ramses II. Paintings and reliefs depicting Ramses and his royal sons with the major deities of Egypt—Osiris, Hathor, Horus, Thoth, and Isis—decorate the tomb walls.

KV5, unfortunately, was robbed within a half century of its construction. The culprit was identified—a workman named Kenena, son of Ruta. But the excavators found a statue of Osiris, god of the afterlife, in a niche at the end of a long corridor. The thief could not remove it because it was fixed to the wall. Weeks's team also discovered a number of small mummy-shaped statuettes called *ushabtis*, which served as servants of the royal sons for eternity. What they have not found are the royal burials themselves. The excavators have postulated that dozens more rooms—the actual burial chambers—may yet be discovered on a lower level. No one knows if Kenena or other thieves removed the presumed treasures buried with the pharaoh's sons or whether they remain to be uncovered. Work by Weeks and his colleagues is likely to continue for decades.

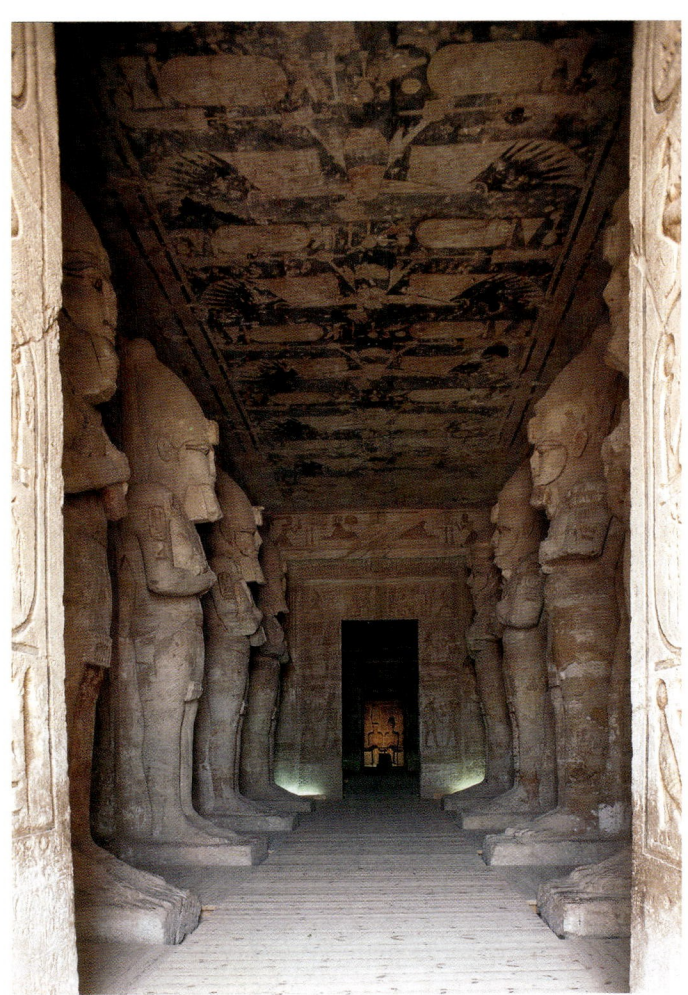

**3-24** Interior of the temple of Ramses II, Abu Simbel, Egypt, Dynasty XIX, ca. 1290–1224 BCE. Sandstone, pillar statues approx. 32' high.

the height of an ancient Egyptian, even though the pharaoh is seated. Spectacular as they are, the rock-cut statues nonetheless lack the refinement of earlier periods, because much was sacrificed to overwhelming size. This is a characteristic of colossal statuary of every period and every place.

**PILLAR STATUES** The grand scale was carried out in the interior (FIG. **3-24**) also, where giant (32-foot-tall) figures of the king in the guise of Osiris, carved as one with the pillars, face each other across the narrow corridor. The pillars, carved from the cliff like the pharaoh's facade portraits, have no load-bearing function. In this respect, they resemble the columns in the tombs at Beni Hasan (FIG. 3-20). The statue-column, in its male (*atlantid*) or female (*caryatid*) variants, reappears throughout the history of art. Often, as here, the human figure is attached to a column or pier (for example, FIGS. 18-6 and 18-16). At other times the figure replaces the architectural member and forms the sole source of support (see FIG. 5-52).

**THE FAMILY OF RAMSES** Ramses, like other pharaohs, had many wives, and he fathered scores of sons. The most important members of his family were honored with immense monuments of their own. At Thebes, for example, north of his own mortuary temple, Ramses ordered the construction of a grand temple for his principal wife, Nefertari. Huge rock-cut statues—four standing images of the king and two of the queen—dominated the temple's facade. For his sons, Ramses constructed a huge underground tomb. The rediscovery of that subterranean complex was one of the major archaeological finds of the 20th century (see "The Tomb of the Sons of Ramses II," above).

**IMMENSE PYLON TEMPLES** Distinct from the pharaonic mortuary temples are the edifices built to honor one or more of the gods. Successive kings often added to them until they reached

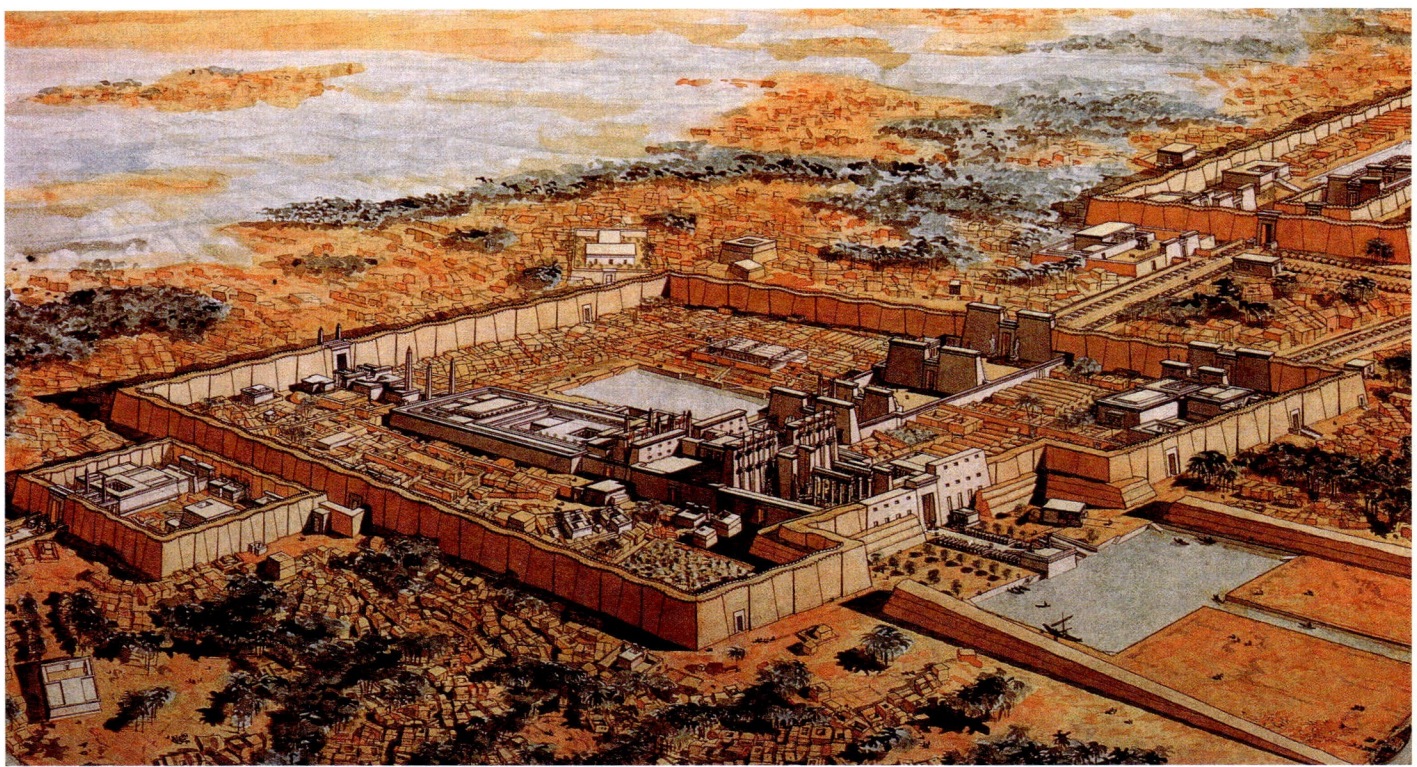

3-25 Restored view of the temple of Amen-Re, Karnak, Egypt, begun 15th century BCE (Jean-Claude Golvin).

gigantic size. The temple of Amen-Re at Karnak (FIG. **3-25**), for example, was largely the work of the 18th-Dynasty pharaohs, including Thutmose I and III and Hatshepsut, but Ramses II (19th Dynasty) and others also contributed sections. Chapels were added to the complex as late as the 26th Dynasty. The artificial sacred lake within the precinct of the Karnak temple is a reference to the primeval waters before creation. The temple rises from the earth as the original sacred mound rose from the waters at the beginning of time.

The New Kingdom *pylon temples* all had similar plans. (The name derives from the simple and massive gateways, or pylons, with sloping walls, as in FIG. 3-28.) A typical pylon temple is bilaterally symmetrical along a single axis that runs from an approaching avenue through a colonnaded court and hall into a dimly lit sanctuary. This Egyptian temple plan evolved from ritualistic requirements. Only the pharaohs and the priests could enter the sanctuary. A chosen few were admitted to the great columnar hall. The majority of the people were allowed only as far as the open court, and a high wall shut off the site from the outside world. The central feature of the New Kingdom pylon temple plan—a narrow axial passageway through the complex—is characteristic of much of Egyptian architecture. Axial corridors are also the approaches to the Old Kingdom pyramids of Gizeh (FIG. 3-10) and to the multilevel mortuary temple of Hatshepsut at Deir el-Bahri (FIG. 3-21).

**HYPOSTYLE HALLS** The dominating feature of the statuary-lined approach to a New Kingdom temple was the monumental facade of the pylon, which was routinely covered with reliefs glorifying Egypt's rulers. Inside was an open court with columns on two or more sides, followed by a hall between the court and sanctuary, its long axis placed at right angles to the corridor of the entire building complex. This *hypostyle hall* (one where columns support the roof) was crowded with massive columns and roofed

by stone slabs carried on lintels. The lintels rested on cubical blocks that in turn rested on giant capitals. In the hypostyle hall at Karnak (FIGS. **3-26** and **3-27**), the central columns are 66 feet high, and the capitals are 22 feet in diameter at the top, large enough to hold a hundred people. The Egyptians, who used no cement, depended on precise cutting of the joints and the weight of the huge stone blocks to hold the columns in place.

In the Amen-Re temple at Karnak and in many other Egyptian hypostyle halls, the builders made the central rows of columns higher than those at the sides. Raising the roof's central section created a *clerestory*. Openings in the clerestory permitted sunlight to filter into the interior, although the stone grilles (FIG. 3-26) would have blocked much of the light. This method of construction appeared in primitive form as early as the Old Kingdom in the valley temple of the Pyramid of Khafre. The clerestory is evidently an Egyptian innovation, and its significance hardly can be overstated. Before the invention of the electric light bulb, illuminating a building's interior was always a challenge for architects. The clerestory played a key role, for example, in Roman basilica and medieval church design and has remained an important architectural feature up to the present.

**SUNKEN RELIEFS ON COLUMNS** In the hypostyle hall at Karnak, the columns are indispensable structurally, unlike the rock-cut columns of the tombs at Beni Hasan (FIGS. 3-19 and 3-20) and Abu Simbel (FIG. 3-24). But their function as vertical supports is almost hidden by horizontal bands of painted *sunken relief* sculpture. To create such reliefs, the New Kingdom sculptors chiseled deep outlines below the stone's surface, rather than cut back the stone around the figures to make the figures project from the surface. Sunken reliefs preserve the contours of the columns they adorn. Otherwise, the Karnak columns would have had an irregular, wavy profile. But despite this effort to maintain sharp architectural lines, the overwhelming of the surfaces with reliefs indicates that the architects'

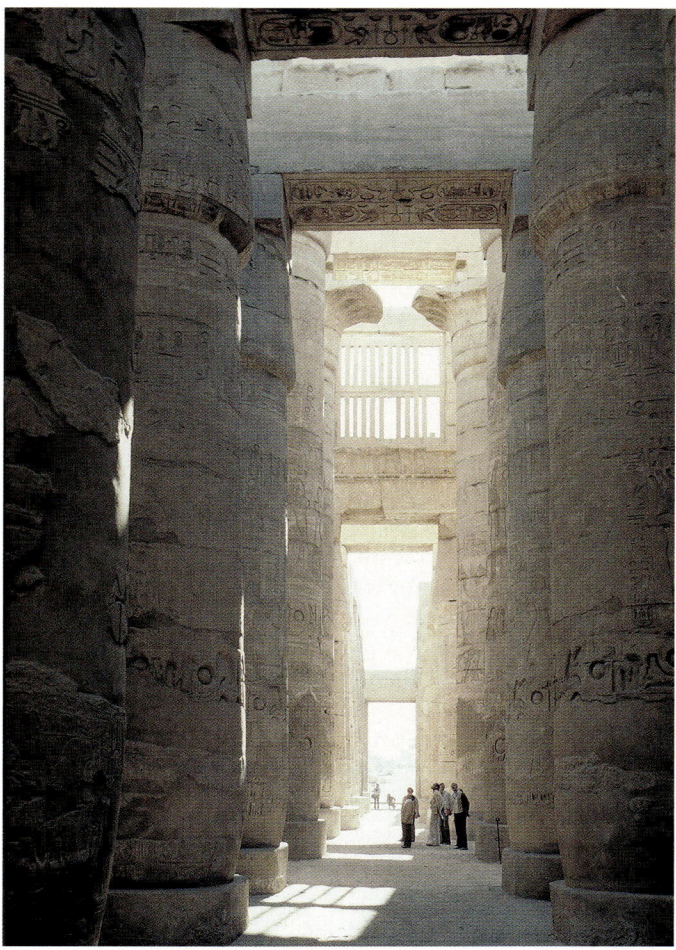

3-26 Hypostyle hall, temple of Amen-Re, Karnak, Egypt, Dynasty XIX, ca. 1290–1224 BCE.

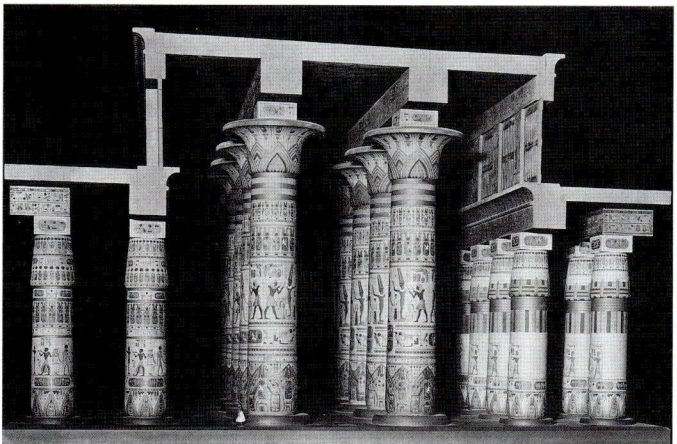

3-27 Model of hypostyle hall, temple of Amen-Re, Karnak, Egypt, Dynasty XIX, ca. 1290–1224 BCE. Metropolitan Museum of Art, New York.

intention was not to emphasize the functional role of the columns. Instead, they used columns as image- and message-bearing surfaces.

Egyptian columns seem to have originated from an early building technique that used firmly bound sheaves of reeds and swamp plants as roof supports in adobe structures. Egyptian masons first translated such early and relatively impermanent building methods into stone in Djoser's funerary precinct at Saqqara (FIGS. 3-6 and 3-7). Evidence of their swamp-plant origin is still seen in the columns at Karnak, which have bud-cluster or bell-shaped capitals resembling lotus or papyrus (the plants of Upper and Lower Egypt).

ARCHITECTURE AFTER ALEXANDER Once formulated, Egyptian traditions tended to have very long lives, in architecture as in the other arts. The pylon temple of Horus at Edfu (FIG. 3-28), built during the third, second, and first centuries BCE, after

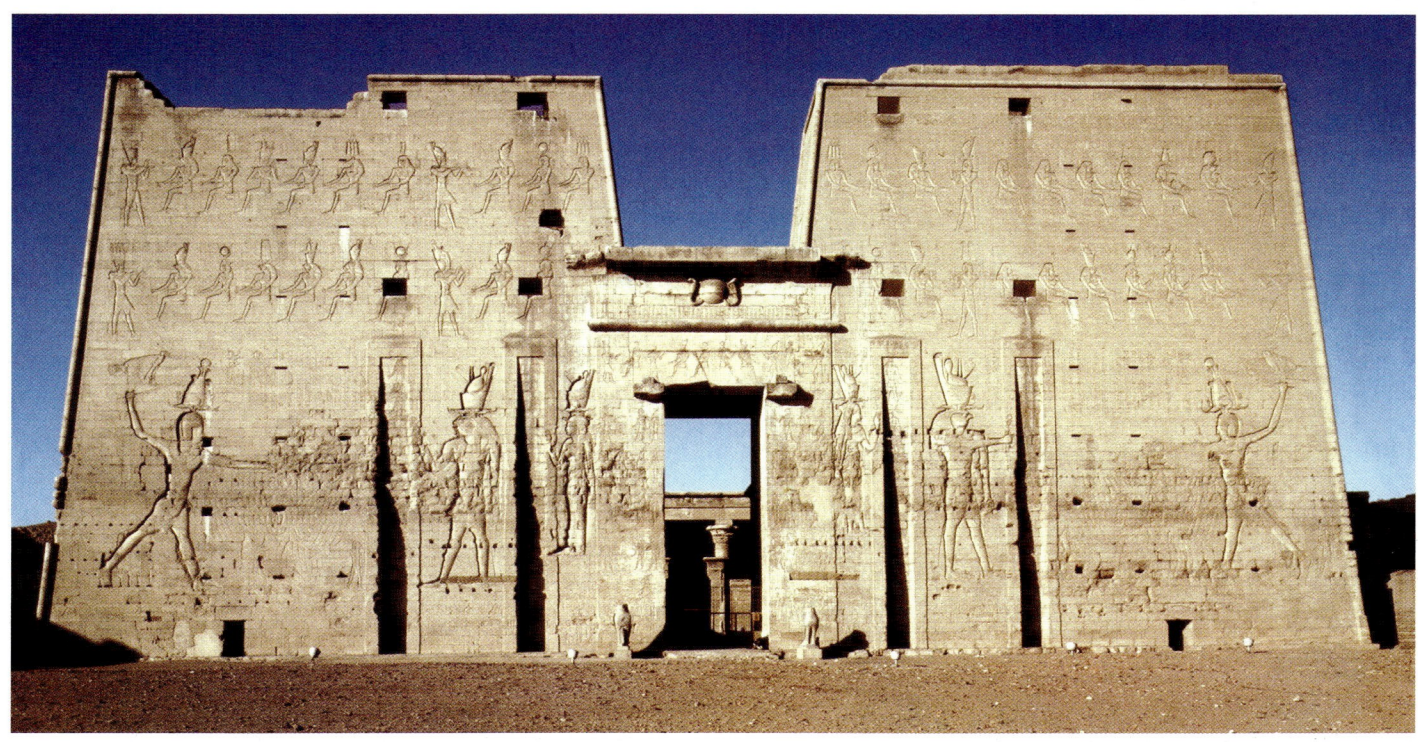

3-28 Temple of Horus, Edfu, Egypt, ca. 237–47 BCE.

Alexander the Great's conquest of Egypt, still follows the basic scheme architects worked out more than a thousand years before. The great entrance pylon at Edfu is especially impressive. The broad surface of its massive facade, with its sloping walls, is broken only by the doorway with its overshadowing cornice, moldings at the top and sides, deep channels to hold great flagstaffs, and sunken reliefs. The reliefs depict Horus and Hathor witnessing an oversized King Ptolemy XIII (r. 51–47 BCE) smiting undersized enemies. It is a striking monument to the persistence of Egyptian architectural and sculptural types, despite many variations over the millennia.

## Sculpture and Painting

SENMUT AND NEFRUA  Extremely popular during the Middle and New Kingdoms were *block statues*. In these works the idea that the ka could find an eternal home in the cubic stone image of the deceased was expressed in an even more radical simplification of form than was common in Old Kingdom statuary. An example of this genre is the block statue of Senmut and Princess Nefrua

(FIG. 3-29). Hatshepsut's chancellor holds the pharaoh's daughter by Thutmose II in his "lap" and envelops the girl in his cloak. The streamlined design concentrates attention on the heads and treats the two bodies as a single cubic block, given over to inscriptions. The polished stone shape has its own simple beauty, with the surfaces turning subtly about smoothly rounded corners. The work—one of many surviving statues depicting Senmut with Hatshepsut's daughter—is also a reflection of the power of Egypt's female ruler. The frequent depiction of Senmut with Nefrua was meant to enhance Senmut's stature through his association with the princess (he was her tutor) and, by implication, with Hatshepsut herself. Toward the end of her reign, however, Hatshepsut believed Senmut had become too powerful, and she had him removed.

PAINTING AT THEBES  The art of adorning tomb walls with paintings, attested already in the Predynastic period (FIG. 3-1), flourished in the New Kingdom. In the 18th-Dynasty Theban tomb of Nebamun, the deceased nobleman, whose official titles were "scribe and counter of grain," is shown standing in his boat, flushing birds from a papyrus swamp (FIG. 3-30). The hieroglyphic text beneath his left arm says that Nebamun is enjoying recreation in his eternal afterlife. (Here, as elsewhere in Egyptian art, the accompanying text amplifies the message of the picture—and vice versa.) In contrast to the static pose of Ti watching others hunt hippopotami (FIG. 3-16), Nebamun is shown striding forward and vigorously swinging his throwing stick. In his right hand, he holds three birds he has caught. A wild cat, impossibly perched on a papyrus stem just in front of and below him, has caught two more in its claws and is holding the wings of a third in its teeth. Nebamun's wife and daughter accompany him on this hunt. They hold the lotuses they have gathered. The artist scaled down their figures in proportion to their rank, as did Old Kingdom artists. And, as in Ti's tomb, the Thebes animals show a naturalism based on careful observation.

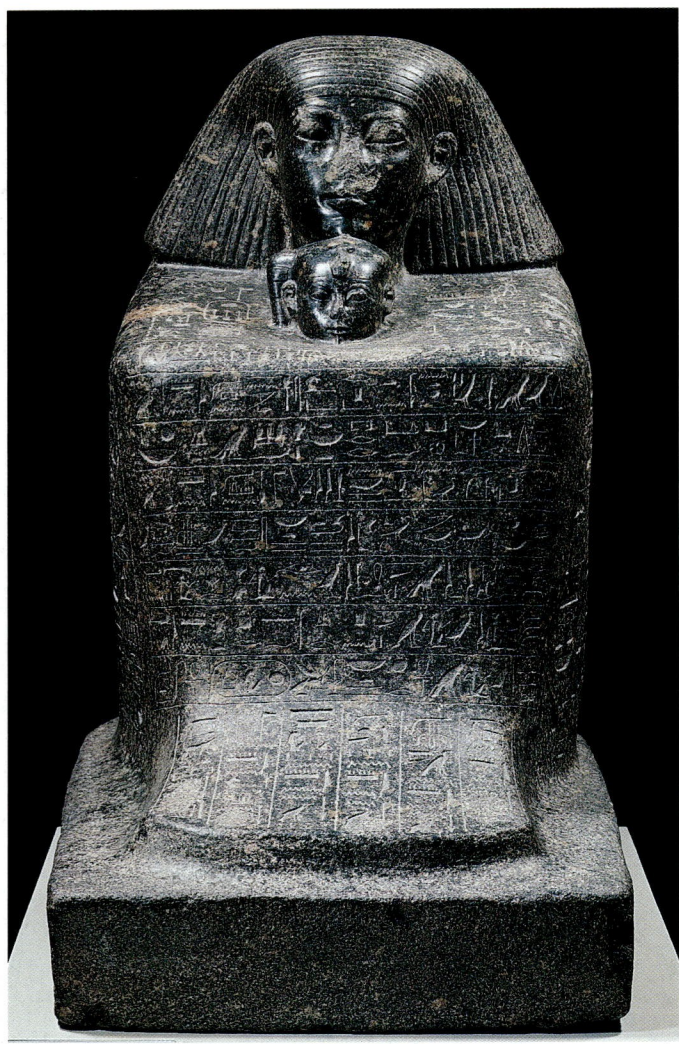

3-29  Senmut with Princess Nefrua, from Thebes, Egypt, Dynasty XVIII, ca. 1470–1460 BCE. Granite, approx. 3′ $\frac{1}{2}$″ high. Ägyptisches Museum, Berlin.

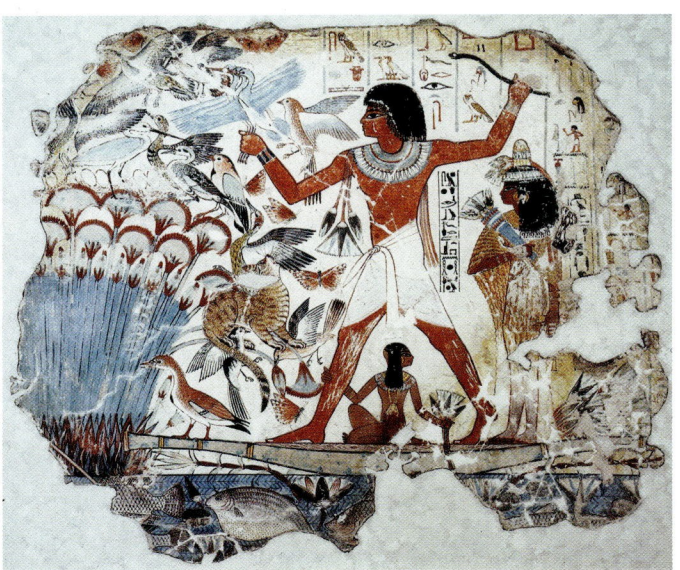

3-30  Fowling scene, from the tomb of Nebamun, Thebes, Egypt, Dynasty XVIII, ca. 1400–1350 BCE. Fresco on dry plaster, approx. 2′ 8″ high. British Museum, London.

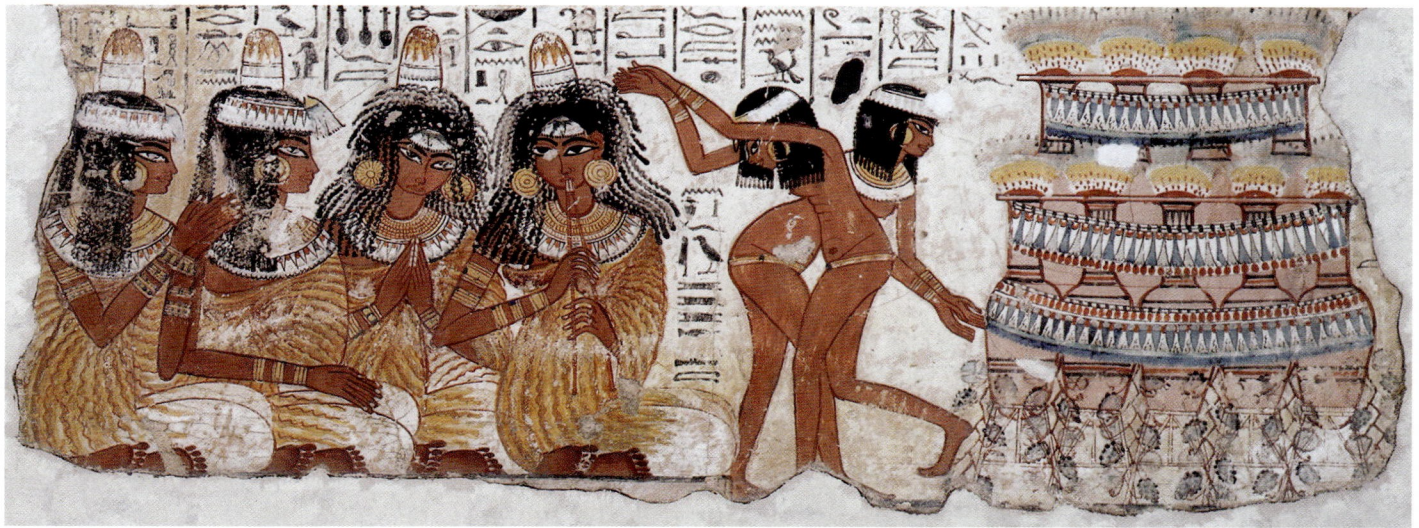

**3-31** Musicians and dancers, detail of a fresco from the tomb of Nebamun, Thebes, Egypt, Dynasty XVIII, ca. 1400–1350 BCE. Fragment approx. 1′ × 2′ 3″. British Museum, London.

The painting technique, also employed in earlier Egyptian tombs, is *fresco secco* (dry fresco), whereby artists let the plaster dry before painting on it. This procedure, in contrast to true fresco painting on wet plaster (see "Fresco Painting," Chapter 19, page 530), permitted slower and more meticulous work than painting on wet plaster, which had to be completed before the plaster dried. Fresco secco, however, is not as durable as true fresco painting, because the colors do not fuse with the wall surface.

**A FEAST FOR THE DEAD** Another fresco fragment from Nebamun's tomb shows four noblewomen watching and apparently participating in a musicale and dance where two nimble and almost nude dancing girls perform at a banquet (FIG. **3-31**). When Nebamun was buried, his family must have eaten the customary ceremonial meal at his tomb. They would have returned one day each year to partake in a commemorative banquet for the living to commune with the dead. This fresco represents just such a funerary feast, with an ample supply of wine jars at the right. It also shows that New Kingdom artists did not always adhere to the old standards for figural representation. The overlapping of the dancers' figures, their facing in opposite directions, and their rather complicated gyrations were carefully and accurately observed and executed, and the result is also a pleasing intertwined motif. The profile view of the dancers is consistent with their lower stature in the Egyptian hierarchy. The composite view is still reserved for Nebamun and his family. Of the four seated women, the artist represented the two at the left conventionally, but the other two face the observer in what is a rarely attempted frontal pose. They clap and beat time to the dance, while one of them plays the reeds. The artist took careful note of the soles of their feet as they sat cross-legged and suggested the movement of the women's heads by the loose arrangement of their hair strands. This informality constituted a relaxation of the Old Kingdom's stiff representational rules.

The frescoes in Nebamun's tomb testify to the luxurious life of the Egyptian nobility, filled with good food and drink, fine musicians, lithe dancers, and leisure time to hunt and fish in the marshes. But, as in the earlier tomb of Ti, the scenes should be read both literally and allegorically. Although Nebamun is shown enjoying himself in the afterlife, the artist symbolically asked viewers to recall how he got there. Hunting scenes reminded Egyptians of Horus, the son of Osiris, hunting down his father's murderer, Seth, the god of disorder, thus ensuring a happy existence for Nebamun. And music and dance were sacred to Hathor, who aided the dead in their passage to the other world. The sensual women at the banquet are a reference to fertility, rebirth, and regeneration—the conquest of death that made the afterlife possible.

## Akhenaton and the Amarna Period

**RELIGIOUS UPHEAVAL** Not long after Nebamun was laid to rest in his tomb at Thebes, a revolution occurred in Egyptian society and religion. In the mid-14th century BCE, the pharaoh Amenhotep IV, later known as Akhenaton (r. 1353–1335 BCE), abandoned the worship of most of the Egyptian gods in favor of Aton, whom he declared to be the universal and only god, identified with the sun disk. He blotted out the name of Amen from all inscriptions and even from his own name and that of his father, Amenhotep III. He emptied the great temples, enraged the priests, and moved his capital downriver from Thebes to a site he named Akhetaton (after his new god), where he built his own city and shrines. It is now called Tell el-Amarna. The pharaoh claimed to be both the son and sole prophet of Aton. To him alone could the god make revelation. Moreover, in stark contrast to earlier practice, Akhenaton's god was represented neither in animal nor in human form but simply as the sun disk emitting life-giving rays. The pharaohs who followed Akhenaton reestablished the cult and priesthood of Amen and restored the temples and the inscriptions. The gigantic temple complex at Karnak (FIG. 3-25), for example, was dedicated to the renewed worship of the Theban god Amen. Akhenaton's brief religious revolution was soon undone, and his new city was largely abandoned.

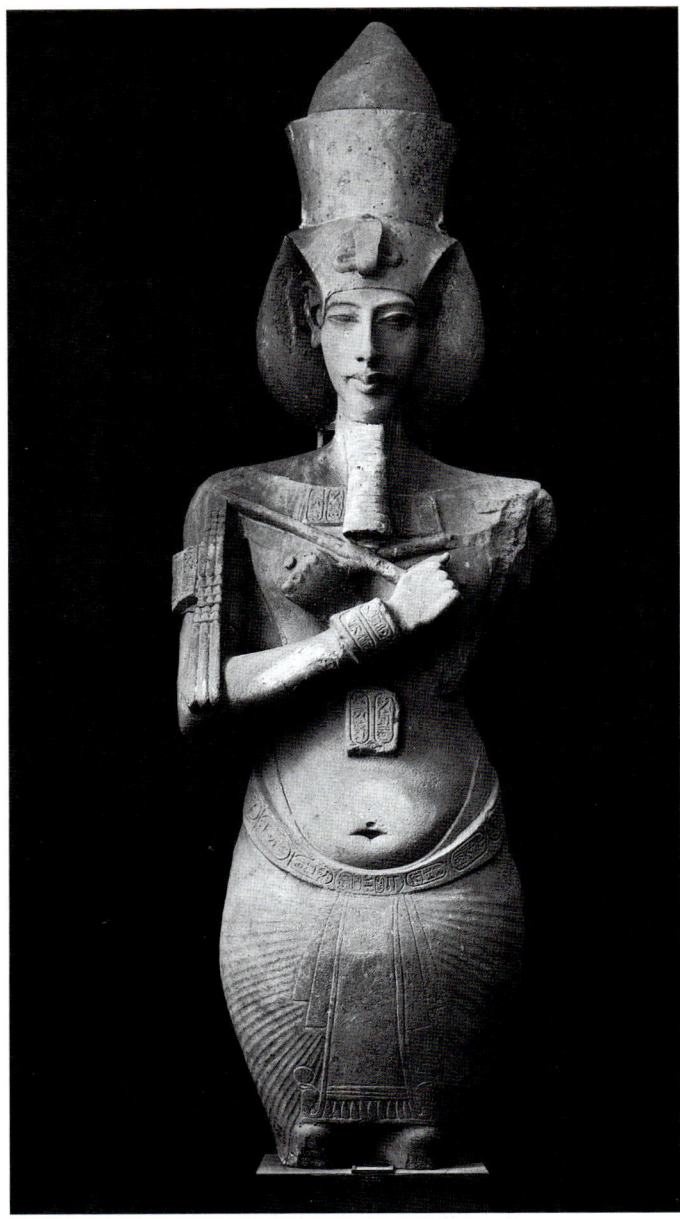

**3-32** Akhenaton, from the temple of Aton, Karnak, Egypt, Dynasty XVIII, ca. 1353–1335 BCE. Sandstone, approx. 13′ high. Egyptian Museum, Cairo.

**ARTISTIC REVOLUTION** During the brief heretical episode of Akhenaton, however, profound changes occurred in Egyptian art. A colossal statue of Akhenaton (FIG. **3-32**) from Karnak, toppled and buried after his death, retains the standard frontal pose of canonical pharaonic portraits. But the effeminate body, with its curving contours, and the long face with full lips and heavy-lidded eyes are a far cry indeed from the heroically proportioned figures of the pharaoh's predecessors (compare FIG. 3-13). Akhenaton's body is curiously misshapen, with weak arms, a narrow waist, protruding belly, wide hips, and fatty thighs. Modern doctors have tried to explain his physique by attributing a variety of illnesses to the pharaoh. They cannot agree on a diagnosis, and their premise—that the statue is an accurate depiction of a physical deformity—is probably faulty. Some art historians think that Akhenaton's portrait is a deliberate artistic reaction against the established style, paralleling the suppression of traditional religion. They argue that Akhenaton's artists tried to formulate a new

androgynous image of the pharaoh as the manifestation of Aton, the sexless sun disk. But no consensus exists other than that the style was revolutionary and short-lived.

**NEFERTITI AND TIYE** A painted limestone bust (FIG. **3-33**) of Akhenaton's queen, Nefertiti (her name means "The Beautiful One Is Here"), exhibits a similar expression of entranced musing and an almost mannered sensitivity and delicacy of curving contour. The piece was found in the workshop of the sculptor THUT-MOSE and is a deliberately unfinished model very likely by the master's own hand. The left eye socket still lacks the inlaid eyeball, making the portrait a kind of before-and-after demonstration piece. With this elegant bust, Thutmose may have been alluding to a heavy flower on its slender stalk by exaggerating the weight of the crowned head and the length of the almost serpentine neck. The Tell el-Amarna sculptor seems to have adjusted the actual likeness of his subject to meet the era's standard of spiritual beauty.

A moving portrait of old age is preserved in the miniature head of Queen Tiye (FIG. **3-34**), mother of Akhenaton. Tiye was the chief wife of Amenhotep III and a commoner by birth, the daughter of a chariot officer. She may have been a sub-Saharan African. The Egyptians were a people of mixed race and frequently married other Africans, although many scholars argue

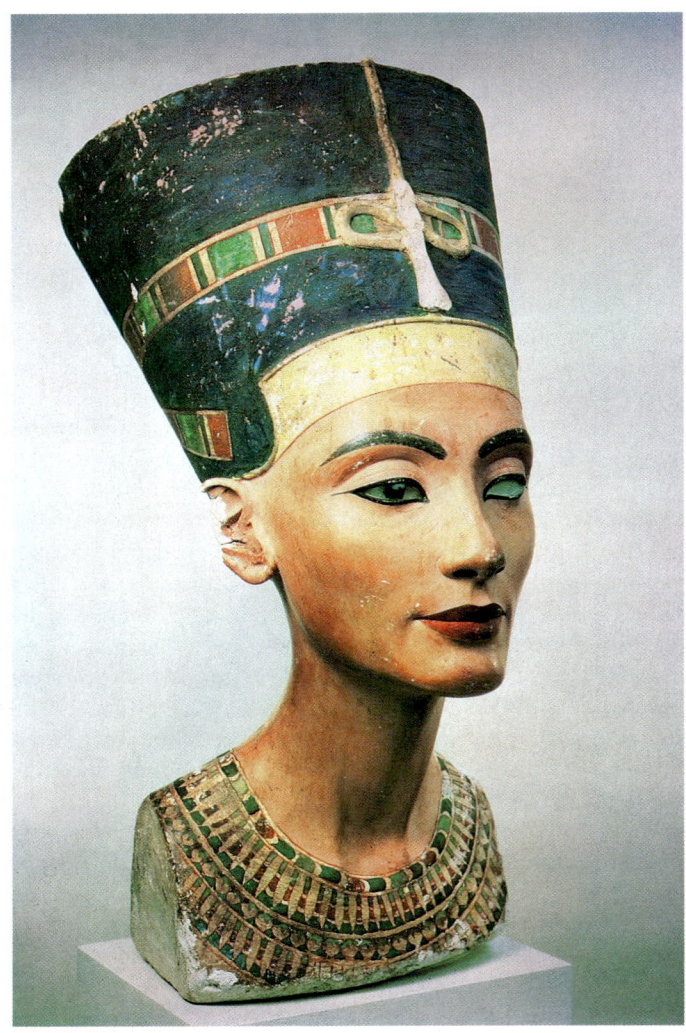

**3-33** THUTMOSE, Nefertiti, from Tell el-Amarna, Egypt, Dynasty XVIII, ca. 1353–1335 BCE. Painted limestone, approx. 1′ 8″ high. Ägyptisches Museum, Berlin.

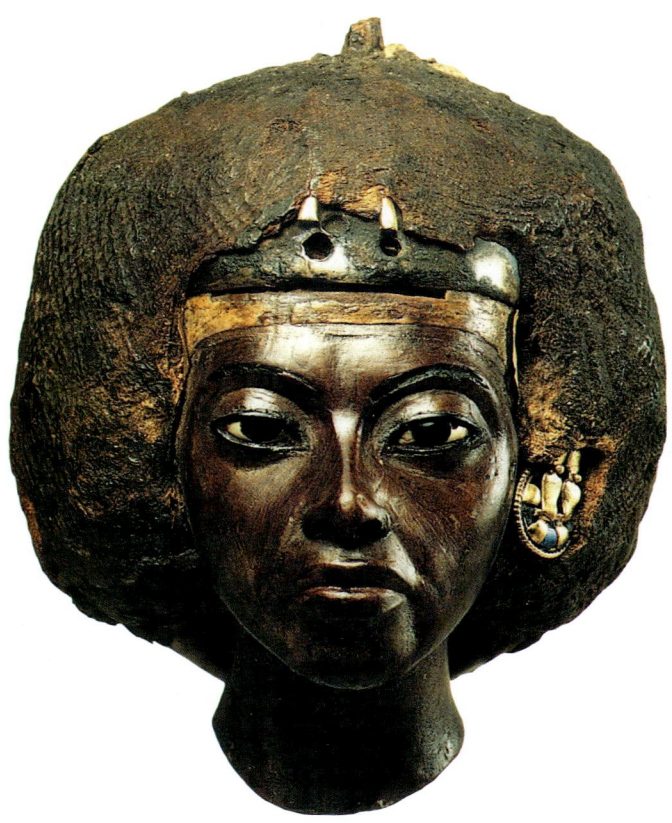

**3-34** Tiye, from Gurob, Egypt, Dynasty XVIII, ca. 1353–1335 BCE. Wood, with gold, silver, alabaster, and lapis lazuli, approx. 3¾″ high. Ägyptisches Museum, Berlin.

that the choice of dark yew wood for Tiye's portrait had no racial implication. The head was found at Gurob with other objects connected with the funerary cult of Amenhotep III. The portrait was probably remodeled during her son's reign to eliminate all reference to deities of the old religion. That is when the head acquired the present wig of plaster and linen with small blue beads. Tiye is shown as an older woman with lines and furrows, consistent with the new relaxation of artistic rules in the Amarna age. Her heavy-lidded slanting eyes are inlaid with alabaster and ebony, the lips are painted red, and the earrings (one is hidden by the later wig) are of gold and lapis lazuli. The wig covers what was originally a silver-foil headdress. A gold band still adorns the forehead. Such luxurious materials were common for royal portraits.

Both Nefertiti and Tiye figured prominently in the art and life of the Amarna age. Tiye, for example, regularly appeared in art beside her husband during his reign, and she apparently played an important role in his administration as well as her son's. Letters survive from foreign rulers advising the young Akhenaton to seek his mother's counsel in the conduct of international affairs. Nefertiti too was an influential woman. She frequently appears in the decoration of the Aton temple at Karnak, and she not only equals her husband in size but also sometimes wears pharaonic headgear.

**ROYAL INTIMACY** A sunken relief stele (FIG. **3-35**), perhaps from a private shrine, provides a rare look at this royal family. The style is familiar from the colossus of Akhenaton (FIG. 3-32) and the portrait head of Nefertiti (FIG. 3-33). Undulating curves replace rigid lines, and the figures possess the prominent bellies that characterize figures of the Amarna school. The pharaoh, his wife, and their three daughters bask in the life-giving rays of Aton, the sun disk. The mood is informal and anecdotal. Akhenaton lifts one of his daughters in order to kiss her. Another daughter sits on Nefertiti's lap and gestures toward her father while the youngest

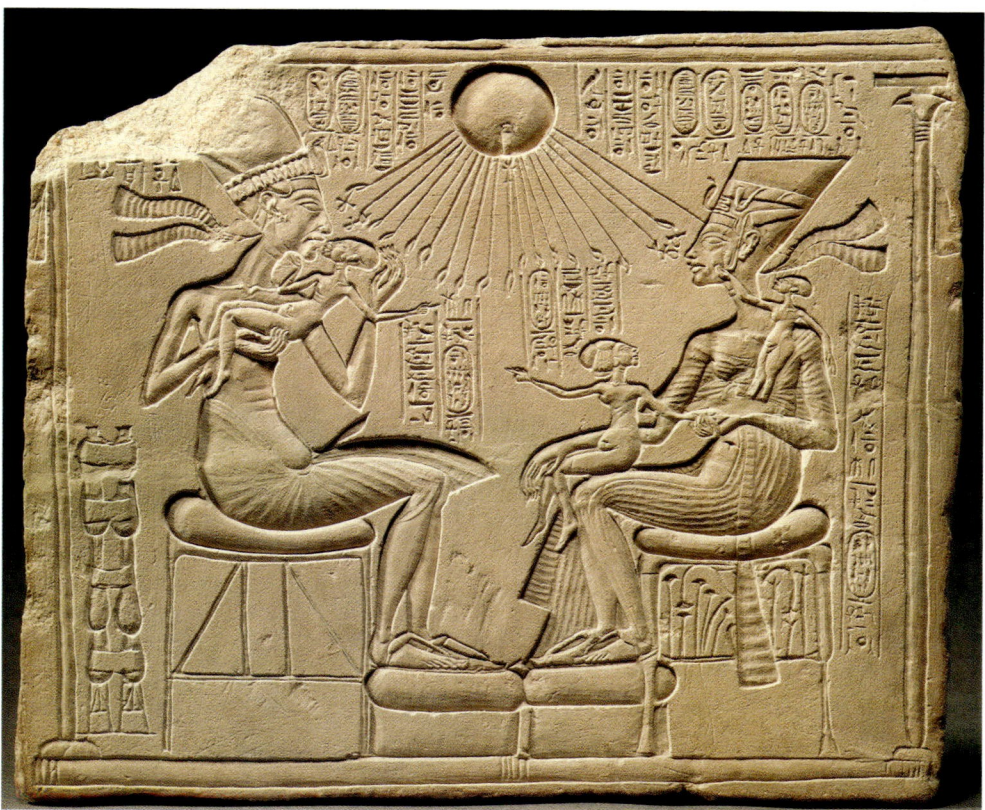

**3-35** Akhenaton, Nefertiti, and three daughters, from Tell el-Amarna, Egypt, Dynasty XVIII, ca. 1353–1335 BCE. Limestone, approx. 12¼″ high. Ägyptisches Museum, Berlin.

daughter reaches out to touch a pendant on her mother's crown. Such an intimate portrayal of the pharaoh and his family is unprecedented in Egyptian art. The political and religious revolution under Akhenaton was matched by an equally radical upheaval in art.

## The Tomb of Tutankhamen and the Post-Amarna Period

**TREASURES OF A BOY KING** The legacy of the Amarna style may be seen in the fabulously rich art and artifacts found in the largely unplundered tomb of Tutankhamen (r. 1333–1323 BCE), who was probably Akhenaton's son by a minor wife. Tutankhamen ruled for a decade and died at age 18. The treasures of his tomb, which include sculpture, furniture, jewelry, and accessories of all sorts, were uncovered in 1922. The adventure of their discovery gained world renown not only for their excavator, Howard Carter, but also for the boy king. Tutankhamen was a very minor figure in Egyptian history. The public remembers him today solely because of the chance survival of his tomb's furnishings.

The principal monument in the collection is the enshrined body of the pharaoh himself. The royal mummy reposed in the innermost of three coffins, nested one within the other. The innermost coffin (FIG. 3-36) was the most luxurious of the three.

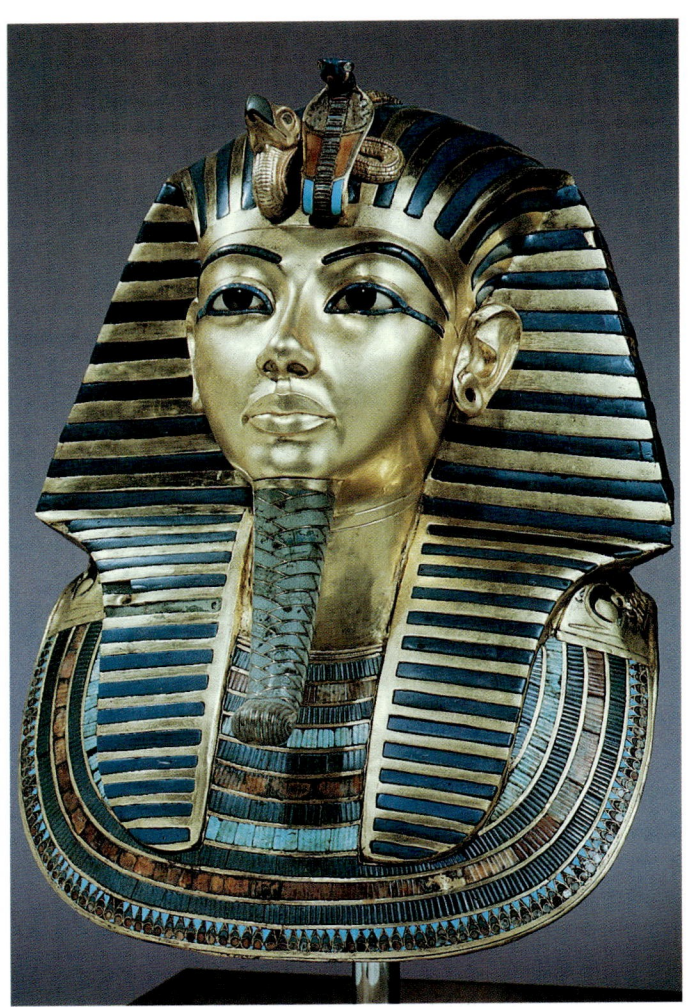

3-37 Death mask of Tutankhamen, from the innermost coffin in his tomb at Thebes, Egypt, Dynasty XVIII, ca. 1323 BCE. Gold with inlay of semiprecious stones, 1′ 9¼″ high. Egyptian Museum, Cairo.

Made of beaten gold (about a quarter ton of it) and inlaid with such semiprecious stones as lapis lazuli, turquoise, and carnelian, it is a supreme monument to the sculptor's and goldsmith's crafts. The portrait mask (FIG. 3-37), which covered the king's face, is also made of gold with inlaid semiprecious stones. It is a sensitive portrayal of the serene adolescent king dressed in his official regalia, including the nemes headdress and false beard. The general effects of the mask and of the tomb treasures as a whole are of grandeur and richness expressive of Egyptian power, pride, and affluence.

**TUTANKHAMEN THE CONQUEROR** Although Tutankhamen probably was considered too young to fight, his position as king required that he be represented as a conqueror. He is shown as such in the panels of a painted chest (FIG. 3-38) deposited in his tomb. The lid panel shows the king as a successful hunter pursuing droves of fleeing animals in the desert, and the side panel shows him as a great warrior. Together, the two panels are a double advertisement of royal power comparable to the later reliefs adorning Assyrian palaces (see FIGS. 2-22 and 2-24). From a war chariot pulled by spirited, plumed horses, Tutankhamen, shown larger than all other figures on the chest, draws his bow against a cluster of bearded Asian enemies, who fall in confusion before him. (The absence of a ground line in an Egyptian painting or relief implies chaos and death.) Tutankhamen slays the enemy, like game, in

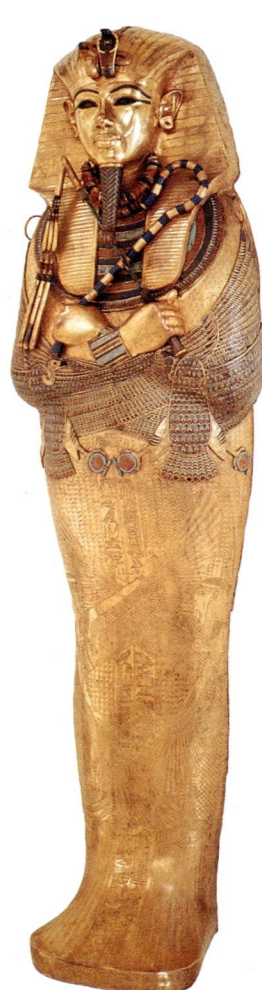

3-36 Innermost coffin of Tutankhamen, from his tomb at Thebes, Egypt, Dynasty XVIII, ca. 1323 BCE. Gold with inlay of enamel and semiprecious stones, approx. 6′ 1″ long. Egyptian Museum, Cairo.

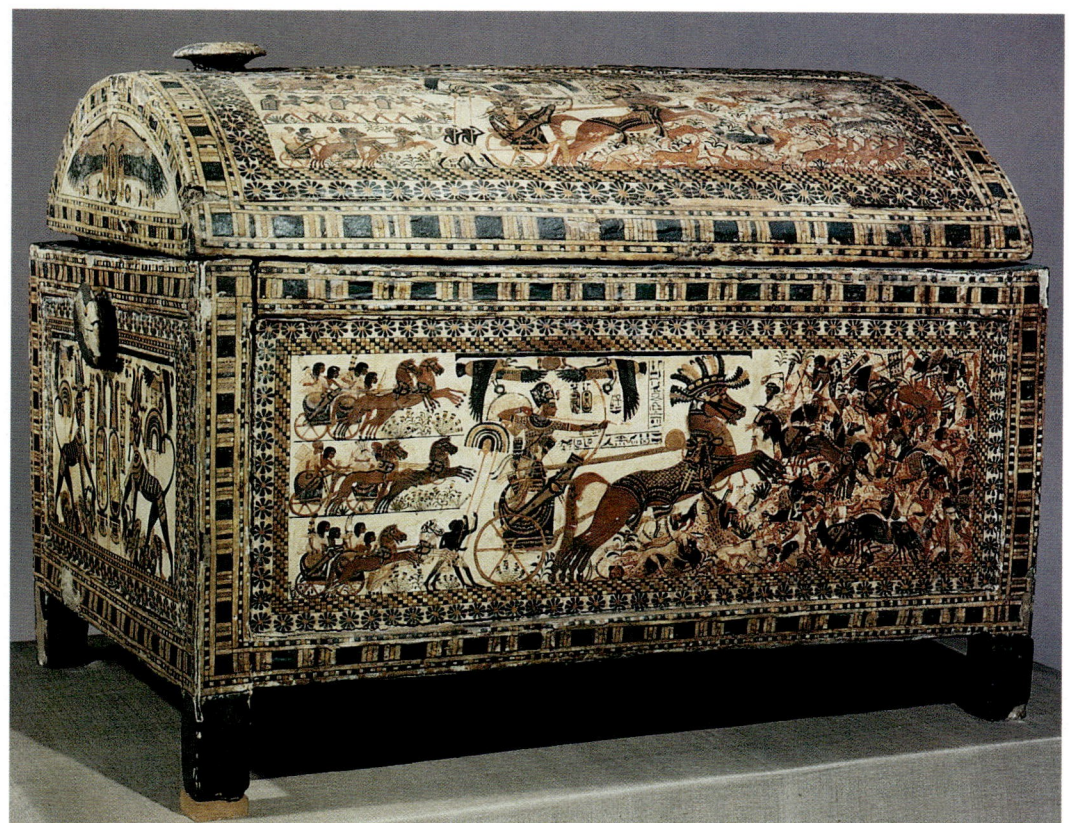

3-38 Painted chest, from the Tomb of Tutankhamen, Thebes, Egypt, Dynasty XVIII, ca. 1333–1323 BCE. Wood, approx. 1′ 8″ long. Egyptian Museum, Cairo.

great numbers. Behind him are three tiers of undersized war chariots, which serve to magnify the king's figure and to increase the count of his warriors. The themes are traditional, but the fluid, curvilinear forms are features reminiscent of the Amarna style.

THE *BOOK OF THE DEAD*  Tutankhamen's mummy case (FIG. 3-36) shows the boy king in the guise of Osiris, god of the dead and king of the underworld, as well as giver of eternal life. The ritual of the cult of Osiris is recorded in the so-called *Book of the Dead*, a collection of spells and prayers. Illustrated papyrus scrolls, some as long as 70 feet, containing these texts were the essential equipment of the tombs of well-to-do persons.

The scroll of Hu-Nefer, the royal scribe and steward of the pharaoh Seti I, was found in his tomb in the Theban necropolis. Our illustration (FIG. 3-39) represents the final judgment of the deceased. At the left, Anubis, the jackal-headed god of embalming,

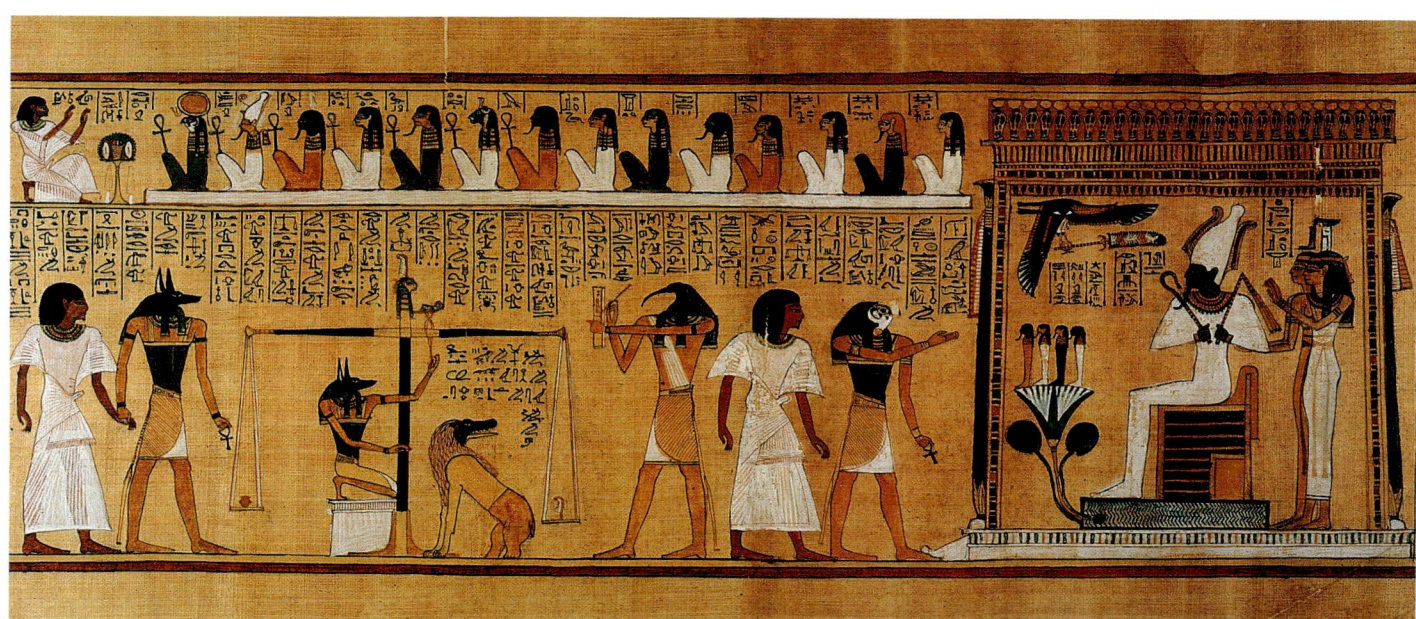

3-39  Last judgment of Hu-Nefer, from his tomb at Thebes, Egypt, Dynasty XIX, ca. 1290–1280 BCE. Painted papyrus scroll, approx. 1′ 6″ high. British Museum, London.

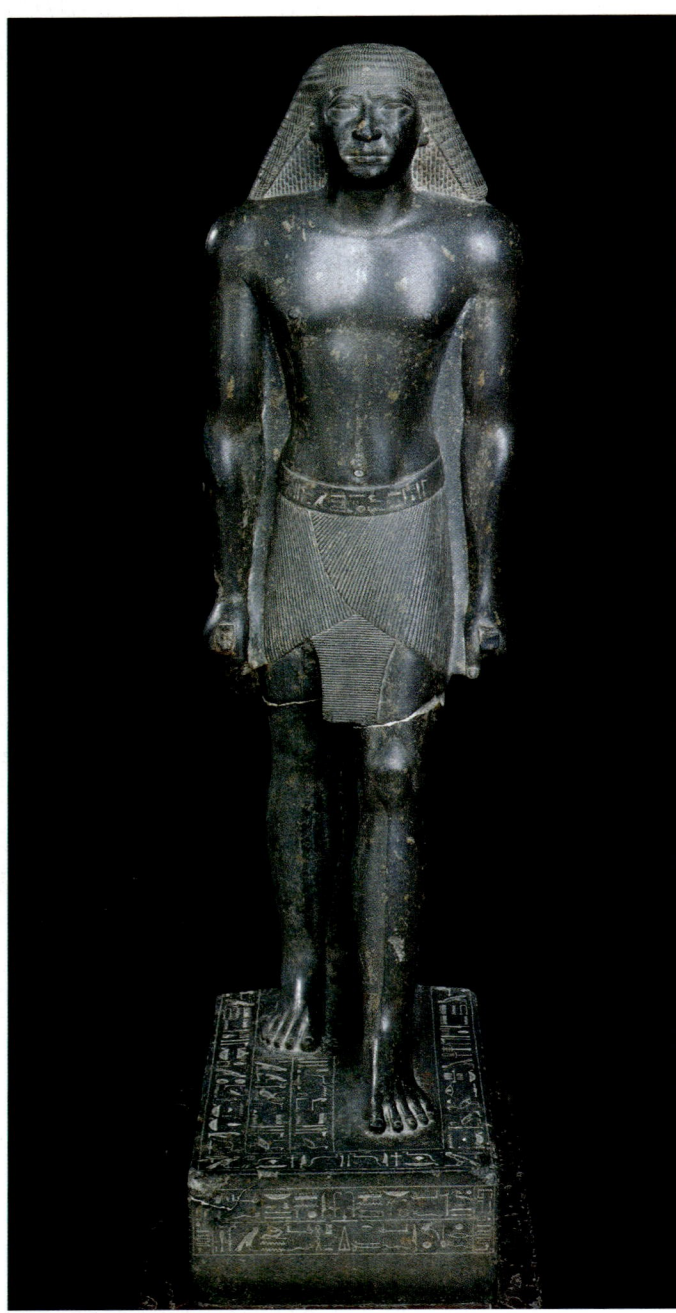

3-40 Mentuemhet, from Karnak, Egypt, Dynasty XXVI, ca. 650 BCE. Granite, approx. 4′ 5″ high. Egyptian Museum, Cairo.

Hu-Nefer kneels in adoration before them. Having been justified by the scales, Hu-Nefer is brought by Osiris's son, the falcon-headed Horus, into the presence of the green-faced Osiris and his sisters Isis and Nephthys to receive the award of eternal life.

In Hu-Nefer's scroll, the figures have all the formality of stance, shape, and attitude of traditional Egyptian art. Abstract figures and hieroglyphs alike are aligned rigidly. Nothing here was painted in the flexible, curvilinear style suggestive of movement that was evident in the art of Amarna and Tutankhamen. The return to conservatism is unmistakable.

## THE LATE PERIOD

**EGYPT IN DECLINE** During the last millennium BCE, Egypt lost the commanding role it once had played in the ancient Near East. The empire dwindled away, and foreign powers invaded, occupied, and ruled the land, until it was taken over by Alexander the Great of Macedon and his Greek successors and, eventually, by the emperors of Rome.

A portrait statue of Mentuemhet (FIG. **3-40**), a rich and powerful man who was Mayor of Thebes and Fourth Priest of Amen during the 26th Dynasty in the seventh century BCE, exemplifies Egyptian sculpture at about the time the Greeks first encountered the art of the Nile Valley (see Chapter 5). The double wig, characteristic of the New Kingdom, and the realism of the head, with its rough and almost brutal characterization, differentiate Mentuemhet's portrait from earlier works. But the rigidity of the stance, the frontality, and the spareness of silhouette with arms at the side and left leg advanced still recall Old Kingdom statuary (FIG. 3-13).

## CONCLUSION

In the Predynastic period, Egyptian sculptors and painters began to formulate the patterns for representing figures and narrating stories that endured for thousands of years. Although there were many divergences from the traditional means of representation, the exceptional longevity of formal traditions in Egypt is one of the marvels of the history of art. It is perhaps the most eloquent testimony of all to the greatness of Egyptian figural art. In architecture too, the Egyptian achievement was extraordinary. From the time of Imhotep, the first master of building in stone, to the architects of the Late Period, the tombs and temples of the Egyptians have expressed the grandeur and permanence of the Kingdom of the Nile. Even after Egypt became a province of the Roman Empire, its prestige remained high. Today, visitors to Rome who enter the city from the airport are greeted by the tomb of a Roman nobleman who died around 12 BCE. His memorial takes the form of a pyramid—2,500 years after the Old Kingdom pharaohs erected the great pyramids of Gizeh, the oldest of the Seven Wonders of the ancient world.

leads Hu-Nefer into the hall of judgment. The god then adjusts the scales to weigh the dead man's heart against the feather of the goddess Maat, protectress of truth and right. A hybrid monster, Ammit, half hippopotamus and half lion, the devourer of the sinful, awaits the decision of the scales. If the weighing had been unfavorable to the deceased, the monster would have eaten his heart. The ibis-headed god Thoth records the proceedings. Above, the gods of the Egyptian pantheon are arranged as witnesses, while

**PREDYNASTIC**

1 | UNION OF UPPER AND LOWER EGYPT, CA. 3000–2920 BCE

2920 BCE

**EARLY DYNASTIC (DYNASTIES I–III)**

| IMHOTEP, FIRST RECORDED NAME OF AN ARTIST, CA. 2625 BCE

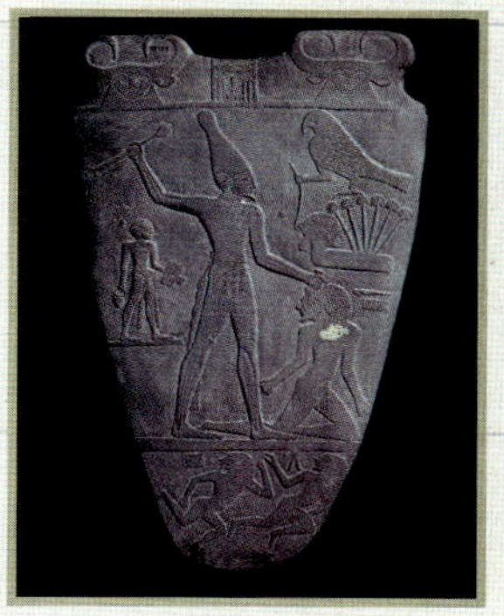

2575 BCE

**OLD KINGDOM (DYNASTIES IV–VIII)**

| SNEFERU, FIRST PHARAOH OF THE OLD KINGDOM, R. 2575–2551 BCE

2 | KHUFU, KHAFRE, AND MENKAURE, BUILDERS OF THE GREAT PYRAMIDS, CA. 2551–2472 BCE

1 Palette of King Narmer, ca. 3000–2920 BCE

2134 BCE

| FIRST INTERMEDIATE PERIOD, 2134–2040 BCE

2040 BCE

**MIDDLE KINGDOM (DYNASTIES XI–XIV)**

| REUNIFICATION OF EGYPT UNDER MENTUHOTEP II, 2040 BCE

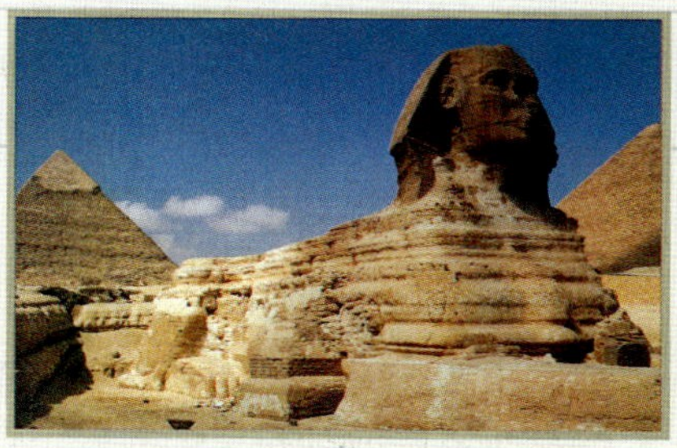

2 Great Sphinx, Gizeh, ca. 2520–2494 BCE

1640 BCE

| SECOND INTERMEDIATE PERIOD, 1640–1550 BCE

1550 BCE

**NEW KINGDOM (DYNASTIES XVII–XX)**

| AHMOSE I DEFEATS THE HYKSOS, 1550 BCE

| HATSHEPSUT, R. 1473–1458 BCE

| AKHENATON AND THE AMARNA PERIOD, 1353–1335 BCE

3 | TUTANKHAMEN, R. 1333–1323 BCE

| RAMSES II, R. 1290–1224 BCE

1070 BCE

| THIRD INTERMEDIATE PERIOD, 1070–712 BCE

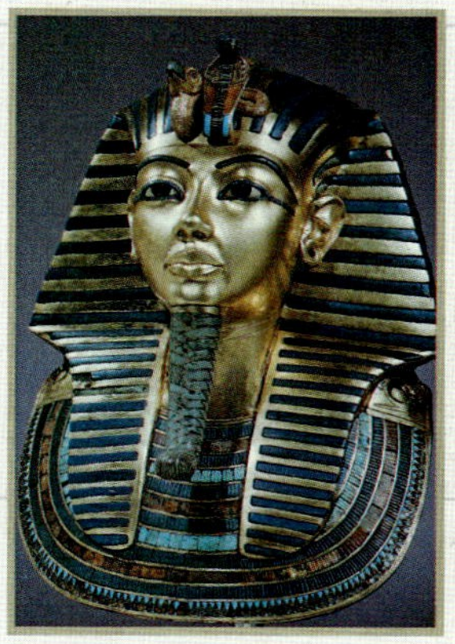

3 Death mask of Tutankhamen, ca. 1323 BCE

712 BCE

**LATE PERIOD (DYNASTIES XXV–XXXI)**

| PERSIA CONQUERS EGYPT, 525 BCE

332 BCE

**GREEK (PTOLEMAIC)**

| ALEXANDER THE GREAT CONQUERS PERSIA AND EGYPT, 332 BCE

| PTOLEMY I, R. 304–284 BCE

4

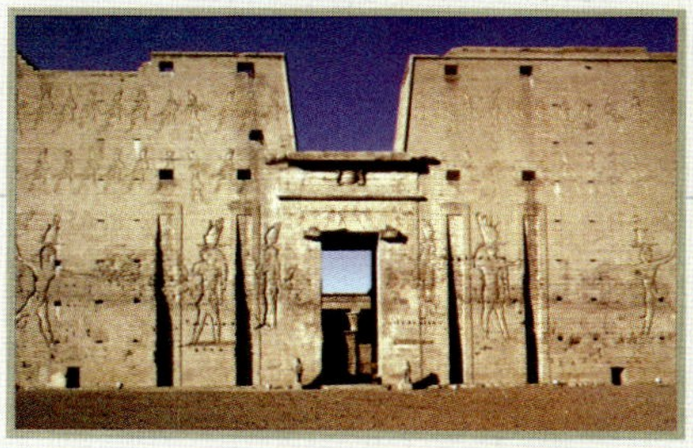

30 BCE

4 Temple of Horus, Edfu, ca. 237–47 BCE

**ROMAN**

| EGYPT BECOMES A ROMAN PROVINCE, 30 BCE

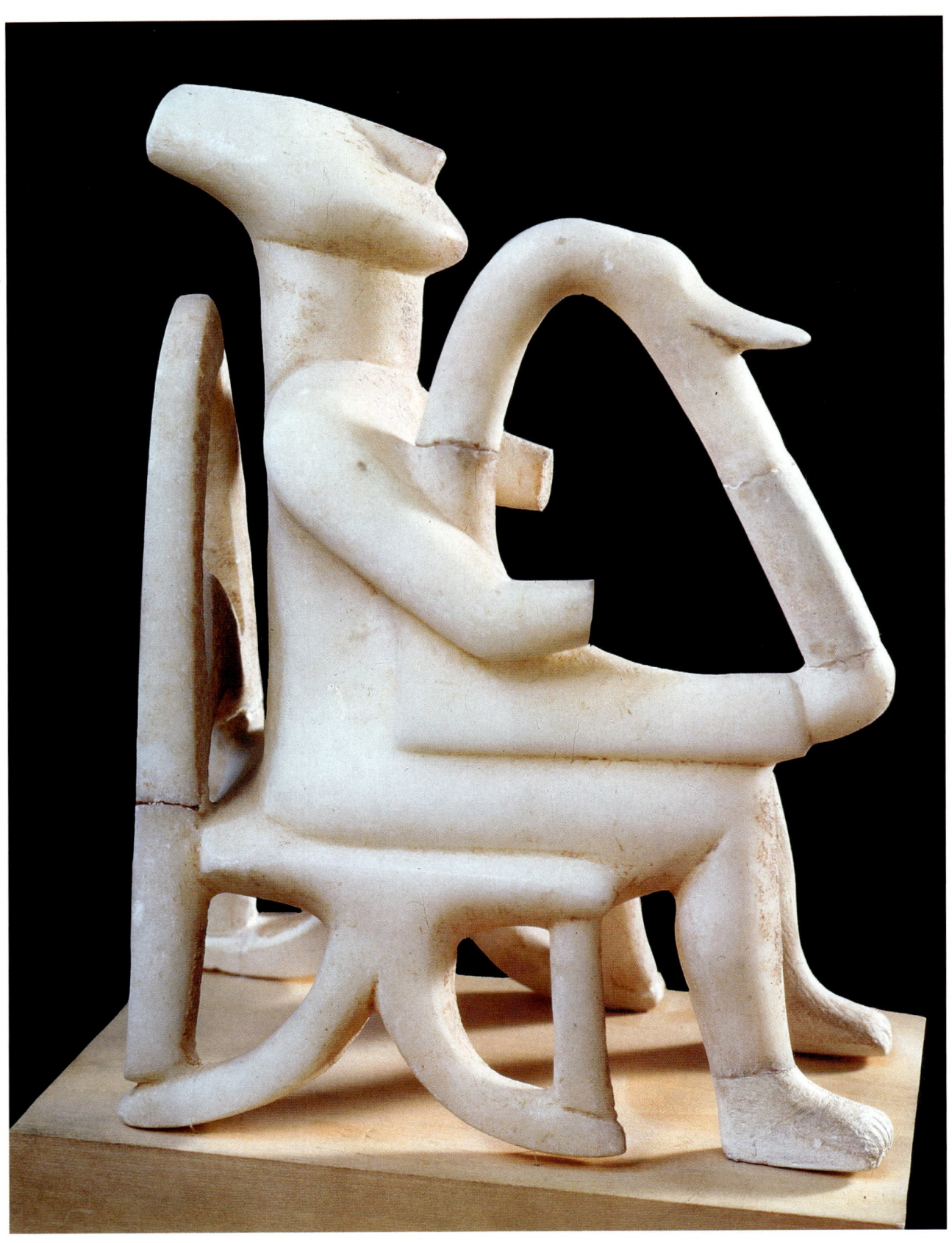

Male lyre player, from Keros (Cyclades), Greece, ca. 2700–2500 BCE. Marble, approx. 9″ high. National Archaeological Museum, Athens.

# 4

# MINOS AND THE HEROES OF HOMER

## THE ART OF THE PREHISTORIC AEGEAN

In the *Iliad,* Homer describes the might and splendor of the Greek armies poised before the walls of Troy.

> Clan after clan poured out from the ships and huts onto the plain . . . innumerable as the leaves and blossoms in their season . . . the Athenians . . . the men of Argos and Tiryns of the Great Walls . . . troops from the great stronghold of Mycenae, from wealthy Corinth . . . from Knossos . . . Phaistos . . . and the other troops that had their homes in Crete of the Hundred Towns.[1]

The Greeks had come from far and wide, from the mainland and the islands (MAP **4-1**), to seek revenge against Paris, the Trojan prince who had abducted Helen, wife of King Menelaus of Sparta. Many consider the *Iliad* to be the finest epic poem ever written. Composed around 750 BCE, it is unquestionably the first great work of Greek literature. In fact, until about 1870 Homer's tale was generally regarded as pure fiction. Scholars discounted the bard as a historian, attributing the profusion of names and places in his writings to the rich abundance of his imagination. The prehistory of Greece in the Bronze Age (the successor of the Stone Age) remained shadowy and lost in an impenetrable world of myth.

**SCHLIEMANN, TROY, AND MYCENAE** In the late 1800s, however, a wealthy German businessman turned archaeologist proved that scholars had done less than justice to the truth of Homer's account. Between 1870 and his death 20 years later, Heinrich Schliemann (whose methods have sometimes been harshly criticized) uncovered some of the very cities Homer named. In 1870, he began work at Hissarlik on the northwestern coast of Turkey, which a British archaeologist, Frank Calvert, had postulated was the site of Homer's Troy. Schliemann dug into a vast mound and found a number of fortified cities built on the remains of one another. One of them had been destroyed by fire in the 13th century BCE. This, scholars now generally agree, was the Troy of King Priam and his son Paris, the city Homer celebrated some 500 years later.

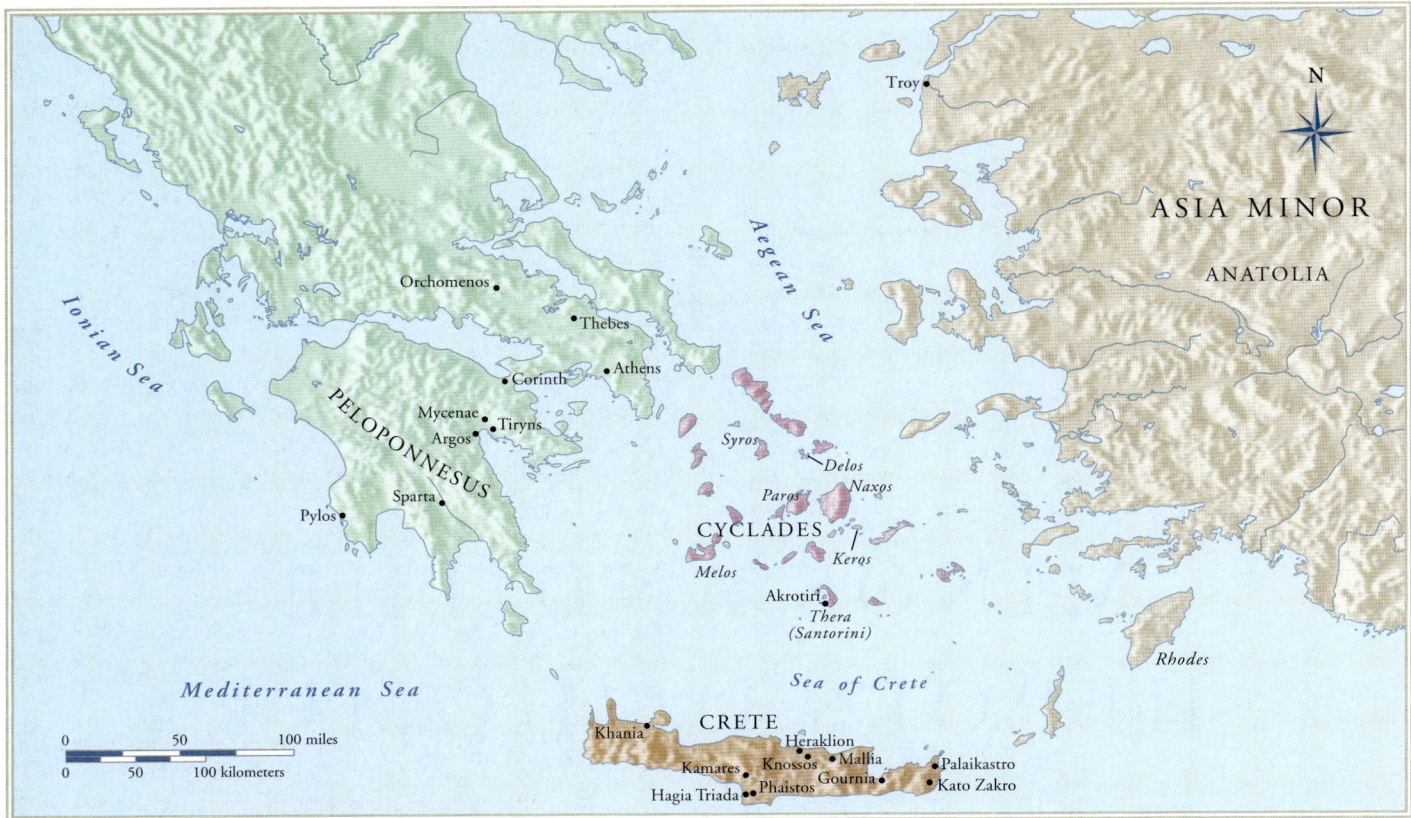

**MAP 4-1** The prehistoric Aegean.

Schliemann continued his excavations at Mycenae on the Greek mainland, where, he believed, King Agamemnon, Menelaus's brother, had once ruled. Here his finds were even more startling. A massive fortress-palace (FIG. 4-20); elaborate tombs (FIGS. 4-21 and 4-22); quantities of gold jewelry, masks (FIG. 4-23), and cups; and inlaid weapons (FIG. 4-24) revealed a magnificent civilization far older than the famous vestiges of classical Greece that had remained visible in Athens and elsewhere. Further discoveries proved that Mycenae had not been the only center of this fabulous civilization.

**KING MINOS AND CRETE** The lesson of Schliemann's success in uncovering Homeric sites was not lost on his successors. Another legendary figure was King Minos of Knossos on the island of Crete. He was said to have exacted from Athens a tribute of youths and maidens to be fed to the Minotaur, a creature half bull and half man housed in a vast labyrinth. Might this story, too, be based on fact? In 1900, an Englishman, Arthur Evans, began work at Knossos. A short time later he uncovered a palace (FIGS. 4-3 and 4-4) that did indeed resemble a maze. Evans named the people who had erected it the Minoans, after their mythological king. His initial findings were soon augmented by additional excavations at Phaistos, Hagia Triada, and other sites, including Gournia, which Harriet Boyd Hawes, an American archaeologist (and one of the first women of any nationality to direct a major excavation), explored between 1901 and 1904.

More recently, important Minoan remains have been excavated at many other locations on Crete, and contemporary sites have been discovered on other islands in the Aegean, most notably on Santorini (ancient Thera). Art historians now have an array of buildings, paintings, and, to a lesser extent, sculptures that attests to the wealth and sophistication of the people who lived in that once obscure heroic age celebrated in later Greek mythology.

**AEGEAN ARCHAEOLOGY TODAY** Less glamorous than the palaces and art objects, but arguably more important for the understanding of Aegean society, are the many documents archaeologists have found written in scripts dubbed Linear A and Linear B. The progress made during the past several decades in deciphering these texts has provided a welcome corrective to the romanticism that characterized the work of Schliemann and Evans. Linear B can now be read, and scholars have begun to reconstruct Aegean civilization by referring to contemporary records and not just to Homer's heroic account.

Historians now also know that humans inhabited Greece as far back as the Lower Paleolithic period and that village life was firmly established in Greece in Neolithic times. But the heyday of the ancient Aegean was not until the second millennium BCE, well after the emergence of the river valley civilizations of Egypt, Mesopotamia, and South Asia (see Chapters 2, 3, and 6).

**AEGEAN GEOGRAPHY** The sea-dominated geography of the Aegean contrasts sharply with that of the Near East (MAP 2-1), as does its temperate climate. The situation of Crete and the Aegean Islands at the commercial crossroads of the ancient Mediterranean had a major effect on their prosperity. The sea also provided a natural defense against the frequent and often disruptive invasions that checker the histories of land-bound civilizations such as those of Mesopotamia.

Historians, art historians, and archaeologists alike divide the prehistoric Aegean into three geographic areas. Each has a distinctive artistic identity. Cycladic art is the art of the Cycladic Islands (so named because they *circle* around Delos), as well as of the adjacent islands in the Aegean, excluding Crete. Minoan art encompasses the art of Crete. Helladic art is the art of the Greek mainland (*Hellas* in Greek). Scholars subdivide each area chronologically into early, middle, and late periods, with the art of the Late Helladic period designated Mycenaean after Agamemnon's great citadel of Mycenae.

# CYCLADIC ART

**"MODERN" SCULPTURE CA. 2500 BCE** Marble was abundantly available in the superb quarries of the Aegean Islands, especially on Naxos and Paros. These same quarries later supplied the master sculptors of classical Greece and Rome with fine marble blocks for monumental statues. But nothing surviving from the classical era is quite like the marble statuettes (FIGS. 4-1 and 4-2) that date from the Early Cycladic period. These sculptures are much revered today (see "Archaeology, Art History, and the Art Market," page 88) because of their striking abstract forms, which call to mind the simple and sleek shapes of some 20th-century statues (see FIGS. 33-16 and 33-71).

Most of the Cycladic sculptures, like many of their Stone Age predecessors in the Aegean, the Near East, and western Europe

(see FIG. 1-4), represent nude women with their arms folded across their abdomens. They vary in height from a few inches to almost life-size. Our example (FIG. **4-1**) is about a foot and a half tall and comes from a grave on the island of Syros. The statuette typifies many of these figures. It is almost flat, and the human body is rendered in a highly schematized manner. Large simple triangles dominate the form—the head, the body itself (which tapers from exceptionally broad shoulders to tiny feet), and the incised triangular pubis. The feet are too fragile to support the figurine. If these sculptures were primarily funerary offerings, as archaeologists believe they were, they must have been placed on their backs in the graves—lying down, like the deceased themselves. Whether they represent those buried with the statuettes or fertility figures or goddesses is still debated. As is true of all such images, the sculptor took pains to emphasize the breasts as well as the pubic area. In the Syros statuette, a slight swelling of the belly may suggest pregnancy.

Traces of paint found on some of the Cycladic figurines indicate that at least parts of these sculptures were colored. The now almost featureless faces would have had painted eyes and mouths in addition to the sculpted noses. Red and blue necklaces and bracelets, as well as painted dots on the cheeks, characterize a number of the surviving figurines.

**MUSIC FOR ETERNITY** Male figures also occur in the Cycladic repertoire. The most elaborate of these take the form of seated musicians, such as the lyre player from Keros (FIG. **4-2**). Wedged between the echoing shapes of chair and instrument, he may be playing for the deceased in the afterlife, although, again, the meaning of these statuettes remains elusive. The harpist

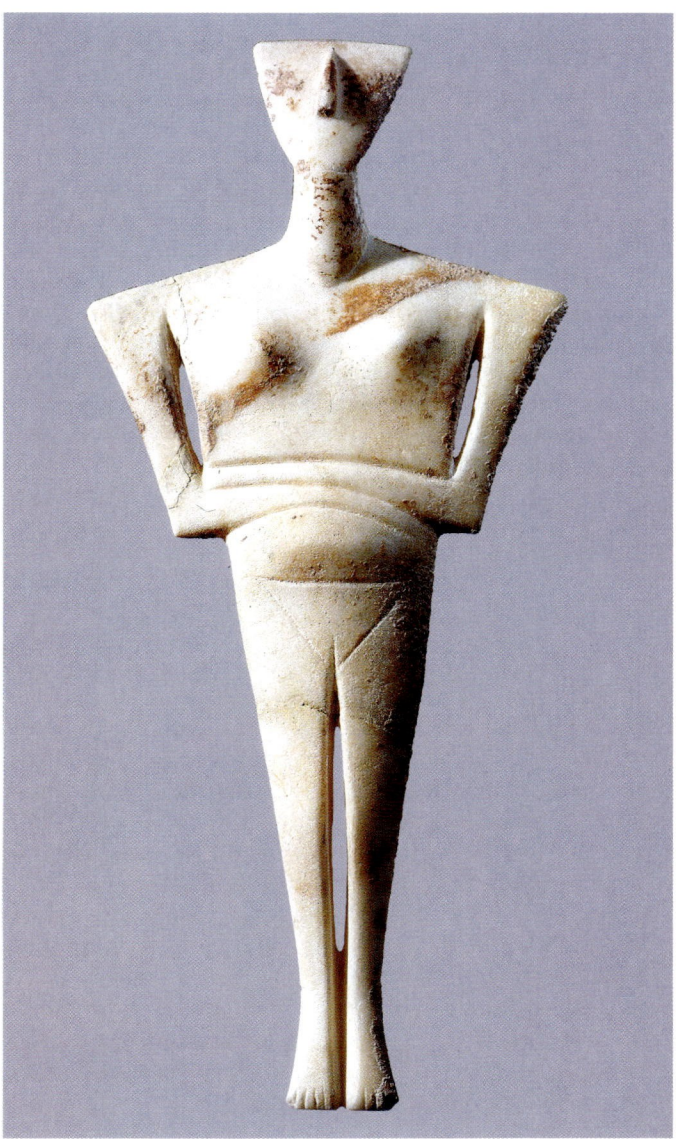

**4-1** Figurine of a woman, from Syros (Cyclades), Greece, ca. 2500–2300 BCE. Marble, approx. 1′ 6″ high. National Archaeological Museum, Athens.

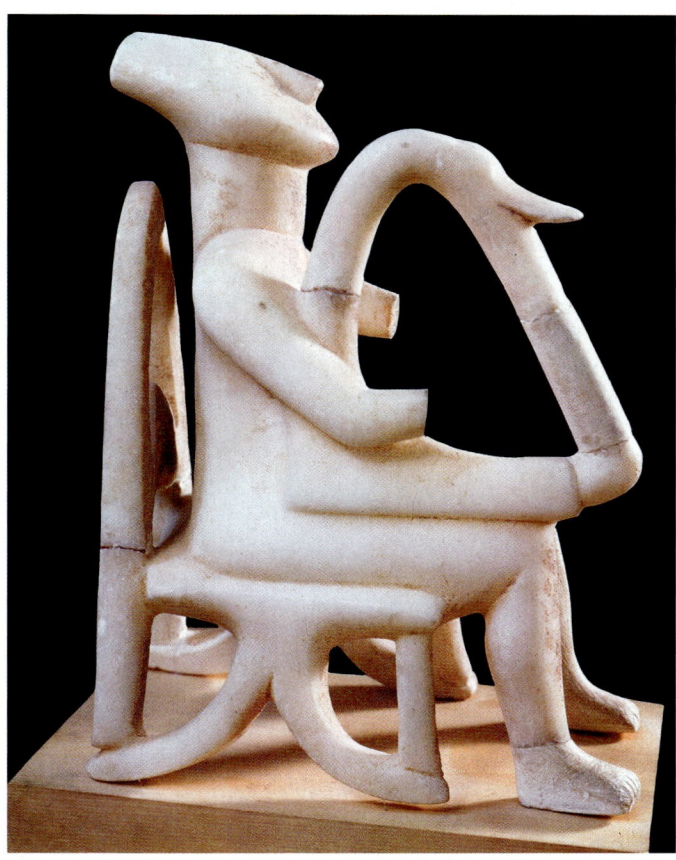

**4-2** Male lyre player, from Keros (Cyclades), Greece, ca. 2700–2500 BCE. Marble, approx. 9″ high. National Archaeological Museum, Athens.

## Archaeology, Art History, and the Art Market

One way the ancient world is fundamentally different from the world today is that ancient art is largely anonymous and undated. No equivalent exists in antiquity for the systematic signing and dating of artworks commonplace in the contemporary world. That is why the role of archaeology in the study of ancient art is so important. Only the scientific excavation of ancient monuments can establish their context. Exquisite and strikingly "modern" sculptures such as the marble Cycladic figurines we illustrate (FIGS. 4-1 and 4-2) may be appreciated as masterpieces when displayed in splendid isolation in glass cases in museums or private homes. But to understand the role these or any other artworks played in ancient society—in many cases, even to determine the date and place of origin of an object—the art historian must know where the piece was uncovered. Only when the context of an artwork is known can one go beyond an appreciation of its formal qualities and begin to analyze its place in art history—and in the society that produced it.

The extraordinary popularity of Cycladic figurines in recent decades has had unfortunate consequences. Clandestine treasure hunters, anxious to meet the insatiable demands of modern collectors, have plundered many sites and smuggled their finds out of Greece to sell to the highest bidder on the international art market. Entire prehistoric cemeteries and towns have been destroyed because of the high esteem in which these sculptures are now held. Two British scholars have calculated that only about 10 percent of the known Cycladic marble statuettes come from secure archaeological contexts. Many of the rest are probably forgeries, produced mostly after World War II when developments in modern art fostered a new appreciation of these abstract renditions of human anatomy and created a boom in demand for "Cycladica" among collectors. For some categories of Cycladic sculptures—those of unusual type or size—not a single piece with a documented provenance exists. Those groups may be 20th-century inventions designed to fetch even higher prices due to their rarity. Consequently, most of the conclusions art historians have drawn about chronology, attribution to different workshops, range of types, and how the figurines were used are purely speculative. The importance of the information the original contexts would have provided cannot be overestimated. That information is, however, probably never recoverable.

---

reflects the same preference for simple geometric shapes and large flat planes as the female figures. Still, the artist showed a keen interest in recording the elegant shape of what must have been a prized possession: the harp with a duck-bill or swan-head ornament at the apex of its sound box. (Animal-headed instruments are well documented in contemporary Mesopotamia [see FIGS. 2-8 *bottom*, 2-9, and 2-10] and Egypt.)

In one instance, figurines of both a musician and a reclining woman were placed in a woman's grave. This suggests that the lyre players are not images of dead men, but it does not prove that the female figurines represent dead women. The man might be entertaining the deceased herself, not her image. Given the absence of written documents in Greece at this date, as everywhere else in prehistoric times, art historians cannot be sure of the meaning of most artworks. Some Cycladic figurines have been found in settlements rather than cemeteries, and it is likely, in fact, that the same form took on different meanings in different contexts.

# MINOAN ART

## Architecture

A PALACE CULTURE EMERGES During the third millennium BCE, both on the Aegean Islands and on the Greek mainland, most settlements were small and consisted only of simple buildings. Only rarely were the dead buried with costly offerings such as the Cycladic statuettes just examined. In contrast, the opening centuries of the second millennium (the Middle Minoan period on Crete) are marked by the construction of large palaces. This first, or Old Palace, period came to an abrupt end around 1700 BCE, when these grand structures were destroyed, probably by an earthquake. Rebuilding began sometime after 1700 BCE, and the ensuing New Palace (Late Minoan) period is the golden age of Crete, an era when the first great Western civilization emerged.

The rebuilt palaces were large, comfortable, and handsome, with ample staircases and courtyards for pageants, ceremonies, and games. They also had storerooms, offices, and shrines that permitted these huge complexes to serve as the key administrative, commercial, and religious centers of Minoan life. The principal palace sites on Crete are at Knossos, Phaistos, Mallia, Kato Zakro, and Khania. All of the complexes were laid out along similar lines. Their size and number, as well as the rich finds they have yielded, attest to the power and prosperity of the Minoans.

THE MINOTAUR'S LABYRINTH The largest of the palaces, at Knossos (FIGS. 4-3 and 4-4), was the legendary home of King Minos. Here, the hero Theseus was said to have battled with the bull-man Minotaur. According to the myth, after defeating the monster, Theseus found his way out of the mazelike complex only with the aid of the king's daughter, Ariadne. She had given Theseus a spindle of thread to mark his path through the labyrinth and then safely out again. In fact, the English word *labyrinth* derives from the intricate plan and scores of rooms of the Knossos palace. *Labrys* means "double ax," and it is a recurring motif in the Minoan palace, referring to sacrificial slaughter. The *labyrinth* was the "House of the Double Axes."

Our aerial view (FIG. 4-3) reveals that the Knossos palace was a rambling structure built against the upper slopes and across the top of a low hill that rises from a fertile plain. All around the palace proper were mansions and villas of the Minoan elite. The great rectangular court (no. 4 in FIG. 4-4), with the palace units grouped around it, had been leveled in the time of the old palace. The new layout suggests that the later palace was carefully planned, with the court serving as the major organizing element.

A secondary organization of the palace plan involves two long corridors. On the west side of the court, a north-south corridor (no. 6) separates official and ceremonial rooms from the magazines (no. 8), where wine, grain, oil, and honey were stored in large jars. On the east side of the court, a smaller east-west corridor (no. 14)

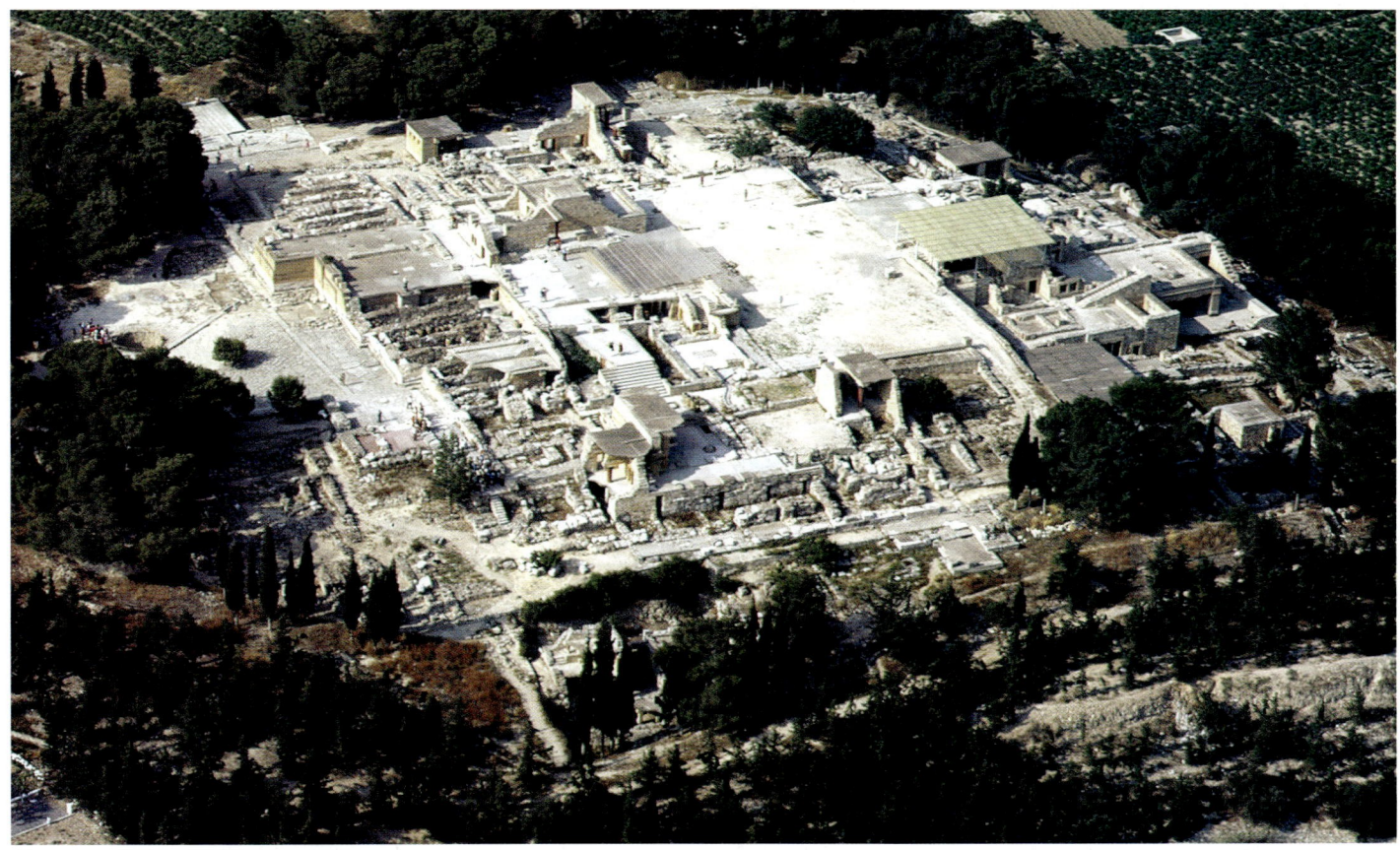

**4-3** Aerial view (looking northeast) of the palace at Knossos (Crete), Greece, ca. 1700–1400 BCE.

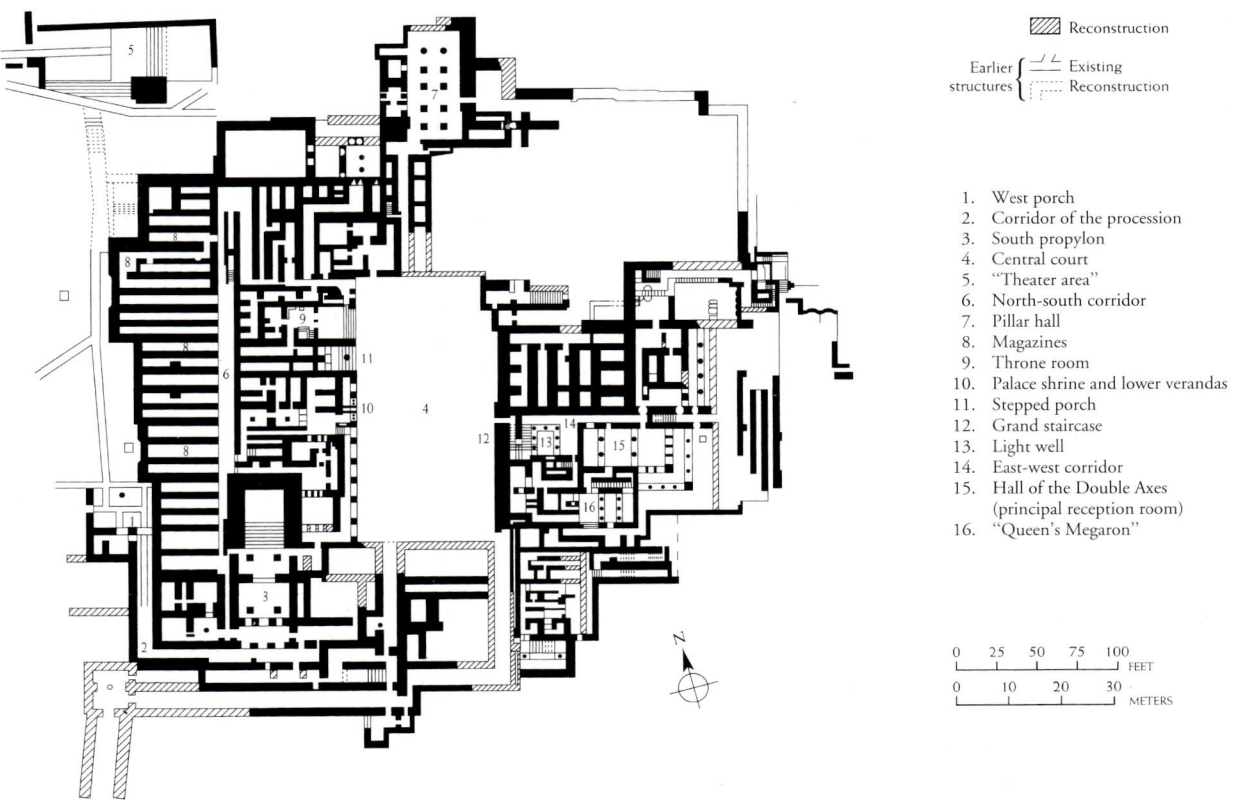

Reconstruction

Earlier structures { Existing / Reconstruction

1. West porch
2. Corridor of the procession
3. South propylon
4. Central court
5. "Theater area"
6. North-south corridor
7. Pillar hall
8. Magazines
9. Throne room
10. Palace shrine and lower verandas
11. Stepped porch
12. Grand staircase
13. Light well
14. East-west corridor
15. Hall of the Double Axes (principal reception room)
16. "Queen's Megaron"

0  25  50  75  100 FEET
0  10  20  30 METERS

**4-4** Plan of the palace at Knossos (Crete), Greece, ca. 1700–1400 BCE.

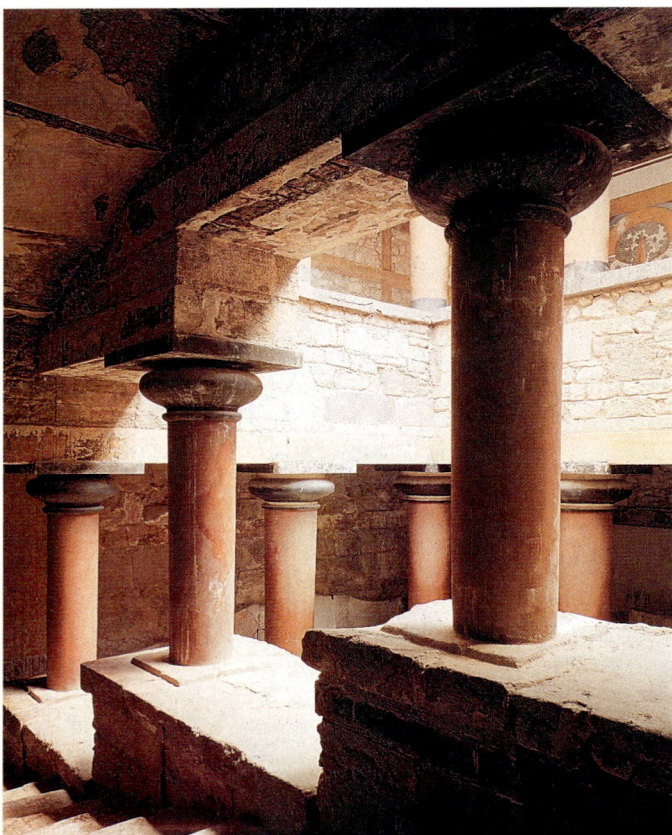

**4-5** Stairwell in the residential quarter of the palace at Knossos (Crete), Greece, ca. 1700–1400 BCE.

effect. The paintings depict many aspects of Minoan life (bull-leaping, processions, and ceremonies) and of nature (birds, animals, flowers, and marine life).

From a ceremonial scene of uncertain significance comes the fragment (FIG. 4-6) dubbed *La Parisienne (The Parisian Woman)* on its discovery because of the elegant dress, elaborate coiffure, and full rouged lips of the young woman (perhaps a priestess or even a goddess) depicted. Although the representation is still convention-bound (note especially the oversized frontal eye in the profile head), the charm and freshness of the mural are undeniable. The painting method used is appropriate to the lively spirit of the Minoans. Unlike the Egyptians, who painted in fresco secco (dry fresco), the Minoans coated the rough fabric of their rubble walls with a fine white lime plaster and used a true (wet) fresco method (see "Fresco Painting," Chapter 19, page 530). The Minoan frescoes required rapid execution and great skill in achieving quick, almost impressionistic effects. The simple, light delicacy of the *Parisienne* painter's technique matches the vivacity of the subject.

**BULL-LEAPING AT KNOSSOS** Liveliness and spontaneity also characterize a fresco (FIG. 4-7) from the palace at Knossos depicting the Minoan ceremony of bull-leaping (see "Minoan Paintings Discovered in Egypt," page 91). Here, too, only fragments of the full composition have been recovered (the dark patches are original; the rest is a modern restoration). The Minoan artist painted the

separates the living quarters and reception rooms (to the south) from the workers' and servants' quarters (to the north). At the northwest corner of the palace is a theater-like area (no. 5) with steps on two sides that may have served as seats. This form is a possible forerunner of the later Greek theater (see FIG. 5-70). Its purpose is unknown, but it is a feature paralleled in the Phaistos palace.

The Cretan palaces were well constructed, with thick walls composed of rough, unshaped fieldstones embedded in clay. Ashlar masonry was used at building corners and around door and window openings. The Minoans also gave thought to such questions as drainage of rainwater. At Knossos, a remarkably efficient system of terracotta pipes underlies the enormous building.

The Knossos palace was complex not only in plan but also in elevation. It had as many as three stories around the central court and even more on the south and east sides where the terrain sloped off sharply. Interior staircases built around light and air wells (FIG. 4-5) provided necessary illumination and ventilation. Painted Minoan columns, originally fashioned of wood but which Evans restored in stone, are characterized by their bulbous, cushionlike capitals and distinctive shafts. The capitals resemble those of the later Greek Doric order (see "Doric and Ionic Temples," Chapter 5, page 116), but the shafts taper from a wide top to a narrower base—the opposite of both Egyptian and later Greek columns.

### *Painting*

**MINOAN PALACE FRESCOES** Mural paintings liberally adorn the palace at Knossos, constituting one of its most striking aspects. The brightly painted walls and the red shafts and black capitals of the wooden columns provided an extraordinarily rich

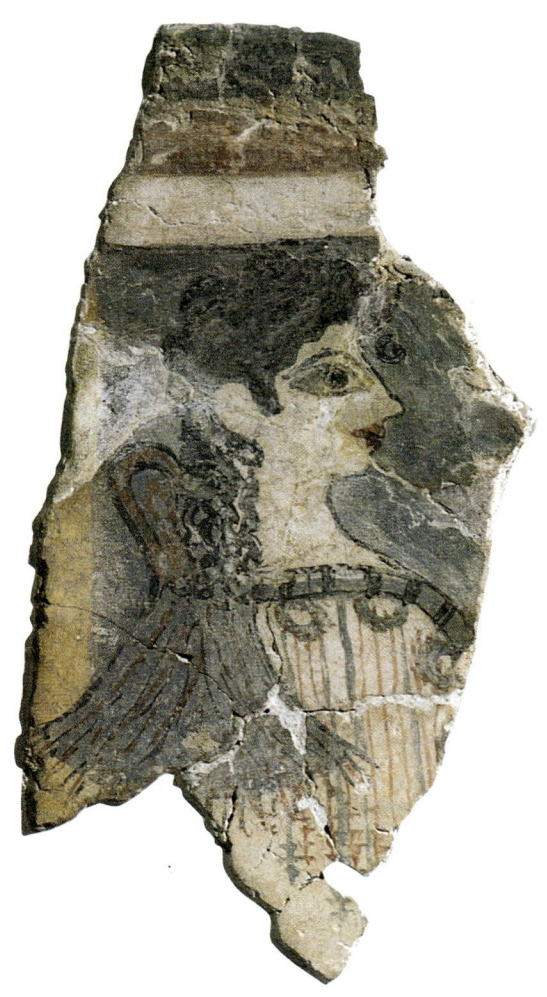

**4-6** Minoan woman or goddess *(La Parisienne)*, from the palace at Knossos (Crete), Greece, ca. 1450–1400 BCE. Fragment of a fresco, approx. 10″ high. Archaeological Museum, Herakleion.

### Minoan Paintings Discovered in Egypt

Knowledge of ancient art and architecture grows daily as archaeologists uncover new paintings, sculptures, pots, and other objects, as well as remains of previously unknown buildings. Although excavators infrequently make a truly astounding discovery, that is what happened when, in the 1980s, an Austrian expedition to Tell el-Daba in the eastern Nile Delta explored a huge palace of the 16th century BCE.

Tell el-Daba, ancient Avaris (see MAP 3-1), was the capital city of the Hyksos. Until Ahmose, founder of the New Kingdom, drove them out around 1530 BCE, the Hyksos ruled the land of the Nile. The palatial complex the Austrians discovered was either built by Ahmose at the beginning of the 18th Dynasty, or built under the last Hyksos pharaoh and destroyed by Ahmose. The archaeologists uncovered the unexpected: pumice from the eruption of the Theran volcano (see "A Volcano Erupts," page 94) and thousands of fragments of Aegean-style wall paintings.

The most impressive of the Avaris murals depicts bull-leapers seen against a maze background that many believe is a topographical reference to the Minoan palace at Knossos. Not only is the subject of the painting Aegean but also the technique (primarily true fresco on lime plaster) and most aspects of style and iconography. Few doubt that Aegean rather than Egyptian artists decorated the palace, although there is little agreement as to why the Egyptians employed foreign painters or chose an Aegean subject.

Whatever the final answer to this archaeological and historical riddle, the excavations at Tell el-Daba have demonstrated that contacts between Egypt and the Aegean world were not confined to trade and politics. In fact, painted walls and floors of Aegean style, technique, and subject also have been discovered in recent years in a Canaanite palace at Tel Kabri in northern Israel. Similar finds had been made much earlier at Alalakh in Syria (see MAP 2-1 for both sites). Together these startling discoveries provide evidence for a rich international exchange of artists and ideas in the Mediterranean world at the middle of the second millennium BCE. Art historians can no longer study the great civilizations of Egypt, the Near East, and the Aegean in isolation.

young women (with fair skin) and the youth (with dark skin) according to the widely accepted ancient convention for distinguishing male and female. The young man is shown in the air, having, it seems, grasped the bull's horns and vaulted over its back in a perilous and extremely difficult acrobatic maneuver. The painter brilliantly suggested the powerful charge of the bull by elongating the animal's shape and using sweeping lines to form a funnel of energy, beginning at the very narrow hindquarters of the bull and culminating in its large, sharp horns and galloping forelegs. The human figures also have stylized shapes, with typically Minoan pinched waists, and are highly animated. Although the profile pose with the full-view eye was a familiar convention in Egypt and Mesopotamia, the elegance of the Cretan figures, with their long, curly hair and proud and self-confident bearing, distinguishes them from all

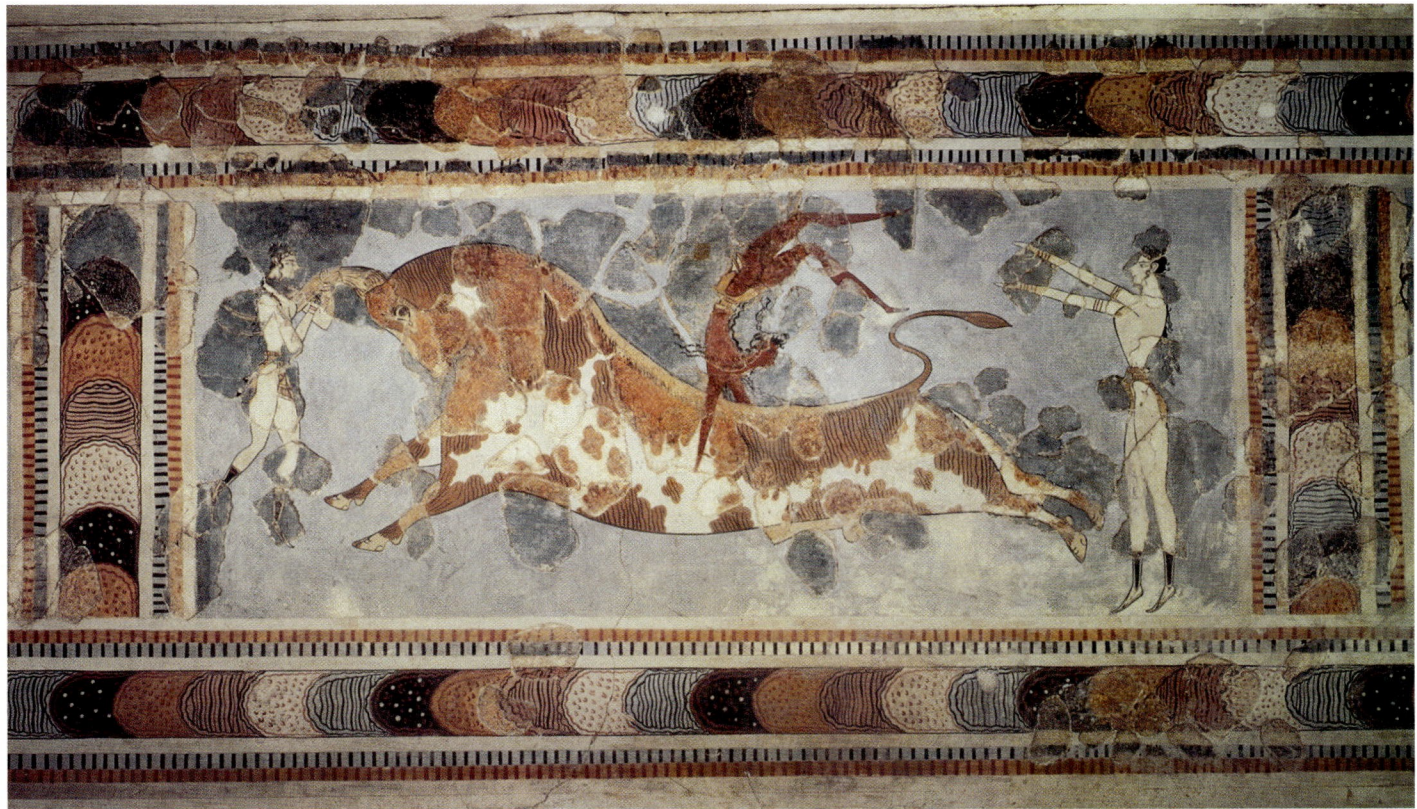

**4-7** Bull-leaping, from the palace at Knossos (Crete), Greece, ca. 1450–1400 BCE. Fresco, approx. 2′ 8″ high, including border. Archaeological Museum, Herakleion.

## A Volcano Erupts, and the History of Art Is Revised

Today, ships bound for the beautiful Greek island of Santorini, with its picture-postcard white houses, churches, shops, and restaurants, weigh anchor in a bay beneath steep, crescent-shaped cliffs. Until about 20,000 BCE, however, ancient Thera had a roughly circular shape and gentler slopes. Then, suddenly, a volcanic eruption blew out the center of the island, leaving behind the moon-shaped main island and several lesser islands grouped around a bay that roughly corresponds to the shape of the gigantic ancient volcano. The volcano erupted again, thousands of years later, during the zenith of Aegean civilization.

Then, the site of Akrotiri, which Greek excavators gradually are uncovering, was buried by a pumice layer more than a yard deep in some areas and by an even larger volume of volcanic ash *(tephra)* that often exceeds five yards in depth, even after nearly 37 centuries of erosion. Tephra filled whole rooms, and boulders the volcano spewed forth pelted the walls of some houses. Closer to the volcano's cone, the tephra is almost 60 yards deep in places. In fact, the force of the eruption was so powerful that sea currents carried the pumice and wind blew the ash throughout the ancient Mediterranean, not only to Crete, Rhodes, and Cyprus but also as far away as Anatolia, Egypt (see "Minoan Paintings Discovered in Egypt," page 91), Syria, and Israel.

Until recently, most scholars embraced the theory formulated decades ago by Spyridon Marinatos, an eminent Greek archaeologist, that the otherwise unexplained demise of Minoan civilization on Crete around 1500 BCE was the by-product of the volcanic eruption on Thera. According to Marinatos, devastating famine followed the rain of ash that fell on Crete. But archaeologists now know that after the eruption, life went on in Crete, if not on Thera. At one Cretan site, the Minoans collected Theran pumice and deposited it in conical cups on a monumental stairway, possibly as a votive offering.

Teams of researchers, working closely in an impressive and most welcome interdisciplinary effort, have pinpointed 1628 BCE as the date of a major climatic event. They have studied tree rings at sites in Europe and in North America for evidence of retarded growth and have examined ice cores in Greenland for peak acidity layers. Both kinds of evidence testify to a significant disruption in weather patterns in that year. Today, most—but not all—scholars believe the cause of this disruption to be the cataclysmic volcanic eruption on Thera.

The revised date of the Theran eruption has profound consequences for the chronology of Aegean art. The Akrotiri frescoes (FIGS. 4-8 and 4-9) are now thought to be at least 150 years older than they were considered not long ago. They predate by many decades the paintings from the Knossos palace (FIGS. 4-6 and 4-7). The discovery has implications for the dating of art objects from other areas as well because of the important interconnections between the Aegean, Egypt, and the Near East during the second millennium BCE.

---

other early figure styles. The angularity of the figures seen in Egyptian wall paintings is modified by the curving Minoan line that suggests the elasticity of the living and moving being.

**BURIED BY A VOLCANO** Much better preserved than the Knossos frescoes are those uncovered much more recently in the excavations of Akrotiri on the volcanic island of Santorini (ancient Thera) in the Cyclades, some 60 miles north of Crete. In the Late Cycladic period, Thera was artistically, and possibly also politically, within the Minoan orbit. The mural paintings from Akrotiri are invaluable additions to the fragmentary and frequently misrestored frescoes from Crete. The excellent condition of the Theran paintings is due to an enormous seismic explosion on Santorini that buried Akrotiri in volcanic pumice and ash, making it a kind of Pompeii of the prehistoric Aegean (see "A Volcano Erupts, and the History of Art Is Revised," above). The Akrotiri frescoes decorated the walls of houses, not the walls of a great palace such as that at Knossos, and therefore the number of painted walls from the site is especially impressive.

**SEAFARING IN THE CYCLADES** One especially interesting Theran fresco is filled with dozens of figures, ships, and buildings. This *Miniature Ships Fresco,* as it has been called, formed a frieze about 17 inches high at the top of at least three walls of a room in the so-called West House at Akrotiri. In our detail of the fresco (FIG. **4-8**), a great fleet sails from one Aegean port headed for

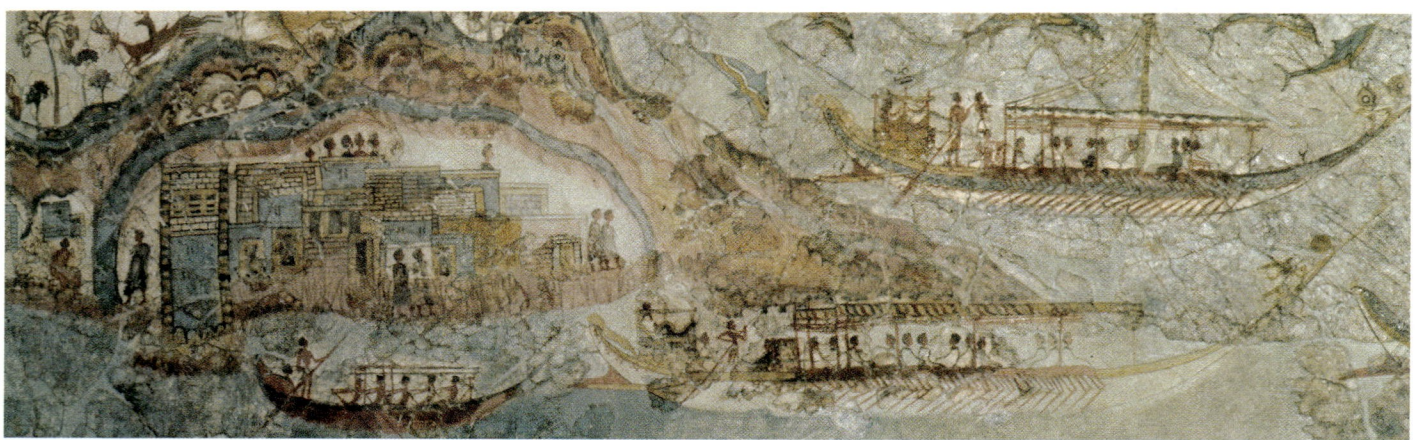

**4-8** Flotilla, detail of *Miniature Ships Fresco,* from Room 5, West House, Akrotiri, Thera (Cyclades), Greece, ca. 1650 BCE. Fresco, approx. 1′ 5″ high. National Archaeological Museum, Athens.

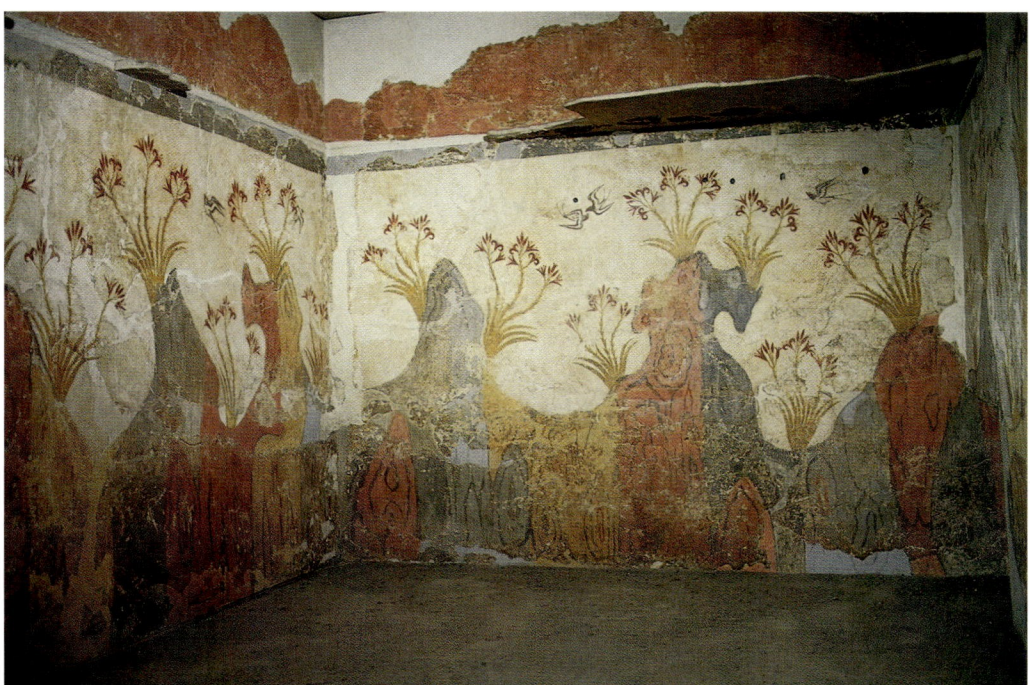

4-9 Landscape with swallows *(Spring Fresco),* from Room Delta 2, Akrotiri, Thera (Cyclades), Greece, ca. 1650 BCE. Fresco, approx. 7′ 6″ high. National Archaeological Museum, Athens.

another (not visible in the illustration), perhaps taking part in a sea festival or perhaps engaged in a naval campaign that calls to mind Homer's much later catalog of ships in the *Iliad.* Such a detailed representation of the movement of ships and people from port to port does not appear again until the Column of the Roman emperor Trajan (see FIG. 10-42) almost two millennia later. The details of ship design and sailing are carefully observed in the fresco, as if it were painted by one who knew ships well. Just as closely studied are the placement and poses of sailors, rowers, and passengers.

Little of the conventional stereotyping and repetition that appear in such representations throughout the history of art is evident in the Akrotiri fresco. Instead, the arrangement of figures and poses varies significantly according to each person's role—steering, tending to the sail, rowing, or simply sitting and conversing. Dolphins frolic about the ships, and on the left shore a lion pursues fleeing deer. The port—encircled by a river represented as arching above it—has quays, houses, and streets filled with men attentive to the coming and going of the ships. The whole composition has an openness and lightness that suggest the freedom of movement of a people born to the sea.

**CELEBRATING NATURE** The almost perfectly preserved mural paintings of another room from Akrotiri capture especially well the freshness and vitality of this vision of the Aegean world. In *Spring Fresco* (FIG. 4-9), nature itself is the sole subject, although the artist's aim was not to render the rocky island terrain realistically but, rather, to capture the landscape's essence and to express joy in the splendid surroundings. The irrationally undulating and vividly colored rocks, the graceful lilies swaying in the cool island breezes, and the darting swallows express the vigor of growth, the delicacy of flowering, and the lightness of birdsong and flight. In the lyrical language of curving line, the artist celebrated the rhythms of spring. This is the first known example of a pure landscape painting, one that not only has no humans but also has no narrative element (compare FIG. 1-18). The Theran *Spring Fresco* represents the polar opposite of the first efforts at mural painting in the caves of Paleolithic Europe, where animals (and occasionally humans) appeared as isolated figures without any indication of setting.

**SEA LIFE ON POTTERY** The love of nature manifested itself in Crete on the surfaces of painted vases even before the period of the new palaces. During the Middle Minoan period, Cretan potters fashioned sophisticated shapes using newly introduced potters' wheels, and decorated their vases in a distinctive and fully polychromatic style. These Kamares Ware vessels, named for the cave on the slope of Mount Ida where they were first discovered, have been found in quantity at Phaistos and Knossos. On our example (FIG. 4-10), as on other Kamares vases, creamy white and reddish-brown

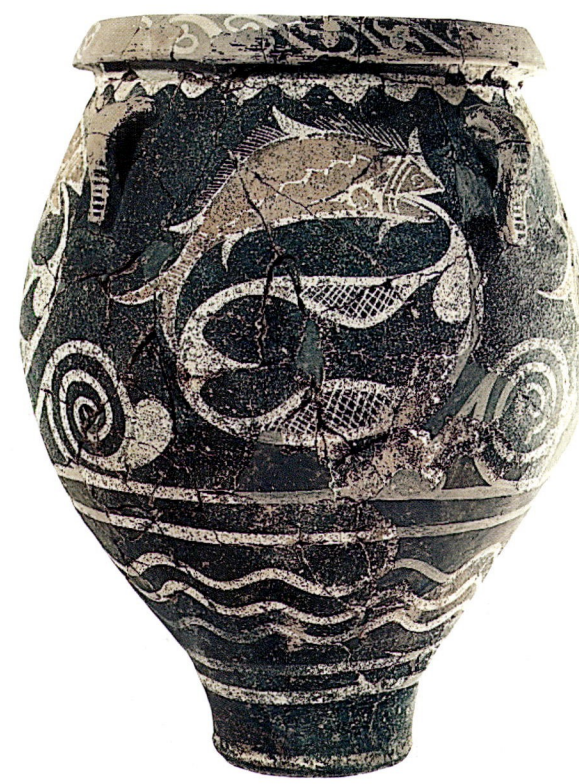

4-10 Kamares Ware jar, from Phaistos (Crete), Greece, ca. 1800–1700 BCE. Approx. 1′ 8″ high. Archaeological Museum, Herakleion.

decoration is set against a rich black ground. The central motif is a great leaping fish—a forerunner of the diving dolphins of Late Minoan and Late Cycladic murals—and perhaps a fishnet surrounded by a host of curvilinear abstract patterns including waves and spirals. The swirling lines evoke life in the sea, and both the abstract and the natural forms beautifully complement the shape of the vessel.

The sea and the creatures that inhabit it also inspired the Late Minoan Marine Style octopus jar (FIG. 4-11) from Palaikastro, which is contemporary with the new palaces at Knossos and elsewhere. The tentacles of the octopus reach out over the curving surfaces of the vessel, embracing the piece and emphasizing its volume. This is a masterful realization of the relationship between the vessel's decoration and its shape, always a problem for the ceramist. This later vase differs markedly from its Kamares Ware predecessor in color. Not only is the octopus jar more muted in tone, but the Late Minoan artist also reversed the earlier scheme and placed dark silhouettes on a light ground. This remained the norm for about a millennium in Greece, until about 530 BCE when, albeit in a very different form, light figures on a dark ground emerged once again as the preferred manner (see FIG. 5-20).

**MINOAN FUNERARY RITUALS** Midway in size and complexity between the decorated clay vessels and the monumental frescoes of Crete and Thera are the paintings on a Late Minoan limestone *sarcophagus* (FIG. 4-12) found at Hagia Triada on the southern coast of Crete. The paintings are closely related in technique, color scheme, and figure style to contemporary palace frescoes, but the subject is foreign to the palace repertoire. Befitting the function of the sarcophagus as a burial container, the paintings illustrate the funerary rites in honor of the dead. They provide welcome information about Minoan religion, which still remains obscure despite more than a century of excavation on Crete. At the right, the dead man appears upright in front of his own tomb, like the New Testament's raised Lazarus in medieval

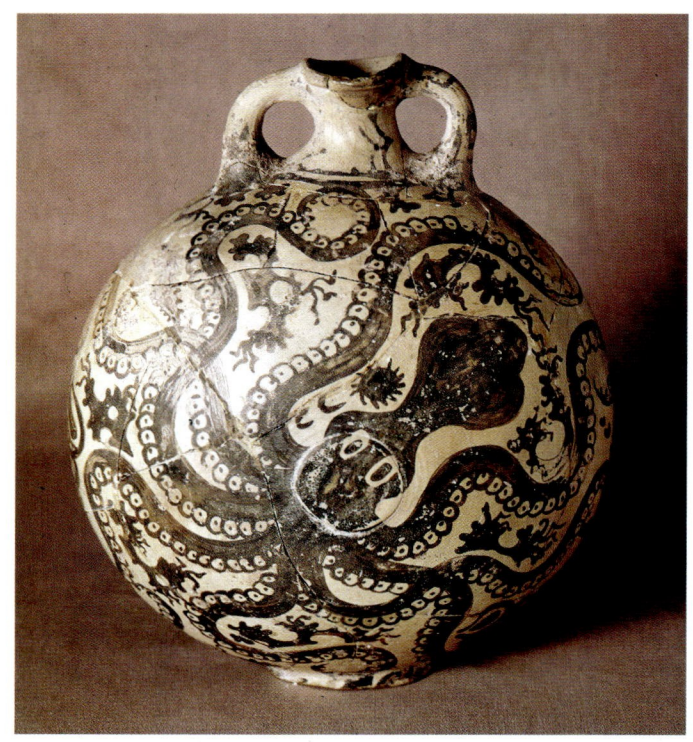

4-11 Marine Style octopus jar, from Palaikastro (Crete), Greece, ca. 1500 BCE. Approx. 11″ high. Archaeological Museum, Herakleion.

art, and watches as three men (note their dark flesh tone) bring offerings to him. At the left, two light-skinned women carry vessels and pour a libation to the deceased while a male musician plays a lyre. The musician immediately brings to mind the Early Cycladic statuettes of lyre players (FIG. 4-2) deposited in tombs, which may indicate some continuity in funerary customs and beliefs from the Early to the Late Bronze Age in the Aegean.

4-12 Sarcophagus, from Hagia Triada (Crete), Greece, ca. 1450–1400 BCE. Painted limestone, approx. 4′ 6″ long. Archaeological Museum, Herakleion.

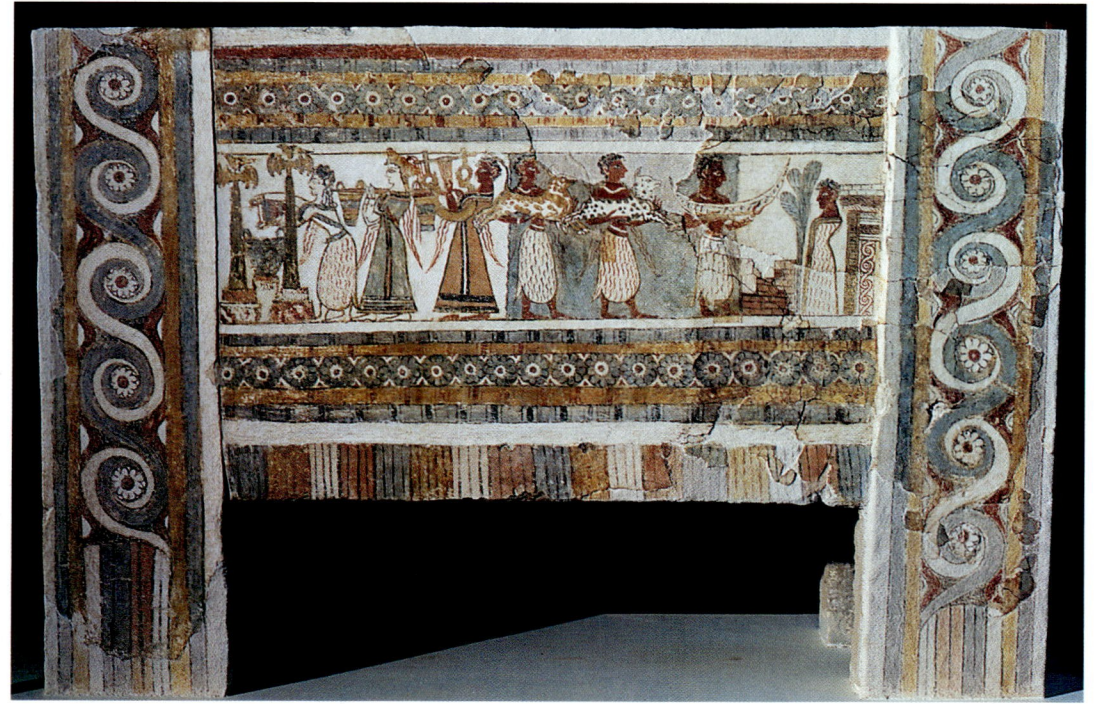

## Sculpture

**JOYFUL FARMERS** Also from Hagia Triada is the so-called *Harvester Vase* (FIG. **4-13**), probably the finest surviving example of Minoan relief sculpture. Only the upper half of the egg-shaped body and neck of the vessel are preserved. Missing are the lower parts of the harvesters (or, as some think, sowers) and the ground on which they stand. Formulaic scenes of sowing and harvesting were staples of Egyptian funerary art (see FIG. 3-17), but the Minoan artist shunned static repetition in favor of a composition that bursts with the energy of its individually characterized figures. The relief shows a riotous crowd singing and shouting as they go to or return from the fields. The artist vividly captured the forward movement and lusty exuberance of the youths.

Although most of the figures conform to the age-old convention of combined profile and frontal views, one figure (at the center of our illustration) is singled out from his companions. He shakes a rattle to beat time, and the artist depicted him in full profile with his lungs so inflated with air that his ribs show. This is one of the first instances in the history of art of a sculptor showing a keen interest in the underlying muscular and skeletal structure of the human body. The artist's painstaking study of human anatomy is a remarkable achievement, especially given the size of the *Harvester Vase,* barely five inches at its greatest diameter. Equally noteworthy is how the sculptor recorded the tension and relaxation of facial muscles with astonishing exactitude. This degree of animation of the human face is without precedent in ancient art.

**GODDESS OR PRIESTESS?** In contrast to Mesopotamia and Egypt, no temples or monumental statues of gods, kings, or monsters have been found in Minoan Crete. Large wooden images may once have existed, but what remains of Minoan sculpture in the round is small in scale, such as the *faience* (glazed earthenware) statuette known as the *Snake Goddess* (FIG. **4-14**), from the palace at Knossos. It is one of several similar figurines that some scholars believe may represent mortal attendants rather than a deity, although the prominently exposed breasts suggest that these figurines stand in the long line of prehistoric fertility images usually considered divinities. (The woman depicted in the Knossos statuette not only holds snakes in her hands but also supports a leopardlike feline peacefully on her head. This implied power over the animal world also seems appropriate for a deity.) The frontality of the figure is reminiscent of Egyptian and Near Eastern statuary, but the costume, with its open bodice and flounced skirt, is distinctly Minoan. If the statuette represents a goddess, as seems likely, then it is yet another example of how human beings fashion their gods in their own image.

**SCULPTURE IN GOLD AND IVORY** British excavations at Palaikastro between 1987 and 1990 yielded fragments of one of the

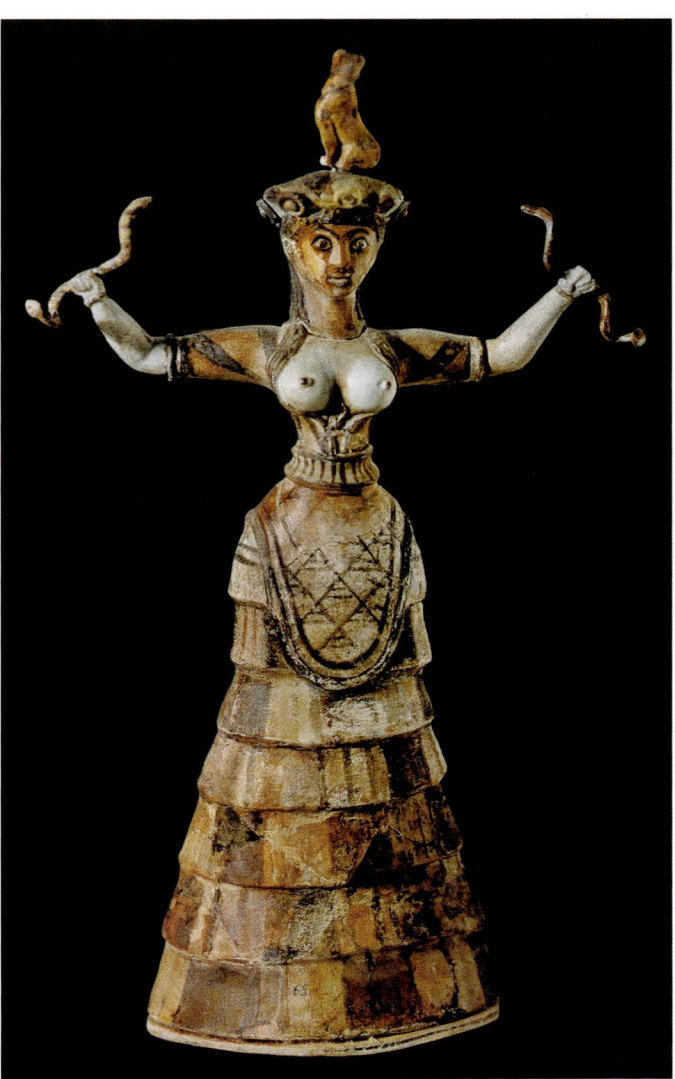

**4-13** *Harvester Vase,* from Hagia Triada (Crete), Greece, ca. 1500 BCE. Steatite, greatest diameter approx. 5″. Archaeological Museum, Herakleion.

**4-14** *Snake Goddess,* from the palace at Knossos (Crete), Greece, ca. 1600 BCE. Faience, approx. 1′ 1½″ high. Archaeological Museum, Herakleion.

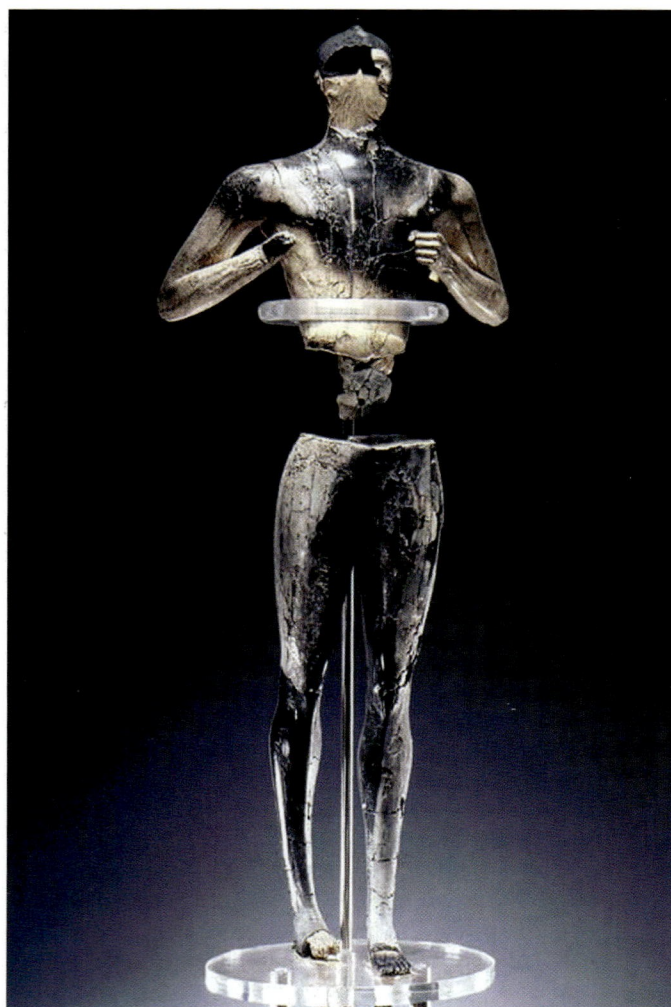

**4-15** Young god(?), from Palaikastro (Crete), Greece, ca. 1500–1475 BCE. Ivory, gold, serpentine, and rock crystal, original height approx. 1′ 7½″. Archaeological Museum, Siteia.

most remarkable objects ever found on Crete. It is a statuette (FIG. 4-15) nearly 20 inches tall, fashioned from hippopotamus tusk ivory, gold, serpentine, and rock crystal. The figurine is a very early example of *chryselephantine* (gold and ivory) sculpture, a technique that the Greeks would later use for their largest and costliest cult images (see FIG. 5-44). The ivory and gold were probably imported from Egypt, the source also of the pose with left foot advanced (see FIGS. 3-13 and 3-15), but the style and iconography are unmistakably Cretan. The work is the creation of a sculptor of extraordinary ability who delighted in rendering minute details of muscles and veins (compare FIG. 4-13). The Palaikastro youth (his coiffure, with shaved head save for a central braid, indicates his age) was displayed alone in a shrine and therefore seems to have been a god rather than a mortal. The statuette's blackened state is the result of fire. The scattered fragments the archaeologists retrieved suggest an act of vandalism in the 15th century BCE.

**MINOAN DECLINE** Scholars dispute the circumstances ending the Minoan civilization, although they now widely believe that Mycenaeans had already moved onto Crete and established themselves at Knossos at the end of the New Palace period. From the palace at Knossos, these intruders appear to have ruled the is-

land for at least half a century, perhaps much longer. Parts of the palace continued to be occupied until its final destruction around 1200 BCE, but its importance as a cultural center faded soon after 1400 BCE, as the focus of Aegean civilization shifted to the Greek mainland.

## MYCENAEAN ART

**HOMER'S MYCENAEANS** The origins of the Mycenaean culture are still debated. The only certainty is the presence of these forerunners of the Greeks on the mainland about the time the old palaces were built on Crete—that is, about the beginning of the second millennium BCE. Doubtless Cretan civilization influenced these people even then, and some believe that the mainland was a Minoan economic dependency for a long time. In any case, Mycenaean power developed on the mainland in the days of the new palaces on Crete, and by 1500 BCE a distinctive Mycenaean culture was flourishing in Greece. Several centuries later, Homer described Mycenae as "rich in gold." The dramatic discoveries of Schliemann and his successors have fully justified this characterization, even if today's archaeologists no longer view the Mycenaeans solely through the heroic eyes of Homer.

### Architecture

**CITADELS GIANTS BUILT** The destruction of the Cretan palaces left the mainland culture supreme. Although this Late Helladic civilization has come to be called Mycenaean, Mycenae was but one of several large citadels. Archaeologists have also unearthed Mycenaean remains at Tiryns, Orchomenos, Pylos, and elsewhere, and Mycenaean fortification walls have even been found on the Acropolis of Athens. The best-preserved and most impressive Mycenaean remains are those of the fortified palaces at Tiryns and Mycenae. Both were built beginning about 1400 BCE and burned (along with all the others) between 1250 and 1200 BCE, when the Mycenaeans seem to have been overrun by northern invaders or to have fallen victim to internal warfare.

Homer knew the citadel of Tiryns (FIG. 4-16), located about 10 miles from Mycenae, as Tiryns of the Great Walls. In the second century CE, when Pausanias, author of an invaluable guidebook to Greece, visited the site, he marveled at the towering fortifications and considered the walls of Tiryns as spectacular as the pyramids of Egypt. Indeed, the Greeks of the historical age believed mere humans could not have erected such edifices and instead attributed the construction of the great Mycenaean citadels to the mythical *Cyclopes,* a race of one-eyed giants. Historians still refer to the huge, roughly cut stone blocks forming the massive fortification walls of Tiryns and other Mycenaean sites as *Cyclopean masonry.*

The heavy walls of Tiryns and other Mycenaean palaces contrast sharply with the open Cretan palaces (FIG. 4-3) and clearly reveal their defensive character. Those of Tiryns average about 20 feet in thickness, and in one section they house a long gallery (FIG. 4-17) covered by a *corbeled vault* (FIG. 4-18*b*). Here the builders piled the large, irregular Cyclopean blocks in horizontal courses and then cantilevered them inward until the two walls met in a pointed arch. No mortar was used, and the vault is held in place only by the weight of the blocks (often several tons each), by the smaller stones used as wedges, and by the clay that fills some of the empty spaces. This primitive but effective vaulting

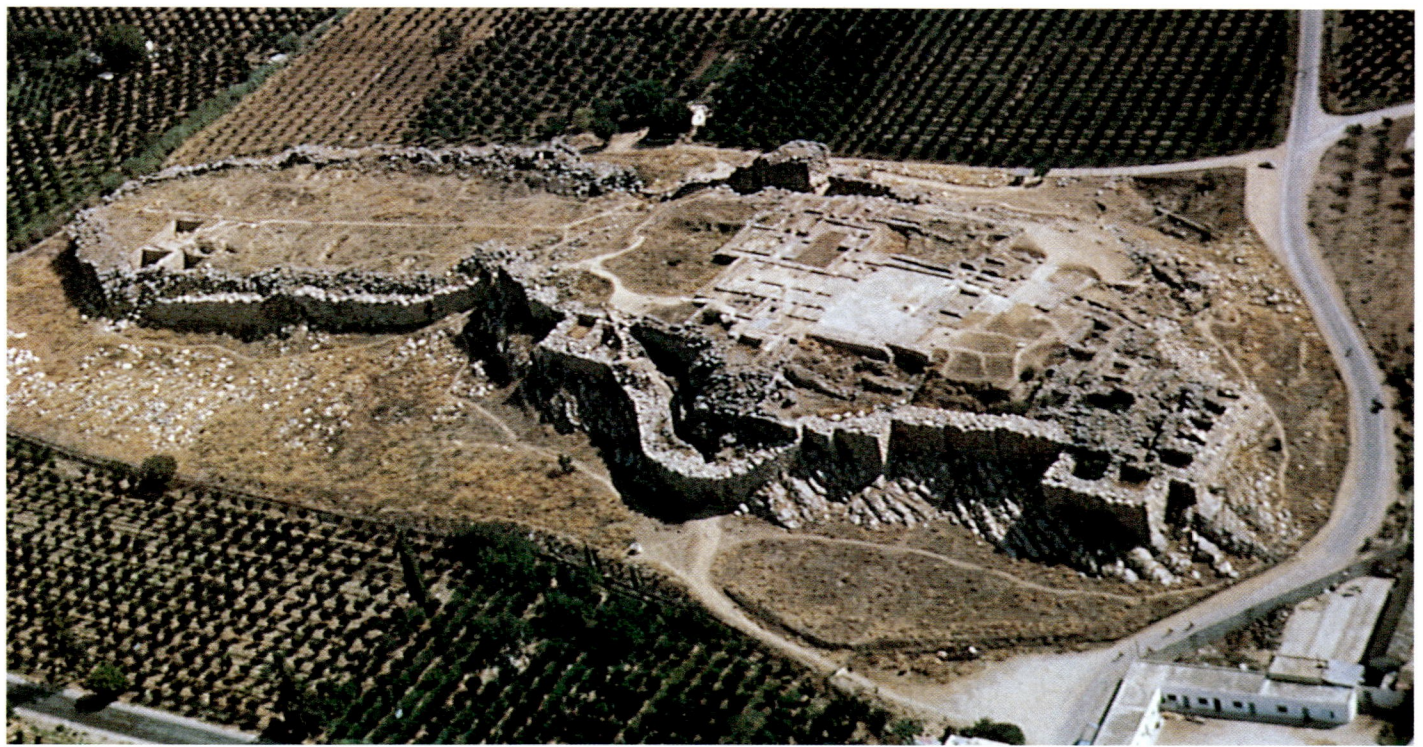

**4-16** Aerial view of the citadel at Tiryns, Greece, ca. 1400–1200 BCE.

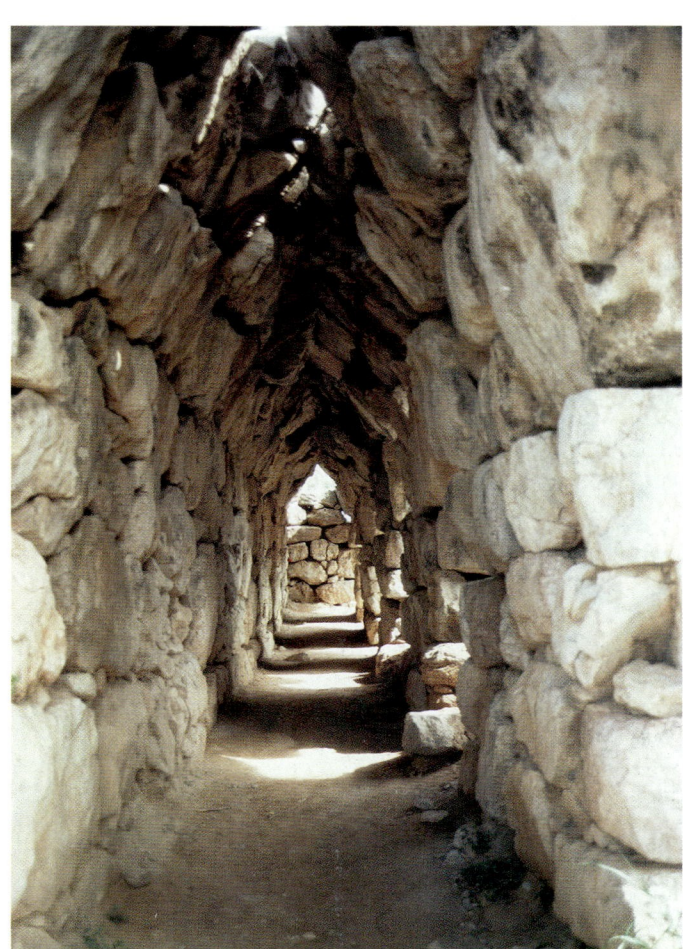

**4-17** Corbeled gallery in the walls of the citadel, Tiryns, Greece, ca. 1400–1200 BCE.

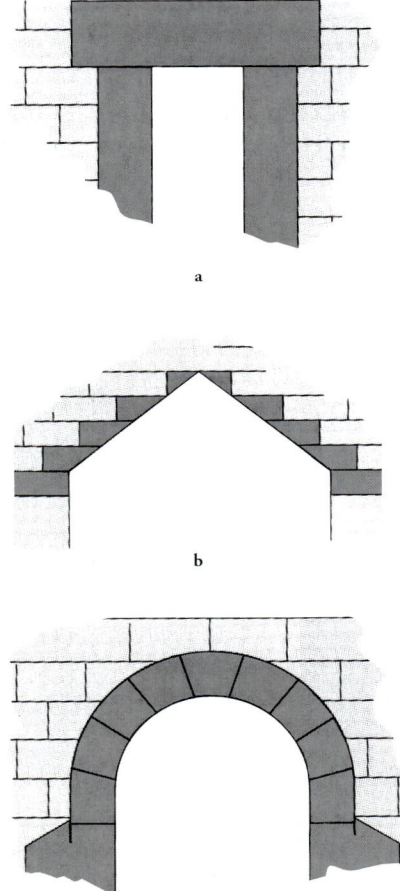

**4-18** Three methods of spanning a passageway: *(a)* post and lintel, *(b)* corbeled arch, *(c)* arch.

scheme possesses an earthy monumentality. It is easy to see how a later age came to believe that the uncouth Cyclopes were responsible for these massive but unsophisticated fortifications.

**THE KING'S HALL** Would-be attackers at Tiryns were compelled to approach the palace (FIG. **4-19**) within the walls via a long ramp that forced the (usually right-handed) soldiers to expose their unshielded sides to the Mycenaean defenders above. Then—if they got that far—they had to pass through a series of narrow gates that also could be defended easily. Inside, at Tiryns as elsewhere, the most important element in the palace plan was the *megaron,* or reception hall, of the king. The main room of the megaron had a throne against the right wall and a central hearth bordered by four Minoan-style wooden columns serving as supports for the roof. A vestibule with a columnar facade preceded the throne room. A variation of this plan later formed the core of some of the earliest Greek temple plans (see FIG. 5-5). This fact suggests some architectural continuity during the so-called Dark Ages that followed the collapse of Mycenaean civilization.

**MYCENAE'S LION GATE** The severity of these fortress-palaces was relieved by frescoes, as in the Cretan palaces, and, at Agamemnon's Mycenae at least, by monumental architectural sculpture. The Lion Gate (FIG. **4-20**) is the outer gateway of the stronghold at Mycenae. It is protected on the left by a wall built on a natural rock outcropping and on the right by a projecting bastion of large blocks. Any approaching enemies would have had to enter this 20-foot-wide channel and face Mycenaean defenders above them on both sides. The gate itself is formed of two great monoliths capped with a huge lintel (FIG. 4-18*a*). Above the lintel, the masonry courses form a *corbeled arch* (FIG. 4-18*b*), leaving an opening that lightens the weight the lintel carries. This *relieving triangle* is filled with a great limestone slab where two lions carved in high relief stand on the sides of a Minoan-type column. The whole design admirably fills its triangular space, harmonizing in dignity, strength, and scale with the massive stones that form the walls and gate. Similar groups appear in miniature on Cretan

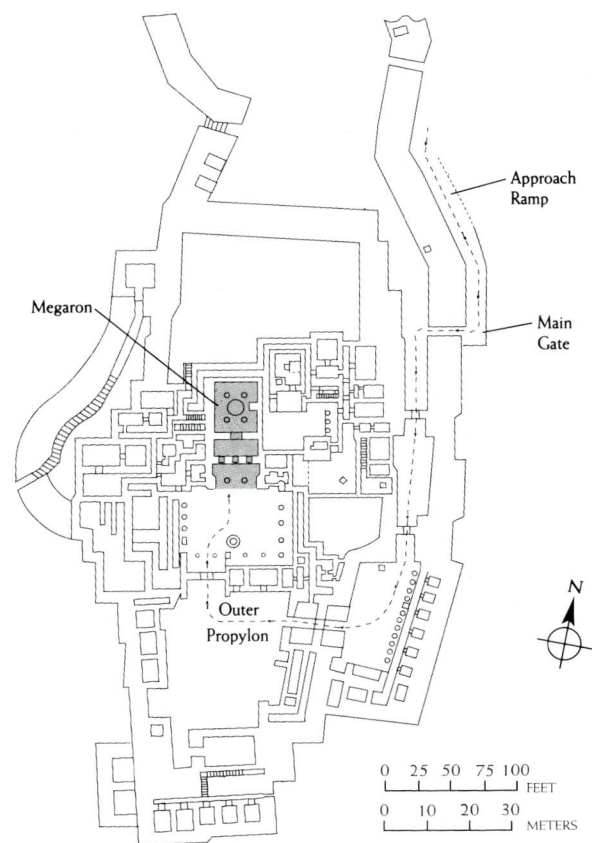

**4-19** Plan of the palace and southern part of the citadel, Tiryns, Greece, ca. 1400–1200 BCE.

seals, but the idea of placing monstrous guardian figures at the entrances to palaces, tombs, and sacred places has its origin in Egypt and the Near East (compare, for example, the Great Sphinx of Gizeh, FIG. 3-11, and the later lion and lamassu gates of Assyria, FIGS. 2-18 and 2-21). At Mycenae the animals' heads were

**4-20** Lion Gate, Mycenae, Greece, ca. 1300–1250 BCE. Limestone, relief panel approx. 9′ 6″ high.

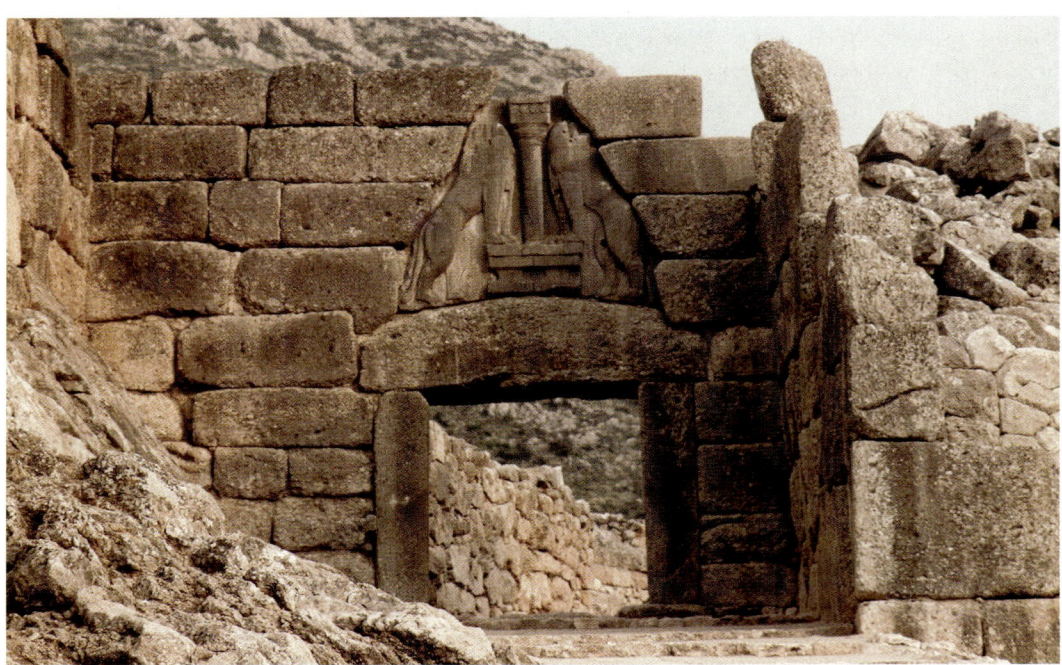

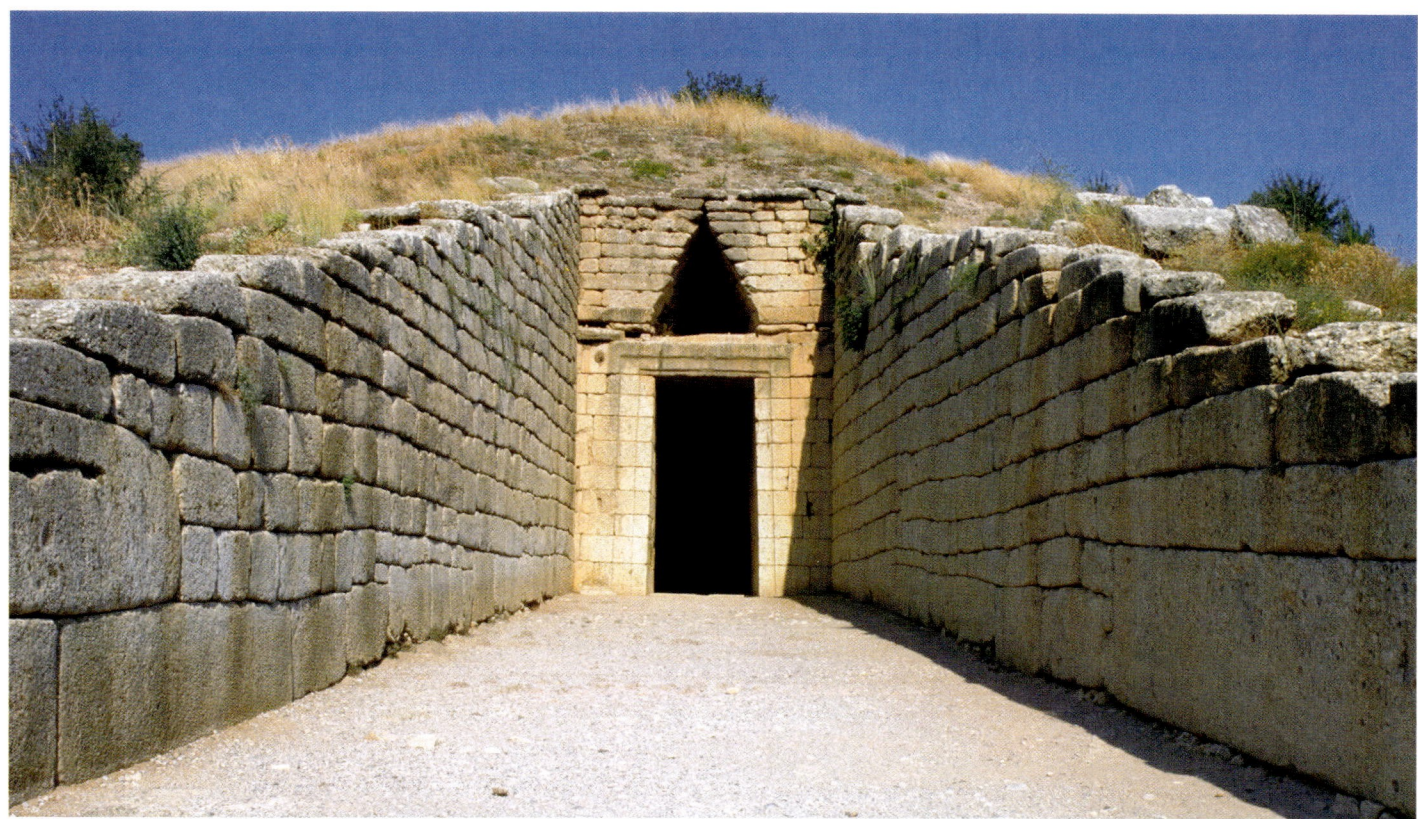

4-21 Treasury of Atreus, Mycenae, Greece, ca. 1300–1250 BCE.

fashioned separately and are lost. Some scholars have suggested that the "lions" were actually composite beasts in the Eastern tradition, possibly sphinxes.

**BEEHIVE TOMBS** The Lion Gate at Mycenae and the towering fortification wall circuit of which it formed a part were constructed a few generations before the presumed date of the Trojan War. At that time, wealthy Mycenaeans were laid to rest outside the citadel walls in beehive-shaped tombs covered by enormous earthen mounds. The best preserved of these *tholos tombs* is the so-called Treasury of Atreus (FIG. **4-21**), which already in antiquity was mistakenly believed to be the repository of the treasure of Atreus, father of Agamemnon and Menelaus. Approached by a long passageway *(dromos)*, the tomb chamber was entered through a doorway surmounted by a relieving triangle similar to that employed in the roughly contemporary Lion Gate. The tholos (FIG. **4-22**) is composed of a series of stone corbeled courses laid on a circular base and ending in a lofty dome. The builders probably constructed the vault using rough-hewn blocks. After they set the stones in place, the masons had to finish the surfaces with great precision to make them conform to both the horizontal and vertical curves of the wall. The principle involved is no different from that of the corbeled gallery of Tiryns (FIG. 4-17). But the problem of constructing a complete dome is much more complicated, and the execution of the vault in the Treasury of Atreus is much more sophisticated than that of the vaulted gallery at Tiryns. About 43 feet high, this is the largest known vaulted space without interior supports that had ever been built. The achievement was not surpassed until the Romans constructed the Pantheon (see FIG. 10-50) almost 1,500 years later using a new technology—concrete construction—unknown to the Mycenaeans.

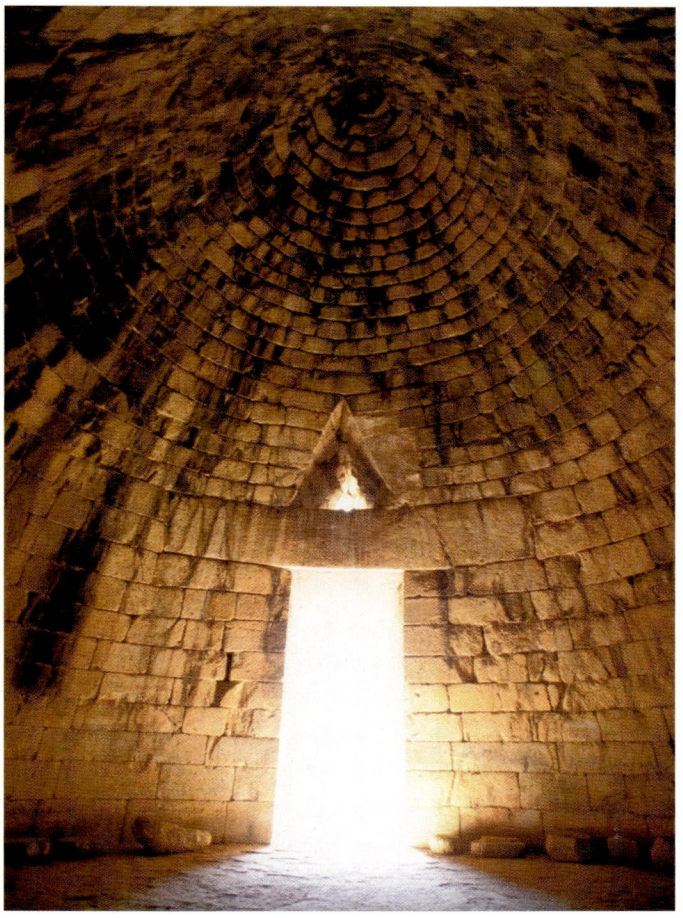

4-22 Vault of the tholos of the Treasury of Atreus, Mycenae, Greece, ca. 1300–1250 BCE. Approx. 43′ high.

## Metalwork, Sculpture, and Painting

**TREASURES OF REVERED KINGS** The Treasury of Atreus had been thoroughly looted long before its modern rediscovery, but excavators have found spectacular grave goods elsewhere at Mycenae. Just inside the Lion Gate, Schliemann uncovered what archaeologists now designate as Grave Circle A. It predates the Lion Gate and the walls of Mycenae by some three centuries. Grave Circle A encloses six deep shafts that had served as tombs for kings and their families. The Mycenaeans laid their dead to rest on the floors of these shaft graves with masks covering their faces, recalling the Egyptian funerary practice. They buried women with their jewelry and men with their weapons and golden cups.

Among the most spectacular of Schliemann's finds is a beaten (repoussé) gold mask (FIG. **4-23**), one of several from the royal burial complex. It often has been compared to the fabulous gold mummy mask of Tutankhamen (see FIG. 3-37). The treatment of the human face is, of course, more primitive in the Mycenaean mask. But this was one of the first known attempts in Greece to render the human face at life-size, whereas Tutankhamen's mask stands in a long line of monumental Egyptian sculptures going back more than a millennium. It is not known whether the Mycenaean masks were intended as portraits, but the goldsmiths recorded different physical types with care. They portrayed youthful faces as well as mature ones. Our example, with its full beard, must depict a mature man, perhaps a king—although not Agamemnon, as Schliemann wished. If Agamemnon was a real king, he lived some 300 years after this mask was fashioned. Clearly the Mycenaeans were "rich in gold" long before Homer's heroes fought at Troy.

Also found in Grave Circle A were several magnificent bronze dagger blades inlaid with gold, silver, and niello (a black metallic alloy), again attesting to the wealth of the Mycenaean kings, as well as to their warlike nature. The largest and most elaborate of the group (FIG. **4-24**) is decorated on one side with a scene of four hunters attacking a lion that has struck down a fifth hunter, while two other lions flee. The other side shows lions attacking deer. The slim-waisted, long-haired figures are Minoan in style, but the artist borrowed the subject from the repertoire of the ancient Near East. It is likely that a Minoan metalworker made the dagger for a Mycenaean patron who admired Minoan art but had different tastes in subject matter than his Cretan counterparts.

**MONUMENTAL SCULPTURE** Large-scale figural art is very rare on the Greek mainland, as on Crete, other than the Minoan-style paintings that once adorned the walls of Mycenaean palaces.

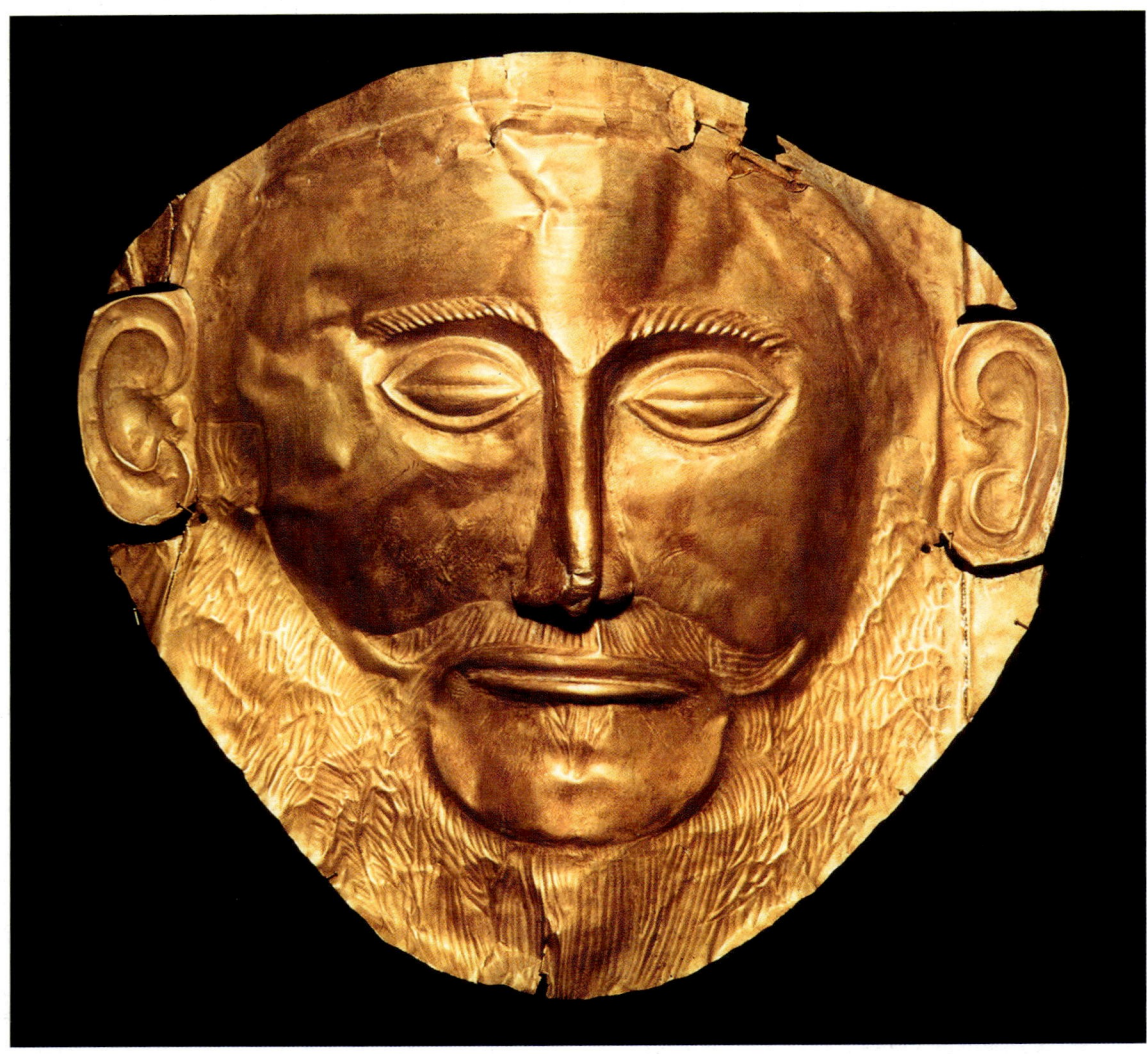

**4-23** Funerary mask, from Grave Circle A, Mycenae, Greece, ca. 1600–1500 BCE. Beaten gold, approx. 1′ high. National Archaeological Museum, Athens.

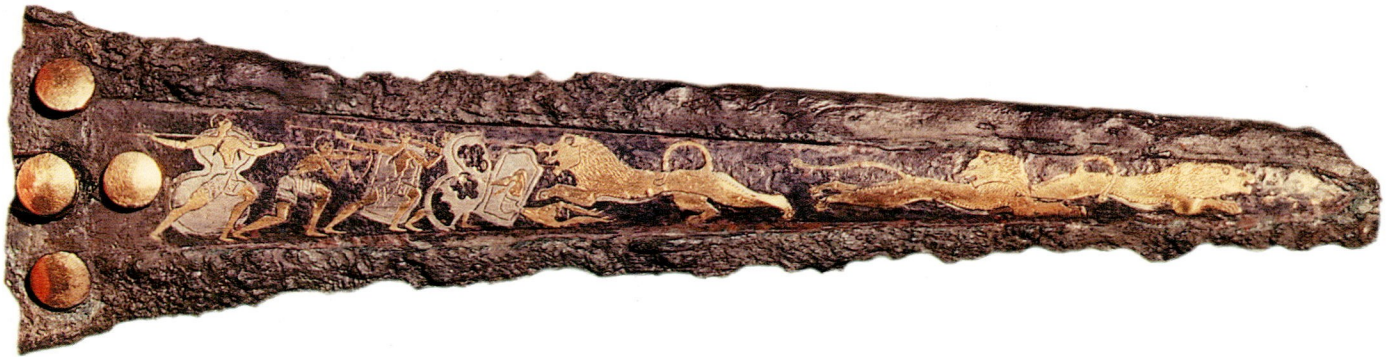

**4-24** Inlaid dagger blade with lion hunt, from Grave Circle A, Mycenae, Greece, ca. 1600–1500 BCE. Bronze, inlaid with gold, silver, and niello, approx. 9″ long. National Archaeological Museum, Athens.

The triangular relief of the Lion Gate at Mycenae is exceptional, as is the painted plaster head (FIG. **4-25**) of a woman, goddess, or, perhaps, sphinx found at Mycenae. The white flesh tone indicates that the head is female. The hair and eyes are dark blue, almost black, and the lips, ears, and headband are red. The artist decorated the cheeks and chin with red circles surrounded by a ring of red dots, recalling the facial paint or tattoos recorded on Early Cycladic figurines of women. Although the large star-ing eyes give the face a menacing, if not terrifying, expression appropriate for a guardian figure such as a sphinx, the closest parallels to this work are terracotta images of goddesses from Mycenaean shrines. This head may therefore be a very early example of a monumental cult statue in Greece.

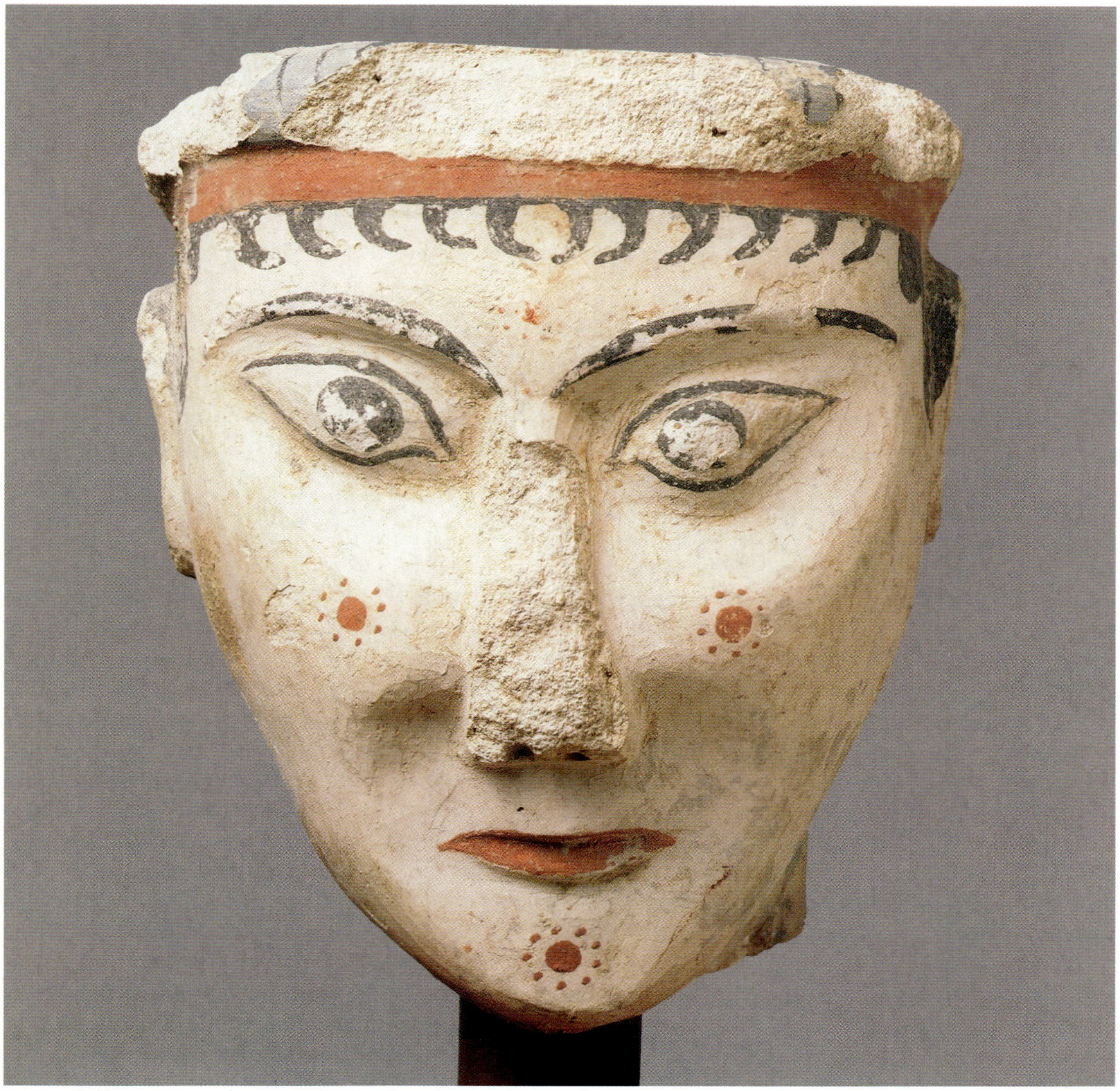

**4-25** Female head, from Mycenae, Greece, ca. 1300–1250 BCE. Painted plaster, approx. $6\frac{1}{2}$″ high. National Archaeological Museum, Athens.

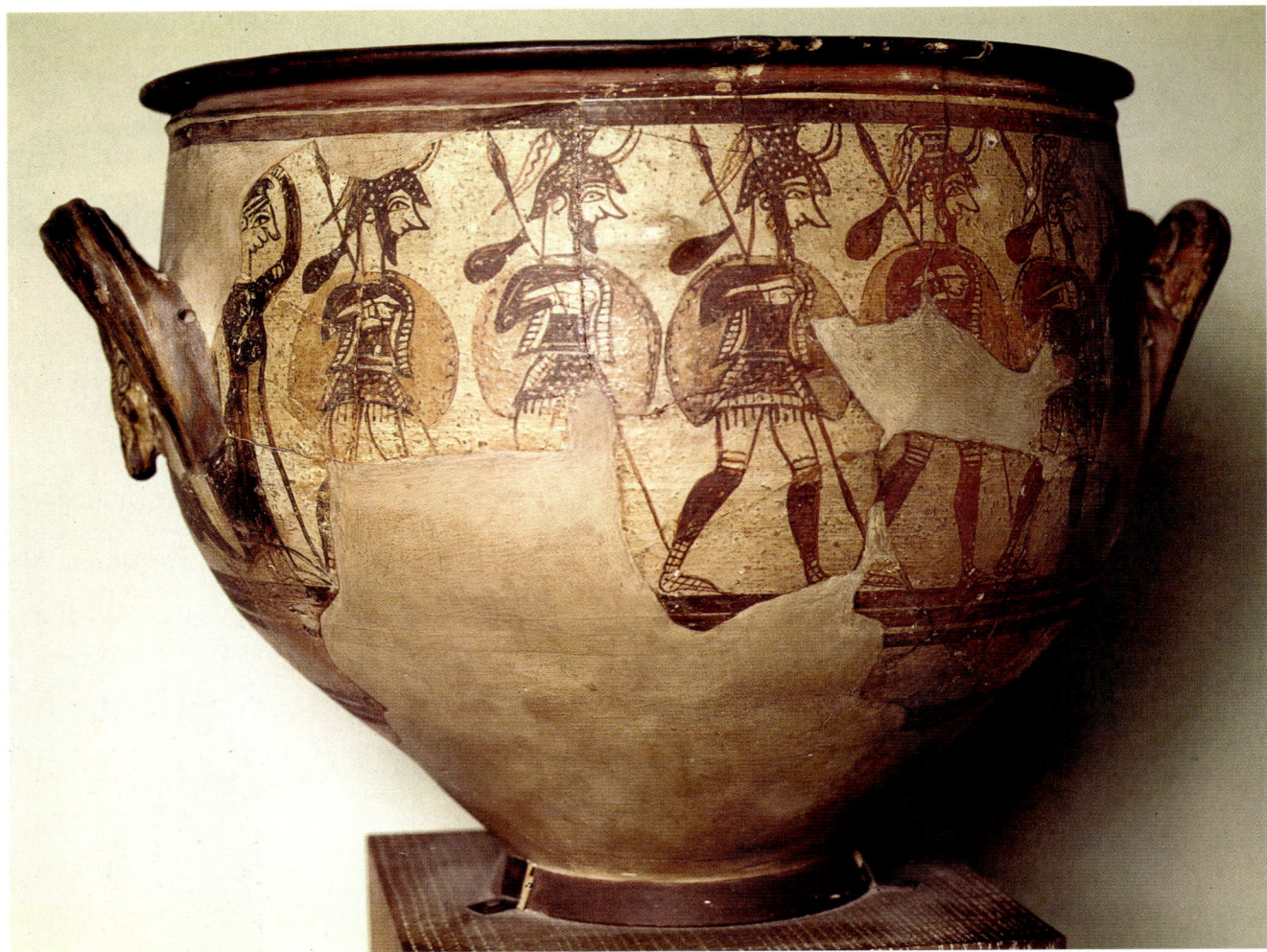

**4-26** *Warrior Vase,* from Mycenae, Greece, ca. 1200 BCE. Approx. 1′ 4″ high. National Archaeological Museum, Athens.

Were it not for this plaster head and a few other exceptional pieces, art historians might have concluded, wrongly, that the Mycenaeans had no monumental freestanding statuary—a reminder that it is always dangerous to generalize from the fragmentary remains of an ancient civilization. Nonetheless, life-size Aegean statuary must have been rare. After the collapse of Mycenaean civilization and for the next several hundred years, no attempts at monumental statuary are evident until, after the waning of the Dark Ages, Greek sculptors were exposed to the great sculptural tradition of Egypt.

**WARRIORS MARCH TO BATTLE** An art form that did continue throughout the period after the downfall of the Mycenaean palaces was vase painting. One of the latest examples of Bronze Age painting is the *krater* (bowl for mixing wine and water) from Mycenae commonly called the *Warrior Vase* (FIG. **4-26**) after its prominent frieze of soldiers marching off to war. At the left a woman bids farewell to the column of heavily armed warriors moving away from her. The painting on this vase has no indication of setting and lacks the landscape elements that characterized earlier Minoan and Mycenaean art. All the soldiers also repeat the same pattern, a far cry from the variety and anecdotal detail of the lively procession of the Minoan *Harvester Vase* (FIG. 4-13).

This simplification of narrative is paralleled in other painted vases by the increasingly schematic and abstract treatment of marine life. The octopus, for example, eventually became a stylized motif composed of concentric circles and spirals that are almost unrecognizable as a sea creature. By the end of the so-called Sub-Mycenaean period, three centuries after the fall of Mycenae, the art of figure painting had been forgotten.

## CONCLUSION

In Homer's time (eighth century BCE), the heyday of Aegean civilization was but a distant memory. The men and women of Crete and Mycenae—Minos and Ariadne, Agamemnon and Helen—had assumed the stature of heroes from a lost golden age. Since the late 19th century, however, archaeologists have been uncovering the remains of that heroic era. The ruins of Cretan palaces, with their open access and mural paintings of palace life and nature itself, attest to the prosperity—and security—of the Minoans. The citadels of Mycenae and Tiryns, with their fortified "Cyclopean" walls, paint a very different picture of Mycenaean society—constantly at war, whether against Troy, northern invaders, or each other. With the destruction of the Mycenaean palaces around 1200 BCE, Greece was plunged into a "Dark Age," when the arts of painting, carving, building, and even writing almost disappeared. The historical Greeks looked back on the achievements of their Minoan and Mycenaean predecessors with awe, but in time they would surpass them and put their stamp on Western civilization and Western art forever.

| CYCLADES | CRETE | MAINLAND GREECE | | |
|---|---|---|---|---|
| Early Cycladic | Early Minoan | Early Helladic | 3000 BCE | |
| | | | | |
| | | | 2000 BCE | |
| Middle Cycladic | Middle Minoan | Middle Helladic | | Old Palace period on Crete, ca. 2000–1700 BCE |
| | | | 1700 BCE | 1 Cycladic lyre player, Keros, ca. 2700–2500 BCE |
| | | | | Linear A script developed, ca. 1700–1600 BCE |
| | | | | New Palace period on Crete, ca. 1700–1400 BCE |
| | | | | |
| | | | 1600 BCE | |
| | | | | Theran eruption, ca. 1628 BCE |
| Late Cycladic | Late Minoan | Late Helladic (Mycenaean) | 1500 BCE | 2 Gold funerary mask, Mycenae, ca. 1600–1500 BCE |
| | | | | Mycenaeans at Knossos, ca. 1450–1400 BCE |
| | | | | |
| | | | 1400 BCE | |
| | | | | Linear B script developed, ca. 1400–1300 BCE |
| | | | | Post-palatial period on Crete, ca. 1400–1200 BCE |
| | | | | 3 Bull-leaping fresco, Knossos, ca. 1450–1400 BCE |
| | | | 1300 BCE | |
| | | | | |
| | | | 1200 BCE | |
| | Sub-Minoan | Sub-Mycenaean | | Destruction of Mycenaean palaces, ca. 1200 BCE |
| | | | | 4 Citadel, Tiryns, ca. 1400–1200 BCE |

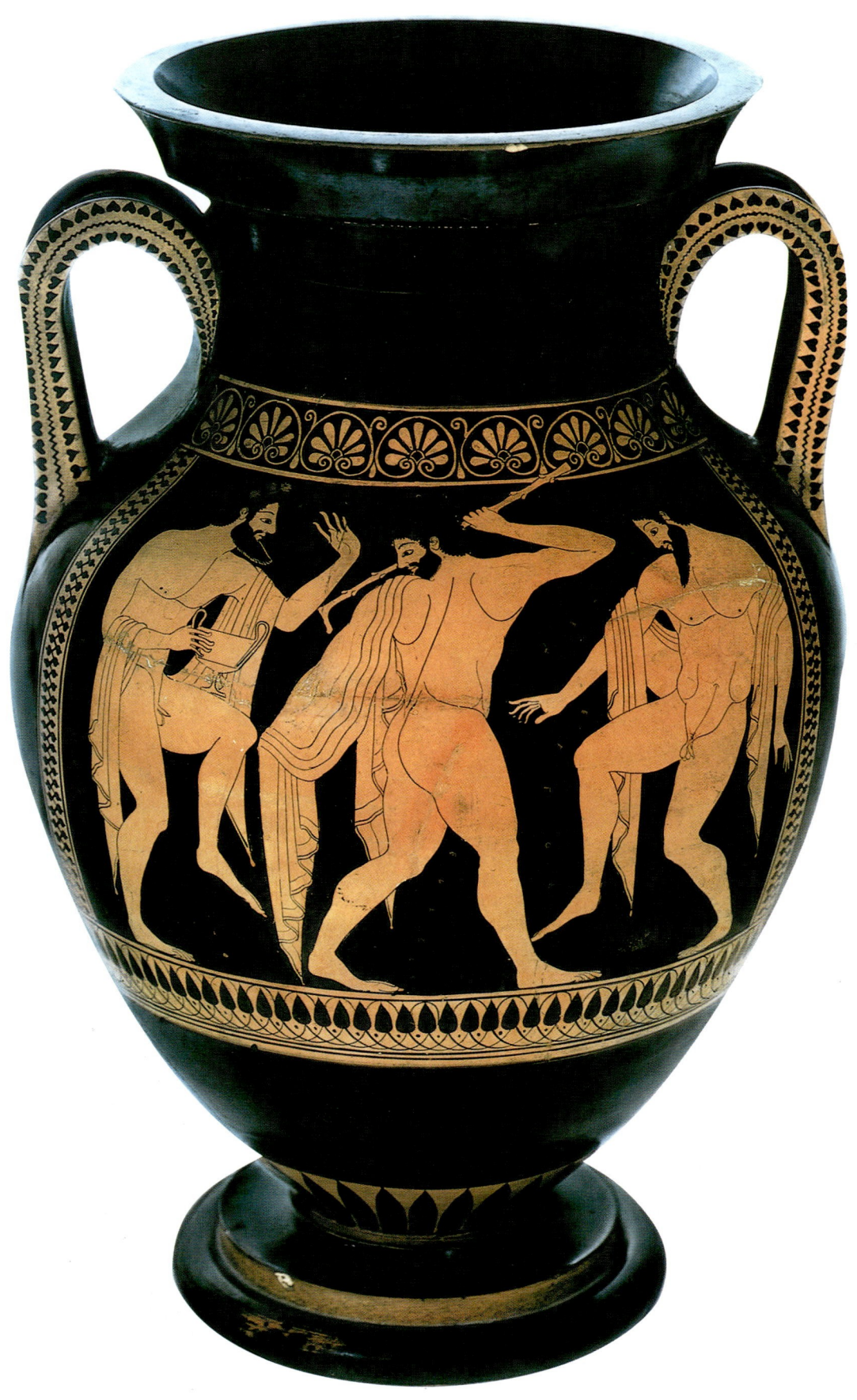

EUTHYMIDES, Three revelers (Attic red-figure amphora), from Vulci, Italy, ca. 510 BCE. Approx. 2′ high. Staatliche Antiken-sammlungen, Munich.

# 5

# GODS, HEROES, AND ATHLETES

## THE ART OF ANCIENT GREECE

"For we are lovers of the beautiful, yet simple in our tastes, and we cultivate the mind without loss of manliness. . . . [We are] the school of Hellas."[1] In the fifth century BCE, the golden age of Athens, the historian Thucydides quoted Pericles, the leader of the Athenians, making this assertion in praise of his fellow citizens. Pericles was comparing the Athenians' open, democratic society with the closed barracks state of their rivals, the Spartans. But Pericles might have been speaking in general of Greek culture and its ideal of humanistic education and life.

## GREEK HUMANISM

For the Greeks, humanity was what mattered, and humans were, in the words of the philosopher Protagoras, the "measure of all things." This humanistic worldview led the Greeks to create the concept of democracy (rule by the *demos,* the people) and to make seminal contributions in the fields of art, literature, and science. The Greek exaltation of humanity and honoring of the individual are so completely part of modern Western habits of mind that most people are scarcely aware that these ideas originated in the minds of the Greeks.

GODS AND HUMANS  Even the gods of the Greeks (see "The Gods and Goddesses of Mount Olympus," page 107), in marked contrast to the divinities of the Near East, assumed human forms whose grandeur and nobility were not free from human frailty. Indeed, unlike the Egyptian and Mesopotamian gods, the Greek deities differed from human beings only in that they were immortal. It has been said that the Greeks made their gods into humans and their humans into gods. Humans, becoming the measure of all things, in turn must represent, if all things in their perfection are beautiful, the unchanging standard of the best. The perfect individual became the Greek ideal.

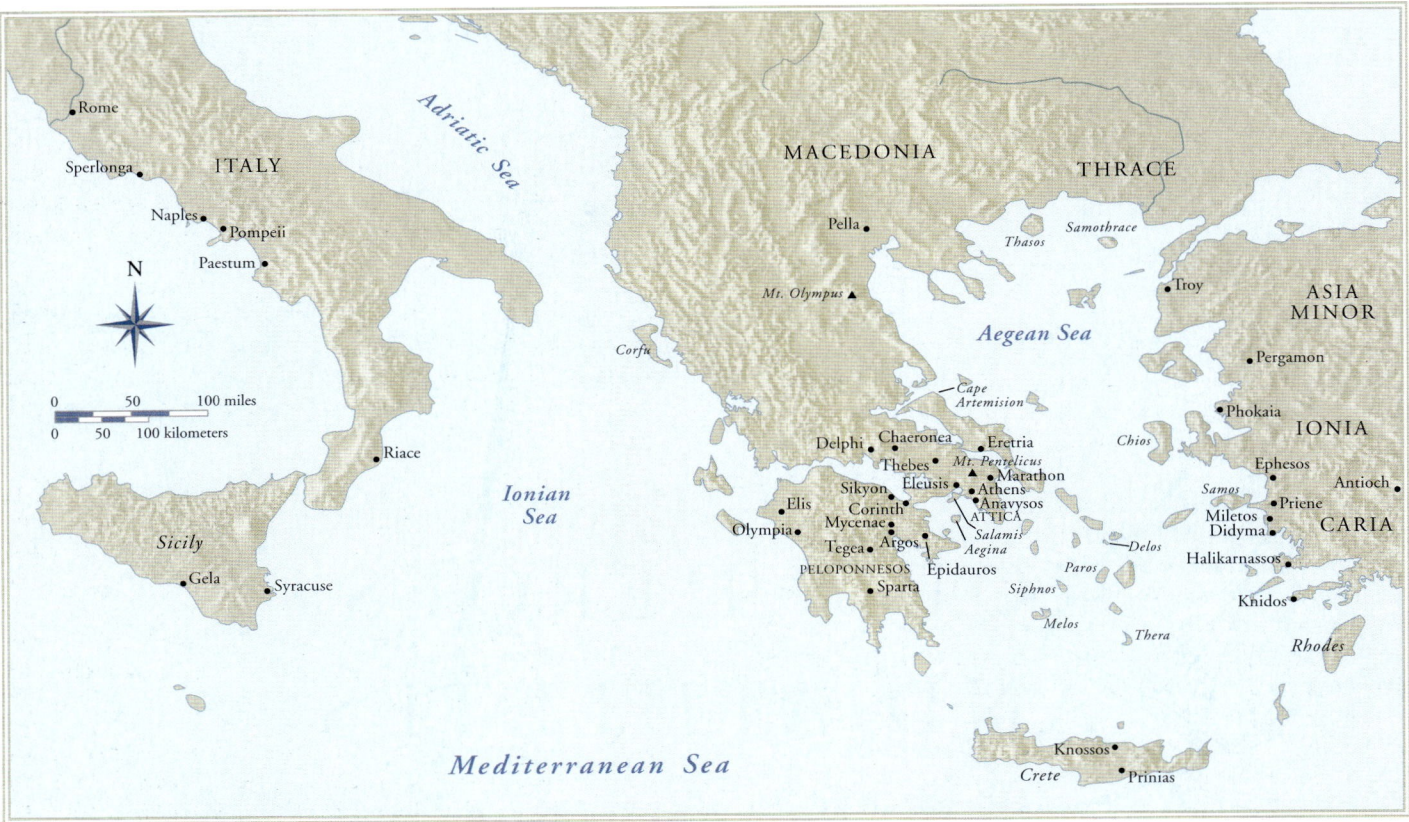

MAP 5-1 The Greek world.

**GREEK ORIGINS** The Greeks, or *Hellenes,* as they called themselves, appear to have been the product of an intermingling of Aegean peoples and Indo-European invaders. They never formed a single nation but instead established independent city-states or *poleis* (singular, *polis*). The Dorians of the north, who many believe brought an end to Mycenaean civilization, settled in the Peloponnesos (MAP 5-1). Across the Aegean, the Ionians settled the western coast of Asia Minor (modern Turkey). The origin of the Ionians is disputed. Some say the northern invaders forced the Ionians out of Greece and that they then sailed from Athens to Asia Minor. Others hold that the Ionians developed in Asia Minor itself between the 11th and 8th centuries BCE out of a mixed stock of settlers. Whatever the origins of the various regional populations, political development differed from polis to polis, although a pattern emerged. Rule was first by kings, then by nobles, and then by tyrants who seized personal power. At last, in Athens, 2,500 years ago, the tyrants were overthrown, and democracy was established.

**OLYMPIA AND HELLAS** In 776 BCE, the separate Greek-speaking states held their first ceremonial games in common at Olympia. The later Greeks calculated their chronology from these first Olympic Games—the first *Olympiad.* From then on, despite their differences and rivalries, the Greeks regarded themselves as citizens of *Hellas,* distinct from the surrounding "barbarians" who did not speak Greek. The enterprising Hellenes, greatly aided by their indented coasts and stepping-stone islands, became a trading and colonizing people who enlarged the geographic and cultural boundaries of Hellas. In fact, today the best preserved of all the grand temples the Greeks erected are found not in Greece proper but in their western colonies in Italy.

**ATHENS AND GREEK CULTURE** Nonetheless, Athens, the capital of Greece today, has justifiably become the symbol of ancient Greek culture. Many of the finest products of Greek civilization were created there. Athens is where the great plays of Aeschylus, Sophocles, and Euripides were first performed. And there, in the city's marketplace (*agora*), covered colonnades (*stoas*), and gymnasiums (*palaestras*), Socrates engaged his fellow citizens in philosophical argument, and Plato formulated his prescription for the ideal form of government in the *Republic.* Complementing the rich intellectual life of ancient Athens was a strong interest in physical exercise, which played a large role in education, as well as in daily life. The Athenian aim of achieving a balance of intellectual and physical discipline, an ideal of humanistic education, is well expressed in the familiar phrase "a sound mind in a sound body."

The distinctiveness and originality of Greek contributions to art, science, and politics should not, however, obscure the enormous debt Greek civilization owed to the earlier great cultures of Egypt and the Near East. Scholars today increasingly recognize this debt, and the ancient Greeks themselves readily acknowledged borrowing ideas, motifs, conventions, and skills from these older civilizations.

**REASSESSING GREEK CIVILIZATION** Nor should a high estimation of Greek art and culture blind historians to the realities of Hellenic life and society. The uncritical admiration in the 18th and 19th centuries of anything Greek has undergone sharp revision in our time. Many modern artists have rejected Greek standards (the late-19th-century French painter Paul Gauguin called Greek art "a lie"). Even Athenian "democracy" was a political reality for only one segment of the demos. Slavery was regarded as

## The Gods and Goddesses of Mount Olympus

The names of scores of Greek gods and goddesses were recorded as early as the eighth century BCE in Homer's epic tales of the war against Troy (*Iliad*) and of the adventures of the Greek hero Odysseus on his long and tortuous journey home (*Odyssey*). Even more are enumerated in the poems of Hesiod, especially his *Theogony (Genealogy of the Gods)* composed around 700 BCE.

The Greek deities most often represented in art are all ultimately the offspring of the two key elements of the Greek universe, Earth (*Gaia/Ge;* we give the names in Greek/Latin form) and Heaven (*Ouranos/Uranus*). Earth and Heaven mated to produce 12 Titans, including Ocean (*Okeanos/Oceanus*) and his youngest brother *Kronos (Saturn)*. Kronos castrated his father in order to rule in his place, married his sister *Rhea*, and then swallowed all his children as they were born, lest one of them seek in turn to usurp him (see FIG. 28-44). When *Zeus (Jupiter)* was born, Rhea deceived Kronos by feeding him a stone wrapped in clothes in place of the infant. After growing to manhood, Zeus forced Kronos to vomit up Zeus's siblings. Together they overthrew their father and the other Titans and ruled the world from their home on Mount Olympus, Greece's highest peak.

This cruel and bloody tale of the origin of the Greek gods has parallels in Near Eastern mythology and is clearly pre-Greek in origin, one of many Greek borrowings from the East. The Greek version of the creation myth, however, appears infrequently in painting and sculpture. Instead, the later 12 Olympian gods and goddesses, the chief deities of Greece, figure most prominently in art—not only in Greek, Etruscan, and Roman times but also in the Middle Ages, the Renaissance, and up to the present.

### THE OLYMPIAN GODS (AND THEIR ROMAN EQUIVALENTS)

**ZEUS (JUPITER)** King of the gods, Zeus (see FIGS. 5-36 and 29-43) ruled the sky and allotted the sea to his brother Poseidon and the Underworld to his other brother Hades. His weapon was the thunderbolt, and with it he led the other gods to victory over the Giants (FIGS. 5-17 and 5-79), who had challenged the Olympians for control of the world.

**HERA (JUNO)** Wife and sister of Zeus, Hera was the goddess of marriage, and Zeus's many love affairs often angered her. Her favorite cities were Mycenae, Sparta, and Argos, and she aided the Greeks in their war against the Trojans.

**POSEIDON (NEPTUNE)** Poseidon (see FIGS. 10-22 and 23-16) was one of the three sons of Kronos and Rhea and was lord of the sea. He controlled waves, storms, and earthquakes with his three-pronged pitchfork *(trident)*.

**HESTIA (VESTA)** Daughter of Kronos and Rhea and sister of Zeus, Poseidon, and Hera, Hestia was goddess of the hearth. In Rome, Vesta had an ancient shrine with a sacred fire in the Roman Forum. Her six Vestal Virgins were the most important priestesses of the state, drawn only from aristocratic families.

**DEMETER (CERES)** Third sister of Zeus, Demeter was the goddess of grain and agriculture. She taught humans how to sow and plow. The English word *cereal* derives from *Ceres*.

**ARES (MARS)** God of war, Ares was the son of Zeus and Hera and the lover of Aphrodite. In the *Iliad* he took the side of the Trojans. Mars, father of the twin founders of Rome, *Romulus* and *Remus* (see FIG. 9-10), looms much larger in Roman mythology and religion than Ares does in Greece.

**ATHENA (MINERVA)** Goddess of wisdom and warfare, Athena (FIGS. 5-32, 5-44, and 5-79) was a virgin (*parthenos* in Greek), born not from a woman's womb but from the head of her father, Zeus. Her city was Athens, and her greatest temple was the Parthenon (FIG. 5-42).

**HEPHAISTOS (VULCAN)** God of fire and of metalworking, Hephaistos fashioned the armor Achilles wore in battle against Troy. He also provided Zeus his scepter and Poseidon his trident, and was the "surgeon" who split open Zeus's head when Athena was born. In some accounts, Hephaistos is the son of Hera without a male partner. In others, he is the son of Hera and Zeus. He was born lame and, uncharacteristically for a god, ugly. His wife Aphrodite was unfaithful to him.

**APOLLO (APOLLO)** God of light and music, and a great archer, Apollo (see FIGS. 5-3, 5-57, and 24-70) was the son of Zeus with *Leto/Latona,* daughter of one of the Titans. His epithet *Phoibos* means "radiant," and the young, beautiful Apollo is sometimes identified with the sun (*Helios/Sol*).

**ARTEMIS (DIANA)** Sister of Apollo, Artemis (see FIGS. 5-57 and 22-47) was goddess of the hunt and of wild animals. As Apollo's twin, she was occasionally regarded as the moon (*Selene/Luna*).

**APHRODITE (VENUS)** Daughter of Zeus and *Dione* (daughter of Okeanos and one of the *nymph*s—the goddesses of springs, caves, and woods), Aphrodite (FIGS. 5-60 and 5-83) was the goddess of love and beauty. In one version of her myth, she was born from the foam (*aphros* in Greek) of the sea (see FIG. 21-27). She was the mother of Eros by Ares and of the Trojan hero *Aeneas* by *Anchises.* Julius Caesar and Augustus traced their lineage to Venus through Aeneas.

**HERMES (MERCURY)** Son of Zeus and another nymph, Hermes (FIGS. 5-58 and 5-62) was the fleet-footed messenger of the gods and possessed winged sandals. He was also the guide of travelers, including the dead journeying to the Underworld. He carried the *caduceus,* a magical herald's rod, and wore a traveler's hat, often also shown with wings.

Equal in stature to the Olympians was *Hades (Pluto),* one of the children of Kronos who fought with his brothers against the Titans but who never resided on Mount Olympus. Hades was the lord of the Underworld and god of the dead.

Other important Greek gods and goddesses were *Dionysos* (*Bacchus,* see FIGS. 10-15 and 22-37), the god of wine and the son of Zeus and a mortal woman; *Eros (Amor* or *Cupid)* (see FIGS. 5-48, 5-84, 22-43, and 28-5), the winged child god of love and the son of Aphrodite and Ares; and *Asklepios (Aesculapius),* son of Apollo and a mortal woman, the Greek god of healing, whose serpent-entwined staff is the emblem of modern medicine.

natural, even beneficial, and was a universal institution among the Greeks. Aristotle, the eminent philosopher who tutored Alexander the Great, declared at the beginning of his *Politics:* "It is clear that some are free by nature, and others are slaves."[2] And Greek women were in no way the equals of Greek men. Women normally remained secluded in their homes, emerging usually only for weddings, funerals, and religious festivals. They played little part in public or political life. Despite the fame of the poet Sappho, only a handful of female artists' names are known, and none of their works survive. The existence of slavery and the exclusion of women from public life are both reflected in Greek art. On many occasions freeborn men and women appear with their slaves in monumental sculpture. The symposium (attended only by men and prostitutes) is a popular subject on painted vases.

Although the Greeks invented and passed on to future generations the concept and practice of democracy, most Greek states, even those constituted as democracies, were dominated by well-born white males, and the most admired virtues were not wisdom and justice but statecraft and military valor. Greek men were educated in the values of Homer's heroes and in the athletic exercises of the palaestra. War among the city-states was chronic and often atrocious. Fighting among themselves, the Greeks eventually fell victim to Macedon's autocracy and Rome's imperialism.

# THE GEOMETRIC AND ORIENTALIZING PERIODS

**OUT OF THE DARK AGE** Disintegration of the Bronze Age social order accompanied the destruction of the Mycenaean palaces. The disappearance of powerful kings and their retinues led to the loss of the knowledge of how to cut masonry, to construct citadels and tombs, to paint frescoes, and to sculpt in stone. Even the arts of reading and writing were forgotten. Depopulation, poverty, and an almost total loss of contact with the outside world characterized the succeeding centuries, sometimes called the Dark Age of Greece.

Only in the eighth century BCE did economic conditions improve and the population begin to grow again. This era was in its own way a heroic age, a time when the poleis of Classical Greece took shape; when the Greeks broke out of their isolation and once again began to trade with cities both in the east and the west; when Homer's epic poems, formerly memorized and passed down from bard to bard, were recorded in written form; and when the Olympic Games were established.

## *Geometric Art*

**FIGURE PAINTING REVIVED** Also during the eighth century the human figure returned to Greek art — not, of course, in monumental statuary, which was exceedingly rare even in Bronze Age Greece, but painted on the surfaces of ceramic pots, which continued to be manufactured after the fall of Mycenae and even throughout the Dark Age. One of the earliest examples is a huge krater (FIG. **5-1**), or mixing bowl, that marked the grave of an Athenian man buried around 740 BCE. At well over three feet tall, this remarkable vase is a considerable technical achievement and testifies both to the potter's skill and to the wealth and position of the deceased's family in the community. The bottom of the great vessel is open, perhaps to permit visitors to the grave to pour

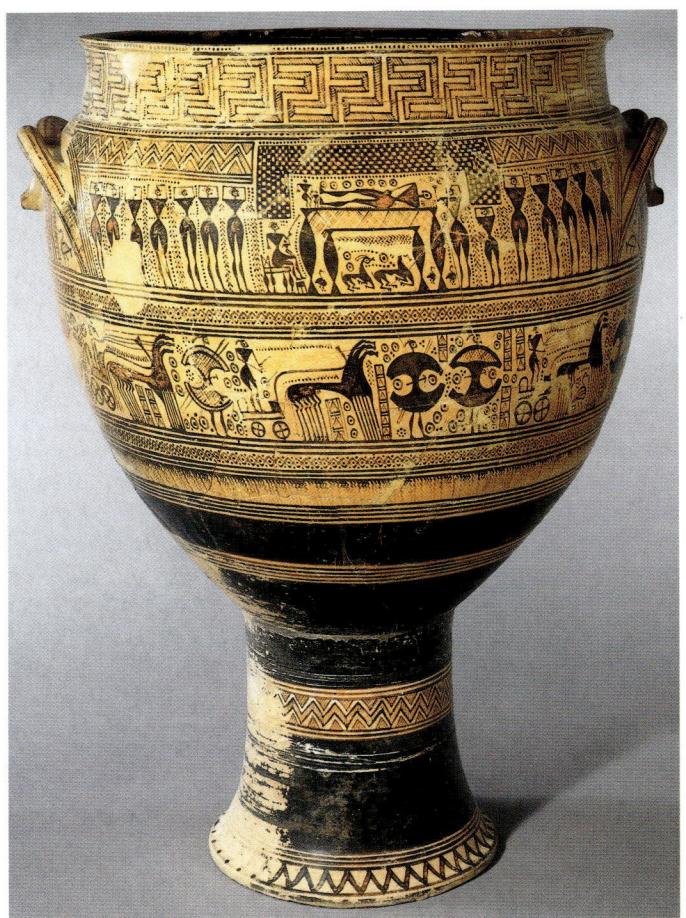

**5-1** Geometric krater, from the Dipylon cemetery, Athens, Greece, ca. 740 BCE. Approx. 3′ 4½″ high. Metropolitan Museum of Art, New York.

libations in honor of the dead, perhaps simply to provide a drain for rainwater, or both. The artist covered much of the surface with precisely painted abstract angular motifs in horizontal bands. Especially prominent is the *meander,* or key, pattern around the rim of the krater. Most early Greek vases were decorated exclusively with abstract motifs. The nature of the ornament has led art historians to designate this formative period of Greek art as *Geometric.* The earliest examples of the Geometric style date to the ninth century BCE.

On our krater, the artist reserved the widest part of the vase for two bands of human figures and horse-drawn chariots, rather than for geometric ornament. Befitting the vase's function as a grave marker, the scenes depict the mourning for a man laid out on his bier and the grand chariot procession in his honor. In the upper band, the shroud, raised to reveal the corpse, is an abstract checkerboard-like backdrop, and the funerary couch has only two legs because the artist had no interest in suggesting depth or representing space. The human figures and the furniture are as two-dimensional as the geometric shapes elsewhere on the vessel. The painter filled every empty surface with circles and M-shaped ornaments, further negating any sense that the mourners inhabit open space. The figures are silhouettes constructed of triangular (frontal) torsos with attached profile arms, legs, and heads (with a single large frontal eye in the center!), following the age-old convention. To distinguish male from female, the painter added a penis growing out of one of the deceased's thighs. The mourning women, who tear their hair out in grief,

### Herakles, Greatest of Greek Heroes

Greek heroes were a class of mortals intermediate between ordinary humans and the immortal gods. Most often the children of gods, some were great warriors, such as those who fought at Troy and were celebrated in Homer's epic poems. Others went from one fabulous adventure to another, ridding the world of monsters and generally benefiting humankind. Many heroes were worshiped after their deaths, and the greatest of them were honored with shrines, especially in the cities most closely associated with them. For example, the bones of Theseus, king of Athens and victor over the Minotaur who inhabited the labyrinthine palace at Knossos (see FIGS. 4-3 to 4-5), were transferred to Athens around 475 BCE from Skyros, where Theseus had been killed, and deposited in his sanctuary near the city center.

The greatest of all the Greek heroes was *Herakles* (the Roman *Hercules*), born in Thebes and the son of Zeus and Alkmene, a mortal woman. Zeus's wife Hera hated Herakles and sent two serpents to attack him in his cradle, but the infant strangled them. Later, Hera caused the hero to go mad and to kill his wife and children. As punishment he was condemned to perform 12 great labors. In the first, he defeated the legendary lion of Nemea and ever after wore its pelt. The lion's skin and his weapon, a club, are Herakles' distinctive attributes (FIGS. 5-63 and 5-66). His last task was to obtain the golden apples Gaia gave to Hera at her marriage (FIG. 5-32). They grew from a tree in the garden of the Hesperides at the farthest western edge of the ocean, and a dragon guarded them. After completion of the 12 seemingly impossible tasks, Herakles was awarded immortality. Athena, who had watched over him carefully throughout his life and assisted him in performing the labors, introduced him into the realm of the gods on Mount Olympus. According to legend, it was Herakles who established the Olympic Games.

---

have breasts emerging beneath their armpits. In both cases the artist was concerned with specifying gender, not with anatomical accuracy. Below are warriors, drawn as though they are walking shields, and several chariots. In the old conceptual manner, both wheels are shown. The horses have the correct number of heads and legs but seem to share a common body, negating any sense of depth. Despite its highly stylized and conventional manner of representation, this vessel marks a significant turning point in the history of Greek art. Not only was the human figure reintroduced into the painter's repertoire, but the art of storytelling also was revived.

**HERO VERSUS MONSTER** Similar schematic figures also appeared in the round at this date, but only at very small scale. One of the most impressive surviving Geometric sculptures is a small solid-cast bronze group (FIG. **5-2**) of a hero, probably Herakles (see "Herakles, Greatest of Greek Heroes," above), battling a *centaur* (a mythological beast that was part man, part horse), possibly Nessos, the centaur who had volunteered to carry the hero's bride across a river and then assaulted her. Whether or not the hero is Herakles and the centaur is Nessos, the mythological nature of the group is certain. The repertoire of the Geometric artist was not limited to scenes inspired by daily life (and death).

Composite monsters were enormously popular in the ancient Near East and Egypt (see Chapters 2 and 3), and renewed contact with foreign cultures may have inspired such figures in Geometric Greece. The centaur is, however, a purely Greek invention—and one that posed a problem for the artist, who had, of course, never seen such a creature. The Geometric centaur was conceived as a man in front and a horse in back, a rather unhappy and unconvincing configuration that results in the forelegs belonging to a different species than the hind legs. In our example, the sculptor rendered the figure of the hero and the human part of the centaur in a similar fashion. Both are bearded and wear helmets, but (contradictory to nature) the man is larger than the horse, probably to suggest that he will be the victor. Like other Geometric male figures, both painted and sculpted, this hero is nude, in contrast to the Near Eastern statuettes that might have inspired such

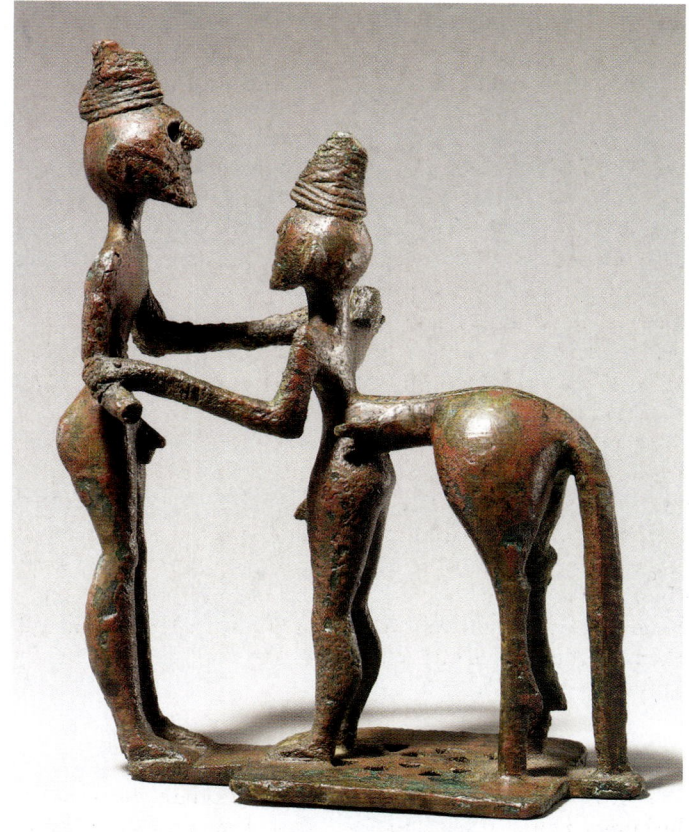

**5-2** Hero and centaur (Herakles and Nessos?), ca. 750–730 BCE. Bronze, approx. $4\frac{1}{2}$″ high. Metropolitan Museum of Art, New York (gift of J. Pierpont).

Greek works. Here, at the very beginning of Greek figural art, one can recognize the Hellenic instinct for the natural beauty of the human figure. In fact, Greek athletes exercised without their clothes and even competed nude in the Olympic Games from very early times.

## Orientalizing Art

**AN OFFERING TO APOLLO** One of the masterworks of the early seventh century BCE is the *Mantiklos Apollo* (FIG. **5-3**), a small bronze statuette dedicated to Apollo at Thebes by an otherwise unknown man named Mantiklos. With characteristic pride in the ability to write, the sculptor (or another) scratched into the thighs of the figure a message from the dedicator to the deity: "Mantiklos dedicated me as a tithe to the far-shooting Lord of the Silver Bow; you, Phoibos [Apollo], might give some pleasing favor in return." Because the Greeks conceived their gods in human form, one cannot be sure whether the figure was meant to represent the youthful Apollo or Mantiklos (or neither). But if the left hand at one time held a bow, then the statuette is certainly an image of the deity. In any case, the purpose of the votive offering is clear. Equally apparent is the increased interest Greek artists at this time had in reproducing details of human anatomy, such as the long hair framing the unnaturally elongated neck, and the pectoral and abdominal muscles, which define the stylized triangular torso. The triangular face has eye sockets that were once inlaid, and the head may have had a separately fashioned helmet on it.

**THE GREEKS LOOK EASTWARD** The *Mantiklos Apollo* was created when the pace and scope of Greek trade and colonization had accelerated and when Greek artists were exposed more than ever before to Eastern artworks, especially small portable objects such as Syrian ivory carvings. The closer contact had a profound effect on the development of Greek art. Indeed, so many motifs borrowed from or inspired by Egyptian and Near Eastern art entered the Greek pictorial vocabulary at this time that historians have dubbed the seventh century BCE the *Orientalizing* period.

An elaborate Corinthian *amphora* (FIG. **5-4**), or two-handled storage jar, typifies the new Greek fascination with the Orient. In a series of bands recalling the organization of Geometric painted vases, animals such as the native boar appear beside exotic lions and panthers and composite creatures inspired by Eastern monsters such as the sphinx and lamassu—in this instance the *siren* (part bird, part woman) prominently displayed on the amphora's neck.

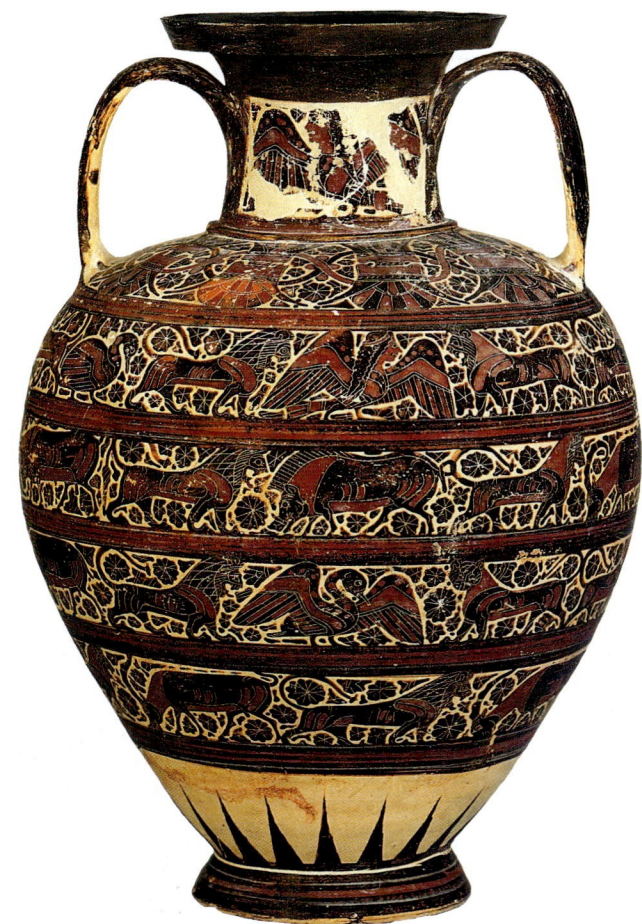

**5-3** *Mantiklos Apollo,* statuette of a youth dedicated by Mantiklos to Apollo, from Thebes, Greece, ca. 700–680 BCE. Bronze, approx. 8″ high. Museum of Fine Arts, Boston.

**5-4** Corinthian black-figure amphora with animal friezes, from Rhodes, Greece, ca. 625–600 BCE. Approx. 1′ 2″ high. British Museum, London.

**BLACK-FIGURE PAINTING** The appeal of such vases was not due solely to their Orientalizing animal friezes but also to a new ceramic technique the Corinthians invented, which art historians call *black-figure painting*. The black-figure painter first put down black silhouettes on the clay surface, as in Geometric times, but then used a sharp pointed instrument to incise linear details within the forms, usually adding highlights in purplish red or white over the black figures before firing the vessel. The combination of the weighty black silhouettes with the delicate detailing and the bright polychrome overlay proved to be irresistible, and Athenian painters soon copied the technique from the Corinthians.

**GREECE'S FIRST STONE TEMPLES** The foundation of the Greek trading colony of Naukratis in Egypt (see MAP 3-1) before 630 BCE brought the Greeks into direct contact with the monumental stone architecture of the Egyptians. Not long after that, the first stone buildings since the fall of the Mycenaean kingdoms began to be constructed in Greece. At Prinias on Crete, for example, a stone temple, called Temple A (FIG. 5-5), was built around 625 BCE to honor an unknown deity. Although the inspiration for the structure came from the East, the form resembles that of a typical Mycenaean megaron, such as that at Tiryns (see FIG. 4-19), with two interior columns flanking a hearth or sacrificial pit. The facade consisted of three great piers; the roof was probably flat.

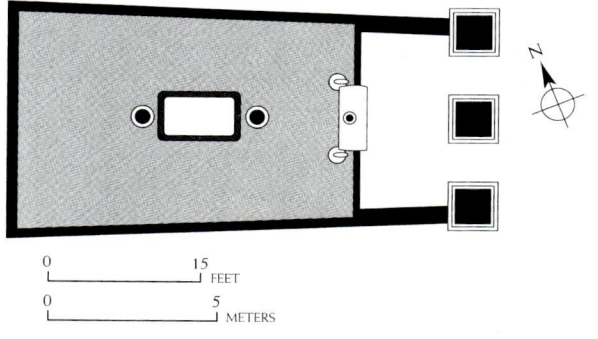

0 ——— 15 FEET
0 ——— 5 METERS

**5-5** Plan of Temple A, Prinias, Greece, ca. 625 BCE.

Above the doorway of the Prinias temple was a huge limestone lintel (FIG. 5-6) supporting confronting statues of seated women, probably goddesses, wearing tall headdresses and capes. Two other similarly dressed, but standing, goddesses are carved in relief on the underside of the block, visible to those entering the temple. On the face of the lintel is a frieze of Orientalizing panthers with frontal heads—the same motif as that on the contemporary Corinthian black-figure amphora (FIG. 5-4). Temple A at Prinias is the earliest known example of a Greek temple with sculptured decoration.

**GODDESS OR WOMAN?** Somewhat earlier and probably also originally from Crete is a limestone statuette of a goddess or maiden (*kore*; plural, *korai*) popularly known as the *Lady of Auxerre* (FIG. 5-7) after the French town that is her oldest recorded location. As with the figure dedicated by Mantiklos, it is uncertain whether the young woman is a mortal or a deity. She wears a long skirt and a cape, as do the women of the Prinias temple, but the Auxerre maiden has no headdress, and the right hand placed across the chest is probably a gesture of prayer, indicating that this is a kore. The style is, however, comparable. Characteristic is the triangular flat-topped head framed by long strands of hair that form complementary triangles to that of the face. Also typical are the small, belted waist and a fondness for pattern. Note the almost Geometric treatment of the long skirt with its incised concentric squares, once brightly painted. Despite its monumental quality, the statue is only a little more than two feet tall—smaller than the seated goddesses of the Prinias lintel but much larger than the bronze statuettes of the era.

**DAEDALUS, MASTER OF ALL ARTS** The *Lady of Auxerre* is the masterpiece of a style usually referred to as *Daedalic*, after the legendary artist DAEDALUS, whose name means "the skillful one." In addition to having been a great sculptor, Daedalus was said to have built the labyrinth in Crete to house the Minotaur and also to have designed a temple at Memphis in Egypt (see MAP 3-1). The historical Greeks attributed to him almost all the great achievements in early sculpture and architecture before the names of artists and architects were recorded. The story that Daedalus worked in Egypt reflects the enormous impact of Egyptian art and architecture on the Greeks of the aptly named Orientalizing age, as well as on their offspring in the succeeding Archaic period.

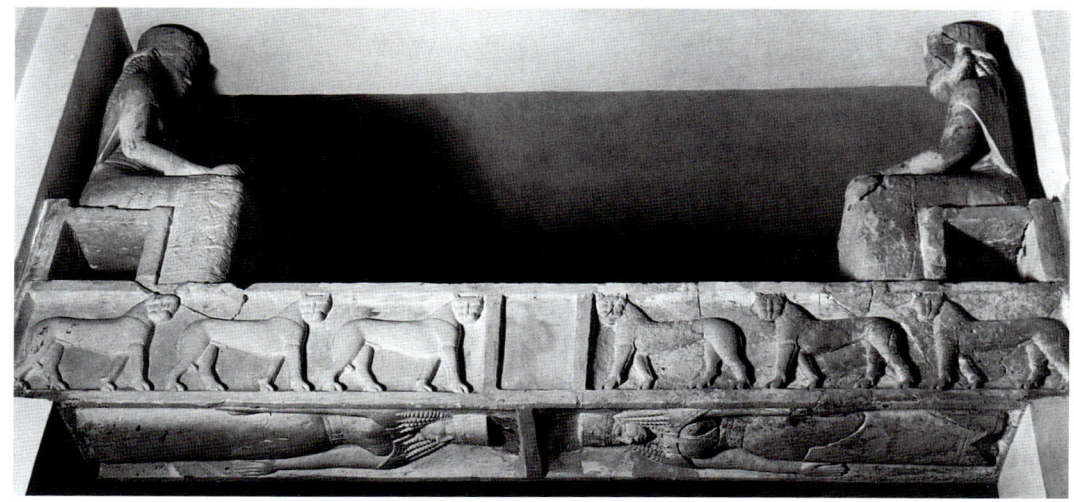

**5-6** Lintel of Temple A, Prinias, Greece, ca. 625 BCE. Limestone, approx. 2′ 9″ high. Archaeological Museum, Herakleion.

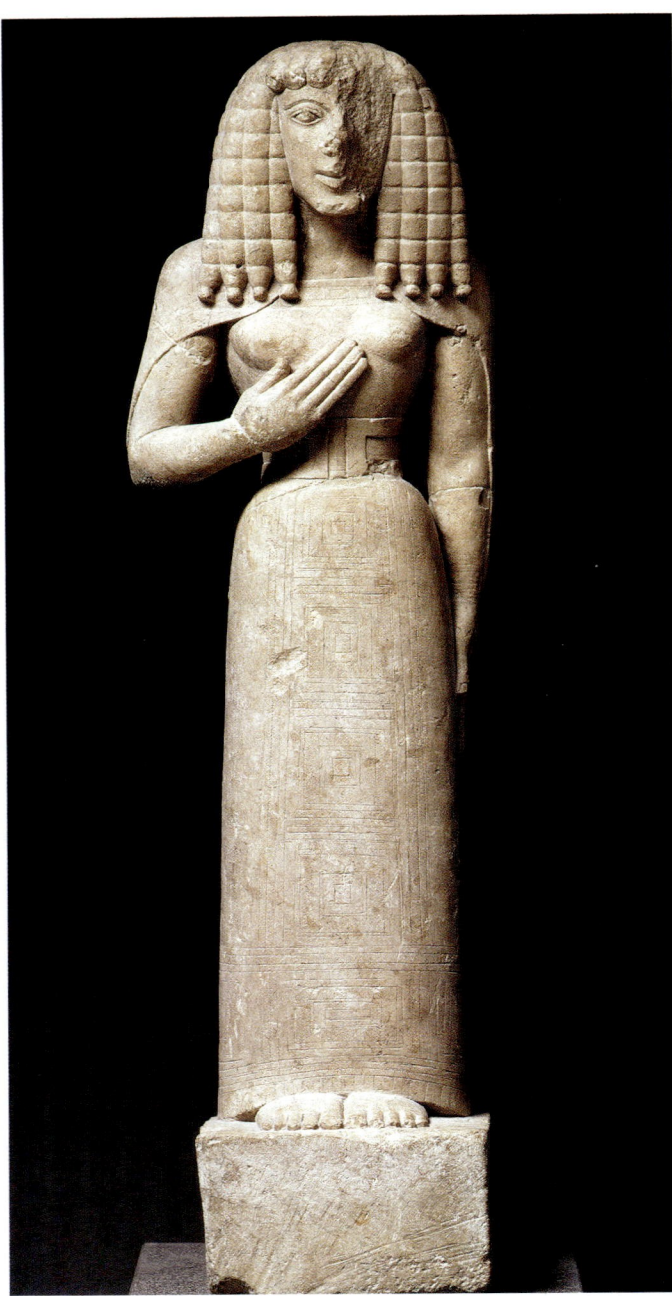

slightly. The arms are held beside the body, and the fists are clenched with the thumbs forward. This kouros even served a funerary purpose. It stood over a grave in the countryside somewhere near Athens. Such statues replaced the huge vases (FIG. 5-1) of Geometric times as the preferred form of grave marker in the sixth century BCE. They also were used as votive offerings in sanctuaries. The kouros type, because of its generic quality, could be employed in several different contexts.

Despite the adherence to Egyptian prototypes, Greek kouros statues differ from their models in two important ways. First, they were liberated from their original stone block. The Egyptian obsession with permanence was alien to the Greeks, who were preoccupied with finding ways to represent motion rather than stability in their sculpted figures. Second, the kouroi are nude, and if

5-7 *Lady of Auxerre*, statue of a goddess or kore, ca. 650–625 BCE. Limestone, approx. 2′ 1½″ high. Louvre, Paris.

## The Archaic Period

### *Statuary*

GREEK KOUROI AND EGYPT According to one Greek writer, Daedalus used the same compositional patterns for his statues as the Egyptians used for their own, and the first truly monumental stone statues of the Greeks follow very closely the canonical Egyptian format. A life-size marble *kouros* ("youth"; plural, *kouroi*) now in New York (FIG. 5-8) emulates the stance of Egyptian statues—for example, the portrait of Mentuemhet (see FIG. 3-40) carved only a half century before the Greek statue. In both cases the figure is rigidly frontal with the left foot advanced

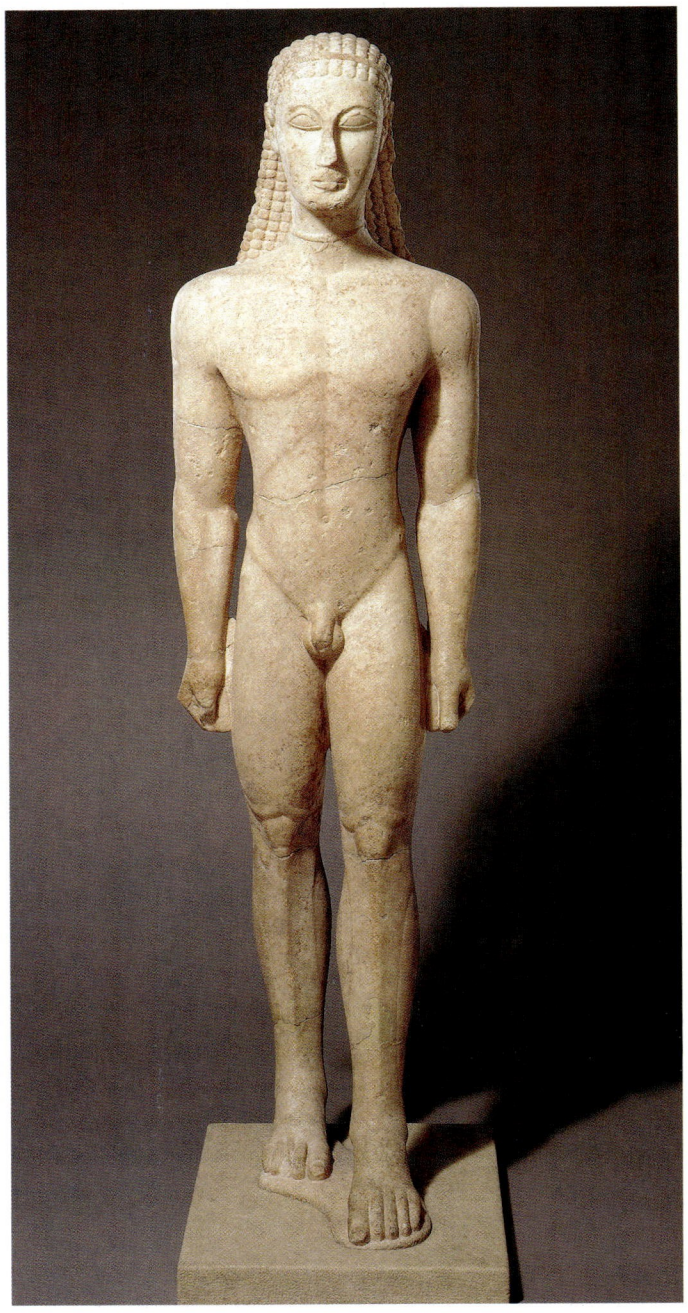

5-8 Kouros, ca. 600 BCE. Marble, approx. 6′ ½″ high. Metropolitan Museum of Art, New York.

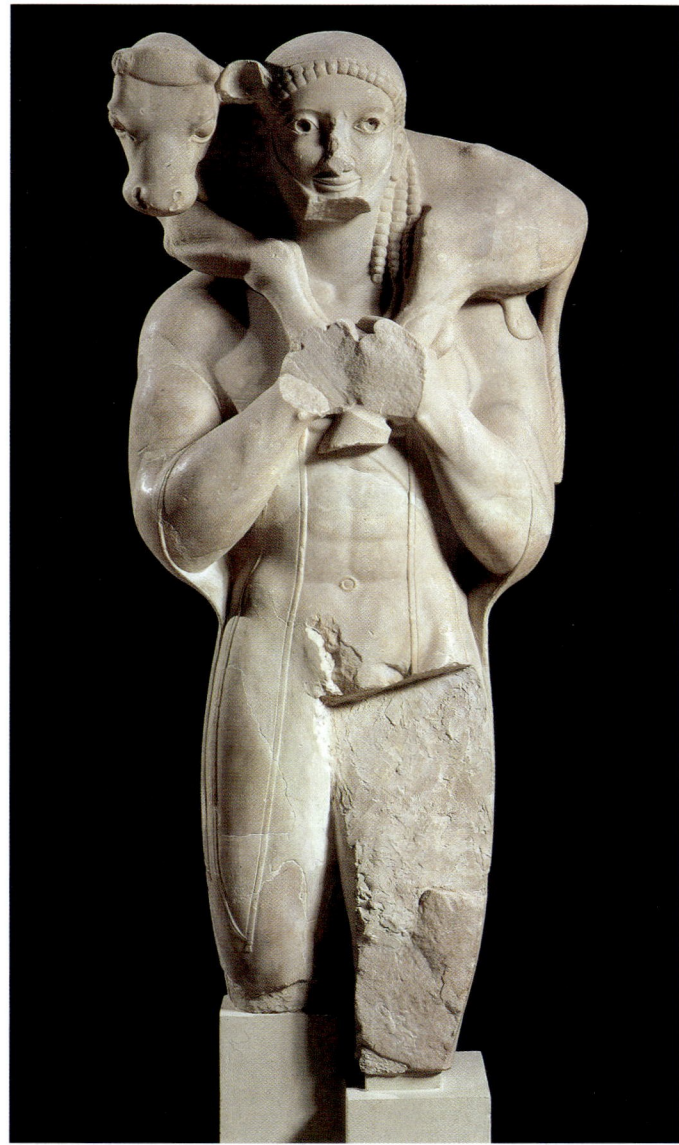

5-9 Calf Bearer, dedicated by Rhonbos on the Acropolis, Athens, Greece, ca. 560 BCE. Marble, restored height approx. 5′ 5″. Acropolis Museum, Athens.

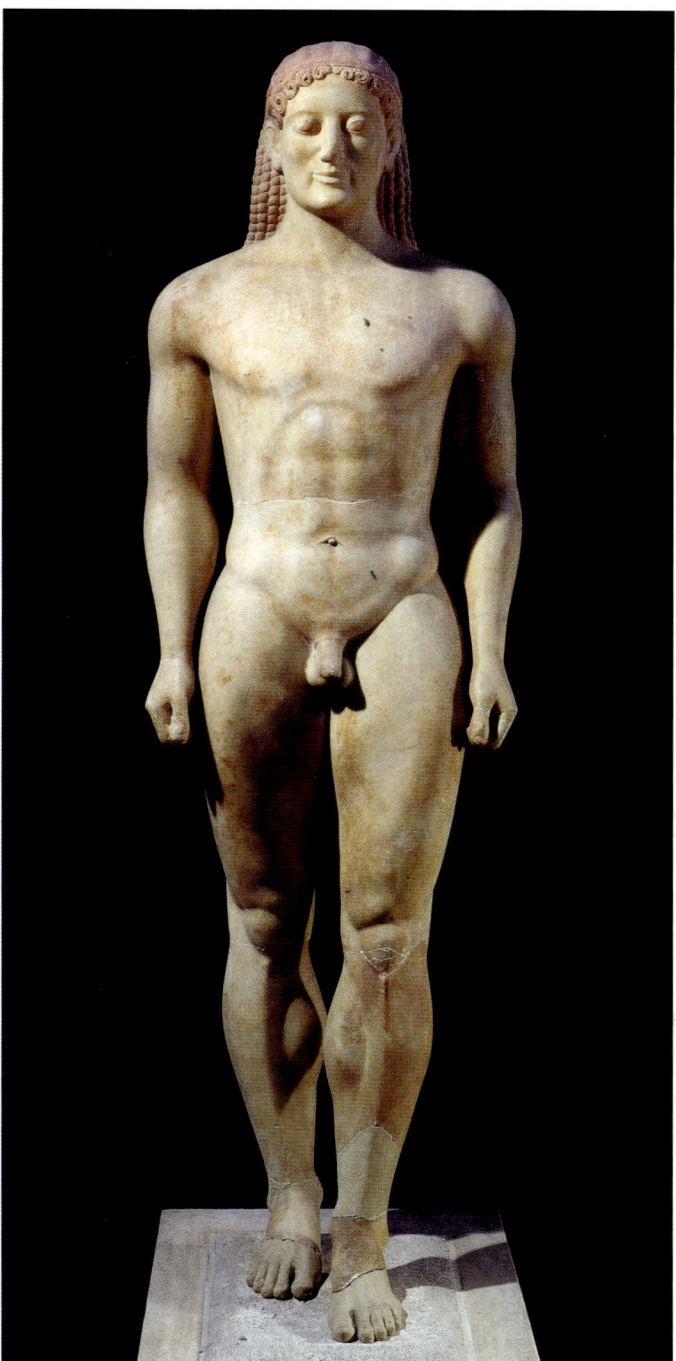

5-10 Kroisos, from Anavysos, Greece, ca. 530 BCE. Marble, approx. 6′ 4″ high. National Archaeological Museum, Athens.

the monumental marble statues lack identifying attributes, they, like the tiny bronze dedicated by Mantiklos (FIG. 5-3), are formally indistinguishable from Greek images of deities with their perfect bodies exposed for all to see.

The New York kouros shares many traits with Greek Orientalizing works such as the *Mantiklos Apollo* and the *Lady of Auxerre,* especially the triangular shape of head and hair and the flatness of the face—the hallmarks of the Daedalic style. Eyes, nose, and mouth all sit on the front of the head, ears were placed on the sides, and the long hair forms a flat backdrop behind the head. In every instance, one sees the result of the sculptor's having drawn these features on four independent sides of the marble block, following the same workshop procedure used in Egypt for millennia. The New York kouros also has the slim waist of earlier Greek statues, and exhibits the same love of pattern. The pointed arch of the rib cage, for example, echoes the V-shaped ridge of the hips, which suggests but does not accurately reproduce the rounded flesh and muscle of the human body.

A SMILING CALF BEARER A generation later than the New York kouros is the statue of a *moschophoros,* or calf bearer (FIG. 5-9), found in fragments on the Athenian Acropolis. Its inscribed base (not visible in our photograph) states that a man whose name has been reconstructed as Rhonbos dedicated the statue. Rhonbos is almost certainly the calf bearer himself, bringing an offering to Athena in thanksgiving for his prosperity. He stands in the left-foot-forward manner of the kouroi, but he is bearded and therefore no longer a youth. He wears a thin cloak (once painted to set it off from the otherwise nude body). No one dressed in such a manner in ancient Athens. The sculptor adhered to the artistic convention of male nudity and attributed to the calf bearer the noble perfection such nudity suggests while also indicating that this mature gentleman is clothed, as any respectable citizen would be in such a context. The Archaic sculptor's love of pattern may be seen once again in the handling of the difficult problem of representing man and animal together. The calf's legs and the moschophoros's arms form a bold X that unites the two bodies both physically and formally.

The calf bearer's face differs markedly from those of earlier Greek statues (and those of Egypt and the Near East) in one notable way. The man smiles—or at least seems to. From this time on, Archaic Greek statues always smile, even in the most inappropriate contexts (see, for example, FIG. 5-27, where a dying warrior with an arrow in his chest grins broadly at the spectator!). This so-called *Archaic smile* has been variously interpreted, but it is not to be taken literally. Rather, the smile seems to be the Archaic sculptor's way of indicating that the person portrayed is alive. By adopting such a convention, the Greek artist signaled a very different intention from any Egyptian counterpart.

**THE GRAVE OF KROISOS** Sometime around 530 BCE a young man named Kroisos died a hero's death in battle, and his grave at Anavysos, not far from Athens, was marked by a kouros statue (FIG. **5-10**). The inscribed base invites visitors to "stay and mourn at the tomb of dead Kroisos, whom raging Ares destroyed one day as he fought in the foremost ranks." The statue, with its distinctive Archaic smile, is no more a portrait of a specific youth than is the New York kouros. But two generations later, without rejecting the Egyptian stance, the Greek sculptor rendered the human body in a far more naturalistic manner. The head is no longer too large for the body, and the face is more rounded, with swelling cheeks replacing the flat planes of the earlier work. The long hair does not form a stiff backdrop to the head but falls naturally over the back. Rounded hips replace the V-shaped ridges of the New York kouros.

Some of the original paint survives on the Kroisos statue, enhancing the sense of life. All Greek stone statues were painted. The modern notion that classical statuary was pure white is mistaken. The Greeks did not, however, color their statues garishly. The flesh was left in the natural color of the stone, which was waxed and polished, while eyes, lips, hair, and drapery were painted in *encaustic* (see "Iaia of Cyzicus and the Art of Encaustic Painting," Chapter 10, page 288). In this technique, the painter mixed the pigment with wax and applied it to the statue while hot.

**BROKEN AND BURIED KORAI** A stylistic "sister" to the Anavysos kouros is the statue of a kore wearing a *peplos* (FIG. **5-11**), a simple, long, woolen belted garment, which gives the female figure a columnar appearance. Traces of paint are preserved here also. As was true of the Kroisos statue, the *Peplos Kore,* as she is known, was buried for more than two millennia, protecting the painted surface from the destructive effects of exposure to the atmosphere and to bad weather. The kore—along with the calf bearer (FIG. 5-9) and many other statues—had been knocked over by the Persians during their sack of the Acropolis in 480 BCE (discussed later). Shortly thereafter, the Athenians buried all the damaged Archaic sculptures. Before that time, they stood as votive offerings in Athena's sanctuary.

The *Peplos Kore*'s missing left arm was extended, a break from the frontal compression of the arms at the sides in Egyptian statues. She once held in her hand an attribute that would identify the

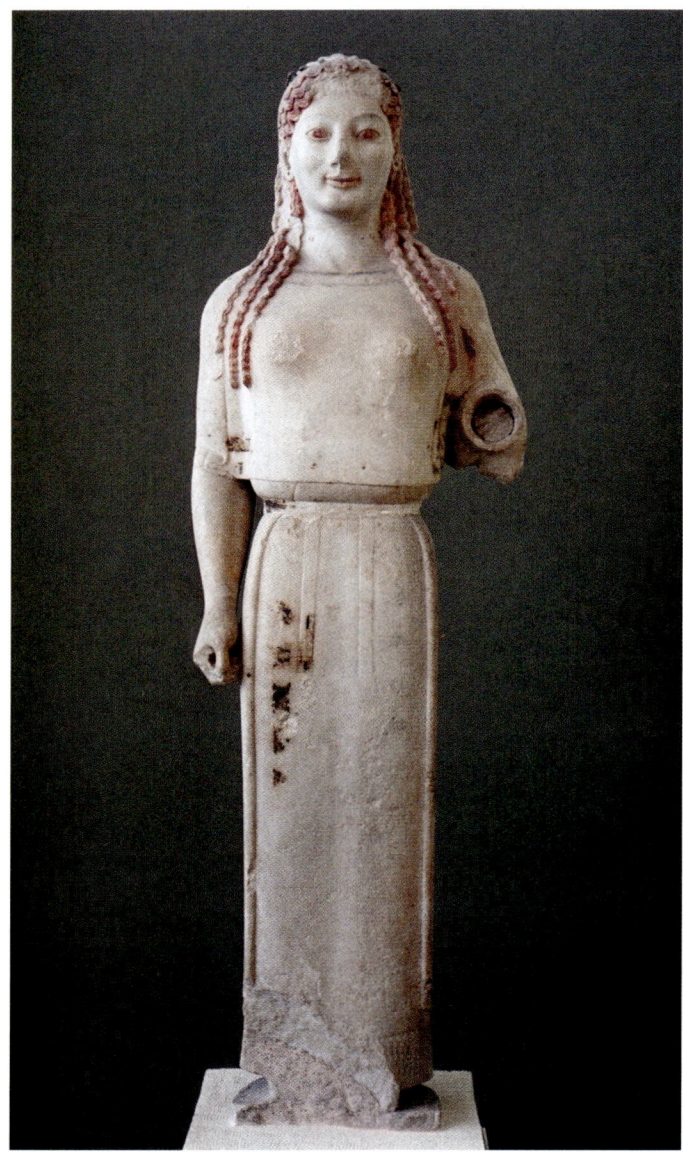

**5-11** *Peplos Kore,* from the Acropolis, Athens, Greece, ca. 530 BCE. Marble, approx. 4′ high. Acropolis Museum, Athens.

figure as a maiden or, as some have suggested, a goddess, perhaps Athena herself. Whatever her identity, the contrast with the *Lady of Auxerre* (FIG. 5-7) is striking. Although in both cases the drapery conceals the entire body save for head, arms, and feet, the sixth-century sculptor rendered the soft female form much more naturally. This softer treatment of the flesh also sharply differentiates later korai from contemporary kouroi, which have hard, muscular bodies.

The *Peplos Kore* is one of the latest peplos-clad dedications on the Acropolis. By the later sixth century, the light linen Ionian *chiton,* worn in conjunction with a heavier *himation* (mantle), was the garment of choice for fashionable women. Archaic sculptors delighted in rendering the intricate patterns created by the cascading folds of thin, soft material, as may be seen in another kore (FIG. **5-12**) the Athenians buried after the Persian destruction of the Acropolis. In this statue the asymmetry of the folds greatly relieves the stiff frontality of the body and makes the figure appear much more lifelike than contemporary kouroi. The sculptor

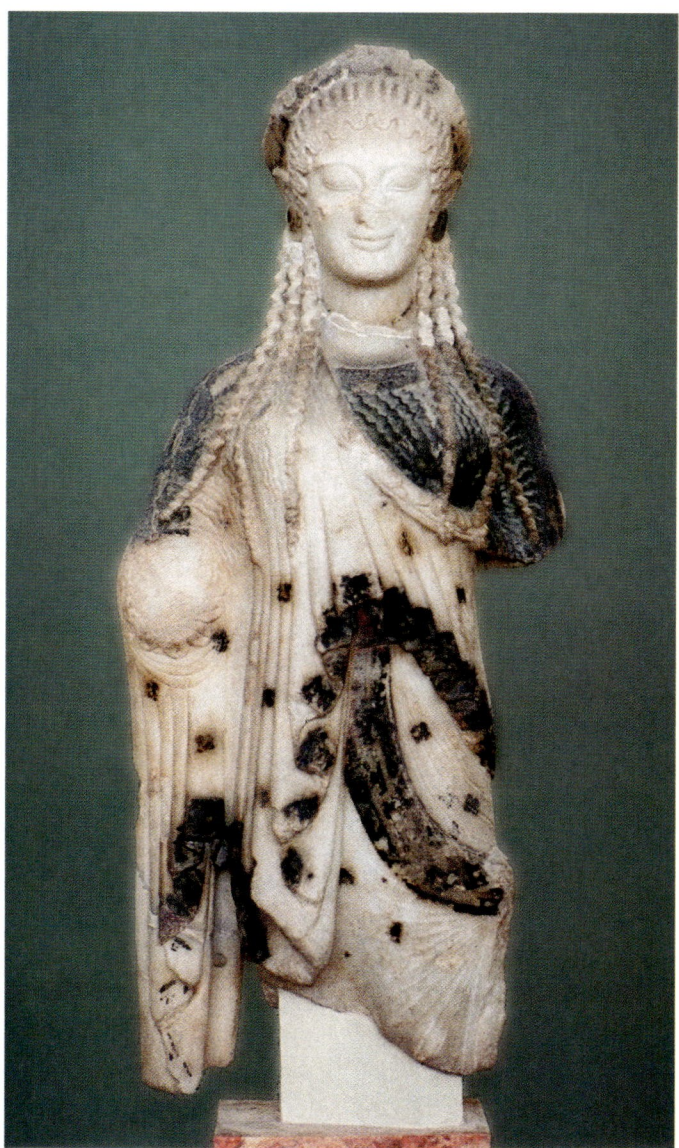

5-12 Kore, from the Acropolis, Athens, Greece, ca. 520–510 BCE. Marble, approx. 1′ 9½″ high. Acropolis Museum, Athens.

limestone, in many cases, and, where it was available, marble, which was more impressive and durable (and more expensive). In Greece proper, if not in its western colonies, marble was readily at hand. Bluish white marble came from Hymettus, just east of Athens. Glittering white marble particularly adapted for carving was brought from Pentelicus, northeast of the city, and from the Aegean Islands, especially Paros (MAP 5-1).

Already in the Orientalizing seventh century BCE, at Prinias, the Greeks had built a stone temple embellished with stone sculptures (FIGS. 5-5 and 5-6). But despite the contemporary Daedalic style of its statues and reliefs, the Cretan temple resembled the megaron of a Mycenaean palace more than anything Greek traders had seen in their travels overseas. In the Archaic age of the sixth century, with the model of Egyptian columnar halls such as that at Karnak (see FIG. 3-25) before them, Greek architects began to build the columnar stone temples that have been more influential on the later history of architecture in the Western world than any other building type ever devised.

Greek temples differed in function from most later religious shrines. The altar lay outside the temple—at the east end, facing the rising sun—and the Greeks gathered outside, not inside, the building to worship. The temple proper housed the so-called *cult statue* of the deity, the grandest of all votive offerings. Both in its early and mature manifestations, the Greek temple was the house of the god or goddess, not of his or her followers.

Figural sculpture played a major role in the exterior program of the Greek temple from early times, partly to embellish the god's shrine, partly to tell something about the deity symbolized within, and partly to serve as a votive offering. But the building itself, with its finely carved capitals and moldings, also was conceived as sculpture, abstract in form and possessing the power of sculpture to evoke human responses. The commanding importance of the sculptured temple, its inspiring function in public life, was emphasized in its elevated site, often on a hill above the city (*acropolis* means "high city"). As Aristotle stipulated: "The site should be a spot seen far and wide, which gives due elevation to virtue and towers over the neighborhood."[3]

achieved added variety by showing the kore grasping part of her chiton in her left hand (unfortunately broken off) to lift it off the ground in order to take a step forward. This is the equivalent of the advanced left foot of the kouroi and became standard for statues of korai. Despite the varied surface treatment of brightly colored garments on the korai, the kore postures are as fixed as those of their male counterparts.

## Architecture and Architectural Sculpture

HOUSES FOR THE GODS  Many of the earliest Greek temples do not survive because they were made of wood and mud brick. Pausanias, who wrote an invaluable guidebook to Greece in the second century CE, noted that in the even-then-ancient Temple of Hera at Olympia, one oak column was still in place. The others had been replaced by stone columns. Archaic and later Greek temples were, however, built of more permanent materials—

PLAN AND PROPORTION  In basic plan, the Greek temple (see "Doric and Ionic Temples," pages 116–117) still discloses a close affinity with the Mycenaean megaron (see FIG. 4-19), and, even in its most elaborate form, it retains the latter structure's basic simplicity. In all cases, the remarkable order, compactness, and symmetry of the Greek scheme strike the eye first, reflecting the Greeks' sense of proportion and their effort to achieve ideal forms in terms of regular numerical relationships and geometric rules. Whether the plan is simple or more complex, no fundamental change occurs in the nature of the units or of their grouping. Classical Greek architecture, like classical music, has a simple core theme with a series of complex, but always quite intelligible, variations developed from it.

The Greeks' insistence on proportional order guided their experiments with the proportions of temple plans. The earliest temples tended to be long and narrow, with the proportion of the ends to the sides roughly expressible as 1:3. From the sixth century on, plans approached but rarely had a proportion of exactly 1:2. Classical temples tended to be a little longer than twice their width. To the Greek mind, proportion in architecture and sculpture was much the same as harmony in music, reflecting and embodying the cosmic order (see "Polykleitos's Prescription for the Perfect Statue," page 133).

## Doric and Ionic Temples

The plan and elevation of Greek temples varied with date, geography, and the requirements of individual projects, but all but the earliest Greek temples have common defining elements that set them apart from both the religious edifices of other civilizations and other kinds of Greek buildings.

*PLAN* The temple core was the *naos*, or *cella*, a room with no windows that usually housed the cult statue of the deity. It was preceded by a *pronaos*, or porch, often with two columns between the *antae*, or extended walls (columns *in antis*). A smaller second room might be placed behind the cella, but in its classical form, the Greek temple had a porch at the rear *(opisthodomos)* set against the blank back wall of the cella. The purpose was not functional but decorative, satisfying the Greek passion for balance and symmetry. A colonnade could be placed across the front of the temple *(prostyle;* FIG. 5-50), across both front and back *(amphiprostyle;* FIG. 5-53), or, more commonly, all around the cella and its porch(es) to form a *peristyle*, as in our diagram (compare FIGS. 5-13 and 5-14). Single *(peripteral)* colonnades were the norm, but double *(dipteral)* colonnades were features of especially elaborate temples (FIG. 5-74).

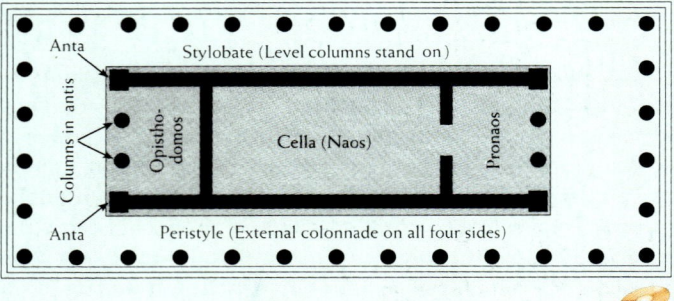

*ELEVATION* The elevation of a Greek temple is described in terms of the platform, the colonnade, and the superstructure *(entablature)*. In the Archaic period, two basic systems evolved for articulating the three units. These are the so-called *orders* of Greek architecture. The orders are differentiated both in the nature of the details and in the relative proportions of the parts. The names of the orders are derived from the Greek regions where they were most commonly employed. The *Doric* was formulated on the mainland and remained the preferred manner there and in the western colonies of the Greeks. The *Ionic* was the order of choice in the Aegean Islands and on the western coast of Asia Minor. The geographical distinctions are by no means absolute. The Ionic order was, for example, often used in Athens (where, according to some, the Athenians were considered Ionians who never migrated).

In both orders, the columns rest on the *stylobate*, the uppermost course of the platform. Metal clamps held together the stone blocks in each horizontal course, and metal dowels joined vertically the blocks of different courses. The columns have two or three parts, depending on the order: the *shaft*, which is marked with vertical channels *(flutes)*; the *capital*; and, in the Ionic order, the *base*. Greek column shafts, in contrast to their Minoan and Mycenaean forebears, taper gradually from bottom to top. They usually are composed of separate *drums* joined by metal dowels to prevent turning as well as shifting, although instances of *monolithic* (single-piece) columns are known. In the Doric order, the top of the shaft is marked with one or several horizontal lines *(necking)* that furnish the transition to the capital. The capital has two elements. The lower part (the *echinus*) varies with the order. In the Doric, it is convex and cushionlike, similar to the echinus of Minoan (see FIG. 4-5) and Mycenaean (see FIG. 4-20) capitals. In the Ionic, it is small and supports a bolster ending in scroll-like spirals (the *volutes*). The upper element, present in both orders, is a flat, square block (the *abacus*) that provides the immediate support for the entablature.

The entablature has three parts: the *architrave* or *epistyle*, the main weight-bearing and weight-distributing element; the *frieze*;

**ORNAMENT AND COLOR** Sculptural ornament was concentrated on the upper part of the building, in the frieze and pediments. Architectural sculpture, like freestanding statuary, was painted and usually was placed only in the building parts that had no structural function. This is true particularly of the Doric order, where decorative sculpture appears only in the metope and pediment "voids." Ionic builders, less severe in this respect as well, were willing to decorate the entire frieze and sometimes even the lower column drums. Occasionally, they replaced their columns with female figures (caryatids; FIGS. 5-16 and 5-52). Capitals, decorative moldings, and other architectural elements were also painted. By painting parts of the building, the designer could bring out more clearly the relationships of the structural parts and soften the stone's glitter at specific points, as well as provide a background to set off the figures.

Although color was used for emphasis and to relieve what might have seemed too bare a simplicity, Greek architecture primarily depended on clarity and balance. To the Greeks, it was

unthinkable to use surfaces in the way the Egyptians used their gigantic columns—as fields for complicated ornamentation (see FIG. 3-25). The history of Greek temple architecture is the history of Greek architects' unflagging efforts to find the most satisfactory (that is, what they believed were perfect) proportions for each part of the building and for the structure as a whole.

**EARLY DORIC IN ITALY** The prime example of early Greek efforts at Doric temple design is not in Greece but in Italy, south of Naples, at Paestum (Greek Poseidonia). The huge (80 × 170 feet) Archaic temple (FIG. 5-13) erected there around 550 BCE retains its entire peripteral colonnade, but most of the entablature, including the frieze, pediment, and all of the roof, has vanished. Called the Basilica after the Roman columnar hall building type that early investigators felt it resembled, the structure is now known to be a temple dedicated to Hera. Scholars refer to it as the Temple of Hera I to distinguish it from the later Temple of Hera II (FIG. 5-29), which stands nearby.

## Doric and Ionic Temples (continued)

and the *cornice*, a molded horizontal projection that together with two sloping *(raking)* cornices forms a triangle that enframes the *pediment.* In the Ionic order, the architrave is usually subdivided into three horizontal bands *(fasciae)*. In the Doric order, the frieze is subdivided into *triglyphs* and *metopes*, whereas in the Ionic the frieze is left open to provide a continuous field for relief sculpture.

Many of the Doric components seem to be translations into stone of an earlier timber architecture. The frieze division into triglyphs and metopes, for example, can be explained best as a stone version of what was originally carpentry. The triglyphs most likely are derived from the ends of crossbeams that rested on

the main horizontal support, the architrave. The metopes then would correspond to the voids between the beam ends in the original wooden structure.

The Doric order is massive in appearance, its sturdy columns firmly planted on the stylobate. Compared with the weighty and severe Doric, the Ionic order seems light, airy, and much more decorative. Its columns are more slender and rise from molded bases. The Doric flutes meet in sharp ridges *(arrises)*, but the Ionic ridges are flat *(fillets)*. The most obvious differences between the two orders are, of course, in the capitals—the Doric, severely plain, and the Ionic, highly ornamental.

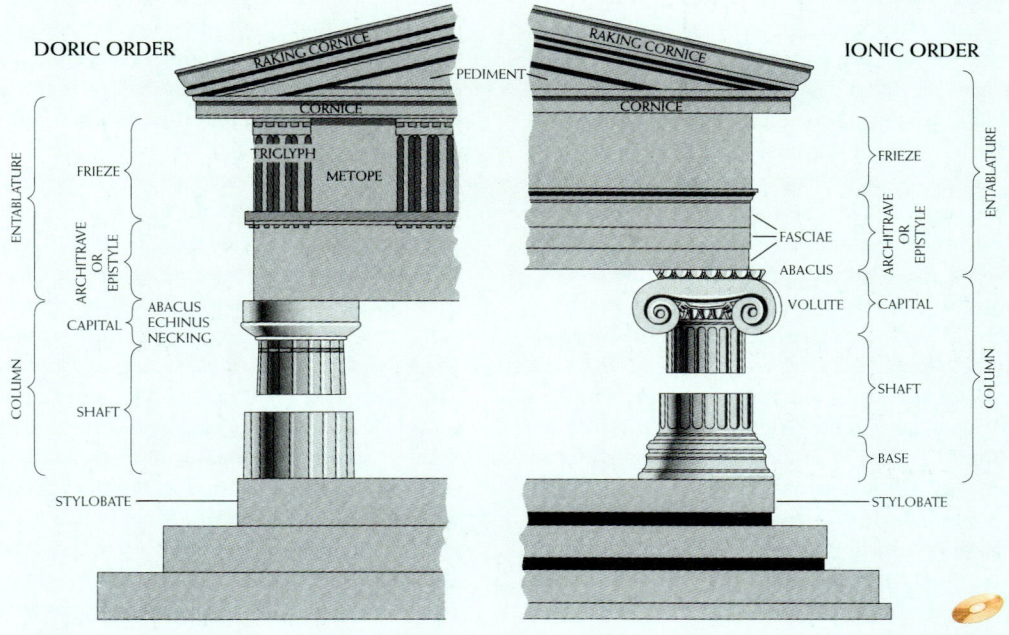

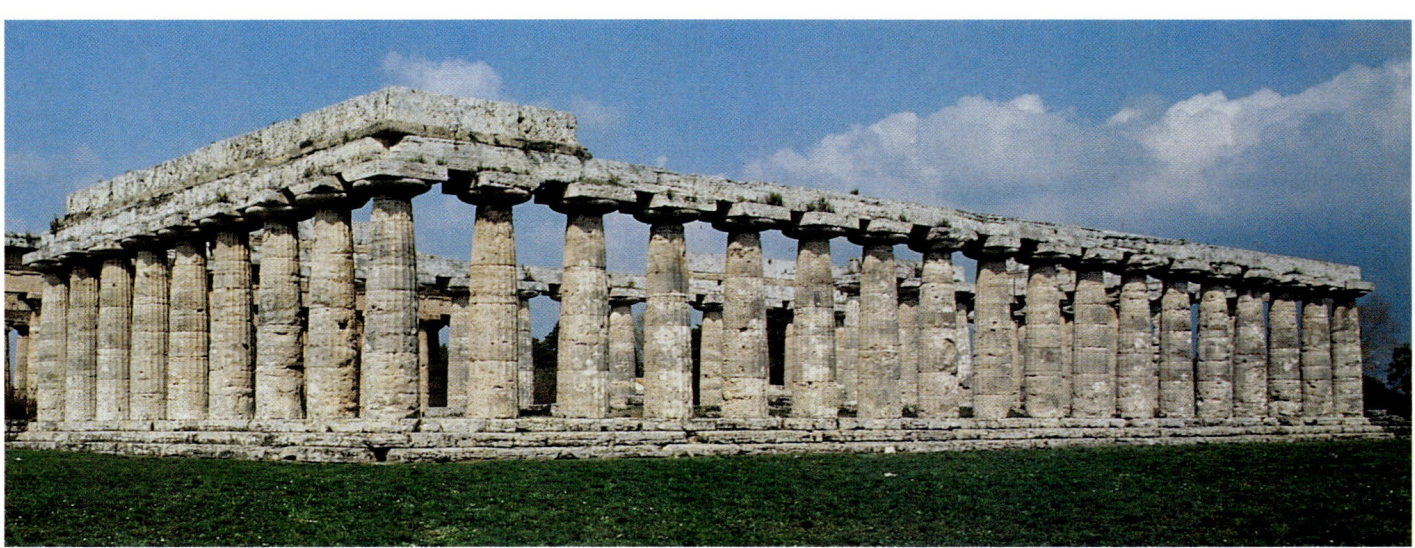

**5-13** Temple of Hera I ("Basilica"), Paestum, Italy, ca. 550 BCE.

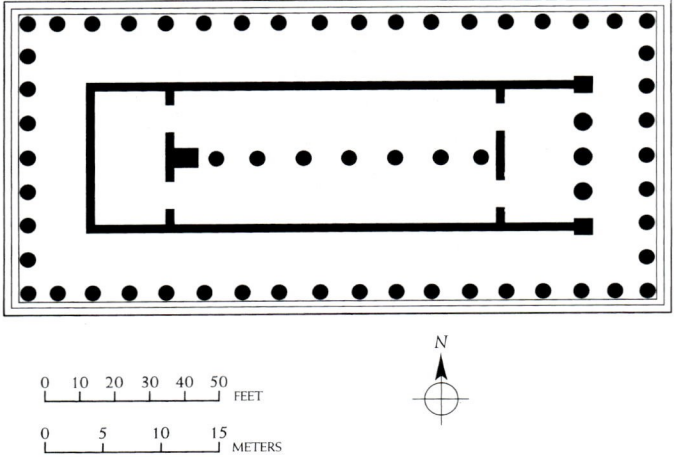

**5-14** Plan of the Temple of Hera I, Paestum, Italy, ca. 550 BCE.

The misnomer is partly due to the building's plan (FIG. **5-14**), which differs from that of most other Greek temples. The unusual feature, found only in early Archaic temples, is the central row of columns that divides the cella into two aisles. Placing columns underneath the *ridgepole* (the timber beam running the length of the building below the peak of the gabled roof) might seem the logical way to provide interior support for the roof structure. But it resulted in several disadvantages. Among these was that this interior arrangement allowed no place for a central statue of the deity to whom the temple was dedicated. Also, the peripteral colonnade, in order to correspond with the interior, had to have an odd number of columns (nine in this case) across the building's facade. At Paestum, three columns were also set in antis instead of the standard two, which in turn ruled out a central doorway for viewing the statue. However, a simple 1:2 ratio of facade and flank columns was achieved by erecting 18 columns on each side of the temple.

The temple's elevation is characterized by heavy, closely spaced columns with a pronounced swelling *(entasis)* at the middle of the shafts, giving the columns a profile akin to that of a cigar. The shafts are topped by large, bulky, pancakelike Doric capitals, which seem compressed by the overbearing weight of the entablature. If the temple's immense roof were preserved, these columns would seem even more compressed, squatting beneath what must have been a high and massive entablature. The columns and capitals thus express in a vivid manner their weight-bearing function. One structural reason, perhaps, for the heaviness of the design and the narrowness of the spans between the columns might be that the Archaic builders were afraid thinner and more widely spaced

columns would result in the superstructure's collapse. In later Doric temples, the columns were placed farther apart, and the forms were gradually refined. The shafts became more slender, the entasis subtler, the capitals smaller, and the entablature lighter. Greek architects sought the ideal proportional relationship among the parts of their buildings. The sculptors of Archaic kouroi and korai grappled with similar problems. Architecture and sculpture developed in a parallel manner in the sixth century.

**THE PEDIMENT PROBLEM** Architects and sculptors were also frequently called on to work together, as at Corfu (ancient Corcyra), where a great Doric temple dedicated to Artemis was constructed early in the sixth century BCE. Corfu is an island off the western coast of Greece and was an important stop on the trade route between the mainland and the Greek settlements in Italy (MAP 5-1). Prosperity made possible the erection of one of the earliest stone peripteral temples in Greece, one also lavishly embellished with sculpture. The metopes were decorated with reliefs (unfortunately very fragmentary today), and both pediments were filled with huge sculptures (more than nine feet high at the center). The pediments on both ends of the temple appear to have been decorated in an identical manner. The west pediment (FIG. **5-15**) is better preserved.

Designing figural decoration for a pediment was never an easy task for the Greek sculptor because of the pediment's awkward triangular shape. The central figures had to be of great size. By contrast, as the pediment tapered toward the corners, the available area became increasingly cramped. At the center of the Corfu pediment is the *gorgon* Medusa, a demon with a woman's body and bird wings. Medusa also had a hideous face and snake hair, and anyone who gazed at her was turned into stone. She is shown in the conventional Archaic bent-leg, bent-arm, pinwheel-like posture that signifies running or, for a winged creature, flying. To her left and right are two great felines. Together they serve as temple guardians, repulsing all enemies from the sanctuary of the goddess. Similar panthers stand sentinel on the lintel of the seventh-century temple at Prinias (FIG. 5-6). The Corfu felines are in the tradition of the guardian lions of the citadel gate at Mycenae (see FIG. 4-20) and the lamassu that stood guard at the entrances to Near Eastern palaces (see FIGS. 2-18 and 2-21). The triad of Medusa and the felines recalls as well Mesopotamian heraldic human-beast compositions (see FIG. 2-10). The Corfu figures are, in short, still further examples of the Orientalizing manner in early Greek sculpture.

Between Medusa and the great beasts are two small figures—the human Chrysaor at her left and the winged horse Pegasus at her right (only the rear legs are preserved). Chrysaor and Pegasus

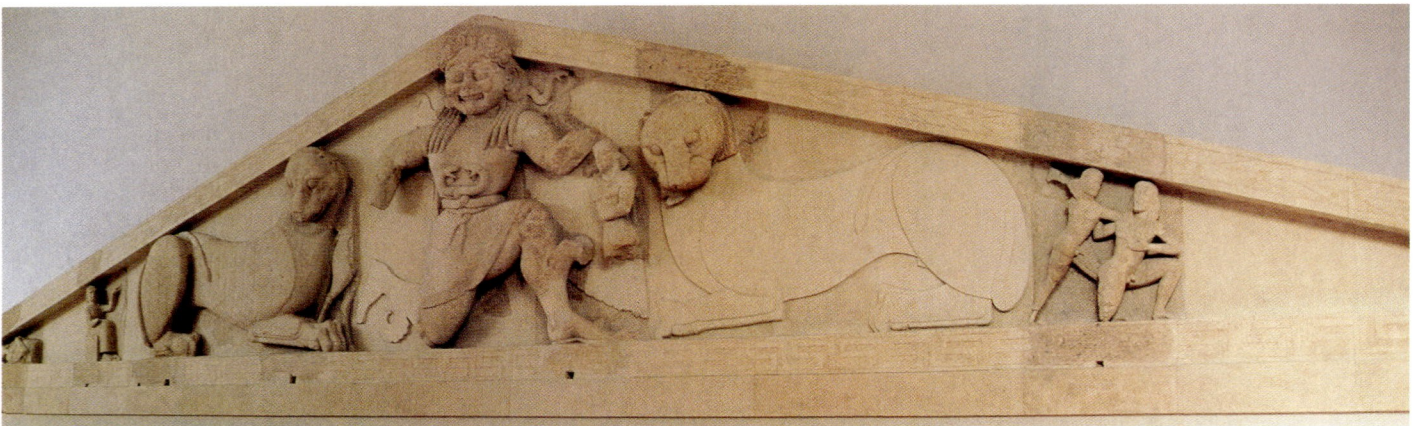

**5-15** West pediment from the Temple of Artemis, Corfu, Greece, ca. 600–580 BCE. Limestone, greatest height approx. 9′ 4″. Archaeological Museum, Corfu.

were Medusa's children. According to legend, they sprang from her head when the Greek hero Perseus severed it with his sword. Their presence here on either side of the living Medusa is therefore a chronological impossibility. The Archaic artist was not interested in telling a coherent story but in identifying the central figure by depicting her offspring.

Narration was, however, the purpose of the much smaller groups situated in the pediment corners. To the viewer's right is Zeus, brandishing his thunderbolt and slaying a kneeling giant. In the extreme corner was a dead giant. The *gigantomachy* (battle of gods and giants) was a popular theme in Greek art from Archaic through Hellenistic times and was a metaphor for the triumph of reason and order over chaos. In the pediment's left corner is one of the Trojan War's climactic events: Achilles' son Neoptolemos kills the enthroned King Priam. The fallen figure to the left of this group may be a dead Trojan.

The master responsible for the Corfu pediments was a pioneer, and the composition shows all the signs of experimentation. The lack of narrative unity in the Corfu pediment and the extraordinary scale diversity of the figures eventually gave way to pedimental designs with figures all acting out a single event and appearing the same size. But the Corfu designer already had shown the way. That sculptor realized, for example, that the area beneath the raking cornice could be filled with gods and heroes of similar size if a combination of standing, leaning, kneeling, seated, and prostrate figures were employed in the composition. And the Corfu master discovered that animals could be very useful space fillers because, unlike humans, they have one end taller than the other.

**CARYATIDS AND GIANTS** The sixth century BCE also saw the erection of grandiose Ionic temples on the Aegean Islands and the west coast of Asia Minor. The gem of Archaic Ionic architecture and architectural sculpture is, however, not a temple but a treasury (FIG. **5-16**) erected by the city of Siphnos in the Sanctuary of Apollo at Delphi. Greek *treasuries* were small buildings set up for the safe storage of votive offerings. At Delphi many poleis expressed their civic pride by erecting these templelike, but nonperipteral, structures. Athens built one with Doric columns in the porch and sculptured metopes in the frieze. The Siphnians equally characteristically employed the Ionic order for their

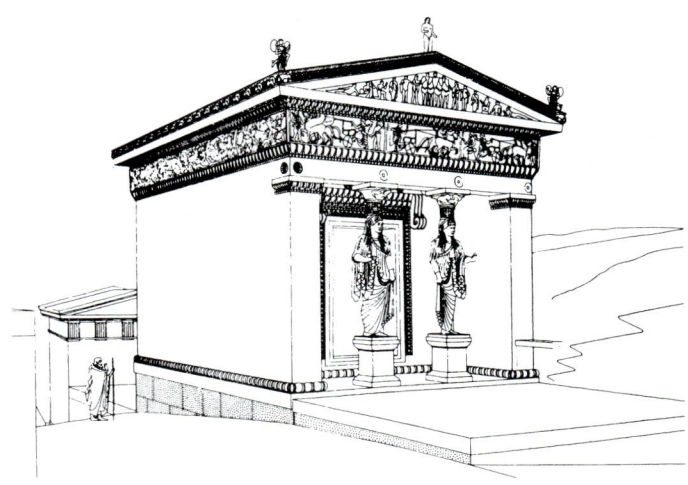

**5-16** Reconstruction drawing of the Siphnian Treasury, Delphi, Greece, ca. 530 BCE.

Delphic treasury. Wealth from the island's gold and silver mines made the luxurious building possible. In the porch, where one would expect to find fluted Ionic columns, far more elaborate caryatids were employed instead. Caryatids are rare, even in Ionic architecture, but they are unknown in Doric architecture, where they would have been discordant elements in that much more severe order. The Siphnian statue-columns resemble contemporary korai dressed in Ionian chitons and himations (FIG. 5-12).

Another Ionic feature of the Siphnian Treasury is the continuous sculptured frieze on all four sides of the building. The north frieze represents the popular theme of the gigantomachy, but it is a much more detailed rendition than that in the corner of the Corfu pediment. In the section reproduced here (FIG. **5-17**), Apollo and Artemis pursue a fleeing giant at the right, while behind them one of the lions pulling a goddess's chariot attacks a giant and bites into his midsection. Paint originally enlivened the crowded composition, and painted labels identified the various protagonists. Some figures had metal weapons. The effect must have been dazzling. On one of the shields the sculptor inscribed his name (unfortunately lost), a clear indication of pride in accomplishment.

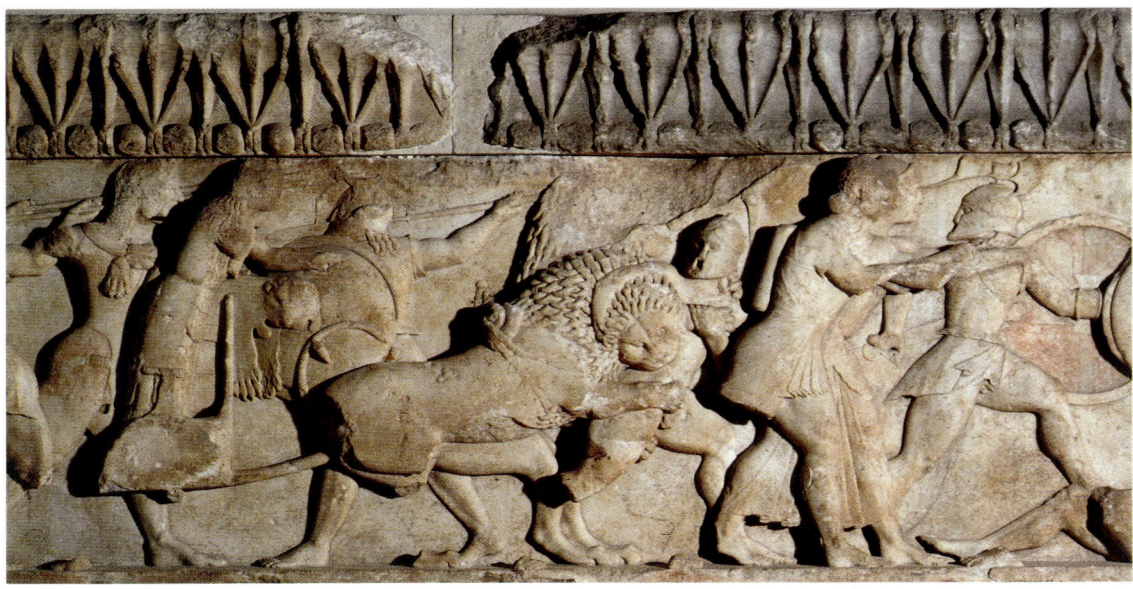

**5-17** Gigantomachy, detail of the north frieze of the Siphnian Treasury, Delphi, Greece, ca. 530 BCE. Marble, approx. 2′ 1″ high. Archaeological Museum, Delphi.

## Vase Painting

**ARTISTS' SIGNATURES** Labeled figures and artists' signatures also appear on Archaic painted vases (see "Greek Vase Painting," page 121). The masterpiece of early black-figure painting is the *François Vase* (FIG. **5-18**), named for the excavator who uncovered it (in an enormous number of fragments) in an Etruscan tomb at Chiusi in Italy (see MAP 9-1), where it had been imported from Athens. This is in itself a testimony to the esteem in which Athenian potters and painters were held at this time. In fact, having learned the black-figure technique from the Corinthians (FIG. 5-4), the Athenians had by the mid-sixth century BCE taken over the export market for fine painted ceramics.

The *François Vase* (a new kind of krater with volute-shaped handles probably inspired by costly metal prototypes) is signed by both its painter ("KLEITIAS painted me") and potter ("ERGOTIMOS made me"). In fact, each signed twice! The krater has more than 200 figures in six registers. Labels abound, naming humans and animals alike, even some inanimate objects. Only one of the bands was given over to the Orientalizing repertoire of animals and sphinxes. The rest constitute a selective encyclopedia of Greek mythology, focusing on the exploits of Peleus and his son Achilles, the great hero of Homer's *Iliad,* and of Theseus, the legendary king of Athens.

In the detail shown here, Lapiths (a northern Greek tribe) and centaurs battle *(centauromachy)* after a wedding celebration where the man-beasts, who were invited guests, got drunk and attempted to abduct the Lapith maidens and young boys. Theseus, also on the guest list, was prominent among the centaurs' Greek adversaries. Kleitias did not fill the space between his figures with decorative ornament, as did his Geometric predecessors (FIG. 5-1). But his heroes conform to the age-old composite type (profile heads with frontal eyes, frontal torsos, and profile legs and arms). His centaurs are much more believable than their Geometric counterparts (FIG. 5-2). The man-horse combination is top/bottom rather than front/back. The lower (horse) portion

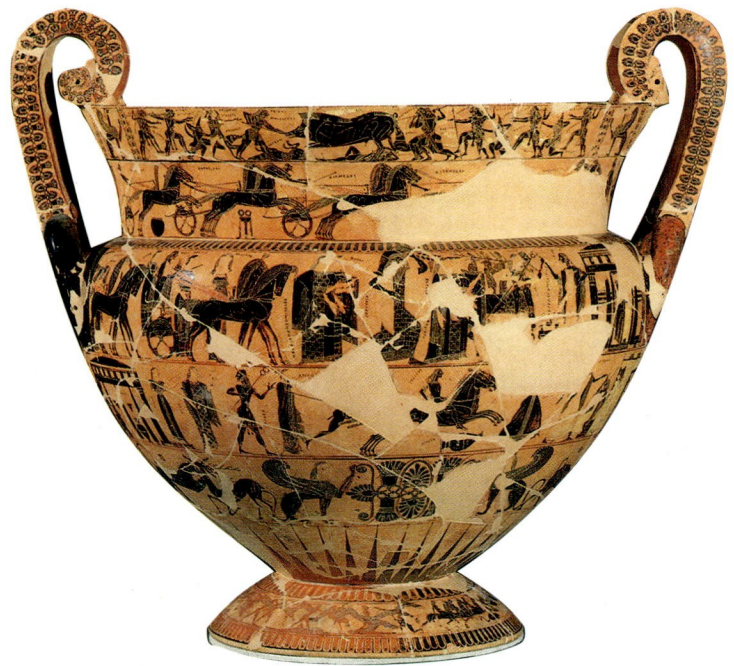

**5-18** KLEITIAS and ERGOTIMOS, *François Vase* (Attic black-figure volute krater), from Chiusi, Italy, ca. 570 BCE. General view *(top)* and detail of centauromachy on other side of vase *(bottom).* Approx. 2′ 2″ high. Museo Archeologico, Florence.

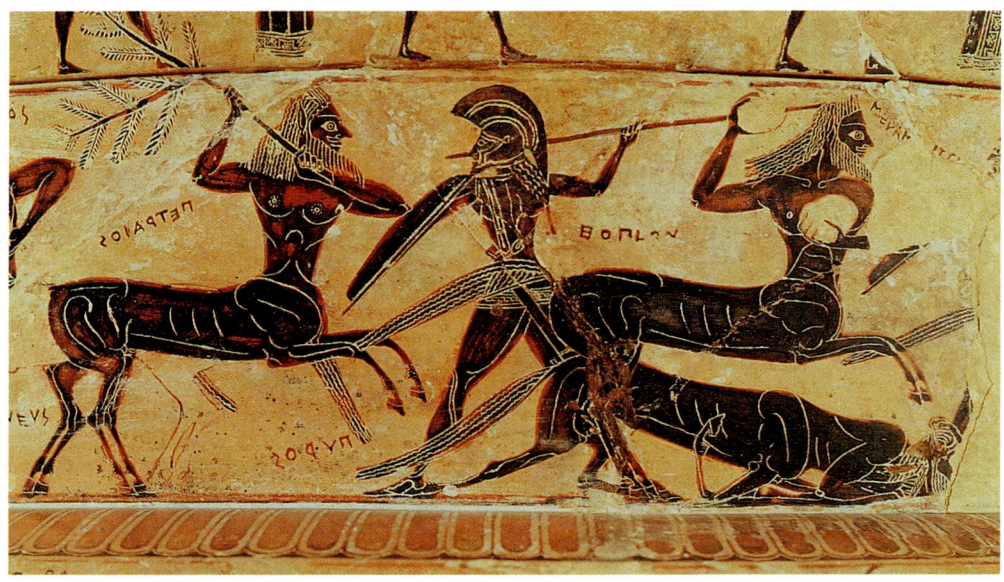

## Greek Vase Painting

The techniques Greek ceramists used to shape and decorate fine vases required a great deal of skill, acquired over many years as apprentices in the workshops of master potters. During the Archaic and Classical periods, when the art of vase painting was at its zenith in Greece, both potters and painters frequently signed their work. These signatures reveal the pride of the artists. They also might have functioned as "brand names" for a large export market. The products of the workshops in Corinth and Athens in particular were much prized and have been found all over the Mediterranean world. The Corinthian amphora we illustrate (FIG. 5-4) was found on Rhodes, an island at the opposite side of the Aegean from mainland Corinth (MAP 5-1). Athenian (Attic) vases were staples in Etruscan tombs in Italy, and all but one of our examples (FIGS. 5-18 to 5-23, 5-57, and 5-58) came from an Etruscan site (see MAP 9-1). Other painted Attic pots have been found as far away as France, Russia, and the Sudan.

The first step in manufacturing a Greek vase was to remove any impurities found in the natural clay and then to knead it, like dough, to remove air bubbles and make it flexible. The Greeks used dozens of different kinds and shapes of pots, and most were fashioned in several parts. The vessel's body was formed by placing the clay on a rotating horizontal wheel. While an apprentice turned the wheel by hand, the potter pulled up the clay with the fingers until the desired shape was achieved. The handles were shaped separately and attached to the vase body by applying *slip* (liquefied clay) to the joints.

Then a specialist, the painter, was called in, although many potters decorated their own work. (Today most people tend to regard painters as more elevated artists than potters, but in Greece the potters owned the shops and employed the painters.) The "pigment" the painter applied to the clay surface is customarily referred to as *glaze*, but the black areas on Greek pots are neither pigment nor glaze but a slip of finely sifted clay that originally was of the same rich red orange color as the clay of the pot. In the three-phase firing process Greek potters used, the first *(oxidizing)* phase turned both pot and slip red. During the second *(reducing)* phase, the oxygen supply into the kiln was shut off, and both pot and slip turned black. In the final *(reoxidizing)* phase, the pot's coarser material reabsorbed oxygen and became red again, while the smoother, silica-laden slip did not and remained black. After long experiment, Greek potters developed a velvety jet-black "glaze" of this kind, produced in kilns heated to temperatures as high as 950° Celsius (about 1,742° Fahrenheit). The firing process was the same whether the painter worked in black-figure or in red-figure. In fact, sometimes both manners were used on the same vase (FIG. 5-20).

---

has four legs of uniform type, and the upper part of the monster is fully human. In characteristic fashion, the animal section of the centaur is shown in strict profile, while the human head and torso are a composite of frontal and profile views. (Kleitias used a consistent profile for the more adventurous detail of the collapsed centaur at the right.)

**EXEKIAS, BLACK-FIGURE MASTER** The acknowledged master of the black-figure technique was an Athenian named EXEKIAS, whose vases were not only widely exported but copied as well. Perhaps his greatest work is an amphora (FIG. **5-19**), found in an Etruscan tomb at Vulci, that Exekias signed as both painter and potter. He did not divide the surface into a series of horizontal

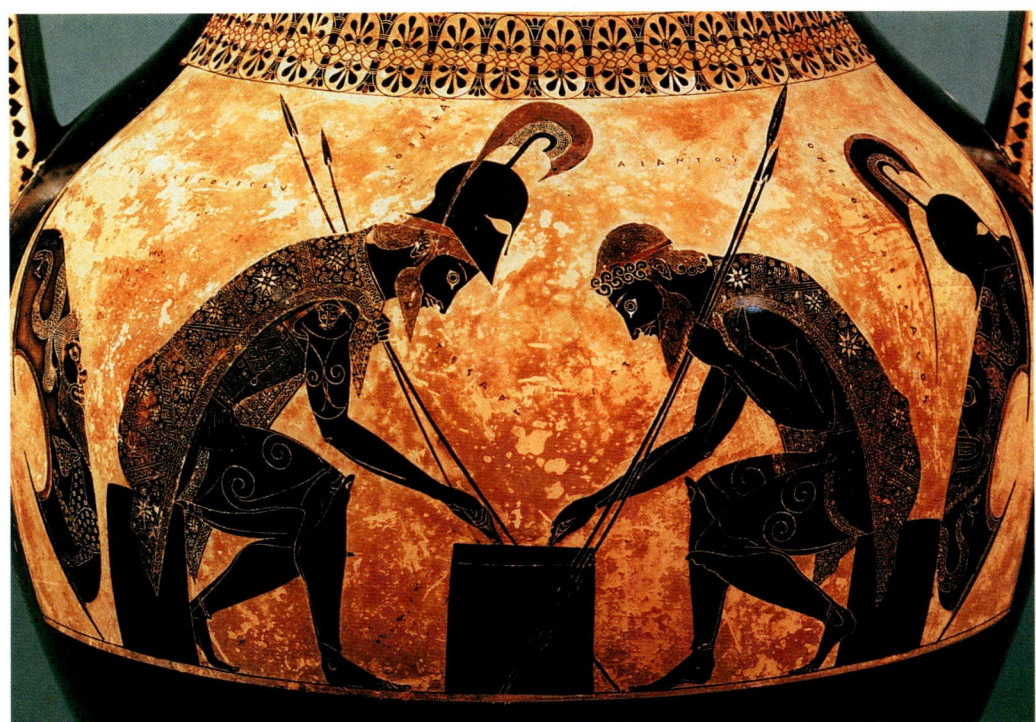

**5-19** EXEKIAS, Achilles and Ajax playing a dice game (detail from an Attic black-figure amphora), from Vulci, Italy, ca. 540–530 BCE. Whole vessel approx. 2′ high. Vatican Museums, Rome.

bands. Instead, he placed figures of monumental stature in a single large framed panel. At the left is Achilles, fully armed. He plays a dice game with his comrade Ajax. Out of the lips of Achilles comes the word *tesara* (four); Ajax calls out *tria* (three). Ajax has taken off his helmet, but both men hold their spears. Their shields are nearby, and each man is ready for action at a moment's notice. It is a classic case of "the calm before the storm." The moment Exekias chose to depict is the antithesis of the Archaic preference for dramatic action. The gravity and tension that will characterize much Classical Greek art of the next century, but are absent in Archaic art, already may be seen here.

Exekias had no equal as a black-figure painter. This may be seen in such details as the extraordinarily intricate engraving of the patterns on the heroes' cloaks (highlighted with delicate touches of white) and in the brilliant composition. The arch formed by the backs of the two warriors echoes the shape of the rounded shoulders of the amphora. The shape of the vessel (compare FIG. 5-4) is echoed again in the void between the heads and spears of Achilles and Ajax. Exekias also used the spears to lead the viewer's eyes toward the thrown dice, where the heroes' eyes are fixed. Of course, those eyes do not really look down at the table but stare out from the profile heads in the old manner. For all his brilliance, Exekias was still wedded to many of the old conventions. Real innovation in figure drawing would have to await the invention of a new ceramic painting technique of greater versatility than black-figure, with its dark silhouettes and incised details.

**"BILINGUAL" PAINTING** The birth of this new technique came around 530 BCE, and the person responsible is known as the ANDOKIDES PAINTER, that is, the anonymous painter who decorated the vases signed by the potter ANDOKIDES. The differences between the two techniques can best be studied on a series of experimental vases with the same composition painted on both sides, once in black-figure and once in the new technique, *red-figure.* Such vases, nicknamed *bilingual vases,* were produced for only a short time. An especially interesting example is an amphora (FIG. 5-20) by the Andokides Painter that features copies of the Achilles and Ajax panel by Exekias, his teacher.

In neither black-figure nor red-figure did the Andokides Painter capture the intensity of the model, and the treatment of details is decidedly inferior. Yet the new red-figure technique had obvious advantages over the old black-figure manner. Red-figure is the opposite of black-figure. What was previously black became red, and vice versa. The artist still employed the same black glaze. But instead of using the glaze to create the silhouettes of figures, the painter outlined the figures and then colored the background black. The red clay was reserved for the figures themselves. Interior details were then drawn with the soft brush in place of the stiff metal graver. The artist could vary the glaze thickness, building it up to give relief to hair curls or diluting it to create brown shades, thereby expanding the chromatic range of the Greek vase painter's craft. The Andokides Painter—many think he was the potter Andokides himself—did not yet appreciate the full potential of

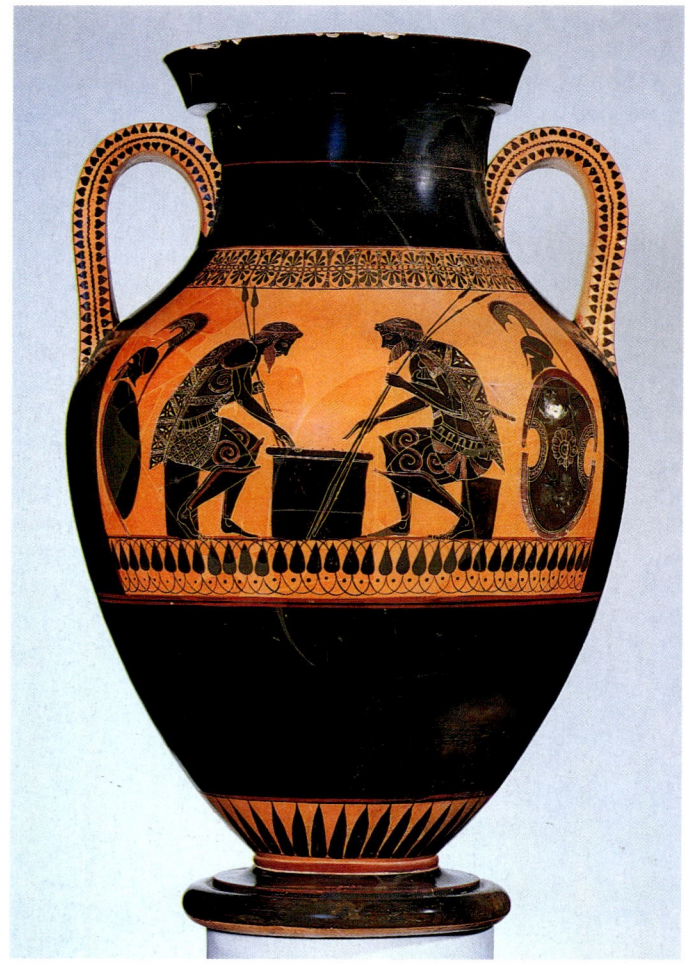 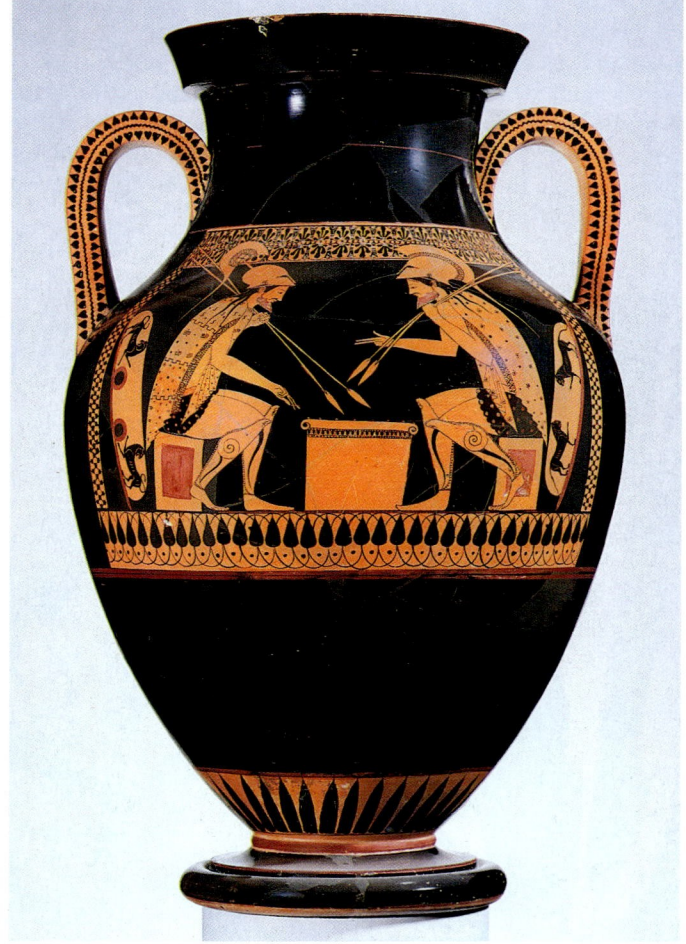

5-20 ANDOKIDES PAINTER, Achilles and Ajax playing a dice game (Attic bilingual amphora), from Orvieto, Italy, ca. 525–520 BCE. Black-figure side *(left)* and red-figure side *(right)*. Approx. 1′ 9″ high. Museum of Fine Arts, Boston.

his own invention. But he created a technique that, in the hands of other, more skilled artists, helped revolutionize the art of drawing.

**EUPHRONIOS AND RED-FIGURE** One of these younger and more adventurous painters was EUPHRONIOS, whose krater depicting the struggle between Herakles and Antaios (FIG. **5-21**) reveals the exciting possibilities of the new red-figure technique. Antaios was a Libyan giant, a son of Earth, and he derived his power from contact with the ground. To defeat him, Herakles had to lift him up into the air and strangle him while no part of the giant's body touched the earth. But Euphronios did not represent the moment of Herakles' triumph. The two wrestle on the ground, and Antaios still possesses enormous strength. Nonetheless, Herakles has the upper hand. The giant's face is a mask of pain. His eyes roll and his teeth are bared. His right arm is paralyzed, with the fingers limp. Euphronios used diluted glaze to show Antaios's unkempt golden brown hair—intentionally contrasted with the neat coiffure and carefully trimmed beard of the emotionless Greek hero.

The artist also used thinned glaze to delineate the muscles of both figures. But Euphronios was interested in more than rendering human anatomy convincingly. He also wished to show that his figures occupy space. Euphronios deliberately rejected the conventional composite posture for the human figure, which communicates so well the specific parts of the human body, and attempted to reproduce how a particular human body is *seen*. He presented, for example, not only Antaios's torso but also his right thigh from the front. The lower leg disappears behind the giant, and one glimpses only part of the right foot. The viewer must mentally make the connection between the upper leg and the foot. The red-figure painter did not create a two-dimensional panel filled with figures in stereotypical postures, as his Archaic and pre-Greek predecessors always did. His panel is a window onto a mythological world with protagonists occupying three-dimensional space—a revolutionary new conception of what a picture was supposed to be.

**RIVALS OF EUPHRONIOS** A preoccupation with the art of drawing per se may be seen in a remarkable amphora (FIG. **5-22**) painted by EUTHYMIDES, a contemporary and competitor of Euphronios. The subject is appropriate for a wine storage jar—three tipsy revelers. But the theme was little more than an excuse for the artist to experiment with the representation of unusual positions of the human form. It is no coincidence that the bodies do not overlap, for each is an independent figure study. Euthymides cast aside the conventional frontal and profile composite views. Instead, he painted torsos that are not two-dimensional surface patterns but are *foreshortened,* that is, drawn in a three-quarter view. Most noteworthy is the central figure, who is shown from the rear with a twisting spinal column and buttocks in three-quarter view. Earlier artists had no interest in attempting such postures because they not only are incomplete but also do not show the "main" side of the human body. But for Euthymides the challenge of drawing the figure from such an unusual viewpoint was a reward in itself. With understandable pride he proclaimed his achievement by adding to the formulaic signature "Euthymides painted me" the phrase "as never Euphronios [could do]"!

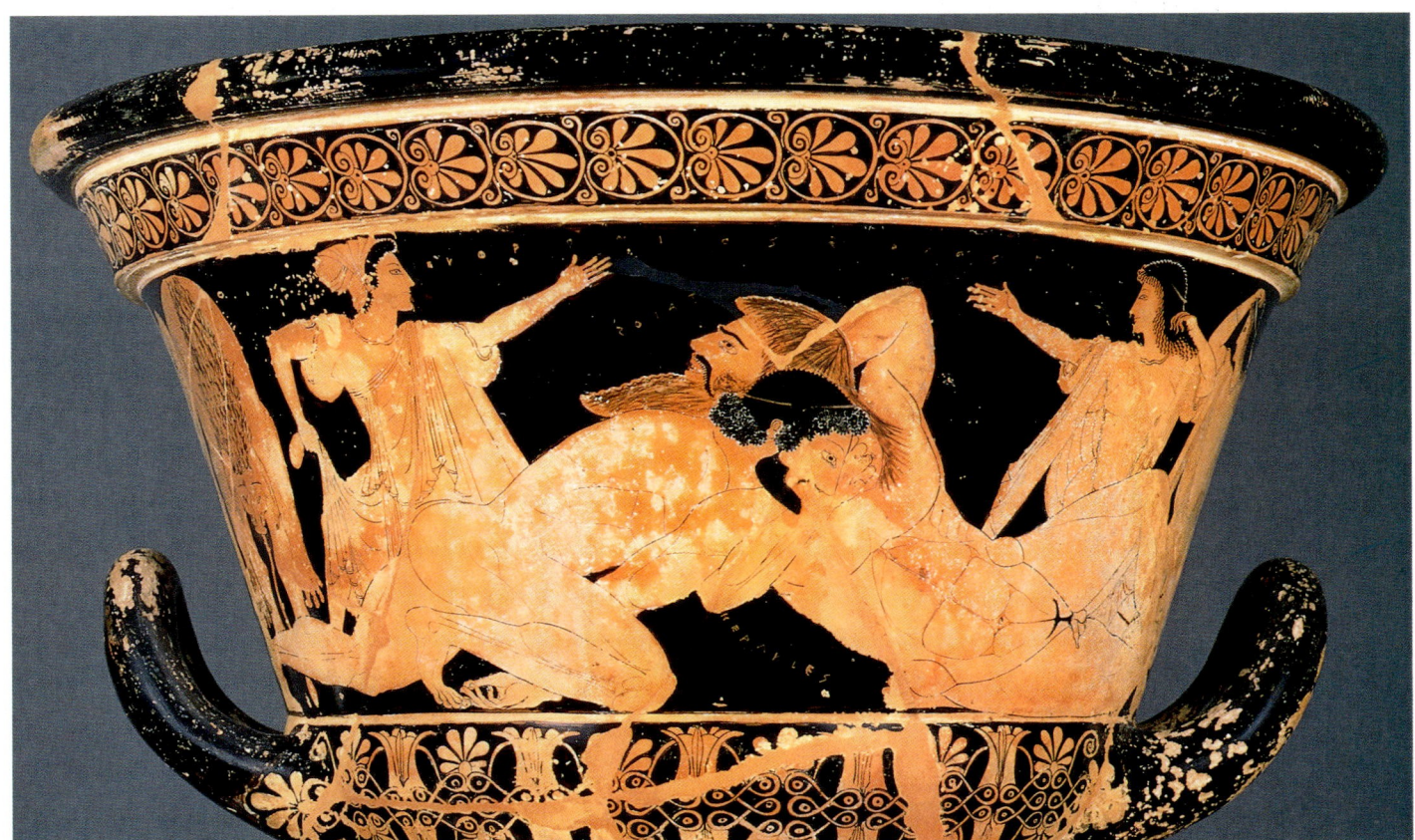

**5-21** EUPHRONIOS, Herakles wrestling Antaios (detail of an Attic red-figure calyx krater), from Cerveteri, Italy, ca. 510 BCE. Whole vessel approx. 1′ 7″ high. Louvre, Paris.

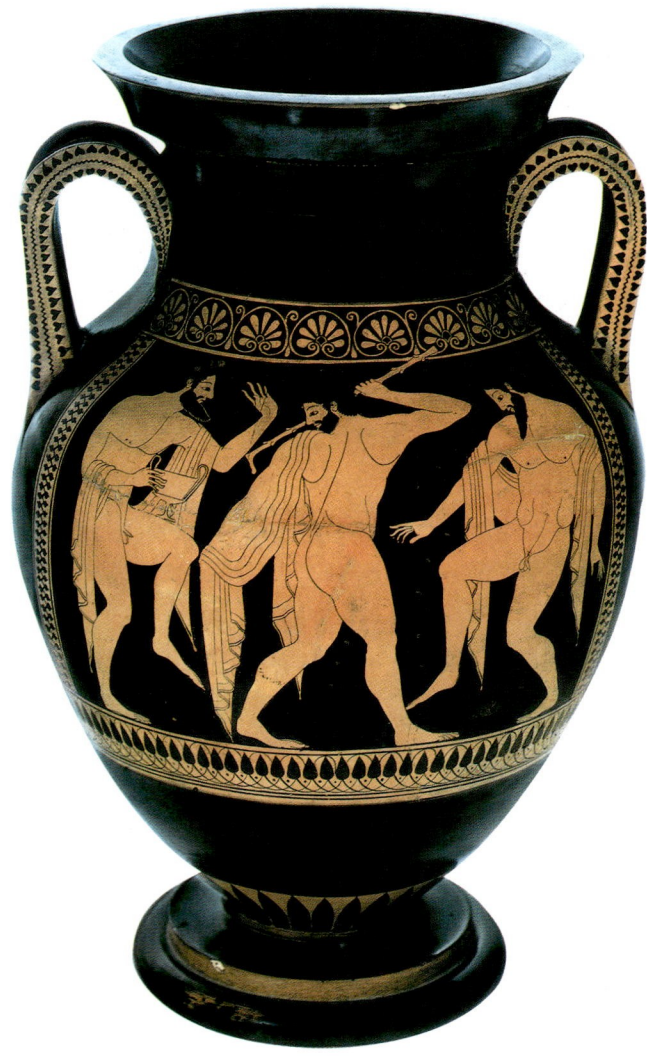

5-22 EUTHYMIDES, Three revelers (Attic red-figure amphora), from Vulci, Italy, ca. 510 BCE. Approx. 2′ high. Staatliche Antikensammlungen, Munich.

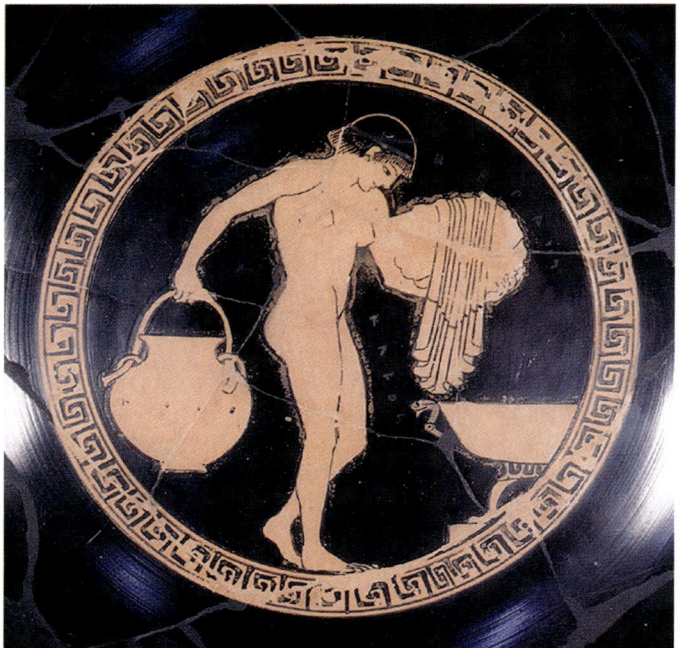

5-23 ONESIMOS, Girl preparing to bathe (interior of an Attic red-figure kylix), from Chiusi, Italy, ca. 490 BCE. Tondo approx. 6″ in diameter. Musées Royaux, Brussels.

THE FEMALE NUDE Interest in the foreshortening of the human figure soon extended to studies of nude women, as on the interior (FIG. 5-23) of a *kylix* (drinking cup) by ONESIMOS. The representation is unusual not only for the successful foreshortening of the girl's torso and breasts, seen in three-quarter view, but also for its subject. This is neither mythology nor a scene of wealthy noblemen partying. This is a servant girl, not the lady of the house, who has removed her clothes to bathe. Such a genre scene, not to mention female nudity, would never have been portrayed publicly in monumental painting or sculpture of this time. Only in the private sphere was such a subject acceptable.

## Aegina and the Transition to the Classical Period

EVOLUTION AND REVOLUTION The years just before and after 500 BCE were also a time of dynamic transition in architecture and architectural sculpture. Some of the changes were evolutionary in nature, others revolutionary. Both kinds are evident in

the Temple at Aegina dedicated to Aphaia, a local goddess. The temple (FIG. 5-24) sits on a prominent ridge with dramatic views out to the sea. The colonnade is 45 × 95 feet and consists of 6 Doric columns on the facade and 12 on the flanks. This is a much more compact structure than the impressive but ungainly Archaic Temple of Hera I at Paestum (FIG. 5-13), even though the ratio of width to length is similar. Doric architects had learned a great deal in the half century that elapsed between construction of the two temples. The columns of the Aegina temple are more widely spaced and more slender. The capitals create a smooth transition from the vertical shafts below to the horizontal architrave above. Gone are the Archaic flattened echinuses and bulging shafts of the Paestum columns.

The Aegina architect also refined the temple plan and internal elevation (FIG. 5-25). In place of a single row of columns down the center of the cella is a double colonnade—and each row has two stories. This arrangement allowed a statue to be placed on the central axis and also gave those gathered in front of the building an unobstructed view through the pair of columns in the pronaos.

Both pediments were filled with life-size statuary (FIG. 5-26) depicting the same subject and using a similar composition. The theme was the battle of Greeks and Trojans, with Athena at the center of the bloody combat. She is larger than all the other figures because she is superhuman, but the sculptors carved all the mortal heroes at the same scale, regardless of the statue's position in the pediment. Unlike the experimental design at Corfu (FIG. 5-15), the Aegina pediments feature a unified theme and consistent size. The latter was achieved by using the whole range of body postures from upright (Athena) to leaning, falling, kneeling, and lying (Greeks and Trojans).

ARCHAISM TO CLASSICISM The sculptures of the Aegina pediments were set in place when the temple was completed

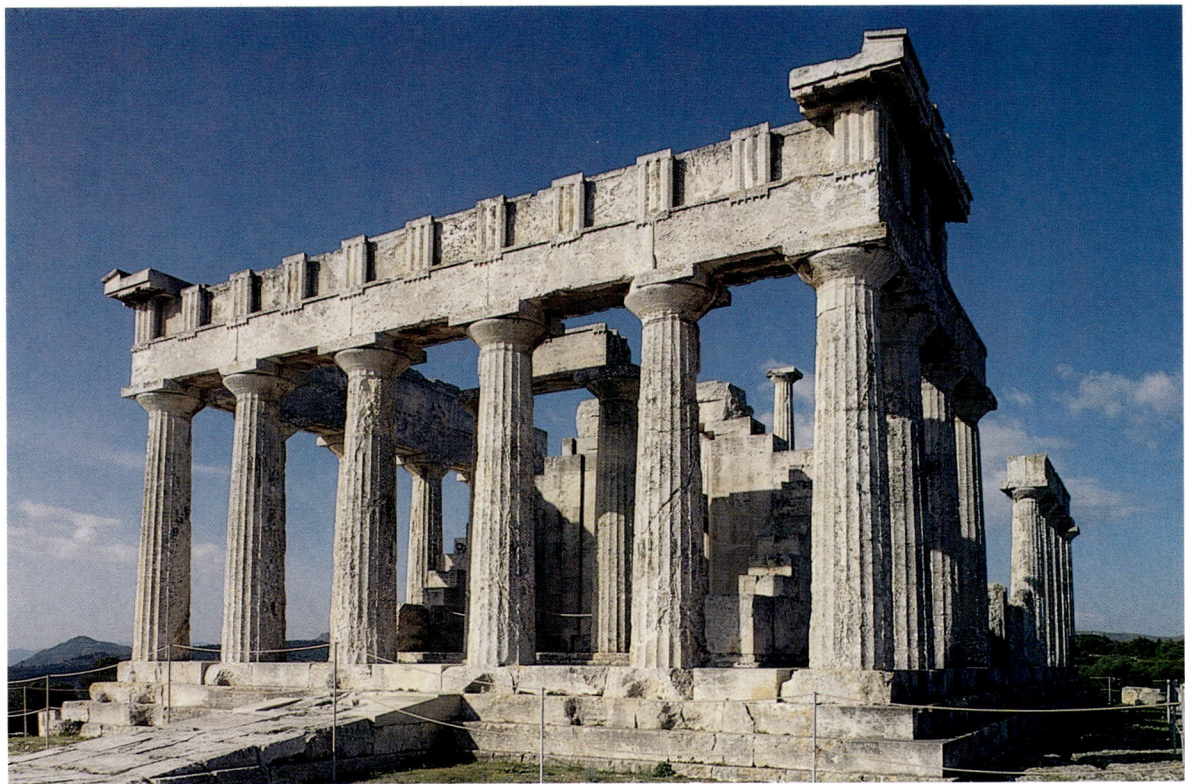

**5-24** Temple of Aphaia, Aegina, Greece, ca. 500–490 BCE.

around 490 BCE. But the pedimental statues at the eastern end were damaged and replaced with a new group a decade or two later. It is very instructive to compare the earlier and later figures. The west pediment's dying warrior (FIG. 5-27) was still conceived in the Archaic mode. His torso is rigidly frontal, and he looks out directly at the spectator. In fact, he smiles at us, in spite of the bronze arrow that punctures his chest. He is like a mannequin in a store window whose arms and legs have been arranged by someone else for effective display. The viewer has no sense whatsoever of a thinking and feeling human being.

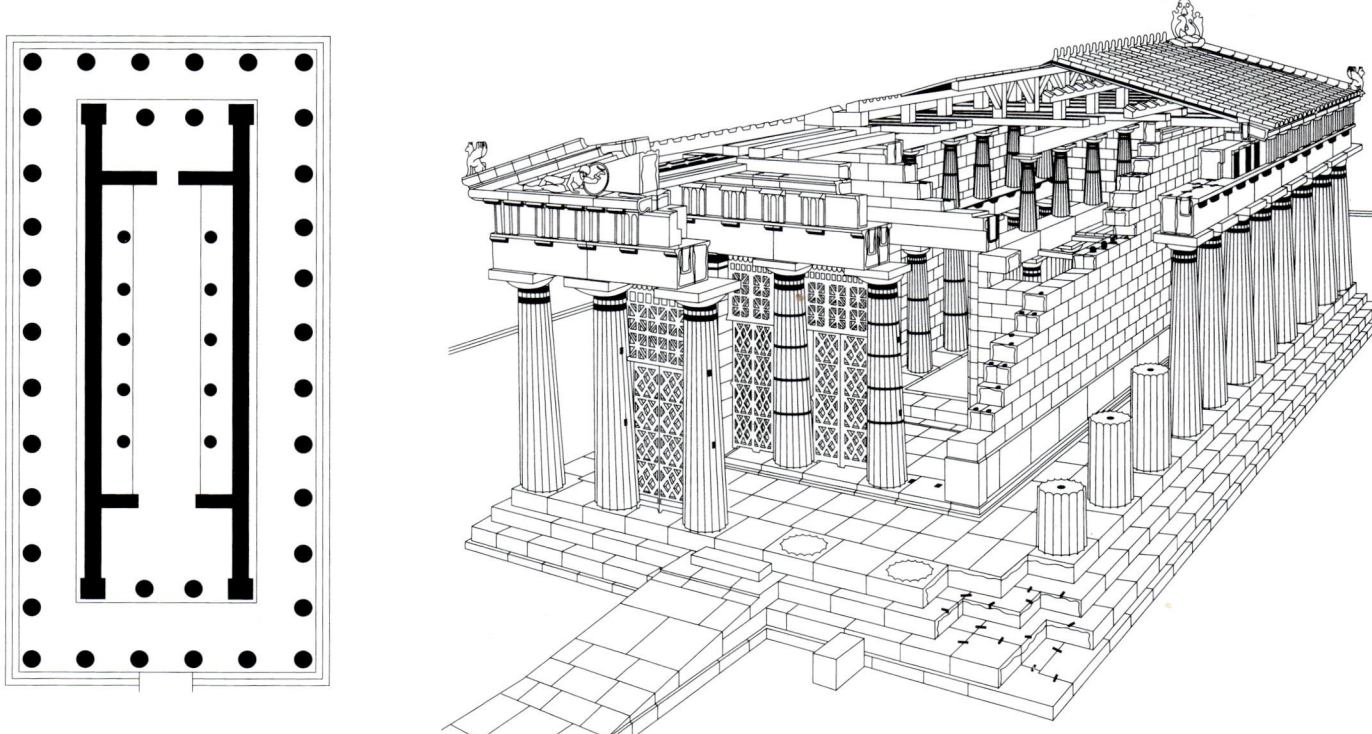

**5-25** Plan (left) and restored cutaway view (right) of the Temple of Aphaia, Aegina, Greece, ca. 500–490 BCE.

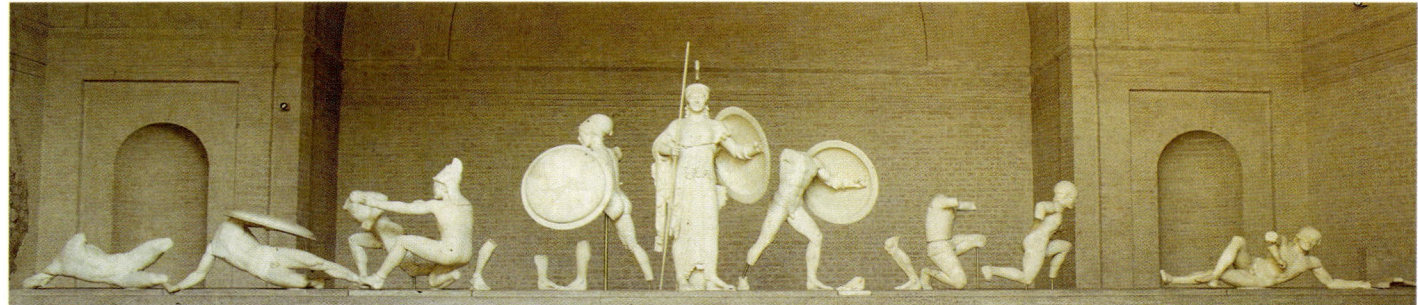

**5-26** West pediment of the Temple of Aphaia, Aegina, Greece, ca. 500-490 BCE. Marble, approx. 5′ 8″ high at center. Glyptothek, Munich.

**5-27** Dying warrior, from the west pediment of the Temple of Aphaia, Aegina, Greece, ca. 500–490 BCE. Marble, approx. 5′ 2½″ long. Glyptothek, Munich.

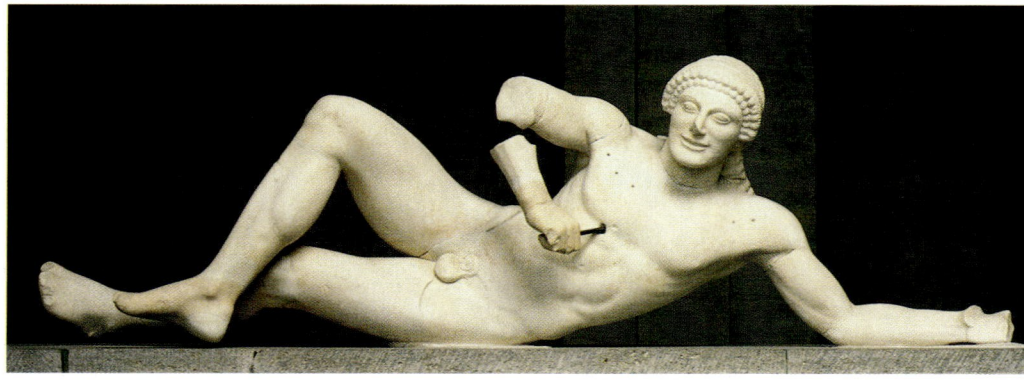

**5-28** Dying warrior, from the east pediment of the Temple of Aphaia, Aegina, Greece, ca. 490–480 BCE. Marble, approx. 6′ 1″ long. Glyptothek, Munich.

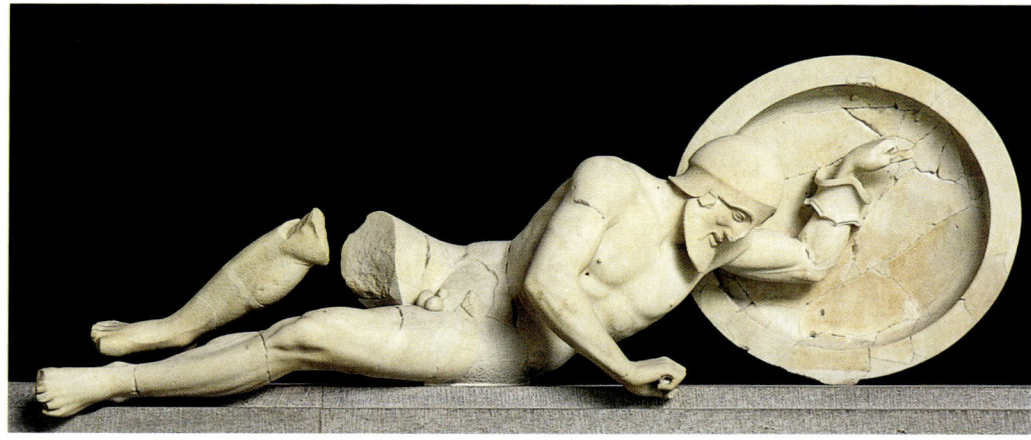

The comparable figure (FIG. 5-28) in the later east pediment is radically different. His posture is more natural and more complex, with the torso placed at an angle to the viewer. (He is on a par with the painted figures of Euphronios, FIG. 5-21.) More-over, he reacts to his wound as a flesh-and-blood human would. He knows that death is inevitable, but he still struggles to rise once again, using his shield for support. And he does not look out at the spectator. He is concerned with his pain, not with the spec-tator. Only a decade, perhaps two, separates the two statues, but they belong to different eras. The later warrior is not a creation of the Archaic world, when sculptors imposed anatomical patterns (and smiles) on statues from without. This statue belongs to the Classical world, where statues move as humans move and possess the self-consciousness of real men and women. This was a radical change in the conception of what a statue was meant to be. In sculpture, as in painting, the Classical revolution had occurred.

# THE EARLY AND HIGH CLASSICAL PERIODS

**THE AFTERMATH OF WAR** Art historians reckon the begin-ning of the Classical* age from a historical event, the defeat of the Persian invaders of Greece by the allied Hellenic city-states. Shortly after Athens was occupied and sacked in 480 BCE, the Greeks won a decisive naval victory over the Persians at Salamis. It had been a difficult war, and at times it had seemed as though

---

*Note: In *Art through the Ages* the adjective "Classical," with uppercase *C*, refers specifically to the Classical period of ancient Greece, 480–323 BCE. Lowercase "classical" refers to Greco-Roman antiquity in general, that is, the period treated in Chapters 5, 9, and 10.

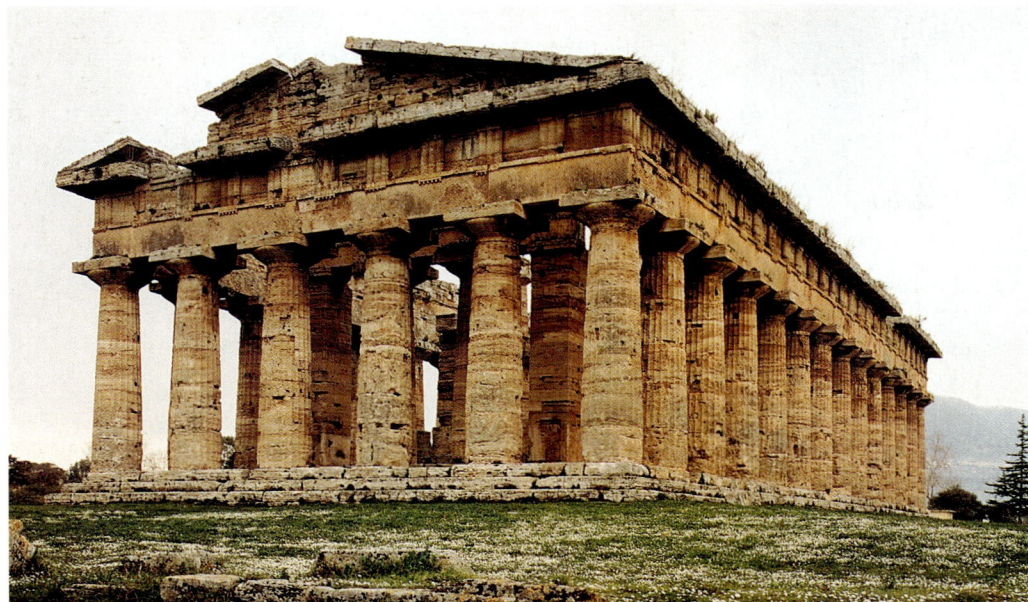

Asia would swallow up Greece, and the Persian king Xerxes (see Chapter 2) would rule over all. When the Persians destroyed the Greek city Miletos in 494 BCE, they killed the male inhabitants and sold the women and children into slavery. The close escape of the Greeks from domination by Asian "barbarians" nurtured a sense of Hellenic identity so strong that from then on the history of European civilization would be distinct from the civilization of Asia, even though they continued to interact.

Typical of the time were the views of the great dramatist Aeschylus, who celebrated, in his *Oresteia,* the triumph of reason and law over barbarous crimes, blood feuds, and mad vengeance. Himself a veteran of the epic battle of Marathon, Aeschylus repudiated in majestic verse all the slavish and inhuman traits of nature that the Greeks at that time of crisis associated with the Persians.

The decades following the removal of the Persian threat are universally considered the high point of Greek civilization. This is the era of the dramatists Sophocles and Euripides, as well as Aeschylus, the historian Herodotus, the statesman Pericles, the philosopher Socrates, and many of the most famous Greek architects, sculptors, and painters.

## Architecture and Architectural Sculpture

**ZEUS'S OLYMPIAN TEMPLE** The first great monument of Classical art and architecture is the Temple of Zeus at Olympia,

site of the Olympic Games. The temple was begun about 470 BCE and was probably completed by 457 BCE. The architect was LIBON OF ELIS. Today the structure is in ruins, its picturesque tumbled column drums an eloquent reminder of the effect of the passage of time on even the grandest monuments humans have built. One can get a good idea of its original appearance, however, by looking at a slightly later Doric temple modeled closely on the Olympian shrine of Zeus—the second Temple of Hera at Paestum (FIG. 5-29). The plans and elevations of both temples follow the pattern of the Temple of Aphaia at Aegina (FIG. 5-25): an even number of columns (six) on the short ends, two columns in antis, and two rows of columns in two stories inside the cella. But the Temple of Zeus was more lavishly decorated than even the Aphaia temple. Statues filled both pediments, and the six metopes over the doorway in the pronaos and the matching six of the opisthodomos were adorned with reliefs.

**TREACHERY AND A CURSE** The subject of the Temple of Zeus's east pediment (FIG. 5-30) had deep local significance: the chariot race between Pelops (from whom the Peloponnesos takes its name) and King Oinomaos. The story is a sinister one. Oinomaos had one daughter, Hippodameia, and it was foretold that he would die if she married. Consequently, Oinomaos challenged any suitor who wished to make Hippodameia his bride to a chariot race from Olympia to Corinth. If the suitor won, he also won the hand of the king's daughter. But if he lost, he was killed. The

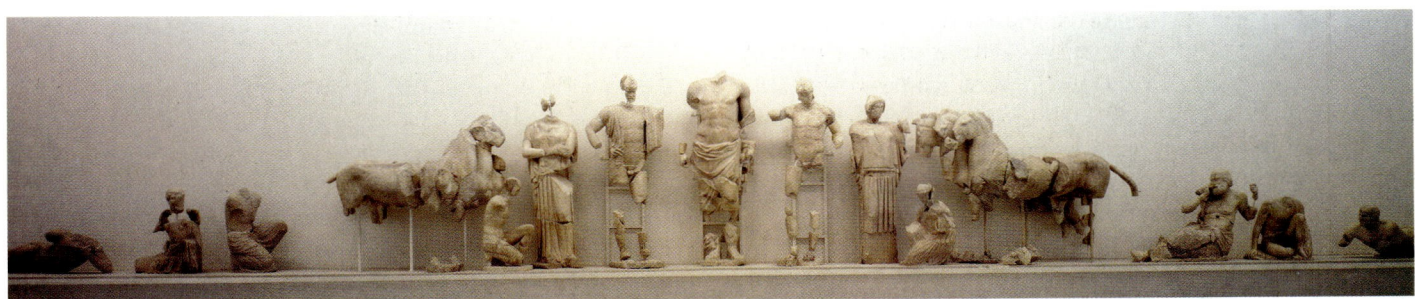

5-30 East pediment from the Temple of Zeus, Olympia, Greece, ca. 470–456 BCE. Marble, approx. 87′ wide. Archaeological Museum, Olympia.

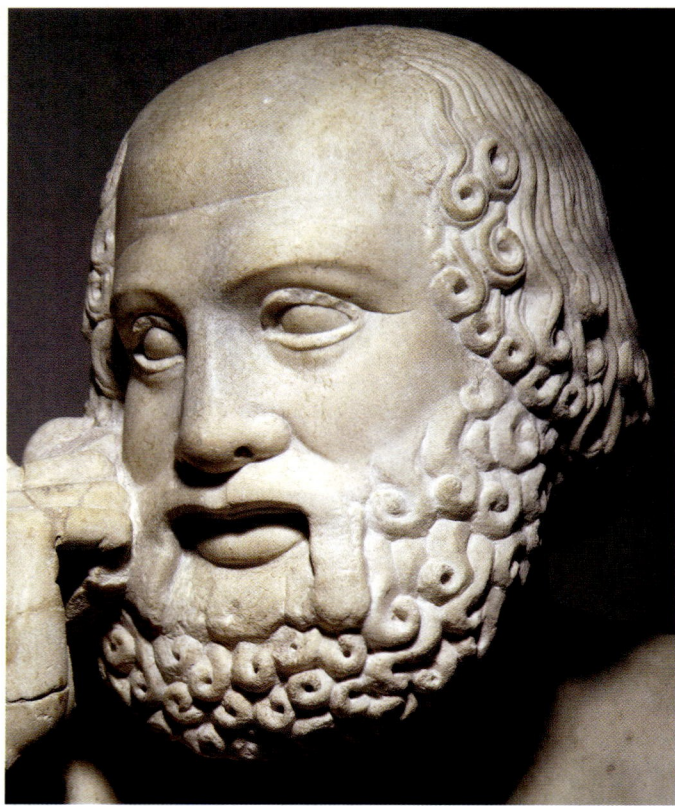

5-31 Seer, from the east pediment of the Temple of Zeus, Olympia, Greece, ca. 470–456 BCE. Marble, full figure approx. 4′ 6″ high. Archaeological Museum, Olympia.

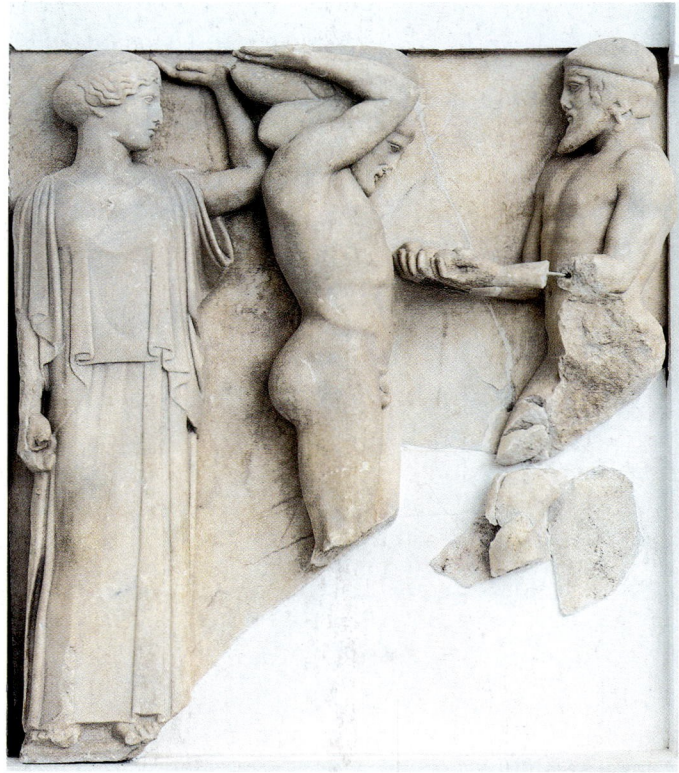

5-32 Athena, Herakles, and Atlas with the apples of the Hesperides, metope from the Temple of Zeus, Olympia, Greece, ca. 470–456 BCE. Marble, approx. 5′ 3″ high. Archaeological Museum, Olympia.

outcome of each race was predetermined, because Oinomaos possessed divine horses his father Ares gave him. To ensure his victory when all others had failed, Pelops resorted to bribing the king's groom, Myrtilos, to rig the royal chariot so that it would collapse during the race. Oinomaos was killed and Pelops won his bride, but he drowned Myrtilos rather than pay his debt to him. Before he died, Myrtilos brought a curse on Pelops and his descendants. This curse led to the murder of Pelops's son Atreus and to events that figure prominently in some of the greatest Greek tragedies of the classical era, Aeschylus's three plays known collectively as the *Oresteia*: the sacrifice by Atreus's son Agamemnon of his daughter Iphigeneia; the slaying of Agamemnon by Aegisthus, lover of Agamemnon's wife Clytaemnestra; and the murder of Aegisthus and Clytaemnestra by Orestes, the son of Agamemnon and Clytaemnestra.

The pedimental statues (which faced toward the starting point of all Olympic chariot races) are, in fact, posed like actors on a stage—Zeus in the center, Oinomaos and his wife on one side, Pelops and Hippodameia on the other, and their respective chariots to each side. All are quiet; the horrible events known to every spectator have yet to occur. Only one man reacts—a seer (FIG. 5-31) who knows the future. He is a remarkable figure. Unlike the gods, heroes, and noble youths and maidens who are the almost exclusive subjects of Archaic and Classical Greek statuary, this seer is a rare depiction of old age. He has a balding, wrinkled head and sagging musculature—and a shocked expression on his face. This is a true show of emotion, unlike the stereotypical "Archaic smile," without precedent in earlier Greek sculpture and not a regular feature of Greek art until the Hellenistic age.

**THE LABORS OF HERAKLES** The metopes of the Zeus temple are also thematically connected with the site, for they depict the 12 labors of Herakles (see "Herakles," page 109), the legendary founder of the Olympic Games. In the metope illustrated here (FIG. 5-32), Herakles holds up the sky (with the aid of the goddess Athena—and a cushion) in place of Atlas, who had undertaken the dangerous journey to fetch the golden apples of the Hesperides for the hero. The load soon will be transferred back to Atlas, but now each of the very high relief figures in the metope stands quietly with the same serene dignity as the statues in the Olympia pediment.

In both attitude and dress (simple Doric peplos for the women), all the Olympia figures display a severity that contrasts sharply with the smiling and elaborately clad figures of the Late Archaic period. Many art historians call this Early Classical phase of Greek art the "Severe Style."

## Statuary

**A NEW WAY TO STAND** Early Classical sculptors were also the first to break away from the rigid and unnatural Egyptian-inspired pose of the Archaic kouroi. This change may be seen in the postures of the Olympia figures and in a somewhat earlier statue from the Athenian Acropolis that, although it is well under life-size, is one of the most important works of Greek sculpture. It is known as the *Kritios Boy* (FIG. 5-33) because it was once thought to have been carved by the sculptor KRITIOS. Never before had a sculptor been concerned with portraying how a human being (as opposed to a stone image) actually stands. Real people do not stand in the stiff-legged pose of the kouroi and korai or their Egyptian predecessors. Humans shift their weight and the position of the main body parts around the vertical, but flexible, axis of the spine. When

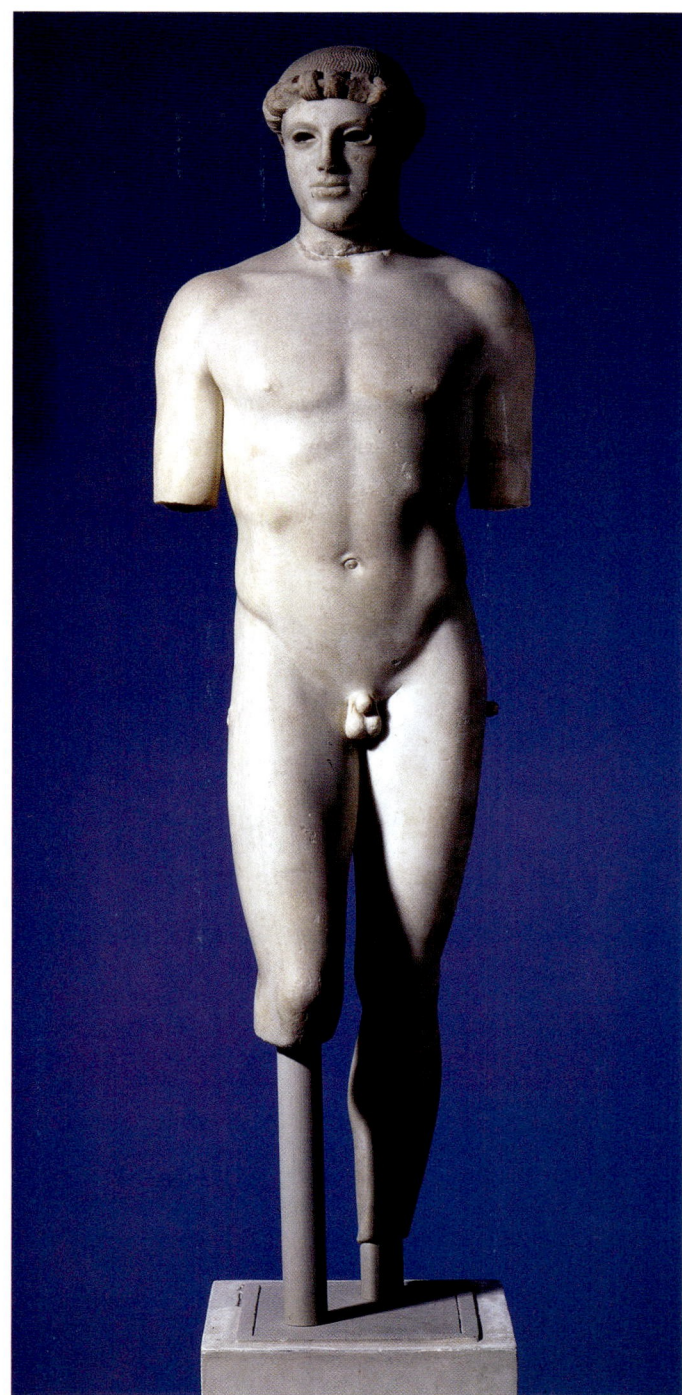

**5-33** *Kritios Boy,* from the Acropolis, Athens, Greece, ca. 480 BCE. Marble, approx. 2′ 10″ high. Acropolis Museum, Athens.

humans move, the body's elastic musculoskeletal structure dictates a harmonious, smooth motion of all its elements. The sculptor of the *Kritios Boy* was among the first to grasp this fact and to represent it in statuary. The youth has a slight dip to the right hip, indicating the shifting of weight onto his left leg. His right leg is bent, at ease. The head also turns slightly to the right and tilts, breaking the unwritten rule of frontality dictating the form of virtually all earlier statues. This weight shift, which art historians describe as *contrapposto* (counterbalance), separates Classical from Archaic Greek statuary. Its reappearance, after a long absence, is one of the hallmarks of the renewed interest in Classical art during the later Middle Ages and Renaissance.

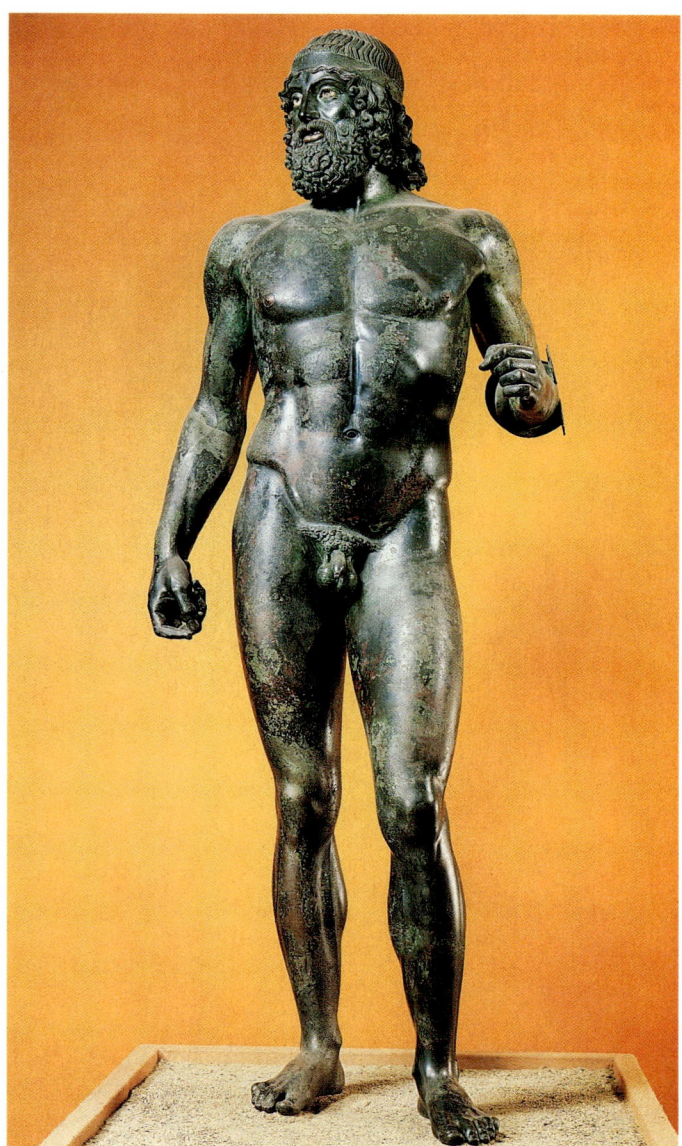

**5-34** Warrior, from the sea off Riace, Italy, ca. 460–450 BCE. Bronze, approx. 6′ 6″ high. Archaeological Museum, Reggio Calabria.

**RESCUED FROM THE SEA** The innovations of the *Kritios Boy* were carried even further in the bronze statue of a warrior (FIG. **5-34**) found in the sea near Riace at the "toe" of the Italian "boot." It is one of a pair of statues a diver accidentally discovered in the cargo of a ship that sank in antiquity on its way from Greece probably to Rome, where Greek sculpture was much admired. Known as the Riace Bronzes, they had to undergo several years of cleaning and restoration after nearly two millennia of submersion in salt water, but they are nearly intact. The statue shown here lacks only its shield, spear, and helmet. It is a masterpiece of hollow-casting (see "Hollow-Casting Life-Size Bronze Statues," page 131), with inlaid eyes, silver teeth and eyelashes, and copper lips and nipples (see FIG. Intro-17). The weight shift is more pronounced than in the *Kritios Boy.* The warrior's head turns more forcefully to the right, his shoulders tilt, his hips swing more markedly, and his arms have been freed from the body. Natural motion in space has replaced Archaic frontality and rigidity.

**VICTORY AT DELPHI** The high technical quality of the Riace warrior is equaled in another bronze statue set up a decade or two earlier to commemorate the victory of the tyrant Polyzalos of

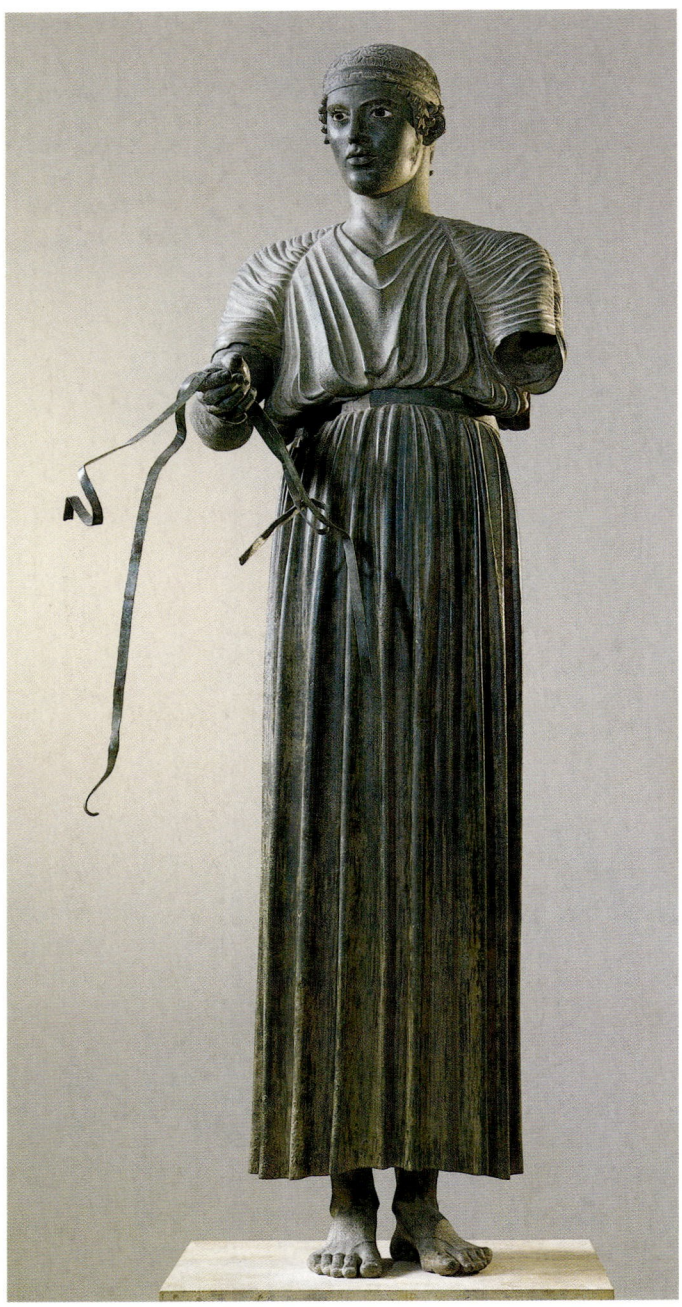

5-35 Charioteer, from a group dedicated by Polyzalos of Gela in the Sanctuary of Apollo, Delphi, Greece, ca. 470 BCE. Bronze, approx. 5′ 11″ high. Archaeological Museum, Delphi.

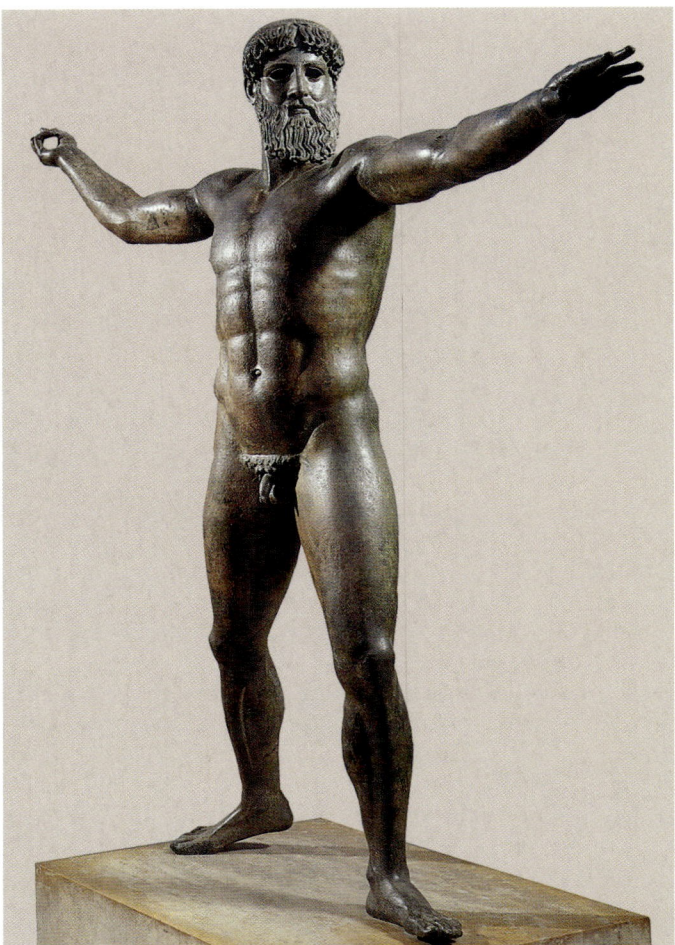

5-36 Zeus (or Poseidon?), from the sea off Cape Artemision, Greece, ca. 460–450 BCE. Bronze, approx. 6′ 10″ high. National Archaeological Museum, Athens.

the head and confines the hair. The eyes are made of glass paste and shaded by delicate bronze lashes.

**ZEUS THE THUNDERER** The male human form in motion is, in contrast, the subject of another Early Classical bronze statue (FIG. 5-36), which, like the Riace warrior, divers found in an ancient shipwreck, this time off the coast of Greece itself at Cape Artemision. The bearded god once hurled a weapon held in his right hand, probably a thunderbolt, in which case he is Zeus. A less likely suggestion is that this is Poseidon with his trident. The pose could be employed equally well for a javelin thrower. Both arms are boldly extended, and the right heel is raised off the ground, underscoring the lightness and stability of hollow-cast monumental statues.

**GREEK STATUES IN ROMAN COPIES** A bronze statue similar to the Artemision Zeus was the renowned *Diskobolos (Discus Thrower)* by MYRON, which is known only through marble copies (FIG. 5-37) made in Roman times. Even when the original was removed from Greece, as were the Riace and Artemision bronzes, only one community or individual could own it. Demand so far exceeded the supply that a veritable industry was born to meet the Roman call for Greek statuary to display in public places and private villas alike. The copies usually were made in less costly marble. The change in medium resulted in a different surface appearance. In most cases, the copyist also had to add an intrusive tree trunk to support the great weight of the stone statue and struts between arms and body to strengthen weak points. The

Gela (Sicily) in a chariot race at Delphi. The statue (FIG. 5-35) is almost all that remains of an enormous group composed of Polyzalos's driver, the chariot, the team of horses, and a young groom. The charioteer stands in an almost Archaic pose, but the turn of the head and feet in opposite directions as well as a slight twist at the waist are in keeping with the Severe Style. The moment chosen for depiction is not during the frenetic race but after, when the driver quietly and modestly holds his horses still in the winner's circle. He grasps the reins in his outstretched right hand (the lower left arm, cast separately, is missing), and he wears the standard charioteer's garment, girdled high and held in at the shoulders and the back to keep it from flapping. The folds emphasize both the verticality and calm of the figure and recall the flutes of a Greek column. A band inlaid with silver is tied around

### Hollow-Casting Life-Size Bronze Statues

Monumental bronze statues such as the Riace warrior (FIG. 5-34), the Delphi charioteer (FIG. 5-35), and the Artemision god (FIG. 5-36) required great technical skill to produce. They could not be manufactured using a single simple mold, as were small-scale Geometric and Archaic figures (FIGS. 5-2 and 5-3). Weight, cost, and the tendency of large masses of bronze to distort when cooling made life-size castings in solid bronze impractical, if not impossible. Instead, large statues were hollow-cast by the *cire perdue* (lost-wax) method. The lost-wax process entailed several steps and had to be repeated many times, because monumental statues were typically cast in parts—head, arms, hands, torso, and so forth.

First, the sculptor fashioned a full-size clay model of the intended statue. Then a clay master mold was made around the model and removed in sections. When dry, the various pieces of the master mold were put back together for each separate body part. Next, a layer of beeswax was applied to the inside of each mold. When the wax cooled, the mold was removed, and the sculptor was left with a hollow wax model in the shape of the original clay model. The artist could then correct or refine details—for example, engrave fingernails on the wax hands or individual locks of hair on the head.

In the next stage, a final clay mold *(investment)* was applied to the exterior of the wax model, and a liquid clay core was poured inside the hollow wax. Metal pins *(chaplets)* then were driven through the new mold to connect the investment with the clay core *(a)*. Now the wax was melted out ("lost") and molten bronze poured into the mold in its place *(b)*. When the bronze hardened and assumed the shape of the wax model, the investment and as much of the core as possible were removed, and the casting process was complete. Finally, the individually cast pieces were fitted together and soldered, surface imperfections and joins smoothed, eyes inlaid, teeth and eyelashes added, attributes such as spears and wreaths provided, and so forth. Such statues were costly to make and much prized.

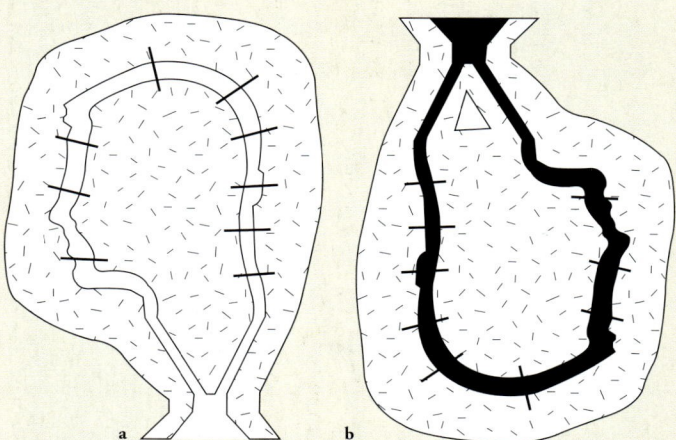

Two stages of the lost-wax method of bronze casting (after S. A. Hemingway[1]): *(a)* clay mold (investment), wax model, and clay core connected by chaplets; *(b)* wax melted out and molten bronze poured into the mold.

[1] Sean A. Hemingway, *How Bronze Statues Were Made in Classical Antiquity* (Cambridge: Harvard University Art Museums, 1996), 4.

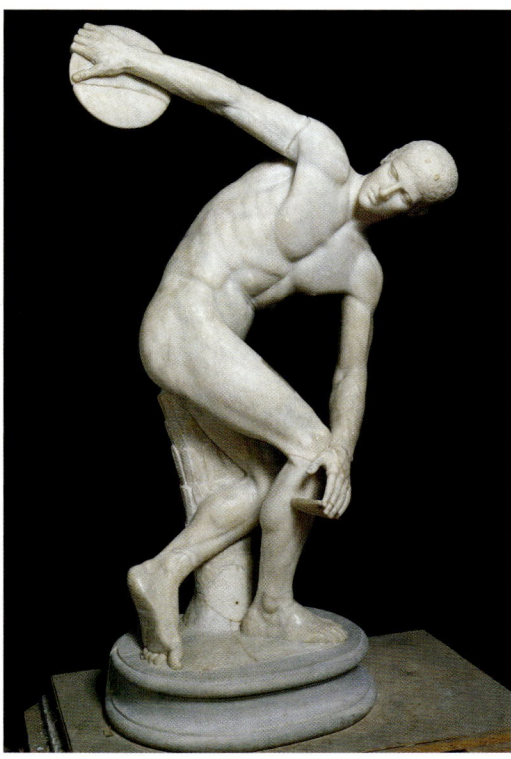

5-37 MYRON, *Diskobolos (Discus Thrower)*. Roman marble copy after a bronze original of ca. 450 BCE, 5′ 1″ high. Museo Nazionale Romano—Palazzo Massimo alle Terme.

copies rarely approach the quality of the originals, and the Roman sculptors sometimes took liberties with their models to conform to their own tastes and needs. Occasionally, for example, a mirror image of the original was created for a specific setting. Nevertheless, the copies are indispensable today. Without them it would be impossible to reconstruct the history of Greek sculpture after the Archaic period.

Myron's *Discus Thrower* is a vigorous action statue, like the Artemision Zeus, but it is composed in an almost Archaic manner, with profile limbs and a nearly frontal chest, suggesting the tension of a coiled spring. Like the arm of a pendulum clock, the right arm of the *Diskobolos* has reached the apex of its arc but has not yet begun to swing down again. Myron froze the action and arranged the body and limbs to form two intersecting arcs, creating the impression of a tightly stretched bow a moment before the string is released. This tension is not, however, mirrored in the athlete's face, which remains expressionless. Once again, as in the later of the two warrior statues from the Aegina pediments (FIG. 5-28), the head is turned away from the spectator. In contrast to Archaic athlete statues, the Classical *Diskobolos* does not perform for the spectator but concentrates on the task at hand.

**THE QUEST FOR IDEAL FORM** One of the most frequently copied Greek statues was the *Doryphoros (Spear Bearer)* by POLYKLEITOS, a work that epitomizes the intellectual rigor of Classical statuary design. The original is lost. We illustrate a marble copy that stood in a palaestra at Pompeii, where it served as a model for

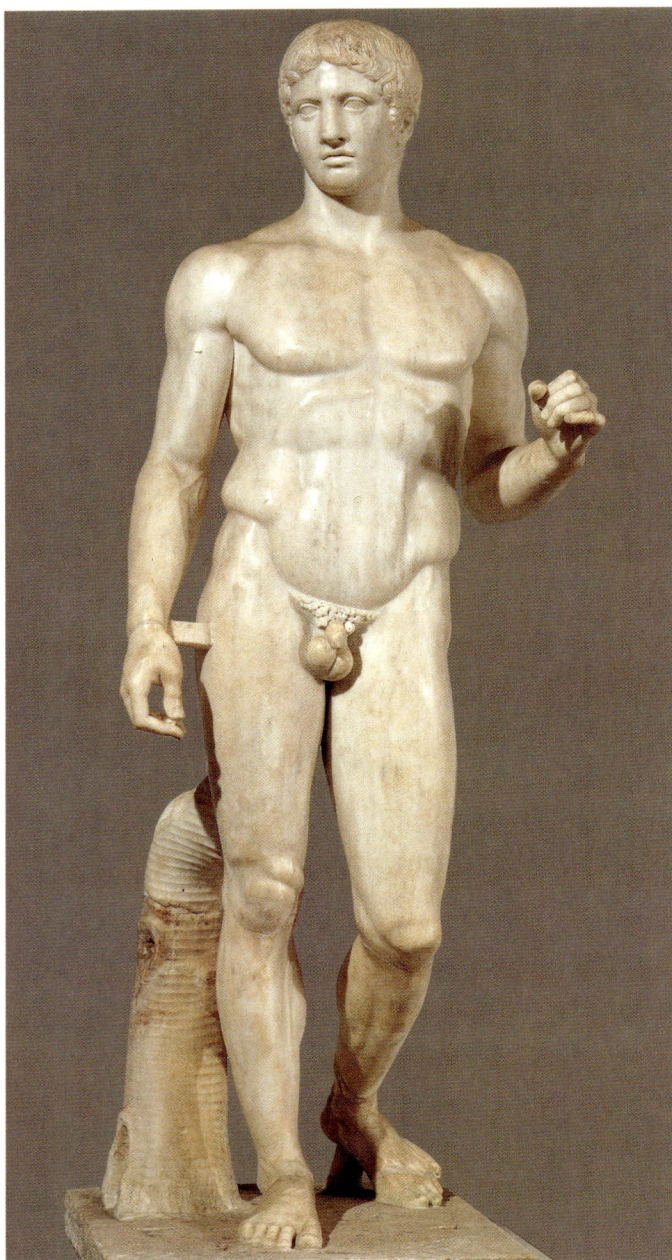

**5-38** POLYKLEITOS, *Doryphoros (Spear Bearer)*. Roman marble copy from Pompeii, Italy, after a bronze original of ca. 450–440 BCE, 6′ 11″ high. Museo Nazionale, Naples.

Roman athletes (FIG. **5-38**). The *Doryphoros* is the embodiment of Polykleitos's vision of the ideal statue of a nude male athlete or warrior. In fact, it was made as a demonstration piece to accompany a treatise on the subject. *Spear Bearer* is but a modern descriptive epithet for the statue. The name Polykleitos assigned to it was *Canon* (see "Polykleitos's Prescription for the Perfect Statue," page 133).

The *Doryphoros* is the culmination of the evolution in Greek statuary from the Archaic kouros to the *Kritios Boy* to the *Riace* warrior. The contrapposto is more pronounced than ever before in a standing statue, but Polykleitos was not content with simply rendering a figure that stands naturally. His aim was to impose order on human movement, to make it "beautiful," to "perfect" it. He achieved this through a system of *chiastic,* or cross, balance. What appears at first to be a casually natural pose is, in fact, the result of an extremely complex and subtle organization of the figure's various parts. Note, for instance, how the rigid supporting leg is echoed by the straight-hanging arm, providing the figure's

right side with the columnar stability needed to anchor the left side's dynamically flexed limbs. If read anatomically, however, the tensed and relaxed limbs may be seen to oppose each other diagonally—the right arm and the left leg are relaxed, and the tensed supporting leg opposes the flexed arm, which held a spear. In like manner, the head turns to the right while the hips twist slightly to the left. And although the *Doryphoros* seems to take a step forward, he does not move. This dynamic asymmetrical balance, this motion while at rest, and the resulting harmony of opposites are the essence of the Polykleitan style.

## The Athenian Acropolis

**ALLIANCE AND TYRANNY** While Polykleitos was formulating his *Canon* in Argos, the Athenians, under the leadership of Pericles, were at work on one of the most ambitious building projects ever undertaken, the reconstruction of the Acropolis after the Persian sack of 480 BCE. Athens, despite the damage it suffered at the hands of the army of Xerxes, emerged from the war with enormous power and prestige. The Athenian commander Themistocles had decisively defeated the Persian navy off the island of Salamis, southwest of Athens, and forced it to retreat to Asia.

In 478 BCE, in the aftermath of the Persians' expulsion from the Aegean, the Greeks formed an alliance for mutual protection against any renewed threat from the east. The new confederacy came to be known as the Delian League, because its headquarters were on the sacred island of Delos, midway between the Greek mainland and the coast of Asia Minor. Although at the outset each league member had an equal vote, Athens was "first among equals," providing the allied fleet commander and determining which cities were to furnish ships and which were instead to pay an annual tribute to the treasury at Delos. Continued fighting against the Persians kept the alliance intact, but Athens gradually assumed a dominant role. In 454 BCE the Delian treasury was transferred to Athens, ostensibly for security reasons. Pericles, who was only in his teens when the Persians laid waste to the Acropolis, was by midcentury the recognized leader of the Athenians, and he succeeded in converting the alliance into an Athenian empire. Tribute continued to be paid, but the surplus reserves were not expended for the common good of the allied Greek states. Instead, they were expropriated to pay the enormous cost of executing Pericles' grand plan to embellish the Acropolis of Athens.

The reaction of the allies—in reality the subjects of Athens—was predictable. Plutarch, who wrote a biography of Pericles in the early second century CE, indicated the wrath the Greek victims of Athenian tyranny felt by recording the protest voiced against Pericles' decision even in the Athenian assembly. Greece, Pericles' enemies said, had been dealt "a terrible, wanton insult" when Athens used the funds contributed out of necessity for a common war effort to "gild and embellish itself with images and extravagant temples, like some pretentious woman decked out with precious stones."[4] This is important to keep in mind when examining those great and universally admired buildings erected on the Acropolis in accordance with Pericles' vision of his polis reborn from the ashes of the Persian sack. They are *not,* as some would wish people to believe, the glorious fruits of Athenian democracy but are instead the by-products of tyranny and the abuse of power. Too often art and architectural historians do not ask how a monument was financed. The answer can be very revealing—and very embarrassing.

**THE "OLYMPIAN PERICLES"** A number of Roman copies are preserved of a famous bronze portrait statue of Pericles fashioned

## Polykleitos's Prescription for the Perfect Statue

One of the most influential philosophers of the ancient world was Pythagoras of Samos, who lived during the latter part of the sixth century BCE. A famous geometric theorem still bears his name. Pythagoras also is said to have discovered that harmonic chords in music are produced on the strings of a lyre at regular intervals that may be expressed as ratios of whole numbers — 2:1, 3:2, 4:3. He and his followers, the Pythagoreans, believed more generally that underlying harmonic proportions could be found in all of nature, determining the form of the cosmos as well as of things on earth, and that beauty resided in harmonious numerical ratios.

By this reasoning, a perfect statue would be one constructed according to an all-encompassing mathematical formula. In the mid-fifth century BCE, the sculptor Polykleitos of Argos set out to make just such a statue (FIG. 5-38). He recorded the principles he followed and the proportions he used in a treatise titled the *Canon*. His treatise is unfortunately lost, but Galen, a physician who lived during the second century CE, summarized the sculptor's philosophy as follows:

[Beauty arises from] the commensurability [*symmetria*] of the parts, such as that of finger to finger, and of all the fingers to the palm and the wrist, and of these to the forearm, and of the forearm to the upper arm, and, in fact, of everything to everything else, just as it is written in the *Canon* of Polykleitos. . . . Polykleitos supported his treatise [by making] a statue according to the tenets of his treatise, and called the statue, like the work, the *Canon*."[1]

This is why Pliny the Elder, writing in the first century CE, maintained that Polykleitos "alone of men is deemed to have rendered art itself [that is, the theoretical basis of art] in a work of art."[2]

Polykleitos's belief that a successful statue resulted from the precise application of abstract principles is reflected in an anecdote (probably a later invention) told by the Roman historian Aelian:

Polykleitos made two statues at the same time, one which would be pleasing to the crowd and the other according to the principles of his art. In accordance with the opinion of each person who came into his workshop, he altered something and changed its form, submitting to the advice of each. Then he put both statues on display. The one was marvelled at by everyone, and the other was laughed at. Thereupon Polykleitos said, "But the one that you find fault with, you made yourselves; while the one that you marvel at, I made."[3]

[1] Galen, *De placitis Hippocratis et Platonis*, 5. Translated by J. J. Pollitt, *The Art of Ancient Greece: Sources and Documents* (New York: Cambridge University Press, 1990), 76.

[2] Pliny the Elder, *Natural History*, 34.55. Translated by Pollitt, 75.

[3] Aelian, *Varia historia*, 14.8. Translated by Pollitt, 79.

**5-39** KRESILAS, Pericles. Roman marble herm copy after a bronze original of ca. 429 BCE, approx. 6′ high. Vatican Museums, Rome.

by KRESILAS, who was born on Crete but who worked in Athens. The portrait was set up on the Acropolis, probably immediately after the leader's death in 429 BCE, and depicted Pericles in heroic nudity. The statue must have resembled the Riace warrior (FIG. 5-34). The copies, in marble, reproduce the head only. Ours (FIG. 5-39) is a *herm* (a bust on a square pillar), a popular format in Roman times for abbreviated copies of famous statues. The herm is inscribed "Pericles, son of Xanthippos, the Athenian," leaving no doubt as to the identification. Pericles wears the helmet of a *strategos* (general), the position he was elected to 15 times. The Athenian leader was said to have had an abnormally elongated skull, and Kresilas recorded this feature (while also concealing it) by providing a glimpse through the helmet's eye slots of the hair at the top of the head. This, together with the unblemished features of Pericles' Classically aloof face and, no doubt, his body's perfect physique, led Pliny to assert that Kresilas had the ability to make noble men appear even more noble in their portraits. This is because this is not a portrait at all in the modern sense of a record of actual features. Pliny refers to Kresilas's "portrait" as "the Olympian Pericles," for in this image Pericles appeared almost godlike.[5]

**PERICLES' ACROPOLIS** The centerpiece of Pericles' great building program on the Acropolis (FIG. 5-40) was the Parthenon (FIG. 5-41, no. 1), or the Temple of Athena Parthenos, erected in the remarkably short period between 447 and 438 BCE. (Work on the great temple's ambitious sculptural ornamentation continued until 432 BCE.) As soon as the Parthenon was completed, construction commenced on a grand new gateway to the Acropolis from the west (the only accessible side of the natural plateau), the Propylaia (FIG. 5-41, no. 2). Begun in 437 BCE, it was left

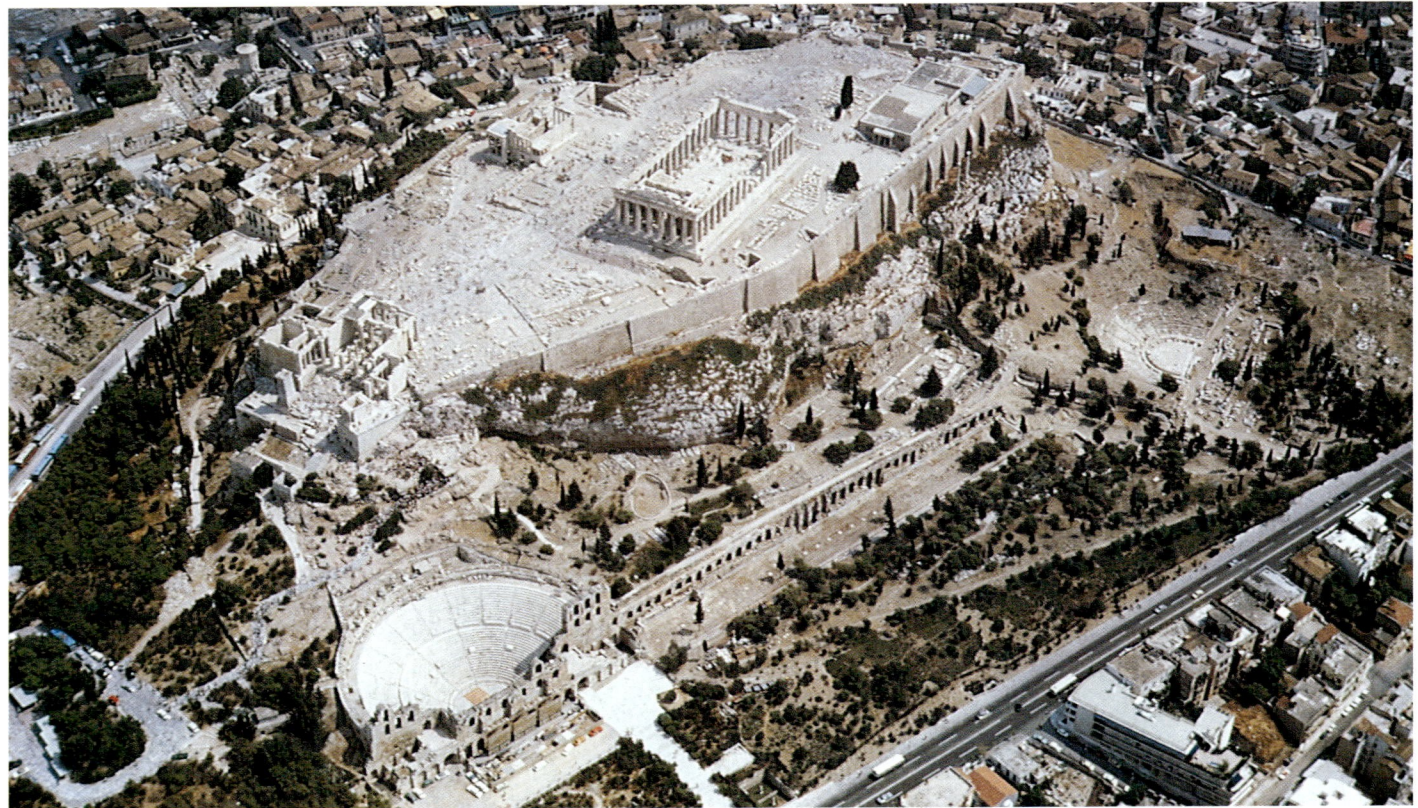

5-40  Aerial view of the Acropolis, Athens, Greece.

unfinished in 431 at the outbreak of the Peloponnesian War between Athens and Sparta. Two later temples, the Erechtheion (FIG. 5-41, no. 3) and the Temple of Athena Nike (FIG. 5-41, no. 4), built after Pericles' death, were probably also part of the original design. The greatest Athenian architects and sculptors of the Classical period focused their attention on the construction and decoration of these four buildings. More human creative genius concentrated on the Periclean Acropolis than at any other place or time in the history of Western civilization.

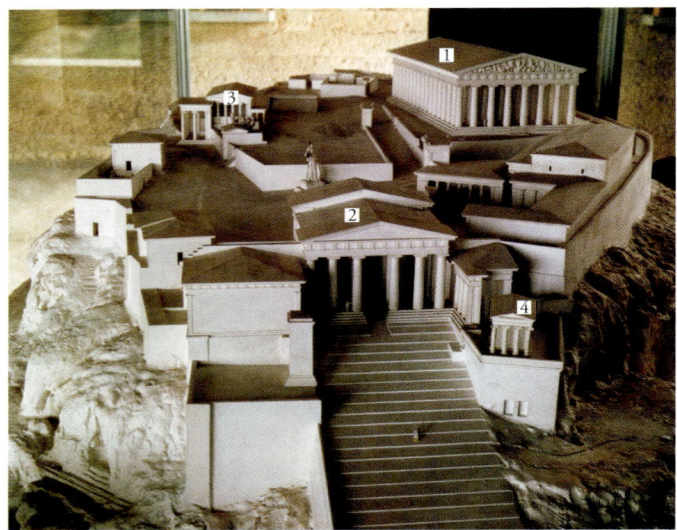

5-41  Model of the Acropolis, Athens, Greece. Acropolis Museum, Athens. 1) Parthenon, 2) Propylaia, 3) Erechtheion, 4) Temple of Athena Nike.

**THE ACROPOLIS TODAY**  That these buildings exist at all today is something of a miracle. In the Middle Ages, the Parthenon, for example, was converted into a Byzantine and later a Roman Catholic church and then, after the Ottoman conquest of Greece, into a mosque. Each time the building was remodeled for a different religion, it was modified structurally. The Christians early on removed the colossal statue of Athena inside. The churches had a great curved *apse* at the east end housing the altar, and the mosque had a *minaret* (tower used to call Muslims to prayer). In 1687, the Venetians besieged the Acropolis, which at that time was in Turkish hands. One of their rockets scored a direct hit on the ammunition depot the Turks had installed in part of the Parthenon. The resultant explosion blew out the building's center. To make matters worse, the Venetians subsequently tried to remove some of the statues from the Parthenon's pediments. In more than one case, statues were dropped and smashed on the ground. Today, a uniquely modern blight threatens the Parthenon and the other buildings of the Periclean age. The corrosive emissions of factories and automobiles are decomposing the ancient marbles. A great campaign has been under way for some time to protect the columns and walls from further deterioration. What little original sculpture remained *in situ* when modern restoration began was transferred to the Acropolis Museum's climate-controlled rooms.

**PARTHENON: IDEAL TEMPLE**  Despite the ravages of time and humanity, most of the Parthenon's peripteral colonnade (FIG. **5-42**) is still standing (or has been reerected), and art historians know a great deal about the building and its sculptural program. The architects were IKTINOS and KALLIKRATES. The statue of Athena (FIG. 5-44) was the work of PHIDIAS, who was also the overseer of the temple's sculptural decoration. In fact, Plutarch

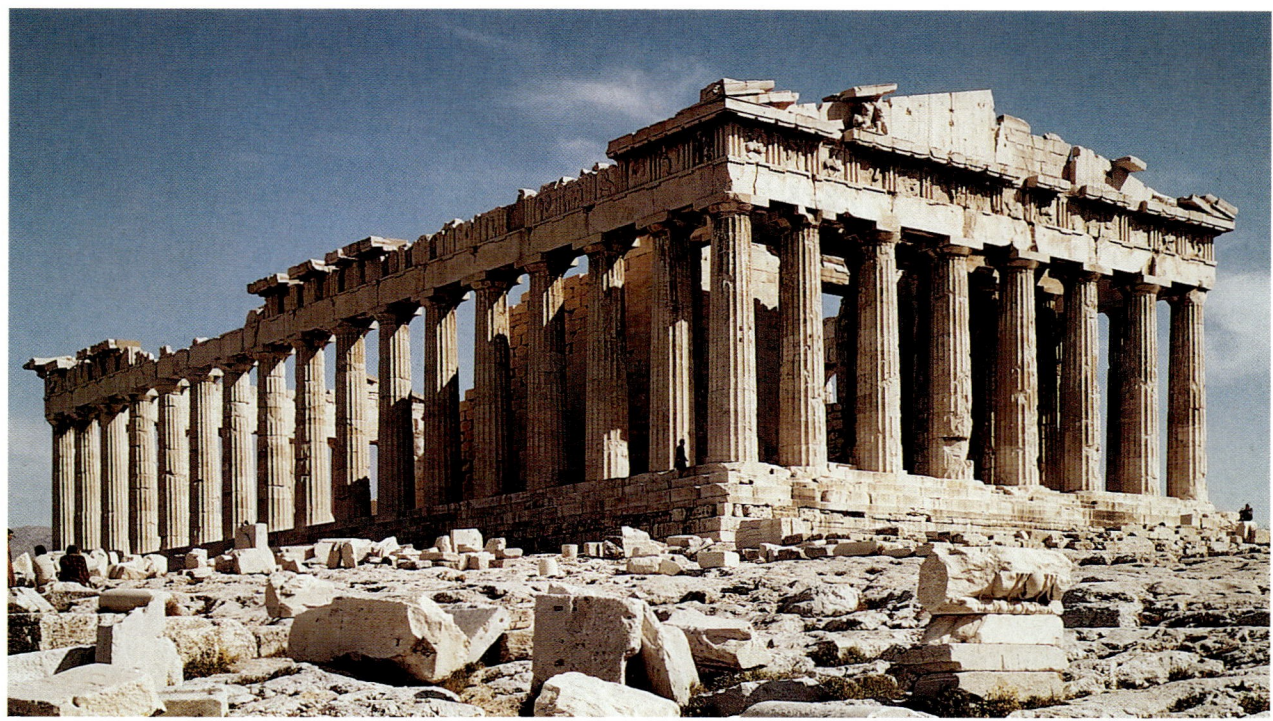

**5-42** Iktinos and Kallikrates, Parthenon, the Temple of Athena Parthenos (view from the northwest), Acropolis, Athens, Greece, 447–438 BCE.

claims that Phidias was in charge of the entire Periclean Acropolis project.

Just as the contemporary *Doryphoros* by Polykleitos may be seen as the culmination of nearly two centuries of searching for the ideal proportions of the various human body parts, so, too, the Parthenon may be viewed as the ideal solution to the Greek architect's quest for perfect proportions in Doric temple design. Its well-spaced columns, with their slender shafts, and the capitals, with their straight-sided conical echinuses, are the ultimate refinement of the bulging and squat Doric columns and compressed capitals of the Archaic Hera temple at Paestum (FIG. 5-13).

**MATHEMATICS AND OPTICS** The Parthenon architects and the *Doryphoros* sculptor were kindred spirits in their belief that beautiful proportions resulted from strict adherence to harmonious numerical ratios, whether they were designing a temple more than 200 feet long or a life-size statue of a nude man. For the Parthenon, the controlling ratio for the *symmetria* of the parts may be expressed algebraically as $x = 2y + 1$. Thus, for example, the temple's short ends have 8 columns and the long sides have 17: $17 = (2 \times 8) + 1$. The stylobate's ratio of length to width is 9:4 ($9 = [2 \times 4] + 1$), and this ratio also characterizes the cella's proportion of length to width, the distance between the centers of two adjacent column drums (the *interaxial*) in proportion to the columns' diameter, and so forth.

The Parthenon's harmonious design and the mathematical precision of the sizes of its constituent elements tend to obscure the fact that this temple, as actually constructed, is quite irregular in shape. Throughout the building are pronounced deviations from the strictly horizontal and vertical lines assumed to be the basis of all Greek post-and-lintel structures. The stylobate, for example, curves upward at the center on both the sides and the facade, forming a kind of shallow dome, and this curvature is carried up into the entablature. Moreover, the peristyle columns lean inward slightly. Those at the corners have a diagonal inclination and are also about two inches thicker than the rest. If their lines were continued, they would meet about 1.5 miles above the temple. These deviations from the norm meant that virtually every Parthenon block and drum had to be carved according to the special set of specifications dictated by its unique place in the structure.

This was obviously a daunting task, and a reason must have existed for these so-called refinements in the Parthenon. Some modern observers note, for example, how the curving of horizontal lines and the tilting of vertical ones create a dynamic balance in the building—a kind of architectural contrapposto—and give it a greater sense of life. The oldest recorded explanation, however, may also be correct. Vitruvius, a Roman architect of the late first century BCE who claims to have had access to the treatise on the Parthenon written by Iktinos—again note the kinship with the *Canon* of Polykleitos—maintains that these adjustments were made to compensate for optical illusions. Vitruvius states, for example, that if a stylobate is laid out on a level surface, it will appear to sag at the center and that the corner columns of a building should be thicker because they are surrounded by light and would otherwise appear thinner than their neighbors.

**MIXING DORIC AND IONIC** The Parthenon is "irregular" in other ways as well. One of the ironies of this most famous of all Doric temples is that it is "contaminated" by Ionic elements (FIG. **5-43**). Although the cella had a two-story Doric colonnade around Phidias's Athena statue (FIG. 5-44), the back room (which housed the goddess's treasury and the tribute collected from the Delian League) had four tall and slender Ionic columns as sole supports for the superstructure. And whereas the temple's exterior had a canonical Doric frieze, the inner frieze that ran around the top of the cella wall was Ionic. Perhaps this fusion of Doric

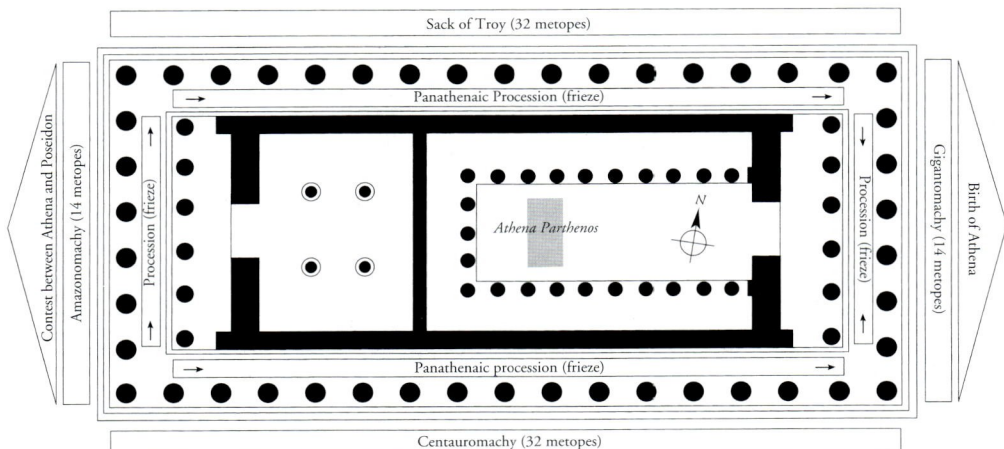

**5-43** Plan of the Parthenon, Acropolis, Athens, Greece, with diagram of sculptural program (after A. Stewart), 447–432 BCE.

Sack of Troy (32 metopes)

Panathenaic Procession (frieze)

Contest between Athena and Poseidon

Amazonomachy (14 metopes)

Procession (frieze)

*Athena Parthenos*

N

Procession (frieze)

Gigantomachy (14 metopes)

Birth of Athena

Panathenaic procession (frieze)

Centauromachy (32 metopes)

and Ionic elements reflects the Athenians' belief that the Ionians of the Cycladic Islands and Asia Minor were descended from Athenian settlers and were therefore their kin. Or it may be Pericles and Iktinos's way of suggesting that Athens was the leader of *all* the Greeks. In any case, a mix of Doric and Ionic features characterizes the fifth-century buildings of the Acropolis as a whole.

**LORD ELGIN'S MARBLES** The costly decision to incorporate two sculptured friezes in the Parthenon's design is symptomatic. This Pentelic-marble temple was more lavishly decorated than any Greek temple before it, Doric or Ionic (FIG. 5-43). Every one of the

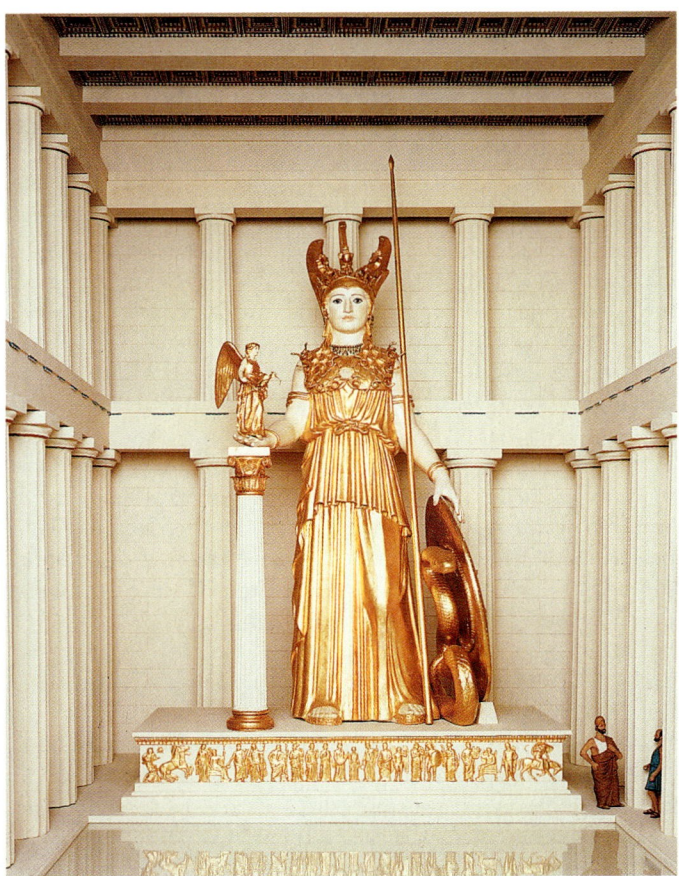

**5-44** PHIDIAS, *Athena Parthenos*, in the cella of the Parthenon, Acropolis, Athens, Greece, ca. 438 BCE. Model of the lost statue, which was approx. 38′ tall. Royal Ontario Museum, Toronto.

92 Doric metopes was decorated with relief sculpture. So, too, was every inch of the 524-foot-long Ionic frieze. The pediments were filled with dozens of larger-than-life-size statues. Most of the Parthenon's reliefs and statues are today exhibited in a special gallery in the British Museum in London, where they are known popularly as the Elgin Marbles. Between 1801 and 1803, while Greece was still under Turkish rule, Lord Elgin, the British ambassador to the Ottoman court at Istanbul, was permitted to dismantle many of the Parthenon sculptures and to ship the best-preserved ones to England. He eventually sold them to the British government at a great financial loss to himself. Although he often has been accused of "stealing" Greece's cultural heritage (the Greek government has long sought the return of the Elgin Marbles to Athens), Lord Elgin must be credited with saving the sculptures from almost certain ruin if they had been left at the site.

**PHIDIAS'S ATHENA** One statue that even Elgin could not recover was Phidias's *Athena Parthenos,* the Virgin, which had been destroyed long before the 19th century. Art historians know a great deal about it, however, from descriptions by Greek and Latin authors and from Roman copies. A model (FIG. **5-44**) gives a good idea of its appearance and setting. It was a chryselephantine statue, that is, fashioned of gold and ivory, the latter used for Athena's exposed flesh. Phidias's statue stood 38 feet tall, and to a large extent the Parthenon was designed around it. To accommodate its huge size, the cella had to be wider than usual. This, in turn, dictated the width of the facade—eight columns at a time when six columns were the norm, as at Aegina (FIGS. 5-24 and 5-25).

Athena was fully armed with shield, spear, and helmet, and she held Nike (the winged female personification of Victory) in her extended right hand. No one doubts that this Nike referred to the victory of 479 BCE. The memory of the Persian sack of the Acropolis was still vivid, and the Athenians were intensely conscious that by driving back the Persians, they were saving their civilization from the eastern "barbarians" who had committed atrocities at Miletos. In fact, the *Athena Parthenos* had multiple allusions to the Persian defeat. On the thick soles of Athena's sandals was a representation of a centauromachy. The exterior of her shield was emblazoned with high reliefs depicting the battle of Greeks and Amazons (*Amazonomachy*), in which Theseus drove the Amazons out of Athens. And Phidias painted a gigantomachy on the shield's interior. Each of these mythological contests was a metaphor for the triumph of order over chaos, of civilization over barbarism, and of Athens over Persia.

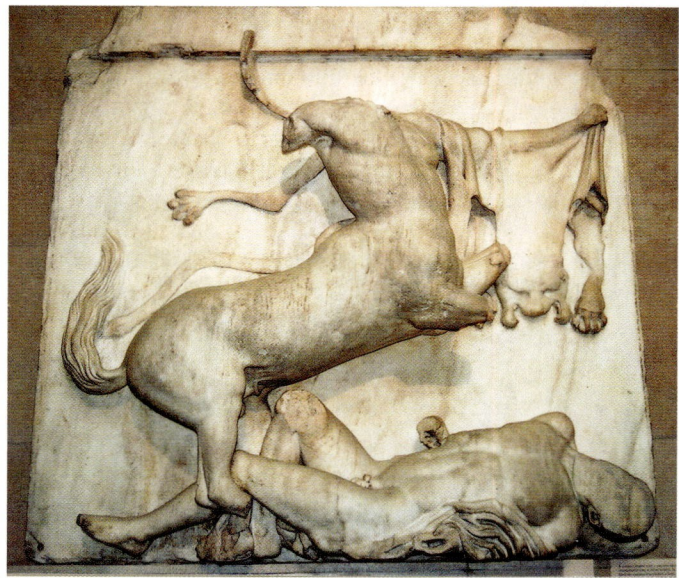

**5-45** Lapith versus centaur, metope from the south side of the Parthenon, Acropolis, Athens, Greece, ca. 447–438 BCE. Marble, approx. 4′ 8″ high. British Museum, London.

**CENTAURS AND PERSIANS** These same themes were taken up again in the Parthenon's Doric metopes (FIG. 5-43). The best-preserved metopes—although the paint on these and all the other Parthenon marbles long ago disappeared—are those of the south side, which depicted the battle of Lapiths and centaurs, a

combat in which Theseus of Athens played a major role. On one extraordinary slab (FIG. 5-45), a triumphant centaur rises up on its hind legs, exulting over the crumpled body of the Greek it has defeated. The relief is so high that parts are fully in the round; some have broken off. The sculptor knew how to distinguish the vibrant, powerful form of the living beast from the lifeless corpse on the ground. In other metopes the Greeks have the upper hand, but the full set suggests that the battle was a difficult one against a dangerous enemy and that losses as well as victories occurred. The same was true of the war against the Persians.

**THE BIRTH OF ATHENA** The subjects of the two pediments were especially appropriate for a temple that celebrated not only Athena but also the Athenians. The east pediment depicted the birth of Athena. At the west was the contest between Athena and Poseidon to determine which one would become the city's patron deity. Athena won, giving her name to the polis and its citizens. It is significant that in the story and in the pediment the Athenians are the judges of the relative merits of the two gods. Here one sees the same arrogance that led to the use of Delian League funds to adorn the Acropolis.

The center of the east pediment was damaged when the apse was added to the Parthenon at the time of its conversion into a church. What remains are the spectators to the left and the right who witnessed Athena's birth on Mount Olympus. At the far left are the head and arms of Helios (the Sun) and his chariot horses rising from the pediment floor (FIG. 5-46). Next to them is a powerful male figure usually identified as Dionysos or possibly Herakles, who entered the realm of the gods on completion of his 12 labors. At the right are three goddesses, probably Hestia, Dione, and Aphrodite (FIG. 5-47), and either Selene (the Moon) or Nyx (Night) and more horses, this time sinking below the pediment's floor. Here, Phidias,

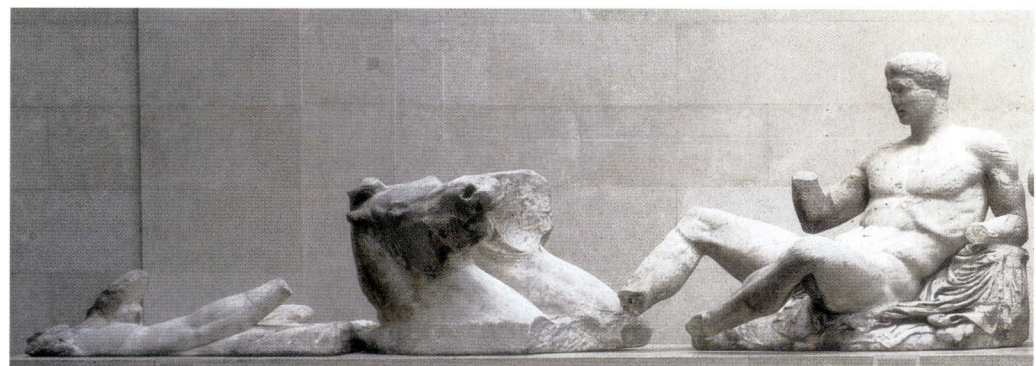

**5-46** Helios and his horses, and Dionysos (Herakles?), from the east pediment of the Parthenon, Acropolis, Athens, Greece, ca. 438–432 BCE. Marble, great-est height approx. 4′ 3″. British Museum, London.

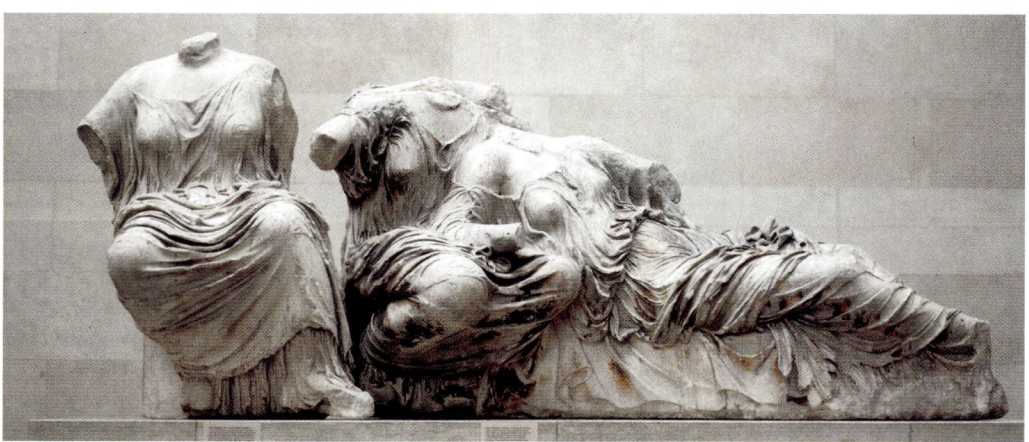

**5-47** Three goddesses (Hestia, Dione, and Aphrodite?), from the east pediment of the Parthenon, Acropolis, Athens, Greece, ca. 438–432 BCE. Marble, greatest height approx. 4′ 5″. British Museum, London.

who designed the composition even if his assistants executed it, discovered an entirely new way to deal with the awkward triangular frame of the pediment. Its bottom line is the horizon line, and charioteers and their horses move through it effortlessly. The individual figures, even the animals, are brilliantly characterized. The horses of the Sun, at the beginning of the day, are energetic. Those of the Moon or Night, having labored until dawn, are weary.

The reclining figures fill the space beneath the raking cornice beautifully. Dionysos/Herakles and Aphrodite in the lap of her mother Dione are monumental Olympian presences yet totally relaxed organic forms. The sculptors fully understood not only the surface appearance of human anatomy, both male and female, but also the mechanics of how muscles and bones make the body move. The Phidian school also mastered the rendition of clothed forms. In the Dione-Aphrodite group, the thin and heavy folds of the garments alternately reveal and conceal the main and lesser body masses while swirling in a compositional tide that subtly unifies the two figures. The articulation and integration of the bodies produce a wonderful variation of surface and play of light and shade.

**ATHENIANS ON THE PARTHENON** In many ways the most remarkable part of the Parthenon's sculptural program is the inner Ionic frieze (FIG. **5-48**). Scholars still debate the subject of the frieze, but most agree that what is represented is the Panathenaic

**5-48** Details of the Panathenaic Festival procession frieze, from the Parthenon, Acropolis, Athens, Greece, ca. 447–438 BCE. Marble, approx. 3′ 6″ high. Horsemen of north frieze *(top)*, British Museum, London; seated gods and goddesses (Poseidon, Apollo, Artemis, Aphrodite, and Eros) of east frieze *(center)*, Acropolis Museum, Athens; and elders and maidens of east frieze *(bottom)*, Louvre, Paris.

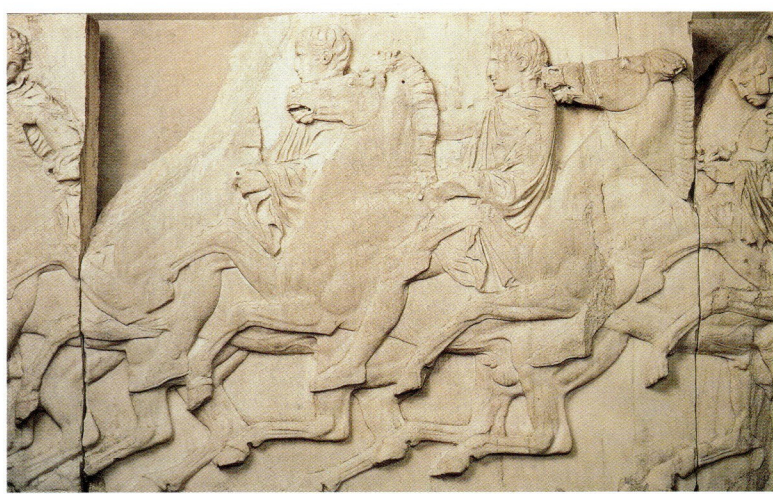

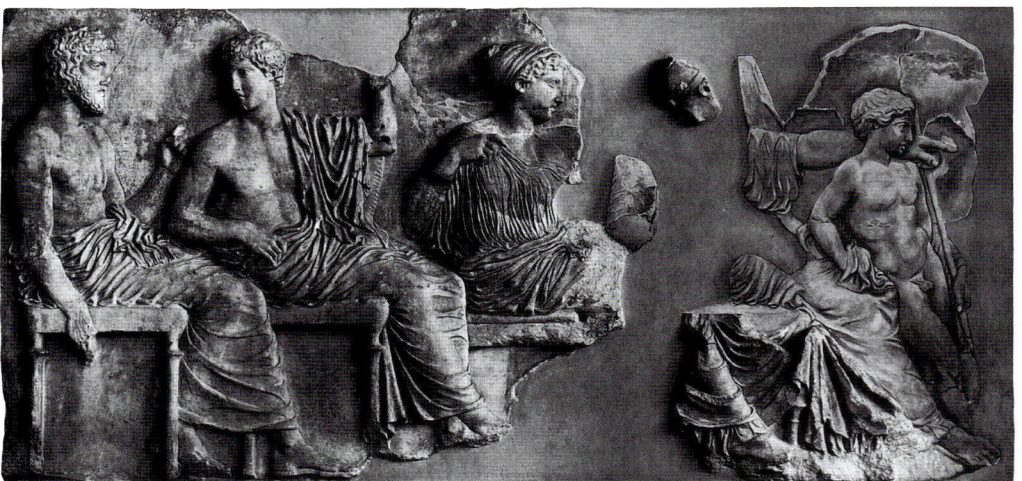

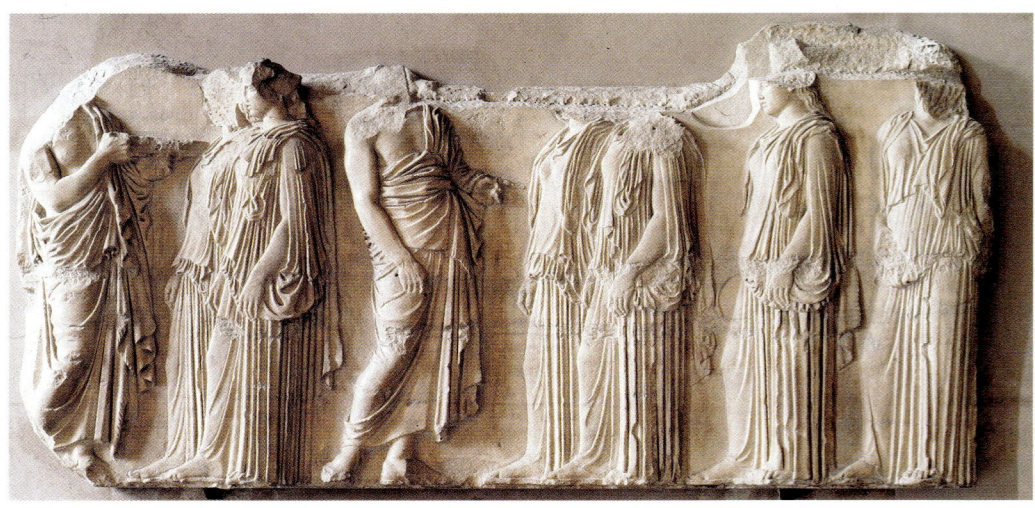

Festival procession that took place every four years in Athens. If this identification is correct, the Athenians judged themselves fit for inclusion in the temple's sculptural decoration. It is another example of the extraordinarily high opinion the Athenians had of their own worth.

The procession began at the Dipylon Gate, passed through the agora (marketplace), and ended on the Acropolis, where a new peplos was placed on an ancient wooden statue of Athena. That statue (probably similar in general appearance to the *Lady of Auxerre,* FIG. 5-7) was housed in the Archaic temple razed by the Persians. The statue had been removed from the Acropolis before the Persian attack for security reasons, and eventually it was installed in the Erechtheion (FIG. 5-51, no. 1). On the Parthenon frieze the procession begins on the west, that is, at the temple's rear, the side facing the gateway to the Acropolis. It then proceeds in parallel lines down the long north and south sides of the building and ends at the center of the east frieze, over the doorway to the cella housing Phidias's statue. It is noteworthy that the upper part of the relief is higher than the lower part so that the more distant and more shaded upper zone is as legible from the ground as the lower part of the frieze. This is another instance of the architects' taking optical effects into consideration.

The frieze vividly communicates the procession's acceleration and deceleration. At the outset, on the west side, marshals gather and youths mount their horses. On the north (FIG. 5-48, *top*) and south, the momentum picks up as the cavalcade moves from the lower town to the Acropolis, accompanied by chariots, musicians, jar carriers, and animals destined for sacrifice. On the east, seated gods and goddesses (FIG. 5-48, *center*), the invited guests, watch the procession slow almost to a halt (FIG. 5-48, *bottom*) as it nears its goal at the shrine of Athena's ancient wooden idol. Most remarkable of all is the role assigned to the Olympian deities. They do not take part in the festival or determine its outcome but are merely spectators. Aphrodite, in fact, extends her left arm to draw her son Eros's attention to the Athenians, just as today a parent at a parade would point out important people to a child. And the Athenian people *were* important—self-important one might say. They were the masters of an empire, and in Pericles' famous funeral oration he painted a picture of Athens that elevated its citizens almost to the stature of gods. The Parthenon celebrated the greatness of Athens and the Athenians as much as it honored Athena.

**PROPYLAIA: ACROPOLIS GATEWAY** Even before all the sculpture was in place on the Parthenon, work began on a new monumental entrance to the Acropolis, the Propylaia (FIG. **5-49**). The architect entrusted with this important commission was MNESIKLES. The site was a difficult one, on a steep slope, but Mnesikles succeeded in disguising the change in ground level by splitting the building into eastern and western sections (FIG. 5-41, no. 2), each one resembling a Doric temple facade. Practical considerations dictated that the space between the central pair of columns on each side be enlarged. This was the path the chariots and animals of the Panathenaic Festival procession took, and they required a wide ramped causeway. To either side of the central ramp were stairs for pedestrian traffic. Inside, tall, slender Ionic columns supported the split-level roof. Once again an Athenian architect mixed the two orders on the Acropolis. But as with the Parthenon, the Doric order was used for the stately exterior and the Ionic only for the interior. It would have been considered unseemly at this date to combine different kinds of columns on one facade. Later Greek architects were not as reticent (FIG. 5-77).

Mnesikles' full plan for the Propylaia was never executed because of a change in the fortunes of Athens after the outbreak of the Peloponnesian War in 431 BCE. Of the side wings that were part of the original project, only the northwest one was completed. That wing is of special importance in the history of art. In Roman times it housed a *pinakotheke* (picture gallery). In it were displayed paintings on wooden panels by some of the major artists of the fifth century BCE. It is uncertain whether or not this was the wing's original function. But if it was, the Propylaia's pinakotheke is the first recorded structure built for the specific purpose of displaying paintings, and it is the forerunner of modern museums.

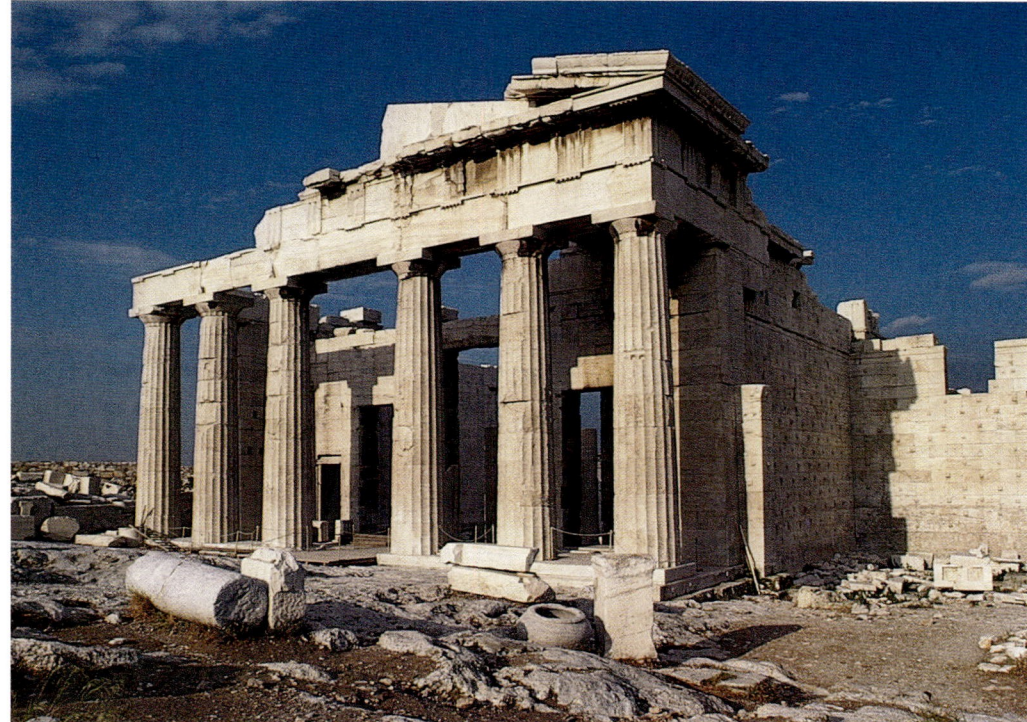

**5-49** MNESIKLES, Propylaia (view from the northeast), Acropolis, Athens, Greece, 437–432 BCE.

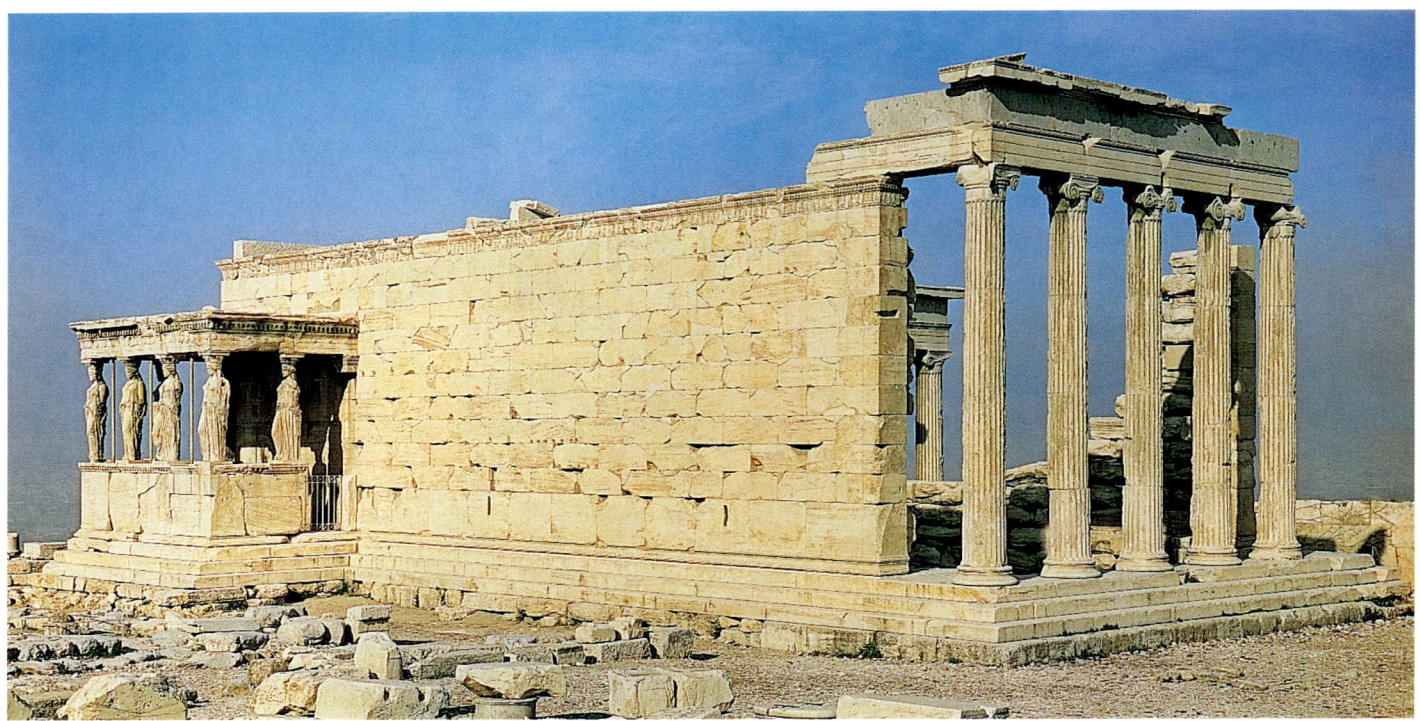

**5-50** Erechtheion (view from the southeast), Acropolis, Athens, Greece, ca. 421–405 BCE.

**ERECHTHEION: MULTIPLE SHRINE** In 421 BCE work finally began on the temple that was to replace the Archaic Athena temple the Persians had razed. The new structure, the Erechtheion (FIGS. 5-50 and 5-51), built to the north of the old temple's remains, was, however, to be a multiple shrine. It honored Athena and housed the ancient wooden image of the goddess that was the goal of the Panathenaic Festival procession. But it also incorporated shrines to a host of other gods and demigods who loomed large in the city's legendary past. Among these were Erechtheus, an early king of Athens, during whose reign the ancient wooden idol of Athena was said to have fallen from the heavens, and Kekrops, another

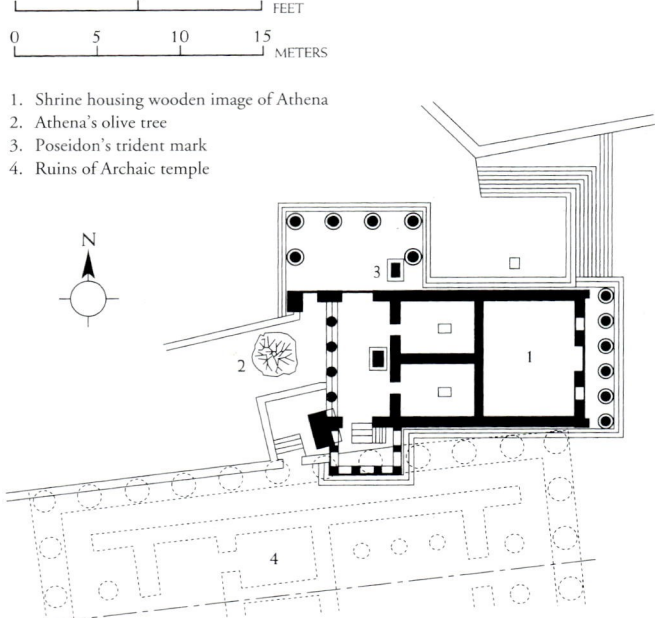

1. Shrine housing wooden image of Athena
2. Athena's olive tree
3. Poseidon's trident mark
4. Ruins of Archaic temple

**5-51** Plan of the Erechtheion, Acropolis, Athens, Greece, ca. 421–405 BCE.

king of Athens, who served as judge of the contest between Athena and Poseidon. In fact, the site chosen for the new temple was the very spot where that contest occurred. Poseidon had staked his claim to Athens by striking the Acropolis rock with his trident and producing a salt-water spring. The imprint of his trident remained for Athenians of the historical period to see. Nearby, Athena had miraculously caused an olive tree to grow. This tree still stood as a constant reminder of her victory over Poseidon.

The asymmetrical plan (FIG. 5-51) of the Ionic Erechtheion is unique for a Greek temple and the antithesis of the simple and harmoniously balanced plan of the Doric Parthenon across the way. Its irregular form reflected the need to incorporate the tomb of Kekrops and other preexisting shrines, the trident mark, and the olive tree into a single complex. The unknown architect responsible for the building also had to struggle with the problem of uneven terrain. The area could not be made level by terracing because that would disturb the ancient sacred sites. As a result, the Erechtheion not only has four sides of very different character, but each side also rests on a different ground level.

Perhaps to compensate for the awkward character of the building as a whole, the architect took great care with the Erechtheion's decorative details. The frieze, for example, was given special treatment. The stone chosen was the dark-blue limestone of Eleusis to contrast with the white Pentelic marble of the walls and columns. Marble relief figures were attached to this dark ground.

**CLASSICAL CARYATIDS** The temple's most striking and famous feature is its south porch, where caryatids (FIGS. 5-50 and 5-52) replaced Ionic columns, as they did a century earlier on the Ionic Siphnian Treasury at Delphi (FIG. 5-16). The Delphi caryatids resemble Archaic korai, and their Classical counterparts equally characteristically look like Phidian-era statues. Although they exhibit the weight shift that was standard for the fifth century, the role of the caryatids as architectural supports for the unusual flat roof is underscored by the vertical flutelike drapery folds concealing their stiff, weight-bearing legs. The Classical

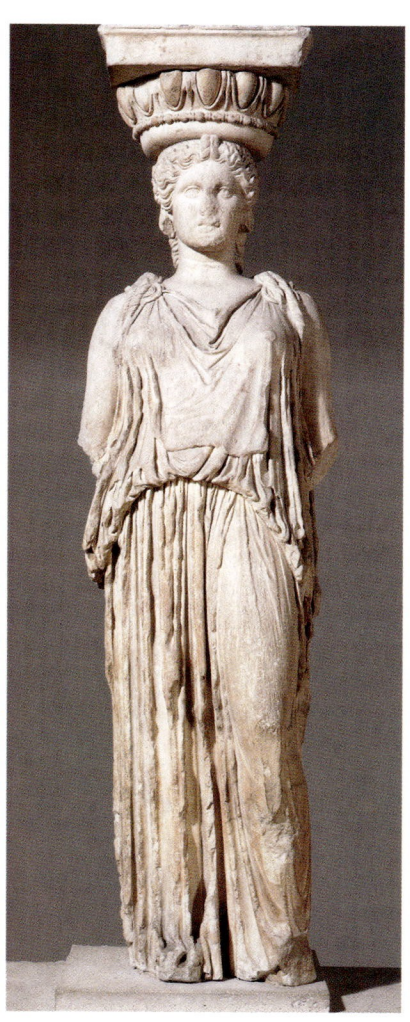

**5-52** Caryatid from the south porch of the Erechtheion, Acropolis, Athens, Greece, ca. 421–405 BCE. Marble, 7′ 7″ high. British Museum, London.

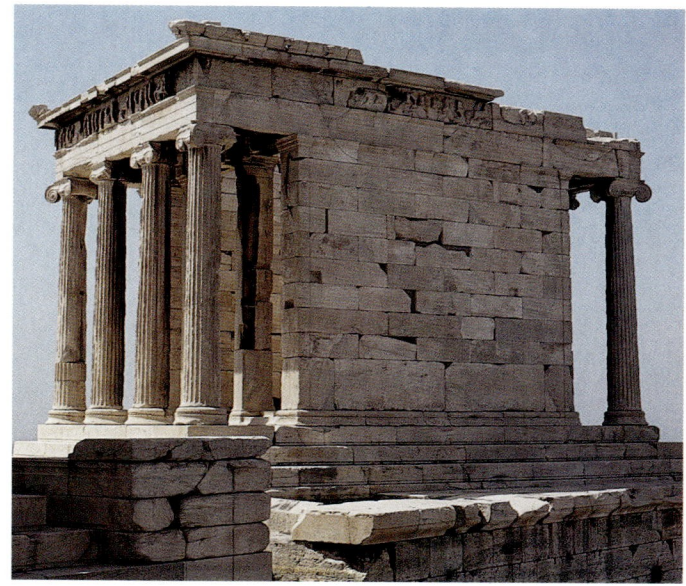

**5-53** KALLIKRATES, Temple of Athena Nike (view from the northeast), Acropolis, Athens, Greece, ca. 427–424 BCE.

architect-sculptor successfully balanced the dual and contradictory functions of these female statue-columns. The figures have enough rigidity to suggest the structural column and just the degree of flexibility needed to suggest the living body.

**ATHENA, BRINGER OF VICTORY** Another Ionic building on the Athenian Acropolis is the little Temple of Athena Nike (FIG. 5-53), designed by Kallikrates, who worked with Iktinos on the Parthenon (and perhaps was responsible for the Ionic elements of that Doric temple). The temple is amphiprostyle with four columns on both the east and west facades. It stands on what used to be a Mycenaean bastion near the Propylaia and greets all visitors entering Athena's great sanctuary. As on the Parthenon, reference was made here to the victory over the Persians—and not just in the temple's name. Part of its frieze was devoted to a representation of the decisive battle at Marathon that turned the tide against the Persians—a human event, as in the Parthenon's Panathenaic Festival procession frieze. But now the sculptors chronicled a specific occasion, not a recurring event acted out by anonymous citizens.

Around the building, at the bastion's edge, a *parapet* was built about 410 BCE and decorated with exquisite reliefs. The theme of the balustrade matched that of the temple proper—Nike (Victory). Her image was repeated dozens of times, always in different attitudes, sometimes erecting trophies bedecked with Persian spoils and sometimes bringing forward sacrificial bulls to Athena. The most beautiful of the reliefs shows Nike adjusting her sandal (FIG. 5-54)—an awkward posture rendered elegant and graceful

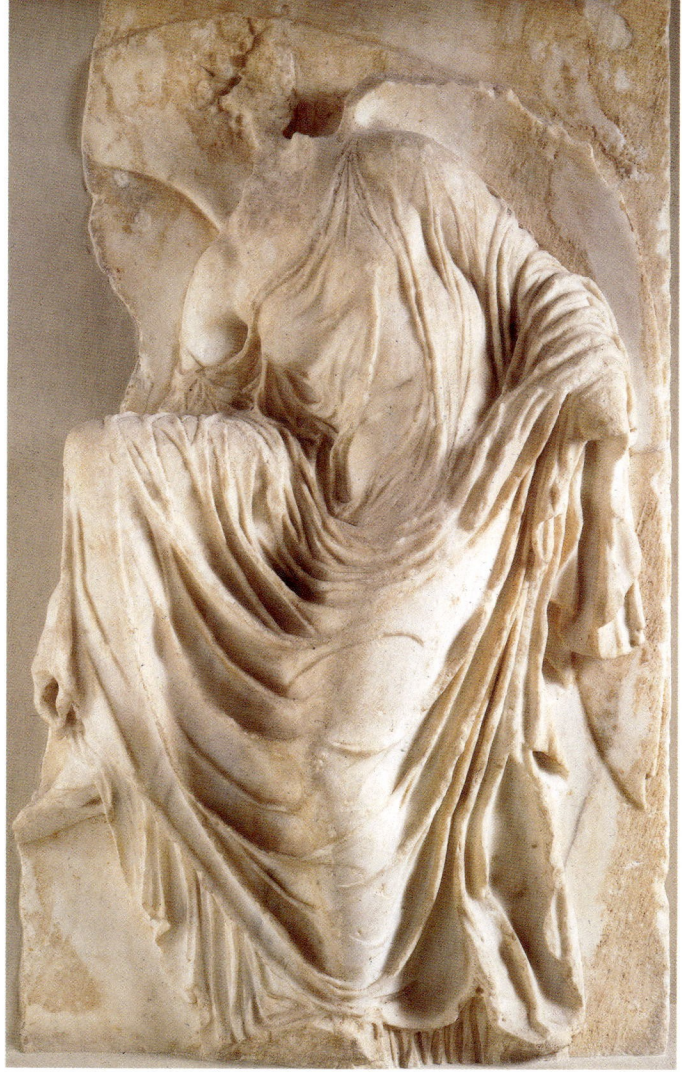

**5-54** Nike adjusting her sandal, from the south side of the parapet of the Temple of Athena Nike, Acropolis, Athens, Greece, ca. 410 BCE. Marble, approx. 3′ 6″ high. Acropolis Museum, Athens.

## A Greek Woman in Her Father's Home: The Hegeso Stele

In Geometric times, huge amphoras and kraters (FIG. 5-1) marked the graves of wealthy Athenians. In the Archaic period, kouroi (FIGS. 5-8 and 5-10) and, to a lesser extent, korai were placed over Greek burials, as were grave stelae ornamented with relief depictions of the deceased. The grave stele of Hegeso (FIG. 5-55) is in this tradition. It was erected at the end of the fifth or beginning of the fourth century BCE to commemorate the death of Hegeso, daughter of Proxenos. Both names are inscribed on the cornice of the pediment that crowns the stele. Antae at left and right complete the architectural framework.

Hegeso is the well-dressed woman seated on an elegant chair (with footstool). She examines a piece of jewelry (once rendered in paint, not now visible) selected from a box a servant girl brings to her. The maid's simple ungirt chiton contrasts sharply with the more elaborate attire of her mistress. The garments of both women reveal the body forms beneath them. The faces are serene, without a trace of sadness. Indeed, both mistress and maid are shown in a characteristic shared moment out of daily life. Only the epitaph reveals that Hegeso is the one who has departed.

The simplicity of the scene on the Hegeso stele is deceptive, however. This is not merely a bittersweet scene of tranquil domestic life before an untimely death. The setting itself is significant—the secluded women's quarters of a Greek house, from which Hegeso rarely would have emerged. Contemporary grave stelae of men regularly show them in the public domain, as warriors. And the servant girl is not so much the faithful companion of the deceased in life as she is Hegeso's possession, like the jewelry box. The slave girl may look solicitously at her mistress, but Hegeso has eyes only for her ornaments. Both slave and jewelry attest to the wealth of Hegeso's father, unseen but prominently cited in the epitaph. (It is noteworthy that the mother's name is not mentioned.) Indeed, even the jewelry box carries a deeper significance, for it probably represents the dowry Proxenos would have provided to his daughter's husband when she left her father's home to enter her husband's home. In the patriarchal society of ancient Greece, the dominant position of men is manifest even when only women are depicted.

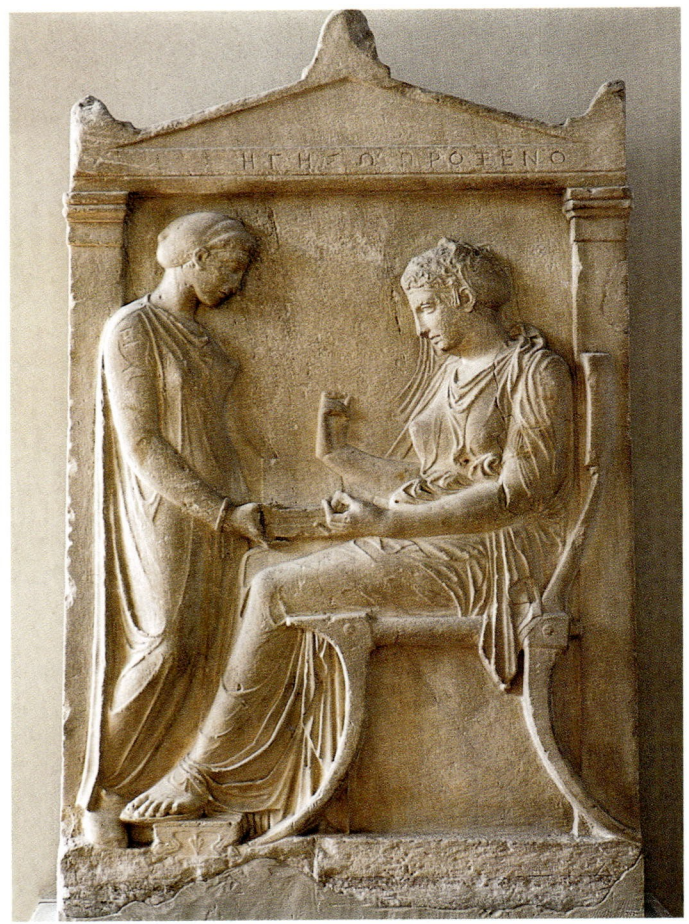

5-55 Grave stele of Hegeso, from the Dipylon cemetery, Athens, Greece, ca. 400 BCE. Marble, 5′ 2″ high. National Archaeological Museum, Athens.

by an anonymous master sculptor. The artist carried the style of the Parthenon pediments (FIG. 5-47) even further and created a figure whose garments cling so tightly to the body that they seem almost transparent, as if drenched with water. The sculptor was, however, interested in much more than revealing the supple beauty of the young female body. The drapery folds form intricate linear patterns unrelated to the body's anatomical structure and have a life of their own as abstract designs. Deep carving produced pockets of shade to contrast with the polished marble surface and enhance the ornamental beauty of the design.

**REMEMBERING THE DEAD** Although the decoration for the great building projects on the Acropolis must have occupied most of the finest sculptors of Athens in the second half of the fifth century BCE, other commissions were available in the city, notably in the Dipylon cemetery. There, around 400 BCE, a beautiful and touching grave stele (FIG. 5-55) in the style of the Temple of Athena Nike parapet reliefs was set up in memory of a woman named Hegeso. Its subject—a young woman in her home, attended by her maid (see "A Greek Woman in Her Father's Home," above)—and its composition have close parallels in contemporary vase painting.

## Painting

**POLYCHROMY IN VASE PAINTING** Art historians know from ancient accounts that in the Classical period some of the most renowned artists were the painters of monumental wooden panels displayed in public buildings, both secular and religious. Such works are by nature perishable, and all of the great panels of the masters are unfortunately lost. Nonetheless, one can get some idea of the polychrome nature of those panel paintings by studying Greek vases such as the *lekythos* (plural *lekythoi;* flasks containing perfumed oil) painted by the so-called ACHILLES PAINTER

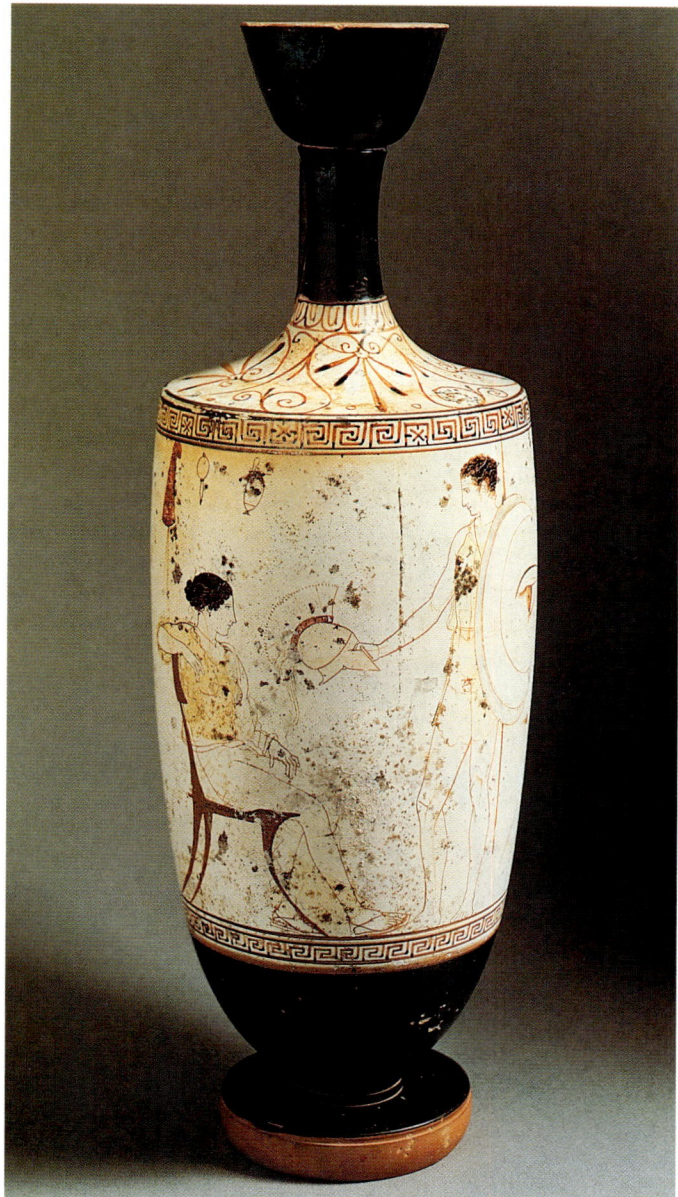

**5-56** ACHILLES PAINTER, Warrior taking leave of his wife (Attic white-ground lekythos), from Eretria, Greece, ca. 440 BCE. Approx. 1′ 5″ high. National Archaeological Museum, Athens.

of white-ground painting were explored almost exclusively on lekythoi, which were commonly placed in Greek graves as offerings to the deceased. For such vessels designed for short-term use, the fragile nature of the white-ground technique was of little concern.

The Achilles Painter's lekythos is decorated with a scene appropriate for its funerary purpose. A youthful warrior takes leave of his wife. The red scarf, mirror, and jug hanging on the wall behind the woman indicate that the setting is the interior of their home. The motif of the seated woman is strikingly similar to that of Hegeso on her grave stele (FIG. 5-55), but here the woman is the survivor. It is her husband, preparing to go to war with helmet, shield, and spear, who will depart, never to return. On his shield is a large painted eye, roughly life-size. Greek shields often were decorated with devices such as the horrific face of Medusa, intended to ward off evil spirits and frighten the enemy. This eye undoubtedly was meant to recall this tradition, but it was little more than an excuse for the Achilles Painter to display superior drawing skills. Since the late sixth century BCE, Greek painters had abandoned the Archaic habit of placing frontal eyes on profile faces and attempted to render the eyes in profile. The Achilles Painter's mastery of this difficult problem in foreshortening is on exhibit here.

**POLYGNOTOS'S REVOLUTION** The leading painter of the first half of the fifth century BCE was POLYGNOTOS OF THASOS, whose works adorned important buildings both in Athens and Delphi. One of these was the pinakotheke of Mnesikles' Propylaia, but the most famous was a portico in the Athenian marketplace that came to be called the Stoa Poikile (Painted Stoa). Descriptions of Polygnotos's paintings make clear that he introduced a revolutionary compositional style, rejecting the scheme used on all the Greek vases examined thus far. Before Polygnotos, figures stood on a common ground line at the bottom of the picture plane, whether they appeared in horizontal bands or single panels. Polygnotos placed his figures on different levels, staggered in tiers in the manner of Ashurbanipal's lion hunt relief (see FIG. 2-24) of two centuries before. He also incorporated landscape elements into his paintings, making his pictures true "windows onto the world" and not simply surface designs peopled with foreshortened figures. The abandonment of a single ground line by Polygnotos and his followers was as momentous a break from the past as the rejection of frontality in statuary by Early Classical Greek sculptors.

**HUBRIS AND MASSACRE** One can visualize Polygnotos's compositions by looking at a red-figure krater (FIG. 5-57) painted around the middle of the fifth century BCE by the NIOBID PAINTER. The painter, whose vases are unsigned, was given this modern nickname from this krater, where one side is devoted to the massacre of the Niobids, the children of Niobe. Niobe, who had at least a dozen children, had boasted that she was superior to the goddess Leto, who had only two offspring, Apollo and Artemis. To punish her *hubris* (arrogance) and teach the lesson that no mortal could be superior to a god or goddess, Leto sent her two children to slay all of Niobe's many sons and daughters. On the Niobid Painter's krater, the influence of Polygnotos is clear. The horrible slaughter occurs in a schematic landscape setting of rocks and trees. The figures are disposed on several levels, and they actively interact with their setting. One slain son, for example, not only has fallen upon a rocky outcropping but is partially hidden by it. The Niobid Painter also drew his face in a three-quarter view, something that even Euphronios and Euthymides had not attempted.

(FIG. **5-56**) about 440 BCE. The artist here employed the *white-ground* technique, which takes its name from the chalky-white slip used to provide a background for the painted figures. Experiments with white-ground painting date back to the Andokides Painter, but the method became popular only toward the middle of the fifth century BCE.

White-ground is essentially a variation of the red-figure technique. First the painter covered the pot with a slip of very fine white clay, then applied black glaze to outline the figures, and diluted brown, purple, red, and white to color them. Other colors—for example, the yellow chosen for the garments of both figures on our lekythos—also could be employed, but these had to be applied after firing because the Greeks did not know how to make them withstand the heat of the kiln. Despite the obvious attractions of the white-ground technique, the impermanence of the expanded range of colors discouraged its use for everyday vessels, such as drinking cups and kraters. In fact, the full polychrome possibilities

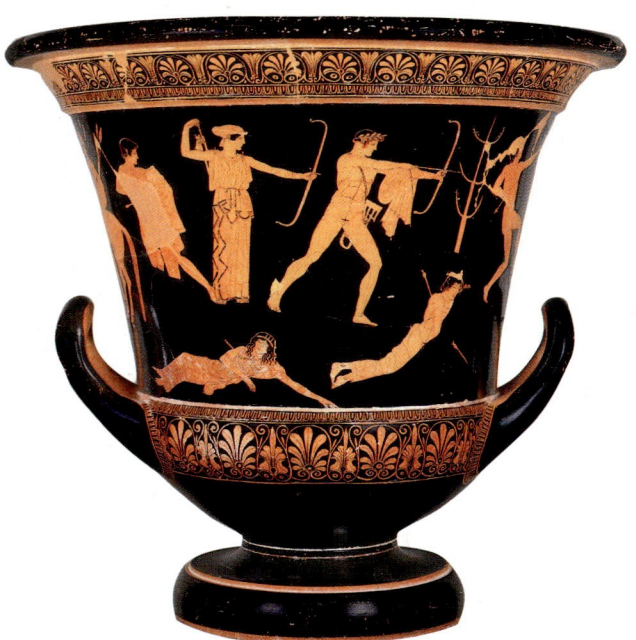

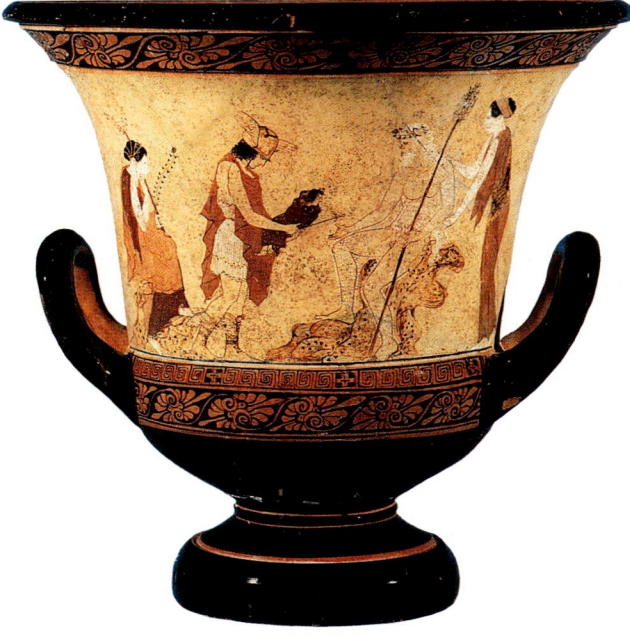

**5-57** NIOBID PAINTER, Artemis and Apollo slaying the children of Niobe (Attic red-figure calyx krater), from Orvieto, Italy, ca. 450 BCE. Approx. 1′ 9″ high. Louvre, Paris.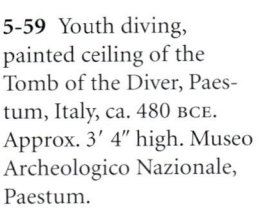

**5-58** PHIALE PAINTER, Hermes bringing the infant Dionysos to Papposilenos (Attic white-ground calyx krater), from Vulci, Italy, ca. 440–435 BCE. Approx. 1′ 2″ high. Vatican Museums, Rome.

**WHITE-GROUND LANDSCAPES** Further insight into the appearance of monumental panel painting of the fifth century BCE comes from a white-ground krater (FIG. **5-58**) by the so-called PHIALE PAINTER. The subject is Hermes handing over his half brother, the infant Dionysos, to Papposilenos ("grandpa-satyr"). The other figures represent the nymphs in the shady glens of Nysa, where Zeus had sent Dionysos, one of his numerous natural sons, to be raised, safe from the possible wrath of his wife Hera. Unlike the decorators of funerary lekythoi, the Phiale Painter used for this krater only colors that could survive the heat of a Greek kiln — reds, brown, purple, and a special snowy white reserved for the flesh of the nymphs and for such details as the hair, beard, and shaggy body of Papposilenos. The use of diluted brown wash to color and shade the rocks may reflect the coloration of Polygnotos's landscapes. This vase and the Niobid krater together provide art

historians with a shadowy idea of the character and magnificence of Polygnotos's great paintings.

**A PLUNGE INTO THE NETHERWORLD** Although all of the panel paintings of the masters were lost long ago, some Greek mural paintings are preserved today. An early example is in the so-called Tomb of the Diver at Paestum in southern Italy. The four walls of this small, coffinlike tomb are decorated with banquet scenes such as appear regularly on Greek vases. On the tomb's ceiling (FIG. **5-59**), a youth dives from a stone platform into a body of water. The scene most likely symbolizes the plunge from this life into the next. Trees resembling those of the Niobid krater are included within the decorative frame. The theme has no parallels on extant Greek vases, but it appears on an Etruscan tomb wall of the late sixth century BCE (see FIG. 9-9). The Greek

**5-59** Youth diving, painted ceiling of the Tomb of the Diver, Paestum, Italy, ca. 480 BCE. Approx. 3′ 4″ high. Museo Archeologico Nazionale, Paestum.

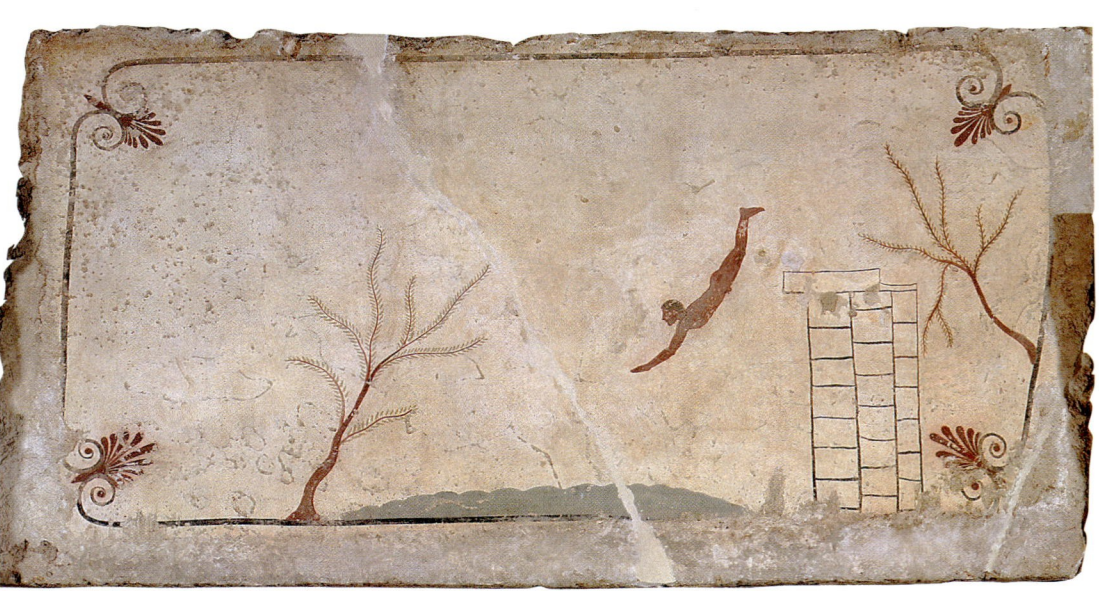

painter of the Tomb of the Diver seems to have been as aware of developments in Etruscan painting in Italy as of the work of contemporaries in mainland Greece.

# THE LATE CLASSICAL PERIOD

**THE RISE OF MACEDON** The Peloponnesian War, which began in 431 BCE, ended in 404 BCE with the complete defeat of a plague-weakened Athens, and left Greece drained of its strength. The victor, Sparta, and then Thebes undertook the leadership of Greece, both unsuccessfully. In the middle of the fourth century, a threat from without caused the rival Greek states to put aside their animosities and unite for their common defense, as they had earlier against the Persians. But at the battle of Chaeronea in 338 BCE, the Greek cities suffered a devastating loss and had to relinquish their independence to Philip II, king of Macedon. Philip was assassinated in 336, and his son, Alexander III, better known simply as Alexander the Great, succeeded him. In the decade before his death in 323 BCE, Alexander led a powerful army on an extraordinary campaign that overthrew the Persian Empire (the ultimate revenge for the Persian invasion of Greece in the early fifth century), wrested control of Egypt, and even reached India.

**NEW DIRECTIONS IN ART** The fourth century BCE was thus a time of political upheaval in Greece, and the chaos had a profound impact on the psyche of the Greeks and on the art they produced. In the fifth century BCE, Greeks had generally believed that rational human beings could impose order on their environment, create "perfect" statues such as the *Canon* of Polykleitos, and discover the "correct" mathematical formulas for constructing temples such as the Parthenon. The Parthenon frieze celebrated the Athenians as a community of citizens with shared values. The Peloponnesian War and the unceasing strife of the fourth century BCE brought an end to the serene idealism of the fifth century. Disillusionment and alienation followed. Greek thought and Greek art began to focus more on the individual and on the real world of appearances rather than on the community and the ideal world of perfect beings and perfect buildings.

## *Sculpture*

**HUMANIZING THE GODS** The new approach to art is immediately apparent in the work of PRAXITELES, one of the great masters of the fourth century BCE. Praxiteles did not reject the themes favored by the sculptors of the High Classical period. His Olympian gods and goddesses retained their superhuman beauty, but in his hands they lost some of their solemn grandeur and took on a worldly sensuousness.

Nowhere is this new humanizing spirit plainer than in the statue of Aphrodite (FIG. **5-60**) that Praxiteles sold to the Knidians after another city had rejected it. The lost original, carved from Parian marble, is known only through copies of Roman date, but Pliny considered it "superior to all the works, not only of Praxiteles, but indeed in the whole world." It made Knidos famous, and many people sailed there just to see the statue in its round temple (compare FIG. 5-71), where "it was possible to view the image of the goddess from every side." According to Pliny, some visitors were "overcome with love for the statue."[6]

The *Aphrodite of Knidos* caused such a sensation in its time because Praxiteles took the unprecedented step of representing the

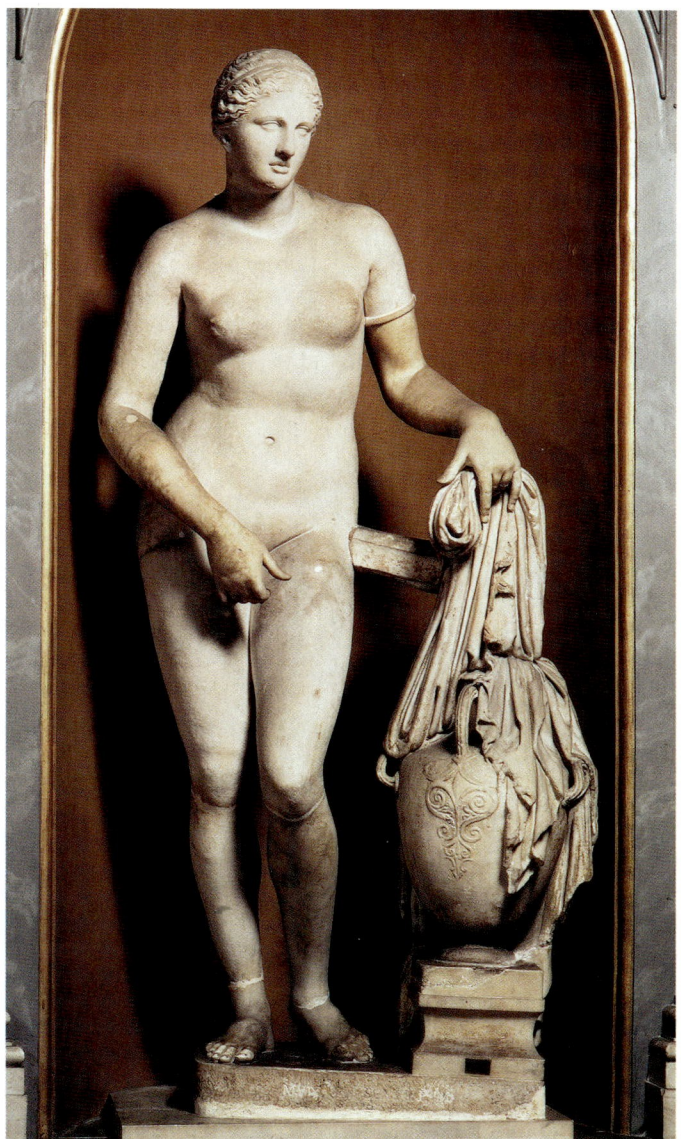

**5-60** PRAXITELES, *Aphrodite of Knidos.* Roman marble copy after an original of ca. 350–340 BCE. Approx. 6′ 8″ high. Vatican Museums, Rome.

goddess of love completely nude. Female nudity was rare in earlier Greek art and had been confined almost exclusively to paintings on vases designed for household use, such as the kylix of Onesimos (FIG. 5-23) discussed earlier. The women so depicted also tended to be courtesans or slave girls, not noblewomen or goddesses, and no one had dared fashion for a temple a statue of a goddess without her clothes. Moreover, Praxiteles' Aphrodite is not a cold and remote image. In fact, the goddess engages in a trivial act out of everyday life. She has removed her garment, draped it over a large *hydria* (water pitcher), and is about to step into the bath. The motif is strikingly similar to the one Onesimos painted.

**DEWY EYES** Although shocking in its day, the *Aphrodite of Knidos* is not openly erotic (the goddess modestly shields her pelvis with her right hand), but she is quite sensuous. Lucian, writing in the second century CE, noted that she has a "welcoming look" and a "slight smile" and that Praxiteles was renowned for his ability to transform marble into soft and radiant flesh. Lucian mentions, for example, the "dewy quality of Aphrodite's eyes."[7] Unfortunately, the rather mechanical Roman copies do not

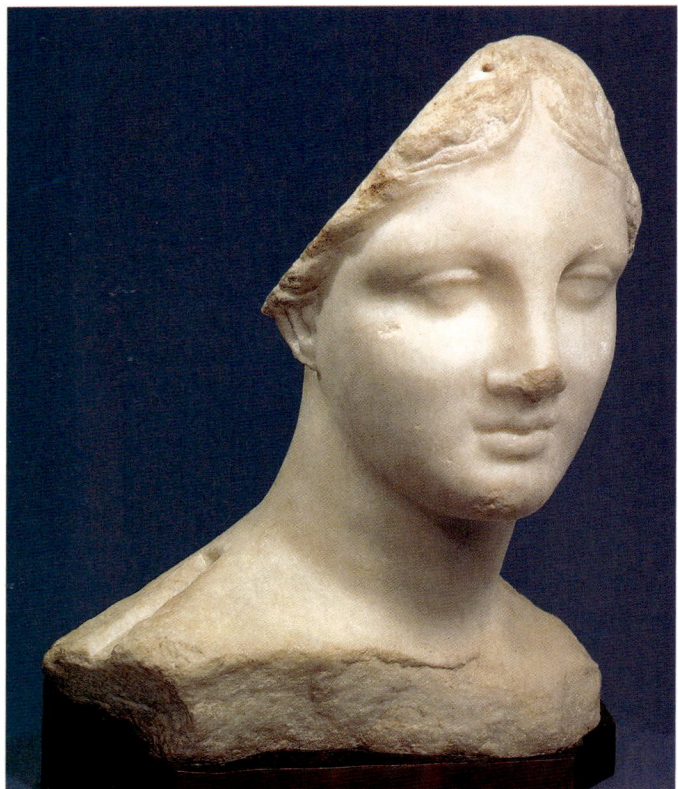

**5-61** Head of a woman, from Chios, Greece, ca. 320–300 BCE. Marble, approx. 1′ 2″ high. Museum of Fine Arts, Boston.

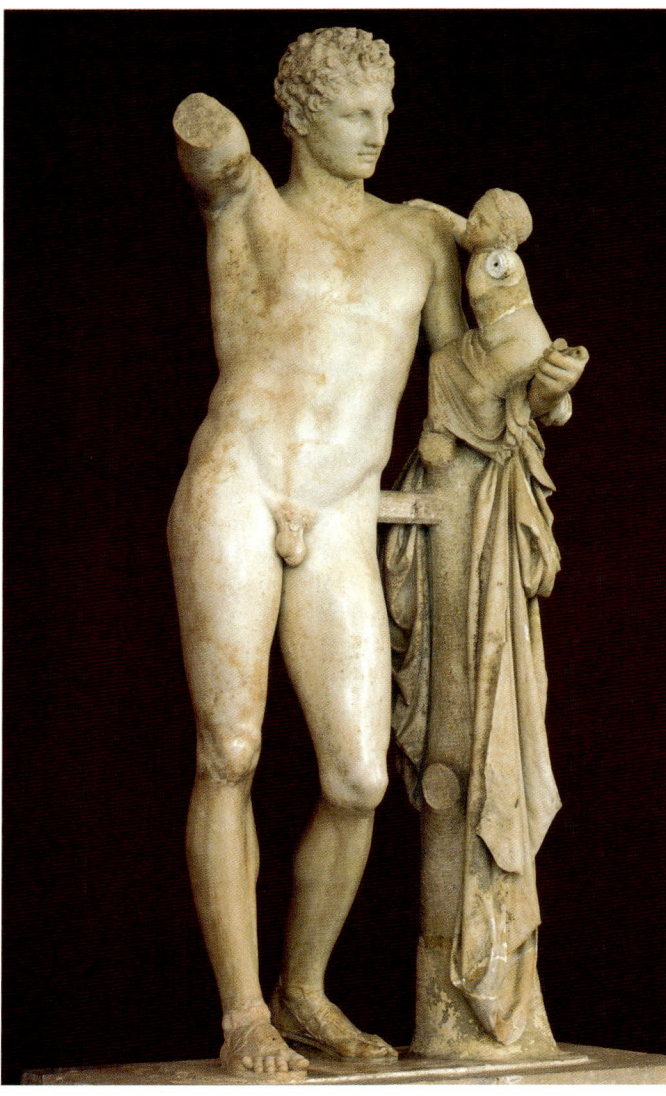

**5-62** PRAXITELES, Hermes and the infant Dionysos, from the Temple of Hera, Olympia, Greece. Marble copy after an original of ca. 340 BCE, approx. 7′ 1″ high. Archaeological Museum, Olympia.

capture the quality of Praxiteles' modeling of the stone, but one can imagine the "look" of the *Aphrodite of Knidos* from original works by sculptors who emulated the master's manner.

One of the finest of these is the head of a woman from Chios (FIG. **5-61**) that was once set into a draped statue. This sculptor wielded the chisel in the Praxitelean manner, suggesting the softness of the young girl's face and the "dewy" gaze of the eyes. The sharp outlining of precisely measured body parts that characterized the work of Polykleitos and his contemporaries gave way to a smooth flow of flesh from forehead to chin, and to a very human sensuousness. In the statues of Praxiteles and his followers, the deities of Mount Olympus still possess a beauty mortals can aspire to, although not achieve, but they are no longer awesome and remote. Praxiteles' gods have stepped off their fifth-century pedestals and entered the fourth-century world of human experience.

**SENSUOUS LANGUOR** The Praxitelean manner also may be seen in a statue once thought to be by the hand of the master himself but now generally considered a copy of the highest quality. The statue of Hermes and the infant Dionysos (FIG. **5-62**) found in the Temple of Hera at Olympia brings to the realm of monumental statuary the theme the Phiale Painter had chosen for a white-ground krater (FIG. **5-58**) a century earlier. Hermes has stopped to rest in a forest on his journey to Nysa to entrust the upbringing of Dionysos to Papposilenos and the nymphs. Hermes leans on a tree trunk (here it is an integral part of the composition and not the copyist's addition), and his slender body forms a sinuous, shallow S-curve that is the hallmark of many of Praxiteles' statues. He looks off dreamily into space while he dangles a bunch of grapes (now missing) as a temptation for the

infant, who is to become the Greek god of the vine. This is the kind of tender and very human interaction between an adult and a child that one encounters frequently in real life but that had been absent from Greek statuary before the fourth century.

The superb quality of the carving appears to be faithful to the Praxitelean original. The modeling is deliberately smooth and subtle, producing soft shadows that follow the planes as they flow almost imperceptibly one into another. The delicacy of the marble facial features stands in sharp contrast to the metallic precision of Polykleitos's bronze *Doryphoros* (FIG. 5-38). Even the *Spear Bearer*'s locks of hair were subjected to the fifth-century sculptor's laws of symmetry and do not violate the skull's perfect curve. One need only compare these two statues to see how broad a change in artistic attitude and intent took place from the mid-fifth to the mid-fourth century BCE. Sensuous languor and an order of beauty that appeals more to the eye than to the mind replaced majestic strength and rationalizing design.

**THE PASSION OF SKOPAS** In the Archaic period and throughout most of the Early and High Classical periods, Greek sculptors generally shared common goals, but in the Late Classical period of the fourth century BCE, distinctive individual styles emerged. The dreamy, beautiful divinities of Praxiteles had enormous appeal, and, as the head of the woman from Chios (FIG. 5-61) attests, the master had many followers. But other sculptors pursued very different interests. One of these was SKOPAS OF PAROS, and although his work reflects the general trend toward the humanization of the Greek gods and heroes, his hallmark is intense emotionalism.

Skopas was an architect as well as a sculptor. He designed the Temple of Athena Alea at Tegea. Fragments of the pedimental statues from that temple are preserved, and they epitomize Skopas's approach to sculpture, even if they are not by his own hand. One of the heads (FIG. 5-63) portrays a hero wearing a lion-skin headdress. It must be either Herakles or his son Telephos, whose battle with Achilles was the subject of the west pediment. The head, like others from the Tegea pediments, is highly dramatic. The hero turns abruptly, and his facial expression shows great psychological tension. His large eyes are set deeply into his head. Fleshy overhanging brows create deep shadows. His lips are slightly parted. The passionate face reveals an anguished soul within. Skopas's work broke with the Classical tradition of benign, serene features and prefigured later Hellenistic depictions of unbridled emotion.

**DEATH AND IRONY** An unprecedented psychological intensity also may be seen in a grave stele (FIG. 5-64) found near the Ilissos River in Athens. The stele was originally set into an architectural frame similar to that of the earlier Hegeso stele (FIG. 5-55). A comparison between the two works is very telling. In the Ilissos stele the relief is much higher, with parts of the figures carved fully in the round. But the major difference is the pronounced change in mood, which reflects the innovations of Skopas. The later work makes a clear distinction between the living and the dead, and depicts overt mourning. The deceased is a young hunter whose features recall those of Skopas's Tegean heroes. At his feet a small boy, either his servant or perhaps a younger brother, sobs openly. The hunter's dog also droops its head in sorrow. Beside the youth an old man, undoubtedly his father, leans on a walking stick and, in a gesture reminiscent of that of the Olympia seer (FIG. 5-31), ponders the irony of fate that has taken the life of his powerful son and preserved him in his frail old age. Most remarkable of all, the hunter himself looks out at the viewer, inviting sympathy and creating an emotional bridge between the spectator and the artwork that was inconceivable in the art of the High Classical period.

**LYSIPPOS AND A NEW CANON** The third great Late Classical sculptor, LYSIPPOS of Sikyon, was so renowned that Alexander the Great selected him to create his official portrait. (Alexander could afford to employ the best. The Macedonian kingdom enjoyed vast wealth. King Philip hired the leading thinker of his age, Aristotle, as the young Alexander's tutor!)

Lysippos introduced a new canon of proportions in which the bodies were more slender than those of Polykleitos—whose own canon continued to exert enormous influence—and the heads roughly one-eighth the height of the body rather than one-seventh, as in the previous century. The new proportions may be seen in one of Lysippos's most famous works, a bronze statue of an *apoxyomenos* (an athlete scraping oil from his body after exercising),

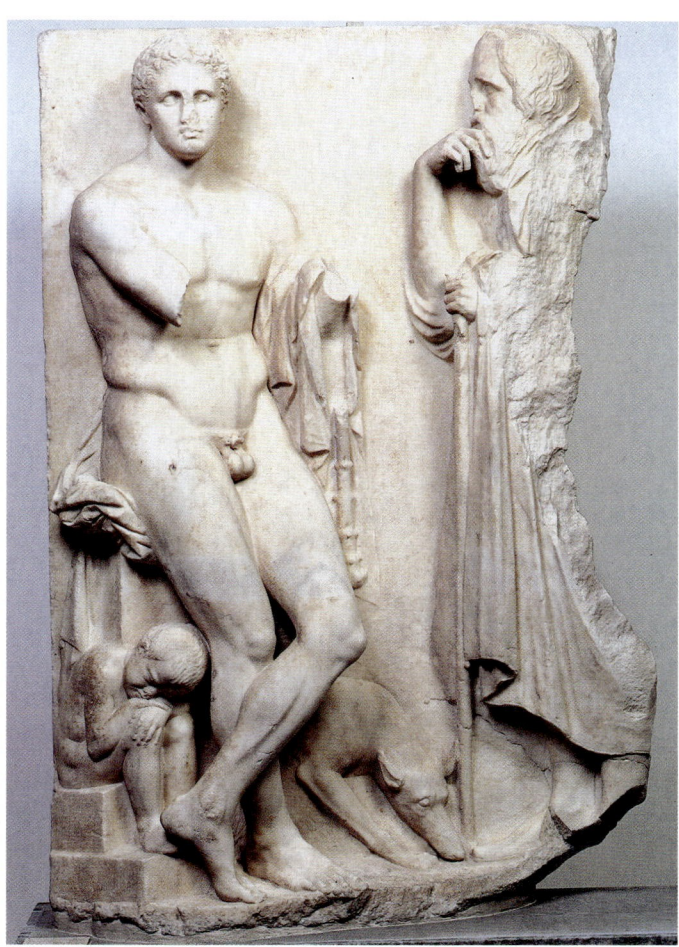

**5-63** Head of Herakles or Telephos, from the west pediment of the Temple of Athena Alea, Tegea, Greece, ca. 340 BCE. Marble, approx. 1′ $\frac{1}{2}$″ high. (Stolen from) Archaeological Museum, Tegea.

**5-64** Grave stele of a young hunter, found near the Ilissos River, Athens, Greece, ca. 340–330 BCE. Marble, approx. 5′ 6″ high. National Archaeological Museum, Athens.

known, as usual, only from Roman copies in marble (FIG. 5-65). A comparison with Polykleitos's *Doryphoros* (FIG. 5-38) reveals more than a change in physique. A nervous energy runs through Lysippos's *Apoxyomenos* that one seeks in vain in the balanced form of the *Doryphoros*. The strigil (scraper) is about to reach the end of the right arm, and at any moment the athlete will switch it to the other hand so that he can scrape his left arm. At the same time, he will shift his weight and reverse the positions of his legs. Lysippos also began to break down the dominance of the frontal view in statuary and encouraged the observer to look at his athlete from multiple angles. Because Lysippos represented the apoxyomenos with his right arm boldly thrust forward, the figure breaks out of the shallow rectangular box that defined the boundaries of earlier statues. To comprehend the action, the observer must move to the side and view Lysippos's work at a three-quarter angle or in full profile.

**COLOSSAL FATIGUE** To grasp the full meaning of another work of Lysippos, a colossal statue (FIG. 5-66) depicting a weary Herakles, the viewer must walk around it. Once again, the original is lost. The most impressive of the surviving marble copies is nearly twice life-size and was exhibited in the Baths of Caracalla in Rome (see FIGS. 10-67 and 10-68). Like the marble copy of Polykleitos's *Doryphoros* (FIG. 5-38) from the Roman palaestra at Pompeii, Lysippos's muscle-bound Greek hero provided inspiration for Romans who came to the baths to exercise. (The statue is signed by the copyist, GLYKON OF ATHENS. Lysippos's name is not mentioned. The educated Roman public did not need a label to identify the famous work.) In the hands of Lysippos, however, the exaggerated muscular development of Herakles is poignantly ironic, for the sculptor depicted the strongman as so weary that he must lean on his club for support. Without that prop Herakles would topple over. Lysippos and other fourth-century BCE artists rejected stability and balance as worthy goals for statuary.

Herakles holds the golden apples of the Hesperides in his right hand behind his back—unseen unless one walks around the statue. Lysippos's subject is thus the same as that of the metope (FIG. 5-32) of the Early Classical Temple of Zeus at Olympia, but the fourth-century BCE Herakles is no longer

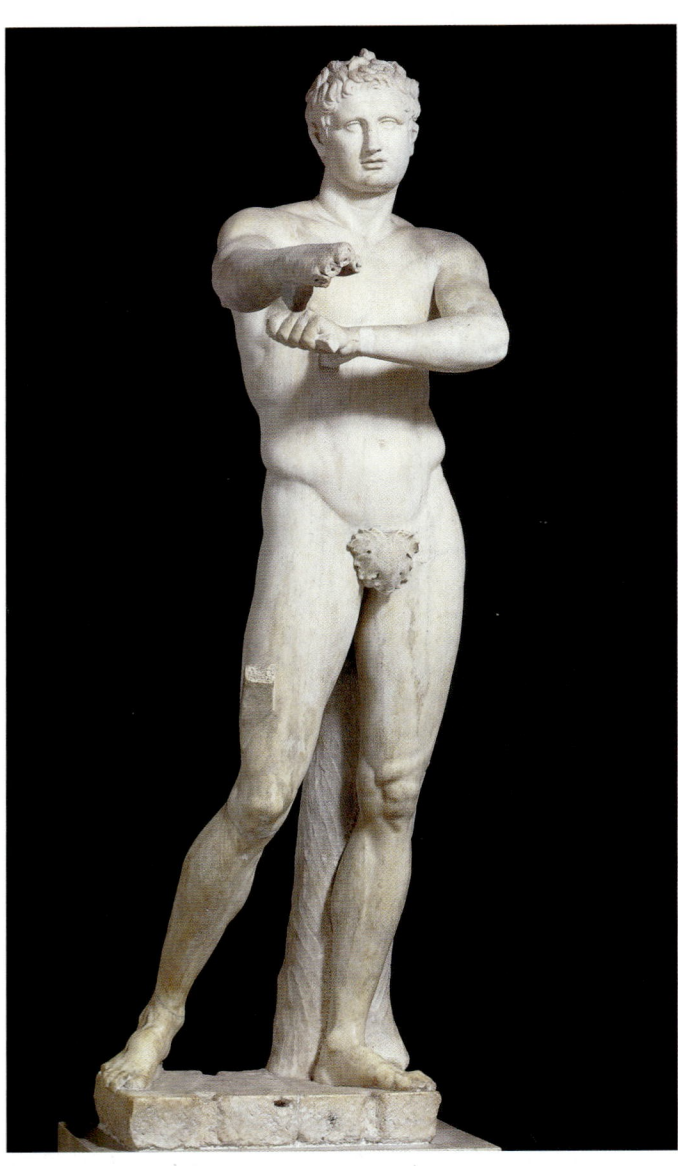

**5-65** LYSIPPOS, *Apoxyomenos (Scraper)*. Roman marble copy after a bronze original of ca. 330 BCE, approx. 6′ 9″ high. Vatican Museums, Rome.

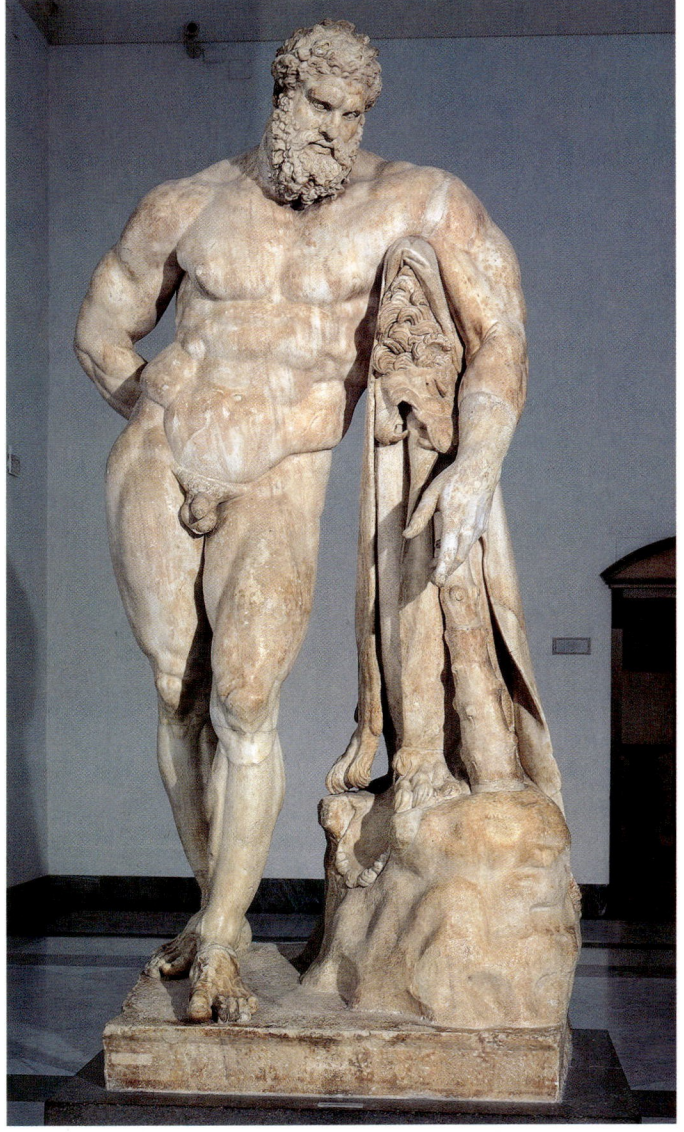

**5-66** LYSIPPOS, Weary Herakles *(Farnese Herakles)*. Roman marble copy from Rome, Italy, signed by GLYKON OF ATHENS, after a bronze original of ca. 320 BCE. Approx. 10′ 5″ high. Museo Nazionale, Naples.

serene. Instead of expressing joy, or at least satisfaction, at having completed one of the impossible 12 labors (see "Herakles," page 109), he is almost dejected. Exhausted by his physical efforts, he can think only of his pain and weariness, not of the reward of immortality that awaits him. Lysippos's portrayal of Herakles in this statue is perhaps the most eloquent testimony yet to Late Classical sculptors' interest in humanizing the great gods and heroes of the Greeks. In this respect, despite their divergent styles, Praxiteles, Skopas, and Lysippos followed a common path.

## Alexander the Great and Macedonian Court Art

ALEXANDER AS EPIC HERO Alexander the Great's favorite book was the *Iliad,* and his own life was very much like an epic saga, full of heroic battles, exotic places, and unceasing drama. Alexander was a man of singular character, an inspired leader with boundless energy and an almost foolhardy courage. He personally led his army into battle on the back of Bucephalus, the wild and mighty steed only he could tame and ride.

Ancient sources reveal that Alexander believed that only Lysippos had captured his essence in a portrait, and that is why only he was authorized to sculpt the king's image. Lysippos's most famous portrait of the Macedonian king was a full-length heroically nude bronze statue of Alexander holding a lance and turning his head toward the sky. Plutarch reported that an epigram was inscribed on the base stating that the statue depicted Alexander gazing at Zeus and proclaiming, "I place the earth under my sway; you, O Zeus, keep Olympus." Plutarch further stated that the portrait was characterized by "leonine" hair and a "melting glance."[8]

The Lysippan original is lost, and because Alexander was portrayed so many times for centuries after his death, it is very difficult to determine which of the many surviving images is most faithful to the fourth-century BCE portrait. A leading candidate is a second-century BCE marble head (FIG. 5-67) from Pella, the capital of Macedonia and Alexander's birthplace. It has the sharp turn of the head and thick mane of hair that were key ingredients of Lysippos's portrait. The sculptor's treatment of the features also is consistent with the style of the later fourth century. The deep-set eyes and parted lips recall the manner of Skopas, and the delicate handling of the flesh brings to mind the faces of Praxitelean statues. Although not a copy, this head very likely approximates the young king's official portrait and provides insight into Alexander's personality as well as the art of Lysippos.

MACEDONIAN OPULENCE Alexander's palace has not been excavated, but one can form an idea of the sumptuousness of life at the Macedonian court from the costly objects found in Macedonian graves and from the abundance of mosaics (see "Mosaics," Chapter 11, page 315) uncovered at Pella in the homes of the wealthy. The Pella mosaics are *pebble mosaics.* The floors are formed of small stones of various colors collected from beaches and riverbanks and set into a thick coat of cement. The finest pebble mosaic yet to come to light has a stag hunt (FIG. 5-68) as its *emblema* (central framed panel), bordered in turn by an intricate floral pattern and a stylized wave motif (not shown in our detail). The artist signed his work in the same manner as proud Greek vase painters and potters did: "Gnosis made it." This is the earliest mosaicist's signature known, and its prominence in the design undoubtedly attests to the artist's reputation. The house owner wanted guests to know that Gnosis himself, and not an imitator, had laid this floor.

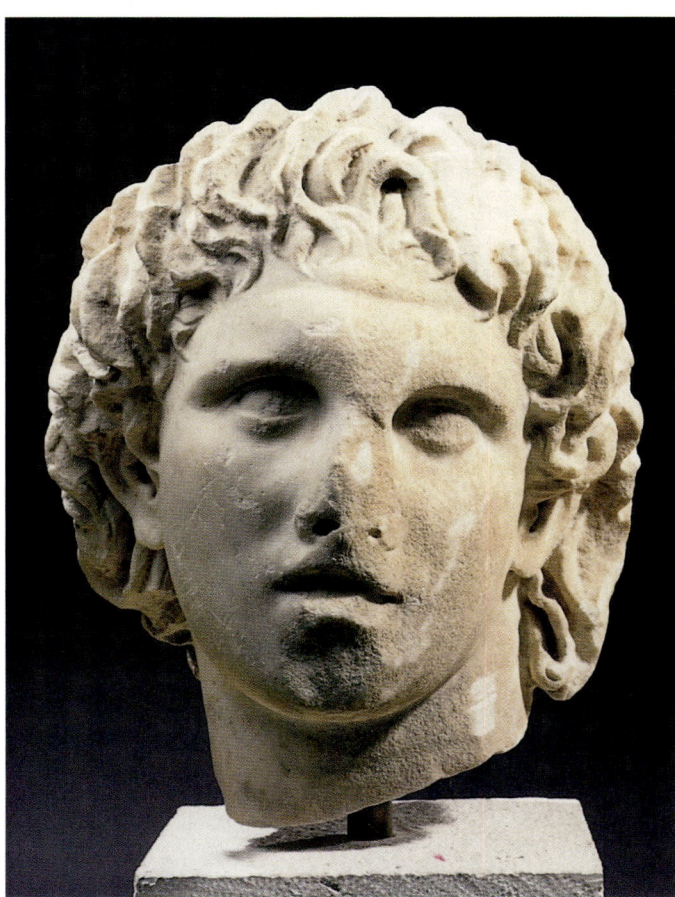

5-67 Head of Alexander the Great, from Pella, Greece, ca. 200–150 BCE. Marble, approx. 1′ high. Archaeological Museum, Pella.

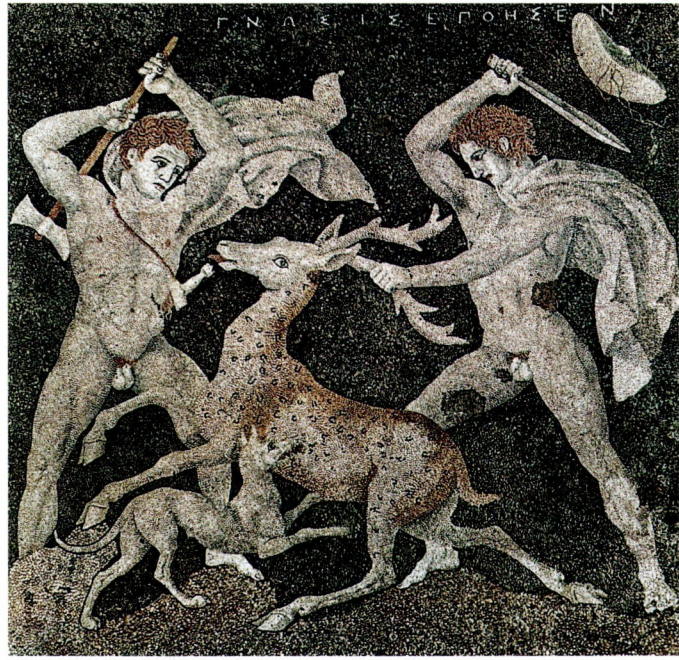

5-68 GNOSIS, Stag hunt, from Pella, Greece, ca. 300 BCE. Pebble mosaic, figural panel 10′ 2″ high. Archaeological Museum, Pella.

The Pella stag hunt, with its light figures against a dark ground, has much in common with red-figure painting. In the pebble mosaic, however, thin strips of lead or terracotta define most of the contour lines and some of the interior details. Subtle gradations of yellow, brown, and red, as well as black, white, and gray pebbles suggest the interior volumes. The musculature of the hunters, and even their billowing cloaks and the animals' bodies, are modeled by shading. Such use of light and dark to suggest volume is rarely seen on Greek painted vases, although examples do exist. Monumental painters, however, commonly used shading. The Greek term for shading was *skiagraphia* (literally, "shadow painting"), and it was said to have been invented by an Athenian painter of the fifth century BCE named APOLLODOROS. Gnosis's emblema, with its sparse landscape setting, probably reflects contemporary panel painting.

**ALEXANDER HUMILIATES DARIUS** A mosaic that decorated the floor of one room of a lavishly appointed Roman house at Pompeii gives an even better idea of monumental painting during Alexander's time. In the *Alexander Mosaic* (FIG. **5-69**), the mosaicist employed *tesserae* (tiny stones or pieces of glass cut to the desired size and shape) instead of pebbles (see "Mosaics," Chapter 11, page 315). The subject is a great battle between the armies of Alexander the Great and the Persian king Darius III, probably the battle of Issus in southeastern Turkey, when Darius fled the battlefield in his chariot in humiliating defeat. The mosaic dates to the late second or early first century BCE. It is widely believed to be a reasonably faithful copy of *Battle of Issus,* a famous panel painting of ca. 310 BCE made by PHILOXENOS OF ERETRIA for King Cassander, one of Alexander's successors.

Philoxenos's painting is notable for its technical mastery of problems that had long fascinated Greek painters. Even Euthymides would have marveled at the fourth-century painter's depiction of the rearing horse seen in a three-quarter rear view below Darius. The subtle modulation of the horse's rump through shading in browns and yellows is precisely what Gnosis was striving to imitate in his pebble mosaic. Other details are even more impressive. The Persian to the right of the rearing horse has fallen to the ground and raises, backwards, a dropped Macedonian shield to protect himself from being trampled. Philoxenos recorded the reflection of the man's terrified face on the polished surface of the shield. Everywhere in the scene, men, animals, and weapons cast shadows on the ground. Philoxenos and other Classical painters' interest in the reflection of insubstantial light on a shiny surface, and in the absence of light (shadows), was far removed from earlier painters' preoccupation with the clear presentation of weighty figures seen against a blank background. The Greek painter here truly opened a window into a world filled not only with figures, trees, and sky but also with light. This Classical Greek notion of what a painting should be characterizes most of the history of art in the Western world from the Renaissance on.

Most impressive about *Battle of Issus,* however, is not the virtuoso details but the psychological intensity of the drama unfolding before the viewer's eyes. Alexander is on horseback leading his army into battle, recklessly one might say, without even a helmet to protect him. He drives his spear through one of Darius's trusted "Immortals," who were sworn to guard the king's life, while the Persian's horse collapses beneath him. The Macedonian king is only a few yards away from Darius, and Alexander directs his gaze at the Persian king, not at the man impaled on his now-useless spear. Darius has called for retreat. In fact, his charioteer is already whipping the horses and speeding the king to safety. Before he escapes, Darius looks back at Alexander and in a pathetic gesture reaches out toward his brash foe. But the victory has

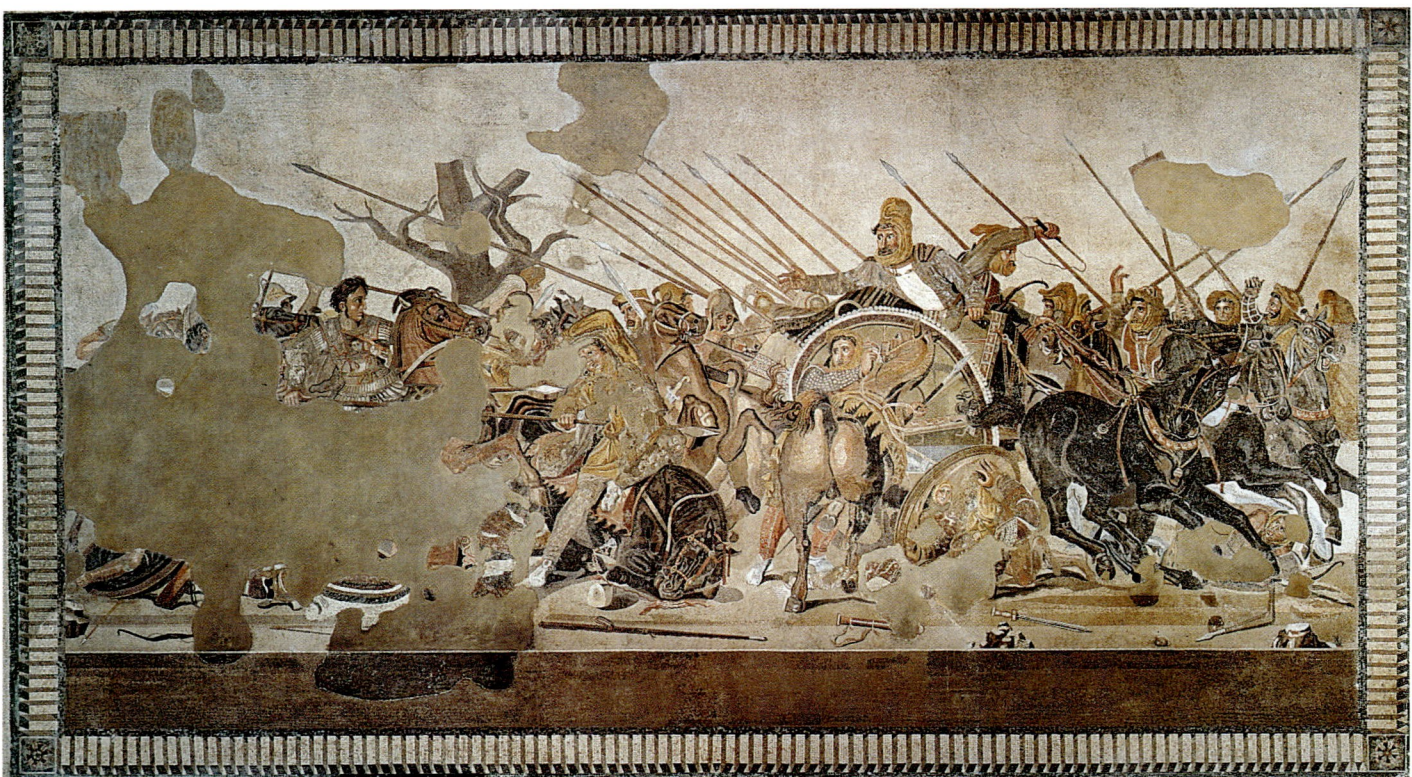

**5-69** PHILOXENOS OF ERETRIA, *Battle of Issus,* ca. 310 BCE. Roman copy *(Alexander Mosaic)* from the House of the Faun, Pompeii, Italy, late second or early first century BCE. Tessera mosaic, approx. 8′ 10″ × 16′ 9″. Museo Nazionale, Naples.

slipped out of his hands. Pliny says Philoxenos's painting of the battle between Alexander and Darius was "inferior to none."[9] It is easy to see how he reached that conclusion.

## Architecture

**A WONDROUS MAUSOLEUM** Five of the Seven Wonders of the ancient world were Greek (see "Babylon: City of Wonders," Chapter 2, page 49), but only one Greek Wonder was a tomb. The tomb built at Halikarnassos for Mausolos, the ruler of Caria in Asia Minor from 377 to 353 BCE, was the only funerary monument the ancients considered worthy of comparison with the pyramids of Egypt (see FIG. 3-8), the solitary Egyptian Wonder. Mausolos's wife, Artemisia, erected the tomb and employed some of the leading sculptors of the day, Skopas among them, to decorate it.

Mausolos's tomb was dismantled long ago, but ancient descriptions have encouraged numerous scholars to attempt a reconstruction. None has won wide acceptance. Nonetheless, the building can be visualized in general terms. It was a multistory structure consisting of a high stepped podium, an Ionic colonnade, and a pyramidal roof capped by a colossal marble group of Mausolos in a four-horse chariot. The height of the tomb, including the chariot, was 140 feet. The fame of the Halikarnassos Wonder was so great that already in Roman times *mausoleum* had become a generic term for any grandiose funerary monument. But the tomb, famous as it was, was only one of the triumphs of Greek architects in the fourth century BCE.

**GREEK THEATERS** In ancient Greece, plays were not performed repeatedly over months or years as they are today, but only once, during sacred festivals. Greek drama was closely associated with religious rites and was not pure entertainment. At Athens in the fifth century BCE, for example, the great tragedies of Aeschylus, Sophocles, and Euripides were performed at the Dionysos festival in the theater dedicated to the god on the southern slope of the Acropolis (FIG. 5-40, far right). The finest theater in Greece, however, is at Epidauros (FIG. **5-70**). It was constructed shortly after Alexander the Great was born. The architect was POLYKLEITOS THE YOUNGER, possibly a nephew of the great fifth-century sculptor. His theater is still used for performances of ancient Greek dramas.

The precursor of the formal Greek theater was a place where ancient rites, songs, and dances were performed. This circular piece of earth with a hard and level surface later became the orchestra of the theater. *Orchestra* literally means "dancing place." The actors and the chorus performed there, and at Epidauros an altar to Dionysos stood at the center of the circle. The spectators sat on a slope overlooking the orchestra—the *theatron,* or "place for seeing." When the Greek theater took architectural shape, the auditorium (*cavea,* Latin for "hollow place, cavity") was always situated on a hillside. The cavea at Epidauros, composed of wedge-shaped sections (*cunei,* singular *cuneus*) of stone benches separated by stairs, is somewhat greater than a semicircle in plan. The auditorium is 387 feet in diameter, and its 55 rows of seats accommodated about 12,000 spectators. They entered the theater via a passageway between the seating area and the scene building *(skene),* which housed dressing rooms for the actors and also formed a backdrop for the plays. The design is simple but perfectly suited to its function. Even in antiquity the Epidauros theater was renowned for the harmony of its proportions. Although spectators sitting in some of the seats would have had a poor view of the skene, all had unobstructed views of the orchestra. Because of the open-air cavea's excellent acoustics, everyone could hear the actors and chorus.

**CORINTHIAN CAPITALS** The theater at Epidauros is situated some 500 yards southeast of the sanctuary of Asklepios, and Polykleitos the Younger worked there as well. He was the architect

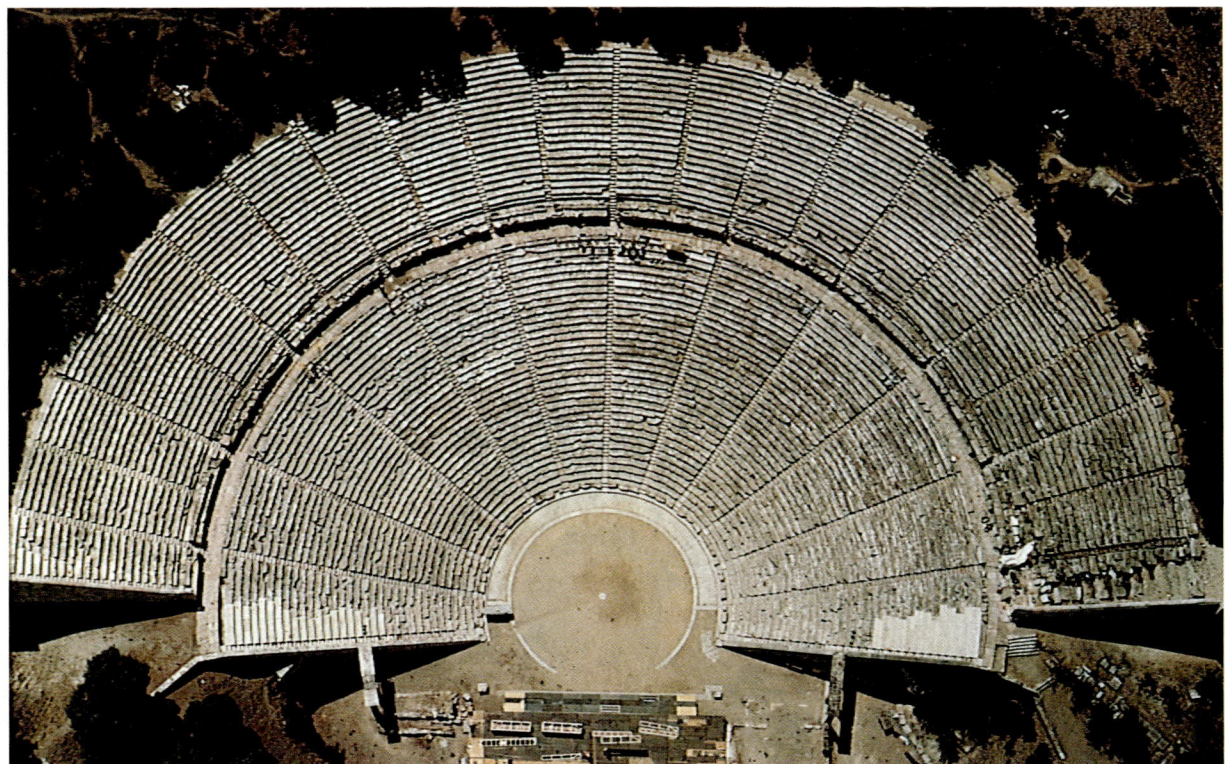

**5-70** POLYKLEITOS THE YOUNGER, Theater, Epidauros, Greece, ca. 350 BCE.

## The Corinthian Capital

The Corinthian capital (FIG. 5-72) is more ornate than either the Doric or Ionic (see "Doric and Ionic Temples," pages 116–117). It consists of a double row of acanthus leaves, from which tendrils and flowers emerge, wrapped around a bell-shaped echinus. Although this capital often is cited as the distinguishing feature of the Corinthian order, strictly speaking no Corinthian order exists. The new capital type was simply substituted for the volute capital in the Ionic order.

The sculptor KALLIMACHOS invented the Corinthian capital during the second half of the fifth century BCE. Vitruvius recorded the circumstances that supposedly led to its creation:

> A maiden who was a citizen of Corinth . . . died. After her funeral, her nurse collected the goblets in which the maiden had taken delight while she was alive, and after putting them together in a basket, she took them to the grave monument and put them on top of it. In order that they should remain in place for a long time, she covered them with a tile. Now it happened that this basket was placed over the root of an acanthus. As time went on the acanthus root, pressed down in the middle by the weight, sent forth, when it was about springtime, leaves and stalks; its stalks growing up along the sides of the basket and being pressed out from the angles because of the weight of the tile, were forced to form volute-like curves at their extremities. At this point, Kallimachos happened to be going by and noticed the basket with this gentle growth of leaves around it. Delighted with the order and the novelty of the form, he made columns using it as his model and established a canon of proportions for it.[1]

Kallimachos worked on the Acropolis. He made the golden lamp that stood beside the ancient wooden statue of Athena in the Erechtheion. Many scholars believe that a Corinthian column supported the outstretched right hand of the Phidian *Athena Parthenos* (FIG. 5-44) because some of the Roman copies of the lost statue have such a column. In any case, the earliest preserved

Corinthian capital dates to the time of Kallimachos. The new type was, however, rarely used before the mid-fourth century BCE and did not become popular until Hellenistic and especially Roman times. Later architects favored the Corinthian capital because of its ornate character and because it eliminated certain problems of both the Doric and Ionic orders.

The Ionic capital, unlike the Doric, has two distinct profiles—the front and back (with the volutes) and the sides. The volutes always faced outward on a Greek temple, but architects met with a vexing problem at the corners of their buildings, which had two adjacent "fronts." They solved the problem by placing volutes on both outer faces of the corner capitals (as on the Erechtheion, FIG. 5-50, and the Temple of Athena Nike, FIG. 5-53), but the solution was an awkward one.

Doric design rules also presented problems for Greek architects at the corners of buildings. The Doric frieze was organized according to three supposedly inflexible rules: (1) A triglyph must be exactly over the center of each column; (2) a triglyph must be over the center of each *intercolumniation* (the space between two columns); and (3) triglyphs at the corners of the frieze must meet so that no space is left over. But the rules are contradictory. If the corner triglyphs must meet, then they cannot be placed over the center of the corner column (see, for example, the Doric temples at Aegina and Paestum and the Parthenon in Athens, FIGS. 5-24, 5-29, and 5-42).

The Corinthian capital eliminated both problems. Because the capital's four sides have a similar appearance, corner Corinthian capitals do not have to be modified, as do corner Ionic capitals. And because the Ionic frieze is used for the Corinthian "order," architects do not have to contend with metopes or triglyphs.

[1] Vitruvius, *De architectura*, 4.1.8–10. Translated by J. J. Pollitt, *The Art of Ancient Greece: Sources and Documents* (New York: Cambridge University Press, 1990), 193–94.

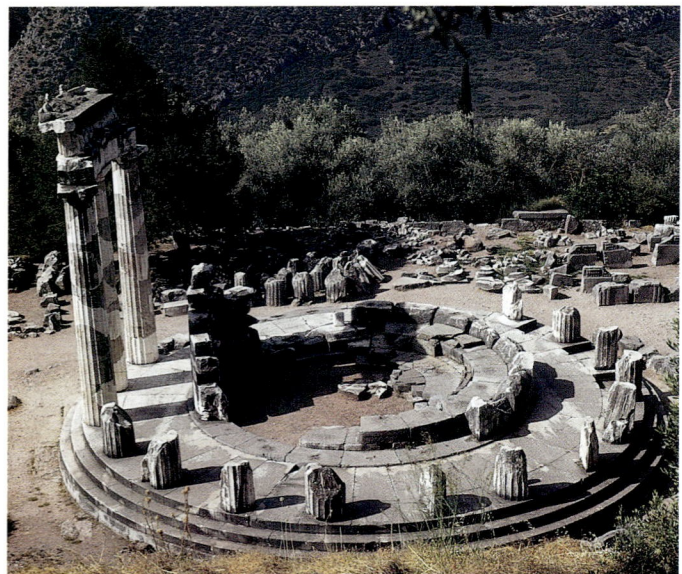

5-71 THEODOROS OF PHOKAIA, Tholos, Delphi, Greece, ca. 375 BCE.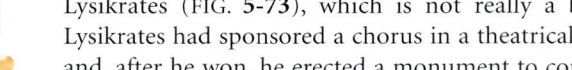

of the *tholos,* the circular shrine that probably housed the sacred snakes of the healing god. That building lies in ruins today, its architectural fragments removed to the local museum, but one can get an approximate idea of its original appearance by looking at the somewhat earlier and partially reconstructed tholos at Delphi (FIG. 5-71) that THEODOROS OF PHOKAIA designed. Both tholoi had an exterior colonnade of Doric columns. Inside, however, both the Delphi and Epidauros columns (FIG. 5-72) were crowned by *Corinthian capitals* (see "The Corinthian Capital," above), an innovation of the second half of the fifth century BCE.

Consistent with the extremely conservative nature of Greek temple design, architects did not readily embrace the Corinthian capital. Until the second century BCE, Corinthian capitals were employed, as at Delphi and Epidauros, only for the interiors of sacred buildings. The earliest instance of a Corinthian capital on the exterior of a Greek building is the Choragic Monument of Lysikrates (FIG. 5-73), which is not really a building at all. Lysikrates had sponsored a chorus in a theatrical contest in 334, and, after he won, he erected a monument to commemorate his

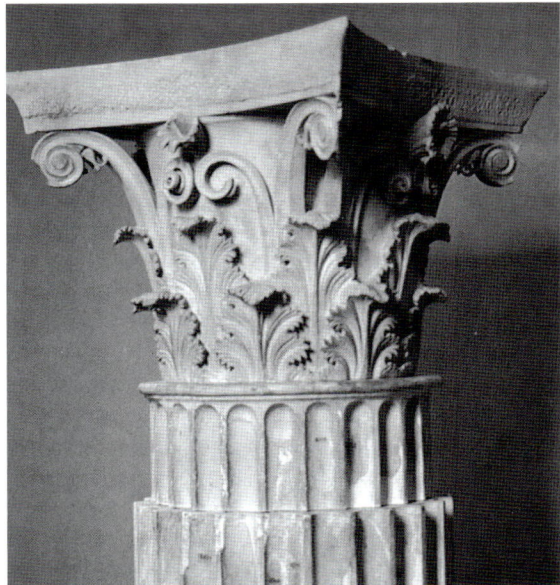

**5-72** POLYKLEITOS THE YOUNGER, Corinthian capital, from the tholos, Epidauros, Greece, ca. 350 BCE. Archaeological Museum, Epidauros.

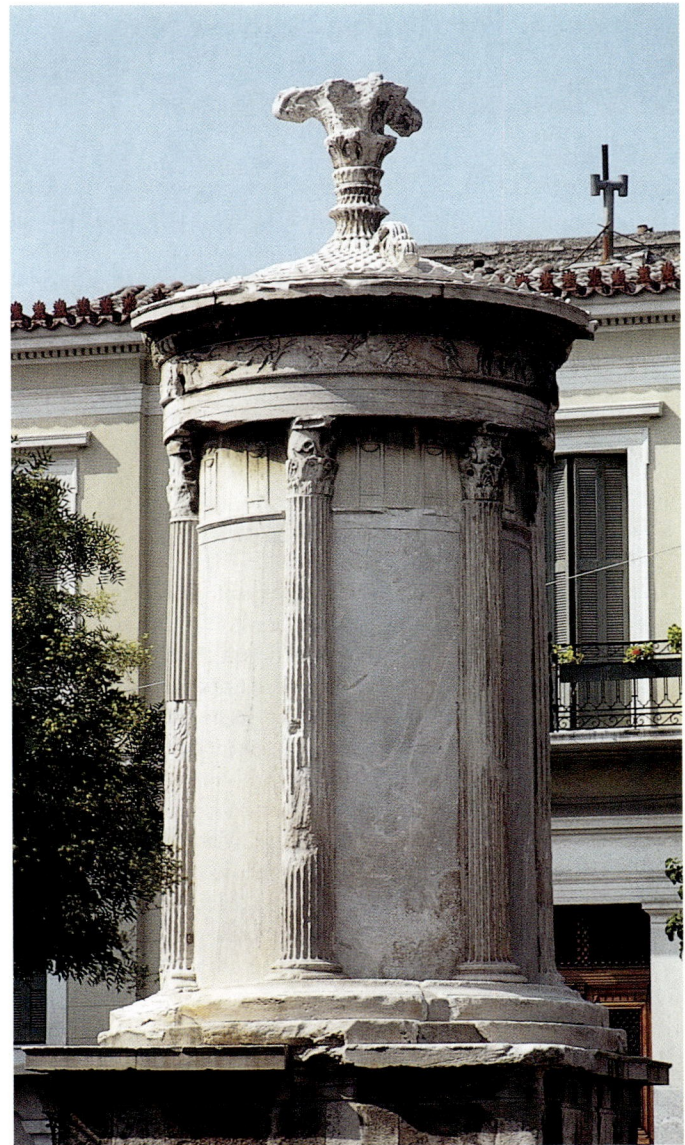

**5-73** Choragic Monument of Lysikrates, Athens, Greece, 334 BCE.

victory. The monument consists of a cylindrical drum resembling a tholos on a rectangular base. Engaged Corinthian columns adorn the drum of Lysikrates' monument, and a huge Corinthian capital sits on top of the roof. The freestanding capital once supported the victor's prize, a bronze tripod.

# THE HELLENISTIC PERIOD

**AFTER ALEXANDER** Alexander the Great's conquest of the Near East and Egypt (where the Macedonian king was buried) ushered in a new cultural age that historians and art historians alike call *Hellenistic.* The Hellenistic period is traditionally reckoned from the death of Alexander in 323 BCE, and lasted nearly three centuries, until 31 BCE, when Queen Cleopatra of Egypt and her Roman consort Mark Antony were decisively defeated at the battle of Actium by Antony's rival Augustus. A year later, Augustus made Egypt a province of the Roman Empire. It is said that when Alexander was on his deathbed, his generals, greedy for the lands their young leader had conquered, asked, "To which one of us do you leave your empire?" He supposedly answered, "To the strongest."[10] Although probably a later invention, this exchange points out the near inevitability of what followed — the division of Alexander's far-flung empire among his Greek generals and their subsequent naturalization among those they subjugated.

The cultural centers of the Hellenistic period were the court cities of the Greek kings — Antioch in Syria, Alexandria in Egypt, Pergamon in Asia Minor, and others (MAP 5-1). An international culture united the Hellenistic world, and its language was Greek. Hellenistic kings became enormously rich on the spoils of the East, priding themselves on their libraries, art collections, scientific enterprises, and skills as critics and connoisseurs, as well as on the learned men they could assemble at their courts. The world of the small, austere, and heroic city-state passed away, as did the power and prestige of its center, Athens. A cosmopolitan ("citizen of the world," in Greek) civilization, much like today's, replaced it.

## Architecture

**BREAKING OLD RULES** The greater variety, complexity, and sophistication of Hellenistic culture called for an architecture on an imperial scale and of wide diversity, something far beyond the requirements of the Classical polis, even beyond that of Athens at the height of its power. Building activity shifted from the old centers on the Greek mainland to the opulent cities of the Hellenistic monarchs in Asia Minor — sites more central to the Hellenistic world.

Great scale, a theatrical element of surprise, and a willingness to break the rules of canonical temple design characterize one of the most ambitious temple projects of the Hellenistic period, the Temple of Apollo at Didyma. The Hellenistic temple was built to replace the Archaic temple at the site the Persians had burned down in 494 BCE when they sacked nearby Miletos. Construction began in 313 BCE according to the design of two architects who were natives of the area, PAIONIOS OF EPHESOS and DAPHNIS OF MILETOS. So vast was the undertaking, however, that work on the temple continued off and on for more than 500 years — and still the project was never completed.

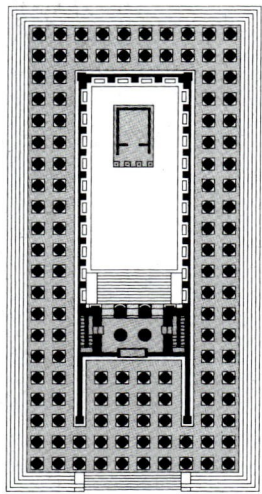

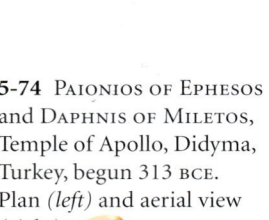

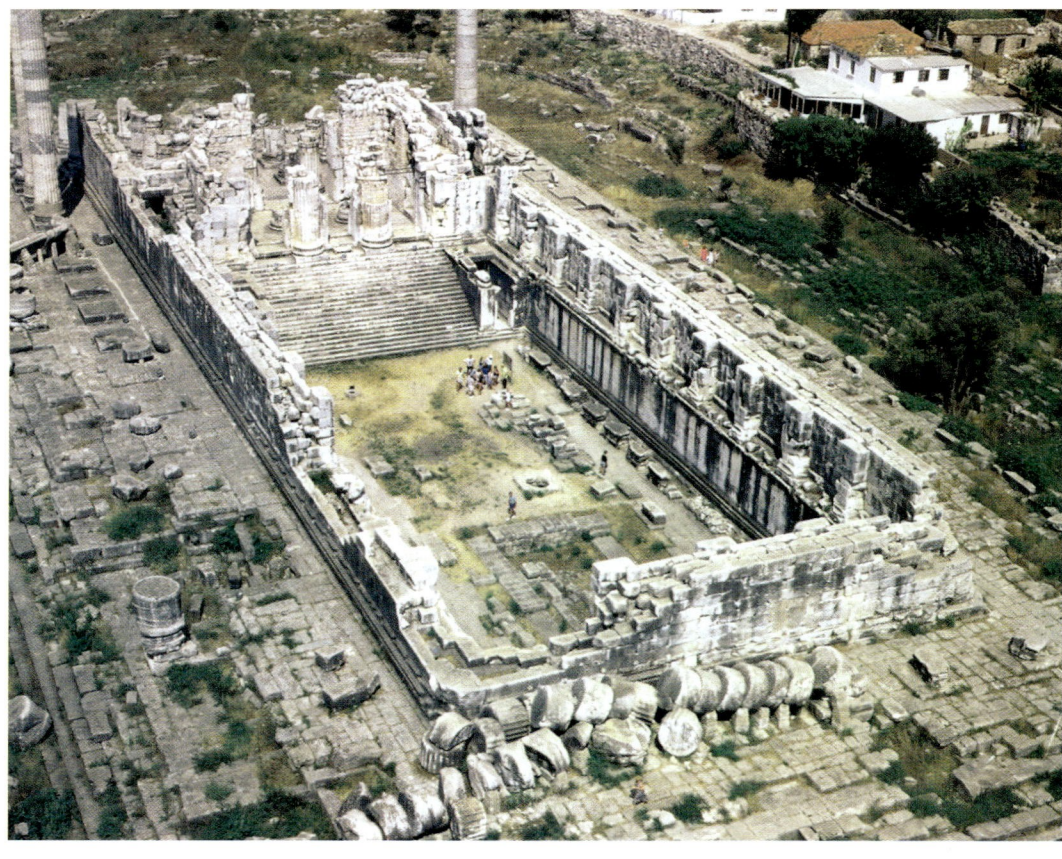

**5-74** Paionios of Ephesos and Daphnis of Miletos, Temple of Apollo, Didyma, Turkey, begun 313 BCE. Plan *(left)* and aerial view *(right)*.

The temple was dipteral in plan (FIG. **5-74,** *left*) and had an unusually broad facade of 10 huge Ionic columns almost 65 feet tall. The sides had 21 columns, consistent with the Classical formula for perfect proportions used for the Parthenon — 21 = (2 × 10) + 1 — but nothing else about the design is Classical. One anomaly immediately apparent to anyone who approached the building was that it had no pediment and no roof — it was *hypaethral,* or open to the sky. And the grand doorway to what should be the temple's cella was elevated nearly five feet off the ground so that it could not be entered. The explanation for these peculiarities is that the doorway served rather as a kind of stage where the oracle of Apollo could be announced to those assembled in front of the temple. The unroofed dipteral colonnade was really only an elaborate frame for a central courtyard (FIG. **5-74,** *right*) that housed a small prostyle shrine that protected a statue of Apollo. Entrance to the interior court was through two smaller doorways to the left and right of the great portal and down two narrow vaulted tunnels that could accommodate only a single file of people. From these dark and mysterious lateral passageways worshipers emerged into the clear light of the courtyard, which contained a sacred spring and was planted with laurel trees in honor of Apollo. Opposite Apollo's inner temple, a stairway some 50 feet wide rose majestically toward three portals leading into the oracular room that also opened onto the front of the temple. This complex spatial planning marked a sharp departure from Classical Greek architecture, which stressed a building's exterior almost as a work of sculpture and left its interior relatively undeveloped.

**THE IDEAL CITY** When the Persians were finally expelled from Asia Minor in 479 BCE, the Greek cities there were in near ruin. Reconstruction of Miletos began after 466 BCE, according to a plan laid out by HIPPODAMOS OF MILETOS, whom Aristotle singled out as the father of rational city planning. Hippodamos imposed a strict grid plan on the site, regardless of the terrain, so that all streets met at right angles. Such *orthogonal* planning actually predates Hippodamos, not only in Archaic Greece but also in the ancient Near East and Egypt. But Hippodamos was so famous that his name has ever since been synonymous with such urban plans. The so-called *Hippodamian plan* also designated separate quarters for public, private, and religious functions. A "Hippodamian city" was logically as well as regularly planned. This desire to impose order on nature and to assign a proper place in the whole to each of the city's constituent parts was very much in keeping with the philosophical tenets of the fifth century BCE. Hippodamos's formula for the ideal city was another manifestation of the same outlook that produced Polykleitos's *Canon* for the human body and Iktinos's treatise on the Parthenon.

Hippodamian planning was still the norm in Late Classical and Hellenistic Greece. The city of Priene (FIG. 5-75), also in Asia Minor, was laid out during the fourth century BCE. It had fewer than 5,000 inhabitants (Hippodamos thought 10,000 was the ideal number). Situated on sloping ground, many of its narrow north-south streets were little more than long stairways. Uniformly sized city blocks, the standard planning unit, were nonetheless imposed on the irregular terrain. The central agora (marketplace) was allotted six blocks. More than one unit also was reserved for major structures such as the Temple of Athena and the theater.

**LIFE IN A GREEK HOME** As in any city, ancient or modern, houses rather than civic or religious buildings occupied most of the area within Priene's walls. Information about the homes of ordinary citizens is scanty, in part because archaeologists have been more interested in uncovering grand edifices, such as

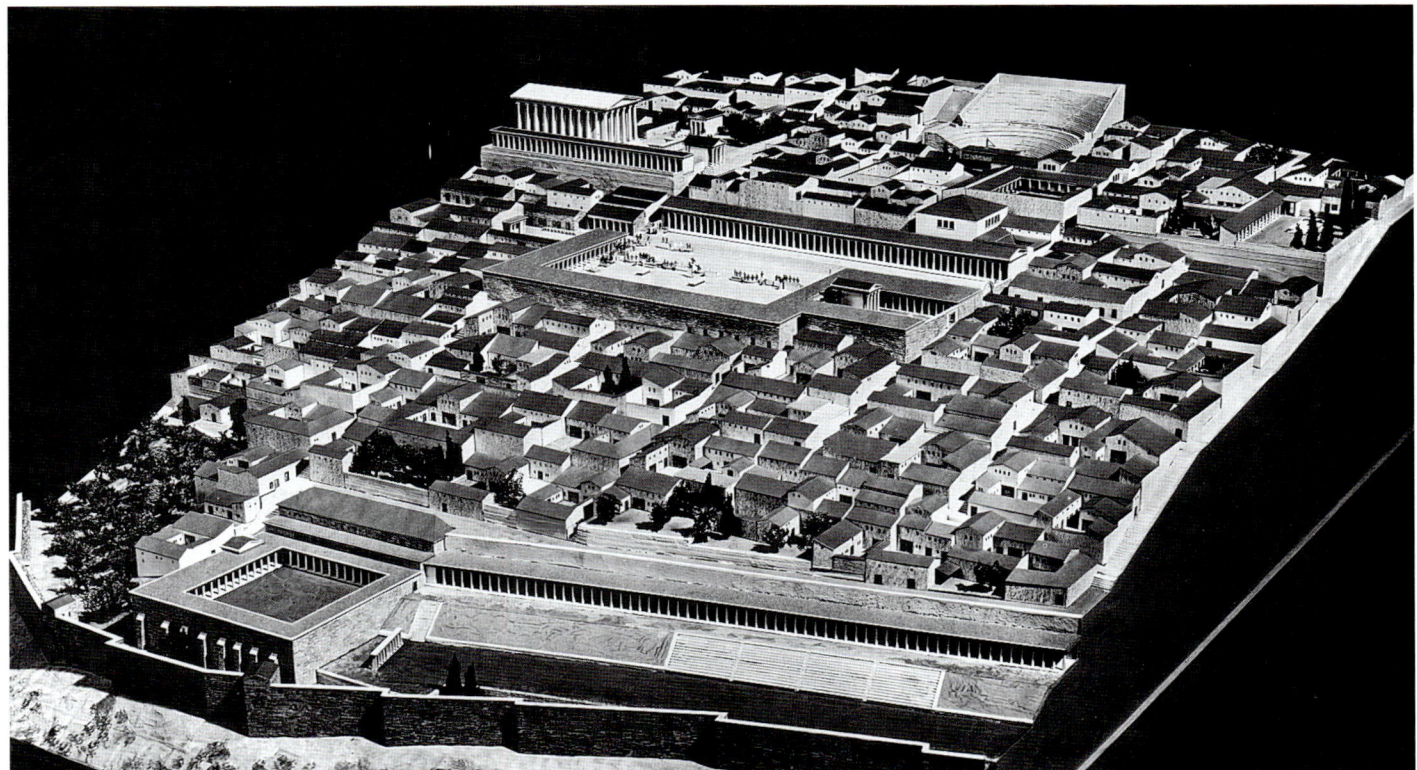

**5-75** Model of the city of Priene, Turkey, fourth century BCE and later. Staatliche Museen, Berlin.

temples and theaters, and in part because ancient authors usually described only exceptional buildings, not common dwellings. The unpretentious Priene houses (for example, FIG. **5-76**) were typical of later Greek times. They were rectangular in plan and fit neatly into the Hippodamian grid, but internally they were not laid out symmetrically. A single entrance from the street led to a modest central court, the largest room in the house, surrounded by several smaller roofed units. In the wealthiest homes, the courtyard was framed by a peristyle and paved with a pebble mosaic. The house illustrated here has columns (of differing dimensions) on only two sides of the court. Exterior windows were rare, because most houses shared walls with their neighbors, and the court provided welcome light and air to the interior. These

courtyards also allowed the collection of rainwater, stored in underground cisterns and used for drinking, cooking, and washing. In most houses a dining room (*andron*) opened onto the court (or onto an anteroom that in turn opened onto the court, as in our example). It was furnished with couches so that the man of the house and his male guests could recline while eating. A kitchen would not be far away. Bedrooms also might open onto the court, but, when a second floor existed, they were normally located upstairs.

**PHILOSOPHERS AND STOAS** The heart of Priene was its agora, bordered by *stoas*. These covered colonnades, or *porticos*, which often housed shops and civic offices, were ideal vehicles for shaping urban spaces, and they were staples of Hellenistic cities. Even the agora of Athens, an ancient city notable for its haphazard, unplanned development, was eventually framed to the east and south by stoas placed at right angles to one another. These new porticos joined the famous Painted Stoa (see page 143), where the Hellenistic philosopher Zeno and his successors taught. The *Stoic* school of Greek philosophy took its name from that building.

The finest of the new Athenian stoas was the Stoa of Attalos II (FIG. **5-77**), a gift to the city by a grateful alumnus, the king of Pergamon, who had studied at Athens in his youth. The stoa was meticulously reconstructed under the direction of the American School of Classical Studies at Athens and today has a second life as a museum housing more than seven decades of finds from the Athenian agora, as well as the offices of the American excavation team. The stoa has two stories, each with 21 shops opening onto the colonnade. The facade columns are Doric on the ground level and Ionic on the second story. Such mixing of the two orders on a single facade had occurred even in the Late Classical period. But it became increasingly common in the Hellenistic period, when

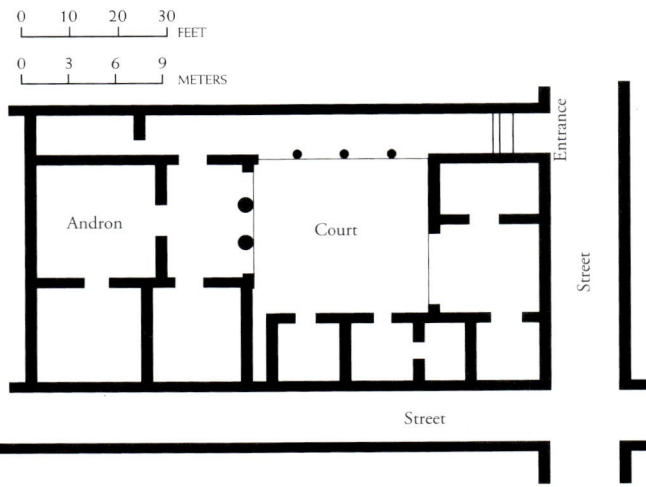

**5-76** Plan of House XXXII, Priene, Turkey, fourth century BCE.

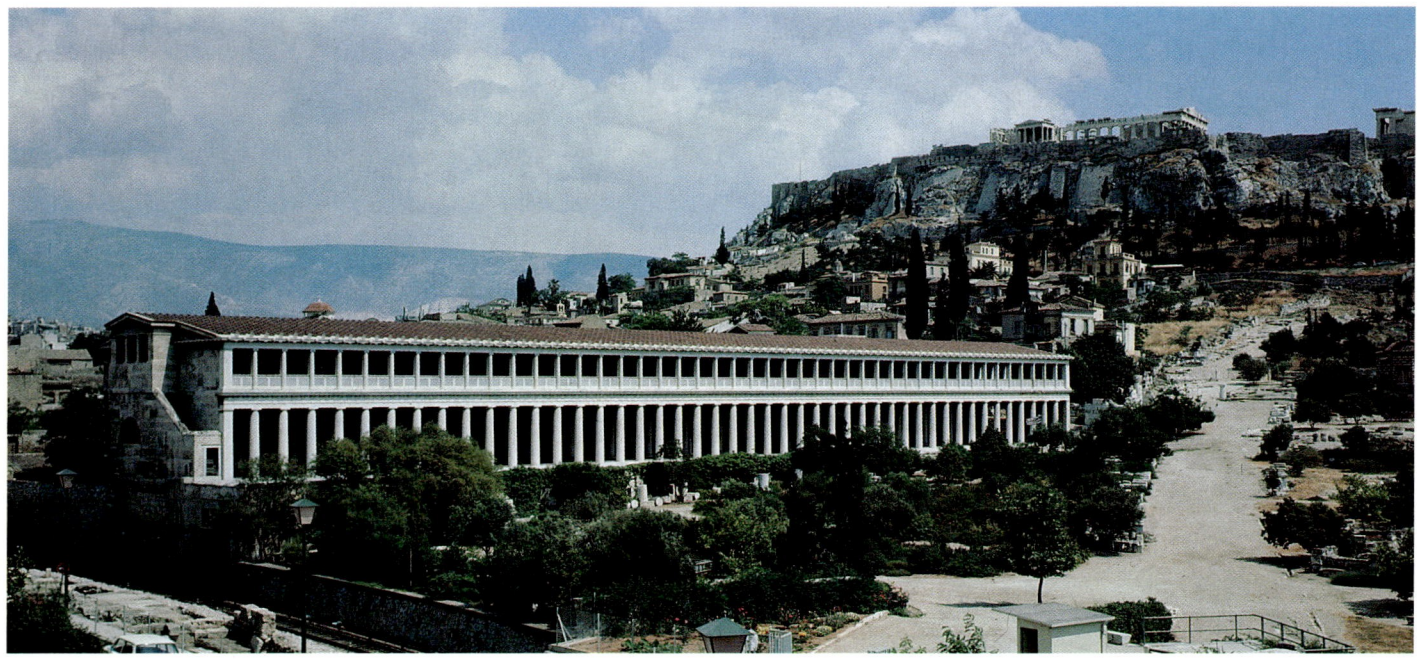

5-77 Stoa of Attalos II, Agora, Athens, Greece, ca. 150 BCE (Acropolis in the background).

respect for the old rules of Greek architecture was greatly diminished and a desire for variety and decorative effects often prevailed. Practical considerations also governed the form of the Stoa of Attalos. The columns are far more widely spaced than in Greek temple architecture, to allow for easy access. And the builders left the lower third of every Doric column shaft unfluted to guard against damage from constant traffic.

## Pergamon

**A HELLENISTIC ACROPOLIS** Pergamon, the kingdom of Attalos II (r. 159–138 BCE), was one of those born in the early third century BCE after the breakup of Alexander's empire. Founded by Philetairos, the Pergamene kingdom embraced almost all of western and southern Asia Minor. Upon the death in 133 BCE of its last king, Attalos III (r. 138–133 BCE), Pergamon was

bequeathed to Rome, which by then was the greatest power in the Mediterranean world. The Attalids enjoyed immense wealth, and much of it was expended on embellishing their capital city, especially its acropolis. Located there were the royal palace, an arsenal and barracks, a great library and theater, an agora, and the sacred precincts of Athena and Zeus. The Altar of Zeus, erected about 175 BCE, is the most famous of all Hellenistic sculptural ensembles. The monument's west front (FIG. 5-78) has been reconstructed in Berlin. The altar proper was on an elevated platform and framed by an Ionic stoalike colonnade with projecting wings on either side of a broad central staircase.

**A GIGANTIC STRUGGLE** All around the altar platform was a sculpted frieze almost 400 feet long, populated by about a hundred larger-than-life-size figures. The subject is the battle of Zeus and the gods against the giants. It is the most extensive representation Greek artists ever attempted of that epic conflict for

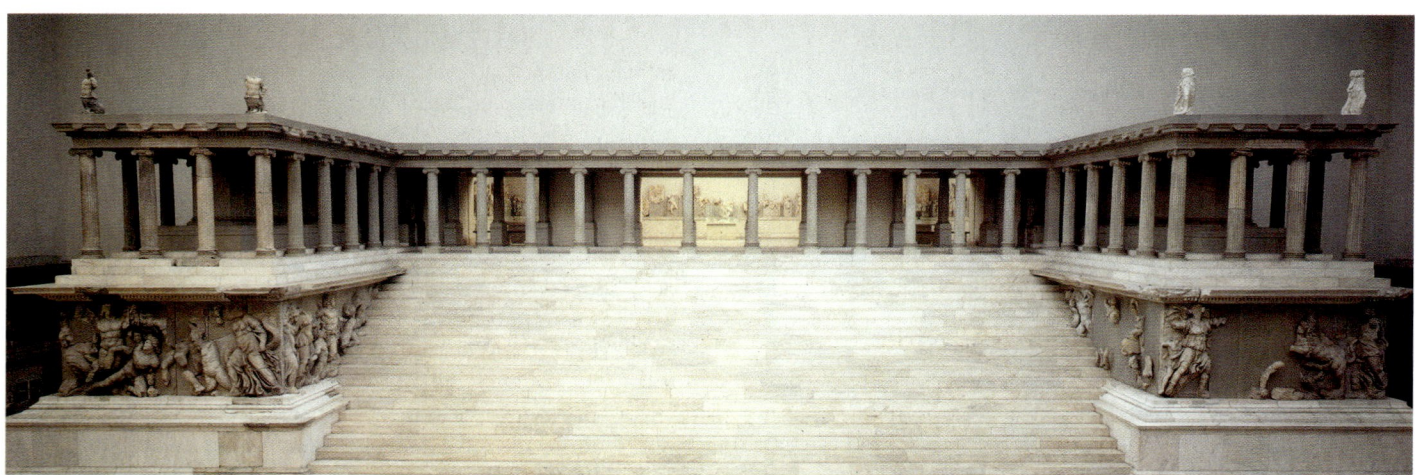

5-78 Reconstructed west front of the Altar of Zeus, from Pergamon, Turkey, ca. 175 BCE. Staatliche Museen, Berlin.

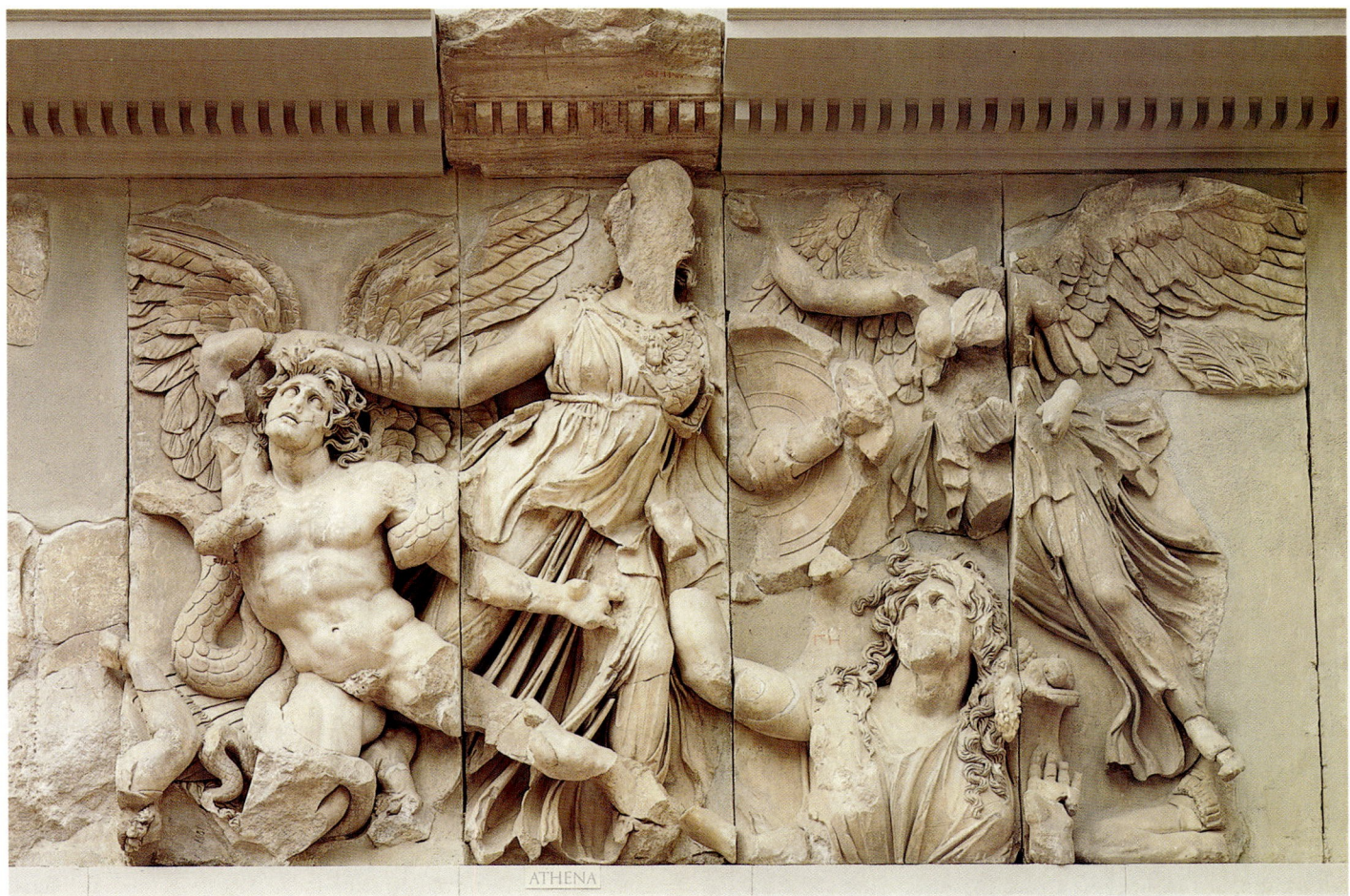

**5-79** Athena battling Alkyoneos, detail of the gigantomachy frieze, from the Altar of Zeus, Pergamon, Turkey, ca. 175 BCE. Marble, approx. 7′ 6″ high. Staatliche Museen, Berlin.

control of the world. A similar subject appeared on the shield of Phidias's *Athena Parthenos* and on some of the Parthenon metopes, where the Athenians wished to draw a parallel between the defeat of the giants and the defeat of the Persians. In the third century, King Attalos I (r. 241–197 BCE) had successfully turned back an invasion by the Gauls in Asia Minor. The gigantomachy of the Altar of Zeus alluded to the Pergamene victory over those barbarians.

A deliberate connection was also made with Athens, whose earlier defeat of the Persians was by then legendary, and with the Parthenon, which already was recognized as a Classical monument—in both senses of the word. The figure of Athena, for example, who grabs the hair of the giant Alkyoneos as Nike flies in to crown her (FIG. **5-79**), is a quotation of the Athena from the Parthenon's east pediment. Zeus himself (not illustrated) was based on the Poseidon of the west pediment. But the Pergamene frieze is not a dry series of borrowed motifs. On the contrary, its tumultuous narrative has an emotional intensity that has no parallel in earlier monuments. The battle rages everywhere, even up and down the very steps one must ascend to reach Zeus's altar (FIG. 5-78). Violent movement, swirling draperies, and vivid depictions of death and suffering are the norm. Wounded figures writhe in pain, and their faces reveal their anguish. When Zeus hurls his thunderbolt, one can almost hear the thunderclap. Deep carving creates dark shadows. The figures project from the background like bursts of light. These features have been justly termed "baroque" and reappear in 17th-century European sculpture (see

Chapter 24). One can hardly imagine a greater contrast than between the Pergamene gigantomachy frieze and that of the Archaic Siphnian Treasury at Delphi (FIG. 5-17).

**NOBILITY IN DEFEAT** On the Altar of Zeus, the victory of Attalos I over the Gauls was presented in mythological disguise. An earlier statuary group set up on Pergamon's acropolis explicitly represented the defeat of the barbarians. Roman copies of some of these figures survive. The sculptor carefully studied and reproduced the distinctive features of the foreign Gauls, most notably their long, bushy hair and mustaches and the *torques* (neck bands) they frequently wore. The Pergamene victors were apparently not included in the group. The viewer saw only their foes and their noble and moving response to defeat.

In what was probably the centerpiece of the Attalid group, a heroic Gallic chieftain (FIG. **5-80**) defiantly drives a sword into his own chest just below the collarbone, preferring suicide to surrender. He already has taken the life of his wife, who, if captured, would have been sold as a slave. In the best Lysippan tradition, the group can be fully appreciated only by walking around it. From one side, the observer sees the Gaul's intensely expressive face, from another his powerful body, and from a third the woman's limp and almost lifeless body. The man's twisting posture, the almost theatrical gestures, and the emotional intensity of the suicidal act are hallmarks of the Pergamene baroque style and were closely paralleled in the later frieze of Zeus's altar.

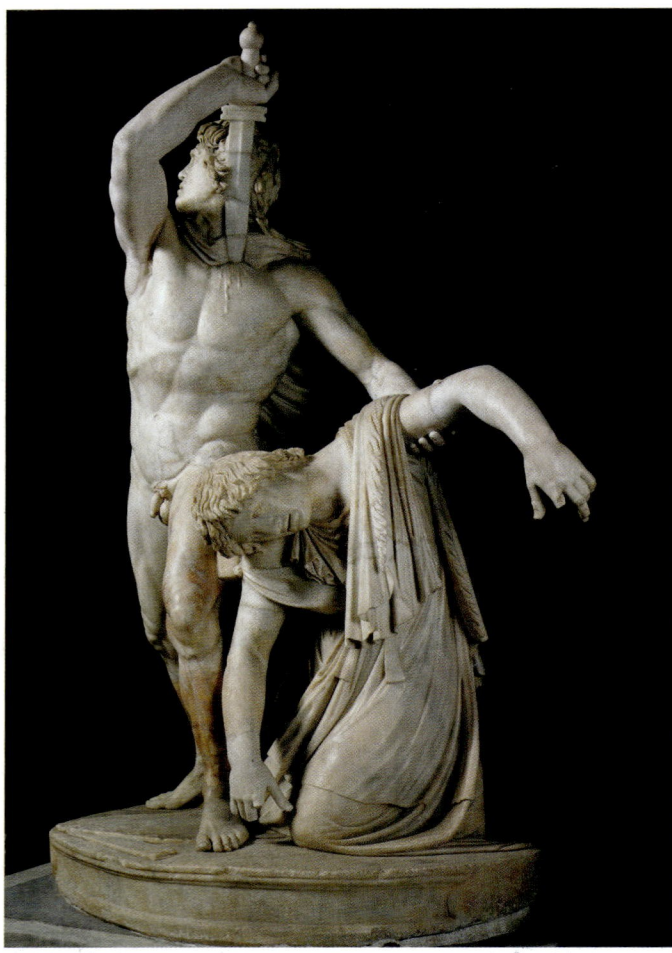

**5-80** EPIGONOS(?), Gallic chieftain killing himself and his wife. Roman marble copy after a bronze original from Pergamon, Turkey, ca. 230–220 BCE, approx. 6′ 11″ high. Museo Nazionale Romano—Palazzo Altemps, Rome.

The third Gaul from this group is a trumpeter (FIG. **5-81**) who collapses upon his large oval shield as blood pours out of the gash in his chest. He stares at the ground with a pained expression on his face. The Hellenistic figure is reminiscent of the dying warrior from the east pediment of the Temple of Aphaia at Aegina (FIG. 5-28), but the pathos and drama of the suffering Gaul are far more pronounced. As in the suicide group and the gigantomachy frieze, the sculptor rendered the male musculature in an exaggerated manner. Note the tautness of the chest and the bulging veins of the left leg—implying that the unseen Attalid hero who has struck down this noble and savage foe must have been an extraordinary man. If this figure is the *tubicen* (trumpeter) Pliny mentioned as the work of the Pergamene master EPIGONOS, then Epigonos may be the sculptor of the entire group and the creator of the dynamic Hellenistic baroque style.

## Sculpture

**VICTORY IN A FOUNTAIN** One of the masterpieces of the Hellenistic baroque style was not created for the Attalid kings but was set up in the Sanctuary of the Great Gods on the island of Samothrace. The *Nike of Samothrace* (FIG. **5-82**) has just alighted on the prow of a Greek warship. Her missing right arm was once raised high to crown the naval victor. (Compare Nike placing a wreath on Athena on the Altar of Zeus, FIG. 5-79). But the Pergamene relief figure seems calm by comparison. The Samothracian Nike's wings still beat, and the wind sweeps her drapery. Her himation bunches in thick folds around her right leg, and her chiton is pulled tightly across her abdomen and left leg. The statue's setting amplified its theatrical effect. The war galley was displayed in the upper basin of a two-tiered fountain. In the lower basin were large boulders. The fountain's flowing water created the illusion of rushing waves dashing up against the prow of the ship. The statue's reflection in the shimmering water below accentuated the sense of lightness and movement. The sound of splashing water added an aural dimension to the visual drama. Art and nature were here combined in one of

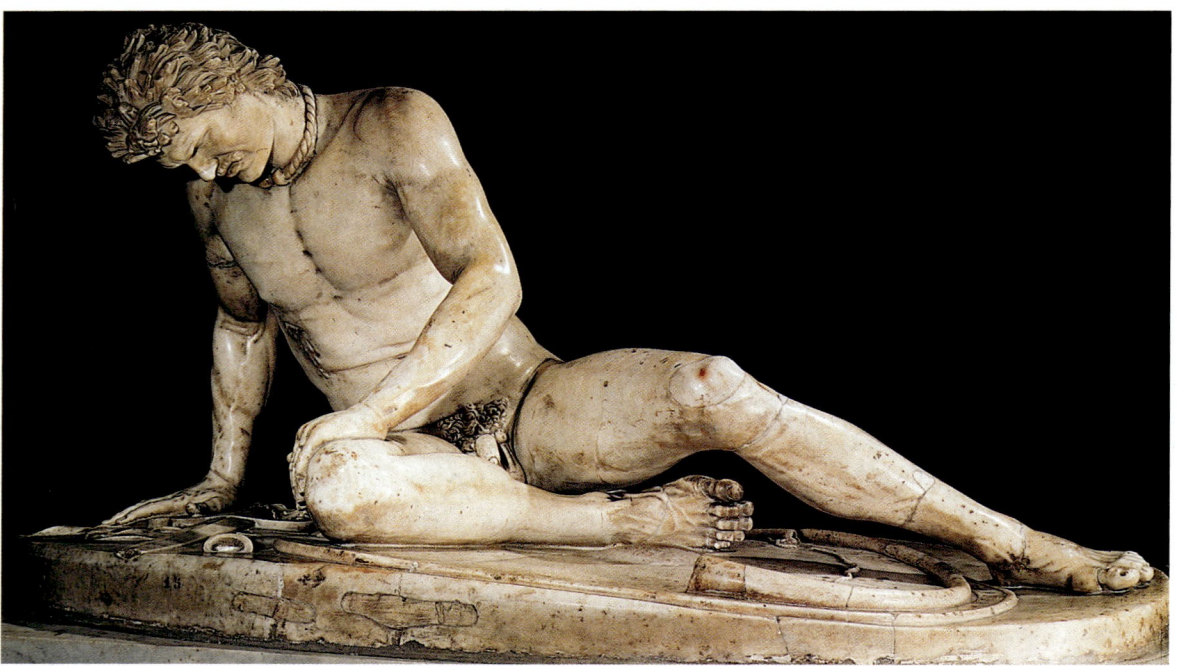

**5-81** EPIGONOS(?), Dying Gaul. Roman marble copy after a bronze original from Pergamon, Turkey, ca. 230–220 BCE, approx. 3′ $\frac{1}{2}$″ high. Museo Capitolino, Rome.

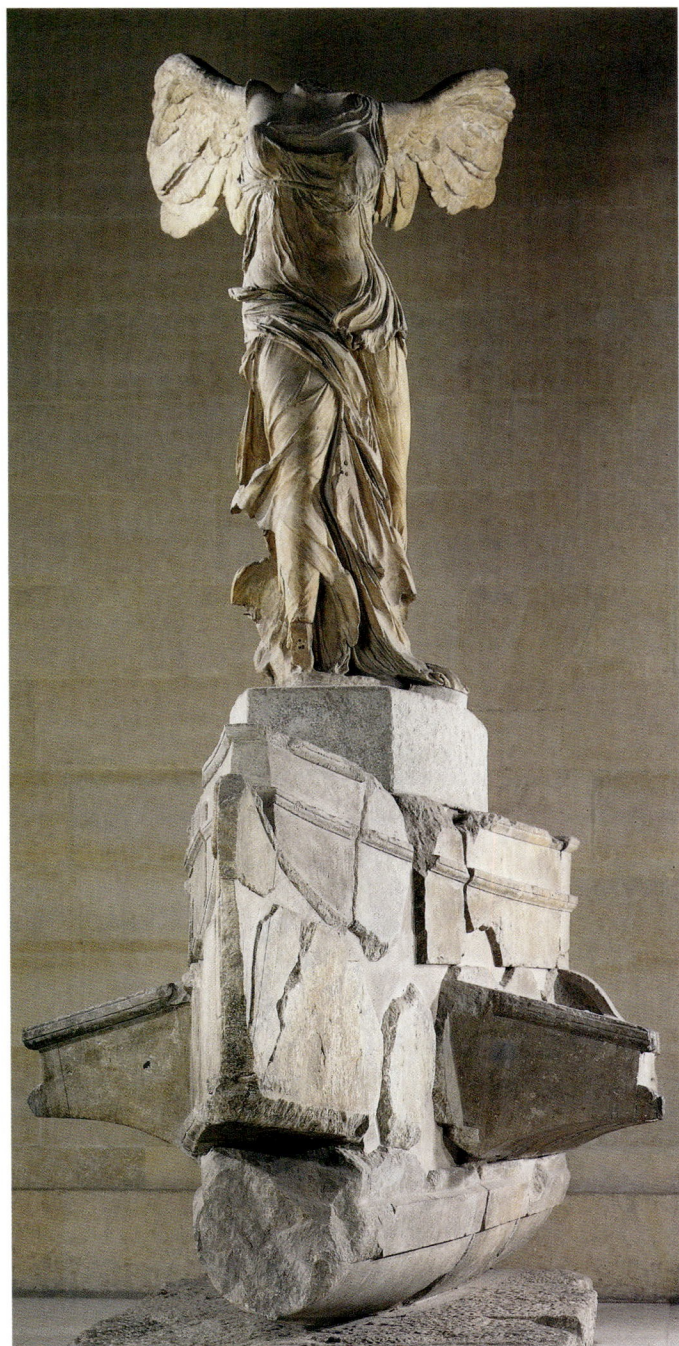

**5-82** Nike alighting on a warship *(Nike of Samothrace)*, from Samothrace, Greece, ca. 190 BCE. Marble, figure approx. 8′ 1″ high. Louvre, Paris.

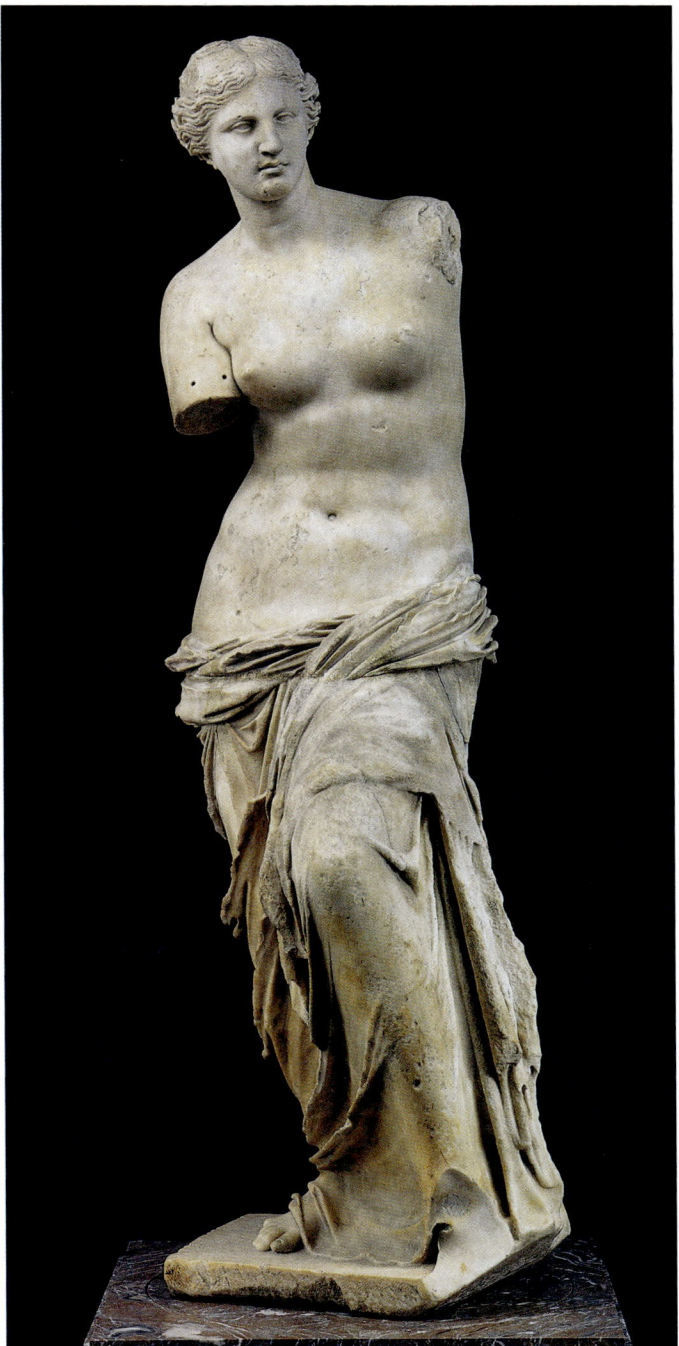

**5-83** ALEXANDROS OF ANTIOCH-ON-THE-MEANDER, Aphrodite *(Venus de Milo)*, from Melos, Greece, ca. 150–125 BCE. Marble, approx. 6′ 7″ high. Louvre, Paris.

the most successful sculptures ever fashioned. In the *Nike of Samothrace* and other works in the Hellenistic baroque manner, sculptors resoundingly rejected the Polykleitan conception of a statue as an ideally proportioned, self-contained entity on a bare pedestal. The Hellenistic statues interact with their environment and appear as living, breathing, and intensely emotive human (or divine) presences.

**HELLENISTIC EROTICISM** In different ways, Praxiteles, Skopas, and Lysippos had already taken bold steps in redefining the nature of Greek statuary. Their distinctive styles continued to influence sculptors throughout the Hellenistic period. The undressing of Aphrodite, for example, became the norm, but Hellenistic sculptors went beyond Praxiteles and openly explored the eroticism of the

nude female form. The famous *Venus de Milo* (FIG. **5-83**) is a larger-than-life-size marble statue of Aphrodite found on Melos together with its inscribed base (now lost) signed by the sculptor, ALEXANDROS OF ANTIOCH-ON-THE-MEANDER. In this statue, the goddess of love is more modestly draped than the *Aphrodite of Knidos* (FIG. 5-60) but more overtly sexual. Her left hand (separately preserved) holds the apple Paris awarded her when he judged her as the most beautiful goddess of all. Her right hand may have lightly grasped the edge of her drapery near the left hip in a halfhearted attempt to keep it from slipping farther down her body. The sculptor intentionally designed the work to tease the spectator. By so doing he imbued his partially draped Aphrodite with a sexuality that is not present in Praxiteles' entirely nude image of the goddess.

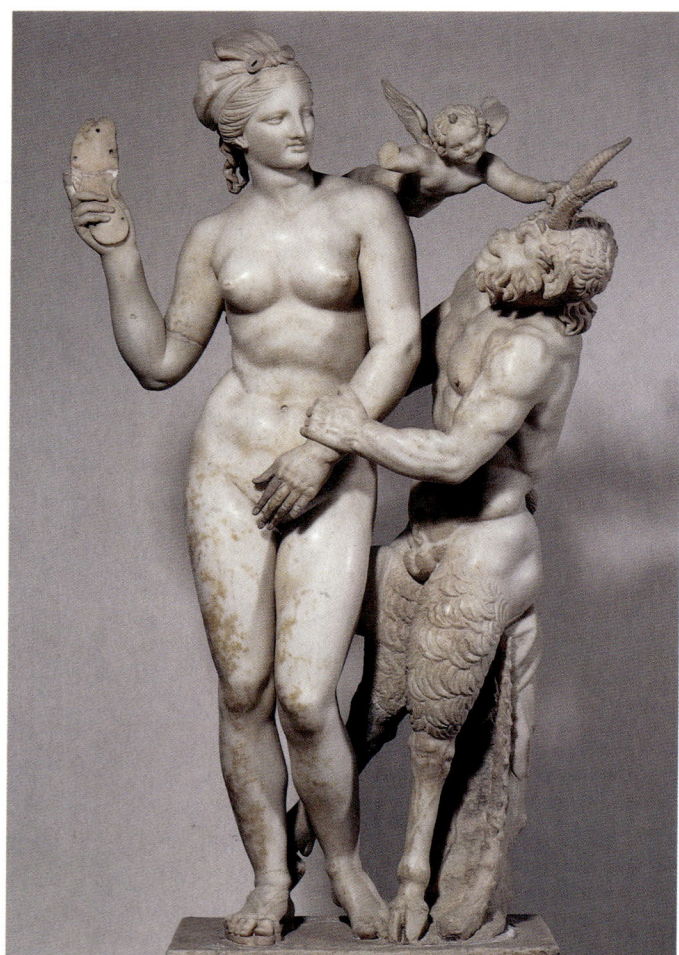

**5-84** Aphrodite, Eros, and Pan, from Delos, Greece, ca. 100 BCE. Marble, 4′ 4″ high. National Archaeological Museum, Athens.

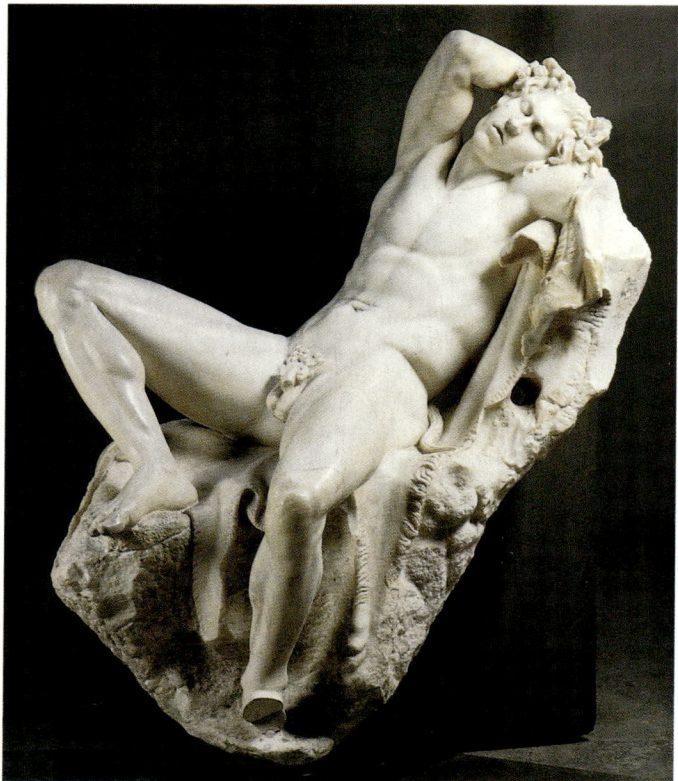

**5-85** Sleeping satyr *(Barberini Faun)*, from Rome, Italy, ca. 230–200 BCE. Marble, approx. 7′ 1″ high. Glyptothek, Munich.

**APHRODITE ATTACKED** The *Aphrodite of Knidos* was directly quoted in an even more playful and irreverent statue of the goddess (FIG. **5-84**) found on Delos. Here, Aphrodite resists the lecherous advances of the semihuman, semigoat Pan, the Greek god of the woods. She defends herself with one of her sandals, while her loyal son Eros flies in to grab one of Pan's horns in an attempt to protect his mother from an unspeakable fate. One may wonder about the taste of Dionysios of Berytos (Beirut), who paid to have this statue erected in a businessmen's clubhouse—especially since both Aphrodite and Eros are portrayed as almost laughing—but such groups were commonplace in Hellenistic times. The combination of eroticism and parody of earlier Greek masterpieces was apparently irresistible. These Hellenistic groups are a far cry from the solemn depictions of the deities of Mount Olympus produced during Classical times.

Also different from earlier periods is the way Eros was represented. In the Hellenistic age he was shown as the pudgy infant Cupid as portrayed in innumerable later artworks, whereas in earlier Greek art he was depicted as an adolescent (FIG. 5-48, *center*). In the history of art, babies are all too frequently rendered as miniature adults—often with adult personalities to match their mature bodies. Hellenistic sculptors knew how to reproduce the soft forms of infants and how to portray the spirit of young children in memorable statues.

**SLEEP AND INTOXICATION** Archaic statues smile at their viewers, and even when Classical statues look away from the viewer they are always awake and alert. Hellenistic sculptors often portrayed sleep. The suspension of consciousness and the entrance into the fantasy world of dreams—the antithesis of the Classical ideals of rationality and discipline—had great appeal for them. This newfound interest can be seen in a statue of a drunken, restlessly sleeping *satyr* (a semihuman follower of Dionysos) known as the *Barberini Faun* (FIG. **5-85**). The statue was found in Rome in the 17th century and restored (not entirely accurately) by Gianlorenzo Bernini, the great Italian Baroque sculptor (see Chapter 24). Bernini no doubt felt that this dynamic statue in the Pergamene manner was the work of a kindred spirit. The satyr has consumed too much wine and has thrown down his panther skin on a convenient rock and then fallen into a disturbed, intoxicated sleep. His brows are furrowed, and one can almost hear him snore.

Eroticism also comes to the fore in this statue. Although men had been represented naked in Greek art for hundreds of years, Archaic kouroi and Classical athletes and gods do not exude sexuality. Sensuality surfaced in the works of Praxiteles in the fourth century BCE. But the dreamy and supremely beautiful Hermes playfully dangling grapes before the infant Dionysos (FIG. 5-62) has nothing of the blatant sexuality of the *Barberini Faun*, whose wantonly spread legs focus attention on his genitals. Homosexuality was common in the man's world of ancient Greece. (In Plato's *Symposium*, Alcibiades refers to Socrates' almost superhuman ability to resist seduction.) It is not surprising that when Hellenistic sculptors began to explore the sexuality of the human body, they turned their attention to both men and women.

**A BATTERED BOXER** Although Hellenistic sculptors tackled an expanded range of subjects, they did not abandon such traditional themes as the Greek athlete. But they often rendered the old subjects in novel ways. This is certainly true of the magnificent bronze statue of a seated boxer (FIG. 5-86), a Hellenistic original

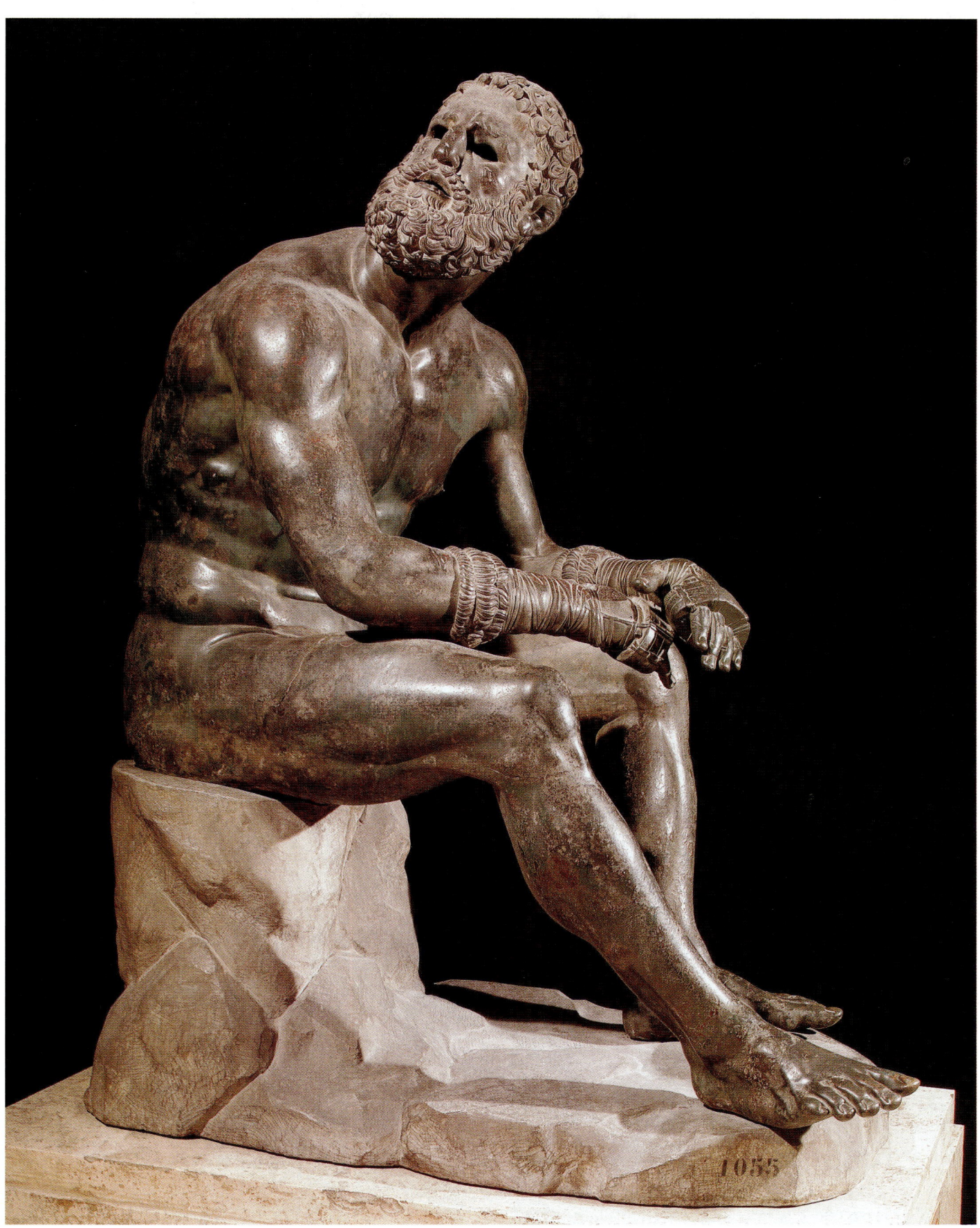

**5-86** Seated boxer, from Rome, Italy, ca. 100–50 BCE. Bronze, approx. 4′ 2½″ high. Museo Nazionale Romano, Rome.

found in Rome and perhaps at one time part of a group. The boxer is not a victorious young athlete with a perfect face and body but a heavily battered, defeated veteran whose upward gaze may have been directed at the man who had just beaten him. Too many punches from powerful hands wrapped in leather thongs — Greek boxers did not use the modern sport's cushioned gloves — have distorted the boxer's face. His nose is broken, as are his teeth. He has smashed "cauliflower" ears. Inlaid copper blood drips from the cuts on his forehead, nose, and cheeks. How different is this rendition of a powerful bearded man from that of the noble warrior from Riace (see FIGS. 5-34 and Intro-17) of the Early Classical period! The Hellenistic sculptor appealed not to the intellect but to the emotions when striving to evoke compassion for the pounded hulk of a once-mighty fighter.

**THE AGED AND THE UGLY** The realistic bent of much of Hellenistic sculpture — the very opposite of the Classical period's idealism — is evident above all in a series of statues of old men and women from the lowest rungs of the social order. Shepherds, fishermen, and drunken beggars are common — the kinds of people who were pictured earlier on red-figure vases but never before were thought worthy of monumental statuary. One of the finest preserved statues of this type (FIG. **5-87**) depicts a haggard old woman bringing chickens and a basket of fruits and vegetables to sell in the market. Her face is wrinkled, her body bent with age,

and her spirit broken by a lifetime of poverty. She carries on because she must, not because she derives any pleasure from life. No one knows the purpose of such statues, but they attest to an interest in social realism absent in earlier Greek statuary.

Statues of the aged and the ugly are, of course, the polar opposites of the images of the young and the beautiful that dominated Greek art until the Hellenistic age, but they are consistent with the period's changed character. The Hellenistic world was a cosmopolitan place, and the highborn could not help but encounter the poor and a growing number of foreigners (non-Greek "barbarians") on a daily basis. Hellenistic art reflects this different social climate in the depiction of a much wider variety

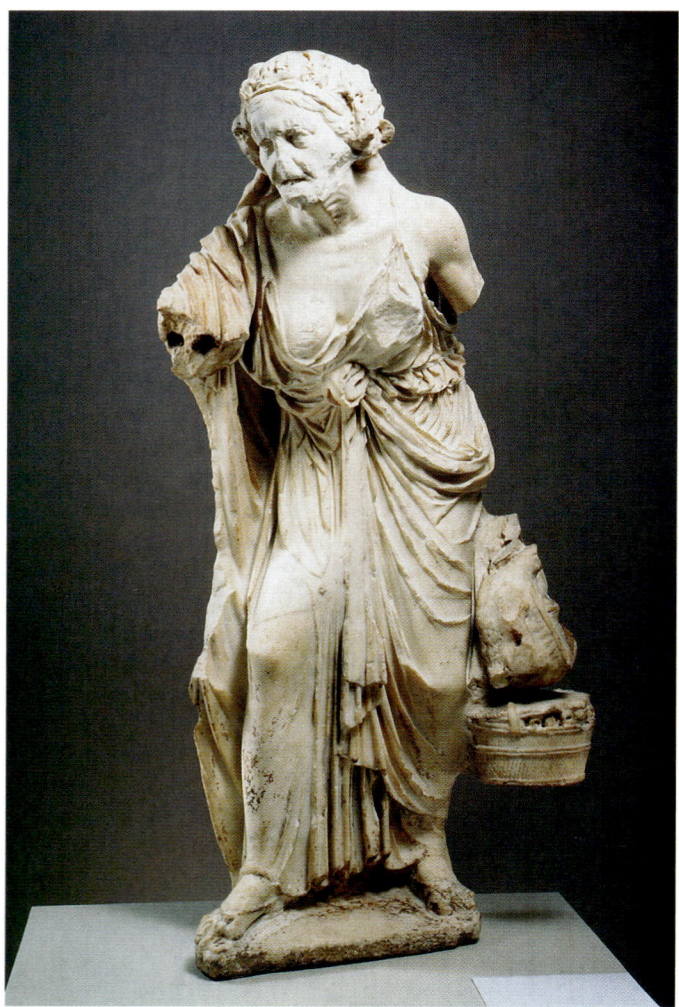

**5-87** Old market woman, ca. 150 – 100 BCE. Marble, approx. 4′ $\frac{1}{2}$″ high. Metropolitan Museum of Art, New York.

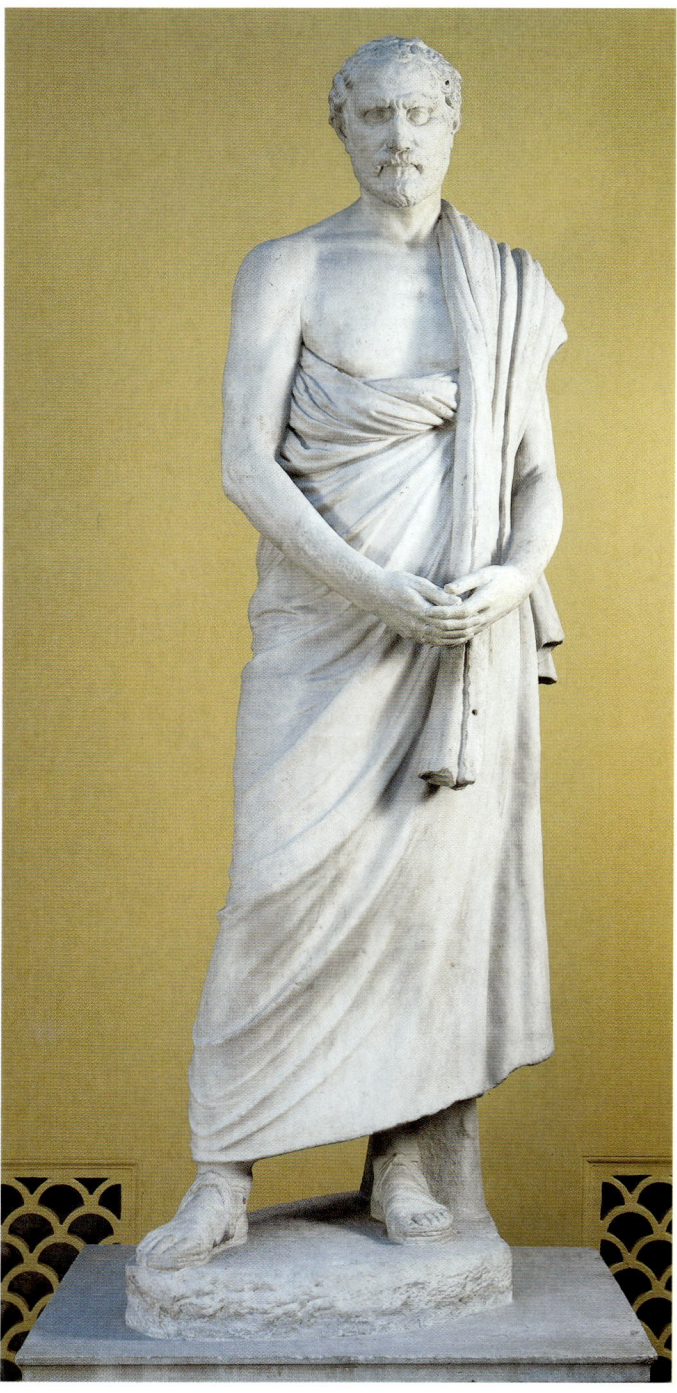

**5-88** Polyeuktos, Demosthenes. Roman marble copy after a bronze original of ca. 280 BCE. 6′ 7$\frac{1}{2}$″ high. Ny Carlsberg Glyptotek, Copenhagen.

of physical types, including different ethnic types. The sensitive portrayal of Gallic warriors with their shaggy hair, strange mustaches, and golden torques (FIGS. 5-80 and 5-81) has already been noted. Africans, Scythians, and others, formerly only the occasional subject of vase painters, also entered the realm of monumental sculpture in Hellenistic art.

**STRONG SPIRIT, WEAK BODY** These sculptures of foreigners and the urban poor, however realistic, are not portraits. Rather, they are sensitive studies of physical types. But the growing interest in the individual beginning in the Late Classical period did lead in the Hellenistic era to the production of true likenesses of specific persons. In fact, one of the great achievements of Hellenistic artists was the redefinition of portraiture. In the Classical period, Kresilas was admired for having made the noble Pericles appear even nobler in his portrait (FIG. 5-39). But in Hellenistic times sculptors sought not only to record the actual appearance of their subjects in bronze and stone but also to capture the essence of their personalities in likenesses that were at once accurate and moving.

One of the earliest of these, perhaps the finest of the Hellenistic age and frequently copied in Roman times, was a bronze portrait statue of Demosthenes (FIG. 5-88) by POLYEUKTOS. The original was set up in the Athenian agora in 280 BCE, 42 years after the great orator's death. Demosthenes was a frail man and in his youth even suffered from a speech impediment, but he had enormous courage and great moral conviction. A veteran of the disastrous battle against Philip II at Chaeronea, he repeatedly tried to rally opposition to Macedonian imperialism, both before and after Alexander's death. In the end, when it was clear the Macedonians would capture him, he took his own life by drinking poison.

Polyeuktos rejected Kresilas's and Lysippos's notions of the purpose of portraiture and did not attempt to portray a supremely confident leader with a magnificent physique. His Demosthenes has an aged and slightly stooped body. Demosthenes clasps his hands nervously in front of him as he looks downward, deep in thought. His face is lined, his hair is receding, and his expression is one of great sadness. Whatever physical discomfort Demosthenes felt is here joined by an inner pain, his deep sorrow over the tragic demise of democracy at the hands of the Macedonian conquerors.

## Hellenistic Art under Roman Patronage

**ROME IN GREECE** In the opening years of the second century BCE, the Roman general Flaminius defeated the Macedonian army and declared the old poleis of Classical Greece as free once again. They never regained their former glory, however. Greece became a Roman province in 146 BCE. When, 60 years later, Athens sided with King Mithridates VI of Pontus (r. 120–63 BCE) in his war against Rome, the general Sulla crushed the Athenians. Thereafter, Athens retained some of its earlier prestige as a center of culture and learning, but politically Athens was just another city in the ever-expanding Roman Empire. Nonetheless, Greek artists continued to be in great demand, both to furnish the Romans with an endless stream of copies of Classical and Hellenistic masterpieces and to create new statues *à la grecque* for Roman patrons.

**LAOCOÖN'S AGONY** One such work is the famous group of the Trojan priest Laocoön and his sons (FIG. 5-89), which was unearthed in Rome in 1506 in the presence of the great Italian

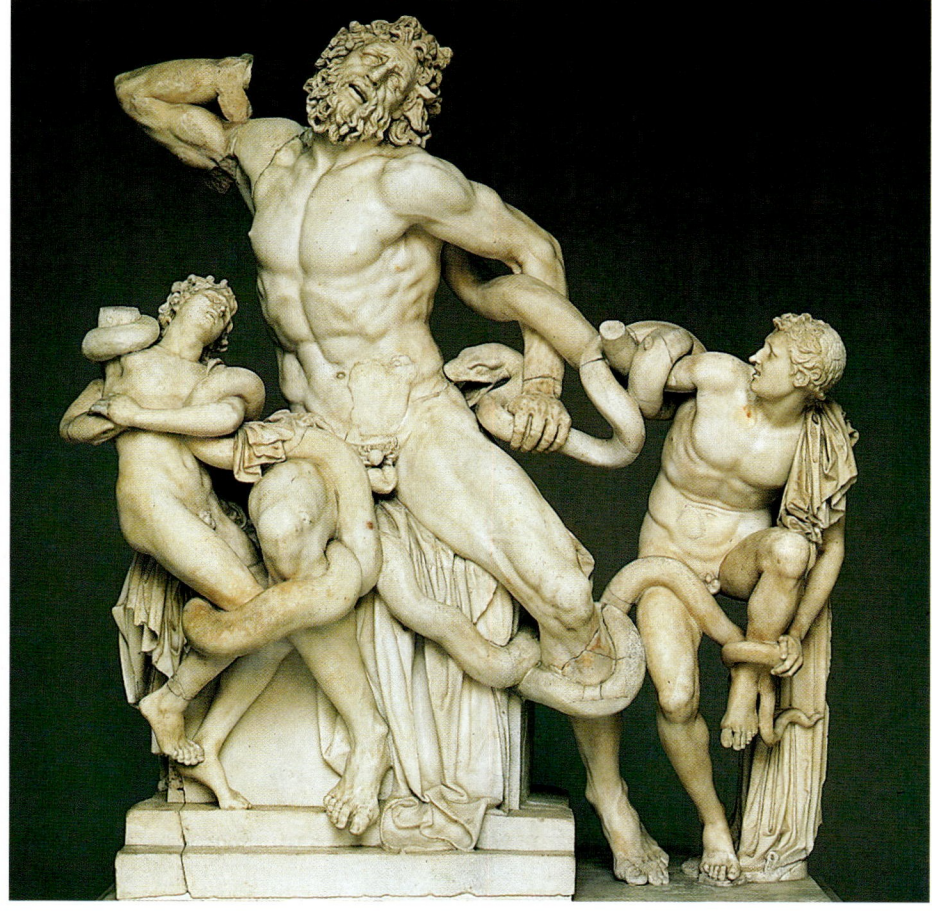

5-89 ATHANADOROS, HAGESANDROS, and POLYDOROS OF RHODES, Laocoön and his sons, from Rome, Italy, early first century CE. Marble, approx. 7′ 10½″ high. Vatican Museums, Rome.

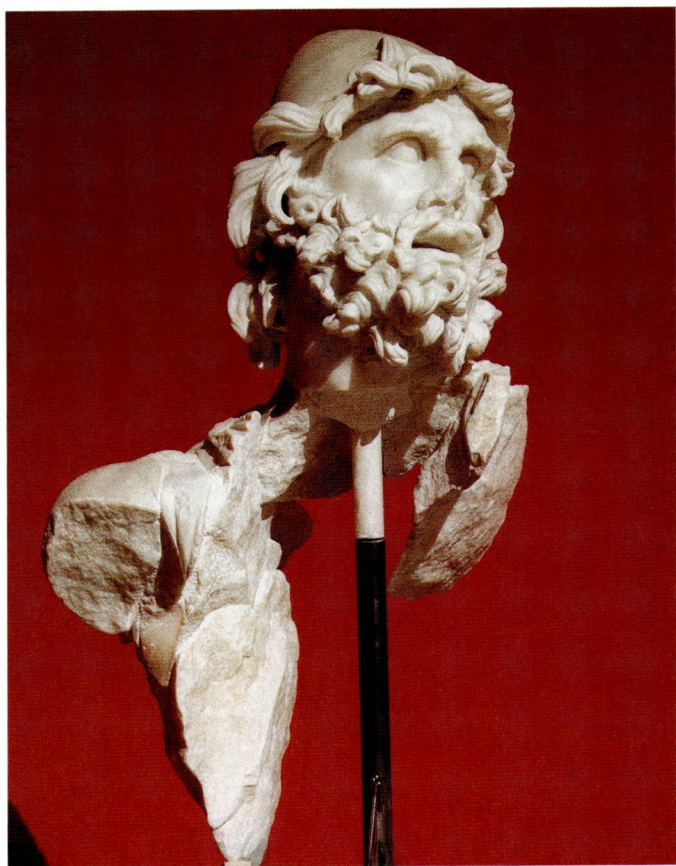

**5-90** ATHANADOROS, HAGESANDROS, and POLYDOROS OF RHODES, *Odysseus*, from Sperlonga, Italy, early first century CE. Marble, full figure approx. 7' high. Museo Archeologico, Sperlonga.

Pergamon, and Laocoön himself is strikingly similar to Alkyoneos (FIG. 5-79), Athena's opponent. In fact, many scholars believe that a Pergamene statuary group of the second century BCE was the inspiration for the three Rhodian sculptors.

**HOMER AT SPERLONGA** That the work seen by Pliny and displayed in the Vatican Museums today was made for Romans rather than Greeks was confirmed in 1957 by the discovery of fragments of several Hellenistic-style groups illustrating scenes from Homer's *Odyssey*. These fragments were found in a grotto that served as the picturesque summer banquet hall of the seaside villa of the Roman emperor Tiberius (r. 14–37 CE) at Sperlonga, some 60 miles south of Rome. One of these groups—depicting the monster Scylla attacking Odysseus's ship—is signed by the same three sculptors Pliny cited as the creators of the Laocoön group. Another of the groups, installed around a central pool in the grotto, depicted the blinding of the Cyclops Polyphemos by Odysseus and his comrades, an incident also set in a cave in the Homeric epic. The figure of Odysseus (FIG. **5-90**) from this theatrical group is one of the finest sculptures of antiquity. The hero's cap can barely contain his swirling locks of hair. Even Odysseus's beard seems to be swept up in the emotional intensity of the moment. The parted lips and the deep shadows produced by sharp undercutting add drama to the head, which was attached to an agitated body. At Tiberius's villa in Sperlonga and in Titus's palace in Rome, the baroque school of Hellenistic sculpture lived on long after Greece ceased to be a political force.

# CONCLUSION

The earliest monumental art and architecture in Greece appeared shortly after the founding of a Greek trading post in the Nile delta, and Egypt provided models for the Greeks' earliest stone sculptures and columnar temples. But in time, the Greeks rejected the Egyptian-inspired Archaic style and revolutionized the history of art.

Greek painters formulated a new way of depicting human figures in space, and Greek sculptors introduced contrapposto into their statues. In the mid-fifth century BCE, Polykleitos developed his *Canon*, a formula for the perfect statue, in the belief that harmonious proportions produced beauty. Similarly, Iktinos and Kallikrates applied numerical ratios to the parts of buildings and constructed their ideal temple, the Parthenon.

In the aftermath of the Peloponnesian War, however, while still adhering to the philosophy that humanity was the "measure of all things," Greek artists began to focus more on the real world of appearances than on the ideal world of perfect beings. Late Classical and Hellenistic sculptors humanized the gods of Mount Olympus and expanded the range of subjects for monumental art to encompass the old, ugly, and foreign, as well as the young, beautiful, and Greek.

By the second century BCE, Greece had come under the sway of the Romans, and when Rome inherited the Pergamene kingdom from the last of the Attalids in 133 BCE, it also became heir to the Greek artistic legacy. What Rome adopted from Greece it passed on to the medieval and modern worlds. If Greece was peculiarly the inventor of the European spirit, Rome was its propagator and amplifier.

Renaissance artist Michelangelo. The marble group, long believed an original of the second century BCE, was found in the remains of the palace of the emperor Titus (r. 79–81 CE), exactly where Pliny had seen it more than 14 centuries before. Pliny attributed the statue to three sculptors—ATHANADOROS, HAGESANDROS, and POLYDOROS OF RHODES—who are now generally thought to have worked in the early first century CE. They probably based their group on a Hellenistic masterpiece depicting Laocoön and only one son. Their variation on the original added the son at Laocoön's left (note the greater compositional integration of the two other figures) to conform with the Roman poet Vergil's account in the *Aeneid*. Vergil vividly described the strangling of Laocoön and his *two* sons by sea serpents while sacrificing at an altar. The gods who favored the Greeks in the war against Troy had sent the serpents to punish Laocoön, who had tried to warn his compatriots about the danger of bringing the Greeks' wooden horse within the walls of their city.

In Vergil's graphic account, Laocoön suffered in terrible agony, and the torment of the priest and his sons is communicated in a spectacular fashion in the marble group. The three Trojans writhe in pain as they struggle to free themselves from the death grip of the serpents. One bites into Laocoön's left hip as the priest lets out a ferocious cry. The serpent-entwined figures recall the suffering giants of the great frieze of the Altar of Zeus at

**900 BCE**

**GEOMETRIC**

| First Olympic Games, 776 BCE
| Homer, fl. ca. 750–700 BCE

**700 BCE**

**ORIENTALIZING**

| Greek trading post established at Naukratis, Egypt, ca. 650–630 BCE
| Draco formulates first written law code for Athens, 621 BCE

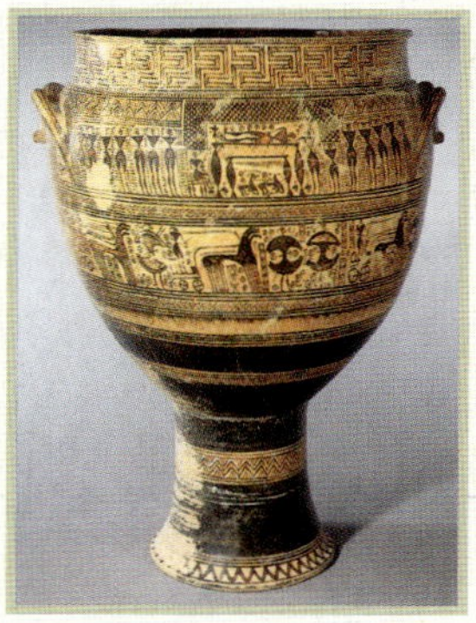

1 Dipylon krater, Athens, ca. 740 BCE

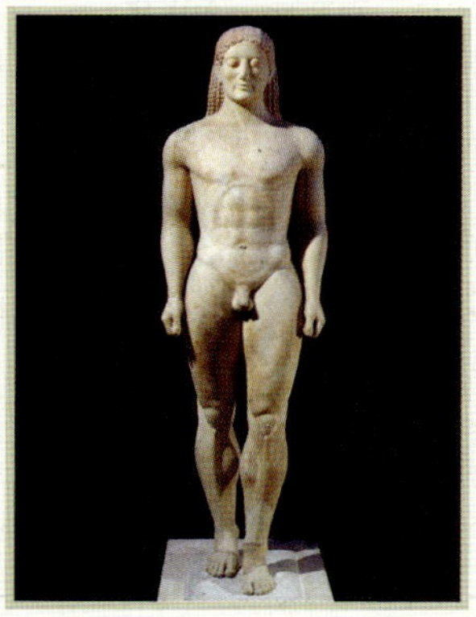

**600 BCE**

**ARCHAIC**

| Sappho, fl. ca. 600 BCE
| Aeschylus, 525–456 BCE
| Democratic reforms of Kleisthenes, 507 BCE
| Persian Wars, 490–479 BCE
| Sophocles, 496–406 BCE
| Pericles, 490–429 BCE
| Herodotus, ca. 485–425 BCE
| Euripides, 485–406 BCE

**480 BCE**

**EARLY CLASSICAL (SEVERE)**

| Persians sack Athenian Acropolis, 480 BCE
| Socrates, 469–399 BCE
| Delian League treasury transferred to Athens, 454 BCE

2 Kroisos, kouros from Anavysos, ca. 530 BCE

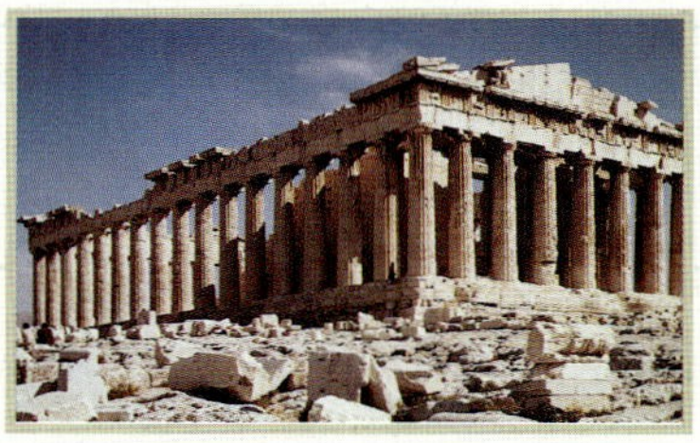

**450 BCE**

**HIGH CLASSICAL**

| Peloponnesian War, 431–404 BCE
| Plato, 429–347 BCE

**400 BCE**

**LATE CLASSICAL**

| Aristotle, 384–322 BCE
| Alexander the Great, r. 336–323 BCE
| Battle of Issus, 333 BCE

3 Parthenon, Acropolis, Athens, 447–438 BCE

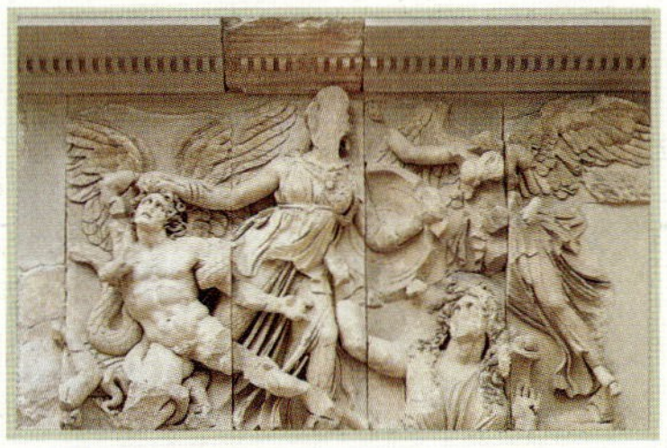

**323 BCE**

**HELLENISTIC**

| Greece becomes a Roman province, 146 BCE
| Attalos III wills Pergamene kingdom to Rome, 133 BCE
| Sulla sacks Athens, 86 BCE

**31 BCE**

| Battle of Actium, 31 BCE

4 Altar of Zeus, Pergamon, ca. 175 BCE

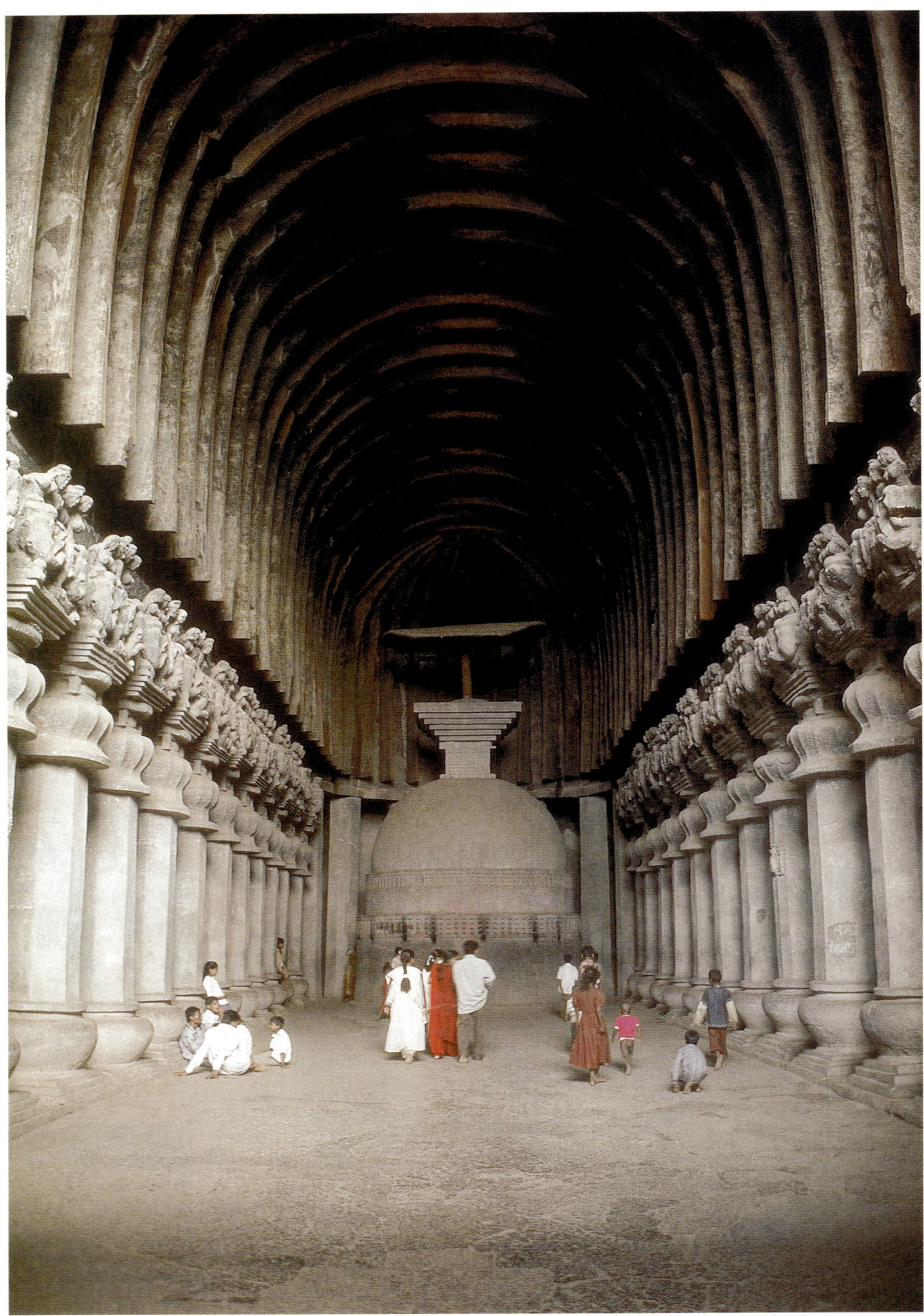

Interior of chaitya hall, Karle, India, ca. 100 CE.

# 6

# PATHS TO ENLIGHTENMENT

## THE ART OF SOUTH AND SOUTHEAST ASIA BEFORE 1200

South and Southeast Asia is a vast geographic area comprising, among others, the modern nations of India, Pakistan, Sri Lanka, Thailand, Vietnam, Cambodia, Bangladesh, and Indonesia (MAP **6-1**). Not surprisingly, the region's inhabitants display tremendous cultural and religious diversity. The people of India alone speak more than 20 different major languages. Those spoken in the north belong to the Indo-European language family, whereas those in the south form a completely separate linguistic family called Dravidian. The art of South and Southeast Asia is equally diverse—and very ancient. When Alexander the Great and his army reached India in 326 BCE, the civilization they encountered was already more than two millennia old. The remains of the first cities in the Indus Valley predate the palaces of Homer's Trojan War heroes (see FIGS. 4-16 and 4-20) by a millennium. This chapter discusses the art and architecture of South and Southeast Asia from their beginnings almost five millennia ago through the 12th century. Chapter 25 treats the later art of the region up to the present day.

## INDIA AND PAKISTAN

### *Indus Civilization*

**URBAN SOPHISTICATION** In the third millennium BCE, the Sumerians were burying their dead in the Royal Cemetery at Ur (see FIGS. 2-8 to 2-11), the Egyptians were erecting the Great Pyramids at Gizeh (see FIG. 3-8), and Aegean sculptors in the Cyclades were carving abstract marble statuettes of women and musicians (see FIGS. 4-1 and 4-2). At the same time, a great civilization arose over a wide geographic area along the Indus River in present-day Pakistan and extended into India as far south as Gujarat and east beyond Delhi. Archaeologists have uncovered impressive remains of this Indus Civilization, as it has come to be called, as well as evidence for active trade between the peoples of the ancient Near East and the Indus Valley.

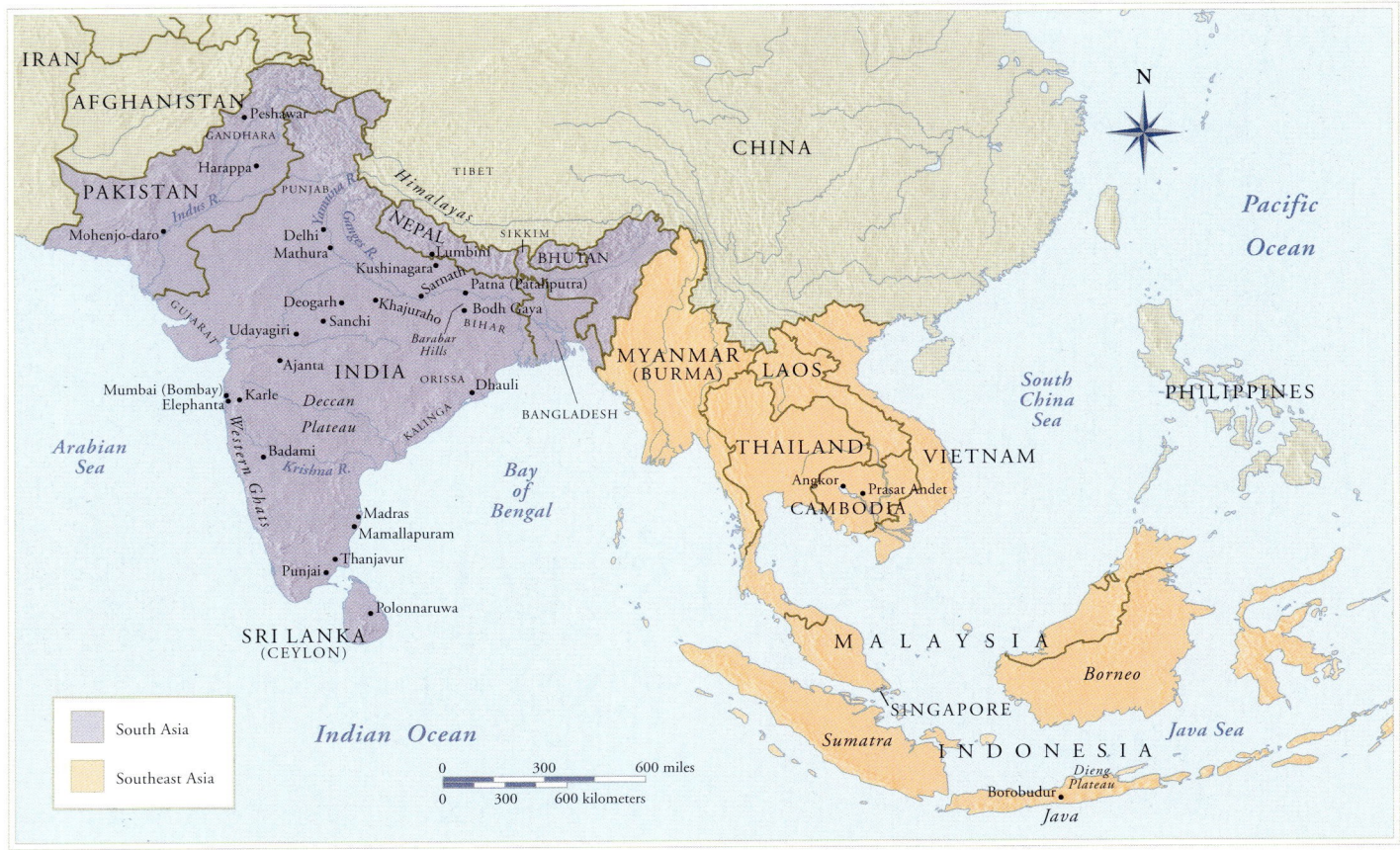

MAP 6-1 South and Southeast Asia.

The most important excavated Indus sites are Harappa and Mohenjo-daro. These early fully developed cities featured streets oriented to compass points, and multistoried houses built of carefully formed and precisely laid kiln-baked bricks. The Indus cities also boasted one of the world's first sophisticated systems of water supply and sewage. In Mohenjo-daro, hundreds of wells throughout the city provided fresh water to homes that featured some of the oldest recorded private bathing areas and toilet facilities, with drainage into public sewers. In the heart of the city stood the so-called Great Bath, a complex of rooms centered on a sunken brick pool (FIG. 6-1) 39 feet long, 23 feet wide, and 8 feet deep. The builders made the pool watertight by sealing the joints between the bricks with bitumen, an asphaltlike material also used in

Mesopotamia. The bath was unlikely to have been a purely recreational facility. Rather, most scholars believe it was designed for ritual bathing of the kind still practiced in the region today.

One intriguing characteristic of the Indus Civilization is that no surviving structures have yet been identified as either temples or palaces. This marks a sharp contrast to the contemporaneous civilizations of Mesopotamia and Egypt.

ELITE SCULPTURE Excavators have discovered surprisingly little art from the long-lived Indus Civilization, and all of the objects found are small. The most impressive is a robed male figure (FIG. 6-2) found at Mohenjo-daro. This steatite (a soft local soapstone) sculpture depicts a figure with half-closed eyes and a closely trimmed beard with shaved upper lip. He wears a headband with a central circular emblem, matched by a similar armband. Holes on each side of his neck suggest that he also wore a necklace of precious metal. *Trefoils* (cloverlike designs with three stylized leaves) decorate his elegant robe. They, as well as the circles of the head- and armbands, originally held red paste and shell inlays, as did the eyes. Scholars often compare the Mohenjo-daro statuette to Sumerian sculptures, where the trefoil motif appears in sacred contexts, and refer to the person portrayed as a "priest-king," the ambiguous term used for some Sumerian leaders. The identity and rank of the Mohenjo-daro figure are, however, uncertain. Nonetheless, the elaborate costume and precious materials make clear that he too was an elite individual.

INDUS SEALS The most common Indus art objects are steatite seals with incised designs. They are similar in many ways to the stamp seals found at contemporaneous sites in Mesopotamia (see "Mesopotamian Seals," Chapter 2, page 40). Most of the Indus

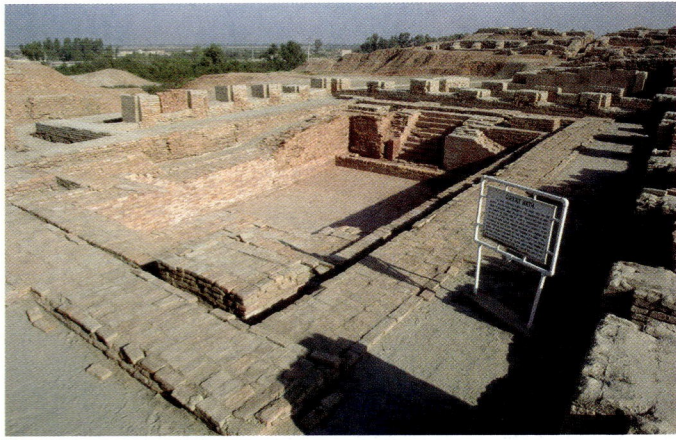

6-1 Great Bath, Mohenjo-daro, Pakistan, ca. 2600–1900 BCE.

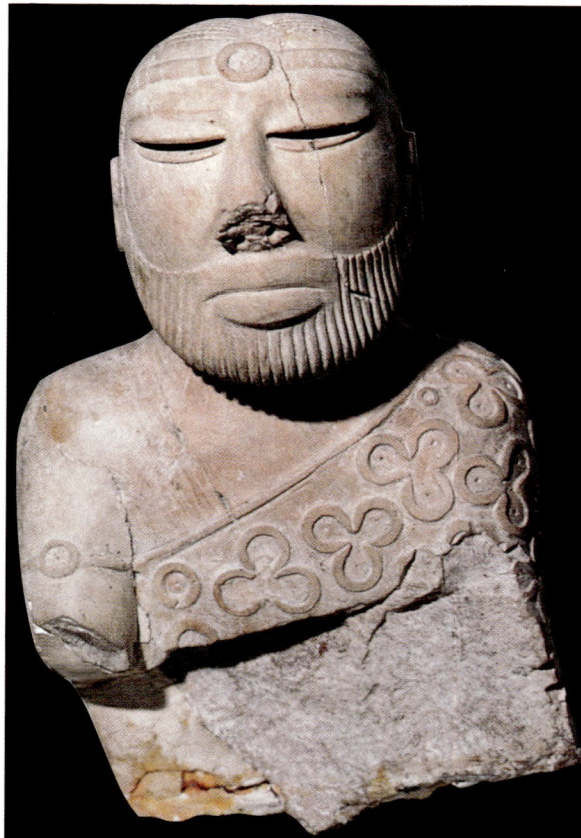

6-2 Robed male figure, from Mohenjo-daro, Pakistan, ca. 2000–1900 BCE. Steatite, $6\frac{7}{8}''$ high. National Museum of Pakistan, Karachi.

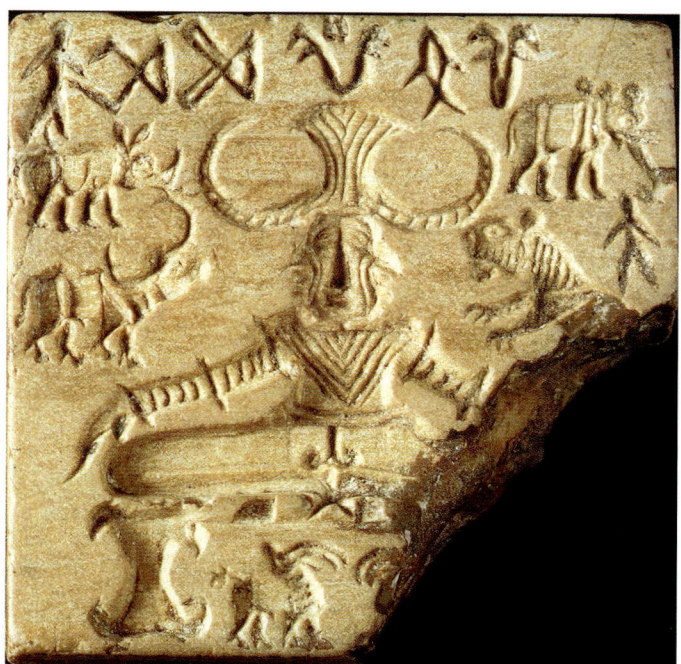

6-3 Seal with seated figure in yogic posture, from Mohenjo-daro, Pakistan, ca. 2600–1900 BCE. Steatite coated with alkali and baked, approx. $1\frac{3}{8}'' \times 1\frac{3}{8}''$. National Museum, New Delhi.

examples have an animal or tiny narrative carved on the face, along with an as yet untranslated script. On the back, a *boss* (circular knob) with a hole permitted insertion of a string so that the seal could be worn or hung on a wall. As in the ancient Near East, the Indus peoples sometimes used the seals to make impressions on clay, apparently for securing trade goods wrapped in textiles. The animals most frequently represented include the humped bull, elephant, rhinoceros, and tiger. Each is portrayed in strict profile. Some of the narrative seals appear to show that the Indus peoples considered trees sacred, as both Buddhists and Hindus later did. Many scholars have suggested that religious and ritual continuities existed between the Indus Civilization and later Indian culture.

One of the most elaborate seals (FIG. **6-3**) depicts a male figure with a horned headdress and, perhaps, three faces, seated (with erect penis) among the profile animals that regularly appear alone on other seals. The figure's folded legs with heels pressed together and his arms resting on the knees suggest a yogic posture (compare FIG. 6-11). *Yoga* (literally "to yoke") is a method for controlling the body and relaxing the mind used in later Indian religions to yoke, or unite, the practitioner to the divine. Although most scholars reject the identification of this figure as a prototype of the multiheaded Hindu god Shiva (FIG. 6-17) as Lord of Beasts, the yogic posture argues that this important Indian meditative practice began as early as the Indus Civilization.

## Vedic and Upanishadic Period

**THE NOBLE ONES** By 1700 BCE, the urban phase of the Indus Civilization had ended in most areas. The production of sculptures, seals, and script gradually ceased, and village life replaced urban culture. Very little art survives from the next thousand years, but the religious foundations laid during this period, based on the oral hymns the Aryans brought to India from Central Asia, helped define most later South and Southeast Asian art. The Aryans were a mobile herding people who occupied the Punjab, an area of northwestern India, in the second millennium BCE. They called themselves *Aryas* (Noble Ones) and spoke Sanskrit, the earliest language yet identified in South Asia.

**VEDAS AND BRAHMINS** Around 1500 BCE, the Aryans composed the first of four *Vedas*. These compilations of religious learning (Veda means "knowledge"), written in Sanskrit, included hymns intended for priests (called *Brahmins*) to chant or sing. The Aryan priests headed a social hierarchy that has come to be called the *caste system,* which still forms the basis of Indian society today. Below the priests were the warriors, traders, and manual laborers (including artists and architects), respectively. The Aryan religion centered on sacrifice, the ritual enactment of often highly intricate and lengthy ceremonies in which the Brahmin priests placed materials, such as milk and *soma* (the sacrificial brew), into a fire that took the sacrifices to the gods in the heavens. It was believed that if the priests performed these rituals accurately, the gods would fulfill the prayers of those who sponsored the sacrifices. These gods, primarily male, included Indra, Varuna, Surya, and Agni, gods associated, respectively, with the rains, the ocean, the sun, and fire. It appears that the Aryans did not make images of these deities.

**SAMSARA, KARMA, AND MOKSHA** The next phase of South Asian urban civilization developed east of the Indus heartland, in the Ganges River Valley. Here, from 800 to 500 BCE, religious thinkers composed a variety of texts called the *Upanishads*. Among the innovative ideas of the Upanishads were *samsara, karma,* and *moksha* (or *nirvana*). Samsara is the belief that individuals are born again after death in an almost endless round of rebirths. The type of rebirth can vary. One can be reborn as a human being, an animal, or even a god. An individual's past actions (karma), either good or bad, determine the nature of future rebirths. The ultimate goal of a person's religious life is to escape from the cycle of birth and death by merging the individual self into the vital force of the universe. This escape is called either moksha (liberation, for Hindus) or nirvana (cessation, for Buddhists).

**HINDUISM AND BUDDHISM** Hinduism and Buddhism, the two major modern religions originating in Asia, developed in the late centuries BCE and the early centuries CE. Hinduism, the dominant religion in India today, discussed in more detail later (see page 178), has its origins in Aryan religion. Buddhism was founded by the Buddha, a historical figure who advocated the path of *asceticism,* or self-discipline and self-denial, as the means to free oneself from attachments to people and possessions, thus ending rebirth (see "Buddhism and Buddhist Iconography," page 171). Unlike their predecessors in South Asia, both Hindus and Buddhists use images of gods and holy persons in religious rituals. Buddhists have the older artistic tradition. Their earliest monuments date to the Maurya period.

## Maurya Dynasty

**CHANDRAGUPTA AND THE GREEKS** When Alexander the Great reached the Indus River in 326 BCE, his troops refused to go further. Reluctantly, Alexander abandoned his dream of conquering India and headed home. After Alexander's death three years later, his generals divided his empire among themselves (see Chapter 5). One of them, Seleucus Nicator, re-invaded India, but Chandragupta Maurya (r. 323–298 BCE), founder of the Maurya dynasty, defeated him in 305 BCE and eventually consolidated almost all of present-day India under his domain. Chandragupta's capital was Pataliputra (modern Patna) in northeastern India, far from the center of the Indus Civilization. Megasthenes, Seleucus's ambassador to the Maurya court, described Pataliputra in his book on India as a large and wealthy city enclosed within mighty wooden walls so extensive that the circuit had 64 gates and 570 towers.

**ASHOKA'S PILLARS** The greatest Maurya ruler was Ashoka (r. 272–231 BCE), who left his imprint on history by converting to Buddhism and spreading the Buddha's teaching throughout and beyond India (see "Ashoka's Conversion to Buddhism," page 173). Ashoka formulated a legal code based on the Buddha's dharma and inscribed his laws on enormous monolithic (one-piece) stone columns erected throughout his kingdom. Ashoka's pillars reached 30 to 40 feet high and are the first monumental stone artworks in India. The pillars penetrated deep into the ground, connecting earth and sky, forming an "axis of the universe," a pre-Buddhist concept that became an important motif in Buddhist architecture. The columns stood along pilgrimage routes to sites associated with the Buddha and on the roads leading to Pataliputra. Capping Ashoka's pillars were elaborate capitals, also carved from a single block of stone. The finest of these is the seven-foot lion capital (FIG. 6-4) at Sarnath, where the Buddha gave his first sermon and set the Wheel of the Law into motion (see "Buddhism," page 171). Stylistically, Ashoka's capital owes much to the ancient Near East, especially the Achaemenid art of Persepolis (see FIG. 2-26), but its iconography is Buddhist. Two pairs of back-to-back lions stand on a round abacus decorated with four wheels and four animals symbolizing the four quarters of the world. The lions once carried a large stone wheel on their backs.

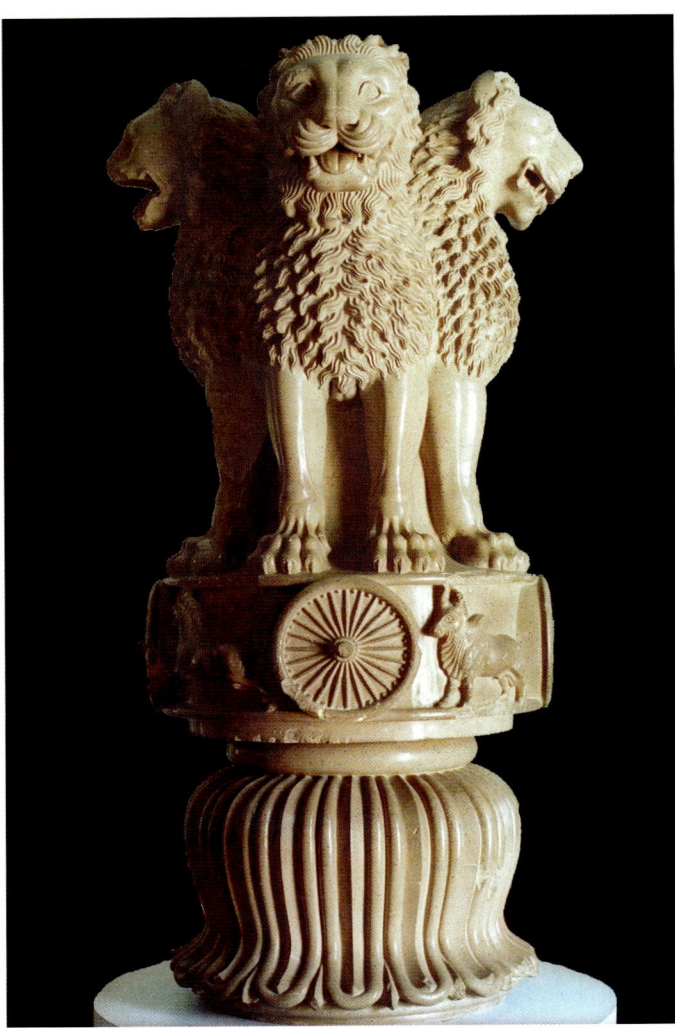

**6-4** Lion capital of column erected by Ashoka at Sarnath, India, ca. 250 BCE. Polished sandstone, approx. 7′ high. Archaeological Museum, Sarnath.

The wheel (chakra) referred to the Wheel of the Law but also indicated Ashoka's stature as a *chakravartin* ("holder of the wheel"), a universal king imbued with divine authority.

## Shunga, Andhra, and Kushan Dynasties

The Maurya Dynasty came to an abrupt end when its last ruler was assassinated by one of his generals, who founded a new dynasty in his own name. The Shungas, however, never ruled an empire as extensive as that of the Mauryas. Their realm was confined to central India. They were succeeded by the Andhras, who also controlled the Deccan plateau to the south. By the middle of the first century CE, an even greater empire, the Kushan, rose in northern India. Its most celebrated king was Kanishka (r. 78–144 CE), whose capital was at Peshawar in Gandhara, a region largely in Pakistan today, close to the Afghanistan border. The Kushans grew rich on trade between China and the west along one of the main caravan routes bringing the luxuries of the Orient to the Roman Empire (see "Silk and the Silk Road," Chapter 7, page 201). Kanishka even struck coins modeled on the imperial coinage of Rome (see Chapter 10), some featuring Greco-Roman deities, but Kanishka's coins also carried portraits of himself and images of the Buddha and various Hindu deities.

### *Buddhism and Buddhist Iconography*

#### THE BUDDHA AND THE EIGHTFOLD PATH

The Buddha (Enlightened One) was born around 563 BCE as Prince Siddhartha Gautama, the eldest son of the king of the Shakya Clan. A prophecy foretold that he would grow up to be either a world conqueror or a great religious leader. His father preferred the secular role for young Siddhartha and groomed him for kingship by shielding the boy from the hardships of the world. When he was 29, however, the prince rode out of the palace, abandoned his wife and family, and encountered firsthand the pain of old age, sickness, and death. Siddhartha responded to the suffering he witnessed by renouncing his opulent life and becoming a wandering ascetic searching for knowledge through meditation. Six years later, he achieved complete enlightenment, or buddhahood, while meditating beneath a pipal tree (the Bodhi tree) at Bodh Gaya ("place of enlightenment") in eastern India. Known from that day on as Shakyamuni (Wise Man of the Shakya Clan), the Buddha preached his first sermon in the Deer Park at Sarnath. There he set in motion the Wheel *(chakra)* of the Law *(dharma)* and expounded the Four Noble Truths that are the core insights of Buddhism: (1) life is suffering; (2) the cause of suffering is desire; (3) one can overcome and extinguish desire; (4) the way to conquer desire and end suffering is to follow the Buddha's Eightfold Path of right understanding, right thought, right speech, right action, right livelihood, right effort, right mindfulness, and right concentration. The Buddha's path leads to nirvana, the cessation of the endless cycle of painful life, death, and rebirth. The Buddha continued to preach until his death at 80 at Kushinagara. His disciples carried on his teaching and established monasteries where others could follow the Buddha's path to enlightenment and nirvana.

#### THE SPREAD OF BUDDHISM

This earliest form of Buddhism is called *Theravada* (the Path of the Elders) Buddhism. The new religion developed and changed over time as the Buddha's teachings spread from India throughout Asia. The second major school of Buddhist thought, *Mahayana* (Great Path) Buddhism, emerged around the beginning of the Christian era. Mahayana Buddhists refer to Theravada Buddhism as *Hinayana* (Lesser Path) Buddhism and believe in a larger goal than nirvana for an individual—namely, buddhahood for all. Mahayana Buddhists also revere *bodhisattvas* ("Buddhas-to-be"), exemplars of compassion who, holding back at the threshold of nirvana, aid others in earning merit and achieving buddhahood (see FIGS. 6-14, 7-12, 8-7, and 8-8). Theravada Buddhism became the dominant sect in southern India, Sri Lanka, and mainland Southeast Asia, whereas Mahayana Buddhism took root in northern India and spread to China, Korea, Japan, and Nepal.

A third important Buddhist sect, especially popular in East Asia, venerates the *Amitabha* Buddha (*Amida* in Japanese), the Buddha of Infinite Light and Life. The devotees of this Buddha hope to be reborn in the Pure Land Paradise of the West (see FIG. 7-13), where the Amitabha resides and can grant them salvation. Pure Land teachings maintain that people have no possibility of attaining enlightenment on their own, but can achieve paradise by faith alone.

#### THE BUDDHA IN ART

When artists began depicting the Buddha in human form, probably in the first century CE, it was as a robed monk. They distinguished the Enlightened One from monks and bodhisattvas by *lakshanas,* body attributes or characteristics indicating the Buddha's superhuman nature. These distinguishing marks include an *urna,* or curl of hair between the eyebrows, shown as a dot; an *ushnisha,* a cranial bump shown as hair on the earliest images (FIGS. 6-9 to 6-11) but later as an actual part of the head (see FIG. 6-12); and, less frequently, palms of hands and soles of feet imprinted with a wheel (FIG. 6-11). The Buddha is also recognizable by his elongated ears, the result of wearing heavy royal jewelry in his youth, but the enlightened Shakyamuni is rarely bejeweled, as are many bodhisattvas. Sometimes the Buddha appears with a halo, or sun disk, behind his head (FIGS. 6-9, 6-11, and 6-12).

Representations of the Buddha also feature a repertory of *mudras,* or hand gestures, conveying fixed meanings. These include the *dhyana* (meditation) mudra, with hands overlapping in the lap, palms upward (FIGS. 6-9 and 25-11); the *bhumisparsha* (earth touching) mudra, right hand down reaching to the ground, calling the earth to witness the Buddha's enlightenment (FIGS. 6-10*b,* and 7-27); the *dharmachakra* (Wheel of the Law, or teaching) mudra, a two-handed gesture with right thumb and index finger forming a circle (FIGS. 6-12 and 8-8); and the *abhaya* (do not fear) mudra, right hand up, palm outward, a gesture of protection or blessing (FIGS. 6-10*c,* 6-11, and 8-7).

Episodes from the Buddha's life are among the most popular subjects in all Buddhist artistic traditions. No single text provides the complete or authoritative narrative of his life and death. Thus, numerous versions and variations exist, allowing for a rich artistic repertory. Four of the most important events are his birth at Lumbini from the side of his mother, Queen Maya (FIG. 6-10*a*) the achievement of buddhahood while meditating beneath the Bodhi tree at Bodh Gaya (FIGS. 6-10*b* and 7-27); the Buddha's first sermon at Sarnath (FIGS. 6-10*c* and 6-12); and his attainment of nirvana when he died *(parinirvana)* at Kushinagara (FIGS. 6-10*d* and 6-25). Buddhists erected monasteries and monuments at the four sites where these key events occurred. Monks and lay pilgrims from throughout the world continue to visit these places today.

**THE GREAT STUPA AT SANCHI** In the world of art and architecture, the unifying characteristic of this age of regional dynasties in South Asia was the patronage of Buddhism. One of the most important Buddhist monasteries, founded during Ashoka's reign and in use for more than a thousand years, is at Sanchi in central India. It consists of many buildings constructed over the centuries, including *viharas* (celled structures where monks live), large *stupas* (see "The Stupa," page 172), *chaitya halls* (halls with rounded, or *apsidal,* ends for housing smaller stupas), and temples for sheltering images.

The Great Stupa at Sanchi dates originally to Ashoka's reign, but its present form, with its tall stone fence and four gates, dates

## The Stupa

An essential element of Buddhist sanctuaries is the *stupa,* a grand circular mound modeled on earlier South Asian burial mounds of a type familiar in many other ancient cultures (see FIGS. 4-21 and 9-5). The stupa was not a tomb, however, but a monument housing relics of the Buddha. When the Buddha died, his cremated remains were placed in eight *reliquaries,* or containers, similar in function to the later reliquaries housed in medieval churches at pilgrimage sites throughout the Christian world (see "Pilgrimages and the Cult of Relics," Chapter 17, page 449). Unlike their Western equivalents, which were meant to be viewed, the Buddha's relics were buried in solid earthen mounds (stupas) that could not be entered. In the mid-third century BCE, Ashoka opened the original eight stupas and spread the Buddha's relics among thousands of stupas in all corners of his realm. Buddhists venerated the Buddha's remains by *circumambulation,* walking around the stupa in a clockwise direction, following the path of the sun, bringing the devotee into harmony with the cosmos. Stupas come in many sizes, from tiny handheld objects to huge structures, such as the Great Stupa at Sanchi (FIG. 6-5) that Ashoka constructed in the third century BCE and later kings enlarged.

The monumental stupas are three-dimensional *mandalas,* or sacred diagrams of the universe. The domed stupa itself represents the world mountain, with the cardinal points marked by *toranas,* or gateways (FIGS. 6-5 and 6-6). The *harmika,* positioned atop the stupa dome, is a stone fence or railing that encloses a square area symbolizing the sacred domain of the gods. At the harmika's center, a *yasti,* or pole, corresponds to the axis of the universe, a motif already present in Ashoka's pillars. Three *chatras,* or stone disks, assigned various meanings, crown the yasti. The yasti rises from the mountain-dome and passes through the harmika, thus uniting this world with the heavenly paradise. A stone fence often encloses the entire structure, clearly separating the sacred space containing the Buddha's relics from the profane world outside.

**6-5** Great Stupa, Sanchi, India, third century BCE to first century CE (view from the east).

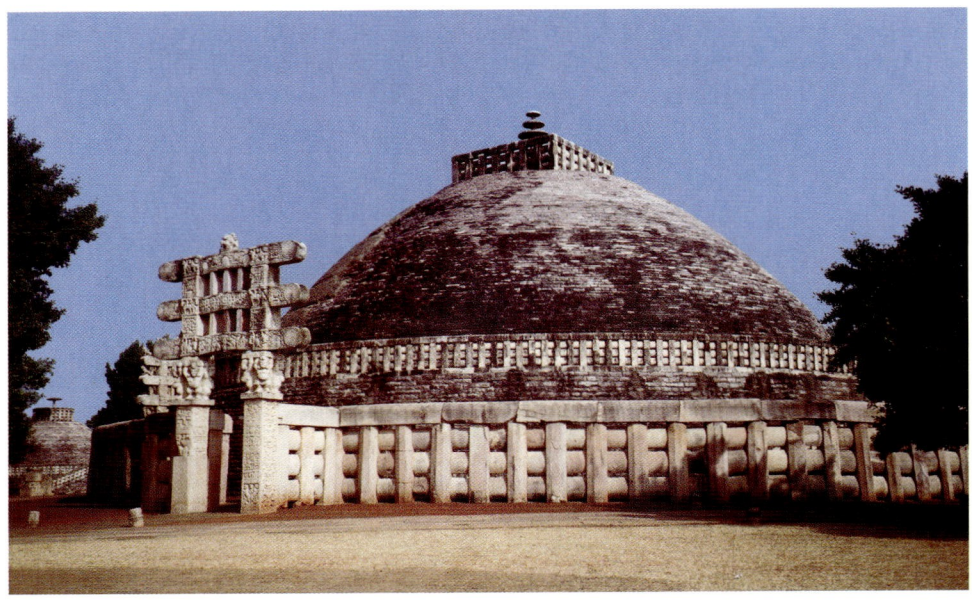

**6-6** Exterior diagram of Great Stupa, Sanchi, India, third century BCE to first century CE.

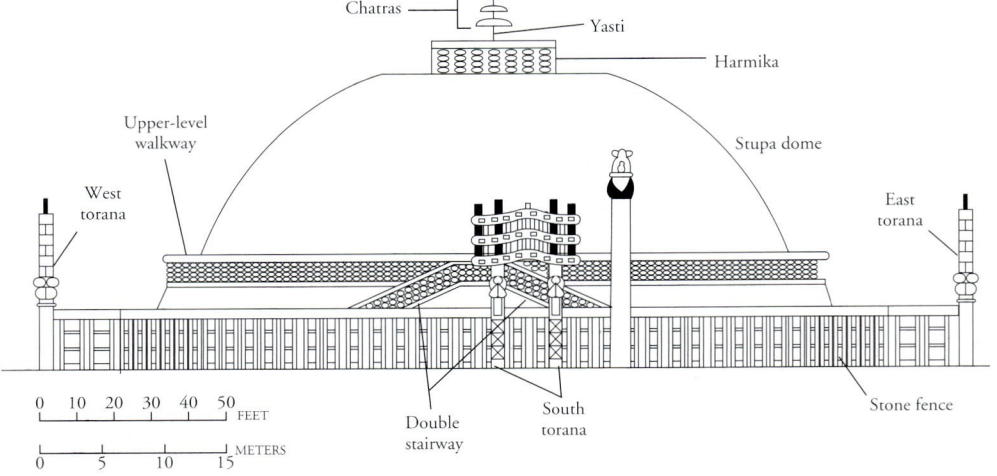

### Ashoka's Conversion to Buddhism

The reign of the Maurya king Ashoka marks both the beginning of monumental stone art and architecture in India (FIG. 6-4) and the first official sponsorship of Buddhism. The impact of Ashoka's conversion to Buddhism on the later history of art and religion in Asia cannot be overstated. An edict carved into a rock at Dhauli in the ancient region of Kalinga (roughly equivalent to the modern state of Orissa on the Bay of Bengal) records Ashoka's embrace of nonviolence and of the teachings of the Buddha after an especially bloody conquest that claimed more than 100,000 lives. The inscription also captures Ashoka's missionary zeal, which spread Buddhism far beyond the boundaries of his kingdom.

> The Beloved of the Gods [Ashoka], conqueror of the Kalingas, is moved to remorse now. For he has felt profound sorrow and regret because the conquest of a people previously unconquered involves slaughter, death, and deportation. . . . [King Ashoka] now thinks that even a person who wrongs him must be forgiven . . .

[and he] considers moral conquest [conquest by dharma] the most important conquest. He has achieved this moral conquest repeatedly both here and among the peoples living beyond the borders of his kingdom. . . . Even in countries which [King Ashoka's] envoys have not reached, people have heard about dharma and about [the king's] ordinances and instructions in dharma. . . . This edict on dharma has been inscribed so that my sons and great-grandsons who may come after me should not think new conquests worth achieving. . . . Let them consider moral conquest the only true conquest.[1]

The story of Ashoka at Kalinga and his renunciation of violence still resonates today. It inspired one of the most important 20th-century Indian sculptors to take up the theme and imbue it with contemporary meaning (see FIG. 25-14).

[1] Rock Edict XIII. Translated by N. A. Nikam and Richard McKeon, *The Edicts of Asoka* (Chicago: The University of Chicago Press, 1959), 27–30.

---

from ca. 50 BCE to 50 CE (FIGS. 6-5 and 6-6). The dome, solid and filled with earth and rubble, stands 50 feet high. Worshipers enter through one of the gateways, walk on the lower circumambulation path, then climb the stairs on the south side to circumambulate at the second level. Carved onto the different parts of the Great Stupa are more than 600 brief inscriptions showing that the donations of hundreds of individuals (more than a third of them women) made the monument's construction possible. Veneration of the Buddha was open to all, not just the monks, and most of the dedications are by common laypeople, who hoped to accrue merit for future rebirths with their gifts.

**THE BUDDHA'S PAST LIVES** The reliefs on the four toranas at Sanchi (FIGS. 6-5 and 6-6) depict not only the Buddha's life story but also the stories of his past lives *(jatakas)*. In Buddhist belief, everyone has had innumerable past lives, including Siddhartha. During Siddhartha's former lives, as recorded in the jatakas, he accumulated sufficient merit to achieve enlightenment and become the Buddha. In the life stories recounted in the Great Stupa reliefs, however, the Buddha never appears as a human being. Instead, the artists indicated his presence by using symbols, for example, footprints, a parasol, or an empty seat. Some scholars regard these symbols as markers of where the Buddha once was, so others can follow in his footsteps.

**YAKSHI AND FLOWERING TREE** Also carved on the eastern gateway is a scantily clad, sensuous woman called a *yakshi* (FIG. 6-7). These goddesses, worshiped throughout India, personified fertility and vegetation. The Sanchi yakshi reaches up to hold on to a mango tree branch while pressing her left foot against the trunk, an action that has brought the tree to flower. Buddhists later adopted this pose, with its rich associations of procreation and abundance, for representing the Buddha's mother, Maya, giving birth (FIG. 6-10a). Thus, the Buddhists adopted pan-Indian symbolism, such as the woman under the tree, when creating their own Buddhist iconography.

**ROCK-CUT MONASTIC HALLS** The best early example of a chaitya hall is the one carved out of the living rock at Karle (FIG. 6-8), datable around 100 CE. The Karle hall has pillared

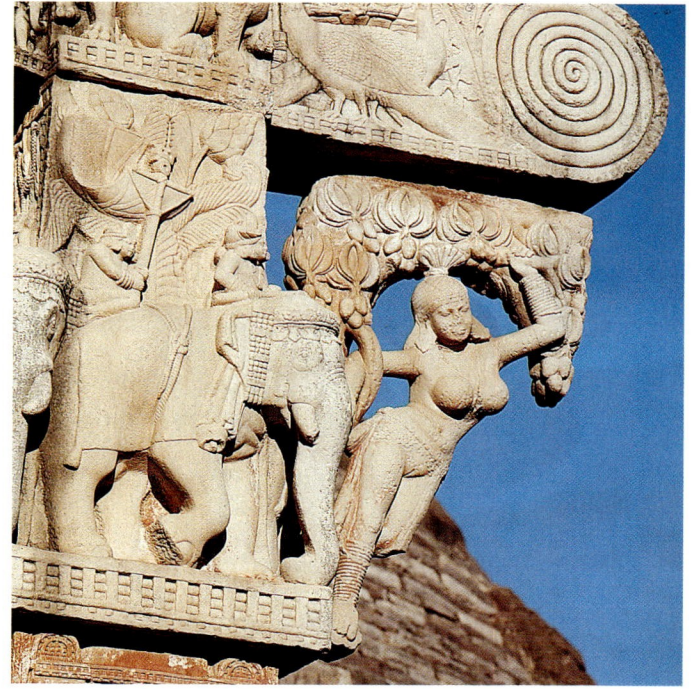

**6-7** Yakshi, detail of eastern gateway, Great Stupa, Sanchi, India, mid-first century BCE to early first century CE.

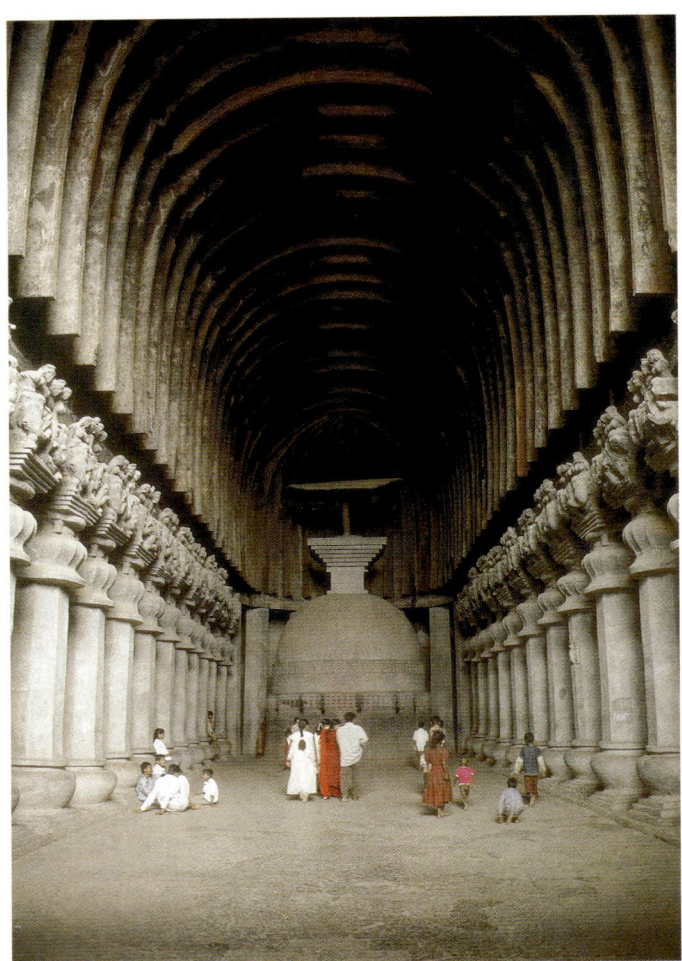

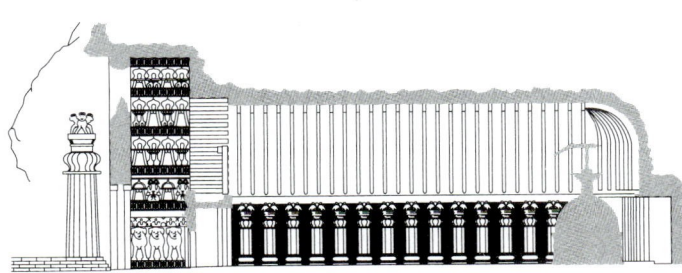

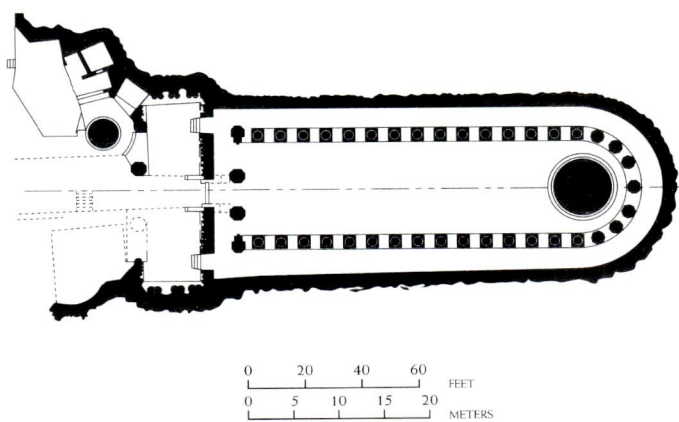

**6-8** Interior *(left)*, section *(top right)*, and plan *(bottom right)* of chaitya hall, Karle, India, ca. 100 CE.

*ambulatories* (walking paths) that allow worshipers to circumambulate the stupa placed at the back of the sacred cave. The hall is nearly 45 feet high and 125 feet long. It surpasses in size even the rock-cut chamber of the temple of the Egyptian pharaoh Ramses II (see FIG. 3-24). Elaborate capitals atop the rock-cut pillars depict men and women riding on elephants. Outside, amorous couples *(mithunas)* flank the entrance. Like the yakshis at Sanchi, these auspicious figures symbolize the creative life force. The Sanchi and Karle figures are early examples of what will become a long tradition of eroticism in Indian religious art (compare FIG. 6-23).

**FIRST BUDDHAS IN HUMAN FORM** The first anthropomorphic representations of the Buddha probably appeared in the first century CE. Scholars still debate what brought about this momentous shift in Buddhist iconography, but one factor may be the changing perception of the Buddha himself. Originally revered as an enlightened mortal, the Buddha increasingly became regarded as a divinity. Consequently, the Buddha's followers desired images of him to worship.

Many of the early portrayals of the Buddha in human form come from the Gandhara region and from Mathura, a city about 90 miles south of Delhi. Both were part of the Kushan Empire during the first three centuries CE.

**GANDHARA AND GRECO-ROMAN ART** In Gandhara, sculptors fashioned representations of the Buddha both in freestanding statuary and narrative reliefs. A second-century CE statue (FIG. 6-9) carved in gray schist, the local stone, shows the Buddha, with ushnisha and urna, dressed in a monk's robe, seated in a cross-legged yogic posture similar to that of the ancient figure on the Indus seal discussed earlier (FIG. 6-3). His hands overlap, palms upward, in the dhyana mudra, the gesture of meditation (see "Buddhism," page 171). Gandhara was part of a widespread region of Hellenized culture and art that stretched across reaches of modern Iran, Russia, Afghanistan, and Pakistan, a legacy of Alexander's incursions in these regions. Gandharan sculpture owes much to Greco-Roman art, both in the treatment of body forms, such as the sharp, arching brows and continuous profile of forehead and nose (see, for example, FIG. 5-39), and in the draping of the togalike garment (see FIG. 10-72).

**LIFE AND DEATH OF THE BUDDHA** One of the earliest pictorial narrative cycles in which the Buddha appears in human form also comes from Gandhara. The schist frieze (FIG. 6-10) depicts, in chronological order from left to right, the Buddha's birth at Lumbini, the enlightenment at Bodh Gaya, the first sermon at Sarnath, and the Buddha's death at Kushinagara. At the left, Queen Maya, in a posture derived from that of earlier South Asian

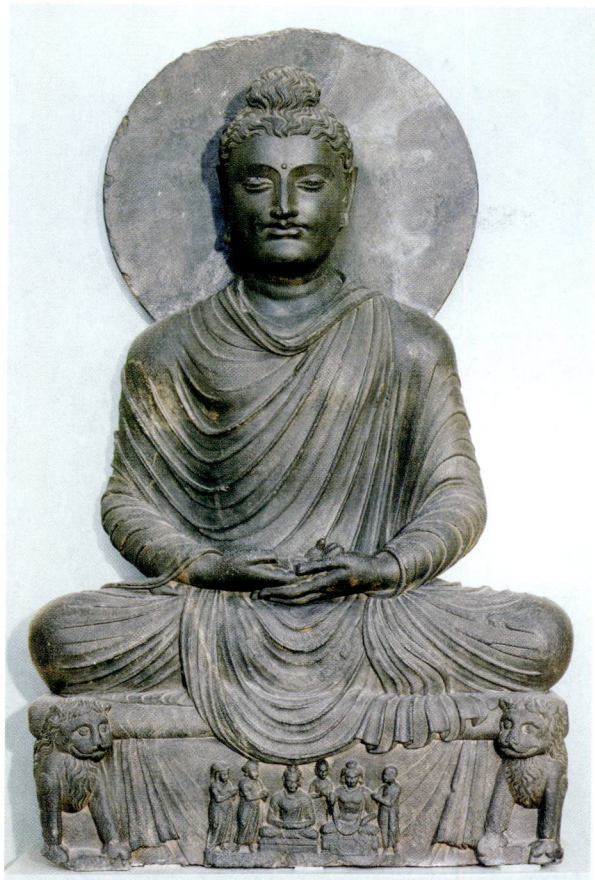

yakshis (FIG. 6-7), gives birth to Prince Siddhartha, who emerges from her right hip, already with his attributes of ushnisha, urna, and halo. Receiving him is the god Indra. Elegantly dressed ladies, one with a fan of peacock feathers, suggest the opulent court life the Buddha left behind. In the next scene, the Buddha sits beneath the Bodhi tree while the soldiers and demons of the evil Mara attempt to distract him from his quest for knowledge. They are unsuccessful, and the Buddha reaches down to touch the earth (bhumisparsha mudra) as witness to his enlightenment. Next, the Buddha preaches the Eightfold Path to nirvana in the Deer Park at Sarnath. The sculptor has set the scene by placing two deer and the Wheel of the Law beneath the figure of the Buddha, who raises his right hand (abhaya mudra) to bless the monks and other devotees who have come to hear his first sermon. In the final section of the frieze, the parinirvana, the Buddha lies dying among his devotees, some of whom wail in grief, while one monk, who realizes that the Buddha has been permanently released from suffering, remains tranquil in meditation.

Although the iconography of the frieze is Buddhist, Roman reliefs must have served as stylistic models for the sculptor. For example, the distribution of standing and equestrian figures over the relief ground, with those behind the first row seemingly suspended in the air, is familiar in Roman art of the second and third centuries CE (see FIGS. 10-66 and 10-71). The figure of the Buddha on his deathbed finds parallels in the reclining figures on the lids of Roman sarcophagi (see FIG. 10-62). The type of hierarchical composition placing a large seated central figure between balanced tiers of smaller onlookers can be seen on the later Arch of the Roman emperor Constantine (see FIG. 10-77), which has precedents in earlier Roman art.

**6-9** Meditating Buddha, from Gandhara, Pakistan, second century CE. Gray schist, 3′ 7½″ high. National Museums of Scotland.

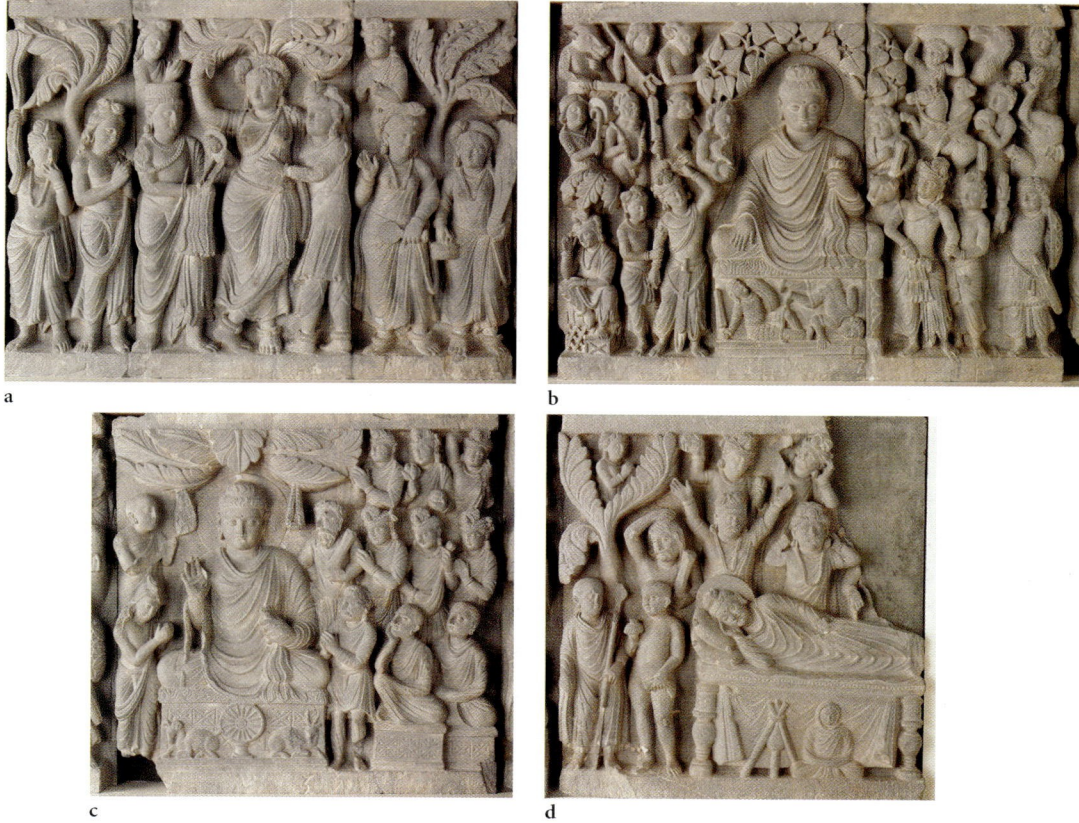

**6-10** The life and death of the Buddha, frieze from Gandhara, Pakistan, second century CE. Schist, 2′ 2⅜″ × 9′ 6⅛″. Freer Gallery of Art, Washington, D.C. a) birth at Lumbini, b) enlightenment at Badh Gaya, c) first sermon at Sarnath, d) death at Kushinagara.

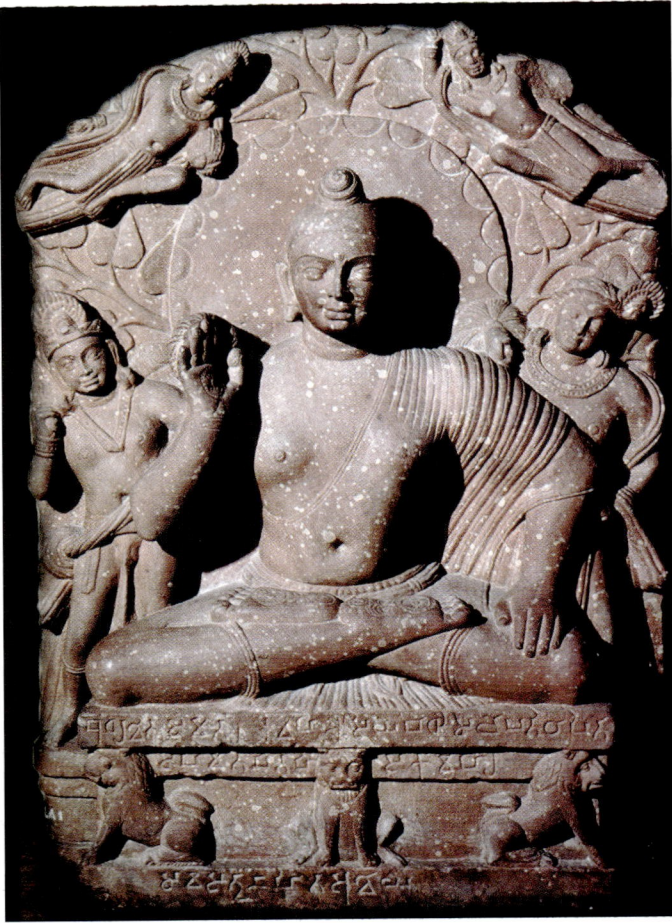

6-11 Buddha seated on lion throne, from Mathura, India, second century CE. Red sandstone, 2′ 3½″ high. Archaeological Museum, Muttra. 💿

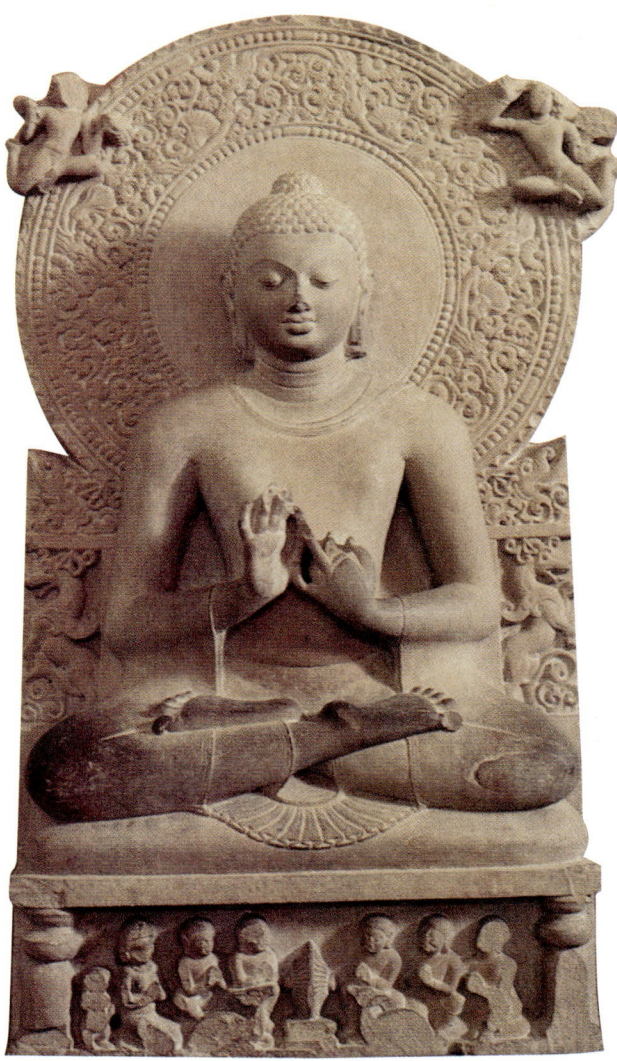

6-12 Seated Buddha preaching first sermon, from Sarnath, India, second half of fifth century. Tan sandstone, 5′ 3″ high. Archaeological Museum, Sarnath.

**BUDDHIST IMAGERY IN MATHURA** Contemporary to the Gandharan sculptures, but stylistically distinct from them, are the Buddha images of Mathura (FIG. **6-11**). The Mathura statues are more closely linked to the Indian portrayals of *yakshas,* the male equivalents of the yakshis. Indian artists represented yakshas as robust, powerful males with broad shoulders and open, staring eyes. Mathura Buddhas, carved from red sandstone, retain these characteristics but wear a monk's robe (with right shoulder bare) and lack the jewelry and other signs of wealth of the yakshas. The robe appears almost transparent, revealing the full, fleshy body beneath. In our example, the Buddha sits in a yogic posture on a lion throne under the Bodhi tree, attended by fly-whisk bearers. He raises his right hand palm-out in the abhaya gesture, indicating to worshipers that they need have no fear. His hands and feet bear the mark of the dharma Wheel.

## The Gupta and Post-Gupta Periods

Around 320* a new empire arose in north central India. The Gupta emperors chose Pataliputra as their capital, deliberately associating themselves with the prestige of the former Maurya Empire. The heyday of this dynasty was under Chandragupta II

(r. 375–415), whose very name recalled the first Maurya emperor. The Guptas were great patrons of art and literature.

**THE CLASSICAL BUDDHA STATUE** Under the Guptas, artists formulated what became the canonical image of the Buddha, combining the Gandharan monastic robe covering both shoulders with the soft, full-bodied Buddha figures with clinging garments of Mathuran sculpture. These disparate styles beautifully merge in a fifth-century Buddha from Sarnath (FIG. **6-12**), whose smooth, unadorned surfaces conform to the Indian notion of perfect bodily form and emphasize the figure's spirituality. The Buddha's eyes are downcast in meditation, and he holds his hands in front of his body in the Wheel-turning gesture, preaching his first sermon, indicated by the tiny Wheel of the Law seen on its edge below the figure. Flanking the Wheel, two now partially broken deer symbolize the Deer Park at Sarnath. Buddha images such as this one became so popular that temples housing Buddha statues seem largely to have displaced the stupa as the norm in Buddhist sacred architecture.

**THE CAVES OF AJANTA** The new popularity of Buddha imagery may be seen in the interior of a chaitya hall (FIG. **6-13**) carved out of the mountainside at Ajanta, northeast of Bombay,

---

* From this point on, all dates in this chapter are CE unless otherwise stated.

### The Painted Caves of Ajanta

Art historians assume India had a rich painting tradition in ancient times, but because early Indian artists often used perishable materials, such as palm leaf and wood, and because of the tropical climate in much of India, nearly all early Indian painting has been lost. At Ajanta in the Deccan, however, paintings cover the walls, pillars, and ceilings of several caves datable to the second half of the fifth century. FIG. 6-14 reproduces a detail of one of the Ajanta murals.

To create these paintings, the artists first applied two layers of clay mixed with straw and other materials to the walls. They then added a third layer of fine white lime plaster. Unlike true fresco painting (see "Fresco," Chapter 19, page 530), in which the painters apply colors to the wet plaster, the Indian painters waited for the lime to dry. This method produces less durable results, and the Ajanta murals have suffered water damage over the centuries. The painters next outlined the figures in dark red and then painted in the details of faces, costumes, and jewelry. The colors used were water soluble and mostly produced from local minerals, including red and yellow ocher. Blue, used sparingly, came from costly lapis lazuli imported from Afghanistan. The last step was to polish the painted surface with a smooth stone.

The Ajanta caves provide a tantalizing glimpse of early Indian painting. Significant later examples of paintings in India are rare before the 13th century (see Chapter 25).

---

at about the same time a Gupta sculptor created the classic Sarnath seated Buddha. Ajanta had been the site of a small Buddhist monastery for centuries, but royal patrons of the local Vakataka dynasty, allied to the Guptas by marriage, added more than 20 new caves in the second half of the fifth century. The typological similarity of the fifth-century Ajanta chaitya halls to the earlier example at Karle (FIG. 6-8) is immediately evident and consistent with the conservative nature of religious architecture in all cultures. At Ajanta, however, sculptors carved a standing Buddha flanked by columns into the front of the stupa.

**PAINTED BODHISATTVAS** Ajanta is renowned above all because the caves retain much of their painted wall and ceiling decoration (see "The Painted Caves of Ajanta," above). We illustrate a detail of one of the restored painted walls in Cave 1 depicting the bodhisattva Padmapani (FIG. **6-14**) among a crowd of devotees, both princes and commoners. With long, dark hair hanging down below a jeweled crown, he stands holding his attribute, a blue lotus flower, in his right hand. The bodhisattva's face shows great compassion as he gazes downward at the actual worshipers passing through the shrine entrance on their way to

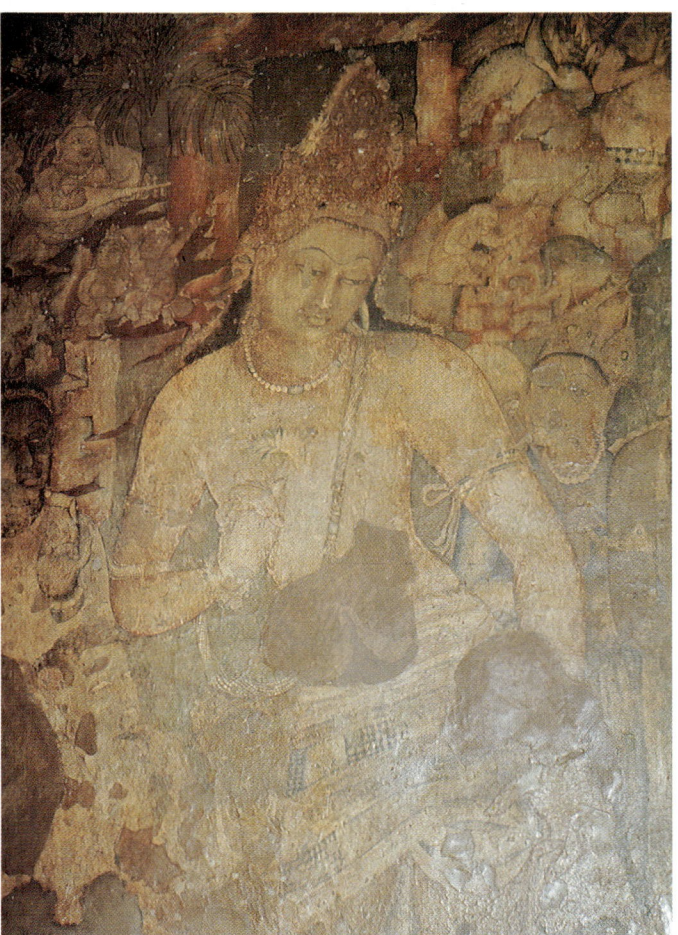

6-13 Interior of Cave 19, Ajanta, India, second half of fifth century.

6-14 Bodhisattva Padmapani, wall painting in Cave 1, Ajanta, India, second half of fifth century.

## *Hinduism and Hindu Iconography*

Unlike Buddhism (and Christianity, Islam, and other religions), Hinduism recognizes no founder or great prophet. Hinduism also has no simple definition, but means "the religion of the Indians." Both "India" and "Hindu" have a common root in the name of the Indus River. The actual practices and beliefs of Hindus vary tremendously, but the literary origins of Hinduism can be traced to the Vedic period, and some aspects of Hindu practice seem already to have been present in the Indus Civilization of the third millennium BCE. Ritual sacrifice by Brahmin priests is central to Hinduism, as it was to the Aryans. The goal of sacrifice is to please a deity in order to achieve release (*moksha*, liberation) from the endless cycle of birth, death, and rebirth (*samsara*) and become one with the universal spirit.

Not only is Hinduism a religion of many gods, but the Hindu deities have various natures and take many forms. This multiplicity suggests the all-pervasive nature of the Hindu gods. The three most important deities are the gods Shiva and Vishnu and the goddess Devi. Each of the three major sects of Hinduism today considers one of these three to be supreme — Shiva in Shaivism, Vishnu in Vaishnavism, and Devi in Shaktism. (*Shakti* is the female creative force.)

*Shiva* (FIGS. 6-16, 6-17, and 6-24) is the Destroyer, but, consistent with the multiplicity of Hindu belief, he is also a regenerative force and, in the latter role, can be represented in the form of a *linga* (a phallus or cosmic pillar). When Shiva appears in human form in Hindu art, he frequently has multiple limbs and heads, signs of his superhuman nature. He often has matted locks piled on top of his head, crowned by a crescent moon. Sometimes he wears a serpent scarf and has a third eye on his forehead (the emblem of his all-seeing nature). Shiva rides the bull *Nandi* (FIG. 6-16) and often carries a trident. His son is the elephant-headed *Ganesha* (FIG. 6-16).

*Vishnu* (FIGS. 6-19 and 6-28) is the Preserver of the Universe. Artists frequently portray him with four arms holding various attributes, including a conch-shell trumpet and discus. He sometimes reclines on a serpent floating on the waters of the cosmic sea. When the evil forces of the universe become too strong, he descends to earth to restore balance and assumes different forms (*avatars,* or incarnations), including a boar (FIG. 6-15), fish, and tortoise, as well as *Krishna,* the divine lover (FIG. 25-6), and even the Buddha himself.

*Devi* is the Great Goddess who takes many forms and has many names. Hindus worship her alone or as a consort of male gods (*Parvati* or *Uma,* wife of Shiva; *Lakshmi,* wife of Vishnu), as well as *Radha,* lover of Krishna (FIG. 25-6). She has both benign and horrific forms; she both creates and destroys. In one manifestation, she is *Durga,* a multiarmed goddess who rides or is accompanied by a lion.

The stationary images of deities in Hindu temples are often made of stone. Hindus periodically remove portable images of their gods, often of bronze (for example, FIG. 6-24), from the temple, particularly during festivals to enable many worshipers to take *darshan* (seeing the deity and being seen by the deity) at one time. In temples dedicated to Shiva, the stationary form is the linga.

---

the monumental rock-cut Buddha image housed in a cell at the back of the cave. The painter has rendered with finesse the sensuous form of the richly attired bodhisattva, gently modeling the figure with gradations of color and delicate highlights and shadows, especially evident in the face and neck.

**BUDDHIST AND HINDU COEXISTENCE** Buddhists and Hindus (and adherents of other faiths) practiced their religions side by side in India, often at the same site. The Hindu Vakataka king Harishena (r. 462–481) and members of his court were the sponsors of the new caves at the Buddhist monastery at Ajanta. Buddhism and Hinduism are not monotheistic religions, such as Judaism, Christianity, and Islam. Instead, Buddhists and Hindus approach the spiritual through many gods and varying paths, which permits mutually tolerated differences. In fact, in Hinduism, the Buddha was one of the 10 incarnations of Vishnu, one of the three principal Hindu deities (see "Hinduism and Hindu Iconography," above). More early Buddhist than Hindu art has survived in India, because the Buddhists constructed large monastic institutions with durable materials such as stone and brick. In the Gupta period, Hindu stone sculpture and architecture began to rival the great Buddhist monuments of South Asia.

**VISHNU RESCUES THE EARTH** The earliest Hindu cave temples are at Udayagiri, near Sanchi. They date to the early fifth century, some 600 years after the first Buddhist examples. Although the Udayagiri temples are architecturally simple and small, the site boasts monumental relief sculptures showing an already fully developed religious iconography. One of these reliefs (FIG. 6-15), carved in a shallow niche of rock, shows a 13-foot-tall Vishnu in his incarnation as the boar Varaha (see "Hinduism," above). The avatar has a human body and a boar's head. Vishnu assumed this form when he rescued the earth — personified as the goddess Bhudevi clinging to the boar's tusk — from being carried off to the bottom of the ocean. Vishnu stands with one foot resting on the coils of a snake king (identified by the multiple hoods behind his human head), who represents the conquered demon that attempted to abduct the earth. Rows of gods and sages form lines to witness the event.

The relief served a political as well as a religious purpose. The patron of the relief was a local king who honored the great Gupta king Chandragupta II in a nearby inscription dated to the year 401. Many scholars believe that the local king wanted viewers to see Chandragupta (he is known to have visited the site) as saving his kingdom by ridding it of its enemies in much the same way Varaha saved the earth. Thus, the Udayagiri sculptors, acting on their patron's wishes, clothed contemporary events in mythological guise, as the Greeks frequently did (see Chapter 5).

**DANCING MANY-ARMED SHIVA** During the sixth century, the Huns brought down the Gupta empire, and various regional dynasties rose to power. In the Deccan, a plateau area in central India, the Chalukya kings ruled from their capital at Badami. There, Chalukya sculptors carved a series of reliefs in the walls of halls cut into the cliff above the city. One relief (FIG. 6-16), datable to the late sixth century, shows Shiva, the second major Hindu

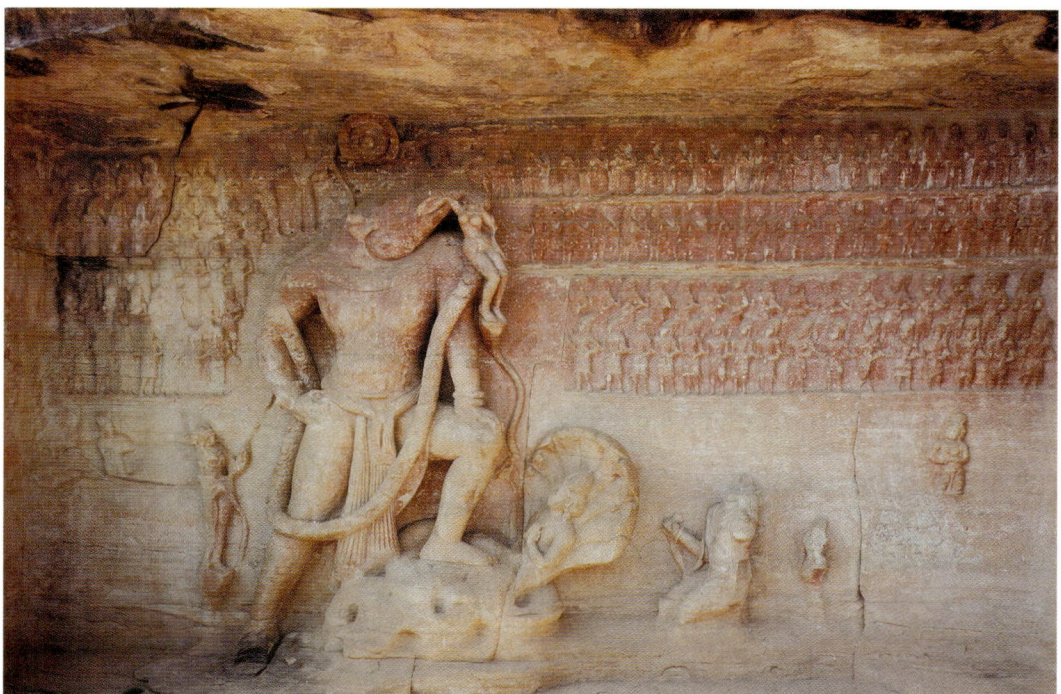

6-15 Boar avatar of Vishnu rescuing the earth, Cave 5, Udayagiri, India, early fifth century. Relief approx. 22′ × 13′; Vishnu 12′ 8″ high.

male deity (see "Hinduism," page 178) dancing the cosmic dance, his 18 arms swinging rhythmically in an arc. Some of the hands hold objects, and others form prescribed mudras. At the right, a drummer (not visible in FIG. 6-16) accompanies the dance, while Shiva's son, the elephant-headed Ganesha, tentatively mimics his father. Nandi, Shiva's bull mount, stands at the left.

Artists often represented Hindu deities as part human and part animal (FIG. 6-15) or, as in the Badami relief, as figures with multiple body parts. Such composite and multilimbed forms indicate that the subjects are not human but more-than-human gods with supernatural powers.

**SHIVA WITH THREE FACES** Another portrayal of Shiva as a superhuman being is found at a third Hindu cave site, on Elephanta, an island in Bombay's harbor named by early Portuguese colonizers who found a life-size stone elephant sculpture there. A king of the Kalachuri dynasty that took control of Elephanta in the sixth century may have commissioned the largest of the island's cave temples. Just inside the cave's west entrance is a shrine housing Shiva's linga, the god's emblem. Deep within the temple, in a niche once closed off with wooden doors, is a nearly 18-foot-high image of Shiva as Mahadeva (FIG. **6-17**), the "Great God" or Lord of Lords. Mahadeva appears to emerge out of the depths of the cave as worshipers' eyes become accustomed to the darkness. This image of Shiva has three faces, each showing a different aspect of the deity. (A fourth, unseen at the back, is implied—the god has not emerged fully from the rock.) The central face expresses Shiva's quiet, balanced demeanor. The clean planes of the face contrast with the richness of the piled hair encrusted with jewels. The two side faces differ significantly. That on the right is female, with framing hair curls. The left face is a grimacing male with a curling mustache who wears a cobra as an earring. The female (Uma) indicates the creative aspect of Shiva. The fierce male (Bhairava) represents Shiva's destructive side. Shiva holds these two opposing forces in check, and the central face expresses their balance. The cyclic destruction and creation of the universe, which the side faces also symbolize, are part of Indian notions of time, matched by the cyclic pattern of death and rebirth (samsara).

**VISHNU'S TOWER AT DEOGARH** The excavated cave shrines just considered are characteristic of early Hindu religious architecture, but temples constructed using quarried stone became more important as Hinduism evolved over the centuries (see "Hindu Temples," page 180). As they did with the cave temples, the Hindus initially built rather small and simple temples but decorated them with narrative reliefs displaying a fully developed

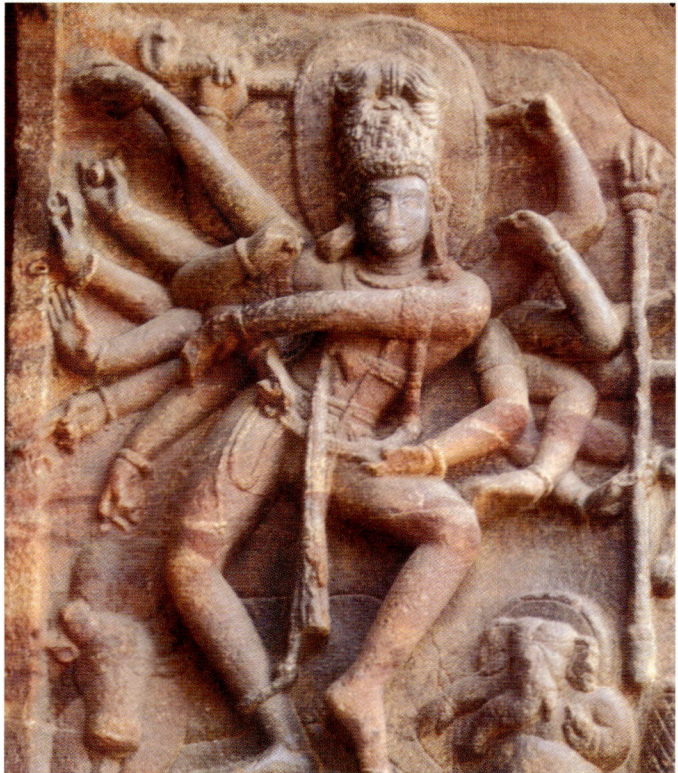

6-16 Dancing Shiva, rock-cut relief in cave temple, Badami, India, late sixth century.

## Hindu Temples

The Hindu temple is the home of the gods on earth and the place where they make themselves visible to humans. At the core of all Hindu temples is the *garbha griha*, the "womb chamber," which houses images or symbols of the deity, for example Shiva's linga (see "Hinduism," page 178). Only the Brahmin priests can enter this inner sanctuary to make offerings to the gods. The worshipers can only stand at the threshold and behold the deity as manifest by its image. In the elaborate multiroomed temples of later Hindu architecture, the worshipers and priests progress through a series of ever more sacred spaces, usually on an east-west axis. Hindu priests and architects attached great importance to each temple's plan and sought to make it conform to the sacred geometric diagram (*mandala*) of the universe.

Architectural historians, following ancient Indian texts, divide Hindu temples into two major typological groups tied to geography. The most important distinguishing feature of the *northern*, or *Nagara*, style of temple (FIG. 6-22) is its beehivelike tower or *shikhara* ("mountain peak"), capped by an *amalaka*, a ribbed cushionlike form, derived from the shape of the amala fruit (believed to have medicinal powers). Amalakas appear on the corners of the lower levels of the shikhara too. Northern temples also have smaller towerlike roofs over the halls (*mandapas*) leading to the garbha griha.

*Southern,* or *Dravida,* temples (FIG. 6-21) can easily be recognized by the flat roofs of their pillared mandapas and by their shorter towered shrines, called *vimanas,* which lack the curved profile of their Nagara counterparts and resemble multilevel pyramids.

---

iconography. The Vishnu Temple at Deogarh (FIG. **6-18**) in north central India, erected in the early sixth century, is among the first Hindu temples constructed with stone blocks. A simple square building on a stone *plinth* (base), it has an elaborately decorated doorway at the front and a relief in a niche on each of the other

three sides. Sculpted guardians and mithuna couples protect the doorway at Deogarh, because it is the transition point between the dangerous outside and the sacred interior, the garbha griha. A small shrine once stood at each corner of the plinth. The temple culminates in a tower (poorly preserved).

**THE CREATION OF THE UNIVERSE** The reliefs in the three niches of the Deogarh temple depict important episodes in the saga of Vishnu. The one we reproduce (FIG. **6-19**) shows Vishnu asleep on the coils of the giant serpent Ananta, whose multiple heads form a kind of umbrella around the god's face. While Lakshmi massages her husband's legs (he has cramps as he gives birth), the four-armed Vishnu dreams the universe into reality. A lotus plant (said

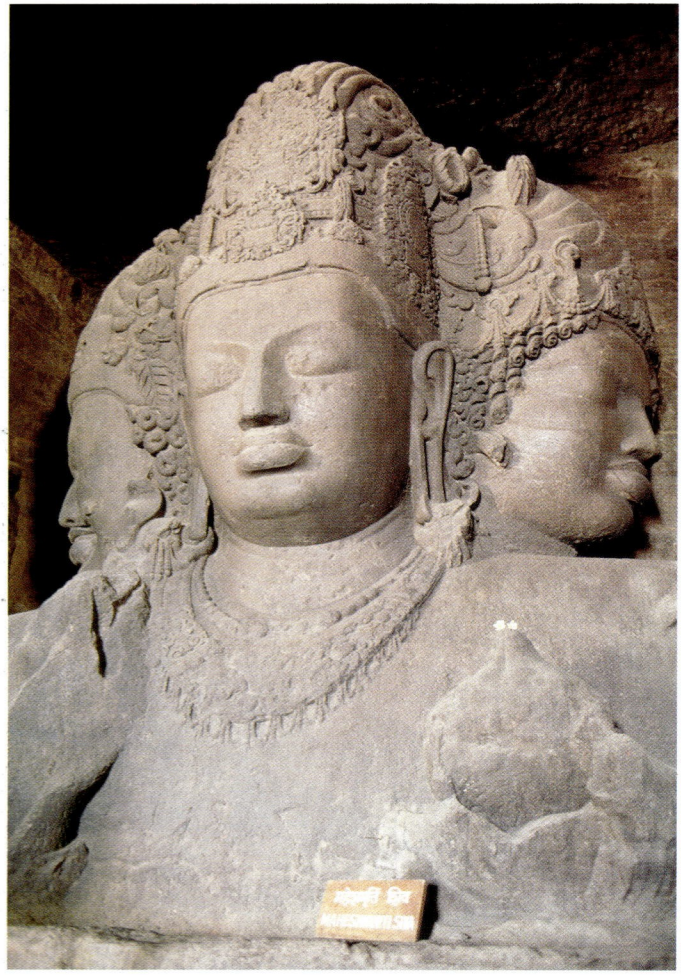

**6-17** Shiva as Mahadeva, Cave 1, Elephanta, India, ca. 550–575. Basalt, Shiva 17′ 10″ high.

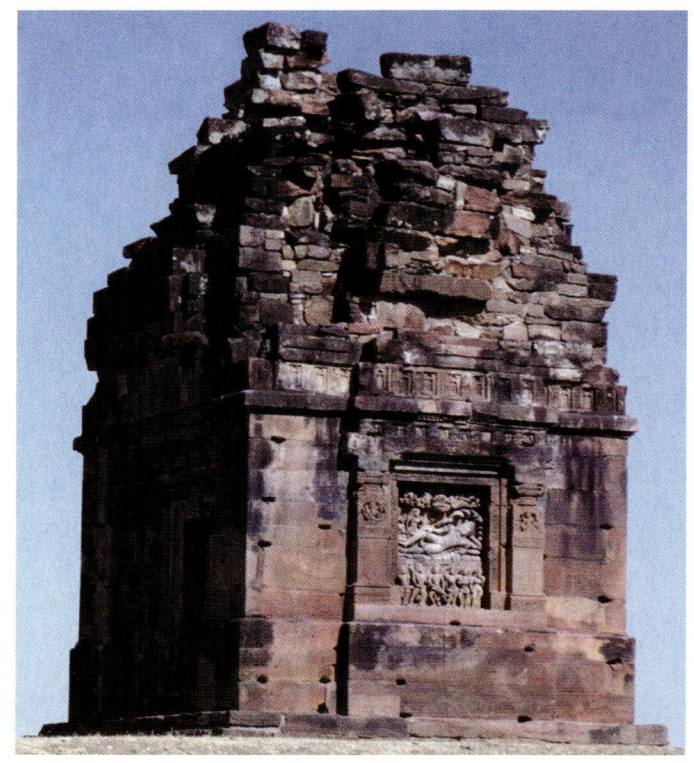

**6-18** Vishnu Temple, Deogarh, India, early sixth century.

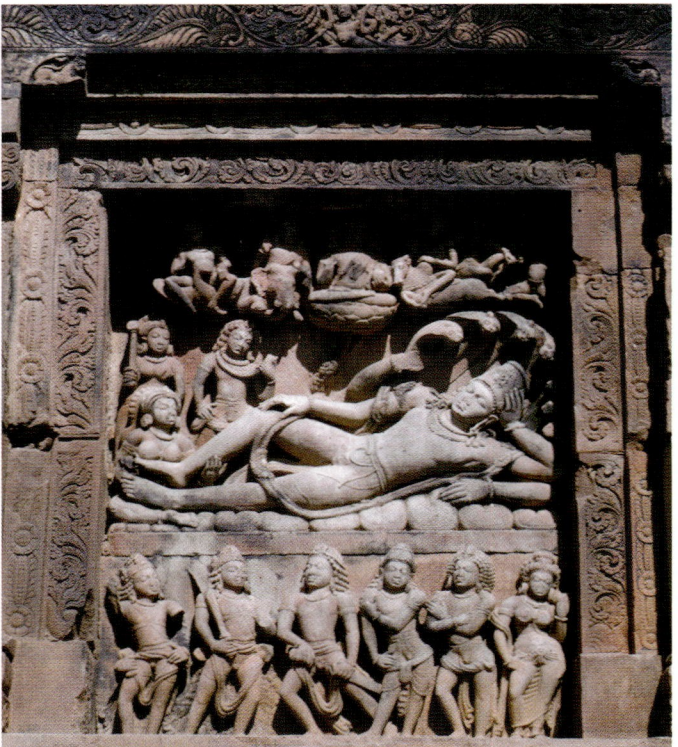

**6-19** Vishnu asleep on the serpent Ananta, detail of facade of the Vishnu Temple, Deogarh, India, early sixth century.

to have grown out of Vishnu's navel) supports the four-headed Hindu god of creation, Brahma. Flanking him are other important Hindu divinities, including Shiva on his bull. Below are six figures. The four at the right are personifications of Vishnu's various powers. They will defeat the two armed demons at the left. The sculptor carved all the figures in the classic Gupta style, with smooth bodies and clinging garments (compare FIG. 6-12).

## Early Medieval Period

During the several centuries corresponding to the early medieval period in western Europe (see Chapter 16), the early Islamic period in the Near East (see Chapter 13), the Tang and Song dynasties in China (see Chapter 7), and the Hakuho, Nara, and Heian periods in Japan (see Chapter 8), regional dynasties ruled parts of India. Among the most important of these kingdoms were the Palas and Chandellas in northern India and the Pallavas and Cholas in the south. Whereas Buddhism spread rapidly throughout eastern Asia, in medieval India it gradually declined, and the various local kings vied with one another to erect glorious shrines to the Hindu gods.

**TEMPLES CARVED FROM BOULDERS** In addition to cave temples and masonry temples, Indian architects created a third type of monument: freestanding temples carved out of rocky outcroppings. Such sculpted temples are rare. Some of the earliest and most impressive of these monolithic temples (FIG. **6-20**) are

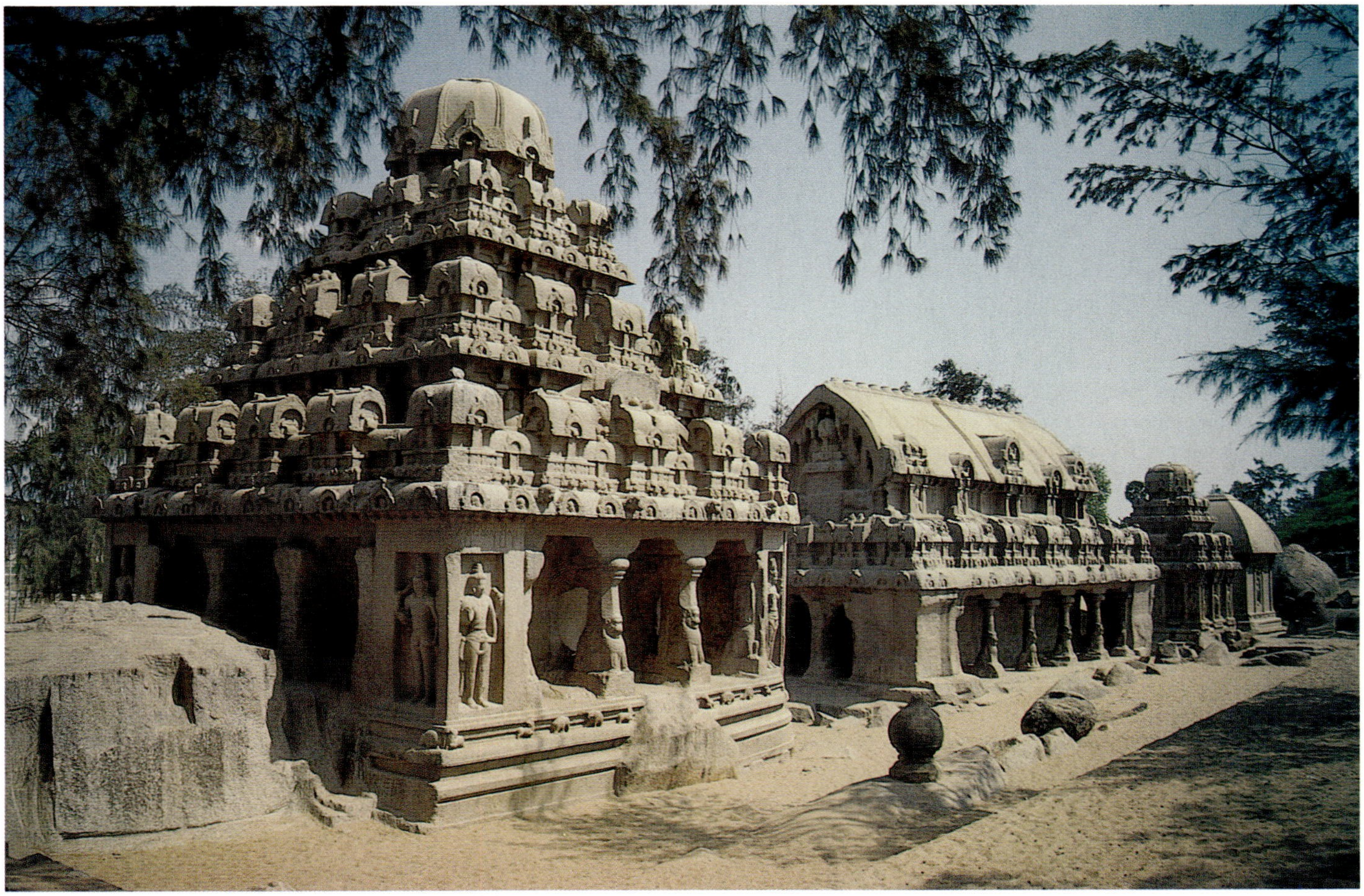

**6-20** Rock-cut temples, Mamallapuram, India, second half of seventh century. From *left* to *right:* Dharmaraja, Bhima, Arjuna, and Draupadi rathas.

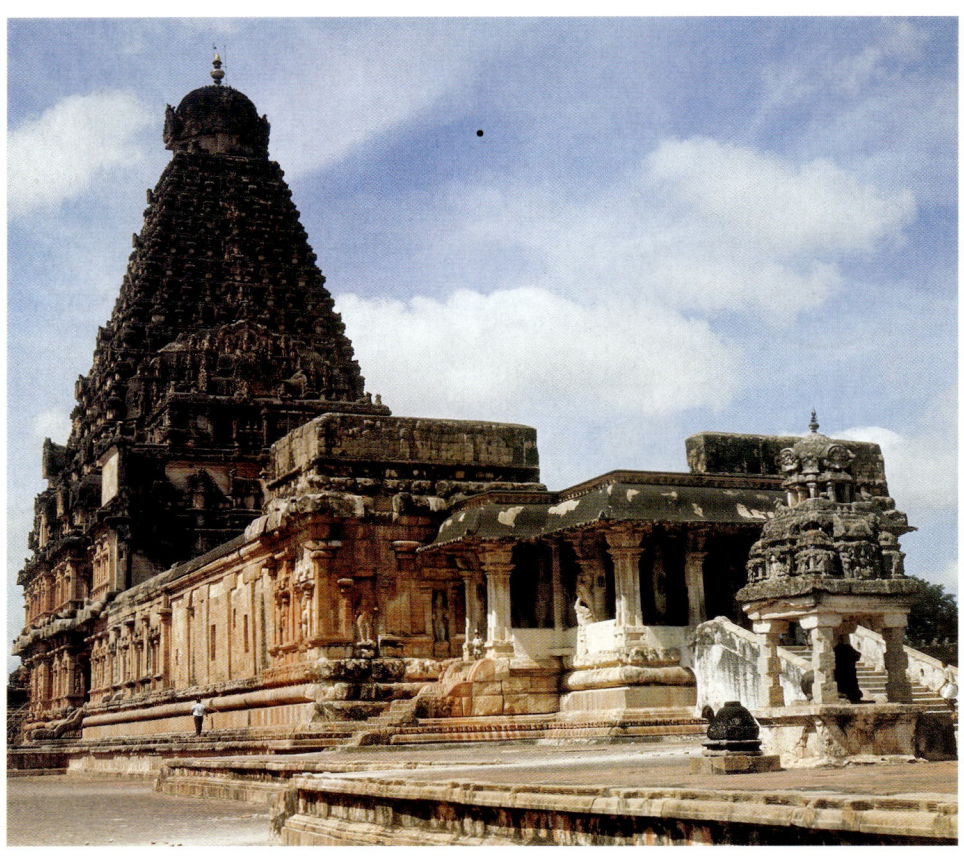

**6-21** Rajarajeshvara Temple, Thanjavur, India, ca. 1010.

at Mamallapuram, south of Madras on the Bay of Bengal, where they are called *rathas,* or "chariots" (that is, vehicles of the gods). In the late seventh century, the Pallava dynasty had five rathas carved out of a single huge granite boulder jutting out from the sand. The group is of special interest because it illustrates the variety of temple forms at this period, based on earlier wooden structures, before a standard masonry type of temple became the rule in southern India. The largest Mamallapuram ratha, the Dharmaraja (in the foreground), dedicated to Shiva, is an early example of the typical southern-style temple with stepped-pyramid vimana (see "Hindu Temples," page 180). The tower ascends in pronounced tiers of cornices decorated with miniature shrines. The lower walls include carved columns and figures of deities inside niches. The Bhima ratha to the right, dedicated to Vishnu, has a rectangular plan and a rounded roof; the next ratha, the Arjuna, is a smaller example of the southern Indian type. At the end of the row sits the very small Draupadi ratha, which was modeled on a thatched hut and is dedicated to Durga, a form of the goddess Devi. The two largest temples were never finished.

**THE APOGEE OF THE SOUTHERN TEMPLE** Under the Cholas, whose territories extended into part of Sri Lanka and even Java, architects constructed temples of unprecedented size and grandeur in the southern Indian tradition. The Rajarajeshvara Temple at Thanjavur (FIG. **6-21**), dedicated in 1010 to Shiva as the lord of Rajaraja, was the largest and tallest temple (210 feet high) in India at its time. The temple stands inside a walled precinct. It consists of a stairway leading to two flat-roofed mandapas, the larger one having 36 pillars, and to the garbha griha in the base of the enormous pyramidal vimana that is as much an emblem of the Cholas' secular power as of their devotion to Shiva. On the exterior walls of the lower stories are numerous reliefs in niches depicting the god in his various forms.

**THE HINDU TEMPLE AS MOUNTAIN** At the same time the Cholas were building the Rajarajeshvara Temple at Thanjavur in the south, the Chandella dynasty was constructing temples—in northern style—at Khajuraho. The Vishvanatha Temple (FIG. **6-22**) is one of more than 20 large and elaborate temples at that site. Vishvanatha ("Lord of the Universe") is another of the many names for Shiva. Dedicated in 1002, the structure has three towers over the mandapas, each rising higher than the preceding one, leading to the tallest tower at the rear, in much the same way the foothills of the Himalayas, Shiva's home, rise to meet their highest peak. The mountain symbolism applies to the interior of the Vishvanatha Temple as well. Under the tallest of the towers, the shikhara, is the garbha griha, the small and dark inner sanctuary chamber, like a cave, which houses the image of the deity. Thus, temples such as the Vishvanatha symbolize constructed mountains with caves, comparable to the actual cave temples at Elephanta and other Indian sites. In all cases, the deity manifests himself or herself within the cave and takes various forms in sculptures. The temple mountains, however, are not intended to appear natural but rather are perfect mountains designed using ideal mathematical proportions.

**THE MITHUNAS OF KHAJURAHO** The reliefs of the Rajarajeshvara Temple at Thanjavur (FIG. 6-21) are typical of southern temple decoration, which is generally limited to images of deities. The exterior walls of Khajuraho's Vishvanatha Temple are equally typical of northern temples in the profusion of sculptures depicting not only gods but mortals, especially pairs of men and women (mithunas) embracing or engaged in sexual intercourse in an extraordinary range of positions (FIG. **6-23**). The use of seminude yakshis and amorous couples as motifs on religious buildings in India has a very long history, going back to the earliest architectural traditions, both Hindu and Buddhist (Sanchi, FIG. 6-7, and

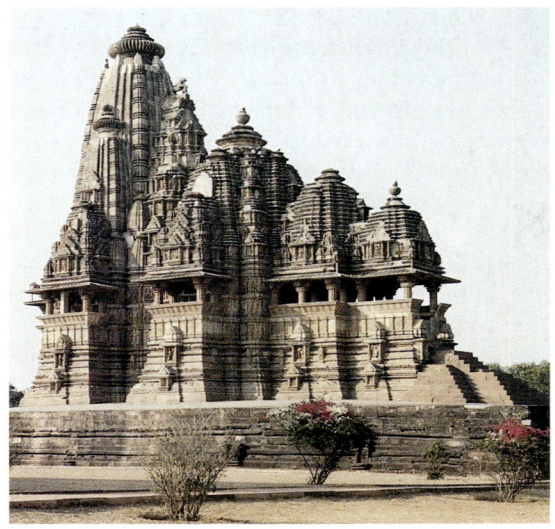

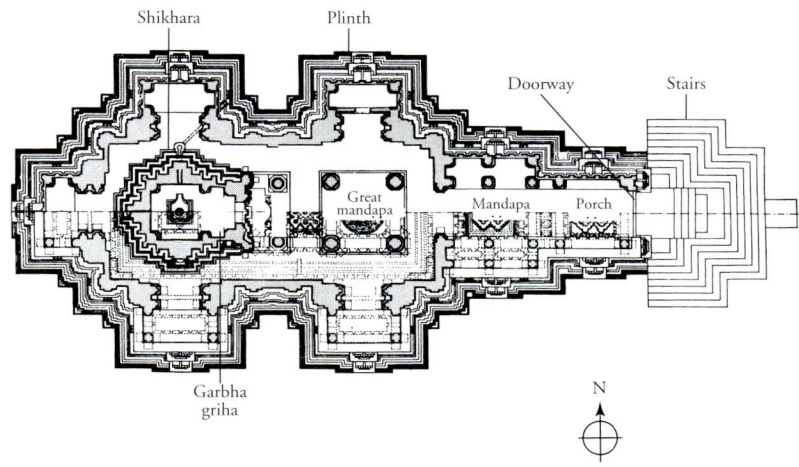

Shikhara  Plinth

Doorway  Stairs

Great
mandapa  Mandapa  Porch

Garbha
griha

N

**6-22** Vishvanatha Temple, Khajuraho, India, ca. 1000. (View looking northwest and plan).

Karle). As in the earlier examples already discussed, the erotic sculptures of Khajuraho suggest fertility and the propagation of life and serve as auspicious protectors of the sacred precinct.

**A PORTABLE BRONZE SHIVA** We conclude our survey of early Indian art with an object quite different in function from anything considered thus far. The statuette of Shiva (FIG. **6-24**) in the Naltunai Ishvaram Temple in Punjai, cast in solid bronze around 1000, recalls the sixth-century relief in the Badami cave (FIG. 6-16). It is one of many examples of portable images of deities created under the Chola kings, the builders of the towering Rajarajeshvara Temple at Thanjavur (FIG. 6-21). Here, Shiva dances as Nataraja ("Lord of the Dance") by balancing on one leg atop a dwarf representing ignorance, which the god stamps out as he dances. Shiva extends all four arms, two of them touching the flaming *nimbus* (light of glory) encircling him. These two upper

hands also hold a small drum (at right) and a flame (at left). Shiva creates the universe to the drumbeat's rhythm, while the small fire represents destruction. His lower left hand points to his upraised foot, indicating the foot as the place where devotees can find refuge and enlightenment. Shiva's lower right hand, raised in the fear-not gesture, tells worshipers to come forward without fear. As Shiva spins, his matted hair comes loose and spreads like a fan on both sides of his head.

This Shiva Nataraja is a movable image (the holes on the base held poles for carrying the statuette), but even when stationary, it would not appear as it does in an art history book. Rather, when Hindus worship the Shiva Nataraja, they dress the image, cover it with jewels, and garland it with flowers. The only bronze part visible is the face, marked with colored powders and scented pastes. Considered the embodiment of the deity, the image is not a symbol of the god but the god itself. All must treat the god/image as a

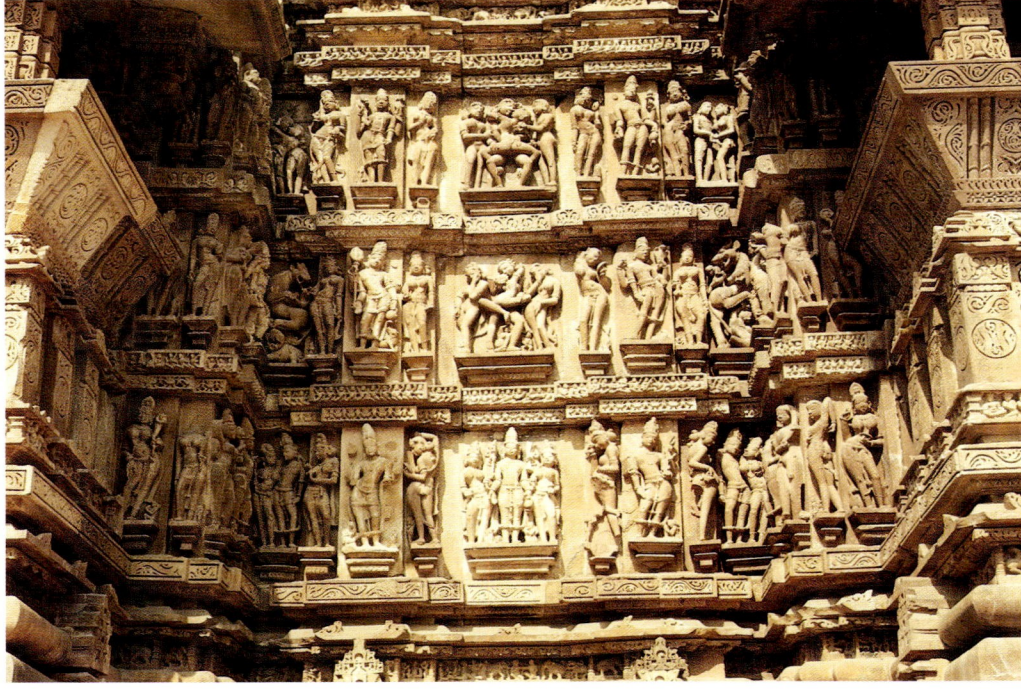

**6-23** Sculptures on temple wall, Vishvanatha Temple, Khajuraho, India, ca. 1000.

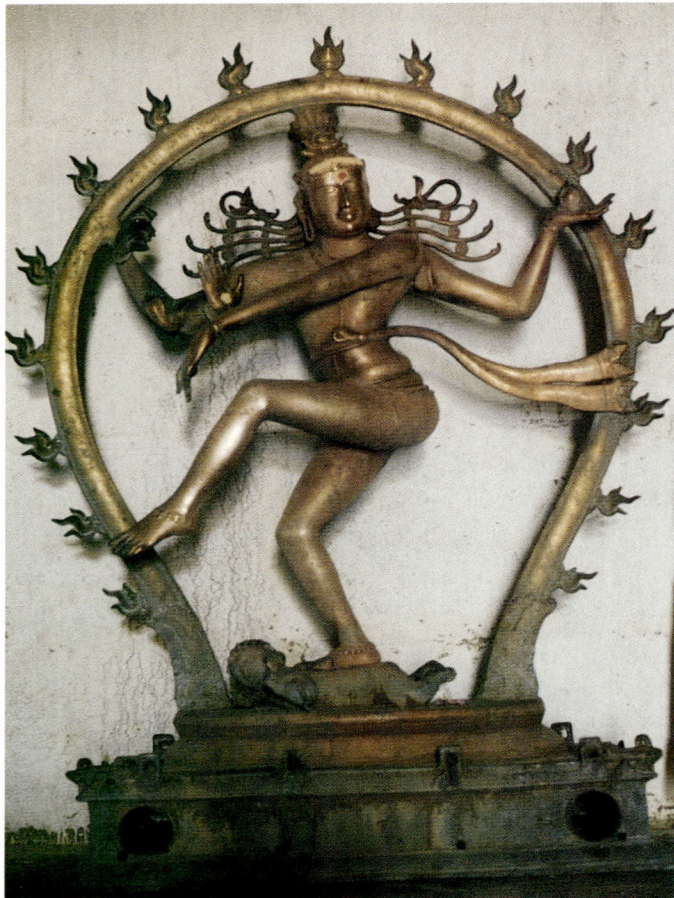

**6-24** Shiva as Nataraja, bronze in the Naltunai Ishvaram Temple, Punjai, India, ca. 1000.

living being. Worship of the deity involves taking care of him as if he were an honored person. Bathed, clothed, given foods to eat, and taken for outings, the image also receives such gifts as songs, lights (lit oil lamps), good smells (incense), and flowers—all things he can enjoy through the senses. The food given to the god is particularly important, as he eats the "essence," leaving the remainder for the worshiper. The food is then *prasada* (grace), sacred because it came in contact with the divine. In an especially religious household, the deity resides as an image and receives the food for each meal before the family eats. When the god resides in a temple, it is then the duty of the priests to feed, clothe, and take care of him.

The Chola dynasty ended in the 13th century, a time of political, religious, and cultural change in South Asia. At this point, Buddhism survived in only some areas of India. It soon died out completely there, although the late form of northern Indian Buddhism continued in Tibet and Nepal. At the same time, Islam, which had arrived in India as early as the eighth century, became a potent political force with the establishment of the Delhi Sultanate in 1206. Hindu and Islamic art assumed preeminent roles in India in the 13th century (see Chapter 25).

## SOUTHEAST ASIA

For scholars of earlier generations, much of the art of Southeast Asia was merely an extension of Indian civilization. Because the Indian character of many Southeast Asian monuments was readily apparent, some researchers hypothesized that Indian artists

had constructed and decorated them and that Indians had colonized Southeast Asia. Today, historians have concluded that such colonization did not occur. The cultural transfer during the first millennium CE was peaceful and nonimperialistic. It appears to have developed almost as a by-product of trade.

In the early centuries CE, extensive trade took place among Rome, India, and China, their ships passing Southeast Asia on the monsoon winds. The tribal chieftains of Southeast Asia quickly saw an opportunity to participate, mainly with their own forest products, such as aromatic woods, bird feathers, and spices. Accompanying the trade goods from India were Sanskrit, Buddhism, and Hinduism—and Buddhist and Hindu art. The Southeast Asian chiefs initially used the transferred elements as a sort of "cultural vocabulary" to compete with one another and to participate in an Indian world. But the Southeast Asian peoples soon modified the Indian cultural material, including the art, to make it their own. Art historians now recognize Southeast Asian art and architecture as a distinctive and important tradition.

### Sri Lanka

Sri Lanka (formerly Ceylon) is an island located at the very tip of the Indian subcontinent. Theravada Buddhism, the oldest form of Buddhism, stressing worship of the historical Buddha, Shakyamuni Buddha (see "Buddhism," page 171), arrived in Sri Lanka as early as the third century BCE. From there it spread to other parts of Southeast Asia. With the demise of Buddhism in India in about the 13th century, Sri Lanka now has the longest-lived Buddhist tradition in the world.

**GAL VIHARA'S GIANT BUDDHA** One of the largest sculptures in Southeast Asia is the 46-foot-long recumbent Buddha (FIG. **6-25**) carved out of a rocky outcropping at Gal Vihara in the 11th or 12th century. To the left of the Buddha, much smaller in scale, stands his cousin and chief disciple, Ananda, arms crossed, mourning Shakyamuni's death. Although more than half a millennium later in date, the Sri Lankan representation of the Buddha's parinirvana reveals its sculptor's debt to the classic Gupta sculptures of India, with their clinging garments, rounded faces, and distinctive renditions of hair (compare FIG. 6-12). Other Southeast Asian monuments, in contrast, exhibit a marked independence from Indian models.

### Java

**BOROBUDUR, COSMIC MOUNTAIN** On the island of Java, part of the modern nation of Indonesia, the period from the 8th to the 10th centuries witnessed the erection of both Hindu and Buddhist monuments. Borobudur (FIG. **6-26**), a Buddhist monument unique in both form and meaning, is the most impressive. Colossal in size, Borobudur measures about 400 feet per side at the base and about 98 feet tall. Built over a small hill on nine terraces accessed by four stairways aligned with the cardinal points, the structure contains literally millions of blocks of volcanic stone. Visitors ascending the massive monument on their way to the summit encounter more than 500 life-size Buddha images, at least 1,000 relief panels, and some 1,500 stupas of various sizes.

Scholars debate the intended meaning of Borobudur. Most think the structure is a constructed cosmic mountain, a three-dimensional mandala where worshipers pass through various realms on their way to ultimate enlightenment. As they

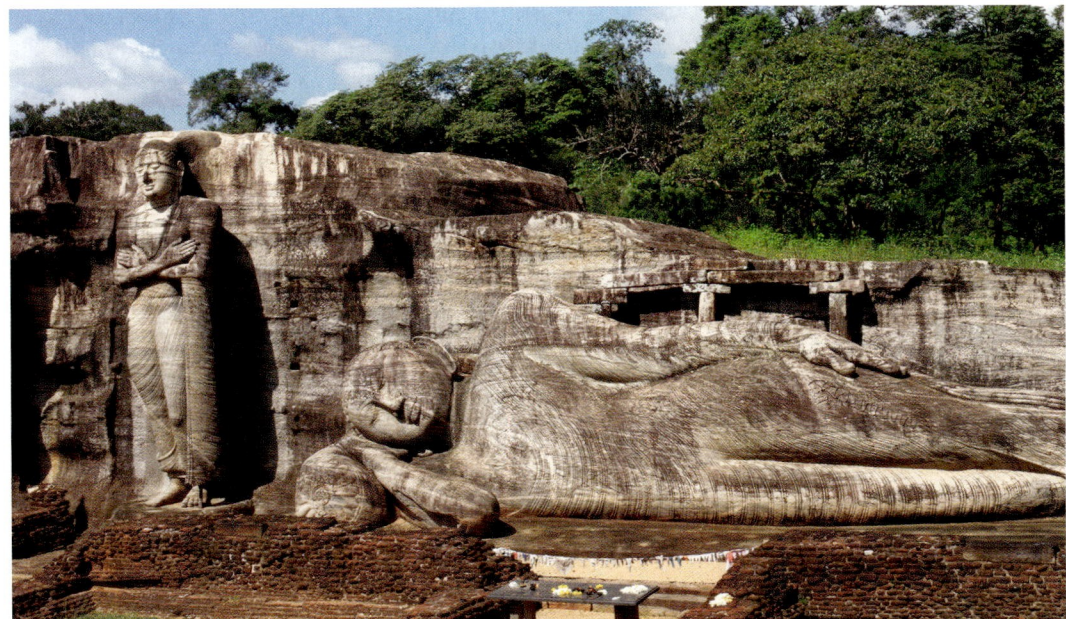

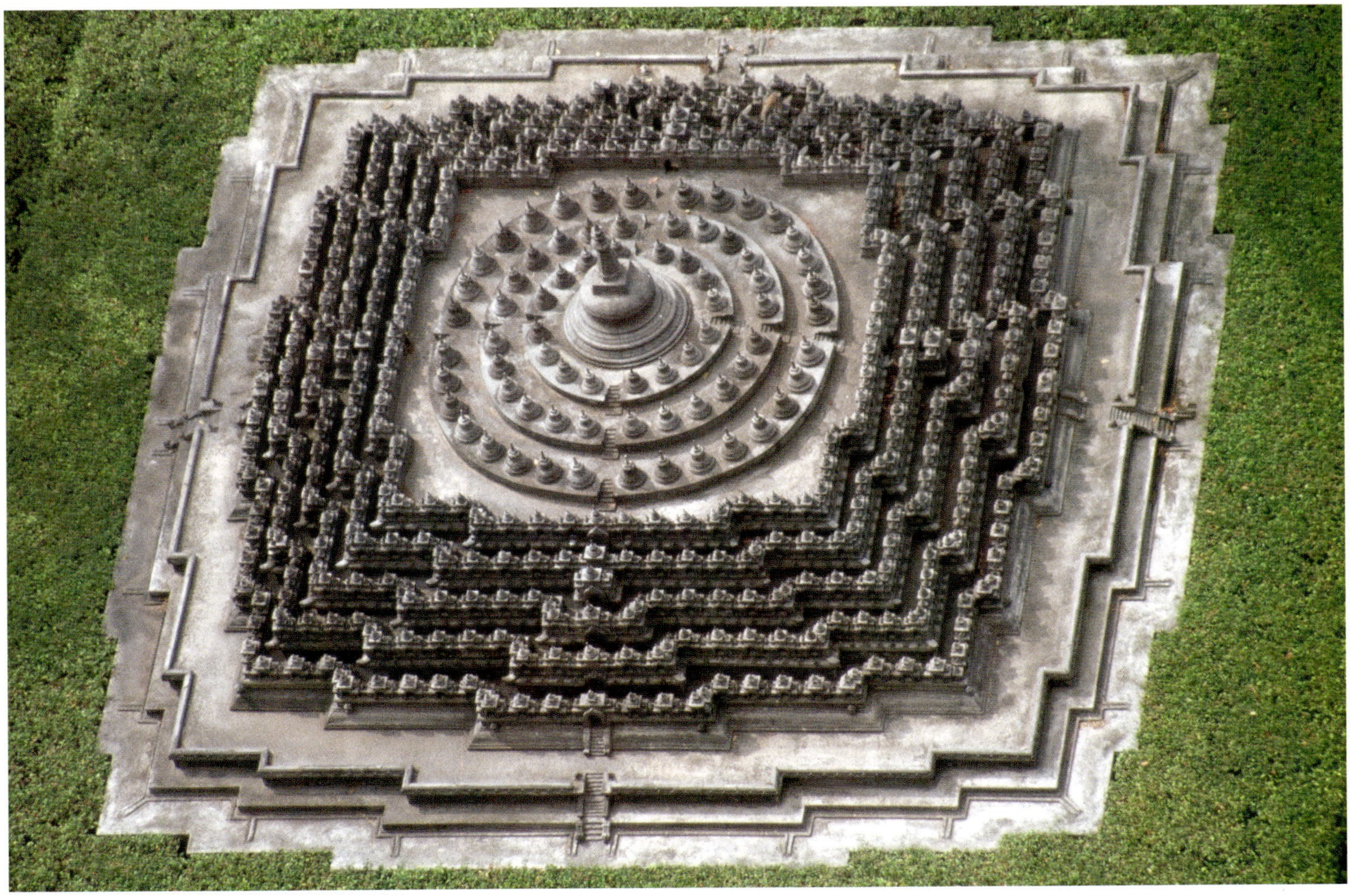

**6-26** Borobudur, Java, Indonesia, ca. 800.

circumambulate Borobudur, pilgrims first see reliefs illustrating the karmic effects of various kinds of human behavior, then reliefs depicting jatakas of the Buddha's earlier lives, and, further up, events from the life of Shakyamuni. On the circular terraces near the summit, each stupa is hollow and houses a statue of the seated Buddha, who has achieved spiritual enlightenment and preaches using the wheel-turning mudra. At the very top is the largest, sealed stupa. It may once have contained another Buddha image, but some think it was left empty to symbolize the formlessness of true enlightenment. Although scholars have interpreted the iconographic program in different ways, all agree on two essential points: the dependence of Borobudur on Indian art, literature, and religion, and the fact that nothing comparable exists in India itself. Borobudur's sophistication, complexity, and originality underline how completely Southeast Asians had absorbed, rethought, and reformulated Indian religion and art by 800.

## Cambodia

In 802, at about the same time the Javanese built Borobudur, the Khmer King Jayavarman II (r. 802–850) founded the Angkor dynasty, which ruled Cambodia for the next 400 years and sponsored the construction of hundreds of monuments. For at least two centuries before the founding of Angkor, the Khmer (the predominant ethnic group in Cambodia) produced Indian-related sculpture of exceptional quality. Images of Vishnu were particularly important during the pre-Angkorian period.

**HARIHARA: SHIVA-VISHNU** A statue (FIG. **6-27**) from Prasat Andet shows Vishnu in his manifestation as Harihara (Shiva-Vishnu). To represent Harihara, the sculptor divided the statue vertically, with Shiva on the god's right side, Vishnu on his left. The tall headgear reflects the division most clearly. The Shiva half, embellished with the winding locks of an ascetic, contrasts with the kingly Vishnu's plain miter. Attributes (now lost) held in the four hands also helped differentiate the two sides. Stylistically, the Cambodian statue, like the Sri Lankan parinirvana group (FIG. 6-25), derives from Indian sculptures of Gupta style (FIG. 6-12). But unlike almost all stone sculpture in India, carved in relief on slabs or steles, this Khmer image is in the round. The Harihara's broken arms and ankles vividly attest to the vulnerability of this format. The Khmer sculptors, however, wanted viewers to see their statues from all sides in the center of the garbha grihas of brick temples.

**VISHNU ON THE COSMIC OCEAN** The Khmer kings were exceedingly powerful and possessed enormous wealth. A now fragmentary statue portraying Vishnu lying on the cosmic ocean (FIG. **6-28**) testifies to both the luxurious nature of much Khmer art and to the mastery of Khmer bronze casters. The surviving portion is about 8 feet long. In complete form, at well over 20 feet long, the Vishnu statue was among the largest bronzes of the ancient and medieval worlds, surpassed only by such lost wonders as the statue of Athena in the Parthenon (FIG. 5-44) and the 120-foot-tall colossus of the Roman emperor Nero (see "An Imperial Pleasure Palace," Chapter 10, page 270). Originally, gold and silver inlays and jewels embellished the image, and the god wore a separate miter on his head. The subject of the gigantic statue is the same as that carved in stone on the early Vishnu temple at Deogarh (FIG. 6-19). Vishnu lies asleep on the cosmic ocean at the moment of the creation of the universe. In the myth, a lotus stem grows from Vishnu's navel, its flower supporting Brahma, the creator god. In this statue, Vishnu had a waterspout emerging from his navel, indicating his ability not only to protect the earth and create Brahma but also to create the waters. In fact, the statue was displayed in an island temple in the western *baray* (reservoir) of Angkor.

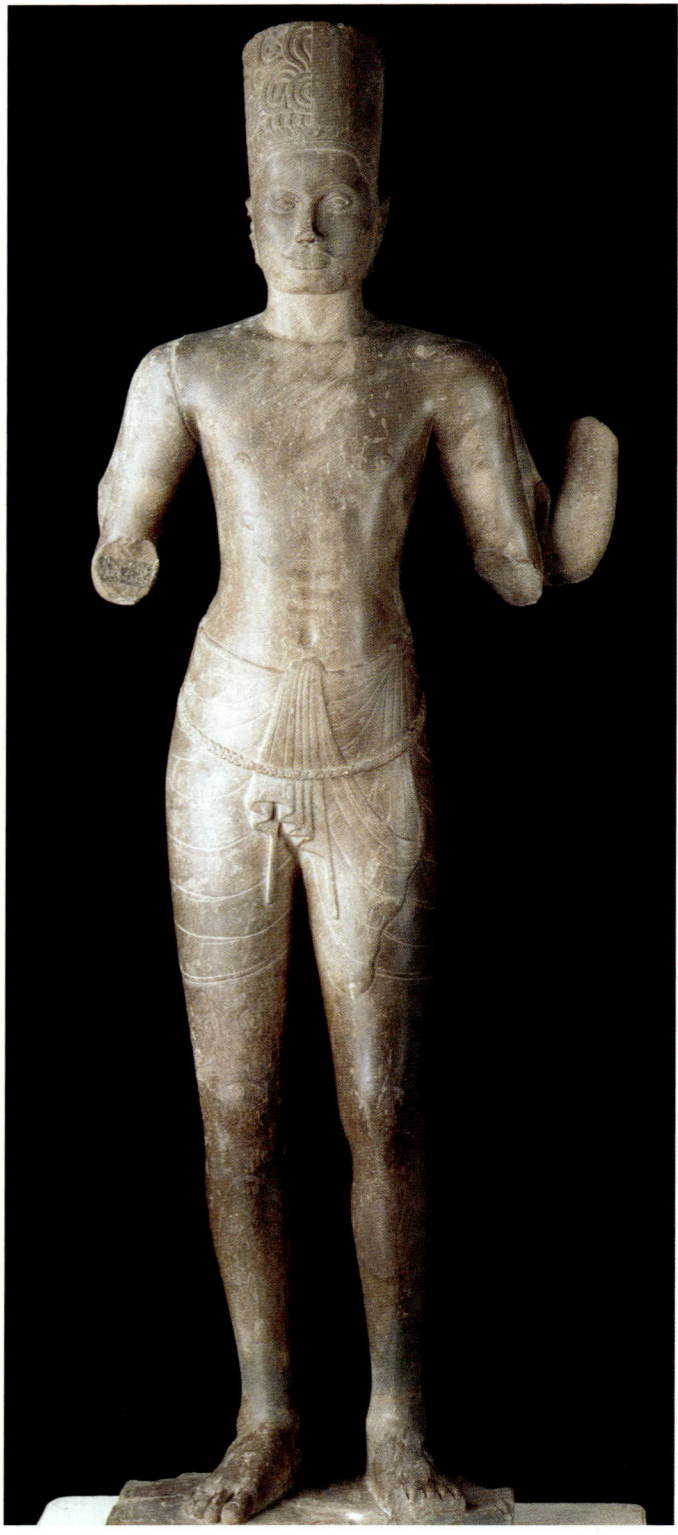

**6-27** Harihara, from Prasat Andet, Cambodia, early seventh century. Stone, 6′ 3″ high. National Museum, Phnom Penh.

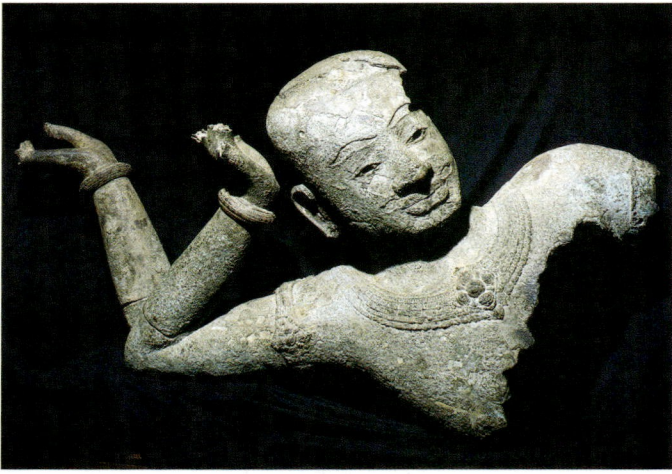

**6-28** Vishnu lying on the cosmic ocean, from Mebon temple on island in Western Baray, Angkor, Cambodia, 11th century. Bronze, approx. 8′ long.

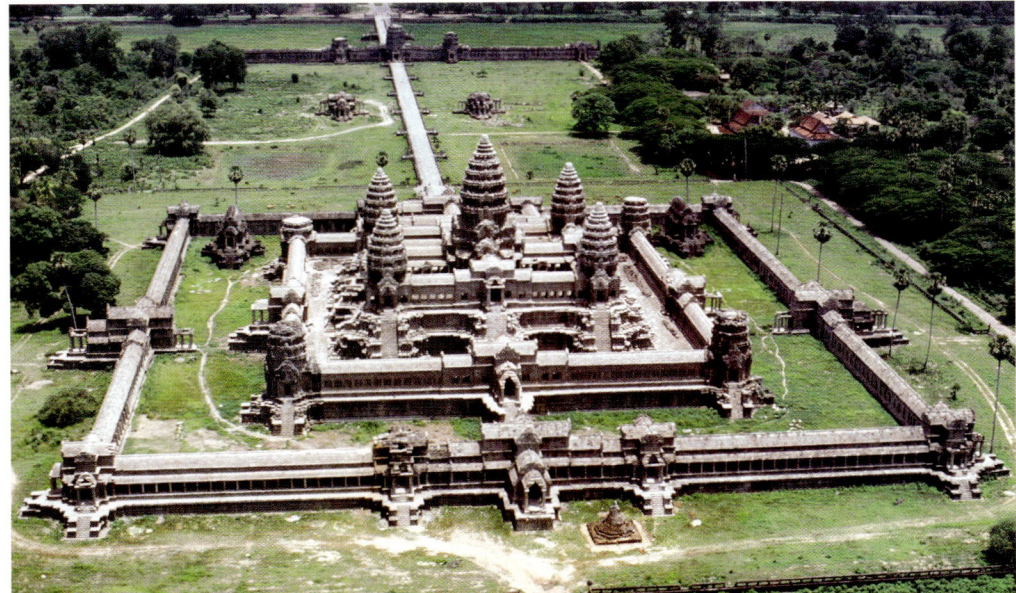

**KHMER KINGSHIP** For more than four centuries, successive kings worked on the construction of the site of Angkor. Founded by Indravarman (r. 877–889), Angkor is an engineering marvel, a grand complex of temples and palaces within a rectangular grid of canals and reservoirs fed by local rivers. Each of the Khmer kings built a temple mountain at Angkor and installed his personal god—Shiva, Vishnu, or the Buddha—on top. He named the image/god with part of his own royal name, implying that the king was a part or manifestation of the deity. When the king died, the Khmer believed that the god reabsorbed him, because he had been the earthly portion of the deity during his lifetime, so they worshiped the king's image posthumously as the god. This concept of kingship approaches an actual deification of the human ruler, familiar in many other societies, such as ancient Egypt (see Chapter 3).

**SURYAVARMAN II AND ANGKOR WAT** Of all the monuments the Khmer kings erected, Angkor Wat (FIG. **6-29**) is the most spectacular. Built by Suryavarman II (r. 1113–1150), it is the largest of the many Khmer temple complexes. Angkor Wat rises from a huge rectangle of land delineated by a moat measuring about 5,000 × 4,000 feet. Like the other Khmer temples, its purpose was to associate the king with his personal god, in this case Vishnu. The centerpiece of the complex is a tall stepped tower surrounded by four smaller towers connected by covered galleries. The five towers symbolize the five peaks of Mount Meru, the sacred mountain at the center of the universe. Two more circuit walls with galleries, towers, and gates enclose the central block. Thus, as one progresses inward through the complex, the towers rise ever higher, like the towers of the Vishvanatha Temple at Khajuraho (FIG. 6-22), but in a more complex sequence and on a much grander scale.

Throughout Angkor Wat, stone reliefs glorify both Vishnu in his various avatars and Suryavarman II. The example we illustrate (FIG. **6-30**), on the inner wall of the lowest gallery, shows the king holding court. Suryavarman II sits on an elaborate wooden throne, its

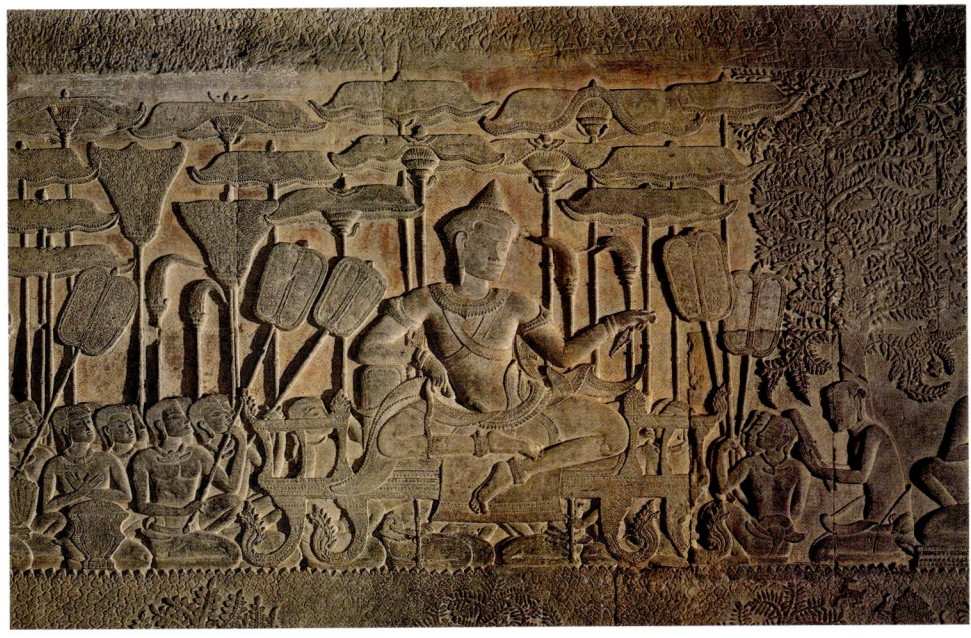

**6-30** King Suryavarman II holding court, lowest gallery, south side, Angkor Wat, Angkor, Cambodia, first half of 12th century. Stone.

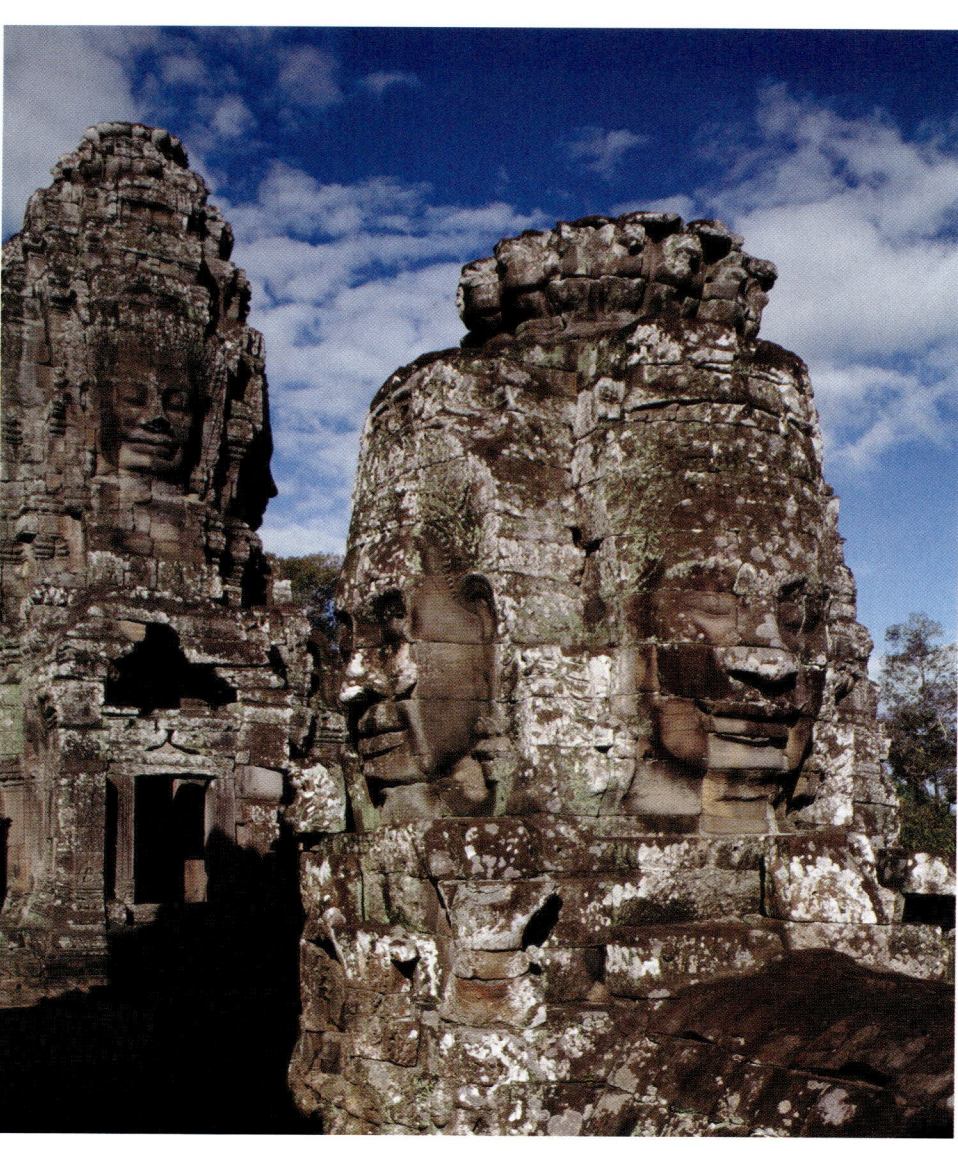

**6-31** Bayon, Angkor Thom, Cambodia, ca. 1200.

bronze legs rising as cobra heads. Kneeling retainers, smaller than the king because they are lesser figures in the Khmer hierarchy, hold a forest of umbrellas and fans, emblems of Suryavarman's exalted rank. In the reliefs of Angkor Wat, religion and politics are united.

**JAYAVARMAN VII AND THE BAYON** Jayavarman VII (r. 1181–1219), Suryavarman II's son, ruled over much of mainland Southeast Asia and built more during his reign than all the Khmer kings preceding him combined. His most important temple, the Bayon, is a complicated monument constructed with unique circular terraces surmounted by towers carved with giant faces (FIG. **6-31**). Jayavarman turned to Buddhism from the Hinduism embraced by the earlier Khmer rulers, but adapted Buddhism so that the Buddha and the bodhisattva Lokeshvara ("Lord of the World") were seen as divine prototypes of the king, in the Khmer tradition. The faces on the Bayon towers perhaps portray Lokeshvara, intended to indicate the watchful compassion emanating in all directions from the capital. Other researchers have proposed that the faces depict Jayavarman himself. Jayavarman's great experiment in religion and art was short-lived, but it also marked the point of change in Southeast Asia when Theravada Buddhism began to dominate most of the mainland.

## CONCLUSION

The Indian subcontinent was the birthplace of Buddhism and Hinduism as well as one of the world's earliest civilizations. Third-millennium BCE sites in the Indus Valley feature monumental architecture and sophisticated water supply and sewage systems. Surviving art objects are few and small, however. The first large-scale sculpture and the first temples in South Asia appeared in connection with the spread of Buddhism at the end of the first millennium BCE. Hindu art and architecture emerged in the mid-first millennium CE. Hindu temples, with their distinctive beehive or pyramidal towers, often covered with elaborate relief sculptures, were built throughout the subcontinent. From India, Buddhist and Hindu art and architecture were exported throughout Southeast Asia.

During the first to fourth centuries, Buddhism also traveled to other parts of Asia—to China, Korea, and Japan. Although the artistic traditions in these countries differ greatly from one another, they share, along with Southeast Asia, a tradition of Buddhist art and an ultimate tie with India. Chapters 7 and 8 trace the changes Buddhist art underwent in East Asia, along with the region's other rich artistic traditions.

| INDIA AND PAKISTAN | SOUTHEAST ASIA | | |
|---|---|---|---|

**INDUS CIVILIZATION**

**2600 BCE**

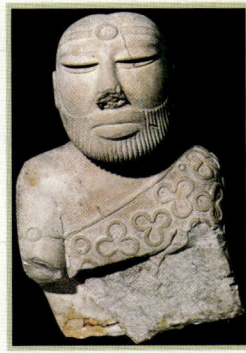

**1500 BCE**

**VEDIC AND UPANISHADIC PERIODS**

- ARYANS compile first of four *Vedas*, CA. 1500 BCE
- *Upanishads* composed, CA. 800–500 BCE
- SIDDHARTHA GAUTAMA, SHAKYAMUNI BUDDHA, CA. 563–483 BCE
- ALEXANDER THE GREAT reaches INDUS RIVER, 326 BCE

**1** Robed male figure, Mohenjo-daro, Pakistan, ca. 2600–1900 BCE

**323 BCE**

**MAURYA DYNASTY**

- CHANDRAGUPTA MAURYA, R. 323–298 BCE
- **2** ASHOKA, MAURYA KING, R. 272–231 BCE

**185 BCE**

**SHUNGA, ANDHRA, AND KUSHAN DYNASTIES**

- SHUNGA DYNASTY, CENTRAL INDIA, 185–72 BCE
- ANDHRA DYNASTY, SOUTHERN INDIA, CA. 50–320 CE
- KUSHAN DYNASTY, NORTHERN INDIA, CA. 50–320 CE
- KANISHKA, KUSHAN KING, R. 78–144 CE

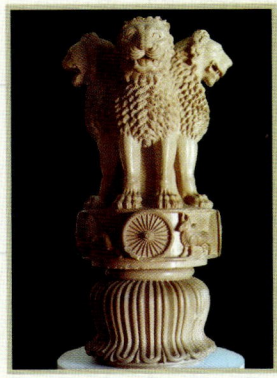

**2** Lion capital of Ashoka, Sarnath, India, ca. 250 BCE

**320 CE**

**GUPTA AND POST-GUPTA PERIODS**

- CHANDRAGUPTA II, GUPTA KING, R. 375–415
- **3** HARISHENA, VAKATAKA KING, R. 462–481
- CHALUKYA DYNASTY, CENTRAL INDIA, 543–743 AND CA. 975–1189
- PALLAVA DYNASTY, SOUTHERN INDIA, CA. 550–728

**647**

- PALA AND SENA DYNASTIES, NORTHERN INDIA, CA. 700–1200
- CHANDELLA DYNASTY, NORTHERN INDIA, 800–1308

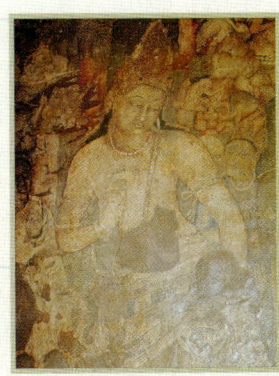

**802**

**MEDIEVAL PERIOD** / **ANGKOR DYNASTY, CAMBODIA**

- JAYAVARMAN II, ANGKOR KING, R. 802–850
- INDRAVARMAN, ANGKOR KING, R. 877–889
- **4** CHOLA DYNASTY, SOUTHERN INDIA, CA. 907–1279
- SURYAVARMAN II, ANGKOR KING, R. 1113–1150

**3** Bodhisattva Padmapani, Ajanta, India, second half of fifth century

**1200**

- MUSLIM SULTANATE, DELHI, 1206

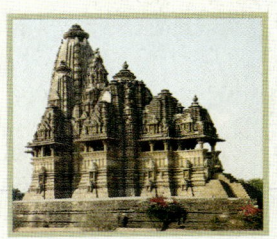

**4** Vishvanatha Temple, Khajuraho, India, ca. 1000

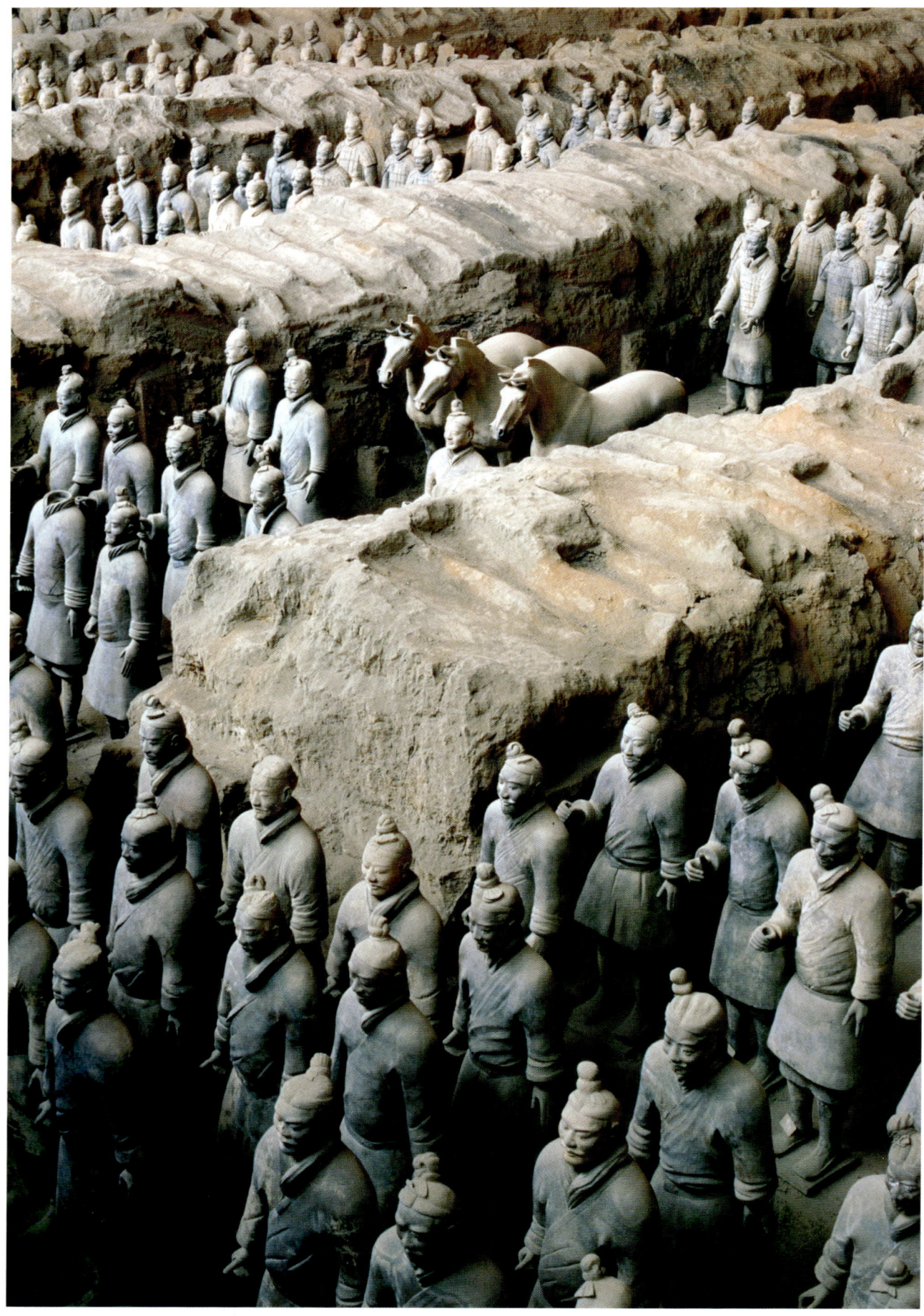

Army of the First Emperor of Qin in pits next to his burial mound, Lintong, China, Qin dynasty, ca. 210 BCE. Painted terracotta, average figure 5′ $10\frac{7}{8}$″ high.

# 7

# THE SILK ROAD AND BEYOND

## THE ART OF EARLY CHINA AND KOREA

East Asia is a vast area, varied both topographically and climatically. Dominated by the huge land mass of China, the region also encompasses the peninsula of Korea and the islands of Japan. In this chapter, we examine the early arts of China and Korea. Early Japanese art and architecture are treated in Chapter 8. Later developments in China and Korea and in Japan are discussed in Chapters 26 and 27.

## CHINA

China's landscape includes sandy plains, mighty rivers, towering mountains, and fertile farmlands (MAP 7-1). Its political and cultural boundaries have varied over the millennia and at times have grown to about twice the area of the United States, encompassing Tibet, Chinese Turkestan (Xinjiang), Mongolia, Manchuria, and parts of Korea. China boasts the world's largest population and is ethnically diverse. The spoken language varies so much that speakers of different dialects do not understand one another. However, the written language, which employs *characters* (signs that record meaning rather than sounds), has permitted different peoples living thousands of miles apart to share literary, philosophic, and religious traditions.

### Neolithic China

China is the only continuing civilization that originated in the ancient world. The Chinese archaeological record, extraordinarily rich, goes back to Neolithic times. Discoveries in recent years have expanded the early record enormously. They have provided evidence of settled village life as far back as the seventh or early sixth millennium BCE. Excavators have uncovered sites with large multifamily houses constructed of wood, bamboo, wattle, daub, and mud plaster, and equipped with hearths. These early villages also had pens for domesticated animals, kilns for pottery production, pits

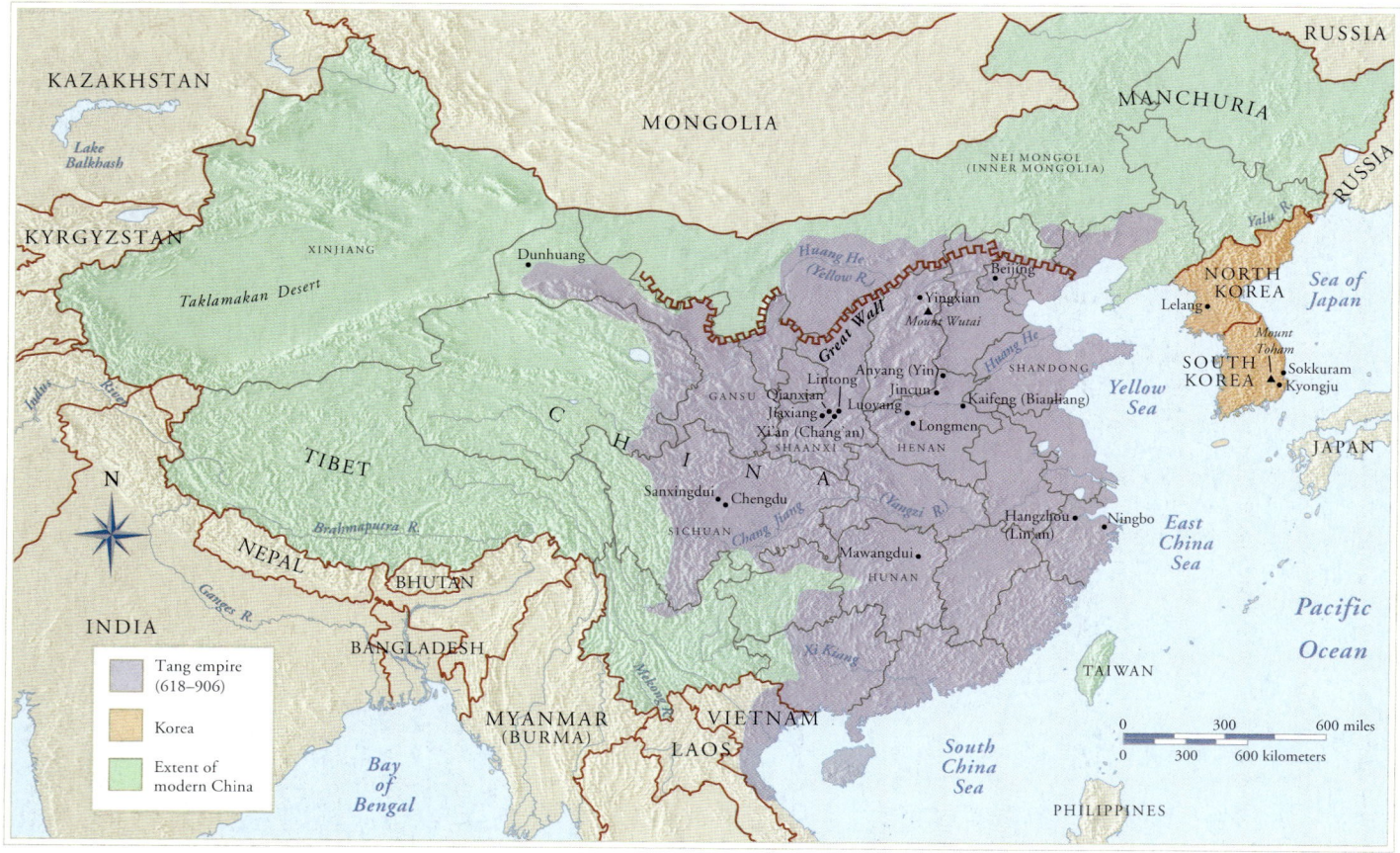

**MAP 7-1** China and Korea.

for storage and refuse, and cemeteries for the dead. Chinese Neolithic artisans produced impressive artworks, especially from jade and clay.

**YANGSHAO POTTERY** Mastery of the art of pottery occurred at a very early date in China. The potters of the Yangshao Culture, which arose along the Yellow River in northeastern China, produced fine decorated *earthenware* bowls (see "Chinese Earthenwares and Stonewares," page 193) even before the invention of the potter's wheel in the fourth millennium BCE. In the third millennium, the Yangshao potters of Gansu Province manufactured painted vessels (FIG. **7-1**) of astonishing sophistication. The multiplicity of shapes suggests that the vessels served a wide variety of functions in daily life, but most of the finds come from graves. Decoration is in red and brownish black on a cream-colored ground. Some pots and bowls have stylized animal motifs, but most feature abstract designs. The painters reveal a highly refined aesthetic sensibility, effectively integrating a variety of angular and curvilinear geometric motifs, including stripes, zigzags, lozenges, circles, spirals, and waves.

## Shang Dynasty

During the past century, China's earliest royal dynasties, long thought to have been mythical, have begun to be confirmed archaeologically. Most recently, excavators have found what they believe to be traces of the Xia (ca. 2000–1600 BCE), China's oldest dynasty. Much better documented, however, is the Shang dynasty (ca. 1600–1050 BCE), the first great Chinese dynasty of the

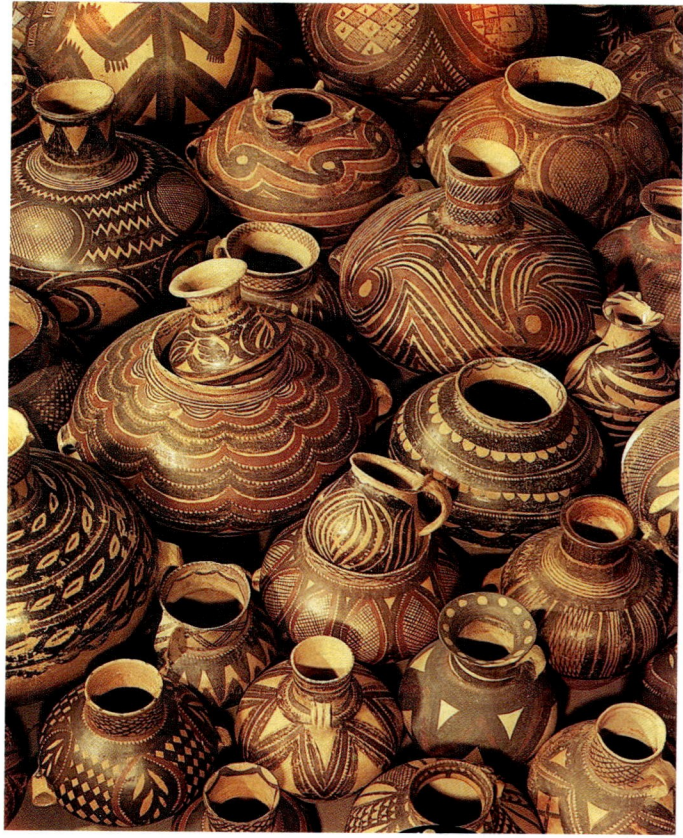

**7-1** Yangshao Culture vases, from Gansu Province, China, mid-third millennium BCE. Earthenware.

### Chinese Earthenwares and Stonewares

China has no rival in the combined length and richness of its ceramic history. Beginning with the makers of the earliest pots in prehistoric villages, ancient Chinese potters showed a flair for shaping carefully prepared and kneaded clay into diverse, often dramatic and elegant vessel forms.

Until Chinese potters developed true *porcelains* (extremely fine, hard white ceramics; see "Chinese Porcelain," Chapter 26, page 767) in about 1300 CE, they produced only two types of clay vessels or objects—earthenwares and stonewares. For both types, potters used clays colored by mineral impurities, especially iron compounds ranging from yellow to brownish black.

The clay bodies of *earthenwares* (FIG. 7-1), fired at low temperatures in open pits or simple kilns, remain soft and porous, thus allowing liquids to seep through. Chinese artists also used the low-fire technique to produce terracotta sculptures, even life-size figures of humans and animals (FIG. 7-5). Over time, Chinese potters developed kilns allowing them to fire their clay vessels at much higher temperatures—more than 2000° Fahrenheit. Such temperatures produce *stonewares,* named for their stonelike hardness and density.

Potters in China excelled at the various techniques commonly used to decorate earthenwares and stonewares. Most of these decorative methods depend on changes occurring in the kiln to chemical compounds found in clay as natural impurities. When fired, many compounds change color dramatically, depending on the conditions in the kiln. For example, if little oxygen remains in a hot kiln, iron oxide (rust) turns either gray or brownish black, whereas an abundance of oxygen produces a reddish hue.

Chinese potters also decorated vessels simply by painting their surfaces. In one of the oldest decorative techniques, the potters applied *slip* (a mixture of clay and water like a fine, thin mud)—by painting, pouring, or dipping—to a clay body not yet fully dry. The natural variety of clay colors produced a broad, if not bright, palette, as seen in Neolithic vessels (FIG. 7-1). But Chinese potters often also added compounds such as iron oxide to the slip to change or intensify the colors. After the vessels had partially dried, the potters could incise lines through the slip down to the clay body to produce designs such as those often seen in later Chinese stonewares (FIG. 7-20).

The slip technique compares with that used by Archaic Greek black-figure painters (see FIGS. 5-4, 5-18, and 5-19). Chinese artists sometimes inlaid designs, too, carving them into plain vessel surfaces and then filling them with slip or soft clay of a contrasting color. Such techniques spread throughout East Asia (FIG. 7-28).

To produce a hard, glassy surface after firing, potters coated plain or decorated vessels with a *glaze,* a finely ground mixture of minerals. Clear or highly translucent glazes best reveal decorated surfaces. More opaque, richly colored glazes (FIG. 7-17) serve as primary decoration.

---

Bronze Age. The Shang kings ruled from a series of royal capitals in the Yellow River valley and vied for power and territory with the rulers of neighboring states.

**ROYAL BURIALS AT ANYANG** In 1928, excavations at Anyang (ancient Yin) brought to light the last Shang capital. There, archaeologists found a large number of objects—turtle shells, animal bones, and bronze containers—inscribed in the earliest form of the Chinese language. These fragmentary records and the other finds at Anyang provide important information about the Shang kings and their affairs. They reveal a warlike, highly stratified society. Walls of pounded earth protected Shang cities. Servants, captives, and even teams of charioteers with chariots and horses accompanied Shang kings to their tombs, a practice noted earlier with regard to the Royal Cemetery at Ur (see Chapter 2). The excavated tomb furnishings include weapons and a great wealth of objects in jade, ivory, lacquer, and bronze. Not only the kings received lavish burials. The tomb of Fu Hao, the wife of Wu Ding (r. ca. 1215–1190 BCE), for example, contained more than a thousand bronze and jade objects, as well as an ivory beaker inlaid with turquoise.

**SHANG BRONZES** Shang artists perfected the casting of elaborate bronze vessels in piece molds (see "Shang Bronze-Casting," page 194). Many of these vessels were used in sacrifices to ancestors and in funerary ceremonies. Shang bronzes held wine, water, grain, or meat for sacrificial rites. Each vessel's shape matched its intended purpose. One of the most dramatic Shang vessel forms is the *guang* (FIG. 7-2), a libation vessel shaped like a covered gravy boat. Preserved examples display the characteristic Shang decorative vocabulary of abstract and animal motifs. These range from

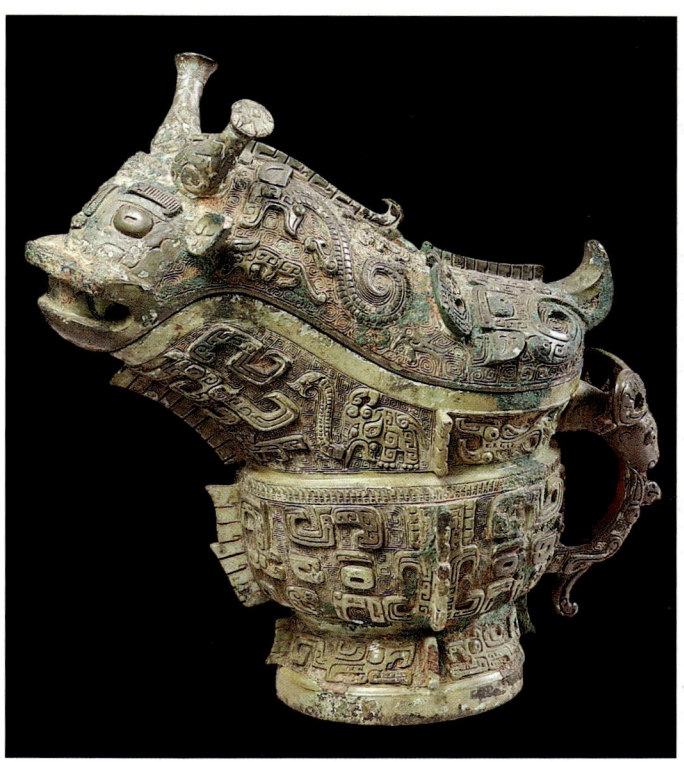

**7-2** Guang, probably from Anyang, China, Shang dynasty, 12th or 11th century BCE. Bronze, $6\frac{1}{2}''$ high. Asian Art Museum of San Francisco (Avery Brundage Collection).

## Shang Bronze-Casting

Among the finest bronzes of the second millennium BCE are those that Shang artists created using piece molds (FIG. 7-2). The Shang bronzeworkers began the process by producing a solid clay model of the desired object and allowing it to dry to durable hardness. Then they pressed damp clay around it to form a mold that hardened but remained somewhat flexible. At that point, they carefully cut the mold in pieces, removed the pieces from the model, and baked the pieces in a kiln to form hard earthenware sections. Sculptors then carved the intricate details of the relief decoration into the inner surfaces of the piece molds. Next, the artists shaved the model to reduce its size to form a core for the piece mold. They then reassembled the mold around the model using bronze spacers to preserve a void between the model and the mold—a space equivalent to the layer of wax used in the lost-wax method (see "Hollow-Casting Life-Size Bronze Statues," Chapter 5, page 131). The Shang bronze casters then added a final clay layer on the outside to hold everything together, leaving open ducts for pouring molten bronze into the space between the model and the mold and to permit gases to escape. Once the mold cooled, they broke it apart, removed the new bronze vessel, and cleaned and polished it.

Shang bronzes show a skill in casting rivaling that of any other ancient civilization and indicating a long developmental period for achieving such mastery. The great numbers of cast-bronze vessels strongly suggest well-organized workshops, but no records provide a clear picture of such matters or of the place the artists held in their society. Bronze-casting may have been a hereditary occupation.

mere suggestions of animal forms emerging out of linear patterns to identifiable representations of specific creatures. Often, distinct motifs stand out against a background of round or squared spirals ending in hooks. Sometimes the same motifs also cover the figures.

In the Shang guang we illustrate (FIG. 7-2), the multiple designs and their fields of background spirals integrate so closely with the form of the vessel that they are not merely an external embellishment but an integral part of the sculptural whole. Some motifs on the vessel's side may represent the eyes of a tiger and the horns of a ram. A horned animal forms the front of the lid, and at the rear is a horned head with a bird's beak. Another horned head appears on the handle. Fish, birds, elephants, rabbits, and more abstract composite creatures swarm over the surface against a background of spirals. The fabulous animal forms, real and imaginary, are unlikely to have been purely decorative. They are probably connected with the world of spirits addressed in the rituals.

**SURPRISING SANXINGDUI** Recent excavations in other regions of China have greatly expanded historical understanding of the Bronze Age. They suggest that at the same time Anyang flourished under its Shang rulers in northern China, so did other major centers with distinct aesthetic traditions. For example, in 1986, pits at Sanxingdui, near Chengdu in southwestern China, yielded a treasure of elephant tusks and objects in gold, bronze, jade, and clay of types never before discovered. They attest to an independent kingdom of enormous wealth contemporary with the better-known Shang dynasty.

The most dramatic find, a bronze statue (FIG. **7-3**) more than eight feet tall, matches anything from Anyang in masterful casting technique. Very different in subject and style from the Shang bronzes, it initially shocked art historians who had formed their ideas about Bronze Age Chinese aesthetics based on Shang material. This figure—of unknown identity—is highly stylized, with elongated proportions and large, staring eyes. It stands on a thin platform supported by four legs formed of fantastic animal heads with horns and trunklike snouts. These, in turn, rest on a thick, heavy square base. The statue as a whole tapers gently as it rises, and the figure gradually becomes rounder. Just below the neck, great arms branch dramatically outward, ending in oversized hands that once held an object, perhaps an attribute revealing its

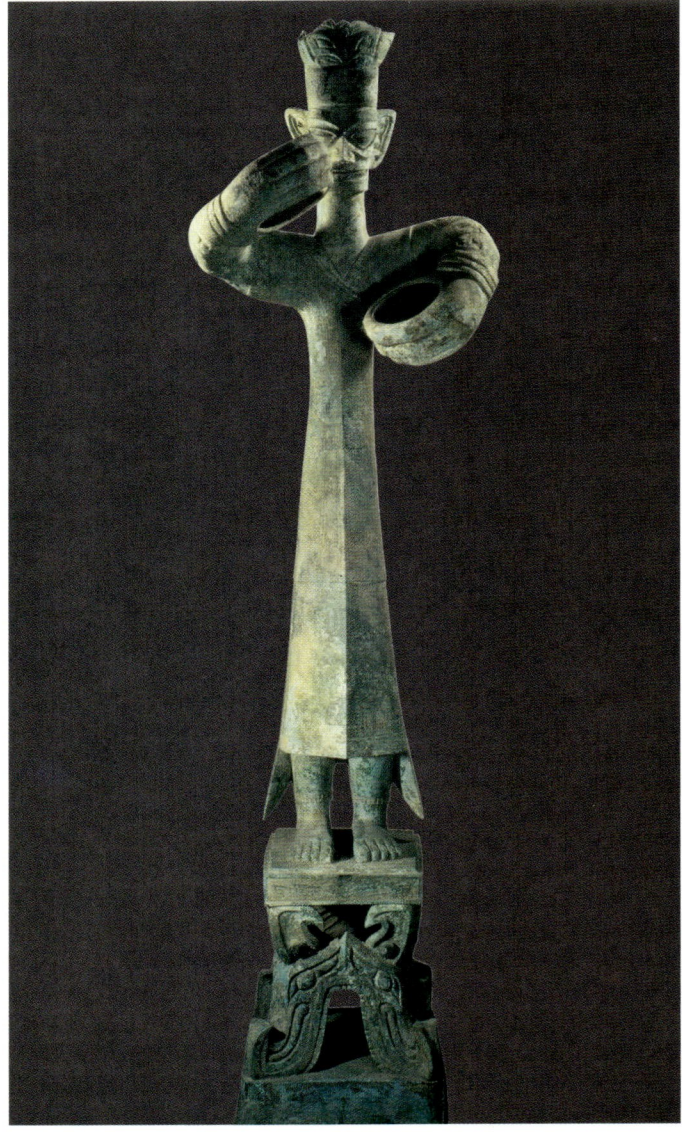

**7-3** Standing figure, from Sanxingdui, China, ca. 1200-1050 BCE. Bronze, 8′ 5″ high, including base. China Cultural Relics Promotional Center, Beijing.

## Chinese Jade

The Chinese first used jade, or more precisely, nephrite, for artworks and ritual objects in the Neolithic period. Nephrite polishes to a more lustrous, slightly buttery finish than jadeite (the stone Chinese sculptors preferred from the 18th century on), which is quite glassy. Both stones come in colors other than the well-known green and are tough, hard, and heavy, as well as beautiful. In China, such qualities became metaphors for the fortitude and moral perfection of superior persons. Jade was also believed to have magical qualities that could protect the dead. Archaeologists have found the tomb of a prince and princess of the Han dynasty (206 BCE–220 CE), each of whom was laid to rest in a suit composed of more than 2,000 jade tablets sewn together with gold wire.

Because of its extreme hardness, jade could not be carved with the Neolithic sculptor's stone tools. Researchers can only speculate on how these early artists were able to cut, shape, and incise the nephrite objects discovered at many Neolithic Chinese sites. The sculptors probably used cords embedded with sand to incise lines into the surfaces. Sand placed in a bamboo tube drill could perforate the hard stone, but the process would have been long and arduous, requiring great patience as well as superior skill. Even after the invention of bronze tools, Chinese sculptors still had to rely on grinding and abrasion rather than simple drilling and chiseling to produce the intricately shaped, pierced, and engraved works such as the *bi* illustrated in FIG. 7-4.

identity. Representations of the human figure on this scale in this period are otherwise unknown. Surface decoration of squared spirals and hook-pointed curves is all that links this gigantic statue with the intricate piece-mold bronze vessels of the Shang (FIG. 7-2). Archaeology will probably continue to produce such surprises and cause art historians to revise once again their picture of Chinese art in the second half of the second millennium BCE.

## Zhou Dynasty

Around 1050 BCE, the Zhou, former vassals of the Shang, captured Anyang and overthrew their Shang overlords. The Zhou dynasty proved to be the longest lasting in China's history—so long that historians divide the Zhou era into two great periods: Western Zhou (ca. 1050–771 BCE) and Eastern Zhou (770–256 BCE). The dividing event is the transfer of the Zhou capital from Chang'an (modern Xi'an) in the west to Luoyang in the east. The closing centuries of Zhou rule include a long period of warfare among competing states (Warring States Period, ca. 475–221 BCE). The Zhou fell to one of these states, the Qin, in 256 BCE. By 221 BCE the Qin had defeated all their other rivals.

Under the Zhou, the decline of old ceremonial rules and the development of markets, together with bronze coinage and the rise of freelance artists, supported a taste for lavish products, such as bronzes inlaid with gold and silver. Late Zhou bronzes featured scenes of hunting, religious rites, and magic practices. These may relate to the subjects and compositions of lost paintings mentioned in Zhou literature. Other materials favored in the late Zhou period were jade (see "Chinese Jade," above) and *lacquer,* a varnishlike substance made from the sap of the Asiatic sumac, used to decorate wood furniture and other objects (see "Lacquered Wood," Chapter 26, page 769).

**JADE DRAGONS** The carving of jade objects for burial with the dead, beginning in Neolithic times, reached a peak of technical perfection during the Zhou dynasty. Among the most common finds in tombs of the period are *bi* disks—thin, flat circular pieces of jade with a hole in the center, which may have symbolized the circle of heaven. Our example (FIG. **7-4**) probably came

from a royal Eastern Zhou tomb at Jincun, near Luoyang in north central China. Rows of raised spirals, created by laborious grinding and polishing, decorate the disk itself. Within the inner circle and around the outer edge of the bi are elegant dragons, which required long hours of work to pierce through the hard jade. The bi testifies to the Zhou sculptor's mastery of this difficult material. The Chinese thought dragons inhabited the water and flew between heaven and earth, bringing rain, so these animals long have been symbols of good fortune in East Asia. They also symbolized the rulers' power to mediate between heaven and earth.

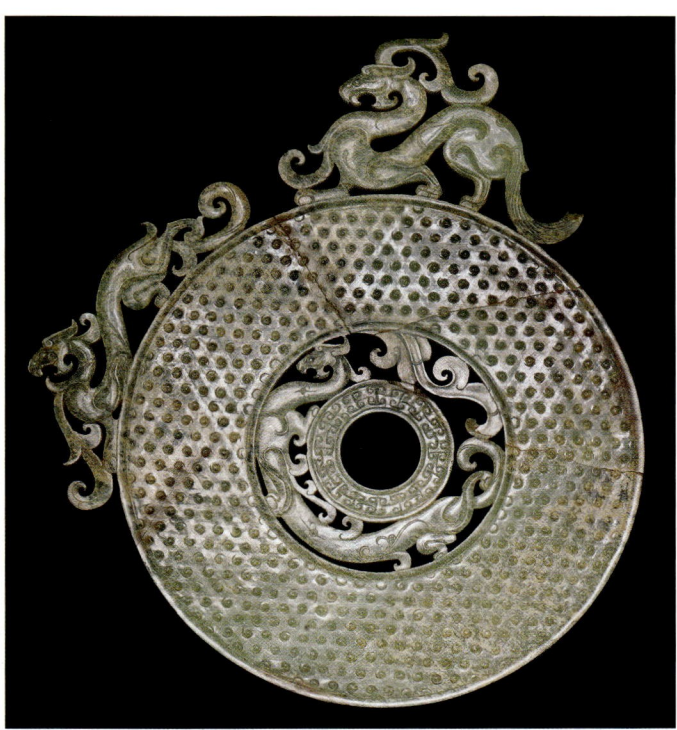

**7-4** *Bi* disk with dragons, from Jincun(?), China, Eastern Zhou dynasty, fourth to third century BCE. Nephrite, $6\frac{1}{2}''$ in diameter. Nelson-Atkins Museum of Art, Kansas City.

## Daoism and Confucianism

Daoism and Confucianism are both philosophies and religions native to China. Both schools of thought attracted wide followings during the Warring States Period (ca. 475–221 BCE), when political turbulence led to social unrest.

Daoism emerged out of the metaphysical teachings attributed to Laozi (604?–531? BCE) and Zhuangzi (370?–301? BCE). It takes its name from Laozi's treatise *Daodejing (The Way and Its Power)*. Daoist philosophy stresses an intuitive awareness, nurtured by harmonious contact with nature, and eschews everything artificial. Daoists seek to follow the universal path, or principle, called the Dao, whose features cannot be described but only suggested through analogies. For example, the Dao is said to be like water, always yielding but eventually wearing away the hard stone that does not yield. For Daoists, strength comes from flexibility and inaction. Historically, Daoist principles encouraged retreat from society in favor of personal cultivation.

Confucius (551–479 BCE) was born in the state of Lu (roughly modern Shandong Province) to an aristocratic family that had fallen on hard times. From an early age, he showed a strong interest in the rites and ceremonies that helped unite people into an orderly society. As he grew older, he developed a deep concern for the suffering caused by the civil conflict of his day. Thus, he adopted a philosophy he hoped would lead to order and stability.

The ideal social order Confucius sought is personified by the *junzi* ("superior person" or "gentleman"), who possesses *ren* ("human-heartedness"). Although the term junzi originally assumed noble birth, in Confucian thought anyone can become a junzi by cultivating the virtues Confucius espoused, especially empathy for suffering, pursuit of morality and justice, respect for ancient ceremonies, and adherence to traditional social relationships, such as those between parent and child, elder and younger sibling, husband and wife, and ruler and subject.

Confucius's disciple Mencius (or Mengzi, 371?–289? BCE), developed the master's ideas further, stressing that the deference to age and rank that is at the heart of the Confucian social order brings a reciprocal responsibility. For example, a king's legitimacy depends on the good will of his people. A ruler should share his joys with his subjects, and will know his laws are unjust if they bring suffering to the people.

Confucius spent much of his adult life trying to find rulers willing to apply his teachings, but he died in disappointment. However, he and Mencius had a profound impact on Chinese thought and social practice. Chinese traditions of venerating deceased ancestors and outstanding leaders encouraged the development of Confucianism as a religion as well as a philosophic tradition. Eventually, Emperor Wu Di (r. 140–87 BCE) of the Han dynasty established Confucianism as the state's official doctrine. Thereafter, it became the primary subject of the civil service exams required for admission into and advancement within government service.

"Confucian" and "Daoist" are broad, imprecise terms scholars often use to distinguish aspects of Chinese culture stressing social responsibility and order (Confucian) from those emphasizing cultivation of individuals, often in reclusion (Daoist). But both philosophies share the idea that anyone can cultivate wisdom or ability, regardless of birth.

## Qin Dynasty

**THE FIRST EMPEROR** During the Warring States Period, China endured more than two centuries of political and social turmoil. This was also a time of intellectual and artistic upheaval, when conflicting schools of philosophy, including Legalism, Daoism, and Confucianism, emerged (see "Daoism and Confucianism," above). Order was finally restored when the powerful armies of the ruler of the state of Qin (from which the modern name "China" derives) conquered all rival states. Qin's ruler took the name Zheng, but he is known to history by his title, Qin Shi Huangdi, the First Emperor of Qin. Between 221 and 210 BCE he controlled an area equal to about half of modern China, much larger than the territories of any of the dynasties before him. During his reign, he ordered the linkage of active fortifications along the northern border of his realm to form the famous Great Wall. The wall defended China against the fierce nomadic peoples of the north, especially the Huns, who eventually made their way to eastern Europe. By sometimes brutal methods, Shi Huangdi consolidated rule through a centralized bureaucracy and adopted standardized written language, weights and measures, and coinage. He also repressed schools of thought other than Legalism, which espoused absolute obedience to the state's authority and advocated strict laws and punishments. Chinese historians long have condemned China's First Emperor, but the bureaucratic system he put in place had a long-lasting impact. Its success was due in large part to Shi Huangdi's decision to replace the feudal lords with talented salaried administrators and to reward merit rather than favor high birth.

**THE EMPEROR'S ARMY** In 1974, excavations started at the site of the immense burial mound of the First Emperor of Qin at Lintong. For its construction, the ruler conscripted many thousands of laborers and had the tomb filled with treasure—a task that continued after his death. The mound itself remains unexcavated, but researchers believe it contains a vast underground funerary palace designed to match the fabulous palace the emperor occupied in life. The historian Sima Qian (136–85 BCE) described both palaces, but scholars did not take his account seriously until the discovery of pits around the tomb filled with more than 6,000 life-size painted terracotta figures of soldiers and horses (FIG. 7-5), as well as bronze horses and chariots. Replicating the emperor's invincible hosts, they served as the immortal imperial bodyguard deployed in trenches outside the First Emperor's tomb.

The terracotta army, comprised of cavalry, chariots, archers, lancers, and hand-to-hand fighters, was one of the 20th century's greatest archaeological discoveries. Lesser versions of Shi Huangdi's army have since been uncovered at other Chinese sites, suggesting that the First Emperor's tomb became the model for many others. The huge assemblage at Lintong testifies to a very high degree of

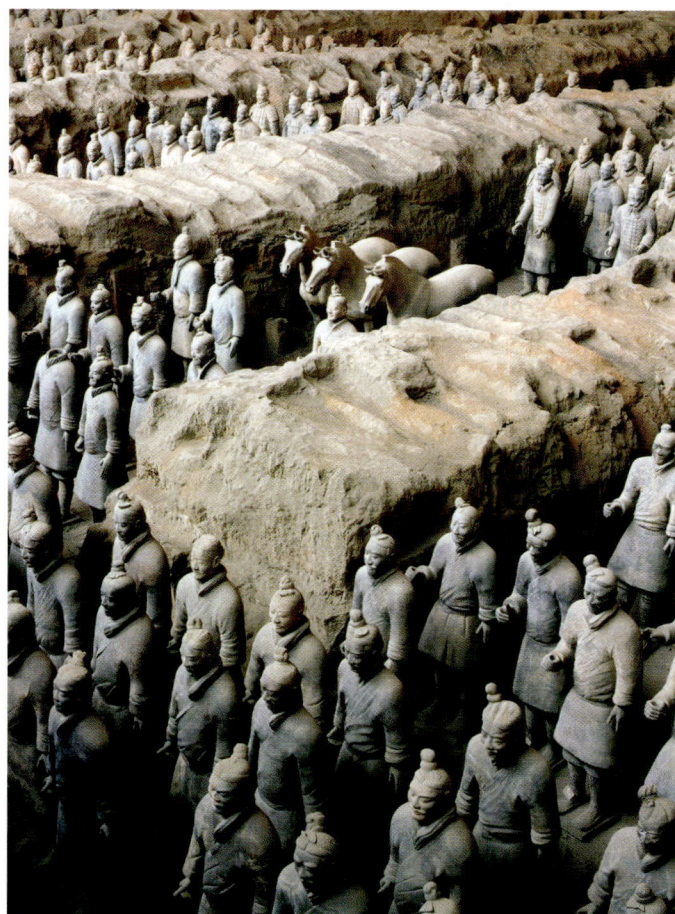

**7-5** Army of the First Emperor of Qin in pits next to his burial mound, Lintong, China, Qin dynasty, ca. 210 BCE. Painted terracotta, average figure 5′ 10$\frac{7}{8}$″ high.

organization in the Qin imperial workshop. Manufacturing this army of statues required a veritable army of sculptors and painters as well as a large number of huge kilns. The First Emperor's artisans could have opted to use the same molds over and over again to produce thousands of identical soldiers standing in strict formation. In fact, they did employ the same molds repeatedly for different parts of the statues, but assembled the parts in many different combinations. Consequently, the stances, arm positions, garment folds, equipment, coiffures, and facial features vary, sometimes slightly, sometimes markedly, from statue to statue. Additional hand modeling of the cast body parts before firing permitted the sculptors to differentiate the figures even more. The Qin painters undoubtedly added further variations to the appearance of the terracotta army. The result of these efforts was a brilliant balance of uniformity and individuality.

## Han Dynasty

Soon after Qin Shi Huangdi's death, the people who had suffered under his reign revolted, assassinated his son, and founded the Han dynasty in 206 BCE. The Han ruled China for four centuries and extended its southern and western boundaries. Chinese armies penetrated far into Central Asia (modern Xinjiang) and even began to trade indirectly with distant Rome via the fabled Silk Road (see "Silk and the Silk Road," page 201).

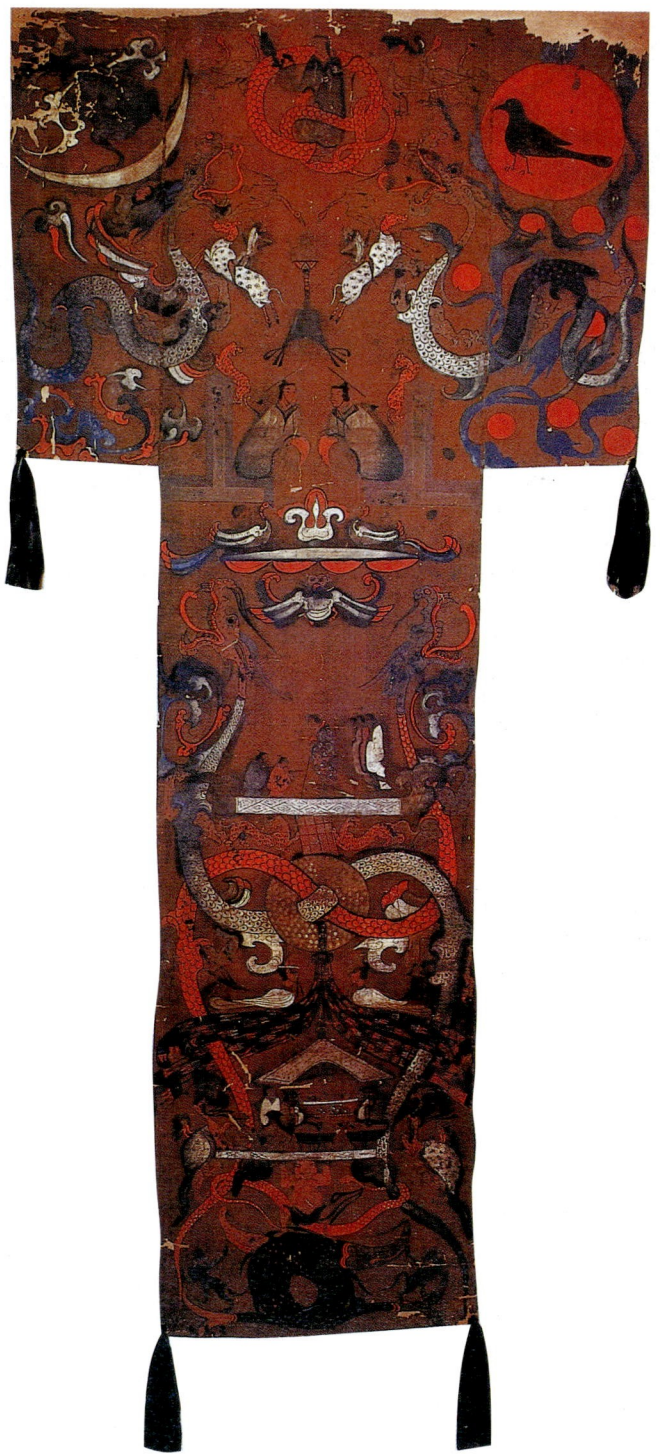

**7-6** Funeral banner, from Tomb 1 (tomb of Dai), Mawangdui, China, Han dynasty, ca. 168 BCE. Painted silk, 6′ 8$\frac{3}{4}$″ × 3′ $\frac{1}{4}$″. Hunan Provincial Museum, Changsha.

**PAINTING ON SILK** In 1972, archaeologists excavated the tomb of the wife of the Marquis of Dai at Mawangdui in Hunan Province. The tomb contained a rich array of burial goods used during the funerary ceremonies and to accompany the deceased into the afterlife. Among the many finds were decorated lacquer utensils, various textiles, and an astonishingly well-preserved corpse in the innermost of four nested sarcophagi. Most remarkable of all, however, was the discovery of a painted **T**-shaped silk banner (FIG. **7-6**) draped over the woman's coffin. Scholars generally agree that

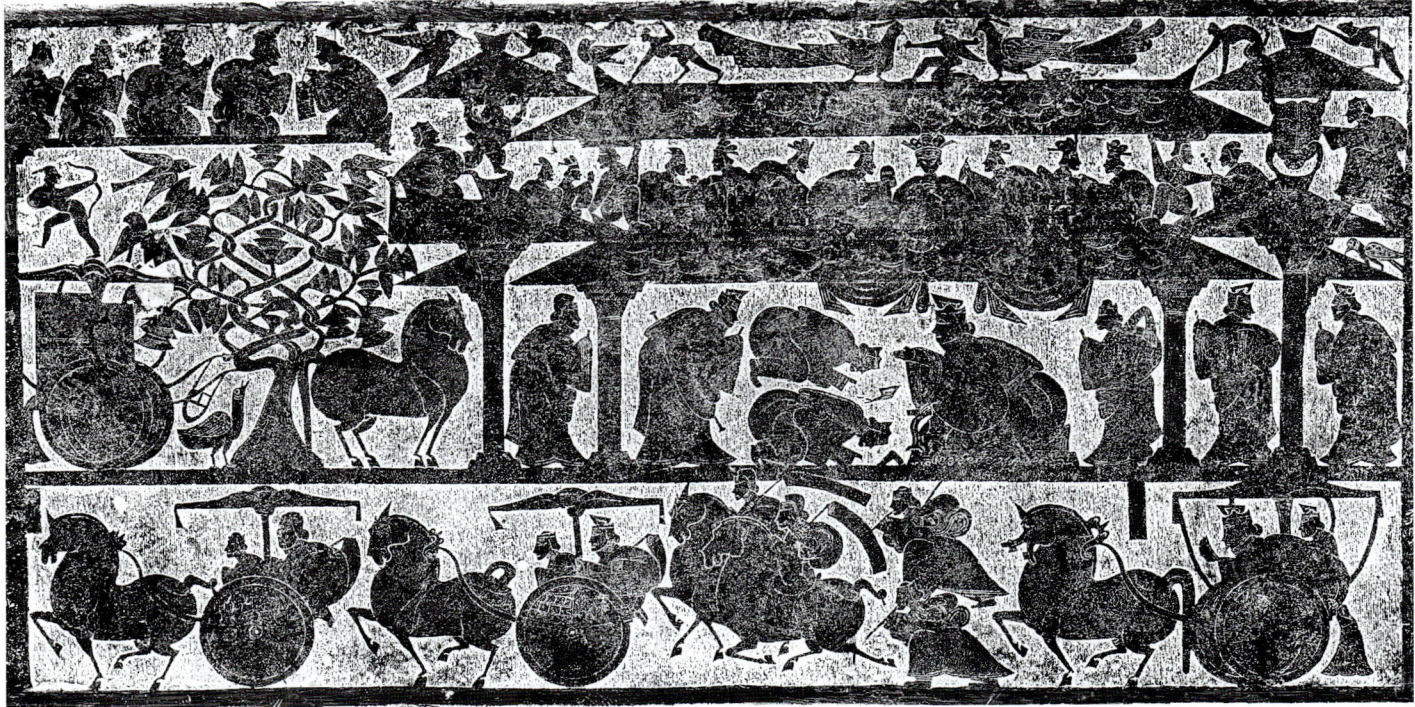

**7-7** The archer Yi(?) and a reception in a mansion, Wu family shrine, Jiaxiang, China, Han dynasty, 147–168 CE. Rubbing of a stone relief, approx. 3′ × 5′.

the area within the cross at the top of the T represents heaven. Most of the vertical section below is the human realm. At the very bottom is the underworld. In the heavenly realm, dragons and immortal beings appear between and below two orbs—the red sun and its symbol, the raven, on the right, and the silvery moon and its symbol, the toad, on the left. Below, the standing figure on the first white platform near the center of the vertical section is probably the Marquise of Dai herself—one of the first portraits in Chinese art. The Marquise awaits her ascent to heaven, where she can attain immortality. Nearer the bottom, the artist depicted the wealthy woman's funeral. Between these two sections is a form resembling a bi disk with two intertwining dragons (compare FIG. 7-4). Their tails reach down to the underworld and their heads point to heaven, unifying the whole composition.

**HAN ANCESTRAL SHRINES** Even more extensive Han pictorial narratives were carved into the stone walls of the Wu family shrines at Jiaxiang in Shandong Province between 147 and 168 CE. The shrines document the emergence of private, nonaristocratic families as patrons of religious and mythological art with political overtones. Dedicated to deceased male family members, the Wu shrines consist of three low walls covered by a pitched roof. On the interior surfaces, images of flat polished stone stand out against an equally flat, though roughly textured, ground. The historical scenes include a representation of the attempt to assassinate the tyrannical First Emperor of Qin by the celebrated third-century BCE hero Jing Ke. On the slab shown here (FIG. 7-7, a rubbing taken from the stone relief) the archer at the upper left is probably the hero Yi, saving the earth from scorching by shooting down the nine extra suns, represented as crows in the Fusang tree. (The small orbs below the sun on the Mawangdui banner probably allude to the same story.) The lowest zone shows a procession of umbrella-carriages moving to the left. Above, underneath the overhanging eaves of a two-story mansion, robed men bearing

gifts pay homage to a central figure of uncertain identity, who is represented as larger and therefore more important. Two men kneel before the larger figure. Women occupy the upper story. Again, one figure is singled out as the most important; she faces forward. Whatever the identities of the individual figures (interpretations vary widely), these scenes of homage and loyalty are consistent with the Confucian ideals of Han society (see "Daoism and Confucianism," page 196).

**HAN HOUSES AND PALACES** No actual remains of Han buildings survive, but ceramic models of houses deposited in Han tombs, together with representations such as those in the Wu family shrines, provide a good idea of Chinese architecture during the early centuries CE. An especially large painted earthenware model (FIG. 7-8) reproduces a Han house with sharply projecting tiled roofs resting on a framework of timber posts, lintels, and brackets. This construction method, in which the walls do not bear the weight of the roof but serve only as screens separating inside from outside and room from room, typifies much Chinese architecture even today (see "Chinese Wooden Construction Methods and Principles," page 200). Descriptions of Han palaces suggest that they were grandiose versions of the type of house reproduced in this model, but with more luxurious decoration, including walls of lacquered wood and mural paintings.

## Period of Disunity

**BUDDHISM REACHES CHINA** For three and a half centuries, from 220 to 589,* civil strife divided China into competing states. Scholars variously refer to this era as the Period of Disunity or the

---

* From this point on, all dates in this chapter are CE unless otherwise stated.

els in the flat, relief-like handling of the robe's heavy concentric folds, the ushnisha (cranial bump) on the head, and the cross-legged position. So new were the icon and its meaning, however, that the Chinese sculptor misrepresented the canonical dhyana mudra, or meditation gesture. Here, the Buddha clasps his hands across his stomach. In South Asian art, they are turned palms upward, with thumbs barely touching in front of the torso.

**PAINTING MATERIALS AND FORMATS** Secular arts also flourished in the Period of Disunity. Rulers sought calligraphers and painters to lend prestige to their courts. Several distinctive materials and formats characterize early Chinese painting. The basic requirements for paintings not on walls are the same as for writing—a round tapered brush, soot-based ink, and either silk or paper. The Chinese were masters of the brush. Sometimes they employed modulated lines that elastically thicken and thin to convey not only outline but depth and mass as well. In other works, they used *iron-wire lines* (thin, unmodulated lines with a suggestion of tensile strength) to define the figures. Chinese painters also used richly colored minerals as pigments, finely ground and suspended in a gluey medium, and watery washes of mineral and vegetable dyes.

The formats of Chinese paintings (other than mural paintings) tend to be personal and intimate. Some pictures were mounted on scrolls for vertical display (unrolled) on appropriate occasions. Others were attached to long, narrow scrolls that viewers unrolled horizontally, section by section. Stiff round or arched folding fans were also popular painting formats. Artists also painted small panels on paper leaves, which were collected in albums. Although some Chinese paintings are monumental in size, most are intimate in scale and best viewed by only one or two people at a time.

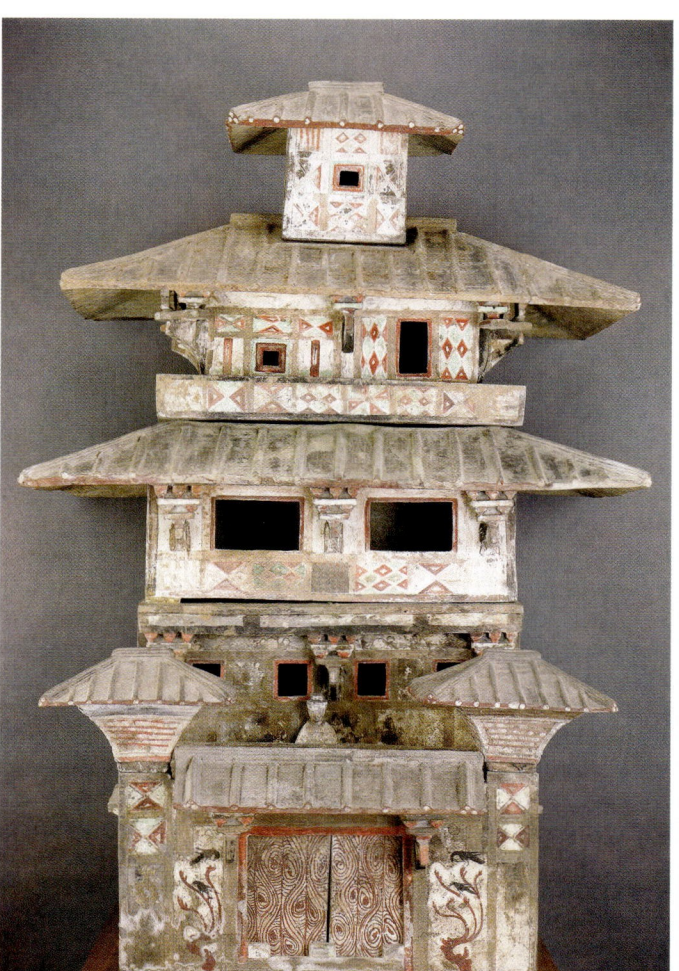

**7-8** Model of a house, Han dynasty, first century CE. Painted earthenware, 4′ 4″ high. Nelson-Atkins Museum of Art, Kansas City.

period of the Six Dynasties or of the Northern and Southern Dynasties. The history of this era is extremely complex, but one development deserves special mention—the occupation of the north by peoples who were not ethnically Han Chinese and who spoke non-Chinese languages. It was in the northern states, connected to India by the desert caravan routes of the Silk Road (see "Silk and the Silk Road," page 201), that Buddhism first took root in China during the Han dynasty (see "Buddhism," Chapter 6, page 171). Certain practices shared with Daoism, such as withdrawal from ordinary society, helped Buddhism gain an initial foothold in the north. But Buddhism's promise of hope beyond the troubles of this world earned it an ever broader audience during the upheavals of the Period of Disunity. In addition, the fully developed Buddhist system of thought attracted intellectuals. Buddhism never fully displaced Confucianism and Daoism, but it did prosper throughout China for centuries and had a profound effect on the further development of the religious forms of those two native traditions.

The earliest extant precisely datable Chinese Buddhist image is a gilded bronze statuette (FIG. 7-9) of Shakyamuni Buddha, the historical Buddha, dated by inscription to the year 338. The oldest Chinese Buddhist texts describe the Buddha as golden and radiating light. This no doubt accounts for the choice of gilded bronze as the sculptor's medium. In both style and iconography, this early Buddha resembles the prototype conceived and developed at Gandhara (see FIG. 6-9). The Chinese figure recalls its presumed South Asian mod-

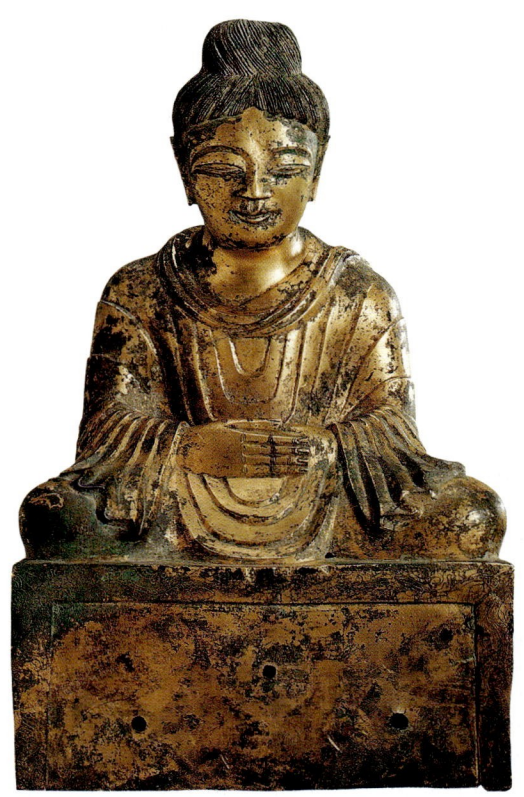

**7-9** Shakyamuni Buddha, Zhao dynasty, Period of Disunity, 338. Gilded bronze, 1′ 3½″ high. Asian Art Museum of San Francisco (Avery Brundage Collection).

## Chinese Wooden Construction Methods and Principles

Although the basic unit of Chinese architecture, the rectangular hall with columns supporting a roof, was common in many ancient civilizations, Chinese buildings are distinguished from Egyptian hypostyle halls (see FIG. 3-27) and Greco-Roman temples (see "Doric and Ionic Temples," Chapter 5, pages 116–117) by the curving silhouettes of their roofs and by their method of construction.

The Chinese, like other ancient peoples, used wood to construct their earliest buildings. Although those structures do not survive, scholars believe that many of the features giving East Asian architecture its specific character may go back to Zhou times. Even the simple buildings reproduced on Han stone carvings (FIG. 7-7) or in clay models (FIG. 7-8) reveal a style and a method of construction long basic to China.

The typical Chinese hall has a pitched roof with projecting eaves. Wooden columns, lintels, and brackets provide the support. The walls serve no weight-bearing function but act only as screens. The colors of Chinese buildings, predominantly red, black, yellow, and white, are also distinctive. Chinese timber architecture is customarily multicolored throughout, save for certain parts left in natural color, such as railings made of white marble. The builders usually painted the screen walls and the columns red. Chinese designers often chose dazzling combinations of colors and elaborate patterns for the beams, brackets, eaves, rafters, and ceilings. The builders painted or lacquered the surfaces to protect the timber from rot and wood parasites, as well as to produce an arresting aesthetic effect.

Our diagram shows the basic construction method of Chinese architecture, with the major components of a Chinese building labeled. The builders laid *beams* (no. 1) between columns, decreasing the length of the beams as the structure rose. The beams supported vertical *struts* (no. 2), which in turn supported higher beams and eventually the *purlins* (no. 3) running the length of the building and carrying the roof's sloping *rafters* (no. 4). Unlike the rigid elements of the triangular trussed timber roof common in the West, which produce flat sloping rooflines, the varying lengths of the Chinese structure's cross beams and the variously placed purlins can create curved profiles. Early Chinese roofs have flat profiles (FIGS. 7-7 and 7-8), but curving rafters later became the norm, not only in China but throughout East Asia (FIGS. 7-14, 7-21, 7-22, 8-6, 8-10, and 8-12). In addition, the interlocking clusters of brackets could cantilever (support with brackets) the roof to allow for broad overhang of the *eaves* (no. 5), another typical feature of Chinese architecture. Multiplication of the *bays* (spaces between the columns) could extend the building's length to any dimension desired, although each bay could be no wider or longer than the length of a single tree trunk. The proportions of the structural elements could be fixed into modules, allowing for standardization of parts. This enabled rapid construction of a building. The workers fit the parts together without using any adhesive substance, such as mortar or glue. Delicately joined as the parts were, they still could easily carry the heavy tiled roofs of Chinese buildings (FIGS. 7-8, 7-14, 7-21, and 26-5).

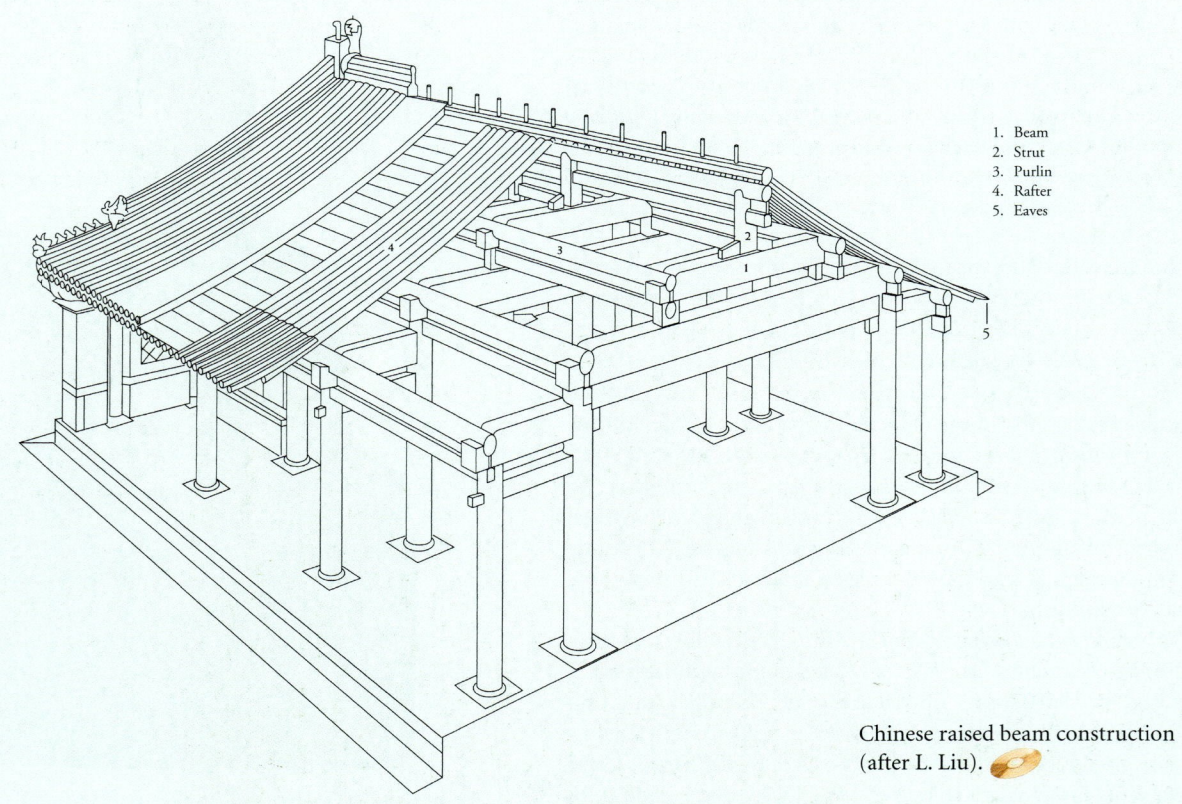

1. Beam
2. Strut
3. Purlin
4. Rafter
5. Eaves

Chinese raised beam construction
(after L. Liu).

## Silk and the Silk Road

Silk is the finest natural fabric ever produced. It comes from the cocoons of caterpillars called silkworms. The manufacture of silk was a well-established industry in China by the second millennium BCE. The basic procedures probably have not changed much since then. Farmers today still raise silkworms from eggs, which they place in trays. The farmers also must grow mulberry trees or purchase mulberry leaves, the silkworms' only food source. Eventually, the silkworms form cocoons out of very fine filaments they extrude as liquid from their bodies. The filaments soon solidify with exposure to air. Before the transformed caterpillars emerge as moths and badly damage the silk, the farmers kill them with steam or high heat. They soften the cocoons in hot water and unwind the filaments onto a reel. The filaments are so fine that workers generally unwind those from 5 to 10 cocoons together to bond into a single strand while the filaments are still soft and sticky. Later, the silkworkers twist several strands together to form a thicker yarn and then weave the yarn on a loom to produce silk cloth. Both the yarn and the cloth can be dyed, and the silk fabric can be decorated by weaving threads of different colors together in special patterns (*brocades*) or by stitching in threads of different colors (*embroidery*). Many Chinese artists painted directly on plain silk (FIGS. 7-6, 7-10, 7-15, 7-18, 7-19, 7-23, 7-24, 26-9, and 26-14).

Greatly admired throughout most of Asia, Chinese silk and the secrets of its production gradually spread throughout the ancient world. The Romans knew of silk as early as the second century BCE and treasured it for garments and hangings. Silk came to the Romans along the ancient fabled Silk Road, actually a network of caravan tracts across Central Asia linking China and the Mediterranean world. The western part, between the Mediterranean region and India, developed first, due largely to the difficult geographic conditions to India's northeast. In Central Asia, the caravans had to skirt the Taklamakan Desert, one of the most inhospitable environments on earth, as well as climb high, dangerous mountain passes. Very few traders actually traveled the entire route. Along the way, goods usually passed through the hands of people from many lands, who often only dimly understood the ultimate origins and destinations of what they traded. The Roman passion for silk ultimately led to the modern name for the caravan tracts, but silk was far from the only product traded along the way. Gold, ivory, gems, glass, lacquer, incense, furs, spices, cotton, linens, exotic animals, and other merchandise precious enough to warrant the risks passed along the Silk Road.

Ideas moved along these trade routes as well. Most important perhaps, travelers on the Silk Road brought Buddhism to China from India in the first century CE, opening up a significant new chapter in both the history of religion and the history of art in China.

---

**LADY FENG'S HEROISM** The most famous early Chinese painter with whom extant works can be associated was Gu Kaizhi (ca. 344–406). Gu was a friend of important members of the Eastern Jin dynasty (317–420) and was renowned as a calligrapher, a painter of court portraits, and a pioneer of landscape painting. A horizontal scroll now in the British Museum, although attributed to Gu Kaizhi in the 11th century, is not actually by his hand, but it provides a good idea of the key elements of his art. Called *Admonitions of the Instructress to the Court Ladies,* the scroll contains painted scenes and accompanying explanatory text. Like all Chinese *handscrolls,* this one was unrolled and read from right to left, with only a small section exposed for viewing at one time. The section we illustrate (FIG. **7-10**) records a well-known act of heroism, the Lady Feng saving her emperor's life by

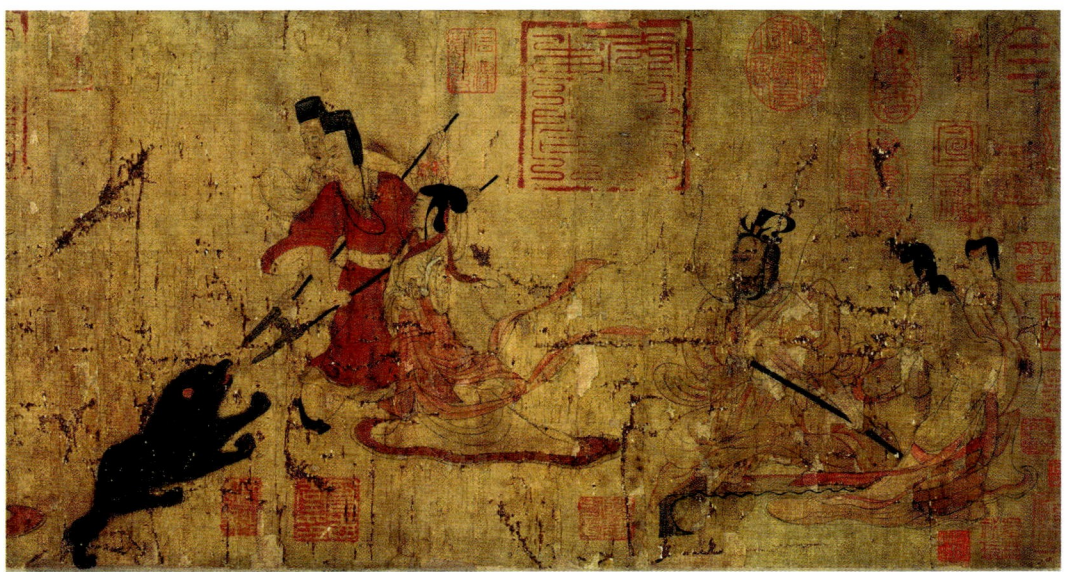

**7-10** Gu Kaizhi, *Lady Feng and the Bear,* detail of *Admonitions of the Instructress to the Court Ladies,* Period of Disunity, late fourth century. Handscroll, ink and colors on silk, $9\frac{3}{4}''$ × 11' $4\frac{1}{2}''$. British Museum, London.

### Xie He's Six Canons

China has a long and rich history of scholarship on painting, preserved today in copies of texts from as far back as the fourth century and in citations to even earlier sources. Few of the first texts on painting survive, but later authors often quoted them, preserving the texts for posterity. Thus, educated Chinese painters and their clients could steep themselves in a rich art historical tradition. Perhaps the most famous subject of later commentary is a set of six "canons" or "laws" of painting formulated in the early sixth century by Xie He. The canons, as translated by James Cahill,[1] are as follows:

1. Engender a sense of movement through spirit consonance.
2. Use the brush with the bone method.
3. Responding to things, depict their forms.
4. According to kind, describe appearances [with color].
5. Dividing and planning, positioning and arranging.
6. Transmitting and conveying earlier models through copying and transcribing.

Several variant translations have also been proposed, and scholars actively debate the precise meaning of these succinct (Xie He employed only four characters for each) and cryptic laws. Interpreting the canons in connection with actual paintings is often difficult, but nonetheless offers valuable insights into what the Chinese valued in painting.

The simplest canons to understand are the third, fourth, and fifth, because they show painters' concern for accuracy in rendering forms and colors and for care in composition, concerns common in many cultures. However, separating form and color into different laws gives written expression to a distinctive feature of early Chinese painting. Painters such as Gu Kaizhi (FIG. 7-10) and Yan Liben (FIG. 7-15) used an outline-and-color technique. Their brushed-ink outline drawings employ flat applications of color. To suggest volume, they used ink shading along edges, such as drapery folds.

Also noteworthy is the order of the laws, suggesting Chinese painters' primary concern: to convey the vital spirit of their subjects and their own sensitivity to that spirit. Next in importance was the handling of the brush and the careful placement of strokes, especially of ink. The sixth canon also speaks to a standard Chinese painting practice: copying. Chinese painters, like painters in other cultures throughout history, trained by copying the works of their teachers and other painters. In addition, artists often copied famous paintings as sources of forms and ideas for their own works and to preserve great works created using fragile materials (FIG. 7-10). In China, as elsewhere, change and individual development occurred in constant reference to the past, the artists always preserving some elements of it.

[1] James Cahill, "The Six Laws and How to Read Them," *Ars Orientalis* 4 (1961), 372–81.

placing herself between him and an attacking bear—a perfect model of Confucian behavior. As in many early Chinese paintings, the figures are set against a blank background with only a minimal setting for the scene, although in other works Gu provided landscape settings for his narratives. The figures' poses and fluttering drapery ribbons, in concert with individualized facial expressions, convey a clear quality of animation. This style accords well with painting ideals expressed in texts of the time, when representing inner vitality and spirit took precedence over reproducing surface appearances (see "Xie He's Six Canons," above).

THE MEETING OF TWO BUDDHAS A gilded bronze statuette (FIG. 7-11) shows how the sculptors of the Northern Wei dynasty (386–534) had transformed the Gandhara-derived style of earlier Buddhist art in China (FIG. 7-9). Dated 518, the piece was probably made for private devotion in a domestic setting or as a votive offering in a temple. It represents the meeting of Shakyamuni Buddha (at the viewer's right) and Prabhutaratna, the Buddha who had achieved nirvana in the remote past, as recounted in the *Lotus Sutra*, an encyclopedic collection of Buddhist thought and poetry. When Shakyamuni was preaching on Vulture Peak, Prabhutaratna's stupa miraculously appeared in the sky. Shakyamuni opened it and revealed Prabhutaratna himself, who had promised to be present whenever the Lotus Law was preached. Shakyamuni sat beside him and continued to expound the Law. The meeting of the two Buddhas symbolized the continuity of Buddhist thought across the ages.

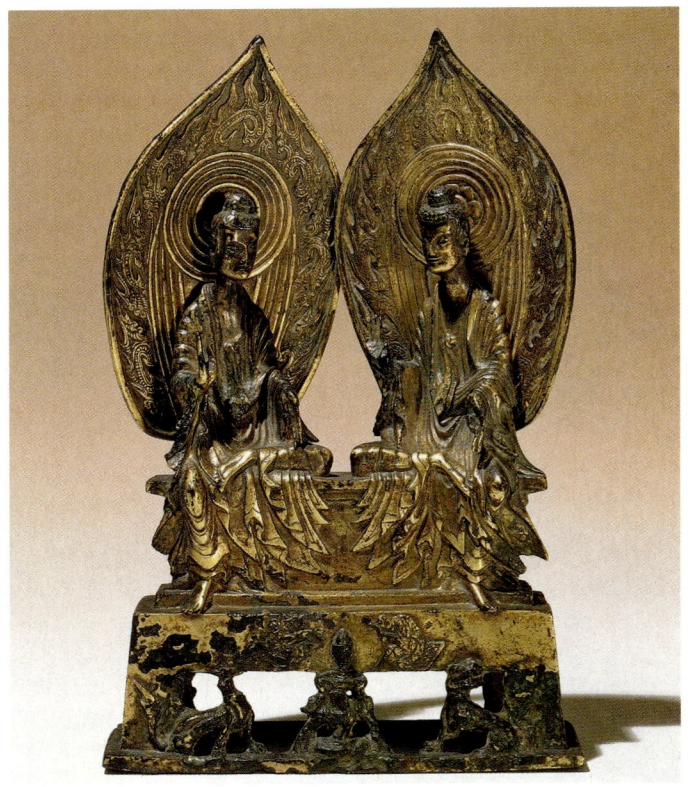

**7-11** Shakyamuni and Prabhutaratna, Northern Wei dynasty, 518. Gilded bronze, 10¼″ high. Musée Guimet, Paris.

Behind each Buddha is a flamelike nimbus (*mandorla*). Both figures sit in the *lalitasana* pose—one leg folded and the other hanging down. This standard pose, which indicates relaxation, underscores the ease of communication between the two Buddhas. Their bodies have elongated proportions, and their smiling faces have sharp noses and almond eyes. The folds of the garments drop like a waterfall from their shoulders to their knees and spill over onto the pedestal, where they form sharp ridges resembling the teeth of a saw. The rhythmic sweep and linear elegance of the folds recall the brushwork of contemporary painting.

## Tang Dynasty

The emperors of the short-lived Sui dynasty (581–618) succeeded in reuniting China and prepared the way for the brilliant Tang dynasty (618–906). Under the Tang emperors, China entered a period of unequaled magnificence (MAP 7-1). Chinese armies marched across Central Asia, prompting an influx of foreign peoples, wealth, and ideas into China. Traders, missionaries, and other travelers journeyed to the cosmopolitan Tang capital at Chang'an, and the Chinese, in turn, ventured westward.

WU ZETIAN'S COSMIC BUDDHA  In its first century, the new dynasty continued to support Buddhism and to sponsor great monuments for Buddhist worshipers. Cave complexes decorated with reliefs and paintings, modeled on those of India (see Chapter 6), were especially popular. One of the most spectacular Tang Buddhist sculptures is carved into the face of a cliff in the great Longmen Cave complex near Luoyang in north central China. Work at Longmen had begun almost two centuries earlier, during the Period of Disunity, under the Northern Wei dynasty (386–534). The site's 1,352 caves, 97,000 statues, 3,600 inscriptions, and 785 carved niches attest to its importance as a Buddhist center.

The colossal relief (FIG. 7-12) that dominates the Longmen complex features a central figure of the Buddha that is 44 feet tall—seated. An inscription records that the project was completed in 675 when Gaozong (r. 649–683) was the Tang emperor and that in 672 the empress Wu Zetian underwrote a substantial portion of the considerable cost with her private funds. Wu Zetian was an exceptional woman by any standard, and when Gaozong died in 683, she declared herself emperor and ruled until 705, when she was forced to abdicate at age 82 (compare "Hatshepsut," Chapter 3, page 71).

Wu Zetian's Buddha is the Vairocana Buddha, not the historical Buddha of FIGS. 7-9 and 7-11 but the Mahayana Cosmic Buddha, the Buddha of Boundless Space and Time (see "Buddhism," Chapter 6, page 171). Flanking him are two of his monks, attendant bodhisattvas, and guardian figures—all smaller than the Buddha but still of colossal size. (FIG. 7-12, which includes two visitors to the site, underscores the scale of the work.) The sculptors represented the Buddha in serene majesty. An almost geometric regularity of contour and smoothness of planes emphasize the volume of the massive figure. The folds of his robes fall in a few concentric arcs. The artists suppressed surface detail in the interest of monumental simplicity and dignity.

THE DUNHUANG GROTTOES  The westward expansion of the Tang Empire increased the importance of Dunhuang, the westernmost gateway to China on the Silk Road. Dunhuang long had been a wealthy, cosmopolitan trade center, a Buddhist pilgrimage destination, and home to thriving communities of Buddhist monks and nuns of varied ethnicity, as well as to adherents of other religions. In the course of several centuries, hundreds of sanctuaries with painted murals were cut into the soft rock of the cliffs near Dunhuang. Known today as the Mogao Grottoes and in antiquity as the Caves of a Thousand Buddhas, the caves also contain images of painted unfired clay and stucco. The earliest recorded cave at Dunhuang was dedicated in 366, but the oldest extant caves date to the late fifth century.

The Dunhuang caves are especially important because in 845 the emperor Wuzong instituted a major persecution, destroying 4,600 Buddhist temples and 40,000 shrines and forcing the return of 260,500 monks and nuns to lay life. Wuzong's policies did not affect Dunhuang, then under Tibetan rule, so the site preserves much of the type of art lost elsewhere.

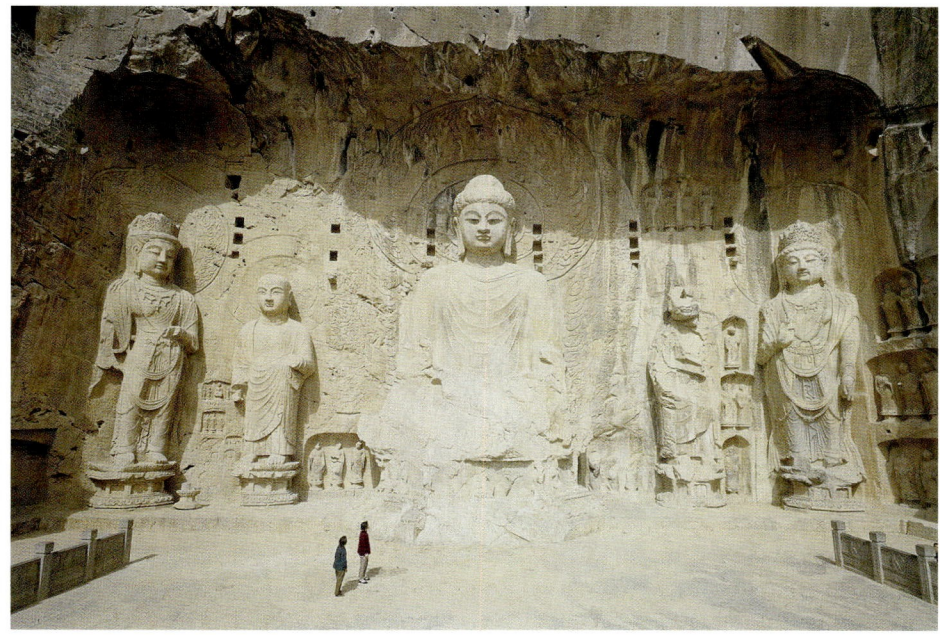

7-12 Vairocana Buddha, disciples, and bodhisattvas, Longmen Caves, Luoyang, China, Tang dynasty, completed 675. Buddha, approx. 44′ high.

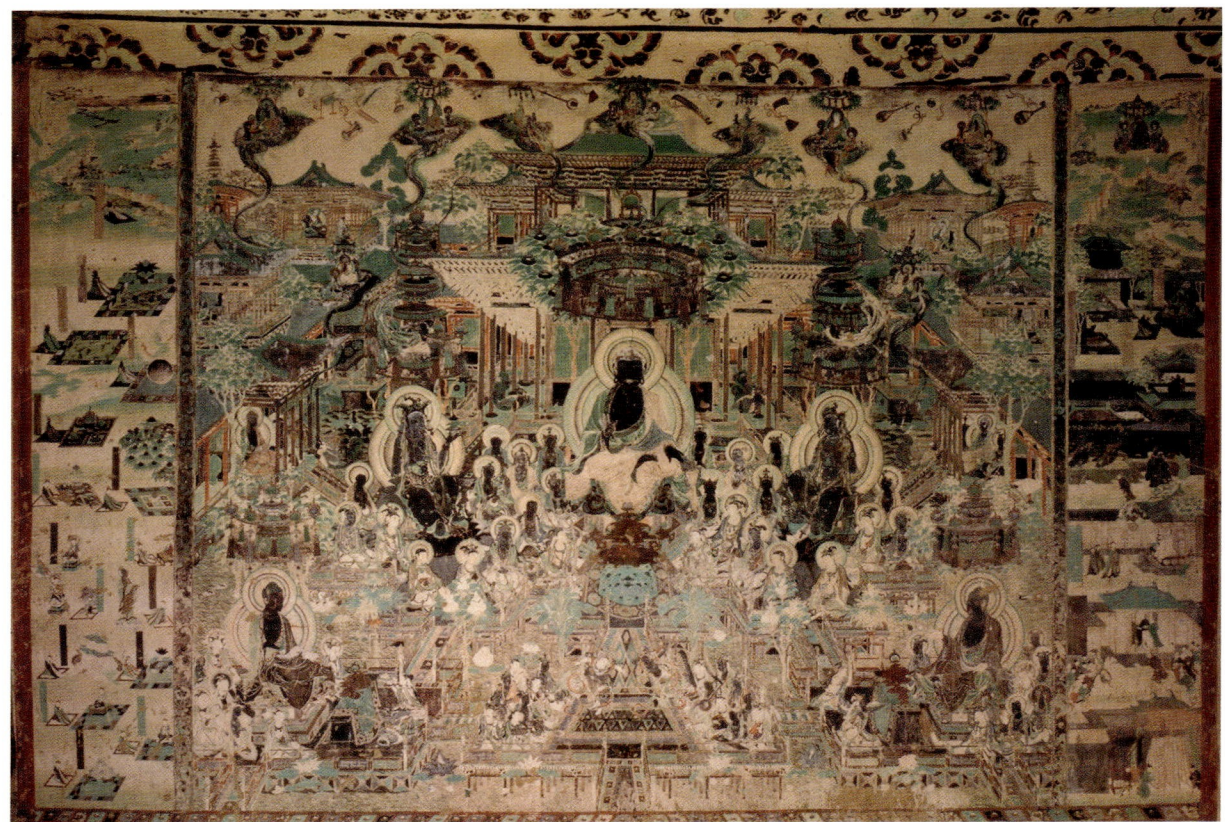

**7-13** Paradise of Amitabha, Cave 172, Dunhuang, China, Tang dynasty, mid-eighth century. Wall painting, approx. 10′ high.

Paradise of Amitabha (FIG. **7-13**), on the wall of one of the Dunhuang caves, shows how the splendor of the Tang era and religious teachings could come together in a powerful image. Buddhist Pure Land sects, especially those centered on Amitabha, Buddha of the West, had captured the popular imagination in the Period of Disunity under the Six Dynasties and continued to flourish during the Tang dynasty. Pure Land teachings asserted that individuals had no hope of attaining enlightenment through their own power because of the waning of the Buddha's Law. Instead, they could obtain rebirth in a realm free from spiritual corruption simply through faith in Amitabha's promise of salvation. Richly detailed, brilliantly colored pictures steeped in the opulence of the Tang dynasty, such as this one, greatly aided worshipers in gaining faith by visualizing the wonders of such a paradise. Amitabha sits in the center of a raised platform, his principal bodhisattvas and lesser divine attendants surrounding him. Before them a celestial dance takes place. Bodhisattvas had strong appeal in East Asia as compassionate beings ready to achieve Buddhahood but dedicated to humanity's salvation. Some received direct worship and became the main subjects of sculpture and painting.

**TANG TEMPLES** In the Dunhuang mural, Amitabha appears against a backdrop of ornate buildings characteristic of the Tang era. The Tang rulers embellished their empire with extravagant wooden structures, colorfully painted and of colossal size, possessing furnishings of great luxury and elaborate gold, silver, and bronze ornaments. Unfortunately, few Tang buildings survive. Among them is the Foguang Si (Buddha Radiance Temple), one of the oldest surviving Buddhist temples in China. It lacks the costly embellishment of imperial structures in the capital, but its east main hall (FIG. **7-14**) displays the distinctive curved roofline

of later Chinese architecture, which was not present in the Han examples (FIGS. 7-7 and 7-8) discussed earlier. A complex grid of beams and purlins, and a thicket of interlocking brackets, support the overhang of the eaves—some 14 feet out from the column faces—as well as the timbered and tiled roof.

**COURT PAINTING** Chang'an, the Tang capital captured from the Sui, was laid out on a grid scheme and occupied more than 30 square miles. It was the greatest city in the world during the seventh and eighth centuries. The Tang emperors also fostered a brilliant tradition of painting. Although few examples are preserved, many art historians regard the early Tang dynasty as the golden age of Chinese figure painting.

In perfect accord with the glowing descriptions of Tang painting style by Chinese poets and critics are the unrestored portions

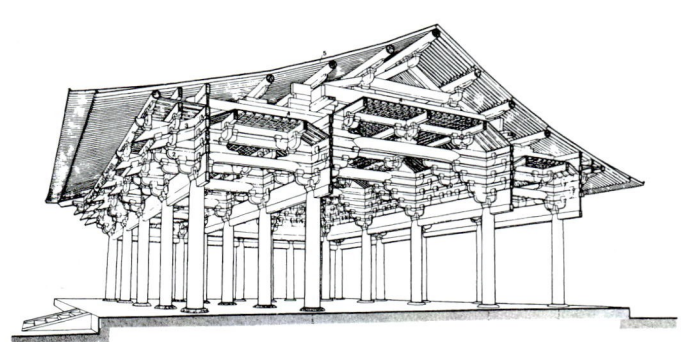

**7-14** Schematic cross-section and perspective drawing of east main hall, Foguang Si (Buddha Radiance Temple), Mount Wutai, China, Tang dynasty, ca. 857 (after L. Liu).

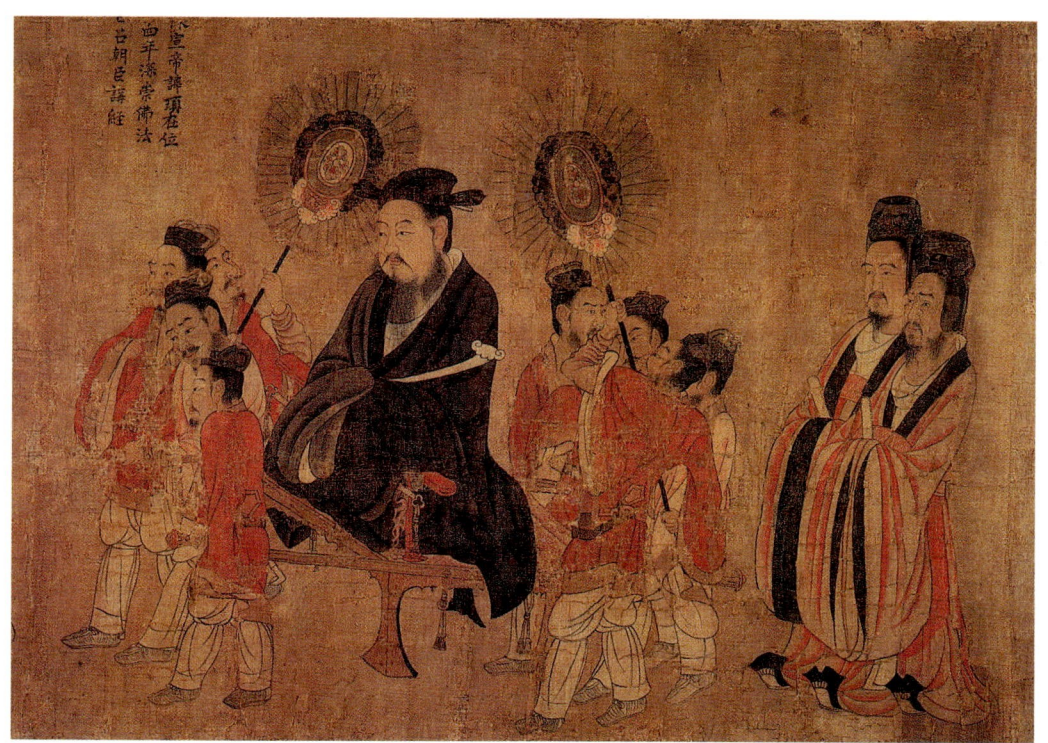

7-15 Attributed to Yan Liben, Emperor Xuan and attendants, detail of *The Thirteen Emperors,* Tang dynasty, ca. 650. Handscroll, ink and colors on silk, detail: $1' 8\frac{1}{4}'' \times 1' 5\frac{1}{2}''$; entire scroll: 17' 5'' long. Museum of Fine Arts, Boston. (Photograph © 2003 Museum of Fine Art, Boston).

of *The Thirteen Emperors* (FIG. 7-15), a masterpiece of line drawing and colored washes. The painting has long been attributed to YAN LIBEN (d. 673). Born into an aristocratic family and the son of a famous artist, Yan Liben was prime minister under the emperor Gaozong as well as a celebrated painter. This handscroll depicts 13 Chinese rulers from the Han to the Sui dynasties. Its purpose was to portray these historical figures as exemplars of moral and political virtue, in keeping with the Confucian ideal of learning from the past. Each emperor stands or sits in an undefined space, his eminence clearly indicated by his great size relative to his attendants. Simple shading in the faces and the robes gives the figures an added semblance of volume and presence. Our detail represents the emperor Xuan of the Chen dynasty (557–589) seated among his attendants, two of whom carry the ceremonial fans that signify his imperial status. The poses of the attendants vary sharply from figure to figure, lending vitality to the composition. Xuan stands out easily from the others not only because of his size and central position but also because of his dark robes and majestic serenity.

**A PRINCESS'S PAINTED TOMB** Wall paintings in the tomb of the Tang princess Yongtai (684–701) at Qianxian, near Chang'an, permit an analysis of court painting styles unobscured by problems of authenticity and reconstruction. When she was 17 years old, Yongtai was either murdered or forced to commit suicide by Wu Zetian. Her underground tomb dates to 706, however, because her formal burial had to await Wu Zetian's own death. The detail illustrated here (FIG. 7-16) depicts palace ladies and their attendants, images of pleasant court life to accompany the princess into her afterlife. The figures appear as if on a shallow stage. The artist did not provide any indications of background or setting, but intervals between the two rows and the figures' grouping in an oval suggest a consistent ground plane. The women assume a variety of poses, seen in full-face and in three-quarter views, from the front or the back. The device of paired figures facing into and out of the space of the picture appears often in paintings of this period and effectively creates depth. Thick, even contour lines describe full-volumed faces

and suggest solid forms beneath the drapery, all with the utmost economy. This simplicity of form and line, along with the measured cadence of the poses, results in an air of monumental dignity.

By the eighth century, China had become an international cultural center, integrating concepts and artistic forms from farther west and affecting developments to the south and east. In particular, Tang artists and craftspeople taught visitors from Korea and Japan, and some even traveled abroad. Thus, fair approximations of the Tang artists' elegant approach to figurative painting, dominated by sweeping brush lines, began to appear elsewhere in East Asia (see FIG. 8-9). They cannot, however, make up for the loss of famous works, including those by the greatest Tang figure painter, Wu Daozi (active ca. 710–760).

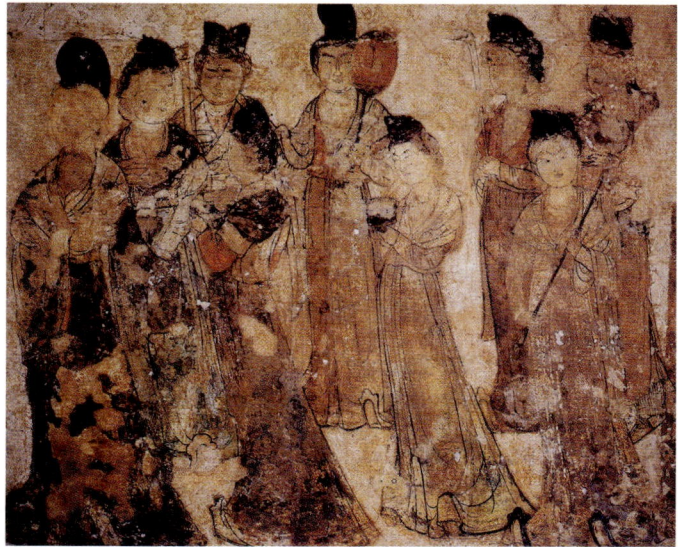

7-16 Palace ladies, detail of a wall painting in the tomb of Princess Yongtai, Qianxian, China, Tang dynasty, 706. Approx. 5' 10'' × 6' 6''.

**GLAZED EARTHENWARE SCULPTURE** Tang ceramists also achieved renown. They produced thousands of earthenware figures of people, domesticated animals, and fantastic creatures for burial in tombs. These statuettes attest to a demand for such objects by a much wider group of patrons than ever before, but terracotta funerary sculpture has a long history in China. The most spectacular example is the ceramic army of the First Emperor of Qin (FIG. 7-5). The subjects of the Tang figurines are also much more diverse than in earlier periods. The depiction of a broad range of foreigners, including Semitic traders and Central Asian musicians on camels, accurately reflects the cosmopolitanism of Tang China.

The artists painted some figurines with colored slips and decorated others, such as the spirited, handsomely adorned neighing horse in FIG. 7-17, with colorful lead glazes that ran in dramatic streams down the objects' sides when fired. The popularity of the horse as a subject of Chinese art reflects the importance the emperors placed on the quality of their stables. The breed represented here is powerful in build. Its beautifully arched neck terminates in a small, elegant head. Richly harnessed and saddled, the horse testifies to its rider's nobility. During the period of Tang power, representing horses in painting and ceramics was a special genre, on equal footing with figural composition and landscape.

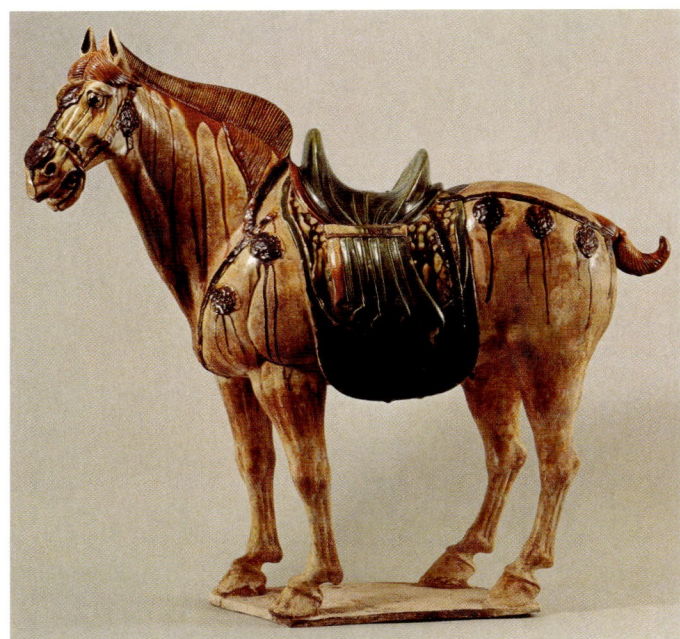

7-17  Neighing Horse, Tang dynasty, eighth to ninth century. Glazed earthenware, 1′ 8″ high. Victoria and Albert Museum, London.

## Song Dynasty

The last century of Tang rule witnessed many popular uprisings and the empire's gradual disintegration. After an interim of internal strife known as the Five Dynasties period (906–960), General Zhao Kuangyin succeeded in consolidating the country once again. He established himself as the first emperor (r. 960–976) of the Song dynasty (960–1279), which ruled China from a capital in the north at Bianliang (modern Kaifeng) during the Northern Song period (960–1127). Under the Song emperors, many of the hereditary privileges of the elite class were curtailed. Political appointments were made on the basis of scores on civil service examinations, and education came to be a more important prerequisite for Song officials than high birth.

The three centuries of Song rule, including the Southern Song period (1127–1279) when the capital was at Lin'an (modern Hangzhou) in southern China, were also a time of extraordinary technological innovation. Under the Song emperors, the Chinese invented the magnetic compass for sea navigation, printing with movable clay type, paper money, and gunpowder. Song China was the most technologically advanced society in the world in the early second millennium.

**FAN KUAN'S LANDSCAPES** For many observers, the Song dynasty also marks the apogee of Chinese landscape painting, which first emerged as a major subject during the Period of Disunity. Although many of the great Northern Song masters worked for the imperial court, FAN KUAN (ca. 960–1030) was a Daoist recluse (see "Daoism and Confucianism," page 196) who shunned the cosmopolitan life of Bianliang. He believed that nature was a better teacher than other artists, and he spent long days in the mountains studying not only configurations of rocks and trees but also the effect of sunlight and moonlight on natural forms. Just as centuries later in Italy, Giorgio Vasari would credit his contemporaries with the conquest of naturalism (see Chapter 21), so did Song critics laud Fan Kuan and other leading painters of the day as the first masters of the recording of light, shade, distance, and texture.

In *Travelers among Mountains and Streams* (FIG. **7-18**), painted in the early 11th century, Fan Kuan presents a vertical landscape of massive mountains rising from the distance. The overwhelming natural forms dwarf the few human and animal figures (for example, the mule train in the lower right corner), which the artist reduced to minute proportions. The nearly seven-foot-long silk hanging scroll cannot contain nature's grandeur, and the landscape continues in all directions beyond its borders. The painter depicted some elements from level ground (for example, the great boulder in the foreground), and others obliquely from the top (the shrubbery on the highest cliff). The shifting perspectives lead viewers on a journey through the mountains. To appreciate such landscapes fully, viewers must focus not only on the larger composition but also on intricate details and on the character of each brush stroke. Numerous "texture strokes" help model massive forms and convey a sense of tactile surfaces. For the face of the mountain, for example, Fan Kuan employed small, pale brush marks, the kind of texture stroke the Chinese call "raindrop strokes."

**HUIZONG, EMPEROR AND PAINTER** A century after Fan Kuan painted in the mountains of Shanxi, the emperor HUIZONG (1082–1135; r. 1101–1125) assumed the Song throne at Bianliang. Less interested in governing than in the arts, he brought the country to near bankruptcy and lost much of China's territory to the armies of the Tartar Jin dynasty (1115–1234), who captured the Song capital in 1126 and took Huizong as a prisoner. He died in their hands several years later. Himself an accomplished poet, calligrapher, and painter, Huizong reorganized the imperial painting academy and required the study of poetry and calligraphy as part of the official training of court painters. *Calligraphy,* or the art of writing, was highly esteemed in China throughout its history, and prominent inscriptions are frequent elements of Chinese paintings (see "Calligraphy and Inscriptions on Chinese Paintings," Chapter 26, page 766). Huizong also promoted the careful study both of

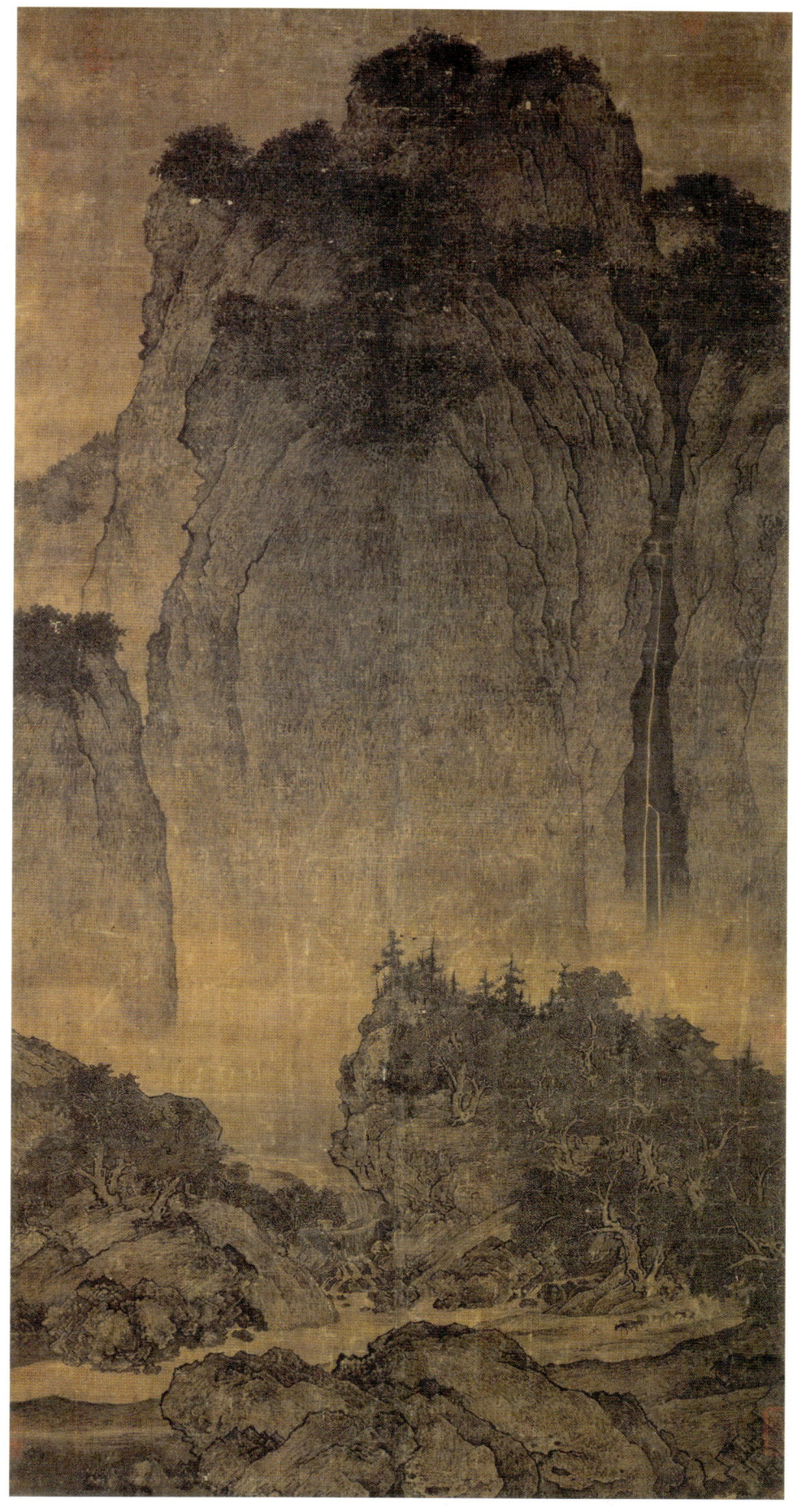

**7-18** FAN KUAN, *Travelers among Mountains and Streams,* Northern Song period, early 11th century. Hanging scroll, ink and colors on silk, 6′ 7$\frac{1}{4}$″ × 3′ 4$\frac{1}{4}$″. National Palace Museum, Taibei.

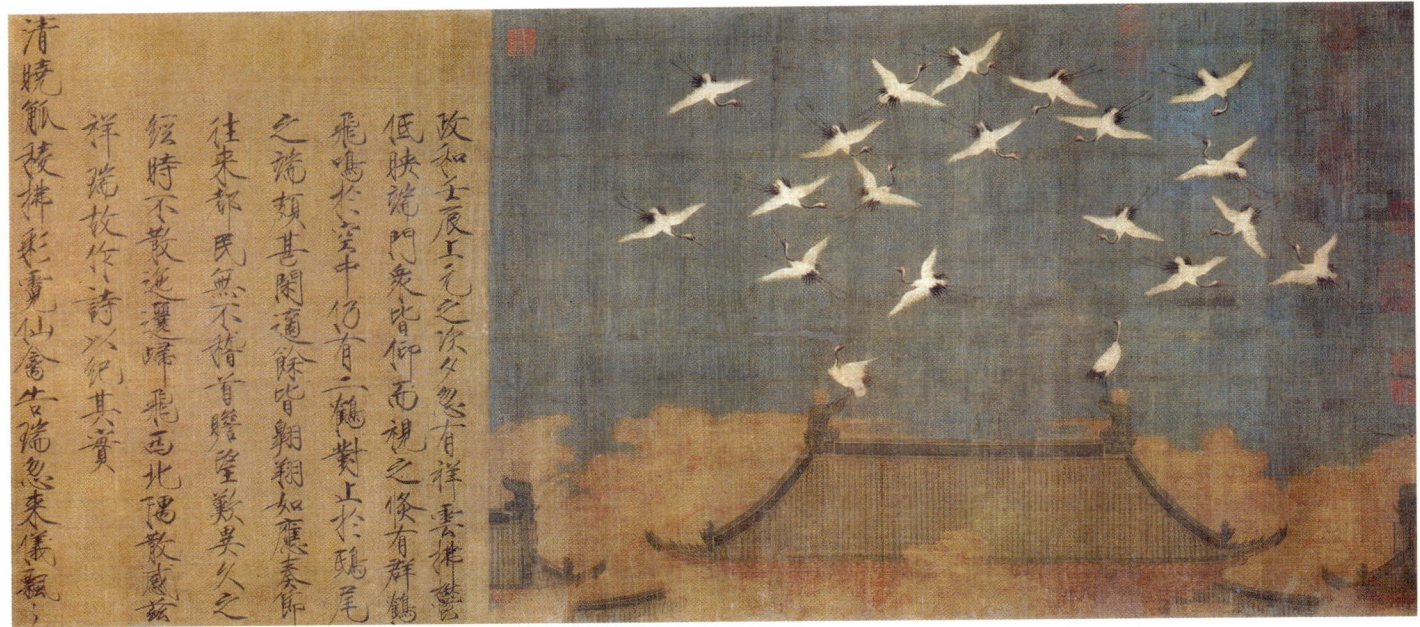

**7-19** Attributed to HUIZONG, *Auspicious Cranes*, Northern Song period, 1112. Section of a handscroll, ink and colors on silk, 1′ 8⅛″ × 4′ 6⅜″. Liaoning Provincial Museum, Shenyang.

nature and of the classical art of earlier periods, and was an avid art collector as well as the sponsor of a comprehensive catalogue of the vast imperial art holdings.

A short handscroll (FIG. **7-19**) usually attributed to Huizong is more likely the work of court painters under his direction, but it displays the emperor's style as both calligrapher and painter. Huizong's characters represent one of many styles of Chinese calligraphy. They are made up of thin strokes, and each character is meticulously aligned with its neighbors to form neat vertical rows. The painting depicts cranes flying over the roofs of Bian-liang. It is a masterful combination of elegant composition and realistic observation. The black and red feathers of the white cranes are carefully recorded, and the birds are depicted from a variety of viewpoints to suggest that they were circling around the roof. Huizong did not, however, choose this subject because of his interest in the anatomy and flight patterns of birds. The painting was a propaganda piece commemorating the appear-ance of 20 white cranes at the palace gates during a festival in 1112. The cranes were regarded as an auspicious sign, proof that Heaven had blessed Huizong's rule. Although few would ever have viewed the handscroll, the cranes were also displayed on painted banners on special occasions, where they could be seen by a larger public.

**CIZHOU POTTERY** Song artists also produced superb ceram-ics. Some reflect their patrons' interests in antiquities and imitate the powerful forms of the Shang and Zhou bronzes. However, Song ceramics more commonly had elegant shapes with fluid sil-houettes. Many featured monochrome glazes, such as the famous celadon wares, also produced in Korea (FIG. 7-28), but a quite dif-ferent kind of pottery, loosely classed as Cizhou, emerged in northern China. The example shown (FIG. **7-20**) is a vase of the high-shouldered shape known as *meiping*. Chinese potters devel-oped the subtle techniques of *sgraffito* (incising the design through a colored slip) during the Northern Song period. They achieved the intricate black-and-white design here by cutting through a black slip (see "Chinese Earthenwares and Stonewares,"

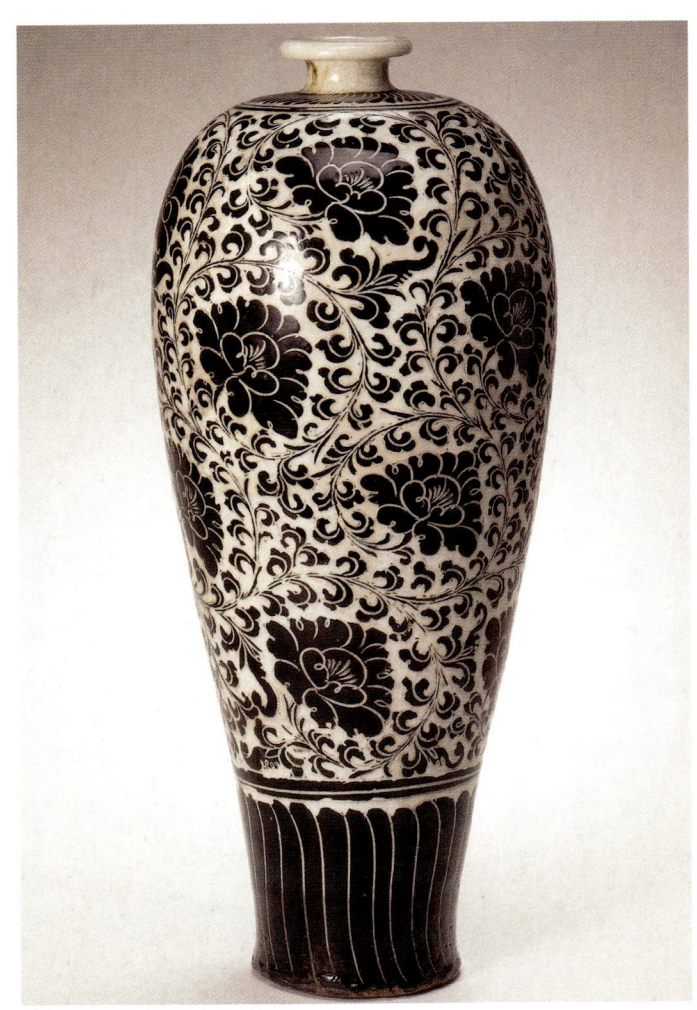

**7-20** Meiping vase, from Xiuwi, China, Northern Song period, 12th century. Stoneware, Cizhou type, with sgraffito decoration, 1′ 7½″ high. Asian Art Museum of San Francisco, San Francisco (Avery Brundage Collection).

page 193). The tightly twining vine and flower petal motifs on this vase closely embrace the vessel in a perfect accommodation of surface design to vase shape.

**CHINESE PAGODAS**  For two centuries during the Northern Song period, the Liao dynasty (907–1125) ruled part of northern China. In 1056, the Liao rulers built the Foguang Si Pagoda (FIGS. **7-21** and **7-22**), the tallest wooden building in the world, at Yingxian in Shanxi Province. The *pagoda*, or tower, the building type most often associated with Buddhism in China and other parts of East Asia, is the most eye-catching feature of a Buddhist temple complex. It somewhat resembles the tall towers of Indian temples (see "Hindu Temples," Chapter 6, page 180) and their distant ancestor, the Indian stupa (see "The Stupa," Chapter 6, page 172). Like stupas, many early pagodas housed relics and provided a focus for devotion to the Buddha. Later pagodas served other functions, such as housing sacred images and texts. The Chinese and Koreans built both stone and brick pagodas, but wooden pagodas were also common and became the standard in Japan.

The nine-story octagonal pagoda at Yingxian is 216 feet tall and made entirely of wood (see "Chinese Wooden Construction," page 200). Sixty giant four-tiered bracket clusters carry the floor beams and projecting eaves of the five main stories. They rest on two concentric rings of columns at each level. Alternating main stories and windowless mezzanines with cantilevered balconies, set back further on each story as the tower rises, form an elevation of nine stories altogether. Along with the open veranda on the ground level and the soaring pinnacle, the balconies visually lighten the building's mass. Our cross-section (FIG. 7-22) shows the symmetrical placement of statues of the Buddha inside, the colossal scale of the ground-floor statue, and the intricacy of the beam-and-bracket system at its most ingenious.

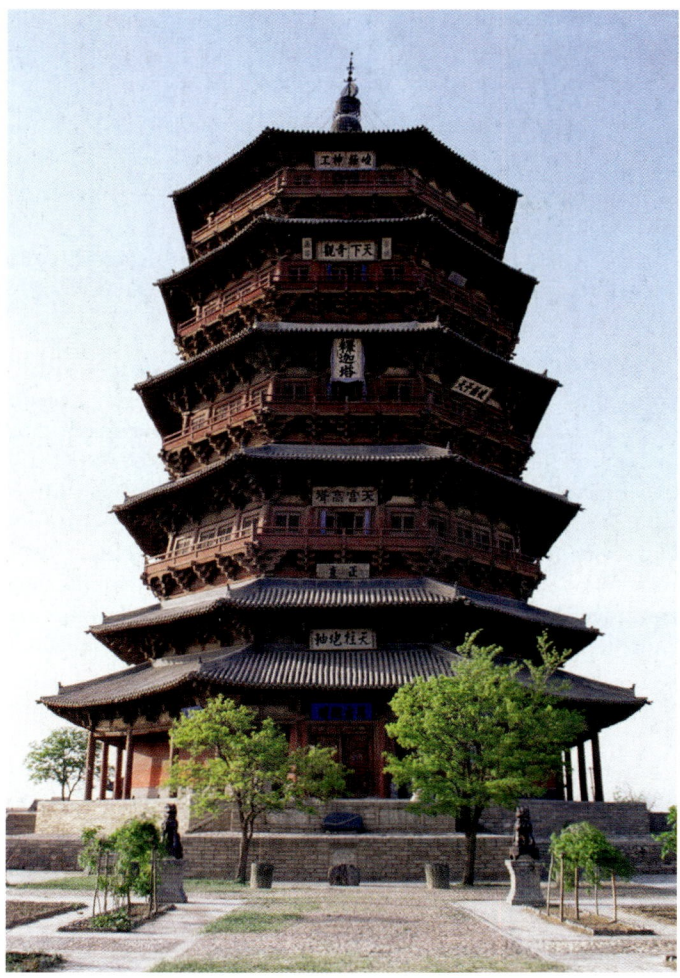

**7-21**  Foguang Si Pagoda, Yingxian, China, Liao dynasty, 1056.

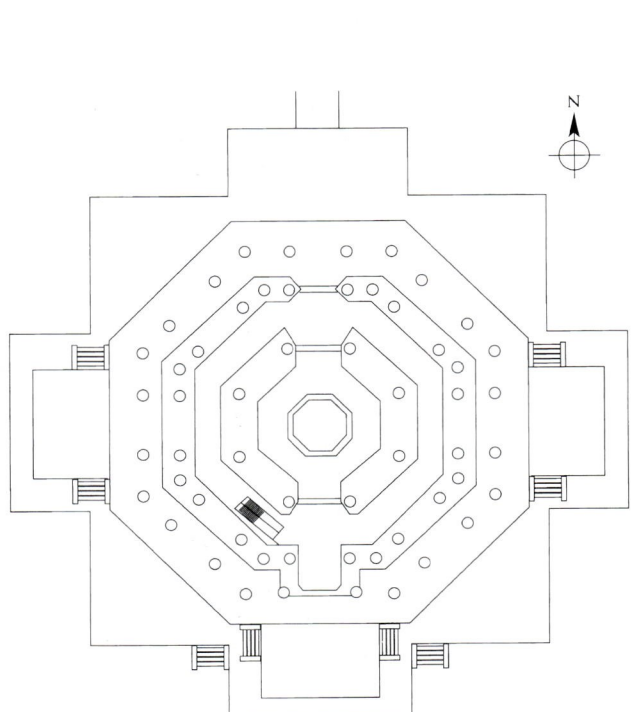

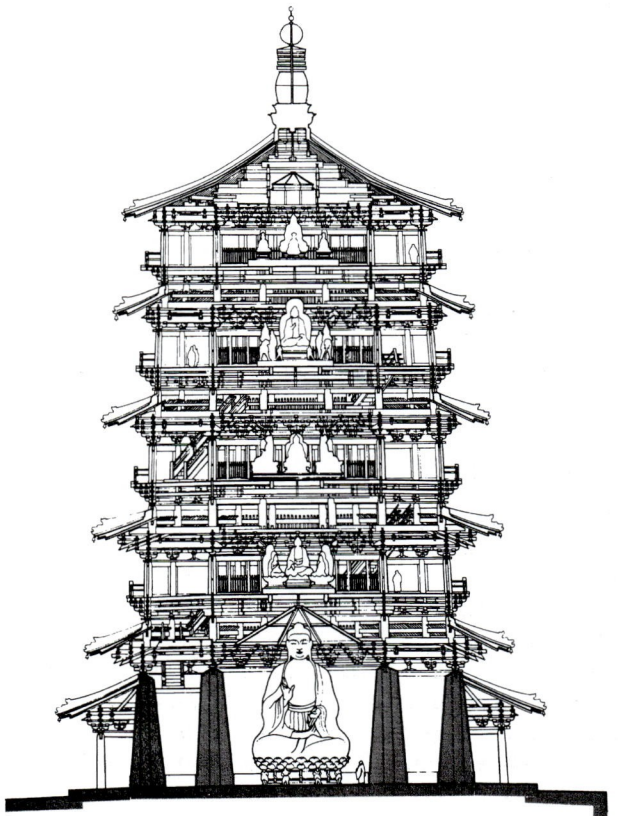

**7-22**  Plan and cross-section of Foguang Si Pagoda, Yingxian, China, Liao dynasty, 1056 (after L. Liu).

## Southern Song Period

When the Jin captured Bianliang and the emperor Huizong in 1126 and took control of northern China, Gaozong (r. 1127–1162), Huizong's sixth son, escaped and eventually established a new Song capital in the south at Lin'an (present-day Hangzhou). From there, he and his successors during the Southern Song period ruled their reduced empire until 1279.

**EMPERORS, POETS, AND PAINTERS** Court sponsorship of painting continued in the new capital and, as in the Northern Song period, some of the emperors were directly involved with the painters of the imperial painting academy. During the reign of Ningzong (r. 1194–1224), members of the court, including Ningzong himself and the empress Yang, frequently added brief poems to the paintings created under their direction. Some of the painters belonged to families that had worked for the Song emperors for several generations. The most famous of these was the Ma family, which began working for the Song dynasty during the Northern Song period.

MA YUAN (ca. 1160–1225) painted *On a Mountain Path in Spring* (FIG. **7-23**), a small silk album leaf, for Ningzong in the early 13th century. In his composition, in striking contrast to Fan Kuan's much larger *Travelers among Mountains and Streams* (FIG. 7-18), the landscape is reduced to a few elements and confined to the foreground and left side of the page. A large, solitary figure gazes out into the infinite distance. Framing him are the carefully placed diagonals of willow branches. Near the upper right corner

a bird flies toward the couplet that Ningzong added in ink, demonstrating his mastery of both poetry and calligraphy (see "Calligraphy and Inscriptions," Chapter 26, page 766):

> *Brushed by his sleeves, wild flowers dance in the wind;*
> *Fleeing from him, hidden birds cut short their songs.*

Some scholars have suggested that the author of the two-line poem is actually the empress Yang, but the inscription is in the emperor's hand. In any case, landscape paintings such as this one are perfect embodiments of the Chinese ideals of peace and unity with nature.

**TWO SPHERES OF BEING** Religious painting also flourished under the Southern Song emperors. Neo-Confucianism, a blend of traditional Chinese thought and selected Buddhist concepts, became the leading philosophy, but Buddhist themes were still the subject of many painters. ZHOU JICHANG (ca. 1130–1190) painted *Arhats Giving Alms to Beggars* (FIG. **7-24**) in 1184 as part of a series of 100 scrolls produced at the southern coastal city of Ningbo for an abbot who invited individual donors to pay for the paintings as offerings in the nearby Buddhist temple. *Arhats* are enlightened disciples of the Buddha who have achieved freedom from rebirth (nirvana) by suppression of all desire for earthly things. They were charged with protecting the Buddhist Law until the arrival of the Buddha of the Future.

In the scroll we illustrate (FIG. 7-24), Zhou Jichang arranged the foreground, middle ground, and background vertically to clarify the arhats' positions relative to one another and to the

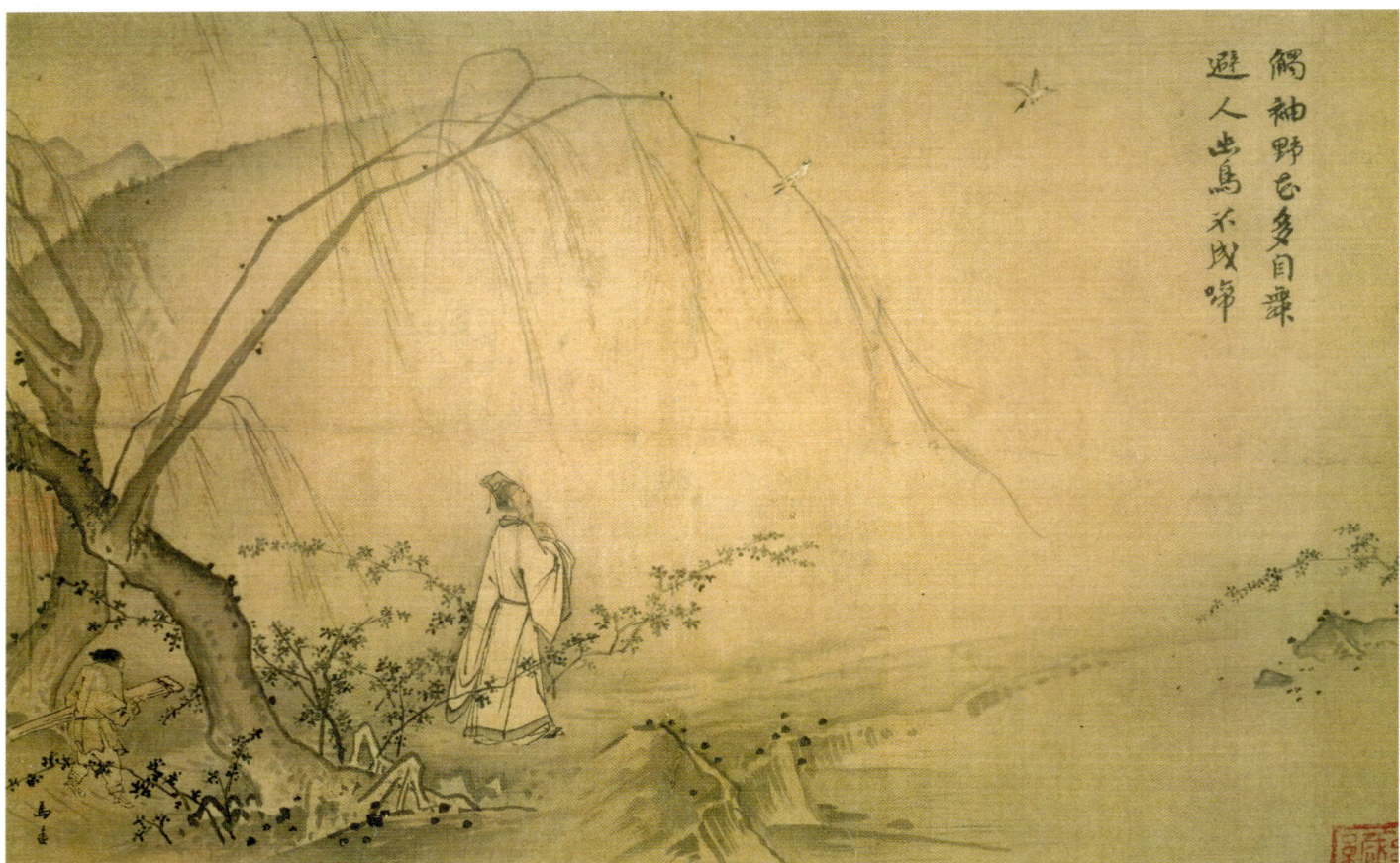

7-23 MA YUAN, *On a Mountain Path in Spring,* Southern Song period, early 13th century. Album leaf, ink and colors on silk, $10\frac{3}{4}'' \times 17''$. National Palace Museum, Taibei.

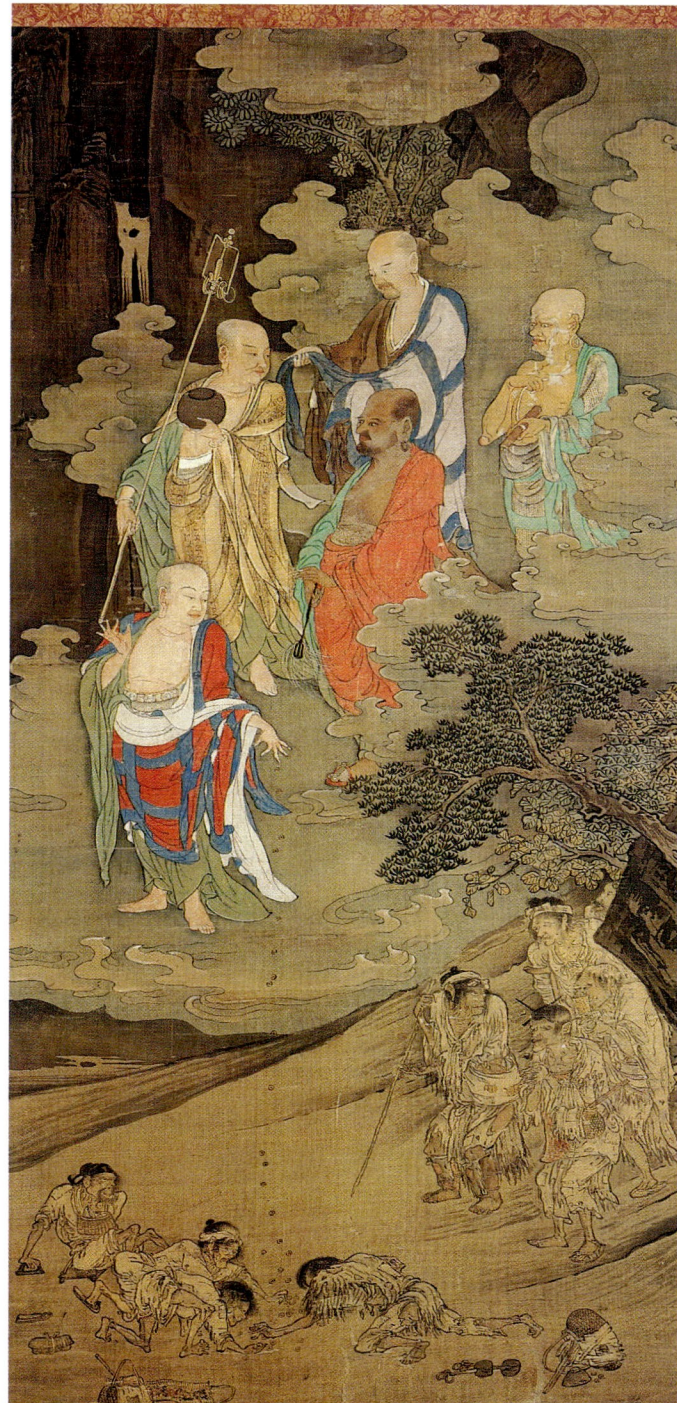

7-24 ZHOU JICHANG, *Arhats Giving Alms to Beggars,* Southern Song period, 1184. Ink and colors on silk, 3′ 8″ × 1′ 9″. Museum of Fine Arts, Boston. (Photograph © 2003 Museum of Fine Art, Boston).

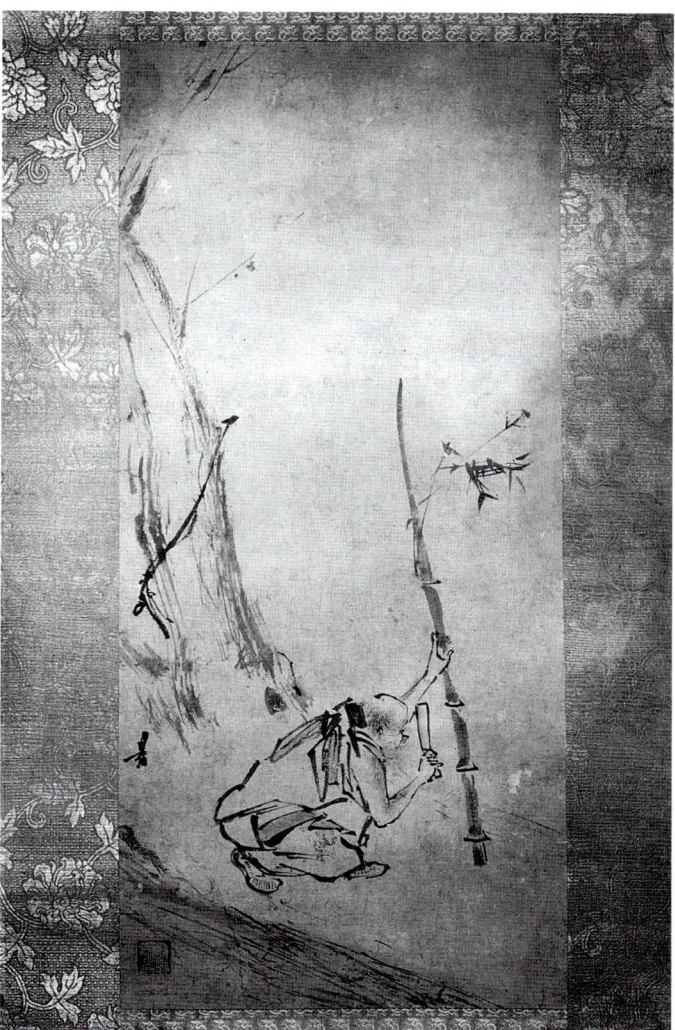

7-25 LIANG KAI, *Sixth Chan Patriarch Chopping Bamboo,* Southern Song period, early 13th century. Hanging scroll, ink on paper, 2′ 5$\frac{1}{4}$″ high. Tokyo National Museum.

beggars. The arhats move with slow dignity in a plane above the ragged wretches who scramble miserably for the alms their serene benefactors throw down. The extreme difference in deportment between the two groups distinguishes their status, as do their contrasting features. The arhats' vividly colored attire, flowing draperies, and quiet gestures set them off from the dirt-colored and jagged shapes of the people physically and spiritually beneath them. The composition of the landscape—the cloudy platform and lofty peaks of the arhats and the desertlike setting of the beggars—also sharply distinguishes the two spheres of being.

**LIANG KAI AND CHAN** Chan Buddhism (see "Chan Buddhism," page 212), which stressed the quest for personal enlightenment through meditation, flourished under the Song dynasty. LIANG KAI (active early 13th century) was a master of an abbreviated, expressive style of ink painting that found great favor among Chan monks in China, Korea, and Japan. He served in the painting academy of the imperial court in Hangzhou, and his early works include poetic landscapes typical of the Southern Song. Later in life, he left the court and concentrated on figure painting, including Chan subjects.

Surviving works attributed to him include an ink painting (FIG. 7-25) of the Sixth Chan Patriarch, Huineng, crouching as he chops bamboo. In Chan thought, the performance of even such mundane tasks had the potential to become a spiritual exercise. More specifically, this scene represents the patriarch's "Chan moment," when the sound of the blade striking the bamboo resonates within his spiritually attuned mind to propel him through the final doorway to enlightenment. The scruffy, caricature-like representation of the revered figure suggests that Huineng's mind is not burdened by worldly matters, such as physical appearance or signs of social status. Liang Kai utilized a variety of brushstrokes in the execution of this deceptively

### Chan Buddhism

Under the Song emperors (960–1279), the new school of *Chan* Buddhism gradually gained importance, until it was second only to Neo-Confucianism. The Chan school traced its origins through a series of patriarchs (the founder and early leaders, joined in a master–pupil lineage). The First Chan Patriarch was Bodhidharma, a semilegendary sixth-century Indian missionary. By the time of the Sixth Chan Patriarch, Huineng (638–713; FIG. 7-25) in the early Tang period, the religious forms and practices of the school were already well established.

Although Chan monks adapted many of the rituals and ceremonies of other schools over the course of time, they focused on the cultivation of the mind or spirit of the individual in order to break through the illusions of ordinary reality, especially by means of meditation. In Chan thought, the means of enlightenment lie within the individual, and direct personal experience with some ultimate reality is the necessary step to its achievement. Meditation is a critical practice. In fact, the word "Chan" is a translation of the Sanskrit word for meditation. Bodhidharma is said to have meditated so long in a cave that his arms and legs withered away. The "Northern School" of Chan holds that enlightenment comes only gradually after long meditation, but the "Southern School" believes that the breakthrough to enlightenment can be sudden and spontaneous.

These beliefs influenced art and aesthetics as they developed in China and spread to Korea and Japan. In Japan, Chan (Japanese *Zen*) had an especially extensive, long-term impact on the arts and remains an important school of Buddhism there today (see "Zen and Zen-Inspired Art," Chapter 27, page 781).

simple picture. Most are pale and wet, ranging from the fine lines of Huineng's beard to the broad texture strokes of the tree. A few darker strokes, which define the vine growing around the tree and the patriarch's clothing, offer visual accents in the painting. This kind of quick and seemingly casual execution of paintings has traditionally been interpreted as a sign of a painter's ability to produce compelling pictures spontaneously as a result of superior training and character, or, in the Chan setting, progress toward enlightenment.

# KOREA

Korea is a northeast Asian peninsula that shares borders with China and Russia, and faces the islands of Japan (MAP 7-1). Korea's pivotal location is a key factor in understanding the relationship of its art to that of China and the influence of its art on that of Japan. Ethnically, the Koreans are related to the peoples of eastern Siberia and Mongolia, as well as to the Japanese. In the early centuries, the Koreans used Chinese characters to write Korean words, but later they invented their own phonetic alphabet. Korean art, although frequently based on Chinese models, is not merely derivative but has, like Korean civilization, a distinct identity.

## Three Kingdoms Period

**CHINA AND THE THREE KINGDOMS** Pottery-producing cultures appeared on the Korean peninsula in the Neolithic period no later than 6000 BCE, and the Korean Bronze Age dates from ca. 1000 BCE. Bronze technology was introduced from the area that is today northeastern China (formerly known as Manchuria). About 100 BCE, during the Han dynasty, the Chinese established outposts in Korea. The most important was Lelang, which became a prosperous commercial center. By the middle of the century, however, three native kingdoms—Koguryo, Paekche, and Silla—controlled most of the Korean peninsula and reigned for more than seven centuries until Silla completed its conquest of its neighbors in 668. During this era, known as the Three Kingdoms period (ca. 57 BCE–688 CE), Korea remained in continuous contact with both China and Japan. Buddhism was introduced into Korea from China in the fourth century CE. The Koreans in turn transmitted it from the peninsula to Japan in the sixth century.

**GOLD CROWNS IN SILLA TOMBS** Tombs of the Silla kingdom have yielded spectacular artifacts representative of the wealth and power of its rulers. Finds in the region of Kyongju justify the city's ancient name—Kumsong ("City of Gold"). The gold-and-jade crown (FIG. **7-26**) from a tomb at Hwangnamdong, near Kyongju, dated to the fifth or sixth century, also attests to the high quality of artisanship among Silla artists. The crown's major elements, the band and the uprights, as well as the myriad spangles adorning them, were cut from sheet gold and embossed along the edges. Gold rivets and wires secure the whole, as do the comma-shaped pieces of jade further embellishing the crown. Archaeologists interpret the uprights as stylized tree and antler forms believed to symbolize life and supernatural power. The Hwangnamdong crown has no counterpart in China, although the technique of working sheet gold may have come to Korea from northeast China.

## Unified Silla Kingdom

Aided by China's emperor, the Silla Kingdom conquered the Koguryo and Paekche kingdoms and unified Korea in 668. The era of the Unified Silla Kingdom (688–935) is roughly contemporary with the Tang dynasty's brilliant culture in China, and many consider it to be Korea's golden age.

**BUDDHIST SOKKURAM** The Silla rulers embraced Buddhism both as a source of religious enlightenment and as a protective force. They considered the magnificent Buddhist temples they constructed in and around their capital of Kyongju to be not only places of worship but also a supernatural defense against external

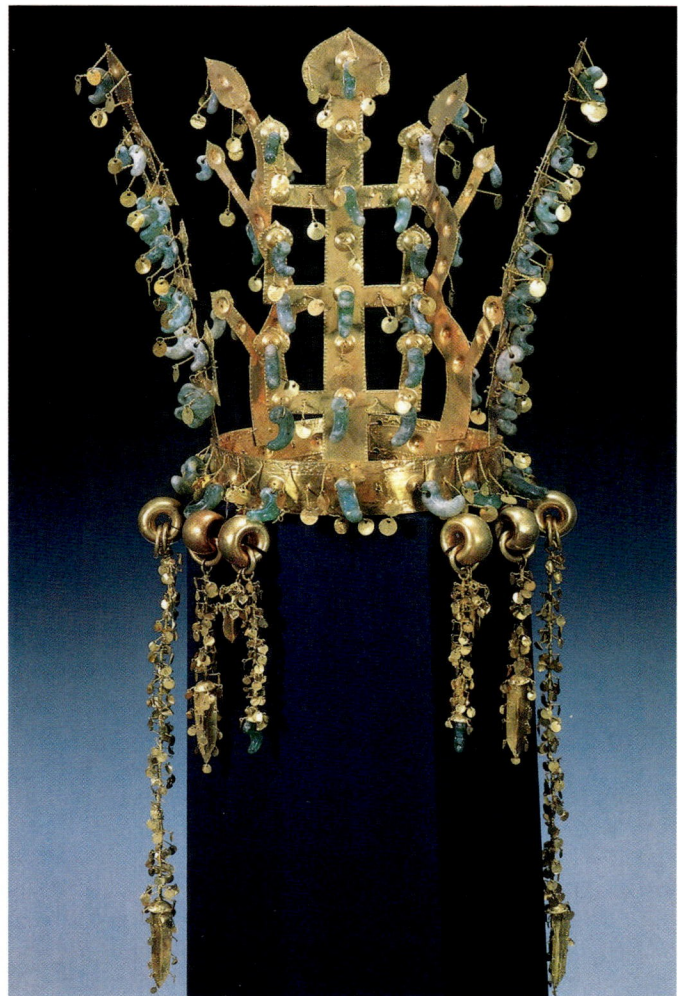

7-26 Crown, from north mound of tomb 98 at Hwangnamdong, near Kyongju, Korea, Silla kingdom, fifth to sixth century. Gold, $10\frac{3}{4}''$ high. Kyongju National Museum, Kyongju.

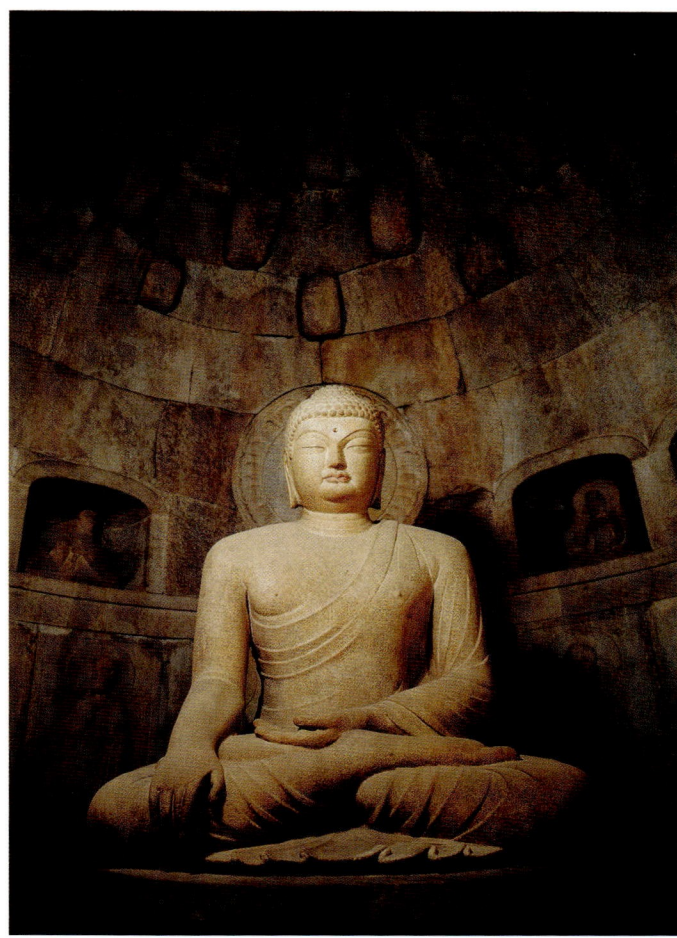

7-27 Shakyamuni Buddha, at entrance to cave temple, Sokkuram, Korea, Great Silla, 751–774. Granite, approx. 11′ high.

threats. Unfortunately, none of these temples survived Korea's turbulent history. However, at Sokkuram, near the summit of Mount Toham, northeast of the city, a splendid granite Buddhist monument is preserved. Scant surviving records suggest that it was built under the supervision of Kim Tae-song, a member of the royal family who served as prime minister. He initiated construction in 742 to honor his parents in his previous life. Certainly the intimate scale of Sokkuram and the quality of its reliefs and freestanding figures support the idea that it was a private chapel for royalty.

The main *rotunda* (circular area under a dome; FIG. **7-27**) measures about 21 feet in diameter. Despite its modest size, the Sokkuram project required substantial resources. Unlike the Chinese Buddhist caves at Longmen (FIG. 7-12), the interior wall surfaces and sculpture were not cut from the rock in the process of excavation. Instead, workers assembled hundreds of granite pieces of various shapes and sizes, attaching them with stone rivets instead of mortar. Sculpted images of bodhisattvas, arhats, and guardians line the lower zone of the wall. Above, 10 niches contain miniature statues of seated bodhisattvas and believers.

All these figures face inward toward the 11-foot-tall statue of Shakyamuni, the historical Buddha, which dominates the cham-

ber as it sits slightly back from center and faces the entrance. Carved from a single block of granite, the image represents the Buddha as he touched the earth to call it to witness the realization of his enlightenment at Bodh Gaya (see FIG. 6-10b). Although remote in time and place from the Sarnath Buddha in India (see FIG. 6-12), this majestic image remains faithful to its iconographic prototype. More immediately, the Korean statue draws on the robust, round-faced figures of Tang China (FIG. 7-12), and its drapery is a more schematic version of the fluid type found in Tang sculpture. However, the figure has a distinctly broad-shouldered dignity combined with harmonious proportions that are without close precedents. It is regarded as one of the finest images of the Buddha in East Asia.

## Koryo Dynasty

Although Buddhism was the established religion of Korea, Confucianism, introduced from China during the Silla era, increasingly shaped social and political conventions. In the ninth century, the three old kingdoms began to reemerge as distinct political entities, but by 935 the Koryo (from Koguryo) had taken control, and they dominated for the next three centuries. The Unified Silla and Koryo kingdoms overlap slightly (the period

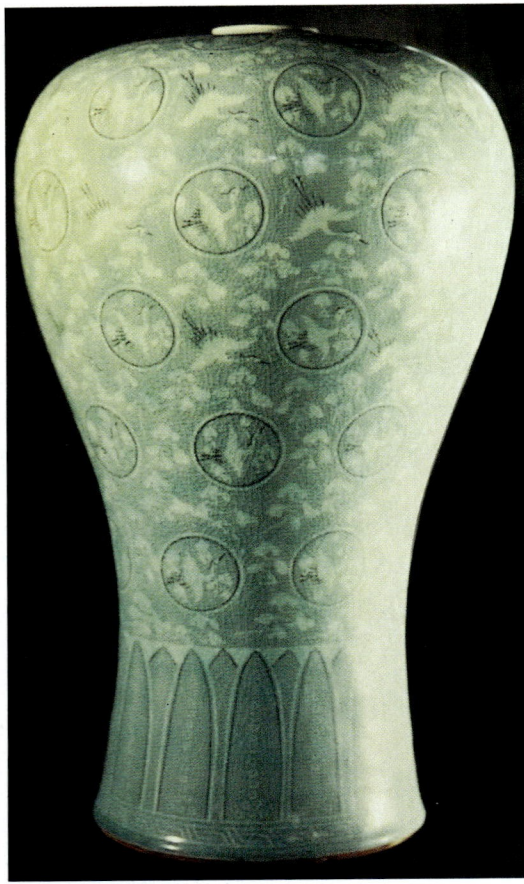

**7-28** Maebyong vase, Koryo period, ca. 918–1000. Celadon with inlaid decoration, 1′ 4½″ tall. Kansong Art Museum, Seoul.

glazes, fired in an oxygen-deprived kiln to become gray, pale blue, pale green, or brownish olive. Incised or engraved designs in the vessel alter the thickness of the glaze to produce elegant tonal variations.

A vase in the shape known as *maebyong* in Korean (FIG. **7-28**; *meiping* in Chinese, FIG. **7-20**) probably dates to early in the Koryo period (ca. 918–1000). It is decorated using the inlay technique for which Koryo potters were famous. On our vase, the artist incised delicate motifs of flying cranes—some flying down and others, in *roundels* (circular frames), flying up—into the clay's surface and then filled the grooves with white and colored slip. Next, the potter covered the incised areas with the celadon green glaze. Variation in the spacing of the motifs shows the potter's sure sense of the dynamic relationship between ornamentation and ceramic volume.

## CONCLUSION

Chinese culture has its roots long before recorded history, and China has often been in the vanguard of technological innovation. The Chinese invented, for example, the magnetic compass, movable type, paper money, and gunpowder, and Chinese silk was treasured in the West.

The Chinese also excelled in the fields of art and architecture. The bronzes of the Shang dynasty are among the finest produced anywhere during the Bronze Age, and Chinese artists were masters in working jade, ivory, and lacquer. Although Chinese artworks of monumental scale, such as the Qin terracotta army, are world renowned, many of the most famous Chinese artists worked on a much more intimate scale, painting landscapes and other subjects in handscrolls and displaying their expertise in recording light, shade, distance, and texture. The Chinese method of bracketed wooden construction, in which walls do not bear weight but serve as screens, was emulated throughout Asia.

China's achievements in virtually every field spread beyond even the boundaries of the vast empires it sometimes controlled. Although Buddhism began in India, the Chinese adaptations and transformations of its teachings, religious practice, and artistic forms were those that spread farther east. The cultural debt of China's neighbors to China is immense. But it was Korea that was the crucial artistic, cultural, and religious link between the mainland and the islands of Japan.

ca. 918–935) because both kingdoms existed as these shifts in power occurred. In 1231, the Mongols, who had invaded China, pushed into Korea, beginning a war lasting 30 years. In the end, the Koryo had to submit to forming an alliance with the Mongols, who eventually conquered all of China (see Chapter 26).

**CELADON WARE** Koryo potters in the 12th century produced the famous Korean *celadon* wares, admired worldwide. Celadon wares are characterized by highly translucent iron-pigmented

| CHINA | KOREA | | |
|---|---|---|---|
| LATE NEOLITHIC | | 5000 BCE | |
| | | 2000 BCE | |
| XIA | | 1600 BCE | |
| SHANG | | | |
| | | 1050 BCE | |
| ZHOU (WARRING STATES, 475–221 BCE) | | | |
| QIN | | 221 BCE | |
| | | 206 BCE | |
| HAN | | 220 CE | |
| PERIOD OF DISUNITY | THREE KINGDOMS PERIOD (57 BCE–668 CE) | | |
| SUI | | 589 | |
| | | 618 | |
| TANG | UNIFIED SILLA KINGDOM (TO 935) | | |
| FIVE DYNASTIES | | 906 | |
| NORTHERN SONG | | 960 | |
| SOUTHERN SONG | KORYO (TO 1392) | 1127 | |
| | | 1279 | |

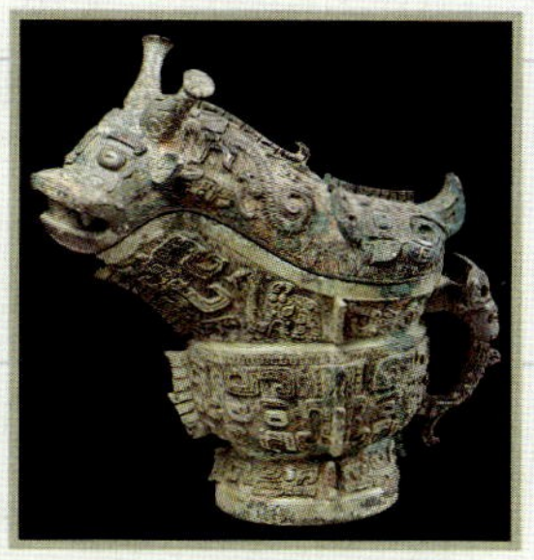

**1** Guang, from Anyang, 12th or 11th century BCE

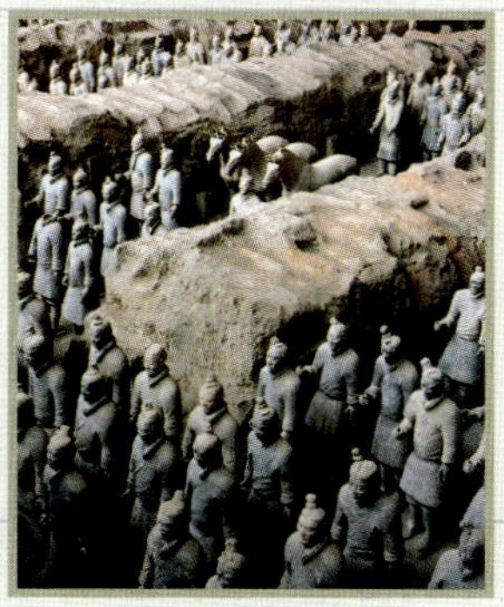

■ Laozi, Daoist philosopher, CA. 604–531 BCE

■ Xie He, *Six Laws of Painting*, early sixth century BCE

■ Shakyamuni Buddha, CA. 563–483 BCE

■ Confucius, 551–479 BCE

■ Mencius, Confucian philosopher, CA. 371–289 BCE

■ Zhuangzi, Daoist philosopher, CA. 370–301 BCE

**2** ■ The First Emperor of Qin, R. 221–210 BCE

**2** Army of the First Emperor of Qin, Lintong, ca. 210 BCE

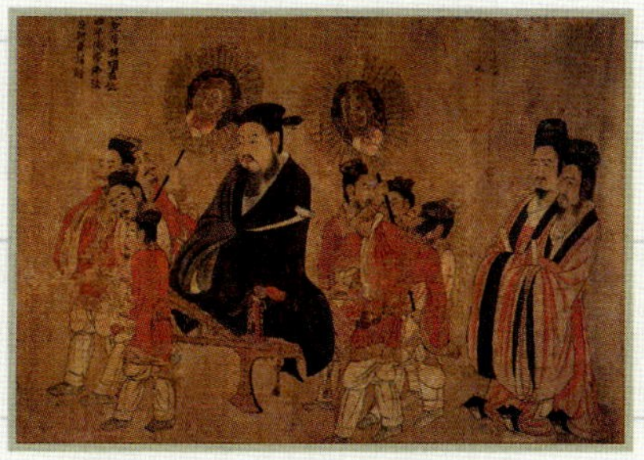

■ Buddhism introduced to Korea, 372

■ Bodhidharma, first Chan Buddhist patriarch, sixth century

**3** ■ Buddhist persecution by Wuzong, 845

**3** Yan Liben, *The Thirteen Emperors*, ca. 650

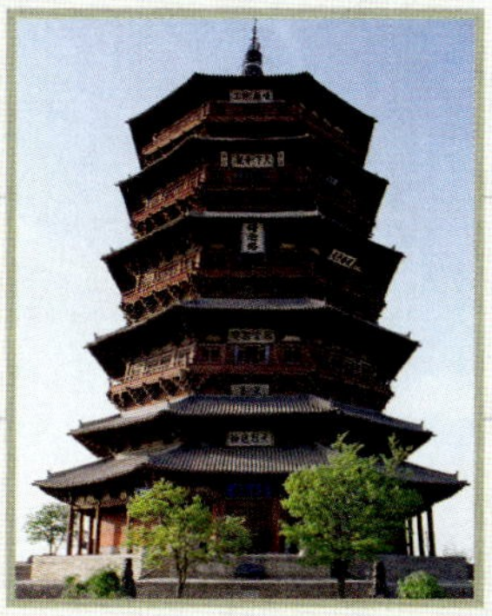

**4** ■ Jin capture Bianliang from Song, 1126

■ Mongols invade Korea, 1231

**4** Foguang Si Pagoda, Yingxian, China, Liao Dynasty, 1056

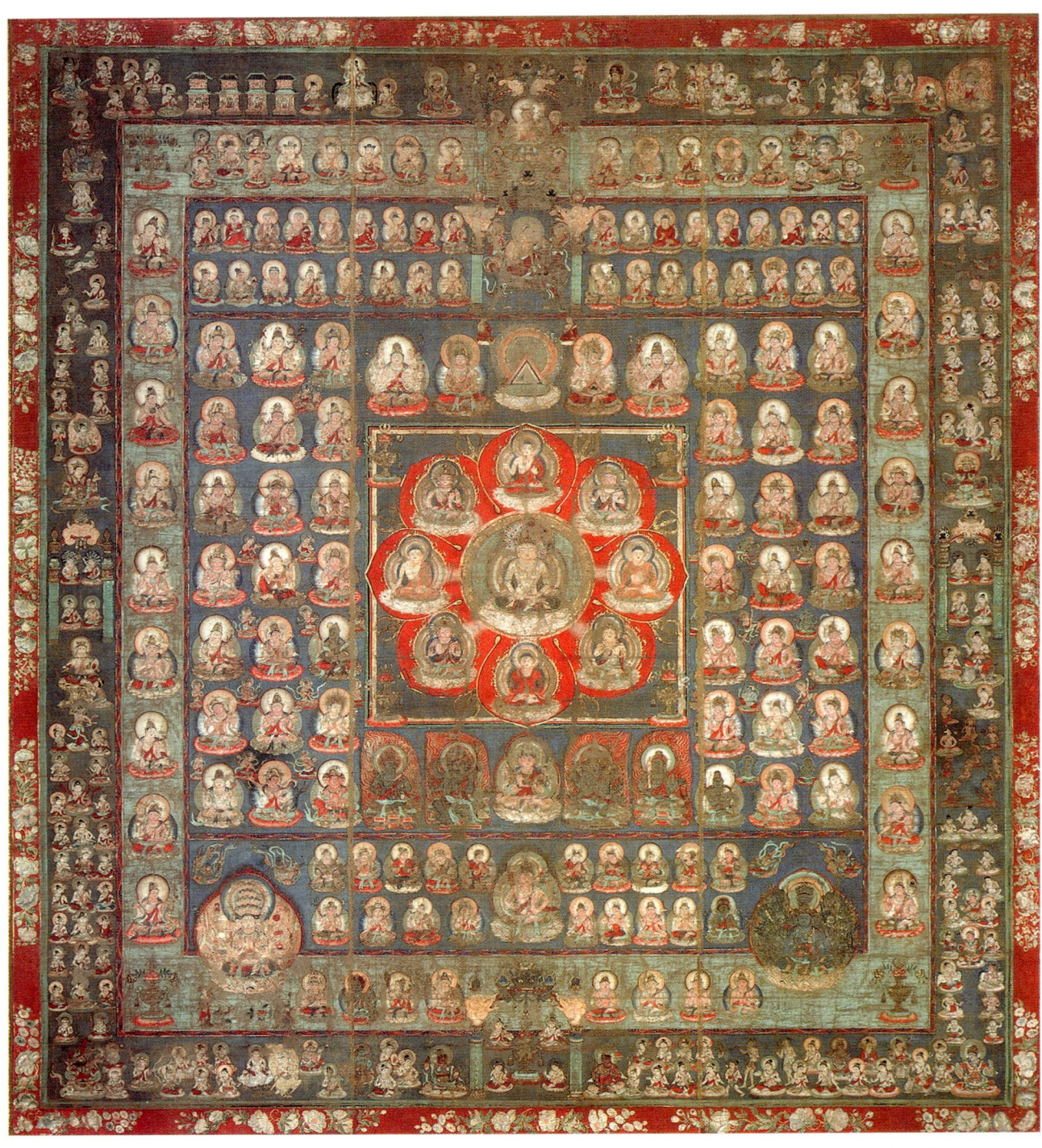

Taizokai (Womb World) of Ryokai Mandara, Kyoogokokuji (Toji), Kyoto, Japan, Early Heian period, second half of ninth century. Hanging scroll, color on silk, 6′ × 5′ $\frac{5''}{8}$.

# 8

# SHRINES, STATUES, AND SCROLLS

## THE ART OF EARLY JAPAN

The Japanese archipelago (MAP **8-1**) consists of four main islands—Hokkaido, Honshu, Shikoku, and Kyushu—and hundreds of smaller ones, a surprising number of them inhabited. Two distinct population groups lived on the islands by earliest historical times, and the great majority of Japan's inhabitants trace their ancestry to one of these two early groups. The history of Japanese art and culture is a history of change and adaptation. Over the centuries, the Japanese have demonstrated a remarkable ability to surmount challenges, such as a mountainous island terrain that made travel and communication difficult. Japanese culture also reveals a responsiveness to imported ideas, such as Buddhism and Chinese writing systems, filtering in from continental eastern Asia. To acknowledge this responsiveness to mainland influences is not to suggest that Japan simply absorbed these imported ideas and practices. Indeed, over the centuries, Japan has developed a truly distinct culture, characterized by wide variety. There are strong regional variations, not just in art but in dialect, cuisine, and local customs—differences that persist to some degree even today. Ultimately, Japan's close proximity to the continent has promoted extensive exchange with mainland cultures, while the sea has helped protect it from outright invasions and allowed it to develop an individual and unique character.

## JAPAN BEFORE BUDDHISM

### Jomon Period (ca. 10,500–300 BCE)

CORD-MARKED POTTERY Japan's earliest distinct culture is the Jomon. The term *jomon*, meaning "cord markings," refers to the technique that this culture used to decorate earthenware vessels. The Jomon people were hunter-gatherers, but in contrast to most hunter-gatherer societies, which were nomadic, the Jomon enjoyed surprisingly

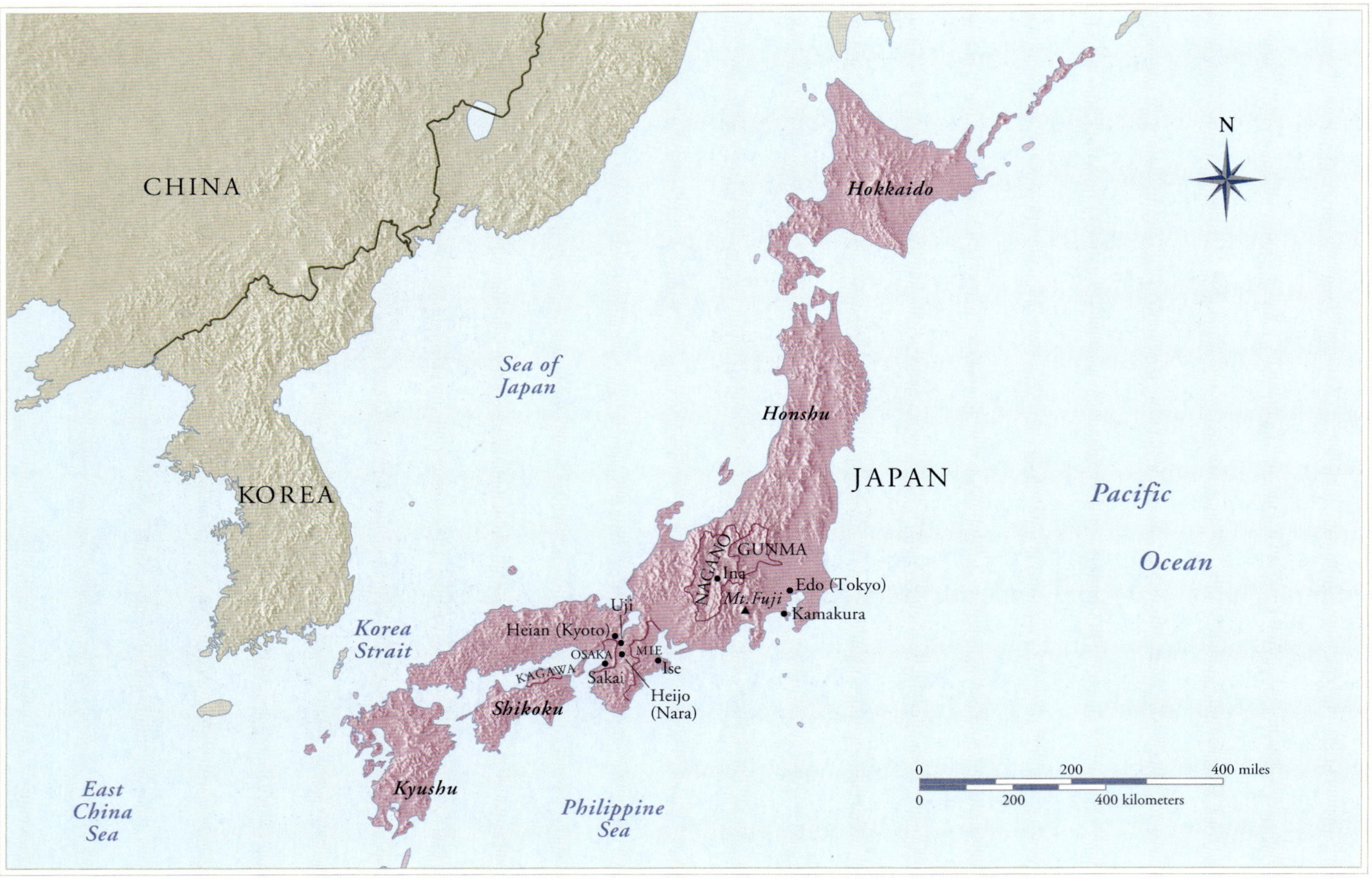

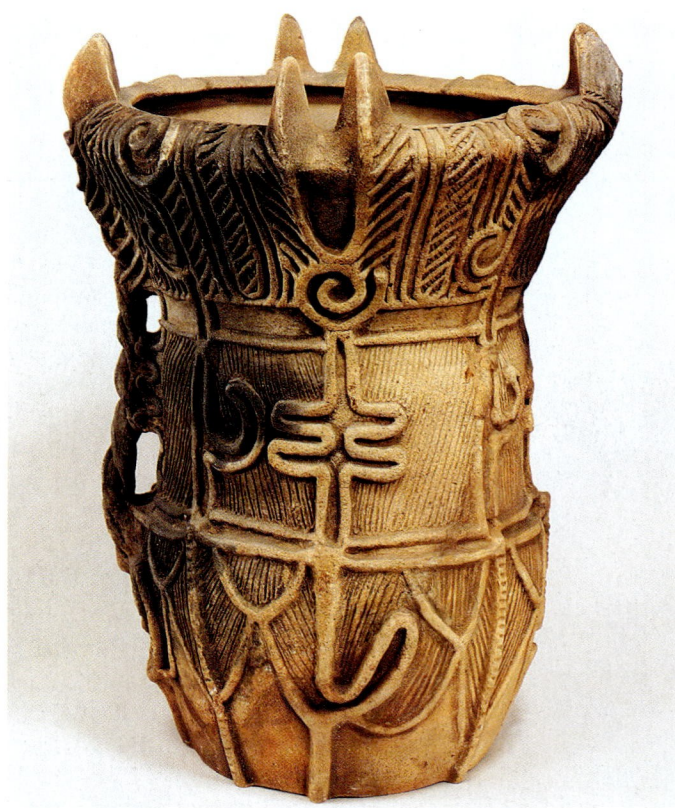

MAP 8-1 Early Japan.

settled lives. Their villages consisted of pit dwellings—shallow round excavations with raised earthen rims and thatched roofs. Their settled existence permitted the Jomon people to develop distinctive ceramic technology, even before their development of agriculture. In fact, archaeologists have dated some ceramic sherds found in Japan to before 10,000 BCE—older than the sherds from any other area of the world.

In addition to rope markings, incised lines and applied coils of clay adorned Jomon pottery surfaces. The most impressive examples come from the Middle Jomon period (2500–1500 BCE). Much of the population then lived in the mountainous inland region, where local variations in ceramic form and surface treatment flourished. However, all Jomon potters shared a highly developed feeling for modeled, rather than painted, ceramic ornament. Jomon pottery displays such a wealth of applied clay coils, striped incisions, and sometimes quasi-figural motifs that the sculptural treatment in certain instances even jeopardizes the basic functionality of the vessel. Jomon vessels served a wide variety of purposes, from storage to cooking to bone burial. Some of the most elaborate pots may have served ceremonial functions.

A dramatic example (FIG. 8-1) from Miyanomae in Nagano Prefecture (a prefecture is a district with a governor) shows a characteristic, intricately modeled surface and a partially sculpted rim. Jomon pottery contrasts strikingly with China's most celebrated Neolithic earthenwares (see FIG. 7-1) in that the Japanese vessels are extremely thick and heavy. The harder, thinner, and lighter Neolithic Chinese earthenware emphasizes basic ceramic form and painted decoration.

8-1 Vessel, from Miyanomae, Nagano Prefecture, Japan, Middle Jomon period, 2500–1500 BCE. Earthenware, 1′ 11⅔″ × 1′ 1¼″. Tokyo National Museum, Tokyo.

## Yayoi (ca. 300 BCE – 300 CE) and Kofun (ca. 330 – 552 CE)* Periods

Jomon culture gradually gave way to Yayoi beginning around 300 BCE in Kyushu, the southernmost of the main Japanese islands. Increased interaction with both China and Korea and immigration from Korea brought dramatic social and technological transformations. People continued to live in pit dwellings, but their villages grew in size, and they developed fortifications, indicating a perceived need for defense. Toward the end of this period, near 300 CE, Chinese visitors noted that Japan had walled towns, many small kingdoms, and a highly stratified social structure. Wet-rice agriculture provided the social and economic foundations for such development.

**BANDED BRONZE BELLS** The Yayoi period was a time of tremendous change in Japanese material culture as well. The Yayoi produced pottery that was less sculptural and sometimes polychrome, a departure from the modeled Jomon ceramic vessels. In addition, they developed bronze casting and loom weaving. Among the most intriguing objects Yayoi artisans produced are the *dotaku,* or bells, based on Han Chinese bell forms. However, the Yayoi eventually abandoned the Chinese use of dotaku as musical instruments, and the bells evolved into treasured ceremonial bronzes. Cast in clay molds, these bronzes generally featured raised geometric decoration presented in bands or blocks. On a few, including one from Kagawa Prefecture (FIG. **8-2**), the ornament consists of simple line drawings of people and animals. Scholars have reached no consensus on the meaning of these images. Whatever their meaning, the dotaku engravings are the earliest surviving examples of pictorial art in Japan.

**TREASURE-FILLED BURIAL MOUNDS** Historians named the succeeding Kofun period (*ko* means "old"; *fun* means "tomb") after the great *tumuli* (pit graves covered by sometimes enormous mounds) that had begun to appear in the third century. These burial mounds were most likely initially built by a horse-riding people

---

* From this point on, all dates in this chapter are CE unless otherwise stated.

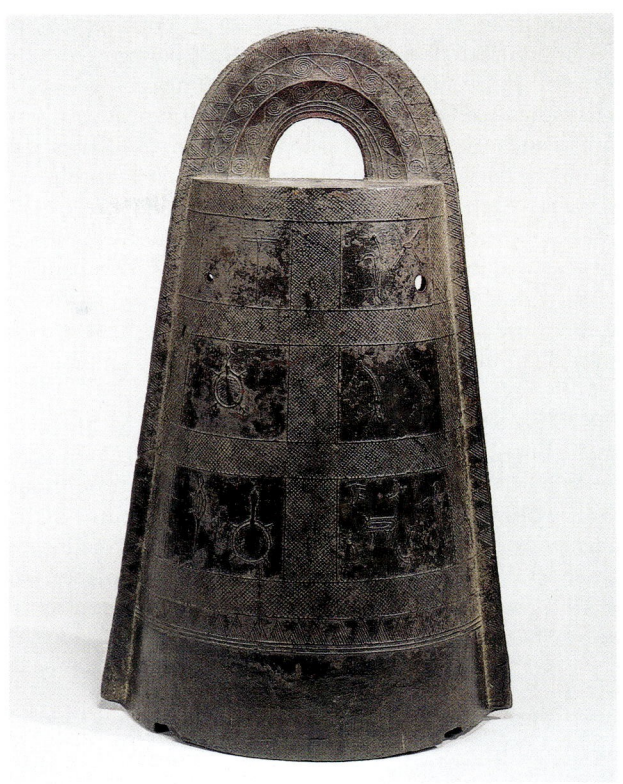

**8-2** *Dotaku* (bell) with incised figural motifs, from Kagawa Prefecture, Japan, late Yayoi period, 100 – 300. Bronze, 1′ 4⅞″ high. Tokyo National Museum, Tokyo.

from the Korean peninsula. The tumuli recall earlier Jomon practices of placing the dead on sacred mountains. The mounds grew dramatically in number and scale in the fourth century. The largest tumulus in Japan (FIG. **8-3**) is believed by scholars to be the tomb of Emperor Nintoku. The central mound, which takes the "keyhole"

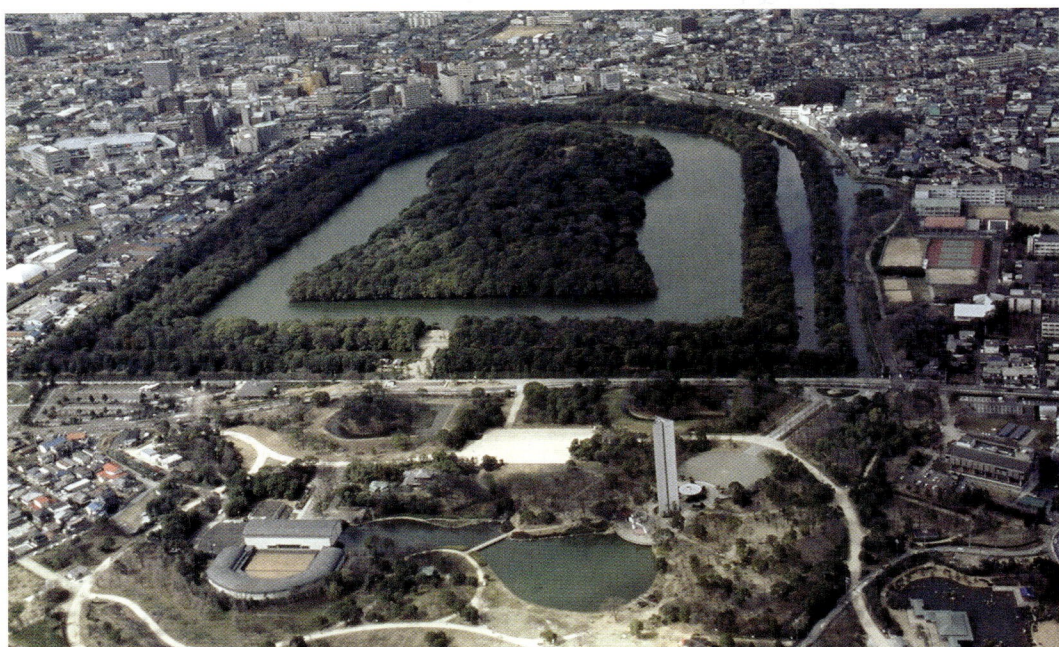

**8-3** Tomb of Emperor Nintoku. Sakai, Osaka Prefecture, Japan, Kofun period, late fourth to early fifth century.

form standard for tumuli during the Kofun period, is approximately 1,600 feet long and rises to a height of 90 feet. Surrounded by three moats, the entire site covers 458 acres. Numerous objects were placed with the coffin in the pit-shaft burial chamber to assist in the transition to the next life. For exalted individuals like Emperor Nintoku, objects buried included important symbolic items and imperial regalia—mirrors, swords, and comma-shaped jewels. Numerous bronze mirrors came from China, but the form of the tombs themselves and many of the buried goods suggest even closer connections with Korea. For example, the comma-shaped jewels closely resemble those found on Korean Silla crowns (see FIG. 7-26), whose simpler gilt bronze counterparts lay in the Japanese tombs.

**CYLINDER-STATUES FOR THE DEAD** Burial practices at Japanese tumuli also included the placement of unglazed ceramic sculptures called *haniwa* on and around the pit grave mounds. These sculptures, such as one from Gunma Prefecture (FIG. **8-4**), are distinctly Japanese. Compared to the terracotta soldiers and horses buried with the Qin emperor in Shaanxi Province, China (see FIG. 7-5), these statues appear deceptively whimsical as variations on a cylindrical theme (*hani* means "clay," *wa* means

"circle"). Yet haniwa sculptors skillfully adapted the basic clay cylinder into a host of forms, from abstract shapes to objects, animals (for example, deer, bears, horses, and monkeys), and human figures, such as warriors and female shamans. These artists altered the shapes of the cylinders, emblazoned them with applied ornaments, excised or built up forms, and then painted the haniwa. The variety of figure types suggests that haniwa functioned not as military guards but as a spiritual barrier protecting both the living and the dead from contamination. The Japanese of the Kofun period set these sculptures, usually several feet in height, both in curving rows and in tableaux, or scenes, around a haniwa house placed directly over the deceased buried in the mound. Presumably, the number of sculptures reflected the status of the deceased; scholars estimate that Emperor Nintoku's tumulus included 20,000 haniwa placed around the mound.

**AMATERASU'S ANCIENT SHRINE** The shrine of the sun goddess, Amaterasu (FIG. **8-5**), at Ise in Mie Prefecture, is the greatest of all monuments associated with the religious system that came to be known as Shinto (see "Pre-Buddhist Beliefs and Rituals in Japan," page 221). The location, use, and ritual reconstruction of this shrine every 20 years (with occasional interruptions) reflect the primary characteristics of Shinto—sacred space, ritual renewal, and purification. The Ise shrine is traditionally dated to the Kofun period. Recent scholarship, however, suggests a later date, but the shrine still serves as a representative example of sacred architecture in ancient Japan. The imperial clan traced its origins to Amaterasu, which reinforced her position as the dominant *kami,* or spiritual being. Although shrine architecture varies tremendously in Japan, scholars believe that the Ise shrine preserves some of the very earliest design elements. Yet the Ise shrine is unique; because of its connection to the Japanese imperial family, no other shrines may be constructed with this same design. The original source of the main sanctuary's form appears to be early granaries, sometimes represented on bronze mirrors or as clay haniwa. This is certainly appropriate, given that granaries were among the most important buildings in Japan's early agrarian society. Although not every aspect of the Ise shrine is equally ancient, the three main structures of the inner shrine convey some sense of Japanese architecture before the introduction of Buddhism and before the development of more elaborately constructed and adorned buildings.

Aside from the thatched roofs and some metallic decorations, the sole construction material at Ise is wood, fitted together in a *mortise-and-tenon* system, in which the wallboards were slipped into slots in the pillars. Two massive freestanding posts (once great cypress trunks), one at each end of the main sanctuary, support most of the weight of the *ridgepole,* the beam at the crest of the roof. The golden-hued cypress columns and planks contrast in color and texture with the white gravel covering the sacred grounds. The roof was originally constructed of thatch, which was smoked, sewn into bundles, and then laid in layers. The smooth shearing of the entire surface produced a gently changing contour. Today, cypress bark covers the roof. Decorative elements enhance the roofline, and include *chigi,* or ridge billets, which were originally extensions of the gable rafters at each end of the roof, and cylindrical wooden weights placed at right angles across the ridgepole. These decorative touches originally had a structural function. This shrine highlights the connection, central to Shinto, between nature and spirit. Not only are the materials derived from the natural world, but the shrine is sited in a specific location at which a kami is believed to have taken up residence.

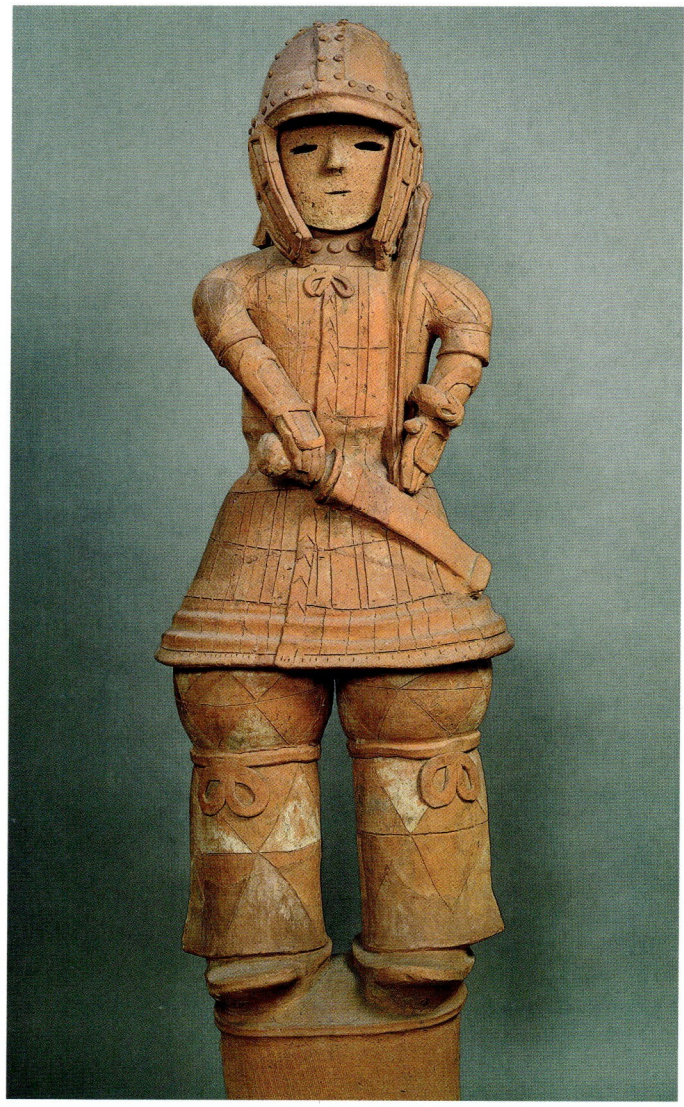

**8-4** *Haniwa* (cylindrical) warrior figure, from Gunma Prefecture, Japan, late Kofun period, fifth to mid-sixth century. Low-fired clay, 4′ 1¼″ high. Aikawa Archaeological Museum, Aikawa.

### Pre-Buddhist Beliefs and Rituals in Japan

The early beliefs and practices of pre-Buddhist Japan, which form a part of the belief system later called Shinto ("Way of the Gods"), did not derive from the teachings of any individual founding figure or distinct leader. Formal scriptures, in the strict sense, do not exist for these beliefs and practices either. Shinto developed in Japan in conjunction with the advent of agriculture during the Yayoi period. Shinto thus originally focused on the needs of this agrarian society, and included agricultural rites surrounding planting and harvesting. Villagers venerated and prayed to a multitude of local, sometimes specialized, deities or spirits called *kami*. The early Japanese believed kami existed in mountains, waterfalls, trees, and other features of nature, as well as in charismatic people, and they venerated not only the kami themselves but also the places the kami occupy, which are considered sacred.

Each clan (a local group claiming a common ancestor, and the basic societal unit during the Kofun period) had its own protector kami, to whom members offered prayers in the spring for successful planting and in the fall for good harvests. Clan members built shrines made up of several buildings, such as the one at Ise (FIG. 8-5), for kami. Priests made offerings of grains and fruits at these shrines and prayed on behalf of the clans. Rituals of divination, water purification, and ceremonial purification at the shrines proliferated. Visitors to the shrine area had to wash before entering in a ritual of spiritual and physical cleansing.

Purity was such a critical aspect of Japanese religious beliefs that people would abandon buildings and even settlements if negative events, such as poor harvests, suggested spiritual defilement. Even the early imperial court moved several times to newly built towns to escape impurity and the trouble it caused. Such purification concepts are also the basis for the cyclical rebuilding of the sanctuaries at grand shrines. The actual buildings of the inner shrine at Ise, for example, have been rebuilt every 20 years—at least 60 times—with few interruptions. Such rebuilding rids the sacred site of physical and spiritual impurities that otherwise might accumulate. During rebuilding, the old structure remains standing until the carpenters erect an exact duplicate next to it. In this way, the Japanese have preserved ancient forms with great precision.

When Buddhism arrived in Japan from the mainland in the sixth century, Shinto practices changed under its influence. For example, until the introduction of Buddhism, painted or carved images of Shinto deities did not exist. Yet despite the eventual predominance of Buddhism in Japan, Shinto continues to exist as a vital religion for many Japanese.

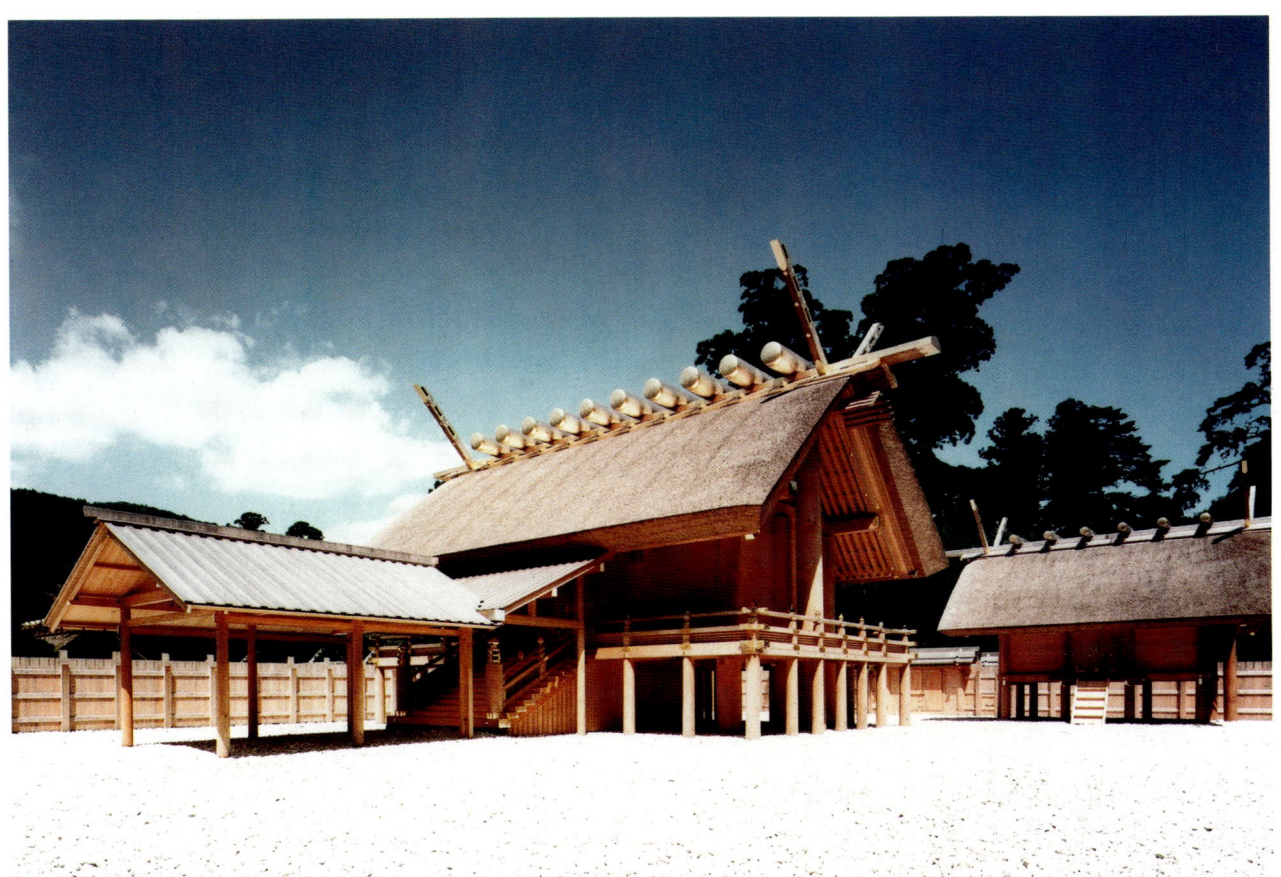

**8-5** Main hall, Ise shrine, Ise, Mie Prefecture, Japan, as rebuilt in 1993.

# Buddhist Japan

## Asuka (552–645), Early Nara (Hakuho; 645–710), and Nara (710–784) Periods

**ESTABLISHING BUDDHISM IN JAPAN** In 552, according to traditional interpretation, the ruler of Paekche, one of Korea's Three Kingdoms (see Chapter 7), sent Japan's ruler a gilded bronze statue of the Buddha along with *sutras* (Buddhist scriptures) translated into Chinese, at the time the written language of eastern Asia. This event marked the beginning of the Asuka period, when Japan's ruling elite embraced major elements of continental culture that had been gradually filtering into Japan. These cultural components became firmly established in Japan and included Chinese writing, Confucianism (see "Daoism and Confucianism," Chapter 7, page 196), and Buddhism (see "Buddhism and Buddhist Iconography," Chapter 6, page 171). The Japanese court, ruling from a series of capitals south of modern Kyoto, increasingly adopted the forms and rites of the Chinese court. In 710, the Japanese finally established what they intended as a permanent capital at Heijo (present-day Nara). City planners laid out the new capital on a symmetrical grid closely modeled on the plan of the Chinese capital of Chang'an. However, Nara remained the capital only until 784; after a transitional period, Heiankyo became the capital in 794.

For half a century after 552, Buddhism met with opposition, but by the end of that time, the new religion was established firmly in Japan. Older beliefs and practices (those that came to be known as Shinto) continued to have significance (and do to the present day), especially as agricultural rituals and imperial court rites. As time passed, Shinto deities even gained new identities as local manifestations of Buddhist deities.

In the arts associated with Buddhist practices, Japan followed Korean and Chinese prototypes very closely, especially during the Asuka, Early Nara (Hakuho), and Nara periods. In fact, early Buddhist architecture in Japan adhered so closely to mainland standards (although generally with a considerable time lag) that surviving Japanese temples have helped greatly in the reconstruction of what was almost completely lost on the continent. Buddhist temples served as monasteries as well and were actually building complexes rather than individual structures.

**A GOLDEN HALL FOR WORSHIP** The main building in a Japanese Buddhist temple complex, the image hall, housed the major sculptural icons and provided a site of worship and prayer. At Horyuji, an important surviving early temple complex located outside Nara, the image hall (FIG. 8-6) is known as the *kondo* (Golden Hall) and dates from around 680. Although periodically repaired and somewhat altered (the covered porch is an eighth-century addition; the upper railing dates to the 17th century), the structure retains its graceful but sturdy forms beneath the modifications. The main pillars (not visible in our illustration due to the porch addition) decrease in diameter from bottom to top, as in classical architecture. The tapering provides an effective transition between the more delicate brackets above and the columns' stout forms. Also somewhat masked by the added porch is the harmonious reduction in scale from the first to the second story. Following Chinese models, the builders used ceramic tiles as roofing material. Other buildings at the site include a five-story pagoda that serves as a reliquary.

**A BRONZE BUDDHA TRIAD** Although wood later became the primary material of Buddhist sculpture through much of Japanese history, bronze was not uncommon. Among the earliest extant examples of Japanese Buddhist sculpture is a bronze *Buddha triad* (Buddha flanked by two bodhisattvas; FIG. **8-7**). Rescued from Horyuji's predecessor, which was destroyed by fire in the seventh century, it became one of the main images in the Horyuji kondo. The central figure in the triad is Shaka (the Indian/Chinese Sakyamuni), the historical Buddha. Despite this identification, this depiction is not, properly speaking, a portrait (in the Western sense of the term). Rather, Shaka is presented in a transhistorical guise, having achieved a higher state of being. Behind the main

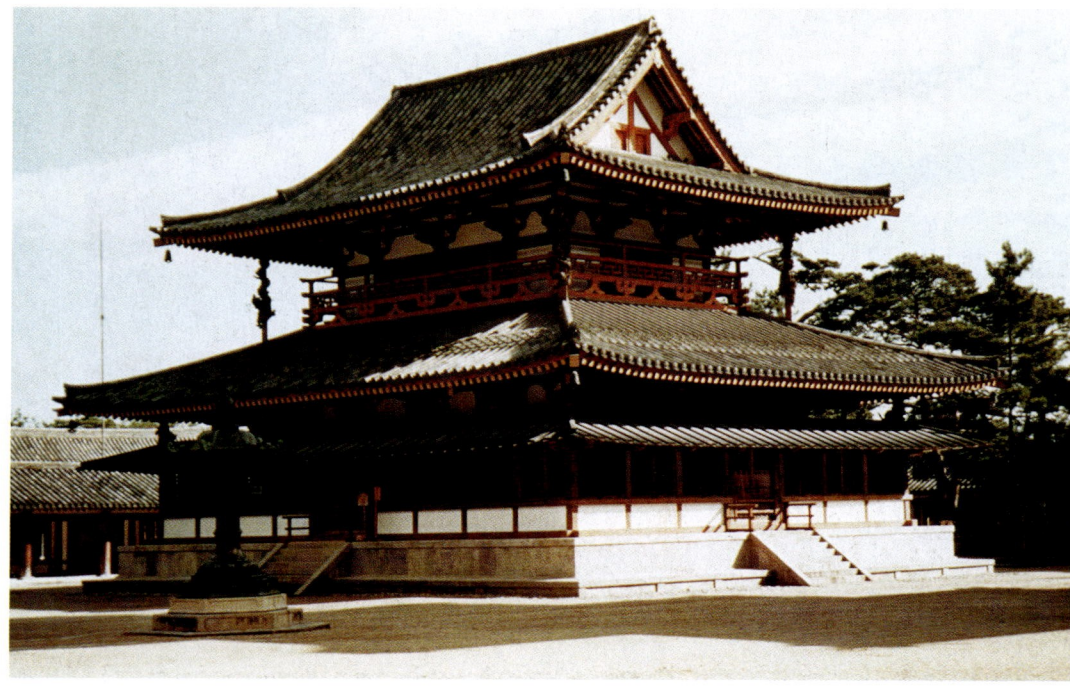

**8-6** Horyuji *kondo* (Golden Hall), Nara, Japan, Early Nara (Hakuho) period, ca. 680.

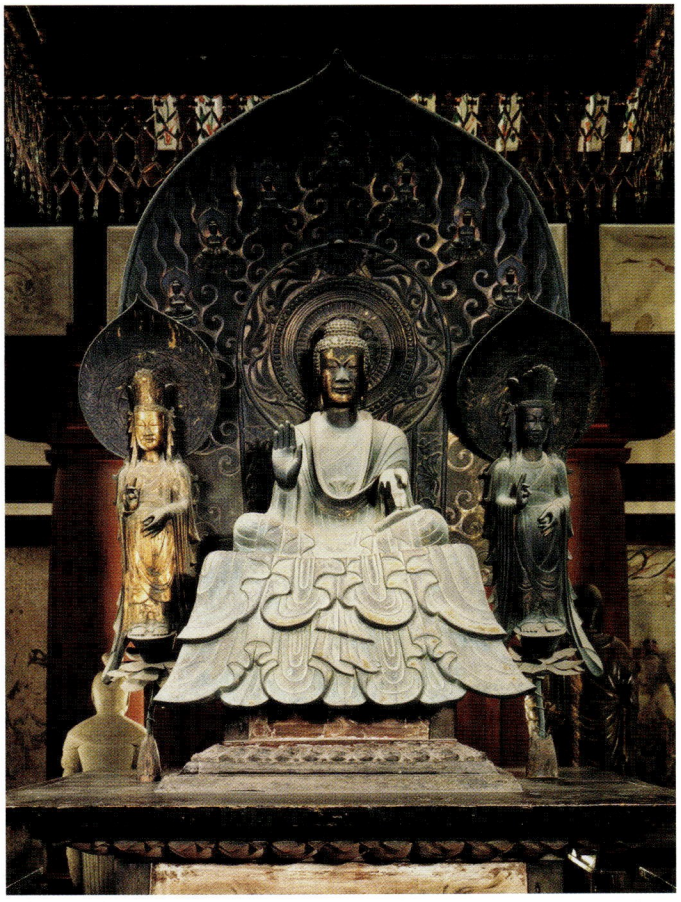

**8-7** Tori Busshi, *Shaka triad*, Horyuji kondo, Nara, Japan, Asuka period, 623. Bronze, 5′ 9½″ high.

image, a flaming mandorla (a lotus-petal-shaped nimbus) bears small figures of other Buddhas. The sculptor, Tori Busshi (*busshi* means "maker of Buddhist images"), was a descendant of a Chinese immigrant. Tori's Buddha triad dates to 623 but reflects the style of the early to mid-sixth century in China and Korea. He elongated the heads and gave greater attention to the drapery's elegantly stylized folds than to a naturalistic modeling of the physical substance of the bodies or their garments.

**MANDORLA-FRAMED STATUES** Within little more than half a century, however, Japan began to move beyond the style of the Asuka period in favor of new ideas and forms coming out of Tang China and Korea. More direct relations with China also narrowed the time lag between developments there and their transfer to Japan. In the triad of Yakushi (Bhaisajyaguru, the Buddha of Healing who presides over the Eastern Pure Land; FIG. **8-8**) in the kondo at the Yakushiji temple of the late seventh century in Nara, the sculptor favored greater anatomical definition and shape-revealing drapery over the dramatic stylizations of the Horyuji statues. The attendant bodhisattvas, especially, reveal the long stylistic trail back through China (see FIG. 7-12) to the sensuous fleshiness of Indian sculpture (see FIG. 6-12). The sculpture's original gilding was destroyed by fire.

**THE PAINTED WALLS OF HORIYUJI** Until a disastrous fire in 1949, the interior walls of the Golden Hall at Horyuji preserved some of the finest examples of Buddhist wall painting in eastern Asia, executed around 710, the beginning of the Nara period. Now the only record of them consists of color photographs. The most important paintings depicted the Buddhas of the four directions. Like the other three, Amida (Amitabha), the Buddha of immeasurable light and infinite life, ruler of the Western Pure

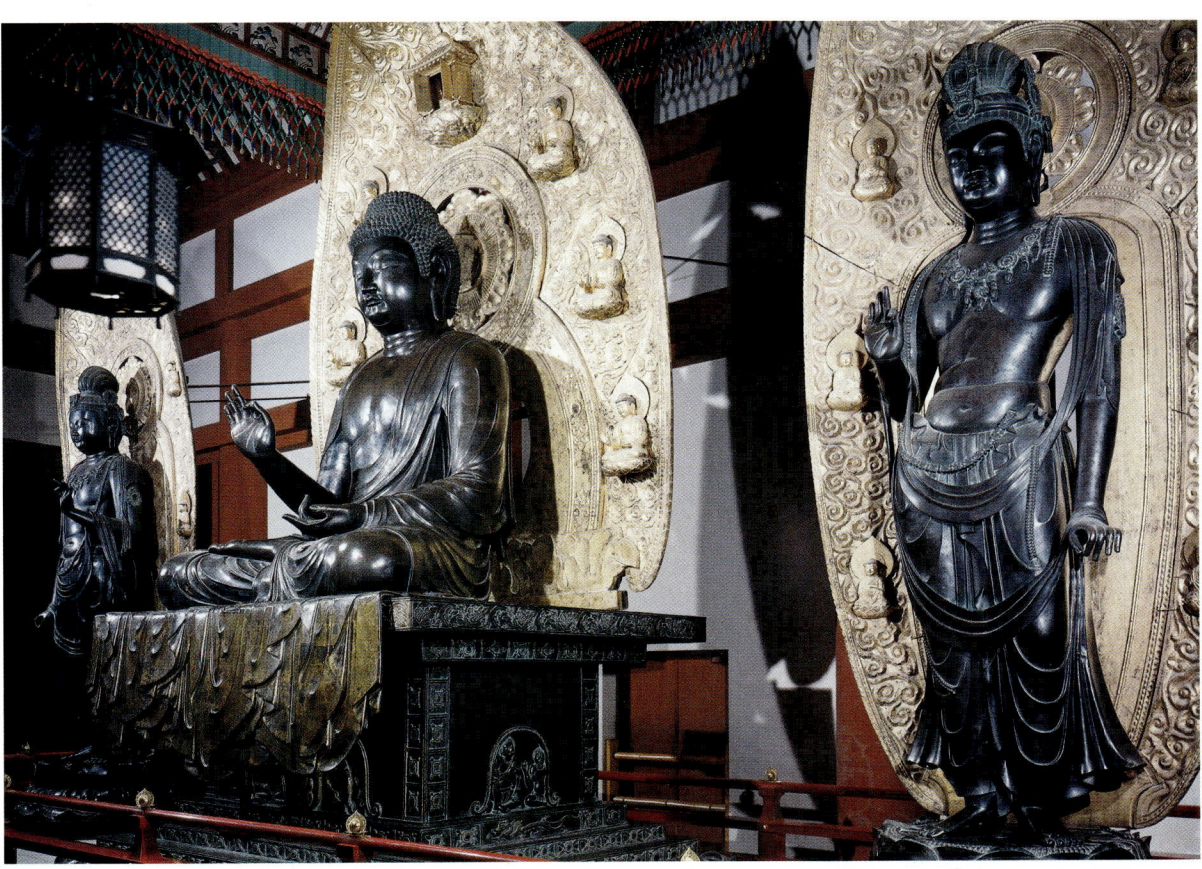

**8-8** *Yakushi triad*, Yakushiji kondo, Nara, Japan, Early Nara (Hakuho) period, late seventh or early eighth century. Bronze, central figure 8′ 4″ high.

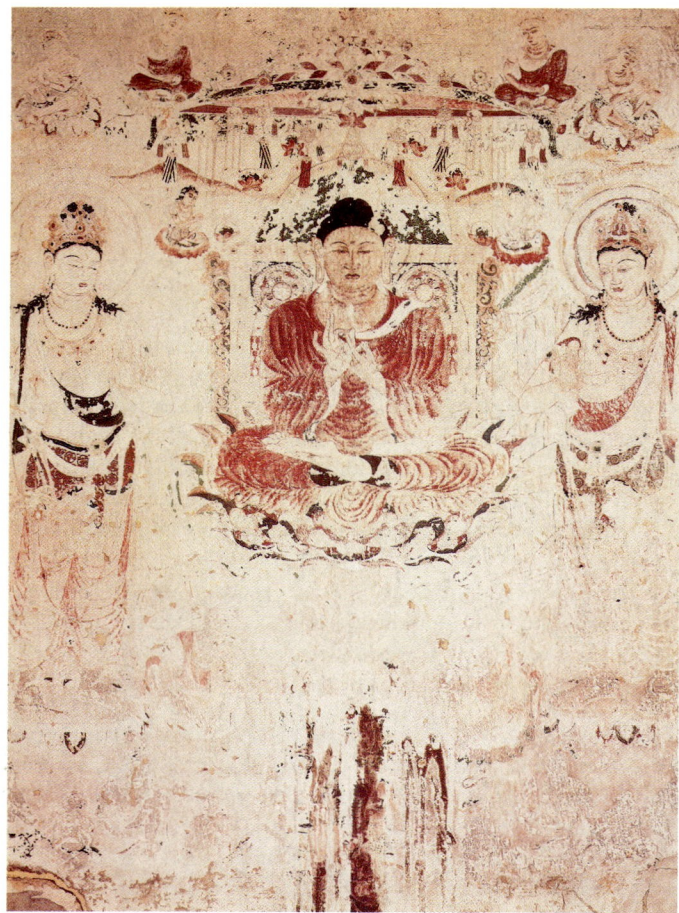

**8-9** Amida triad, wall painting (damaged), from Horyuji kondo, Nara, Japan, Early Nara (Hakuho) period, ca. 710. Ink and colors, 10′ 3″ × 8′ 6″. Horyuji Treasure House, Nara.

743 was historically important as part of an imperial attempt to unify and strengthen the country by utilizing religious authority to reinforce imperial power. The temple served as the administrative center of a network of branch temples built in every province. Thus, the consolidation of imperial authority and thorough penetration of Buddhism throughout the country went hand in hand. The dissemination of a common religion contributed to the eventual disruption of the clan system and the unification of disparate political groups. So important was the construction of both the building and the Daibutsu that court and government officials as well as Buddhist dignitaries from China and India were present at the opening ceremonies in 752. Sadly, the current building does not match the original—it is significantly smaller (the current building has 7 bays; the original had 11). Yet it still radiates enormous presence. Even in its diminished size, the Daibutsuden is still the largest wooden building in the world. The treasures that Todaiji houses serve today as almost a museum of eighth-century pan-Asian culture. Many of the temple's sculptures were inspired by the finest Tang Chinese art forms.

## Heian Period (794–1185)

In 784, possibly to escape the power of the Buddhist priests in Nara, the imperial house moved its capital north, eventually relocating in 794 in what became its home until modern times. Originally called Heiankyo ("capital of peace and tranquility"), it is known today as Kyoto. In the early Heian period, Japan maintained fairly close ties with China, but from the middle of the ninth century on, relations between Japan and China deteriorated so rapidly that, by that century's end, court-sponsored contacts had ceased. Japanese culture, especially at court, became much more self-directed than it had been in the preceding few centuries.

**ESOTERIC BUDDHISM** Among the major developments during the early Heian period was the introduction of Esoteric Buddhism to Japan from China. Esoteric, or secret, Buddhism is so named because of the secret transmission of its teachings. Two Esoteric sects made their appearance in Japan during the early Heian period: Tendai in 805 and Shingon in 806. The teachings of Tendai were based on the *Myohorenge kyo*, the *Lotus Sutra*, one of the Buddhist scriptural narratives. Tendai was brought to Japan by a Buddhist priest who traveled to China specifically to study Tendai Buddhism. He believed that all individuals possessed buddha nature and could become enlightened to this reality through such acts as meditation and careful living.

The introduction of Shingon (True Word) Buddhism had a wider impact. Conveyed by a Japanese student-priest, after a trip to the Chinese capital of Chang'an, Shingon is based on the various sutras. Shingon followers believe that anyone can achieve enlightenment through contemplation and rituals. To aid focus during meditation, Shingon disciples use special hand gestures (mudras; see FIG. 6-12) and recite particular words or syllables (mantras in Sanskrit, shingon in Japanese). Shingon became the primary form of Buddhism in Japan through the mid-10th century.

Because of the emphasis on ritual and meditation in Shingon, the arts flourished during the early Heian period. Both paintings and sculptures provided followers with visualizations of specific Buddhist deities and allowed them to contemplate the transcendental concepts central to the religion. Of particular importance in Shingon meditation was the mandala (mandara in Japanese), a diagram of the cosmic universe. Among the most famous mandalas is the Womb World (Taizokai), which was usually hung on

Land (FIG. 8-9), sits enthroned in his paradisical land, attended by bodhisattvas. The exclusive worship of Amida later became a major trend in Japanese Buddhism, and much grander depictions of his paradise appeared, resembling those at Dunhuang in China (see FIG. 7-13). Here, however, the representation is simple and iconic. Although executed on a dry wall, the painting process involved techniques similar to fresco, such as transferring designs from paper to wall by piercing holes in the paper and pushing colored powder through the perforations. As with the Buddha triad at Yakushiji, the mature Tang style, with its echoes of Indian sensuality, surfaces in this work. The smooth brush lines, thoroughly East Asian, give the figures their substance and life. Such lines belong to a particular type, often seen in Buddhist painting, called iron-wire lines because they are thin and even with a suggestion of tensile strength. Also, as in many other Buddhist paintings, the lines are red instead of black. The identity of the painters of these pictures is unknown, but some scholars have suggested they were Chinese or Korean rather than Japanese.

**THE GREAT BUDDHA** During the Nara period, the imperial court sponsored the construction in Nara of a temple complex, the Golden Hall (FIG. 8-10) at the Todaiji temple. Later destroyed, it was rebuilt in the early 18th century. Also known as the Great Buddha Hall (*Daibutsuden*), it housed a 53-foot bronze image of the Cosmic Buddha, Roshana (Vairocana), inspired by colossal stone statues of this type in China (see FIG. 7-12). The commissioning of Todaiji and its Great Buddha (*Daibutsu*) by Emperor Shomu in

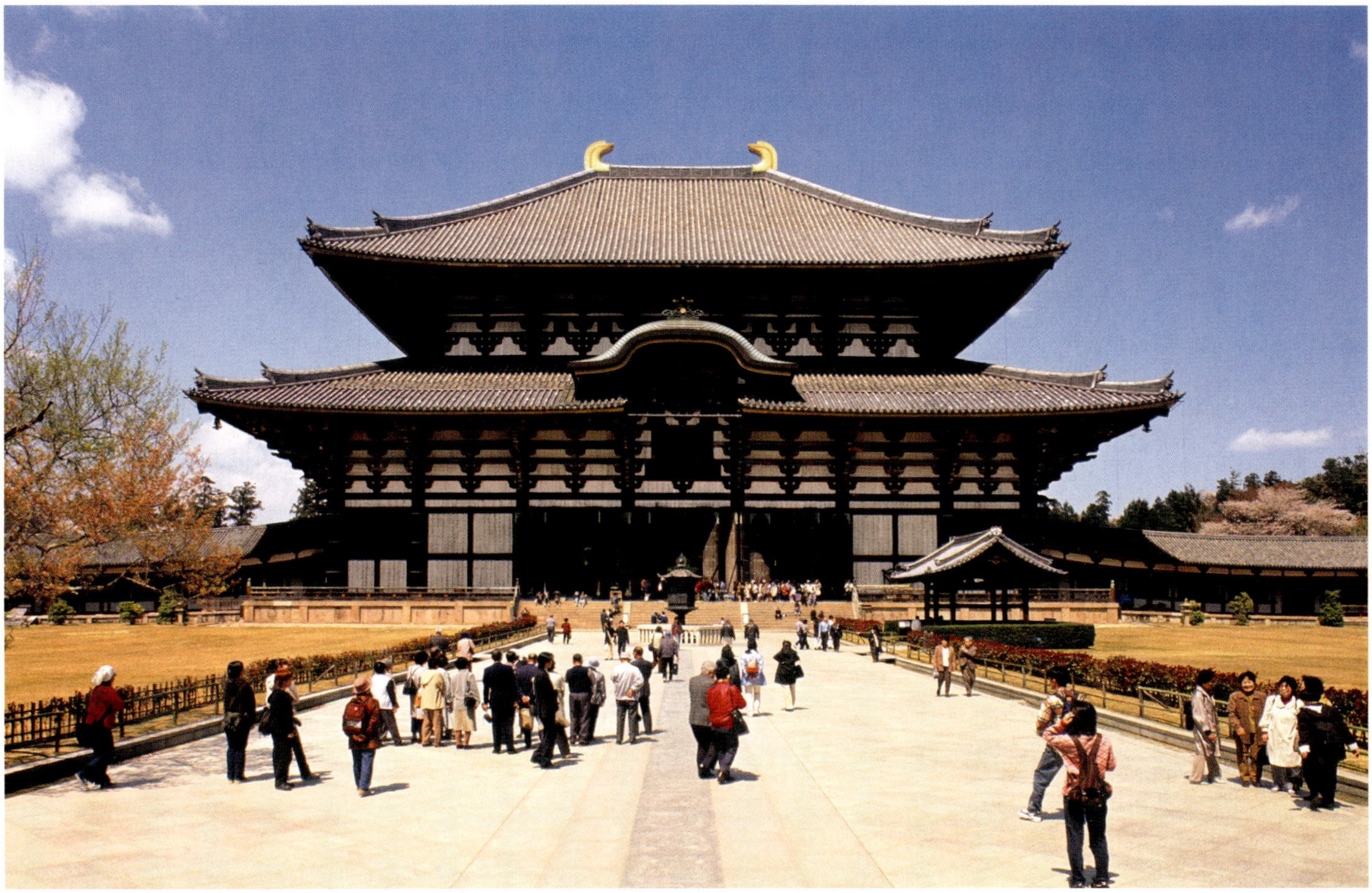

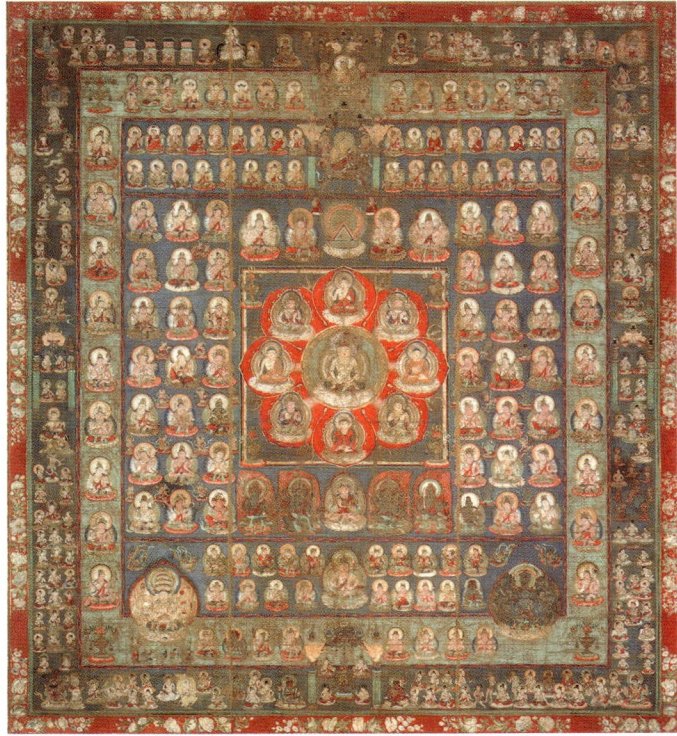

**8-10** Daibutsuden, Todaiji, Japan, Nara period, eighth century, rebuilt ca. 1700.

the wall of a Shingon kondo. The Womb World is composed of 12 zones, each representing one of the various dimensions of buddha nature (for example, universal knowledge, wisdom, achievement, and purity). The mandala we illustrate here (FIG. **8-11**) is among the best preserved in Japan, and is located at Kyoogokokuji (Toji), the Shingon teaching center established in 823.

**SUGGESTING CELESTIAL ARCHITECTURE** During the middle and later Heian period, belief in the vow of Amida, the Buddha of the Western Pure Land, to save believers through rebirth in his realm gained great prominence among the Japanese aristocracy. Eventually, the simple message of Pure Land Buddhism—universal salvation—facilitated the spread of Buddhism to all classes of Japanese. The most important surviving monument in Japan related to Pure Land beliefs is the so-called Phoenix Hall of the Byodoin (FIG. **8-12**), a temple built by Fujiwara Yorimichi (r. 990–1074) in memory of his father Michinaga on the grounds of Michinaga's summer villa at Uji. Dedicated in 1053, the Phoenix Hall houses a wooden statue of Amida carved from multiple joined blocks, the predominant wooden sculpture technique by this time. The building's elaborate winged form evokes images of the Buddha's palace in his Pure Land, as depicted in East Asian paintings (see FIG. 7-13) based on the design of great Chinese palaces. By placing only light pillars on the exterior, elevating the wings, and situating the whole on a reflective pond, the Phoenix Hall builders suggested the floating weightlessness of a celestial architecture. The building's name derives

**8-11** Taizokai (Womb World) of Ryokai Mandara, Kyoogokokuji (Toji), Kyoto, Japan, Early Heian period, second half of ninth century. Hanging scroll, color on silk, $6' \times 5' \frac{5}{8}''$. Tokyo National Museum.

## Japanese Literature and Court Culture

During the Nara and Heian periods (710–1185), the Japanese imperial court developed as the center of an elite culture. Both men and women produced literature, paintings, calligraphy, and decorative arts that critics generally consider "classical" today. Heian court members, especially those from the great Fujiwara clan that dominated the court for a century and a half, compiled the first great anthologies of Japanese poetry and wrote Japan's most influential secular prose.

Japanese poetry and related painting and decorative art emphasize human sentiments intertwined with responses to nature, seasonality, and a body of standard metaphors and symbols. For example, the full moon, flying geese, crying deer, and certain plants symbolize autumn, which in turn evokes somber emotions, fading love, and dying. Such concrete but evocative images frequently appear in paintings. Exchanging poems was a common Japanese social practice and a frequent preoccupation of lovers.

A lady-in-waiting to an empress of the early 11th century wrote the best-known and longest-admired work of literature in Japan, *Tale of Genji*. Known as Lady Murasaki, the author is one of many important Heian women writers, including especially diarists and poets. Generally considered the world's first lengthy novel, *Tale of Genji* tells of the life and loves of Prince Genji and, after his death, of his heirs. The novel and much of Japanese literature consistently display a sensitivity to the sadness in the world caused by the transience of love and life. Illustrated scrolls of *Tale of Genji* (FIG. 8-13) rely on key poetic motifs and careful compositions to convey such feelings.

from its overall birdlike shape and from two bronze phoenixes decorating the ridgepole ends. In eastern Asia, these birds were believed to alight on lands properly ruled. Here, they represented imperial might, sometimes associated especially with the empress. The authority of the Fujiwara family derived primarily from the marriage of daughters to the imperial line.

**A TALE OF LOVE AND INTRIGUE** Japan's most admired literary classic is *Tale of Genji* (see "Japanese Literature and Court Culture," below), written around 1000 by Murasaki Shikubu (usually referred to as Lady Murasaki), a lady-in-waiting at the court. Recounting the lives and loves of Prince Genji and his descendants, *Tale of Genji* provides readers with a view of Heian court culture. The oldest extant examples of illustrated copies are fragments from a deluxe set of early-12th-century handscrolls. From textual and physical evidence, scholars have suggested that the set originally consisted of about 10 handscrolls produced by about five teams of artisans. Each team consisted of a nobleman talented in calligraphy, a chief painter, and assistants. The script is primarily *hiragana,* a sound-based writing system developed in Japan from Chinese characters. Hiragana originally served the needs of women (who were not taught Chinese) and became the primary script for Japanese court poetry. In these handscrolls, pictures alternate with text, as in Gu Kaizhi's *Admonitions* scrolls (see FIG. 7-10). However, the Japanese work focuses on emotionally charged moments in personal relationships, rather than on lessons in exemplary behavior. In the scene illustrated here (FIG. **8-13**), for example, Genji meets with his greatest love near the time of her death. The bush-clover in the garden identifies the season as autumn, the season associated with the fading of life and love.

Here, a radically upturned ground plane and strong diagonal lines suggest three-dimensional space rather than depict it illusionistically. Further, these features convey an elevated viewpoint; the painter omitted roofs and ceilings to allow a privileged view of the emotionally charged moments typically represented in the interiors. Flat fields of unshaded color emphasize the painting's two-

**8-12** Phoenix Hall, Byodoin, Uji, Japan, Heian period, 1053.

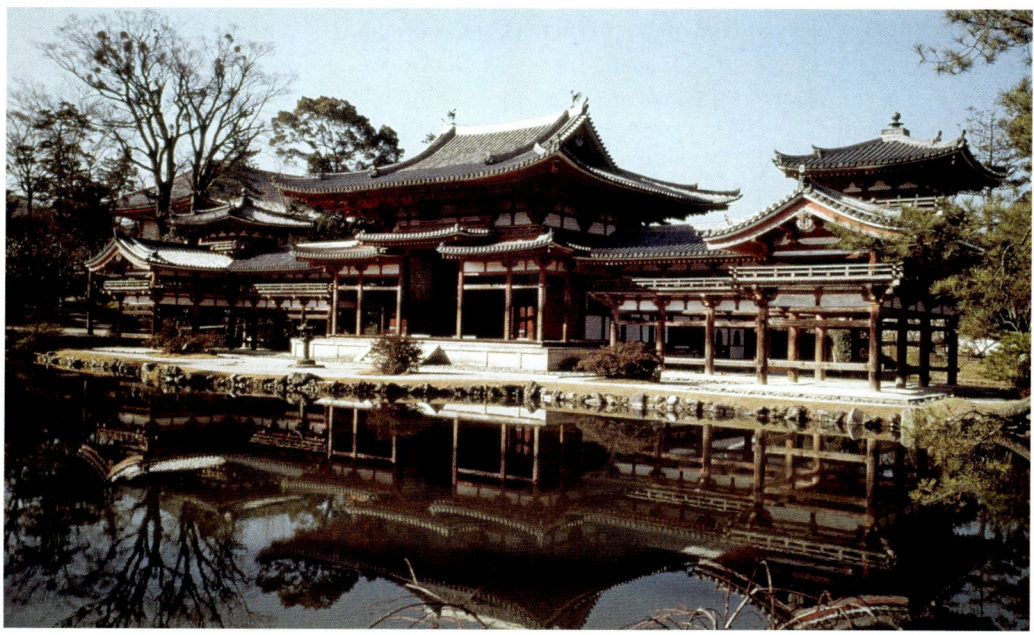

dimensional character, but rich patterns in the textiles and architectural ornament give a feeling of sumptuousness. The human figures appear constructed of stiff layers of contrasting fabrics, and the artist simplified and generalized the aristocratic faces, using a technique called "line for eye and hook for nose." This lack of individualization may reflect societal restrictions on looking directly at exalted persons, or it may have served to ease viewers' identification with a character in the story. Several formal features of the *Genji* illustrations—native subjects, bright mineral pigments, lack of emphasis on strong

brushwork, and general flatness—were later considered typical of *yamato-e* (native-style painting; the term *yamato* means "Japan" and is used to describe anything that is characteristically Japanese). In the early Heian period before this example was made, however, *yamato-e* probably referred only to Japanese subject matter.

**PAINTINGS OF BUDDHIST TALES** Painted during the late 12th century, at the end of the Heian period, *The Legends of Mount Shigi* (FIG. 8-14) represents a different facet of narrative

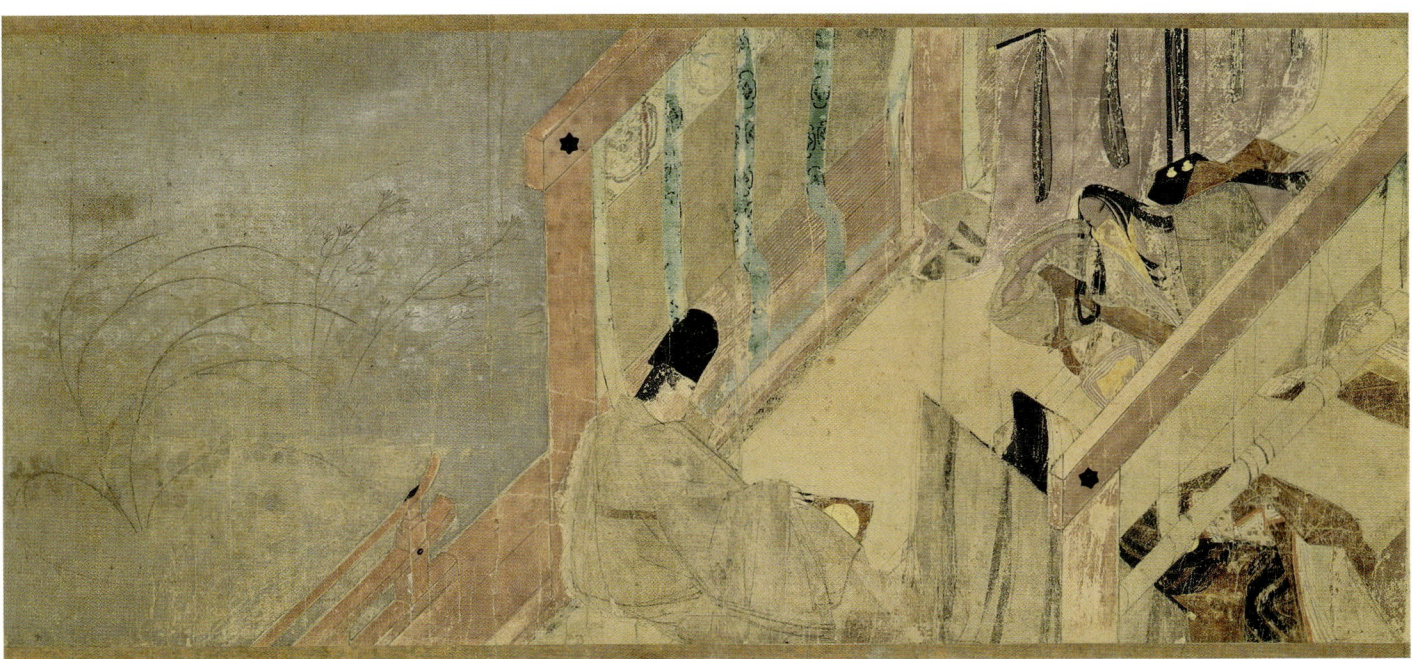

**8-13** Scene from Minori chapter, *Tale of Genji,* Late Heian period, first half of 12th century. Handscroll, ink and color on paper, $8\frac{5}{8}''$ high. Goto Art Museum, Tokyo.

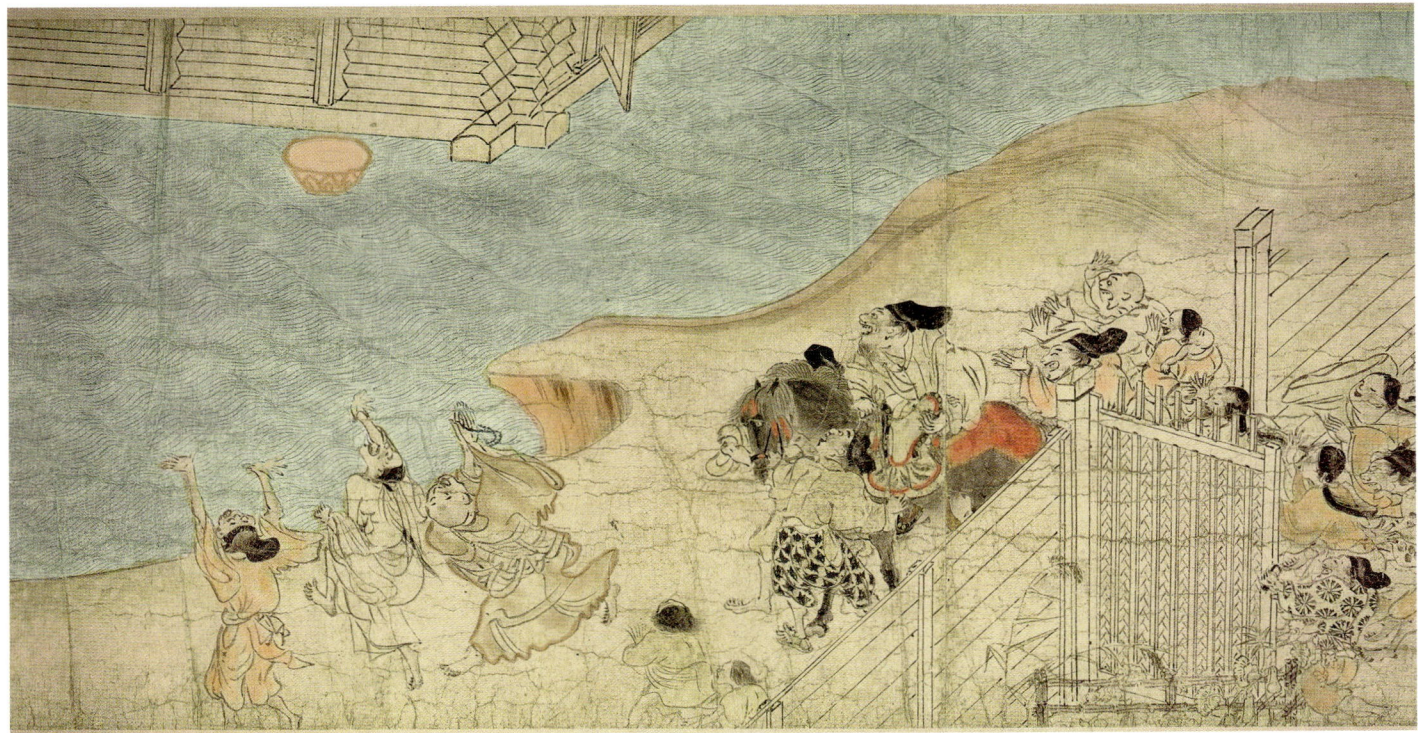

**8-14** Detail of the Flying Storehouse, from *The Legends of Mount Shigi,* Late Heian period, late 12th century. Handscroll, ink and colors on paper, $1'\frac{1}{2}''$ high. Chogosonshiji, Nara.

handscroll painting. The stories belong to a genre of pious Buddhist tales devoted to miraculous events involving virtuous individuals. Unlike the *Genji* scrolls, short segments of text and pictures do not alternate. Instead, the painters took advantage of the scroll format to present several scenes in a long, unbroken stretch. For example, the first scroll shows the same travelers at several stages of their journey through a continuous landscape.

The *Mount Shigi* scrolls illustrate three miracles associated with a Buddhist monk named Myoren and his mountaintop temple. The first relates the story of the flying storehouse and depicts Myoren's begging bowl lifting the rice-filled storehouse of a wealthy landowner and carrying it off to the monk's hut in the mountains (FIG. 8-14). The painter depicted the astonished landowner, his attendants, and several onlookers in various poses—some grimacing, others gesticulating wildly and scurrying about in frantic amazement. The artist exaggerated each feature of the painted figures, in striking contrast to the *Genji* scroll figures.

## Kamakura Period (1185–1332)

In the late 12th century, a series of civil wars between rival warrior families led to the end of the Japanese imperial court as a major political and social force. The victors, headed by the Minamoto family, established their *shogunate* (military government) at Kamakura in eastern Japan. The imperial court remained in Kyoto as the theoretical source of political authority but without actual power. During the Kamakura period, more frequent and positive contact with China brought with it an appreciation for more recent cultural developments there, ranging from new architectural styles to Zen Buddhism.

**A PRIESTLY PORTRAIT** Rebuilding in Nara presented an early opportunity for architectural experimentation. A leading figure in planning and directing the reconstruction efforts was the priest Shunjobo Chogen (1121–1206), who is reputed to have made three trips to China between 1166 and 1176. After learning about contemporary Chinese architecture, he oversaw the rebuilding of Todaiji, among other projects. His portrait statue (FIG. **8-15**) is one of the most striking examples of the high level of naturalism prevalent in the early Kamakura period. Characterized by finely painted details, a powerful rendering of the signs of aging, and the inclusion of such personal attributes as prayer beads, the statue of Chogen exhibits the carving skill and style of the Kei school of sculptors (see "Japanese Artists, Workshops, and Patrons," page 229). The Kei school traced its lineage to Jocho, a famous sculptor of the mid-11th century. Its works display fine Heian carving

**8-15** Detail of the priest Shunjobo Chogen, Todaiji, Nara, Japan, Kamakura period, early 13th century. Painted cypress wood, 2′ 8$\frac{3}{8}$″ high.

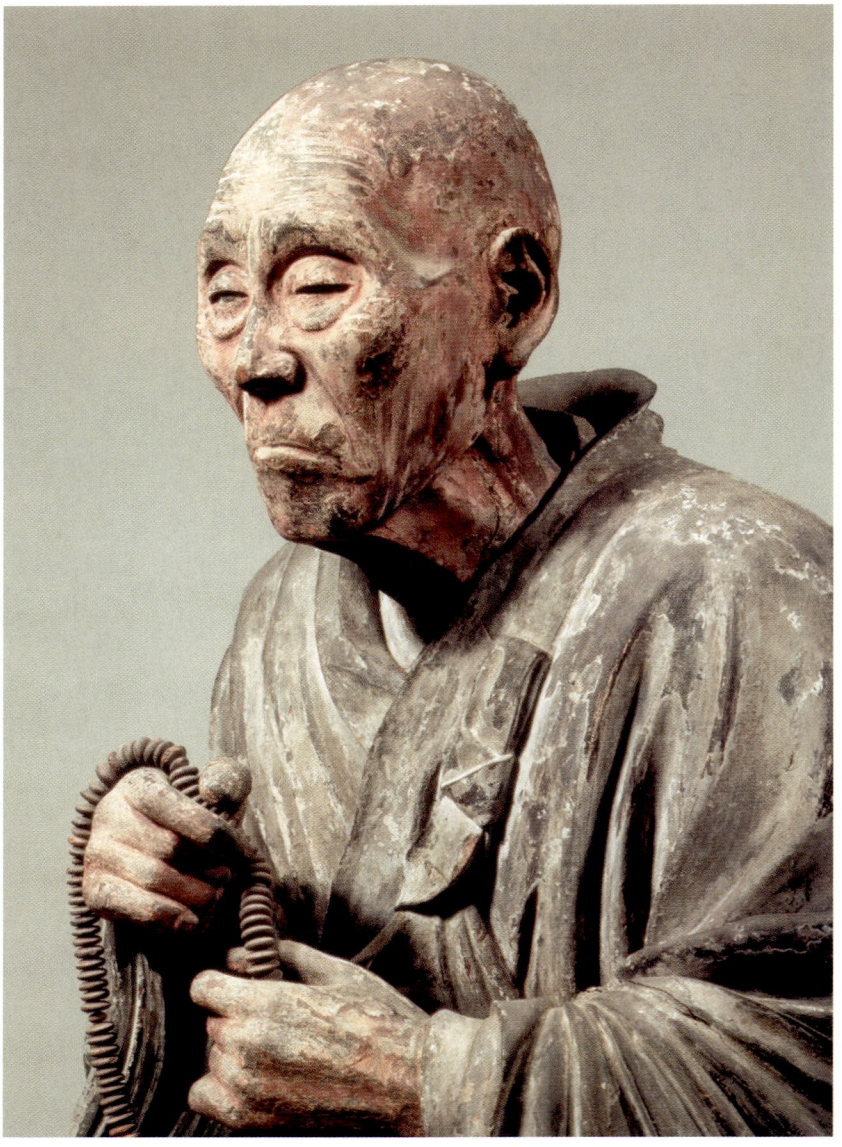

## Japanese Artists, Workshops, and Patrons

For much of early Japanese history, art production was largely dependent on commissions. Until the Late Heian period (1086–1185), major commissions came almost exclusively from the imperial court or the great temples. As warrior families gained wealth and power, they too extended great commissions—in many cases closely following the aristocrats' precedents in subject and style.

Artists, for the most part, did not work independently, but rather were affiliated with workshops. Indeed, until recently, hierarchically organized male workshops produced most Japanese art. Membership in these workshops was often based on familial relationships. Each workshop was dominated by a master, and many of his main assistants and apprentices were relatives. Outsiders of considerable skill sometimes joined workshops, often through marriage or adoption. The eldest son usually inherited the master's position, after rigorous training in the necessary skills from a very young age. Therefore, one meaning of the term "school of art" in Japan is a network of workshops tracing their origins back to the same master, a kind of artistic clan. Inside the workshops, the master and senior assistants handled the most important production stages, but artists of lower rank helped with the more routine work. The portrait statue of Chogen (FIG. 8-15), for example, was created by a workshop based on familial ties.

Artistic cooperation also surfaced in court bureaus, an alternative to family workshops. These official bureaus, located at the imperial palace, had emerged by the Heian period. The painting bureau accrued particular fame; teams of court painters, led by the bureau director, produced pictures such as the scenes in the *Tale of Genji* handscrolls (FIG. 8-13). This system remained vital into the Kamakura period and well beyond. Under the direction of a patron or the patron's representative, the master painter laid out the composition by brushing in the initial outlines and contours. Under his supervision, junior painters applied the colors. The master then completed the work by brushing in fresh contours and details such as facial features. Very junior assistants and apprentices assisted in the process by preparing paper, ink, and pigments. Unlike mastership in hereditarily run workshops, competition among several families determined control of the Court Painting Bureau during the Heian and Kamakura periods.

Not all art was controlled by the bureaus or family workshops. Priest-artists were trained in temple workshops; these artists produced Buddhist art objects for public viewing as well as images for private priestly meditation. Amateur painting was common among aristocrats of all ranks. As they did for poetry composition and calligraphy, aristocrats frequently held elegant competitions in painting. Both women and men participated in such activities. In fact, court ladies probably played a significant role in developing the painting style seen in the *Genji* scrolls, and a few participated in public projects.

---

techniques combined with an increased concern for natural volume and detail learned from studying, among other sources, surviving Nara period works and works imported from Song China. Enhancing the natural quality of Japanese portrait statues is the use of inlaid rock crystal for the eyes, a technique found only in Japan.

**MOUNTED WARRIORS ON A HANDSCROLL** All the painting types flourishing in the Heian period continued to prosper in the Kamakura period. A striking example of narrative handscroll painting is *The Burning of the Sanjo Palace* (FIG. **8-16**), a fragment of a work illustrating some of the battles in the civil wars at the end of the Heian period. Here, the viewer sees the drama unfold in swift and violent staccato brushwork and vivid flashes of color. At the beginning of the scroll (read from right to left), the eye focuses first on a mass of figures rushing toward a blazing building (not shown here)—the painting's crescendo—and then moves at a slowed pace through swarms of soldiers, horses, and bullock

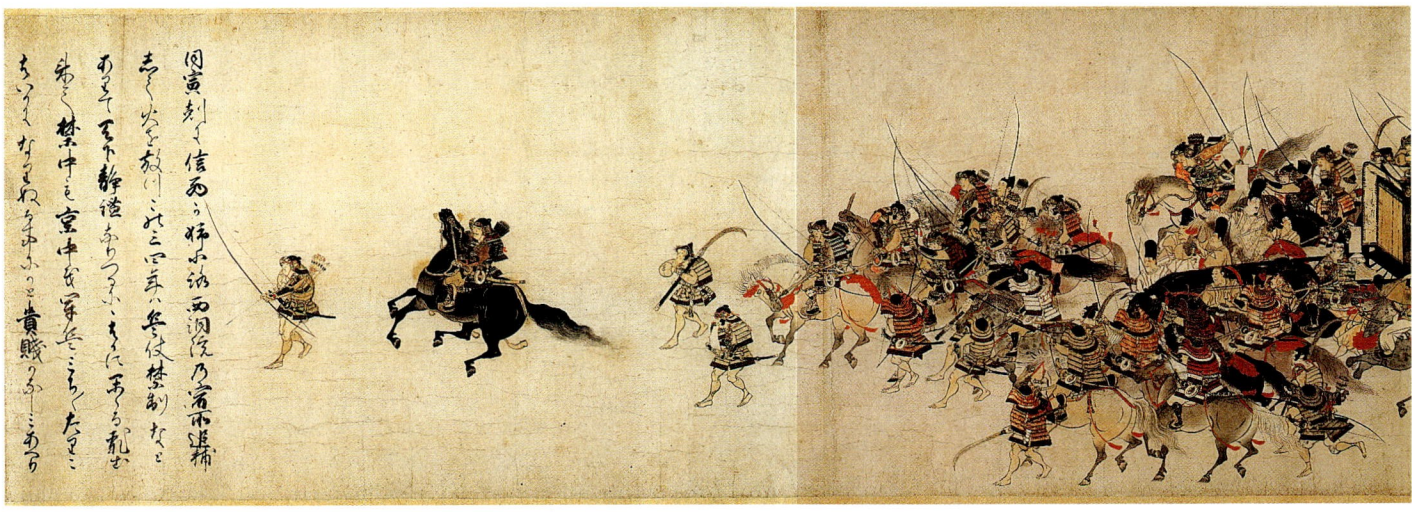

**8-16** Detail of *The Burning of the Sanjo Palace*, Kamakura period, 13th century. Handscroll, ink and colors on paper, 1′ 4¼″ high; complete scroll, 22′ 10″ long. Museum of Fine Arts, Boston (Fenollosa-Weld Collection).

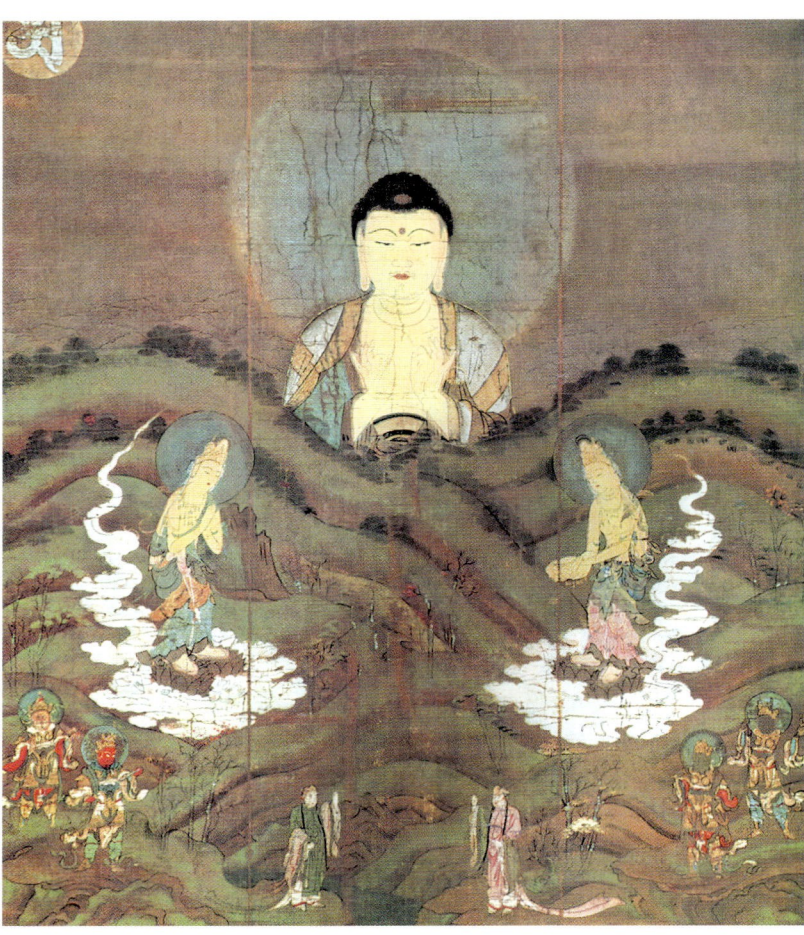

carts. Finally, a warrior on a rearing horse arrests the viewer's gaze. The horse and rider, however, serve as a *deceptive cadence* (false ending). They are merely a prelude to the single figure of an archer, who picks up and completes the soldiers' mass movement, drawing the turbulent narrative to a quiet close.

**THE SAVING POWER OF AMIDA** Buddhism and Buddhist painting remained vital in the Kamakura period. Evangelical monks spread Pure Land beliefs throughout Japan to people from all levels of society, and new Pure Land sects emerged that the lower ranks of society, including peasants, found especially appealing. But elite patrons continued to commission major Pure Land artworks. Pure Land Buddhism in Japan stressed the saving power of Amida, who, if called on, hastened to believers at the moment of death and conveyed them to his Pure Land. Pictures of this scene often hung in the presence of a dying person, who recited Amida's name to ensure salvation.

In *Amida Descending over the Mountains* (FIG. **8-17**), a gigantic Amida appears to move directly toward the viewer. His two main attendant bodhisattvas have already made the passage. The grand frontal presentation of Amida gives the painting an iconic quality even as the bodhisattvas' movement continues his descent. Particularly striking in this painting is the way in which Amida's halo resembles a rising moon, an image long admired in Japan for its spiritual beauty.

## CONCLUSION

Striking transformations mark the long history of Japanese art as the country's population received, responded to, and developed new forms and ideas from continental eastern Asia. Early metalwork, Buddhist architecture, and the basic painting formats and media, to name only a few examples, readily reveal Japan's close ties to the continent. However, from earliest times, Japan maintained distinctive aesthetic ideals and preferences. For instance, the dynamic forms of Jomon pottery and haniwa figures suggest that the early Japanese derived a deep pleasure from allowing the colors and textures of their raw materials to remain prominent in the final objects. This tendency may not have been exclusive to Japanese art and certainly did not dominate in later centuries, but it did remain a vital part of Japan's aesthetic heritage, helping determine what people accepted from the continent and how they adapted it. In the end, however, the most distinctive feature of Japanese art is its great variety. This reflects the people's capacity to embrace radically different aesthetics simultaneously, appreciating their separate contributions to a richly diverse material culture. Chapter 27 shows how this cultural flexibility continued after several decades of upheaval, the Kamakura rulers' downfall in the early 14th century (1332), and the establishment of a new shogunate by the end of the century.

| | | |
|---|---|---|
| JOMON | 10,500 BCE | |
| | | ▍ HUNTING AND FISHING |
| MIDDLE JOMON | 2500 BCE | |
| | | **1** |
| | 1500 BCE | |
| | 300 BCE | |
| | | ▍ RICE GROWING AND METALWORKING |
| YAYOI | 100 CE | |
| | | **2** |
| | 300 | |
| | | ▍ EMERGENCE OF IMPERIAL FAMILY |
| KOFUN | 552 | |
| ASUKA | | **3** ▍ BUDDHISM OFFICIALLY INTRODUCED, 552 |
| | 645 | |
| EARLY NARA (HAKUHO) | 710 | |
| NARA | | ▍ TRANSFER OF CAPITAL TO NARA, 710 |
| | 794 | |
| HEIAN | | ▍ TRANSFER OF CAPITAL TO HEIANKYO (KYOTO), 794 |
| | | ▍ NEW SECTS OF ESOTERIC BUDDHISM INTRODUCED, CA. 805 |
| | | ▍ SUSPENSION OF DIPLOMATIC RELATIONS WITH CHINA, 894 |
| | | ▍ PURE LAND BUDDHISM TEACHINGS GAIN IMPORTANCE, FROM 10TH CENTURY |
| | | ▍ WARRIOR CLANS RISE IN POWER, 12TH CENTURY |
| | 1185 | |
| KAMAKURA | | ▍ KAMAKURA SHOGUNATE ESTABLISHED, 1185 |
| | | ▍ POPULAR PURE LAND SECTS EMERGE, 13TH CENTURY |
| | | **4** |
| | 1332 | |

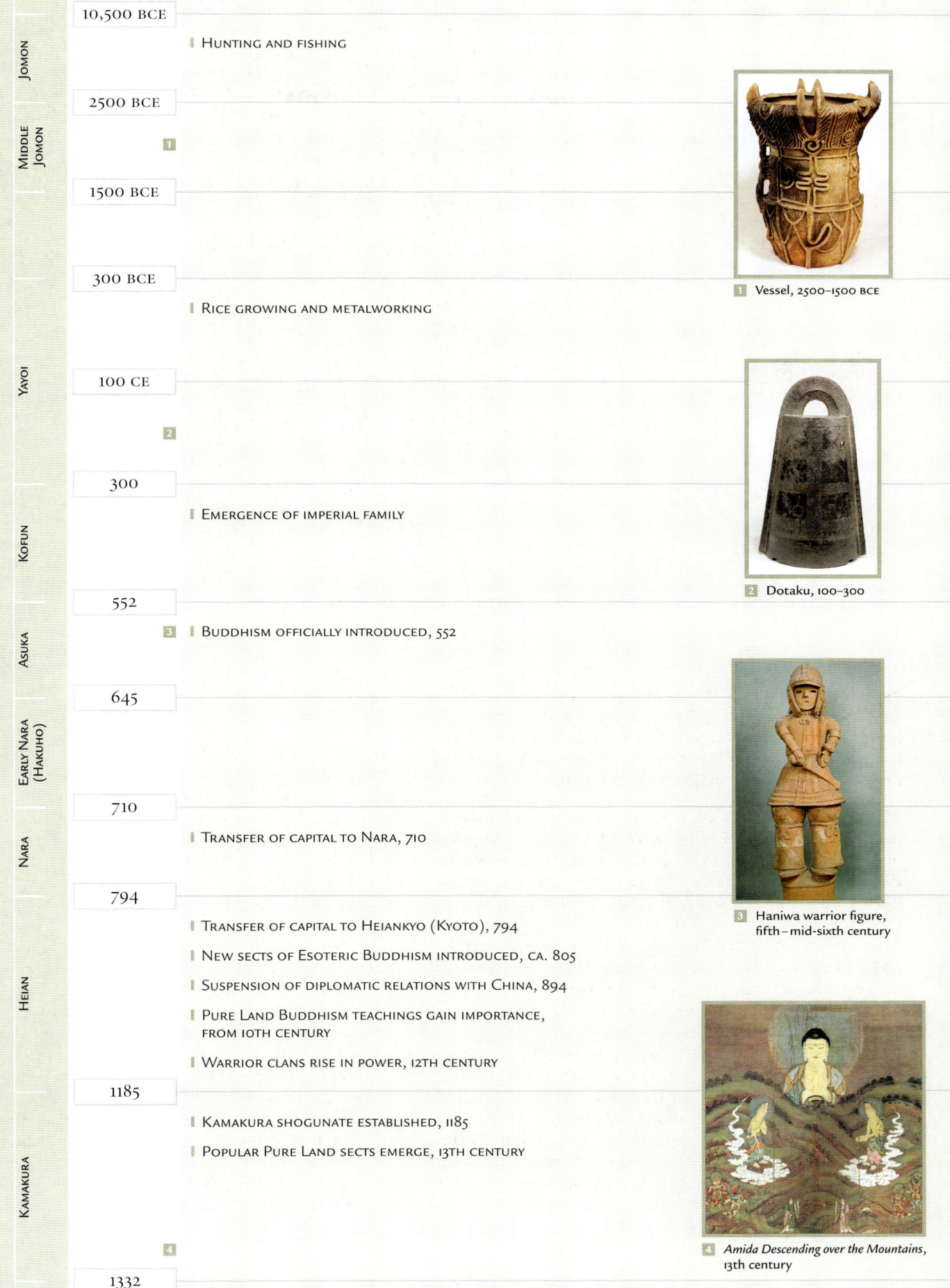

**1** Vessel, 2500–1500 BCE

**2** Dotaku, 100–300

**3** Haniwa warrior figure, fifth–mid-sixth century

**4** *Amida Descending over the Mountains,* 13th century

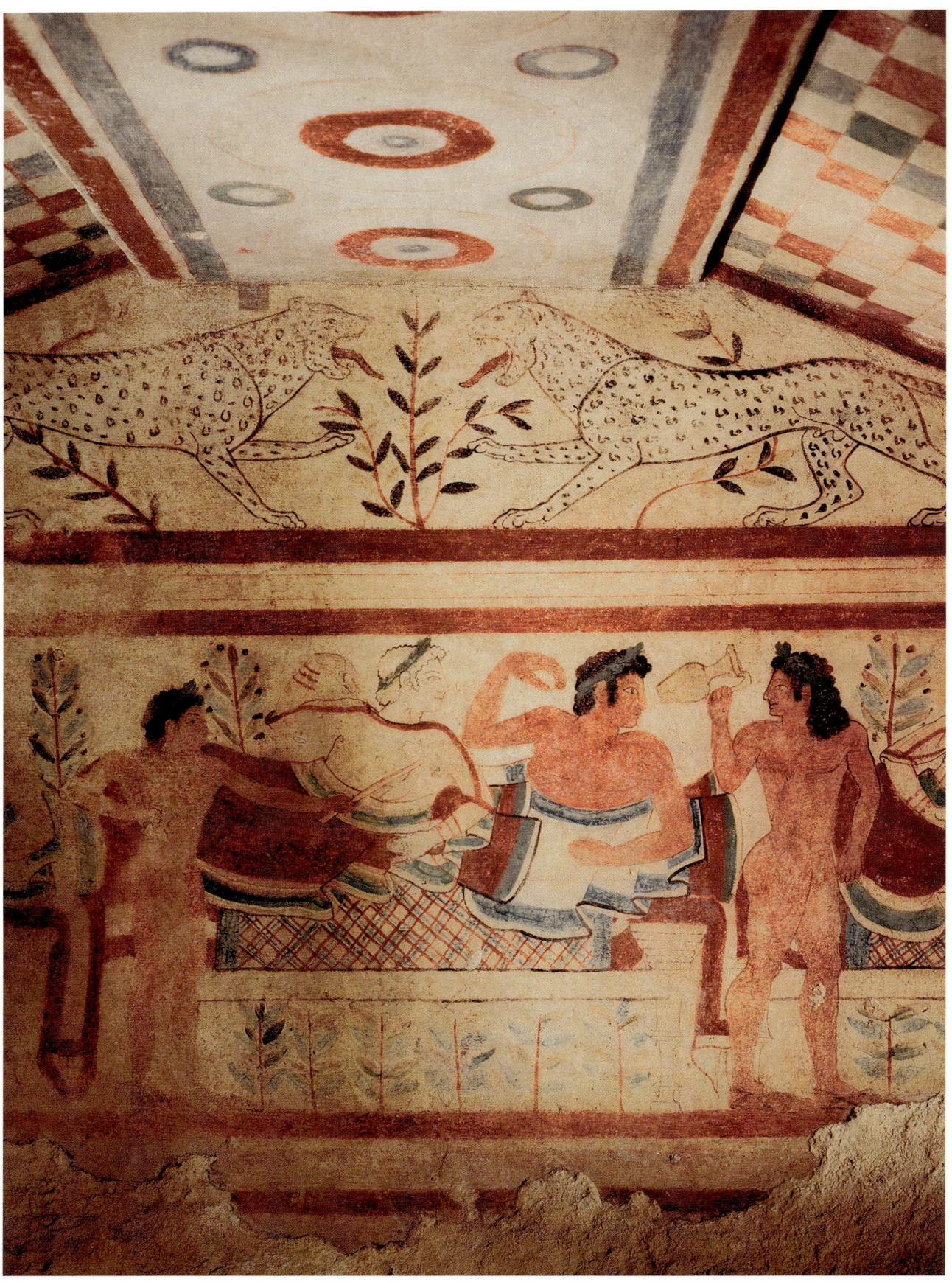

Banqueters, detail of a mural painting in the Tomb of the Leopards, Tarquinia, Italy, ca. 480–470 BCE.

# 9

# ITALY BEFORE THE ROMANS

## THE ART OF THE ETRUSCANS

"The Etruscans, as everyone knows, were the people who occupied the middle of Italy in early Roman days, and whom the Romans, in their usual neighbourly fashion, wiped out entirely." So opens D. H. Lawrence's witty and sensitive *Etruscan Places* (1929), one of the earliest modern essays that highly values Etruscan art and treats it as much more than a debased form of the art of the contemporary city-states of Greece and southern Italy. ("Most people despise everything B.C. that isn't Greek, for the good reason that it ought to be Greek if it isn't," Lawrence goes on to say!) Today it is no longer necessary to argue the importance and originality of Etruscan art. Deeply influenced by, yet different from, Greek art, Etruscan sculpture, painting, and architecture not only provided the models for early Roman art and architecture but also had an impact on the art of the Greek colonies in Italy.

ETRUSCAN ORIGINS The heartland of the Etruscans was the territory between the Arno and Tiber rivers of central Italy (MAP **9-1**). The lush green hills still bear their name — Tuscany, the land of the people the Romans called *Tusci,* the region centered on Florence, birthplace of Renaissance art. So do the blue waters that splash up against the western coastline of the Italian peninsula, for the Greeks referred to the Etruscans as *Tyrrhenians* and gave their name to the sea off Tuscany. The origin of the Tusci people — the enduring "mystery of the Etruscans" — is, however, not clear at all. Their language, although written in a Greek-derived script and extant in inscriptions that are still in large part obscure, is unrelated to the Indo-European linguistic family. Ancient authors, as fascinated by the puzzle as modern scholars are, generally felt that the Etruscans emigrated from the east. Herodotus, the fifth-century BCE Greek historian, specifically declared that they came from Lydia in Asia Minor and were led by King Tyrsenos — hence their Greek name. But Dionysius of Halicarnassus, writing at the end of the first century BCE, maintained that the Tusci were native Italians. And some modern researchers have theorized that the Etruscans came into Italy from the north.

All these theories are current today, and no doubt some truth exists in each of them. The Etruscan people of historical times were very likely the result of a gradual

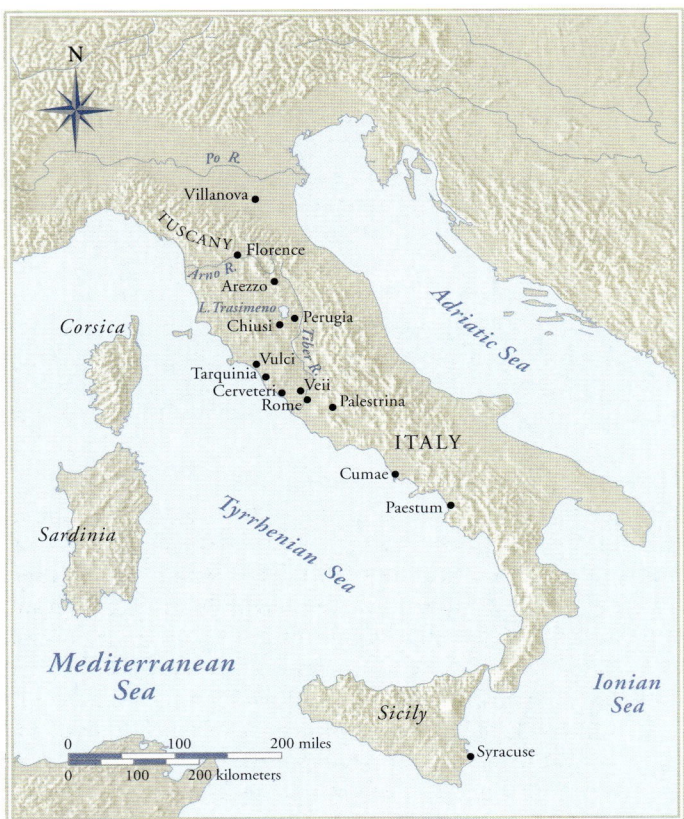

MAP 9-1 Italy in Etruscan times.

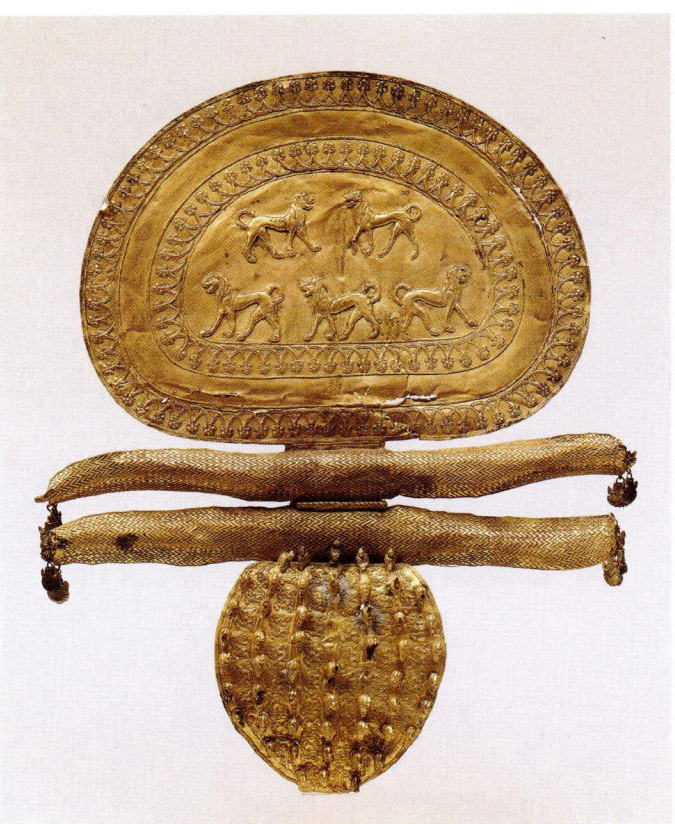

9-1 Fibula with Orientalizing lions, from the Regolini-Galassi Tomb, Cerveteri, Italy, ca. 650–640 BCE. Gold, approx. 1' ½″ high. Vatican Museums, Rome.

fusion of native and immigrant populations. This mixing of peoples occurred between the end of the Bronze Age and the so-called Villanovan era (named after an important northern Italian site, and contemporary with the Geometric period in Greece). At that time the Etruscans emerged as a people with a culture related to but distinct from those of other Italic peoples and from the civilizations of Greece and the Orient.

**THE CITIES OF ETRURIA** During the eighth and seventh centuries BCE, the Etruscans, as highly skilled seafarers, enriched themselves through trade abroad. By the sixth century, they controlled most of northern and central Italy from such strongholds as Tarquinia (ancient Tarquinii), Cerveteri (Caere), Vulci, and Veii. But these cities never united to form a state, so it is improper to speak of an Etruscan "nation" or "kingdom," only of *Etruria,* the territory occupied by the Etruscans. The cities coexisted, flourishing or fading independently. Any semblance of unity among them was based primarily on common linguistic ties and religious beliefs and practices. This lack of political cohesion eventually made the Etruscans relatively easy prey for Lawrence's Roman aggressors.

# EARLY ETRUSCAN ART

## Orientalizing Art

**ETRUSCAN WEALTH** Iron, tin, copper, and silver were all successfully mined in Etruria. This great mineral wealth transformed Etruscan society during the seventh century BCE. The modest Villanovan villages and their agriculturally based economies gave

way to prosperous cities engaged in international commerce. Such cities as Cerveteri, blessed with rich mines, could acquire foreign goods, and Etruscan aristocrats quickly developed a taste for luxury objects incorporating Eastern motifs. To satisfy the demand, local artisans, inspired by imported goods, produced magnificent objects for both homes and tombs. As is true of Greece at the same time, art historians speak of an Orientalizing period of Etruscan art followed by an Archaic period. And, as in Greece, the local products cannot be mistaken for the foreign models.

**GOLD JEWELRY** About the middle of the seventh century BCE, a wealthy Etruscan family stocked the so-called Regolini-Galassi Tomb (named for its excavators) at Cerveteri with bronze cauldrons and gold jewelry of Etruscan manufacture and Orientalizing style. The most spectacular of the many luxurious objects in the family tomb is a golden *fibula* (clasp or safety pin; FIG. **9-1**) of unique shape used to fasten a woman's gown at the shoulder. The giant fibula is in the Italic tradition, but the five lions that walk across the gold surface were borrowed from the Orient. The technique, also emulating Eastern imports, is masterful, combining hammered relief *(repoussé)* and *granulation* (the fusing of tiny metal balls, or granules, to a metal surface). The Regolini-Galassi fibula equals or exceeds in quality anything that might have served as a model.

The jewelry from the Regolini-Galassi Tomb also includes a golden *pectoral* that covered a deceased woman's chest, and two gold circlets that may be earrings, although they are large enough to be bracelets. Such a taste for ostentatious display is frequently the hallmark of newly acquired wealth, and this was certainly the case in seventh-century BCE Etruria.

## Etruscan Counterparts of Greco-Roman Gods and Heroes

| ETRUSCAN | GREEK | ROMAN |
|----------|-------|-------|
| Tinia | Zeus | Jupiter |
| Uni | Hera | Juno |
| Menrva | Athena | Minerva |
| Apulu | Apollo | Apollo |
| Artumes | Artemis | Diana |
| Hercle | Herakles | Hercules |

## Archaic Art and Architecture

**ETRUSCAN TEMPLES** Etruscan artists looking eastward for inspiration were also greatly impressed by the art and architecture of Greece. But however eager they may have been to emulate Greek works, the distinctive Etruscan temperament always manifested itself. The vast majority of Archaic Etruscan artworks depart markedly from their prototypes. This is especially true of religious architecture. The design of Etruscan temples superficially owes much to Greece, but the differences far outweigh the similarities. Because of the materials Etruscan architects employed, usually only the foundations of Etruscan temples have survived. These are nonetheless sufficient to reveal the plans of the edifices. Supplementing the archaeological record is the Roman architect Vitruvius's treatise on architecture written near the end of the first century BCE. In it, Vitruvius provided an invaluable chapter on Etruscan temple design.

Archaeologists have constructed a model (FIG. 9-2) of a typical Archaic Etruscan temple based on Vitruvius's account. The sixth-century Etruscan temple resembled contemporary Greek stone gable-roofed temples (see "Doric and Ionic Temples," Chapter 5, pages 116–117), but it had wooden columns and a wooden roof, and its walls were of sun-dried brick. Entrance was possible only via a narrow staircase at the center of the front of the temple, which sat on a high podium, the only part of the building made of stone. Columns also were restricted to the front of the building, creating a deep porch that occupied roughly half the podium and setting off one side of the structure as the main side. In contrast, the front and rear of Greek temples were indistinguishable, and steps and columns were placed on all sides. The Etruscan temple was not meant to be seen as a sculptural mass from the outside and from all directions, as Greek temples were. Instead it functioned primarily as an ornate home for grand statues of Etruscan gods. It was a place of shelter, protected by the wide overhang of its roof.

Etruscan temples differed in other ways from those of Greece. Etruscan (or *Tuscan*) columns resembled Greek Doric columns, but they were made of wood, were unfluted, and had bases. Because of the lightness of the superstructure they had to support, Etruscan columns were, as a rule, much more widely spaced than Greek columns. Unlike their Greek counterparts, Etruscan temples frequently had three cellas—one for each of their chief gods, Tinia, Uni, and Menrva (see "Etruscan Counterparts of Greco-Roman Gods and Heroes," above). And pedimental statuary was exceedingly rare in Etruria. The Etruscans normally placed narrative statuary—in terracotta instead of stone—on the peaks of their temple roofs.

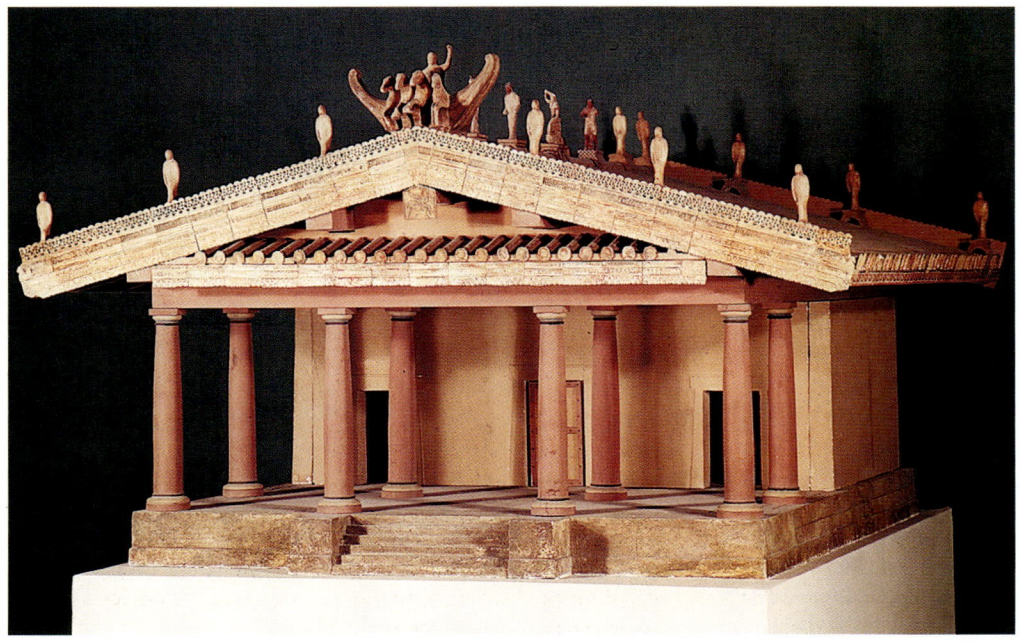

**9-2** Model of a typical Etruscan temple of the sixth century BCE, as described by Vitruvius. Istituto di Etruscologia e di Antichità Italiche, Università di Roma, Rome.

### Etruscan Artists in Rome

In 616 BCE, according to the traditional chronology, Tarquinius Priscus of Tarquinia became Rome's first Etruscan king. He ruled for almost 40 years. His grandson, Tarquinius Superbus ("the Arrogant"), was Rome's last king. Outraged by his tyrannical behavior, the Romans drove him out in 509 BCE. Before his expulsion, however, Tarquinius Superbus embarked on a grand program to embellish the modest city of huts Romulus had founded two centuries before.

The king's most ambitious undertaking was the erection of a magnificent temple (see FIG. 10-1, no. 4) on the Capitoline Hill for the joint worship of Jupiter, Juno, and Minerva. For this great commission, he summoned architects, sculptors, and workers from all over Etruria. Rome's first great religious shrine was Etruscan in patronage, in manufacture, and in form. The architect's name is unknown, but several sources preserve the identity of the Etruscan sculptor brought in to adorn the temple. His name was Vulca of Veii. Pliny the Elder describes his works as "the finest images of deities of that era . . . more admired than gold."[1] The Romans entrusted Vulca with making the statue of Jupiter that stood in the central of the Capitoline temple's three cellas. He also fashioned the enormous terracotta statuary group of Jupiter in a four-horse chariot, which was placed on the roof at the highest point directly over the center of

the temple facade. The fame of Vulca's red-faced (painted terracotta) portrayal of Jupiter was so great that Roman generals would paint their faces red in emulation of his Jupiter when they paraded in triumph through Rome after a battlefield victory. (One can get an approximate idea of the appearance of this early Jupiter temple and of Vulca's roof statue from the model reproduced in FIG. 9-2.)

One story told about Vulca's chariot group underscores both its tremendous size and the reverent awe in which it was held by later generations. Terracotta statuary normally condenses and contracts in the furnace as the clay's moisture evaporates in the heating process. Vulca's statue swelled instead and could be removed from the furnace only by dismantling its walls and lifting off its roof.[2]

Vulca is the only Etruscan artist named by any ancient writer, but the signatures of other Etruscan artists appear on surviving artworks. One of these is Novios Plautios (FIG. 9-12), who also worked in Rome, although a few centuries later. By then the Etruscan kings of Rome were a distant memory, and the Romans had captured Veii and annexed its territory.

[1] Pliny, *Natural History*, 35.157.

[2] Plutarch, *Life of Poplicola*, 13.

**AN EPIC ROOFTOP CONTEST** The finest of these rooftop statues to survive today is the life-size image of Apulu (FIG. **9-3**), which displays the energy and excitement that characterize Archaic Etruscan art in general. The statue comes from a temple in the Portonaccio sanctuary at Veii. It is but one of a group of at least four painted terracotta figures that adorned the top of the temple roof. The god confronts Hercle for possession of the Ceryneian hind, a wondrous beast with golden horns that was sacred to Apulu's sister Artumes. The bright paint and the rippling folds of Apulu's garment call to mind the Ionian korai of the Acropolis (see FIG. 5-12). But this vital figure's extraordinary force, huge swelling contours, plunging motion, gesticulating arms, fanlike calf muscles, and animated face are distinctly Etruscan. Some scholars have attributed the Apulu to VULCA OF VEII, the most famous Etruscan sculptor of the time (see "Etruscan Artists in Rome," above). The statue's discovery in 1916 was instrumental in prompting a reevaluation of the originality of Etruscan art.

**DINING IN THE AFTERLIFE** Although life-size terracotta statuary was known in Greece, this medium was especially favored in Etruria. Another Archaic Etruscan terracotta masterwork is the sarcophagus in the form of a husband and wife reclining on a banqueting couch (FIG. **9-4**), from a tomb in the Cerveteri necropolis. The sarcophagus was cast in four sections and is of monumental size, but it contained only the ashes of the deceased. Cremation was the most common means of disposing of the dead in Italy at this time. This kind of funerary monument had no parallel at this date in Greece, where there were no monumental tombs that could house such sarcophagi. The Greeks buried their dead in simple graves marked by a stele or a statue. Moreover, although banquets were commonly depicted on Greek vases (which, by the late sixth century BCE, the Etruscans

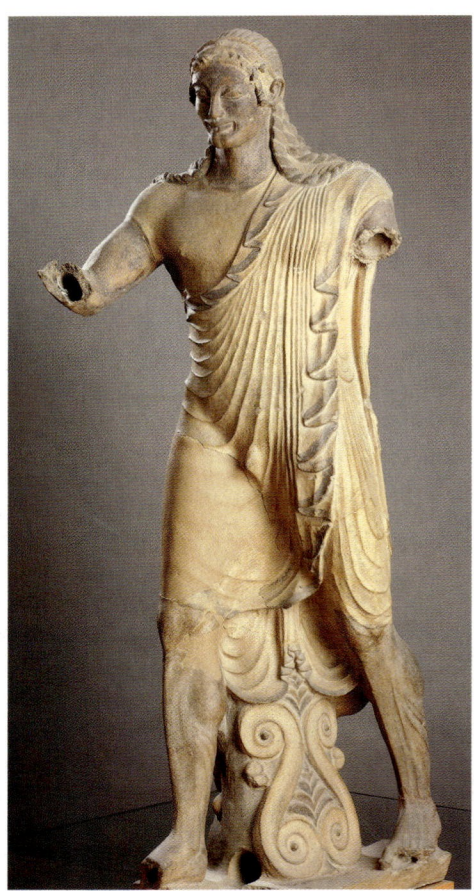

**9-3** Apulu (Apollo), from the roof of the Portonaccio Temple, Veii, Italy, ca. 510–500 BCE. Painted terracotta, approx. 5′ 11″ high. Museo Nazionale di Villa Giulia, Rome. ◑

### The "Audacity" of Etruscan Women

At the instigation of the emperor Augustus at the end of the first century BCE, Titus Livy wrote a history of Rome from its legendary founding in 753 BCE to his own day. In the first book of his great work, Livy recounted the tale of Tullia, daughter of Servius Tullius, an Etruscan king of Rome in the sixth century. The princess had married the less ambitious of two brothers of the royal Tarquinius family, while her sister had married the bolder of the two princes. Together, Tullia and her brother-in-law, Tarquinius Superbus, arranged for the murder of their spouses. They then married each other and plotted the overthrow and death of Tullia's father. After the king's murder, Tullia ostentatiously drove her carriage over her father's corpse, spraying herself with his blood. (The Roman road where the evil deed occurred is still called the Street of Infamy.) Livy, though condemning Tullia's actions, placed them in the context of the famous "audacity" of Etruscan women.

The independent spirit and relative freedom women enjoyed in Etruscan society similarly horrified (and threatened) other Greco-Roman male authors. The stories the fourth-century BCE Greek historian Theopompus heard about the debauchery of Etruscan women appalled him. Etruscan women epitomized immorality for Theopompus, but much of what he reported is untrue. Etruscan women did not, for example, exercise naked alongside Etruscan men. But archaeological evidence confirms the accuracy of at least one of his "slurs": Etruscan women did attend banquets and recline with their husbands on a common couch (FIGS. 9-4 and 9-8). Aristotle also remarked on this custom. It was so foreign to the Greeks that it both shocked and frightened them. Only men, boys, slave girls, and prostitutes attended Greek symposia. The wives remained at home, excluded from most aspects of public life. In Etruscan Italy, in striking contrast to contemporary Greece, women also regularly attended sporting events with men. This, too, is well documented in Etruscan paintings and reliefs.

Etruscan inscriptions also reflect the higher status of women in Etruria as compared to Greece. They often give the names of both the father and mother of the person commemorated (for example, the inscribed portrait of Aule Metele, FIG. 9-15), a practice unheard of in Greece (witness the grave stele of "Hegeso, daughter of Proxenos," FIG. 5-55). Etruscan women, moreover, retained their own names and could legally own property independently of their husbands. The frequent use of inscriptions on Etruscan mirrors and other toilet items (FIG. 9-12) buried with women seems to attest to a high degree of female literacy as well.

imported in great quantities and regularly deposited in their tombs), only men dined at Greek symposia. The image of a husband and wife sharing the same banqueting couch is uniquely Etruscan (see "The 'Audacity' of Etruscan Women," above).

The man and woman on the Cerveteri sarcophagus are as animated as the Apulu of Veii (FIG. 9-3), even though they are at rest. They are the antithesis of the stiff and formal figures encountered in Egyptian tomb sculptures (compare the portraits of Menkaure and Khamerernebty[?] from Gizeh, FIG. 3-13). Also typically Etruscan, and in striking contrast to contemporary Greek statues with their emphasis on proportion and balance, is the manner in which the Cerveteri sculptor rendered the upper and lower parts of each body. The legs were only summarily modeled, and the transition to the torso at the waist is unnatural. The Etruscan artist's interest focused on the upper half of the figures, especially on the vibrant faces and gesticulating arms. Gestures are still an important ingredient of Italian conversation today, and the Cerveteri banqueters and the Veii Apulu speak to viewers in a way that Greek statues of similar date, with their closed contours and calm demeanor, never do.

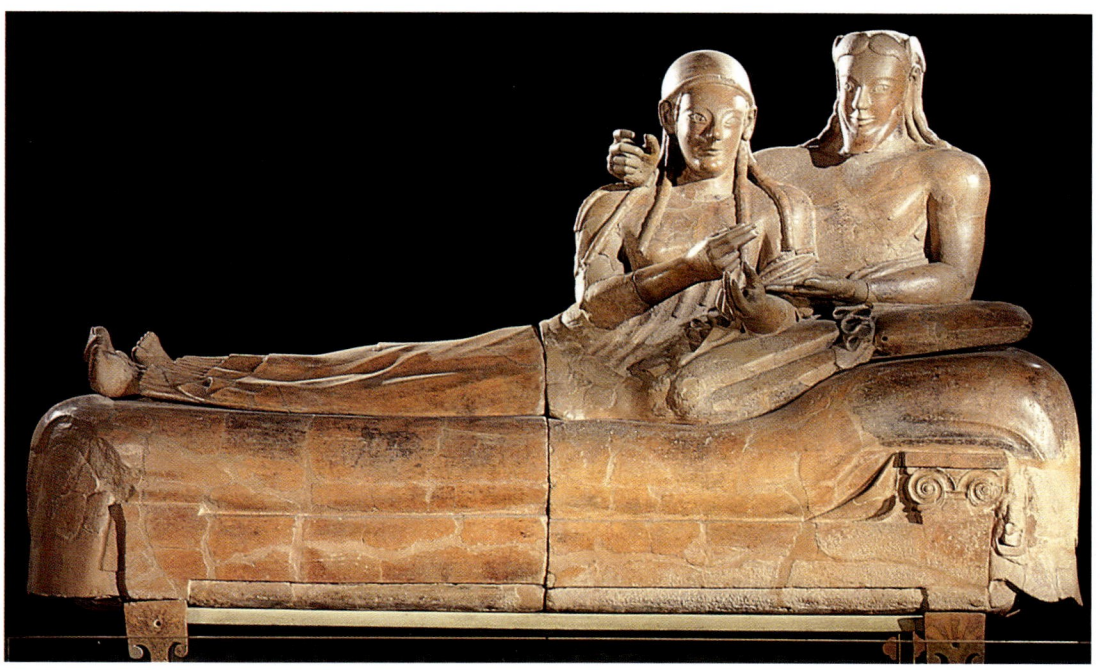

**9-4** Sarcophagus with reclining couple, from Cerveteri, Italy, ca. 520 BCE. Painted terracotta, approx. 6′ 7″ × 3′ 9½″. Museo Nazionale di Villa Giulia, Rome.

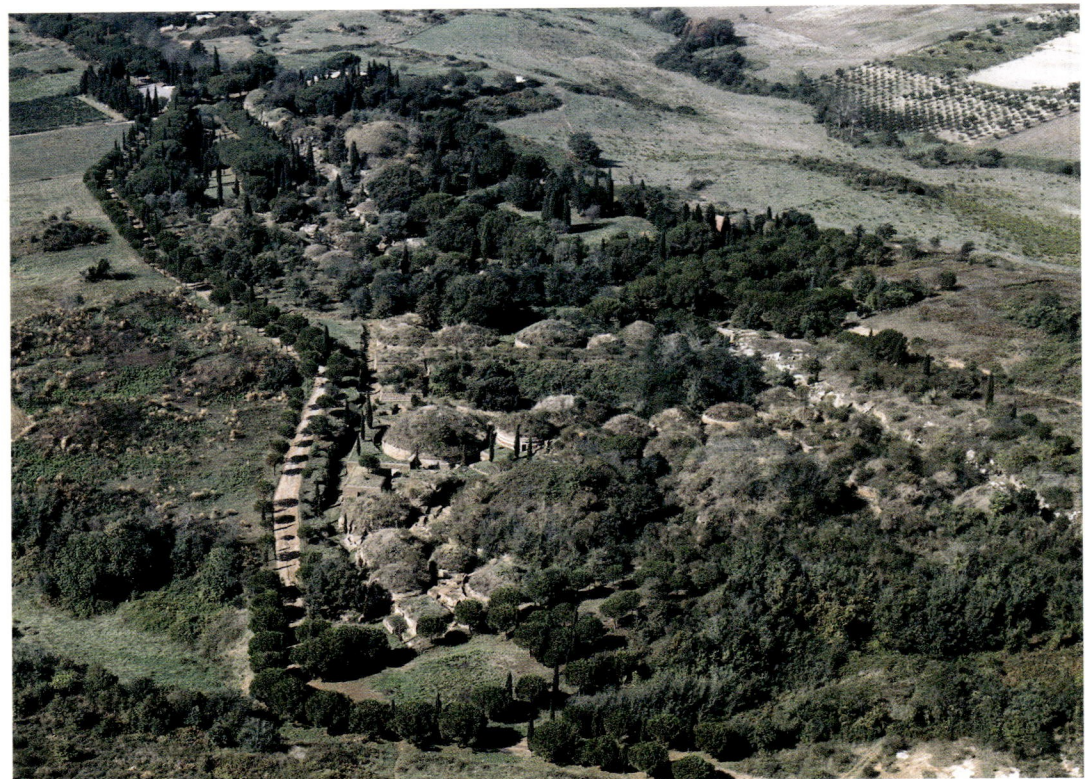

**9-5** Aerial view of Banditaccia necropolis, Cerveteri, Italy, seventh to second centuries BCE.

**HOUSES FOR THE DEAD** The exact findspot of the Cerveteri sarcophagus is not known, but the kind of tomb that housed such sarcophagi is well documented. The typical tomb at Cerveteri (FIG. **9-5**) took the form of a mound, or *tumulus* (plural *tumuli*), not unlike the Mycenaean Treasury of Atreus (see FIG. 4-21). But whereas the Mycenaean tholos tomb was constructed of masonry blocks and then covered by an earthen mound, each Etruscan tumulus covered one or more subterranean multichambered tombs cut out of the dark local limestone called tufa. These burial mounds sometimes reached colossal size, with diameters in excess of 130 feet. They were arranged in cemeteries in an orderly manner along a network of streets, producing the effect of veritable cities of the dead (which is the literal meaning of the Greek word *necropolis*), and were always located some distance from the cities of the living.

The underground tomb chambers cut into the rock resembled the houses of the living. In the plan of the sixth-century BCE Tomb of the Shields and Chairs at Cerveteri (FIG. **9-6**), for example, the central entrance and the smaller chambers opening onto a large central space mirror the axial sequence of rooms in actual Etruscan houses of the time. The effect of a domestic interior was enhanced by the beds and grand armchairs with curved backs and footstools (clearly visible on the plan), as well as the ceiling beams, framed doorways, and even windows that were cut out of the rock. The technique recalls that of the rock-cut Egyptian tombs at Beni Hasan (see FIG. 3-20). One cannot help but notice the very different values of the Etruscans and the Greeks. The Etruscans' temples no longer stand because they were constructed of wood and mud brick, but their grand subterranean tombs are as permanent as the bedrock itself. The Greeks employed stone for the shrines of their gods but only rarely built monumental tombs for their dead.

The most elaborate of the Cerveteri underground tombs, in decoration if not in plan, is the so-called Tomb of the Reliefs (FIG. **9-7**). Like the much earlier Tomb of the Shields and Chairs, it accommodated several generations of a single family. The walls and

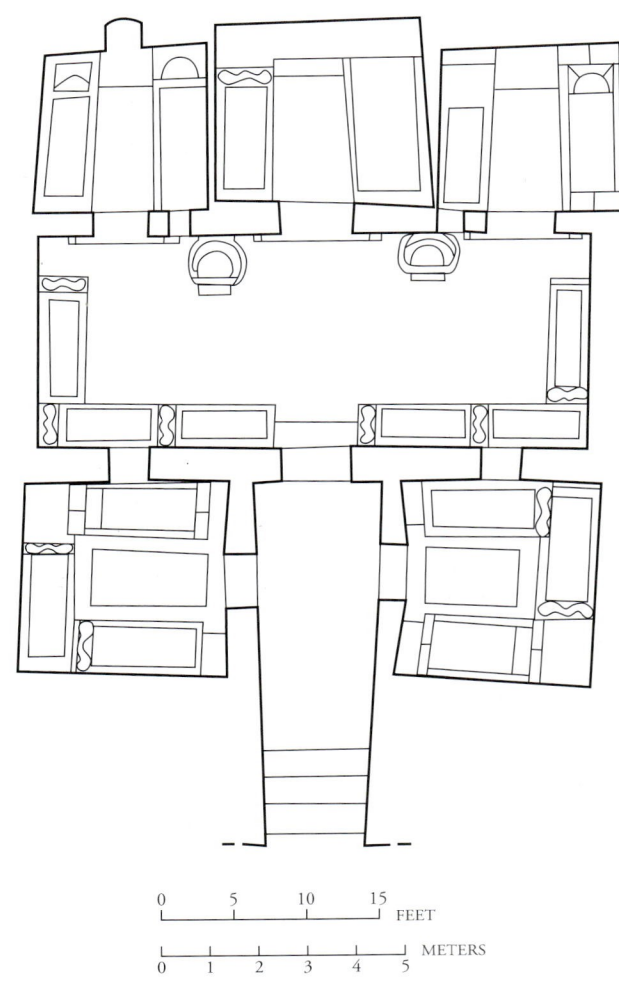

**9-6** Plan of the Tomb of the Shields and Chairs, Cerveteri, Italy, second half of the sixth century BCE.

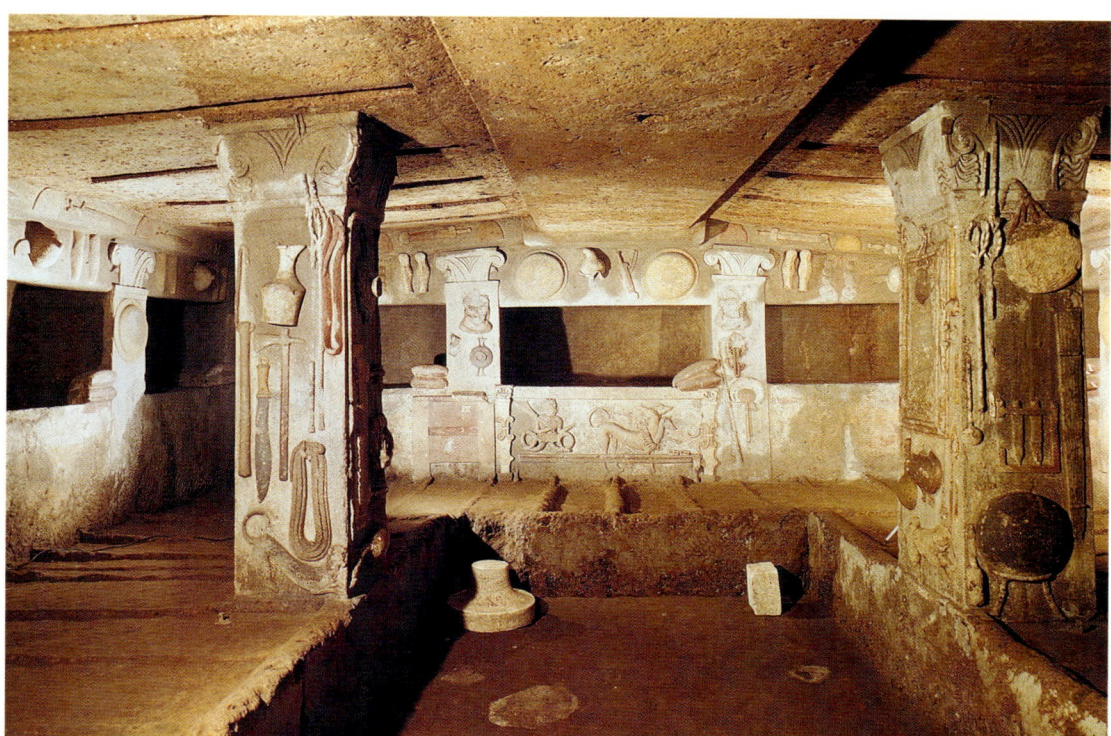

9-7 Interior of the Tomb of the Reliefs, Cerveteri, Italy, third century BCE.

piers of this tomb were, as usual, gouged out of the tufa bedrock, but in this instance brightly painted stucco reliefs covered the stone. The stools, mirrors, drinking cups, pitchers, and knives effectively suggest a domestic context, underscoring the connection between Etruscan houses of the dead and those of the living.

**TARQUINIA'S PAINTED TOMBS** Large underground burial chambers hewn out of the natural rock were also the norm at Tarquinia. But tumuli do not cover the Tarquinian tombs, and the interiors do not have carvings imitating the appearance of Etruscan houses. In some cases, however, paintings decorate the tomb chamber walls. Painted tombs are statistically rare, the privilege of only the wealthiest Etruscan families. Nevertheless, archaeologists have discovered many at Tarquinia by using periscopes to explore tomb contents from the surface before considering time-consuming and costly excavation. Consequently, art historians have an almost unbroken record of monumental painting in Etruria from Archaic to Hellenistic times.

**LEOPARDS AND A FEAST** A characteristic example dating to the early fifth century BCE is the Tomb of the Leopards (FIG. 9-8), named for the beasts that guard the interior of the painted

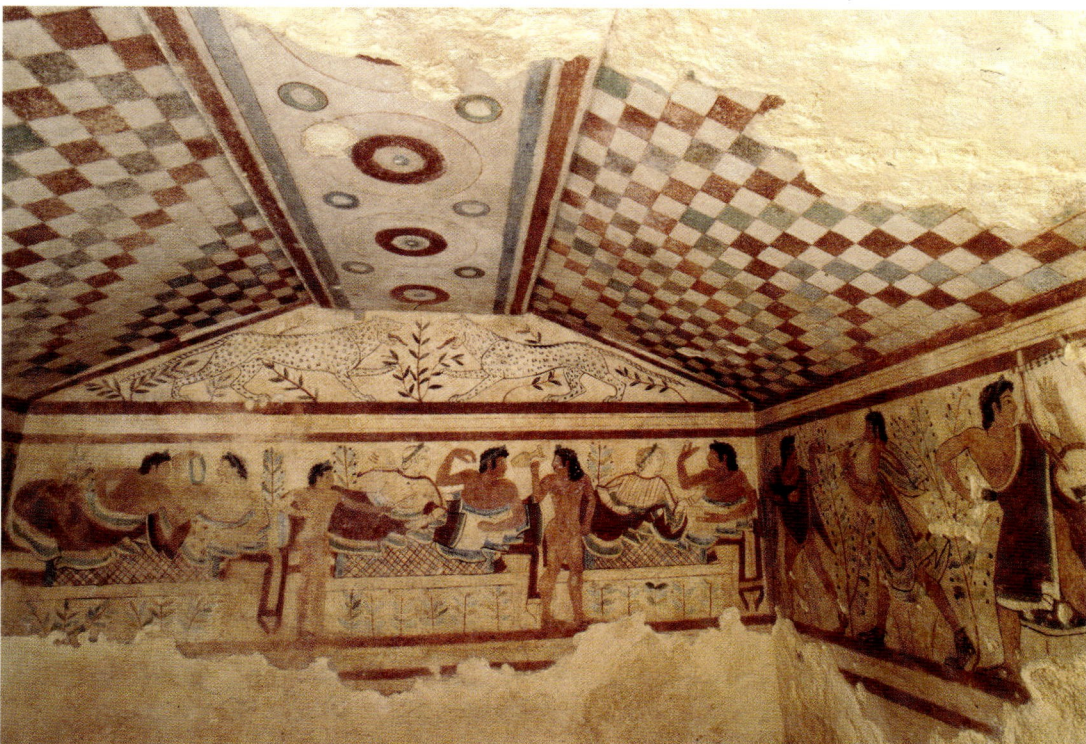

9-8 Leopards, banqueters, and musicians, mural paintings in the Tomb of the Leopards, Tarquinia, Italy, ca. 480–470 BCE.

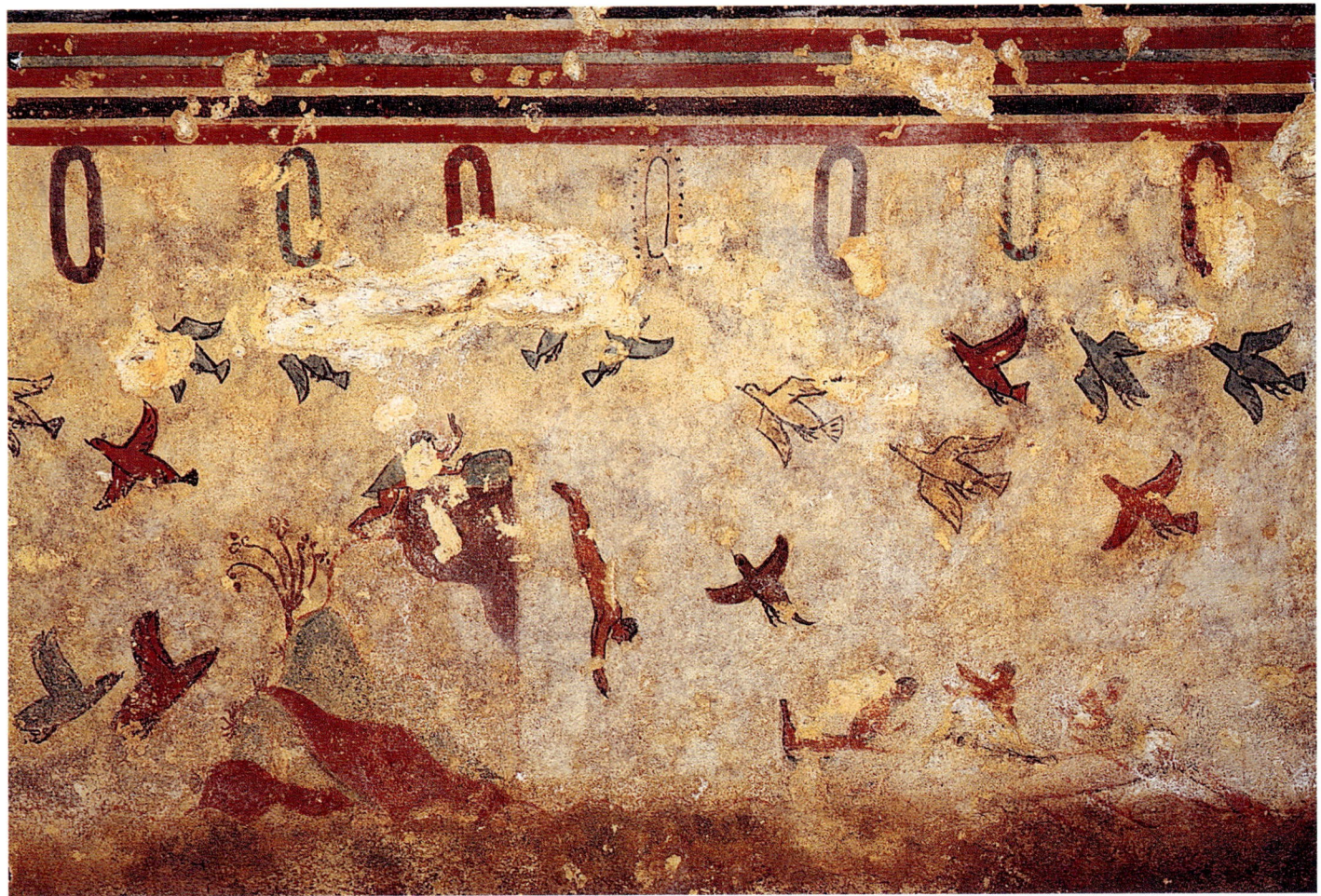

**9-9** Diving and fishing, mural painting in the Tomb of Hunting and Fishing, Tarquinia, Italy, ca. 530–520 BCE.

chamber from their perch within the rear wall pediment. They are reminiscent of the panthers on each side of Medusa in the pediment of the Archaic Greek Temple of Artemis at Corfu (see FIG. 5-15). But mythological figures, whether Greek or Etruscan, are uncommon in Tarquinian murals, and the Tomb of the Leopards has none. Instead, banqueting couples (the men with dark skin, the women with light skin, in conformity with the age-old convention) adorn the walls—painted versions of the terracotta sarcophagus from Cerveteri (FIG. 9-4). Pitcher- and cupbearers serve them, and musicians entertain them. The banquet takes place in the open air or perhaps in a tent set up for the occasion. In characteristic Etruscan fashion, the banqueters, servants, and entertainers all make exaggerated gestures with unnaturally enlarged hands. The man on the couch at the far right on the rear wall holds up an egg, the symbol of regeneration. The tone is joyful. The painting is a celebration of life, food, wine, music, and dance, rather than a somber contemplation of death.

**ETRUSCAN LANDSCAPES** In stylistic terms, the Etruscan figures are comparable to those on sixth-century Greek vases before Late Archaic painters became preoccupied with the problem of foreshortening. Etruscan painters may be considered somewhat backward in this respect, but in other ways they seem to have outpaced their counterparts in Greece, especially in their interest in rendering nature. In the Tomb of the Leopards, the landscape is but a few trees and shrubs placed between the entertainers (and leopards) and behind the banqueting couches. But elsewhere the natural environment was the chief interest of Tarquinian painters.

Scenes of Etruscans enjoying the pleasures of nature decorate all the walls of the main chamber of the aptly named Tomb of Hunting and Fishing at Tarquinia. In our detail (FIG. **9-9**), a youth dives off a rocky promontory, while others fish from a boat and birds fill the sky all around. On another wall, youthful hunters aim their slingshots at the brightly painted birds. The scenes of hunting and fishing recall the painted reliefs in the Old Kingdom Egyptian Tomb of Ti (see FIG. 3-16) and the mural paintings from the New Kingdom Tomb of Nebamun (see FIG. 3-30), and may indicate knowledge of this Egyptian funerary tradition. The multicolored rocks may be compared to those of the Aegean *Spring Fresco* from Thera (see FIG. 4-9), but art historians know of nothing similar in contemporary Greek art save the Tomb of the Diver at Paestum (see FIG. 5-59). The latter is, however, exceptional and is from a Greek tomb in Italy about a half century *later* than the Tarquinian tomb. In fact, it is likely that the Paestum composition emulated older Etruscan designs, undermining the now outdated art historical judgment that Etruscan art was merely derivative and that Etruscan artists never set the standard for Greek artists.

The fifth century BCE was a golden age in Greece but not in Etruria. In 509 BCE, the Romans expelled the last of their Etruscan kings, Tarquinius Superbus (see "Etruscan Artists in Rome," page 236), replacing the monarchy with a republican form of government. In 474 BCE, an alliance of Cumaean Greeks and Hieron I of Syracuse (Sicily) defeated the Etruscan fleet off Cumae, effectively ending Etruscan dominance of the seas, and with it Etruscan prosperity. These events had important consequences in the world of art and architecture. The number of Etruscan tombs, for example, decreased sharply, and the quality of the furnishings declined markedly. No longer were tombs filled with golden jewelry and imported Greek vases or decorated with mural paintings of the first rank. But Etruscan art did not cease. Indeed, in the areas in which Etruscan artists excelled, especially the casting of statues in bronze and terracotta, they continued to produce impressive works, even though fewer in number.

## Classical Art

ROME'S ETRUSCAN WOLF The best-known of these later Etruscan statues—one of the most memorable portrayals of an animal in the history of world art—is the *Capitoline Wolf* (FIG. 9-10). The statue is a somewhat larger than life-size hollow-cast bronze portrayal of the she-wolf that, according to legend, nursed Romulus and Remus after they were abandoned as infants. When the twins grew to adulthood, they quarreled, and Romulus killed his brother. On April 21, 753 BCE, Romulus founded Rome on the Palatine Hill and became the city's king. The statue of the she-wolf seems to have been made, however, for the new Roman Republic after the expulsion of Tarquinius Superbus. It became the new government's totem. The appropriately defiant image has remained the emblem of Rome to this day.

The *Capitoline Wolf* is not, however, a work of Roman art, which had not yet developed a distinct identity, but the product of an Etruscan workshop. (The suckling infants are additions by the Italian Renaissance sculptor Antonio Pollaiuolo.) The vitality noted in the human figure in Etruscan art is here concentrated in the tense, watchful animal body of the she-wolf, with her spare flanks, gaunt ribs, and taut, powerful legs. The lowered neck and head, alert ears, glaring eyes, and ferocious muzzle capture the psychic intensity of the fierce and protective beast as danger approaches. Not even the great animal reliefs of Assyria (see FIG. 2-24) match, much less surpass, this profound rendering of animal temper.

AREZZO'S BRONZE CHIMERA Another masterpiece of Etruscan bronze-casting, found in 1553 and greatly admired during the Renaissance, is the *Chimera of Arezzo* (FIG. 9-11), which dates about a century later than the *Capitoline Wolf*. The *chimera* is a monster of Greek invention with a lion's head and body and a serpent's tail. A second head, that of a goat, grows out of the lion's left side. The goat's neck bears the wound the Greek hero Beller-ophon inflicted when he hunted and slew the composite beast. As rendered by the Etruscan sculptor, the chimera, although injured and bleeding, is nowhere near defeated. Like the earlier she-wolf statue, the bronze chimera has muscles that are stretched tightly over its rib cage. It prepares to

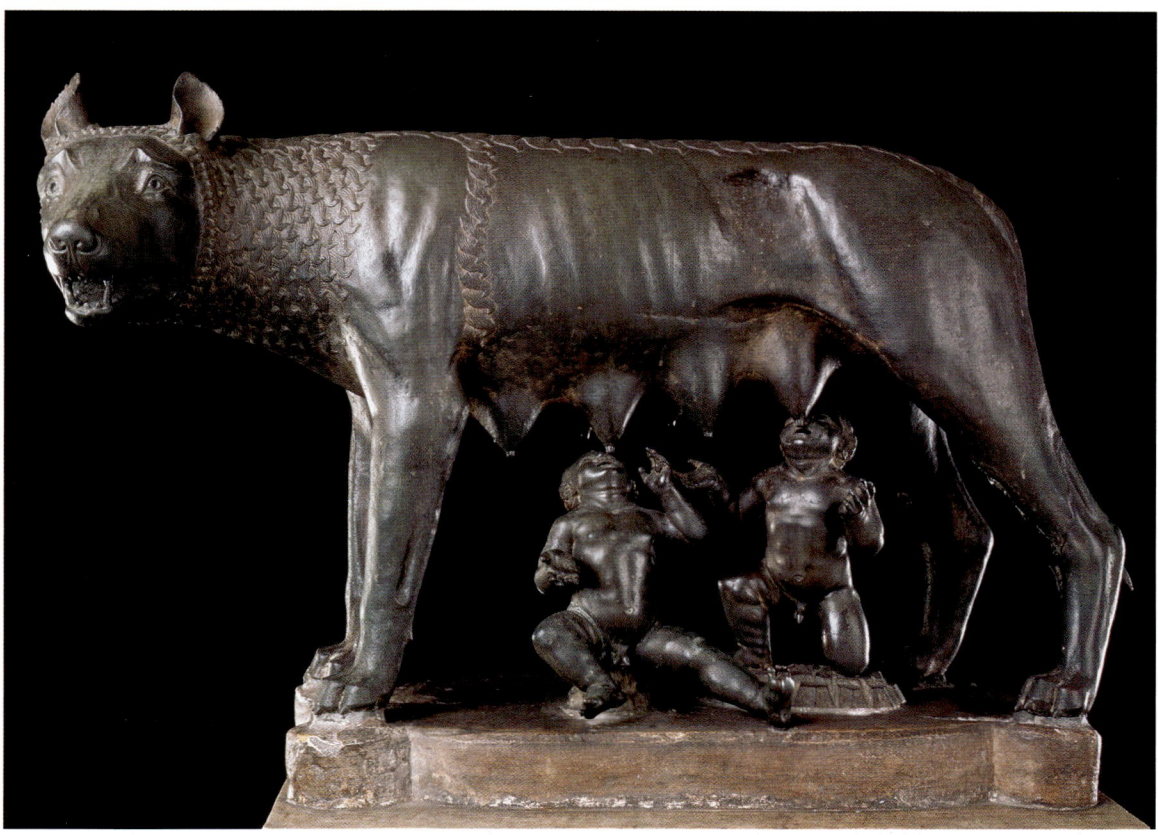

**9-10** *Capitoline Wolf,* from Rome, Italy, ca. 500–480 BCE. Bronze, approx. 2′ 7½″ high. Palazzo dei Conservatori, Rome.

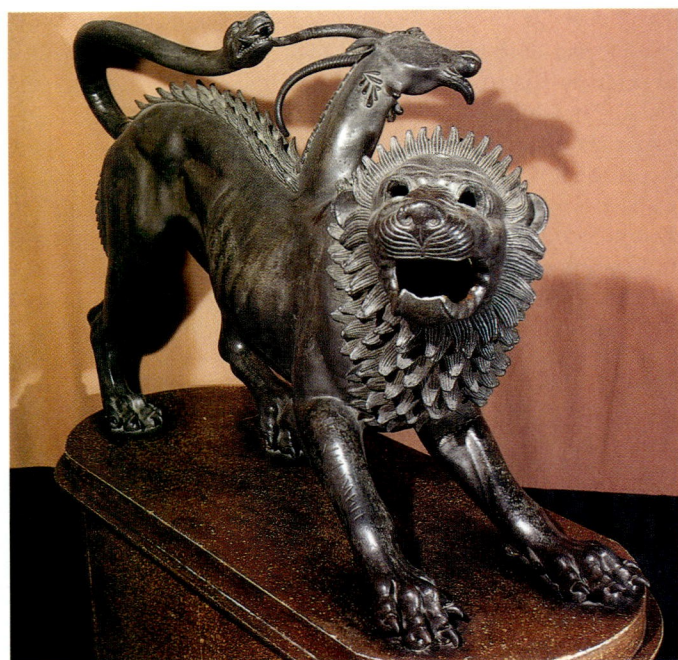

**9-11** *Chimera of Arezzo,* from Arezzo, Italy, first half of fourth century BCE. Bronze, approx. 2′ 7½″ high. Museo Archeologico Nazionale, Florence.

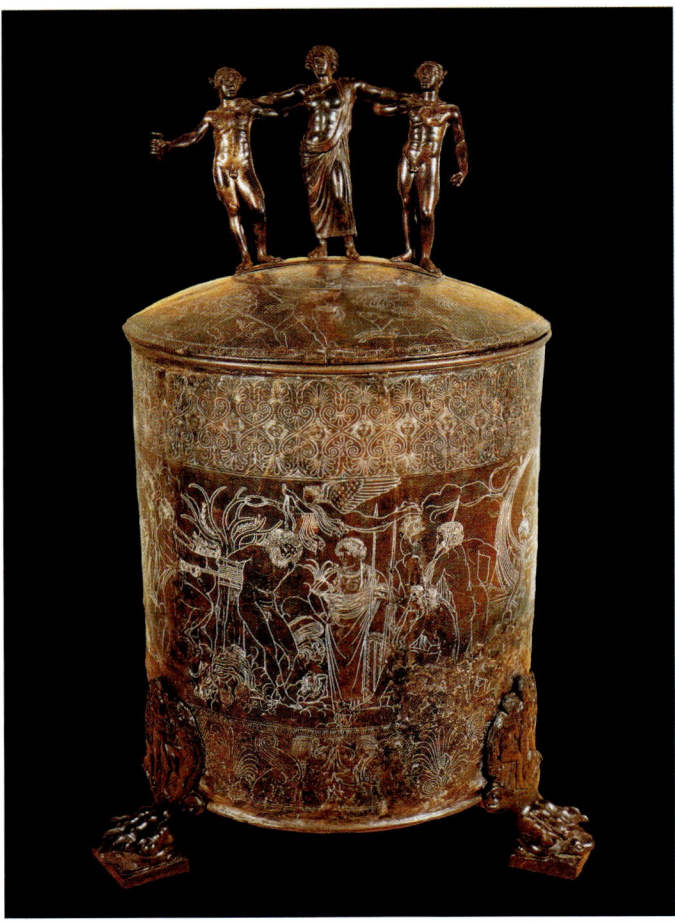

**9-12** NOVIOS PLAUTIOS, *Ficoroni Cista,* from Palestrina, Italy, late fourth century BCE. Bronze, approx. 2′ 6″ high. Museo Nazionale di Villa Giulia, Rome.

attack, and a ferocious cry emanates from its open jaws. Some scholars have postulated that the statue was part of a group that originally included Bellerophon, but the chimera could have just as well stood alone. The menacing gaze upward toward an unseen adversary need not have been answered. In this respect, too, the chimera is in the tradition of the guardian nurse of Romulus and Remus.

### Etruscan Art and the Rise of Rome

**ROME OVERWHELMS ETRURIA** At about the time the *Chimera of Arezzo* was fashioned, Rome began to appropriate Etruscan territory. Veii fell to the Romans in 396 BCE, after a terrible 10-year siege. Peace was concluded with Tarquinia in 351, but by the beginning of the next century, Tarquinia, too, was annexed by Rome, and Cerveteri was conquered in 273 BCE. Rome's growing power in central Italy is indicated indirectly by the engraved inscription on the *Ficoroni Cista* (FIG. **9-12**). Etruscan artists produced such *cistae* (cylindrical containers for a woman's toilet articles), made of sheet bronze with cast handles and feet and elaborately engraved bodies, in large numbers from the fourth century BCE forward. Along with engraved bronze mirrors, they were popular gifts for both the living and the dead. The Etruscan bronze cista industry centered in Palestrina (ancient Praeneste), where the *Ficoroni Cista* was found. The inscription on the cista's handle states that Dindia Macolnia, a local noblewoman, gave the bronze container to her daughter and that the artist was one NOVIOS PLAUTIOS. According to the inscription, his workshop was not in Palestrina but in Rome, which by this date was becoming an important Italian cultural, as well as political, center.

The engraved frieze of the *Ficoroni Cista* depicts an episode from the Greek story of the expedition of the Argonauts in search of the Golden Fleece. Scholars generally agree that the composition is an adaptation of a lost Greek panel painting, perhaps one on display in Rome—another testimony to the burgeoning wealth and prestige of the city once ruled by Etruscan kings. The Greek source for Novios Plautios's engraving is evident in the figures seen entirely from behind or in three-quarter view, and in the placement of the protagonists on several levels in the Polygnotan manner (see FIG. 5-57).

**THE GATE OF MARS** In the third century BCE, the Etruscan city of Perugia (ancient Perusia) formed an alliance with Rome and was spared the destruction suffered by Veii, Cerveteri, and other Etruscan towns. Portions of Perugia's ancient walls are still standing, as are some of its gates. One of these, the so-called Porta Marzia (Gate of Mars), was dismantled by the Renaissance architect Antonio da Sangallo, but the upper part of the gate is preserved, embedded in a later wall (FIG. **9-13**). The archway is formed by a series of trapezoidal stone *voussoirs* held in place by being pressed against each other (see FIG. 4-18c). Such arches were built earlier in Greece as well as in Mesopotamia (see FIG. 2-25), but Italy, first under the Etruscans and later under the Romans, is where *arcuated* (arch-shaped) gateways and freestanding ("triumphal") arches became a major architectural type.

The use of Hellenic-inspired pilasters to frame the rounded opening of the Porta Marzia typifies the Etruscan adaptation of Greek motifs. Arches bracketed by engaged columns or pilasters have a long and distinguished history in Roman and later times. In the Porta Marzia, sculpted half-figures of Jupiter and his sons Castor and Pollux and their steeds look out from between the

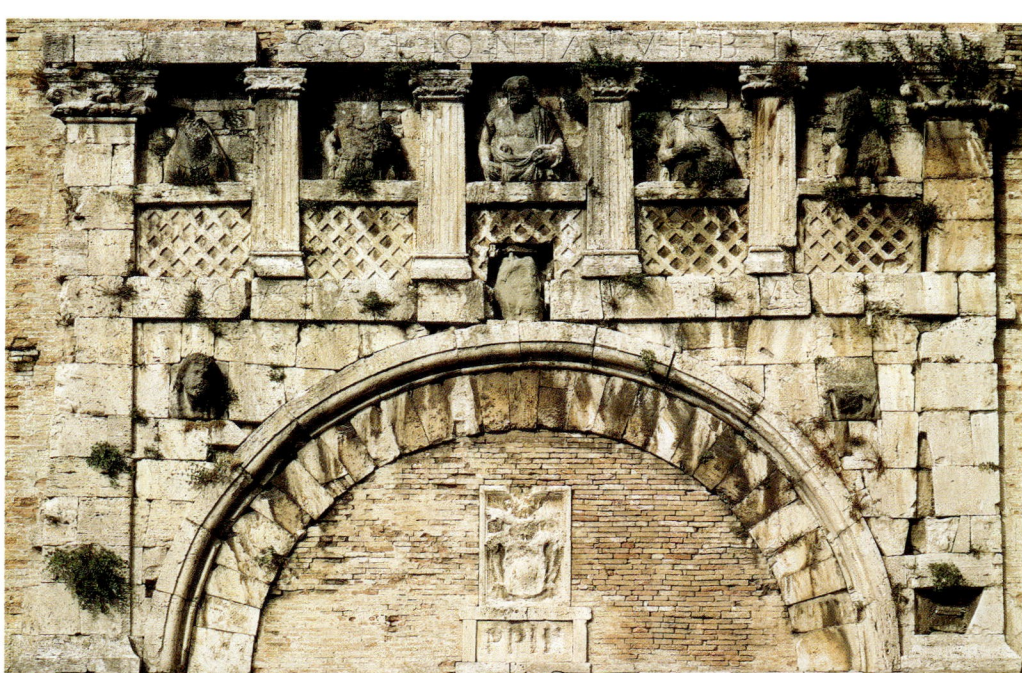

fluted pilasters. The divine twins had appeared miraculously on a battlefield in 484 BCE to turn the tide in favor of the Romans. The presence of these three deities at the apex of the Porta Marzia may reflect the new Roman practice of erecting triumphal arches crowned by gilded bronze statues.

**TORMENT IN THE UNDERWORLD** In Hellenistic Etruria, the descendants of the magnificent Archaic terracotta sarcophagus from Cerveteri (FIG. 9-4) were made of local stone. The leading production center was Tarquinia, and that is where the sar-cophagus of Lars Pulena (FIG. **9-14**) was fashioned early in the second century BCE and placed in his family's tomb. The deceased is shown in a reclining position, but he is not at a festive banquet, and his wife is not present. His expression is somber, a far cry from the smiling, confident faces of the Archaic era when Etruria enjoyed its greatest prosperity. Similar heads—realistic but generic types, not true portraits—are found on all later Etruscan sarcophagi and in tomb paintings. They are symptomatic of the economic and political decline of the once-mighty Etruscan city-states.

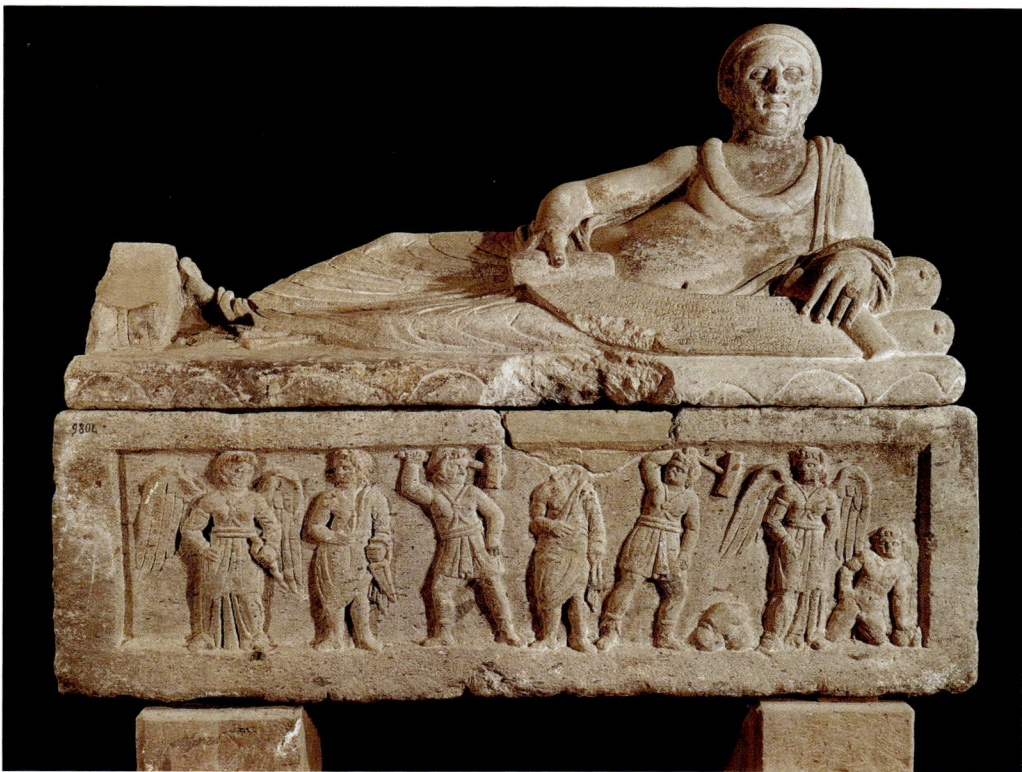

**9-14** Sarcophagus of Lars Pulena, from Tarquinia, Italy, early second century BCE. Tufa, approx. 6′ 6″ long. Museo Archeologico Nazionale, Tarquinia.

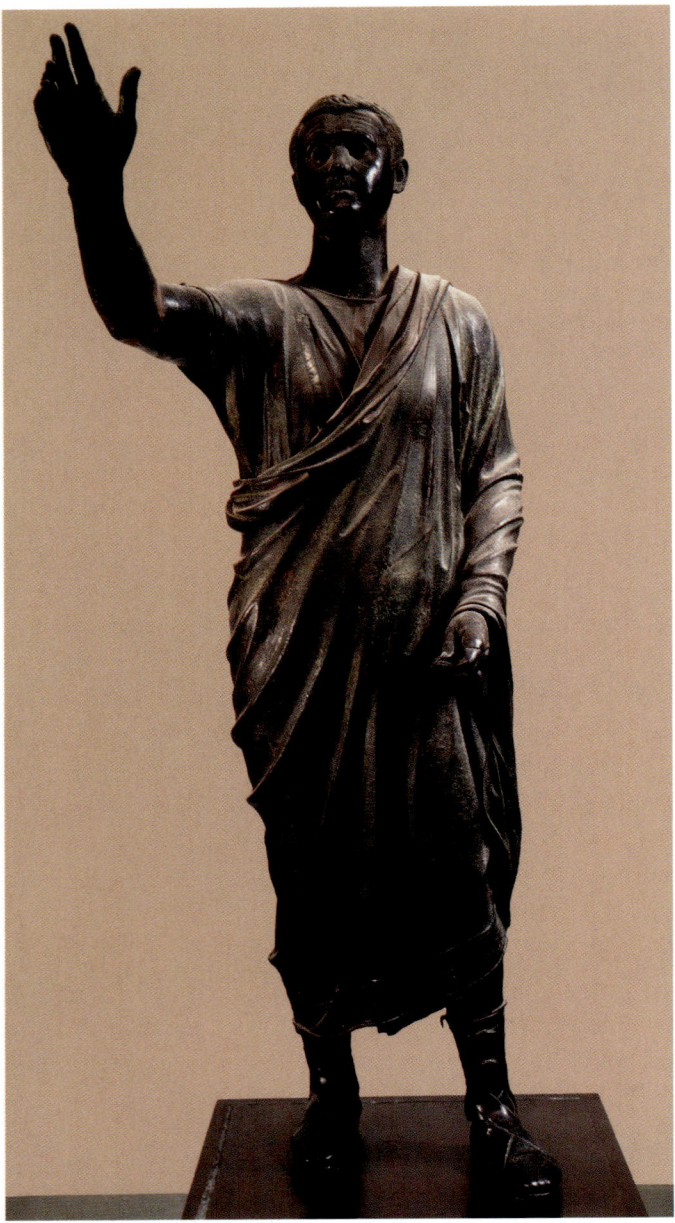

**9-15** Aule Metele *(Arringatore),* from Cortona, near Lake Trasimeno, Italy, early first century BCE. Bronze, approx. 5′ 7″ high. Museo Archeologico Nazionale, Florence.

Also attesting to a gloomy assessment of the future is the theme chosen for the coffin proper. The deceased is shown in the underworld, attacked by two *Charuns* (Etruscan death demons) swinging lethal hammers. Above, on the lid, Lars Pulena exhibits a partially unfurled scroll inscribed with the record of his life's accomplishments. Lacking confidence in a happy afterlife, he dwells instead on the past.

**ETRUSCAN OR ROMAN?** In striking contrast, the portrait of Aule Metele (FIG. **9-15**) is a supremely self-confident image. He is portrayed as a magistrate raising his arm to address an assembly—hence his modern nickname *Arringatore* (Orator). This life-size bronze statue was discovered in 1566 near Lake Trasimeno and is yet another Etruscan masterpiece known to Italian Renaissance sculptors. The statue of the orator proves that Etruscan artists continued to be experts at bronze-casting long after the heyday of Etruscan prosperity.

The *Arringatore* was most likely produced at about the time that Roman hegemony over the Etruscans became total. The so-called Social War of the early first century BCE ended in 89 BCE with the conferring of Roman citizenship on all of Italy's inhabitants. In fact, Aule Metele—his Etruscan name and his father's and mother's names are inscribed on the hem of his garment—wears the short toga and high laced boots of a Roman magistrate. His head, with its close-cropped hair and signs of age in the face, resembles portraits produced in Rome at the time. This orator is Etruscan in name only.

## CONCLUSION

In the Archaic period, the Etruscans dominated the Italian peninsula. Although they imported Greek objects, especially painted vases, in great numbers, their art, while influenced by that of Greece, was distinctive and innovative. No Greek parallels exist for Etruscan tombs with mural paintings, temples with rooftop statuary, or sarcophagi depicting married couples.

By the first century BCE, however, Etruria had been incorporated into the ever-expanding empire of Rome. The portrait of Aule Metele (FIG. 9-15), for example, is indistinguishable from contemporary Roman portraits. If the origin of the Etruscans remains debatable, the question of their demise has a ready answer. Aule Metele and his compatriots became Romans, and Etruscan art became Roman art.

900 BCE

VILLANOVAN

▎ GREEK COLONIZATION OF SOUTHERN ITALY AND SICILY BEGINS, MID-EIGHTH CENTURY BCE

▎ FOUNDING OF ROME, 753 BCE

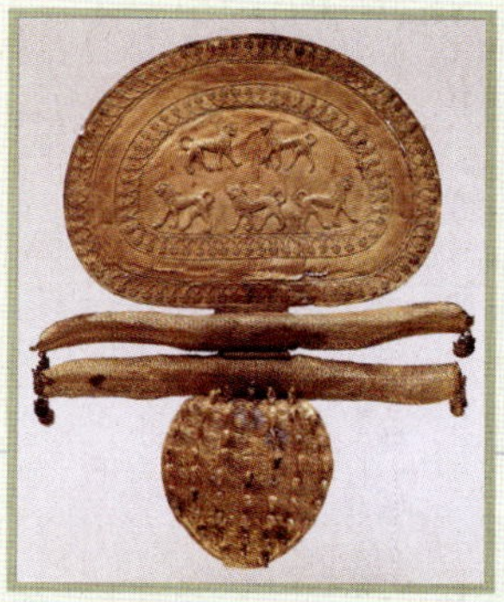

700 BCE

ORIENTALIZING

▎ TARQUINIUS PRISCUS, FIRST ETRUSCAN KING OF ROME, (R. 616–578 BCE)

**1**

**1** Regolini-Galassi fibula, Cerveteri, ca. 650–640 BCE

600 BCE

ARCHAIC

▎ EXPULSION OF ETRUSCAN KINGS FROM ROME, 509 BCE

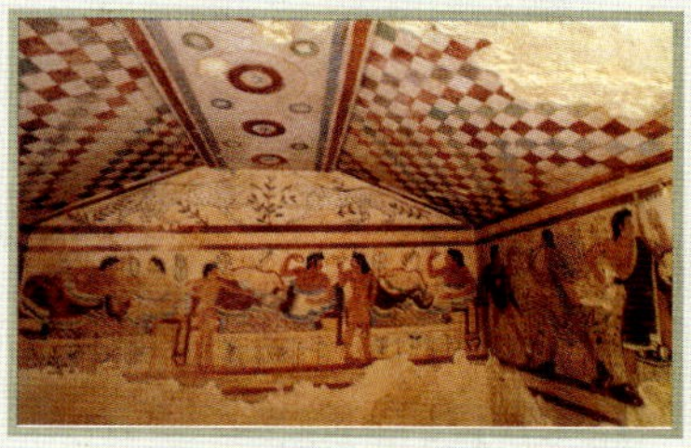

**2** Tomb of the Leopards, Tarquinia, ca. 480–470 BCE

480 BCE

**2** ▎ GREEKS DEFEAT THE ETRUSCAN NAVY AT CUMAE, 474 BCE

▎ ROMANS DESTROY VEII, 396 BCE

▎ PEACE BETWEEN ROME AND TARQUINIA, 351 BCE

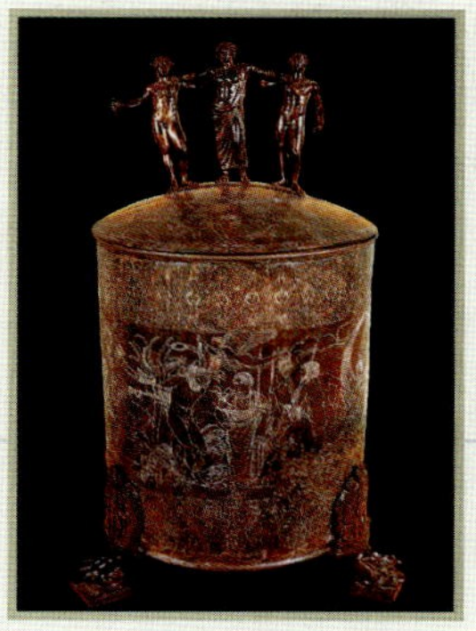

CLASSICAL

**3**

323 BCE

▎ ROMAN CONQUEST OF CERVETERI, 273 BCE

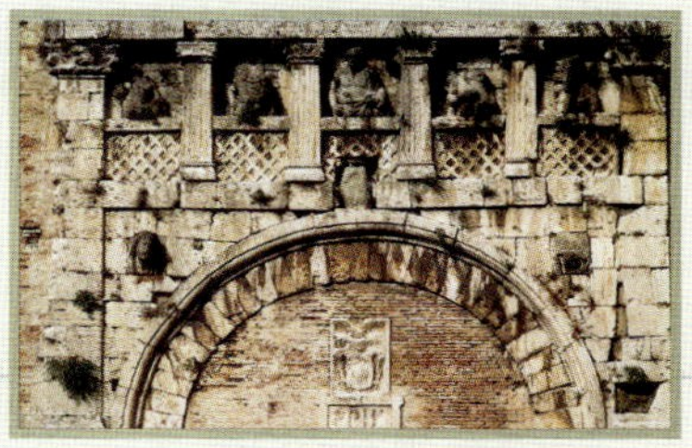

**3** Ficoroni Cista, late fourth century

HELLENISTIC

**4**

89 BCE

▎ END OF SOCIAL WAR AND COMPLETION OF ROMANIZATION OF ITALY, 89 BCE

**4** Porta Marzia, Perugia, second century BCE

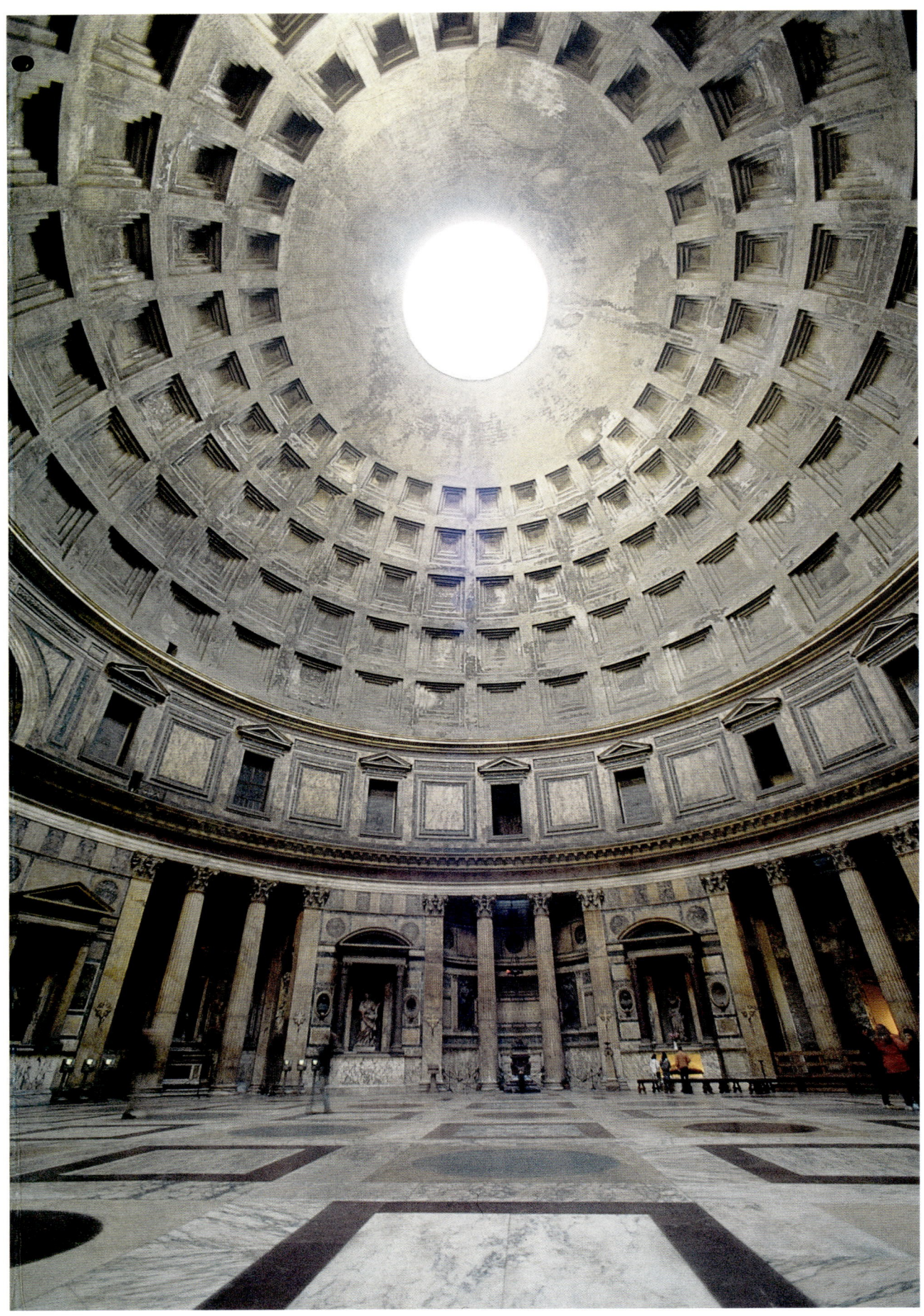

Interior of the Pantheon, Rome, Italy, 118–125 CE.

# 10

# FROM SEVEN HILLS
# TO THREE CONTINENTS

## THE ART OF ANCIENT ROME

With the rise and triumph of Rome, a single government ruled, for the first time in human history, from the Tigris and Euphrates to the Thames and beyond, from the Nile to the Rhine and Danube (MAP 10-1). Within the Roman Empire's borders lived people of numerous races, religions, tongues, traditions, and cultures: Britons and Gauls, Greeks and Egyptians, Africans and Syrians, Jews and Christians, to name but a few. Of all the ancient civilizations, only the Roman approximates today's world in its multicultural character.

Roman monuments of art and architecture, spread throughout the vast territory the Romans governed, are the most conspicuous and numerous of all the remains of ancient civilization. Many, converted to other uses, are part of the fabric of modern life, not merely ruins that spark the curiosity of tourists, students, and scholars. Even in North America, where no Roman remains exist save for imported statues, paintings, and mosaics, modern versions of Roman buildings such as the Pantheon (FIG. 10-48) may be found in cities and on college campuses.

**FROM VILLAGE TO WORLD CAPITAL** The far-flung Roman Empire centered on the city on the Tiber River that, according to legend, Romulus founded as a modest village of huts on April 21, 753 BCE. Nine centuries later, Rome was the capital of the greatest empire the world had ever known. The imperial city (FIG. 10-1) awed foreign kings and even later Roman rulers. The historian Ammianus Marcellinus reported that when the emperor Constantius visited Rome in 357 CE and entered the Forum of Trajan (FIG. 10-41), constructed 250 years earlier, he "stopped in his tracks, astonished" and marveled at the Forum's opulence and size, "which cannot be described by words and could never again be attempted by mortal men."[1]

## REPUBLIC

**KINGS, SENATORS, AND CONSULS** Our story, however, begins long before Roman art and architecture embodied the imperial ideal of the Roman state, at a time when that "state" encompassed no territory beyond one of its famous seven hills. The

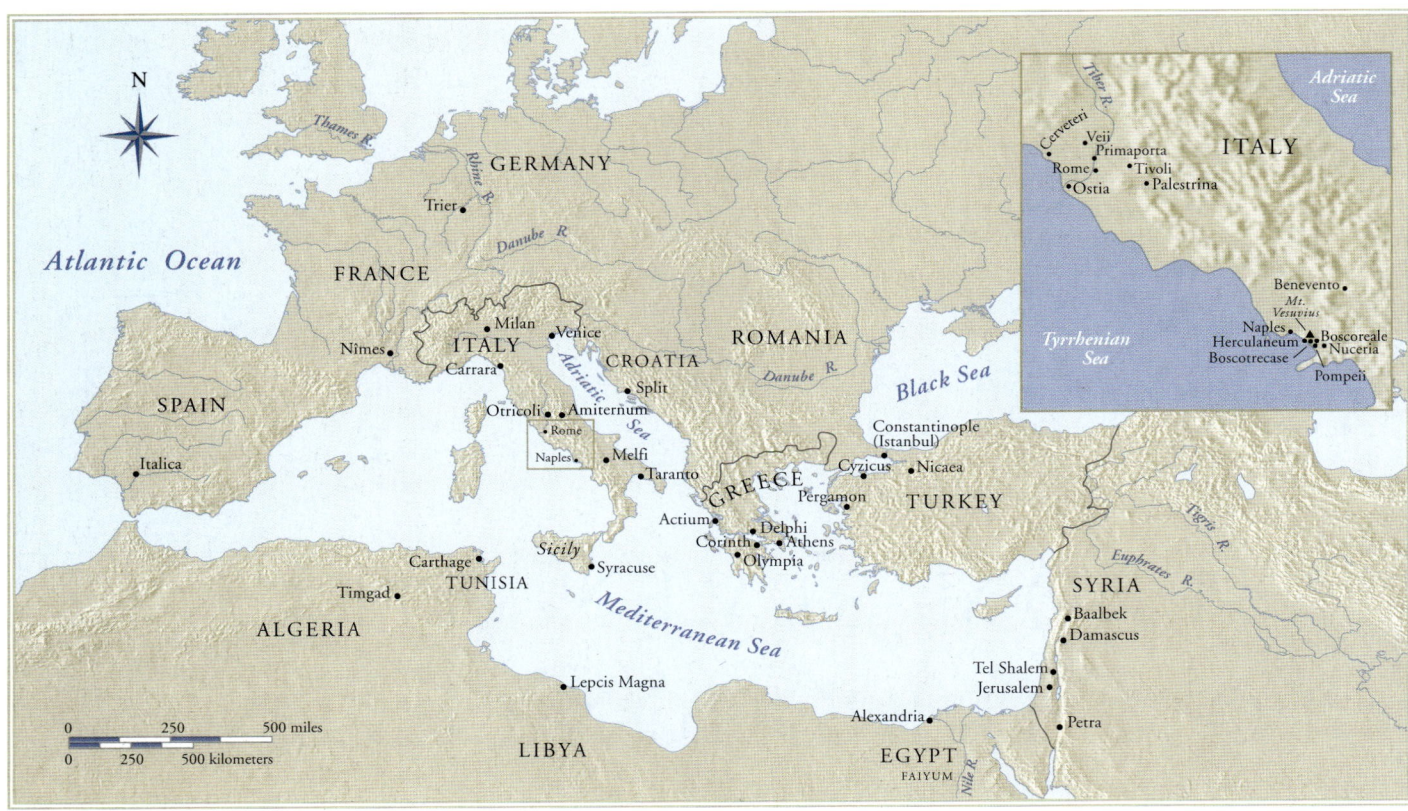

**MAP 10-1** The Roman world.

## ART AND SOCIETY

### *An Outline of Roman History*

#### Monarchy (753–509 BCE)

Latin and Etruscan kings ruled Rome from the city's foundation by Romulus until the revolt against Tarquinius Superbus (exact dates of rule unreliable).

#### Republic (509–27 BCE)

The Republic lasted from the expulsion of Tarquinius Superbus until the bestowing of the title of Augustus on Octavian, the grandnephew of Julius Caesar and victor over Mark Antony in the Civil War that ended the Republic. Some major figures were:

- Marcellus, b. 268(?), d. 208 BCE, consul
- Marius, b. 157, d. 86 BCE, consul
- Sulla, b. 138, d. 79 BCE, consul and dictator
- Pompey, b. 106, d. 48 BCE, consul
- Julius Caesar, b. 100, d. 44 BCE, consul and dictator
- Mark Antony, b. 83, d. 30 BCE, consul

#### Early Empire (27 BCE–96 CE)

The Early Empire began with the rule of Augustus and his Julio-Claudian successors and continued until the end of the Flavian dynasty. Selected emperors and their dates of rule (with names of the most influential empresses in parentheses) were:

- Augustus (Livia), r. 27 BCE–14 CE
- Tiberius, r. 14–37
- Caligula, r. 37–41
- Claudius (Agrippina the Younger), r. 41–54
- Nero, r. 54–68
- Vespasian, r. 69–79

- Titus, r. 79–81
- Domitian, r. 81–96

#### High Empire (96–192 CE)

The High Empire began with the rule of Nerva and the Spanish emperors, Trajan and Hadrian, and ended with the last emperor of the Antonine dynasty. The emperors (and empresses) of this period were:

- Nerva, r. 96–98
- Trajan (Plotina), r. 98–117
- Hadrian (Sabina), r. 117–138
- Antoninus Pius (Faustina the Elder), r. 138–161
- Marcus Aurelius (Faustina the Younger), r. 161–180
- Lucius Verus, co-emperor, r. 161–169
- Commodus, r. 180–192

#### Late Empire (192–337 CE)

The Late Empire began with the Severan dynasty and included the so-called soldier emperors of the third century, the tetrarchs, and Constantine, the first Christian emperor. Selected emperors (and empresses) were:

- Septimius Severus (Julia Domna), r. 193–211
- Caracalla (Plautilla), r. 211–217
- Severus Alexander, r. 222–235
- Trajan Decius, r. 249–251
- Trebonianus Gallus, r. 251–253
- Diocletian, r. 284–305
- Constantine I, r. 306–337

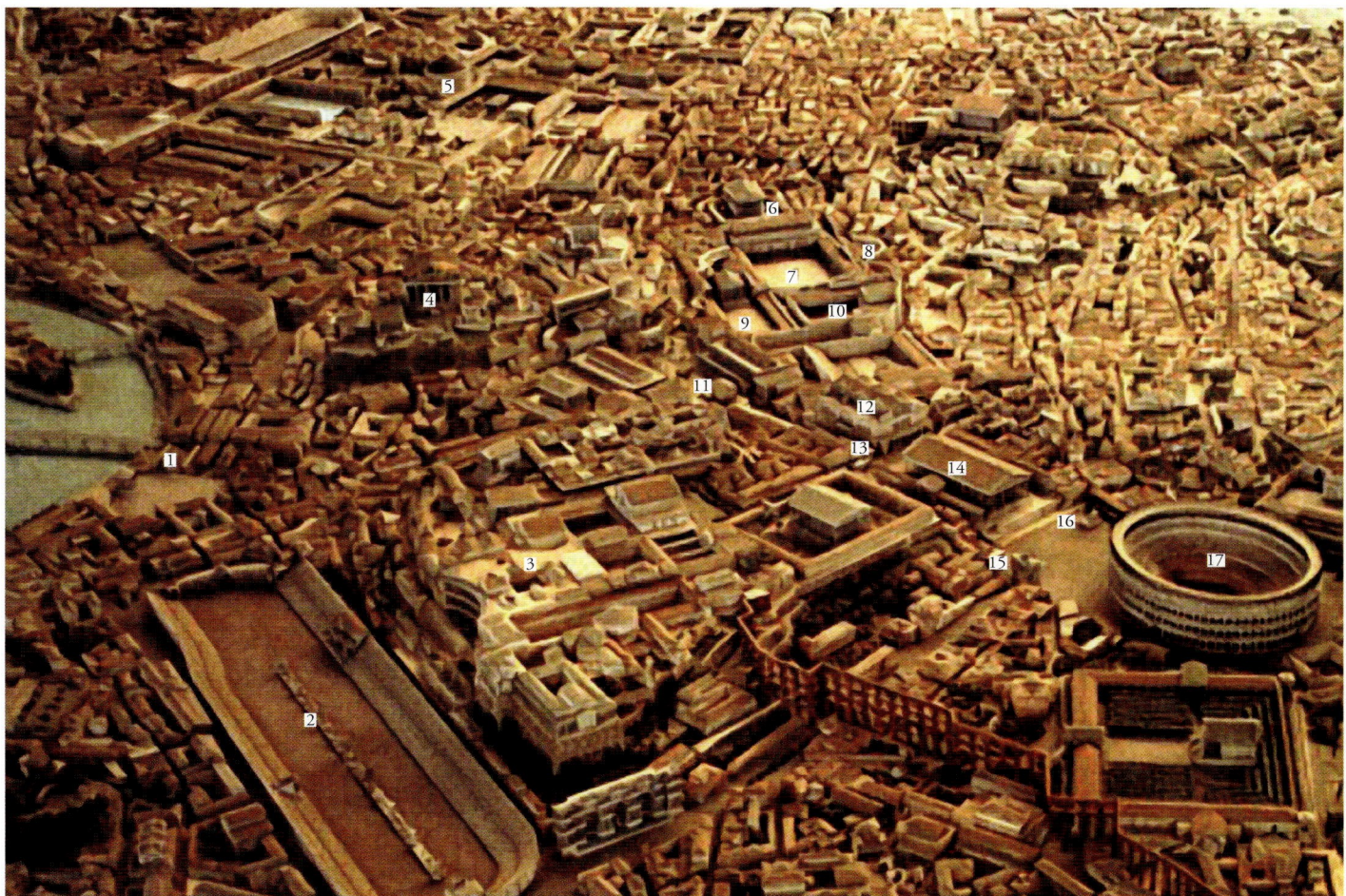

**10-1** Model of the city of Rome during the early fourth century CE. Museo della Civiltà Romana, Rome. 1) Temple of Fortuna Virilis, 2) Circus Maximus, 3) Palatine Hill, 4) Temple of Jupiter Capitolinus, 5) Pantheon 6) Column of Trajan, 7) Forum of Trajan, 8) Markets of Trajan, 9) Forum of Julius Caesar, 10) Forum of Augustus, 11) Forum Romanum, 12) Basilica Nova, 13) Arch of Titus, 14) Temple of Venus and Roma, 15) Arch of Constantine, 16) Colossus of Nero, 17) Colosseum.

Rome of Romulus in the eighth century BCE comprised only small huts of wood, wattle, and daub, clustered together on the Palatine Hill (FIG. 10-1, no. 3) overlooking what was then uninhabited marshland. In the Archaic period, Rome was essentially an Etruscan city, both politically and culturally. Its greatest shrine, the Temple of Jupiter Optimus Maximus (Best and Greatest) on the Capitoline Hill, was built by an Etruscan king, designed by an Etruscan architect, made of wood and mud brick in the Etruscan manner, and decorated with terracotta statuary by an Etruscan sculptor (see "Etruscan Artists in Rome," Chapter 9, page 236).

In 509 BCE, the Romans threw out Tarquinius Superbus, the last of Rome's Etruscan kings, and established a constitutional government (see "An Outline of Roman History," page 248) The new Roman Republic vested power mainly in a *senate* (literally, "a council of elders," *senior* citizens) and in two elected *consuls*. Under extraordinary circumstances a *dictator* could be appointed for a specified time and a specific purpose, such as commanding the army during a crisis. All leaders came originally from among the wealthy landowners, or *patricians*, but later also from the *plebeian* class of small farmers, merchants, and freed slaves.

Before long, the descendants of Romulus conquered Rome's neighbors one by one: the Etruscans and the Gauls to the north, the Samnites and the Greek colonists to the south. Even the Carthaginians of North Africa, who under Hannibal's dynamic leadership had annihilated some of Rome's legions and almost brought down the Republic, fell before the might of Roman armies.

**THE CRAZE FOR GREEK ART** The year 211 BCE was a turning point both for Rome and for Roman art. Breaking with precedent, Marcellus, conqueror of the fabulously wealthy Sicilian Greek city of Syracuse, brought back to Rome not only the usual spoils of war—captured arms and armor, gold and silver coins, and the like—but also the city's artistic patrimony. Thus began, in the words of the historian Livy, "the craze for works of Greek art."[2] According to the biographer Plutarch, the Romans, "who had hitherto been accustomed only to fighting or farming," now began "affecting urbane opinions about the arts and about artists, even to the point of wasting the better part of a day on such things."[3] Ships filled with plundered Greek statues and paintings became a frequent sight in the harbor of Ostia at the mouth of the Tiber River.

Exposure to Greek sculpture and painting and to the splendid marble temples of the Greek gods increased as the Romans expanded their conquests beyond Italy. Greece became a Roman province in 146 BCE, and in 133 BCE the last Attalid king of Pergamon willed his kingdom to Rome (see Chapter 5). Nevertheless, although the Romans developed a virtually insatiable taste for Greek "antiques," their own monuments were not slavish imitations of Greek masterpieces. The Etruscan basis of Roman art and architecture was never forgotten, and the statues and buildings of the Roman Republic are highly eclectic, drawing on both Greek and Etruscan traditions. The resultant mix, however, is distinctly Roman.

## The Roman Architectural Revolution
### Concrete Construction

The history of Roman architecture would be very different if the Romans had been content to use the same building materials the Greeks, Etruscans, and other ancient peoples did. Instead, the Romans developed concrete construction, which revolutionized architectural design. Roman *concrete* was made from a changing recipe of lime mortar, volcanic sand, water, and small stones (*caementa,* from which the English word *cement* is derived). Builders placed the mixture in wooden frames and left it to dry and to bond with a brick or stone facing. When the concrete dried completely, the wooden molds were removed, leaving behind a solid mass of great strength, though rough in appearance. The Romans often covered the rough concrete with stucco or with marble *revetment* (facing). Despite this lengthy procedure, concrete walls were much less costly to construct than walls of imported Greek marble or even local tufa and travertine.

The advantages of concrete go well beyond cost, however. It is possible to fashion concrete shapes that masonry construction cannot achieve, especially huge vaulted and domed rooms without internal supports. The Romans came to prefer these over the Greek and Etruscan post-and-lintel structures. Concrete enabled Roman builders to think of architecture in radical new ways. Roman concrete architecture became an architecture of space rather than of sheer mass.

To cover and give shape to these new "spatial envelopes," the Romans employed a variety of vaulting systems. The following were the most common types:

**BARREL VAULTS** Also called the *tunnel vault,* the *barrel vault* is an extension of a simple arch, creating a semicylindrical ceiling over parallel walls. Pre-Roman builders constructed barrel vaults using traditional ashlar masonry (see FIG. 2-25), but those earlier vaults and all later stone vaults (see, for example, FIG. 17-6) are less stable than concrete barrel vaults. If any of the blocks of a cut-stone vaults comes loose, the whole may collapse. Also, masonry barrel vaults can be illuminated only by light entering at either end of the tunnel. In contrast, windows can be placed at any point in concrete barrel vaults, because once the concrete hardens, it forms a seamless sheet of "artificial stone" that may be punctured

almost at will. Whether made of stone or concrete, barrel vaults require *buttressing* (lateral support) of the walls below the vaults to counteract their downward and outward *thrust.*

**GROIN VAULTS** A *groin* or *cross vault* is formed by the intersection at right angles of two barrel vaults of equal size. Besides appearing lighter than the barrel vault, the groin vault needs less buttressing. The barrel vault's thrust is concentrated along the entire length of the supporting wall. The groin vault's thrust, however, is concentrated along the groins, and buttressing is needed only at the points where the groins meet the vault's vertical supports, usually *piers.* The system leaves the area between the supports open, permitting light to enter. Groin vaults, like barrel vaults, can be built using stone blocks—but with the same structural limitations when compared to concrete vaulting.

When a series of groin vaults covers an interior hall, as in our diagram and in FIGS. 10-44, 10-68, and 10-79, the open lateral arches of the vaults form the equivalent of a *clerestory* of a traditional timber-roofed structure (for example, see FIG. 11-8). Such a *fenestrated* (with openings or windows) sequence of groin vaults has a major advantage over wooden clerestories. Concrete vaults are relatively fireproof, always an important consideration given that fires were common occurrences (see "Timber Roofs and Stone Vaults," Chapter 17, page 451).

**HEMISPHERICAL DOMES** The largest domed space in the ancient world for more than a millennium was the corbeled, beehive-shaped tholos of the Treasury of Atreus at Mycenae (see FIG. 4-22). The Romans were able to surpass the Mycenaeans by using concrete to construct hemispherical *domes,* which usually rested on concrete cylindrical *drums.* If a barrel vault is described as a round arch extended in a line, then a hemispherical dome may be described as a round arch rotated around the full circumference of a circle. Masonry domes (compare FIG. 10-73), like masonry vaults, cannot accommodate windows without threatening their stability. Concrete domes can be opened up even at their apex with a circular "eye" *(oculus),* as in our diagram and FIGS. 10-33, 10-49, and 10-50, allowing much-needed light to reach the vast spaces beneath.

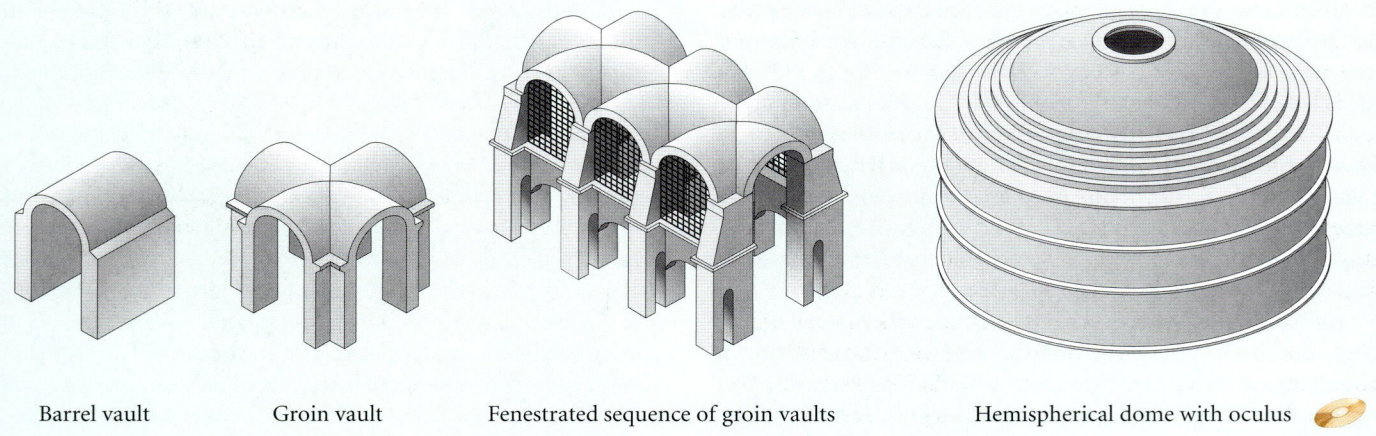

Barrel vault          Groin vault          Fenestrated sequence of groin vaults          Hemispherical dome with oculus

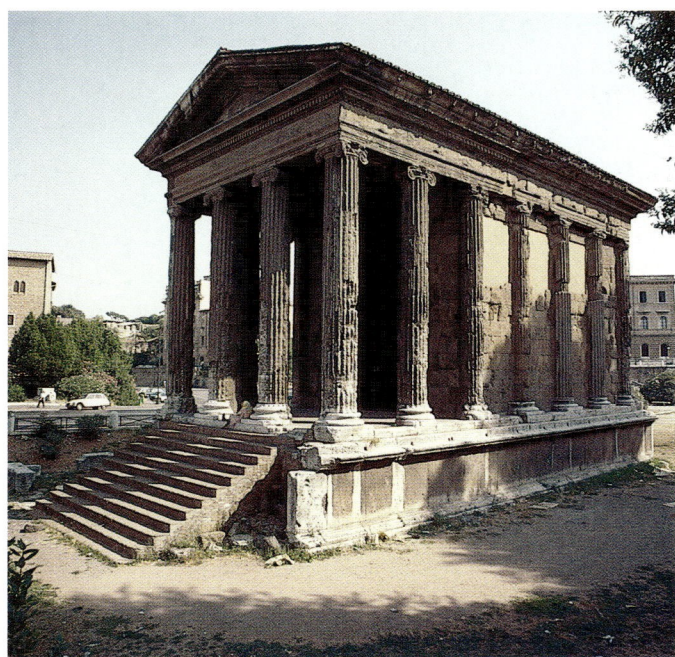

10-2 Temple of "Fortuna Virilis" (Temple of Portunus), Rome, Italy, ca. 75 BCE.

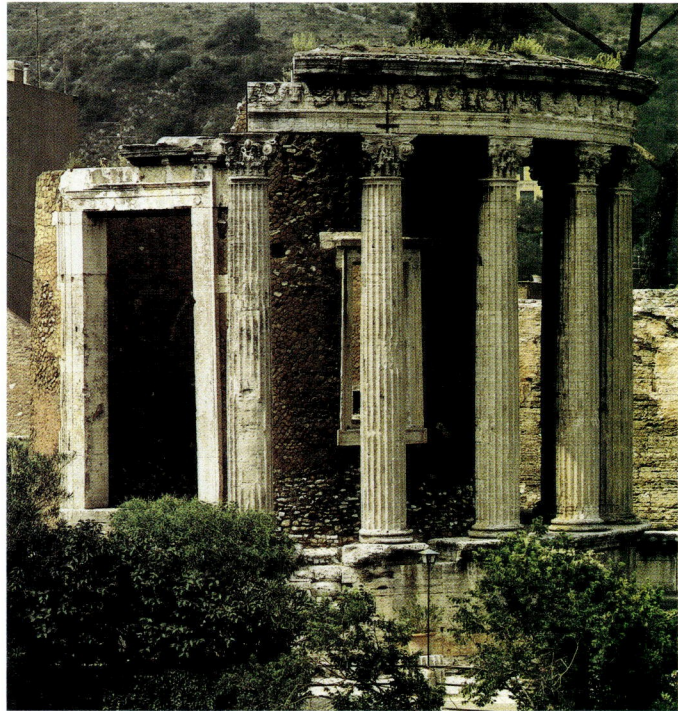

10-3 Temple of Vesta(?), Tivoli, Italy, early first century BCE.

## Architecture

**ECLECTICISM ON THE TIBER** Eclecticism is the primary characteristic of the Republican temple on the east bank of the Tiber known as the Temple of "Fortuna Virilis" (FIGS. **10-2** and 10-1, no. 1), actually the Temple of Portunus, the Roman god of harbors. In plan it follows the Etruscan pattern. The high podium is accessible only at the front, with its wide flight of steps. Freestanding columns are confined to the deep porch. But the structure is built of stone (local tufa and travertine), overlaid originally with stucco in imitation of the gleaming white marble temples of the Greeks. The columns are not Tuscan but Ionic, complete with flutes and bases, and a matching Ionic frieze. Moreover, in an effort to approximate a peripteral Greek temple while maintaining the basic Etruscan plan, the architect added a series of engaged Ionic half-columns on the sides and back of the cella. The result was a *pseudoperipteral* temple. Although the design combines Etruscan and Greek elements, it is uniquely Roman.

**TIVOLI'S TEMPLE ON A CLIFF** The Romans' admiration for the Greek temples they encountered in their conquests also led to the importation into Republican Italy of a temple type unknown in Etruscan architecture—the round, or tholos, temple. At Tivoli (ancient Tibur), on a dramatic site overlooking a deep gorge, a Republican architect erected such a Greek-inspired temple early in the first century BCE. Usually called the Temple of Vesta (FIG. **10-3**), it is circular in plan and has travertine Corinthian columns. The frieze is carved with garlands held up by oxen heads, also in emulation of Greek models. But the high podium can be reached only via a narrow stairway leading to the cella door. This arrangement introduced an axial alignment not found in Greek tholoi (see FIG. 5-71), where, as in Greek rectangular temples, steps continue all around the structure. Also in contrast with the Greeks, the Roman builders did not construct the cella wall using masonry blocks but a new material of recent invention: concrete (see "The Roman Architectural Revolution: Concrete Construction," page 250).

**CONCRETE TRANSFORMS A HILLSIDE** The most impressive and innovative use of concrete during the Republic was in the Sanctuary of Fortuna Primigenia (FIG. **10-4**), the goddess of good fortune, at Palestrina (ancient Praeneste, formerly an Etruscan city). The great complex was constructed in the late second century BCE. Spread out over several terraces leading up the hillside

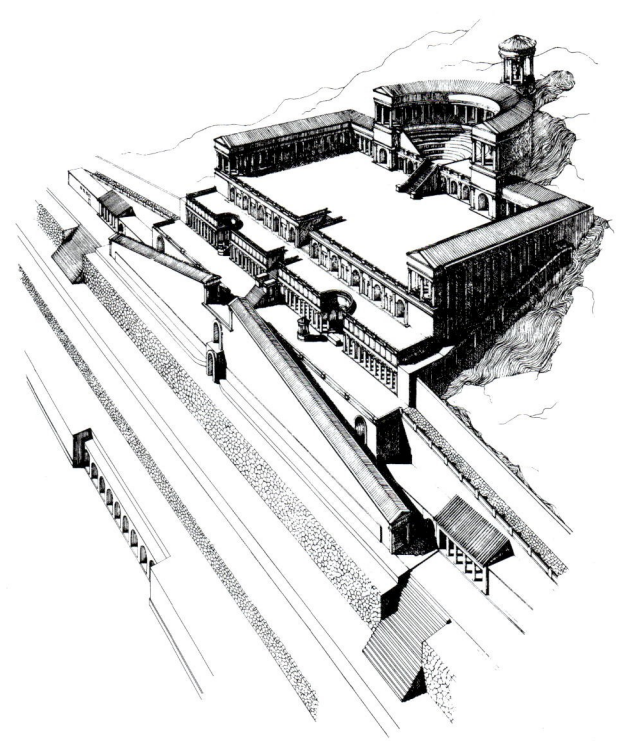

10-4 Reconstruction drawing of the Sanctuary of Fortuna Primigenia, Palestrina, Italy, late second century BCE.

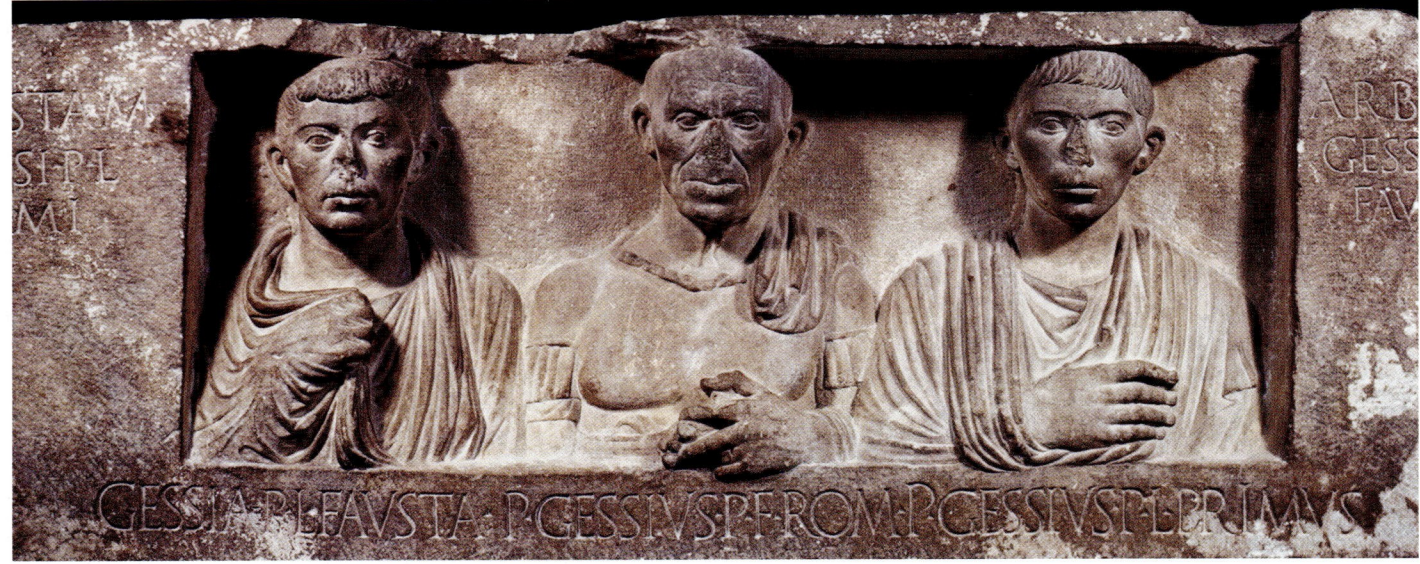

**10-5** Funerary relief with portraits of the Gessii, from Rome(?), Italy, ca. 30 BCE. Marble, approx. 2′ 1½″ high. Museum of Fine Arts, Boston.

to a tholos at the peak of an ascending triangle, the layout reflects the Republican taste for colossal Hellenistic designs. The means of construction, however, was distinctly Roman.

The builder used concrete barrel vaults of enormous strength to support the imposing terraces and to cover the great ramps leading to the grand central staircase, as well as to give shape to the shops aligned on two consecutive levels. In this way, the unknown architect transformed the entire hillside into a grandiose complex symbolic of Roman power. This subjection of nature to human will and rational order was the first full-blown manifestation of the Roman imperial spirit. It contrasts with the more restrained Greek practice of simply crowning a hill with sacred buildings, as opposed to converting the hill itself into architecture.

## Sculpture

**PORTRAITS AND SOCIETY** The patrons of the Roman Republic's great temples and sanctuaries were in almost all cases men from old and distinguished families, often victorious generals who used the spoils of war to finance public works. These aristocratic patricians were fiercely proud of their lineage. They kept

likenesses (*imagines*) of their ancestors in wooden cupboards in their homes and paraded them at the funerals of prominent relatives. Marius, a renowned Republican general who lacked a long and distinguished genealogy, was ridiculed by his patrician colleagues as a man who had no ancestral portraits in his home. Slaves and former slaves could not possess *any* family portraits, because, under Roman law, their parents and grandparents were not people but property. Freed slaves often ordered portrait reliefs (FIGS. **10-5** and **10-6**) for their tombs to commemorate their new status as Roman citizens (see "Art for Former Slaves," page 253).

**REPUBLICAN VERISM** The surviving portraits of prominent Roman Republican figures, which appear to be literal reproductions of individual faces, must be seen in this context. Although their style derives to some degree from Hellenistic and Etruscan, and perhaps even Ptolemaic Egyptian, portraits, Republican portraits are one way the patrician class celebrated its elevated position in society. The subjects of these portraits were almost exclusively men (and to a lesser extent women) of advanced age, for generally only elders held power in the Republic. These patricians did not ask sculptors to make them appear nobler than they were, as Kresilas portrayed Pericles (see FIG. 5-39). Instead, they requested

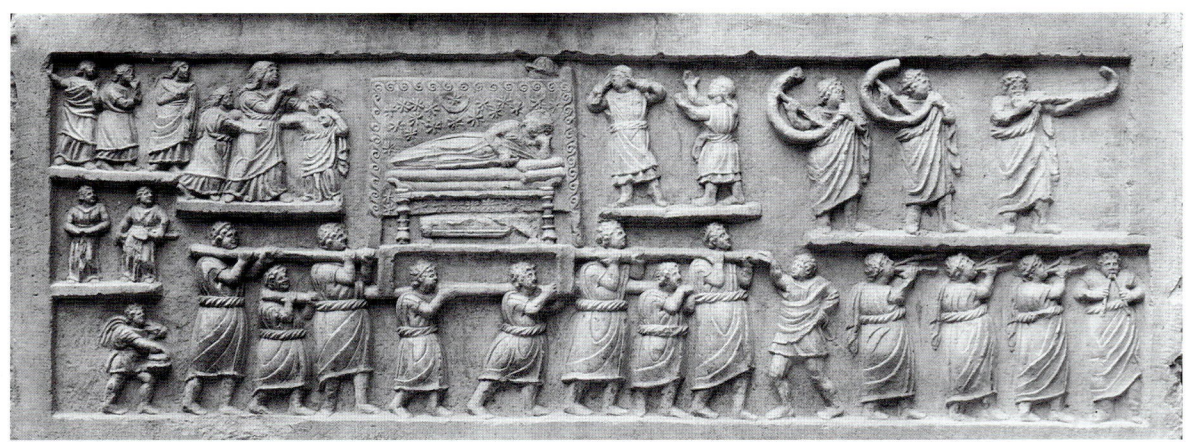

**10-6** Relief with funerary procession, from Amiternum, Italy, second half of first century BCE. Limestone, approx. 2′ 2″ high. Museo Nazionale d'Abruzzo, L'Aquila.

## Art for Former Slaves

Historians and art historians alike tend to focus on the lives and monuments of famous individuals, but some of the most interesting remains of ancient Roman civilization are the artworks commissioned by ordinary people, especially former slaves, or *freedmen* and *freedwomen.* Slavery was common in the Roman world. It is estimated that Italy at the end of the Republic had some two million slaves, or roughly one slave for every three citizens. The very rich might own hundreds of slaves, but slaves could be found in all but the poorest households. The practice was so much a part of Roman society that even slaves often became slave owners when their former masters freed them. Some gained freedom in return for meritorious service. Others were only freed in their masters' wills. Most slaves died as slaves in service to their original or new owners.

The most noteworthy of all the artworks commissioned by Roman freedmen and freedwomen are the stone reliefs that regularly adorned their tomb facades. One of these reliefs (FIG. 10-5) depicts three people, all named Gessius. At the left is Gessia Fausta and at the right Gessius Primus. Both are the freed slaves of Publius Gessius, the freeborn citizen in the center, shown wearing a general's *cuirass* (breastplate) and portrayed in the standard Republican superrealistic fashion (FIGS. 10-7 to 10-9). As slaves this couple had no legal standing; they were the property of Publius Gessius. After they were freed, however, in the eyes of the law the ex-slaves became people. These stern frontal portraits proclaim their new status as legal members of Roman society—and their gratitude to Publius Gessius for granting them that status.

As was the custom, the two ex-slaves bear their patron's name, but whether they are sister and brother, wife and husband, or unrelated is unclear. The inscriptions on the relief explicitly state that the monument was paid for with funds provided by the will

of Gessius Primus and that the work was directed by Gessia Fausta, the only survivor of the three. The relief thus depicts the living and the dead side by side, indistinguishable except by the accompanying message. This theme is common in Roman art (compare FIGS. 10-46 and 10-57) and proclaims that death does not break bonds formed in life.

More rarely, freed slaves commissioned tomb reliefs that were narrative in character. A relief from Amiternum (FIG. 10-6) depicts the cortege in honor of the deceased, complete with musicians, professional female mourners who pull their hair in a display of feigned grief, and the deceased's wife and children. The deceased is laid out on a bier with a canopy as a backdrop, much like the figures on Greek Geometric vases (see FIG. 5-1). Here, however, the dead man surprisingly props himself up as if still alive, surveying his own funeral. This may be an effigy, like the reclining figures on the lids of Etruscan sarcophagi (see FIGS. 9-4 and 9-14), rather than the deceased himself.

Compositionally, the relief is also not what one would expect. Mourners and musicians stand on floating ground lines, as if on flying carpets. They are not to be viewed as suspended in space, however, but as situated behind the front row of pallbearers and musicians. This sculptor, in striking contrast to the (usually Greek) artists employed by the patrician aristocracy, had little regard for the rules of classical art. The Amiternum artist studiously avoided overlapping and placed the figures wherever they fit, so long as they were clearly visible. This approach to making pictures was characteristic of preclassical art, but it had been out of favor for several centuries. One looks in vain for similar compositions in the art commissioned by the consuls and senators of the Roman Republic. In ancient Rome's cosmopolitan world, as today, stylistic tastes often were tied to a person's political and social status.

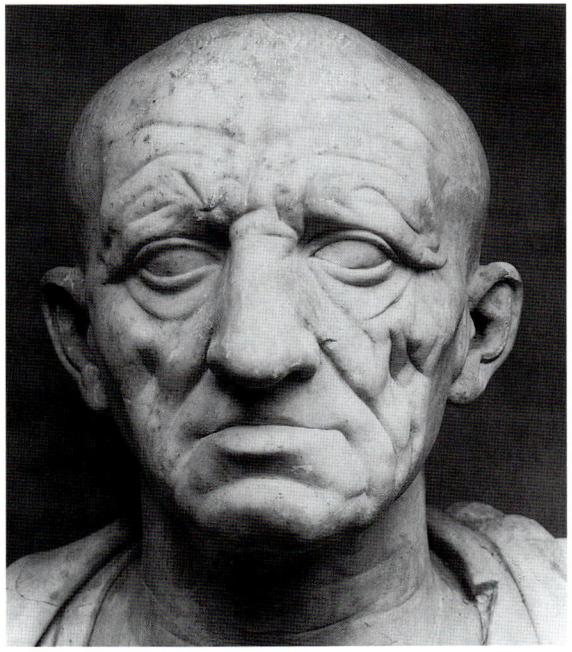

**10-7** Head of a Roman patrician, from Otricoli, Italy, ca. 75–50 BCE. Marble, approx. 1′ 2″ high. Museo Torlonia, Rome.

brutally realistic images of distinctive features, in the tradition of the treasured household *imagines.*

One of the most striking of these so-called *veristic* (superrealistic) portraits is the head of an unidentified patrician (FIG. 10-7) found near Otricoli. The sculptor painstakingly recorded each rise and fall, each bulge and fold, of the facial surface, like a mapmaker who did not want to miss the slightest detail of surface change. Scholars debate whether such portraits were truly blunt records of actual features or exaggerated types designed to make a statement about personality: serious, experienced, determined, loyal to family and state—virtues that were much admired during the Republic.

**OLD HEADS ON YOUNG BODIES** The portrait from Otricoli is in bust form. The Romans believed that the head alone was enough to constitute a portrait. The Greeks, in contrast, believed that head and body were inseparable parts of an integral whole, so their portraits were always full length (see FIG. 5-88). In fact, in Republican portraiture veristic heads were often, although incongruently, placed on bodies to which they could not possibly belong.

Such is the case in the curious and discordant portrait of a general (FIG. 10-8) found at Tivoli. The cuirass at his side, which acts as a prop for the heavy marble statue, is the emblem of his

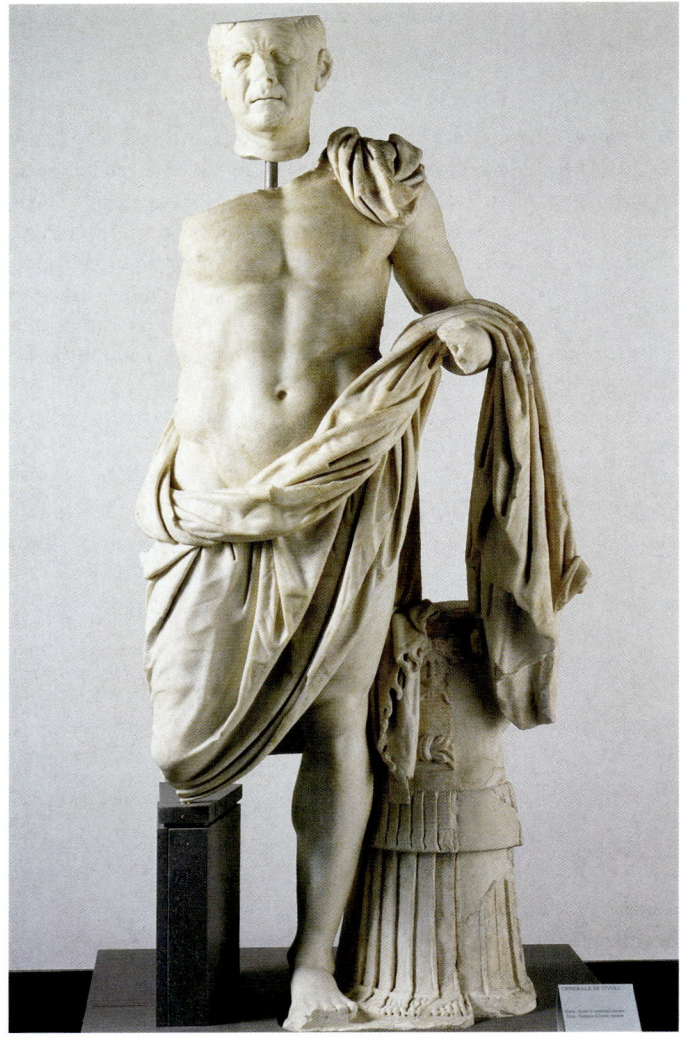

10-8 Portrait of a Roman general, from the Sanctuary of Hercules, Tivoli, Italy, ca. 75–50 BCE. Marble, approx. 6′ 2″ high. Museo Nazionale Romano-Palazzo Massimo alle Terme, Rome.

rank. But the general does not appear as he would in life. Although he has a typically stern and lined Republican head, it sits atop a powerful, youthful, almost nude body. The sculptor modeled the portrait on the statues of Greek athletes and heroes the Romans admired so much and often copied (see Chapter 5). The incorporation of references to Greek art in these portrait statues evoked the notion of patrician cultural superiority as well as heroicized the person portrayed. In the Tivoli statue, however, the patron's modesty dictated that a mantle shield the genitals.

**CAESAR BREAKS THE RULES** Beginning early in the first century BCE, the Roman desire to advertise distinguished ancestry led to the placement of portraits of illustrious forebears on Republican coins. These ancestral portraits supplanted the earlier Roman tradition (based on Greek convention) of using images of divinities on coins. No Roman, however, dared to place his own likeness on a coin until 44 BCE, when Julius Caesar, shortly before his assassination on the Ides of March, issued coins featuring his portrait and his newly acquired title, *dictator perpetuus* (dictator for life). The *denarius* (the standard Roman silver coin, from which the word *penny* ultimately derives) illustrated here (FIG. **10-9**) records Caesar's aging face and receding hairline in conformity with the Republican veristic tradition. But placing the likeness of a living person on a coin violated all the norms of

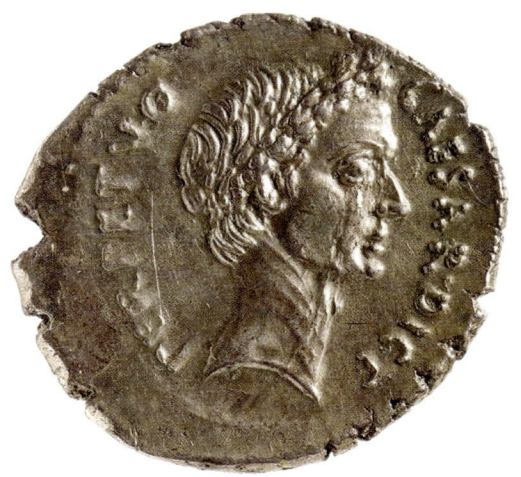

10-9 Denarius with portrait of Julius Caesar, 44 BCE. Silver, diameter approx. $\frac{3}{4}$″. American Numismatic Society, New York.

Republican propriety. Henceforth, Roman coins, which circulated throughout the vast territories under Roman control, would be used to mold public opinion in favor of the ruler by announcing his achievements—both real and fictional.

## POMPEII AND THE CITIES OF VESUVIUS

**BURIED BY A VOLCANO** On August 24, 79 CE, Mount Vesuvius, a long-dormant volcano whose fertile slopes were covered with vineyards during the Late Republic and Early Empire, suddenly erupted (see "An Eyewitness Account of the Eruption of Mount Vesuvius," page 255). Many prosperous towns around the Bay of Naples (the ancient Greek city of Neapolis), among them Pompeii, were buried in a single day. This catastrophe for the inhabitants of the Vesuvian cities has, however, been a boon for archaeologists and art historians. When researchers first explored the buried cities in the 18th century, the ruins had been undisturbed for nearly 1,700 years (see "Rising from the Ashes: The Excavation of Herculaneum and Pompeii," Chapter 28, page 815). The Vesuvian sites are still being excavated, but the remains already uncovered permit a reconstruction of the art and life of Roman towns of the Late Republic and Early Empire with a completeness far beyond that possible anywhere else.

**OSCANS, SAMNITES, AND ROMANS** The Oscans, one of the many Italic tribes that occupied Italy during the heyday of the Etruscans, were the first to settle at Pompeii. Toward the end of the fifth century BCE, the Samnites, another Italic people, took over the town. Under the influence of their Greek neighbors, the Samnites greatly expanded the original settlement and gave monumental shape to the city center. Pompeii fought with other Italian cities on the losing side against Rome in the Social War, and in 80 BCE Sulla founded a new Roman colony on the site, with Latin as its official language. The colony's population had grown to between 10,000 and 20,000 when, in February 62 CE, an earthquake shook the city, causing extensive damage. When Mount Vesuvius erupted 17 years later, repairs were still in progress.

**AN ARCHAEOLOGICAL PARK** Walking through Pompeii today is an experience that cannot be approximated at any other site.

### An Eyewitness Account of the Eruption of Mount Vesuvius

Pliny the Elder, whose *Natural History* is one of the most important sources for the history of Greek art, was among those who tried to rescue others from danger when Mount Vesuvius erupted. He was overcome by fumes the volcano spewed forth, and died. His nephew, Pliny the Younger, a government official under the emperor Trajan, left an account of the eruption and his uncle's demise:

> [The volcanic cloud's] general appearance can best be expressed as being like a pine . . . for it rose to a great height on a sort of trunk and then split off into branches. . . . Sometimes it looked white, sometimes blotched and dirty, according to the amount of soil and ashes it carried with it. . . . The buildings were now shaking with

violent shocks, and seemed to be swaying to and fro as if they were torn from their foundations. Outside, on the other hand, there was the danger of falling pumice-stones, even though these were light and porous. . . . Elsewhere there was daylight, [but around Vesuvius, people] were still in darkness, blacker and denser than any night that ever was. . . . When daylight returned on the 26th—two days after the last day [my uncle] had been seen—his body was found intact and uninjured, still fully clothed and looking more like sleep than death.[1]

[1] Betty Radice, trans., *Pliny the Younger: Letters and Panegyricus,* vol. 1 (Cambridge, Mass.: Harvard University Press, 1969), 427–33.

---

The streets, with their heavy flagstone pavements and sidewalks, are still there, as are the stepping stones that enabled pedestrians to cross the streets without having to step in puddles. Ingeniously, the city planners placed these stones in such a way that vehicle wheels could straddle them, enabling supplies to be brought directly to the shops, taverns, and bakeries. Tourists still can visit the impressive concrete-vaulted rooms of Pompeii's public baths and sit in the seats of its open-air theater and indoor concert hall, even walk among the tombs outside the city walls. The sights include private homes with magnificently painted walls and pleasant gardens. Some still have their kitchen utensils in place. Pompeii has been called the living city of the dead for good reason.

## Architecture

**THE HEART OF POMPEII** The center of civic life in any Roman town was its *forum,* or public square, usually located at the city's geographic center at the intersection of the main north-south street, the *cardo,* and the main east-west avenue, the *decumanus* (FIG. 10-40). The forum, however, generally was closed to all but pedestrian traffic. Pompeii's forum (FIG. **10-10**) lies in the southwest corner of the expanded Roman city but at the heart of the original town. The forum took on monumental form in the second century BCE when the Samnites, inspired by Hellenistic architecture, erected two-story colonnades on three sides of the long and narrow plaza. At the north end they constructed a Temple of Jupiter (FIG. 10-10, no. 2). When Pompeii became a Roman colony in 80 BCE, the Romans converted the temple into a *Capitolium*—a triple shrine of Jupiter, Juno, and Minerva (see "The Gods and Goddesses of Mount Olympus," Chapter 5, page 107). The temple is of standard Republican type, constructed of tufa covered with fine white stucco and combining an Etruscan plan with Corinthian columns. It faces into the civic square, dominating the area. This is very different from the siting of Greek temples (see FIGS. 5-40 and 5-41), which stood in isolation and could be approached and viewed from all sides, like colossal statues on giant stepped pedestals. The Roman forum, like the Etrusco-Roman temple, has a chief side, a focus of attention.

The area within the porticos of the forum at Pompeii was empty, except for statues commemorating local dignitaries and, later, Roman emperors. This is where the citizens conducted daily commerce and held festivities. All around the square, behind

the colonnades, were secular and religious structures, including the town's administrative offices. Most noteworthy is the *basilica* (FIG. 10-10, no. 3) at the southwest corner, the earliest well-preserved building of its kind. Constructed during the late second century BCE, the basilica housed the law court of Pompeii and also was used for other official purposes. In plan it resembles the forum itself: long and narrow, with two stories of internal columns dividing the space into a central *nave* and flanking *aisles.* This scheme had a long afterlife in architectural history and will be familiar to anyone who has ever entered a Christian church.

**GLADIATORS AND WILD ANIMALS** The forum was an oasis in the heart of Pompeii—an open, airy plaza. Throughout the rest of the city, every square foot of land was developed. Shortly after the Romans took control of Pompeii, two of the town's wealthiest officials, Quinctius Valgus and Marcus Porcius, used their own

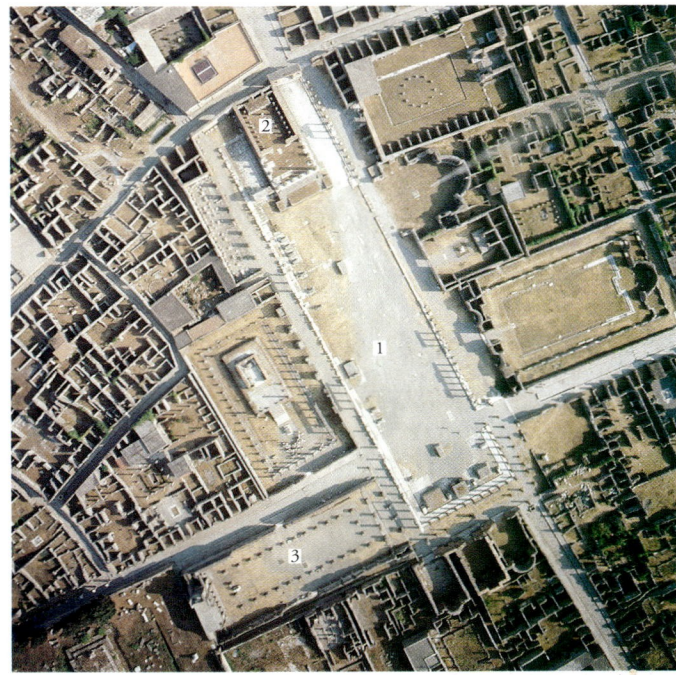

**10-10** Aerial view of the forum (1), with Temple of Jupiter (Capitolium, 2) and Basilica (3), Pompeii, Italy, second century BCE and later.

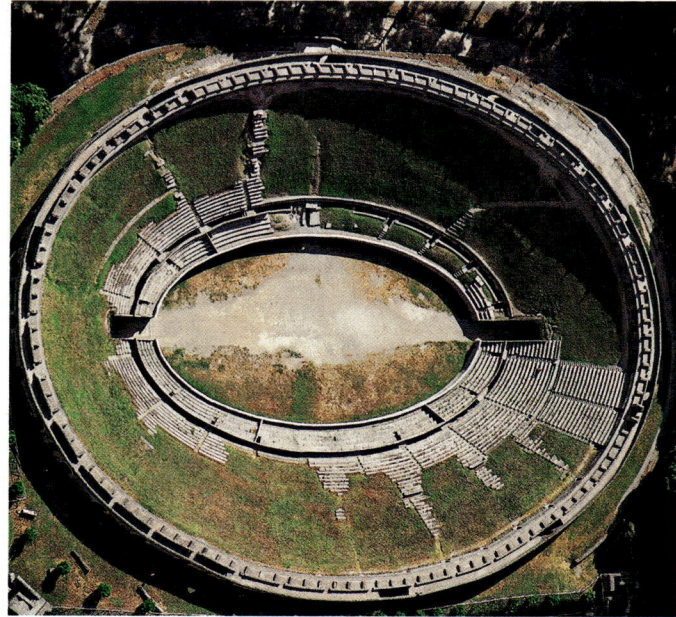

10-11 Aerial view of the amphitheater, Pompeii, Italy, ca. 70 BCE.

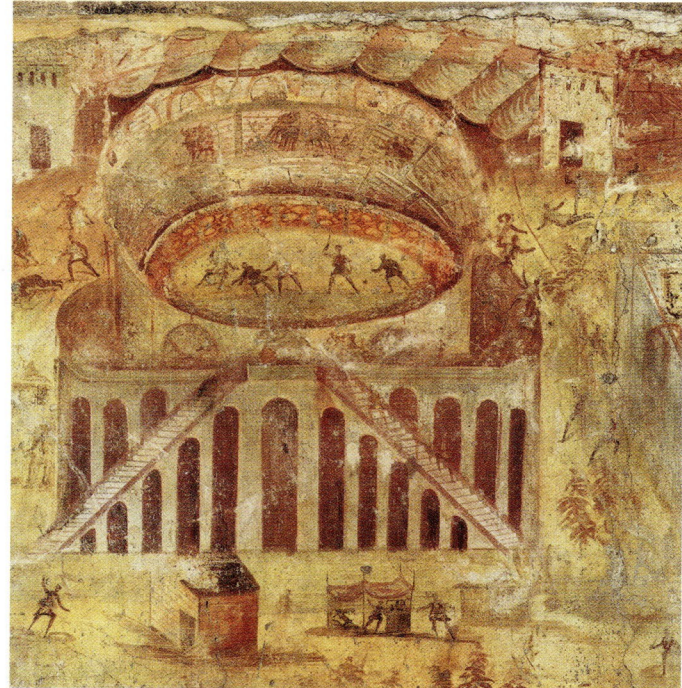

10-12 Brawl in the Pompeii amphitheater, wall painting from House I,3,23, Pompeii, Italy, ca. 60–79 CE. Approx. 5′ 7″ × 6′ 1″. Museo Nazionale, Naples.

funds to erect a large amphitheater (FIG. **10-11**) at the southeastern end of town. It is the earliest such structure known and could seat some 20,000 spectators—more than the entire population of the town even a century and a half after it was built! The donors would have had choice reserved seats in the new entertainment center. In fact, seating was assigned by rank, both civic and military, so that the Roman social hierarchy was on display at every event.

The word *amphitheater* means "double theater," and the Roman structures closely resemble two Greek theaters put together, although the Greeks never built amphitheaters. Greek theaters were situated on natural hillsides (see FIGS. 5-40 and 5-70), but supporting an amphitheater's continuous elliptical *cavea* (seating area) required building an artificial mountain. Only concrete, unknown to the Greeks, was capable of such a job. In the Pompeii amphitheater, a series of radially disposed concrete barrel vaults forms a giant retaining wall that holds up the earthen mound and stone seats. Barrel vaults also form the tunnels leading to the *arena,* the central area where bloody gladiatorial combats and wild animal hunts occurred. (*Arena* is Latin for "sand," which soaked up the blood of the wounded and killed.) The Roman amphitheater stands in sharp contrast, both architecturally and functionally, to the Greek theater, home of refined performances of comedies and tragedies.

A painting (FIG. **10-12**) on the wall of a Pompeian house records an unfortunate incident that occurred in the amphitheater. A brawl broke out between the Pompeians and their neighbors, the Nucerians, during a gladiatorial contest in 59 CE. The fighting left many seriously wounded and led to the closing of the amphitheater for a decade. The painting shows the cloth awning (*velarium*) that could be rolled down from the top of the cavea to shield spectators from sun and rain. It also features the distinctive external double staircases (not visible in FIG. 10-11) that enabled large numbers of people to enter and exit the cavea in an orderly fashion.

**TOWNHOUSES FOR THE WEALTHY** At Pompeii, as in modern cities and towns, private homes occupied most of the area outside the civic center. The evidence from Pompeii regarding Roman domestic architecture (see "The Roman House," page 257) is unparalleled anywhere else and is the most precious

by-product of the catastrophic volcanic eruption of 79 CE. One of the best preserved houses at Pompeii, partially rebuilt and an obligatory stop on every tourist's itinerary today, is the House of the Vettii, an old Pompeian house remodeled and repainted after the earthquake of 62 CE. Our photograph (FIG. **10-13**) was taken

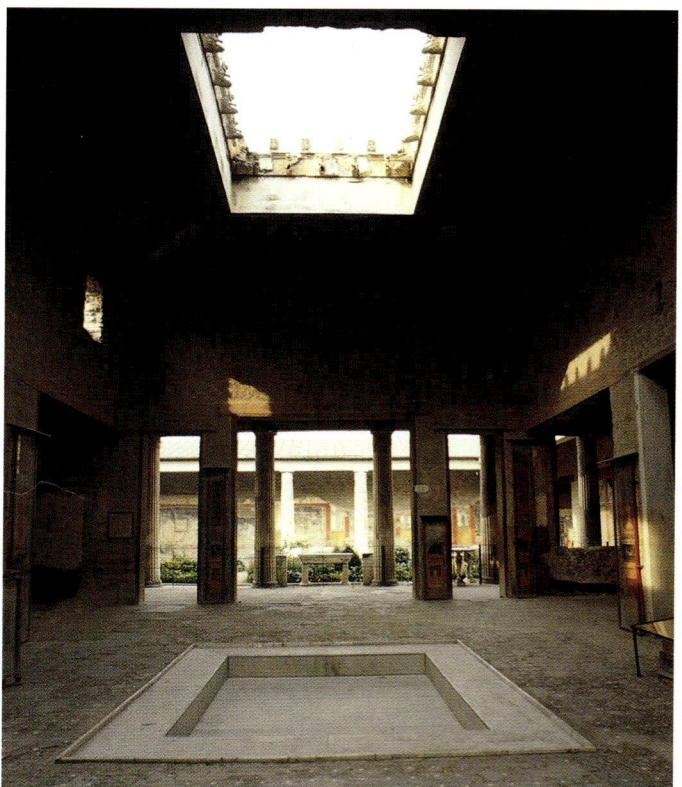

10-13 Atrium of the House of the Vettii, Pompeii, Italy, second century BCE, rebuilt 62–79 CE.

### The Roman House

The Roman house was more than just a place to live. It played an important role in Roman societal rituals. In the Roman world, individuals were frequently bound to others in a patron-client relationship whereby a wealthier, better-educated, and more powerful *patronus* would protect the interests of a *cliens*, sometimes large numbers of them. The standing of a patron in Roman society often was measured by clientele size. Being seen in public accompanied by a crowd of clients was a badge of honor. In this system, a plebeian might be bound to a patrician, a freed slave to a former owner, or even one patrician to another. Regardless of rank, all clients were obligated to support their patron in political campaigns and to perform specific services on request, as well as to call on and salute the patron at the patron's home.

A client calling on a patron would enter the typical Roman *domus* (private house) through a narrow foyer (*fauces,* the "throat" of the house), which led to a large central reception area, the *atrium.* The rooms flanking the fauces could open inward, as in our diagram, or outward, in which case they were rented out as shops. The roof over the atrium was partially open to the sky, not only to admit light but also to channel rainwater into a basin (*impluvium*) below. The water could be stored in cisterns for household use. Opening onto the atrium was a series of small bedrooms called *cubicula* (cubicles). At the back were the patron's *tablinum* or "home office," a dining room (*triclinium*), a kitchen, and sometimes a small garden.

Endless variations of the same basic plan exist, dictated by the owners' personal tastes and means, the nature of the land plot, and so forth, but all Roman houses of this type were inward-looking in nature. The design shut off the street's noise and dust, and all internal activity focused on the brightly illuminated atrium at the center of the residence. This basic module (only the front half of the typical house in our diagram) resembles the plan of the typical Etruscan house as reflected in the Tomb of the Shields and Chairs (see FIG. 9-6) and other tombs at Cerveteri. Thus, few doubt that the early Roman house, like the early Roman temple, grew out of the Etruscan tradition.

During the second century BCE, when Roman architects were beginning to construct stone temples with Greek columns, the Roman house also took on Greek airs. Builders added a peristyle garden behind the Etruscan-style house, providing a second internal illumination source as well as a pleasant setting for meals served in a summer triclinium. The axial symmetry of the plan meant that on entering the fauces of the house, a visitor could be greeted by a vista through the atrium directly into the peristyle garden (as in FIG. 10-13), which often boasted a fountain or pool, marble statuary, mural paintings, and mosaic floors.

Such houses were not, of course, the norm. While they were typical of Pompeii and other towns, they were very rare in large cities such as Rome, where the masses lived instead in multistory apartment houses (FIG. 10-53).

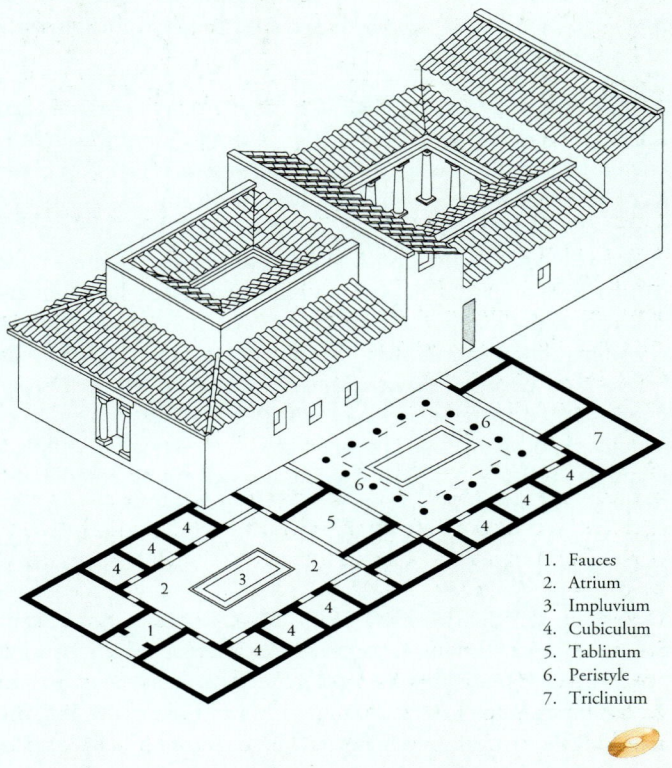

1. Fauces
2. Atrium
3. Impluvium
4. Cubiculum
5. Tablinum
6. Peristyle
7. Triclinium

in the *fauces.* It shows the *impluvium* in the center of the *atrium,* the opening in the roof above, and, in the background, the *peristyle* garden with its marble tables and splendid mural paintings dating to the last years of the Vesuvian city. At that time, two brothers, Aulus Vettius Restitutus and Aulus Vettius Conviva, probably freedmen who had made their fortune as merchants, owned the house. Their wealth enabled them to purchase and furnish the kind of fashionable townhouse that in an earlier era only patricians could have acquired.

One such house, a luxurious Pompeian mansion of the second century BCE, the so-called House of the Faun, epitomizes Livy's Republican "craze for things Greek." The house takes its nickname from the Hellenistic-style bronze statue that stood in one of its two atriums. The mansion, which occupied an entire city block, also had two huge peristyle gardens. First Style murals (see page 258) of Greek type covered most of the walls, and mosaics decorated the floors of many rooms. The most spectacular mosaic panel found in the house depicts Alexander the Great battling Darius of Persia (see FIG. 5-69) and is a copy of a fourth-century BCE Greek panel painting.

## Painting

**PAINTED WALLS EVERYWHERE** The houses and villas around Mount Vesuvius have yielded a treasure trove of mural paintings, the most complete record of the changing fashions in interior decoration found anywhere in the ancient world. The sheer quantity of these paintings tells a great deal about both the prosperity and the tastes of the times. How many homes today, even of the very wealthy, have custom-painted murals in nearly every room? Roman wall paintings were true frescoes (see "Fresco Painting," Chapter 19, page 530), with the colors applied while the plaster was still damp. The process was a painstaking one. First the painter had to prepare the wall by applying the plaster (mixed with marble dust if the patron could afford it) in several layers with a smooth trowel. Only then could painting begin. Finally, when the surface dried, the painter polished the wall to achieve a marblelike finish.

In the early years of exploration at Pompeii and nearby Herculaneum, excavators focused almost exclusively on the figural panels that formed part of the overall mural designs, especially those depicting Greek heroes and famous myths. These were cut out of the walls and transferred to the Naples Archaeological Museum. (The painting of the brawl in the amphitheater, FIG. 10-12, suffered this fate.) In time, more enlightened archaeologists put an end to the practice of cutting pieces out of the walls, and gave serious attention finally to the mural designs as a whole. Toward the end of the 19th century, August Mau, a German art historian, divided the various mural painting schemes into four so-called Pompeian Styles, numbered in the order they were introduced. Mau's classification system, although later refined and modified in detail, still serves as the basis for the study of Roman painting.

**THE FIRST STYLE AND GREECE** The *First Style* also has been called the Masonry Style because the decorator's aim was to imitate costly marble panels using painted stucco relief. (For walls faced with real marble slabs, see FIGS. 10-50 and 17-18.) In the fauces (FIG. **10-14**) of the Samnite House at Herculaneum, the visitor is greeted at the doorway by a stunning illusion of walls constructed, or at least faced, with marbles imported from quarries all over the Mediterranean. This approach to wall decoration is comparable to the modern practice, employed in private libraries and corporate meeting rooms alike, of using cheaper manufactured materials to approximate the look and shape of genuine wood paneling. The practice is not, however, uniquely Pompeian or Roman. First Style walls are well documented in the Greek world from the late fourth century BCE on. The use of the First Style in Republican houses is yet another example of the Hellenization of Roman architecture.

**SECOND STYLE ILLUSIONISM** The First Style never went completely out of fashion, but after 80 BCE a new approach to mural design became more popular. The *Second Style* is in most respects the antithesis of the First Style. Some scholars have argued that the Second Style also has precedents in Greece, but most believe it is a Roman invention. Certainly, the Second Style evolved in Italy and was popular until around 15 BCE, when Roman painters introduced the Third Style. Second Style painters aimed not to create the illusion of an elegant marble wall, as First Style painters sought to do. Rather, they wanted to dissolve a room's confining walls and replace them with the illusion of an imaginary three-dimensional world. They did this purely pictorially. The First Style's modeled stucco panels gave way to the Second Style's flat wall surfaces.

**DIONYSIAC MYSTERIES AT POMPEII** An early example of the new style is the room (FIG. 10-15) that gives its name to the Villa of the Mysteries at Pompeii. Many scholars believe that this chamber was used to celebrate, in private, the rites of the Greek god Dionysos (Roman Bacchus). Dionysos was the focus of an unofficial mystery religion popular among women in Italy at this time. The precise nature of the Dionysiac rites is unknown, but the figural cycle in the Villa of the Mysteries, illustrating mortals (all female save for one boy) interacting with mythological figures, probably provides some evidence for the cult's initiation rites. In these rites young women, emulating Ariadne, daughter of King Minos (see Chapter 4), were united in marriage with Dionysos.

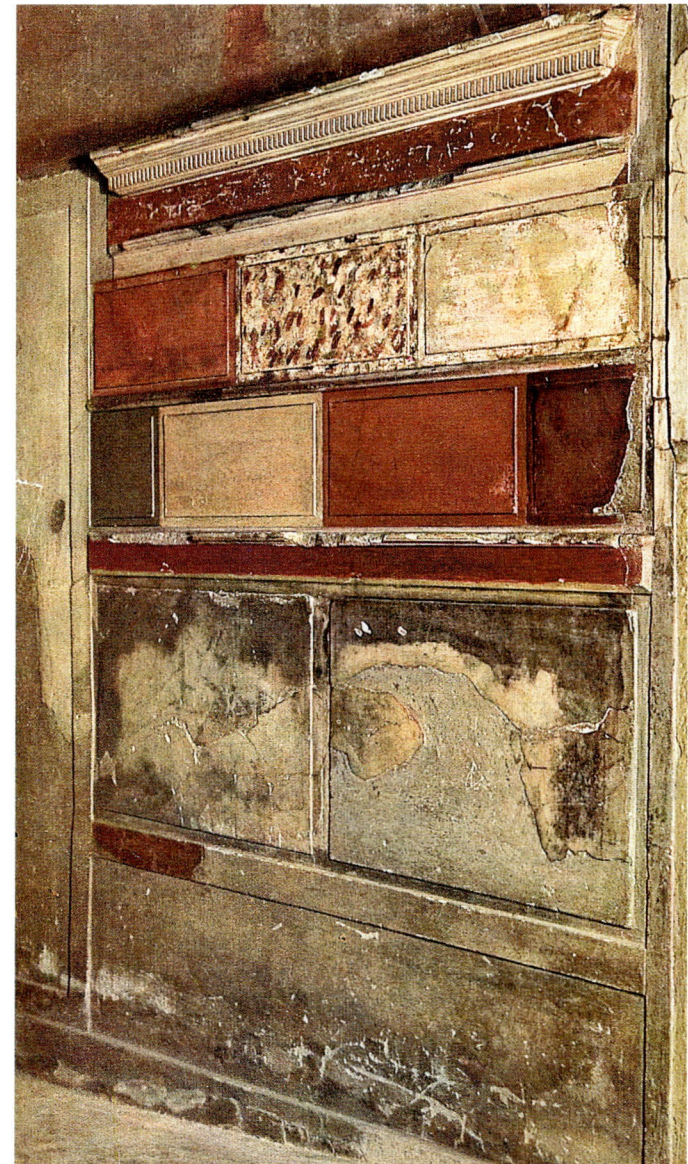

**10-14** First Style wall painting in the fauces of the Samnite House, Herculaneum, Italy, late second century BCE.

The backdrop for the nearly life-size figures is a series of painted panels imitating marble revetment, just as in the First Style but without the modeling in relief. In front of this marble wall (but actually on the same two-dimensional surface), the painter created the illusion of a shallow ledge on which the human and divine actors move around the room. Especially striking is the way some of the figures interact across the corners of the room. For example, a seminude winged woman at the far right of the rear wall lashes out with her whip across the space of the room at a kneeling woman with a bare back (the initiate and bride-to-be of Dionysos) on the left end of the right wall. Nothing comparable to this room existed in Hellenistic Greece. Despite the presence of Dionysos, satyrs, and other figures from Greek mythology, this is a Roman design.

**PERSPECTIVE PAINTING** In the early Second Style Dionysiac mystery frieze, the spatial illusionism is confined to the painted platform that projects into the room. But in mature Second Style designs, painters created a three-dimensional setting that also extends beyond the wall. An example is a cubiculum (FIG. **10-16**) from the Villa of Publius Fannius Synistor at Boscoreale, near

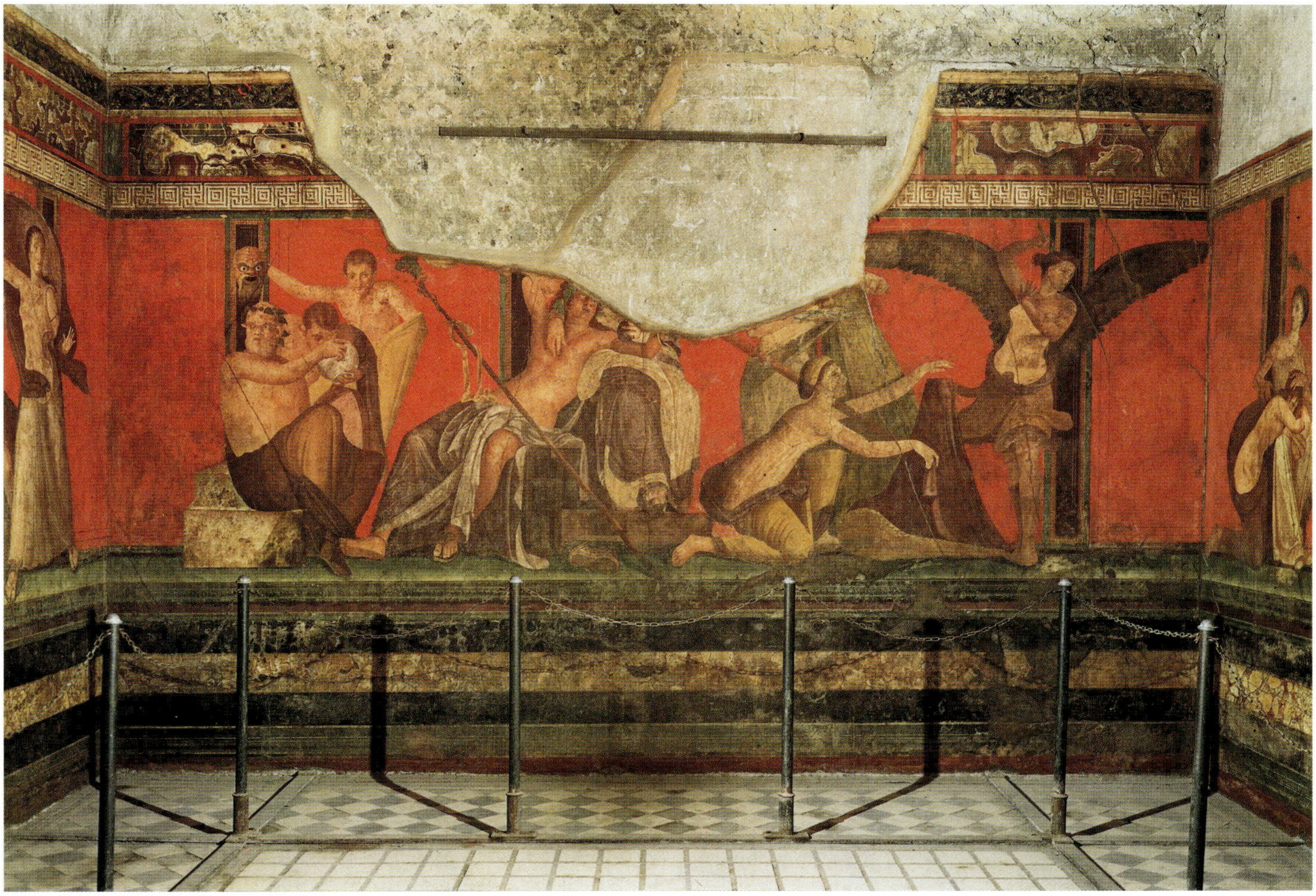

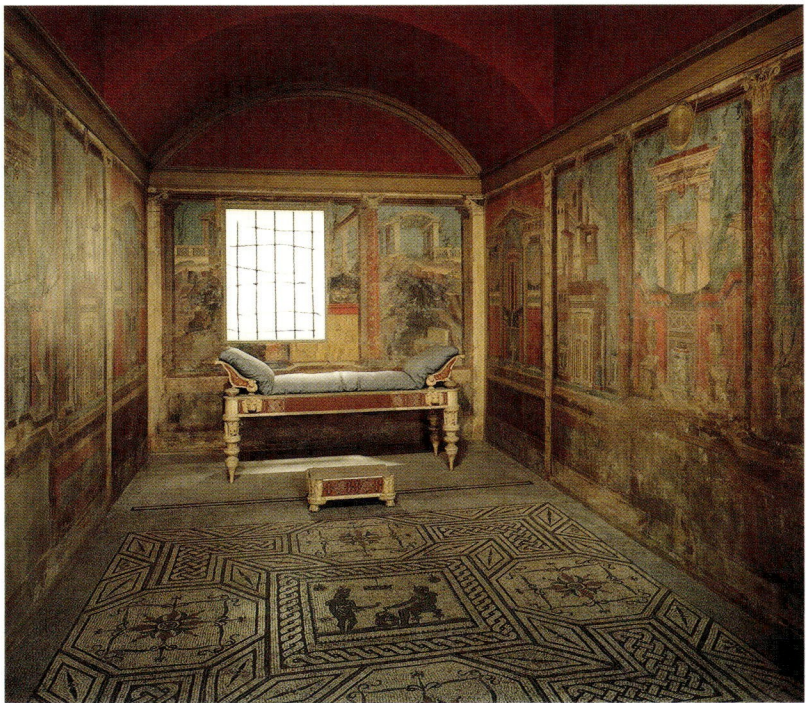

**10-15** Dionysiac mystery frieze, Second Style wall paintings in Room 5 of the Villa of the Mysteries, Pompeii, Italy, ca. 60–50 BCE. Frieze approx. 5′ 4″ high.

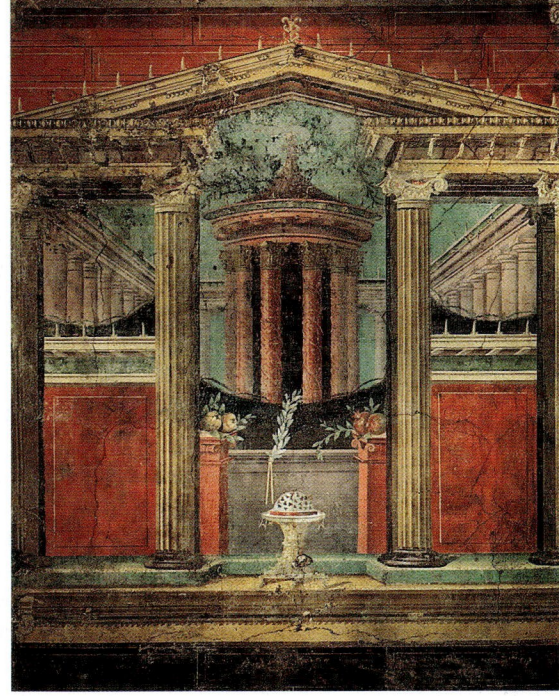

**10-16** Second Style wall paintings (general view, *left*, and detail of tholos, *right*) from Cubiculum M of the Villa of Publius Fannius Synistor, Boscoreale, Italy, ca. 50–40 BCE. Approx. 8′ 9″ high. Metropolitan Museum of Art, New York.

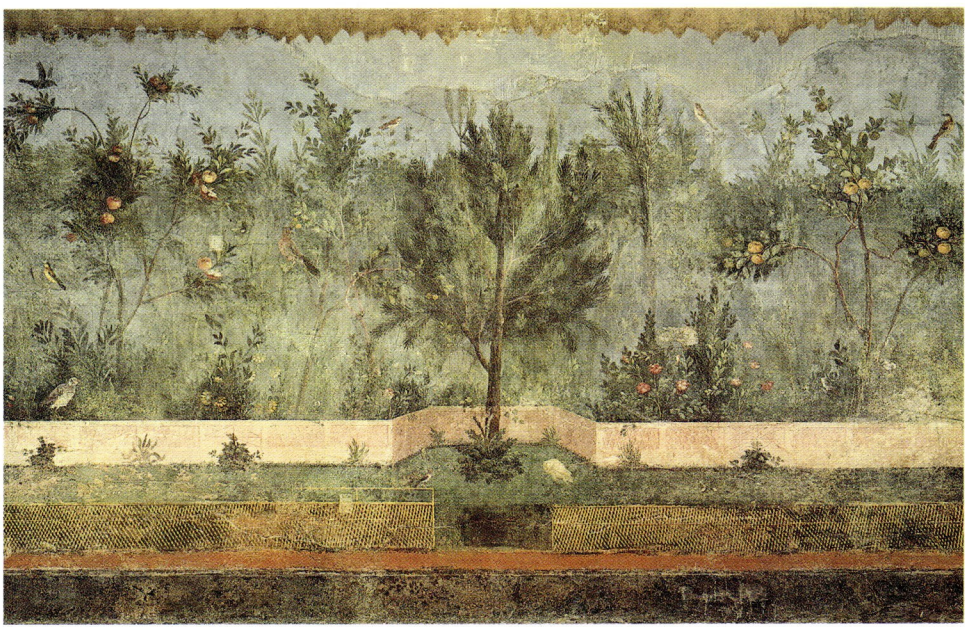

**10-17** Gardenscape, Second Style wall painting, from the Villa of Livia, Primaporta, Italy, ca. 30–20 BCE. Approx. 6′ 7″ high. Museo Nazionale Romano-Palazzo Massimo alle Terme, Rome.

Pompeii, decorated between 50 and 40 BCE. The frescoes were removed soon after their discovery, and today they are part of a reconstructed Roman bedroom in the Metropolitan Museum of Art. All around the room the Second Style painter opened up the walls with vistas of Italian towns, marble temples, and colonnaded courtyards. Painted doors and gates invite the viewer to walk through the wall into the magnificent world the painter created.

Although the Boscoreale painter was inconsistent in applying it, this Roman artist, like many others in the towns Vesuvius buried, demonstrated a knowledge of single-point *linear perspective,* often incorrectly said to be an innovation of Italian Renaissance artists (see "Depicting Objects in Space," Chapter 21, page 578). In this kind of perspective, all the receding lines in a composition converge on a single point along the painting's central axis to show depth and distance. Ancient writers state that Greek painters of the fifth century BCE first used linear perspective for the design of Athenian stage sets (hence its Greek name, *skenographia,* "scene painting"). In the Boscoreale cubiculum the device is most successfully employed in the far corners, where a low gate leads to a peristyle framing a tholos temple (FIG. 10-16, detail). Roman painters used one-point linear perspective more consistently and on an even grander scale in the somewhat later Room of the Masks in what was probably the house of the emperor Augustus on the Palatine Hill in Rome. Linear perspective was a favored tool of Second Style painters seeking to transform the usually windowless walls of Roman houses into "picture-window" vistas that expanded the apparent space of the rooms.

**AN EMPRESS'S PAINTED GARDEN** The ultimate example of a Second Style picture-window wall (FIG. **10-17**) was found in the Villa of Livia, wife of the emperor Augustus, at Primaporta, just north of Rome. There, imperial painters decorated a vaulted, partly underground room on all sides with lush gardenscapes. The only architectural element is the flimsy fence of the garden itself. To suggest recession, the painter mastered another kind of perspective, *atmospheric perspective,* indicating depth by the increasingly blurred appearance of objects in the distance. At Livia's villa, the fence, trees, and birds in the foreground are precisely painted, while the details of the dense foliage in the background are indistinct. Among the wall paintings examined so far, only the landscape

fresco from Thera (see FIG. 4-9) offers a similar wraparound view of nature. But the Aegean fresco's white sky and red, yellow, and blue rock formations do not create a successful illusion of a world filled with air and light just a few steps away.

**THIRD STYLE ELEGANCE** The open, verdant Primaporta gardenscape is the polar opposite of First Style designs, which reinforce, rather than deny, the heavy presence of confining walls. But tastes changed rapidly in the Roman world, as in society today. Not long after Livia had her villa painted, Roman patrons began to favor mural designs that reasserted the primacy of the wall surface. In the *Third Style* of Pompeian painting, artists no longer attempted to replace the walls with three-dimensional worlds of their own creation. Nor did they seek to imitate the appearance of the marble walls of Hellenistic kings. Instead they decorated walls with delicate linear fantasies sketched on predominantly monochromatic (one-color) backgrounds.

One of the earliest examples of the new style is a room (FIG. **10-18**) in the Villa of Agrippa Postumus at Boscotrecase, near Pompeii, also a property owned by the imperial family. The villa was probably painted just before 10 BCE. Nowhere did the artist use illusionistic painting to penetrate the wall. In place of the stately columns of the Second Style are insubstantial and impossibly thin *colonnettes* supporting featherweight canopies barely reminiscent of pediments. In the center of this delicate and elegant architectural frame is a tiny floating landscape painted directly on the jet-black ground. It is hard to imagine a sharper contrast with the panoramic gardenscape at Livia's villa. On other Third Style walls, landscapes and mythological scenes appear in frames, like modern canvas paintings hung on walls. Never could these framed panels be mistaken for windows opening onto a world beyond the room.

**ROMAN PAINTING AND LATIN POETRY** Despite the differences in style, the landscapes of the Primaporta and Boscotrecase villas reveal a love of country life and idealization of nature that also appear in the pastoral poetry of Vergil, a contemporary of Livia and Augustus. Horace, another renowned Augustan poet, also proclaimed in one of his odes the satisfaction afforded the city dweller by a villa in the countryside, where life is beautiful, simple, and natural, in contrast with the urban greed for gold and

### *The Roman Illustrated Book*

The hundreds of paintings uncovered in the cities buried by the eruption of Mount Vesuvius give the false impression that the history of Roman painting is well documented and that art historians can trace its development decade by decade. But Pompeii, Herculaneum, and the other towns around the Bay of Naples have yielded only frescoes. As in Greece, no Roman paintings on wooden panels have been discovered, save for the special case of Roman Egypt (FIGS. 10-63 and 10-64). Nor has anyone found any of the grand tableaux of battles and besieged cities that were exhibited in Roman triumphal processions and then displayed in public buildings to perpetuate the memory of a general's great achievements on the state's behalf.

Also apparently lost are virtually all illustrated Roman books, although art historians know they once existed in great numbers. The oldest preserved painted manuscript, itself very incomplete, is the *Vatican Vergil,* which dates from the early fifth century CE. It

originally contained more than 200 pictures illustrating all of Vergil's works. Today only 50 painted *folios* (pages) of the *Aeneid* and *Georgics* survive.

The page illustrated here (FIG. 10-19) includes a section of text from the *Georgics* at the top and a framed illustration below. Vergil recounts his visit to a modest farm near Tarentum (Taranto, in southern Italy) belonging to an old man from Corycus in Asia Minor. In the illustration, the old farmer is seated at the left. His rustic farmhouse is in the background, rendered in a three-quarter view. The farmer speaks about the pleasures of the simple life in the country and on his methods of gardening. His audience is two laborers and, at the far right, Vergil himself in the guise of a farmhand. The style is reminiscent of Pompeian landscapes, with quick touches that suggest space and atmosphere. In fact, the heavy, dark frame has close parallels in the late Pompeian styles of mural painting (FIG. 10-20).

power. A fifth-century CE illustrated manuscript (FIG. 10-19) containing some of Vergil's pastoral poems also provides invaluable evidence about the nature of Roman illustrated books (see "The Roman Illustrated Book," above).

**NERO AND THE FOURTH STYLE** In the *Fourth Style,* a taste for illusionism returned once again. This style became popular around the time of the Pompeian earthquake of 62 CE, and it was the preferred manner of mural decoration when the town was buried in volcanic ash in 79. The earliest examples, such as

**10-18** Detail of a Third Style wall painting, from Cubiculum 15 of the Villa of Agrippa Postumus, Boscotrecase, Italy, ca. 10 BCE. Approx. 7′ 8″ high. Metropolitan Museum of Art, New York.

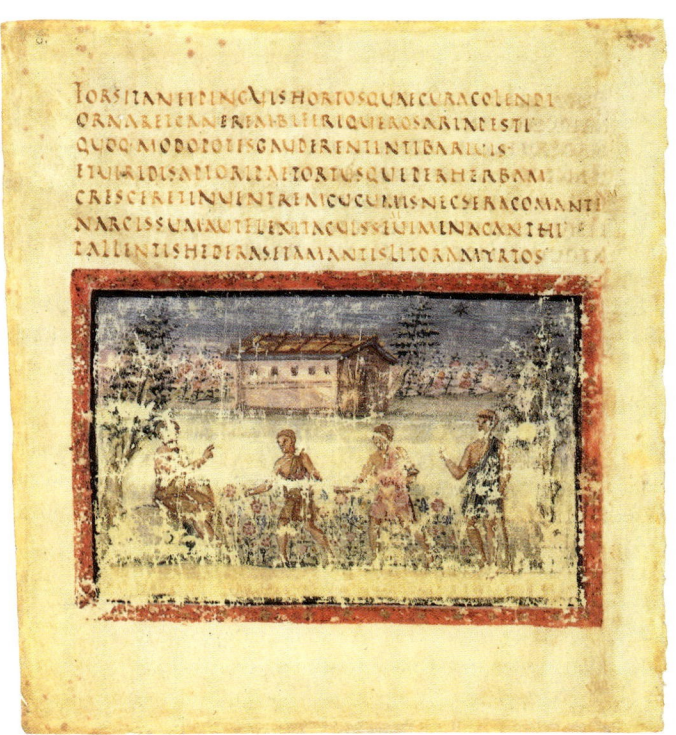

**10-19** The old farmer of Corycus, folio 7 verso of the *Vatican Vergil,* ca. 400–420 CE. Tempera on parchment, approx. 1′ 1½″ × 1′. Biblioteca Apostolica Vaticana, Rome.

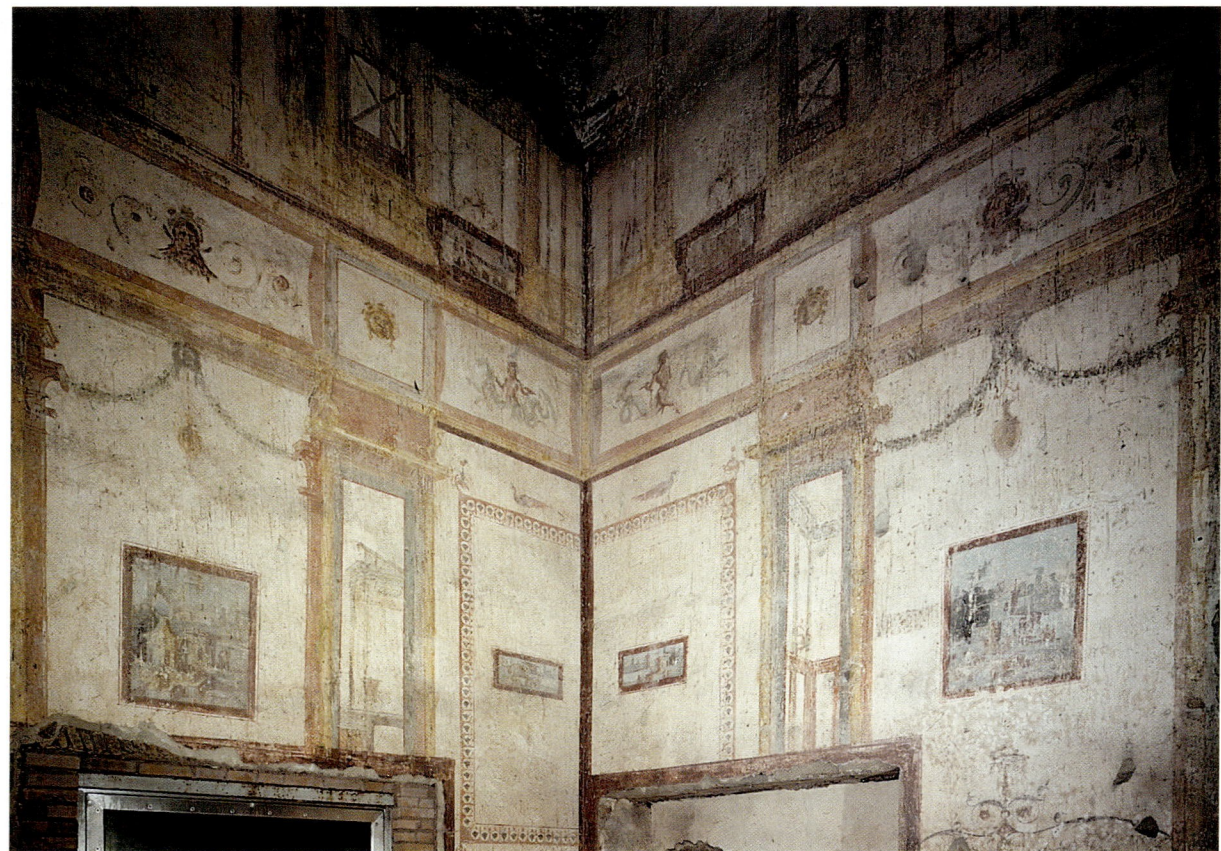

10-20 Fourth Style wall paintings in Room 78 of the Domus Aurea (Golden House) of Nero, Rome, Italy, 64–68 CE.

Room 78 (FIG. **10-20**) in the emperor Nero's fabulous Domus Aurea, or Golden House, in Rome (see "An Imperial Pleasure Palace: The Golden House of Nero," page 270), display a kinship with the Third Style. All the walls are an austere creamy white. In some areas the artist painted sea creatures, birds, and other motifs directly on the monochromatic background, much like the landscape in the Boscotrecase villa (FIG. 10-18). Landscapes appear here also—as framed paintings in the center of each large white subdivision of the wall. But views through the wall are also part of the design, although the Fourth Style architectural vistas are irrational fantasies. The viewer looks out not on cityscapes or round temples set in peristyles but at fragments of buildings—columns supporting half-pediments, double stories of columns supporting nothing at all—painted on the same white ground as the rest of the wall. In the Fourth Style, architecture became just another motif in the painter's ornamental repertoire.

**PAINTING BEFORE THE ERUPTION** In the latest Fourth Style designs, Pompeian painters rejected the quiet elegance of the Third Style and early Fourth Style in favor of crowded and confused compositions and sometimes garish color combinations. The Ixion Room (FIG. **10-21**) of the House of the Vettii at Pompeii was decorated in this manner just before the eruption of Mount Vesuvius. The room served as a triclinium in the house the Vettius brothers remodeled after the earthquake. It opened onto the peristyle seen in the background of FIG. 10-13.

The decor of the dining room is a kind of résumé of all the previous styles, another instance of the eclecticism noted earlier as characteristic of Roman art in general. The lowest zone, for example, is one of the most successful imitations anywhere of costly multicolored imported marbles, despite the fact that the illusion is created without recourse to relief, as in the First Style. The large white panels in the corners of the room, with their delicate floral frames and floating central motifs, would fit naturally into the most elegant Third Style design. Unmistakably Fourth Style, however, are the fragmentary architectural vistas of the central and upper zones of the Ixion Room walls. They are unrelated to one another, do not constitute a unified cityscape beyond the wall, and are peopled with figures that would tumble into the room if they took a single step forward.

**GREEK MYTHS ON ROMAN WALLS** The Ixion Room takes its nickname from the mythological panel painting at the center of the rear wall (FIG. 10-21). Ixion had attempted to seduce Hera, and Zeus punished him by binding him to a perpetually spinning wheel. The panels on the two side walls also have Greek myths as subjects. The Ixion Room may be likened to a small private art gallery with paintings decorating the walls, as in many modern homes. Scholars long have believed that these and the many other mythological paintings on Third and Fourth Style walls were based on lost Greek panels. They attest to the Romans' continuing admiration for Greek artworks three centuries after Marcellus brought the treasures of Syracuse to Rome. But few, if any, of these mythological paintings can be described as true copies of "Old Masters," as are the many Roman replicas of famous Greek statues that have been found throughout the Roman world, including Pompeii (see FIG. 5-38).

Mythological figures were on occasion also the subject of Roman mosaics. In the ancient world, mosaics were usually confined to floors (as was the *Battle of Issus,* FIG. 5-69), where the tesserae formed a durable as well as decorative surface. In Roman times, however, mosaics also decorated walls and even ceilings, foreshadowing the extensive use of wall and vault mosaics in the Middle Ages

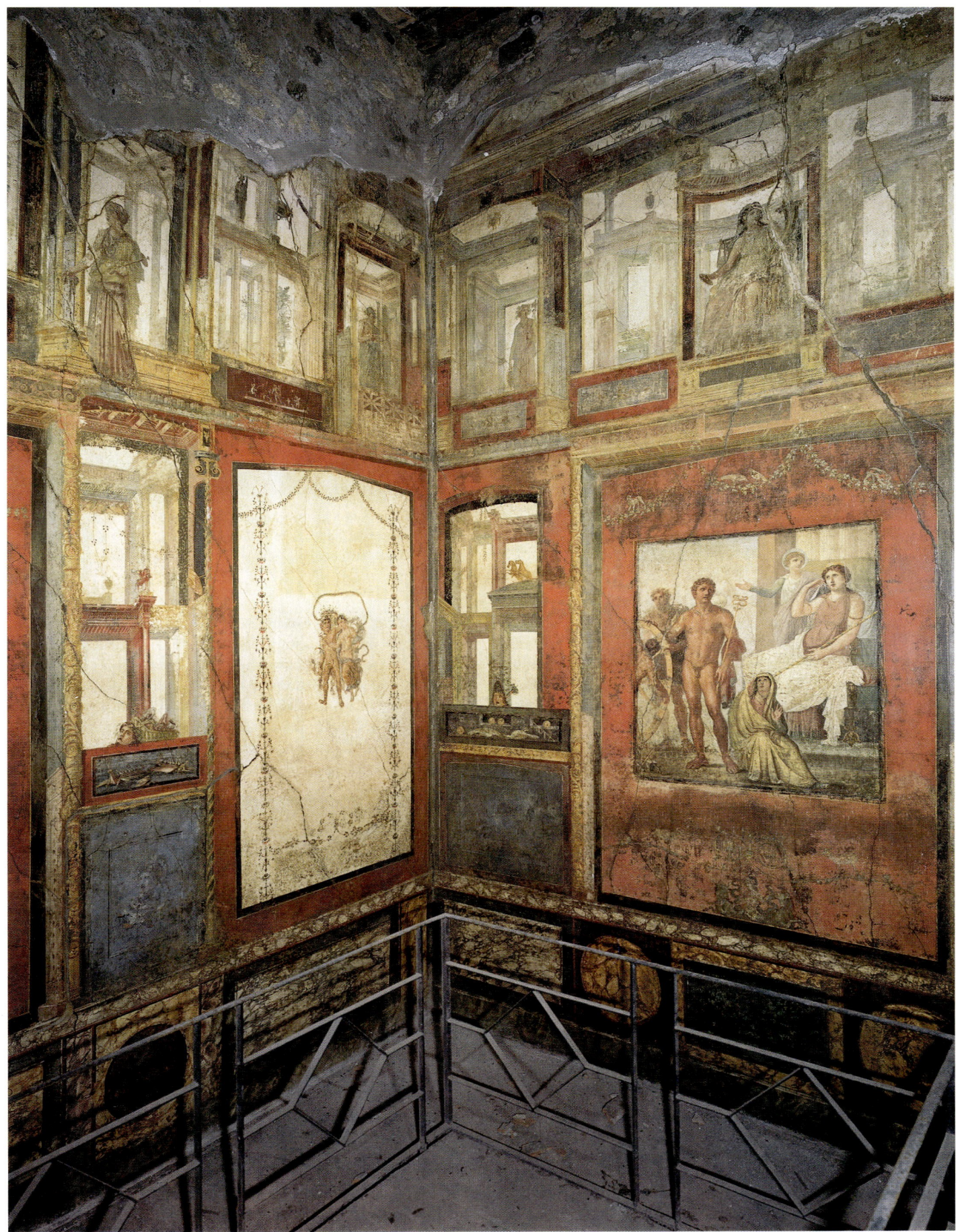

10-21 Fourth Style wall paintings in the Ixion Room (Triclinium P) of the House of the Vettii, Pompeii, Italy, ca. 70–79 CE.

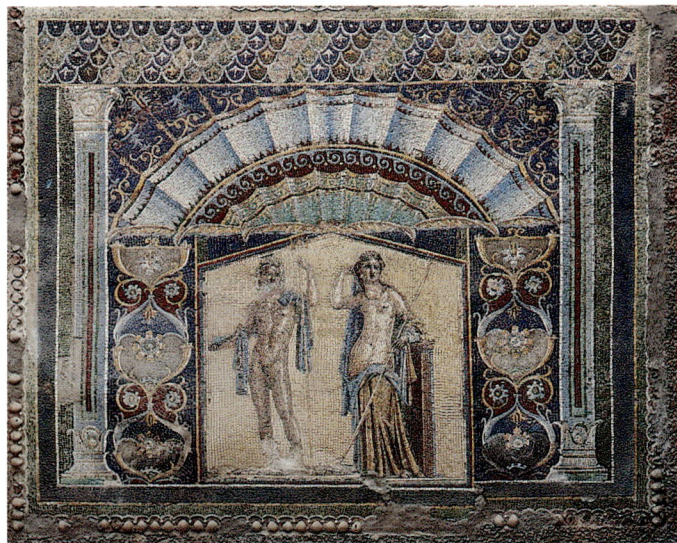

**10-22** Neptune and Amphitrite, wall mosaic in the summer triclinium of the House of Neptune and Amphitrite, Herculaneum, Italy, ca. 62–79 CE.

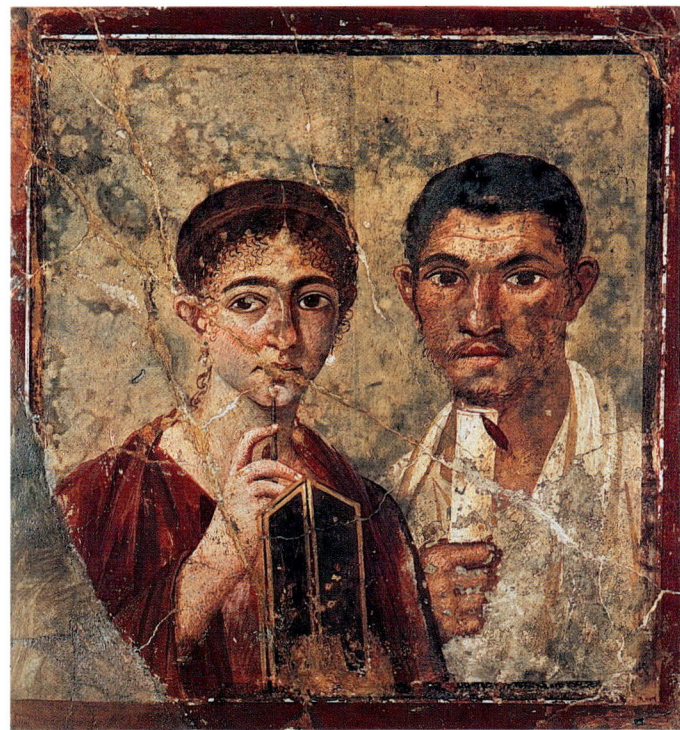

**10-23** Portrait of a husband and wife, wall painting from House VII,2,6, Pompeii, Italy, ca. 70–79 CE. Approx. 1′ 11″ × 1′ 8½″. Museo Nazionale, Naples.

(see "Mosaics," Chapter 11, page 315). The mosaic shown in FIG. **10-22** adorns a wall in the House of Neptune and Amphitrite at Herculaneum. The sea god and his wife preside over the running water of the fountain in the courtyard in front of them where the house's owners and guests enjoyed outdoor dining in warm weather.

**PRETENTIOUS PRIVATE PORTRAITS** The subjects chosen for Roman wall paintings and mosaics were diverse. Although mythological themes were immensely popular, Romans commissioned a vast range of other subjects. As noted, landscape paintings frequently appear on Second, Third, and Fourth Style walls. Paintings and mosaics depicting scenes from history include the *Battle of Issus* mosaic and the mural painting of the brawl in the amphitheater of Pompeii (FIG. 10-12). Given the Roman custom of keeping *imagines* of illustrious ancestors in atriums, it is not surprising that painted portraits also appear in Pompeian houses. The portrait of a husband and wife illustrated here (FIG. **10-23**) originally formed part of a Fourth Style wall of an *exedra* (recessed area) opening onto the atrium of a Pompeian house. The man holds a scroll and the woman a stylus (writing instrument) and a wax writing tablet, standard attributes in Roman marriage portraits. They suggest the fine education of those depicted—even if, as was sometimes true, the individuals were uneducated or even illiterate. Such portraits were thus the Roman equivalent of modern wedding photographs of the bride and groom posing in rented formal garments never worn by them before or afterward. In contrast, the heads are not standard types but sensitive studies of the man and woman's individual faces. This is another instance of a realistic portrait placed on a conventional figure type, a recurring phenomenon in Roman portraiture (see "Role Playing in Roman Portraiture," page 265), first seen here in the statue of the Republican general found at Tivoli (FIG. 10-8).

**PAINTING THE INANIMATE** The Roman interest in recording individual appearance extended to everyday objects. This explains the frequent inclusion of still-life paintings in the mural schemes of the Second, Third, and Fourth Styles. A still life with peaches and a carafe (FIG. **10-24**), a detail of a painted wall from Herculaneum, demonstrates that Roman painters sought to create illusionistic effects when depicting small objects, as well as buildings and landscapes. The artist paid scrupulous attention to shad-

ows and highlights, working directly from an arrangement made specifically for this painting. The fruit, the stem and leaves, and the glass jar were set out on shelves to give the illusion of the casual, almost accidental, relationship of objects in a cupboard. Art historians have not found evidence of anything like these Roman studies of food and other inanimate objects until the Dutch still lifes of the 17th and 18th centuries (see FIGS. 24-55 and 24-56). The

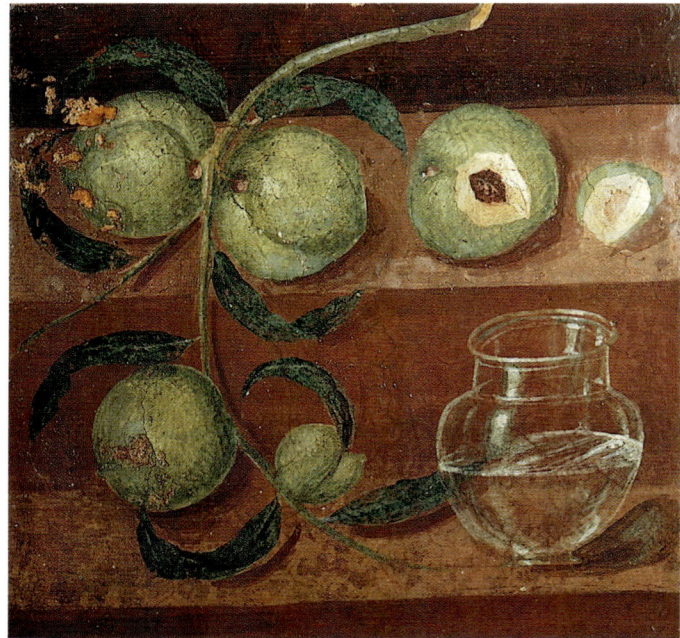

**10-24** Still life with peaches, detail of a Fourth Style wall painting, from Herculaneum, Italy, ca. 62–79 CE. Approx. 1′ 2″ × 1′ 1½″. Museo Nazionale, Naples.

## Role Playing in Roman Portraiture

In every town throughout the vast Roman Empire, portraits of the emperors and empresses and their families were on display—in forums, basilicas, baths, and markets; in front of temples; atop triumphal arches—anywhere a statue could be placed. The rulers' heads varied little from Britain to Syria. All were replicas of official images, either imported or scrupulously copied by local artists. But the portrait heads were placed on many types of bodies. The type chosen depended on the position the person held in Roman society or the various fictitious guises assumed by imperial family members. Portraits of Augustus, for example, show him not only as armed general (FIG. 10-25) but also as recipient of the civic crown for saving the lives of fellow citizens (see FIG. Intro-9), veiled priest, toga-clad magistrate, traveling commander on horseback, heroically nude warrior, and various Roman gods, including Jupiter, Apollo, and Mercury.

Such role playing was not confined to emperors and princes but extended to their wives, daughters, sisters, and mothers.

Statues of Livia (FIG. 10-26) portray her as many goddesses, including Ceres, Juno, Venus, and Vesta. She also appears as the personification of Health, Justice, and Piety. In fact, it was common for imperial women to appear on Roman coins not only as goddesses but also as embodiments of feminine virtue. Faustina the Younger, for example, the wife of Marcus Aurelius and mother of 13 children, appears as Venus and Fecundity, among many other roles. Julia Domna (FIG. 10-64), Septimius Severus's wife, is Juno, Venus, Peace, or Victory in some portraits.

Ordinary citizens also engaged in role playing. Some assumed literary pretensions, as did a husband and wife (FIG. 10-23) in their Pompeian home. Others equated themselves with Greek heroes (FIG. 10-61) or Roman deities (FIG. 10-62) on their coffins. The common people followed the lead of the emperors and empresses.

---

Roman murals are not as exact in drawing, perspective, or rendering of light and shade as the Dutch canvases. Still, the ancient painter understood that the look of things is a function of light. The goal was to paint light as one would strive to paint the touchable object that reflects and absorbs it.

## EARLY EMPIRE

ANTONY AND CLEOPATRA The murder of Julius Caesar on the Ides of March, 44 BCE, plunged the Roman world into a bloody civil war. The fighting lasted 13 years and ended only when Octavian (better known as Augustus), Caesar's grandnephew and adopted son, crushed the naval forces of Mark Antony and Queen Cleopatra of Egypt at Actium in northwestern Greece. Antony and Cleopatra committed suicide, and in 30 BCE, Egypt, once the wealthiest and most powerful kingdom of the ancient world, became another province in the ever-expanding Roman Empire.

Historians reckon the passage from the old Roman Republic to the new Roman Empire from the day in 27 BCE when the Senate conferred the majestic title of Augustus (r. 27 BCE–14 CE) on Octavian. The Empire was ostensibly a continuation of the Republic, with the same constitutional offices, but in fact Augustus, who was recognized as *princeps* (first citizen), occupied all the key positions. He was consul and *imperator* (commander in chief; root of the word *emperor*) and even, after 12 BCE, *pontifex maximus* (chief priest of the state religion). These offices gave Augustus control of all aspects of Roman public life.

THE PAX ROMANA With powerful armies keeping order on the Empire's frontiers and no opposition at home, Augustus brought peace and prosperity to a war-weary Mediterranean world. Known in his own day as the *Pax Augusta* (Augustan Peace), the peace Augustus established prevailed for two centuries. It came to be called simply the *Pax Romana*. During this time the emperors commissioned a huge number of public works throughout the Empire: roads, bridges, forums, temples, basilicas, theaters, amphitheaters, market halls, and bathing complexes, all

on an unprecedented scale. And the erection of imperial portraits and arches covered with reliefs recounting the emperor's great deeds reminded people everywhere of the source of this beneficence. These portraits and reliefs often presented a picture of the emperor and his achievements that bore little resemblance to historical fact. Their purpose, however, was not to provide an objective record but to mold public opinion. The Roman emperors and the artists they employed have had few equals in the effective use of art and architecture for propagandistic ends.

## Augustus and the Julio-Claudians (27 BCE–68 CE)

AUGUSTUS, SON OF A GOD When Octavian inherited Caesar's fortune in 44 BCE, he was not yet 19 years old. When he vanquished Antony and Cleopatra at Actium in 31 BCE and became undisputed master of the Mediterranean world, he had not reached his 32nd birthday. The rule by elders that had characterized the Roman Republic for nearly half a millennium came to an abrupt end. Suddenly, Roman portraitists were called on to produce images of a *youthful* head of state. But Augustus was more than young. Caesar had been made a god after his death, and Augustus, though never claiming to be a god himself, widely advertised himself as the son of a god. His portraits—produced in great numbers by anonymous artists paid by the state—were designed to present the image of a godlike leader, a superior being who, miraculously, never aged. Although Augustus lived until 14 CE, even official portraits made near the end of his life continued to show him as a handsome youth (see FIG. Intro-9). Such a notion may seem ridiculous today, when television, the Internet, magazines, and newspapers portray world leaders as they truly appear, but in antiquity few people had actually seen the emperor. His official image was all most knew. It therefore could be manipulated at will.

The models for Augustus's idealized portraits cannot be found in the veristic likenesses of the Roman Republic. Rather, Classical Greek art inspired the emperor's sculptors. The portrait

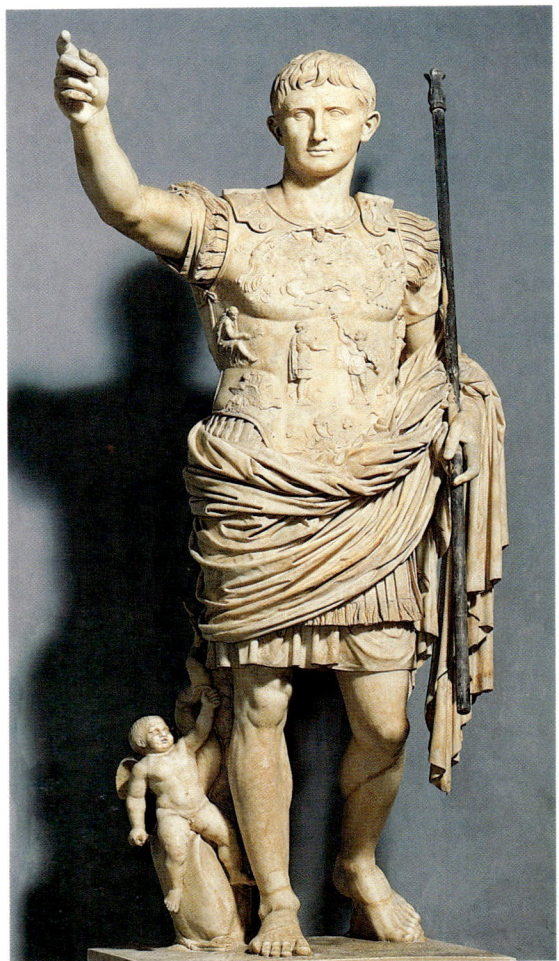

**10-25** Portrait of Augustus as general, from Primaporta, Italy, early first century CE copy of a bronze original of ca. 20 BCE. Marble, 6′ 8″ high. Vatican Museums, Rome.

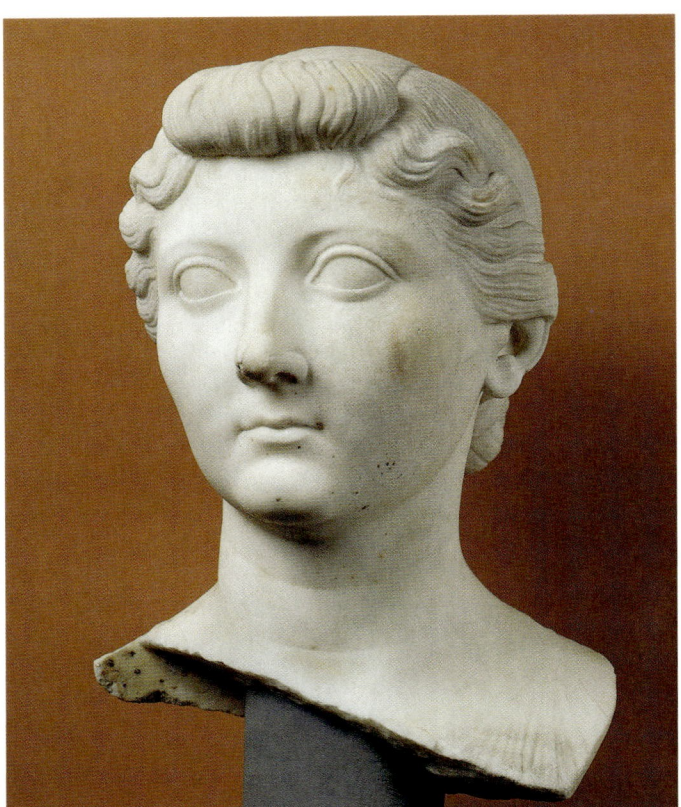

**10-26** Portrait bust of Livia, from Faiyum, Egypt, early first century CE. Marble, approx. 1′ 1½″ high. Ny Carlsberg Glyptotek, Copenhagen.

statue of Augustus (FIG. **10-25**) found at his wife Livia's villa at Primaporta (FIG. 10-17) depicts the emperor as general. (Others portray him in different roles. See "Role Playing in Roman Portraiture," page 265.) It is based closely on Polykleitos's *Doryphoros* (see FIG. 5-38). Here, however, the emperor addresses his troops with his right arm extended in the manner of the orator Aule Metele (see FIG. 9-15). Although the head is that of an individual and not a nameless athlete, its overall shape, the sharp ridges of the brows, and the tight cap of layered hair emulate the Polykleitan style. The reliefs on the emperor's cuirass advertise an important diplomatic victory—the return of the Roman military standards the Parthians had captured from a Republican general. The Cupid at Augustus's feet proclaims his divine descent. Caesar's family, the Julians, traced their ancestry back to Venus. Cupid was the goddess's son. Thus, the sculptor designed every facet of the Primaporta statue to carry a political message.

**LIVIA, NEVER-AGING EMPRESS** A marble portrait of Livia (FIG. **10-26**) shows that the imperial women of the Augustan age shared the emperor's eternal youthfulness. Although she sports the latest Roman coiffure, with the hair rolled over the forehead and knotted at the nape of the neck, Livia's blemish-free skin and sharply defined features derive from images of Classical Greek goddesses. Livia outlived Augustus by 15 years, dying at age 87. In her portraits, the coiffure changed with the introduction of each

new fashion, but her face remained ever young, as befitted her exalted position in the Roman state.

**A SHRINE TO PEACE** On Livia's birthday in 9 BCE, Augustus dedicated the Ara Pacis Augustae (Altar of Augustan Peace), the monument celebrating his most important achievement, the establishment of peace. The altar (FIG. **10-27**) was reconstructed during the Fascist era in Italy in connection with the 2,000th anniversary of Augustus's birth, when Mussolini was seeking to build a modern Roman Empire. Figural reliefs and acanthus tendrils adorn the altar's marble precinct walls. Four panels on the east and west ends depict carefully selected mythological subjects, including (at the right in FIG. 10-27) a relief of Aeneas making a sacrifice. Aeneas was the son of Venus and one of Augustus's forefathers. The connection between the emperor and Aeneas was a key element of Augustus's political ideology for his new Golden Age. It is no coincidence that the *Aeneid* was written during the rule of Augustus. Vergil's epic poem glorified the young emperor by celebrating the founder of the Julian line.

A second panel (FIG. **10-28**), on the other end of the altar enclosure, depicts a seated matron with two lively babies on her lap. Her identity is uncertain. She is usually called Tellus (Mother Earth), although some have named her Pax (Peace), Ceres (goddess of grain), or even Venus. Whoever she is, she epitomizes the fruits of the Pax Augusta. All around her the bountiful earth is in bloom, and animals of different species live peacefully side by side. Personifications of refreshing breezes (note their windblown drapery) flank her. One rides a bird, the other a sea creature. Earth, sky, and water are all elements of this picture of peace and fertility in the Augustan cosmos.

Processions of the imperial family and other important dignitaries appear on the long north and south sides of the Ara Pacis (FIG. **10-29**). These parallel friezes were clearly inspired to some

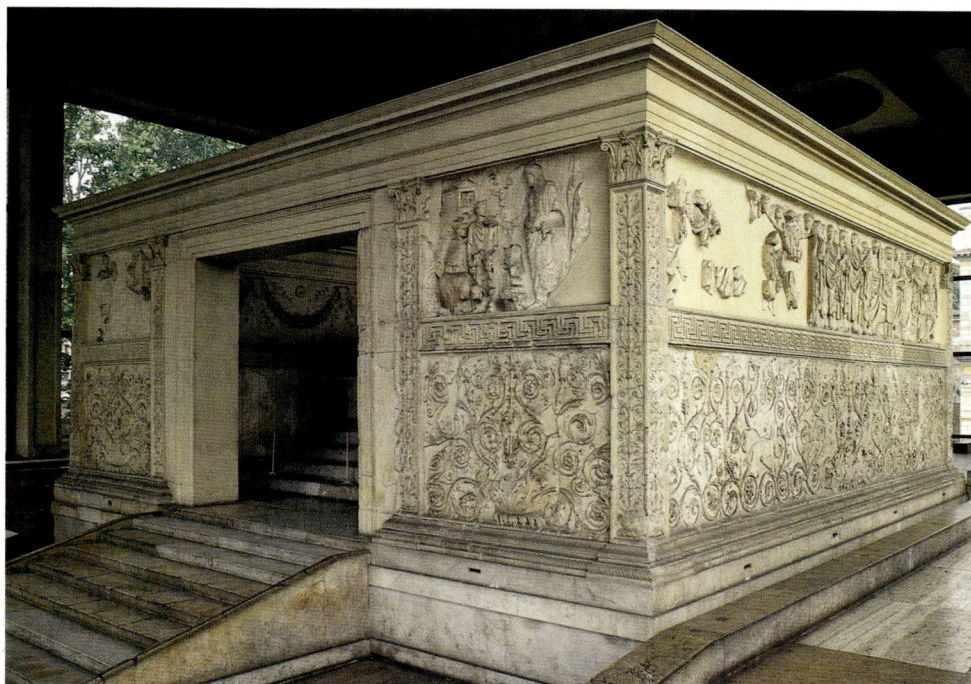

**10-27** Ara Pacis Augustae (Altar of Augustan Peace), view from the south-west, Rome, Italy, 13–9 BCE.

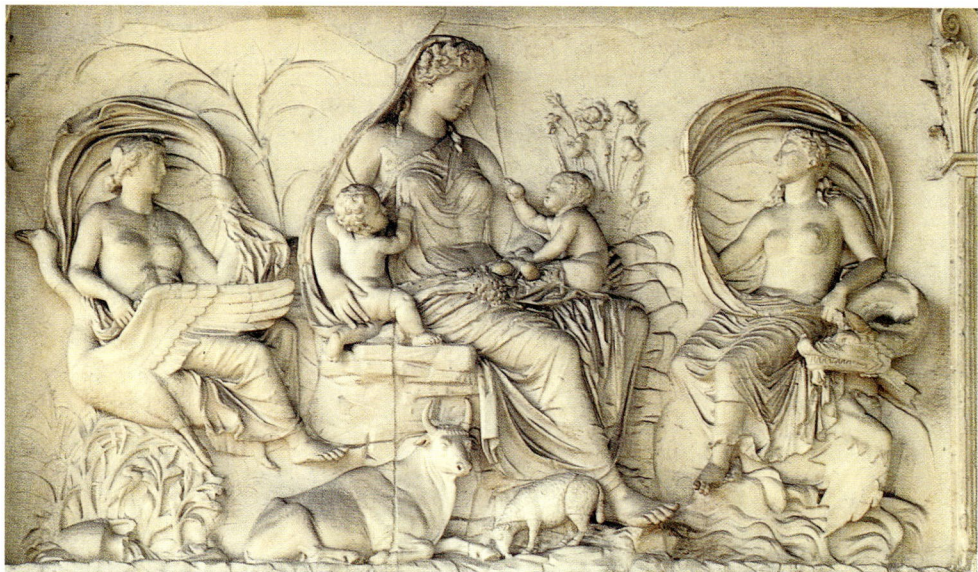

**10-28** Female personification (Tellus?), panel from the east facade of the Ara Pacis Augustae, Rome, Italy, 13–9 BCE. Marble, approx. 5′ 3″ high.

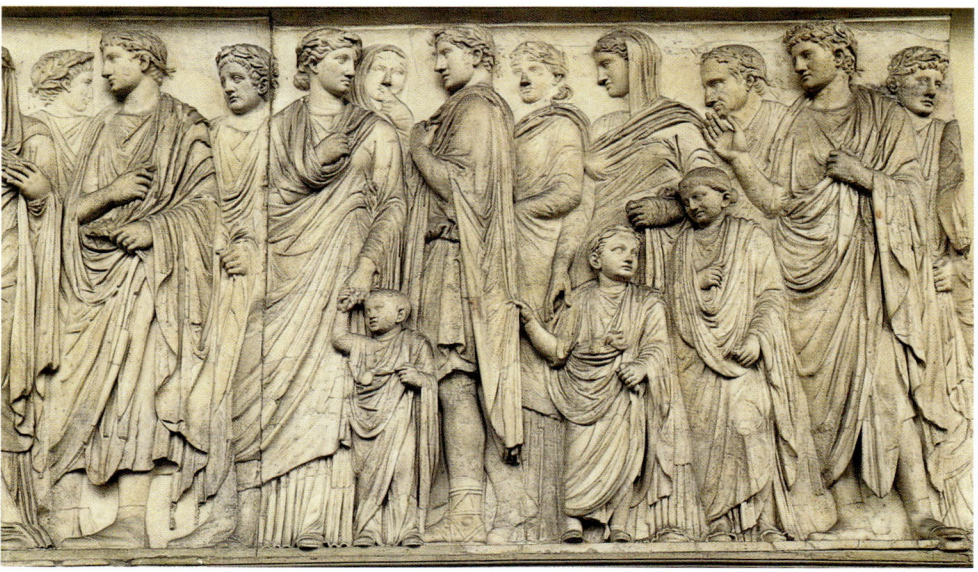

**10-29** Procession of the imperial family, detail of the south frieze of the Ara Pacis Augustae, Rome, Italy, 13–9 BCE. Marble, approx. 5′ 3″ high.

degree by the Panathenaic procession frieze of the Parthenon (see FIG. 5-48, *bottom*). Augustus sought to present his new order as a Golden Age equaling that of Athens under Pericles in the middle of the fifth century BCE. The emulation of Classical models thus made a political statement, as well as an artistic one.

Even so, the Roman procession is very different in character from the Greek. On the Parthenon, anonymous figures act out an event that recurred every four years. The frieze stands for *all* Panathenaic Festival processions. The Ara Pacis depicts a specific event—probably the inaugural ceremony of 13 BCE when work on the altar began—and recognizable contemporary figures. Among those portrayed are children, who restlessly tug on their elders' garments and talk to one another when they should be quiet on a solemn occasion—in short, children who act like children and not like miniature adults, as they frequently do in the history of art. Their presence lends a great deal of charm to the procession, but that is not why children were included on the Ara Pacis when they had never before appeared on any Greek or Roman state monument. Augustus was concerned about a decline in the birthrate among the Roman nobility, and he enacted a series of laws designed to promote marriage, marital fidelity, and raising children. The portrayal of men with their families on the Altar of Peace was intended as a moral exemplar. Once again, the emperor used art to further his own political and social agendas.

**ROME, THE MARBLE CITY** Augustus's most ambitious project in the capital was the construction of a new forum (FIG. 10-1, no. 10) next to Julius Caesar's forum (FIG. 10-1, no. 9), which Augustus completed. Both forums were made of white marble from Carrara (ancient Luna), the same source used by the great sculptors of the Italian Renaissance. Prior to the opening of these quarries in the second half of the first century BCE, marble had to be imported at great cost from abroad, and it was used sparingly. The ready availability of Italian marble under Augustus made

possible the emperor's famous boast that he had found Rome a city of brick and transformed it into a city of marble.

The extensive use of Carrara marble for public monuments (including the Ara Pacis) must be seen as part of Augustus's larger program to make his city the equal of Periclean Athens. In fact, the Forum of Augustus incorporated several explicit references to Classical Athens and to the Acropolis in particular, most notably copies of the caryatids of the Erechtheion (see FIG. 5-52) in the upper story of the porticos. Roman history also was evoked. The porticos contained dozens of portrait statues, including images of all the major figures of the Julian family going back to Aeneas. Augustus's forum became a kind of public atrium filled with *imagines*. His family history thus became part of the Roman state's official history. The Forum of Augustus and those of his successors did serve a practical function by providing alternative areas to the old and overcrowded Republican Forum Romanum for the conduct of state business. Yet they also gave the emperors the opportunity to present their own version of history to the Roman people.

**ROME IN FRANCE** The Forum of Augustus is in ruins today, but the conservative neoclassical Augustan style it epitomizes may be seen in an exceptionally well preserved temple at Nîmes (ancient Nemausus) in southern France (ancient Gaul). The so-called Maison Carrée (FIG. 10-30) dates to the opening years of the first century CE. Larger than the Temple of "Fortuna Virilis" in Rome (FIG. 10-2), this Corinthian pseudoperipteral temple was patterned on the Temple of Mars in the Forum of Augustus. In fact, many scholars believe that some of the artisans who worked on the Roman temple went immediately afterward to Nîmes to work on the Maison Carrée.

Vitruvius, whose treatise, *The Ten Books of Architecture*, dedicated to Augustus, became the bible of Renaissance architects, preferred the classicizing architectural style of the Maison Carrée and

**10-30** Maison Carrée, Nîmes, France, ca. 1–10 CE.

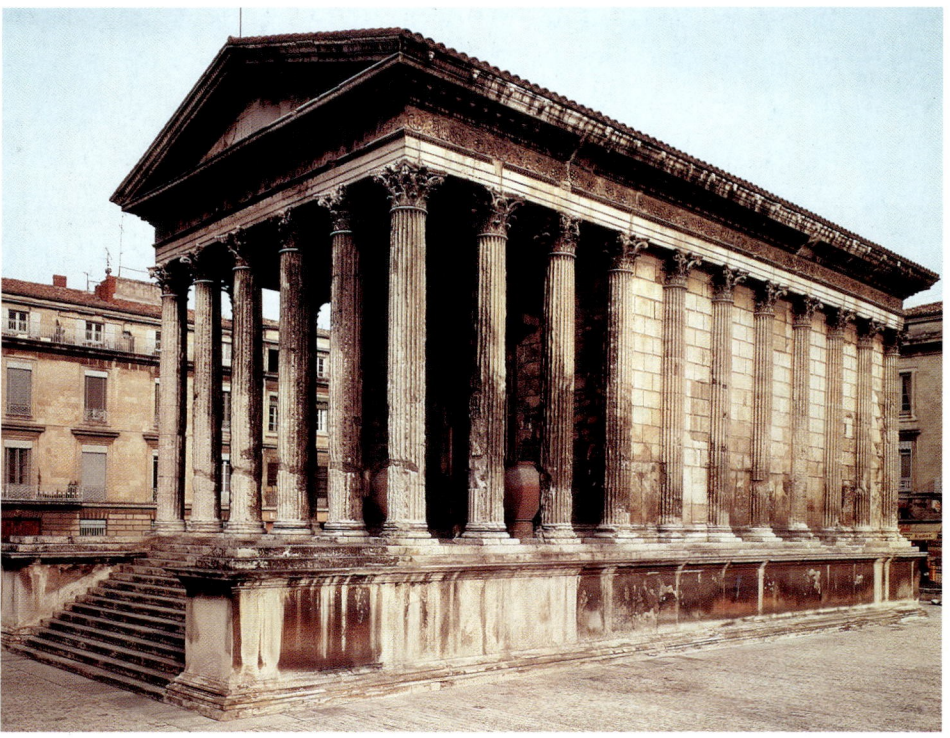

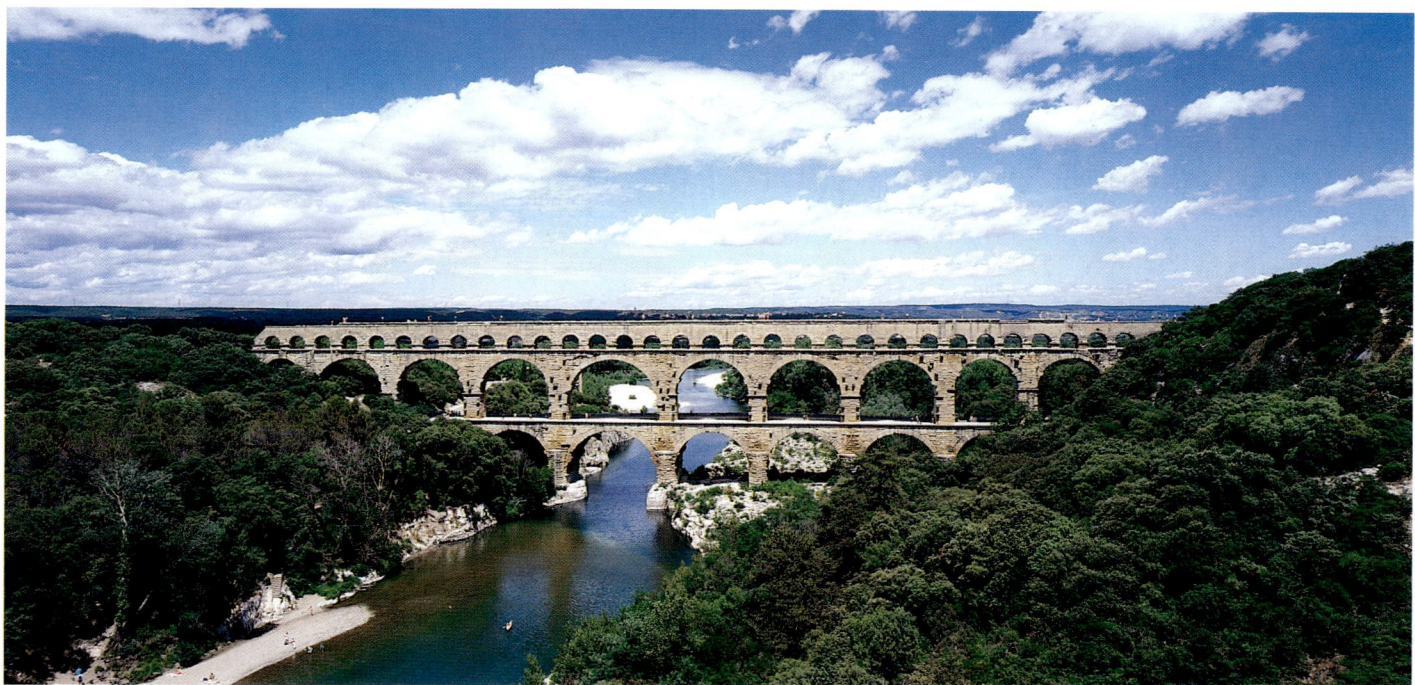

**10-31** Pont-du-Gard, Nîmes, France, ca. 16 BCE.

the Forum of Augustus to the newer Roman vaulted concrete technology. (Another admirer of classical architecture was Thomas Jefferson, U.S. president and architect. He modeled his design for the State Capitol in Richmond, Virginia, on the Nîmes temple.)

An earlier Augustan project at Nîmes was the construction of the great aqueduct-bridge known today as the Pont-du-Gard (FIG. **10-31**). Beginning in the fourth century BCE, the Romans built aqueducts to carry water from mountain sources to their city on the Tiber River. As Rome's power spread through the Mediterranean world, its architects constructed aqueducts, roads, and bridges to serve colonies throughout the far-flung empire. The Pont-du-Gard demonstrates the skill of Rome's engineers. The aqueduct provided about 100 gallons of water a day for each inhabitant of Nîmes from a source some 30 miles away. The water was carried over the considerable distance by gravity flow, which required channels built with a continuous gradual decline over the entire route from source to city. The three-story bridge at Nîmes was erected to maintain the height of the water channel where the water crossed the Gard River. Each large arch spans some 82 feet and is constructed of blocks weighing up to two tons each. The bridge's uppermost level consists of a row of smaller arches, three above each of the large openings below. They carry the water channel itself. Their quickened rhythm and the harmonious proportional relationship between the larger and smaller arches reveal that the Roman engineer had a keen aesthetic, as well as practical, sense.

**CLAUDIAN RUSTICATION** Many aqueducts were required to meet the demand for water in the capital. Under the emperor Claudius (r. 41–54 CE), a grandiose gate, the Porta Maggiore (FIG. **10-32**), was constructed at the point where two of Rome's water lines (and two intercity trunk roads) converged. Its huge *attic* (uppermost story) bears a wordy dedicatory inscription that conceals the conduits of both aqueducts, one above the other. The gate is the outstanding example of the Roman *rusticated* (rough) masonry

style. Instead of using the precisely shaped blocks favored by Greek and Augustan architects, the designer of the Porta Maggiore combined smooth and rusticated surfaces. These created an exciting, if eccentric, facade with crisply carved pediments resting on engaged columns composed of rusticated drums.

**NERO'S GOLDEN HOUSE** In 64 CE, when Nero (r. 54–68 CE), stepson and successor of Claudius, was emperor, a great fire destroyed large sections of Rome. Rebuilding was carried out in accordance with a new code that required greater fireproofing, resulting in the widespread use of concrete, which was both cheap and fire resistant. Increased use of concrete gave Roman architects

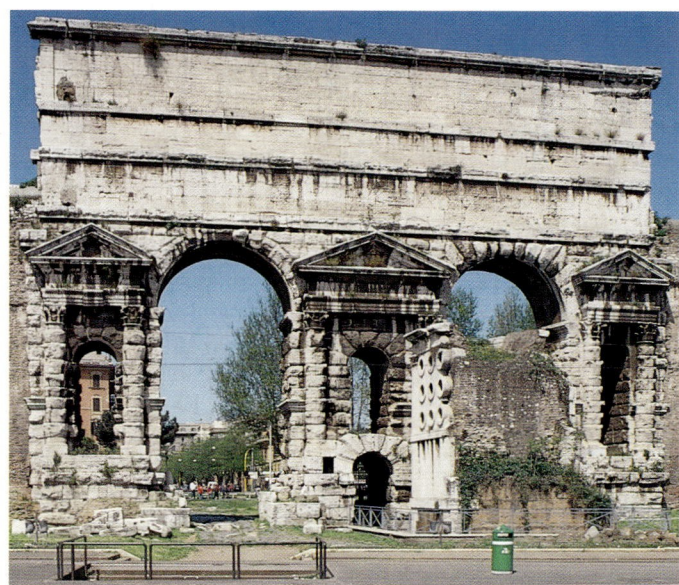

**10-32** Porta Maggiore, Rome, Italy, ca. 50 CE.

### An Imperial Pleasure Palace: The Golden House of Nero

Nero's Domus Aurea, or Golden House, was a vast and notoriously extravagant country villa in the heart of Rome. The second-century CE Roman biographer Suetonius described it vividly:

The entrance-hall was large enough to contain a huge statue [of Nero in the guise of Sol, the sun god; FIG. 10-1, no. 16], 120 feet high; and the pillared arcade ran for a whole mile. An enormous pool, like a sea, was surrounded by buildings made to resemble cities, and by a landscape garden consisting of ploughed fields, vineyards, pastures, and woodlands—where every variety of domestic and wild animal roamed about. Parts of the house were overlaid with gold and studded with precious stones and mother-of-pearl. All the dining-rooms had ceilings of fretted ivory, the panels of which could slide back and let a rain of flowers, or of perfume from hidden sprinklers, shower upon [Nero's] guests. The main

dining-room was circular, and its roof revolved, day and night, in time with the sky. Sea water, or sulphur water, was always on tap in the baths. When the palace had been decorated throughout in this lavish style, Nero dedicated it, and condescended to remark: "Good, now I can at last begin to live like a human being!"[1]

Suetonius's description is a welcome reminder that the Roman ruins tourists flock to see are but a dim reflection of the magnificence of the original structures. Only in rare instances, such as the Pantheon, with its marble-faced walls and floors (FIG. 10-50), can visitors experience anything approaching the architects' intended effects. Even there, much of the marble paneling is of later date, and the gilding is missing from the dome.

[1] Suetonius, *Nero*, 31. Translated by Robert Graves, *Suetonius: The Twelve Caesars* (New York: Penguin, 1957; illustrated edition, 1980), 197–98.

---

the opportunity to explore the possibilities opened up by the still relatively new material.

After the great fire, Nero asked SEVERUS and CELER, two brilliant architect-engineers, to build a grand new palace for him on a huge confiscated plot of fire-ravaged land near the Forum Romanum (see "An Imperial Pleasure Palace: The Golden House of Nero," above). Nero's Domus Aurea has been excavated only in part, but traces of rich decorations, with marble paneling and painted and gilded stucco, have been found in some rooms, while others are adorned with frescoes (FIG. 10-20) in the latest style. Structurally, most of these chambers, although built of concrete, are unremarkable. One octagonal hall (FIG. **10-33**), however, stands apart from the rest and testifies to Severus and Celer's entirely new approach to architectural design.

The ceiling of the octagonal room is a dome that modulates from an eight-sided to a hemispherical form as it rises toward the oculus—the circular opening that admitted light to the room. Radiating outward from the five inner sides (the other three, directly or indirectly, face the outside) are smaller, rectangular rooms, covered by concrete vaults. Decorative recesses enlivened these satellite rooms. The middle one contained a waterfall. The architects ingeniously lit the rooms by leaving spaces between their vaulted ceilings and the central dome's exterior. But the most significant aspect of the design is that here, for the first time, the architects appear to have thought of the walls and vaults not as limiting space but as shaping it.

Today, the octagonal hall is deprived of its stucco decoration and marble *incrustation* (veneer). The concrete shell stands bare, but this serves to focus the visitor's attention on the design's spatial complexity. When one walks through the rooms, one sees that the central domed octagon is defined not by walls but by eight angled piers. The wide square openings between the piers are so large that the rooms beyond look like extensions of the central hall. The grouping of spatial units of different sizes and proportions under a variety of vaults creates a dynamic three-dimensional composition that is both complex and unified. Nero's architects were not

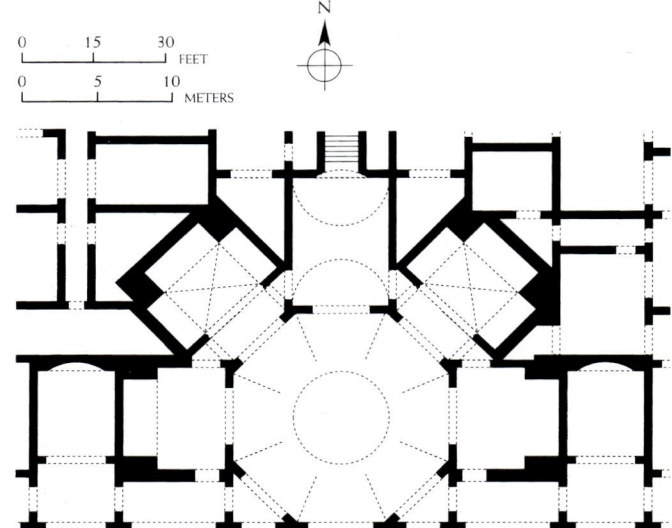

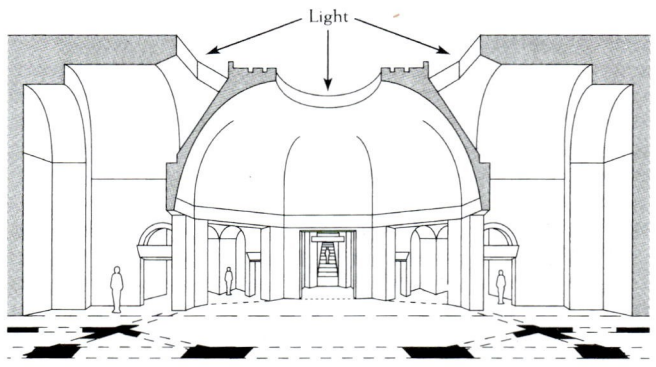

**10-33** SEVERUS and CELER, plan *(above)* and section *(below)* of the octagonal hall of the Domus Aurea (Golden House) of Nero, Rome, Italy, 64–68 CE.

only inventive but also progressive in their recognition of the malleable nature of concrete, a material not limited to the rectilinear forms of traditional post-and-lintel construction.

## The Flavians (69–96 CE)

Because of his outrageous behavior, Nero was forced to commit suicide in 68 CE, bringing the Julio-Claudian dynasty to an end. A year of renewed civil strife followed. The man who emerged triumphant in this brief but bloody conflict was Vespasian (r. 69–79 CE), a general who had served under Claudius and Nero. Vespasian, whose family name was Flavius, had two sons, Titus (r. 79–81 CE) and Domitian (r. 81–96 CE). The Flavian dynasty ruled Rome for more than a quarter century.

COLOSSUS AND COLOSSEUM The Flavians left their mark on the capital in many ways, not the least being the construction of the Colosseum (FIGS. **10-34** and 10-1, no. 17), the monument

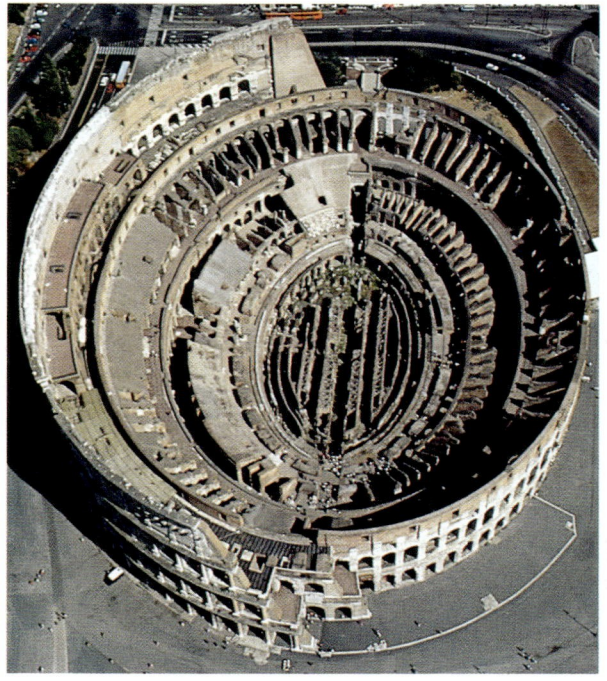

that, for most people, still represents Rome more than any other building. In the past it was identified so closely with Rome and its empire that in the early Middle Ages there was a saying, "While stands the Colosseum, Rome shall stand; when falls the Colosseum, Rome shall fall; and when Rome falls—the World."[4] The Flavian Amphitheater, as it was known in its own day, was one of Vespasian's first undertakings after becoming emperor. The decision to build the Colosseum was very shrewd politically. The site chosen was the artificial lake on the grounds of Nero's Domus Aurea, which was drained for the purpose. By building the new amphitheater there, Vespasian reclaimed for the public the land Nero had confiscated for his private pleasure and provided Romans with the largest arena for gladiatorial combats and other lavish spectacles that had ever been constructed. The Colosseum takes its name, however, not from its size—it could hold more than 50,000 spectators—but from its location beside the Colossus of Nero (FIG. 10-1, no. 16), the huge statue of the emperor portrayed as the sun god, at the entrance to his urban villa.

Vespasian, who died in 79 CE, did not live to see the Colosseum in use. Titus completed and formally dedicated the amphitheater in 80. To mark the opening, games were held for 100 days, at extravagant cost but to the people's delight. The highlight was the flooding of the arena to stage a complete naval battle with more than 3,000 participants. Later emperors would compete to see who could put on the most elaborate spectacles, and over the years many thousands of lives were lost in the gladiatorial and animal combats staged in the amphitheater. Many of those who died were Christians, and the Colosseum has never quite outlived its infamy in this respect.

AN ENGINEERING MARVEL The Colosseum, like the much earlier amphitheater at Pompeii (FIG. 10-11), could not have been built without concrete. A complex system of barrel-vaulted corridors holds up the enormous oval seating area. This concrete "skeleton" reveals itself today to anyone who enters the amphitheater. In the centuries following the fall of Rome, the Colosseum served as a convenient quarry for ready-made building materials. Almost all its marble seats were hauled away, exposing the network of vaults below. Hidden in antiquity but visible today are the arena substructures, which housed waiting rooms for the gladiators, animal cages, and machinery for raising and lowering stage sets as well as animals and humans. Cleverly designed lifting devices brought beasts from their dark dens into the arena's bright light. Above the seats a great velarium, as at Pompeii (FIG. 10-12), once shielded the spectators. Poles affixed to the Colosseum's facade held up the giant awning.

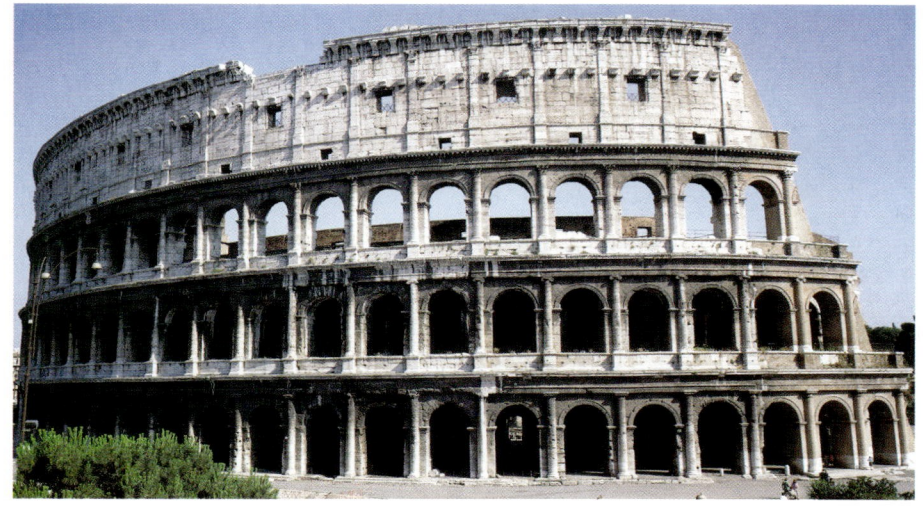

**10-34** Aerial view (*top*) and facade (*bottom*) of the Colosseum (Flavian Amphitheater), Rome, Italy, ca. 70–80 CE.

The exterior travertine shell is approximately 160 feet high, the height of a modern 16-story building. Numbered entrances led to the cavea, where the spectators sat according to their place in the social hierarchy. The relationship of the 76 gateways to the tiers of seats within was carefully thought out and resembles that seen in modern sports stadiums. The decor of the exterior, however, had nothing to do with function. The facade is divided into four bands, with large arched openings piercing the lower three. Ornamental Greek orders frame the arches in the standard Roman sequence for multistoried buildings: from the ground up, Tuscan Doric, Ionic, and then Corinthian. This sequence is based on the proportions of the orders, with the Tuscan viewed as capable of supporting the heaviest load. The uppermost story is circled with Corinthian pilasters (and between them the brackets for the wooden poles that held up the velarium).

The use of engaged columns and a lintel to frame the openings in the Colosseum's facade is a variation of the scheme used on the Etruscan Porta Marzia at Perugia (see FIG. 9-13). The Romans commonly used this scheme from Late Republican times on. Like the pseudoperipteral temple, which is an eclectic mix of Greek orders and Etruscan plan, this way of decorating a building's facade combined Greek orders with an architectural form foreign to Greek post-and-lintel architecture, namely the arch. Revived in the Italian Renaissance, the motif had a long, illustrious history in classical architecture. The Roman practice of framing an arch with an applied Greek order had no structural purpose, but it added variety to the surface. It also unified a multistoried facade by casting a net of verticals and horizontals over it.

**THE REVIVAL OF VERISM** Vespasian was an unpretentious career army officer who desired to distance himself from Nero's extravagant misrule. His portraits (FIG. **10-35**) reflect his much simpler tastes. They also made an important political statement. Breaking with the tradition Augustus established of depicting the Roman emperor as an eternally youthful god on earth, Vespasian's sculptors resuscitated the veristic tradition of the Republic, possibly at his specific direction. Although not as brutally descriptive as many Republican likenesses, Vespasian's portraits frankly recorded his receding hairline and aging, leathery skin—proclaiming his traditional Republican values in contrast to Nero's.

**AN ELEGANT FLAVIAN WOMAN** Portraits of people of all ages survive from the Flavian period, in contrast to the Republic, when only elders were deemed worthy of depiction. A portrait bust of a young woman (FIG. **10-36**), probably a Flavian princess, is a case in point. Its purpose was not to project Republican virtues but rather idealized beauty—through contemporary fashion rather than by reference to images of Greek goddesses. The portrait is notable for its elegance and delicacy and for the virtuoso way the sculptor rendered the differing textures of hair

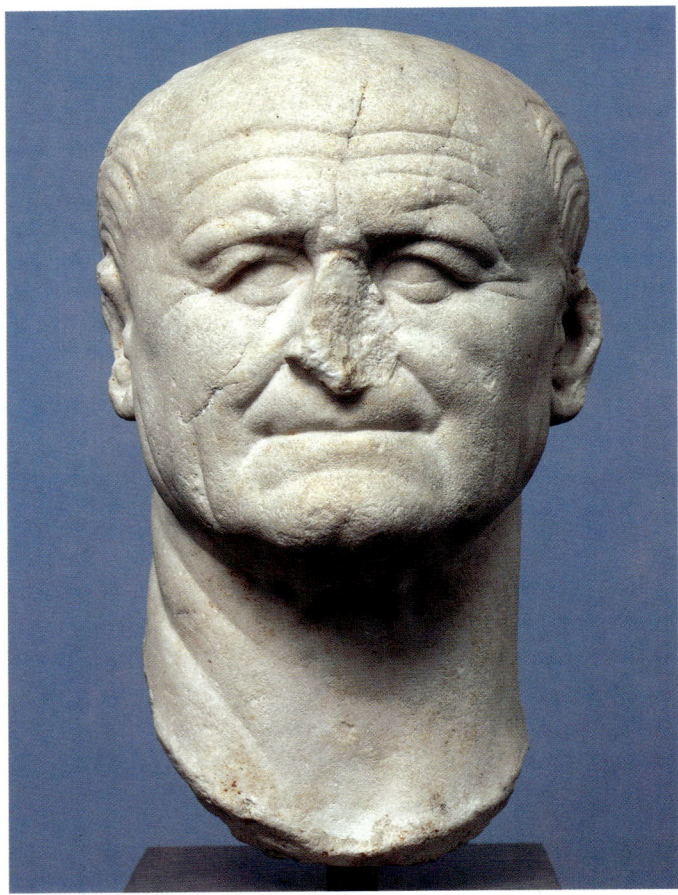

**10-35** Portrait of Vespasian, ca. 75-79 CE. Marble, approx. 1′ 4″ high. Ny Carlsberg Glyptotek, Copenhagen.

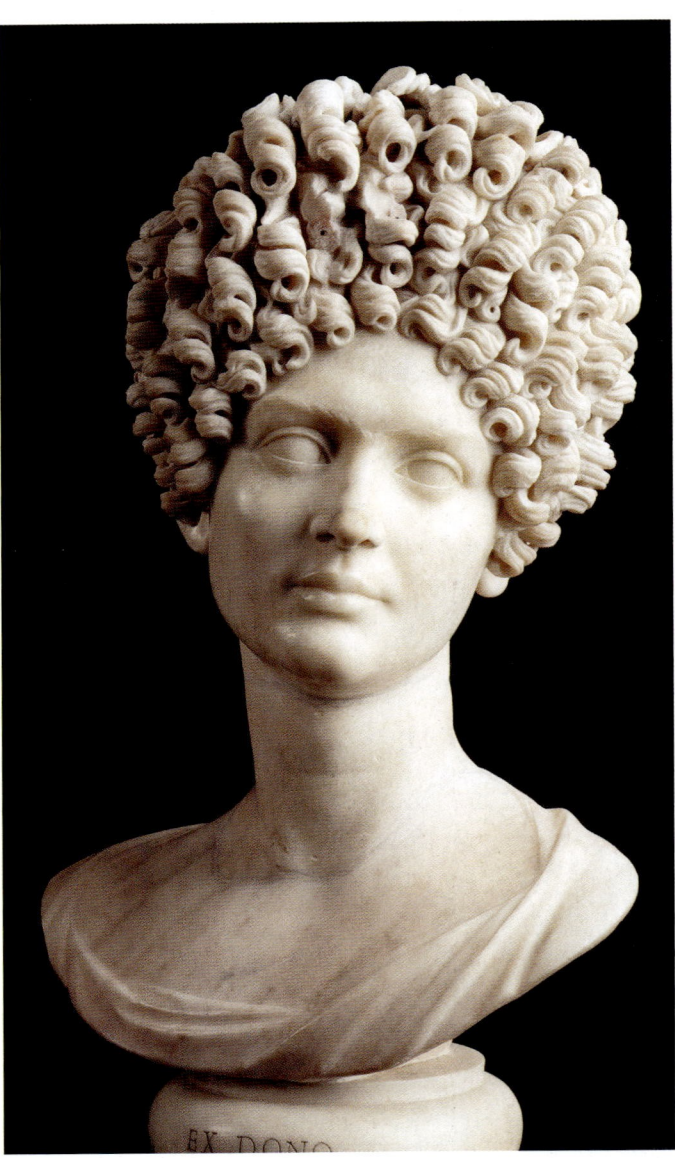

**10-36** Portrait bust of a Flavian woman, from Rome, Italy, ca. 90 CE. Marble, approx. 2′ 1″ high. Museo Capitolino, Rome.

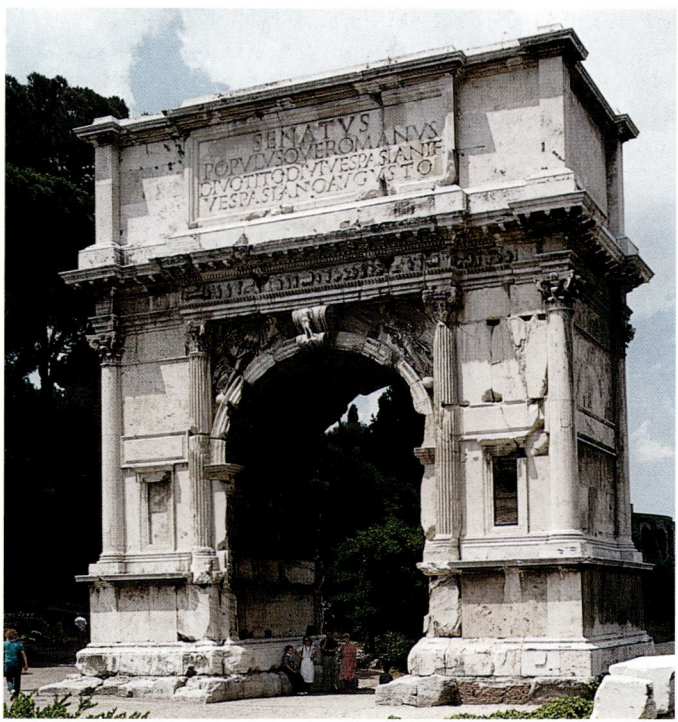

**10-37** Arch of Titus, Rome, Italy, after 81 CE.

and flesh. The elaborate Flavian coiffure, with its corkscrew curls punched out by skilled hands using a drill instead of a chisel, creates a dense mass of light and shadow set off boldly from the softly modeled and highly polished skin of the face and swanlike neck. The drill played an increasing role in Roman sculpture in succeeding periods and in time was used even for portraits of men, when much longer hair and full beards were fashionable.

**A NEW ARCH FOR A NEW GOD** When Titus died in 81 CE, only two years after becoming emperor, his younger brother, Domitian, succeeded him. Domitian erected an arch (FIGS. **10-37** and 10-1, no. 13) in Titus's honor on the Sacred Way leading into the Republican Forum Romanum (FIG. 10-1, no. 11). This type of arch, the so-called *triumphal arch,* has a long history in Roman

art and architecture, beginning in the second century BCE and continuing even into the era of Christian Roman emperors. The term is something of a misnomer, however, because Roman arches celebrated more than just military victories. Such free-standing arches, usually crowned by gilded bronze statues, commemorated a wide variety of events, ranging from victories abroad to the building of roads and bridges at home.

The Arch of Titus is typical of the early triumphal arch and consists of one passageway only. As on the Colosseum, engaged columns frame the arcuated opening, but their capitals are the *Composite* type, an ornate combination of Ionic volutes and Corinthian acanthus leaves that became popular at about the same time as the Fourth Style in Roman painting. Reliefs depicting personified Victories (winged women, as in Greek art) fill the *spandrels* (the area between the arch's curve and the framing columns and entablature). A dedicatory inscription stating that the arch was set up to honor the god Titus, son of the god Vespasian, dominates the attic. Roman emperors normally were proclaimed gods after they died, unless they ran afoul of the Senate and were damned. The statues of those who suffered *damnatio memoriae* were torn down, and their names were erased from public inscriptions. This was Nero's fate.

**THE SPOILS OF JERUSALEM** Inside the passageway of the Arch of Titus are two great relief panels. They represent the triumphal parade of Titus down the Sacred Way after his return from the conquest of Judaea at the end of the Jewish Wars in 70 CE. One of the reliefs (FIG. **10-38**) depicts Roman soldiers carrying the spoils—including the sacred seven-branched candelabrum, the *menorah*—from the Temple in Jerusalem. Despite considerable damage to the relief, the illusion of movement is convincing. The parade moves forward from the left background into the center foreground and disappears through the obliquely placed arch in the right background. The energy and swing of the column of soldiers suggest a rapid march. The sculptor rejected the classicizing low relief of the Ara Pacis (FIG. 10-29) in favor of extremely deep carving, which produces strong shadows. The heads of the forward figures have broken off because they stood free from the block. Their high relief emphasized their different placement in space compared to the heads in low relief, which are intact. The play of light and shade across the protruding foreground and receding background figures enhances the sense of movement.

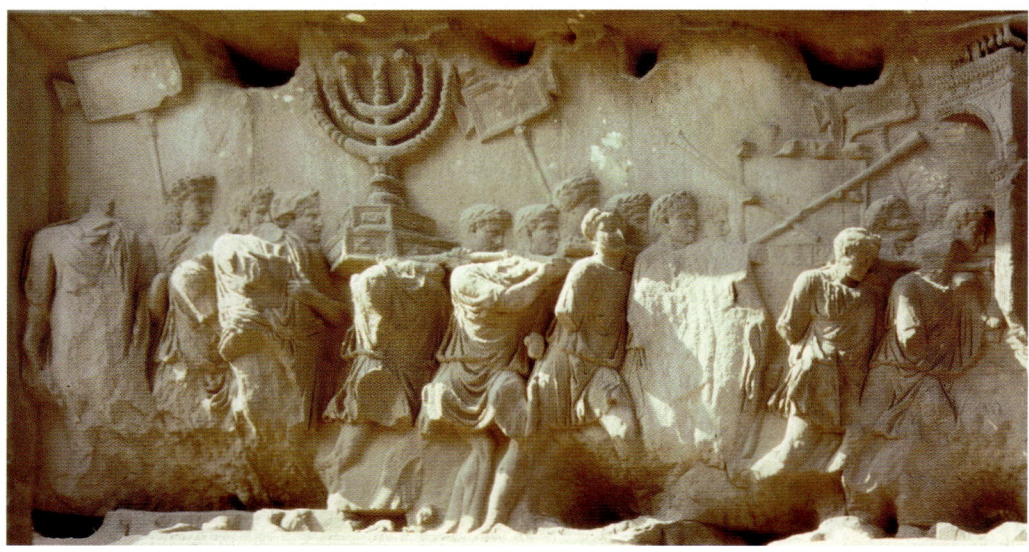

**10-38** Spoils of Jerusalem, relief panel from the Arch of Titus, Rome, Italy, after 81 CE. Marble, approx. 7′ 10″ high.

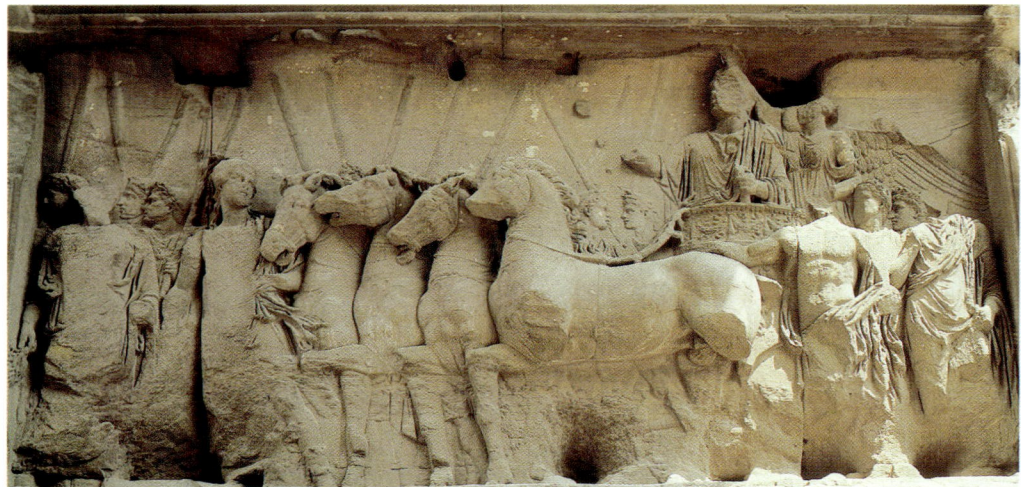

**TITUS IN TRIUMPH** The panel on the other side of the passageway shows Titus in his triumphal chariot (FIG. **10-39**). The seeming historical accuracy of the spoils panel (FIG. 10-38)—it closely corresponds to the contemporary description of Titus's triumph by the Jewish historian Josephus—gave way in this panel to allegory. Victory rides with Titus in the four-horse chariot and places a wreath on his head. Below her is a bare-chested youth who is probably a personification of Honor *(Honos)*. A female personification of Valor *(Virtus)* leads the horses. These allegorical figures transform the relief from a record of Titus's battlefield success into a celebration of imperial virtues. Such an intermingling of divine and human figures occurs on the Republican Villa of the Mysteries frieze at Pompeii (FIG. 10-15), but the Arch of Titus panel is the first known instance of divine beings interacting with humans on an official Roman historical relief. (On the Ara Pacis, FIG. 10-27, Aeneas and "Tellus" appear in separate framed panels and were carefully segregated from the procession of living Romans.) The Arch of Titus was erected after the emperor's death, and its reliefs were carved when Titus was already a god. Soon afterward, however, this kind of interaction between mortals and immortals became a staple of Roman narrative relief sculpture, even on monuments honoring a living emperor.

# HIGH EMPIRE

**THE ROMAN EMPIRE AT ITS PEAK** In the second century CE, under Trajan, Hadrian, and the Antonines, the Roman Empire reached its greatest geographic extent (MAP 10-1) and the height of its power. Rome's might was unchallenged in the Western world, although the Germanic peoples in Europe, the Berbers in Africa, and the Parthians and Persians in the Near East constantly applied pressure. Within the empire's secure boundaries, the Pax Romana meant unprecedented prosperity for all who came under Roman rule.

## *Trajan (98–117 CE)*

**THE FIRST SPANISH EMPEROR** Domitian's extravagant lifestyle and ego resembled Nero's. He demanded to be addressed as *dominus et deus* (lord and god), and so angered the senators that he was assassinated in 96 CE. The Senate chose the elderly Nerva, one of its own, as emperor. Nerva ruled for only 16 months, but before he died he established a pattern of succession by adoption that lasted for almost a century. Nerva picked Trajan, a capable and popular general born in Italica (Spain), as the next emperor. Trajan was the first non-Italian to rule Rome. Under Trajan, imperial armies brought Roman rule to ever more distant areas, and the imperial government took on ever greater responsibility for its people's welfare by instituting a number of far-sighted social programs. Trajan was so popular that he was granted the title *Optimus* (the Best), an epithet he shared with Jupiter (who was said to have instructed Nerva to choose Trajan as his successor). In late antiquity, Augustus, the founder of the Roman Empire, and Trajan became the yardsticks for success. The goal of new emperors was to be *felicior Augusto, melior Traiano* (luckier than Augustus, better than Trajan).

**A NEW COLONY IN AFRICA** In 100 CE, Trajan founded a new colony for army veterans at Timgad, ancient Thamugadi (FIG. **10-40**), in what is today Algeria. Timgad was built along a major road about 100 miles from the sea. Like other colonies, it became the physical embodiment of Roman authority and civilization for the local population and served as a key to the Romanization of the provinces. The town was planned with great precision, its design resembling that of a Roman military encampment or *castrum*. (Scholars still debate which came first. The castrum may have been based on the layout of Roman colonies.) Unlike the sprawling unplanned cities of Rome and Pompeii, Timgad is a square divided into equal quarters by its two main streets, the cardo and the decumanus. They cross at right angles and are bordered by colonnades. Monumental gates in the colony's original walls mark the ends of the two avenues. The forum is located at the point where the streets intersect. The quarters are subdivided into square blocks, and the forum and public buildings, such as the theater and baths, occupy areas sized as multiples of these blocks. The Roman plan is a modification of the Hippodamian plan of Greek cities (see FIG. 5-75), though more rigidly ordered.

The fact that most of these colonial settlements were laid out in the same manner, regardless of whether they were in North Africa, Mesopotamia, or England, expresses concretely the unity and centralized power of the Roman Empire at its height. But even the Romans could not regulate human behavior completely. As the population of Timgad grew sevenfold and burst through

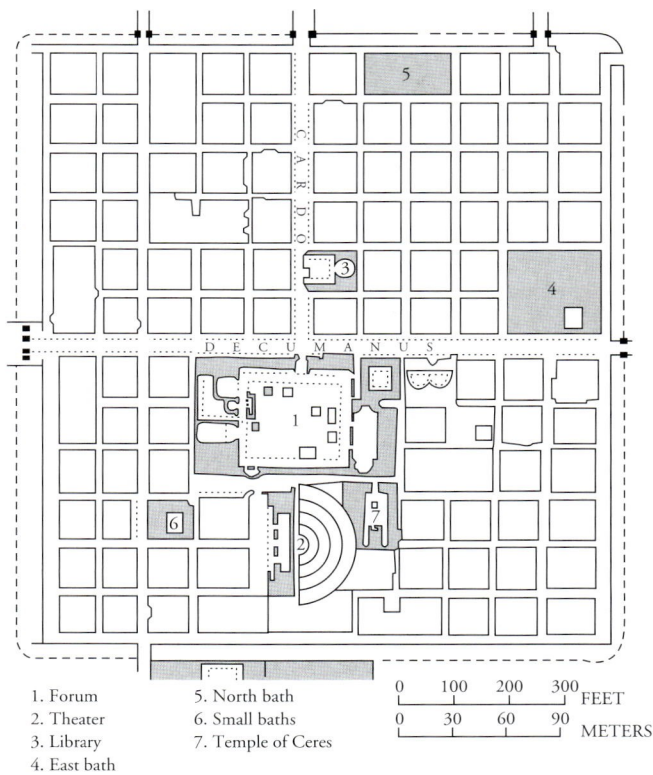

| | |
|---|---|
| 1. Forum | 5. North bath |
| 2. Theater | 6. Small baths |
| 3. Library | 7. Temple of Ceres |
| 4. East bath | |

**10-40** Plan of Timgad (Thamugadi), Algeria, founded 100 CE.

the Trajanic settlement walls, rational planning was ignored, and the city and its streets branched out haphazardly.

**ROME'S GREATEST FORUM** Trajan's major building project in Rome was a huge new forum (FIGS. **10-41** and 10-1, no. 7), roughly twice the size of the forum Augustus built (FIG. 10-1, no. 10) a century before—even if the enormous market complex next to the forum is excluded. The new forum glorified Trajan's victories in his two wars against the Dacians (who lived in what is now Romania) and was paid for with the spoils of those campaigns. The architect was APOLLODORUS OF DAMASCUS, Trajan's chief military engineer during the Dacian wars, who had constructed a world-famous bridge across the Danube River. Apollodorus's plan incorporated the main features of most early forums (FIG. 10-10), except that a huge basilica, not a temple, dominated the colonnaded open square. The temple (completed after the emperor's death and dedicated to the newest god in the Roman pantheon, Trajan himself) was set instead behind the basilica. It stood at the rear end of the forum in its own courtyard, with two libraries and a giant commemorative column, the Column of Trajan (FIGS. 10-41, no. 2, and 10-42).

One entered Trajan's forum through an impressive gateway resembling a triumphal arch. Inside the forum were other reminders of Trajan's military prowess. A larger-than-life-size gilded-bronze equestrian statue of the emperor stood at the center of the great court in front of the basilica. Statues of captive Dacians stood above the columns of the forum porticos.

The Basilica Ulpia (Trajan's family name was Ulpius) was a much larger and far more ornate version of the basilica in the

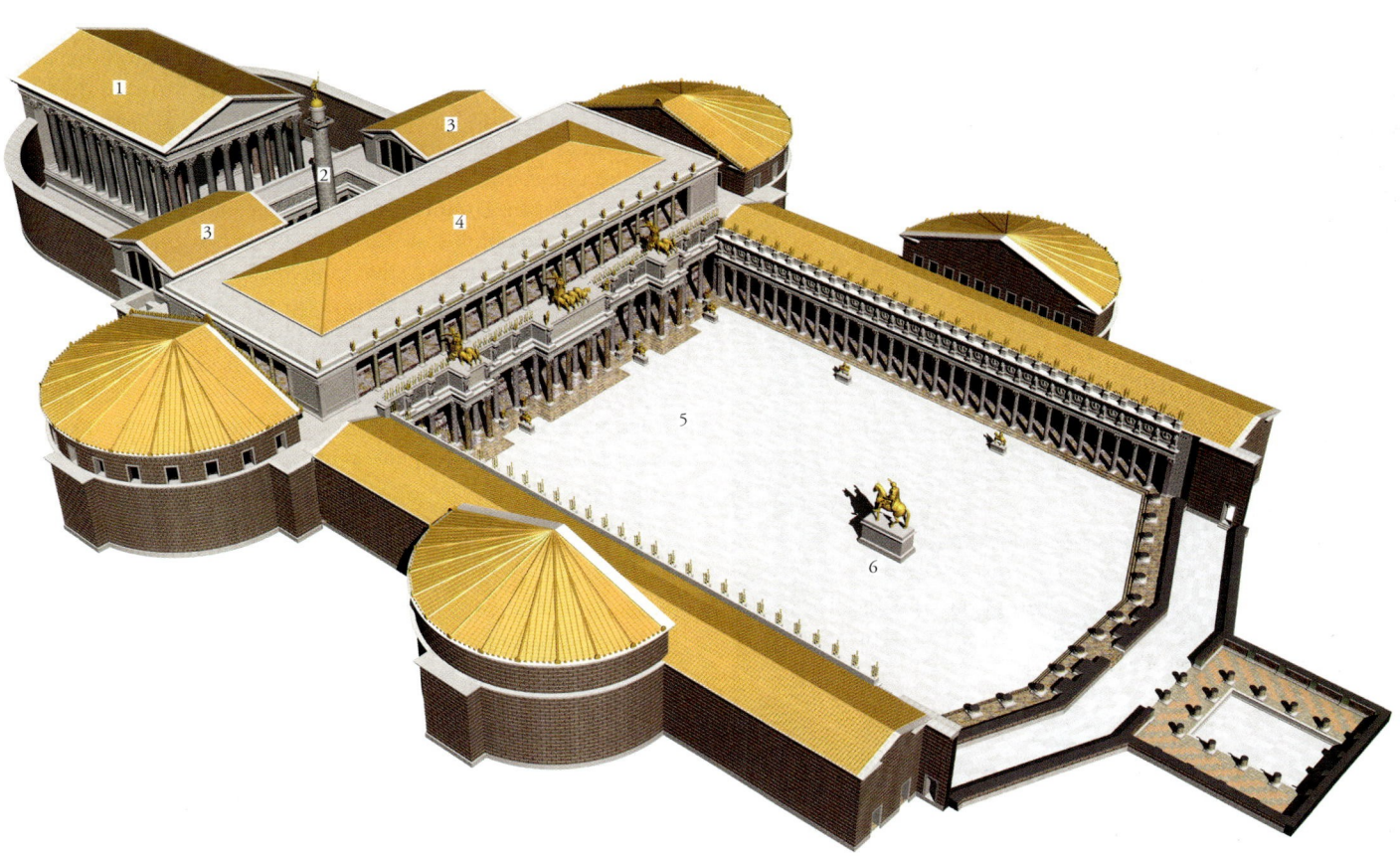

**10-41** APOLLODORUS OF DAMASCUS, Forum of Trajan, Rome, Italy, dedicated 112 CE. Reconstruction by James E. Packer and John Burge. 1) Temple of Trajan, 2) Column of Trajan, 3) Libraries, 4) Basilica Ulpia, 5) Forum, 6) Equestrian statue of Trajan.

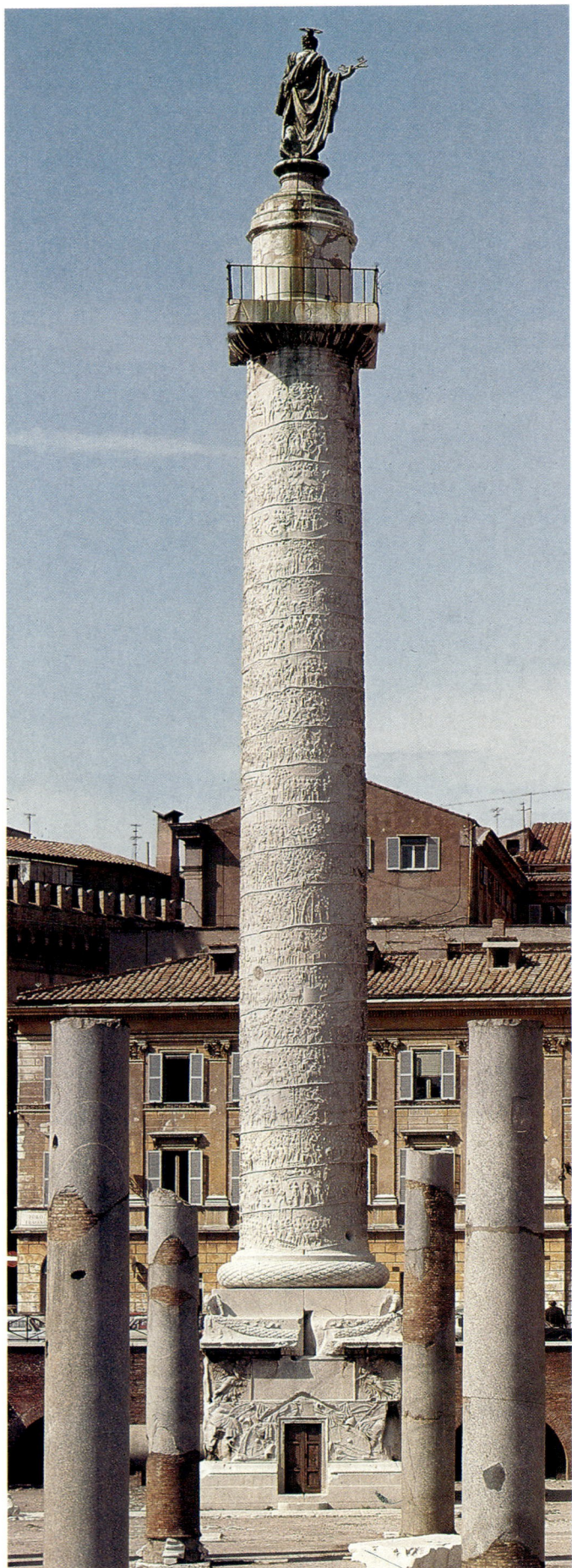

**10-42** Column of Trajan, Forum of Trajan, Rome, Italy, dedicated 112 CE.

forum of Pompeii (FIG. 10-10, no. 3). As shown in FIG. 10-41, no. 4, it had *apses*, or semicircular recesses, on each short end. Two aisles flanked the nave on each side. In contrast to the Pompeian basilica and later Christian churches, the entrances were on the long side facing the forum. The building was vast: about 400 feet long (without the apses) and 200 feet wide. Light entered through clerestory windows, made possible by elevating the timber-roofed nave above the colonnaded aisles. In the Republican basilica at Pompeii, light reached the nave only indirectly through aisle windows. The clerestory (used millennia before at Karnak in Egypt, see FIGS. 3-25 and 3-26) was a much better solution. Early Christian architects embraced this feature of the Basilica Ulpia for the design of the first churches (see FIGS. 11-8 and 11-16).

**TRAJAN'S COLUMNAR TOMB** The Column of Trajan (FIG. 10-42) was probably also the brainchild of Apollodorus of Damascus. The idea of covering the shaft of a colossal freestanding column with a continuous spiral narrative frieze seems to have been invented here, but it was often copied. As late as the 19th century, a column inspired by the Column of Trajan was erected in the Place Vendôme in Paris in commemoration of the victories of Napoleon. The type even appeared in Christian settings with reliefs illustrating the life of Christ (see FIG. 16-25).

Trajan's Column is 128 feet high. Coins indicate that it was once topped by a heroically nude statue of the emperor. Trajan's portrait was lost in the Middle Ages, and in the 16th century a statue of Saint Peter replaced it. The square base, decorated with captured Dacian arms and armor, served as Trajan's tomb. His ashes and those of his wife, Plotina, were placed inside it in golden urns.

The 625-foot band that winds around the column has been likened to an illustrated scroll of the type housed in the neighboring libraries (and that Lars Pulena holds on his sarcophagus, see FIG. 9-14). The reliefs depict Trajan's two successful campaigns against the Dacians. The story is told in more than 150 episodes in which some 2,500 figures appear. The band increases in width as it winds to the top of the column, so that it is easier to see the upper portions. Throughout, the relief is very low so as not to distort the contours of the shaft. Legibility was enhanced in antiquity by paint, but it still would have been very difficult for anyone to follow the narrative from beginning to end.

Much of the spiral frieze is given over to easily recognizable compositions like those found on coin reverses and on historical relief panels: Trajan addressing his troops, sacrificing to the gods, and so on. The narrative is not a reliable chronological account of the Dacian Wars, as was once thought. The sculptors nonetheless accurately recorded the general character of the campaigns. Notably, battle scenes take up only about a quarter of the frieze. As is true of modern military operations, the Romans spent more time constructing forts, transporting men and equipment, and preparing for battle than fighting. The focus is always on the emperor, who appears again and again in the frieze, but the enemy is not belittled. The Romans won because of their superior organization and more powerful army, not because they were inherently superior beings.

**SHOPPING IN IMPERIAL ROME** On the Quirinal Hill overlooking the forum, Apollodorus built the Markets of Trajan (FIGS. 10-43 and 10-1, no. 8) to house both shops and administrative offices. As earlier at Palestrina (FIG. 10-4), the transformation of a natural slope into a multilevel complex was possible here only by using concrete. Trajan's architect was a master of this modern

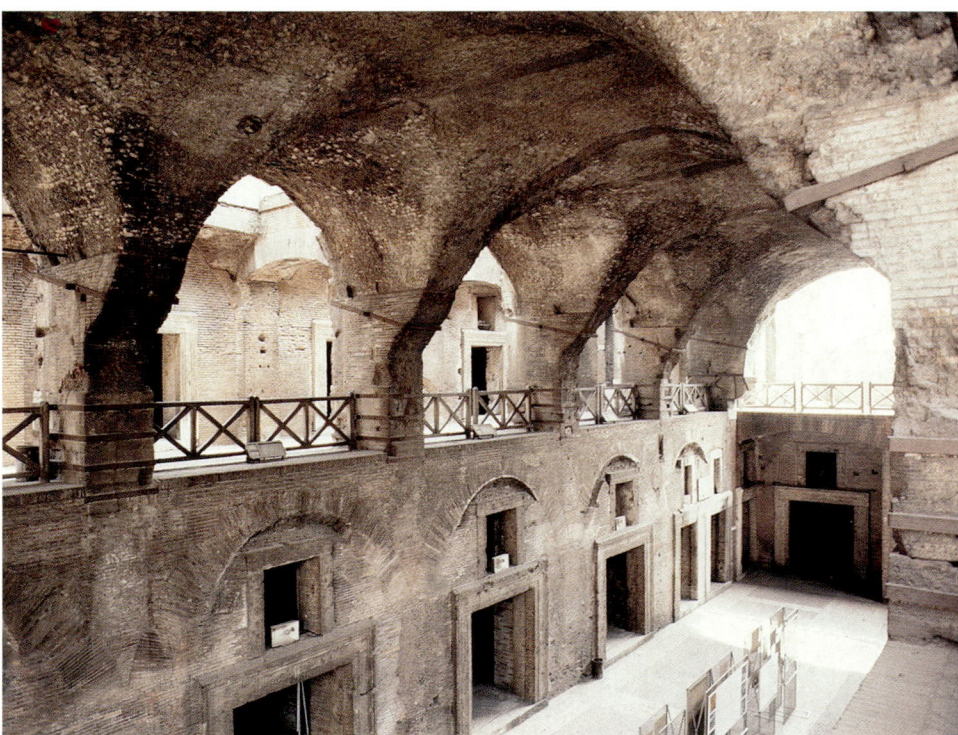

**10-43** Apollodorus of Damascus, aerial view of Markets of Trajan, Rome, Italy, ca. 100–112 CE.

medium as well as of the traditional stone-and-timber post-and-lintel architecture of the forum below.

The basic unit was the *taberna,* a single-room shop covered by a barrel vault. Each taberna had a wide doorway, usually with a window above it that allowed light to enter a wooden inner attic used for storage. The shops were on several levels. They opened either onto a hemispherical facade winding around one of the great exedras of Trajan's forum, onto a paved street farther up the hill, or onto a great indoor market hall (FIG. **10-44**) resembling a modern shopping mall. The hall housed two floors of shops, with

**10-44** Apollodorus of Damascus, interior of the great hall, Markets of Trajan, Rome, Italy, ca. 100–112 CE.

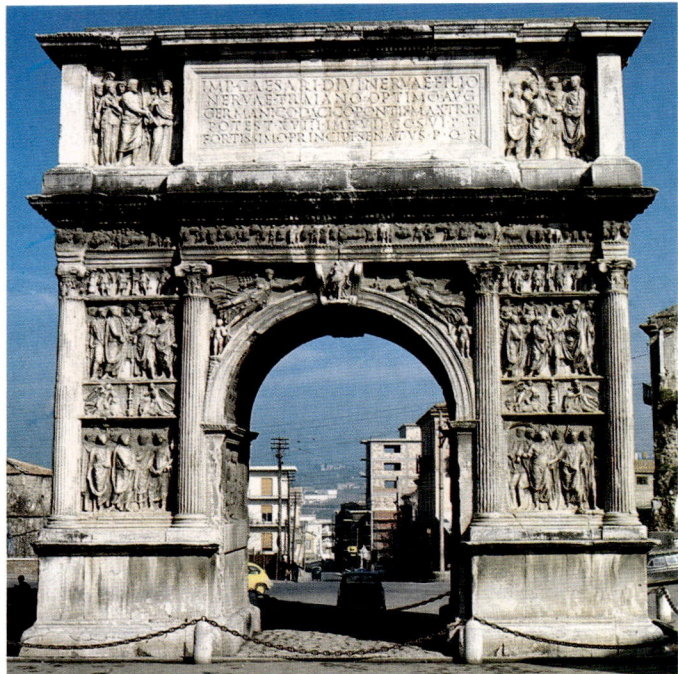

**10-45** Arch of Trajan, Benevento, Italy, ca. 114–118 CE.

founder of colonies for army veterans and as the builder of a new port at Ostia, Rome's harbor at the mouth of the Tiber. The reliefs present Trajan as the guarantor of peace and security in the Empire, the benefactor of the poor, and the patron of soldiers and merchants alike. In short, the emperor was "all things to all people."

In several of the panels, Trajan freely intermingles with divinities, and on the arch's attic (which may have been completed after his death and deification) Jupiter hands his thunderbolt to the emperor, awarding him dominion over the earth. Such scenes, depicting the "first citizen" of Rome as a divinely sanctioned ruler in the company of the gods, henceforth became the norm, not the exception, in official Roman art.

**RACING IN THE CIRCUS MAXIMUS** One of Trajan's other benefactions to the Roman people was the restoration of the Circus Maximus (FIG. 10-1, no. 2), where the world's best horse teams competed in chariot races. A relief (FIG. **10-46**) that once decorated a circus official's tomb gives a partial view of the refurbished racecourse. The relief is not a product of one of the emperor's official sculptural workshops. It illustrates once again how different the art produced for Rome's huge working class was from the art commissioned by the state and old aristocratic families.

The relief shows the Circus Maximus in distorted perspective. Only one team of horses races around the central island, but the charioteer is shown twice, once driving the horses and a second time holding the palm branch of victory. Art historians refer to such representations as *continuous narration;* that is, the same figure appears more than once in the same space at different stages of a story. This is not the first instance of continuous narration, but few earlier examples exist, and only much later did this way of telling a story in pictures become common. (The emperor's appearance in different settings in the Column of Trajan's frieze is not an example of continuous narration.)

In fact, the charioteer may appear a third time within the same relief, for he may be, later in life, the toga-clad official who appears at the panel's left end. There the recently deceased official clasps hands with his wife. (The handshake between man and woman is a symbol of marriage in Roman art.) She is of smaller stature—and less important than her husband in this context, for it is *his* career in the circus commemorated on *his* tomb—and

the upper shops set back on each side and lit by skylights. Light from the same sources reached the ground-floor shops through arches beneath the great umbrella-like groin vaults covering the hall (see "The Roman Architectural Revolution," page 250).

**TRIUMPHAL ARCH BILLBOARDS** In 109 CE, Trajan opened a new road, the Via Traiana, in southern Italy. Several years later a great arch (FIG. **10-45**) honoring Trajan was built at the point where the road entered Benevento (ancient Beneventum). Architecturally, the Arch of Trajan at Benevento is almost identical to Titus's arch (FIG. 10-37) on the Sacred Way in Rome, but relief panels cover both facades of the Trajanic arch, giving it a billboardlike function. Every inch of the surface was used to advertise the emperor's achievements. In one panel, he enters Rome after a successful military campaign. In another, he distributes largess to needy children. In still others, he was portrayed as the

**10-46** Funerary relief of a circus official, from Ostia, Italy, ca. 110–130 CE. Marble, approx. 1′ 8″ high. Vatican Museums, Rome.

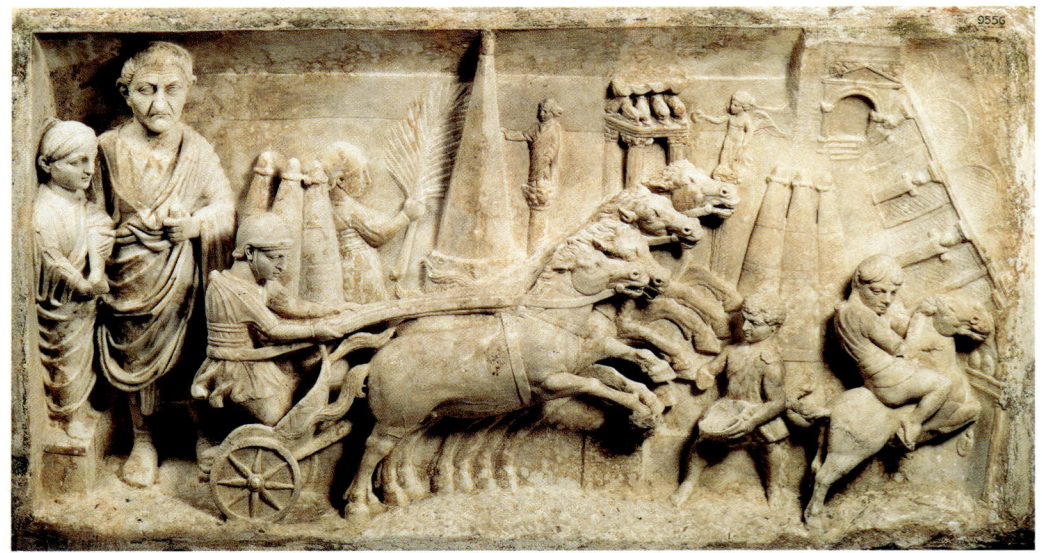

she is shown standing on a base. The base indicates that she is not a living person but a statue. The handshake between man and statue is the plebeian artist's shorthand way of saying the wife died before the husband, that her death had not broken their marriage bond, and that, because the husband has now died, the two will be reunited in the afterlife. The rules of classical design, which still guided the artists employed by the Roman state, were ignored here, as in the funerary relief from Amiternum (FIG. 10-6), also made for a non-elite patron. Later in the century, however, some of these nonclassical elements appeared in official art as well.

## *Hadrian (117–138 CE)*

**HADRIAN AND GREECE** Hadrian, Trajan's chosen successor and fellow Spaniard, was a connoisseur and lover of all the arts, as well as an author and architect. He greatly admired Greek culture and traveled widely as emperor, often in the Greek East. Everywhere he went, statues and arches were set up in his honor. More portraits of Hadrian exist today than of any other emperor except Augustus. Hadrian, who was 41 years old at the time of Trajan's death and who ruled for more than two decades, is always depicted in his portraits as a mature adult who never ages.

A rare bronze portrait of Hadrian is the fragmentary statue (FIG. **10-47**) of the emperor wearing a cuirass found at Tel Shalem, Israel, several miles south of the ancient city of Scythopolis. The portrait probably was erected toward the end of Hadrian's lifetime, when Rome put down a second Jewish revolt and Judaea was reorganized as a new province called Syria Palaestina. Hadrian's portraits more closely resemble Kresilas's portrait of Pericles (see FIG. 5-39) than those of any Roman emperor before him, and no one doubts that Classical Greek statuary inspired his likenesses. Fifth-century BCE statues also provided the prototypes for the idealizing official portraits of Augustus, but the Augustan models were Greek images of young athletes. The models for Hadrian's artists were statues of mature Greek men. Hadrian himself wore a beard—a habit that, in its Roman context, must be viewed as a Greek affectation. Beards then became the norm for all subsequent Roman emperors for more than a century and a half.

**THE TEMPLE OF ALL GODS** Soon after Hadrian became emperor, work began on the Pantheon (FIGS. **10-48** and 10-1, no. 5), the temple of all the gods, one of the best-preserved buildings of antiquity. It also has been one of the most influential designs in architectural history. The Pantheon reveals the full potential of concrete, both as a building material and as a means for shaping architectural space. The temple originally was approached from a columnar courtyard and, like temples in Roman forums, stood at one narrow end of the enclosure. Its facade of eight Corinthian columns—almost all that could be seen from ground level in antiquity—was a bow to tradition. Everything else about the Pantheon was revolutionary. Behind the columnar porch is an immense concrete cylinder covered by a huge hemispherical dome 142 feet in diameter. The dome's top is also 142 feet from the floor (FIG. **10-49**). The design is thus based on the intersection of two circles (one horizontal, the other vertical) so that the interior space can be imagined as the orb of the earth and the dome as the vault of the heavens.

**10-47** Portrait bust of Hadrian as general, from Tel Shalem, Israel, ca. 130–138 CE. Bronze, approx. 2′ 11″ high. Israel Museum, Jerusalem.

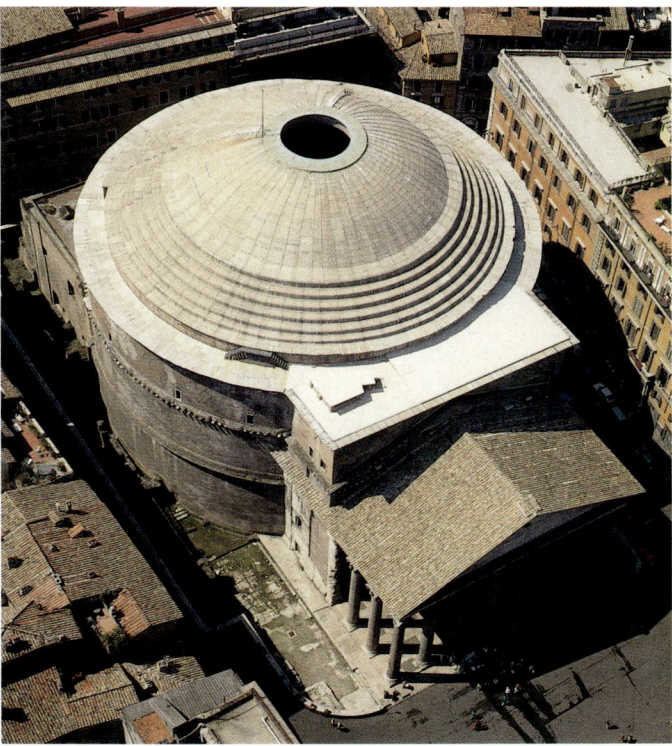

**10-48** Aerial view of the Pantheon, Rome, Italy, 118–125 CE.

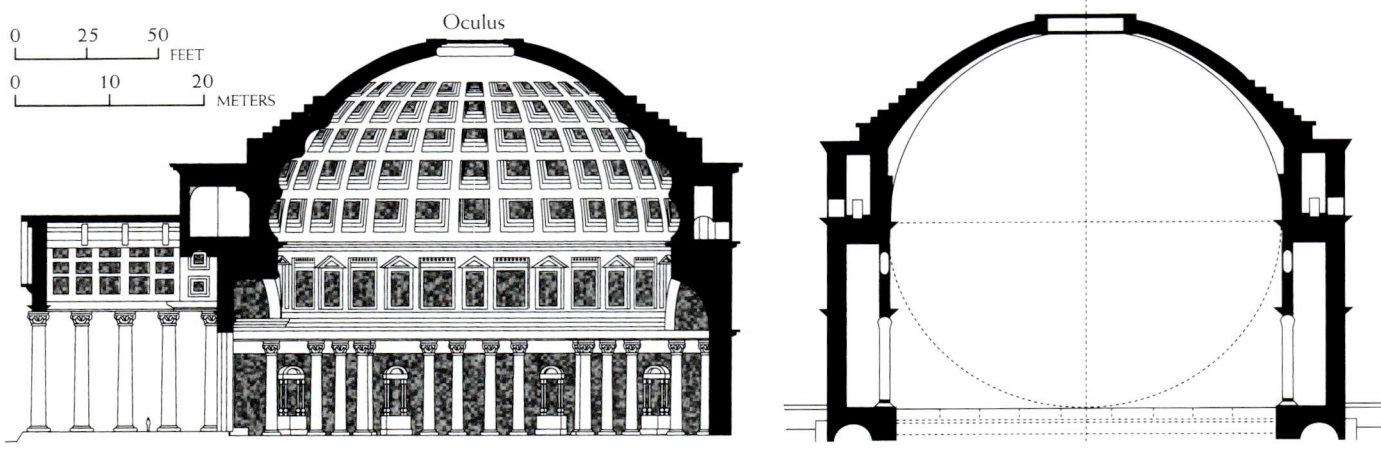

10-49 Longitudinal and lateral sections of the Pantheon, Rome, Italy, 118–125 CE.

If the Pantheon's design is simplicity itself, executing that design took all the ingenuity of Hadrian's engineers. The cylindrical drum was built up level by level using concrete of varied composition. Extremely hard and durable basalt was employed in the mix for the foundations, and the "recipe" was gradually modified until, at the top, featherweight pumice replaced stones to lighten the load. The dome's thickness also decreases as it nears the oculus, the

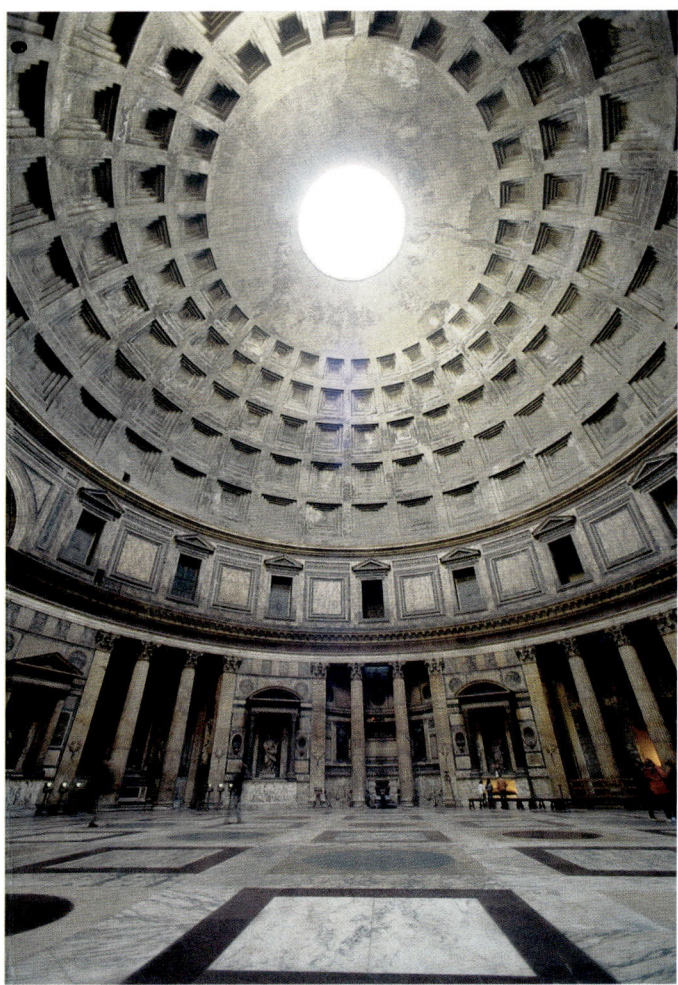

10-50 Interior of the Pantheon, Rome, Italy, 118–125 CE.

circular opening 30 feet in diameter that is the only light source for the interior (FIG. 10-50). The dome's weight was lessened, without weakening its structure, through the use of *coffers* (sunken decorative panels). These further reduced the dome's mass and also provided a handsome pattern of squares within the vast circle. Renaissance drawings suggest that each coffer once had a glistening gilded-bronze rosette at its center, enhancing the symbolism of the dome as the starry heavens.

Below the dome, much of the original marble veneer of the walls, niches, and floor has survived (FIG. 10-50). In the Pantheon, visitors can get a sense, as almost nowhere else, of how magnificent the interiors of Roman concrete buildings could be. But despite the luxurious skin of the Pantheon's interior, on first entering the structure one senses not the weight of the enclosing walls but the space they enclose. In pre-Roman architecture, the form of the enclosed space was determined by the placement of the solids, which did not so much shape space as interrupt it. Roman architects were the first to conceive of architecture in terms of units of space that could be shaped by the enclosures. The Pantheon's interior is a single unified, self-sufficient whole, uninterrupted by supporting solids. It encloses visitors without imprisoning them, opening through the oculus to the drifting clouds, the blue sky, the sun, and the gods. In this space, the architect used light not just to illuminate the darkness but to create drama and underscore the symbolism of the interior shape. On a sunny day, the light that passes through the oculus forms a circular beam, a disk of light that moves across the coffered dome in the course of the day as the sun moves across the sky itself. Escaping from the noise and torrid heat of a Roman summer day into the Pantheon's cool, calm, and mystical immensity is an experience almost impossible to describe and one that should not be missed.

HADRIAN'S COUNTRY RETREAT Although some have suggested that Hadrian himself was the architect of the Pantheon, the amateur builder does not deserve credit for the design. Hadrian was, however, deeply involved with the construction of his own country villa at Tivoli, where building activity seems never to have ceased until the emperor's death.

One of his projects was the construction of a pool and an artificial grotto, called the Canopus and Serapeum (FIG. 10-51), respectively. Canopus was an Egyptian city connected to Alexandria by a canal. Its most famous temple was dedicated to the god

## Hadrian: Emperor and Architect

Dio Cassius, a third-century CE senator who wrote a history of Rome from its foundation to his own day, recounted a revealing anecdote about Hadrian and Apollodorus of Damascus, architect of the Forum of Trajan (FIG. 10-41):

> Hadrian first drove into exile and then put to death the architect Apollodorus who had carried out several of Trajan's building projects.... When Trajan was at one time consulting with Apollodorus about a certain problem connected with his buildings, the architect said to Hadrian, who had interrupted them with some advice, "Go away and draw your pumpkins. You know nothing about these problems." For it so happened that Hadrian was at that time priding himself on some sort of drawing. When he became emperor he remembered this insult and refused to put up with Apollodorus's outspokenness. He sent him [his own] plan for the temple of Venus and Roma [FIG. 10-1, no. 14], in order to demonstrate that it was possible for a great work to be conceived without his [Apollodorus's] help, and asked him if he thought the building was well designed. Apollodorus sent a [very critical] reply. . . . [The emperor did not] attempt to restrain his anger or hide his pain; on the contrary, he had the man slain.[1]

The story says a great deal both about the absolute power Roman emperors wielded and about how seriously Hadrian took his architectural designs. But perhaps the most interesting detail is the description of Hadrian's drawings of "pumpkins." These must have been drawings of concrete domes like the one in the Serapeum (FIG. 10-51) at Hadrian's Tivoli villa. Such vaults were too adventurous for Apollodorus, or at least for a public building in Trajanic Rome, and Hadrian had to try them out later at home at his own expense.

[1] Dio Cassius, *Roman History*, 69.4.1–5. Translated by J. J. Pollitt, *The Art of Rome, c. 753 B.C.–A.D. 337: Sources and Documents* (New York: Cambridge University Press, 1983), 175–76.

---

Serapis. Nothing about the Tivoli design, however, derives from Egyptian architecture. The grotto at the end of the pool is made of concrete and has an unusual pumpkin-shaped dome that Hadrian probably designed himself (see "Hadrian: Emperor and Architect," above). Yet, in keeping with the persistent eclecticism of Roman art and architecture, Greek columns and marble copies of famous Greek statues lined the pool, as one would expect from a lover of Greek art. The Corinthian colonnade at the curved end of the pool is, however, of a type unknown in Classical Greek architecture. The colonnade not only lacks a superstructure but has arcuated (curved or arched) lintels, as opposed to traditional Greek horizontal lintels, between alternating pairs of columns. This simultaneous respect for Greek architecture and willingness to break Greek design rules typifies much Roman architecture of the High and Late Empire.

**A BAROQUE TOMB IN A MOUNTAIN** An even more extreme example of what many have called Roman "baroque" architecture (because of the striking parallels with 17th-century Italian buildings) is the second-century CE tomb nicknamed

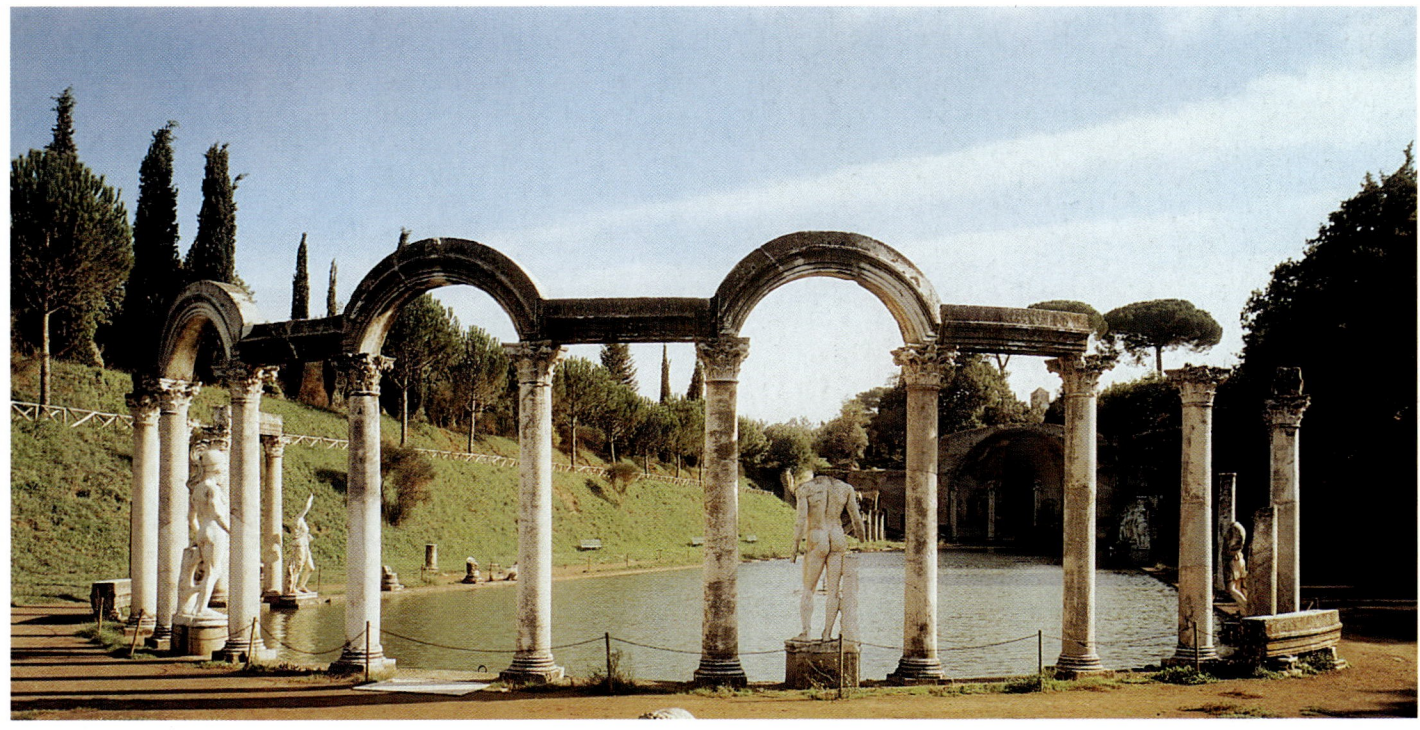

10-51 Canopus and Serapeum, Hadrian's Villa, Tivoli, Italy, ca. 125–128 CE.

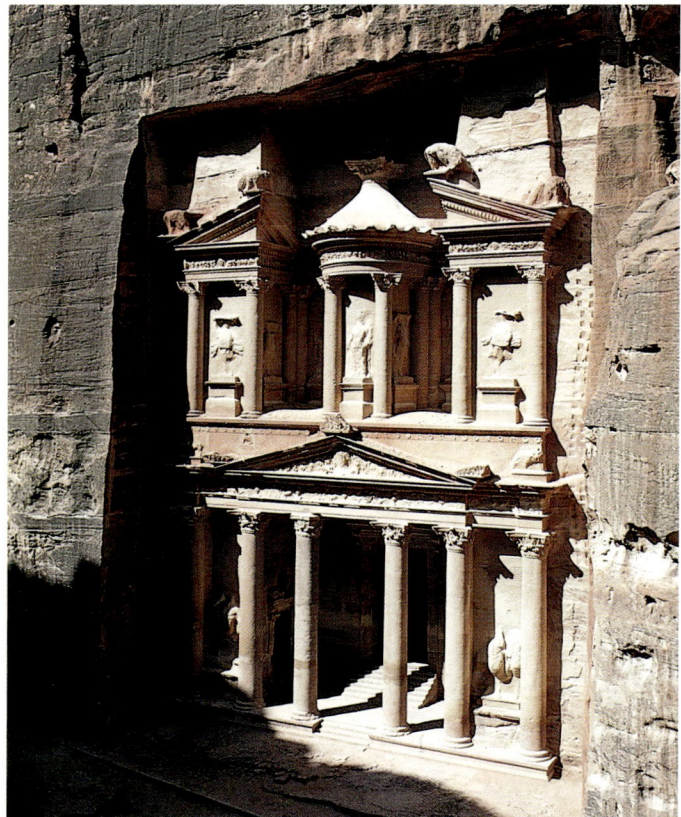

**10-52** Al-Khazneh ("Treasury"), Petra, Jordan, second century CE.

Al-Khazneh, the "Treasury" (FIG. **10-52**), at Petra, Jordan. It is one of the most elaborate of many tomb facades cut into the sheer rock faces of the local rose-colored mountains. As at Hadrian's villa, classical architectural elements are used here in a purely ornamental fashion and with a studied disregard for classical rules.

The Treasury's facade is more than 130 feet high and consists of two stories. The lower story resembles a temple facade with six columns, but the columns are unevenly spaced and the pediment is only wide enough to cover the four central columns. On the upper level, a temple-within-a-temple is set on top of the lower temple. Here the facade and roof split in half to make room for a central tholoslike cylinder, which contrasts sharply with the rectangles and triangles of the rest of the design. On both levels,

the rhythmic alternation of deep projection and indentation creates dynamic patterns of light and shade. At Petra, as at Tivoli, the vocabulary of Greek architecture was maintained, but the syntax is new and distinctively Roman. In fact, the design recalls some of the architectural fantasies painted on the walls of Roman houses—for example, the tholos seen through columns surmounted by a broken pediment (FIG. 10-16, detail) in the Second Style cubiculum from Boscoreale.

## Ostia

**THE CROWDED LIFE OF THE CITY**  The average Roman, of course, did not own a luxurious country villa and was not buried in a grand tomb. About 90 percent of Rome's population of close to one million lived in multistory apartment blocks (*insulae*). After the great fire of 64 CE, these were built of brick-faced concrete. The rents were not cheap, as the law of supply and demand in real estate was just as valid in antiquity as it is today. Juvenal, a Roman satirist of the early second century CE, commented that people willing to give up chariot races and the other diversions Rome had to offer could purchase a fine home in the countryside "for a year's rent in a dark hovel" in a city so noisy that "the sick die mostly from lack of sleep."[5]

Conditions were much the same for the inhabitants of Ostia, Rome's harbor city. After its new port opened under Trajan, Ostia's prosperity increased dramatically and so did its population. A burst of building activity began under Trajan and continued under Hadrian and throughout the second century CE. Many multistory second-century insulae (FIG. **10-53**) have been preserved at Ostia. Shops occupied the ground floors. Above were up to four floors of apartments. Although many of the insula apartments were large, they had neither the space nor the light of the typical Pompeian private domus (see "The Roman House," page 257). In place of peristyles, the insulae of Ostia and Rome had only narrow light wells or small courtyards. Consequently, instead of looking inward, large numbers of glass windows faced the city's noisy streets. Only deluxe apartments had private toilets. Others shared latrines, often on a different floor from the apartment. Still, these insulae were quite similar to modern apartment houses, which also sometimes have shops on the ground floor.

Another strikingly modern feature of these multifamily residences is their brick facades, which were not concealed by stucco

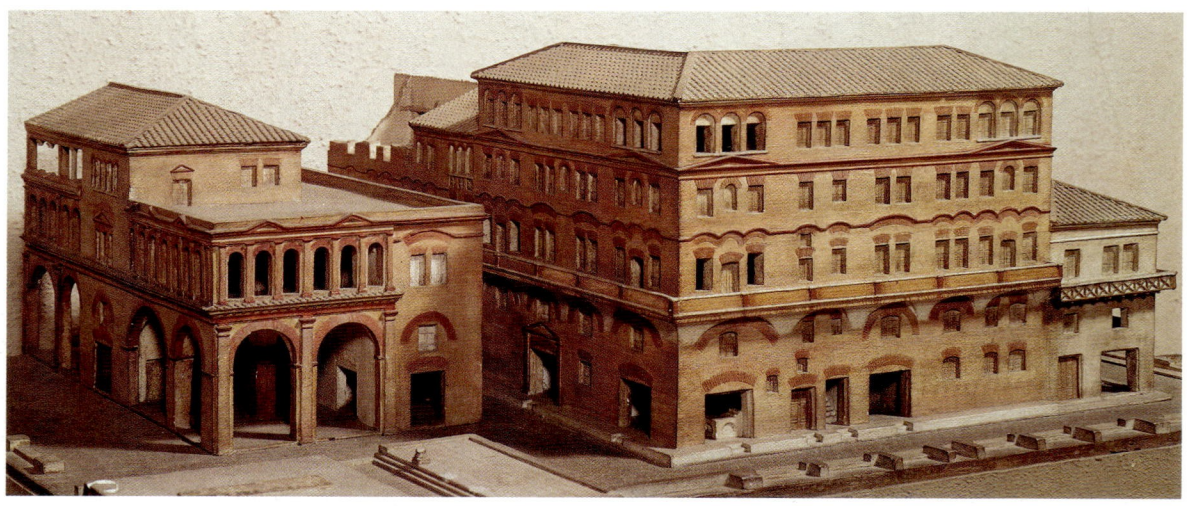

**10-53**  Model of an insula, Ostia, Italy, second century CE. Museo della Civiltà Romana, Rome.

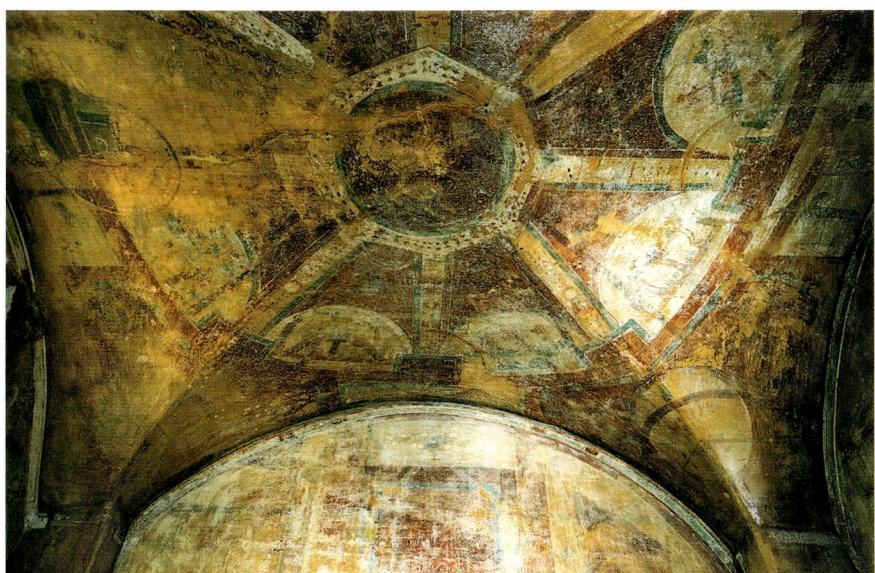

or marble veneers. When a classical motif was desired, brick pilasters or engaged columns could be added, but the brick was always left exposed. Ostia and Rome have many examples of apartment houses, warehouses, and tombs with intricate moldings and contrasting colors of brick. In the second century CE, brick came to be appreciated as attractive in its own right.

**FRESCOED WALLS AND VAULTS** Although the decoration of Ostian insulae tended to be more modest than that of the private houses of Pompeii, the finer apartments had mosaic floors and painted walls and ceilings. The frescoed groin vaults of Ostia are of special interest, because few painted ceilings are preserved in the cities buried by the eruption of Mount Vesuvius, and they are rarely of the vaulted type. Room IV (FIG. **10-54**) in the aptly named Insula of the Painted Vaults is typical of painted ceiling design of the second and third centuries CE. Such designs appear both in urban buildings and in the underground Christian catacombs (see FIG. 11-3). The painter treated the groin vault as if it were a dome, with a central oculus-like medallion surrounded by eight wedge-shaped segments resembling wheel spokes. In each segment is a white lunette with delicate paintings of birds and flowers, motifs also common earlier at Pompeii.

**NEPTUNE'S MOSAICS** The most popular choice for elegant pavements at Ostia in both private and public edifices was the black-and-white mosaic. One of the largest and best preserved examples is in the so-called Baths of Neptune, named for the grand mosaic floor (FIG. **10-55**) showing four seahorses pulling the Roman god of the sea across the waves. Neptune needs no chariot to support him as he speeds along, his mantle blowing in the strong wind. All about the god are other sea denizens, positioned so that wherever a visitor enters the room, some figures appear right side up. The artist rejected the complex polychrome modeling of figures seen in Pompeian mosaics such as the *Battle of Issus* (see FIG. 5-69) and used simple black silhouettes enlivened by white interior lines. Roman black-and-white mosaics were conceived as surface decorations and not as three-dimensional windows and thus were especially appropriate for floors.

**WORKERS' TOMBS** Ostian tombs of the second century CE were usually constructed of brick-faced concrete, and the facades of these houses of the dead resembled those of the contemporary insulae of the living. These were normally communal tombs, not the final resting places of the very wealthy. Many of them were adorned with small painted terracotta plaques immortalizing the activities of middle-class merchants and professional people.

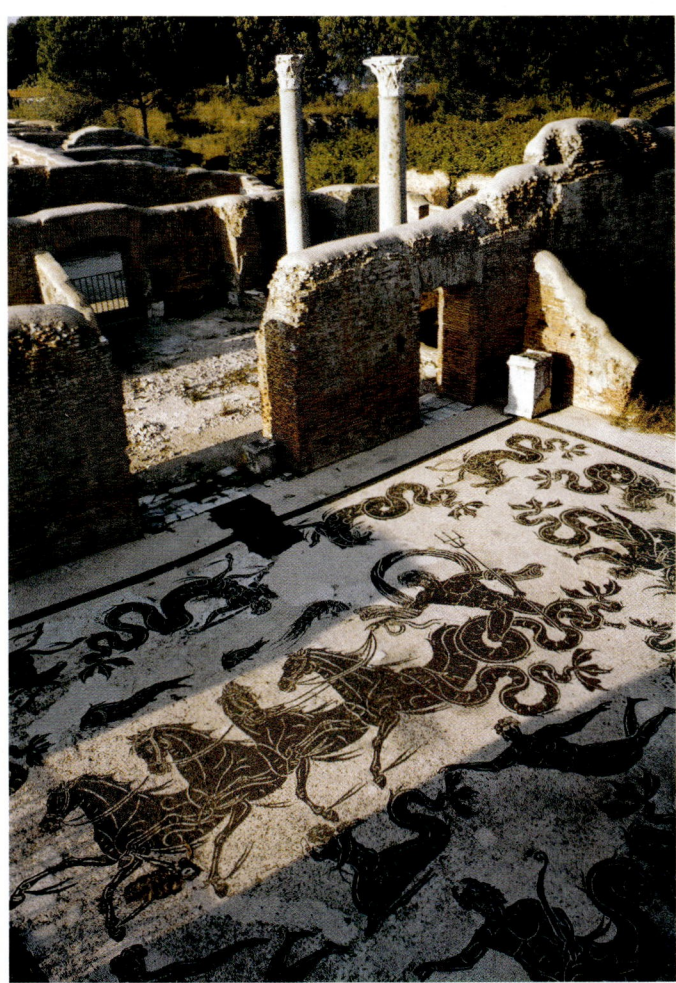

10-55 Neptune and creatures of the sea, floor mosaic in the Baths of Neptune, Ostia, Italy, ca. 140 CE.

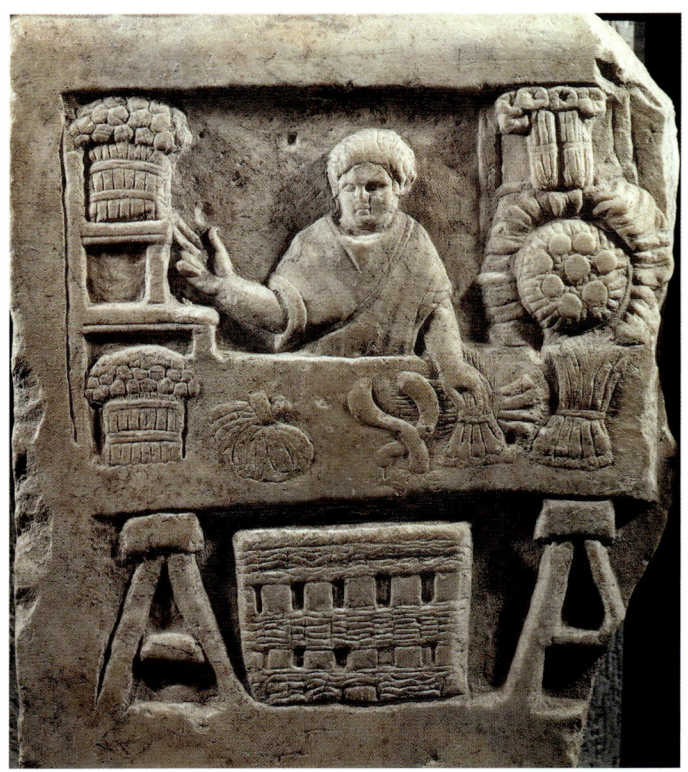

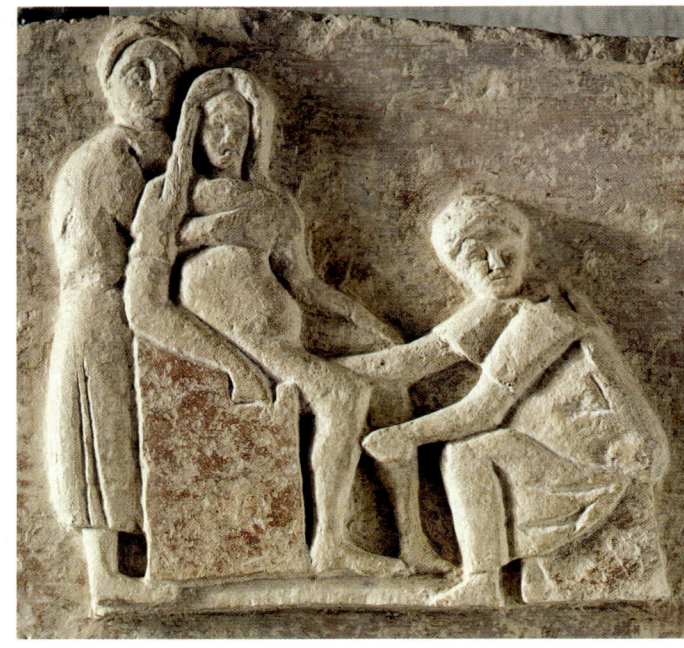

**10-56** Funerary reliefs of a vegetable vendor *(left)* and a midwife *(right)*, from Ostia, Italy, second half of second century CE. Painted terracotta, approx. 1′ 5″ and 11″ high, respectively. Museo Ostiense, Ostia.

We illustrate two of these plaques (FIG. **10-56**). One depicts a vegetable seller behind a counter (which has been tilted forward so that the observer can see the produce clearly). The other shows a midwife delivering a baby. Because she looks out at the viewer rather than at what she is doing and because almost all these reliefs focus on the livelihoods of the deceased, it is likely that the relief commemorates the midwife rather than the mother. Scenes of daily life such as these appeared on Roman funerary reliefs all over western Europe. Centuries later they may have served as the models for some medieval illustrations of the "labors of the months." They were as much a part of the classical legacy to the later history of art as the monuments commissioned by Roman emperors, which until recently were the exclusive interest of art historians.

## The Antonines (138–192 CE)

**SUCCESSION BY ADOPTION** Early in 138 CE, Hadrian adopted the 51-year-old Antoninus Pius (r. 138–161 CE). At the same time, he required that Antoninus adopt Marcus Aurelius (r. 161–180 CE) and Lucius Verus (r. 161–169 CE), thereby assuring a peaceful succession for at least another generation. When Hadrian died later in the year, he was proclaimed a god, and Antoninus Pius became emperor. Antoninus ruled the Roman world with distinction for 23 years. After his death and deification, Marcus Aurelius and Lucius Verus became the Roman Empire's first coemperors.

**CLASSICAL AND NONCLASSICAL** Shortly after Antoninus Pius's death, Marcus and Lucius erected a memorial column in his honor. Its pedestal has a dedicatory inscription on one side and a relief (FIG. **10-57**) illustrating the *apotheosis* (ascent to the heavens) of Antoninus and his wife Faustina the Elder on the opposite side. On the adjacent sides are two identical representations

of the *decursio* (FIG. **10-58**), or ritual circling of the imperial funerary pyre.

The two figural compositions are very different. The apotheosis relief remains firmly in the classical tradition with its elegant, well-proportioned figures, personifications, and single ground line corresponding to the panel's lower edge. The Campus Martius (Field of Mars), personified as a youth holding the Egyptian obelisk that stood in that area of Rome, reclines at the lower left corner. Roma (Rome personified) leans on a shield decorated with the she-wolf suckling Romulus and Remus (compare FIG. 9-10). Roma bids farewell to the couple being lifted into the realm of the gods on the wings of a personification of uncertain identity. All this was familiar from earlier scenes of apotheosis. New to the imperial repertoire, however, was the fusion of time the joint apotheosis represents. Faustina had died 20 years before Antoninus Pius. By depicting the two as ascending together, the artist wished to suggest that Antoninus had been faithful to his wife for two decades and that now they would be reunited in the afterlife. This notion had been employed before in the funerary reliefs of freed slaves and the middle class (FIG. 10-46) but had never been used in an elite context.

The decursio reliefs break even more strongly with classical convention. The figures are much stockier than those in the apotheosis relief, and the panel was not conceived as a window onto the world. The ground is the whole surface of the relief, and marching soldiers and galloping horses alike are shown on floating patches of earth. This, too, had not occurred before in imperial art, only in plebeian art (FIG. 10-6). After centuries of following classical design rules, elite Roman artists and patrons finally became dissatisfied with them. When seeking a new direction, they adopted some of the nonclassical conventions of the art of the lower classes.

**IMPERIAL MAJESTY ON HORSEBACK** Another break with the past occurred in the official portraits of Marcus Aurelius, although the pompous trappings of imperial iconography were

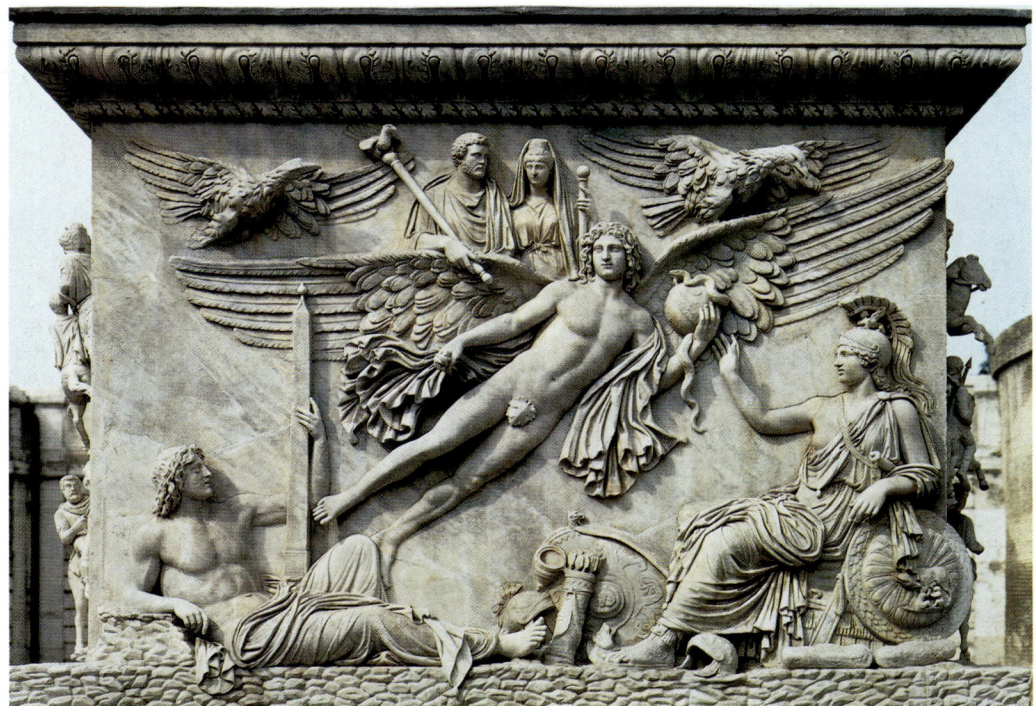

**10-57** Apotheosis of Antoninus Pius and Faustina, pedestal of the Column of Antoninus Pius, Rome, Italy, ca. 161 CE. Marble, approx. 8′ 1½″ high. Vatican Museums, Rome.

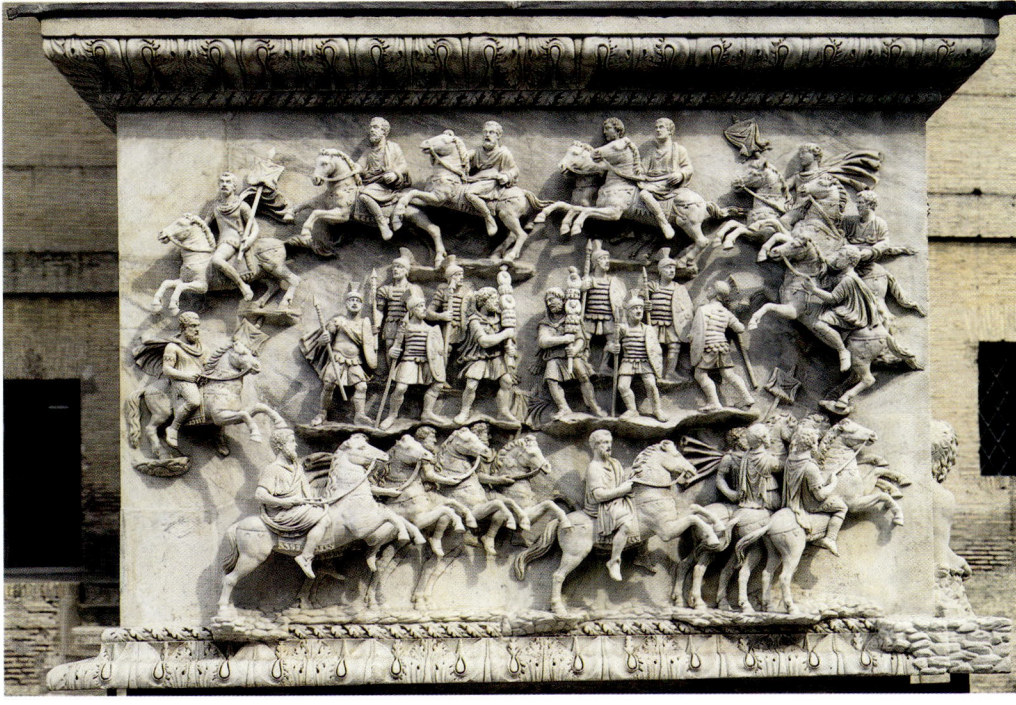

**10-58** Decursio, pedestal of the Column of Antoninus Pius, Rome, Italy, ca. 161 CE. Marble, approx. 8′ 1½″ high. Vatican Museums, Rome.

retained. In a larger-than-life-size gilded-bronze equestrian statue (FIG. **10-59**), the emperor possesses a superhuman grandeur and is much larger than any normal human would be in relation to his horse. Marcus stretches out his right arm in a gesture that is both a greeting and an offer of clemency. Some evidence suggests that beneath the horse's raised right foreleg an enemy once cowered, begging the emperor for mercy. The statue conveys the awesome power of the godlike Roman emperor as ruler of the whole world.

In the 16th century, Pope Paul III selected this statue as the centerpiece for Michelangelo's new design for the Capitoline Hill in Rome (see FIGS. 22-26 and 22-27). The statue inspired many Renaissance sculptors to portray their patrons on horseback (see FIGS. 21-29 and 21-30). Recently removed from its Renaissance site and painstakingly restored, Marcus's portrait owed its preservation throughout the Middle Ages to the fact that it was mistakenly thought to portray Constantine, the first Christian emperor of Rome. Most ancient bronze statues were melted down for their metal value, because they were regarded as impious images from the pagan world. Even today, after centuries of new finds, only a very few bronze equestrian statues are known. The type was, however, often used for imperial portraits—an equestrian statue of

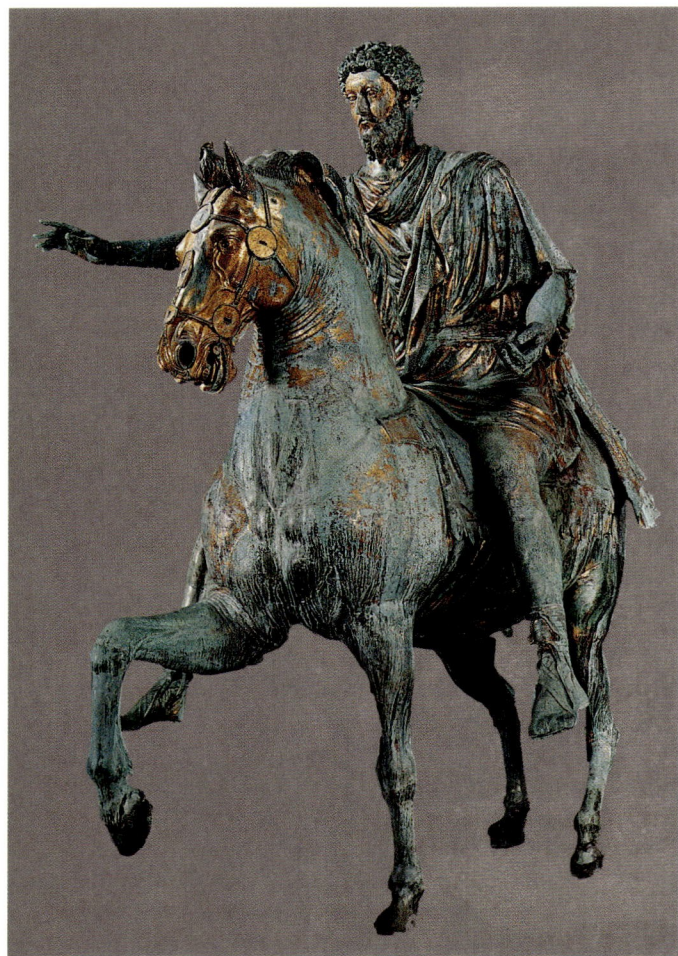

**10-59** Equestrian statue of Marcus Aurelius, from Rome, Italy, ca. 175 CE. Bronze, approx. 11′ 6″ high. Musei Capitolini, Rome.

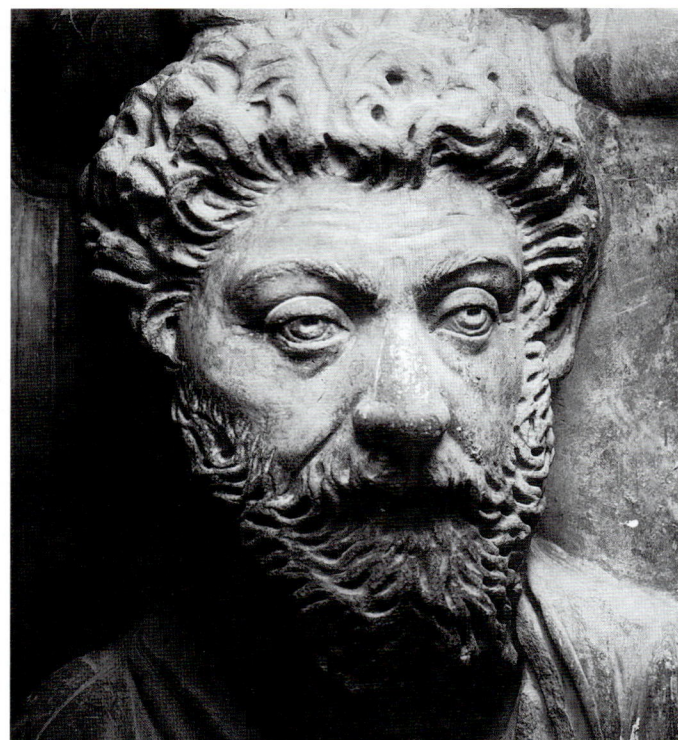

**10-60** Portrait of Marcus Aurelius, detail of a relief from a lost arch, Rome, Italy, ca. 175–180 CE. Marble, approx. life-size. Palazzo dei Conservatori, Rome.

Trajan stood in the middle of his forum (FIG. 10-41). Perhaps more than any other statuary type, the equestrian portrait expresses the Roman emperor's majesty and authority.

**DISQUIETING ANTONINE PORTRAITS** This message of supreme confidence is not, however, conveyed by the portrait head of Marcus's equestrian statue or by the late portraits of the emperor in marble, such as the one illustrated here (FIG. **10-60**). The latter is a detail of a panel from a lost arch that probably resembled Trajan's arch at Benevento (FIG. 10-45). The emperor rides in a triumphal chariot, and, like Titus before him (FIG. 10-39), he is crowned by Victory. The Antonine sculptor, in keeping with contemporary practice, used a drill to render the emperor's long hair and beard and even to accentuate the pupils of his eyes, creating bold patterns of light and shadow across his face. A chisel was used to carve the lines in Marcus's forehead and the deep ridges running from his nostrils to the corners of his mouth.

Portraits of aged emperors were not new (FIG. 10-35), but Marcus's were the first ones in which a Roman emperor appears weary, saddened, and even worried. For the first time, the strain of constant warfare on the frontiers and the burden of ruling a worldwide empire show in the emperor's face. The Antonine sculptor ventured beyond Republican verism. The ruler's character, his thoughts, and his soul were exposed for all to see, as Marcus revealed them himself in his *Meditations,* a deeply moving philo-

sophical treatise setting forth the emperor's personal worldview. This was a major turning point in the history of ancient art, and, coming as it did when the classical style was being challenged in relief sculpture (FIG. 10-58), it marked the beginning of the end of classical art's domination in the Greco-Roman world.

**FROM CREMATION TO BURIAL** Other profound changes also were taking place in Roman art and society at this time. Beginning under Trajan and Hadrian and especially during the rule of the Antonines, Romans began to favor burial over cremation. This reversal of funerary practices may reflect the influence of Christianity and other Eastern religions, whose adherents believed in an afterlife for the human body. Although the emperors themselves continued to be cremated in the traditional Roman manner, many private citizens opted for burial. Thus they required larger containers for their remains than the ash urns that were the norm until the second century CE. This in turn led to a sudden demand for sarcophagi, which are more similar to modern coffins than any other ancient type of burial container.

**ORESTES ON ROMAN SARCOPHAGI** Greek mythology was one of the most popular subjects for the decoration of these sarcophagi. In many cases, especially in the late second and third centuries CE, the Greek heroes and heroines were given the portrait features of the deceased Roman men and women in the marble coffins. These private patrons were following the model of imperial portraiture, where emperors and empresses frequently masqueraded as gods and goddesses and heroes and heroines (see "Role Playing in Roman Portraiture," page 265). An early example of the type (although it lacks any portraits) is the sarcophagus (FIG. **10-61**) now in Cleveland, one of many decorated with the story of the tragic Greek hero Orestes. All the examples of this type

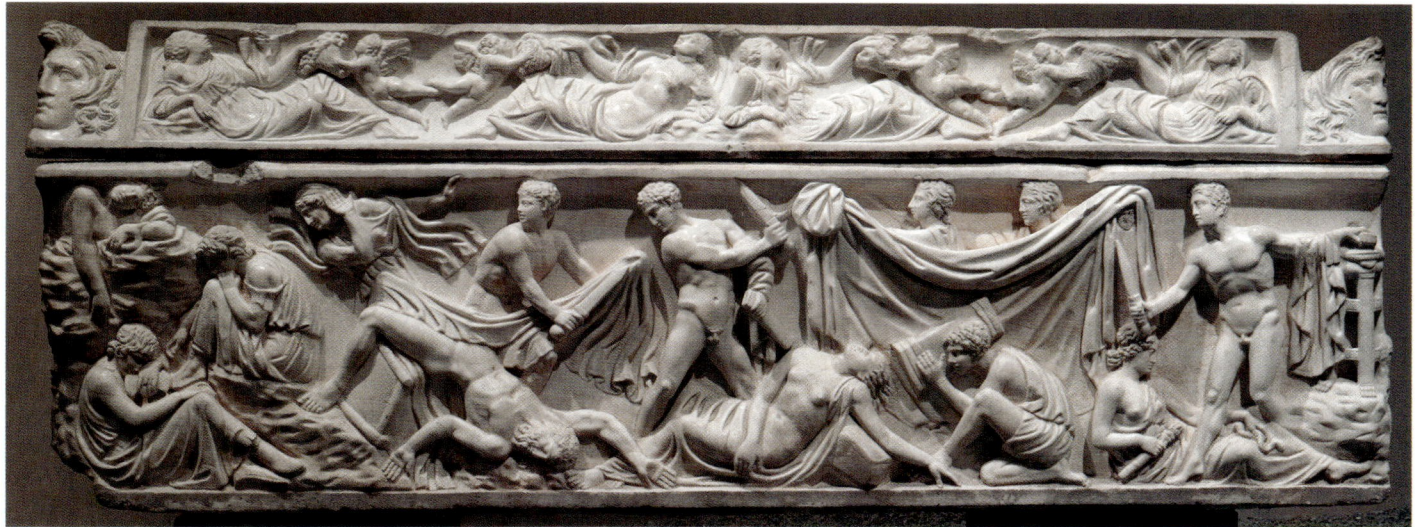

**10-61** Sarcophagus with the myth of Orestes, ca. 140–150 CE. Marble, 2′ 7½″ high. Cleveland Museum of Art, Cleveland.

use the same basic composition. Orestes appears several times: slaying his mother Clytaemnestra and her lover Aegisthus to avenge their murder of his father Agamemnon, taking refuge at Apollo's sanctuary at Delphi (symbolized by the god's tripod at the right), and so forth.

The repetition of sarcophagus compositions indicates that sculptors had access to pattern books. In fact, sarcophagus production was a major industry during the High and Late Empire. Several important regional manufacturing centers existed. The sarcophagi produced in the Latin West, such as the Cleveland Orestes sarcophagus, differ in format from those made in the Greek-speaking East. Western sarcophagi have reliefs only on the front and sides, because they were placed in floor-level niches inside Roman tombs. Eastern sarcophagi have reliefs on all four sides and stood in the center of the burial chamber. This contrast parallels the essential difference between the Etrusco-Roman and the Greek temple. The former was set against the wall of a forum or sanctuary and approached from the front, whereas the latter could be reached (and viewed) from every side.

**A MORTAL VENUS'S COFFIN** An elaborate example (FIG. 10-62) of a sarcophagus of the Eastern type comes from Rapolla, near Melfi in southern Italy. It was manufactured, however, in Asia Minor and attests to the vibrant export market for such luxury items in Antonine times. The decoration of all four sides of the marble box with statuesque images of Greek gods and heroes in

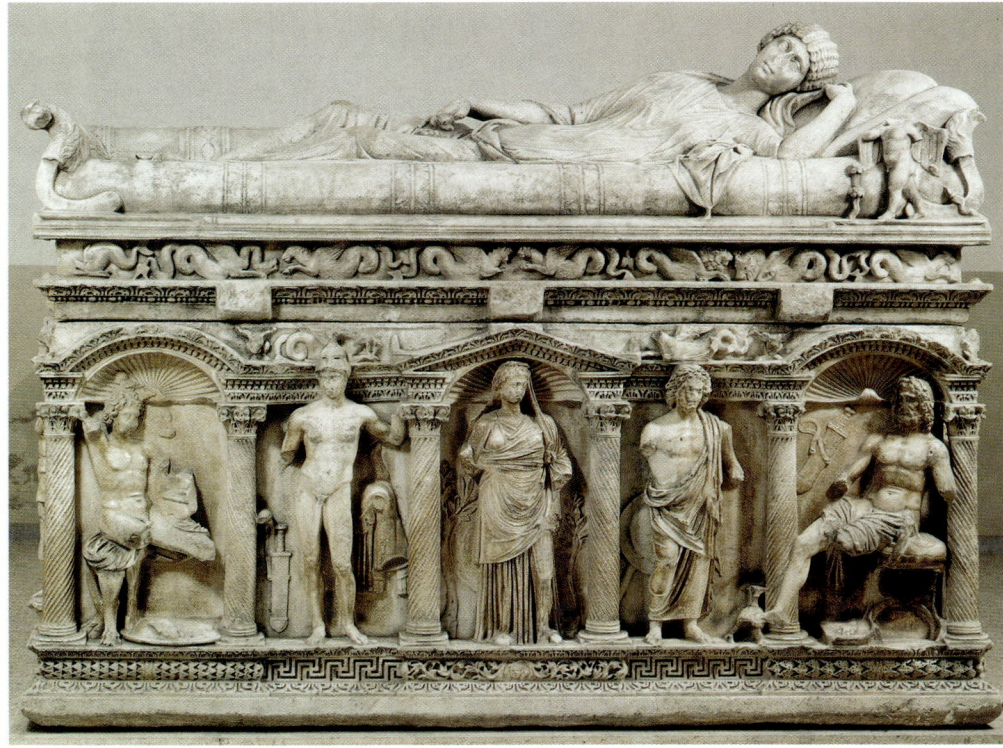

**10-62** Asiatic sarcophagus with *kline* portrait of a woman, from Rapolla, near Melfi, Italy, ca. 165–170 CE. Marble, approx. 5′ 7″ high. Museo Nazionale Archeologico del Melfese, Melfi.

### Iaia of Cyzicus and the Art of Encaustic Painting

The names of very few Roman artists are known. Those that are tend to be names of artists and architects who directed major imperial building projects (Severus and Celer, Domus Aurea; Apollodorus of Damascus, Forum of Trajan), worked on a gigantic scale (Zenodorus, Colossus of Nero), or made precious objects for famous patrons (Dioscurides, gem cutter for Augustus).

An interesting exception to this rule is Iaia of Cyzicus. Pliny the Elder, who died in the eruption of Mount Vesuvius (see "An Eyewitness Account," page 255), reported the following about this renowned painter from Asia Minor who worked in Italy during the Republic:

> Iaia of Cyzicus, who remained a virgin all her life, painted at Rome during the time when M. Varro [116–27 BCE] was a youth, both with a brush and with a cestrum on ivory, specializing mainly in portraits of women; she also painted a large panel in Naples representing an old woman and a portrait of herself done with a mirror. Her hand was quicker than that of any other painter, and her artistry was of such high quality that she commanded much higher prices than the most celebrated painters of the same period.[1]

The *cestrum* Pliny mentioned is a small spatula used in *encaustic* painting, a technique of mixing colors with hot wax and then applying them to the surface. Pliny knew of encaustic paintings of considerable antiquity, including those of Polygnotos of Thasos, a famous fifth-century BCE Greek painter (see Chapter 5, page 143). The best evidence of the technique comes, however, from Roman Egypt, where mummies were routinely furnished with portraits painted with encaustic on wooden panels (FIG. 10-63).

Artists applied encaustic to marble as well as to wood. According to Pliny, when Praxiteles was asked which one of his statues he preferred, the fourth-century BCE Greek artist, perhaps the ancient world's greatest marble sculptor, replied: "Those that Nikias painted."[2] This anecdote underscores the importance of coloration in ancient statuary.

[1] Pliny the Elder, *Natural History*, 35.147–148. Translated by J. J. Pollitt, *The Art of Rome, c. 753 B.C.–A.D. 337: Sources and Documents* (New York: Cambridge University Press, 1983), 87.

[2] Pliny the Elder, *Natural History*, 35.133.

architectural frames is distinctively Asiatic. But the lid portrait, which carries on the tradition of Etruscan sarcophagi (see FIGS. 9-4 and 9-14), is also a feature of the most expensive Western Roman coffins. Here the deceased, a woman, reclines on a *kline* (bed). With her are her faithful little dog (only its forepaws remain at the left end of the lid) and Cupid (at the right). The winged infant god mournfully holds a downturned torch, a reference to the death of a woman whose beauty rivaled that of his mother, Venus (who appears in one of the niches on the back of the sarcophagus).

**ROMAN MUMMY PORTRAITS** In Egypt, burial had been practiced for millennia. Even after the Kingdom of the Nile was reduced to a Roman province in 30 BCE, Egyptians continued to bury their dead in mummy cases. Recent excavations at the Bahariya Oasis have dramatically demonstrated the persistence of these burial customs. In Roman times, however, painted portraits on wood often replaced the traditional stylized portrait masks (see "Iaia of Cyzicus and the Art of Encaustic Painting," above). Hundreds of Roman mummy portraits have been preserved in the cemeteries of the Faiyum district. One of them (FIG. **10-63**) depicts a man who, following the lead of Marcus Aurelius, has long, curly hair and a full beard. Such portraits, which mostly date to the second and third centuries CE, were probably painted while the subjects were still alive. Art historians use them to trace the evolution of portrait painting after Mount Vesuvius erupted in 79 CE (compare FIG. 10-23). Our example exhibits the painter's refined use of the brush and spatula, mastery of the depiction of varied textures and of the play of light over the soft and delicately modeled face, and sensitive portrayal of the deceased's calm demeanor.

The Western and Eastern Roman sarcophagi and the mummy cases of Roman Egypt all served the same purpose, despite their differing shape and character. In an empire as vast as Rome's, regional differences are to be expected. As will be discussed later, geography also played a major role in the Middle Ages, when Western and Eastern Christian art differed sharply.

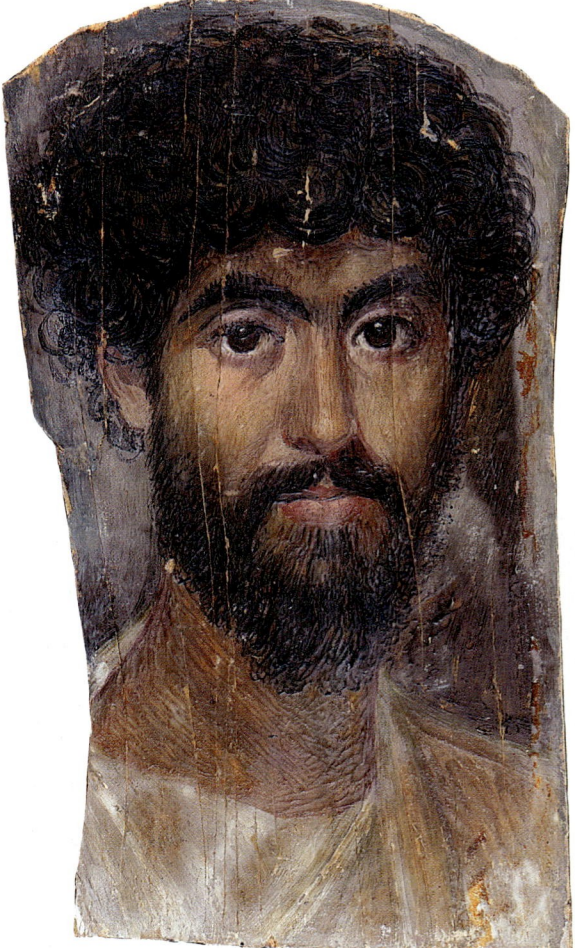

**10-63** Mummy portrait of a man, from Faiyum, Egypt, ca. 160–170 CE. Encaustic on wood, approx. 1′ 2″ high. Albright-Knox Art Gallery, Buffalo.

# LATE EMPIRE

**A CIVILIZATION IN TRANSITION** By the time of Marcus Aurelius, two centuries after Augustus established the Pax Romana, Roman power was beginning to erode. It was more and more difficult to keep order on the frontiers, and even within the Empire the authority of Rome was being challenged. Marcus's son Commodus (r. 180–192 CE), who succeeded his father, was assassinated, bringing the Antonine dynasty to an end. The economy was in decline, and the efficient imperial bureaucracy was disintegrating. Even the official state religion was losing ground to Eastern cults, Christianity among them, which were beginning to gain large numbers of converts. The Late Empire was a pivotal era in world history during which the pagan ancient world was gradually transformed into the Christian Middle Ages.

## The Severans (193–235 CE)

**AN AFRICAN RULES THE EMPIRE** Civil conflict followed Commodus's death. When it ended, an African-born general named Septimius Severus (r. 193–211 CE) was master of the Roman world. The new emperor, anxious to establish his legitimacy, adopted himself into the Antonine dynasty, proclaiming himself as Marcus Aurelius's son. It is not surprising, then, that official portraits of Septimius Severus depict him with the long hair and beard of his Antonine "father"—whatever his actual appearance may have been. Many portraits in marble and bronze exist today of the African emperor and of his wife, Julia Domna, the daughter of a Syrian priest, and their two sons, Caracalla and Geta. But only one painted portrait of the family has been found. In fact, the portrait (FIG. **10-64**), discovered in Egypt and painted in *tempera* (pigments in egg yolk) on wood (as were many of the mummy portraits from Faiyum), is the only surviving painted likeness of any Roman emperor. Such portraits, however, must have been quite common all over the empire. Their perishable nature explains their almost total loss.

The Severan family portrait is of special interest for two reasons beyond its mere survival. The emperor's hair is tinged with gray, suggesting that his marble portraits—which, like all marble sculptures in antiquity, were painted—also may have revealed his advancing age in this way. (The same was very likely true of the marble likenesses of the old and tired Marcus Aurelius, FIG. 10-60.) The group portrait is also notable because the face of the emperor's younger son, Geta, was erased. When Caracalla (r. 211–217 CE) succeeded his father as emperor, he had his brother murdered and his memory damned. (Caracalla also ordered the death of his own wife, Plautilla.) The painted *tondo* (circular format) portrait from Egypt is an eloquent testimony to that damnatio memoriae and to the long arm of Roman authority. This kind of defacement of a political rival's portrait is not new. As noted earlier, for example, Thutmose III of Egypt destroyed the portraits of Hatshepsut after her death (see FIG. 3-22). But the Romans employed damnatio memoriae as a political tool more often and more systematically than any other civilization.

**PORTRAYING A RUTHLESS EMPEROR** One of the finest marble portraits of the ruthless Caracalla is illustrated in FIG. **10-65**. The sculptor brilliantly suggested the texture of the emperor's short hair and close-cropped beard through deft handling of the chisel and incisions into the marble surface. More remarkable, however, is the moving characterization of Caracalla's suspicious nature, a further development from the groundbreaking introspection of the portraits of Marcus Aurelius. Caracalla's brow is knotted, and he abruptly turns his head over his left shoulder, as if he suspects danger from behind. The emperor had reason to be fearful. He was felled by an assassin's dagger in the sixth year of his rule. Assassination would be the fate of many Roman emperors during the turbulent third century CE.

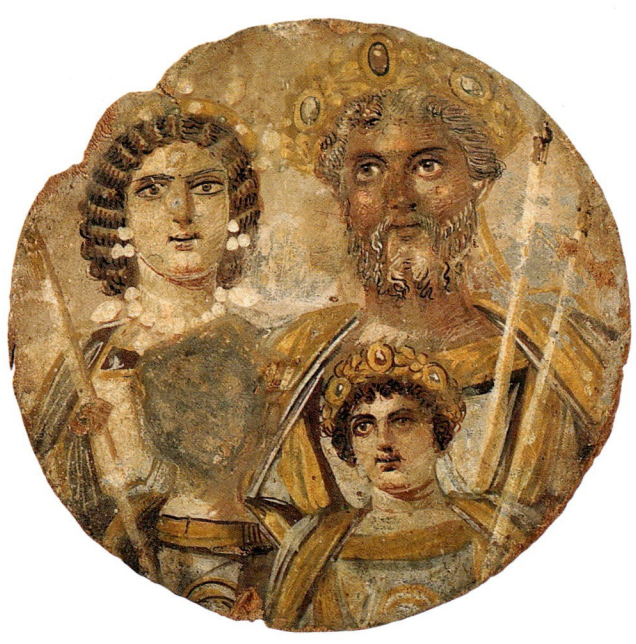

**10-64** Painted portrait of Septimius Severus and his family, from Egypt, ca. 200 CE. Tempera on wood, approx. 1′ 2″ diameter. Staatliche Museen, Berlin.

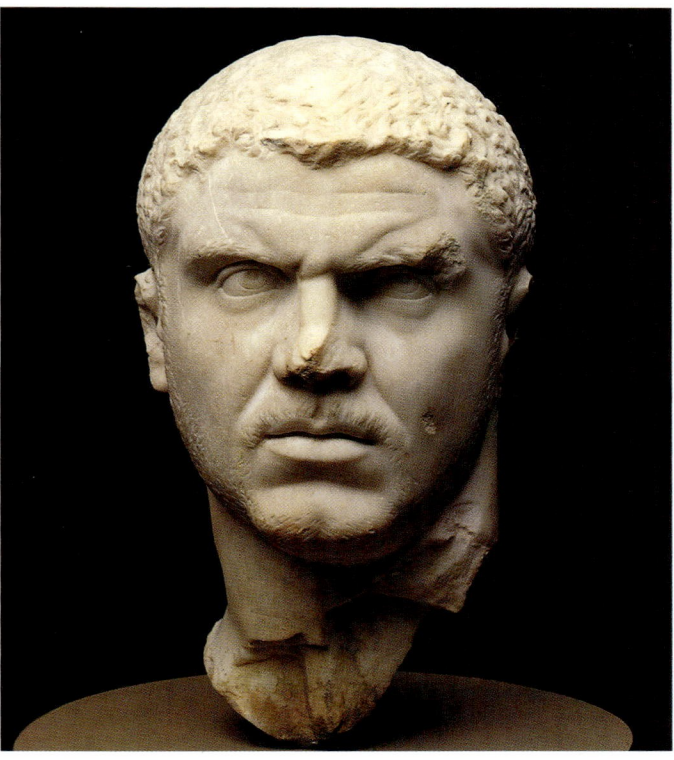

**10-65** Portrait of Caracalla, ca. 211–217 CE. Marble, approx. 1′ 2″ high. Metropolitan Museum of Art, New York.

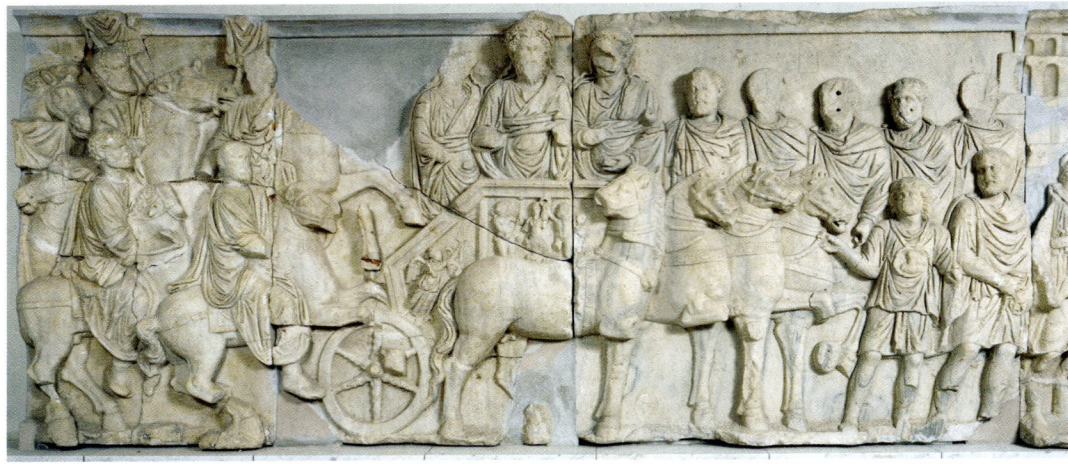

**10-66** Chariot procession of Septimius Severus, relief from the Arch of Septimius Severus, Lepcis Magna, Libya, 203 CE. Marble, approx. 5′ 6″ high. Castle Museum, Tripoli.

**THE NONCLASSICAL STYLE TAKES ROOT** The hometown of the Severans was Lepcis Magna, on the coast of what is now Libya. In the late second and early third centuries CE, imperial funds were used to construct a modern harbor there, as well as a new forum, basilica, arch, and other monuments. The Arch of Septimius Severus, erected in 203 at the intersection of two major streets, lay in ruins for centuries but has recently been rebuilt. It has friezes on the attic on all four sides. One of these (FIG. **10-66**) shows the chariot procession of Septimius and his two sons. Unlike the triumph panel (FIG. 10-39) from the Arch of Titus in Rome, this relief gives no sense of rushing motion. Rather, it has a stately stillness. The chariot and the horsemen behind it are moving forward, but the emperor and his sons are detached from the procession and facing the viewer. Also different is the way the figures in the second row have no connection with the ground and are elevated above the heads of those in the first row so that they can be seen more clearly.

Both the frontality and the floating figures were new to official Roman art in Antonine and Severan times, but both appeared long before in the private art of freed slaves (compare FIGS. 10-5 and 10-6). Once sculptors in the emperor's employ embraced these nonclassical elements, they had a long afterlife, appearing in medieval art in frontal images of Christ and the saints. As is often true in the history of art, the emergence of a new aesthetic was a by-product of a period of social, political, and economic upheaval. Art historians call this new non-naturalistic, more abstract style the Late Antique style.

**CARACALLA'S GIGANTIC BATHS** The Severans were also active builders in the capital. The Baths of Caracalla in Rome (FIG. **10-67**) were the greatest in a long line of bathing and recreational complexes erected with imperial funds to win the public's favor. Made of brick-faced concrete and covered by enormous vaults springing from thick walls up to 140 feet high, Caracalla's baths covered an area of almost 50 acres. They dwarfed the typical baths of cities and towns such as Ostia and Pompeii and even Rome itself. The design was symmetrical along a central axis, facilitating the Roman custom of taking sequential plunges in cold-, warm-, and hot-water baths in, respectively, the *frigidarium, tepidarium,* and *caldarium.*

The caldarium (FIG. 10-67, no. 4) of Caracalla's baths was a circular chamber so large that until recently it seated hundreds of spectators at open-air performances of Italian operas. Its dome was almost as large as the Pantheon's (FIG. 10-50), and the

**10-67** Plan of the central section of the Baths of Caracalla, Rome, Italy, 212–216 CE. 1) Natatio, 2) Frigidarium, 3) Tepidarium, 4) Caldarium, 5) Palaestra. The bathing, swimming, and exercise areas were surrounded by landscaped gardens, lecture halls, and other rooms, all enclosed within a great concrete perimeter wall.

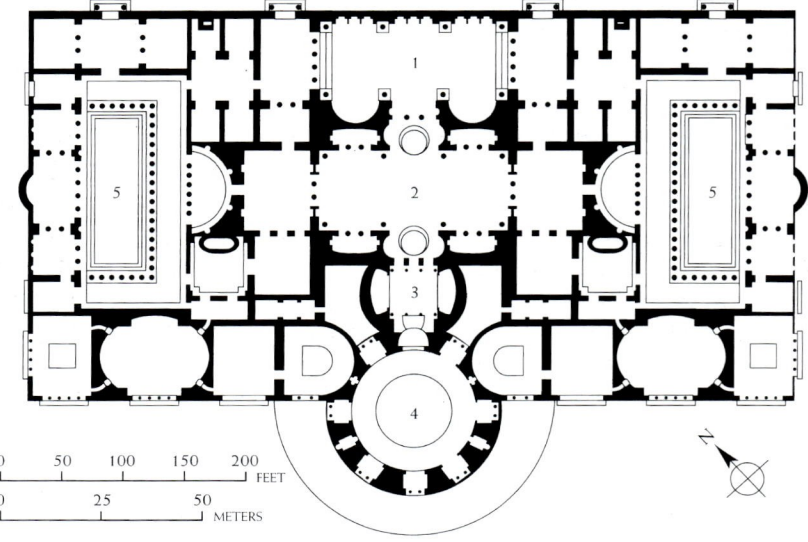

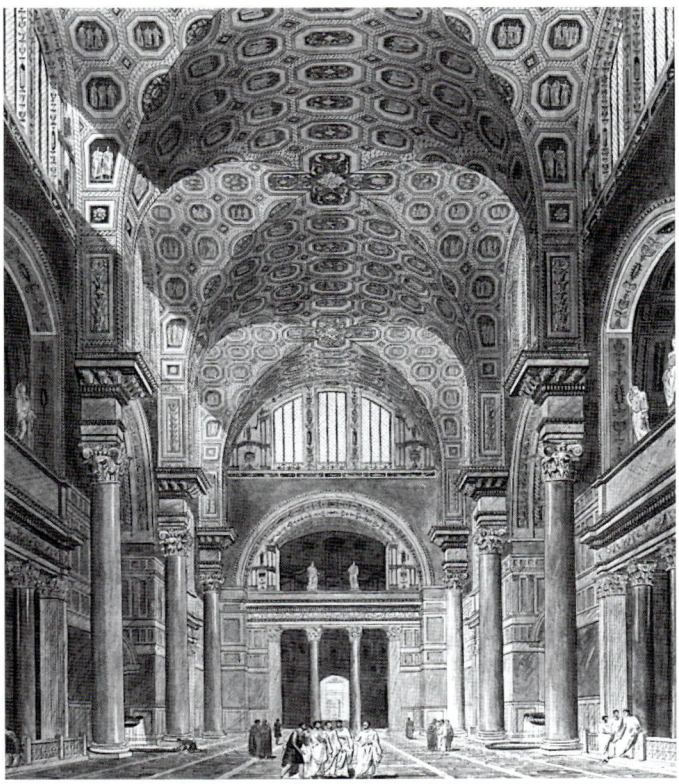

**10-68** Reconstruction drawing of the central hall (*frigidarium*) of the Baths of Caracalla, Rome, Italy, 212–216 CE.

concrete drum that supported it was much taller. Our reconstruction of the frigidarium (FIG. **10-68**), which was also the central hall of the baths, shows not only the scale of the architecture and the way light entered through fenestrated groin vaults but also how lavishly the rooms were decorated. Stuccoed vaults, mosaic floors (both black-and-white and polychrome), marble-faced walls, and colossal statuary were found throughout the complex. Although the vaults themselves collapsed long ago, many of the mosaics and statues are preserved. Among these is the 10-foot-tall copy of Lysippos's Herakles (see FIG. 5-66), whose muscular body must have inspired Romans to exercise vigorously.

Caracalla's baths also had landscaped gardens, lecture halls, libraries, colonnaded exercise courts (*palaestras*), and a giant swimming pool (*natatio*). Archaeologists estimate that up to 1,600 bathers at a time could enjoy this Roman equivalent of a modern health spa. A branch of one of the city's major aqueducts supplied water, and furnaces circulated hot air through hollow floors and walls throughout the complex.

## The Soldier Emperors (235–284 CE)

**A STORMY HALF CENTURY** The Severan dynasty ended when Severus Alexander (r. 222–235 CE) was murdered. The next half century was one of almost continuous civil war. One general after another was declared emperor by his troops, only to be murdered by another general a few years or even a few months later. (In the year 238, two coemperors the Senate chose were dragged from the imperial palace and murdered in public after only three months in office.) In these unstable times, no emperor could begin ambitious architectural projects. The only significant building activity in Rome during the "soldier emperors" era occurred under Aurelian (r. 270–275 CE). He constructed a new defensive

wall circuit for the capital—a military necessity and a poignant commentary on the decay of Roman power.

**IMPERIAL SOUL PORTRAITS** If architects went hungry in third-century Rome, sculptors and engravers had much to do. Great quantities of coins (in debased metal) were produced so that the troops could be paid with money stamped with the current emperor's portrait and not with that of his predecessor or rival. Each new ruler set up portrait statues and busts everywhere to assert his authority.

The sculpted portraits of the third century CE are among the most moving ever produced. Following the lead of the sculptors of the Marcus Aurelius and Caracalla portraits, artists fashioned likenesses of the soldier emperors that are as notable for their emotional content as they are for their technical virtuosity. Trajan Decius (r. 249–251), for example, whose brief reign is best known for persecution of Christians, was portrayed as an old man with bags under his eyes and a sad expression (FIG. **10-69**). In his eyes, which glance away nervously rather than engage viewers directly, is the anxiety of a man who knows he can do little to restore order to an out-of-control world. The sculptor modeled the marble as if it were pliant clay, compressing the sides of the head at the level of the eyes, etching the hair and beard into the stone, and chiseling deep lines in the forehead and around the mouth. The portrait reveals the anguished soul of the man—and of the times.

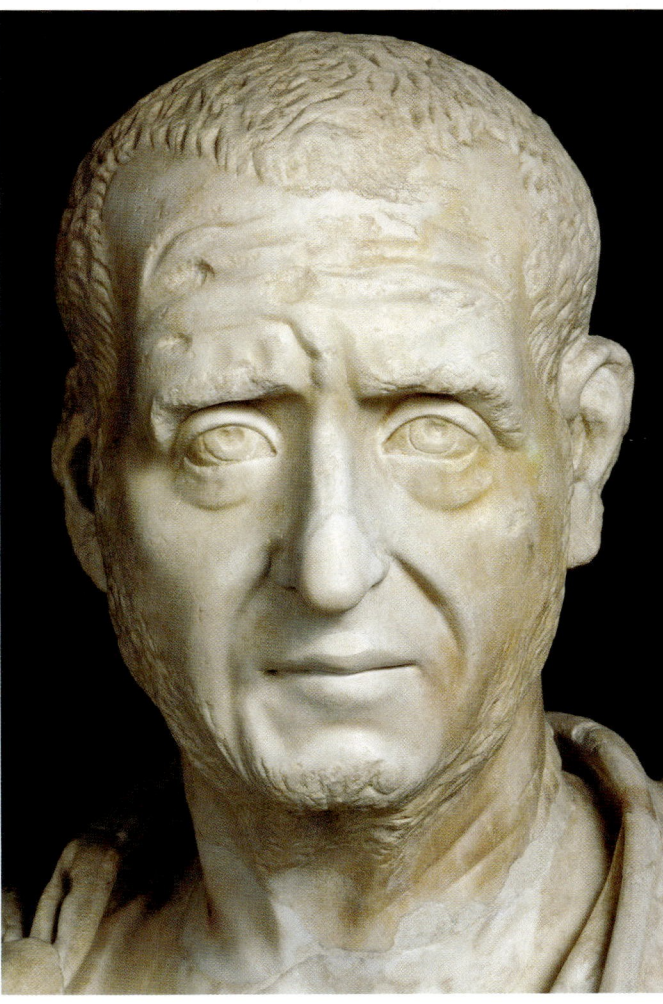

**10-69** Portrait bust of Trajan Decius, 249–251 CE. Marble, full bust approx. 2′ 7″ high. Museo Capitolino, Rome.

Decius's successor was Trebonianus Gallus (r. 251–253 CE), another short-lived emperor. In a larger-than-life-size bronze portrait (FIG. **10-70**), Trebonianus appears in heroic nudity, as had so many emperors and generals before him. His physique is not, however, that of the strong but graceful Greek athletes Augustus and his successors admired so much. Instead, his is a wrestler's body with massive legs and a swollen trunk. The heavy-set body dwarfs his head, with its nervous expression. In this portrait, the Greek ideal of the keen mind in the harmoniously proportioned body gave way to an image of brute force, an image well suited to the era of the soldier emperors.

**BARBARIANS AND MITHRAS** By the third century, burial of the dead had become so widespread that even the imperial family was practicing it in place of cremation. Sarcophagi were more popular than ever. An unusually large sarcophagus (FIG. **10-71**), discovered in Rome in 1621 and purchased by Cardinal Ludovisi, is decorated on the front with a chaotic scene of battle between Romans and one of their northern foes, probably the Goths. The sculptor spread the writhing and highly emotive figures evenly across the entire relief, with no illusion of space behind them. This piling of figures is an even more extreme rejection of classical perspective than was the use of floating ground lines on the pedestal of the Column of Antoninus Pius (FIG. 10-58). It underscores the increasing dissatisfaction Late Roman artists felt with the classical style.

Within this dense mass of intertwined bodies, the central horseman stands out vividly. He wears no helmet, and thrusts out his open right hand to demonstrate that he holds no weapon. Several scholars have identified him as one of the sons of Trajan Decius. In an age when the Roman army was far from invincible and Roman emperors were constantly felled by other Romans, the young general on the *Ludovisi Battle Sarcophagus* is boasting that he is a fearless commander assured of victory. His self-assurance may stem from his having embraced one of the increasingly popular Oriental mystery religions. On the youth's forehead is carved the emblem of Mithras, the Persian god of light, truth, and victory

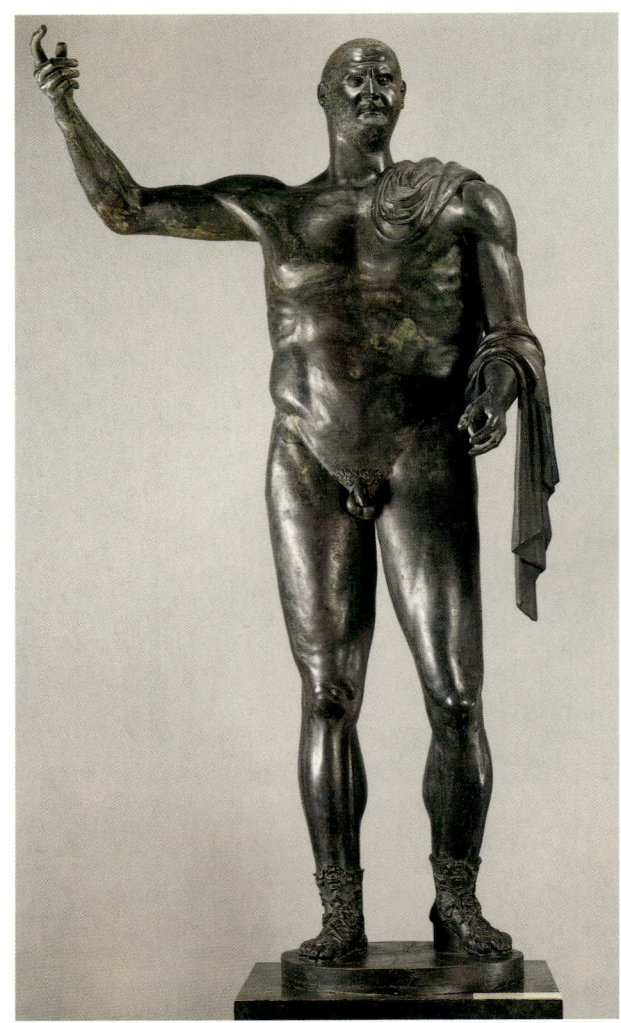

**10-70** Heroic portrait of Trebonianus Gallus, from Rome, Italy, 251–253 CE. Bronze, approx. 7′ 11″ high. Metropolitan Museum of Art, New York.

**10-71** Battle of Romans and barbarians *(Ludovisi Battle Sarcophagus),* from Rome, Italy, ca. 250–260 CE. Marble, approx. 5′ high. Museo Nazionale Romano-Palazzo Altemps, Rome.

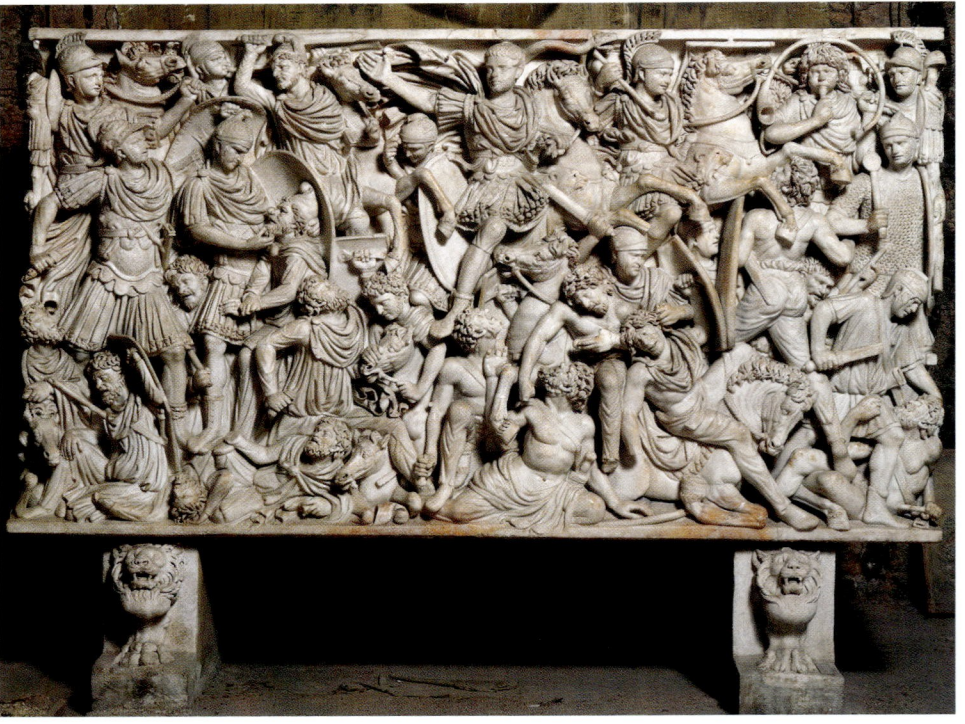

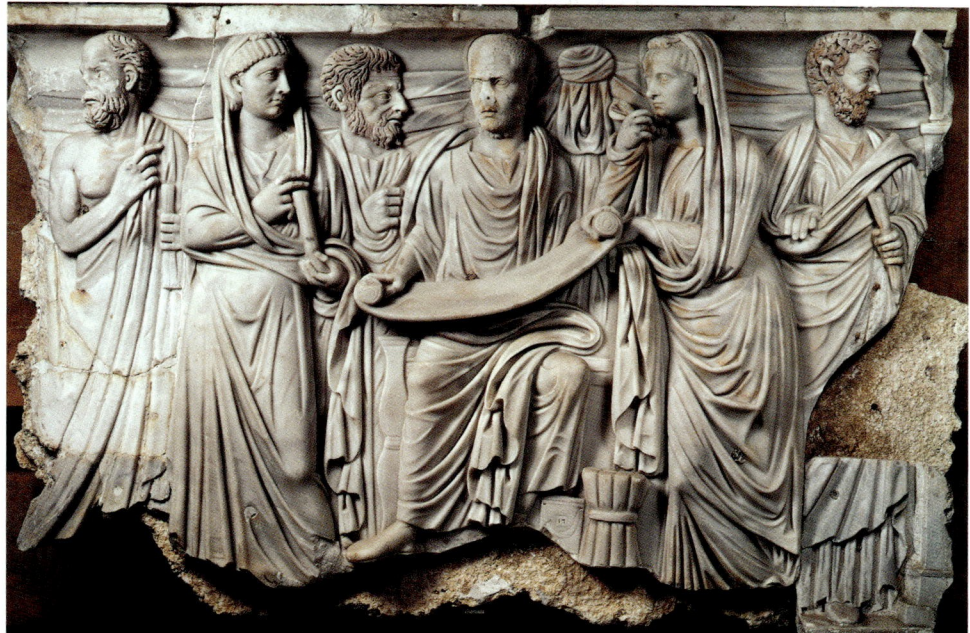

**10-72** Sarcophagus of a philosopher, ca. 270–280 CE. Marble, approx. 4′ 11″ high. Vatican Museums, Rome.

over death. Many shrines to Mithras dating to this period have been found at Rome and Ostia.

**PHILOSOPHERS AND STUDENTS** The insecurity of the times led many Romans to seek solace in philosophy. On many third-century sarcophagi, the deceased assumes the role of the learned intellectual. (Others continued to masquerade as Greek heroes or Roman generals.) One especially large example (FIG. **10-72**) depicts a seated Roman philosopher holding a scroll. Two standing women (also with portrait features) look to him for wisdom. In the background are other philosophers, students of the central deceased teacher. This type of sarcophagus became very popular for Christian burials, where the wise-man motif was used not only to portray the deceased (see FIG. 11-4) but also Christ flanked by his apostles (see FIG. 11-5). Compositions with a central frontal figure and subordinate flanking figures, such as on this sarcophagus and on the Severan arch at Lepcis Magna (FIG. 10-66), are also quite common in Early Christian art (see FIGS. 11-5 and 11-17).

**A CRITIQUE OF THE PANTHEON** The decline in respect for classical art also can be seen in architecture. At Baalbek (ancient Heliopolis) in modern Lebanon, the architect of the Temple of Venus (FIG. **10-73**), following in the "baroque" tradition of the Treasury at Petra (FIG. 10-52), ignored almost every rule of classical design. Although made of stone, the third-century building, with its circular domed cella set behind a gabled columnar facade, was in many ways a critique of the concrete Pantheon (FIG. 10-48), which by then had achieved the status of a "classic." Many features of the Baalbek temple intentionally depart from the norm. The platform, for example, is scalloped all around the cella. The columns—the only known instance of *five*-sided Corinthian capitals with corresponding pentagonal bases—support a matching scalloped entablature (which serves to buttress the shallow stone dome). These concave forms and those of the niches in the cella walls play off against the cella's convex shape. Even the "traditional" facade of the Baalbek temple is eccentric. The unknown architect inserted an arch within the triangular pediment.

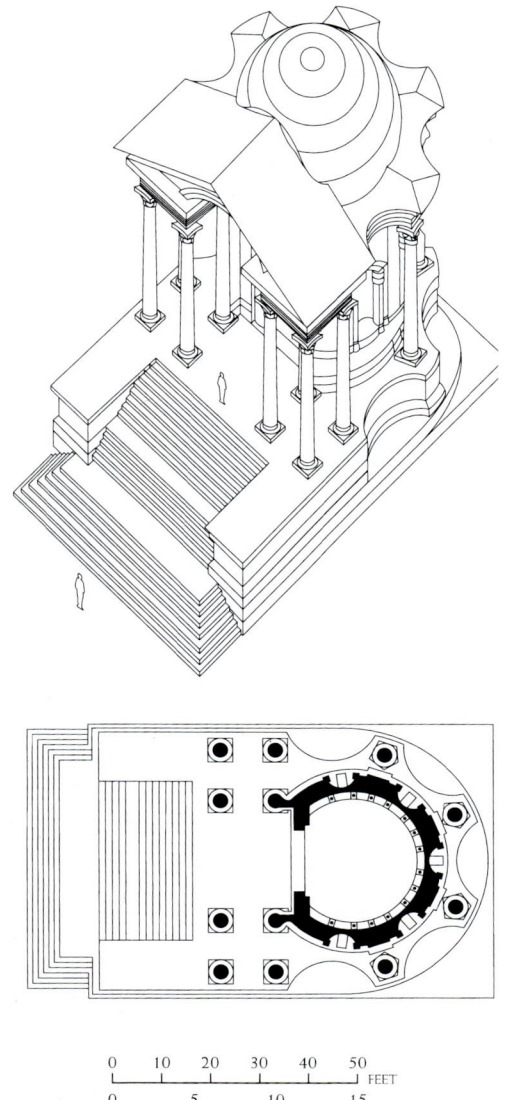

0 10 20 30 40 50 FEET

0 5 10 15 METERS

**10-73** Restored view (*top*) and plan (*bottom*) of the Temple of Venus, Baalbek, Lebanon, third century CE.

## Diocletian and the Tetrarchy (284–306 CE)

**POWER SHARED, ORDER RESTORED** In an attempt to restore order to the Roman Empire, Diocletian (r. 284–305 CE), whose troops proclaimed him emperor, decided to share power with his potential rivals. In 293, he established the *tetrarchy* (rule by four) and adopted the title of Augustus of the East. The other three tetrarchs were a corresponding Augustus of the West, and Eastern and Western Caesars (whose allegiance to the two Augusti was cemented by marriage to their daughters). Together, the four emperors ruled without strife until Diocletian retired in 305. Without his leadership, the new tetrarchs began fighting among themselves, and the tetrarchic form of government collapsed. The division of the Roman Empire into eastern and western spheres survived, however. It persisted throughout the Middle Ages, setting the Latin West apart from the Byzantine East.

**INDIVIDUALITY LOST** The four tetrarchs often were portrayed together, both on coins and in the round. Artists did not try to capture their individual appearances and personalities but sought instead to represent the nature of the tetrarchy itself—that is, to portray four equal partners in power. In the two pairs of porphyry (purple marble) portraits of the tetrarchs we illustrate (FIG. 10-74), it is impossible to name the rulers. Each of the four emperors has lost his identity as an individual and been subsumed into the larger entity of the tetrarchy. All the tetrarchs are identically clad in cuirass and cloak. Each grasps a sheathed sword in the left hand. With their right arms they embrace one another in an overt display of concord. The figures, like those on the decursio relief (FIG. 10-58) of the Column of Antoninus Pius, have large cubical heads on squat bodies. The drapery is schematic and the bodies are shapeless. The faces are emotionless masks, distinguished only by the beard on two of the figures (probably the older Augusti, distinguishing them from the younger Caesars). Nonetheless, each pair is as alike as freehand carving can achieve. In this group portrait, carved eight centuries after Greek sculptors first freed the human form from the formal rigidity of the Egyptian-inspired kouros stance, the human figure was once again conceived in iconic terms. Idealism, naturalism, individuality, and personality now belonged to the past.

**DIOCLETIAN'S FORTRESS-PALACE** When Diocletian abdicated in 305, he returned to Dalmatia (roughly the area of the

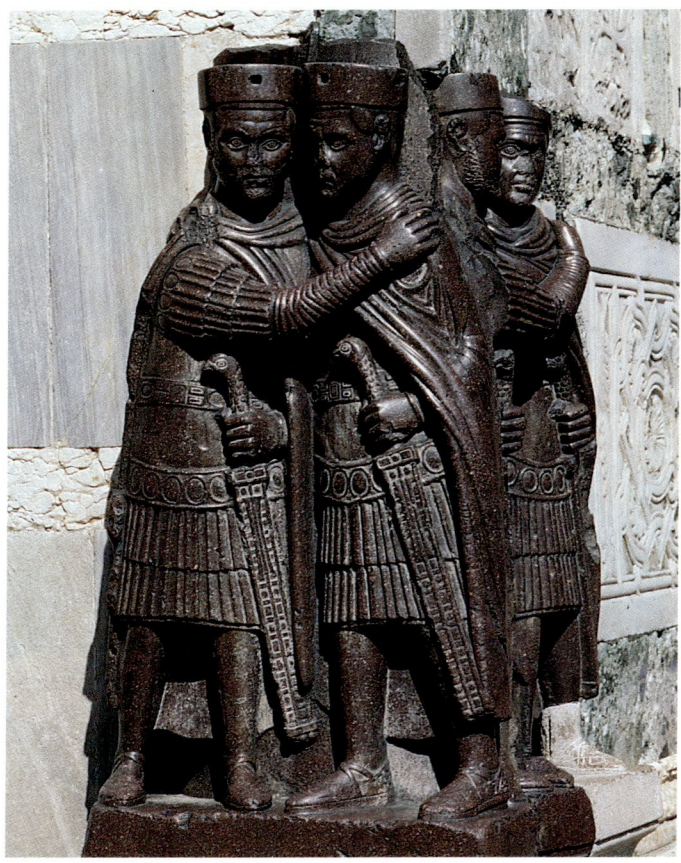

**10-74** Portraits of the four tetrarchs, from Constantinople, ca. 305 CE. Porphyry, approx. 4′ 3″ high. Saint Mark's, Venice.

former Yugoslavia), where he was born. There he built a palace (FIG. 10-75) for himself at Split, near ancient Salona on the Adriatic coast in Croatia. Just as Aurelian had felt it necessary to girdle Rome with fortress walls, Diocletian instructed his architects to provide him with a well-fortified suburban palace. The complex, which covers about 10 acres, was laid out like a Roman castrum, complete with watchtowers flanking the gates. It gave the emperor a sense of security in the most insecure of times.

Within the high walls, two avenues (comparable to the cardo and decumanus in a provincial colony such as Timgad, FIG. 10-40)

**10-75** Model of the Palace of Diocletian, Split, Croatia, ca. 300–305 CE. Museo della Civiltà Romana, Rome.

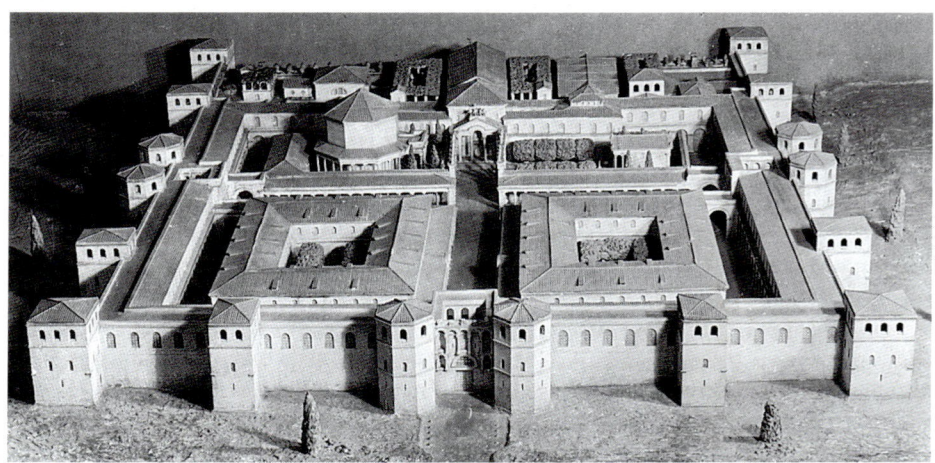

intersected at the palace's center. Where a city's forum would have been situated, Diocletian's palace had a colonnaded court leading to the entrance to the imperial residence. If admitted to the emperor's private quarters, a visitor passed through a templelike facade with an arch within its pediment, as in the Temple of Venus at Baalbek (FIG. 10-73). The formal purpose of this motif was undoubtedly to emphasize the design's central axis, but symbolically it became the "gable of glorification" under which Diocletian appeared before those who gathered in the court to pay homage to him. On one side of the court was a Temple of Jupiter; on the other side, Diocletian's mausoleum (left rear in FIG. 10-75), which towered above all the other structures in the complex. The emperor's huge domed tomb was a type that would become very popular in Early Christian times not only for mausoleums but eventually also for churches, especially in the Byzantine East. It is, in fact, used as a church today.

## Constantine (306–337 CE)

**CONSTANTINE AND CHRISTIANITY** The short-lived concord among the tetrarchs that ended with Diocletian's abdication was followed by an all-too-familiar period of conflict. This latest civil war among rival Roman armies lasted two decades. The eventual victor was Constantine I ("the Great"), son of Constantius Chlorus, Diocletian's Caesar of the West. After the death of his father, Constantine invaded Italy in 312. At the battle of the Milvian Bridge, the gateway to Rome, he defeated and killed Maxentius and took control of the capital. Constantine attributed his victory to the aid of the Christian god. In 313, he and Licinius, Constantine's coemperor in the East, issued the Edict of Milan, ending the persecution of Christians.

In time, Constantine and Licinius became foes, and in 324 Constantine defeated and executed Licinius near Byzantium (modern Istanbul, Turkey). Constantine was now unchallenged ruler of the whole Roman Empire. Shortly after the death of Licinius, he founded a "New Rome" on the site of Byzantium and named it Constantinople ("City of Constantine"). A year later, in 325, at the Council of Nicaea, Christianity became the de facto official religion of the Roman Empire. From this point on, paganism declined rapidly. Constantinople was dedicated on May 11, 330, "by the commandment of God." In succeeding decades, many Christian churches were erected there. Constantine himself was baptized on his deathbed in 337. For many scholars, the transfer of the seat of power from Rome to Constantinople and the recognition of Christianity mark the beginning of the Middle Ages.

Constantinian art is a mirror of this transition from the classical to the medieval world. In Rome, for example, Constantine was a builder in the grand tradition of the emperors of the first, second, and early third centuries, erecting public baths, a basilica on the Sacred Way leading into the Roman Forum, and a triumphal arch. But he was also the patron of the city's first churches, including Saint Peter's (see FIG. 11-7).

**A NEW ARCH WITH OLD RELIEFS** After his decisive victory at the Milvian Bridge, Constantine erected a great triple-passageway arch (FIG. **10-76** and 10-1, no. 15) in the shadow of the Colosseum to commemorate his defeat of Maxentius. The arch was the largest erected in Rome since the end of the Severan dynasty nearly a century before. Much of the sculptural decoration, however, was taken from earlier monuments of Trajan, Hadrian, and Marcus Aurelius. The columns also date to an earlier era. Sculptors refashioned the second-century reliefs to honor Constantine by recutting the heads of the earlier emperors with the features of the new ruler. They also added labels to the old reliefs, such as *Fundator Quietus* (bringer of peace) and *Liberator Urbis* (liberator of the city), references to the downfall of Maxentius and the end of civil war.

The reuse of statues and reliefs on the Arch of Constantine has often been cited as evidence of a decline in creativity and technical skill in the waning years of the pagan Roman Empire. Although such a judgment is in large part deserved, it ignores the fact that the reused sculptures were carefully selected to associate Constantine with the "good emperors" of the second century. That message is underscored in one of the new Constantinian reliefs above the arch's lateral passageways. It shows Constantine on the speaker's platform in the Roman Forum, flanked by statues of Hadrian and Marcus Aurelius.

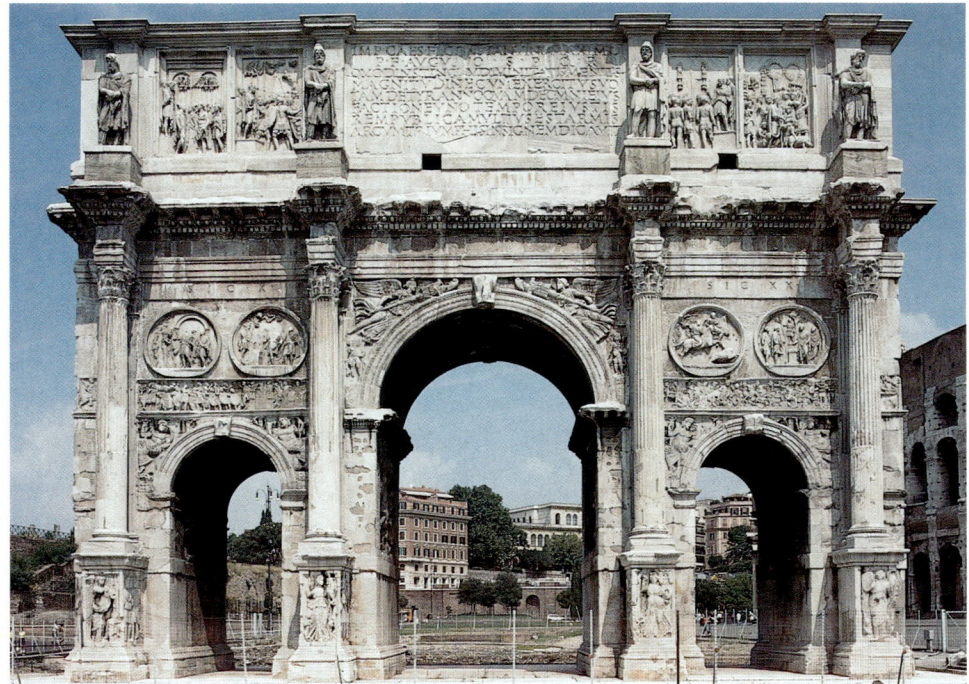

**10-76** Arch of Constantine (south side), Rome, Italy, 312–315 CE.

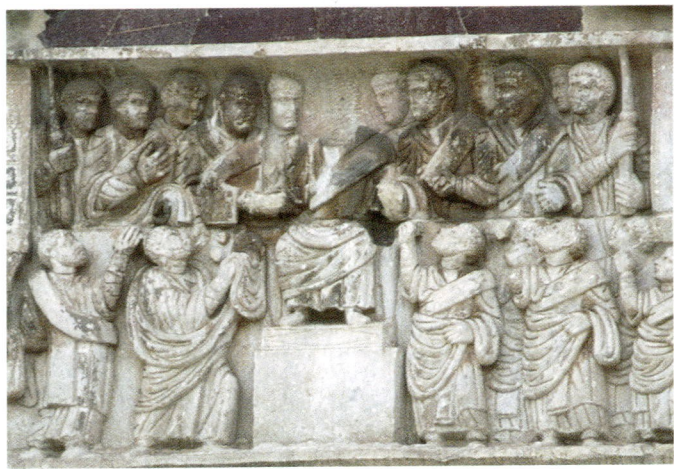

**10-77** Distribution of largess, detail of the north frieze of the Arch of Constantine, Rome, Italy, 312–315 CE. Marble, approx. 3′ 4″ high.

In another Constantinian relief (FIG. **10-77**), the emperor is shown with attendants, distributing largess to grateful citizens who approach him from right and left. Constantine is a frontal and majestic presence, elevated on a throne above the recipients of his munificence. The figures are squat in proportion, like the tetrarchs (FIG. 10-74). They do not move according to any classical principle of naturalistic movement but, rather, with the mechanical and repeated stances and gestures of puppets. The relief is very shallow, the forms were not fully modeled, and the details were incised. The heads were not distinguished from one another. The sculptor depicted a crowd, not a group of individuals. (Constantine's head, which was carved separately and set into the relief, has been lost.) The frieze is less a narrative of action than a picture of actors frozen in time so that the viewer can distinguish instantly the all-important imperial donor (at the center on a throne) from his attendants (to the left and right above) and the recipients of the largess (below and of smaller stature).

This approach to pictorial narrative was once characterized as a "decline of form," and when judged by classical art standards, it was. But the composition's rigid formality, determined by the rank of those portrayed, was consistent with a new set of values. It soon became the preferred mode, supplanting the classical notion that a picture is a window onto a world of anecdotal action. Comparing this Constantinian relief with a Byzantine icon (see FIG. 12-16) reveals that the new compositional principles of the Late Antique style are those of the Middle Ages. They were very different from, but not necessarily "better" or "worse" than, those of classical antiquity. The Arch of Constantine was the quintessential monument of its era, exhibiting a respect for the classical past in its reuse of second-century sculptures while rejecting the norms of classical design in its frieze, paving the way for the iconic art of the Middle Ages.

**CONSTANTINE'S COLOSSUS** After Constantine's victory over Maxentius, his official portraits broke with tetrarchic tradition as well as with the style of the soldier emperors, and resuscitated the Augustan image of an eternally youthful head of state. The most impressive by far of Constantine's preserved portraits is an eight-and-one-half-foot-tall head (FIG. **10-78**), one of several marble fragments of a colossal enthroned statue of the emperor that was composed of a brick core, a wooden torso covered with bronze, and a head and limbs of marble. Constantine's artist modeled the semi-nude seated portrait on Roman images of Jupiter. The emperor held an orb (possibly surmounted by the cross of Christ), the

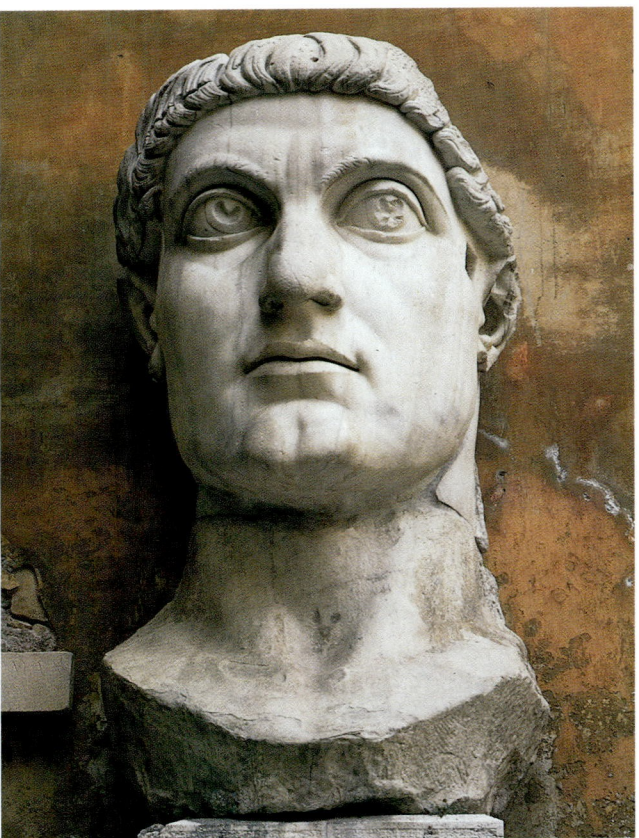

**10-78** Portrait of Constantine, from the Basilica Nova, Rome, Italy, ca. 315–330 CE. Marble, approx. 8′ 6″ high. Palazzo dei Conservatori, Rome.

symbol of global power, in his extended left hand. The nervous glance of third-century portraits is absent, replaced by a frontal mask with enormous eyes set into the broad and simple planes of the head. The emperor's personality is lost in this immense image of eternal authority. The colossal size, the likening of the emperor to Jupiter, the eyes directed at no person or thing of this world—all combine to produce a formula of overwhelming power appropriate to Constantine's exalted position as absolute ruler.

**ROME'S NEW BASILICA** Constantine's gigantic portrait sat in the western apse of the Basilica Nova ("New Basilica") in Rome (FIGS. **10-79** and 10-1, no. 12), a project Maxentius had begun on a site not far from the Arch of Titus. Constantine completed the building after his rival's death. From its position in the apse, the emperor's image dominated the interior of the basilica in much the same way that enthroned statues of Greco-Roman divinities loomed over awestruck mortals who entered the cellas of pagan temples.

The Basilica Nova ruins never fail to impress tourists with their size and mass. The original structure was 300 feet long and 215 feet wide. Brick-faced concrete walls 20 feet thick supported coffered barrel vaults in the aisles. These vaults also buttressed the groin vaults of the nave, which was 115 feet high. The walls and floors were richly marbled and stuccoed, and could be readily admired by those who came to the basilica to conduct business, because the groin vaults permitted ample light to enter the nave directly. Our reconstruction effectively suggests the immensity of the interior, where the great vaults dwarf not only humans but also even the emperor's colossal portrait. The drawing also clearly reveals the fenestration of the groin vaults, a lighting system akin to the clerestory of a traditional stone-and-timber basilica. The

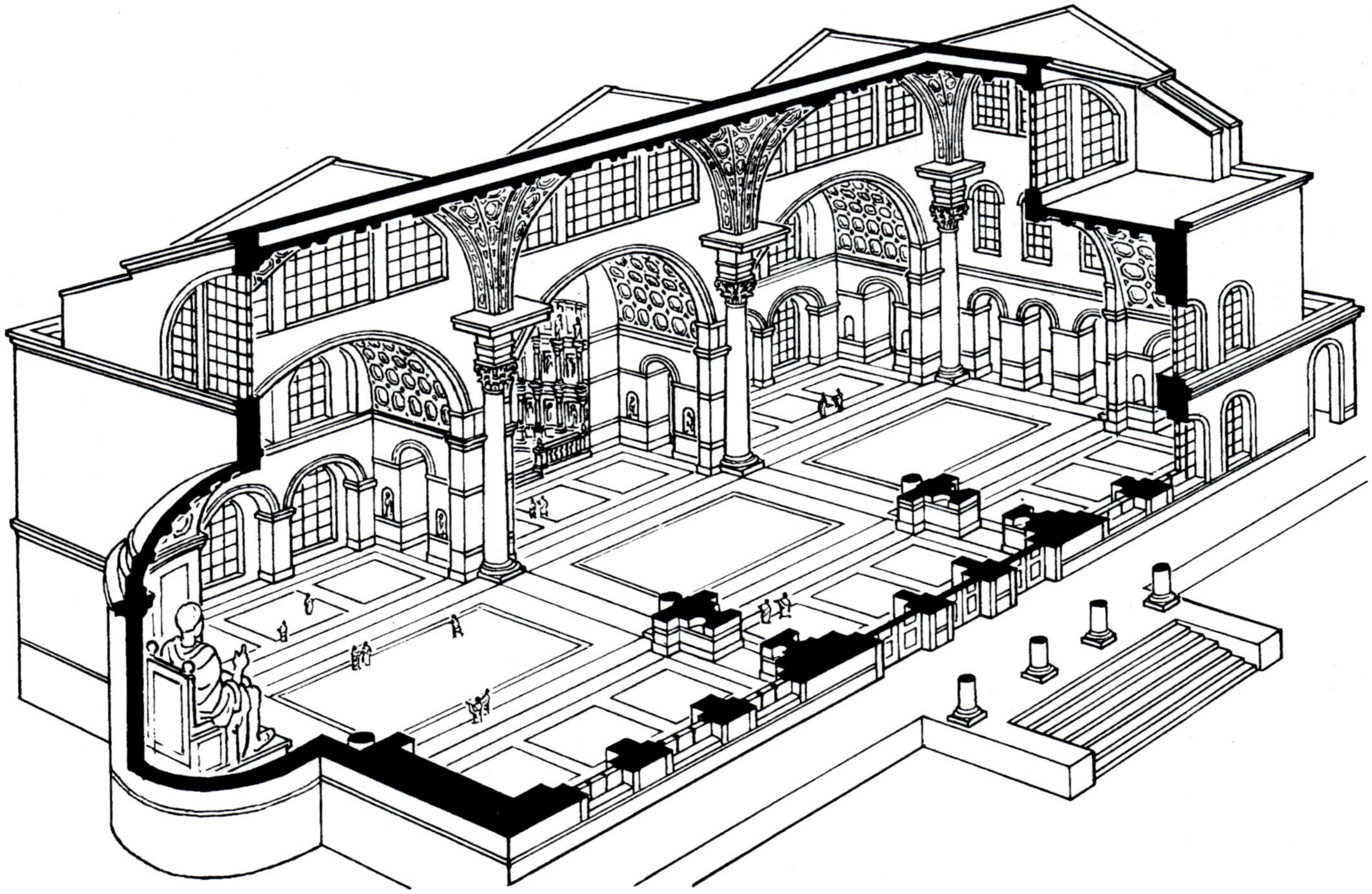

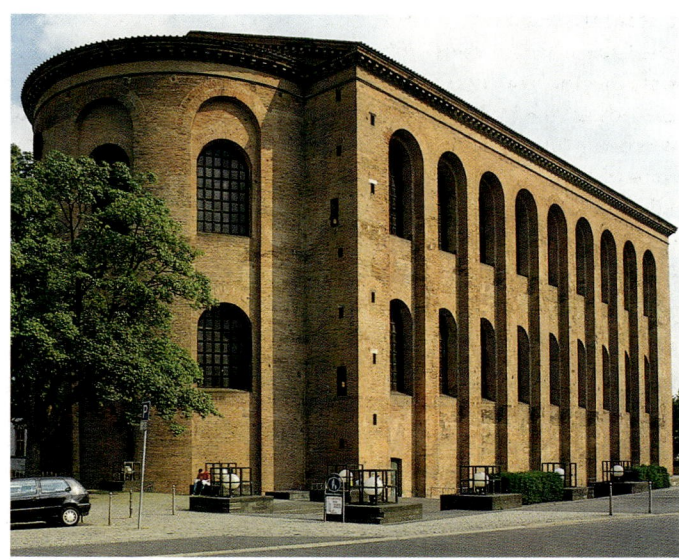

**10-79** Reconstruction drawing of the Basilica Nova (Basilica of Constantine), Rome, Italy, ca. 306–312 CE.

lessons learned in the design and construction of buildings such as Trajan's great market hall (FIG. 10-43) and the Baths of Caracalla (FIG. 10-68) were applied here to the Roman basilica.

Although one could argue that the Basilica Nova was the ideal solution to the problem of basilica design with its spacious, well-lit interior and economical, fire-resistant concrete frame, it became the exception rather than the rule. The traditional basilica form exemplified by Trajan's Basilica Ulpia (FIG. 10-41) remained the norm for centuries.

**CONSTANTINE IN GERMANY** At Trier (ancient Augusta Treverorum) on the Moselle River in Germany, the imperial seat of Constantius Chlorus as Caesar of the West, Constantine built a new palace complex. It included a basilica-like audience hall, the Aula Palatina (FIG. **10-80**), of traditional form and materials. The Aula Palatina measures about 190 feet long and 95 feet wide. Its austere brick exterior characterized much later Roman—and Early Christian—architecture. The verticality of the building's boldly projecting buttresses originally was lessened by horizontal timber galleries, which permitted the servicing of the windows. The brick wall was stuccoed in grayish white. The use of lead-framed panes of glass for the windows enabled Late Roman builders to give life and movement to blank exterior surfaces.

Inside (FIG. **10-81**), the audience hall was also very simple. Its flat, wooden, coffered ceiling is some 95 feet above the floor. The interior has no aisles, just a wide space with two stories of large windows that provide ample light. At the narrow north end, the main hall is divided from the semicircular apse (which also has a flat ceiling) by a so-called *triumphal arch*. The Aula Palatina's interior is quite severe, although the arch and apse originally were covered with marble veneer and mosaics to provide a magnificent environment for the enthroned emperor. The design of both the interior and exterior was closely paralleled in many Early Christian basilicas (for example, see FIG. 11-8). The Aula Palatina itself was later converted into a Christian church.

**10-80** Aula Palatina (exterior), Trier, Germany, early fourth century CE.

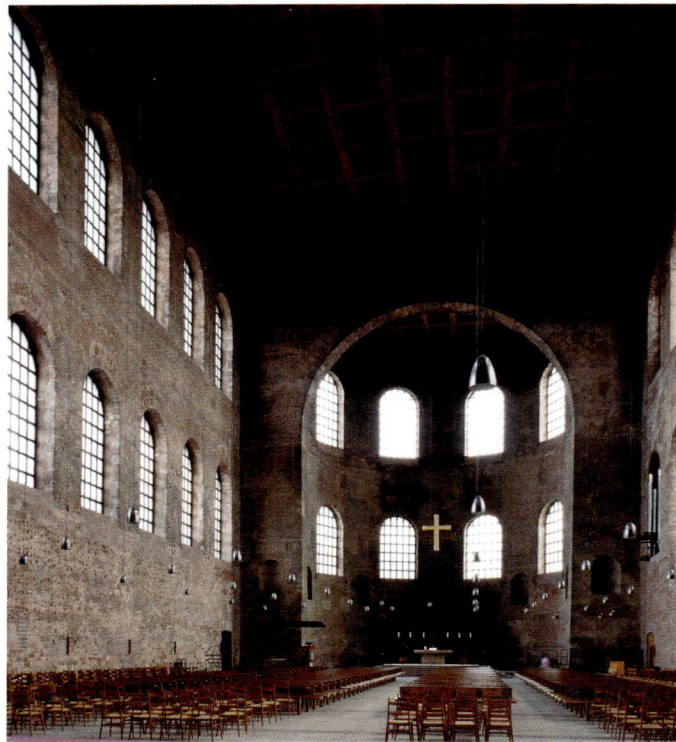

**10-81** Aula Palatina (interior), Trier, Germany, early fourth century CE.

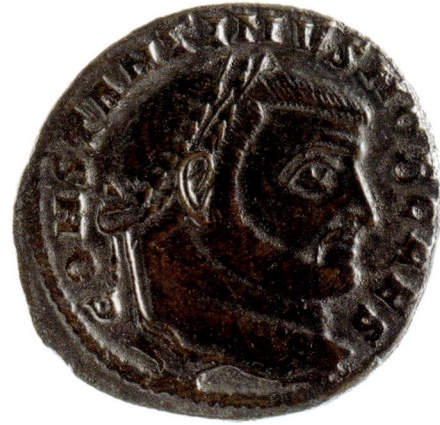

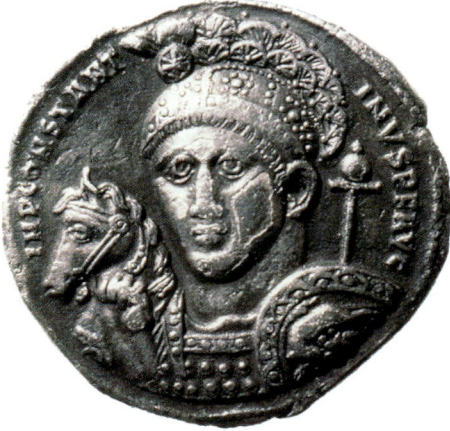

**10-82** Coins with portraits of Constantine. Nummus *(top)*, 307 CE. Billon, diameter approx. 1″. American Numismatic Society, New York. Medallion *(bottom)*, ca. 315 CE. Silver, diameter approx. 1″. Staatliche Münzsammlung, Munich.

**TWO FACES OF CONSTANTINE** We close our survey of ancient Roman art with two portraits of Constantine stamped on Roman coins. These images reveal both the essential character of Roman imperial portraiture and the special nature of Constantinian art. The first (FIG. **10-82,** *top*) was struck shortly after the death of Constantine's father, when Constantine was in his early 20s and his position was still insecure. Here, in his official portrait, he appears considerably older, because he adopted the imagery of the tetrarchs. Indeed, were it not for the accompanying label identifying this Caesar as Constantine, it would be impossible to know who was portrayed.

Eight years later, after the defeat of Maxentius and the issuance of the Edict of Milan, Constantine's portrait (FIG. 10-82, *bottom*) was transformed. Clean-shaven and looking his actual 30 years of age, the unchallenged Augustus of the West rejected the mature tetrarchic "look" in favor of youth. Eternal youthfulness henceforth characterized all the emperor's portraits (compare FIG. 10-78) until his death more than two decades later. These two coins should dispel any uncertainty about the often fictive nature of imperial portraiture and the ability of Roman emperors to choose any official image that suited their needs. In Roman art, "portrait" is often not synonymous with "likeness."

**CLASSICAL AND MEDIEVAL** The later coin is also an eloquent testimony to the dual nature of Constantinian rule. The emperor appears in his important role as imperator (general), dressed in armor, wearing an ornate helmet, and carrying a shield bearing the enduring emblem of the Roman state—the she-wolf nursing Romulus and Remus (compare FIG. 9-10 and Roma's shield in FIG. 10-57). Yet he does not carry the scepter of the pagan Roman emperor. Rather, he holds a cross crowned by an orb. And at the crest of his helmet, at the front, just below the grand plume, is a disk containing the *Christogram*, the monogram made up of *chi* (X), *rho* (P), and *iota* (I), the initial letters of Christ's name in Greek (compare the shield one of the soldiers holds in FIG. 12-10).

Constantine was at once portrayed as Roman emperor and as a soldier in the army of the Lord. The coin, like Constantinian art in general, belongs both to the classical and to the medieval world.

## CONCLUSION

In Europe, the Middle East, and Africa today, the remains of Roman civilization are everywhere. Roman temples and basilicas have an afterlife as churches. The powerful concrete vaults of ancient Roman buildings form the cores of modern houses, stores, restaurants, factories, and museums. Bullfights, sports events, operas, and rock concerts are staged in Roman amphitheaters. Roman aqueducts continue to supply water to some modern towns. Ships dock in what were once Roman ports, and western Europe's highway system still closely follows the routes of Roman roads.

Roman civilization also lives on in law and government, in languages, in the calendar—even in the coins used daily. Roman art speaks in a language almost everyone can readily understand. Its diversity and eclecticism foreshadowed the modern world. The Roman use of art, especially portraits and historical relief sculptures, to manipulate public opinion is similar to the carefully crafted imagery of contemporary political campaigns. And the Roman mastery of concrete construction began an architectural revolution still felt today. Indeed, the Roman Empire is the bridge—in politics, the arts, and religion—between the ancient and the medieval and modern Western worlds.

**Kings**

753 BCE

▮ FOUNDATION OF ROME BY ROMULUS, 753 BCE

509 BCE

**Republic**

▮ EXPULSION OF ETRUSCAN KINGS FROM ROME, 509 BCE

▮ MARCELLUS BRINGS SPOILS OF SYRACUSE TO ROME, 211 BCE

▮ ROMAN CONQUEST OF GREECE, 146 BCE

▮ ROME INHERITS KINGDOM OF PERGAMON, 133 BCE

▮ FOUNDATION OF ROMAN COLONY AT POMPEII, 80 BCE

▮ ASSASSINATION OF JULIUS CAESAR, 44 BCE

▮ BATTLE OF ACTIUM, 31 BCE

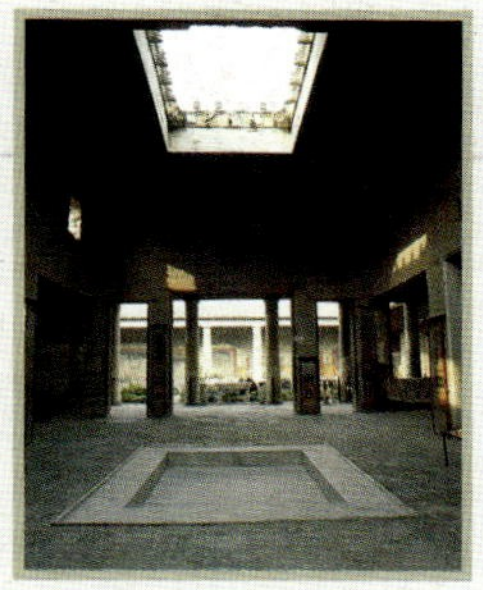

**1** House of the Vettii, Pompeii, second century BCE

27 BCE

**Early Empire**

**2** AUGUSTUS, R. 27 BCE–14 CE

▮ VITRUVIUS, *The Ten Books of Architecture,* CA. 25 BCE

▮ VERGIL, 70–19 BCE

▮ JULIO-CLAUDIANS, R. 14–68 CE

▮ FLAVIANS, R. 69–96

▮ ERUPTION OF MOUNT VESUVIUS, 79

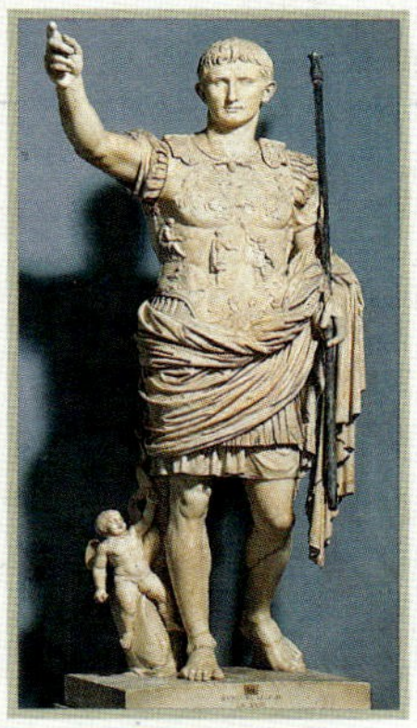

**2** Portrait of Augustus, from Primaporta, ca. 20 BCE

96 CE

**High Empire**

▮ TRAJAN, R. 98–117

**3** HADRIAN, R. 117–138

▮ ANTONINES, R. 138–192

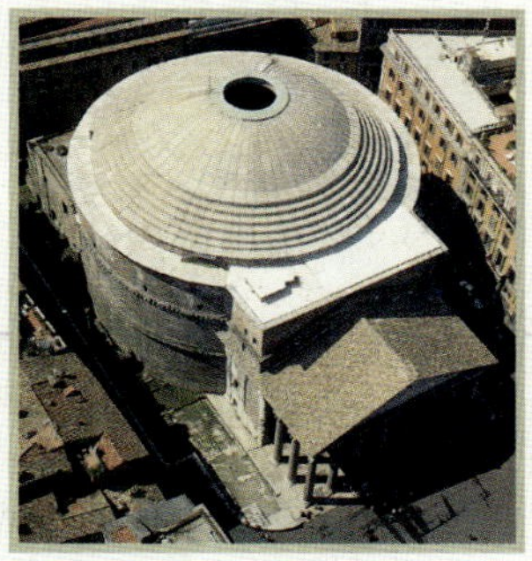

192

**Late Empire**

▮ SEVERANS, R. 193–235

▮ SOLDIER EMPERORS, R. 235–284

▮ DIOCLETIAN, R. 284–305

▮ CONSTANTINE, R. 306–337

▮ DEDICATION OF CONSTANTINOPLE, 330

**3** Pantheon, Rome, 118–125

**4**

337

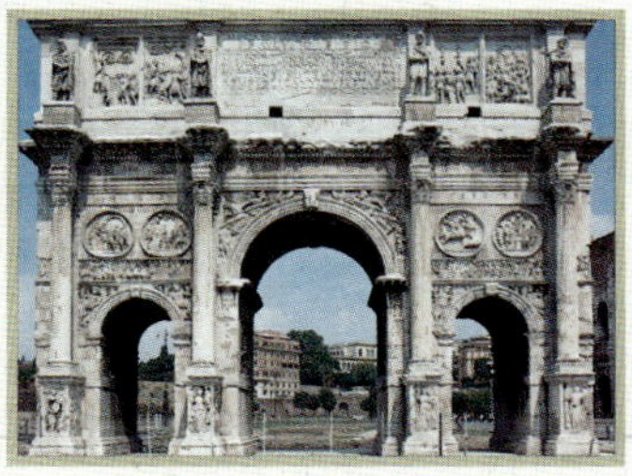

**4** Arch of Constantine, Rome, 312–315

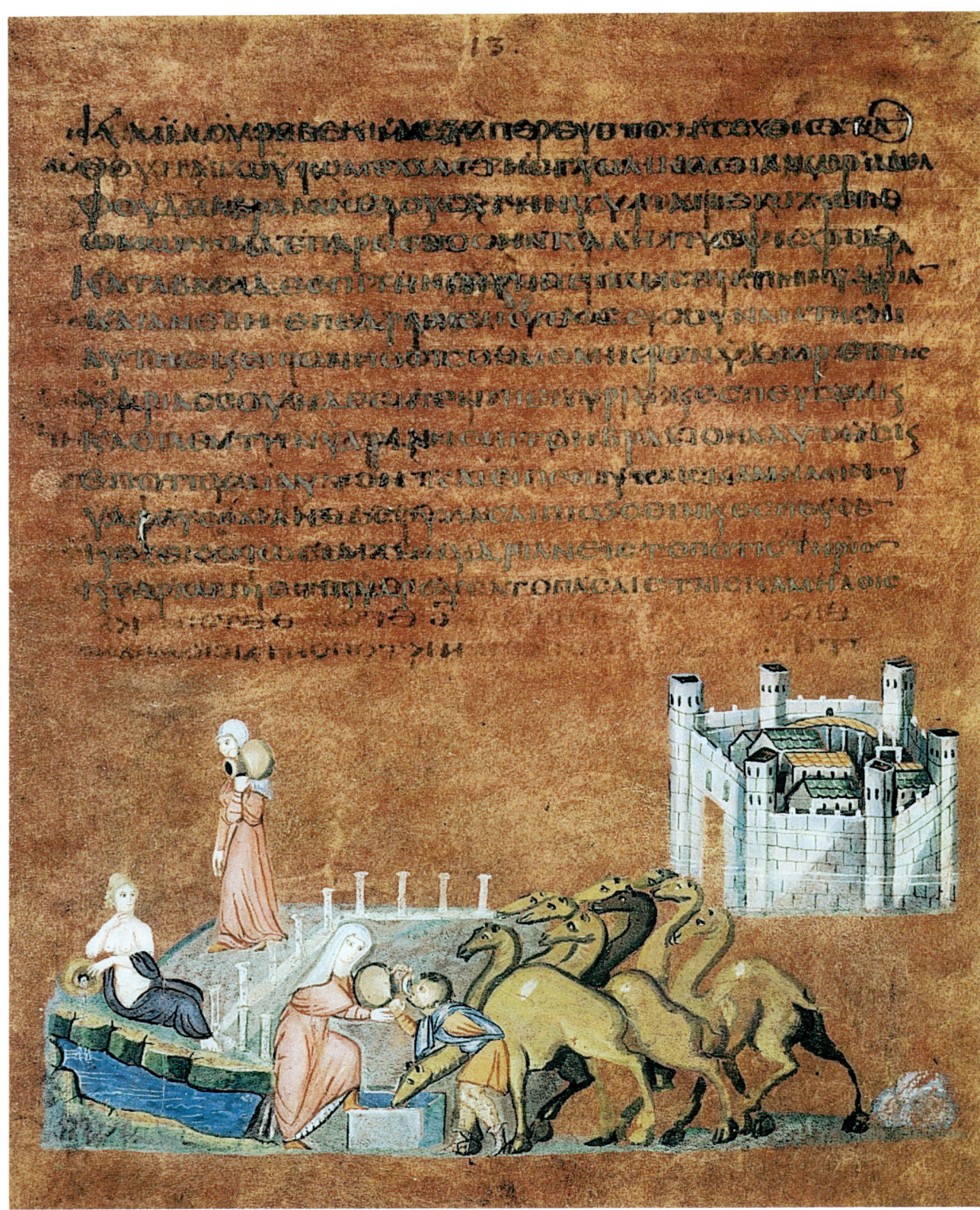

Rebecca and Eliezer at the well, folio 7 recto of the *Vienna Genesis*, early sixth century. Tempera, gold, and silver on purple vellum, approx. $1' \frac{1}{4}'' \times 9\frac{1}{4}''$. Österreichische Nationalbibliothek, Vienna.

# 11

# PAGANS, CHRISTIANS, AND JEWS

## THE ART OF LATE ANTIQUITY

The Roman Empire was home to an extraordinarily diverse population. In Rome alone on any given day, someone walking through the city's various quarters would have encountered people of an astonishing range of social, ethnic, racial, linguistic, and religious backgrounds. And the multicultural character of Roman society became only more pronounced as the empire grew. The previous chapter focused on the rich legacy of art and architecture bequeathed by the pagan Roman world. But during the third and fourth centuries a rapidly growing number of people rejected the emperors' polytheism (belief in multiple gods) in favor of monotheism (the worship of a single all-powerful god). This chapter addresses the Jewish and Christian art produced under Roman rule. These Late Antique sculptures, paintings, mosaics, and buildings occupy a special place in our account of art through the ages because they formed the foundation of the art and architecture of the Middle Ages.

**DURA-EUROPOS**  The powerful religious crosscurrents of late antiquity may be seen in microcosm in a distant outpost of the Roman Empire on a promontory overlooking the Euphrates River in Syria (MAP **11-1**). Called Europos by the Greeks and Dura by the Romans, the town probably was founded shortly after the death of Alexander the Great by one of his successors. By the end of the second century BCE, Dura-Europos was in the hands of the Parthians. The Roman emperor Trajan captured the city in 115 CE, but Dura reverted to Parthian control shortly thereafter.* In 165, under Marcus Aurelius, the Romans retook the city and placed a permanent garrison there. Dura-Europos fell in 256 to Rome's new enemy in the East, the Sasanians, heirs to the Parthian Empire (see Chapter 2). The Sasanian victory at Dura is an important fixed point in the chronology of late antiquity because the fortified town's population was evacuated and its buildings left largely intact. This "Pompeii of the desert" has revealed the remains of more than a dozen different cult buildings, including many shrines of the polytheistic religions of the Mediterranean and Near East. But the excavators also discovered worship places for the monotheistic creeds of Judaism and Christianity, even though neither was an approved religion in the Roman state.

---

* From this point on, all dates in this chapter are CE unless otherwise stated.

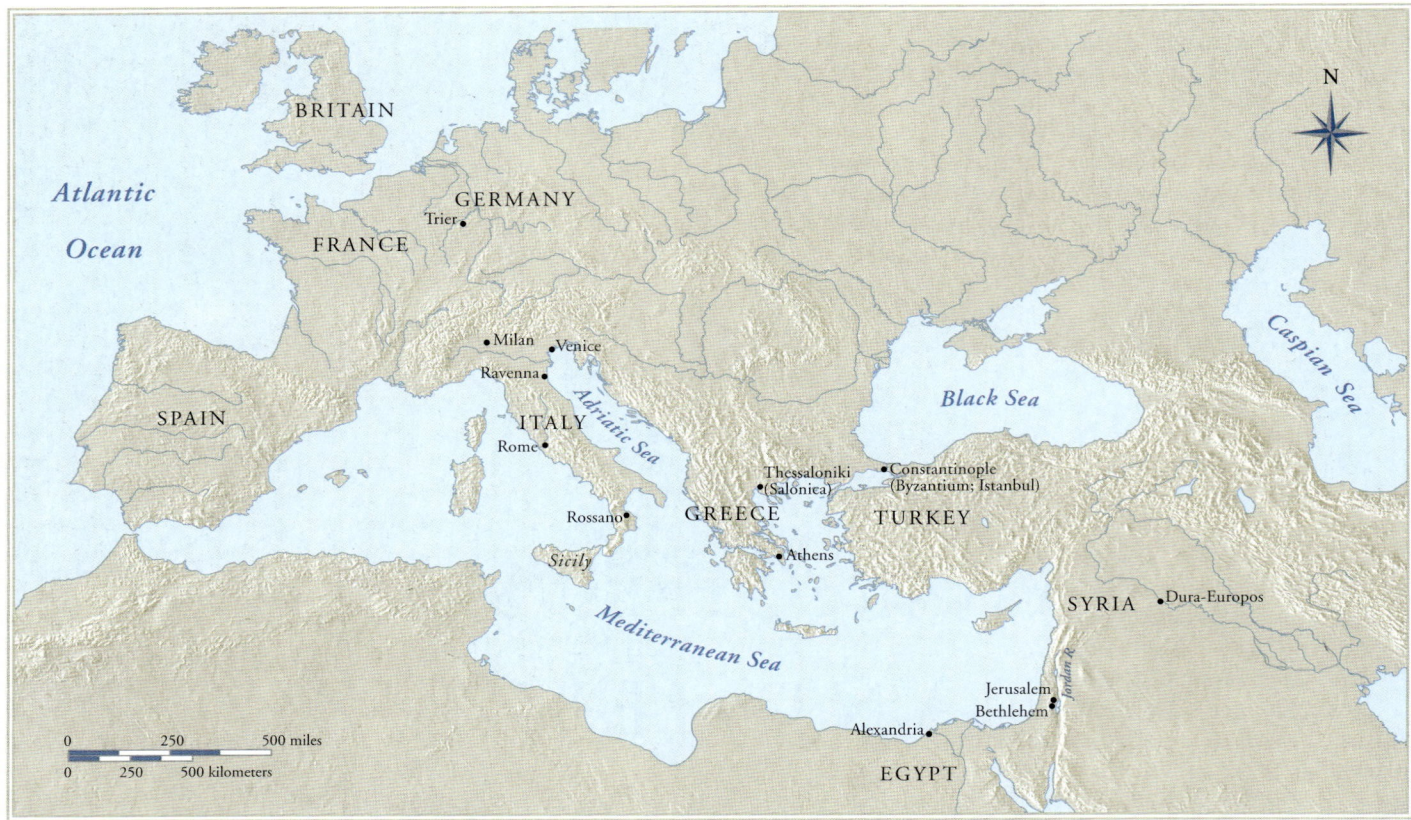

**MAP 11-1** Europe and the Near East in late antiquity.

**SYNAGOGUE PAINTINGS** The synagogue at Dura-Europos is remarkable not only for its very existence in a Roman garrison town but also for its extensive cycle of mural paintings (FIG. **11-1**) depicting biblical themes. The building, originally a private house with a central courtyard, was converted into a synagogue during the latter part of the second century. The paintings surprised scholars when they were first reported, because they seem to defy the Bible's Second Commandment prohibiting the making of graven images. It is now apparent that although the Jews of the Roman Empire did not worship idols as did their pagan contemporaries, biblical stories appeared on the painted walls of synagogues and probably also in painted manuscripts, although no illustrated Bible of this period survives. God (YHWH, or Yahweh in the Old Testament), however, never appears in the Dura paintings, except as a hand emerging from the top of the framed panels.

The Dura murals are mostly devoid of action, even when the subject is a narrative theme. The artists tell the stories through stylized gestures, and the figures, which have expressionless features and lack both volume and shadow, tend to stand in frontal rows. This Late Antique style, discussed in Chapter 10, is characteristic of much pagan art during the third and fourth centuries, including the friezes of the Arch of Septimius Severus at Lepcis Magna (see FIG. 10-66) and the Arch of Constantine in Rome (FIG. 10-77). The style of the Dura synagogue paintings is thus consistent with a major artistic trend in pagan, Jewish, and Christian art alike during the Late Roman Empire.

The Dura painting of Samuel anointing David (FIG. 11-1, center) exemplifies the Late Antique style. The episode is depicted just to the right of the niche that housed the sacred Jewish *Torah* (the scroll containing the *Pentateuch,* the first five books of the Hebrew Scriptures). The prophet anoints the future king of Israel, while David's six older brothers look on. The painter drew attention to

Samuel by depicting him larger than all the rest, a familiar convention of Late Antique art. David and his brothers are emotionless and almost disembodied spiritual presences. Their bodies do not even have enough feet! David, however, is distinguished from his brothers by the purple toga he wears. Purple was the color associated with the Roman emperor. The Dura artist borrowed the imperial toga to signify David's royalty.

**BAPTISM IN AN OLD HOUSE** The Christian community house (FIG. **11-2**) at Dura-Europos was also a remodeled private residence with a central courtyard. Its meeting hall (created by breaking down the partition between two rooms on the court's south side) could accommodate no more than about 70 people at a time. It had a raised platform at one end where the congregation leader sat or stood. Another room, on the opposite side of the courtyard, had a canopy-covered font for baptismal rites, the all-important ceremony initiating a new convert into the Christian community. Upstairs a communal dining room may have existed for the celebration of the *Eucharist,* when the faithful partook of the bread and wine symbolic of the body and blood of Christ (see "The Life of Jesus in Art," pages 308–309).

Although the baptistery had mural paintings (poorly preserved), the place where Christians gathered to worship at Dura, as elsewhere in the Roman Empire, was a modest secondhand house, in striking contrast to the grand temples of the Roman gods. Without the approval of the state, Christian communities remained small in number and often attracted the most impoverished classes of society. They found the promise of an afterlife where rich and poor were judged on equal terms especially appealing. Nonetheless, the emperor Diocletian was so concerned by the growing popularity of Christianity in the Roman army ranks that he ordered a fresh round of persecutions in 303 to 305, a half

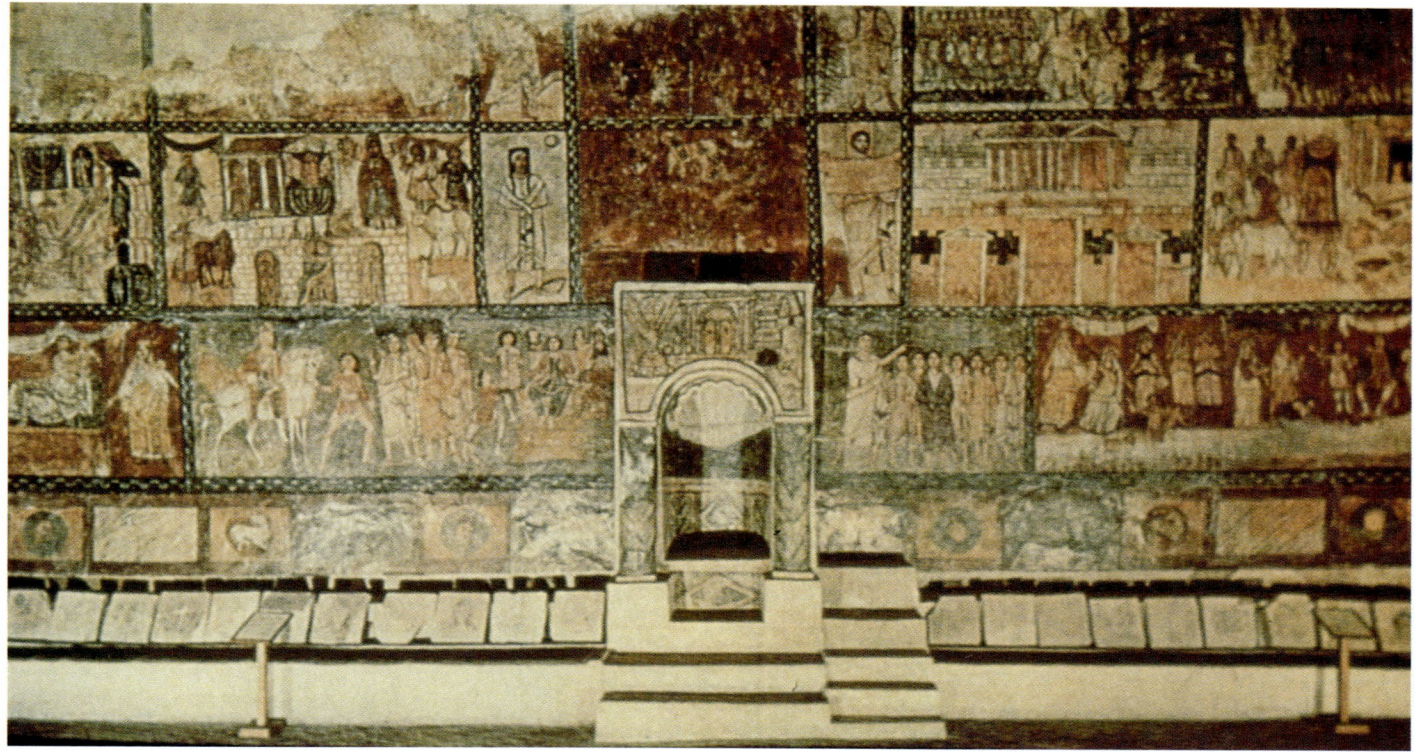

11-1 Interior of the synagogue at Dura-Europos, Syria, with wall paintings of Old Testament themes, ca. 245–256. Tempera on plaster. Reconstruction in National Museum, Damascus.

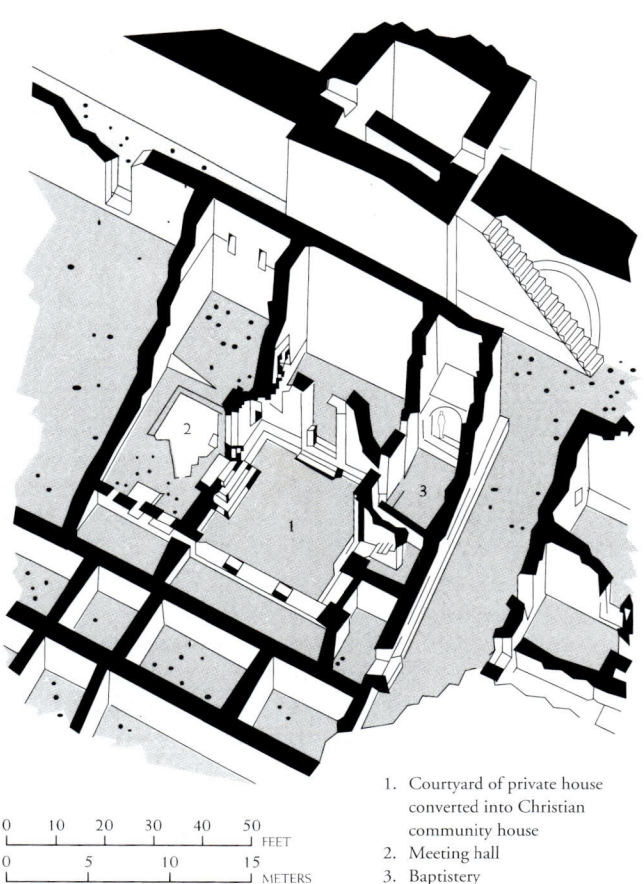

1. Courtyard of private house converted into Christian community house
2. Meeting hall
3. Baptistery

11-2 Reconstruction of the Christian community house at Dura-Europos, Syria, ca. 240–256.

century after the last great persecutions under Trajan Decius. The Romans hated the Christians because of their alien beliefs—that their god had been incarnated in the body of a man and that the death and Resurrection of the god-man Christ made possible the salvation and redemption of all. But they also hated them because they refused to pay even token homage to the Roman state's official gods (which included deified emperors as well as the traditional pantheon of classical gods and goddesses). As Christianity's appeal grew, so too did the Roman state's fear of weakening imperial authority. Persecution ended only when Constantine, after defeating Maxentius at the Milvian Bridge in Rome in 312, came to believe that the Christian god was the source of his power rather than a threat to it. A year after that victory, the Edict of Milan brought an end to the official mistreatment of Christians.

## THE CATACOMBS AND FUNERARY ART

THE "HOLLOWS" OF ROME  Very little is known about the art of the first Christians. When we speak of "Early Christian art," we mean the earliest preserved works with Christian subjects, not the art of Christians at the time of Jesus. Most Early Christian art in Rome dates to the third and fourth centuries and is found in the *catacombs*—vast subterranean networks of galleries (passageways) and chambers designed as cemeteries for burying the Christian dead, many of them sainted martyrs. To a much lesser extent, the catacombs also housed the graves of Jews and others. The builders tunneled the catacombs out of the tufa bedrock, much as the Etruscans created the underground tomb chambers in the necropolis at Cerveteri (see FIG. 9-7). The catacombs are less elaborate than the Etruscan tombs, but much more extensive. The name derives from the Latin *ad catacumbas,* which means "in the hollows." The catacombs in Rome (others exist elsewhere) comprise galleries estimated to run for 60 to 90 miles—and additional catacombs may be discovered yet. From the second through the fourth centuries, these catacombs were in constant use, housing as many as four million bodies.

In accordance with Roman custom, Christians had to be buried outside a city's walls on private property, usually purchased by a *confraternity,* or association, of Christian families pooling funds. Each of the catacombs was initially of modest extent. First, the builders dug a gallery three to four feet wide around the perimeter of the burial ground at a convenient level below the surface. In the walls of these galleries, they cut openings to receive the bodies of the dead. These openings, called *loculi,* were placed one above another, like shelves. Often, the Christians carved small rooms out of the rock, called *cubicula* (as in Roman houses of the living), to serve as mortuary chapels. Once the original perimeter galleries were full of loculi and cubicula, they cut other galleries at right angles to them. This process continued as long as lateral space permitted. They then dug lower levels connected by staircases. Some catacomb systems extended as deep as five levels. When adjacent burial areas belonged to members of the same Christian confraternity, or by gift or purchase fell into the same hands, the owners opened passageways between the respective cemeteries. The galleries thus spread laterally and gradually acquired a vast extent. After Christianity received official approval, churches rose on the land above the catacombs so that the pious could worship openly at the grave sites of some of the earliest Christian martyrs.

## Painting

**JONAH AND JESUS** The frescoes that decorated many cubicula were Roman in style but Christian in subject. The ceiling (FIG. 11-3) of a cubiculum in the Catacomb of Saints Peter and Marcellinus in Rome, for example, is similar to the second-century frescoed vault (see FIG. 10-54) in the Insula of the Painted Vaults at Ostia. In the catacomb, the polygonal frame of the Ostian spoked-wheel design became a large circle with the symbol of the Christian faith, the cross, at its center. The arms of the cross terminate in four *lunettes* (semicircular frames), which also find parallels in the Ostian composition.

The lunettes contain the key episodes from the Old Testament story of Jonah. The sailors throw him from his ship on the left. He emerges on the right from the "whale" (the Greek word is *ketos,* or sea dragon, and that is how the artist represented the monstrous marine creature that swallowed Jonah). And, safe on land at the bottom, Jonah contemplates the miracle of his salvation and the mercy of God. Jonah was a popular figure in Early Christian painting and sculpture, especially in funerary contexts. The Christians honored him as a *prefiguration* (prophetic forerunner) of Christ, who rose from death as Jonah had been delivered from the belly of the ketos, also after three days. Old Testament miracles prefiguring

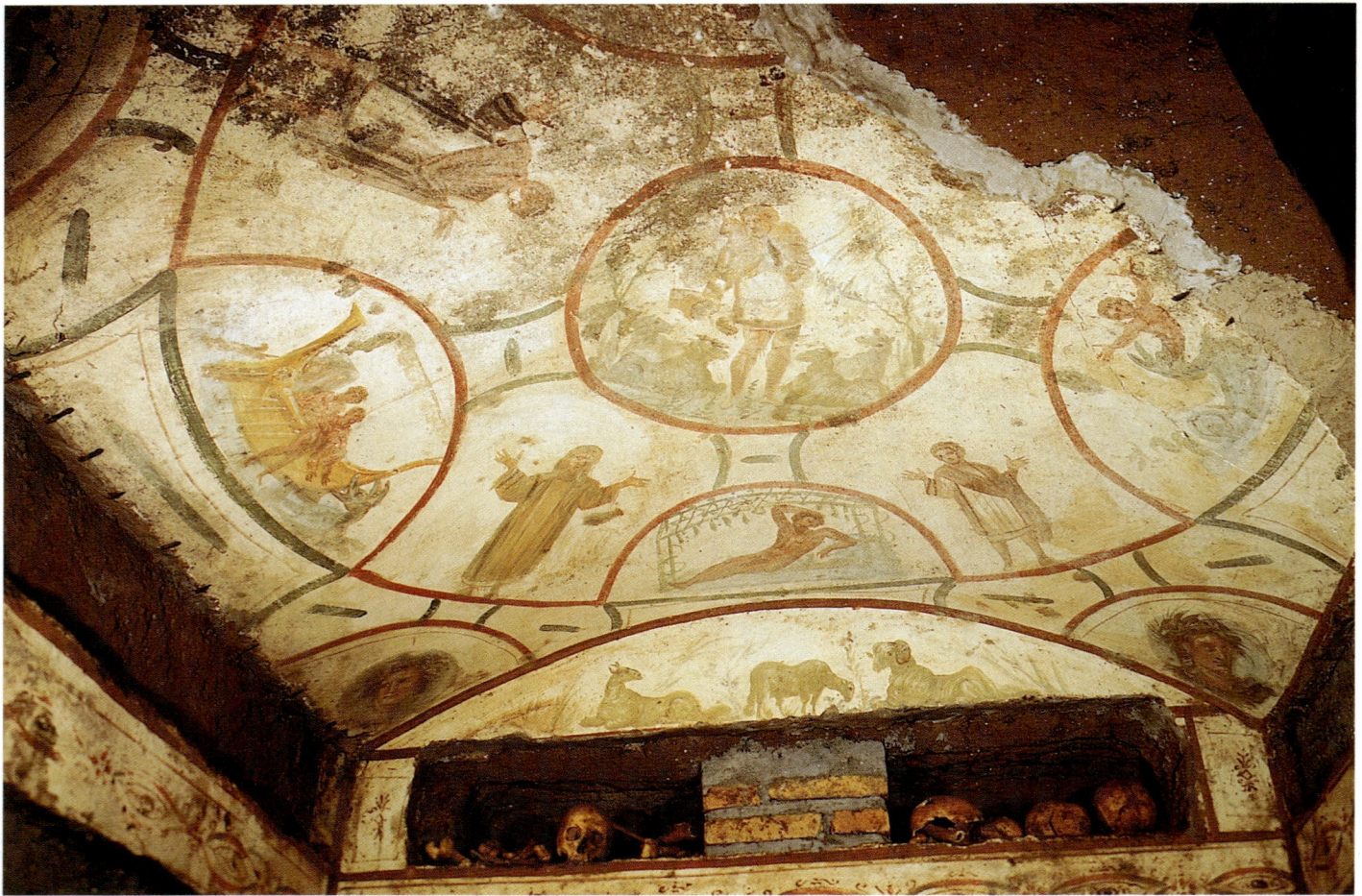

**11-3** The Good Shepherd, the story of Jonah, and orants, painted ceiling of a cubiculum in the Catacomb of Saints Peter and Marcellinus, Rome, Italy, early fourth century.

### Jewish Subjects in Christian Art

From the beginning, the Old Testament played an important role in Christian life and Christian art, in part because Jesus was a Jew and so many of the first Christians were converted Jews, but also because Christians came to view many of the persons and events of the Old Testament as prefigurations of New Testament persons and events. Christ himself established the pattern for this kind of biblical interpretation when he compared Jonah's spending three days in the belly of the sea monster (usually translated as "whale" in English) to the comparable time he would be entombed in the earth before his Resurrection (Matt. 12:40). In the fourth century, Saint Augustine (354–430) confirmed the validity of this approach to the Old Testament when he stated that "the New Testament is hidden in the Old; the Old is clarified by the New."[1]

Thus the Old Testament figured prominently in Early Christian art in all media. Biblical tales of Jewish faith and salvation were especially common in funerary contexts but appeared also in churches and on household objects. The Old Testament stories depicted in paintings, sculptures, and mosaics discussed in Chapters 11 and 12 are listed here.

**JONAH** (FIGS. 11-3 and 11-4) Jonah, an Old Testament prophet, had disobeyed God's command. In his wrath, the Lord caused a storm while Jonah was at sea. Jonah asked the sailors to throw him overboard, and the storm subsided. A sea dragon then swallowed Jonah, but God answered his prayers, and the monster spat out Jonah after three days and nights, foretelling Christ's Resurrection.

**ABRAHAM AND THE THREE ANGELS** (see FIGS. 12-8, upper right, and 12-34) Sarah, wife of Abraham, the father of the Hebrew nation, was 90 years old and childless when three angels visited Abraham. They announced that Sarah would bear a son, and she later miraculously gave birth to Isaac. Christians believe the Old Testament angels symbolized the Holy Trinity.

**SACRIFICE OF ISAAC** (FIGS. 11-5 and 12-8, upper right) God instructed Abraham to sacrifice Isaac, his only son, as proof of his faith. When it became clear that Abraham would obey, the Lord sent an angel to restrain him and provided a ram for sacrifice in Isaac's place. Christians view this episode as a prefiguration of the sacrifice of God's only son, Jesus.

**DANIEL** (FIG. 11-5) Daniel, one of the most important Jewish prophets, violated a Persian decree against prayer, and the Persians threw him into a den of lions. God sent an angel to shut the lions' mouths, and Daniel emerged unharmed. Like Jonah's story, this is an Old Testament salvation tale, a precursor of Christ's triumph over death.

**ADAM AND EVE** (FIG. 11-5) Eve, the first woman, tempted by a serpent, ate the forbidden fruit of the tree of knowledge. She also fed some to Adam, the first man. As punishment, God expelled Adam and Eve from Paradise. This "Original Sin" ultimately led to Christ's sacrifice on the cross so that all humankind could be saved. Christian theologians often consider Christ the new Adam and his mother, Mary, the new Eve.

[1] Augustine, *City of God*, 16.26.

---

Christ's Resurrection abound in the catacombs and in Early Christian art in general (see "Jewish Subjects in Christian Art," above).

**CHRIST AND HIS SHEEP** A man, a woman, and at least one child occupy the compartments between the Jonah lunettes. They are *orants* (praying figures), raising their arms in the ancient attitude of prayer. Together they make up a cross-section of the Christian family seeking a heavenly afterlife. The cross's central medallion shows Christ as the Good Shepherd, whose powers of salvation are underscored by his juxtaposition with Jonah's story. The motif can be traced back to Archaic Greek art (see FIG. 5-9), but there the pagan calf bearer offered his sheep in sacrifice to Athena. In Early Christian art, Christ is the youthful and loyal protector of the Christian flock, who said to his disciples, "I am the good shepherd; the good shepherd gives his life for the sheep" (John 10:11). In the Christian motif, the sheep on Christ's shoulders is one of the lost sheep he has retrieved, symbolizing a sinner who has strayed and been rescued.

Prior to the fourth century, artists almost invariably represented Christ either as the Good Shepherd or as a teacher. Only after Christianity became the Roman Empire's official religion did Christ take on in art such imperial attributes as the halo, the purple robe, and the throne, which denoted rulership. Eventually artists depicted Christ with the beard of a mature adult, which has been the standard form for centuries, supplanting the youthful imagery of most Early Christian portrayals of Christ.

### Sculpture

**COFFINS FOR THE FAITHFUL** All Christians rejected cremation, and the wealthiest Christian faithful, like their pagan contemporaries, favored impressive marble sarcophagi. Many of these coffins have survived in the catacombs and elsewhere. As one would expect, the most common themes painted on the walls and vaults of the Roman subterranean cemeteries were also the subjects that appeared on Early Christian sarcophagi. Often, the decoration of the marble coffins was a collection of significant Christian themes, just as on the painted ceiling in the Catacomb of Saints Peter and Marcellinus (FIG. 11-3).

On the front of a sarcophagus (FIG. **11-4**) in Santa Maria Antiqua in Rome, the story of Jonah takes up the left third. At the center are an orant and a seated philosopher, the latter a motif borrowed directly from contemporary pagan sarcophagi (see FIG. 10-72). The heads of both the praying woman and the seated man reading from a scroll are unfinished. Roman workshops often produced sarcophagi before knowing who would purchase them. The sculptors added the portraits at the time of burial, if they added them at all. This practice underscores the universal appeal of the themes chosen. At the right are two different, yet linked, representations of Jesus—as the Good Shepherd and as a child receiving baptism in the Jordan River, though he really was baptized at age 30 (see "The Life of Jesus in Art," pages 308–309). The sculptor suggested the future

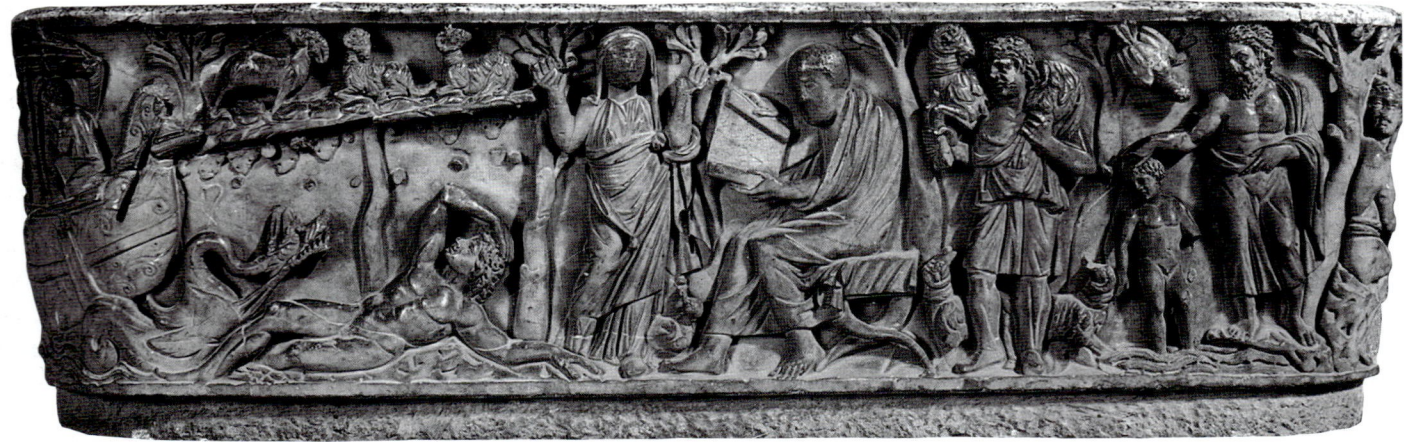

**11-4** Sarcophagus with philosopher, orant, and Old and New Testament scenes, Santa Maria Antiqua, Rome, Italy, ca. 270. Marble, 1′ 11¼″ × 7′ 2″.

ministry of the baptized Jesus by turning the child's head toward the Good Shepherd and by placing his right hand on one of the sheep. In the early centuries of Christianity, baptism was usually delayed almost to the moment of death because it cleansed the Christian of all sin. One of those who was baptized on his deathbed was the emperor Constantine (see Chapter 10).

**A CONVERT'S SARCOPHAGUS** Another pagan convert to Christianity was the city prefect of Rome, Junius Bassus, who, according to the inscription on his sarcophagus (FIG. **11-5**), was baptized just before he died in 359. The sarcophagus, decorated only on three sides in the western Roman manner (see Chapter 10), is, however, divided into two registers of five compartments, each framed by columns in the tradition of Asiatic sarcophagi (see FIG. 10-62). In contrast to the Santa Maria Antiqua sarcophagus, the deceased does not appear on the body of the coffin. Instead, stories from the Old and New Testaments fill the 10 niches. Christ has pride of place and appears in the central compartment of each register: as a teacher enthroned between his chief apostles, Saints Peter and Paul (above), and triumphantly entering Jerusalem on a donkey (below). Appropriately, the scene of Christ's heavenly triumph is situated above that of his earthly triumph. Both compositions owe a great deal to

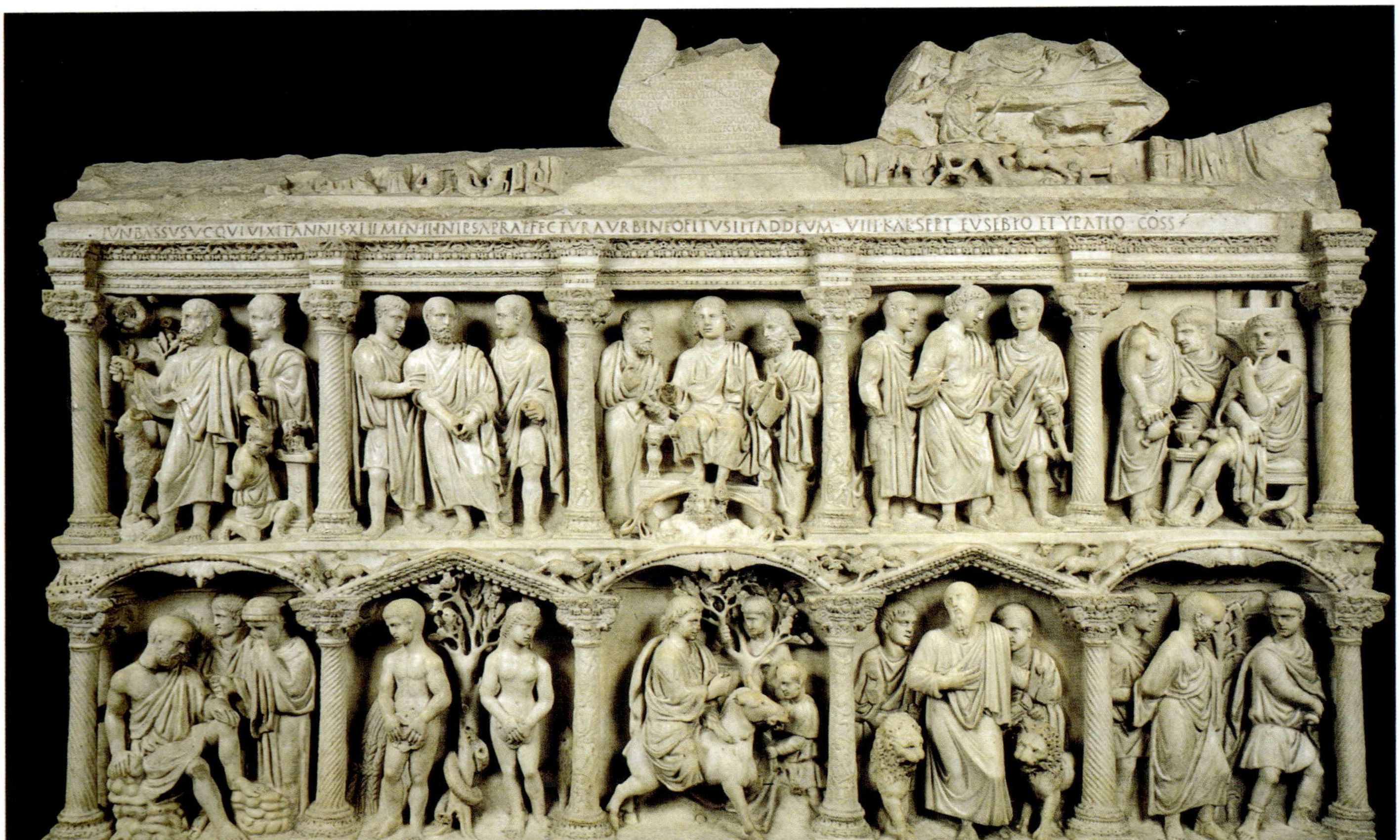

**11-5** Sarcophagus of Junius Bassus, from Rome, Italy, ca. 359. Marble, 3′ 10½″ × 8′. Museo Storico del Tesoro della Basilica di San Pietro, Rome.

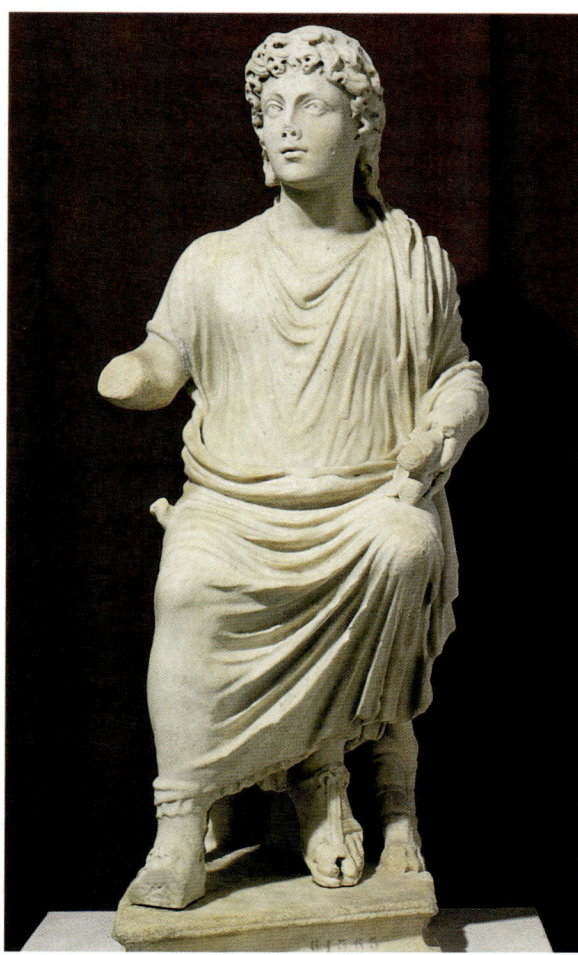

**11-6** Christ seated, from Civita Latina, Italy, ca. 350–375. Marble, approx. 2′ 4½″ high. Museo Nazionale Romano—Palazzo Massimo alle Terme, Rome.

Bassus and other Christians, whether they were converts from paganism or from Judaism, hoped for a similar salvation.

**AN "IDOL" OF CHRIST**  Apart from the reliefs on privately commissioned sarcophagi, monumental sculpture became increasingly uncommon in the fourth century. Portrait statues of Roman emperors and other officials continued to be erected, and statues of pagan gods and mythological figures were still made, but their numbers decreased sharply. In his *Apologia,* Justin Martyr, a second-century philosopher who converted to Christianity and was mindful of the Second Commandment's admonition to shun graven images, accused the pagans of worshiping statues as gods. Christians tended to suspect the freestanding statue, linking it with the false gods of the pagans, so Early Christian houses of worship had no "cult statues." Nor did the first churches have any equivalent of the pedimental statues and relief friezes of Greco-Roman temples.

The Greco-Roman experience, however, was still a living part of the Mediterranean mentality, and many Christians like Junius Bassus were recent converts from paganism who retained some of their classical values. This may account for those rare instances of Early Christian "idols," such as the marble statuette of the seated Christ shown here (FIG. **11-6**). Less than three feet tall, the sculpture is a freestanding version of the Christ between Saints Peter and Paul on the Junius Bassus sarcophagus (FIG. 11-5). As on the relief, Christ's head is that of a long-haired Apollo-like youth, but the statuary type was one employed for bearded Roman philosophers of advanced age. Like those learned men, Christ wears the Roman tunic, toga, and sandals, and holds an unopened scroll in his left hand. The piece is unique and, unfortunately, of unknown provenance, so art historians only can speculate about its original context and function. Several third- and fourth-century marble statuettes of Christ as the Good Shepherd and of Jonah also survive, but they too are exceptional. Monumental sculpture of Christian character was not significant in the history of art until the 12th century (see Chapter 17).

## ARCHITECTURE AND MOSAICS

**IMPERIAL PATRONAGE**  Although some Christian ceremonies were held in the catacombs, regular services took place in private community houses of the type found at Dura-Europos (FIG. 11-2). Once Christianity achieved imperial sponsorship under Constantine, an urgent need suddenly arose to construct churches. The new buildings had to meet the requirements of Christian liturgy, provide a suitably monumental setting for the celebration of the Christian faith, and accommodate the rapidly growing numbers of worshipers.

Constantine was convinced that the Christian god had guided him to victory over Maxentius, and in lifelong gratitude he protected and advanced Christianity throughout the empire, as well as in the obstinately pagan capital city of Rome. As emperor, he was, of course, obliged to safeguard the ancient Roman religion, traditions, and monuments, and, as noted in Chapter 10, he was (for his time) a builder on a grand scale in the heart of the city. But eager to provide buildings to house the Christian rituals and venerated burial places, especially the memorials of founding saints, Constantine also was the first major patron of Christian architecture. He constructed elaborate basilicas, memorials, and mausoleums not only in Rome but also in Constantinople, his "New Rome" in the East, and at sites sacred to Christianity, most notably Bethlehem, the birthplace of Jesus, and Jerusalem, the site of his crucifixion.

pagan Roman art. In the upper zone, Christ, like an enthroned Roman emperor, sits above a personification of the sky god holding a billowing mantle over his head, indicating that Christ is ruler of the universe. The scene below derives in part from portrayals of Roman emperors entering cities on horseback, but Christ's steed and the absence of imperial attributes contrast sharply with the imperial models the sculptor used as compositional sources.

The Old Testament scenes on the Junius Bassus sarcophagus were chosen for their significance in the early Christian Church. Adam and Eve, for example, are in the second niche from the left on the lower level. Their Original Sin of eating the apple in the Garden of Eden ultimately necessitated Christ's sacrifice for the salvation of humankind. To the right of the entry into Jerusalem is Daniel, unscathed by flanking lions, saved by his faith. At the upper left, Abraham is about to sacrifice Isaac. Christians believe that this Old Testament story was a prefiguration of God's sacrifice of his own son, Jesus.

The Crucifixion itself, however, does not appear on the Junius Bassus sarcophagus. Indeed, the subject was very rare in Early Christian art, and unknown prior to the fifth century. Artists emphasized Christ's divinity and exemplary life as teacher and miracle worker, not his suffering and death at the hands of the Romans. This sculptor, however, alluded to the Crucifixion in the scenes in the two compartments at the upper right depicting Jesus being led before Pontius Pilate for judgment. The Romans condemned Jesus to death, but he triumphantly overcame it. Junius

## The Life of Jesus in Art

Christians believe that Jesus of Nazareth is the son of God, the *Messiah* (Savior, *Christ*) of the Jews prophesied in the Old Testament. His life—his miraculous birth from the womb of a virgin mother, his preaching and miracle working, his execution by the Romans and subsequent ascent to heaven—has been the subject of countless artworks from Roman times through the present day. The primary literary sources for these representations are the Gospels of the New Testament attributed to the Four Evangelists, Saints Matthew, Mark, Luke, and John (see "The Four Evangelists," Chapter 16, page 426); later apocryphal works; and commentaries on these texts by medieval theologians.

The life of Jesus dominated the subject matter of Christian art to a far greater extent than Greco-Roman religion and mythology ever did classical art. Whereas images of athletes, portraits of statesmen and philosophers, narratives of war and peace, genre scenes, and other secular subjects were staples of the classical tradition, Christian iconography held a near monopoly in the art of the Western world in the Middle Ages.

Although many of the events of Jesus' life were rarely or never depicted during certain periods, the cycle as a whole has been one of the most frequent subjects of Western art, even after the revival of classical and secular themes in the Renaissance. Thus it is useful to summarize the entire cycle here in one place, giving selected references to illustrations of the various episodes, from late antiquity to the 17th century. We describe the events as they usually appear in the artworks.

### INCARNATION AND CHILDHOOD

The first "cycle" of the life of Jesus consists of the events of his conception, birth, infancy, and childhood.

**ANNUNCIATION TO MARY** (see FIGS. 12-33, 19-12, and 21-36) The archangel Gabriel announces to the Virgin Mary that she will miraculously conceive and give birth to God's son Jesus. God's presence at the *Incarnation* is sometimes indicated by a dove, the symbol of the Holy Spirit, the third "person" of the Trinity with God the Father and Jesus.

**VISITATION** (see FIG. 18-22) The pregnant Mary visits Elizabeth, her older cousin, who is pregnant with the future Saint John the Baptist. Elizabeth is the first to recognize that the baby Mary is bearing is the Son of God, and they rejoice.

**NATIVITY** (see FIGS. 13-30, 19-3, and 19-4), **ANNUNCIATION TO THE SHEPHERDS** (see FIG. 16-28), and **ADORATION OF THE SHEPHERDS** (see FIG. 24-64) Jesus is born at night in Bethlehem and placed in a basket. Mary and her husband Joseph marvel at the newborn in a stable or, in Byzantine art, in a cave. An angel announces the birth of the Savior to shepherds in the field, who rush to Bethlehem to adore the child.

**ADORATION OF THE MAGI** (see FIG. 21-9) A bright star alerts three wise men (*magi*) in the East that the King of the Jews has been born. They travel 12 days to find the Holy Family and present precious gifts to the infant Jesus.

**PRESENTATION IN THE TEMPLE** (see FIG. 13-30) In accordance with Jewish tradition, Mary and Joseph bring their firstborn son to the temple in Jerusalem, where the aged Simeon, who God said would not die until he had seen the Messiah, recognizes Jesus as the prophesied Savior of humankind.

**MASSACRE OF THE INNOCENTS** and **FLIGHT INTO EGYPT** King Herod, fearful that a rival king has been born, orders the massacre of all infants in Bethlehem, but an angel warns the Holy Family and they escape to Egypt.

**DISPUTE IN THE TEMPLE** Joseph and Mary travel to Jerusalem for the feast of Passover (the celebration of the release of the Jews from bondage to the pharaohs of Egypt). Jesus, only 12 years old at the time, engages in learned debate with astonished Jewish scholars in the temple, foretelling his ministry.

### PUBLIC MINISTRY

The public ministry cycle comprises the teachings of Jesus and the miracles he performed.

**BAPTISM** (FIG. 11-4) The beginning of Jesus' public ministry is marked by his baptism at age 30 by John the Baptist in the Jordan River, where the dove of the Holy Spirit appears and God's voice is heard proclaiming Jesus as his son.

**CALLING OF MATTHEW** (see FIG. 24-19) Jesus summons Matthew, a tax collector, to follow him, and Matthew becomes one of his 12 disciples, or *apostles* (from the Greek for "messenger"), and later the author of one of the four Gospels.

**MIRACLES** In the course of his teaching and travels, Jesus performs many miracles, revealing his divine nature. These include acts of healing and the raising of the dead, the turning of water into wine, walking on water and calming storms, and the creation of wondrous quantities of food. In the miracle of loaves and fishes (FIG. 11-17), for example, Jesus transforms a few loaves of bread and a handful of fishes into enough food to feed several thousand people.

**DELIVERY OF THE KEYS TO PETER** (see FIG. 21-40) The fisherman Peter was one of the first Jesus summoned as a disciple. Jesus chooses Peter (whose name means "rock") as his successor. He declares that Peter is the rock on which his church will be built, and symbolically delivers to Peter the keys to the kingdom of heaven.

**TRANSFIGURATION** (see FIG. 12-13) Jesus scales a high mountain and, in the presence of Peter and two other disciples, James and John the Evangelist, is transformed into radiant light. God, speaking from a cloud, discloses that Jesus is his son.

**CLEANSING OF THE TEMPLE** Jesus returns to Jerusalem, where he finds money changers and merchants conducting business in the temple. He rebukes them and drives them out of the sacred precinct.

## The Life of Jesus in Art (continued)

### PASSION

The Passion (from Latin *passio,* "suffering") cycle includes the episodes leading to Jesus' death, Resurrection, and ascent to heaven.

**ENTRY INTO JERUSALEM** (FIGS. 11-5 and 13-30) On the Sunday before his Crucifixion (Palm Sunday), Jesus rides triumphantly into Jerusalem on a donkey, accompanied by disciples. Crowds of people enthusiastically greet Jesus and place palm fronds in his path.

**LAST SUPPER** (see FIGS. 20-9, 21-37, 22-3, 22-52, and 23-4) and **WASHING OF THE DISCIPLES' FEET** In Jerusalem, Jesus celebrates Passover with his disciples. During this Last Supper, Jesus foretells his imminent betrayal, arrest, and death and invites the disciples to remember him when they eat bread (symbol of his body) and drink wine (his blood). This ritual became the celebration of *Mass (Eucharist)* in the Christian Church. At the same meal, Jesus sets an example of humility for his apostles by washing their feet.

**AGONY IN THE GARDEN** Jesus goes to the Mount of Olives in the Garden of Gethsemane, where he struggles to overcome his human fear of death by praying for divine strength. The apostles who accompanied him there fall asleep despite his request that they stay awake with him while he prays.

**BETRAYAL** and **ARREST** (see FIG. 19-11) One of the disciples, Judas Iscariot, agrees to betray Jesus to the Jewish authorities in return for 30 pieces of silver. Judas identifies Jesus to the soldiers by kissing him, and Jesus is arrested. Later, a remorseful Judas hangs himself from a tree (FIG. 11-21).

**TRIALS OF JESUS** (FIGS. 11-5 and 11-20) and **DENIAL OF PETER** Jesus is brought before Caiaphas, the Jewish high priest, and is interrogated about his claim to be the Messiah. Meanwhile, the disciple Peter thrice denies knowing Jesus, as Jesus predicted he would. Jesus is then brought before the Roman governor of Judaea, Pontius Pilate, on the charge of treason because he had proclaimed himself as King of the Jews. Pilate asks the crowd to choose between freeing Jesus or Barabbas, a murderer. The people choose Barabbas, and the judge condemns Jesus to death. Pilate washes his hands, symbolically relieving himself of responsibility for the mob's decision.

**FLAGELLATION** and **MOCKING** The Roman soldiers who hold Jesus captive whip (flagellate) him and mock him by dressing him as King of the Jews and placing a crown of thorns on his head.

**CARRYING OF THE CROSS, RAISING OF THE CROSS** (see FIG. 24-34), and **CRUCIFIXION** (see FIGS. 11-21, 12-22, 16-15, and 16-26) The Romans force Jesus to carry the cross on which he will be cruci-fied from Jerusalem to Mount Calvary (Golgotha, the "place of the skull," where Adam was buried). He falls three times and gets stripped along the way. Soldiers erect the cross and nail his hands and feet to it. Jesus' mother, John the Evangelist, and Mary Magdalene mourn at the foot of the cross, while soldiers torment Jesus. One of them (the centurion Longinus) stabs his side with a spear. After suffering great pain, Jesus dies. The Crucifixion occurred on a Friday, and Christians celebrate the day each year as Good Friday.

**DEPOSITION** (see FIGS. 20-7 and 22-42), **LAMENTATION** (see FIGS. 12-27 and 19-9), and **ENTOMBMENT** (see FIG. 17-33) Two disciples, Joseph of Arimathea and Nicodemus, remove Jesus' body from the cross (the Deposition); sometimes those present at the Crucifixion look on. They take Jesus to the tomb Joseph had purchased for himself, and Joseph, Nicodemus, the Virgin Mary, Saint John the Evangelist, and Mary Magdalene mourn over the dead Jesus (the Lamentation). (When in art the isolated figure of the Virgin Mary cradles her dead son in her lap, it is called a *Pietà* [Italian for "pity"; see FIG. 18-51].) In portrayals of the Entombment, his followers lower Jesus into a sarcophagus in the tomb.

**DESCENT INTO LIMBO** (see FIG. 12-31) During the three days he spends in the tomb, Jesus (after death, Christ) descends into Hell, or Limbo, and triumphantly frees the souls of the righteous, including Adam, Eve, Moses, David, Solomon, and John the Baptist. In Byzantine art, this episode is often labeled *Anastasis* (Greek, *resurrection*), although it refers to events preceding Christ's emergence from the tomb and reappearance on earth.

**RESURRECTION** and **THREE MARYS AT THE TOMB** On the third day (Easter Sunday), Christ rises from the dead and leaves the tomb while the guards outside are sleeping. The Virgin Mary, Mary Magdalene, and Mary, the mother of James, visit the tomb, find it empty, and learn from an angel that Christ has been resurrected.

**NOLI ME TANGERE, SUPPER AT EMMAUS,** and **DOUBTING OF THOMAS** During the 40 days between Christ's Resurrection and his ascent to heaven, he appears on several occasions to his followers. Christ warns Mary Magdalene, weeping at his tomb, with the words "Don't touch me" (*Noli me tangere* in Latin), but he tells her to inform the apostles of his return. At Emmaus he eats supper with two of his astonished disciples. Later, Thomas, who cannot believe that Christ has risen, is invited to touch the wound in his side that he received at his Crucifixion.

**ASCENSION** (see FIGS. 12-15 and 17-26) On the 40th day, on the Mount of Olives, with his mother and apostles as witnesses, Christ gloriously ascends to heaven in a cloud.

## Rome

**CONSTANTINE AND PETER** Constantine's dual role as both Roman emperor and champion of the Christian faith was reflected in his decision to locate the new churches of Rome on the city's outskirts to avoid any confrontation between Christian and pagan ideologies. The greatest of Constantine's churches in Rome was Old Saint Peter's (FIG. **11-7**), probably begun as early as 319. The present-day church (see FIG. 24-4), one of the masterpieces of Italian Renaissance and Baroque architecture, is a replacement for the Constantinian structure. Old Saint Peter's stood on the western side of the Tiber River on the spot where Constantine and Pope Sylvester believed Peter, the first apostle and founder of the Christian community in Rome, had been buried (see "Constantine and Old Saint Peter's," page 311). Excavations in the Roman cemetery beneath the church have in fact revealed a second-century memorial erected in honor of the Christian martyr at his reputed grave. The great Constantinian church, capable of housing 3,000 to 4,000 worshipers at one time, was raised, at immense cost, upon a terrace over the ancient cemetery on the irregular slope of the Vatican Hill. It enshrined one of the most hallowed sites in Christendom, second only to the Holy Sepulcher in Jerusalem, the site of Christ's Resurrection. The project also fulfilled the figurative words of Christ himself, when he said, "Thou art Peter, and upon this rock I will build my church" (Matt. 16:18). Peter was Rome's first bishop and also the head of the long line of popes that extends to the present.

**BASILICA TO CHURCH** The plan and elevation of Old Saint Peter's resemble those of Roman basilicas and audience halls, such as the Basilica Ulpia in the Forum of Trajan (FIG. 10-41) and the Aula Palatina at Trier (see FIGS. 10-80 and 10-81), rather than the design of any Greco-Roman temple. The Christians, understandably, did not want their houses of worship to mimic the form of pagan shrines, but practical considerations also contributed to their shunning the pagan temple type. The Greco-Roman temple housed only the cult statue of the deity. All rituals took place outside at open-air altars. The classical temple, therefore, could have been adapted only with great difficulty as a building that accommodated large numbers of people within it. The Roman basilica, in contrast, was ideally suited as a place for congregation.

Like Roman basilicas, Old Saint Peter's (FIG. 11-7) had a wide central *nave* (300 feet long) with flanking *aisles* and an *apse* at the

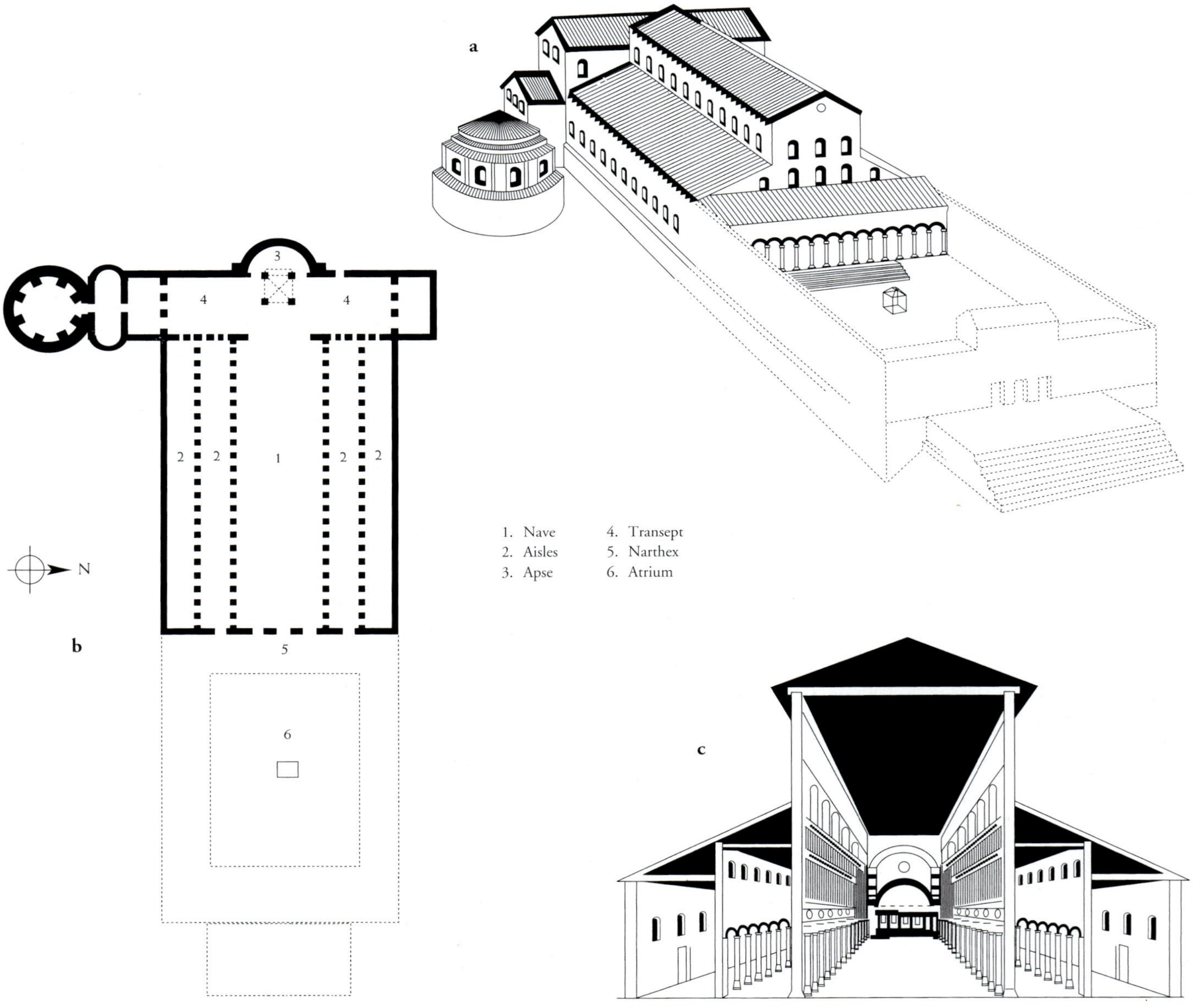

1. Nave    4. Transept
2. Aisles   5. Narthex
3. Apse    6. Atrium

**11-7** Restored view *(a)*, plan *(b)*, and section *(c)* of Old Saint Peter's, Rome, Italy, begun ca. 320. (The restoration of the forecourt is conjectural.)

## Constantine and Old Saint Peter's

Constantine the Great was the first emperor to sponsor the construction of churches in Rome. His generosity went well beyond providing land and erecting edifices. It extended to outfitting the interiors with costly altars, chandeliers, candlesticks, pitchers, goblets, and plates fashioned of gold and silver and sometimes embellished with jewels and pearls. The *Liber pontificalis,* or *Book of the Pontiffs (Popes),* compiled by an anonymous sixth-century author, provides a vivid picture of the emperor's involvement with the building of Old Saint Peter's (FIG. 11-7) and of his gifts to the new basilica, as well as a list of the income from imperial properties in cities in various parts of the Empire that was donated as an endowment for the new church. The information is contained in the life of Pope Sylvester, 34th bishop of Rome (r. 314–335).

> The emperor Constantine built a basilica to St. Peter the Apostle . . . where he buried the tomb with St. Peter's body. . . . He sealed [the tomb] on all sides with copper. . . . Above he decorated it with porphyry and other vine-scroll columns which he brought from Greece. He also built the basilica's apse-vault of shining gold-foil; and over St. Peter's body . . . he provided a cross of finest gold weighing 150 lb. . . . He also provided 4 brass candelabra, 10 ft in size, finished in silver . . . , each weighing 300 lb; 3 gold chalices with . . . jewels . . . ; 20 silver chalices . . . ; a gold paten . . . adorned with . . . jewels and with pearls, 215 in number . . . ; 5 silver patens; . . . a gold crown . . . , which is a chandelier, with 50 dolphins . . . ; 32 silver lights in the centre of the basilica, with dolphins . . . ; on the right of the basilica, 30 silver lights . . . ; the altar itself, of silver chased with gold, weighing 350 lb, decorated on all sides with . . . jewels and pearls, the jewels 400 in number; [and] a censer of finest gold, decorated on all sides with jewels, 60 in number.[1]

[1] Raymond Davis, trans., *The Book of Pontiffs* (Liverpool: Liverpool University Press, 1989), 18–19.

end. Preceding it was an open colonnaded courtyard, very much like the forum proper in the Forum of Trajan but called an *atrium,* like the central room in a private house. Worshipers entered the basilica through a *narthex,* or vestibule. When they emerged in the nave, they had an unobstructed view of the altar in the apse, framed by the so-called *triumphal arch* dividing the nave from the transept. The *transept,* or transverse aisle, an area perpendicular to the nave between the nave and apse, was a special feature of the Constantinian church. It housed the relics of Saint Peter that hordes of pilgrims came to see. (*Relics* are the body parts, clothing, or objects associated with a saint or Christ himself; see "Pilgrimages and the Cult of Relics," Chapter 17, page 449.) The transept became a standard element of church design in the West only much later, when it also took on, with the nave and apse, the symbolism of the Christian cross.

**INSIDE AN EARLY CHURCH** Unlike pagan temples, Old Saint Peter's was not adorned with lavish exterior sculptures. Its brick walls were as austere as those of the Aula Palatina at Trier (see FIG. 10-80). Inside, however, were frescoes and mosaics, marble columns (taken from pagan buildings, as was customary at the time), grandiose chandeliers, and gold and silver vessels on jeweled altar cloths for use in the Mass. A huge marble *baldacchino* (domical canopy over an altar), supported by four spiral columns, marked the spot of Saint Peter's tomb.

One can get some idea of the character of the timber-roofed interior of Old Saint Peter's by comparing our section drawing (FIG. 11-7c) with the photograph of the interior (FIG. **11-8**) of Santa Sabina in Rome. Santa Sabina, built a century later, is a basilican church of much more modest proportions, but it still retains its Early Christian character. The Corinthian columns of Santa

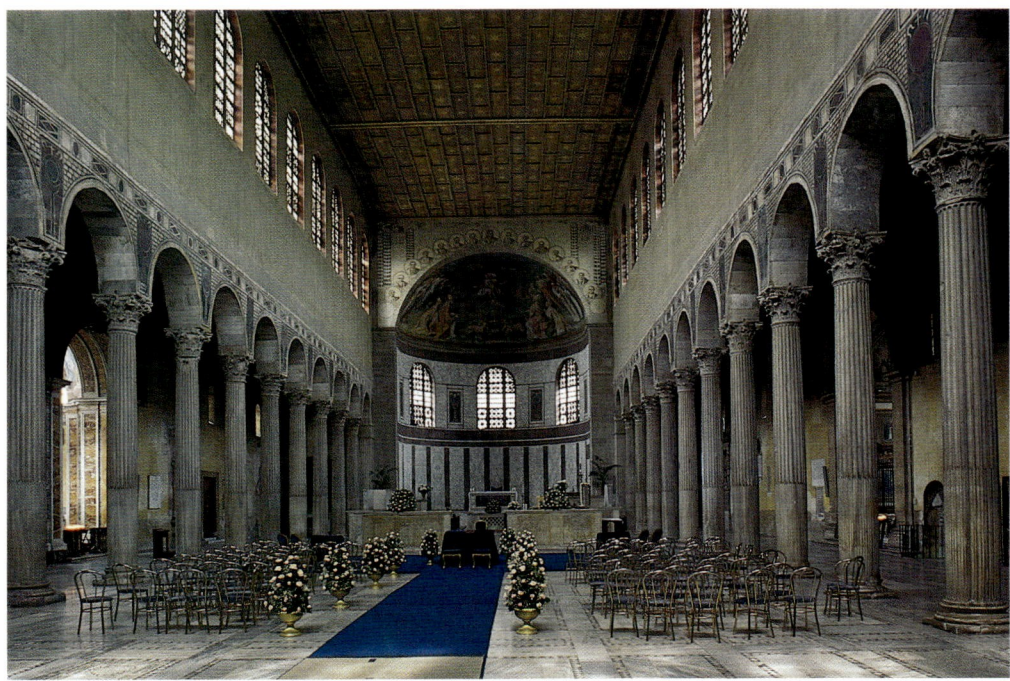

**11-8** Interior of Santa Sabina, Rome, Italy, 422–432.

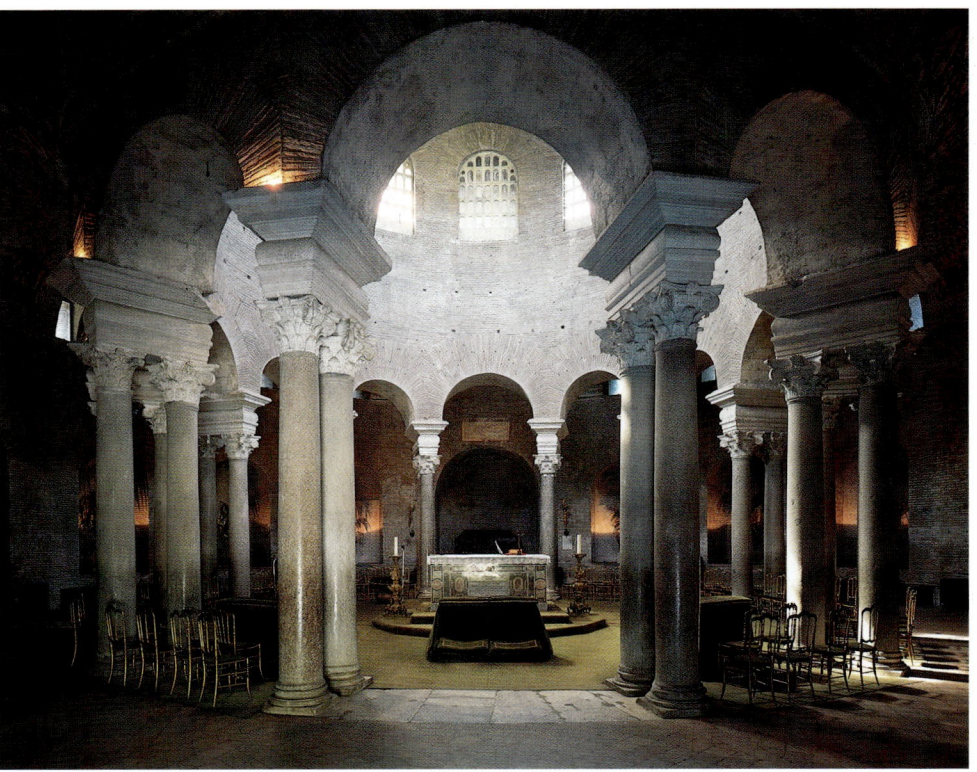

**11-9** Interior of Santa Costanza, Rome, Italy, ca. 337–351.

Sabina's nave produce a steady rhythm that focuses all attention on the apse, which frames the altar. In Santa Sabina, as in Old Saint Peter's, the nave is drenched with light from the *clerestory* windows piercing the thin upper wall beneath the timber roof. The same light would have illuminated the frescoes and mosaics that commonly adorned the nave and apse of Early Christian churches. Outside, Santa Sabina has plain brick walls. They closely resemble the exterior of Trier's Aula Palatina (FIG. 10-80).

**THE CENTRAL PLAN** The rectangular basilican church design was long the favorite of the Western Christian world, but Early Christian architects also adopted another classical architectural type: the *central-plan* building. The type is so named because the building's parts are of equal or almost equal dimensions around the center. Roman central-plan buildings were usually round or polygonal domed structures. Byzantine architects developed this form to monumental proportions and amplified its theme in numerous ingenious variations. In the West, the central plan was used generally for structures adjacent to the main basilicas, such as mausoleums, baptisteries, and private chapels, rather than for actual churches, as in the East (see Chapter 12).

A highly refined example of the central-plan design is Santa Costanza in Rome (FIGS. **11-9** and **11-10**), built in the mid-fourth century, possibly as the mausoleum for Constantina, the emperor Constantine's daughter. Recent excavations have called the traditional identification into question, but Constantina's monumental porphyry sarcophagus was placed in the building, even if the structure was not built as her tomb. The mausoleum, later converted into a church, stood next to the basilican church of Saint Agnes, whose tomb was in a nearby catacomb. Santa Costanza has antecedents that can be traced back to the beehive tombs of the Mycenaeans (see FIGS. 4-21 and 4-22), but its immediate predecessors were the domed structures of the Romans, such as the Pantheon (see FIGS. 10-48 to 10-50) and especially imperial mausolea such as Diocletian's at Split (see FIG. 10-75). At Santa Costanza, the interior design of the Roman buildings was modified to accommodate an

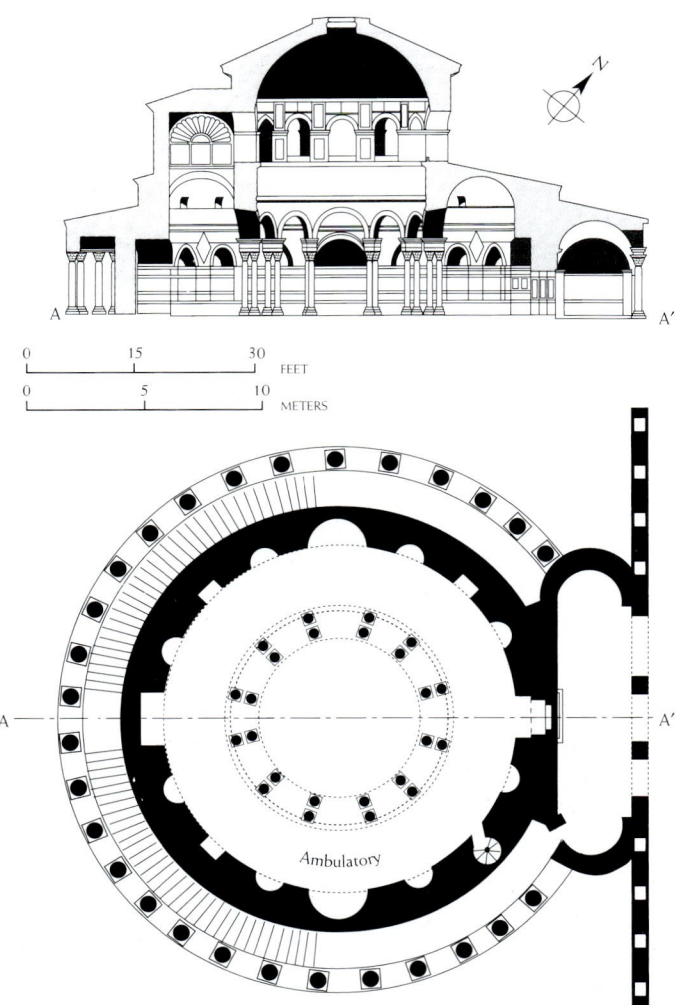

**11-10** Longitudinal section *(top)* and plan *(bottom)* of Santa Costanza, Rome, Italy, ca. 337–351.

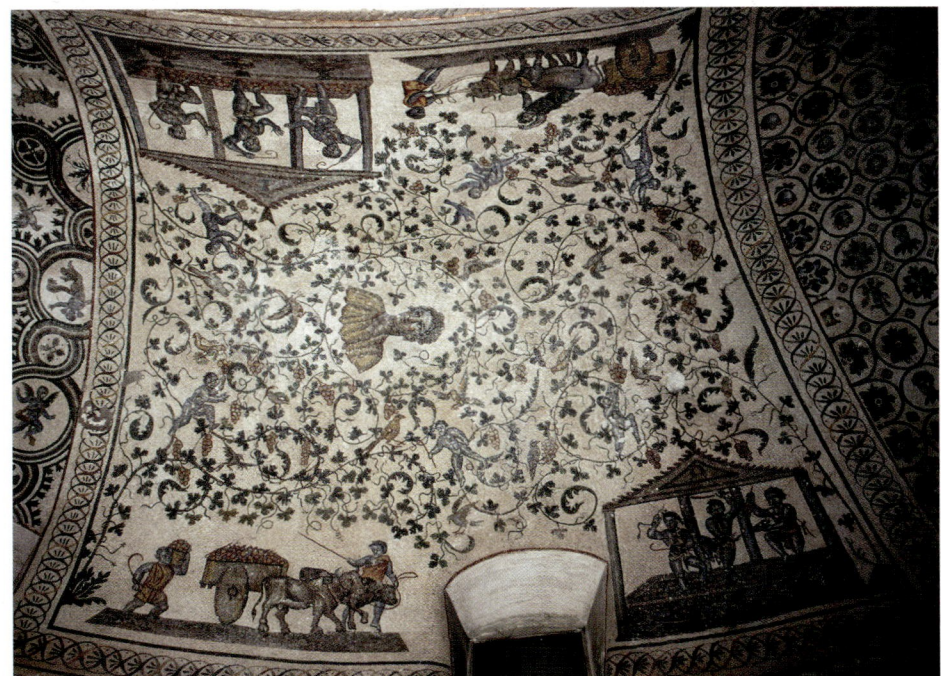

*ambulatory,* a ringlike barrel-vaulted corridor separated from the central domed cylinder by a dozen pairs of columns. It is as if the nave of the Early Christian basilica with its clerestory wall were bent around a circle, the ambulatory corresponding to the basilican aisles.

**A MOSAIC VINEYARD** Like Early Christian basilicas, Santa Costanza has a severe brick exterior. Its interior was once richly adorned with mosaics, although most are lost. Old and New Testament themes appeared side by side, as in the catacombs and on Early Christian sarcophagi. The Santa Costanza mosaic program, however, also included pagan subjects, although they were susceptible to a Christian interpretation. In our detail (FIG. **11-11**) of a mosaic in the ambulatory vault, a portrait bust is at the center of a rich vine scroll. There is a second bust in another section of the mosaic vault, but both are heavily restored, and the identification of the pair as Constantina and her husband is uncertain. Scenes of putti harvesting grapes and producing wine, echoing the decoration of Constantina's sarcophagus (not shown), surround the portraits. In the Roman world, wine was primarily associated with Bacchus, but for a Christian, the imagery of the Santa Costanza mosaics brought to mind the wine of the Eucharist and the blood of Christ.

Mosaic decoration played an important role in the interiors of Early Christian buildings (see "Mosaics," page 315). When, under Constantine, Christianity suddenly became a public and official religion in Rome, not only were new buildings required in order to house the faithful, but wholesale decoration programs for the churches also became necessary. To advertise the new faith in all its diverse aspects—its dogma, scriptural narrative, and symbolism—and to instruct and edify believers, acres of walls in dozens of new churches had to be filled in the style and medium that would carry the message most effectively.

**CHRIST AS SUN GOD** The earliest known mosaic of explicitly Christian content is the late-third-century vault mosaic (FIG. **11-12**) in a small Christian mausoleum not far from Saint Peter's tomb in the Roman cemetery beneath Old Saint Peter's. It depicts Christ in the guise of a familiar pagan deity, Sol Invictus (in Greek, Helios), the Invincible Sun, driving the sun chariot through the golden heavens. All about Christ are vines, as in Santa

Costanza (FIG. 11-11). He holds an orb in his left hand, characterizing him as ruler of the universe, another borrowing from the repertory of pagan Roman art. But viewers could easily distinguish the Christian charioteer from Sol by the halo around his head. The halo's rays suggest the pattern of a cross. This is a far more grandiose conception of Christ than the role of Good Shepherd, and a fitting theme for the vaulted ceiling above the deceased. Christ does appear, however, as the caretaker of the Christian flock below, on the west wall of the tomb. On the east wall, in typical Early Christian fashion, is the story of Jonah.

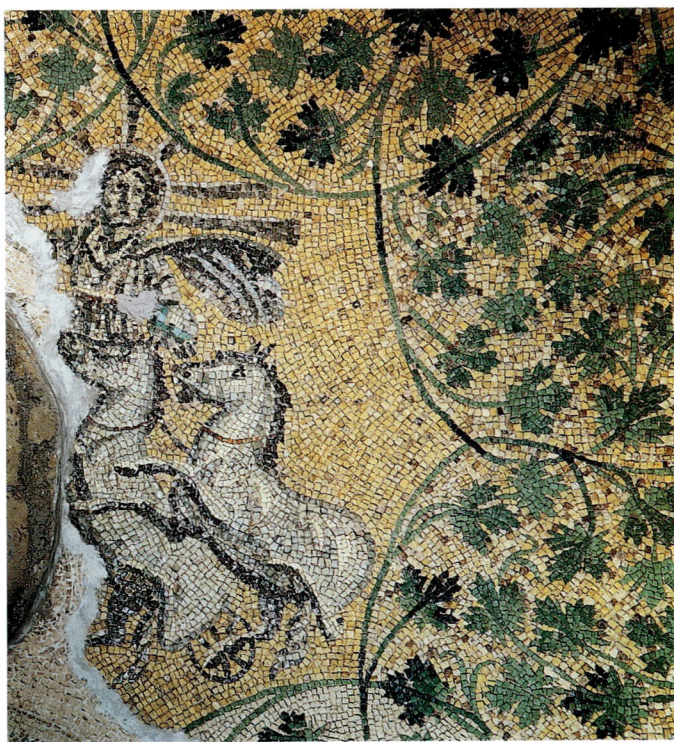

11-12 Christ as Sol Invictus, detail of a vault mosaic in the Mausoleum of the Julii, Rome, Italy, late third century.

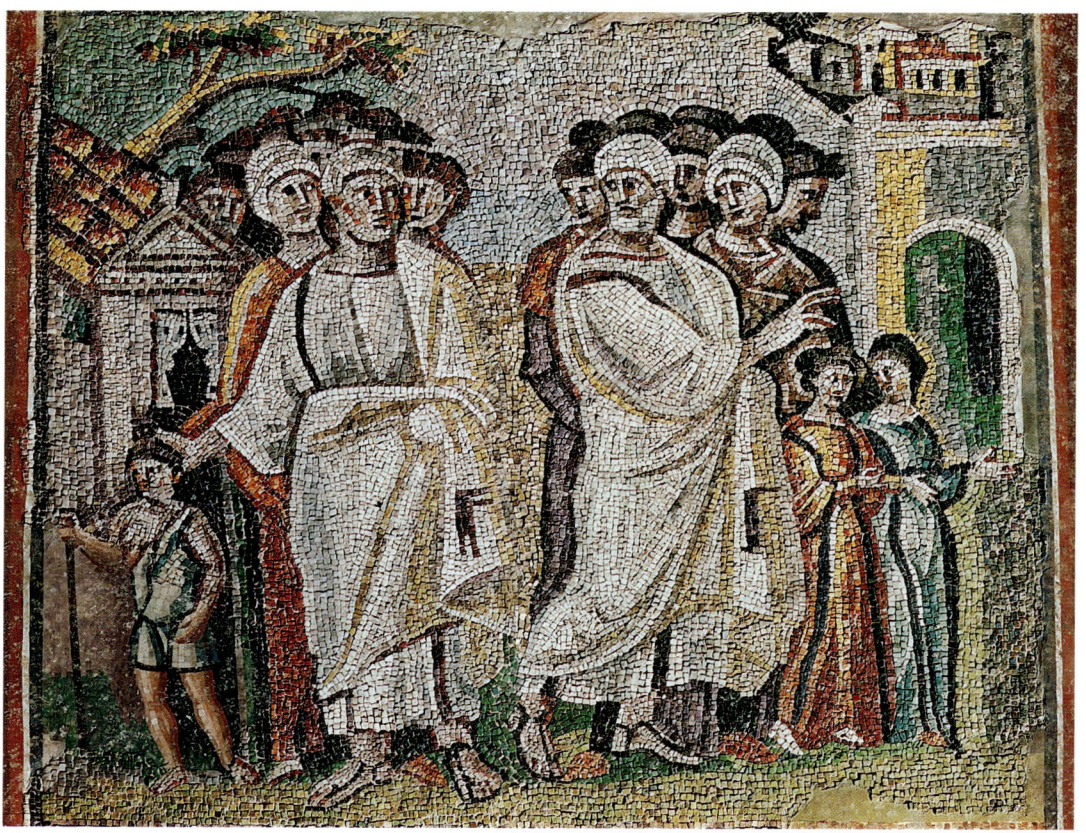

**11-13** The parting of Lot and Abraham, mosaic in the nave of Santa Maria Maggiore, Rome, Italy, 432–440.

**ABRAHAM AND LOT** Old Testament themes are the focus of the extensive fifth-century mosaic cycle in the nave of the basilican church of Santa Maria Maggiore in Rome, the first major church in the West dedicated to the Virgin Mary. The church was begun in 432, the year after Mary had been officially designated as the Mother of God (*Theotokos,* "bearer of god" in Greek) at the Council of Ephesus. A characteristic panel (FIG. **11-13**) of great dramatic power represents the parting of Abraham and his nephew Lot, as set forth in Genesis, the Bible's opening book. Agreeing to disagree, Lot leads his family and followers to the right, toward the city of Sodom, while Abraham heads for Canaan, moving toward a building (perhaps symbolizing the Christian Church) on the left. Lot's is the evil choice, and the instruments of the evil (his two daughters) are in front of him. The figure of the yet unborn Isaac, the instrument of good (and, as noted earlier, a prefiguration of Christ), stands before his father, Abraham.

The cleavage of the two groups is emphatic, and each group was represented by a shorthand device that could be called a "head cluster," which had precedents in antiquity and had a long history in Christian art. The figures turn from each other in a sharp dialogue of glance and gesture. The wide eyes, turned in their sockets; the broad gestures of enlarged hands; and the opposed movements of the groups all may remind viewers of a silent, expressive chorus that comments on the drama's action only with hands and bodies. Such simplified motion, characteristic of Late Antique narrative art of both pagan and Christian subject matter, has great power to communicate without ambiguity.

The heritage of classical art is, however, still apparent in the Santa Maria Maggiore mosaics. In the Abraham and Lot mosaic, for example, the background town and building would not be out of place in the spiral frieze of Trajan's Column (see FIG. 10-42).

The figures themselves also still loom with massive solidity. They cast shadows and were modeled in dark and light to give them their three-dimensional appearance. Another century had to pass before Western Christian mosaicists portrayed figures entirely as flat images, rather than as plastic bodies, finally rejecting the norms of classical art in favor of a style better suited for a focus on the spiritual instead of the natural world.

## Ravenna

**A CRUMBLING EMPIRE** In the decades following the foundation in 324 of Constantinople, the New Rome in the East, and the death of Constantine in 337, the pace of Christianization of the Roman Empire quickened. In 380 the emperor Theodosius I issued an edict finally establishing Christianity as the state religion. In 391 he enacted a ban against pagan worship. In 394 the Olympic Games, the enduring symbol of the classical world and its values, were abolished. Theodosius died in 395, and imperial power passed to his two sons, Arcadius, who became Emperor of the East, and Honorius, Emperor of the West. The problems that plagued the last pagan emperors, most notably the threat of invasion from the north, did not, however, disappear with the conversion to Christianity.

In 404, when the Visigoths, under their king, Alaric, threatened to overrun Italy from the northwest, Honorius moved the capital of his crumbling empire from Milan to Ravenna, an ancient Roman city (perhaps founded by the Etruscans) near Italy's Adriatic coast, some 80 miles south of Venice. There, in a city surrounded by swamps and thus easily defended, his imperial authority survived the fall of Rome to Alaric in 410. Honorius died in 423, and the reins of government were taken by his half sister,

### Mosaics

As an art form, mosaic had a rather simple and utilitarian beginning, seemingly invented primarily to provide an inexpensive and durable flooring. Originally, small beach pebbles were set, unaltered from their natural form and color, into a thick coat of cement. Artisans soon discovered, however, that the stones could be arranged in decorative patterns. At first, these *pebble mosaics* were uncomplicated and were confined to geometric shapes. Generally, the artists used only black and white stones. Examples of this type, dating back to the eighth century BCE, have been found at Gordion in Asia Minor. Eventually, artists arranged the stones to form more complex pictorial designs, and by the fourth century BCE the technique had developed to a high level of sophistication. Mosaicists depicted elaborate figural scenes using a broad range of colors—yellow, brown, and red in addition to black, white, and gray—and shaded the figures, clothing, and setting to suggest volume. Thin strips of lead provided linear definition (see FIG. 5-68).

By the middle of the third century BCE, artists had invented a new kind of mosaic that permitted the best mosaicists to create designs that more closely approximated true paintings. The new technique employed *tesserae* (Latin for "cubes" or "dice"). These tiny cut stones gave the artist much greater flexibility because their size and shape could be adjusted at will, eliminating the need for lead strips to indicate contours and interior details. Much more gradual gradations of color also became possible, and

mosaicists finally could aspire to rival the achievements of panel painters (see FIG. 5-69).

In Early Christian mosaics, the tesserae are usually made of glass, which reflects light and makes the surfaces sparkle. Glass tesserae were occasionally used in ancient mosaics, but the Romans preferred opaque marble pieces. Mosaics quickly became the standard means of decorating walls and vaults in Early Christian buildings, although mural paintings were also used. The mosaics caught the light flooding through the windows in vibrant reflection, producing sharp contrasts and concentrations of color that could focus attention on a composition's central, most relevant features. Mosaics worked in the Early Christian manner were not meant to incorporate the subtle tonal changes a naturalistic painter's approach would require. Color was *placed*, not blended. Bright, hard, glittering texture, set within a rigorously simplified pattern, became the rule. For mosaics situated high in an apse or ambulatory vault or over the nave colonnade, far above the observer's head, the painstaking use of tiny tesserae seen in Roman floor mosaics would be meaningless. Early Christian mosaics, designed to be seen from a distance, employed larger tesserae. The pieces were also set unevenly so that their surfaces could catch and reflect the light. Artists favored simple designs for optimal legibility. For several centuries, mosaic, in the service of Christian theology, was the medium of some of the supreme masterpieces of medieval art.

Galla Placidia, whom the Visigoths had captured in Rome in 410. Galla Placidia had married a Visigothic chieftain before returning to Ravenna and the Romans after the chieftain's death six years later. In 476 Ravenna fell to Odoacer, the first Germanic king of Italy, who was overthrown in turn by Theodoric, king of the Ostrogoths, who established his capital at Ravenna in 493. The subsequent history of the city belongs with that of the Byzantine Empire (see Chapter 12).

**MOSAICS FOR A MARTYR** The so-called Mausoleum of Galla Placidia (FIG. **11-14**) in Ravenna is a rather small *cruciform* (cross-shaped) structure with barrel-vaulted arms and a tower at the crossing. Built shortly after 425, almost a quarter century before Galla Placidia's death in 450, it was probably intended as a chapel to the martyred Saint Lawrence. The building was, however, once thought to be Galla Placidia's tomb, hence its name today. Originally the building adjoined the narthex of the now greatly altered palace-church of Santa Croce (Holy Cross), which was also cruciform in plan. Although the chapel's plan is that of a Latin cross, the cross arms are very short and appear as little more than apselike extensions of a square. The emphasis is on the tall *crossing tower* with its vault resembling a dome. The chapel is in essence a central-plan structure. Yet this small, unassuming building also represents one of the earliest successful fusions of the two basic Late Antique plans, the *longitudinal,* used for basilican churches, and the *central,* used primarily for baptisteries and mausoleums. It introduced, on a small scale, a building type that

was to have a long history in church architecture: the basilican plan with a vaulted or domed crossing.

The chapel's unadorned brick shell encloses one of the richest mosaic ensembles in Early Christian art. Mosaics cover every square inch of the interior surfaces above the marble-faced walls. Garlands and decorative medallions resembling snowflakes on a dark blue ground adorn the barrel vaults of the nave and

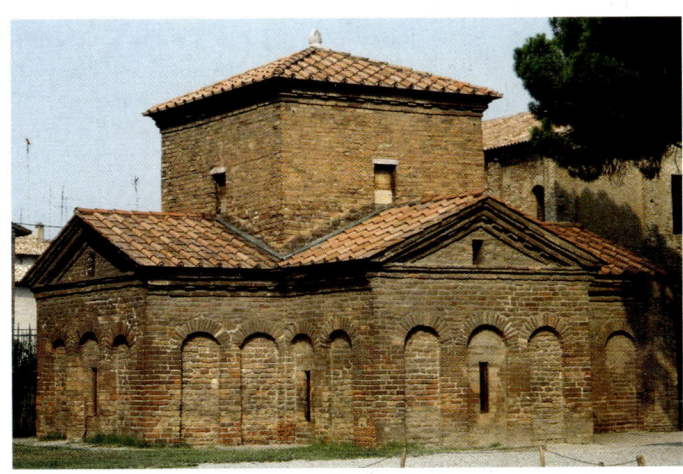

11-14 Mausoleum of Galla Placidia, Ravenna, Italy, ca. 425.

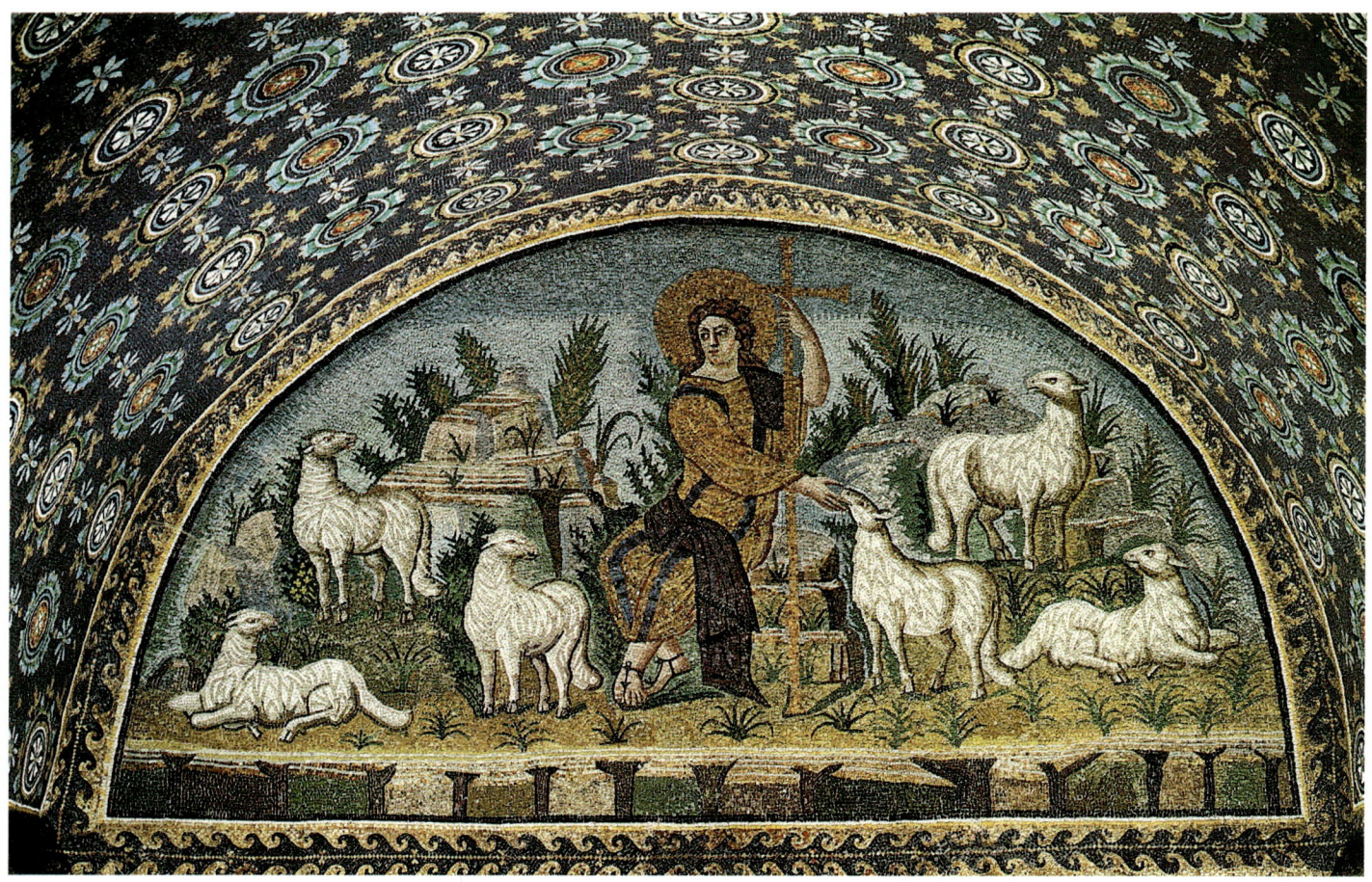

**11-15** Christ as the Good Shepherd, mosaic from the entrance wall of the Mausoleum of Galla Placidia, Ravenna, Italy, ca. 425.

cross arms. The tower has a large golden cross set against a star-studded sky. Representations of saints and apostles cover the other surfaces.

Christ as Good Shepherd is the subject of the lunette (FIG. **11-15**) above the entrance. No earlier version of the Good Shepherd is as regal as this one. Instead of carrying a lamb on his shoulders, Jesus sits among his flock, haloed and robed in gold and purple. To his left and right, the sheep are distributed evenly in groups of three. But their arrangement is rather loose and informal, and they occupy a carefully described landscape that extends from foreground to background beneath a blue sky. All the forms have three-dimensional bulk and cast shadows. In short, the panel is full of Greco-Roman illusionistic devices. The mosaicist was still deeply rooted in the classical tradition. Some 50 years later, this artist's successors in Ravenna worked in a much more abstract and formal manner.

**THEODORIC'S PALACE-CHURCH** Around 504, soon after Theodoric settled in Ravenna, he ordered the construction of his own palace-church, a three-aisled basilica dedicated to the Savior. In the ninth century, the relics of Saint Apollinaris were transferred to this church. The building was rededicated and has been known since that time as Sant'Apollinare Nuovo. The rich mosaic decorations of the interior nave walls (FIG. **11-16**) are divided into three zones. Only the upper two date from Theodoric's time. Old Testament patriarchs and prophets stand between the clerestory windows. Above them, scenes from Christ's life alternate with decorative panels.

The mosaic depicting the miracle of the loaves and fishes (FIG. **11-17**) illustrates well the stylistic change that had occurred since the decoration of the Mausoleum of Galla Placidia. Jesus, beardless, in the imperial dress of gold and purple, and now distinguished by the cross-inscribed *nimbus* (halo) that signifies his divinity, faces directly toward the viewer. With extended arms he directs his disciples to distribute to the great crowd the miraculously increased supply of bread and fish he has produced. The artist made no attempt to supply details of the event. The emphasis is instead on the holy character of it, the spiritual fact that Jesus is performing a miracle by the power of his divinity. The fact of the miracle takes it out of the world of time and of incident. The presence of almighty power, not anecdotal narrative, is the important aspect of this scene. The mosaicist told the story with the least number of figures necessary to make its meaning explicit. The artist aligned the figures laterally, moved them close to the foreground, and placed them in a shallow picture box cut off by a golden screen close behind their backs. The landscape setting, which the artist who worked for Galla Placidia so explicitly described, is here merely a few rocks and bushes that enclose the figure group like parentheses. The blue sky of the physical world has given way to the otherworldly splendor of heavenly gold, the standard background color for mosaics from this point on. Remnants of Roman illusionism appear only in the handling of the individual figures, which still cast shadows and retain some of their former volume. But the shadows of the drapery folds already are only narrow bars. Soon afterward, they disappeared in Christian art.

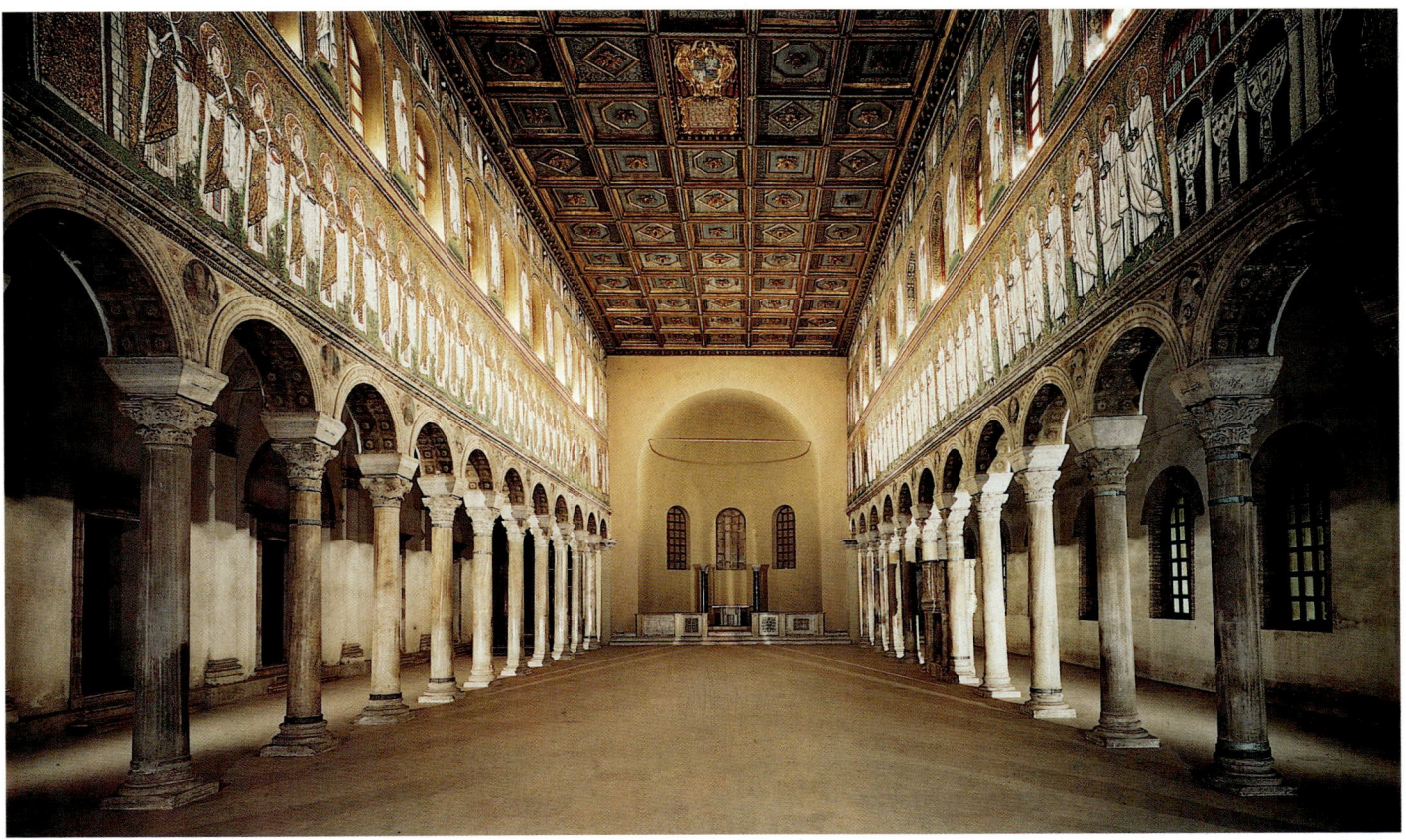

**11-16** Interior of Sant'Apollinare Nuovo, Ravenna, Italy, dedicated 504.

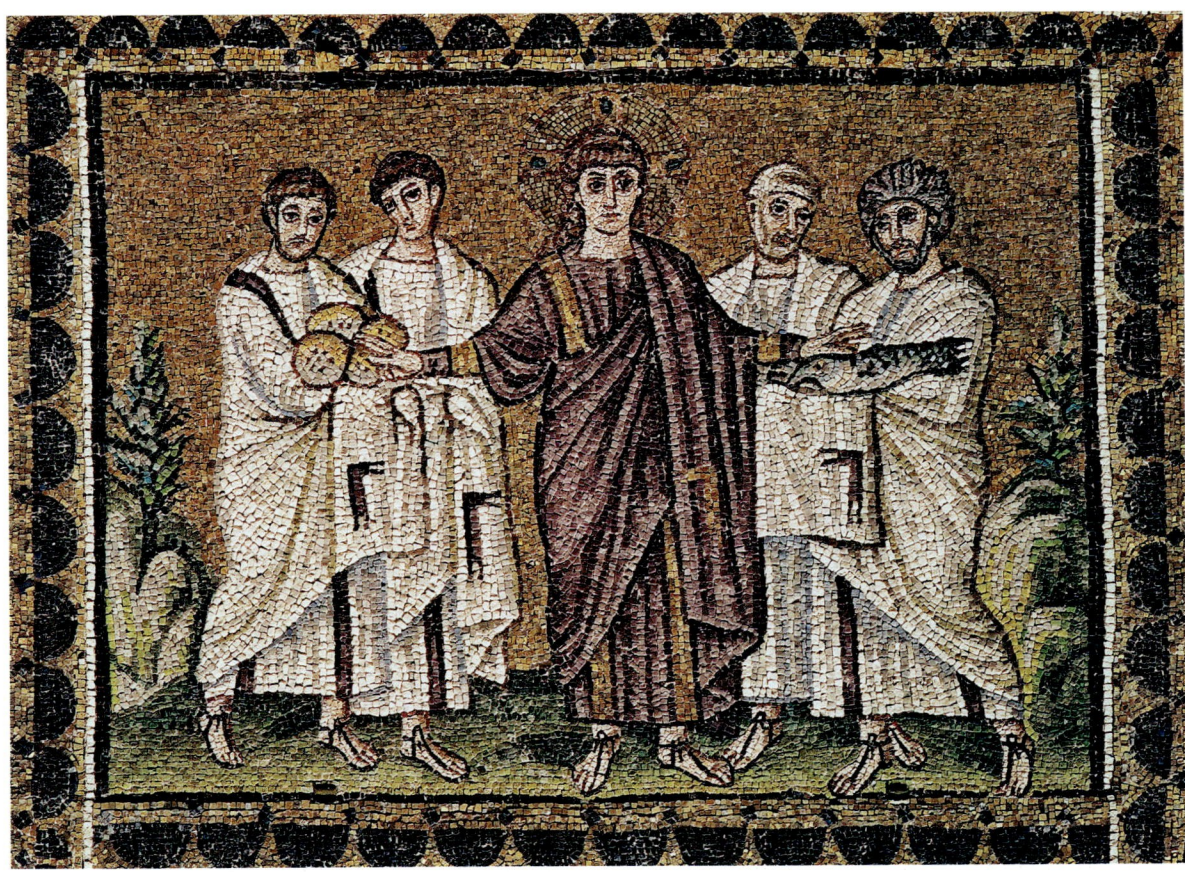

**11-17** Miracle of the loaves and fishes, mosaic from the top register of the nave wall (above the clerestory windows) of Sant'Apollinare Nuovo, Ravenna, Italy, ca. 504.

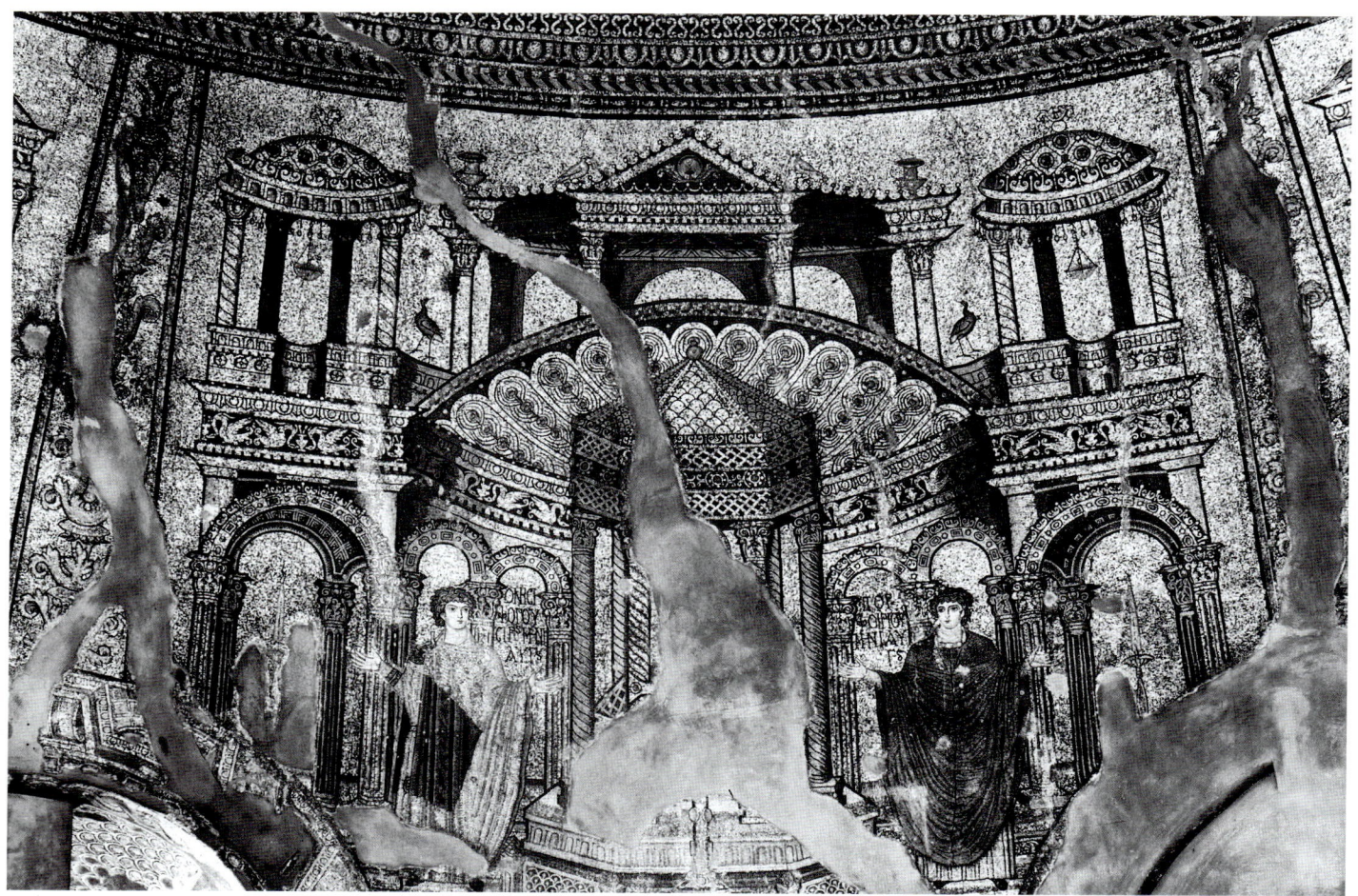

**11-18** Saints Onesiphorus and Porphyrius, detail of the dome mosaic, Church of Saint George, Thessaloniki, Greece, ca. 390–450.

**A CITY NOT OF THIS WORLD** In the eastern Roman Empire, the pace of stylistic change was even more rapid. Many of the features of the Sant'Apollinare Nuovo mosaic may be seen, in more advanced form and created perhaps as much as a century earlier, in the mosaics of the dome of the Church of Saint George at Thessaloniki (Salonica) in northern Greece. The church, of the central-plan type, was originally built around 300 as the mausoleum of Galerius, the tetrarchic Caesar of the East under Diocletian. It was converted into a church sometime between 390 and 450.

Only part of the mosaic decoration of the Church of Saint George is preserved. The detail we illustrate here (FIG. **11-18**) comes from the lower of two bands of mosaics, which had eight panels. Seven are fairly well preserved. In each one, two saints with their arms raised in prayer stand before two-story architectural fantasies that resemble Roman mural paintings (see FIG. 10-16) and the facades of the rock-cut tombs of Petra (see FIG. 10-52). In this respect, the Thessaloniki mosaics are more closely tied to the classical past than are those of Sant'Apollinare Nuovo. Yet figures and architecture alike have lost almost all substance, and it is increasingly difficult to imagine, for example, rounded torsos and limbs beneath the flat, curtainlike garments the saints wear. A new aesthetic is on exhibit here, one quite foreign to classical art, with its worldly themes, naturalism, perspective illusionism, modeling in light and shade, and proportionality. The formality of the poses and the solemn, priestly demeanor of the Thessaloniki figures, as well as the ethereal golden background,

became prominent features of Byzantine art (see Chapter 12). The Saint George dome mosaic seems to have completed the change from the naturalistic images of the pagan floor mosaic, which are literally under the feet and of this world, to the floating images of a celestial world high above the Christian's wondering gaze.

## Luxury Arts

### Illuminated Manuscripts

**THE FIRST ILLUSTRATED BIBLES** Although few examples survive, illustrated books were popular in the ancient world. The long tradition of placing pictures in manuscripts began in pharaonic Egypt (see FIG. 3-39). The oldest well-preserved painted manuscript containing biblical scenes is the early sixth-century *Vienna Genesis,* so called because of its present location. The book is sumptuous. The pages are fine calfskin dyed with rich purple, the same dye used to give imperial cloth its distinctive color, and the Greek text is written in silver ink (see "Medieval Manuscript Illumination," page 319).

The page we reproduce (FIG. **11-19**) illustrates the story of Rebecca and Eliezer in the Book of Genesis (24:15–61). When Isaac, Abraham's son, was 40 years old, his parents sent their servant Eliezer to find a wife for him. Eliezer chose Rebecca because

## Medieval Manuscript Illumination

Rare as medieval books are, they are far more numerous than their ancient predecessors (see "The Roman Illustrated Book," Chapter 10, page 261). The dissemination of manuscripts, as well as their preservation, was aided greatly by an important invention of the Early Empire period, the codex. The *codex* is much like a modern book, composed of separate leaves (*folios*) enclosed within a cover and bound together at one side. The new format superseded the long manuscript scroll (*rotulus*) used by the Egyptians, Greeks, Etruscans, and Romans. (The Etruscan magistrate Lars Pulena, FIG. 9-14; the philosophers on Roman and Early Christian sarcophagi, FIGS. 10-72 and 11-4; and Christ himself in his role as teacher, FIGS. 11-5 and 11-6, all hold rotuli in their hands.) Much more durable *vellum* (calfskin) and *parchment* (lambskin), which provided better surfaces for painting, also replaced the comparatively brittle papyrus used for ancient scrolls. As a result, luxuriousness of ornament became more and more typical of sacred books in the Middle Ages, and at times the material beauty of the pages and their illustrations overwhelm or usurp the spiritual beauty of the text. Art historians refer to the luxurious painted books produced before the invention of the printing press as *illuminated manuscripts,* from the Latin *illuminare,* meaning "to adorn, ornament, or brighten."

Such books were costly to produce and involved many steps. Numerous artisans performed very specialized tasks, beginning with the curing and cutting (and sometimes the dyeing) of the animal skin, followed by the sketching of lines to guide the scribe and to set aside spaces for illumination, the lettering of the text, the addition of paintings, and finally the binding of the pages and attachment of covers, buckles, and clasps. The covers could be even more sumptuous than the book itself. Many covers survive that are fashioned of gold and decorated with jewels, ivory carvings, and repoussé reliefs (see FIG. 16-15).

---

when he stopped at a well, she was the first woman to draw water for him and his camels. The *Vienna Genesis* illustration presents two episodes of the story within a single frame. In the first episode, at the left, Rebecca leaves the city of Nahor to fetch water from the well. In the second episode, she gives water to Eliezer and his 10 camels, while one of them already laps water from the well.

The artist painted Nahor as a walled city seen from above, in the manner of the cityscapes on the Santa Maria Maggiore mosaics (FIG. 11-13), which maintained Roman pictorial conventions in widespread use in painting, mosaic, and relief sculpture. Rebecca walks to the well along the colonnaded avenue of a Roman city. A seminude female personification of a spring is the source of the well water. These are further reminders of the persistence of classical motifs and stylistic modes in Early Christian art. The painter presented the action with all possible simplicity but included convincing touches, such as the drinking camel and Rebecca bracing herself with her raised left foot on the rim of the well as she tips up her jug for Eliezer. The figures appear as silhouetted against a blank landscape except for the miniature city and the road to the well. Everything necessary for bare narrative is present and nothing else.

**JESUS BEFORE PILATE** Closely related to the *Vienna Genesis* is another early-sixth-century Greek manuscript, the *Rossano Gospels,* the earliest preserved illuminated book that contains illustrations of the New Testament. By this time a canon of New Testament iconography had been fairly well established. Like that of the *Vienna Genesis,* the text of the *Rossano Gospels* is in silver on purple vellum. The Rossano artist, however, attempted with considerable success to harmonize the colors with the purple background.

The subject of our illustration (FIG. **11-20**) is the appearance of Jesus before Pilate, who asks the Jews to choose between Jesus and Barabbas (Matt. 27:2–26). In the fashion of the continuous narrative of the *Vienna Genesis,* the separate episodes of the story appear in the same frame, but in this case without repeating any of the protagonists. The vividly gesturing figures are on two levels separated by a simple ground line. In the upper level, Pilate presides over the tribunal. He sits on an elevated dais, following a long-established pattern in Roman art (compare Constantine in the distribution-of-largess frieze on the Arch of Constantine,

**11-19** Rebecca and Eliezer at the well, folio 7 recto of the *Vienna Genesis,* early sixth century. Tempera, gold, and silver on purple vellum, approx. $1' \frac{1}{4}'' \times 9\frac{1}{4}''$. Österreichische Nationalbibliothek, Vienna.

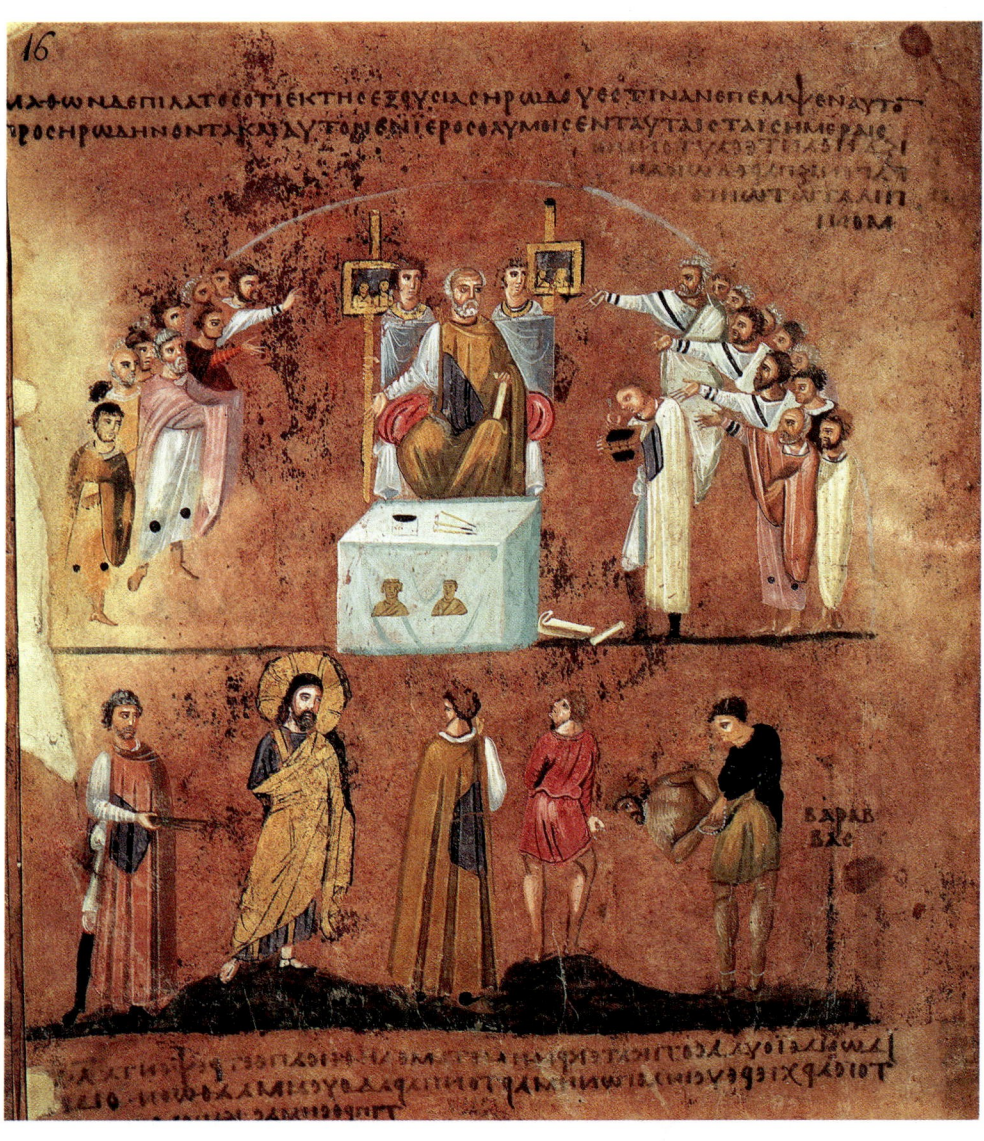

**11-20** Christ before Pilate, folio 8 verso of the *Rossano Gospels*, early sixth century. Tempera on purple vellum, approx. 11″ × 10¼″. Museo Diocesano d'Arte Sacra, Rossano.

FIG. 10-77). The people form an arch around Pilate (the artist may have based the composition on a painting in an apse) and demand the death of Jesus, while a court scribe records the proceedings. Jesus (here a bearded adult, as soon became the norm for medieval and later depictions of Christ) and the bound Barabbas appear in the lower level. The painter explicitly labeled Barabbas to avoid any possible confusion so that the picture would be as readable as the text. The haloed Christ and Pilate on his magistrate's dais, flanked by painted imperial portraits, needed no further identification.

## Ivory Carving

**CHRIST'S PASSION IN IVORY** A century before the pages of the *Rossano Gospels* were illuminated with scenes from the Passion cycle, a Roman or northern Italian sculptor produced a series of panels for an ivory box dramatically recounting the suffering and triumph of Christ. Ivory carving (see "Ivory Carving in Antiquity and the Early Middle Ages," page 321) was another luxury art much admired in the Early Christian period, and these plaques, now in the British Museum, are among the finest known. The narrative on the box begins with Pilate washing his hands, Jesus carrying the cross on the road to Calvary, and the denial of Peter, all compressed into a single panel. The plaque we illustrate (FIG. **11-21**) is the next in the sequence and shows, at the left, Judas hanging from a tree with his open bag of silver dumped on the ground beneath his feet. The Crucifixion is at the right. The Virgin Mary and Joseph of Arimathea are to the left of the cross. On the other side Longinus thrusts his spear into the side of the "King of the Jews" (*REX IVD* is inscribed above Jesus' head). The two remaining panels show two Marys and two soldiers at the open doors of a tomb with an empty coffin within and the doubting Thomas touching the wound of the risen Christ. The series is one of the oldest cycles of Passion scenes preserved today. The artist who fashioned the ivory box helped establish the iconographical types for medieval narratives of Christ's life.

On the London ivories, Jesus appears once again as a beardless youth. In the Crucifixion (FIG. 11-21), the earliest known rendition of the subject in the history of art, he exhibits a superhuman imperviousness to pain. The Savior is a muscular, nearly nude, heroic figure who appears virtually weightless. He does not *hang* from the cross; he is *displayed* on it, a divine being with open eyes who has conquered death. The striking contrast between the powerful frontal unsuffering Jesus on the cross and the limp hanging body of his betrayer with his snapped neck is very effective, both visually and symbolically.

## Ivory Carving in Antiquity and the Early Middle Ages

Ivory has been prized since the earliest times, when the tusks of Ice Age European mammoths were fashioned into pendants, beads, and other items for bodily adornment, and, occasionally, statuettes (see FIG. 1-3). The primary ivory sources in the historical period are the elephants of India and especially Africa, where the species is larger than the Asian counterpart and the tusks longer, heavier, and of finer grain. African elephant tusks 5 to 6 feet in length and weighing 10 pounds are common, but tusks of male elephants can be 10 feet long or more and weigh well over 100 pounds. Carved ivories are familiar, if precious, finds at Mesopotamian and Egyptian sites, and ivory objects were manufactured and coveted in the prehistoric Aegean and throughout the classical world. Most frequently employed then for household objects, small votive offerings, and gifts to the deceased, ivory also could be used for grandiose statues such as Phidias's *Athena Parthenos* (see FIG. 5-44).

In the Greco-Roman world, people admired ivory both for its beauty and because of its exotic origin. Elephant tusks were costly imports, and Roman generals proudly displayed them in triumphal processions when they paraded the spoils of war before the people. (In FIG. 12-1, a barbarian brings tribute to a Byzantine emperor in the form of an ivory tusk.) Adding to the expense of the material itself was the fact that only highly skilled artisans were capable of working in ivory. The tusks were very hard and of irregular shape, and the ivory workers needed a full toolbox of saws, chisels, knives, files, and gravers close at hand to cut the tusks into blocks for statuettes or thin plaques decorated with relief figures and ornament.

In late antiquity and the early medieval period, ivory was employed most frequently for book covers, boxes and chests (FIG. 11-21), and diptychs (FIGS. 11-22 and 12-2). A *diptych* is a pair of hinged tablets, usually of wood, with a wax layer on the inner sides for writing letters and other documents. (The court scribe recording Jesus' trial in the *Rossano Gospels*, FIG. 11-20, and the woman in a painted portrait from Pompeii, FIG. 10-23, both hold wooden diptychs.) Diptychs fashioned out of ivory generally were created for ceremonial and official purposes—for example, to announce the election of a consul or a marriage between two wealthy families or to commemorate the death of an elevated member of society.

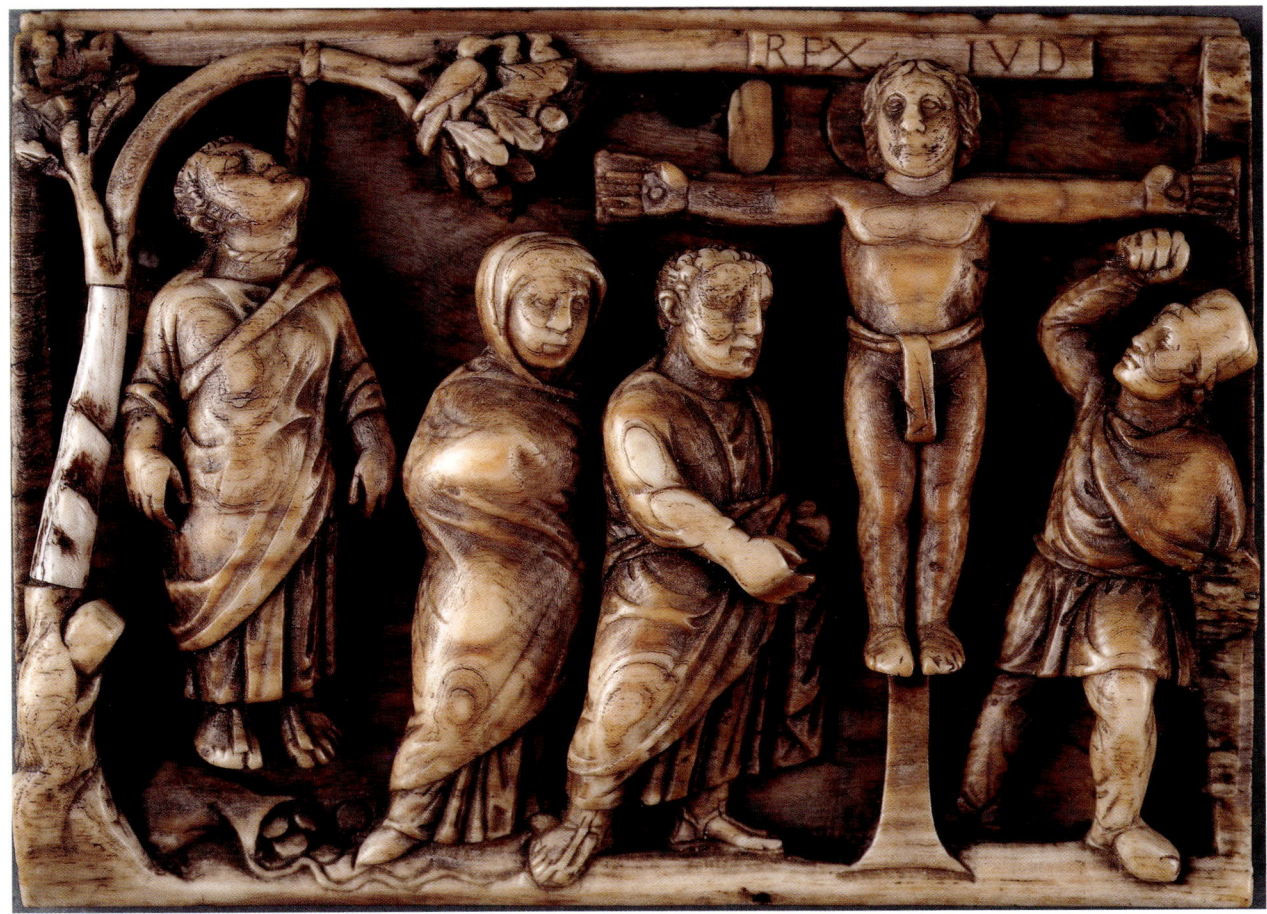

**11-21** Suicide of Judas and Crucifixion of Christ, plaque from a box, ca. 420. Ivory, $3'' \times 3\frac{7}{8}''$. British Museum, London.

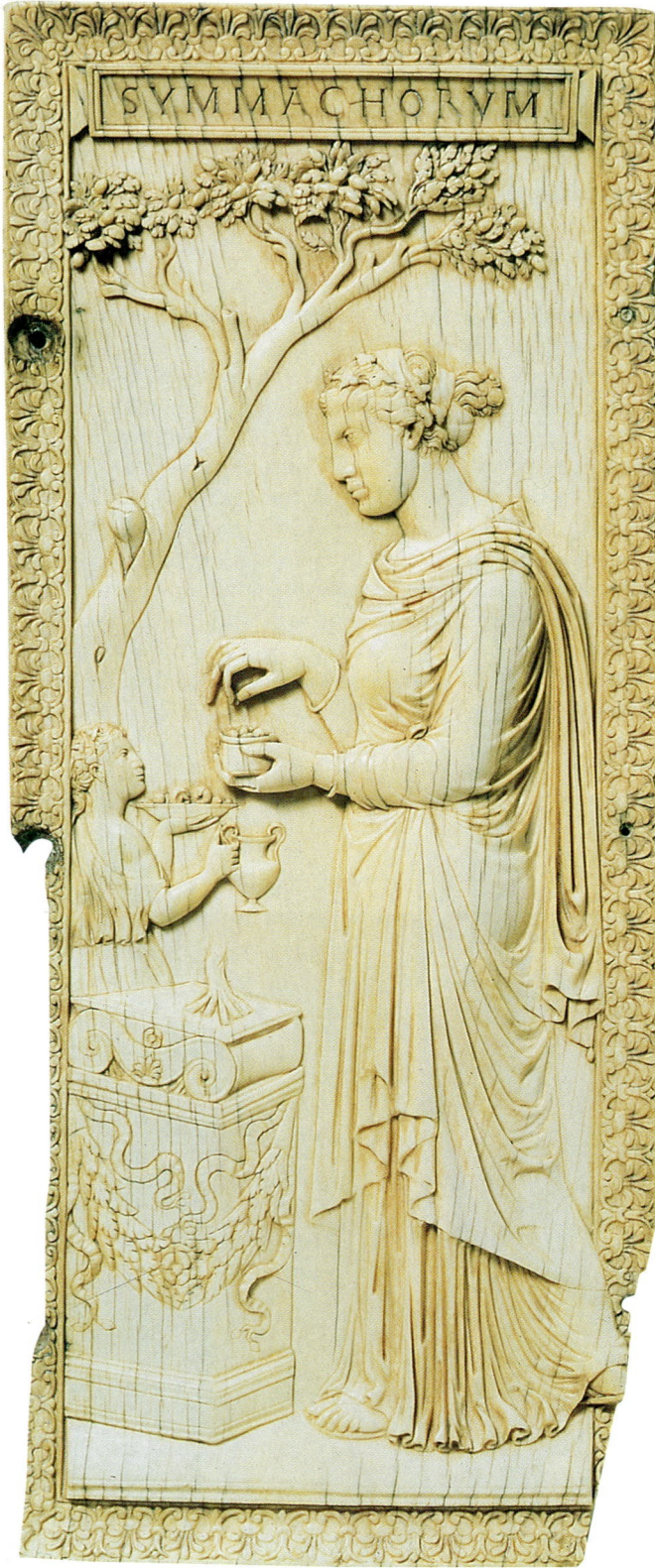

**11-22** Woman sacrificing at an altar, right leaf of the Diptych of the Nicomachi and the Symmachi, ca. 400. Ivory, $11\frac{3}{4}'' \times 5\frac{1}{2}''$. Victoria and Albert Museum, London.

**THE ENDURING PAGAN GODS**  It is important to remember that although after Constantine all the most important architectural projects in Italy were Christian in character, not everyone converted to the new religion, even after Theodosius closed all

temples and banned all pagan cults in 391. An ivory plaque (FIG. **11-22**), probably produced in Rome around 400, strikingly exhibits the endurance of pagan themes and patrons and of the classical style. The ivory, one of a pair of leaves of a diptych, may commemorate either the marriage of members of two powerful Roman families of the senatorial class, the Nicomachi and the Symmachi, or the passing within a decade of two prominent male members of the two families. Whether or not the diptych was connected with any specific event(s), the Nicomachi and the Symmachi here ostentatiously reaffirmed their faith in the old pagan gods. Certainly, they favored the aesthetic ideals of the classical past, as exemplified by such works as the stately processional friezes of the Greek Parthenon (see FIG. 5-48) and the Roman Ara Pacis (see FIG. 10-29).

The leaf we reproduce, inscribed "of the Symmachi," represents a woman sacrificing at an altar in front of a tree. She wears ivy in her hair and seems to be celebrating the rites of Bacchus, although scholars dispute the identity of the divinity honored. The other diptych panel, inscribed "of the Nicomachi," also shows a woman at an open-air altar. On both panels, the precise yet fluent and graceful line; the easy, gliding poses; and the mood of spiritual serenity reveal an artist who practiced within a still-vital classical tradition that idealized human beauty as its central focus.

The great senatorial magnates of Rome, who resisted the empirewide imposition of the Christian faith at the end of the fourth century, probably deliberately sustained the classical tradition. Despite the great changes that had occurred in art during the later third and fourth centuries, classical values lived on. Many artists had turned away from Greco-Roman naturalism to something archaic, abstract, and bluntly expressive—as seen even in official imperial commissions such as the portraits of the tetrarchs (see FIG. 10-74) and the frieze of the Arch of Constantine (see FIG. 10-77). But for other artists and patrons, classical art was still the standard for measuring success. The classical tradition was never fully extinguished in the Middle Ages. It survived in intermittent revivals, renovations, and restorations side by side and in contrast with the opposing nonclassicizing medieval styles. The rise of classical art to dominance in the Renaissance would be one of the signs of the end of the medieval world.

## CONCLUSION

Under Constantine, Christianity became an imperially sponsored religion, and Christian themes have ever since been the subjects of many of the greatest works of Western art. Although Old Testament themes were popular because they were frequently interpreted as prefigurations of events in the New Testament, Early Christian artists established much of the iconography of the life of Jesus in art. In architecture, too, Early Christian basilican churches stand at the head of a long line of shrines of similar plan extending to the present day.

The conversion of the pagan world to Christianity was accompanied by the rejection of the classical style in sculpture and painting and the emergence of a new non-naturalistic, hieratic aesthetic featuring wafer-thin, frontal figures and gold backgrounds. This Late Antique style was ideally suited to a focus on the spiritual world rather than the natural one, and became the norm in Byzantine art (see Chapter 12).

**29**

PRE-CONSTANTINIAN

▌ CRUCIFIXION OF CHRIST, 29

▌ PERSECUTION OF THE CHRISTIANS UNDER TRAJAN DECIUS, 249–251

▌ PERSECUTION OF THE CHRISTIANS UNDER DIOCLETIAN, 303–305

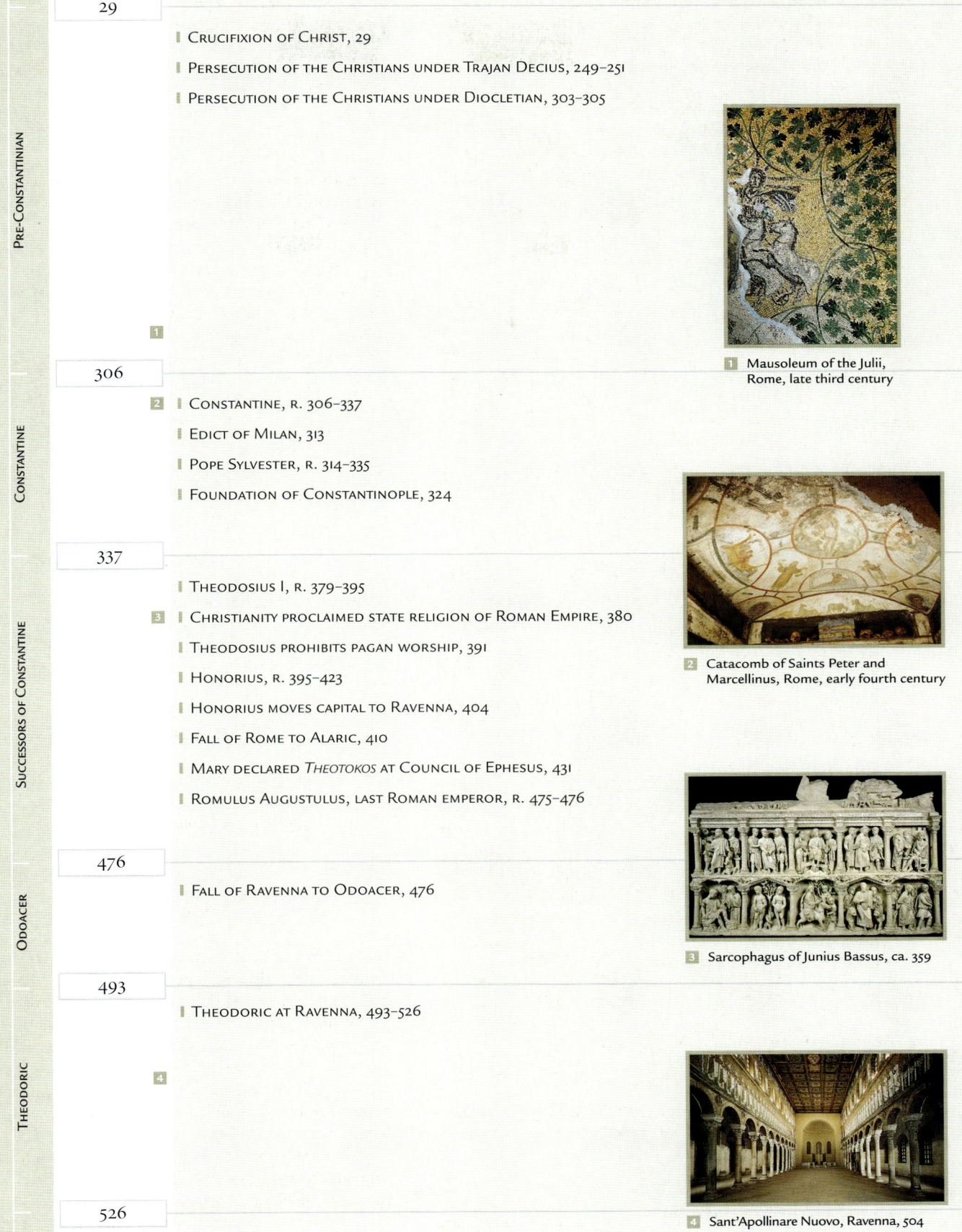

**1** Mausoleum of the Julii, Rome, late third century

**306**

CONSTANTINE

**2** ▌ CONSTANTINE, R. 306–337

▌ EDICT OF MILAN, 313

▌ POPE SYLVESTER, R. 314–335

▌ FOUNDATION OF CONSTANTINOPLE, 324

**337**

SUCCESSORS OF CONSTANTINE

▌ THEODOSIUS I, R. 379–395

**3** ▌ CHRISTIANITY PROCLAIMED STATE RELIGION OF ROMAN EMPIRE, 380

▌ THEODOSIUS PROHIBITS PAGAN WORSHIP, 391

▌ HONORIUS, R. 395–423

▌ HONORIUS MOVES CAPITAL TO RAVENNA, 404

▌ FALL OF ROME TO ALARIC, 410

▌ MARY DECLARED *THEOTOKOS* AT COUNCIL OF EPHESUS, 431

▌ ROMULUS AUGUSTULUS, LAST ROMAN EMPEROR, R. 475–476

**2** Catacomb of Saints Peter and Marcellinus, Rome, early fourth century

**476**

ODOACER

▌ FALL OF RAVENNA TO ODOACER, 476

**3** Sarcophagus of Junius Bassus, ca. 359

**493**

THEODORIC

▌ THEODORIC AT RAVENNA, 493–526

**4**

**526**

**4** Sant'Apollinare Nuovo, Ravenna, 504

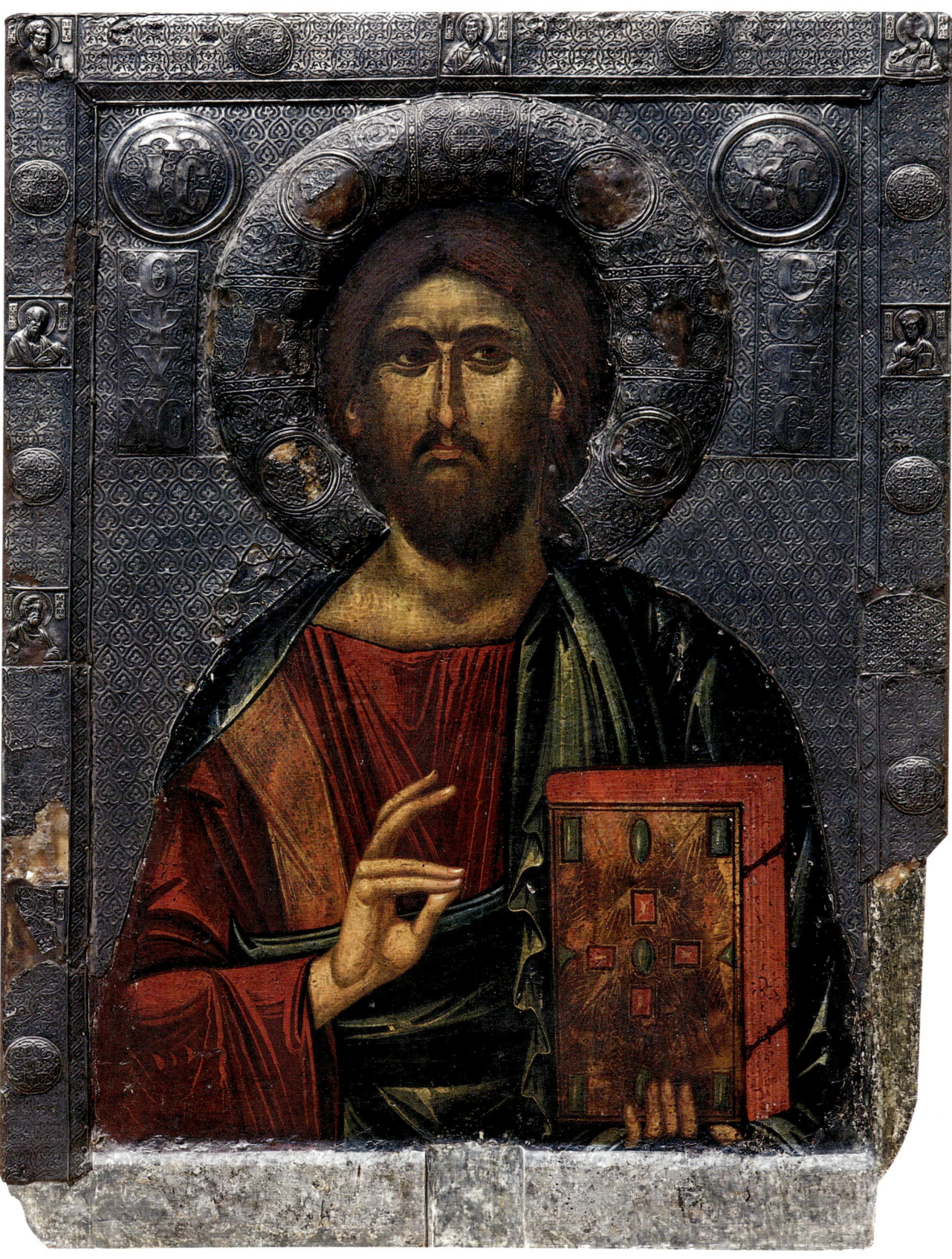

Christ as Savior of Souls, icon from the church of Saint Clement, Ohrid, Macedonia, early 14th century. Tempera, linen, and silver on wood, $3' \frac{1}{4}'' \times 2' 2\frac{1}{2}''$. Icon Gallery of Saint Clement, Ohrid.

# 12

# ROME IN THE EAST

## THE ART OF BYZANTIUM

When Constantine I founded a "New Rome" in the East in 324 on the site of the ancient Greek city of Byzantium and called it Constantinople in honor of himself, he legitimately could claim to be ruler of a united Roman Empire. In the fifth century, however, that empire, by then officially a Christian state, fell apart. After the sack of Rome in 410, an Emperor of the West ruled first from Milan and then from Ravenna, and an Emperor of the East ruled from Constantinople. Though not formally codified, the division of the Roman Empire became permanent. Centralized government disintegrated in the western half and was replaced by warring kingdoms that, during the Middle Ages, formed the foundations of the modern Western European nations (MAP 12-1). The eastern half of the Roman Empire, only loosely connected by religion to the west and with only minor territorial holdings there, had a long and complex history of its own. Centered at New Rome, the Eastern Christian Empire remained a cultural and political entity for a millennium, until the last of a long line of Eastern Roman emperors, ironically named Constantine XI, died at Constantinople in 1453, defending it in vain against the Ottoman Turks.

Historians call that Eastern Christian Roman Empire "Byzantium," employing Constantinople's original name, and use the term *Byzantine* to identify whatever pertains to Byzantium—its territory, its history, and its culture. The Byzantine emperors, however, did not use these terms to define themselves. They called their empire "Rome" *(Romania)* and themselves "Romans" *(Romaioi)*. Though they spoke Greek and not Latin, the Eastern Roman emperors never relinquished their claim as the legitimate successors to the ancient Roman emperors. Nevertheless, *Byzantium* and *Byzantine*, though inexact terms, have become in modern times the accepted designations for the Eastern Roman Empire, and we shall use them here.

Byzantium preserved its identity throughout alternating periods of good rule and misrule, stability and instability, expansion and contraction, victory and defeat. When its shrinking borders reduced it to a mere fragment of the once mighty Byzantine Empire, when it became only a small medieval Greek kingdom, an enclave around the city of Constantinople, it still was stubbornly "Rome." As such, it had resisted successive

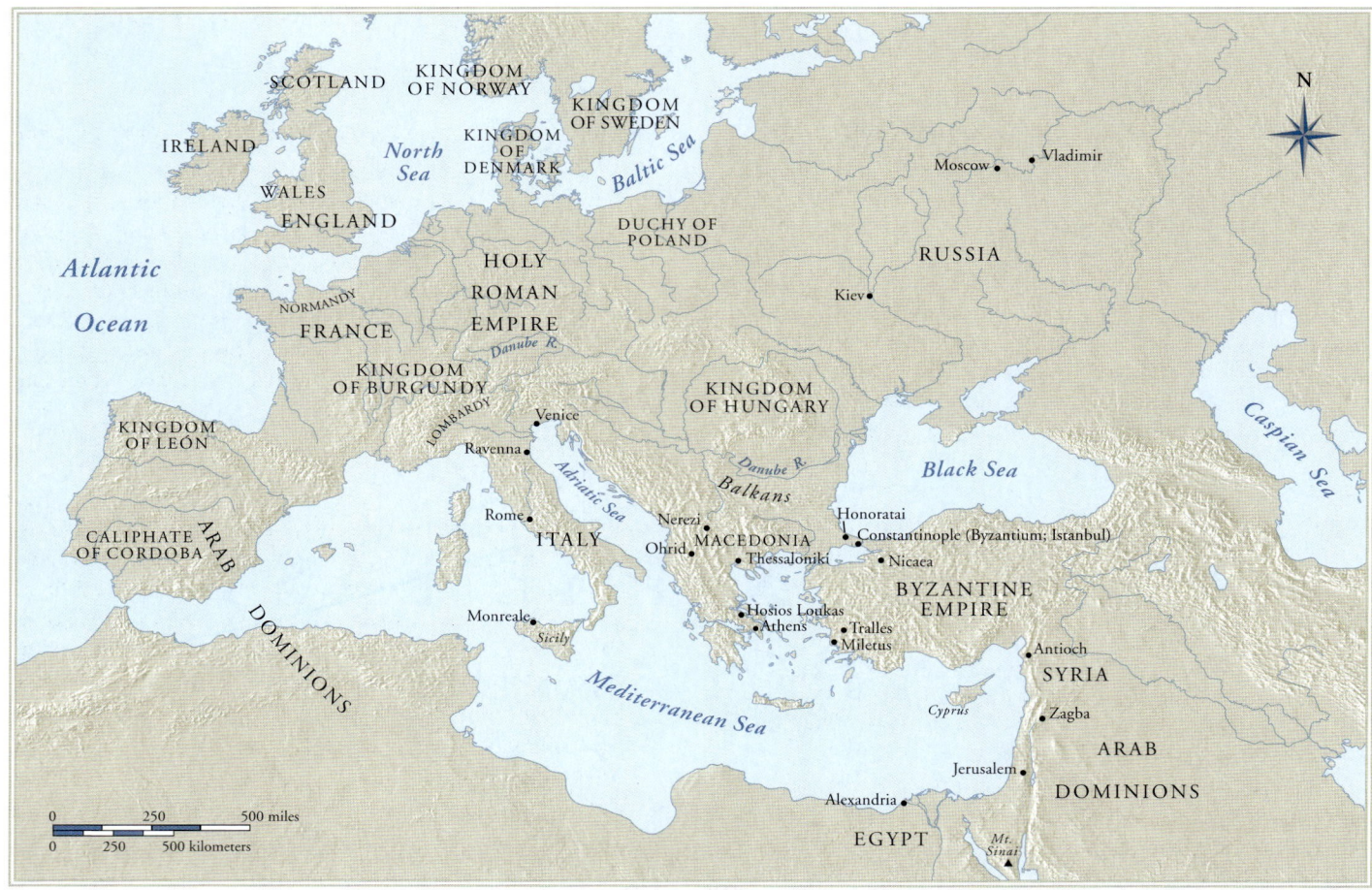

**MAP 12-1** Europe and the Byzantine Empire ca. 1000.

assaults of Sasanian Persians, Arabs, Russians, Serbs, Normans, Franks, Venetians, and others, until Ottoman armies finally captured Constantinople. During the long course of its history, Byzantium was the Christian buffer against the expansion of Islam into central and northern Europe, and its cultural influence was felt repeatedly in Europe throughout the Middle Ages. Byzantium Christianized the Slavic peoples of the Balkans and of Russia, giving them its Orthodox religion and alphabet, its literary culture, and its art and architecture. Byzantium's collapse in 1453 brought the Ottoman Empire into Europe as far as the Danube River, but the effect of Constantinople's fall was felt even further to the west. The westward flight of Byzantine scholars from the Rome of the East introduced the study of classical Greek to Italy and helped inspire there the new consciousness of antiquity that historians call the Renaissance.

**CHURCH AND STATE UNITED** Constantine recognized Christianity at the beginning of the fourth century, Theodosius established it as the Roman Empire's official religion at the end of the fourth century, and Justinian, in the sixth century, proclaimed it New Rome's only *lawful* religion. By that time it was not simply the Christian religion but the *Orthodox* Christian doctrine that the Byzantine emperor asserted as the only permissible faith for his subjects. This Orthodox Christianity was *trinitarian*. Its central article of faith was the equality of the three aspects of the Trinity of Father, Son, and Holy Spirit (as stated in Roman Catholic, Protestant, and Eastern Orthodox creeds today). All other versions of Christianity were called heresies, especially the *Arian*, which asserted that Christ had a human nature and was

therefore not equal to God but only one of his creations, and the *Monophysite*, which insisted that Christ had only one nature, which was divine. Justinian considered it his first duty not only to stamp out the few surviving pagan cults but also to crush all those who professed any Christian doctrine other than the Orthodox.

The Byzantine emperors considered themselves the earthly vicars of Jesus Christ. Their will was God's will. They exercised the ultimate spiritual as well as temporal authority. As sole executives for church and state, the emperors shared power with neither senate nor church council. They reigned supreme, combining the functions of both pope and caesar, which the Western Christian world would keep strictly separate. The Byzantine emperors' exalted position made them quasidivine. The imperial court, with its hierarchy of lesser and greater functionaries converging upward to the throne, was an image of the Kingdom of Heaven.

In practice, the Byzantine emperors' attempt to make real the ideal of absolute political and religious unity was a failure. They ruled over peoples of great ethnic, religious, cultural, and linguistic diversity, with varying histories and institutions—Armenians, Syrians, Egyptians, Jews, and Arabs, as well as Greeks, Italians, Germans, Slavs, and many others. Many of these were heretical Christians, and Byzantine efforts to force Orthodoxy on them in the interest of political and doctrinal unity led to bitter resistance, especially in Monophysite Egypt and Syria. When Islam made its way into the Byzantine Empire in the seventh century, the disaffected peoples of these provinces gave it ready support. Religious intolerance lost the great Eastern provinces. The same rigid Orthodoxy also eventually severed its last ties to the Latin Christianity of the West.

## The Emperors of New Rome

Byzantine art is generally, and properly, considered to belong to the Middle Ages rather than to the ancient world, but the emperors of Byzantium, New Rome, considered themselves the direct successors of the emperors of Old Rome. Although the official state religion was Christianity and all pagan cults were suppressed, the political imagery of Byzantine art displays a striking continuity between ancient Rome and medieval Byzantium. Artists continued to portray emperors sitting on thrones holding the orb of the earth in their hands, battling foes while riding on mighty horses, and receiving tribute from defeated enemies. In the Early Byzantine period, official portraits continued to be set up in great numbers throughout the territories Byzantium controlled. But, as was true of the classical world, much of imperial Byzantine statuary is forever lost. Nonetheless, some of the lost portraits of the Byzantine emperors can be visualized from miniature versions of them on ivory reliefs such as the *Barberini Ivory* (FIG. 12-1) and from descriptions in surviving texts.

One especially impressive portrait in the Roman imperial tradition, melted down long ago, depicted the emperor Justinian on horseback atop a grandiose column. Cast in glittering bronze, like the equestrian statue of Marcus Aurelius (see FIG. 10-59) set up nearly 400 years earlier, it attested to the continuity between the art of Old and New Rome, where pompous imperial images were commonly displayed at the apex of freestanding columns. (Compare FIG. 10-42, where a statue of Saint Peter has replaced a lost statue of the emperor Trajan.) Procopius, the sixth-century historian who chronicled Justinian's wars and who wrote, at the

emperor's behest, a treatise on his ambitious building program, described the equestrian portrait:

> Finest bronze, cast into panels and wreaths, encompasses the stones [of the column] on all sides, both binding them securely together and covering them with adornment. . . . This bronze is in color softer than pure gold, while in value it does not fall much short of an equal weight of silver. At the summit of the column stands a huge bronze horse turned towards the east, a most noteworthy sight. . . . Upon this horse is mounted a bronze image of the Emperor like a colossus. . . . He wears a cuirass in heroic fashion and his head is covered with a helmet . . . and a kind of radiance flashes forth from there. . . . He gazes towards the rising sun, steering his course, I suppose, against the Persians. In his left hand he holds a globe, by which the sculptor has signified that the whole earth and sea were subject to him, yet he carries neither sword nor spear nor any other weapon, but a cross surmounts his globe, by virtue of which alone he has won the kingship and victory in war. Stretching forth his right hand towards the regions of the East and spreading out his fingers, he commands the barbarians that dwell there to remain at home and not to advance any further.[1]

Statues such as this are the missing links in an imperial tradition that never really died and that lived on also in the Holy Roman Empire of the Western medieval world (see FIG. 16-11) and in the Renaissance (see FIGS. 21-29 and 21-30).

[1] Cyril Mango, trans., *The Art of the Byzantine Empire, 312–1453: Sources and Documents* (Upper Saddle River, NJ: Prentice Hall, 1972), 110–11.

---

**A THRICE GLORIOUS EMPIRE**  The Byzantine Empire's unity, fragmented from invasions by hostile peoples and hostile creeds, also was regularly disrupted by events at home: palace intrigues, conspiracies and betrayals, bureaucratic corruption, violent religious controversy, civil commotion, rebellions, and assassinations. Yet with characteristic resilience, Byzantium, in three periods of revived energy, recovered from dismal defeats, disunity, and stagnation. At those times intelligent, able, and successful rulers in war and peace guided the state. Under them Byzantium prospered and its culture flourished. These were the periods when the unique stylistic features of Byzantine art and architecture were shaped and refined.

Art historians divide the history of Byzantine art into the three periods of its greatest glory, sometimes referred to as "golden ages." The first, *Early Byzantine*, extends from the age of the emperor Justinian (r. 527–565) to the onset of *Iconoclasm* (the destruction of images used in religious worship) under Leo III in 726. The *Middle Byzantine* period begins with the renunciation of Iconoclasm in 843 and ends with the western Crusaders' occupation of Constantinople in 1204. *Late Byzantine* corresponds to a third golden age in the 14th and early 15th centuries after the Byzantines recaptured Constantinople in 1261 until its final loss in 1453 to the Ottoman Turks and the conversion of many churches to mosques (see Chapter 13).

# EARLY BYZANTINE ART (527–726)

**THE GOLDEN AGE OF JUSTINIAN**  The reign of Justinian and his politically astute consort, the Empress Theodora, marks

the end of the Late Roman Empire and the beginning of the Byzantine Empire. At this time Byzantine art emerged as a recognizably novel and distinctive style, leaving behind the uncertainties and hesitations of Early Christian artistic experiment. Though still revealing its sources in Late Antique art, it definitively expressed, with a new independence and power of invention, the unique character of the Eastern Christian culture centered at Constantinople.

Justinian briefly restored the Roman Empire's power and extent. His generals, Belisarius and Narses, drove the Ostrogoths out of Italy, expelled the Vandals from the African provinces, beat back the Bulgars on the northern frontier, and held the Sasanians at bay on the eastern borders. At home, the emperor put down a dangerous rebellion of political and religious factions in the city, and Orthodoxy triumphed over the Monophysite heresy. In Constantinople alone Justinian built or restored more than 30 churches of the Orthodox faith, and his activities as builder extended throughout the Byzantine Empire. The historian of his reign, Procopius, declared that the emperor's ambitious building program was an obsession that cost his subjects dearly in taxation. But his grand monuments defined the Byzantine style in architecture forever after. Justinian also supervised the codification of Roman law in a great work known as the *Corpus juris civilis (Code of Civil Law)*, which became the foundation of the law systems of many modern European nations. Justinian could claim, with considerable justification, to have revived the glory of "Old Rome" in New Rome (see "The Emperors of New Rome," above).

## Luxury Arts

**JUSTINIAN THE CONQUEROR** The triumphant image of Justinian's New Rome was set forth for all to see on an ivory plaque known today as the *Barberini Ivory* (FIG. **12-1**). Carved in five parts (one is lost), the *Barberini Ivory* shows at the center an emperor, usually identified as Justinian, riding triumphantly on a rearing horse, while a startled, half-hidden barbarian recoils in fear behind him. The dynamic twisting postures of both horse and rider and the motif of the spear-thrusting equestrian emperor are survivals of the pagan Roman Empire, as are the personifications of bountiful Earth (below the horse) and palm-bearing Victory (flying in to crown the conqueror). Also borrowed from pagan art are the barbarians at the bottom of the plaque bearing tribute and seeking clemency. They are juxtaposed with a lion, elephant, and tiger—exotic animals native to Africa and Asia, sites of Justinianic conquest. At the left, a Roman soldier carries a statuette of another Victory, reinforcing the central panel's message.

The source of the emperor's strength, however, comes not from his earthly armies but from God. The uppermost panel depicts two angels holding aloft a youthful image of Christ carrying a cross in his left hand. Christ blesses Justinian with a gesture of his right hand, indicating approval of Justinian's rule. Still conceived in the language of classical art, the *Barberini Ivory* announced Byzantium's theocratic state.

**VICTORY BECOMES AN ARCHANGEL** Another ivory panel (FIG. **12-2**), created somewhat earlier than the *Barberini Ivory* and likewise carved in the Eastern Christian Empire, perhaps in Constantinople, offers further evidence of the persistence of classical art. The panel, the largest extant Byzantine ivory, is all that is preserved of what was once a hinged diptych in the Early Christian tradition. It depicts Saint Michael the Archangel, patron of the imperial church of Hagia Sophia (FIGS. 12-3 to 12-5), and is inscribed "Receive these gifts." The dedication is perhaps a reference to the cross-surmounted orb of power that the archangel once offered to a Byzantine emperor depicted on the missing diptych leaf. The prototype of Michael must have been a pagan winged Victory, although Victory was personified as a woman in Greco-Roman art and usually carried the palm branch of victory, as does the Victory on the *Barberini Ivory*.

The archangel's flowing drapery, which reveals the body's shape, the delicately incised wings, and the facial type and coiffure are other indications that the artist who carved this ivory was still working in the tradition of classical art. Nonetheless, the Byzantine ivory carver had little concern for the rules of naturalistic representation. The archangel dwarfs the architectural setting. Michael's feet, for example, rest on three steps at once, and his upper body, wings, and arms are in front of the column shafts while his lower body is behind the column bases at the top of the reced-

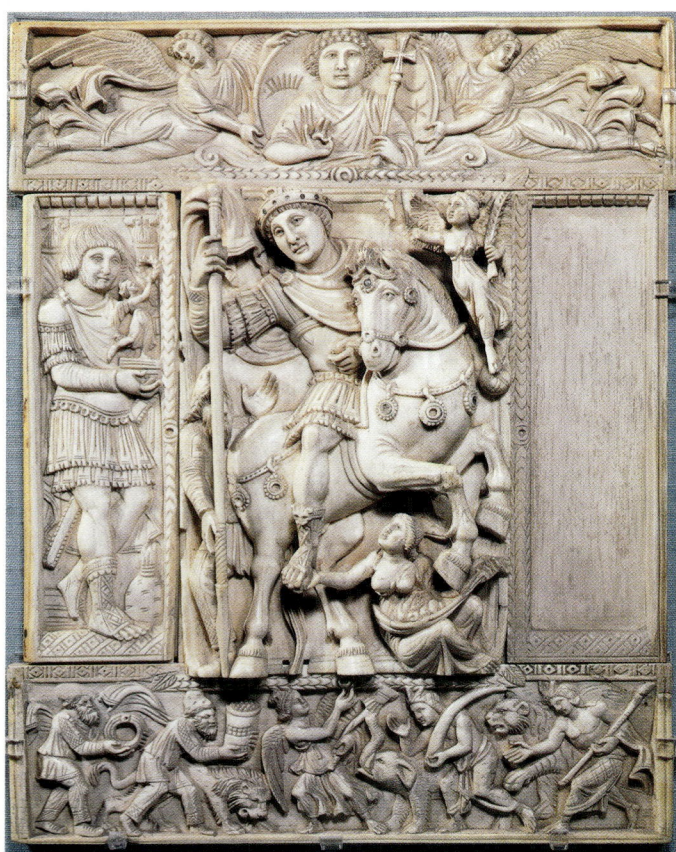

**12-1** Justinian as world conqueror (*Barberini Ivory*), mid-sixth century. Ivory, 1′ 1½″ × 10½″. Louvre, Paris.

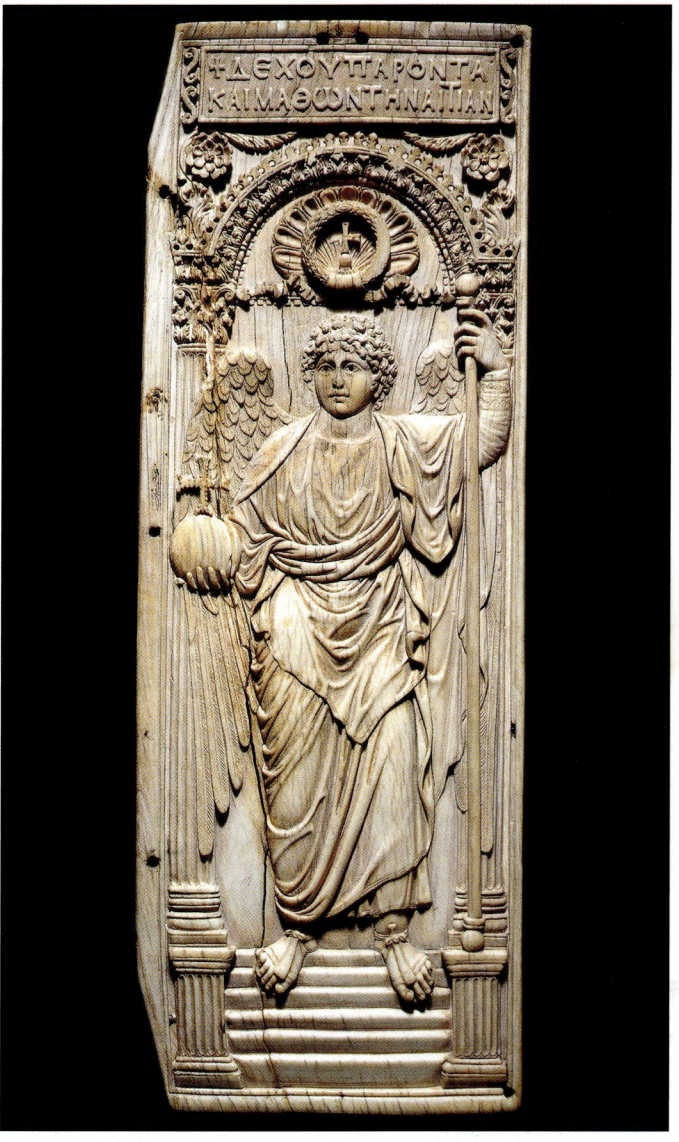

**12-2** Saint Michael the Archangel, right leaf of a diptych, early sixth century. Ivory, approx. 1′ 5″ × 5½″. British Museum, London.

ing staircase. These spatial ambiguities, of course, do not detract from the figure's striking beauty, but they do signify the emergence of a new aesthetic that characterized Byzantine art for centuries. Here, the sculptor has rejected the goal of most classical artists: to render the three-dimensional world in convincing and consistent fashion and to people that world with fully modeled figures firmly rooted on the ground. Michael seems more to float in front of the architecture than to stand in it.

## Architecture and Mosaics

**BYZANTIUM'S GREATEST CHURCH** The most important monument of early Byzantine art is Hagia Sophia (FIG. 12-3), the church of Holy Wisdom, in Constantinople. ANTHEMIUS OF TRALLES and ISIDORUS OF MILETUS—a mathematician and a physicist rather than architects in the modern sense of the word—designed and built the church for Justinian between 532 and 537. It is Byzantium's grandest building and one of the supreme accomplishments of world architecture. Its dimensions are formidable for any structure not made of steel. In plan (FIG. 12-4), it is about 270 feet long and 240 feet wide. The dome is 108 feet in diameter, and its crown rises some 180 feet above the pavement. (The first dome collapsed in 558 and was replaced. It required repair again in the 9th and 14th centuries. The present dome is greater in height and more stable than the original.) In scale, Hagia Sophia rivals the architectural wonders of Rome: the Pantheon, the Baths of Caracalla, and the Basilica of Constantine. In exterior view, the great dome dominates the structure, but the building's present external aspects are much changed from their original appearance. Huge buttresses were added to the Justinianic design, and four towering Turkish minarets were constructed after the Ottoman conquest of 1453, when Hagia Sophia became a mosque. The building was secularized in the 20th century and is now a museum.

The characteristic Byzantine plainness and unpretentiousness of the exterior (which, in this case, also disguise the great scale) scarcely prepare visitors for the building's interior (FIG. 12-5), which was once richly appointed. A poet and member of Justinian's court, Paul the Silentiary, recorded his impressions of Hagia Sophia. His words allow readers to visualize the original magnificence of the interior, whose walls and floors were clad with colored stones from all over the known world:

> Who . . . shall sing the marble meadows gathered upon the mighty walls and spreading pavement. . . . [There is stone] from the green flanks of Carystus [and] the speckled Phrygian stone, sometimes rosy mixed with white, sometimes gleaming with purple and silver flowers. There is a wealth of porphyry stone, too, besprinkled with little bright stars. . . . You may see the bright green stone of Laconia and the glittering marble with wavy veins found in the deep gullies of the Iasian peaks, exhibiting slanting streaks of blood-red and livid white; the pale yellow with swirling red from the Lydian headland; the glittering crocus-like golden stone [of Libya]; . . . glittering [Celtic] black [with] here and there an abundance of milk; the pale onyx with glint of precious metal; and [Thessalian marble] in parts vivid green not unlike emerald. . . . It has spots resembling snow next to flashes of black so that in one stone various beauties mingle.[1]

**THE MYSTICISM OF LIGHT** What distinguishes Hagia Sophia from the equally lavishly revetted and paved interiors of Roman buildings such as the Pantheon (see FIG. 10-50) is the special mystical quality of the light that floods the interior (FIG. 12-5). The soaring canopy-like dome that dominates the inside as well as the outside of the church rides on a halo of light from windows in the dome's base. Visitors to Hagia Sophia from Justinian's time to today have been struck by the light within the church and its effect on the human spirit. The 40 windows at the base of the dome create the illusion that the dome is resting on the light that pours through them. The historian Procopius observed that the dome looked as if it were suspended by "a golden chain from Heaven." Said he: "You might say that the space is not illuminated

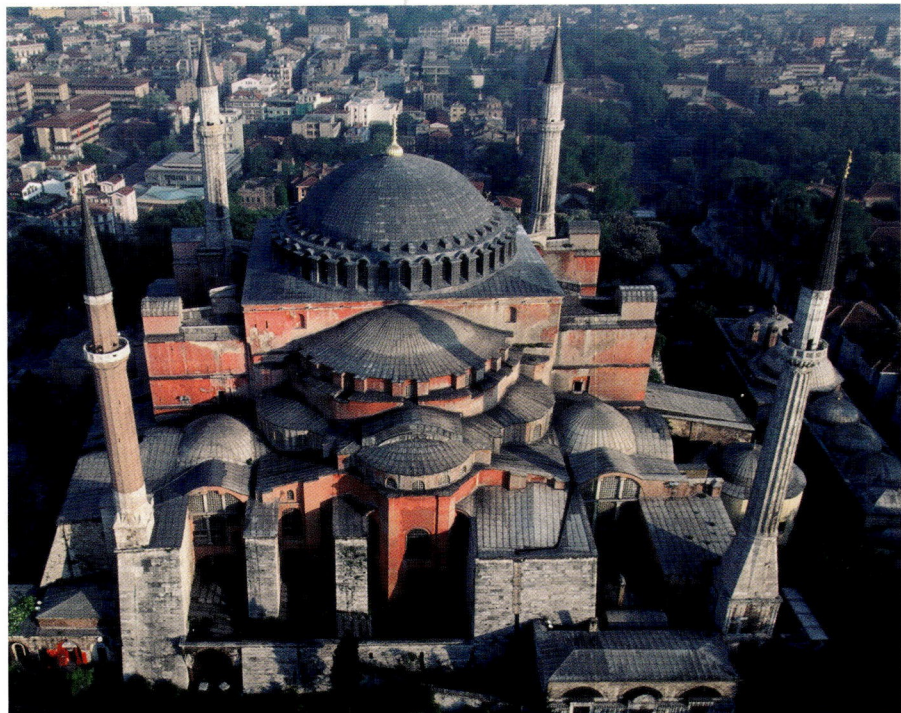

12-3 ANTHEMIUS OF TRALLES and ISIDORUS OF MILETUS, Hagia Sophia (view facing north), Constantinople (Istanbul), Turkey, 532–537.

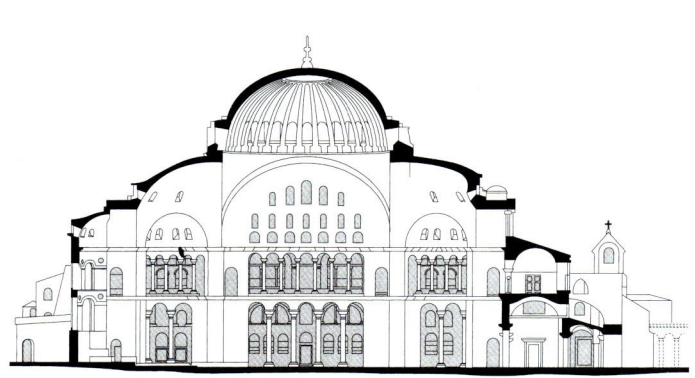

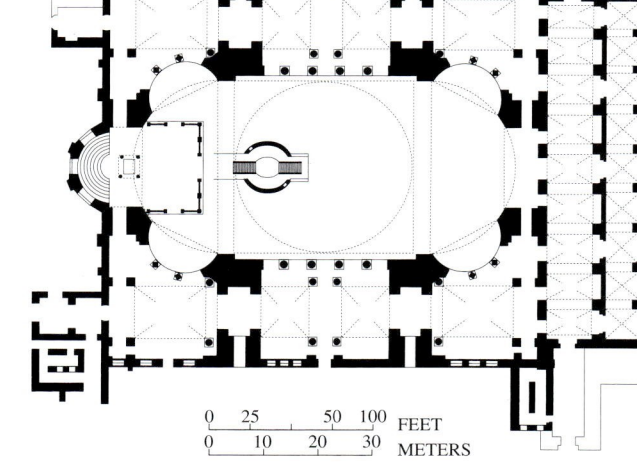

**12-4** ANTHEMIUS OF TRALLES and ISIDORUS OF MILETUS, longitudinal section *(left)* and plan *(right)* of Hagia Sophia, Constantinople (Istanbul), Turkey, 532–537 (after drawings by Van Nice and Antoniades). 

0 25 50 100 FEET
0 10 20 30 METERS
N

**12-5** ANTHEMIUS OF TRALLES and ISIDORUS OF MILETUS, interior of Hagia Sophia (view facing southwest), Constantinople (Istanbul), Turkey, 532–537. 

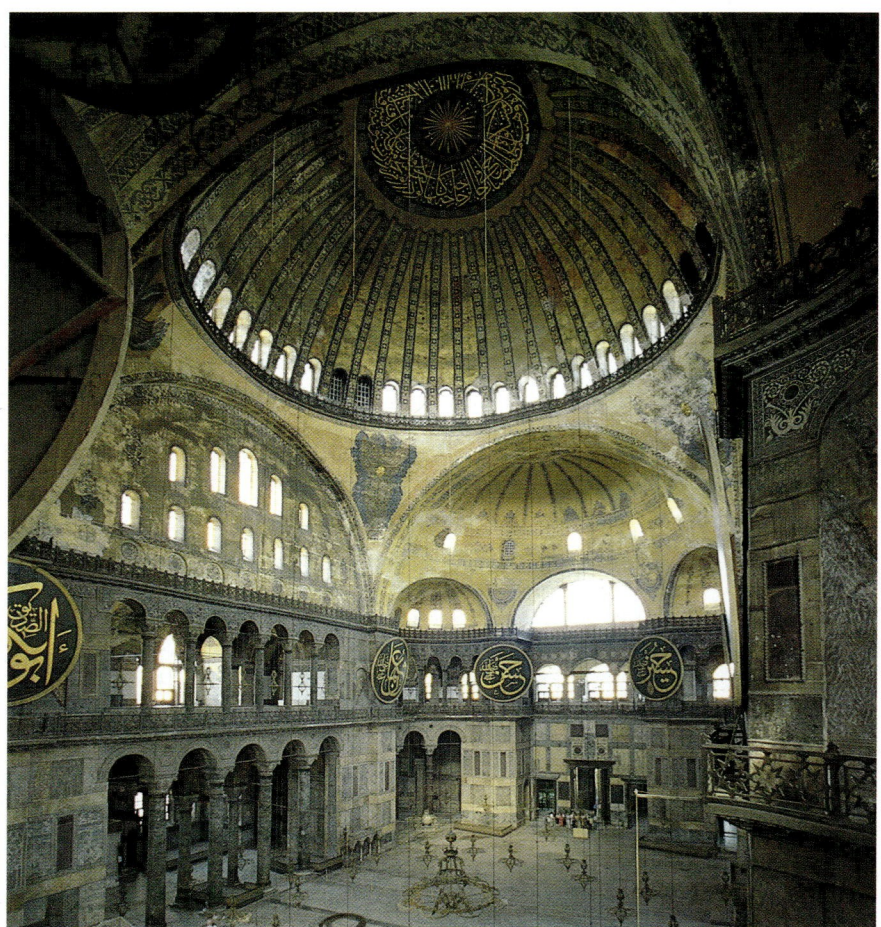

by the sun from the outside, but that the radiance is generated within, so great an abundance of light bathes this shrine all around."[2]

Paul the Silentiary compared the dome to "the firmament which rests on air" and described the vaulting as covered with "gilded tesserae from which a glittering stream of golden rays pours abundantly and strikes men's eyes with irresistible force. It is as if one were gazing at the midday sun in spring."[3] Thus, Hagia Sophia has a vastness of space shot through with light,

and a central dome that appears to be supported by the light it admits. Light is the mystic element—light that glitters in the mosaics, shines forth from the marbles, and pervades and defines spaces that, in themselves, seem to escape definition. Light seems to dissolve material substance and transform it into an abstract spiritual vision. Pseudo-Dionysius, perhaps the most influential mystic philosopher of the age, wrote in *The Divine Names:* "Light comes from the Good and . . . light is the visual image of God."[4]

### Pendentives and Squinches

Perhaps the most characteristic feature of Byzantine architecture is the placement of a dome, which is circular at its base, over a square, as in the Justinianic church of Hagia Sophia (FIGS. 12-3 to 12-5) and countless later structures (for example, FIGS. 12-20 and 12-23). Two structural devices that are the hallmark of Byzantine engineering made this feat possible: *pendentives* and *squinches.*

In pendentive construction (from the Latin *pendere,* "to hang") a dome rests on what is, in effect, a second, larger dome. The top portion and four segments around the rim of the larger dome are omitted so that four curved triangles, or pendentives, are formed. The pendentives join to form a ring and four arches whose planes bound a square. The weight of the dome is thus transferred through the pendentives and arches to the four piers from which the arches spring, instead of to the walls. The first use of pendentives on a monumental scale was in Hagia Sophia in the mid-sixth century, although Near Eastern architects had experimented with them earlier. In Roman and Early Christian central-plan buildings, such as the Pantheon (see FIG. 10-50) and Santa Costanza (see FIGS. 11-9 and 11-10), the domes spring directly from the circular top of a cylinder (see "The Roman Architectural Revolution," Chapter 10, page 250).

The pendentive system is a dynamic solution to the problem of setting a round dome over a square or rectangular space, making possible a union of centralized and longitudinal or basilican structures. A similar effect can be achieved using squinches—arches, corbels, or lintels—that bridge the corners of the supporting walls and form an octagon inscribed within a square. To achieve even greater height, a builder can rest a dome on a cylindrical drum that in turn rests on either pendentives or squinches, but the principle of supporting a dome over a square is the same.

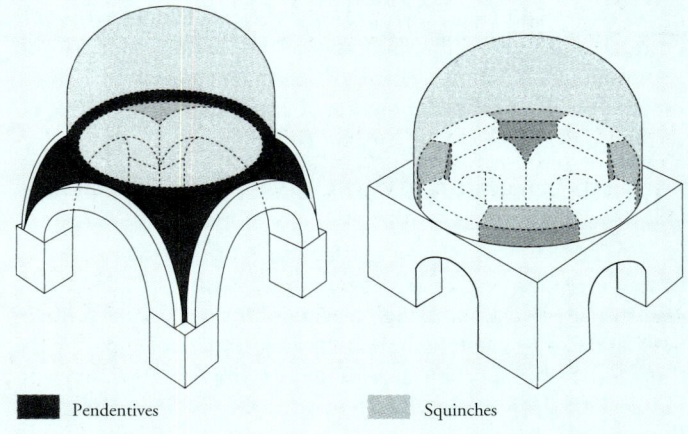

Pendentives      Squinches

Domes on pendentives *(left)* and squinches *(right)*

**PENDENTIVES** How was this illusion of a floating "dome of Heaven" achieved? Justinian's architects used *pendentives* (see "Pendentives and Squinches," above) to transfer the weight from the great dome to the piers beneath, rather than to the walls. With pendentives, not only could the space beneath the dome be unobstructed but scores of windows could puncture the walls themselves. This created the impression of a dome suspended above, not held up by, walls. Experts today can explain the technical virtuosity of Anthemius and Isidorus, but it remained a mystery to their contemporaries. Procopius communicated the sense of wonderment experienced by those who entered Justinian's great church: "No matter how much they concentrate their attention on this and that, and examine everything with contracted eyebrows, they are unable to understand the craftsmanship and always depart from there amazed by the perplexing spectacle."[5]

**THE DOMED BASILICA** By placing a hemispherical dome on a square base instead of on a circular base, as in the Pantheon, Anthemius and Isidorus succeeded in fusing two previously independent and seemingly mutually exclusive architectural traditions: the vertically oriented central-plan building and the longitudinally oriented basilica. Hagia Sophia is, in essence, a domed basilica (FIGS. 12-4 and 12-5)—a uniquely successful conclusion to several centuries of experimentation in Christian church architecture. However, the thrusts of the pendentive construction at Hagia Sophia made external buttresses necessary, as well as huge internal northern and southern wall piers and eastern and western half-domes. The semidomes' thrusts descend, in turn, into still smaller half-domes surmounting columned exedrae that give a curving flow to the design.

The diverse vistas and screenlike ornamented surfaces mask the structural lines. The columnar *arcades* of the nave and galleries have no real structural function. Like the walls they pierce, they are only part of a fragile "fill" between the huge piers. Structurally, although Hagia Sophia may seem Roman in its great scale and majesty, it does not have Roman organization of its masses. The very fact that the "walls" in Hagia Sophia are actually concealed (and barely adequate) piers indicates that the architects sought Roman monumentality as an *effect* and did not design the building according to Roman principles. Using brick in place of concrete marked a further departure from Roman practice and characterizes Byzantine architecture as a distinctive structural style. Hagia Sophia's eight great supporting piers are ashlar masonry, but the screen walls are brick, as are the vaults of the aisles and galleries and the dome and semicircular half-domes known as *conches.*

**BYZANTINE LITURGY** The ingenious design of Hagia Sophia provided the illumination and the setting for the solemn liturgy of the Orthodox faith. The large windows along the rim of the great dome poured light down upon the interior's jeweled splendor, where priests staged the sacred spectacle. Sung by clerical choirs, the Orthodox equivalent of the Latin Mass celebrated the sacrament of the Eucharist at the altar in the apsidal sanctuary, in spiritual reenactment of Jesus' Crucifixion. Processions of chanting priests, accompanying the *patriarch* (archbishop) of Constantinople, moved slowly to and from the sanctuary and the vast nave. The gorgeous array of their vestments (compare FIG. 12-35) rivaled the interior's polychrome marbles, metals, and mosaics, all glowing in shafts of light from the dome.

The nave of Hagia Sophia was reserved for the clergy, not the congregation. The laity, segregated by sex, were confined to the shadows of the aisles and galleries, restrained in most places by marble parapets. The complex spatial arrangement allowed only partial views of the brilliant ceremony. The emperor was the only lay person privileged to enter the sanctuary. When he participated with the patriarch in the liturgical drama, standing at the pulpit beneath the great dome, his rule was again sanctified and his person exalted. Church and state were symbolically made one, as in fact they were. The church building was then the earthly image of the court of Heaven, its light the image of God and God's holy wisdom.

At Hagia Sophia, the intricate logic of Greek theology, the ambitious scale of Rome, the vaulting tradition of the Near East, and the mysticism of Eastern Christianity combined to create a monument that is at once a summation of antiquity and a positive assertion of the triumph of Christian faith.

**RAVENNA, SACRED FORTRESS** In 493, Theodoric, the Ostrogoths' greatest king, chose the Italian city of Ravenna as the capital of his kingdom, which encompassed much of the Balkans and all of Italy (see Chapter 11). During the short history of Theodoric's unfortunate successors, the importance of the city declined. But in 539, Justinian's general Belisarius captured Ravenna, initiating the third and most important stage of the city's history. Reunited with the Eastern Empire, Ravenna remained the "sacred fortress" of Byzantium, a Byzantine foothold in Italy for two centuries, until the Lombards and then the Franks overtook it.

Ravenna enjoyed its greatest cultural and economic prosperity during Justinian's reign, at a time when repeated sieges, conquests, and sackings threatened the "eternal city" of Rome with complete extinction. As the seat of Byzantine dominion in Italy,

ruled by Byzantine *exarchs* (governors), Ravenna and its culture became an extension of Constantinople. Its art, even more than that of the Byzantine capital (where relatively little outside of architecture has survived), clearly reveals the transition from the Early Christian to the Byzantine style.

**SAN VITALE, MARTYR'S SHRINE** San Vitale (FIGS. **12-6** and **12-7**), dedicated by Bishop Maximianus in 547 in honor of Saint Vitalis, who was martyred at Ravenna in the second century, is the most spectacular building in Ravenna. The church is an unforgettable experience for all who have entered it and marveled at its intricate design and magnificent golden mosaics. Construction of San Vitale began under Bishop Ecclesius shortly after Theodoric's death in 526. Julianus Argentarius (Julian the Banker) provided the enormous sum of 26,000 gold *solidi* (weighing in excess of 350 pounds) required to proceed with the work. The church is unlike any of the other sixth-century churches of Ravenna (see FIG. 11-16). Indeed, it is unlike any other church in Italy. Although it has a traditional plain exterior and a polygonal apse, San Vitale is not a basilica. It is centrally planned, like Justinian's churches in Constantinople, and it seems, in fact, to have been loosely modeled on the earlier Church of Saints Sergius and Bacchus there.

The design features two concentric octagons. The dome-covered inner octagon rises above the surrounding octagon to provide the interior with clerestory lighting. The central space is defined by eight large piers that alternate with curved, columned exedrae, pushing outward into the surrounding two-story ambulatory and creating, on the plan, an intricate eight-leafed design. The exedrae closely integrate the inner and outer spaces that otherwise would have existed simply side by side as independent units. A cross-vaulted *choir* preceding the apse interrupts the ambulatory and gives the plan some axial stability. This effect is weakened, however, by the off-axis placement of the narthex, whose odd angle never has been explained fully. (The atrium, which no longer exists, may have paralleled a street that ran in the same direction as the angle of the narthex.)

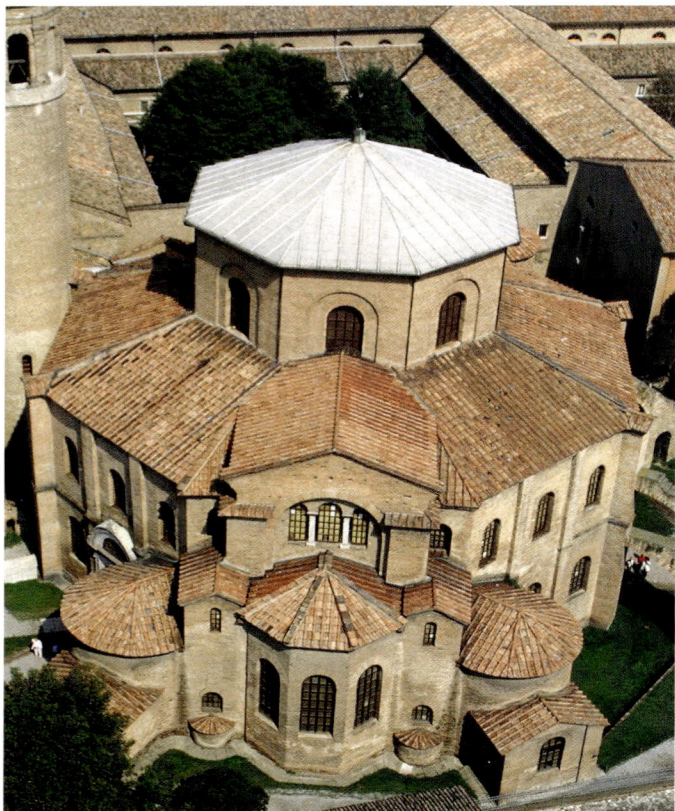

**12-6** Aerial view of San Vitale (view facing northwest), Ravenna, Italy, 526–547.

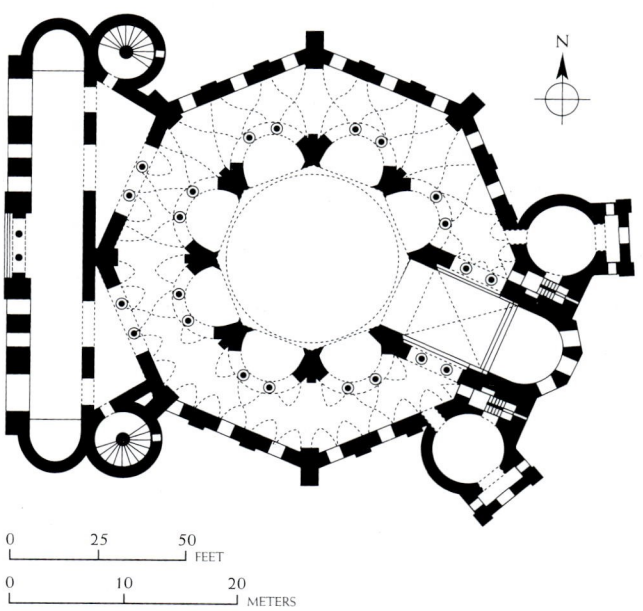

0 25 50 FEET
0 10 20 METERS

**12-7** Plan of San Vitale, Ravenna, Italy, 526–547.

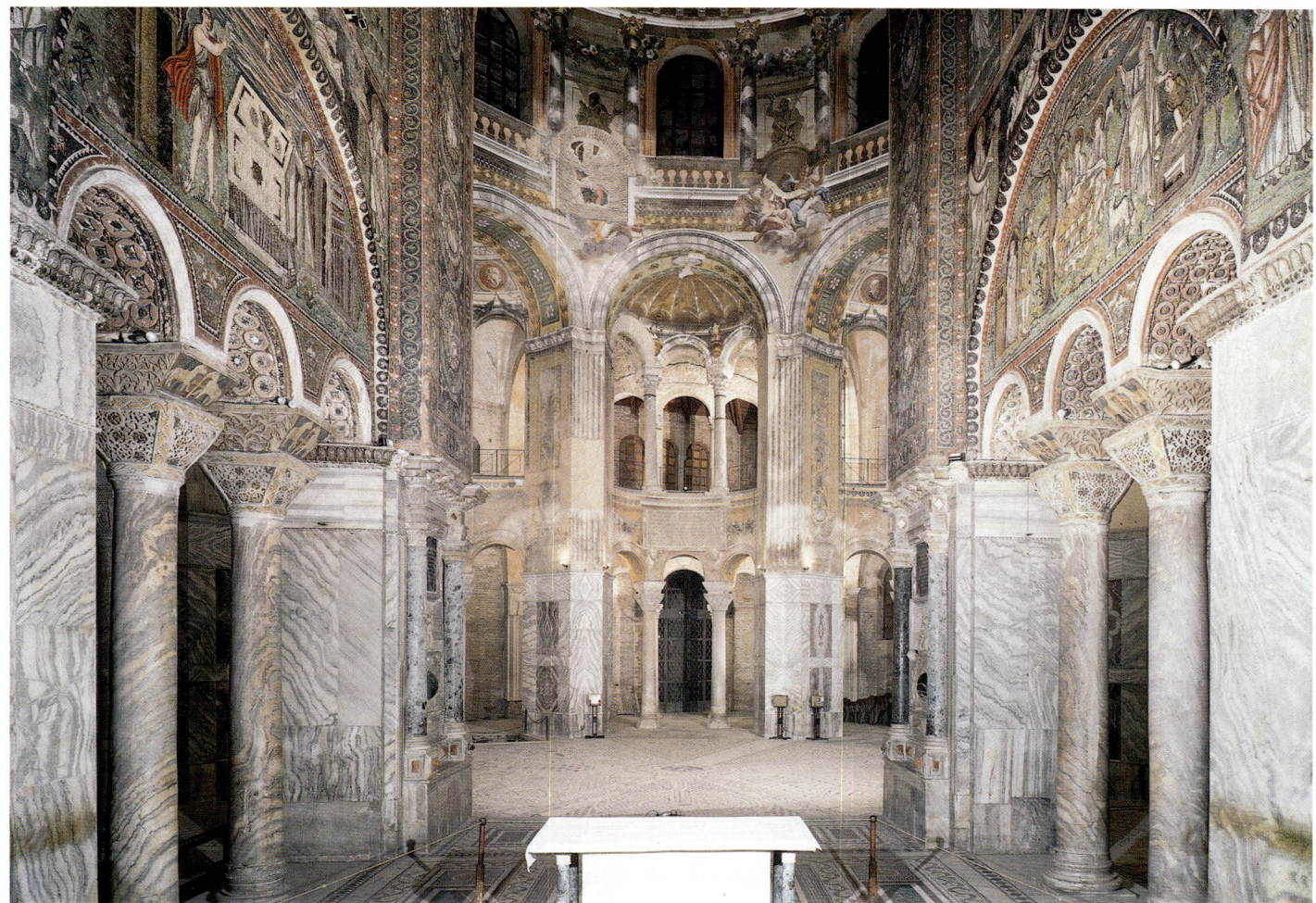

**12-8** Interior of San Vitale (view from the apse into the choir), Ravenna, Italy, 526–547.

San Vitale's intricate plan and elevation combine to produce an effect of great complexity. The exterior's octagonal regularity is not readily apparent inside. A rich diversity of ever-changing perspectives greets visitors walking through the building (FIG. **12-8**). Arches looping over arches, curving and flattened spaces, and wall and vault shapes seem to change constantly with the viewer's position. Light filtered through alabaster-paned windows plays over the glittering mosaics and glowing marbles that cover the building's complex surfaces, producing a sumptuous effect.

**THE SECOND COMING** The mosaics that decorate San Vitale's choir and apse (FIG. **12-9**), like the building itself, must be regarded as one of the climactic achievements of Byzantine art. Completed less than a decade after the Ostrogoths surrendered Ravenna, the apse and choir decorations form a unified composition, whose theme is the holy ratification of Justinian's right to rule.

In the apse vault, Christ, youthful in the Early Christian tradition, holds a scroll with seven seals (Rev. 5:1) and sits on the orb of the world at the time of his Second Coming. The four rivers of Paradise flow beneath him, and rainbow-hued clouds float above. Christ extends the golden martyr's wreath to Vitalis, the patron saint of the church, introduced here by an angel. At Christ's left, another angel introduces Bishop Ecclesius, in whose time the church foundations were laid. Ecclesius offers a model of San Vitale to Christ. The arrangement recalls Christ's prophecy of the last days of the world: "And then shall they see the Son of Man coming in the clouds with great power and glory. And then shall he send his angels, and shall gather together his elect from the four winds, from the uttermost part of Heaven" (Mark 13:26–27).

Images and symbols covering the entire sanctuary express the single idea of Christ's redemption of humanity and the reenactment of it in the Eucharist. Below the apse mosaic (at the right in FIG. 12-8), for example, the lunette mosaic over the two columns of the choir depicts Abraham and the three angels and the sacrifice of Isaac, prefigurations of the Trinity and of the Crucifixion, respectively (see "Jewish Subjects in Christian Art," Chapter 11, page 305).

**JUSTINIAN AND MAXIMIANUS** On the choir wall to the left of the apse mosaic appears Justinian (FIG. **12-10**). He stands on the Savior's right side. The two are united visually and symbolically by the imperial purple they wear and by their haloes. Justinian is also accompanied by a dozen attendants, paralleling Christ's Twelve Apostles. Thus, the mosaic program underscores the dual political and religious roles of the Byzantine emperor. The laws of the Eastern Church and the laws of the state, united in the laws of God, were manifest in the person of the emperor, whose right to rule was God-given.

The positions of the figures are all-important. They express the formulas of precedence and rank. Justinian is at the center, distinguished from the other dignitaries by his purple robe and halo. At his left (at right in the mosaic) is Bishop Maximianus, the man responsible for San Vitale's completion. The mosaicist stressed the bishop's importance by labeling his figure with the

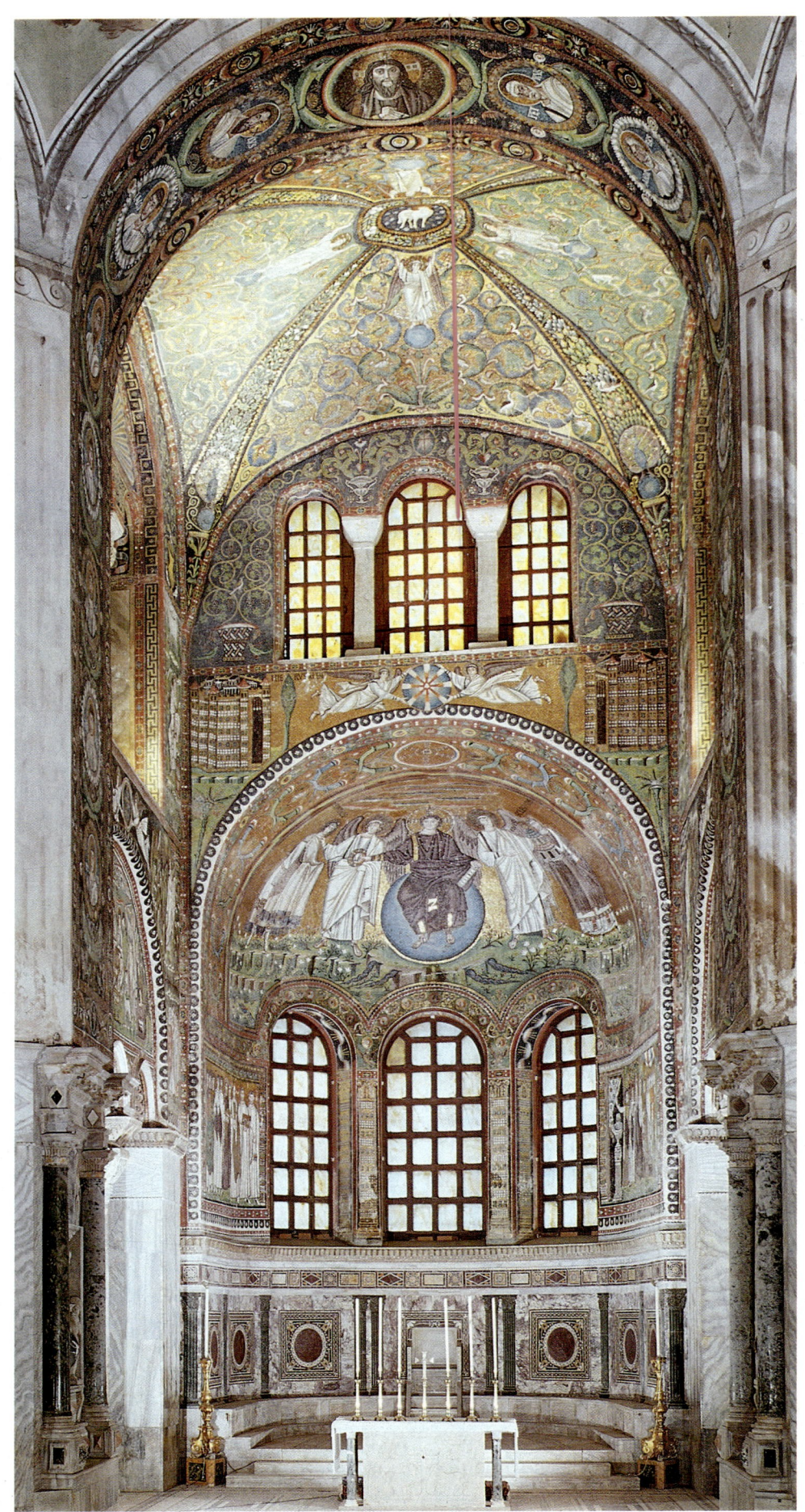

**12-9** Choir and apse of San Vitale with mosaic of Christ between two angels, Saint Vitalis, and Bishop Ecclesius, Ravenna, Italy, 526–547.

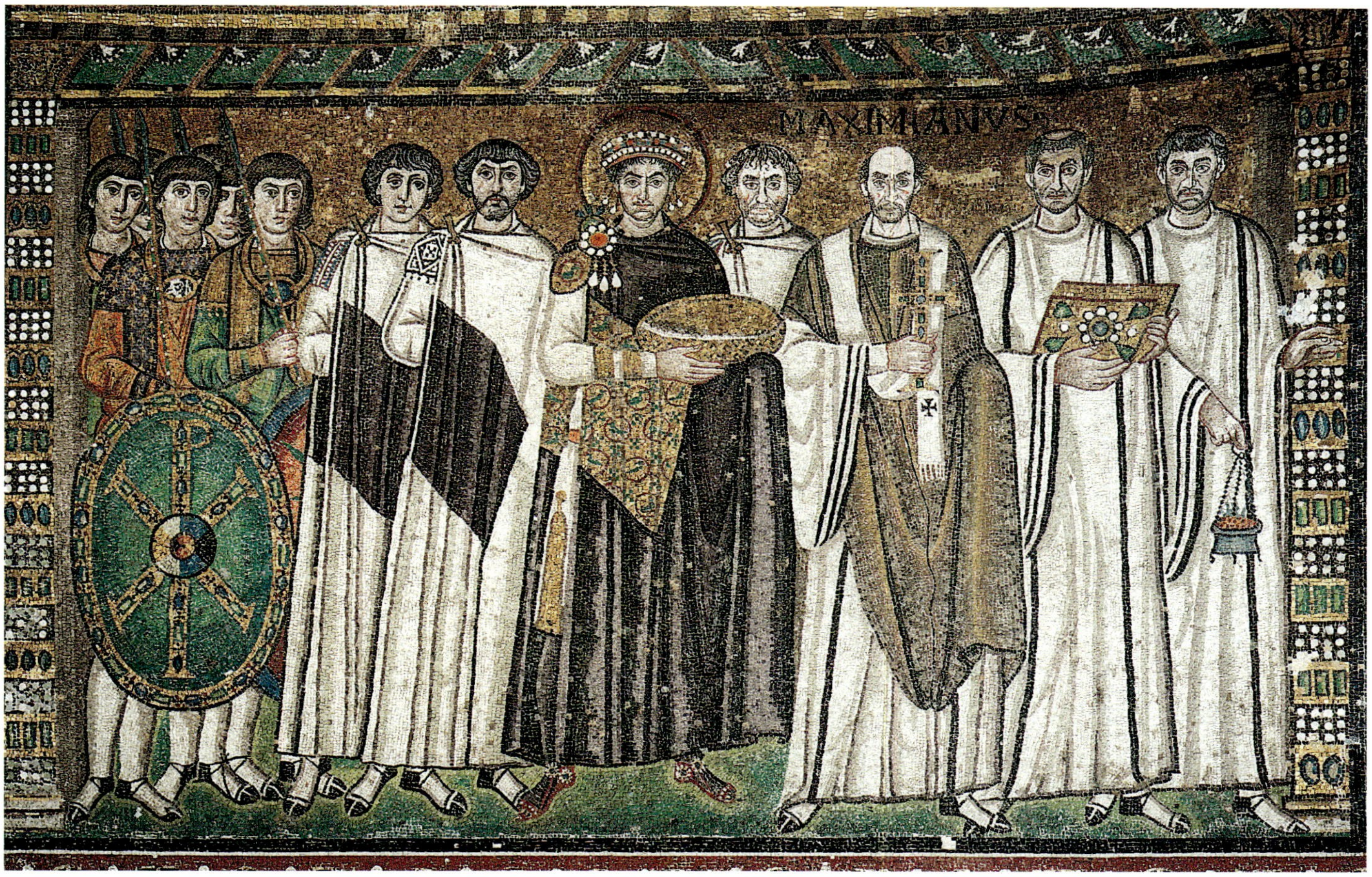

**12-10** Justinian, Bishop Maximianus, and attendants, mosaic from the north wall of the apse, San Vitale, Ravenna, Italy, ca. 547.

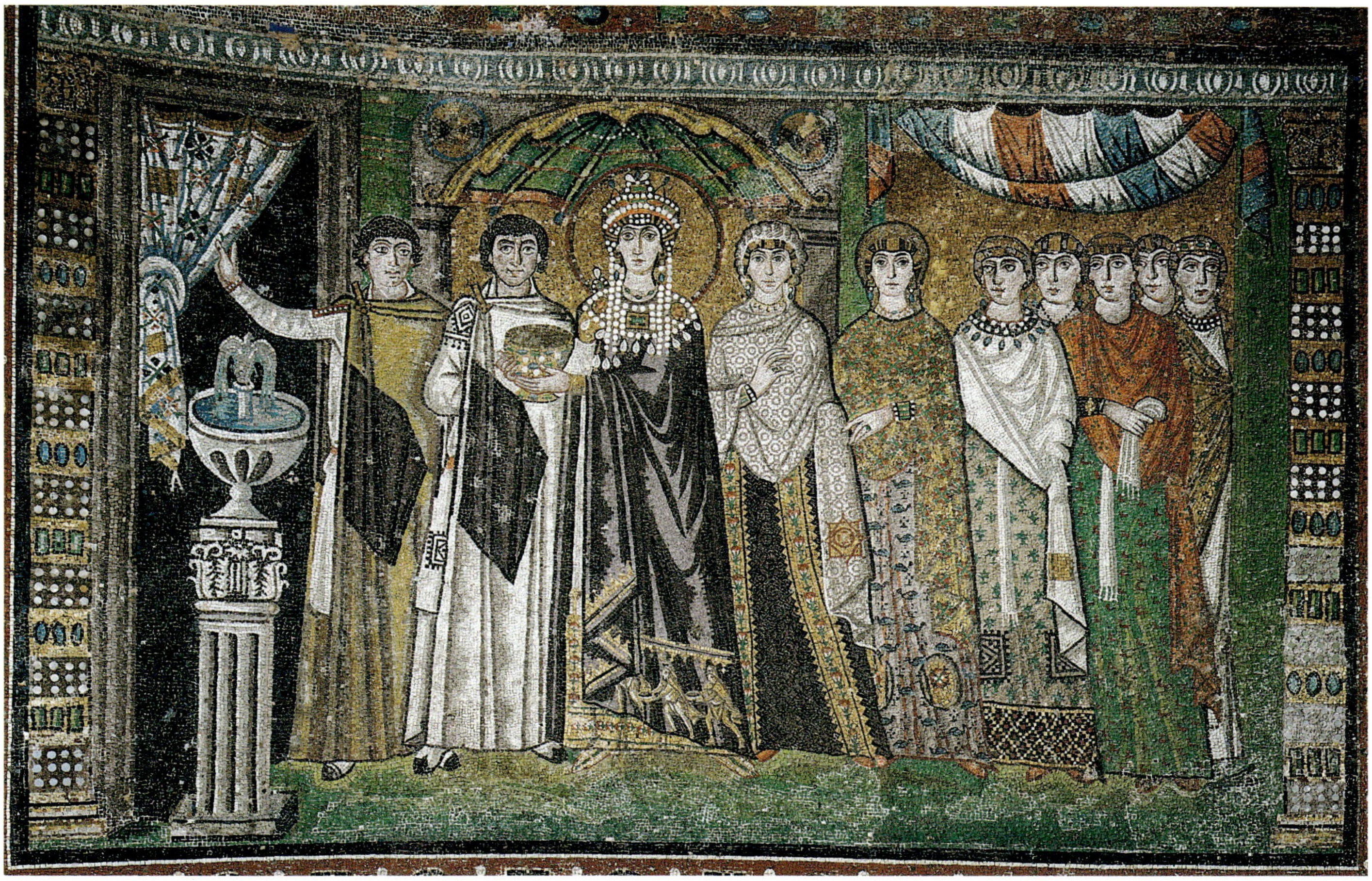

**12-11** Theodora and attendants, mosaic from the south wall of the apse, San Vitale, Ravenna, Italy, ca. 547.

## Theodora: A Most Unusual Empress

Theodora (FIG. 12-11), wife of Justinian and empress of Byzantium, was not born into an aristocratic family. Her father, who died when she was a child, was the "keeper of bears" for one of the circus *factions* (teams, distinguished by color) at Constantinople. His responsibility was to prepare these animals for bear fights, bear hunts, and acrobatic performances involving bears in a long tradition rooted in ancient Rome. Theodora's mother was an actress, and after the death of her father the young Theodora took up the same career. Acting was not a profession the highborn held in esteem. At Byzantium, actresses often doubled as prostitutes, and the beautiful Theodora was no exception. In fact, actresses were so low on the Byzantine social ladder that the law prohibited senators from marrying them.

Justinian met Theodora when he was about 40 years old, she only 25. She became his mistress, but before they could wed, as they did in 525, ignoring all the social norms of the day, Justinian's uncle, the emperor Justin, first had to rewrite the law against senatorial marriages to actresses to permit wedlock with an *ex-actress*. When Justin died in April 527, Justinian was crowned emperor by the patriarch of Constantinople, and Theodora became empress of Byzantium, capping what can be fairly described as one of the most remarkable and improbable "success stories" of any age. By all accounts, even of those openly hostile to the imperial couple, Justinian and Theodora remained faithful to each other for the rest of their lives.

It was not Theodora's beauty alone that attracted Justinian. John the Lydian, a civil servant at Constantinople at the time, described her as "surpassing in intelligence all men who ever lived." As her husband's trusted adviser, she repaid him for elevating her from poverty and disgrace to riches and prestige. During the Nika revolt in Constantinople in 532, when all of her husband's ministers counseled flight from the city, Theodora, by the sheer force of her personality, persuaded Justinian and his generals to hold their ground. The revolt was suppressed.

---

only identifying inscription in the composition. Some have identified the figure behind and between Justinian and Maximianus as Julius Argentarius, the church's benefactor.

The artist divided the figures into three groups: the emperor and his staff; the clergy; and the imperial guard, bearing a shield with the *chi-rho-iota* monogram of Christ. Each group has a leader whose feet precede (by one foot overlapping) the feet of those who follow. The positions of Justinian and Maximianus are curiously ambiguous. Although the emperor appears to be slightly behind the bishop, the golden *paten* (large bowl holding the Eucharist bread) he carries overlaps the bishop's arm. Thus, symbolized by place and gesture, the imperial and churchly powers are in balance. Justinian's paten, Maximianus's cross, and the attendant clerics' book and censer produce a slow forward movement that strikingly modifies the scene's rigid formality. No background is indicated. The artist wished the observer to understand the procession as taking place in this very sanctuary. Thus, the emperor appears forever as a participant in the sacred rites and as the proprietor of this royal church, the very symbol of his rule of the Western Empire.

**THE NEW BYZANTINE AESTHETIC** The procession at San Vitale recalls but contrasts with that of Augustus and his entourage on the Ara Pacis (see FIG. 10-29), erected more than half a millennium earlier in Rome. There the fully modeled marble figures have their feet planted firmly on the ground. The Romans talk among themselves, unaware of the viewer's presence. All is anecdote, all very human and of this world, even if the figures themselves conform to a classical ideal of beauty that cannot be achieved in reality. The frontal figures of the Byzantine mosaic, however, hover before viewers, weightless and speechless. Their positions in space are as uncertain as that of Saint Michael on the ivory diptych examined earlier (FIG. 12-2). Tall, spare, angular, and elegant, the figures have lost the rather squat proportions characteristic of much Early Christian work. The garments fall straight, stiff, and thin from the narrow shoulders. The organic body has dematerialized, and, except for the heads, some of which seem to be true portraits, viewers see a procession of solemn spir-

its gliding silently in the presence of the sacrament. This mosaic reveals the Byzantine world's new aesthetic, one very different from that of the classical world but equally compelling. Blue sky has given way to heavenly gold, and matter and material values are disparaged. Byzantine art is an art without solid bodies or cast shadows, with blank golden spaces, and with the perspective of Paradise, which is nowhere and everywhere.

**THEODORA AT SAN VITALE** Justinian's counterpart on the opposite wall of the apse is his empress, Theodora (FIG. **12-11**), one of the most remarkable women of the Middle Ages (see "Theodora: A Most Unusual Empress," above). She too is accompanied by her retinue. Both processions move into the apse, Justinian proceeding from left to right and Theodora from right to left, in order to take part in the Eucharist. Justinian carries the paten containing the bread and Theodora the golden cup with the wine. The portraits in the Theodora mosaic exhibit the same stylistic traits as those in the Justinian mosaic, but the women are represented within a definite architecture, perhaps the atrium of San Vitale. The empress stands in state beneath an imperial canopy, waiting to follow the emperor's procession. An attendant beckons her to pass through the curtained doorway. The fact that she is outside the sanctuary in a courtyard with a fountain and only about to enter attests that, in the ceremonial protocol, her rank was not quite equal to her consort's. But the very presence of Theodora at San Vitale is significant. Neither she nor Justinian ever visited Ravenna. Their participation in the liturgy at San Vitale is pictorial fiction. The mosaics are proxies for the absent sovereigns. Justinian was represented because he was the head of the Byzantine state, and by his presence he exerted his authority over his territories in Italy. But Theodora's portrayal is more surprising and testifies to her unique position in Justinian's court. Theodora's prominent role in the mosaic program of San Vitale is proof of the power she wielded at Constantinople and, by extension, at Ravenna. In fact, the representation of the Three Magi on the border of her robe suggests that she belongs in the elevated company of the three monarchs who approached the newborn Jesus bearing gifts.

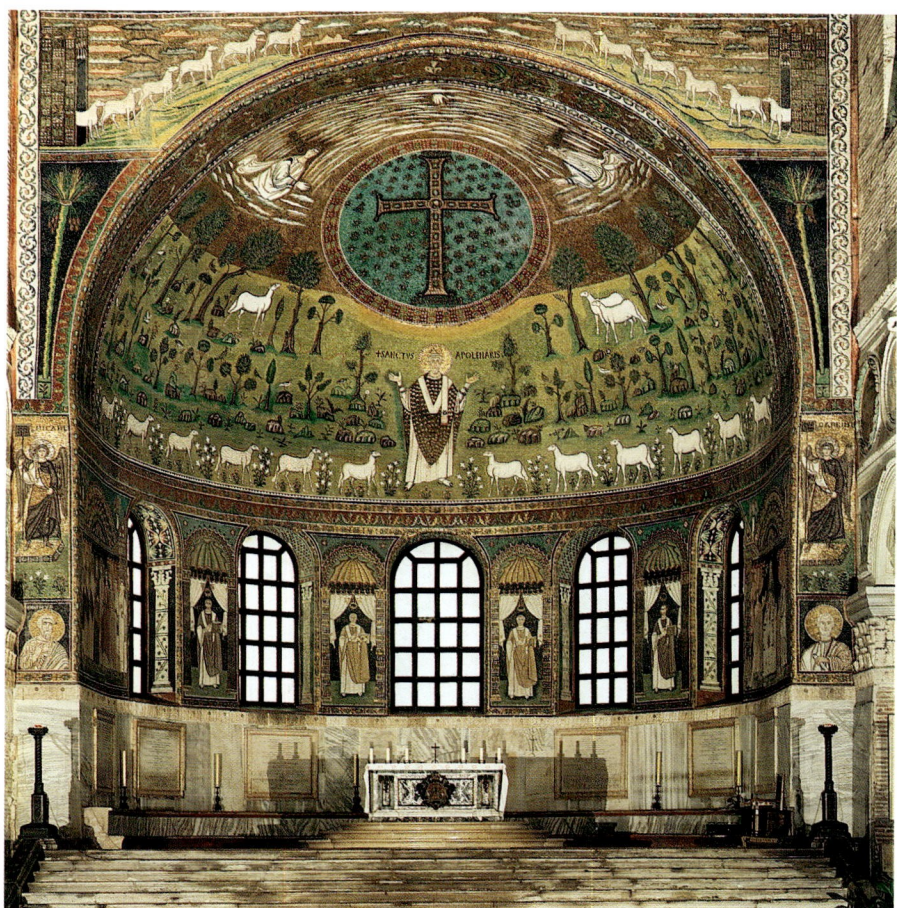

**12-12** Saint Apollinaris amid sheep, apse mosaic, Sant'Apollinare in Classe, Ravenna, Italy, ca. 533–549.

**SAINT APOLLINARIS** Until the ninth century, the Church of Sant'Apollinare in Classe housed the body of Saint Apollinaris, who suffered his martyrdom in Classe, Ravenna's port. The building itself is Early Christian in type, a basilica with a nave and flanking aisles, like Theodoric's palace-church dedicated to the same saint in Ravenna (see FIG. 11-16). As in the earlier church, the Justinianic building's outside is plain and unadorned, but the interior is decorated with sumptuous mosaics, although in this case they are confined to the apse (FIG. **12-12**).

The mosaic decorating the semivault above the apse probably was completed by 549, when the church was dedicated. (The mosaics of the framing arch were added later.) Against a gold ground, a large medallion with a jeweled cross (symbol of the transfigured Christ) dominates the composition. This may represent the cross Constantine erected on the hill of Calvary to commemorate the martyrdom of Jesus. Visible just above the cross is the hand of God. On either side of the medallion, in the clouds, are Moses and Elijah, who appeared before Christ during his Transfiguration. Below these two figures are three sheep, the three disciples who accompanied Christ to the foot of the Mount of the Transfiguration. Beneath, amid green fields with trees, flowers, and birds, stands the church's patron saint, Apollinaris. He is portrayed in the Early Christian manner as an orant with uplifted arms. Accompanying him are 12 sheep, perhaps representing the Christian congregation under the protection of Saint Apollinaris, and forming, as they march in regular file across the apse, a wonderfully decorative base.

**BYZANTINE ART AND DOGMA** Comparison of the Early Byzantine Sant'Apollinare in Classe mosaic with the Galla Placidia mosaic (see FIG. 11-15) from the Early Christian period at Ravenna shows how the style and artists' approach to the subject changed during the course of a century. Both mosaics portray a human figure and some sheep in a landscape. But in Classe, in the mid-sixth century, the artist did not try to re-create a segment of the physical world, telling the story instead in terms of flat symbols, lined up side by side. The mosaicist carefully avoided overlapping in what must have been an intentional effort to omit all reference to the three-dimensional space of the material world and physical reality. Shapes have lost the volume seen in the earlier mosaic and instead are flat silhouettes with linear details. The effect is that of an extremely rich, flat tapestry without illusionistic devices. This new Byzantine style became the ideal vehicle for conveying the extremely complex symbolism of the fully developed Christian dogma.

The Sant'Apollinare in Classe apse mosaic, for example, has much more meaning than first meets the eye. The Transfiguration of Christ—here, into the cross—symbolizes not only his own death, with its redeeming consequences, but also the death of his martyrs (in this case, Saint Apollinaris). The lamb, also a symbol of martyrdom, appropriately represents the martyred apostles. The whole scene expands above the altar, where the priests celebrated the sacrament of the Eucharist—the miraculous recurrence of the supreme redemptive act. The very altars of Christian churches were, from early times, sanctified by the bones and relics of martyrs (see "Pilgrimages and the Cult of Relics," Chapter 17, page 449). Thus, the mystery and the martyrdom were joined in one concept. The death of the martyr, in imitation of Christ, is a triumph over death that leads to eternal life. The images above the altar present an inspiring vision to the eyes of believers. The way of the martyr is open to them, and the reward of eternal life is within their reach. The organization of the symbolism and the images is *hieratic,* and the graphic message must have been delivered to the faithful with overwhelming force. Looming above their eyes is the apparition of a great mystery, ordered to make perfectly simple and clear that humankind's duty is to seek salvation. The anonymous artist, working under the direction of the priests, made sure that the devout could read the pictorial message as easily as an inscription—more easily, in fact, for many of the faithful were illiterate.

**MONASTICISM IN EGYPT** During Justinian's reign, almost continuous building took place, not only in Constantinople and Ravenna but all over the Byzantine Empire. At about the time mosaicists in Ravenna were completing their work at San Vitale and Sant'Apollinare in Classe, Justinian's builders were rebuilding an important early monastery at Mount Sinai in Egypt where Moses received the Ten Commandments from God. Now called Saint Catherine's, the monastery marked the spot at the foot of the mountain where the Bible says God first spoke to the Hebrew prophet from a burning bush.

The monastic movement began in Egypt in the third century and spread rapidly to Palestine and Syria in the East and as far as Ireland in the West. It began as a migration to the wilderness by those who sought a more spiritual way of life, far from the burdens, distractions, and temptations of town and city. In desert places these refuge seekers lived austerely as hermits, in contemplative isolation, cultivating the soul's perfection. So many thousands fled the cities that the authorities became alarmed—noting the effect on the tax base, military recruitment, and business in general.

The origins of organized monasticism are associated with Saint Anthony and Saint Pachomius in Egypt in the fourth century. By the fifth century, regulations governing monastic life began to be codified. Individual monks were brought together to live according to a rule within a common enclosure, a community under the direction of an abbot (see "Medieval Monasteries and Benedictine Rule," Chapter 16, page 434). The monks typically lived in a walled monastery, an architectural complex that included the monks' residence (an alignment of single cells), a *refectory* (dining hall), a kitchen, storage and service quarters, a guest house for pilgrims, and, of course, an *oratory* or monastery church (see FIG. 16-19).

**TRANSFIGURATION AT MOUNT SINAI** Justinian rebuilt the monastery at Mount Sinai between 548 and 565 and enclosed it within protective walls. The site had been an important pilgrimage destination since the fourth century, and Justinian's fortress was intended to protect not only the hermit-monks but also the lay pilgrims during their visits. The Mount Sinai church was dedicated to the Virgin Mary, whom the Orthodox Church had officially recognized in the mid-fifth century as the Mother of God (*Theotokos,* "bearer of God" in Greek), putting to rest a controversy about the divine nature of Christ. The church's apse mosaic (FIG. **12-13**) depicts the Transfiguration. Jesus appears in a deep-blue almond-shaped *mandorla* (aureole of light). Flanking him are the Old Testament prophets Elijah and Moses. (Other mosaics in the church depict Moses receiving the Law and standing before the burning bush.) At Christ's feet are the disciples John, Peter, and James. Portrait busts of saints and prophets in medallions frame the whole scene. The artist stressed the intense whiteness of Jesus' transfigured, spiritualized form, from which rays stream down on the disciples. The stately figures of Elijah and Moses and the static frontality of Jesus set off the frantic terror and astonishment of the gesticulating disciples. This effectively contrasts the eternal composure of heavenly beings with the distraught responses of the earthbound.

In this apse the mosaicist swept away all traces of landscape and architectural setting for a depthless field of gold, fixing the

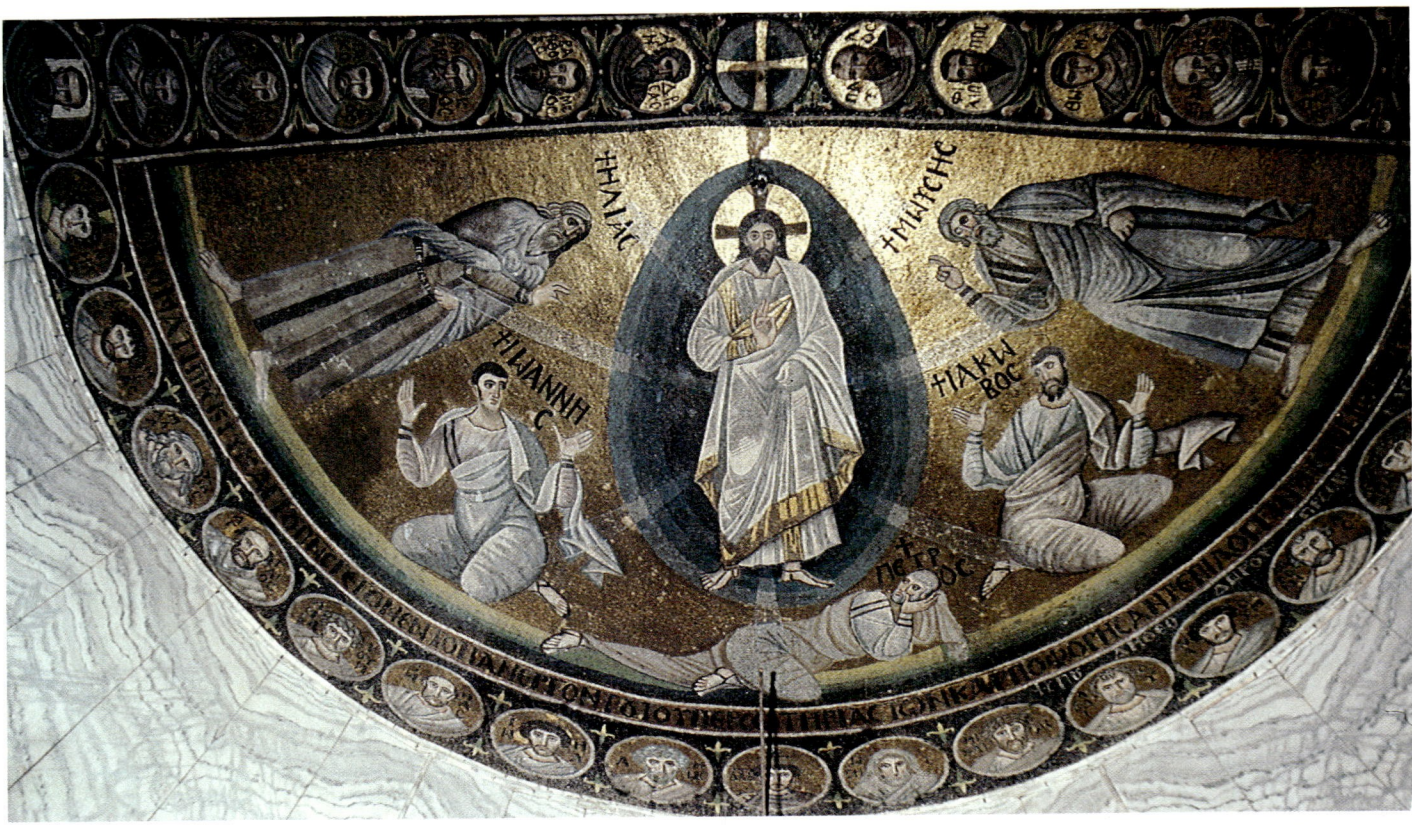

**12-13** Transfiguration of Jesus, apse mosaic, Church of the Virgin, monastery of Saint Catherine, Mount Sinai, Egypt, ca. 548–565.

figures and their labels in isolation from one another. A rainbow band of colors graduating from yellow to blue bounds the golden field at its base. The figures are ambiguously related to this multi-color ground line. Sometimes they are placed behind it; sometimes they overlap it. The bodies cast no shadows, even though supernatural light streams over them. This is a world of mystical vision, where the artist subtracted all substance that might suggest the passage of time or motion through physical space so that the devout can contemplate the eternal and motionless world of religious truth.

## Painting

**ANICIA JULIANA AND THE ARTS** The physical world was, however, the focus of one of the rare secular books to survive from the early Middle Ages, either in Byzantium or the West. In the mid-first century, a Greek physician named Dioskorides compiled an encyclopedia of medicinal herbs called *De materia medica*. An early-sixth-century copy of this medical manual, nearly a thousand pages in length, is in the Austrian National Library. The *Vienna Dioskorides* (FIG. **12-14**), as it is called, was a gift from the people of Honoratai, near Constantinople, to Anicia Juliana, daughter of the short-lived Emperor of the West, Anicias Olybrias (r. 472). Anicia Juliana was a leading patron of the arts in and around Constantinople. She had built a church dedicated to the Virgin Mary at Honoratai in 512. She also provided the funds to erect Saint Polyeuktos in Constantinople between 524 and 527.

The excavated ruins of that church indicate that it was a domed basilica—an important forerunner of the pioneering design of Justinian's Hagia Sophia (FIGS. 12-3 to 12-5).

The *Vienna Dioskorides* contains 498 illustrations, almost all images of plants rendered with a scientific fidelity to nature that stands in stark contrast to contemporary Byzantine paintings and mosaics of religious subjects. It is likely that the *Vienna Dioskorides* painters copied the illustrations as well as the text of a classical manuscript. One page, however, cannot be a copy—the dedication page (FIG. 12-14) featuring a portrait of Anicia Juliana in an eight-pointed star and circle frame. She is enthroned between personifications of Magnanimity and Prudence, with a kneeling figure labeled Gratitude of the Arts at her feet. The shading and modeling of the figures, the heads seen at oblique angles, the perspectival rendering of the throne's footstool, and the use of personifications establish that the painter still worked in the classical tradition that most other Byzantine artists had rejected.

**MARY AT THE ASCENSION** One of the essential Christian beliefs is that following his Crucifixion and entombment, Christ rose from the dead after three days and, on the 40th day, ascended from the Mount of Olives to Heaven. The Ascension is the subject of a full-page painting (FIG. **12-15**) in a manuscript known as the *Rabbula Gospels*. Written in Syriac by the monk Rabbula at the monastery of Saint John the Evangelist at Zagba in Syria, it dates to the year 586. The composition shows Christ, bearded and in a mandorla, as in the Mount Sinai Transfiguration (FIG. 12-13), but the mandorla is here borne aloft by angels. Below, Mary, other

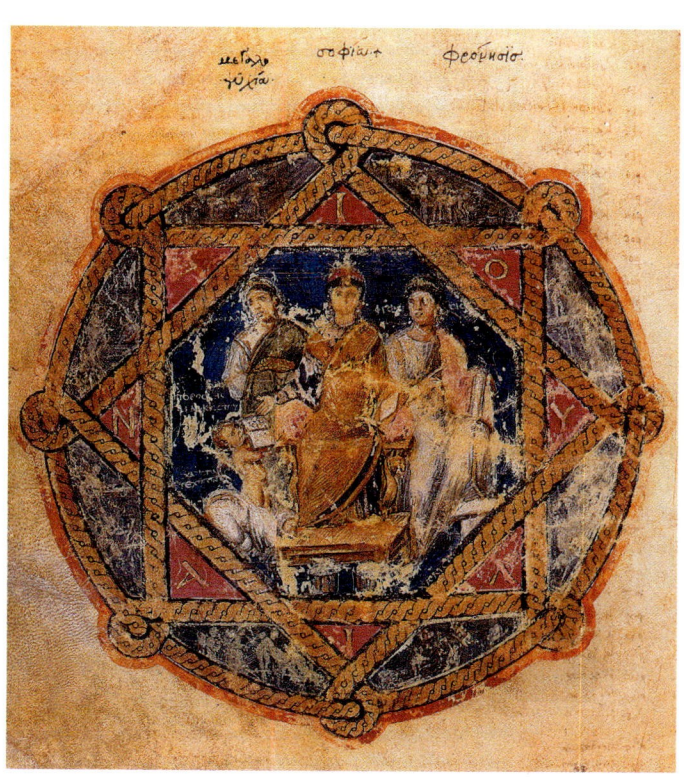

**12-14** Anicia Juliana between Magnanimity and Prudence, folio 6 verso of the *Vienna Dioskorides,* from Honoratai, near Constantinople (Istanbul), Turkey, ca. 512. Tempera on parchment, approx. 1′3″ × 1′11″. Österreichische Nationalbibliothek, Vienna.

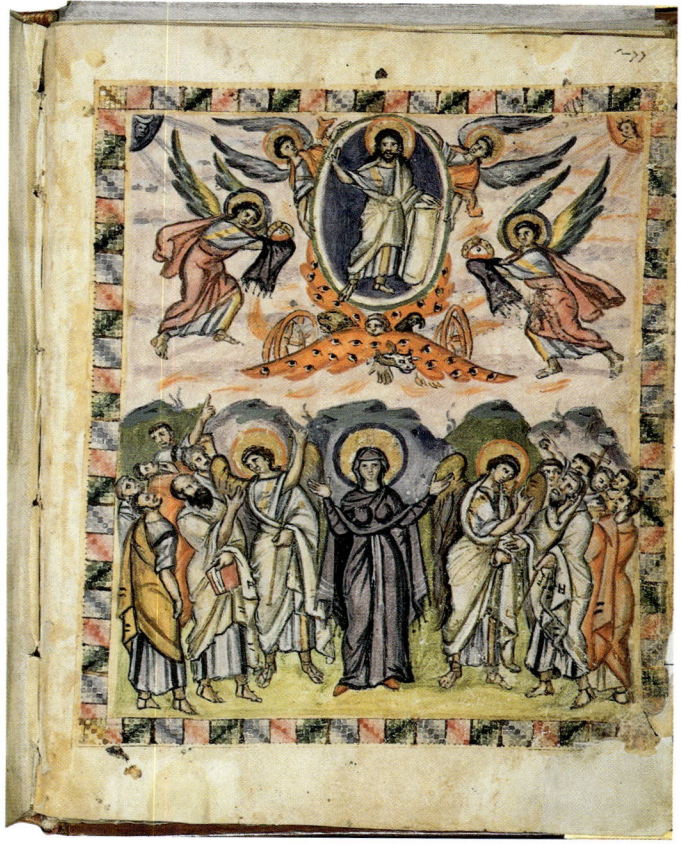

**12-15** Ascension of Christ, folio 13 verso of the *Rabbula Gospels,* from Zagba, Syria, 586. Approx. 1′ 1″ × 10½″. Biblioteca Medicea-Laurenziana, Florence.

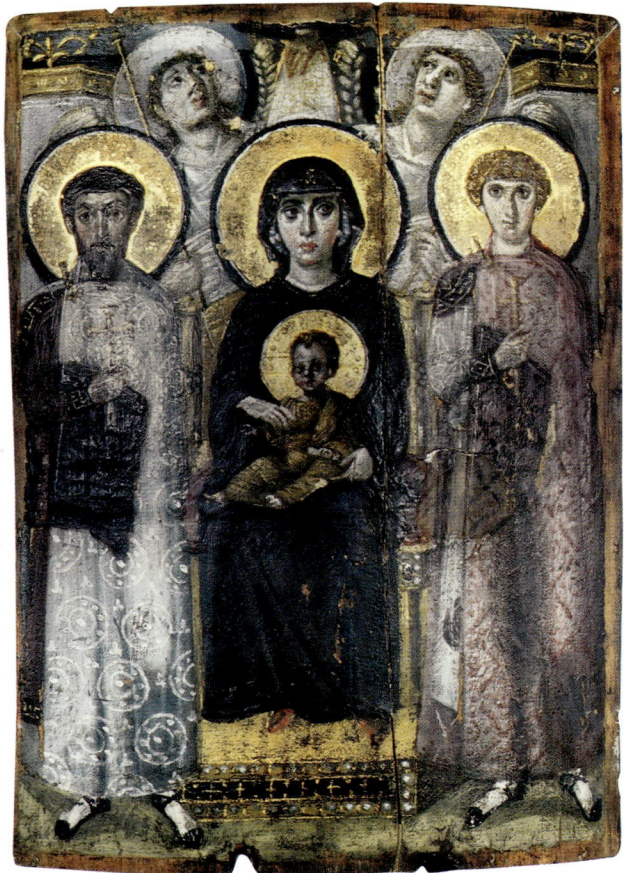

**12-16** Virgin (Theotokos) and Child between Saints Theodore and George, icon, sixth or early seventh century. Encaustic on wood, 2′ 3″ × 1′ 7⅜″. Monastery of Saint Catherine, Mount Sinai, Egypt.

angels, and various apostles look on. The artist set the figures into a mosaic-like frame (compare FIGS. 12-10 and 12-11), and many think the manuscript page was modeled after a mural painting or mosaic in a Byzantine church somewhere in the Eastern Empire.

The account of Christ's Ascension is not part of the accompanying text of the *Rabbula Gospels* but is borrowed from the Book of Acts. And even Acts omits mention of the Virgin's presence at the miraculous event. Here, however, the Theotokos occupies a very prominent position, central and directly beneath Christ. It is an early example of the prominent role the Mother of God played in later medieval art, both in the East and in the West. Frontal, with a nimbus, and posed as an orant, Mary stands apart from the commotion all about her and looks out at the viewer. Other details also depart from the Gospel texts. Christ, for example, does not rise in a cloud. Rather, as in the vision of Ezekiel in the book of Revelation, he ascends in a mandorla above a fiery winged chariot. The chariot carries the symbols of the Four Evangelists—the man, lion, ox, and eagle (see "The Four Evangelists," Chapter 16, page 426). This page is not therefore an *illustration* of the Gospels but an independent *illumination* presenting one of the central tenets of Christian faith. Similar compositions appear on pilgrims' flasks from Palestine that were souvenir items reproducing important monuments visited. They reinforce the theory that the *Rabbula Gospels* Ascension was based on a lost painting or mosaic in a major church.

**ICONS FOR THE DEVOUT** Gospel books such as the *Rabbula Gospels* played an important role in monastic religious life. So, too, did *icons*, which also figured prominently in private devotion. Unfortunately, few early icons survive because of the wholesale destruction of images *(iconoclasm)* that occurred in the eighth century (see "Icons and Iconoclasm," page 341). Some of the finest early examples come from Saint Catherine's monastery at Mount Sinai. The one we illustrate (FIG. **12-16**) was painted in encaustic on wood, continuing a tradition of panel painting in Egypt that, like so much else in the Byzantine world, goes back to the Roman Empire (see FIG. 10-63).

In a composition reminiscent of the portrait of Anicia Juliana in the *Vienna Dioskorides* (FIG. 12-14), the Sinai icon painter represented the enthroned Theotokos and Child with Saints Theodore and George. The two guardian saints intercede with the Virgin on the viewer's behalf. Behind them, two angels look upward to a shaft of light where the hand of God appears. The foreground figures are strictly frontal and have a solemn demeanor. Background details are few and suppressed. The forward plane of the picture dominates. Space is squeezed out. It is a perfect example of Byzantine hieratic style. Traces of the Greco-Roman illusionism noted in the Anicia Juliana portrait remain in the Virgin's rather personalized features, in her sideways glance, and in the posing of the angels' heads. But the painter rendered the saints in the new Byzantine manner.

# ICONOCLASM (726–843)

**BYZANTIUM IN CRISIS** The preservation of the Early Byzantine icons at the Mount Sinai monastery is fortuitous but ironic, for opposition to icon worship was especially prominent in the Monophysite provinces of Syria and Egypt. And there, in the seventh century, a series of calamities erupted, indirectly causing the imperial ban on images. The Sasanians (see Chapter 2), chronically at war with Rome, swept into the eastern provinces early in the seventh century. Between 611 and 617 they captured the great cities of Antioch, Jerusalem, and Alexandria. Hardly had the Byzantine emperor Heraclius (r. 610–641) pressed them back and defeated them in 627 when a new and overwhelming power appeared unexpectedly on the stage of history. The Arabs, under the banner of the new Islamic religion, conquered not only Byzantium's eastern provinces but also Persia itself, replacing the Sasanians in the age-old balance of power with the Christian West (see Chapter 13). In a few years the Arabs were launching attacks on Constantinople, and Byzantium was fighting for its life.

These were catastrophic years for the Eastern Roman Empire. They terminated once and for all the long story of imperial Rome, closed the Early Byzantine period, and inaugurated the medieval era of Byzantine history. Almost two-thirds of the Byzantine Empire's territory was lost—many cities and much of its population, wealth, and material resources. The shock of these events persuaded the emperor Leo III (r. 717–741) that God had punished the Christian Roman Empire for its idolatrous worship of icons by setting upon it the merciless armies of the infidel. In 726 he formally prohibited the use of images, and for more than a century Byzantine artists produced little new religious figurative art. In place of images, the iconoclasts used symbolic forms already familiar in Early Christian art—the cross (FIG. 12-12), the vacant Throne of Heaven, the cabinet with the scriptural scrolls, and so forth. Stylized floral, animal, and architectural motifs provided decorative fill.

## Icons and Iconoclasm

*Icons* ("images" in Greek) are small portable paintings depicting Christ, the Virgin, or saints (or a combination of all three, as in FIG. 12-16). Icons survive from as early as the fourth century. From the sixth century on, they became enormously popular in Byzantine worship, both public and private. Eastern Christians considered icons a personal, intimate, and indispensable medium for spiritual transaction with holy figures. Some icons (for example, FIG. 12-29) came to be regarded as wonder-working, and believers ascribed miracles and healing powers to them.

Icons, however, were by no means universally accepted. From the beginning, many Christians were deeply suspicious of the practice of imaging the divine, whether on portable panels, on the walls of churches, or especially as statues that reminded them of pagan idols. The opponents of Christian figural art had in mind the Old Testament prohibition of images the Lord dictated to Moses in the Second Commandment: "Thou shalt not make unto thee any graven image or any likeness of anything that is in heaven above, or that is in the earth beneath, or that is in the water under the earth. Thou shalt not bow down thyself to them, nor serve them" (Exod. 20:4, 5).

When, early in the fourth century, Constantia, sister of the emperor Constantine, requested an image of Christ from Eusebius, the first great historian of the Christian Church, he rebuked her, referring to the Second Commandment:

> Can it be that you have forgotten that passage in which God lays down the law that no likeness should be made of what is in heaven or in the earth beneath? . . . Are not such things banished and excluded from churches all over the world, and is it not common knowledge that such practices are not permitted to us . . . lest we appear, like idol worshipers, to carry our God around in an image?[1]

Opposition to icons became especially strong in the eighth century, when the faithful often burned incense and knelt before them in prayer to seek protection or a cure for illness. Although icons were intended only to evoke the presence of the holy figures addressed in prayer, in the minds of many, icons became identified with the personages represented. Icon veneration became confused with idol worship, and this brought about an imperial ban on *all* sacred images. The term for this destruction of holy pictures is *iconoclasm*. The *iconoclasts* (breakers of images) and the *iconophiles* (lovers of images) became bitter and irreconcilable enemies. The anguish of the latter can be read in a graphic description of the deeds of the iconoclasts, written in about 754:

> In every village and town one could witness the weeping and lamentation of the pious, whereas, on the part of the impious, [one saw] sacred things trodden upon, [liturgical] vessels turned to other use, churches scraped down and smeared with ashes because they contained holy images. And wherever there were venerable images of Christ or the Mother of God or the saints, these were consigned to the flames or were gouged out or smeared over.[2]

The consequences of iconoclasm for the history of Byzantine art are difficult to overstate. For more than a century not only did the portrayal of Christ, the Virgin, and the saints cease, but the iconoclasts also systematically destroyed countless works from the early centuries of Christendom. Knowledge of Byzantine art before the revival of image making in the ninth century is therefore very fragmentary. Writing a history of Early Byzantine art presents a great challenge to art historians.

[1] Cyril Mango, trans., *The Art of the Byzantine Empire, 312–1453: Sources and Documents* (Upper Saddle River, N.J.: Prentice Hall, 1972), 17–18.
[2] Ibid., 152.

# MIDDLE BYZANTINE ART (843–1204)

**THE IMAGE MAKERS RETURN** In the ninth century, a powerful reaction against iconoclasm set in. The destruction of images was condemned as a heresy, and restoration of the images began in 843. Shortly thereafter, under a new line of emperors, the Macedonian dynasty, art, literature, and learning sprang to life once again. In this great renovation, as historians have called it, Byzantine culture recovered something of its ancient Hellenistic sources and accommodated them to the forms inherited from the Justinianic age.

Basil I (r. 867–886), head of the new dynasty, thought of himself as the restorer of the Roman Empire. He denounced as usurpers the Frankish Carolingian monarchs of the West (see Chapter 16) who, since 800, had claimed the title "Roman Empire" for their realm. Basil bluntly reminded their emissary that the only true emperor of Rome reigned in Constantinople. They were not Roman emperors but merely "kings of the Germans." Iconoclasm had forced Byzantine artists westward, where doubtless they found employment at the courts of these Germanic kings. They strongly influenced the character of Western European art. But under Basil and his successors, mural painters, mosaicists, book illuminators, ivory carvers, and metalworkers once again received commissions aplenty.

## Architecture and Mosaics

**UNDOING ICONOCLASM** Basil I and his successors undertook the laborious and costly task of refurbishing the churches the iconoclasts defaced and neglected, Hagia Sophia first among them. There, in 867, the Macedonian dynasty dedicated a new mosaic (FIG. 12-17) in the apse depicting the enthroned Virgin with the Christ Child in her lap. In the vast space beneath the dome of the great church, the figures look undersized, but the

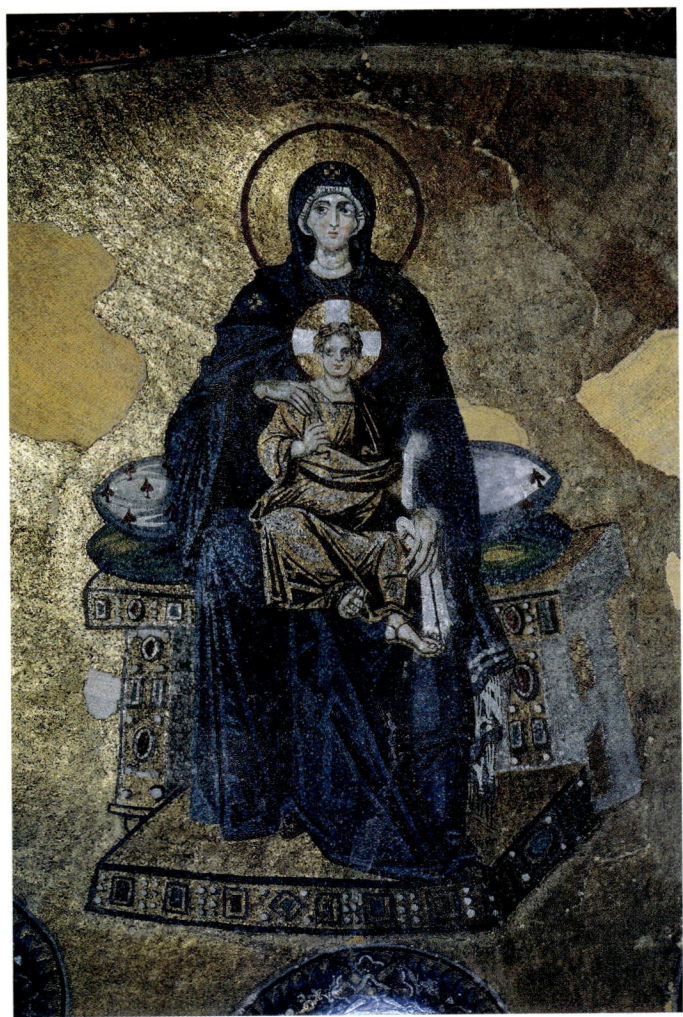

**12-17** Virgin (Theotokos) and Child enthroned, apse mosaic, Hagia Sophia, Constantinople (Istanbul), Turkey, dedicated 867.

seated Theotokos is actually more than 16 feet tall. An accompanying inscription, now fragmentary, announced that "pious emperors" (the Macedonians) had commissioned the mosaic to replace one the "impostors" (the iconoclasts) had destroyed.

The original mosaic's subject is uncertain, but the ninth-century work echoes the style and composition of the Early Byzantine Mount Sinai icon (FIG. 12-16) of the Theotokos, Christ, and saints. Here, the strict frontality of Mother and (much older) Child is alleviated by the angular placement of the throne and footstool. The mosaicist rendered the furnishings in a perspective that, although imperfect, recalls once more the Greco-Roman roots of Byzantine art. The treatment of the folds of Christ's robes is, by contrast, even more schematic and flatter than in earlier mosaics. These seemingly contradictory stylistic features are not uncommon in Byzantine paintings and mosaics. Most significant about the images in the Hagia Sophia apse is their very existence. The iconophiles had triumphed over the iconoclasts.

**NEW CHURCHES FOR THE OLD FAITH** Although the new emperors did not wait very long to redecorate the churches of their predecessors, they undertook little new church construction in the decades following the renunciation of iconoclasm in 843. But in the 10th century and through the 12th, a number of monastic churches arose that are the flowers of Middle Byzantine architecture. They feature a brilliant series of variations on the domed central plan. From the exterior, the typical later Byzantine church building is a domed cube, with the dome rising above the square on a kind of cylinder or drum. The churches are small, vertical, high shouldered, and, unlike earlier Byzantine buildings, have exterior wall surfaces with vivid decorative patterns, probably reflecting the impact of Islamic architecture.

**VISUAL DRAMA AT HOSIOS LOUKAS** The monastery Church of the Theotokos (FIGS. **12-18**, *right*, and **12-19**, *top*) at Hosios Loukas (Saint Luke) in Greece, near ancient Delphi, dates

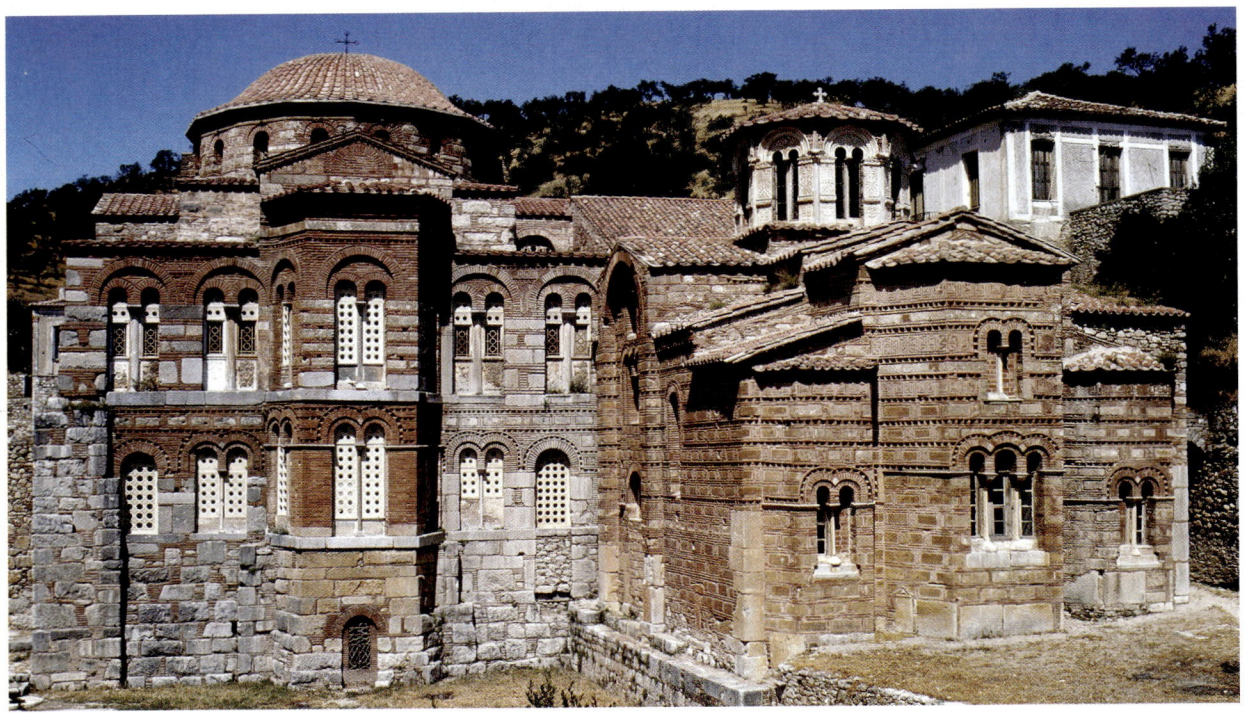

**12-18** Monastery churches at Hosios Loukas, Greece (view from the east). Katholikon *(left),* first quarter of 11th century, and Church of the Theotokos *(right),* second half of 10th century.

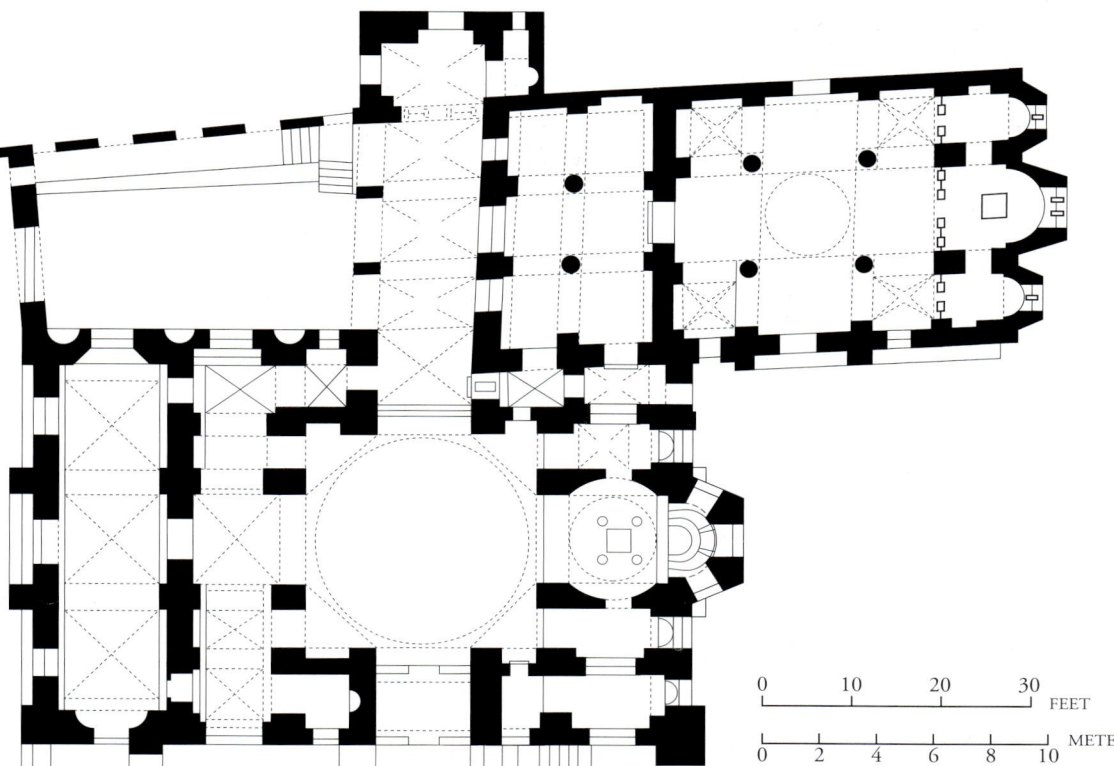

**12-19** Plans of Church of the Theotokos (*top*) and Katholikon (*bottom*), Hosios Loukas, Greece, second half of 10th and first quarter of 11th century.

0    10    20    30    FEET

0    2    4    6    8    10    METERS

to the second half of the 10th century. One of two churches at the site, it exemplifies church design during this second golden age of Byzantine art and architecture. Light stones framed by dark red bricks—the so-called *cloisonné* technique, a term borrowed from enamel work (see FIG. 16-2)—make up the walls. The interplay of arcuated windows, projecting apses, and varying roof lines further enhances this surface dynamism. The plan (FIG. 12-19) shows the form of a domed cross in square with four equal-length, vaulted cross arms (the Greek cross). The dome rests on pendentives. Around this unit, and by the duplication of it, Byzantine architects developed dynamic intersecting spaces.

In the adjacent, larger Katholikon (FIGS. 12-18, *left*, and 12-19, *bottom*), built in the early 11th century, the architect placed a dome over an octagon inscribed within a square. The octagon was formed by squinches, which, as noted earlier (see "Pendentives and Squinches," page 331), play the same role as pendentives in making the transition from a square base to a round dome but create a different visual effect on the interior (FIG. **12-20**). This arrangement departs from the older designs, such as Santa Costanza's circular plan (see FIG. 11-10), San Vitale's octagonal plan (FIG. 12-7), and Hagia Sophia's dome on pendentives rising from a square (FIG. 12-4). The Katholikon's complex core lies within two rectangles, the outermost one forming the exterior walls. Thus, in plan from the center out, a circle-octagon-square-oblong series exhibits an intricate interrelationship that is at once complex and unified.

The interior elevation of the Katholikon reflects its involved plan. Like earlier Byzantine buildings, the church creates a mystery out of space, surface, light, and dark. High and narrow, it forces one's gaze to rise and revolve. The eye is drawn upward toward the dome, but much can distract it in the interplay of flat walls and concave recesses; wide and narrow openings; groin and barrel vaults; single, double, and triple windows; and illuminated and dark spaces. Middle Byzantine architects seem to have aimed for the creation of complex interior spaces with dramatically shifting perspectives.

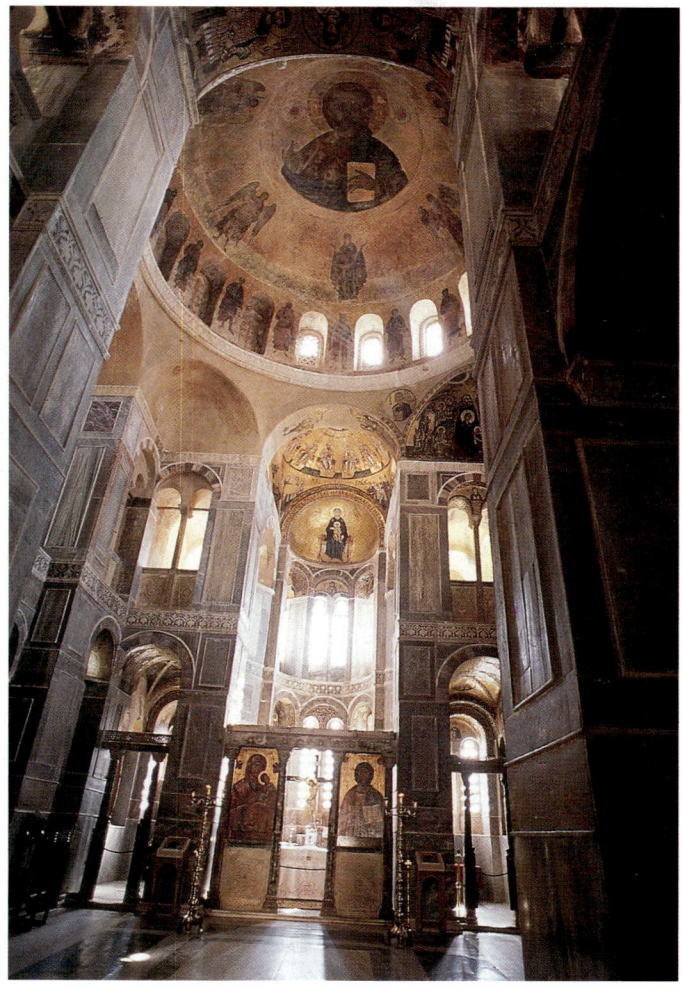

**12-20** Interior of Katholikon (view facing east), Hosios Loukas, Greece, first quarter of 11th century.

Christ as Pantokrator, dome mosaic in the Church of the Dormition, Daphni, Greece, ca. 1090–1100.

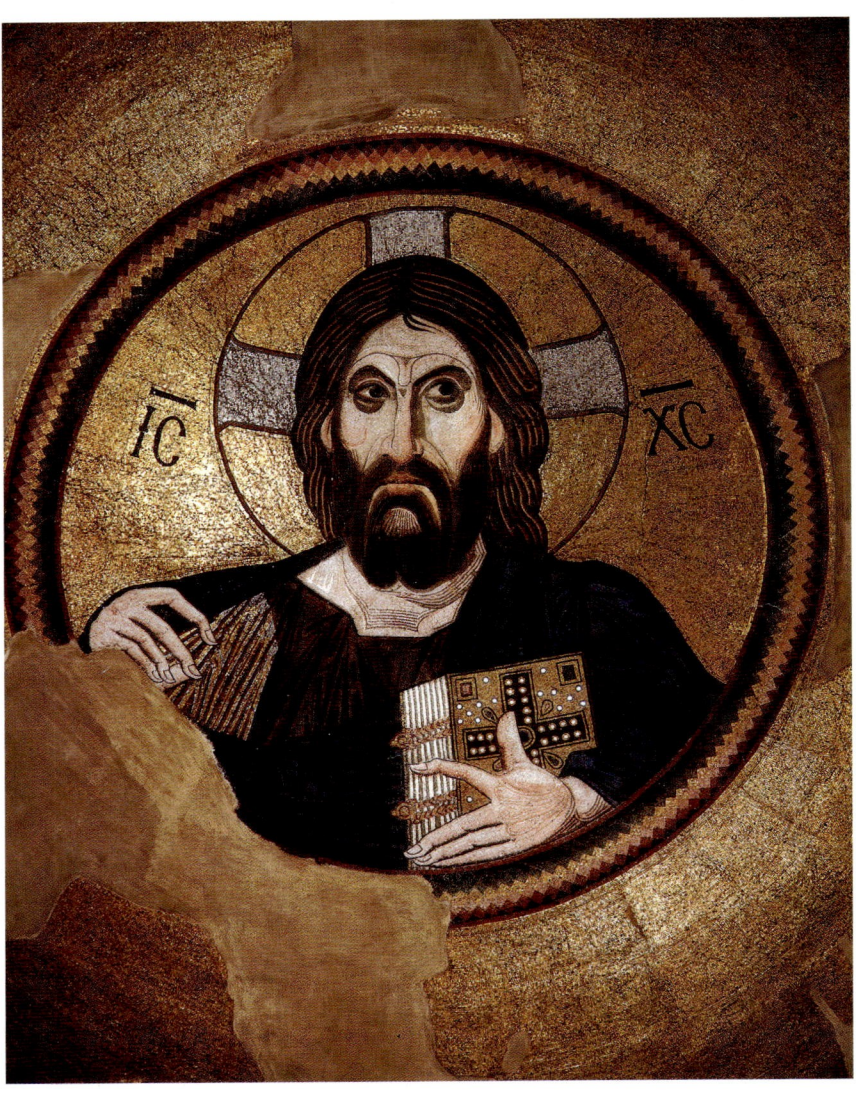

**CHRIST, PANTOKRATOR** Much of the original mosaic decoration of the Hosios Loukas Katholikon does not survive, but at Daphni, near Athens, the mosaics produced during Byzantium's second golden age fared much better. In the monastery Church of the Dormition (from the Latin for "sleep," referring to the ascension of the Virgin Mary to Heaven at the moment of her death), the main elements of the late-11th-century pictorial program are intact, although the mosaics were restored in the 19th century. Gazing down from on high in the central dome (FIG. **12-21**) is the fearsome image of Christ as *Pantokrator* (literally "ruler of all" in Greek but usually applied to Christ in his role as Last Judge of humankind). The dome mosaic is the climax of an elaborate hierarchical pictorial program including several New Testament episodes below. The Daphni Pantokrator is like a gigantic icon hovering dramatically in space. The mosaic serves to connect the awestruck worshiper in the church below with heaven through Christ. The Pantokrator theme was a common one in churches throughout the Byzantine Empire. There was also a mosaic of the Pantokrator in the dome of the Hosios Loukas Katholikon. Today a painting replaces it. The most famous Pantokrator of all was the work of Eulalios, who decorated the dome of the Church of the Holy Apostles in Constantinople (see "Eulalios: Painter of Christ," page 345).

On one of the walls below the Daphni dome, beneath the barrel vault of one arm of the Greek cross, an unknown artist depicted Christ's Crucifixion (FIG. **12-22**) in a pictorial style characteristic of the post-Iconoclastic Middle Byzantine period. Like the Pantokrator mosaic in the dome, the Daphni Crucifixion is a subtle blend of the painterly, Hellenistic style and the later more abstract and formalistic Byzantine style. The Byzantine artist fully assimilated classicism's simplicity, dignity, and grace into a perfect synthesis with Byzantine piety and pathos. The figures have regained the classical organic structure to a surprising degree, particularly compared to figures from the Justinianic period (compare FIGS. 12-9 and 12-10). The style is a masterful adaptation of classical statuesque qualities to the linear Byzantine manner.

In quiet sorrow and resignation, the Virgin and Saint John flank the crucified Christ. A skull at the foot of the cross indicates Golgotha, the "place of skulls." Nothing else was needed to set the scene. Symmetry and closed space combine to produce an effect of the motionless and unchanging aspect of the deepest mystery of the Christian religion. The timeless presence is, as it were, beheld in unbroken silence. The picture is not a narrative of the historical event of the Crucifixion, the approach taken by the carver of the Early Christian ivory panel (see FIG. 11-21) examined in the previous chapter. Nor is Christ a triumphant, beardless youth, oblivious to pain and defiant of the laws of gravity. Rather, he has a tilted head and sagging body, and blood spurts from the wound Longinus inflicted on him, although he is not overtly in pain. The Virgin and John point to the figure on the cross as if to a devotional object. They act as intercessors between the viewer below and Christ, who, in the dome, appears as the Last Judge of all humans.

### Eulalios: Painter of Christ

Most of the art of Byzantium, and of the Middle Ages in general, is anonymous. The names of the builders of Justinian's great sixth-century church of Hagia Sophia in Constantinople (FIG. 12-3) are known. But the mosaicist who adorned its apse (FIG. 12-17) in the ninth century is nameless, even though the homily the patriarch Photius delivered for the building's dedication in 867 survives. The scribe Rabbula signed the *Gospels* he wrote in Syriac in 586, but the identity of the painter of its full-page miniatures (FIG. 12-15) is unknown.

Medieval authors did, however, record the name of Eulalios, a painter who worked in the 12th century. So great was his fame that more than one writer notes his name and describes his paintings. Eulalios's most important commission was the decoration of the dome of the Church of the Holy Apostles in Constantinople with an image of Christ as Pantokrator. Nicephorus Callistus, an early-14th-century poet, historian, and author of saints' lives, was so struck by Eulalios's portrayal of Christ that he speculated that the painter had actually seen the Pantokrator:

> Either Christ himself came down from heaven and showed the exact traits of his face to [the painter] or else the famous Eulalios mounted up to the very skies to paint with his skilled hand Christ's exact appearance.[1]

Nicholas Mesarites, who visited the Church of the Holy Apostles around the year 1200, left a more precise description of Eulalios's Christ:

[The dome] exhibits an image of the God-man Christ looking down, as it were, from the rim of heaven towards the floor of the church and everything that is in it. . . . His head is in proportion to his body that is represented down to the navel, his eyes are joyful and welcoming to those who are not reproached by their conscience, but to those who are condemned by their own judgment, they are wrathful and hostile. . . . The right hand blesses those who walk a straight path, while it admonishes those who do not and, as it were, checks them and turns them back from their disorderly course. The left hand, with its fingers spread as far apart as possible, supports the Gospel.[2]

It is easy to visualize Eulalios's Pantokrator by comparing Nicholas Mesarites' description with surviving representations of the same theme: for example, the mosaic dome of the Church of the Dormition at Daphni (FIG. 12-21), or even the apse of the Cathedral at Monreale (FIG. 12-24) in faraway Sicily. Both conform to the same basic iconographic type—an image of the stern but benevolent judge of human worth who can strike fear into sinners who come before him but who can reward the blessed.

[1] Cyril Mango, trans., *The Art of the Byzantine Empire, 312–1453: Sources and Documents* (Upper Saddle River, N.J.: Prentice Hall, 1972), 231–32.

[2] Ibid., 232.

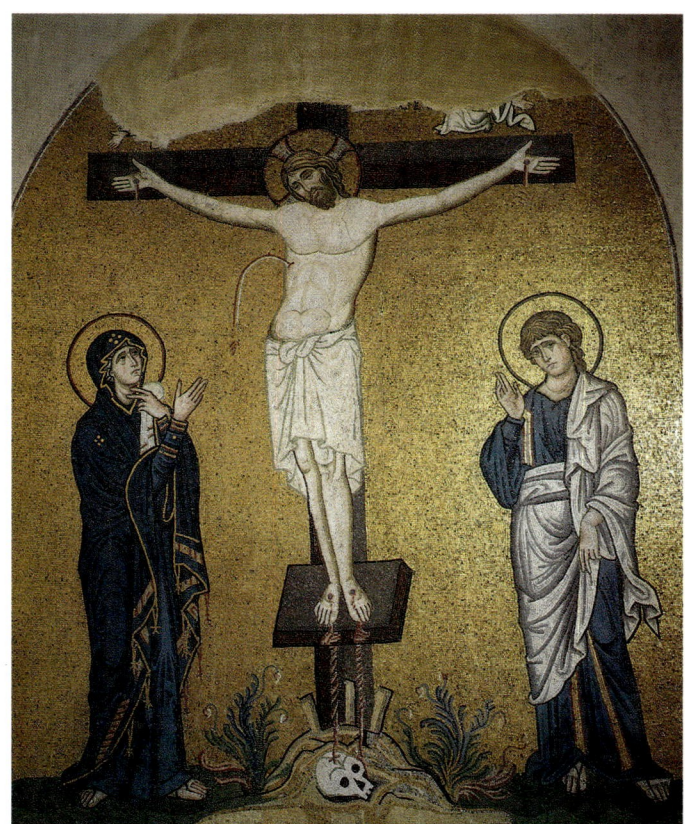

**12-22** Crucifixion, mosaic in the Church of the Dormition, Daphni, Greece, ca. 1090–1100.

**VENICE AND BYZANTIUM** The revival on a grand scale of church building, featuring vast stretches of mosaic-covered walls, was not confined to the Greek-speaking Byzantine East in the 10th to 12th centuries. A resurgence of religious architecture and of the mosaicist's art also occurred in areas of the former Western Roman Empire where the ties with Constantinople were the strongest. In the Early Byzantine period, Venice, about 80 miles north of Ravenna on the eastern coast of Italy, was a dependency of that Byzantine stronghold. In 751, Ravenna fell to the Lombards, and they wrested control of most of northern Italy from Constantinople. Venice, however, became an independent power. Its *doges* (dukes) enriched themselves and the city through seaborn commerce, serving as the crucial link between Byzantium and the West.

Venice had obtained the relics of Saint Mark from Alexandria in Egypt in 829, and the doges constructed the first Venetian shrine dedicated to the evangelist—a palace chapel and martyrium—shortly thereafter. Fire destroyed the ninth-century chapel in 976. The Venetians then built a second shrine on the site, but a grandiose new church begun in 1063 by Doge Domenico Contarini replaced it. This building was modeled on the Church of the Holy Apostles at Constantinople, built in Justinian's time. The Constantinopolitan church no longer exists, but its key elements were a cruciform plan with a central dome over the crossing and four other domes over the four equal arms of the Greek cross, as at Saint Mark's. Because of its importance to the city, the doges repeatedly remodeled the 11th-century structure, in time disguising its lower levels with Romanesque and Gothic additions. In 1807 St. Mark's was consecrated as the Cathedral of Venice.

**12-23** Interior of Saint Mark's (view facing east), Venice, Italy, begun 1063.

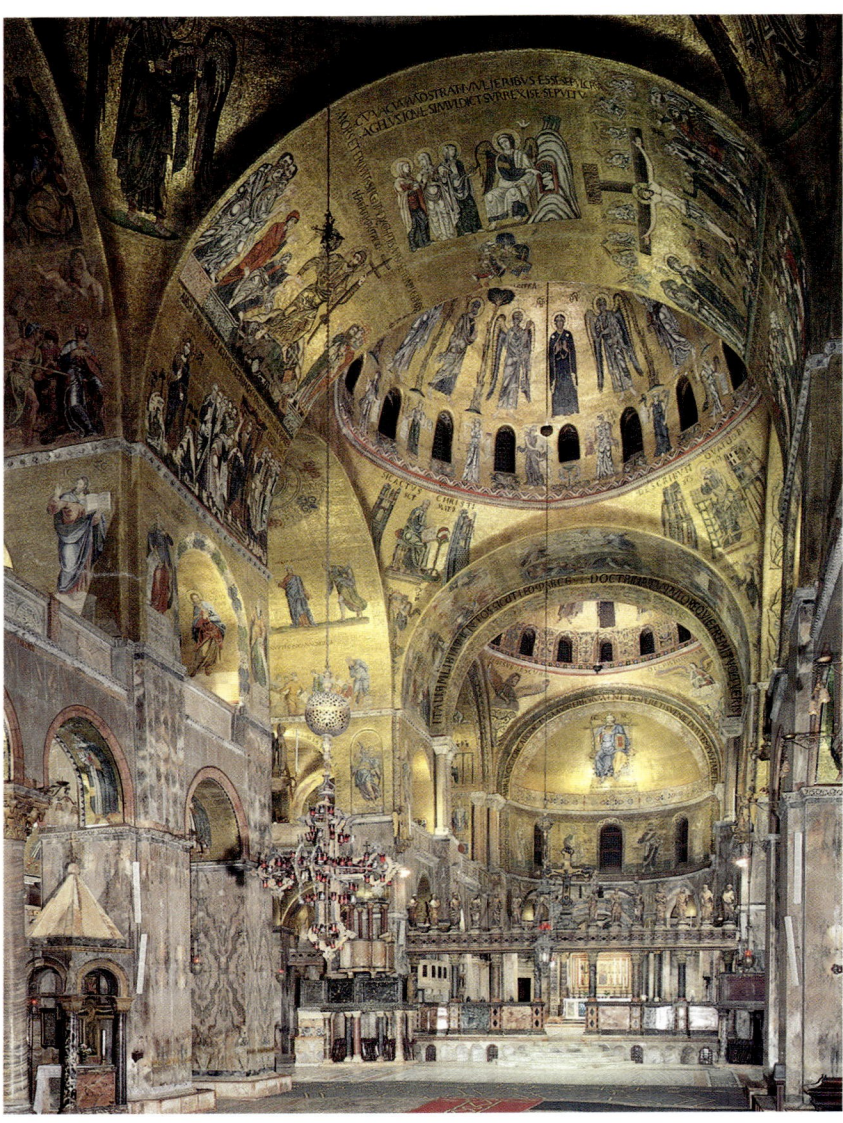

**SAINT MARK'S MOSAICS** The interior (FIG. **12-23**) of Saint Mark's is, like its plan, Byzantine in effect. Light enters through a row of windows at the bases of all five domes, vividly illuminating a rich cycle of mosaics. Both Byzantine and local artists worked on Saint Mark's mosaics over the course of several centuries. Most of the mosaics date to the 12th and 13th centuries. Cleaning and restoration on a grand scale have returned the mosaics to their original splendor, enabling visitors to experience the full radiance of mosaic (some 40,000 square feet of it) as it covers, like a gold-brocaded and figured fabric, all the walls, arches, vaults, and domes.

In the vast central dome, 80 feet above the floor and 42 feet in diameter, Christ ascends to heaven in the presence of the Virgin Mary and the Twelve Apostles. The great arch framing the church crossing bears a narrative of the Crucifixion and Resurrection of Christ and of his liberation from death (Anastasis) of Adam and Eve, Saint John the Baptist, and other biblical figures. The mosaics have explanatory labels in both Latin and Greek, reflecting Venice's position as the key link between eastern and western Christendom in the later Middle Ages. The insubstantial figures on the walls, vaults, and domes appear weightless, and they project no farther from their flat field than do the elegant Latin and Greek letters above them. Nothing here reflects on the world of matter, of solids, of light and shade, of perspective space. Rather, the mosaics reveal the mysteries of the Christian faith.

**A ROYAL CHURCH IN SICILY** Venetian success was matched in the western Mediterranean by the Normans, who, having driven the Arabs from Sicily, set up a powerful kingdom there, whose resources equaled those of Venice. Though they were the enemies of Byzantium, the Normans, like the Venetians, assimilated Byzantine culture and even employed Byzantine artisans. The mosaics of the great basilican church of Monreale, not far from Palermo, are striking evidence of Byzantium's presence in Sicily. They rival those of Saint Mark's in both quality and extent. One scholar has estimated that more than 100 million glass and stone tesserae were required for the Monreale mosaics.

The Norman king William II paid for the mosaics, and he is portrayed twice, continuing the theme of royal presence and patronage of the much earlier Ravenna portraits of Justinian and Theodora at San Vitale (FIGS. 12-10 and 12-11). In one panel, William, clearly labeled, unlike Justinian or his consort, stands next to the enthroned Christ, who places his hand on William's crown. In the second, the king kneels before the Virgin and presents her with a model of the Monreale church, a role that at San Vitale was played by Bishop Ecclesius (FIG. 12-9) rather than by the emperor or empress. As in the Ravenna church, the mosaic program commemorates both the piety and power of the ruler who reigns with divine authority.

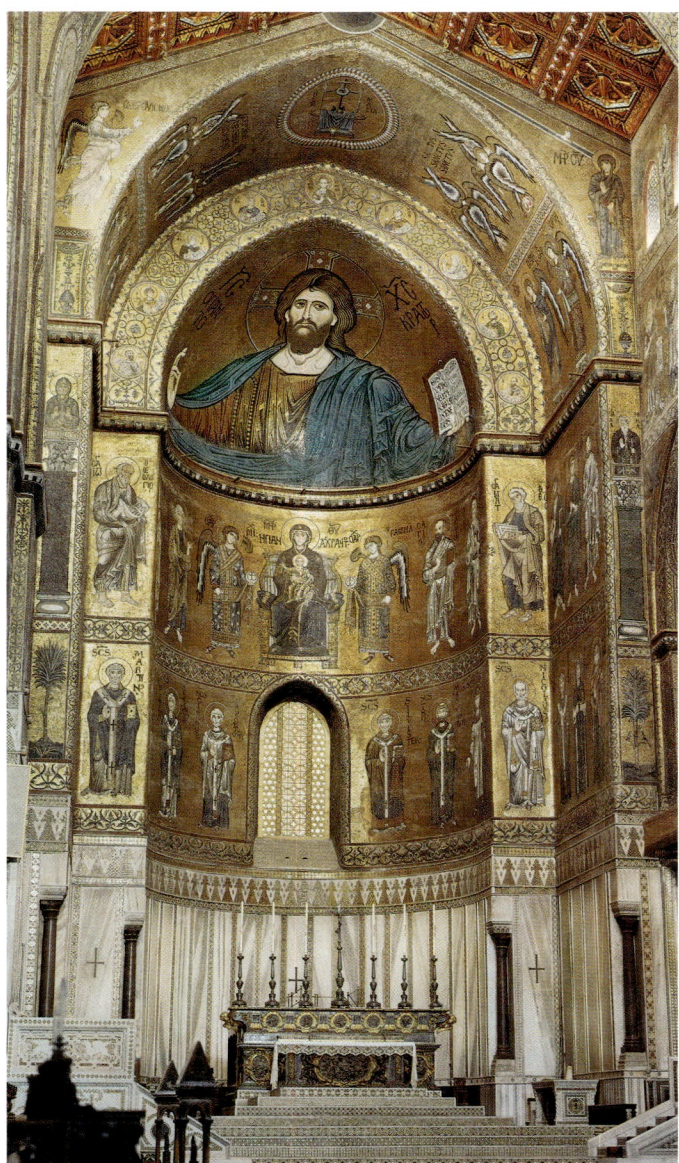

**12-24** Pantokrator, Theotokos and Child, angels, and saints, apse mosaic in the cathedral at Monreale, Italy, ca. 1180–1190.

The apse mosaics (FIG. **12-24**) are especially impressive. The image of Christ as Pantokrator, as ruler and judge of heaven and earth, looms menacingly in the vault, a colossal allusion to William's kingly power and a challenge to all who would dispute the royal right. In Byzantium proper, the Pantokrator's image usually appears in the main dome of centralized churches such as those at Hosios Loukas (FIG. 12-20) and Daphni (FIG. 12-21), but the Greek churches are monastic churches and were not built for the glorification of monarchs. Monreale, moreover, is a basilica—longitudinally planned in the Western tradition. The semidome of the apse, the only vault in the building and its architectural focus, was the most conspicuous place for the vast image with its political overtones. Below the Pantokrator in rank and dignity, the enthroned Theotokos is flanked by archangels and the Twelve Apostles symmetrically arranged in balanced groups. Lower on the wall (and less elevated in the hierarchy) are popes, bishops, and other saints. The artists observed the stern formalities of style characteristic of Byzantine hieraticism here, far from Constantinople. The Monreale mosaics, like those at Saint Mark's in Venice (FIG. 12-23), testify to the stature of Byzantium and of Byzantine art in medieval Italy.

## Luxury Arts

**AN EMPRESS AT SAINT MARK'S**  The wealth and pretensions of the Venetian dukes and the Norman kings of Sicily are revealed not only by their ambitious building programs with their acres of mosaic-covered walls, vaults, and domes but also by the sometimes extravagant furnishings of their churches. In 976, the Venetian doge Pietro Orseolo ordered from Constantinople a set of gold-and-enamel plaques nailed on wood for the second church of Saint Mark in Venice. In 1105, under Doge Ordelafo Falier, the plaques were refashioned into a *pala* (*altarpiece,* or panel placed behind and over the altar) that was again augmented in 1209 with booty from the Crusaders' sack of Constantinople. The altarpiece was modified once more in 1345. In its final form the Venetian *Pala d'Oro (Golden Pala)* reflects contemporaneous (Gothic) taste in Italy and unites plaques of several different periods featuring narrative scenes from Christ's life and dozens of saints, angels, prophets, and temporal rulers in golden niches surrounded by jewels of many different hues.

Among the figures added in 1105 were Doge Falier and probably also the Byzantine Emperor Alexius I Comnenus (r. 1081–1118), although the latter's portrait does not survive. Preserved, however, is the portrait of his wife, the Empress Irene (FIG. **12-25**). The regally attired and haloed gold-and-enamel Irene is a frontal, wafer-thin, weightless figure, a stylistic cousin to the mosaic saints and apostles of Monreale, despite the enormous differences in scale and technique. The portrayal of the empress (and the emperor?) suggests that the *Pala d'Oro* in its 1105 form was an imperial gift to the Venetian church. The inclusion of Irene's haloed

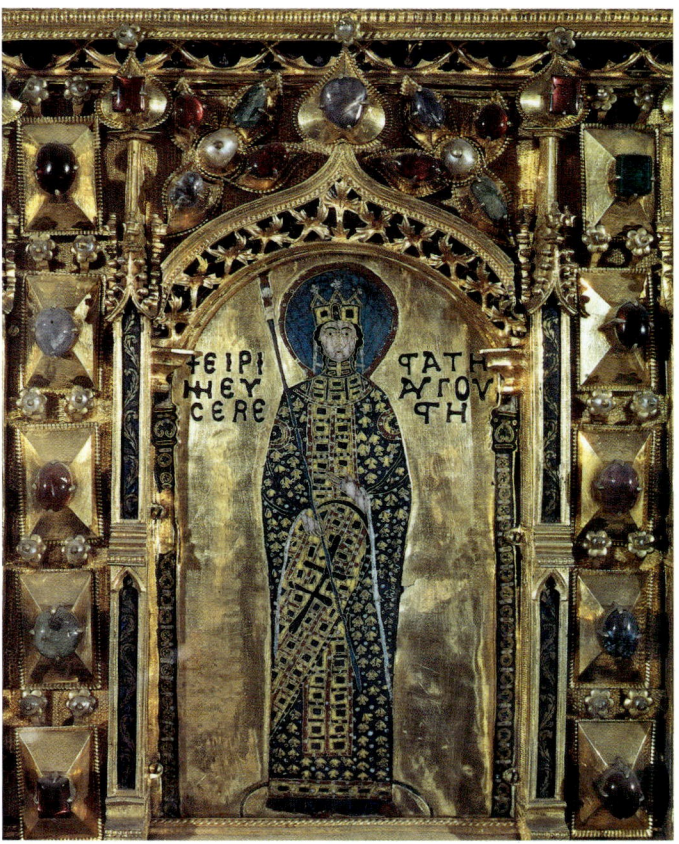

**12-25** Empress Irene, detail of the *Pala d'Oro,* Saint Mark's, Venice, Italy, ca. 1105. Gold cloisonné inlaid with precious stones, detail approx. $7'' \times 4\frac{1}{2}''$.

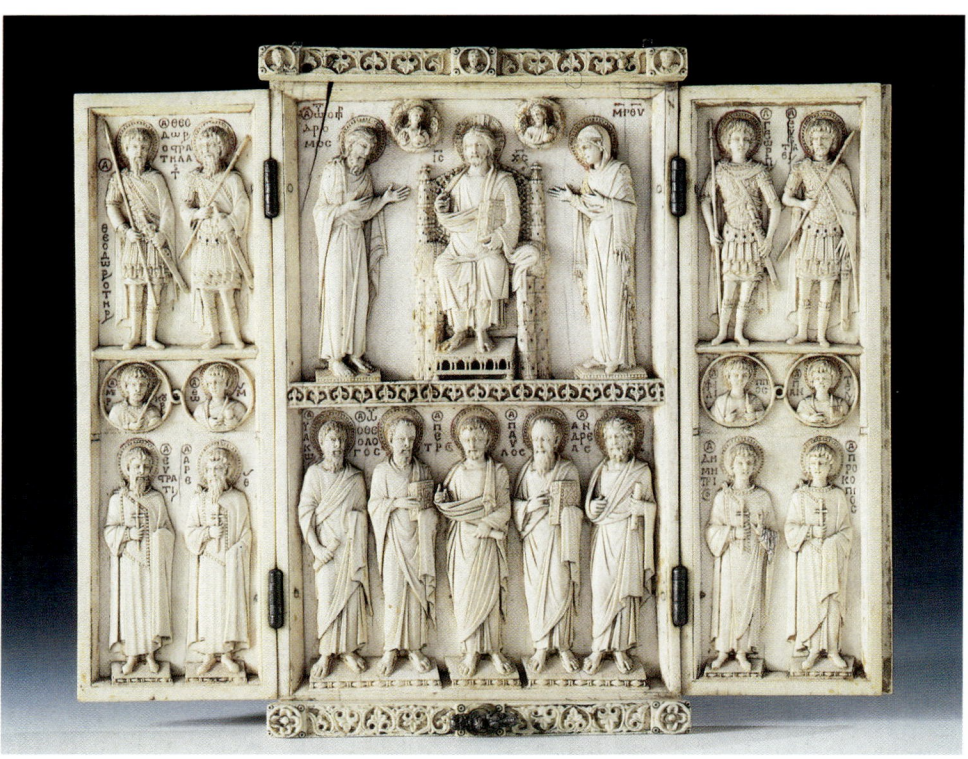

**12-26** *Christ enthroned with saints (Harbaville Triptych)*, ca. 950. Ivory, central panel $9\frac{1}{2}'' \times 5\frac{1}{2}''$. Louvre, Paris.

portrait in the pictorial program of Saint Mark's carried on a tradition that goes back to the sixth-century mosaic of Theodora (FIG. 12-11) at Ravenna. The *Pala d'Oro* Irene once again testifies to the important role the Byzantine empresses played in both life and art, as well as to continuing commercial, political, and artistic exchanges between Italy and Byzantium.

**DIPTYCH TO TRIPTYCH** Costly carved ivories also were produced in large numbers in the Middle Byzantine period, but after iconoclasm the three-part *triptych* replaced the earlier diptych as the standard format for ivory panels. One example of this type is the *Harbaville Triptych* (FIG. **12-26**), a portable shrine with hinged wings that was used for private devotion. Such triptychs were very popular—among those who could afford such luxurious items—and they often replaced icons for use in personal prayer. Carved on the wings of the *Harbaville Triptych*, both inside and out, are four pairs of full-length figures and two pairs of medallions depicting saints. A cross dominates the central panel on the back of the triptych (not illustrated). On the inside is a scene of *Deësis* (supplication). Saint John the Baptist and the Theotokos appear as intercessors, praying on behalf of the viewer to the enthroned Savior. Below them are five apostles.

The hieratic formality and solemnity associated with Byzantine art, visible in the mosaics of Ravenna and Monreale and in the *Pala d'Oro* enamel plaques, yielded here to a softer, more fluid technique. The figures may lack true classical contrapposto, but the looser stances (most stand on bases, like freestanding statues) and three-quarter views of many of the heads relieve the hard austerity of the customary frontal pose. This more natural, classicizing spirit was a second, equally important, stylistic current of the Middle Byzantine period. It also surfaced in mural painting and book illumination.

## Painting

**BYZANTIUM IN THE BALKANS** When the emperors lifted the ban against religious images and again encouraged religious painting at Constantinople, the impact was felt far and wide. The style varied from region to region, but a renewed enthusiasm for picturing the key New Testament figures and events was universal.

In 1164, at Nerezi in Macedonia, Byzantine painters embellished the church of Saint Pantaleimon with murals of great emotional power. One of these represents the Lamentation over the dead Christ (FIG. 12-27). It is an image of passionate grief. The artist captured Christ's followers in attitudes, expressions, and gestures of quite human bereavement. Joseph of Arimathea and the disciple Nicodemus kneel at his feet, while Mary presses her cheek against her dead son's face and Saint John clings to Christ's left hand. In the Gospels, neither Mary nor John was present at the entombment of Christ. Their presence here, as elsewhere in Middle Byzantine art, was designed to intensify for the viewer the emotional impact of Christ's death. Such representations parallel the development of liturgical hymns recounting the Virgin's lamenting her son's death on the Cross.

At Nerezi, the scene is set in a hilly landscape below a blue sky—a striking contrast to the abstract golden world of the mosaics favored for church walls elsewhere in the Byzantine Empire. The artist strove to make utterly convincing an emotionally charged realization of the theme by staging the Lamentation in a more natural setting and peopling it with fully modeled actors. This alternate representational mode is no less Byzantine than the hieratic style of Ravenna or the poignant melancholy of Daphni.

**DAVID AS GREEK HARPIST** Another example of this classicizing style is a page from a book of the Psalms of David. The

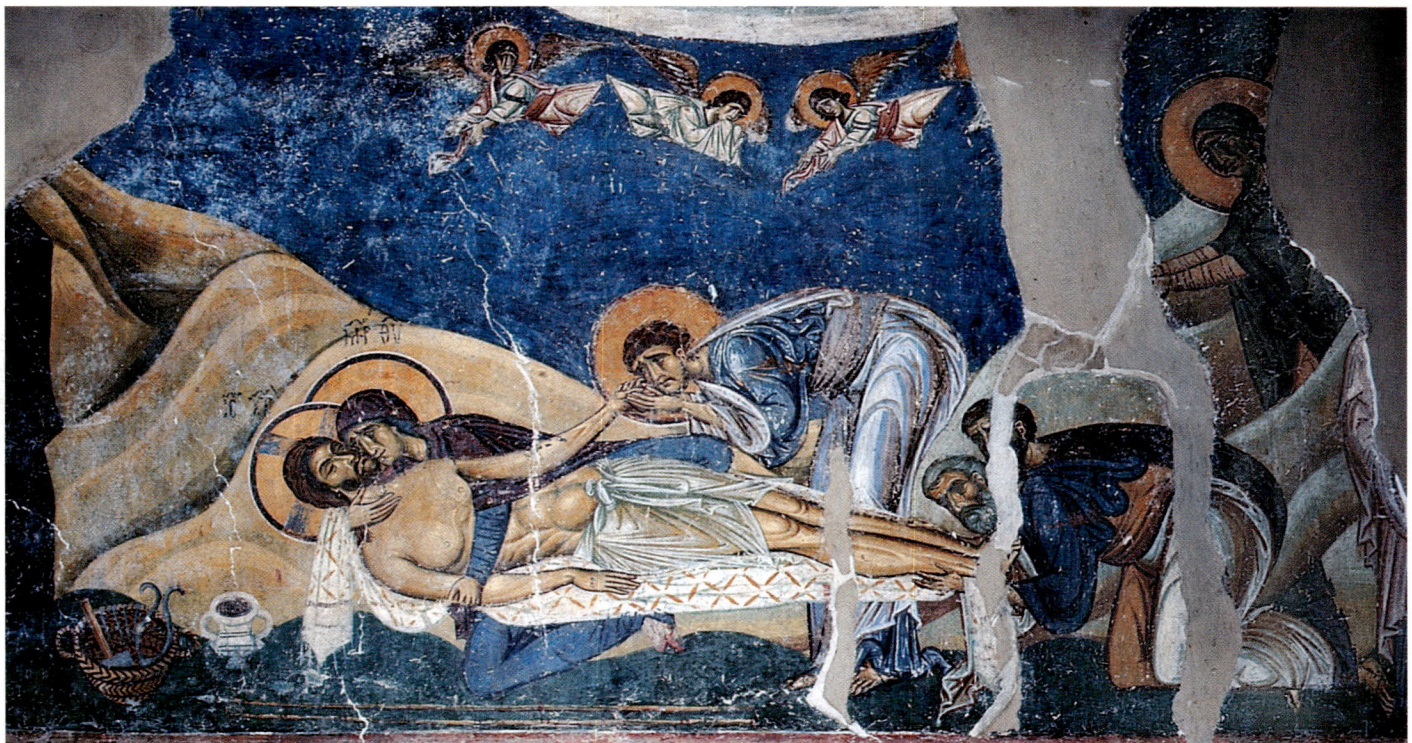

12-27 Lamentation over the Dead Christ, wall painting, Saint Pantaleimon, Nerezi, Macedonia, 1164.

so-called *Paris Psalter* (FIG. 12-28) reasserts the artistic values of the Greco-Roman past with astonishing authority. Art historians believe the manuscript dates from the mid-10th century—the so-called Macedonian Renaissance, a time of enthusiastic and careful study of the language and literature of ancient Greece, and of humanistic reverence for the classical past. It was only natural that artists would once again draw inspiration from the Hellenistic naturalism of the pre-Christian Mediterranean world.

David, the psalmist, surrounded by sheep, goats, and his faithful dog, plays his harp in a rocky landscape with a town in the background. Similar settings appeared frequently in Pompeian murals. Befitting an ancient depiction of Orpheus, the Greek hero who could charm even inanimate objects with his music, allegorical figures accompany the Old Testament harpist. Melody looks over his shoulder, and Echo peers from behind a column. A reclining male figure points to a Greek inscription that identifies him as representing the mountain of Bethlehem. These allegorical figures do not appear in the Bible. They are the stock population of Greco-Roman painting. Apparently, the artist had seen a work from late antiquity or perhaps earlier and partly translated it into a Byzantine pictorial idiom. In works such as this, Byzantine artists kept the classical style alive in the Middle Ages.

**A MIRACLE-WORKING ICON** Nothing in Middle Byzantine art better demonstrates the rejection of the iconoclastic viewpoint than the painted icon's return to prominence. After the restoration of images, such icons multiplied by the thousands to meet public and private demand. In the 11th century, the clergy began to display icons in hieratic order (Christ, the Theotokos, John the Baptist, and then other saints, as on the *Harbaville Triptych*) in tiers on the *templon,* the low columnar screen separating the sanctuary from the main body of a Byzantine church.

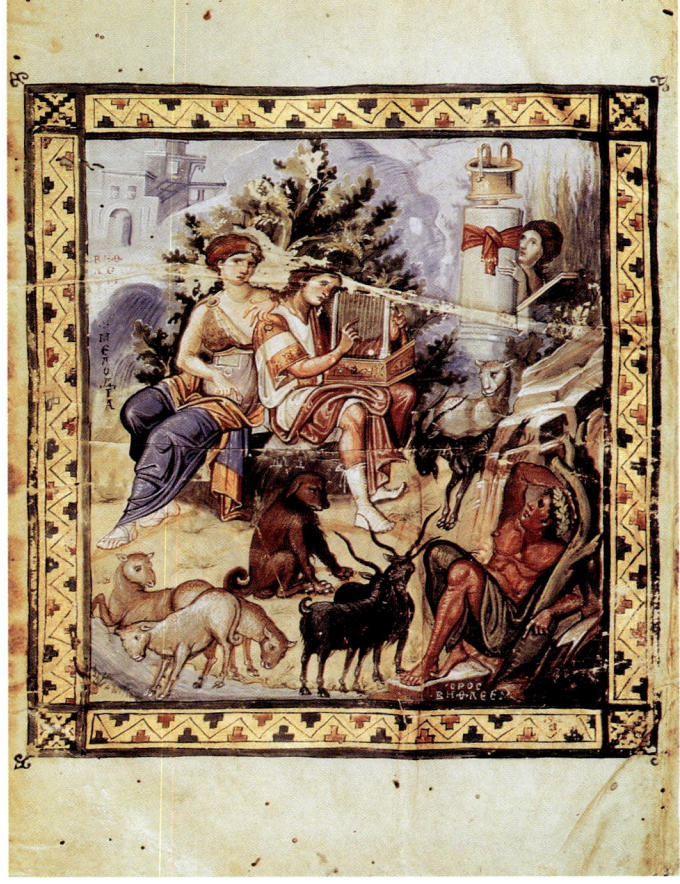

12-28 David composing the Psalms, folio 1 verso of the *Paris Psalter,* ca. 950–970. Tempera on vellum, $1' 2\frac{1}{8}'' \times 10\frac{1}{4}''$. Bibliothèque Nationale, Paris.

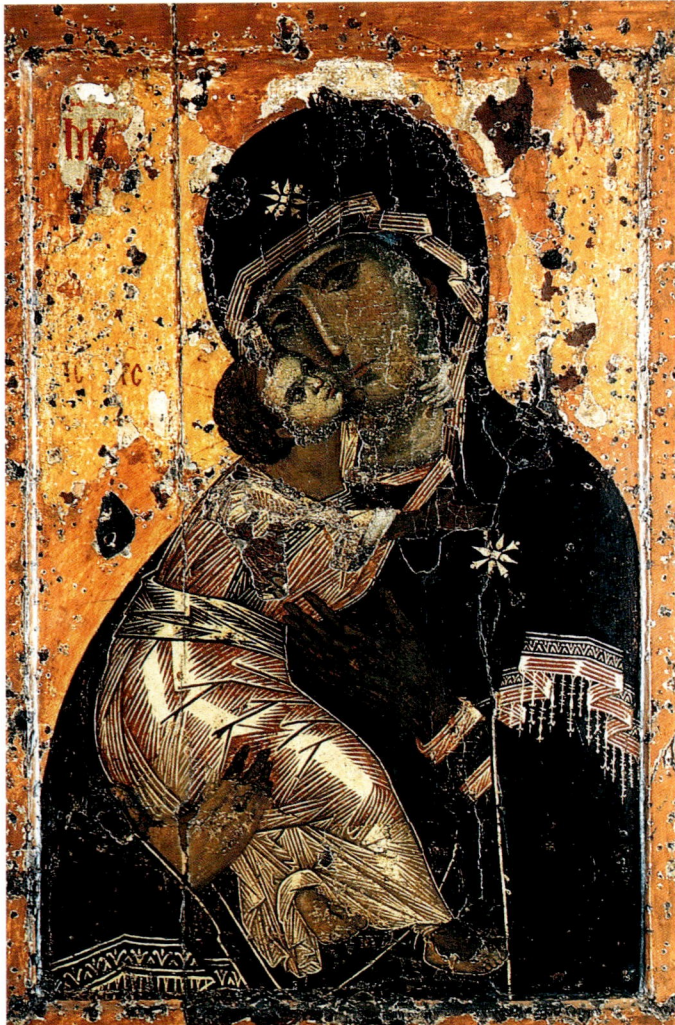

**12-29** Virgin (Theotokos) and Child, icon *(Vladimir Virgin)*, late 11th to early 12th century. Tempera on wood, original panel approx. 2′ 6½″ × 1′ 9″. Tretyakov Gallery, Moscow.

Our example, the renowned *Vladimir Virgin* (FIG. **12-29**), is a masterpiece of its kind. Descended from works such as the Mount Sinai icon (FIG. 12-16), the *Vladimir Virgin* clearly reveals the stylized abstraction resulting from centuries of working and reworking the conventional image. Probably painted by a Constantinopolitan artist, the characteristic traits of the Byzantine icon of the Virgin and Child are all present: the Virgin's long, straight nose and small mouth; the golden rays in the infant's drapery; the decorative sweep of the unbroken contour that encloses the two figures; and the flat silhouette against the golden ground. But this is a much more tender and personalized image of the Virgin than that in the Mount Sinai icon. Here Mary is depicted as the Virgin of Compassion, who presses her cheek against her son's in an intimate portrayal of Mother and Child. The image is also infused with a deep pathos as Mary contemplates the future sacrifice of her son. (The back of the icon bears images of the instruments of Christ's Passion.)

The icon of Vladimir, like most icons, has seen hard service. Placed before or above altars in churches or private chapels, the icon was blackened by the incense and smoke from candles that burned before or below it. It was frequently repainted, often by inferior artists, and only the faces show the original surface. First painted in the late 11th or early 12th century, it was taken to Kiev (Ukraine) in 1131, then to Vladimir (Russia) in 1155 (hence its

name), and in 1395, as a wonder-working image, to Moscow to protect that city from the Mongols. The Russians believed that the sacred picture saved the city of Kazan from later Tartar invasions and all of Russia from the Poles in the 17th century. The *Vladimir Virgin* is a historical symbol of Byzantium's religious and cultural mission to the Slavic world.

# LATE BYZANTINE ART (1204–1453)

THE SACK OF CONSTANTINOPLE When rule passed from the Macedonian to the Comnenian dynasty in the later 11th and the 12th centuries, three events of fateful significance changed Byzantium's fortunes for the worse. The Seljuk Turks conquered most of Anatolia. The Byzantine Orthodox Church broke finally with the Church of Rome. And the Crusades brought the Latins (a generic term for the peoples of the West) into Byzantine lands on their way to fight for the Cross against the Saracens (Muslims) in the Holy Land (see "The Crusades," Chapter 17, page 466).

Crusaders had passed through Constantinople many times en route to "smite the infidel" and had marveled at its wealth and magnificence. Envy, greed, religious fanaticism (the Latins called the Greeks "heretics"), and even ethnic enmity motivated the Crusaders when, during the Fourth Crusade in 1203 and 1204, the Venetians persuaded them to divert their expedition against the Muslims in Palestine and to attack Constantinople instead. They took the city and atrociously sacked it. Nicetas Choniates, a contemporaneous historian, expressed the feelings of the Byzantines toward the Crusaders: "The accursed Latins would plunder our wealth and wipe out our race. . . . Between us there can be only an unbridgeable gulf of hatred. . . . They bear the Cross of Christ on their shoulders, but even the Saracens are kinder."[6]

The Latins set up kingdoms within Byzantium, notably in Constantinople itself. What remained of Byzantium was split into three small states. The Palaeologans ruled one of these, the kingdom of Nicaea. In 1261, Michael VIII Palaeologus (r. 1259–1282) succeeded in recapturing Constantinople. But his empire was no more than a fragment, and even that disintegrated during the next two centuries. Isolated from the Christian West by Muslim conquests in the Balkans and besieged by Muslim Turks to the east, Byzantium sought help from the West. It was not forthcoming. In 1453, the Ottoman Turks, then a formidable power, took Constantinople and brought to an end the long history of Byzantium (see Chapter 13). But despite the state's grim political condition under the Palaeologan dynasty, the arts flourished well into the 14th century.

## *Architecture*

A MULTIPLICATION OF DOMES Late Byzantine architecture did not depart radically from the characteristic plans and elevations of Middle Byzantine architecture. But the number of domes and drums increased, and their groupings became more and more dramatic. Elevations became narrower and steeper. Wall and drum arcades were more deeply cut back into overlapping arches. The eaves curved rhythmically and varied brick patterns ornamented the external walls.

The church of Saint Catherine (FIG. **12-30**) in Thessaloniki, second city to Constantinople in rank, shows all these Palaeologan variations on the grand stylistic theme of Middle Byzantine architecture. The plan is an inscribed cross with a central dome

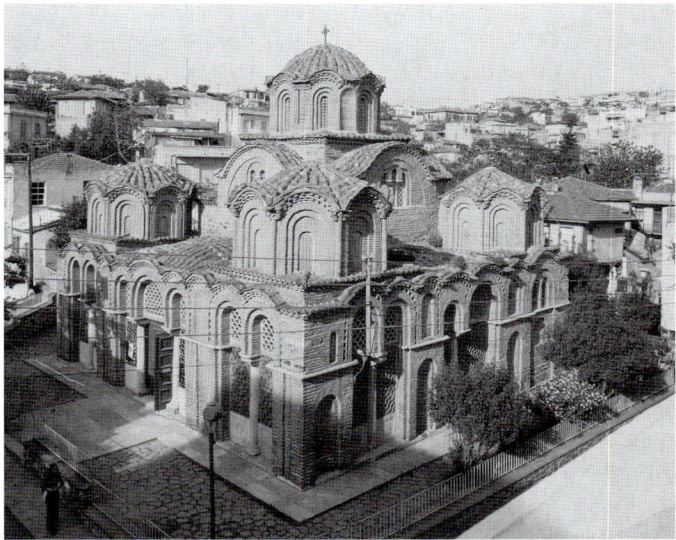

**12-30** Church of Saint Catherine, Thessaloniki, Greece, ca. 1280.

and four additional domes at the corners. On the exterior these appear as *cupolas,* drums with shallow caps, the central drum rising a level above the others. Thus the church has a vertical gradation from a rectilinear base to the superstructure's cylindrical volumes, culminating in the dominant central unit. Wall and drum arcades are grouped rhythmically in alternating pairs and triads. Lively patterning face and punctuate the enframements of arches and niches and the scalloped eaves. The intricate harmonizing by alternation and repetition of walls and openings and of verticals, half-circles, and cylinders produces a lively rhythm.

## Painting

**RESURRECTION AND REDEMPTION** A new burst of creative energy also enlivened Late Byzantine painting. Artists produced masterpieces of mural and icon painting rivaling those of the earlier periods. A fresco (FIG. **12-31**) in the apse of the *parekklesion* (side chapel, in this instance a funerary chapel) of the Church of Christ in Chora (now the Kariye Museum, formerly the Kariye Camii mosque) in Constantinople depicts the Anastasis. One of many subsidiary subjects making up the complex mosaic program of Saint Mark's in Venice (FIG. 12-23), the Anastasis is here central to a cycle of pictures portraying the themes of human mortality and redemption by Christ and of the intercession of the Virgin, both appropriate for a funerary chapel.

In the Kariye fresco, Christ, trampling Satan and all the locks and keys of his prison house of Hell, raises Adam and Eve from their tombs. Looking on are John the Baptist, King David, and King Solomon on the left, and various martyr saints on the right. Christ, central and in a luminous mandorla, reaches out equally to Adam and Eve. The action is swift and smooth, the supple

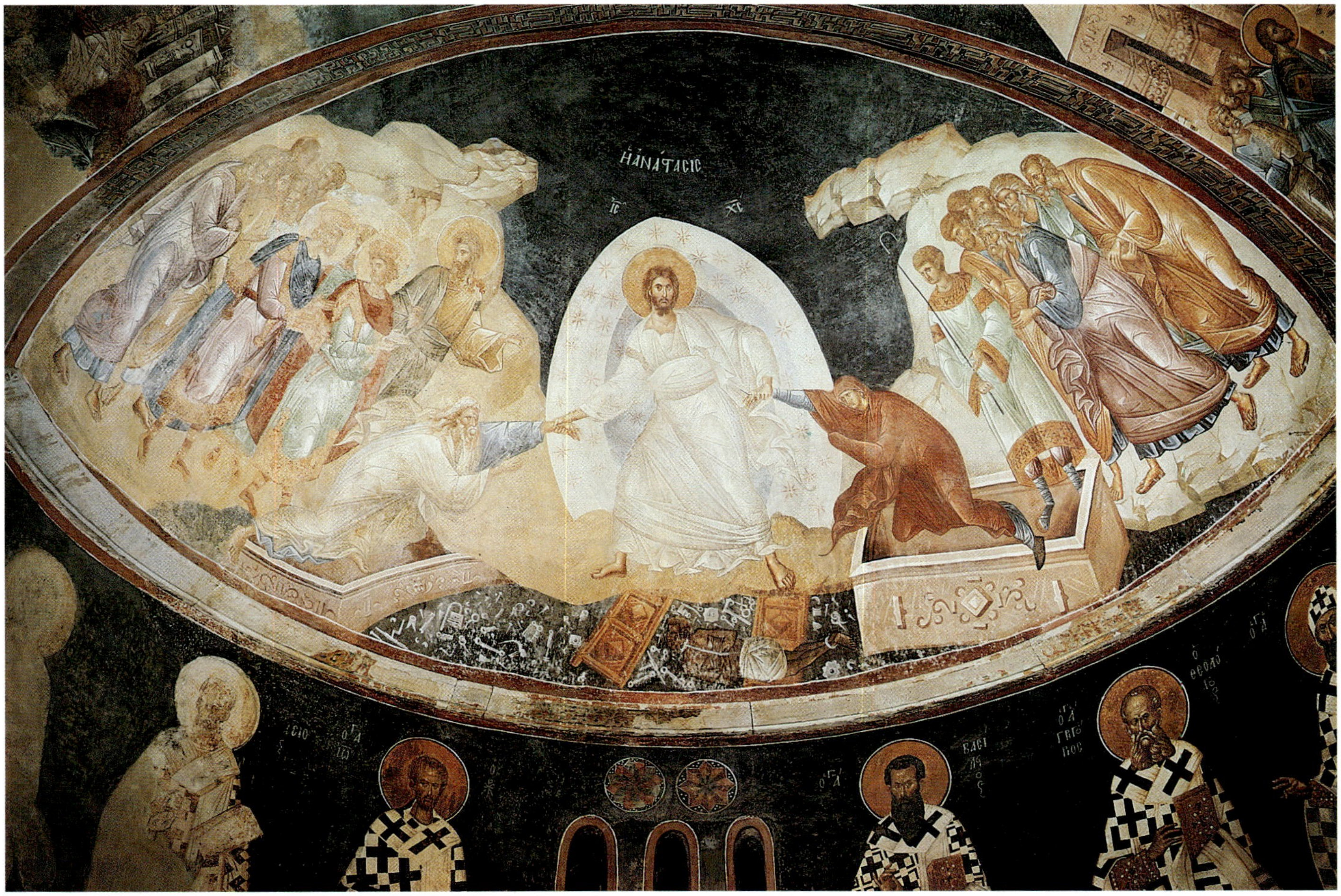

**12-31** Anastasis, apse fresco in the *parekklesion* of the Church of Christ in Chora (now the Kariye Museum), Constantinople (Istanbul), Turkey, ca. 1310–1320.

motions executed with the grace of a ballet. The figures float in a spiritual atmosphere, spaceless and without material mass or shadow-casting volume. This same smoothness and lightness can be seen in the modeling of the figures and the subtly nuanced coloration. The jagged abstractions of drapery found in many earlier Byzantine frescoes and mosaics are gone in a return to the fluid delineation of drapery characteristic of the long tradition of classical illusionism.

Throughout the centuries, Byzantine artists looked back to Greco-Roman illusionism. But unlike classical artists, Byzantine painters and mosaicists were not concerned with the systematic observation of material nature as the source of their representations of the eternal. They drew their images from a persistent and conventionalized vision of a spiritual world unsusceptible to change. That consistent vision is what unites works as distant in date as the sixth-century apse mosaic at Mount Sinai (FIG. 12-13) and the 14th-century Kariye fresco.

**ICONS AND ICONOSTASIS** Byzantine spirituality was perhaps most intensely revealed in icon painting. In the Late Byzantine period, the Early Byzantine templon developed into an *iconostasis* (icon stand), a high screen with doors. As its name implies, the iconostasis supported tiers of painted devotional images, which began to be produced again in large numbers, both in Constantinople and throughout the diminished Byzantine Empire.

Our example (FIG. **12-32**), notable for the lavish use of finely etched silver foil to frame the tempera figure of Christ as Savior of Souls, dates to the beginning of the 14th century. It comes from the church of Saint Clement at Ohrid in Macedonia, where many Late Byzantine icons imported from the capital have been preserved. The painter of the Ohrid Christ, in a manner consistent with Byzantine art's conservative nature, adhered to an iconographical and stylistic tradition that went back to the earliest icons from the monastery at Mount Sinai. As elsewhere (for example, FIG. 12-21), the Savior holds a bejeweled Bible in his left hand while he blesses the faithful with his right hand. The style is typical of Byzantine eclecticism. Note especially the juxtaposition of Christ's fully modeled head and neck, which reveal the Byzantine painter's Greco-Roman heritage, with the schematic linear folds of Christ's garment, which do not envelop the figure but rather seem to be placed in front of it.

**A PARADE OF ICONS** In the Late Byzantine period, icons often were painted on two sides because they were intended to be carried in processions. When they were deposited in the church, they were not mounted on the iconostasis but were exhibited on stands so they could be viewed from both sides. The Ohrid icon of Christ has a painting of the Crucifixion on its reverse. Another double icon from Saint Clement's, also imported from Constantinople, represents the Virgin on the front as Christ's counterpart as Savior of Souls. The Annunciation (FIG. 12-33) is the subject of

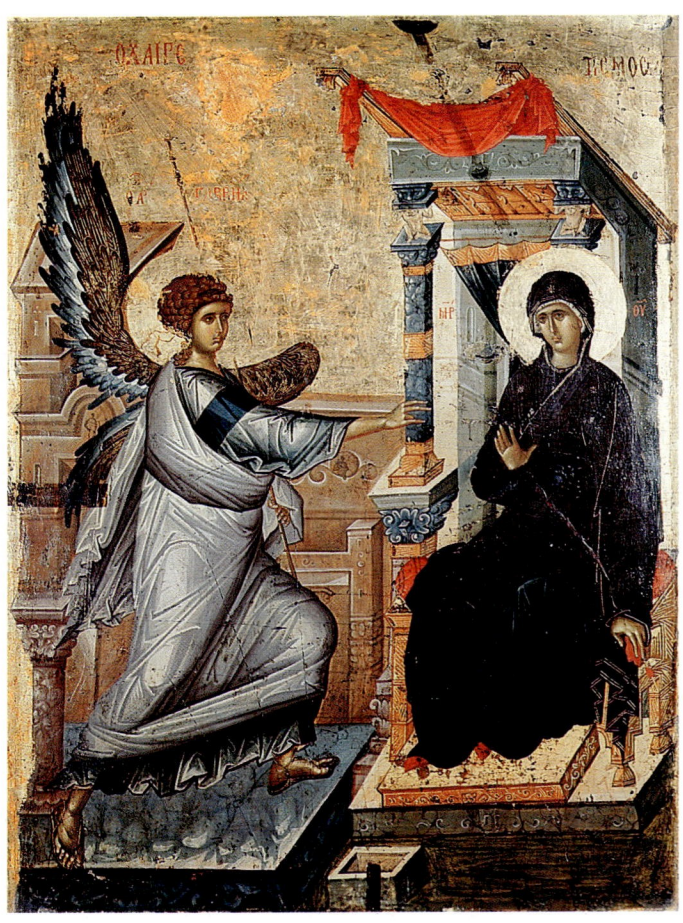

**12-32** Christ as Savior of Souls, icon from the church of Saint Clement, Ohrid, Macedonia, early 14th century. Tempera, linen, and silver on wood, 3′ $\frac{1}{4}$″ × 2′ 2$\frac{1}{2}$″. Icon Gallery of Saint Clement, Ohrid.

**12-33** Annunciation, reverse of two-sided icon from the church of Saint Clement, Ohrid, Macedonia, early 14th century. Tempera and linen on wood, 3′ $\frac{1}{4}$″ × 2′ 2$\frac{3}{4}$″. Icon gallery of Saint Clement, Ohrid.

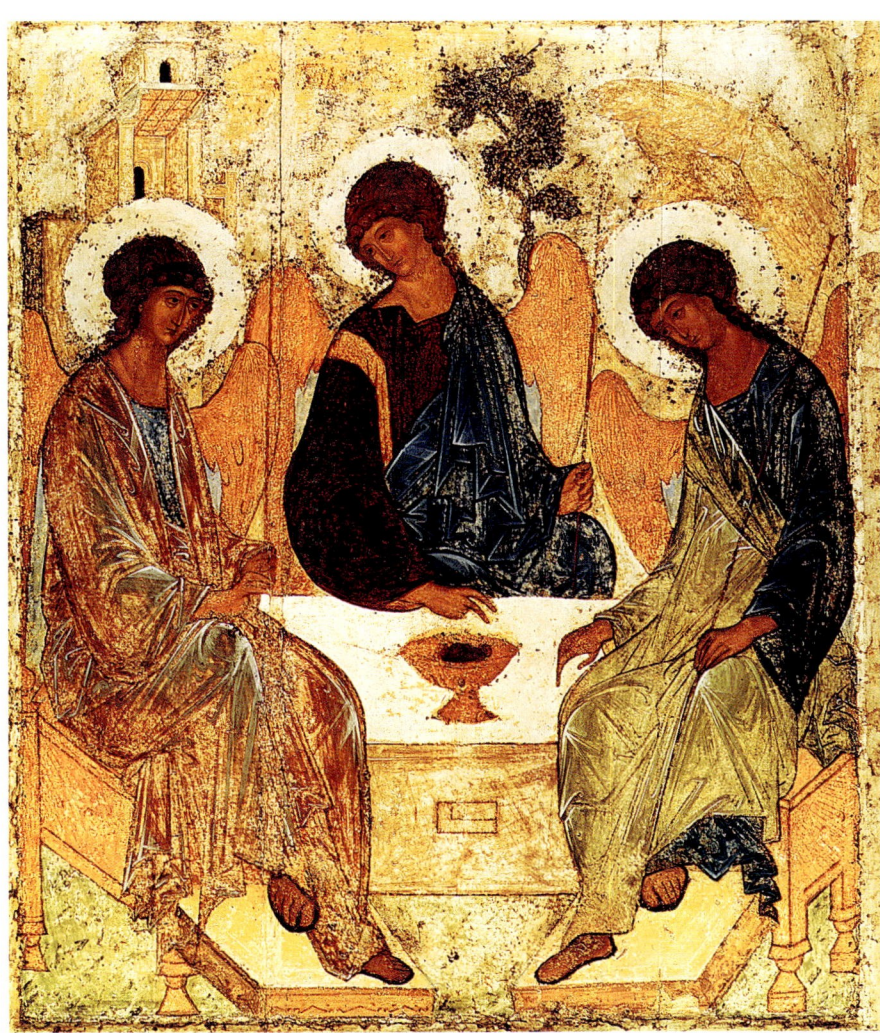

**12-34** ANDREI RUBLYEV, Three angels (Old Testament Trinity), ca. 1410. Tempera on wood, 4′ 8″ × 3′ 9″. Tretyakov Gallery, Moscow.

the reverse. With a commanding gesture of heavenly authority, the angel Gabriel announces to Mary that she is to be the Mother of God. She responds with a simple gesture conveying both astonishment and acceptance. The gestures and attitudes of the figures are again conventional, as are the highly simplified architectural props. The latter are rendered in inconsistent perspective derived from classical prototypes, but the sturdy three-dimensional forms have been set against an otherworldly gold sky, suggesting the sacred space in which the narrative unfolds. This icon also exemplifies the eclecticism that characterizes Byzantine art throughout its long history.

**RUSSIAN ICON PAINTING** In Russia, icon painting flourished for centuries, extending the life of the Byzantine painting style well beyond the collapse of the Byzantine Empire in 1453. Russian paintings usually had strong patterns, firm lines, and intense contrasting colors. All served to heighten the legibility of the icons in the wavering candlelight and clouds of incense that worshipers encountered in church interiors. For many art historians, Russian painting reached a climax in the work of ANDREI RUBLYEV (ca. 1370–1430). His rendition of the three Old Testament angels who appeared to Abraham (FIG. **12-34**) is a work of great spiritual power, as well as an unsurpassed example of subtle line in union with intensely vivid color. The angels sit about a table, each framed with a halo and sweeping wings, three nearly identical figures dis-

tinguished only by their garment colors. The light linear play of the draperies sets off the tranquil demeanor of the figures. Color defines the forms and becomes more intense by the juxtaposition of complementary hues. The intense blue and green folds of the central figure's cloak, for example, stand out starkly against the deep-red robe and the gilded orange of the wings. In the figure on the left, the highlights of the orange cloak are an opalescent blue green. The unmodulated saturation, brilliance, and purity of the color harmonies are the hallmark of Rublyev's style.

## Luxury Arts

**PRIESTLY ROBES** In Byzantium, other arts also played an indispensable part in the ensemble of a church interior—the carvings and rich metalwork of the iconostasis, serving to frame icons that themselves often were ornamented with precious metals and jewels; the finely wrought, gleaming candlesticks and candelabra; the illuminated books bound in gold or ivory and inlaid with jewels and enamels; and the crosses, croziers, sacred vessels, and processional banners. Each, with its great richness of texture and color, contributed to the total ambience of the Byzantine church. And amid these opulent inanimate treasures, the solemn clergy celebrated the liturgy of the Orthodox faith in magnificent embroidered and bejeweled robes.

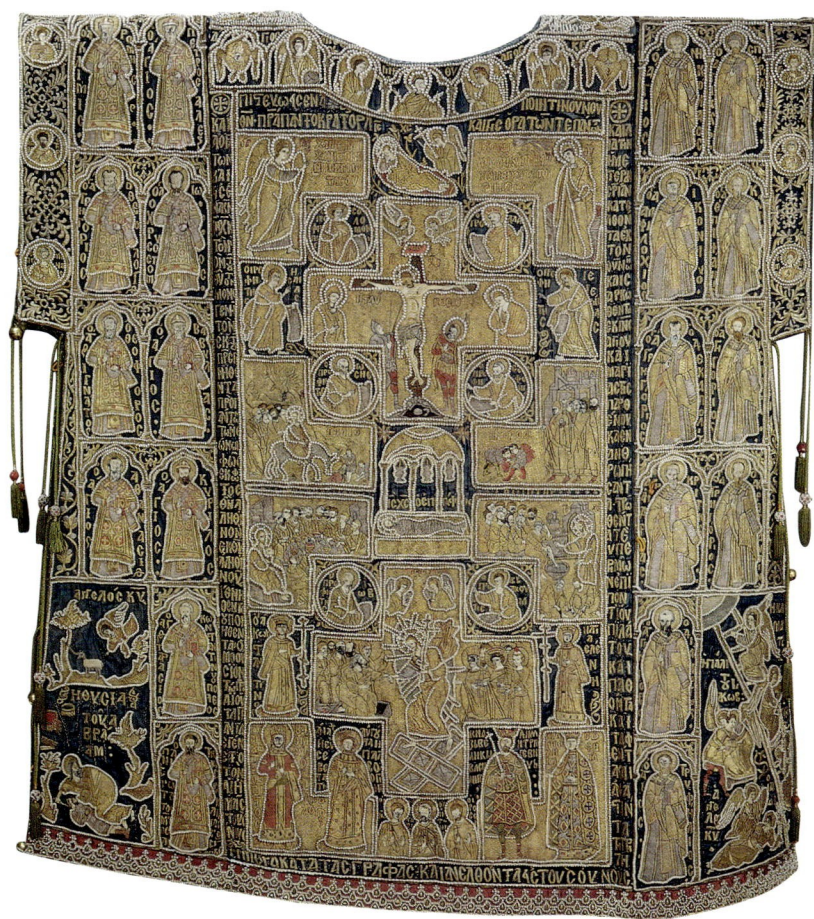

**12-35** Large sakkos of Photius, ca. 1417. Satin embroidered with gold and silver thread and silk with pearl ornament, approx. 4′ 5″ long. Kremlin Armory, Moscow.

Fortunately some of these vestments have been reverently preserved through centuries of political and social upheaval in Russia. One of them is the so-called large *sakkos* (a magnificent "small sakkos" also exists) or tunic (FIG. **12-35**) of Photius, the early-15th-century Metropolitan (Orthodox archbishop) of Russia. It can represent here this whole branch of the "minor arts" and remind readers of how incomplete the story of art through the ages would be if the narrative were confined to monumental works of painting, sculpture, and architecture.

Photius's satin sakkos is embroidered with gold and silver thread and colored silks outlined with pearls. Dozens of religious and secular figures appear in a dazzling array of rectilinear, L-shaped, cruciform, and circular frames. The Crucifixion dominates the center of the front, and below is the Anastasis. All around are various Orthodox Church feasts and figures of saints, as well as Old Testament scenes, including the sacrifice of Abraham, linked with the Crucifixion. Also portrayed are the Grand Prince of Moscow, Vasily Dimitrievich, and his wife Sophia Vitovtovna (labeled in Russian), as well as the future emperor John VIII Palaeologus (r. 1425–1448) and his wife Anna Vasilyevna (named in Greek). Beside John is Photius, "Metropolitan of Kiev and all Russia." Needleworkers most likely embroidered the sakkos between the time of John's marriage in 1416 and Anna Vasilyevna's death in 1418. The couple probably sent the sakkos to Photius as a gift. In 15th-century Russia, as in sixth-century Ravenna, the rulers of Byzantium, as the vicars of God on earth, joined the clergy in celebration of the liturgy of the Christian Church.

**THE THIRD ROME** A third of a century after Photius first donned his sakkos, Constantinople fell to the Ottoman Turks, never to be recovered. With the passing of Byzantium, Russia became its self-appointed heir, defending Christendom against the infidel. The court of the tsar (derived from the word *caesar*) declared: "Because the Old Rome has fallen, and because the Second Rome, which is Constantinople, is now in the hands of the godless Turks, thy kingdom, O pious Tsar, is the Third Rome. . . . Two Romes have fallen, but the Third stands, and there shall be no more."[7] Rome, Byzantium, Russia—Old Rome, New Rome, and Third Rome—were a continuum, where artistic change was slow and the old ways never really died.

## CONCLUSION

In the centuries following the foundation of Constantinople (Byzantium) in 330, the Christian world became divided into the Latin West, centered in Rome, and the Greek Orthodox East, with its capital at Constantinople. Under Justinian, Byzantine art reached an early pinnacle, setting the pattern for much of later Byzantine art. Justinianic mosaicists carried on and codified the formal, hieratic style of late antiquity. Justinian's architects also pioneered the distinctive form of Byzantine churches. Mirroring the schism in Christianity, Byzantine churches are centrally planned, dome-covered structures, in contrast to the longitudinal basilicas favored in the West. The New Rome of the East lasted for more than a millennium until its final defeat at the hands of the Muslims in 1453. By then, however, Byzantine artists had already made a major impact on the art of the West (see Chapter 19).

**527**

EARLY BYZANTINE

[1] | JUSTINIAN, R. 527–565
| NIKA RIOTS IN CONSTANTINOPLE, 532
| BELISARIUS CAPTURES RAVENNA, 539
| HERACLIUS DEFEATS PERSIANS, 627
| ARABS BESIEGE CONSTANTINOPLE, 717–718

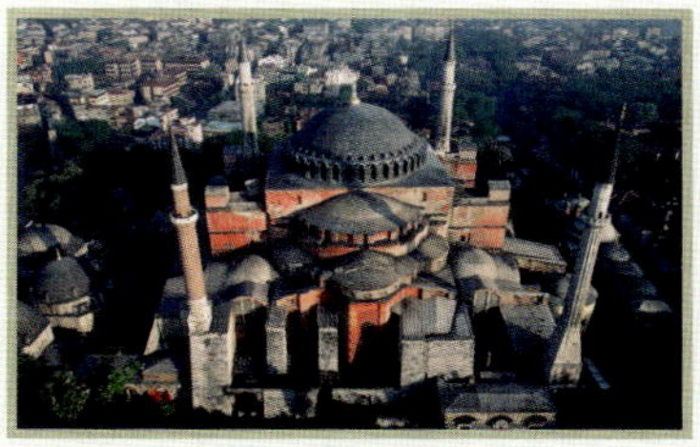

[1] Hagia Sophia, Constantinople, 532–537

**726**

ICONOCLASM

| LEO III PROHIBITS IMAGE MAKING, 726
| RAVENNA FALLS TO THE LOMBARDS, 751

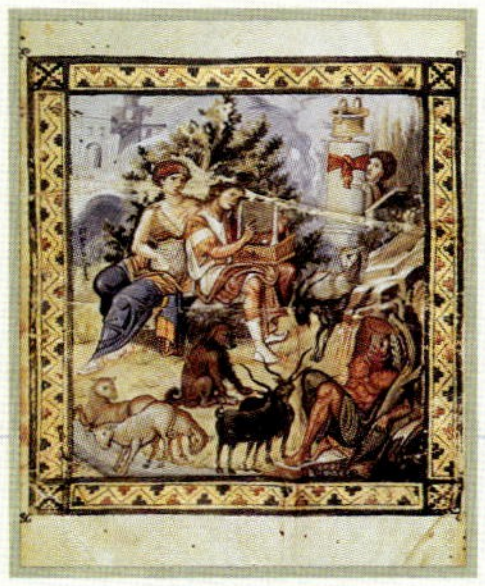

**843**

| RESTORATION OF IMAGES, 843
| BASIL I, R. 867–886, FOUNDER OF MACEDONIAN DYNASTY
[2] | BASIL II, R. 980–1001, REVIVAL OF BYZANTINE POWER
| SCHISM BETWEEN BYZANTINE AND ROMAN CHURCHES, 1054
| NORMAN CONQUEST OF SICILY, 1060–1092
| SELJUK TURKS CAPTURE BYZANTINE ASIA MINOR, 1073
[3] | FIRST CRUSADE, 1095–1099
| FOURTH CRUSADE AND THE FRANKISH CONQUEST, 1202–1204

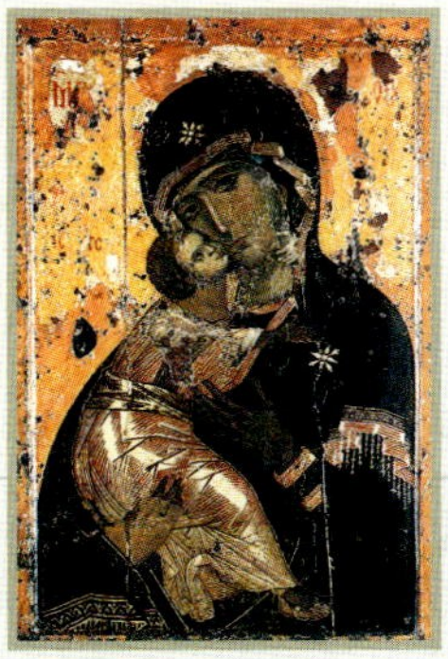

[2] *Paris Psalter,* ca. 950–970

MIDDLE BYZANTINE

**1204**

| MICHAEL VIII PALAEOLOGUS RECAPTURES CONSTANTINOPLE
FROM THE FRANKS, 1261

[3] Vladimir Virgin, late
11th–early 12th century

LATE BYZANTINE

[4]

**1453**

| OTTOMAN TURKS CAPTURE CONSTANTINOPLE;
END OF BYZANTINE EMPIRE, 1453

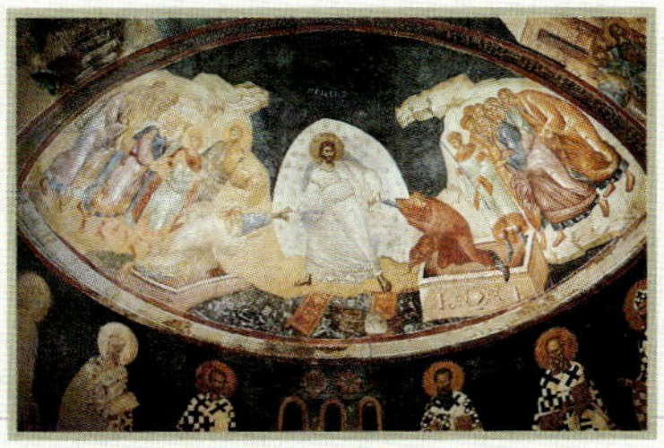

[4] Church of Christ in Chora,
Constantinople, ca. 1310–1320

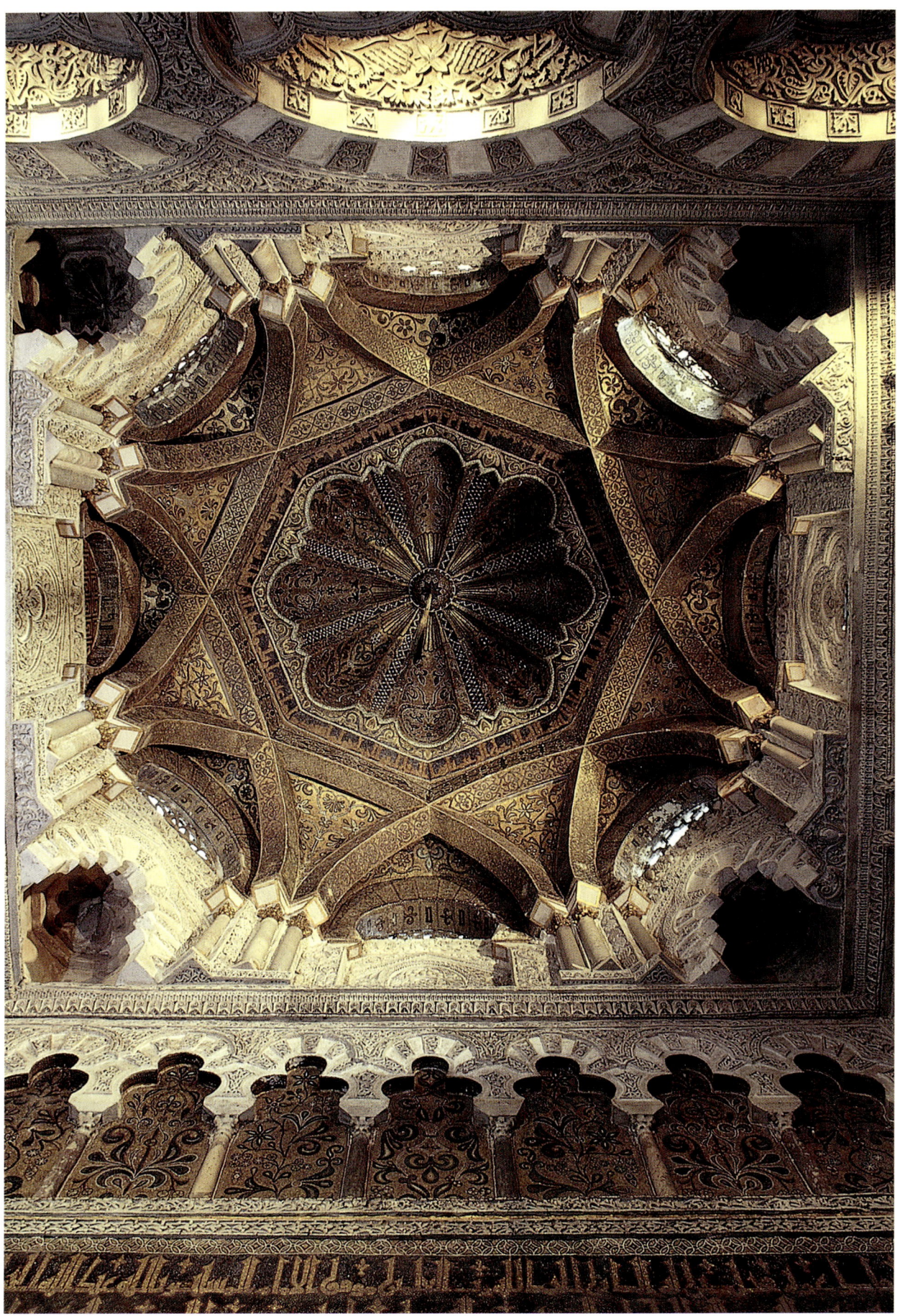

Dome in front of the mihrab of the Great Mosque, Córdoba, Spain, 961–965.

# 13

# IN PRAISE OF ALLAH

## THE ART OF THE ISLAMIC WORLD

The religion of *Islam* (an Arabic word meaning "submission to God") arose among the peoples of the Arabian peninsula early in the seventh century (see "Muhammad and Islam," page 359). The Arabs were nomadic herders and caravan merchants traversing, from ancient times, the wastes and oases of the vast Arabian desert and settling and controlling its coasts. When Islam arose, the Arabs were peripheral to the Byzantine and Persian empires. Yet within little more than a century, the Mediterranean, once ringed and ruled by Byzantium, had become an Islamic lake, and the armies of Islam had subdued the Middle East, long the seat of Persian dominance and influence.

The swiftness of the Islamic advance is among the wonders of world history. By 640, Muslims ruled Syria, Palestine, and Iraq in the name of Allah. In 642, the Byzantine army abandoned Alexandria, marking the Muslim conquest of Lower (northern) Egypt. In 651, the successors of Muhammad brought more than 400 years of Sasanian rule in Iran to an end (see Chapter 2). By 710, all of North Africa was under Muslim control. A victory at Jerez de la Frontera in southern Spain in 711 seemed to open all of western Europe to the Muslims. By 732, they had advanced north to Poitiers in France. There, however, an army of Franks under Charles Martel, the grandfather of Charlemagne, opposed them successfully (see Chapter 16). Although Islamic forces continued to conduct raids in France, they could not extend their control beyond the Pyrenees along the French-Spanish border. But in Spain, the Muslim rulers of Córdoba flourished until 1031, and not until 1492 did Islamic influence and power in the Iberian Peninsula end. That year the caliphs of Granada fell to King Ferdinand and Queen Isabella, the sponsors of Columbus's voyage to the New World. In the East, the Muslims reached the Indus River by 751, and only in Anatolia could stubborn Byzantine resistance slow their advance. Relentless Muslim pressure against the shrinking Byzantine Empire eventually caused its collapse in 1453, when the Ottoman Turks entered Constantinople (see Chapter 12).

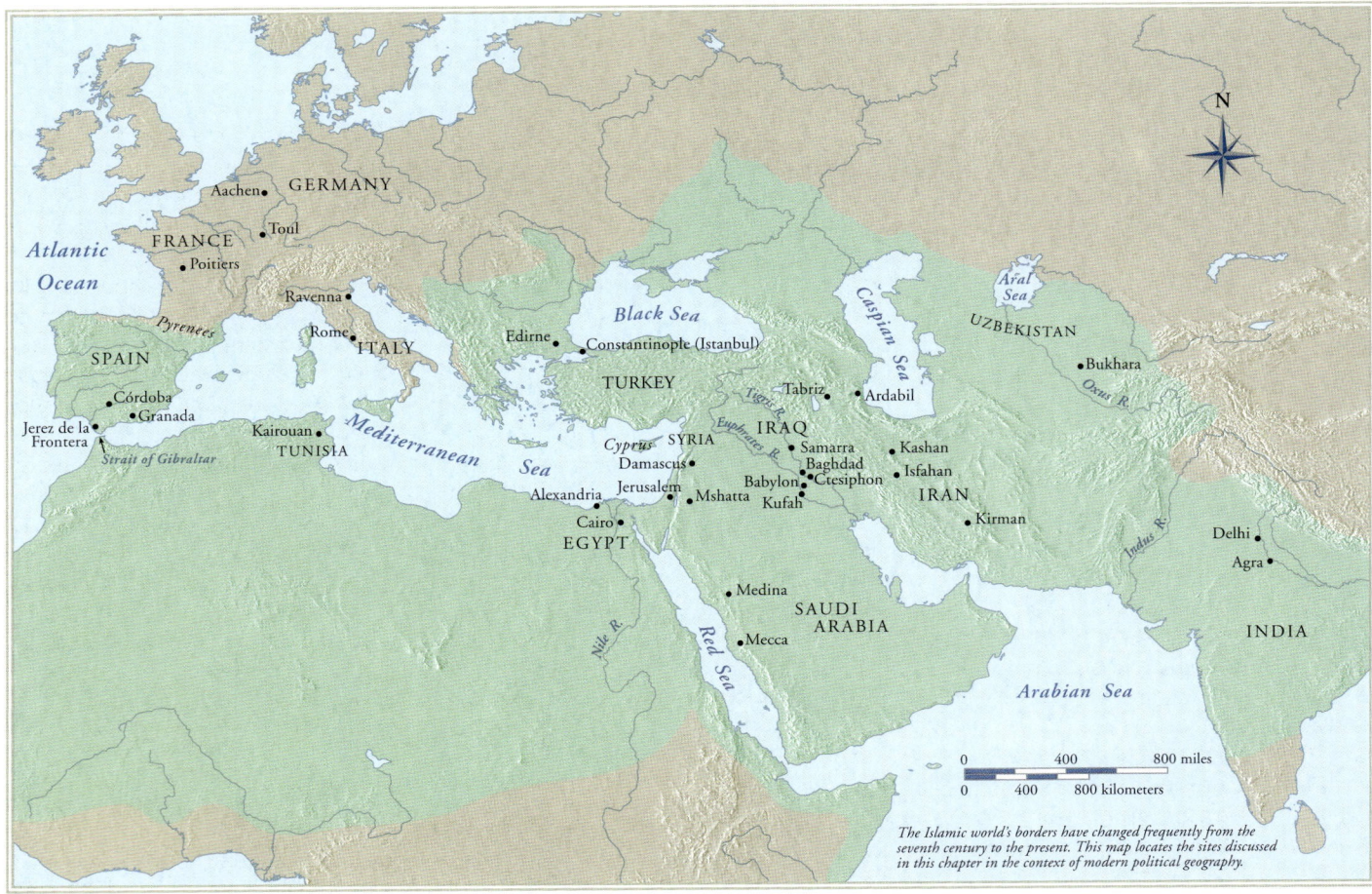

**MAP 13-1** The Islamic world.

**THE IMPACT OF ISLAM** The irresistible and far-ranging sweep of Islam from Arabia to India to North Africa and Spain (MAP **13-1**) was not due to military might alone. That the initial victories had effects that endured for centuries can be explained only by the nature of Islamic faith and its appeal to millions of converts. Islam remains today one of the world's great religions, with adherents on all continents. And the sophistication of its culture has had a profound impact around the globe. Christian scholars in the West during the 12th and 13th centuries eagerly studied Arabic translations of Aristotle and other Greek writers of antiquity (see Chapter 18). Arabic love lyrics and poetic descriptions of nature inspired the early French troubadours. Arab scholars laid the foundations of arithmetic and algebra, and their contributions to astronomy, medicine, and the natural sciences have made a lasting impression in the Western world.

The triumph of Islam also brought a new and compelling tradition to the history of world art and architecture. Like Islam itself, Islamic art spread quickly both eastward and westward from the land once inhabited by the peoples of the ancient Near East and their Sasanian successors (see MAP 2-1). In the Middle East and North Africa, Islamic art largely replaced Late Antique art. And from a foothold in the Iberian peninsula, Islamic art made an impact on Western medieval art, although Islamic art stands in sharp contrast both to the figural art of Europe and the Mediterranean and to the Western architectural vocabulary. Islamic artists and architects also brought their distinctive style to South Asia, where a Muslim sultanate was established at Delhi in India in the early 13th century (see Chapter 25). In fact, perhaps the most famous building in Asia, the Taj Mahal (see FIG. 25-5) at Agra, is an Islamic mausoleum.

# EARLY ISLAMIC ART

During the early centuries of Islamic history, the Muslim world's political and cultural center was the Fertile Crescent of ancient Mesopotamia. This crescent-shaped area of cultivable land was strewn with impressive ruins of earlier cultures, from the Sumerians to the Sasanians (see Chapter 2). The caliphs of Damascus (capital of modern Syria) and Baghdad (capital of Iraq) appointed provincial governors to rule the vast territories they controlled. These governors eventually gained relative independence by setting up dynasties in various territories and provinces: the Umayyads in Syria (661–749) and in Spain (756–1031), the Abbasids in Iraq (750–1258, largely nominal after 945), the Fatimids in Egypt (909–1171), and so on. Like other potentates before and after, the Islamic rulers were builders on a grand scale.

## Architecture

**TRIUMPH IN JERUSALEM** The first great achievement of Islamic architecture is the Dome of the Rock (FIG. **13-1**) in Jerusalem. The Muslims had taken the city from the Byzantines in 638, and the Umayyad caliph Abd al-Malik (r. 685–705) erected the monumental sanctuary between 687 and 692 as an architectural tribute to the triumph of Islam. The Dome of the Rock marked the coming of the new religion to the city that had been, and still is, sacred to both Jews and Christians. The structure rises from a huge platform known as the Noble Enclosure. Even today it dominates the skyline of the holy city. The sanctuary was erected

## Muhammad and Islam

Muhammad, founder of Islam and revered as its Final Prophet, was a native of Mecca on the west coast of Arabia. Born around 570 into a family of merchants in the great Arabian caravan trade, Muhammad was inspired to prophecy. Critical of the polytheistic religion of his fellow Arabs, he preached a religion of the one and only God (*Allah* in Arabic), whose revelations Muhammad received beginning in 610 and for the rest of his life. Opposition to Muhammad's message among the Arabs was strong enough to prompt the Prophet and his growing number of followers to flee from Mecca to a desert oasis eventually called Medina ("City of the Prophet"). Islam dates its beginnings from this flight in 622, known as the *Hijra* (emigration).[1] Barely eight years later, in 630, Muhammad returned to Mecca with 10,000 soldiers. He took control of the city, converted the population to Islam, and destroyed all the idols. But he preserved as the Islamic world's symbolic center the small cubical building that had housed the idols, the *Kaaba* (from the Arabic for "cube"). The Arabs associated the Kaaba with the era of Abraham and Ishmael, the common ancestors of Jews and Arabs. Muhammad died in Medina in 632.

The essential meaning of Islam is acceptance of and submission to Allah's will. Believers in Islam are called *Muslims* ("those who submit"). Islam requires living according to the rules laid down in the collected revelations communicated through Muhammad during his lifetime. These are recorded in the *Koran,* Islam's sacred book, codified by the Muslim ruler Uthman (r. 644–656). The word "Koran" means "recitations"—a reference to the archangel Gabriel's instructions to Muhammad in 610 to "recite in the name of Allah." The Koran is composed of 114 *surahs* (chapters) divided into verses.

The profession of faith in the one God, Allah, is the first of five obligations binding all Muslims. In addition, the faithful must worship five times daily, facing in Mecca's direction; give alms to the poor; fast during the month of Ramadan; and once in a lifetime—if possible—make a pilgrimage to Mecca. Muslims are guided not only by the revelations in the Koran but also by Muhammad's life. The Prophet's exemplary ways and customs, collected in the *Sunnah,* are supplemental to the Koran, offering guidance to the faithful on ethical problems of everyday life. The reward for the Muslim faithful is Paradise.

Islam has much in common with Judaism and Christianity. Its adherents think of it as a continuation, completion, and in some sense a reformation of those other great monotheisms. Islam incorporates many of the Old Testament teachings, with their sober ethical standards and hatred of idol worship, and those of the New Testament Gospels. Adam, Abraham, Moses, and Jesus are acknowledged as the prophetic predecessors of Muhammad, the final and greatest of the prophets. Muhammad did not claim to be divine, as did Jesus, and he did not perform miracles. Rather, he was God's messenger, the purifier and perfecter of the common faith of Jews, Christians, and Muslims in one God. Islam also differs from Judaism and Christianity in its simpler organization. Muslims worship God directly, without a hierarchy of rabbis, priests, or saints acting as intermediaries.

In Islam, as Muhammad defined it, religious and secular authority were united even more completely than in Byzantium. Muhammad established a new social order, replacing the Arabs' old decentralized tribal one. In this he was influenced, no doubt, by the examples of the emperors and kings reigning in the lands his people would occupy. He took complete charge of his community's temporal, as well as spiritual, affairs. After Muhammad's death, the *caliphs* (from the Arabic for "successor") continued this practice of uniting religious and political leadership in one ruler.

[1] Muslims date events beginning with the Hijra in the same way Christians reckon events from Christ's birth and the Romans before them began their calendar with Rome's founding by Romulus in 753 BCE. The Muslim year is, however, a 354-day year of 12 lunar months, and dates cannot be converted by simply adding 622 to Christian-era dates.

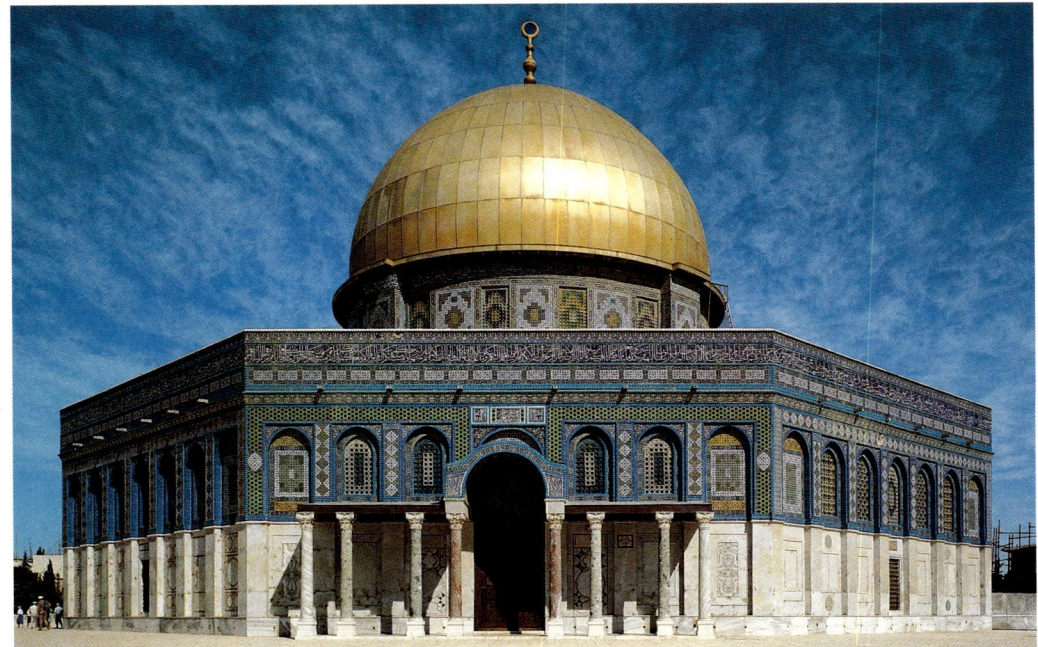

**13-1** Dome of the Rock, Jerusalem, 687–692.

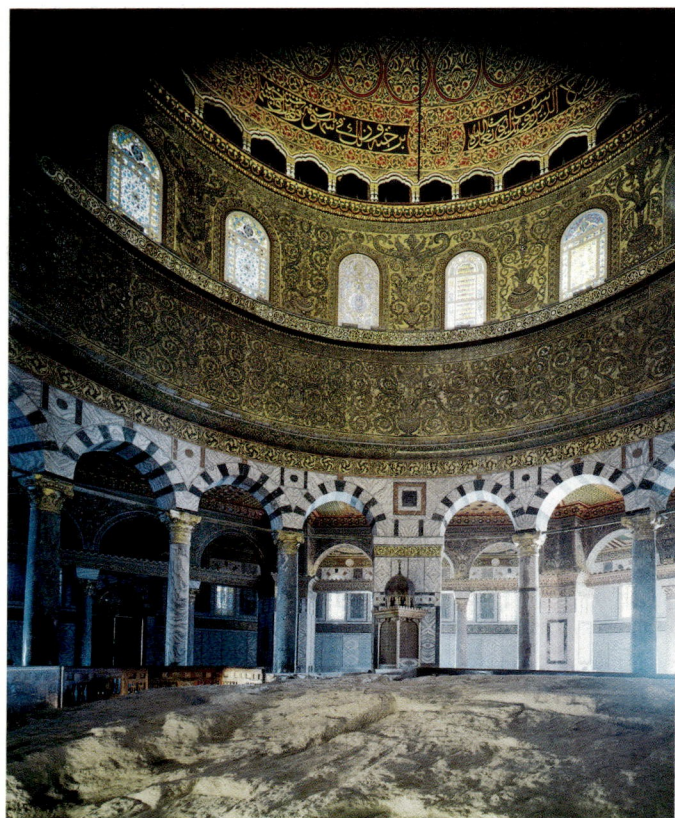

**13-2** Interior of the Dome of the Rock, Jerusalem, 687–692.

design, construction, and ornamentation principles that had long been applied in, and were still current in, Byzantium and the Middle East. The Dome of the Rock is a domed octagon resembling San Vitale in Ravenna (see FIG. 12-6) in its basic design. In all likelihood, a neighboring Christian monument, Constantine the Great's Rotunda of the Holy Sepulchre, inspired the Dome of the Rock's designers. That fourth-century rotunda bore a family resemblance to the roughly contemporary Constantinian mausoleum (later rededicated as Santa Costanza) in Rome (see FIGS. 11-9 and 11-10). The Dome of the Rock is a member of the same extended family. Its double-shelled wooden dome, however, some 60 feet across and 75 feet high, so dominates the elevation as to reduce the octagon to function merely as its base. This soaring, majestic unit creates a decidedly more commanding effect than that of Late Roman and Byzantine domical structures (see, for example, FIGS. 11-10 and 12-3). The silhouettes of those domes are comparatively insignificant when seen from the outside.

The building's exterior has been much restored. Tiling from the 16th century and later has replaced the original mosaic. Yet the vivid, colorful patterning that wraps the walls like a textile is typical of Islamic ornamentation. It contrasts markedly with Byzantine brickwork and Greco-Roman sculptured profiling and carved decoration. The interior's rich mosaic ornament (FIG. 13-2) has been preserved. From it one can imagine how the exterior walls originally appeared. Islamic practice does not significantly distinguish interior and exterior decor. The splendor of infinitely various surfaces is given to public gaze both within and outside buildings.

**NEW CAPITAL, NEW MOSQUE** The Umayyads transferred their capital from Mecca to Damascus in 661. There, Abd al-Malik's son, the caliph al-Walid (r. 705–715), purchased a Byzantine church (formerly a Roman temple) and built an imposing new mosque for the expanding Muslim population (see "The Mosque," page 361). The Umayyads demolished the church, but they used the Roman precinct walls as a foundation for their own construction. Like the Dome of the Rock, the Great Mosque of Damascus (FIG. **13-3**) owes much to the architecture of the

on the traditional site of Adam's burial, of Abraham's preparation for Isaac's sacrifice, and of the Temple of Solomon the Romans destroyed in 70. It houses the rock (FIG. **13-2**) from which Muslims later came to believe Muhammad ascended to Heaven.

As Islam took much of its teaching from Judaism and Christianity, so its architects and artists borrowed and transformed

**13-3** Aerial view of the Great Mosque, Damascus, Syria, 706–715.

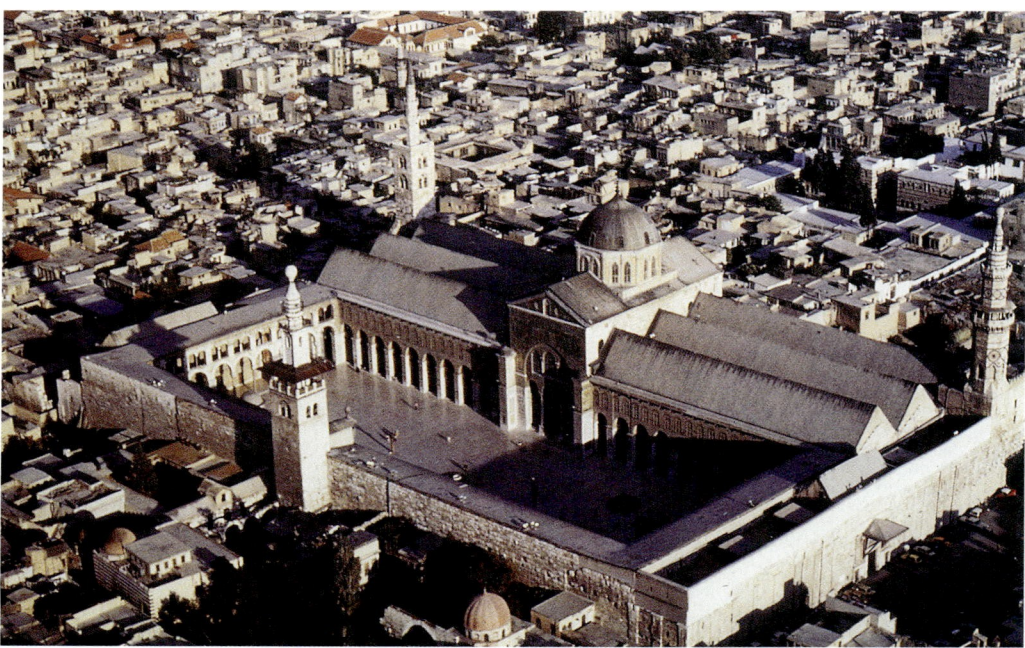

## The Mosque

Islamic religious architecture is closely related to Muslim prayer, an obligation laid down in the Koran for all Muslims. In Islam, worshiping can be a private act. It requires neither prescribed ceremony nor a special locale. Only the *qibla*—the direction (toward Mecca) Muslims face while praying—is important. But worship also became a communal act when the first Muslim community established a simple ritual for it. To celebrate the Muslim sabbath, which occurs on Friday, the community convened each Friday at noon, probably in the Prophet's house in Medina. The main feature of Muhammad's house was a large square court with rows of palm trunks supporting thatched roofs along the north and south sides. The southern side was wider and had a double row of trunks. It faced Mecca. During these communal gatherings, the *imam,* or leader of collective worship, stood on a stepped pulpit, or *minbar,* set up in front of the southern (qibla) wall.

These features became standard in the Islamic house of worship, the *mosque* (from Arabic *masjid,* a place of prostration), where the faithful gathered for the five daily prayers. The *congregational mosque* (also called the *Friday mosque* or *great mosque*), was ideally large enough to accommodate a community's entire population for the Friday noonday prayer. A very important feature both of ordinary mosques and of congregational mosques is the *mihrab,* a semicircular niche usually set into the qibla wall (FIG. 13-8). Often a dome over the bay in front of it marked its position (FIGS. 13-3, 13-8, and 13-13). The niche was a familiar Greco-Roman architectural feature, generally enclosing a statue. But for Islamic architecture, its origin, purpose, and meaning are still debated. Some scholars believe the mihrab originally may have honored the place where the Prophet stood in his house at Medina when he led communal worship. It thus would have been a revered religious memorial.

In some mosques, a *maqsura* precedes the mihrab. The maqsura is the area generally reserved for the ruler or his representative and can be quite elaborate in form (FIG. 13-12). Many mosques also have one or more *minarets* (FIGS. 13-3, 13-9, and 13-20), towers from which the faithful are called to worship. When buildings of other faiths were converted into mosques, the change was clearly signaled on the exterior by the erection of minarets (see FIG. 12-3). Early mosques are generally characterized by *hypostyle halls,* communal worship halls with roofs held up by a multitude of columns (FIGS. 13-8 and 13-11). Later variations of the early mosque formulation include mosques with four *iwans* (vaulted rectangular recesses), one on each side of the courtyard (FIG. 13-23), and *central-plan* mosques with a single large dome-covered interior space (FIGS. 13-20 to 13-22), as in Byzantine churches, some of which were later converted to mosques (see FIGS. 12-3 to 12-5).

The mosque's origin is still in dispute, although one prototype may well have been the Prophet's house in Medina. Once the Muslims had firmly established themselves in their acquired territories, they began to build on a large scale, impelled, perhaps, by a desire to create such visible evidence of their power as would surpass in size and splendor that of their non-Islamic predecessors. Today, mosques continue to be erected throughout the world. Despite many variations in design and detail and the employment of modern building techniques and materials unknown in Muhammad's day, the mosque's essential features are unchanged. All mosques, wherever they are built and whatever their plan, are oriented toward Mecca, and the faithful worship facing the qibla wall.

Greco-Roman and Early Christian East. It is constructed of masonry blocks, columns, and capitals salvaged from the Roman and Early Christian structures on the land al-Walid acquired for his mosque. The courtyard is bounded by pier arcades reminiscent of Roman aqueducts. The minarets, two at the southern corners and one at the northern side of the enclosure—the earliest in the Islamic world—are modifications of the preexisting Roman square towers. The grand prayer hall, taller than the rest of the complex, is on the south side of the courtyard (facing Mecca). Its main entrance is distinguished by a facade with a pediment and arches, recalling classical and Byzantine models, respectively. The facade faces into the courtyard, like a Roman forum temple (see FIG. 10-10), a plan maintained throughout the long history of mosque architecture. The Damascus mosque synthesizes elements received from other cultures into a novel architectural unity, which includes the distinctive Islamic elements of mihrab, mihrab dome, minbar, and minaret.

An extensive cycle of mosaics once covered the walls of the Great Mosque. In one of the surviving sections (FIG. **13-4**), a conch shell niche "supports" an arcaded pavilion with a flowering rooftop flanked by structures shown in classical perspective. Like the architectural design, the mosaics owe much to Roman, Early Christian, and Byzantine art (compare FIGS. 10-22 and 11-18). Indeed, some evidence indicates that the Great Mosque mosaics were the work of Byzantine mosaicists. Characteristically, tem-

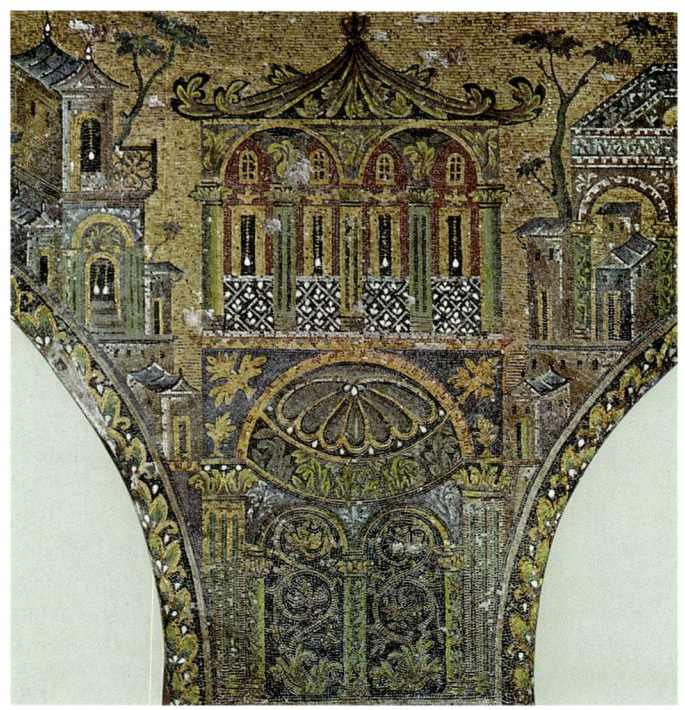

**13-4** Detail of a mosaic in the courtyard arcade of the Great Mosque, Damascus, Syria, 706–715.

ples, clusters of houses, trees, and rivers compose the pictorial fields, bounded by stylized vegetal design, familiar in Roman, Early Christian, and Byzantine ornament. No zoomorphic forms, human or animal, appear either in the pictorial or ornamental spaces. This is true of all the mosaics in the Great Mosque as well as the mosaics in the earlier Dome of the Rock (FIG. 13-2). Islamic tradition shuns the representation of fauna of any kind in sacred places. The world shown in the Damascus mosaics, suspended miragelike in a featureless field of gold, was explained in accompanying (but now lost) inscriptions as an image of Paradise. Many passages from the Koran describe the gorgeous places of Paradise awaiting the faithful—gardens, groves of trees, flowing streams, and "lofty chambers." Indeed, the abundant luxurious images and ornament, floating free of all human reference, create a vision of Paradise appealing to the spiritually oriented imagination, whatever its religion.

**AN UMAYYAD DESERT PALACE** The Umayyad rulers of Damascus constructed numerous palatial residences throughout the vast territories they governed. The urban palaces are lost, but some rural palaces survive. The latter were not merely idyllic residences removed from the congestion, noise, and disease of the cities. They seem to have served as nuclei for the agricultural development of acquired territories and possibly as hunting lodges. In addition, the Islamic palaces were symbols of authority over new lands, as well as expressions of their owners' wealth.

One of the most impressive Umayyad palaces, despite the fact that it was never completed, is at Mshatta in the Jordanian desert. Its plan (FIG. **13-5**) resembles that of Diocletian's palace at Split (see FIG. 10-75), which in turn reflects the layout of a Roman fortified camp. The high walls of the Mshatta palace incorporate 25 towers but lack parapet walkways for patrolling guards. The walls, nonetheless, offered safety from marauding nomadic tribes and provided privacy for the caliph and his entourage. Visitors entered the palace through a large portal on the south side. To the right was a mosque (the plan shows the mihrab niche in the qibla wall), in which the rulers and their guests could fulfill their obligation to pray five times a day. The mosque was separated from the palace's residential wing and official audience hall by a small ceremonial area and an immense open courtyard. Most Umayyad palaces also were provided with fairly elaborate bathing facilities that displayed technical features, such as heating systems, adopted from Roman baths. Just as under the Roman Empire, these baths probably served more than merely hygienic purposes. Indeed, in several Umayyad palaces, excavators have uncovered in the baths paintings and sculptures of hunting and other secular themes, including depictions of dancing women—themes traditionally associated with royalty in the Near East. Large halls frequently attached to many of these baths seem to have been used as places of entertainment, as was the case in Roman times. Thus, the bath-spa-social center, a characteristic amenity of Roman urban culture that died out in the Christian world, survived in Islamic culture.

The architectural ornamentation of many of the early Islamic palaces was confined to simply molded stucco and decorative brickwork, but at Mshatta the facade is enlivened by a richly carved stone frieze (FIG. **13-6**). The long band is more than 16 feet high and consists of a series of triangles framed by elaborately carved moldings. Each triangle contains a large rosette that

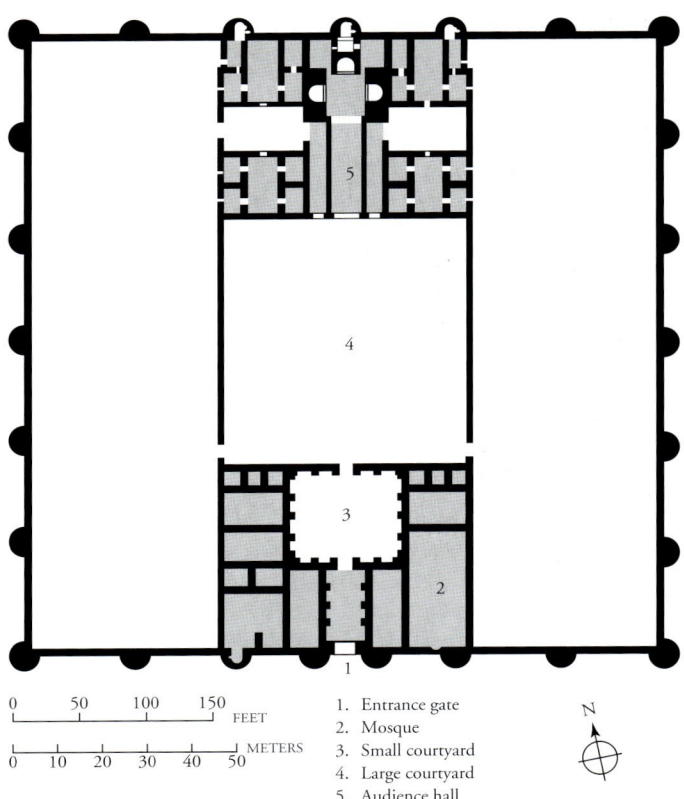

**13-5** Plan of the Umayyad palace, Mshatta, Jordan, ca. 740–750 (after Alberto Berengo Gardin).

projects from a field densely covered with curvilinear, vegetal designs. No two triangles were treated the same way, and animal figures appear in some of them. Similar compositions of birds, felines, and vegetal scrolls can be found in Roman, Byzantine, and Sasanian art. The Mshatta frieze, however, has no animal figures to the right of the entrance portal—that is, on the part of the facade corresponding to the mosque's qibla wall.

**THE ABBASID CITY OF PEACE** In 750, after years of civil war, the Abbasids, who claimed descent from Abbas, an uncle of Muhammad, overthrew the Umayyad caliphs. The new rulers moved the capital from Damascus to a site in Iraq near the old Sasanian capital of Ctesiphon (see FIG. 2-28). There the caliph al-Mansur (r. 754–775) established a new capital, Baghdad, which he called Madina al-salam, the City of Peace. The city was laid out in 762 at a time astrologers determined as favorable. It was round in plan, about a mile and a half in diameter. The shape signified that the new capital was the center of the universe. At the city's center was the caliph's palace, oriented to the four compass points.

For almost 300 years Baghdad was the hub of Arab power and of a brilliant Islamic culture. The Abbasid caliphs were renowned throughout the world and even established diplomatic relations with Charlemagne at Aachen in Germany. The Abbasids lavished their wealth on art, literature, and science and were responsible for the translation of numerous Greek texts that otherwise would

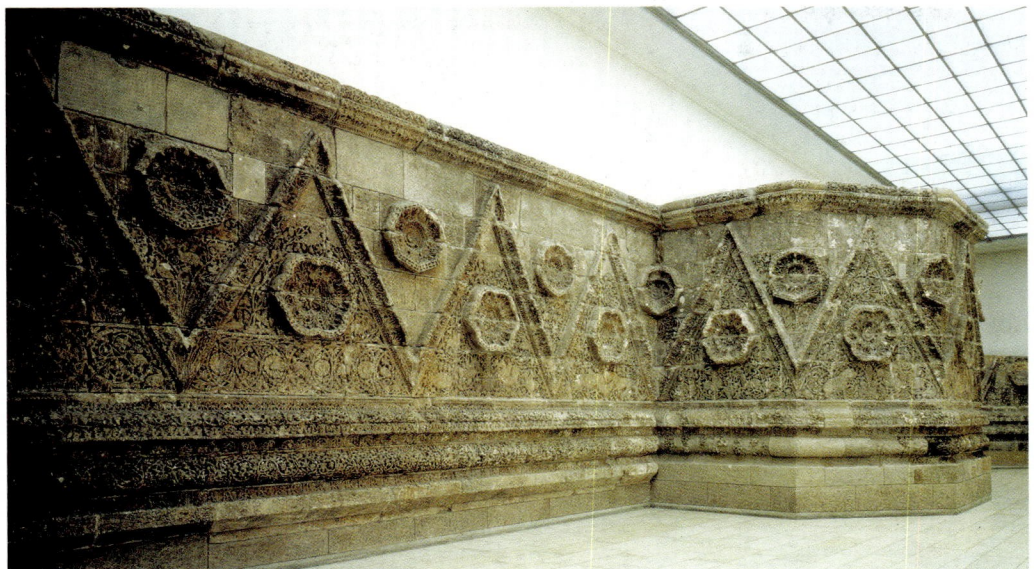

**13-6** Frieze of the Umayyad palace, Mshatta, Jordan, ca. 740–750. Limestone, 16′ 7″ high. Museum für Islamische Kunst, Staatliche Museen, Berlin.

have been lost. Many of these works were introduced to the medieval West through their Arabic versions.

**KAIROUAN'S HYPOSTYLE MOSQUE** Of all the variations in mosque plans, the hypostyle mosque most closely reflects the mosque's supposed origin, Muhammad's house in Medina (see "The Mosque," page 361). One of the finest hypostyle mosques, still in use today, is the mid-eighth-century Great Mosque at Kairouan (FIGS. **13-7** and **13-8**) in Abbasid Tunisia. It still houses its carved wooden minbar of 862, the oldest known. The precinct takes the form of a slightly askew parallelogram of huge scale, some 450 × 260 feet. Built of stone, its walls have sturdy buttresses, square in profile. A series of lateral entrances on the east and west lead to an arcaded forecourt (no. 7 on the plan), oriented north-south on axis with the mosque's impressive minaret

(no. 8) and the two domes (nos. 3 and 6) of the hypostyle prayer hall (no. 4). The first dome (no. 6) is over the entrance bay, the second (no. 3) over the bay that fronts the mihrab (no. 2) set into the qibla wall (no. 1). A raised nave connects the domed spaces and prolongs the north-south axis of the minaret and courtyard. Eight columned aisles flank the nave on either side, providing space for a large congregation.

**SAMARRA'S SPIRAL MINARET** The three-story minaret of the Kairouan mosque is square in plan and believed to be a near copy of a Roman lighthouse, but minarets can take a variety of forms. Perhaps the most striking and novel is that of the immense (more than 45,000 square yards) Great Mosque at Samarra, Iraq, the largest mosque in the world. The Abbasid caliph al-Mutawakkil (r. 847–861) erected it between 848 and

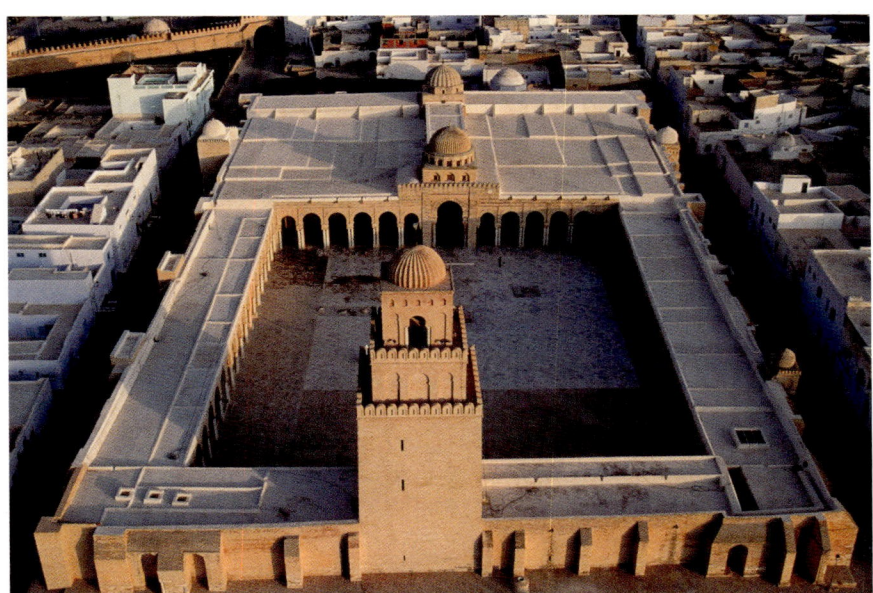

**13-7** Aerial view of the Great Mosque, Kairouan, Tunisia, ca. 836–875.

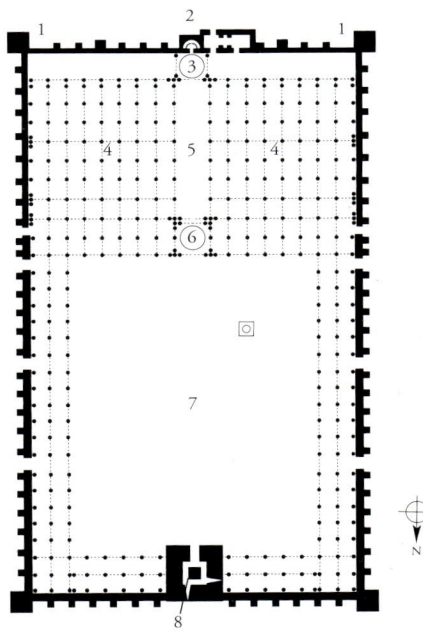

1. Qibla wall
2. Mihrab
3. Mihrab dome
4. Hypostyle prayer hall
5. Nave
6. Entrance dome
7. Forecourt
8. Minaret

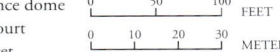

**13-8** Plan of the Great Mosque, Kairouan, Tunisia, ca. 836–875.

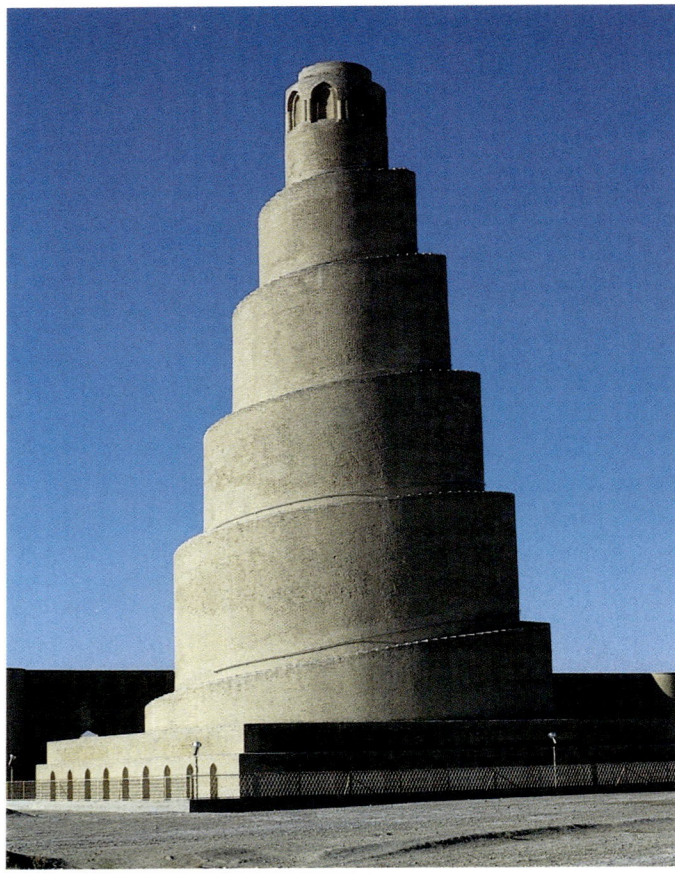

13-9 *Malwiya* minaret of the Great Mosque, Samarra, Iraq, 848–852.

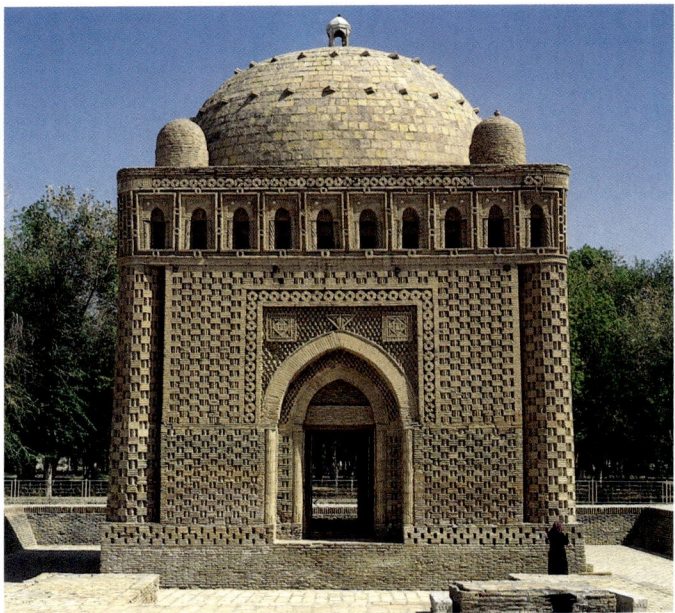

13-10 Mausoleum of the Samanids, Bukhara, Uzbekistan, early 10th century.

852. Known as the *Malwiya* ("snail shell" in Arabic) minaret (FIG. 13-9) and more than 165 feet tall (note how it dwarfs the modern fence), it now stands alone, but originally a bridge linked it to the mosque. The brick tower is distinguished by its stepped spiral ramp, which increases in slope from bottom to top. Many have compared its form to the ziggurats of ancient Mesopotamia (see FIGS. 2-2 and 2-14), but those rectilinear stepped platforms bear very little resemblance to the Samarran minaret. Nonetheless, the minaret inspired some later European depictions of the biblical Tower of Babel (Babylon's ziggurat; see "Babylon: City of Wonders," Chapter 2, page 49). Too tall to have been used to call Muslims to prayer, the *Malwiya* minaret, visible from a considerable distance in the flat plain around Samarra, was probably intended to announce the presence of Islam in the Tigris Valley.

**MEMORIALIZING THE DEAD** The eastern realms of the Abbasid empire were overseen by dynasties of governors who exercised considerable independence while recognizing the ultimate authority of the Baghdad caliphs. One of these dynasties, the Samanids (r. 819–1005), presided over the eastern frontier beyond the Oxus River (Transoxiana) on the border with India. In the early 10th century, they erected an impressive domed brick mausoleum (FIG. 13-10) at Bukhara in modern Uzbekistan. Monumental tombs were virtually unknown in the early Islamic period. Muhammad had been opposed to elaborate burials and instructed his followers to bury him in a simple unmarked grave. In time, however, the Prophet's resting place in Medina was enclosed by a wooden screen and covered by a dome. By the ninth century, Abbasid caliphs were laid to rest in dynastic mausoleums.

The Samanid mausoleum at Bukhara is one of the earliest preserved tombs in the Islamic world. It is constructed of baked bricks and takes the form of a cube with slightly sloping sides capped by a dome. With exceptional skill, the builders painstakingly shaped the bricks to create a vivid and varied surface pattern. Some of the bricks form engaged columns at the corners. A brick *blind arcade* (a series of arches in relief, with blocked openings) runs around all four sides. Inside, the walls are as elaborate as the exterior. The brick dome rests on arcuated brick squinches (see "Pendentives and Squinches," Chapter 12, page 331) framed by engaged colonnettes. The dome-on-cube form had a long and distinguished future in Islamic funerary architecture.

**UMAYYAD CÓRDOBA** At the opposite end of the Muslim world, Abd-al-Rahman I, the only Umayyad notable to escape the Abbasid massacre of his clan in Syria, fled to Spain in 750. There, the Arabs had overthrown the Christian kingdom of the Visigoths in 711. The Arab military governors of the peninsula accepted the fugitive as their overlord, and he founded the Spanish Umayyad dynasty, which lasted for almost three centuries. The capital of the Spanish Umayyads was Córdoba, which became the center of a brilliant culture rivaling that of the Abbasids at Baghdad and exerting major influence on the civilization of the Christian West.

The jewel of the capital at Córdoba was its Great Mosque, begun in 784 and enlarged several times during the 9th and 10th centuries. It eventually became one of the largest mosques in the Islamic West. The additions followed the original style and arrangement of columns and arches, and the builders maintained a striking stylistic unity for the entire building. The hypostyle prayer hall (FIG. 13-11) has 36 piers and 514 columns topped by a unique system of double-tiered arches that carried a wooden roof (now replaced by vaults). The two-story system was the builders' response to the need to raise the roof to an acceptable height using short columns that had been employed earlier in other structures. The lower arches are horseshoe-shaped, a form perhaps adapted from earlier Near Eastern architecture or of Visigothic origin (see FIG. 16-10). In the West, the horseshoe arch quickly became closely associated with Muslim architecture. Visually, these arches seem to

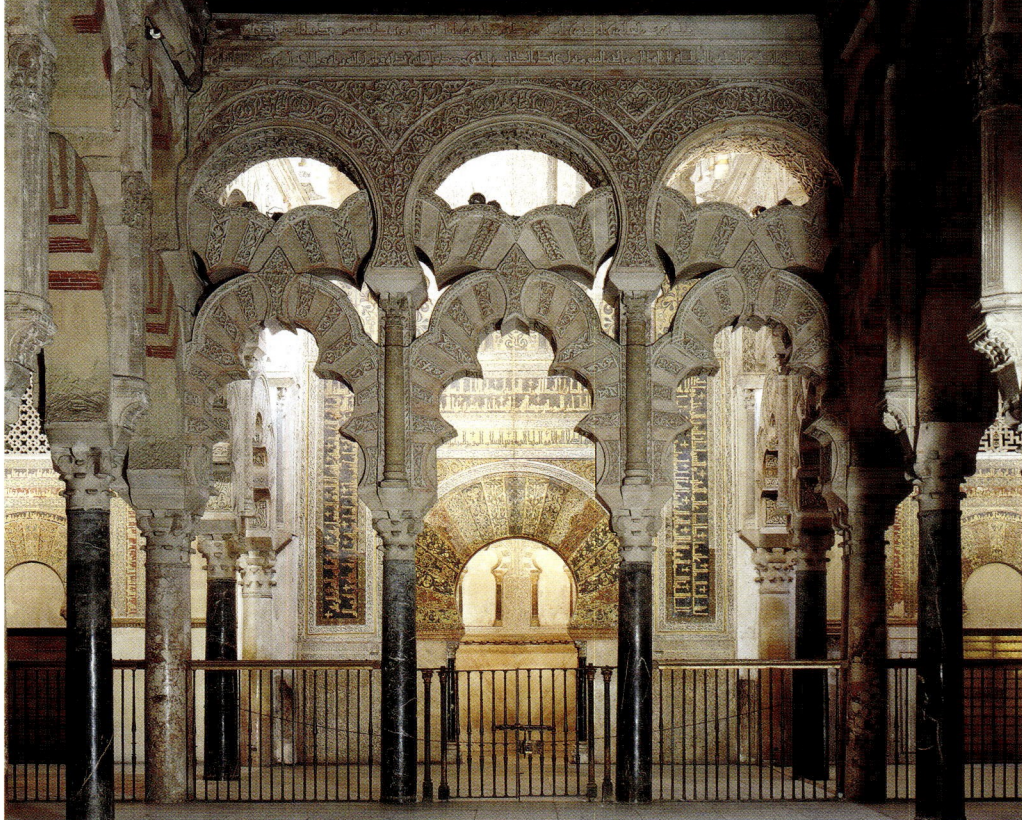

**13-11** Prayer hall of the Great Mosque, Córdoba, Spain, 8th to 10th centuries.

billow out like sails blown by the wind, and they contribute greatly to the light and airy effect of the Córdoba mosque's interior.

The caliph al-Hakam II (r. 961–976) undertook major renovations to the mosque. His builders expanded the prayer hall and added a series of domes. They also erected the elaborate maqsura (FIG. **13-12**), the area reserved for the caliph and connected to his palace by a corridor in the qibla wall. The Córdoba maqsura is a prime example of Islamic experimentation with highly decorative multilobed arches. The builders created rich and varied abstract patterns and further enhanced the magnificent effect of the complex arches by sheathing the walls with marbles and mosaics. The mosaicists and even the tesserae were brought to Spain from

**13-12** Maqsura of the Great Mosque, Córdoba, Spain, 961–965.

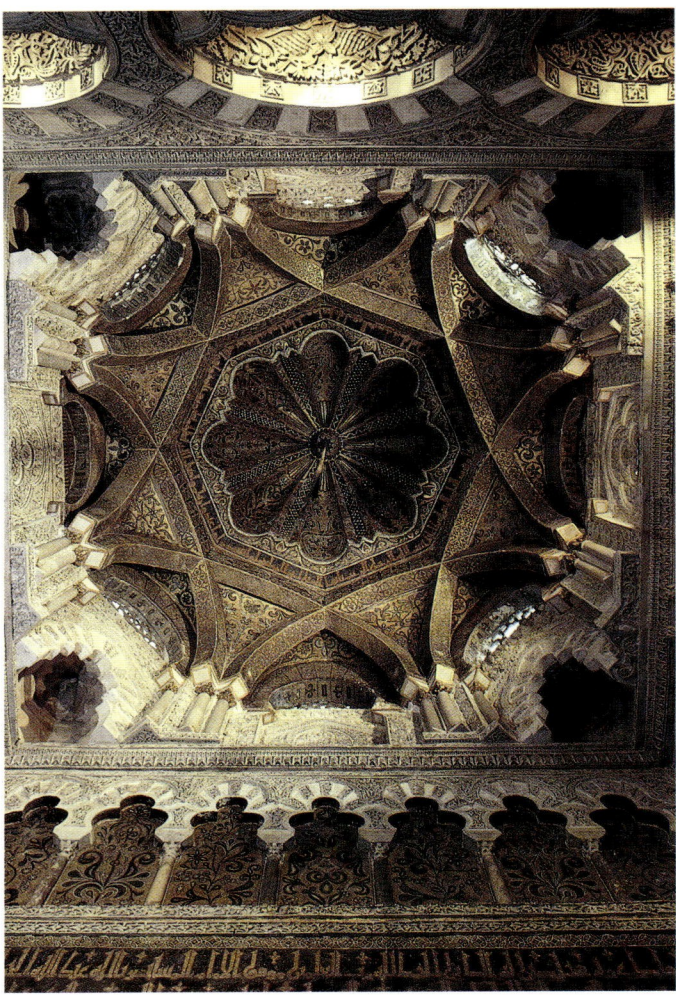

**13-13** Dome in front of the mihrab of the Great Mosque, Córdoba, Spain, 961–965.

Constantinople by al-Hakam II, who wished to emulate the great mosaic-clad monuments his Umayyad predecessors had erected in Jerusalem (FIG. 13-2) and Damascus (FIG. 13-4).

The same desire for decorative effect also inspired the design of the dome (FIG. **13-13**) that covers the area in front of the mihrab, one of the four domes built during the 10th century to emphasize the axis leading to the mihrab. The dome rests on an octagonal base of arcuated squinches and is crisscrossed by ribs that form an intricate pattern centered on two squares set at 45-degree angles to each other. The mosaics are the work of the same Byzantine artists responsible for the maqsura's decoration.

## Luxury Arts

**ARABESQUES** In the mosaics at Córdoba, as elsewhere in the Islamic world, most of the design elements are based on plant motifs, which are sometimes intermingled with abstract geometric shapes and, in secular settings, with animal figures. Often the natural forms are so stylized that they are lost in the purely decorative tracery of the tendrils, leaves, and stalks. These *arabesque*s—so called because they are one of the most distinctive features of Islamic ("Arab") art—form abstract patterns of extraordinary beauty and complexity, usually covering an entire surface, whether that of a small utensil or the wall of a building. This ornamental system offers a potential for unlimited growth, as it

permits extension of the designs in any desired direction. Most characteristic, perhaps, is the arabesque's independence of its carrier. Neither its size (within limits) nor its forms are dictated by anything but the design itself.

**ISLAMIC SILK** Both arabesques and figural patterns appear frequently on movable furnishings, such as rugs and hangings. Wood is scarce in most of the Islamic world, and the kind of furniture used in the West—beds, tables, and chairs—is rarely found in Muslim structures. Architectural spaces, therefore, are not defined by the type of furniture placed in them. A room's function (eating or sleeping, for example) can change simply by rearranging the carpets and cushions.

Silk textiles and wool carpets are among the glories of Islamic art. Unfortunately, because of their fragile nature and the heavy wear carpets endure, early Islamic textiles are rare today and often fragmentary. Silk thread was also very expensive. Silk is produced by silkworms, which can flourish only in certain temperate regions. Silk textiles were manufactured first in China in the third millennium BCE. They were shipped over what came to be called the Silk Road through Asia to the Middle East and Europe (see "Silk and the Silk Road," Chapter 7, page 201).

One of the earliest Islamic silks (FIG. **13-14**) is found today in Nancy, France. Unfortunately, it is fragmentary, and its colors, once rich blues, greens, and oranges, faded long ago. The silk survives because it was associated with the relics of Saint Amon housed in Toul Cathedral. The precious fabric may have been used to wrap the treasures when they were transported to France in 820. It probably dates to the eighth century and is said to come from Zandana near Bukhara. The design consists of repeated medallions with confronting lions flanking a palm tree. Other animals scamper across the silk between the roundels. Such zoomorphic

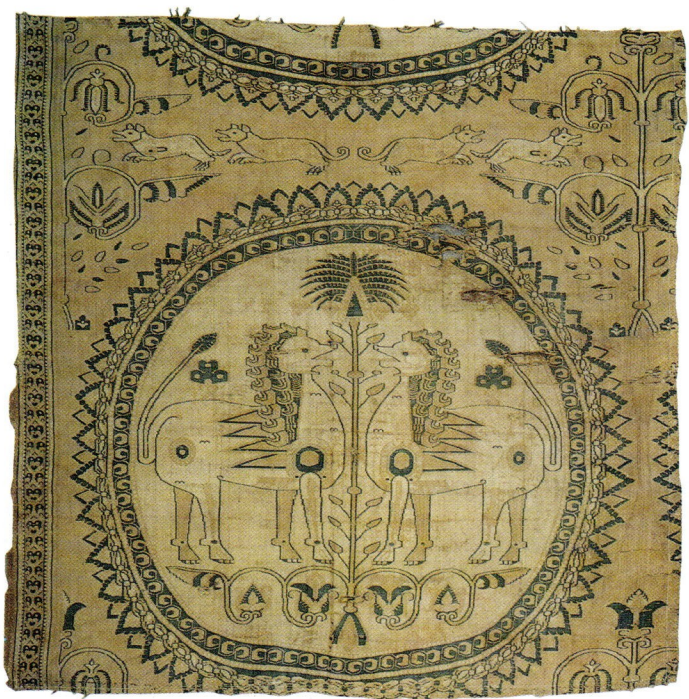

**13-14** Confronting lions and palm tree, fragment of a textile said to be from Zandana, near Bukhara, Uzbekistan, eighth century. Silk compound twill, 2′ 11″ × 2′ 9½″. Musée Historique de Lorraine, Nancy, France.

motifs are foreign to the decorative vocabulary of mosque architecture, but they could be found in Muslim households—even in Muhammad's in Medina. The Prophet, however, was said to have objected to curtains decorated with figures and permitted only cushions adorned with animals or birds.

**A SIGNED ZOOMORPHIC EWER** The furnishings of Islamic palaces and mosques reflected a love of sumptuous materials and rich decorative patterns. Metal, wood, glass, and ivory were artfully worked into a great variety of objects for the mosque or home. Colored glass was used with striking effect in mosque lamps. Ornate ceramics of high quality were produced in large numbers. Basins, ewers, jewel cases, writing boxes, and other decorative items were made of bronze or brass, engraved, and inlaid with silver.

One of the most striking examples of the metalworker's art is the cast brass ewer in the form of a bird (FIG. **13-15**) signed by SULAYMAN and dated 796. (The place of origin also was inscribed but is illegible today.) Some 15 inches tall, the ewer is nothing less than a freestanding statuette, although the holes between the eyes and beak function as a spout and betray its utilitarian purpose. The decoration on the body, which bears traces of silver and copper inlay, takes a variety of forms. In places, the etched lines seem

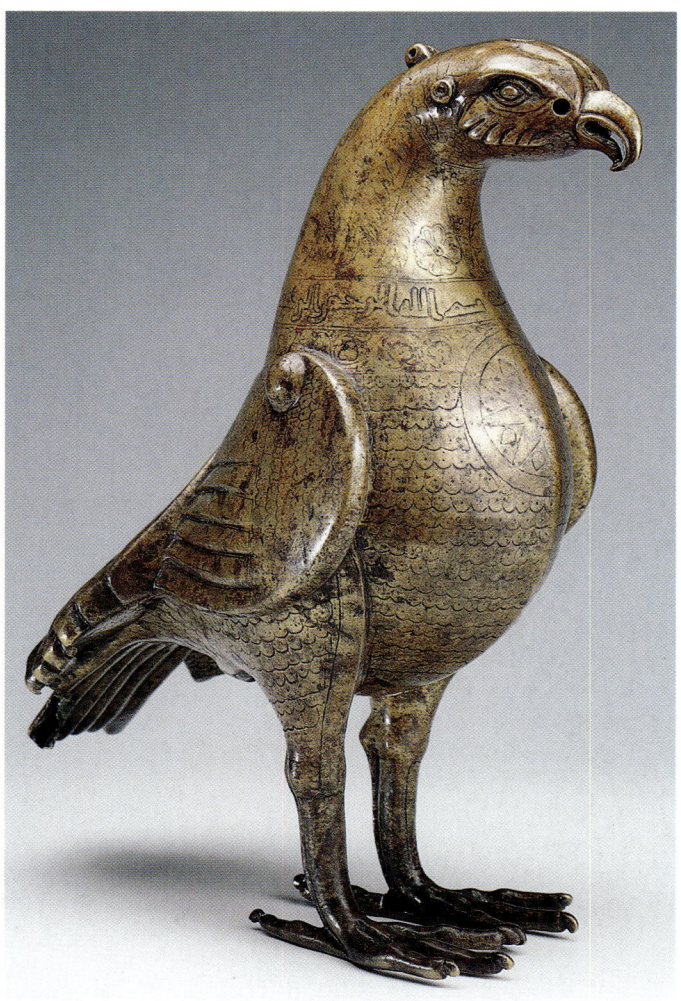

**13-15** SULAYMAN, *Ewer in the form of a bird*, 796. Brass with silver and copper inlay, 1′ 3″ high. Hermitage, Saint Petersburg.

to suggest natural feathers, but the rosettes on the neck, the large medallions on the breast, and the inscribed collar have no basis in anatomy. Similar motifs can be found in Islamic textiles, pottery, and architectural tiles. The ready adaptability of motifs to various scales and to various techniques again illustrates both the flexibility of Islamic design and its relative independence from its carrier.

**THE ART OF THE KORAN** In the Islamic world, the art of *calligraphy,* ornamental writing, was more revered even than the art of textiles. The faithful wanted to reproduce the Koran's sacred words in as beautiful a script as human hands could contrive. And these words were displayed not only on the fragile pages of books but also on the walls of buildings. Quotations from the Koran appear, for example, in a mosaic band above the outer ring of columns inside the Dome of the Rock (FIG. 13-2). The practice of calligraphy was itself a holy task and required long and arduous training. The scribe had to possess exceptional spiritual refinement. An ancient Arabic proverb proclaims, "Purity of writing is purity of soul." Only in China does calligraphy hold so supreme a position among the arts (see "Calligraphy and Inscriptions on Chinese Paintings," Chapter 26, page 766).

Arabic script predates Islam. It is written from right to left with certain characters connected by a baseline. Although the chief Islamic book, the sacred Koran, was codified in the mid-seventh century, the earliest preserved Korans are datable to the ninth century. Koran pages were either bound into books or stored as loose sheets in boxes. Most of the early examples are written in the script form called *Kufic,* after the city of Kufah, one of the renowned centers of Arabic calligraphy. Kufic script is quite angular, with the uprights forming almost right angles with the baseline. As with Hebrew and other Semitic languages, the usual practice was to write in consonants only. But to facilitate recitation of the Koran, scribes often indicated vowels by red or yellow symbols above or below the line.

All of these features can be seen on a 9th- or early 10th-century page (FIG. **13-16**) in Dublin that carries the heading and opening lines of surah 18 of the Koran. Five text lines in black ink with red vowels appear below a decorative band incorporating the chapter title in gold and ending in a palm-tree *finial* (a crowning ornament). This approach to page design has parallels at the extreme northwestern corner of the then-known world—in the early medieval manuscripts of the British Isles, where text and ornament are similarly united (see FIG. 16-8). But the stylized human and animal forms that populate those Christian books never appear in Korans.

# LATER ISLAMIC ART

## Architecture

**THE NASRIDS' RED FORTRESS** In the early years of the 11th century, the Umayyad caliphs' power in Spain unraveled, and their palaces fell prey to Berber soldiers from North Africa. The Berbers ruled southern Spain for several generations but could not resist the pressure of Christian forces from the north. Córdoba fell to the Christians in 1236. From then until the final Christian triumph in 1492, the Nasrids, an Arab dynasty that had established its capital at Granada in 1230, ruled the remaining Muslim territories in Spain.

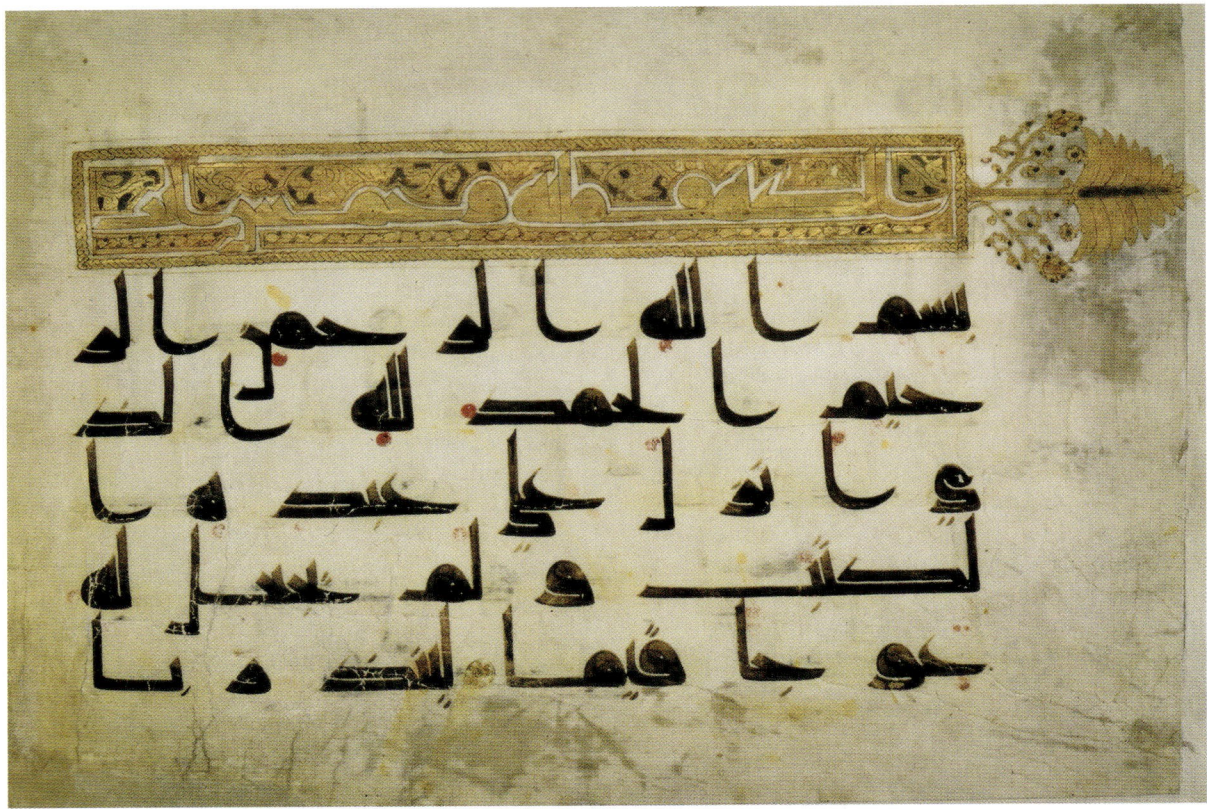

**13-16** Koran page with beginning of surah 18, *al-Kahf (The Cave),* 9th or early 10th century. Ink and gold on vellum, $7\frac{1}{4}'' \times 10\frac{1}{4}''$. Chester Beatty Library and Oriental Art Gallery, Dublin.

On a rocky spur at Granada, the Nasrids constructed a huge palace-fortress called the Alhambra ("the Red" in Arabic) because of the rose color of the stone used for its walls and 23 towers. By the end of the 14th century, the complex, a veritable city with a population of 40,000, included at least a half dozen royal residences. Only two of these fared well over the centuries. They present a vivid picture of court life in Islamic Spain before the Christian reconquest. Paradoxically, the two palaces owe their preservation to the Christian victors, who maintained a few of the buildings as trophies commemorating the expulsion of the Nasrids.

**PARADISE AND HEAVEN** One of those palaces is the Palace of the Lions, named for the courtyard fountain with marble lions carrying its water basin on their backs. It is an unusual instance of freestanding stone sculpture in the Islamic world. The palace was the residence of Muhammad V (r. 1354–1391), and its courtyards, lush gardens, and luxurious carpets and other furnishings were designed to conjure the image of Paradise. The complex is noteworthy also for its elaborate stucco ceilings and walls, which never fail to impress visitors.

We reproduce a view of the ceiling of the so-called Hall of the Two Sisters (FIG. **13-17**) in the Palace of the Lions. The dome of the square room rests on an octagonal drum supported by squinches and pierced by eight pairs of windows, but its structure is difficult to discern because of the intricate carved stucco decoration. The ceiling is covered with some 5,000 *muqarnas*—tier after tier of stalactite-like prismatic forms that seem aimed at denying the structure's solidity. The muqarnas ceiling was intended to catch and reflect sunlight as well as form beautiful abstract patterns. The lofty vault in this hall and others in the palace were meant to symbolize the dome of heaven. The flickering light

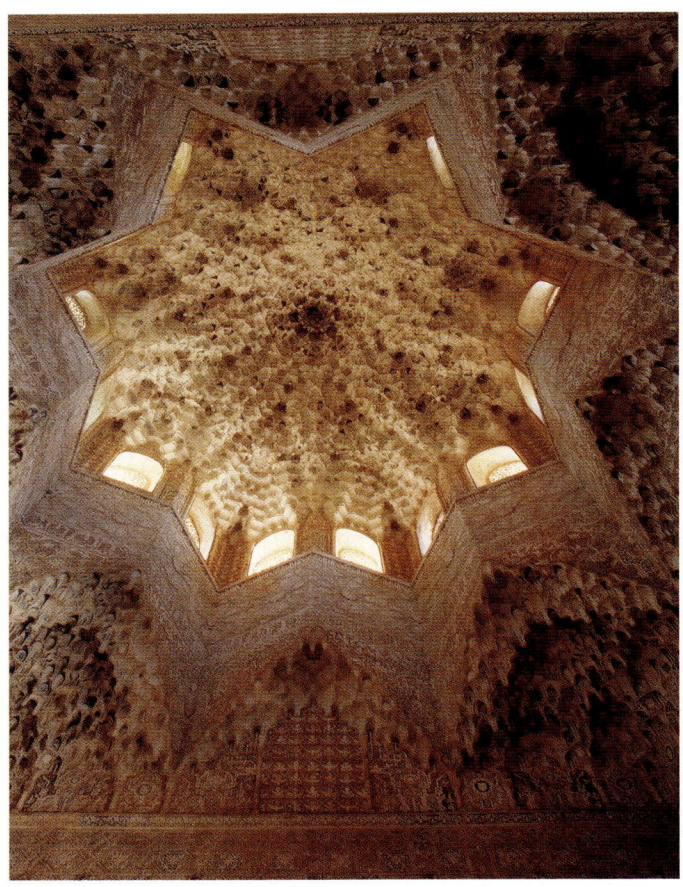

**13-17** Muqarnas dome, Hall of the Two Sisters, Alhambra palace, Granada, Spain, 1354–1391.

and shadows create the effect of a starry sky as the sun's rays move from window to window during the day. To underscore the symbolism, the palace walls were inscribed with verses by the court poet Ibn Zamrak, who compared the Alhambra's lacelike muqarnas ceilings to "the heavenly spheres whose orbits revolve."

**THE SLAVE SULTANS OF EGYPT** In the mid-13th century, the Mongols from east-central Asia (see Chapter 26) conquered much of the eastern Islamic world. The center of Islamic power moved from Baghdad to Egypt. The lords of Egypt at the time were former Turkish slaves (*mamluks* in Arabic) who converted to Islam. The capital of the Mamluk *sultans* (rulers) was Cairo, which became the largest Muslim city of the late Middle Ages. The Mamluks were prolific builders, and Sultan Hasan, although not an important figure in Islamic history, was the most ambitious of all. He ruled briefly as a child and was deposed, but regained the sultanate from 1354 until 1361, when he was assassinated.

**MADRASA AND MAUSOLEUM** Hasan's major building project in Cairo was a huge madrasa complex (FIGS. **13-18** and **13-19**) on a plot of land about 8,000 square yards in area. A *madrasa* ("place of study" in Arabic) is a theological college devoted to the teaching of Islamic law. Hasan's complex was so large that it housed not only four such colleges for the study of the four major schools of Islamic law but also a mosque, mausoleum, orphanage, and hospital, as well as shops and baths. Like all Islamic building complexes incorporating religious, educational, and charitable functions, this one was supported by an endowment funded by rental properties. The income from these paid the salaries of attendants and faculty, provided furnishings and supplies such as oil for the lamps or free food for the poor, and supported scholarships for needy students.

The grandiose structure has a large central courtyard with a monumental fountain in the center and four iwans (rectangular vaulted recesses) opening onto it, a design used earlier for Iranian mosques (FIG. 13-23). In each corner of the main courtyard (FIG. 13-19), between the iwans, is a madrasa with its own courtyard and four or five stories of rooms for the students. The largest iwan in the complex, on the southern side, served as a mosque. Contemporaries believed the soaring vault that covered this iwan was taller than the arch of the Sasanian palace at Ctesiphon (see FIG. 2-28), which was then one of the most admired engineering feats in the world. Behind the qibla wall stands the sultan's mausoleum, a gigantic version of the type of tomb the Samanids erected at Bukhara (FIG. 13-10). The siting of the dome-covered cube south of the mosque was carefully calculated. The prayers of the faithful facing Mecca, therefore, were directed toward Hasan's tomb. (Only the sultan's two sons are actually buried there. Hasan's body was not returned when he was killed.)

A muqarnas cornice crowns the exterior walls of the complex, and marble plaques of several colors cover the mihrab in the mosque and the walls of Hasan's mausoleum. But the complex as a whole is relatively austere, characterized by its massiveness and geometric clarity. It presents a striking contrast to the filigreed elegance of the contemporary Alhambra, and testifies to the diversity of regional styles within the Islamic world, especially after the end of the Umayyad and Abbasid dynasties.

**THE OTTOMANS COME TO POWER** During the course of the 9th to 11th centuries, the Turkic people, of central Asian origin, largely converted to Islam. They moved into Iran and the Near East in the 11th century, and by 1055 the Seljuk Turkish dynasty had built an extensive, although short-lived, empire that stretched from India to western Anatolia. By the end of the 12th

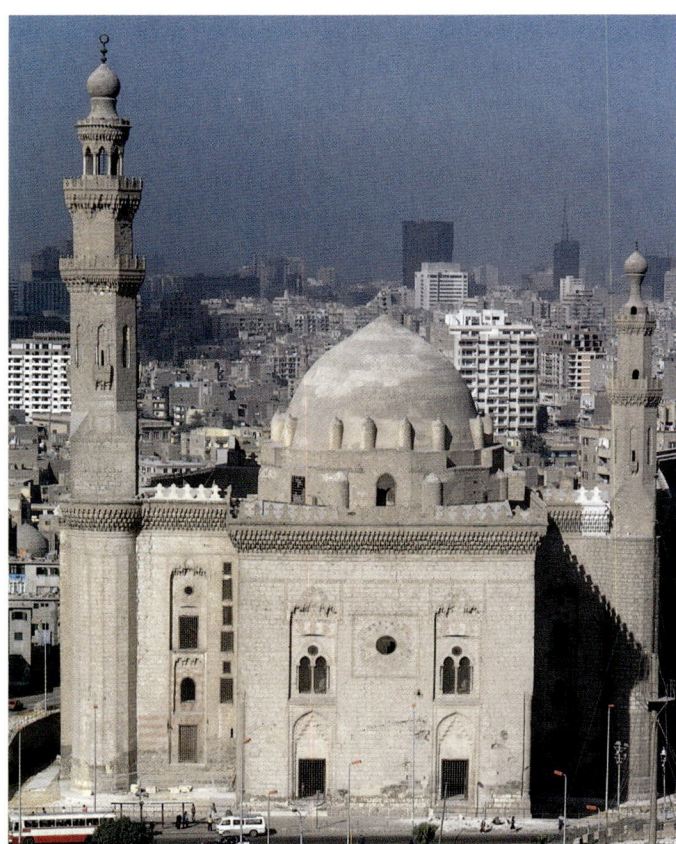

**13-18** Madrasa-mosque-mausoleum complex of Sultan Hasan (view from the south with the mausoleum in the foreground), Cairo, Egypt, begun 1356.

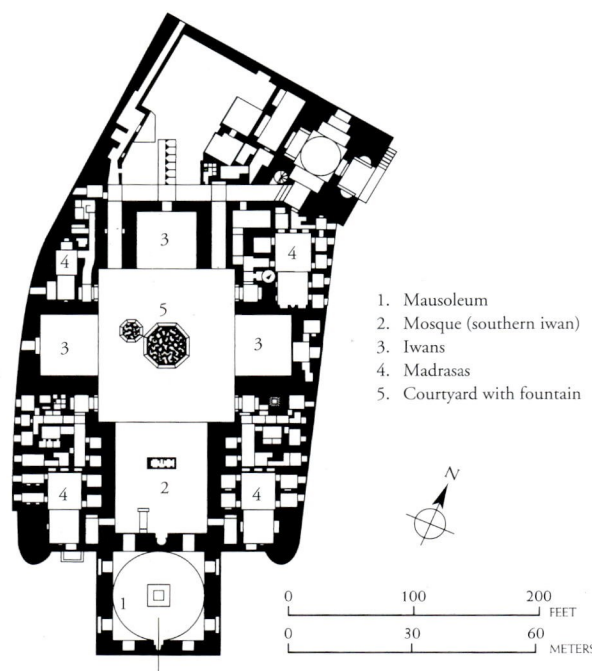

1. Mausoleum
2. Mosque (southern iwan)
3. Iwans
4. Madrasas
5. Courtyard with fountain

0    100    200 FEET
0    30    60 METERS

**13-19** Plan of the madrasa-mosque-mausoleum complex of Sultan Hasan, Cairo, Egypt, begun 1356.

century, this empire had broken up into regional states, and in the early 13th century it came under the sway of the Mongols, led by Genghis Khan (see Chapter 26). After the Seljuks fell, several local dynasties established themselves in Anatolia, among them the Ottomans, founded by Osman I (r. 1281–1326). Under Osman's successors, the Ottoman state expanded for a period of two and a half centuries throughout vast areas of Asia, Europe, and North Africa to become, by the middle of the 15th century, one of the great world powers.

The Ottoman emperors were lavish patrons of architecture. Ottoman builders developed a new type of mosque with a square prayer hall covered by a dome as its core. In fact, the dome-covered square, which had been a dominant form in Iran and was employed for the 10th-century mausoleum at Bukhara (FIG. 13-10), became the nucleus of all Ottoman architecture. The combination had an appealing geometric clarity. At first used singly, the domed units came to be used in multiples, a turning point in Ottoman architecture.

After the Ottoman Turks conquered Constantinople (Istanbul) in 1453, they firmly established their architectural code. The new lords of Constantinople were impressed by Hagia Sophia (see FIGS. 12-3 to 12-5), which, in some respects, conformed to their own ideals. They converted the Byzantine church into a mosque with minarets. But the longitudinal orientation of Hagia Sophia's interior never satisfied Ottoman builders, and Anatolian development moved instead toward the central-plan mosque.

**SINAN THE GREAT** The first examples of the central-plan mosque were built in the 1520s, eclipsed later only by the works of the most famous Ottoman architect, SINAN (ca. 1491–1588). A contemporary of the great Italian Renaissance sculptor, painter, and architect Michelangelo (see Chapter 22), and with equal aspirations to immortality, Sinan perfected the Ottoman architectural style. By his time, the basic domed unit was universally used. It could be multiplied, enlarged, or contracted as needed, and almost any number of units could be used together. Thus, the typical Ottoman building of Sinan's time was a creative assemblage of domical units and artfully juxtaposed geometric spaces. Builders usually erected domes with an extravagant margin of structural safety that has since served them well in earthquake-prone Istanbul and other Ottoman cities. (The sound construction of the Ottoman mosques was vividly demonstrated in August 1999 when a powerful earthquake centered 65 miles east of Istanbul toppled hundreds of modern buildings and killed thousands of people but caused no damage to the centuries-old mosques.) Working within this architectural tradition, Sinan searched for solutions to the problems of unifying the additive elements and of creating a monumental centralized space with harmonious proportions.

**THE CENTRAL PLAN AT EDIRNE** Sinan's efforts to overcome the limitations of a segmented interior found their ultimate expression in the Mosque of Selim II at Edirne (FIGS. **13-20** to **13-22**), which had been the capital of the Ottoman Empire from 1367 to 1472 and where Selim II (r. 1566–1574) maintained a palace. There, Sinan created a structure that made it possible to see the mihrab from almost any spot in the mosque. The massive dome, effectively set off by four slender pencil-shaped minarets (each more than 200 feet high, among the tallest ever constructed), dominates the city's skyline (FIG. 13-20). Various dependent structures were placed around the mosque. Most important Ottoman mosques had numerous annexes, including libraries and schools, hospices, baths, soup kitchens for the poor,

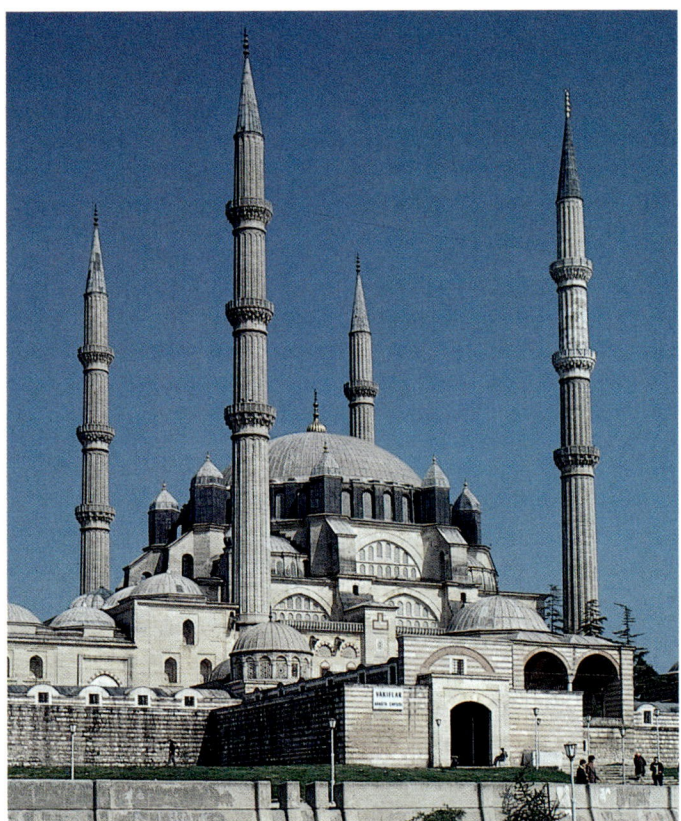

**13-20** SINAN, Mosque of Selim II, Edirne, Turkey, 1568–1575.

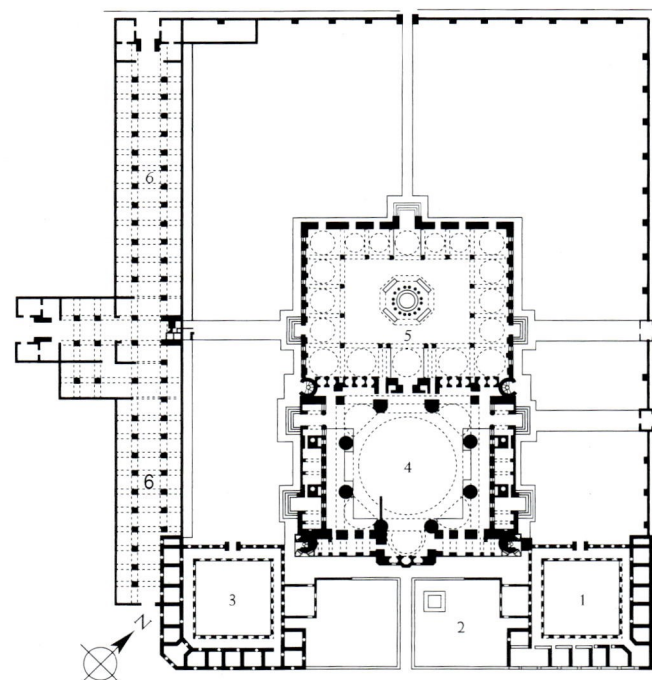

1. Madrasa
2. Cemetery
3. Darül-Kurra (house for the readers of the Quran)
4. Mosque
5. Avlu (courtyard forming summer extension of mosque)
6. Arasta (covered market)

```
0        250       500
|         |         | FEET
0     75      150
|     |       | METERS
```

**13-21** SINAN, plan of the Mosque of Selim II, Edirne, Turkey, 1568–1575.

### Sinan the Great, the Mosque of Selim II, and Hagia Sophia

Sinan (ca. 1491–1588), called Sinan the Great, was in fact the greatest Ottoman architect. Born a Christian, he was recruited for service in the Ottoman government, converted to Islam, and was trained in engineering and the art of building while in the Ottoman army. His talent was quickly recognized, and he was entrusted with increasing responsibility until, in 1538, he was appointed the chief court architect for Suleyman the Magnificent (r. 1520–1566), a generous patron of art and architecture. Hundreds of building projects, both sacred and secular, have been attributed to Sinan, although he could not have been involved with all that bear his name.

The capstone of Sinan's distinguished career was the Edirne mosque (FIGS. 13-20 to 13-22) of Suleyman's son, Selim II, which Sinan designed when he was almost 80 years old. There, he sought to surpass the greatest achievements of Byzantine architects just as Sultan Hasan's builders in Cairo attempted to rival and exceed the Sasanian architects of antiquity. Sa'i Mustafa Çelebi, Sinan's biographer, recorded the architect's accomplishment in his own words:

Sultan Selim Khan ordered the erection of a mosque in Edirne. . . . His humble servant [I, Sinan] prepared for him a drawing depicting, on a dominating site in the city, four minarets on the four corners of a dome. . . . Those who consider themselves architects among Christians say that in the realm of Islam no dome can equal that of the Hagia Sophia; they claim that no Muslim architect would be able to build such a large dome. In this mosque, with the help of God and the support of Sultan Selim Khan, I erected a dome six cubits higher and four cubits wider than the dome of the Hagia Sophia.[1]

The Edirne dome is, in fact, higher than Hagia Sophia's (see FIG. 12-5) when measured from its base, but its crown is not as far above the pavement as that of the dome of Justinian's church. Nonetheless, Sinan's feat was universally acclaimed as a triumph, and the Mosque of Selim II was considered proof that the Ottomans finally had outshone the Christian emperors of Byzantium in the realm of architecture.

[1] Aptullah Kuran, *Sinan: The Grand Old Master of Ottoman Architecture* (Washington, D.C.: Institute of Turkish Studies, 1987), 168–69.

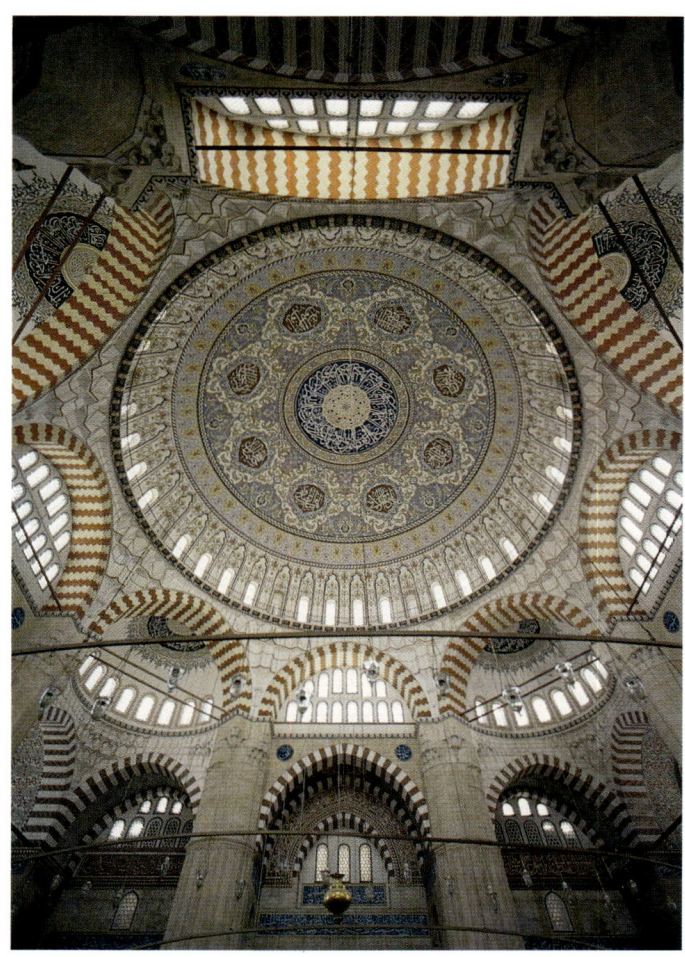

**13-22** SINAN, interior of the Mosque of Selim II, Edirne, Turkey, 1568–1575.

markets, and hospitals, as well as a cemetery containing the mausoleum of the sultan responsible for building the mosque (compare Hasan's complex in Cairo, FIG. 13-19). These utilitarian buildings were grouped around the mosque and axially aligned with it if possible. More generally, they were adjusted to their natural site and linked with the central building by planted shrubs and trees.

The Edirne mosque is preceded by a rectangular court covering an area equal to that of the building (FIG. 13-21). Porticos formed by domed squares surround the courtyard. Behind it, the building rises majestically to its climactic dome, whose height surpasses that of Hagia Sophia (see "Sinan the Great, the Mosque of Selim II, and Hagia Sophia," above). But it is the organization of this mosque's interior space (FIG. 13-22) that reveals the genius of its builder. The mihrab is recessed into an apselike alcove deep enough to permit window illumination from three sides, making the brilliantly colored tile panels of its lower walls sparkle as if with their own glowing light. The plan of the main hall is an ingenious fusion of an octagon with the dome-covered square (FIG. 13-21). The octagon, formed by the eight massive dome supports, is pierced by the four half-dome-covered corners of the square. The result is a fluid interpenetration of several geometric volumes that represents the culminating solution to Sinan's lifelong search for a monumental unified interior space. Sinan's forms are clear and legible, like mathematical equations. Height, width, and masses are related to one another in a simple but effective ratio of 1:2. The building is generally regarded as the climax of Ottoman architecture. Sinan proudly proclaimed it his masterpiece.

**ISFAHAN'S GREAT MOSQUE** The Mosque of Selim II at Edirne was erected during a single building campaign under the direction of a single master architect, but many other major

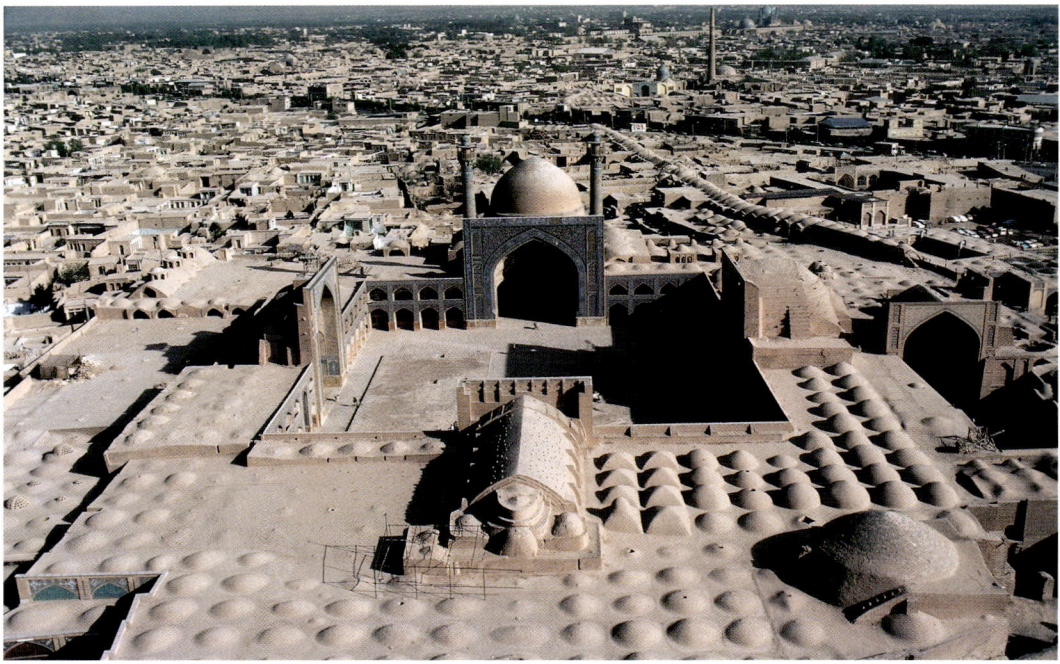

**13-23** Aerial view of the Great Mosque (looking southwest), Isfahan, Iran, 11th to 17th centuries.

Islamic architectural projects were built or remodeled over several centuries. A case in point is the Great Mosque at Isfahan (FIG. **13-23**) in Iran. The earliest mosque on the site, of the hypostyle type, was constructed in the eighth century during the caliphate of the Abbasids. But Sultan Malik Shah I (r. 1072–1092), whose capital was at Isfahan, transformed the structure in the 11th century. Later remodeling further altered the mosque's appearance. The present mosque, which retains its basic 11th-century plan, consists of a large courtyard bordered by a two-story arcade on each side. As in the 14th-century complex of Sultan Hasan in Cairo (FIG. 13-19), four iwans open onto the courtyard, one at the center of each side. The southwestern iwan leads into a dome-covered room in front of the mihrab. It func-

tioned as a maqsura reserved for the sultan and his attendants. It is uncertain whether this plan, with four iwans and a dome before the mihrab, was employed for the first time in the Great Mosque at Isfahan, but it became standard in Iranian mosque design. In four-iwan mosques the qibla iwan is always the largest. Its size (and the dome that often accompanied it) immediately indicated to worshipers the proper direction for prayer.

**IRANIAN TILEWORK** The iwans of the Isfahan mosque feature soaring pointed arches framing tile-sheathed muqarnas vaults. The muqarnas ceilings probably were installed in the 14th century, and the ceramic-tile revetment on the walls and vaults is the work of the 17th-century Safavid rulers of Iran. The use of glazed

**13-24** Winter prayer hall of the Shahi (Imam) Mosque, Isfahan, Iran, 1611–1638.

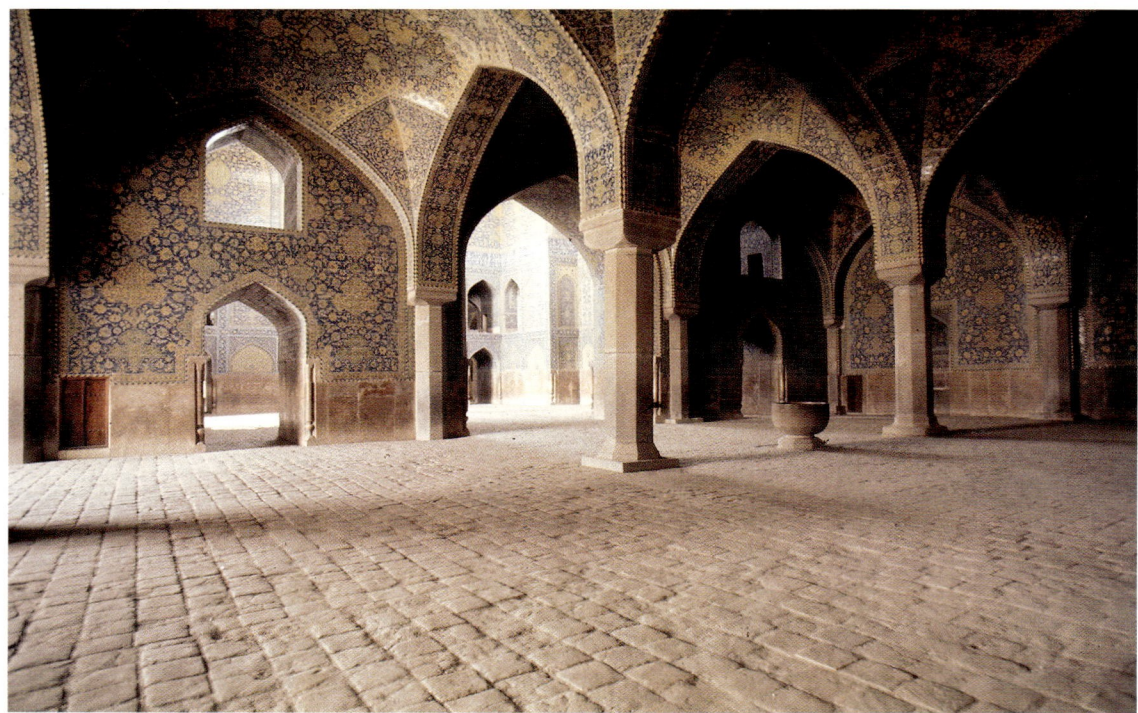

### Islamic Tilework

From the Dome of the Rock (FIGS. 13-1 and 13-2), the earliest major Islamic building, to the present day, mosaics or ceramic tiles have been used to decorate the walls and vaults of mosques, madrasas, palaces, and tombs. The golden age of Islamic tilework was the 16th and 17th centuries. At that time, Islamic artists used two basic techniques to enliven building interiors with brightly colored tiled walls and to sheathe their exteriors with gleaming tiles that reflected the sun's rays.

In *mosaic tilework* (for example, FIG. 13-25), large ceramic panels of single colors are fired in the potter's kiln and then cut into smaller pieces and set in plaster in a manner similar to the laying of mosaic tesserae of stone or glass (see "Mosaics," Chapter 11, page 315).

*Cuerda seca* (dry cord) tilework was introduced in Umayyad Spain during the 10th century—hence its Spanish name even in Middle Eastern and Central Asian contexts. Cuerda seca tiles (for example, FIG. 13-24) are polychrome and can more easily bear complex arabesque patterns as well as Arabic script. They are more economical to use because vast surfaces can be covered with large tiles much more quickly than they can with thousands of smaller mosaic tiles. But when such tiles are used to sheathe curved surfaces, the ceramists must fire the tiles in the exact shape required. Polychrome tiles have other drawbacks. Because all the glazes are fired at the same temperature, cuerda seca tiles are not as brilliant in color as mosaic tiles and do not reflect light the way the more irregular surfaces of tile mosaics do. The preparation of the multicolored tiles also requires greater care. To prevent the colors from running together during firing, the potters outline the motifs on cuerda seca tiles with greased cords containing manganese, which leaves a matte black line between the colors after firing.

tiles has a long history in the Middle East. Even in ancient Mesopotamia, gates and walls were sometimes covered with colorful baked bricks (see FIGS. 2-23 and 2-25). In the Islamic world, the art of ceramic tilework reached its peak in the 16th and 17th centuries in Iran and Turkey (see "Islamic Tilework," above). Employed as a veneer over a brick core, tiles could sheathe entire buildings, including domes and minarets.

The Shahi (or Royal) Mosque in Isfahan, recently renamed the Imam Mosque, which dates from the early 17th century, is widely recognized as one of the masterpieces of Islamic tilework. Its dome is a prime example of tile mosaic, and its winter prayer hall (FIG. 13-24) houses one of the finest ensembles of cuerda seca tiles in the world. Covering the walls, arches, and vaults of the prayer hall presented a special challenge to the Isfahan ceramists. They had to manufacture a wide variety of shapes with curved surfaces to sheathe the complex forms of the hall. The result was a technological triumph as well as a dazzling display of abstract ornament.

CERAMIC CALLIGRAPHY We noted earlier the Koran's central importance to the Islamic world and how its verses appeared in the mosaics of the earliest great Islamic building, the Dome of the Rock in Jerusalem (FIG. 13-2). Excerpts from the Koran appear on the walls of numerous other Islamic structures in a variety of media. Indeed, some of the masterworks of Arabic calligraphy are found not in manuscripts but on walls. A 14th-century mihrab (FIG. 13-25) from the Madrasa Imami in Isfahan exemplifies the perfect aesthetic union between the calligrapher's art and arabesque ornament. The pointed arch that immediately enframes the mihrab niche bears an inscription from the Koran in Kufic, the stately rectilinear script employed for the early Koran page illustrated (FIG. 13-16). Many supple cursive styles also make up the repertoire of Islamic calligraphy. One of these styles, known as *Muhaqqaq,* fills the mihrab's outer rectangular frame. The mosaic tile ornament on the curving surface of the niche and the area above the pointed arch are composed of tighter and looser networks of geometric and abstract floral motifs. The mosaic technique is masterful. Every piece

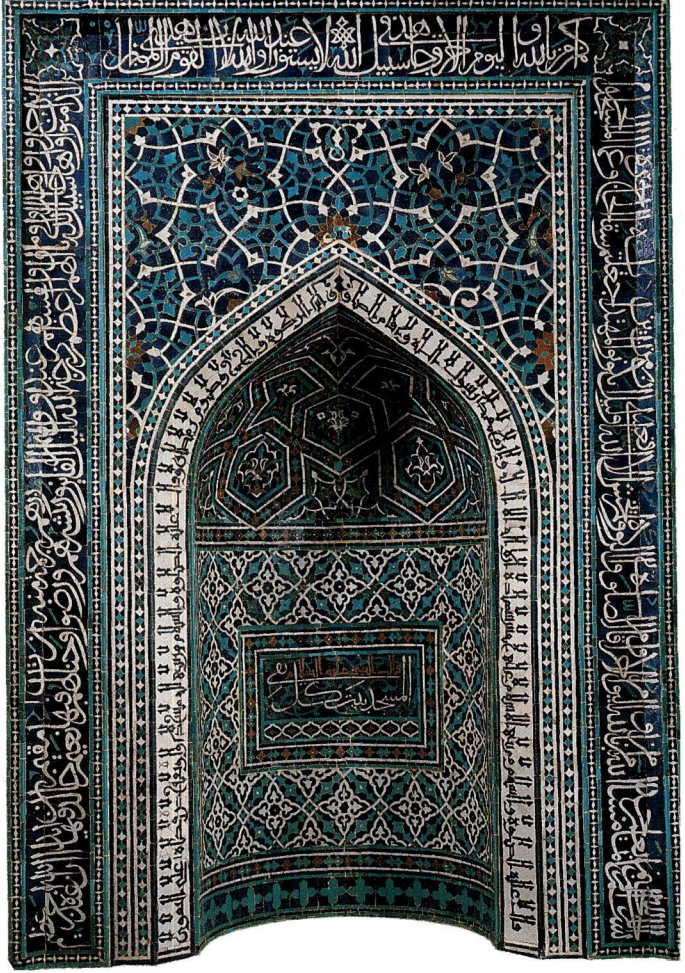

**13-25** Mihrab from the Madrasa Imami, Isfahan, Iran, ca. 1354. Glazed mosaic tilework, 11′ 3″ × 7′ 6″. Metropolitan Museum of Art, New York.

had to be chiseled and cut to fit its specific place in the mihrab—even the tile inscriptions. The framed inscription in the center of the niche—proclaiming that the mosque is the domicile of the pious believer—is smoothly integrated with the subtly varied patterns. The mihrab's outermost inscription—detailing the five pillars of Islamic faith—serves as a fringelike extension, as well as a boundary, for the entire design. The calligraphic and geometric elements are so completely unified that only the practiced eye can distinguish them. The artist transformed the architectural surface into a textile surface, the three-dimensional wall into a two-dimensional hanging, weaving the calligraphy into it as another cluster of motifs within the total pattern.

## Luxury Arts

The tile-covered mosques of Isfahan, Sultan Hasan's madrasa complex in Cairo, and the architecture of Sinan the Great in Edirne are enduring testaments to the brilliant artistic culture of the Safavid, Mamluk, and Ottoman rulers of the Muslim world. But these are just some of the most conspicuous public manifestations of the greatness of later Islamic art and architecture (see Chapter 25 for the achievements of the Muslim rulers of India). In the smaller-scale, and often private, realm of the luxury arts, Muslim artists also excelled. From the vast array of manuscript paintings, ceramics, textiles, and metalwork, five masterpieces may serve to suggest both the range and the quality of the inappropriately dubbed Islamic "minor arts" of the 13th to 16th centuries.

**MILLIONS OF KNOTS** The first of these artworks (FIG. **13-26**) is by far the largest, one of a pair of carpets from Ardabil in Iran. They come from the funerary mosque of Shaykh Safi al-Din (1252–1334), the founder of the Safavid line, but were made in 1540, two centuries after the erection of the mosque, during the reign of Shah Tahmasp (r. 1524–1576). Tahmasp elevated carpet weaving to a national industry and set up royal factories at Isfahan, Kashan, Kirman, and Tabriz. The name of MAQSUD OF KASHAN is woven into the design of the carpet we illustrate. He must have been the designer who supplied the master pattern to two teams of royal weavers (one for each of the two carpets). The carpet, almost 35 × 18 feet, consists of roughly 25 million knots, some 340 to the square inch. (Its twin has even more knots.)

The design consists of a central sunburst medallion, representing the inside of a dome, surrounded by 16 pendants. Mosque lamps (appropriate motifs for the Ardabil funerary mosque) are suspended from two pendants on the long axis of the carpet. The lamps are of different sizes, and some scholars have suggested that this is an optical device to make the two appear equal in size when viewed from the end of the carpet at the room's threshold (the bottom end in our illustration). The rich blue background is covered with leaves and flowers attached to delicate stems that spread over the whole field. The entire composition presents the illusion of a heavenly dome with lamps reflected in a pool of water full of floating lotus blossoms. No human or animal figures appear, as befits a carpet intended for a mosque, although they can be found on other Islamic textiles used in secular contexts, both earlier (FIG. 13-14) and later.

**THE BOOK OF KINGS** Shah Tahmasp was also a great patron of books. Around 1525 he commissioned an ambitious decade-long project to produce an illustrated 742-page copy of the *Shahnama (Book of Kings)*. The *Shahnama* is the Persian national epic poem by Firdawsi (940–1025). It recounts the history of Iran from the Creation until the Muslim conquest. Tahmasp's *Shahnama*

contains 258 illustrations by many artists, including some of the most renowned painters of the day. It was eventually presented as a gift to Selim II, the Ottoman sultan who was the patron of Sinan's mosque at Edirne (FIGS. 13-20 to 13-22). The manuscript later entered a private collection in the West and ultimately was auctioned off as a series of individual pages, destroying its integrity—an unfortunate consequence of the esteem in which Islamic art is held throughout the world.

The page we reproduce (FIG. 13-27) is the work of SULTAN-MUHAMMAD and depicts Gayumars, the legendary first king of Iran, and his court. Gayumars was said to have ruled from a mountaintop when humans first learned to cook food and clothe themselves in leopard skins. In Sultan-Muhammad's representation of the story, Gayumars presides over his court (all the figures

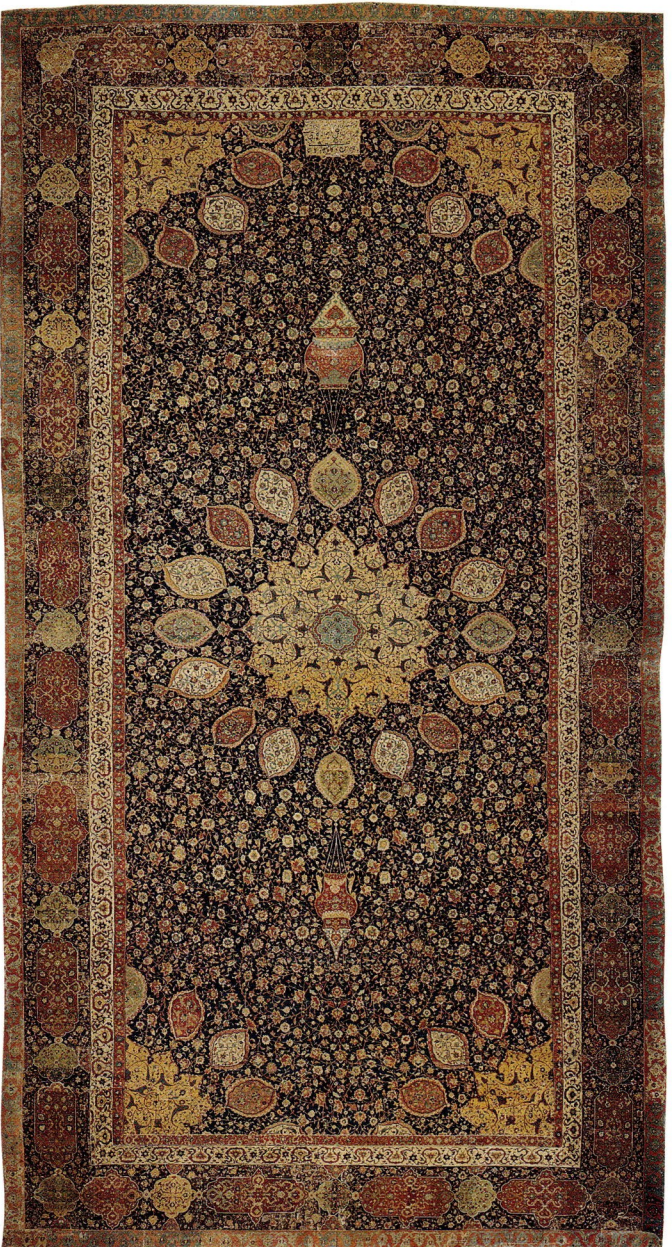

**13-26** MAQSUD OF KASHAN, carpet from the funerary mosque of Shaykh Safi al-Din, Ardabil, Iran, 1540. Knotted pile of wool and silk, 34′ 6″ × 17′ 7″. Victoria and Albert Museum, London.

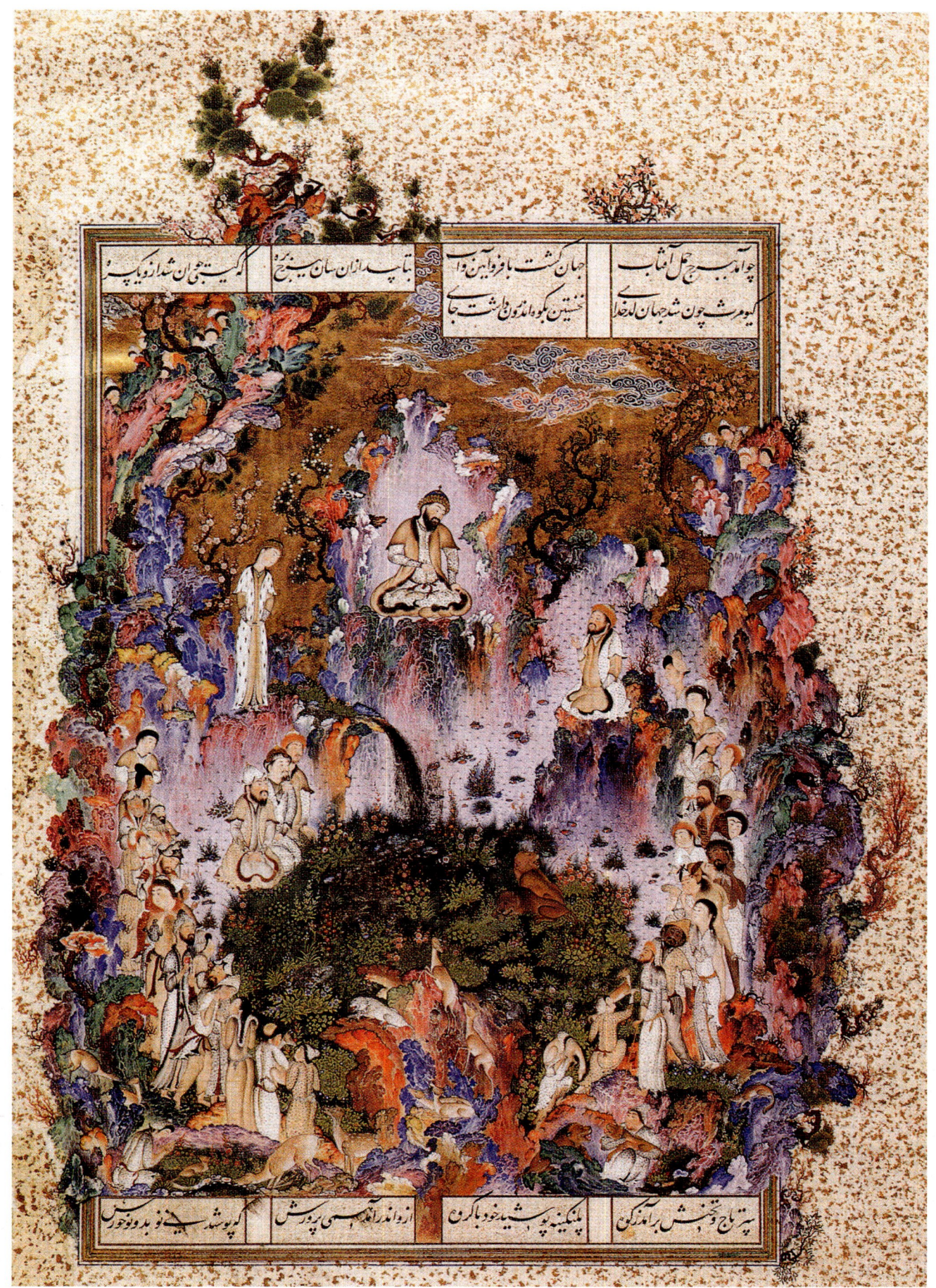

**13-27** SULTAN-MUHAMMAD, *the court of Gayumars*, detail of folio 20 verso of the *Shahnama* of Shah Tahmasp, from Tabriz, Iran, ca. 1525–1535. Ink, watercolor, and gold on paper, full page approx. 1′ 1″ × 9″. Prince Sadruddin Aga Khan Collection, Geneva.

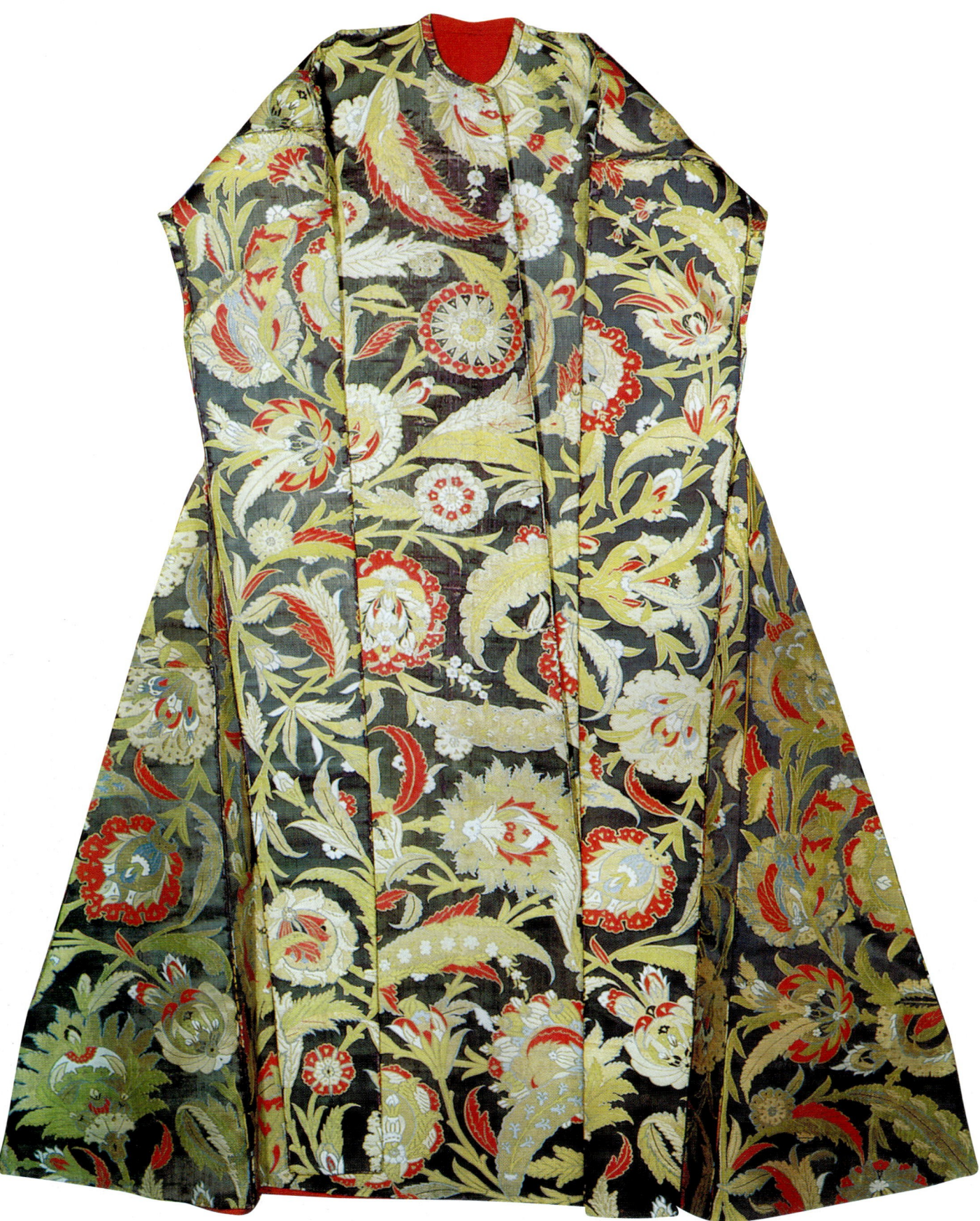

**13-28** Ottoman royal ceremonial caftan, from Istanbul, Turkey, ca. 1550. Polychrome silk and gilt-metal thread, 4′ 9″ high. Topkapi Palace Museum, Istanbul.

wear leopard skins) from his mountain throne. The king is surrounded by light amid a golden sky. His son and grandson are perched on multicolored rocky outcroppings to the viewer's left and right, respectively. The court encircles the ruler and his heirs. Dozens of human faces are portrayed within the rocks themselves. Many species of animals populate the lush landscape. According to the *Shahnama,* wild beasts became instantly tame in the presence of Gayumars. Sultan-Muhammad rendered the figures, animals, trees, rocks, and sky with an extraordinarily delicate touch. The sense of lightness and airiness that permeates the painting is enhanced by its placement on the page—floating, off center, on a speckled background of gold leaf. The painter gave his royal patron a singular vision of Iran's fabled past.

**A ROYAL OTTOMAN CAFTAN** When Tahmasp's *Shahnama* was presented to Selim II, the Ottoman sultan would have received the precious gift with due pomp and circumstance, perhaps wearing a majestic ceremonial caftan like the one illustrated here (FIG. **13-28**). It was woven of silk thread around 1550, perhaps for Suleyman the Magnificent's son Bayezid. More than a thousand such caftans are preserved in the Ottoman Topkapi Palace, now a museum. But this caftan was one of the most difficult to create on a loom because of its large number of colors and because of the complexity of its floral designs. This kind of

distinctive Ottoman design of sinuous curved leaves and complex blossoms is known as *saz,* a Turkish term recalling an enchanted forest. The saz design is never repeated on this garment, a remarkable feat. The designer, nonetheless, made sure the pattern matched across the front opening. Court protocol dictated that Ottoman rulers stood absolutely motionless in the presence of visitors. This explains why the caftan has no fastenings to prevent it from opening. The wearer's arms protruded through slits at the shoulders. The sleeves are ankle length; they served only for decoration and were draped over the back. The rich saz arabesque of the Ottoman robe presents a telling contrast with the Byzantine sakkos of Photius (see FIG. 12-35), which is covered with Jewish and Christian narratives, saints, and Russian royalty, as well as a portrait of Photius himself.

**ISLAMIC ART FOR CHRISTIANS** Figures and animals do adorn a brass basin (FIG. **13-29**) from Egypt inlaid with gold and silver and signed—six times—by the Mamluk artist MUHAMMAD IBN AL-ZAYN. The basin, used for washing hands at official ceremonies, must have been fashioned for a specific Mamluk patron. Some scholars think a court official named Salar ordered the piece as a gift for his sultan, but no inscription identifies him. The central band depicts Mamluk hunters and Mongol enemies. Running animals fill the friezes above and below. Arabesques of

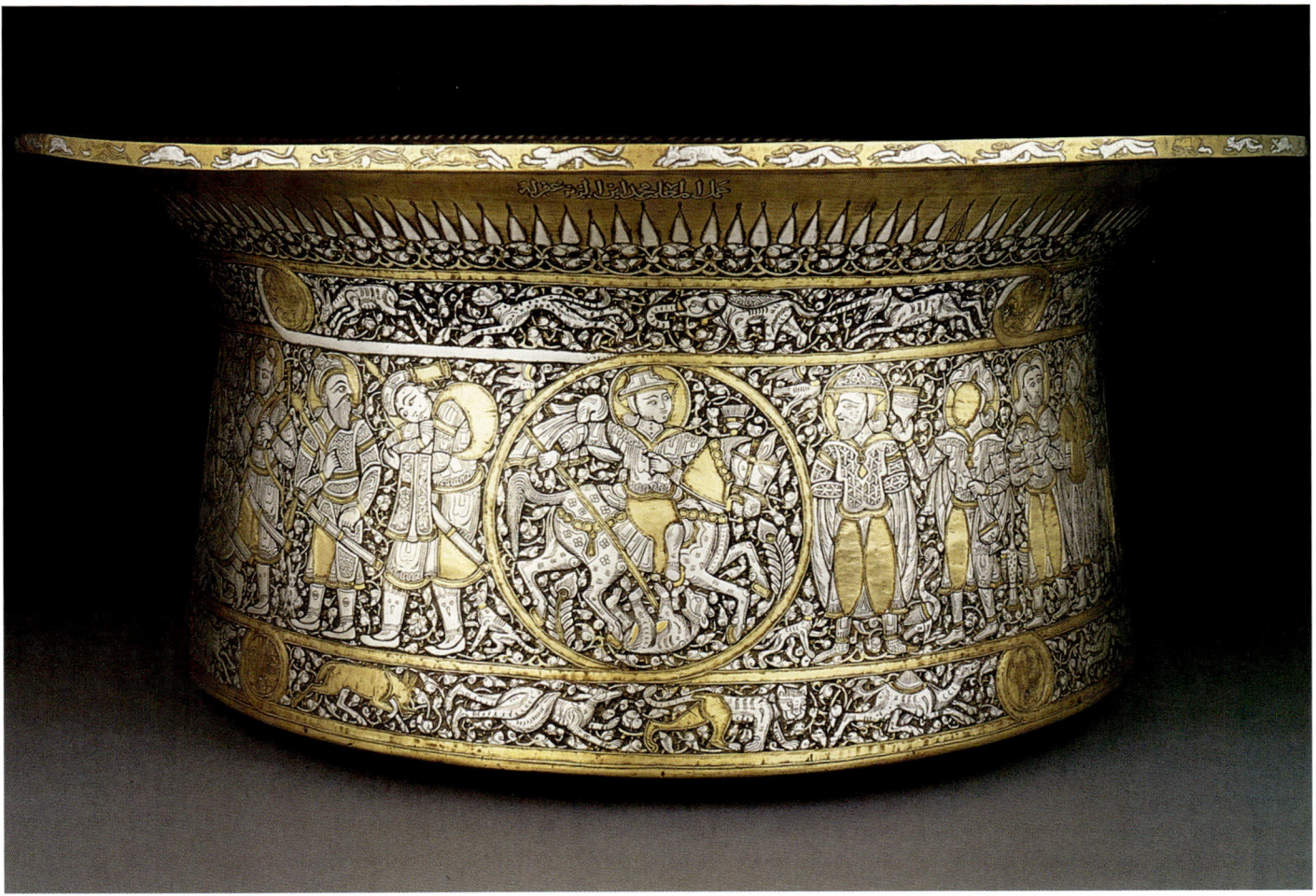

**13-29** MUHAMMAD IBN AL-ZAYN, basin *(Baptistère de Saint Louis),* from Egypt, ca. 1300. Brass, inlaid with gold and silver, $8\frac{3}{4}''$ high. Louvre, Paris.

### Christian Patronage of Islamic Art

During the 11th, 12th, and 13th centuries, large numbers of Christians traveled to Islamic lands, especially to the Christian holy sites in Jerusalem and Bethlehem, either as pilgrims (see "Pilgrimages," Chapter 17, page 449) or as Crusaders (see "The Crusades," Chapter 17, page 466). Many returned with mementos of their journey, usually in the form of inexpensive mass-produced souvenirs. But some wealthy individuals commissioned local Islamic artists to produce custom-made pieces using costly materials.

A unique brass canteen (FIG. 13-30) inlaid with silver and decorated with scenes of the life of Christ appears to be the work of a 13th-century Ayyubid metalsmith in the employ of a Christian patron. The canteen is a luxurious version of the "pilgrim flasks" Christian visitors to the Holy Land often brought back to Europe. Four inscriptions in Arabic promise eternal glory, secure life, perfect prosperity, and increasing good luck to the canteen's owner, who is unfortunately not named. That the owner was a Christian is suggested not only by the type of object but by the choice of scenes engraved into the canteen. The Madonna and Christ Child appear enthroned in the central medallion, and three panels depicting New Testament events (see "The Life of Jesus in Art," Chapter 11, pages 308–309) fill most of the band around the medallion. The narrative unfolds in a counterclockwise sequence (Arabic is read from right to left), beginning with the Nativity (at 2 o'clock) and continuing with the Presentation in the Temple (10 o'clock) and the Entry into Jerusalem (6 o'clock). The scenes may have been chosen because the patron had visited their locales (Bethlehem and Jerusalem). Most scholars believe that the artist used Syrian Christian manuscripts as the source for the canteen's Christian iconography. Many of the decorative details, however, are common in contemporary Islamic metalwork inscribed with the names of Muslim patrons. Whoever the owner was, the canteen testifies to the fruitful artistic interaction between Christians and Muslims in 13th-century Syria.

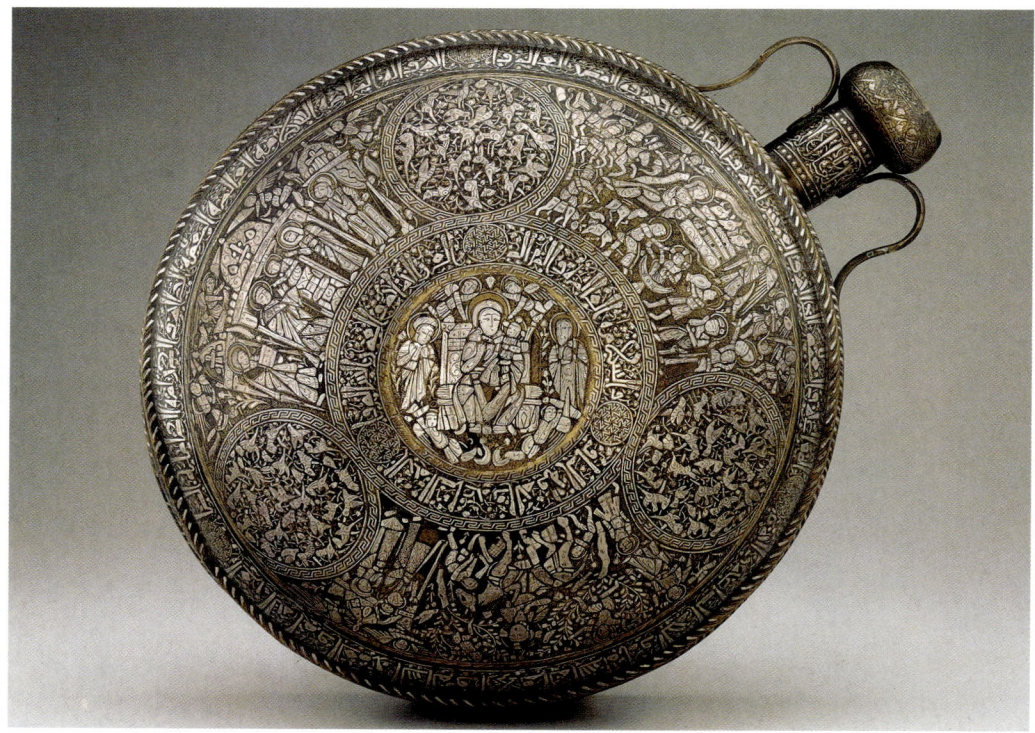

**13-30** Canteen with episodes from the life of Christ, from Syria, ca. 1240–1250. Brass, inlaid with silver, 1′ 2½″ diameter. Freer Gallery of Art, Washington, D.C.

inlaid silver fill the background of all the bands and roundels. Figures and animals also decorate the inside and underside of the basin.

The basin has long been known as the *Baptistère de Saint Louis,* but the association with the famous French king (see "Louis IX: The Saintly King," Chapter 18, page 498) is a myth, for he died before the piece was made. Nonetheless, the *Baptistère,* brought to France long ago, was used in the baptismal rites of newborns of the French royal family as early as the 17th century. Like the Zandana silk in Toul Cathedral (FIG. 13-14) and a canteen (FIG. **13-30**) with scenes of the life of Christ (see "Christian Patronage of Islamic Art," above), Muhammad ibn al-Zayn's basin testifies to the prestige of Islamic art in western Europe.

## CONCLUSION

The irresistible and far-ranging sweep of Islam from Arabia to India to North Africa and Spain brought a new and compelling tradition to the history of world art and architecture. Like Islam itself, Islamic art spread quickly. In the Middle East and North Africa, Islamic art largely replaced Late Antique art. And from a foothold in the Iberian peninsula, it made an impact on Western medieval art, although Islamic art stands in sharp contrast both to the figural art of Europe and the Mediterranean and to the Western architectural vocabulary. Islamic artists and architects also brought their distinctive style to South Asia, where a Muslim sultanate was established at Delhi in India in the early 13th century (see Chapter 25).

| | | | | | |
|---|---|---|---|---|---|
| SYRIA AND IRAQ | SPAIN | IRAN AND CENTRAL ASIA | EGYPT | TURKEY | INDIA |

Birth of Muhammad in Mecca, ca. 570

**600**

Muhammad's first revelation, 610

Muhammad's flight to Medina (Hijra), 622

Death of Muhammad in Medina, 632

Muslims capture Jerusalem, 638

Muslim conquest of Lower Egypt, 642

Umayyad Caliphate established, 661

**700**

Muslim armies enter Spain, 711

Charles Martel defeats Muslims at Poitiers, 732

Abbasid caliphate established, 750

Umayyad caliphate established in Spain, 756

Abbasids found Baghdad, 762

**800**

Samanid dynasty established in Transoxiana, 819

**900**

Fatimid dynasty established in Egypt, 909

Fatimids found Cairo, 969

**1000**

Fall of Umayyad caliphate in Spain, 1031

Seljuk dynasty established in Iran, 1038

First Crusade captures Jerusalem, 1099

**1100**

Saladin founds Ayyubid dynasty in Egypt, 1171

Saladin captures Jerusalem from Crusaders, 1187

**1200**

Sultanate of Delhi established, 1206

Nasrid dynasty established at Granada, 1230

Mamluk dynasty established in Egypt, 1250

Mongols sack Baghdad, 1258

Ottoman Empire founded, 1281

**1300**

**1400**

Ottomans capture Constantinople, 1453

Fall of Granada to the Christians, 1492

**1500**

Safavid dynasty established in Iran, 1501

Mughal dynasty established in India, 1526

Ottomans capture Baghdad, 1534

**1600**

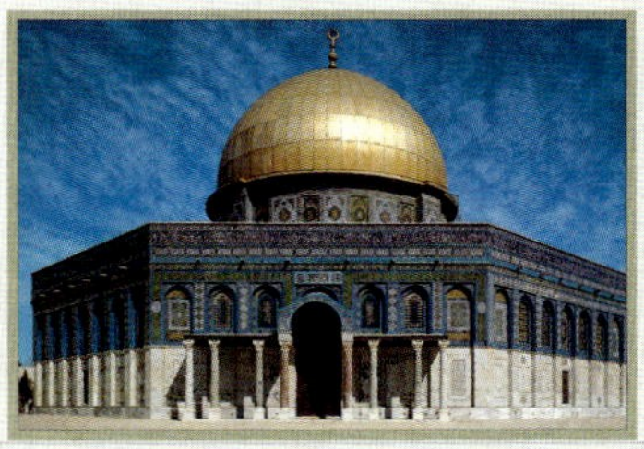

1 Dome of the Rock, Jerusalem, 687–692

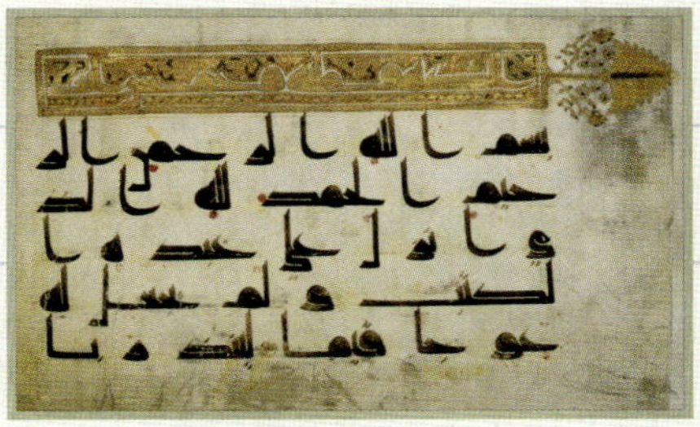

2 Koran page, Dublin, ca. 900

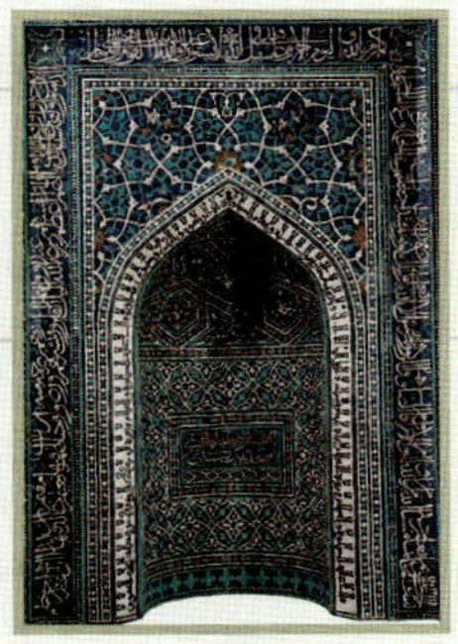

3 Great Mosque, Isfahan, begun late 11th century

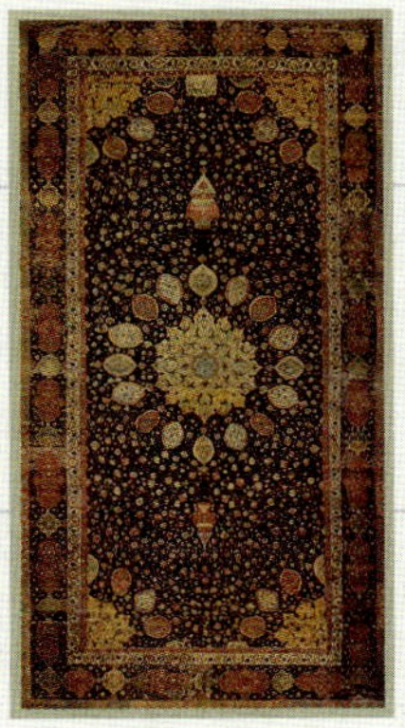

4 Maqsud of Kashan, Ardabil carpet, 1540

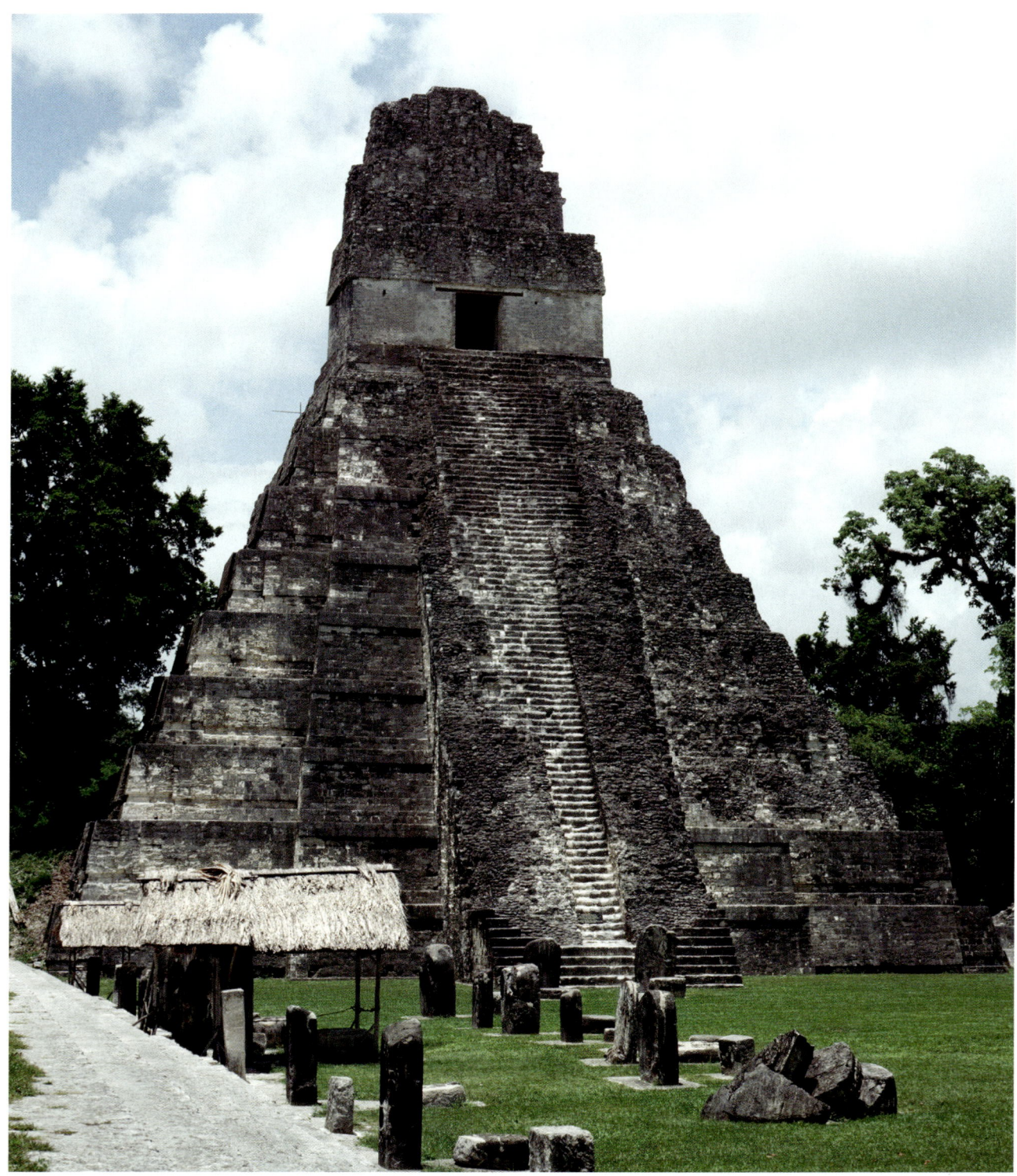

Temple I (Temple of the Giant Jaguar), Maya, Tikal, Petén, Guatemala, ca. 732 CE.

# 14

# FROM ALASKA
# TO THE ANDES

## NATIVE ARTS OF THE AMERICAS BEFORE 1300

The origins of the indigenous peoples of the Americas are still disputed. Sometime no later than 30,000 to 10,000 BCE these first Americans probably crossed the now submerged land bridge called Beringia, which connected the shores of the Bering Strait between Asia and North America (MAP **14-1**). Some scholars also have proposed that at least some migrants reached the Western Hemisphere via boats traveling along the Pacific coast of North America.

These Stone Age nomads were hunter-gatherers. They made tools only of bone, pressure-flaked stone, and wood. They had no knowledge of agriculture but possibly some of basketry. They could control fire and probably built simple shelters. For many centuries, they spread out until they occupied the two American continents. But they were always few in number. When the first Europeans arrived at the end of the 15th century (see Chapter 30), the total population of the Western Hemisphere may not have exceeded 40 million.

Between 8000 and 2000 BCE, a number of the migrants learned to fish, farm cotton, and domesticate such plants as squash and maize (corn). The nomads settled down in villages and learned to make clay pottery utensils and lively figurines. Metal technology, although extremely sophisticated when it existed, developed only in the Andean region of South America (eventually spreading north into modern-day Mexico) and generally met only the need for ornament, not for tools. With these skills as a base, many cultures rose and fell over long periods.

Several of the peoples of North, Central, and South America had already reached a high level of social complexity and technological achievement by the early centuries CE. Although most relied on stone tools, did not use the wheel (except for toys), and had no pack animals but the llama (in South America), the early Americans developed complex agricultural techniques and excelled in the engineering arts associated with the planning and construction of cities, civic and domestic buildings, roads and bridges, and irrigation and drainage systems. They carved monumental stone statues and reliefs, painted extensive murals, and mastered the arts of weaving, pottery, and metalwork. The Maya of Mesoamerica even had a highly developed writing system and knowledge of mathematical calculation that allowed them to keep precise

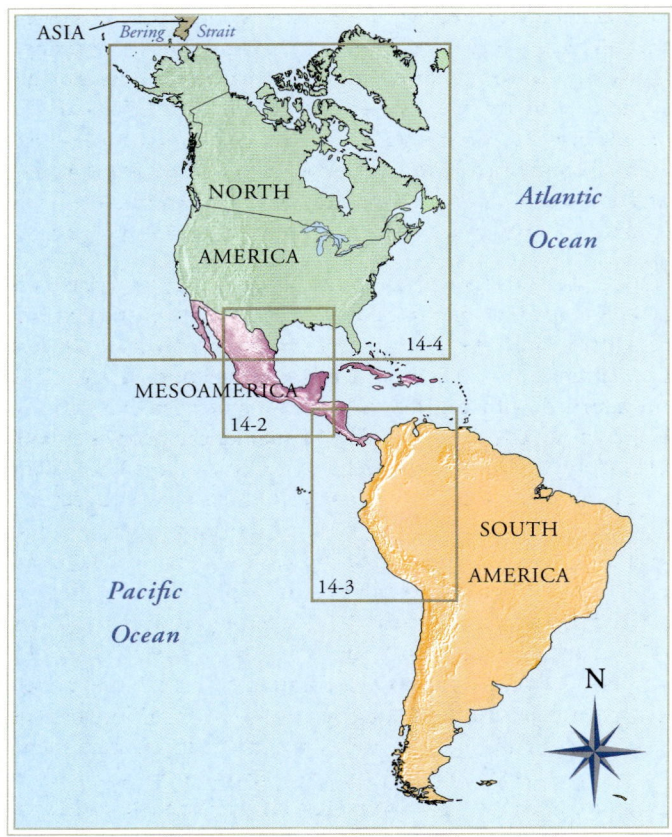

**MAP 14-1** The Americas.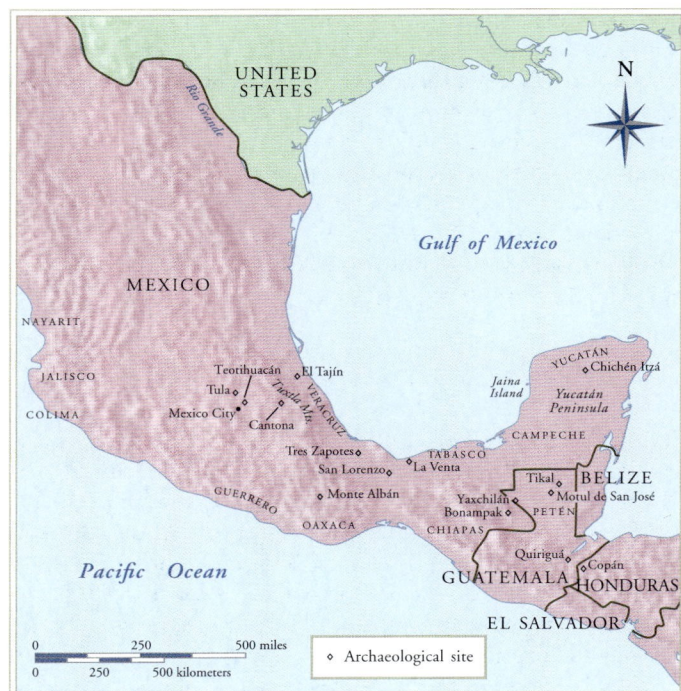

records and create a sophisticated calendar and a highly accurate astronomy.

**DESTRUCTION AND RECONSTRUCTION** These advanced civilizations abruptly collapsed, however, in the 16th century when Hernan Cortés, Francisco Pizarro, and their armies conquered the Aztec and Inka empires. Most of the once-glorious American cities were destroyed in the Spaniards' zeal to obliterate all traces of pagan beliefs. Other sites were abandoned to the forces of nature—erosion and the encroachment of tropical forests. But despite the ruined state of the pre-Hispanic cities today, archaeologists and art historians have been able to reconstruct much of the art and architectural history of ancient America. This chapter examines in turn the artistic achievements of the native peoples of Mesoamerica, South America, and North America before 1300. Chapter 30 treats the art and architecture of the Americas from 1300 to the present.

# MESOAMERICA

**GEOGRAPHY AND CLIMATE** The term *Mesoamerica* names the region that comprises part of present-day Mexico, Guatemala, Belize, Honduras, and the Pacific coast of El Salvador (MAP **14-2**). Mesoamerica was the homeland of several of the great civilizations that flourished before the arrival of Christopher Columbus and the subsequent European invasion. The principal regions of *pre-Columbian* Mesoamerica are the Gulf Coast region (Olmec culture); the states of Jalisco, Colima, and Nayarit, collectively known as West Mexico; Chiapas, Yucatán, Quintana Roo, and Campeche states in Mexico and the Petén area of Guatemala (Maya culture); southwestern Mexico and the state of Oaxaca (Zapotec and Mixtec cultures); and the central plateau surrounding

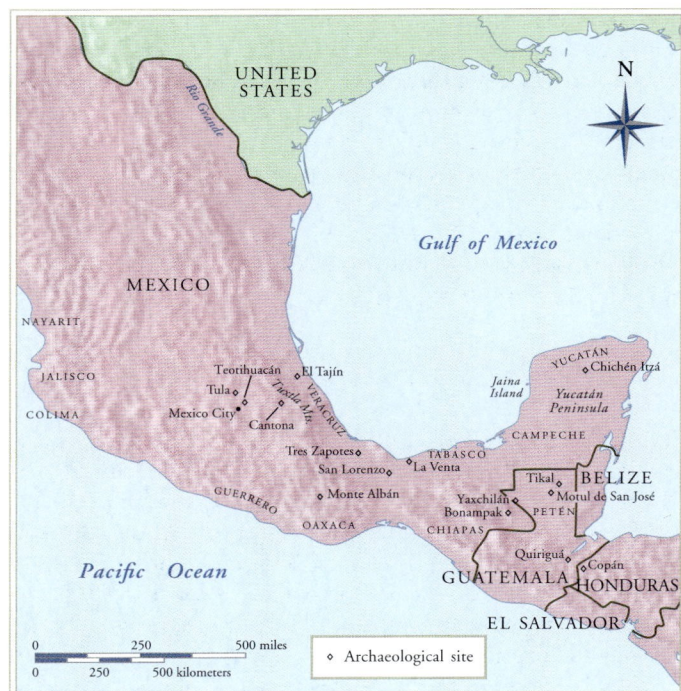

**MAP 14-2** Mesoamerica.

modern-day Mexico City (Teotihuacán, Toltec, and Aztec cultures). These cultures were often influential over extensive areas.

The Mexican highlands are a volcanic and seismic region. In highland Mexico, great reaches of arid plateau land, fertile for maize and other crops wherever water is available, lie between heavily forested mountain slopes, which at some places rise to a perpetual snow level. The moist tropical rain forests of the coastal plains yield rich crops, when the land can be cleared. In Yucatán, a subsoil of limestone furnishes abundant material for both building and carving. This limestone tableland merges with the vast Petén region of Guatemala, which separates Mexico from Honduras. Yucatán and the Petén, where dense rain forest alternates with broad stretches of grassland, host some of the most spectacular Maya ruins. The great mountain chains of Mexico and Guatemala extend into Honduras and slope sharply down to tropical coasts. Highlands and mountain valleys, with their chill and temperate climates, alternate dramatically with the humid climate of tropical rain forest and coastlines.

**LANGUAGE AND CHRONOLOGY** The variegated landscape of Mesoamerica may have much to do with the diversity of languages its native populations speak. Numerous languages are distributed among no fewer than 14 linguistic families. Many of the languages spoken in the preconquest periods survive to this day. Various Mayan languages linger in Guatemala and southern Mexico. The Náhuatl of the Aztecs endures in the Mexican highlands. The Zapotec and Mixtec languages persist in Oaxaca and its environs. Diverse as the languages of these peoples were, their cultures otherwise had much in common. The Mesoamerican peoples shared maize cultivation, religious beliefs and rites, myths, social structures, customs, and arts.

Archaeologists, with ever-increasing refinement of technique, have been uncovering, describing, and classifying Mesoamerican monuments for more than a century. Since the 1950s, when linguists made important breakthroughs in deciphering the Maya hieroglyphic script, evidence for a detailed account of Maya history and art has emerged. Many Maya rulers now can be listed by name and the dates of their reigns fixed with precision. Other writing systems, such as that of the Zapotec, who began to record dates at a very early time, are less well understood, but researchers are making rapid progress in their interpretation. The general Mesoamerican chronology is now well established and widely accepted. The standard chronology, divided into three epochs, involves some overlapping of subperiods—the Preclassic (Formative) extends from 2000 BCE to about 300 CE; the Classic period runs from about 300 to 900; and the Postclassic begins ca. 900 and ends with the Spanish conquest of 1521.

## Preclassic (ca. 2000 BCE–300 CE)

**THE OLMEC** The Olmec culture of the present-day states of Veracruz and Tabasco is often called the "mother culture" of Mesoamerica, because many distinctive Mesoamerican religious, social, and artistic traditions can be traced to it. Although little is known of Olmec origins, history, or language, the wide diffusion of Olmec institutional forms, monuments, arts, and artifacts reflects the culture's broad influence. Excavations in and around not only the principal Gulf Coast sites of Olmec culture—Tres Zapotes, San Lorenzo, and La Venta—but also in central Mexico and along the Pacific coast from the Mexican state of Guerrero to El Salvador indicate that Olmec influence was far more widespread than scholars once supposed.

Settling in the tropical lowlands of the Gulf of Mexico, the Olmec peoples cultivated a terrain of rain forest and alluvial lowland washed by numerous rivers flowing into the gulf. Here, between approximately 1500 and 400 BCE, social organization assumed the form that later Mesoamerican cultures adapted and developed. The mass of the population—food-producing farmers scattered in hinterland villages—provided the sustenance and labor that maintained a hereditary caste of rulers, hierarchies of priests, functionaries, and artisans. The nonfarming population presumably lived, arranged by rank, within precincts that served ceremonial, administrative, and residential functions, and perhaps also as marketplaces. At regular intervals, the whole community convened for ritual observances at the religious-civic centers of towns such as San Lorenzo and La Venta. These centers were the formative architectural expressions of the structure and ideals of Olmec society.

**COLOSSAL RULER PORTRAITS** At La Venta, low clay-and-earthen platforms and stone fences enclosed two great courtyards. At one end of the larger area was a mound almost 100 feet high. Although now very eroded, this early pyramid, built of earth and adorned with colored clays, may have been intended to mimic a mountain, held sacred by Mesoamerican peoples as both a life-giving source of water and a feared destructive force. (Volcanic eruptions and earthquakes still wreak havoc in this region.) The La Venta layout is an early form of the temple-pyramid and plaza complex aligned on a north-south axis that characterized later Mesoamerican ceremonial center design.

Four colossal basalt heads (FIG. **14-1**), weighing about 10 tons each and standing between 6 and 10 feet high, face out from the plaza. More than a dozen similar heads have been found at San Lorenzo and Tres Zapotes. Almost as much of an achievement as the carving of these huge stones with stone tools was their transportation across the 60 miles of swampland from the nearest known basalt source, the Tuxtla Mountains. Although the identities of the colossi are uncertain, their individualized features and distinctive headgear and ear ornaments, as well as the later Maya practice of carving monumental ruler portraits, suggest that the Olmec heads portray rulers rather than deities. The sheer size of the heads and their intensity of expression evoke great power, whether mortal or divine.

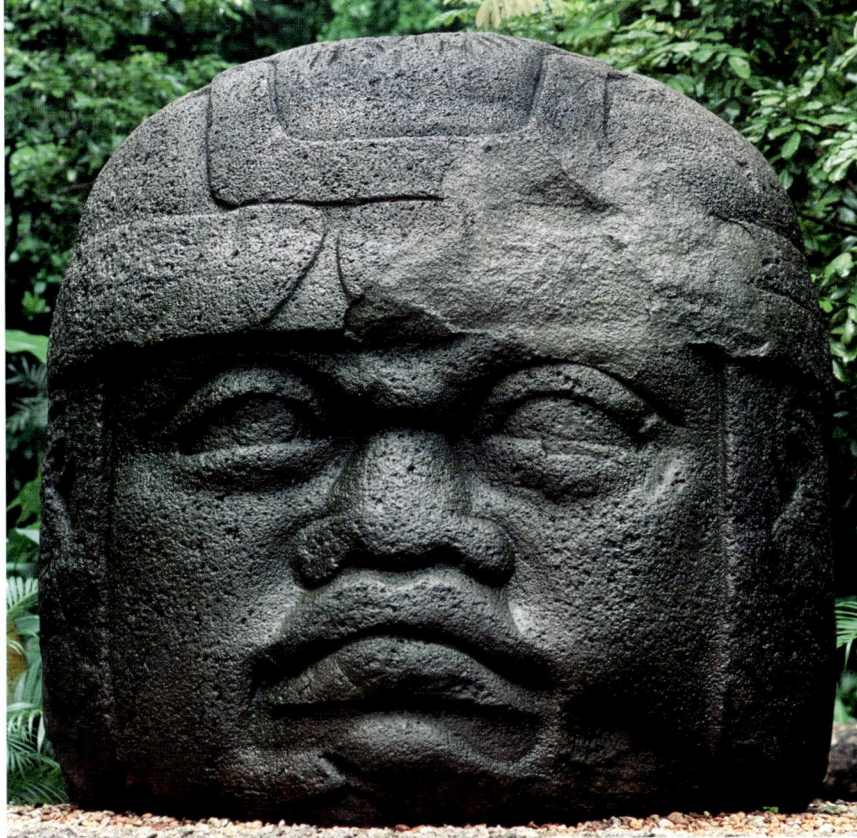

**14-1** Colossal head, Olmec, La Venta, Mexico, 900–400 BCE. Basalt, 9'4" high. Museo-Parque La Venta, Villahermosa.

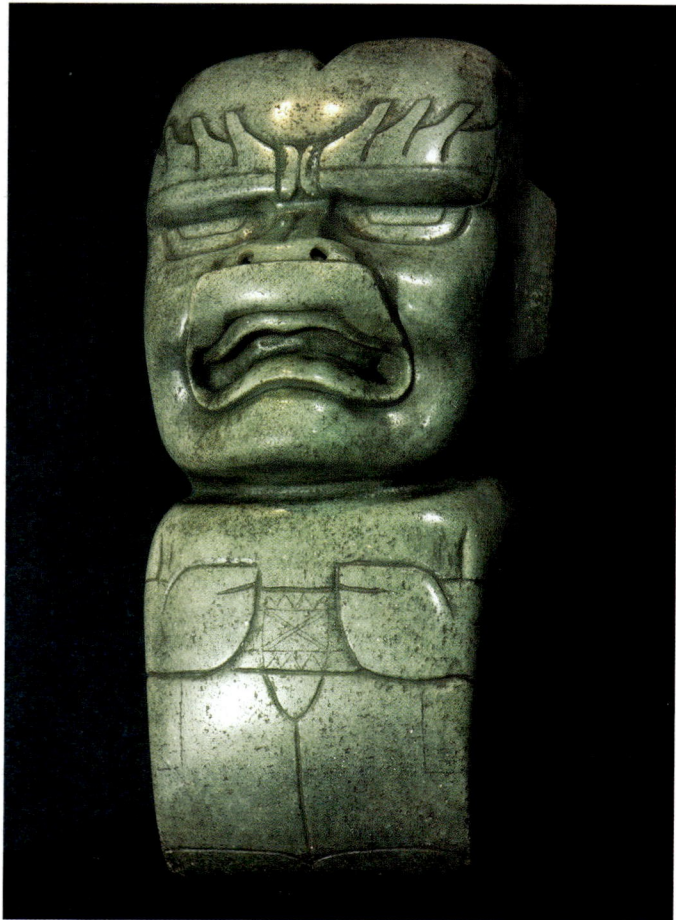

**14-2** Ceremonial ax in the form of a jaguar-human, Olmec, from La Venta, Mexico, 900–400 BCE. Jadeite, 11$\frac{1}{2}$" high. British Museum, London.

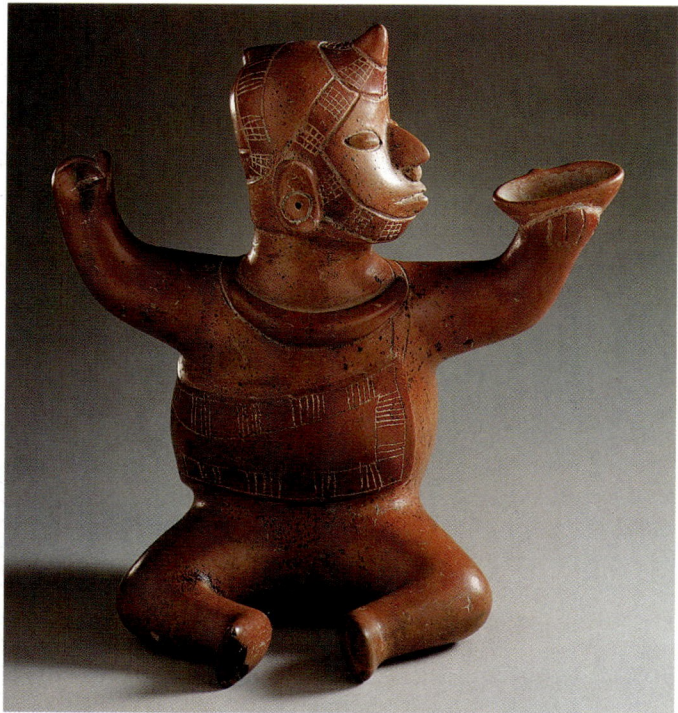

**14-3** *Drinker* (seated figure with raised arms), from Colima, Mexico, ca. 200 BCE – 500 CE. Clay with orange and red slip, 1′ 1″ high. Los Angeles County Museum of Art (The Proctor Stafford Collection, purchased with funds provided by Mr. and Mrs. Allan C. Balch).

**JADE CELTS** The Olmec also carved sculptures in jade, an extremely hard dark green stone they acquired from unknown sources far from their homeland. All Mesoamerican peoples prized jade, as did the ancient Chinese (see "Chinese Jade," Chapter 7, page 195). Sometimes the Olmec carved it into ax-shaped polished forms called *celts,* which they then buried as votive offerings under their ceremonial courtyards or platforms. The celt shape could be modified into a figural form, combining relief carving with incising. Stone-tipped drills and abrasive materials, such as sand, were used to carve jade. Subjects represented include crying babies (of unknown significance) and figures combining human and animal features and postures (FIG. **14-2**). Although Olmec religious beliefs and practices are little known, such human-animal representations may refer to the belief that religious practitioners underwent dangerous transformations to wrest power from supernatural forces and harness it for the good of the community.

**WEST MEXICAN SCULPTURE** Far to the west of the tropical heartland of the Olmec are the Preclassic sites along Mexico's Pacific coast. The ancient peoples of the modern West Mexican states of Nayarit, Jalisco, and Colima were long thought to have existed at Mesoamerica's geographic and cultural fringes. Recent archaeological discoveries, however, have revealed that although the West Mexicans did not produce large-scale stone sculpture, they did build permanent structures. These included tiered platforms and ball courts (see "The Mesoamerican Ball Game," page 389), architectural features found in nearly all Mesoamerican

cultures. Yet West Mexico is best known for its rich tradition of clay sculpture.

The sculptures come from tombs consisting of shafts as deep as 50 feet with chambers at their base. Because scientific excavations began only recently, much of what is known about West Mexican tomb contents derives primarily from the artifacts found and sold by grave robbers. Researchers believe, however, that most of these tombs were built and filled with elaborate offerings during the late Preclassic period, the half millennium before 300 CE.

The large ceramic figures found in the Colima tombs are consistently a highly burnished red orange, in contrast with the distinctive polychrome surfaces of the majority of other West Mexican ceramics. The area also is noted for small-scale clay narrative scenes that include modeled houses and temples and numerous solid figurines shown in a variety of lively activities. These sculptures, which may provide informal glimpses of daily life, are not found in any other ancient Mesoamerican culture. Although their subjects are often described as anecdotal and secular rather than religious, the Mesoamerican belief system did not recognize such a division. Consequently, scholars are unsure whether the figure we illustrate (FIG. **14-3**) is a religious practitioner with a horn on his forehead (a common indigenous symbol of special powers) or a political leader wearing a shell ornament (often a Mesoamerican emblem of rulership) — or a person serving both roles.

## Teotihuacán (ca. 100 BCE – 750 CE)

**THE PLACE OF THE GODS** At Olmec sites, the characteristic later Mesoamerican temple-pyramid-plaza layout appeared in embryonic form. At Teotihuacán (FIG. **14-4**), northeast of modern Mexico City, the Preclassic scheme underwent a monumental

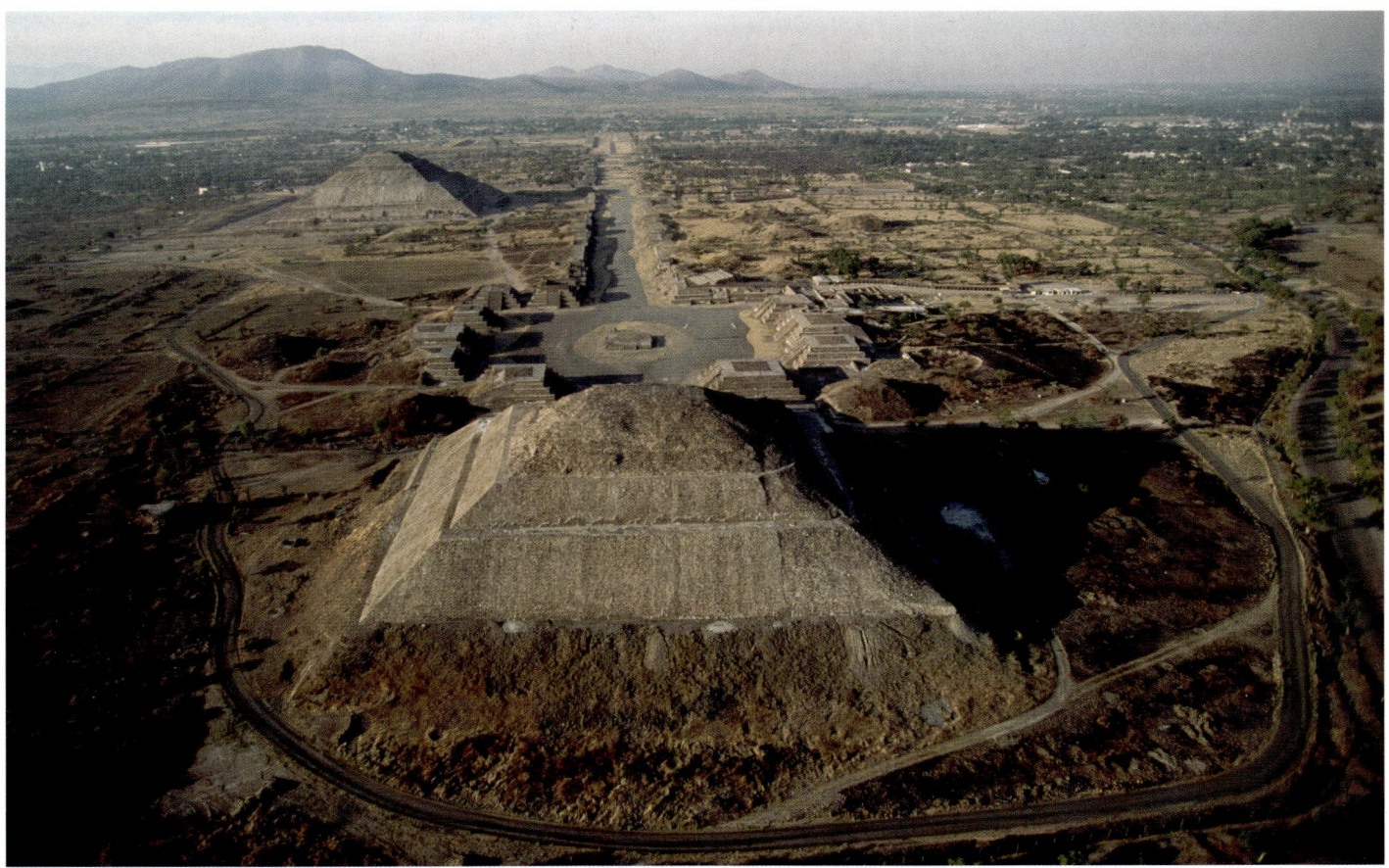

**14-4** Aerial view of Teotihuacán (from the north), Valley of Mexico, Mexico. Pyramid of the Moon *(foreground)*, Pyramid of the Sun *(top left)*, and the Citadel *(background)*, all connected by the Avenue of the Dead; main structures ca. 50–200 CE; site ca. 100 BCE–750 CE.

expansion into a genuine city. Teotihuacán was a large, densely populated metropolis that fulfilled a central civic, economic, and religious role for the region and indeed for much of Mesoamerica. Built up during nearly a millennium, ca. 100 BCE to 750 CE, the site's major monuments were constructed between 50 and 250 CE, during the late Preclassic period. Teotihuacán covers nine square miles, laid out in a grid pattern with the axes oriented by sophisticated surveying. The city's orientation, as well as the placement of some of its key pyramids, also appear to have been related to astronomical phenomena.

At its peak, around 600 CE, Teotihuacán may have had as many as 125,000–200,000 residents, which would have made it the sixth largest city in the world at that time. Divided into numerous wardlike sectors, this metropolis must have had a uniquely cosmopolitan character, with Zapotec peoples located in the city's western wards, and merchants from Veracruz living in the eastern wards, importing their own pottery and building their houses and tombs in the style of their homelands. The city's urbanization did nothing to detract from its sacred nature. In fact, it vastly augmented Teotihuacán's importance as a religious center. The Aztecs, who visited Teotihuacán regularly and reverently long after it had been abandoned, gave it its current name, which means "the place of the gods." Because the city's inhabitants left only a handful of undeciphered hieroglyphs and linguists do not yet even know what language they spoke, the names of many major features of the site are unknown. The Avenue of the Dead and the Pyramids of the Sun and Moon are later Aztec designations that do not necessarily relate to the original names of these entities.

The grid plan is quartered by a north-south and an east-west axis, each four miles in length. The rational scheme recalls Hellenistic and Roman urban planning (compare FIGS. 5-75 and 10-40) and is very unusual in Mesoamerica before the Aztecs. The main north-south axis, the Avenue of the Dead (FIG. 14-4), is 130 feet wide and connects the Pyramid of the Moon complex with the Citadel and its Temple of Quetzalcoatl. This two-mile stretch is not a continuously flat street but is broken by sets of stairs, giving pedestrians a constantly changing view of the surrounding buildings and landscape.

**TEOTIHUACÁN'S PYRAMIDS** The Pyramid of the Sun (FIG. 14-4, *top left*), facing west on the east side of the Avenue of the Dead, was erected in the first century CE during the late Preclassic period. It is the city's centerpiece and its largest structure, rising to a height of more than 200 feet. The Pyramid of the Moon (FIG. 14-4, *foreground*) was built a century or more later, ca. 150–250 CE. The shapes of the monumental structures at Teotihuacán echo the surrounding mountains. Their imposing mass and scale surpass those of all other Mesoamerican sites. Rubble-filled and faced with the local volcanic stone, the pyramids consist of stacked squared platforms diminishing in perimeter from the base to the top, much like the Stepped Pyramid of Djoser in Egyptian Saqqara (see FIG. 3-4). Ramped stairways led to crowning temples constructed of perishable materials such as wood and thatch, no longer preserved.

The Teotihuacanos built the Pyramid of the Sun over a cave, which they reshaped and filled with ceramic offerings. The pyramid may have been constructed to honor a sacred spring within

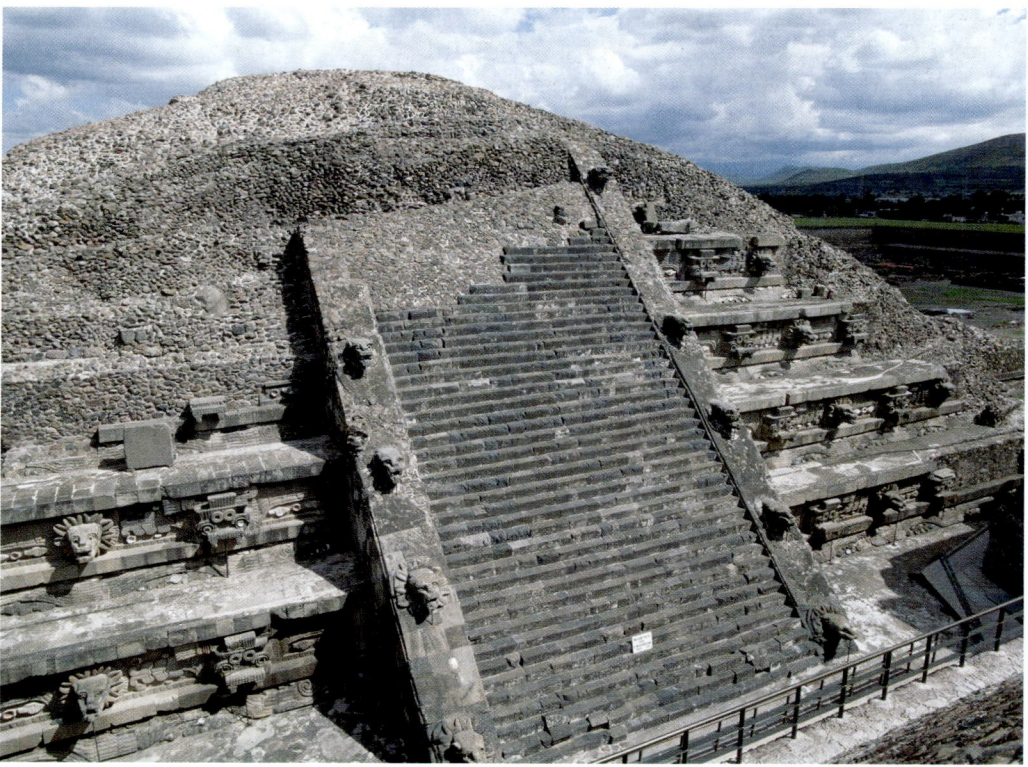

**14-5** Detail of Temple of Quetzalcoatl, the Citadel, Teotihuacán, Valley of Mexico, Mexico, third century CE.

the now-dry cave. The excavators found children buried at the four corners of each of the pyramid's tiers. The later Aztec sacrificed children to bring rainfall, and Teotihuacán art abounds with references to water, so the Teotihuacanos may have shared the Aztec preoccupation with rain and agricultural fertility. The city's inhabitants rebuilt the Pyramid of the Moon (currently being excavated) at least five times in Teotihuacán's early history. It may have been positioned to mimic the shape of Cerro Gordo, the volcanic mountain behind it, undoubtedly an important source of life-sustaining streams.

**THE FEATHERED SERPENT** At the south end of the Avenue of the Dead is the great quadrangle of the Citadel (FIG. 14-4, *background*). It encloses a smaller pyramidal shrine datable to the third century CE, the Temple of Quetzalcoatl (FIG. **14-5**). Quetzalcoatl, the "feathered serpent," was a major god in the Mesoamerican pantheon at the time of the Spanish conquest, hundreds of years after the fall of Teotihuacán. The later Aztecs associated him with wind, rain clouds, and life. Beneath the temple, archaeologists found a tomb looted in antiquity, perhaps that of a Teotihuacán ruler. The discovery has led them to speculate that like the Maya, the Teotihuacanos also buried their elite in or under pyramids. Surrounding the tomb both beneath and around the pyramid were the remains of at least a hundred sacrificial victims. Some were adorned with necklaces made of strings of human jaws, both real and sculpted from shell. Like most other Mesoamerican groups, the Teotihuacanos invoked and appeased their gods through human sacrifice. The presence of such a large number of victims also may reflect Teotihuacán's militaristic expansion—throughout Mesoamerica, the victors often sacrificed captured warriors.

The temple's sculptured panels, which feature projecting stone heads of Quetzalcoatl alternating with heads of a long-snouted scaly creature with rings on its forehead, decorate each of the temple's six terraces. This is the first unambiguous representation of the feathered serpent in Mesoamerica. The scaly creature's identity is unclear. Linking these alternating heads are low-relief carvings of feathered-serpent bodies and seashells. The latter reflect Teotihuacán contact with the peoples of the Mexican coasts and also symbolize water, an essential ingredient for the sustenance of an agricultural economy.

**MURAL PAINTING** Like those of most ancient Mesoamerican cities, Teotihuacán's buildings and streets were once stuccoed over and brightly painted. In a treatment unique to Teotihuacán during the Classic period, however, elaborate murals covered the walls of the rooms of its elite residential compounds. The paintings chiefly depict deities, ritual activities, and processions of priests, warriors, and even animals. Experimenting with a variety of surfaces, materials, and techniques over the centuries, Teotihuacán muralists finally settled on applying pigments to a smooth lime-plaster surface coated with clay. They then polished the surface to a high sheen. Although some Teotihuacán paintings have a restricted palette of varying tones of red (largely derived from the mineral hematite), creating subtle contrasts between figure and ground, most employ vivid hues arranged in flat, carefully outlined patterns. One mural (FIG. 14-6) depicts an earth or nature goddess who some scholars think was the city's principal deity. Always shown frontally with her face covered by a jade mask, she is dwarfed by her large feathered headdress and reduced to a bust placed upon a stylized pyramid. She stretches her hands out to provide liquid streams filled with bounty (compare the Sumerian mural at Zimri-Lim's palace, FIG. 2-17), but the stylized human hearts that flank the frontal bird mask in her headdress reflect her dual nature. They remind viewers that the ancient Mesoamericans saw human sacrifice as essential to agricultural renewal.

The influence of Teotihuacán was all-pervasive in Mesoamerica. Colonies were established as far away as the southern borders of Maya civilization, in the highlands of Guatemala, some 800 miles from Teotihuacán.

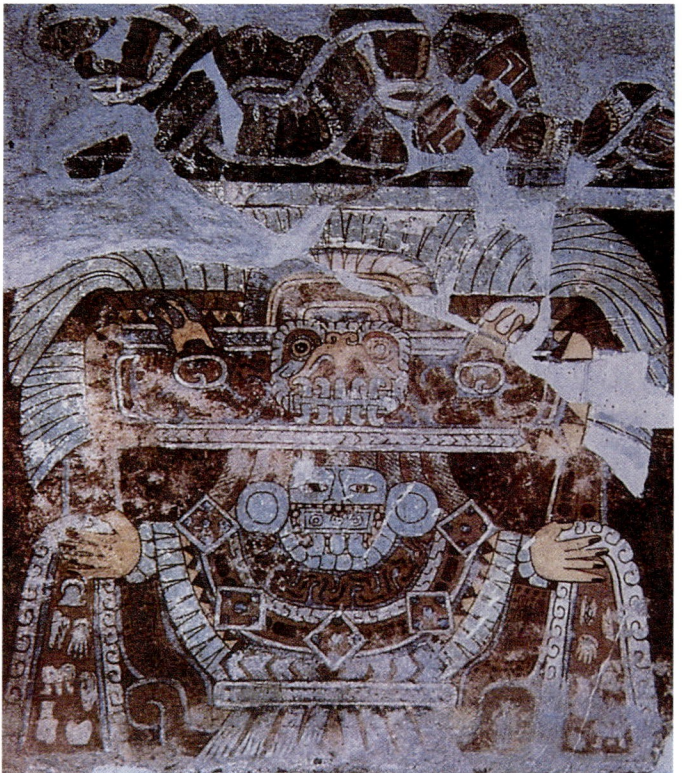

**14-6** Goddess, mural painting from Tetitla apartment complex at Teotihuacán, Valley of Mexico, Mexico, 650–750 CE. Pigments over clay and plaster.

## Classic (ca. 300–900 CE)

**THE MAYA** Strong cultural influences stemming from the Olmec tradition and from Teotihuacán contributed to the development of Classic Maya culture. As was true of Teotihuacán, the foundations of Maya civilization were laid in the Preclassic period, perhaps by 600 BCE or even earlier. At that time, the Maya, who occupied the moist lowland areas of Belize, southern Mexico, Guatemala, and Honduras, seem to have abandoned their early somewhat egalitarian pattern of village life and adopted a hierarchical autocratic society. This system evolved into the typical Maya city-state governed by hereditary rulers and ranked nobility. How and why this happened is still uncertain.

Stupendous building projects signaled the change. Vast complexes of terraced temple-pyramids, palaces, plazas, ball courts (see "The Mesoamerican Ball Game," page 389), and residences of the governing elite dotted the Maya area. Unlike the Teotihuacán civilization, no one site ever achieved complete dominance as the single center of power. The new architecture, and the art embellishing it, advertised the power of the rulers, who appropriated cosmic symbolism and stressed their descent from gods to reinforce their claims to legitimate rulership. The unified institutions of religion and kingship were established so firmly, their hold on life and custom was so tenacious, and their meaning was so fixed in the symbolism and imagery of art that the rigidly conservative system of the Classic Maya lasted almost a thousand years. Maya civilization began to decline in the eighth century. By 900, it had vanished.

Although the causes of the beginning and end of Classic Maya civilization are obscure, researchers are gradually revealing its history, beliefs, ceremonies, conventions, and patterns of daily life. Long romanticized, the Maya now enter the world history stage as believably as the peoples of other great civilizations. No longer viewed as a peaceful, benign society under theocratic rule, the Maya are now seen as flesh-and-blood peoples who glorified their rulers and oppressed the lower classes, undertook (and broke) strategic political alliances, waged war, and practiced human sacrifice. This more accurate picture is the consequence of modern interdisciplinary scholarship. Archaeologists, epigraphers (scholars who decipher writing systems), art historians, and ethnographers (those who study contemporary societies) all have contributed to a clearer understanding of ancient Maya culture.

**DECODING MAYAN SCRIPT** Like the decipherment of Egyptian writing early in the 19th century (see Chapter 3), the decoding of the Mayan script has been an exciting intellectual adventure. By the end of the 19th century, numbers, dates, and some astronomical information could be read, but little else, leading scholars to conclude that the Maya were obsessed with time and religion and uninterested in recording the mundane events of human lives. Two important breakthroughs beginning in the 1950s radically altered the understanding of both Mayan writing and the Maya worldview. The first was the realization that the Maya depicted their rulers (rather than gods or anonymous priests) in their art and noted their rulers' achievements in their texts. The second was that Mayan writing is largely phonetic; that is, the hieroglyphs are made up of signs representing sounds in the Mayan language. Fortunately, the various Mayan languages were recorded in colonial texts and dictionaries, and most are still spoken today. Although perhaps only half of the ancient Mayan script can be translated accurately into spoken Mayan, today scholars can at least grasp the general meaning of many more hieroglyphs.

**ASTRONOMY AND CALENDARS** The Maya possessed a highly developed knowledge of arithmetic calculation and the ability to observe and record the movements of the sun, the moon, and numerous planets. They contrived an intricate but astonishingly accurate calendar, and although their calendric structuring of time was radically different in form from the Western calendar used today, it was just as precise and efficient. With their calendar, the Maya established the all-important genealogical lines of their rulers, which certified their claim to rule, and created the only true written history in ancient America. Although other ancient Mesoamerican societies, even in the Preclassic period, also possessed calendars, only the Maya calendar can be translated directly into today's calendrical system.

**ARCHITECTURE AND RITUAL** The most sacred and majestic buildings of Maya cities were raised in enclosed, centrally located precincts. The religious-civic transactions that guaranteed the order of the state and the cosmos occurred in these settings. The Maya held dramatic rituals within a sculptured and painted environment, where huge symbols and images proclaimed the nature and necessity of that order. Maya builders designed spacious plazas for vast audiences who were exposed to overwhelming propaganda. The programmers of that propaganda, the ruling families and troops of priests, nobles, and retainers, wore its symbolism in their costumes. In Maya paintings and sculptures, the Maya elite wear extravagant profusions of vividly colorful cotton textiles, feathers, jaguar skins, and jade, all emblematic of their rank and wealth. On the different levels of the painted and polished temple platforms, the ruling classes performed the offices of their rites in clouds of incense to the music of maracas, flutes, and drums. The Maya transformed the architectural complex at each city's center into a theater of religion and statecraft. In the stagelike layout of a characteristic Maya city

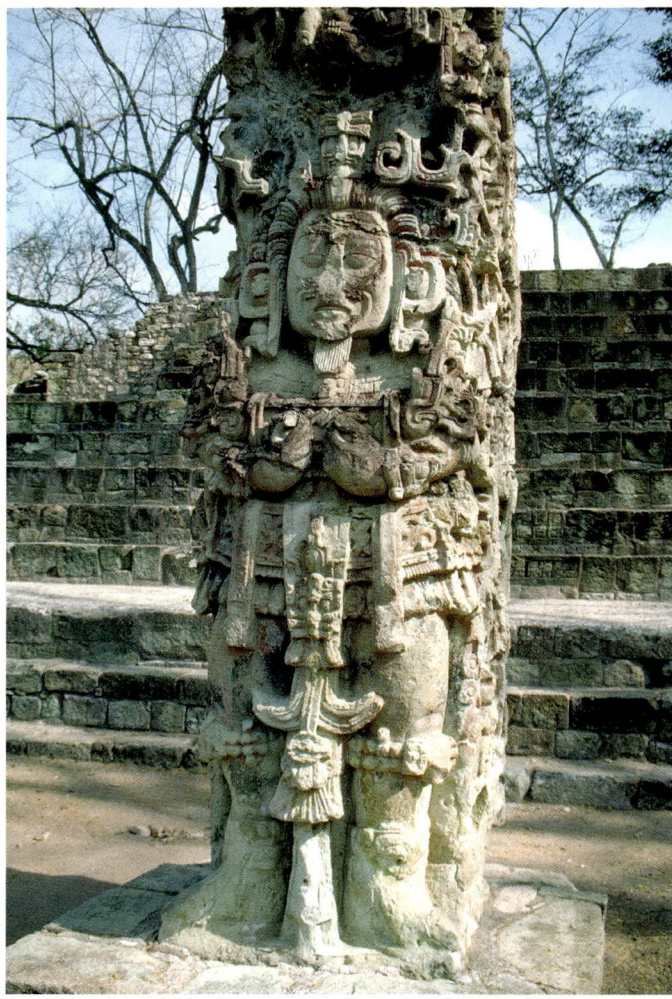

**14-7** Stele D portraying the ruler 18-Rabbit, Maya, Great Plaza at Copán, Honduras, 736 CE. Stone, 11′ 9″ high. 🔴

center, its principal group, or "site core," was the religious and administrative nucleus for a population of dispersed farmers settled throughout a suburban area of many square miles.

**COPÁN'S PORTRAIT STELAE** Because Copán, on the western border of Honduras, has more hieroglyphic inscriptions and well-preserved carved monuments than any other site in the Americas, it was one of the first Maya sites excavated. It also has proved one of the richest in the trove of architecture, sculpture, and artifacts recovered. Conspicuous plazas dominated the heart of the city. In Copán's Great Plaza, the Maya set up tall, sculpted stone stelae. Carved with the portraits of the rulers who erected them, these stelae also recorded their names, dates of reign, and notable achievements in glyphs on the front, sides, or back.

Stele D (FIG. **14-7**), erected in 736 CE, represents one of the city's foremost rulers, Waxaklahun-Ubah-K'awil, known as 18-Rabbit (r. 695–738). In a dynastic succession of 16 rulers, 18-Rabbit was the 13th. During his long reign, Copán may have reached its greatest physical extent and range of political influence. On Stele D, 18-Rabbit wears an elaborate headdress and ornamented kilt and sandals. He holds across his chest a double-headed serpent bar, symbol of the sky and of his absolute power. His features have the quality of a portrait likeness, although highly idealized. The Maya elite, like the Egyptian pharaohs (see Chapter 3), tended to have themselves portrayed in a conventionalized manner and as eternally youthful. The dense, deeply carved ornamental details that frame the face and figure in florid profusion stand almost clear of the block and wrap around the sides of the stele. The high relief, originally painted, gives the impression of a freestanding statue, although a hieroglyphic text is carved on the flat back side of the stele. Although a powerful ruler who erected many stelae and buildings at Copán, including one of Mesoamerica's best-preserved (and carefully restored) ball courts (FIG. **14-8**; see "The Mesoamerican Ball Game," page 389), 18-Rabbit eventually was captured and beheaded by the king of neighboring Quiriguá.

**CLASSIC TIKAL** Another great Maya site of the Classic period is Tikal in Guatemala, some 150 miles north of Copán. Tikal is one of the oldest and largest of the Maya cities. Together with its suburbs, Tikal originally covered some 75 square miles and served as the ceremonial center of a population of perhaps 75,000. The Maya did not lay out central Tikal on a grid plan as did the designers of contemporary Teotihuacán. Instead, causeways connected irregular groupings. Modern surveys have uncovered the remains of as many as 3,000 separate structures in an area of about six square miles. The site's nucleus, the Great Plaza, is studded with stelae and defined by numerous architectural complexes. The most prominent monuments are the two soaring

**14-8** Ball court (view looking north), Middle Plaza, Copán, Maya, Copán Valley, Honduras, 738 CE. 🔴

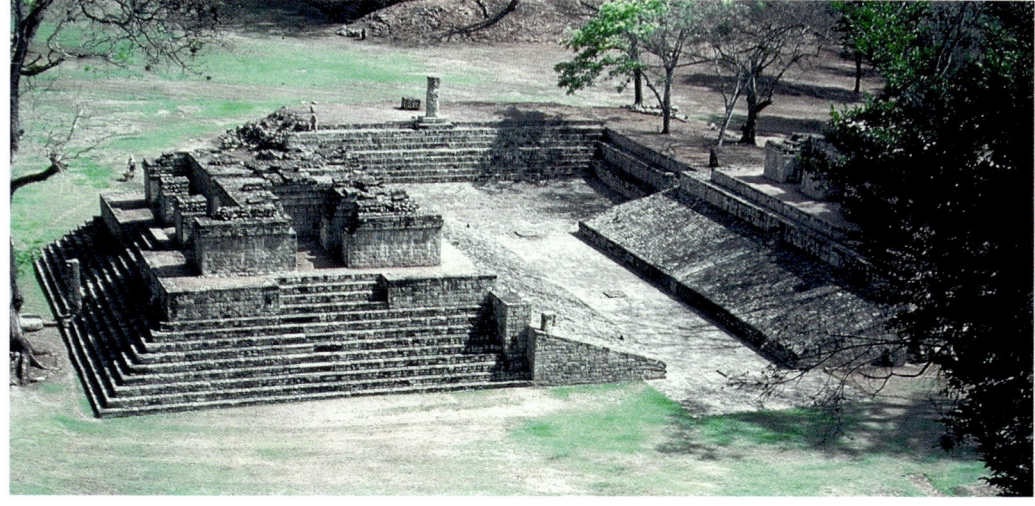

## The Mesoamerican Ball Game

After witnessing the native ball game of Mexico soon after their arrival in the 16th century, the Spanish conquerors took Aztec ball players back to Europe to demonstrate the novel sport. Their chronicles remark on the athletes' great skill, the heavy wagering that accompanied the competition, and the ball itself, made of rubber, a substance the Spaniards had never seen before.

The game was played throughout Mesoamerica and into the southwestern United States, beginning at least 3,400 years ago, the date of the earliest known ball court. The Olmec were apparently avid players. Their very name—a modern invention in Nahuatl, the Aztec language—means "rubber people," after the latex-growing region they inhabited. Not only are ball players represented in Olmec art, but remnants of sunken earthen ball courts and even rubber balls have been found at Olmec sites.

The Olmec earthen playing field evolved in other Mesoamerican cultures into a plastered masonry surface, I- or T-shaped in plan, flanked by two parallel sloping or straight walls. Sometimes the walls were wide enough to support small structures on top, as at Copán (FIG. 14-8). At other sites, temples stood at either end of the ball court. These structures were common features of Mesoamerican cities. At Cantona, for example, archaeologists have uncovered 22 ball courts even though only a small portion of the site has been excavated. Teotihuacán (FIG. 14-4) is an exception. The excavators have not yet found a ball court there, but mural paintings at the site illustrate people playing the game with portable markers and sticks. Most ball courts were adjacent to the important civic structures of Mesoamerican cities, such as palaces and temple-pyramids, as at Copán.

Surprisingly little is known about the rules of the ball game itself—how many players were on the field, how goals were scored and tallied, and how competitions were arranged. Unlike a modern soccer field with its standard dimensions, Mesoamerican ball courts vary widely in size. The largest known—at Chichén Itzá—is nearly 500 feet long; Copán's is about 93 feet long. Some have stone rings, which a ball conceivably could have been tossed through, set high up on their walls at right angles to the ground, but many courts lack this feature. Alternatively, the ball may have been bounced against the walls and into the end zones. As in soccer, players could not touch the ball with their hands but used their heads, elbows, hips, and legs. They wore thick leather belts, and sometimes even helmets, and padded their knees and arms against the blows of the fast-moving solid rubber ball. Typically, the Maya portrayed ball players wearing heavy protective clothing and kneeling, poised to deflect the ball (FIG. 14-10).

Although widely enjoyed as a competitive spectator sport, the ball game did not serve solely for entertainment. The ball, for example, may have represented a celestial body such as the sun, its movements over the court imitating the sun's daily passage through the sky. Reliefs on the walls of ball courts at certain sites make clear that the game sometimes culminated in human sacrifice, probably of captives taken in battle and then forced to participate in a game they were predestined to lose.

Ball playing also had a role in Mesoamerican mythology. In the ancient Maya epic known as the *Popol Vuh (Council Book)*, first written down in Spanish in the colonial period, a legendary pair of twins is forced to play ball with the evil lords of the Underworld. The brothers lose and are sacrificed. The sons of one twin eventually travel to the Underworld and, after a series of trials including a ball game, outwit the lords and kill them. They revive their father, buried in the ball court after his earlier defeat at the hands of the Underworld gods. The younger twins rise to the heavens to become the sun and the moon, and the father becomes the god of maize, principal sustenance of all Mesoamerican peoples. The ball game and its aftermath, then, were a metaphor for the cycle of life, death, and regeneration that permeated Mesoamerican religion.

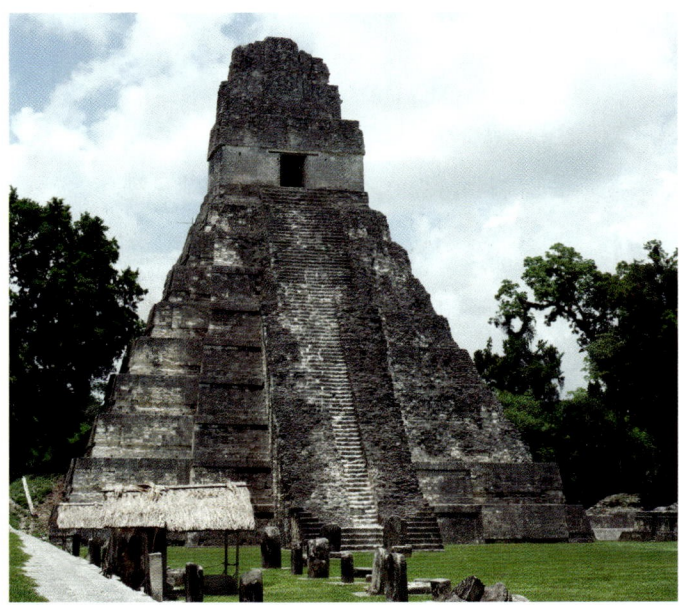

**14-9** Temple I (Temple of the Giant Jaguar), Maya, Tikal, Petén, Guatemala, ca. 732 CE.

pyramids, taller than the surrounding rain forest, that face each other across an open square. The larger pyramid (FIG. **14-9**), Temple I (also called the Temple of the Giant Jaguar after a motif on one of its carved wooden lintels), reaches a height of about 150 feet. It is the temple-mausoleum of a great Tikal ruler, Hasaw Chan K'awil, who died in 732 CE. His body was placed in a vaulted chamber under the pyramid's base. The towering structure is made up of nine sharply inclining platforms, probably a reference to the nine levels of the Underworld. A narrow stairway leads up to a three-chambered temple. The temple is surmounted by an elaborately sculpted *roof comb*, a vertical architectural projection that once bore the ruler's giant portrait modeled in stucco. The entire structure exhibits most concisely the ancient Mesoamerican formula for the stepped temple-pyramid and the compelling aesthetic and psychological power of Maya architecture.

**JAINA CLAY SCULPTURE** The almost unlimited variety of figural attitude and gesture permitted in the modeling of clay explains the profusion of Maya ceramic figurines that, like their West Mexican predecessors (FIG. 14-3), may illustrate aspects of everyday life. Small-scale freestanding figures in the round, they are remarkably lifelike, carefully descriptive, and even comic at times.

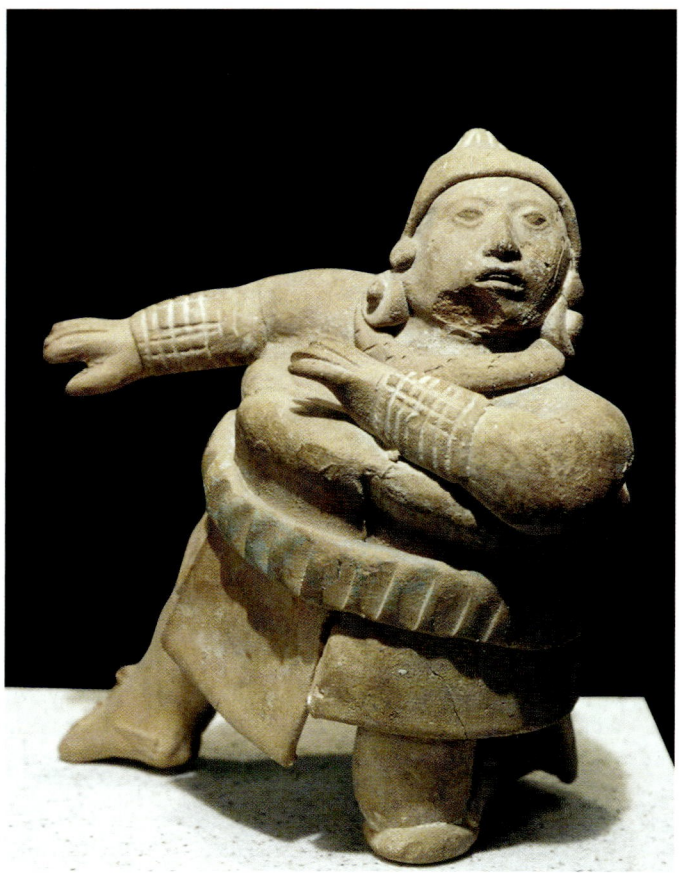

**14-10** Ball player, Maya, from Jaina Island, Mexico, 700–900 CE. Painted clay, 6¼″ high. National Museum of Anthropology, Mexico City.

They represent a wider range of human types and activities than is commonly depicted on Maya stelae. Ball players (FIG. **14-10**), women weaving, older men, dwarves, supernatural beings, and amorous couples, as well as elaborately attired rulers and warriors, make up the figurine repertory. Many of the hollow figurines are also whistles. They were made in ceramic workshops on the mainland, often with molds, but burials on the island cemetery of Jaina, off the western coast of Yucatán, yielded hundreds of such figures, including the ball player we illustrate. Traces of blue remain on the figure's belt, remnants of the vivid pigments that once covered many of these figurines. The Maya used "Maya blue," a combination of a particular kind of clay and indigo, a vegetable dye, to paint both ceramics and murals. This pigment has proven virtually indestructible, unlike the other colors that largely have disappeared over time. Like the larger terracotta figures of West Mexico, these figurines were made to accompany the dead on their inevitable voyage to the Underworld. The excavations at Jaina, however, have revealed nothing more that might clarify the meaning and function of the figures. Male figurines were not found exclusively in the burials of male individuals, for example.

**HISTORY PAINTING AT BONAMPAK** The vivacity of the Jaina figurines and their variety of pose, costume, and occupation were reinterpreted in two dimensions at Bonampak (Mayan for "painted walls") in southeastern Mexico. Three chambers in one Bonampak structure contain mural paintings that record important aspects of Maya court life. The example we reproduce (FIG. **14-11**) shows warriors surrounding captives on a terraced platform. The figures represented have naturalistic proportions and overlap, twist, turn, and gesture. The artists used fluid and calligraphic line to outline the figures, working with color to indicate both texture and

**14-11** Presentation of captives to Lord Chan Muwan, Maya, Room 2, Structure 1, Bonampak, Mexico, ca. 790 CE. Mural, approx. 17′ × 15′; watercolor copy by Antonio Tejeda. Peabody Museum, Harvard University, Cambridge.

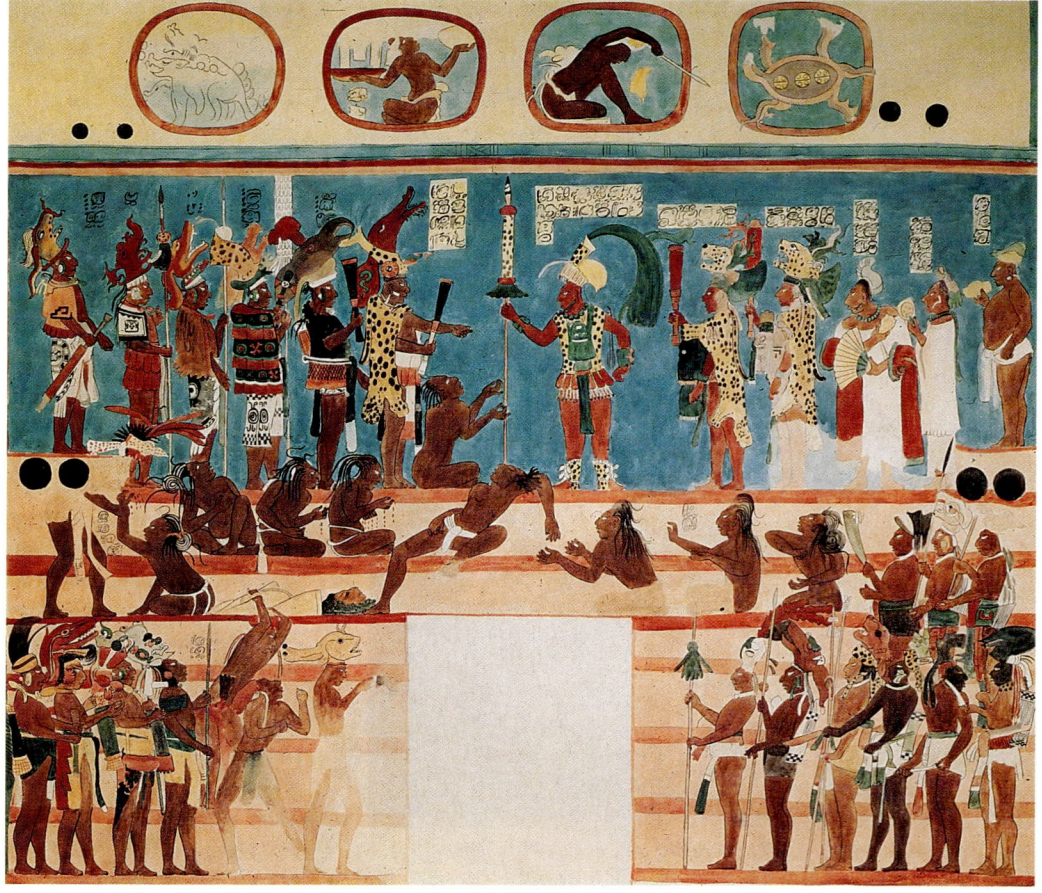

volume. The Bonampak painters combined their pigments—both mineral and organic—with a mixture of water, crushed limestone, and vegetable gums and applied them to their stucco walls in a technique best described as a cross between fresco and tempera.

The Bonampak murals are filled with circumstantial detail. The information given is comprehensive, explicit, and presented with the fidelity of an eyewitness report. The royal personages are identifiable by both their physical features and their costumes, and accompanying inscriptions provide the precise day, month, and year for the events recorded. All the scenes at Bonampak relate the events and ceremonies that welcome a new royal heir (shown as a toddler in some scenes). They include presentations, preparations for a royal fete, dancing, battle, and the taking and sacrificing of prisoners. On all occasions of state, public bloodletting was an integral part of Maya ritual. The ruler, his consort, and certain members of the nobility drew blood from their own bodies and sought union with the supernatural world. The slaughter of captives taken in war regularly accompanied this ceremony. Indeed, Mesoamerican cultures undertook warfare largely to provide victims for sacrifice. The torture and eventual execution of prisoners served both to nourish the gods and to strike fear into enemies and the general populace.

The scene in Structure I, Room 2, depicts the presentation of prisoners to Lord Chan Muwan (FIG. 14-11). The painter arranged the figures in registers that may represent a pyramid's steps. On the uppermost step, against a blue background, is a file of gorgeously

appareled nobles wearing animal headgear. Conspicuous among them on the right are retainers clad in jaguar pelts and jaguar headdresses. Also present is Chan Muwan's wife (third from right). The ruler himself, in jaguar jerkin and high-backed sandals, stands at the center, facing a crouching victim who appears to beg for mercy. Naked captives, anticipating death, crowd the middle level. One of them, already dead, sprawls at the ruler's feet. Others dumbly contemplate the blood dripping from their mutilated hands. The lower zone, cut through by a doorway into the structure housing the murals, shows clusters of attendants who are doubtless of inferior rank to the lords of the upper zone. The stiff formality of the victors contrasts graphically with the supple imploring attitudes and gestures of the hapless victims. The Bonampak victory was short-lived. The murals were never finished, and shortly after the dates written on the walls the site seems to have been abandoned.

**SHIELD JAGUAR AND LADY XOC** A rare representation in monumental art of a woman playing an important role in Maya ritual appears on the painted lintels of a temple (Structure 23) at Yaxchilán. Lintel 24 (FIG. **14-12**) depicts the ruler Itzamna Balam II (r. 681–742 CE), known as Shield Jaguar, and his principal wife, Lady Xoc. Lady Xoc is magnificently outfitted in an elaborate woven garment, headdress, and jewels. She pierces her tongue with a barbed cord in a bloodletting ceremony that, according to accompanying inscriptions, celebrated the birth of a son to one of

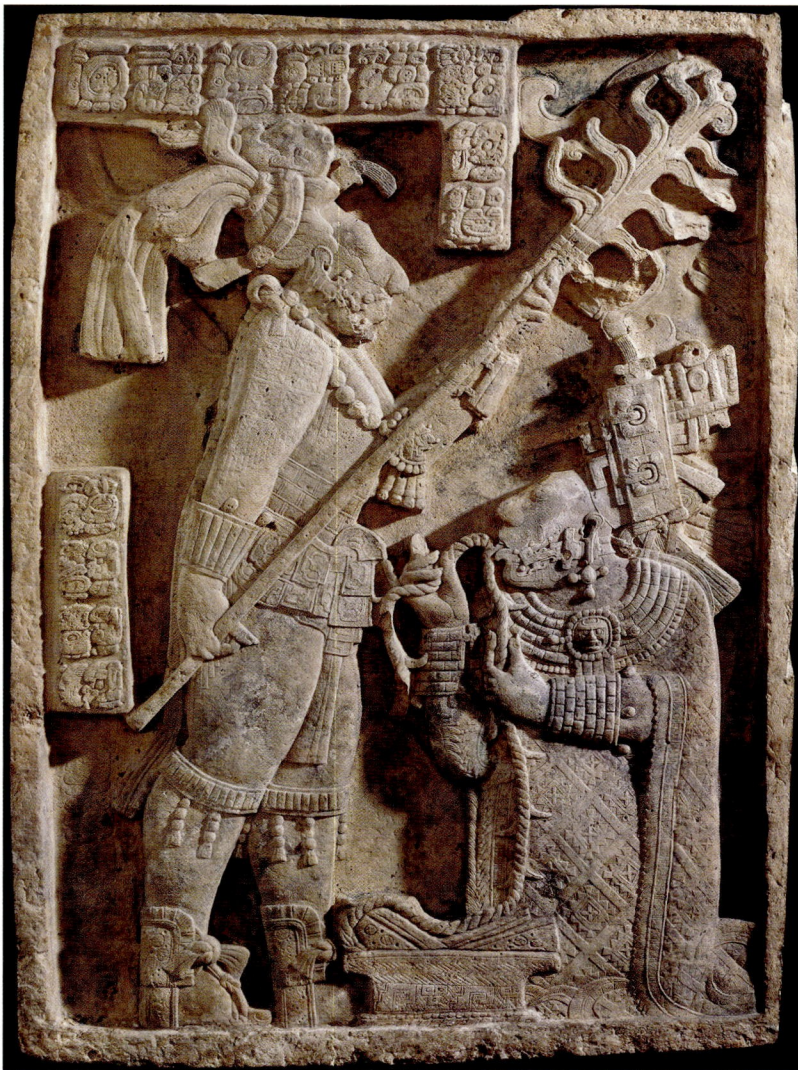

14-12 Shield Jaguar and Lady Xoc, Maya, Lintel 24, Temple 23, Yaxchilán, Mexico, ca. 725 CE. Limestone, 3′ 7″ × 2′ 6$\frac{1}{2}$″. British Museum, London.

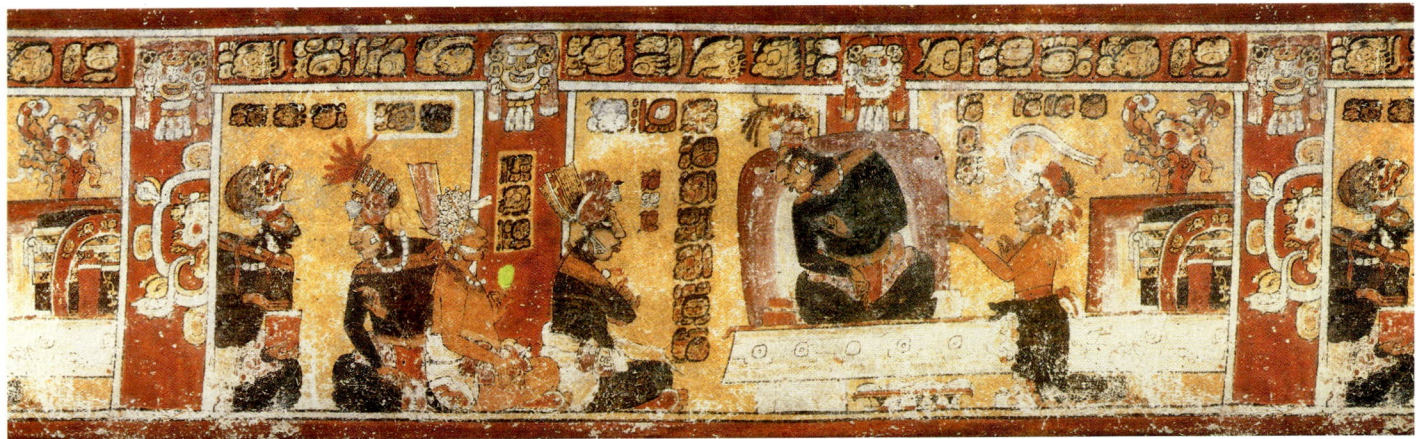

**14-13** Enthroned Maya lord and courtiers, cylinder vase (rollout view), Maya, from Motul de San José region, Guatemala, 672–830 CE. Ceramic with red, rose, orange, white, and black on cream slip, approx. 8″ high. Dumbarton Oaks Research Library and Collections, Washington, D.C.

the ruler's other wives as well as an alignment between the planets Saturn and Jupiter. The celebration must have taken place in a dark chamber or at night because Shield Jaguar provides illumination with a blazing torch. These ceremonies were intended to produce hallucinations. (Lintel 25 depicts Lady Xoc and her vision of an ancestor emerging from the mouth of a serpent.)

**MAYA VASE PAINTING** Vivid narratives also appear on the much smaller surfaces of painted cylinder vases. A rollout view of a typical vase design (FIG. **14-13**) shows a palace scene where an enthroned lord sits surrounded by courtiers and attendants. In this scene, at once regal and intimate, the participants gesture and talk. The elaborate costumes of the Copán stele, the Bonampak paintings, and the Yaxchilán lintel are absent. Instead, the figures wear simple loincloths, turbans of wrapped cloth and feathers, and black body paint. The red frame that surrounds the scene suggests an architectural setting. The painter provided a glimpse of the event through the open doorways of a palace.

The horizontal band of hieroglyphs at the top describes the vessel and names the artist. Although this particular name has not been completely deciphered, the names of a handful of Maya vase painters, all male, are now known. Some texts even list the contents of the vessel. One pot marked with the glyph for cacao, or chocolate, still contained remnants of the prestigious drink when it was discovered. In our example, the artist may have portrayed himself among the participants. He repeats his name in one of the vertical texts, which refer to both the figures and ritual events. Some artists even recorded their parentage, clearly stating they were of noble birth and high status. Vases such as this one may have been used as drinking and food vessels for noble Maya, but their final destination was the tomb, where they accompanied the deceased to the Underworld. They likely were commissioned by the deceased before his death or by his survivors and occasionally were sent from distant sites as funerary offerings. (The Maya intermarried with other powerful families to consolidate power between important cities, and both trade and gift exchanges were common.)

## Terminal Classic and Early Postclassic (ca. 800–1250 CE)

Throughout Mesoamerica, the Classic period ended at different times with the disintegration of the great civilizations. Teotihuacán's political and cultural empire, for example, was disrupted around 600, and its influence waned. About 650 the center of the great city was destroyed by fire, but the cause is still unknown. Within a century, however, Teotihuacán was deserted. Around 900, many of the great Maya sites were abandoned to the jungle, leaving a few northern Maya cities to flourish for another century or two before they, too, became depopulated. The Classic culture of the Zapotecs, centered at Monte Albán in the state of Oaxaca, came to an end around 700, and the neighboring Mixtec peoples assumed supremacy in this area during the Postclassic period. Classic El Tajín, later heir to the Olmec in the Veracruz plain, survived the general crisis that afflicted the others but was burned sometime in the 12th century. The war and confusion that followed the collapse of the Classic civilizations broke the great states up into small, local political entities isolated in fortified sites. The collapse encouraged even more warlike regimes and chronic aggression. The militant city-state of Chichén Itzá dominated Yucatán, while in central Mexico the Toltec and the later Aztec peoples, both ambitious migrants from the north, forged empires by force of arms.

**CHICHÉN ITZÁ AND THE NORTH** Yucatán, a flat, low limestone peninsula covered with scrub vegetation, lies north of the rolling and densely forested region of the Guatemalan Petén. During the Classic period, Mayan-speaking peoples sparsely inhabited this northern region. For reasons that are still the subject of debate, when the southern Classic Maya sites were abandoned after 900, the northern Maya continued to build many new temples in this area. They also experimented with building construction and materials to a much greater extent than their cousins farther south. Piers and columns appeared in doorways, and stone mosaics enlivened outer facades. The northern groups also invented a new type of construction, a solid core of coarse rubble faced inside and out with a veneer of square limestone plates.

**CARACOL AND CASTILLO** The design of the structure known as the Caracol ("snail" in Spanish) at Chichén Itzá (FIG. **14-14**, *foreground*) suggests that the northern Maya were as inventive of architectural form as they were experimental with construction and materials. A cylindrical tower rests on a broad terrace that is in turn supported by a larger rectangular platform measuring 169 × 232 feet. The tower, composed of two concentric walls, encloses a circular staircase that leads to a small chamber near the top of the structure. In plan, the building recalls the cross-section of a conch shell. The conch shell was an attribute of the feathered serpent, and round temples were dedicated to him in central Mexico.

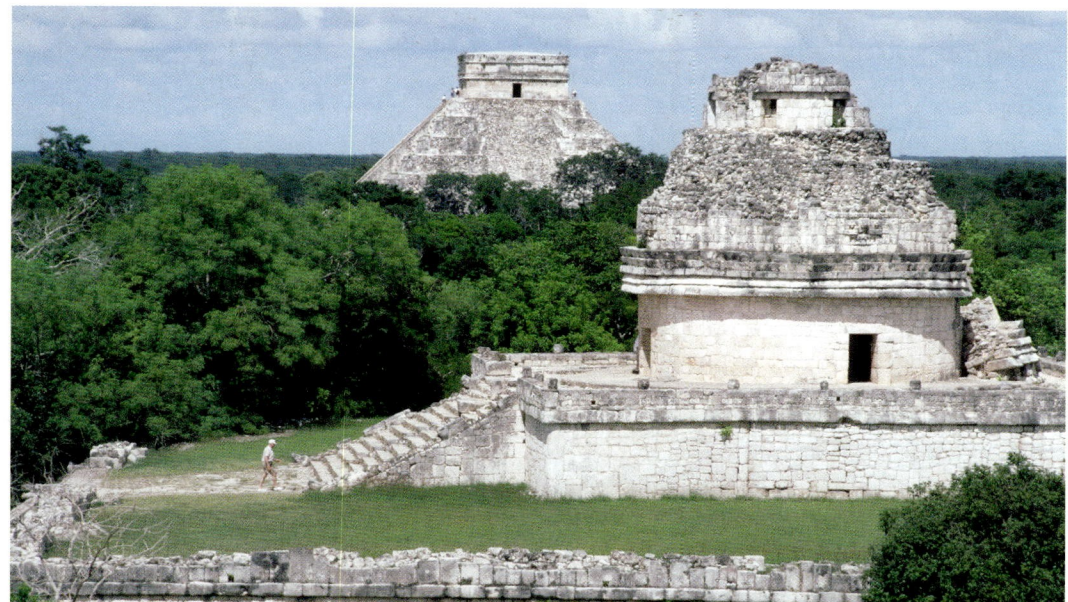

14-14 The Caracol (foreground) and the Castillo (background), Maya, Chichén Itzá, Yucatán, Mexico, ca. 800–900 CE.

This building may therefore have been a temple to Kukulkan, the Maya equivalent of Quetzalcoatl. Windows along the Caracol's staircase and an opening at the summit probably were used for astronomical observation, which has given the building another nickname—the Observatory. Noted astronomers, the Maya tracked celestial events closely, both for practical reasons, such as determining when to plant and the date of the next eclipse, and to foretell and attempt to manipulate the future.

Behind the Caracol in our photograph (FIG. 14-14) is the Castillo ("Castle"), 98 feet high and 182 feet wide at the base. The monument is a temple dedicated to Kukulkan atop a great pyramid, the signature form of sacred architecture throughout Mesoamerica. Steps on four sides of the nine-tiered pyramid converge on the temple level. Painted reliefs throughout the structure relating to the cult of Quetzalcoatl are signatures of Central Mexican influence on the northern Maya of Yucatán.

**TOLTEC GUARDIANS** The name *Toltec*, which signifies "makers of things," generally refers to a powerful tribe of invaders from the north, whose arrival in central Mexico coincided with the great disturbances that must have contributed to the fall of the Classic civilizations. The Toltec capital at Tula flourished from about 900 to 1200. The Toltecs were great political organizers and military strategists, dominating large parts of north and central Mexico. They also were respected both as master artisans and farmers, and later peoples such as the Aztec looked back on them admiringly, proud to claim descent from them.

At Tula, four colossal *atlantids* (male statue-columns; FIG. 14-15) portraying armed warriors reflect the grim, warlike regime of the Toltecs. These images of brutal authority stand eternally at attention, warding off all hostile threats. Built up of four stone drums each, the sculptures stand atop Pyramid B. They wear feathered headdresses and, as breastplates, stylized butterflies, heraldic symbols of the

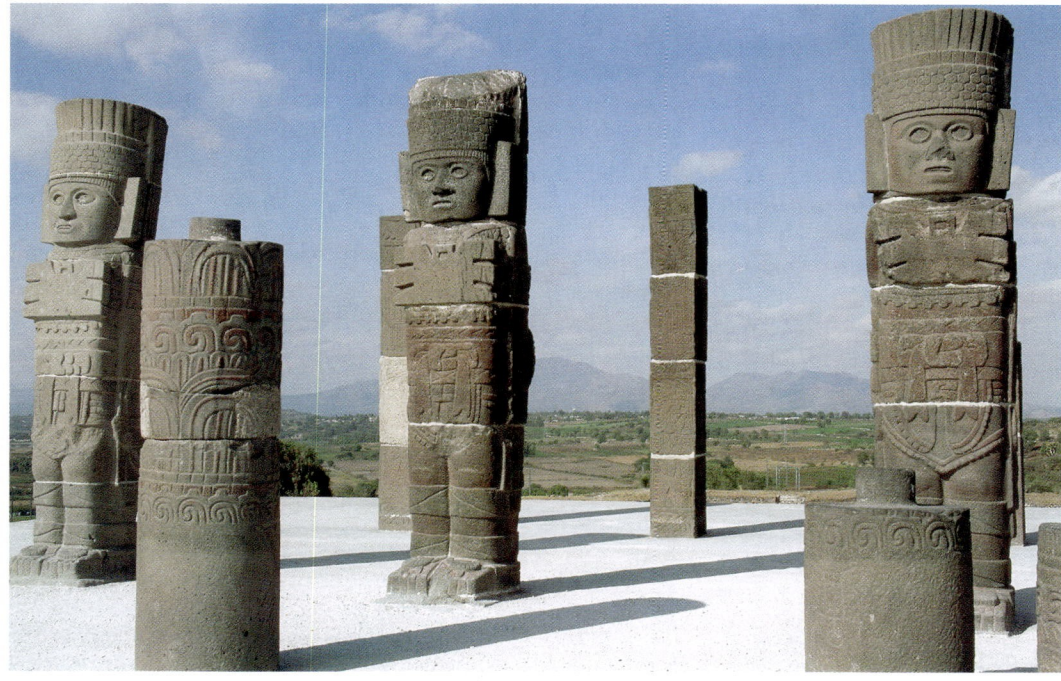

14-15 Colossal atlantids, Pyramid B, Toltec, Tula, Hidalgo, Mexico, ca. 900–1180 CE. Stone, each approx. 16′ high.

Toltec. In one hand they clutch a bundle of darts and in the other an *atlatl* (spear-thrower), typical weapons of highland Mexico. The figures originally supported a temple roof, now missing. Such an architectural function requires rigidity of pose, compactness, and strict simplicity of contour. The unity and regularity of architectural mass and silhouette here combine perfectly with abstraction of form.

By 1180, the last Toltec ruler abandoned Tula, followed by most of his people. Some years later, the city was catastrophically destroyed, its ceremonial buildings burned to their foundations, its walls thrown down, and the straggling remainder of its population scattered. The exact reasons for the Toltecs' departure and for their city's destruction are unknown. Although the stage was set for the rise of the last great civilization of Mesoamerica, the Aztecs (see Chapter 30), they did not reach the height of their power for another 300 years.

## INTERMEDIATE AREA

Between the highly developed civilizations of Mesoamerica and the South American Andes (MAPS 14-2 and 14-3) lies a region archaeologists have dubbed the "Intermediate Area." Comprising parts of El Salvador, Honduras, Ecuador, and Venezuela, and all of Panama, Costa Rica, Nicaragua, and Colombia, at the time of the European invasion it was by no means a unified political territory but rather was occupied by many small rival chiefdoms. Although the people of the Intermediate Area did not produce monumental architecture on the scale of their neighbors to the north and south and, unlike the Mesoamericans, left no written records, they too were consummate artists. Potters in the Intermediate Area made some of the earliest ceramics of the Americas, and they continued to create an astonishing variety of terracotta vessels and figures until the time of the Spanish conquest. Among the other arts practiced in the Intermediate Area was stone sculpture, including large-scale figures and elaborately carved *metates* (ceremonial grinding stones, possibly used as thrones). The ancient Costa Ricans excelled at carving jade as well, particularly anthropomorphic and zoomorphic celts. Throughout the area, goldworking was prized, and the first Europeans to make contact here were astonished to see the inhabitants nearly naked but covered in gold jewelry. The legend of El Dorado, a Colombian chief who coated himself in gold as part of his accession rites, was largely responsible for the Spanish invaders' ruthless plunder of the region.

**TAIRONA GOLD** In northern Colombia, the Sierra Nevada de Santa Marta rises above the Caribbean. The topography of lofty mountains and river valleys allowed for considerable isolation and the independent development of various groups. Late inhabitants of this region (from about 1000 to contact with the Spanish conquerors, in the poorly documented chronology of the area) included a group known as the Tairona, whose metalwork is among the finest of all the ancient American goldworking styles.

Goldsmiths in Peru, Ecuador, and southern Colombia produced technologically advanced and aesthetically sophisticated work in gold mostly by cutting and hammering thin gold sheets. The Tairona smiths, however, who had to obtain gold by trade, used the lost-wax process (see "Hollow-Casting," Chapter 5, page 131) in part to preserve the scarce amount of the precious metal available to them. They cast small works of the highest quality in both fabrication and design.

Tairona pendants were not meant to be worn simply as rich accessories to costume but as amulets or talismans representing

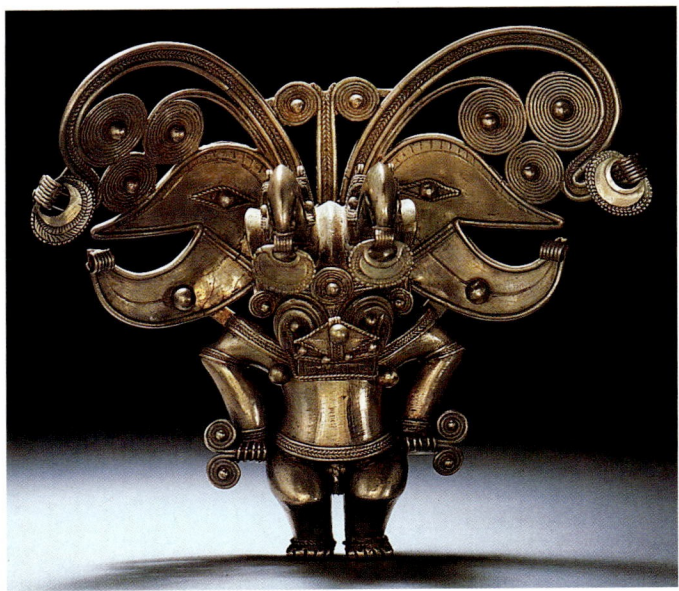

**14-16** Pendant in the form of a bat-faced man, Tairona, from northeastern Colombia, after 1000 CE. Gold, $5\frac{1}{4}$" high. Metropolitan Museum of Art, New York (Jan Mitchell and Sons Collection).

powerful beings who gave the wearer protection and status. Our example (FIG. 14-16) shows a bat-faced man—perhaps a masked man rather than a composite being, or a man in the process of spiritual transformation. In local mythology, the bat was the first animal to be created. This bat-man wears an immense headdress made up of two birds in the round, two great beaked heads, and a series of spirals crowned by two overarching stalks. The harmony of repeated curvilinear motifs, the rhythmic play of their contours, and the precise delineation of minute detail bespeak the anonymous artist's technical control and aesthetic sensitivity.

## SOUTH AMERICA

As in Mesoamerica, the indigenous civilizations of Andean South America (MAP 14-3) jarred against and stimulated one another, produced towering monuments and sophisticated paintings, sculptures, ceramics, and textiles, and were exterminated in violent confrontations with the Spanish conquistadors. Although less well studied than the ancient Mesoamerican cultures, those of South America are actually older, and in some ways they surpassed the accomplishments of their northern contemporaries. Andean peoples, for example, mastered metalworking much earlier, and their monumental architecture predates that of the earliest Mesoamerican culture, the Olmec, by more than a millennium. The peoples of northern Chile even began to mummify their dead at least 500 years before the Egyptians (see "Mummification," Chapter 3, page 59).

**GEOGRAPHY** The Central Andean region of South America lies between Ecuador and northern Chile, its western border the Pacific Ocean. It consists of three well-defined geographic zones, running north and south and roughly parallel to one another. The narrow western coastal plain is a hot desert crossed by rivers, creating habitable fertile valleys. Next, the high peaks of the great Cordillera of the Andes hem in plateaus of a temperate climate. The region's inland border, the eastern slopes of the Andes, is a hot and humid jungle.

**CHRONOLOGY** Andean civilizations flourished both in the highlands and on the coast. Highland cave dwellers fashioned the

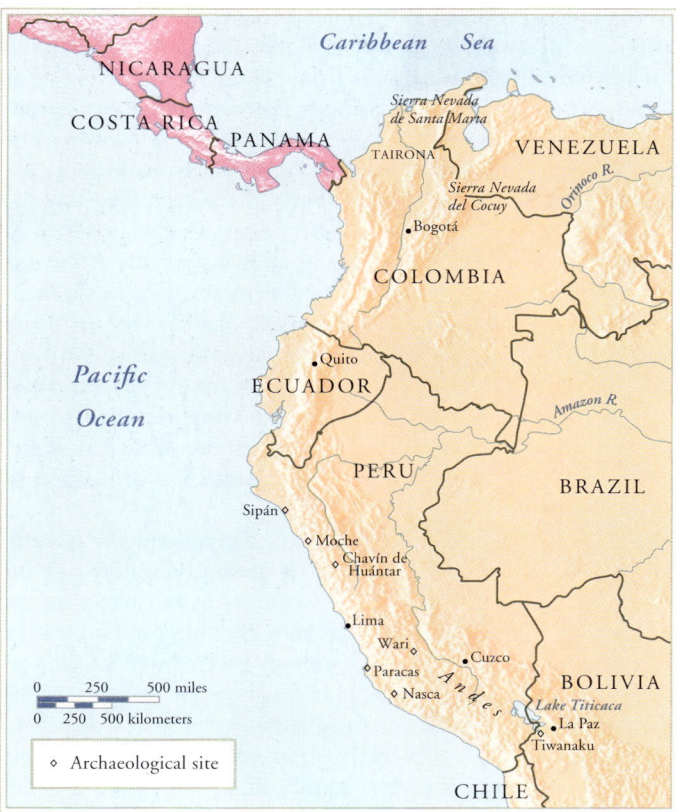

MAP 14-3 Andean region of South America.

first rudimentary art objects by 8800 BCE. Sophisticated textiles started to be produced as early as 2500 BCE during the Preceramic period. The firing of clay began around 1800 BCE during the so-called Initial period. Beginning about 800 BCE, Andean chronology alternates between periods known as "horizons," when a single culture appears to have dominated a broad geographic area for a relatively long period, and "intermediate periods" characterized by more independent regional development. The first period, Early Horizon, is represented by the Chavín culture (ca. 800–200 BCE); the Middle Horizon by the Tiwanaku and Wari cultures (ca. 600–1000 CE); and the Late Horizon by the Inka Empire (see Chapter 30). Among the many regional styles that flourished between these horizons, the most important are the Early Intermediate period (ca. 200 BCE–700 CE) Paracas and Nasca cultures of the south coast of Peru, and the Moche in the north.

## Early Cultures (ca. 3000–800 BCE)

The discovery of complex ancient communities documented by radiocarbon dating is changing the picture of early South American cultures. Planned communities boasting organized labor systems and monumental architecture dot the narrow river valleys that drop from the Andes to the Pacific Ocean. In the Central Andes, these early sites began to develop around 3000 BCE, about a millennium before the invention of pottery there. Carved gourds and some fragmentary cotton textiles survive from this early period. They depict composite creatures, such as crabs turning into snakes, as well as doubled and then reversed images, both hallmarks of later Andean art.

**CEREMONIAL ARCHITECTURE** The architecture of the early coastal sites typically consists of large U-shaped flat-topped plat-

forms—some as high as a 10-story building—around sunken courtyards. Many had numerous small chambers on top. Construction materials included both uncut fieldstones and handmade *adobes* (sun-dried mud bricks) in the shape of cones, laid point to point in coarse mud plaster to form walls and platforms. These complexes almost always faced toward the Andes mountains, source of the life-giving rivers on which these communities depended for survival. Mountain worship, which continues in the Andean region to this day, was probably the focus of early religious practices as well. In the highlands, archaeologists also have discovered large ceremonial complexes. In place of the numerous interconnecting rooms found on top of many coastal mounds, the highland examples have a single small chamber at the top, often with a stone-lined firepit in the center. These pits probably played a role in ancient fire rituals. Burnt offerings, often of exotic objects such as marine shells and tropical bird feathers, have been found in the pits.

## Chavín (ca. 800–200 BCE)

**CHAVÍN DE HUÁNTAR** Named after the ceremonial center of Chavín de Huántar, located in the northern highlands of Peru, the Chavín culture developed and spread throughout much of the coastal region and the highlands during the first millennium BCE. Once thought to be the "mother culture" of the Andean region, the Chavín horizon style is now seen as the culmination of developments that began some 2,000 years earlier elsewhere.

The main temple of Chavín de Huántar (FIG. **14-17**) resembles some sacred complexes of the Preceramic and Initial periods. It is a U-shaped, stone-faced structure facing east between two rivers. Although at first glance its three stories appear to be a solid stepped platform, in fact a labyrinth of narrow passageways, small chambers, and stairways penetrate the temple. No windows, however, light the interior spaces. The few members of Chavín society with access to these rooms must have witnessed secret and sacred torch-lit ceremonies. The temple is fronted by sunken courts, an arrangement also adopted from earlier coastal sites. Modifications to the structure during the centuries have resulted in the asymmetrical shape seen today.

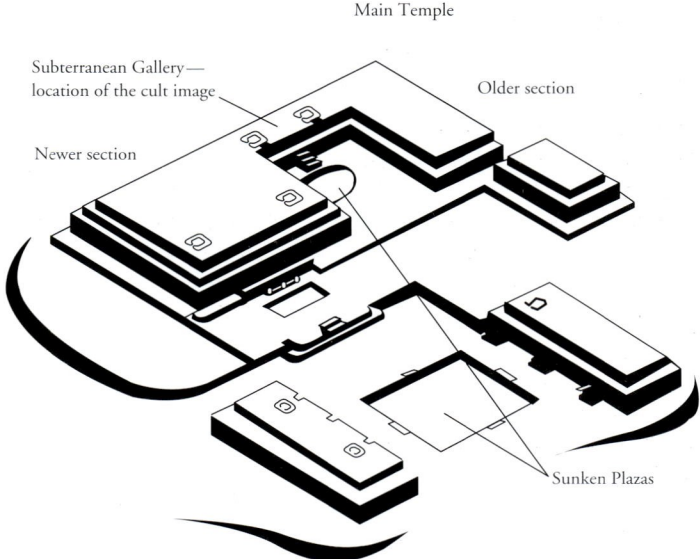

14-17 Reconstructed drawing of sacred center showing temple and associated sunken courtyards, Chavín de Huántar, Peru, first millennium BCE.

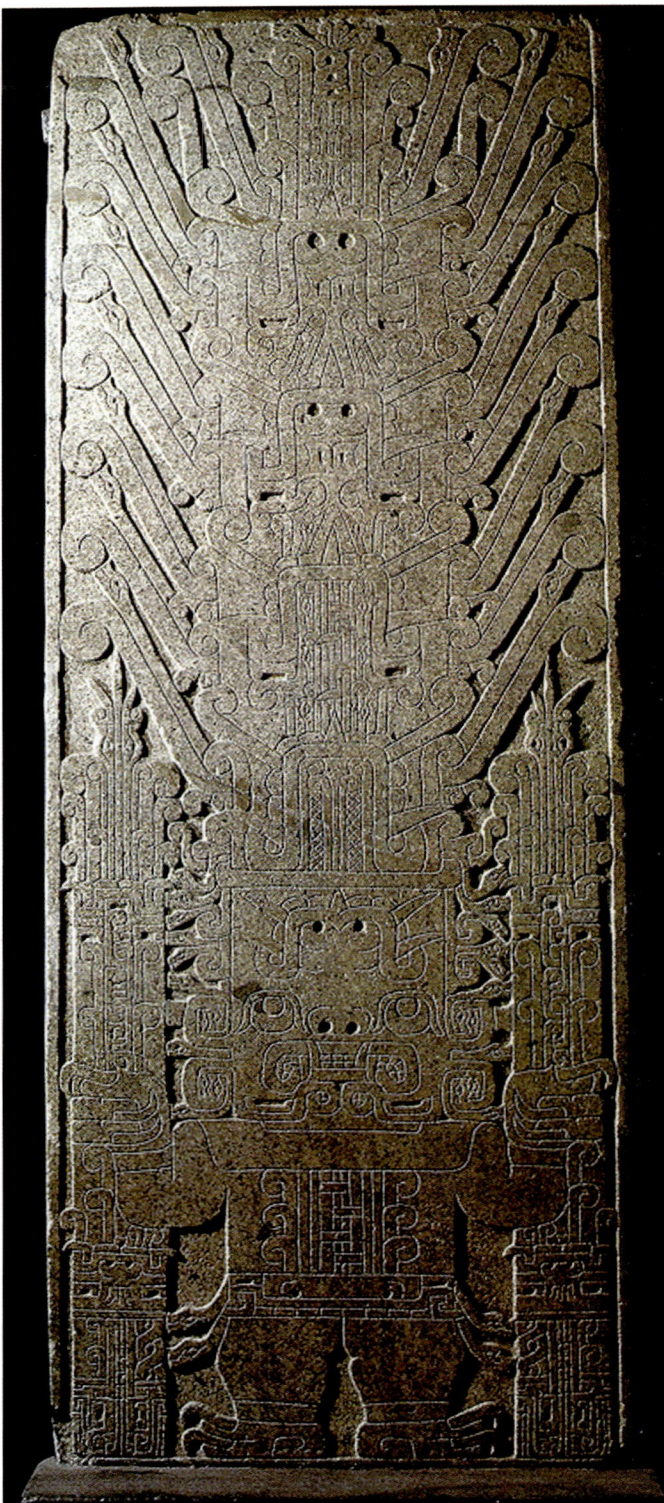

**14-18** *Raimondi Stele*, from main temple, Chavín de Huántar, Peru, first millennium BCE. Incised green diorite, 6′ high. Instituto Nacional de Cultura, Lima.

The temple complex at Chavín de Huántar is famous for its extensive stone carvings. The most common subjects are composite creatures that combine feline, avian, reptilian, and human features. Consisting largely of low relief on panels, cornices, and columns, and some rarer instances of freestanding sculpture, Chavín carving is essentially shallow, linear incision. An immense oracular cult image stood in the center of the temple's oldest part. Other examples of sculpture in the round include heads of mythological creatures *tenoned* (attached by stone pegs) into the exterior walls.

**A REVERSIBLE GOD** The *Raimondi Stele* (FIG. **14-18**), named after its discoverer, represents a figure called the "staff god." He appears in various versions from Colombia to northern Bolivia but always holds staffs. Seldom, however, do the representations have the degree of elaboration found at Chavín. The Chavín god bares his teeth and gazes upward. His elaborate headdress dominates the upper two-thirds of the slab. Inverting the image reveals that the headdress is composed of a series of fanged jawless faces, each emerging from the mouth of the one above it. Snakes abound. They extend from the deity's belt, make up part of the staffs, serve as whiskers and hair for the deity and the headdress creatures, and form a braid at the apex of the composition. The *Raimondi Stele* clearly illustrates the Andean artistic tendency toward both multiplicity and dual readings. Upside down, the god's face turns into not one but two faces. The ability of gods to transform before the viewer's eyes is a core aspect of Andean religion.

Chavín iconography spread widely throughout the Andean region through portable media such as goldwork, textiles, and ceramics. For example, more than 300 miles from Chavín on the south coast of Peru, archaeologists have discovered cotton textiles with imagery recalling Chavín sculpture. Painted staff-bearing female deities, apparently local manifestations or consorts of the highland staff god, decorate these large cloths, which may have served as wall hangings in temples. Ceramic vessels found on the north coast of Peru also carry motifs much like those found on Chavín stone carvings.

## Paracas (ca. 400 BCE–200 CE)

Several coastal traditions developed during the period between about 500 BCE and 600 CE. Together they exemplify the great variations within Peruvian art styles. The Paracas culture, which lasted about six centuries (ca. 400 BCE–200 CE), occupied a desert peninsula and a nearby river valley on the south coast of Peru.

**FUNERARY MANTLES** Outstanding among the Paracas arts are the funerary textiles used to wrap the bodies of the dead in multiple layers. The dry desert climate preserved the textiles, buried in shaft tombs beneath the sands. These textiles are among the enduring masterpieces of Andean art (see "Andean Weaving," page 397). Most are of woven cotton with designs embroidered onto the fabric in alpaca or vicuña wool imported from the highlands. The weavers used more than 150 vivid colors, the majority derived from plants.

Feline, bird, and serpent motifs appear on many of the textiles, but the human figure, real or mythological, predominates. A common theme on the grave mantles is humans dressed up as or changing into animals—consistent with the Andean transformation theme noted on the *Raimondi Stele* (FIG. 14-18). On the example we illustrate (FIG. 14-19) is a figure with prominent eyes, who appears scores of times over the surface. The flowing hair and the slow kicking motion of the legs suggest airy, hovering movement. The flying or floating being carries what some have identified as batons and fans and others as knives and hallucinogenic mushrooms. On other mantles the figures carry the skulls or severed heads of enemies. Some scholars have interpreted the flying figures as Paracas religious practitioners dancing or flying during an ecstatic trance. Others believe they are images of the deceased. Despite endless repetitions of the figure, variations of detail occur throughout each textile, notably in the figures' positions and in subtle color changes.

## Andean Weaving

When the Inka first encountered the Spanish conquistadors, they were puzzled by the Europeans' fixation on gold and silver. The Americans valued finely woven cloth just as highly as precious metal. Textiles and clothing dominated every aspect of their existence. Storing textiles in great warehouses, their leaders demanded cloth as tribute, gave it as gifts, exchanged it during diplomatic negotiations, and even burned it as a sacrificial offering. Although both men and women participated in cloth production, the Inka rulers selected the best women weavers from around the empire and sequestered them for life to produce textiles exclusively for the rulers.

The Andean weavers manufactured their textiles by spinning into yarn the cotton grown in five different shades on the warm coast and the fur sheared from highland llamas, alpacas, vicuñas, or guanacos, and then weaving the yarn into cloth. Rare tropical bird feathers and small plaques of gold and silver were sometimes sewn onto cloth destined for the nobility. Andean weavers mastered nearly every textile technique known today, many executed with a simple device known as a *backstrap loom*. Such looms are still in use in the Andes. The weavers stretch the long *warp* (vertical) threads between two wooden bars. The top one is tied to an upright. A belt or backstrap, attached to the bottom bar, encircles the waist of the seated weaver, who maintains the tension of the warp threads by leaning back. The weaver passes the *weft* (horizontal) threads over and under the warps and pushes them tightly against each other to produce the finished cloth. In ancient textiles, the sturdy cotton often formed the warp, and the wool, which can be dyed brighter colors, served to create complex designs in the weft. *Embroidery* (see

"Embroidery and Tapestry," Chapter 17, page 476), the sewing of threads onto a finished ground cloth to form contrasting designs, was the specialty of the Paracas culture (FIG. 14-19).

The dry deserts of coastal Peru have preserved not only numerous textiles from different periods but also hundreds of finely worked baskets containing spinning and weaving implements. These tools are invaluable sources of information about Andean textile production processes. The baskets found in documented contexts came from women's graves, attesting to the close identity between weaving and women, the reverence for the cloth-making process, and the Andean belief that textiles were necessary in the afterlife.

A special problem all weavers confront is that they must visualize the entire design in advance and cannot easily change it during the weaving process. No records exist of how Andean weavers learned, retained, and passed on the elaborate patterns they wove into cloth, but some painted ceramics depict weavers at work, apparently copying designs from finished models. However, the inventiveness of individual weavers is evident in the endless variety of colors and patterns in surviving Andean textiles. This creativity often led Andean artists to design textiles that are highly abstract and geometric. Paracas embroideries (FIG. 14-19), for example, may depict humans, down to the patterns on the tunics they wear, yet the figures are reduced to their essentials in order to focus on their otherworldly role. The culmination of this tendency toward abstraction may be seen in the Wari compositions (FIG. 14-25) in which figural motifs become stunning blocks of color that overwhelm the subject matter itself.

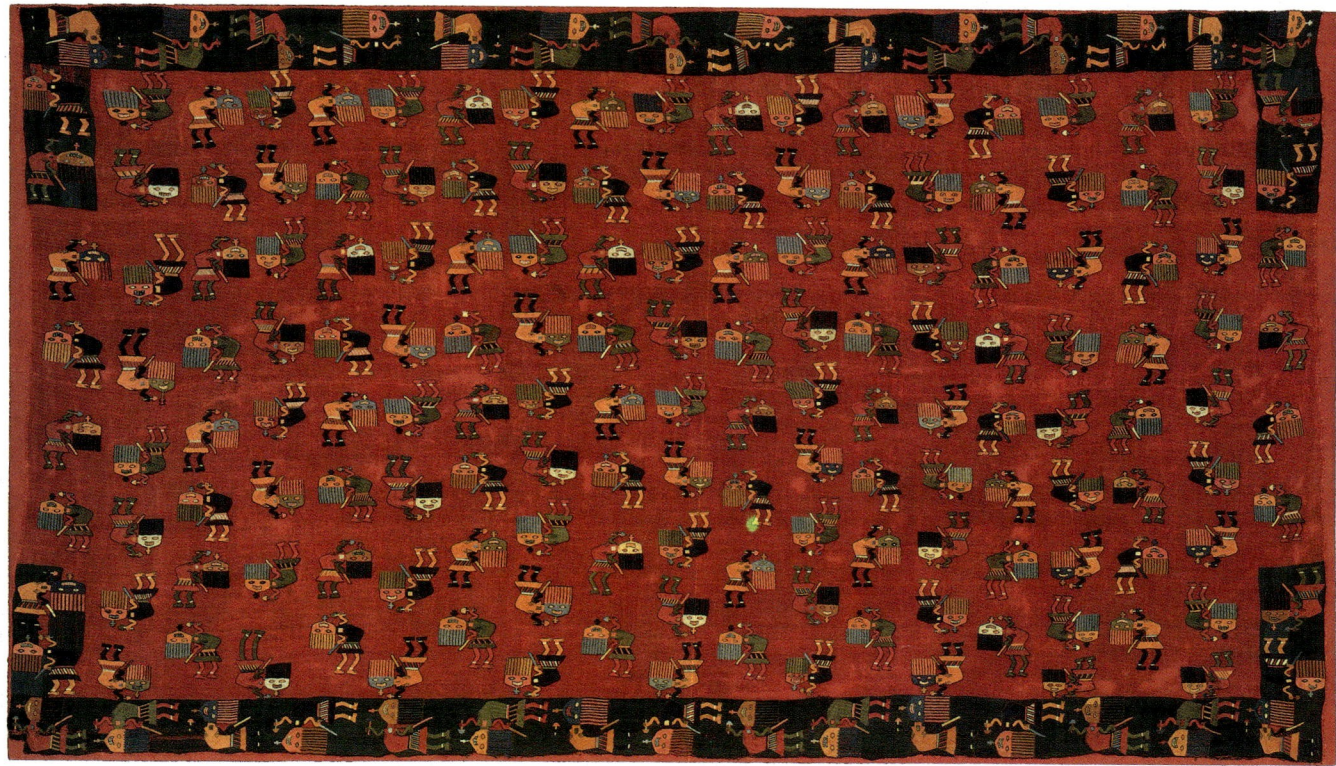

**14-19** Embroidered funerary mantle, Paracas, from southern coast of Peru, first century CE. Plain weave camelid fiber with stem-stitch embroidery embroidered with camelid wool, 4′ 7⅞″ × 7′ 10⅞″. Museum of Fine Arts, Boston (William A. Paine Fund. Photograph © 2003 Museum of Fine Arts, Boston).

## Nasca (ca. 200 BCE–600 CE)

**NASCA PAINTED POTTERY** The Nasca culture takes its name from the Nasca River Valley south of Paracas. The early centuries of the Nasca civilization are contemporary with the closing centuries of the Paracas culture, and Nasca style followed closely the Paracas flowing line and strong emphasis on color. The Nasca were renowned for their pottery. Thousands of their ceramic vessels survive. The vases usually have round bottoms, double spouts connected by bridges, and smoothly burnished polychrome surfaces. The subjects vary greatly, but plants, animals, and composite mythological creatures, partly human and partly animal, are most common. Nasca painters often represented ritual impersonators, some of whom, like the Paracas flying figures, hold trophy heads and weapons. In the example we illustrate (FIG. **14-20**), two such costumed figures fly around the vessel. The painter reduced their bodies and limbs to abstract appendages and focused on the heads. The figures wear a multicolored necklace, a whiskered gold mouthpiece, circular disks hanging from the ears, and a rayed crown on the forehead. Masks or heads with streaming hair, possibly more trophy heads, flow over the impersonators' backs, increasing the sense of motion.

**EARTH DRAWINGS** Nasca artists also depicted figures on a gigantic scale. Some 800 miles of lines drawn in complex networks on the dry surface of the Nasca Plain have long attracted world attention because of their colossal size, which defies human perception from the ground. Preserved today on the Nasca Plain are about three dozen images of birds, fish, and plants. Our illustration (FIG. **14-21**) shows a hummingbird several hundred feet long. The Nasca artists also drew geometric forms, such as trapezoids, spirals, and straight lines running for miles.

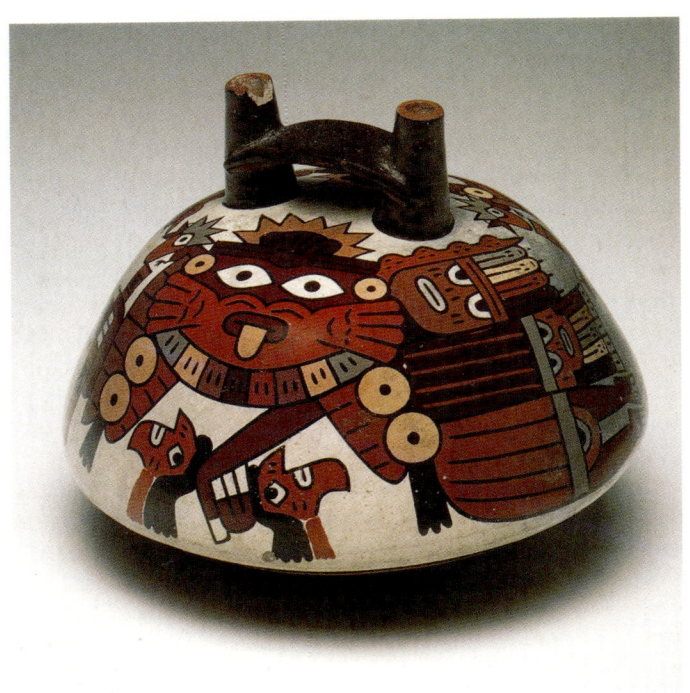

**14-20** Bridge-spouted vessel with flying figures, Nasca, from Nasca River valley, Peru, ca. 50–200 CE. Painted ceramic, approx. 5½″ high. Art Institute of Chicago, Chicago (Kate S. Buckingham Endowment).

These Nasca Lines, as the immense earth drawings are called, were produced when the artists selectively removed the dark top layer of stones to expose the light clay and calcite below. The lines were constructed quite easily from available materials and with

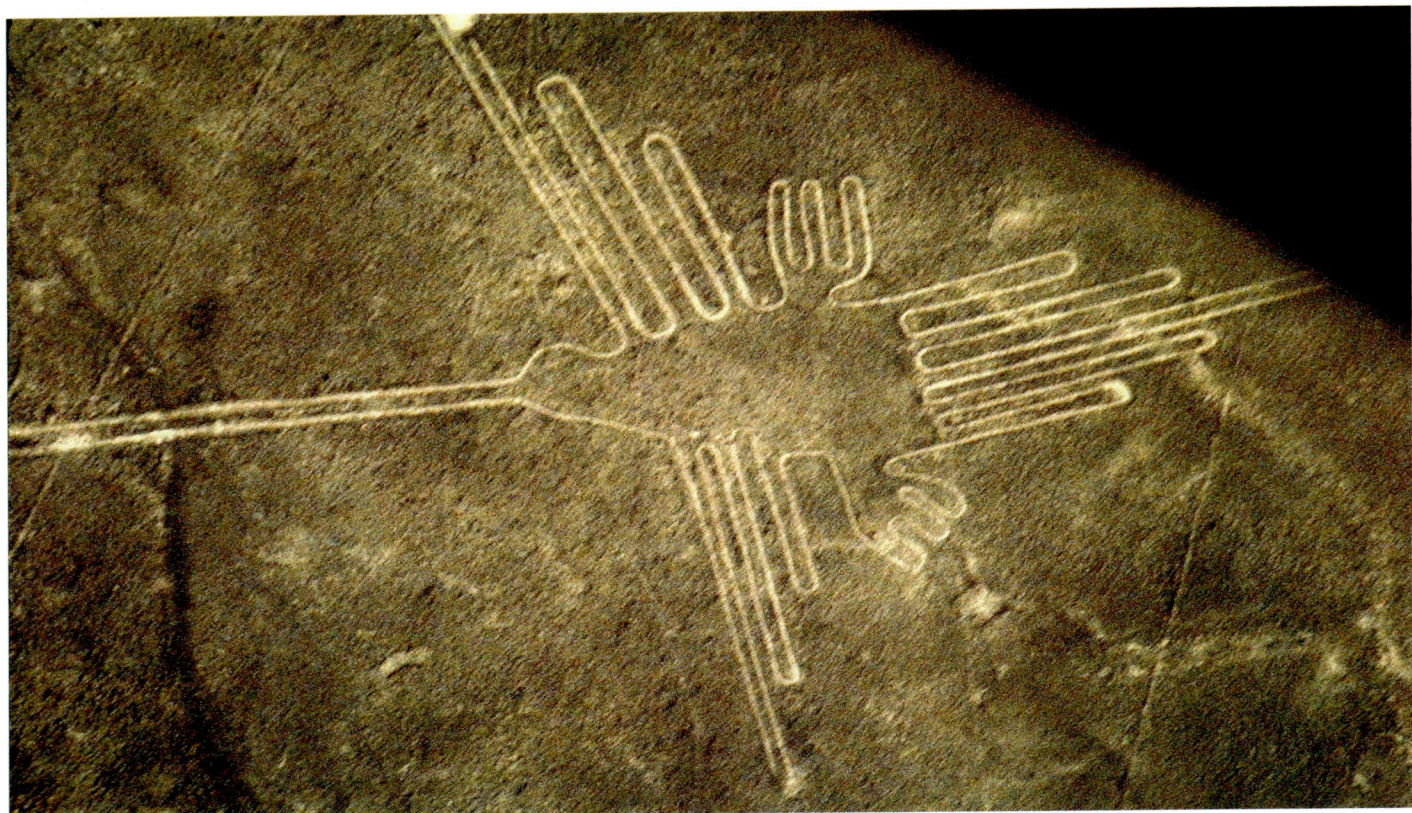

**14-21** Hummingbird, Nasca Plain, Nasca, Peru, ca. 500 CE. Dark layer of pebbles scraped aside to reveal lighter clay and calcite beneath.

some rudimentary geometry. Small groups of workers have made modern reproductions of them with relative ease. The lines seem to be paths laid out using simple stone-and-string methods. Some lead in traceable directions across the deserts of the Nasca River drainage. Others are punctuated by many shrinelike nodes, like the knots on a cord. Some lines converge at central places usually situated close to water sources and seem to be associated with water supply and irrigation. They may have marked pilgrimage routes for those who journeyed to local or regional shrines on foot. Altogether, the vast arrangement of the Nasca Lines is a system—not a meaningless maze but a traversable map that plotted out the whole terrain of Nasca material and spiritual concerns. Remarkably, until quite recently similar ritual pathways were made and used in association with shrines in highland Bolivia, demonstrating the tenacity of the Andean indigenous belief systems.

## Moche (ca. 1 – 700 CE)

**MOCHE CERAMICS** Among the most famous art objects the ancient Peruvians produced are the painted clay vessels of the Moche, who occupied a series of river valleys on the north coast of Peru around the same time the Nasca flourished to the south. Among ancient civilizations, only the Greeks and the Maya surpassed the Moche in the information recorded on their ceramics.

Moche pots illustrate architecture, metallurgy, weaving, the brewing of *chicha* (fermented maize beer), human deformities and diseases, and even sexual acts. Moche vessels are predominantly flat-bottomed stirrup-spouted jars derived from Chavín prototypes. They are generally decorated with a bichrome (two-color) slip. Although the Moche made early vessels by hand without the aid of a potter's wheel, they fashioned later ones in two-piece molds. Thus, numerous near-duplicates survive. Moche potters continued to refine the stirrup spout, making it an elegant slender tube, much narrower than the Chavín examples. This refinement may be seen in the portrait vessel illustrated here (FIG. **14-22**), an elaborate example of a common Moche type. It may depict the face of a warrior, a ruler, or even a royal retainer whose image may have been buried with many other pots to accompany his dead master. The realistic rendering of the physiognomy is particularly striking.

**THE LORD OF SIPÁN** Elite men, along with retinues of sacrificial victims, appear to be the occupants of several rich Moche tombs excavated near the village of Sipán on the arid northwest coast of Peru. The Sipán burials have yielded a treasure of golden artifacts and more than a thousand ceramic vessels. The discovery of the tombs in the late 1980s made a great stir in the archaeological world, contributing significantly to the knowledge of Moche culture. Beneath a large adobe platform adjacent to two high but greatly eroded pyramids, excavators found several lavish burials, including the tomb of a man known today as the Lord of Sipán or the Warrior Priest. The splendor of the funeral trappings that adorned his body, the quantity and quality of the sumptuous accessories, and the bodies of the retainers buried with him indicate that he was a personage of the highest rank. Indeed, he may have been one of the warrior priests so often pictured on Moche ceramic wares and murals (and in this tomb on a golden pyramid-shaped rattle) assaulting his enemies and participating in sacrificial ceremonies.

An ear ornament of turquoise and gold (FIG. **14-23**) found in one Sipán tomb shows a warrior priest clad much like the Lord of Sipán. Two retainers appear in profile to the left and right of the

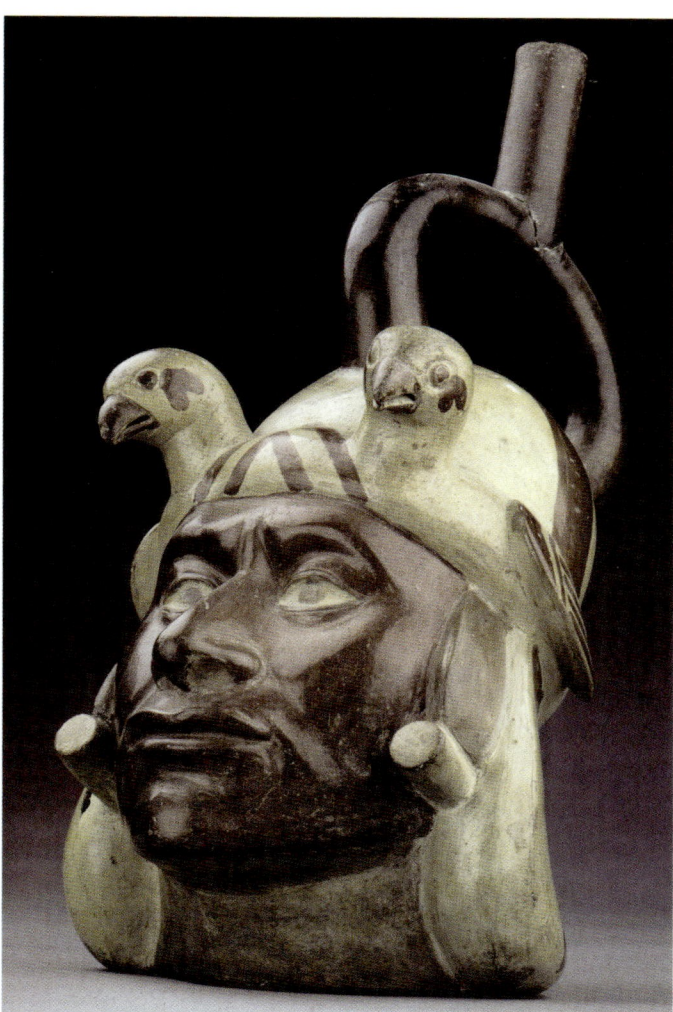

**14-22** Vessel in the shape of a portrait head, Moche, from north coast Peru, fifth to sixth century CE. Painted clay, $12\frac{1}{2}''$ high. Museu Arqueológico Rafael Larco Herrera, Lima.

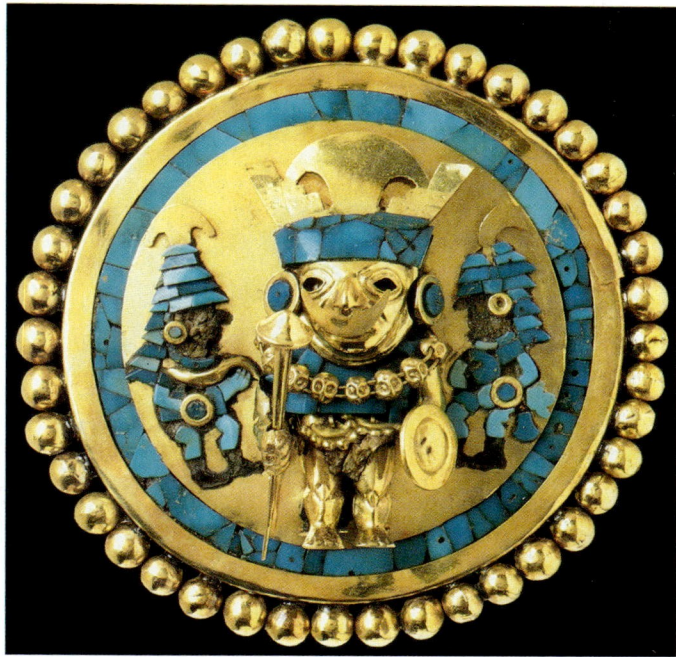

**14-23** Ear ornament, from a tomb at Sipán, Moche, Peru, ca. 300 CE. Gold and turquoise, approx. $4\frac{4}{5}''$. Bruning Archaeological Museum, Lambayeque.

central figure. Represented frontally, he carries a war club and shield and wears a necklace of owl-head beads. The figure's blade-like crescent-shaped helmet is a replica of the large golden one buried with the Sipán lord. The war club and shield also match finds in the Warrior Priest's tomb. The ear ornament of the jewelry image is a simplified version of the piece itself. Other details also correspond to actual finds—for example, the removable nose ring that hangs down over the mouth. The value of the Sipán find is incalculable for what it reveals about elite Moche culture and for its confirmation of the accuracy of the iconography of Moche artworks.

## Tiwanaku (ca. 100–1000 CE)

The bleak highland country of southeastern Peru and southwestern Bolivia contrasts markedly with the warm valleys of the coast. In the mountains, another culture developed beginning in the second century CE. Named Tiwanaku after its principal archaeological site on the southern shore of Lake Titicaca, the culture flourished for nearly a millennium, spreading to the adjacent coastal area as well as to other highland areas, eventually extending from southern Peru to northern Chile.

**THE GATEWAY OF THE SUN** Tiwanaku was an important ceremonial center. Its inhabitants constructed grand buildings using the region's fine sandstone, andesite, and diorite. Tiwanaku's imposing Gateway of the Sun (FIG. **14-24**) is a huge monolithic block of andesite pierced by a single doorway. Moved in ancient times from its original location within the site, the gateway now forms part of an enormous walled platform. The gate is crowned with relief sculpture. The central figure is a Tiwanaku version of the Chavín staff god (FIG. **14-18**). Larger than all the other figures and presented frontally, he dominates the composition and presides over the passageway. Rays project from his head. Many terminate in puma heads, representing the power of the highlands' fiercest predator. The staff god—possibly a sky and weather deity rather than the sun deity the rayed head suggests—appears in art throughout the Tiwanaku horizon, associated with smaller attendant figures. Those of the Gateway of the Sun are winged and have human or condor heads. Like the puma, the condor is an impressive carnivore, the largest raptor in the world. Sky and earth beings thus converge on the gate, which probably served as the doorway to a sacred area, a place of transformation. The reliefs were once colorfully painted. The figures' eyes were apparently also inlaid with turquoise, and the surfaces covered with gold, producing a dazzling effect.

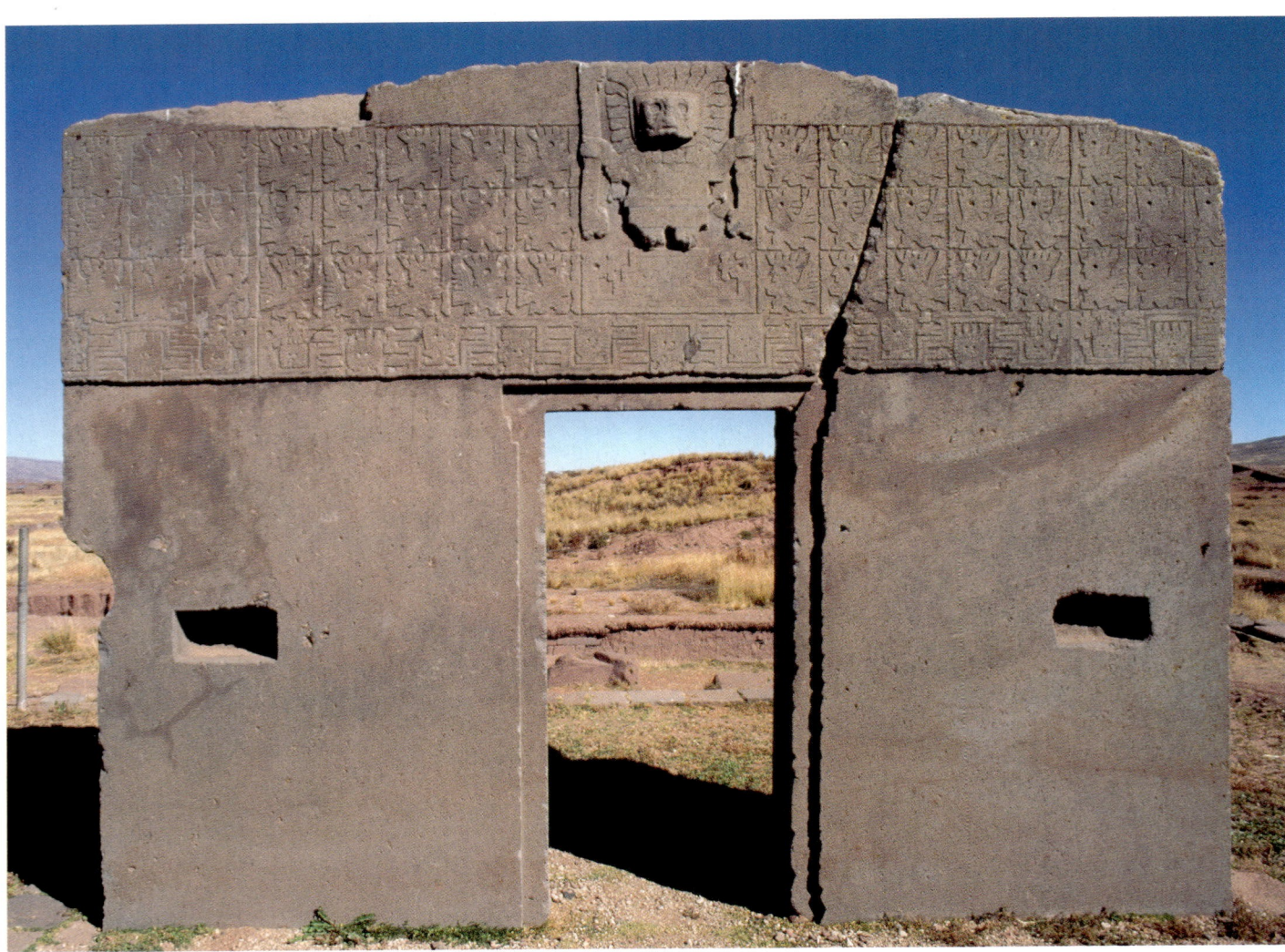

**14-24** Gateway of the Sun, Tiwanaku, Bolivia, ca. 375–700 CE. Stone, 9′ 10″ high.

## Wari (ca. 500–800 CE)

The flat, abstract, and repetitive figures surrounding the central figure on the Gateway of the Sun recall woven textile designs. Indeed, the people of the Tiwanaku culture, like those of Paracas, were consummate weavers, although many fewer textiles survive from the damp highlands. However, from a contemporaneous Peruvian culture known as Wari, which dominated parts of the dry coast, many examples of weaving, especially tunics, have been recovered.

**ABSTRACTION IN TAPESTRY** Although Wari weavers fashioned cloth, like the earlier Paracas textiles (FIG. 14-19), from both wool and cotton fibers, the resemblance between the two textile styles ends there. Whereas Paracas motifs were embroidered onto the plain woven surface, Wari designs were woven directly into the fabric, the weft threads packed densely over the warp threads in a technique known as *tapestry* (see "Embroidery and Tapestry," Chapter 17, page 476). Some particularly fine pieces have more than 200 weft threads per inch. Furthermore, unlike the relatively naturalistic individual figures depicted on Paracas mantles, those appearing on Wari textiles are so closely connected and so abstract as to be nearly unrecognizable. In the tunic shown here, the so-called *Lima Tapestry* (FIG. 14-25), the Wari designer expanded or compressed each figure in a different way and placed them in vertical rows pressed between narrow red bands of plain cloth. Elegant tunics such as this must have been prestige garments made for the elite.

# North America

**REGIONS AND PEOPLES** In many parts of the United States and Canada, indigenous cultures have been discovered that reach back as far as 12,000 years ago. Most of the surviving art objects, however, come from the past 2,000 years. Scholars divide the vast and varied territory of North America (MAP 14-4) into cultural regions based on the relative homogeneity of language and social and artistic patterns. Native lifestyles varied widely over the continent, ranging from small bands of migratory hunters to settled — at times even urban — agriculturalists. Among the art-producing peoples who inhabited the continent before the arrival of Europeans are the Eskimos of Alaska and the Inuits of Canada, who hunted and fished across the Arctic from Greenland to Siberia, and the maize farmers of the American Southwest, who wrested water from their arid

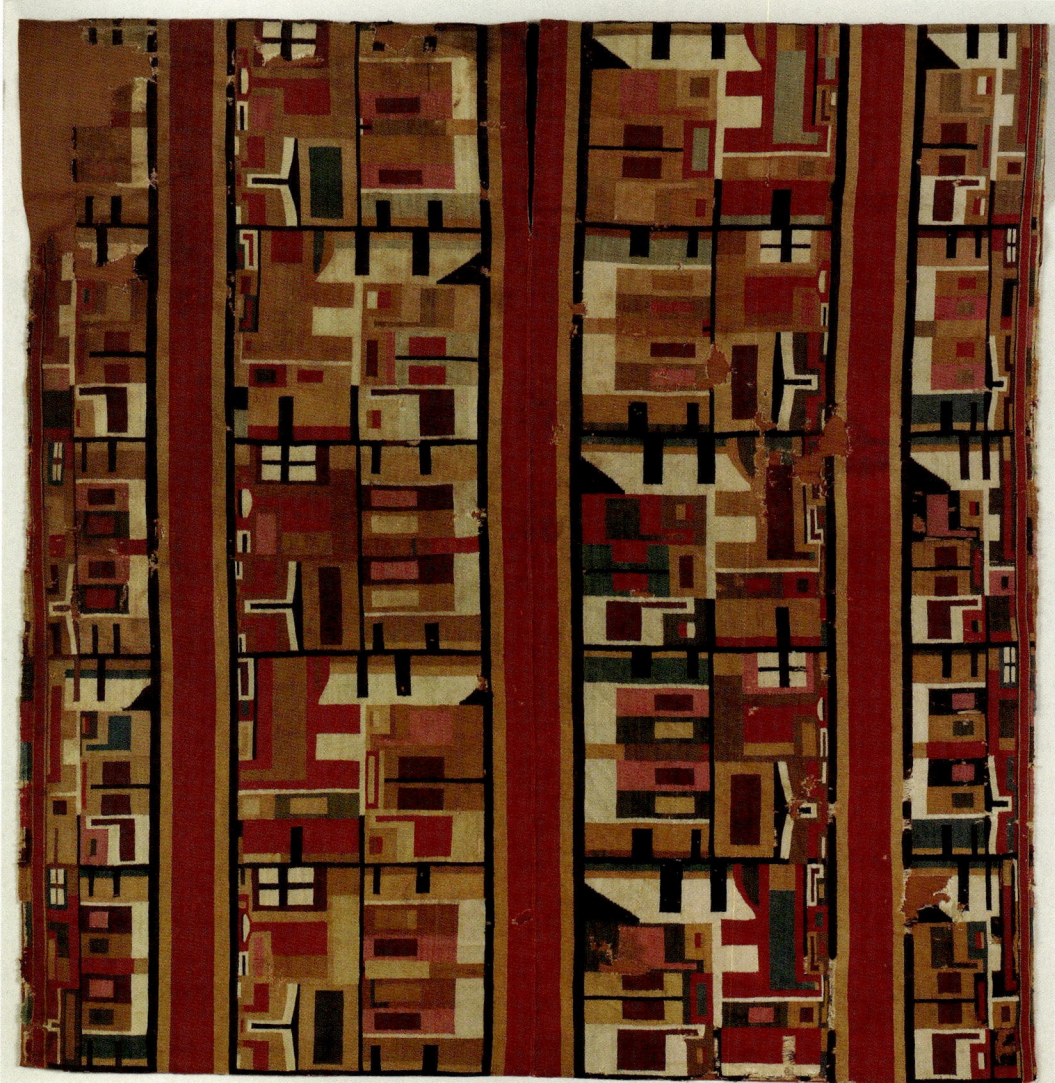

**14-25** *Lima Tapestry* (tunic), Wari, from Peru, ca. 500–800 CE. 3′ 3$\frac{3}{8}$″ × 2′ 11$\frac{3}{8}$″. National Museum of Archaeology, Anthropology, and History of Peru, Lima.

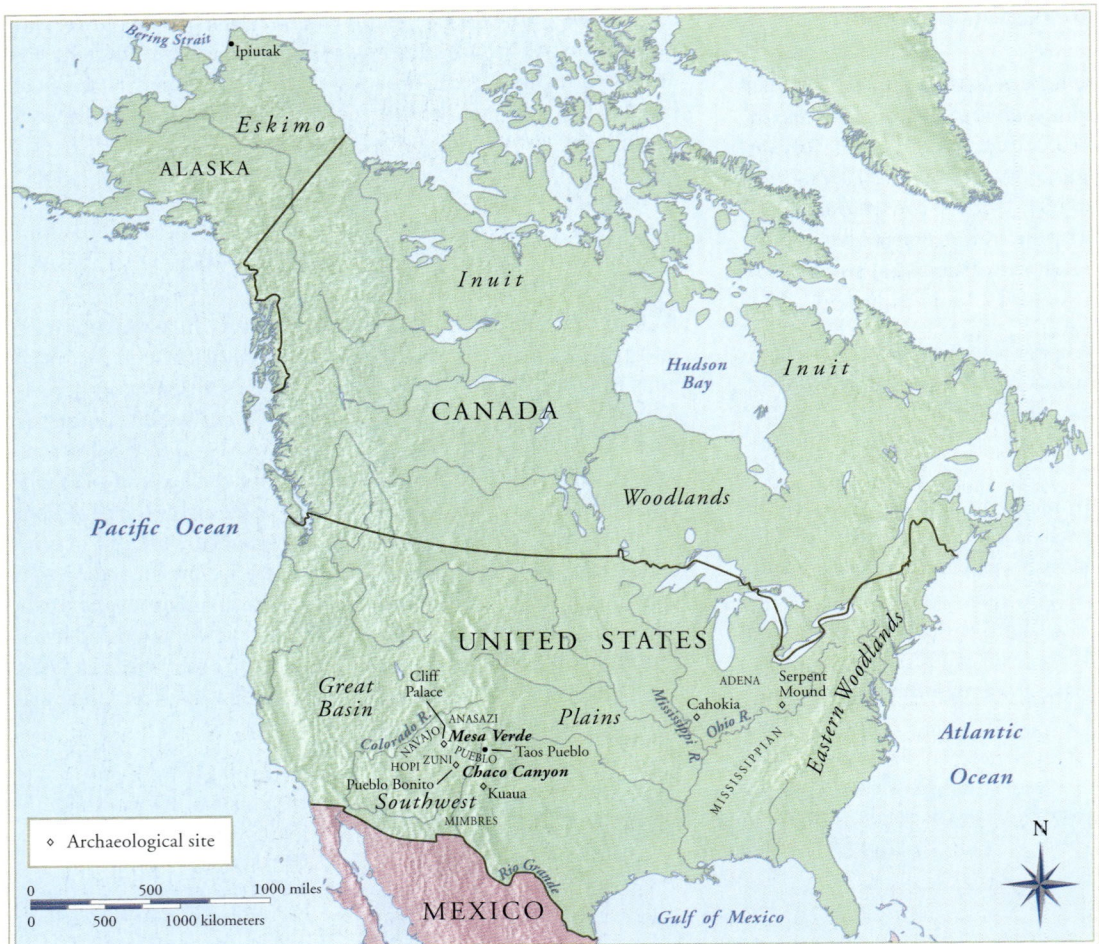

MAP 14-4 North America.

environment and built effective irrigation systems as well as roads and spectacular cliff dwellings. The vast, temperate Eastern Woodlands—ranging from eastern Canada to Florida and from the Atlantic to the Great Plains west of the Mississippi—also were home to farmers. Some of them left behind great earthen mounds that once functioned as their elite residences or burial places.

## Eskimo

**A MASK OF SEVERAL FACES** The Eskimoan peoples originally migrated to North America across the Bering Strait. During the early first millennium CE, a community of Eskimo sea mammal hunters and tool makers occupied the Ipiutak site at Point Hope in Alaska during the Norton, or Old Bering Sea, culture that began around 500 BCE. Finds from the site include a variety of burial goods as well as tools. Of special interest is a burial mask (FIG. **14-26**) datable to ca. 100 CE, fashioned, like most Arctic artworks, out of walrus ivory because of the scarcity of wood in the region. The mask is composed of nine carefully shaped parts that are interrelated to produce several faces, both human and animal, echoing the transformation theme noted in other ancient American cultures. The confident, subtle composition in shallow relief is a tribute to the artist's imaginative control over the material. The mask's abstract circles and curved lines are common motifs on the decorated tools discovered at Point Hope. For centuries, the Eskimo also carved human and animal figures, always at small scale, reflecting a nomadic lifestyle that required the creation of portable objects.

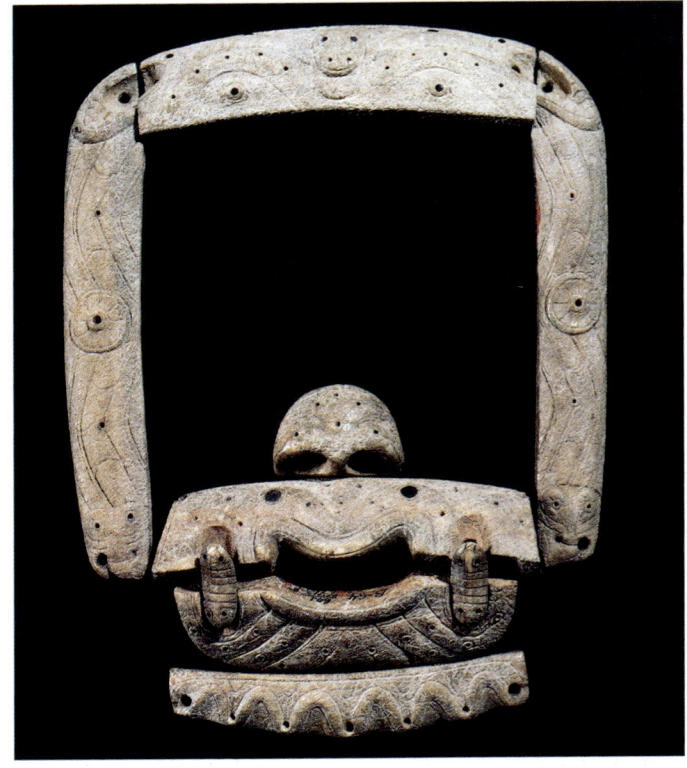

**14-26** Burial mask, Ipiutak, from Point Hope, Alaska, ca. 100 CE. Ivory, greatest width $9\frac{1}{2}''$. American Museum of Natural History, New York.

## Woodlands

**ADENA PIPES** Early Native American artists also excelled in working stone into a variety of utilitarian and ceremonial objects. A pipe in the shape of a man (FIG. **14-27**) is a product of the Adena culture of Ohio, documented at about 500 sites in the Central Woodlands. Carved between 500 BCE and the end of the millennium, the pipe is related in form and costume (note the prominent ear spools) to some Mesoamerican sculptures. The Adena buried their elite in great earthen mounds and often placed ceremonial pipes such as this one in the graves. Smoking was an important social and religious ritual in many Native American cultures, and pipes were treasured status symbols that men wanted to take with them into the afterlife. The standing figure on the illustrated pipe has naturalistic joint articulations and musculature, a lively flexed-leg pose, and an alert facial expression—all combining to suggest movement.

**MISSISSIPPIAN MOUNDS** The Adena were the first great mound builders of North America, but the Mississippian culture, which emerged around 800 CE and eventually encompassed much of the eastern United States, surpassed all earlier Woodlands peoples in the size and complexity of their communities. One Mississippian mound site, Cahokia in southern Illinois, was the largest city in North America in the early second millennium CE, with a population of at least 20,000 and an area of more than six square miles. There were approximately 120 mounds at Cahokia. The grandest, 100 feet tall and built in stages between ca. 900 and 1200 CE, was Monk's Mound. It is aligned with the position of the sun at the equinoxes and may have served as an astronomical observatory as well as the site of agricultural ceremonies. Each stage was topped by wooden structures that then were destroyed in preparation for the building of a new layer.

The Mississippians also constructed *effigy mounds* (mounds built in the form of animals or birds). One of the best preserved is Serpent Mound (FIG. **14-28**), a twisting earthwork on a bluff overlooking a creek in Ohio. It measures nearly a quarter mile

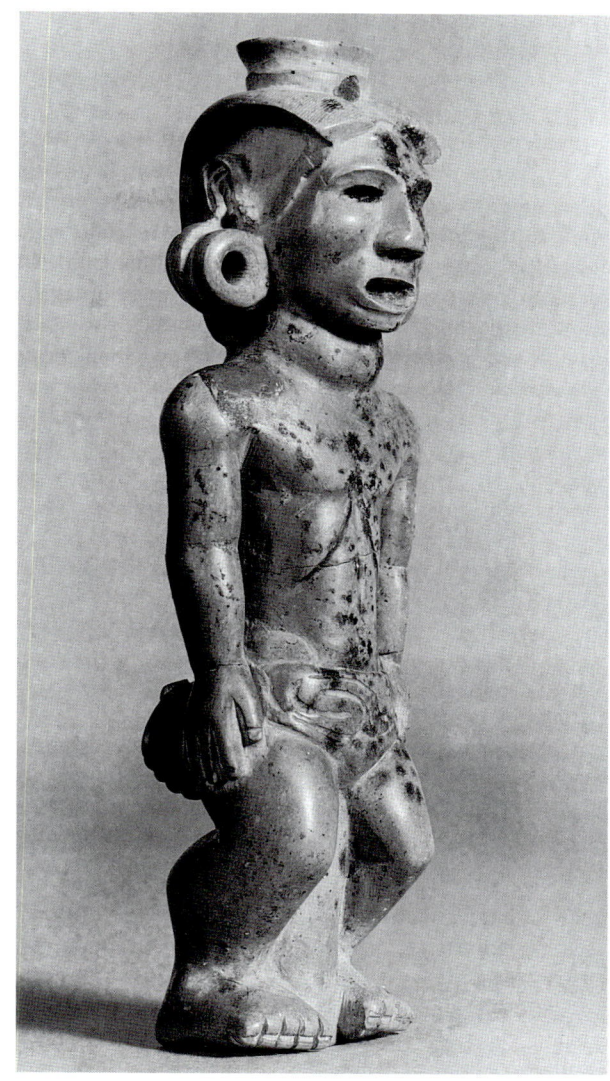

**14-27** Pipe, Adena, from a mound in Ohio, ca. 500–1 BCE. Stone, 8″ high. Ohio Historical Society, Columbus.

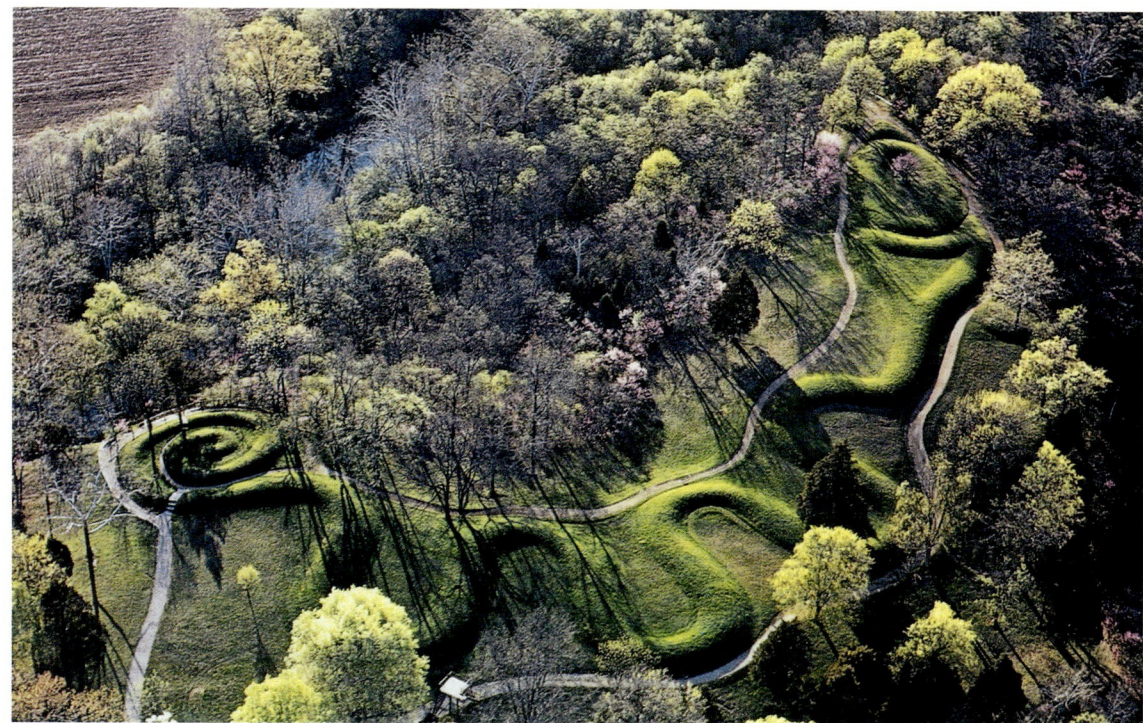

**14-28** Serpent Mound, Mississippian, Ohio, ca. 1070 CE. 1200′ long, 20′ wide, 5′ high.

### Serpent Mound

Serpent Mound (FIG. 14-28) is one of the largest and best known of the Woodlands effigy mounds, but it is the subject of considerable controversy. The mound was first excavated in the 1880s and represents one of the first efforts at preserving a Native American site from destruction at the hands of pot hunters and farmers. For a long time after its exploration, archaeologists attributed its construction to the Adena culture, which flourished in the Ohio area during the last several centuries BCE. New radiocarbon dates taken from the mound, however, indicate that it was built much later by the people known as Mississippians. Unlike most other ancient mounds, Serpent Mound contained no evidence of burials or temples. Serpents, however, were important in Mississippian iconography, appearing, for example, etched on shell gorgets similar to the one illustrated in FIG. 14-29. Snakes were strongly associated with the earth and the fertility of crops.

A stone figurine found at one site, for example, depicts a woman digging her hoe into the back of a large serpentine creature whose tail turns into a vine of gourds.

Another possible meaning for the construction of Serpent Mound, however, has been proposed recently. The new date suggested for it is 1070, not long after the brightest appearance in recorded history of Halley's Comet in 1066. Could Serpent Mound have been built in response to this important astronomical event? It even has been suggested that the serpentine form of the mound replicates the comet itself streaking across the night sky. Whatever its meaning, such a large and elaborate earthwork only could have been built by a large labor force under the firm direction of a powerful elite eager to leave its mark on the landscape forever.

---

from its open jaw (at the top right in our photograph), which seems to clasp an oval-shaped mound in its mouth, to its tightly coiled tail (at the far left). Both its date and meaning are controversial (see "Serpent Mound," above).

**MISSISSIPPIAN GORGETS** The Mississippian peoples, like their predecessors in North America, also manufactured small portable art objects. The shell *gorget*, or neck pendant, was a favorite item. Our example (FIG. **14-29**) was found at a site in Tennessee and dates from ca. 1250 to 1300 CE. The incised gorget

depicts a running warrior, shown in the same kind of composite profile and frontal view with bent arms and legs used to suggest motion in other ancient cultures (compare, for example, FIG. 5-15). The Tennessee warrior wears an elaborate headdress incorporating an arrow. He carries a mace in his left hand and a severed human head in his right. On his face is the painted forked eye of a falcon. Most Mississippian gorgets come from burial and temple mounds and are thought to have been gifts to the dead to ensure their safe arrival and prosperity in the land of the spirits. Other art objects found in such contexts include fine mica

**14-29** Incised shell gorget, Mississippian, from Sumner County, Tennessee, ca. 1250–1300 CE. 4″ wide. Courtesy National Museum of the American Indian, Smithsonian Institution.

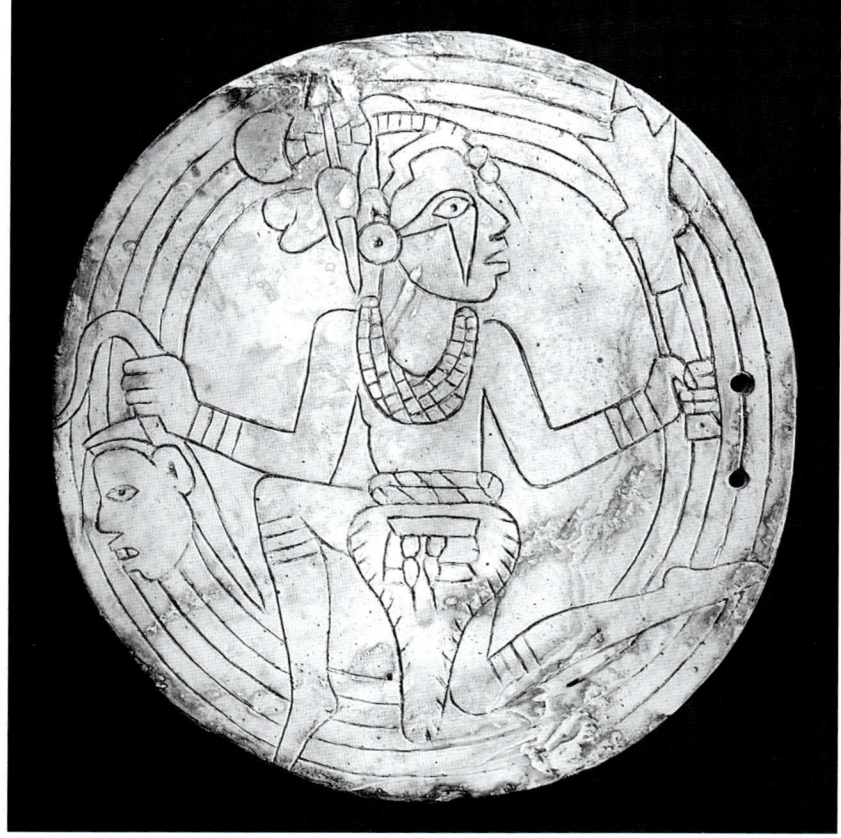

cutouts and embossed copper cutouts of hands, bodies, snakes, birds, and other presumably symbolic forms.

## Southwest

**MIMBRES POTTERY** In the Southwest, Native Americans have been producing pottery since before the beginning of the common era. The most impressive examples of decorated pottery, however, date after 1000 CE. The Mimbres culture of southwestern New Mexico, which flourished between ca. 1000 and 1250 CE, is renowned for its black-on-white painted bowls. The one we illustrate (FIG. **14-30**) dates to ca. 1250 and features an animated graphic rendering of two black cranes on a white ground. The contrast between the bowl's abstract border designs and the birds creates a dynamic tension. Thousands of different compositions are known from Mimbres pottery. They range from lively and complex geometric patterns to abstract pictures of humans, animals, and composite mythological beings. Almost all are imaginative creations by artists who seem to have been bent on not repeating themselves. Their designs emphasize linear rhythms balanced and controlled within a clearly defined border. Because the potter's wheel was unknown in the Americas, the artists used

the coiling method to build countless sophisticated shapes of varied size, always characterized by technical excellence. Although historians have no direct knowledge about the potters' identities, the fact that pottery making was usually women's work in the Southwest during the historic period (see "Gender Roles in Native American Art," Chapter 30, page 913) suggests that the Mimbres potters also may have been women.

Mimbres bowls have been found in burials under house floors, inverted over the head of the deceased and ritually "killed" by puncturing a small hole at the base, perhaps to allow the spirits of the deceased to join their ancestors in the sky (viewed as a dome by contemporary Southwestern peoples).

**ANASAZI PUEBLOS** The Anasazi (Navajo for "enemy ancestors"), northern neighbors of the Mimbres, emerged as an identifiable culture around 200 CE, but the culture did not reach its peak until about 1000. The Anasazi constructed architectural complexes that reflect masterful building skills. Many ruined Anasazi *pueblos* (urban settlements) are scattered throughout the Southwest. In Chaco Canyon, New Mexico, the Anasazi built a great semicircle of 800 rooms reaching to five stepped-back stories, the largest of several such sites in and around the canyon. Chaco Canyon was the center of a wide trade network extending as far as Mexico.

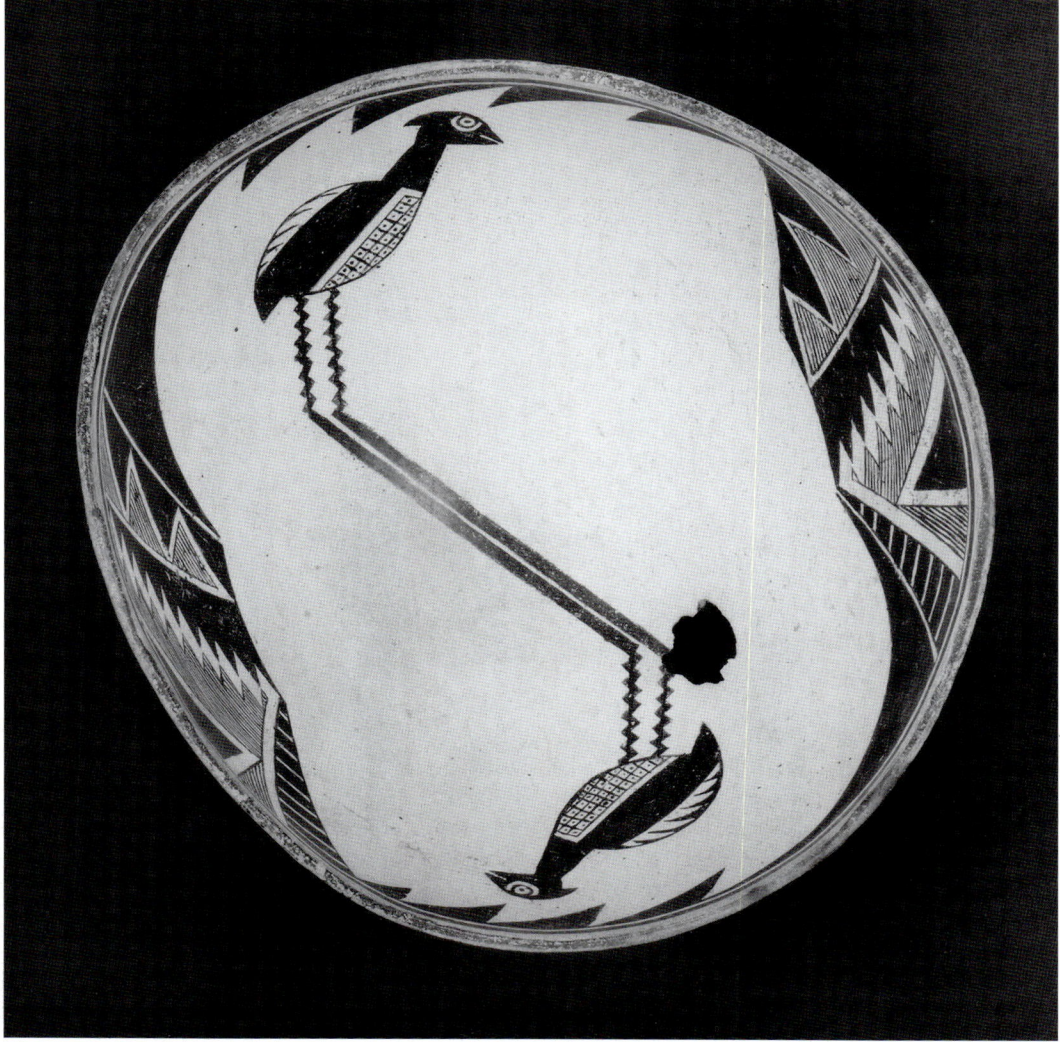

**14-30** Bowl with two cranes and geometric forms, Mimbres, from New Mexico, ca. 1250 CE. Ceramic, black-on-white, diameter approx. 1′ $\frac{1}{2}$″. Art Institute of Chicago, Chicago (Hugh L. and Mary T. Adams Fund).

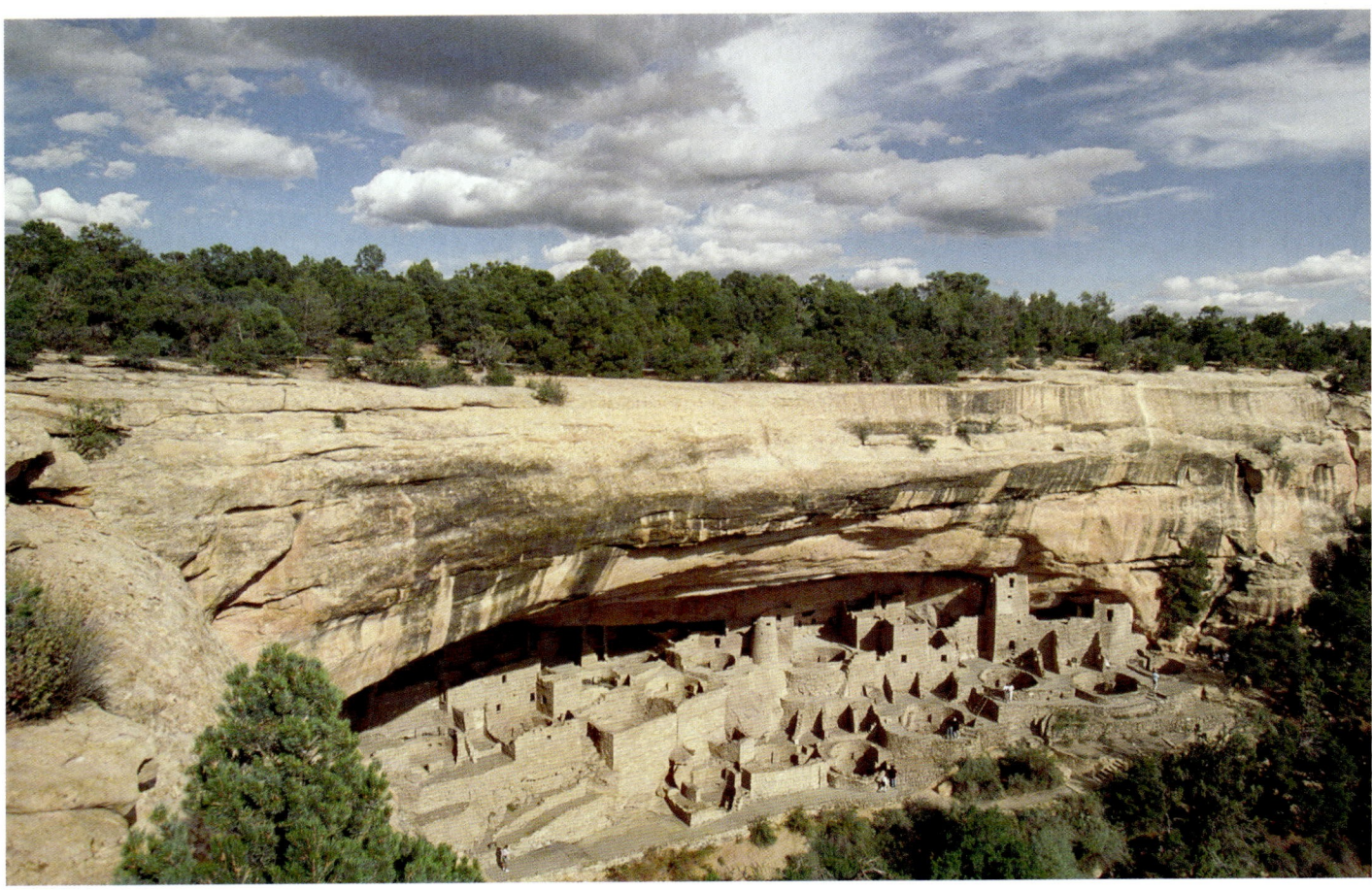

**14-31** Cliff Palace, Anasazi, Mesa Verde National Park, Colorado, ca. 1150–1300 CE.

Sometime in the late 12th century, a drought occurred, and the Anasazi largely abandoned their open canyon-floor dwelling sites to move farther north to the steep-sided canyons and lusher environment of Mesa Verde in southwestern Colorado. Cliff Palace (FIG. **14-31**) is wedged into a sheltered ledge above a valley floor. It contains about 200 rectangular rooms (mostly communal dwellings) of carefully laid stone and timber, once plastered inside and out with adobe. The location for Cliff Palace was not accidental. The Anasazi designed it to take advantage of the sun to heat the pueblo in winter and shade it during the hot summer months.

Scattered in the foreground of our Cliff Palace photograph are two dozen large circular semisubterranean structures, called *kivas,* which once were roofed over and entered with a ladder through a hole in the flat roof. These chambers were (and remain) the spiritual centers of native Southwest life, male council houses where ritual regalia are stored and private rituals and preparations for public ceremonies take place.

The Anasazi did not disappear but gradually evolved into the various Pueblo peoples who still live in Arizona, New Mexico, Colorado, and Utah. They continue to speak their native languages, practice deeply rooted rituals, and make pottery in the traditional manner. Their art is discussed in Chapter 30.

## CONCLUSION

When Europeans first arrived in the Americas in the late 15th and early 16th centuries, they encountered native peoples whose artistic traditions were at least as ancient as those of classical Greece and Rome. In Mesoamerica, the Olmec erected great earthen pyramids and colossal stone portraits between ca. 900 and 400 BCE. At Teotihuacán, a great city featuring a grid plan and towering stone pyramids arose between 100 BCE and 750 CE. The Classic Maya (ca. 300–900 CE) built vast complexes of temple-pyramids, palaces, plazas, and ball courts, and decorated them with monumental sculptures and mural paintings. In Andean South America, the Chavín culture erected monumental ceremonial complexes with extensive stone carvings between 800 and 200 BCE. The Paracas, Nasca, Moche, and Wari cultures (ca. 400 BCE–800 CE) have left behind fabulous ceramics and textiles. In North America, the Mississippian culture constructed huge earthen mounds beginning around 900 CE. From an early date, the native peoples of the American Southwest lived in sophisticated urban communities and excelled in the art of pottery. The extraordinary diversity of American art and architecture before contact with Europeans reflects the enormous variety and vitality of the native cultures of the Western Hemisphere.

| MESOAMERICA | SOUTH AMERICA | NORTH AMERICA | | |
|---|---|---|---|---|

**MESOAMERICA** **SOUTH AMERICA** **NORTH AMERICA**

| Column A | Column B | Column C | |
|---|---|---|---|

PRECLASSIC (FORMATIVE) — PRECERAMIC — 3000 BCE

2000 BCE

INITIAL PERIOD — 1200 BCE

□1 ▎OLMEC CULTURE, CA. 1200–400 BCE (M)

800 BCE

EARLY HORIZON

▎CHAVÍN CULTURE, CA. 800–200 BCE (S)

▎BEGINNINGS OF MAYA CIVILIZATION, CA. 600 BCE (M)

▎EARLIEST MESOAMERICAN WRITING, CA. 500 BCE (M)

▎ADENA CULTURE, CA. 500–1 BCE (N)

▎NORTON (OLD BERING SEA) CULTURE, 500 BCE–1000 CE (N)

▎PARACAS CULTURE, CA. 400 BCE–200 CE (S)

▎SHAFT-TOMB CULTURES OF WEST MEXICO, CA. 200 BCE–250 CE (M)

▎NASCA CULTURE, CA. 200 BCE–600 CE (S)

▎FOUNDATION OF TEOTIHUACÁN, CA. 100 BCE (M)

1 CE

□2 ▎MOCHE CULTURE, CA. 1–700 (S)

▎TIWANAKU CULTURE, CA. 100–1000 (S)

▎ANASAZI CULTURE, CA. 200–1400 (N)

EARLY INTERMEDIATE PERIOD — 300

CLASSIC — MIDDLE HORIZON — 400

VARIOUS OVERLAPPING INDIGENOUS CULTURES (SEE LIST)

▎WARI CULTURE, CA. 500–800 (S)

▎ITZAMNA BALAM II, YAXCHILÁN, R. 681–742 (M)

▎HASAW CHAN K'AWIL, TIKAL, R. 682–732 (M)

▎WAXAKLAHUN-UBAH-K'AWIL, COPÁN, R. 695–738 (M)

□3 ▎ABANDONMENT OF TEOTIHUACÁN, CA. 750 (M)

800

▎ASCENDANCE OF CHICHÉN ITZÁ, CA. 800 (M)

▎MISSISSIPPIAN CULTURE, CA. 800–1500 (N)

EARLY POSTCLASSIC — LATE INTERMEDIATE PERIOD — 900

▎ABANDONMENT OF SOUTHERN MAYA SITES, CA. 900 (M)

▎TOLTEC DOMINATION AT TULA, CA. 900–1200 (M)

1000

□4 ▎MIMBRES CULTURE, CA. 1000–1250 (N)

1300

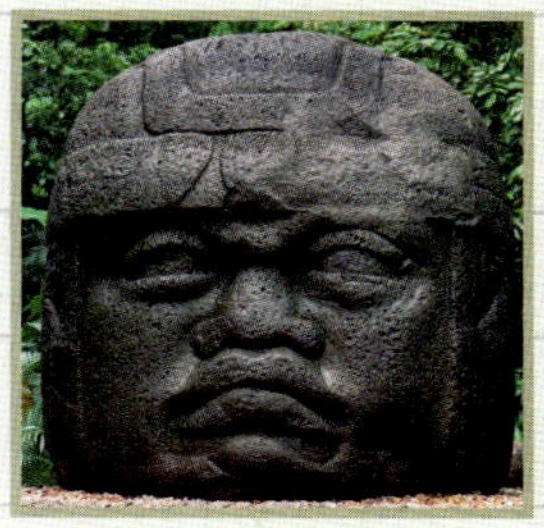

1 Olmec colossal head, La Venta, ca. 900–400 BCE

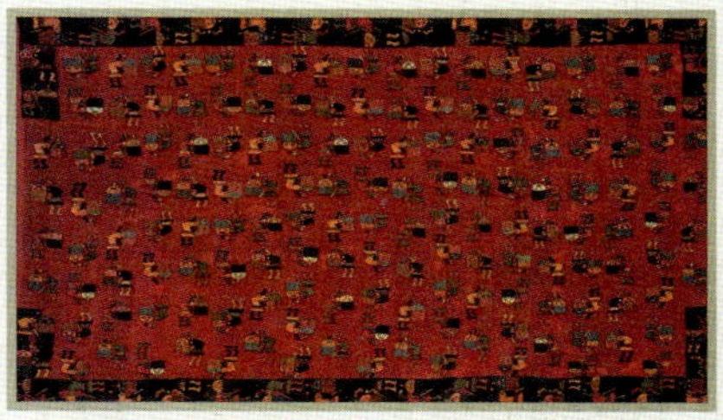

2 Embroidered funerary mantle, Paracas, first century CE

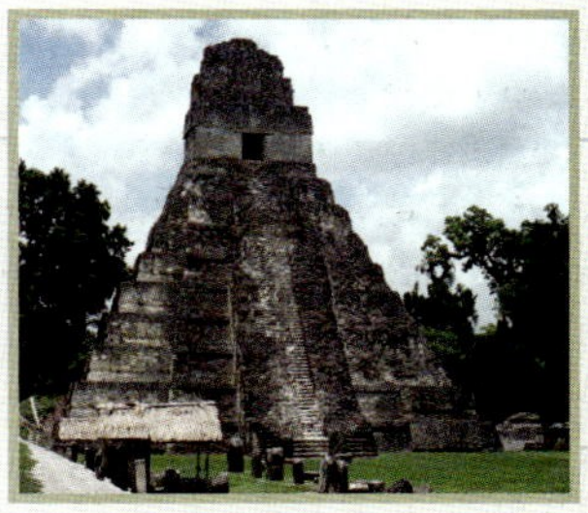

3 Temple I, Tikal, ca. 732

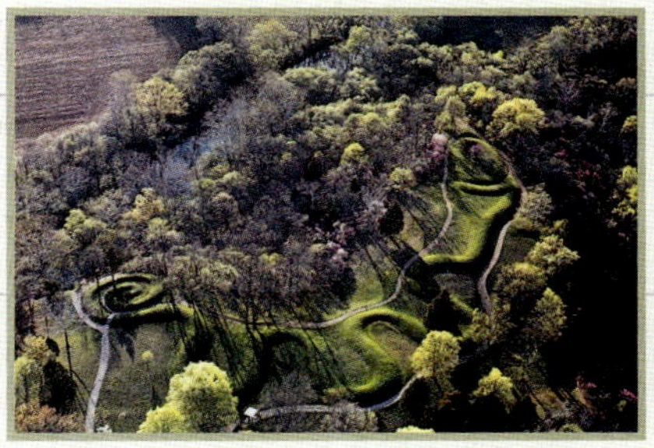

4 Serpent Mound, Ohio, ca. 1070

KEY: M = MESOAMERICA / N = NORTH AMERICA / S = SOUTH AMERICA

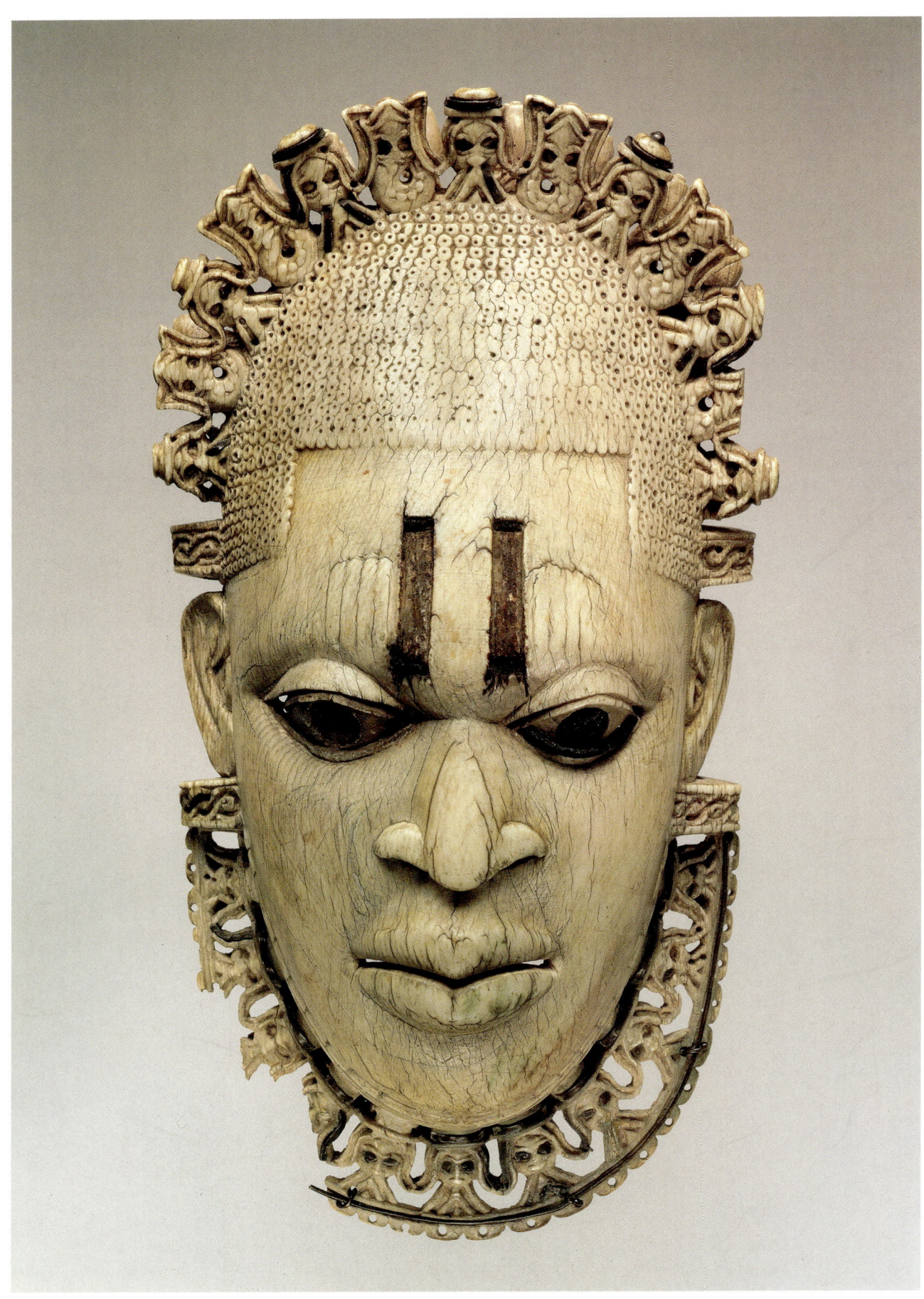

Ivory belt mask of a Queen Mother, from Benin, Nigeria, mid-16th century. Ivory and iron, 9⅜″ high. Metropolitan Museum of Art, New York (The Michael C. Rockefeller Memorial Collection, gift of Nelson A. Rockefeller, 1972. Photograph © 1995 The Metropolitan Museum of Art).

# 15

# SOUTH FROM
# THE SAHARA

## EARLY AFRICAN ART

Africa is a vast continent comprising more than one-fifth of the world's land mass and many distinct topographical and ecological zones. Parched deserts occupy northern and southern regions, high mountains rise in the east, and three great rivers—the Niger, the Congo, and the Nile—and their lush valleys support agriculture and large settled populations (MAP **15-1**). It is not yet possible to present a coherent, continent-wide history of early African art. A few areas have been fairly well surveyed archaeologically, but most of the continent remains little known in periods prior to European contact, which began along the seacoasts in the late 15th century. Many inland areas were virtually unknown to outsiders before 1850 or 1900.

Hundreds of distinct ethnic, cultural, and linguistic groups, often but inaccurately called "tribes," long have inhabited this enormous continent. Currently comprising more than 52 nations, such population groups historically have ranged in size from a few hundred, in hunting and gathering bands, to several million, in kingdoms and empires. Councils of elders often governed smaller groups, whereas larger populations sometimes have joined with other ethnic groups within a centralized state under a king. Kingdoms and empires headed by sacred rulers are known from several parts of Africa from about 1000 CE onward.

Within this great variety of African peoples are many shared core beliefs and practices. These include honoring ancestors and worshiping nature deities, often with blood sacrifice, and a tendency to elevate rulers to sacred status. Most peoples also consult diviners or fortune tellers. These beliefs have given rise to many richly expressive art traditions: rock engraving and painting, personal decoration, masquerades and other lavish festivals, the display of court arts and regalia, figural sculpture (often in shrines), elaborate architecture, and domestic arts, among other forms.

All the hundreds of ethnic groups in Africa, speaking as many mutually unintelligible languages, made visual arts that differ according to economy, lifestyle, ideology, and the materials available to them. Rock engravings and paintings in the Sahara and southern Africa, for example, depict thousands of animals as well as rituals held by the hunting and gathering or herding peoples who created most of the art. These nomadic and semi-nomadic peoples also excelled in the arts of personal adornment. Among farmers, in

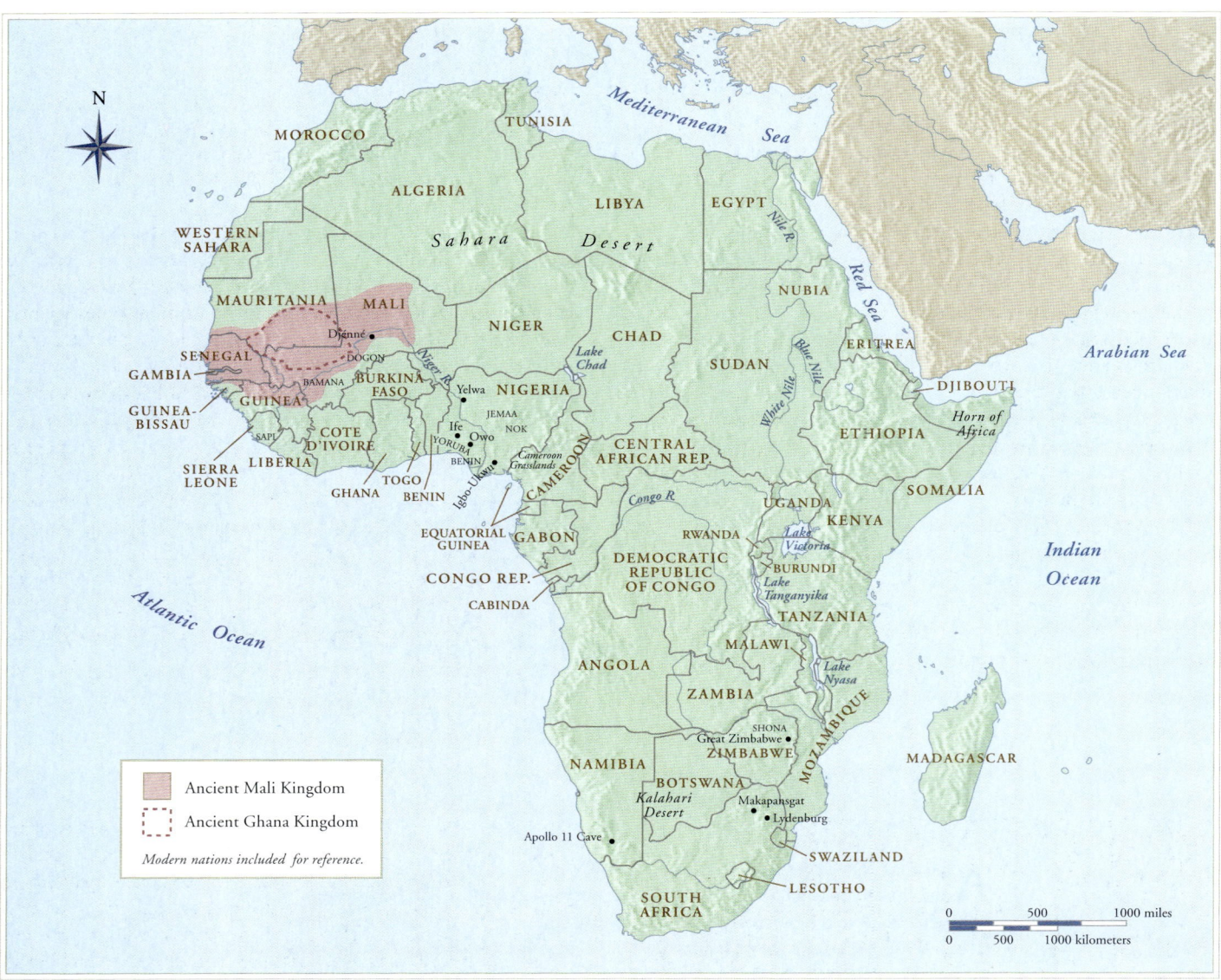

**MAP 15-1** Africa before 1800.

contrast, figural sculpture in terracotta, wood, and metal was often housed in shrines to legendary ancestors or nature deities held responsible for the health of crops and the well-being of the people. The regalia, art, and architecture of kings and their courts project ideas of wealth and power. Nearly all African peoples lavished artistic energy on the decoration of their own bodies to express their identity and status, and many communities mounted richly layered festivals, including masquerades, to celebrate harvests, the New Year, and the deaths of great people. In Africa, art helps define and create culture. It is integrated within African life and thought, and was not created solely for display until the final decades of the 20th century.

This chapter provides a chronological survey of sub-Saharan African art through the 18th century (see "Dating African Art and Identifying African Artists," page 411). Chapter 32 treats the past two centuries. The art and architecture of Egypt and of Roman and Islamic North Africa were examined in Chapters 3, 10, and 13 respectively.

## PREHISTORIC AFRICAN ART

**AFRICA'S EARLIEST ART** Thousands of rock engravings and paintings found in hundreds of sites across the continent constitute the earliest known African art. Some painted animals from the Apollo 11 Cave in southwestern Africa (see FIG. 1-2) date to perhaps as long ago as 25,000 years, earlier than all but the oldest Paleolithic art of Europe (see Chapter 1). As humankind apparently originated in Africa, the world's earliest art may yet be discovered there as well. The greatest concentrations of rock art are in what are now dry desert regions—the Sahara to the north, the Horn in the east, and the Kalahari to the south—as well as in caves and on rock outcroppings in southern Africa. Probably because rock artists were more often hunter-gatherers or herders than farmers, these are precisely *not* the areas where most African sculpture is found. Accurately naturalistic renderings as well as stylized images on rock surfaces show animals and humans in many different positions and activities, singly or in groups, stationary or in motion. Most of these works date to within the past 4,000 to 6,000 years or slightly more, and they provide a rich record of the environment, human activities, and animal species.

The central Saharan painting shown here (FIG. **15-1**), for example, depicts a running woman with convincing animation and significant detail. The dotted marks on her shoulders, legs, and torso probably show body painting applied for a ritual. The white parallel patterns attached to her arms and waist appear to

## Dating African Art and Identifying African Artists

Most African objects are unlabeled and unsigned and, consequently, insecurely dated. Early collectors did not bother to ask the names of artists or when the works were made. Organizing the vast array of African artworks into a firm chronology is therefore extremely difficult. Broad historical trends are reasonably clear, but more extensive archaeological work is needed in numerous parts of the continent before many artworks and even cultures can be firmly dated.

Some African peoples have left written documents that help date their artworks, even when their methods of measuring time differ from those used today. Other cultures, such as the Benin kingdom, preserve complex oral records of past events. Historians can check these against the accounts of Portuguese, German, and Dutch travelers and traders who visited the kingdom and recorded their observations.

The work of individual artists is now also being recognized, even if their names are often lost. Biographies have been compiled for some famous sculptors who worked in the late 19th or early 20th centuries. When artists are members of craft or occupational guilds—such as blacksmiths and brass casters in the Western Sudan—commissions go to the group chief, and the

specific artist who worked on the commission may never be known. Nevertheless, individual hands can be identified if their work is distinctive. Documentation now exists for several hundred individual artists.

Where documentation on authorship or dating is fragmentary or unavailable, art historians sometimes try to establish chronology from an object's style, determining what sorts of changes occurred over time to forms of a similar type. Scientific techniques such as *radiocarbon dating* (measuring the decay rate of carbon isotopes in organic matter to provide dates for wood, fiber, and ivory) and *thermoluminescence* (dating the amounts of radiation found in fired clay objects) have also proved useful. The history of African art is slowly being written, but there are still large gaps that need to be filled in. One of the major problems impeding compilation of an accurate African art history is illegal and uncontrolled excavation. By removing artworks from the ground, treasure hunters disturb or ruin their original contexts, and the possibility of establishing accurate chronologies is compromised or wholly lost. (This last problem is not unique to Africa; see "Archaeology, Art History, and the Art Market," Chapter 4, page 88.)

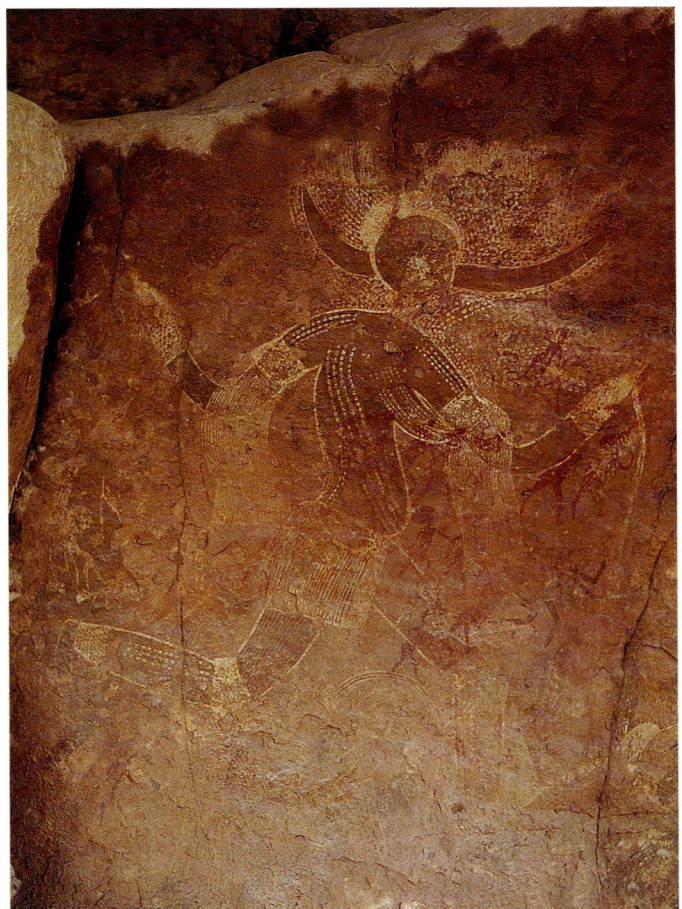

**15-1** Running woman, rock painting, from Tassili (Inauouanrhat), Algeria, ca. 6000–4000 BCE.

represent flowing raffia decorations and her skirt, also probably raffia. Horns are part of her ceremonial attire. Notably, this detailed image was painted over a field of much smaller painted human beings, an indication of why it is often so difficult to date and interpret art on rock surfaces, as superimpositions are frequent.

Although both the precise dating and meaning are problematic for much rock art, a considerable literature exists that describes, analyzes, and interprets the varied human and animal activities shown, as well as the evidently symbolic, more abstract patterns. Overall meanings and uses probably coincide with those of the later arts—references to ideas and rituals about the origin, survival, health, and continuity of human populations. The human and humanlike renderings depict people and a host of spirits and other supernatural beings and gods.

# AFRICAN ART, CA. 500 BCE–1000 CE

## Nok Art (Central Sudan)

**NOK TERRACOTTA HEADS** Outside Egypt and neighboring Nubia, the earliest African sculptures in the round have been found at several sites in the Central Sudan, part of a broad band of grassland that spans the continent south of the Sahara. These dispersed sites are collectively designated the Nok culture, but there is no reason to believe that they were unified politically or socially. Named after the site where such sculptures were first discovered in 1928, Nok art dates between 500 BCE and 200 CE. Hundreds of Nok-style human and animal heads, body parts, and figures have been found accidentally during tin mining operations, as well as in archaeological excavations.

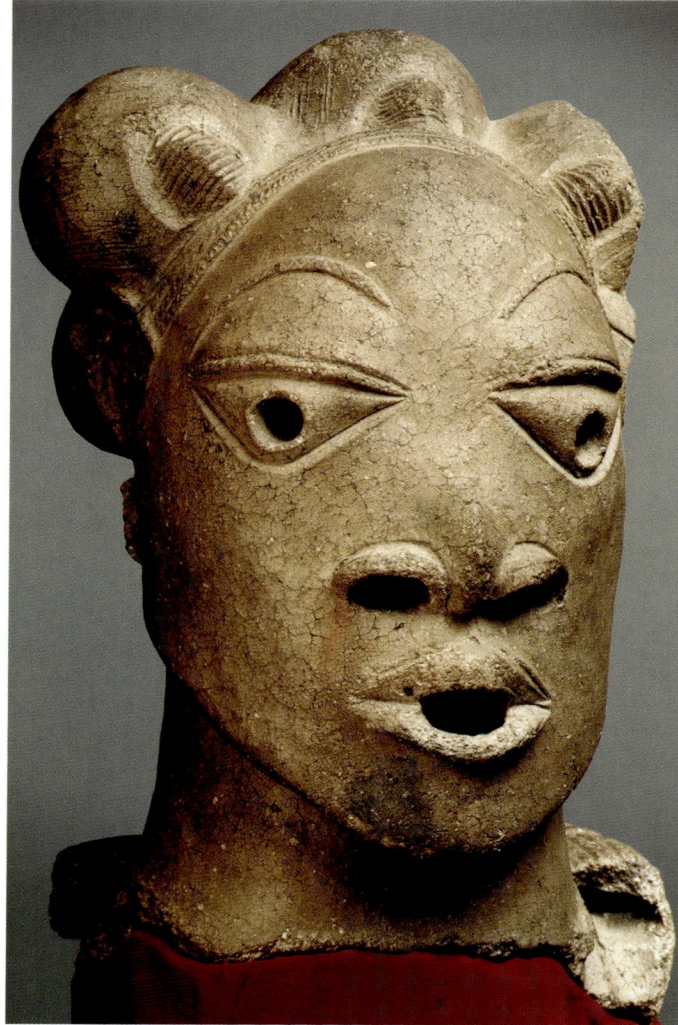

**15-2** Nok head, from Rafin Kura, Nigeria, ca. 500 BCE – 200 CE. Terracotta, 1′ 2 3/16″ high. National Museum, Lagos.

A representative Nok terracotta head (FIG. **15-2**), a fragment of a full figure, depicts an expressive face with large alert eyes, flaring nostrils, and parted lips. The sculptor probably pierced the eyes, mouth, and ear holes—a characteristic of Nok style—to help equalize the heating of the hollow clay head during the firing process. The coiffure with incised grooves, the raised eyebrows, the deeply cut triangular eyes, and the sharp jaw line suggest that the sculptor carved some details of the head while modeling the rest. A probable earlier artistic tradition of woodcarving that has not survived may explain the lack of any known art tradition leading to the highly sophisticated Nok sculptures. The gender of Nok artists is unknown. Because the primary ceramists and clay sculptors across the continent are women, Nok sculptors may have been as well (see "Gender Roles in African Art Production," Chapter 32, page 955). Researchers are unclear about the function of these objects, but a ritual context is more likely than a simply decorative one.

### Lydenburg Art (Southern Africa)

**SCULPTURE IN SOUTH AFRICA** Later in date than the Nok examples are the seven life-size (or nearly life-size) terracotta heads discovered outside the town of Lydenburg in present-day South Africa. They date to the later centuries of the first millennium of our era, although dating is controversial and still imprecise. The head shown here (FIG. **15-3**), reconstructed from frag-

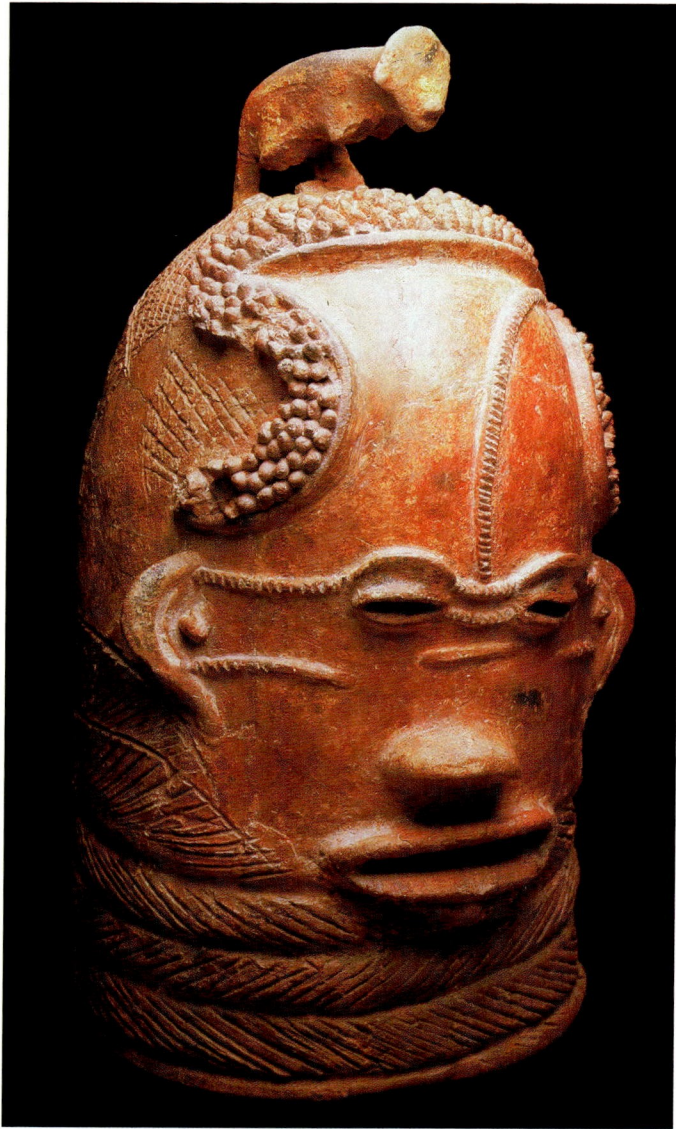

**15-3** Head, from Lydenburg, South Africa, sixth to eighth century CE. Terracotta, 1′ 2 15/16″ high. IZIKO Museums of Cape Town.

ments, has a humanlike form, although its inverted pot shape differs markedly from the sculptural Nok heads. The artist created the eyes, ears, nose, and mouth, as well as the hairline, by applying thin clay fillets onto the head. The same method produced what are probably *scarification* marks (scars intentionally created to form patterns on the flesh) on the forehead, temples, and between the eyes. The horizontal neck bands, with their incised surfaces, resemble the ringed or banded necks that are considered signs of beauty in many parts of the continent. A small, unidentifiable animal sits atop the head. One can only guess at the uses and meanings of these heads, but a ritual function is again more likely than a purely secular one.

### Igbo-Ukwu Art (Lower Niger Region)

**EARLY BRONZE CASTING** By the 9th or 10th century, a West African bronze-casting tradition of great sophistication had developed in the lower Niger area, just east of that great river. Dozens of refined, varied objects in an extremely intricate style were excavated in a family compound near the community of Igbo-Ukwu.

### Art and Leadership in Africa

The relationships between leaders and art forms are strong, complex, and universal in Africa. Political, spiritual, and social leaders—kings, chiefs, titled people, and religious specialists—have the power and wealth to command the best artists and to require the richest, most durable materials to adorn themselves, furnish their homes, and make visible the cultural and religious organizations they lead. Leaders dispense art or the prerogative to use it. They use it instrumentally both to maintain existing patterns and to cause change. Thus the uses and meanings of leaders' arts are varied, whether overt or subtle, active or passive.

A number of formal or structural principles or trends characterize leaders' arts and thus set them off from the popular arts owned and used by ordinary people. Leaders' arts—for example, the sumptuous and layered regalia of chiefs and kings—tend to be durable and are often made of expensive materials, such as ivory, beads, copper alloys, and other rich metals. The art and architecture commissioned by African leaders also tend to be larger and more complex than those of other patrons. A palace, for example, is more extensive, with more rooms and finer decoration, than an ordinary dwelling. The arts often elevate leaders and draw attention to their superior status: stools or chairs, ornate clothing, and special weaponry serve these purposes. A leader's reach is often extended by handheld objects: staff, spear, or knife; pipe, fly whisk (FIG. 15-4), or scepter. Such forms also serve to magnify gestures. These and other objects, such as fans (see FIG. Intro-16), shields, umbrellas, and architectural forms, protect leaders physically or spiritually. Many of these forms have the effect of magnifying the apparent size and grandeur of the leader, further setting him or her off from the people at large. Sometimes a person is overloaded with regalia and implements to the point of virtual immobility, suggesting that the temporary holder of an office is less significant than the eternal office itself. Still, these arts render both the office and its holder visibly prominent and grand, thus contributing to the person's place at the center and top of the hierarchy.

Although it is easier to see leaders' arts in centralized, hierarchical societies (such as Benin, FIG. 15-11), leaders among less centralized peoples are no less conversant with the power of art to move people and effect change. Masquerades and religious cults, for example, are usually established and run by leaders who themselves may be less visible than the forms they commission and manipulate: shrines, altars, festivals, and rites of passage such as funerals, the last being especially elaborate and festive in many parts of Africa. Arts controlled by leaders thus help create pageantry, mystery, and spectacle, enriching and changing the lives of the people.

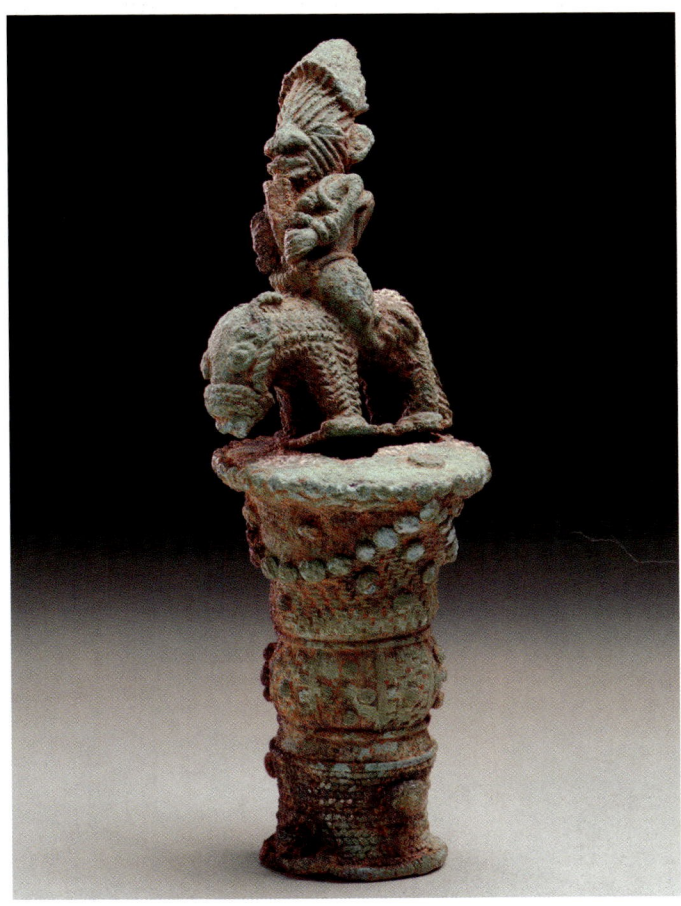

**15-4** Equestrian figure on fly-whisk hilt, from Igbo-Ukwu, Nigeria, 9th to 10th century CE. Copper-alloy bronze, figure $6\frac{3}{16}''$ high. National Museum, Lagos.

The ceramic, copper, cast bronze, and iron artifacts included basins, bowls, altar stands, staffs, swords, scabbards, knives, and pendants. In one burial, the grave goods consisted of numerous prestige objects—copper anklets, armlets, spiral ornaments, a fan handle, and thousands of beads. The tomb also contained three elephant tusks, a beaded armlet, a crown, and a bronze leopard's skull. These items, doubtless the regalia of a leader (see "Art and Leadership in Africa, above), are the earliest metal castings known from regions south of the Sahara.

A lost-wax cast bronze (FIG. **15-4**), the earliest found in Africa, depicts an equestrian figure on a fly-whisk handle. The handle was made by a casting method similar to that used much earlier in the Mediterranean and Near East (see "Hollow-Casting," Chapter 5, page 131). The sculpture's upper section comprises a figure seated on a horselike animal, and the lower is an elaborately embellished handle with beaded and threadlike patterns. The facial stripes on the human figure probably represent marks of titled status, as can still be found among contemporary Igbo-speaking peoples in the same region today.

## AFRICAN ART, CA. 1000–1800*

### Inland Niger Delta Art (Western Sudan)

The inland floodplain of the Niger River in the Western Sudan was for the African continent a kind of "fertile crescent," analogous to that of ancient Mesopotamia (see Chapter 2). The metal-casting techniques used in Igbo-Ukwu, for example, may have come from this region. Although firm evidence for bronze casting

---

* From this point on, all dates in this chapter are CE unless otherwise stated.

## Idealized Naturalism at Ile-Ife

When the German anthropologist Leo Frobenius first "discovered" the refined and naturalistic sculpture of Ile-Ife just after the turn of the 19th century in the Lower Niger River region, he could not believe that such works were locally made. Rather, he ascribed authorship to ancient Greece, where similarly lifelike art was well known. Other scholars traced such works to ancient Egypt, along with patterns of sacred kingship that were also believed to have been diffused several thousand miles from the Nile Valley to Yorubaland. Kings are known in numerous Yoruba city-states, all of which trace their origin to Ile-Ife, where Yoruba legends recount the world, its peoples, and sacred kingship began. Many careful archaeological excavations in and around the contemporary city of Ile-Ife, especially near the king's palace, moreover, confirm that the Yoruba ancestors of present-day residents were indeed the artists who made the extraordinary sculptures in stone, terracotta, and copper alloys ascribed to Ile-Ife. A number of these works were employed in the service of kingship, in ceremonies of installation, in funerals, and probably in annual festivals that reaffirmed the sacred power of the ruler and the allegiance of his people. Radiocarbon dates associated with several excavated Ife sites and with works of idealized naturalism place most of this art between the 11th or 12th and the 15th centuries.

Like the king figure we illustrate (FIG. 15-6), most Ife heads and figures are modeled with focused attention on naturalistic detail, apart from blemishes or signs of age, which are absent. Thus Ife style is lifelike but at the same time idealized, as if most of the people were portrayed as young adults in the prime of life and without any disfiguring warts or wrinkles. Some life-size heads,

although still idealized, take naturalism to the point of descriptive, imitative portraiture. This is especially true of a group of about 30 heads cast in copper alloys. Many of these are sufficiently individualized that scholars are quite certain specific persons were being portrayed, although nearly all their names are lost. Among the most convincing portraits, however, is a mask of almost pure copper that has long carried the name of a famous early king, Obalufon. Until it became a holding of the Ife museum, the mask was apparently kept in the palace of the *oni* (king) from the time that it was made. Several very naturalistic heads have small holes above the forehead and around the lips and jaw, where black beads were found. These suggest that some heads were fitted with beaded veils, such as those known among Yoruba kings today, and perhaps human hair as well. Elaborate beadwork, a Yoruba royal prerogative, is also seen on the Ife king's image we illustrate (FIG. 15-6).

The hundreds of terracotta and copper-alloy heads, body parts and fragments, animals, and ritual vessels from Ile-Ife attest to a remarkable period in African art history, a period during which sensitive, meticulously rendered idealized naturalism prevailed. To this day works in this style stand in contrast to the vast majority of African objects, which show the human figure in many different quite strongly conventionalized styles. Also clear is the distinction between the "perceptual naturalism" of most Ife works and the "conceptual naturalism" of most other African art. The latter suggests that for the most part, the representation of human forms conformed to local conventions passed down from one artist to another, whereas Ife style came about when artists actually perceived the human faces and bodies they portrayed.

---

in the Inland Delta has yet to be discovered, a copper industry is known to have flourished there from around 500, and sophisticated sculpture dates from around 1000.

**JENNE TERRACOTTAS** By about 800, a walled town, called Jenne-Jeno by archaeologists, had been built on high ground left dry during the flooding season. The archaeological evidence suggests the presence of several ethnic groups and many specialist workshops of blacksmiths, sculptors, potters, and others. Hundreds of accomplished, confidently modeled terracotta sculptures dating to between 1000 and 1500 have been found at numerous unmapped sites in the Jenne region. Unfortunately, as is true of the Nok terracottas, the vast majority of these sculptures were excavated illegally, and contextual information about them has been destroyed. The subject matter includes equestrians, male and female couples, emaciated and diseased people with lesions and swellings, and snake-entwined figures. There are seated, reclining, kneeling, and standing human figures. Some wear elaborate jewelry, but many are without adornment. The group we illustrate (FIG. **15-5**) appears at first to be a mother and her children, but the "children" clambering up their "mother's" torso are in fact adults, easily discerned as such by their proportions. In some similar groups the "children" have beards. The woman therefore seems to be a metaphorical or legendary mother and the group is not a common family, although everyday genre scenes also occur among the preserved ceramic sculptures from the Inland Niger Delta.

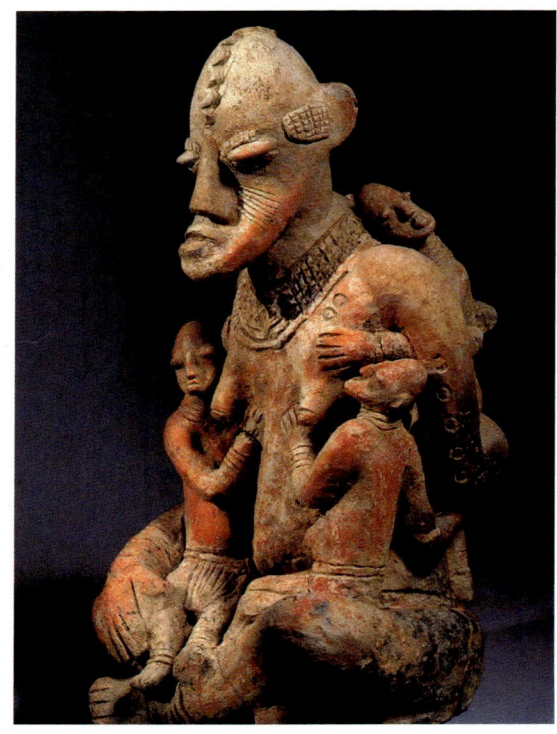

**15-5** Mother with children(?), from the Inland Niger Delta, Mali, ca. 1000–1500. Terracotta, 1' 1¾" high. Private collection.

## Ile-Ife Art (West of the Lower Niger)

By the 11th and 12th centuries, a very naturalistic style had appeared at Ile-Ife, about 200 miles west of Igbo Ukwu. Ile-Ife has long been considered the cradle of Yoruba civilization, the place where the gods created the universe. Origin stories also account for a line of divine Yoruba rulers extending from the legendary past until today.

**SACRED KINGS** An early work (FIG. **15-6**), cast in a zinc-brass alloy, undoubtedly represents a ruler. This finely rendered figure, unlike most later African wood sculpture, shows fleshlike modeling in the torso and the kind of idealized naturalism in facial features that approaches portraiture (see "Idealized Naturalism at Ile-Ife," page 414). Its proportions are less lifelike, however, than they are ideological. For modern Yoruba, the head is the locus of wisdom, destiny, and the essence of being. Such ideas probably developed at least 800 years ago. The sculptor accurately recorded the precise details of the heavily beaded costume, crown, and jewelry worn by both ancient and contemporary kings in Ile-Ife and other Yoruba city-states. The Ile-Ife figures and related works from the Yoruba kingdom of Owo to the southeast served mainly in rituals focused on sacred kingship. Many of these rituals have survived into the 21st century.

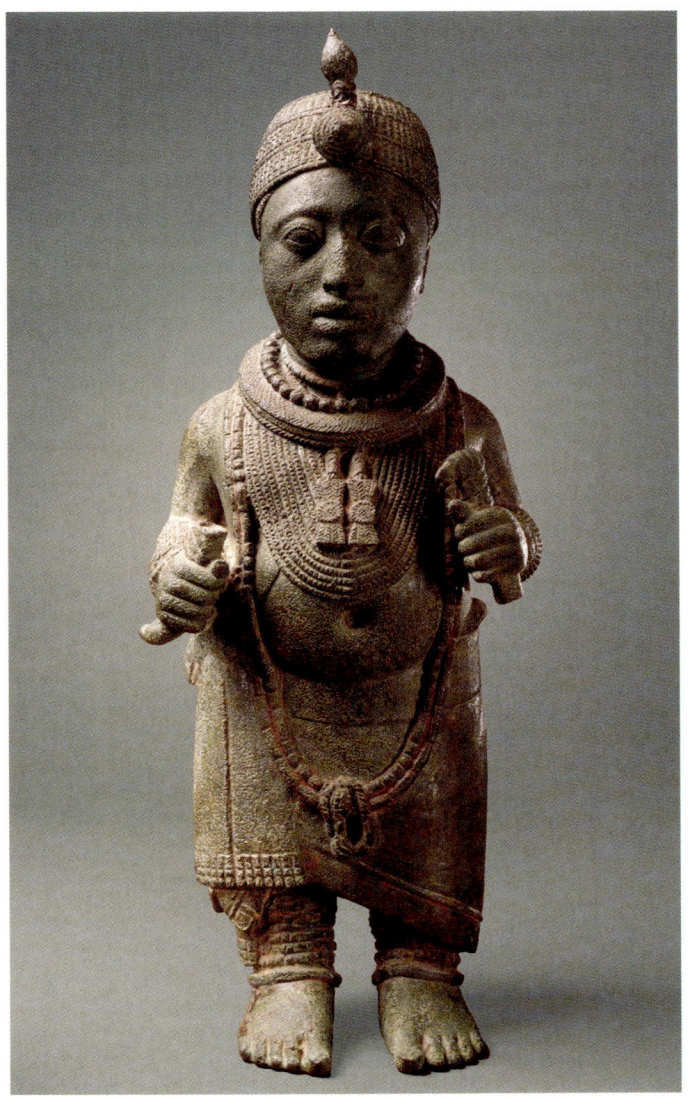

**15-6** King, from Ife, Nigeria, 11th to 12th century. Zinc brass, 1′ 6½″ high. Ife Museum, Ife.

## Great Zimbabwe Art (Southern Africa)

**RUINS OF A LOST EMPIRE** The most famous southern African site is a complex of stone ruins at the large southeastern political center called Great Zimbabwe. First occupied in the 11th century, the site features walled enclosures and towers that date from about the late 13th to the middle of the 15th century, when the Great Zimbabwe empire had a wide trade network. Finds of beads and pottery from Persia, the Near East, and China, along with copper and gold objects, underscore that Great Zimbabwe was a prosperous trade center well before Europeans began their coastal voyaging in the late 15th century. Most archaeologists and historians agree that the rulers at Great Zimbabwe and other nearby royal towns were ancestors of the area's present Shona-speaking peoples.

Using ethnographic information gathered from Portuguese accounts of the 16th to early 19th centuries and more recent studies of Shona culture, scholars have tried to interpret the meanings of the buildings and artifacts found at Great Zimbabwe. Most agree that the complex was a royal residence with special areas for the ruler (the royal hill complex), his wives, and nobles, including an open court for ceremonial gatherings. At the zenith of the empire's power, as many as 18,000 people may have lived in the surrounding area, with most of the commoners living outside the enclosed structures reserved for royalty. Although the actual habitations are gone, the remaining enclosures are unusual for their size and the excellence of their stonework. Some perimeter walls reach heights of 30 feet. One of these, known as the Great Enclosure (FIG. **15-7**), houses one large

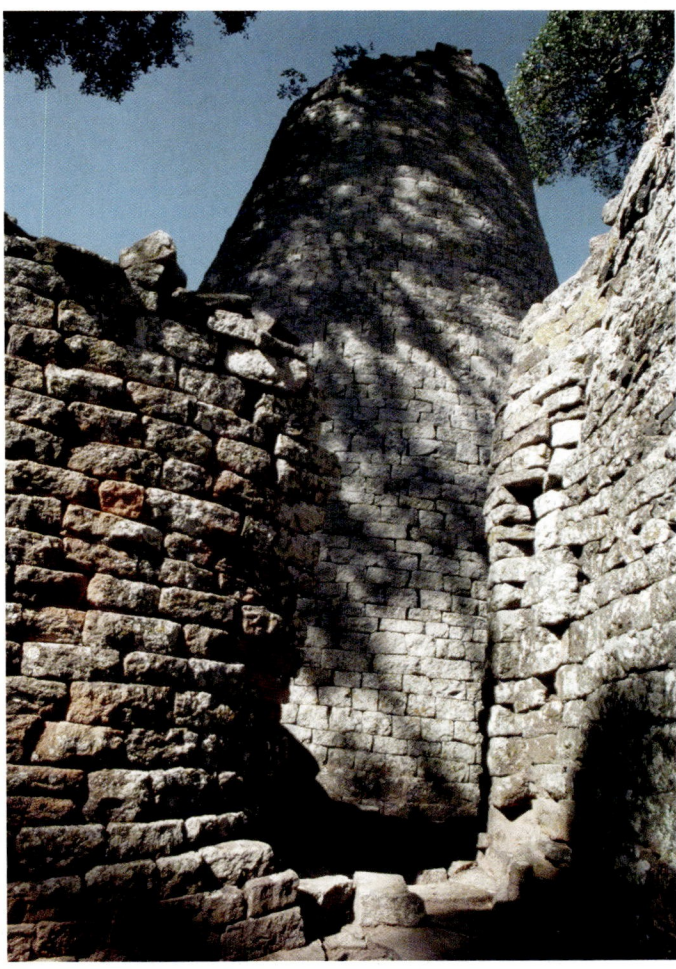

**15-7** Walls and tower, Great Enclosure, Great Zimbabwe, Zimbabwe, 14th century.

and several small conical towerlike stone structures. Scholars have interpreted these symbolically as masculine (large) and feminine (small) forms, but their precise significance is unknown. The form of the largest tower suggests a granary. Such grain bins were symbols of royal power and generosity, as the ruler received tribute in grain and dispensed it to the people in times of need.

**SOAPSTONE BIRDS** Explorations at Great Zimbabwe have yielded eight soapstone monoliths. Seven came from the royal hill complex and probably were set up as part of shrines to ancestors. The eighth bird monolith (FIG. **15-8**), found in an area now considered the ancestral shrine of the ruler's first wife, stands several feet tall. Some have interpreted the bird as symbolizing the first wife's ancestors. (Ancestral spirits among the present-day Shona take the form of birds, especially eagles, believed to communicate between the sky and the earth.) The crocodile on the front of the monolith may represent the wife's elder male ancestors. The circles beneath the bird are called the "eyes of the crocodile" in Shona and may symbolically represent elder female ancestors. The double- and single-chevron motifs may represent young male and young female ancestors, respectively. The bird perhaps represents some form of bird of prey, such as an eagle, although this and other bird sculptures from the site have feet with five humanlike toes, rather than an eagle's three-toed talons. In fact, the species of the birds cannot be identified. Some researchers have speculated that the bird and crocodile symbolize previous rulers who would have acted as messengers between the living and the dead, as well as between the sky and the earth.

## Lalibela Art and Architecture (Ethiopia)

**CHRISTIAN ETHIOPIA** The rugged highlands of present-day Ethiopia, where land travel is difficult, nevertheless played host to a Christian kingdom in the 13th to 15th centuries. Christianity had arrived in Ethiopia in the early fourth century, when the region was part of the indigenous Aksum Empire, where some fine stone monoliths were made. In the early 13th century, a ruler of the Zagwe dynasty, named Lalibela, commissioned a series of churches to be cut from living bedrock at his capital, today also called Lalibela. The largest of these rock-cut churches (FIG. **15-9**), Beta Medhane Alem ("House of the Savior of the World"), has a nave and

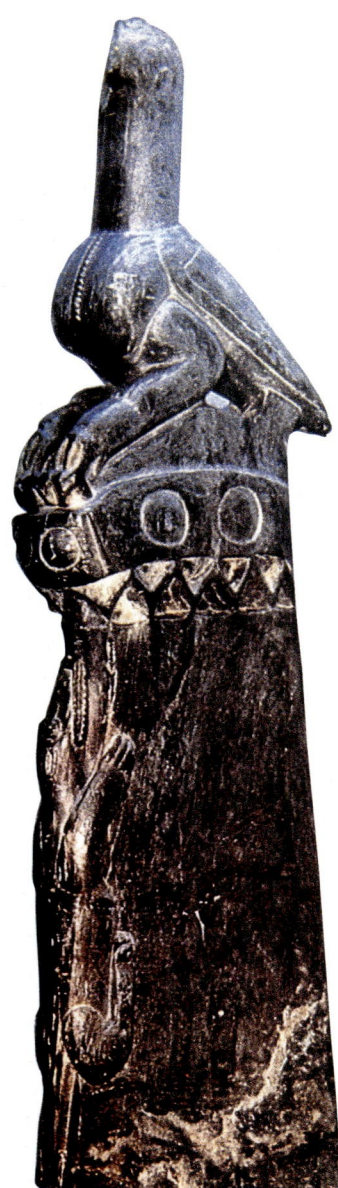

**15-8** Bird with crocodile image on top of stone monolith, from Great Zimbabwe, Zimbabwe, 15th century. Soapstone, bird image 1′ 2½″ high. Great Zimbabwe Site Museum, Great Zimbabwe. 🥏

**15-9** Beta Medhane Alem church, Lalibela, Ethiopia, 14th century. 🥏

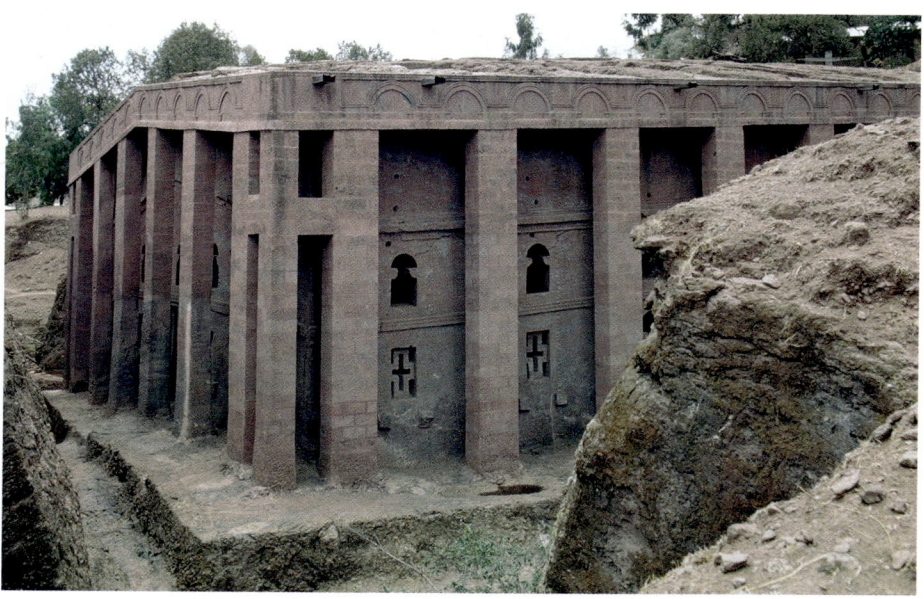

four flanking aisles. The exterior takes the form of a colonnade of closely set square pillars, with a crowning pitched roof decorated with semicircular motifs in relief, one each above and between every column, reinforcing the rhythm of the pillars. The planning and skilled labor needed to carve from the bedrock a complex building such as this, with all its details, is truly astonishing. The bedrock tufa is soft and easily worked. Nonetheless, the entire design had to be visualized before the work began because there was no possibility of revision or correction. More amazing still is the fact that more than 1,500 such sculpted churches exist in Ethiopia. Churches are being "constructed" in this manner as acts of devotion even today.

## Benin Art (Lower Niger)

The Benin kingdom was established just west of the lower reaches of the Niger River before 1400, most likely in the 13th century. It reached its greatest power and geographical extent in the 15th and 16th centuries. The kingdom's vicissitudes and slow decline thereafter culminated in the burning and sacking of the Benin palace and city by the British in 1897. Benin City thrives today, however, and the palace, where the Benin king continues to live, has been partially rebuilt. By observing current rituals and regalia and talking with elderly specialists who understand the significance of these cultural features, researchers continue to learn about earlier royal Benin art.

Benin artists have produced many complex, finely cast copper-alloy sculptures, as well as artworks in ivory, wood, ceramic, and wrought iron. Royalty commissioned (and sometimes still do) cast-metal pieces and ivory carvings from guilds of highly trained professional men. The hereditary *oba*, or sacred king, and his court still use and dispense art objects as royal favors to title holders and other chiefs (see "Art and Leadership," page 413). Benin kings to this day maintain ritual relationships with their Yoruba counterparts at Ile-Ife, and Benin oral tradition says that the first king of the new dynasty in the 14th century was the grandson of a Yoruba king. Other traditions, although contested, credit the Yoruba with the introduction of copper-alloy casting to Benin.

**IVORY FOR A KING** The ivory masquette we illustrate (FIG. **15-10**) was almost certainly worn by a Benin king at his waist. Probably this and the few other known naturalistic ivory carvings of human "masks" were commissioned by Oba Esigie (r. ca. 1504–1550), under whom, with the help of the Portuguese, the Benin kingdom flourished and expanded. Esigie's mother, Idia, helped him in warfare, and in return he created for her the title of Queen Mother, Iy'oba, and built her a separate palace and court. The mask probably represents Idia. Its sensitive naturalism places it in the 16th century. On its crown are alternating Portuguese heads and mudfish, respectively symbolic references to Benin's trade and diplomatic relationships with the Portuguese and to Olokun, god of the sea, wealth, and creativity. Another series of Portuguese heads also adorns the lower part of the carving. In the late 15th and 16th centuries, Benin people probably associated the Portuguese, with their large ships from across the sea, their powerful weapons, and their wealth in metals, cloth, and other goods, with Olokun, the deity they deem responsible for abundance and prosperity.

**THE HAND AND ARM** The centrality of the sacred oba in Benin culture is well demonstrated by his depiction twice on a cast-brass royal shrine called an *ikegobo* (FIG. **15-11**). It features symmetrical hierarchical compositions centered on the dominant king. Flanking and supporting him are smaller, lesser members of

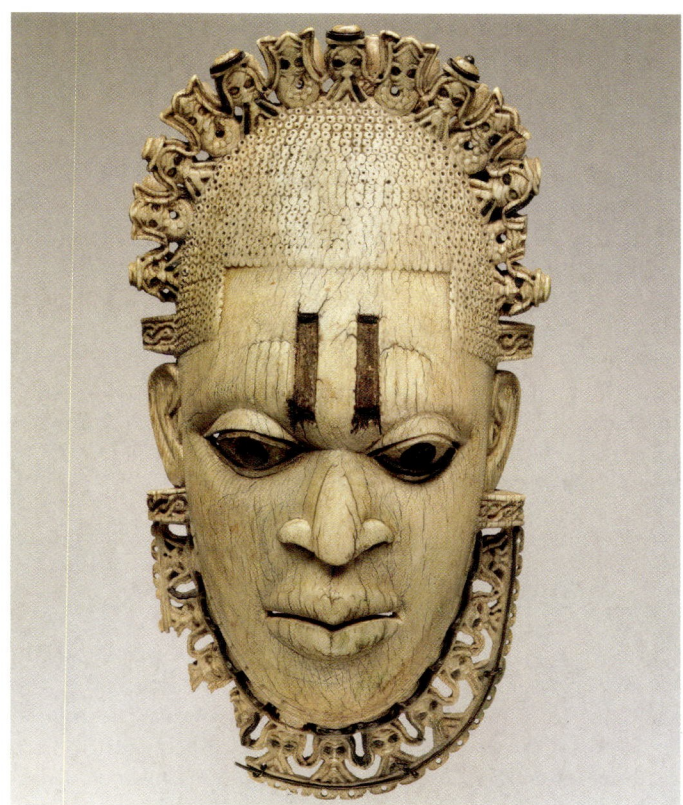

**15-10** Ivory belt mask of a Queen Mother, from Benin, Nigeria, mid-16th century. Ivory and iron, $9\frac{3}{8}''$ high. Metropolitan Museum of Art, New York (The Michael C. Rockefeller Memorial Collection, gift of Nelson A. Rockefeller, 1972. © 1995 The Metropolitan Museum of Art).

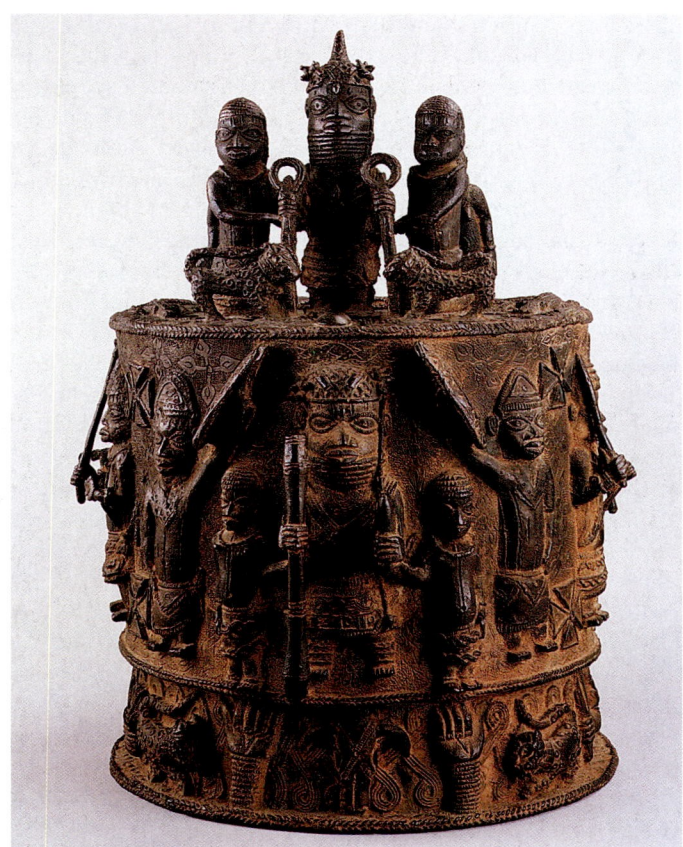

**15-11** Altar to the Hand and Arm (*ikegobo*), from Benin, Nigeria, 17th to 18th century(?). Bronze, $1'\ 5\frac{1}{2}''$ high. British Museum, London.

the court, and in front, a pair of leopards, animals sacrificed by the sacred king and symbolic of his power over all creatures. Similar compositions are common in Benin arts, as exemplified by the royal plaque from Benin discussed in the Introduction (see FIG. Intro-16). Notably, too, the proportions of the king are distorted to emphasize his head, the seat of his will and power. One of the king's praise names is "great head." The treatment of human faces on this altar is more conventionalized than on the ivory, attesting to its later manufacture (17th or 18th century).

At such personal altars, the king and other high-ranking officials made sacrifices to their own powers of success and accomplishment—symbolized by the hand and arm. The altar invokes power, both in the ritual's anticipated outcome and in the shrine's iconography. The inclusion of leopards on the top and around the base, along with ram and elephant heads and crocodiles (not all visible in FIG. 15-11), reiterates this power.

## Sapi Art (West Atlantic Coast)

During the 15th and 16th centuries, the Sapi people on the Atlantic coast of Africa carved stone, wood, and ivory images for their own use. Between 1490 and 1540, however, Portuguese explorers and traders commissioned Sapi artists to create objects exclusively for export to Europe: delicate spoons, forks, and elaborate containers usually referred to as saltcellars, as well as boxes, hunting horns, and knife handles. All were meticulously carved from elephant tusk ivory with refined and even elegant detail and careful finish. Ivory was plentiful in those early days and was one of the coveted exports in early West and Central Africa trade with Europe. The Sapi export ivories are a fascinating hybrid art form. They are the earliest examples of African tourist art.

The saltcellar shown here (FIG. **15-12**), almost 17 inches high, has been attributed to the MASTER OF THE SYMBOLIC EXECUTION, one of the three major Sapi ivory carvers during the period 1500–1540. It is his name piece and depicts an extraordinary execution scene. A kneeling figure with a shield in one hand holds an axe in the other hand over another sitting figure about to lose his head. On the ground before the executioner, six severed heads (five visible here) grimly testify to the executioner's power. A double zigzag line separates the lid of the globular container from the rest of the vessel. This vessel rests in turn on a circular platform held up by slender rods adorned with crocodile images. Two male and two female figures sit between these rods, grasping them. The men wear European-style pants, and the women wear skirts, but the women have elaborate raised patterns, surely decorative scars, on their upper chests. The European components of this saltcellar are the overall design of a spherical container on a pedestal and some of the geometric patterning on the base and the sphere, as well as certain elements of dress such as the shirts and hats. What is distinctly African is the style of the human heads and figures and their proportions, the latter skewed here to emphasize the head, as so often seen in African art. Identical large noses with flaring nostrils, as well as the conventions for rendering eyes and lips, can be seen on Sapi stone figures from the same region and period. Scholars cannot be sure whether it was the African carver or the European patron who specified the subject matter and the configurations of various parts.

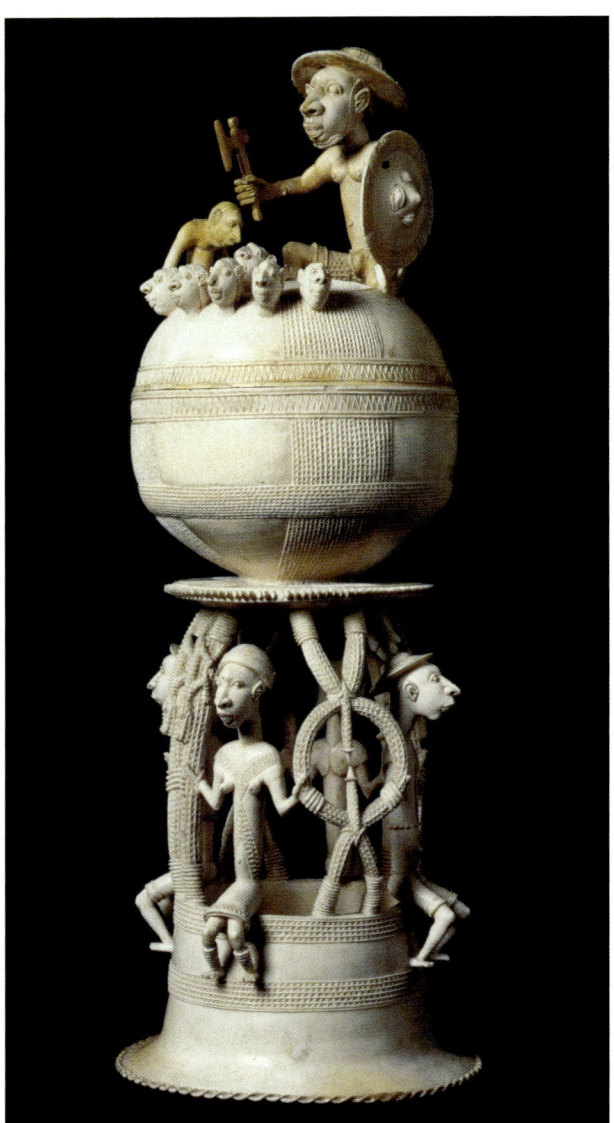

**15-12** MASTER OF THE SYMBOLIC EXECUTION, saltcellar, Sapi-Portuguese, from Sierra Leone, 15th to 16th century. Ivory, 1′ 4⅞″ high. Museo Nazionale Preistorico e Etnografico Luigi Pigorini, Rome.

## CONCLUSION

The art forms discussed in this chapter have survived for many centuries in large measure because they are made of durable materials such as terracotta, ivory, and cast metal (bronze or one of several copper alloys). It is clear that many of these art forms were used in elite contexts and were associated with kings and chieftains. Some of these traditions still continue in altered form. In Benin, for example, there is virtually no break between 16th- and 17th-century art forms and those that survive on kings' ancestral altars today. The same is true for Christian Ethiopia, where both painted icons and rock-cut churches are still being made. In the cases of Igbo Ukwu and Ile-Ife, recent forms are somewhat different from ancient ones, but the connections between the two eras are nevertheless clear. Some of the more recent versions of these art forms are examined in Chapter 32.

**500 BCE**

■ FIRST SUB-SAHARAN CERAMICS, FIFTH CENTURY BCE

**1** ■ NOK CULTURE, CA. 500 BCE–200 CE

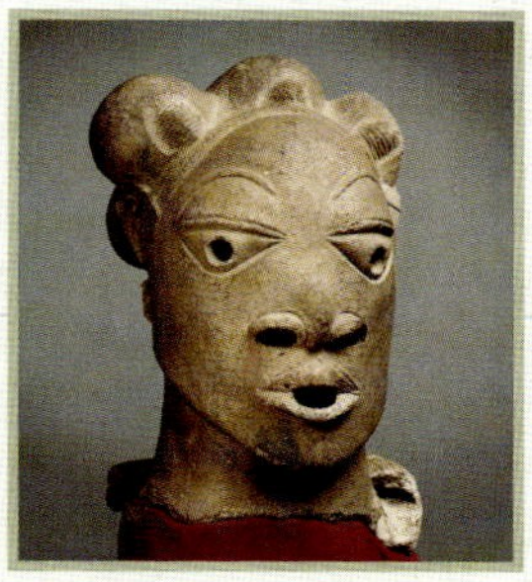

**200 CE**

■ CHRISTIANITY **INTRODUCED** TO ETHIOPIA, FOURTH CENTURY

**1** Nok head, Nigeria, ca. 500 BCE–200 CE

**500**

■ ISLAM SPREADS THROUGHOUT NORTH AFRICA, SEVENTH CENTURY

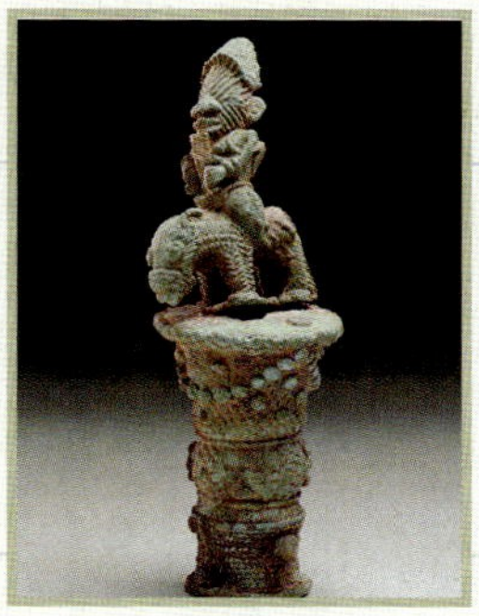

**800**

■ FIRST BRONZE CASTINGS, 9TH CENTURY

**2** ■ IGBO-UKWU CULTURE, 9TH–10TH CENTURIES

■ JENNE CULTURE, 9TH–15TH CENTURIES

**2** Igbo-Ukwu fly-whisk hilt, Nigeria, 9th to 10th century

**1000**

■ ILE-IFE CULTURE, 11TH–12TH CENTURIES

■ GREAT ZIMBABWE CULTURE, 11TH–15TH CENTURIES

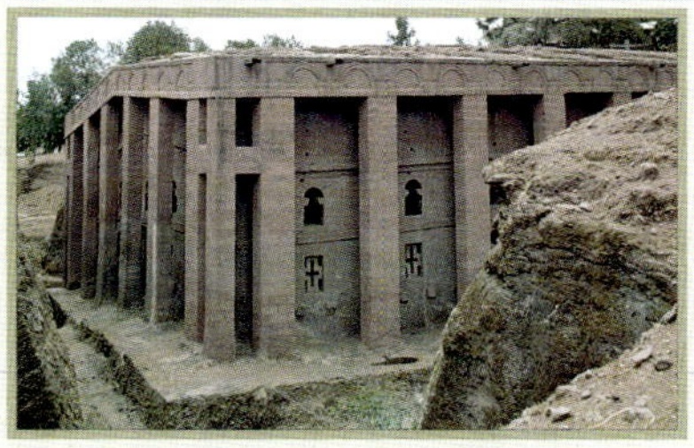

**1200**

■ BENIN KINGDOM, FOUNDED 13TH CENTURY

**3**

**3** Beta Medhane Alem church, Lalibela, Ethiopia, 14th century

**1400**

■ SAPI CULTURE, 15TH–16TH CENTURIES

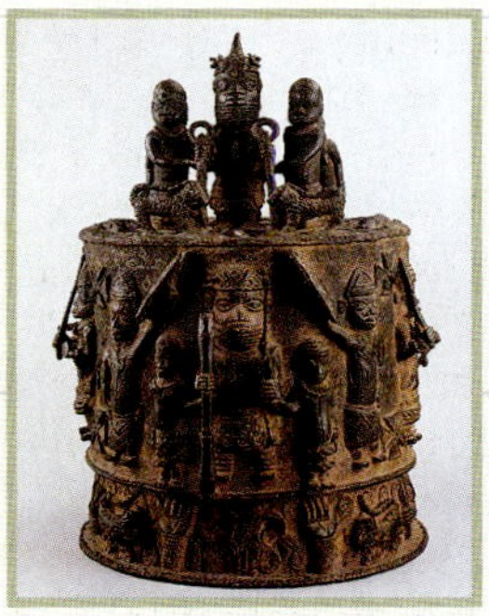

**1600**

**4**

**4** Altar of the Hand and Arm, Benin, Nigeria, 17th to 18th century

**1800**

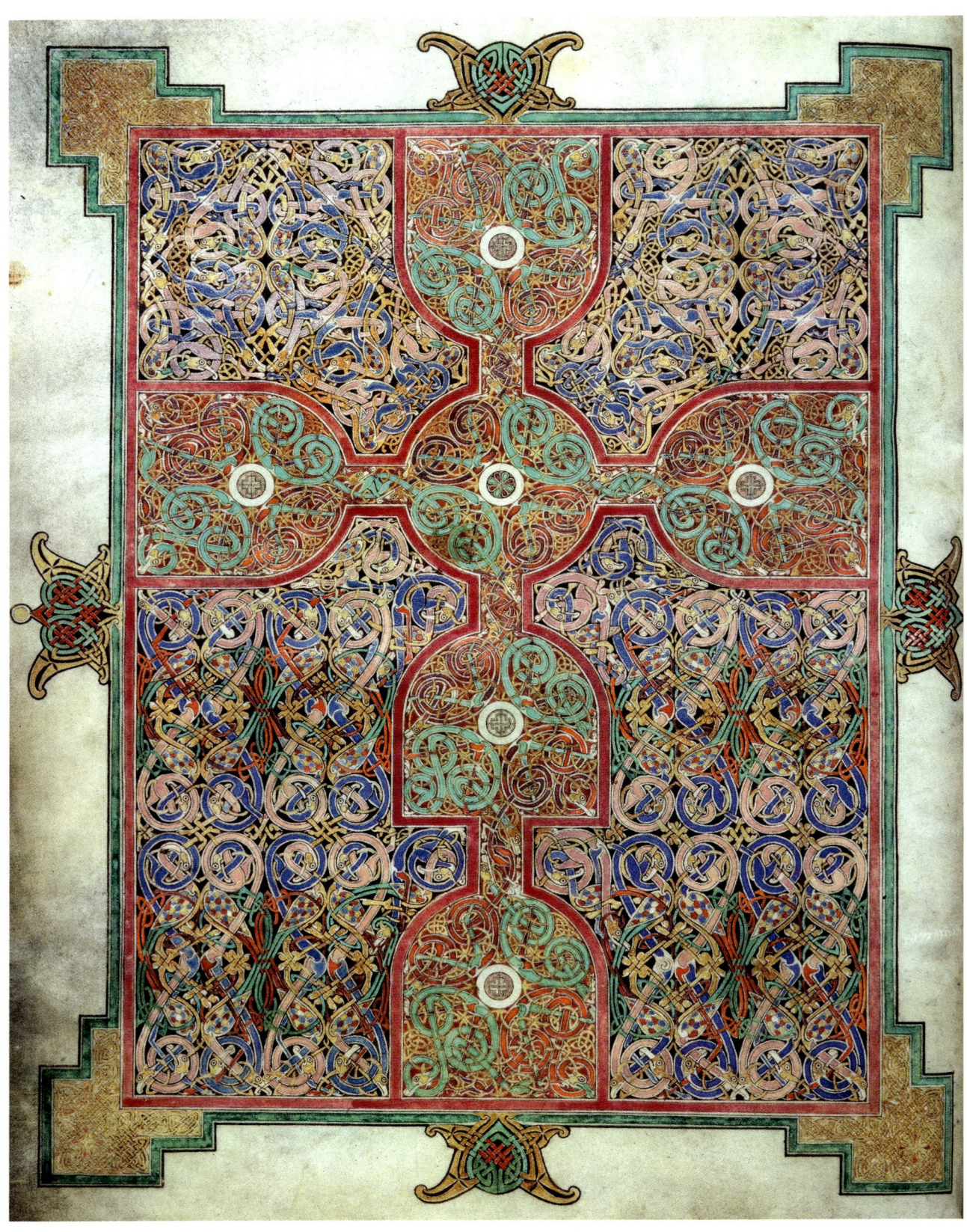

Cross and carpet page, folio 26 verso of the *Lindisfarne Gospels,* from Northumbria, England, ca. 698–721. Tempera on vellum, 1′ 1$\frac{1}{2}$″ × 9$\frac{1}{4}$″. British Library, London.

# 16

# EUROPE AFTER THE FALL OF ROME

## EARLY MEDIEVAL ART IN THE WEST

Historians once referred to the thousand years (roughly 400 to 1400) between the dying Roman Empire's adoption of Christianity as its official religion and the rebirth (Renaissance) of interest in classical antiquity as the Dark Ages. Scholars and laypersons alike thought this long "interval"—between the ancient and what was perceived as the beginning of the modern European world—was rough and uncivilized, and crude and primitive artistically. They viewed these centuries—dubbed the Middle Ages—as simply a blank between (in the middle of) two great civilizations.

This negative assessment, a legacy of the humanist scholars of Renaissance Italy, persists today in the retention of the noun *Middle Ages* and the adjective *medieval* to describe this period and its art. The force of tradition dictates that we continue to use those terms, even though modern scholars long ago ceased to see the art of medieval Europe as unsophisticated or inferior.

**THE MEDIEVAL FUSION** Art historians date the art of the early Middle Ages to the half millennium from about 500 to 1000. Early medieval civilization in western Europe represents a fusion of Christianity, the Greco-Roman heritage, and the cultures of the non-Roman peoples north of the Alps. Although the Romans called everyone who lived beyond the classical world's frontiers "barbarians," many northerners had risen to prominent positions within the Roman army and government during the later Roman Empire. Others established their own areas of rule, sometimes with Rome's approval, sometimes in opposition to imperial authority. In time, these non-Romans merged with the citizens of the former northwestern provinces of Rome and slowly developed political and social institutions that have continued into modern times. Over the centuries a new order gradually replaced what had been the Roman Empire, resulting eventually in the foundation of today's European nations (MAP **16-1**).

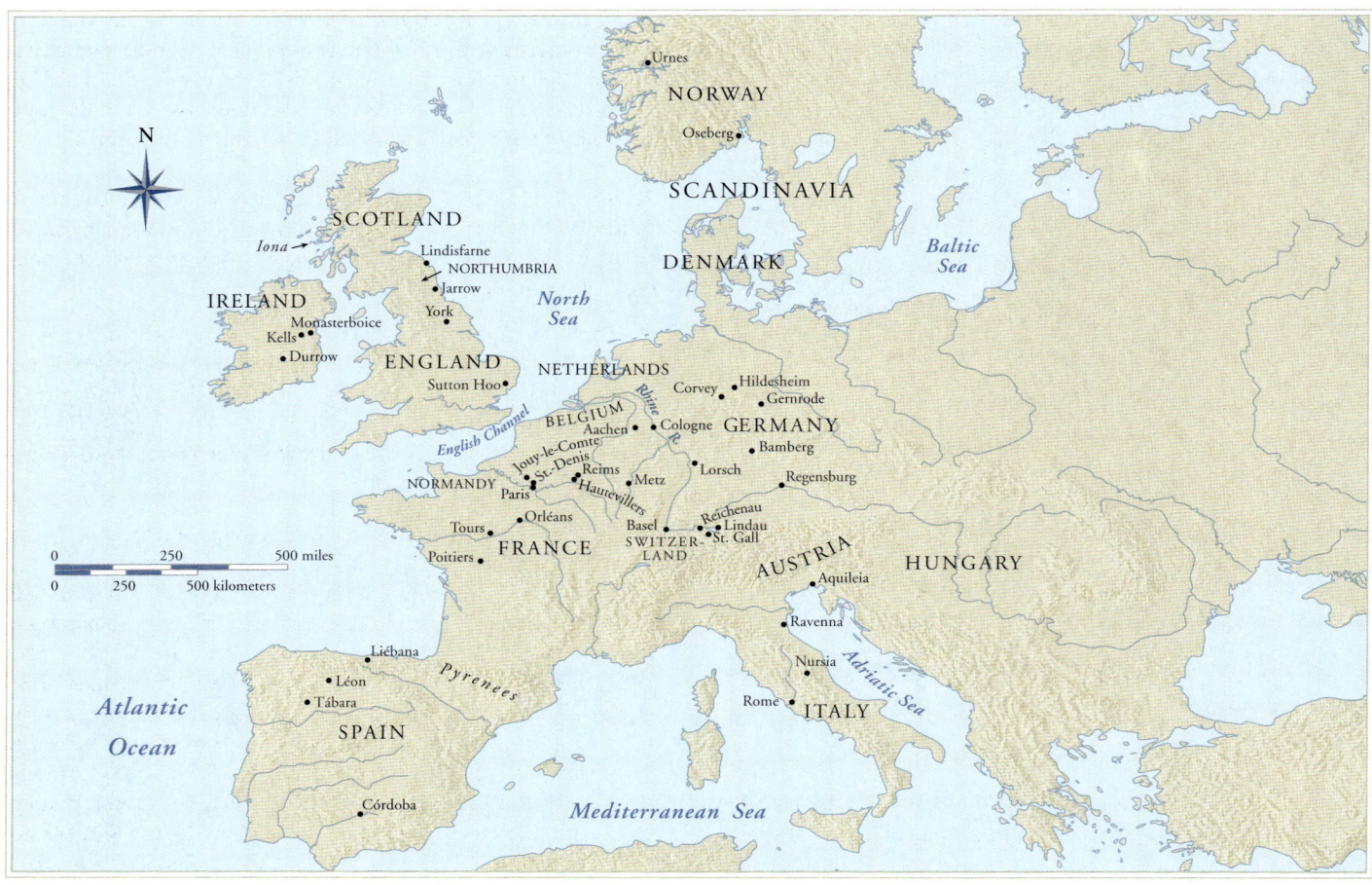

MAP 16-1 Early medieval sites in Europe.

# THE ART OF THE WARRIOR LORDS

As Rome's power waned in late antiquity, armed conflicts and competition for political authority became commonplace among the non-Roman peoples of Europe—Huns, Vandals, Merovingians, Franks, Goths, and others. Once one group established itself in Italy or in one of Rome's European provinces, another often pressed in behind and compelled it to move on. The Visigoths, for example, who at one time controlled part of Italy and formed a kingdom in what is today southern France, were forced southward into Spain under pressure from the Franks, who had crossed the lower Rhine River and established themselves firmly in France, Switzerland, the Netherlands, and parts of Germany. The Ostrogoths moved from Pannonia (at the junction of modern Hungary, Austria, and the former Yugoslavia) to Italy. Under Theodoric, they established their kingdom there, only to have it fall less than a century later to the Lombards, the last of the early Germanic powers to occupy land within the limits of the old Roman Empire (see Chapter 12). In the North, Anglo-Saxons controlled what had been Roman Britain. Celts inhabited France and parts of the British Isles, including Ireland, the one area of western Europe the Romans never colonized. In Scandinavia the great seafaring Vikings held sway.

**ART AND STATUS** Art historians do not know the full range of art and architecture these non-Roman peoples produced. What has survived is not truly representative and consists almost exclusively of small "status symbols"—weapons and items of personal adornment such as bracelets, pendants, and belt buckles that archaeologists have discovered in lavish burials. Earlier scholars, who viewed medieval art through a Renaissance lens, ignored these "minor arts" because of their small scale, seeming utilitarian nature, and abstract ornament, and because the people who made them rejected the classical idea that the representation of organic nature should be the focus of artistic endeavor. In their own time, these objects, which often display a high degree of technical and stylistic sophistication, were regarded as treasures. They enhanced the prestige of those who owned them and testified to the stature of those who were buried with them. In the great early (possibly seventh-century) Anglo-Saxon epic *Beowulf,* the hero is cremated and his ashes placed in a huge tumulus overlooking the sea. As an everlasting tribute to Beowulf's greatness, his people "buried rings and brooches in the barrow, all those adornments that brave men had brought out from the hoard after Beowulf died. They bequeathed the gleaming gold, treasure of men, to the earth."[1]

**MEROVINGIAN FIBULAE** Most characteristic, perhaps, of the prestige adornments was the *fibula,* a decorative pin favored by the Romans (and the Etruscans before them; see FIG. 9-1). Fibulae were usually used to fasten the garments of men and women alike. Made of bronze, silver, or gold, they were often decorated profusely, sometimes with inlaid precious or semiprecious stones. The fibula we illustrate (FIG. **16-1**) is one of a pair found in France with other Merovingian jewelry of the mid-sixth century. It once must have been the proud possession of a wealthy Merovingian woman and seems to have been buried with her. The pin resembles, in its general form, the roughly contemporary but plain fibulae used to

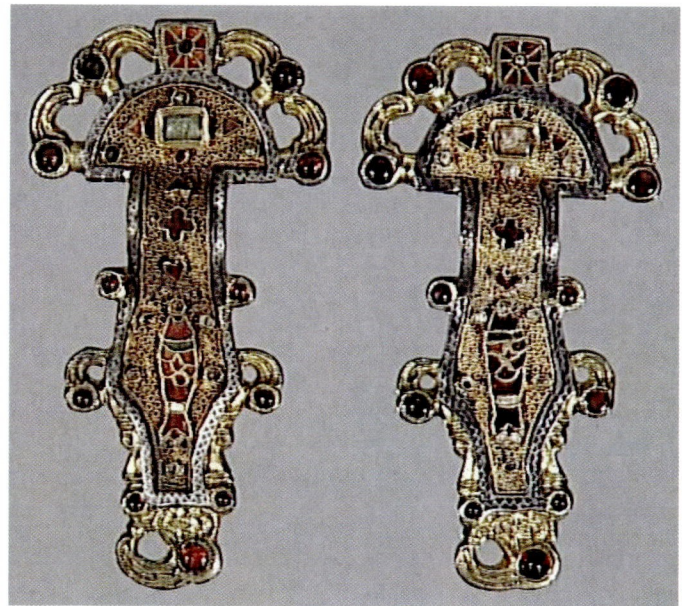

**16-1** Merovingian looped fibula, from Jouy-le-Comte, France, mid-sixth century. Silver gilt worked in filigree, with inlays of garnets and other stones, 4″ long. Musée des Antiquités Nationales, Saint-Germain-en-Laye.

fasten the outer garments of some of the attendants flanking the Byzantine emperor Justinian in the apse mosaic of San Vitale in Ravenna (see FIG. 12-10). (Note how much more elaborate is the emperor's clasp. In Rome, New Rome, and early medieval Europe alike, these fibulae were emblems of office and of prestige.)

Almost the entire surface of the Merovingian fibula is covered with decorative patterns adjusted carefully to the basic shape of the object they adorn. They thus describe and amplify its form and structure, becoming an organic part of the object itself. Often zoomorphic elements were so successfully integrated into this type

of highly disciplined, abstract decorative design that they became almost unrecognizable. One must examine our fibula carefully to discover that it contains animal forms. A fish may be discerned just below the center of the fibula. The looped forms around the edges are stylized eagles' heads with red garnets forming the eyes.

**A KING'S FINAL VOYAGE** The *Beowulf* saga also recounts the funeral of the warrior lord Scyld, who was laid to rest in a ship set adrift in the North Sea overflowing with arms and armor and costly adornments:

> They laid their dear lord, the giver of rings, deep within the ship by the mast in majesty; many treasures and adornments from far and wide were gathered there. I have never heard of a ship equipped more handsomely with weapons and war-gear, swords and corselets; on his breast lay countless treasures that were to travel far with him into the waves' domain.[2]

In 1939, a treasure-laden ship was discovered in a burial mound at Sutton Hoo in Suffolk, England. Although unique, it epitomizes the early medieval tradition of burying great lords with rich furnishings, as recorded in *Beowulf*. Among the many precious finds were a gold belt buckle, 10 silver bowls, a silver plate with the imperial stamp of the Byzantine emperor Anastasius I (r. 491–518), and 40 gold coins (perhaps to pay the 40 oarsmen who would row the deceased across the sea on his final voyage). Also placed in the ship were two silver spoons inscribed "Saulos" and "Paulos," Saint Paul's names in Greek before and after his baptism. They may allude to a conversion to Christianity. Some historians have associated the site with the East Anglian king Raedwald, who was baptized a Christian before his death in 625, but the identity of the king buried at Sutton Hoo is uncertain.

**CLOISONNÉ** Most extraordinary of all the Sutton Hoo finds is a purse cover (FIG. 16-2) decorated with cloisonné-enamel plaques. The *cloisonné* technique is documented at least as early as the New Kingdom in Egypt, and was favored by early medieval

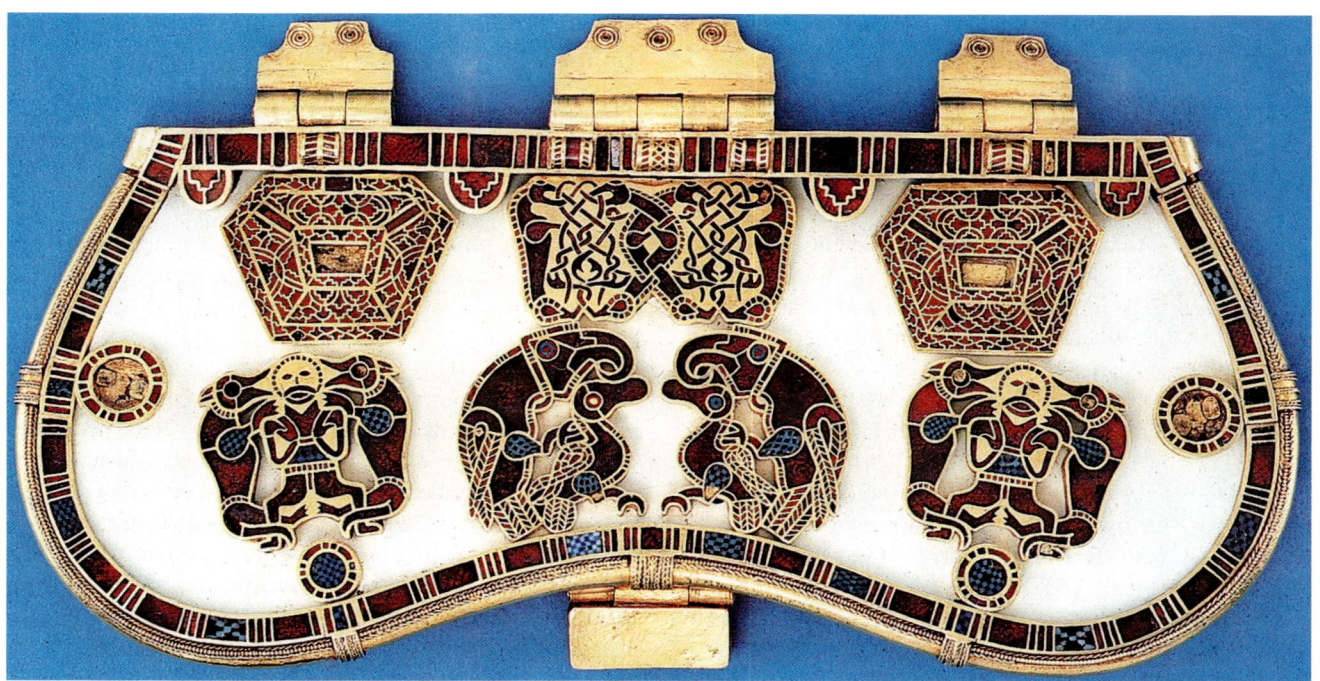

**16-2** Purse cover, from the Sutton Hoo ship burial in Suffolk, England, ca. 625. Gold, glass, and enamel cloisonné with garnets and emeralds, $7\frac{1}{2}$″ long. British Museum, London.

"treasure givers." Metalworkers produced cloisonné jewelry by soldering small metal strips or *cloisons* (French for "partitions"), edge-up, to a metal background, and then filling the compartments with semiprecious stones, pieces of colored glass, or glass paste fired to resemble sparkling jewels. The edges of the cloisons are an important part of the design. Cloisonné is a cross between mosaic (see "Mosaics," Chapter 11, page 315) and stained glass (see "Stained-Glass Windows," Chapter 18, page 492), but was employed only on a miniature scale.

On the Sutton Hoo purse cover (FIG. 16-2), four symmetrically arranged groups of figures make up the lower row. The end groups consist of a man standing between two beasts. He faces front, and they appear in profile. This heraldic type of grouping has a venerable heritage in the ancient world (see FIG. 2-10), but must have delivered a powerful contemporary message. It is a pictorial parallel to the epic sagas of the era in which heroes like Beowulf battle and conquer horrific monsters. The two center groups represent eagles attacking ducks. The animal figures are cunningly composed. For example, the convex beaks of the eagles (compare the Merovingian fibula, FIG. 16-1) fit against the concave beaks of the ducks. The two figures fit together so snugly that they seem at first to be a single dense abstract design. This is true also of the man-animals motif.

Above these figures are three geometric designs. The outer ones are clear and linear in style. In the central design, an interlace pattern, the interlacements turn into writhing animal figures. Elaborate interlace patterns are characteristic of many times and places, notably in the art of the Islamic world (see Chapter 13). But the combination of interlace with animal figures was uncommon outside the realm of the early medieval warlords. In fact, metalcraft with a vocabulary of interlace patterns and other motifs beautifully integrated with the animal form was, without doubt, *the* art of the early Middle Ages in the West. Interest in it was so great that the colorful effects of jewelry designs were imitated in the painted decorations of manuscripts, in stone sculpture, in the masonry of churches, and in sculpture in wood, an especially important medium of Viking art.

**THE PIRATES OF THE NORTH** In 793 the pagan traders and pirates known as Vikings (named after the *viks*—coves or "trading places"—of the Norwegian shoreline) set sail from Scandinavia and landed in the British Isles. They destroyed the Christian monastic community on Lindisfarne Island off the Northumbrian (northeastern) coast of England (see page 425). Shortly after, these *Norsemen* (North men) attacked the monastery at Jarrow in England as well as that on Iona Island, off the west coast of Scotland. From this time until the mid-11th century, the Vikings were the terror of western Europe. From their great ships they seasonally harried and plundered the coasts, harbors, and river settlements of the West. Their fast, seaworthy longboats took them on wide-ranging voyages, from Ireland eastward to Russia and westward to Iceland and Greenland and even, briefly, to Newfoundland in North America, long before Columbus arrived in the "New World."

The Vikings were not intent merely on a hit-and-run strategy of destruction but on colonizing the lands they occupied by conquest. Their exceptional talent for organization and administration, as well as for war, enabled them to take and govern large territories in Ireland, England, and France, as well as in the Baltic regions and Russia. For a while, in the early 11th century, the whole of England was part of a Danish empire. When Vikings settled in northern France in the early 10th century, their territory came to be called Normandy—home of the Norsemen who

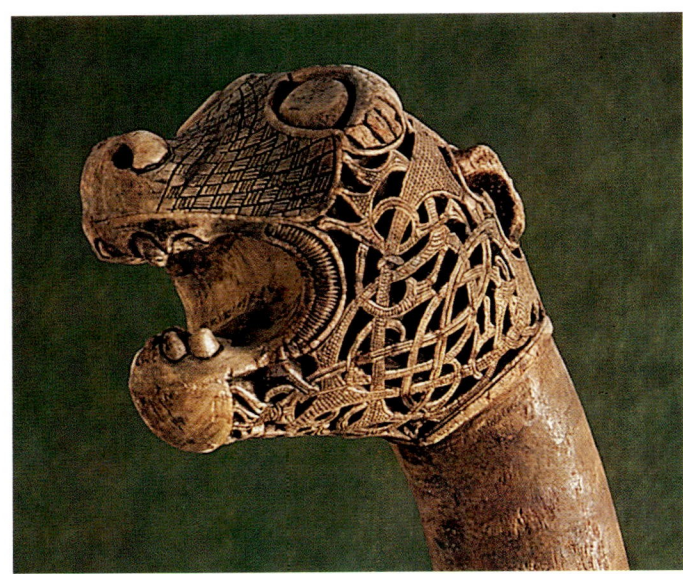

**16-3** Animal-head post, from the Viking ship burial, Oseberg, Norway, ca. 825. Wood, head approx. 5″ high. University Museum of National Antiquities, Oslo.

became *Normans*. (Later, a Norman duke, William the Conqueror, sailed across the English Channel and invaded and became the master of Anglo-Saxon England; see FIGS. 17-39 and 17-40.)

**BURIAL IN A VIKING SHIP** The art of the Viking sea rovers was early associated with their great wooden ships. Striking examples of Viking wood carving were found in a ship burial near Oseberg, Norway. The ship, which was covered by a mound like the earlier Sutton Hoo burial, was more than 70 feet long. When the vessel was found, it contained the remains of two women. The size of the burial alone and the lavishly carved wooden ornament of the sleek ship attest to the importance of those laid to rest there. The vessel also once must have carried many precious objects that robbers removed long before its modern discovery.

We illustrate a wooden animal-head post (FIG. 16-3) from the Oseberg ship that, like the other animal forms in the carved bands that follow the prow's gracefully curving lines, expresses dynamic energy. This head combines in one composition the image of a roaring beast with protruding eyes and flaring nostrils and the deftly carved, controlled, and contained pattern of tightly interwoven animals that writhe, gripping and snapping, in serpentine fashion. The Oseberg animal head is a powerfully expressive example of the union of two fundamental motifs of the art of the warrior lords on the northern frontiers of the former Roman Empire—the animal form and the interlace pattern.

**ANIMAL ART ON A CHURCH** By the 11th century, much of Scandinavia had become Christian, but Viking artistic traditions persisted. Nowhere is this more evident than in the decoration of the portal (FIG. 16-4) of the stave church (*staves* are wedge-shaped timbers placed vertically) at Urnes, Norway. The portal and a few staves are almost all that is preserved of a mid-11th-century church whose fragments were incorporated in the walls of a 12th-century church. Gracefully elongated animal forms intertwine with flexible plant stalks and tendrils in spiraling rhythm. The effect of natural growth is astonishing, yet it has been subjected to the designer's highly refined abstract sensibility. This intricate Urnes style was the culmination of three centuries (the 8th to the 11th) of Viking inventiveness.

### Medieval Books

The central role books played in the medieval Christian Church led to the development of a large number of specialized types for priests, monks and nuns, and laypersons.

The primary sacred text came to be called the Bible ("the Book"), consisting of the Old Testament of the Jews, originally written in Hebrew, and the Christian New Testament, written in Greek. In the late fourth century, Saint Jerome produced the canonical Latin, or *Vulgate* (vulgar, or common tongue), version of the Bible, which incorporates 46 Old and 27 New Testament books. Before the invention of the printing press in the 15th century, all books were written by hand ("manuscripts," from the Latin *manu scriptus*). Bibles were extremely difficult to produce, and few early medieval monasteries possessed a complete Bible. Instead, several biblical books often were gathered in separate volumes.

The *Pentateuch* contains the first five books of the Old Testament, beginning with the Creation of Adam and Eve (Genesis). The *Gospels* ("good news") are the New Testament works of Saints Matthew, Mark, Luke, and John (see "The Four Evangelists," page 426) and tell the story of the life of Christ (see "The Life of Jesus in Art," Chapter 11, pages 308–309). Medieval Gospel books often contained *canon tables*—a concordance, or matching, of the corresponding passages of the four Gospels as compiled by Eusebius of Caesarea in the fourth century. *Psalters* contained the 150 psalms of King David, written in Hebrew and translated into both Greek and Latin.

Other types of books also were frequently employed in the Christian liturgy. The *lectionary* contains passages from the Gospels reordered to appear in the sequence they were read during the celebration of Mass throughout the liturgical year. *Breviaries* include the texts required for the daily recitations of monks. *Sacramentaries* were used by priests and incorporate the prayers they recited during Mass. *Benedictionals* contain bishops' blessings.

In the later Middle Ages, religious books were developed for the private devotions of the laity, patterned after monks' readers. The most popular was the *Book of Hours,* so called because it contains the prayers to be read at specified times of the day.

Many other types of books were written and copied in the Middle Ages—theological treatises, secular texts on history and science, and even some classics of Greco-Roman literature—but these were illustrated less frequently than the various sacred texts.

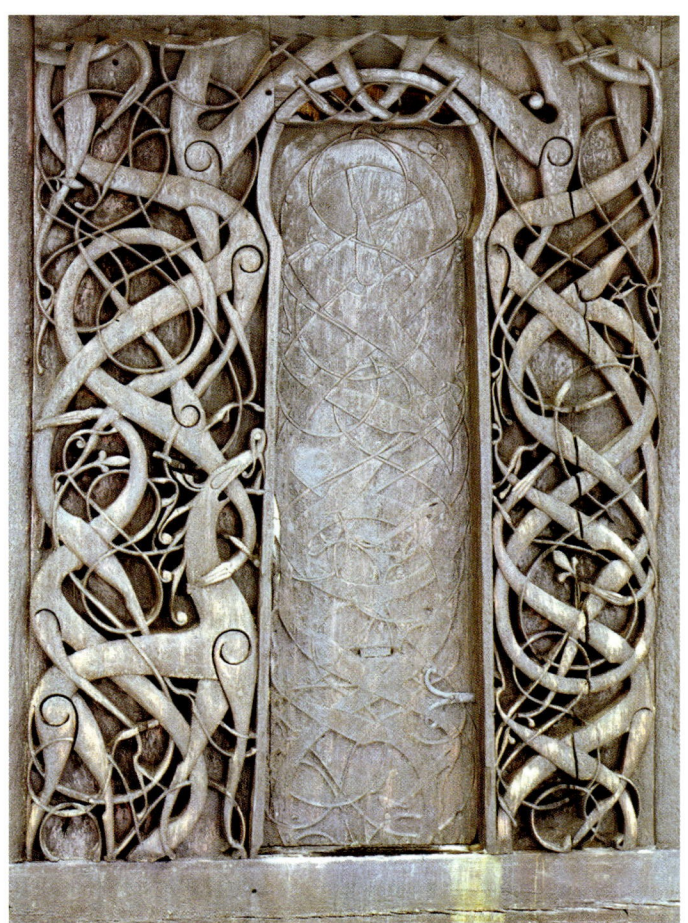

**16-4** Wooden portal of the stave church at Urnes, Norway, ca. 1050–1070.

## HIBERNO-SAXON ART

**CHRISTIAN MISSIONARIES** In 432 Saint Patrick established a church in Ireland and began the Christianization of the Celts. The new converts, although nominally subject to the popes of Rome, quickly developed a form of monastic organization that differed from the Church of Rome in its liturgical practices and even in its calendar of holidays. The relative independence of the Irish monasteries was due in part to their isolation. They often were situated in inaccessible and inhospitable places where the monks could carry on their duties far from worldly temptations and distractions.

Before long, Irish monks, filled with missionary zeal, set up monastic establishments in Britain and Scotland. In 563 Saint Columba founded an important monastery on the Scottish island of Iona, where he successfully converted the native Picts to Christianity. Iona monks established the monastery at Lindisfarne off the northern coast of Britain in 635. From these and other later foundations, which became great centers of learning for both Scotland and England, Irish and Anglo-Saxon missionaries journeyed through Europe, establishing great monasteries in Italy, Switzerland, Germany, the Low Countries, and France.

**HIBERNO-SAXON BOOKS** A style art historians designate as *Hiberno-Saxon* (Hibernia was the ancient name of Ireland), or sometimes as *Insular* to denote the Irish-English islands where it was produced, flourished within the monasteries of the British Isles. Its most distinctive products were the illuminated manuscripts of the Christian Church (see "Medieval Books," above). Liturgical books were the primary vehicles in the effort to Christianize the British Isles. They literally brought the Word of God to a predominantly illiterate population who regarded the monks' sumptuous volumes with awe. Books were scarce, jealously

## The Four Evangelists

*E*vangelist derives from the Greek word for "one who announces good news," namely the Gospel of Christ. The authors of the Gospels, the first four books of the New Testament, are Saints Matthew, Mark, Luke, and John, collectively known as the Four Evangelists. The Gospel books provide the authoritative account of the life of Jesus, differing in some details, but together constituting the literary basis for the iconography of Christ throughout the long history of Christian art (see "The Life of Jesus in Art," Chapter 11, pages 308–309).

Matthew was a tax collector in Capernaum before Christ called him to become one of his apostles. Little else is known about him, and there are differing accounts as to how he became a martyr. Mark was the first bishop of Alexandria in Egypt, where he was martyred. He was a companion of both Saint Peter and Saint Paul. One tradition says that Peter dictated the Gospel to Mark, or at least inspired him to write it. Luke was a disciple of Saint Paul. Paul refers to him as a physician, but Luke is also said to have painted a portrait of the Virgin Mary and the Christ Child. In the later Middle Ages he was often chosen as the patron saint of painters' guilds. John was one of the most important of Christ's apostles. He sat next to Jesus at the Last Supper and was present at the Crucifixion, Lamentation, and Transfiguration.

John was also the author of the Apocalypse, the last book of the New Testament, which he wrote in exile on the Greek island of Patmos. The Apocalypse records John's visions of the end of the world, the Last Judgment, and the Second Coming.

Each of the Evangelists has a unique symbol derived from passages in Ezekiel (1:5–14) and the Apocalypse (4:6–8). Matthew's symbol is the winged man or angel, because his Gospel opens with a description of the human ancestry of Christ. Because Mark's Gospel begins with a voice crying in the wilderness, his symbol is the lion, the king of the desert. Luke's symbol is the ox, because his Gospel opens with a description of the priest Zacharias sacrificing an ox. John's symbol is the eagle, the soaring bird connected with his apocalyptic visions.

The Four Evangelists appear frequently in medieval art, especially in illuminated Gospel books where they regularly serve as frontispieces to their respective Gospels. Often they are represented as seated authors, with or without their symbols (see FIGS. Intro-7, 16-7, 16-12, and 16-13). In some instances, all Four Evangelists are shown together (see FIG. Intro-7). Frequently, both in painting and in sculpture, only the symbols are represented (see FIGS. 12-15, 16-5, 17-21, 17-23, 17-27, 17-32, and 18-5).

---

guarded treasures. Most of them were housed in the libraries and *scriptoria* (writing studios) of monasteries or major churches. Illuminated books are the most important extant monuments of the brilliant artistic culture that flourished in Ireland and Northumbria during the seventh and eighth centuries.

**A CHECKERBOARD EVANGELIST** Among the earliest Hiberno-Saxon illuminated manuscripts is the *Book of Durrow,* a Gospel book that may have been written and decorated in the monastic scriptorium at Iona, although its provenance is not documented. In the late Middle Ages it was housed in Durrow, Ireland—hence its modern nickname. The Durrow Gospels already display one of the most characteristic features of Insular book illumination: full pages devoted neither to text nor to illustration but to pure embellishment. Interspersed between the Durrow text pages are so-called *carpet pages,* resembling textiles, made up of decorative panels of abstract and zoomorphic forms. The *Book of Durrow* also contains pages where the initial letters of an important passage of sacred text are enormously enlarged and transformed into elaborate decorative patterns. Examples of Hiberno-Saxon carpet pages (FIG. 16-6) and initial pages (FIG. 16-8) will be examined later. It is important to note at the outset that this type of manuscript decoration had no precedent in classical art. It is one of many indications of the independence of Insular art from the classical tradition.

In the *Book of Durrow,* each of the four Gospel books has a carpet page facing a page dedicated to the symbol of the Evangelist who wrote that Gospel, framed by an elaborate interlace border. These pages served to highlight the major divisions of the text for liturgical use. The symbol of Saint Matthew (FIG. **16-5**) is a man (more commonly represented later as winged; see "The Four Evangelists," above), but the only human parts that the artist, a seventh-century

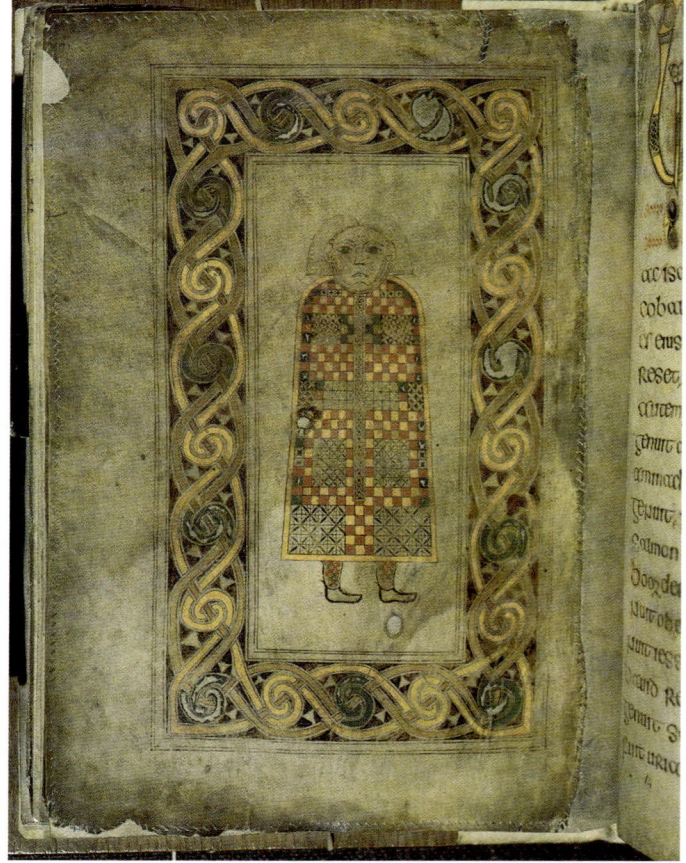

**16-5** Man (symbol of Saint Matthew), folio 21 verso of the *Book of Durrow,* possibly from Iona, Scotland, ca. 660–680. Ink and tempera on parchment, $9\frac{5}{8}'' \times 6\frac{1}{8}''$. Trinity College Library, Dublin.

monk, chose to render are a schematic frontal head and two profile feet. The rest of the "body" is enveloped by a checkerboard cloak of yellow, red, and green squares filled with intricate abstract designs and outlined in dark brown or black. The cloak, as well as the prominent frame around the figure, resemble the cloisonné decoration of contemporary belt buckles, brooches, and purse ornaments. The *Book of Durrow* weds the abstraction of early medieval personal adornment with Early Christian pictorial imagery. The vehicle for the transmission of those Mediterranean forms was the illustrated book itself, brought to the North by Christian missionaries.

**CARPETS AND CROSSES** The marriage between Christian imagery and the animal-interlace style of the North may be seen in the cross-inscribed carpet page (FIG. **16-6**) of the *Lindisfarne Gospels*. The book, produced in the Northumbrian monastery on Lindisfarne Island, contains several ornamental pages and exemplifies Hiberno-Saxon art at its best. According to a later *colophon* (an inscription, usually on the last page, providing information regarding a book's manufacture), Eadfrith, Bishop of Lindisfarne between 698 and his death in 721, wrote the *Lindisfarne Gospels* "for God and Saint Cuthbert." Cuthbert's relics (see "Pilgrimages and the Cult of Relics," Chapter 17, page 449) recently had been deposited in the Lindisfarne church.

The patterning and detail of the Lindisfarne ornamental page are much more intricate and compact than those of the *Book of Durrow*. Serpentine interlacements of fantastic animals devour each other, curling over and returning on their writhing, elastic shapes. The rhythm of expanding and contracting forms produces a most vivid effect of motion and change. But it is held in check by

the regularity of the design and by the dominating motif of the inscribed cross. The cross—the all-important symbol of the imported religion—stabilizes the rhythms of the serpentines and, perhaps by contrast with its heavy immobility, seems to heighten the effect of motion. The illuminator placed the motifs in detailed symmetries, with inversions, reversals, and repetitions that must be studied closely to appreciate not so much their variety as their mazelike complexity. The zoomorphic forms intermingle with clusters and knots of line, and the whole design vibrates with energy. The color is rich yet cool. The painter adroitly adjusted shape and color to achieve a smooth and perfectly even surface.

**SAINT MATTHEW AT WORK** All the works examined thus far, whether jeweled metalwork, wooden panels, or painted books, display the northern artists' preference for small, infinitely complex, and painstaking designs. Even the Matthew symbol in the *Book of Durrow* (FIG. 16-5) reveals that the illuminator's concern was abstract design, not the depiction of the natural world. But exceptions exist. In some Insular manuscripts it is clear that the northern artists based their compositions on classical pictures in imported Mediterranean books. Such is the case with the author portrait of Saint Matthew in the *Lindisfarne Gospels* (FIG. **16-7**). The Hiberno-Saxon illuminator's model must have been one of the illustrated Gospel books a Christian missionary brought from Italy to England. Author portraits were familiar features of Greek and Latin books, and similar representations of seated philosophers or poets writing or reading abound in ancient art (see FIGS. 10-72 and 11-4). Unlike the cross page of the same book, the Lindisfarne Evangelist portrait follows a long tradition of Mediterranean manuscript illumination.

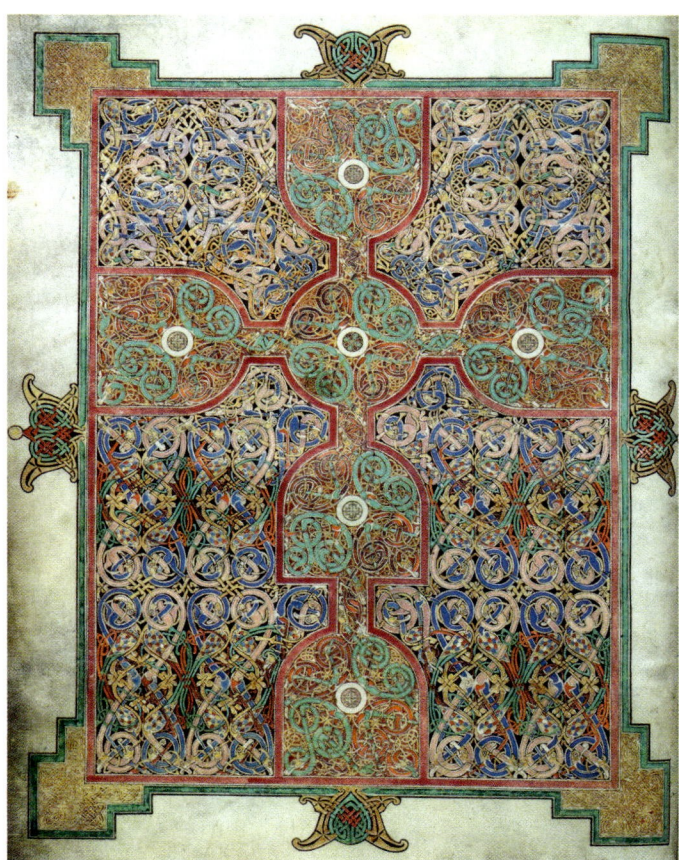

**16-6** Cross and carpet page, folio 26 verso of the *Lindisfarne Gospels*, from Northumbria, England, ca. 698–721. Tempera on vellum, $1' 1\frac{1}{2}'' \times 9\frac{1}{4}''$. British Library, London.

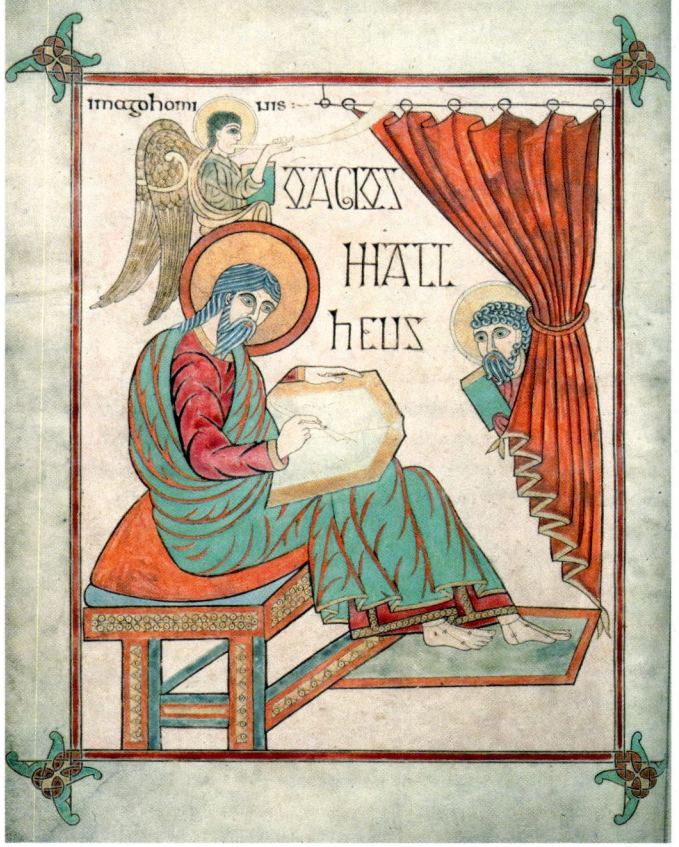

**16-7** Saint Matthew, folio 25 verso of the *Lindisfarne Gospels*, from Northumbria, England, ca. 698–721. Tempera on vellum, $1' 1\frac{1}{2}'' \times 9\frac{1}{4}''$. British Library, London.

Matthew sits in his study composing his account of the life of Christ. A curtain sets the scene indoors, as in classical art (compare FIG. 5-56), and the Evangelist's seat is shown at an angle, which also suggests a Mediterranean model employing classical perspective. The painter (or the scribe) labeled Matthew in a curious combination of Greek (*O Agios,* saint—written in Roman rather than Greek characters) and Latin (*Mattheus*), perhaps to lend the prestige of two classical languages to the page. The former was the language of the New Testament, the latter that of the Church of Rome. Matthew is accompanied by his symbol, the winged man (labeled *imago hominis,* image of the man). The figure—actually just a disembodied head and shoulders—behind the curtain has been variously identified. He is probably Moses, holding the closed book of the Old Testament in contrast with the open book of Matthew's New Testament, a common juxtaposition in medieval Christian art and thought.

Although a southern manuscript inspired the Lindisfarne composition, the Northumbrian painter's goal was not to copy the model faithfully. Instead, uninterested in the emphasis on volume, shading, and perspective that are the hallmarks of the pictorial illusionism of classical and Late Antique painting, the Lindisfarne illuminator conceived his subject in terms of line and color exclusively. In the Hiberno-Saxon manuscript, the drapery folds are a series of sharp, regularly spaced, curving lines filled in with flat colors. The painter converted fully modeled forms bathed in light into the linear idiom of northern art. The result is not an inferior imitation of a Mediterranean prototype but a vivid new vision of the Evangelist.

**ILLUMINATING THE WORD** The greatest achievement of Hiberno-Saxon art in the eyes of almost all modern observers is the *Book of Kells* (FIG. 16-8), the most elaborately decorated of the Insular Gospel books. Medieval commentators shared this high opinion, and one wrote in the *Annals of Ulster* for the year 1003 that this "great Gospel [is] the chief relic of the western world." The *Book of Kells* (named after the monastery in southern Ireland that owned it) was written and decorated either at Iona or a closely related Irish monastery. The manuscript probably was created for display on a church altar. From an early date it was housed in an elaborate metalwork box, befitting a greatly revered "relic." The *Book of Kells* boasts an unprecedented number of full-page illuminations, including carpet pages, evangelist symbols, portrayals of the Virgin Mary and of Christ, New Testament narrative scenes, canon tables, and several instances of monumentalized and embellished words from the Bible.

The page we reproduce (FIG. 16-8) opens the account of the nativity of Jesus in the Gospel of Saint Matthew. The initial letters of Christ in Greek (XPI, *chi-rho-iota*) occupy nearly the entire page, although two words—*autem* (abbreviated simply as *h*) and *generatio*—appear at the lower right. Together they read: "Now this is how the birth of Christ came about." The page corresponds to the opening of Matthew's Gospel, the passage read in church on Christmas Day. The illuminator transformed the holy words into extraordinarily intricate abstract designs that recall Celtic and Anglo-Saxon metalwork. But the cloisonné-like interlace is not purely abstract pattern. The letter *rho,* for example, ends in a male head, and animals are at its base to the left of *h generatio.* Half-figures of winged angels appear to the left of *chi,* accompanying the monogram as if accompanying Christ himself. Close observation reveals many other figures, human and animal.

When the priest Giraldus Cambrensis visited Ireland in 1185, he described a manuscript he saw that, if not the *Book of Kells* itself, must have been very much like it:

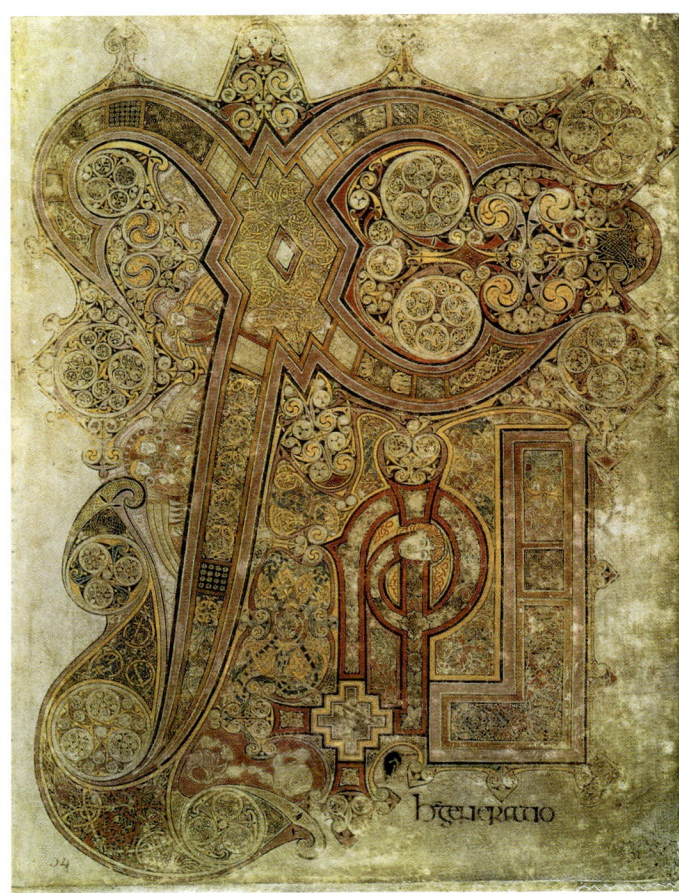

**16-8** Chi-rho-iota page, folio 34 recto of the *Book of Kells,* probably from Iona, Scotland, late eighth or early ninth century. Tempera on vellum, $1' \ 1'' \times 9\frac{1}{2}''$. Trinity College Library, Dublin.

Fine craftsmanship is all about you, but you might not notice it. Look more keenly at it and you . . . will make out intricacies, so delicate and subtle, so exact and compact, so full of knots and links, with colors so fresh and vivid, that you might say that all this was the work of an angel, and not of a man. For my part, the oftener I see the book, the more carefully I study it, the more I am lost in ever fresh amazement, and I see more and more wonders in the book.[3]

**IRELAND'S HIGH CROSSES** The preserved art of the early Middle Ages is, as has been noted, confined almost exclusively to small and portable works. The high crosses of Ireland, erected between the 8th and 10th centuries, are exceptional in their mass and scale. These majestic monuments, some more than 20 feet in height, preside over burial grounds adjoining the ruins of monasteries at sites widely distributed throughout the Irish countryside, and in some instances also in England. Freestanding and unattached to any architectural fabric, the high crosses have the imposing unity, weight, and presence of both building and statue—architecture and sculpture combined.

The *High Cross of Muiredach* (FIG. 16-9) at Monasterboice, Ireland, is one of the largest and finest Irish crosses. An inscription on the bottom of the west face of the shaft asks a prayer for a man named Muiredach. Most scholars identify him as the influential Irish cleric of the same name who was abbot of Monasterboice and died in 923. The monastery he headed was one of Ireland's oldest, founded in the late fifth century. The cross probably marked the abbot's grave.

The concave arms of Muiredach's cross are looped by four arcs that form a circle. The arms expand into squared terminals

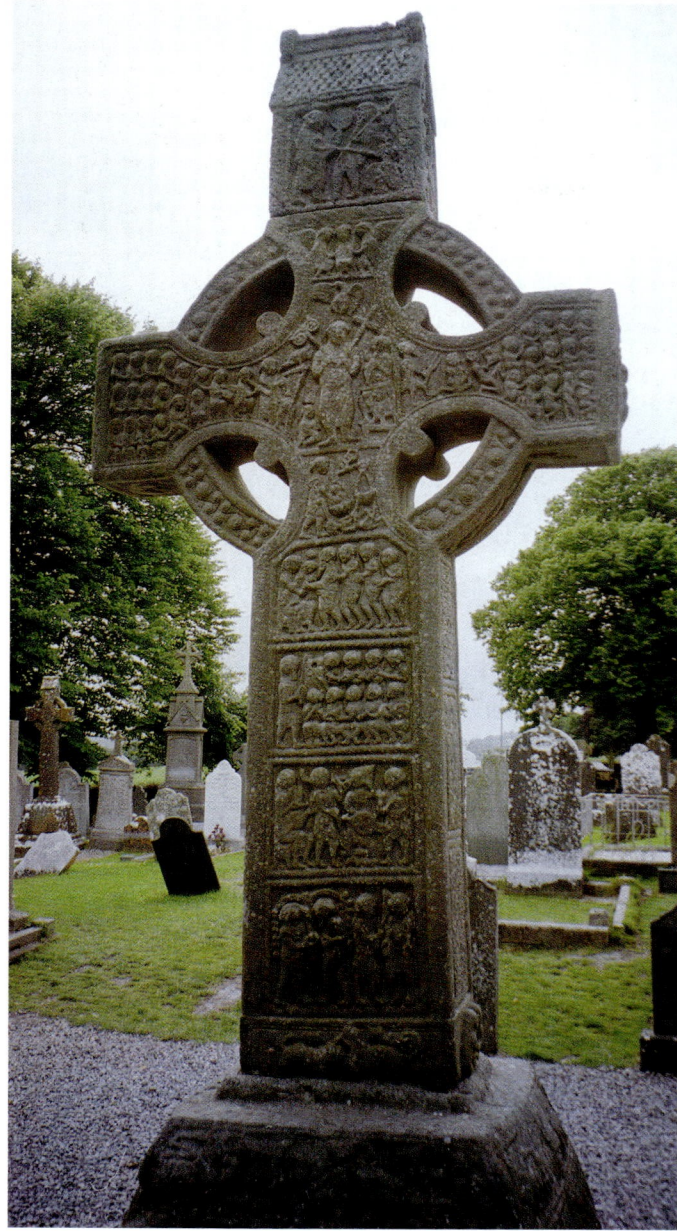

**16-9** *High Cross of Muiredach* (east face), Monasterboice, Ireland, 923. Sandstone, approx. 18′ high.

(compare FIG. 16-6). The circle intersecting the cross identifies the type as Celtic. The early high crosses bear abstract designs, especially the familiar interlace pattern. But the later ones, like Muiredach's, have figured panels, with scenes from the life of Christ or, occasionally, fantastic animals or events from the life of some Celtic saint. At the center of the west side of Muiredach's cross is a depiction of the Crucified Christ. On the east side (FIG. 16-9) the risen Christ stands as judge of the world, the hope of the dead. Below him the souls of the dead are being weighed on scales—a theme that sculptors of 12th-century church portals (see FIGS. Intro-6 and 17-25) took up with extraordinary force.

# MOZARABIC ART

**VISIGOTHS AND MUSLIMS** When Muslim armies crossed into Spain from North Africa in 711 (see Chapter 13), they brought Islam to a land that the Romans had ruled for centuries. Roman sovereignty had brought new roads to the Iberian peninsula and new cities with Roman temples, forums, theaters, and aqueducts. But in the early fifth century, the Roman cities fell to Germanic invaders, most notably the Visigoths, who had converted to Christianity. The stone churches the Visigoths built in the sixth and seventh centuries were basilican in form and regularly incorporated horseshoe arches, a form usually associated with Islamic architecture (see FIG. 13-11), but which predates the Muslim conquest. Although the Islamic caliphs of Córdoba swept the Visigoths away, they never succeeded in gaining control of the northernmost parts of the peninsula. There, the Christian culture of Iberia, called *Mozarabic* (referring to Christians living in Arab territories), continued to flourish, centered in the monasteries of the various Christian kingdoms.

**THE TÁBARA SCRIPTORIUM** One northern Spanish monk, Beatus, abbot of San Martín at Liébana, wrote *Commentary on the Apocalypse* around 776. This influential work was widely copied and illustrated in the monastic scriptoria of medieval Europe. One such copy was produced at the monastery of San Salvador at Tábara in the Kingdom of Léon in 970. The colophon (FIG. **16-10**) to the illustrated *Commentary* presents the earliest known depiction of a medieval scriptorium. Because the artist provided a composite of exterior and interior views of the building, it is especially informative. At the left is a great bell tower with a monk on the ground floor ringing the bells. The painter carefully recorded the Islamic-style glazed-tile walls of the tower, its interior ladders, and its

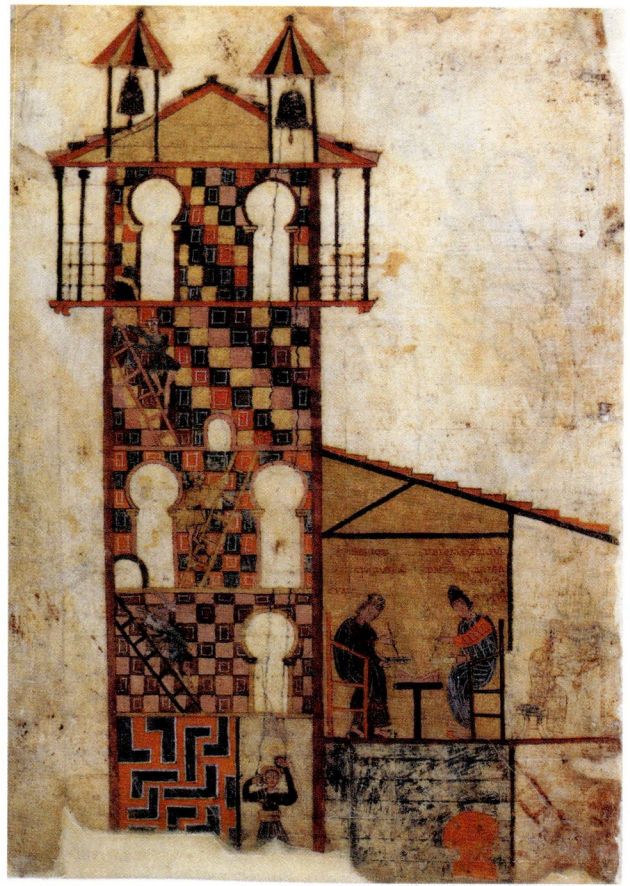

**16-10** EMETERIUS, the tower and scriptorium of San Salvador de Tábara, colophon (folio 168) of the *Commentary on the Apocalypse* by Beatus, from Tábara, Spain, 970. Tempera on parchment, $1′2\frac{1}{8}″ \times 10″$. Archivo Histórico Nacional, Madrid.

elegant windows with their horseshoe arches, the legacy of the Visigoths. To the right, in the scriptorium proper, three monks are performing their respective specialized duties. The colophon identifies the two monks in the main room as the scribe Senior and the painter EMETERIUS. To the right, a third monk uses shears to cut sheets of parchment. The colophon also pays tribute to Magius, "the worthy master painter . . . May he deserve to be crowned with Christ,"[4] who died before he could complete his work on the book. His pupil Emeterius took his place and brought the project to fruition. He must be the painter of the colophon.

# CAROLINGIAN ART

**ROME RISES AGAIN** On Christmas Day of the year 800, Pope Leo III crowned Charles the Great (Charlemagne), King of the Franks since 768, as emperor of Rome (r. 800–814). In time Charlemagne came to be seen as the first Holy (that is, Christian) Roman Emperor, a title his successors in the West did not formally adopt until the 12th century. The setting for Charlemagne's coronation, fittingly, was Saint Peter's basilica in Rome (see FIG. 11-7), built by Constantine, the first Roman emperor to embrace Christianity. Born in 742, when northern Europe was still in chaos, Charlemagne consolidated the Frankish kingdom his father and grandfather bequeathed him and defeated the Lombards in Italy. He thus united Europe and laid claim to reviving the glory of the ancient Roman Empire. He gave his name (Carolus Magnus in Latin) to an entire era, the *Carolingian* period.

Charlemagne's official seal bore the words *renovatio imperii Romani* (renewal of the Roman Empire). The "Carolingian Renaissance" was a remarkable historical phenomenon, an energetic, brilliant emulation of the art, culture, and political ideals of Early Christian Rome. Charlemagne's (Holy) Roman Empire, waxing and waning for a thousand years and with many hiatuses, existed in central Europe until Napoleon destroyed it in 1806.

**IMPERIAL IMAGERY REVIVED** When Charlemagne returned home from his coronation in Rome, he ordered the transfer of an equestrian statue of the Ostrogothic king Theodoric from Ravenna to the Carolingian palace complex at Aachen. That portrait is lost, as is the grand gilded bronze statue of the Byzantine emperor Justinian that once crowned a column in Constantinople (see "The Emperors of New Rome," Chapter 12, page 327). But in the early Middle Ages both statues stood as reminders of ancient Rome's glory and of the pretensions and aspirations of the medieval successors of Rome's Christian emperors. The portrait of Theodoric may have been the inspiration for a ninth-century bronze statuette (FIG. **16-11**) of a Carolingian emperor on horseback. Charlemagne greatly admired Theodoric, the first Germanic ruler of Rome. Many have identified the small bronze figure as Charlemagne himself, although others think it portrays his grandson, Charles the Bald (r. 840–877).

The ultimate model for the statuette was the equestrian portrait of Marcus Aurelius (see FIG. 10-59) in Rome. In the Middle Ages, it was mistakenly thought to represent Constantine, the first Christian emperor, another revered predecessor of Charlemagne and his Carolingian successors. The medieval sculptor portrayed the ninth-century emperor, like Marcus Aurelius, as overly large so that he, not the horse, is the center of attention. But unlike the Roman emperor, the Carolingian monarch sits rigidly upright. Quiet dignity replaced the torsion of Marcus Aurelius's body and the bold gesture of his right arm. Charlemagne (or Charles the Bald) is on parade, wearing imperial robes rather than a general's

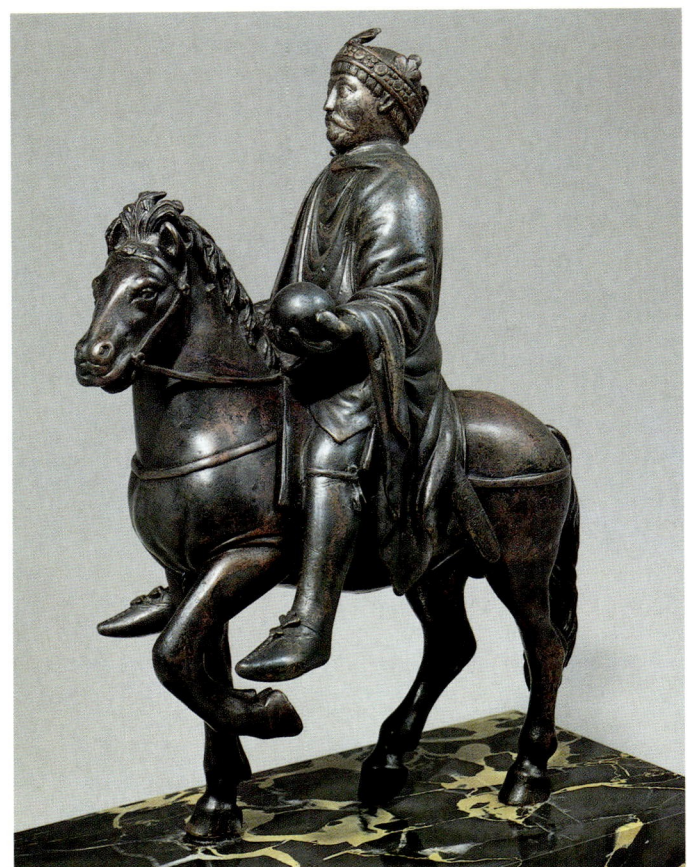

**16-11** Equestrian portrait of Charlemagne or Charles the Bald, from Metz, France, ninth century. Bronze, originally gilt, $9\frac{1}{2}''$ high. Louvre, Paris.

cloak, although his sheathed sword is visible. On his head is the imperial crown, and in his outstretched left hand he holds a globe, symbol of world dominion. The portrait proclaimed the *renovatio* of the Roman Empire's power and trappings.

## The Art of the Book

**CHARLEMAGNE'S BOOKS** Charlemagne was a sincere admirer of learning, the arts, and classical culture (see "The Revival of Learning at Charlemagne's Court," page 431). He, his successors, and the scholars under their patronage placed a very high value on books, both sacred and secular, importing many and producing far more. One of these is the famous *Coronation Gospels* (also known as the *Gospel Book of Charlemagne*). An old (and probably inaccurate) legend says that the book was found on Charlemagne's knees when, in the year 1000, Otto III had the emperor's tomb opened. The text is written in handsome gold letters on purple vellum.

The major full-page illuminations show the four Gospel authors at work. The page we reproduce (FIG. **16-12**) depicts Saint Matthew and may be compared to the portrait of the same Evangelist in the *Lindisfarne Gospels* (FIG. 16-7). The Carolingian painter's technique is markedly different from that of the Northumbrian painter. Deft, illusionistic brushwork defines the massive drapery folds wrapped around the body beneath. The illuminator used color and modulation of light and shade, not line, to create shapes. The cross-legged chair, the lectern, and the saint's toga are familiar Roman accessories. The landscape background is classicizing, and the frame is filled with the kind of

## The Revival of Learning at Charlemagne's Court

To make his empire as splendid as Rome's, Charlemagne invited to his court at Aachen the best minds and the finest artisans of western Europe and the Byzantine East. Among them were Theodulf of Orléans, Paulinus of Aquileia, and Alcuin, master of the cathedral school at York, the center of Northumbrian learning. Alcuin brought Anglo-Saxon scholarship to the Carolingian court.

Charlemagne himself, according to Einhard, his biographer, could read and speak Latin fluently, in addition to Frankish, his native tongue. He also could understand Greek, and he studied rhetoric and mathematics with the learned men he gathered around him. But he never learned to write properly—that was a task best left to professional scribes. In fact, one of Charlemagne's

dearest projects was the recovery of the true text of the Bible, which, through centuries of errors in copying, had become quite corrupt. Various scholars undertook the great project at the emperor's behest, but Alcuin of York's revision of the Bible, prepared at the new monastery at Tours, became the most widely used.

Charlemagne's scribes also were responsible for the development of a new, more compact, and more easily written and legible version of Latin script called *Caroline minuscule.* The letters on this page are descended from the alphabet Carolingian scribes perfected. Later generations also owe to Charlemagne's patronage the restoration and copying of important classical texts. The earliest known manuscripts of many Greek and Roman authors are Carolingian in date.

acanthus leaves found in Roman temple capitals and friezes (see FIG. 10-30). Almost nothing is known in the Hiberno-Saxon or Frankish West that could have prepared the way for such a classicizing portrayal of Saint Matthew. If a Frank, rather than an Italian or a Byzantine, painted the Saint Matthew and the other Evangelist portraits of the *Coronation Gospels,* the northern artist had fully absorbed the classical manner. Classical painting style was one of the many components of Charlemagne's program to establish Aachen as the capital of a renewed Christian Roman Empire.

**AN IMPASSIONED EVANGELIST** The classicizing style evident in the *Coronation Gospels* was by no means the only one that appeared suddenly in the Carolingian world. Court schools and monasteries employed a wide variety of styles derived from Late Antique prototypes. Another Saint Matthew (FIG. **16-13**), in a Gospel book made for Archbishop Ebbo of Reims, France, may be an interpretation of an author portrait very similar to the one the *Coronation Gospels* master used as a model. It resembles it in pose and in brushwork technique, but there the resemblance stops. The *Ebbo Gospels* illuminator replaced the classical calm and

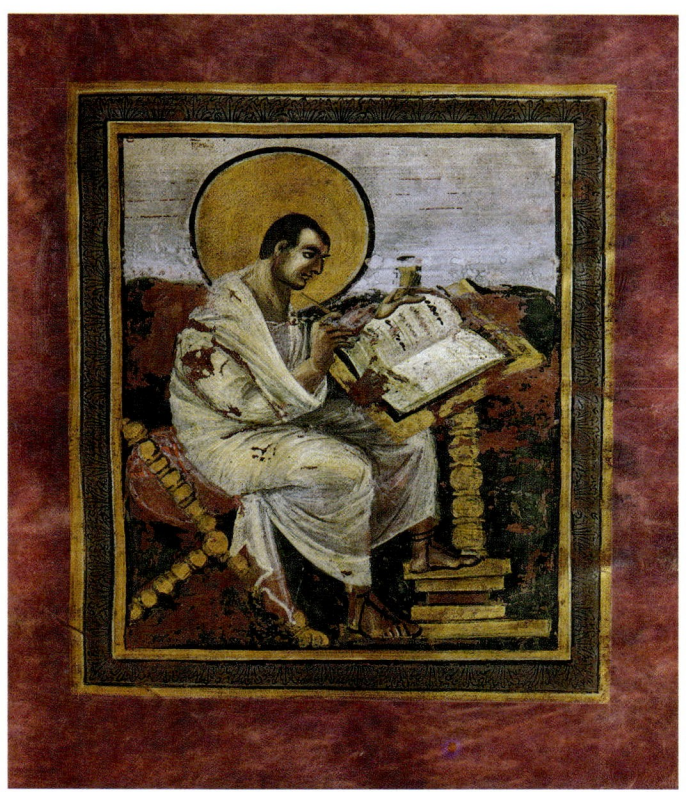

**16-12** Saint Matthew, folio 15 recto of the *Coronation Gospels (Gospel Book of Charlemagne),* from Aachen, Germany, ca. 800–810. Ink and tempera on vellum, $1' \frac{3}{4}'' \times 10''$. Schatzkammer, Kunsthistorisches Museum, Vienna.

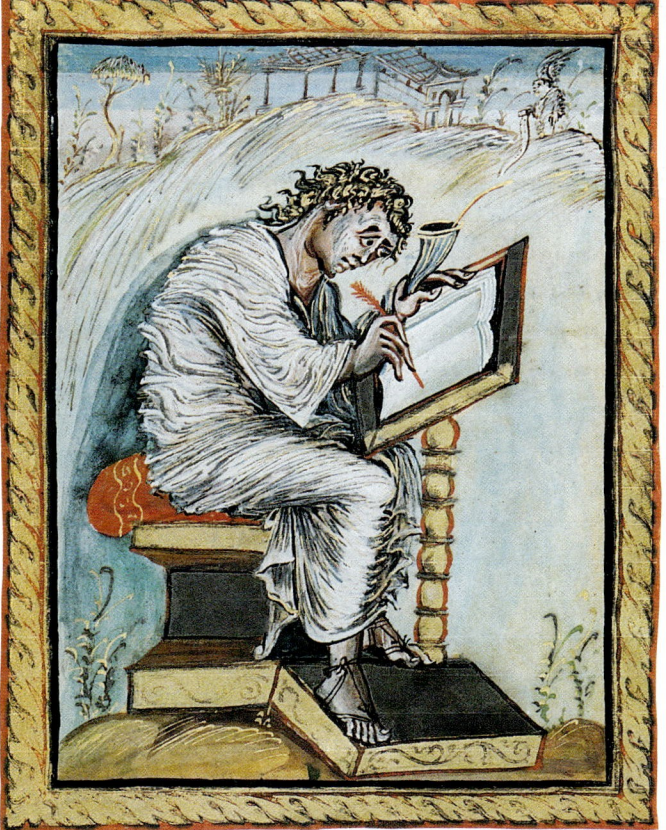

**16-13** Saint Matthew, folio 18 verso of the *Ebbo Gospels (Gospel Book of Archbishop Ebbo of Reims),* from Hautvillers (near Reims), France, ca. 816–835. Ink and tempera on vellum, $10\frac{1}{4}'' \times 8\frac{3}{4}''$. Bibliothèque Municipale, Épernay.

solidity of the *Coronation Gospels* with an energy that amounts to frenzy, and the frail saint almost leaps under its impulse. Matthew (the winged man in the upper right corner identifies him) writes in frantic haste. His hair stands on end, his eyes open wide, the folds of his drapery writhe and vibrate, the landscape behind him rears up alive. The painter even set the page's leaf border in motion. Matthew's face, hands, inkhorn, pen, and book are the focus of the composition. This presentation contrasts strongly with the settled pose of the Saint Matthew of the *Coronation Gospels* with its even stress so that no part of the composition starts out at viewers to seize their attention. Just as the painter of the *Lindisfarne Gospels* Matthew (FIG. 16-7) transformed an imported model into something original, translating the classicizing manner of a southern manuscript into a Hiberno-Saxon idiom, so the *Ebbo Gospels* artist translated a classical prototype into a new Carolingian vernacular. This master painter brilliantly merged classical illusionism and the North's linear tradition.

### ILLUSTRATING THE PSALMS
One of the most extraordinary medieval manuscripts is the *Utrecht Psalter* (book of psalms). The text reproduces the Psalms of David in three columns of Latin capital letters emulating the script and page organization of ancient books. The artist illustrated each psalm with a pen-and-ink drawing stretching across the entire width of the page. Our example (FIG. **16-14**) depicts figures acting out—literally and with a genius for anecdotal detail—Psalm 44 (Psalm 43 of the Vulgate text of the Carolingian era), in which the psalmist laments the plight of the oppressed Israelites. Where the text says, "we are counted as sheep for slaughter," the artist drew some slain sheep fallen to the ground in front of a walled city reminiscent of cities on the Column of Trajan in Rome (see FIG. 10-42) and in Early Christian mosaics and manuscripts (see FIG. 11-19). At the left, the faithful grovel on the ground before a temple because the psalm reads "our soul is bowed down to the dust; our belly cleaveth unto the earth." The artist's response to "Awake, why sleepest thou, O Lord" was to depict the Lord (as Christ instead of the Hebrew God, complete with cruciform halo), flanked by six pleading angels, reclining in a canopied bed overlooking the slaughter below.

The drawing shows a vivid animation of much the same kind as the Saint Matthew of the *Ebbo Gospels,* and the *Utrecht Psalter* may have been produced in the same "school of Reims." As in the *Ebbo Gospels,* even the earth heaves up around the figures. The bodies are tense, shoulders hunched, heads thrust forward. The rapid, sketchy techniques used to render the figures convey the same nervous vitality as the Evangelists in the *Ebbo Gospels.* Some scholars have argued that the costumes and other details indicate that the artist followed one or more manuscripts compiled 400 years before. Even if the *Utrecht Psalter* is not a copy, it certainly was designed to evoke earlier artworks and to appear "ancient."

### BEJEWELED GOLDEN BOOKS
The taste for sumptuously wrought and portable objects, shown previously in the art of the early medieval warrior lords, persisted under Charlemagne and his successors. They commissioned numerous works employing costly materials, including book covers made of gold and jewels, and sometimes also ivory or pearls. Gold and gems not only glorified the Word of God but also evoked the heavenly Jerusalem.

One of the most luxurious Carolingian book covers (FIG. **16-15**) is the one later added to the *Lindau Gospels.* The gold cover was fashioned in one of the workshops of Charles the Bald's court and is monumental in conception. A youthful Christ in the Early Christian tradition is shown nailed to the cross, surrounded by pearls and jewels (raised on golden claw feet so that they can catch and reflect the light even more brilliantly and protect the delicate metal relief from denting). The statuesque open-eyed figure, rendered in *repoussé* (hammered or pressed relief), brings to mind the beardless unsuffering Christ of the fifth-century ivory casket from Italy in the British Museum (see FIG. 11-21). In contrast, the four angels and the personifications of the Moon and the Sun above and the crouching figures of the Virgin Mary and Saint John (and two other figures of uncertain identity) in the quadrants below display the vivacity and nervous energy of the *Utrecht Psalter* figures. This eclectic work highlights the stylistic diversity of early medieval art in Europe. Here, however, the translated figural style of the Mediterranean prevails, in keeping with the classical tastes and imperial aspirations of the Frankish "emperors of Rome."

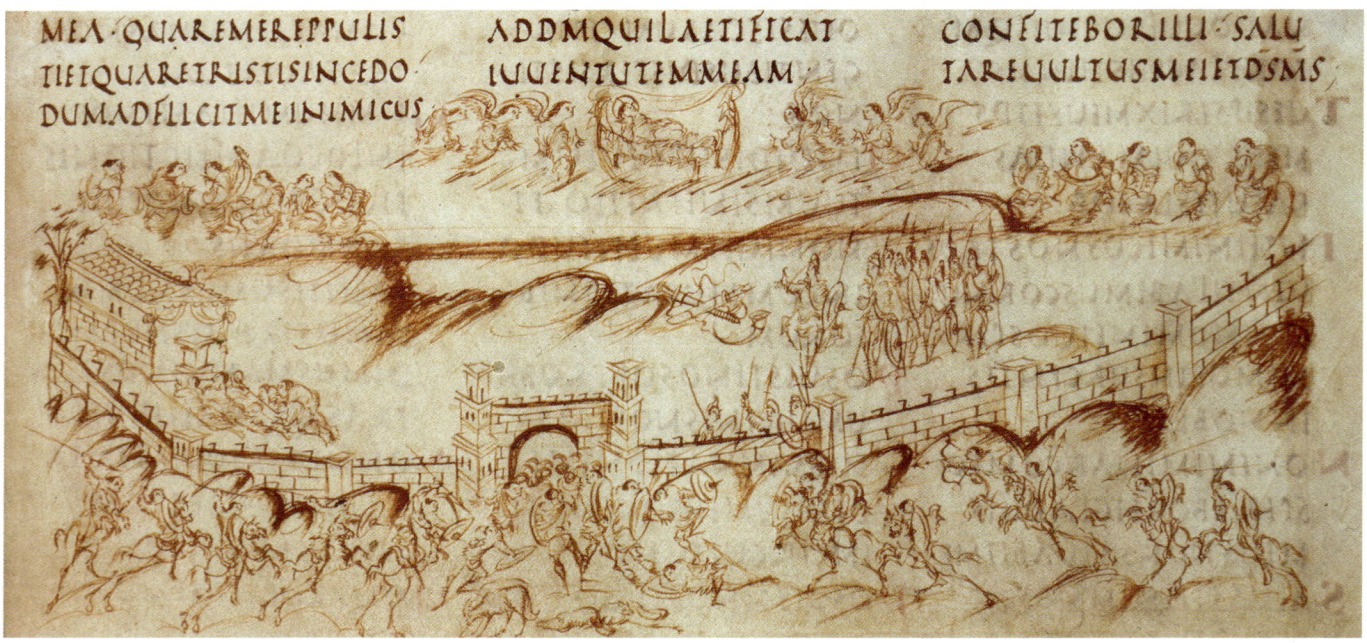

**16-14** Psalm 44, detail of folio 25 recto of the *Utrecht Psalter,* from Hautvillers (near Reims), France, ca. 820–835. Ink on vellum, full page, $1' 1'' \times 9\frac{7}{8}''$. University Library, Utrecht.

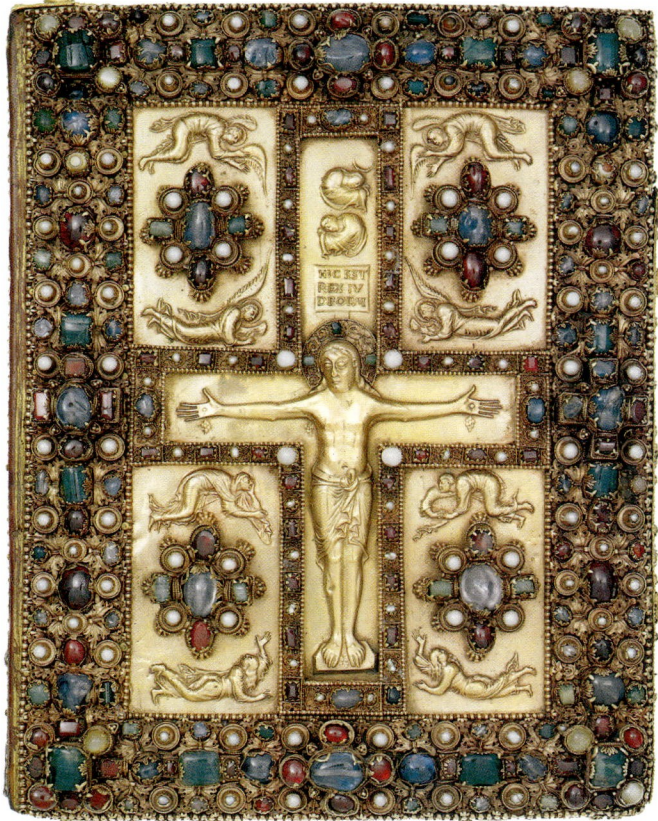

16-15 Crucifixion, front cover of the *Lindau Gospels,* from Saint Gall, Switzerland, ca. 870. Gold, precious stones, and pearls, 1′ $1\frac{3}{8}″$ × $10\frac{3}{8}″$. Pierpont Morgan Library, New York.

## Architecture

In his eagerness to reestablish the imperial past, Charlemagne also encouraged the use of Roman building techniques. In architecture, as in sculpture and painting, innovations made in the reinterpretation of earlier Roman Christian sources became fundamental to the subsequent development of northern European architecture. For his models, Charlemagne went to Rome and Ravenna. One was the former heart of the Roman Empire, which he wanted to

"renew." The other was the long-term western outpost of Byzantine might and splendor, which he wanted to emulate in his own capital at Aachen, a site chosen because of its renowned hot springs.

**AACHEN AND RAVENNA** Charlemagne often visited Ravenna, and, as already noted, he brought an equestrian statue of Theodoric from there to display in his palace complex at Aachen, where it served as a model for Carolingian equestrian portraits (FIG. 16-11). Charlemagne also imported porphyry (purple marble) columns from Ravenna to adorn his Palatine Chapel, and historians long have thought he chose one of Ravenna's churches as the model for the new structure. The plan (FIG. **16-16**) of the Aachen chapel resembles that of San Vitale (see FIG. 12-7), and a direct relationship very likely exists between the two.

A comparison between the northern building, the first vaulted structure of the Middle Ages in the West, and its southern counterpart is instructive. The Aachen plan is simpler. Omitted were San Vitale's apselike extensions reaching from the central octagon into the ambulatory. At Aachen, the two main units stand in greater independence of each other. This solution may lack the subtle sophistication of the Byzantine building, but the Palatine Chapel gains geometric clarity. A view of the interior of the Palatine Chapel (FIG. **16-17**) shows that the "floating" quality of San Vitale (see FIG. 12-8) was converted into massive geometric form.

The Carolingian conversion of a complex and subtle Byzantine prototype into a building that expresses robust strength and clear structural articulation foreshadows the architecture of the 11th and 12th centuries and the style called Romanesque (see Chapter 17). So, too, does the treatment of the Palatine Chapel's

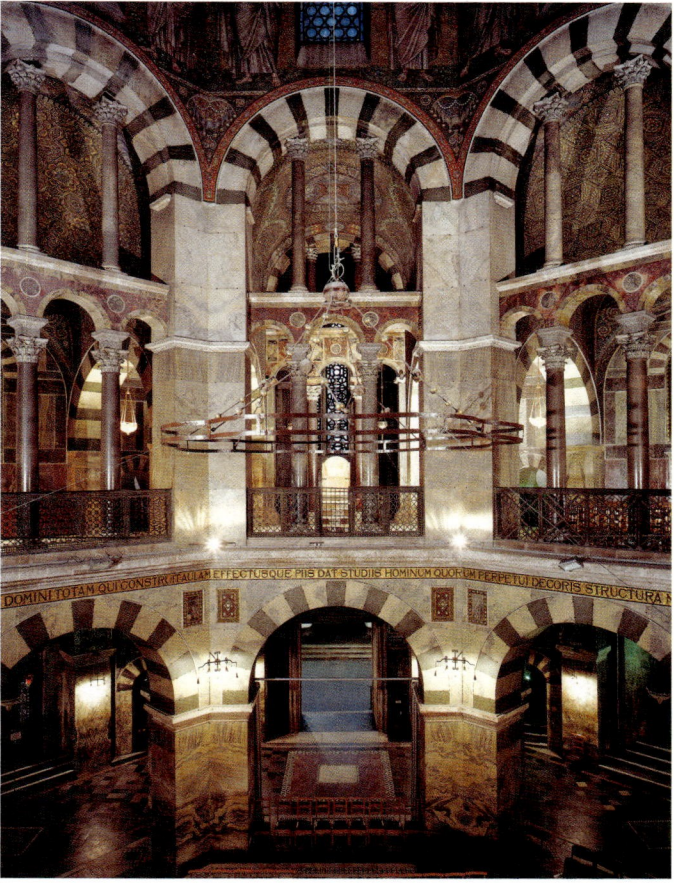

16-17 Interior of the Palatine Chapel of Charlemagne, Aachen, Germany, 792–805.

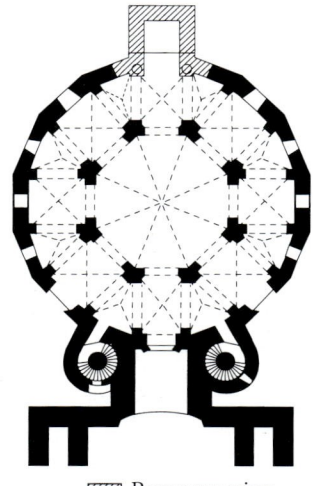

0   50   100 FEET
0   15   30 METERS
▨ Reconstruction

16-16 Restored plan of the Palatine Chapel of Charlemagne, Aachen, Germany, 792–805.

## Medieval Monasteries and Benedictine Rule

Monastic foundations appeared in the West beginning in Early Christian times. The monks who established monasteries also made the rules that governed them. The most significant of these monks was Benedict of Nursia (Saint Benedict), who founded the Benedictine Order in 529. By the ninth century, the "Rule" Benedict wrote *(Regula Sancti Benedicti)* had become standard for all Western monastic establishments, in part because Charlemagne had encouraged its adoption throughout the Frankish territories.

Saint Benedict believed that the corruption of the clergy that accompanied the increasing worldliness of the Christian Church was rooted in the lack of firm organization and regulation. Neglect of the commandments of God and of the Church was due, as he saw it, to idleness and selfishness. The cure for this was communal association in an *abbey* under the absolute rule of an *abbot* the monks elected (or an *abbess* the nuns chose), who would see to it that each hour of the day was spent in useful work and in sacred reading. The emphasis was on work and study and not on meditation and austerity. This is of great historical significance. Since antiquity, manual labor had been considered disgraceful, the business of the lowborn or of slaves. Benedict raised it to the dignity of religion. The core idea of what many people today call the "work ethic" found early expression here as an essential feature of spiritual life. By thus exalting the virtue of manual labor, Benedict not only rescued it from its age-old association with slavery but also recognized it as the way to self-sufficiency for the entire religious community.

Whereas some of Saint Benedict's followers emphasized spiritual "work" over manual labor, others, most notably the Cistercians (see "Bernard of Clairvaux," Chapter 17, page 461), put his teachings about the value of physical work into practice. These monks reached into their surroundings and helped reduce the vast areas of daunting wilderness of early medieval Europe. They cleared dense forest teeming with wolves, bear, and wild boar; drained swamps; cultivated wastelands; and built roads, bridges, and dams, as well as monastic churches and their associated living and service quarters.

An ideal monastery (FIG. 16-19) provided all the facilities necessary for the conduct of daily life—a mill, bakery, infirmary, vegetable garden, and even a brewery—so that the monks felt no need to wander outside its protective walls. Such religious communities were centrally important to the revival of learning. The clergy, who were also often scribes and scholars, had a monopoly on the skills of reading and writing in an age of almost universal illiteracy. The monastic libraries and scriptoria (FIG. 16-10), where books were read, copied, illuminated, and bound with ornamented covers, became centers of study. These were almost the sole repositories of what remained of the literary culture of the Greco-Roman world and early Christianity. Saint Benedict's requirements of manual labor and sacred reading were expanded to include writing and copying books, studying music for chanting the day's offices, and—of great significance—teaching. The monasteries were the schools of the early Middle Ages, as well as self-sufficient communities and production centers.

---

exterior, where two cylindrical towers with spiral staircases flank the entrance portal (FIG. 16-16). This was a first step toward the great dual-tower facades of churches in the West from the 10th century to the present. Above the portal, Charlemagne could appear in a large framing arch and be seen by those gathered in the atrium in front of the chapel. (Only part of the atrium is included in our plan.) Directly behind that second-story arch was Charlemagne's marble throne. From there he could peer down at the altar in the apse. Charlemagne's imperial gallery followed the model of the imperial gallery at Hagia Sophia in Constantinople (see FIGS. 12-4 and 12-5). The Palatine Chapel was in every sense a royal chapel. Charlemagne's son, Louis the Pious (r. 814–840), was crowned there when he succeeded his father as emperor.

**THE GATEWAY TO LORSCH** The Carolingian evocation of the Roman past is illustrated by a remarkable survival from the ninth century, the Torhalle (FIG. **16-18**), or gatehouse, of the monastery at Lorsch, Germany. The gate is difficult to date because it is unique. Long thought to be from Charlemagne's time, it recently has been placed later in the century. Built as a freestanding structure in the atrium of the monastic church, the Lorsch Torhalle is a distant relative of the Arch of Constantine (see FIG. 10-76). But it follows more closely the design of Roman city gates, with its second-story windows and flanking towers (which also recall the arrangement of the Palatine Chapel's facade at Aachen). Also inspired by Roman architecture are the fairly close copies of Composite capitals and the framing of the arcuated passageways by engaged columns. The decorative treatment of the flat wall surfaces with colored inlays of cream and pink stone imitates

Roman *opus reticulatum,* a method of facing concrete walls with lozenge-shaped bricks or stones to achieve a netlike ornamental surface pattern. However, the columns support a decorative *stringcourse* (raised horizontal *molding,* or band) instead of a full entablature, and the second level has no parallel in classical

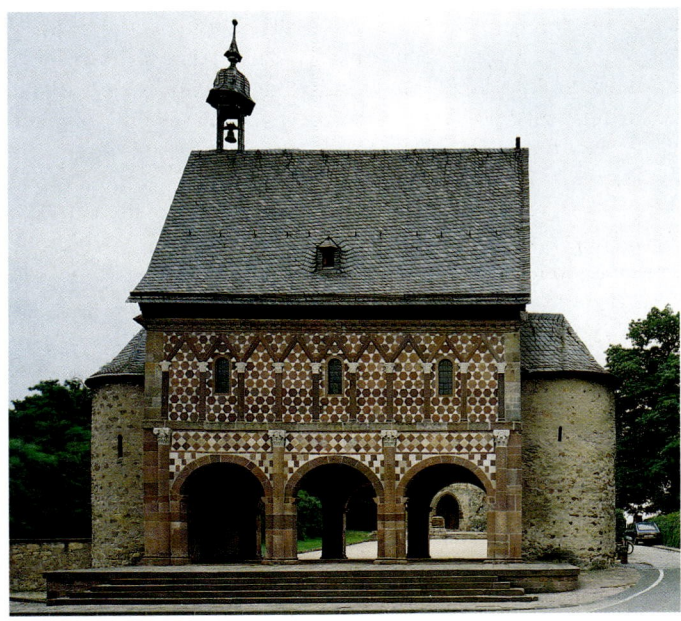

**16-18** Torhalle (gatehouse), Lorsch, Germany, ninth century.

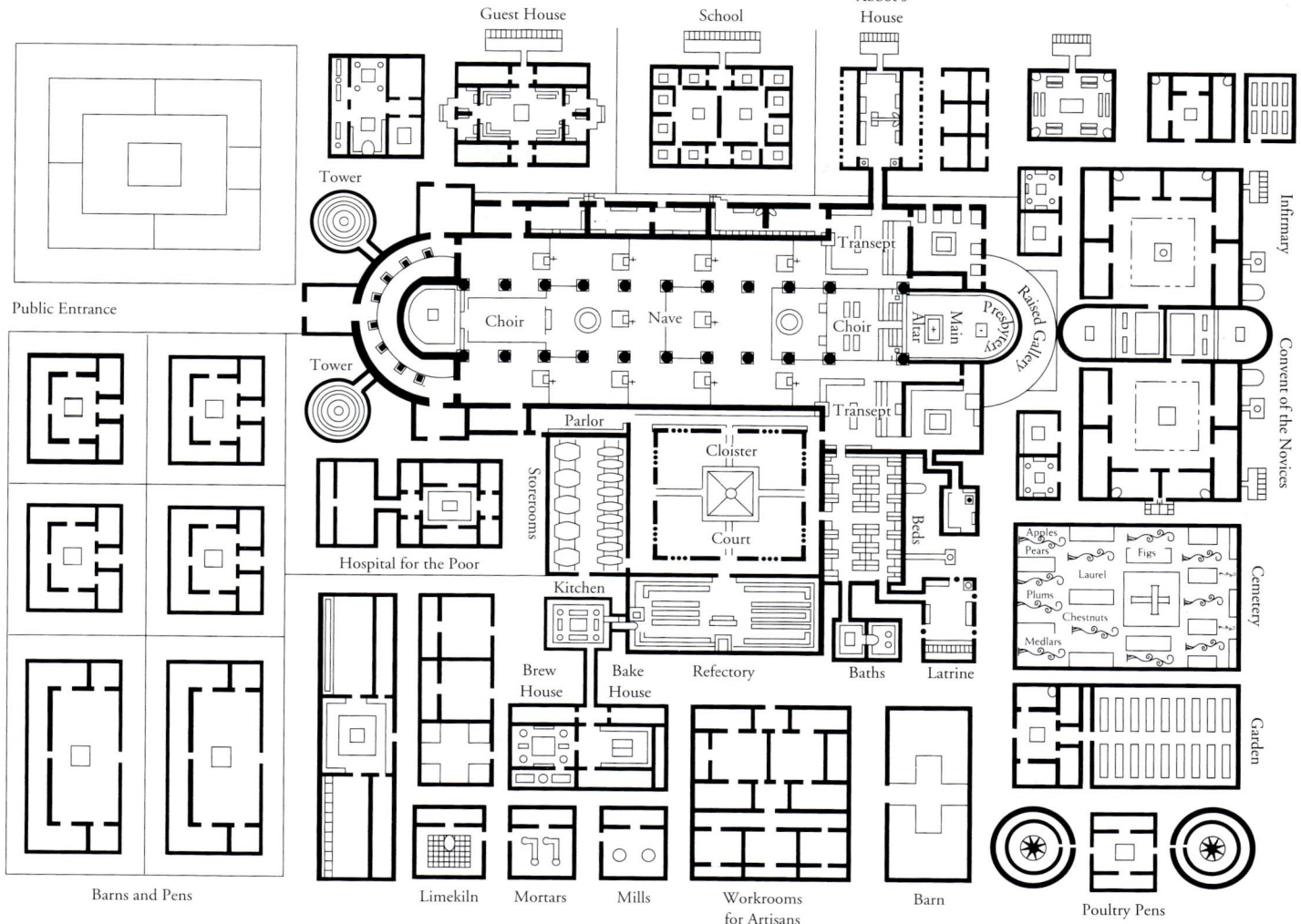

**16-19** Schematic plan for a monastery at Saint Gall, Switzerland, ca. 819. (Redrawn after a ninth-century manuscript; original in red ink on parchment, 2′ 4″ × 3′ 8⅛″. Stiftsbibliothek, Saint Gall.)

The image labels include: Guest House, School, Abbot's House, Tower, Public Entrance, Tower, Infirmary, Convent of the Novices, Transept, Raised Gallery, Choir, Nave, Choir, Main Altar, Presbytery, Parlor, Cloister, Court, Beds, Storerooms, Hospital for the Poor, Kitchen, Apples, Pears, Figs, Laurel, Plums, Chestnuts, Medlars, Cemetery, Brew House, Bake House, Refectory, Baths, Latrine, Garden, Barns and Pens, Limekiln, Mortars, Mills, Workrooms for Artisans, Barn, Poultry Pens

architecture. Pseudo-Ionic pilasters carry a zigzag of ornamental moldings, and the opus reticulatum was converted into a decorative pattern of hexagons and triangles that form star shapes. Finally, the steeply pitched timber roof that shelters a chapel dedicated to Saint Michael unmistakably stamps this gatehouse as a northern building. Still, the source of inspiration is clear, and if the final product no longer closely resembles the original, it is due to the fact that it is not a copy but a free interpretation of its model.

**THE IDEAL MONASTERY** The Lorsch monastery itself is not preserved, but a fascinating contemporary document, the ideal plan (FIG. **16-19**) for a monastery at Saint Gall in Switzerland, provides precious information about the design of Carolingian monastic communities. About 819, a schematic plan for a Benedictine community (see "Medieval Monasteries and Benedictine Rule," page 434) was drawn for Haito, the abbot of Reichenau and bishop of Basel, and sent to the abbot of Saint Gall. The plan provided a coherent arrangement of all the buildings of a monastic community and was intended as a guide in the rebuilding of the Saint Gall monastery. The design's fundamental purpose was to separate the monks from the *laity,* or nonclergy, who also inhabited the community. Variations of the scheme may be seen in later monasteries all across western Europe.

Near the center, dominating everything, was the church with its *cloister,* a colonnaded courtyard (see FIG. 17-20) not unlike the Early Christian atrium (see FIG. 11-7) but situated to the side of the church rather than in front of its main portal. Reserved for the monks alone, the cloister provided the peace and quiet necessary for contemplation and was regarded as a kind of earthly paradise removed from the world at large. Around the cloister were grouped the most essential buildings: dormitory, refectory, kitchen, and storage rooms. Other structures, including an infirmary, school, guest house, bakery, brewery, and workshops, were grouped around this central core of church and cloister.

Haito invited the abbot of Saint Gall to adapt the plan as he saw fit, and the Saint Gall builders did not, in fact, follow the Reichenau model exactly. Nonetheless, if the abbot had wished, Haito's plan *could* have served as a practical guide for the Saint Gall masons because it was laid out using a *module* (standard unit) of two and a half feet. Parts or multiples of this module were employed consistently throughout the plan. For example, the nave's width, indicated on the plan as 40 feet, was equal to 16 modules; the length of each monk's bed to two and a half modules; and the width of paths in the vegetable garden to one and a quarter modules. This systematic building up of the plan from a prescribed module parallels the Carolingian invention of that most convenient device, the division of books into chapters and subchapters.

**CAROLINGIAN BASILICAS** The models that carried the greatest authority for Charlemagne and his builders were those from the Christian phase of the Late Roman Empire. The widespread adoption of the Early Christian basilica, at Saint Gall and elsewhere, rather than the domed central plan of Byzantine churches, was crucial to the subsequent development of Western church architecture. Unfortunately, no Carolingian basilica has survived in anything approaching its original form. Nevertheless, it is possible to reconstruct the appearance of some of them with fair accuracy. Several of these structures appear to have followed their Early Christian models quite closely. But in other instances Carolingian builders significantly modified the basilica plan, converting it into a much more complex form. The monastery church at Saint Gall (FIG. 16-19), for example, was essentially a traditional basilica, but it had features not found in any Early Christian church. Most obvious is the addition of a second apse on the west end of the building, perhaps to accommodate additional altars and relics (see "Pilgrimages and the Cult of Relics," Chapter 17, page 449). Whatever its purpose, this feature remained a characteristic regional element of German churches until the 11th century.

Not quite as evident but much more important to the subsequent development of church architecture in the North was the presence of a transept at Saint Gall, a very rare feature, but one that characterized the two greatest Early Christian basilicas in Rome, Saint Peter's (see FIG. 11-7) and Saint Paul's. The Saint Gall transept is as wide as the nave on the plan and was probably the same height. Early Christian builders had not been concerned with proportional relationships. They assembled the various portions of their buildings only in accordance with the dictates of liturgical needs. On the Saint Gall plan, however, the various parts of the building are related to one another by a geometric scheme that ties them together into a tight and cohesive unit. Equalizing the widths of nave and transept automatically makes the area where they cross (the *crossing*) a square. Most Carolingian churches shared this feature. But Haito's planner also used the crossing square as the unit of measurement for the remainder of the church plan. The transept arms are equal to one crossing square, the distance between transept and apse is one crossing square, and the nave is four and a half crossing squares long. The fact that the two aisles are half as wide as the nave integrates all parts of the church in a rational, lucid, and orderly plan.

**TOWERS AND WESTWORKS** The Saint Gall plan also reveals another important feature of many Carolingian basilicas: towers framing the end(s) of the church. Haito's plan shows only two towers, both cylindrical and on the west side of the church, as at the Palatine Chapel at Aachen (FIG. 16-16), but they stand apart from the church facade. If a tower existed above the crossing, the silhouette of Saint Gall would have shown three towers altering the horizontal profile of the traditional basilica and identifying the church even from afar.

Other Carolingian basilicas had towers that were incorporated in the fabric of the west end of the building, thereby creating a unified monumental facade that greeted all those who entered the church. Architectural historians call this feature of Carolingian and some later churches the *westwork* (German *Westwerck*, western entrance structure). In contemporary documents it is referred to as a *castellum* (Latin, castle or fortress) or *turris* (tower). The sole surviving example is the abbey church at Corvey (FIG. **16-20**). The uppermost parts are 12th-century additions (easily distinguishable from the

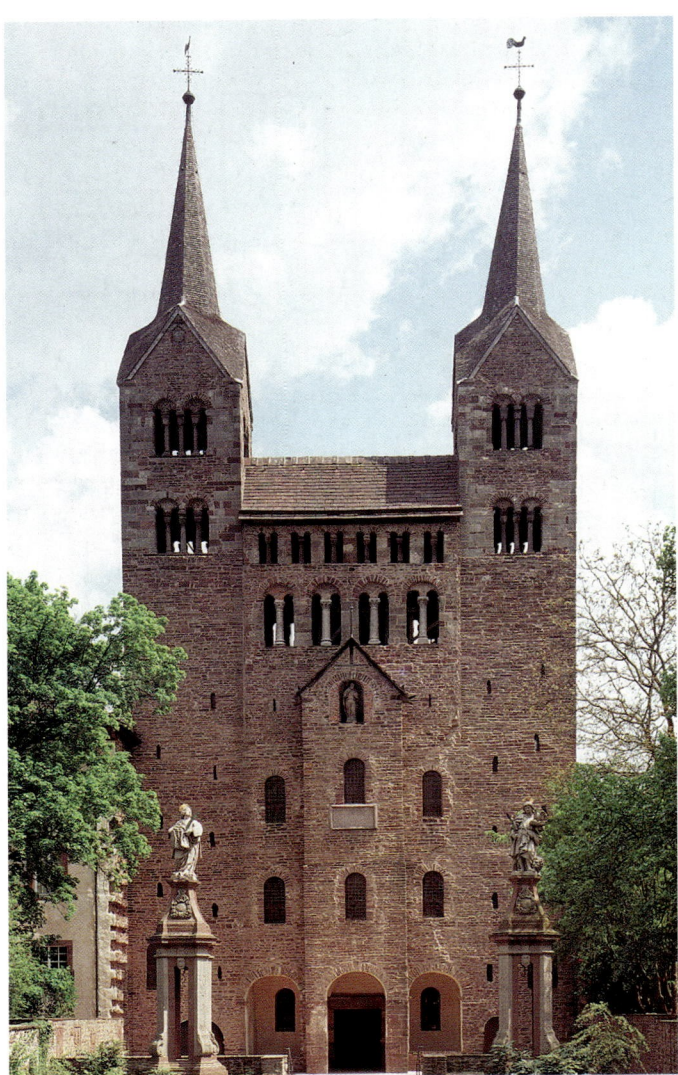

**16-20** Westwork of the abbey church, Corvey, Germany, 873–885.

original westwork by the differing masonry technique). Stairs in each tower provided access to the upper stories of the westwork. On the second floor was a two-story chapel with an aisle and a gallery on three sides. As at Aachen, the chapel opened onto the nave, and from it, on occasion, the emperor and his entourage could watch and participate in the service below. Not all Carolingian westworks, however, served as seats for the visiting emperor. They also functioned as churches within churches, housing a second altar for special celebrations on major feast days. Boys' choirs stationed in the westwork chapel participated from above in the services conducted in the church's nave.

# OTTONIAN ART

**AFTER CHARLEMAGNE** Charlemagne was buried in the Palatine Chapel at Aachen. His empire survived him by fewer than 30 years. When his son Louis the Pious died in 840, the Carolingian Empire was divided among Louis's sons, Charles the Bald, Lothair, and Louis the German. After bloody conflicts among the brothers, a treaty was signed in 843 partitioning the Frankish lands into western, central, and eastern areas, very roughly foreshadowing the later nations of France and Germany and a third realm corresponding to a long strip of land stretching from the Netherlands and Belgium to

Rome. Intensified Viking incursions in the West helped bring about the collapse of the Carolingians. The empire's breakup into weak kingdoms, ineffectual against the invasions, brought a time of confusion to Europe. The Viking scourge in the West was complemented by the invasions of the Magyars in the East and by the plundering and piracy of the Saracen (Muslim) corsairs in the Mediterranean.

Only in the mid-10th century did the eastern part of the former empire consolidate under the rule of a new Saxon line of German emperors called, after the names of the three most illustrious family members, the *Ottonians*. The first Otto (r. 936–973) was crowned emperor in Rome by the pope in 962, assuming the title Charlemagne's weak successors held during most of the previous century. The three Ottos made headway against the invaders from the East, remained free from Viking depredations, and not only preserved but also enriched the culture and tradition of the Carolingian period. The Christian Church, which had become corrupt and disorganized, recovered in the 10th century under the influence of a great monastic reform encouraged and sanctioned by the Ottonians, who also cemented ties with Italy and the papacy.

By the time the last of the Ottonian line, Henry II, died in the early 11th century, the pagan marauders had become Christianized and settled, and the monastic reforms had been highly successful.

## Architecture

**THE BASILICA TRANSFORMED** Ottonian architects followed the course of their Carolingian predecessors, building basilican churches with towering spires and imposing westworks. The best preserved 10th-century Ottonian basilica is Saint Cyriakus at Gernrode. The church was the centerpiece of a convent that Margrave (military governor) Gero founded on the site in 961. Construction of the church began the same year. In the 12th century, a large apse replaced the western entrance, but the upper parts of the westwork, including the two cylindrical towers, were left intact. The interior (FIG. **16-21**), although heavily restored in the 19th century, retains its 10th-century character. Saint Cyriakus reveals how Ottonian architects enriched the form of the

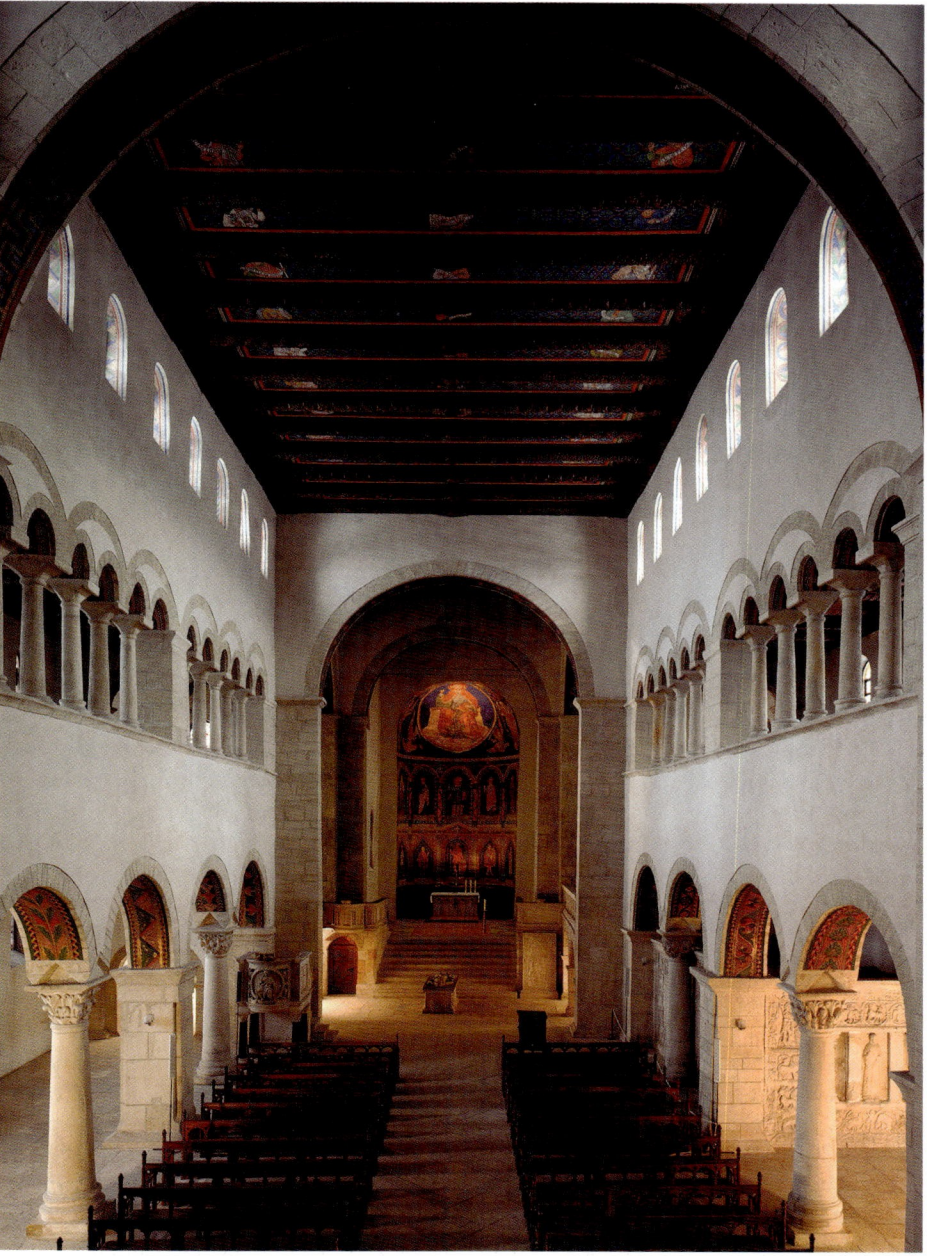

**16-21** Nave of the church of Saint Cyriakus, Gernrode, Germany, 961–973.

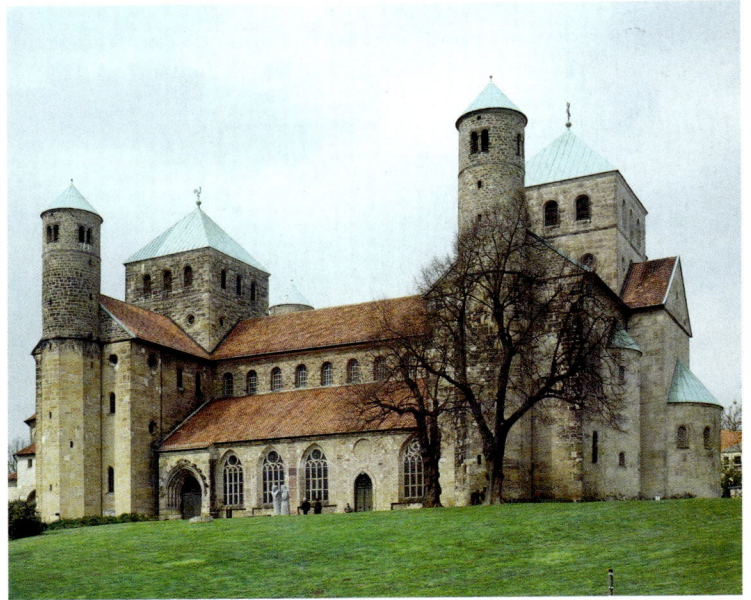

16-22 Saint Michael's, Hildesheim, Germany, 1001–1031.

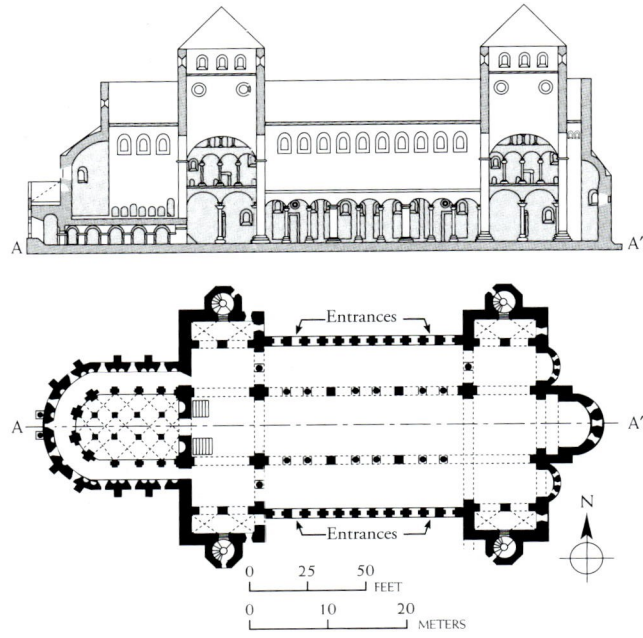

16-23 Longitudinal section (top) and plan (bottom) of the abbey church of Saint Michael's, Hildesheim, Germany, 1001–1031.

Early Christian basilica. The church has a transept at the east with a square choir in front of the apse. The nave is one of the first in the West to incorporate a gallery between the ground-floor arcade and the clerestory, a design that became very popular in the succeeding Romanesque era (see Chapter 17). Scholars have reached no consensus on the function of these galleries in Ottonian churches. They cannot have been reserved for women, as some think they were in Byzantium, because Saint Cyriakus is a nuns' church. One suggestion is that the galleries housed additional altars, as in the westwork at Corvey. They may also have been where the choirs sang.

The nave arcade itself was also transformed at Gernrode by the adoption of the *alternate-support system.* Heavy square piers alternate with columns, dividing the nave into vertical units and mitigating the tunnel-like horizontality of the Early Christian basilica. The division continues into the gallery level, breaking the smooth rhythm of an all-column arcade and leading the eye upward. Later architects would carry this "verticalization" of the basilican nave much further (see, for example, FIG. 18-17).

BISHOP BERNWARD One of the great patrons of Ottonian art and architecture was Bishop Bernward of Hildesheim, Germany. He was the tutor of Otto III (r. 983–1002) and builder of the abbey church of Saint Michael at Hildesheim (FIGS. **16-22** and **16-23**). Bernward, who made Hildesheim a center of learning, was an eager scholar, a lover of the arts, and, according to Thangmar of Heidelberg, his biographer, an expert craftsman and bronze caster. In 1001, he traveled to Rome as the guest of Otto III. During this stay, Bernward studied at first hand the monuments of the empire the Carolingian and Ottonian emperors revered.

Constructed between 1001 and 1031 (and rebuilt after being bombed during World War II), Bernward's Saint Michael's has a double-transept plan, tower groupings, and a westwork. The two transepts create eastern and western centers of gravity. The nave merely seems to be a hall that connects them. Lateral entrances leading into the aisles from the north and south (FIG. 16-23) additionally make for an almost complete loss of the traditional

basilican orientation toward the east. Some ancient Roman basilicas, such as the Basilica Ulpia in Trajan's Forum (see FIG. 10-41), also had two apses and were entered from the side, and Bernward probably was familiar with this variant basilican plan.

At Hildesheim, as in the plan of the monastery at Saint Gall (FIG. 16-19), the builders adopted a modular approach. The crossing squares, for example, were used as the basis for the nave's dimensions—three crossing squares long and one square wide. The three units were emphasized visually by the placement of heavy piers at the corners of each square. These piers alternate with pairs of columns as wall supports in a design similar to that of the earlier Ottonian church at Gernrode (FIG. 16-21).

## Sculpture

COLOSSAL BRONZE DOORS In 1001, when Bishop Bernward was in Rome visiting the young Otto III, he resided in Otto's palace on the Aventine Hill in the neighborhood of Santa Sabina (see FIG. 11-8), an Early Christian church renowned for its carved wooden doors. Those doors, decorated with episodes from both the Old and New Testaments, may have inspired the remarkable bronze doors the bishop had cast for his new church in Germany. The colossal doors (FIG. **16-24**) for Saint Michael's, dated by inscription to 1015, are more than 16 feet tall. Each was cast in a single piece with the figural sculpture, a technological tour de force of lost-wax casting (see "Hollow-Casting," Chapter 5, page 131). Carolingian sculpture, like most sculpture since late antiquity, consisted primarily of small-scale art executed in ivory and precious metals, so the 16 individual panels of the Hildesheim doors may be compared to the covers of Carolingian (FIG. 16-15) and Ottonian books. Bernward's doors are more public than any book cover, but they were situated at the entrance to the church from the cloister, where only the monks could pass through them.

The panels of the left door illustrate highlights from the biblical Book of Genesis, beginning with the creation of Adam (at the

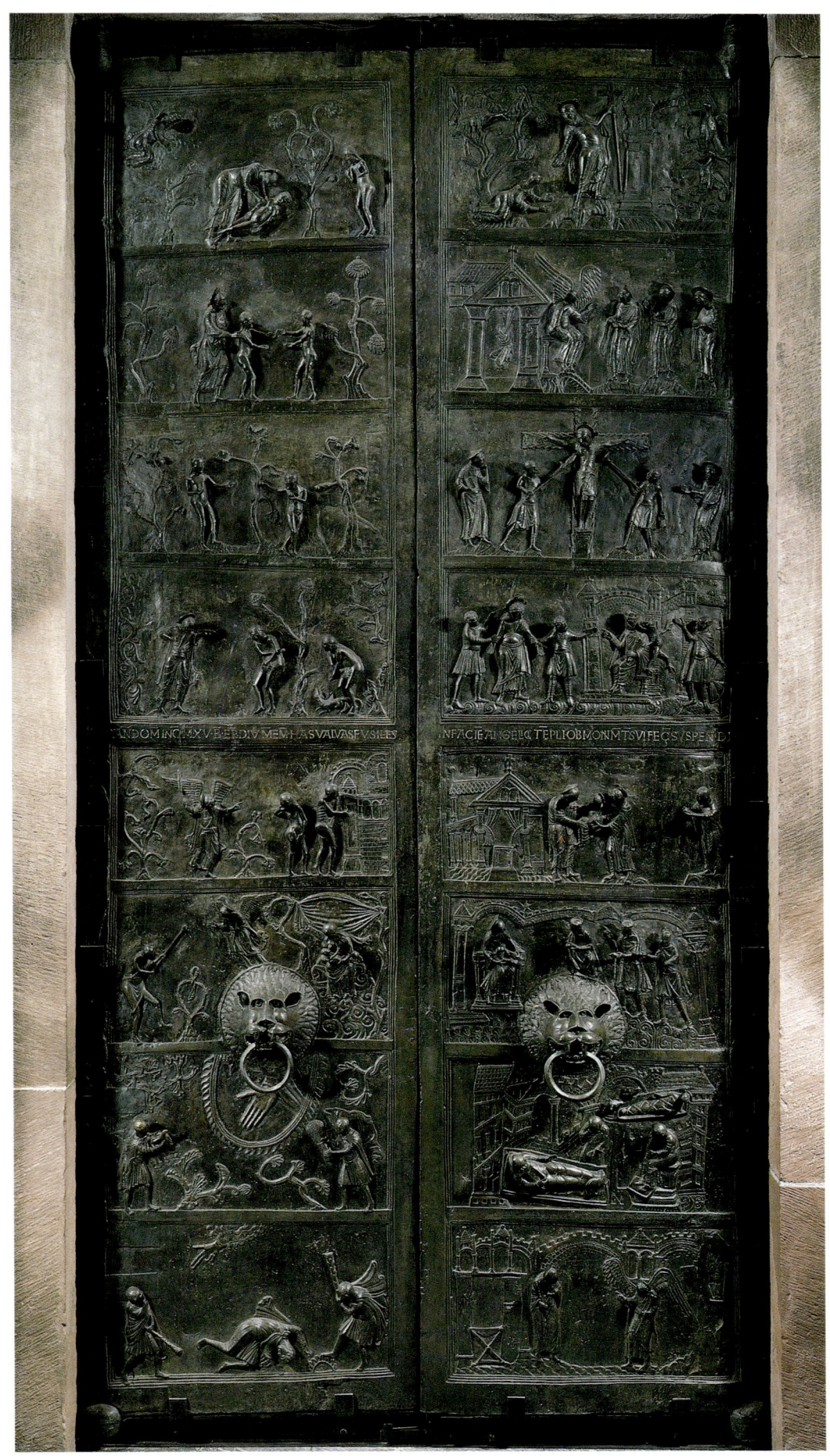

**16-24** Doors with relief panels (Genesis, left door; life of Christ, right door), commissioned by Bishop Bernward for Saint Michael's, Hildesheim, Germany, 1015. Bronze, 16′ 6″ high. Dom-Museum, Hildesheim.

top) and ending with the murder of Adam and Eve's son Abel by his brother Cain (at the bottom). The right door recounts the life of Christ (reading from the bottom up), starting with the Annunciation and terminating with the appearance to Mary Magdalene of Christ after the Resurrection (see "The Life of Jesus in Art," Chapter 11, pages 308–309). Together, the doors tell the story of Original Sin and ultimate redemption, showing the expulsion from the Garden of Eden and the path back to Paradise through the Christian Church. As in Early Christian times, the Old Testament was interpreted as prefiguring the New Testament (see "Jewish Subjects in Christian Art," Chapter 11, page 305). The panel depicting the Fall of Adam and Eve, for example, is juxtaposed with the Crucifixion on the other door. Eve nursing the infant Cain is opposite Mary with the Christ Child in her lap.

The composition of many of the scenes on the doors derives from Carolingian manuscript illumination, and the style of the figures has an expressive strength that brings to mind the illustrations in the *Utrecht Psalter* (FIG. 16-14). For example, in the fourth panel from the top on the left door, God, portrayed as a man, accuses Adam and Eve after their fall from grace. As he lays on them the curse of mortality, the primal condemnation, he jabs his finger at them with the force of his whole body. The force is concentrated in the gesture, which becomes the psychic focus of the whole composition. The frightened pair crouch, not only to hide their shame but also to escape the lightning bolt of divine wrath. Each passes the blame—Adam pointing backward to Eve and Eve pointing downward to the deceitful serpent. The starkly flat setting throws into relief the gestures and attitudes of rage, accusation, guilt, and fear. The sculptor presented the story with simplicity, although with great emotional impact, as well as a flair for anecdotal detail. Adam and Eve both struggle to point with one arm while attempting to shield their bodies from sight with the other. With an instinct for expressive pose and gesture, the artist brilliantly communicated their newfound embarrassment at their nakedness and their unconvincing denials of wrongdoing.

**CHRIST'S TRIUMPH** The great doors of Saint Michael's were not the only large-scale examples of bronze-casting Bernward commissioned. Within the church stood a bronze spiral column (FIG. **16-25**) that is preserved intact, save for its later capital and missing surmounting cross. It probably was begun sometime after the doors were set in place and completed before the bishop's death in 1022. The seven spiral bands of relief tell the story of Jesus' life in 24 scenes, beginning with his baptism and concluding with his entry into Jerusalem. These are the missing episodes from the story told on the church's doors.

The narrative reads from bottom to top, exactly as on the Column of Trajan in Rome (see FIG. 10-42). That triumphal column was unmistakably the model for the Hildesheim column, even though the Ottonian narrative unfolds from right to left instead of from left to right. Once again, a monument in Rome provided the inspiration for the Ottonian artists working under Bernward's direction. Both the doors and the column of Saint Michael's lend credence to the Ottonian emperors' claim to be the heirs to Charlemagne's *renovatio imperii Romani*.

**MONUMENTAL SUFFERING** Nowhere was the revival of interest in monumental sculpture more evident than in the crucifix (FIG. **16-26**) Archbishop Gero commissioned and presented to Cologne Cathedral in 970. Carved in oak and then painted and gilded, the six-foot-tall image of Christ nailed to the cross is both statue and *reliquary* (a shrine for sacred relics; see "Pilgrimages

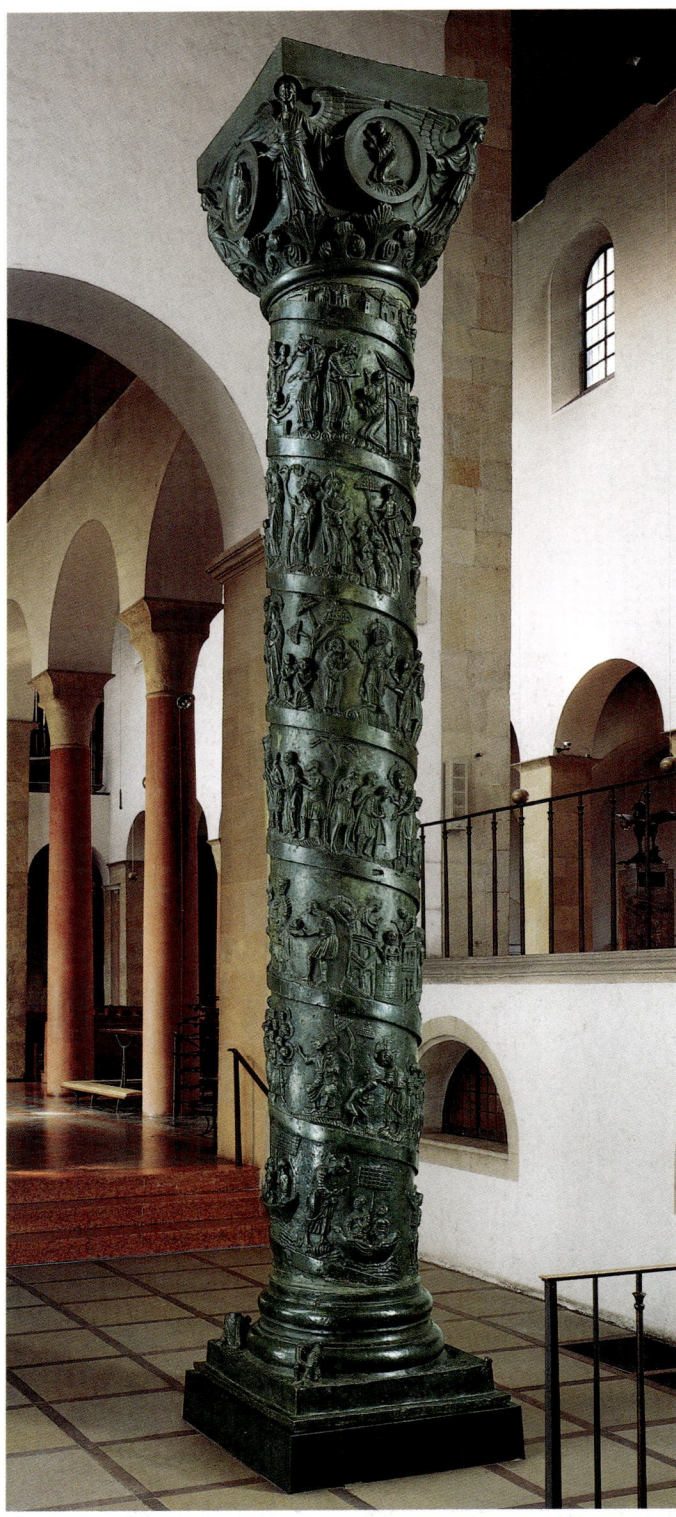

**16-25** Column with reliefs illustrating the life of Christ, commissioned by Bishop Bernward for Saint Michael's, Hildesheim, Germany, ca. 1015–1022. Bronze, 12′ 6″ tall. Dom-Museum, Hildesheim.

and the Cult of Relics," Chapter 17, page 449). A compartment in the back of the head held the Host. A later story tells how a crack developed in the wood of Gero's crucifix but was miraculously healed. Similar tales of miracles are attached to many sacred Christian objects, for example, some Byzantine icons (see "Icons," Chapter 12, page 341).

The Gero crucifix presents a dramatically different conception of the Savior from that seen on the cover of the *Lindau Gospels*

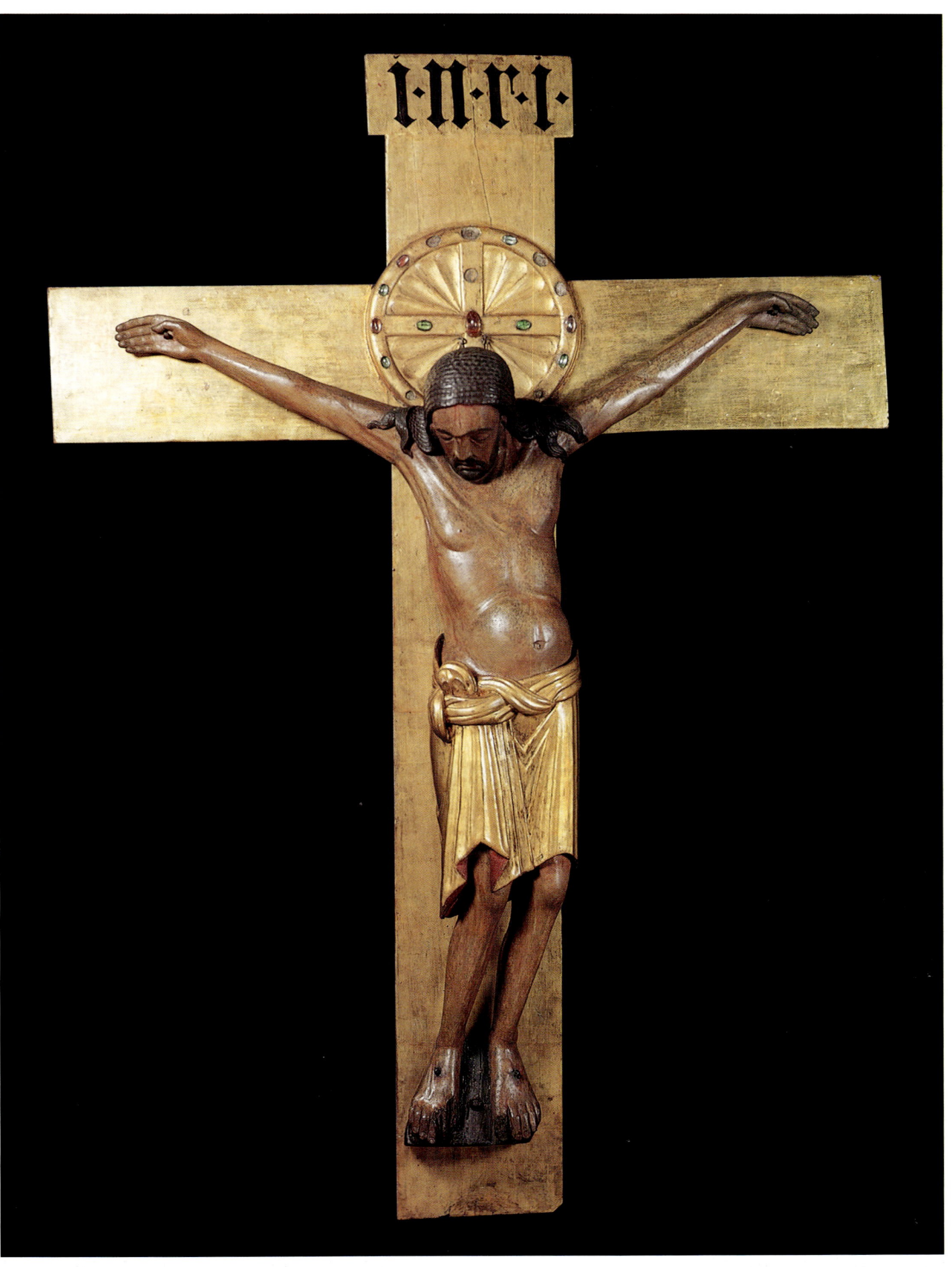

**16-26** Crucifix commissioned by Archbishop Gero for Cologne Cathedral, Cologne, Germany, ca. 970. Painted wood, height of figure 6′ 2″, Rheimisches Bildarchiv.

(FIG. 16-15), with its Early Christian imagery of the youthful Christ triumphant over death. The bearded Christ of the Cologne crucifix is more akin to Byzantine representations of the suffering Jesus (see FIG. 12-22), but the emotional power of the Ottonian work is greater still. The sculptor depicted Christ as an all-too-human martyr. Blood streaks down his forehead from the (missing) crown of thorns. His eyelids are closed, and his face is contorted in pain. Christ's body sags under its own weight. The muscles are stretched to the limit—those of his right shoulder and chest seem almost to rip apart. The halo behind Christ's head may foretell his subsequent Resurrection, but all the worshiper can sense is his pain. Gero's crucifix is the most powerful characterization of intense agony of the early Middle Ages.

## The Art of the Book

**UTA AND THE VIRGIN** Ottonian artists carried on the Carolingian tradition of producing sumptuous books for the clergy and royalty alike. One of the finest is the lectionary produced at Regensburg, Germany, for Uta, abbess of Niedermünster. The *Uta Codex* illustrates the important role that women could play both in religious life and as patrons of the arts during the early Middle Ages (see "Romanesque Countesses, Queens, and Nuns," Chapter 17, page 473). Uta was instrumental in bringing Benedictine reforms to the Niedermünster convent (see "Medieval Monasteries," page 434), whose nuns were usually the daughters of the local nobility. Uta herself was well known in Ottonian royal circles. Near the end of her life, she presented the nunnery with a luxurious codex containing many full-page illuminations interspersed with Gospel readings. The lectionary's gold, jewel, and enamel case also survives, underscoring the nature of medieval books as sacred objects to be venerated in their own right as well as embodiments of the eternal Word of God.

The dedicatory page (FIG. **16-27**) at the front of the *Uta Codex* depicts the Virgin Mary with the Christ Child in her lap in the central medallion. Labeled *Virgo Virginum,* Virgin of Virgins, Mary is the model for Uta and Niedermünster's nuns. Uta is, in fact, present. She is the full-length figure presenting a new book—*this* book—to the Virgin. An inscription accompanies

**16-27** Abbess Uta dedicating her codex to the Virgin, folio 2 recto of the *Uta Codex,* from Regensburg, Germany, ca. 1025. Tempera on parchment, approx. $9\frac{5}{8}'' \times 5\frac{1}{8}''$. Bayerische Staatsbibliothek, Munich.

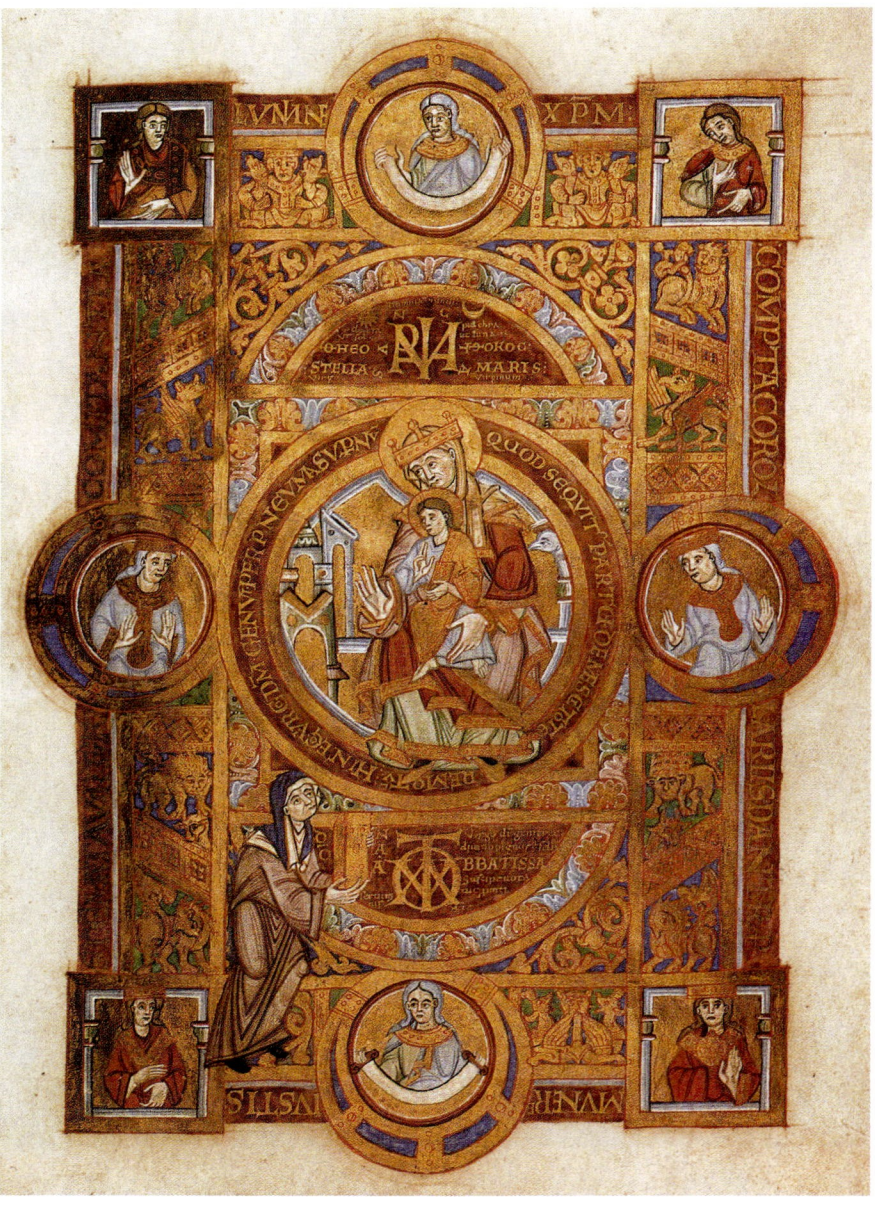

## Theophanu: A Byzantine Princess in Ottonian Germany

Otto I was crowned king of the Saxons by the bishop of Mainz at Aachen in 936, but it was not until 962 that Pope John XII conferred the title of Emperor of Rome upon him in Saint Peter's basilica. Otto, known as the Great, had ambitions to restore the glory of Charlemagne's Christian Roman Empire and to enlarge the territory under his rule. In 951 he defeated a Roman noble who had taken prisoner Adelaide, the widow of the Lombard king Lothar. Otto then married Adelaide, assumed the title of King of the Lombards, and extended his power south of the Alps. Looking eastward, in 972 he arranged the marriage of his son, Otto II, to Theophanu (ca. 955–991), the daughter of the Byzantine emperor Romanos II. Otto II was 60, Theophanu 17. They wed in Saint Peter's, with Pope John XIII presiding. When Otto the Great died the next year, Otto II succeeded him. The second Otto died in Italy in 983 and was buried in the atrium of Saint Peter's. His son, Otto III, only three years old at the time, nominally became king, but it was his mother, Theophanu, co-regent with Adelaide until 985 and sole regent thereafter, who wielded power in the Ottonian Empire until her own death in 991. Adelaide then served as regent until Otto III was old enough to rule on his own. He was crowned Emperor of Rome in 996.

Theophanu brought the prestige of Byzantium to Germany, and also Byzantine culture and art. The Ottonian court emulated much of the splendor and pomp of Constantinople and imported Byzantine luxury goods in great quantities. One surviving ivory panel, carved in the West but of Byzantine style and labeled in Greek, depicts Christ simultaneously crowning Otto II and Theophanu. The impact of Byzantine art in Ottonian Germany can also be seen in manuscript illumination (FIG. 16-28).

---

the dedicatory image: "Virgin Mother of God, happy because of the divine Child, receive the votive offerings of your Uta of ready service."[5] The artist painted Uta last, superimposing her figure upon the design and carefully placing it so that Uta's head touches the Virgin's medallion but does not penetrate it, suggesting the interplay between, but also the separation of, the divine and human realms (FIG. 16-24).

**A ROYAL LECTIONARY** Uta presented her codex to the Niedermünster convent about the time the last Ottonian emperor, Henry II (r. 1002–1024), died. He also commissioned a book of Gospel readings for the Mass, the *Lectionary of Henry II,* a gift to Bamberg Cathedral. We reproduce the full-page illumination of the Annunciation of Christ's birth to the shepherds (FIG. **16-28**). The angel has just alighted on a hill, his wings still beating, and the wind of his landing agitates his draperies. Although the angel is a far cry from the dynamic marble *Nike of Samothrace* (see FIG. 5-82) of Hellenistic times, the framed panel still incorporates much that was at the heart of the classical tradition, including the rocky landscape setting with grazing animals, common also in Early Christian art (see FIG. 11-15). The golden background betrays, however, knowledge of Byzantine book illumination and mosaic decoration. (Otto II, r. 973–983, married a Byzantine princess; see "Theophanu: A Byzantine Princess in Ottonian Germany," above). The angel looms immense above the startled and terrified shepherds, filling the golden sky, and bends on them a fierce and menacing glance as he extends his hand in the gesture of authority and instruction. Emphasized more than the message itself are the power and majesty of God's authority. The artist portrayed it here with the same emotional impact as the electric force of God's violent pointing in the Hildesheim doors (FIG. 16-24).

**THE IMPERIAL IDEAL** Henry II's predecessor was his cousin, Otto III, son of Otto II and Theophanu. Of the three Ottos, the last dreamed the most of a revived Christian Roman Empire. Indeed, it was his life's obsession. Otto III was keenly aware of his descent from both German and Byzantine imperial lines. It is said that he was more proud of his Constantinopolitan than his German roots. He moved his court, with its Byzantine rituals, to Rome and there set up theatrically the symbols and trappings of Roman imperialism. Otto's romantic dream of imperial unity for Europe never materialized. He died prematurely, at age 21, and, at his own request, was buried beside Charlemagne at Aachen.

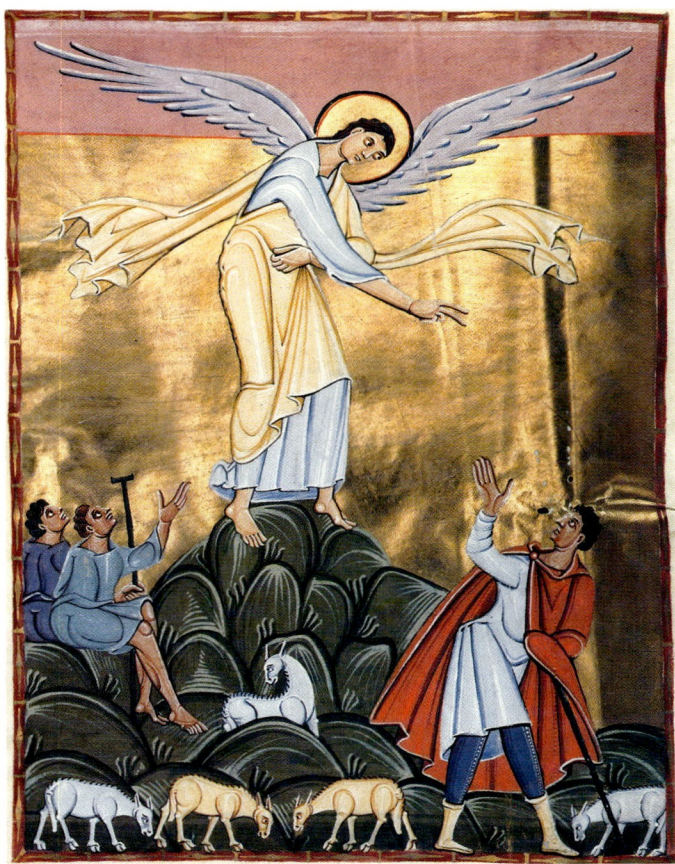

**16-28** Annunciation to the Shepherds, folio in the *Lectionary of Henry II,* from Reichenau, Germany, 1002–1014. Tempera on vellum, approx. 1′ 5″ × 1′ 1″. Bayerische Staatsbibliothek, Munich.

**16-29** Otto III enthroned, folio 24 recto of the *Gospel Book of Otto III*, from Reichenau, Germany, 997–1000. Tempera on vellum, 1′ 1″ × 9⅜″. Bayerische Staatsbibliothek, Munich.

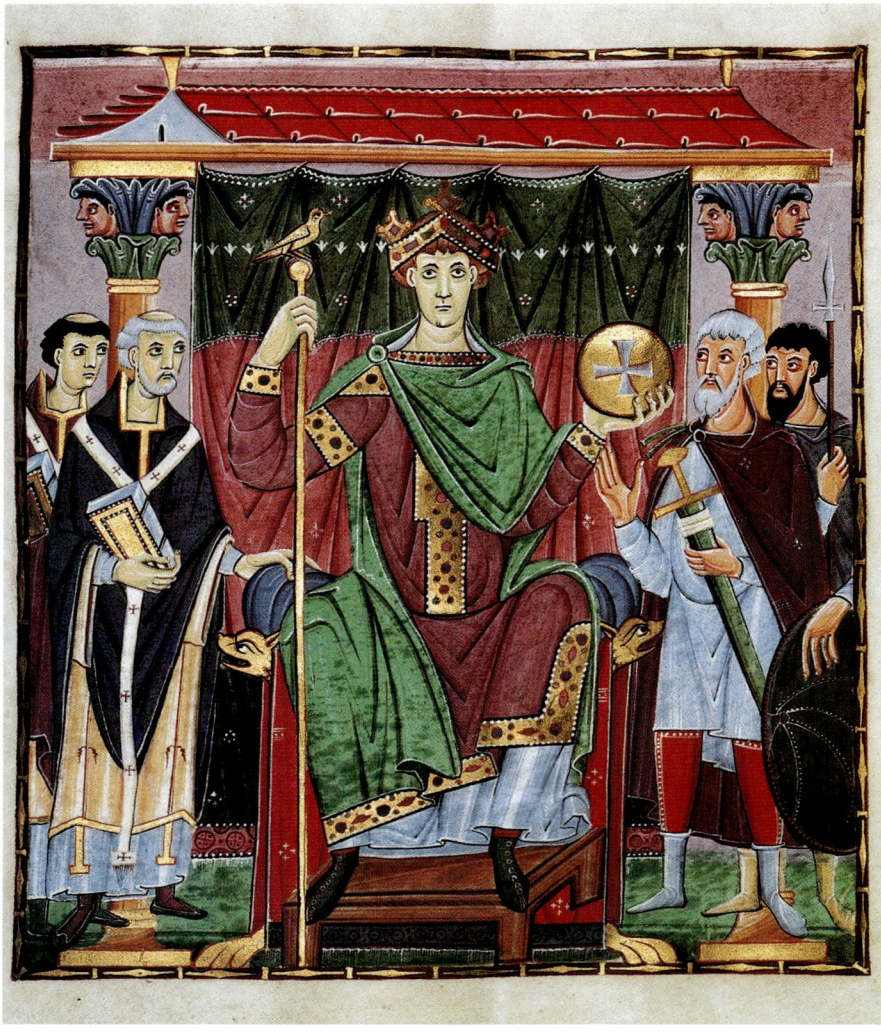

Otto III is portrayed in a Gospel book (FIG. **16-29**) that takes his name. The illuminator represented the emperor enthroned, holding the scepter and cross-inscribed orb that represent his universal authority, conforming to a Christian imperial iconographic tradition that went back to Constantine (see FIG. 10-82, *right*). At his sides are the clergy and the barons (the Christian Church and the state), both aligned in his support. On the facing page (not illustrated), classicizing female personifications of Slavinia, Germany, Gaul, and Rome—the provinces of the Ottonian Empire—bring tribute to the young emperor. Stylistically remote from Byzantine art, the picture still has a clear political resemblance to the Justinianic mosaic in San Vitale (see FIG. 12-10).

## CONCLUSION

The last emperor of the Western Roman Empire died in 476. For centuries, western Europe, save for the Byzantine Empire's stronghold at Ravenna, was home to competing groups of non-Romans—Franks, Anglo-Saxons, and Vikings, among others. Constantly on the move, these peoples left behind monuments that are all of small scale, but often of costly materials, expert workmanship, and sophisticated design. The permanent centers of artistic culture in the early Middle Ages were the monasteries that Christian missionaries established beyond the Alps and across the English Channel. There, master painters illuminated liturgical books in a distinctive style that fused the abstract and animal interlace forms of the native peoples with Christian iconography. When the Frankish Charlemagne was crowned Emperor of Rome in 800, imperial rule was reestablished in the former Roman provinces. With it came a revival of interest in the classical style and monumental architecture, a tradition carried on by Charlemagne's Carolingian and Ottonian successors.

The ideal of a Christian Roman Empire gave partial unity to western Europe in the 9th, 10th, and early 11th centuries. To this extent, ancient Rome lived on to the millennium, culminating in the frustrated ambition of Otto III. The Romanesque period that followed, however, denied the imperial spirit that had prevailed for centuries—but not the notion of Western Christendom. A new age was about to begin, and Rome—an august memory—ceased to be the deciding influence. Europe found unity, rather, in a common religious heritage and a missionary zeal. By the year 1000, even remote Iceland had adopted Christianity. The next task for the kings and church leaders of Europe was to take up the banner of Christ and attempt to wrest control of the Holy Land from the Muslims.

FRANCE AND GERMANY

NORTHERN EUROPE

MEROVINGIAN

CAROLINGIAN

OTTONIAN

HIBERNO-SAXON PERIOD IN THE BRITISH ISLES, VIKING PERIOD IN SCANDINAVIA

**476**

- END OF WESTERN ROMAN EMPIRE, 476
- ANGLO-SAXONS TAKE OVER ROMAN BRITAIN, CA. 480
- MEROVINGIAN DYNASTY, 482–751
- SAINT BENEDICT ESTABLISHES BENEDICTINE RULE FOR MONASTERIES, 529
- MUSLIMS DEFEAT VISIGOTHS IN SPAIN, 711
- CHARLES MARTEL DEFEATS MUSLIMS AT POITIERS, 732

1 Sutton Hoo purse cover, ca. 625

**751**

- BEATUS OF LIÉBANA, *Commentary on the Apocalypse*, CA. 776
- CHARLEMAGNE, R. 768–814, CROWNED EMPEROR IN ROME, 800
- VIKING RAIDS BEGIN IN BRITAIN, 793
- 2 LOUIS THE PIOUS, R. 814–840
- CHARLES THE BALD, R. 840–875
- CLUNIAC ORDER FOUNDED, 910

2 Ebbo Gospels, ca. 816–835

**936**

- OTTO I, R. 936–973, CROWNED EMPEROR IN ROME, 962
- OTTO II, R. 973–983; MARRIES BYZANTINE PRINCESS THEOPHANU, 972
- OTTO III, R. 983–1002
- HUGH CAPET, KING OF FRANCE, R. 987–996
- BERNWARD, BISHOP OF HILDESHEIM, 993–1022

3 Gero Crucifix, ca. 970

**1000**

- 4 HENRY II, R. 1002–1024, LAST OTTONIAN EMPEROR
- UTA, ABBESS OF NIEDERMÜNSTER, 1002–1025

**1024**

- EDWARD THE CONFESSOR, ANGLO-SAXON KING OF ENGLAND, R. 1042–1066

**1050**

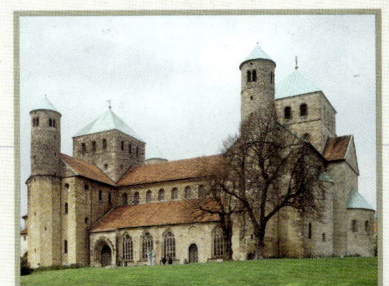

4 Saint Michael's, Hildesheim, Germany, 1001–1031

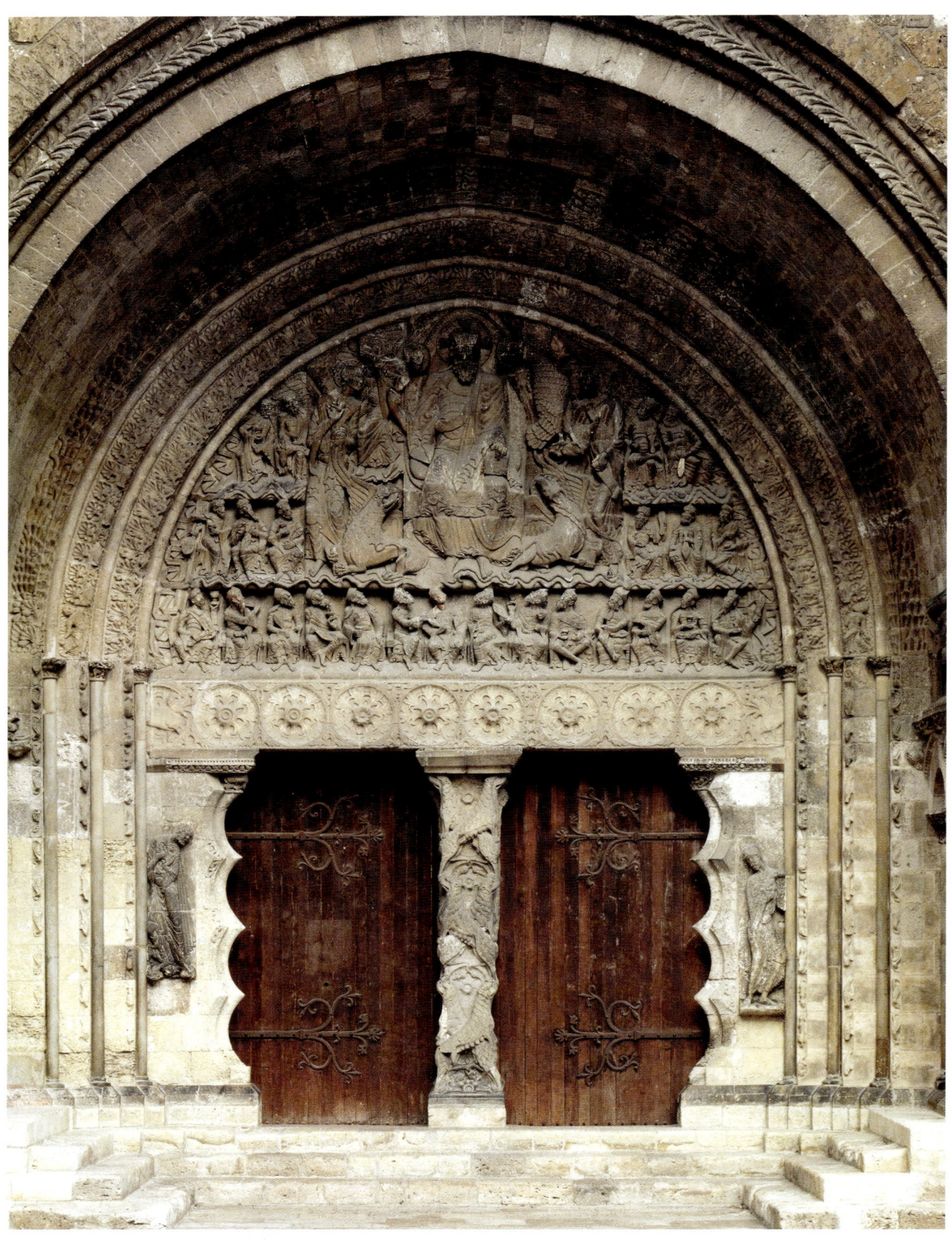

South portal of Saint-Pierre, Moissac, France, ca. 1115–1135.

# 17

# THE AGE OF PILGRIMAGES
## ROMANESQUE ART

The Romanesque era is the first since Archaic and Classical Greece to take its name from an artistic style rather than from politics or geography. Unlike Carolingian and Ottonian art, named for emperors, or Hiberno-Saxon art, a regional term, Romanesque is a title art historians invented to describe an artistic phenomenon. *Romanesque* means "Romanlike" and was first applied in the early 19th century to describe European architecture of the 11th and 12th centuries. Scholars noted that certain architectural elements of this period, principally barrel and groin vaults based on the round arch, resembled those of ancient Roman architecture. Thus, the word distinguished most Romanesque buildings from earlier medieval timber-roofed structures, as well as from later Gothic churches with vaults resting on pointed arches. Scholars in other fields quickly borrowed the term. Today "Romanesque" broadly designates the history and culture of western Europe between about 1050 and 1200.

**THE RISE OF TOWNS** In the early Middle Ages, the focus of life was the *manor,* or estate, of a landholding *liege lord,* who might grant tenure of a portion of his land to *vassals.* The vassals swore allegiance to their liege and rendered him military service in return for the land and the promise of protection. But in the Romanesque period, a sharp increase in trade encouraged the growth of towns and cities, gradually displacing *feudalism* as the governing political, social, and economic system of late medieval Europe (MAP **17-1**). The new towns were granted independence from the feudal lords in the form of *charters,* which enumerated the communities' rights, privileges, immunities, and exemptions beyond the feudal obligations they owed the lords. Often located on navigable rivers, the new urban centers naturally became the nuclei of networks of maritime and overland commerce.

**MONASTERIES AND CHURCHES** Separated by design from the busy secular life of Romanesque towns were the monasteries (see "Medieval Monasteries," Chapter 16, page 434) and their churches. During the 11th and 12th centuries, thousands of ecclesiastical buildings were remodeled or newly constructed. This immense building

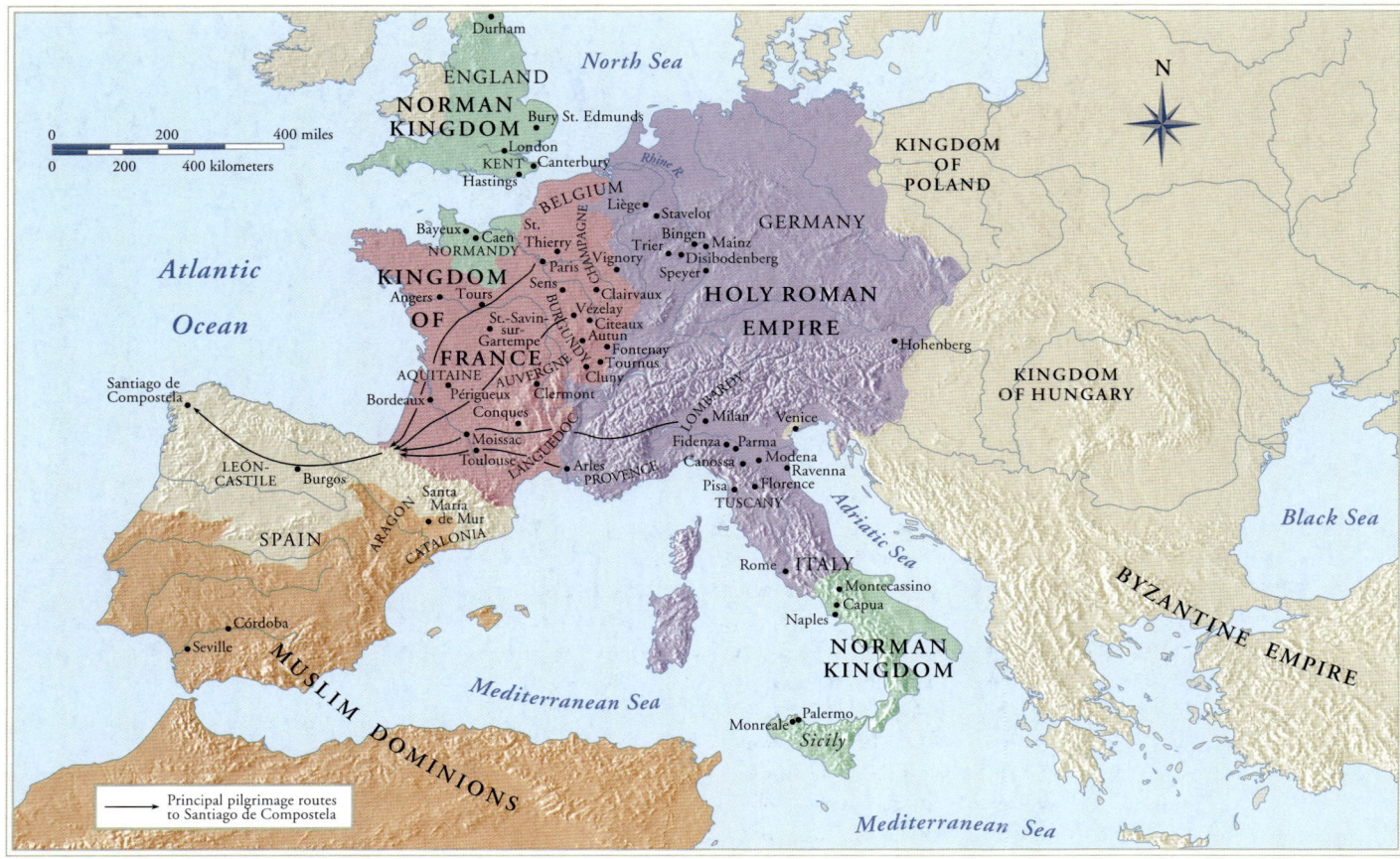

MAP 17-1 Europe about 1100.

enterprise reflected in part the rise of independent cities and the prosperity they enjoyed. But it also was an expression of the widely felt relief and thanksgiving that the conclusion of the first Christian millennium in the year 1000 had not brought an end to the world, as many had feared. In the Romanesque age, the construction of churches became almost an obsession. Raoul Glaber (ca. 985–ca. 1046), a monk who witnessed the coming of the new millennium, noted the beginning of it:

> [After the] year of the millennium, which is now about three years past, there occurred, throughout the world, especially in Italy and Gaul, a rebuilding of church basilicas. Notwithstanding, the greater number were already well established and not in the least in need, nevertheless each Christian people strove against the others to erect nobler ones. It was as if the whole earth, having cast off the old by shaking itself were clothing itself everywhere in the white robe of the church.[1]

PILGRIMAGES The enormous investment in ecclesiastical buildings and furnishings also reflected a significant increase in pilgrimage traffic in Romanesque Europe (see "Pilgrimages and the Cult of Relics," page 449). Pilgrims were important sources of funding for those monasteries that possessed the relics of venerated saints. The clergy of the various monasteries vied with one another to provide magnificent settings for the display of their relics. Justification for such heavy investment to attract donations could be found in the Bible itself, for example in Psalm 26:8, "Lord, I have loved the beauty of your house, and the place where your glory dwells." Traveling pilgrims fostered the growth of towns as well as monasteries. Pilgrimages were, in fact, the primary economic and conceptual catalyst for the art and architecture of the Romanesque period.

## ARCHITECTURE

Although the widespread use of stone vaults in 11th- and 12th-century churches inspired the term "Romanesque," Romanesque architecture was, in fact, highly varied and not always vaulted. Some Romanesque churches, especially in Italy, retained the wooden roofs of their Early Christian predecessors long after stone vaulting had become commonplace elsewhere. Nonetheless, despite pronounced regional differences, almost all Romanesque buildings manifest a new widely shared method of architectural thinking, a new logic of design and construction. To a certain extent, Romanesque architecture can be compared to the Romance languages of Europe, which vary regionally but have a common core in Latin, the language of the Romans.

### France

WOOD AND STONE AT VIGNORY This regional diversity is evident even in the earliest Romanesque buildings. The church of Saint-Étienne (Saint Stephen) at Vignory (FIGS. 17-1 and 17-2) in the Champagne region of central France exemplifies the northern style of French Romanesque architecture in which builders used large sawn blocks of stone to construct the walls of their buildings but roofed them with timber. Many elements of the Vignory church have strong ties to the past. Other features became widely adopted only in later Romanesque architecture. The interior (FIG. 17-1), for example, reveals a kinship with the three-story wooden-roofed churches of the Ottonian era (see FIG. 16-21). At Vignory, however, the second story is not a true *tribune* (upper

## Pilgrimages and the Cult of Relics

The cult of relics was not new in the Romanesque era. For centuries, Christians had traveled to sacred shrines housing the body parts of, or objects associated with, the holy family or the saints. The faithful had long believed that such relics—bones, clothing, instruments of martyrdom, and the like—had the power to heal body and soul. The veneration of relics reached a high point in the 11th and 12th centuries.

In Romanesque times, pilgrimage was the most conspicuous feature of public devotion, proclaiming the pilgrim's faith in the power of saints and hope for their special favor. The major shrines—Saint Peter's and Saint Paul's in Rome and the Church of the Holy Sepulcher in Jerusalem—drew pilgrims from all over Europe. The visitors braved, for salvation's sake, bad roads and hostile wildernesses infested with robbers who preyed on innocent travelers. The journeys could take more than a year to complete—when they were successful. People often undertook pilgrimage as an act of repentance or as a last resort in their search for a cure for some physical disability. Hardship and austerity were means of increasing pilgrims' chances for the remission of sin or of disease. The distance and peril of the pilgrimage were measures of pilgrims' sincerity of repentance or of the reward they sought.

For those with less time or money than required for a pilgrimage to Rome or Jerusalem, holy destinations could be found closer to home. In France, for example, the church at Vézelay housed the bones of Mary Magdalene. Saint Foy's remains were enshrined at Conques, Lazarus's at Autun, Saint Martin's at Tours, and Saint Saturninus's at Toulouse. Each of these great shrines was also an important way station en route to the most venerated shrine in the West, the tomb of Saint James at Santiago de Compostela in northwestern Spain (MAP 17-1; see "A Pilgrim's Guide to Santiago de Compostela," page 450).

Hordes of pilgrims paying homage to saints placed a great burden on the churches that stored their relics, but they also provided significant revenues, making possible the erection of ever grander and more luxuriously appointed structures. The popularity of pilgrimages led to changes in church design, necessitating longer and wider naves and aisles, transepts and ambulatories with additional chapels (FIG. 17-5), and second-story galleries (FIG. 17-6). Pilgrim traffic also established the routes that later became the major avenues of European commerce and communication.

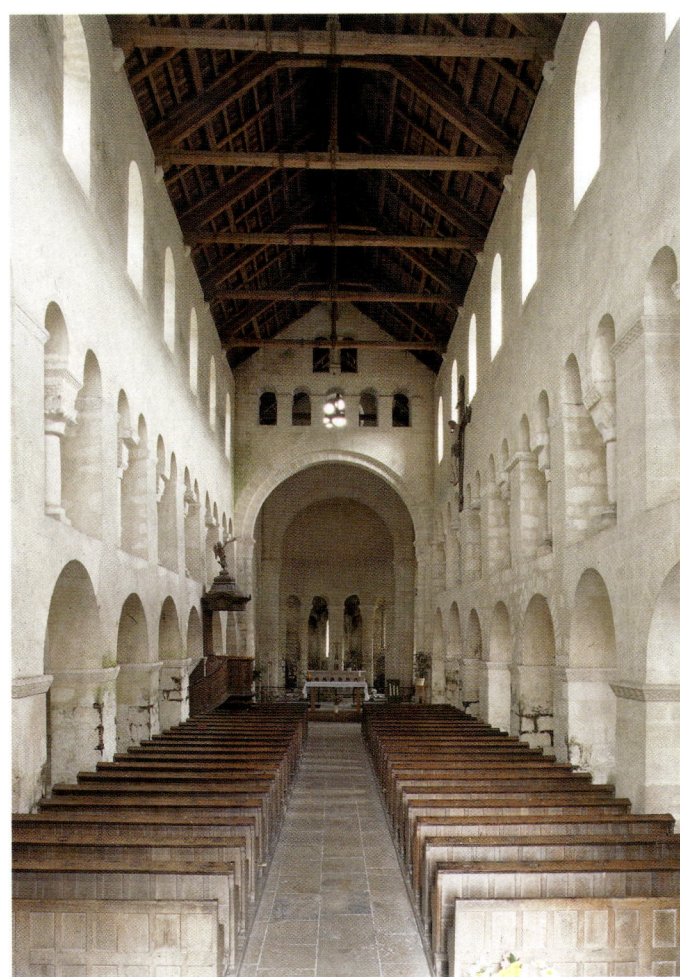

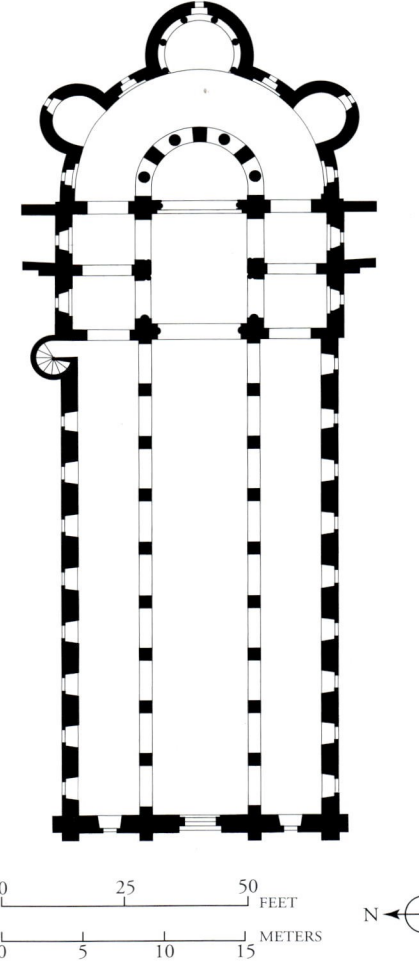

17-1 Interior of Saint-Étienne, Vignory, France, 1050–1057.

17-2 Plan of Saint-Étienne, Vignory, France, 1050–1057.

## *A Pilgrim's Guide to Santiago de Compostela*

The volume of traffic along the major pilgrimage roads of western Europe gave rise to travel guides that, like modern guidebooks, provided pilgrims not only with information about saints and shrines but also with practical information about roads, accommodations, food, and drink. The most famous Romanesque guidebook described the four roads leading to the church of Saint James at Santiago de Compostela through Arles and Toulouse; Conques and Moissac; Vézelay and Périgueux; and Tours and Bordeaux (MAP 17-1). James was the symbol of Christian resistance to Muslim expansion in western Europe, and his relics, discovered in the ninth century, drew pilgrims from far and wide. The guidebook's anonymous 12th-century author, possibly Aimery Picaud, a Cluniac monk, was himself a well-traveled pilgrim. The text states that it was written "in Rome, in the lands of Jerusalem, in France, in Italy, in Germany, in Frisia and mainly in Cluny."[1]

Pilgrims reading the guidebook learned about the saints and their shrines at each stop along the way to Spain. Saint Saturninus of Toulouse, for example, endured a martyr's death at the hands of pagans when he "was tied to some furious and wild bulls and then precipitated from the height of the citadel. . . . His head crushed, his brains knocked out, his whole body torn to pieces, he rendered his worthy soul to Christ. He is buried in an excellent location close to the city of Toulouse where a large basilica [FIGS. 17-4 to 17-6] was erected by the faithful in his honor."[2]

Given the competition among monasteries and cities for the possession of saints' relics, the *Pilgrim's Guide to Santiago de Compostela* also included comments on authenticity. About Saint James's tomb, the author stated: "May therefore the imitators from beyond the mountains blush who claim to possess some portion of him or even his entire relic. In fact, the body of the Apostle is here in its entirety, divinely lit by paradisiacal carbuncles, incessantly honored with immaculate and soft perfumes, decorated with dazzling celestial candles, and diligently worshipped by attentive angels."[3]

[1] William Melczer, *The Pilgrim's Guide to Santiago de Compostela* (New York: Italica Press, 1993), 133.

[2] Ibid., 103.

[3] Ibid., 127.

---

gallery over the aisle opening onto the nave) but rather a screen with alternating piers and columns opening onto very tall flanking aisles. The east end of the church, in contrast, has an innovative and influential plan (FIG. 17-2) with an ambulatory around the choir and three semicircular chapels opening onto it. These *radiating chapels* probably housed the church's relics, which the faithful could view without having to enter the choir where the main altar was situated.

Saint-Étienne is also an early example of the introduction of stone sculpture into Romanesque ecclesiastical architecture, one of the period's defining features. Here the sculptures were confined to relief decoration of the capitals of the ambulatory and false tribunes where abstract and vegetal ornament, lions, and other quadrupeds are the exclusive motifs. The earliest Romanesque sculptures appeared in Romanesque churches constructed with ashlar masonry, and the two traditions are closely allied.

**VAULTING AT TOURNUS** Further south, in southern France, Spain, and Lombardy, early Romanesque builders generally preferred to construct their edifices with brick or small bricklike blocks of stone and to cover the nave and aisles with vaults. The church of Saint-Philibert (FIG. 17-3) at Tournus in Burgundy is an example of this southern tradition. Originally, Saint-Philibert, like Saint-Étienne, had a fire-prone timber roof (see "Timber Roofs and Stone Vaults," page 451). Around 1060, masonry vaults replaced the wooden roof. In the nave, cylindrical piers support barrel vaults that run perpendicular to the nave's axis, one in each bay, separated by *transverse arches*. This scheme made possible the opening of clerestory windows at the ends of the vaults, providing ample illumination to the nave. As at Vignory, the aisles are almost as tall as the nave, and they are covered by groin vaults that help buttress the barrel vaults.

**TOULOUSE'S PILGRIMAGE CHURCH** Around 1070, not long after Saint-Philibert was vaulted, the counts of Toulouse began construction of a great new church in honor of the city's first bishop, Saint Saturninus (Saint Sernin in French), who was

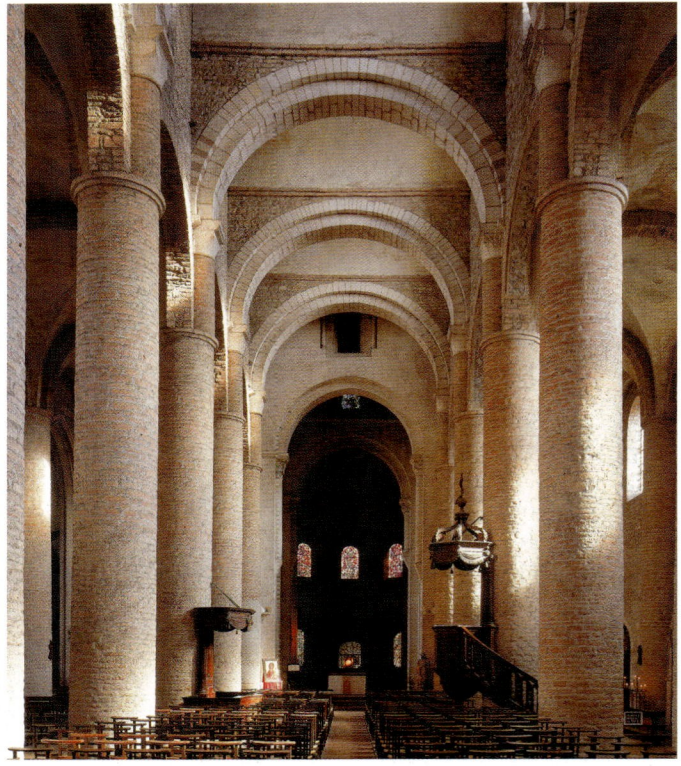

**17-3** Interior of Saint-Philibert, Tournus, France. Nave vaults, ca. 1060.

## Timber Roofs and Stone Vaults

The perils of wooden construction are well documented by the chroniclers of medieval ecclesiastical history. In some cases, churches burned over and over again in the course of a single century and repeatedly had to be extensively repaired or completely rebuilt. In September 1174, for example, Canterbury Cathedral, which had been dedicated only 44 years earlier, was accidentally set ablaze and destroyed. A vivid eyewitness account is preserved in the *Chronica* of Gervase of Canterbury (1141–1210), who entered the monastery at Canterbury in 1163 and wrote a history of the archbishopric from 1100 to 1199:

> During an extraordinarily violent south wind, a fire broke out before the gate of the church, and outside the walls of the monastery, by which three cottages were half destroyed. From thence, while the citizens were assembling and subduing the fire, cinders and sparks carried aloft by the high wind, were deposited upon the church, and being driven by the fury of the wind between the joints of the lead, remained there amongst the half-rotten planks, and shortly glowing with increased heat, set fire to the rotten rafters; from these the fire was communicated to the larger beams and their braces, no one yet perceiving or helping. For the well-painted ceiling below, and the sheet-lead covering above, concealed between them the fire that had arisen within. . . . But beams and braces burning, the flames arose to the slopes of the roof; and the sheets of lead yielded to the increasing heat and began to melt. Thus the raging wind, finding a freer entrance, increased the fury of the fire. . . . And now that the fire had loosened the beams from the pegs that bound them together, the half-burnt timbers fell into the choir below upon the seats of the monks; the seats, consisting of a great mass of woodwork, caught fire, and thus the mischief grew worse and worse. And it was marvellous, though sad, to behold how that glorious choir itself fed and assisted the fire that was destroying it. For the flames multiplied by this mass of timber, and extending upwards full fifteen cubits [about twenty-five feet], scorched and burnt the walls, and more especially injured the columns of the church. . . . In this manner the house of God, hitherto delightful as a paradise of pleasures, was now made a despicable heap of ashes, reduced to a dreary wilderness.[1]

After the fire, the Canterbury monks summoned a master builder from Sens, a French city 75 miles southeast of Paris, to supervise the construction of their new church. Gervase reports that the first task William of Sens tackled was "the procuring of stone from beyond the sea."

A quest for fireproof structures, however, seems not to have been the primary rationale for stone vaulting. Although protection from devastating conflagrations was no doubt one of the attractions of building stone roofs in an age when candles provided interior illumination, other factors probably played a greater role in the decision to make the enormous investment that stone masonry required. A desire to provide a suitably majestic setting for the display of relics—and the competition for pilgrimage traffic and the donations pilgrims brought with them—as well as enhanced acoustics for the Christian liturgy and the music that accompanied it, probably better explain the rapid spread of stone vaulting throughout Romanesque Europe. Some contemporary texts, in fact, comment on the visual impact of costly stone vaults. For example, in 1150 at Angers in northwestern France, a church chronicler explained why the bishop replaced the timber roof of his cathedral with stone vaults:

> [He] took down the timber beams of the nave of the church, threatening to fall from sheer old age, and began to build stone vaults of wondrous effect.[2]

[1] Quoted in Elizabeth Gilmore Holt, *A Documentary History of Art,* 2nd ed. (Princeton, N.J.: Princeton University Press, 1981), 1: 52–54.

[2] Roger Stalley, *Early Medieval Architecture* (New York: Oxford University Press, 1999), 132.

---

martyred in the middle of the third century. Toulouse was an important stop on the pilgrimage road through southwestern France to Santiago de Compostela in northwestern Spain (see "A Pilgrim's Guide to Santiago de Compostela," page 450). Large congregations were common at the shrines along the great pilgrimage routes, and Saint-Sernin was designed to accommodate them. The grand scale of the building is highlighted in our aerial view (FIG. 17-4), which includes automobiles, trucks, and nearly invisible pedestrians. The church's 12th-century exterior is still largely intact, although the two towers of the western facade (at the left in FIG. 17-4) were never completed, and the prominent crossing tower is largely Gothic and later.

Saint-Sernin's plan (FIG. 17-5) closely resembles those of the churches of Saint James at Santiago de Compostela and Saint Martin at Tours, and exemplifies what has come to be called the "pilgrimage church" type. At Toulouse one clearly can see how the builders provided additional space for curious pilgrims, worshipers, and liturgical processions alike. They increased the length of the nave, doubled the side aisles, and added a transept, ambulatory, and radiating chapels. Radiating chapels opening onto an ambulatory already were a feature of the abbey church at Vignory (FIG. 17-2), but at Toulouse the chapels are greater in number and are attached to the transept as well as the ambulatory, to accommodate the hordes of pilgrims who had journeyed from afar to view the church's relics.

GEOMETRY AND VAULTING The Saint-Sernin plan is extremely regular and geometrically precise. The crossing square, flanked by massive piers and marked off by heavy arches, served as the module for the entire church. Each nave bay, for example, measures exactly one-half of the crossing square, and each aisle bay measures exactly one-quarter. The builders employed similar simple ratios throughout the building. The first suggestion of such a planning scheme in medieval Europe was the Saint Gall monastery plan (see FIG. 16-19), almost three centuries earlier. The Toulouse solution was a crisply rational and highly refined

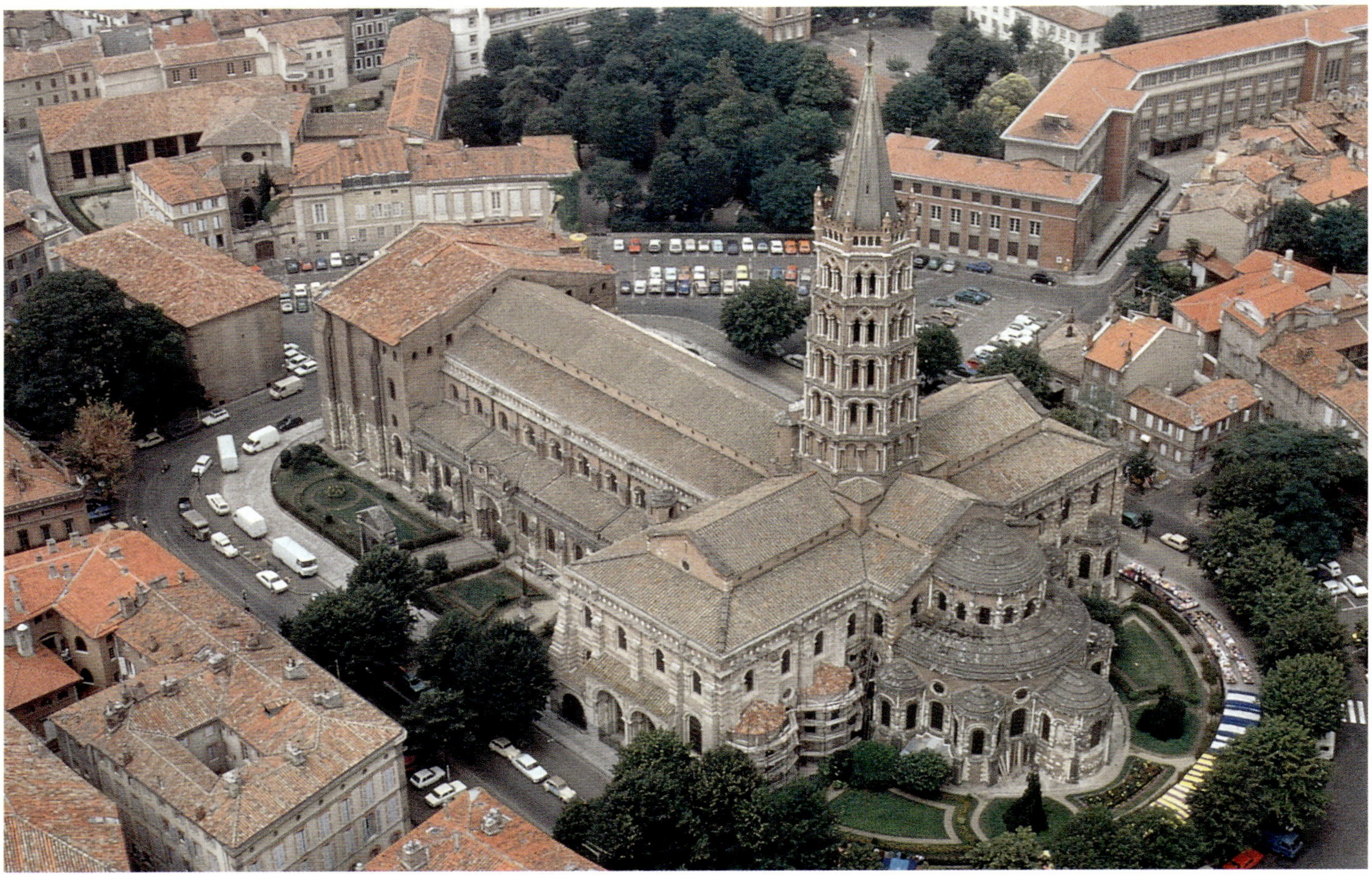

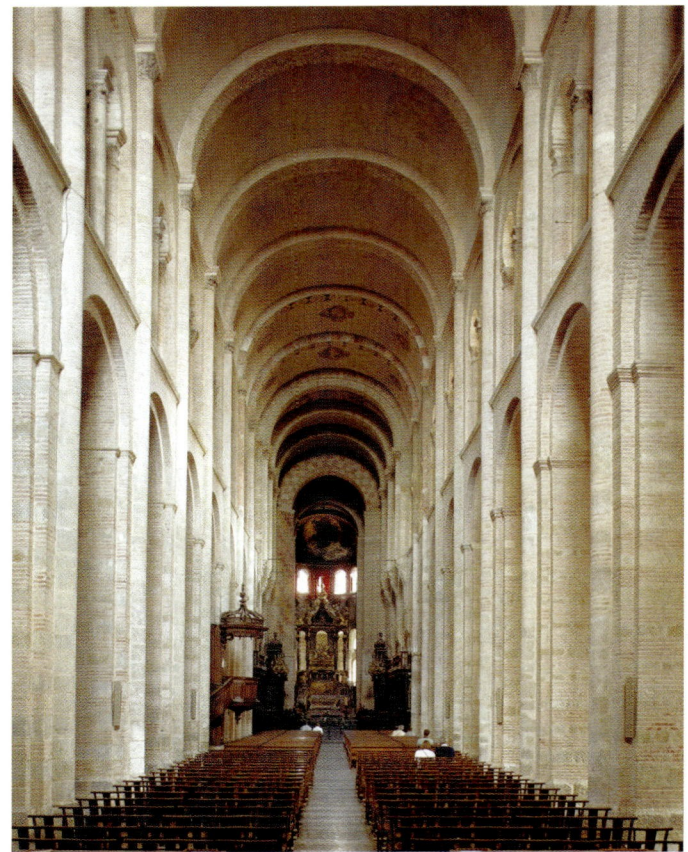

17-4 Aerial view of Saint-Sernin (from the southeast), Toulouse, France, ca. 1070–1120.

realization of an idea first seen in Carolingian architecture. This approach to design became increasingly common in the Romanesque period.

Saint-Sernin, unlike the more modestly sized churches at Vignory (FIG. 17-1) and Tournus (FIG. 17-3), has tribunes over the inner aisle and opening onto the nave (FIG. **17-6**), which housed overflow crowds on special occasions. The tribunes also played an important role in buttressing the continuous semicircular cut-stone barrel vault that covers Saint-Sernin's nave. Groin vaults (indicated by Xs on the plan, FIG. 17-5) in the tribunes as well as in the ground-floor aisles absorbed the pressure exerted by the barrel vault along the entire length of the nave. The groin vaults

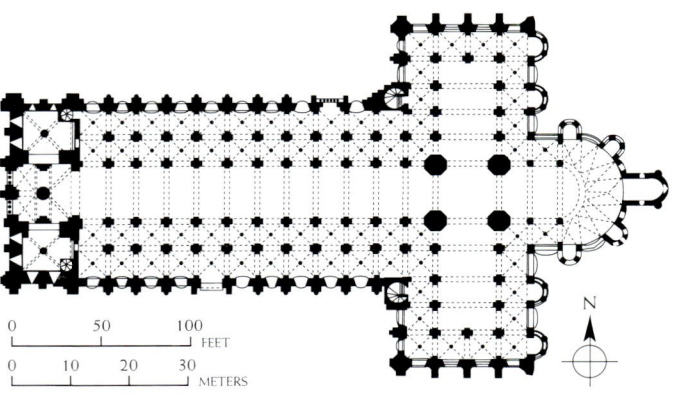

17-5 Plan of Saint-Sernin, Toulouse, France, ca. 1070–1120 (after Kenneth John Conant).

17-6 Interior of Saint-Sernin, Toulouse, France, ca. 1070–1120.

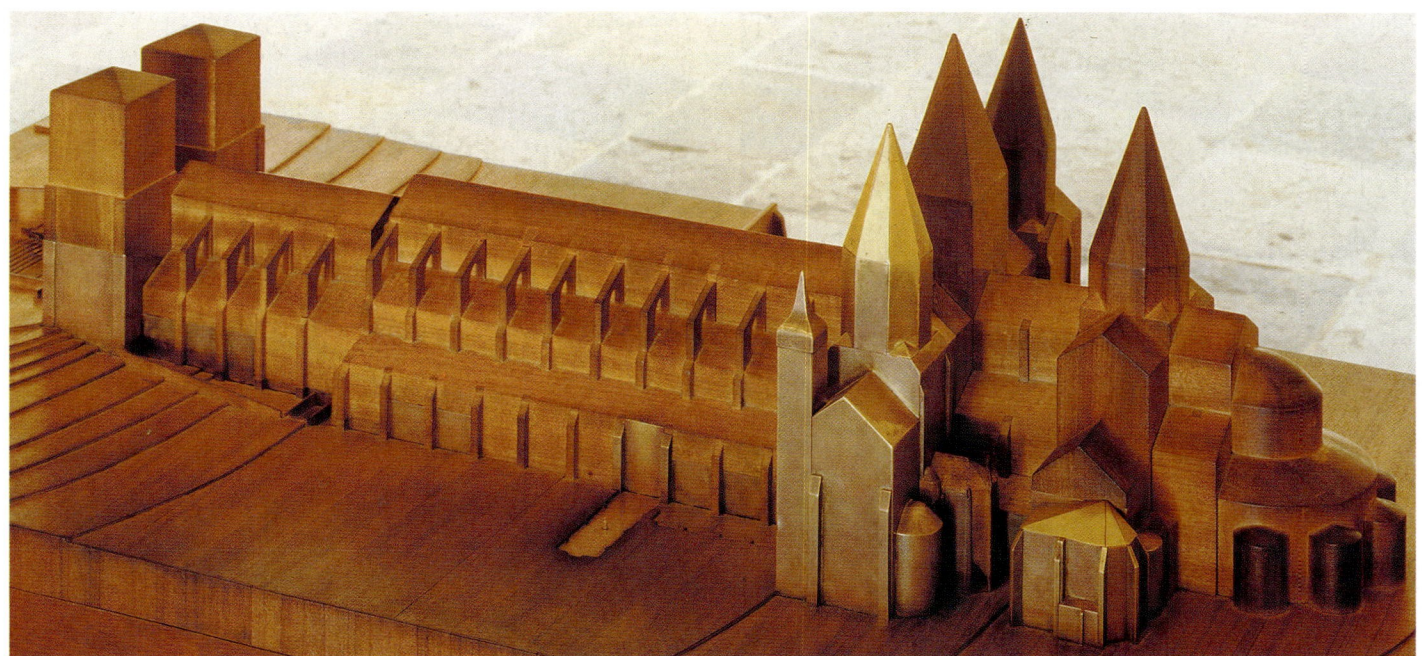

**17-7** Model of the third abbey church ("Cluny III"), Cluny, France, 1088–1130. Musée du Farinier, Cluny.

served as buttresses for the barrel vault and transferred the main thrust to the thick outer walls.

The builders of Saint-Sernin were not content with just buttressing the massive nave vault. They also carefully coordinated the design of the vault with that of the nave arcade below and with the modular plan of the building as a whole. Our view of the interior (FIG. 17-6) shows that the geometric floor plan (FIG. 17-5) is fully reflected in the nave walls, where the piers marking the corners of the bays are embellished with engaged half-columns. Architectural historians refer to piers with columns or pilasters attached to their rectangular cores as *compound piers*. At Saint-Sernin the engaged columns rise from the bottom of the compound piers to the vault's *springing* (the lowest stone of an arch) and continue across the nave as transverse arches.

As a result, the Saint-Sernin nave seems to be composed of numerous identical vertical volumes of space placed one behind the other, marching down the building's length in orderly procession, an effect also characteristic of the Tournus nave (FIG. 17-3), although achieved by using transverse barrel vaults. Saint-Sernin's spatial organization corresponds to and renders visually the plan's geometric organization. The segmentation of the nave also is reflected in the building's exterior walls (FIG. 17-4), where buttresses frame each bay. This rationally integrated scheme, with repeated units decorated and separated by moldings, had a long future in later church architecture in the West.

**EUROPE'S LARGEST CHURCH** In 909 William, Duke of Aquitaine, donated land near Cluny to a community of reform-minded Benedictine monks under Berno of Baume's leadership. Because William waived his feudal rights to the land, the abbot of Cluny was subject only to the pope in Rome, a unique privilege. Berno founded a new order at Cluny according to the rules of Saint Benedict (see "Medieval Monasteries and Benedictine Rule," Chapter 16, page 434). Under Berno's successors, the Cluniac monks became famous for their scholarship, music, and art. Their influence and wealth grew rapidly, and they built a series of ever more elaborate monastic churches at Cluny.

The third church at Cluny was erected between 1088 and 1130, when Hugh of Semur was abbot. Called Cluny III by art historians,

the building is, unfortunately, largely destroyed today. It has, however, been reconstructed on paper and in models (FIG. 17-7). At the time of its erection, Cluny III was the largest church in Europe, and it retained that distinction for almost 500 years until the new Saint Peter's in Rome was completed in the early 17th century (see FIGS. 24-2 to 24-4). Contemporaries considered Cluny III a place worthy for angels to dwell if they lived on earth. The church had an innovative and influential design, with a barrel-vaulted nave, four aisles, and radiating chapels, as at Saint-Sernin, but with a three-story nave elevation (arcade-tribune-clerestory) and slightly pointed nave vaults. With a nave more than 500 feet long and more than 100 feet high (both dimensions are about 50 percent greater than at Saint-Sernin), it epitomized the grandiose scale of the new stone-vaulted Romanesque churches and was a symbol of the power and prestige of the Cluniac order.

**CISTERCIAN AUSTERITY** Underlying Hugh of Semur's decision to make the huge expenditure that Cluny III required was the conviction that a magnificent setting for the Christian liturgy was a fitting tribute to the Lord. In the minds of many medieval monks, especially those of the Cluniac order, the construction of beautiful churches and the dedication of luxurious reliquaries were equated with piety. But one of the founding principles of monasticism was the rejection of worldly pleasures in favor of a life of contemplation. Some monks were appalled by the costly churches being erected all around them. One group founded a new order at Cîteaux in eastern France in 1098. The Cistercians (so called from the Latin name for Cîteaux) were Benedictine monks who split from the Cluniac order to return to the strict observance of the Rule of Saint Benedict, changing the color of their habits from Cluniac Benedictine black to unbleached white. These so-called White Monks emphasized productive manual labor, and their systematic farming techniques stimulated the agricultural transformation of Europe. The Cistercian movement expanded with astonishing rapidity. Within a half century, more than 500 Cistercian monasteries had been established.

The Cistercians' rejection of worldly extravagance and their emphasis on poverty, labor, and prayer are reflected in the austerity of their churches. The abbey at Cîteaux itself no longer was also aesthetically pleasing. The system used at Tournus (FIG. 17-3) met the first test but apparently failed the second, because the design was almost never adopted elsewhere.

Covering the nave with groin vaults instead of barrel vaults became the solution. Ancient Roman builders had used the groin vault widely, because they realized that its concentration of thrusts at four supporting points permitted clerestory windows (see "The Roman Architectural Revolution," Chapter 10, page 250, and FIGS. 10-68 and 10-79). The great Roman vaults were made possible by the use of concrete, which could be poured into forms, where it solidified into a homogeneous mass. But the technique of mixing concrete had not survived into the Middle Ages. The technical problems of building groin vaults of cut stone and heavy rubble, which had very little cohesive quality, at first limited their use to the covering of small areas, such as the individual bays of the aisles of Saint-Philibert (FIG. 17-3) and Saint-Sernin (FIG. 17-5). But during the 11th century, masons, using ashlar blocks joined by mortar, developed a groin vault of monumental dimensions.

**THE SPEYER SOLUTION** Speyer Cathedral (FIG. **17-9**) in the German Rhineland is an early example of groin vaults used over a nave. The church was begun in 1030 and was the burial place of the Holy Roman Emperors until the beginning of the 12th century. Like all cathedrals, Speyer was also the seat (*cathedra* in Latin) of the powerful local bishop. In its earliest form, Speyer Cathedral was a timber-roofed structure. When the emperor Henry IV rebuilt it between 1082 and 1106, his masons covered the nave with groin vaults, which made possible the insertion of a small clerestory window above each pair of tribune arches. Scholars disagree about where the first comprehensive use of groin vaulting occurred in

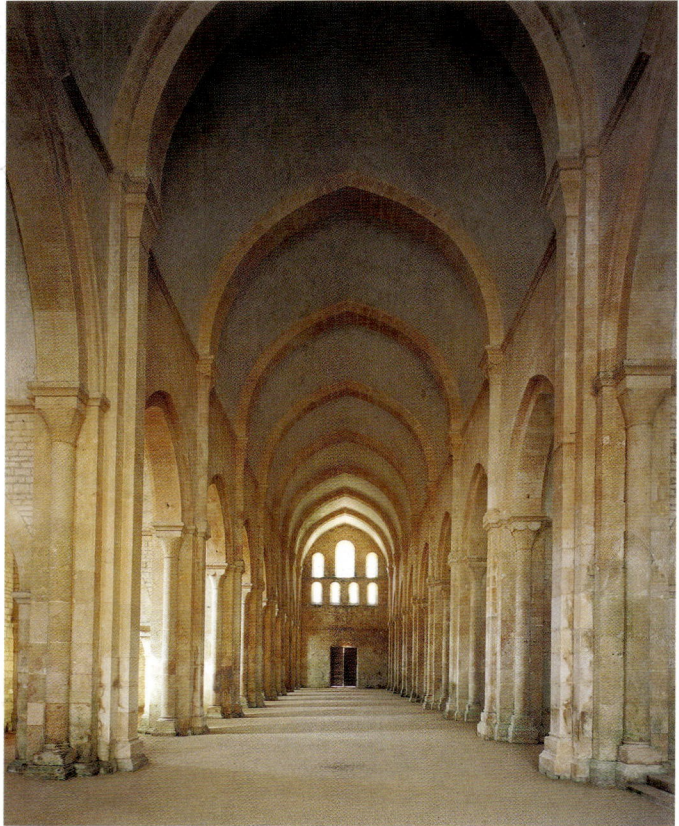

**17-8** Interior of abbey church of Notre-Dame, Fontenay, France, 1139–1147.

stands, but the nearby church of Notre-Dame at Fontenay (FIG. **17-8**) is representative of the Cistercian approach to architectural design. The church has a square east end, without an ambulatory or chapels. The walls are devoid of ornament, and the column capitals are plain. The nave has a single-story elevation with neither clerestory nor gallery. Light, however, reaches the nave through the large windows in the flat east wall and because the aisle bays have transverse barrel vaults like those in the Tournus nave (FIG. 17-3). Pointed arches—a feature of Cluny III—were used both in the nave arcade and in the barrel vault. This forward-looking structural device would permit later architects to increase the height of the nave dramatically. Pointed arches transfer the thrust of the vaults more directly downward to the piers and require less buttressing on the sides.

## Germany and Lombardy

GROIN VAULTS IN NAVES The continuous barrel-vaulted naves of Cluny III, Saint-Sernin at Toulouse (FIG. 17-6), and Notre-Dame at Fontenay (FIG. 17-8) provided an impressive setting as well as excellent acoustics for church services, and were relatively fireproof. But the barrel vaults often failed in one critical requirement—lighting. Due to the great outward thrust the barrel vaults exerted along their full length, even when pointed instead of semicircular, a clerestory was difficult to construct. (The Toulouse and Fontenay designers did not even attempt to introduce a clerestory, although their counterparts at Cluny III succeeded.) A more complex and efficient type of vaulting was needed. Structurally, the central problem of Romanesque architecture was the need to develop a masonry vault system that admitted light and

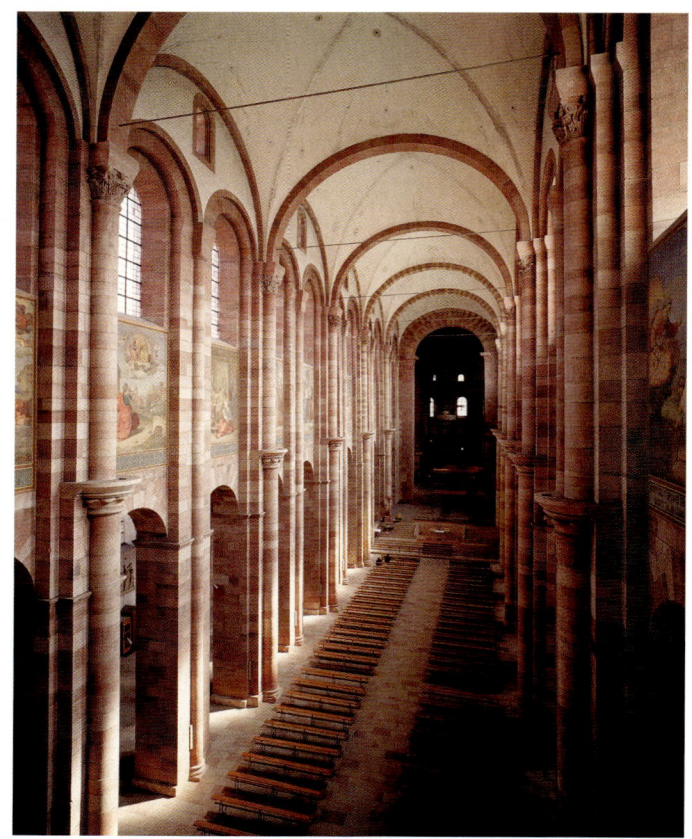

**17-9** Interior of Speyer Cathedral, Speyer, Germany, begun 1030; nave vaults, ca. 1082–1106.

Romanesque times, and nationalistic concerns sometimes color the debate. We will not argue here for the precedence of any one region. But no one doubts that the large groin vaults covering the nave of Speyer Cathedral represent one of the most daring and successful engineering experiments of the time. The nave is 45 feet wide, and the crowns of the vaults are 107 feet high.

Also in contrast to Saint-Sernin, Speyer Cathedral employs an alternate-support system in the nave, as in the Ottonian church of Saint Cyriakus at Gernrode (see FIG. 16-21). At Speyer, however, the alternation continues all the way up into the vaults, with the nave's more richly molded compound piers marking the corners of the groin vaults. Speyer's interior shows the same striving for height and the same compartmentalized effect seen in Saint-Sernin (FIG. 17-6). By virtue of the alternate-support system, the rhythm of the Speyer nave is a little more complex. Because each compartment is individually vaulted, the effect of a sequence of vertical spatial blocks is even more convincing.

**LOMBARD INNOVATION** Ever since Charlemagne crushed the Lombards in 773, German kings held sway over Lombardy, and the Rhineland and northern Italy cross-fertilized each other artistically. No agreement exists as to which source of artistic influence was dominant in the Romanesque age, the northern or the southern. The question, no doubt, will remain the subject of controversy until the construction date of Sant'Ambrogio in Milan (FIGS. **17-10** and **17-11**) can be established unequivocally. The church, erected in honor of Saint Ambrose, Milan's first bishop (d. 397), is the central monument of Lombard Romanesque architecture.

Whether or not it was a prototype for Speyer Cathedral, Sant'Ambrogio remains a remarkable building. It has an atrium

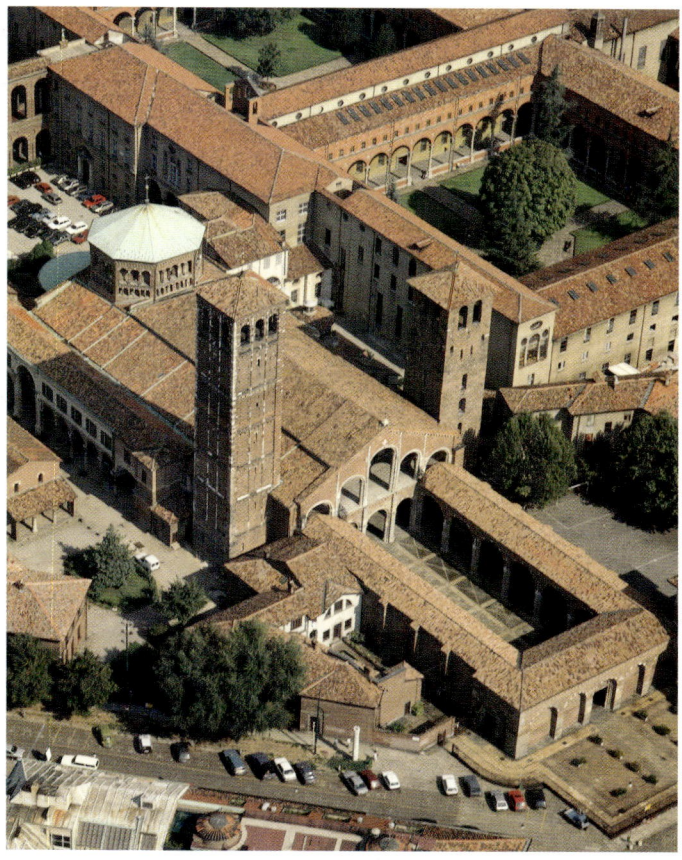

**17-10** Aerial view of Sant'Ambrogio, Milan, Italy, late 11th to early 12th century.

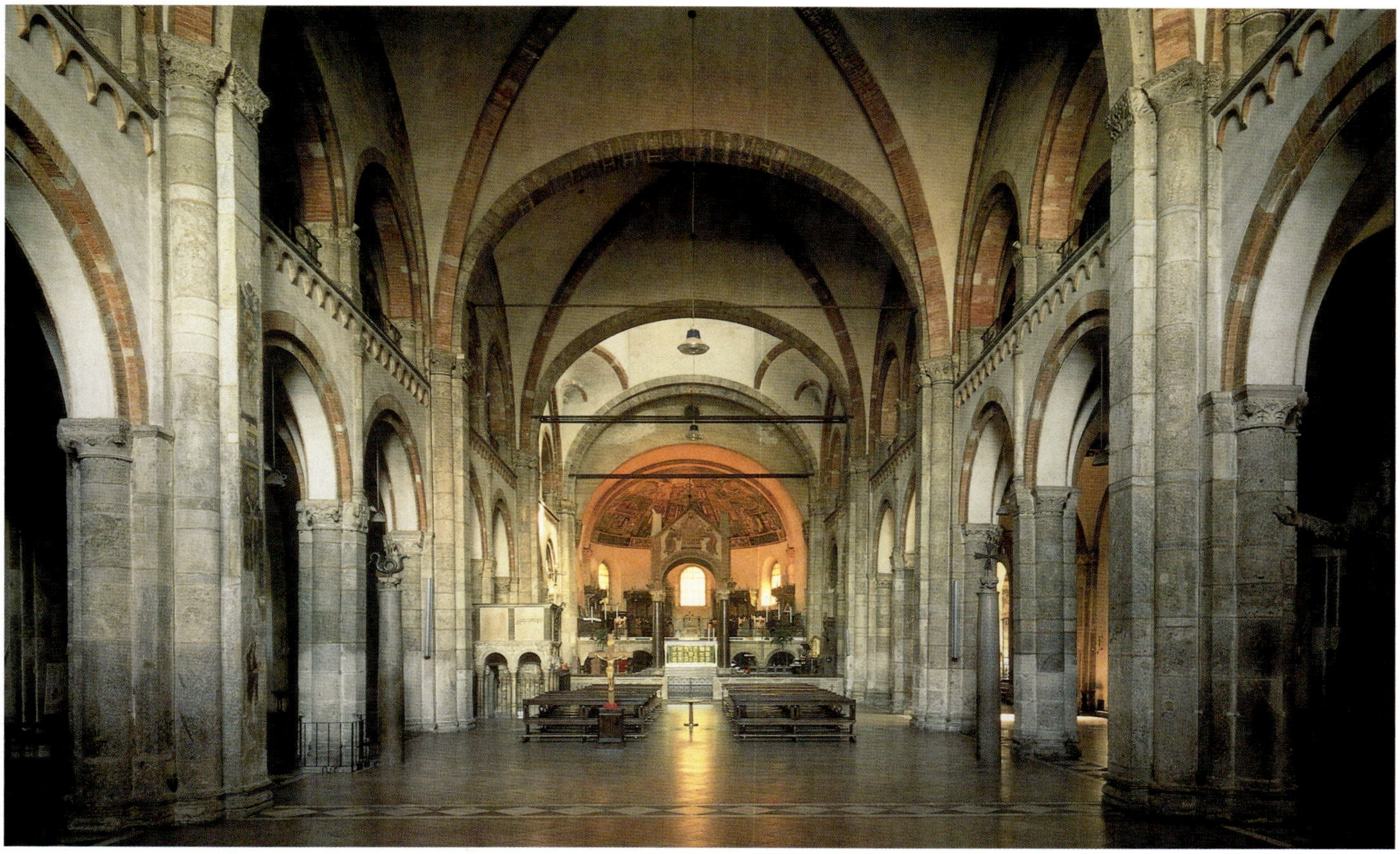

**17-11** Interior of Sant'Ambrogio, Milan, Italy, late 11th to early 12th century.

in the Early Christian tradition (one of the last to be built), a two-story narthex pierced by arches on both levels, two bell towers *(campaniles)* joined to the building, and, over the nave's east end, an octagonal tower that recalls the crossing towers of German churches. Of the facade bell towers, the shorter one dates back to the 10th century, and the taller north campanile is a 12th-century addition.

Sant'Ambrogio has a nave and two aisles, but no transept. Each bay consists of a full square in the nave flanked by two small squares in each aisle, all covered with groin vaults. The main vaults are slightly domical, rising higher than the transverse arches. An octagonal dome covers the last bay, its windows providing the major light source (the building lacks a clerestory) for the otherwise rather dark interior. The emphatic alternate-support system perfectly reflects the geometric regularity of the plan. The lightest pier moldings are interrupted at the gallery level, and the heavier ones rise to support the main vaults. At Sant'Ambrogio, the compound piers even continue into the ponderous vaults, which have supporting arches, or *ribs,* along their groins. This is one of the first instances of rib vaulting, a salient characteristic of mature Romanesque and of later Gothic architecture (see "The Gothic Rib Vault," Chapter 18, page 482).

The regional character of Romanesque architecture can be seen clearly by comparing the proportions of Sant'Ambrogio with those of both Speyer Cathedral (FIG. 17-9) and Saint-Sernin at Toulouse (FIGS. 17-4 and 17-6). The Milanese building does not aspire to the soaring height of the French and German churches. Save for the later of the two towers, Sant'Ambrogio's proportions are low and broad and remain close to those of Early Christian basilicas. Italian architects, with their firm roots in the venerable Early Christian style, never accepted the verticality found in northern architecture, not even during the Gothic period.

## Normandy and England

After their conversion to Christianity in the early 10th century, the Vikings (see Chapter 16) settled on the northern coast of France in present-day Normandy. Almost at once, they proved themselves not only aggressive warriors but also skilled administrators and

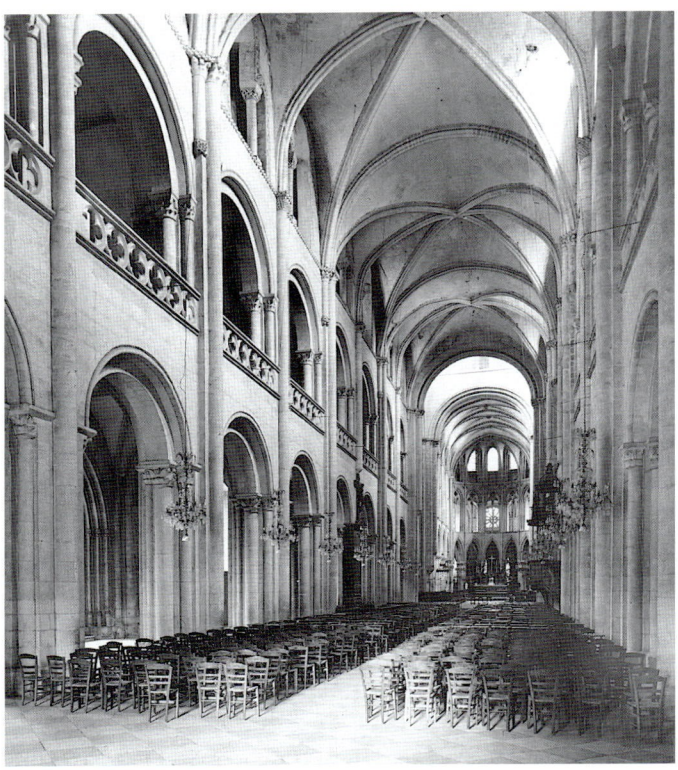

**17-13** Interior of Saint-Étienne, Caen, France, vaulted ca. 1115–1120.

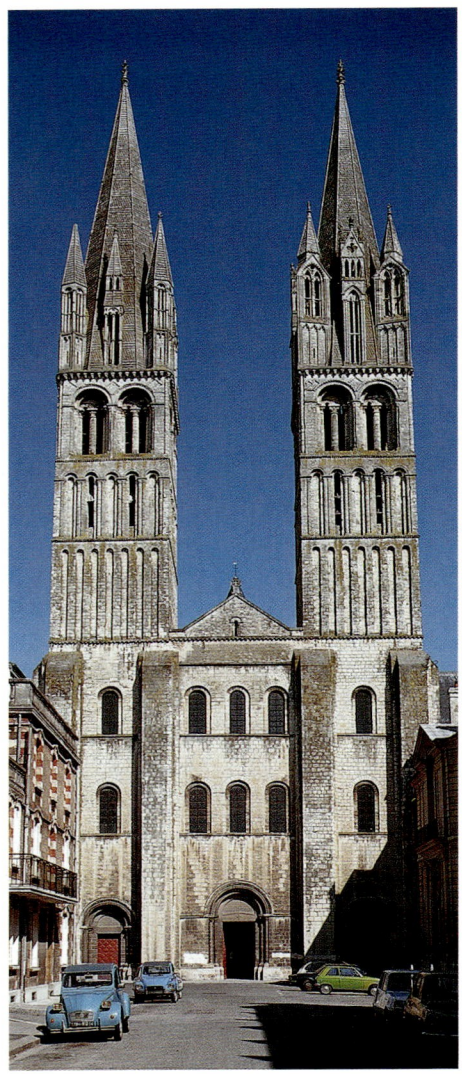

**17-12** West facade of Saint-Étienne, Caen, France, begun 1067.

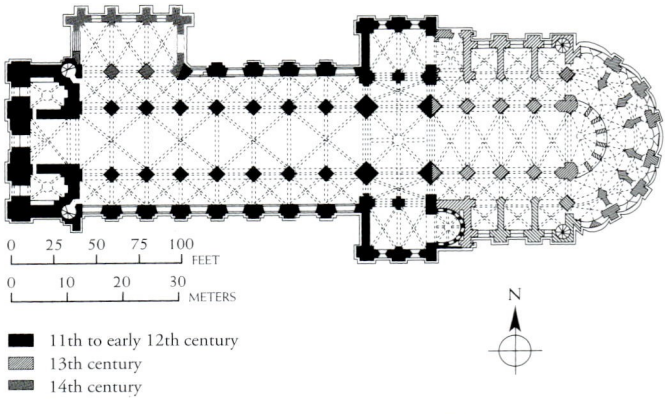

■ 11th to early 12th century
▨ 13th century
▧ 14th century

**17-14** Plan of Saint-Étienne, Caen, France.

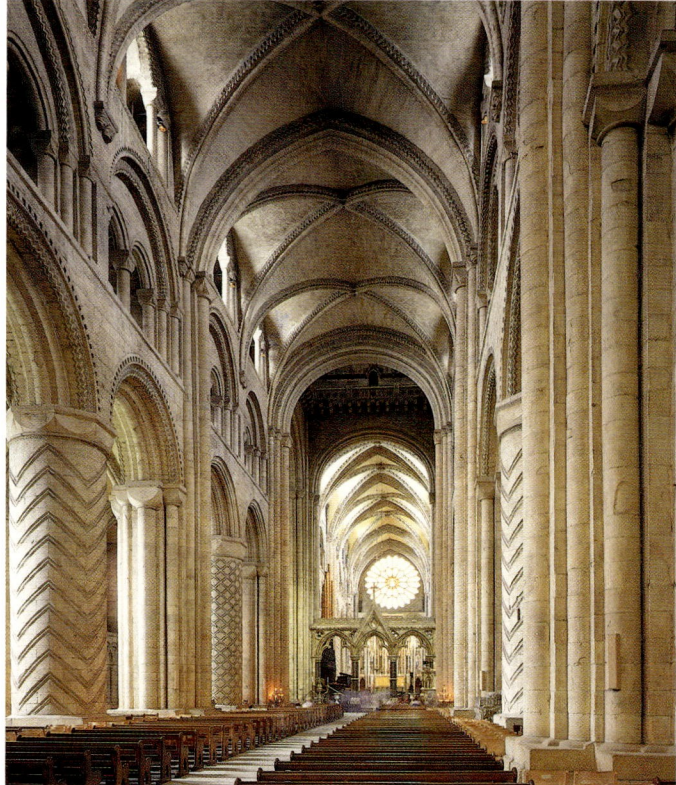

17-15 Interior of Durham Cathedral, England, begun ca. 1093.

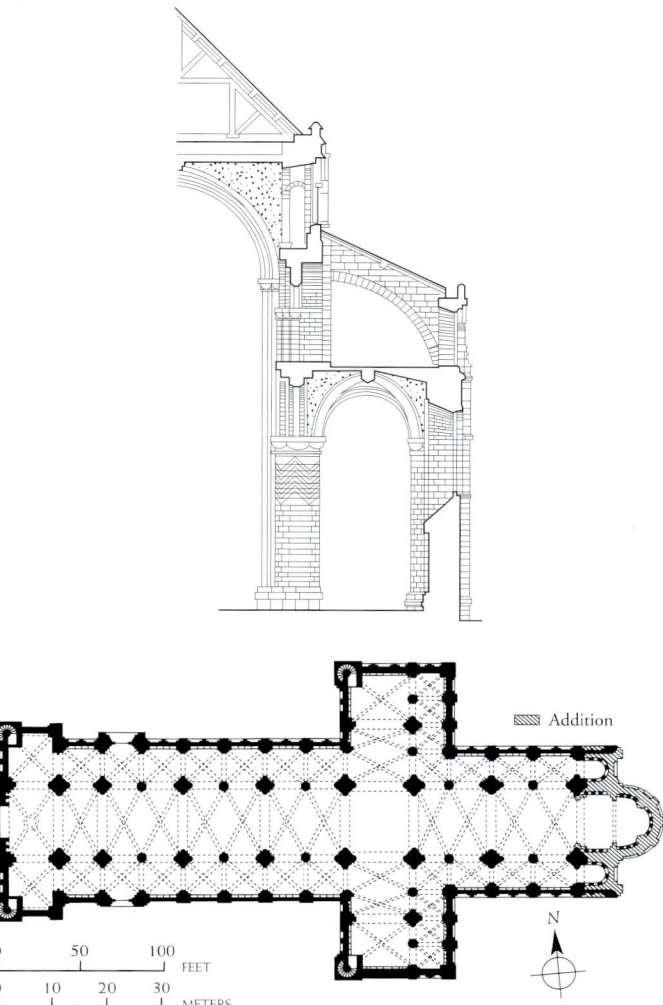

Addition

17-16 Lateral section *(top)* and plan *(bottom)* of Durham Cathedral, England (after Kenneth John Conant).

builders, active in Sicily (see FIG. 12-24) as well as in northern Europe. The Normans quickly developed a distinctive Romanesque architectural style that became the major source of French Gothic architecture.

THE CONQUEROR'S CHURCH Most critics consider the abbey church of Saint-Étienne at Caen the masterpiece of Norman Romanesque architecture. It was begun by William of Normandy (William the Conqueror; see page 476) in 1067 and must have advanced rapidly, as he was buried there in 1087. Saint-Étienne's west facade (FIG. 17-12) is a striking design rooted in the tradition of Carolingian and Ottonian westworks, but it displays the increased rationalism of Romanesque architecture. Four large buttresses divide the facade into three bays that correspond to the nave and aisles. Above the buttresses, the towers also display a triple division and a progressively greater piercing of their walls from lower to upper stages. (The culminating spires are a Gothic addition.) The tripartite division is employed throughout the facade, both vertically and horizontally, organizing it into a close-knit, well-integrated design that reflects the careful and methodical planning of the entire structure.

The original design of Saint-Étienne called for a wooden roof, as originally at Speyer and Tournus. But the Caen nave (FIG. 17-13) has compound piers with simple engaged half-columns alternating with piers with half-columns attached to pilasters. When groin vaults were introduced around 1115, the varied nave piers proved an ideal match. The alternating compound piers soar all the way to the vaults' springing. Their branching ribs divide the large square-vault compartments into six sections, making a *sexpartite vault* (FIG. 17-14). These vaults rise high enough to provide room for an efficient clerestory. The resulting three-story elevation, with its large arched openings, provides more light to the interior. It also makes the nave appear even taller than it actually is. As in the Milanese church of Sant'Ambrogio (FIG. 17-11), the Norman building has rib vaults. The diagonal and transverse ribs compose a structural skeleton that partially supports the still fairly massive paneling between them. But despite the heavy masonry, the large windows and reduced interior wall surface give Saint-Étienne's nave a light and airy quality that is unusual in the Romanesque period.

ENGLISH ROMANESQUE William of Normandy's conquest of Anglo-Saxon England in 1066 began a new epoch in English history. In architecture, it signaled the importation of French Romanesque building and design methods. Durham Cathedral (FIGS. 17-15 and 17-16) sits majestically on a cliff overlooking the Wear River in northern England. It was begun around 1093, in the generation following the Norman conquest, and is the centerpiece of a monastery, cathedral, and fortified-castle complex on the Scottish frontier.

Unlike Speyer Cathedral and Saint-Étienne, Durham Cathedral, which predates the remodeled Caen church, was conceived from the very beginning as a vaulted structure. Consequently, the pattern of the ribs of the nave's groin vaults is reflected in the design of the arcade below. Each seven-part nave vault covers two bays. Large, simple pillars ornamented with abstract designs (diamond, chevron, and cable patterns, all originally painted) alternate with compound piers that carry the transverse arches of the vaults. The pier-vault relationship scarcely could be more visible or the building's structural rationale better expressed.

The bold surface patterning of the Durham nave is a reminder that the raising of imposing stone edifices such as the Romanesque churches of England and Normandy required more than just the talents of master designers. A corps of expert masons had to transform rough stone blocks into the precise shapes necessary for their specific place in the church's fabric. Although thousands of simple quadrangular ashlar blocks make up the great walls of these buildings, much more complex shapes also needed to be produced in large numbers. To cover the nave and aisles, the stonecutters had to carve blocks with concave faces to conform to the curve of the vault. Also required were blocks with projecting moldings for the ribs, blocks with convex surfaces for the pillars or with multiple profiles for the compound piers, and so forth. It was an immense undertaking, and it is no wonder that medieval building campaigns often lasted for decades.

The plan (FIG. 17-16, *bottom*) of Durham Cathedral is typically English with its long, slender proportions. It does not employ the modular scheme with the same care and logic seen at Caen. But in other ways this English church is even more innovative than the French church. It is the earliest example known of a ribbed groin vault placed over a three-story nave. And in the nave's western parts, completed before 1130, rib vaults were combined with slightly pointed arches, bringing together for the first time two of the key elements that determined the structural evolution of Gothic architecture. Also of great significance is the way the nave vaults were buttressed. Our lateral section (FIG. 17-16, *top*) reveals that simple *quadrant arches* (arches whose curve extends for one quarter of a circle's circumference) were used in place of groin vaults in the tribune. The structural descendants of the Durham quadrant arches are the flying buttresses that epitomize the mature Gothic solution to church construction (see "The Gothic Cathedral," Chapter 18, page 488).

## Tuscany

South of the Lombard region, Italy retained its ancient traditions and, for the most part, produced Romanesque architecture that was structurally less experimental than that of Lombardy. The buildings of Tuscany, along with those of Rome itself, adhered closely to the traditions of the Early Christian basilica. They underscore that diversity is the rule, not the exception, in Romanesque Europe.

**ROMANESQUE PISA** The cathedral complex at Pisa (FIG. **17-17**) dramatically testifies to the prosperity the busy maritime city enjoyed. The cathedral, its freestanding bell tower, and the *baptistery*, where infants and converts were initiated into the Christian community, present a rare opportunity to study a coherent group of three Romanesque buildings. Save for the upper portion of the baptistery, with its remodeled Gothic exterior, the three structures are stylistically homogeneous.

Construction of Pisa Cathedral began first — in 1063, the same year work began on Saint Mark's in Venice (see FIG. 12-23), another powerful maritime city. The Pisan project was funded by the spoils of a naval victory over the Muslims off Palermo in Sicily in 1062. The cathedral is large, with a nave and four aisles, and is one of the most impressive and majestic of all Romanesque churches. The Pisans, according to a document of the time, wanted their bishop's church not only to be a monument to the glory of God

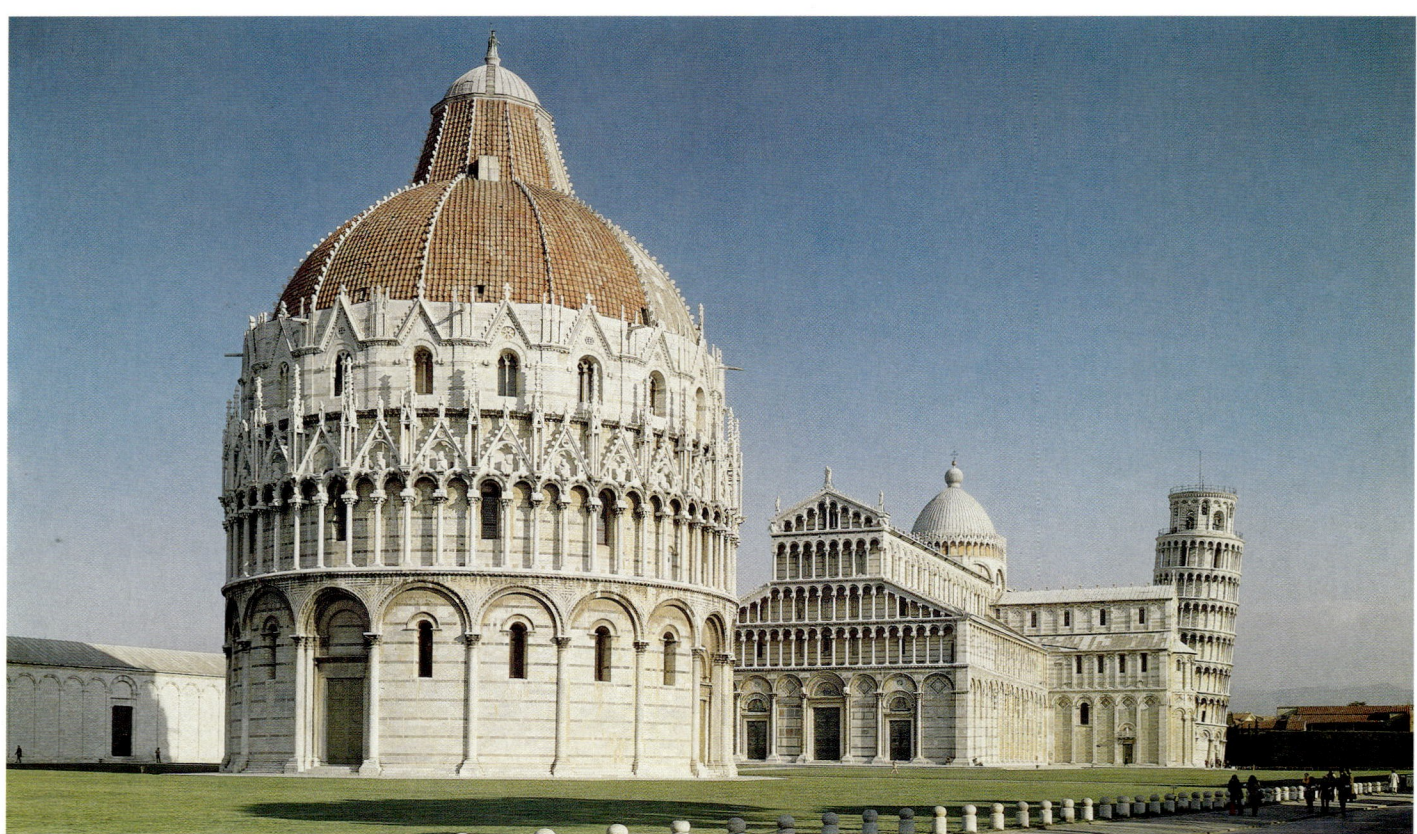

**17-17** Cathedral complex, Pisa, Italy; cathedral begun 1063; baptistery begun 1153; campanile begun 1174.

but also to bring credit to the city. At first glance, Pisa Cathedral resembles an Early Christian basilica. But the broadly projecting transept, the crossing dome, and the facade's multiple arcaded galleries distinguish it as Romanesque. So too does the rich marble *incrustation* (wall decoration consisting of bright panels of different colors, as in the Pantheon's interior, FIG. 10-50).

The cathedral's campanile, detached in the standard Italian fashion, is the famous Leaning Tower of Pisa (FIG. 17-17, *right*). The tilted vertical axis is the result of a settling foundation. It began to "lean" even while under construction and now inclines some 21 perilous feet out of plumb at the top. Graceful arcaded galleries mark the tower's stages and repeat the cathedral's facade motif, effectively relating the round campanile to its mother building.

**FLORENCE BAPTISTERY** Florence is always associated with the Renaissance of the 15th and 16th centuries, but it was already an important independent city-state in the Romanesque period. The gem of Florentine Romanesque architecture is the baptistery of San Giovanni (FIG. **17-18**). Dedicated to Saint John, the city's patron saint, by Pope Nicholas II in 1059, it was constructed during the succeeding century. Like Pisa's baptistery (FIG. 17-17, *left*), which it predates, Florence's baptistery faces that city's great cathedral. These freestanding Italian baptisteries are unusual and reflect the great significance the Florentines and Pisans attached to baptisms. On the day of a newborn child's anointment, the citizenry gathered in the baptistery to welcome a new member into their community. The Tuscan baptisteries therefore were important civic, as well as religious, structures. Some of the most renowned artists of the late Middle Ages and the Renaissance were employed to provide the Florentine and Pisan baptisteries with pulpits (see FIG. 19-2), bronze doors (see FIGS. 21-1, 21-2, and 21-4), and mosaics.

The simple and serene classicism of San Giovanni's design recalls ancient Roman architecture. The baptistery stands in a direct line of descent from the Pantheon (see FIG. 10-48) and imperial mausoleums such as Diocletian's (see FIG. 10-75) to the Early Christian Santa Costanza (see FIG. 11-9), the Byzantine San Vitale (see FIG. 12-6), and other central-plan structures, pagan or Christian, including Charlemagne's Palatine Chapel at Aachen (see FIG. 16-17). The distinctive Tuscan Romanesque marble incrustation that patterns the walls stems ultimately from Roman wall designs (see FIGS. 10-14 and 10-50). The simple oblong and arcuated panels assert the building's structural lines and its elevation levels.

In plan, San Giovanni is a domed octagon, wrapped on the exterior by an elegant arcade, three arches to a bay. It has three entrances, one each on the north, south, and east sides. On the west side an oblong sanctuary replaces the original semicircular apse. The domical vault is some 90 feet in diameter, its construction a feat remarkable for its time.

**THE BASILICAN TRADITION** Contemporaneous with the baptistery and also featuring elaborate marble incrustation is the Benedictine abbey church of San Miniato al Monte (FIG. **17-19**). It sits, as its name implies, on a hillside overlooking the Arno River and the heart of Florence. The body of the church was completed by 1090, its facade not until the early 13th century. Even more than Pisa Cathedral, the structure recalls the Early Christian basilica, but *diaphragm arches* divide its nave into three equal compartments. The arches rise from compound piers and brace the rather high, thin walls. They also provide firebreaks beneath the wooden roof and compartmentalize the basilican interior in the manner so popular with most Romanesque builders. The compound piers alternate with pairs of simple columns with Roman-revival Composite capitals.

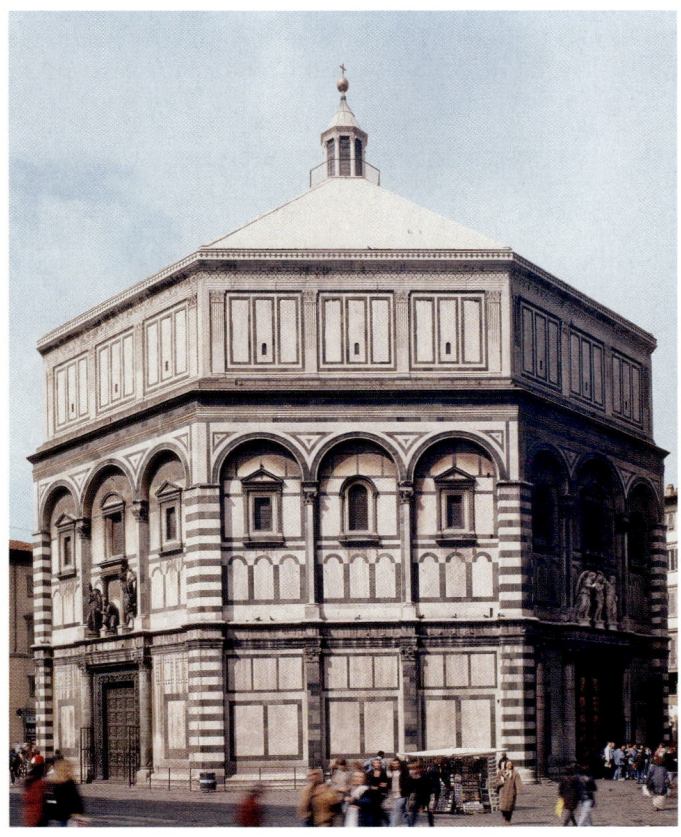

**17-18** Baptistery of San Giovanni, Florence, Italy, dedicated 1059.

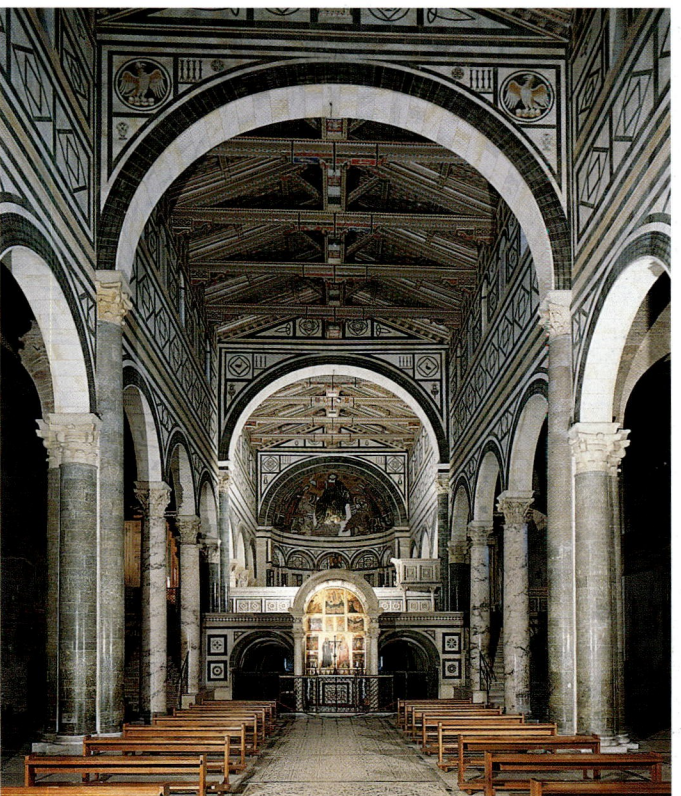

**17-19** Interior of San Miniato al Monte, Florence, Italy, ca. 1062–1090.

# SCULPTURE

## Architectural Sculpture

**STONE SCULPTURE REVIVED** Stone sculpture, with some notable exceptions, such as the great crosses of the British Isles (see FIG. 16-9), had almost disappeared from the art of western Europe during the early Middle Ages. The revival of stonecarving is one of the hallmarks of the Romanesque age—and one of the reasons the period is aptly named. The inspiration for stone sculpture no doubt came, at least in part, from the abundant remains of ancient statues and reliefs throughout Rome's northwestern provinces. As one would expect, individual Romanesque sculptural motifs and compositions often originated in Carolingian and Ottonian ivory carving, metalwork, and manuscript illumination. But Roman sculptures throughout France, Italy, Germany, and Spain provided a powerful spur to the imaginations of Romanesque patrons and artists alike.

**CLOISTER SCULPTURE** The beginnings of a revived tradition of stonecarving can be seen in the carved capitals of northern Romanesque churches such as Saint-Étienne at Vignory (FIG. 17-1), and the practice of decorating capitals with reliefs continued in the 12th century. The most extensive preserved ensemble of sculptured early Romanesque capitals is found in the cloister (FIG. **17-20**) of Saint-Pierre at Moissac in southwestern France. The Moissac abbey had joined the Cluniac order in 1047 and was an important stop along the pilgrimage route to the tomb of Saint James at Santiago de Compostela. The monks, enriched by the gifts of pilgrims and noble benefactors, adorned their church with an elaborate series of relief sculptures.

*Cloister* (from the Latin word *claustrum,* an enclosed place) connotes being shut away from the world. Architecturally, the medieval church cloister expressed the seclusion of the spiritual life, the *vita contemplativa.* At Moissac, as elsewhere, the cloister provided the monks (and nuns) with a foretaste of Paradise. In its garden or the timber-roofed walkway supported by piers and columns that framed the garden, they could read their devotions, pray, and meditate in an atmosphere of calm serenity, each monk withdrawn into the private world where the soul communes only with God. The physical silence of the cloister was one with the silence that the more austere monastic communities required of their members. The monastery cloisters of the 12th century are monuments to the vitality, popularity, and influence of monasticism at its peak.

Moissac's cloister sculpture program consists of large figural reliefs on the piers as well as *historiated* (ornamented with figures) capitals on the columns. The pier reliefs portray the Twelve Apostles and the first Cluniac abbot of Moissac, Durandus (1047–1072), who was buried in the cloister. The 76 capitals alternately crown single and paired column shafts. They are variously decorated, some with abstract patterns, many with biblical scenes or the lives of saints, others with fantastic monsters of all sorts—basilisks, griffins, lizards, gargoyles, and more. Such *bestiaries* became very popular in the Romanesque age. The monstrous forms were reminders of the chaos and deformity of a world without God's order. Medieval artists delighted in inventing composite beasts with multiple heads and other fantastic creations. Historiated capitals were also a feature of Moissac's mother church, Cluny III, and were common in Cluniac monasteries. The Cistercians, not surprisingly, rejected such extravagances as distractions from their devotions. The most outspoken Cistercian critic of the new Romanesque sculptures was Abbot Bernard of Clairvaux (see "Bernard of Clairvaux on Cloister Sculpture," page 461).

**ART AND THE LAITY** The Romanesque period also witnessed the spread of sculpture to other areas of the church, both inside and out. Many art historians have noted that the reemergence of monumental stone sculpture in western Europe coincided with the introduction of stone vaulting in Romanesque churches. But stone-walled churches and monumental westworks had been built for centuries, even if the structures bore timber ceilings and roofs. The addition of stone vaults to basilican churches is not in itself an explanation for the resurgence of stonecarving in the Romanesque period. The earliest Romanesque sculptures, in fact, appear in

**17-20** Cloister of Saint-Pierre, Moissac, France, ca. 1100–1115. Limestone with marble relief panels, piers approx. 6′ high.

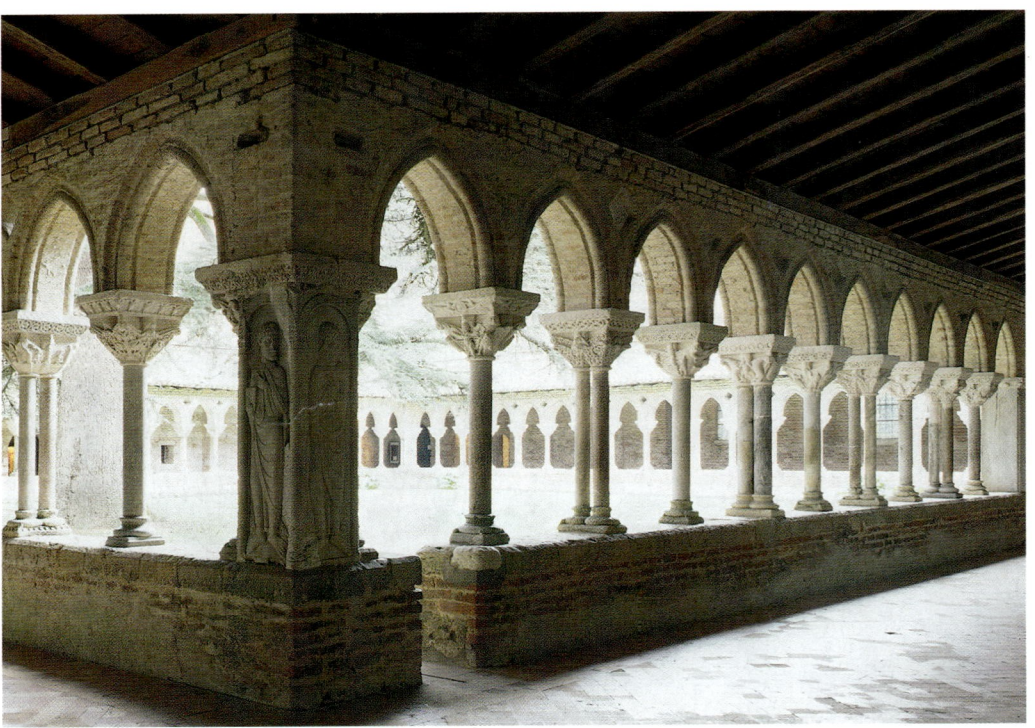

## Bernard of Clairvaux on Cloister Sculpture

The most influential theologian of the Romanesque era was Bernard of Clairvaux (1090–1153). A Cistercian monk and abbot of the monastery he founded at Clairvaux in northern Burgundy, he embodied not only the reforming spirit of the Cistercian order but also the new religious fervor awakening in the West. Bernard's impassioned eloquence made him a European celebrity and drew him into the stormy politics of the Romanesque era. He intervened in high ecclesiastical and secular matters, defended and sheltered embattled popes, counseled kings, denounced heretics, and preached Crusades against the Muslims—all in defense of papal Christianity and spiritual values. He was declared a saint in 1174, barely two decades after his death.

In a letter Bernard wrote in 1127 to William, abbot of Saint-Thierry, he complained about the rich outfitting of non-Cistercian churches in general and the sculptural adornment of monastic cloisters in particular.

> I will overlook the immense heights of the places of prayer, their immoderate lengths, their superfluous widths, the costly refinements, and painstaking representations which deflect the attention ... of those who pray and thus hinder their devotion. ... But so be it, let these things be made for the honor of God ... [But] in the cloisters, before the eyes of the brothers while they read—what ... are the filthy apes doing there? The fierce lions? The monstrous centaurs? The creatures, part man and part beast? ... You may see many bodies under one head, and conversely many heads on one body. On one side the tail of a serpent is seen on a quadruped, on the other side the head of a quadruped is on the body of a fish. Over there an animal has a horse for the front half and a goat for the back ... Everywhere so plentiful and astonishing a variety of contradictory forms is seen that one would rather read in the marble than in books, and spend the whole day wondering at every single one of them than in meditating on the law of God. Good God! If one is not ashamed of the absurdity, why is one not at least troubled at the expense?[1]

[1] *Apologia* 12.28–29. Translated by Conrad Rudolph, *The "Things of Greater Importance": Bernard of Clairvaux's* Apologia *and the Medieval Attitude toward Art* (Philadelphia: University of Pennsylvania Press, 1990), 279, 283.

timber-roofed early Romanesque churches like Saint-Étienne at Vignory (FIG. 17-1). Stonecarving is, however, consistent with the widespread desire in the Romanesque period (the Cistercians were notable exceptions) to beautify the house of the Lord.

The proliferation of stone sculpture in the 12th century also reflects the changing role of many churches in Western Christendom. In the early Middle Ages, most churches served small monastic communities, and the worshipers were primarily or exclusively clergy. With the rise of towns in the Romanesque period, churches, especially those on the major pilgrimage routes, increasingly served the lay public. To reach this new, largely illiterate audience and to draw a wider population into their places of worship, church officials decided to display Christian symbols and stories throughout their churches, especially in portals. Stone, rather than painting or mosaic, was the most suitable durable medium for such exterior decorative programs.

**SCULPTURE AT TOULOUSE** One of the earliest precisely dated series of large Romanesque figure reliefs is a group of seven marble slabs, representing angels, apostles, and Christ, made for the great pilgrimage church of Saint-Sernin at Toulouse (FIGS. 17-4 to 17-6). An inscription states that the reliefs date to the year 1096 and that the artist was a certain BERNARDUS GELDUINUS. Today the plaques are affixed to the ambulatory wall. Their original location is uncertain. Some scholars have suggested that they once formed part of a shrine dedicated to Saint Saturninus that stood in the *crypt* of the grand structure. Others believe the reliefs once decorated a choir screen or an exterior portal.

We illustrate the centerpiece of the group, the figure of Christ in Majesty (FIG. **17-21**). Christ sits in a mandorla, his right hand raised in blessing, his left hand resting on an open book inscribed with the words *Pax vobis* ("peace be unto you"). The signs of the Four Evangelists (see "The Four Evangelists," Chapter 16, page 426) occupy the corners of the slab. Art historians debate the sources of Gelduinus's style, but one easily can imagine such a composition

used for a Carolingian or Ottonian work in metal or ivory, perhaps a book cover. The polished marble has the gloss of both materials, and the sharply incised lines and the ornamentation of Christ's aureole are characteristic of pre-Romanesque metalwork.

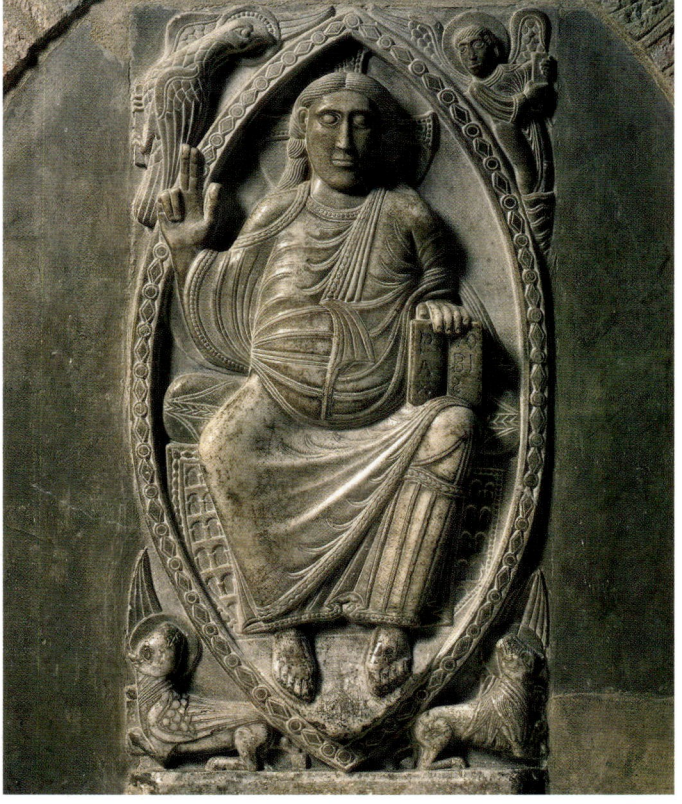

**17-21** BERNARDUS GELDUINUS, Christ in Majesty, relief in the ambulatory of Saint-Sernin, Toulouse, France, ca. 1096. Marble, 4′ 2″ high.

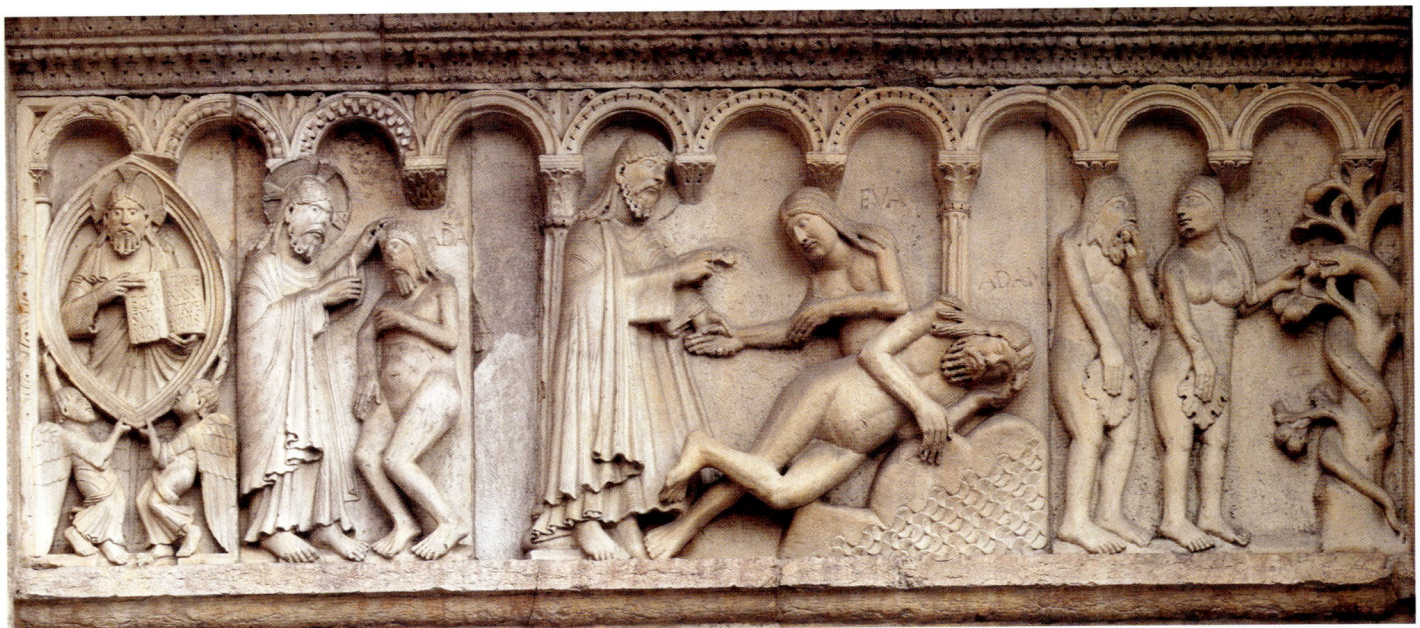

**17-22** WILIGELMO, creation and temptation of Adam and Eve, frieze on the west facade, Modena Cathedral, Modena, Italy, ca. 1110. Marble, approx. 3' high.

**GENESIS AT MODENA** Some 15 years later, around 1110, another sculptor carved one of the first fully developed narrative reliefs in Romanesque art. The facade of Modena Cathedral in northern Italy has a marble frieze that extends on two levels across three of its bays. It represents scenes from Genesis set against an architectural backdrop of a type common on Late Roman and Early Christian sarcophagi, which were plentiful in the area. The segment shown (FIG. **17-22**) illustrates the creation and temptation of Adam and Eve (Gen. 2, 3:1–8), the theme employed almost exactly a century earlier on Bishop Bernward's bronze doors to Saint Michael's at Hildesheim (see FIG. 16-24). At Modena, as at Hildesheim, the faithful entered the house of the Lord with a reminder of Original Sin and the suggestion that the only path to salvation is through the Christian Church.

On the Modena frieze, Christ is at the far left, framed by a mandorla held up by angels—a variation on the motif of the Saint-Sernin ambulatory relief (FIG. 17-21). The creation of Adam, then Eve, and the serpent's temptation of Eve are to the right. The relief carving is high, and some parts are almost entirely in the round. The frieze is the work of a master craftsman whose name, WILIGELMO, is given in an inscription on another relief on the facade. There he boasts, "Among sculptors, your work shines forth, Wiligelmo." The inscription is also an indication of the pride of Wiligelmo's patrons in obtaining the services of such an accomplished sculptor for their city's cathedral.

**THE SECOND COMING** At Modena, the frieze recounts the beginning of the human race. Some 25 years later, the south portal (FIG. **17-23**) of Saint-Pierre at Moissac, facing the town square, announced its end. The portal's vast *tympanum* (see "The Romanesque Portal," page 463) depicts the Second Coming of Christ as King and Judge of the world in its last days. As befits his majesty, the enthroned Christ is at the center, reflecting a compositional rule followed since Early Christian times. The signs of the Four Evangelists flank him. To one side of each pair of signs is an attendant angel holding scrolls to record human deeds for judgment.

The figures of crowned musicians, which complete the design, are the Twenty-Four Elders who accompany Christ as the kings of this world and make music in his praise. Each turns to face him, much as would the courtiers of a Romanesque monarch in attendance on their lord. Two courses of wavy lines symbolizing the clouds of Heaven divide the Elders into three tiers.

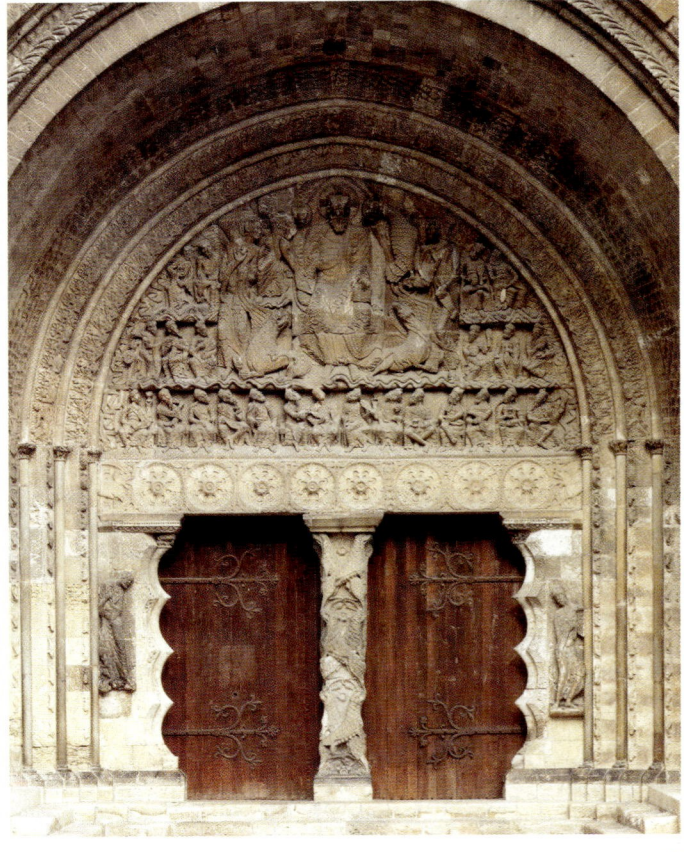

**17-23** South portal of Saint-Pierre, Moissac, France, ca. 1115–1135.

## The Romanesque Portal

One of the most significant and distinctive features of Romanesque art is the revival of monumental sculpture in stone. Because of the Second Commandment's prohibition of graven images, large-scale carved Old and New Testament figures (and later saints) were almost unknown in Christian art before the Romanesque period. But in the late 11th and early 12th centuries, rich ensembles of figural reliefs began to appear again. Freestanding statuary, however, still associated with pagan idol worship, remained very rare.

Although sculpture in a variety of materials adorned different areas of Romanesque churches, it was most often found in the grand stone portals through which the faithful had to pass. Sculpture had been employed in church doorways before. For example, carved wooden doors greeted Early Christian worshipers as they entered Santa Sabina in Rome. And Ottonian bronze doors decorated with Old and New Testament scenes marked the entrance to Saint Michael's at Hildesheim (see FIG. 16-24). But these were exceptions. And in the Romanesque era (and during the Gothic period that followed), sculpture usually appeared in the area *around,* rather than *on,* the doors.

Our drawing shows the parts of church portals that Romanesque sculptors regularly decorated with figural reliefs:

- *Tympanum* (FIGS. 17-23 and 17-25 to 17-27), the prominent semicircular *lunette* above the doorway proper, comparable in importance to the triangular pediment of a Greco-Roman temple
- *Voussoirs* (FIG. 17-26), the wedge-shaped blocks that together form the *archivolts* of the arch framing the tympanum

- *Lintel* (FIG. 17-27), the horizontal beam above the doorway
- *Trumeau* (FIGS. 17-23 and 17-24), the center post supporting the lintel in the middle of the doorway
- *Jambs* (FIGS. 17-23 and 17-27), the side posts of the doorway

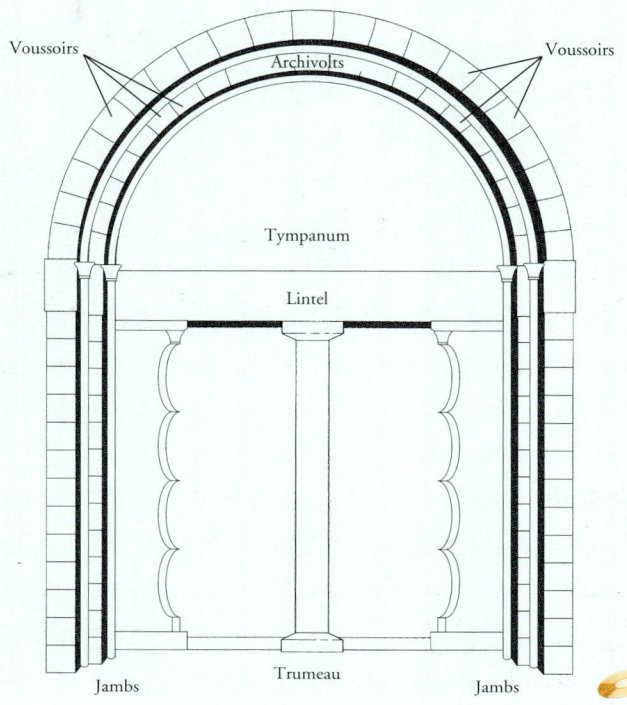

Many variations exist within the general style of Romanesque sculpture, as within Romanesque architecture. The figures of the Moissac tympanum contrast sharply with those of the reliefs previously examined. The extremely elongated bodies of the recording angels, the cross-legged dancing pose of Saint Matthew's angel, and the jerky, hinged movement of the Elders' heads are characteristic of the nameless Moissac master's style of representing the human figure. The zigzag and dovetail lines of the draperies, the bandlike folds of the torsos, the bending back of the hands against the body, and the wide cheekbones are also common features of this distinctive style. The animation of the individual figures, however, contrasts with the stately monumentality of the composition as a whole, producing a dynamic tension in the tympanum.

**A PROPHET AT THE DOOR** Below the tympanum are a richly decorated trumeau and elaborate door jambs with scalloped contours (FIG. 17-23), the latter a borrowing from Islamic architecture (see FIG. 13-12). On the trumeau's right face is a prophet (FIG. **17-24**) whom some identify as Jeremiah, others as Isaiah. Whoever the prophet is, he displays the scroll where his prophetic vision is written. His position below the apparition of Christ as the apocalyptic Judge is yet another instance of the pairing of Old and New Testament themes. This is in keeping with

an iconographic tradition established in Early Christian times (see "Jewish Subjects in Christian Art," Chapter 11, page 305).

The prophet's figure is very tall and thin, in the manner of the tympanum angels, and, like Matthew's angel, he executes a cross-legged step. The animation of the body reveals the passionate nature of the soul within. The flowing lines of the drapery folds ultimately derive from manuscript illumination and here play gracefully around the elegant figure. The long, serpentine locks of hair and beard frame an arresting image of the dreaming mystic. The prophet seems entranced by his vision of what is to come, the light of ordinary day unseen by his wide eyes.

Six roaring interlaced lions fill the trumeau's outer face (FIG. 17-23). The animal world was never far from the medieval mind. Kings and barons often were associated with animals thought to be the most fiercely courageous — for example, Richard the Lionheart, Henry the Lion, and Henry the Bear. Lions were the church's ideal protectors. In the Middle Ages, people believed lions slept with their eyes open. But the idea of placing fearsome images at the gateways to important places has a very ancient origin. The lions and composite monsters that guarded the palaces of Near Eastern and Mycenaean kings (see FIGS. 2-18, 2-21, and 4-20) and the panthers and leopards in Greek temple pediments (see FIG. 5-15) and Etruscan tombs (see FIG. 9-8) are the ancestors of the interlaced lions at Moissac.

**JUDGMENT DAY AT AUTUN** In 1132, the Cluniac bishop Étienne de Bage consecrated the Burgundian cathedral of Saint-Lazare (Saint Lazarus) at Autun. For its tympanum (FIG. **17-25**) he commissioned a dramatic vision of the Last Judgment, announced by four trumpet-blowing angels. In the tympanum's center, far larger than any other figure, is Christ, enthroned in a mandorla. He dispassionately presides over the separation of the Blessed from the Damned. At the left, an obliging angel boosts one of the Blessed into the heavenly city. Below, the souls of the dead line up to await their fate. Two of the men near the center of the lintel carry bags emblazoned with a cross and a shell. These are the symbols of pilgrims to Jerusalem and Santiago de Compostela. Those who had made the difficult journey would be judged favorably. To their right, three small figures beg an angel to intercede on their behalf. The angel responds by pointing to the Judge above. On the right side are those who will be condemned to Hell (see FIG. Intro-6). One poor soul is plucked from the earth by giant hands. Directly above, in the tympanum, is one of the most unforgettable renditions of the weighing of souls in the history of art. Angels and devils contest at the scales, each trying to manipulate the balance for or against a soul. Hideous demons guffaw and roar. Their gaunt, lined bodies, with legs ending in sharp claws, writhe and bend like long, loathsome insects. A devil, leaning from the dragon mouth of Hell, drags souls in, while, above him, a howling demon crams souls headfirst into a furnace. The resources of the Romanesque imagination, heated by a fearful faith, conjured up an appalling scene.

One can appreciate the terror the Autun tympanum must have inspired in the believers who passed beneath it as they entered the cathedral. Even those who could not read could, in the words of Bernard of Clairvaux, "read in the marble." For the literate, the Autun clergy composed explicit written warnings to reinforce the pictorial message, and had the words engraved in Latin on the tympanum. For example, beneath the weighing of souls, the inscription reads, "May this terror terrify those whom

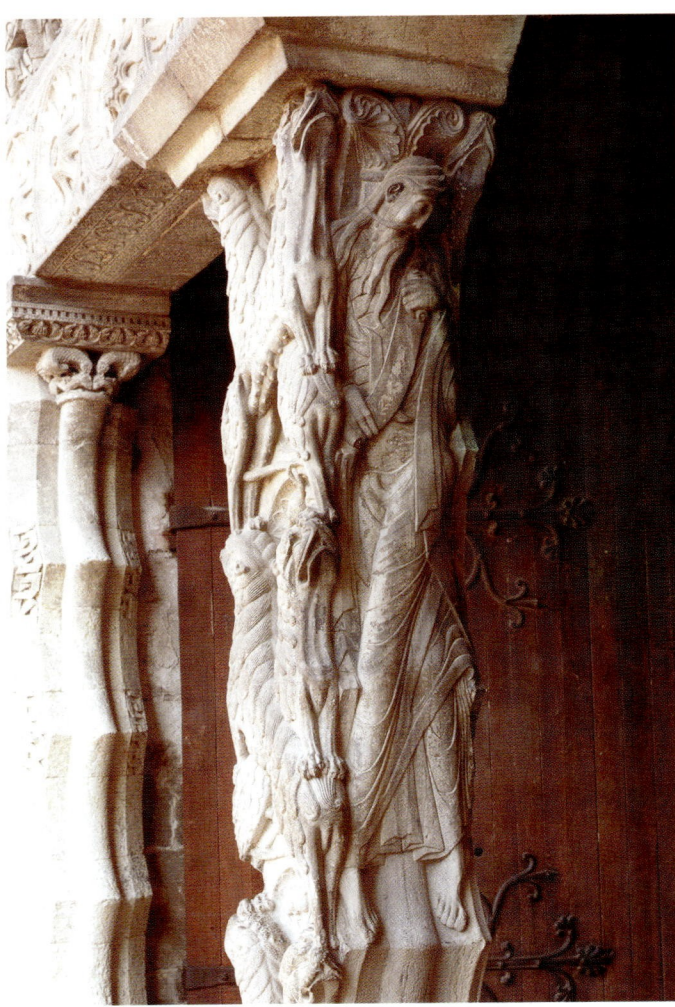

**17-24** Lions and Old Testament prophet (Jeremiah or Isaiah?), from the trumeau of the south portal of Saint-Pierre, Moissac, France, ca. 1115–1130. Marble, approx. life-size.

**17-25** GISLEBERTUS, Last Judgment, west tympanum of Saint-Lazare, Autun, France, ca. 1120–1135. Marble, approx. 21' wide at base.

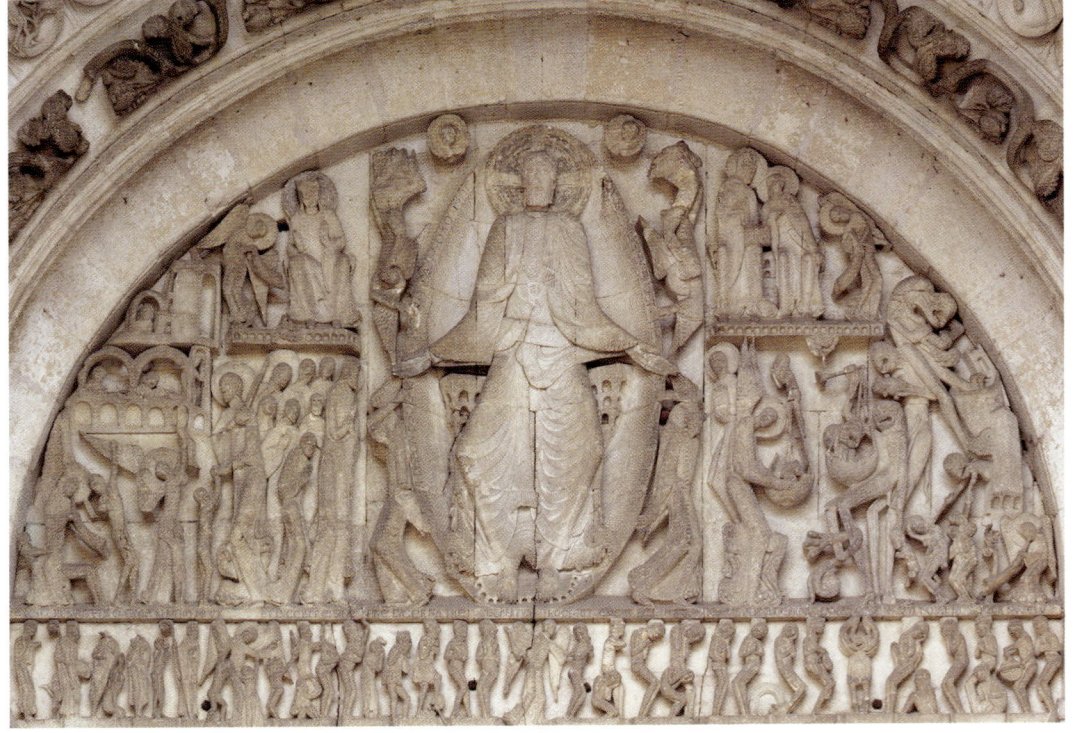

earthly error binds, for the horror of these images here in this manner truly depicts what will be."[2] The admonition echoes the sentiment expressed in the colophon of a mid-10th-century illustrated copy of Beatus of Liébana's *Commentary on the Apocalypse.* There, the painter Magius (teacher of Emeterius; see FIG. 16-10) explained the purpose of his work: "I have painted a series of pictures for the wonderful words of [the Apocalypse's] stories, so that the wise may fear the coming of the future judgment of the world's end."[3]

A second prominent inscription on the Autun portal, directly beneath the feet of Christ, names GISLEBERTUS as the sculptor. It has been suggested that Gislebertus placed his signature on the tympanum not to advertise his own fame but as a kind of request to spectators to pray for his salvation on Judgment Day. Pride in individual accomplishment was nonetheless an important factor in the increasing number of artists' signatures in Romanesque times, as witnessed by Wiligelmo's boast at Modena.

**VÉZELAY AND THE CRUSADES** Another large tympanum (FIG. **17-26**), this one at the church of La Madeleine (Mary Magdalene) at Vézelay, not far from Autun, depicts the Ascension of Christ and the Mission of the Apostles. As related in Acts 1:4–9, Christ foretold that the Twelve Apostles would receive the power of the Holy Spirit and become the witnesses of the truth of the Gospels throughout the world. The light rays emanating from Christ's hands represent the instilling of the Holy Spirit in the apostles (Acts 2:1–42) at the Pentecost (the seventh Sunday after Easter). The apostles, holding the Gospel books, receive their spiritual assignment, to preach the Gospel to all nations. The Christ figure is a splendid essay in calligraphic theme and variation. The drapery lines shoot out in rays, break into quick zigzag rhythms, and spin into whorls, wonderfully conveying the spiritual light and energy that flow from Christ over and into the equally animated apostles. The overall composition, as well as the detailed treatment of the figures, contrasts with the much more sedate representation of the Second Coming at Moissac, where almost all the figures are contained within a grid of horizontal and vertical lines. The sharp differences between the two tympana once again highlight the regional diversity of Romanesque art.

The world's heathen, the objects of the apostles' mission, appear on the lintel below and in eight compartments around the tympanum. The portrayals of the yet-to-be-converted constitute a medieval anthropological encyclopedia. Present are the legendary giant-eared Panotii of India, Pygmies (who require ladders to mount horses), and a host of other races, some characterized by a dog's head, others by a pig's snout, and still others by flaming hair. The assembly of agitated figures also includes hunchbacks, mutes, blind men, and lame men. Humanity, still suffering, awaits the salvation to come. The whole world is electrified by the promise of the ascended Christ, who looms above human misery and deformity. Again, as at Autun, as worshipers entered the portal, the tympanum established God's omnipotence and presented the Church as the road to salvation.

The Mission of the Apostles theme was an ideal choice for the Vézelay tympanum. Vézelay is more closely associated with the Crusades (see "The Crusades," page 466) than any other church in Europe. Pope Urban II had intended to preach the launching of the First Crusade at Vézelay in 1095, a generation before the tympanum was carved. In 1147, Bernard of Clairvaux called for the Second Crusade at Vézelay, and King Louis VII of France took up the cross there. In 1190, it was from Vézelay that King Richard the Lionheart of England and King Philip Augustus of France set out on the Third Crusade. The spirit of the Crusades determined in part the iconography of the Vézelay tympanum. The Crusades were a kind of "second mission of the apostles" to convert the infidel.

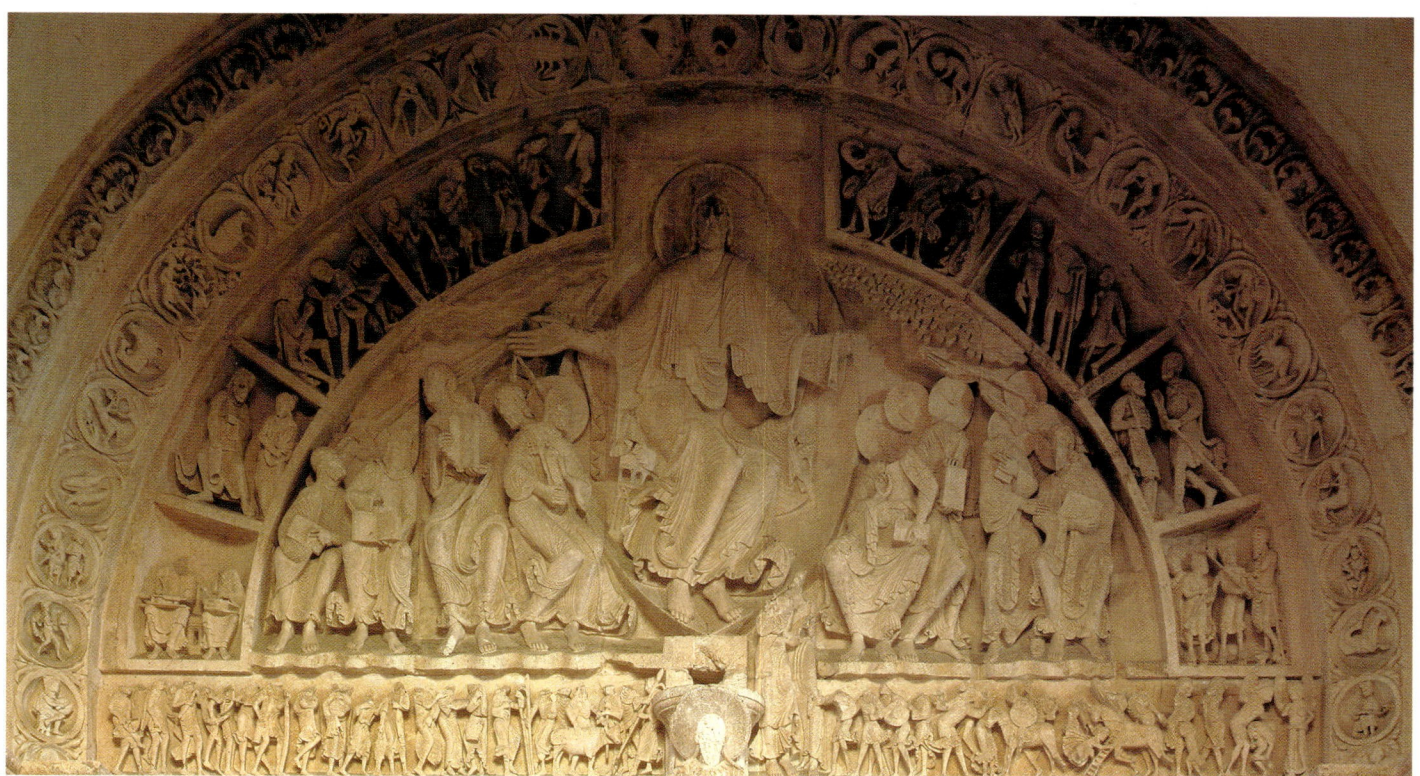

**17-26** Ascension of Christ and Mission of the Apostles, tympanum of the center portal of the narthex of La Madeleine, Vézelay, France, 1120–1132.

### The Crusades

B etween 1095, when Pope Urban II called for an assault on the Holy Land at the Council of Clermont, and 1190, Christians launched three great Crusades from France. The *Crusades* ("taking of the Cross") were mass armed pilgrimages, whose stated purpose was to wrest the Christian shrines of the Holy Land from Muslim control. Crusaders and pilgrims were bound by similar vows. They hoped not only to atone for sins and win salvation but also to glorify God and extend the power of the Christian Church. The joint action of the papacy and the barons—mostly French—in this type of holy war strengthened papal authority over the long run and created an image of Christian solidarity.

The joining of religious and secular forces in the Crusades was symbolically embodied in the Christian warrior, the fighting priest, or the priestly fighter. From the early medieval warrior evolved the Christian knight, who fought for the honor of God rather than in defense of his chieftain. The first and most typical of the crusading knights were the Knights Templar. After the Christian conquest of Jerusalem in 1099, they stationed themselves next to the Dome of the Rock (see FIG. 13-1), that is, on the site of Solomon's Temple, the source of their name. Their mission was to protect pilgrims visiting the recovered Christian shrines. Formally founded in 1118, the Knights Templar order was blessed by Bernard of Clairvaux, who gave them a rule of organization based on that of his own Cistercians. Bernard justified their militancy by declaring that "the knight of Christ" is "glorified in slaying the infidel . . . because thereby Christ is glorified," and the Christian knight then wins salvation. The Cistercian abbot saw the Crusades as part of the general reform of the Church and as the defense of the supremacy of Christendom. He himself preached the Second Crusade in 1147.

The Crusaders achieved little in the East. They established a few unstable kingdoms and princely states in Syria and the Holy Land, which the Muslims later overthrew and assimilated. But in western Europe, the Crusades' impact was much greater. They increased the power and prestige of the towns. Many communities purchased their charters from the barons when the barons needed to finance their campaigns in the Holy Land. A middle class of merchants and artisans arose to rival the power of the feudal lords and the great monasteries. Italian maritime towns such as Pisa (FIG. 17-17) thrived on the commercial opportunities presented by the transportation of Crusaders overseas. The Crusades, together with pilgrimages, contributed significantly to the growth of trade and the rise of cities in the Romanesque era.

**PROVENCE AND ROME** The core of what once was Roman Gaul is the French region of Provence ("the [Roman] Province"). It is rich in the remains of Roman art and architecture, and some of the ancient monuments directly inspired the articulation of Provençal church facades. One example is the mid-12th-century church of Saint-Trophîme (FIG. **17-27**) at Arles, a site described in the *Pilgrim's Guide to Santiago de Compostela* (see page 450).

Arles was an important Roman colony founded by Julius Caesar, and Saint Trophimus was an early bishop in Roman Gaul. The western entrance to the church has a projecting portal resembling a Roman arch "attached" to the building's otherwise simple facade. The frieze above the freestanding columns recalls the sculptured fronts of Late Antique sarcophagi. The figures in high relief between the columns emulate classical statuary.

**17-27** Central portal, west facade, Saint-Trophîme, Arles, France, mid-12th century.

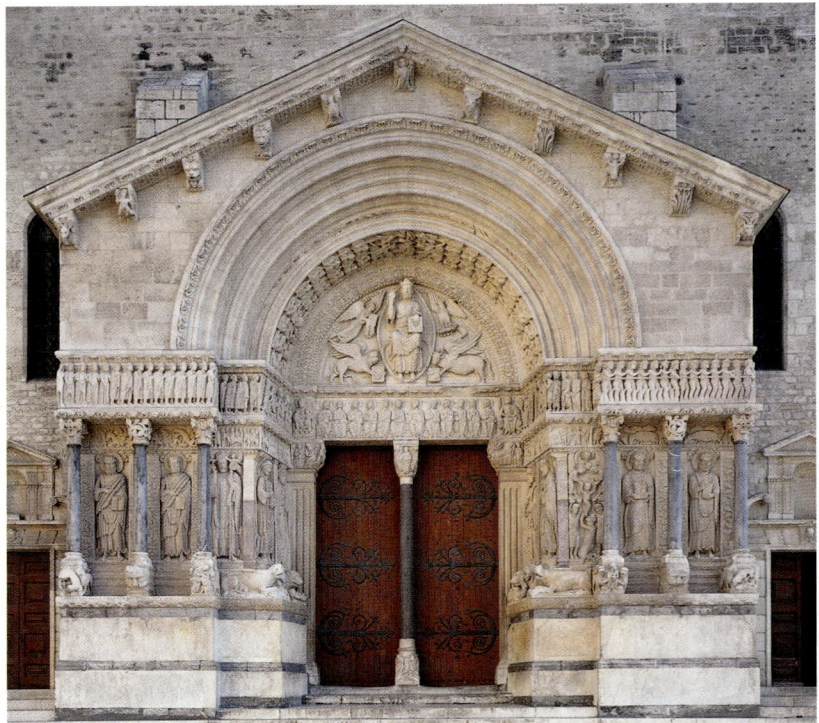

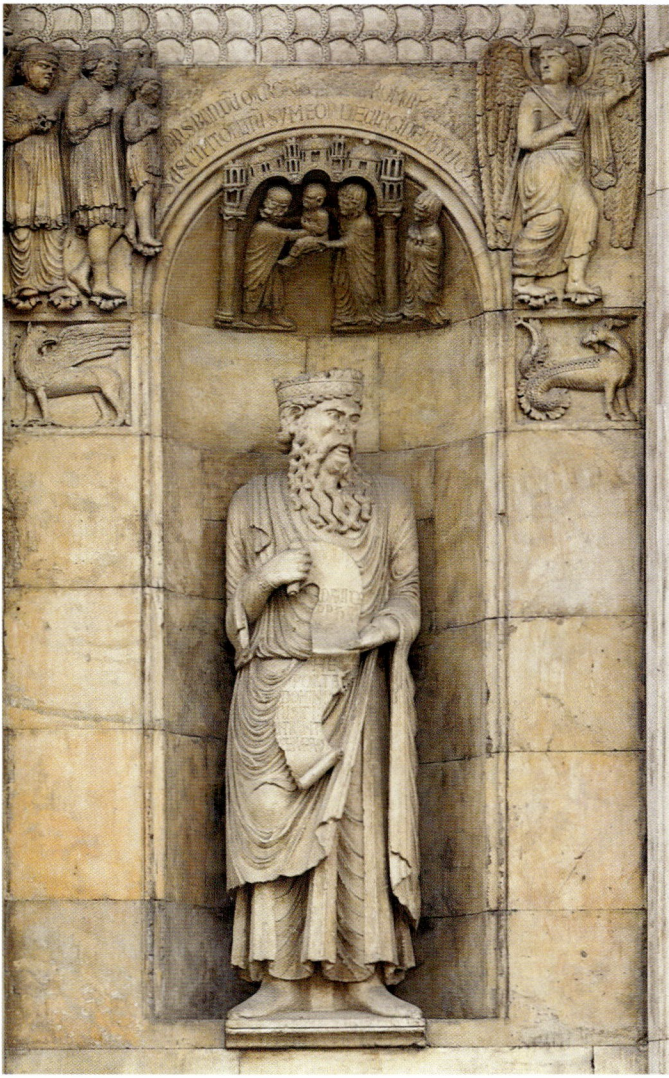

**17-28** BENEDETTO ANTELAMI, *King David*, statue in a niche on the west facade of Fidenza Cathedral, Fidenza, Italy, ca. 1180–1190. Marble, approx. life-size.

The subject matter is, however, strictly Christian and typically Romanesque. The tympanum shows Christ surrounded by the signs of the Four Evangelists. On the lintel, directly below him, the Twelve Apostles appear at the center of a continuous frieze depicting the Last Judgment. The outermost parts of the frieze represent the Saved (on Christ's right) and the Damned in the flames of Hell (on his left). Below, in the jambs and the front bays of the portals, stand grave figures of saints draped in classical garb. The sculptor gave pride of place to Saint Trophimus, the third figure from the left. Across the doorway is a depiction of the stoning of Saint Stephen, whose relics were housed at Arles. It is the only narrative relief on the facade's lower part.

The quiet stances of the saints of Saint-Trophîme contrast with the spinning, twisting, and dancing figures seen at Autun and Vézelay. The Arles draperies, modeled on ancient stone sculpture rather than medieval manuscripts and metalwork, are also less agitated and show nothing of the dexterous linear play of the earlier portals. But the statuesque treatment of the figures on the Arles jambs has parallels in French Gothic art. In fact, in the north of France, near Paris, sculptors already had begun to adorn

church portals with jamb figures that approximated freestanding statuary (see FIGS. 18-5 and 18-6).

**BENEDETTO ANTELAMI** The reawakening of interest in stone sculpture in the round also may be seen in northern Italy, where the sculptor BENEDETTO ANTELAMI was active in the last quarter of the 12th century. Several reliefs by his hand exist, including Parma Cathedral's pulpit and the portals of that city's baptistery. But his most unusual works are the monumental marble statues of two Old Testament figures he carved for the west facade of Fidenza Cathedral. Antelami's *King David* (FIG. **17-28**) seems confined within his niche. His elbows are kept close to his body. Absent is the weight shift that is the hallmark of classical statuary. Yet the sculptor's conception of this prophet is undeniably rooted in Greco-Roman art. One need only compare the Fidenza David with the prophet on the Moissac trumeau (FIG. 17-24), who also displays an unfurled scroll, to see how much the Italian sculptor freed his figure from its architectural setting. Antelami's classical approach to portraying biblical figures in stone was not immediately emulated. But the idea of placing freestanding statues in niches would be taken up again in Italy by Early Renaissance sculptors (see FIG. 21-7).

## Metalwork and Wood Sculpture

**RAINER OF HUY** Another Romanesque sculptor whose name is known is RAINER OF HUY, a bronzeworker from the Meuse River valley in Belgium, an area renowned for its metalwork. In 1118 he masterfully cast in a single piece the baptismal font (FIG. 17-29) for Notre-Dame-des-Fonts in Liège. The bronze basin rests on the foreparts of a dozen oxen, a reference to the "molten sea . . . on twelve oxen" cast in bronze for King Solomon's temple (1 Kings 7 : 23 – 25). The Old Testament story was thought to prefigure Christ's baptism (the oxen were equated with the Twelve Apostles), which is the central scene on Rainer's font.

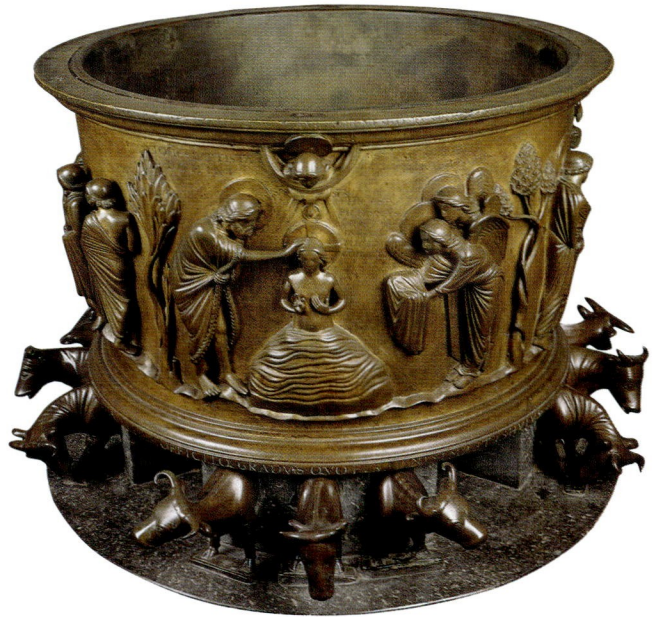

**17-29** RAINER OF HUY, *baptism of Christ*, baptismal font from Notre-Dame-des-Fonts, Liège, Belgium, 1107–1118. Bronze, 2′ 1″ high. Saint-Barthélémy, Liège.

The style is classicizing. The figures are softly rounded, with idealized bodies and faces and heavy clinging drapery. One figure (at the left in our photo) is even shown in a three-quarter view from the rear, a popular motif in classical art. Some of Rainer's figures, including Christ himself, are naked. In Romanesque art, the classical spirit lived on both north and south of the Alps.

**THE THRONE OF WISDOM** Despite the widespread use of stone relief sculptures to adorn Romanesque church portals, resistance to the creation of statues in the round—in any material—continued. The avoidance of anything that might be construed as an idol was still the rule, in keeping with the Second Commandment. Two centuries after Archbishop Gero commissioned a monumental wooden image of the crucified Christ for Cologne Cathedral (see FIG. 16-26), freestanding statues of Christ, the Virgin Mary, and the saints were still quite rare. The veneration of relics, however, brought with it a demand for small-scale images of the holy family and saints to be placed on the chapel altars of churches along the pilgrimage roads. Reliquaries in the form of saints (or parts of saints), tabletop crucifixes, and small wooden devotional images began to be produced in great numbers.

One of the most popular types, a specialty of the workshops of Auvergne, France, was a wooden statuette depicting the Virgin Mary with the Christ Child in her lap. The *Morgan Madonna* (FIG. **17-30**), so named because it once belonged to the financier and collector J. Pierpont Morgan, is one example. The type—known as the Throne of Wisdom, *sedes sapientia*e—is a western European freestanding version of the Byzantine Theotokos theme popular in icons and mosaics (see FIGS. 12-16 and 12-17). Christ holds a Bible in his left hand and raises his right arm in blessing (both hands are broken off). He is the embodiment of the divine wisdom contained in the Holy Scriptures. His mother, seated on a wooden chair, is in turn the Throne of Wisdom because her lap is the Christ Child's throne. As in Byzantine art, familiar to many Romanesque painters and sculptors, both Mother and Child sit rigidly upright and are strictly frontal, emotionless figures. But the intimate scale, the gesture of benediction, the once-bright coloring of the garments, and the soft modeling of the Virgin's face make the group seem much less remote than its counterparts in Byzantium.

**WIBALD'S SILVER RELIQUARY** Far more costly, but also created for private devotional purposes, is the reliquary of Saint Alexander (FIG. **17-31**), made in 1145 for Abbot Wibald of Stavelot in Belgium to house the hallowed pope's relics. The idealized head, which resembles portraits of youthful Roman emperors such as Augustus (see FIG. Intro-9) and Constantine (see FIG. 10-78), is almost life-size and was fashioned in beaten (repoussé) silver with bronze gilding for the hair. The saint wears a collar of jewels and enamel plaques around his neck. Enamels and gems also adorn the box on which the head is mounted. The reliquary rests on four bronze dragons—mythical animals of the kind that populated Romanesque cloister capitals. Not surprisingly, Bernard of Clairvaux was as critical of lavish church furnishings like the Alexander reliquary as he was of Romanesque cloister sculpture:

[Men's] eyes are fixed on relics covered with gold and purses are opened. The thoroughly beautiful image of some male or female saint is exhibited and that saint is believed to be the more holy the more highly colored the image is. People rush to kiss it, they are invited to donate, and they admire the beautiful more than they

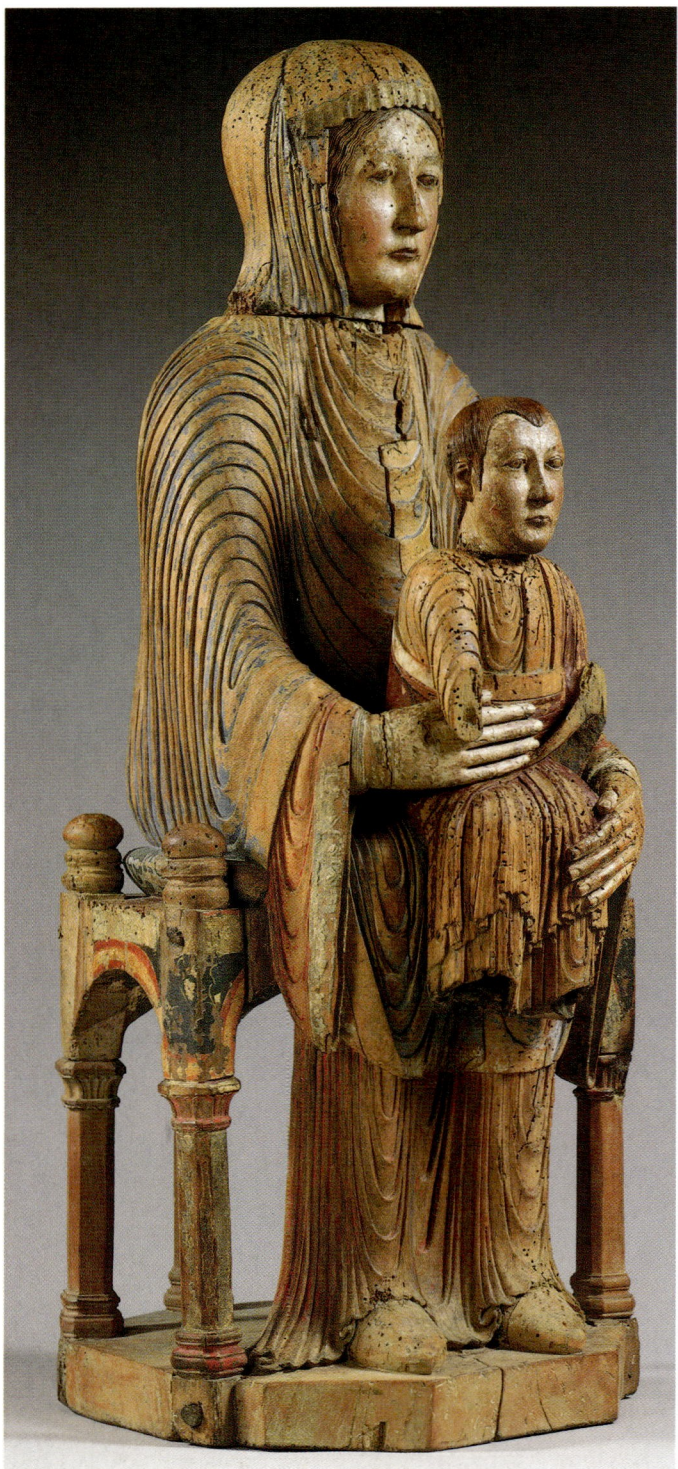

**17-30** Virgin and Child *(Morgan Madonna),* from the Auvergne, France, second half of 12th century. Painted wood, 2′ 7″ high. Metropolitan Museum of Art, New York (gift of J. Pierpont Morgan, 1916).

venerate the sacred. . . . O vanity of vanities, but no more vain than insane! The Church . . . dresses its stones in gold and it abandons its children naked. It serves the eyes of the rich at the expense of the poor.[4]

The central plaque on the front of the Stavelot reliquary depicts Pope Alexander II (r. 1061–1073). Saints Eventius and Theodolus flank him. The nine plaques on the other three sides

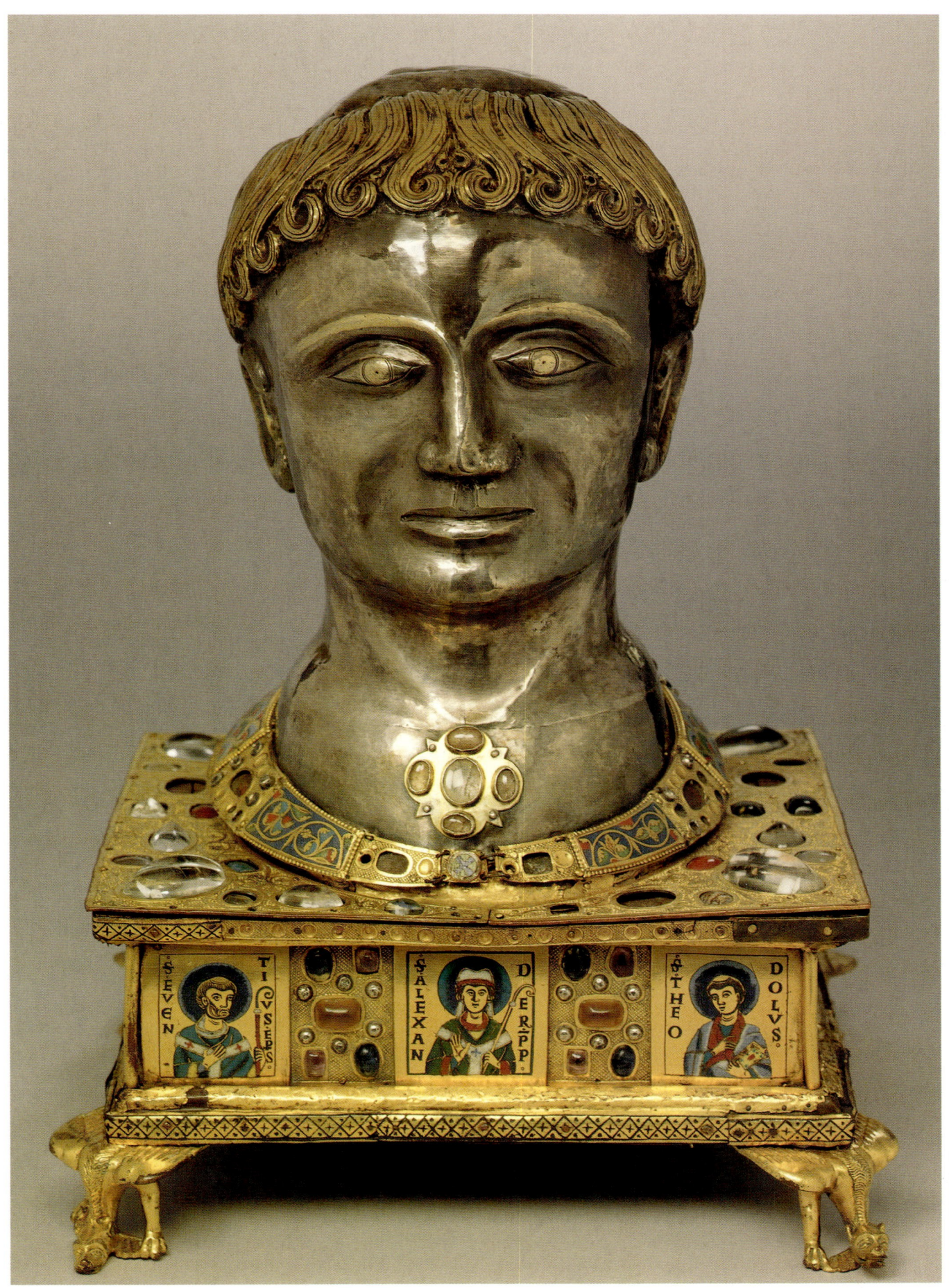

**17-31** Head reliquary of Saint Alexander, from Stavelot Abbey, Belgium, 1145. Silver repoussé (partly gilt), gilt bronze, gems, pearls, and enamel, approx. 1′ 5½″ high. Musées Royaux d'Art et d'Histoire, Brussels.

represent female allegorical figures—Wisdom, Piety, and Humility among them. Although a local artist produced these enamels in the Meuse River region, the models were surely Byzantine (compare FIG. 12-25). Saint Alexander's reliquary underscores the multiple sources of Romanesque art, as well as its stylistic diversity. Not since antiquity had people journeyed as extensively as they did in the Romanesque period, and artists regularly saw works of wide geographic origin. Abbot Wibald himself epitomizes the well-traveled 12th-century clergyman. He was abbot of Montecassino in southern Italy, took part in the Second Crusade, and was sent by Frederick Barbarossa (Holy Roman Emperor, r. 1152–1190) to Constantinople to arrange Frederick's wedding to the niece of the Byzantine emperor Manuel Comnenus.

## PAINTING

Unlike the practices of placing vaults over naves and aisles and decorating building facades with monumental stone reliefs, the art of painting did not need to be "revived" in the Romanesque period. Illuminated manuscripts had been produced in large numbers in the early Middle Ages, and even the Roman tradition of mural painting had never died, especially in Italy. But the quantity of preserved frescoes and illustrated books from the Romanesque era is unprecedented. As is true of Romanesque architecture and sculpture, painting of this period exhibits considerable regional and stylistic diversity. We discuss here a representative sample of Romanesque paintings from several regions in different media and formats.

### *Mural Painting*

**CHRISTIAN SPAIN**  In the eighth century, Muslim armies from North Africa defeated the Visigoths and occupied almost all of the Iberian Peninsula, bringing with them both Islam and Islamic art (see Chapter 13). But in northern Spain, the Muslim conquerors never completely controlled many areas, and Christianity and Christian art still flourished (see FIG. 16-10). In fact, Catalonia in northeastern Spain has more Romanesque mural paintings today than anywhere else.

One of the most impressive is the fresco (FIG. **17-32**), now in Boston, that once filled the apse of Santa María de Mur, a monastery church not far from Lérida. The formality, symmetry, and placement of the figures are Byzantine—compare the 6th-century apse of Saint Catherine's at Mount Sinai in Egypt (see FIG. 12-13) and the late-12th-century apse of the basilica at Monreale (see FIG. 12-24). But the Spanish artist rejected Byzantine mosaic in favor of direct painting on plaster-coated walls. And the iconographic scheme in the semidome of the apse is more closely tied to those of the Romanesque church portals of France (FIGS. 17-23 and 17-27).

In the Santa María de Mur fresco, Christ in a star-strewn mandorla is flanked by the signs of the Four Evangelists—the Apocalypse theme that so fascinated the Romanesque imagination. Seven lamps between Christ and the Evangelist signs symbolize the seven Christian communities where Saint John addressed his revelation (the Apocalypse) at the beginning of his book (Rev. 1:4, 12, 20). Below stand apostles, paired off in formal frontality, much like the saints on the facade of Saint-Trophîme at Arles

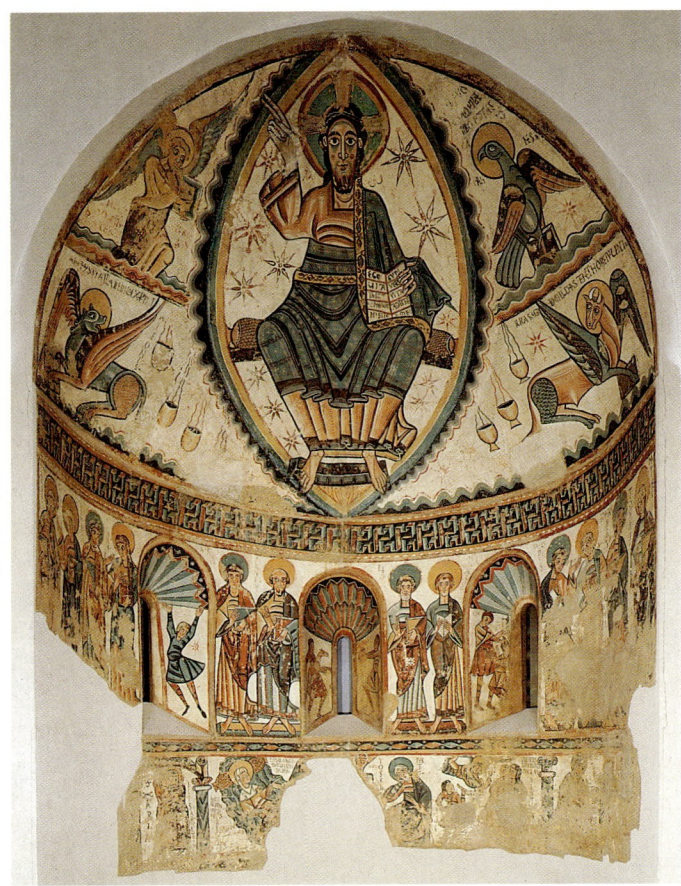

**17-32**  Christ in Majesty, apse fresco from Santa María de Mur, near Lérida, Spain, mid-12th century. 24′ × 22′. Museum of Fine Arts, Boston.

(FIG. 17-27), as well as in the apse at Monreale (see FIG. 12-24). The principal figures are rendered with partitioning of the drapery into volumes, here and there made tubular by local shading. The painter stiffened the irregular shapes of actual cloth into geometric patterns. The effect overall is one of simple, strong, and even blunt directness of statement, reinforced by harsh, bright color, appropriate for a powerful icon.

**ITALY AND BYZANTIUM**  The tradition of decorating church apses with imposing images of Christ and saints is a venerable one, going back to Early Christian art. So, too, is the idea of illustrating episodes from the Old and New Testaments above the nave arcade of basilican churches, as at Santa Maria Maggiore (see FIG. 11-13) and Sant'Apollinare Nuovo (see FIG. 11-17). In the late 11th century, Romanesque artists used fresco rather than mosaic to create framed scenes from Christ's life along both sides of the nave of Sant'Angelo in Formis, near Capua in southern Italy.

Our detail (FIG. **17-33**) shows the panel illustrating the entombment of Christ, with Mary cradling the head of her dead son as Joseph of Arimathea and Nicodemus lower him into his coffin. The weeping Saint John the Evangelist (with nimbus) watches. The fully modeled figures, the three-dimensional architectural setting, and the natural blue sky provide a sharp contrast with the Catalonian mural. But a comparison with the painted lamentation scene in Saint Pantaleimon in Macedonia (see FIG. 12-27)

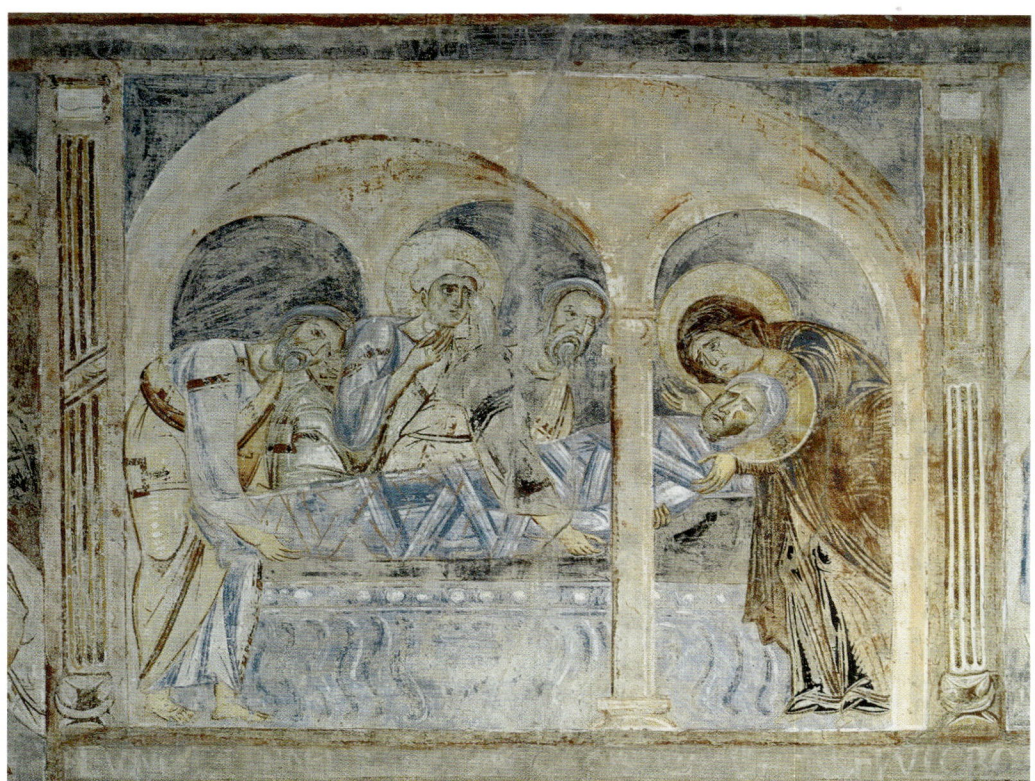

17-33 Entombment of Christ, fresco above the nave arcade, Sant'Angelo in Formis, near Capua, Italy, ca. 1085.

underscores that the Italian painters used Byzantine artworks as models. Sant'Angelo in Formis was constructed and decorated under the direction of Abbot Desiderius (later Pope Victor III) of Montecassino, the great monastery Saint Benedict founded in the sixth century. For the church at Montecassino, Desiderius imported artisans from Constantinople and instructed them to train his monks in mosaic and other arts. Sant'Angelo in Formis displays the work of these Italian pupils of Desiderius's Greek masters.

**PAINTED VAULTS** The Santa María de Mur and Sant'Angelo in Formis frescoes easily could be moved to an Early Christian basilica, where they would find ready homes in the apse and nave. But the murals of the Benedictine abbey church of Saint-Savin-sur-Gartempe (FIG. **17-34**) were inconceivable before the mastering of stone vaulting in the Romanesque period. Saint-Savin is a *hall church,* a church where the aisles are approximately the same height as the nave (as at Tournus, FIG. 17-3). The tall windows in the aisles provided more illumination to the nave than in churches that had low aisles and tribunes. This may explain why paintings (not true frescoes) decorate the nave's continuous barrel vault.

The subjects were all drawn from the Pentateuch, the opening five books of the Old Testament, in contrast to the New Testament themes of Sant'Angelo in Formis. They also bear little resemblance stylistically to the Byzantine-inspired murals of the Capuan and Catalonian churches. The elongated, agitated cross-legged figures of the Saint-Savin paintings are northern both in spirit and in form. They have stylistic affinities both to the reliefs of southern French portals and to some of the illuminated manuscripts discussed next.

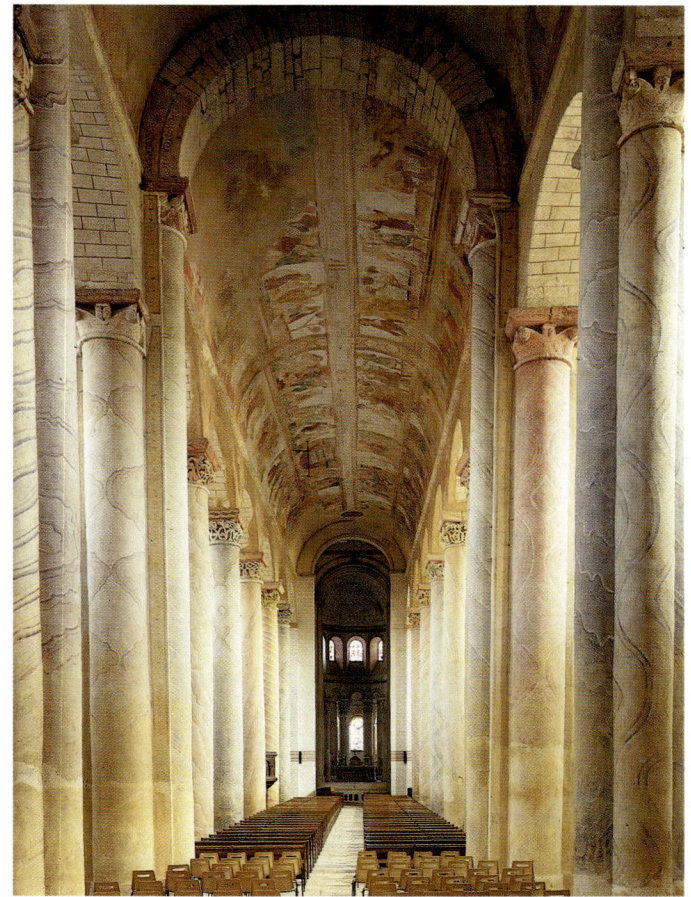

17-34 Nave of the abbey church, Saint-Savin-sur-Gartempe, France. Painted barrel vault, ca. 1100.

## Manuscript Illumination

**HILDEGARD'S VISIONS** The number and variety of illuminated manuscripts dating to the Romanesque era attest to the great demand for illustrated religious tomes in the abbeys of western Europe and to the extraordinary productivity of the scribes and painters, almost exclusively monks and nuns, working in the scriptoria of these isolated religious communities. One manuscript, however, stands apart from all the rest: the *Scivias (Know the Ways [Scite vias] of God)* of Hildegard of Bingen. Hildegard was a German nun and eventually the abbess of the convent at Disibodenberg in the Rhineland (see "Romanesque Countesses, Queens, and Nuns," page 473). The manuscript, lost in 1945, is known today only through a facsimile. The original probably was written and illuminated at the monastery of Saint Matthias at Trier between 1150 and Hildegard's death in 1179, but it is possible the book was produced at Bingen under Hildegard's supervision. The *Scivias* contains a record of Hildegard's vision of the divine order of the cosmos and of humankind's place in it. The vision came to her as a fiery light that poured into her brain from the open vault of heaven.

On the opening page (FIG. **17-35**) of the Trier manuscript, Hildegard sits within the monastery walls, with her feet resting on a footstool, in much the same way the Evangelists of the *Coronation* and *Ebbo Gospels* (see FIGS. 16-12 and 16-13) were portrayed. This Romanesque page is a link in a chain of author portraits that goes back to classical antiquity. The painter showed Hildegard experiencing her divine vision by depicting five long tongues of fire emanating from above and entering her brain, just as she describes the experience in the accompanying text. Hildegard immediately sets down what has been revealed to her on a wax tablet resting on her left knee. Nearby, the monk Volmar, Hildegard's confessor, copies into a book all she has written. Here, in a singularly dramatic context, is a picture of the essential nature of ancient and medieval book manufacture—individual scribes copying and recopying texts by hand (compare FIG. 16-10).

**KNIGHT VERSUS DRAGONS** One of the major Romanesque scriptoria was at the abbey of Cîteaux, France, mother church of the Cistercian order. Just before Bernard joined the monastery in 1112, the monks completed work on an illuminated copy of Saint Gregory's *Moralia in Job*. It is an example of Cistercian illumination before Bernard's passionate opposition to figural art in monasteries led in 1134 to a Cistercian ban on elaborate paintings in manuscripts. After 1134, full-page illustrations were prohibited, and even initial letters had to be nonfigurative and of a single color.

The historiated initial we reproduce (FIG. **17-36**) clearly would have been in violation of Bernard's ban if it had not been painted before his prohibitions took effect. A knight, his squire, and two roaring dragons form an intricate letter *R*, the initial

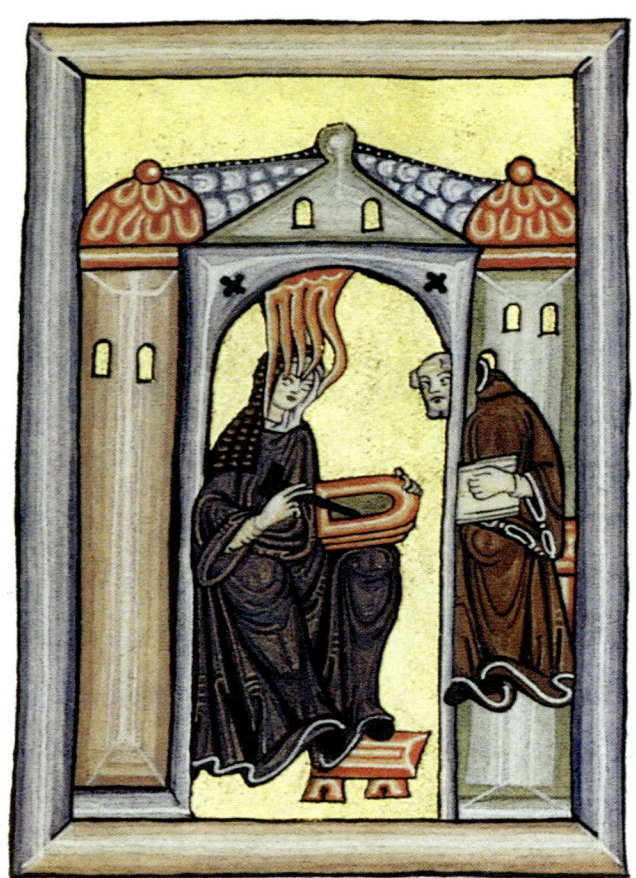

**17-35** The vision of Hildegard of Bingen, detail of a facsimile of a lost folio in the *Scivias* by Hildegard of Bingen, from Trier or Bingen, Germany, ca. 1050–1179. Formerly in Hessische Landesbibliothek, Wiesbaden.

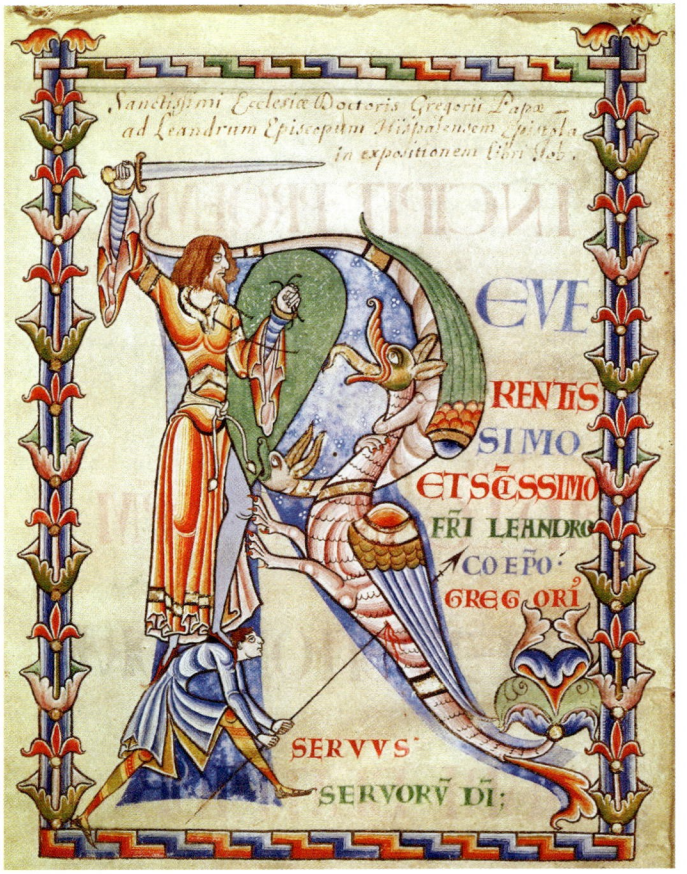

**17-36** Initial *R* with knight fighting a dragon, folio 4 verso of the *Moralia in Job*, from Cîteaux, France, ca. 1115–1125. Ink and tempera on vellum, 1′ 1¾″ × 9¼″. Bibliothèque Municipale, Dijon.

## Romanesque Countesses, Queens, and Nuns

Romanesque Europe was still a man's world, but women could and did have power and influence. Countess Matilda of Canossa (1046–1115), who ruled Tuscany after 1069, was sole heiress of vast holdings in northern Italy. She was a key figure in the political struggle between the popes and the German emperors who controlled Lombardy. With unflagging resolution she defended Pope Gregory's reforms and at her death willed most of her lands to the papacy.

More famous and more powerful was Eleanor of Aquitaine (1122–1204), wife of Henry II of England. She married Henry after her marriage to Louis VII, king of France, was annulled. She was queen of France for 15 years and queen of England for 35 years. During that time she bore three daughters and five sons. Two became kings—Richard I (Lionheart) and John. She prompted her sons to rebel against their father, so Henry imprisoned her. Released at Henry's death, she lived on as dowager queen, managing England's government and King John's holdings in France.

Of quite different stamp was Hildegard of Bingen (1098–1179), the most prominent nun of the 12th century and one of the greatest religious figures of the Middle Ages. Hildegard was born into an aristocratic family that owned large estates in the German Rhineland. At a very early age she began to have visions. When she was eight, her parents placed her in the Benedictine *double monastery* (for monks *and* nuns) at Disibodenberg. She became a nun at 15. In 1141, God instructed Hildegard in a vision to disclose her visions to the world. Before then she had revealed them only to close confidants at the monastery. One of these was the monk Volmar, and Hildegard chose to dictate her visions to him (FIG. 17-35) for posterity. No less a figure than Bernard of Clairvaux certified in 1147 that her visions were authentic. Archbishop Heinrich of Mainz joined him in endorsing Hildegard. In 1148, the Cistercian pope Eugenius III formally authorized Hildegard "in the name of Christ and Saint Peter to publish all that she had learned from the Holy Spirit." At this time Hildegard became the abbess of a new convent built for her near Bingen. As reports of Hildegard's visions spread, kings, popes, barons, and prelates sought her counsel. All of them were attracted by her spiritual insight into the truth of the mysteries of the Christian faith.

In addition to her visionary works—the most important is the *Scivias* (FIG. 17-35)—Hildegard also wrote two scientific treatises. *Physica* is a study of the natural world, and *Causae et curae (Causes and Cures)* is a medical encyclopedia. Hildegard also composed the music and wrote the lyrics of 77 songs, which appeared under the title *Symphonia*.

Hildegard was the most famous of all Romanesque nuns, but she was by no means the only learned woman of her age. A younger contemporary, the abbess Herrad (d. 1195) of Hohenberg, Austria, was also the author of an important medieval encyclopedia. Herrad's *Hortus deliciarum (Garden of Delights)* is a history of the world intended for instructing the nuns under her supervision, but it was more widely read.

---

letter of the salutation *Reverentissimo*. This page is the opening of Gregory's letter to "the very reverent" Leandro, Bishop of Seville. The knight is a slender, regal figure who raises his shield and sword against the dragons while the squire, crouching beneath him, runs a lance through one of the monsters. Although the duel between knight and dragons was intended as an allegory of the spiritual struggle of monks, Bernard's opposition to this kind of illumination is clear from his condemnation of carvings of monstrous creatures and "fighting knights" on contemporary cloister capitals (see "Bernard of Clairvaux," page 461).

Ornamented initials go back to the Hiberno-Saxon period (see FIG. 16-8), but here the artist translated the theme into Romanesque terms. This page may be a reliable picture of a medieval baron's costume. The typically Romanesque banding of the torso and partitioning of the folds (especially the servant's skirts) are evident, but the master painter deftly avoided stiffness and angularity. The partitioning actually accentuates the knight's verticality and elegance and the thrusting action of his servant. The flowing sleeves add a spirited flourish to the swordsman's gesture. The knight, handsomely garbed, cavalierly wears no armor and aims a single stroke with proud disdain, unmoved by the ferocious dragons lunging at him.

**MASTER HUGO** The *Bury Bible,* produced at the Bury Saint Edmunds abbey in England around 1135, exemplifies the sumptuous illustration common to the large Bibles produced in wealthy Romanesque abbeys not subject to the Cistercian ban. Such costly books lent prestige to monasteries that could afford them (see "Medieval Books," Chapter 16, page 425).

The artist responsible for the *Bury Bible* is known: MASTER HUGO, who was also a sculptor and metalworker. He joins Bernardus Gelduinus (FIG. 17-21), Wiligelmo (FIG. 17-22), Gislebertus (FIG. 17-25), Benedetto Antelami (FIG. 17-28), and Rainer of Huy (FIG. 17-29) in the small but growing company of Romanesque artists who signed their works or whose names were recorded. In the 12th century, artists, illuminators as well as sculptors, increasingly began to identify themselves. Although most medieval artists remained anonymous, the contrast of the Romanesque period with the early Middle Ages is striking. Hugo seems to have been a secular artist, one of the emerging class of professional artists and artisans who depended for their livelihood on commissions from well-endowed monasteries. These artists resided in towns rather than within secluded abbey walls, and they traveled frequently to find work. They were the exception, however, and the typical Romanesque scribes and illuminators continued to be monks and nuns working anonymously in the service of God. The Benedictine Rule, for example, specified that "craftsmen in the monastery . . . should pursue their crafts with all humility after the abbot has given permission."

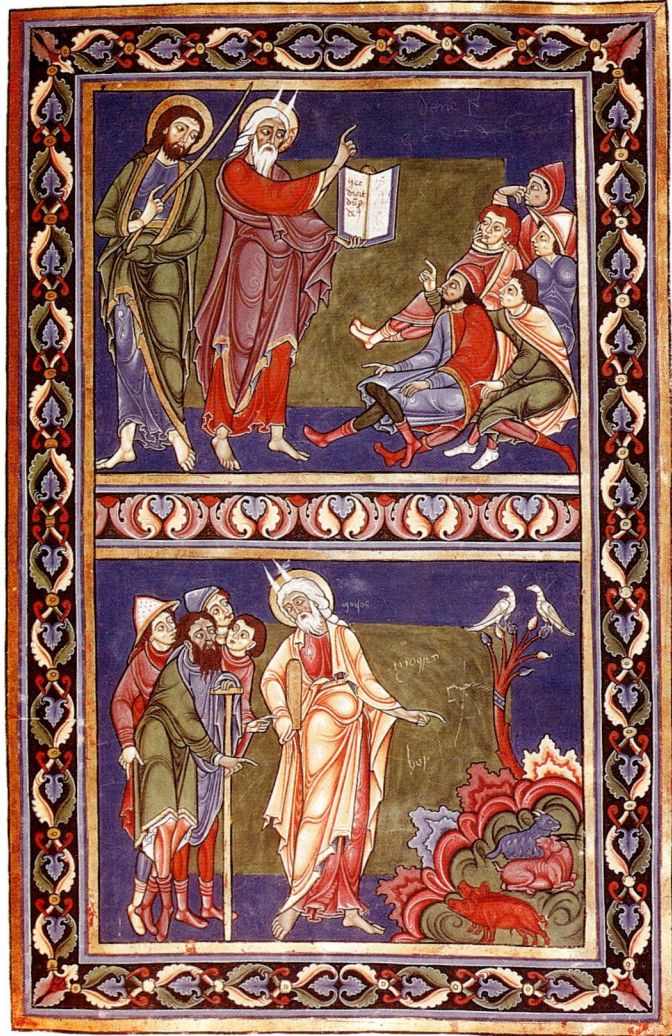

**17-37** MASTER HUGO, *Moses expounding the Law,* folio 94 recto of the *Bury Bible,* from Bury Saint Edmunds, England, ca. 1135. Ink and tempera on vellum, approx. 1′ 8″ × 1′ 2″. Corpus Christi College, Cambridge.

Our page of the *Bury Bible* (FIG. **17-37**) shows two scenes from Deuteronomy framed by symmetrical leaf motifs in softly glowing harmonized colors. The upper register depicts Moses and Aaron proclaiming the law to the Israelites. Master Hugo represented Moses with horns, consistent with Saint Jerome's translation of the Hebrew word that also means "rays" (compare Michelangelo's similar conception of the Hebrew prophet, FIG. 22-10). The lower panel portrays Moses pointing out the clean and unclean beasts. The gestures are slow and gentle and have quiet dignity. The figures of Moses and Aaron seem to glide. This presentation is quite different from the abrupt emphasis and spastic movement seen in earlier Romanesque paintings. The movements of the figures appear more integrated and smooth. Yet patterning remains in the multiple divisions of the draped limbs, the lightly shaded volumes connected with sinuous lines and ladderlike folds. Hugo still thought of the drapery and body as somehow the same. The frame has a quite definite limiting function, and the painter carefully fit the figures within it.

**THE PRINCE OF SCRIBES** The *Eadwine Psalter* is the masterpiece of an English monk known as EADWINE THE SCRIBE. It contains 166 illustrations, and many are variations of those in

the Carolingian *Utrecht Psalter* (see FIG. 16-14). The last page (FIG. **17-38**), however, presents a rare picture of a Romanesque artist at work. The "portrait" of Eadwine—it is probably a generic type and not a specific likeness—also has models in the past. It is in the long tradition of author portraits in ancient and medieval manuscripts (see FIGS. 16-7, 16-12, 16-13, and 17-35), although the true author of the *Eadwine Psalter* is King David. Eadwine exaggerated his importance by likening his image to that of an Evangelist writing his gospel and by including an inscription within the inner frame that identifies him and proclaims that he is a "prince among scribes." He declares that, due to the excellence of his work, his fame will endure forever and that he can offer his book as an acceptable gift to God. Eadwine, like other Romanesque sculptors and painters who signed their works, may have been concerned for his fame, but these artists, whether monks or laity, were not yet aware of the concepts of fine art and fine artist. To them, their work existed not for its own sake but for God's.

The style of the Eadwine portrait is related to that of the *Bury Bible,* but, although the patterning is still firm (notably in the cowl and the thigh), the drapery falls more softly and follows the movements of the body beneath it. Here, the arbitrariness of many Romanesque painted and sculpted garments yielded slightly, but clearly, to the requirements of more naturalistic representation. The Romanesque artist's instinct for decorating the surface remained, as is apparent in the gown's whorls and spirals. But, significantly, these were painted in very lightly so that they would not conflict with the functional lines that contain them.

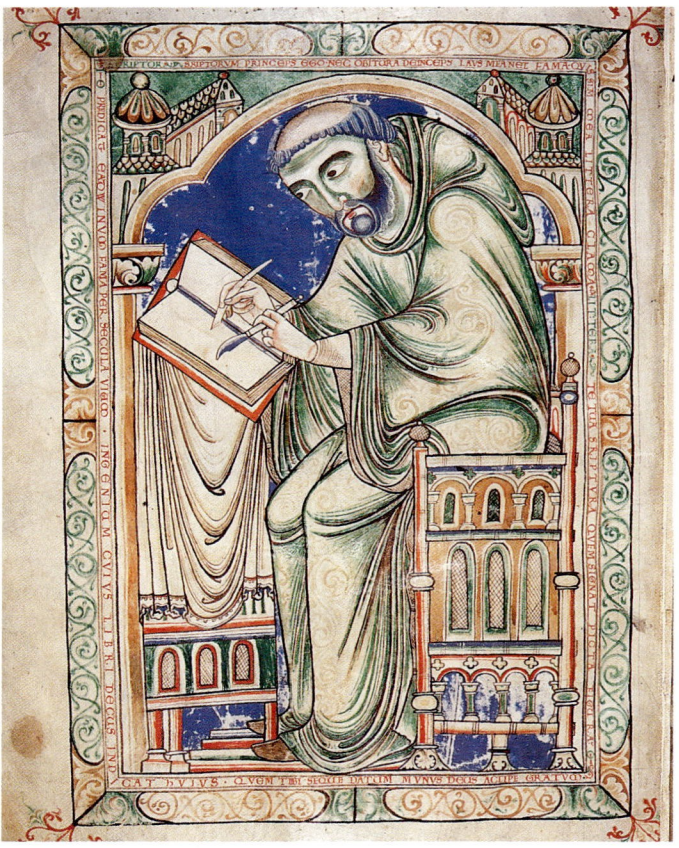

**17-38** EADWINE THE SCRIBE(?), Eadwine the Scribe at work, folio 283 verso of the *Eadwine Psalter,* ca. 1160–1170. Ink and tempera on vellum. Trinity College, Cambridge.

**THE CONQUEST OF ENGLAND** This account of Romanesque painting concludes with a work that is *not* a painting. Nor is the so-called *Bayeux Tapestry* (FIGS. **17-39** and **17-40**) a woven tapestry. It is, instead, an embroidered fabric made of wool sewn on linen (see "Embroidery and Tapestry," page 476). But the *Bayeux Tapestry* is closely related to Romanesque manuscript illumination. Its borders are populated by the kinds of real and imaginary animals found in contemporaneous books, and an explanatory Latin text sewn in thread accompanies many of the pictures.

Some 20 inches high and about 230 feet long, the *Bayeux Tapestry* is a continuous, friezelike, pictorial narrative of a crucial moment in England's history and of the events that led up to it. The Norman defeat of the Anglo-Saxons at Hastings in 1066 brought England under the control of the Normans, uniting all of England and much of France under one rule. The dukes of Normandy became the kings of England. Commissioned by Bishop Odo, the half brother of the conquering Duke William, the embroidery may have been sewn by women at the Norman court. Many art historians, however, believe it was the work of English

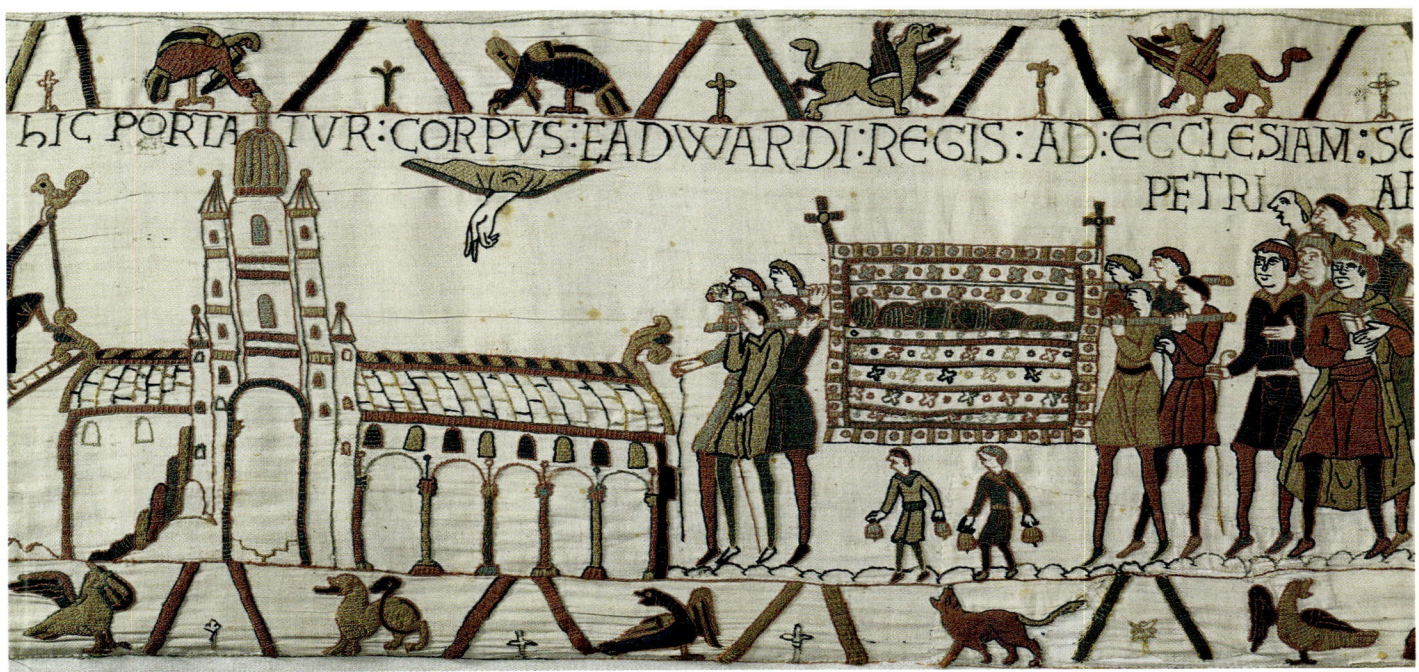

**17-39** Funeral procession to Westminster Abbey, detail of the *Bayeux Tapestry,* from Bayeux Cathedral, Bayeux, France, ca. 1070–1080. Embroidered wool on linen, 1′ 8″ high (entire length of fabric 229′ 8″). Centre Guillaume le Conquérant, Bayeux.

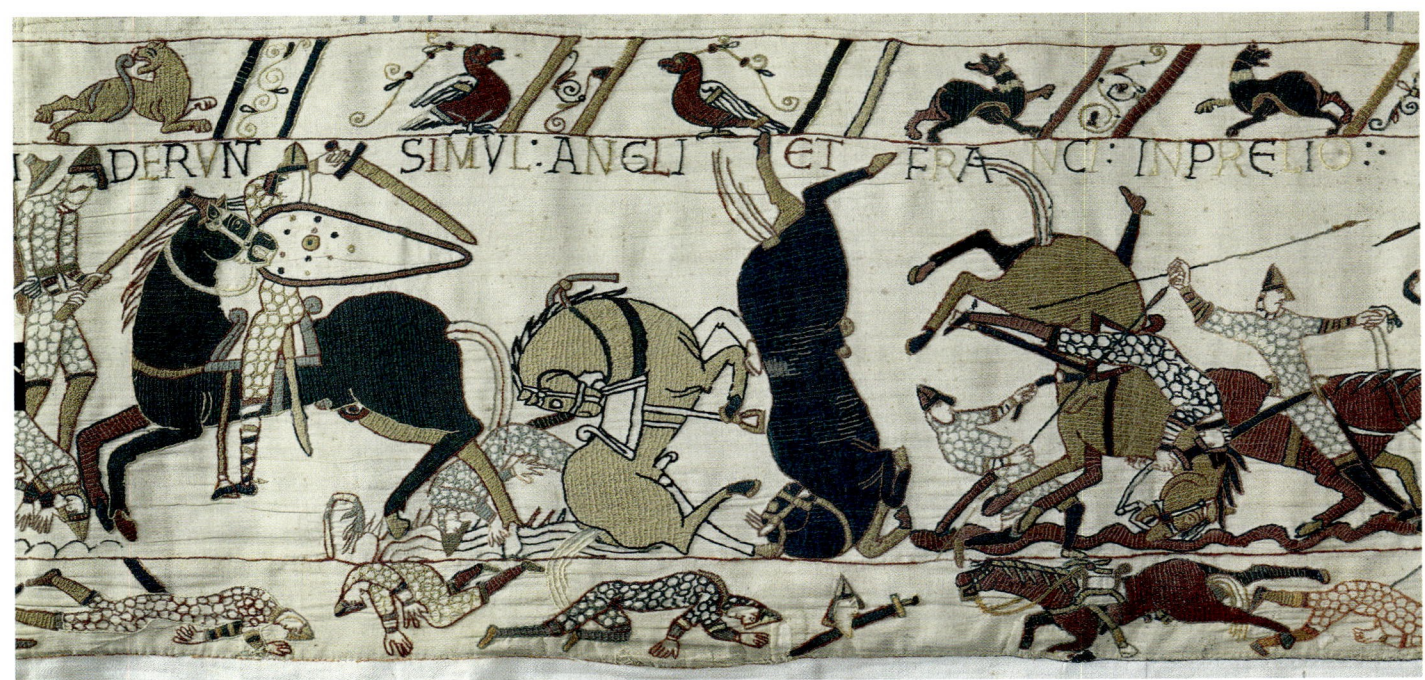

**17-40** Battle of Hastings, detail of the *Bayeux Tapestry,* from Bayeux Cathedral, Bayeux, France, ca. 1070–1080. Embroidered wool on linen, 1′ 8″ high (entire length of fabric 229′ 8″). Centre Guillaume le Conquérant, Bayeux.

## Embroidery and Tapestry

The most famous embroidery of the Middle Ages is, ironically, known as the *Bayeux Tapestry* (FIGS. 17-39 and 17-40). Embroidery and tapestry are related, but different, means of decorating textiles. *Tapestry* designs are woven on a loom as part of the fabric. *Embroidery* patterns are sewn with threads.

The needleworkers who fashioned the *Bayeux Tapestry* were either Norman or English women. They employed eight colors of dyed wool—two varieties of blue, three shades of green, yellow, buff, and terracotta red—and two kinds of stitches. In *stem stitching,* short overlapping strands of thread form jagged lines.

*Laid-and-couched work* creates solid blocks of color. In the latter technique, the needleworker first lays down a series of parallel and then a series of cross stitches. Finally, the stitcher tacks down the cross-hatched threads using couching (knotting). On the *Bayeux Tapestry,* the natural linen color was left exposed for the background, human flesh, building walls, and other "colorless" design elements. Stem stitches define the contours of figures and buildings and delineate interior details, such as facial features, body armor, and roof tiles. Laid-and-couched work was employed for clothing, animal bodies, and other solid areas.

stitchers in Kent, where Odo was earl after the Norman conquest. Odo donated the work to Bayeux Cathedral (hence its nickname), but it is uncertain whether it was originally intended for display in the church's nave, where the theme would have been a curious choice.

The circumstances leading to the Norman invasion of England are well documented. In 1066, Edward the Confessor, the Anglo-Saxon king of England, died. The Normans believed Edward had recognized William of Normandy as his rightful heir. But the crown went to Harold, earl of Wessex, the king's Anglo-Saxon brother-in-law, who had sworn an oath of allegiance to William. The betrayed Normans, descendants of the seafaring Vikings, boarded their ships, crossed the English Channel, and crushed Harold's forces.

We illustrate two episodes of the epic tale as represented in the *Bayeux Tapestry.* The first detail (FIG. 17-39) depicts King Edward's funeral procession. The hand of God points the way to the church where he was buried—Westminster Abbey, consecrated on December 28, 1065, just a few days before Edward's death. The church was one of the first Romanesque buildings erected in England, and the embroiderers took pains to record its main features, including the imposing crossing tower and the long nave with tribunes. Here William was crowned king of England on Christmas Day, 1066. (The coronation of every English monarch since then also has occurred in Westminster Abbey.)

The second detail (FIG. 17-40) shows the Battle of Hastings in progress. The Norman cavalry cuts down the English defenders. The lower border is filled with the dead and wounded, although the upper register continues the animal motifs of the rest of the embroidery. The Romanesque artist co-opted some of the characteristic motifs of Greco-Roman battle scenes. Note, for example, the horses with twisted necks and contorted bodies (compare FIG. 5-69). But the artists rendered the figures in the Romanesque manner. Linear patterning and flat color replaced classical three-dimensional volume and modeling in light and dark hues.

The *Bayeux Tapestry* is unique in Romanesque art in that it depicts an event in full detail at a time shortly after it occurred, recalling the historical narratives of ancient Roman art. The Norman embroidery often has been likened to the scroll-like frieze of the Column of Trajan (see FIG. 10-42). Like the Roman account, the story told on the *Bayeux Tapestry* is the conqueror's version of history, a proclamation of national pride. And as on Trajan's Column, the narrative is not confined to battlefield successes. It is a complete chronicle of events. Included are the preparations for war, with scenes depicting the felling and splitting of trees for ship construction; the loading of equipment onto the vessels; the cooking and serving of meals; and so forth. In this respect, the *Bayeux Tapestry* is the most *Roman*-esque of all Romanesque artworks.

## CONCLUSION

With the death of the last Ottonian emperor in 1024, the greatest patrons of art and architecture in Europe became the monasteries, especially those along the pilgrimage routes leading to the tomb of Saint James at Santiago de Compostela in Spain. In the Romanesque age, immense churches with stone vaults rose throughout Europe, didactic relief sculptures adorned church portals and cloisters, and the relics of saints were housed in gold and silver and enamel reliquaries.

Not everyone embraced the new artistic trends. The Cistercians in particular shunned elaborate churches designed to accommodate multitudes of pilgrims, and banned figural adornment in their sacred books. Bernard of Clairvaux, the influential Cistercian abbot who was later beatified, protested as fervently against the decoration of monastic churches with sculpture as he preached Crusades to capture the Holy Land from the Muslims. But for most clergy and laity alike, the appeal of the new churches with their sculpted reliefs and glittering relics was irresistible. Each region had a characteristic style, but the revival of monumental architecture and sculpture was Europe-wide.

1000

  HUGH OF SEMUR, 1024–1109, ABBOT OF CLUNY

  COUNTESS MATILDA OF CANOSSA, 1046–1115

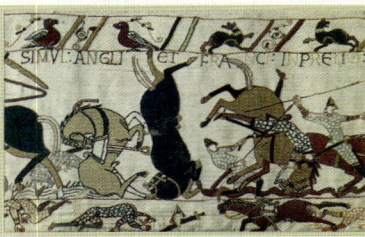

1050

  FINAL SEPARATION OF LATIN (ROMAN) CHURCH FROM THE BYZANTINE (GREEK ORTHODOX) CHURCH, 1054

  NORMAN CONQUEST OF SOUTHERN ITALY AND SICILY, 1060–1101

  NORMAN CONQUEST OF ENGLAND (BATTLE OF HASTINGS), 1066

1075

  POPE GREGORY VII (1073–1085) ASSERTS SPIRITUAL SUPREMACY OF PAPACY OVER KINGS AND EMPERORS, 1075

  BERNARD OF CLAIRVAUX, CA. 1090–1153

  POPE URBAN II PREACHES THE FIRST CRUSADE, 1095

  HILDEGARD OF BINGEN, 1098–1179

  CISTERCIAN ORDER FOUNDED, 1098

  CRUSADERS CAPTURE JERUSALEM, 1099

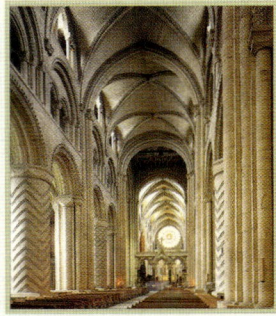

1100

  FOUNDATION OF THE KNIGHTS TEMPLAR, 1118

  ELEANOR OF AQUITAINE, 1122–1204

  KING LOUIS VII OF FRANCE, R. 1137–1180

  GERVASE OF CANTERBURY, 1141–1210

  KORAN TRANSLATED INTO LATIN, 1143

  SECOND CRUSADE, 1147–1148

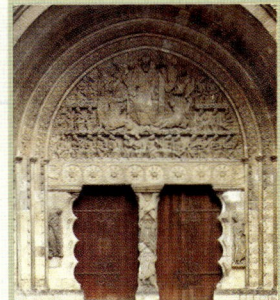

1150

  FREDERICK BARBAROSSA, HOLY ROMAN EMPEROR, R. 1152–1190

  KING HENRY II PLANTAGENET OF ENGLAND, R. 1154–1189

  KING PHILIP AUGUSTUS OF FRANCE, R. 1180–1223

  KING RICHARD THE LIONHEART OF ENGLAND, R. 1189–1199

  THIRD CRUSADE, 1190–1192

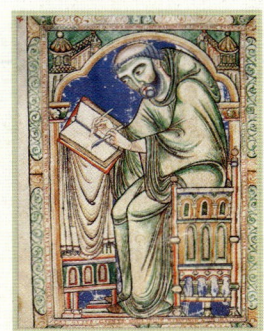

1200

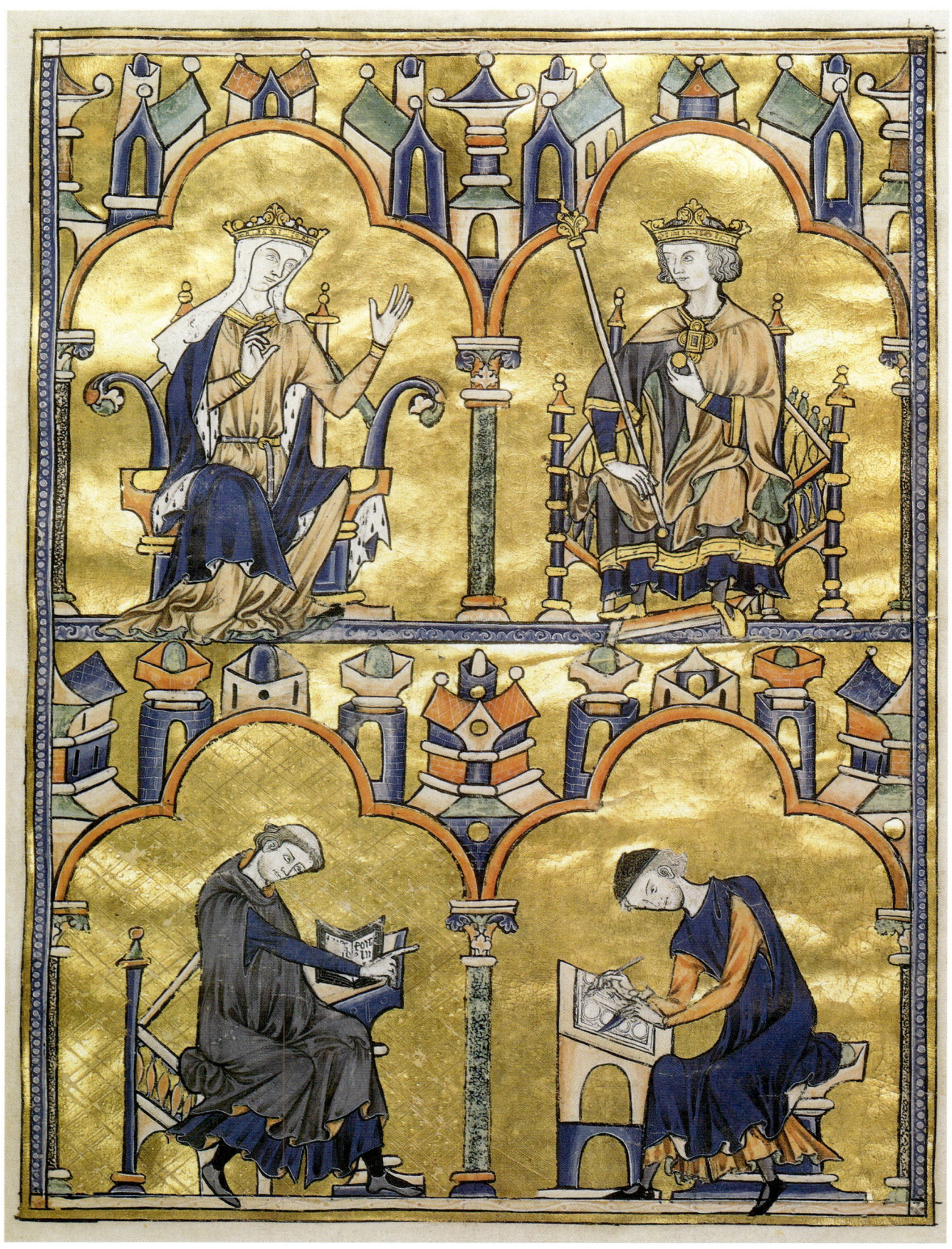

Blanche of Castile, Louis IX, and two monks, dedication page (folio 8 recto) of a moralized Bible, from Paris, France, 1226–1234. Ink, tempera, and gold leaf on vellum, 1′ 3″ × 10$\frac{1}{2}$″. Pierpont Morgan Library, New York.

# 18

# THE AGE OF GREAT CATHEDRALS

## GOTHIC ART

In the mid-16th century, Giorgio Vasari (1511–1574), the "father of art history," used "Gothic" as a term of ridicule to describe late medieval art and architecture. For him, Gothic art was "monstrous and barbarous," invented by the Goths.[1] With the publication of his famous treatise, Vasari codified for all time the notion already advanced by the early Renaissance artist Lorenzo Ghiberti (1378–1455), who, in his *Commentarii,* characterized the Middle Ages as a period of decline. The humanists of the Italian Renaissance, who placed Greco-Roman art on a pedestal, believed that the uncouth Goths were responsible not only for the downfall of Rome but also for the destruction of the classical style in art and architecture. They regarded "Gothic" art with contempt and considered it ugly and crude.

In the 13th and 14th centuries, however, when the Gothic style was the rage in most of Europe, especially north of the Alps, contemporary commentators considered Gothic buildings *opus modernum* (modern work) or *opus francigenum* (French work). They recognized that the great cathedrals towering over their towns displayed an exciting and new building and decoration style—and that the style originated in France. Clergy and the lay public alike regarded their new cathedrals not as distortions of the classical style but as images of the City of God, the Heavenly Jerusalem, which they were privileged to build on earth.

The Gothic style first appeared in northern France around 1140. In southern France (see FIG. 17-27) and elsewhere in Europe, the Romanesque style still flourished. But by the 13th century, the opus modernum of the region around Paris had spread throughout western Europe, and in the next century further still (MAP **18-1**). The Cathedral of Saint Vitus in Prague (Czech Republic), for example, begun in 1344, closely emulated French Gothic architecture.

Although it became an internationally acclaimed style, Gothic art was, nonetheless, a regional phenomenon. To the east and south of Europe, the Islamic and Byzantine styles still held sway. And many regional variants existed within European Gothic, just as distinct regional styles characterized the Romanesque period. Gothic began and ended at different dates in different places. When the banker Jacques

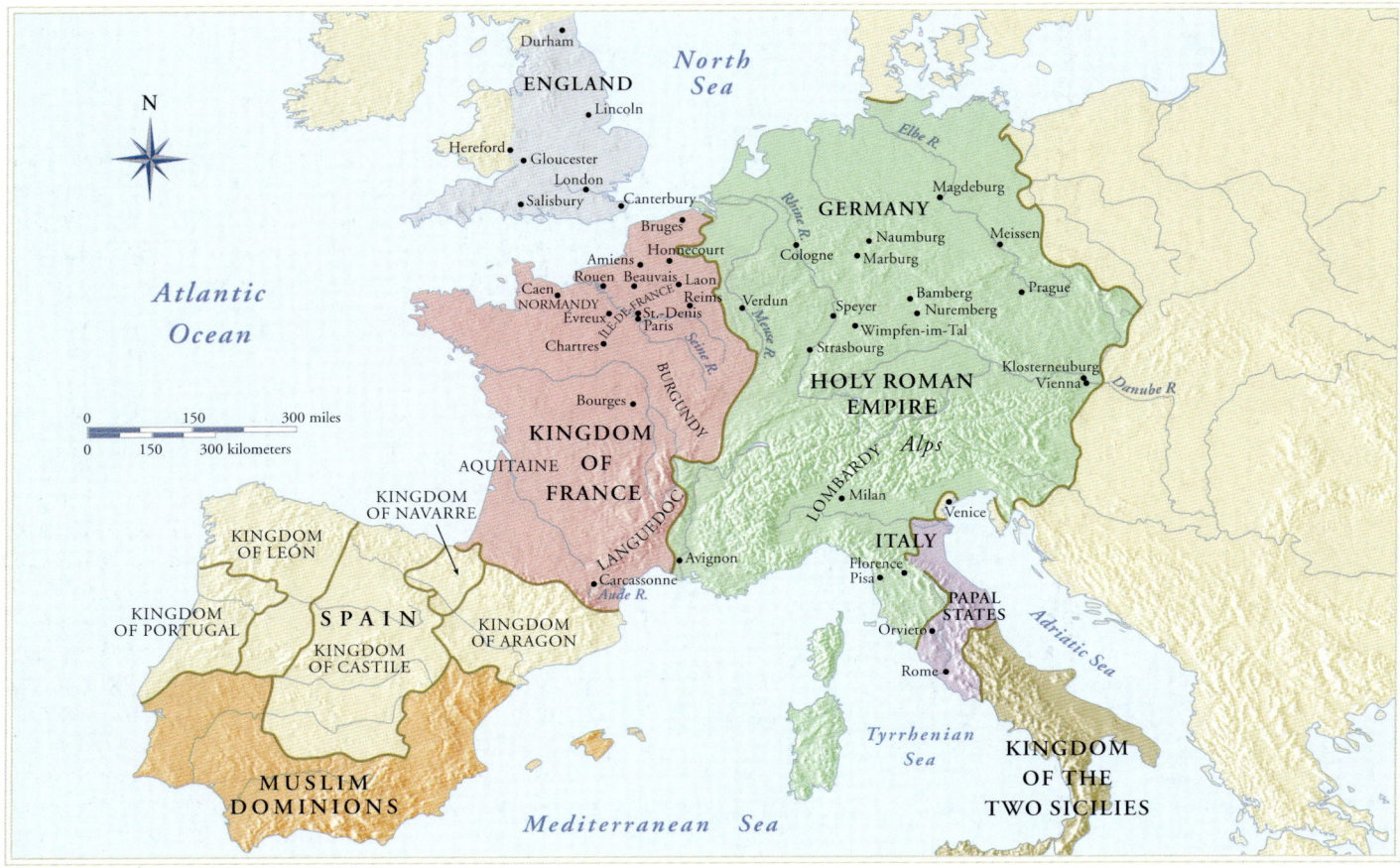

**MAP 18-1** Europe about 1200.

Coeur built his home in Bourges (FIG. 18-28) in the Gothic style in the mid-15th century, classicism already reigned supreme in Italy. While the Gothic church of Saint-Maclou (FIG. 18-25) was under construction in Rouen in the early years of the 16th century, Michelangelo was painting the ceiling of the Sistine Chapel in Rome.

**TURMOIL AND CHANGE** The Gothic period was a time of great prosperity yet also one of turmoil in Europe. In 1337, the Hundred Years' War began, shattering the peace between France and England. In the 14th century, a great plague, the Black Death, swept over western Europe and killed at least a quarter of its people. From 1378 to 1417, opposing popes resided in Rome and in Avignon in southern France during the political-religious crisis known as the Great Schism (see Chapter 19).

Above all, the Gothic age was a time of profound change in European society. The focus of both intellectual and religious life shifted definitively from monasteries in the countryside and pilgrimage churches to rapidly expanding secular cities with great new cathedrals reaching to the sky. In these new Gothic urban centers, prosperous merchants made their homes, universities run by professional guilds of scholars formed, and minstrels sang of chivalrous knights and beautiful maidens at royal "courts of love." Although the papacy was at the height of its power and knights throughout Europe still gathered to wage Crusades against the Muslims, the independent secular nations of modern Europe were beginning to take shape. Foremost among them was France.

# FRENCH GOTHIC

## Architecture and Architectural Decoration

**SUGER AND SAINT-DENIS** On June 11, 1144, King Louis VII of France, Queen Eleanor of Aquitaine, royal court members, and a host of distinguished clergy, including five archbishops, converged on the Benedictine abbey church of Saint-Denis for the dedication of its new east end (FIGS. **18-1** and **18-2**). Saint Dionysius (Denis in French) was the apostle who brought Christianity to Gaul and who died a martyr's death there in the third century. The church, just a few miles north of Paris, housed the saint's tomb and those of the French kings, as well as the crimson military banner said to have belonged to Charlemagne. The Carolingian basilica was France's royal church, the very symbol of the monarchy (just as Speyer Cathedral [see FIG. 17-9] was the burial place of the German rulers of the Holy Roman Empire). But the old building was in disrepair and had become too small to accommodate the growing number of pilgrims. Its abbot, Suger, also believed it was of insufficient grandeur to serve as the official church of the French kings (see "Abbot Suger and the Rebuilding of Saint-Denis," page 481). Thus, Suger began to rebuild the church in 1135 by erecting a new west facade with sculptured portals. In 1140, work began on the east end. Suger died before he could remodel the nave, but he attended the 1144 dedication of the new choir, ambulatory, and radiating chapels.

## Abbot Suger and the Rebuilding of Saint-Denis

Abbot Suger of Saint-Denis (1081–1151) rose from humble parentage to become the right-hand man of both Louis VI (r. 1108–1137) and Louis VII (r. 1137–1180). When the latter, accompanied by his queen, Eleanor of Aquitaine, left to join the Second Crusade (1147–1149), Suger served as regent of France. From his youth, Suger wrote, he had dreamed of the possibility of embellishing the church in which French monarchs had been buried since the ninth century. In 1122, he became abbot of Saint-Denis and within 15 years began rebuilding the monastery founded in the Merovingian age. In Suger's time, the power of the French kings, except for scattered holdings, extended over an area not much larger than the Île-de-France, the region centered on Paris. But the kings had pretensions to rule all of France. Suger aimed to increase the prestige both of his abbey and of the monarchy by rebuilding France's royal church in grand fashion.

Suger wrote three detailed treatises about his activities as abbot of Saint-Denis. He recorded that he summoned masons and artists from many regions to help design and construct his new church. And in one important passage he described the special qualities of the new east end (FIGS. 18-1 to 18-3) dedicated in 1144:

> [I]t was cunningly provided that—through the upper columns and central arches which were to be placed upon the lower ones built in the crypt—the central nave of the old [Carolingian church] should be equalized, by means of geometrical and arithmetical instruments, with the central nave of the new addition; and, likewise, that the dimensions of the old side-aisles should be equalized with the dimensions of the new side-aisles, except for that elegant and praiseworthy extension in [the form of] a circular string of chapels, by virtue of which the whole [church] would shine with the wonderful and uninterrupted light of most sacred windows, pervading the interior beauty.[1]

The abbot's brief discussion of Saint Denis's new ambulatory and chapels is key to the understanding of Early Gothic architecture. But he wrote at much greater length about his church's glorious golden and gem-studded furnishings. Here, for example, is Suger's description of the *altar frontal* (hanging in front of the altar) in the choir:

> Into this panel, which stands in front of [Saint Denis's] most sacred body, we have put . . . about forty-two marks of gold [and] a multifarious wealth of precious gems, hyacinths, rubies, sapphires, emeralds and topazes, and also an array of different large pearls.[2]

The costly furnishings and the light-filled space caused Suger to "delight in the beauty of the house of God" and "called [him] away from external cares." The new church made him feel as if he was "dwelling . . . in some strange region of the universe which neither exists entirely in the slime of the earth nor entirely in the purity of Heaven." In Suger's eyes, then, his splendid new church, permeated with light and outfitted with gold and precious gems, was a way station on the road to Paradise, which "transported [him] from this inferior to that higher world."[3] He regarded a lavish investment in art as a spiritual aid, not as an undesirable distraction for the pious monk, as did Bernard of Clairvaux (see "Bernard of Clairvaux," Chapter 17, page 461). Suger's forceful justification of art in the church set the stage for the proliferation of costly stained-glass windows and sculptures in the great cathedrals of the Gothic age.

[1] Erwin Panofsky, trans., *Abbot Suger on the Abbey Church of Saint-Denis and Its Art Treasures,* 2nd ed. (Princeton: Princeton University Press, 1979), 101.

[2] Ibid., 55.

[3] Ibid., 65.

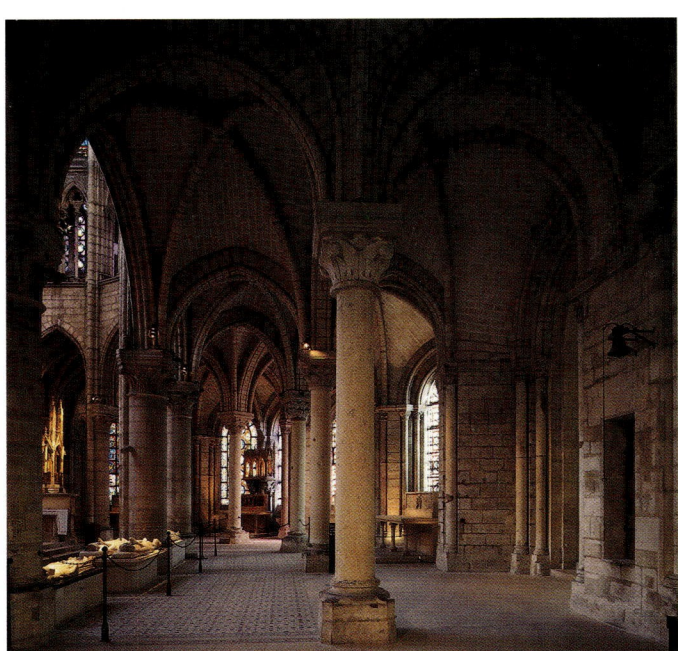

**18-1** Ambulatory and radiating chapels, abbey church, Saint-Denis, France, 1140–1144.

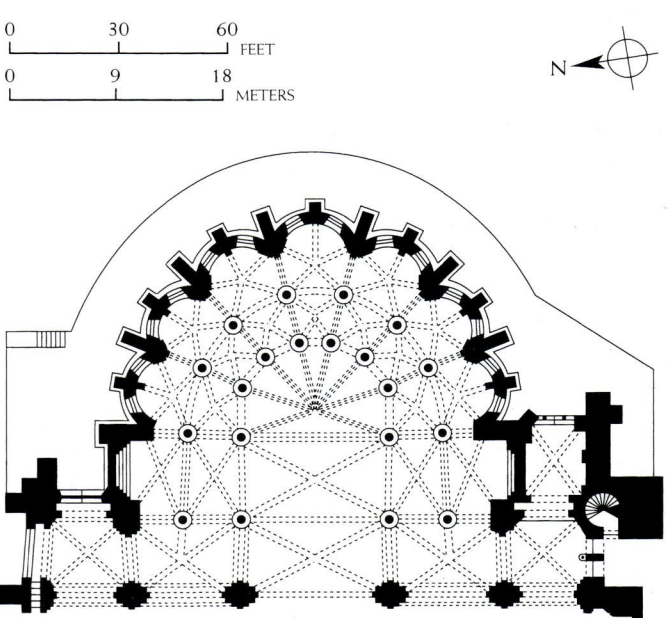

**18-2** Plan of the east end, abbey church, Saint-Denis, France, 1140–1144 (after Sumner Crosby).

## The Gothic Rib Vault

The ancestors of the Gothic *rib vault* are the Romanesque vaults found at Caen (see FIG. 17-13), Durham (see FIG. 17-15), and elsewhere. The rib vault's distinguishing feature is the crossed, or diagonal, arches under its groins, as seen in the Saint-Denis ambulatory and chapels (FIG. 18-3; compare FIG. 18-18). These arches form the *armature,* or skeletal framework, for constructing the vault. Gothic vaults generally have more thinly vaulted *webs* between the arches than Romanesque vaults have. But the chief difference between Romanesque and Gothic rib vaults is the *pointed arch,* an integral part of the Gothic skeletal armature. Pointed arches were first widely used in Sasanian architecture (see FIG. 2-28), and Islamic builders later adopted them. French Romanesque architects (see FIG. 17-8) borrowed the form from Muslim Spain and passed it to their Gothic successors. Pointed arches allowed Gothic builders to make the crowns of all the vault's arches approximately the same level, regardless of the space to be vaulted. The Romanesque architects could not achieve this with their semicircular arches.

Our diagrams illustrate this key difference. In diagram *a,* the rectangle *ABCD* is an oblong nave bay to be vaulted. *AC* and *DB* are the diagonal ribs; *AB* and *DC,* the transverse arches; and *AD* and *BC,* the nave arcade's arches. If the architect uses semicircular arches (*AFB,*

*BJC,* and *DHC),* their radii and, therefore, their heights (*EF, IJ,* and *GH),* will be different, because the height of a semicircular arch is determined by its width. The result will be a vault (diagram *b*) with higher transverse arches (*DHC*) than the arcade's arches (*CJB*). The vault's crown (*F*) will be still higher. If the builder uses pointed arches, the transverse (*DLC*) and arcade (*BKC*) arches can have the same heights (*GL* and *IK* in diagram *a*). The result will be a Gothic rib vault (diagram *c*), where the points of the arches (*L* and *K*) are at the same level as the vault's crown (*F*).

A major advantage of the Gothic vault is its flexibility, which permits the vaulting of compartments of varying shapes, as may be seen at Saint-Denis (FIGS. 18-2 and 18-3). Pointed arches also channel the weight of the vaults more directly downward than do semicircular arches. The vaults, therefore, require less buttressing to hold them in place, in turn permitting the opening up of the walls with large windows beneath the arches. Because pointed arches also lead the eye upward, they make the vaults appear taller than they actually are. In our diagrams, the crown (*F*) of both the Romanesque (diagram *b*) and Gothic (diagram *c*) vaults is the same height from the pavement, but the Gothic vault seems taller. Both the physical and visual properties of rib vaults with pointed arches aided Gothic builders in their quest for soaring height in church interiors.

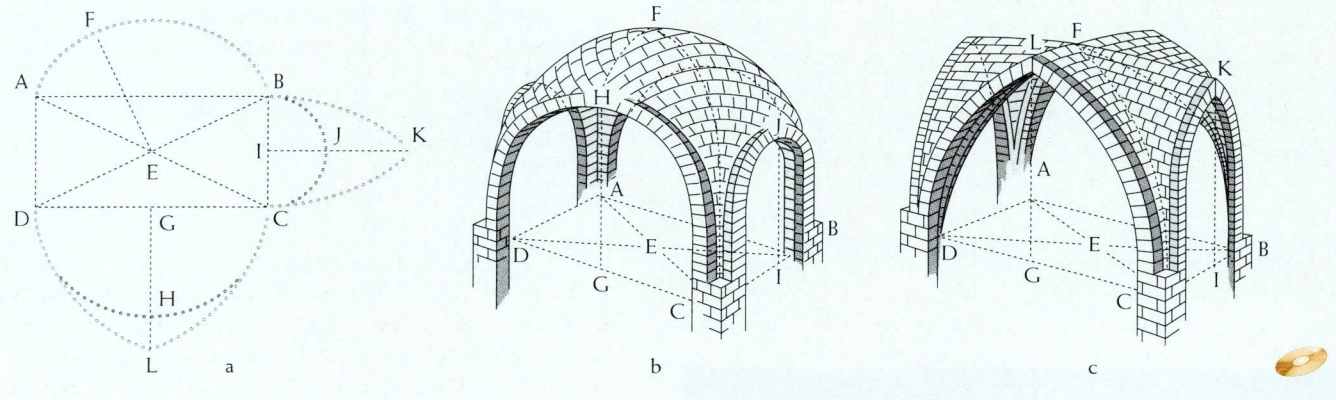

18-3 Vaults of the ambulatory and radiating chapels of the choir, abbey church, Saint-Denis, France, 1140–1144.

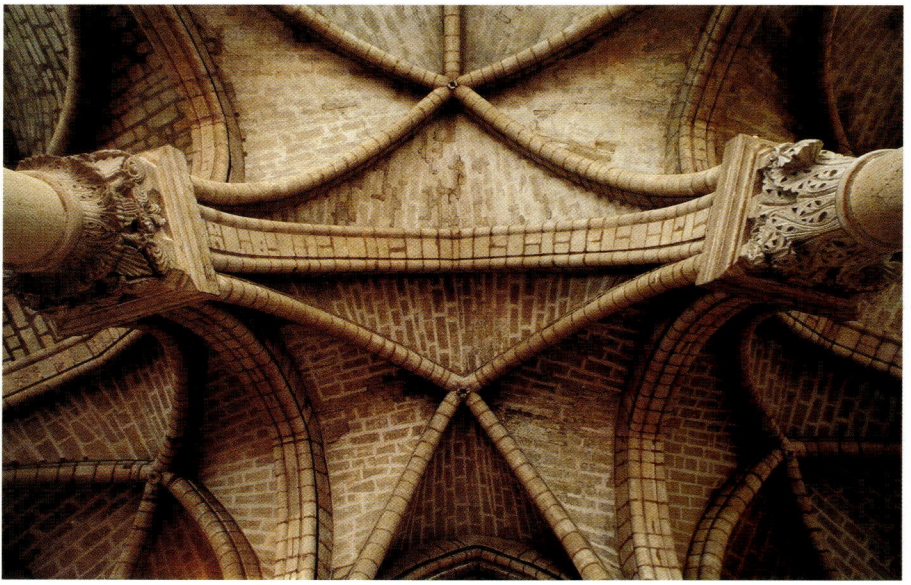

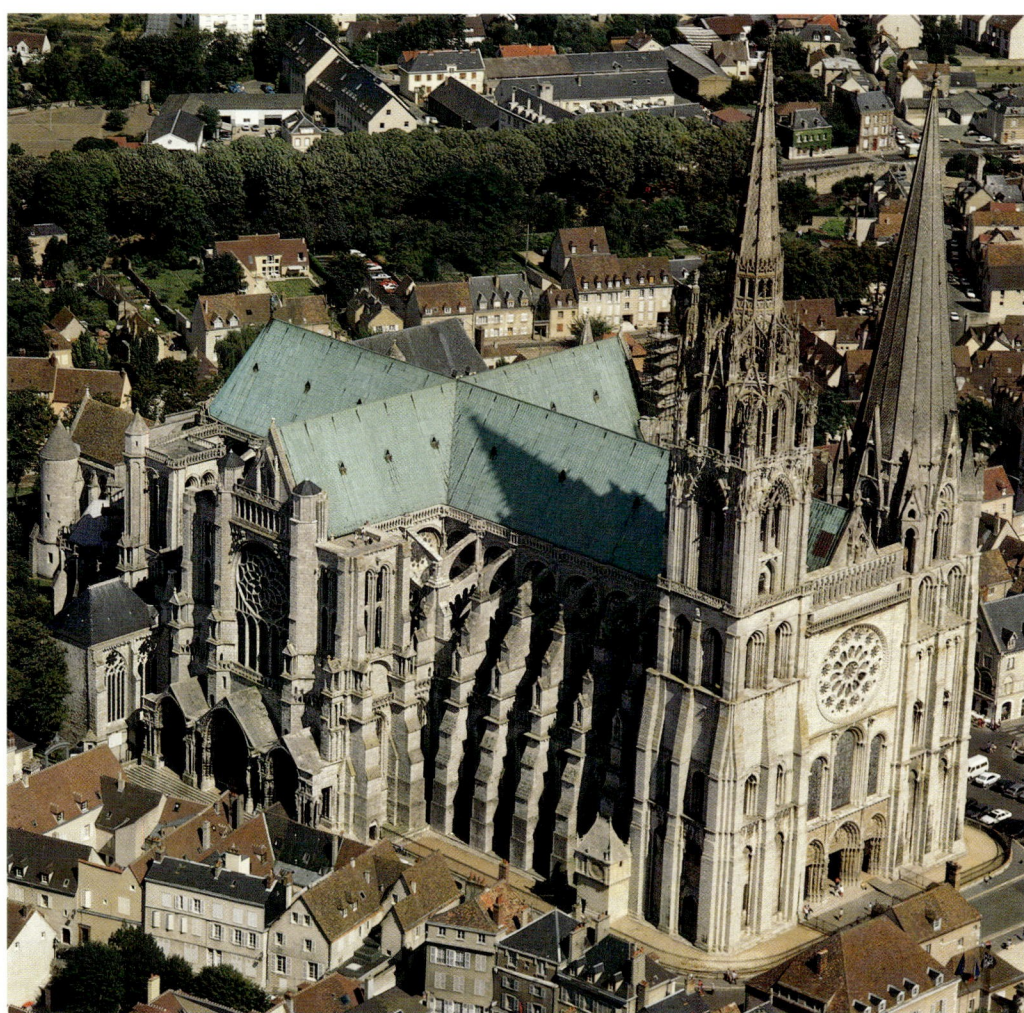

**LUX NOVA** Because the French considered the old church a relic in its own right, the new east end had to conform to the dimensions of the crypt below it. Nevertheless, the remodeled portion of Saint-Denis represented a sharp break from past practice. There, one can already see the basic features of the new Gothic style of architecture. Innovative rib vaults resting on *pointed arches* (see "The Gothic Rib Vault," page 482) cover the ambulatory and chapels (FIGS. 18-1 and **18-3**). These pioneering, exceptionally light vaults spring from slender columns in the ambulatory and from the thin masonry walls framing the chapels. The lightness of the vaults enabled the builders to eliminate the walls between the chapels and open up the outer walls and fill them with stained-glass windows (see "Stained-Glass Windows," page 492). Suger and his contemporaries marveled at the "wonderful and uninterrupted light" that poured in through the "most sacred windows." The abbot called the colored light *lux nova,* "new light." The multicolored rays coming through the windows shone on the walls and columns, almost dissolving them. Both the new type of vaulting and the use of stained glass became hallmarks of French Gothic architecture.

**SCULPTURE AT SAINT-DENIS** Saint-Denis is also the key monument of Early Gothic sculpture. Little of the sculpture that Suger commissioned for the west facade of the abbey church survived the French Revolution, but much of the mid-12th-century structure is intact. It consists of a double-tower westwork as at Saint-Étienne at Caen (see FIG. 17-12) and has massive walls in the Romanesque tradition. A restored large central *rose window*

(a circular stained-glass window), a new feature that became standard in French Gothic architecture, punctuates the facade's upper story. For the three portals, Suger imported sculptors to carry on the rich heritage of Romanesque Burgundy (see "The Romanesque Portal," Chapter 17, page 463). But at Saint-Denis, the sculptors introduced statues of Old Testament kings, queens, and prophets attached to columns, which screened the jambs of all three doorways.

**THE ROYAL PORTAL** This innovative treatment of the portals of Suger's church appeared immediately afterward at the Cathedral of Notre Dame ("Our Lady," that is, the Virgin Mary) at Chartres (FIG. **18-4**), also in the Île-de-France. Work on the west facade, the "Royal Portal" (FIG. **18-5**), began around 1145. (The Royal Portal is so named because of the statue-columns of kings and queens flanking its three doorways.) The lower parts of the massive west towers at Chartres and the portals between them are all that remain of a cathedral begun in 1134 and destroyed by fire in 1194 before it had been completed. Reconstruction of the cathedral began immediately, but in the High Gothic style (discussed later). The west portals, however, constitute the most complete and impressive surviving ensemble of Early Gothic sculpture. Thierry of Chartres, chancellor of the Cathedral School of Chartres (see "Paris: The Intellectual Capital of Gothic Europe," page 487) from 1141 until his death 10 years later, may have conceived the complex iconographical program. The archivolts of the right portal, for example, depict the seven female Liberal Arts and

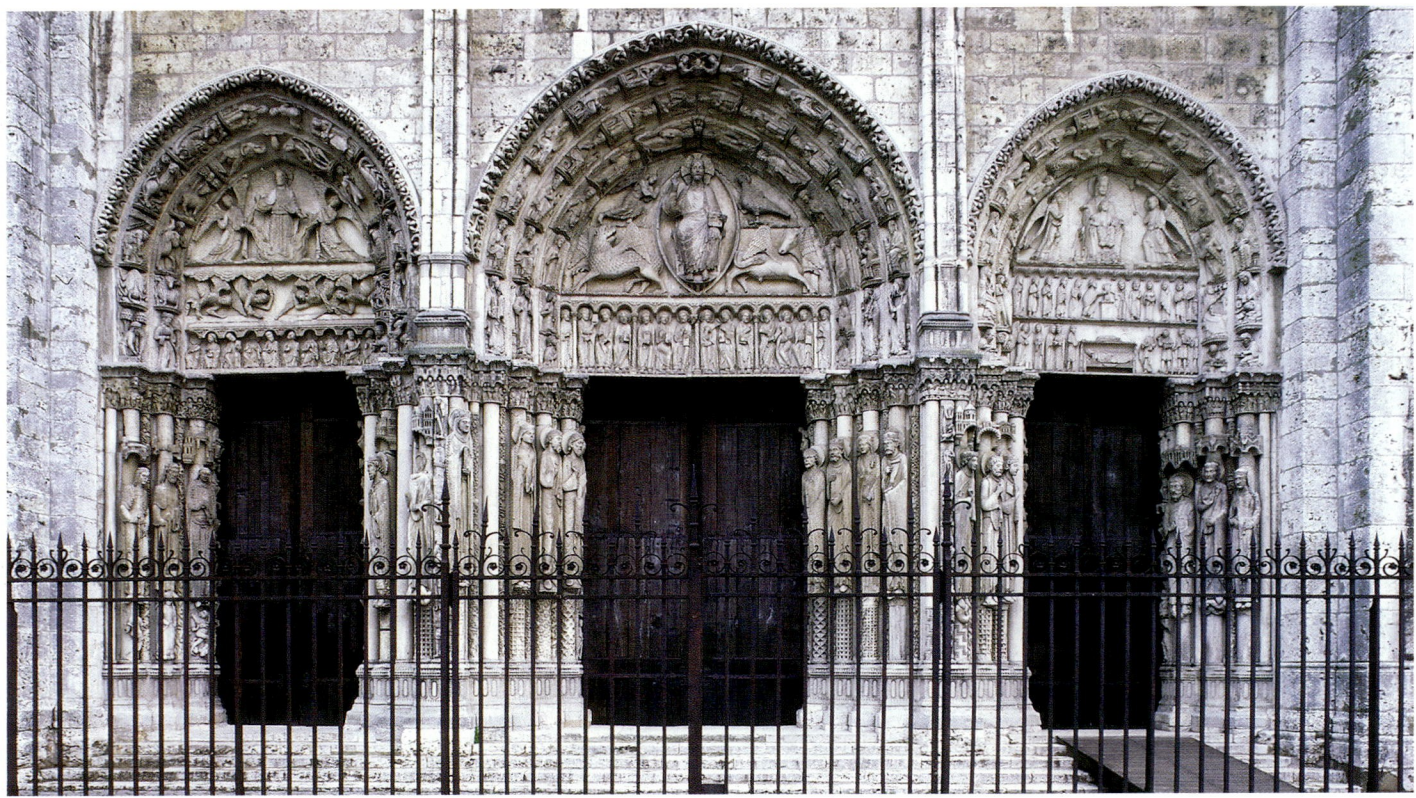

18-5 Royal Portal, west facade, Chartres Cathedral, Chartres, France, ca. 1145–1155.

their male champions. The figures represent the core of medieval learning and symbolize human knowledge, which Thierry and others believed led to true faith.

**CHRIST AND THE VIRGIN AT CHARTRES** The sculptures of the west facade (FIG. 18-5) proclaim the majesty and power of Christ. To unite the three doorways iconographically and visually, the sculptors carved episodes from Christ's life on the capitals, which form a kind of frieze linking one entrance to the next. In the tympanum of the right portal, Christ appears in the lap of the Virgin Mary (Notre Dame). Scenes of his birth and early life fill the lintel below. The tympanum's theme and composition recall Byzantine representations of the Theotokos (see FIGS. 12-16 and 12-17), as well as the Romanesque Throne of Wisdom (see FIG. 17-30). But Mary's prominence on the Chartres facade has no parallel in the decoration of Romanesque church portals. At Chartres the designers gave her a central role in the sculptural program, a position she maintained throughout the Gothic period. The cult of the Virgin Mary reached a high point in the Gothic age. As the Mother of Christ, she stood compassionately between the Last Judge and the horrors of Hell, interceding for all her faithful. Worshipers in the later 12th and 13th centuries sang hymns to her, put her image everywhere, and dedicated great cathedrals to her. Soldiers carried the Virgin's image into battle on banners, and her name joined that of Saint Denis as part of the French king's battle cry. Mary became the spiritual lady of chivalry, and the Christian knight dedicated his life to her. The severity of Romanesque themes stressing the Last Judgment yielded to the gentleness of Gothic art, in which Mary is the kindly Queen of Heaven.

Christ's Ascension into Heaven appears in the tympanum of the left portal. All around, in the archivolts, are the signs of the

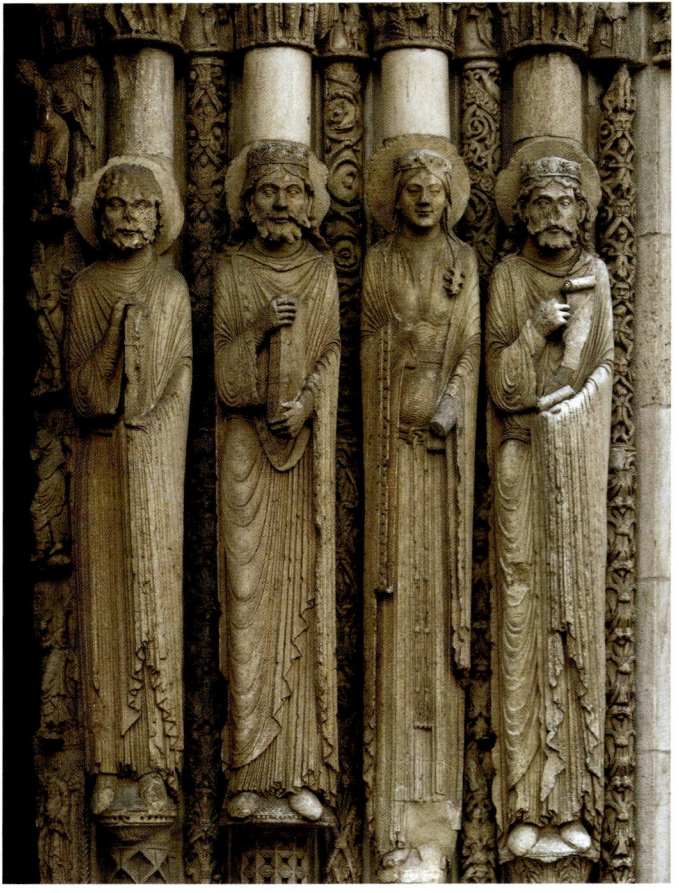

18-6 Old Testament kings and queen, jamb statues, central doorway of Royal Portal, Chartres Cathedral, Chartres, France, ca. 1145–1155.

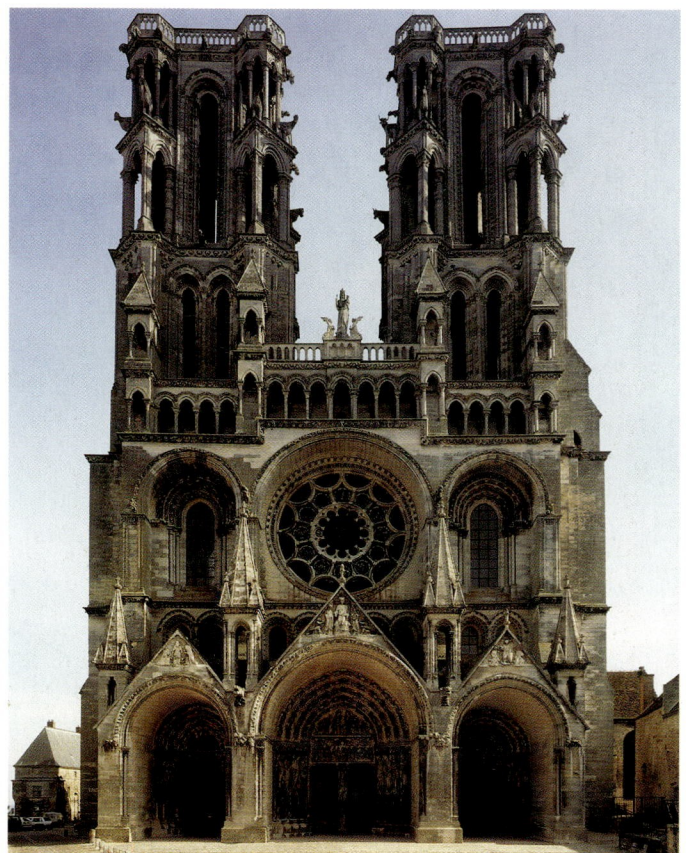

**18-7** West facade of Laon Cathedral, Laon, France, begun ca. 1190.

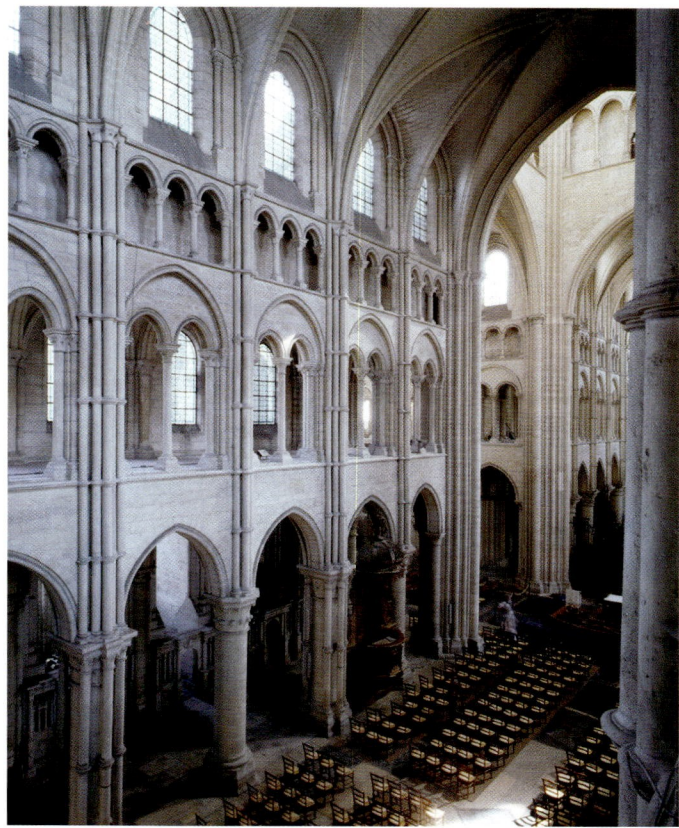

**18-8** Interior of Laon Cathedral (view facing northeast), Laon, France, begun ca. 1190.

zodiac and scenes representing the various labors of the months of the year. They are symbols of the cosmic and earthly worlds. The Second Coming is the subject of the central tympanum. The signs of the Four Evangelists, the Twenty-Four Elders of the Apocalypse, and the Twelve Apostles appear around Christ or on the lintel. The Second Coming—in essence, the Last Judgment theme—was still of central importance, as it was in Romanesque portals. But at Early Gothic Chartres the theme became a symbol of salvation rather than damnation.

**STATUE-COLUMNS** Statues of Old Testament kings and queens (FIG. **18-6**) decorate the jambs flanking each doorway of the Royal Portal. They are the royal ancestors of Christ and, both figuratively and literally, support the New Testament figures above the doorways. They wear 12th-century clothes, and medieval observers also regarded them as images of the kings and queens of France, symbols of secular as well as of biblical authority. (This was the motivation for vandalizing the comparable figures at Saint-Denis during the French Revolution.)

Seen from a distance, the statue-columns appear to be little more than vertical decorative accents within the larger designs of the portals and facade (FIG. **18-5**). The figures stand rigidly upright with their elbows held close against their hips. The linear folds of their garments—inherited from the Romanesque style, along with the elongated proportions—generally echo the vertical lines of the columns behind them. (In this respect, Gothic jamb statues differ significantly from classical caryatids; see FIG. 5-52. The Gothic figures are *attached* to columns. The classical statues *replaced* the columns.) And yet, within and despite this architectural straitjacket, the statues display the first signs of a new

naturalism. They stand out from the plane of the wall. The sculptors conceived and treated the statues as three-dimensional volumes, so the figures "move" into the space of observers. The new naturalism is noticeable particularly in the statues' heads, where kindly human faces replace the masklike features of most Romanesque figures. At Chartres, a personalization of appearance began that was transformed first into idealized portraits of the perfect Christian and finally, by 1400, into the portraiture of specific individuals. The sculptors of the Royal Portal statues initiated an era of artistic concern with personality and individuality.

**EARLY GOTHIC AT LAON** Both Chartres Cathedral and the abbey church of Saint-Denis had long building histories, and only small portions of the structures date to the Early Gothic period. Laon Cathedral (FIGS. **18-7** and **18-8**), however, begun about 1160 and finished shortly after 1200, provides a comprehensive picture of French church architecture of the second half of the 12th century. Although the Laon builders retained many Romanesque features in their design, they combined them with the rib vault resting on pointed arches, the essential element of Early Gothic architecture.

Among the plan's Romanesque features are the nave bays with their large sexpartite rib vaults, flanked by two small groin-vaulted squares in each aisle. The vaulting system (except for the pointed arches), as well as the vaulted gallery above the aisles, derived from Norman Romanesque churches such as Saint-Étienne at Caen (see FIG. 17-13), which enjoyed great prestige in northern France throughout the 12th century. A new feature found in the Laon interior, however, is the *triforium,* the band of arcades below the clerestory (FIG. 18-8). The triforium occupies the space

**18-9** Nave elevations of four French Gothic cathedrals at the same scale (after Louis Grodecki).

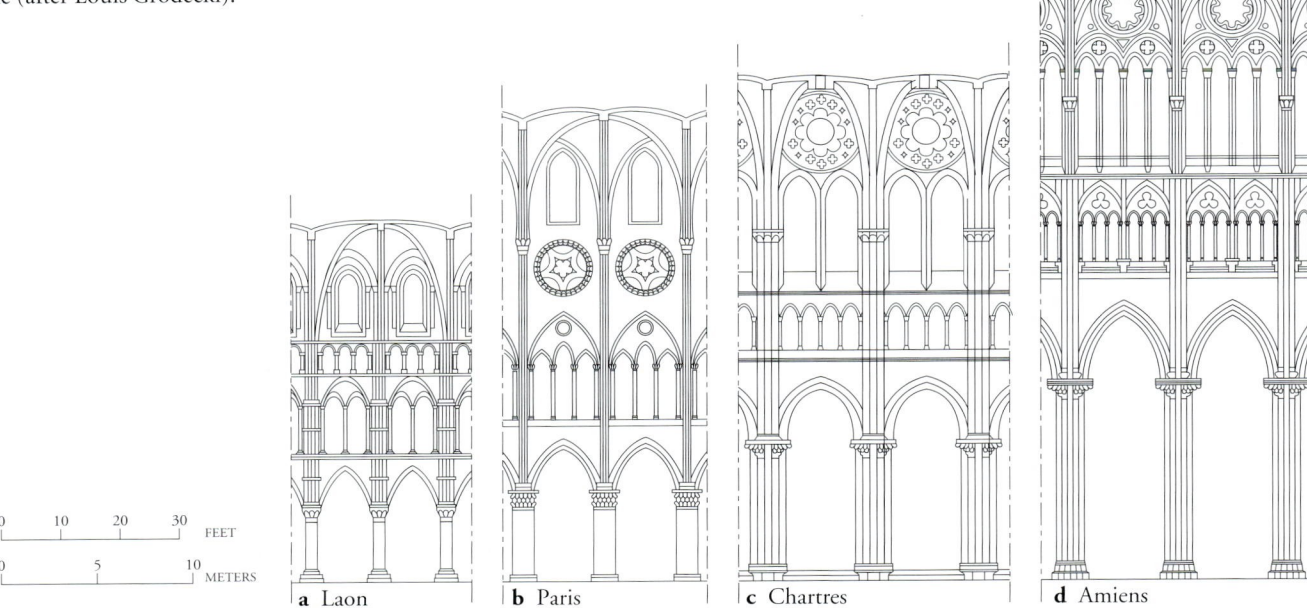

0    10    20    30    FEET

0         5         10    METERS

**a** Laon   **b** Paris   **c** Chartres   **d** Amiens

corresponding to the exterior strip of wall covered by the sloping timber roof above the galleries. The insertion of the triforium into the Romanesque three-story nave-wall elevation reflected a growing desire to break up and eliminate all continuous wall surfaces. The new horizontal zone produced the characteristic four-story Early Gothic interior elevation: nave arcade, vaulted gallery, triforium, and clerestory with single *lancets* (tall, narrow windows ending in pointed arches). FIG. **18-9** compares the Laon nave elevation (FIG. 18-9*a*) with those of another four-story Early Gothic cathedral (FIG. 18-9*b*) and two three-story High Gothic cathedrals (FIGS. 18-9*c* and 18-9*d*).

The Laon architect also employed the alternate-support system of Caen and other Romanesque churches. In the nave arcade, compound piers alternate with simple piers. In the gallery and

triforium, bundles of three and five shafts alternate in framing the aisle bays. The Laon designer moved away from the compartmentalized effect of Romanesque interiors, which tends to make visitors pause as they advance from unit to unit. Gothic architects aimed, even if rather timidly at Laon, to create a unified interior space that sweeps uninterruptedly from west to east. The level crowns of the successive nave vaults, made possible by pointed arches, enhance this longitudinal continuity (FIG. 18-8).

Laon Cathedral's west facade (FIG. 18-7) signals an even more pronounced departure from the Romanesque style still lingering at Saint-Denis and the Chartres Royal Portal. Typically Gothic are the huge central rose window, the deep porches in front of the doorways, and the open structure of the towers. A comparison of the facades of Laon Cathedral and Saint-Étienne at Caen (see

**18-10** Notre-Dame (view from the south), Paris, France, begun 1163; nave and flying buttresses, ca. 1180–1200; remodeled after 1225.

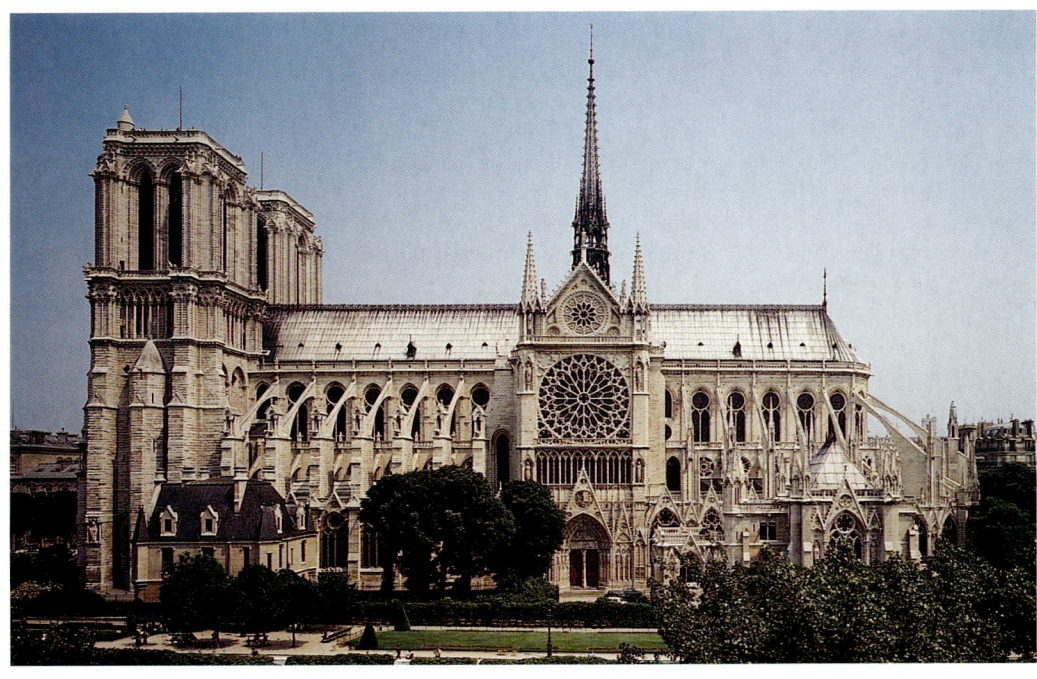

### Paris: The Intellectual Capital of Gothic Europe

A few years before the formal consecration of the altar of Notre-Dame in Paris (FIG. 18-10), Philip II (Philip Augustus, r. 1180–1223) succeeded to the throne. Philip brought the barons under his control and expanded the royal domains to include Normandy in the north and most of Languedoc in the south, laying the foundations for the modern nation of France. Renowned as "the maker of Paris," he gave the city its walls, paved its streets, and built the palace of the Louvre (now one of the world's great museums) to house the royal family. Although Rome remained the religious center of Western Christendom, Paris became its intellectual capital. The University of Paris attracted the best minds from all over Europe. Virtually every thinker of note in the Gothic world at some point studied or taught at Paris.

Even in the Romanesque period, Paris was a center of learning. Its Cathedral School professors were known as Schoolmen and the philosophy they developed as Scholasticism. The greatest of the early Schoolmen was Peter Abelard (1079–1142), a champion of logical reasoning. Abelard and his contemporaries had been introduced to the writings of the Greek philosopher Aristotle through the Arabic scholars of Islamic Spain. Abelard applied Aristotle's system of rational inquiry to the interpretation of religious belief. Until the 12th century, truth had been considered the exclusive property of divine revelation as given in the Holy Scriptures. But the Schoolmen, using Aristotle's method, sought to demonstrate that reason alone could lead to certain truths. Their goal was to prove the central articles of Christian faith by argument (disputatio). In Scholastic argument, a possibility is stated, an authoritative view is cited in objection, the positions are reconciled, and, finally, a reply is given to each of the rejected original arguments.

One of Abelard's greatest critics was Bernard of Clairvaux (see "Bernard of Clairvaux," Chapter 17, page 461), who believed Scholasticism was equivalent to questioning Christian dogma. Although Bernard succeeded in 1140 in having the Church officially condemn Abelard's doctrines, the Schoolmen's philosophy developed systematically until it became the dominant Western philosophy of the late Middle Ages. By the 13th century, the Schoolmen of Paris already had organized as a professional guild of master scholars, separate from the numerous Church schools overseen by the bishop of Paris. The structure of the Parisian guild served as the model for many other European universities.

The greatest exponent of Abelard's Scholasticism was Thomas Aquinas (1225–1274), an Italian monk who became a saint. Aquinas settled in Paris in 1244. There, the German theologian Albertus Magnus instructed him in Aristotelean philosophy. Aquinas went on to become an influential teacher at the University of Paris. His most famous work, the *Summa Theologica* (left unfinished at his death), is a model of the Scholastic approach to knowledge. Aquinas divided his treatise into books, the books into questions, the questions into articles, each article into objections with contradictions and responses, and, finally, answers to the objections. He set forth five ways to prove the existence of God by rational argument. Aquinas's work remains the foundation of contemporary Catholic teaching.

The earliest manifestations of the Gothic spirit in art and architecture—the sculptured portals and vaulted east end of Suger's Saint-Denis (FIGS. 18-1 to 18-3)—are contemporary with the first stages of Scholastic philosophy. Both also originated in Paris and its environs. Many art historians have noted the parallels between them, how the logical thrust and counterthrust of Gothic construction, the geometric relationships of building parts, and the systematic organization of the iconographical programs of Gothic church portals coincide with Scholastic principles and methods. Although no documents exist linking the scholars, builders, and sculptors, Gothic art and architecture shared with Scholasticism an insistence on systematic design and procedure. They both sought stable, coherent, consistent, and structurally intelligible solutions.

---

FIG. 17-12) reveals a much deeper penetration of the wall mass in the later building. At Laon, as in Gothic architecture generally, the operating principle was to reduce sheer mass and replace it with intricately framed voids.

**PARIS AND NOTRE-DAME** About 1130, Louis VI moved his official residence to Paris, spurring much commercial activity and a great building boom. Paris soon became the leading city of France, indeed of all northern Europe (see "Paris: The Intellectual Capital of Gothic Europe," above), making a new cathedral a necessity. Notre-Dame of Paris (FIG. **18-10**) occupies a picturesque site on an island in the Seine River called the Île-de-la-Cité. The Gothic church replaced a large Merovingian basilica and has a complicated building history. The choir and transept were completed by 1182; the nave, by ca. 1225; and the facade not until ca. 1250–1260. Sexpartite vaults covered the nave, as at Laon. The original elevation (the builders modified the design as work progressed) had four stories, but the scheme (FIG. 18-9b) differed from Laon's (FIG. 18-9a). In place of the triforium over the gallery, stained glass *oculi* (singular *oculus*, a small round window) opened up the wall below the clerestory lancets. As a result, two of the four stories were now filled by windows, further reducing the masonry area. (This four-story nave elevation can be seen in only one bay in FIG. 18-10, immediately to the right of the south transept and partially hidden by it.)

**FLYING BUTTRESSES** To hold the much thinner—and taller (compare FIGS. 18-9a and 18-9b)—walls of Notre-Dame in place, the unknown architect introduced *flying buttresses,* exterior arches that spring from the lower roofs over the aisles and ambulatory (FIG. 18-10) and counter the outward thrust of the nave vaults. Flying buttresses seem to have been employed as early as 1150 in a few smaller churches, but at Notre-Dame in Paris they circle a great urban cathedral. The internal quadrant arches beneath the aisle roofs at Durham (see FIG. 17-16, *top*), also employed at Laon, perform a similar function and may be regarded as precedents for exposed Gothic flying buttresses. The combination of precisely positioned flying buttresses and rib vaults with pointed arches was the ideal solution to the problem of constructing towering naves with huge windows filled with stained glass. The flying buttresses, like slender extended fingers holding up the walls, also are important elements contributing to the distinctive "look" of Gothic cathedrals (see "The Gothic Cathedral," page 488).

## The Gothic Cathedral

The great cathedrals erected throughout Europe in the later 12th and 13th centuries are the enduring symbols of the Gothic age. These towering structures are eloquent testimonies to the extraordinary skill of the architects, engineers, carpenters, masons, sculptors, glassworkers, and metalsmiths who constructed and decorated the buildings.

Most of the architectural components of Gothic cathedrals appeared in earlier structures, but the way Gothic architects combined the elements made the buildings unique expressions of medieval faith. The key ingredients of the Gothic "recipe" were rib vaults with pointed arches, flying buttresses, and huge colored-glass windows (see "Stained-Glass Windows," page 492). Our "exploded" view of a typical Gothic cathedral illustrates how these and other important Gothic architectural devices worked together.

### THE VOCABULARY OF GOTHIC ARCHITECTURE

1. *Pinnacle:* A sharply pointed ornament capping the piers or flying buttresses; also used on cathedral facades.

2. *Flying buttresses:* Masonry struts that transfer the thrust of the nave vaults across the roofs of the side aisles and ambulatory to a tall pier rising above the church's exterior wall. Compare the cross-section of Beauvais Cathedral (see FIG. Intro-18).

3. *Vaulting web:* The masonry blocks that fill the area between the ribs of a groin vault.

4. *Diagonal rib:* In plan, one of the ribs that form the X of a groin vault. In the diagrams of rib vaults on page 482, the diagonal ribs are the lines *AC* and *DB*.

5. *Transverse rib:* A rib that crosses the nave or aisle at a 90-degree angle (lines *AB* and *DC* in the diagrams on page 482).

6. *Springing:* The lowest stone of an arch; in Gothic vaulting, the lowest stone of a diagonal or transverse rib.

7. *Clerestory:* The windows below the vaults that form the nave elevation's uppermost level. By using flying buttresses and rib vaults on pointed arches, Gothic architects could build huge clerestory windows and fill them with *stained glass* held in place by ornamental stonework called *tracery*.

8. *Oculus:* A small round window.

9. *Lancet:* A tall, narrow window crowned by a pointed arch.

10. *Triforium:* The story in the nave elevation consisting of arcades, usually blind (FIGS. 18-9*c* and 18-12), but occasionally filled with stained glass (see FIG. Intro-2).

11. *Nave arcade:* The series of arches supported by piers separating the nave from the side aisles.

12. *Compound pier with shafts (responds):* Also called the *cluster pier,* a pier with a group, or cluster, of attached shafts, or *responds,* extending to the springing of the vaults.

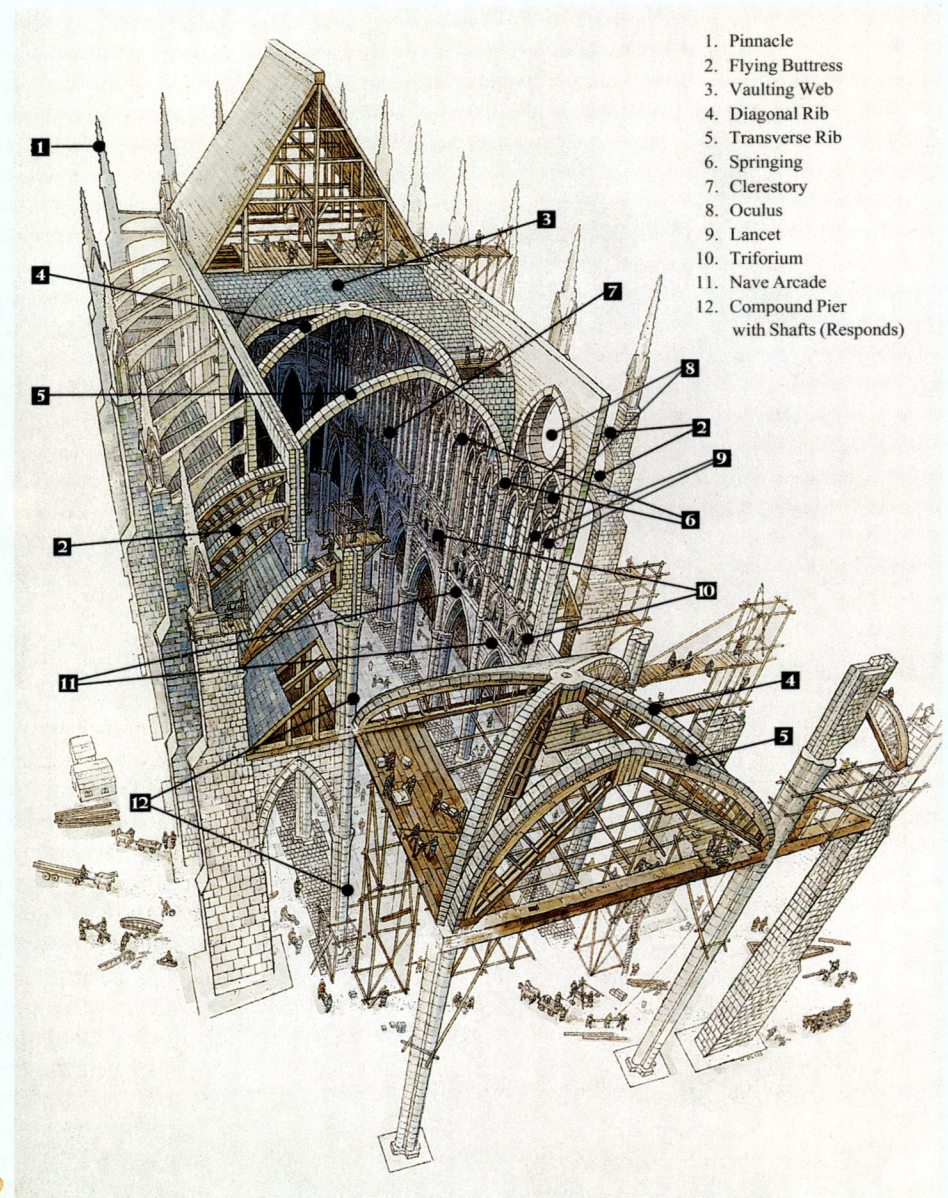

1. Pinnacle
2. Flying Buttress
3. Vaulting Web
4. Diagonal Rib
5. Transverse Rib
6. Springing
7. Clerestory
8. Oculus
9. Lancet
10. Triforium
11. Nave Arcade
12. Compound Pier with Shafts (Responds)

**FIRES AND FUNDRAISING** Churches burned frequently in the Middle Ages (see "Timber Roofs," Chapter 17, page 451), and church officials often had to raise money suddenly for new building campaigns. In contrast to monastic churches, which usually were small and completed fairly quickly, the building histories of urban cathedrals often extended over decades and sometimes over centuries. Their financing depended largely on collections and public contributions (not always voluntary), and a lack of funds often interrupted building programs. Unforeseen events, such as wars, famines, or plagues, or friction between the town and cathedral authorities would often stop construction, which then might not resume for years. At Reims (FIG. 18-21), the clergy offered *indulgences* (pardons for sins committed) to those who helped underwrite the enormous cost of erecting the cathedral. The rebuilding of Chartres Cathedral after the devastating fire of 1194 took a relatively short 27 years, but at one point the townspeople revolted against the prospect of a heavier tax burden. They stormed the bishop's residence and drove him into exile for four years.

**CHARTRES AFTER 1194** Chartres Cathedral's mid-12th-century west facade (FIGS. 18-4 and 18-5) and the masonry of the crypt to the east were all that were left standing after the 1194 conflagration. The crypt housed the most precious relic of Chartres — the mantle of the Virgin, which miraculously survived the fire. For piety and economy, the builders used the crypt for the foundation of the new structure. The incorporation of the old crypt and west facade in the new building determined the church's dimensions, but not its plan or elevation. Architectural historians usually consider the post-1194 Chartres Cathedral the first High Gothic building.

**THE HIGH GOTHIC PLAN** The Chartres plan (FIG. 18-11) reveals a new kind of organization. Rectangular nave bays replaced the square bays with sexpartite vaults and the alternate-support system, still present in Early Gothic churches such as Laon Cathedral (FIG. 18-8). The new system, in which a rectangular unit in the nave, defined by its own vault, was flanked by a single square in each aisle rather than two, as before, became the High Gothic norm. A change in vault design and the abandonment of the alternate-support system usually accompanied this new bay arrangement. The High Gothic vault, which covered a relatively smaller area and therefore was braced more easily than its Early Gothic predecessor, had only four parts. The visual effect of these changes was to unify the interior (FIG. 18-12). The High Gothic architect aligned identical units so that viewers saw them in too rapid a sequence to perceive them as individual volumes of space. The nave became a vast, continuous hall.

**THE HIGH GOTHIC ELEVATION** The 1194 Chartres Cathedral was also the first church to have been planned from the beginning with flying buttresses, another key High Gothic feature. The flying buttresses made it possible to eliminate the tribune

0  25  50  75  100
FEET
0  10  20  30
METERS

**18-11** Plan of Chartres Cathedral, Chartres, France, as rebuilt after 1194 (after Paul Frankl).

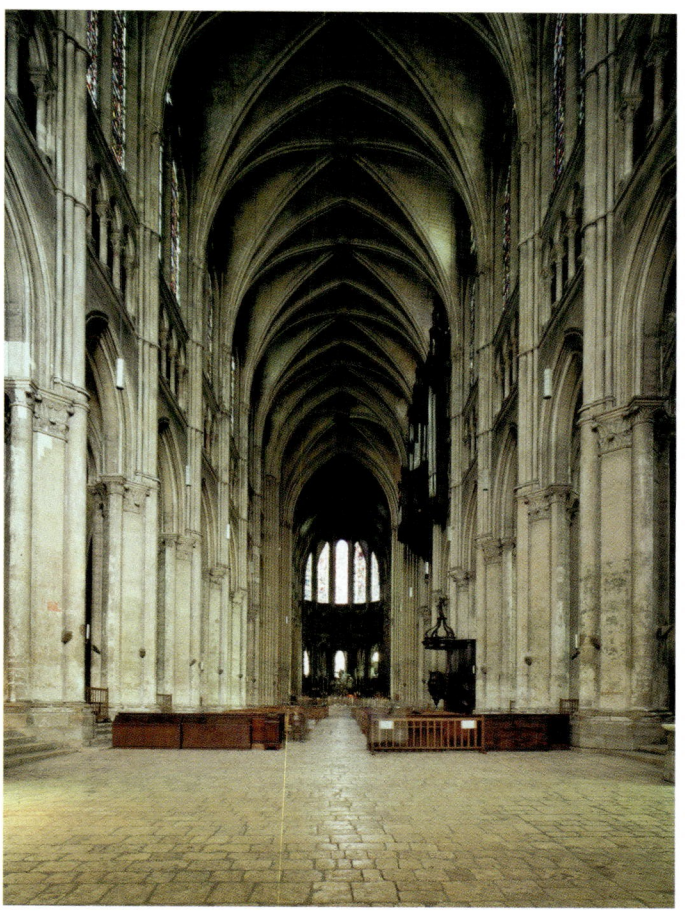

**18-12** Interior of Chartres Cathedral (view facing east), Chartres, France, begun 1194.

above the aisle, which had partially braced Romanesque and Early Gothic naves (compare FIG. 18-9c with FIGS. 18-9a and 18-9b). The new High Gothic tripartite nave elevation consisted of arcade, triforium, and clerestory with greatly enlarged windows. The Chartres windows are almost as high as the main arcade and consist of double lancets crowned by a single oculus. The strategic placement of flying buttresses permitted the construction of nave walls with so many voids that heavy masonry played a minor role.

**STAINED GLASS** Despite the vastly increased size of the clerestory windows, the Chartres nave (FIG. 18-12) is relatively dark. The explanation for this seeming contradiction is that light-muffling colored glass fills the windows. These windows were not meant to illuminate the interior with bright sunlight but to transform natural light into Suger's mystical *lux nova* (see "Stained-Glass Windows," page 492). Chartres retains almost the full complement of its original stained glass, which, although it has a dimming effect, transforms the character of the interior in dramatic fashion. Gothic churches that have lost their original stained-glass windows give a false impression of what their designers intended.

**THE VIRGIN'S WINDOW** One Chartres window that survived the fire of 1194 and was subsequently reused in the High Gothic cathedral is the tall single lancet the French call *Notre Dame de la Belle Verrière* (Our Lady of the Beautiful Window, FIG. 18-13). The central section, depicting the Virgin Mary enthroned with the Christ Child in her lap, dates to ca. 1170 and has a red background. The framing angels seen against a blue ground were added when the window was reinstalled in the 13th-century choir. The artist represented Mary as the beautiful, young, rather worldly Queen of Heaven, haloed, crowned, and accompanied by the dove of the Holy Spirit. The frontal composition is traditional. Comparing this Virgin and Child with the Theotokos and Child of Hagia Sophia (see FIG. 12-17) highlights not only the greater severity and aloofness of the Byzantine image but also the sharp difference between the light-reflecting mosaic medium and Gothic light-filtering stained glass. Gothic and Byzantine builders used light to transform the material world into the spiritual, but in opposite ways. In Gothic architecture, light entered from outside the building through a screen of stone-set colored glass. In Byzantine architecture, light was reflected from myriad glass tesserae set into the thick masonry wall.

**A QUEEN'S GIFT TO CHARTRES** Chartres's 13th-century Gothic windows are even more spectacular than the *Belle Verrière* because they were designed from the outset to fill entire walls, thanks to the introduction of flying buttresses. The immense rose window (approximately 43 feet in diameter) and tall lancets of Chartres Cathedral's north transept (FIGS. 18-4 and 18-14) were the gift of the Queen of France, Blanche of Castile, around 1220. The royal motifs of yellow castles on a red ground and yellow *fleurs-de-lis*—three-petaled iris flowers—on a blue ground fill the eight narrow windows in the rose's lower spandrels. The iconography is also fitting for a queen. The enthroned Virgin and Child appear in the roundel at the center of the rose, which resembles a gem-studded book cover or cloisonné brooch. Around her are four doves of the Holy Spirit and eight angels. Twelve square panels contain images of Old Testament kings, including David and Solomon (at the 12 and 1 o'clock

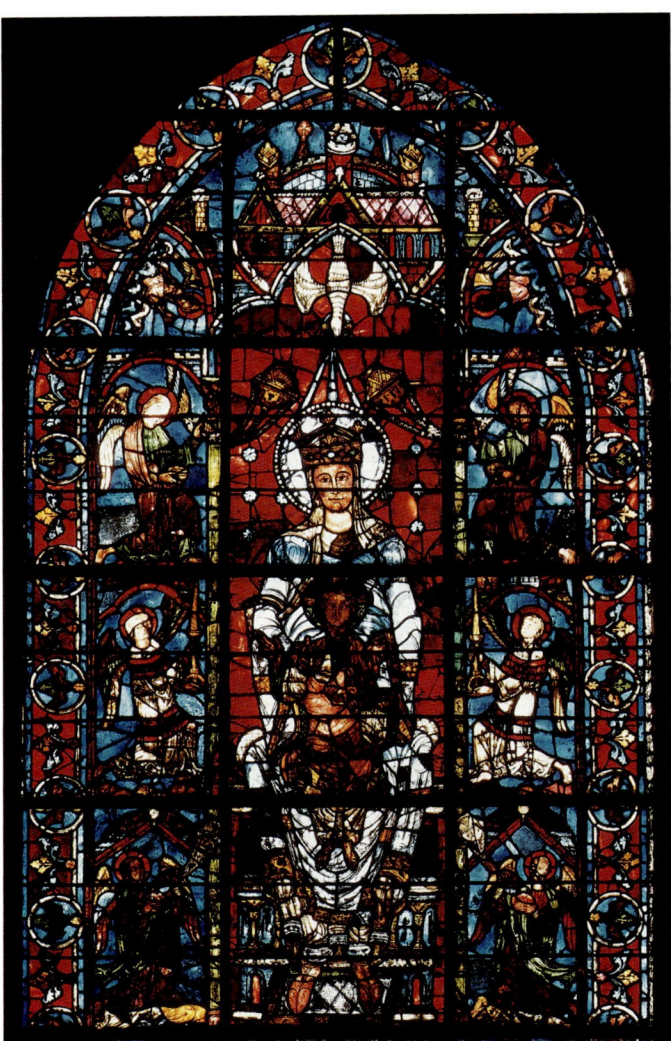

**18-13** Virgin and Child and angels *(Notre Dame de la Belle Verrière)*, window in the choir of Chartres Cathedral, Chartres, France, ca. 1170, with 13th-century side panels. Stained glass, 16′ × 7′ × 8″.

positions respectively). These are the royal ancestors of Christ. Isaiah (11:1–3) had prophesied that the Messiah would come from the family of the patriarch Jesse, father of David. The genealogical "tree of Jesse" is a familiar motif in medieval art. Below, in the lancets, are Saint Anne and the baby Virgin flanked by four of Christ's Old Testament ancestors, Melchizedek, David, Solomon, and Aaron, echoing the royal genealogy of the rose, but at a larger scale. Many Gothic stained-glass windows also present narrative scenes, and their iconographical programs are sometimes as complex as those of the sculptured church portals.

The rose and lancets change in hue and intensity with the hours, turning solid architecture into a floating vision of the celestial heavens. Almost the entire mass of wall opens up into stained glass, which is held in place by an intricate stone armature of bar tracery. Here, the Gothic passion for luminous colored light led to a most daring and successful attempt to subtract all superfluous material bulk just short of destabilizing the structure. That this vast, complex fabric of stone-set glass has maintained its structural integrity for almost 800 years attests to the Gothic builders' engineering genius.

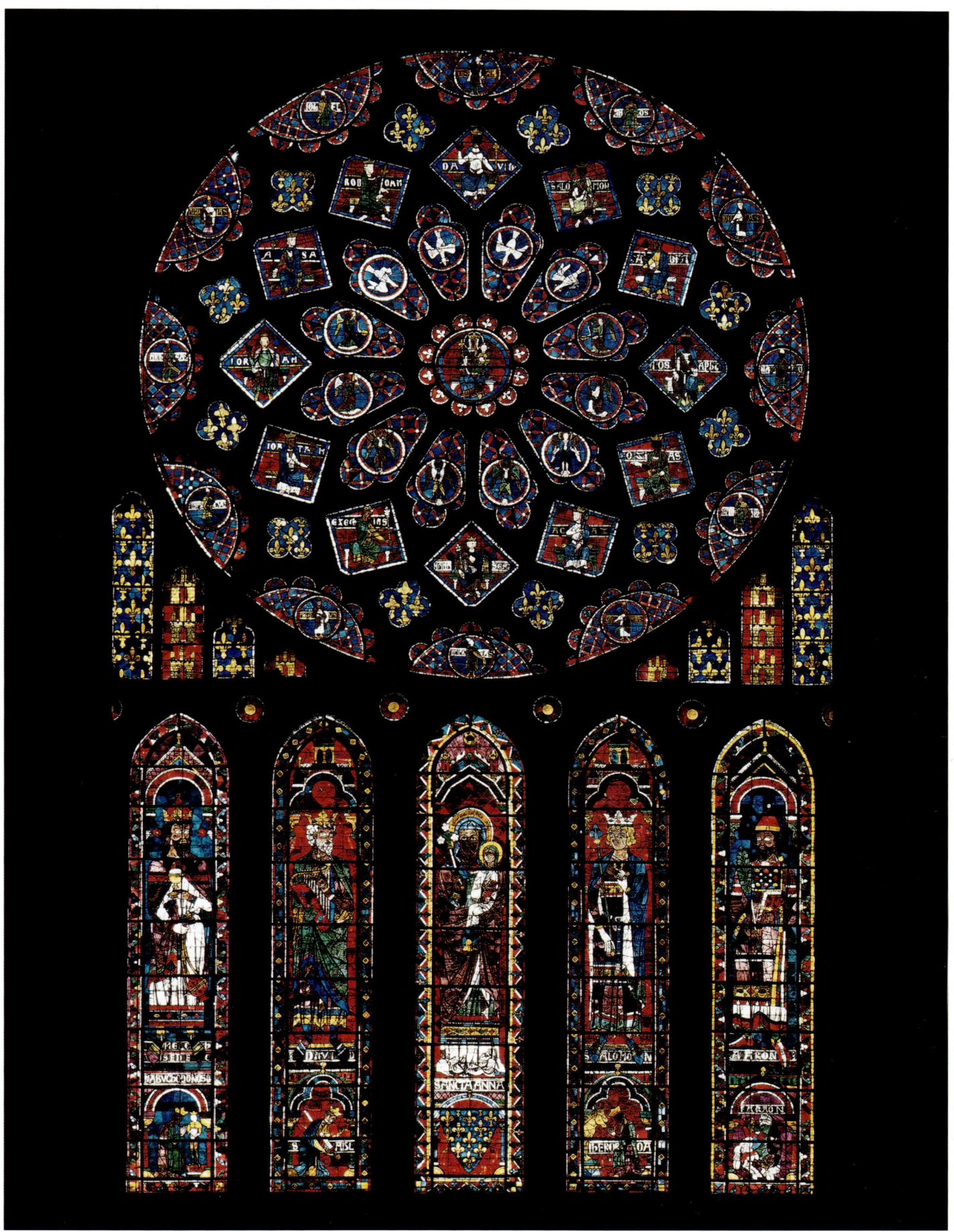

**18-14** Rose window and lancets, north transept, Chartres Cathedral, Chartres, France, ca. 1220. Stained glass, rose window approx. 43′ in diameter.

## Stained-Glass Windows

Stained glass is almost synonymous with Gothic architecture. No other age produced windows of such rich color and beauty. The art of making colored glass is, however, very old. Egyptian artists excelled at fashioning colorful glass vessels and other objects for both home and tomb. Archaeologists also have uncovered thousands of colored-glass artifacts at hundreds of sites throughout the classical world.

Although the technology of manufacturing colored glass was ancient, the way artists used stained glass in the Gothic period was new. Stained-glass windows were not just installed to introduce color and religious iconography into church interiors. That could have been done—and was done much earlier—with both mural paintings and mosaics, often with magnificent effect. But stained-glass windows differ from those earlier techniques in one all-important respect. They do not conceal walls; they replace them. And they transmit rather than reflect light, filtering and transforming the natural sunlight as it enters the building. Abbot Suger called this colored light "lux nova" (see "Abbot Suger," page 481). Hugh of Saint-Victor (1096–1142), a prominent Parisian theologian who died while Suger's Saint-Denis was under construction, also commented on the special mystical quality of stained-glass windows. "Stained-glass windows," he wrote, "are the Holy Scriptures . . . and since their brilliance lets the splendor of the True Light pass into the church, they enlighten those inside."[1] William Durandus, Bishop of Mende, expressed a similar sentiment at the end of the 13th century: "The glass windows in a church are Holy Scriptures, which expel the wind and the rain, that is, all things hurtful, but transmit the light of the True Sun, that is, God, into the hearts of the faithful."[2]

As early as the fourth century, architects used colored glass for church windows. Perfection of the technique came gradually. The stained-glass windows in the Saint-Denis ambulatory (FIG. 18-1) already show a high degree of skill. According to Suger, they were "painted by the exquisite hands of many masters from different regions," proving that the art was known widely at that time.[3]

The manufacture of stained-glass windows was costly and labor-intensive. The full process was recorded around 1100 in a treatise on the arts written by a Benedictine monk named Theophilus. First, the master designer drew the exact composition of the planned window on a wooden panel, indicating all the linear details and noting the colors for each section. Glassblowers provided flat sheets of glass of different colors to *glaziers* (glassworkers), who cut the windowpanes to the required size and shape with special iron shears. Glaziers produced an even greater range of colors by *flashing* (fusing one layer of colored glass to another). Purple, for example, resulted from the fusing of red and blue (compare the color triangle, FIG. Intro-10). Next, painters added details such as faces, hands, hair, and clothing in enamel by tracing the master design on the wood panel through the colored glass. Then they heated the painted glass to fuse the enamel to the surface. The glaziers then *leaded* the various fragments of glass; that is, they joined them by strips of lead called *cames*. The leading not only held the (usually quite small) pieces together but also separated the colors to heighten the effect of the design as a whole. The distinctive character of Gothic stained-glass windows is largely the result of this combination of fine linear details with broad flat expanses of color framed by black lead. Finally, the glassworkers strengthened the completed window with an armature of iron bands, which in the 12th century formed a grid over the whole design (FIG. 18-13). In the 13th century, the bands followed the outlines of the medallions and of the surrounding areas (FIGS. 18-14 and 18-23).

The form of the stone window frames into which the glass was set also evolved throughout the Gothic era. Early rose windows, such as the one on Chartres Cathedral's west facade (FIG. 18-4), have stained glass held in place by *plate tracery*. The glass fills only the "punched holes" in the heavy ornamental stonework. *Bar tracery* (FIG. 18-14), a later development, is much more slender. The stained-glass windows fill almost the entire opening, and the stonework is unobtrusive, more like delicate leading than masonry wall.

[1] Attributed to Hugh of Saint-Victor, *Speculum de mysteriis ecclesiae,* Sermon 2.

[2] William Durandus, *Rationale divinorum officiorum,* 1.1.24. Translated by John Mason Neale and Benjamin Webb, *The Symbolism of Churches and Church Ornaments* (Leeds, England: T. W. Green, 1843), 28.

[3] Erwin Panofsky, trans., *Abbot Suger on the Abbey Church of Saint-Denis and Its Art Treasures,* 2nd ed. (Princeton: Princeton University Press, 1979), 73.

**PORCH OF THE CONFESSORS** The sculptures adorning the portals of the two new Chartres transepts erected after the 1194 fire are also prime examples of the new High Gothic spirit. As at Laon (FIG. 18-7) and Paris (FIG. 18-10) Cathedrals, the Chartres transept portals project more forcefully from the church than do the Early Gothic portals of its west facade (compare FIGS. 18-4 and 18-5). Similarly, the statues of saints on the portal jambs are more independent from the architectural framework. Three figures from the Porch of the Confessors (FIG. **18-15**) in the south transept reveal the great changes Gothic sculpture underwent since the Royal Portal statues (FIG. 18-6) of the mid-12th century. These changes recall in many ways the revolutionary developments in ancient Greek sculpture during the transition from the Archaic to the Classical style (see Chapter 5). The Chartres transept statues we illustrate date from 1220 to 1230 and represent Saints Martin, Jerome, and Gregory. Although the figures are still attached to columns, the architectural setting does not determine their poses as much as it did on the west portals. The saints communicate quietly with one another, like waiting dignitaries. They turn slightly toward and away from each other, breaking the rigid vertical lines that, on the Royal Portal, fix the figures immovably. The drapery folds are not stiff and shallow vertical accents, as on the west facade. The fabric falls and laps over the bodies in soft, if still regular, folds.

The treatment of the faces is even more remarkable. The sculptor gave the figures individualized features and distinctive

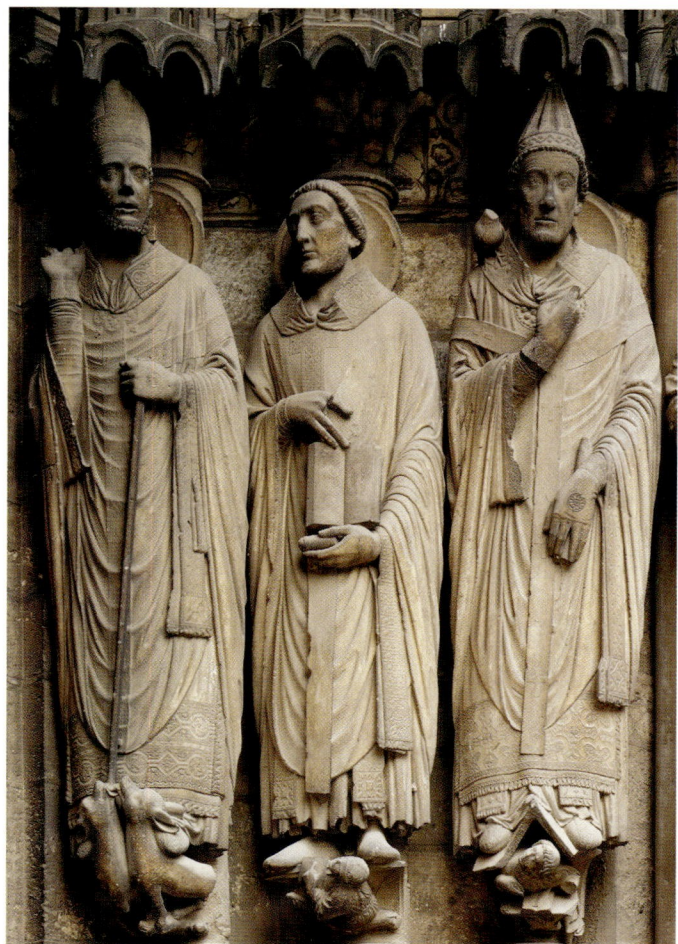

**18-15** Saints Martin, Jerome, and Gregory, jamb statues, Porch of the Confessors (right doorway), south transept, Chartres Cathedral, Chartres, France, ca. 1220–1230.

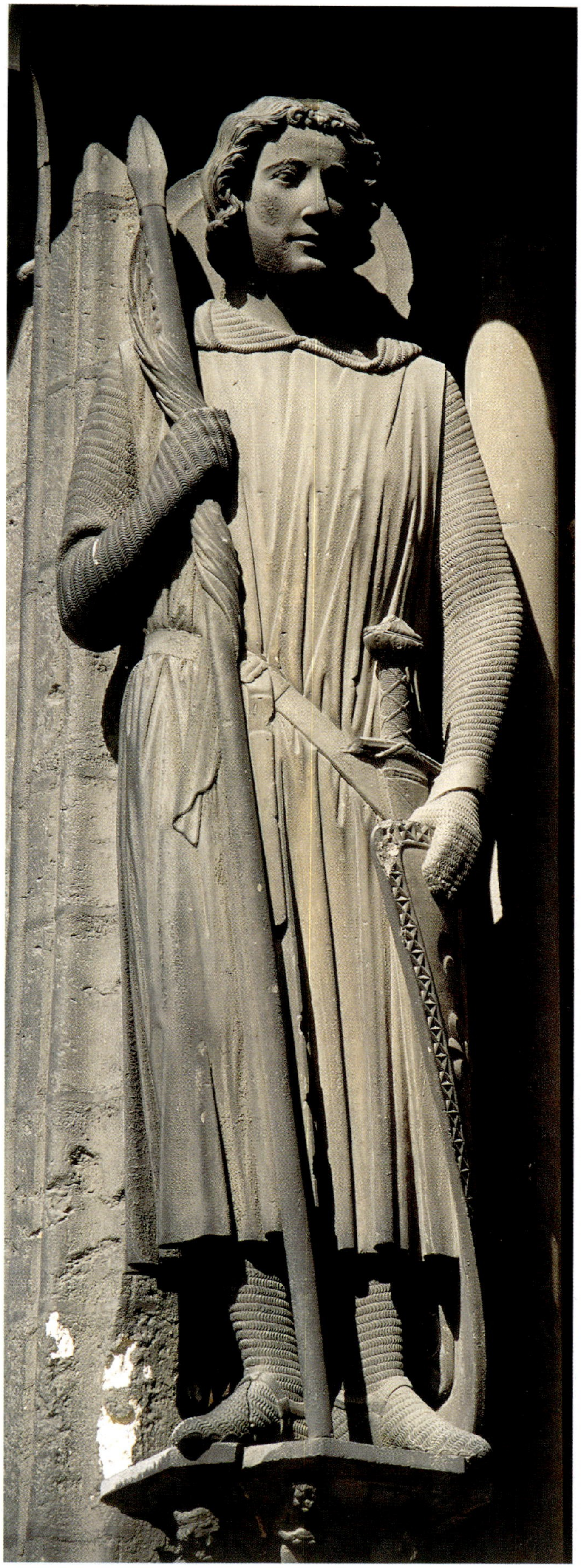

personalities and clothed them in the period's liturgical costumes. Saint Martin is a tall, intense priest with gaunt features (compare the spiritually moved but not particularized face of the Moissac prophet in FIG. 17-24). Saint Jerome appears as a kindly, practical administrator-scholar, holding his copy of the Scriptures. At the right, the introspective Saint Gregory seems lost in thought as he listens to the dove of the Holy Ghost on his shoulder. Thus, the sculptor did not contrast the three men simply in terms of their poses, gestures, and attributes but, most particularly and emphatically, as persons. Personality, revealed in human faces, makes the real difference.

**THE IDEAL WARRIOR** The south-transept figure of Saint Theodore (FIG. **18-16**), the martyred warrior on the Porch of the Martyrs, presents an even sharper contrast with Early Gothic jamb statues. The sculptor portrayed Theodore as the ideal Christian knight and clothed him in the cloak and chain-mail armor of Gothic Crusaders. The handsome, long-haired youth holds his spear firmly in his right hand and rests his left hand on his shield. He turns his head to the left and swings out his hip to the right. The body's resulting torsion and pronounced sway call to mind Classical Greek statuary, especially the contrapposto stance of Polykleitos's *Spear Bearer* (see FIG. 5-38). It is not inappropriate to speak of the changes that occurred in 13th-century Gothic sculpture as a second "Classical revolution."

**18-16** Saint Theodore, jamb statue, Porch of the Martyrs (left doorway), south transept, Chartres Cathedral, Chartres, France, ca. 1230.

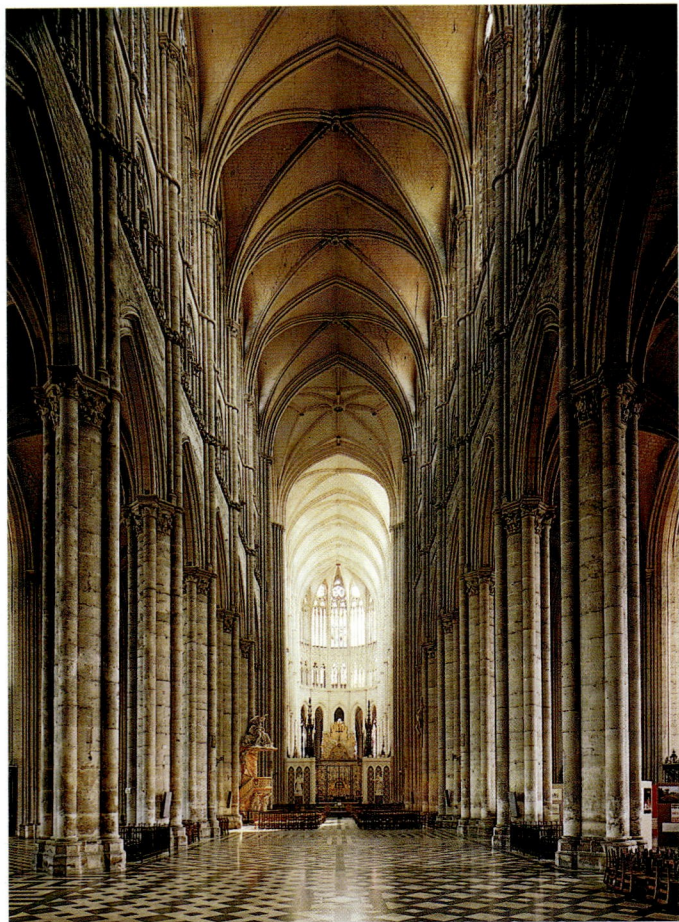

**18-17** ROBERT DE LUZARCHES, THOMAS DE CORMONT, and RENAUD DE CORMONT, interior of Amiens Cathedral (view facing east), Amiens, France, begun 1220.

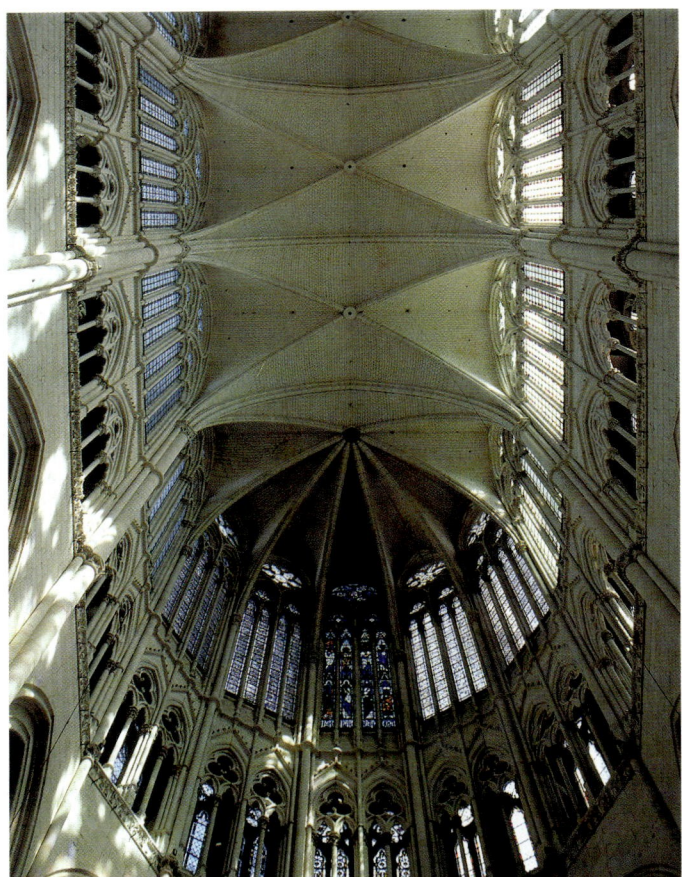

**18-18** ROBERT DE LUZARCHES, THOMAS DE CORMONT, and RENAUD DE CORMONT, vaults, clerestory, and triforium of the choir of Amiens Cathedral, Amiens, France, begun 1220.

**THE QUEST FOR HEIGHT** Chartres Cathedral was one of the most influential buildings in the history of architecture. Its builders set a pattern that many other Gothic architects followed, even if they refined the details. Construction of Amiens Cathedral (FIGS. **18-17** to **18-19**) began in 1220, while work was still in progress at Chartres. The architects were ROBERT DE LUZARCHES, THOMAS DE CORMONT, and RENAUD DE CORMONT. The builders finished the nave by 1236 and the radiating chapels by 1247, but work on the choir continued until almost 1270. The Amiens elevation (FIGS. 18-9*d* and 18-17) derived from the High Gothic formula established at Chartres (FIGS. 18-9*c* and 18-12). But Amiens Cathedral's proportions are even more elegant, and the number and complexity of the lancet windows in both its clerestory and triforium are even greater. The whole design reflects the builders' confident use of the complete High Gothic structural vocabulary: the rectangular-bay system, the four-part rib vault, and a buttressing system that permitted almost complete dissolution of heavy masses and thick weight-bearing walls. At Amiens, the concept of a self-sustaining skeletal architecture reached full maturity. What remained as walls was stretched like a skin between the piers and seems to serve no purpose other than to provide a weather screen for the interior (FIG. 18-18).

Amiens Cathedral is one of the most impressive examples of the French Gothic obsession with constructing ever taller cathedrals. Using their new skeletal frames of stone, French builders attempted goals almost beyond limit, pushing to new heights with ever more slender supports. The nave vaults at Laon rise to a height of about 80 feet; at Paris, to 107 feet; and at Chartres, to 118 feet.

Those at Amiens are 144 feet above the floor (FIG. 18-9). The tense, strong lines of the Amiens vault ribs converge to the colonnettes and speed down the shell-like walls to the compound piers. Almost every part of the superstructure has its corresponding element below. The overall effect is of effortless strength, of a buoyant lightness one normally does not associate with stone architecture. Viewed directly from below, the choir vaults (FIG. 18-18) seem like a canopy, tentlike and suspended from bundled masts. The light flooding in from the clerestory makes the vaults seem even more insubstantial. The effect recalls another great building, one utterly different from Amiens but where light also plays a defining role: Hagia Sophia in Constantinople (see FIG. 12-5). Once again, the designers reduced the building's physical mass by structural ingenuity and daring, and light dematerializes further what remains. If Hagia Sophia is the perfect expression of Byzantine spirituality in architecture, Amiens, with its soaring vaults and giant windows admitting divine colored light, is its Gothic counterpart.

**THE HIGH GOTHIC FACADE** Work began on the Amiens west facade (FIG. 18-19) at the same time as the nave (1220). Its lower parts seem to reflect the influence of Laon Cathedral (FIG. 18-7) in the spacing of the funnel-like and gable-covered portals. But the Amiens builders punctured the upper parts of the facade to an even greater degree than did the Laon designer. The deep piercing of walls and towers at Amiens seems to have left few continuous surfaces for decoration, but the ones that remained were covered with a network of colonnettes, arches, pinnacles, rosettes, and other decorative stonework that visually screens and nearly dissolves the structure's solid core. Sculpture also extends to the

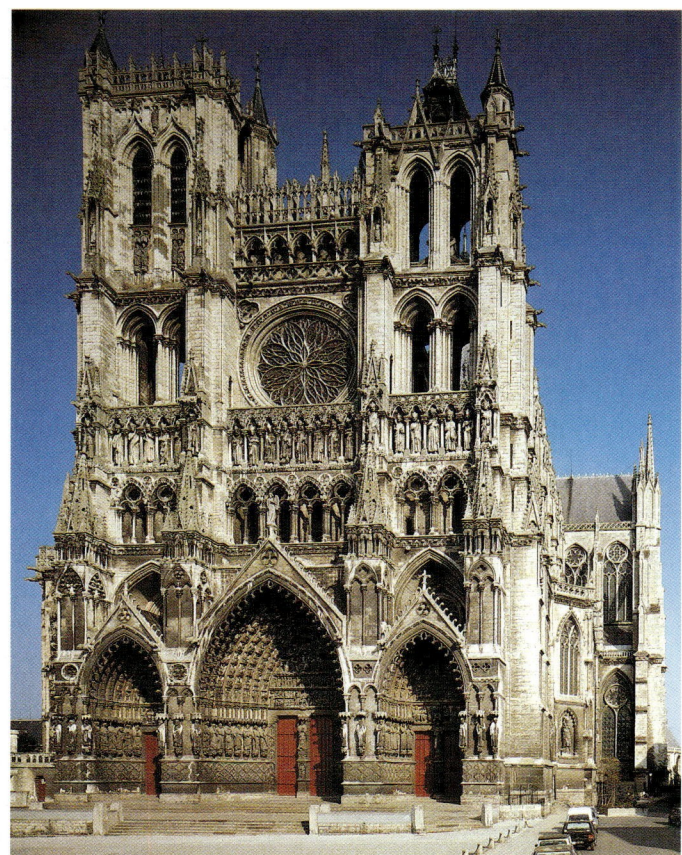

**18-19** Robert de Luzarches, Thomas de Cormont, and Renaud de Cormont, west facade of Amiens Cathedral, Amiens, France, begun 1220.

areas above the portals, especially the band of statues (the so-called kings' gallery) running the full width of the facade directly below the rose window (with 15th-century tracery). The uneven towers were later additions. The shorter one dates from the 14th century, the taller one from the 15th century.

THE BEAUTIFUL GOD The most prominent statue on the Amiens facade is of Christ (the *Beau Dieu,* or Beautiful God) on the central doorway's trumeau (FIG. **18-20**). The sculptor fully modeled Christ's figure, enveloping his body with massive drapery folds cascading from his waist. The statue stands freely and is as independent of its architectural setting as any Gothic facade statue ever was. Nonetheless, the sculptor still placed an architectural canopy over the figure's head. It is in the latest Gothic style, mimicking the east end of a 13th-century cathedral with a series of radiating chapels pierced by elegant lancet windows. Above the canopy is the great central tympanum with the representation of Christ as Last Judge. But the *Beau Dieu* is a handsome, kindly figure who does not strike terror into sinners. Instead he blesses those who enter the church and tramples a lion and a dragon symbolizing the evil forces in the world. This image of Christ gives humankind hope in salvation. The *Beau Dieu* epitomizes the bearded, benevolent image of Christ that replaced the youthful Early Christian Christ (see FIG. 11-6) and the stern Byzantine Pantocrator (see FIGS. 12-21 and 12-24) as the preferred representation of the Savior in later European art. The figure's quiet grace and grandeur also contrast sharply with the emotional intensity of the twisting Romanesque prophet carved in relief on the Moissac trumeau (see FIG. 17-24).

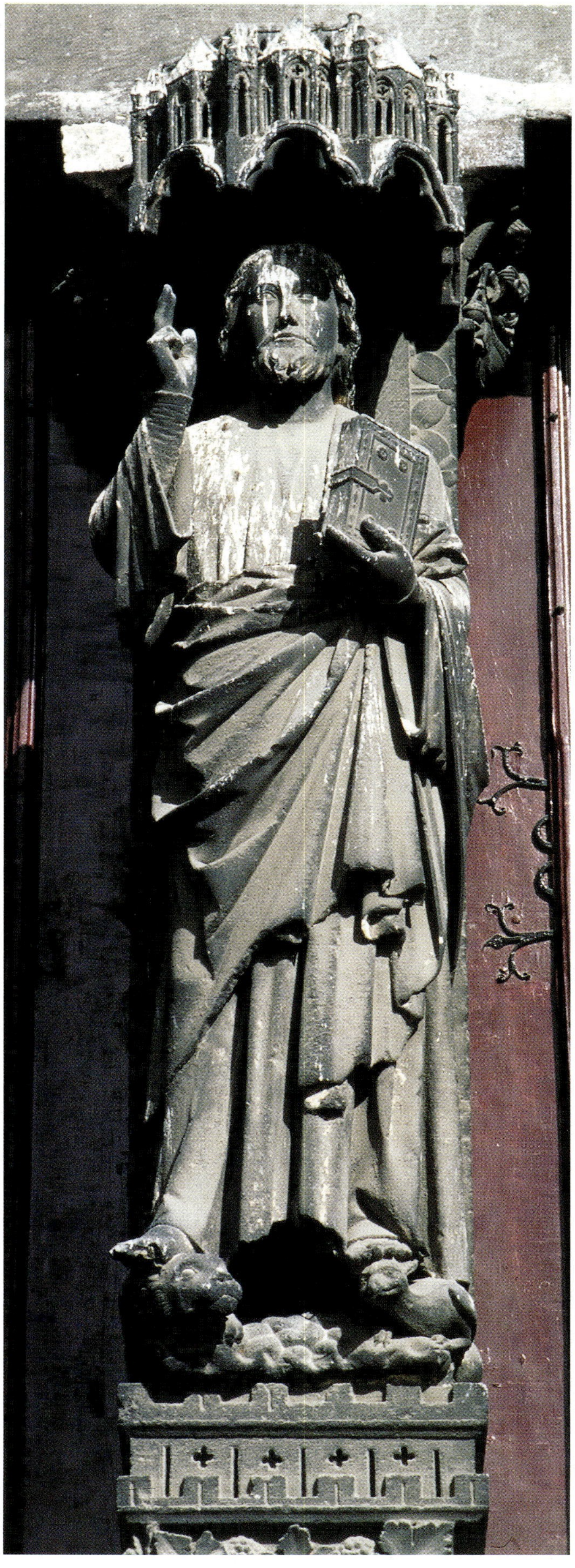

**18-20** Christ *(Beau Dieu),* trumeau statue of central doorway, west facade, Amiens Cathedral, Amiens, France, ca. 1220–1235.

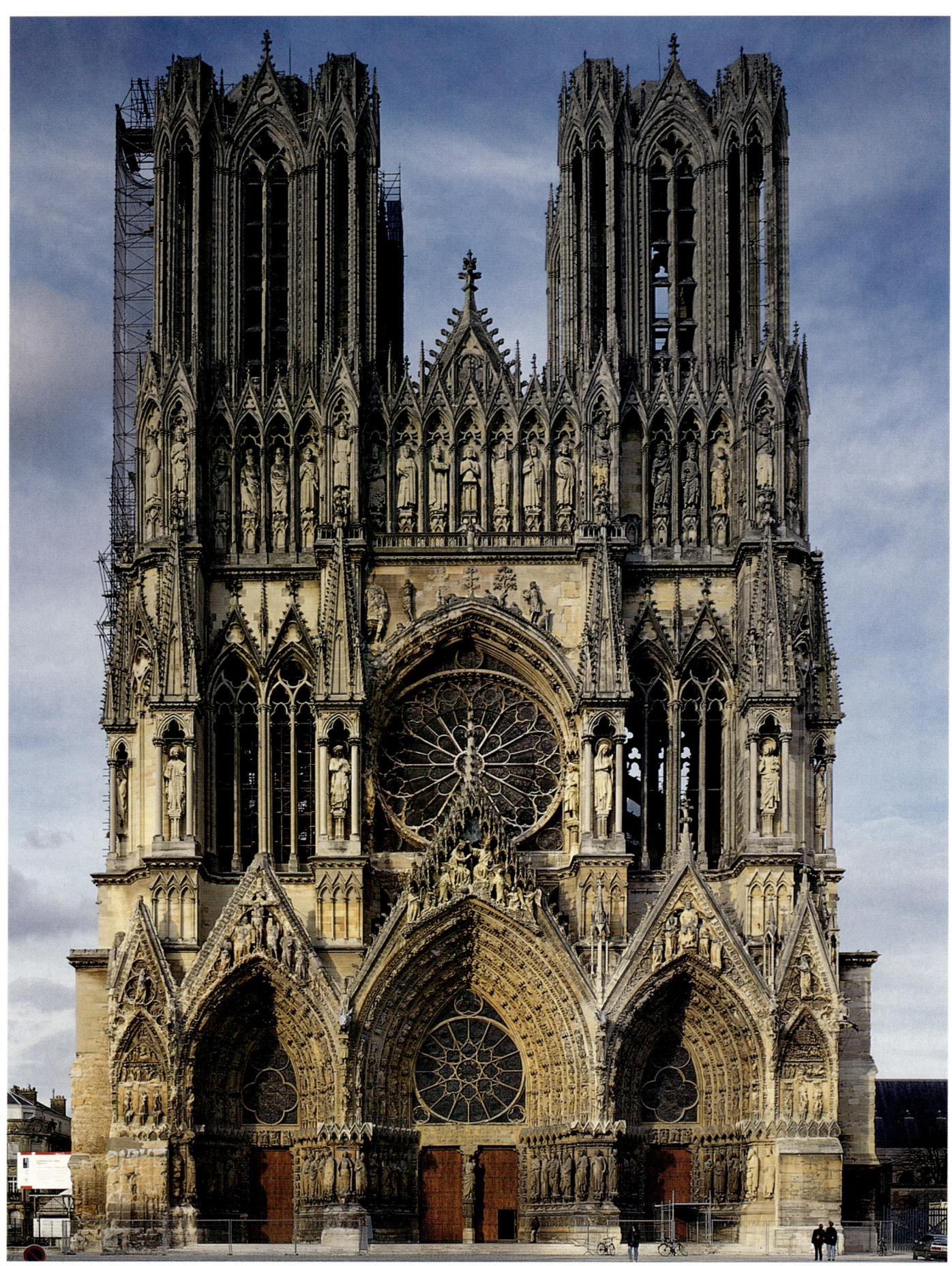

**18-21** West facade of Reims Cathedral, Reims, France, ca. 1225–1290.

**GLASS REPLACES STONE** Construction of Reims Cathedral (FIG. **18-21**) began only a few years after work commenced at Amiens. The Reims builders carried the High Gothic style of the Amiens west facade still further, both architecturally and sculpturally. The two facades, although similar, display some significant differences. The kings' gallery of statues at Reims is *above* the great rose window, and the figures stand in taller and more ornate frames. In fact, the designer "stretched" every detail of the facade. The openings in the towers and those to the left and right of the rose window are taller, narrower, and more intricately decorated, and they more closely resemble the elegant lancets of the clerestory within. A pointed arch also frames the rose window itself, and the pinnacles over the portals are taller and more elaborate than those at Amiens. Most striking, however, is the treatment of the tympanums over the doorways, where stained-glass windows replaced the stone relief sculpture of earlier facades. The contrast with Romanesque heavy masonry construction (see FIG. 17-12) is extreme. But the rapid transformation of the Gothic facade since the 12th-century designs of Saint-Denis and Chartres (FIG. 18-4) and even Laon (FIG. 18-7) is no less noteworthy.

**STATUES BEGIN TO CONVERSE** At Reims the fully ripened Gothic style also can be seen in sculpture. At first glance, the jamb statues of the west portals of Reims Cathedral (FIG. **18-22**)

appear to be completely detached from their architectural background. The sculptors shrank the supporting columns into insignificance so that they in no way restrict the free and easy movements of the full-bodied figures. (Compare the Reims statue-columns with those of the Royal Portal of Chartres, FIG. 18-6, where the background columns occupy a volume equal to that of the figures.) The two Reims jamb statues we illustrate portray Saint Elizabeth visiting the Virgin Mary before the birth of Jesus. They are two of a series of statues celebrating Mary's life and are further testimony to the Virgin's central role in Gothic iconography.

The sculptor of the Visitation group reveals a classicizing bent startlingly unlike anything seen since Roman times. The artist probably studied actual classical statuary in France. Although art historians have been unable to pinpoint specific models, the heads of both women look like ancient Roman portraits. The youthful Mary, for example, resembles the women of the Antonine dynasty, especially Faustina the Younger, Marcus Aurelius's wife. Whatever the sculptor's source, the statues are astonishing approximations of the classical naturalistic style. The Reims master even incorporated the Greek contrapposto posture, going far beyond the stance of the Chartres Saint Theodore (FIG. 18-16). At Reims, the swaying of the hips is much more pronounced. The right legs bend, and the knees press through the rippling folds of the garments. The sculptor also set the figures' arms in motion. Mary and Elizabeth turn their faces toward each other and they converse through gestures. In the Reims Visitation group, the formerly isolated Gothic jamb statues became actors in a biblical narrative.

**A RADIANT ROYAL CHAPEL** The stained-glass windows inserted into the portal tympanums of Reims Cathedral exemplify the wall-dissolving High Gothic architectural style. The architect of Sainte-Chapelle (FIG. **18-23**) in Paris extended this style to an entire building. Louis IX built Sainte-Chapelle, joined to the royal palace, as a repository for the crown of thorns and other relics of Christ's Passion he had purchased in 1239 from his cousin Baldwin II, the Latin emperor of Constantinople. The chapel is a masterpiece of the so-called *Rayonnant* (radiant) style of the High Gothic age, which dominated the second half of the century. It was associated with the royal Parisian court of Saint Louis (see "Louis IX: The Saintly King," page 498). In Sainte-Chapelle, the dissolution of walls and the reduction of the bulk of the supports were carried to the point that some 6,450 square feet of stained glass make up more than three-quarters of the structure. The supporting elements were reduced so much that they are hardly more than large *mullions*, or vertical stone bars. The emphasis is on the extreme slenderness of the architectural forms and on linearity in general. Although the chapel was heavily restored in the 19th century (after damage during the French Revolution), it has retained most of its original 13th-century stained glass. Sainte-Chapelle's enormous windows filter the light and fill the interior with an unearthly rose-violet atmosphere. Approximately 49 feet high and 15 feet wide, they were the largest designed up to their time.

**THE VIRGIN AS QUEEN** The "court style" of Saint Louis was not confined to architecture. Indeed, the elegance and delicacy displayed in Sainte-Chapelle's design permeated the pictorial arts as well. By the early 14th century, a mannered elegance that marks Late Gothic art in general had replaced the monumental and

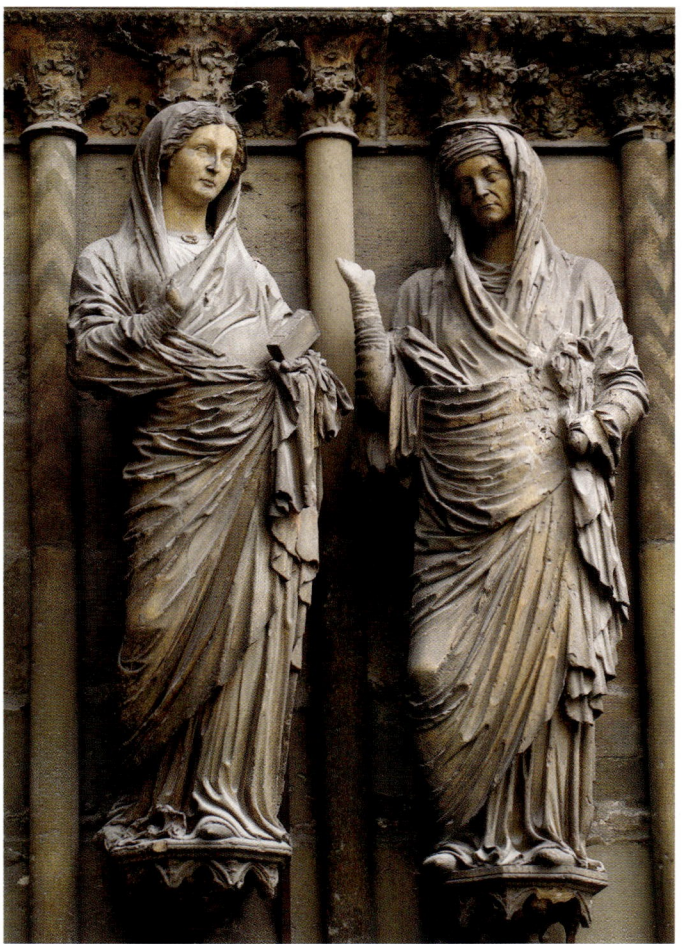

**18-22** Visitation, jamb statues of central doorway, west facade, Reims Cathedral, Reims, France, ca. 1230.

### *Louis IX: The Saintly King*

The royal patron behind the Parisian "court style" of Gothic art and architecture was King Louis IX (1215–1270; r. 1226–1270), grandson of Philip Augustus. Louis inherited the throne when he was only 12 years old, so until he reached adulthood six years later, his mother, Blanche of Castile, granddaughter of Eleanor of Aquitaine (see "Romanesque Countesses, Queens, and Nuns," Chapter 17, page 473), served as France's regent.

The French regarded Louis as the ideal king, and in 1297, 27 years after Louis's death, Pope Boniface VIII declared him a saint. In his own time, Louis was revered for his piety, justice, truthfulness, and charity. His almsgiving and his donations to religious foundations were extravagant. He especially favored the *mendicant* (begging) orders, the Dominicans and Franciscans (see "Mendicant Orders and Confraternities," Chapter 19, page 524). He admired their poverty, piety, and self-sacrificing disregard of material things.

Louis launched two unsuccessful Crusades, the Seventh (1248–1254, when, in her son's absence, Blanche was again French regent) and the Eighth (1270). He died in Tunisia during the latter. As a crusading knight who lost his life in the service of the Church, Louis personified the chivalric virtues of courage, loyalty, and self-sacrifice. Saint Louis united in his person the best qualities of the Christian knight, the benevolent monarch, and the holy man. He became the model of medieval Christian kingship.

Louis's political accomplishments were also noteworthy. He subdued the unruly French barons, and between 1243 and 1314 no one seriously challenged the crown. He negotiated a treaty with Henry III, king of France's traditional enemy, England. Such was his reputation for integrity and just dealing that he served as arbiter in at least a dozen international disputes. So successful was he as peacekeeper that despite civil wars through most of the 13th century, international peace prevailed. Under Saint Louis, medieval France was at its most prosperous, and its art and architecture were admired and imitated throughout Europe.

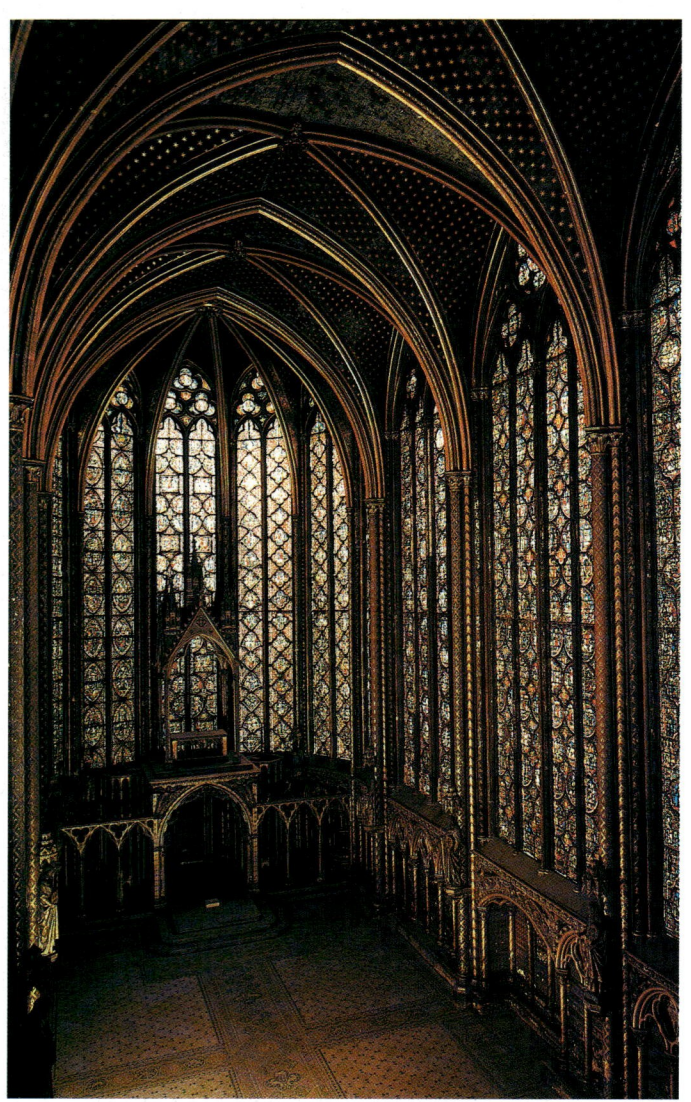

**18-23** Interior of the upper chapel, Sainte-Chapelle, Paris, France, 1243–1248.

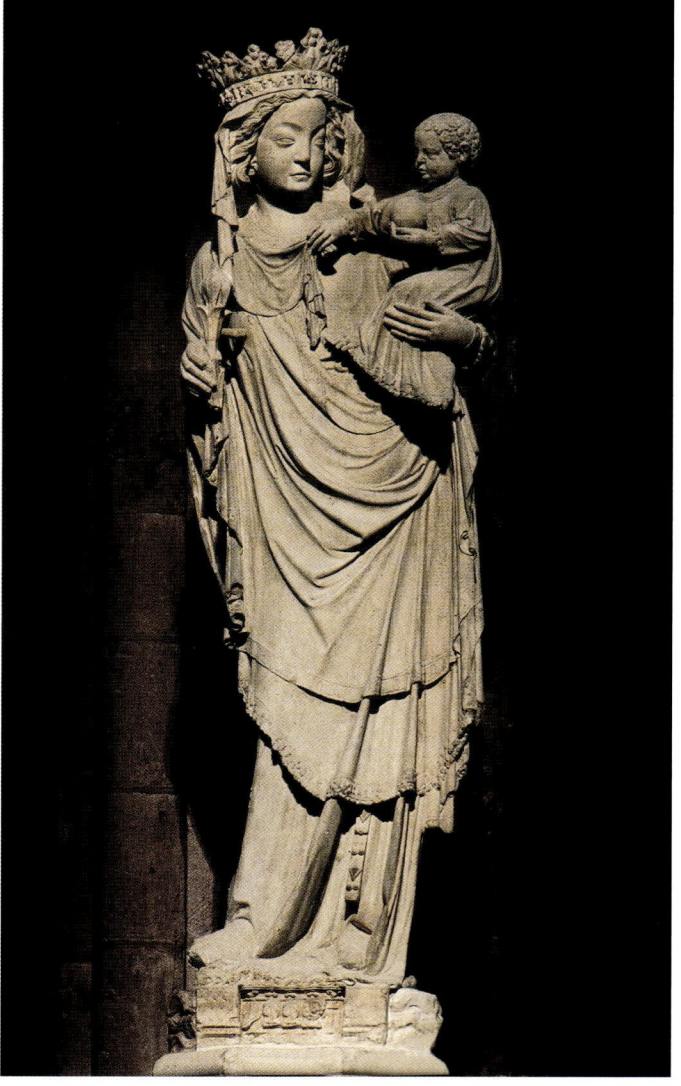

**18-24** Virgin and Child *(Virgin of Paris),* Notre-Dame, Paris, France, early 14th century.

solemn sculptural style of the High Gothic portals. Perhaps the best example of the late French court style in sculpture is the statue nicknamed the *Virgin of Paris* (FIG. **18-24**) because of its location in the Parisian Cathedral of Notre-Dame. The sculptor portrayed Mary as a worldly queen, decked out in royal garments and wearing a heavy gem-encrusted crown. The Christ Child is equally richly attired and is very much the infant prince in the arms of his young mother. The tender, anecdotal characterization of mother and son represents a further humanization of the portrayal of religious figures in Gothic sculpture.

The playful interaction of an adult and an infant in the *Virgin of Paris* may be compared with the similarly composed statuary group of Hermes and the infant Dionysos (see FIG. 5-62) by the Greek sculptor Praxiteles. Indeed, the exaggerated swaying S curve of the Virgin's body superficially resembles the shallow S curve Praxiteles introduced in the fourth century BCE. But unlike its Late Classical predecessor, the Late Gothic S curve was not organic (derived from within the figure), nor was it a rational, if pleasing, organization of human anatomical parts. Rather, the Gothic curve was an artificial form imposed on figures, a decorative device that produced the desired effect of elegance but that had nothing to do with body structure. In fact, in our example, the body is quite lost behind the heavy drapery, which, deeply cut and hollowed, almost denies the figure a solid existence. The ornamental line the sculptor created with the flexible fabric is analogous to the complex tracery of the Late Gothic style in architecture, which dominated northern Europe in the 14th and 15th centuries.

**FLAMBOYANT ARCHITECTURE** The change from Rayonnant architecture to the Late Gothic, or *Flamboyant,* style (named for the flamelike appearance of its pointed bar tracery), occurred in the 14th century. The style reached its florid maturity nearly a century later. This period was a difficult one for the French monarchy. Long wars against England and the duchy of Burgundy sapped its economic and cultural strength, and building projects in the royal domain either ceased or never began. Architects accepted the new style most enthusiastically in regions outside the Île-de-France.

Normandy is particularly rich in Flamboyant architecture, and the church of Saint-Maclou (FIG. **18-25**) in Rouen, its capital, is a masterpiece of the Flamboyant style. The church is tiny (only about 75 feet high and 180 feet long) compared to the great Gothic cathedrals. Its facade presents a sharp contrast with the High Gothic style of the 13th century (compare FIGS. 18-19 and 18-21). The five portals (two of them blind) bend outward in an arc. Ornate gables crown the doorways, pierced through and filled with wiry, "flickering" Flamboyant tracery made up of curves and countercurves that form brittle decorative webs and mask the building's structure. The transparency of the pinnacles over the doorways permits visitors to see the central rose window and the flying buttresses, even though they are set well back from the facade. The overlapping of all features, pierced as they are, confuses the structural lines and produces a bewildering complexity of views that is the hallmark of the Flamboyant style.

**A DOUBLY FORTIFIED TOWN** The Gothic age was truly the age of great cathedrals, but people, of course, also needed and built secular structures such as town halls, palaces, and private residences. In an age of frequent warfare, the feudal barons often constructed fortified castles in places enemies could not easily access. Sometimes thick defensive wall circuits or *ramparts* enclosed entire towns. In time, however, purely defensive wars became ob-

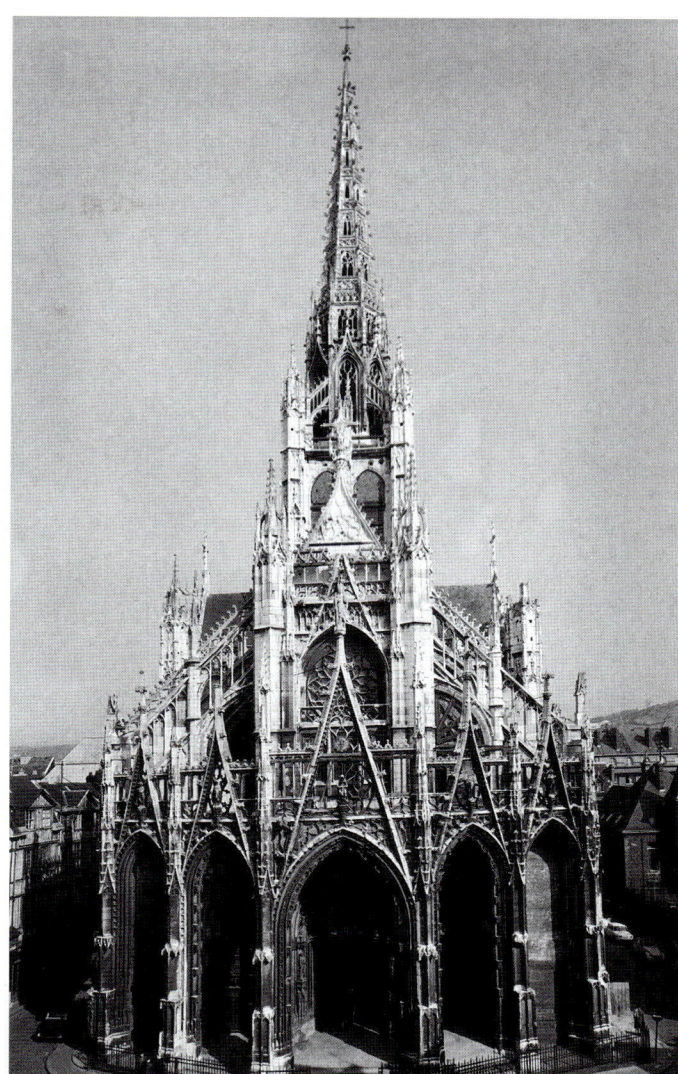

**18-25** West facade of Saint-Maclou, Rouen, France, ca. 1500–1514.

solete due to the invention of artillery and improvements in siege craft. The fortress era gradually passed, and throughout Europe once-mighty ramparts fell into ruin.

One of the most famous Gothic fortified towns is Carcassonne (FIG. **18-26**) in Languedoc in southern France. It was the regional center of resistance to the northern forces of royal France. Built on a hill bounded by the Aude River, Carcassonne had been fortified since Roman times. It had Visigothic walls dating from the 6th century, but in the 12th century masons reinforced them. *Battlements* (low parapets) with *crenellations* (composed of alternating solid *merlons* and open *crenels*) protected guards patrolling the stone ring surrounding the town. Carcassonne might be forced to surrender but could not easily be taken by storm.

Within the town's double walls was a fortified castle (FIG. 18-26, *left*) with a massive attached *keep,* a secure tower that could serve as a place of last refuge. Balancing that center of secular power was the bishop's seat, the Cathedral of Saint-Nazaire (FIG. 18-26, *right*). The small church, built between 1269 and 1329, may have been the work of an architect brought in from northern France. In any case, Saint-Nazaire's builders were certainly familiar with the latest developments in architecture in the Île-de-France. Today, Carcassonne provides a rare glimpse of what was once a familiar sight in Gothic France: a tightly contained complex of castle, cathedral, and town within towered walls.

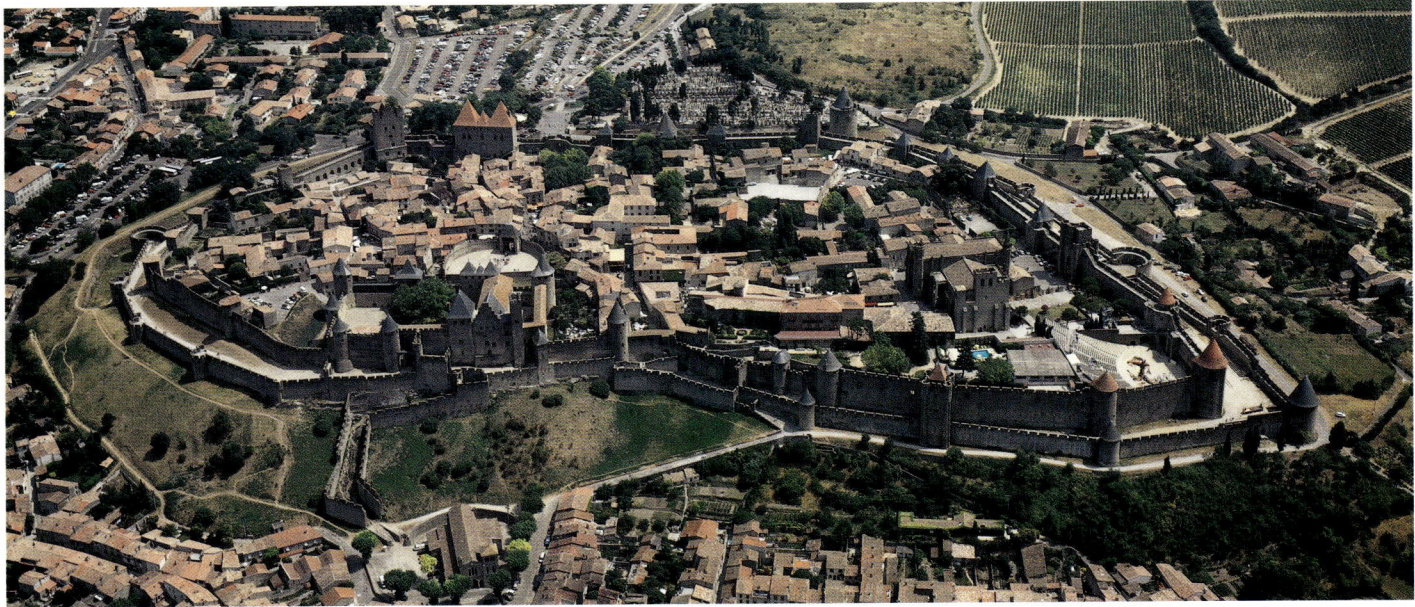

18-26  Aerial view of the fortified town of Carcassonne, France. Bastions and towers, 12th–13th centuries, restored by EUGÈNE VIOLLET-LE-DUC in the 19th century.

**TOWERING GUILD HALLS** One of the many signs of the growing secularization of urban life in the late Middle Ages was the erection of monumental meeting halls and warehouses for the increasing number of craft guilds that were being formed throughout Europe. An early example is the imposing guild hall and market (FIG. **18-27**) of the clothmakers of Bruges, begun in 1230. Situated in the city's major square, it was a forceful reminder of the important role of artisans and merchants in Gothic Europe. The design combines features of military (the corner "watch-towers" with their crenellations) and church (lancet windows with crowning oculi) architecture. The uppermost, octagonal portion of the tower with its flying buttresses and pinnacles dates to the 15th century, but even the original two-story tower is taller than the rest of the hall. Lofty towers were a common feature of late medieval guild and town halls and were intended to compete for attention and prestige with the towers of city cathedrals.

**PROSPERITY AT HOME** The fortunes of the new class of wealthy merchants that rose to prominence throughout Europe in the late Middle Ages may not have equaled those of the hereditary royalty, but their power and influence were still enormous. One such figure was the French trader and financier Jacques Coeur (1395–1456), whose astonishing career illustrates how wealth and power could be won and lost by enterprising private citizens. Coeur had banking houses in every city of France and many abroad. He employed more than 300 agents and competed with the great trading republics of Italy. His merchant ships filled the Mediterranean. With the papacy's permission, he traded widely with the Muslims of Egypt and the Middle East and gained concessions there that benefited French commerce for centuries. He was financial adviser to King Charles VII of France and a friend of Pope Nicholas V. The animosity of hundreds of his highborn debtors and competitors eventually led to Coeur's downfall. His enemies framed him on an absurd charge of having poisoned Agnes Sorel, the king's mistress, and he was imprisoned. His vast wealth and property were confiscated and distributed among the king's people. Coeur escaped from prison and made his way to Rome, where the pope warmly received him. He died of fever while leading a fleet of papal war galleys in the eastern Mediterranean.

Jacques Coeur's great town house (FIG. **18-28**), built between 1443 and 1451 in his native city of Bourges, still stands. It is the best-preserved example of Late Gothic domestic architecture.

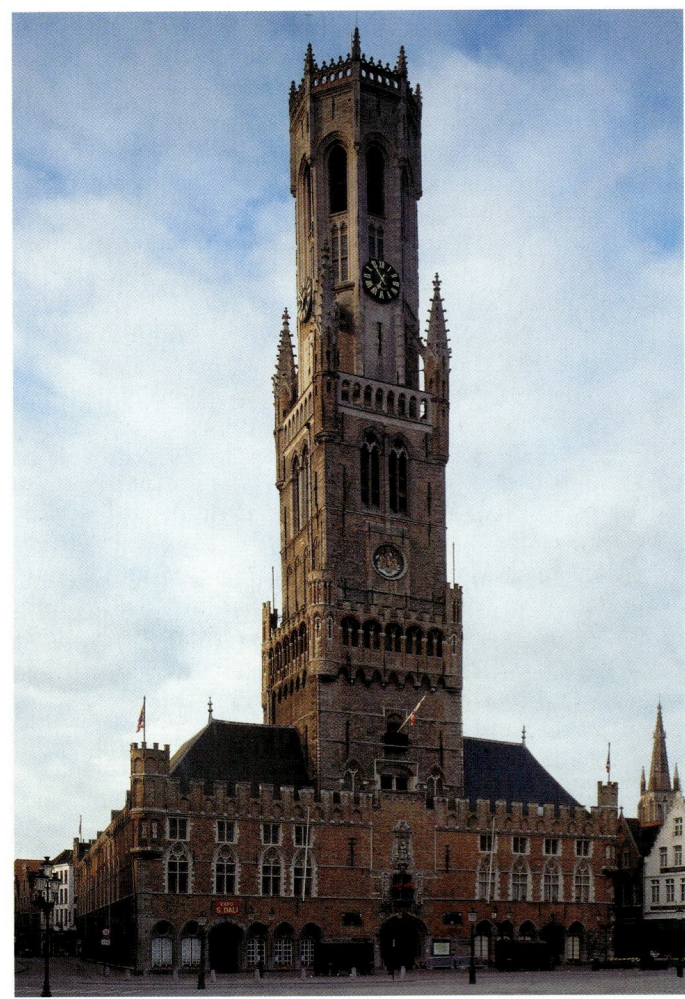

18-27  Hall of the cloth guild, Bruges, Netherlands, begun 1230.

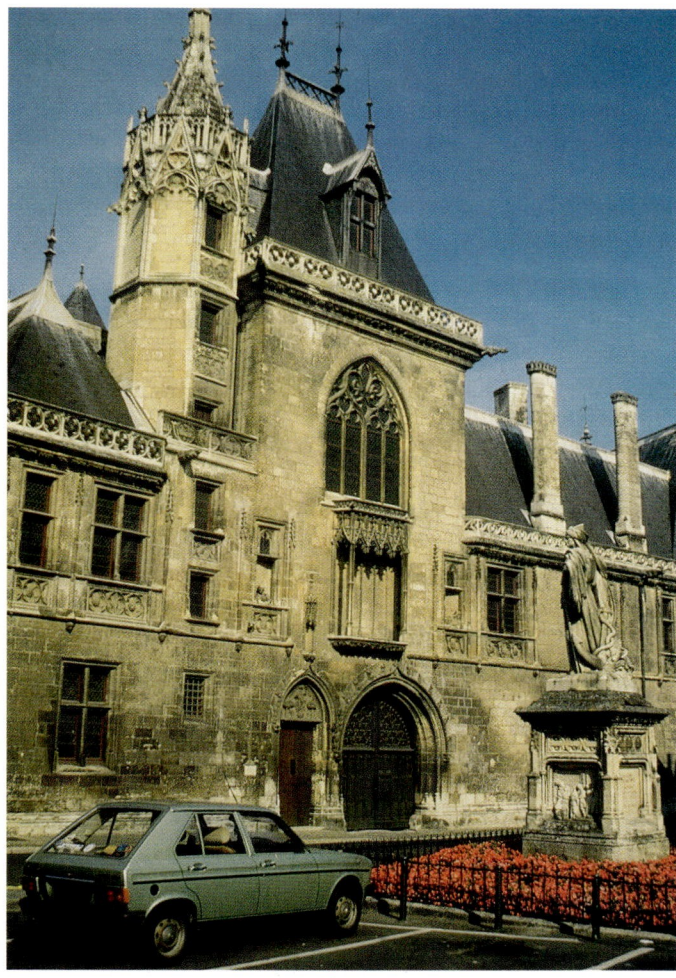

**18-28** House of Jacques Coeur, Bourges, France, 1443–1451.

The house's plan is irregular, with the units arranged around an open courtyard. The service areas (maintenance shops and storage, servants' quarters, baths) occupy the ground level. The upper stories house the great hall and auxiliary rooms used for offices and family living rooms.

The focus of the broad facade is a tall central section with a very steep pyramidal roof, a spire-capped tower with Flamboyant tracery, a large pointed-arch stained-glass window, and two doorways (one for pedestrians and the larger one for horses and carriages). The elegant canopied niche beneath the great window once housed a royal equestrian statue. A comparable statue of Coeur on horseback dominated the facade opening onto the interior courtyard. An unusual feature of the external facade is the pair of false windows with life-size relief sculptures of a male and a female servant looking down upon passersby in the street. Jacques Coeur's house is both a splendid example of Late Gothic architecture and a monumental symbol of the period's new secular spirit — an expression of the triumph of city culture, of capital accumulation, and of the desire for worldly convenience and proud display.

## Book Illumination and Luxury Arts

Paris's claim as the intellectual center of Gothic Europe (see "Paris," page 487) did not rest solely on the stature of its university faculty and on the reputation of its architects, masons, sculptors, and stained-glass makers. The city was also a renowned center for the production of fine books. The famous Florentine poet Dante Alighieri (1265–1321), in fact, referred to Paris in his *Divine Comedy* of ca. 1310–1320 as the city famed for the art of illumination.[2] Indeed, the Gothic period is when book manufacture shifted from monastic scriptoria shut off from the world to urban workshops staffed by laypersons. The owners of these new for-profit secular businesses sold their products to the royal family, scholars, and prosperous merchants. Concentrated in Paris, these Gothic shops were the forerunners of modern publishing houses.

**THE ART OF GEOMETRY** One of the most intriguing Parisian manuscripts preserved today was not, however, produced for sale. It is the personal sketchbook compiled by VILLARD DE HONNECOURT, an early 13th-century master mason. Its pages contain details of buildings, plans of choirs with radiating chapels, church towers, lifting devices, a sawmill, stained-glass windows, and other subjects of obvious interest to architects and masons. But also sprinkled liberally throughout the pages are drawings depicting religious and worldly figures, as well as animals, some realistic and others purely fantastic.

On the page we illustrate (FIG. **18-29**), Villard demonstrated the value of the *ars de geometria* (art of geometry) to artists. He showed that both natural forms and buildings are based on simple geometric shapes such as the square, circle, and triangle. Even where he

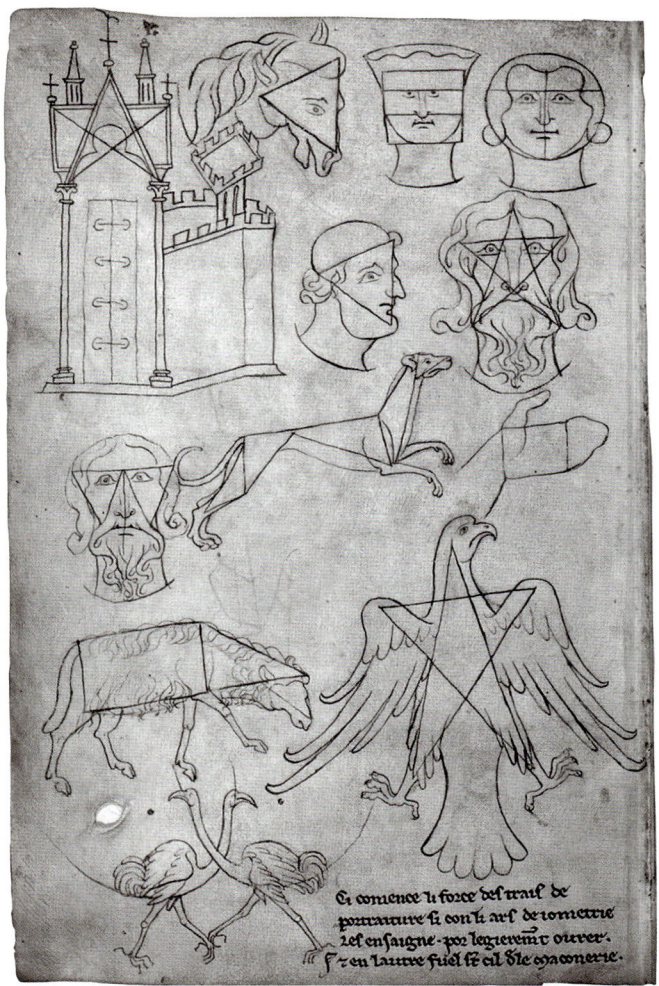

**18-29** VILLARD DE HONNECOURT, figures based on geometric shapes, folio 18 verso of a sketchbook, from Paris, France, ca. 1220–1235. Ink on vellum, $9\frac{1}{4}'' \times 6''$. Bibliothèque Nationale, Paris.

claimed to have drawn his animals from nature, he composed his figures around a skeleton not of bones but of abstract geometric forms. Geometry was, in Villard's words, "strong help in drawing figures."

But geometry played a symbolic as well as a practical role in Gothic art and architecture. Gothic artists, architects, and theologians alike thought the triangle, for example, embodied the idea of the Trinity of God the Father, Christ, and the Holy Spirit. The circle, which has neither a beginning nor an end, symbolized the eternity of the one God. When Gothic architects based their designs on the art of geometry, building their forms out of abstract shapes laden with symbolic meaning, they believed they were working according to the divinely established laws of nature.

**GOD AS ARCHITECT** A vivid illustration of this concept appears as the frontispiece (FIG. **18-30**) of a moralized Bible produced in Paris during the 1220s. *Moralized Bibles* are heavily illustrated, each page pairing paintings of Old and New Testament episodes with explanations of their moral significance. The page we show does not conform to this formula because it is the introduction to all that follows. Above the illustration, the scribe wrote (in French rather than Latin): "Here God creates heaven and earth, the sun and moon, and all the elements." God appears as the architect of the world, shaping the universe with the aid of a compass. Within

the perfect circle already created are the spherical sun and moon and the unformed matter that will become the earth once God applies the same geometric principles to it. In contrast to the biblical account of Creation, in which God created the sun, moon, and stars after the earth had been formed, and made the world by sheer force of will and a simple "Let there be . . ." command, the Gothic artist portrayed God as an industrious architect, creating the universe with some of the same tools used by mortal builders.

**A BIBLE FIT FOR A QUEEN** Not surprisingly, most of the finest Gothic books known today belonged to the French monarchy. Saint Louis in particular was an avid collector of both secular and religious books. The library he and his royal predecessors and successors formed was vast. It eventually became the core of France's national library, the Bibliothèque Nationale. One of the books the royal family commissioned is a moralized Bible now in the collection of New York's Pierpont Morgan Library. Louis's mother, Blanche of Castile, ordered the Bible during her regency (1226–1234) for her teenage son. The dedication page (FIG. **18-31**) has a costly gold background and depicts Blanche and Louis enthroned beneath triple-lobed arches and miniature cityscapes. The latter can be compared to the architectural canopies above the heads of contemporaneous French portal statues (FIG. 18-20). Below, in

**18-30** God as architect of the world, folio 1 verso of a moralized Bible, from Paris, France, ca. 1220–1230. Ink, tempera, and gold leaf on vellum, $1' 1\frac{1}{2}'' \times 8\frac{1}{4}''$. Österreichische Nationalbibliothek, Vienna.

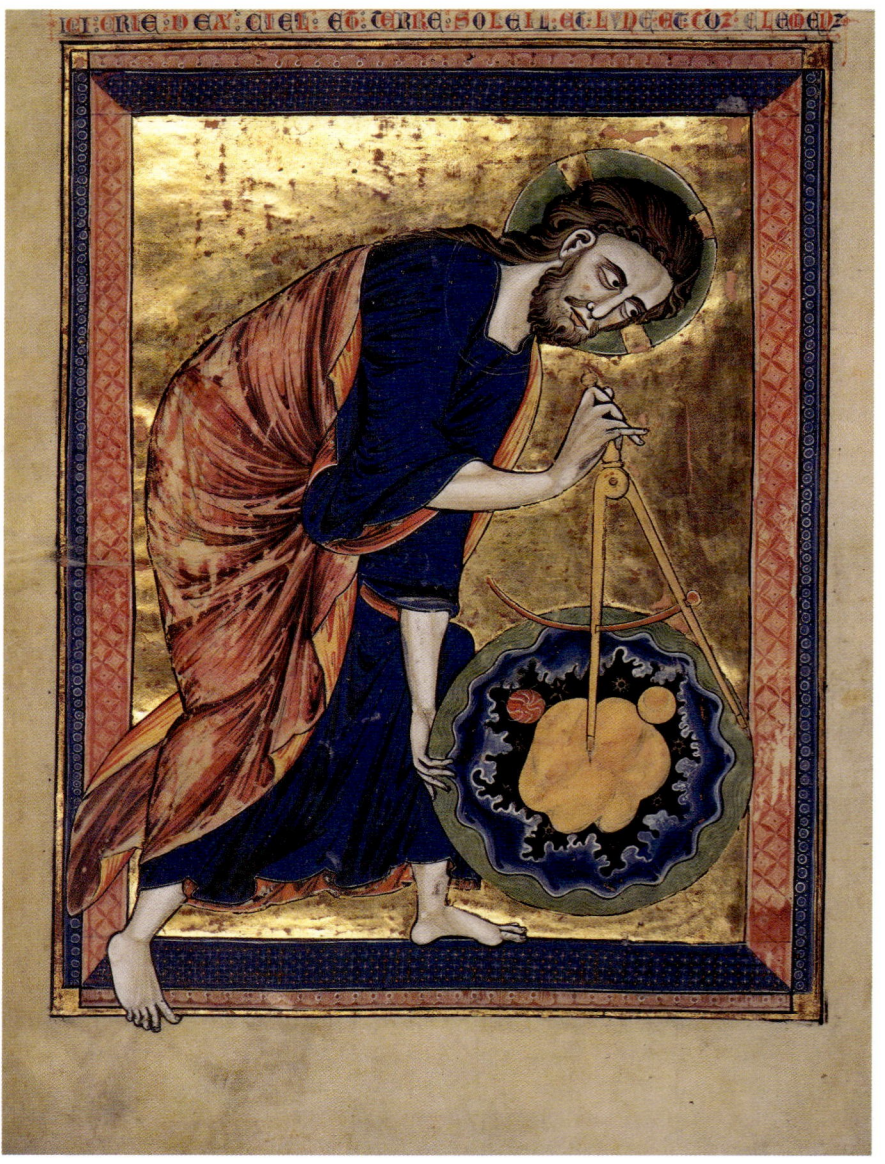

The preparation of the illuminated pages also involved several hands. Some artists, for example, specialized in painting borders or initials. Only the workshop head or one of the most advanced assistants would paint the main figural scenes. Given this division of labor and the assembly-line nature of Gothic book production, it is astonishing how uniform the style is on a single page, as well as from page to page, in most illuminated manuscripts.

**SAINT LOUIS'S PSALTER** The golden background of Blanche's Bible is unusual and has no parallel in Gothic windows. But the radiance of stained glass probably inspired the glowing color of other 13th-century Parisian illuminated manuscripts. In some cases, masters in the same urban workshop produced both glass and books. Many art historians believe that the *Psalter of Saint Louis* (FIG. 18-32) is one of several books produced in Paris for Louis IX by artists associated with those who made the stained glass for his Sainte-Chapelle. Certainly, the painted architectural setting in Louis's psalter reflects the pierced screenlike lightness and transparency of royal buildings such as Sainte-Chapelle. The painted figures also express the same aristocratic elegance as the Rayonnant "court style" of architecture favored by royal Paris. The intense colors, especially the blues, emulate glass. The borders resemble glass partitioned by leading. And the gables, pierced by rose windows with bar tracery, are standard Rayonnant architectural features.

The page from the *Psalter of Saint Louis* shown here (FIG. 18-32) represents Abraham and the three angels. Christians believe that the Old Testament story prefigures the Christian Trinity (see "Jewish Subjects in Christian Art," Chapter 11, page 305). The subject was

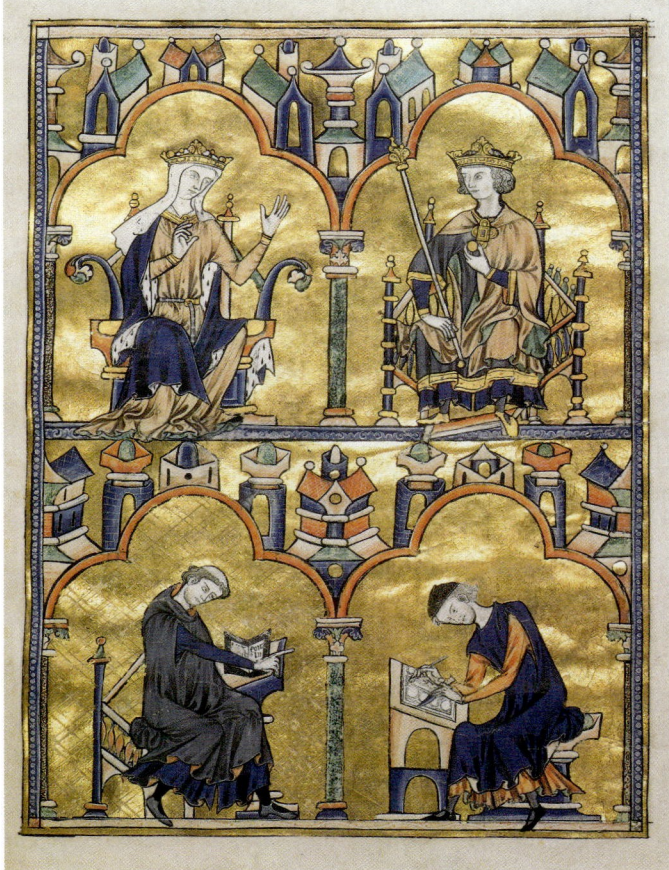

**18-31** Blanche of Castile, Louis IX, and two monks, dedication page (folio 8 recto) of a moralized Bible, from Paris, France, 1226–1234. Ink, tempera, and gold leaf on vellum, 1' 3" × 10½". Pierpont Morgan Library, New York.

similar architectural frames, are a monk and a scribe. The older clergyman dictates a sacred text to his young apprentice. The scribe already has divided his page into two columns of four roundels each, a format often used for the paired illustrations of moralized Bibles. The inspirations for such designs were probably the roundels of Gothic stained-glass windows (compare the borders of the *Belle Verrière* window at Chartres, FIG. 18-13, and the windows of Louis's own, later, Sainte-Chapelle, FIG. 18-23).

The picture of Gothic book production on the dedication page of Blanche of Castile's moralized Bible is a very abbreviated one, as was the view of a monastic scriptorium discussed earlier (see FIG. 16-10). The manufacturing process used in the workshops of 13th-century Paris did not differ significantly from that of 10th-century Tábara. It involved many steps and numerous specialized artists, scribes, and assistants of varying skill levels. The Benedictine abbot Johannes Trithemius (1462–1516) described the way books were still made in his day in his treatise *In Praise of Scribes:*

> If you do not know how to write, you still can assist the scribes in various ways. One of you can correct what another has written. Another can add the rubrics [headings] to the corrected text. A third can add initials and signs of division. Still another can arrange the leaves and attach the binding. Another of you can prepare the covers, the leather, the buckles and clasps. All sorts of assistance can be offered the scribe to help him pursue his work without interruption. He needs many things which can be prepared by others: parchment cut, flattened and ruled for script, ready ink and pens. You will always find something with which to help the scribe.[3]

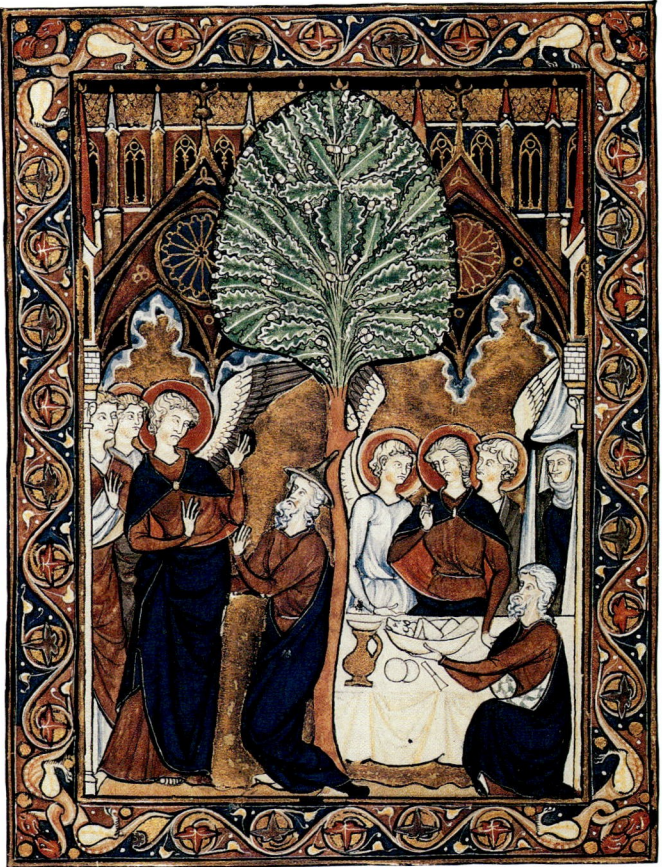

**18-32** Abraham and the three angels, folio 7 verso of the *Psalter of Saint Louis,* from Paris, France, 1253–1270. Ink, tempera, and gold leaf on vellum, 5" × 3½". Bibliothèque Nationale, Paris.

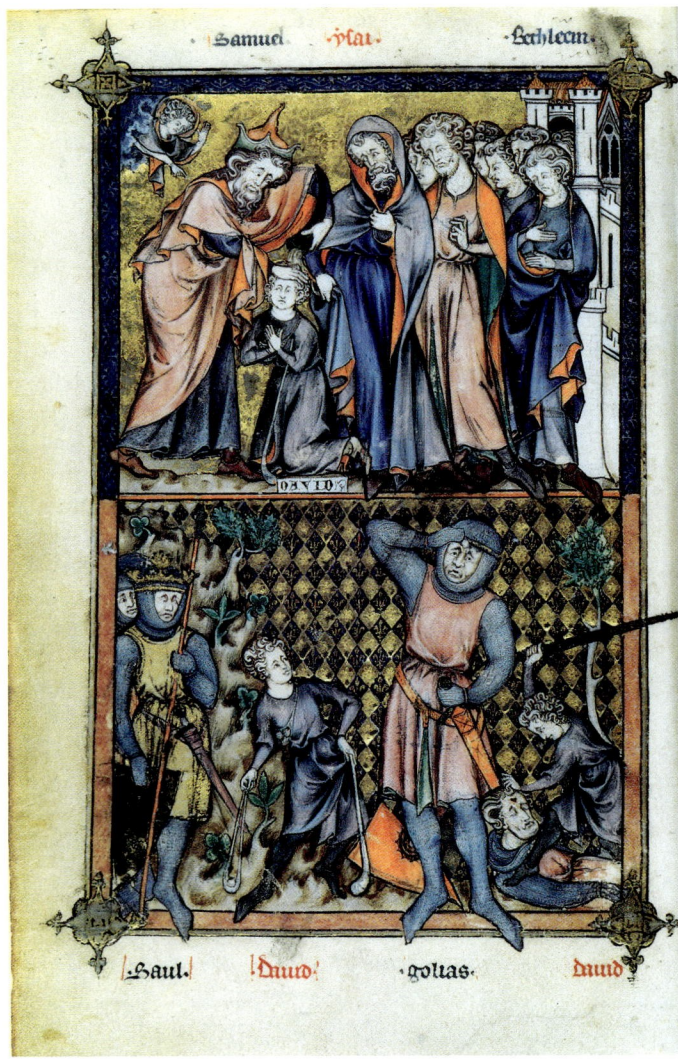

**18-33** MASTER HONORÉ, David anointed by Samuel and battle of David and Goliath, folio 7 verso of the *Breviary of Philippe le Bel,* from Paris, France, 1296. Ink and tempera on vellum, $7\frac{7}{8}'' \times 4\frac{7}{8}''$. Bibliothèque Nationale, Paris.

popular in Byzantine art (see FIGS. 12-8 and 12-34). The Gothic artist included two episodes on the same page, separated by the tree of Mamre mentioned in the Bible. At the left, Abraham greets the three angels. In the other scene, he entertains them while his wife Sarah peers at them from a tent. The figures' delicate features and the linear wavy strands of their hair have parallels in Blanche of Castile's moralized Bible, as well as in Parisian stained glass. The elegant proportions, facial expressions, theatrical gestures, and swaying poses are characteristic of the Parisian court style admired throughout Europe. A later example of this mannered style in sculpture, complete with the exaggerated contrapposto of the angel in the left foreground, is the *Virgin of Paris* (FIG. 18-24).

**PRAYERS FOR A KING** As in the Romanesque period, some Gothic manuscript illuminators signed their work. The names of others appear in royal accounts of payments made and similar official documents. One of the artists who produced books for the French court was MASTER HONORÉ, whose Parisian workshop was on the street known today as rue Boutebrie. Honoré illuminated a *breviary* (a book of selected prayers and psalms) for Philippe le Bel (Philip the Fair, r. 1285–1314) in 1296. The page we illustrate (FIG. 18-33) features two Old Testament scenes involving David. In the

upper panel, Samuel anoints the youthful David. Below, while King Saul looks on, David prepares to hurl his slingshot at his most famous opponent, the giant Goliath (who already touches the wound on his forehead!). And then, in a classic example of continuous narration, David slays Goliath with his sword.

Master Honoré's linear treatment of hair, his figures' delicate hands and gestures, and their elegant swaying postures are typical of Parisian painting of the time. But this painter was much more interested than most of his colleagues in giving his figures sculptural volume and showing the play of light on their bodies. Honoré was not concerned with locating his figures in space, however. The Goliath panel in the *Breviary of Philippe le Bel* has a textilelike decorative background, and the feet of Honoré's figures frequently overlap the border. Compared to his contemporaries, Master Honoré pioneered naturalism in figure painting. But he still approached the art of book illumination as a decorator of two-dimensional pages. He did not embrace the classical notion that a painting should be an illusionistic window into a three-dimensional world.

**JEAN PUCELLE AND ITALY** David and Saul also are the subjects of a miniature painting at the top left of an elaborately decorated text page in the *Belleville Breviary* (FIG. **18-34**). JEAN PUCELLE of Paris illuminated it around 1325. He went far beyond Honoré and other French artists by placing his fully modeled

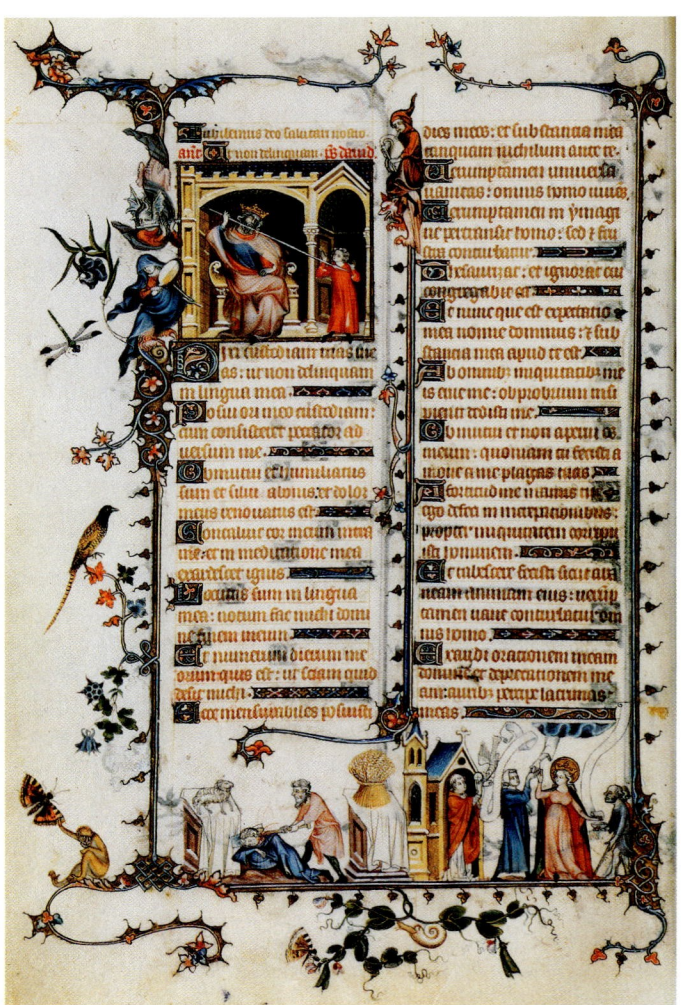

**18-34** JEAN PUCELLE, David before Saul, folio 24 verso of the *Belleville Breviary,* from Paris, France, ca. 1325. Ink and tempera on vellum, $9\frac{1}{2}'' \times 6\frac{3}{4}''$. Bibliothèque Nationale, Paris.

figures in three-dimensional architectural settings rendered in convincing perspective. For example, Pucelle painted Saul as a weighty figure seated on a throne seen in a three-quarter view, and he meticulously depicted the receding coffers of the barrel vault over the young David's head. Such "stage sets" already had become commonplace in Italian painting, and Pucelle seems to have visited Italy and studied Duccio's work in Siena (see Chapter 19). Pucelle's (or one of his assistants') renditions of plants, a bird, butterflies, a dragonfly, a fish, a snail, and a monkey also reveal a keen interest in and close observation of the natural world. Nonetheless, in the *Belleville Breviary* the text still dominates the figures, and the artist (and his patron) delighted in ornamental flourishes, fancy initial letters, and abstract patterns. In that respect, comparisons to monumental panel paintings are inappropriate. Pucelle's breviary remains firmly in the tradition of book illumination.

The *Belleville Breviary* is of special interest because Pucelle's name and those of some of his assistants appear at the end of the book, in a memorandum recording the payment they received for their work. Inscriptions in other Gothic illuminated books regularly state the production costs—the prices paid for materials, especially gold, and for the execution of initials, figures, flowery script, and other embellishments. By this time, illuminators were professional guild members, and their personal reputation, like modern "brand names," guaranteed the quality of their work. Though the cost of materials was still the major factor determining a book's price, individual skill and reputation increasingly decided the value of the illuminator's services. The centuries-old monopoly of the Christian Church in book production had ended.

**A VIRGIN FOR SAINT-DENIS** The royal family also patronized goldsmiths, silversmiths, and other artists specializing in the production of luxury works in metal and enamel for churches, palaces, and private homes. Especially popular among the wealthy were statuettes of sacred figures, which were purchased either for private devotion or as gifts to churches. The Virgin Mary was a favored subject, reflecting her new prominence in the iconography of Gothic portal sculpture.

Perhaps the finest of these costly statuettes is the large silver-gilt figurine known as the *Virgin of Jeanne d'Evreux* (FIG. **18-35**). The queen, wife of Charles IV (r. 1322–1328), donated the image of the Virgin and Child to the royal abbey church of Saint-Denis in 1339. Mary stands on a rectangular base decorated with enamel scenes of Christ's Passion. (Some art historians think the enamels are Jean Pucelle's work.) But no hint of grief appears in the beautiful young Mary's face. The Christ Child, also without a care in the world, playfully reaches for his mother. The elegant proportions of the two figures, Mary's swaying posture, the heavy drapery folds, and the intimate human characterization of the holy figures are also features of the roughly contemporary *Virgin of Paris* (FIG. 18-24). The carver of large stone statues and the royal silversmith working at small scale approached the representation of the Virgin and Child in a similar fashion.

In the *Virgin of Jeanne d'Evreux,* as in the *Virgin of Paris,* Mary appears not only as the Mother of Christ but also as the Queen of Heaven. The Saint-Denis Mary also originally had a crown on her head, and the scepter she holds is in the form of the fleur-de-lis, the French monarchy's floral emblem. The statuette also served as a reliquary. The Virgin's scepter contained hairs believed to come from Mary's head.

**THE CASTLE OF LOVE** Gothic artists produced luxurious objects for secular, as well as religious, contexts. Sometimes they

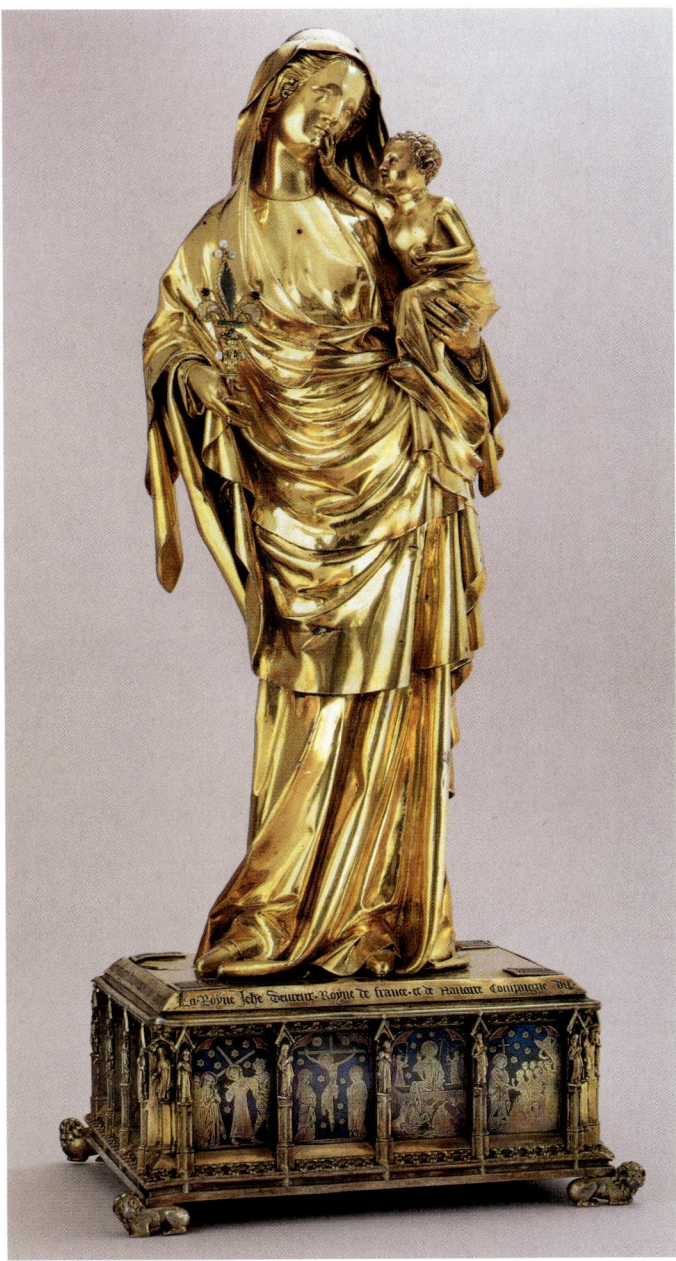

**18-35** *Virgin of Jeanne d'Evreux,* from the abbey church of Saint-Denis, France, 1339. Silver gilt and enamel, 2′ 3½″ high. Louvre, Paris.

decorated these costly pieces with stories of courtly love inspired by the romantic literature of the day, such as the famous story of Lancelot and Queen Guinevere, wife of King Arthur of Camelot. The French poet Chrétien de Troyes recorded their love affair in the late 12th century.

One of the most interesting objects of this type is a woman's jewelry box adorned with ivory relief panels. The theme of the panel illustrated here (FIG. **18-36**) is related to the *Romance of the Rose* by Guillaume de Lorris, written ca. 1225–1235 and completed by Jean de Meung between 1275 and 1280. At the left the sculptor carved the allegory of the siege of the Castle of Love. Gothic knights attempt to capture love's fortress by shooting flowers from their bows and hurling baskets of roses over the walls from catapults. Among the castle's defenders is Cupid, who aims his arrow at one of the knights while a comrade scales the walls on a ladder. The scene in the lid's two central sections shows two knights jousting on

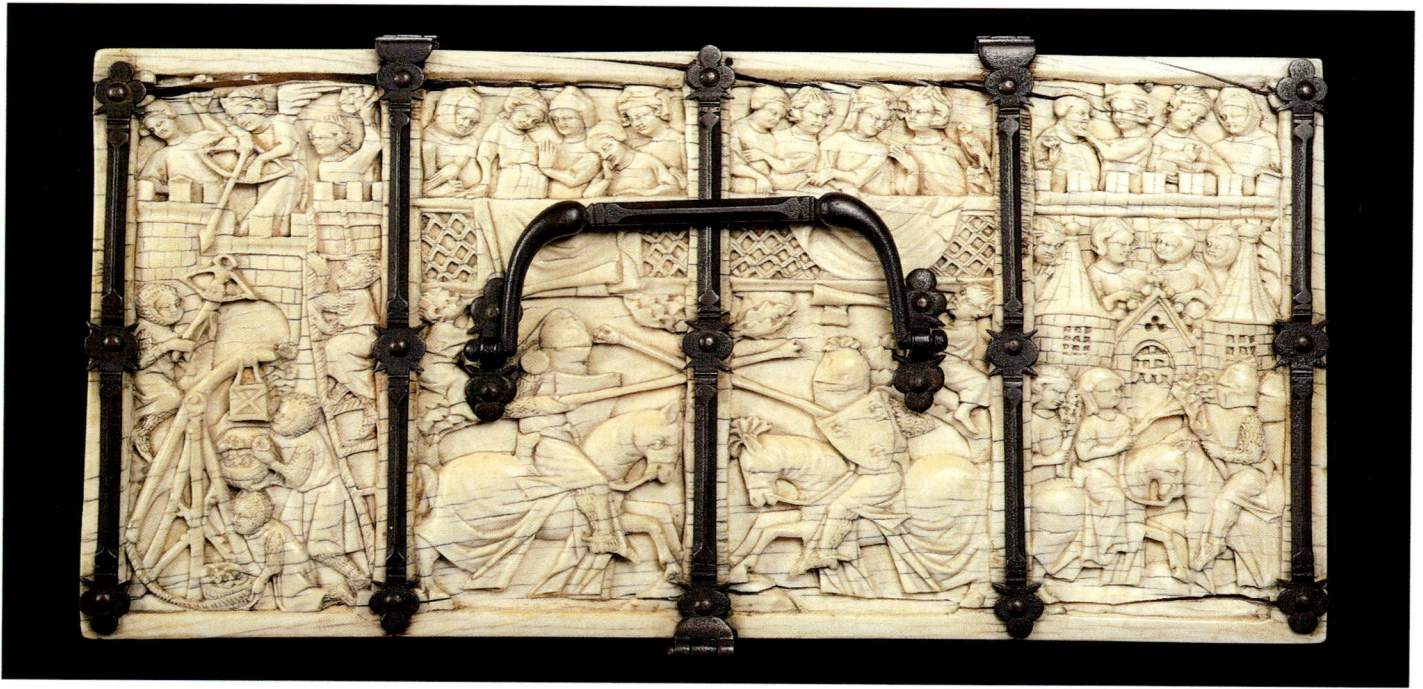

**18-36** The Castle of Love and knights jousting, lid of a jewelry casket, from Paris, France, ca. 1330–1350. Ivory and iron, $4\frac{1}{2}'' \times 9\frac{3}{4}''$. Walters Art Museum, Baltimore.

horseback. Several maidens look down on the contest from a balcony and cheer the knights on, as trumpets blare. A youth in the crowd holds a hunting falcon. The sport was a favorite pastime of the leisure class in the late Middle Ages. At the right, the victorious knight receives his prize (a bouquet of roses) from a chastely dressed maiden on horseback. The scenes on the casket's sides include the famous medieval allegory of female virtue, the legend of the unicorn, a white horse with a single ivory horn. Only a virgin could attract the rare animal, and any woman who could do so thereby also demonstrated her moral purity. Religious themes may have monopolized artistic production for churches in the Gothic age, but secular themes figured prominently in private contexts. Unfortunately, very few examples of the latter survive.

## GOTHIC OUTSIDE OF FRANCE

**OPERE FRANCIGENO** In 1269, the prior (deputy abbot) of the church of Saint Peter at Wimpfen-im-Tal in the German Rhineland hired "a very experienced architect who had recently come from the city of Paris" to rebuild his monastery church.[4] The architect reconstructed the church *opere francigeno* (in the French manner)—that is, in the Gothic style of the Île-de-France. The spread of the Parisian Gothic style had begun even earlier, but in the second half of the 13th century the new style became dominant throughout western Europe. European architecture did not, however, turn Gothic all at once nor in a uniform way. Almost everywhere, patrons and builders modified the "court style" of the Île-de-France according to local preferences. Because the old Romanesque traditions lingered on in many places, each area, marrying its local Romanesque design to the new style, developed its own brand of Gothic architecture.

## *England*

**FRENCH TRANSLATED INTO ENGLISH** Salisbury Cathedral (FIGS. **18-37** to **18-39**) embodies the essential characteristics of English Gothic architecture. Begun in 1220, the same year work started on Amiens Cathedral (FIGS. 18-17 to 18-19), Salisbury Cathedral was mostly completed in about 40 years. The two cathedrals are, therefore, almost exactly contemporary, and the differences between them are very instructive. Although Salisbury's facade has lancet windows and blind arcades with pointed arches, as well as statuary, it presents a striking contrast to French designs (compare Amiens, FIG. 18-19, and Reims, FIG. 18-21). The English facade is a squat screen in front of the nave, wider than the building behind it. The soaring height of the French facades is absent. The Salisbury facade also does not correspond to the three-part division of the interior (nave and two aisles). Different too is the emphasis on the great crossing tower (added ca. 1320–1330), which dominates the silhouette. Salisbury's height is modest compared with that of Amiens and Reims. And because height is not a decisive factor in the English building, the architect used the flying buttress sparingly and as a rigid prop, rather than as an integral part of the vaulting system within the church. In short, the English builders adopted some of the superficial motifs of French Gothic architecture but did not embrace its structural logic or emphasis on height.

Equally distinctive is the long rectilinear plan (FIG. 18-38), with its double transept and flat eastern end. The latter feature was characteristic of Cistercian churches (see FIG. 17-8) and had been favored in England since Romanesque times. The interior (FIG. 18-39), although Gothic in its three-story elevation, pointed arches, four-part rib vaults, and compound piers, conspicuously departs from the French Gothic style. The pier colonnettes stop at the springing of the nave arches and do not connect with the

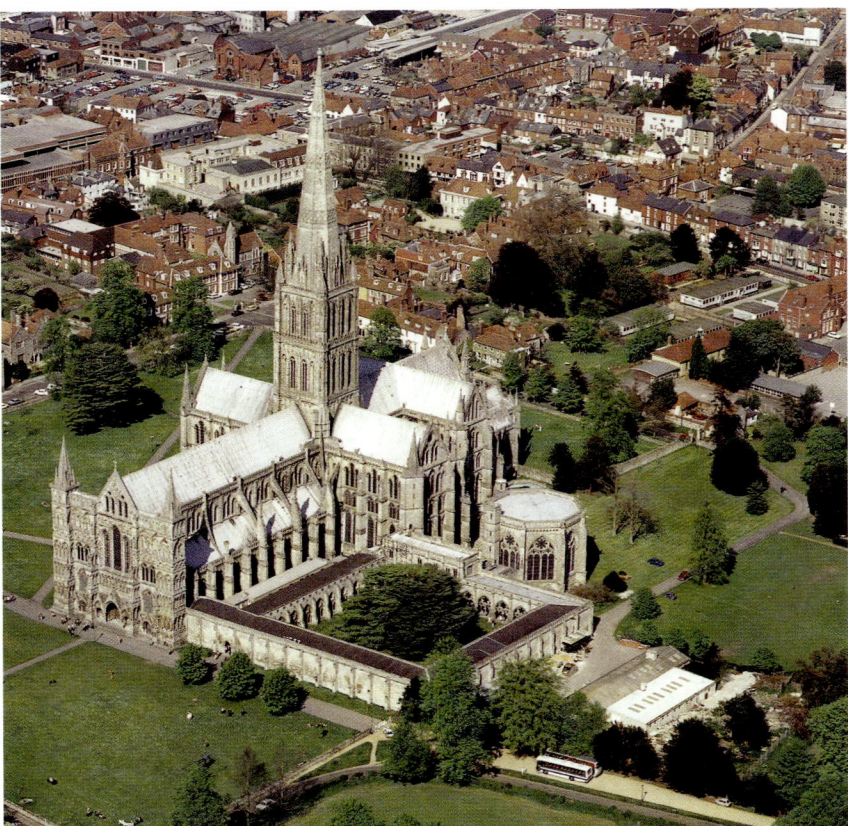

18-37 Aerial view of Salisbury Cathedral, Salisbury, England, 1220–1258; west facade completed 1265; spire ca. 1320–1330.

vault ribs (compare FIGS. 18-17 and 18-18). Instead, the vault ribs rise from corbels in the triforium, producing a strong horizontal emphasis. Underscoring this horizontality is the rich color contrast between the light stone of the walls and vaults and the dark Purbeck marble used for the triforium moldings and corbels, compound pier responds, and other details. Once again, however, the impact of the French Gothic style is clearly visible in the decorative details, especially the tracery of the triforium. Nonetheless, visitors to Salisbury could not mistake the English cathedral for a French one.

**DECORATED AND PERPENDICULAR** Early on, English architecture found its native language in the elaboration of architectural pattern for its own sake (for example, the decorative patterning of the Romanesque piers of Durham Cathedral; see FIG. 17-15). Structural logic, expressed in the building fabric, was secondary. The pier, wall, and vault elements, still relatively simple at Salisbury, became increasingly complex and decorative in

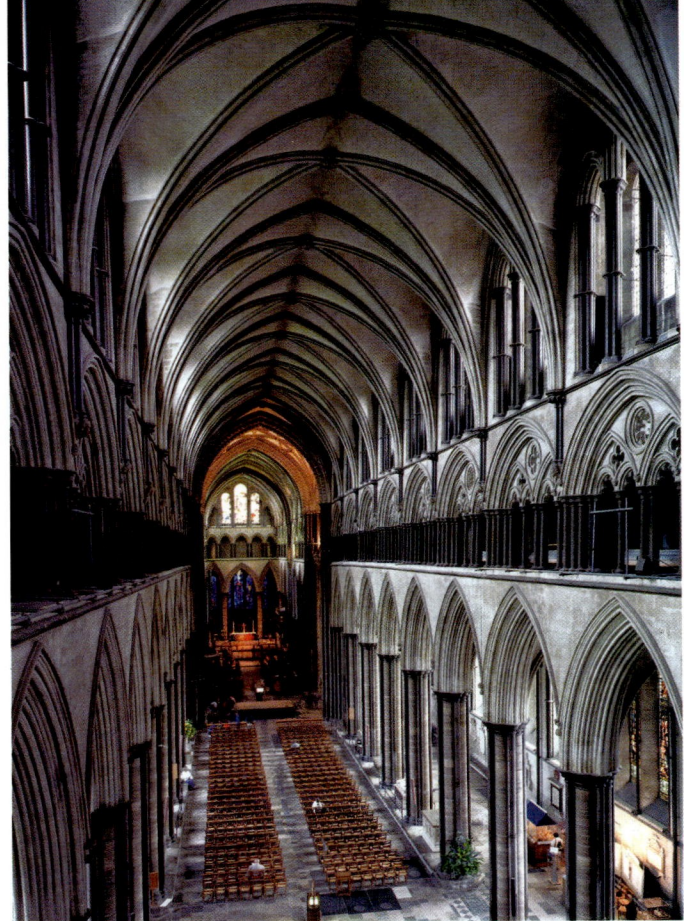

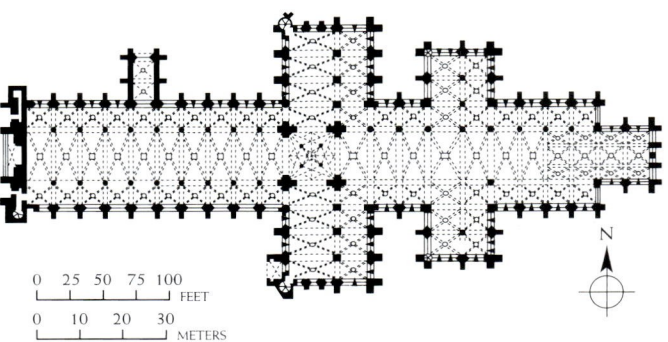

18-38 Plan of Salisbury Cathedral, Salisbury, England, 1220–1258.

18-39 Interior of Salisbury Cathedral (view facing east), Salisbury, England, 1220–1258.

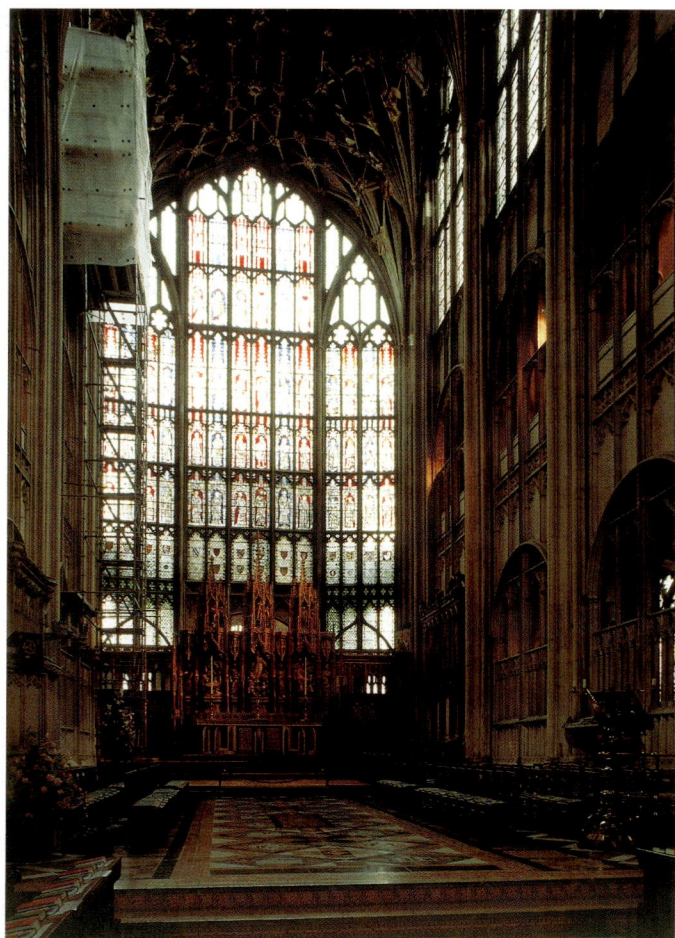

18-40 Choir of Gloucester Cathedral (view facing east), Gloucester, England, 1332–1357.

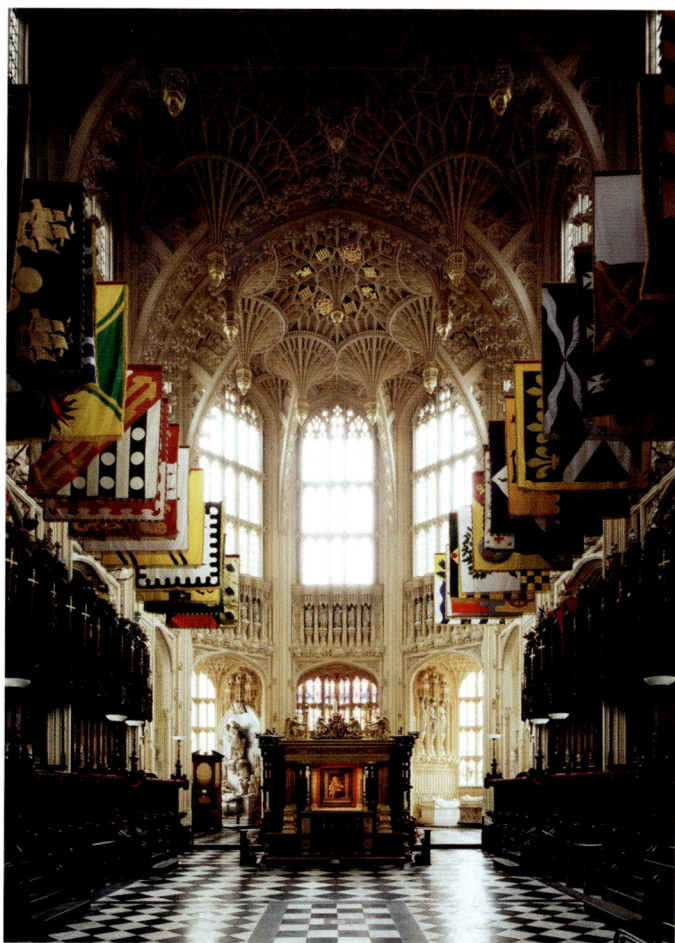

18-41 ROBERT and WILLIAM VERTUE, Chapel of Henry VII, Westminster Abbey, London, England, 1503–1519.

the 14th century. Architectural historians usually call the English Gothic architectural style of that period the Decorated style. The choir of Gloucester Cathedral (FIG. **18-40**), remodeled about a century after Salisbury, illustrates the transition from the Decorated to the last English Gothic style, the Perpendicular style. The newer style took its name from the pronounced verticality of its decorative details, in contrast to the horizontal emphasis of Salisbury and early English Gothic.

A single enormous window divided into tiers of small windows of like shape and proportion fills the characteristically flat east end of Gloucester Cathedral. At the top, two slender lancets flank a wider central section that also ends in a pointed arch. The design has much in common with the screen facade of Salisbury, but the proportions are different. Vertical, as opposed to horizontal, lines dominate. In the choir wall, the architect also erased Salisbury's strong horizontal accents, as the vertical wall elements lift directly from the floor to the vaulting, unifying the walls with the vaults in the French manner. The vault ribs, which designers had begun to multiply soon after Salisbury, are at Gloucester a dense thicket of entirely ornamental strands that serve no structural purpose. The choir, in fact, is not covered by rib vaults at all but by a continuous Romanesque barrel vault with applied Gothic ornament. In the Gloucester choir, the taste for decorative surfaces triumphed over structural "honesty."

**FAN VAULTS** The decorative and structure-disguising qualities of the Perpendicular style became even more pronounced in its late phases. A primary example is the early 16th-century ceiling of the chapel of Henry VII (FIG. **18-41**) adjoining Westminster Abbey in London. In this chapel, the earlier linear play of ribs became a kind of architectural embroidery. The architect pulled the ribs into uniquely English *fan vault* shapes with large hanging *pendants* resembling stalactites. The vault looks like something organic that hardened in the process of melting. Intricate tracery recalling lace overwhelms the cones hanging from the ceiling. The chapel represents the dissolution of structural Gothic into decorative fancy. The architect released the Gothic style's original lines from their function and multiplied them into the uninhibited architectural virtuosity and theatrics of the Perpendicular style. A contemporaneous phenomenon in France was the Flamboyant style seen in such churches as Saint-Maclou at Rouen (FIG. 18-25).

**ROYAL TOMBS** Henry VII's chapel also houses the king's tomb in the form of a large stone coffin with sculpted portraits of Henry and his queen, Elizabeth of York, lying on their backs. This type of tomb is a familiar feature of the churches of Late Gothic England—indeed, of Late Gothic Europe. Though not strictly part of the architectural fabric, as are tombs set into niches in the church walls, freestanding tombs with recumbent images of the deceased are permanent and immovable units of church furniture. They preserve both the remains and the memory of the person entombed and testify to the deceased's piety as well as prominence.

Services for the dead were a vital part of the Christian liturgy. The Christian hope for salvation in the hereafter prompted the

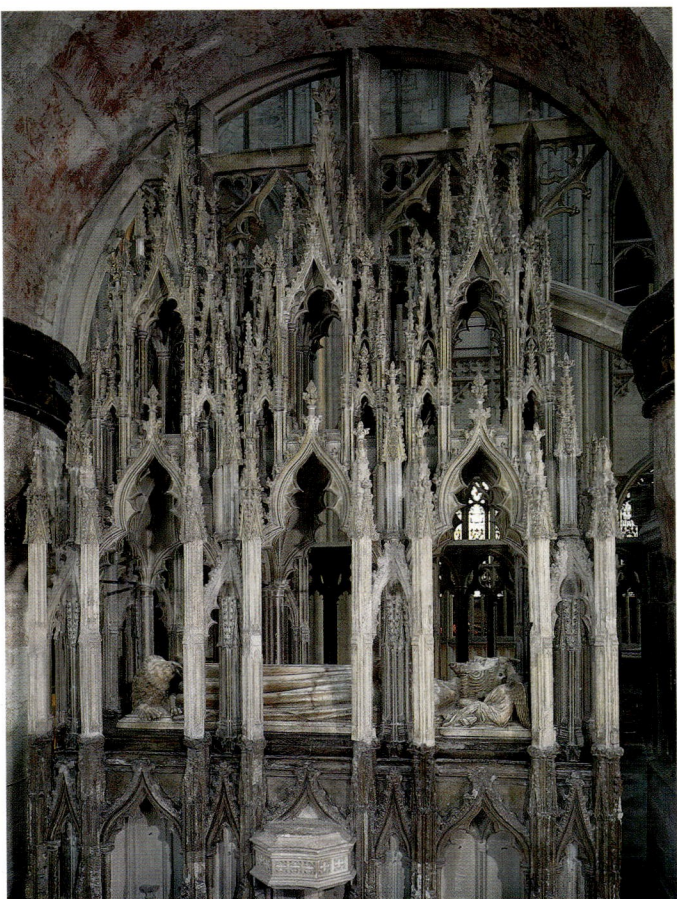

**18-42** Tomb of Edward II, Gloucester Cathedral, Gloucester, England, ca. 1330–1335.

dying faithful to request masses sung, sometimes in perpetuity, for the eternal repose of their souls. Toward that end, the highborn and wealthy endowed whole chapels for the chanting of masses *(chantries),* and made rich bequests of treasure and property to the Church. Many also required that their tombs be placed as near as possible to the choir or at some other important location in the church, if not in a chapel especially designed and endowed to house it, such as Henry's chapel at Westminster Abbey. Freestanding tombs, accessible to church visitors, had a moral as well as a sepulchral and memorial purpose. The silent image of the deceased, cold and still, was a solemn reminder of human mortality, all the more effective because the remains of the person depicted were directly below the portrait. The tomb of an illustrious person could bring distinction, pilgrims, and patronage to the church in which it was placed, just as relics of saints attracted pilgrims from far and wide (see "Pilgrimages," Chapter 17, page 449).

**EDWARD II AS RELIC** A very elaborate example of a freestanding tomb (FIG. **18-42**) is that of Edward II (r. 1307–1327), installed in Gloucester Cathedral several years after the king's murder. Edward's successor, his son Edward III, paid for the memorial to his father, who reposes in regal robes with his crown on his head. The sculptor portrayed the dead king as an idealized Christlike figure (compare FIG. 18-20). On each side of Edward's head is an attentive angel tenderly touching his hair. At his feet is a guardian lion, emblem also of the king's strength and valor. An intricate Perpendicular Gothic canopy encases the coffin, forming a kind of miniature chapel protecting the deceased. It is a fine example of the English manner with its forest of delicate alabaster and Purbeck marble

gables, buttresses, and pinnacles. A distinctive feature is the use of *ogee arches* (arches made up of two double-curved lines meeting at a point), a characteristic Late Gothic form. Art historians often have compared tombs like Edward's to reliquaries. Indeed, the shrinelike frame and the church setting transform the deceased into a kind of saintly relic worthy of veneration.

**GOTHIC MAPS** We conclude our survey of Gothic England with a monument of a very different kind—a large vellum map of the world (FIG. **18-43**) displayed in Hereford Cathedral. This *mappamundi* ("cloth of the world" in Latin) is probably the work of RICHARD DE BELLO, a priest attached to Lincoln Cathedral from 1264 to 1283. It exemplifies the art of cartography (mapmaking) in the 13th century. Cartography had its roots in antiquity, especially in the imperially commissioned geographic surveys of the known world. In fact, at the bottom left of the Hereford map is a picture of the Roman emperor Augustus handing a document to three surveyors and instructing them to "Go into the whole world and report back to the Senate on each continent."

The orientation of the Hereford map and of many other medieval maps is unlike that of most modern maps. North is at the left and east at the top. The explanation is that Christians believed that on Judgment Day Christ would rise in the east, like the sun. At the gabled top of the Hereford map, Christ appears as the enthroned Last Judge of humankind. An angel leads the Saved to Paradise on the left (Christ's right), while grotesque demons pull the Damned into the mouth of Hell. This iconographical theme recalls the tympanum of the Romanesque church of Saint-Lazare at Autun (see FIGS. Intro-6 and 17-25). A distinctive Gothic element is the presence of the Virgin Mary below Christ, interceding with her son on behalf of those who prayed to her.

At the world's exact center is Jerusalem, not because medieval mapmakers believed the earth was a flat disk with Jerusalem at its

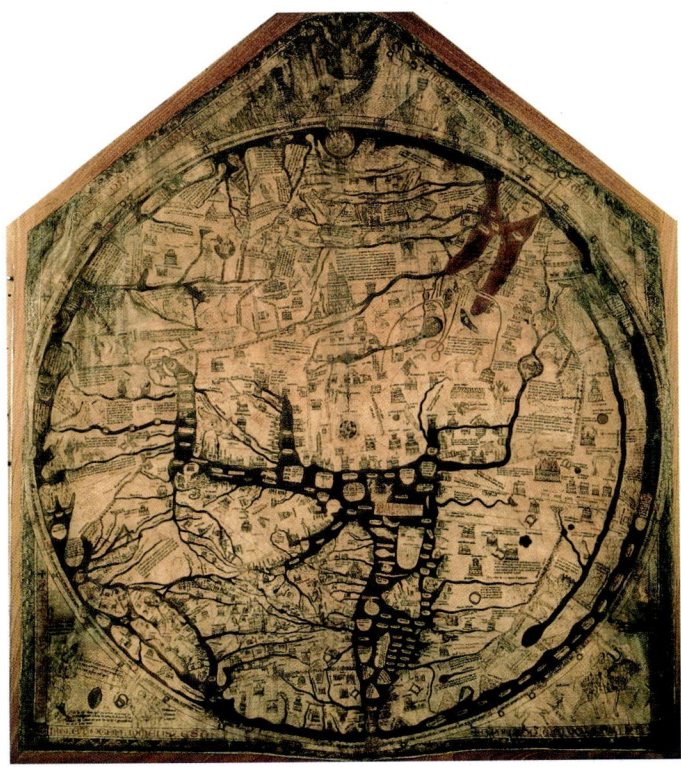

**18-43** RICHARD DE BELLO(?), *Mappamundi* (world map) of Henry III, ca. 1277–1289. Tempera on vellum, approx. 5′ 2″ × 4′ 4″. Hereford Cathedral, Hereford, England.

center but because of the central importance of the holy city in medieval thought. Jerusalem appears as a circular walled city accompanied by a picture of Christ on the cross. As was the norm, the Hereford artist characterized most of the world's famous places by their chief buildings. Crete's major feature, for example, is a circular maze, the legendary labyrinth of the Minoan palace at Knossos (see FIGS. 4-3 and 4-4). Babylon's Tower of Babel (see "Babylon: City of Wonders," Chapter 2, page 49) is a multistory fortress with crenellated battlements of the kind found at Carcassonne (FIG. 18-26). Alexandria's lighthouse, one of the Seven Wonders of the ancient world, stands at the mouth of the Nile River in Egypt. In some places, the mapmaker provided pictures of the monstrous races that were said to inhabit the far corners of the earth, just as the sculptor of the Vézelay tympanum (see FIG. 17-26) did in the previous century. The Gothic artist also answered the question of what a traveler would find beyond the oceans that bounded the continents—*MORS* (death).

## *Germany*

**COLOGNE'S SOARING VAULTS**  The architecture of Germany remained conservatively Romanesque well into the 13th century. In many German churches, the only Gothic feature was the rib vault, buttressed solely by the heavy masonry of the walls. By mid-century, though, the French Gothic style began to make a profound impact, as Cologne Cathedral (FIGS. **18-44** and **18-45**) demonstrates. Begun in 1248 under the direction of GERHARD OF COLOGNE, the cathedral was not completed until more than 600 years later, making it one of the longest building projects on record. Work halted entirely from the mid-16th to the mid-19th century, when the 14th-century design for the facade was unexpectedly found. Gothic Revival architects then completed the building according to the Gothic plans, adding the nave, towers, and facade to the east end that had stood alone for several centuries. The Gothic/Gothic Revival structure is the largest cathedral in northern Europe and boasts a giant (422-foot-long) nave with two aisles on each side.

The 150-foot-high 14th-century choir (FIG. 18-45) is a skillful variation of the Amiens Cathedral choir (FIGS. 18-17 and 18-18) design, with double lancets in the triforium and tall, slender single windows in the clerestory above and choir arcade below. Completed four decades after Gerhard's death, but according to his plans, the choir expresses the Gothic quest for height even more emphatically than many French Gothic buildings. Despite the cathedral's seeming lack of substance, the stability of the structure was proven during World War II, when the city of Cologne suffered from extremely heavy aerial bombardments.

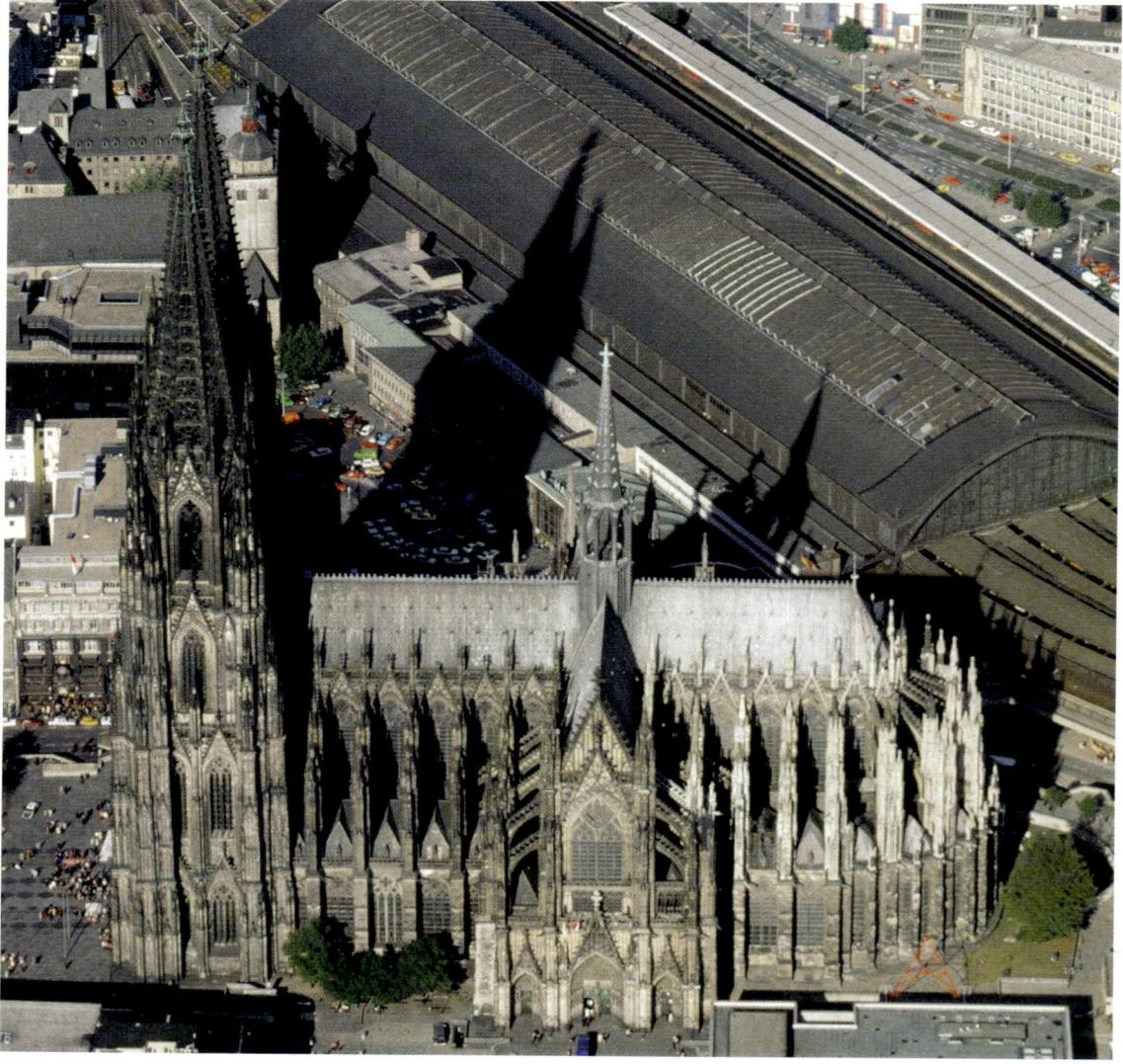

**18-44** GERHARD OF COLOGNE, aerial view of Cologne Cathedral (from the south), Cologne, Germany, begun 1248; nave, facade, and towers completed 1880.

The church survived the war by virtue of its Gothic skeletal design. Once the first few bomb blasts had blown out all of its windows, subsequent explosions had no adverse effects, and the skeleton remained intact and structurally sound.

**MARBURG'S HALL CHURCH** A different type of design, also probably of French origin (see FIG. 17-34) but developed especially in Germany, is the *Hallenkirche,* or hall church, in which the aisles are the same height as the nave. Hall churches, consequently, have no tribune, triforium, or clerestory. An early German example of this type is the church of Saint Elizabeth at Marburg (FIGS. **18-46** and **18-47**), built between 1235 and 1283. It incorporates French-inspired rib vaults with pointed arches and tall lancet windows. The facade has two spire-capped towers in the French manner but no tracery arcades or portal sculpture. Because the aisles provide much of the bracing for the nave vaults, the exterior of Saint Elizabeth is without the dramatic parade of flying buttresses that typically circles French Gothic churches. But the German interior, lighted by double rows of tall windows in the aisle walls, is more unified and free flowing, less narrow and divided, and more brightly illuminated than the interiors of French and English Gothic churches.

**HIGH DRAMA AT STRASBOURG** Like French Gothic architects, French sculptors also often set the standard for their counterparts abroad. In the German Rhineland, which the successors of the Carolingian and Ottonian emperors still ruled, work began in 1176 on a new cathedral for Strasbourg, today a French city. The apse, choir, and transepts were in place by around 1240. Stylistically, these sections of the new church are Romanesque. But the reliefs of the two south-transept portals are fully Gothic and reveal the impact of contemporary French sculpture, especially that of Reims.

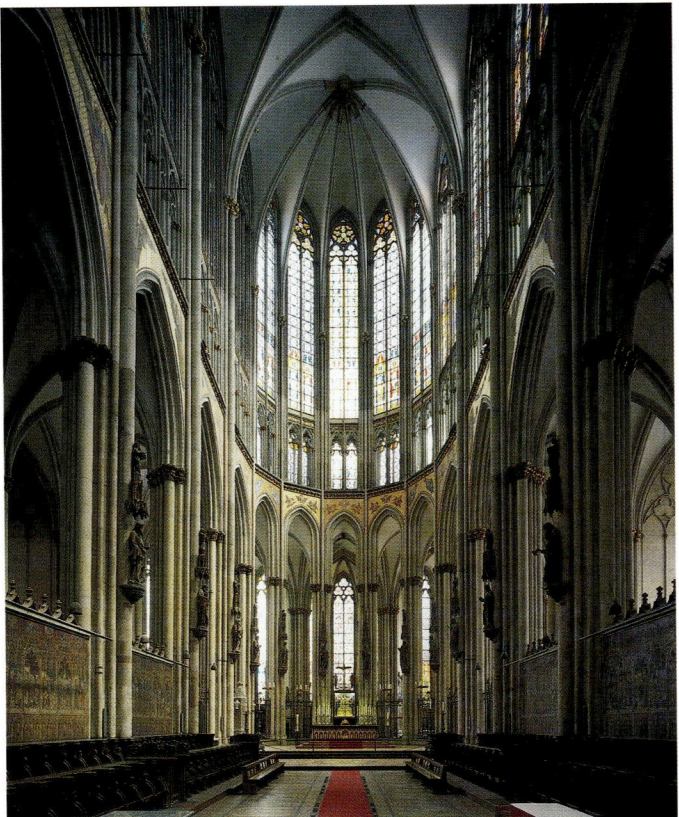

**18-45** GERHARD OF COLOGNE, Choir of Cologne Cathedral (view facing east), Cologne, Germany, completed 1322.

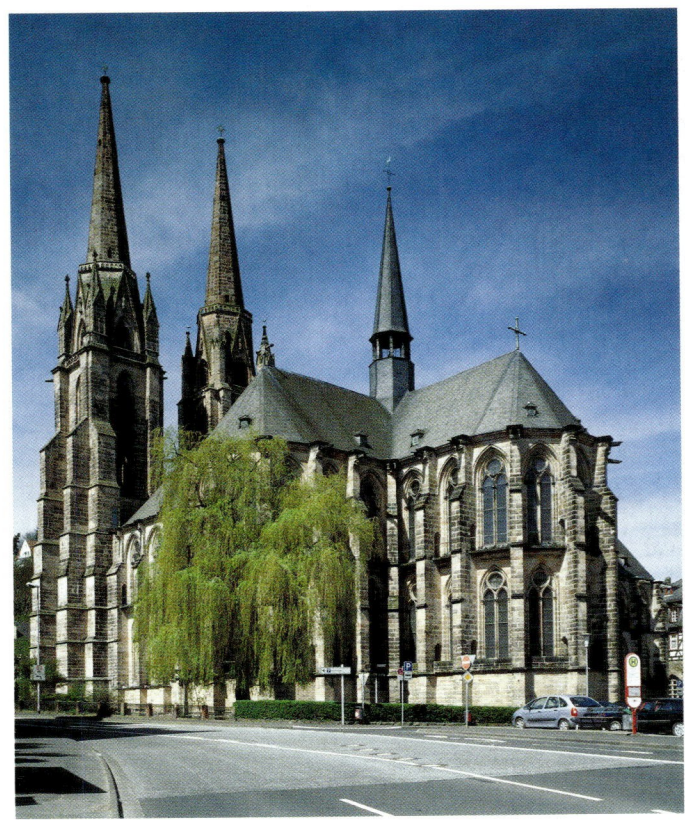

**18-46** Saint Elizabeth (view facing northwest), Marburg, Germany, 1235–1283.

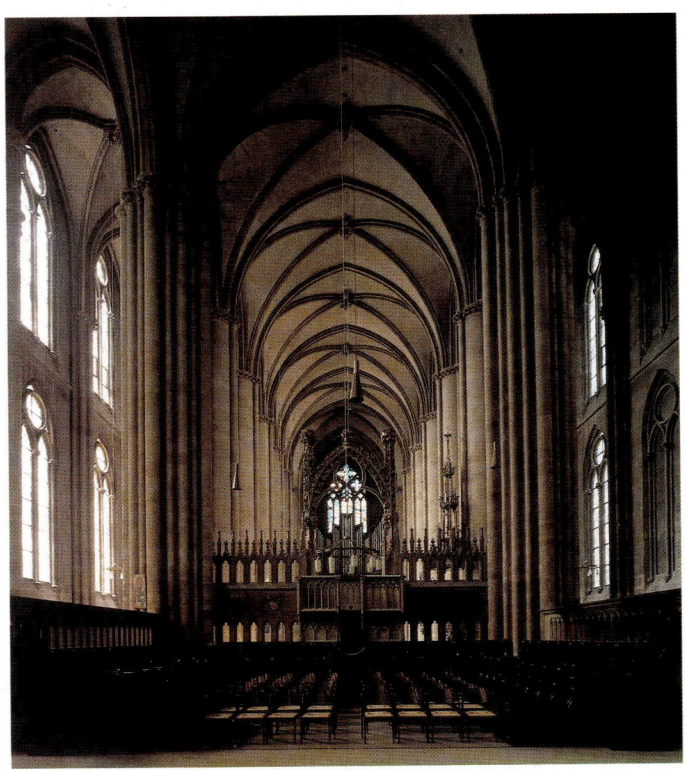

**18-47** Interior of Saint Elizabeth (view facing west), Marburg, Germany, 1235–1283.

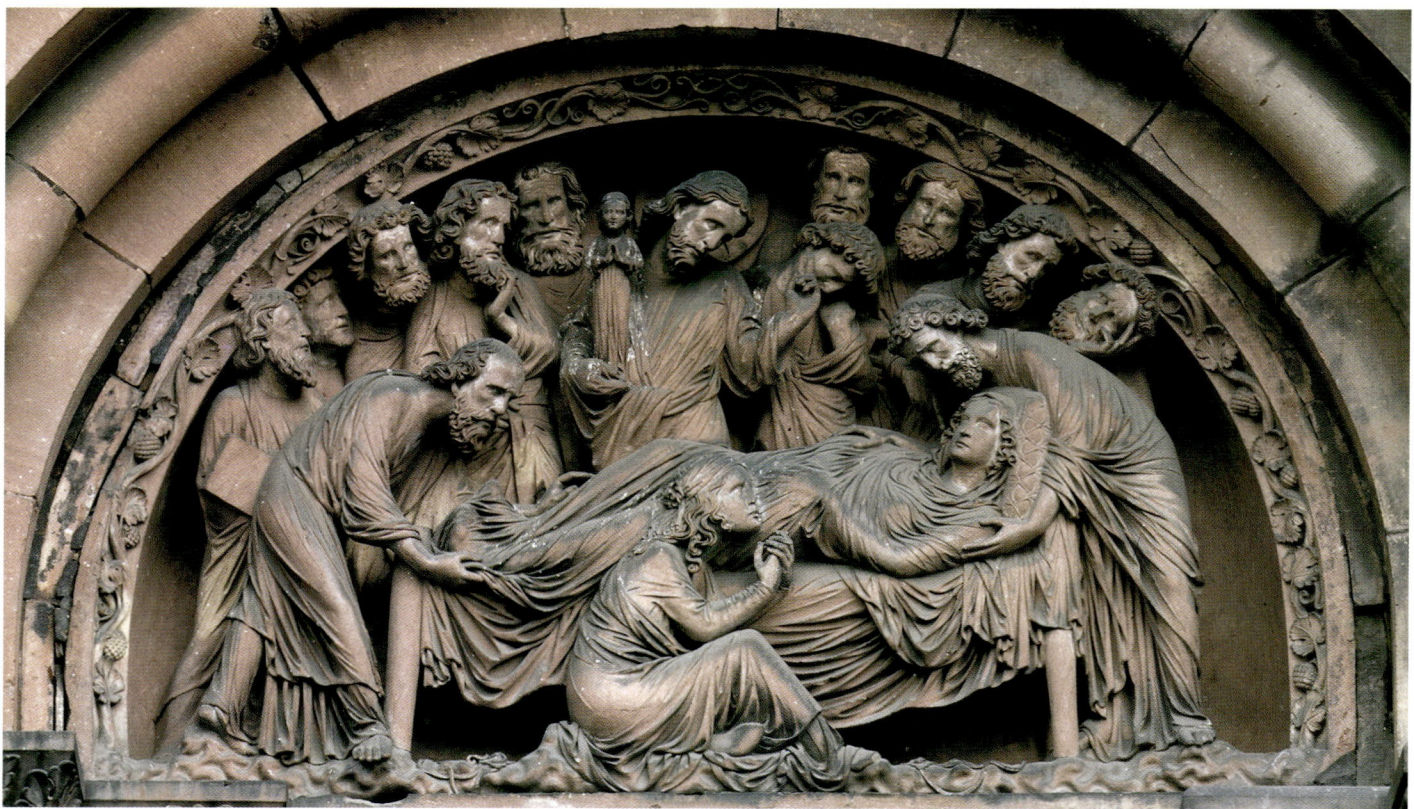

**18-48** Death of the Virgin, tympanum of left doorway, south transept, Strasbourg Cathedral, Strasbourg, France, ca. 1230.

We illustrate the left tympanum (FIG. **18-48**), where the theme is the death of the Virgin Mary. A comparison of the Strasbourg Mary on her deathbed with the Mary of the Reims Visitation group (FIG. 18-22) suggests that the German master had studied the recently installed French jamb statues. The Twelve Apostles gather around the Virgin, forming an arc of mourners well suited to the semicircular frame. At the center Christ receives his mother's soul (the doll-like figure he holds in his left hand). Mary Magdalene, wringing her hands in grief, crouches beside the deathbed. The sorrowing figures express emotion in varying degrees of intensity, from serene resignation to gesturing agitation. The sculptor organized the group by dramatic pose and gesture but also by the rippling flow of deeply incised drapery that passes among them like a rhythmic electric pulse. The sculptor's objective was to imbue the sacred figures with human emotions and to stir emotional responses in observers. In Gothic France, as already noted, art became increasingly humanized and natural. In Gothic Germany, artists carried this humanizing trend even further by emphasizing passionate drama.

**DONOR "PORTRAITS"** The Strasbourg style, with its feverish emotionalism, was particularly appropriate for narrating dramatic events in relief. The sculptor entrusted with the decoration of the west choir of Naumburg Cathedral faced a very different challenge. The task was to carve statues of the 12 benefactors of the original 11th-century church on the occasion of a new fundraising campaign. The vivid gestures and agitated faces in the Strasbourg tympanum contrast with the quiet solemnity of the Naumburg statues. Two of the figures stand out from the group because of their exceptional quality. They represent the margrave (German military governor) Ekkehard II of Meissen and his wife

Uta (FIG. **18-49**). The statues are attached to columns and stand beneath architectural canopies, following the pattern of French Gothic portal statuary. Their location indoors accounts for the preservation of much of the original paint. Ekkehard and Uta give an idea of how the facade and transept sculptures of Gothic cathedrals once looked.

The period costumes and the individualized features and personalities of the margrave and his wife give the impression that they sat for their own portraits, although the subjects lived well before the sculptor's time. Ekkehard, the intense and somewhat stout knight, contrasts with the beautiful and aloof Uta. With a wonderfully graceful gesture, she draws the collar of her gown partly across her face while she gathers up a soft fold of drapery with a jeweled, delicate hand. The sculptor understood that the drapery and the body it enfolds are distinct. The artist subtly revealed the shape of Uta's right arm beneath her cloak and rendered the fall of drapery folds with an accuracy that indicates the use of a model. The two statues are arresting images of real people, even if they bear the names of aristocrats the artist never met. By the mid-13th century, life-size images of secular personages had found their way into churches.

**EQUESTRIAN STATUARY** Somewhat earlier in date than the Naumburg "portraits" is the equestrian statue known as the *Bamberg Rider* (FIG. **18-50**). For centuries this statue has been mounted against a pier in Bamberg Cathedral beneath an architectural canopy that frames the rider's body but not his horse. Scholars debate whether the statue was made for this location or moved there, perhaps from the church's exterior. A similar equestrian statue of the same period stood in the market square of Magdeburg, Germany. Both statues revive the imagery of the

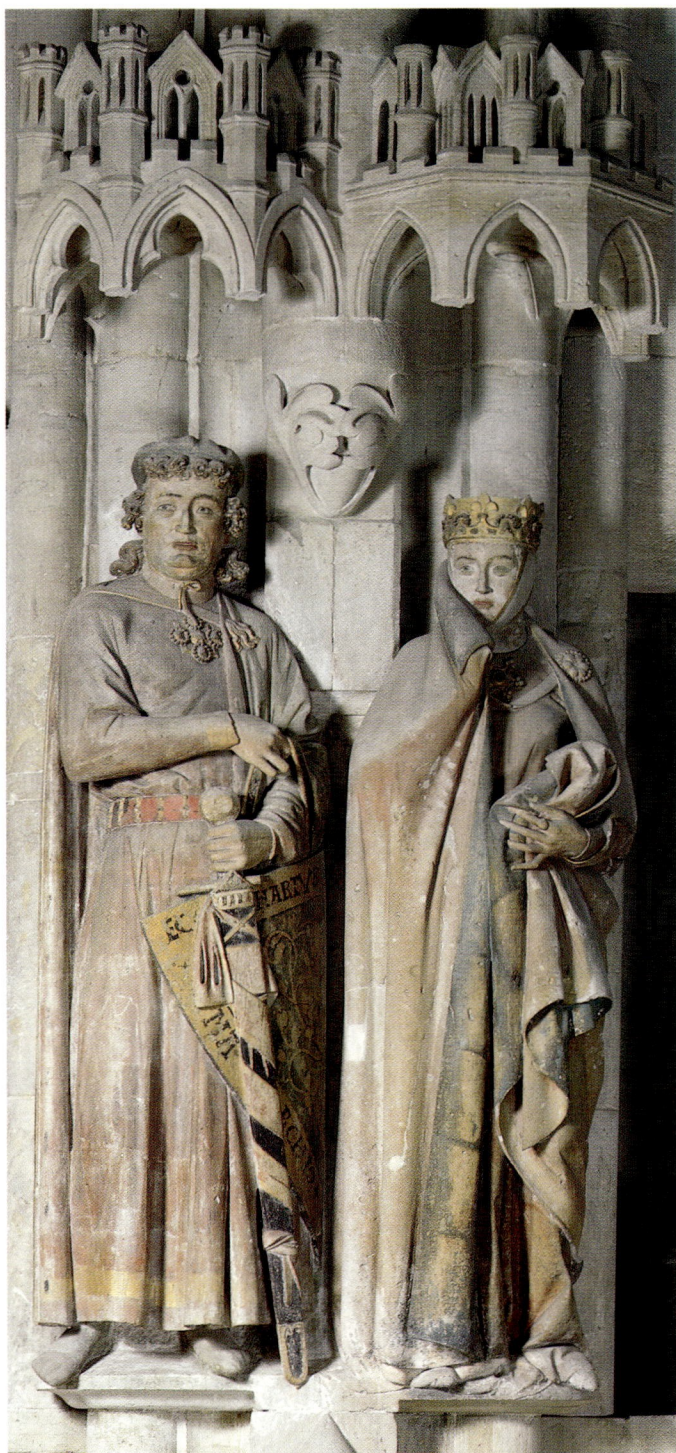

18-49 Ekkehard and Uta, statues in the west choir, Naumburg Cathedral, Naumburg, Germany, ca. 1249–1255. Painted limestone, approx. 6′ 2″ high.

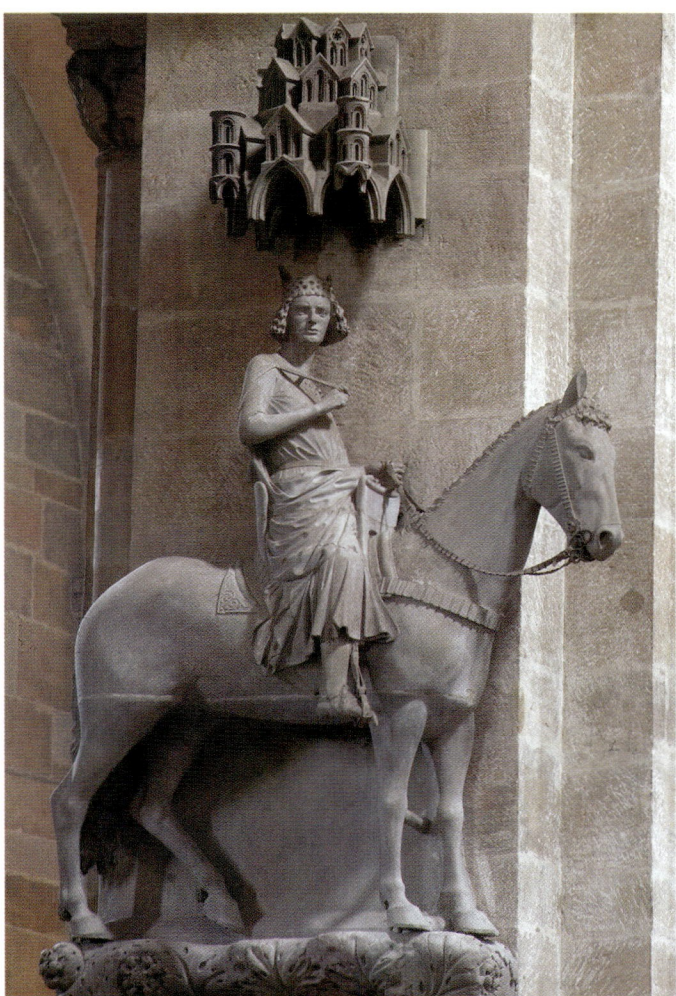

18-50 Equestrian portrait (Bamberg Rider), statue in the east choir, Bamberg Cathedral, Germany, ca. 1235–1240. Sandstone, 7′ 9″ high.

Carolingian Empire (see FIG. 16-11), derived in turn from that of ancient Rome (see FIG. 10-59).

Like Ekkehard and Uta, the *Bamberg Rider* seems to be a true portrait. Some believe it represents a German emperor, perhaps Frederick II (r. 1220–1250), who was a benefactor of Bamberg Cathedral. The many other identifications include Saint George and one of the three magi, but a historical personality is most likely the subject. The presence of a Holy Roman Emperor in the

cathedral would have underscored the unity of church and state in 13th-century Germany. The artist carefully represented the rider's costume, the high saddle, and the horse's trappings. The proportions of horse and rider are correct, although the sculptor did not quite understand the animal's anatomy, so its shape is rather stiffly schematic. The rider turns toward the observer, as if presiding at a review of troops. The torsion of this figure seems to reflect the same impatience with subordination to architecture found in the Reims portal statues (FIG. 18-22).

**MARY GRIEVES FOR CHRIST** The confident 13th-century figures at Naumburg and Bamberg stand in marked contrast to a haunting 14th-century German image of the Virgin Mary holding the dead Christ in her lap (FIG. 18-51). The widespread troubles of the 14th century—war, plague, famine, and social strife—brought on an ever more acute awareness of suffering. This found its way readily into religious art. The Dance of Death, Christ as the Man of Sorrow, and the Seven Sorrows of the Virgin Mary became favorite themes. A fevered and fearful piety sought comfort and reassurance in the reflection that Christ and the Virgin Mother shared humanity's woes. To represent this, artists emphasized the traits of human suffering in powerful, expressive exaggeration. In the illustrated carved and painted wood group (called a *Pietà*, "pity" or "compassion" in Italian), the sculptor portrayed

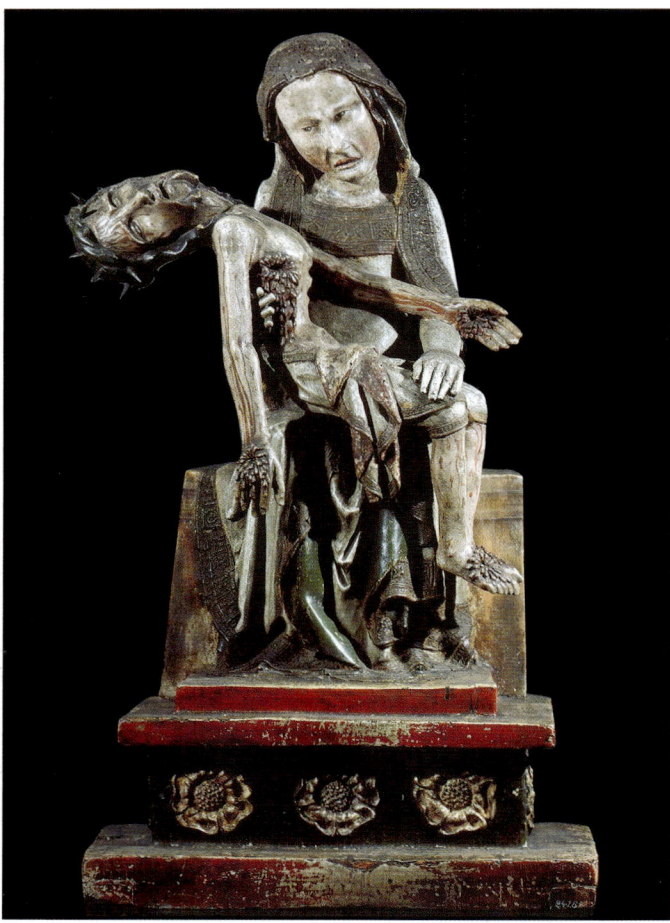

Christ as a stunted, distorted human wreck, stiffened in death and covered with streams of blood gushing from a huge wound. The Virgin Mother, who cradles him like a child in her lap, is the very image of maternal anguish, her oversized face twisted in an expression of unbearable grief.

This statue expresses nothing of the serenity of Romanesque and earlier Gothic depictions of Mary (see FIGS. 17-30 and 18-5, right tympanum). Nor does the *Röttgen Pietà* (named after a collector) have anything in common with the aloof, iconic images of the Theotokos with the infant Jesus in her lap common in Byzantine art (see FIGS. 12-16 and 12-17). Here the artist forcibly confronts the devout with an appalling icon of agony, death, and sorrow that humanizes, almost to the point of heresy, the sacred personages. The work calls out to the horrified believer, "What is your suffering compared to this?"

The humanizing of religious themes and religious images accelerated steadily from the 12th century. By the 14th century, art addressed the private person (often in a private place) in a direct appeal to the emotions. The expression of feeling accompanied the representation of the human body in motion. As the figures of the church portals began to twist on their columns, then move within their niches, and then stand independently, their details became more outwardly related to the human audience as expressions of recognizable human emotions.

**NICHOLAS OF VERDUN**  When Abbot Suger wanted to install a magnificent crucifix in the new Gothic choir of Saint-Denis, he selected artists from Germany's Meuse River Valley for the job. The Mosan region long had been famous for the quality of its metalworkers and enamelers (see FIGS. 17-29 and 17-31). The Saint-Denis crucifix is lost, but Suger described it in one of his treatises on the building and adorning of the royal abbey church. The cross stood on a sumptuous base decorated with 68 enamel

**18-51**  Virgin with the Dead Christ *(Röttgen Pietà),* from the Rhineland, Germany, ca. 1300–1325. Painted wood, 2′ 10½″ high. Rheinisches Landemuseum, Bonn.

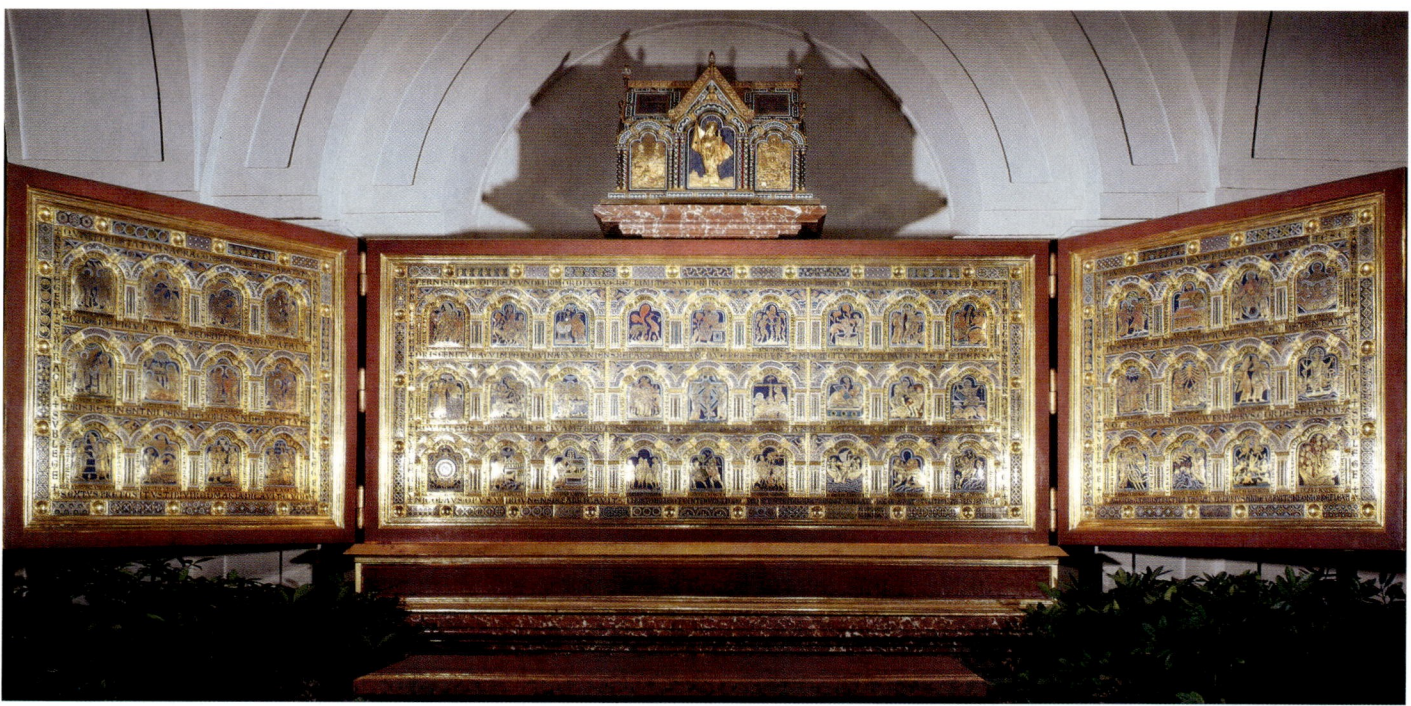

**18-52**  NICHOLAS OF VERDUN, the *Klosterneuburg Altar,* from the abbey church at Klosterneuburg, Austria, 1181. Gilded copper and enamel, 3′ 6¾″ high. Stiftsmuseum, Klosterneuburg.

scenes pairing Old and New Testament episodes. Costly furnishings such as this crucifix were key ingredients in Suger's plan to make his new church an earthly introduction to the splendors of Paradise (see "Abbot Suger," page 481).

The leading Mosan artist of the late 12th and early 13th centuries was NICHOLAS OF VERDUN. In 1181 he completed work on a gilded-copper and enamel *ambo* (a pulpit for biblical readings) for the Benedictine abbey church at Klosterneuburg, near Vienna in Austria. After a fire damaged the pulpit in 1330, the church hired artists to convert the pulpit into an altarpiece. The pulpit's sides became the wings of a triptych. The 14th-century artists also added 6 scenes to Nicholas's original 45.

We illustrate the *Klosterneuburg Altar* in its final form (FIG. 18-52), with its 51 enamels set into trefoil-arched niches framed by explanatory inscriptions. The central row of enamels depicts New Testament episodes, beginning with the Annunciation, and bears the label *sub gracia,* or the world "under grace," that is, after the coming of Christ. The upper and lower registers contain Old Testament scenes labeled, respectively, *ante legem,* "before the law" Moses received on Mount Sinai, and *sub lege,* "under the law" of the Ten Commandments. In this scheme, prophetic Old Testament events appear above and below the New Testament episodes they prefigure. This organization was unlikely to have been Nicholas's invention. Provost Wernher of Klosterneuburg or another church official probably formulated the iconographical program, consistent with a long tradition going back to the earliest Christian art (see "Jewish Subjects in Christian Art," Chapter 11, page 305).

On the *Klosterneuburg Altar,* the Annunciation to Mary of the coming birth of Jesus, for example, is framed above and below by enamels of angels announcing the births of Isaac and Samson. In the central section of the triptych, the Old Testament counterpart of Christ's Crucifixion is Abraham's sacrifice of Isaac (FIG. 18-53), a parallel already established in Early Christian times in both art (see FIG. 11-5) and literature. Nicholas of Verdun's gold figures stand out vividly from the blue enamel background. The biblical actors twist and turn, make emphatic gestures, and wear garments that are almost overwhelmed by the intricate linear patterns of their folds. In the Abraham and Isaac panel, the angel flies in at the very last moment to grab the blade of Abraham's sword

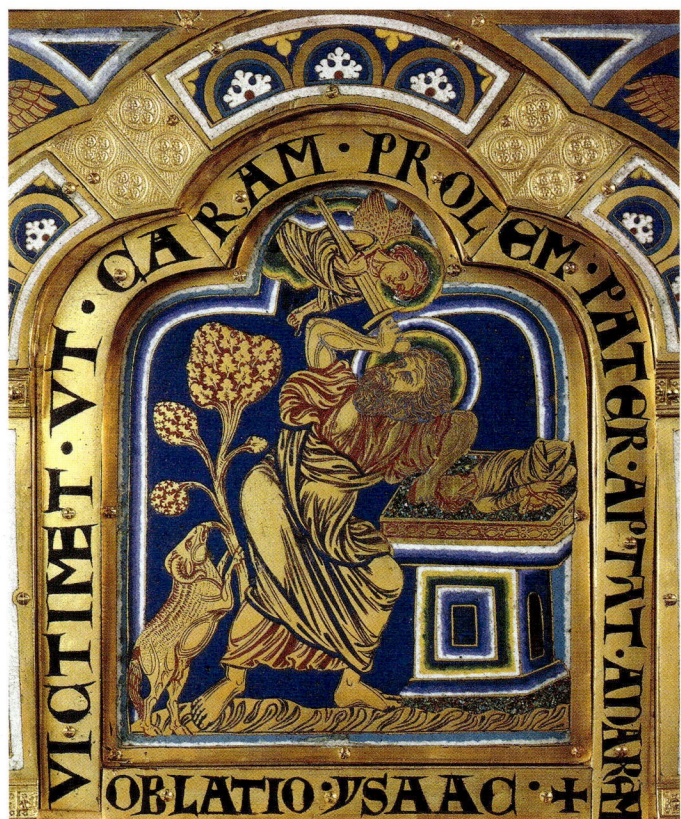

**18-53** NICHOLAS OF VERDUN, Sacrifice of Isaac, detail of the *Klosterneuburg Altar,* from the abbey church at Klosterneuburg, Austria, 1181. Gilded copper and enamel, $5\frac{1}{2}''$ high. Stiftsmuseum, Klosterneuburg.

before he can kill the bound Isaac on the altar. The intense emotionalism of the representation and the linear complexity of the garments foreshadowed the tone and style of the Strasbourg tympanum depicting the death of the Virgin (FIG. 18-48).

**THE MAGI'S RELICS** Sculpted versions of the Klosterneuburg figures appear on the *Shrine of the Three Kings* (FIG. 18-54) in

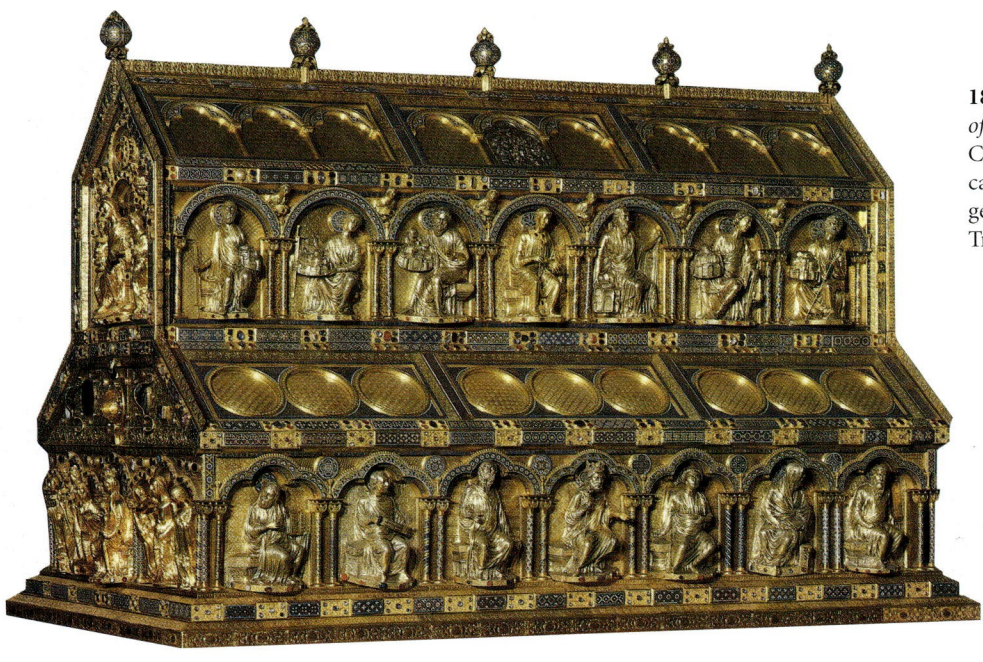

**18-54** NICHOLAS OF VERDUN, *Shrine of the Three Kings,* from Cologne Cathedral, Cologne, Germany, begun ca. 1190. Silver, bronze, enamel, and gemstones, 5′ 8″ × 6′ × 3′ 8″. Cathedral Treasury, Cologne.

Cologne Cathedral. Nicholas of Verdun probably began work on the huge reliquary (six feet long and almost as tall) in 1190. Philip von Heinsberg, archbishop of Cologne from 1167 to 1191, commissioned the shrine to contain relics of the three magi. The Holy Roman Emperor Frederick Barbarossa acquired them in the conquest of Milan in 1164 and donated them to the German cathedral. Possession of the magi's relics gave the Cologne archbishops the right to crown German kings. Nicholas's reliquary, made of silver and bronze with ornamentation in enamel and gemstones, is one of the most luxurious ever fashioned, especially considering its size. The shape resembles that of a basilican church. Repoussé figures of the Virgin Mary, the three magi, Old Testament prophets, and New Testament apostles in arcuated frames are variations of those on the Klosterneuburg pulpit. The deep channels and tight bunches of the drapery folds are hallmarks of Nicholas's style. A similar figural style appeared a half-century later in Strasbourg Cathedral's *Death of the Virgin* tympanum (FIG. 18-48).

Nicholas of Verdun's *Klosterneuburg Altar* and his *Shrine of the Three Kings,* together with Suger's treatises on the furnishings of Saint-Denis, are welcome reminders of how magnificently outfitted medieval church interiors were. The so-called minor arts played a defining role in creating a special otherworldly atmosphere for Christian ritual. These Gothic examples continued a tradition that dates back to the Roman emperor Constantine and the first imperial patronage of Christianity (see "Constantine and Old Saint Peter's," Chapter 11, page 311).

## *Italy*

Nowhere is the regional diversity of Gothic architecture more evident than in Italy. In the Romanesque period, as already discussed, Italian architects stood apart from developments north of the Alps. Many Italian Romanesque churches more closely resemble Early Christian basilicas than contemporary buildings in France, Germany, or England. Similarly, few Italian architects accepted the northern Gothic style. Some architectural historians even have questioned whether it is proper to speak of late medieval Italian buildings as Gothic structures.

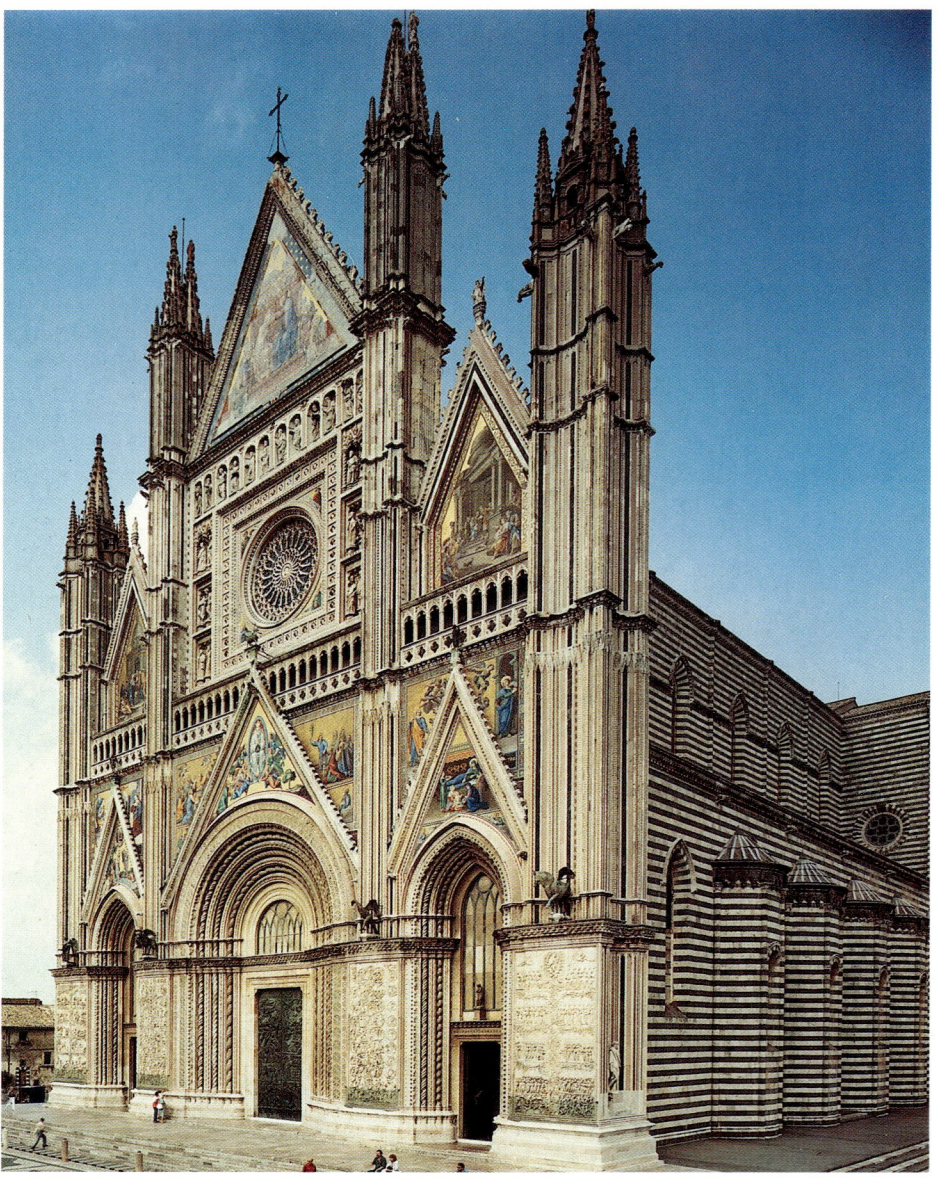

18-55 LORENZO MAITANI, west facade of Orvieto Cathedral, Orvieto, Italy, begun 1310.

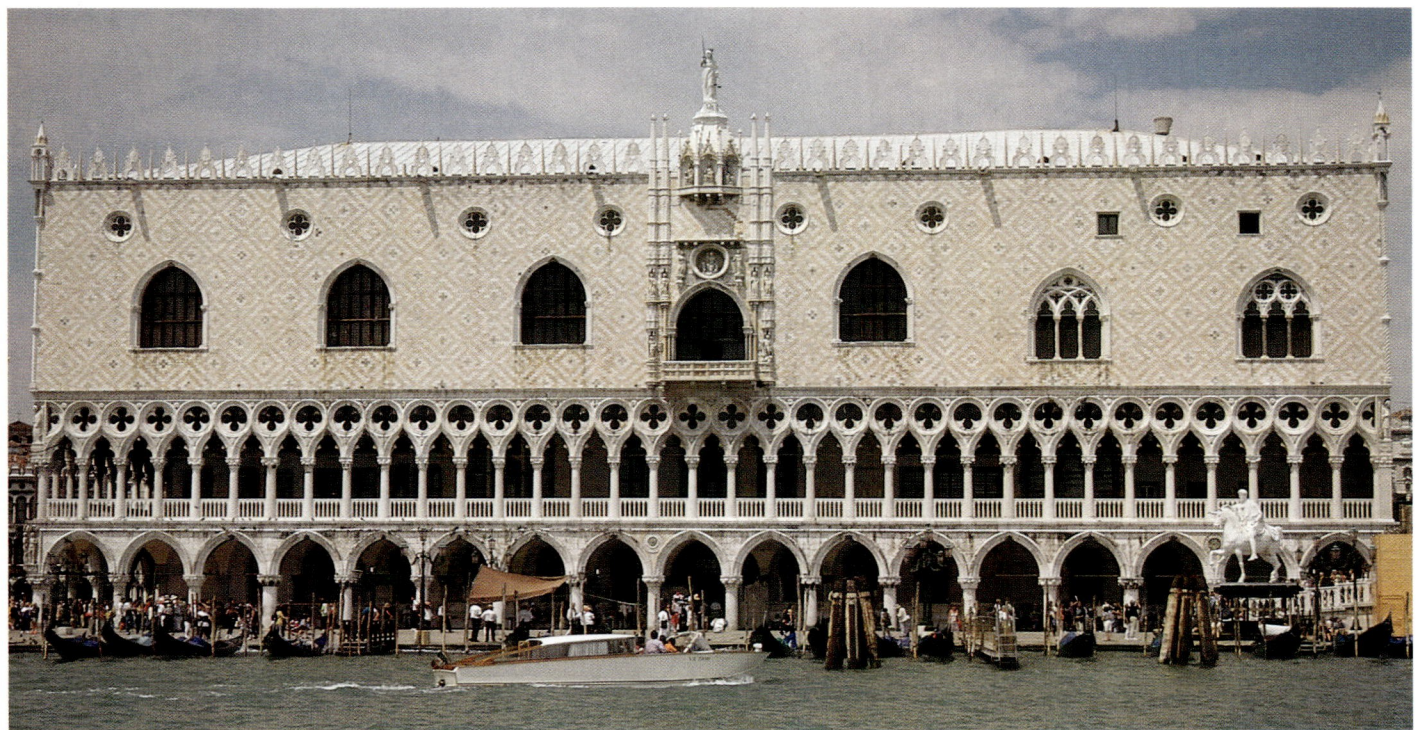

**18-56** Doge's Palace, Venice, Italy, begun ca. 1340–1345; expanded and remodeled, 1424–1438.

**ORVIETO CATHEDRAL** The west facade of Orvieto Cathedral (FIG. **18-55**) is typical of late medieval architecture in Italy. Designed in the early 14th century by LORENZO MAITANI, an architect from nearby Siena, the Orvieto facade imitates some elements of the French Gothic architectural vocabulary. French influence is especially noticeable in the pointed gables over the three doorways, in the rose window in the upper zone framed by statues in niches, and in the four large pinnacles that divide the facade into three bays. The outer pinnacles serve as miniature substitutes for the big northern European west-front towers. Maitani's facade is, however, merely a Gothic overlay masking a marble-revetted basilican structure in the Tuscan Romanesque tradition, as our three-quarter view of the cathedral reveals. The Orvieto facade resembles a great altar screen, its single plane covered with carefully placed carved and painted ornament. In principle, Orvieto belongs with Pisa Cathedral (see FIG. 17-17) and other Italian buildings, rather than with Amiens (FIG. 18-19) or Reims (FIG. 18-21) Cathedrals. Inside, Orvieto Cathedral has a timber-roofed nave with a two-story elevation (columnar arcade and clerestory) in the Early Christian manner. Both the triumphal arch framing the apse and the nave arcade's arches are round as opposed to pointed.

**A PALACE ON A LAGOON** One of the wealthiest cities of late medieval Italy—and of Europe—was Venice, renowned for its streets of water. Situated on a lagoon on the northeastern coast of Italy, Venice was secure from land attack and could rely on a powerful navy for protection against invasion from the sea. Internally, Venice was a tight corporation of ruling families who, for centuries, provided stable rule and fostered economic growth. The Venetian republic's seat of government was the Doge's (Duke's) Palace (FIG. **18-56**). Begun around 1340–1345 and significantly

remodeled after 1424, it was the most ornate public building in medieval Italy. In a stately march, the first level's short and heavy columns support rather severe pointed arches that look strong enough to carry the weight of the upper structure. Their rhythm is doubled in the upper arcades, where more-slender columns carry ogee arches, which terminate in flamelike tips between medallions pierced with quatrefoils. Each story is taller than the one beneath it, the topmost as high as the two lower arcades combined. Yet the building does not look top-heavy. This is due in part to the complete absence of articulation in the top story and in part to the walls' delicate patterning, in cream- and rose-colored marbles, which makes them appear paper thin. The Doge's Palace is the monumental representative of a delightful and charming variant of Late Gothic architecture. Colorful, decorative, light and airy in appearance, and not overloaded, the Venetian Gothic is ideally suited to Venice, which floats between water and air.

**MILAN'S ECLECTIC CATHEDRAL** Since Romanesque times, northern European influences had been felt more strongly in Lombardy than in the rest of Italy. When Milan's citizens decided to build their own cathedral (FIG. **18-57**) in 1386, they invited experts from France, Germany, and England, as well as from Italy. These masters argued among themselves and with the city council, and no single architect ever played a dominant role. The result of this attempt at "architecture by committee" was, not surprisingly, a compromise. The building's proportions, particularly the nave's, became Italian (that is, wide in relation to height), and the surface decorations and details remained Gothic. Clearly derived from France are the cathedral's multitude of pinnacles and the elaborate tracery on the facade, flank, and transept. But even before the building was half finished, the new classical style of the

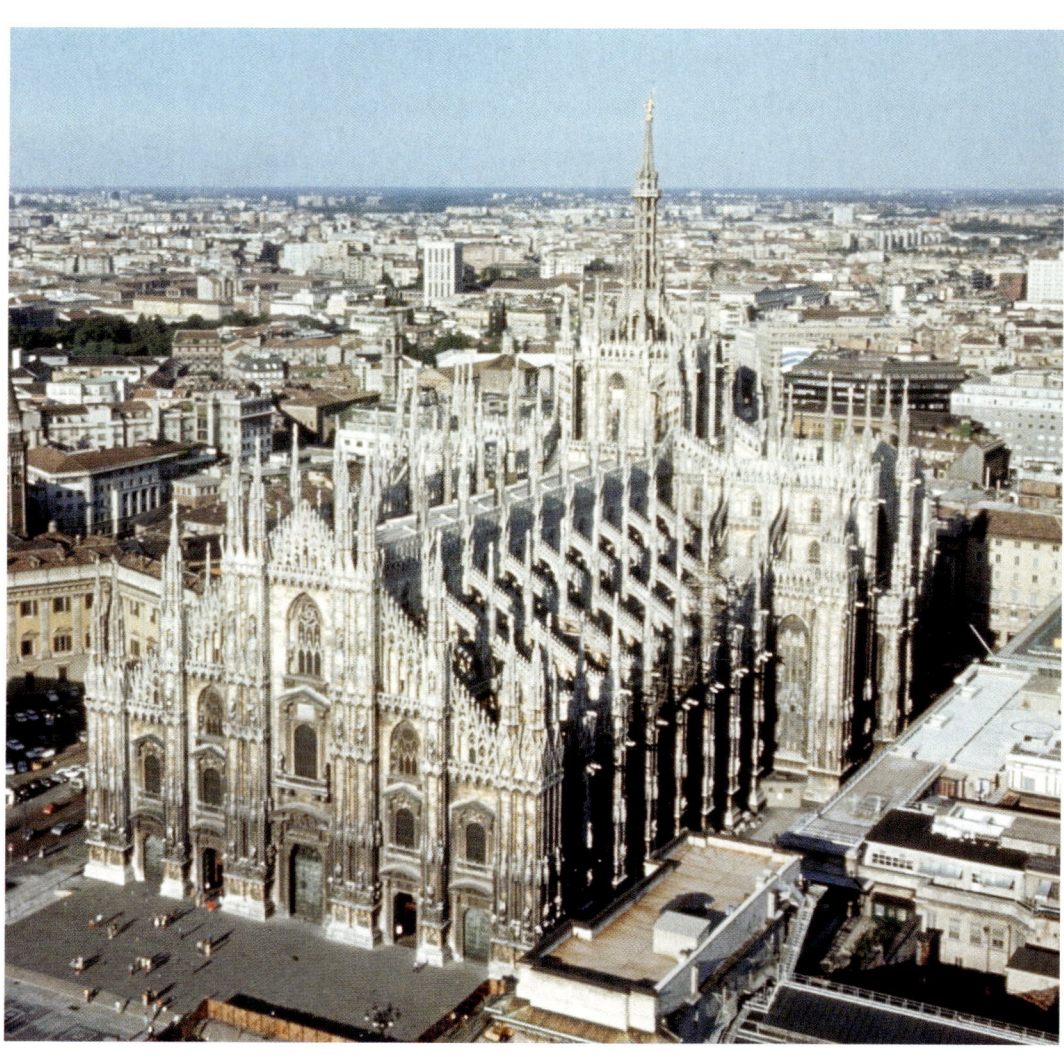

Italian Renaissance had been well launched (see Chapter 21), and the Gothic design had become outdated. Thus, Milan Cathedral's elaborate facade represents a confused mixture of Late Gothic and classicizing Renaissance elements. With its pediment-capped rectilinear portals amid Gothic pinnacles, the cathedral stands as a symbol of the waning of the Gothic style.

## CONCLUSION

The story of Gothic art and architecture begins in the Île-de-France around 1140. At Saint-Denis, Paris, Chartres, and elsewhere, French architects pioneered a new building style. Using rib vaults with pointed arches, flying buttresses, and stained-glass windows, French builders constructed towering cathedrals with statue-lined portals and interiors flooded with mystical multicolored light. Contemporaries regarded the new Gothic churches as images of the City of God on earth.

The French architectural style spread quickly throughout Europe, and with it the Parisian court style of book illumination and freestanding sculpture. As in the Romanesque period, however, regional diversity was the norm. In England, for example, Gothic architects embraced many of the characteristic motifs of contemporary French architecture, but not its structural logic or emphasis on height. South of the Alps, Italian builders adhered so tenaciously to the Early Christian basilican tradition that some scholars do not consider late medieval Italian architecture to be "Gothic" at all. But the Italians were pioneers in other fields, especially painting, and it was Italy, not France, that was shortly to become the birthplace of the new age known as the Renaissance.

**EARLY GOTHIC**

1140

Peter Abelard, 1079–1142

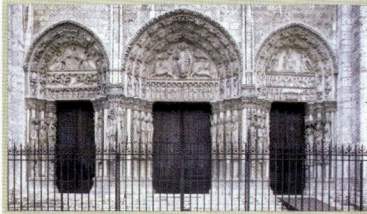 Suger, abbot of Saint-Denis, 1122–1151

King Louis VII of France, r. 1137–1180

Second Crusade, 1147–1149

Frederick Barbarossa, Holy Roman Emperor, r. 1152–1190

Chrétien de Troyes, fl. ca. 1160–1190

King Philip Augustus of France, r. 1180–1223

Saint Francis of Assisi, 1182–1226

1 Royal Portal, Chartres Cathedral, France, ca. 1145–1155

1194

University of Paris founded, ca. 1200

Capture of Constantinople by Latins (Fourth Crusade), 1204

King John of England signs Magna Carta, 1215

**HIGH GOTHIC**

2 Frederick II, Holy Roman Emperor, r. 1220–1250

*Romance of the Rose,* Part I, ca. 1225–1235

Saint Thomas Aquinas, 1225–1274

King Louis IX (Saint Louis) of France, r. 1226–1270

Blanche of Castile, regent of France, 1226–1234

Treaty of Paris between Louis IX and Henry III of England, 1259

Byzantines retake Constantinople, 1261

3 Dante Alighieri, 1265–1321

Marco Polo in China, 1271–1292

*Romance of the Rose,* Part II, ca. 1275–1280

King Philippe le Bel of France, r. 1285–1314

Pope Boniface VIII canonizes Louis IX, 1297

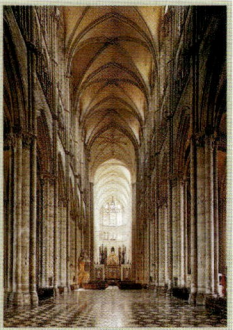

2 Amiens Cathedral, France, begun 1220

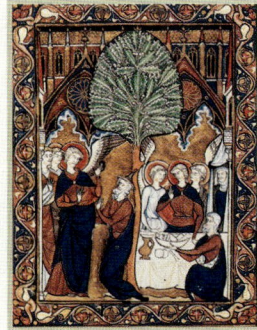

3 Psalter of St. Louis, 1253–1270

1300

King Edward II of England, r. 1307–1327

King Charles IV of France, r. 1322–1328

Hundred Years' War between France and England, 1337–1453

Geoffrey Chaucer, ca. 1343–1400

**LATE GOTHIC**

Black Death first sweeps over Europe, 1347–1350

Great Schism, 1378–1417

Fall of Constantinople to the Ottoman Turks, 1453

King Henry VII of England, r. 1471–1509

1500

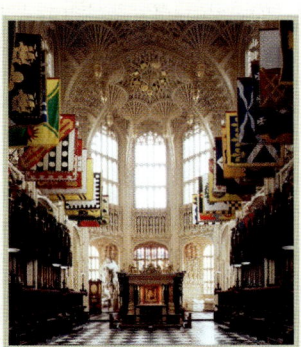

4 Chapel of Henry VII, London, England, 1503–1519

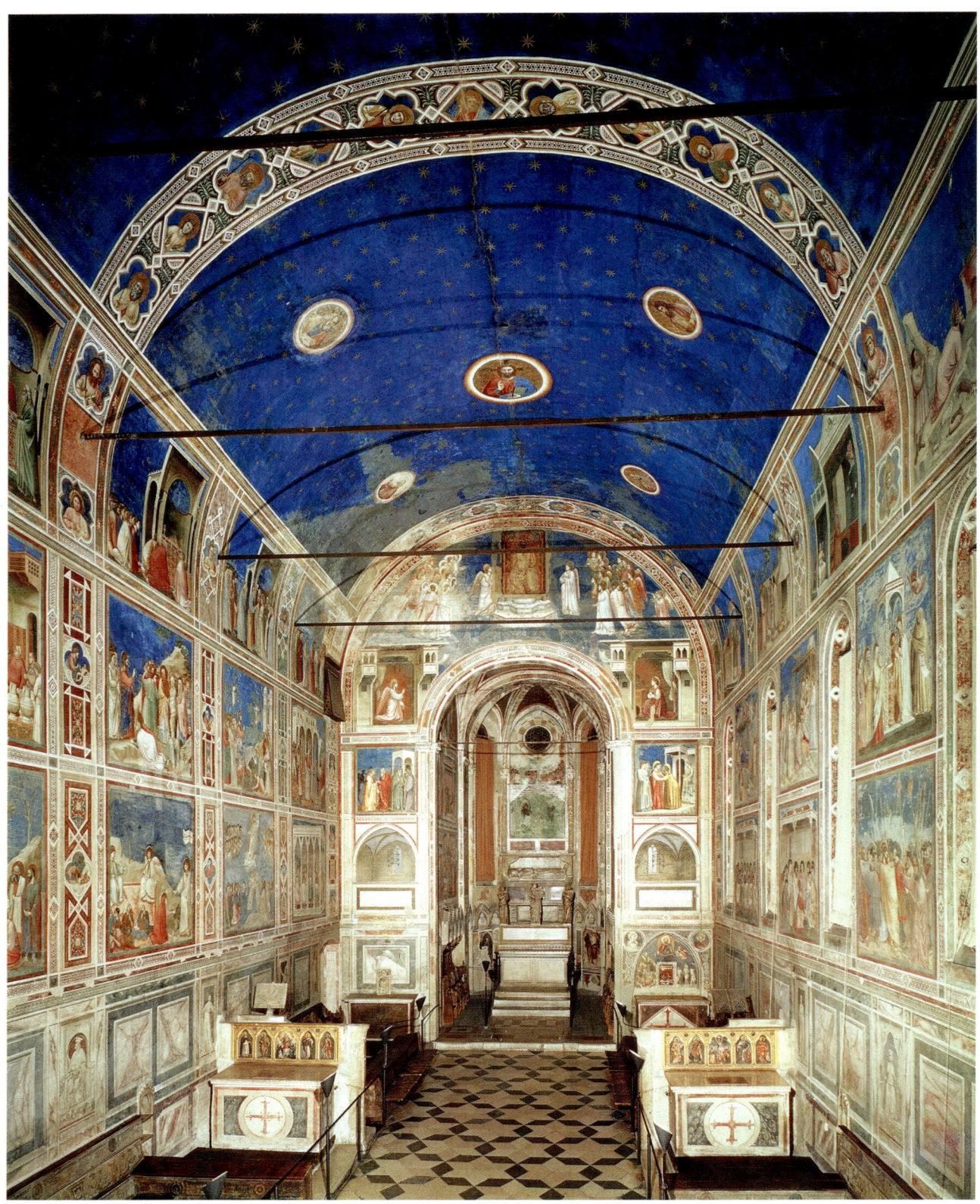

Interior of the Arena Chapel (Cappella Scrovegni), Padua, Italy, 1305–1306.

# 19

# FROM GOTHIC TO RENAISSANCE

## 14TH-CENTURY ITALIAN ART

The essentially religious view of the world that dominated medieval Europe began to change dramatically in what we call the European Renaissance. Although religion continued to occupy a primary position in the lives of Europeans, a growing concern with the natural world, the individual, and humanity's worldly existence characterized the Renaissance period. Derived from the French word *renaissance* and the Italian word *rinascita*, both meaning "rebirth," the Renaissance extends roughly from the 14th through the 16th centuries. In the 14th century, scholars and artists began to cultivate what they believed to be a rebirth of art and culture. A revived interest in classical* cultures—indeed, the veneration of classical antiquity as a model—was central to this rebirth, hence the notion of the Middle Ages, or medieval period, as the age in between antiquity and the Renaissance. The transition from the medieval to the Renaissance, though dramatic, did not come about abruptly. The Renaissance had its roots in epochs that even preceded the Middle Ages, and much that is medieval persisted in the Renaissance and in later periods. The Renaissance eventually gave way to the modern era; the continuous nature of this development is revealed in the use of the term "early modern" by many scholars to describe the Renaissance. We begin our examination of the Renaissance in Italy.

## THE CITY-STATES: POLITICS AND ECONOMICS

In the 14th century, Italy (MAP **19-1**) consisted of numerous city-states, each functioning independently. Each city-state consisted of a geographic region, varying in size, dominated by a major city. Most of the city-states, such as Venice, Florence, Lucca, and Siena, were republics. These republics were constitutional oligarchies—governed by executive bodies, advisory councils, and special commissions. Other powerful city-states included the Papal States, the Kingdom of Naples, and the Duchies of Milan, Modena, Ferrara, and Savoy. As their names indicate, these city-states were politically distinct from the republics.

---

*Note: In *Art through the Ages* the adjective "Classical," with uppercase *C*, refers specifically to the Classical period of ancient Greece, 480–323 BCE. Lowercase "classical" refers to Greco-Roman antiquity in general, that is, the period treated in Chapters 5, 9, and 10.

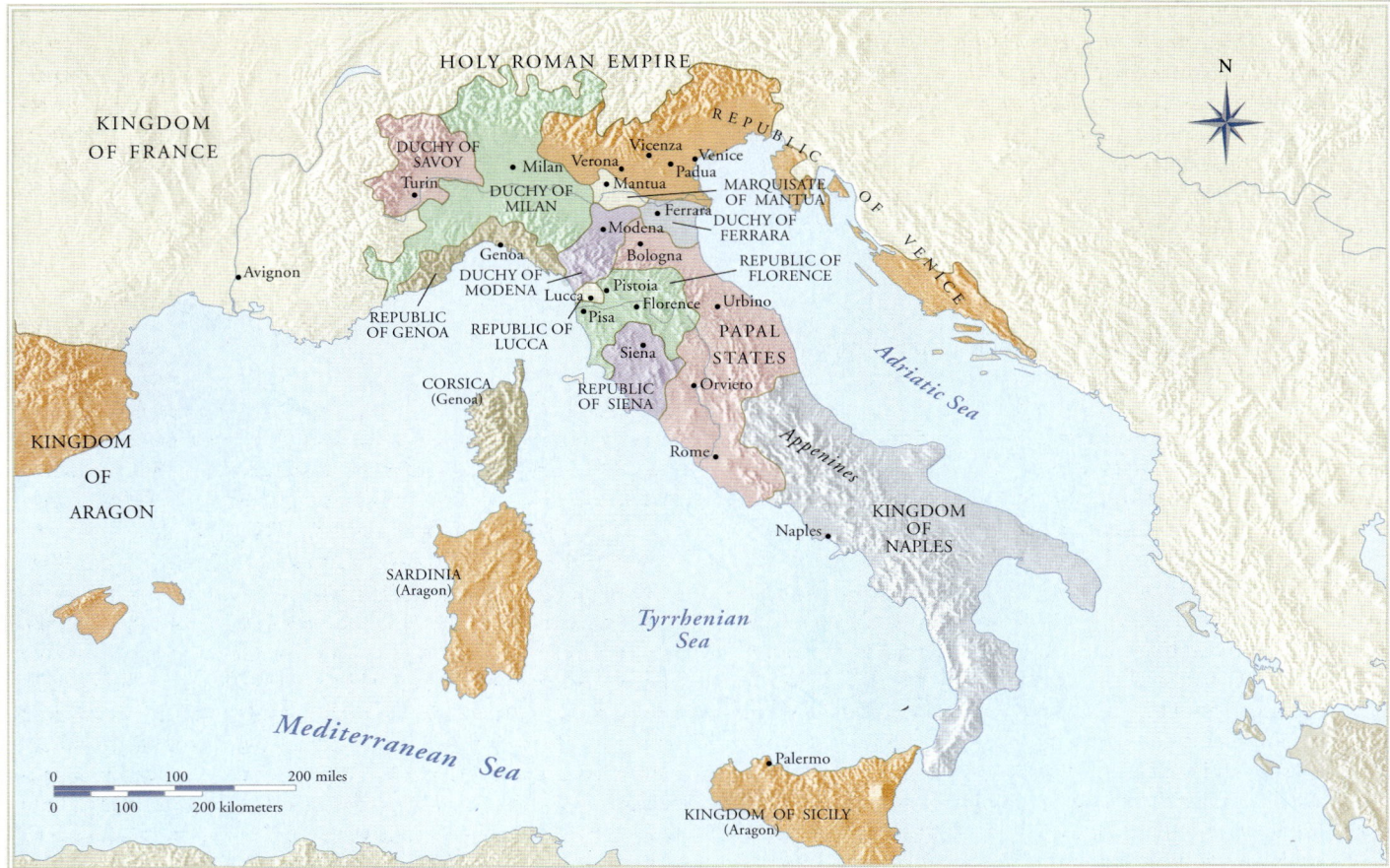

MAP 19-1 Italy around 1400.

The uniqueness and independence of each city-state were underscored by their separate economies; for example, Italy's port cities expanded maritime trade, whereas the economies of other cities centered on such flourishing industries as arms, banking, or textiles.

As a result of this economic prosperity, Italy had established a thriving international trade and held a commanding position in the Mediterranean world by the beginning of the 14th century. The structured organization of economic activity extended to the many trades and professions. Guilds (associations of master craftspeople, apprentices, and tradespeople), which had emerged during the 12th century, became prominent. These associations not only protected members' common economic interests against external pressures, such as taxation, but also provided them with the means to regulate their internal operations (for example, work quality and membership training). Although members' personal security and welfare were the guilds' primary concerns, these organizations dominated city governments as well.

## DISRUPTION AND CHANGE

**THE BLACK DEATH** Despite the relative stability and prosperity established throughout the Italian peninsula, the eruption of the Black Death (bubonic plague) in the late 1340s threw this delicate balance into chaos. Originating in China, the Black Death swept across the entire European continent. The most devastating natural disaster in European history, the Black Death eliminated between 25 and 50 percent of Europe's population in about five years. Italy was particularly hard hit. In large cities,

where people lived in relatively close proximity, the death tolls climbed as high as 50 or 60 percent of the population.

The Black Death had a significant effect on art. It stimulated religious bequests and encouraged the commissioning of devotional images. The focus on sickness and death also led to a burgeoning in hospital construction.

**THE GREAT SCHISM** Disruptions in the religious realm also contributed to the societal upheaval. In 1305, the College of Cardinals (the collective body of all cardinals) elected a French pope, Clement V, who settled in Avignon. Subsequent French popes remained in Avignon, despite their announced intentions to return to Rome. Understandably, this did not sit well with Italians, who saw Rome as the rightful capital of the universal church. The conflict between the French and Italians resulted in the election in 1378 of two popes—Clement VII, who resided in Avignon (and who does not appear on historical lists of popes compiled by the Catholic Church), and Urban VI (r. 1378–1389), who remained in Rome. Thus began what became known as the Great Schism. After 40 years, a council convened by the Holy Roman Emperor Sigismund managed to resolve this crisis in the church by electing a new Roman pope, Martin V (r. 1417–1431), who was acceptable to all.

## LETTERS AND LEARNING

**A VERNACULAR LITERATURE** Concurrent with these momentous shifts in the economic, social, and religious realms was the development of a vernacular (commonly spoken) literature, which dramatically affected Italy's intellectual and cultural life. Latin remained the official language of church liturgy and state documents. However, the creation of an Italian vernacular literature (based on the Tuscan dialect common in Florence) expanded the audience for philosophical and intellectual concepts because of its greater accessibility. Dante Alighieri (1265–1321; the author of *The Divine Comedy*), the poet and scholar Francesco Petrarch (1304–1374), and Giovanni Boccaccio (1313–1375; the author of *Decameron*) were among those most responsible for establishing this vernacular literature.

**REVIVING CLASSICAL VALUES** Fundamental to the development of the Italian Renaissance was humanism, which emerged during the 14th century and became a central component of much of Italian art and culture in the 15th and 16th centuries. Humanism was more a code of civil conduct, a theory of education, and a scholarly discipline than a philosophical system. As the word *humanism* suggests, the chief concerns of its proponents were human values and interests as distinct from—but not opposed to—religion's otherworldly values. Humanists held up classical cultures as particularly laudatory. This enthusiasm for antiquity, represented by Cicero's elegant Latin and the Augustan age, involved study of Latin classics and a conscious emulation of what proponents thought were the Roman civic virtues. These included self-sacrificing service to the state, participation in government, defense of state institutions (especially the administration of justice), and stoic indifference to personal misfortune in the performance of duty. With the help of a new interest in and knowledge of Greek, the humanists of the late 14th and 15th centuries recovered a large part of the Greek as well as the Roman literature and philosophy that had been lost, left unnoticed, or cast aside in the Middle Ages. What classical cultures provided to humanists was a model for living in this world, a model primarily of human focus that derived not from an authoritative and traditional religious dogma but from reason.

Ideally, humanists sought no material reward for services rendered. The sole reward for heroes of civic virtue was fame, just as the reward for leaders of the holy life was sainthood. For the educated, the lives of heroes and heroines of the past became as edifying as the lives of the saints. Petrarch wrote a book on illustrious men, and his colleague Boccaccio complemented it with biographies of famous women—from Eve to his contemporary, Joanna, queen of Naples. Both Petrarch and Boccaccio were famous in their own day as poets, scholars, and men of letters—their achievements equivalent in honor to those of the heroes of civic virtue. In 1341, Petrarch was crowned in Rome with the laurel wreath, the ancient symbol of victory and merit. The humanist cult of fame emphasized the importance of creative individuals and their role in contributing to the renown of the city-state and of all Italy.

Yet humanism, with its revival of interest in antiquity's secular culture, was only part of the general humanizing tendency in life and art that began in the 14th century and became dominant in subsequent centuries. Italy, crowded with classical monuments and memorials, was the natural setting for receiving humanistic values recovered from antiquity's omnipresent influence.

**AN ARTISTIC TRANSITION** Humanism—particularly the renewed interest in the classical—was an essential component of Italian Renaissance art and culture that developed in the 14th century and reached its zenith in the 15th and 16th centuries.

Although some scholars refer to late-13th- and 14th-century Italian art as Late Gothic, connecting it with the medieval culture that preceded it, other scholars describe it as Early Renaissance. Both of these characterizations have merit. Medieval conventions dominated late-13th- and 14th-century art and architecture, but artists more assertively attempted to break away from these conventions.

## THE MOVEMENT AWAY FROM MEDIEVALISM IN ART

**MANIERA GRECA** The fundamentally medieval nature of much of Italian art of this period is evident in a panel of the *Saint Francis Altarpiece* (FIG. **19-1**) by BONAVENTURA BERLINGHIERI (active ca. 1235–1244). Throughout the Middle Ages, the Byzantine style dominated Italian painting. This Italo-Byzantine style, or *maniera greca* (Greek style), surfaced in Berlinghieri's altarpiece. Painted in tempera on wood panel, Saint Francis wears the belted clerical garb of the order he founded. He holds a large book and displays the *stigmata*—marks like Christ's wounds—that appeared on his hands and feet. The saint is flanked by two angels, whose presentation—the frontality of their poses, prominent halos, and lack of modeling—indicates that Berlinghieri borrowed from Byzantine models. The painter enhanced this connection to earlier art forms with gold leaf (gold beaten into tissue-paper-thin sheets that then can be applied to surfaces), which emphasizes the image's flatness and spiritual nature. Other scenes from Francis's life depicted on the panel strongly suggest that their source is Byzantine illuminated manuscripts (compare FIG. 12-15). The central scene on the saint's right depicts Saint Francis preaching to the birds. The saint and his two attendants are aligned carefully against a shallow tower and wall, from Early Christian times a stylized symbol of a town or city. In front of the saint is another stage-scenery image of nested birds and twinkling plants. The composition's strict formality (relieved somewhat by the lively stippling—applied small dots or paint flecks—of the plants), the shallow space, and the linear flatness in the rendering of the forms are all familiar traits of a long and venerated tradition, soon suddenly and dramatically replaced. Despite the limited means of pictorial illusion at his disposal, Berlinghieri imbued this painting with an emotional resonance. The narrative scenes that run along the sides of the *Saint Francis Altarpiece* contribute to this resonance by providing an active contrast to the stiff formality of the large central image of Francis. For example, the scene on the upper left depicts Francis receiving the stigmata from a seraph and reveals the emotion of the Stigmatization.

Berlinghieri's depiction of Saint Francis sheds light on more than aspects of style—it also highlights the increasingly prominent role of religious orders in Italy (see "Mendicant Orders and Confraternities," page 524). The Franciscan order, named after its founder, Saint Francis of Assisi (ca. 1181–1226), worked diligently to impress on the public the saint's valuable example and to demonstrate its commitment to teaching and to alleviating suffering. Berlinghieri's altarpiece, commissioned for the church of San Francesco (Saint Francis) in Pescia, was created nine years after the saint's death and is the earliest known signed and dated representation of Saint Francis. Appropriately, this image focuses on the aspects of the saint's life that the Franciscans wanted to promote, thereby making visible (and thus more credible) the

## Mendicant Orders and Confraternities

The pope's absence from Italy during much of the 14th century (the Avignon papacy) contributed to an increase in prominence of monastic orders and confraternities. Such orders as the Augustinians, Carmelites, and Servites became very active, ensuring a constant religious presence in the daily life of Italians. Of the monastic orders, the largest and most influential were the *mendicants* (begging friars)—the Franciscans, founded by Francis of Assisi (FIG. 19-1), and the Dominicans, founded by the Spaniard Dominic de Guzman (ca. 1170–1221). These mendicants renounced all worldly goods and committed themselves to spreading God's word, performing good deeds, and ministering to the sick and dying. The Dominicans, in particular, contributed significantly to establishing urban educational institutions. The Franciscans and Dominicans became very popular among Italian citizens because of their devotion to their faith and the more personal relationship with God they encouraged.

Although both mendicant orders were working for the same purpose—the glory of God—a degree of rivalry nevertheless existed between the two. They established their churches on opposite sides of Florence—Santa Croce (see FIG. Intro-3), the Franciscan church, on the eastern side, and the Dominicans' Santa Maria Novella (FIGS. 19-19 and 21-34) on the western.

*Confraternities,* organizations consisting of laypersons who dedicated themselves to strict religious observance, also grew in popularity during the 14th and 15th centuries. The mission of confraternities included tending the sick, burying the dead, singing hymns, and performing other good works.

The mendicant orders and confraternities continued to play an important role in Italian religious life through the 16th century. Further, the numerous artworks and monastic churches they commissioned ensured their enduring legacy.

**19-1** BONAVENTURA BERLINGHIERI, panel from the *Saint Francis Altarpiece,* San Francesco, Pescia, Italy, 1235. Tempera on wood, approx. 5′ × 3′ × 6″.

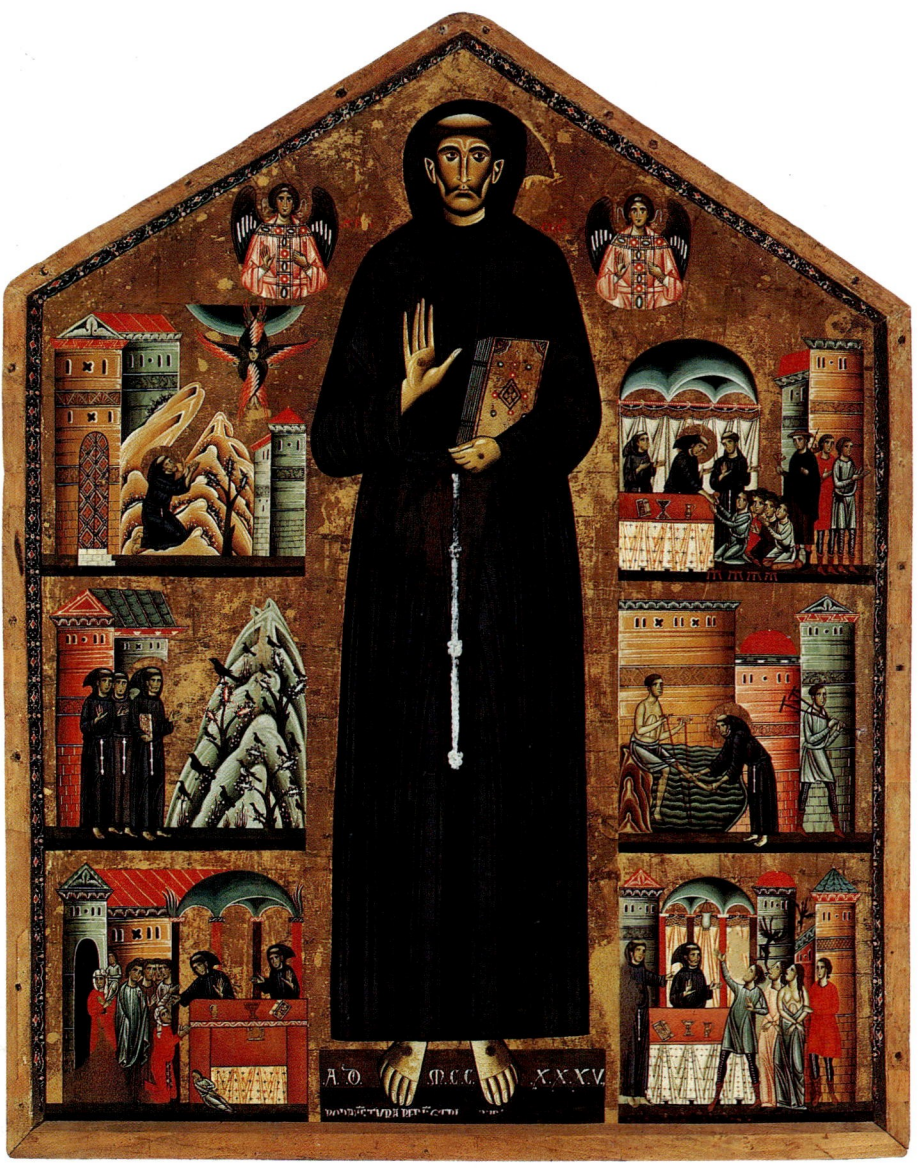

## Artists' Names in Renaissance Italy

In contemporary societies, people have become accustomed to a standardized method of identifying individuals. Given names are coupled with family names, although the order of the two (or more) names sometimes varies. This standardization has been necessitated by increased reliance on "official" documentation such as birth certificates, driver's licenses, and wills.

However, such regularity in names was not the norm in Italy during the 14th and 15th centuries. Often, individuals adopted their hometowns as one of their names. For example, sculptor Nicola Pisano (FIGS. 19-2 and 19-3) was from Pisa, Giulio Romano (see FIG. 22-49) was from Rome, and painter Domenico Veneziano was from Venice. Leonardo da Vinci (see FIGS. 22-1 to 22-5) hailed from the small town of Vinci, Andrea del Castagno (see FIG. 21-37) from Castagno. This information was particularly valuable when meeting someone for the first time, especially once

mobility and travel increased in the 14th century. Such artists are often referred to by their given names, such as *Leonardo*.

Nicknames were also common. Masaccio (see FIGS. 21-10, 21-11, and 21-12) was "Big Thomas," and his fellow artist, Masolino, was "Small Thomas." Guido di Pietro is better known today as Fra Angelico (the Angelic Friar; FIG. 21-36), and Cenni di Pepo (FIG. 19-6) is remembered as Cimabue, meaning "bull's head." Artists sometimes derived their names from their renowned works. Jacopo della Quercia was familiar to early-15th-century Italians as Jacopo del Fonte (Jacopo of the Fountain) for his impressive Fonte Gaia (Gay Fountain) in the public square in front of the Palazzo Pubblico in Siena.

Names were not only nonstandardized but also impermanent and could be changed at will. This flexibility has resulted in significant challenges for historians, who often must deal with archival documents and records.

legendary life of this holy man. Saint Francis believed he could get closer to God by rejecting worldly goods, and to achieve this he stripped himself bare in a public square and committed himself to a strict life of fasting, prayer, and meditation. The appearance of stigmata on his hands and feet (visible in Berlinghieri's painting) was perceived as God's blessing and led some followers to see Francis as a second Christ. Fittingly, four of the six scenes that surround the central figure of Saint Francis depict miraculous healings, connecting him more emphatically to Christ. The coarse habit he wears, tied at the waist with a rope, became the garb of the Franciscans.

**THE INFLUENCE OF CLASSICAL ART** Interest in the art of classical antiquity was not unheard of during the medieval period. For example, the Visitation group statues on the west facade of Reims Cathedral (see FIG. 18-22) show an unmistakable interest in Roman sculpture, even though the facial modeling reveals their Gothic origin. However, the 13th-century sculpture of NICOLA PISANO (active ca. 1258–1278), contemporary with the Reims statues, exhibits an interest in classical forms unlike that found in the works of his predecessors. This interest was perhaps due in part to the influence of the humanistic culture of Sicily under its king, Holy Roman Emperor Frederick II. The king was known in his own time as "the wonder of the world" for his many intellectual gifts and other talents. Frederick's nostalgia for the past grandeur of Rome fostered a revival of Roman sculpture and decoration in Sicily and southern Italy before the mid-13th century. Because Nicola Pisano (see "Artists' Names in Renaissance Italy," above) may have received his early training in this environment, he may have been influenced by Roman artworks. After Frederick's death in 1250, Nicola Pisano traveled northward and eventually settled in Pisa. Then at the height of its political and economic power, Pisa was recognized by artists as a locale for lucrative commissions (see "Art to Order: Commissions and Patronage," page 526).

Nicola Pisano's sculpture, unlike the French sculpture of the period, was not part of the extensive decoration of great portals. He carved marble reliefs and ornament for large pulpits, completing the first in 1260 for the baptistery of Pisa Cathedral (FIG. 19-2). Some elements of the pulpit's design carried on medieval

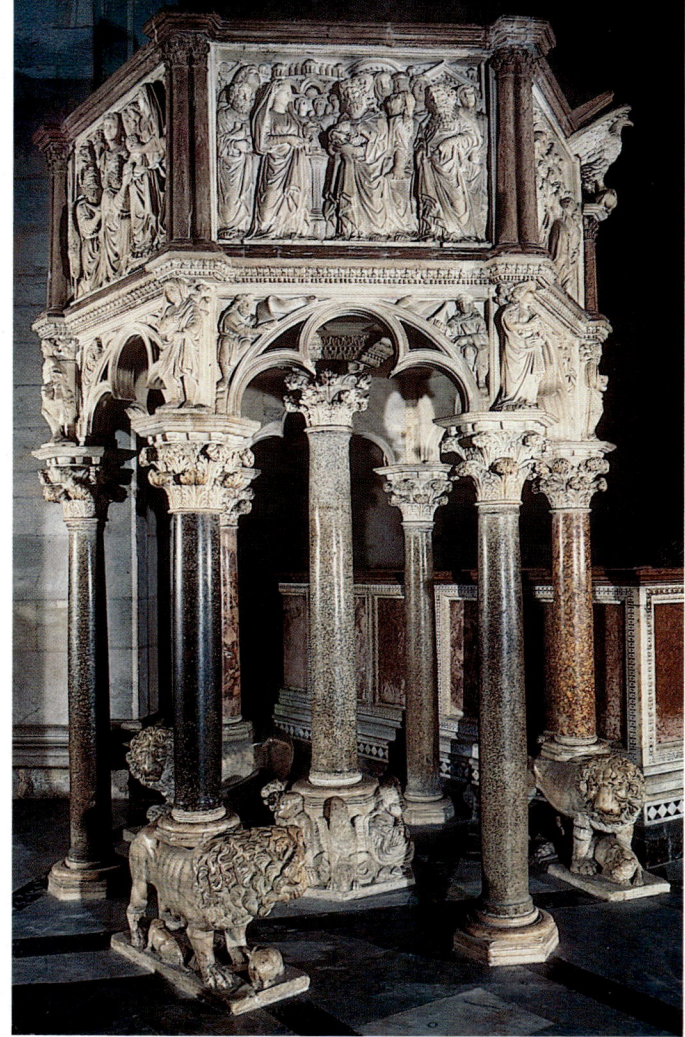

**19-2** NICOLA PISANO, pulpit of Pisa Cathedral baptistery, Pisa, Italy, 1259–1260. Marble, approx. 15′ high.

### Art to Order
#### Commissions and Patronage

Because of today's international open art market, the general public tends to see art as the creative expression of an individual—the artist. However, artists did not always enjoy this degree of freedom. Historically, artists rarely undertook major artworks without a patron's concrete commission.

The patron could be a civic group, religious entity, or private individual. Guilds, although primarily economic commercial organizations, contributed to their city's religious and artistic life by subsidizing the building and decoration of numerous churches and hospitals. For example, the Arte della Lana (wool manufacturers' guild) oversaw the start of the Florence Cathedral (FIGS. 19-17 and 19-18) in 1296, and the Arte di Calimala (wool merchants' guild) supervised the completion of its dome (see FIG. 21-13).

Religious groups, such as the monastic orders, were also major art patrons. Of course, the papacy had long been an important patron, and artists vied for the pope's prestigious commissions. The papacy's patronage became even more visible during the 16th and 17th centuries, and today the Vatican Museums hold one of the world's most spectacular art collections.

Wealthy families and individuals commissioned artworks for a wide variety of reasons. Besides the aesthetic pleasure these patrons derived from art, the images often also served as testaments to the patron's wealth, status, power, and knowledge. Art was commissioned for propagandistic, philanthropic, or commemorative purposes as well.

Because artworks during this period were the product of what was, in effect, a service contract, viewers must consider the patrons' needs or wishes when looking at commissioned art and architecture. From the few extant contracts, it appears that artists normally were asked to submit drawings or models to their patrons for approval. Patrons expected artists to adhere to the approved designs fairly closely. Surviving contracts do not have the detail one might expect from a legal document. These contracts usually stipulate certain conditions, such as the insistence on the artist's own hand in the production of the work, the pigment quality and amount of gold or other precious items to be used, completion date, payment terms, and penalties for failure to meet the contract's terms. Although it is clear that patrons could have been very specific about the details of projects and often made many decisions about the works, those expectations are often absent from the written contracts. Regardless, the patron's role looms large in any discussion of art created before the 17th century, when an open art market developed.

---

traditions (for example, the trilobed arches and the lions supporting some of the columns), but Nicola Pisano also incorporated classical elements into this medieval type of structure. The large, bushy capitals are a Gothic variation of the Corinthian capital; the arches are round rather than pointed *(ogival)*; and the large rectangular relief panels, if their proportions were altered slightly, could have come from the sides of Roman sarcophagi. The densely packed large-scale figures of the individual panels also seem to derive from the compositions found on Roman sarcophagi. In one of these panels, *The Annunciation and the Nativity* (FIG. 19-3), the Virgin reclines in a manner reminiscent of the lid figures on Etruscan (see FIGS. 9-4 and 9-14) and Roman (see

FIG. 10-62) sarcophagi, and the face types, beards, coiffures, and draperies, as well as the bulk and weight of the figures, were clearly inspired by classical relief sculpture. (For information on the Annunciation and the Nativity, see "The Life of Jesus in Art," Chapter 11, pages 308–309 or xvi–xvii in Volume II.) Scholars have even been able to pinpoint the models of some of Nicola's figures on Roman sarcophagi the sculptor would have known.

A SON'S SCULPTURAL RESPONSE Nicola Pisano's classicizing manner was countered by his son GIOVANNI PISANO (ca. 1250–1320). Giovanni's version of *The Annunciation and the Nativity* (FIG. 19-4), from the pulpit in Sant'Andrea at Pistoia, was

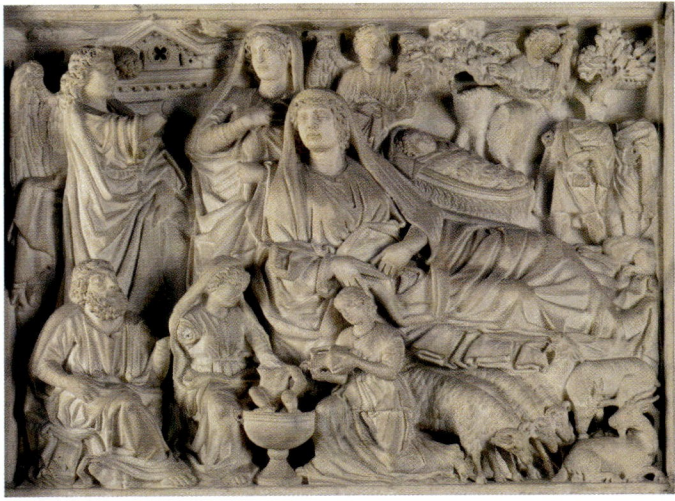

**19-3** NICOLA PISANO, *The Annunciation and the Nativity,* detail of pulpit of Pisa Cathedral baptistery, Pisa, Italy, 1259–1260. Marble relief, approx. 2′ 10″ × 3′ 9″.

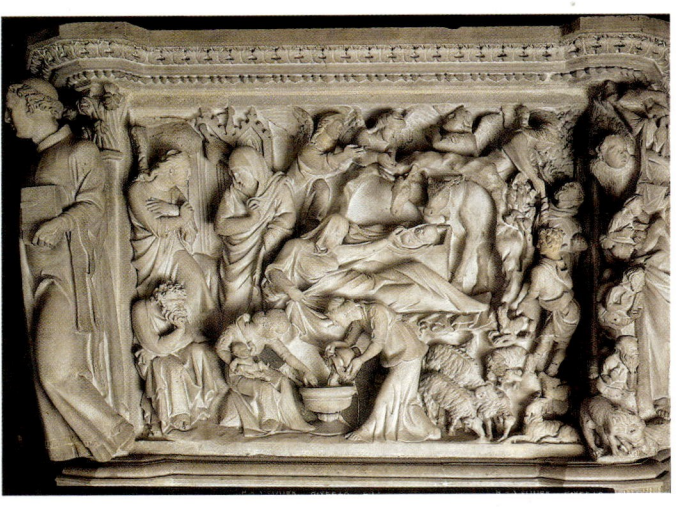

**19-4** GIOVANNI PISANO, *The Annunciation and the Nativity,* detail of the pulpit of Sant'Andrea, Pistoia, Italy, 1297–1301. Marble relief, approx. 2′ 10″ × 3′ 4″.

finished some 40 years after the one by his father in the Pisa baptistery. It offers a striking contrast to Nicola Pisano's thick carving and placid, almost stolid, presentation of the theme. Giovanni Pisano arranged the figures loosely and dynamically. An excited animation twists and bends them, and their motion is suggested by spaces that open deeply between them. In the Annunciation episode, which is combined with the Nativity (as in the older version), the Virgin shrinks from the angel's sudden appearance in a posture of alarm touched with humility. The same spasm of apprehension contracts her supple body as she reclines in the Nativity scene. The drama's principals share in a peculiar nervous agitation, as if they all suddenly are moved by spiritual passion. Only the shepherds and the sheep, appropriately, do not yet share in the miraculous event. The swiftly turning, sinuous draperies; the slender figures they enfold; and the general emotionalism of the scene are features not found in Nicola Pisano's interpretation. Thus, the father's and son's works show, successively, two novel trends of great significance for subsequent art— a new interest in classical antiquity and a burgeoning naturalism.

**SCULPTURAL FORM IN PAINTING** The art of Pietro Cavallini (active ca. 1273–1308) represented one style of the Roman school of painting. A great interest in the sculptural rendering of form characterized the style, as evidenced in a detail (FIG. **19-5**) from Cavallini's badly damaged fresco, *Last Judgment,* in the church of Santa Cecilia in Trastevere in Rome. Cavallini, perhaps under the influence of Roman paintings now lost, abandoned Byzantine stylized dignity and replaced it with a long-lost impression of solidity and strength in *Seated Apostles.* He achieved this effect through careful depiction of light that illuminates the figures, throwing them into relief, along with his presentation of drapery, which envelops the figures and enhances their three-dimensionality.

**A SUMMARY OF BYZANTINE STYLE** Like Cavallini, Cenni di Pepo, better known as Cimabue (ca. 1240–1302; see "Artists' Names in Renaissance Italy," page 525), moved beyond the limits of the Italo-Byzantine style. Although his works reveal the unmistakable influence of Gothic sculpture, Cimabue was inspired by the same impulse toward naturalism as Giovanni Pisano, and challenged the conventions that dominated earlier art. The formality evident in Cimabue's *Madonna Enthroned with Angels and Prophets* (FIG. **19-6**) is appropriate to the dignity of the theme represented. The artist modeled his large image on Byzantine examples (see FIG. 12-16), revealed in the painting's careful structure and symmetry.

He also used the gold embellishments common to Byzantine art to enhance the folds and three-dimensionality of the drapery. However, Cimabue constructed a deeper space for the Madonna and the surrounding figures to inhabit. Despite such departures from Byzantine convention, this vast altarpiece is a final summary of centuries of Byzantine art before its utter transformation.

**AN EMPIRICAL ART** A naturalistic approach based on observation was the major contribution of Giotto di Bondone (ca. 1266–1337), who made a much more radical break with the past. Scholars still debate the sources of Giotto's style, although one source must have been the style of the Roman school of painting Cavallini represented. Another formative influence on Giotto may have been the work of the man presumed to be his teacher, Cimabue. The art of the French Gothic sculptors (perhaps seen by Giotto himself but certainly familiar to him from the sculpture of Giovanni Pisano, who had spent time in Paris) and ancient Roman art, both sculpture and painting, must have contributed to Giotto's artistic education. Some believe that new developments in contemporaneous Byzantine art further influenced him.

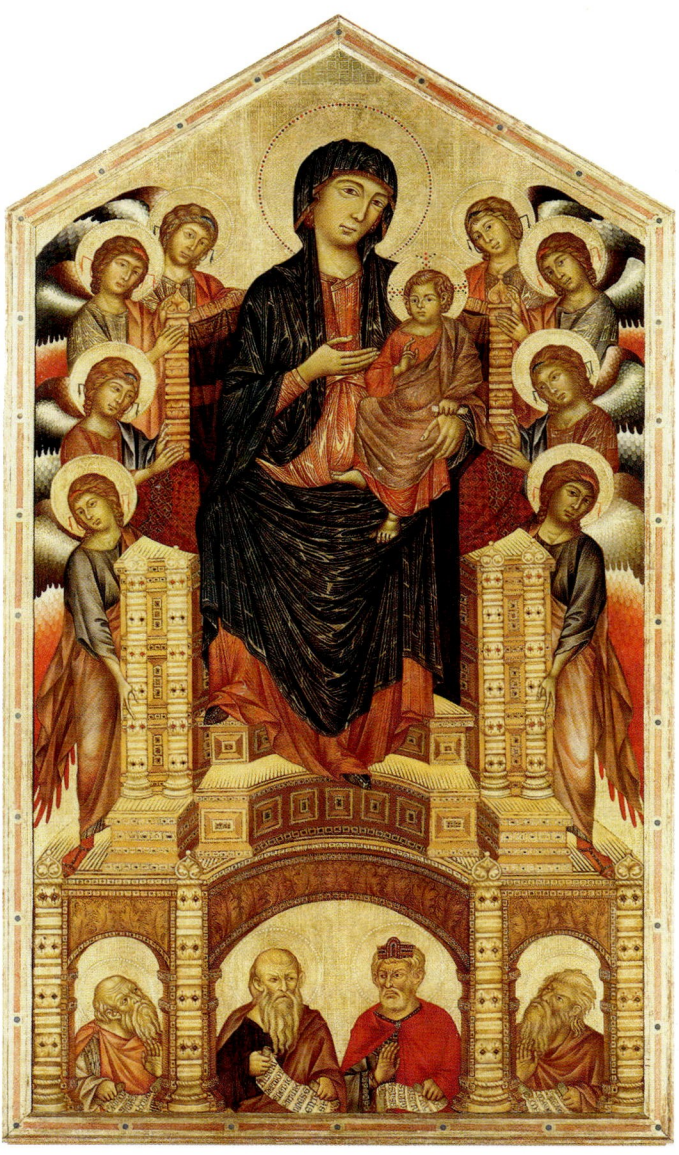

**19-6** Cimabue, *Madonna Enthroned with Angels and Prophets,* ca. 1280–1290. Tempera on wood, 12′ 7″ × 7′ 4″. Galleria degli Uffizi, Florence.

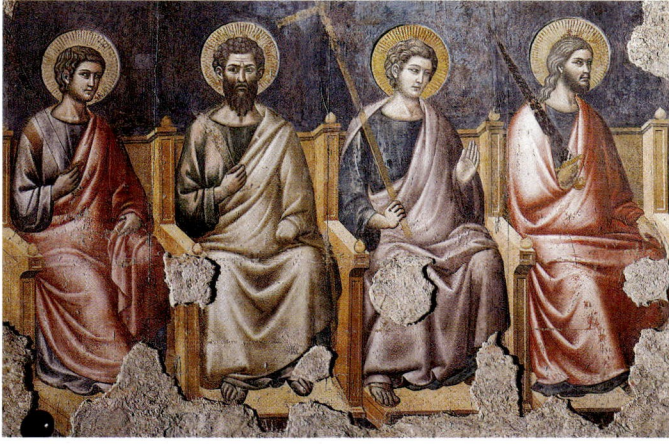

**19-5** Pietro Cavallini, *Seated Apostles,* detail of the *Last Judgment,* Santa Cecilia in Trastevere, Rome, Italy, ca. 1291. Fresco.

Yet no mere synthesis of these varied influences could have produced the significant shift in artistic approach that has led some scholars to describe Giotto as the father of Western pictorial art. Renowned in his own day, his reputation has never faltered. Regardless of the other influences on his artistic style, his true teacher was nature—the world of visible things.

Giotto's revolution in painting did not consist only of displacing the Byzantine style, establishing painting as a major art form for the next seven centuries, and restoring the naturalistic approach developed by the ancients and largely abandoned in the Middle Ages. He also inaugurated a method of pictorial expression based on observation and initiated an age that might be called "early scientific." By stressing the preeminence of sight for gaining knowledge of the world, Giotto and his successors contributed to the foundation of empirical science. They recognized that the visual world must be observed before it can be analyzed and understood. Praised in his own and later times for his fidelity to nature, Giotto was more than a mere imitator of it. He revealed nature while observing it and divining its visible order. In fact, he showed his generation a new way of seeing. With Giotto, Western artists turned resolutely toward the visible world as their source of knowledge of nature.

On nearly the same great scale as the Madonna painted by Cimabue, Giotto depicted her (FIG. 19-7) in a work that offers an opportunity to appreciate his perhaps most telling contribution to representational art—sculptural solidity and weight. The Madonna, enthroned with angels, rests within her Gothic throne with the unshakable stability of an ancient marble goddess (see FIG. 10-28). Giotto replaced Cimabue's slender Virgin, fragile beneath the thin ripplings of her drapery, with a sturdy, queenly mother, bodily of this world, even to the swelling of her bosom. Her body is not lost; it is asserted. The new art aimed, before all else, to construct a figure that has substance, dimensionality, and bulk. Works painted in the new style portray figures, like those in sculpture, that project into the light and give the illusion that they could throw shadows. In Giotto's *Madonna Enthroned*, the throne is deep enough to contain the monumental figure and breaks away from the flat ground to project and enclose her.

**19-7** GIOTTO DI BONDONE, *Madonna Enthroned*, ca. 1310. Tempera on wood, 10′ 8″ × 6′ 8″. Galleria degli Uffizi, Florence.

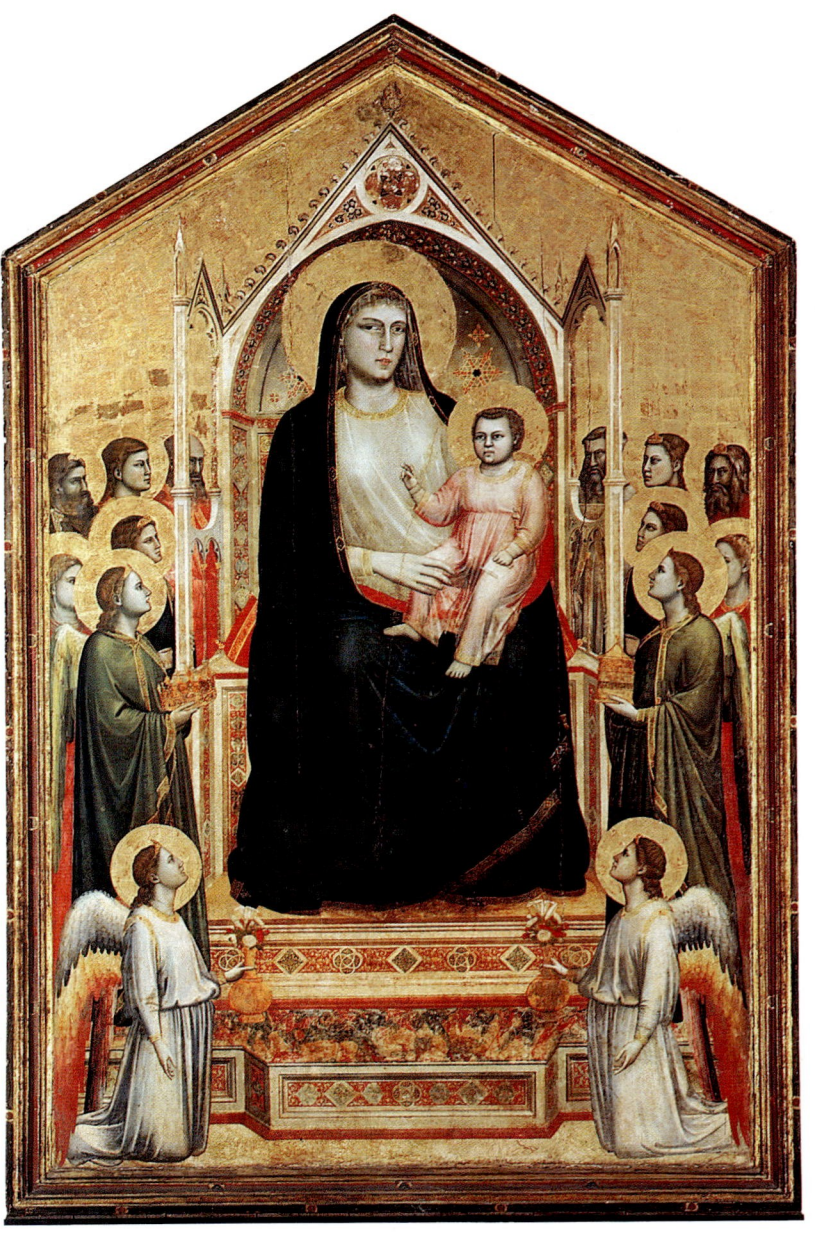

**CHRONICLING THE LIVES OF THE VIRGIN AND CHRIST**
Projecting on a flat surface the illusion of solid bodies moving through space presents a double challenge. Constructing the illusion of a body also requires constructing the illusion of a space sufficiently ample to contain that body. In Giotto's fresco cycles (he was primarily a muralist), he constantly strove to reconcile these two aspects of illusionistic painting. His frescoes (paintings on wet plaster; see "Fresco Painting," page 530) in the Arena Chapel (Cappella Scrovegni) at Padua (FIG. 19-8) show his art at its finest. The Arena Chapel, which takes its name from an ancient Roman amphitheater nearby, was built for Enrico Scrovegni, a wealthy Paduan merchant, on a site adjacent to his now razed palace. This building, intended for the Scrovegni family's private use, was consecrated in 1305, and its design is so perfectly suited to its interior decoration that some scholars have suggested that Giotto himself may have been its architect.

The rectangular barrel-vaulted hall has six narrow windows in its south wall only, which left the entire north wall an unbroken and well-illuminated surface for painting. The entire building seems to have been designed to provide Giotto with as much flat surface as possible for presenting one of the most impressive and complete pictorial cycles of Christian Redemption ever rendered. With 38 framed pictures, arranged on three levels, the artist related the most poignant incidents from the lives of the Virgin and her parents, Joachim and Anna (top level); the life and mission of Christ (middle level); and his Passion, Crucifixion, and Resurrection (bottom level). These three pictorial levels rest on a coloristically neutral base. Imitation marble veneer—reminiscent of ancient Roman decoration (see FIG. 10-50), which Giotto may have seen—alternates with the Virtues and Vices painted in *grisaille* (monochrome grays, often used for modeling in paintings) to resemble sculpture. The climactic event of the cycle of human salvation, the Last Judgment, covers most of the west wall above the chapel's entrance.

The hall's vaulted ceiling is blue, an azure sky symbolic of Heaven. It is dotted with golden stars and medallions bearing images of Christ, Mary, and various prophets. Giotto painted the same blue in the backgrounds of the narrative panels on the walls below (some now faded or flaked). The color thereby functions as

## Fresco Painting

Fresco has a long history, particularly in the Mediterranean region (see FIGS. 4-6 to 4-9), where the Minoans used it as early as 1650 BCE. Fresco (Italian for "fresh") is a mural-painting technique that involves applying permanent limeproof pigments, diluted in water, on freshly laid lime plaster. Because the pigments are absorbed into the surface of the wall as the plaster dries, fresco is one of the most permanent painting techniques. The stable condition of frescoes such as those in the Arena Chapel (FIGS. 19-8 and 19-9) and in the Sistine Chapel (see FIGS. 22-12, 22-13, and 22-14), now hundreds of years old, testify to the longevity of this painting method. The colors have remained vivid (although dirt and soot have necessitated cleaning) because of the chemically inert pigments the artists used. In addition to this *buon fresco* ("true" fresco) technique, artists used *fresco secco* (dry fresco). Fresco secco involves painting on dried lime plaster. Although the finished product visually approximates buon fresco, the pigments are not absorbed into the wall and simply adhere to the surface, so fresco secco does not have buon fresco's longevity. Compare, for example, the current condition of Michelangelo's buon fresco Sistine Ceiling (see FIG. 22-13) with Leonardo da Vinci's *Last Supper* (see FIG. 22-3), executed largely in fresco secco (with experimental techniques and pigments).

The buon fresco process is time-consuming and demanding and requires several layers of plaster. Although buon fresco methods vary, generally the artist prepares the wall with a rough layer of lime plaster called the *arriccio* (brown coat). The artist then transfers the composition to the wall, usually by drawing directly on the arriccio with a burnt-orange pigment called *sinopia* (most popular during the 14th century), or by transferring a *cartoon* (a full-sized preparatory drawing). Cartoons increased in usage in the 15th and 16th centuries, largely replacing sinopia underdrawings. Finally, the *intonaco* (painting coat) is laid smoothly over the drawing in sections (called *giornate*, Italian for "days") only as large as the artist expects to complete in that session. The artist must paint fairly quickly, because once the plaster is dry, it will no longer absorb the pigment. Any areas of the intonaco that remain unpainted after a session must be cut away so that fresh plaster can be applied for the next giornata.

In areas of high humidity, such as Venice, fresco was less appropriate because of the obstacle the moisture presented to the drying process. Over the centuries, fresco became less popular, although it did experience a revival in the 1930s with the Mexican muralists (see FIGS. 33-80 and 33-81). Many of the older frescoes have been transferred from their original walls by lifting off the intonaco layer of plaster and readhering the images to other supports.

---

a unifying agent for the entire decorative scheme and renders the scenes more realistic.

The individual panels are framed with decorative borders, which, with their delicate tracery, offer a striking contrast to the sparse simplicity of the images they surround. Subtly scaled to the chapel's space (only about half life-size), Giotto's stately and slow-moving actors present their dramas convincingly and with great restraint. *Lamentation* (FIG. **19-9**) reveals the essentials of his style. In the presence of angels darting about in hysterical grief, a congregation mourns over the dead body of the Savior just before its entombment. Mary cradles her son's body, while Mary Magdalene looks solemnly at the wounds in Christ's feet and Saint John the Evangelist throws his arms back dramatically. Giotto arranged a shallow stage for the figures, bounded by a thick diagonal rock incline that defines a horizontal ledge in the foreground. Though rather narrow, the ledge provides firm visual support for the figures, and the steep slope indicates the picture's dramatic focal point at the lower left. The rocky landscape also links this scene with the adjoining one. Giotto connected the framed scenes throughout the fresco cycle with such formal elements. The figures are sculpturesque, simple, and weighty, but this mass did not preclude motion and emotion. Postures and gestures that might have been only rhetorical and mechanical convey, in *Lamentation*, a broad spectrum of grief. They range from Mary's almost fierce despair to the passionate outbursts of Mary Magdalene and John to the philosophical resignation of the two disciples at the right and the mute sorrow of the two hooded mourners in the foreground (compare FIG. 12-27). Giotto constructed a kind of stage that served as a model for artists who depicted human dramas in many subsequent paintings. His style was far removed from the isolated episodes and figures seen in art until the late 13th century. In *Lamentation*, a single event provokes an intense response. This combination of compositional complexity and emotional resonance was rarely attempted, let alone achieved, in art before Giotto.

The formal design of the *Lamentation* fresco, the way the figures are grouped within the constructed space, is worth close study. Each group has its own definition, and each contributes to the rhythmic order of the composition. The strong diagonal of the rocky ledge, with its single dead tree (the tree of knowledge of good and evil, which withered at the Fall of Adam), concentrates the viewer's attention on the group around the head of Christ, whose positioning is dynamically off center. All movement beyond this group is contained, or arrested, by the massive bulk of the seated mourner in the painting's left corner. The seated mourner to the right establishes a relation with the center group, who, by their gazes and gestures, draw the viewer's attention back to Christ's head. Figures seen from the back, which are frequent in Giotto's compositions, represent an innovation in the development away from the formal Italo-Byzantine style. These figures emphasize the foreground, aiding the visual placement of the intermediate figures farther back in space. This device, the very contradiction of the old frontality, in effect puts viewers behind the "observer" figures, who, facing the action as spectators, reinforce the sense of stagecraft as a model for painting.

Giotto's new devices for depicting spatial depth and bodily mass could not, of course, have been possible without his management of light and shade. He shaded his figures to indicate both the direction of the light that illuminates them and the shadows (the diminished light), giving the figures volume. In *Lamentation*, light falls upon the upper surfaces of the figures (especially the two central bending figures) and passes down to dark in their

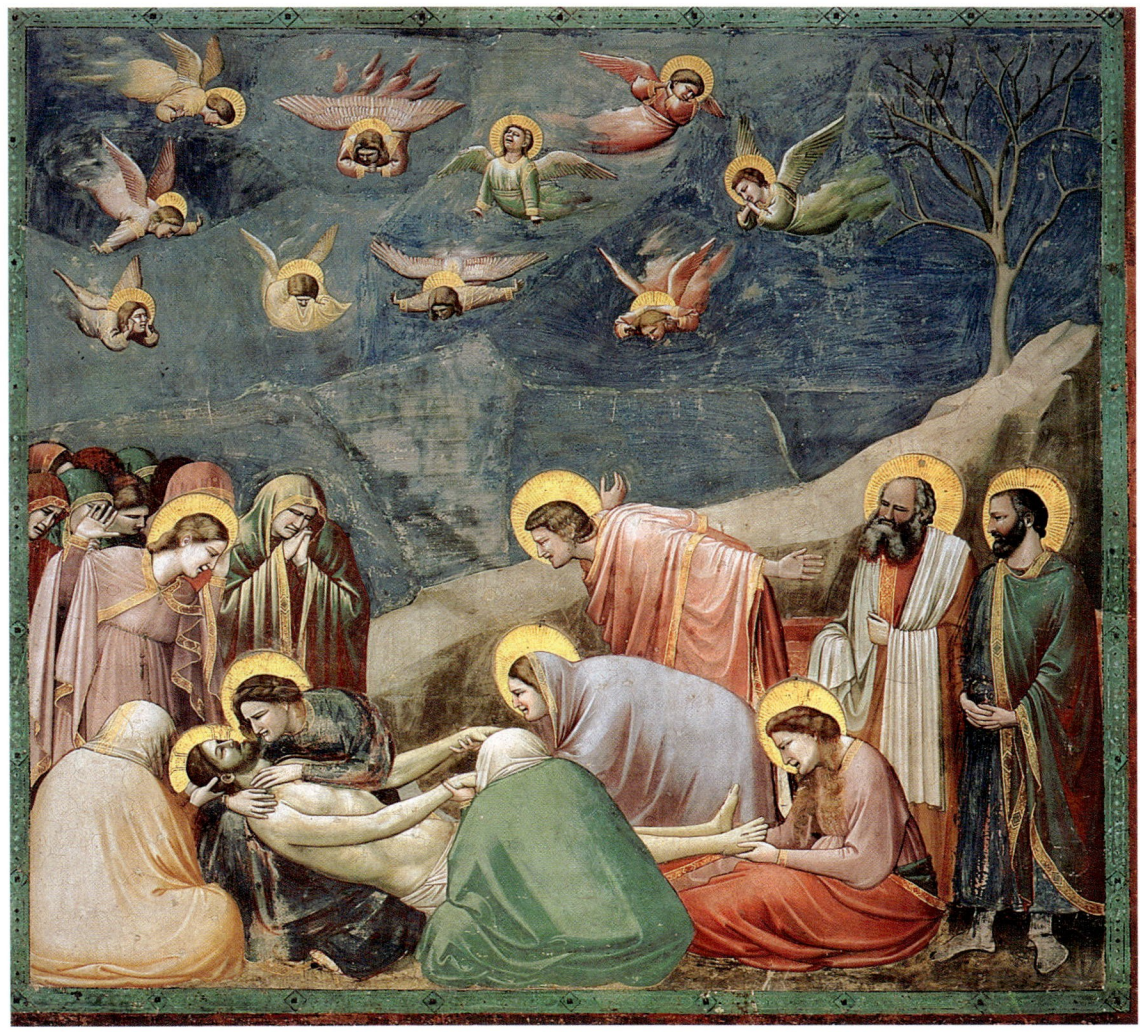

**19-9** Giotto di Bondone, *Lamentation*, Arena Chapel (Cappella Scrovegni), Padua, Italy, ca. 1305. Fresco, 6' 6¾" × 6'¾".

draperies, separating the volumes one from the other and pushing one to the fore, the other to the rear. The graded continuum of light and shade, directed by an even neutral light from a single steady source—not shown in the picture—was the first step toward the development of *chiaroscuro* (the use of dramatic contrasts of dark and light to produce modeling).

The stagelike settings made possible by Giotto's innovations in *perspective* (the depiction of three-dimensional objects in space on a two-dimensional surface) and lighting suited perfectly the dramatic narrative the Franciscans emphasized then as a principal method for educating the faithful in their religion. In the humanizing age, the old stylized presentations of the holy mysteries had evolved into what were called the "mystery" plays. The drama of the Mass was extended into one- and two-act tableaus and scenes and then into simple narratives offered at church portals and in city squares. (Eventually, confraternities also presented more elaborate religious dramas called *sacre rappresentazioni*—sacred representations.) The great increase in popular sermons to huge city audiences prompted a public taste for narrative, recited as dramatically as possible. The arts of illusionistic painting, of drama, and of sermon rhetoric with all their theatrical flourishes were developing simultaneously and were mutually influential. Giotto's art masterfully—perhaps uniquely—synthesized dramatic narrative, holy lesson, and truth to human experience in a visual idiom of his own inven-

tion, accessible to all. Not surprisingly, Giotto's frescoes served as textbooks for generations of Renaissance painters from Masaccio to Michelangelo and beyond.

## *The Republic of Siena*

Among 14th-century Italian city-states, the Republics of Siena and Florence were notable for their strong commitment to art. Both Siena and Florence (the major cities of these two republics) were urban centers of bankers and merchants with widespread international contacts. Chroniclers and historians recognized early on the importance of these two cities for the development of art; discussions comparing their artistic contributions extend back into the 14th century.

**MARY IN MAJESTY**  Siena was a commanding presence in 14th-century Italy. Particularly proud of their victory over the Florentines at the battle of Monteperti in 1260, the Sienese believed that the Virgin Mary had sponsored their victory. This belief reinforced Sienese devotion to the Virgin, which was paramount in the religious life of the city. Sienese citizens could boast of Siena's dedication to the Queen of Heaven as more ancient and venerable than that of all others. It is important that loyalty to the secular republican city-state was linked with devotion to its favorite saint. The Virgin became protector not only of every citizen but also of the city itself.

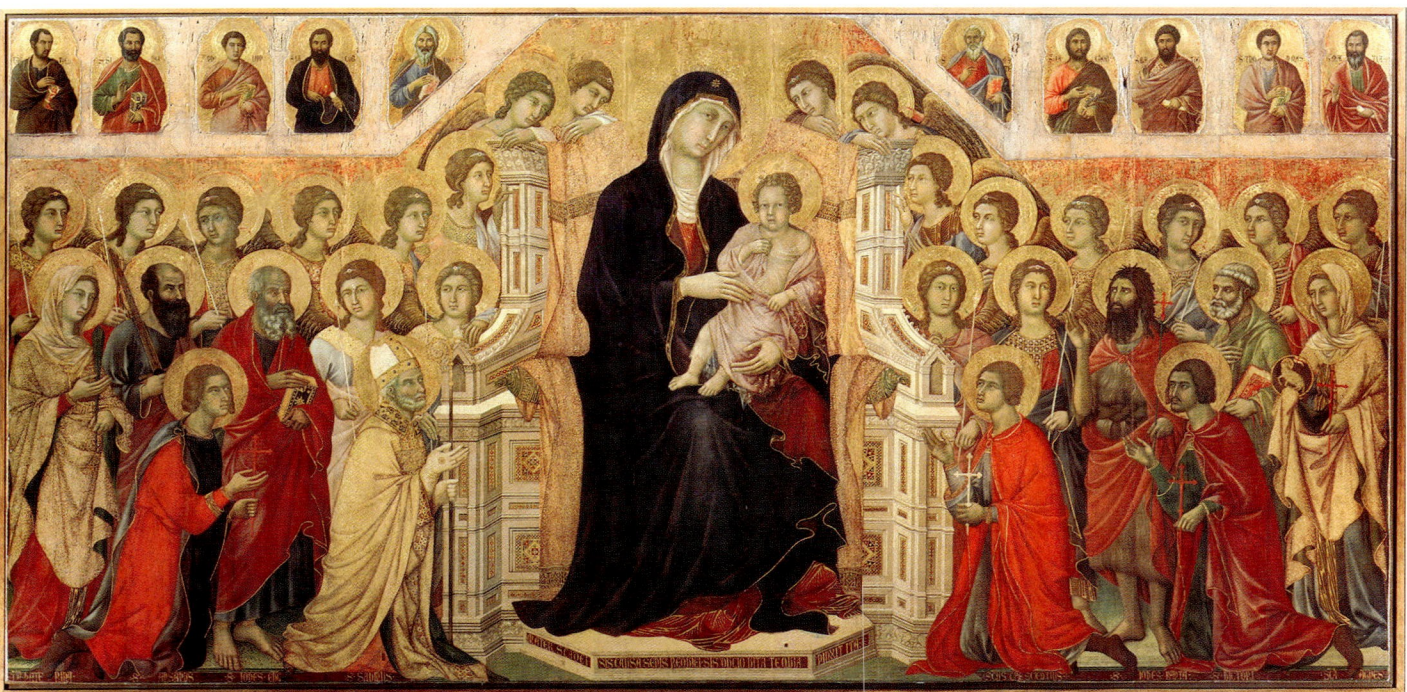

**19-10** DUCCIO DI BUONINSEGNA, *Virgin and Child Enthroned with Saints,* principal panel of the *Maestà* altarpiece, from the Siena Cathedral, Siena, Italy, 1308–1311. Tempera on wood, 7' × 13' (center panel). Museo dell'Opera del Duomo, Siena.

The works of DUCCIO DI BUONINSEGNA (active ca. 1278–1318) represent Sienese art in its supreme achievement. His immense altarpiece, the *Maestà,* was designed to replace a much smaller painting of the Virgin Mary. Duccio's inscription of his name at the base of the Virgin's throne in the *Maestà* is part of a prayer for himself and for the city of Siena, its cathedral, and its churches.

The *Maestà,* painted in tempera front and back and composed of many panels, was commissioned for the high altar of the Siena Cathedral in 1308 and completed by Duccio and his assistants in 1311. As originally executed, it consisted of a seven-foot-high central panel (FIG. **19-10**), surmounted by seven pinnacles above, and a *predella,* or raised shelf, of panels at the base, altogether some 13 feet high. Unfortunately, the work no longer can be seen in its entirety. It was dismantled in subsequent centuries, and many of its panels are now scattered as single masterpieces among the world's museums.

The main panel of the front side represents the Virgin enthroned in majesty (maestà) as Queen of Heaven amid choruses of angels and saints. Duccio derived the composition's formality and symmetry, along with the figures and facial types of the principal angels and saints, from Byzantine tradition. But the artist relaxed the strict frontality and rigidity of the figures in the typical Byzantine icon and iconostasis, or apse mosaic; they turn to each other in quiet conversation. Further, Duccio individualized the faces of the four saints kneeling in the foreground, who perform their ceremonial gestures without stiffness. Similarly, Duccio softened the usual Byzantine hard body outlines and drapery patterning. The drapery, particularly that of the female saints at both ends of the panel, falls and curves loosely. This is a feature familiar in northern Gothic works (see FIG. 18-35) and is a mark of the artistic dialogue that occurred between Italy and the north in the 14th century.

Despite these changes that reveal Duccio's interest in the new naturalism, he respected the age-old requirement that as an altarpiece, the *Maestà* would occupy the very center of the sanctuary as the focus of worship. As such, he knew it should be an object holy in itself—a work of splendor to the eyes, precious in its message and its materials. Duccio thus recognized that the function of this work naturally limited experimentation with depicting narrative action and producing illusionistic effects (such as Giotto's) by modeling forms and adjusting their placement in pictorial space.

Instead, the Queen of Heaven panel is a miracle of color composition and texture manipulation, unfortunately not apparent in a photo. Close inspection of the original reveals what the Sienese artists learned from other sources. In the 13th and 14th centuries, Italy was the distribution center for the great silk trade from China and the Middle East (see "Silk and the Silk Road," Chapter 7, page 201). After processing in city-states such as Lucca and Florence, the silk was exported throughout Europe to satisfy an immense market for sumptuous dress. (Dante, Petrarch, and many of the humanists decried the appetite for luxury in costume, which to them represented a decline in civic and moral virtue.) People throughout Europe (Duccio and other artists among them) prized fabrics from China, Persia, Byzantium, and the Islamic realms. In the *Maestà* panel, Duccio created the glistening and shimmering effects of textiles, adapting the motifs and design patterns of exotic materials.

On the front panel of the *Maestà* Duccio showed himself as the great master of the formal altarpiece. However, he allowed himself greater latitude for experimentation in the small accompanying panels, front and back. It is these images that reveal his powers as a narrative painter. In the numerous panels on the back, he illustrated the later life of Christ—his ministry (on the predella), his Passion (on the main panel), and his Resurrection

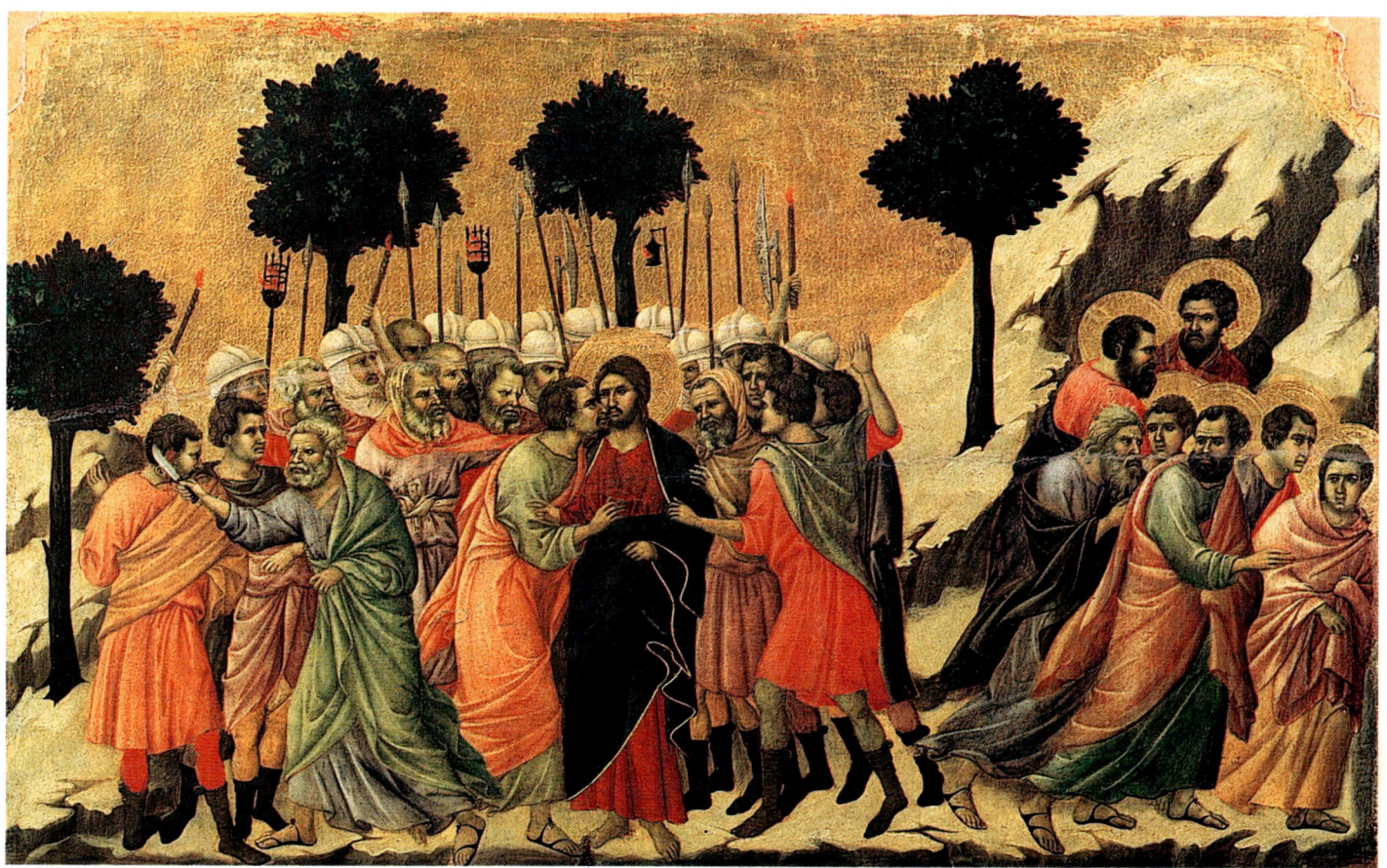

**19-11** DUCCIO DI BUONINSEGNA, *Betrayal of Jesus*, detail from the back of the *Maestà* altarpiece, from the Siena Cathedral, Siena, Italy, 1309–1311. Tempera on wood, detail approx. 1′ 10½″ × 3′ 4″. Museo dell'Opera del Duomo, Siena.

and appearances to the disciples (on the pinnacles). In the small narrative pictures, Duccio relaxed the formalism appropriate to the iconic, symbolic representation of the maestà and displayed his ability not only as a narrator but also as an experimenter with new pictorial ideas. In a synoptic sequence on one of the small panels, *Betrayal of Jesus* (FIG. **19-11**), the artist represented several episodes of the event—the betrayal of Jesus by Judas's false kiss, the disciples fleeing in terror, and Peter cutting off the ear of the high priest's servant. Although the background, with its golden sky and rock formations, remains traditional, the style of the figures before it has changed quite radically. The bodies are not the flat frontal shapes of earlier Byzantine art. Duccio imbued them with mass, modeled them with a range from light to dark, and arranged their draperies around them convincingly. Even more novel and striking is how the figures seem to react to the central event. Through posture, gesture, and even facial expression, they display a variety of emotions. Duccio carefully differentiated among the anger of Peter, the malice of Judas (echoed in the faces of the throng about Jesus), and the apprehension and timidity of the fleeing disciples. These figures are actors in a religious drama that the artist interpreted in terms of thoroughly human actions and reactions. In this and similar narrative panels, Duccio took another decisive step toward the humanization of religious subject matter. The greatness of the *Maestà* did not have to wait for modern acclaim. A Sienese chronicler noted that nothing like it had been done anywhere else in Italy (see "A Majestic Altarpiece: Duccio's *Maestà*," page 534).

**AN "INTERNATIONAL STYLE"** Duccio's successors in the Sienese school displayed even greater originality and assurance than Duccio. SIMONE MARTINI (ca. 1285–1344) was a pupil of Duccio and a close friend of Petrarch, who praised him highly for his portrait of "Laura" (the woman to whom Petrarch dedicated his sonnets). Martini worked for the French kings in Naples and Sicily and, in his last years, produced paintings for the papal court at Avignon, where he came in contact with northern painters. By adapting the insubstantial but luxuriant patterns of the French Gothic manner to Sienese art and, in turn, by acquainting northern painters with the Sienese style, Martini was instrumental in forming the so-called *International Style*. This new style swept Europe during the late 14th and early 15th centuries because it appealed to the aristocratic taste for brilliant colors, lavish costumes, intricate ornamentation, and themes involving splendid processions.

Martini's own style did not quite reach the full exuberance of the developed International Style, but his famous *Annunciation* altarpiece (FIG. **19-12**) provides a counterpoint to Giotto's style. Elegant shapes and radiant color; flowing, fluttering line; and weightless figures in a spaceless setting characterize the *Annunciation*. The complex etiquette of the European chivalric courts dictated the presentation. The angel Gabriel has just alighted, the breeze of his passage lifting his mantle, his iridescent wings still beating. The gold of his sumptuous gown heraldically represents the celestial realm whence he bears his message. The Virgin, putting down her book of devotions, shrinks demurely from

### A Majestic Altarpiece
### *Duccio's Maestà*

Agnolo di Tura del Grasso provided one of the most complete records of the completion and installation of the *Maestà* in the Siena Cathedral. Scholars consider his account reliable, as he was the keeper of the record books of Siena's chief financial magistracy. He described the pomp and ceremony that accompanied the transport of the altarpiece to the cathedral:

This *[Maestà]* was painted by master Duccio di Niccolò, painter of Siena, who was in his time the most skillful painter one could find in these lands. The panel was painted outside the Porta a Stalloreggi in the Borgo a Laterino, in the house of the Muciatti. The Sienese took the panel to the Cathedral at noontime on the ninth of June [1311], with great devotions and processions, with the bishop of Siena, Ruggero da Casole, with all of the clergy of the Cathedral, and with all the monks and nuns of Siena, and the Nove [the ruling council of Siena], with the city officials, the Podestà and the Captain, and all the citizens with coats of arms and those with more

distinguished coats of arms, with lighted lamps in hand. And thus, the women and children went through Siena with much devotion and around the Campo in procession, ringing all the bells for joy, and this entire day the shops stayed closed for devotions, and throughout Siena they gave many alms to the poor people, with many speeches and prayers to God and to his mother, Madonna ever Virgin Mary, who helps, preserves and increases in peace the good state of the city of Siena and its territory, as advocate and protectress of that city, and who defends the city from all danger and all evil. And so, this panel was placed in the Cathedral on the high altar. The panel is painted on the back with the Old Testament [sic], with the Passion of Jesus Christ, and on the front is the Virgin Mary with her son in her arms and many saints at the side. Everything is ornamented with fine gold; it cost three thousand gold florins.[1]

[1] Quoted in James H. Stubblebine, *Duccio di Buoninsegna and His School* (Princeton, N.J.: Princeton University Press, 1979), 1: 33–34.

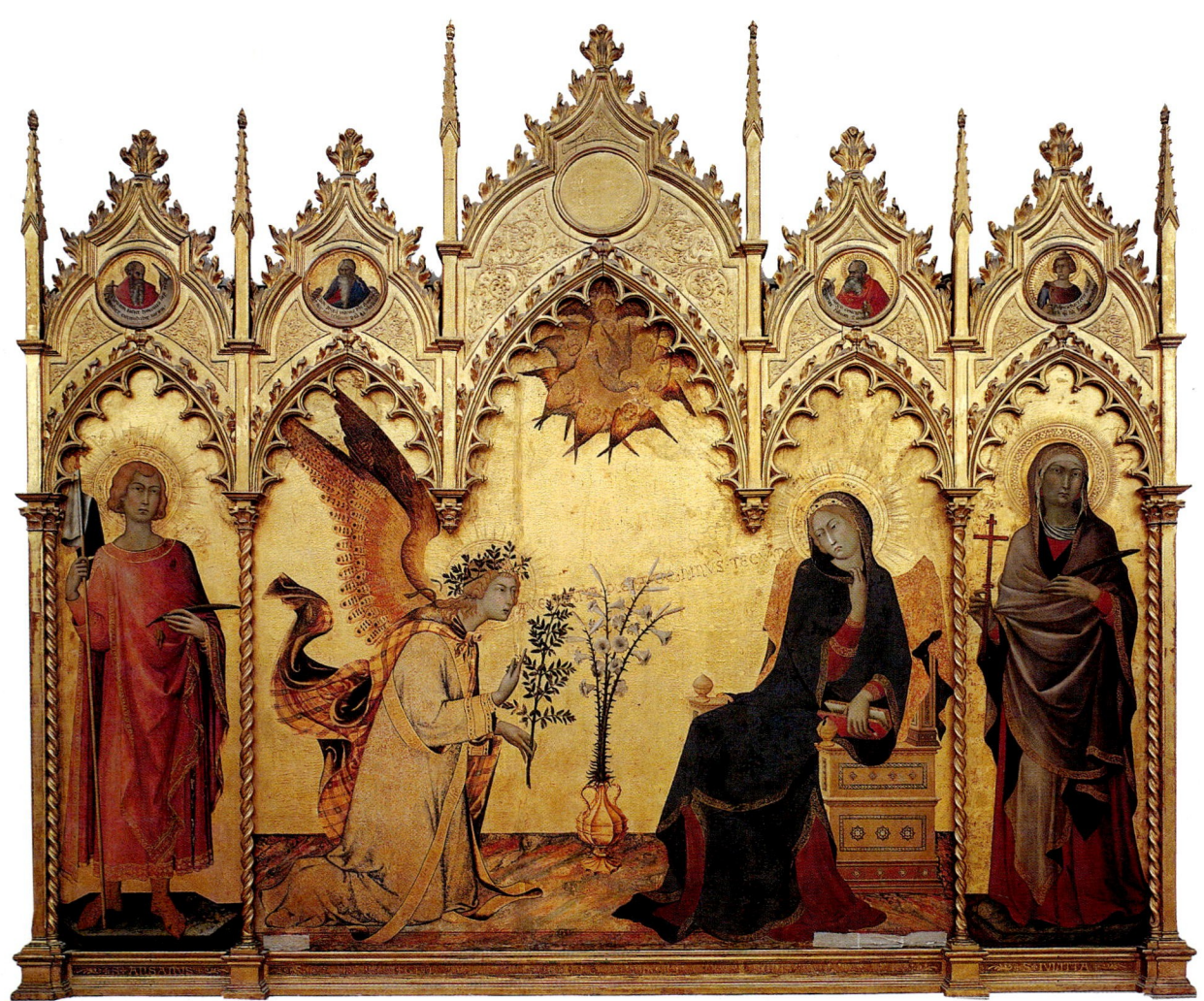

**19-12** Simone Martini and Lippo Memmi(?), *Annunciation,* 1333 (frame reconstructed in the 19th century). Tempera and gold leaf on wood, approx. 10′ 1″ × 8′ 8¾″ *(center panel).* Galleria degli Uffizi, Florence.

## Mastering a Craft
### Artistic Training in the Renaissance

In 14th- through 16th-century Italy, training to become a professional artist (earning membership in the appropriate guild) was a laborious and lengthy process. Because Italians perceived art as a trade, they expected artists to be trained as they would in any other profession. Accordingly, aspiring artists started their training at an early age, anywhere from 7 to 15 years old. Their fathers would negotiate arrangements with specific master artists, whereby each youth lived with a master for a specified number of years, usually five or six. During that time, they served as apprentices to the masters in the workshop, learning the trade. This living arrangement served as a major obstacle for aspiring female artists, as it was considered inappropriate for young girls to live in a master's household.

The skills apprentices learned varied with the type of studio they joined. Those apprenticed to painters learned to grind pigments, draw, prepare wood panels for painting, gild, and lay plaster for fresco. Sculptors in training learned to manipulate different materials (for example, wood, stone, terracotta, wax, bronze, or stucco), although many sculpture workshops specialized in only one or two of these materials. For stone carving, apprentices learned their craft by blocking out the master's designed sculpture.

The guilds supervised this rigorous training. They wanted not only to ensure their professional reputations by admitting only the most talented members but also to control the number of artists (to limit undue competition). Toward this end they frequently tried to regulate the number of apprentices working under a single master. Surely the quality of the apprentices a master trained reflected the master's competence. When encouraging a prospective apprentice to join his studio, the Paduan painter Francesco Squarcione boasted he could teach "the true art of perspective and everything necessary to the art of painting. . . . I made a man of Andrea Mantegna [see FIGS. 21-45, 21-46, 21-47, and 21-48] who stayed with me and I will also do the same to you."[1]

As their skills developed, apprentices took on increasingly difficult tasks. After completing their apprenticeships, artists entered the appropriate guilds. For example, painters, who ground pigments, joined the guild of apothecaries; sculptors were members of the guild of stoneworkers; and goldsmiths entered the silk guild, because gold often was stretched into threads wound around silk for weaving. Such memberships served as certification of the artists' competence. Once "certified," artists often affiliated themselves with established workshops, as assistants to master artists. This was largely for practical reasons. New artists could not expect to receive many commissions, and the cost of establishing their own workshops was high. In any case, this arrangement was not permanent, and workshops were not necessarily static enterprises. Although well-established and respected studios existed, workshops could be organized around individual masters (with no set studio locations) or organized for a specific project, especially an extensive decoration program.

Generally, assistants were charged with gilding frames and backgrounds, completing decorative work, and, occasionally, rendering architectural settings. Artists regarded figures, especially those central to the represented subject, as the most important and difficult parts of a painting, and the master retained responsibility for such figures. Assistants were allowed to paint some of the less important or marginal figures, but only under the master's close supervision.

Eventually, of course, artists hoped to attract patrons and establish themselves as masters. Artists, who were largely anonymous during the medieval period, began to enjoy greater emancipation during the 15th and 16th centuries, when they rose in rank from artisan to artist-scientist. The value of their individual skills—and their reputations—became increasingly important to their patrons and clients. This apprentice system—the passing of knowledge from one generation to the next—accounts for the sense of continuity people experience when reviewing Italian Renaissance art.

[1] Quoted in Giuseppe Fiocco, *Mantegna: La cappella Ovetari nella chiesa degli Eremitani* (Milan: A. Pizzi, 1974), 7.

---

Gabriel's reverent genuflection, an appropriate gesture in the presence of royalty. She draws about her the deep blue, golden-hemmed mantle, the heraldic colors she wears as Queen of Heaven. Despite the Virgin's modesty and diffidence and the tremendous import of the angel's message, the scene subordinates drama to court ritual, and structural experimentation to surface splendor. The intricate tracery of the richly tooled Late Gothic frame enhances the painted magnificence. Of French inspiration, it replaced the more sober, clean-cut shapes traditional in Italy, and its appearance here is eloquent testimony to the two-way flow of transalpine influences that fashioned the International Style.

Simone Martini and his student and assistant, LIPPO MEMMI, signed the altarpiece and dated it (1333). Lippo's contribution to the *Annunciation* is still a matter of debate, but historians now generally agree he painted the two lateral saints, Saint Ansanus and Saint Margaret(?). Lippo drew these figures, which are reminiscent of the jamb statues of Gothic church portals, with greater solidity and without the linear elegance of Martini's central pair. Given the nature of medieval and Renaissance workshop practices, it is often next to impossible to distinguish the master's hand from those of assistants, especially if the master corrected or redid part of the latter's work (see "Mastering a Craft: Artistic Training in the Renaissance," above). This uncertainty is exacerbated by the fact that *Annunciation*'s current architectural enframements are dated much later than the central panel.

**CONCERN FOR SPATIAL ILLUSION** The Lorenzetti brothers, also Duccio's students, shared in the general experiments in pictorial realism that characterized the 14th century, especially in their search for convincing spatial illusions. Going well beyond his master, PIETRO LORENZETTI (active 1320–1348) achieved remarkable success in a large panel, *The Birth of the Virgin*

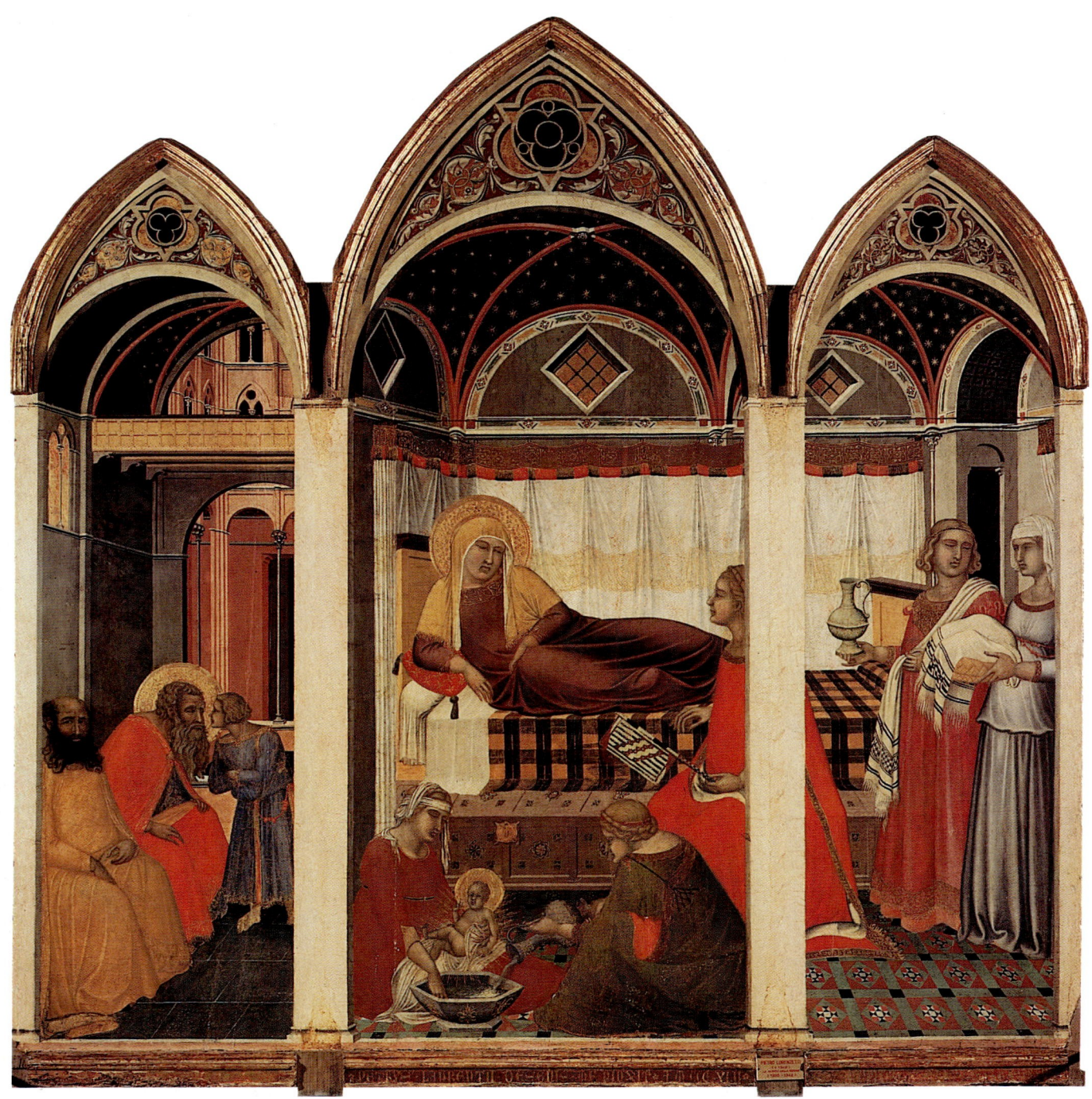

**19-13** Pietro Lorenzetti, *The Birth of the Virgin,* from Altar of Saint Savinus, Siena Cathedral, Siena, Italy, 1342. Tempera on wood, approx. 6′ 1″ × 5′ 11″. Museo dell'Opera del Duomo, Siena.

(FIG. **19-13**). Like Duccio's *Maestà* and Simone Martini's *Annunciation,* the panel was painted for the Siena Cathedral as part of a program honoring the Virgin Mary, heavenly Queen of the Republic. Pietro Lorenzetti painted the wooden architectural members that divide the panel as though they extend back into the painted space, as if viewers were looking through the wooden frame (apparently added later) into a boxlike stage, where the event takes place. That one of the vertical members cuts across one of the figures, blocking part of it from view, strengthens the illusion. In subsequent centuries, artists exploited this use of architectural elements to enhance pictorial illusion. A long, successful history of such visual illusions produced by unifying both real and simulated architecture with painted figures evolved from these experiments.

Pietro Lorenzetti did not make just a structural advance here; his very subject represents a marked step in the advance of worldly realism. Saint Anne, reclining wearily as the midwives wash the child and the women bring gifts, is the center of an episode that occurs in an upper-class Italian house of the period. A number of carefully observed domestic details and the scene at the left, where Joachim eagerly awaits the news of the delivery, place the event in an actual household, as if viewers had moved the panels of the walls back and peered inside. Pietro Lorenzetti joined structural innovation in illusionistic space with the new curiosity that led to careful inspection and recording of what lay directly before the artist's eye in the everyday world.

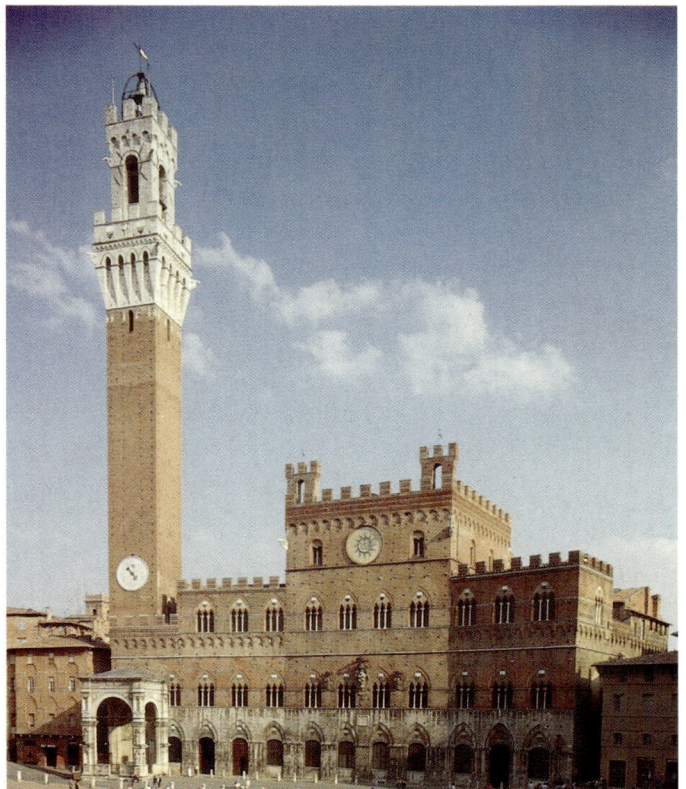

19-14 Palazzo Pubblico, Siena, Italy, 1288–1309.

most buildings of its type and period, it abuts a lofty tower, which (along with Giotto's campanile in Florence; see FIG. 19-17, left of image) is one of the finest in Italy. This tall structure served as lookout over the city and the countryside around it and as a bell tower for ringing signals of all sorts to the populace. The city, a self-contained political unit, had to defend itself against neighboring cities and often against kings and emperors. In addition, it had to be secure against internal upheavals common in the history of the Italian city-republics. Class struggle, feuds between rich and powerful families, even uprisings of the whole populace against the city governors were constant threats. The heavy walls and battlements of the Italian town hall eloquently express how frequently the city governors needed to defend themselves against their own citizens. The high tower, out of reach of most missiles, includes machicolated galleries (galleries with holes in their floors to allow stones or hot liquids to be dumped on enemies below). These were built out on corbels around the top of the structures to provide openings for a vertical (downward) defense of the tower's base.

**DEPICTING GOVERNMENTAL EFFECTS** Pietro Lorenzetti's brother AMBROGIO LORENZETTI (active 1319–1348) both elaborated the advances in illusionistic representation in spectacular fashion and gave visual form to Sienese civic concerns in a vast fresco program in the Palazzo Pubblico. Ambrogio Lorenzetti produced three frescoes: *Allegory of Good Government, Bad Government and the Effects of Bad Government in the City,* and *Effects of Good Government in the City and in the Country.* The turbulent politics of the Italian cities—the violent party struggles, the overthrow and reinstatement of governments—certainly would have called for solemn reminders of fair and just administration. And the city hall was just the place for paintings such as Ambrogio Lorenzetti's. Indeed, the leaders of the Sienese government who commissioned this fresco series had undertaken the "ordering and reformation of the whole city and *contado* ('countryside') of Siena."

In *Effects of Good Government in the City and in the Country,* the artist depicted the urban and rural effects of good government. *Peaceful City* (FIG. 19-15) is a panoramic view of Siena, with its clustering palaces, markets, towers, churches, streets, and walls.

**A BASTION OF POWER** The Sienese were concerned about matters of both church and state. The city-state was a proud commercial and political rival of Florence. The secular center of the community, the town hall, was almost as great an object of civic pride as the cathedral. A building such as the Palazzo Pubblico of Siena (FIG. **19-14**) must have earned the admiration of Siena's citizens as well as of visiting strangers, inspiring in them respect for the city's power and success. More symmetrical in its design than

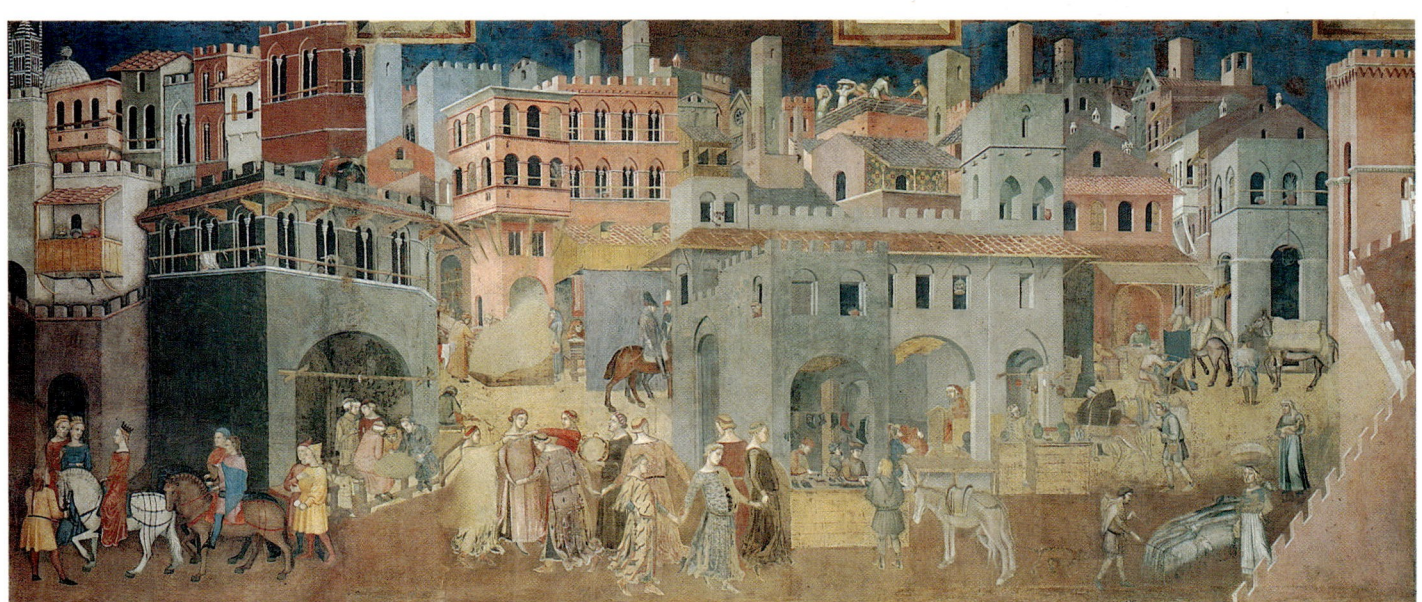

19-15 AMBROGIO LORENZETTI, *Peaceful City,* detail from *Effects of Good Government in the City and in the Country,* Sala della Pace, Palazzo Pubblico, Siena, Italy, 1338–1339. Fresco.

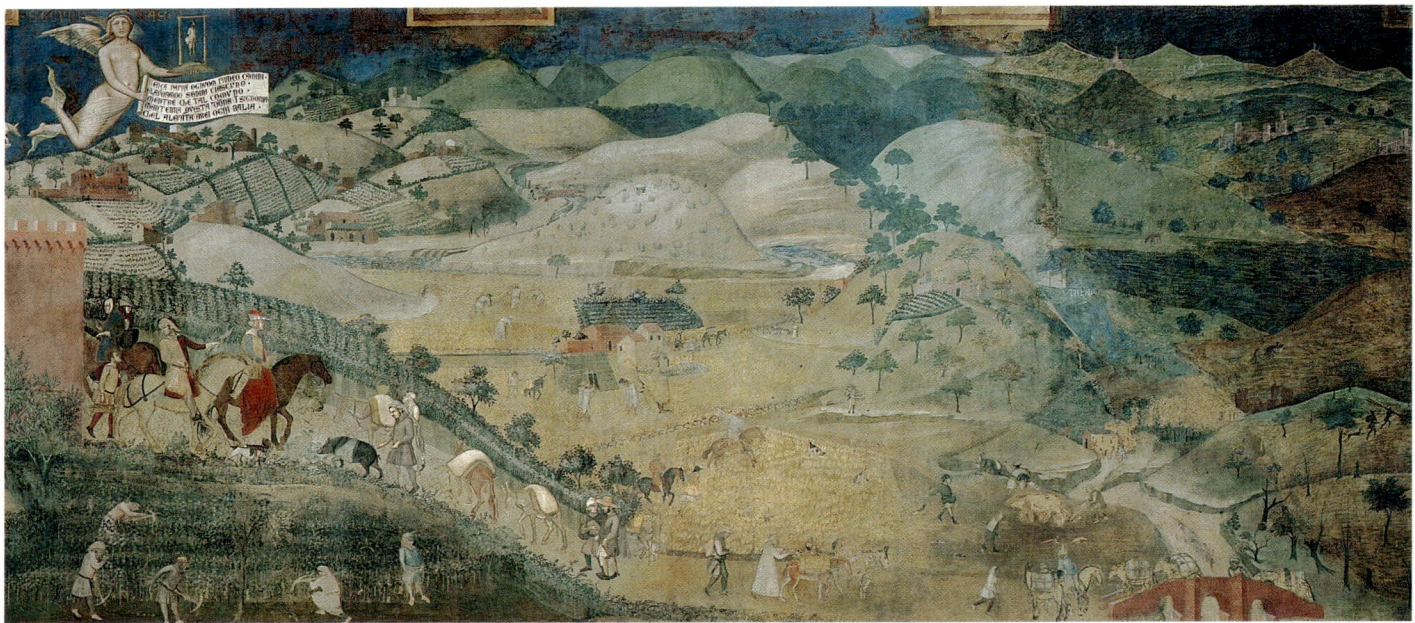

**19-16** AMBROGIO LORENZETTI, *Peaceful Country,* detail from *Effects of Good Government in the City and in the Country,* Sala della Pace, Palazzo Pubblico, Siena, Italy, 1338–1339. Fresco.

The city's traffic moves peacefully, guild members ply their trades and crafts, and a cluster of radiant maidens, hand in hand, performs a graceful circling dance. Such dancers were part of festive springtime rituals; here, their presence also serves as a metaphor for a peaceful commonwealth. The artist fondly observed the life of his city, and its architecture gave him an opportunity to apply Sienese artists' rapidly growing knowledge of perspective. Passing through the city gate to the countryside beyond its walls, Ambrogio Lorenzetti's *Peaceful Country* (FIG. **19-16**) presents a bird's-eye view of the undulating Tuscan countryside—its villas, castles, plowed farmlands, and peasants going about their seasonal occupations. An allegorical figure of Security hovers above the landscape, unfurling a scroll that promises safety to all who live under the rule of the law. In this sweeping view of an actual countryside, *Peaceful Country* represents one of the first appearances of landscape in Western art since antiquity. Whereas earlier ancient depictions were fairly generic, Lorenzetti particularized the landscape—as well as the city view—by careful observation and endowed the painting with the character of a portrait of a specific place and environment. By combining some of Giotto's analytical powers with Duccio's narrative talent, Ambrogio Lorenzetti achieved more spectacular results than those of either of his two great predecessors.

The Black Death may have ended the careers of both Lorenzettis. They disappear from historical records in 1348, the year that brought so much horror to defenseless Europe.

## The Republic of Florence

THE "MOST BEAUTIFUL" TUSCAN CHURCH Like Siena, the Republic of Florence was a dominant city-state during the 14th century, as evidenced by such statements as one by the early historian Giovanni Villani (ca. 1270–1348). Villani wrote that Florence was "the daughter and the creature of Rome," suggesting a preeminence inherited from the Roman Empire. Florentines prided themselves on what they perceived as economic and cultural superiority. The city-state assured its centrality to banking operations by making its gold florin the standard coin of exchange everywhere, and its economic prosperity was further enhanced by its control of the textile industry. Florentines translated their pride in their predominance into such landmark buildings as Florence Cathedral (FIG. **19-17**). Recognized as the center for the most important religious observances in the city, the cathedral was begun in 1296 by ARNOLFO DI CAMBIO. Intended as the "most beautiful and honorable church in Tuscany," this structure reveals the competitiveness Florentines felt with such cities as Siena and Pisa. Cathedral authorities planned for the church to hold the city's entire population, and although it holds only about 30,000 (Florence's population at the time was slightly less than 100,000), it seemed so large that even the noted architect Leon Battista Alberti commented that it seemed to cover "all of Tuscany with its shade." The architects ornamented the building's surfaces, in the old Tuscan fashion, with marble-encrusted geometric designs. This matched it to the 11th-century Romanesque baptistery of San Giovanni nearby (see FIG. 17-18). The vast gulf that separates this Italian church from its northern European counterparts is strikingly evident when the former is compared with a full-blown German representative of the High Gothic style, such as Cologne Cathedral (see FIG. 18-44).

Cologne Cathedral's emphatic stress on the vertical produces an awe-inspiring upward rush of almost unmatched vigor and intensity. The building has the character of an organic growth shooting heavenward, its toothed upper portions engaging the sky. The pierced, translucent stone tracery of the spires merges with the atmosphere.

Florence Cathedral, in contrast, clings to the ground and has no aspirations to flight. All emphasis is on the horizontal elements of the design, and the building rests firmly and massively on the ground. Simple geometric volumes are defined clearly and show no tendency to merge either into each other or into the sky. The dome, though it may seem to be rising because of its ogival section, has a crisp, closed silhouette that sets it off emphatically against the sky behind it. But because this dome is the monument with which

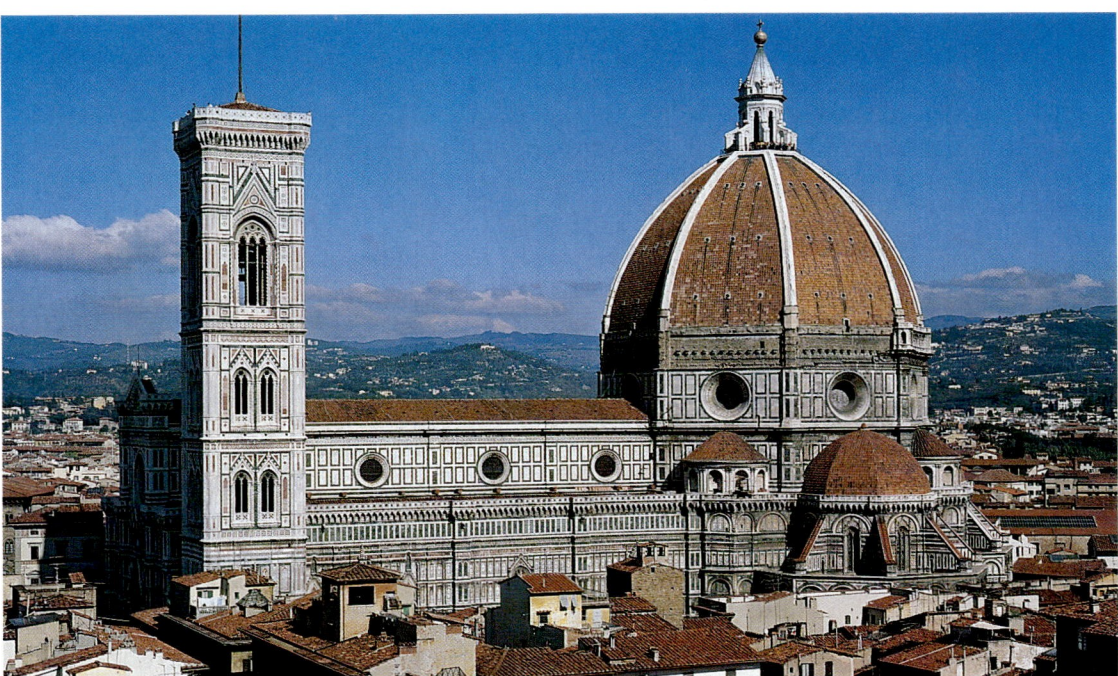

19-17 ARNOLFO DI CAMBIO and others, Florence Cathedral (view from the south), Florence, Italy, begun 1296.

architectural historians usually introduce the Renaissance (it was built by Filippo Brunelleschi between 1420 and 1436), the following comparison of the campanile with the Cologne towers may be somewhat more appropriate in this discussion of 14th-century Italian art and architecture.

**A TOWER OF BUILDING BLOCKS** Designed by the painter Giotto di Bondone in 1334 (and completed with some minor modifications after his death), the Florence campanile (FIG. 19-17) stands apart from the cathedral, in keeping with Italian tradition. In fact, it could stand anywhere else in Florence without looking out of place; it is essentially self-sufficient. The same hardly can be said of the Cologne towers (see FIG. 18-44). They are essential elements of the building behind them, and it would be unthinkable to detach one of them and place it somewhere else. No individual element in the Cologne grouping seems capable of an independent existence. One form merges into the next in a series of rising movements that pull the eye upward and never permit it to rest until it reaches the sky. The beauty of this structure is formless rather than formal—a beauty that speaks to the heart rather than to the intellect.

The Italian tower is entirely different. Neatly subdivided into cubic sections, Giotto's tower is the sum of its clearly distinguished parts. Not only could this tower be removed from the building without adverse effects, but also each of the component parts—cleanly separated from each other by continuous moldings—seems capable of existing independently as an object of considerable aesthetic appeal. This compartmentalization is reminiscent of the Romanesque style, but it also forecasts the ideals of Renaissance architecture. Artists hoped to express structure in the clear, logical relationships of the component parts and to produce self-sufficient works that could exist in complete independence. Compared to Cologne's north towers, Giotto's campanile has a cool and rational quality that appeals more to the intellect than to the emotions.

In Florence Cathedral's plan, the nave appears almost to have been added to the crossing complex as an afterthought. In fact, the nave was built first, mostly according to Arnolfo's original plans (except for the vaulting), and the crossing was redesigned midway through the 14th century to increase the cathedral's interior space.

In its present form, the area beneath the dome is the design's focal point, and the nave leads to it. To visitors from the north, the nave may seem as strange as the plan; neither has a northern European counterpart. The Florence nave bays (FIG. 19-18) are twice as deep as those of Amiens (see FIG. 18-17), and the wide arcades permit

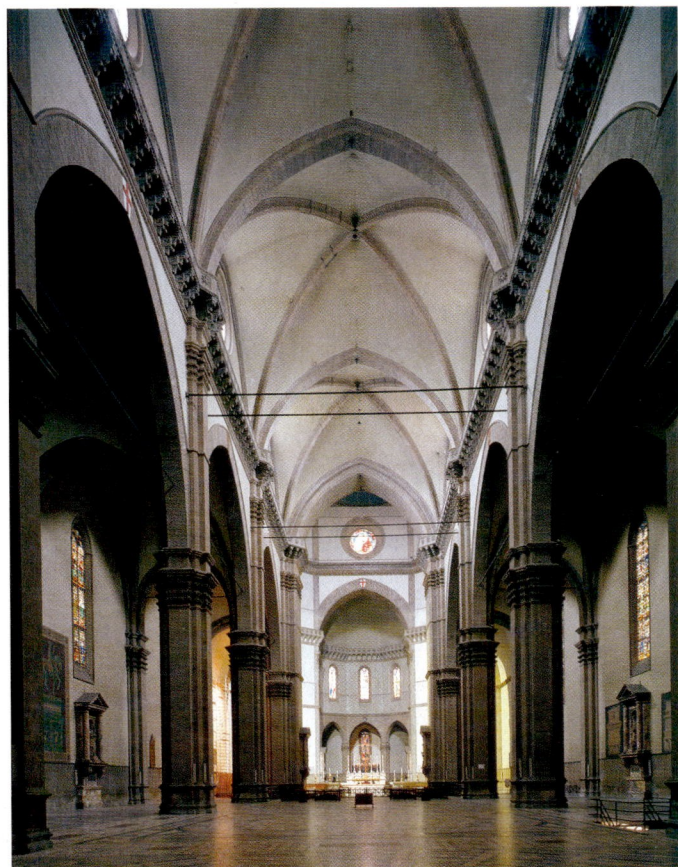

19-18 Nave of Florence Cathedral (view facing east), Florence, Italy, begun 1296.

the shallow aisles to become part of the central nave. The result is an interior of unmatched spaciousness. The accent here, as it is on the exterior, is on the horizontal elements. The substantial capitals of the piers prevent them from soaring into the vaults and emphasize their function as supports.

The facade of Florence Cathedral was not completed until the 19th century and then in a form much altered from its original design. In fact, until the 17th century, Italian builders exhibited little concern for the facades of their churches, and dozens remain unfinished to this day. One reason for this may be that the facades were not conceived as integral parts of the structures but as screens that could be added to the church exterior at any time.

**ACCOMMODATING THE FAITHFUL** The increased importance of the mendicant orders during the 14th century led to the construction of large churches by the Franciscans (Santa Croce; see FIG. Intro-3) and the Dominicans (see "Mendicant Orders and Confraternities," page 524) in Florence. The Florentine government and contributions from private citizens subsidized the commissioning of the Dominicans' Santa Maria Novella (FIG. 19-19) around 1246. The large congregations these orders attracted necessitated the expansive scale of this church. Small *oculi* (round openings) and marble striping along the ogival arches punctuate the nave. Originally, a screen *(tramezzo)* placed across the nave separated the friars from the lay audience; the Mass was performed on separate altars on each side of the screen. Church officials removed this screen in the mid-16th century to encourage greater lay participation in the Mass. A powerful Florentine family, the Rucellai, commissioned the facade for Santa Maria Novella from architect Leon Battista Alberti in the mid-15th century.

**A MEMORIAL TO THE BLACK DEATH** The tabernacle of the Virgin Mary in Florence's Or San Michele (FIG. 19-20) is the work of two "Giotteschi" (followers of Giotto), Andrea di Cione, known as ORCAGNA (active 1343–1368), and BERNARDO DADDI (ca. 1290–1348). Orcagna produced the work's architecture and sculpture, and Bernardo Daddi painted the panel of the Madonna, which the tabernacle enshrines. Or San Michele was originally a grain market, a *loggia* (open-sided arcade) into the street; it was transformed into a church, confraternity building, and center for the city's guilds. Around mid-century, upper stories were added to house a granary. Or San Michele also functioned as a guild church, and each guild was assigned a niche on the building's exterior for a commissioned statue of its patron saint.

Construction of Orcagna's tabernacle was prompted by the plague, which decimated Europe in the late 1340s. Italy was particularly hard hit by this Black Death. With death tolls climbing as

**19-19** Nave of Santa Maria Novella, Florence, Italy, ca. 1246–1470.

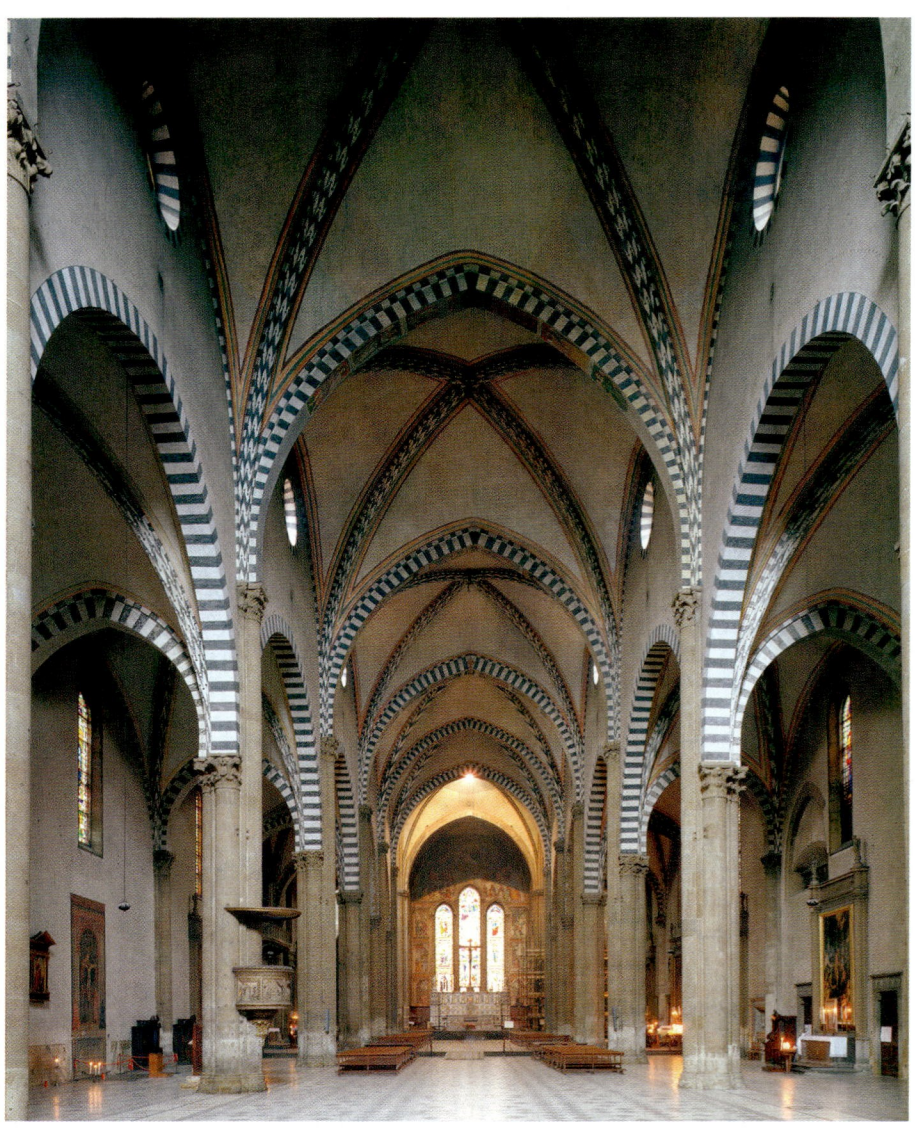

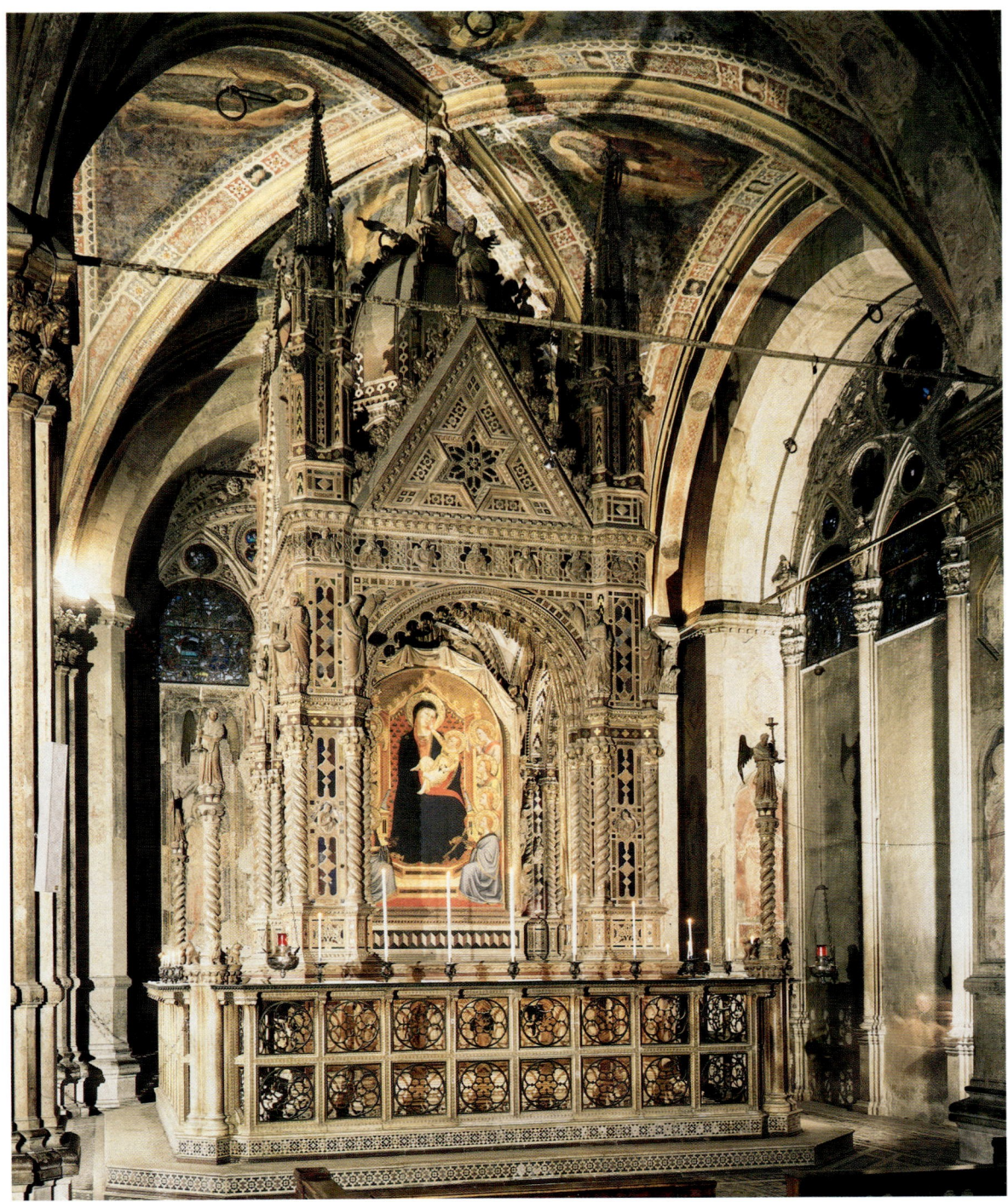

**19-20** Orcagna, tabernacle, Or San Michele, Florence, Italy, begun 1349. Mosaic, gold, marble, lapis lazuli. Bernardo Daddi, *Madonna and Child with Saints,* painted panel insert, 1346–1347.

high as 50 or 60 percent of the population in large cities, the plague wreaked havoc on all levels of society. This disaster prompted the commission of religious and devotional artworks. Such donations funded Orcagna's tabernacle, which donors no doubt perceived as a kind of memorial to both the dead and the survivors. Individuals made bequests to a supposed miraculous portrait of the Virgin, which later burned and was replaced with the image by Bernardo Daddi. The entire tabernacle, started in 1349, took 10 years to complete, costing the vast sum of 87,000 gold florins.

Orcagna, an artistic virtuoso, was an architect, sculptor, and painter; he was familiar with the styles and practice of all the arts in post-Giotto Florence. The architectural enframement of the tabernacle recalls the polygonal piers and the slender spiral colonnettes of the Florence Cathedral and campanile (FIG. 19-17), as well as the triangular pediment, fenestration, and pinnacles of a typical Italian Gothic facade (see FIG. 18-55). The planar surfaces sparkle with gold, lapis lazuli, mosaic, and finely cut marble, all inlaid in geometric patterns called *Cosmato work* (from *Cosmati,* the name given to craftsmen who worked in marble and mosaic in the 12th to 14th centuries, many belonging to a family of that name). The effect is that of a gem-encrusted, scintillating shrine or reliquary, more the work of a jeweler than an architect.

The lavish ornamentation and costly materials recall the medieval association of precious material with holy things and

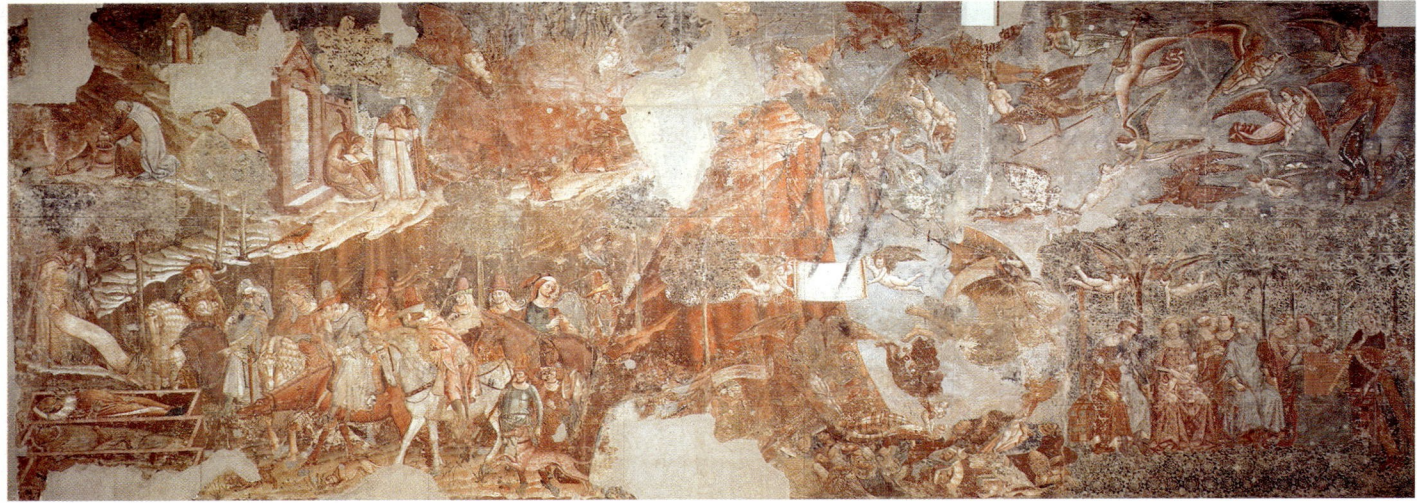

**19-21** Francesco Traini(?) or Buonamico Buffalmacco(?), *Triumph of Death*, 1330s. Fresco, 18′ 6″ × 49′ 2″. Camposanto, Pisa.

themes, in this case with the original miracle-working image of the Virgin, which the new *Madonna and Child* replaced. Bernardo Daddi interpreted this most popular of Gothic subjects in a light, delicate manner appropriate to the humanizing of religion and to the emotional requirements of private devotion. Flanked by angels, two of whom swing censers filled with incense, the enthroned Virgin sits within a round arch with sculptured curtains. The Christ Child playfully touches his mother's face. The composition is conventional but softened by sentiment. The architectural enframement provides an illusionistic stage for the image, composing an ensemble of architecture, painting, and sculpture to serve devotion to the Virgin Mary. This tabernacle attests to the versatility of Florentine artists after Giotto as they followed the various paths suggested by his original inspiration. The ideas that gained momentum in the 14th century—humanism, direct observation, greater concern with the solidity of forms, and the interest in illusion—became prominent in the following centuries.

## Pisa

Italy's port cities—Genoa, Pisa, and Venice—controlled the ever busier and more extended avenues of maritime commerce that connected the West with the lands of Islam, with Byzantium and Russia, and overland with China. As a port city, Pisa established itself as a major shipping power and thus as a dominant Italian city-state. Yet Pisa was not immune from the disruption that the Black Death wreaked across all of Italy and Europe in the late 1340s. Concern with death was a significant theme in art even before the onset of the plague and became more prominent in the years after mid-century.

**DEALING WITH DEATH** *Triumph of Death* (FIG. **19-21**) is a tour de force of death imagery. The creator of this large-scale (over 18 × 49 feet) fresco remains disputed; some attribute the work to FRANCESCO TRAINI (active c. 1321–1363), while others argue for BUONAMICO BUFFALMACCO (active 1320–1336). Painted on the wall of the Camposanto ("holy field"), the enclosed burial ground adjacent to the Pisa Cathedral, the fresco captures the horrors of death and forces viewers to confront their mortality.

In the left foreground, young aristocrats, mounted in a stylish cavalcade, encounter three coffin-encased corpses in differing stages of decomposition. As the horror of the confrontation with death strikes them, the ladies turn away with delicate and ladylike disgust, while a gentleman holds his nose (the animals, horses and dogs, sniff excitedly). At the far left, the hermit Saint Macarius unrolls a scroll whose inscription speaks of the folly of pleasure and the inevitability of death. In contrast with this mournful scene, hermits who have come to terms with their mortality exist peacefully in the background of the fresco. On the far right, ladies and gentlemen ignore dreadful realities, occupying themselves in an orange grove with music and amusements while all around them angels and demons struggle for the souls of the corpses heaped in the middle foreground.

As direct and straightforward as these scenes seem, more subtle messages are also embedded in the imagery. For example, those in *Triumph of Death* who appear unprepared for death and thus unlikely to see salvation after death are depicted as wealthy and reveling in luxury. Given that the Dominicans—an order committed to a life of poverty—participated in the design for this fresco program, this imagery surely was intended to warn against greed and lust.

Although *Triumph of Death* consists of a compilation of disparate scenes, the artist rendered each scene with naturalism and emotive power. It is an irony of history that, as Western humanity drew both itself and the world into ever sharper visual focus, it perceived ever more clearly that corporeal things are perishable.

## CONCLUSION

In the early 14th century, people began to manifest a growing interest in the natural world. Accordingly, artists such as Giotto and Duccio, for example, began to abandon some of the conventions of medieval art and increasingly based their artworks on their worldly observations, resulting in a greater naturalism in art. Greater illusionism, more emphatic pictorial solidity and spatial depth, and stronger emotional demonstrations from depicted figures were among the developments. This changing worldview came to be known as the Renaissance. Instrumental in the germination of Renaissance art was the humanists' revived veneration of classical cultures. The subsequent maturation of Renaissance art and thought will be chronicled in Chapters 20, 21, 22, and 23.

SAINT DOMINIC, CA. 1170–1221

SAINT FRANCIS OF ASSISI, CA. 1181–1226

**1200**

FRANCISCAN ORDER FOUNDED, 1209

DOMINICAN ORDER FOUNDED, 1215

FREDERICK II (HOLY ROMAN EMPEROR)

**1225**

SAINT THOMAS AQUINAS, CA. 1225–1274 (SCHOLASTICISM)

**1**

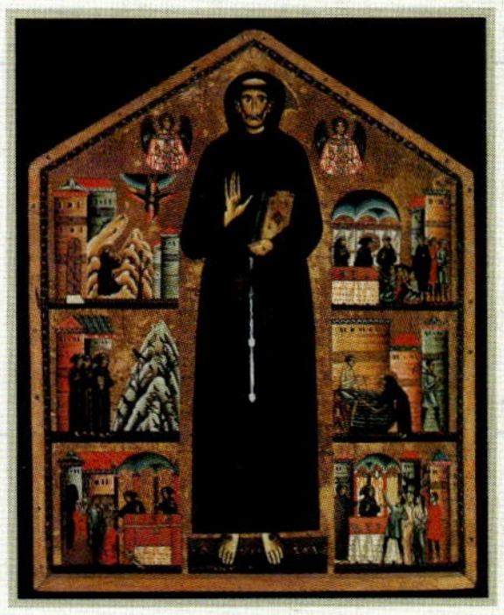

**1** Bonaventura Berlinghieri, panel from Saint Francis Altarpiece, 1235

**1250**

DANTE ALIGHIERI, 1265–1321, *The Divine Comedy*

TRIUMPH OF THE PAPACY
FALL OF HOHENSTAUFEN HOLY ROMAN EMPERORS

**2**
**3**

**1300**

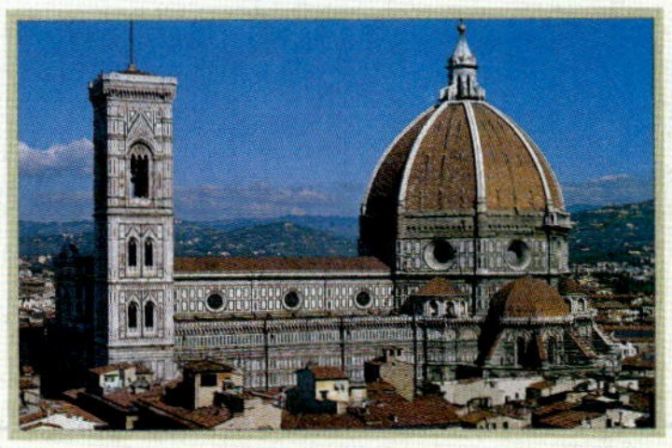

**2** Florence Cathedral, 1296–1436

FRANCESCO PETRARCH, 1304–1374, HUMANIST POET

**1305**

PAPACY MOVED TO AVIGNON, 1305

GIOVANNI BOCCACCIO, 1313–1375, HUMANIST SCHOLAR AND NOVELIST

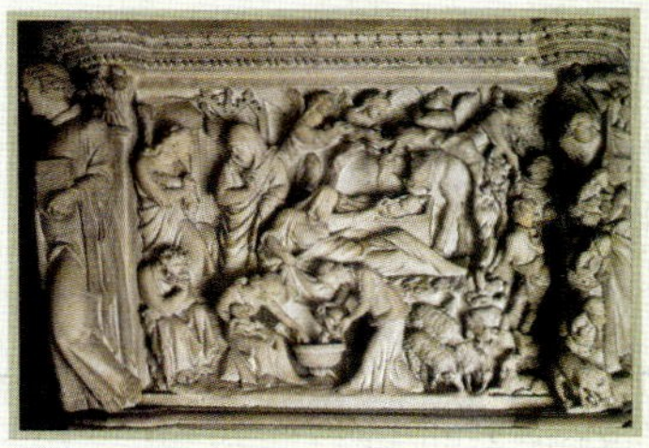

AVIGNON PAPACY

**1338**

**4**

SAINT CATHERINE OF SIENA, 1347–1380

BLACK DEATH, 1348–MID 1350S

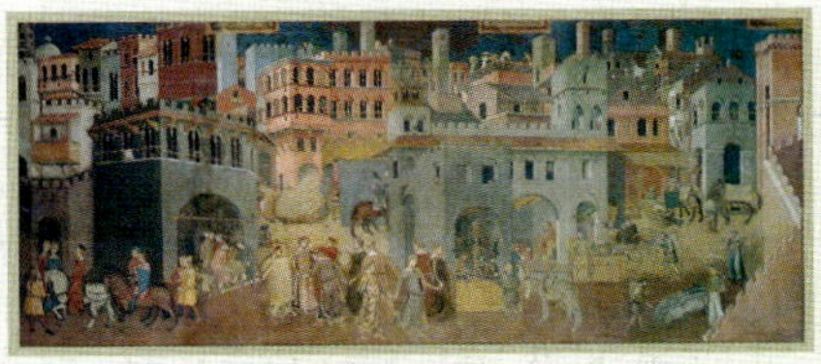

HUNDRED YEARS' WAR BETWEEN FRANCE AND ENGLAND

**3** Giovanni Pisano, *The Annunciation and the Nativity*, Pistoia, Italy, 1297–1301

**1378**

BEGINNING OF GREAT SCHISM, 1378

ELECTION OF CLEMENT VII (AVIGNON), 1378

ELECTION OF URBAN VI (ROME), 1378

GREAT SCHISM IN THE CHRISTIAN CHURCH

**4** Ambrogio Lorenzetti, *Peaceful City*, Siena, Italy, 1338–1339

**1400**

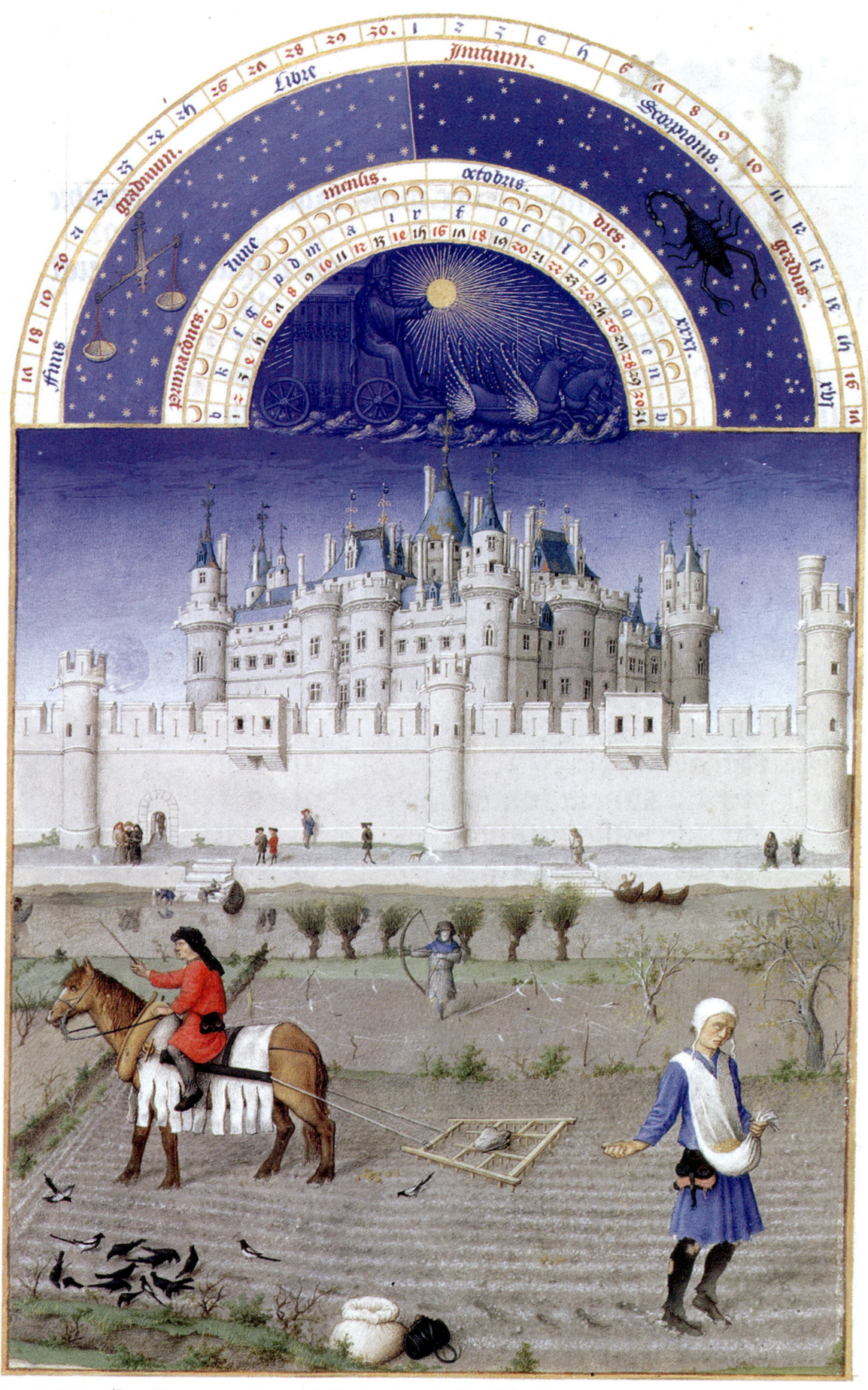

LIMBOURG BROTHERS (POL, HENNEQUIN, HERMAN), *October,* from *Les Très Riches Heures du Duc de Berry,* 1413–1416. Ink on vellum, approx. $8\frac{1}{2}'' \times 5\frac{1}{2}''$. Musée Condé, Chantilly.

were thus didactic (especially for the illiterate). They also reinforced Church doctrines for viewers and stimulated devotion. Given their function as backdrops to the Mass, it is not surprising that many altarpieces depict scenes directly related to Christ's sacrifice (for example, FIG. 20-7). These public altarpieces most often took the form of *polyptychs* (hinged multipaneled paintings) or carved relief panels. The hinges allowed users to close the polyptych's side wings over the central panel(s). Artists decorated both the exterior and interior of the altarpieces. This multi-image format provided artists the opportunity to construct narratives through a sequence of images, somewhat like manuscript illustration. Although scholars do not have concrete information about the specific circumstances in which these altarpieces were opened or closed, evidence suggests that they remained closed on regular days and were opened on Sundays and feast days. This schedule would have allowed viewers to see both the interior and exterior—diverse imagery at various times according to the liturgical calendar. As will be discussed in Chapter 23, differing Protestant conceptions of the Eucharist led, ultimately, to a decline of the altarpiece as a dominant art form in northern Europe.

**REDEMPTION AND SALVATION** The *Ghent Altarpiece* in Saint Bavo Cathedral in Ghent (FIG. 20-5) is one of the largest and most admired Flemish altarpieces of the 15th century. Jodocus

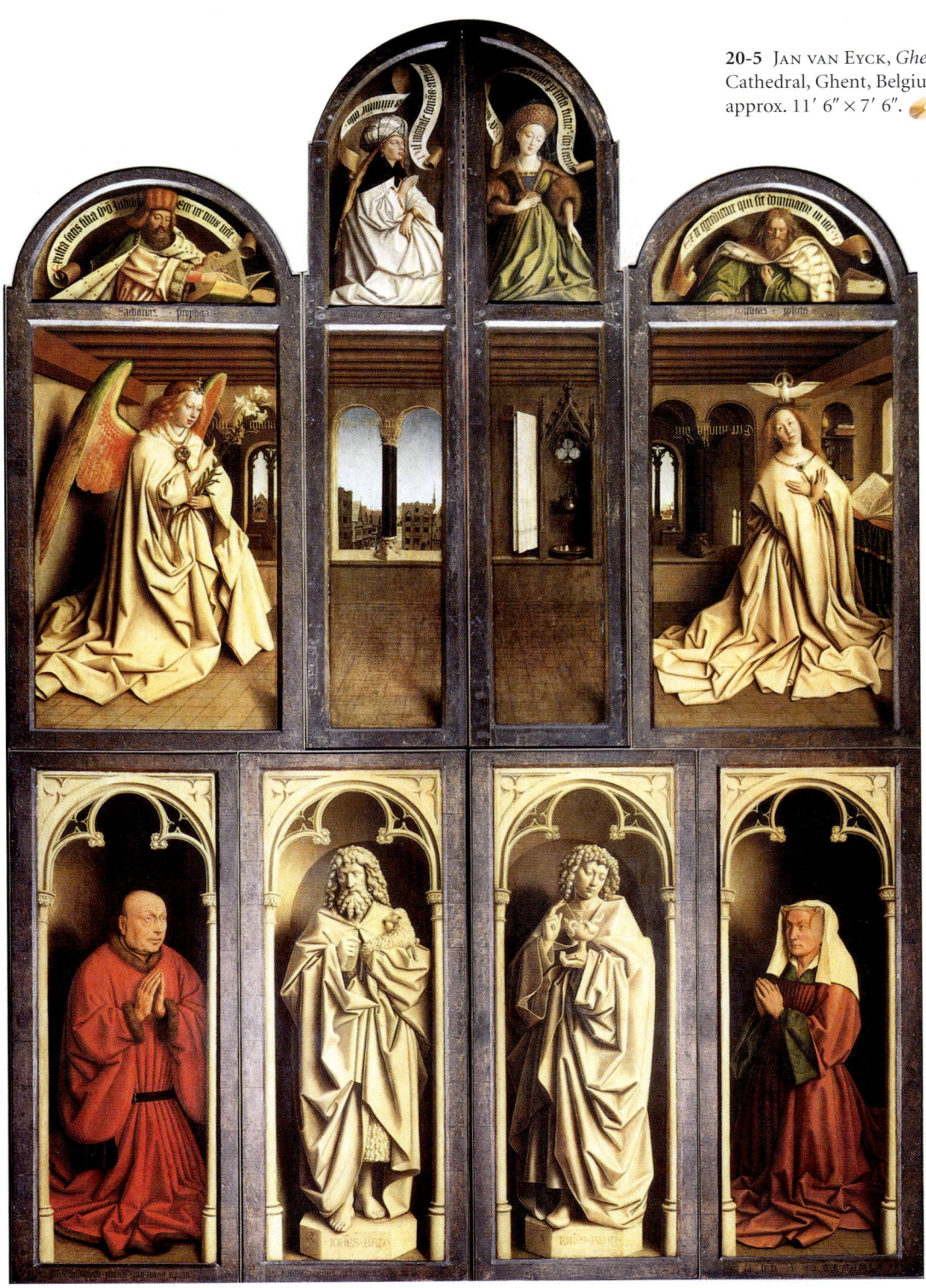

**20-5** JAN VAN EYCK, *Ghent Altarpiece* (closed), Saint Bavo Cathedral, Ghent, Belgium, completed 1432. Oil on wood, approx. 11′ 6″ × 7′ 6″.

Vyd and his wife Isabel Borluut commissioned this polyptych from JAN VAN EYCK (ca. 1390–1441). That van Eyck was, at the time, Philip the Good's court painter reveals the powerful circles in which Vyd (diplomat-retainer of Philip the Good) traveled. Certainly, Vyd's largess and the political and social connections that this work revealed to its audience contributed to Vyd's appointment as burgomeister (chief magistrate) of Ghent shortly after this work was unveiled. Completed in 1432, the *Ghent Altarpiece* functioned as the liturgical centerpiece of the endowment established in the chapel that Vyd and Borluut built. This chapel is located in the local church dedicated to Saint John the Baptist (now Saint Bavo Cathedral).

Two of the exterior panels of the *Ghent Altarpiece* depict the donors at the bottom. The husband and wife, painted in illusionistically rendered niches, kneel with their hands clasped in prayer. They gaze piously at illusionistic stone sculptures of Ghent's patron saints, Saint John the Baptist and Saint John the Evangelist (who was probably also Vyd's patron saint). An Annunciation scene appears on the upper register, with a careful representation of a Flemish town outside the painted window of the center panel. In the uppermost arched panels, van Eyck depicted images of the Old Testament prophets Zachariah and Micah, along with sibyls, classical mythological prophetesses whose writings the Christian Church interpreted as prophecies of Christ.

When opened, the altarpiece (FIG. **20-6**) reveals a sumptuous, superbly colored painting of the medieval conception of humanity's Redemption. In the upper register, God the Father—wearing the pope's triple tiara, with a worldly crown at his feet, and resplendent in a deep-scarlet mantle—presides in majesty. To God's right is the Virgin, represented as the Queen of Heaven, with a crown of 12 stars upon her head. Saint John the Baptist sits to God's left. To either side is a choir of angels, on the right an angel playing an organ. Adam and Eve appear in the far panels. The inscriptions in the arches above Mary and Saint John extol the Virgin's virtue and purity and Saint John's greatness as the forerunner of Christ. The particularly significant inscription above the Lord's head translates as "This is God, all-powerful in his divine majesty; of all the best, by the gentleness of his goodness; the most liberal giver, because of his infinite generosity." The step behind the crown at the Lord's feet bears the inscription, "On his head, life without death. On his brow, youth without age. On his right, joy without sadness. On his left, security without fear." The entire altarpiece amplifies the central theme of salvation—even though humans, symbolized by Adam and Eve, are sinful, they will be saved because God, in his infinite love, will sacrifice his own son for this purpose.

The panels of the lower register extend the symbolism of the upper. In the central panel, the community of saints comes from the four corners of the earth through an opulent, flower-spangled landscape. They proceed toward the altar of the Lamb and toward the octagonal fountain of life. The Lamb symbolizes the sacrificed Son of God, whose heart bleeds into a chalice, while into the fountain spills the "pure river of water of life, clear as crystal, proceeding out of the throne of God and of the Lamb" (Rev. 22:1). On the right, the Twelve Apostles and a group of martyrs in red robes advance; on the left appear prophets. In the right background come the virgin martyrs, and in the left background the holy confessors approach. On the lower wings, other approaching groups symbolize the four cardinal virtues: the hermits, Temperance; the pilgrims, Prudence; the knights, Fortitude; and the

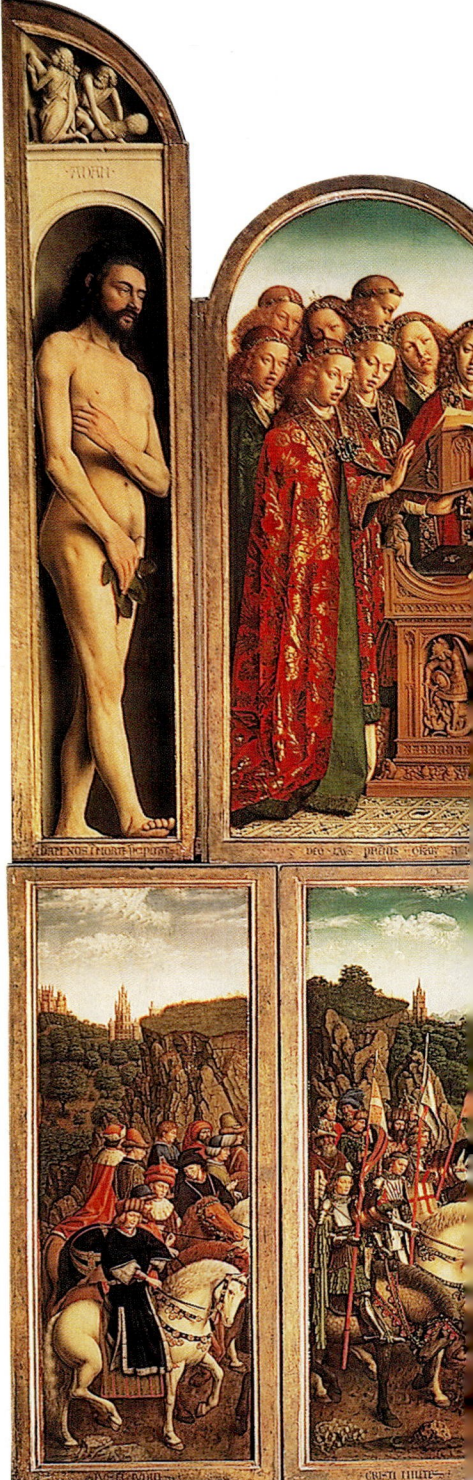

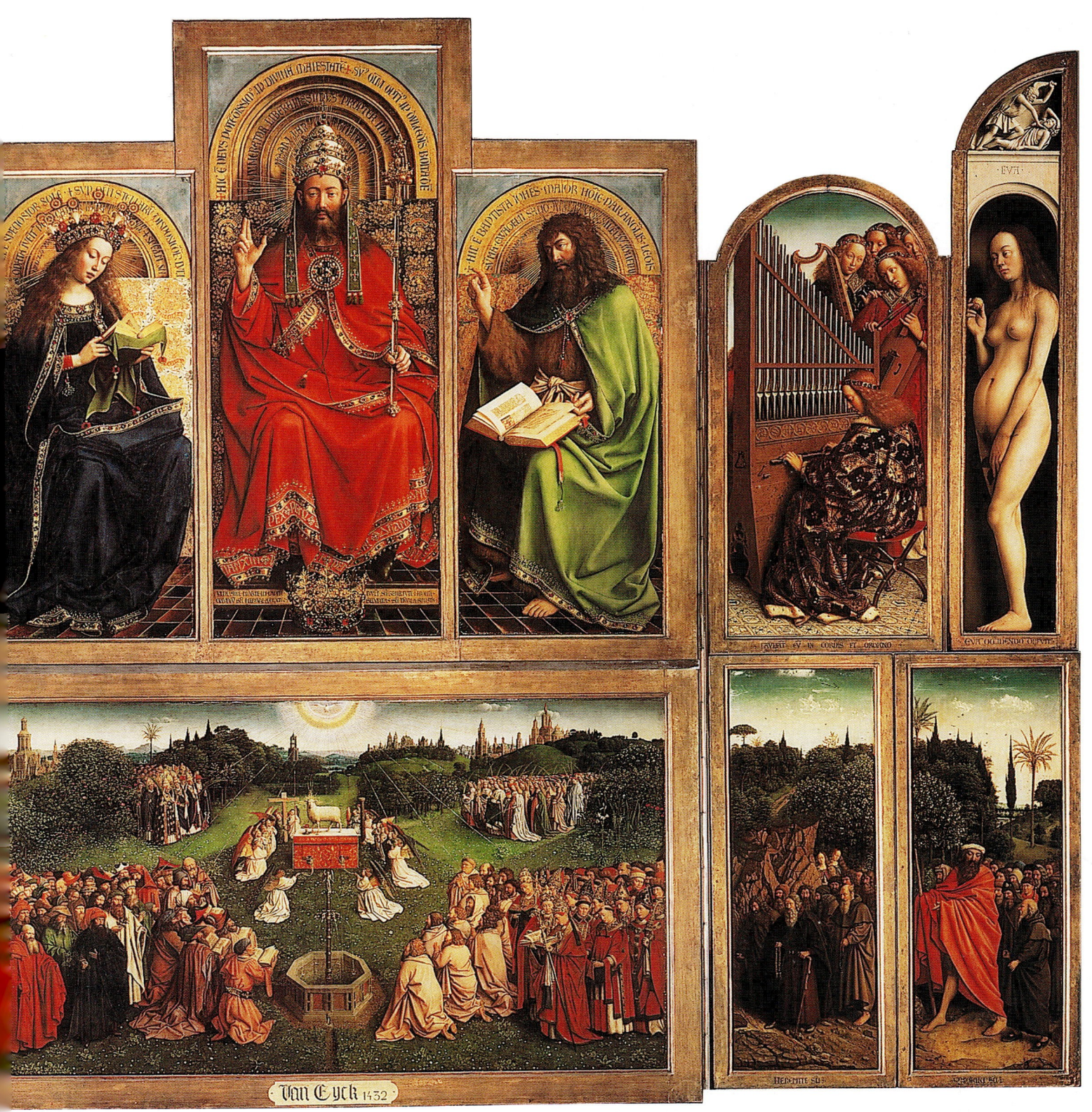

**20-6** Jan van Eyck, *Ghent Altarpiece* (open), Saint Bavo Cathedral, Ghent, Belgium, completed 1432. Oil on wood, approx. 11′ 6″ × 15′.

judges, Justice. The altarpiece celebrates the whole Christian cycle from the Fall to the Redemption, presenting the Church triumphant in heavenly Jerusalem.

Van Eyck rendered the entire altarpiece in a shimmering splendor of color that defies reproduction. No small detail escaped van Eyck, trained as a miniaturist. With pristine specificity, he revealed the beauty of the most insignificant object as if it were a work of piety as much as a work of art. He depicted the soft texture of hair, the glitter of gold in the heavy brocades, the luster of pearls, and the flashing of gems, all with loving fidelity to appearance.

**OIL PAINTS AND GLAZES** Oil paints facilitated the exactitude found in the work of van Eyck and others. Although traditional scholarship credited Jan van Eyck with the invention of oil painting, recent evidence has revealed that oil paints had been known for some time and that Melchior Broederlam was using oils in the 1390s. Flemish painters built up their pictures by superimposing translucent paint layers, called *glazes,* on a layer of underpainting, which in turn had been built up from a carefully planned drawing made on a panel prepared with a white ground. With the rediscovered medium, painters created richer colors than previously had been possible. Thus, a deep, intense tonality; the illusion of glowing light; and hard, enamel-like surfaces characterized 15th-century Flemish painting. These traits differed significantly from the high-keyed color, sharp light, and rather matte surface of tempera (see "Painters, Pigments, and Panels," page 555). The brilliant and versatile oil medium suited perfectly the formal intentions of the Flemish painters, who aimed for sharply focused, hard-edged, and sparkling clarity of detail in their representation of thousands of objects ranging in scale from large to almost invisible.

The apprentice training system throughout the continent (see "The Artist's Profession in Flanders," page 556) ensured the transmission of information about surfaces and pigments from generation to generation, thereby guaranteeing the continued viability of the painting tradition.

**THE DRAMA OF CHRIST'S DEATH** Like the art of van Eyck, that of ROGIER VAN DER WEYDEN (ca. 1400–1464) had a great impact on northern painting during the 15th century. In particular, Rogier (as scholars refer to him) created fluid and dynamic compositions stressing human action and drama. He concentrated on such themes as the Crucifixion and the Pietà, moving observers emotionally by relating the sufferings of Christ.

*Deposition* (FIG. **20-7**) was the center panel of a *triptych* (three-paneled painting) commissioned by the Archers' Guild of Louvain for the church of Notre-Dame hors-les-murs (Notre-Dame "outside the [town] walls") in Louvain. Rogier acknowledged the

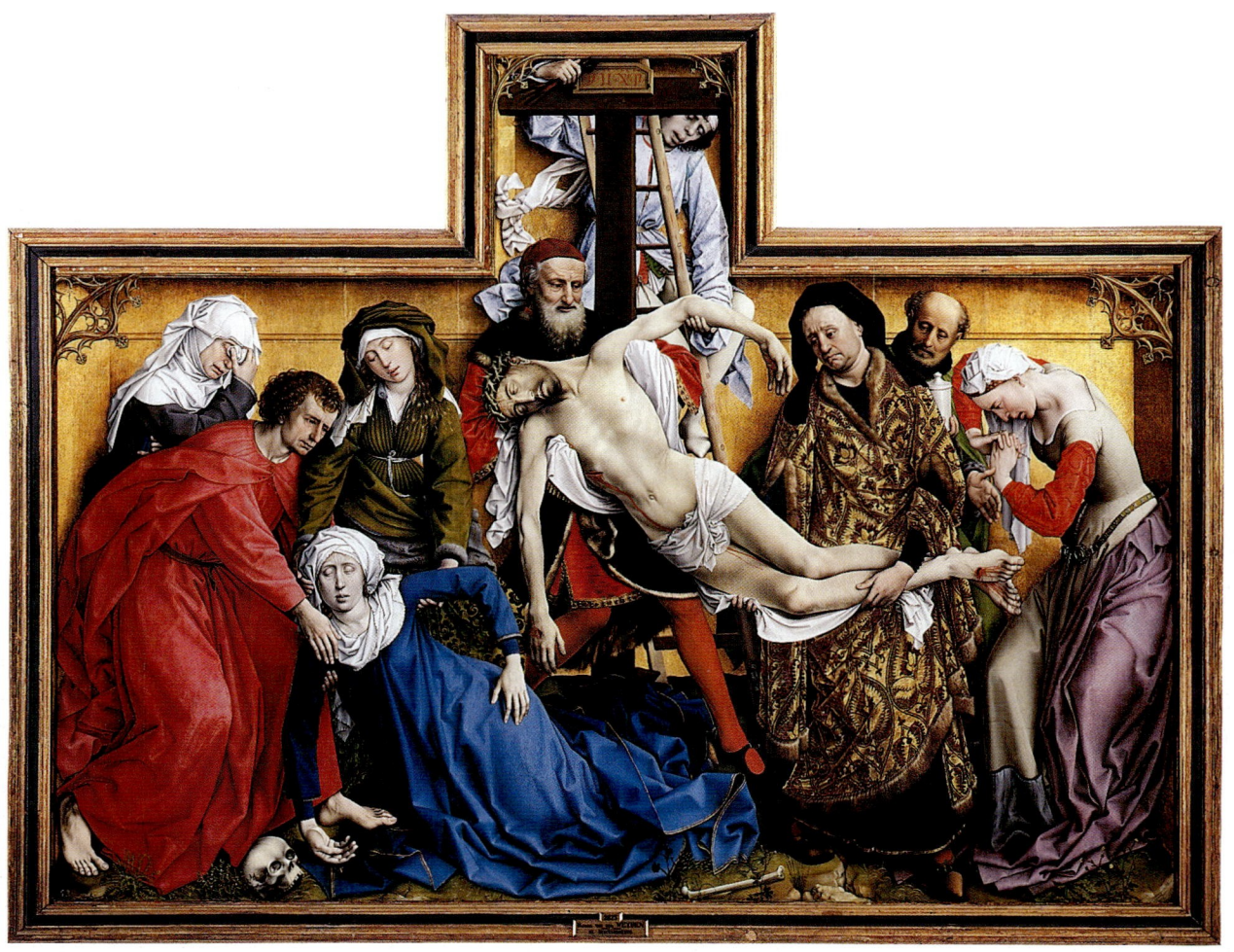

**20-7** ROGIER VAN DER WEYDEN, *Deposition,* from Notre-Dame hors-les-murs, Louvain, Belgium, ca. 1435. Oil on wood, approx. 7′ 3″ × 8′ 7″. Museo del Prado, Madrid.

## Painters, Pigments, and Panels

The generic word *paint* or *pigment* encompasses a wide range of substances artists have used over the years. Fresco aside (see "Fresco Painting," Chapter 19, page 530), during the 14th century, egg *tempera* was the material of choice for most painters, both in Italy and northern Europe. Tempera consists of egg combined with a wet paste of ground pigment. In his influential guidebook *Il Libro dell'Arte (The Craftsman's Handbook)*, Cennino Cennini, a contemporaneous painter, mentioned that artists mixed only the egg yolk with the ground pigment, but analysis of paintings from this period has revealed that some artists chose to use the whole egg. Images painted with tempera have a velvety sheen to them and exhibit a lightness of artistic touch because thick application of the pigment mixture results in premature cracking and flaking.

Scholars have discovered that artists used oil paints as far back as the 8th century, but not until the early 15th century did painting with this material become widespread. Flemish artists were among the first to employ oils extensively (often mixing them with tempera), and Italian painters quickly followed suit. The discovery of better drying components in the early 15th century enhanced the setting capabilities of oils. Rather than apply these oils in the light, flecked brushstrokes that tempera encouraged, artists laid the oils down in transparent *glazes* over opaque or semiopaque underlayers. In this manner, painters could build up deep tones through repeated glazing. Unlike tempera, whose surface dries quickly due to water evaporation, oils dry more uniformly and slowly, providing the artist time to rework areas. This flexibility must have been particularly appealing to artists who worked very deliberately, such as Leonardo da Vinci (Chapter 22, pages 613–618). Leonardo also preferred oil paint because its gradual drying process and consistency permitted him to blend the pigments, thereby creating the impressive *sfumato* (smoky effect) that contributed to his fame.

Both tempera and oils can be applied to various surfaces. Through the early 16th century, wooden panels served as the foundation for most paintings. Italians painted on poplar; northern artists used oak, lime, beech, chestnut, cherry, pine, and silver fir. Availability of these timbers determined the choice of wood. Linen canvas became increasingly popular in the late 16th century. Although evidence suggests that artists did not intend permanency for their early images on canvas, the material proved particularly useful in areas such as Venice where high humidity warped wood panels and made fresco unfeasible. Further, until canvas paintings were stretched on wooden stretcher bars before framing or affixed to a surface, they were more portable than wood panels.

---

patrons of this large painting by incorporating the crossbow (the guild's symbol) into the decorative spandrels in the corners.

This altarpiece nicely sums up Rogier's early style and content. Instead of creating a deep landscape setting, as Jan van Eyck might have, he compressed the figures and action onto a shallow stage to concentrate the observer's attention. Here, Rogier imitated the large sculptured shrines so popular in the 15th century, especially in Germany, and the device admirably serves his purpose of expressing maximum action within a limited space. The painting, with the artist's crisp drawing and precise modeling of forms, resembles a stratified relief carving. A series of lateral undulating movements gives the group a compositional unity, a formal cohesion that Rogier strengthened by psychological means—by depicting the desolating anguish shared by many of the figures. The similar poses of Christ and the Virgin Mary further unify *Deposition*. Few painters have equaled Rogier in the rendering of passionate sorrow as it vibrates through a figure or distorts a tear-stained face. His depiction of the agony of loss is among the most authentic in religious art. The emotional impact on the viewer is immediate and direct.

**SAVING LIVES AND SOULS** Rogier further demonstrated his immense talent for producing compositionally complex and emotionally intense images in the *Last Judgment Altarpiece* (FIG. **20-8**). Nicholas Rolin, whom Philip the Good had appointed chancellor of the Burgundian territories, commissioned this polyptych. Created for the Hôtel-Dieu (hospital) in Beaune (also founded by Rolin), this image served an important function in the treatment of hospital patients. The public often attributed the horrific medical maladies affecting people of all walks of life to God's displeasure, and perceived such afflictions as divine punishment. Thus, the general populace embraced praying to patron saints as a viable component of treatment. On the altarpiece's exterior (not illustrated), Rogier depicted Saints Anthony and Sebastian, both considered plague saints—saints whose legends made them appropriate intercessors for warding off or curing the plague. Chancellor Rolin and his wife also appear on the exterior, in perpetual prayer to the two saints. This work served many purposes. It demonstrated Nicholas Rolin's devotion and generosity, aided in patient therapy, and warned of the potential fate of people's souls should they turn away from the Christian Church.

Rogier gave visual form to this warning on the altarpiece's interior (FIG. 20-8), where he depicted the Last Judgment, a reminder of larger issues beyond earthly life and death—everlasting life or consignment to Hell. A radiant Christ appears in the center panel, above the archangel Michael, who holds the scales to weigh souls. The panels on both sides include numerous saints above the dead. On the ends, the saved are ushered into Heaven on the left, and the damned tumble into the fires of Hell on the right. Because this altarpiece is largely horizontal, for the artist to rely solely on the common convention of distinguishing the spiritual from the mundane by placing the figures in a vertical hierarchy would not have been very effective. Therefore, Rogier used both hierarchy and scale to emphasize the relative importance of the figures. Christ appears as the largest and highest figure in the altarpiece, whereas the naked souls are minuscule.

## The Artist's Profession in Flanders

As in Italy (see "Mastering a Craft," Chapter 19, page 534), guilds controlled the Flemish artist's profession. To pursue a craft, individuals had to belong to the guild controlling that craft. Painters, for example, sought admission to the Guild of Saint Luke, which included saddlers, glassworkers, and mirror-workers as well. The path to eventual membership in the guild began, for men, at an early age, when the father apprenticed his son in boyhood to a master, with whom the young aspiring painter lived. The master taught the fundamentals of his craft—how to make implements; how to prepare panels with gesso (plaster mixed with a binding material); and how to mix colors, oils, and varnishes. Once the youth mastered these procedures and learned to work in the master's traditional manner, he usually spent several years working as a journeyman in various cities, observing and absorbing ideas from other masters. He then was eligible to become a master and applied for admission to the guild. Through the guild, he obtained commissions. The guild also inspected his paintings to ensure that he used quality materials and to evaluate workmanship. It also secured him adequate payment for his labor. As a result of this quality control, Flemish artists soon gained a favorable reputation for their solid artisanship.

It is clear that women had many fewer opportunities than men to train as artists, in large part because of social and moral constraints that would have forbidden women's apprenticeship in the homes of male masters. Moreover, from the 16th century, when academic training courses supplemented and then replaced guild training, until the 20th century, women would not as a rule expect or be permitted instruction in figure painting, insofar as it involved dissection of cadavers and study of the nude male model. Flemish women interested in pursuing art as a career most often received tutoring from fathers and husbands who were professionals and whom the women assisted in all the technical procedures of the craft. Despite these obstacles, a substantial number of Flemish women in the 15th century were able to establish themselves as artists (revealed by membership records of the art guilds of cities such as Bruges). That these female artists were able to negotiate the difficult path to acceptance as professionals is a testament to both their tenacity and their artistic skill.

**20-8** ROGIER VAN DER WEYDEN, *Last Judgment Altarpiece* (open), Hôtel-Dieu, Beaune, France, ca. 1444–1448. Oil on wood, 7′ 4$\frac{5}{8}$″ × 17′ 11″. Musée de l'Hôtel-Dieu, Beaune.

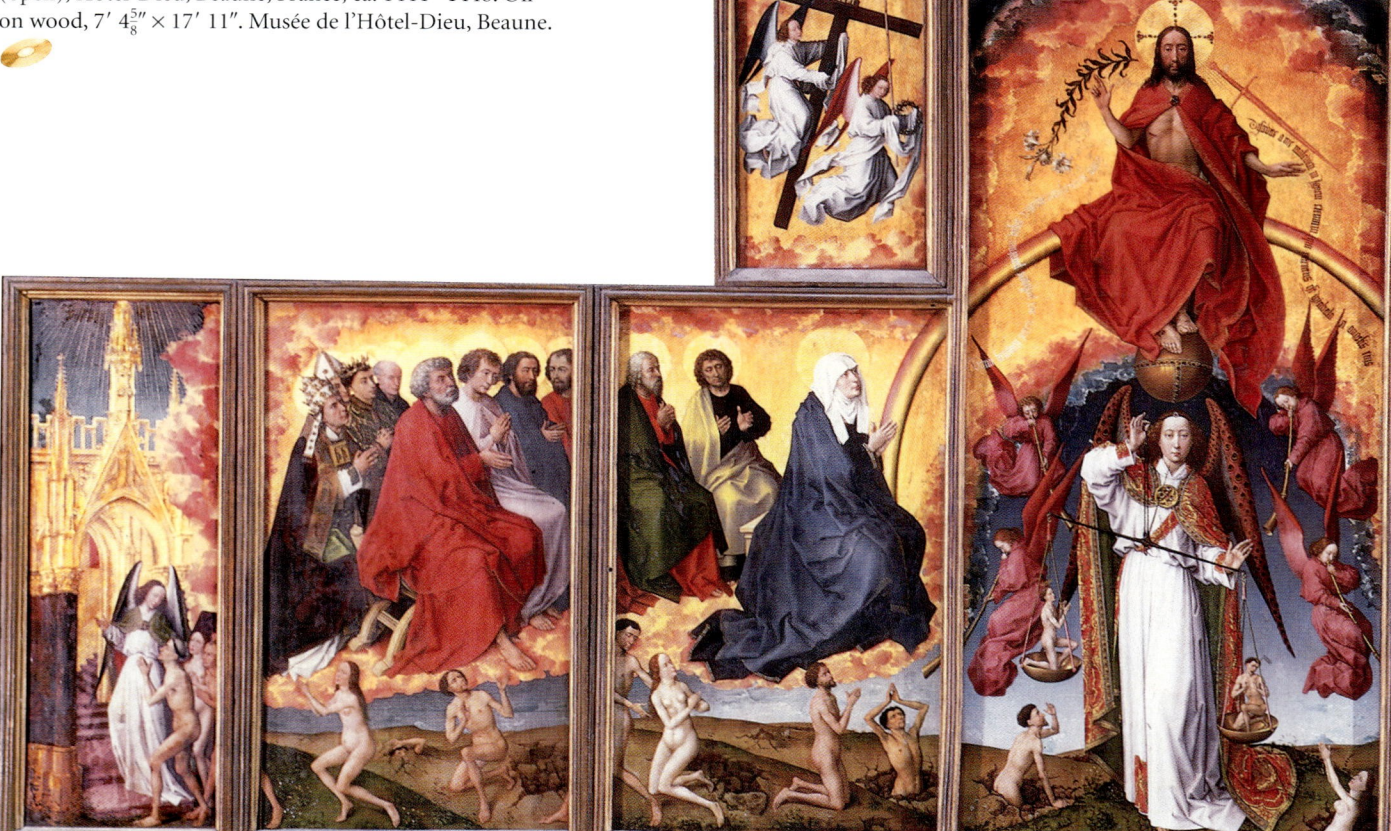

**A FLEMISH LAST SUPPER** Among the first northern paintings to demonstrate the use of a single vanishing point (see "Depicting Objects in Space," Chapter 21, page 578) is *Last Supper* (FIG. **20-9**) by DIRK BOUTS (ca. 1415–1475). *Last Supper* is the central panel of *Altarpiece of the Holy Sacrament*, commissioned from Bouts by the Louvain Confraternity of the Holy Sacrament in 1464. All of the central room's *orthogonals* (lines imagined to be behind and perpendicular to the picture plane that converge at a vanishing point) lead to a single vanishing point in the center of the mantelpiece above Christ's head. However, the small side room has its own vanishing point, and neither it nor the vanishing point of the main room falls on the horizon of the landscape seen through the windows.

Scholars also have noted that Bouts's *Last Supper* was the first Flemish panel painting depicting this event. In this central panel, Bouts did not focus on the biblical narrative itself but instead presented Christ in the role of a priest performing a ritual from the liturgy of the Christian Church—the consecration of the Eucharistic wafer. This contrasts strongly with other Last Supper depictions, which often focused on Judas's betrayal or on Christ's comforting of John. Bouts also added to the complexity of this image by including four servants (two in the window and two standing), all dressed in Flemish attire. These servants are most likely portraits of the confraternity's members responsible for commissioning the altarpiece.

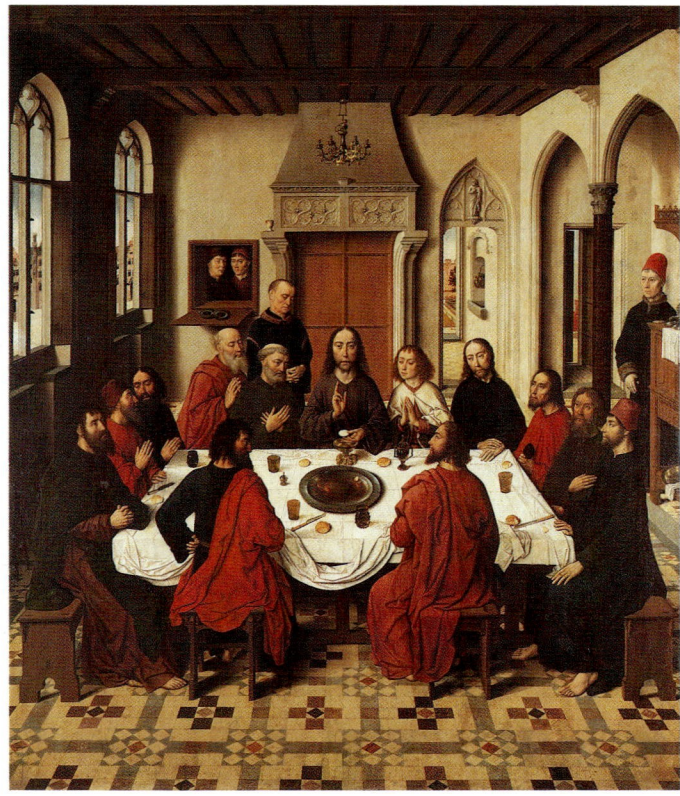

**20-9** DIRK BOUTS, *Last Supper,* center panel of the *Altarpiece of the Holy Sacrament,* Saint Peter's, Louvain, Belgium, 1464–1468. Oil on wood, approx. 6′ × 5′.

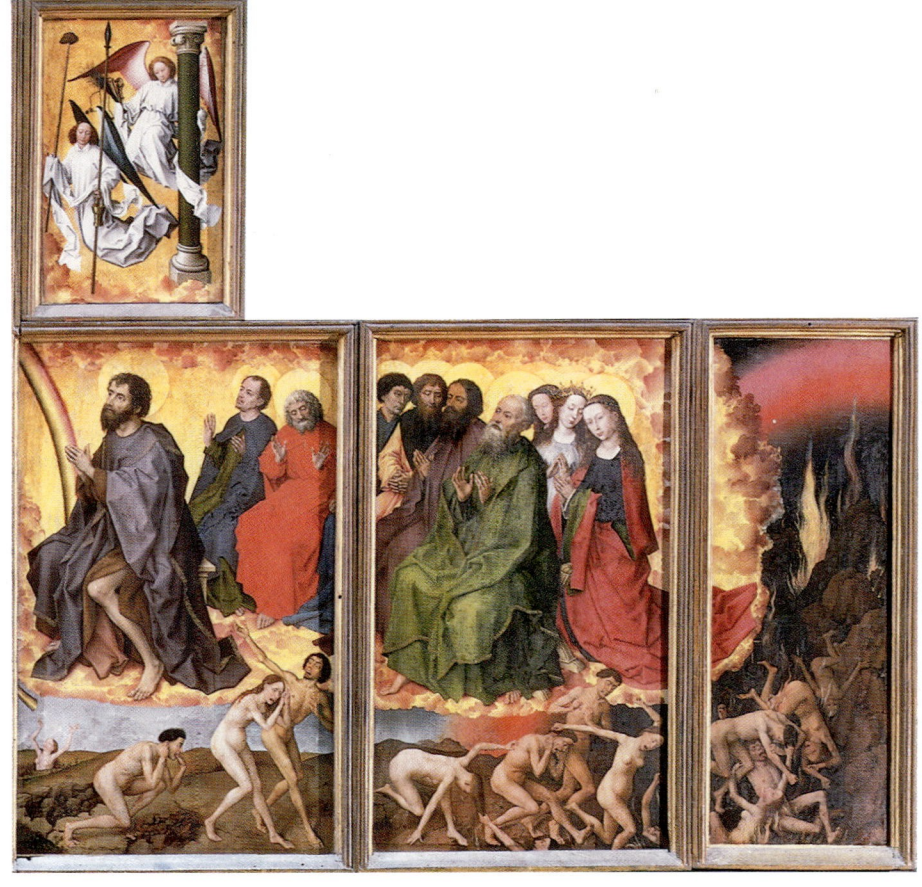

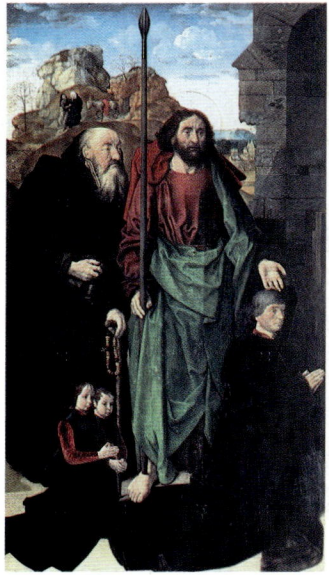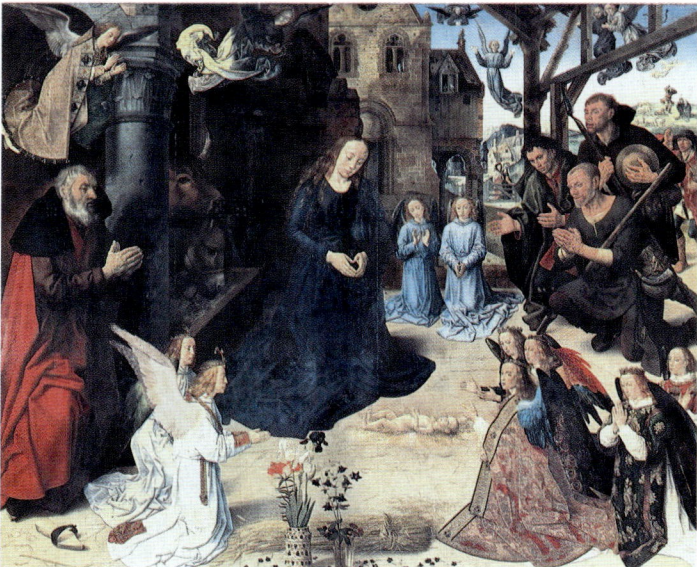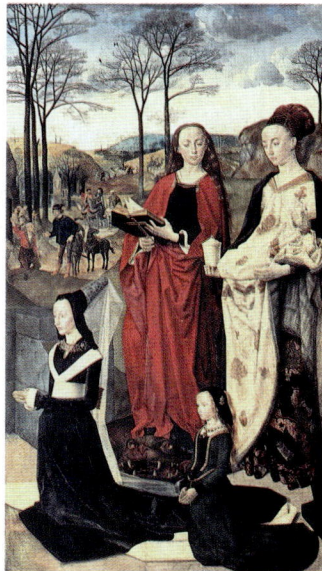

**20-10** HUGO VAN DER GOES, *Portinari Altarpiece* (open), from Sant'Egidio, Florence, Italy, ca. 1476. Tempera and oil on wood, 8′ 3 ½″ × 10′ (center panel), 8′ 3½″ × 4′ 7½″ (each wing). Galleria degli Uffizi, Florence.

**FROM FLANDERS TO FLORENCE** Artists and patrons throughout Europe expressed great interest in Flemish art. Indeed, the *Portinari Altarpiece* (FIG. **20-10**) is just one example of a Flemish painting that made its way out of Flanders. A large-scale altarpiece installed in a family chapel in Florence, the *Portinari Altarpiece* was the creation of Flemish artist HUGO VAN DER GOES (ca. 1440–1482). As the dean of the painters' guild of Ghent from 1468 to 1475, Hugo was an extremely popular painter.

Hugo painted the triptych for Tommaso Portinari, an Italian shipowner and agent for the powerful Medici family of Florence. Portinari appears on the wings of the altarpiece with his family and their patron saints. The central panel is titled *Adoration of the Shepherds.* On this large surface, Hugo displayed a scene of solemn grandeur, muting the high drama of the joyous occasion. The Virgin, Joseph, and the angels seem to brood on the suffering to come rather than to meditate on the Nativity miracle. Mary kneels, somber and monumental, on a tilted ground that has the expressive function of centering the main actors. From the right rear enter three shepherds, represented with powerful realism in attitudes of wonder, piety, and gaping curiosity. Their lined plebeian faces, work-worn hands, and uncouth dress and manner seem immediately familiar. The symbolic architecture and a continuous wintry northern landscape unify the three panels. Symbols surface throughout the altarpiece. Iris and columbine flowers symbolize the Sorrows of the Virgin; the 15 angels represent the Fifteen Joys of Mary; a sheaf of wheat stands for Bethlehem (the "house of bread" in Hebrew), a reference to the Eucharist; and the harp of David, emblazoned over the building's portal in the middle distance (just to the right of the Virgin's head), signifies the ancestry of Christ.

To stress the meaning and significance of the depicted event, Hugo revived medieval pictorial devices. Small scenes shown in the background of the altarpiece represent (from left to right) the flight into Egypt, the Annunciation to the Shepherds, and the arrival of the Magi. Hugo's variation in the scale of his figures to differentiate them by their importance to the central event also reflects older traditions. Still, he put a vigorous, penetrating realism

to work in a new direction, characterizing human beings according to their social level while showing their common humanity.

After Portinari placed his altarpiece in the family chapel in the Florentine church of Sant'Egidio, it created a considerable stir among Italian artists. Although the painting as a whole may have seemed unstructured to them, Hugo's masterful technique and what they thought of as incredible realism in representing drapery, flowers, animals, and, above all, human character and emotion made a deep impression on them. At least one Florentine artist, Domenico Ghirlandaio, paid tribute to the northern master by using Hugo's most striking motif, the adoring shepherds, in one of his own Nativity paintings.

**CELEBRATING A MYSTIC MARRIAGE** The artistic community in Flanders held Hugo's contemporary, HANS MEMLING (ca. 1430–1494), in high esteem as well. Memling specialized in images of the Madonna; the many that survive are young, slight, pretty princesses, each holding a doll-like infant Christ. One such painting is the *Saint John Altarpiece,* the center panel of which is *Virgin with Saints and Angels* (FIG. **20-11**). The patrons of this altarpiece—two brothers and two sisters of the order of the Hospital of Saint John in Bruges—appear on the exterior side panels (not illustrated). In the central panel, two angels, one playing a musical instrument and the other holding a book, flank the Virgin. To the sides of Mary's throne stand Saint John the Baptist on the left and Saint John the Evangelist on the right, and in the foreground are Saints Catherine and Barbara. This gathering celebrates the Mystic Marriage of Saint Catherine of Alexandria; a number of virgin saints were believed to have entered into a special spiritual marriage (Mystic Marriage) with Christ. As one of the most revered virgins of Christ, Saint Catherine (and the celebration of her Mystic Marriage in paintings such as this) provided a model of devotion especially resonant with women viewers (particularly nuns). The altarpiece exudes an opulence that results from the rich colors, carefully depicted tapestries and brocades, and the serenity of the figures. The composition is balanced and serene; the color, sparkling and luminous; and the

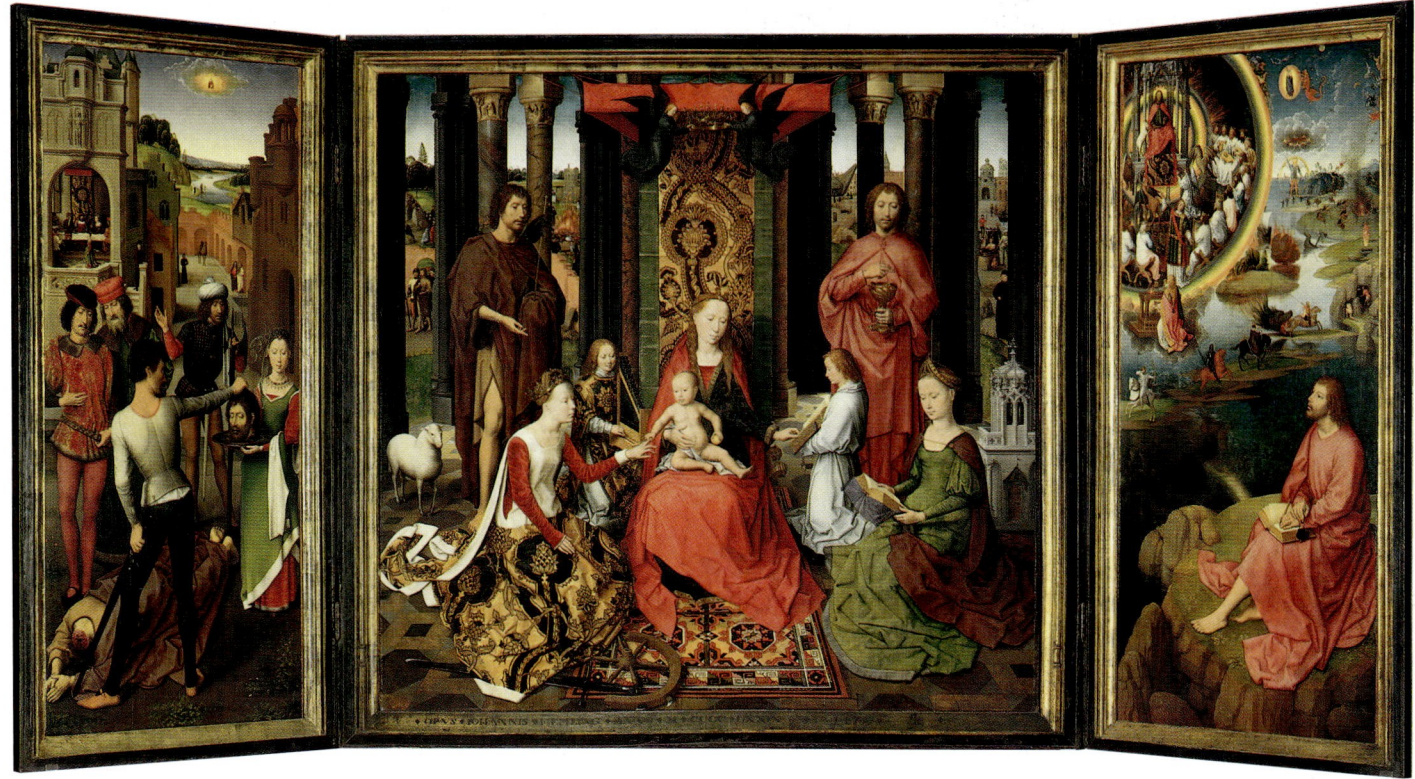

**20-11** HANS MEMLING, *Virgin with Saints and Angels,* center panel of the *Saint John Altarpiece,* Hospitaal Sint Jan, Bruges, Belgium, 1479. Oil on wood, approx. 5′ 7¾″ × 5′ 7¾″ (center panel), 5′ 7¾″ × 2′ 7⅛″ (each wing).

execution, of the highest technical quality. Works such as this earned Memling the following tribute after his death: "Johannes Memlinc [Memling] was the most accomplished and excellent painter in the entire Christian world."[1] Fortunately for contemporary viewers, Memling's paintings are among the best preserved from the 15th century.

## *Private Devotional Imagery*

**IN THE PRIVACY OF THE HOME** The Flemish did not limit their demonstrations of piety to the public realm, relying increasingly on private devotional practices. The expanding use of prayer books and Books of Hours (such as *Les Très Riches Heures;* FIGS. 20-1 and 20-2) was one manifestation of this commitment to private prayer. Individuals commissioned artworks for private devotional use in the home as well. So strong was the impetus for private devotional imagery that it seems, based on an accounting of extant Flemish religious paintings, that lay patrons outnumbered clerical patrons by a ratio of two to one. Dissatisfaction with the clergy accounted, in part, for this commitment to private prayer. In addition, popular reform movements advocated personal devotion, and in the years leading up to the Protestant Reformation in the early 16th century, private devotional exercises and prayer grew in popularity.

One of the more prominent features of these images commissioned for private use is the integration of religious and secular concerns. For example, biblical scenes were often presented as transpiring in a Flemish house. Although this may seem inappropriate or even sacrilegious, religion was such an integral part of Flemish life that separating the sacred from the secular became

virtually impossible. Further, the presentation in religious art of familiar settings and objects no doubt strengthened the direct bond the patron or viewer felt with biblical figures.

**THE SYMBOLIC AND THE SECULAR** The *Mérode Altarpiece* (FIG. **20-12**) is representative of triptychs commissioned for private use. Scholars generally agree that the artist, referred to as the "Master of Flémalle," is ROBERT CAMPIN (ca. 1378–1444), the leading painter of the city of Tournai. Similar in format to large-scale Flemish public altarpieces, the *Mérode Altarpiece* is considerably smaller (the central panel is roughly two feet square), which allowed the owners to close the wings and move the painting when necessary. The popular Annunciation theme (as prophesied in Isa. 7:14) occupies the triptych's central panel. The archangel Gabriel approaches Mary, who sits reading. The artist depicted a well-kept middle-class Flemish home as the site of the event. The carefully rendered architectural scene in the background of the right wing confirms this identification of the locale.

The depicted accessories, furniture, and utensils contribute to the identification of the setting as Flemish. However, the objects represented are not merely decorative. They also function as religious symbols, thereby reminding viewers of the event's miraculous nature. The book, extinguished candle, lilies, copper basin (in the corner niche), towels, fire screen, and bench symbolize, in different ways, the Virgin's purity and her divine mission. In the right panel, Joseph has made a mousetrap, symbolic of the theological tradition that Christ is bait set in the trap of the world to catch the Devil. The painter completely inventoried a carpenter's shop. The ax, saw, and rod in the foreground are not only tools of the carpenter's trade but also mentioned in Isaiah 10:15. In the left panel, the altarpiece's donor, Peter Inghelbrecht, and his wife

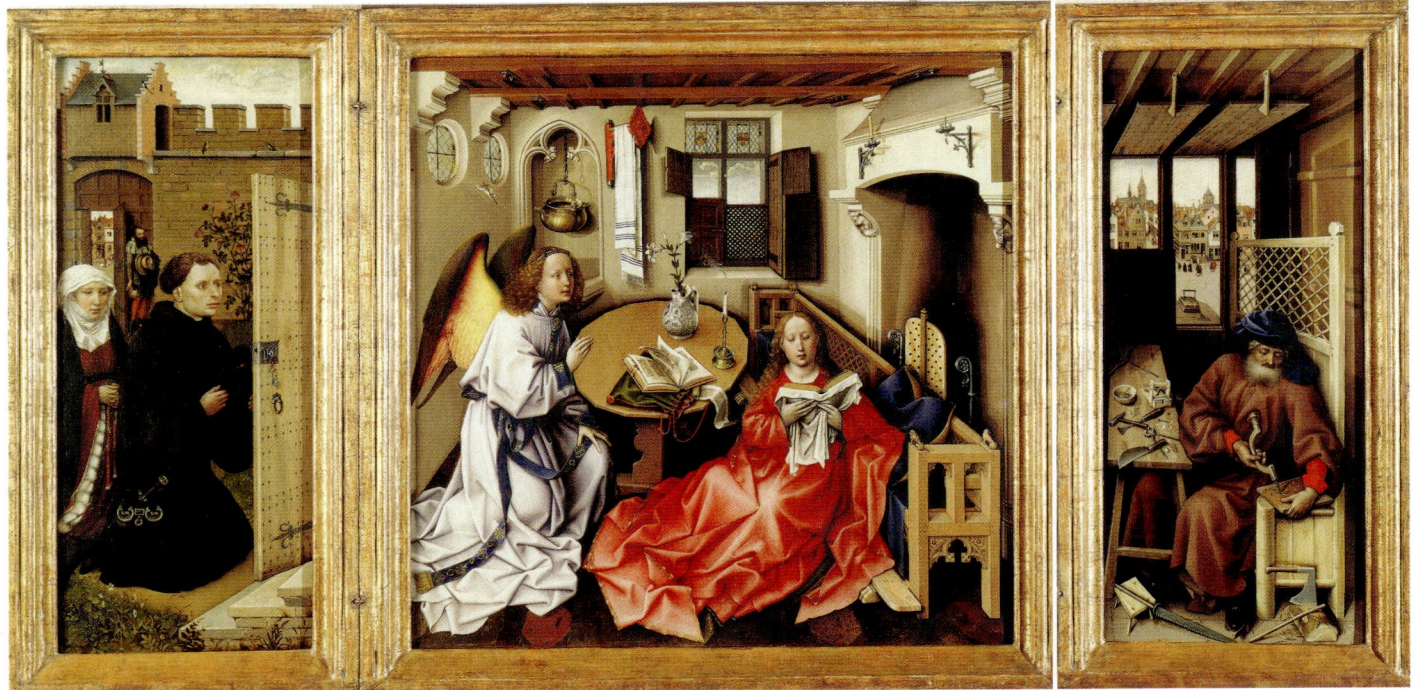

**20-12** ROBERT CAMPIN (Master of Flémalle), *Mérode Altarpiece* (open), *The Annunciation* (center panel), ca. 1425–1428. Oil on wood, center panel approx. 2′ 1″ × 2′ 1″. Metropolitan Museum of Art, New York (The Cloisters Collection, 1956).

kneel and seem to be permitted to witness this momentous event through an open door. The Inghelbrechts, a devout, middle-class couple, appear in a closed garden, symbolic of Mary's purity, and the flowers depicted (such as strawberries and violets) all relate to Mary's virtues, especially humility.

The careful personalization of this entire altarpiece is further suggested by the fact that the Annunciation theme refers to the patron's name, Inghelbrecht (angel bringer), and the workshop scene in the right panel also refers to his wife's name, Schrin-mechers (shrine maker).

**FOR BETTER, FOR WORSE** References to both the secular and the religious in Flemish painting also surface in Jan van Eyck's double portrait *Giovanni Arnolfini and His Bride* (FIG. **20-13**). Van Eyck depicted the Lucca financier (who had established himself in Bruges as an agent of the Medici family) and his betrothed in a Flemish bedchamber that is simultaneously mundane and charged with the spiritual. As in the *Mérode Altarpiece,* almost every object portrayed conveys the sanctity of the event, specifically, the holiness of matrimony. Arnolfini and his bride, Giovanna Cenami, hand in hand, take the marriage vows. The cast-aside clogs indicate that this event is taking place on holy ground. The little dog symbolizes fidelity (the common canine name Fido orig-inated from the Latin *fido,* "to trust"). Behind the pair, the curtains of the marriage bed have been opened. The bedpost's *finial* (crowning ornament) is a tiny statue of Saint Margaret, patron saint of childbirth. From the finial hangs a whisk broom, symbolic of domestic care. The oranges on the chest below the window may refer to fertility, and the all-seeing eye of God seems to be referred to twice. It is symbolized once by the single candle burning in the left rear holder of the ornate chandelier, and again by the mirror, in which the viewer sees the entire room reflected (FIG. **20-14**). The small medallions set into the mirror frame show tiny scenes

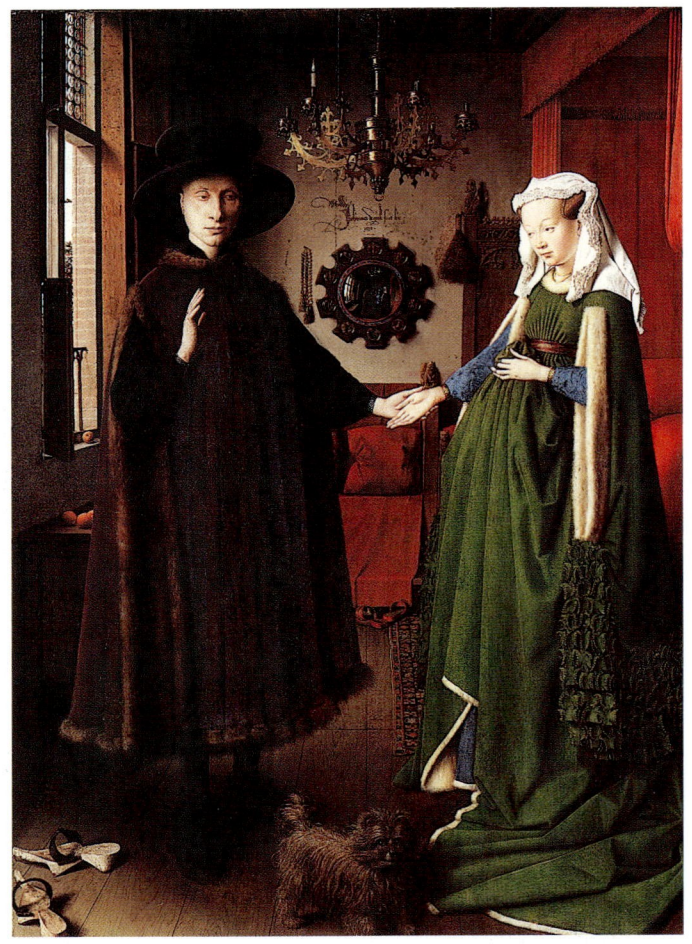

**20-13** JAN VAN EYCK, *Giovanni Arnolfini and His Bride,* 1434. Oil on wood, approx. 2′ 8″ × 1′ 11½″. National Gallery, London.

from the Passion of Christ and represent God's promise of salvation for the figures reflected on the mirror's convex surface.

Flemish viewers would have been familiar with many of the objects included in *Giovanni Arnolfini and His Bride* because of traditional Flemish customs. Husbands traditionally presented brides with clogs, and the solitary lit candle in the chandelier was also part of Flemish marriage practices. Van Eyck's placement of the two figures suggests conventional gender roles—the woman stands near the bed and well into the room, whereas the man stands near the open window, symbolic of the outside world.

Van Eyck enhanced the documentary nature of this scene by exquisitely painting each object. He carefully distinguished textures and depicted the light from the window on the left reflecting off various surfaces. The artist augmented the scene's credibility by including the convex mirror (FIG. 20-14), because viewers can see not only the principals, Arnolfini and his wife, but also two persons who look into the room through the door. One of these must be the artist himself, as the florid inscription above the mirror, "Johannes de Eyck fuit hic" (Jan van Eyck was here), announces he was present. The picture's purpose, then, seems to have been to record and sanctify this marriage. Although this has been the traditional interpretation of the image, some scholars recently have taken issue with this reading, suggesting that Arnolfini is conferring legal privileges on his wife to conduct business in his absence. Despite the lingering questions about the precise purpose of *Giovanni Arnolfini and His Bride*, the painting provides viewers today with great insight into both van Eyck's remarkable skill and Flemish life in the 15th century.

**SAINT OR GOLDSMITH?** Like *Giovanni Arnolfini and His Bride*, *A Goldsmith in His Shop, Possibly Saint Eligius* (FIG. **20-15**) by PETRUS CHRISTUS (ca. 1410–1472) testifies to the incorporation of references to both the religious and the secular realms that characterizes much of 15th-century Flemish art. Traditional scholarship posited a religious interpretation of this painting. According to this interpretation, *A Goldsmith in His Shop, Possibly Saint Eligius* conveys the importance and sacredness of the sacrament of marriage. In the painting, Saint Eligius (initially a master goldsmith before committing his life to God) sits in his stall, showing an elegantly attired couple a selection of rings. The bride's betrothal girdle lies on the table as a symbol of chastity, and the woman reaches for the ring the goldsmith weighs. The artist's inclusion of a crystal container for Eucharistic wafers (on the lower shelf to the right of Saint Eligius) and the scales (a reference to the Last Judgment) supports a religious interpretation of this painting. A halo that at one time circled Saint Eligius's head seemingly emphasized the religious nature of this scene. However, scientific analysis revealed that the halo was added later by an artist other than Christus, and it has been removed.

Although not completely dismissing this religious reading of *A Goldsmith in His Shop, Possibly Saint Eligius,* more recent scholarship has argued that this painting was more likely commissioned as part of the tradition of vocational paintings produced for installation in guild chapels. Although the couple's presence suggests a marriage portrait, most scholars now believe that the goldsmiths' guild in Bruges commissioned this painting. Saint Eligius was the patron saint of gold- and silversmiths, blacksmiths, and metalworkers, all of whom shared a chapel in a building adjacent to their meetinghouse. Because we know that this chapel was reconsecrated in 1449, the same date as this painting, it seems probable that *A Goldsmith in His Shop, Possibly Saint*

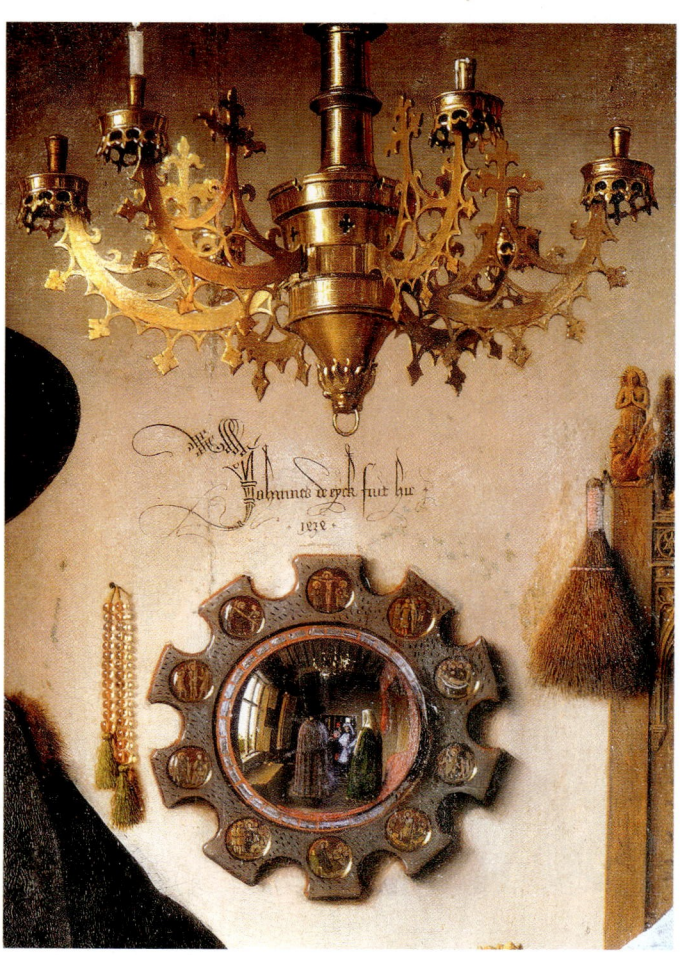

**20-14** JAN VAN EYCK, detail of *Giovanni Arnolfini and His Bride*, 1434.

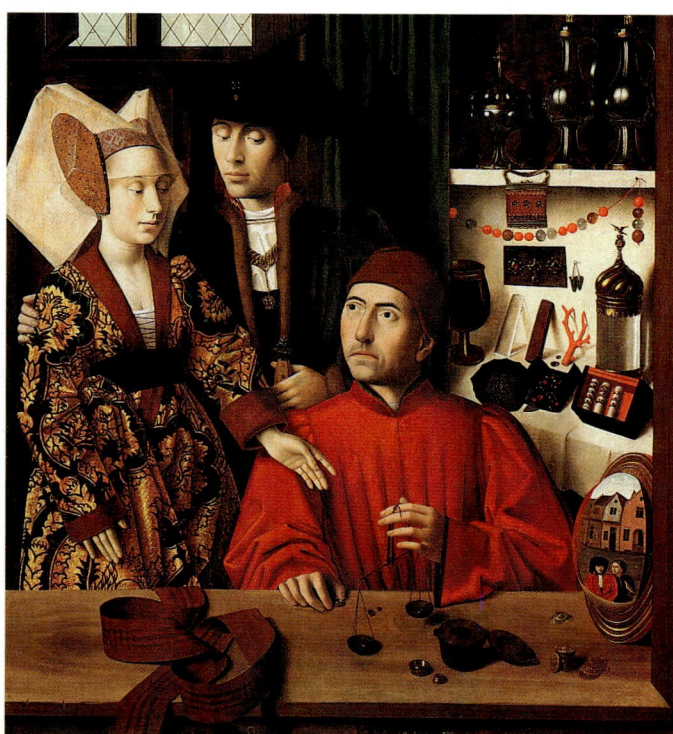

**20-15** PETRUS CHRISTUS, *A Goldsmith in His Shop, Possibly Saint Eligius,* 1449. Oil on wood, approx. 3′ 3″ × 2′ 10″. Metropolitan Museum of Art, New York (the Robert Lehman Collection, 1975).

*Eligius,* which depicts an economic transaction and focuses on the goldsmith's profession, was commissioned for this chapel. Scrutiny of this painting reveals that Christus went to great lengths to produce a historically credible image. For example, the variety of objects depicted in the painting serves as advertisement for the goldsmiths' guild. The raw materials—precious stones, beads, crystal, coral, and seed pearls—are scattered among finished products, including rings, buckles, and brooches. The cast pewter vessels on the upper shelves were donation pitchers, given to distinguished guests by town leaders. All these objects attest to the centrality and importance of the goldsmiths to both the secular and sacred communities. The naturalism of this painting is enhanced by such elements as the meticulously painted convex mirror in the foreground, which extends the painting's space into that of the viewer, creating a greater sense of involvement.

## Portraiture

**MEETING THE VIEWER'S GAZE** Emerging capitalism led to an urban prosperity that fueled the growing bourgeois market for art objects, particularly in Bruges, Antwerp, and, later, Amsterdam.

This prosperity contributed to a growing interest in secular art, such as landscapes and portraits, in addition to religious artworks. Two Flemish works shown so far, the *Ghent Altarpiece* (FIG. 20-5) and the *Mérode Altarpiece* (FIG. 20-12), include painted portraits of their donors. These paintings marked a significant revival of portraiture, a genre that had languished since antiquity. Jan van Eyck's *Man in a Red Turban* (FIG. 20-16) is a completely secular portrait without the layer of religious interpretation common to Flemish painting. In this work (possibly a van Eyck self-portrait), the image of a living individual apparently required no religious purpose for being—only a personal one. These private portraits began to multiply as both artists and patrons became interested in the reality (both physical and psychological) such portraits revealed. As human beings confronted themselves in painted portraits, they objectified themselves as people. In this confrontation, the man van Eyck portrayed looks directly at the viewer or, perhaps, at himself in a mirror. So far as studies show, this was the first Western painted portrait in a thousand years to do so. The level, composed gaze, directed from a true three-quarter head pose, must have impressed observers deeply. The painter created the illusion that from whatever angle

**20-16** JAN VAN EYCK, *Man in a Red Turban,* 1433. Oil on wood, approx. $10\frac{1}{4}'' \times 7\frac{1}{2}''$. National Gallery, London.

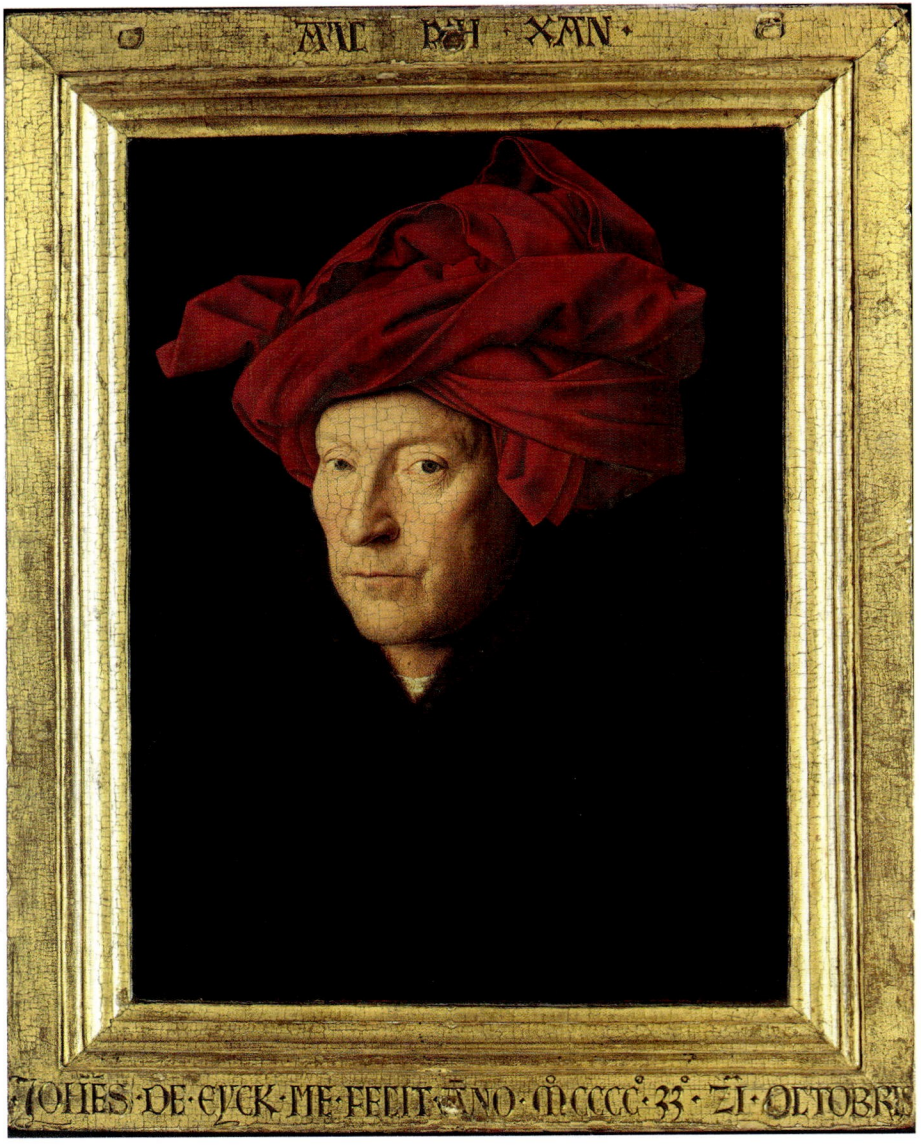

### Edges and Borders
*Framing Paintings*

Until recent decades, when painters began to complete their works by simply affixing canvas to wooden stretcher bars, artists considered the frame an integral part of the painting. Frames served a number of functions, some visual, others conceptual. For paintings such as large-scale altarpieces that were part of a larger environment, frames were often used to integrate the painting with its surroundings. Frames could also be used to reinforce the illusionistic nature of the painted image. For example, Giovanni Bellini (see FIG. 22-31) and Andrea Mantegna (see Chapter 21, pages 605–608) duplicated the carved pilasters of their architectural frames in their paintings, thereby enhancing the illusion of space and rendering their painted images more "real." Or, conversely, a frame could be used specifically to distance the viewer from the (often otherworldly) scene by calling attention to the separation of the image from the viewer's space.

Most 15th- and 16th-century paintings included elaborate frames that artists helped design and construct. Frames were frequently polychromed (painted) or gilded, adding to the expense. Surviving contracts reveal that as much as half of an altarpiece's cost derived from the frame. For small works, artists sometimes affixed the frames to the panels before painting, creating an insistent visual presence as they worked. Occasionally, a single piece of wood served as both panel and frame, and the artist carved the painting surface from the wood, leaving the edges as a frame.

Larger images with elaborate frames, such as altarpieces, required the services of a woodcarver or stonemason. The painter worked closely with the individual constructing the frame to ensure its appropriateness for the image(s) produced.

Unfortunately, over time, many frames were removed from paintings. For instance, most scholars believe that individuals concerned with conserving the *Ghent Altarpiece* (FIG. 20-5) removed its elaborately carved frame and dismantled the altarpiece in 1566 to protect it from Protestant iconoclasts. As ill luck would have it, when the panels were reinstalled in 1587, no one could find the frame, which probably had been destroyed. Sadly, the absence of many of the original frames deprives viewers today of the complete artistic vision of painters and, sometimes, of their hired woodcarvers.

---

a viewer observes the face, the eyes return that gaze. Van Eyck, with his considerable observational skill and controlled painting style, injected a heightened sense of specificity into this portrait by including beard stubble, veins in the bloodshot left eye, and weathered and aged skin.

Although a definitive identification of the sitter has yet to be made, the possibility that *Man in a Red Turban* is a van Eyck self-portrait seems reinforced by the inscriptions on the frame (see "Edges and Borders: Framing Paintings," above). Across the top, van Eyck wrote "As I can" in Flemish using Greek letters, and across the bottom in Latin appears the statement "Jan van Eyck made me" and the date.

Admired artists, such as van Eyck, established portraiture among their principal tasks. For various reasons, great patrons embraced the opportunity to have their likenesses painted. They wanted to memorialize themselves in their dynastic lines; to establish their identities, ranks, and stations with images far more concrete than heraldic coats of arms; or to represent themselves at state occasions when they could not attend. They even used such paintings when arranging marriages. Royalty, nobility, and the very rich would send painters to "take" the likeness of a prospective bride or groom. Evidence reveals that when young King Charles VI of France sought a bride, a painter journeyed to three different royal courts to make portraits of the candidates for the king to use in making his choice.

**CAPTURING CLASS AND CHARACTER** The commission details for Rogier van der Weyden's portrait of an unknown young lady (FIG. **20-17**) remain unclear. Her dress and bearing imply noble rank. The artist created a portrait that not only presented a faithful likeness of her somewhat plain features but also revealed her individual character. Her lowered eyes, tightly locked thin fingers, and fragile physique bespeak a reserved and pious demeanor. This style contrasted with the formal Italian approach

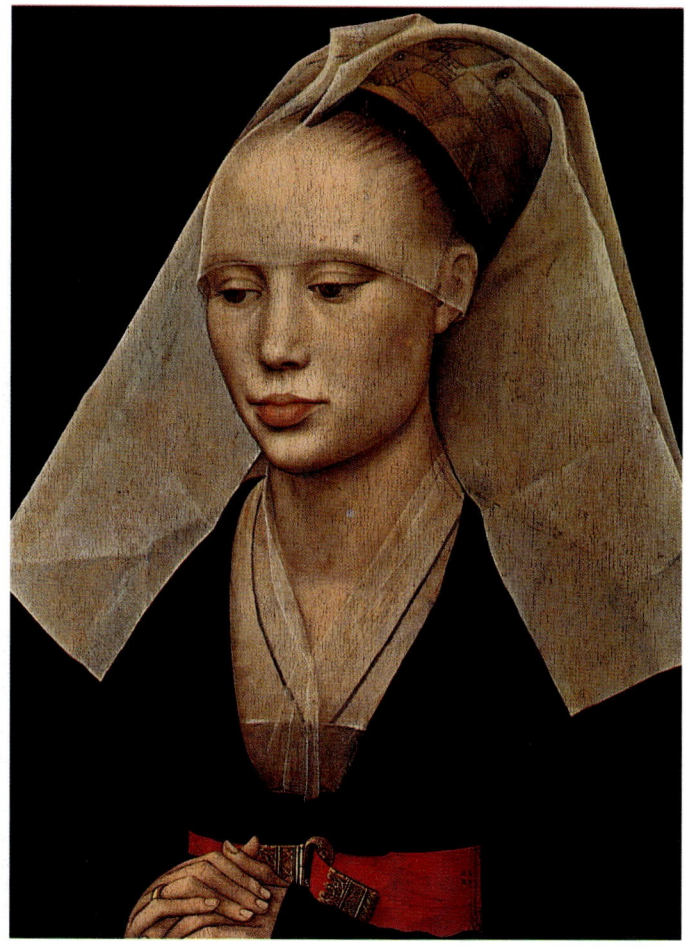

**20-17** ROGIER VAN DER WEYDEN, *Portrait of a Lady*, ca. 1460. Oil on panel, 1′ 1⅜″ × 10 1/16″. National Gallery, Washington (Andrew W. Mellon Collection).

(see FIG. 21-31), derived from the profiles common to coins and medallions, which was sterner and conveyed little of the sitter's personality. Rogier was perhaps chief among the Flemish in his penetrating readings of his subjects, and, as a great pictorial composer, he made beautiful use here of flat, sharply pointed angular shapes that so powerfully suggest this subject's composure. Unlike Jan van Eyck, Rogier placed little emphasis on minute description of surface detail. Instead, he defined large, simple planes and volumes, achieving an almost "abstract" effect, in the modern sense, of dignity and elegance.

## An Enigmatic Flemish Painter

**LOVE AND MARRIAGE OR SEX AND SIN?** Although certain genres and themes in painting emerged so frequently during the 15th century in Flanders as to qualify as conventions, this country also produced one of the most fascinating and puzzling painters in history, HIERONYMUS BOSCH (ca. 1450–1516). Interpretations of Bosch differ widely. Was he a satirist, an irreligious mocker, or a pornographer? Was he a heretic or an orthodox fanatic like Girolamo Savonarola, his Italian contemporary? Was he obsessed by guilt and the universal reign of sin and death?

Bosch's most famous work, the so-called *Garden of Earthly Delights* (FIG. **20-18**), is also his most enigmatic, and no interpretation of it is universally accepted. This large-scale work takes the familiar form of a triptych. More than 7 feet high, the painting extends to more than 12 feet wide when opened. This triptych format seems to indicate a religious function for this work, but documentation reveals that *Garden of Earthly Delights* resided in the palace of Henry III of Nassau, regent of the Netherlands, seven years after its completion. This suggests a secular commission for private use. Scholars have proposed that such a commission, in conjunction with the central themes of marriage, sex, and procreation, points to a wedding commemoration, which, as seen in *Giovanni Arnolfini and His Bride* (FIG. 20-13) and in *A Goldsmith in His Shop, Possibly Saint Eligius* (FIG. 20-15), was not uncommon. Any similarity to these paintings ends there, however. Whereas van Eyck and Christus grounded their depictions of betrothed couples in contemporary Flemish life and custom, Bosch's image portrays a visionary world of fantasy and intrigue.

In the left panel, God presents Eve to Adam in a landscape, presumably the Garden of Eden. Bosch complicated his straightforward presentation of this event by placing it in a wildly imaginative setting that includes an odd pink fountainlike structure in a body of water and an array of fanciful and unusual animals, which may hint at an interpretation involving alchemy—the medieval study of seemingly magical changes, especially chemical changes. The right panel, in contrast, bombards viewers with the horrors of Hell. Beastly creatures devour people, while others are impaled or strung on musical instruments, as if on a medieval rack. A gambler is nailed to his own table. A spidery monster embraces a girl while toads bite her. A sea of inky darkness envelops all of these horrific scenes. Observers must search through the hideous enclosure of Bosch's Hell to take in its fascinating though repulsive details.

Sandwiched between Paradise and Hell is the huge central panel, with nude people blithely cavorting in a landscape dotted with bizarre creatures and unidentifiable objects. The numerous fruits and birds (fertility symbols) in the scene suggest procreation, and, indeed, many of the figures are paired off as couples. The orgiastic overtones of *Garden of Earthly Delights*, in conjunction with the terrifying image of Hell, have led some scholars to interpret this triptych, like other Last Judgment images, as a warning to viewers of the fate awaiting the sinful, decadent, and immoral.

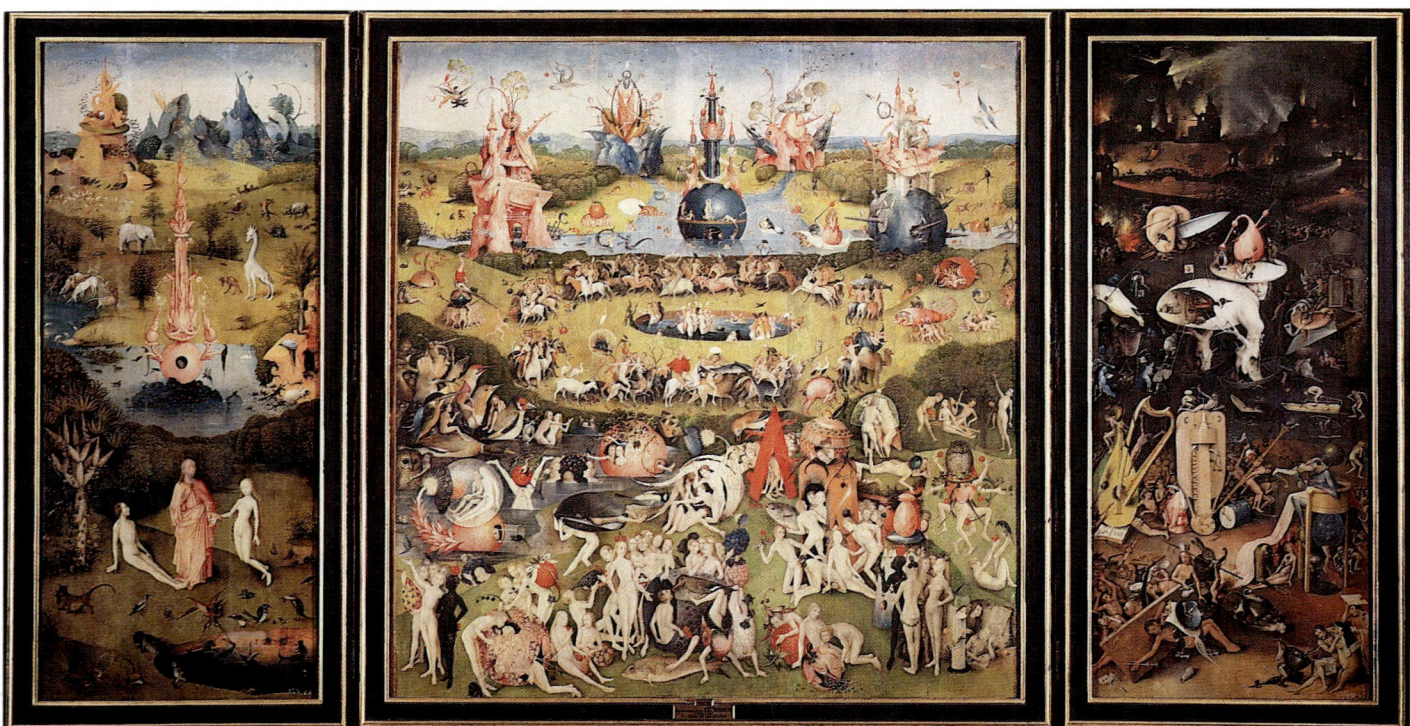

**20-18** HIERONYMUS BOSCH, *Garden of Earthly Delights. Creation of Eve* (left wing), *Garden of Earthly Delights* (center panel), *Hell* (right wing), 1505–1510. Oil on wood, center panel 7′ $2\frac{5}{8}$″ × 6′ $4\frac{3}{4}$″. Museo del Prado, Madrid.

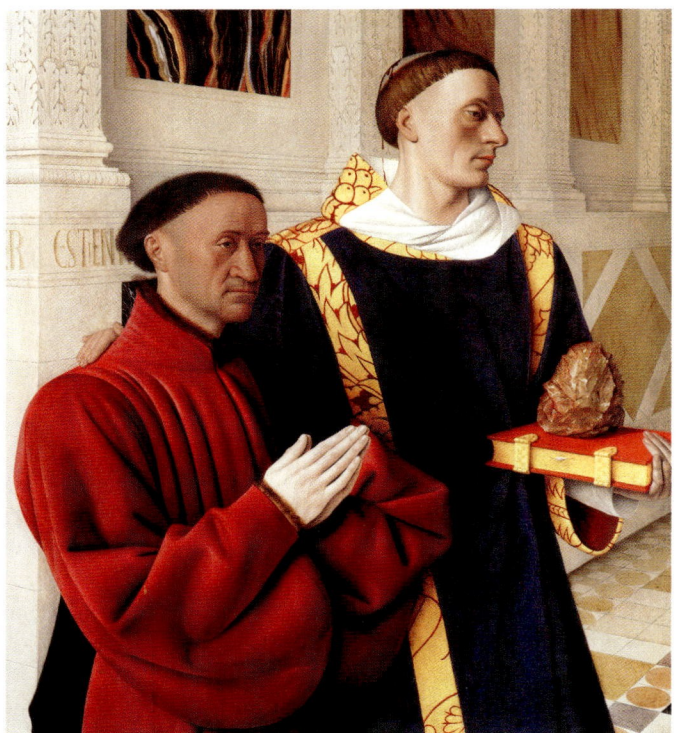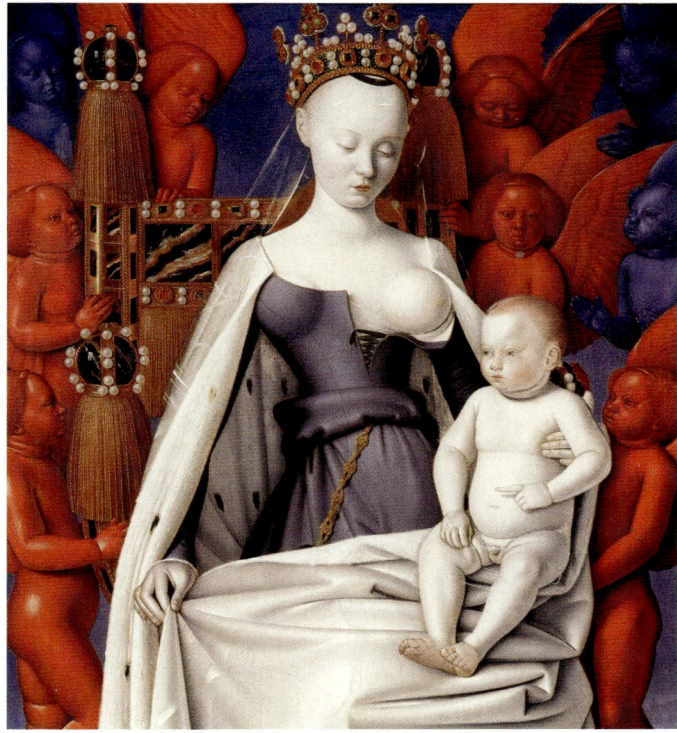

**20-19** Jean Fouquet, *Melun Diptych. Étienne Chevalier and Saint Stephen* (left wing), ca. 1450. Oil on wood, $3' \frac{1}{2}'' \times 2' 9\frac{1}{2}''$. Gemäldegalerie, Staatliche Museen, Berlin. *Virgin and Child* (right wing), ca. 1451. Oil on wood, $3' 1\frac{1}{4}'' \times 2' 9\frac{1}{2}''$. Koninklijk Museum voor Schone Kunsten, Antwerp, Belgium.

## 15TH-CENTURY FRENCH ART

In France, the Hundred Years' War decimated economic enterprise and prevented political stability. The anarchy of war and the weakness of the kings gave rise to a group of duchies, each with significant power. The strongest of these, as mentioned earlier, was the Duchy of Burgundy. Despite this instability, French artists joined the retinues of the wealthiest nobility—the dukes of Berry, Bourbon, and Nemours and sometimes the royal court—where they could continue to develop their art.

**PORTRAYING THE PIOUS** Images for private devotional use were popular in France, as in Flanders. Among the French artists whose paintings were in demand was JEAN FOUQUET (ca. 1420–1481), who worked for King Charles VII (the patron and client of Jacques Coeur; see FIG. 18-28) and for the duke of Nemours. Fouquet painted a diptych (two-paneled painting; FIG. **20-19**) for Étienne Chevalier. Despite lowly origins, Chevalier elevated himself in French society, and in 1452 Charles VII named him treasurer of France. In the left panel, Chevalier appears with his patron saint, Saint Stephen (Étienne in French), in a format commonly referred to as a donor portrait because an individual commissioned (or "gave") the portrait as evidence of devotion. Appropriately, Fouquet depicted Chevalier as devout—kneeling, with hands clasped in prayer. The representation of the pious donor with his standing saint recalls Flemish art, as do the three-quarter stances and the sharp, clear focus of the portraits. The artist depicted Saint Stephen holding the stone of his martyrdom (death by stoning) atop a volume of the Scriptures, thereby ensuring that viewers properly identify the saint. Fouquet rendered the entire image in meticulous detail and included a highly ornamented architectural setting.

In its original diptych form (the two panels were separated some time ago and now reside in different museums), the viewer would follow the gaze of Chevalier and Saint Stephen over to the right panel, which depicts the Virgin Mary and Christ Child. The juxtaposition of these two images allowed the patron to bear witness to the sacred. However, other interpretations present themselves. The integration of sacred and secular (especially the political or personal) prevalent in other Northern European artworks also emerges here, complicating the reading of this diptych. The depiction of the Virgin Mary was modeled after Agnès Sorel, the mistress of King Charles VII. Sorel was respected as a pious individual, and, according to an inscription, Chevalier commissioned this painting to fulfill a vow he made after Sorel's death in 1450. Thus, in addition to the religious interpretation of this diptych, there is surely a personal narrative here as well.

## 15TH-CENTURY GERMAN ART

Whereas the exclusive authority of the monarchies in France, England, and Spain fostered cohesive and widespread developments in the arts of those countries, the lack of a strong centralized power in the Holy Roman Empire (whose core was Germany) led to provincial artistic styles that the strict guild structure perpetuated. Because the Holy Roman Empire did not participate in the long, drawn-out saga of the Hundred Years' War, its economy was stable and prosperous. Without a dominant court culture to commission artworks and with the flourishing of the middle class, wealthy merchants and clergy became the primary German patrons during the 15th century.

## German Piety

**A ROSE AMONG THORNS** Most of the early years of STEPHAN LOCHNER (ca. 1400–1451) remain a mystery. Scholars have documented his artistic activity in Cologne in 1440, and by 1447 he had accrued sufficient respect to be named city councilor, representing the painters' guild. Lochner's painting from the 1430s, *Madonna in the Rose Garden* (FIG. **20-20**), presents an extremely popular theme in the Rhineland. The artist depicted the Virgin Mary and Christ Child in a rose arbor, a traditional reference to Mary's holiness ("a rose among thorns") and a symbol of her purity. Increasing interest in Rosary devotion no doubt contributed to the popularity of this theme. The Rosary, a devotional exercise in which one meditates on aspects of the lives of Christ and Mary while reciting prayers, particularly served the needs of the laity in a time of growing privatization of religion. Lochner presented this subject using stylized conventions. He established a symmetrical and very structured composition, and the exquisite gold background recalls Byzantine and medieval artworks. His use of established conventions can be attributed, in part, to the new patronage. Wealthy laypersons who desired such images for private devotional purposes or as status symbols relied on a familiar, recognizable iconography and presentation.

**FISHING IN LAKE GENEVA** As in Flanders, large-scale altarpieces were familiar sights in the Holy Roman Empire. Among the most notable of these is the *Altarpiece of Saint Peter* painted in 1444 for the chapel of Notre-Dame des Maccabées in the Cathedral of Saint Peter in Geneva. On one exterior wing of this triptych appears *Miraculous Draught of Fish* (FIG. **20-21**) by the Swiss

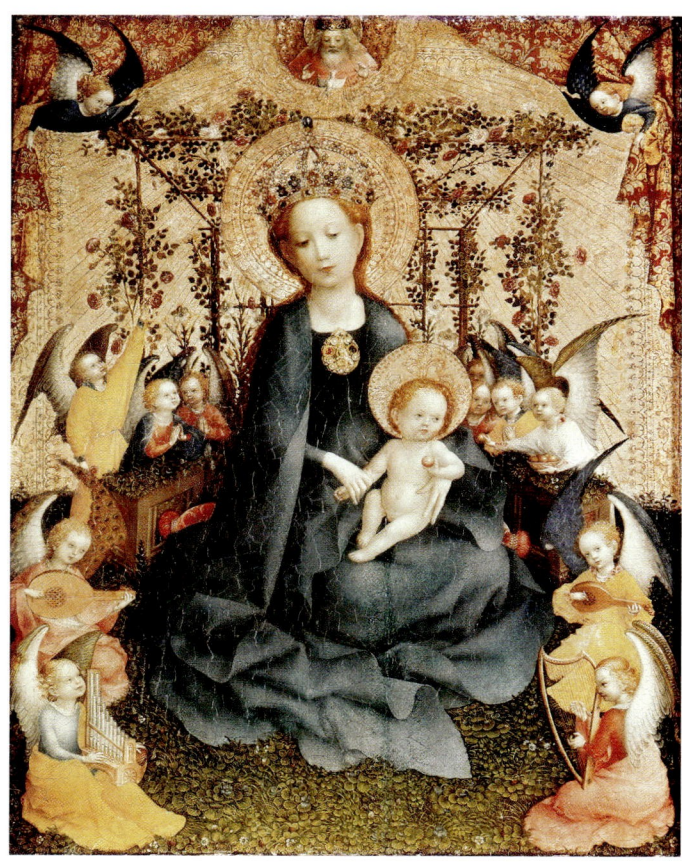

**20-20** STEPHAN LOCHNER, *Madonna in the Rose Garden,* ca. 1430–1435. Tempera on wood, approx. 1′ 8″ × 1′ 4″. Wallraf-Richartz Museum, Cologne.

**20-21** KONRAD WITZ, *Miraculous Draught of Fish,* from the *Altarpiece of Saint Peter,* from Chapel of Notre-Dame des Maccabées in the Cathedral of Saint Peter, Geneva, Switzerland, 1444. Oil on wood, approx. 4′ 3″ × 5′ 1″. Musée d'art et d'histoire, Geneva.

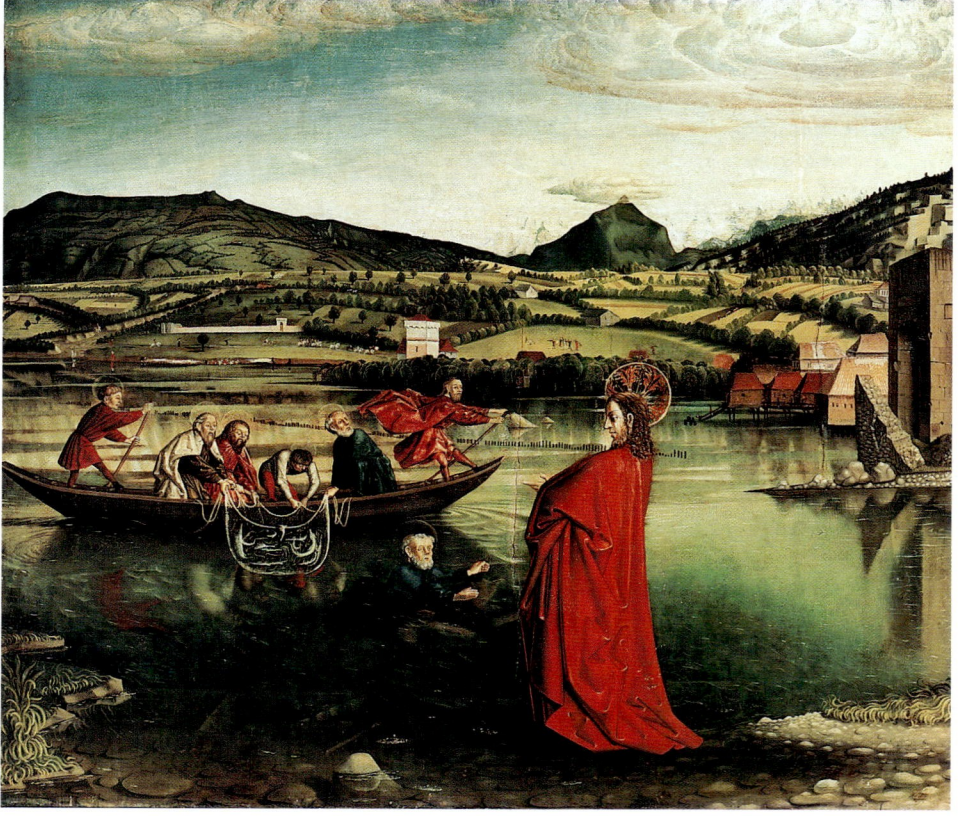

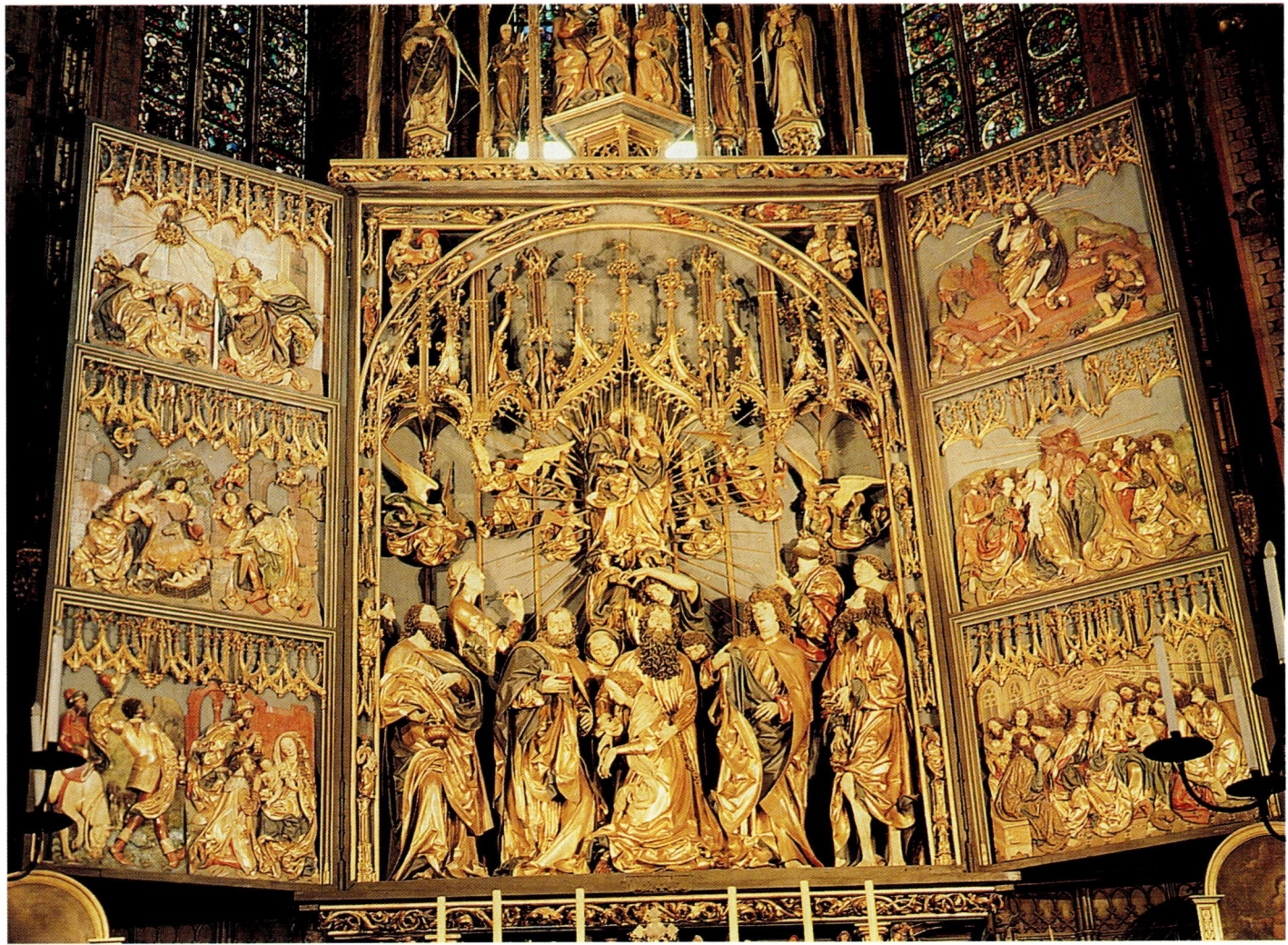

**20-22** Veit Stoss, *The Death and Assumption of the Virgin* (wings open), altar of the Virgin Mary, church of Saint Mary, Kraków, Poland, 1477–1489. Painted and gilded wood, 43′ × 35′.

painter Konrad Witz (ca. 1400–1446). The other exterior wing (not illustrated) depicts the release of Saint Peter from prison. The central panel has been lost. On the interior wings, Witz painted scenes of the Adoration of the Magi and of Saint Peter's presentation of the donor (Bishop François de Mies) to the Virgin and Child. *Miraculous Draught of Fish* is particularly significant because of the landscape's prominence. Witz showed precocious skill in the study of water effects—the sky glaze on the slowly moving lake surface, the mirrored reflections of the figures in the boat, and the transparency of the shallow water in the foreground. He observed and depicted the landscape so carefully that art historians have determined the exact location shown. Witz presented a view of the shores of Lake Geneva, with the town of Geneva on the right and Le Môle Mountain in the distance behind Christ's head. This painting is one of the first 15th-century works depicting a specific site.

**WITNESSING THE VIRGIN'S ASSUMPTION** The works of German artists who specialized in carving large wooden *retables* (altarpieces) reveal most forcefully the power of the Late Gothic style. The sculptor Veit Stoss (1447–1533) carved a great altarpiece (FIG. 20-22) for the church of Saint Mary in Kraków, Poland.

In the central boxlike shrine, huge figures (some are nine feet high) represent the Virgin's death and Assumption, and on the wings Stoss portrayed scenes from the lives of Christ and Mary. The altar expresses the intense piety of Gothic culture in its late phase, when artists used every figural and ornamental design resource from the vocabulary of Gothic art to heighten the emotion and to glorify the sacred event. In *The Death and Assumption of the Virgin*, the disciples of Christ congregate around the Virgin, who sinks down in death. One of them supports her, while another, just above her, wrings his hands in grief. Stoss posed others in attitudes of woe and psychic shock, striving for realism in every minute detail. Moreover, he engulfed the figures in restless, twisting, and curving swaths of drapery whose broken and writhing lines unite the whole tableau in a vision of agitated emotion. The artist's massing of sharp, broken, and pierced forms that dart flamelike through the composition—at once unifying and animating it— recalls the design principles of Late Gothic architecture (see FIG. 18-25). Indeed, in the Kraków altarpiece, Stoss merged sculpture and architecture, enhancing their union with paint and gilding.

**AN ORNATE SPIRITUAL VISION** Tilman Riemenschneider (ca. 1460–1531) depicted the Virgin's Assumption in the center

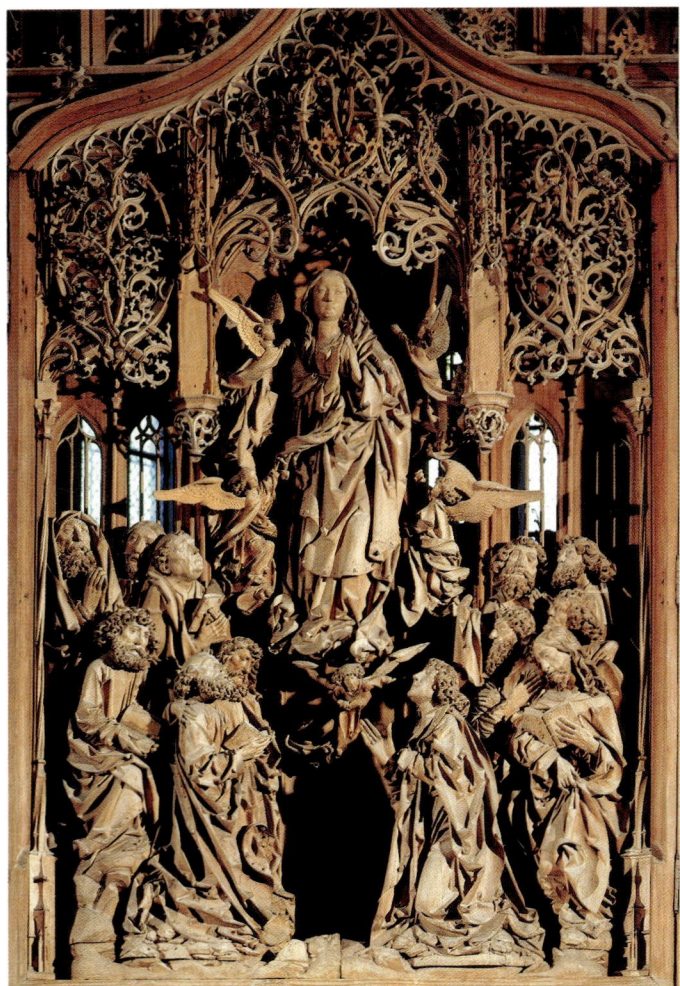

**20-23** TILMAN RIEMENSCHNEIDER, *The Assumption of the Virgin,* center panel of the *Creglingen Altarpiece,* parish church, Creglingen, Germany, ca. 1495–1499. Carved lindenwood, 6′ 1″ wide.

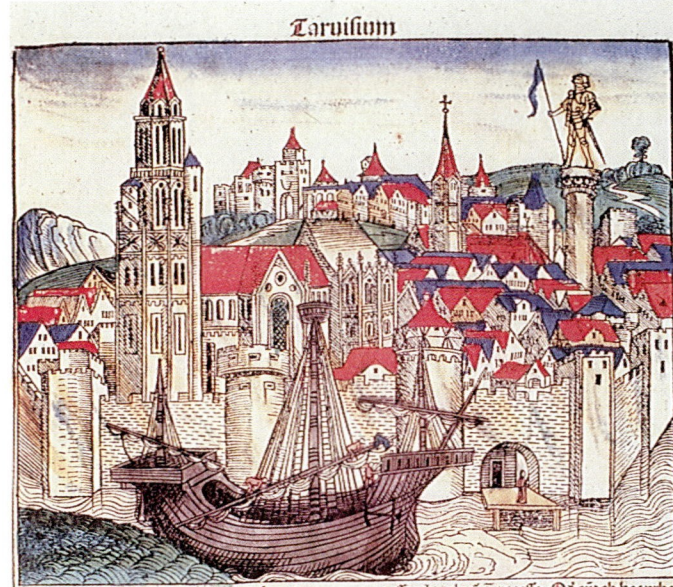

**20-24** MICHEL WOLGEMUT and Shop, "Tarvisium," page from the so-called *Nuremberg Chronicle,* 1493. Woodcut, approx. 1′ 2″ × 9″. Printed by Anton Koberger.

panel of the *Creglingen Altarpiece* (FIG. **20-23**), created for a parish church in Creglingen. He also incorporated intricate Gothic forms, especially in the altarpiece's elaborate canopy. By employing an endless and restless line that runs through the draperies of the figures in *The Assumption of the Virgin,* Riemenschneider succeeded in setting the whole design into fluid motion, and no individual element functions without the rest. The draperies float and flow around bodies lost within them, serving not as descriptions but as design elements that tie the figures to one another and to the framework. A look of psychic strain, a facial expression common to Riemenschneider's figures and consonant with the emerging age of disruption, heightens the spirituality of the figures, immaterial and weightless as they appear.

## Graphic Art

**GOING AGAINST THE GRAIN** A new age blossomed in the 15th century with a sudden technological advance that had widespread effects—the German invention of the *letterpress,* printing with movable type. Printing had been known in China centuries before but had never developed, as it did in 15th-century Europe, into a revolution in written communication and in the generation and management of information. Printing provided new and challenging media for artists, and the earliest form was the *woodcut*

(see "Graphic Changes: The Development of Printmaking," page 569). Using a gouging instrument, artists remove sections of wood blocks, sawing along the grain. They ink the ridges that carry the designs, and the hollows remain dry of ink and do not print. Artists produced woodcuts well before the development of movable-type printing. But when a rise in literacy and the improved economy necessitated production of illustrated books on a grand scale, artists met the challenge of bringing the woodcut picture onto the same page as the letterpress.

The illustrations (more than 650 of them!) for the so-called *Nuremberg Chronicle,* a history of the world produced in the shop of the Nuremberg artist MICHEL WOLGEMUT (1434–1519), document this achievement. The hand-colored page illustrated (FIG. **20-24**) represents Tarvisium (modern Tarvisio), a town in the extreme northeast of Italy, as it was in the "fourth age of the world" (according to the Latin inscription at top). The blunt, simple lines of the woodcut technique give a detailed perspective of Tarvisium, its harbor and shipping, its walls and towers, its churches and municipal buildings, and the baronial castle on the hill. Despite the numerous architectural structures, historians cannot determine whether this illustration represents the artist's accurate depiction of the city or his fanciful imagination. Artists often reprinted the same image as illustrations of different cities; hence, this depiction of Tarvisium was likely fairly general. Regardless, the work is a monument to a new craft, which expanded in concert with the art of the printed book.

### *Graphic Changes*
#### *The Development of Printmaking*

The popularity of prints over the centuries attests to the medium's enduring appeal. Generally speaking, a print is an artwork on paper, usually produced in multiple impressions. The set of prints an artist creates from a single print surface is often referred to as an *edition*. The printmaking process involves the transfer of ink from a printing surface to paper, which can be accomplished in several ways. During the 15th and 16th centuries, artists most commonly used the *relief* and *intaglio* methods of printmaking.

Artists produce relief prints by carving into a surface, usually wood. The oldest and simplest of the printing methods, relief printing requires artists to conceptualize their images negatively; that is, they remove the surface areas around the images. Thus, when the printmaker inks the surface, the carved-out areas remain clean, and a positive image results when the artist presses the printing block against paper. Because artists produce *woodcuts* through a subtractive process (removing parts of the material), it is difficult to create very thin, fluid, and closely spaced lines. As a result, woodcut prints tend to exhibit stark contrasts and sharp edges (see FIGS. Intro-8, 23-1, and 23-4).

In contrast to the production of relief prints, the intaglio method involves a positive process; the artist incises or scratches an image on a metal plate, often copper. The image can be created on the plate manually *(engraving* or *drypoint)* using a tool (a *burin* or *stylus;* see FIGS. 20-25, 21-26, 23-6, and 23-8) or chemically *(etching)*. In the latter process, an acid bath eats into the exposed parts of the plate where the artist has drawn through an acid-resistant coating. When the artist inks the surface of the intaglio plate and wipes it clean, the ink is forced into the incisions. Then the artist runs the plate and paper through a roller press, and the paper absorbs the remaining ink, creating the print. Because the artist "draws" the image onto the plate, intaglio prints possess a character different from that of relief prints. Engravings, drypoints, and etchings generally present a wider variety of linear effects. They also often reveal to a greater extent evidence of the artist's touch, the result of the hand's changing pressure and shifting directions.

The paper and inks artists use also affect the finished look of the printed image. During the 15th and 16th centuries, European printmakers had papers produced from cotton and linen rags that papermakers mashed with water into a pulp. The papermakers then applied a thin layer of this pulp to a wire screen and allowed it to dry to create the paper. As contact with the Far East increased, printmakers made greater use of what was called Japan paper (of mulberry fibers) and China paper. Artists, then as now, could select from a wide variety of inks. The type and proportion of the ink ingredients affect the consistency, color, and oiliness of inks, which various papers absorb differently. The portability of prints—paper is lightweight, and, until recently, the size of presses precluded large prints—has appealed to artists over the years. Further, the opportunity to produce many impressions from the same print surface is an attractive option. Relatively speaking, prints can be sold at cheaper prices than paintings or sculptures, significantly expanding the buying audience. Recently, scholars have attempted to ascertain the audience for prints as well as their market value during the 15th and 16th centuries. The limited amount of extant documentation, however, has hindered these efforts. Regardless, the number and quality of existing prints, both from northern Europe and Italy, attest to the importance of the print medium during the Renaissance.

**DRAWING ON METAL** The woodcut medium hardly had matured when the technique of engraving (inscribing on a hard surface), begun in the 1430s and well developed by 1450, proved much more flexible (see "Graphic Changes," above). Predictably, in the second half of the century, engraving began to replace the woodcut process, for making both book illustrations and widely popular single prints. Metal engraving produces an intaglio (incised) surface for printing; the incised lines (hollows) of the design, rather than the ridges, take the ink. It is the reverse of the woodcut technique, which produces *rilievo* (relief).

MARTIN SCHONGAUER (ca. 1430–1491) was the most skilled and subtle northern master of metal engraving. His *Saint Anthony Tormented by Demons* (FIG. **20-25**) shows both the versatility of the medium and the artist's mastery of it. The stoic saint is caught in a revolving thornbush of spiky demons, who claw and tear at him furiously. With unsurpassed skill and subtlety, Schongauer created marvelous distinctions of tonal values and textures—from smooth skin to rough cloth, from the furry and feathery to the hairy and scaly. The use of *hatching* to describe forms, probably developed by Schongauer, became standard among German graphic artists. The Italians preferred parallel hatching (compare Antonio Pollaiuolo's engraving, FIG. 21-26) and rarely adopted the other method, which, in keeping with the general northern approach to art, tends to describe the surfaces of things rather than their underlying structures.

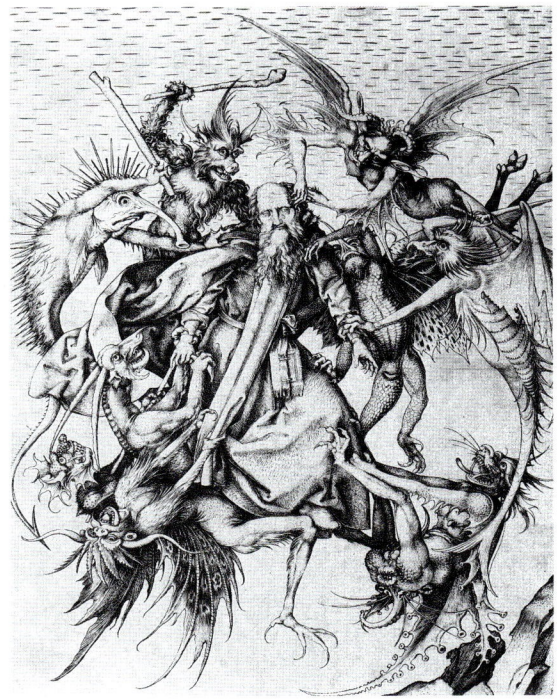

**20-25** MARTIN SCHONGAUER, *Saint Anthony Tormented by Demons*, ca. 1480–1490. Engraving, approx. 1′ 1″ × 11″. Metropolitan Museum of Art, New York (Rogers Fund, 1920).

**20-26** Portal, Colegio de San Gregorio, Valladolid, Spain, ca. 1498.

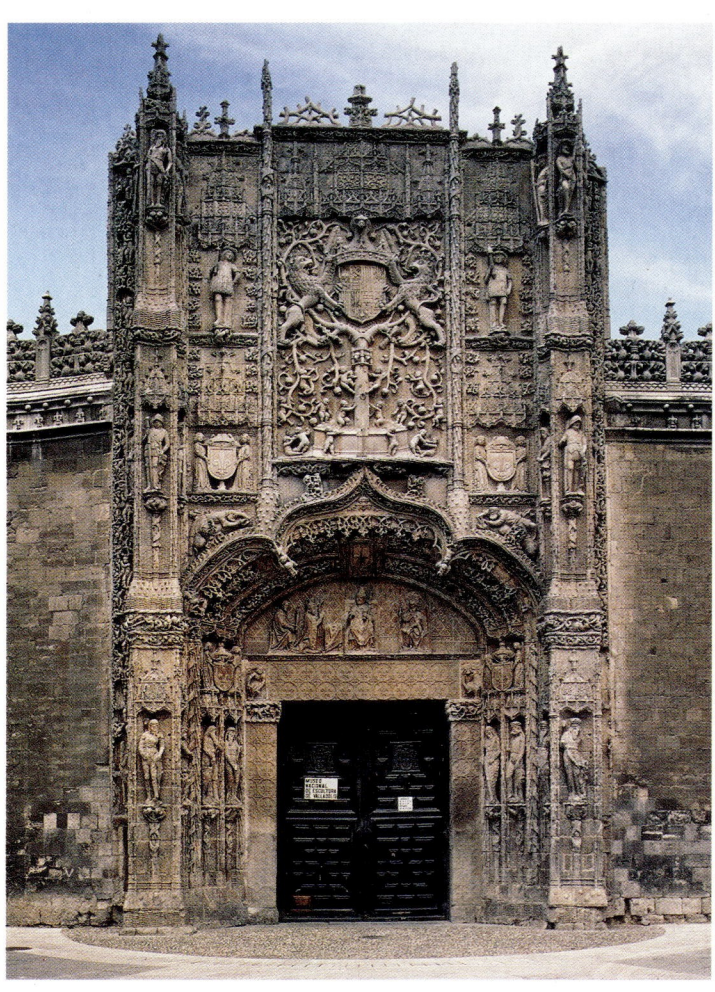

## 15TH-CENTURY SPANISH ART

Spain's ascent to power in Europe began in the mid-15th century with the marriage of Isabella of Castile (1451–1504) and Ferdinand of Aragon (1452–1516) in 1469. Together, Ferdinand and Isabella worked to strengthen royal control of the Spanish government. Eventually, their descendants became the most powerful monarchs in Europe.

**SILVERWORK-INSPIRED ARCHITECTURE** During the 15th century and well into the 16th, a Late Gothic style of architecture, the Plateresque, prevailed in Spain. *Plateresque* derives from the Spanish word *platero,* meaning silversmith, and relates to the style because of the delicate execution of its ornament. The Colegio de San Gregorio (Seminary of Saint Gregory; FIG. **20-26**) in the Castilian city of Valladolid handsomely exemplifies the Plateresque manner. Great carved retables, like the German altarpieces that influenced them (see FIGS. 20-22 and 20-23), appealed to church patrons and architects in Spain. They thus made such retables a conspicuous decorative feature of their exterior architecture, dramatizing a portal set into an otherwise blank wall. The Plateresque entrance of San Gregorio is a lofty sculptured stone screen that bears no functional relation to the architecture behind it. On the entrance level, lacelike tracery reminiscent of Moorish design hems the flamboyant ogival arches. A great screen, paneled into sculptured compartments, rises above the tracery. In the center, the branches of a huge pomegranate tree (symbolizing Granada, the Moorish capital of Spain captured by the Habsburgs in 1492) wreathe the coat of arms of King Ferdinand and Queen Isabella. Cupids play among the tree branches, and, flanking the central panel, niches enframe armed pages of the court, heraldic wild men (wild men symbolized aggression, and here as heralds announce the royal intentions), and armored soldiers, attesting to Spain's proud new militancy. In typical Plateresque and Late Gothic fashion, the activity of a thousand intertwined motifs unifies the whole design, which, in sum, creates an exquisitely carved panel greatly expanded in scale from the retables that inspired it.

## CONCLUSION

Northern and Spanish art in the 15th century was the product of political, religious, social, and economic changes. Among the notable transformations in art were the increased use of oil paints in Flanders, a greater illusionism in manuscript illumination, and the invention of movable-type printing in Germany. Flanders, in particular, was at the forefront of artistic developments, in part because of the power and patronage of the Burgundian dukes. This situation did not last long. Charles the Bold, who had assumed the title of duke of Burgundy in 1467, died in 1477, bringing to an end the dominance of the Burgundian Netherlands. France and the Holy Roman Empire divided the Burgundian territories. Eventually, through a series of fortuitous marriages, untimely deaths, and political shifts, Charles I, the grandson of Ferdinand and Isabella of Spain, united the three major dynastic lines — Habsburg, Burgundian, and Spanish.

| HUNDRED YEARS' WAR BEGINS, 1337 |
| THE PAPACY IN AVIGNON, 1305–1378 |

1375

| THE GREAT SCHISM IN THE CHURCH, 1378–1417 |
| THE NETHERLANDS UNDER THE DUKES OF BURGUNDY, 1384–1477 |

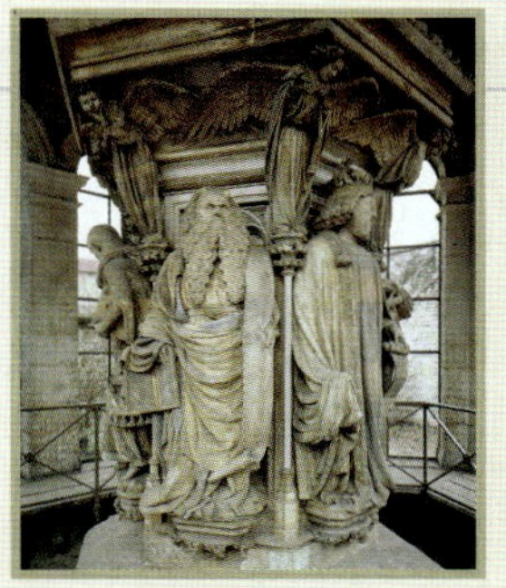

1  Claus Sluter, *Well of Moses,*
1395–1406

PHILIP THE BOLD (BURGUNDY)

JOHN THE FEARLESS

1425

2  | HUNDRED YEARS' WAR ENDS, 1453 |

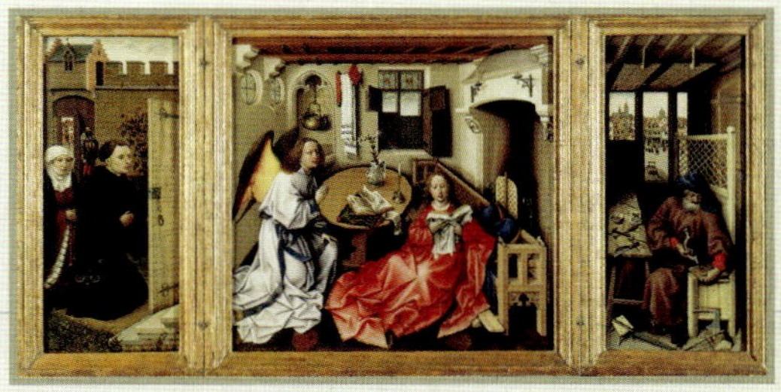

2  Robert Campin (Master of Flémalle), *Mérode Altarpiece,*
ca. 1425–1428

PHILIP THE GOOD

1467

CHARLES THE BOLD

1477

| BURGUNDY AND BURGUNDIAN NETHERLANDS PASS TO
HOLY ROMAN EMPIRE; MAXIMILIAN I, HABSBURG EMPEROR, 1486 |

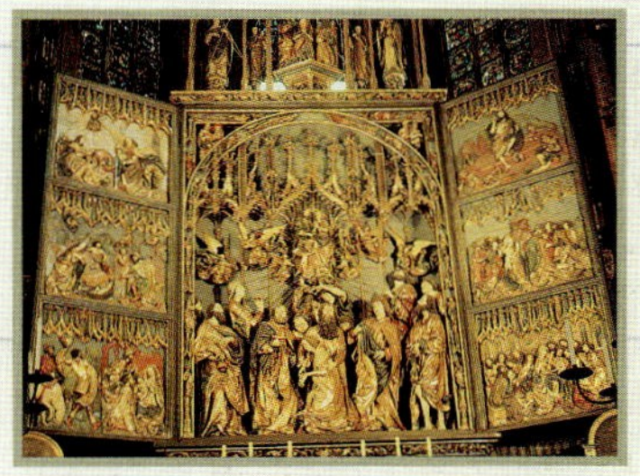

3  Veit Stoss, *The Death and Assumption
of the Virgin Mary,* 1477–1489

| MOORISH KINGDOM OF GRANADA FALLS TO SPAIN, 1492 |
3  | COLUMBUS ARRIVES IN WEST INDIES, 1492 |
| FRENCH INVADE ITALY, 1494 |

4

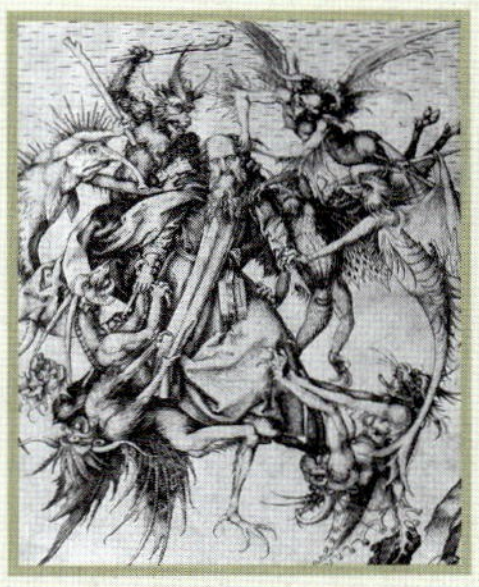

FERDINAND (ARAGON) AND ISABELLA (CASTILE), CATHOLIC RULERS OF SPAIN

4  Martin Schongauer,
*Saint Anthony Tormented
by Demons,* ca. 1480–1490

1500

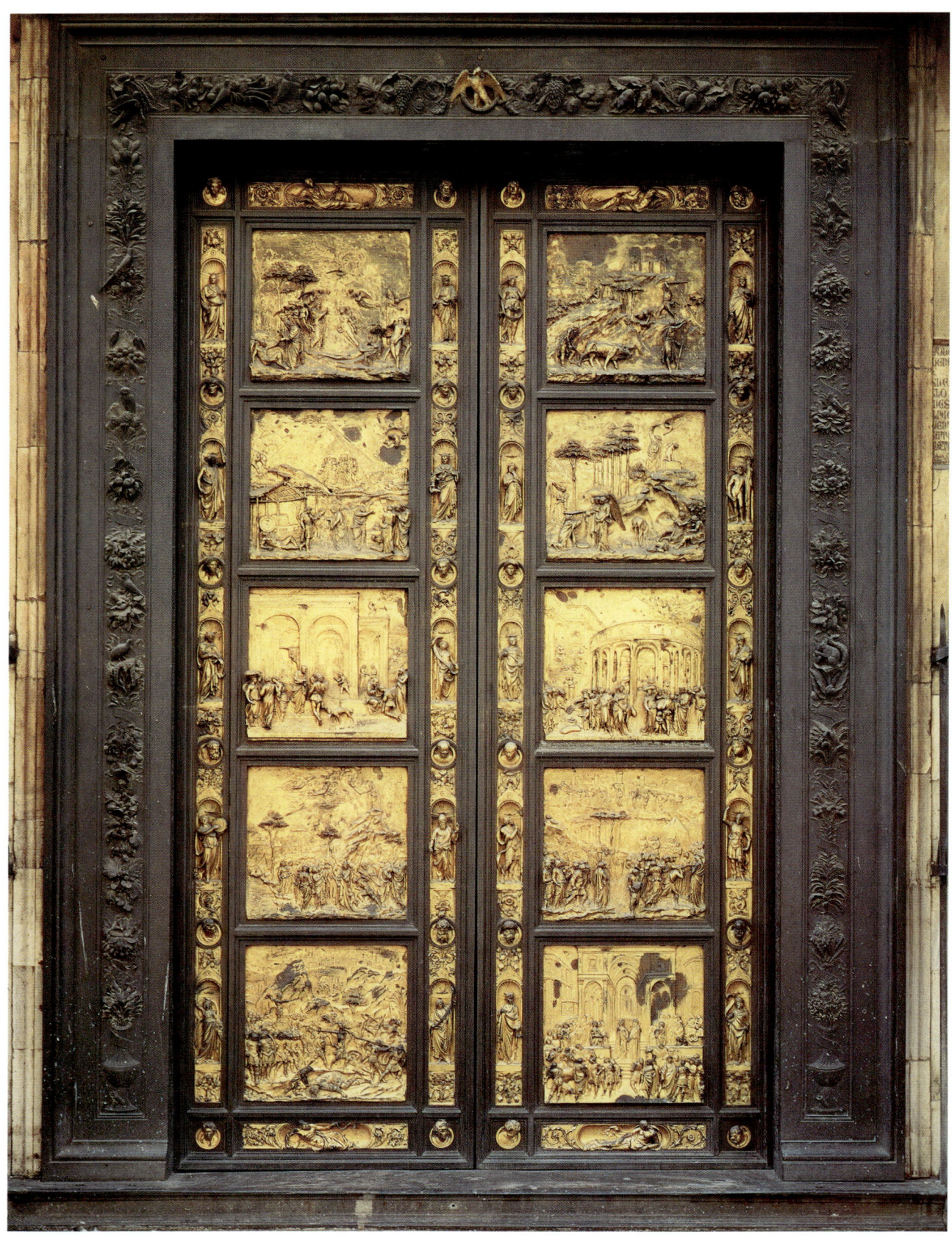

Lᴏʀᴇɴᴢᴏ Gʜɪʙᴇʀᴛɪ, east doors ("Gates of Paradise"), baptistery of Florence Cathedral, Florence, Italy, 1425–1452. Gilded bronze relief, approx. 17′ high. Modern copy, ca. 1980. Original panels in Museo dell'Opera del Duomo, Florence.

# 21

# HUMANISM AND THE ALLURE OF ANTIQUITY

## 15TH-CENTURY ITALIAN ART

The 15th century in Italy witnessed the flourishing of a significantly new and expanded artistic culture—the Renaissance—whose early development was chronicled in Chapter 19. The continued maturation of this culture was due to several factors, among them the spread of humanism, political and economic fluctuations throughout Italy, and a fortunate abundance of artistic talent.

**THE SPREAD OF HUMANISM** The humanism disseminated by Petrarch and Boccaccio during the 14th century had greater impact as the 15th century progressed. Increasingly, Italians in elite circles embraced the tenets underlying humanism—an emphasis on education and on expanding knowledge (especially of classical antiquity), the exploration of individual potential and a desire to excel, and a commitment to civic responsibility and moral duty.

For humanists, the quest for knowledge began with the legacy of the Greeks and Romans—the writings of Plato, Socrates, Aristotle, Ovid, and others. The development of a literature based on a vernacular (commonly spoken) Tuscan dialect expanded the audience for humanist writings. Further, the invention of movable metal type by the German Johann Gutenberg around 1445 facilitated the printing and wide distribution of books. Italians enthusiastically embraced this new printing process; by 1464 Subiaco (near Rome) boasted a press, and by 1469 Venice had established one as well. Among the first books printed in Italy using this new press was Dante's vernacular epic, *Divine Comedy*. The production of editions in Foligno (1472), Mantua (1472), Venice (1472), Naples (1477 and 1478–1479), and Milan (1478) testifies to the widespread popularity during the 15th century of Dante's epic poem about Heaven, Purgatory, and Hell.

The humanists did not restrict their learning to antique writings. They avidly acquired information in a wide range of fields, including science (such as botany, geology, geography, and optics), medicine, and engineering. Leonardo da Vinci's phenomenal expertise in many fields—from art and architecture to geology, aerodynamics, hydraulics, botany, and military science, among many others—serves to define the modern notion of a "Renaissance man."

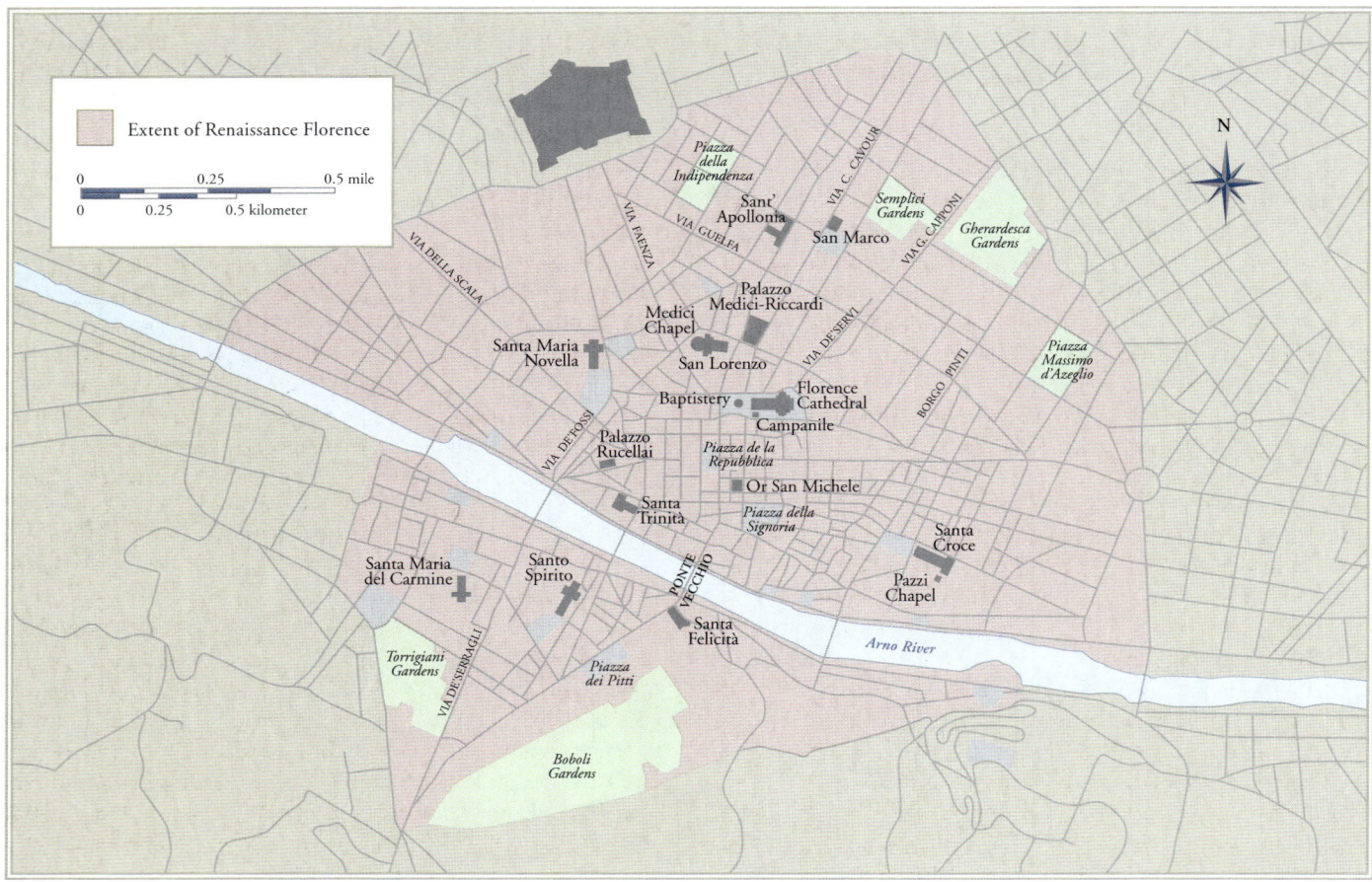

MAP 21-1 Renaissance Florence.

RECOGNIZING ACHIEVEMENT Humanism also fostered a belief in individual potential and encouraged individual achievement, along with civic responsibility. Whereas people in medieval society accorded great power to divine will in determining the events that affected lives, those in Renaissance Italy adopted a more secular stance. Humanists not only encouraged individual improvement but also rewarded excellence with fame and honor. Achieving and excelling through hard work became moral imperatives.

OF WEALTH AND POWER Fifteenth-century Italy witnessed constant fluctuations in its political and economic spheres, including shifting power relations among the numerous city-states and the rise of princely courts. *Condottieri* (military leaders) with large numbers of mercenary troops at their disposal played a major role in the ongoing struggle for power. Princely courts, such as those in Urbino and Mantua, emerged as cultural and artistic centers (see "Cultivating Culture: The Princely Courts and Artistic Patronage," page 575). The association of humanism with education and culture appealed to accomplished individuals of high status, and humanism had its greatest impact among the elite and powerful, such as those associated with these courts. It was these individuals who were in the best position to commission art. As a result, much of Italian Renaissance art was infused with humanist ideas. The intersection of art with humanist doctrines during the Renaissance can be seen in the popularity of subjects selected from classical history or mythology, in the increased concern with developing perspectival systems and depicting anatomy accurately, in the revival of portraiture and other self-aggrandizing forms of patronage, and in citizens' extensive participation in civic and religious art commissions.

Because high-level patronage required significant accumulated wealth, the individuals and families who had managed to prosper economically came to the fore in artistic circles. Among the best known was the Medici family, which acquired its vast fortune from banking. Although they were not a court family, the Medici used their tremendous wealth to wield great power and to commission art and architecture on a scale rarely seen, then or since. The Medici were such lavish patrons of art and learning that, to this day, the term *Medici* is widely used to refer to a generous patron of the fine arts.

The historical context that gave rise to the Renaissance and the importance of patronage account for the character of 15th-century Italian art. In addition, the sheer serendipity of the abundance of exceedingly talented artists also must be considered. Renaissance Italy experienced major shifts in artistic models, such as increased interest in perspective and illusionism. In part, these shifts were due to a unique artistic environment in which skilled artists, through industriousness and dialogue with others, forever changed the direction and perception of art.

# FLORENCE

## Sculpture and Civic Pride in the Early Renaissance

We begin our discussion of 15th-century Italian art with a competition in 1401 for a design for the east doors of the Florence baptistery (see FIG. 17-18). Artists and public alike considered this

## Cultivating Culture
### The Princely Courts and Artistic Patronage

The absence of a single authoritative sovereign ruling all of Italy and the fragmented nature of the independent city-states provided a fertile breeding ground for the ambitions of the power-hungry. In the 15th century, Italian society witnessed the expansion of princely courts throughout the peninsula. A prince was in essence the lord of a territory, and, despite this generic title, he could have been a duke, marquis, cardinal, pope, tyrant, or papal vicar. At this time, major princely courts emerged in Milan, Naples, Ferrara, Savoy, Mantua, and papal Rome. Rather than denoting a specific organizational structure or physical entity, the term *princely court* referred to a power relationship between the prince and the territory's inhabitants based on imperial models. Each prince worked tirelessly not just to preserve but also to extend his control and authority, seeking to establish a societal framework of people who looked to him for jobs, favors, protection, prestige, and leadership. The importance of these princely courts derived from their role as centers of power and culture.

The efficient functioning of a princely court required a sophisticated administrative structure. Each prince employed an extensive household staff, ranging from counts, nobles, cooks, waiters, stewards, footmen, stable hands, and ladies-in-waiting to dog handlers, leopard keepers, pages, and runners (who did menial fetching chores). The duke of Milan had more than 40 chamberlains to attend to his personal needs alone. Each prince also needed an elaborate bureaucracy to oversee political, economic, and military operations and to ensure his continued control. These officials included secretaries, lawyers, captains, ambassadors, and condottieri. Burgeoning international diplomacy and trade made each prince the center of an active and privileged sphere. Their domains extended to the realm of culture, for they saw themselves as more than political, military, and economic leaders. The princes felt responsible for the vitality of cultural life in their territories, and art was a major component for developing a cultured populace. Visual imagery also appealed to them as effective propaganda for reinforcing their control. As undoubtedly the wealthiest individuals in their regions, princes possessed the means to commission numerous artworks and buildings. Thus, art functioned in several capacities—as evidence of princely sophistication and culture, as a form of prestige or commemoration, as public education and propaganda, as a demonstration of wealth, and as a source of visual pleasure.

Princes often researched in advance the reputations and styles of the artists and architects they commissioned. Such assurances of excellence were necessary, because the quality of the work reflected not just on the artist but on the patron as well. Yet despite the importance of individual style, princes sought artists who also were willing, at times, to subordinate their personal styles to work collaboratively on large-scale projects.

Princes bestowed on selected individuals the title of "court artist." Serving as a court artist had its benefits, among them a guaranteed salary (not always forthcoming), living quarters in the palace, liberation from guild restrictions, and, on occasion, status as a member of the prince's inner circle, perhaps even a knighthood. For artists struggling to elevate their profession from the ranks of craftspeople, working for a prince presented a marvelous opportunity. Until the 16th century, artists had limited status and were in the same class as small shopkeepers and petty merchants. Indeed, at court dinners, artists most often were seated with other members of the salaried household: tailors, cobblers, barbers, and upholsterers. Thus, the possibility of advancement was a powerful and constant incentive.

Princes demanded a great deal from court artists. Artists not only created the frescoes, portraits, and sculptures that have become their legacies but also designed tapestries, seat covers, costumes, masks, and decorations for various court festivities. Because princes constantly entertained, received ambassadors and dignitaries, and needed to maintain a high profile to reinforce their authority, lavish social functions were the norm. Artists often created gifts for visiting nobles and potentates. Recipients judged such gifts on the quality of both the work and the materials. By using expensive materials—gold leaf, silver leaf, lapis lazuli, silk, and velvet brocade—princes could impress others with their wealth and good taste.

The experiences of court artists varied widely; some princes treated them as mere servants, others as trusted colleagues. At one end of the spectrum was Perino del Vaga, whose life at the papal court was described by biographer Giorgio Vasari: "[He had] to draw day and night and to meet the demands of the Palace, and, among other things, to make the designs of embroideries, of engravings for banner-makers, and of innumerable ornaments required by the caprice of Farnese and other Cardinals and noblemen. In short, . . . being always surrounded by sculptors, masters in stucco, wood-carvers, seamsters, embroiderers, painters, gilders, and other suchlike craftsmen, he had never an hour of repose."[1] In contrast was Leonardo da Vinci's treatment at the hands of his last patron, King Francis I of France, in whose arms the great artist is said to have died.

For princes who harbored dreams of expanding their control and who wanted to craft suitable legacies, art was indispensable. Hence, the history of Renaissance art cannot be fully understood without serious consideration of courtly culture.

[1] Giorgio Vasari, *Lives of the Painters, Sculptors and Architects,* translated by Gaston du C. de Vere (New York: Knopf, 1996), 2: 184.

---

commission particularly prestigious because of the intended placement of the doors on the baptistery's east side, facing the cathedral entrance. Even at this early date, many of the traits that characterized Renaissance art were evident. These include the development of a new pictorial illusionism, patronage as both a civic imperative and a form of self-promotion, and the esteem increasingly accorded to artists.

Andrea Pisano (ca. 1270–1348), unrelated to the 13th-century Italian sculptors Nicola (see FIGS. 19-2 and 19-3) and Giovanni (see FIG. 19-4), had designed the south doors of the same structure between 1330 and 1335. In 1401, the Arte di Calimala (wool merchants' guild) sponsored the competition for the second set of doors, requiring each entrant to submit a relief panel depicting the sacrifice of Isaac. This biblical event centers on God's order to Abraham that he sacrifice his son Isaac as a demonstration of Abraham's devotion to God. Just as Abraham is about to comply, an angel intervenes and stops him from plunging the knife into his son's throat. Because of the parallel between Abraham's willingness to sacrifice Isaac and God's sacrifice of his Son, Jesus Christ, to redeem mankind, the sacrifice of Isaac was often linked to the Crucifixion. Both refer to covenants, and given that the sacrament of baptism initiates the neonate, or convert, into the possibilities of these covenants, Isaac's sacrifice was certainly appropriate for representation on a baptistery.

The selection of this theme may also have been influenced by historical developments. In the late 1390s, Giangaleazzo Visconti of Milan began a military campaign to take over the Italian peninsula. By 1401, when the directors of the cathedral's artworks initiated this competition, Visconti's troops had virtually surrounded Florence (MAP 21-1), and its independence was in serious jeopardy. Despite dwindling water and food supplies, Florentine officials exhorted the public to defend the city's freedom. For example, the humanist chancellor, Coluccio Salutati, whose Latin style of writing was widely influential, urged his fellow citizens to adopt the republican ideal of civil and political liberty associated with ancient Rome and to identify themselves with its spirit. To be Florentine was to be Roman; freedom was the distinguishing virtue of both. (Florentine faith and sacrifice were rewarded in 1402, when Visconti died suddenly, ending the invasion threat.) The story of Abraham and Isaac, with its theme of sacrifice, paralleled the message city officials had conveyed to inhabitants. It is certainly plausible that the Arte di Calimala, asserting both its preeminence among Florentine guilds and its civic duty, selected the subject with this in mind.

Those supervising this project selected as semifinalists seven artists from among the many who entered the widely advertised competition for the commission. Only the panels of the two finalists, LORENZO GHIBERTI (1378–1455) and FILIPPO BRUNELLESCHI (1377–1446), have survived. In 1402, the selection committee awarded the commission to Ghiberti. Both artists used the same

French Gothic *quatrefoil* frames Andrea Pisano had used for the baptistery's south doors and depicted the same moment of the narrative—the angel's halting of the action. Examining these two panels provides insight into some stylistic indications of the direction Early Renaissance art was to take during the 15th century.

**ABRAHAM'S SACRIFICE** Brunelleschi's panel (FIG. 21-1) shows a sturdy and vigorous interpretation of the theme, with something of the emotional agitation favored by Giovanni Pisano (see FIG. 19-4). Abraham seems suddenly to have summoned the dreadful courage needed to kill his son at God's command—he lunges forward, draperies flying, exposing Isaac's throat to the knife. Matching Abraham's energy, the saving angel darts in from the left, grabbing Abraham's arm to stop the killing. Brunelleschi's figures demonstrate his ability to observe carefully and represent faithfully all the elements in the biblical narrative.

**EMULATING ANTIQUE MODELS** Where Brunelleschi imbued his image with dramatic emotion, Ghiberti emphasized grace and smoothness. In Ghiberti's panel (FIG. 21-2), Abraham appears in the familiar Gothic S-curve pose and seems to contemplate the act he is about to perform, even as he draws his arm back to strike. The figure of Isaac, beautifully posed and rendered, recalls Greco-Roman statuary and could be regarded as the first truly classicizing nude since antiquity. (Compare, for example, the torsion of Isaac's body and the dramatic turn of his head with those of the Hellenistic statue of a Gaul thrusting a sword into his own chest, FIG. 5-80). Unlike his medieval predecessors, Ghiberti revealed a genuine appreciation of the nude male form and a deep interest in how the muscular system and skeletal structure move the human body. Even the altar on which Isaac kneels displays Ghiberti's emulation of antique models. It is decorated with acanthus scrolls of a type that commonly adorned Roman temple friezes in Italy and throughout the former Roman Empire (see, for example, FIG. 10-30). These classical references reflect the increasing influence of humanism.

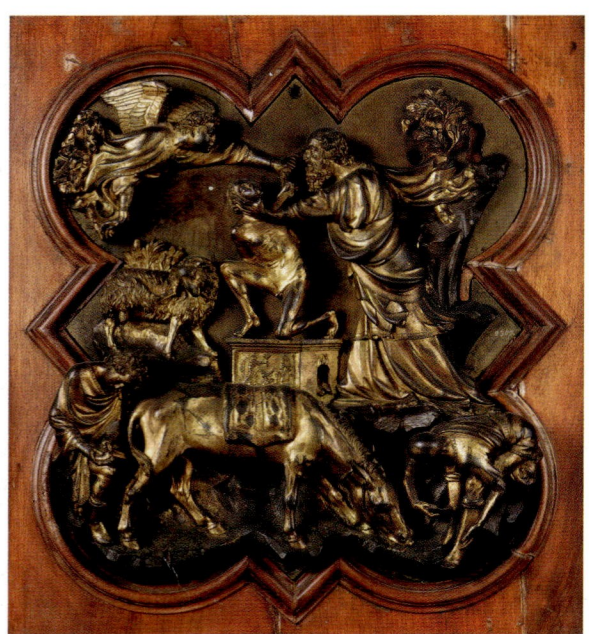

21-1 FILIPPO BRUNELLESCHI, *Sacrifice of Isaac,* competition panel for east doors, baptistery of Florence Cathedral, Florence, Italy, 1401–1402. Gilded bronze relief, 1′ 9″ × 1′ 5″. Museo Nazionale del Bargello, Florence.

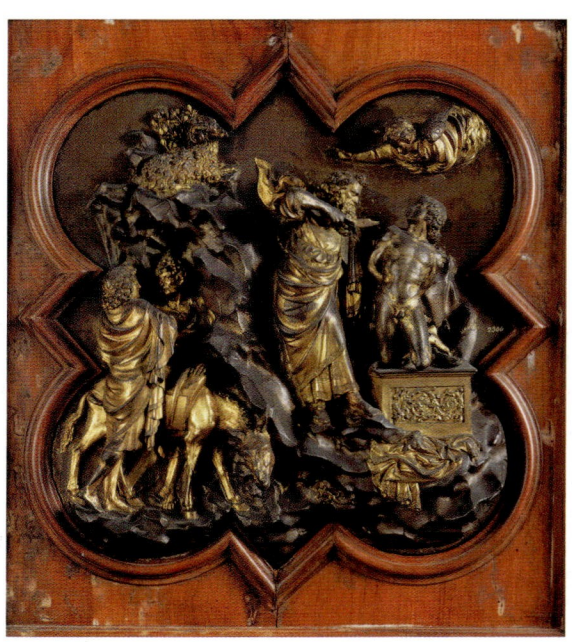

21-2 LORENZO GHIBERTI, *Sacrifice of Isaac,* competition panel for east doors, baptistery of Florence Cathedral, Florence, Italy, 1401–1402. Gilded bronze relief, 1′ 9″ × 1′ 5″. Museo Nazionale del Bargello, Florence.

Ghiberti's training included both painting and goldsmithery. His careful treatment of the gilded bronze surfaces, with their sharply and accurately incised detail, proves his skill as a goldsmith. As a painter, he was interested in spatial illusion. The rocky landscape seems to emerge from the blank panel toward the viewer, as does the strongly foreshortened angel. Brunelleschi's image, in contrast, emphasizes the planar orientation of the surface.

That Ghiberti cast his panel in only two pieces (thereby reducing the amount of bronze needed) no doubt impressed the selection committee. Ghiberti's construction method differed from that of Brunelleschi, who built his from several cast pieces. Thus, not only would Ghiberti's doors, as proposed, be lighter and more impervious to the elements, but they also represented a significant cost savings.

Ghiberti's submission clearly had much to recommend it, both stylistically and technically. Although Ghiberti's image was perhaps less overtly emotional than Brunelleschi's, it was more cohesive and presented a more convincing spatial illusion. Ghiberti further developed these pictorial effects, sometimes thought alien to sculpture, in his later work.

Ghiberti's pride in winning the commission is evident in his description of the award, which also reveals the fame and glory increasingly accorded to individual achievement during the Early Renaissance:

> To me was conceded the palm of the victory by all the experts and by all . . . who had competed with me. To me the honor was conceded universally and with no exception. To all it seemed that I had at that time surpassed the others without exception, as was recognized by a great council and an investigation of learned men. . . . The testimonial of the victory was given in my favor by all. . . . It was granted to me and determined that I should make the bronze door for this church.[1]

Ghiberti completed the 28 door panels depicting scenes from the New Testament in 1424. Church officials eventually decided to move the doors to the baptistery's north side.

**A FEAST IN PERSPECTIVE** Like Ghiberti, DONATELLO (ca. 1386–1466) was another sculptor who carried forward most dramatically the search for innovative forms capable of expressing the new ideas of the Early Renaissance. Donatello shared the humanist enthusiasm for Roman virtue and form. His greatness lies in an extraordinary versatility and a depth that led him through a spectrum of themes fundamental to human experience and through stylistic variations that express these themes with unprecedented profundity and force. Donatello understood the different aesthetic conventions artists routinely invoked at the time to distinguish their depictions of the real from those of the ideal and the earthly from the spiritual. His expansive knowledge and skill allowed him to portray this sweeping range with great facility. Further, as an astute observer of human life, Donatello could, with ease, depict figures of diverse ages, ranks, and human conditions. Few artists could match this range. That Donatello advanced both naturalistic illusion and classical idealism in sculpture remains a remarkable achievement.

This illusionism, like that Ghiberti pursued in his *Sacrifice of Isaac* panel, is evident in Donatello's bronze relief, *Feast of Herod* (FIG. **21-3**), on the baptismal font in the Siena baptistery. Salome (to the right) still dances even though she already has delivered the severed head of John the Baptist, which the kneeling executioner offers to King Herod. The other figures recoil in horror

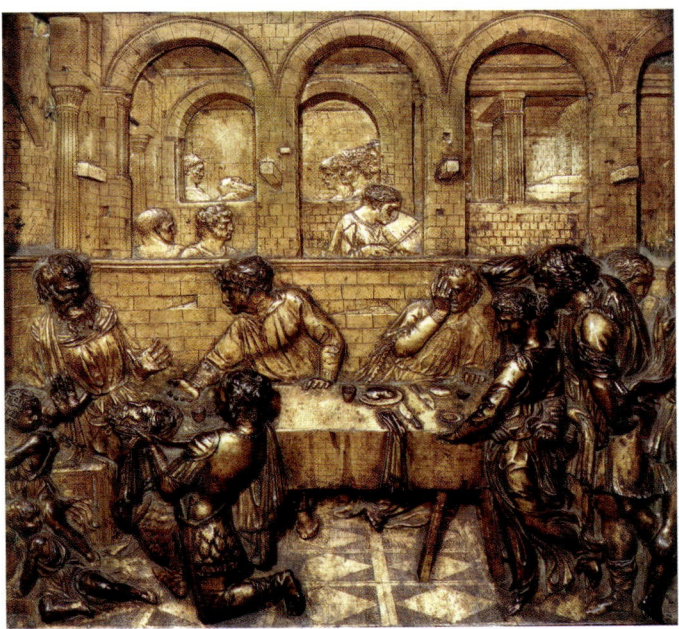

21-3 DONATELLO, *Feast of Herod,* from the baptismal font of Siena Cathedral, Siena, Italy, ca. 1425. Gilded bronze relief, approx. 1′ 11″ × 1′ 11″.

into two groups. At the right, one man covers his face with his hand; at the left, Herod and two terrified children shrink back in dismay. The psychic explosion drives the human elements apart, leaving a gap across which the emotional electricity crackles. This masterful stagecraft obscures another drama Donatello was playing out on the stage itself. The *Feast* marked the advent of rationalized perspective space, long prepared for in 14th-century Italian art and recognized by Donatello and his generation as a way to intensify the optical reality of the action and the characterization of the actors. Donatello, using pictorial perspective, opened the space of the action well into the distance, showing two arched courtyards and groups of attendants in the background. This penetration of the panel surface by spatial illusion replaced the flat grounds and backdrop areas of the medieval past. Ancient Roman illusionism (compare FIG. 10-16) had returned.

**KEEPING PERSPECTIVE** Fourteenth-century Italian artists, such as Duccio and the Lorenzetti brothers, had used several devices to indicate distance, but with the invention of "true" linear perspective (a discovery generally attributed to Brunelleschi), Early Renaissance artists acquired a way to make the illusion of distance mathematical and certain (see "Depicting Objects in Space: Perspectival Systems in the Early Renaissance," page 578). In effect, they thought of the picture plane as a transparent window through which the observer looks to see the constructed pictorial world. This discovery was enormously important, for it made possible what has been called the "rationalization of sight." It brought all our random and infinitely various visual sensations under a simple rule that could be expressed mathematically.

Indeed, the Renaissance artists' interest in perspective (based on principles already known to the ancient Greeks and Romans) reflects the emergence of science itself, which is, put simply, the mathematical ordering of our observations of the physical world. The observer's position of looking "through" a picture into the painted "world" is precisely that of scientific observers fixing their gaze on the carefully placed or located datum of their research. Of

## Depicting Objects in Space
### Perspectival Systems in the Early Renaissance

Scholars long have noted the Renaissance fascination with perspective. In essence, portraying perspective involves constructing a convincing illusion of space in two-dimensional imagery while unifying all objects within a single spatial system. Renaissance artists were not the first to focus on depicting illusionistic space; both the Greeks and the Romans were well versed in perspectival rendering. However, the perspectival systems developed during the Renaissance contrasted sharply with the portrayal of space during the preceding medieval period, when spiritual concerns superseded interest in the illusionistic presentation of objects.

Renaissance perspectival systems included both linear perspective and atmospheric perspective. Developed by Brunelleschi, *linear perspective* allows artists to determine mathematically the relative size of rendered objects to correlate them with the visual recession into space, and can be either one-point or two-point (see diagrams below). In one-point linear perspective, the artist first must identify a horizontal line that marks, in the image, the horizon in the distance (hence the term *horizon line*). The artist then selects a *vanishing point* on that horizon line (often located at the

exact center of the line). By drawing *orthogonals* (diagonal lines) from the edges of the picture to the vanishing point, the artist creates a structural grid that organizes the image and determines the size of objects within the image's illusionistic space. Under this system of linear perspective, artists often foreshorten a figure as the body recedes back into an illusionistic space, as seen in Andrea Mantegna's *Dead Christ* (FIG. 21-48). Among the works that provide clear examples of one-point linear perspective are Masaccio's *Holy Trinity* (FIG. 21-12), Leonardo da Vinci's *Last Supper* (see FIG. 22-3), and Raphael's *School of Athens* (see FIG. 22-17). Two-point linear perspective also involves the establishment of a horizon line. Rather than utilizing a single vanishing point along this horizon line, the artist identifies two of them. The orthogonals that result from drawing lines from an object to each of the vanishing points creates, as in one-point perspective, a grid that indicates the relative size of objects receding into space. An example of two-point perspective is Titian's *Madonna of the Pesaro Family* (see FIG. 22-36).

Rather than rely on a structured mathematical system (as does linear perspective), *atmospheric perspective* involves optical phenomena. Artists using atmospheric (sometimes called *aerial*) perspective exploit the principle that the farther back the object is in space, the blurrier, less detailed, and bluer it appears. Further, color saturation and value contrast diminish as the image recedes into the distance. Leonardo da Vinci used atmospheric perspective to great effect, as seen in works such as *Virgin of the Rocks* (see FIG. 22-1) and *Mona Lisa* (see FIG. 22-4).

These two methods of creating the illusion of space in pictures are not exclusive, and Renaissance artists often used both to heighten the sensation of three-dimensional space, as visible in Raphael's *Marriage of the Virgin* (see FIG. 22-18).

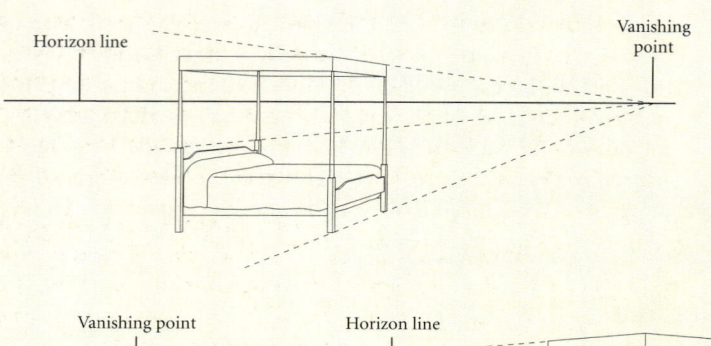

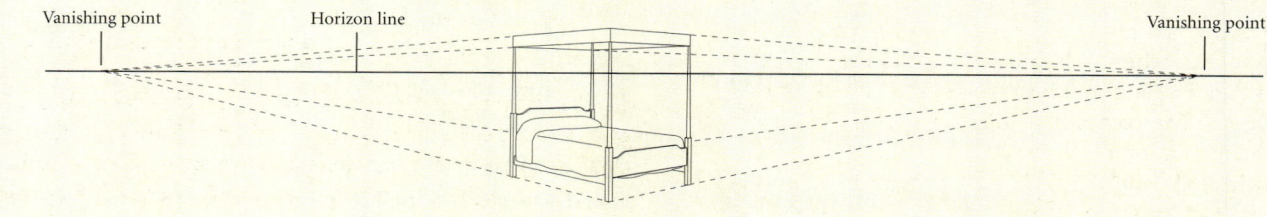

course, Early Renaissance artists were not primarily scientists; they simply found perspective an effective way to order and clarify their compositions.

Nonetheless, the art viewer cannot doubt that perspective, with its new mathematical certitude, conferred a kind of aesthetic legitimacy on painting by making the picture *measurable* and exact. According to Plato, measure is the basis of beauty. The art of Greece certainly was based on this belief. In the Renaissance, when humanists rediscovered Plato and eagerly read his works, artists once again exalted the principle of measure as the foundation of the beautiful in the fine arts. The projection of measurable objects on flat surfaces influenced the character of Renaissance paintings and made possible scale drawings, maps, charts, graphs, and diagrams—means of exact representation that laid the foundation

for modern science and technology. Mathematical truth and formal beauty conjoined in the minds of Renaissance artists.

**THE "GATES OF PARADISE"** Ghiberti was among the Italian artists in the 15th century who embraced a unified system for representing space; his enthusiasm for perspectival illusion is particularly evident in the famous east doors (FIG. **21-4**) commissioned from him by church officials in 1425 for the baptistery of Florence Cathedral. Michelangelo later declared these as "so beautiful that they would do well for the gates of Paradise."[2] Three sets of doors provide access to the baptistery (see FIG. 17-18). Andrea Pisano created the first set, on the south side, between 1330 and 1335. Ghiberti's first pair of doors (1403–1424), the result of the competition, was moved to the north doorway

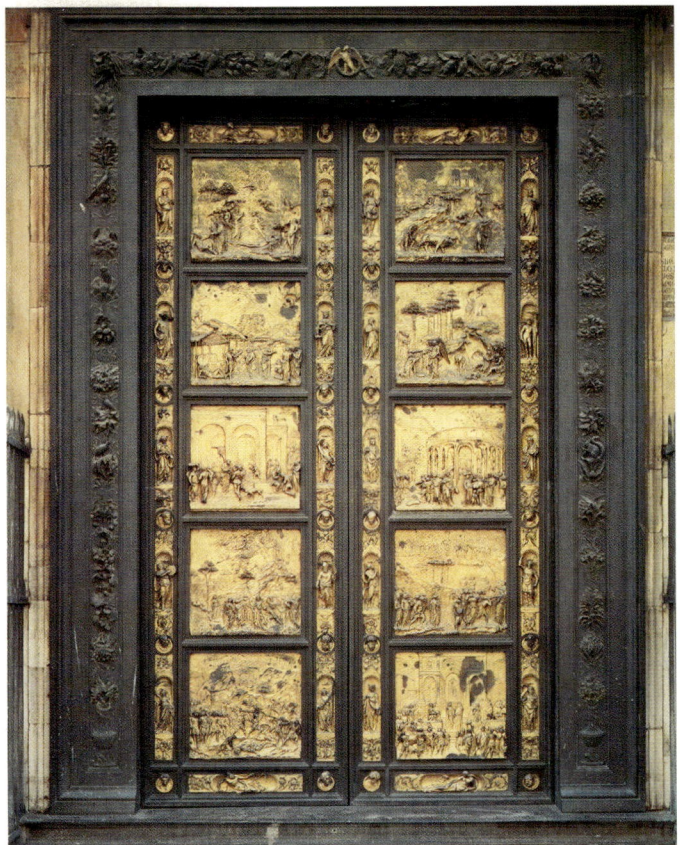

21-4 LORENZO GHIBERTI, east doors ("Gates of Paradise"), baptistery of Florence Cathedral, Florence, Italy, 1425–1452. Gilded bronze relief, approx. 17′ high. Modern copy, ca. 1980. Original panels in Museo dell'Opera del Duomo, Florence.

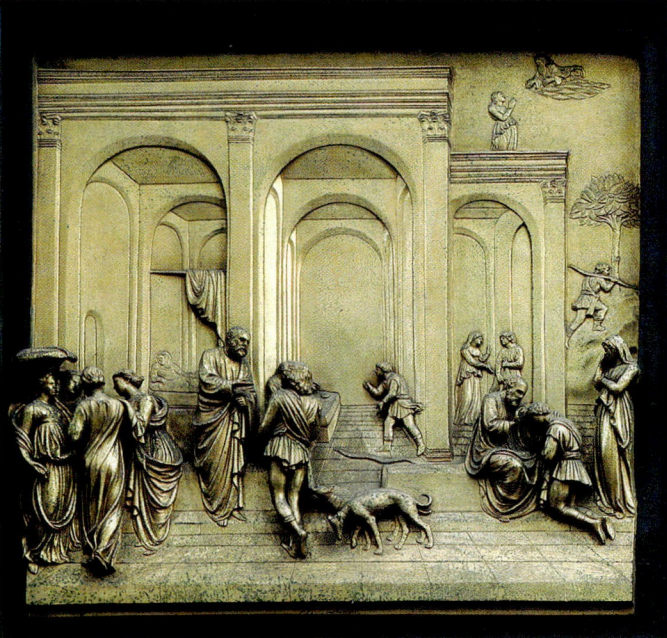

21-5 LORENZO GHIBERTI, *Isaac and His Sons* (detail of FIG. 21-4), east doors, baptistery of Florence Cathedral, Florence, Italy, 1425–1452. Gilded bronze relief, approx. 2′ 7½″ × 2′ 7½″. Museo dell'Opera del Duomo, Florence.

so that his second pair of doors (1425–1452) could be placed in the east doorway. In these "Gates of Paradise," Ghiberti abandoned the quatrefoil pattern that frames the reliefs on the south and north doors and reduced the number of panels from 28 to 10, possibly at the behest of his patrons. Each of the panels contains a relief set in plain moldings and depicts a scene from the Old Testament. The complete gilding of the reliefs creates an effect of great splendor and elegance.

The individual panels of Ghiberti's east doors, such as *Isaac and His Sons* (FIG. 21-5), clearly recall painting techniques in their depiction of space as well as in their treatment of the narrative. Some exemplify more fully than painting many of the principles formulated by the architect and theorist Leon Battista Alberti in his 1435 treatise, *On Painting*. In his relief, Ghiberti created the illusion of space partly through the use of pictorial perspective and partly by sculptural means. He represented buildings according to a painter's one-point perspective construction, but the figures (in the bottom section of the relief, which actually projects slightly toward the viewer) appear almost in the full round, some of their heads standing completely free. As the eye progresses upward, the relief increasingly flattens, concluding with the architecture in the background, which Ghiberti depicted in barely raised lines. In this manner, the artist created a sort of sculptor's aerial perspective, with forms appearing less distinct the deeper they are in space. Ghiberti described the east doors as follows:

> I strove to imitate nature as closely as I could, and with all the perspective I could produce [to have] excellent compositions rich with

many figures. In some scenes I placed about a hundred figures, in some less, and in some more. . . . There were ten stories, all [sunk] in frames because the eye from a distance measures and interprets the scenes in such a way that they appear round. The scenes are in the lowest relief and the figures are seen in the planes; those that are near appear large, those in the distance small, as they do in reality.[3]

In these panels, Ghiberti achieved a greater sense of depth than had seemed possible in a relief. His principal figures do not occupy the architectural space he created for them; rather, the artist arranged them along a parallel plane in front of the grandiose architecture. (According to Leon Battista Alberti, in his *De re aedificatoria*—*On the Art of Building*—the grandeur of the architecture reflects the dignity of the events shown in the foreground.) Ghiberti's figure style mixes a Gothic patterning of rhythmic line; classical poses and motifs; and a new realism in characterization, movement, and surface detail. The medieval narrative method of presenting several episodes within a single frame persisted. In *Isaac and His Sons* (FIG. 21-5), the group of women in the left foreground attends the birth of Esau and Jacob in the left background; in the central foreground, Isaac sends Esau and his dogs to hunt game; and, in the right foreground, Isaac blesses the kneeling Jacob as Rebecca looks on (Gen. 25–27). Yet viewers experience little confusion because of Ghiberti's careful and subtle placement of each scene. The figures, in varying degrees of projection, gracefully twist and turn, appearing to occupy and move through a convincing stage space, which Ghiberti deepened by showing some figures from behind. The classicism derives from the artist's close study of ancient art. According to his biography, he admired and collected classical sculpture, bronzes, and coins. Their influence is seen throughout the panel, particularly in the figure of Rebecca, which Ghiberti based on a popular Greco-Roman statuary type. The emerging practice of collecting classical art in the 15th century had much to do with the appearance of classicism in Renaissance humanistic art.

## Exemplary Lives
### The Path to Sainthood

Saints are a ubiquitous element in modern society, surfacing in the names of geographic locations and churches, as well as appearing in artworks. Why is this, and what purpose do saints serve? What is the history of saints, and how does one achieve sainthood?

The word *saint* derives from the Latin word *sanctus*, meaning "made holy to God," or *sacred*. Thus, saints are people who have demonstrated a dedication to God's service. The first saints were martyrs—individuals who suffered and died for Christianity—selected by public acclaim. The faithful called on these martyrs to intercede on their behalf. By the end of the fourth century CE, the group of saints expanded to include confessors, individuals who merited honor for the Christian devotion they demonstrated while alive.

A more formal process of canonization emerged in the 12th century (although the procedures in use today were established in 1634). The Roman Catholic Church derived the term *canonization* from the idea of a canon, or list, of approved saints. Canonization is a lengthy and involved process. Normally several years must pass before the Church will consider a deceased Catholic for sainthood. After a panel of theologians and cardinals of the Congregation for the Causes of Saints thoroughly evaluates the candidate's life, the pope proclaims an approved candidate "venerable" (worthy of reverence). Evidence of the performance of a miracle earns the candidate beatification (from the word *beatus,* meaning "blessed"). After proof of another miracle, the pope canonizes the candidate as a saint.

Despite the concept of a canon, no such thing as an authoritative register of all saints exists. Different groups have compiled various lists. For example, the Roman Martyrology, which is not comprehensive, contains more than 4,500 names. Indeed, during John Paul II's papacy alone (1978–), over 500 people have been canonized.

Saints provided inspiration to the faithful and were greatly respected for their teaching ability. For these reasons, representations of saints were popular in art, especially in eras when religion dominated the lives of the populace. This was not idolatry, because viewers did not worship the images. The images simply encouraged and facilitated personal devotion. The pious called on saints to intercede on behalf of sinners (themselves or others).

The faithful admired each saint for certain traits or qualities, often having to do with the particulars of the saint's life or death. For example, the devout remembered Saint Teresa (see FIG. 24-9) for her transverberation (the piercing of her heart by the arrow of Divine Love); they associated Saint Bartholomew (see FIGS. 22-25 and 24-28) with the manner of his martyrdom (he was flayed alive). Art viewers recognized saints by their attributes. For example, artists usually depicted Saint Sebastian—a Roman guard the emperor Diocletian ordered shot by archers for refusing to deny Christ—bound to a post or tree, his body pierced by numerous arrows. Other saints and their attributes follow:

| SAINT | DEPICTED |
|---|---|
| Francis of Assisi (see FIG. 19-1) | In a long robe tied at waist with rope; with stigmata |
| Peter (see FIG. 23-5) | With keys signifying the power to "bind and loose" (Matt. 16:19) |
| Jerome (see FIG. 23-21) | As either a scholar at his desk or a hermit in the wilderness |
| Stephen (see FIGS. 20-19 and 23-26) | With a stone, referring to his death by stoning |
| Augustine (see FIG. 23-26) | In a mitre (tall pointed hat) and bishop's vestments |

**STATUE-FILLED NICHES** Ghiberti was just one of numerous artists who acknowledged Donatello's prodigious talent. Donatello's enviable skill at creating visually credible and engaging relief sculptures extended to sculpture in the round. His artistry impressed those in a position to commission art, as demonstrated by his participation, along with other esteemed sculptors, such as Ghiberti, in another major civic art program of the early 1400s—the decoration of Or San Michele.

Or San Michele was an early-14th-century building that at various times housed a granary, the headquarters of the guilds, a church, and Orcagna's tabernacle (see FIG. 19-20). After construction of Or San Michele, city officials assigned each of the niches on the building's exterior to a specific guild for decoration with a sculpture of its patron saint (see "Exemplary Lives: The Path to Sainthood," above). Most of the niches languished empty. By 1406, guilds had placed statues in only 5 of the 14 niches. Between 1406 and 1423, however, guilds filled the 9 vacant niches with statues by Donatello, Ghiberti, and Nanni di Banco. How might historians account for this flurry of activity? First, city officials issued a dictum in 1406 requiring the guilds to comply with the original plan and fill their assigned niches. Second, Florence was once again under siege, this time by King Ladislaus (r. 1399–1414) of Naples. Ladislaus had marched north, had occupied Rome and the Papal States by 1409, and then had threatened to overrun Florence. As they had previously, Florentine officials urged citizens to stand firm and defend their city-state from tyranny. As had Visconti a few years earlier, Ladislaus, on the verge of military success in 1414, fortuitously died, and Florence found itself spared yet again. The guilds may well have viewed this threat as an opportunity to perform their civic duty by rallying their fellow Florentines while also promoting their own importance and position in Florentine society. The early-15th-century niche sculptures thus served various purposes, and their public placement provided an ideal vehicle for presenting political, artistic, and economic messages to a wide audience. Examining a few of these Or San Michele sculptures will reveal the stylistic and historical significance of all these works.

**FOUR MARTYRED SCULPTORS** Among the niches filled in the early 15th century was that assigned to the Florentine guild of sculptors, architects, and masons, who chose NANNI DI BANCO (ca. 1380–1421) to create four life-size marble statues of the guild's martyred patron saints. These four Christian sculptors had defied an order from the Roman emperor Diocletian to make a statue of a pagan deity. In response, the emperor ordered them put to death. Because they placed their faith above all else, these saints were perfect role models for the 15th-century Florentines whom city leaders exhorted to stand fast in the face of the invasion threat by Ladislaus.

Nanni's sculptural group, *Four Crowned Saints* (FIG. **21-6**), also represented an early attempt to solve the Renaissance problem of integrating figures and space on a monumental scale. The artist's positioning of the figures, which stand in a niche that is *in* but confers some separation *from* the architecture, furthered the gradual emergence of sculpture from its architectural setting. This process began with such works as the 13th-century statues of the west front of Reims Cathedral (see FIG. 18-22). The niche's spatial recess permitted a new and dramatic possibility for the

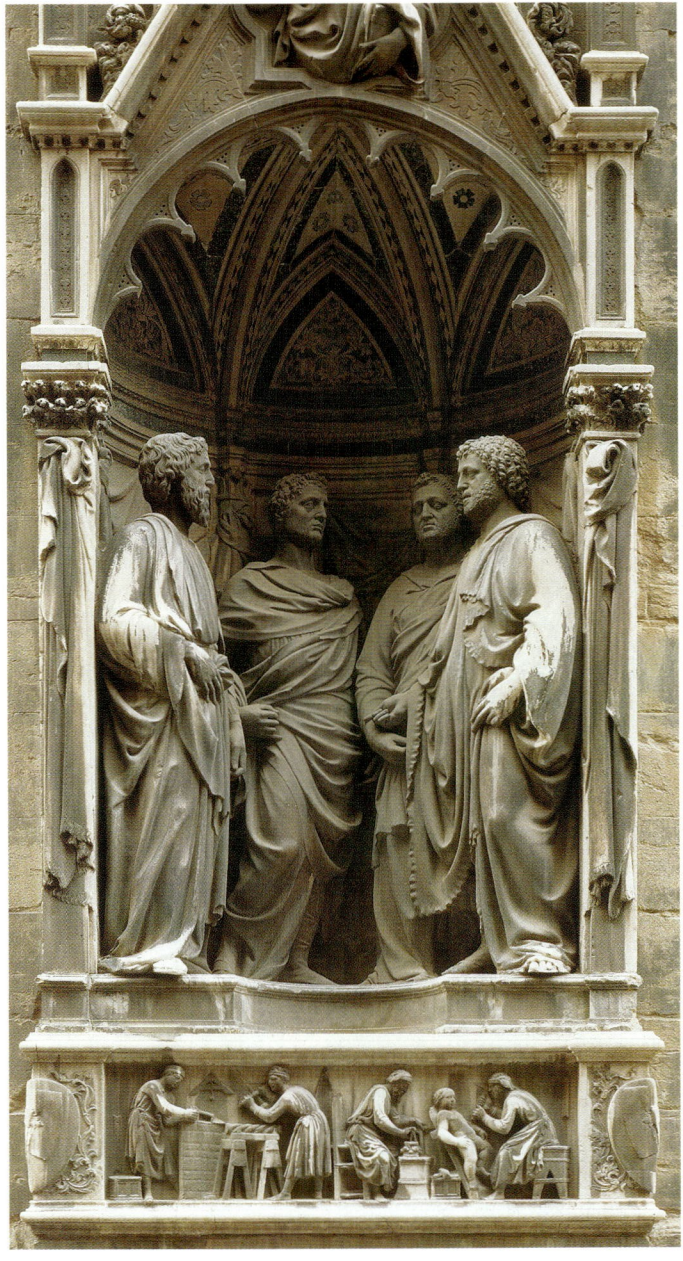

**21-6** NANNI DI BANCO, *Four Crowned Saints,* Or San Michele, Florence, Italy, ca. 1408–1414. Marble, figures approx. life-size. Modern copy in exterior niche. Original sculpture in museum on second floor of Or San Michele.

interrelationship of the figures. By placing them in a semicircle within their deep niche and relating them to one another by their postures and gestures, as well as by the arrangement of draperies, Nanni arrived at a unified spatial composition. Further, a remarkable psychological unity connects these unyielding figures, whose bearing expresses the discipline and integrity necessary to face adversity. While the figure on the right speaks, pointing to his right, the two men opposite listen and the one next to him looks out into space, pondering the meaning of the words. Later Renaissance artists, particularly Leonardo, exploited this technique of reinforcing the formal unity of a figural group with psychological cross-references.

In *Four Crowned Saints,* Nanni also displayed a deep respect for and close study of Roman portrait statues. The emotional intensity of the faces of the two inner saints owes much to the extraordinarily moving portrayals in stone of Roman emperors of the third century CE (see FIG. 10-69), and the bearded heads of the outer saints reveal a familiarity with second-century CE imperial portraiture (see FIG. 10-60). Early Renaissance artists, such as Donatello and Nanni di Banco, sought to portray individual personalities and characteristics. Roman models served as inspiration, but Renaissance artists did not simply copy them. Rather, they strove to interpret or offer commentary on their classical models in the manner of humanist scholars dealing with classical texts.

**SUGGESTING MOTION IN STONE** Donatello's incorporation of Classical Greek and Roman principles surfaced in *Saint Mark* (FIG. **21-7**), commissioned for Or San Michele by the guild of linen drapers and completed in 1413. In this sculpture, Donatello took a fundamental step toward depicting motion in the human figure by recognizing the principle of weight shift. Earlier chapters have established the importance of weight shift in the ancient world; Greek sculptors grasped the essential principle that the human body is not rigid, as they demonstrated in works such as the *Kritios Boy* (see FIG. 5-33) and the *Doryphoros* (see FIG. 5-38). It is a flexible structure that moves by continuously shifting its weight from one supporting leg to the other, its main masses moving in consonance. Donatello reintroduced this concept (known as *contrapposto;* see Chapter 5, page 129).

As the saint's body "moves," its drapery "moves" with it, hanging and folding naturally from and around bodily points of support so that the viewer senses the figure as a draped nude, not simply as an integrated column with arbitrarily incised drapery. This separates Donatello's *Saint Mark* from all medieval portal statuary. It was the first Renaissance figure whose voluminous drapery (the pride of the Florentine guild that paid for the statue) did not conceal but accentuated the movement of the arms, legs, shoulders, and hips. This development further contributed to the sculpted figure's independence from its architectural setting. Saint Mark's stirring limbs, shifting weight, and mobile drapery suggest impending movement out of the niche.

**ELEVATED FIGURES** Between 1416 and 1435, the officials in charge of cathedral projects commissioned from Donatello five statues for niches on the *campanile* (bell tower) adjacent to Florence Cathedral—a project that, like the figures for Or San Michele, had originated in the preceding century. Unlike the Or San Michele figures, however, which were installed only slightly above eye level, these sculptures were designed for niches some 30 feet above the ground. At that distance, delicate descriptive details (hair, garments, and features) cannot be recognized readily.

The campanile figures thus required massive garment folds that could be read from afar and a much broader, summary treatment of facial and anatomical features, all of which Donatello used to great effect. In addition, he took into account the elevated position of his figures and, with subtly calculated distortions, created images that are at once realistic and dramatic when seen from below.

The most striking of the five figures is a prophet who is probably Habbakuk but is generally known by the nickname Zuccone, or "pumpkin-head" (FIG. 21-8). This figure shows Donatello's power of characterization at its most original. The artist represented all his prophets with a harsh, direct realism reminiscent of some ancient Roman portraits (compare FIGS. 10-7, 10-35, and 10-69). Their faces are bony, lined, and taut; Donatello carefully individualized each of them. The Zuccone is also bald, a departure from the conventional representation of the prophets but in keeping with many Roman portrait heads. Donatello's prophet wears an awkwardly draped and crumpled mantle with deeply undercut folds—a far cry from the majestic prophets of medieval portals. The head discloses a fierce personality; the deep-set eyes glare under furrowed brows, the nostrils flare, and the broad mouth is agape, as if the prophet were in the very presence of disasters that would prompt dire warnings.

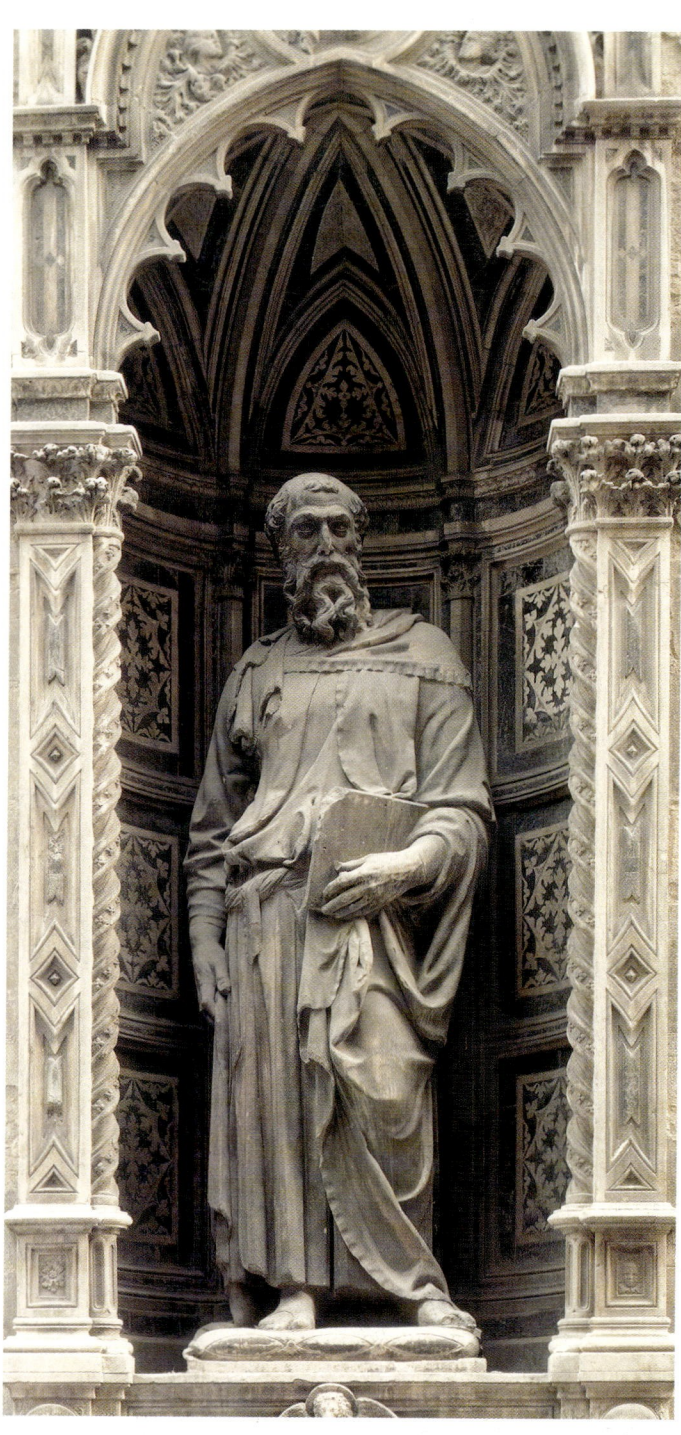

**21-7** DONATELLO, *Saint Mark,* Or San Michele, Florence, Italy, 1411–1413. Marble, approx. 7′ 9″ high. Modern copy in exterior niche. Original sculpture in museum on second floor of Or San Michele.

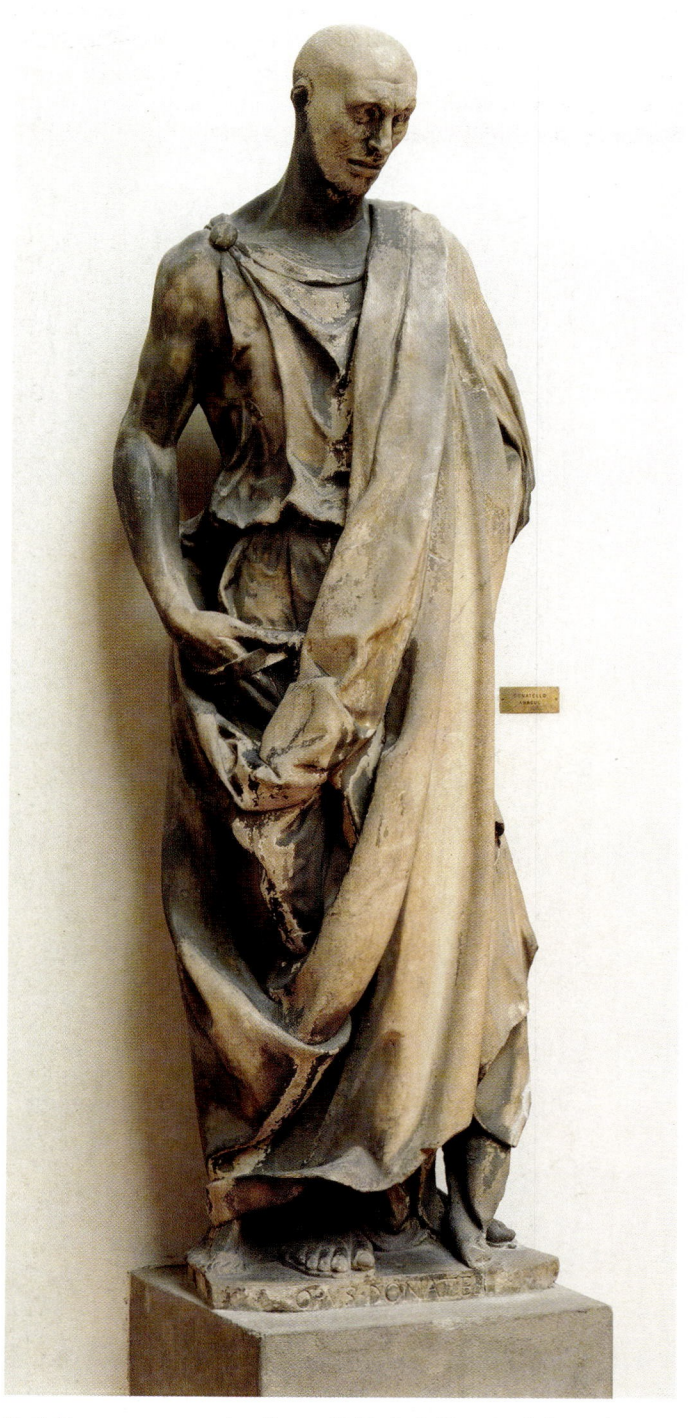

**21-8** DONATELLO, prophet figure, Habbakuk (Zuccone), from the campanile of Florence Cathedral, Florence, Italy, 1423–1425. Marble, approx. 6′ 5″ high. Museo dell'Opera del Duomo, Florence.

## Painting, Perspective, and Patronage

**INSPIRED BY THE GOTHIC** The International Style (see FIG. 19-12), the dominant style in painting around 1400 that persisted well into the 15th century, developed side by side with the new styles. GENTILE DA FABRIANO (ca. 1370–1427) produced a work representative of the International Style—*Adoration of the Magi* (FIG. **21-9**), an altarpiece in the sacristy of the church of Santa Trinità in Florence. Gentile's patron was Palla Strozzi, the wealthiest Florentine of his day, and the altarpiece, with its elaborate gilded Gothic frame, is testimony to Strozzi's lavish tastes. So too is the painting itself, with its gorgeous surface and sumptuously costumed kings, courtiers, captains, and retainers accompanied by a menagerie of exotic and ornamental animals. Gentile portrayed all these elements in a rainbow of color with extensive use of gold. The painting presents all the pomp and ceremony of chivalric etiquette in a scene that sanctifies the aristocracy in the presence of the Madonna and Child. Although the style is fundamentally Late Gothic, Gentile inserted striking bits of radical naturalism. The artist depicted animals from a variety of angles, and he foreshortened their forms convincingly. He did the same with human figures, such as the man removing the spurs from the standing magus in the center foreground. On the right side of the predella (the ledge at the base of an altarpiece), Gentile placed the Presentation scene in a "modern" architectural setting. And on the left side of the predella, he painted what may have been the very first nighttime Nativity with the central light source—the radiant Christ Child—introduced into the picture itself. Although predominantly conservative, Gentile demonstrated that he was not oblivious to contemporary experimental trends and that he could blend naturalistic and inventive elements skillfully and subtly into a traditional composition without sacrificing Late Gothic coloristic splendor.

**REVOLUTIONIZING REPRESENTATION** A leading innovator in early-15th-century painting was Tommaso Guidi (or Tommaso di ser Giovanni), known as MASACCIO (1401–1428).

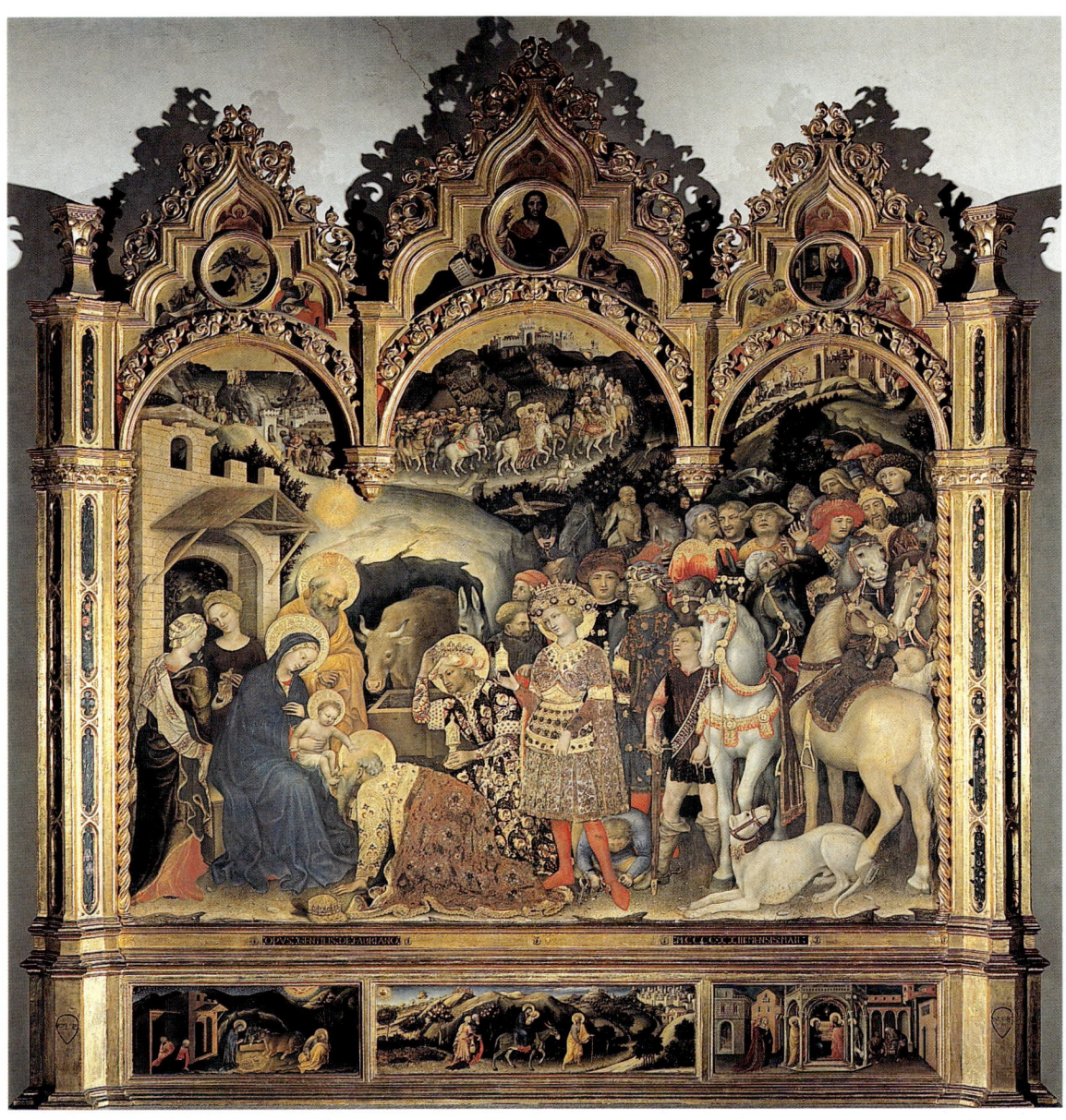

**21-9** GENTILE DA FABRIANO, *Adoration of the Magi*, altarpiece from Santa Trinità, Florence, Italy, 1423. Tempera on wood, approx. 9′ 11″ × 9′ 3″. Galleria degli Uffizi, Florence.

Although his presumed teacher, Masolino da Panicale, had worked in the International Style, Masaccio moved suddenly, within the short span of six years, into wide-open and unexplored territory (see "Imitation and Emulation: Artistic Values in the Renaissance," page 585). Most art historians recognize no other painter in history to have contributed so much to the development of a new style in so short a time as Masaccio, whose creative career was cut short by his death at age 27. Masaccio was the artistic descendant of Giotto, whose calm, monumental style he revolutionized with a whole new repertoire of representational devices that generations of Renaissance painters later studied and developed. Masaccio also knew and understood the innovations of his great contemporaries, Donatello and Brunelleschi, and he introduced new possibilities for both form and content.

The frescoes Masaccio painted in the Brancacci Chapel of Santa Maria del Carmine in Florence provide excellent examples of his innovations. In *Tribute Money* (FIG. **21-10**), painted shortly before his death, Masaccio depicted a seldom-represented narrative from the Gospel of Matthew (17:24–27). As the tax collector confronts Christ at the entrance to the Roman town of Capernaum, Christ directs Saint Peter to the shore of Lake Galilee. There, as foreseen by Christ, Peter finds the half-drachma tribute in the mouth of a fish and returns to pay the tax. Art historians have debated the reason for the selection of this particular biblical story. Most scholars believe that Felice Brancacci, owner of the family chapel in the early 15th century, commissioned the fresco. Why such an obscure narrative appealed to Brancacci or Masaccio is unclear. Some scholars have suggested that *Tribute Money,* in which Christ condones taxation, served as a commentary on the *catasto* (state income tax) whose implementation

Florentines were considering at the time. However, Brancacci's considerable wealth makes it unlikely he would have supported the catasto. Moreover, this fresco's placement in a private family chapel meant that the public had only limited access. Therefore, because this fresco lacked the general audience enjoyed by, for example, the Or San Michele niche sculptures, it seems ill-suited for public statements.

Masaccio presented this narrative in three episodes within the fresco. In the center, Christ, surrounded by his disciples, tells Saint Peter to retrieve the coin from the fish, while the tax collector stands in the foreground, his back to spectators and hand extended, awaiting payment. At the left, in the middle distance, Saint Peter extracts the coin from the fish's mouth, and, at the right, he thrusts the coin into the tax collector's hand. Masaccio's figures recall Giotto's in their simple grandeur, but they convey a greater psychological and physical credibility. Masaccio realized the bulk of the figures through modeling not with a flat, neutral light lacking an identifiable source but with a light coming from a specific source outside the picture. The light strikes the figures at an angle, illuminating the parts of the solids that obstruct its path and leaving the rest in deep shadow. This chiaroscuro gives the illusion of deep sculptural relief. Between the extremes of light and dark, the light appears as a constantly active but fluctuating force highlighting the scene in varying degrees, almost a tangible substance independent of the figures. In Giotto's frescoes, light is revealed only by the modeling of masses. In Masaccio's, light has its own nature, and the masses are visible only because of its direction and intensity. The viewer can imagine the light as playing over forms—revealing some and concealing others, as the artist directs it.

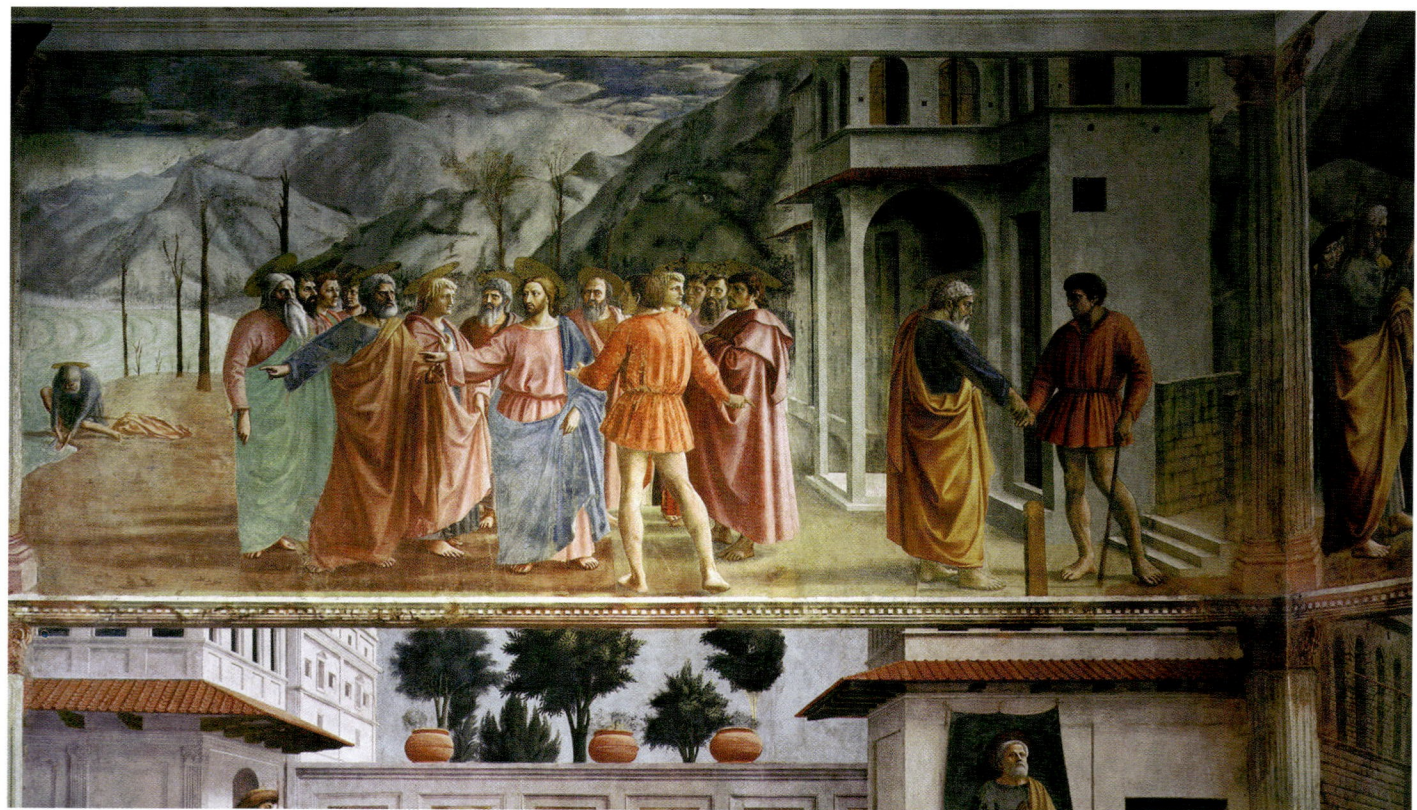

**21-10** MASACCIO, *Tribute Money,* Brancacci Chapel, Santa Maria del Carmine, Florence, Italy, ca. 1427. Fresco, 8′ 1″ × 19′ 7″.

## Imitation and Emulation
### Artistic Values in the Renaissance

The familiar premium that current Western society seems to place on artistic originality is actually a fairly recent phenomenon. Among the concepts Renaissance artists most valued were *imitation* and *emulation*. Although many Renaissance artists did develop unique, recognizable styles, convention, both in terms of subject matter and representational practices, predominated. In a review of Italian Renaissance art, certain themes, conceits, and artistic formats surface with great regularity, and the traditional training practices reveal the importance of imitation and emulation to aspiring Renaissance artists.

Imitation was the starting point in a young artist's training (see "Mastering a Craft," Chapter 19, page 535). Renaissance Italians believed that the best way to learn was to copy the works of masters. Accordingly, much of an apprentice's training consisted of copying exemplary artworks. Leonardo filled his sketchbooks with drawings of well-known sculptures and frescoes, and Michelangelo spent hours visiting churches around Florence and Rome and sketching the artworks he found there.

The next step was emulation, which involved modeling one's art after that of another artist. Although imitation still provided the foundation for this practice, an artist used features of another's art only as a springboard for improvements or innovations. Thus, developing artists went beyond previous artists and attempted to prove their own competence and skill by improving on established and recognized masters. Comparison and a degree of competition were integral to emulation. To evaluate the "improved" artwork, viewers had to know the original "model."

Renaissance artists believed that developing artists would ultimately arrive at their own unique style through this process of imitation and emulation. Cennino Cennini (ca. 1370–1440) explained the value of this training procedure in a book he published in 1400, *Il Libro dell'Arte (The Craftsman's Handbook)*, which served as a practical guide to making art:

> Having first practiced drawing for a while as I have taught you above, that is, on a little panel, take pains and pleasure in constantly copying the best things which you can find done by the hand of great masters. And if you are in a place where many good masters have been, so much the better for you. But I give you this advice: take care to select the best one every time, and the one who has the greatest reputation. And, as you go on from day to day, it will be against nature if you do not get some grasp of his style and of his spirit. For if you undertake to copy after one master today and after another one tomorrow, you will not acquire the style of either one or the other, and you will inevitably, through enthusiasm, become capricious, because each style will be distracting your mind. You will try to work in this man's way today, and in the other's tomorrow, and so you will not get either of them right. If you follow the course of one man through constant practice, your intelligence would have to be crude indeed for you not to get some nourishment from it. Then you will find, if nature has granted you any imagination at all, that you will eventually acquire a style individual to yourself, and it cannot help being good; because your hand and your mind, being always accustomed to gather flowers, would ill know how to pluck thorns.[1]

[1] Cennino Cennini, *The Craftsman's Handbook (Il Libro dell'Arte),* translated by Daniel V. Thompson Jr. (New York: Dover Publications, 1960), 14–15.

---

The individual figures in *Tribute Money* are solemn and weighty, but they also express bodily structure and movement, as do Donatello's statues. Masaccio's representations adeptly suggest bones, muscles, and the pressures and tensions of joints. Each figure conveys a maximum of contained energy. The figure of Christ and the two appearances of the tax collector make the viewer understand what the Renaissance biographer Giorgio Vasari* meant when he said, "the works made before his [Masaccio's] day can be said to be painted, while his are living, real, and natural."[4]

Masaccio's arrangement of the figures is equally inventive. They do not appear as a stiff screen in the front planes. Instead, the artist grouped them in circular depth around Christ, and he placed the whole group in a spacious landscape, rather than in the confined stage space of earlier frescoes. The group itself generates the foreground space that the architecture on the right amplifies. Masaccio depicted this architecture in one-point perspective, locating the vanishing point, where all the orthogonals converge, to coincide with Christ's head. Aerial perspective, the diminishing of light and the blurring of outlines as the distance increases, unites the foreground with the background. Although ancient Roman painters used aerial perspective, medieval artists had abandoned it. Thus it virtually disappeared from art until Masaccio and his contemporaries rediscovered it, apparently independently. They came to realize that the light and air interposed between viewers and what they see are two parts of the visual experience called "distance."

**SINNERS' ANGUISH** In an awkwardly narrow space at the entrance to the Brancacci Chapel, Masaccio painted the *Expulsion of Adam and Eve from Eden* (FIG. **21-11**), another fresco displaying the representational innovations of *Tribute Money*. For example, the sharply slanted light from an outside source creates deep relief, with lights placed alongside darks, and acts as a strong unifying agent. Masaccio also presented the figures with convincing structural accuracy, thereby suggesting substantial bodily weight. Further, the hazy, atmospheric background

---

* Giorgio Vasari (1511–1574) established himself as both a painter and architect during the 16th century. However, people today usually associate him with his landmark book, *Lives of the Most Eminent Painters, Sculptors and Architects,* first published in 1550. Scholars long have considered this book a major source of information about Italian art and artists, although many of the details have proven inaccurate. Regardless, Vasari's *Lives* remains a tour de force—an ambitious, comprehensive book dedicated to recording the biographies of artists.

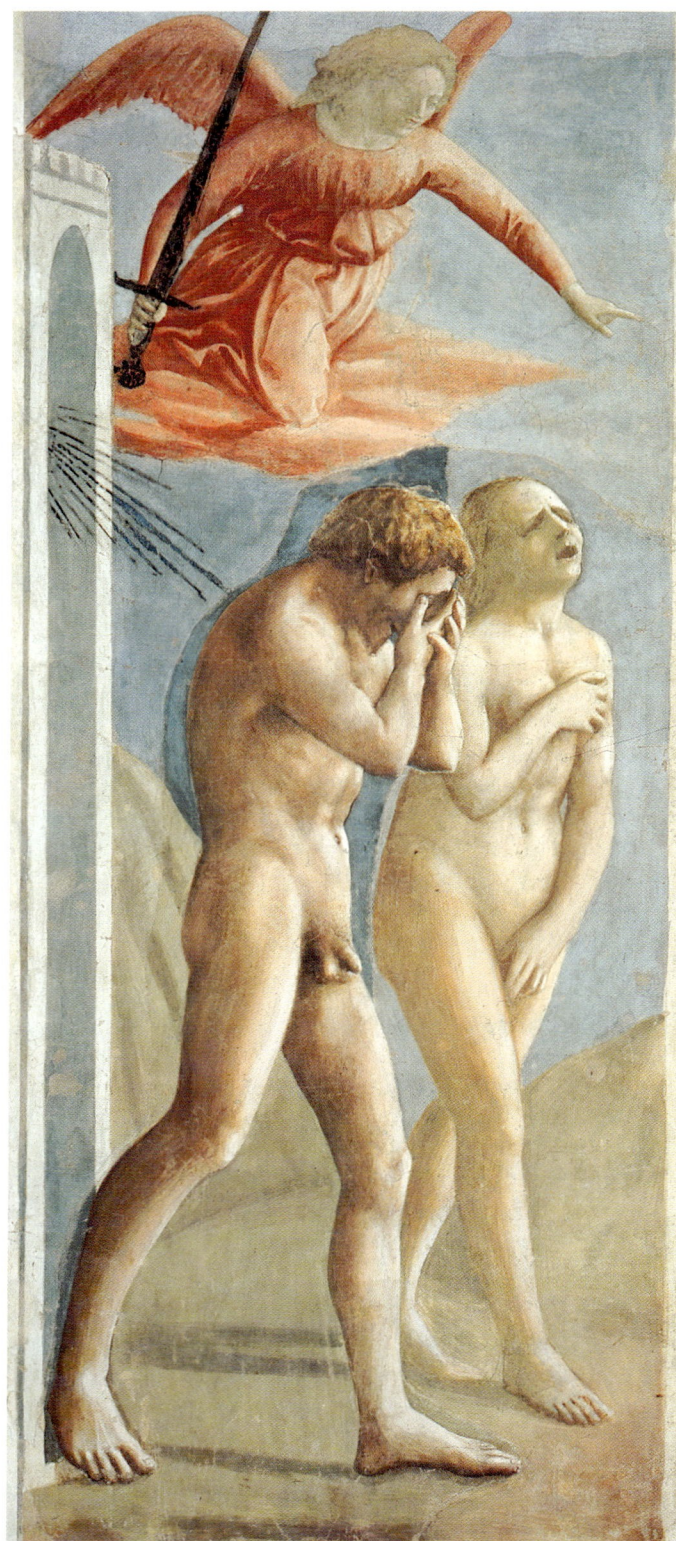

21-11 MASACCIO, *Expulsion of Adam and Eve from Eden,* Brancacci Chapel, Santa Maria del Carmine, Florence, Italy, ca. 1425. Fresco, 7′ × 2′ 11″.

specifies no locale but suggests a space around and beyond the figures. Adam's feet, clearly in contact with the ground, mark the human presence on earth, and the cry issuing from Eve's mouth voices her anguish. The angel does not force them physically from Eden. Rather, they stumble on blindly, driven by the angel's will and their own despair. The composition is starkly simple, its message incomparably eloquent.

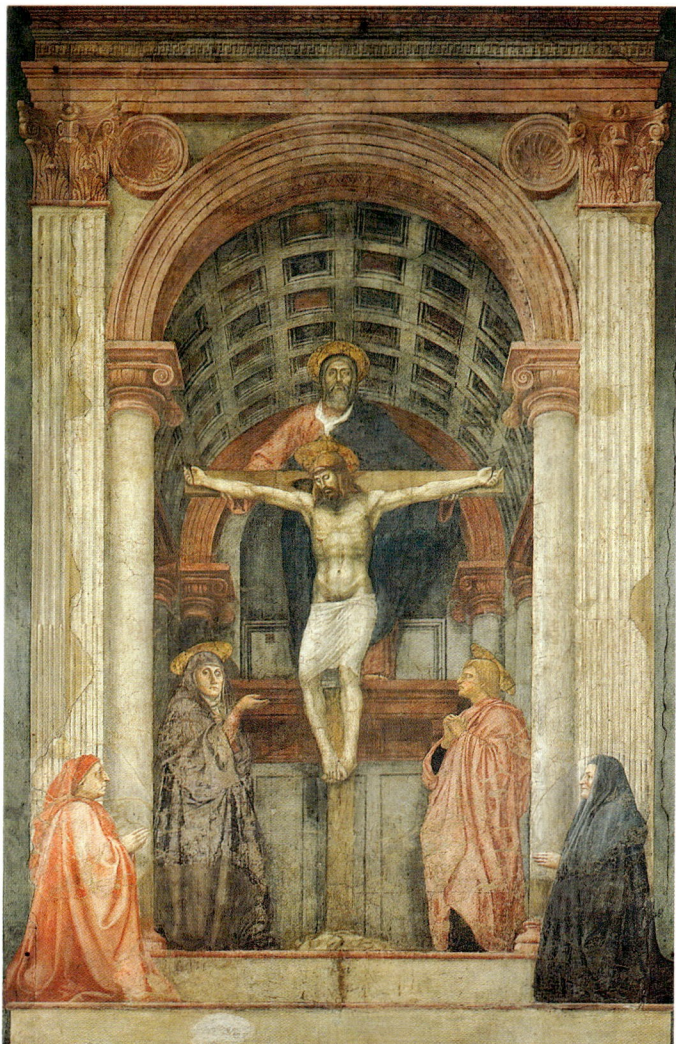

21-12 MASACCIO, *Holy Trinity,* Santa Maria Novella, Florence, Italy, ca. 1428. Fresco, 21′ × 10′ 5″.

**FATHER, SON, AND HOLY SPIRIT** Masaccio's *Holy Trinity* fresco (FIG. **21-12**) in Santa Maria Novella, whose dating is still disputed, embodies two principal Renaissance interests. One is realism based on observation, and the other is the application of mathematics to pictorial organization in the new science of perspective. The artist painted the composition on two levels of unequal height. Above, in a *coffered* barrel-vaulted chapel reminiscent of a Roman triumphal arch, the Virgin Mary and Saint John appear on either side of the crucified Christ. God the Father emerges from behind Christ, supporting the arms of the cross. The dove of the Holy Spirit hovers between God's head and Christ's head. Masaccio also included portraits of the donors of the painting, Lorenzo Lenzi and his wife, who kneel just in front of the pilasters that enframe the chapel. Below the altar—a masonry insert in the depicted composition—the artist painted a tomb containing a skeleton. An inscription in Italian painted above the skeleton reminds the spectator that "I was once what you are, and what I am you will become."

Although the subject matter of *Holy Trinity* may not be dramatically innovative, the illusionism of Masaccio's depiction is breathtaking. He brilliantly demonstrated the principles of Brunelleschi's perspective. Indeed, this work is so much in the Brunelleschian manner that some historians have suggested that

Brunelleschi may have collaborated with Masaccio. Masaccio placed the vanishing point at the foot of the cross. With this point at eye level, spectators look up at the Trinity and down at the tomb. About five feet above the floor level, the vanishing point pulls the two views together, creating the illusion of an actual structure that transects the wall's vertical plane. Whereas the tomb appears to project forward into the church, the chapel recedes visually behind the wall and appears as an extension of the spectator's space. This adjustment of the pictured space to the position of the viewer was a first step in the development of illusionistic painting, which fascinated many artists of the Renaissance and the later Baroque period. Masaccio was so exact in his metrical proportions that it is actually possible to calculate the dimensions of the chapel (for example, the span of the painted vault is seven feet; the depth of the chapel, nine feet). Thus, he achieved not only a successful illusion but also a rational measured coherence that is responsible for the unity and harmony of this monumental composition.

Masaccio's commitment to pictorial illusionism resulted in a powerful fresco that instructs the faithful through its images. The ascending pyramid of figures leads viewers from the despair of death to the hope of resurrection and eternal life.

## *Early-15th-Century Architecture*

**ROMAN ARCHITECTURAL APPEAL** Filippo Brunelleschi's ability to codify a system of linear perspective derived in part from his skill as an architect. Although his biographer, Manetti, reported that Brunelleschi turned to architecture out of disappointment over the loss of the baptistery commission, he continued to work as a sculptor for several years and received commissions for sculpture as late as 1416. It is true, however, that as the 15th century progressed, Brunelleschi's interest turned increasingly toward architecture. Several trips to Rome (the first in 1402, probably with his friend Donatello), where he was captivated by the Roman ruins, heightened his fascination with architecture. It may well be in connection with his close study of Roman monuments and his effort to make an accurate record of what he saw that Brunelleschi developed his revolutionary system of geometric linear perspective that 15th-century artists so eagerly adopted. It made him the first acknowledged Renaissance architect.

**A CROWNING ACHIEVEMENT** Brunelleschi's broad knowledge of Roman construction principles, combined with an analytical and inventive mind, permitted him to solve an engineering problem that no other 15th-century architect could solve. The challenge was the design and construction of a dome for the huge crossing of the unfinished Florence Cathedral (FIGS. **21-13** and 19-17). The problem was staggering; the space to be spanned (140 feet) was much too wide to permit construction with the aid of traditional wooden centering. Nor was it possible (because of the crossing plan) to support the dome with buttressed walls. Brunelleschi seems to have begun work on the problem about 1417. In 1420, officials overseeing cathedral projects awarded Brunelleschi and Ghiberti a joint commission. The latter, however, soon retired from the project and left the field to his associate.

With exceptional ingenuity, Brunelleschi not only discarded traditional building methods and devised new ones but also invented much of the machinery necessary for the job. Although he might have preferred the hemispheric shape of Roman domes, Brunelleschi raised the center of his dome and designed it around an ogival (pointed arch) section (FIG. **21-14**), which is inherently more stable

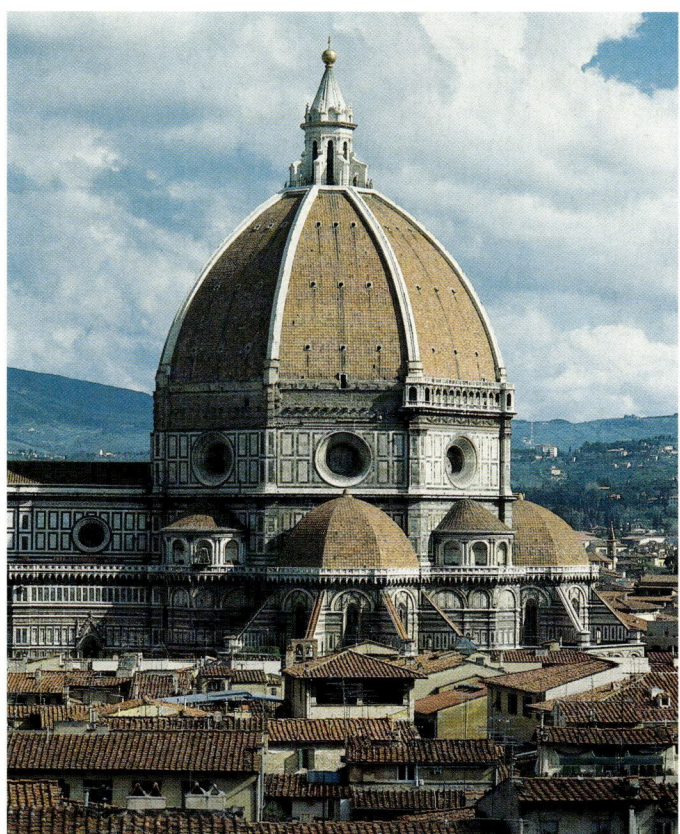

**21-13** FILIPPO BRUNELLESCHI, dome of Florence Cathedral (view from the south), Florence, Italy, 1420–1436.

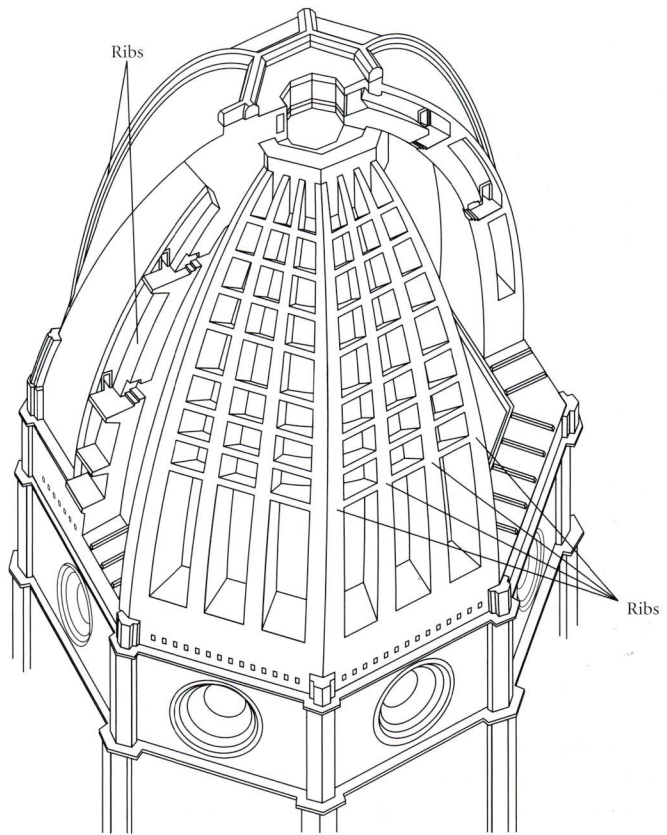

Ribs

Ribs

**21-14** Cutaway view of dome of Florence Cathedral (after P. Sanpaolesi).

because it reduces the outward thrust around the dome's base. To minimize the structure's weight, he designed a relatively thin double shell (the first in history) around a skeleton of 24 ribs. The 8 most important are visible on the exterior. Finally, in almost paradoxical fashion, Brunelleschi anchored the structure at the top with a heavy lantern, built after his death but from his design.

Despite Brunelleschi's knowledge of and admiration for Roman building techniques and even though the Florence Cathedral dome was his most outstanding engineering achievement, he arrived at the solution to this most critical structural problem through what were essentially Gothic building principles. Thus, the dome, which also had to harmonize in formal terms with the century-old building, does not really express Brunelleschi's architectural style. That is more apparent in subsequent designs when his ideas had matured.

**A MODULAR DESIGN** San Lorenzo and Santo Spirito, the two basilican churches Brunelleschi built in Florence, echo the clarity and classically inspired rationality that characterized much of his architecture. Of the two, the later Santo Spirito (FIGS. **21-15** and **21-16**), begun around 1436 and completed, with some changes, after Brunelleschi's death, shows the architect's mature style. Brunelleschi laid out this cruciform building in either multiples or segments of the dome-covered crossing square. The aisles, subdivided into small squares covered by shallow, saucer-shaped vaults, run all the way around the flat-roofed central space. They have the visual effect of compressing the longitudinal design into a centralized one, because the various aspects of the interior resemble one another, no matter where observers stand. Originally, this centralization effect would have been even stronger; Brunelleschi had planned to extend the aisles across the front of the nave as well, as shown on the plan (FIG. 21-16, *left*). Because of the design's modular basis, adherence to such a design would have demanded four entrances in the facade, instead of the traditional and symbolic three, a feature hotly debated

during Brunelleschi's lifetime and changed after his death. The appearance of the exterior walls also was modified later (compare the two plans in FIG. 21-16), when the recesses between the projecting semicircular chapels were filled in to convert the original highly sculpted wall surface into a flat one.

The major features of the interior (FIG. 21-15), however, are much as Brunelleschi designed them. He identified a mathematical unit that served to determine the dimensions of every aspect of Santo Spirito. This unit, repeated throughout the interior, creates a rhythmic harmony. For example, the nave is twice as high as it is wide; the arcade and clerestory are of equal height, which means that the height of the arcade equals the nave's width; and so on. Crisp joinings highlight these basic characteristics of the building for observers so that they can read them like mathematical equations. The austerity of the decor enhances the restful and tranquil atmosphere. Brunelleschi left no space for expansive wall frescoes that only would interrupt the clarity of his architectural scheme. The calculated logic of the design echoes that of classical buildings, such as Roman basilicas. Further, the rationality of Santo Spirito contrasts sharply with the soaring drama and spirituality of the vaults and nave arcades of Gothic churches. It even deviates from those in Italy, such as the Florence Cathedral nave (see FIG. 19-18), whose verticality is restrained in comparison to their northern counterparts. Santo Spirito fully expressed the new Renaissance spirit that placed its faith in reason rather than in the emotions.

**A CENTRAL-PLAN CHAPEL** Brunelleschi's apparent effort to impart a centralized effect to the interior of Santo Spirito suggests that he was intrigued by the compact and self-contained qualities of earlier central-plan buildings, such as the Roman Pantheon (see FIG. 10-50). The Pazzi chapel presented Brunelleschi with the opportunity to explore this interest, in a structure much better suited to such a design than a basilican church. The chapel (FIGS. **21-17** to **21-19**) was the Pazzi family's gift to the church of Santa Croce in Florence (see "Honoring God and Family: Family Chapel Endowments," page 589) and served as Santa Croce's chapter house. Brunelleschi began to design the Pazzi Chapel around 1440. It was not completed until the 1460s, long after his

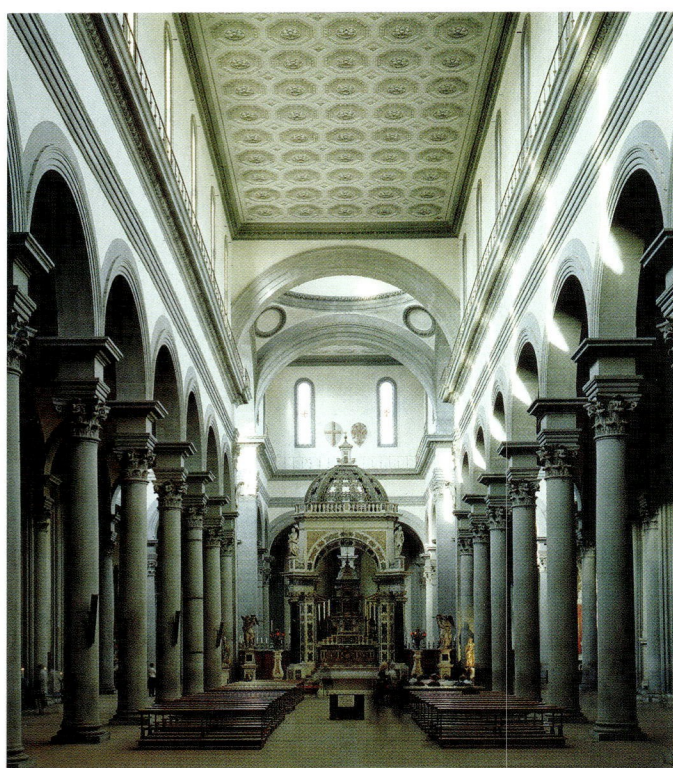

**21-15** FILIPPO BRUNELLESCHI, interior of Santo Spirito (view facing northeast), Florence, Italy, begun ca. 1436.

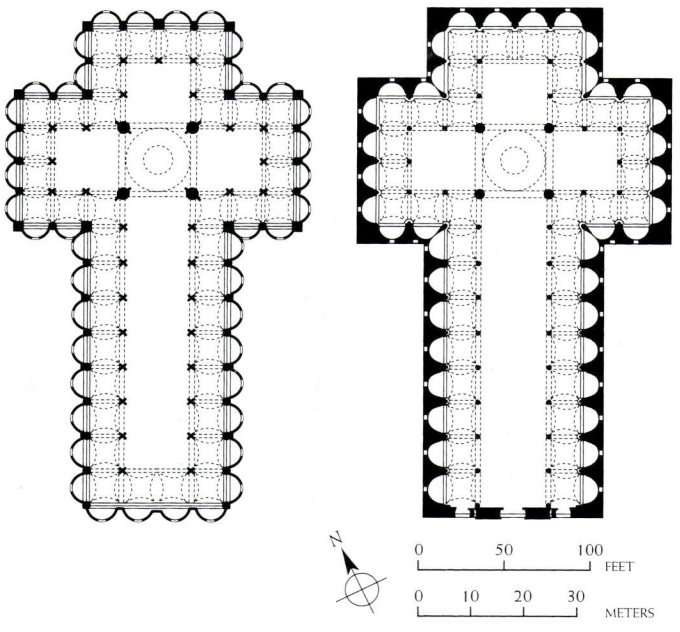

**21-16** FILIPPO BRUNELLESCHI, early plan of Santo Spirito *(left)* and plan as constructed *(right)*, Florence, Italy.

## *Honoring God and Family*
### *Family Chapel Endowments*

During the 14th through 16th centuries in Italy, wealthy families regularly endowed chapels in or adjacent to major churches. These family chapels usually were located on either side of the choir near the altar at the church's east end. Particularly wealthy families endowed chapels in the form of separate buildings constructed adjacent to churches. For example, the Medici chapel (Old Sacristy) abuts San Lorenzo in Florence. Powerful banking families, such as the Baroncelli, Bardi, and Peruzzi, each sponsored chapels in the Florentine church of Santa Croce. The Pazzi commissioned a chapel (FIGS. 21-17, 21-18, and 21-19) adjacent to Santa Croce, and the Brancacci family sponsored the decorative program (FIGS. 21-10 and 21-11) of their chapel in Santa Maria del Carmine.

These families sponsored such chapels as expressions of piety and devotion. The chapels also served as burial sites for important family members and as spaces for liturgical celebrations and commemorative services. Chapel owners sponsored Masses for the dead, praying to the Virgin Mary and the saints for intercession on behalf of their deceased loved ones. Changes in Christian doctrine prompted these concerted efforts to improve individuals' chances for eternal salvation. Until the 13th century,

Christians believed that after death, souls went either to Heaven or Hell. After that time, the concept of Purgatory—a way station between Heaven and Hell where souls could atone for sins before Judgment Day—increasingly won favor. Pope Innocent III recognized the existence of such a place in 1215 at the Fourth Lateran Council (a major church council that dealt with redefining church doctrine). Because Purgatory represented a chance for the faithful to improve their chances of eventually gaining admittance to Heaven, they eagerly embraced this opportunity. They extended this idea to improving their chances while alive, so charitable work, good deeds, and devotional practices proliferated. Family chapels provided the space necessary for the performance of devotional rituals. Most chapels included altars, as well as chalices, vestments, candlesticks, and other objects used in the Mass. Most patrons also commissioned decorations, such as painted altarpieces, frescoes on the walls, and sculptural objects.

Thus, families endowed these chapels to ensure the well-being of the souls of individual family members and ancestors. The gifts also honored the families themselves and burnished their images in the larger community.

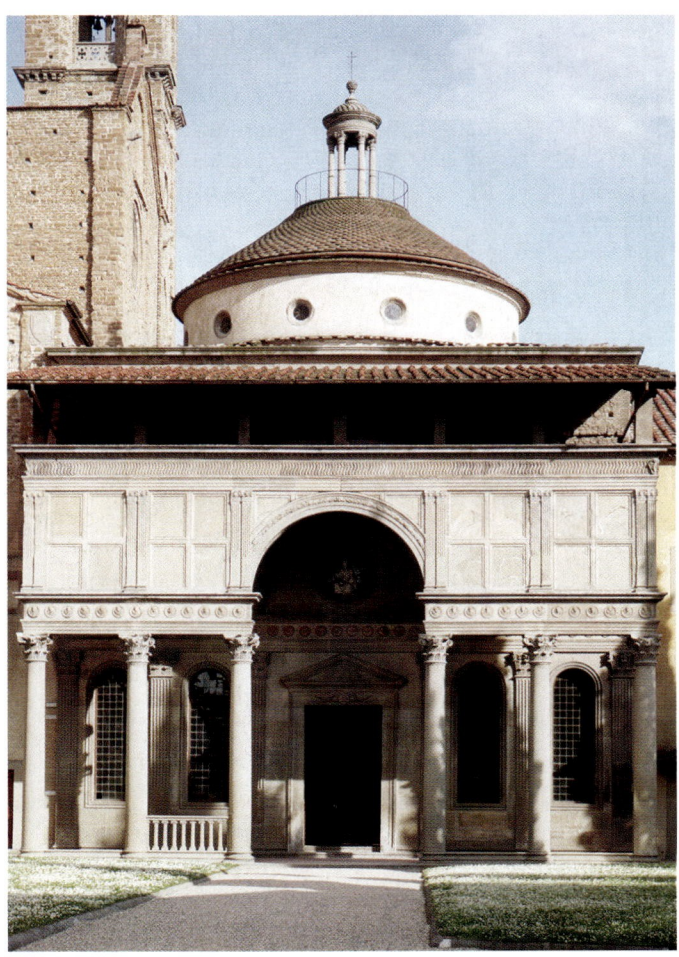

**21-17** FILIPPO BRUNELLESCHI, facade of the Pazzi Chapel, Santa Croce, Florence, Italy, begun ca. 1440.

death. The exterior (FIG. 21-17) probably does not reflect Brunelleschi's original design. The loggia, admirable as it is, seems to have been added as an afterthought, perhaps by the sculptor-architect Giuliano da Maiano (1432–1490). Historians have suggested that the local chapter of Franciscan monks who held meetings in the chapel needed the expansion. Behind the loggia stands one of the first independent Renaissance buildings

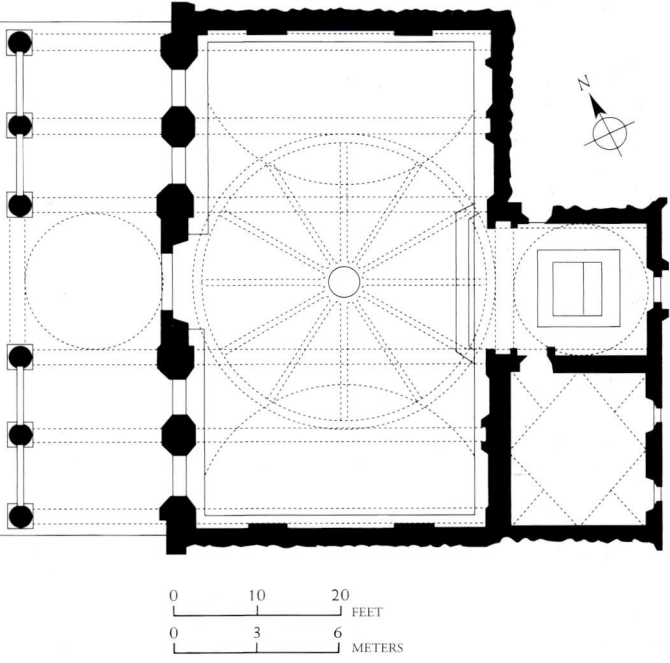

**21-18** FILIPPO BRUNELLESCHI, plan of the Pazzi Chapel, Santa Croce, Florence, Italy.

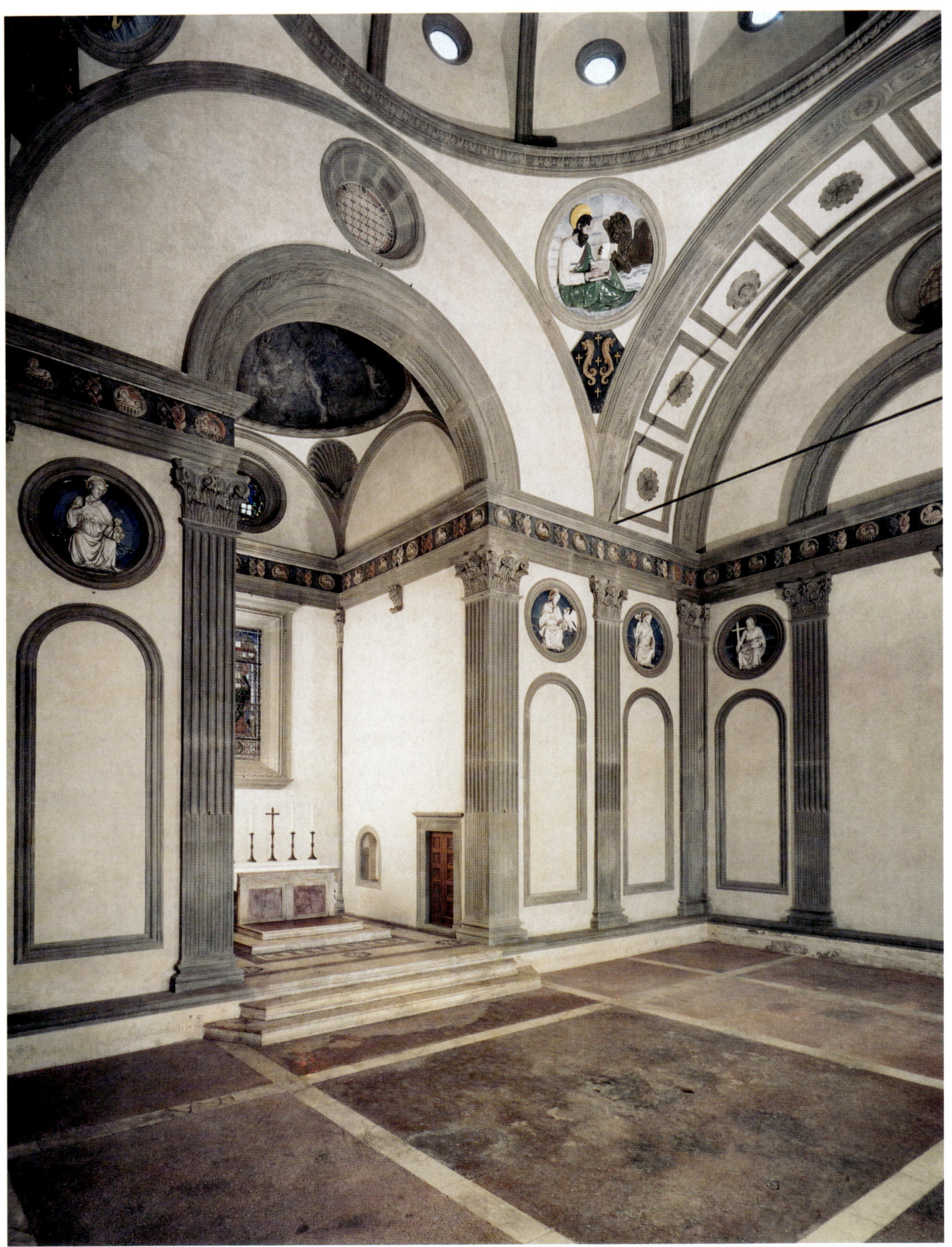

**21-19** Filippo Brunelleschi, interior of the Pazzi Chapel (view facing northeast), Santa Croce, Florence, Italy, begun ca. 1440.

conceived basically as a central-plan structure. Although the plan (FIG. 21-18) is rectangular, rather than square or round, the architect placed all emphasis on the central dome-covered space. The short barrel-vault sections that brace the dome on two sides appear to be incidental appendages. The interior trim (FIG. 21-19) is done in gray stone, so-called *pietra serena* ("serene stone"), which stands out against the white stuccoed walls and crisply defines the modular relationships of plan and elevation. As he did in his design for Santo Spirito, Brunelleschi used a basic unit that allowed him to construct a balanced, harmonious, and regularly proportioned space. Medallions in the dome's *pendentives* consist of glazed terracotta reliefs representing the Four Evangelists. These medallions, together with the images of the Twelve Apostles on the pilaster-framed wall panels, add striking color accents to the tranquil interior.

## *The Medici as Patrons*

**A PALACE FIT FOR A MEDICI** It seems curious that Brunelleschi, the most renowned architect of his time, did not participate in the upsurge of palace building that Florence experienced in the 1430s and 1440s. This proliferation of palazzi testified to the stability of the Florentine economy and to the affluence and confidence of the city's leading citizens. Brunelleschi, however, confined his efforts in this field to work on the Palazzo di Parte Guelfa (headquarters of Florence's then ruling "party") and to a rejected model for a new palace that Cosimo de' Medici intended to build.

Early in the 15th century, Giovanni de' Medici (ca. 1360–1429) had established the family fortune. Cosimo (1389–1464) expanded his family's financial control, which led to considerable political power as well. This consolidation of power in a city that prided itself on its republicanism did not go unchallenged. In the early 1430s, a power struggle with other wealthy families led to the Medici's expulsion from Florence. In 1434, the Medici returned, but Cosimo, aware of the importance of public perception, attempted to maintain a lower profile and to wield his power from behind the scenes. In all probability, this attitude accounted for his rejection of Brunelleschi's design for the Medici residence, which he evidently found too imposing and ostentatious to be politically wise. Cosimo eventually awarded the commission to MICHELOZZO DI BARTOLOMMEO (1396–1472), a young architect who had been Donatello's collaborator in several sculptural enterprises. Although Cosimo chose Michelozzo instead of Brunelleschi, Brunelleschi's architectural style in fact deeply influenced the young architect. To a limited extent, the Palazzo Medici-Riccardi (FIG. 21-20) reflects Brunelleschian principles.

Later bought by the Riccardi family (hence the name Palazzo Medici-Riccardi), who almost doubled the facade's length in the 18th century, the palace, both in its original and extended form, is a simple, massive structure. Heavy rustication on the ground floor accentuates its strength. Michelozzo divided the building block into stories of decreasing height by using long, unbroken stringcourses (horizontal bands), which give it coherence. Dressed stone on the upper levels produces a smoother surface with each successive story and modifies the severity of the ground floor. The building thus appears progressively lighter as the eye moves upward. The extremely heavy cornice, which Michelozzo related not to the top story but to the building as a whole, dramatically reverses this effect. Like the ancient Roman cornices that served as Michelozzo's models (compare, for example, FIGS. 10-30, 10-37, and 10-45), the Palazzo Medici-Riccardi cornice is a very effective lid for the structure, clearly and

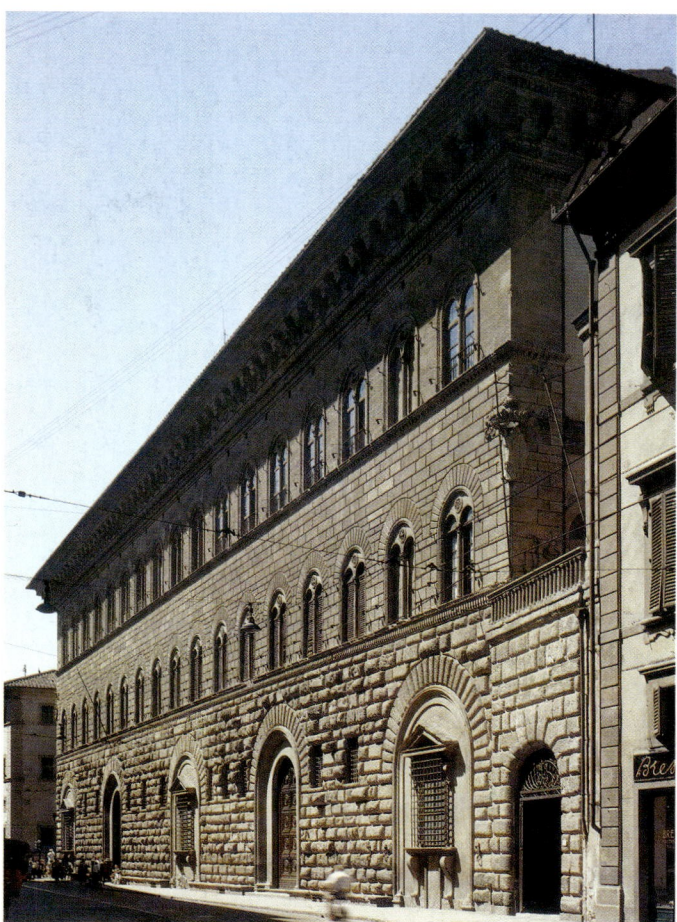

21-20 MICHELOZZO DI BARTOLOMMEO, facade of the Palazzo Medici-Riccardi, Florence, Italy, begun 1445.

emphatically defining its proportions. Michelozzo also may have been inspired by the many extant examples of Roman rusticated masonry, and Roman precedents even exist for the juxtaposition of rusticated and dressed stone masonry on the same facade (see FIG. 10-32). However, nothing in the ancient world precisely compares to Michelozzo's design. The Palazzo Medici-Riccardi is an excellent example of the simultaneous respect for and independence from the antique that characterize the Early Renaissance in Italy.

The Palazzo Medici-Riccardi is built around an open colonnaded court (FIG. 21-21) that clearly shows Michelozzo's debt to Brunelleschi. The round-arched colonnade, although more massive in its proportions, closely resembles other buildings by Brunelleschi. This internal court surrounded by an arcade was the first of its kind and influenced a long line of descendants in Renaissance domestic architecture.

**THE MEDICI: CULTIVATED HUMANISTS** The references to classical architecture in the Palazzo Medici-Riccardi's design were entirely appropriate for its patrons. The Medici were avid humanists. Cosimo began the first public library since the ancient world, and historians estimate that in some 30 years he and his descendants expended the equivalent of almost $20 million for manuscripts and books. Beyond their enthusiastic collecting of classical and Renaissance literature, the Medici eventually became voracious art collectors. Scarcely a great architect, painter, sculptor, philosopher, or humanist scholar escaped the Medici's notice.

Cosimo was the very model of the cultivated humanist. His grandson Lorenzo (1449–1492), called "the Magnificent," was a

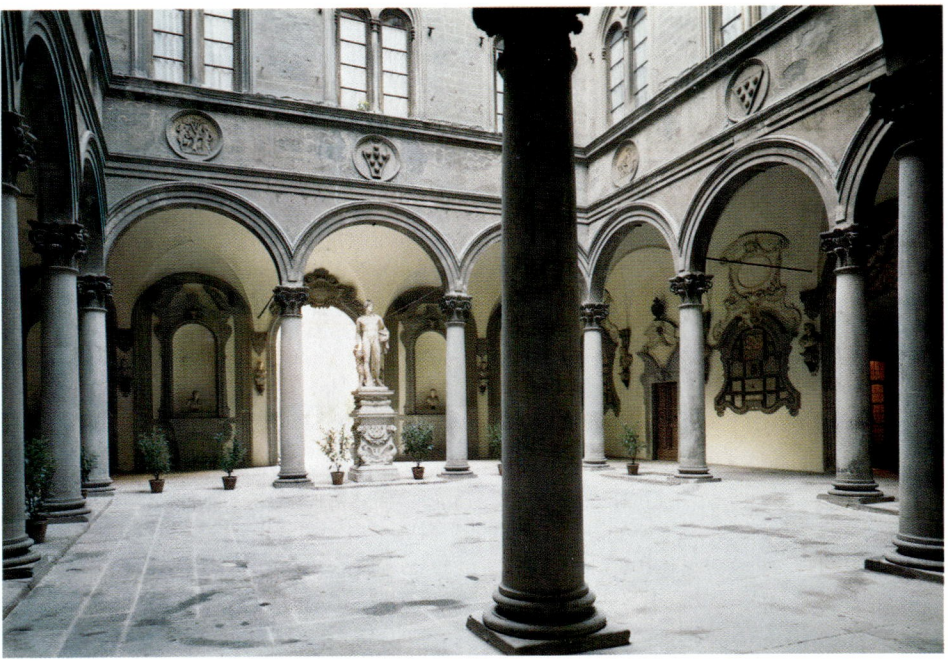

**21-21** MICHELOZZO DI BARTOLOMMEO, interior court of the Palazzo Medici-Riccardi, Florence, Italy, begun 1445.

talented poet himself and gathered about him a galaxy of artists and gifted men in all fields, extending the library Cosimo had begun and revitalizing his academy for instructing artists. He also participated in what some have called the Platonic Academy of Philosophy (most likely an informal reading group), and lavished funds (often the city's own) on splendid buildings, festivals, and pageants. A review here of some of the hundreds of artworks the Medici commissioned reveals the family's interest in humanist ideas and its concern about its public image.

**BOTH CHAOTIC AND ORDERED** PAOLO UCCELLO (1397–1475), a Florentine painter trained in the International Style, received a commission from the Medici to produce a series of panel paintings. Uccello painted *Battle of San Romano* (FIG. **21-22**), one of three wood panels (all with the same title), to decorate Lorenzo the Magnificent's bedchamber. The scenes commemorate the Florentine victory over the Sienese in 1432. In the panel illustrated, Niccolò da Tolentino, a friend and supporter of Cosimo, leads the charge against the Sienese. This particular image may have been selected to commemorate Tolentino, whose subsequent death

perhaps was due to his friendship with the Medici. Although the painting focuses on Tolentino's military exploits, it also acknowledges the Medici. The reference appears in symbolic form. The bright orange fruit (appropriately placed) behind the unbroken and sturdy lances on the left were known as *mela medica* (medicinal apples). Given that the name Medici means "doctor," this fruit was a fitting symbol (one of many) of the family.

Uccello's obsession with perspective undoubtedly appealed to the Medici. The development of perspectival systems intrigued the humanists, because perspective represented the rationalization of vision. As staunch humanists, the Medici pursued all facets of expanding knowledge. In *Battle of San Romano*, Uccello created a composition that recalls the processional splendor of Gentile's *Adoration of the Magi* (FIG. 21-9). But in contrast with Gentile's International Style, characterized by surface decoration, Uccello's world is constructed from immobilized solid forms. He foreshortened broken spears, lances, and a fallen soldier and carefully placed them along the converging orthogonals of the perspectival system to create a base plane like a checkerboard, on which he then placed the larger volumes in measured intervals.

**21-22** PAOLO UCCELLO, *Battle of San Romano,* ca. 1455. Tempera on wood, approx. 6′ × 10′ 5″. National Gallery, London.

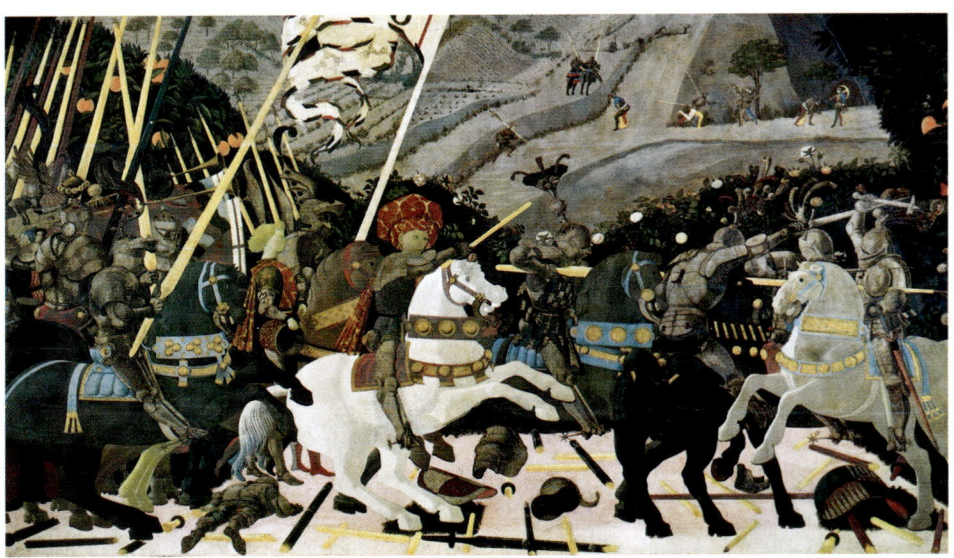

This diligently created space recedes to a landscape that resembles the low cultivated hillsides between Florence and Lucca. The rendering of three-dimensional form, used by other painters for representational or expressive purposes, became for Uccello a preoccupation. For him, it had a magic of its own, which he exploited to satisfy his inventive and original imagination.

**A CLASSICALLY INSPIRED DAVID** The Medici acquired art from the most esteemed artists, and they identified Donatello as among those worthy of receiving their coveted commissions. The bronze statue *David* (FIG. **21-23**), created sometime between the late 1420s and the late 1450s by Donatello for the Palazzo Medici courtyard, was the first freestanding nude statue since ancient times. The nude, as such, proscribed in the Christian Middle Ages as both indecent and idolatrous, had been shown only rarely—and then only in biblical or moralizing contexts, such as the story of Adam and Eve or descriptions of sinners in Hell. Donatello reinvented the classical nude, even though his subject is not a pagan god, hero, or athlete but the biblical David, the young slayer of Goliath and the symbol of the independent Florentine republic. David possesses both the relaxed classical contrapposto stance and the proportions and sensuous

beauty of Greek Praxitelean gods (see FIG. 5-62), qualities absent from medieval figures. The invoking of classical poses and formats appealed to the humanist Medici.

The Medici were aware of Donatello's earlier *David,* a sculpture located in the Palazzo della Signoria, the center of political activity in Florence. The artist had produced it during the threat of invasion by King Ladislaus, and it had become a symbol of Florentine strength and independence. Their selection of the same subject suggests that the Medici identified themselves with Florence or, at the very least, saw themselves as responsible for Florence's prosperity and freedom.

**CELEBRATING FAMILY AND CITY** Another David sculpture produced by one of the most important sculptors during the second half of the century, ANDREA DEL VERROCCHIO (1435–1488), reaffirms this identification of the Medici with Florence. A painter as well as a sculptor, Verrocchio directed a flourishing *bottega* (studio-shop) in Florence that attracted many students, among them Leonardo da Vinci. Verrocchio, like Donatello, also had a broad repertoire. His *David* (FIG. **21-24**) contrasts strongly in its narrative realism with the quiet, aesthetic classicism of Donatello's

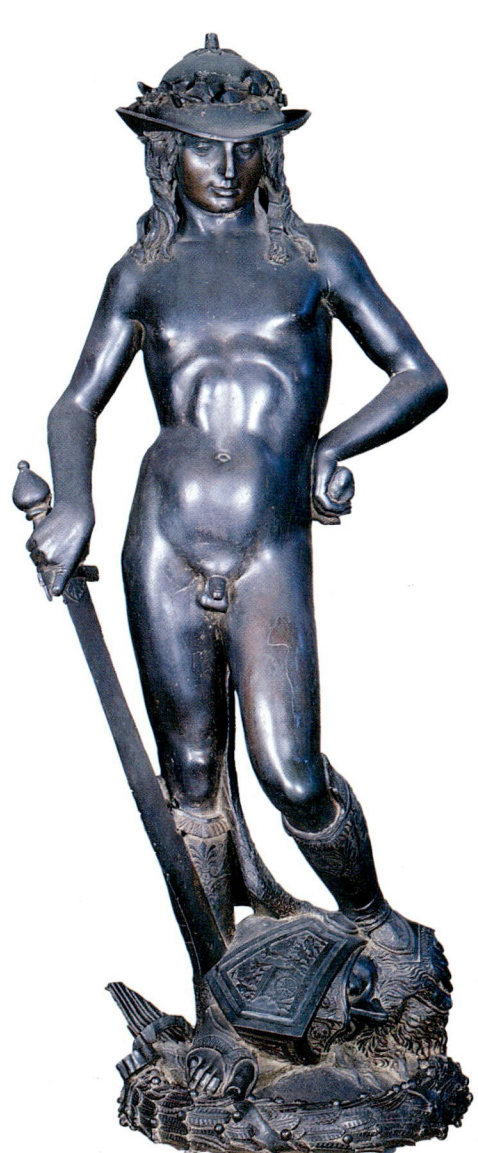

**21-23** DONATELLO, *David,* late 1420s–late 1450s. Bronze, 5′ 2¼″ high. Museo Nazionale del Bargello, Florence.

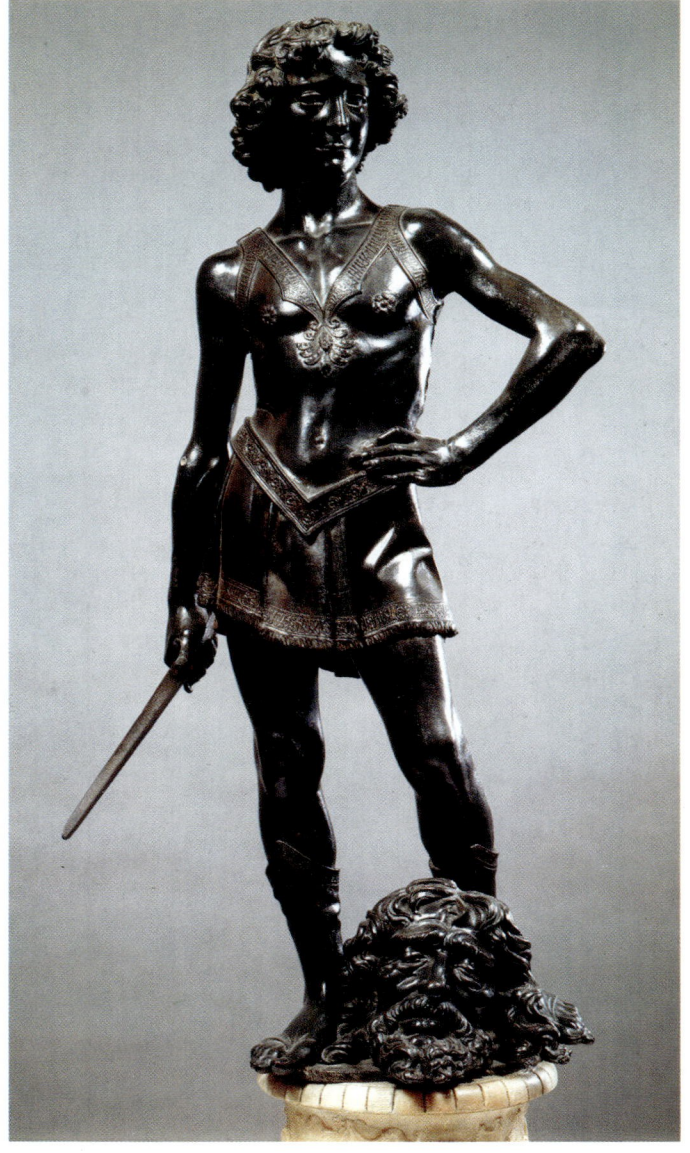

**21-24** ANDREA DEL VERROCCHIO, *David,* ca. 1465–1470. Bronze, approx. 4′ 1½″ high. Museo Nazionale del Bargello, Florence.

*David*. Verrocchio's *David* is a sturdy, wiry young apprentice clad in a leathern doublet who stands with a jaunty pride. As in Donatello's version, Goliath's head lies at David's feet. He poses like a hunter with his kill. The easy balance of the weight and the lithe, still thinly adolescent musculature, with prominent veins, show how closely Verrocchio read the biblical text and how clearly he knew the psychology of brash and confident young men.

Lorenzo and Giuliano de' Medici eventually sold Verrocchio's bronze *David* to the Florentine *signoria* (a governing body) for placement in the Palazzo della Signoria. After the Medici were expelled from Florence, city officials appropriated Donatello's *David* for civic use and moved it to the Palazzo as well.

**A MYTHIC WRESTLING MATCH** Closely related in stylistic intent to Verrocchio's work is that of Antonio Pollaiuolo (ca. 1431–1498). Pollaiuolo, who is also important as a painter and engraver, received a Medici commission in the 1470s to produce a small-scale sculpture, *Hercules and Antaeus* (FIG. **21-25**). In contrast to the placid presentation of Donatello's *David, Hercules and Antaeus* exhibits the stress and strain of the human figure in violent action. This sculpture departs dramatically from the convention of frontality that had dominated statuary art during the Middle Ages and the Early Renaissance. Not quite 18 inches high, *Hercules and Antaeus* embodies the ferocity and vitality of elemental physical conflict. The group illustrates the Greek myth of a wrestling match between Antaeus (Antaios), a giant and son of Earth, and Hercules (Herakles). As seen earlier, Euphronios represented this story on an ancient Greek vase (see FIG. 5-21). Each time Hercules threw him down, Antaeus sprang up again, his strength renewed by contact with the earth. Finally, Hercules held him aloft, so that he could not touch the earth, and strangled him around the waist. Pollaiuolo strove to convey the final excruciating moments of the struggle—the straining and cracking of sinews, the clenched teeth of Hercules, and the kicking and screaming of Antaeus. The figures intertwine and interlock as they fight, and the flickering reflections of light on the dark gouged bronze surface contribute to a fluid play of planes and the effect of agitated movement. The subject matter, derived from Greek mythology, and the emphasis on human anatomy reflect the Medici preference for humanist imagery. Even more specifically, Hercules had been represented on Florence's state seal since the end of the 13th century. As was demonstrated by commissions such as the two *David* sculptures, the Medici clearly embraced every opportunity to associate themselves with the glory of the Florentine republic, surely claiming much of the credit for it.

**BATTLING NUDES** Although not commissioned by the Medici, Pollaiuolo's engraving *Battle of the Ten Nudes* (FIG. **21-26**) further demonstrates the artist's sustained interest in the realistic presentation of human figures in action. Earlier artists, such as Donatello and Masaccio, had dealt effectively with the problem of rendering human anatomy, but they usually depicted their figures at rest or in restrained motion. As is evident in his *Hercules and Antaeus,* Pollaiuolo took delight in showing violent action and found his opportunity in subjects dealing with combat. He conceived the body as a powerful machine and liked to display its mechanisms, such as knotted muscles and taut sinews that activate the skeleton as ropes pull levers. To show this to best effect, Pollaiuolo developed a figure so lean and muscular that it appears *écorché* (as if without skin), with strongly accentuated delineations at the wrists, elbows, shoulders, and knees. His *Battle of the Ten Nudes* shows this figure type in a variety of poses and from numerous viewpoints, allowing Pollaiuolo to demonstrate his prowess in rendering the nude male figure. In this, he was a kindred spirit of late-sixth-century Greek vase painters, such as Euthymides (see FIG. 5-22), who had experimented with foreshortening for the first time in history. If Pollaiuolo's figures, even though they hack and slash at each other without mercy, seem somewhat stiff and frozen, it is because Pollaiuolo shows *all* the muscle groups at maximum tension. Not until several decades later did an even greater anatomist, Leonardo, observe that only part of the body's muscle groups are involved in any one action, while the others are relaxed.

The medium that Pollaiuolo used for *Battle of the Ten Nudes*—engraving—was probably developed by northern European artists around the middle of the 15th century. But whereas German graphic artists, such as Martin Schongauer (see FIG. 20-25), described their forms with hatching that follows the forms, Italian engravers, such as Pollaiuolo, preferred parallel hatching. The former method was in keeping with the general northern approach to art, which tended to describe surfaces of forms rather than their underlying structures, whereas the latter was better suited for the anatomical studies that preoccupied Pollaiuolo and his Italian contemporaries.

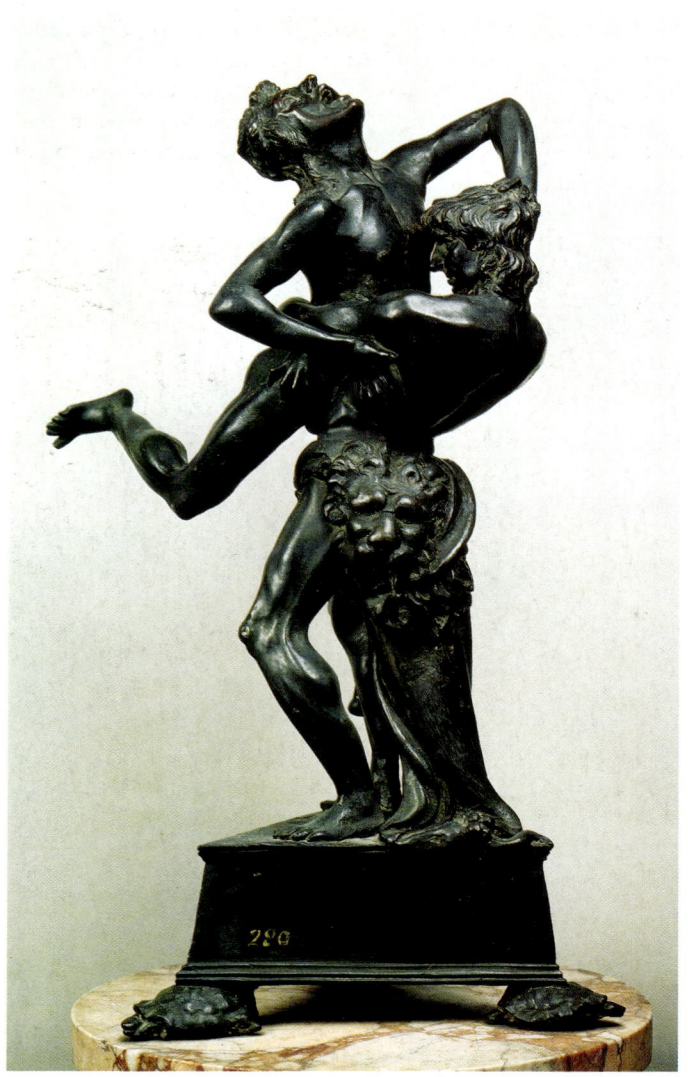

**21-25** Antonio Pollaiuolo, *Hercules and Antaeus,* ca. 1475. Bronze, approx. 1′ 6″ high with base. Museo Nazionale del Bargello, Florence.

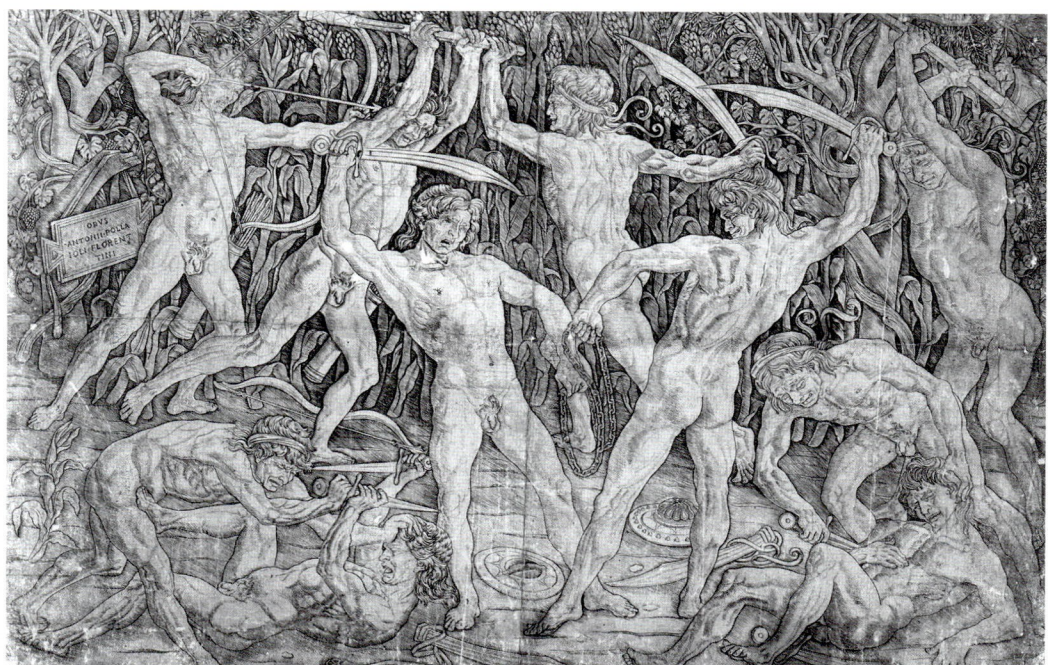

**21-26** Antonio Pollaiuolo, *Battle of the Ten Nudes*, ca. 1465. Engraving, approx. 1′ 3″ × 1′ 11″. Metropolitan Museum of Art, New York (bequest of Joseph Pulitzer, 1917).

**VISUAL POETRY** Sandro Botticelli (1444–1510) remains among the best known of the artists who produced works for the Medici. One of the works he painted in tempera on canvas for the Medici was his famous *Birth of Venus* (FIG. **21-27**). A poem on that theme by Angelo Poliziano, one of the leading humanists of the day, inspired Botticelli to create this lyrical image. Zephyrus (the west wind) blows Venus, born of the sea foam and carried on a cockle shell, to her sacred island, Cyprus. There, the nymph Pomona runs to meet her with a brocaded mantle. The lightness and bodilessness of the winds move all the figures without effort. Draperies undulate easily in the gentle gusts, perfumed by rose petals that fall on the whitecaps. Botticelli's nude presentation of

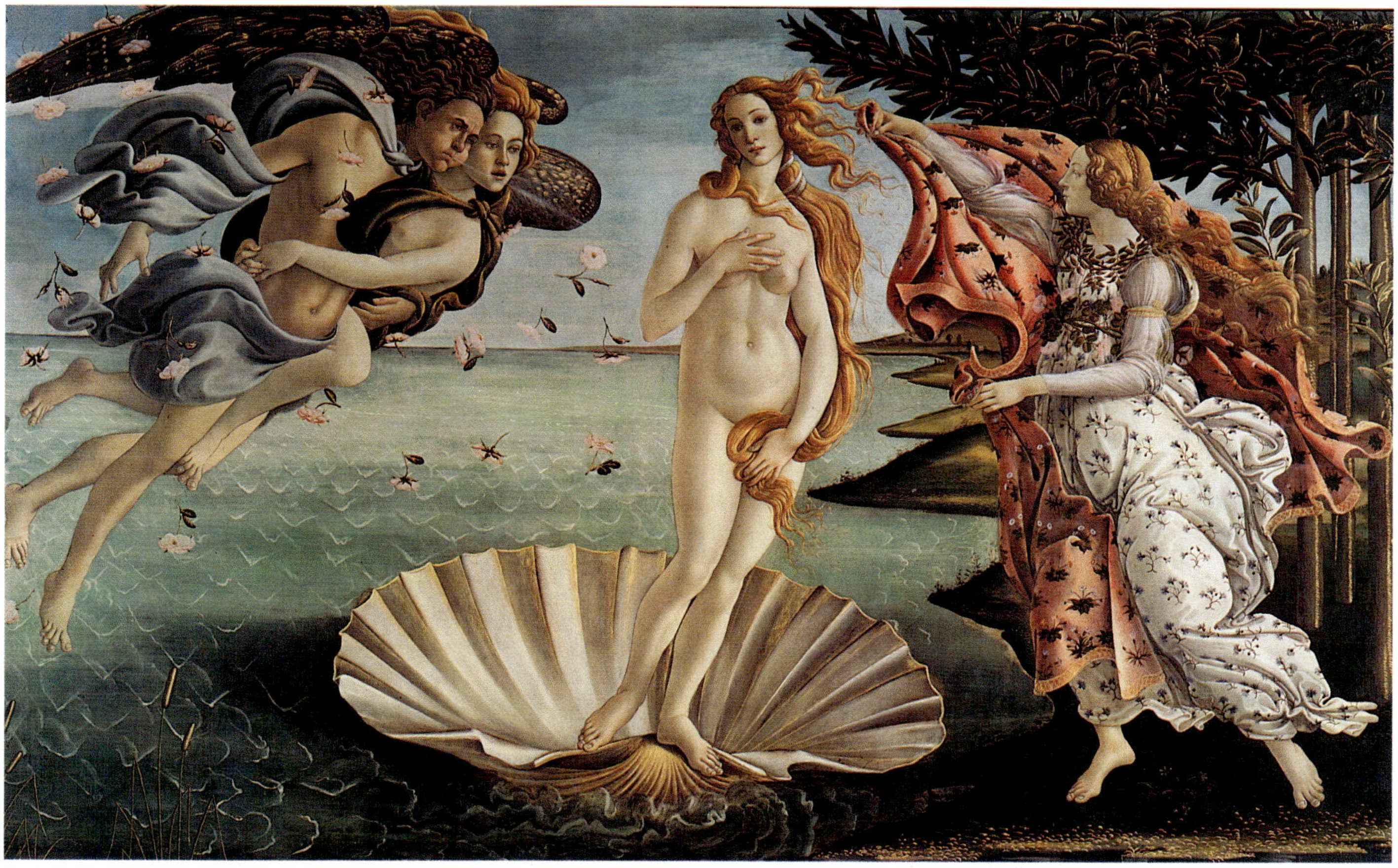

**21-27** Sandro Botticelli, *Birth of Venus*, ca. 1482. Tempera on canvas, approx. 5′ 8″ × 9′ 1″. Galleria degli Uffizi, Florence.

the Venus figure was in itself an innovation. As mentioned earlier, the nude, especially the female nude, had been proscribed during the Middle Ages. The artist's use (especially on such a large scale) of an ancient Venus statue of the Venus *pudica* (modest Venus) type—a Hellenistic variant of Praxiteles' famous *Aphrodite of Knidos* (see FIG. 5-60)—as a model could have drawn the charge of paganism and infidelity. But in the more accommodating Renaissance culture and under the protection of the powerful Medici, the depiction went unchallenged.

Botticelli's style is clearly distinct from the earnest search many other artists pursued to comprehend humanity and the natural world through a rational and empirical order. Indeed, Botticelli's elegant and beautiful style seems to have ignored all of the scientific knowledge experimental art had gained (for example, in the areas of perspective and anatomy). His style paralleled the allegorical pageants that were staged in Florence as chivalric tournaments but were structured around allusions to classical mythology; the same trend is evident in the poetry of the 1470s and 1480s. Artists and poets at this time did not directly imitate classical antiquity but used the myths, with delicate perception of their charm, in a way still tinged with medieval romance. Ultimately, Botticelli created a style of visual poetry, parallel to the Petrarchan love poetry written by Lorenzo de' Medici. His paintings possess a lyricism and courtliness that appealed to cultured patrons such as the Medici.

As evidenced by these Medici commissions, the Florentine family did not restrict their collecting to any specific style or artist. Their acquisitions, as already noted, often incorporated elements associated with humanism, from mythological subject matter to concerns with anatomy and perspective. Collectively, the art of the Medici also makes a statement about the patrons themselves. Careful businessmen that they were, the Medici were not sentimental about their endowment of art and scholarship. Cosimo acknowledged that his good works were not only for the honor of God but also to construct his own legacy. This is not to suggest that the Medici were solely self-serving—throughout the century, Medici family members demonstrated a sustained and sincere love of learning.

## THE RISE OF PORTRAITURE

Given the increased emphasis on individual achievement and recognition that humanism fostered, it is not surprising that portraiture enjoyed a revival in the 15th century. Commemorative portraits of the deceased were common, and patrons also commissioned portraits of themselves. The profile pose was customary in Florence until about 1470, when three-quarter and full-face portraits began to replace it. Bust-length portraits based on Roman precedents also became prominent.

**A PSYCHOLOGICAL PROFILE** In about the last decade of the 15th century, Sandro Botticelli painted the nearly full-face *Portrait of a Youth* (FIG. **21-28**). Painters of northern Europe (see FIGS. 20-16 and 20-17) popularized three-quarter and full-face views earlier in the century. Such poses increased the information available to viewers about the subject's appearance. Further, these poses permitted greater exploration of the subject's character, although Italian artists and patrons continued to favor an impersonal formality that concealed the private psychological person. An apparent exception, Botticelli's young man is highly expressive psychologically. The delicacy of the pose, the head's graceful tilt,

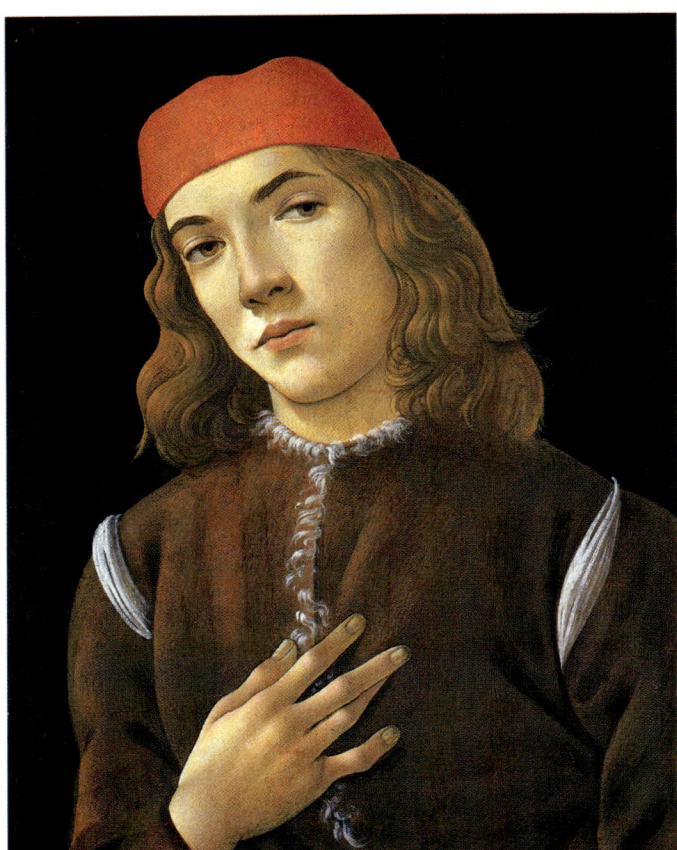

21-28 SANDRO BOTTICELLI, *Portrait of a Youth*, early 1480s. Tempera on panel, 1′ 4″ × 1′. National Gallery of Art, Washington (Andrew W. Mellon Collection).

the sidelong glance, and the elegant hand gesture compose an equivocal expression half musing and half insinuating.

Botticelli was the pupil of Fra Filippo Lippi (FIG. 21-38), who must have taught him the method of "drawing" firm, pure outline with light shading within the contours. The effect is apparent in the portrait's explicit and sharply elegant form. Botticelli infinitely refined this method, and art historians recognize him as one of the great masters of line.

**A CAT ON A HORSE** In 1443, Donatello left Florence for northern Italy to accept a rewarding commission from the Republic of Venice to create a commemorative monument in honor of the recently deceased Venetian condottiere Erasmo da Narni, nicknamed Gattamelata ("honeyed cat," a wordplay on his mother's name, Melania Gattelli). City officials asked Donatello to portray Gattamelata on horseback in a statue (FIG. **21-29**) to be erected in the square of Sant'Antonio in Padua. Although equestrian statues occasionally had been set up in Italy in the late Middle Ages, Donatello's *Gattamelata* is the first to rival the grandeur of the mounted portraits of antiquity, such as that of Marcus Aurelius (see FIG. 10-59), which the artist must have seen in Rome. Donatello's contemporaries, one of whom described Gattamelata as sitting "there with great magnificence like a triumphant Caesar,"[5] recognized this reference to antiquity. The figure stands high on a lofty elliptical base, set apart from its surroundings, and almost celebrates sculpture's liberation from architecture. Massive and majestic, the great horse bears the armored general easily, for, unlike the sculptor of Marcus Aurelius, Donatello did not represent the Venetian commander as superhuman and more

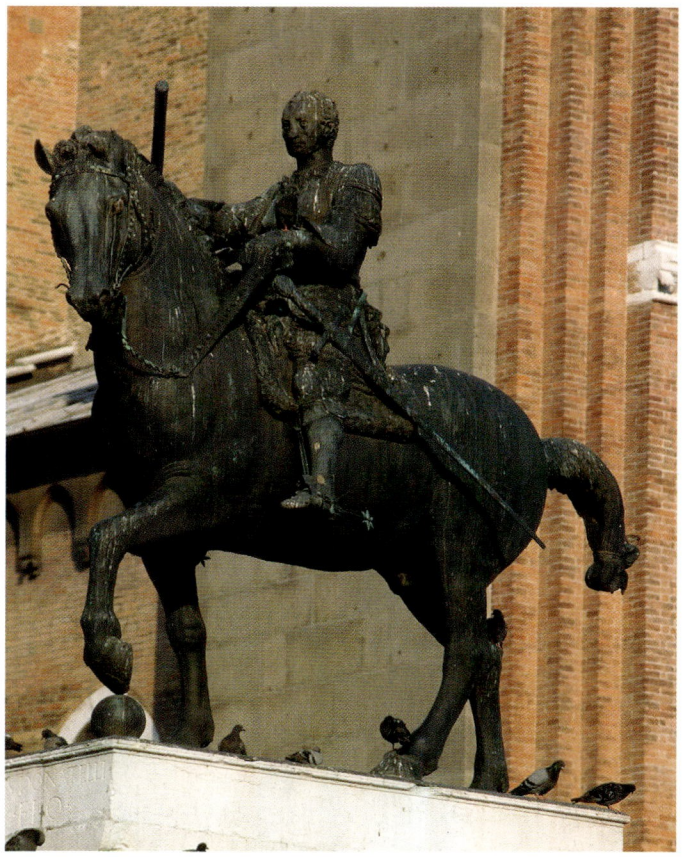

**21-29** Donatello, *Gattamelata* (equestrian statue of Erasmo da Narni), Piazza del Santo, Padua, Italy, ca. 1445–1450. Bronze, approx. 11′ × 13′.

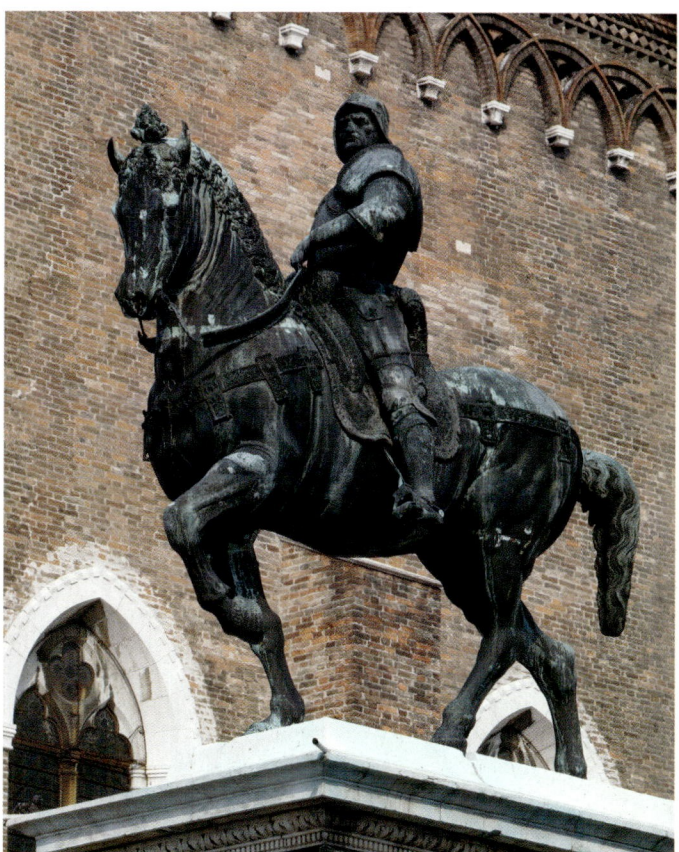

**21-30** Andrea del Verrocchio, *Bartolommeo Colleoni* (equestrian statue), Campo dei Santi Giovanni e Paolo, Venice, Italy, ca. 1483–1488. Bronze, approx. 13′ high.

than life-size. The officer dominates his mighty steed by force of character rather than sheer size. Together, man and horse convey an overwhelming image of irresistible strength and unlimited power—an impression Donatello reinforced visually by placing the left forehoof of the horse on an orb, reviving a venerable ancient symbol for hegemony over the earth. The Italian rider, his face set in a mask of dauntless resolution and unshakable will, is the very portrait of the male Renaissance individualist. Such a man—intelligent, courageous, ambitious, and frequently of humble origin—could, by his own resourcefulness and on his own merits, rise to a commanding position in the world.

**A DOMINATING MILITARY LEADER** Verrocchio's equestrian statue of another condottiere of Venice, Bartolommeo Colleoni (FIG. **21-30**), provides a counterpoint to *Gattamelata*. Eager to garner the fame of *Gattamelata* by emulating Donatello's sculpture, Colleoni provided for the statue in his will. Both artists executed the statues after the death of their subjects, so neither Donatello nor Verrocchio knew personally the individual he portrayed. The result is a fascinating difference of interpretation (like that between the two *Davids*, FIGS. 21-23 and 21-24) as to the demeanor of a professional captain of armies. Verrocchio placed the statue of the bold equestrian general on a pedestal even higher than that Donatello used for *Gattamelata* so that viewers could see the dominating, aggressive figure from all major approaches to the piazza (the Campo dei Santi Giovanni e Paolo). In contrast with the near repose of *Gattamelata*, the *Colleoni* horse moves in a prancing stride, arching and curving its powerful neck, while the commander seems suddenly to shift his whole weight to the

stirrups and rise from the saddle with a violent twist of his body. The artist depicted the figures with an exaggerated tautness—the animal's bulging muscles and the man's fiercely erect and rigid body together convey brute strength. In *Gattamelata*, Donatello created a portrait of grim sagacity; Verrocchio's *Bartolommeo Colleoni* is a portrait of merciless might. Machiavelli wrote in his famous political treatise of 1513, *The Prince,* that the successful ruler must combine the traits of the lion and the fox. It seems that Donatello's *Gattamelata* is a little like the latter and that Verrocchio's *Bartolommeo Colleoni* is much like the former.

**A WOMAN OF CULTURE** Women were also portrait subjects. Domenico Ghirlandaio (1449–1494) produced a portrait of an aristocratic young woman (FIG. **21-31**), probably Giovanna Tornabuoni, a member of the powerful Albizzi family and wife of Lorenzo Tornabuoni. Although artists did not often employ the profile pose to convey a character reading, this portrait reveals the proud bearing of a sensitive and beautiful young woman. It tells viewers much about the advanced state of culture in Florence, the value and careful cultivation of beauty in life and art, the breeding of courtly manners, and the great wealth behind it all. The painting also shows the powerful attraction classical literature held for Italian humanists; in the background, an epitaph (Giovanna Tornabuoni died in childbirth in 1488) quotes the ancient Roman poet Martial.

**SUMMARIZING FLORENTINE ART** Domenico Ghirlandaio's art summarizes the state of Florentine art toward the end of the 15th century. Giovanni Tornabuoni, one of the wealthiest

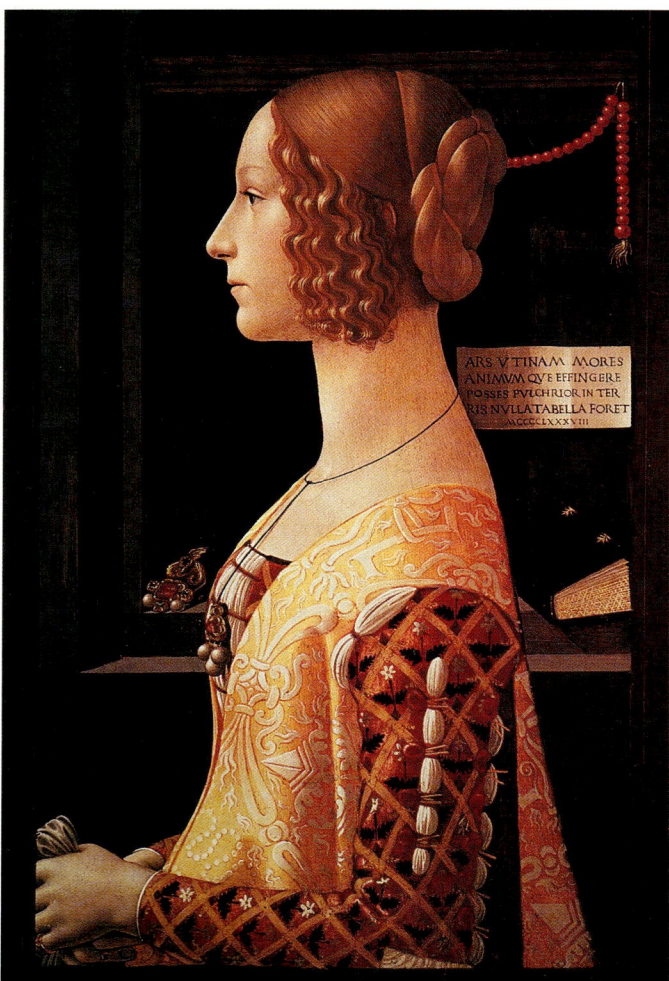

Florentines of his day, commissioned Ghirlandaio's most representative pictures, a cycle of frescoes depicting scenes from the lives of the Virgin and Saint John the Baptist, for the choir of Santa Maria Novella. In the illustrated painting, *Birth of the Virgin* (FIG. **21-32**), Mary's mother, Saint Anne, reclines in a palace room embellished with fine *intarsia* (wood inlay) and sculpture, while midwives prepare the infant's bath. From the left comes a grave procession of women led by a young Tornabuoni family member, probably Ludovica, Giovanni's daughter. Ludovica holds as prominent a place in the composition (close to the central axis) as she must have held in Florentine society. Her appearance in the painting (a different female member of the house appears in each fresco) is conspicuous evidence of the secularization of sacred themes—commonplace in art by this time. Artists depicted living persons of high rank not only as present at biblical dramas but also, as here, often stealing the show from the saints. The display of patrician elegance tempers the biblical narrative and subordinates the tableau's devotional nature.

Ghirlandaio's composition epitomizes the achievements of Early Renaissance painting: clear spatial representation; statuesque, firmly constructed figures; and rational order and logical relations among these figures and objects. If anything of earlier traits remains here, it is the arrangement of the figures, which still cling somewhat rigidly to layers parallel to the picture plane.

## FURTHER DEVELOPMENTS
## IN ARCHITECTURE

LEON BATTISTA ALBERTI (1404–1472) entered the profession of architecture rather late in life, but nevertheless made a remarkable contribution to architectural design. He was the first to study seriously the treatise of Vitruvius (*De architectura*), and his knowledge of it, combined with his own archaeological investigations, made him the first Renaissance architect to understand Roman

**21-31** DOMENICO GHIRLANDAIO, *Giovanna Tornabuoni*(?), 1488. Oil and tempera on wood, approx. 2′ 6″ × 1′ 8″. Thyssen-Bornemisza Collection, Madrid, Spain.

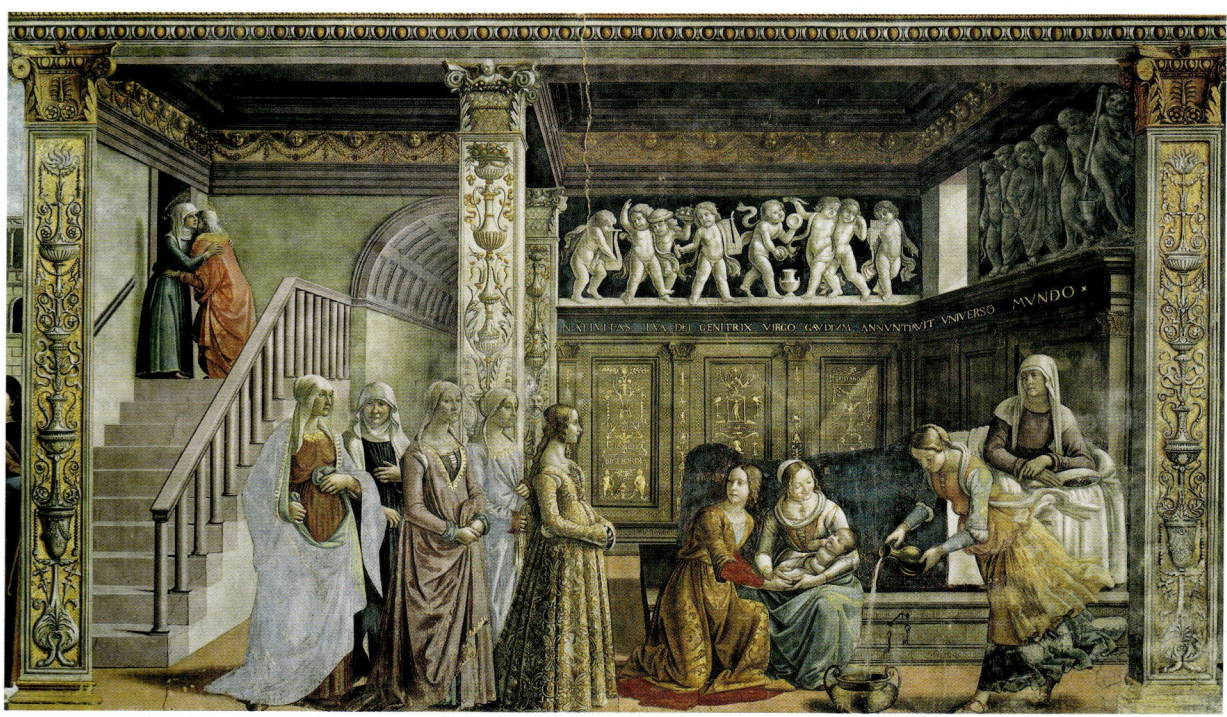

**21-32** DOMENICO GHIRLANDAIO, *Birth of the Virgin,* Cappella Maggiore, Santa Maria Novella, Florence, Italy, 1485–1490. Fresco.

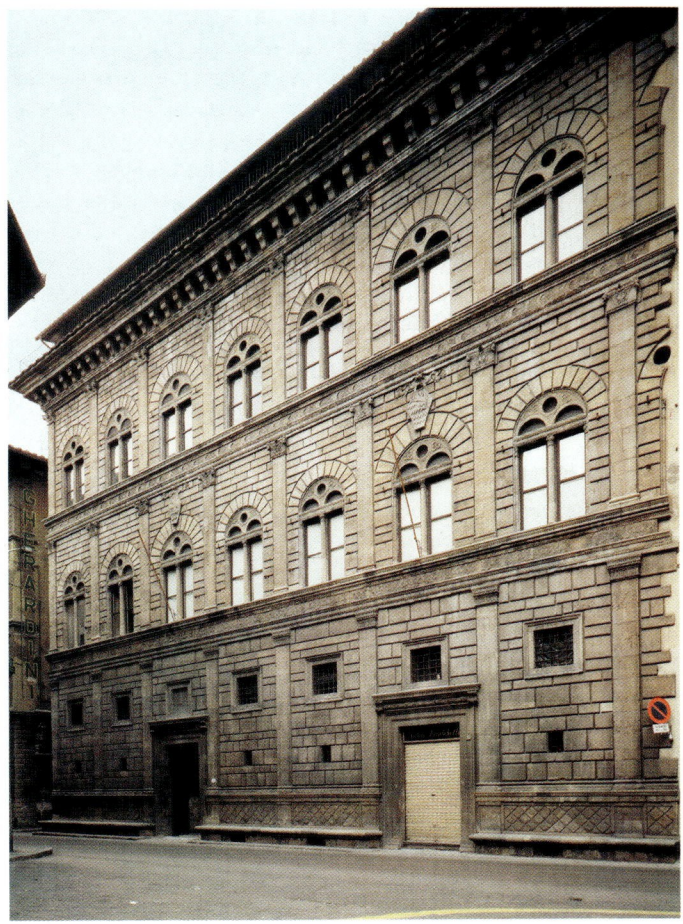

**21-33** LEON BATTISTA ALBERTI, Palazzo Rucellai, Florence, Italy, ca. 1452–1470.

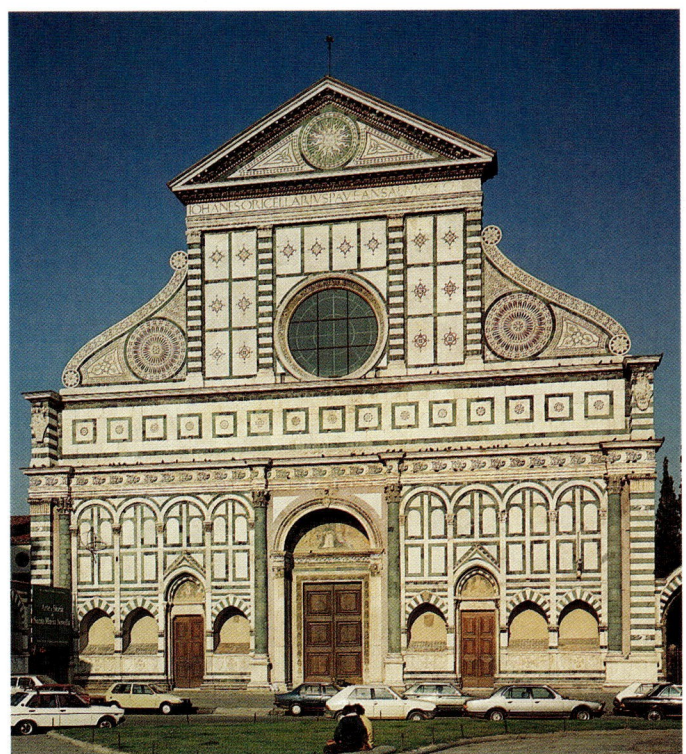

**21-34** LEON BATTISTA ALBERTI, west facade of Santa Maria Novella, Florence, Italy, ca. 1458–1470.

architecture in depth. Alberti's most important and influential theoretical work, *De re aedificatoria* (written about 1450, published 1486), although inspired by Vitruvius, contains much original material. Alberti advocated a system of ideal proportions and argued that the central plan was the ideal form for a Christian church. He also considered incongruous the combination of column and arch, which had persisted since Roman times (see FIG. 10-51). By arguing that the arch is a wall opening that should be supported only by a section of wall (a pier), not by an independent sculptural element (a column), Alberti (with a few exceptions) disposed of the medieval arcade used for centuries.

**BUILDING ON CLASSICISM** Alberti's own architectural style represents a scholarly application of classical elements to contemporary buildings. His Palazzo Rucellai in Florence (FIG. **21-33**) probably dates from the mid-1450s. Alberti organized the facade, built over a number of medieval houses, in a much more severe fashion than the Palazzo Medici-Riccardi facade (FIG. 21-20), another classically inspired building. Flat pilasters, which support full entablatures, define each story of the Palazzo Rucellai. A classical cornice crowns the palace. The rustication of the wall surfaces between the smooth pilasters is subdued and uniform. Alberti created the sense that the structure becomes lighter in weight toward its top by adapting the ancient Roman manner of using different capitals for each story. He chose Tuscan (the Etruscan variant of the Greek Doric order) for the ground floor, Composite (the Roman combination of Ionic volutes with the acanthus leaves of the Corinthian) for the second story, and Corinthian for the third floor. Alberti modeled his facade on the most imposing Roman ruin of all, the Colosseum (see FIG. 10-34), but he was no slavish copyist. On the Colosseum's facade the capitals employed are, from the bottom up, Tuscan, Ionic, and Corinthian. Moreover, Alberti adapted the Colosseum's varied surface to a flat facade, which does not allow the deep penetration of the building's mass that is so effective in the Roman structure. By converting his ancient model's *engaged columns* (half-round columns attached to a wall) into shallow pilasters that barely project from the wall, Alberti created a large-meshed linear net. Stretched tightly across the front of his building, it not only unifies the three levels but also emphasizes the wall's flat, two-dimensional qualities.

**OF RATIOS AND RATIONALITY** The Rucellai family also commissioned from Alberti the design for the facade of the 13th-century Gothic church of Santa Maria Novella in Florence (FIGS. **21-34** and **21-35**). Here, Alberti took his cue (just as Brunelleschi did occasionally) from a pre-Gothic medieval design—that of

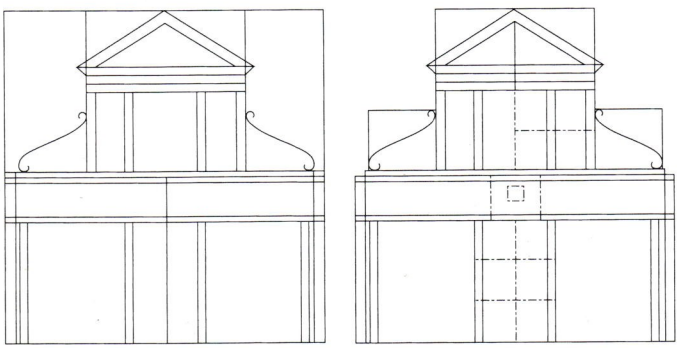

**21-35** LEON BATTISTA ALBERTI, diagrams of west facade, Santa Maria Novella, Florence, Italy.

San Miniato al Monte. Following this Romanesque model, he designed a small, pseudoclassical, pediment-capped temple front for the facade's upper part and supported it with a broad base of pilaster-enframed arcades that incorporate the six tombs and three doorways of the extant Gothic building. But in the organization of these elements, Alberti took a long step beyond the Romanesque planners. The height of Santa Maria Novella (to the pediment tip) equals its width so that the entire facade can be inscribed in a square (FIG. 21-35, *left*). Throughout the facade, Alberti defined areas and related them to one another in terms of proportions that can be expressed in simple numerical ratios (1:1, 1:2, 1:3, 2:3, and so on). For example, the upper structure can be encased in a square one-fourth the size of the main square (for other squares, see the right diagram). The cornice of the entablature that separates the two levels halves the major square so that the lower portion of the building is a rectangle twice as wide as it is high. Further, the areas outlined by the columns on the lower level are squares with sides about one-third the width of the main unit. In his treatise, Alberti wrote at length to promote the necessity of such harmonic relationships for designing beautiful buildings.

Alberti shared this conviction with Brunelleschi, and this fundamental dependence on classically derived mathematics distinguished their architectural work from that of their medieval predecessors. They believed in the eternal and universal validity of numerical ratios as the source of beauty. In this respect, Alberti and Brunelleschi revived the true spirit of the High Classical age of ancient Greece, as epitomized by the sculptor Polykleitos and the architect Iktinos, who produced canons of proportions for the perfect statue and the perfect temple. But it was not only a desire to emulate Vitruvius and the Classical masters that motivated Alberti to turn to mathematics in his quest for beauty. His contemporary, the Florentine humanist Giannozzo Manetti, had argued that Christianity itself possessed the order and logic of mathematics; in his 1452 treatise, *On the Dignity and Excellence of Man,* Manetti stated that Christian religious truths were as self-evident as mathematical axioms.

The Santa Maria Novella facade was an ingenious solution to a difficult design problem. On one hand, it adequately expressed the organization of the structure attached to it. On the other hand, it subjected preexisting and quintessentially medieval features, such as the large round window on the second level, to a rigid geometrical order that instilled a quality of classical calm and reason. This facade also introduced a feature of great historical consequence — the scrolls that simultaneously unite the broad lower and narrow upper level and screen the sloping roofs over the aisles. With variations, such spirals appeared in literally hundreds of church facades throughout the Renaissance and Baroque periods.

## IMAGES OF PIETY AND DEVOTION

**A VISUAL CALL TO PRAYER** As is evident from the plethora of religious imagery produced during the 15th century, humanism and religion were not mutually exclusive. For many artists, humanist concerns were not a primary consideration. FRA ANGELICO (ca. 1400–1455) was among those; his art focused on serving the Roman Catholic Church. In the late 1430s, the abbot of the Dominican monastery of San Marco in Florence asked Fra Angelico to produce a series of frescoes for the monastery. The Dominicans of San Marco had dedicated themselves to lives of prayer and work, and the religious compound was mostly spare and austere to encourage the monks to immerse themselves in their devotional lives. Fra Angelico's frescoes illustrated a 13th-century text, *De modo orandi* (*The Way of Prayer*), which describes the nine ways of prayer used by Saint Dominic, the order's founder.

Among the works he completed was *Annunciation* (FIG. **21-36**), which appears at the top of the stairs leading to the friars' cells. Appropriately, Fra Angelico presented the scene of the Virgin Mary and the Archangel Gabriel with simplicity and serenity. The two figures appear in a plain loggia, and the artist painted all the fresco elements with a pristine clarity. As an admonition to heed the devotional function of the images, Fra Angelico included a small

**21-36** FRA ANGELICO, *Annunciation,* San Marco, Florence, Italy, ca. 1440–1445. Fresco, 7′ 1″ × 10′ 6″.

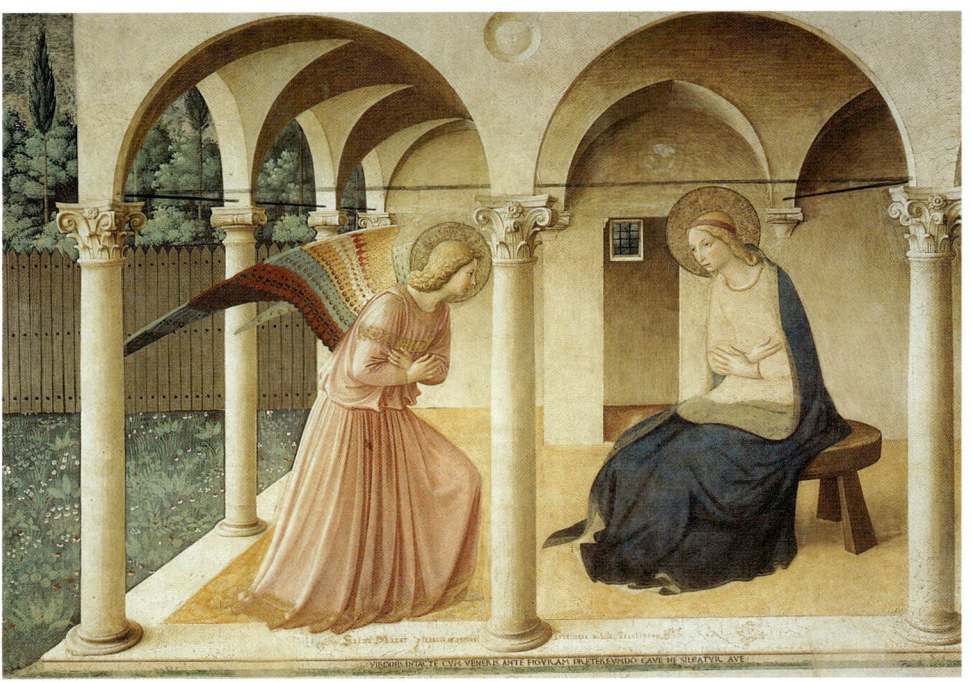

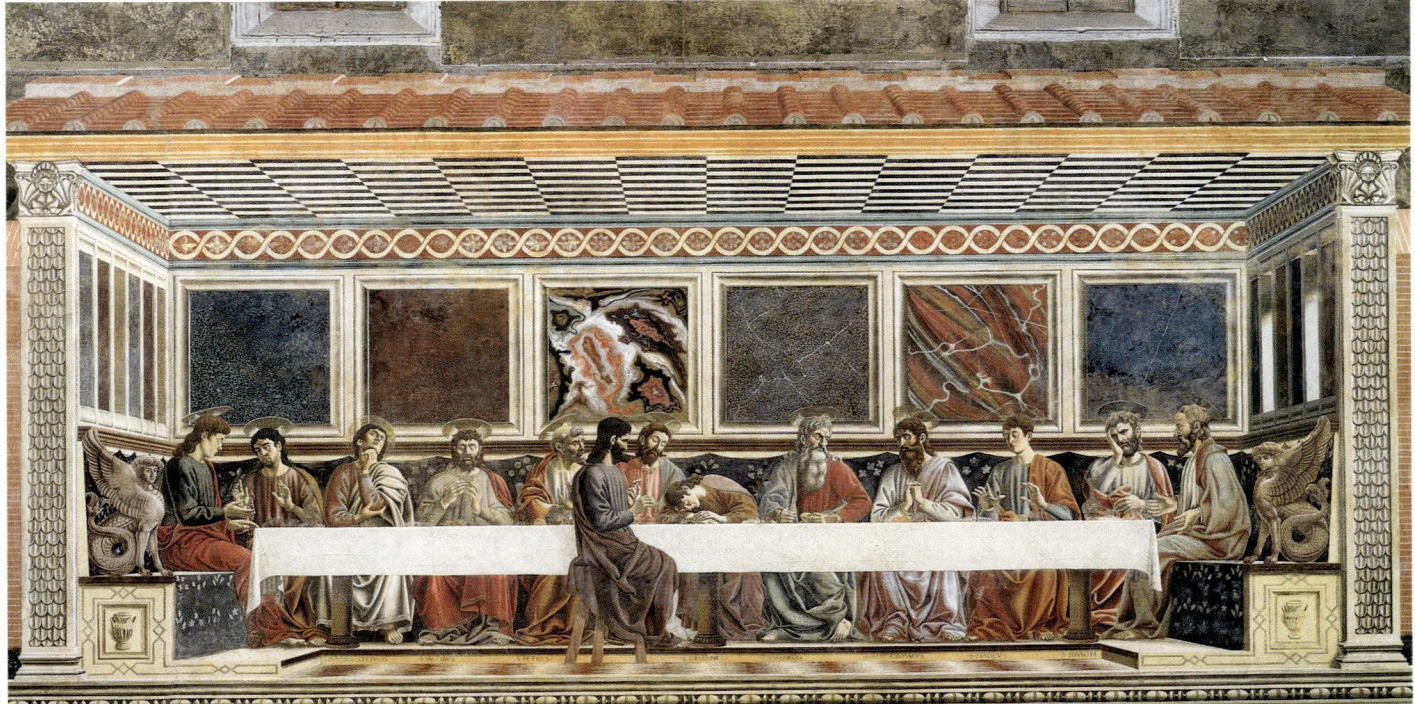

**21-37** ANDREA DEL CASTAGNO, *Last Supper*, the refectory, monastery of Sant'Apollonia, Florence, Italy, 1447. Fresco, approx. 15′ × 32′.

inscription at the base of the image that reads, "As you venerate, while passing before it, this figure of the intact Virgin, beware lest you omit to say a Hail Mary." Like most of Fra Angelico's paintings, *Annunciation*'s simplicity and directness still has an almost universal appeal and fully reflects the artist's simple and humble character.

**THE LAST SUPPER IN PERSPECTIVE** ANDREA DEL CASTAGNO (ca. 1421–1457), like Fra Angelico, accepted a commission to produce a series of frescoes for a religious establishment. His *Last Supper* (FIG. **21-37**), painted in the refectory (dining hall) of Sant'Apollonia in Florence, a convent for Benedictine nuns, manifests both a commitment to the biblical narrative and an interest in perspective. The lavishly painted space that Christ and his 12 disciples occupy suggests Castagno's absorption with creating the illusion of three-dimensional space. However, closer scrutiny reveals inconsistencies, such as the fact that Renaissance perspectival systems make it impossible to see both the ceiling and the roof, as Castagno depicted. Further, the two side walls do not appear parallel.

The artist chose a conventional compositional format, with the figures seated at a horizontally placed table. Castagno derived the apparent self-absorption of most of the disciples and the malevolent features of Judas (who sits alone on the outside of the table) from the Gospel of Saint John, rather than the more familiar version of the Last Supper recounted in the Gospel of Saint Luke. The exploration of perspective so prevalent in 15th-century Italian art clearly influenced Castagno's depiction of the Last Supper, which no doubt was a powerful presence for the nuns during their daily meals.

**A FACILITY WITH LINE** A younger contemporary of Fra Angelico, FRA FILIPPO LIPPI (ca. 1406–1469), was also a friar—but there all resemblance ends. According to reports, Fra Filippo seems to have been an amiable man unsuited for monastic life. He indulged in misdemeanors ranging from forgery and embezzlement to the abduction of a pretty nun, Lucretia, who became his mistress and the mother of his son, the painter Filippino Lippi (1457–1504). Only the Medici's intervention on his behalf at the papal court preserved Fra Filippo from severe punishment and total disgrace. An orphan, Fra Filippo spent his youth in a monastery adjacent to the church of Santa Maria del Carmine, and, when about 18, he must have met Masaccio there and witnessed the decoration of Brancacci Chapel. Fra Filippo's early work survives only in fragments, but these show that he tried to work with Masaccio's massive forms. Later, probably under the influence of Ghiberti's and Donatello's relief sculptures, he developed a linear style that emphasized the contours of his figures and permitted him to suggest movement through flying and swirling draperies.

A painting from Fra Filippo's later years, *Madonna and Child with Angels* (FIG. **21-38**), shows his skill in manipulating line. A wonderfully fluid line unifies the composition and contributes to the precise and smooth delineation of forms. Few artists have surpassed Fra Filippo's skill in using line. He interpreted his subject here in a surprisingly worldly manner. The Madonna, a beautiful young mother, is not at all spiritual or fragile, and neither is the Christ Child, whom two angels hold up. One of the angels turns with the mischievous, puckish grin of a boy refusing to behave for the pious occasion. Significantly, all figures reflect the use of live models (that for the Madonna even may have been Lucretia). Fra Filippo plainly relished the charm of youth and beauty as he found it in this world. He preferred the real in landscape also; the background, seen through the window, incorporates recognizable features of the Arno River Valley. Compared with the earlier Madonnas by Giotto (see FIG. 19-7) and Duccio (see FIG. 19-10), this work shows how far artists had carried the humanization of the theme. Whatever the ideals of spiritual perfection may have meant to artists in past centuries, Renaissance artists realized such ideals in terms of the sensuous beauty of this world.

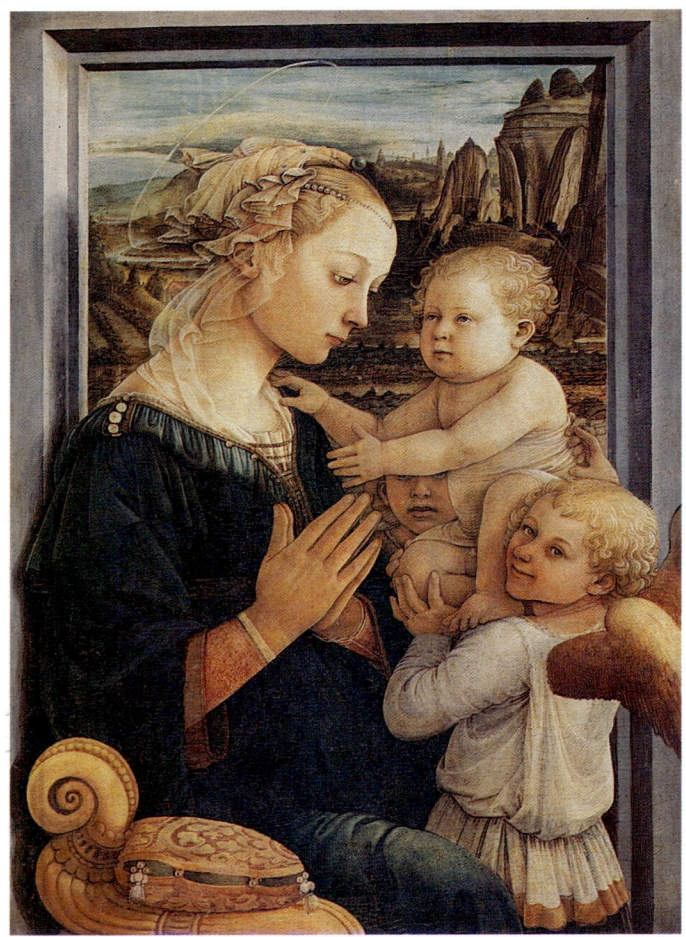

**21-38** Fra Filippo Lippi, *Madonna and Child with Angels,* ca. 1455. Tempera on wood, approx. 3′ × 2′ 1″. Galleria degli Uffizi, Florence.

**21-39** Luca della Robbia, *Madonna and Child,* Or San Michele, Florence, Italy, ca. 1455–1460. Terracotta with polychrome glaze, diameter approx. 6′.

**RELIEF SCULPTURE FOR THE MASSES** During the latter half of the 15th century, increasing demand for devotional images for private chapels and shrines (rather than for large public churches) contributed to a growing secularization of traditional religious subject matter. Luca della Robbia (1400–1482) discovered a way to produce Madonna images so that persons of modest means could buy them. His discovery (around 1430), involving the application of vitrified (heat-fused) potters' glazes to sculpture, led to his production, in quantity, of glazed terracotta reliefs. He is best known for these works. Inexpensive, durable, and decorative, they became extremely popular and provided the basis for a flourishing family business. Luca's nephew Andrea della Robbia (1435–1525) and Andrea's sons, Giovanni della Robbia (1469–1529) and Girolamo della Robbia (1488–1566), carried on this tradition well into the 16th century; people still refer to it as "della Robbia ware."

An example of Luca's specialty is the *Madonna and Child* (FIG. 21-39), commissioned by a guild and set into a wall of Or San Michele. The figures appear within a *tondo* (a circular painting or relief sculpture), a format that became popular with both sculptors and painters in the later part of the century. For example, Brunelleschi incorporated it into his design of the Pazzi Chapel's interior (FIG. 21-19), where most of the roundels are the work of Luca della Robbia himself. In his tondo for Or San Michele, Luca's introduction of high-key color into sculpture added a certain worldly gaiety to the Madonna and Child theme, and his customary light blue ground (and here the green and white of lilies and the white architecture) suggests in this work the festive Easter season and the freshness of May, the Virgin's month. The somber majesty of the old Byzantine style had long since disappeared. The young mothers who prayed before images in this new form could easily identify with the Madonna and doubtless did. The distance between the observed and observers had vanished.

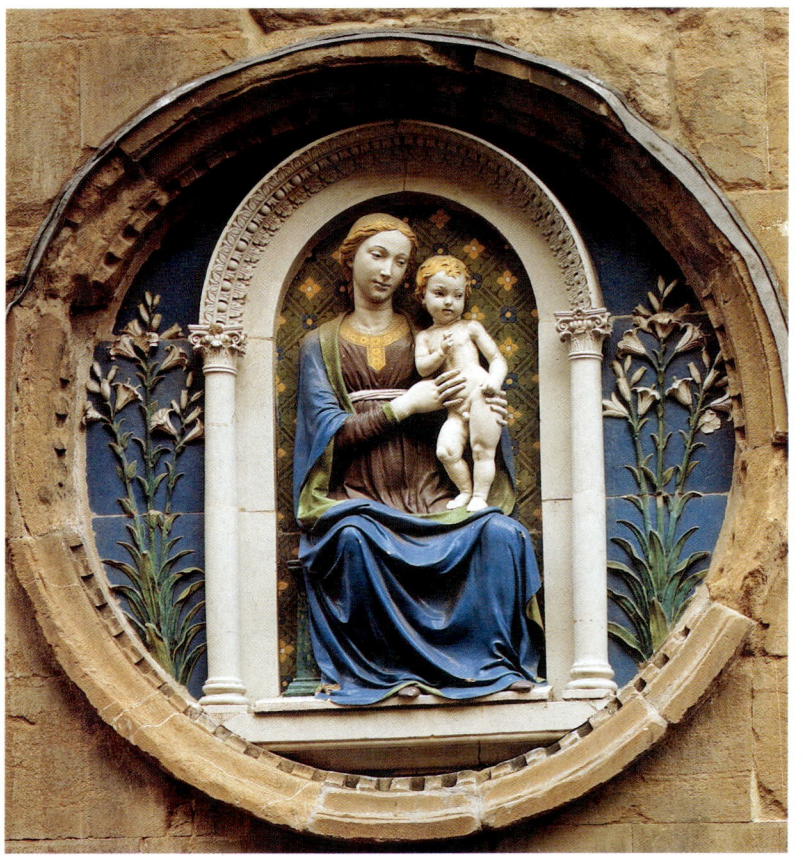

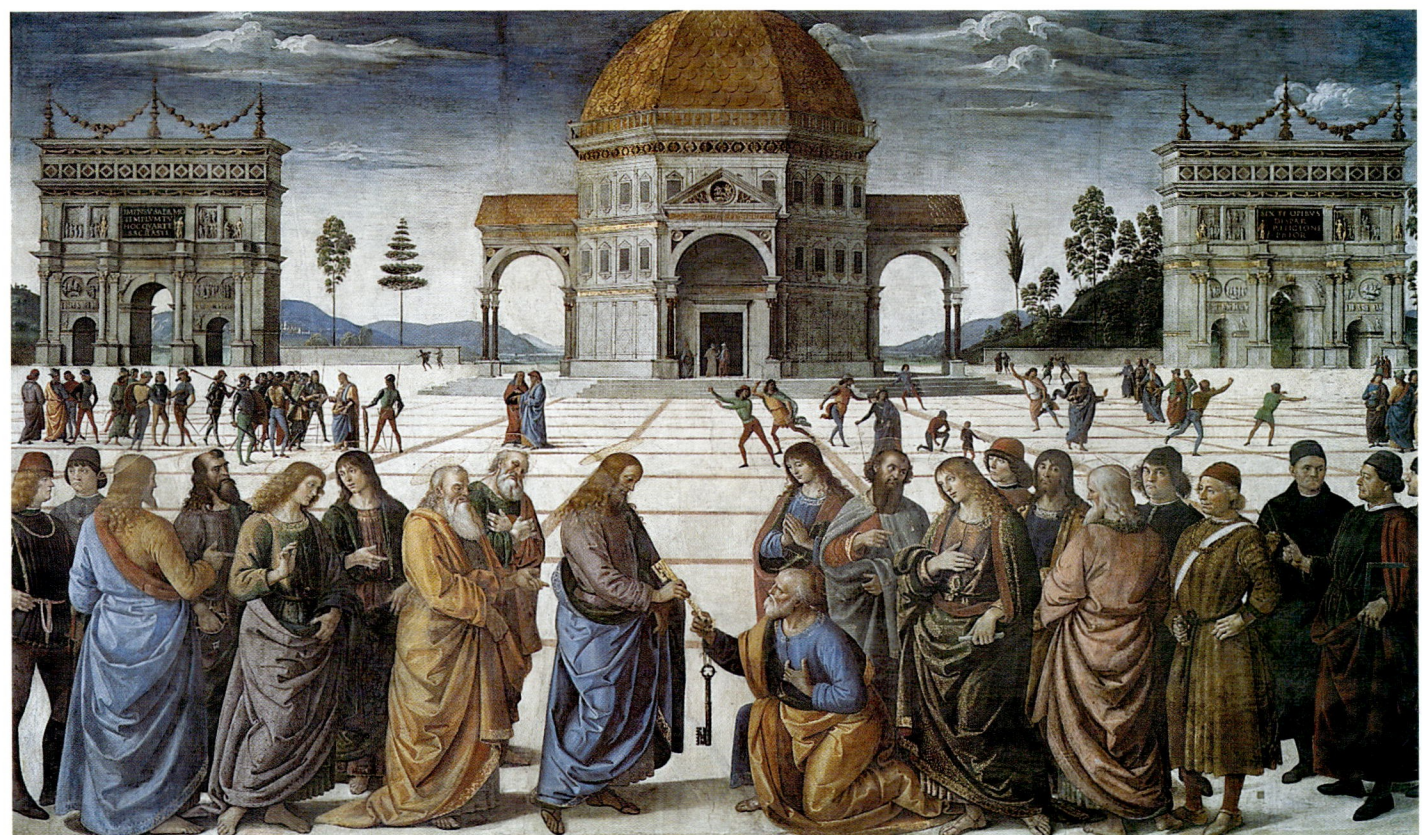

**21-40** PERUGINO, *Christ Delivering the Keys of the Kingdom to Saint Peter,* Sistine Chapel, Vatican, Rome, Italy, 1481–1483. Fresco, 11′ 5½″ × 18′ 8½″, Vatican Museums.

**THE ESTABLISHMENT OF PAPAL AUTHORITY** Of course, the production of religious art extended beyond Florence. The pope's presence in Rome ensured an active artistic scene there as well. Between 1481 and 1483, Pope Sixtus IV summoned a group of artists, including Botticelli, Ghirlandaio, and Luca Signorelli, to Rome to decorate with frescoes the walls of the newly completed Sistine Chapel. Pietro Vannucci, known as PERUGINO (ca. 1450–1523), was among this group and painted *Christ Delivering the Keys of the Kingdom to Saint Peter* (FIG. **21-40**). The papacy had, from the beginning, based its claim to infallible and total authority over the Roman Catholic Church on this biblical event. In Perugino's version, Christ hands the keys to Saint Peter, who stands amidst an imaginary gathering of the Twelve Apostles and Renaissance contemporaries. These figures occupy the apron of a great stage space that extends into the distance to a point of convergence in the doorway of a central-plan temple. (Perugino used parallel and converging lines in the pavement to mark off the intervening space.) Figures in the middle distance complement the near group, emphasizing its density and order by their scattered arrangement. At the corners of the great piazza, duplicate triumphal arches serve as the base angles of a distant compositional triangle whose apex is in the central building. Perugino modeled the arches very closely on the Arch of Constantine (see FIG. 10-76) in Rome. Although an anachronism in a painting depicting a scene from Christ's life, the arches remind viewers of the close ties between Constantine and Saint Peter and of the great basilica the first Christian emperor built over Saint Peter's tomb in Rome. Christ and Peter flank the triangle's central axis, which runs through the temple's doorway, the perspective's vanishing point. Thus, the composition interlocks both two-dimensional and three-dimensional space, and the placement of central actors emphasizes the axial center. This spatial science allowed the artist to organize the action systematically. Perugino, in this single picture, incorporated the learning of generations.

## THE PRINCELY COURTS

Although virtually all the artworks discussed thus far in this chapter are Florentine, art production flourished throughout Italy in the 15th century. In particular, the princely courts that rulers established in such cities as Naples, Urbino, Milan, Ferrara, and Mantua deserve much credit for nurturing the arts. These princely courts consisted of the prince (lord of a territory), his consort and children, courtiers, household staff, and administrators (see "Cultivating Culture," page 575). The considerable wealth these princes possessed, coupled with their desire for recognition, fame, and power, resulted in major art commissions.

### Mantua

Marquis Ludovico Gonzaga (1412–1478) ruled one of these princely courts, the marquisate of Mantua in northern Italy. A famed condottiere, Gonzaga established his reputation as a fierce military leader while general of the Milanese armies. A visit to Mantua by Pope Pius II in 1459 stimulated the Marquis's determination to transform Mantua into a spectacular city. After the pope's departure, Gonzaga set about building a city that would be the envy of all of Italy.

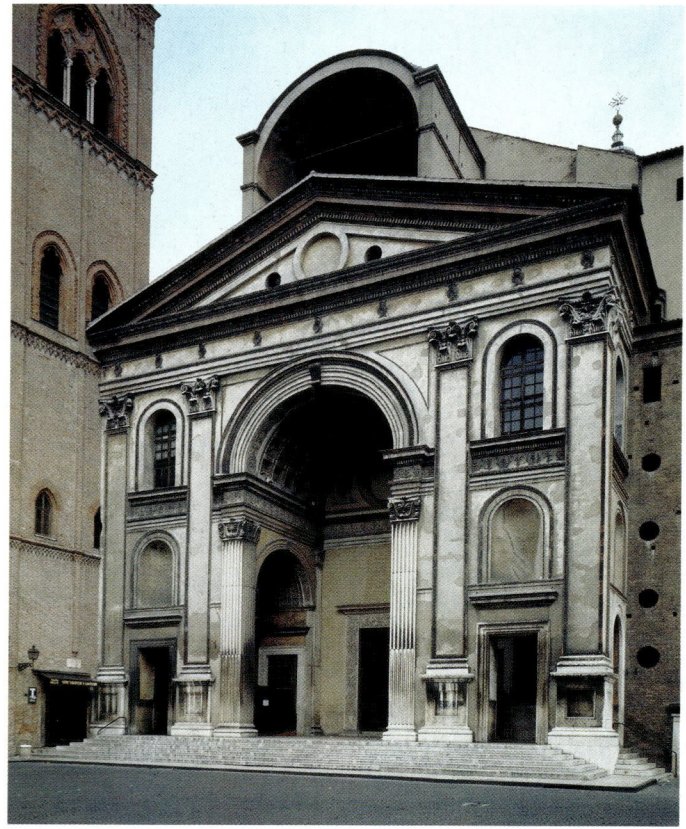

21-41 LEON BATTISTA ALBERTI, west facade of Sant'Andrea, Mantua, Italy, designed ca. 1470.

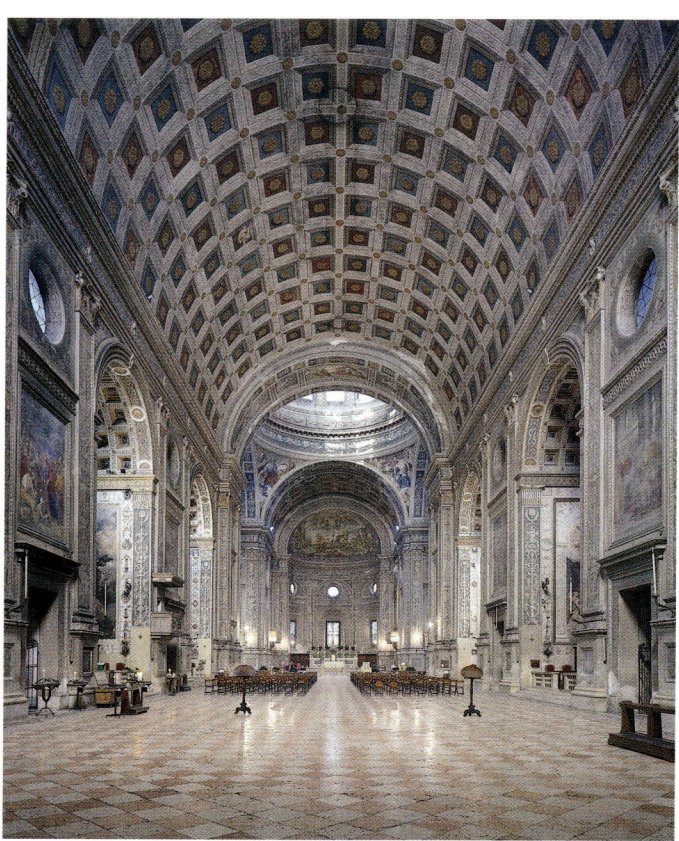

21-43 LEON BATTISTA ALBERTI, interior of Sant'Andrea, Mantua, Italy, designed ca. 1470.

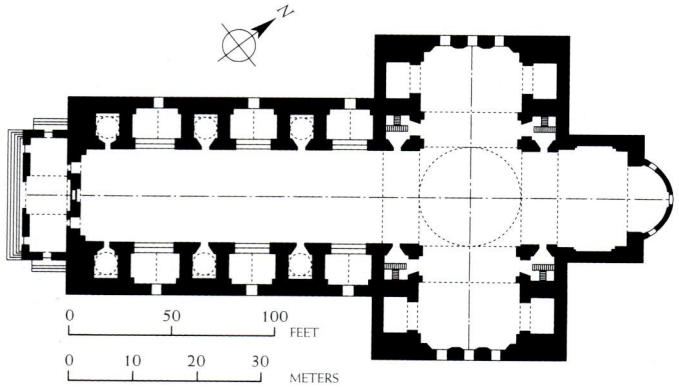

21-42 LEON BATTISTA ALBERTI, plan of Sant'Andrea, Mantua, Italy, designed ca. 1470.

AN EXPANSIVE MANTUAN CHURCH One of the major projects Gonzaga instituted was the redesigning of the church of Sant'Andrea in Mantua (FIGS. 21-41 to 21-43) to replace an 11th-century church. Gonzaga turned to Alberti for this important commission. In the ingeniously planned facade, which illustrates the culmination of Alberti's experiments, the architect locked together two complete Roman architectural motifs—the temple front and the triumphal arch. The combination was already a feature of classical architecture. Many Roman triumphal arches incorporated a pediment over the arcuated passageway and engaged columns, including the Augustan arch at Rimini (FIG. 21-44), illustrated here for comparison. Alberti's concern for proportion led him to equalize the facade's vertical and horizontal

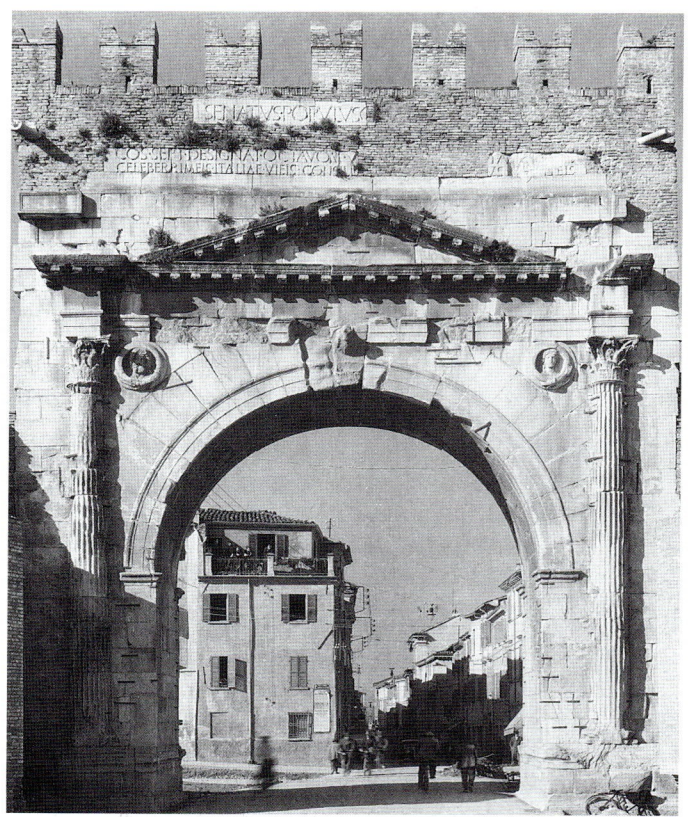

21-44 Arch of Augustus, Rimini, Italy, 27 BCE.

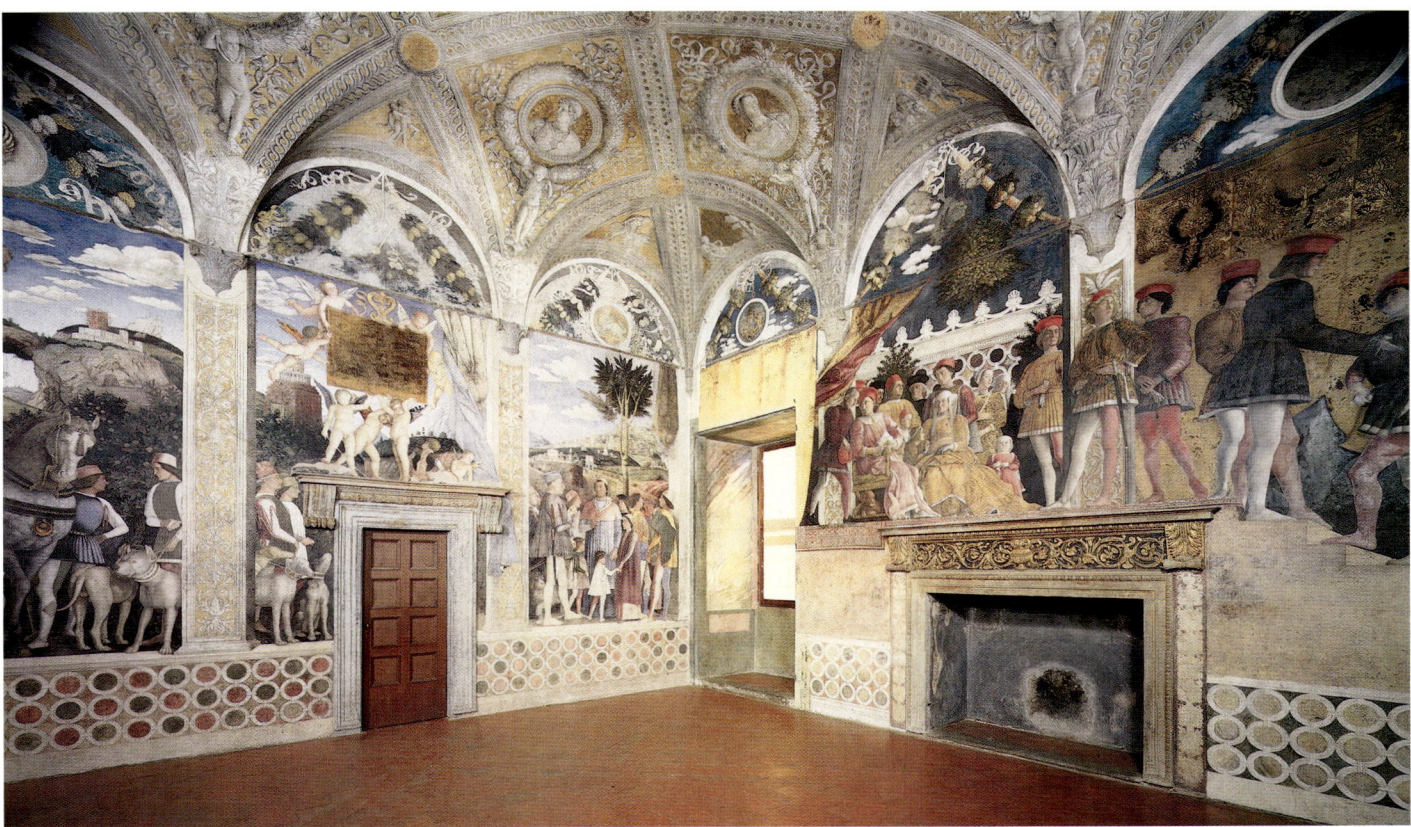

21-45 ANDREA MANTEGNA, interior of the Camera degli Sposi (Room of the Newlyweds), Palazzo Ducale, Mantua, Italy, 1474. Fresco.

dimensions, which left it considerably lower than the church be-hind it. Because of the primary importance of visual appeal, many Renaissance architects made this concession not only to the demands of a purely visual proportionality in the facade but also to the facade's relation to the small square in front of it, even at the expense of continuity with the body of the building. Yet struc-tural correspondences to the building do exist in the Sant'Andrea facade. The facade pilasters are the same height as those on the nave's interior walls, and the central barrel vault over the main ex-terior entrance, with smaller barrel vaults branching off at right angles, introduces (in proportional arrangement but on a smaller scale) the interior system. The facade pilasters, as part of the wall, run uninterrupted through three stories in an early application of the "colossal" or "giant" order that became a favorite motif of Michelangelo.

The tremendous vaults in the interior of Sant'Andrea (FIG. 21-43) suggest that Alberti may have been inspired by the ruined Basilica Nova of Constantine in Rome (see FIG. 10-79) — erro-neously thought in the Middle Ages and Renaissance to be a Roman temple. He abandoned the medieval columned arcade Brunelleschi used in Santo Spirito (FIG. 21-15). Thick walls alter-nating with vaulted chapels and interrupted by a massive dome over the crossing support the huge barrel vault. Because Filippo Juvara added the present dome in the 18th century, the effect may be somewhat different than Alberti planned. Regardless, the vault calls to mind the vast interior spaces and dense enclosing masses of Roman architecture. In his treatise, Alberti criticized the tradi-tional basilican plan (with continuous aisles flanking the central nave) as impractical because the colonnades conceal the cere-monies from the faithful in the aisles. For this reason, he designed a single huge hall (FIG. 21-42) with independent chapels branch-ing off at right angles. This break with a Christian building tradi-tion that had endured for a thousand years was extremely influen-tial in later Renaissance and Baroque church planning.

PAINTING AWAY THE WALLS Like other princes, Ludovico Gonzaga believed that an impressive palace was an important visual expression of his authority. One of the most spectacular rooms in Palazzo Ducale was the so-called Camera degli Sposi (Room of the Newlyweds; FIG. 21-45), originally the Camera Picta (Painted Room), decorated by ANDREA MANTEGNA (ca. 1431–1506) of Padua, near Venice. Taking almost nine years to complete the extensive fresco program, Mantegna produced a se-ries of images that aggrandize Ludovico Gonzaga and his family, and reveal the activities and rhythm of courtly life. The scenes depict vignettes that include Ludovico, his wife, his children, courtiers, and attendants, among others; the particulars of each scene are still a matter of scholarly debate. Standing in the Cam-era degli Sposi, surrounded by the spectacle and majesty of these scenes, the viewer cannot help but be thoroughly impressed by both the commanding presence and elevated status of the patron and the dazzling artistic skills of Mantegna.

Mantegna performed a triumphant feat of pictorial illusion-ism, producing the first completely consistent illusionistic decora-tion of an entire room. Using actual architectural elements, Man-tegna painted away the room's walls in a manner that foretold later Baroque decoration. It recalls the efforts of Italian painters more than 15 centuries earlier at Pompeii and elsewhere to integrate mural painting and actual architecture in frescoes of the so-called Second Style of Roman painting (see FIGS. 10-15 and 10-16).

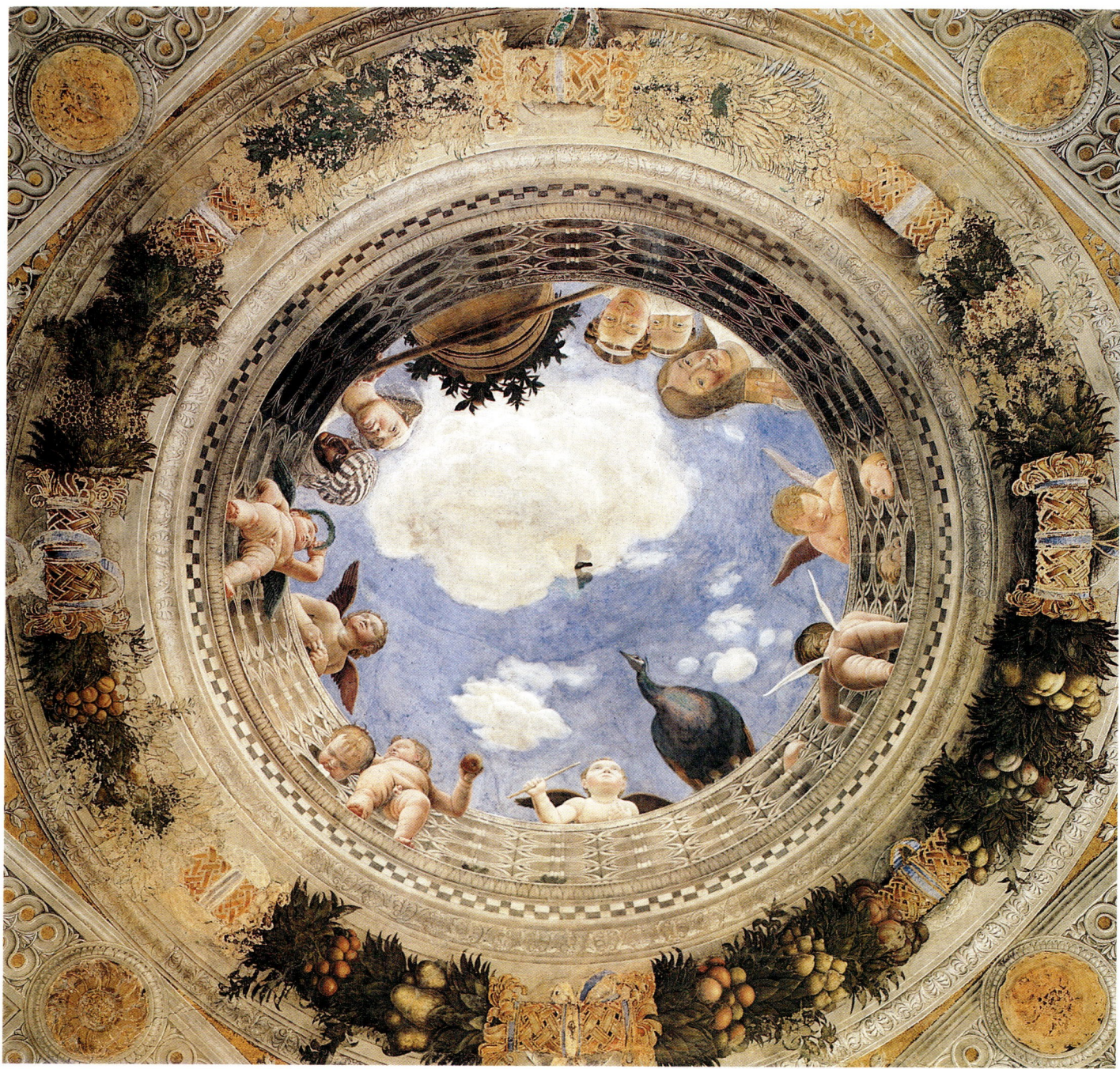

**21-46** ANDREA MANTEGNA, ceiling of the Camera degli Sposi (Room of the Newlyweds), Palazzo Ducale, Mantua, Italy, 1474. Fresco, 8′ 9″ in diameter.

Mantegna's *trompe l'oeil* (French, "deceives the eye") design, however, went far beyond anything preserved from ancient Italy. The Renaissance painter's daring experimentalism led him to complete the room's decoration with the first *di sotto in sù* (from below upwards) perspective of a ceiling (FIG. 21-46). Baroque ceiling decorators later broadly developed this technique. Inside the Room of the Newlyweds, the viewer becomes the viewed as figures look down into the room. The oculus is itself an "eye" looking down. Cupids (the sons of Venus), strongly foreshortened, set the amorous mood as the painted spectators (who are not identified) smile down on the scene. The peacock is an attribute of Juno, Jupiter's bride, who oversees lawful marriages. This tour de force of illusionism climaxes almost a century of experimentation with perspective.

**A SAINT VIEWED FROM BELOW** Whereas the Gonzaga frescoes showcase Mantegna's mature style, his earlier frescoes in the Ovetari Chapel in the Church of the Eremitani (largely destroyed in World War II) in Padua reveal Mantegna's early interest in illusionism and highlight the breadth of his literary, archaeological, and pictorial learning. *Saint James Led to Martyrdom* (FIG. 21-47) depicts the condemned saint stopping, even on the way to his own death, to bless a man who has rushed from the crowd and kneels before him (while a Roman soldier restrains others from coming forward). Yet narrative does not seem to have been Mantegna's primary concern in this fresco. The painter strove for historical authenticity, much like the antiquarian scholars of the University of Padua. He excerpted the motifs (such as those that appear on the barrel-vaulted triumphal arch) from the classical

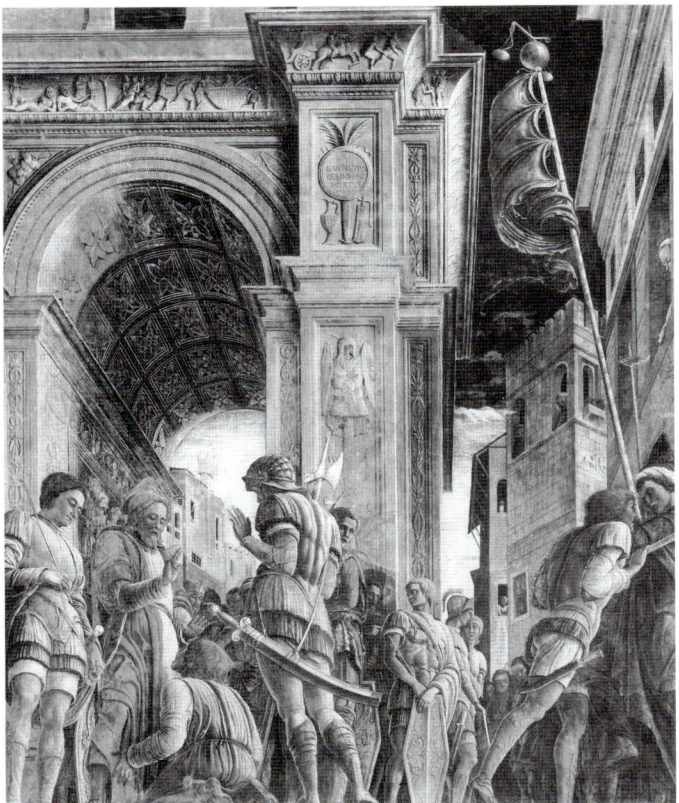

**21-47** ANDREA MANTEGNA, *Saint James Led to Martyrdom,* Ovetari Chapel, Church of the Eremitani (largely destroyed, 1944), Padua, Italy, ca. 1455. Fresco, 10′ 9″ wide.

ornamental vocabulary. Antique attire served as the model for the soldiers' costumes.

Perspective also occupied Mantegna's attention. Indeed, he seemed to set up for himself difficult problems in perspective for the joy of solving them. Here, the observer views the scene from a very low point, almost as if looking up out of a basement window at the vast arch looming above. The lines of the building to the right plunge down dramatically. Several significant deviations from true perspective are apparent, however, and establish that Mantegna did not view the scientific organization of pictorial space as an end in itself. Using artistic license, he ignored the third vanishing point (seen from below, the buildings should converge toward the top). Disregarding perspectival facts, he preferred to work toward a unified, cohesive composition whose pictorial elements relate to the picture frame. Mantegna partly compensated for the lack of perspectival logic by inserting strong diagonals in the right foreground (the banner staff, for example).

**EXAMINING CHRIST'S WOUNDS** One of Mantegna's later paintings, *Dead Christ* (FIG. **21-48**), is a work of overwhelming power. At first glance, this painting seems to be a strikingly realistic study in foreshortening. Careful scrutiny, however, reveals that the artist reduced the size of the figure's feet, which, as he must have known, would cover much of the body if properly represented. Thus, tempering naturalism with artistic license, Mantegna presented both a harrowing study of a strongly foreshortened cadaver and an intensely poignant depiction of a biblical tragedy. The painter's harsh, sharp line seems to cut the surface as if it were metal and conveys, by its grinding edge, the theme's corrosive emotion. Remarkably, all the science of the 15th century here serves the purpose of devotion.

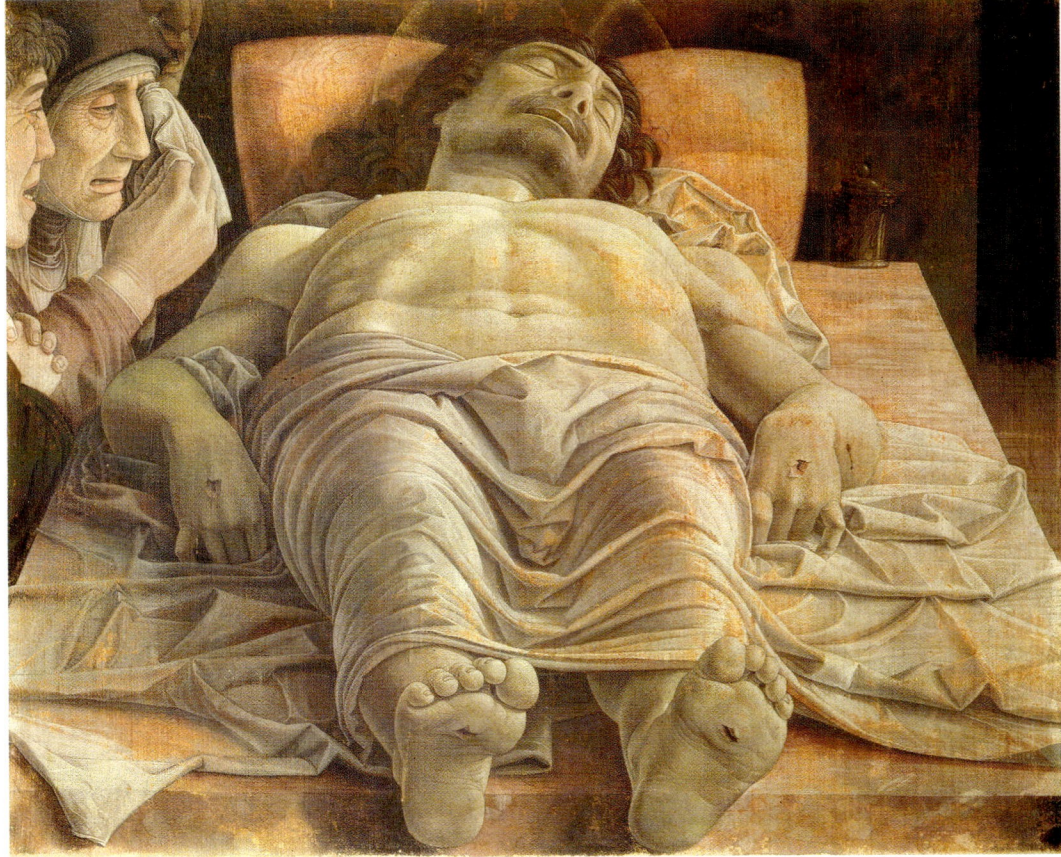

**21-48** ANDREA MANTEGNA, *Dead Christ,* ca. 1501. Tempera on canvas, 2′ 2¾″ × 2′ 7⅞″. Pinacoteca di Brera, Milan.

Artists in northern Italy, not only in Mantua but in Ferrara and Venice as well, attempted to follow in Mantegna's footsteps. His influence went even further, however, for he was also a great engraver (the line in the *Dead Christ* certainly suggests engraving). His prints found their way across the Alps to Germany, where they influenced Albrecht Dürer (see FIGS. 23-4 to 23-8 and Intro-8), a leading figure in 16th-century art.

## Urbino

Urbino, southeast of Florence across the Appenines, was another princely court; the patronage of Federico da Montefeltro (1422–1482) accounted for its status as a center of Renaissance art and culture. In fact, the humanist writer Paolo Cortese described Federico as one of the two greatest artistic patrons of the 15th century (the other was Cosimo de' Medici). Federico, like Ludovico Gonzaga, was a well-known condottiere. So renowned was Federico for his military skills that he was in demand by popes and kings across Europe, and soldiers came from across the continent to study with this military expert. One of the artists who received several commissions from Federico was PIERO DELLA FRANCESCA (ca. 1420–1492). His art projected a mind cultivated by mathematics. Piero believed that the highest beauty resides in forms that have the clarity and purity of geometric figures. Toward the end of his long career, Piero, a skilled geometrician, wrote the first theoretical treatise on systematic perspective, after having practiced the art with supreme mastery for almost a lifetime. His association with the architect Alberti at Ferrara and at Rimini around 1450–1451 probably turned his attention fully to perspective (a science in which Alberti was an influential pioneer) and helped determine his later, characteristically architectonic, compositions. This approach appealed to Federico, a patron fascinated by architectural space and its depiction. Observers can say fairly that Piero established his compositions almost entirely by his sense of the exact and lucid structures defined by mathematics.

**A LEGENDARY FRESCO STYLE** Piero produced many memorable works before he came to the attention of Federico da Montefeltro. One of these earlier works is the fresco cycle in the apse of the church of San Francesco in Arezzo, southeast of Florence on the Arno. Painted between 1452 and 1456, the cycle represents 10 episodes from the legend of the True Cross (the cross on which Christ died) and is based on a 13th-century popularization of the Scriptures, the *Golden Legend,* by Jacobus de Voragine. In the climactic scene of Piero's Arezzo cycle, the *Finding of the True Cross and Proving of the True Cross* (FIG. **21-49**), Saint Helena, mother of Constantine, accompanied by her retinue, oversees the unearthing of the buried crosses (at left), and witnesses (at right) how the True Cross miraculously restores a dead man (the nude figure) to life. The architectural background organizes and controls the grouping of the figures; its medallions, arches, and rectangular panels are the two-dimensional counterparts of the ovoid, cylindrical, and cubic forms placed in front of it. The careful delineation of architecture suggests an architect's vision, certainly that of a man entirely familiar with compass and straightedge. As the architectonic nature of the abstract shapes controls the grouping, so too does it impart a mood of solemn stillness to the figures.

Piero's work shows, in addition, an unflagging interest in the properties of light and color. In his effort to make the clearest possible distinction between forms, he flooded his pictures with light, imparting a silver-blue tonality. To avoid heavy shadows, he illuminated the dark sides of his forms with reflected light. By moving the darkest tones of his modeling toward the centers of his volumes, he separated them from their backgrounds. Because of this technique, Piero's paintings lack some of Masaccio's relief-like qualities but gain in spatial clarity, as each shape forms an independent unit surrounded by an atmospheric envelope and movable to any desired position, like a figure on a chessboard.

**A PIOUS PATRON** Piero deployed all his skills for the paintings commissioned by Federico da Montefeltro. One of those works is *Enthroned Madonna and Saints Adored by Federico da Montefeltro,* also called the *Brera Altarpiece* (FIG. **21-50**). The clarity of Piero's

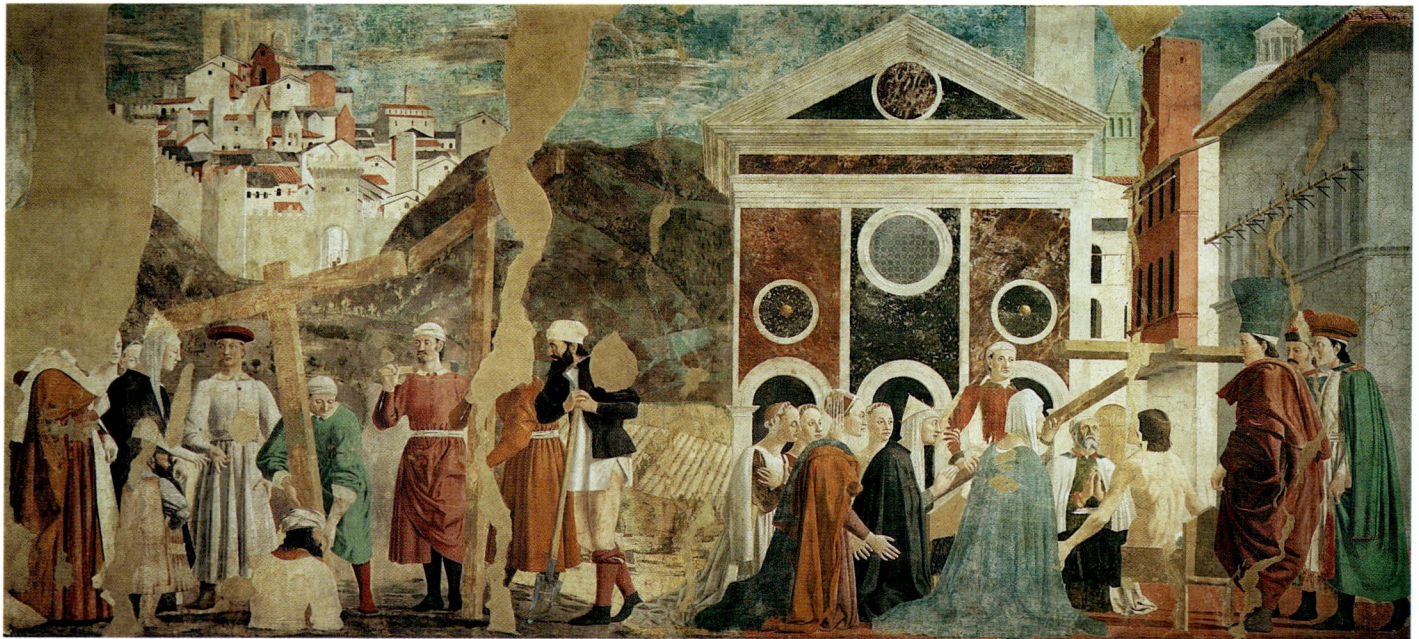

**21-49** PIERO DELLA FRANCESCA, *Finding of the True Cross and Proving of the True Cross,* San Francesco, Arezzo, Italy, ca. 1455. Fresco, 6′ 4″ × 11′ 8$\frac{3}{8}$″.

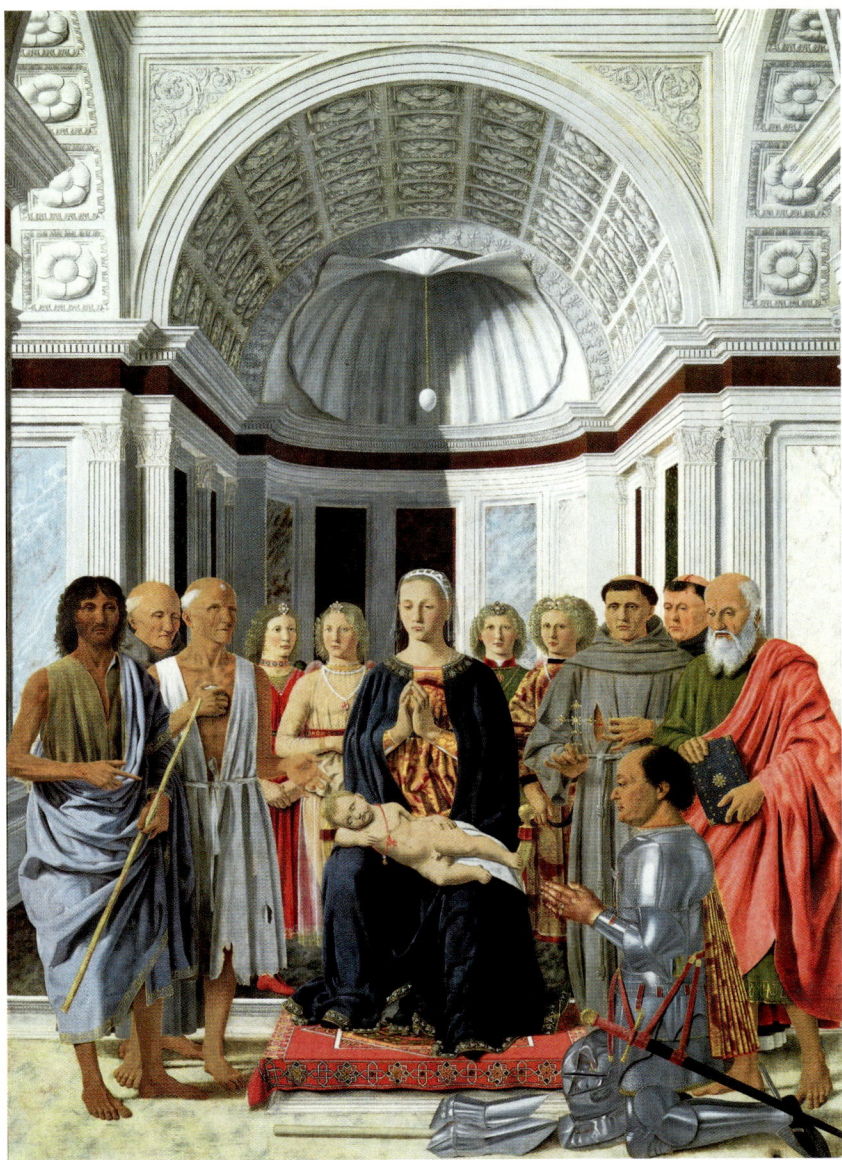

**21-50** Piero della Francesca, *Enthroned Madonna and Saints Adored by Federico da Montefeltro (Brera Altarpiece)*, ca. 1472–1474. Oil on panel, 8′ 2″ × 5′ 7″. Pinacoteca di Brera, Milan.

earlier works is in full view here, as Federico, clad in armor, kneels piously at the Virgin's feet. Directly behind him stands Saint John the Evangelist, his patron saint. Where the viewer would expect to see his wife, Battista Sforza (on the lower left, as a mirror image to Federico), no figure is present. Battista had died in 1472, shortly before Federico commissioned this painting. Thus, her absence clearly announces his loss. Piero further called attention to it by depicting Saint John the Baptist, Battista's patron saint, at the far left. The ostrich egg that hangs suspended from a shell over the Virgin's head was a common presence over altars dedicated to Mary. The figures appear in an illusionistically painted coffered barrel vault, which may have reflected the actual architecture of the painting's intended location, the church of San Bernadino degli Zoccolanti near Urbino. If such were the case, it would have enhanced the illusion, and the viewer would be compelled to believe in Federico's presence before the Virgin, Christ Child, and saints. That Piero depicted Federico in profile was undoubtedly a concession to the patron. The right side of Federico's face had been badly injured in a tournament, and the resulting deformity made him reluctant to show that side of his face. The number of works (including other portraits) that Piero executed for Federico reflects his success in accommodating his patron's wishes.

## TURMOIL AT THE END OF THE CENTURY

In the 1490s, Florence underwent a political, cultural, and religious upheaval. Florentine artists and their fellow citizens responded then not only to humanist ideas but also to the incursion of French armies and especially to the preaching of the Dominican monk Girolamo Savonarola, the reforming priest-dictator who denounced the paganism of the Medici and their artists, philosophers, and poets. Savonarola exhorted the people of Florence to repent their sins, and, when Lorenzo de' Medici died in 1492 and the Medici fled, he prophesied the downfall of the city and of Italy and assumed absolute control of the state. Together with a large number of citizens, Savonarola believed that the Medici's political, social, and religious power had corrupted Florence and had invited the scourge of foreign invasion. Savonarola denounced humanism and encouraged "bonfires of the vanities" for citizens to burn their classical texts, scientific treatises, and philosophical publications. Modern scholars still debate the significance of Savonarola's brief span of power. Apologists for the undoubtedly sincere monk deny that his actions played a role in

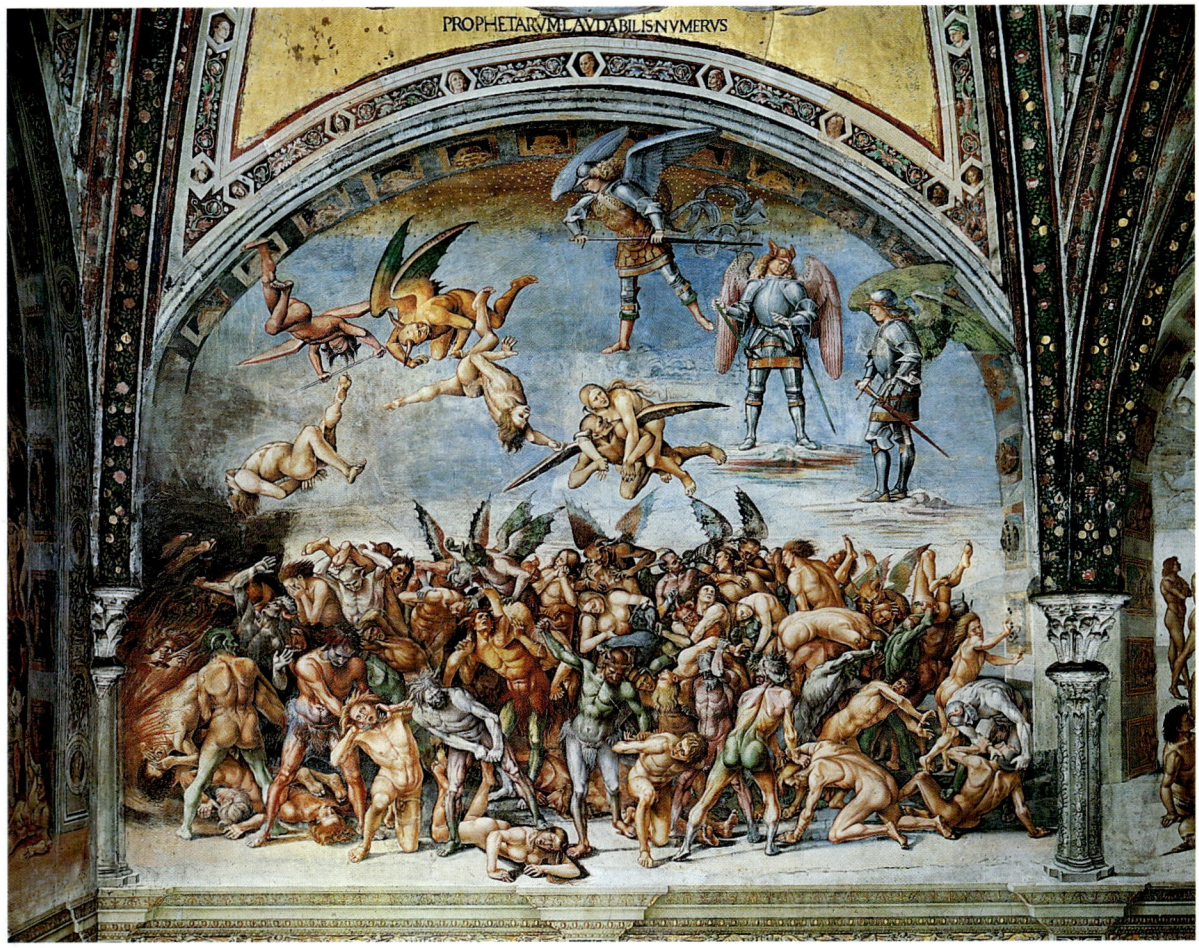

**21-51** LUCA SIGNORELLI, *Damned Cast into Hell*, San Brizio Chapel, Orvieto Cathedral, Orvieto, Italy, 1499–1504. Fresco, approx. 23′ wide.

the decline of Florentine culture at the end of the 15th century. But he did condemn humanism as heretical nonsense, and his banishing of the Medici, Tornabuoni, and other wealthy families from Florence deprived local artists of some of their major patrons. Certainly, the puritanical spirit that moved Savonarola must have dampened considerably the neopagan enthusiasm of the Florentine Early Renaissance.

**A VISION OF THE DAMNED** Outside Florence, the fiery passion of the sermons of Savonarola found its pictorial equal in the work of the Umbrian painter LUCA SIGNORELLI (ca. 1445–1523). The artist further developed Antonio Pollaiuolo's interest in the depiction of muscular bodies in violent action in a wide variety of poses and foreshortenings. In the San Brizio Chapel in Orvieto Cathedral, Signorelli's painted scenes depicting the end of the world include *Damned Cast into Hell* (FIG. **21-51**). Few figure compositions of the 15th century have the same awesome psychic impact. Saint Michael and the hosts of Heaven hurl the damned into Hell, where, in a dense, writhing mass, they are vigorously tortured by demons. The horrible consequences of a sinful life had not been so graphically depicted since Gislebertus carved his vision of the Last Judgment in the west tympanum of Saint-Lazare at Autun (see FIGS. 17-25 and Intro-6) around 1130. The figures—nude, lean, and muscular—assume every conceivable posture of anguish. Signorelli's skill at foreshortening the human figure was one with his mastery of its action, and, although each figure is clearly a study from a model, he fit his theme to the

figures in an entirely convincing manner. Terror and rage pass like storms through the wrenched and twisted bodies. The fiends, their hair flaming and their bodies the color of putrefying flesh, lunge at their victims in ferocious frenzy.

## CONCLUSION

Expanding interest in humanism provided a foundation for much of the art produced in 15th-century Italy. The pronounced fascination with perspectival systems, along with the popularity of subjects derived from classical history and mythology, are evidence of the influence of humanism. Another factor in the development of 15th-century Italian art was the continuing political instability, which facilitated the consolidation of power by princely courts (such as those in Urbino and Mantua) and dominant families (such as the Medici). Such powerful individuals and families saw themselves not just as political and economic leaders but as cultural ones as well. For this reason, art patronage was a priority for many of them, and their commissions—in terms of quantity, scale, choice of subject and artist, and, often, visibility—affected the direction that art took in Italy. The flourishing of art during the 15th century continued the "rebirth" of Italian culture begun in the previous century, and the artworks produced served as important models for Leonardo, Michelangelo, Raphael, and the other masters of the 16th century.

■ Giangaleazzo Visconti dies; Milanese armies withdraw
from Tuscany, 1402

■ King Ladislaus of Naples dies, 1414

■ End of Great Schism in Catholic Church, 1417

1420

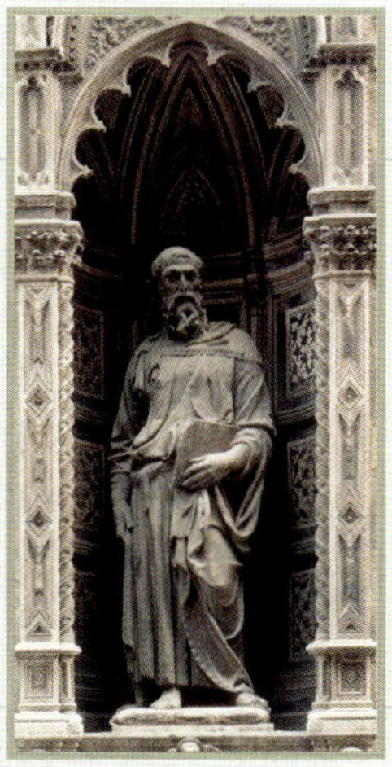

1425

1   Donatello, *Saint Mark*,
Or San Michele,
Florence, Italy, 1411–1413

1430

■ Battle of San Romano, 1432

■ Marsilio Ficino, Neoplatonic philosopher, 1433–1499

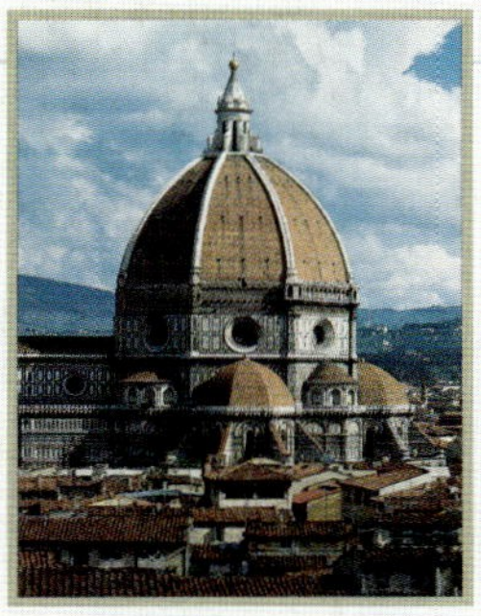

2   Filippo Brunelleschi,
dome of Florence
Cathedral, 1420–1436

1440

■ Invention of movable metal type
by Johann Gutenberg, ca. 1445

■ Lorenzo de' Medici, 1449–1492

■ Conquest of Constantinople by Turks, 1453

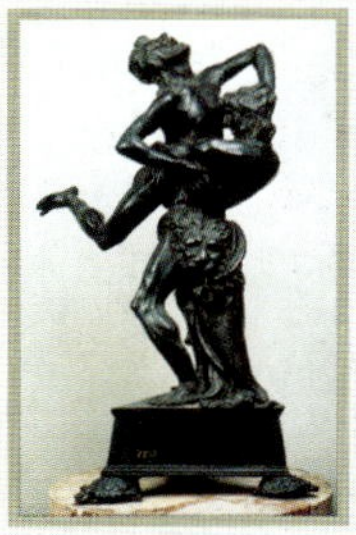

3   Antonio Pol-
laiuolo, *Hercules
and Antaeus*,
ca. 1475

1470

1475

1480

■ Medici expelled from Florence, 1494

■ Girolamo Savonarola assumes power, 1496;
is burned at stake, 1498

■ France captures Milan, 1499

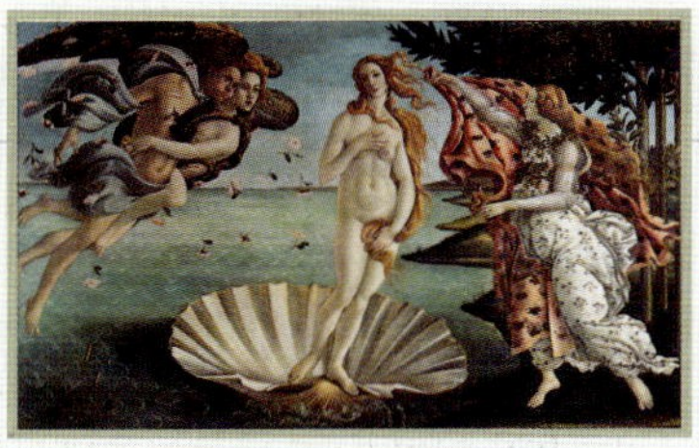

4   Sandro Botticelli, *Birth of Venus*,
ca. 1482

1500

EARLY RENAISSANCE

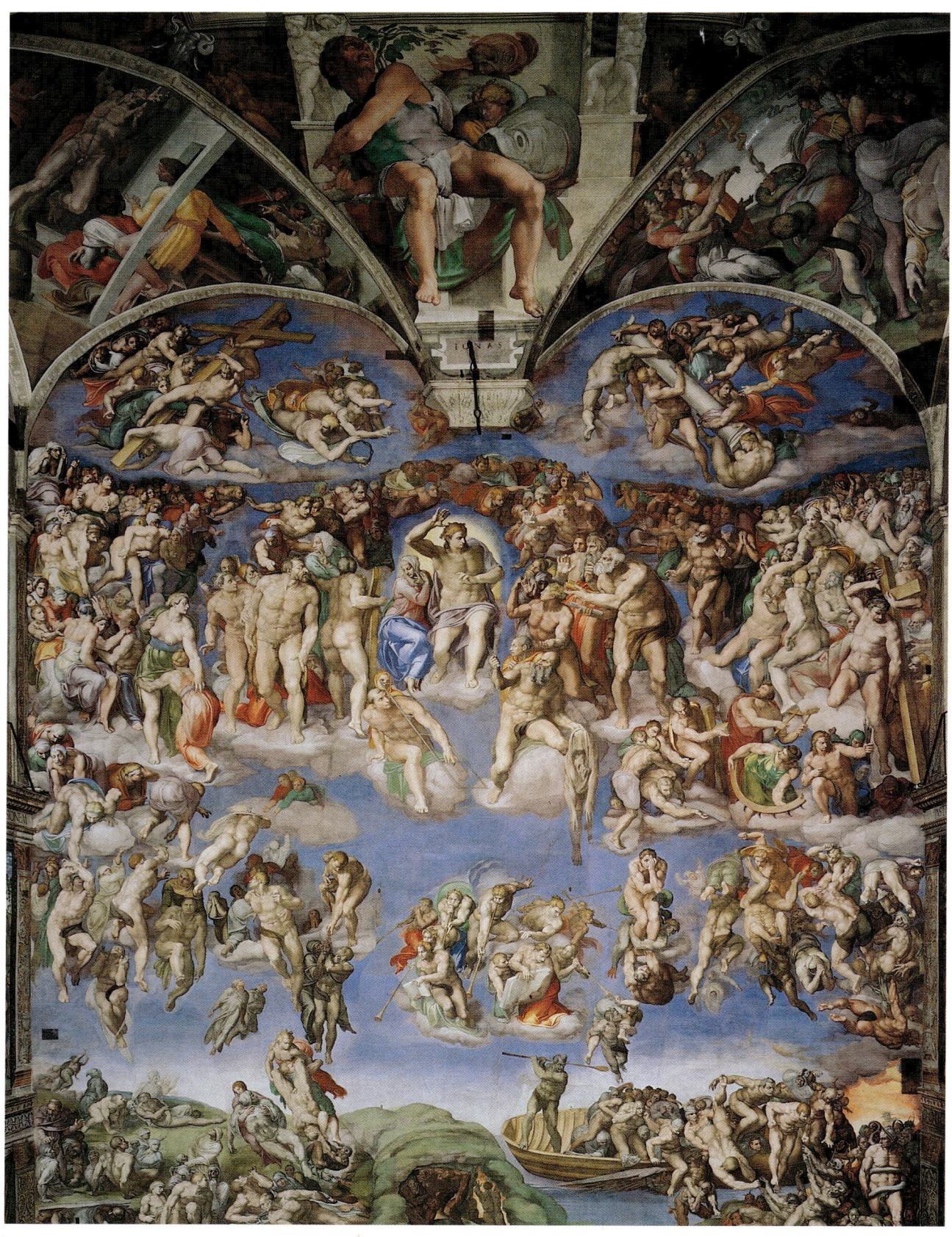

MICHELANGELO BUONARROTI, *Last Judgment,* fresco on the altar wall of the Sistine Chapel, Vatican City, Rome, Italy, 1534–1541.
Copyright © Nippon Television Network Corporation, Tokyo.

# 22

# BEAUTY, SCIENCE, AND SPIRIT IN ITALIAN ART

## THE HIGH RENAISSANCE AND MANNERISM

The 15th-century artistic developments in Italy (for example, the interest in perspectival systems, in depicting anatomy, and in classical cultures) matured during the 16th century, accounting for the designations "Early Renaissance" for the 15th century and "High Renaissance" for the 16th century. Although no singular style characterizes the High Renaissance, the art of those most closely associated with this period—Leonardo da Vinci, Raphael, Michelangelo, and Titian—exhibits an astounding mastery, both technical and aesthetic. High Renaissance artists created works of such authority that generations of later artists relied on these artworks for instruction.

These exemplary artistic creations further elevated the prestige of artists. Artists could claim divine inspiration, thereby raising visual art to a status formerly given only to poetry. Thus, painters, sculptors, and architects came into their own, successfully claiming for their work a high position among the fine arts. In a sense, 16th-century masters created a new profession with its own rights of expression and its own venerable character.

## THE HIGH RENAISSANCE

### The Transition from Early Renaissance to High Renaissance

FROM A(NATOMY) TO Z(OOLOGY) Among the Italian Renaissance artists who have never ceased to captivate the public's interest is LEONARDO DA VINCI (1452–1519). Born in the small town of Vinci, near Florence, Leonardo trained in the studio of Andrea del Verrocchio. Art was but one of Leonardo's innumerable interests. The scope and depth of these interests were without precedent—so great as to frustrate any hopes he might have had of realizing all his feverishly inventive imagination could conceive. Still, his immense intellect, talent, and foresight allowed him to map the routes art and science were to take in the future.

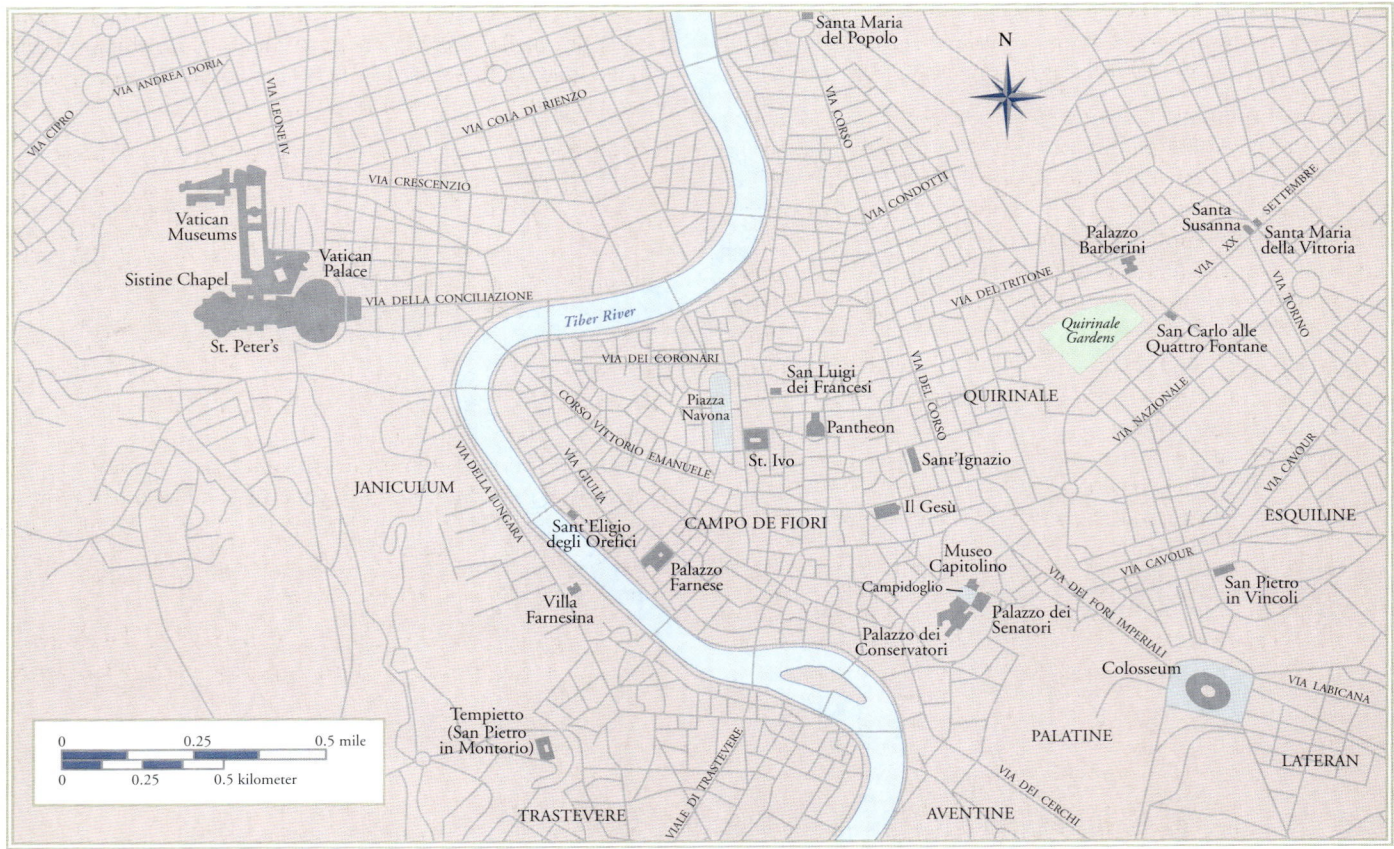

MAP 22-1 Rome with Renaissance and Baroque monuments.

Although the discussion here focuses on Leonardo as an artist, exploring his art in conjunction with his other interests considerably enhances an understanding of his artistic production. Leonardo revealed his unquenchable curiosity in his voluminous notes, liberally interspersed with sketches dealing with botany, geology, geography, cartography, zoology, military engineering, animal lore, anatomy, and aspects of physical science, including hydraulics and mechanics. These studies informed his art. For example, Leonardo's in-depth exploration of optics gave him an understanding of perspective, light, and color that he used in his painting. His scientific drawings are themselves artworks.

Leonardo's great ambition in his painting, as well as in his scientific endeavors, was to discover the laws underlying the processes and flux of nature. With this end in mind, he also studied the human body and contributed immeasurably to knowledge of physiology and psychology. Leonardo believed that reality in an absolute sense is inaccessible and that humans can know it only through its changing images. He considered the eyes the most vital organs and sight the most essential function, as, through these, individuals could grasp the images of reality most directly and profoundly. In his notes, he stated repeatedly that all his scientific investigations made him a better painter.

Around 1481, Leonardo left Florence, offering his services to Ludovico Sforza, duke of Milan, who accepted them. The political situation in Florence was uncertain, and Leonardo may have felt that his particular skills would be in greater demand in Milan, providing him with the opportunity for increased financial security. He devoted most of a letter to the duke of Milan to advertising his competence and his qualifications as a military engineer, mentioning only at the end his abilities as a painter and sculptor:

> And in short, according to the variety of cases, I can contrive various and endless means of offence and defence. . . . In time of peace I believe I can give perfect satisfaction and to the equal of any other in architecture and the composition of buildings, public and private; and in guiding water from one place to another. . . . I can carry out sculpture in marble, bronze, or clay, and also I can do in painting whatever may be done, as well as any other, be he whom he may.[1]

This letter illustrates the 15th-century artist's relation to patrons, as well as Leonardo's breadth of competence. That he should select military engineering and design to interest a patron is an index of the period's instability.

**PAINTING THE SOUL'S INTENTION** During his first sojourn in Milan, Leonardo painted *Virgin of the Rocks* (FIG. **22-1**) as the central panel of an altarpiece for the chapel of the Confraternity of the Immaculate Conception (see "Mendicant Orders and Confraternities," Chapter 19, page 524) in San Francesco Grande. The painting builds on Masaccio's understanding and usage of chiaroscuro, the subtle play of light and dark. Modeling with light and shadow and expressing emotional states were, for Leonardo, the heart of painting:

> A good painter has two chief objects to paint—man and the intention of his soul. The former is easy, the latter hard, for it must be

expressed by gestures and the movement of the limbs. . . . A painting will only be wonderful for the beholder by making that which is not so appear raised and detached from the wall.[2]

Leonardo presented the figures in *Virgin of the Rocks* in a pyramidal grouping and, more notably, as sharing the same environment. This groundbreaking achievement—the unified representation of objects in an atmospheric setting—was a manifestation of his scientific curiosity about the invisible substance surrounding things. The Madonna, Christ Child, infant John the Baptist, and angel emerge through nuances of light and shade from the half-light of the cavernous visionary landscape. Light simultaneously veils and reveals the forms, immersing them in a layer of atmosphere that exists between them and the viewer's eye. Leonardo's effective use of atmospheric perspective is in full view here. The figures pray, point, and bless, and these acts and gestures, although their meanings are not certain, visually unite the individuals portrayed. The angel points to the infant John and, through his outward glance, involves spectators in the tableau. John prays to the Christ Child and is blessed in return. The Virgin herself completes the series of interlocking gestures, her left hand reaching toward the Christ Child and her right hand resting protectively on John's shoulder. The melting mood of

tenderness, enhanced by the caressing light, suffuses the entire composition. By creating an emotionally compelling, visually unified, and spatially convincing image, Leonardo succeeded in expressing "the intention of his soul."

**A MAJESTIC CARTOON** Leonardo's style fully emerges in a cartoon (a full-size preliminary drawing; see "Disegno: Drawing on Design Fundamentals," page 617), *Virgin and Child with Saint Anne and the Infant Saint John* (FIG. 22-2). Here, the glowing light falls gently on the majestic forms, on a scene of tranquil grandeur and balance. Leonardo ordered every part of his cartoon with an intellectual pictorial logic that results in an appealing visual unity. The figures are robust and monumental, the stately grace of their movements reminiscent of the Phidian statues of goddesses in the pediments of the Parthenon (see FIG. 5-47). Leonardo's infusion of Greek principles into his designs cannot be attributed to specific knowledge of Greek monuments; he and his contemporaries never saw those particular sculptures, because their acquaintance with classical art was limited to Etruscan and Roman monuments and Roman copies of Greek masterpieces.

**A DRAMATIC BETRAYAL** For the refectory of the church of Santa Maria delle Grazie in Milan, Leonardo painted *Last Supper*

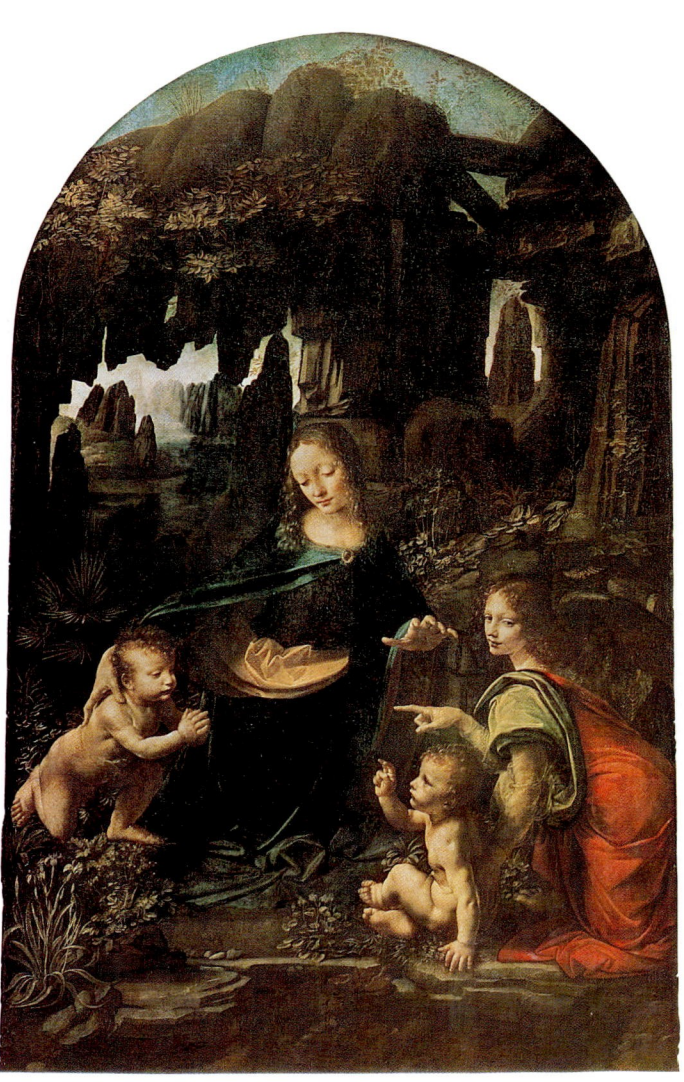

22-1 LEONARDO DA VINCI, *Virgin of the Rocks,* ca. 1485. Oil on wood (transferred to canvas), approx. 6′ 3″ × 3′ 7″. Louvre, Paris.

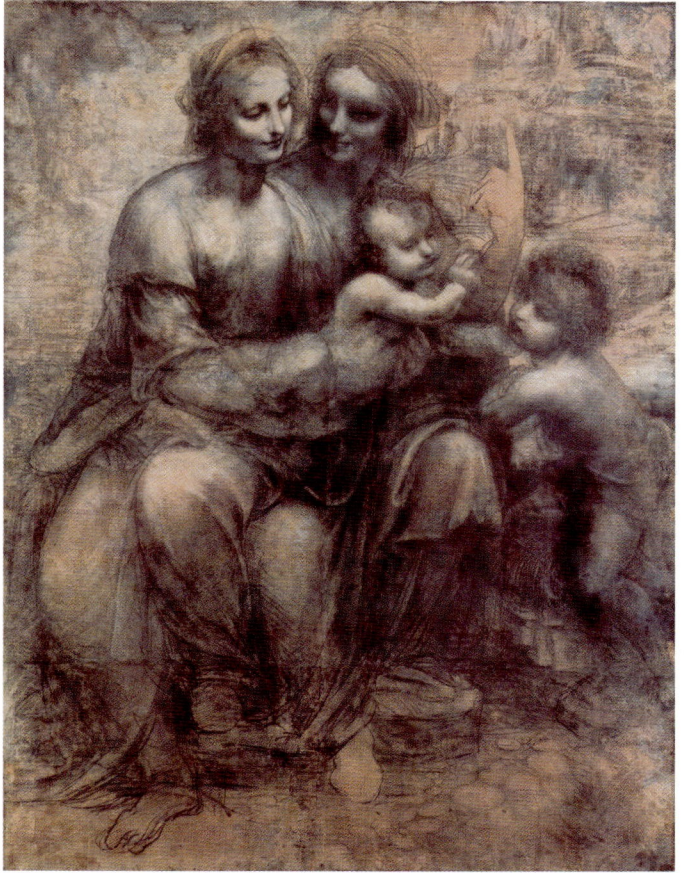

22-2 LEONARDO DA VINCI, cartoon for *Virgin and Child with Saint Anne and the Infant Saint John,* ca. 1505–1507. Charcoal heightened with white on brown paper, approx. 4′ 6″ × 3′ 3″. National Gallery, London.

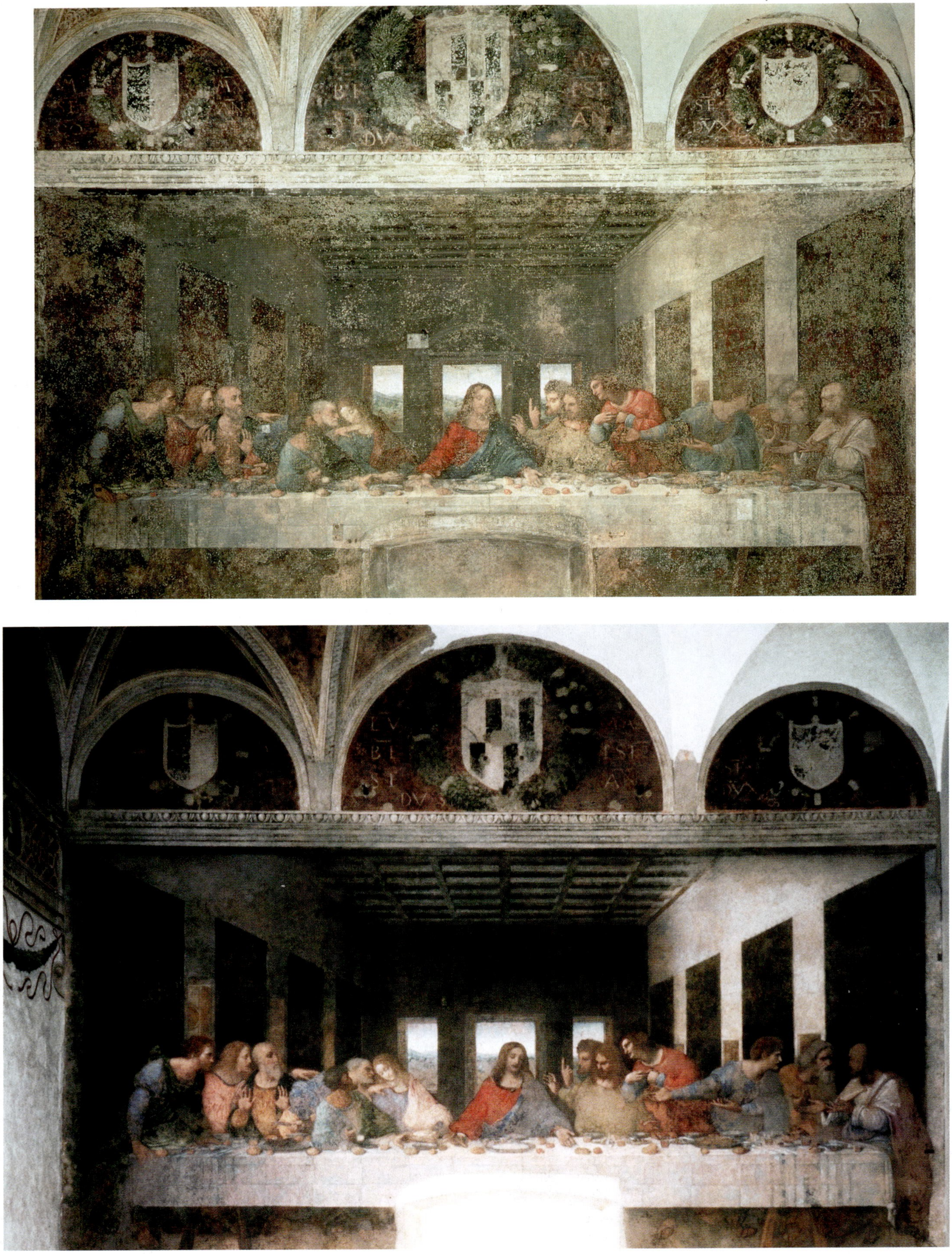

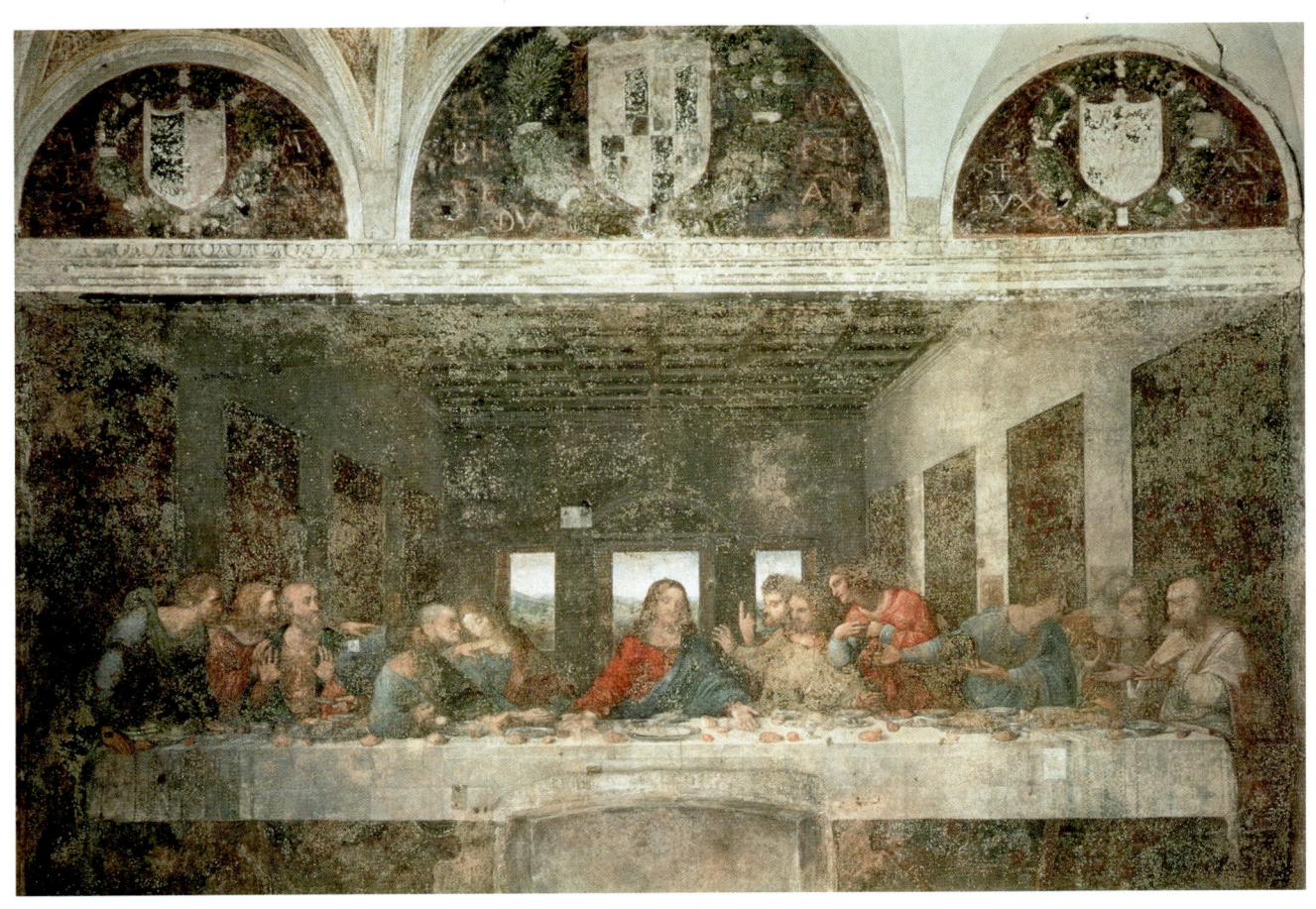

**22-3** Leonardo da Vinci, *Last Supper* (*top*, uncleaned; *bottom*, cleaned), ca. 1495–1498. Fresco (oil and tempera on plaster), 13′ 9″ × 29′ 10″. Refectory, Santa Maria delle Grazie, Milan.

## Disegno
### Drawing on Design Fundamentals

In the 16th century in Italy, drawing (or *disegno*) assumed a position of greater prominence than ever before in artistic production. Until the late 15th century, the expense of drawing surfaces and their lack of availability limited the production of preparatory sketches. Most artists drew on parchment (prepared from the skins of calves, sheep, and goats) or on vellum (made from the skins of young animals and therefore very expensive). Because of the cost of these materials, drawings in the 14th and 15th centuries tended to be extremely detailed and meticulously executed. Artists often drew using *silverpoint* (a stylus made of silver) because of the fine line it produced and the sharp point it maintained. The introduction in the late 15th century of less expensive paper made of fibrous pulp, from the developing printing industry, allowed artists to experiment more and to draw with greater freedom. As a result, sketches abounded. Artists executed these drawings in pen and ink, chalk, charcoal, brush, and graphite or lead.

The importance of drawing extended beyond the mechanical or technical possibilities that drawing afforded artists, however. The term *disegno* also referred to design, an integral component of good art. Design was the foundation of art, and drawing was the fundamental element of design. A statement by the artist Federico Zuccaro that drawing is the external physical manifestation (*disegno esterno*) of an internal intellectual idea or design (*disegno interno*) confirms this connection.

The design dimension of art production became increasingly important as artists cultivated their own styles. The early stages of artistic training largely focused on imitation and emulation (see "Imitation and Emulation," Chapter 21, page 585), but, to achieve widespread recognition, artists were expected to move beyond this dependence on previous models and develop their own styles. Although the artistic community and public at large acknowledged technical skill, the conceptualization of the artwork—its theoretical and formal development—was paramount. *Disegno,* or *design* in this case, represented an artist's conceptualization and intention. In the literature of the period, the terms writers and critics often invoked to praise esteemed artists included *invenzione* (invention), *ingegno* (ingenuity), *fantasia* (imagination), and *capriccio* (originality).

---

(FIG. **22-3**). Despite its ruined state (in part from the painter's unfortunate experiments with his materials) and although it often has been restored ineptly (see "Restoring the Glory of Renaissance Art," page 628), the painting is both formally and emotionally his most impressive work. Christ and his 12 disciples are seated at a long table set parallel to the picture plane in a simple, spacious room. Leonardo amplified the painting's highly dramatic action by placing the group in an austere setting. Christ, with outstretched hands, has just said, "One of you is about to betray me" (Matt. 26:21). A wave of intense excitement passes through the group as each disciple asks himself and, in some cases, his neighbor, "Is it I?" (Matt. 26:22). Leonardo visualized a sophisticated conjunction of the dramatic "One of you is about to betray me" with the initiation of the ancient liturgical ceremony of the Eucharist, when Christ, blessing bread and wine, said, "This is my body, which is given for you. Do this for a commemoration of me. . . . This is the chalice, the new testament in my blood, which shall be shed for you" (Luke 22:19–20). The artist's careful conceptualization of the composition imbued this dramatic moment with force and lucidity.

In the center, Christ appears isolated from the disciples and in perfect repose, the still eye of the swirling emotion around him. The central window at the back, whose curved pediment arches above his head, frames his figure. The pediment is the only curve in the architectural framework, and it serves here, along with the diffused light, as a halo. Christ's head is the focal point of all converging perspective lines in the composition. Thus, the still, psychological focus and cause of the action is also the perspectival focus, as well as the center of the two-dimensional surface. One could say that the two-dimensional, the three-dimensional, and the psychodimensional focuses are the same. Leonardo presented the agitated disciples in four groups of three, united among and within themselves by the figures' gestures and postures. The artist sacrificed traditional iconography to pictorial and dramatic consistency by placing Judas on the same side of the table as Jesus and the other disciples. His face in shadow, Judas clutches a money bag in his right hand and reaches his left forward to fulfill the Master's declaration: "But yet behold, the hand of him that betrayeth me is with me on the table" (Luke 22:21). The two disciples at the table ends are more quiet than the others, as if to bracket the energy of the composition, which is more intense closer to Christ, whose calm both halts and intensifies it.

The disciples register a broad range of emotional responses, including fear, doubt, protestation, rage, and love. Leonardo's numerous preparatory studies suggest that he thought of each figure as carrying a particular charge and type of emotion. Like a skilled stage director (perhaps the first, in the modern sense), he read the Gospel story carefully, and scrupulously cast his actors as the New Testament described their roles. In this work, as in his other religious paintings, Leonardo revealed his extraordinary ability to apply his voluminous knowledge about the observable world to the pictorial representation of a religious scene, resulting in a psychologically complex and compelling painting.

**A SMILE FOR THE AGES** Leonardo's *Mona Lisa* (FIG. **22-4**) is probably the world's most famous portrait. The sitter's identity is still the subject of scholarly debate, but Renaissance biographer Giorgio Vasari asserted that she is Lisa di Antonio Maria Gherardini, the wife of Francesco del Giocondo, a wealthy Florentine—hence, "Mona (an Italian contraction of *ma donna,* "my lady") Lisa." Despite the uncertainty of this identification, this portrait is notable because it stands as a convincing representation of an individual, rather than serving as an icon of status. Mona Lisa appears in half-length view, her hands quietly folded and her gaze directed at observers, engaging them psychologically. The ambiguity of the famous "smile" is really the consequence of Leonardo's fascination and skill with chiaroscuro and atmospheric perspective, which he revealed in his *Virgin of the Rocks* (FIG. 22-1) and *Virgin and Child with Saint Anne and the Infant Saint John* (FIG. 22-2) groups. Here, they serve to disguise rather than reveal a human psyche. The

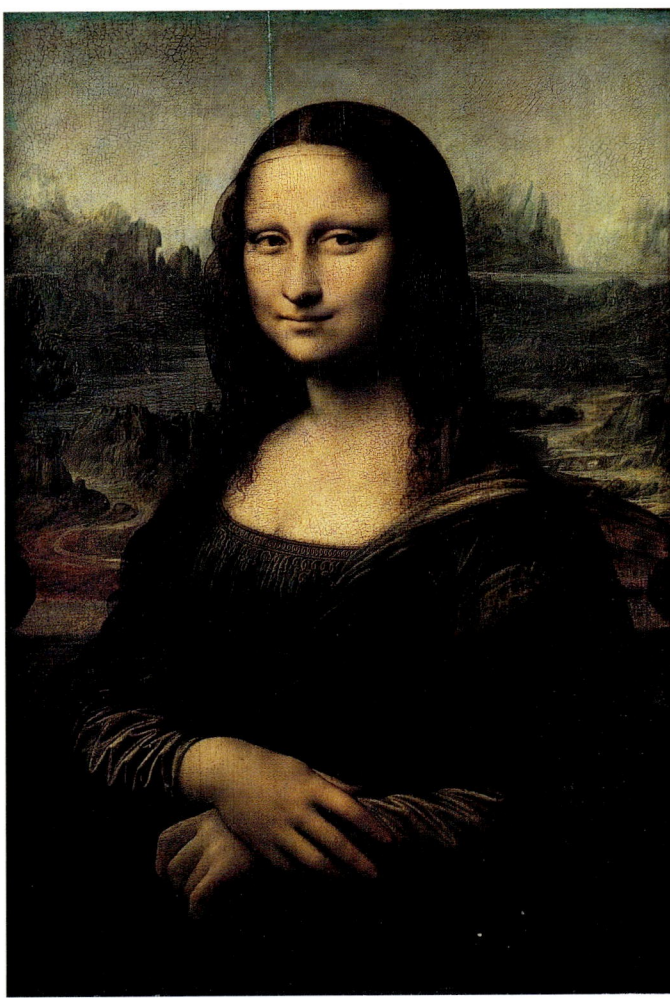

22-4 LEONARDO DA VINCI, *Mona Lisa,* ca. 1503–1505. Oil on wood, approx. 2′ 6″ × 1′ 9″. Louvre, Paris. 

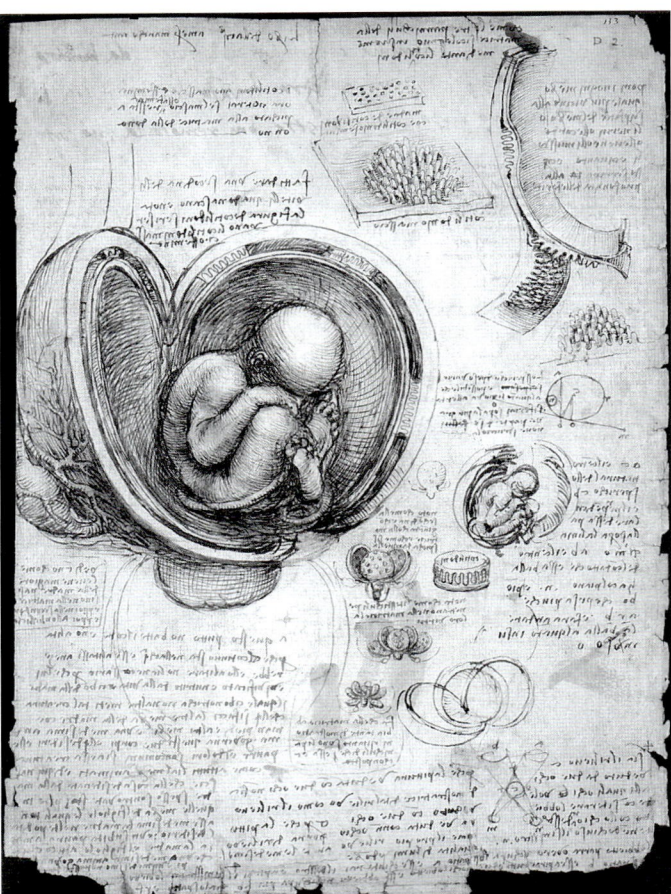

22-5 LEONARDO DA VINCI, *The Fetus and Lining of the Uterus,* ca. 1511–1513. Pen and ink with wash, over red chalk and traces of black chalk on paper, 1′ × 8⅝″. Royal Library, Windsor Castle. 

artist subtly adjusted the light and blurred the precise planes—Leonardo's famous smoky *sfumato* (misty haziness)—rendering the facial expression hard to determine.

The lingering appeal of *Mona Lisa* derives in large part from Leonardo's decision to set his subject against the backdrop of a mysterious uninhabited landscape. This landscape, with roads and bridges that seem to lead nowhere, is reminiscent of his *Virgin of the Rocks.* It also recalls Fra Filippo Lippi's "portrait," *Madonna and Child with Angels* (FIG. 21-38), with figures seated in front of a window that the viewer looks through into a distant landscape. Originally, the artist represented Mona Lisa in a *loggia* with columns. When the painting was trimmed (not by Leonardo), these columns were eliminated. (The remains of the column bases may still be seen to the left and right of Mona Lisa's shoulders.)

**ANATOMICAL DRAWING** Leonardo completed very few paintings; his perfectionism, relentless experimentation, and far-ranging curiosity diffused his efforts. However, the drawings in his notebooks preserved an extensive record of his ideas. His interests focused increasingly on science in his later years, and he embraced knowledge of all facets of the natural world. His investigations in anatomy yielded drawings of great precision and beauty of execution. *The Fetus and Lining of the Uterus* (FIG. 22-5), although it does not meet 21st-century standards for accuracy (for example, Leonardo regularized the uterus's shape to a sphere, and his char-

acterization of the lining is incorrect), was an astounding achievement in its day. Analytical anatomical studies such as this epitomized the scientific spirit of the Renaissance, establishing that era as a prelude to the modern world and setting it in sharp contrast to the preceding Middle Ages. Although Leonardo may not have been the first scientist of the modern world (at least not in the modern sense of the term), he certainly originated a method of scientific illustration, especially cutaway and exploded views. Scholars have long recognized the importance of these drawings for the development of anatomy as a science, especially in an age predating photographic methods such as X rays.

Leonardo was well known in his time as both architect and sculptor, although no actual buildings or surviving sculptures can be definitively attributed to him. From his many drawings of central-plan buildings, it appears he shared the interest of other Renaissance architects in this building type. As for sculpture, Leonardo left numerous drawings of monumental equestrian statues, and one resulted in a full-scale model for a monument to Francesco Sforza (Ludovico's father). The French used it as a target and shot it to pieces when they occupied Milan in 1499. Due to the French presence, Leonardo left Milan and served for a while as a military engineer for Cesare Borgia, who, with the support of his father, Pope Alexander VI, tried to conquer the cities of the Romagna region in north-central Italy and create a Borgia duchy. At a later date, Leonardo returned to Milan in the service of the French. At the invitation of King Francis I, he then went to France, where he died at the château of Cloux in 1519.

## Julius II: A Warrior-Pope's Quest for Authority

Another individual whose interests and activities affected the course of the High Renaissance was Pope Julius II (Giuliano della Rovere, r. 1503–1513). Beyond his responsibility as the spiritual leader of Christendom, Julius II extended his quest for authority to the temporal realm, as other medieval and Renaissance popes had done. An immensely ambitious man, Julius II indulged his enthusiasm for engaging in battle, which earned him a designation as the "warrior-pope." In addition, his selection of the name Julius, after Julius Caesar, reinforces the perception that the Roman Empire served as his governmental model.

Julius II's papacy is notable for his contributions to the arts. He was an avid art patron and understood well the propagandistic value of visual imagery. After his election as pope, he immediately commissioned artworks that would present an authoritative image of his rule and reinforce the primacy of the Catholic Church. Among the many projects he commissioned were a new design for Saint Peter's basilica, the construction of his tomb, the painting of the Sistine Chapel ceiling, and the decoration of the papal apartments. These large-scale projects clearly required considerable financial resources. Many Church members perceived the increasing sale of indulgences as a revenue-generating mechanism to fund papal art, architecture, and lavish lifestyles. This perception, accurate or not, prompted disgruntlement among the faithful. Thus, Julius II's patronage, despite its exceptional artistic legacy, also contributed to the rise of the Reformation.

RE-CREATING THE CAESARS' ROME One of the most important artistic projects Julius II initiated was his plan to replace the Constantinian basilica, Old Saint Peter's (see FIG. 11-7 or page xxii in Volume II), with a new structure. The earlier building had fallen into considerable disrepair and, in any event, did not suit this ambitious pope's taste for the colossal. Julius wanted to gain control over the whole of Italy and to make the Rome of the popes reminiscent of (if not more splendid than) the Rome of the caesars. As the symbolic seat of the papacy, Saint Peter's represented the history of the Church. Given this importance, Julius II carefully chose the architect DONATO D'ANGELO BRAMANTE (1444–1514) for this commission. Born in Urbino and trained as a painter (perhaps by Piero della Francesca), Bramante went to Milan in 1481 and, like Leonardo, stayed there until the French arrived in 1499. In Milan, he abandoned painting to become one of his generation's most renowned architects. Under the influence of Filippo Brunelleschi, Leon Battista Alberti, and perhaps Leonardo, all of whom strongly favored the art and architecture of classical antiquity, Bramante developed the High Renaissance form of the central-plan church.

Bramante originally designed the new Saint Peter's (FIG. 22-6) to consist of a cross with arms of equal length, each terminated by an apse. Julius II intended the new building to serve as a martyrium to mark Saint Peter's grave and also hoped to have his own tomb in it. A large dome would have covered the crossing, and smaller domes over subsidiary chapels would have covered the diagonal axes of the roughly square plan. Bramante's ambitious plan called for a boldly sculptural treatment of the walls and piers under the dome. His design for the interior space was complex in the extreme, with the intricate symmetries of a crystal. It is possible to detect in the plan some nine interlocking crosses, five of them supporting domes. The scale was titanic; according to sources, Bramante boasted he would place the dome of the Pantheon (see FIG. 10-48) over the Basilica Nova (Basilica of Constantine; FIG. 10-79).

A commemorative medal by CHRISTOFORO FOPPA CARADOSSO (FIG. 22-7) shows how Bramante's scheme would have attempted to do just that. The dome is hemispherical, like that of the Pantheon, but the massive unity of that building is broken up here by two towers and a medley of domes and porticos. In light of Julius II's interest in the Roman Empire, using the Pantheon as a model was entirely appropriate. That Bramante's design for the new Saint Peter's was commemorated on a medal is in itself significant. Such medals proliferated in the 15th century, reviving the ancient

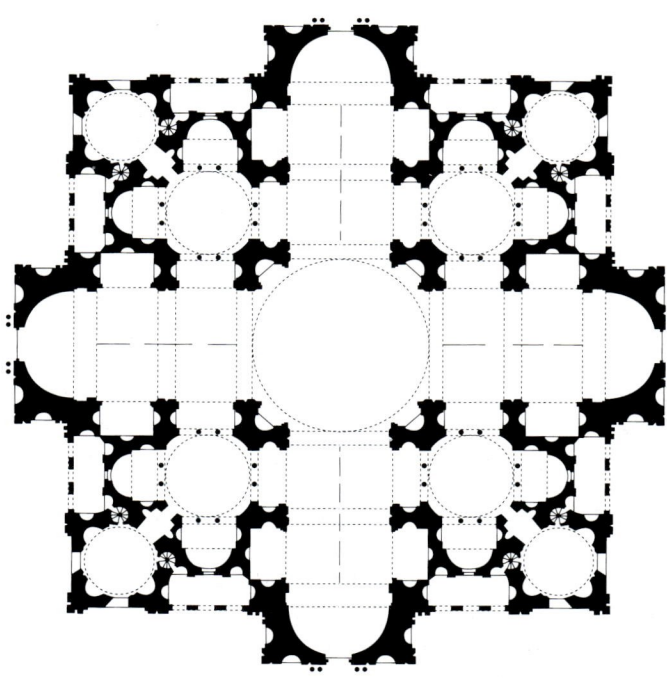

22-6 DONATO D'ANGELO BRAMANTE, plan for the new Saint Peter's, the Vatican, Rome, Italy, 1505.

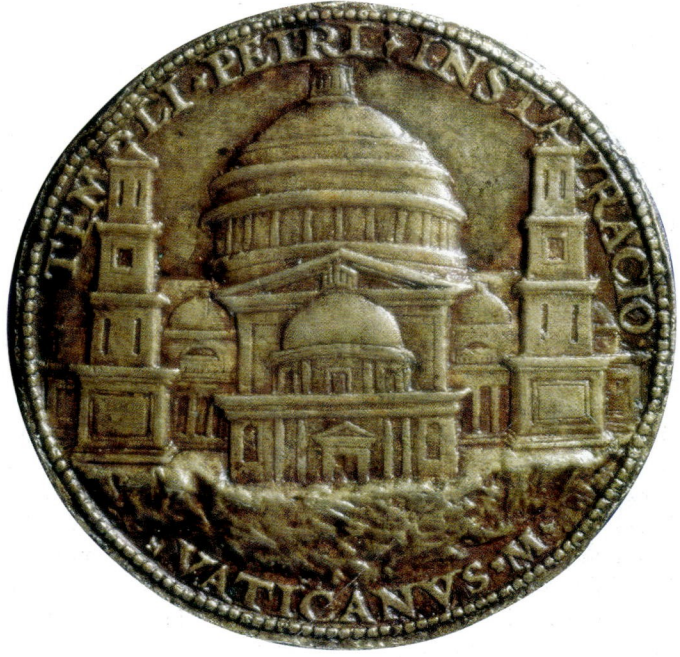

22-7 CHRISTOFORO FOPPA CARADOSSO, medal showing Bramante's design for the new Saint Peter's, 1506. British Museum, London.

Roman practice of placing images of important imperial building projects on the reverses of Roman coins. Renaissance humanists prized these coins and avidly collected them; the Medici family's collection still forms the core of the coin cabinet of Florence's Archaeological Museum.

During Bramante's lifetime, the actual construction of the new Saint Peter's basilica did not advance beyond the building of the crossing piers and the lower choir walls. After his death, the work passed from one architect to another and finally to Michelangelo (FIGS. 22-28 and 22-29), whom Pope Paul III appointed in 1546 to complete the building. Not until the 17th century, however, did the Church oversee the completion of Saint Peter's.

**A SCULPTURED MONUMENT** Julius II's selection of Bramante for this important commission reflected his confidence in the architect's ability to find a suitable architectural vocabulary to convey the pope's vision of a temporal humanist authority. This vocabulary, based on Greek and Roman models, emerged in an earlier building by Bramante, a structure often considered the perfect prototype of classical domed architecture for the Renaissance and subsequent periods. This building—the Tempietto (FIG. **22-8**)—received its name because, to contemporaries, it had the look of a small pagan temple from antiquity. "Little Temple" is, in fact, a perfectly appropriate nickname for the structure, because its lower story was directly inspired by the round temples of Roman Italy that Bramante would have known in Rome and its environs (see FIG. 10-3).

King Ferdinand and Queen Isabella of Spain commissioned the Tempietto to mark the conjectural location of Saint Peter's

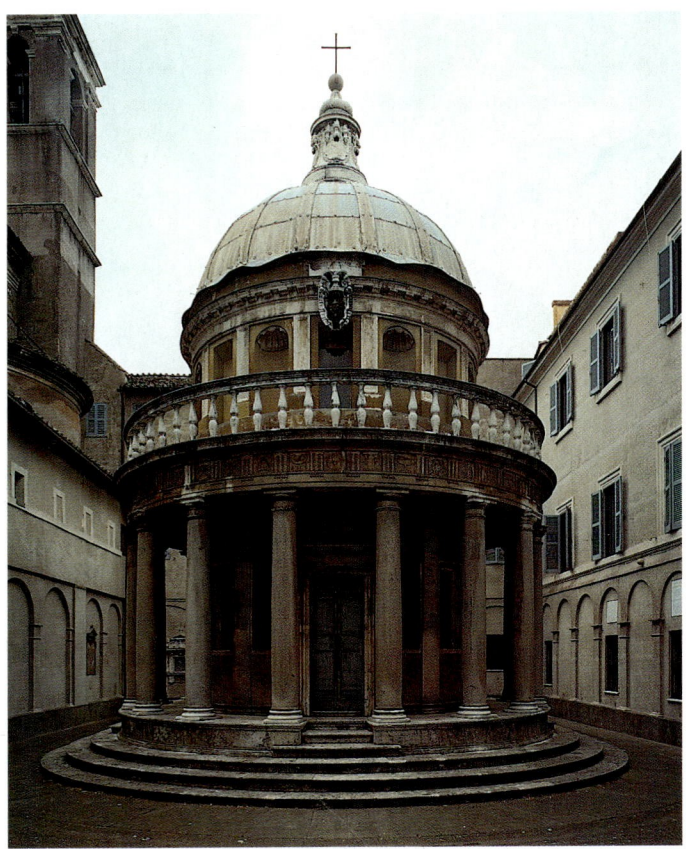

22-8 DONATO D'ANGELO BRAMANTE, Tempietto, San Pietro in Montorio, Rome, Italy, 1502(?).

crucifixion. Available information suggests that the patrons asked Bramante to undertake the project in 1502, but some scholars have disputed that traditional dating of the building. In any case, evidence reveals that Bramante began construction of the Tempietto during the first decade of the 16th century.

The architect relied on the composition of volumes and masses and on a sculptural handling of solids and voids to set apart this building, all but devoid of ornament, from structures built in the preceding century. Standing inside the cloister alongside the church of San Pietro in Montorio, Rome, the Tempietto resembles a sculptured reliquary and would have looked even more like one inside the circular colonnaded courtyard Bramante planned for it but never executed.

At first glance, the structure may seem severely rational with its sober circular stylobate and the cool Tuscan style of the colonnade, neither giving any indication of the placement of an interior altar or of the entrance. However, Bramante achieved a truly wonderful balance and harmony in the relationship of the parts (dome, drum, and base) to one another and to the whole. Conceived as a tall domed cylinder projecting from the lower wider cylinder of its colonnade, this small building incorporates all the qualities of a sculptured monument. Bramante's sculptural eye is most evident in the rhythmical play of light and shadow, seen around the columns and balustrade and across the deep-set rectangular windows alternating with shallow shell-capped niches in the cella walls and drum. Although the Tempietto, superficially at least, may resemble a Greek *tholos* (a circular shrine; FIG. 5-71), and although antique models provided the inspiration for all its details, the combination of parts and details was new and original. (Classical tholoi, for instance, had neither drum nor balustrade.)

If one of the main differences between the Early and High Renaissance styles of architecture was the former's emphasis on detailing flat wall surfaces versus the latter's sculptural handling of architectural masses, then the Tempietto certainly broke new ground and stood at the beginning of a new High Renaissance era. Renaissance architects understood the significance of the Tempietto. The architect Andrea Palladio, an artistic descendant of Bramante, included it in his survey of ancient temples because Bramante was "the first to bring back to light the good and beautiful architecture that from antiquity to that time had been hidden."[3] Round in plan and elevated on a base that isolates it from its surroundings, the Tempietto conforms to Alberti's and Palladio's strictest demands for an ideal church.

**NOVEL AND LOFTY THINGS** In addition to initiating the redesign of Saint Peter's, Pope Julius II commissioned numerous paintings and sculptures. The artist whom he deemed best able to convey his message was MICHELANGELO BUONARROTI (1475–1564), who received some of the most coveted commissions from the pope. Although he was an architect, sculptor, painter, poet, and engineer, Michelangelo thought of himself first as a sculptor, regarding that calling as superior to that of a painter because the sculptor shares in something like the divine power to "make man" (see "The Merits of Painting versus Sculpture: The Views of Leonardo and Michelangelo," page 621). Drawing a conceptual parallel to Plato's ideas, Michelangelo believed that the image produced by the artist's hand must come from the idea in the artist's mind. The idea, then, is the reality that the artist's genius has to bring forth. But artists are not the creators of the ideas they conceive. Rather, they find their ideas in the natural world, reflecting the absolute idea, which, for the artist, is beauty.

### The Merits of Painting versus Sculpture
#### The Views of Leonardo and Michelangelo

Leonardo da Vinci and Michelangelo each produced work in a variety of artistic media, earning enviable reputations not just as painters and sculptors but as architects and draughtsmen as well. The two disagreed, however, on the relative merits of the different media. In particular, Leonardo, with his intellectual and analytical mind, preferred painting to sculpture, which he denigrated as manual labor. In contrast, Michelangelo, who worked in a more intuitive manner, saw himself primarily as a sculptor. Two excerpts from their writings reveal their positions on the relationship between the two media.

Leonardo da Vinci wrote the following in "Comparison of Painting and Sculpture" from his so-called *Treatise on Painting:*

Painting is a matter of greater mental analysis, of greater skill, and more marvelous than sculpture, since necessity compels the mind of the painter to transform itself into the very mind of nature, to become an interpreter between nature and art. Painting justifies by reference to nature the reasons of the pictures which follow its laws: in what ways the images of objects before the eye come together in the pupil of the eye; which, among objects equal in size, looks larger to the eye; which, among equal colors will look more or less dark or more or less bright; which, among things at the same depth, looks more or less low; which, among those objects placed at equal height, will look more or less high, and why, among objects placed at various distances, one will appear less clear than the other.

This art comprises and includes within itself all visible things such as colors and their diminution which the poverty of sculpture cannot include. Painting represents transparent objects but the sculptor will show you the shapes of natural objects without artifice. The painter will show you things at different distances with variation of color due to the air lying between the objects and the eye; he shows you mists through which visual images penetrate with difficulty; he shows you rain which discloses within it clouds with mountains and valleys; he shows the dust which discloses within it and beyond it the combatants who stirred it up; he shows streams of greater or lesser density; he shows fish playing between the surface of the water and its bottom; he shows the polished pebbles of various colors lying on the washed sand at the bottom of rivers, surrounded by green plants; he shows the stars at various heights above us, and thus he achieves innumerable effects which sculpture cannot attain.

The sculptor says that bas-relief is a kind of painting. This may be accepted in part, insofar as design is concerned, because it shares in perspective. But with regard to shadows and lights, it is false.[1]

Michelangelo wrote these excerpts in a letter to Benedetto Varchi in the late 1540s:

I believe that painting is considered excellent in proportion as it approaches the effect of relief, while relief is considered bad in proportion as it approaches the effect of painting.

I used to consider that sculpture was the lantern of painting and that between the two things there was the same difference as that between the sun and the moon. But . . . I now consider that painting and sculpture are one and the same thing. . . .

Suffice that, since one and the other (that is to say, both painting and sculpture) proceed from the same faculty, it would be an easy matter to establish harmony between them and to let such disputes alone, for they occupy more time than the execution of the figures themselves. As to that man [Leonardo] who wrote saying that painting was more noble than sculpture, if he had known as much about the other subjects on which he has written, why, my serving-maid would have written better![2]

[1] Quoted in Robert Klein and Henri Zerner, *Italian Art 1500–1600: Sources and Documents* (Evanston, Ill.: Northwestern University Press, 1966), 7–8.

[2] Michelangelo to Benedetto Varchi, ca. 1547; ibid., 13–14.

---

One of Michelangelo's best-known observations about sculpture is that the artist must proceed by finding the idea—the image locked in the stone, as it were. Thus, by removing the excess stone, the sculptor extricates the idea (see FIG. Intro-15), like Pygmalion bringing forth the living form. The artist, Michelangelo felt, works through many years at this unceasing process of revelation and "arrives late at novel and lofty things."[4]

Michelangelo did indeed arrive "at novel and lofty things," for he broke sharply from the lessons of his predecessors and contemporaries in one important respect. He mistrusted the application of mathematical methods as guarantees of beauty in proportion. Measure and proportion, he believed, should be "kept in the eyes." Biographer Vasari quotes Michelangelo as declaring that "it was necessary to have the compasses in the eyes and not in the hand, because the hands work and the eye judges."[5] Thus, Michelangelo set aside the ancient Roman architect Vitruvius, Alberti, Leonardo, and others who tirelessly sought the perfect measure, and asserted that the artist's inspired judgment could identify other pleasing proportions. In addition, Michelangelo argued that the artist must not be bound, except by the demands made by realizing the idea. This insistence on the artist's own authority was typical of Michelangelo and anticipated the modern concept of the right to a self-expression of talent limited only by the artist's own judgment. The artistic license to aspire far beyond the "rules" was, in part, a manifestation of the pursuit of fame and success that humanism fostered. In this context, Michelangelo created works in architecture, sculpture, and painting that departed from High Renaissance regularity. He put in its stead a style of vast, expressive strength conveyed through complex, eccentric, and often titanic forms that loom before the viewer in tragic grandeur. Michelangelo's self-imposed isolation, creative furies, proud independence, and daring innovations led Italians to speak of the dominating quality of the man and his works in one word—*terribilità*, the sublime shadowed by the awesome and the fearful.

**"THE GIANT"** In 1501, the Florence Cathedral building committee asked Michelangelo to work a great block of marble left over from an earlier aborted commission. From this stone, Michelangelo crafted *David* (FIG. 22-9), which assured his reputation then and now as an extraordinary talent. This early work reveals Michelangelo's fascination with the human form, and *David*'s formal references to classical antiquity surely appealed to Julius II, who associated himself with the humanists and with Roman emperors. Thus, this sculpture and the fame that accrued to Michelangelo on its completion called the artist to the pope's attention, leading to major papal commissions.

For *David*, Michelangelo took up the theme Donatello (see FIG. 21-23) and Andrea del Verrocchio (see FIG. 21-24) had used successfully. Like other David sculptures, Michelangelo's version had a political dimension. It seems certain that with the stability

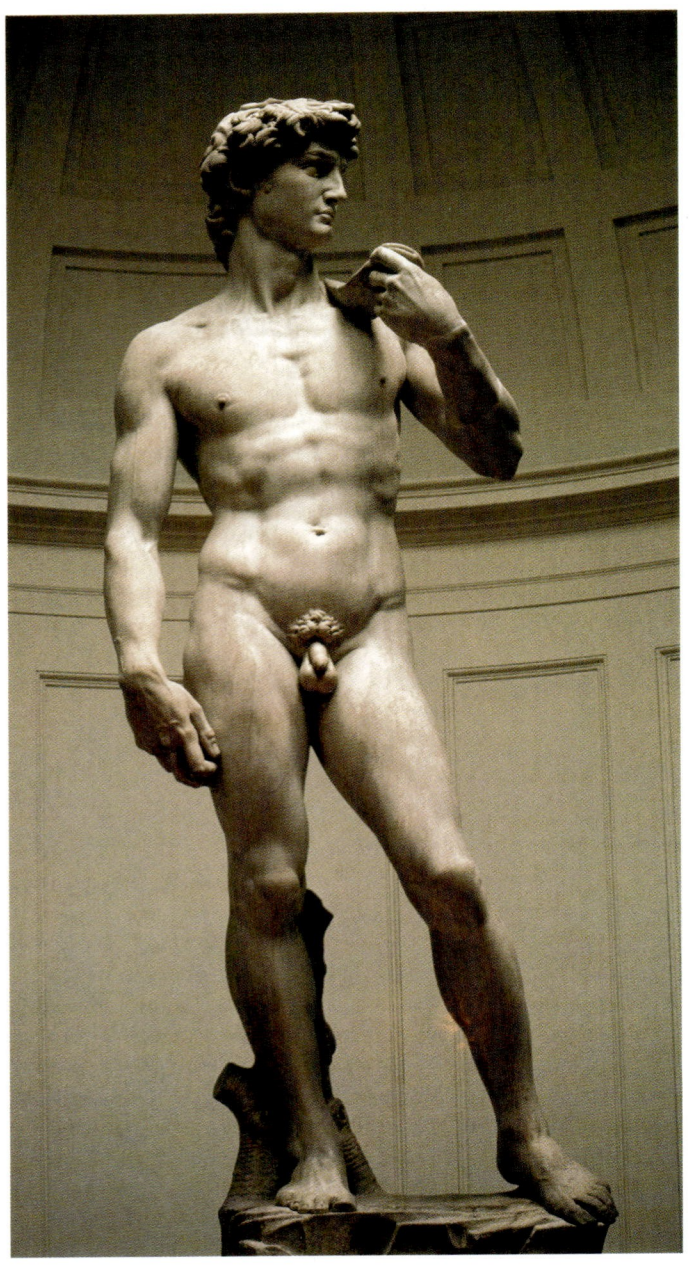

22-9 MICHELANGELO BUONARROTI, *David*, 1501–1504. Marble, 13′ 5″ high. Galleria dell'Accademia, Florence.

of the republic in some jeopardy, Florentines viewed David as the symbolic defiant hero of the Florentine republic, especially given the statue's placement near the west door of the Palazzo della Signoria. Michelangelo was surely cognizant of the political symbolism associated with the figure of David and other public sculptures in Florentine history. However, the degree to which the artist intended a specific political message is unknown. Regardless, only 40 years after *David*'s completion, biographer Giorgio Vasari extolled the political value of the colossal statue, claiming that "without any doubt the figure has put in the shade every other statue, ancient or modern, Greek or Roman—this was intended as a symbol of liberty for the Palace, signifying that just as David had protected his people and governed them justly, so whoever ruled Florence should vigorously defend the city and govern it with justice."[6]

Despite the traditional association of David with heroism, Michelangelo chose to represent David not after the victory, with Goliath's head at his feet, but turning his head to his left, sternly watchful of the approaching foe. His whole muscular body, as well as his face, is tense with gathering power. *David* exhibits the characteristic representation of energy in reserve that imbues Michelangelo's later figures with the tension of a coiled spring. The young hero's anatomy plays an important part in this prelude to action. His rugged torso, sturdy limbs, and large hands and feet alert viewers to the strength to come. Each swelling vein and tightening sinew amplifies the psychological energy of the monumental David's pose.

Michelangelo doubtless had the classical nude in mind. He, like many of his colleagues, greatly admired Greco-Roman statues, his knowledge limited mostly to Roman sculptures and Roman copies of Greek art. In particular, classical sculptors' skillful and precise rendering of heroic physique impressed Michelangelo. In his *David*, Michelangelo, without strictly imitating the antique style, captured the tension of Lysippan athletes (see FIG. 5-65) and the psychological insight and emotionalism of Hellenistic statuary (see FIGS. 5-80 and 5-81). This David differs from those of Donatello and Verrocchio in much the same way later Hellenistic statues departed from their Classical predecessors. Michelangelo abandoned the self-contained compositions of the 15th-century David statues by giving David's head the abrupt turn toward his gigantic adversary. Michelangelo's *David* is compositionally and emotionally connected to an unseen presence beyond the statue; this, too, is evident in Hellenistic sculpture (see FIG. 5-86). As early as *David*, then, Michelangelo invested his efforts in presenting towering pent-up emotion rather than calm ideal beauty. He transferred his own doubts, frustrations, and passions into the great figures he created or planned. And this resulted in works like *David*—a truly titanic sculpture (referred to as "the Giant" by Florentines) with immense physical and symbolic presence.

**IN MEMORY OF A WARRIOR-POPE** The first project Julius II commissioned from Michelangelo in 1505 was the pontiff's own tomb. The original design called for a freestanding two-story structure with some 28 statues. This colossal monument would have given Michelangelo the latitude to sculpt numerous human figures while providing the pope with a grandiose memorial (which Julius II intended to locate in Saint Peter's). Shortly after Michelangelo began work on this project, the pope, for unknown reasons, interrupted the commission, possibly because funds had to be diverted to Bramante's rebuilding of Saint Peter's. After

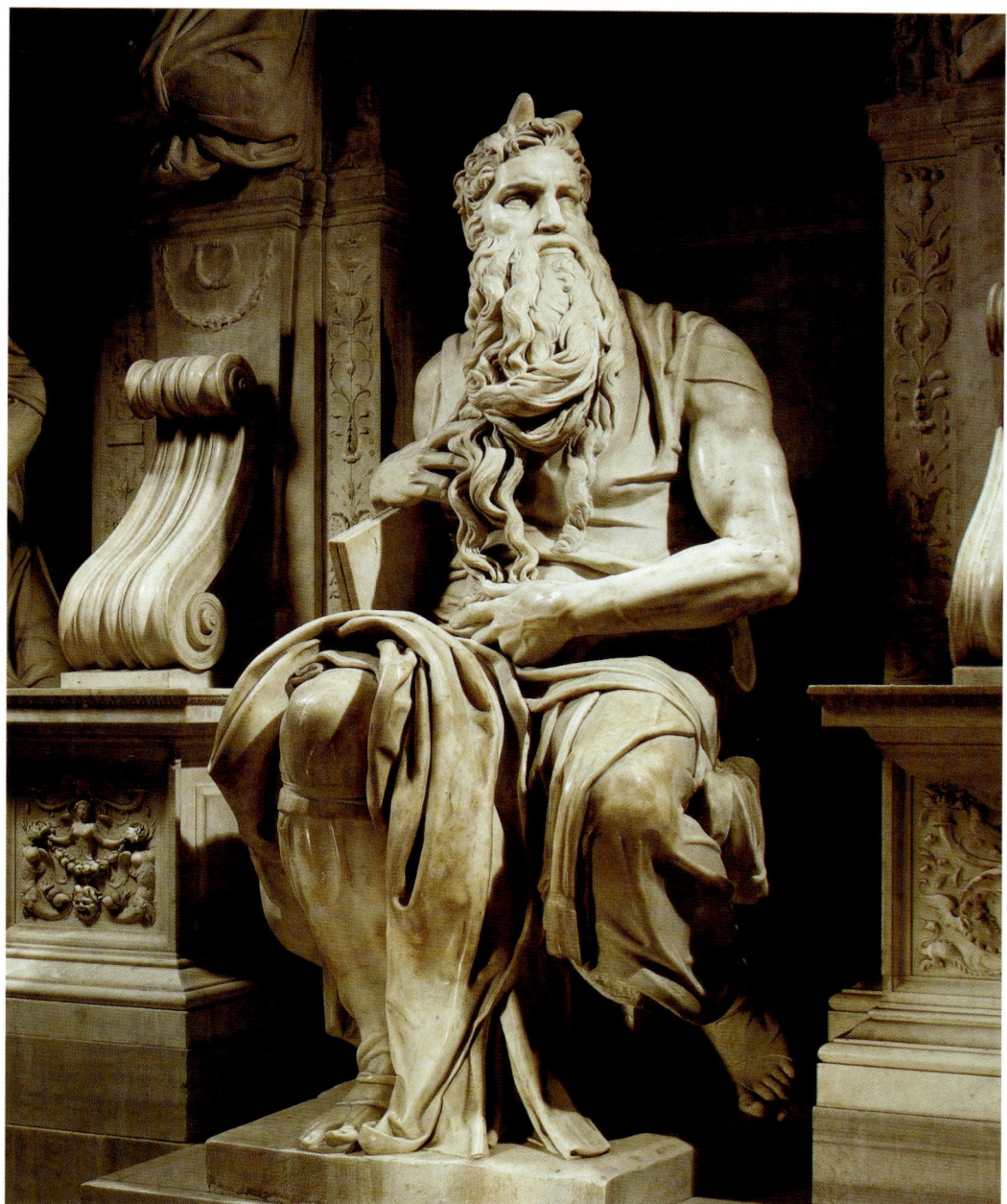

**22-10** MICHELANGELO BUONARROTI, *Moses,* San Pietro in Vincoli, Rome, Italy, ca. 1513–1515. Marble, approx. 8′ 4″ high.

Julius II's death in 1513, Michelangelo was forced to reduce the scale of the project step-by-step until, in 1542, a final contract specified a simple wall tomb with fewer than one-third of the originally planned figures. Michelangelo completed the tomb in 1545 and saw it placed in San Pietro in Vincoli, Rome, where Julius II had served as a cardinal before his accession to the papacy. Given Julius's ambitions, it is safe to say that had he seen the final design of his tomb, or known where it was eventually located, he would have been bitterly disappointed.

The spirit of the tomb may be summed up in the figure *Moses* (FIG. **22-10**), which Michelangelo completed during one of his sporadic resumptions of the work in 1513. Meant to be seen from below and to be balanced with seven other massive forms related to it in spirit, the *Moses* now, in its comparatively paltry setting, does not have its originally intended impact. Michelangelo

depicted the Old Testament prophet seated, the Tablets of the Law under one arm and his hands gathering his voluminous beard. The horns that appear on Moses's head were a sculptural convention in Christian art and helped Renaissance viewers identify Moses (see FIG. 17-37). Here again, Michelangelo used the turned head, which concentrates the expression of awful wrath that stirs in the mighty frame and eyes. The muscles bulge, the veins swell, and the great legs seem to begin slowly to move. If this titan ever rose to his feet, one writer said, the world would fly apart. To find such pent-up energy—both emotional and physical—in a seated statue, historians must turn once again to Hellenistic statuary (see FIG. 5-86).

**REPRESENTING OPPRESSION** Originally, Michelangelo intended for some 20 sculptures of slaves, in various attitudes of revolt and exhaustion, to appear on the tomb. One such figure is *Bound Slave* (FIG. 22-11). (Another such figure is shown in FIG. Intro-15.) Considerable scholarly uncertainty about this sculpture (and three other "slave" figures) exists. Although conventional scholarship connected these statues with the Julius tomb, some art historians now doubt this. A lively debate also continues about the subject of these figures; many scholars reject

their identification as "slaves" or "captives." Despite these unanswered questions, the "slaves," like *David* and *Moses*, represent definitive statements. Michelangelo created figures that do not so much represent an abstract concept, as in medieval allegory, but embody powerful emotional states associated with oppression. Indeed, Michelangelo communicated his expansive imagination through every plane and hollow of the stone. In *Bound Slave*, the defiant figure's violent contrapposto is the image of frantic but impotent struggle. Michelangelo based his whole art on his conviction that whatever can be said greatly through sculpture and painting must be said through the human figure.

**A GRAND BIBLICAL DRAMA** Julius II's artistic program continued unabated, despite the obstacles he encountered. With the suspension of the tomb project, Julius II gave the bitter and reluctant Michelangelo the commission to paint the ceiling of the Sistine Chapel (FIGS. **22-12** and **22-13**) in 1508. The artist, insisting that painting was not his profession (a protest that rings hollow after the fact, but Michelangelo's major works until then had been in sculpture, and painting was of secondary interest to him), assented in the hope that the tomb project could be revived. Michelangelo faced enormous difficulties in painting the Sistine ceiling. He had to address his relative inexperience in the fresco technique; the ceiling's dimensions (some 5,800 square feet); its height above the pavement (almost 70 feet); and the complicated perspective problems presented by the vault's height and curve. Yet, in less than four years, Michelangelo produced an unprecedented work—a monumental fresco incorporating the patron's agenda, Church doctrine, and the artist's interests. Depicting the

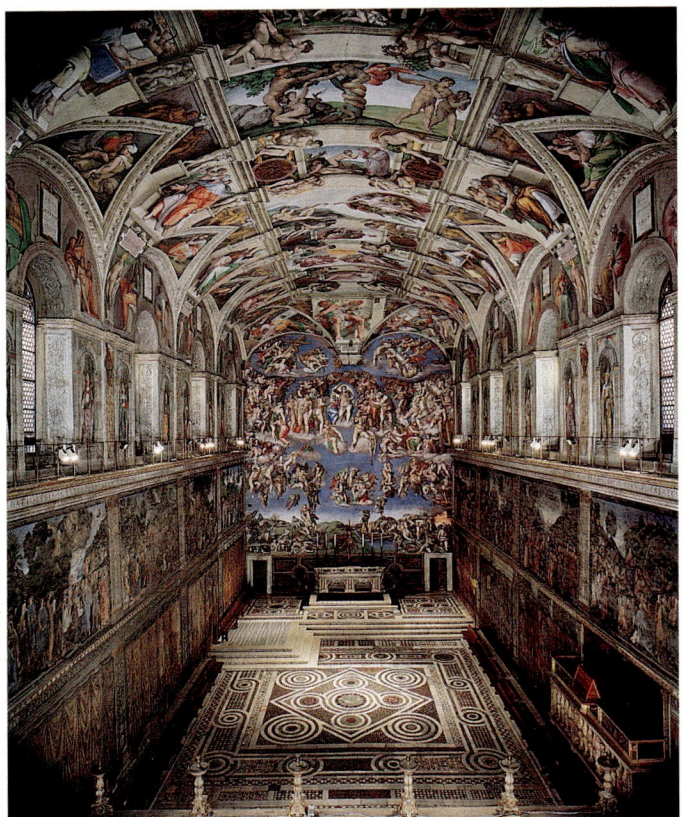

22-12 Interior of the Sistine Chapel (view facing east), Vatican City, Rome, Italy, built 1473. Copyright © Nippon Television Network Corporation, Tokyo. 🔎

22-11 MICHELANGELO BUONARROTI, *Bound Slave*, 1513–1516. Marble, approx. 6′ 10½″ high. Louvre, Paris. 🔎

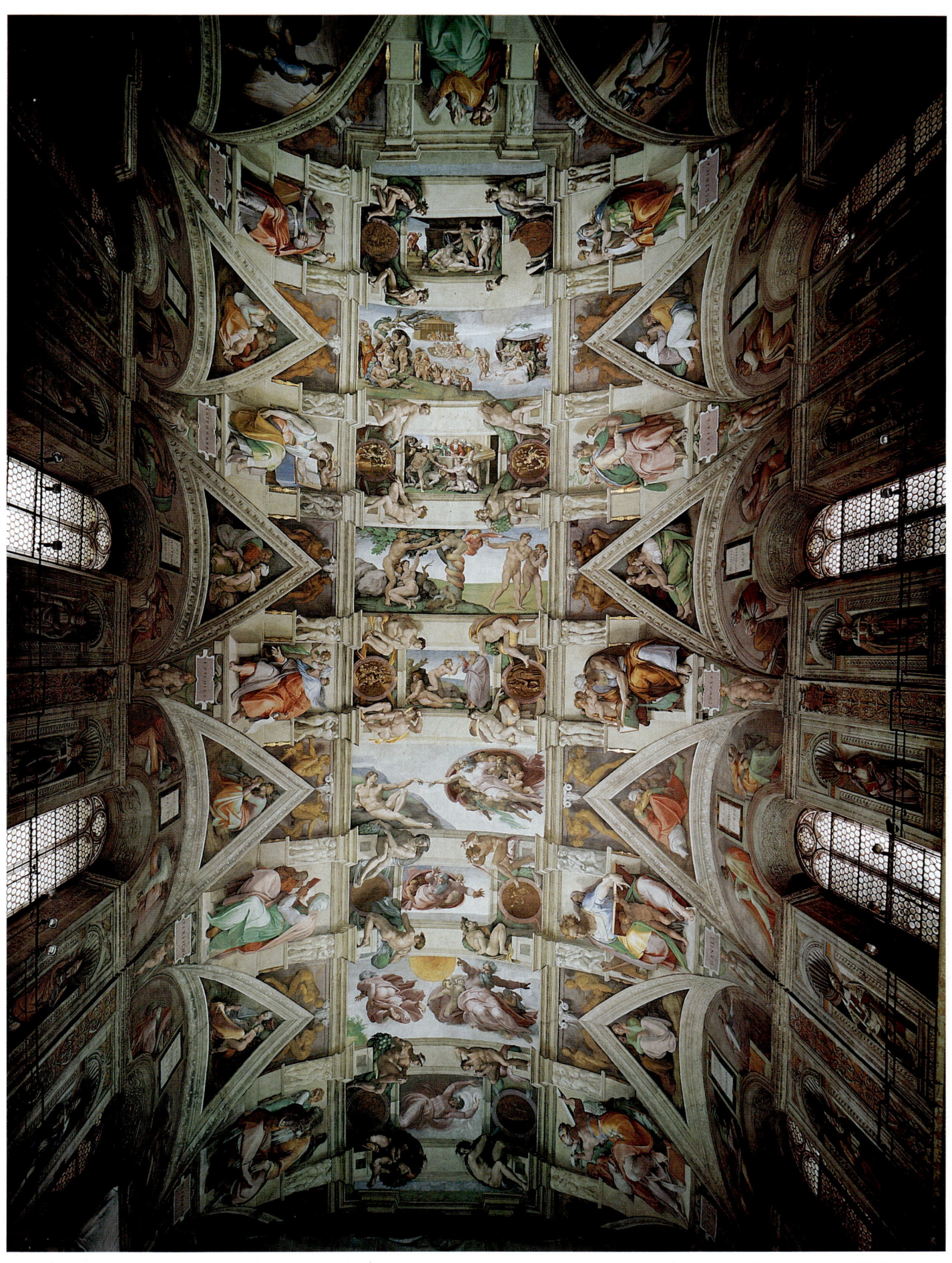

**22-13** MICHELANGELO BUONARROTI, ceiling of the Sistine Chapel, Vatican City, Rome, Italy, 1508–1512. Fresco, approx. 128′ × 45′. 🔊

most august and solemn themes of all, the Creation, Fall, and Redemption of humanity (most likely selected by Julius II with input from Michelangelo and a theological adviser), Michelangelo spread a colossal decorative scheme across the vast surface. He succeeded in weaving together more than 300 figures in an ultimate grand drama of the human race.

A long sequence of narrative panels describing the Creation, as recorded in the biblical book Genesis, runs along the crown of the vault, from *God's Separation of Light and Darkness* (above the altar) to *Drunkenness of Noah* (nearest the entrance to the chapel). Thus, as viewers enter the chapel, look up, and walk toward the altar, they review, in reverse order, the history of the fall of humankind. The Hebrew prophets and pagan sibyls who foretold the coming of Christ appear seated in large thrones on both sides of the central row of scenes from Genesis, where the vault curves down. In the four corner pendentives, Michelangelo placed four Old Testament scenes with David, Judith, Haman, and Moses and the Brazen Serpent. Scores of lesser figures also appear. The ancestors of Christ fill the triangular compartments above the windows, nude youths punctuate the corners of the central panels, and small pairs of putti (cherubic little boys) in grisaille support the painted cornice surrounding the entire central corridor. The overall conceptualization of the ceiling's design and narrative structure not only presents a sweeping chronology of Christianity but also is in keeping with Renaissance ideas about Christian history. Such ideas include interest in the conflict between good and evil and between the energy of youth and the wisdom of age. The conception of the entire ceiling was astounding in itself, and the articulation of it in its thousand details was a superhuman achievement.

Unlike Andrea Mantegna's decoration of the Camera degli Sposi in Mantua (see FIG. 21-45), the strongly marked unifying architectural framework in the Sistine Chapel does not construct "picture windows" enframing illusions just within. Rather, the viewer focuses on figure after figure, each sharply outlined against the neutral tone of the architectural setting or the plain background of the panels. Here, as in his sculpture, Michelangelo relentlessly concentrated his expressive purpose on the human figure. To him, the body was beautiful not only in its natural form but also in its spiritual and philosophical significance. The body was simply the manifestation of the soul or of a state of mind and character. Michelangelo represented the body in its most simple, elemental aspect—in the nude or simply draped, with no background and no ornamental embellishment. He always painted with a sculptor's eye for how light and shadow communicate volume and surface. It is no coincidence that many of the figures seem to be tinted reliefs or full-rounded statues.

**DEPICTING MAN'S CREATION** One of the ceiling's central panels is *Creation of Adam* (FIG. 22-14). Michelangelo did not paint the traditional representation but a bold, entirely humanistic interpretation of the momentous event. God and Adam confront each other in a primordial unformed landscape of which Adam is still a material part, heavy as earth. The Lord transcends the earth, wrapped in a billowing cloud of drapery and borne up by his powers. Life leaps to Adam like a spark from the extended and mighty hand of God. The communication between gods and heroes, so familiar in classical myth, is here concrete. This blunt depiction of the Lord as ruler of Heaven in the Olympian pagan sense indicates how easily High Renaissance thought joined classical and Christian traditions. Yet the classical trappings do not obscure the essential Christian message.

Beneath the Lord's sheltering left arm is a female figure, apprehensively curious but as yet uncreated. Scholars traditionally

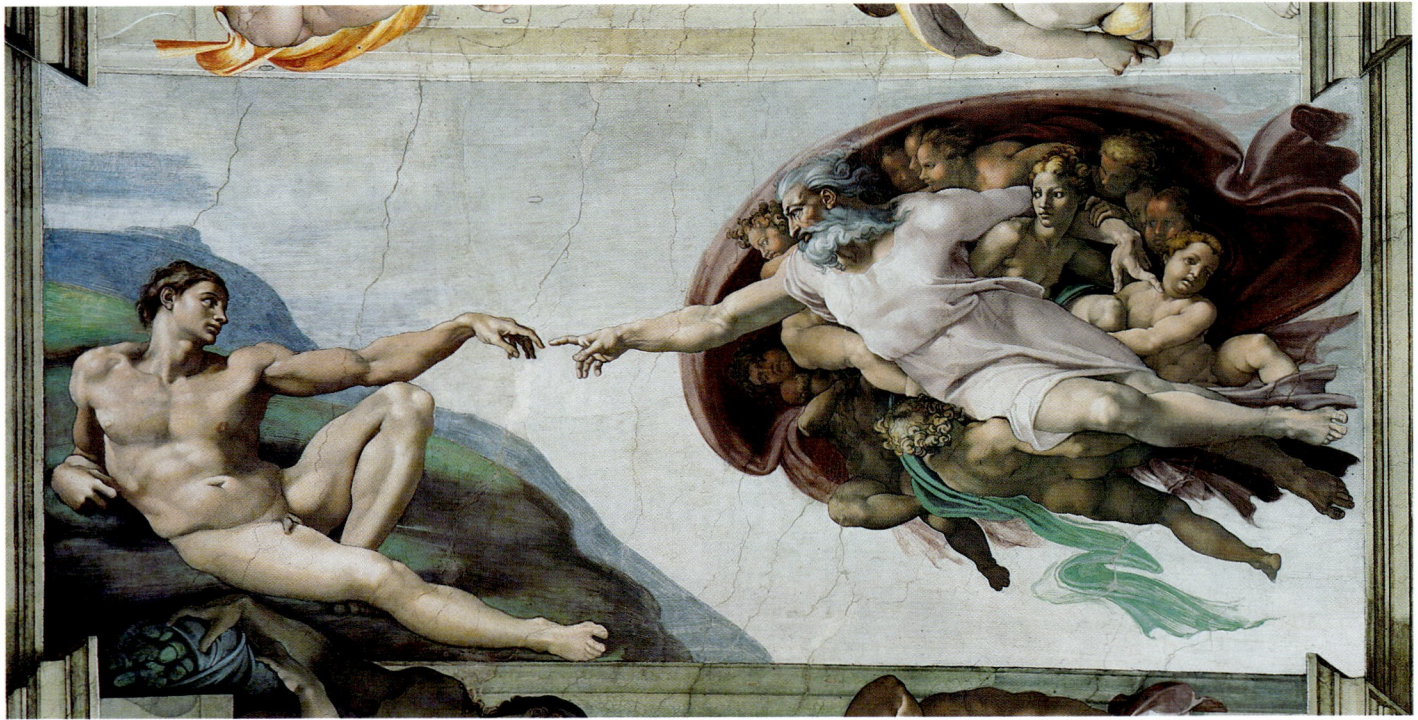

22-14 MICHELANGELO BUONARROTI, *Creation of Adam* (detail), ceiling of the Sistine Chapel, Vatican City, Rome, Italy, 1511–1512. Fresco, approx. 9′ 2″ × 18′ 8″.

believed her to represent Eve but recently have suggested she may be the Virgin Mary (with the Christ Child at her knee). If the new identification is correct, it suggests that Michelangelo incorporated into his fresco one of the essential tenets of Christian faith. This is the belief that Adam's original sin eventually led to the sacrifice of Christ, which in turn made possible the redemption of all humankind.

As God reaches out to Adam, the viewer's eye follows the motion from right to left, but Adam's extended left arm leads the eye back to the right, along the Lord's right arm, shoulders, and left arm to his left forefinger, which points to the Christ Child's face. The focal point of this right-to-left-to-right movement—the fingertips of Adam and the Lord—is dramatically off-center. Michelangelo replaced the straight architectural axes found in Leonardo's compositions with curves and diagonals. For example, the bodies of the two great figures are complementary—the concave body of Adam fitting the convex body and billowing "cloak" of God. Thus, motion directs not only the figures but also the whole composition. The reclining positions of the figures, the heavy musculature, and the twisting poses are all intrinsic parts of Michelangelo's style.

Visitors to the Sistine Chapel will encounter a cleaned ceiling (FIGS. 22-13 and **22-15**), revealing much brighter colors (see "Restoring the Glory of Renaissance Art," page 628). Controversy accompanied the execution of this restoration, and the vivid colors (FIG. **22-16**) take many viewers aback. That reaction, however, probably derives from familiarity with the formerly soot- and grime-covered ceiling.

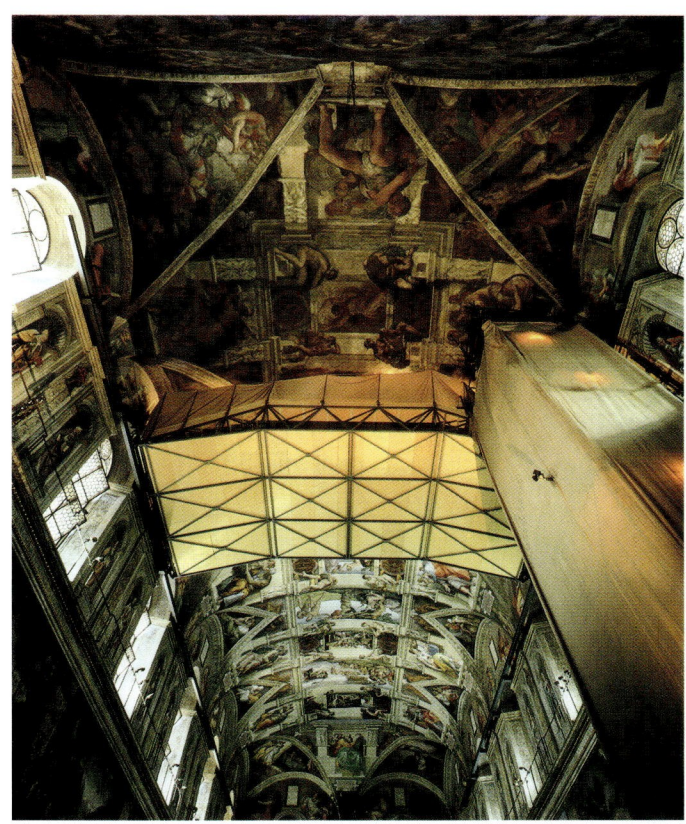

**22-15** Cleaning of the ceiling of the Sistine Chapel, Vatican City, Rome, Italy, 1977–1989.

**22-16** Detail of the Azor-Sadoch lunette's left side over one of the Sistine Chapel windows at various stages of the restoration process, Vatican City, Rome, Italy, 1977–1989. Copyright © Nippon Television Network Corporation, Tokyo.

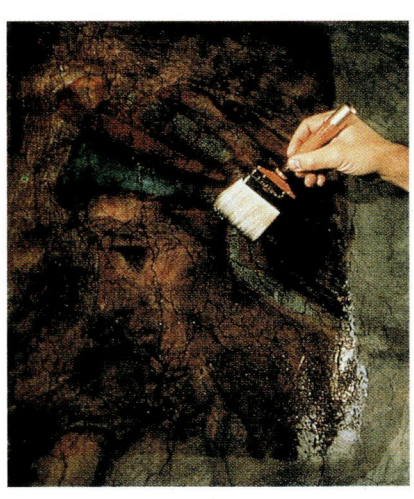

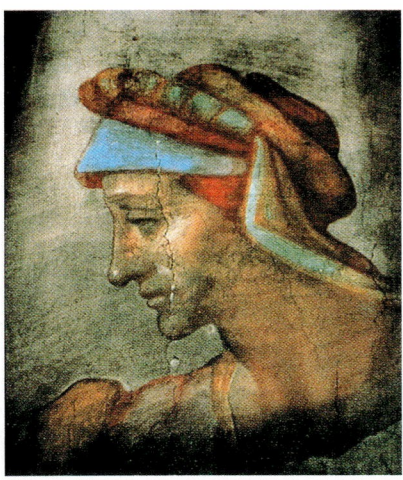

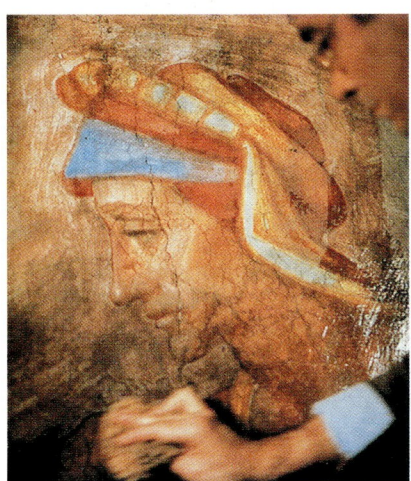

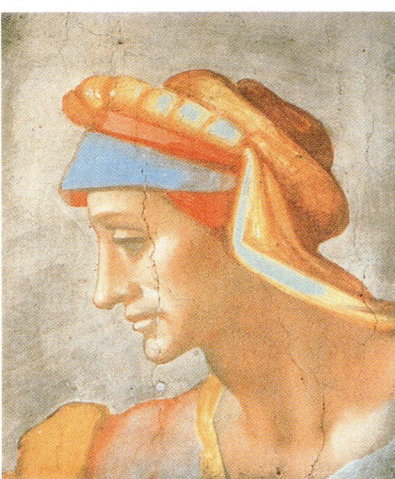

### Restoring the Glory of Renaissance Art

The year 1989 marked the completion of the cleaning and restoration of the Sistine Chapel ceiling—after 12 years of painstaking work. Restorers removed centuries of accumulated grime, overpainting, and protective glue, uncovering much of the artist's original craft in form, color, style, and procedure. Our before-and-after details of one of the lunettes over the windows (FIG. 22-16) depict four stages of the restoration process. In these semicircular spaces, Michelangelo painted figures representing the ancestors of Christ (Matt. 1:1–17). After computer assessment of the damage (including use of infrared and ultraviolet lights), the restorers worked carefully and slowly to clean the fresco of soot, dirt, dissolved salts, and various types of gums and varnishes made of animal glues. Over the centuries, restorers had used such varnishes to brighten the darkening fresco; unfortunately, over time the varnishes deteriorated, making the painting even darker. For the latest cleaning effort, the restorer first wet a small section of the fresco with distilled, deionized water. The application of a cleaning solution made of bicarbonates of sodium and ammonium and supplemented with an antibacterial, antifungal agent followed. Adding carboxymethylcellulose and water to this solution created a gel that clung to the ceiling fresco. After three minutes, restorers removed the gel. Our details (of the Azor-Sadoch lunette) reveal the startling product of the restorers' procedure, as the original work emerged from the dark film of time and faulty repairs.

These figures, once thought purposefully dark, now show brilliant colors of high intensity, brushed on with an astonishing freedom and verve. The fresh, luminous hues, boldly joined in unexpected harmonies, seem uncharacteristically dissonant to some experts and have aroused brisk controversy. Some believe that the restorers removed Michelangelo's work along with the accumulated layers and that the apparently strident coloration cannot possibly be his. Others insist that the restoration effort has revealed to modern eyes the artist's real intentions and effects—that in the Sistine Chapel Michelangelo already had paved the way for the Mannerist reaction to the High Renaissance, examined later in this chapter. In any event, due to the restoration, scholars are now restudying and reassessing Michelangelo's pictorial art and its influence.

The restoration also has shed light on Michelangelo's manner of painting, because restorers constructed a bridgelike scaffolding (FIG. 22-15) similar to that the artist designed and used. Despite the persistence of stories that Michelangelo painted the ceiling lying on his back, those are merely myths. In his journals, Michelangelo complained bitterly of his pain and suffering from working on an overhead fresco while standing. One sonnet by the artist included a litany of complaints, among others: "In front my skin grows loose and long; behind, By bending it becomes more taut and strait; Crosswise I strain me like a Syrian bow."[1]

On completion of this monumental cleaning project, restorers turned their attention to Michelangelo's *Last Judgment* (FIG. 22-25) behind the altar in the Sistine Chapel. They completed their restoration of that large fresco in 1994.

The recent treatment of Leonardo's *Last Supper* (FIG. 22-3) in the refectory of Santa Maria delle Grazie in Milan presented restorers with an even greater challenge. Leonardo had mixed oil and tempera, applying much of it *a secco* (to dried, rather than wet, plaster). Thus, the wall did not absorb the pigment as in the *buon fresco* technique, and the paint quickly began to flake. The humidity of Milan further accelerated the deterioration. Over the centuries, the fresco has been subjected to frequent alterations. Napoleonic troops attacked the fresco; at other times, it was cleaned with a variety of materials. Consequently, current restorers confronted a monumental task. Their efforts, like those of the Sistine Chapel restorers, were painstaking and slow, involving extensive scholarly, chemical, and computer analysis. Their work took more than two decades, and they unveiled the cleaned fresco to the public in May 1999.

Like other restorations, this one was not without controversy. Dr. Pinin Brambilla Barcilon, who oversaw the cleaning project, declared: "What we have brought to light are Leonardo's original and brilliant colors. Nothing has been removed from the original painting, and nothing has been added."[2] Yet Dr. James Beck, a professor of art history at Columbia University and a vocal critic of the cleaning, charges the painting is now "18–20 percent Leonardo and 80 percent by the restorer."[3] Viewers will have to judge the results for themselves. But to minimize future deterioration, viewing time is limited, and visitors are ushered through areas outfitted with special filtration systems and dust-absorbing carpets before entering the refectory.

The controversies have not put a damper on other restoration projects. After the cleaning of *Last Judgment*, the Vatican continued the restoration of the remaining frescoes in the Sistine Chapel (including those by Perugino, Botticelli, and Ghirlandaio), and the cleaned frescoes were unveiled to the public in December 1999. Restorers cleaned the frescoes in the Stanza della Segnatura in the Vatican Apartments in Rome (the restored *School of Athens*, FIG. 22-17, was unveiled in 1996). Still in progress is the work on the frescoes in the Stanza d'Eliodoro.

Of course, restoration has also been critical for artworks other than frescoes. Michelangelo's *Moses* (FIG. 22-10) in San Pietro in Vincoli was cleaned in 2001; live video links provided by three Web cams allowed the public to monitor the cleaning via the Internet for the duration of the restoration. Currently, Michelangelo's *David* is undergoing cleaning. Begun in September 2002, the restoration was originally scheduled to be finished at the end of March 2003. However, controversy about the cleaning techniques being used erupted in spring 2003, and as a result, completion has been delayed. During the process, the sculpture (and restoration) will be visible to visitors to the Galleria dell'Accademia (where the statue was moved in 1837 to protect it from vandalism and the elements).

[1] Quoted in Robert Goldwater and Marco Treves, eds., *Artists on Art*, 3rd ed. (New York: Pantheon Books, 1958), 59.

[2] Piero Valsecchi, "It's Art, but Is It Leonardo's?" Milan Associated Press Wire, 28 May 1999.

[3] Ibid.

**A CONGREGATION OF GREAT THINKERS** While Michelangelo was hard at work on the Sistine Chapel ceiling, Pope Julius II turned his attention to the papal apartments. In 1508, the pope called Raffaello Santi (or Sanzio), known as RAPHAEL (1483–1520), to the papal court in Rome, perhaps on the recommendation of Raphael's fellow townsman, Bramante. Born in a small town in Umbria near Urbino, Raphael probably learned the rudiments of his art from his father, Giovanni Santi, a painter connected with the ducal court of Federico da Montefeltro.

Once in Rome, in competition with older artists such as Perugino and Luca Signorelli, Raphael received one of the largest commissions of the time—the decoration of the papal apartments in the Vatican. Of the suite's several rooms (*stanze*), Raphael painted the Stanza della Segnatura (Room of the Signature—the papal library) and the Stanza d'Eliodoro (Room of Heliodorus). His pupils completed the others, following his sketches. On the four walls of the Stanza della Segnatura, under the headings of Theology (called *Disputà*), Law (*Justice*), Poetry (*Parnassus*), and Philosophy (*School of Athens*), Raphael presented images that symbolize and sum up Western learning as Renaissance society understood it. The frescoes refer to the four branches of human knowledge and wisdom while pointing out the virtues and the learning appropriate to a pope. Given Julius II's desire for recognition as both a spiritual and temporal leader, it is appropriate that the Theology and Philosophy frescoes face each other. The two images present a balanced picture of the pope—as a cultured, knowledgeable individual, on the one hand, and as a wise, divinely ordained religious authority, on the other hand.

On one wall, in Raphael's Philosophy mural (the so-called *School of Athens*, FIG. **22-17**), the setting is not a "school" but a congregation of the great philosophers and scientists of the ancient world. Raphael depicted these luminaries—rediscovered by Renaissance thinkers—conversing and explaining their various theories and ideas. In a vast hall covered by massive vaults that recall Roman architecture (and approximate the appearance of the new Saint Peter's in 1509, when the painting was executed), colossal statues of Apollo and Athena, patron gods of the arts and of wisdom, oversee the interactions. Plato and Aristotle serve as the central figures around whom Raphael carefully arranged the others. Plato holds his book *Timaeus* and points to heaven, the source of his inspiration, while Aristotle carries his book *Nichomachean Ethics* and gestures toward the earth, from which his observations of reality sprang. Appropriately, ancient philosophers, men concerned with the ultimate mysteries that transcend this world, stand on Plato's side. On Aristotle's side are the philosophers and scientists concerned with nature and human affairs. At the lower left, Pythagoras writes as a servant holds up the harmonic scale. In the foreground, Heraclitus (probably a portrait of Michelangelo) broods alone. Diogenes sprawls on the steps. At the right, students surround Euclid, who demonstrates a theorem. This group is especially interesting; Euclid may be a portrait of the aged Bramante. At the extreme right, just to the right of the astronomers Zoroaster and Ptolemy, both holding globes, Raphael included his own portrait.

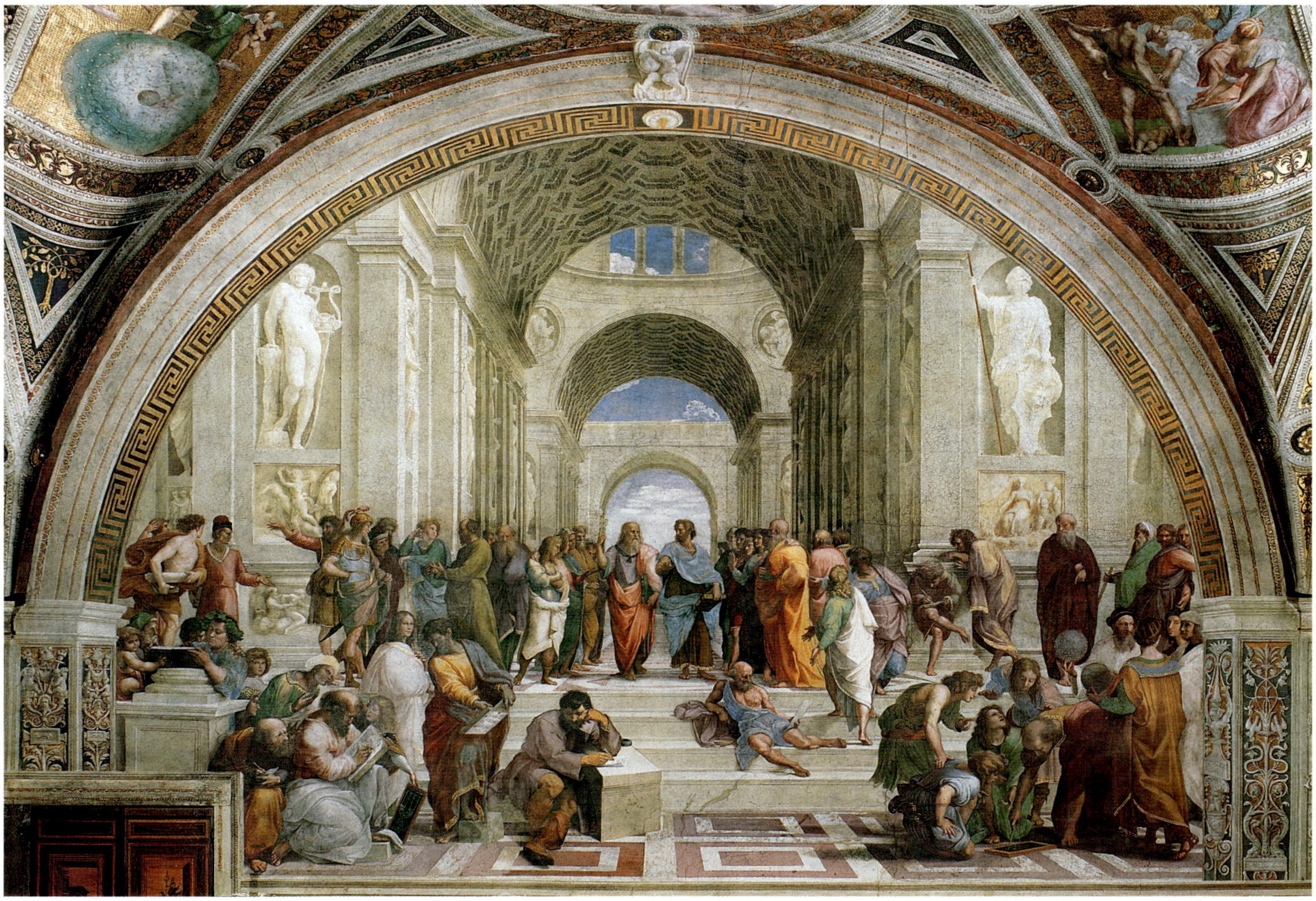

**22-17** RAPHAEL, Philosophy (*School of Athens*), Stanza della Segnatura, Vatican Palace, Rome, Italy, 1509–1511. Fresco, approx. 19′ × 27′.

The groups appear to move easily and clearly, with eloquent poses and gestures that symbolize their doctrines and present an engaging variety of figural positions. Their self-assurance and natural dignity convey the very nature of calm reason, that balance and measure the great Renaissance minds so admired as the heart of philosophy.

Significantly, in this work Raphael placed himself among the mathematicians and scientists, and certainly the evolution of pictorial science came to its perfection in *School of Athens*. Raphael's convincing depiction of a vast perspectival space on a two-dimensional surface was the consequence of the union of mathematics with pictorial science, here mastered completely.

The artist's psychological insight matured along with his mastery of the problems of physical representation. All characters in Raphael's *School of Athens,* like those in Leonardo's *Last Supper* (FIG. 22-3), communicate moods that reflect their beliefs, and the artist's placement of each figure tied these moods together. Raphael carefully considered his design devices for relating individuals and groups to one another and to the whole. These compositional elements demand close study. From the center, where Plato and Aristotle stand, Raphael arranged the groups of figures in an elliptical movement. It seems to swing forward, looping around two foreground groups on both sides and then back again to the center. Moving through the wide opening in the foreground along the floor's perspectival pattern, the viewer's eye penetrates the assembly of philosophers and continues, by way of the reclining Diogenes, up to the here-reconciled leaders of the two great opposing camps of Renaissance philosophy. The perspectival vanishing point falls on Plato's left hand, drawing the viewer's attention to *Timaeus*. In the Stanza della Segnatura, Raphael reconciled and harmonized not only the Platonists and Aristotelians but also paganism and Christianity, surely a major factor in his appeal to Julius II.

Pope Julius II was clearly a formidable force, and his selection of artists and art projects reveals his interests and agenda. Likewise, these projects—Saint Peter's, the Sistine ceiling, his tomb, and the papal apartments—provide insights into the unique contributions and skills of the artists and architects involved, individuals such as Bramante, Michelangelo, and Raphael.

## Synthesizing the Period's Excellence

**HIGH RENAISSANCE IDEALS** Raphael's artistic development recapitulated the 15th-century sequence of artistic tendencies. Although strongly influenced by Leonardo and Michelangelo, Raphael developed an individual style that, in itself, clearly depicts the ideals of High Renaissance art. His powerful originality prevailed while he learned from everyone. He assimilated what he best could use and rendered into form the classical instinct of his age. Among Raphael's early works was *Marriage of the Virgin* (FIG. **22-18**), which he painted for the Chapel of Saint Joseph in the church of San Francesco in Città di Castello, southeast of Florence. The subject is a fitting one for a chapel dedicated to Saint Joseph. According to the *Golden Legend* (a 13th-century collection of stories about the lives of the saints), Joseph competed with other suitors for Mary's hand. The high priest was to give the Virgin to whichever suitor presented to him a rod that had miraculously bloomed. Raphael depicted Joseph with his flowering rod and about to place Mary's wedding ring on her extended hand. Other virgins congregate at the left, and the unsuccessful suitors stand on the right. One of them breaks his rod in

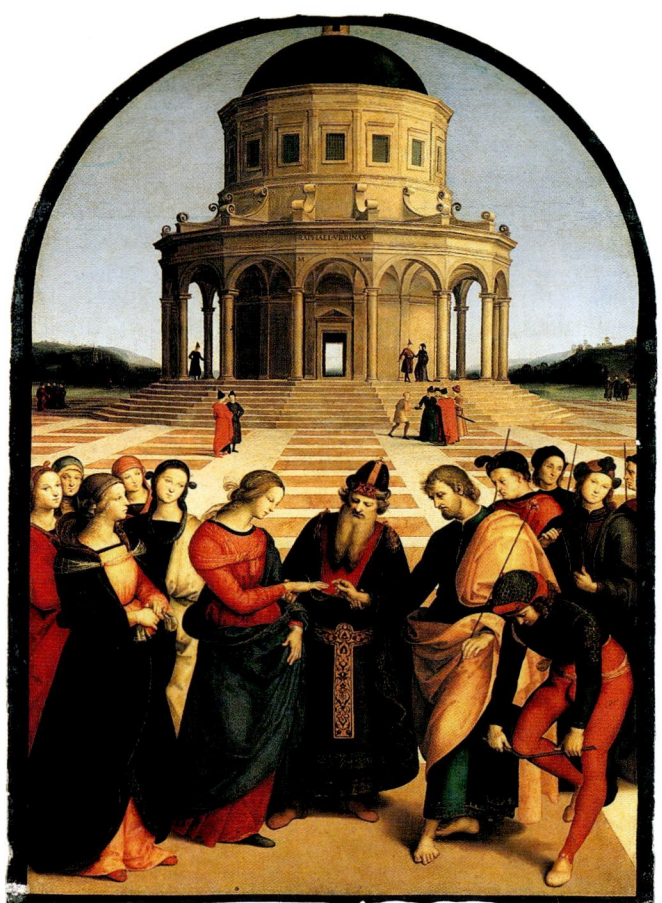

**22-18** RAPHAEL, *Marriage of the Virgin,* from the Chapel of Saint Joseph in San Francesco in Città di Castello, near Florence, Italy, 1504. Oil on wood, 5′ 7″ × 3′ 10½″. Pinacoteca di Brera, Milan.

half over his knee in frustration, giving Raphael an opportunity to demonstrate his mastery of foreshortening and of the perspective system he learned from Perugino (see FIG. 21-40), his teacher. The temple in the background is Raphael's version of a centrally planned building. The painting is almost exactly contemporary to Bramante's Tempietto (FIG. 22-8), but Raphael employed Brunelleschian arcades rather than Bramante's more "modern" classicizing post-and-lintel system.

Raphael spent the four years from 1504 to 1508 in Florence. There, he discovered that the painting style he had learned so painstakingly from Perugino already was, like Brunelleschi's architectural style, outmoded. An artistic battle had developed between the two archrivals, Leonardo and Michelangelo. Crowds flocked to Santissima Annunziata to see Leonardo's recently unveiled cartoon of the Virgin, Christ Child, Saint Anne, and Saint John (probably an earlier version of *Virgin and Child with Saint Anne and the Infant Saint John,* FIG. 22-2). Michelangelo responded with the *Doni Madonna* (not illustrated). Around this time, Florentine officials commissioned both artists to decorate the council hall in the Palazzo Vecchio with frescoes memorializing Florentine victories of the past. Although neither artist completed his fresco and only some small preparatory sketches and small copies survive, this project must have had a considerable effect on artists in Florence, especially on one as gifted as Raphael.

**UNIFYING DEVOTION AND BEAUTY** Under Leonardo's influence, Raphael began to modify the Madonna compositions

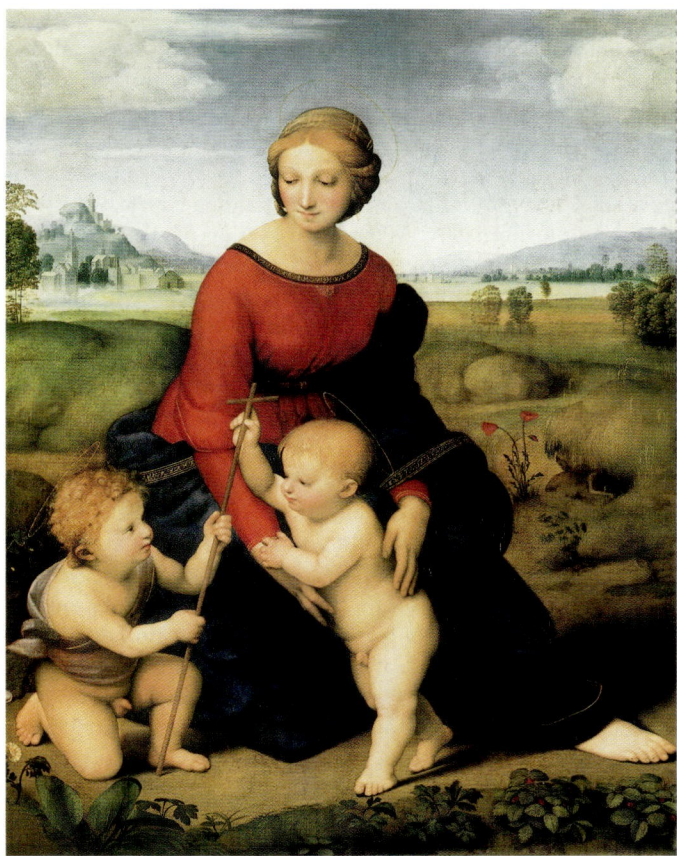

**22-19** RAPHAEL, *Madonna in the Meadow*, 1505–1506. Oil on panel, 3′ 8½″ × 2′ 10¼″. Kunsthistorisches Museum, Vienna.

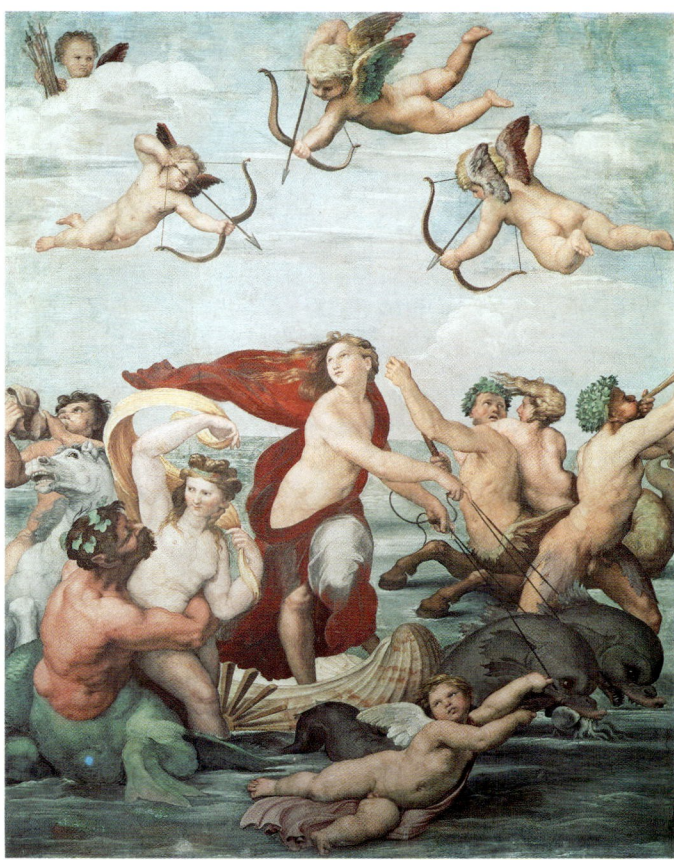

**22-20** RAPHAEL, *Galatea*, Sala di Galatea, Villa Farnesina, Rome, Italy, 1513. Fresco, 9′ 8″ × 7′ 5″.

he had learned in Umbria. In the *Madonna in the Meadow* (FIG. 22-19) of 1505–1506, Raphael used the pyramidal composition of Leonardo's *Virgin of the Rocks* (FIG. 22-1). Further, Raphael may have based his modeling of faces and figures in subtle chiaroscuro on an earlier version of the theme in Leonardo's cartoon for *Virgin and Child with Saint Anne and the Infant Saint John* (FIG. 22-2). Yet Raphael placed the large, substantial figures in a Peruginesque landscape, with the older artist's typical feathery trees in the middle ground. Although Raphael experimented with Leonardo's dusky modeling, he tended to return to Perugino's lighter tonalities. Raphael preferred clarity to obscurity, not fascinated, as Leonardo was, with mystery.

**A MONUMENTAL MYTH** Pope Leo X (Giovanni de' Medici, r. 1513–1521), the son of Lorenzo de' Medici, succeeded Julius II as Raphael's patron. Leo was a worldly, pleasure-loving prince who spent huge sums on the arts; as a true Medici, he was a sympathetic connoisseur. Raphael moved in the highest circles of the papal court, the star of a brilliant society. He was young, handsome, wealthy, and adulated, not only by his followers but also by Rome and all of Italy. Genial, even-tempered, generous, and highminded, Raphael's personality contrasted strikingly with that of the aloof, mysterious Leonardo or the tormented and obstinate Michelangelo. The pope was not Raphael's only patron. His friend Agostino Chigi, an immensely wealthy banker who managed the papal state's financial affairs, commissioned Raphael to decorate his palace on the Tiber with scenes from classical mythology. Outstanding among the frescoes Raphael painted in the small but

splendid Villa Farnesina is *Galatea* (FIG. **22-20**), which Raphael based on *Metamorphoses*, by the ancient Roman poet Ovid.

In Raphael's fresco, Galatea flees from her uncouth lover, the Cyclops Polyphemus, on a shell drawn by leaping dolphins. Sea creatures and playful cupids surround her. The painting erupts in unrestrained pagan joy and exuberance, an exultant song in praise of human beauty and zestful love. Compositionally, Raphael enhanced the liveliness of the image by placing the sturdy figures around Galatea in bounding and dashing movements that always return to her as the energetic center. The cupids, skillfully foreshortened, repeat the circling motion. Raphael conceived his figures sculpturally, and Galatea's body—supple, strong, and vigorously in motion—contrasts with Botticelli's delicate, hovering, almost dematerialized Venus (see FIG. 21-27) while suggesting the spiraling compositions of Hellenistic statuary (see FIG. 5-80). Pagan myth presented in monumental form, in vivacious movement, and in a spirit of passionate delight resurrects the naturalistic art and poetry of the classical world.

**COUNTING ON GENTILITY** Raphael also excelled at portraiture. His subjects were the illustrious scholars and courtiers who surrounded Pope Leo X, among them his close friend Count Baldassare Castiglione (1478–1529), the author of a handbook on High Renaissance criteria for genteel behavior. In *Book of the Courtier*, Castiglione enumerated the attributes of the perfect courtier: impeccable character, noble birth, military achievement, classical education, and knowledge of the arts. Castiglione then described a way of life based on cultivated rationality in imitation

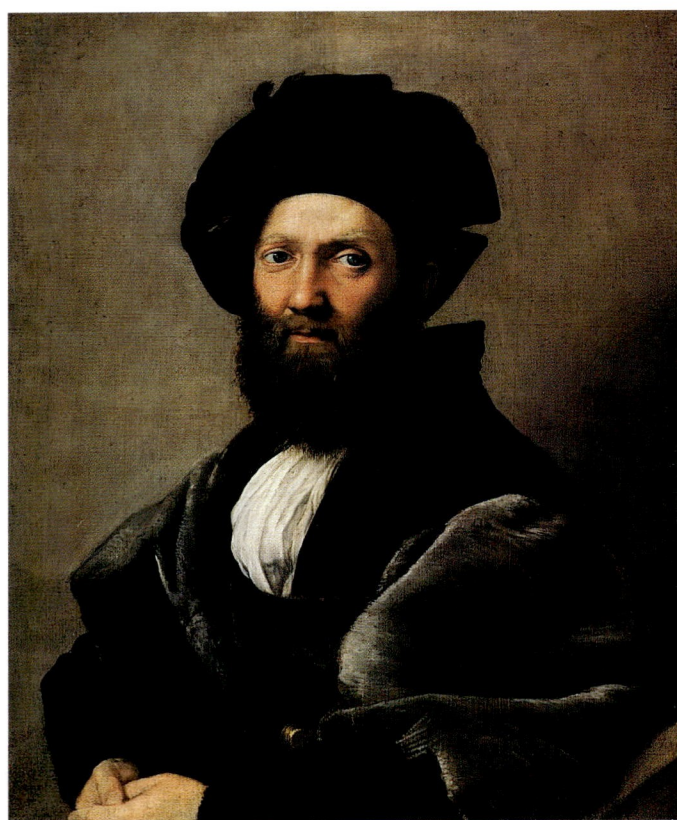

22-21 RAPHAEL, *Baldassare Castiglione,* ca. 1514. Oil on wood transferred to canvas, approx. 2′ 6¼″ × 2′ 2½″. Louvre, Paris.

(1492–1519), duke of Urbino, son and grandson of Lorenzo the Magnificent. Giuliano's tomb (FIG. 22-22) is compositionally the twin of Lorenzo's. Michelangelo finished neither tomb. Scholars believe he intended to place pairs of recumbent river gods at the bottom of the sarcophagi, balancing the pairs of figures that rest on the sloping sides. However, despite this contention, the composition of the tombs has been a long-standing puzzle. How were they to look ultimately? What do they signify? Unfortunately, scholars possess insufficient evidence to answer these questions.

Traditional art historical scholarship suggested that the arrangement Michelangelo planned, but never completed, can be interpreted as the soul's ascent through the levels of the Neoplatonic universe. Neoplatonism, a school of thought based on Plato's idealistic, spiritualistic philosophy, experienced a renewed popularity in the 16th-century humanist community. The lowest level of the tomb, represented by the river gods, would have signified the underworld of brute matter, the source of evil. The two statues on the sarcophagi would symbolize the realm of time—the specifically human world of the cycles of dawn, day, evening, and night. Humanity's state in this world of time was considered one of pain and anxiety, of frustration and exhaustion. At left, the female figure of Night and, at right, the male figure of Day appear to be chained into never-relaxing tensions. Both exhibit that anguished twisting of the body's masses in contrary directions, known as *figura serpentinata,* seen in the artist's *Bound Slave* (FIG. 22-11) and in his Sistine Chapel paintings. This contortion is a staple of Michelangelo's figural art. Day, with a body the thickness of a great tree and the anatomy of Hercules (or of a reclining Greco-Roman river god that may have inspired Michelangelo's

of the ancients. In Raphael's portrait of him (FIG. 22-21), Castiglione, splendidly yet soberly garbed, looks directly at viewers with a philosopher's grave and benign expression, clear-eyed and thoughtful. The figure is in half-length and three-quarter view, a pose made popular by *Mona Lisa* (FIG. 22-4). Both portraits exhibit the increasing attention High Renaissance artists paid to the subject's personality and psychic state. The muted and low-keyed tones befit the temper and mood of this reflective middle-aged man—the background is entirely neutral, without the usual landscape or architecture. The head and the hands wonderfully reveal the man, who himself had written so eloquently in *Courtier* of enlightenment from the love of beauty. Such love animated Raphael, Castiglione, and other artists of their age, and Michelangelo's poetry suggests he shared in this widespread appreciation for the beauty found in the natural world.

## Michelangelo in the Service of the Medici

Following the death of Julius II, Michelangelo, like Raphael, went into the service of the Medici popes, Leo X and his successor Clement VII (Giulio de' Medici, r. 1523–1534). These Medici chose not to perpetuate their predecessor's fame by letting Michelangelo complete Julius's tomb; instead, they (Pope Leo X and the then cardinal Giulio de' Medici) commissioned him in 1519 to build a funerary chapel, the New Sacristy, in San Lorenzo in Florence.

**TWO DUKES FACING OFF** At opposite sides of the New Sacristy stand Michelangelo's sculpted tombs of Giuliano (1478–1516), duke of Nemours (south of Paris), and Lorenzo

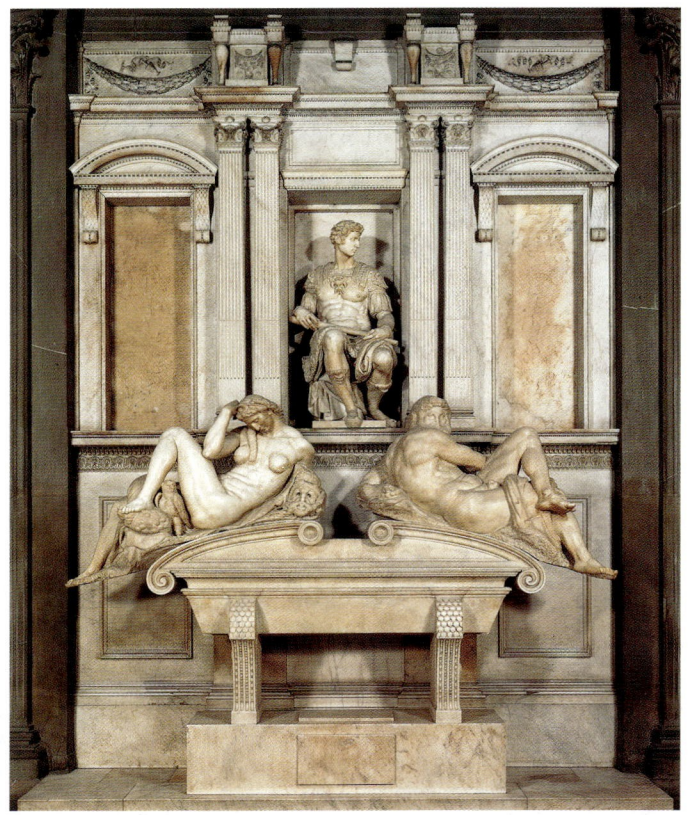

22-22 MICHELANGELO BUONARROTI, tomb of Giuliano de' Medici, New Sacristy (Medici Chapel), San Lorenzo, Florence, Italy, 1519–1534. Marble, central figure approx. 5′ 11″ high.

statue), strains his huge limbs against each other, his unfinished visage rising menacingly above his shoulder. Night, the symbol of rest, twists as if in troubled sleep, her posture wrenched and feverish. The artist surrounded her with an owl, poppies, and a hideous mask symbolic of nightmares. Recent scholarship challenges this interpretation. These scholars argue that the personifications of night and day allude not to humanity's pain but to the life cycle and the passage of time leading ultimately to death.

On their respective tombs, sculptures of Lorenzo and Giuliano appear in niches at the apex of the structures. Transcending worldly existence, they represent the two ideal human types—the contemplative man (Lorenzo) and the active man (Giuliano). Giuliano (FIG. 22-22) sits clad in the armor of a Roman emperor and holding a commander's baton, his head turned alertly as if in council (he looks toward the statue of the Virgin at one end of the chapel). Across the room, Lorenzo appears wrapped in thought, his face in deep shadow. Together, they symbolize the two ways human beings might achieve union with God—through meditation or through the active life fashioned after that of Christ. In this sense, they are not individual portraits. Indeed, Michelangelo declined to make portraits of the actual dukes; who, he asked, would care what they looked like in a thousand years? This attitude is consistent with Michelangelo's interests; throughout his career he demonstrated less concern for facial features and expressions than for the overall human form. The rather generic visages of the two Medici captains of the Church attest to this. For the artist, the contemplation of what lies beyond the corrosion of time counted more.

## The Papacy of Pope Paul III

**A PALACE FIT FOR A POPE** Pope Paul III (Alessandro Farnese, r. 1534–1549) maintained the lavish lifestyle previous popes enjoyed. Paul III also continued the papal tradition of extensive art patronage. An early major project he commissioned when he was still Cardinal Farnese was the construction of the Palazzo Farnese in Rome (FIG. **22-23**). To design the palazzo, the pope selected ANTONIO DA SANGALLO THE YOUNGER (1483–1546), who established himself as the favorite architect of Pope Paul III and

therefore received many commissions that might have gone to Michelangelo. Antonio, the youngest of a family of architects, went to Rome around 1503 and became Bramante's draftsman and assistant. He is the perfect example of the professional architect; indeed, his family constituted an architectural firm, often planning and drafting for other architects. Antonio built fortifications for almost the entire papal state and received more commissions for military than for civilian architecture. Although he may not have invented it, Antonio certainly contributed significantly to the modern method of constructing bastioned fortifications.

The Palazzo Farnese set the standard for the High Renaissance palazzo and fully expresses the classical order, regularity, simplicity, and dignity of the High Renaissance. The broad, majestic front of the Palazzo Farnese asserts to the public the exalted station of a great family. This impressive facade encapsulates the aristocratic epoch that followed the stifling of the nascent middle-class democracy of European cities (especially the Italian cities) by powerful kings heading centralized states. It is thus significant that Paul chose to enlarge greatly the original rather modest palace to its present form after his accession to the papacy in 1534, reflecting his ambitions both for his family and for the papacy. At Antonio's death in 1546, Michelangelo assumed control of the building's completion.

Facing a spacious paved square, the facade is the very essence of princely dignity in architecture. The *quoins* (rusticated building corners) and cornice frame firmly anchor the rectangle of the smooth front, and lines of windows (the central row with alternating triangular and segmental pediments, in Bramante's fashion) mark a majestic beat across it. The window casements are not flush with the wall, as in the Palazzo Medici-Riccardi (see FIG. 21-20), but project from its surface, so instead of being a flat, thin plane, the facade is a spatially active three-dimensional mass. The rusticated doorway and second-story balcony, surmounted by the Farnese coat of arms, emphasize the central axis and bring the design's horizontal and vertical forces into harmony. This centralizing feature, absent from the palaces of Michelozzo di Bartolommeo (see FIG. 21-20) and Leon Battista Alberti (see FIG. 21-33), is the external opening of a central corridor axis that runs through the entire building and continues in the garden beyond. Around this axis, Antonio arranged the rooms with strict regularity. The

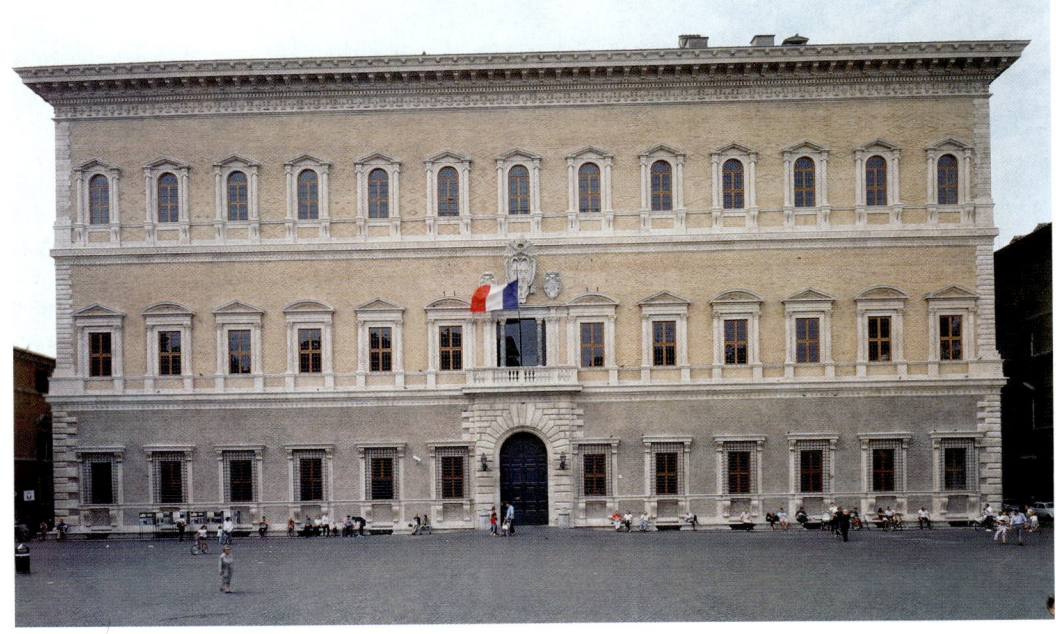

22-23 ANTONIO DA SANGALLO THE YOUNGER, Palazzo Farnese (view from the northwest), Rome, Italy, ca. 1530–1546.

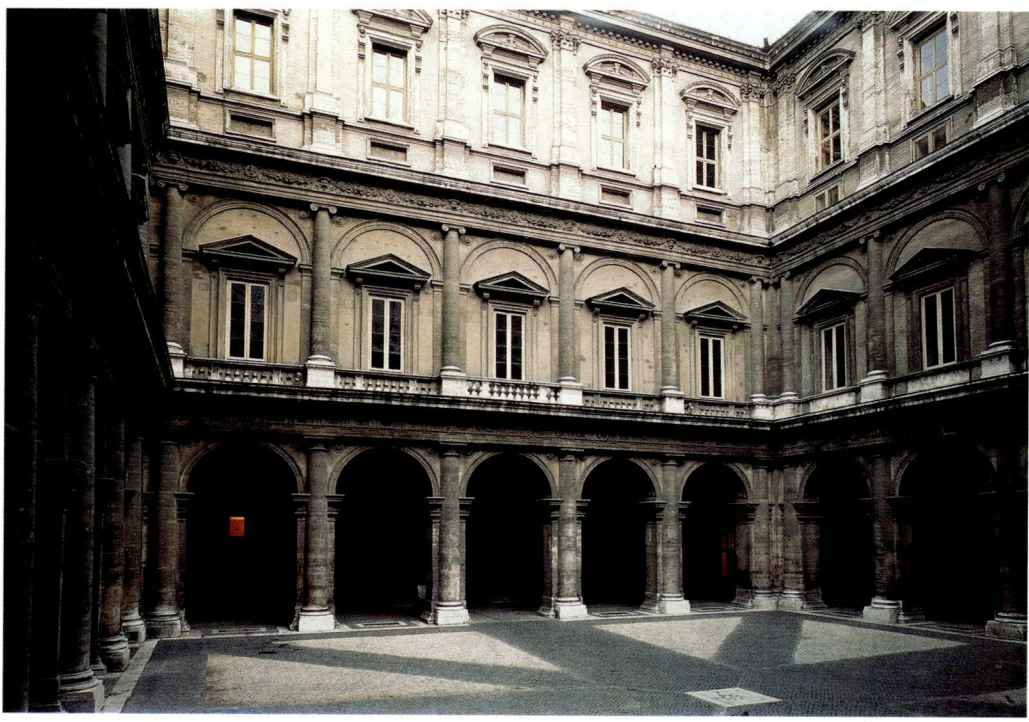

**22-24** ANTONIO DA SANGALLO THE YOUNGER, courtyard of the Palazzo Farnese, Rome, Italy, ca. 1530–1546. Third story and attic by MICHELANGELO BUONARROTI, 1548.

interior courtyard (FIG. **22-24**) displays stately column-enframed arches on the first two levels, as in the Roman Colosseum (see FIG. 10-34). On the third level, Michelangelo incorporated his sophisticated variation on that theme (based in part on the Colosseum's fourth-story Corinthian pilasters), with overlapping pilasters replacing the weighty columns of Antonio's design.

**CHRIST ON JUDGMENT DAY** Although many of Paul III's commissions were personal, he also extended numerous commissions to artists in his capacity as pope. Many of these commissions were part of an orchestrated campaign to restore the prominence of the Catholic Church in the wake of the Protestant Reformation. The Reformation (see Chapter 23, pages 663–665) was the result of widespread dissatisfaction with the leadership and policies of the Roman Catholic Church. Led by clerics such as Martin Luther (1483–1546) and John Calvin (1509–1564) in the Holy Roman Empire, early-16th-century reformers directly challenged papal authority, especially regarding secular issues. Disgruntled Catholics voiced concerns about the sale of indulgences (pardons for sins, reducing the time a soul spent in purgatory), nepotism (the appointment of relatives to important positions), and high Church officials pursuing personal wealth. This reform movement resulted in the establishment of Protestantism, with sects such as Lutheranism and Calvinism. Central to Protestantism was a belief in personal faith rather than adherence to decreed Church practices and doctrines. Because the Protestants believed that the only true religious relationship was the personal relationship between an individual and God, they were, in essence, eliminating the need for Church intercession central to Catholicism.

The Catholic Church, in response, mounted a full-fledged campaign to counteract the defection of its members to Protestantism. Led by Pope Paul III, this response, the Counter-Reformation, consisted of numerous initiatives. The Council of Trent, which met intermittently from 1545 through 1563, was a major component of this effort. Composed of cardinals, archbishops, bishops, abbots, and theologians, the Council of Trent dealt with issues of Church doctrine, including many the Protestants contested.

Many papal commissions during this period can be viewed as an integral part of the Counter-Reformation effort. Popes long had been aware of the power of visual imagery to construct and reinforce ideological claims, and 16th-century popes exploited this capability (see "The Role of Religious Art in Counter-Reformation Italy," page 636). Among Paul III's first papal commissions was a large fresco for the Sistine Chapel. Michelangelo agreed to paint the large-scale *Last Judgment* fresco (FIG. **22-25**; like the Sistine ceiling, newly cleaned and restored—see "Restoring the Glory of Renaissance Art," page 628) on the chapel's altar wall. Here, Michelangelo depicted Christ as the stern judge of the world—a giant whose mighty right arm is lifted in a gesture of damnation so broad and universal as to suggest he will destroy all creation, Heaven and earth alike. The choirs of Heaven surrounding him pulse with anxiety and awe. Crowded into the space below are trumpeting angels, the ascending figures of the just, and the downward-hurtling figures of the damned. On the left, the dead awake and assume flesh; on the right, demons, whose gargoyle masks and burning eyes revive the demons of Romanesque tympana (see FIG. 17-25), torment the damned.

Michelangelo's terrifying vision of the fate that awaits sinners goes far beyond even Signorelli's gruesome images (see FIG. 21-51). Martyrs who suffered especially agonizing deaths crouch below the Judge. One of them, Saint Bartholomew, who was skinned alive, holds the flaying knife and the skin, its face a grotesque self-portrait of Michelangelo. The figures are huge and violently twisted, with small heads and contorted features. Yet while this immense fresco impresses on viewers Christ's wrath on Judgment Day, it also holds out hope. A group of saved souls— the elect—crowd around Christ, and on the far right appears a figure with a cross, most likely the Good Thief (crucified with Christ) or a saint martyred by crucifixion, such as Saint Andrew.

**CAPITALIZING ON ROMAN HISTORY** Driven by his restive genius, Michelangelo was rarely content to grapple with only a single commission. While he was executing the *Last Judgment* fresco, he received another flattering and challenging commission

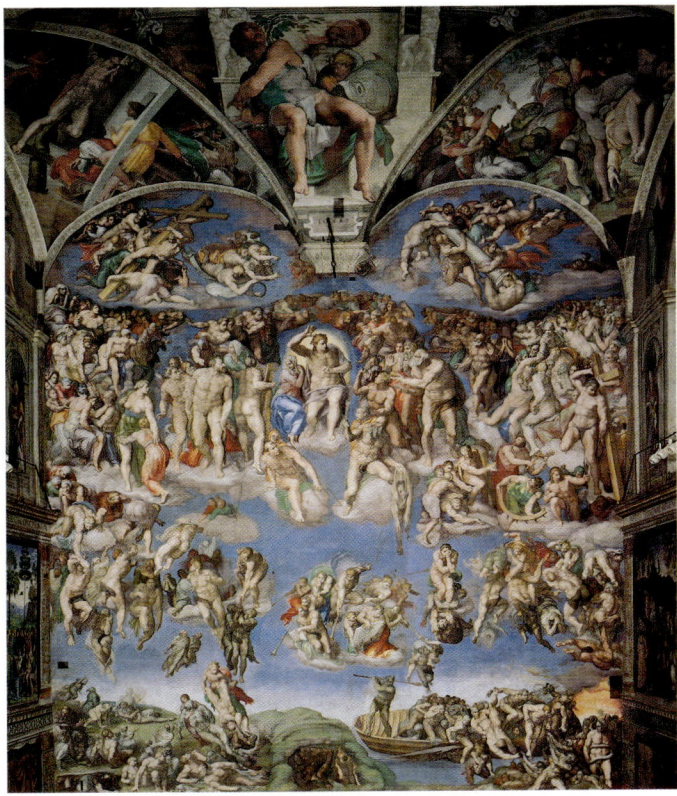

22-25 MICHELANGELO BUONARROTI, *Last Judgment*, fresco on the altar wall of the Sistine Chapel, Vatican City, Rome, Italy, 1534–1541. Copyright © Nippon Television Network Corporation, Tokyo.

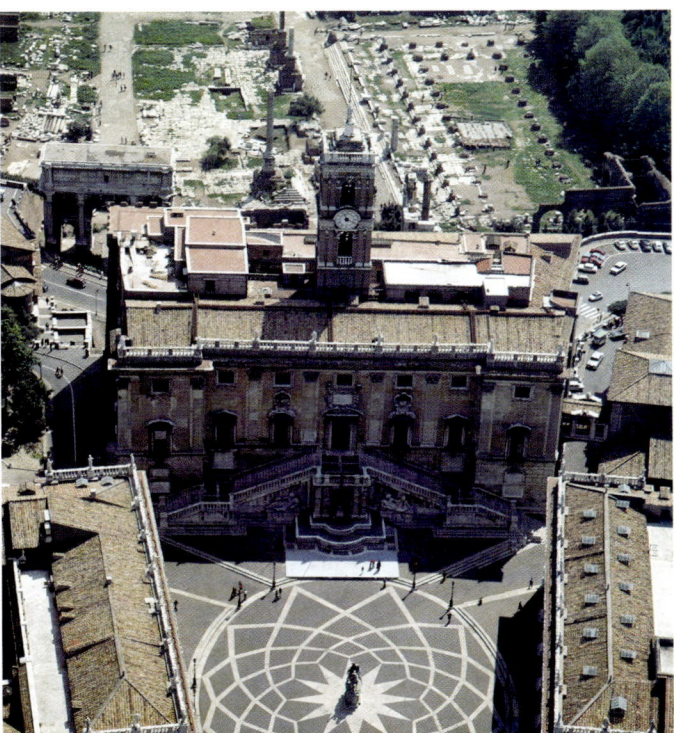

22-26 MICHELANGELO BUONARROTI, aerial view of Capitoline Hill (Campidoglio), Rome, Italy, designed ca. 1537.

from Pope Paul III. In 1537, he undertook the reorganization of the Capitoline Hill (the Campidoglio) in Rome (FIG. 22-26). The pope wished to transform the ancient hill, which once had been the site of the Roman Empire's spiritual capitol, the greatest temple to Jupiter in the Roman world, into a symbol of the power of the new Rome of the popes. Michelangelo confronted an immense challenge. He had to incorporate into his design two existing buildings—the medieval Palazzo dei Senatori (Palace of the Senators) on the east and the 15th-century Palazzo dei Conservatori (Palace of the Conservators) on the south. These buildings formed an 80-degree angle. Such preconditions might have defeated a lesser architect, but Michelangelo converted what seemed a limitation into the most impressive design for a civic unit formulated during the entire Renaissance.

He carried his obsession with human form over to architecture and reasoned that buildings should follow the form of the human body. This meant organizing their units symmetrically around a central and unique axis, as the arms relate to the body or the eyes to the nose. "For it is an established fact," he once wrote, "that the members of architecture resemble the members of man. Whoever neither has been nor is a master at figures, and especially at anatomy, cannot really understand architecture."[7] It must have been with such arguments that he convinced his sponsors of the need to balance the Palazzo dei Conservatori, whose facade he was to redesign, with a similar unit on the square's north side. To achieve balance and symmetry in design, Michelangelo placed the new building (the Museo Capitolino, originally planned only as a portico with single rows of offices above and behind it) so that it stood at the same angle to the Palazzo dei Senatori as the Palazzo dei Conservatori. This yielded a trapezoidal plan, rather than a rectangular one, for the piazza.

Michelangelo subsequently adjusted all other design elements to this unorthodox but basic feature.

The ancient statue of Marcus Aurelius (see FIG. 10-59), the only equestrian statue of a Roman emperor to survive the Middle Ages, became the focal point for the whole design. The pope ordered it moved to the Capitoline Hill against the advice of Michelangelo, who might have preferred to carve his own centerpiece. The symbolic significance of the famous monument must have appealed to Paul III. Although the 15th-century humanists had rediscovered the statue's true identity (by comparison with Roman coins), the medieval identification of the portrait as Constantine the Great, the first Christian emperor, still lingered and was an integral part of its fabled history. In the 16th century, the image of Marcus Aurelius on horseback carried a double significance. It was the ultimate symbol of the pagan Roman Empire over which Christianity had triumphed, but Italians also associated it with Constantine, Saint Peter, and the establishment of the papacy. In short, this equestrian portrait of an omnipotent yet benevolent Roman emperor encapsulated the city's whole history from antiquity to the early Christian Church to the 16th-century papacy. It was the ideal centerpiece for the new civic center of Renaissance Rome (MAP 22-1) and beautifully served the needs of a humanist pope during the Counter-Reformation.

To connect this central monument with the surrounding buildings, Michelangelo provided it with an oval base and placed it centrally in an oval pavement design. Michelangelo's choice of the oval is noteworthy, as other Renaissance architects considered it an unstable geometric figure and therefore shunned it. Given the piazza's trapezoidal shape, however, Michelangelo deemed the oval (which combines centralizing and axial qualities) best suited to relate the design's various elements to one another. Later artists

## The Role of Religious Art in Counter-Reformation Italy

**B**oth Catholics and Protestants took seriously the role of devotional imagery in religious life. However, their views differed dramatically. Whereas Catholics deemed art as valuable for cultivating piety, Protestants believed such visual imagery could produce idolatry and could distract the faithful from their goal—developing a personal relationship with God (see "Iconoclasm and the Reaction against Religious Art," Chapter 23, page 667). As part of the Counter-Reformation effort, Pope Paul III convened the Council of Trent in 1545 and directed them to review controversial Church doctrines. At its conclusion in 1563, the council issued the following edict on the invocation (plea or call for help) of saints, the veneration of saints' relics, and the role of sacred images, published in *Canons and Decrees of the Council of Trent:*

> The holy council commands all bishops and others who hold the office of teaching and have charge of the *cura animarum* [literally, "cure of souls"—the responsibility of laboring for the salvation of souls], that in accordance with the usage of the Catholic and Apostolic Church, received from the primitive times of the Christian religion, and with the unanimous teaching of the holy Fathers and the decrees of sacred councils, they above all instruct the faithful diligently in matters relating to intercession and invocation of the saints, the veneration of relics, and the legitimate use of images. . . . Moreover, that the images of Christ, of the Virgin Mother of God, and of the other saints are to be placed and retained especially in the churches, and that due honor and veneration is to be given them; . . . because the honor which is shown them is referred to the prototypes which they represent, so that by means of the images which we kiss and before which we uncover the head and prostrate ourselves, we adore Christ and venerate the saints whose likeness they bear. That is what was defined by the decrees of the councils, especially of the Second Council of Nicaea, against the opponents of images.

Moreover, let the bishops diligently teach that by means of the stories of the mysteries of our redemption portrayed in paintings and other representations the people are instructed and confirmed in the articles of faith, which ought to be borne in mind and constantly reflected upon; also that great profit is derived from all holy images, not only because the people are thereby reminded of the benefits and gifts bestowed on them by Christ, but also because through the saints the miracles of God and salutary examples are set before the eyes of the faithful, so that they may give God thanks for those things, may fashion their own life and conduct in imitation of the saints and be moved to adore and love God and cultivate piety. . . .

And if at times it happens, when this is beneficial to the illiterate, that the stories and narratives of the Holy Scriptures are portrayed and exhibited, the people should be instructed that not for that reason is the divinity represented in picture as if it can be seen with bodily eyes or expressed in colors or figures. Furthermore, in the invocation of the saints, the veneration of relics, and the sacred use of images, all superstition shall be removed, all filthy quest for gain eliminated, and all lasciviousness avoided, so that images shall not be painted and adorned with a seductive charm, or the celebration of saints and the visitation of relics be perverted by the people into boisterous festivities and drunkenness, as if the festivals in honor of the saints are to be celebrated with revelry and with no sense of decency. . . .

That these things may be the more faithfully observed, the holy council decrees that no one is permitted to erect or cause to be erected in any place or church, howsoever exempt, any unusual image unless it has been approved by the bishop; . . .[1]

[1] Quoted in Robert Klein and Henri Zerner, *Italian Art 1500–1600: Sources and Documents* (Evanston, Ill.: Northwestern University Press, 1966), 120–21.

during the Baroque period adopted the oval as their favorite geometric figure.

Facing the piazza, the two lateral palazzi, the Palazzo dei Conservatori and Museo Capitolino (FIG. **22-27**), have identical two-story facades. Michelangelo introduced viewers again to the giant order, the tall pilasters first seen in more reserved fashion in Alberti's Sant'Andrea in Mantua (see FIG. 21-41). Michelangelo used the giant order with much greater authority. The huge pilasters not only tie the two stories together but also provide a sturdy skeleton that actually functions as the structure's main support. Michelangelo all but eliminated walls. At ground level, he interposed columns to soften the transition from the massive bulk of the pilaster-faced piers to the deep voids between them. These columns carry straight lintels, in the manner Alberti earlier advocated, but Michelangelo used them with even greater logic and consistency than Alberti did.

For the third building on the piazza, the three-storied Palazzo dei Senatori (FIG. 22-26), the architect added a double flight of steps to the entrance. He also embellished the facade, incorporating the same design elements that he had employed for the other two palazzi but in a less sculptural fashion. The axial building, with its greater height, thus became a distinctive and commanding accent for the ensemble, providing variety within the design without disrupting its unity.

Michelangelo might have made the piazza a roomlike enclosure, as Alberti, in his treatise, had advised for all piazze. But the architect chose to leave one side open. He merely suggested a fourth wall with a balustrade and a thin screen of Classical statuary that effectively defines the piazza's limits without obstructing a panoramic view across the city roofs toward the Vatican. The symbolism of this axis must have pleased the pope just as much as the piazza's dynamic design.

**A SCULPTOR'S FINISHING TOUCH** In 1546, Michelangelo undertook his last project for Pope Paul III—the supervision of the building of the new Saint Peter's. With the Church facing challenges to its supremacy, Paul III surely felt a sense of urgency about the completion of this project. Michelangelo's work on Saint Peter's, after efforts by a succession of architects following Bramante's death, apparently became a long-term show of dedication, thankless and without pay.

Among Michelangelo's difficulties was his struggle to preserve and carry through Bramante's original plan (FIG. 22-6), which he praised (although he did modify it). Michelangelo recognized the strength of the initial design (as he had with Antonio's project for the Palazzo Farnese, FIGS. 22-23 and 22-24) and chose to retain it as the basis for his design. With Bramante's plan for Saint Peter's,

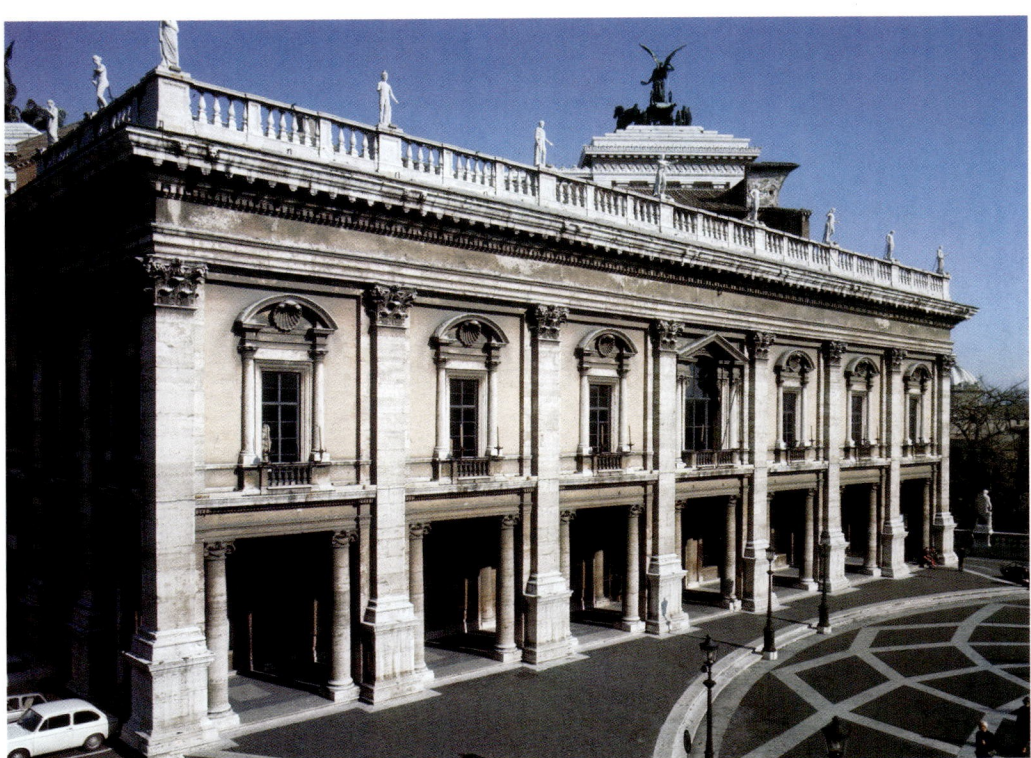

Michelangelo reduced the central component from a number of interlocking crosses to a compact domed Greek cross inscribed in a square and fronted with a double-columned portico (FIG. 22-28). Without destroying the centralizing features of Bramante's plan, Michelangelo, with a few strokes of the pen, converted its snowflake complexity into massive, cohesive unity.

Michelangelo's treatment of the building's exterior further reveals his interest in creating a unified and cohesive design. Because of later changes to the front of the church, the west (apse) end (FIG. 22-29) offers the best view of his style and intention. The colossal order again served him nobly, as the giant pilasters seem to march around the undulating wall surfaces, confining the

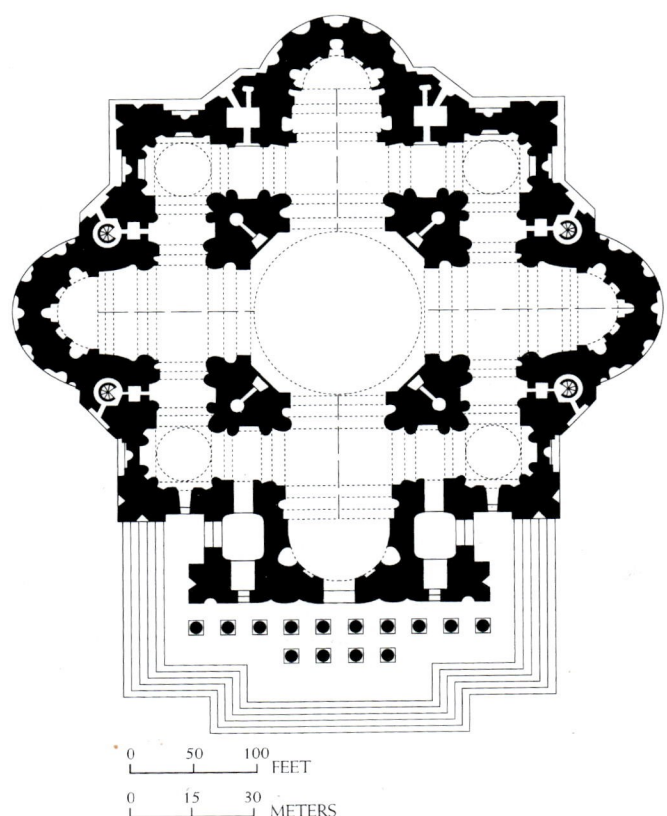

0    50    100
                FEET
0    15    30
                METERS

22-28 MICHELANGELO BUONARROTI, plan for Saint Peter's, Vatican City, Rome, Italy, 1546.

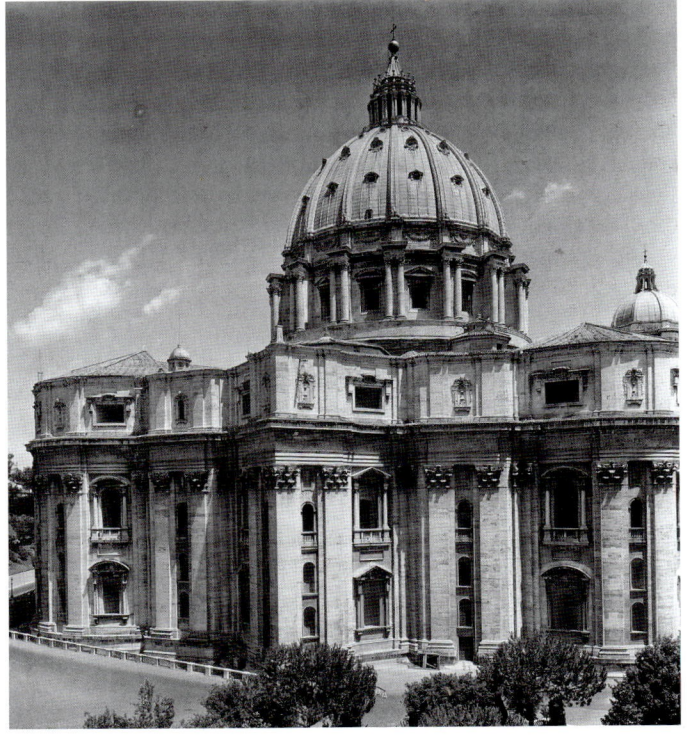

22-29 MICHELANGELO BUONARROTI, Saint Peter's (view from the northwest), Vatican City, Rome, Italy, 1546–1564. Dome completed by GIACOMO DELLA PORTA, 1590.

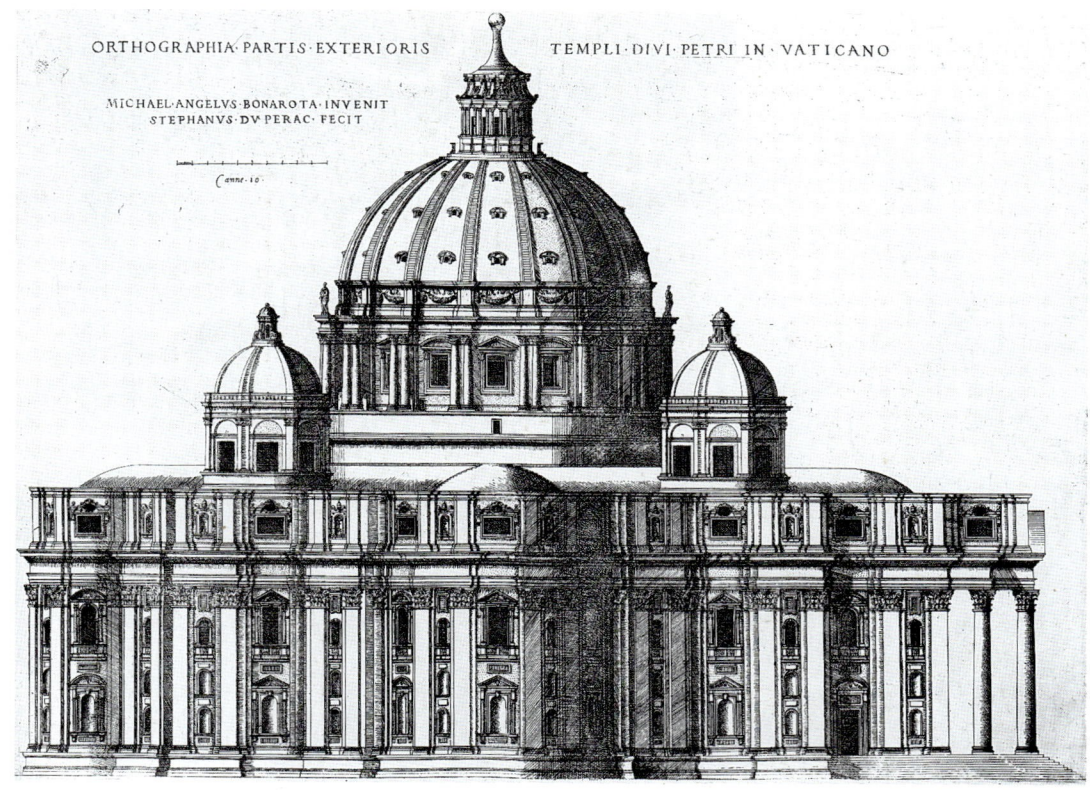

**22-30** MICHELANGELO BUONARROTI, drawing of south elevation of Saint Peter's, Vatican City, Rome, Italy, 1546–1564 (engraving by ÉTIENNE DUPÉRAC, ca. 1569). Metropolitan Museum of Art, New York (Harris Brisbane Dick Fund, 1941).

movement without interrupting it. The architectural sculpturing here extends up from the ground through the attic stories and into the drum and the dome, unifying the whole building from base to summit. Baroque architects later learned much from this kind of integral design, which Michelangelo based on his conviction that architecture is one with the organic beauty of the human form.

The domed west end—as majestic as it is today and as influential as it has been on architecture throughout the centuries—is not quite as Michelangelo intended it. Originally, Michelangelo had planned a dome with an ogival section (raised silhouette), like that of Florence Cathedral (see FIG. 21-13). But in his final version he decided on a hemispheric (semicircular silhouette) dome (FIG. 22-30) to temper the verticality of the design of the lower stories and to establish a balance between dynamic and static elements. However, when GIACOMO DELLA PORTA (ca. 1533–1602) executed the dome after Michelangelo's death, he restored the earlier high design, ignoring Michelangelo's later version. Giacomo's reasons were probably the same ones that had impelled Brunelleschi to use an ogival section for his Florentine dome—greater stability and ease of construction. The result is that the dome seems to rise from its base, rather than rest firmly on it—an effect Michelangelo might not have approved. Nevertheless, Saint Peter's dome is probably the most impressive in the world and has served as a model for generations of architects to this day.

Michelangelo's art began in the style of the 15th century, developed into the epitome of High Renaissance art, and, at the end, moved toward Mannerism and the Baroque. He was 89 when he died in 1564, still hard at work on both the Capitoline Hill and Saint Peter's. Few artists, then or since, could escape his influence, and variations of his style provided the foundation of art production for centuries.

## Early-16th-Century Venetian Art

Venice long had been a major Mediterranean coastal port and served as the gateway to the Orient. Reaching the height of its commercial and political power during the 15th century, Venice saw its fortunes decline in the 16th century. Even so, Venice and the Papal States were the only Italian sovereignties to retain their independence during the century of strife; either France or Spain dominated all others. Although the discoveries in the New World and the economic shift from Italy to such areas as the Netherlands were largely responsible for the decline of Venice, even more immediate and pressing events drained its wealth and power. After their conquest of Constantinople, the Turks began to vie with Venice for control of the eastern Mediterranean and evolved into a constant threat to Venice. Early in the century, the European powers of the League of Cambrai also attacked Venice. Formed and led by Pope Julius II, who coveted Venetian holdings on Italy's mainland, the League included Spain, France, and the Holy Roman Empire, in addition to the Papal States. Despite these challenges, Venice developed a flourishing, independent, and influential school of artists.

**THE PRIMACY OF COLOR** The effect of Venice's soft-colored light was of particular interest to artists in the maritime republic. Venetian artist GIOVANNI BELLINI (ca. 1430–1516) played an important role in developing the evocative use of color and contributed significantly to creating what is known as the Venetian style. Trained in the International Style (see Chapter 19, pages 533–535) by his father, Jacopo, a student of Gentile da Fabriano, Bellini worked in the family shop and did not develop his own style until after his father's death in 1470. His early independent works show the dominant influence of his brother-in-law Andrea Mantegna. But in the late 1470s, he came into contact with the work of the Sicilian-born painter Antonello da Messina

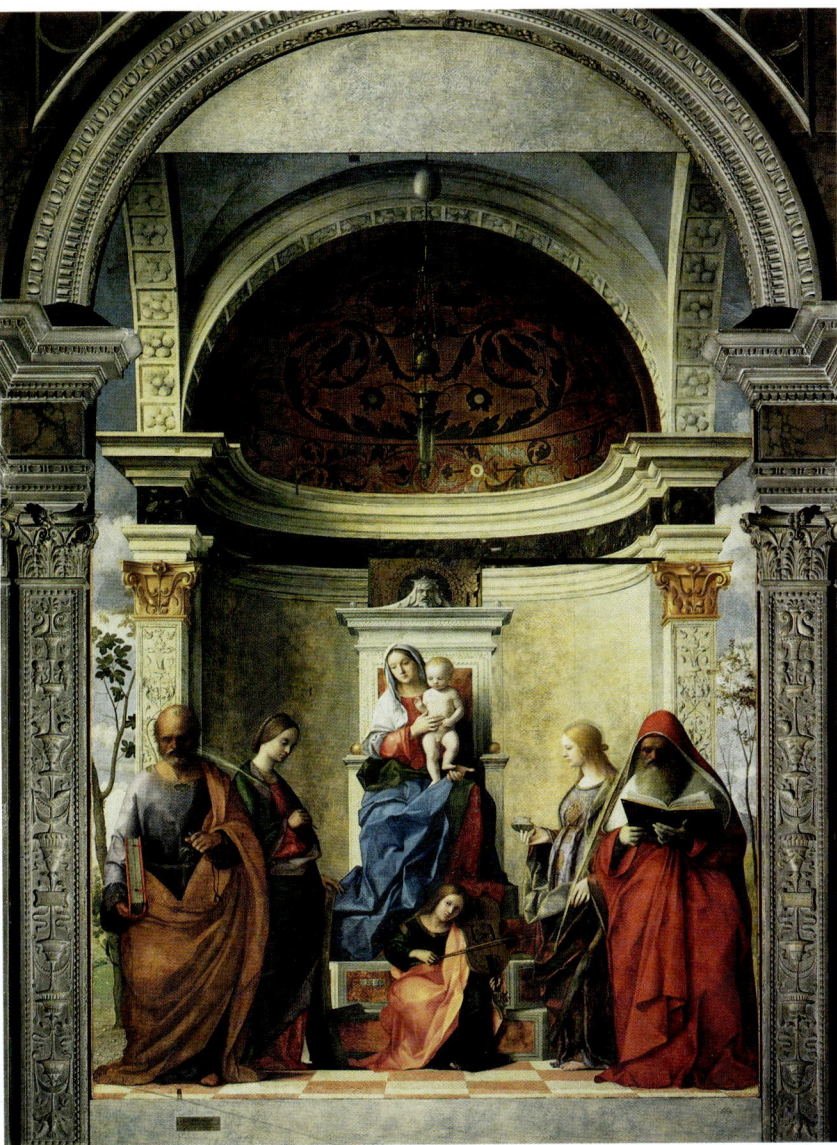

**22-31** GIOVANNI BELLINI, *San Zaccaria Altarpiece,* San Zaccaria, Venice, Italy, 1505. Oil on wood transferred to canvas, approx. 16′ 5″ × 7′ 9″.

(ca. 1430–1479), which impressed him. Antonello received his early training in Naples, where he must have come in close contact with Flemish painting and mastered using mixed oil (see Chapter 20, page 554). This more flexible medium is wider in coloristic range than either tempera or fresco (see "Fresco Painting," Chapter 19, page 530). Antonello arrived in Venice in 1475 and during his two-year stay introduced his Venetian colleagues to the possibilities the new oil technique offered. As a direct result of Bellini's contact with Antonello, Bellini abandoned Mantegna's harsh linear style and developed a sensuous coloristic manner that was to characterize Venetian painting in the late-15th and 16th centuries.

Bellini earned great recognition for his many Madonnas, which he painted both in half-length (with or without accompanying saints) on small devotional panels and in full-length on large, monumental altarpieces of the *sacra conversazione* (holy conversation) type. In the sacra conversazione, which gained great popularity as a theme for religious paintings from the middle of the 15th century on, a unified space joins saints from different epochs who seem to converse either with each other or with the audience. (Raphael employed much the same conceit in his *School of Athens,* FIG. 22-17, where he gathered Greek philosophers of different eras.) Bellini carried on the tradition in one of his large altarpieces, the *San Zaccaria Altarpiece* (FIG. 22-31).

In the *San Zaccaria Altarpiece,* Bellini refined many of the compositional elements of his earlier altarpieces. As was conventional, the Virgin Mary sits enthroned, holding the Christ Child, with saints flanking her. Here, attributes aid the identification of all the saints but Saint Lucy: Saint Peter with his key and book, Saint Catherine with the palm of martyrdom and the broken wheel, and Saint Jerome with a book (representing his translation of the Bible into Latin). At the foot of the throne sits an angel playing a viol. Bellini placed the group in a carefully painted shrine. The sophistication of his style is best seen in his use of color and light. The painting radiates a feeling of serenity and spiritual calm. Viewers derive this sense less from the figures (no interaction occurs among them) than from the harmonious and balanced presentation of color and light. Bellini's method of painting here became softer and more luminous than in his earlier works. Line is not the chief agent of form; indeed, outlines dissolve in light and shadow. The impact of this work is due largely to glowing color—a soft radiance that envelops the forms with an atmospheric haze and enhances their majestic serenity.

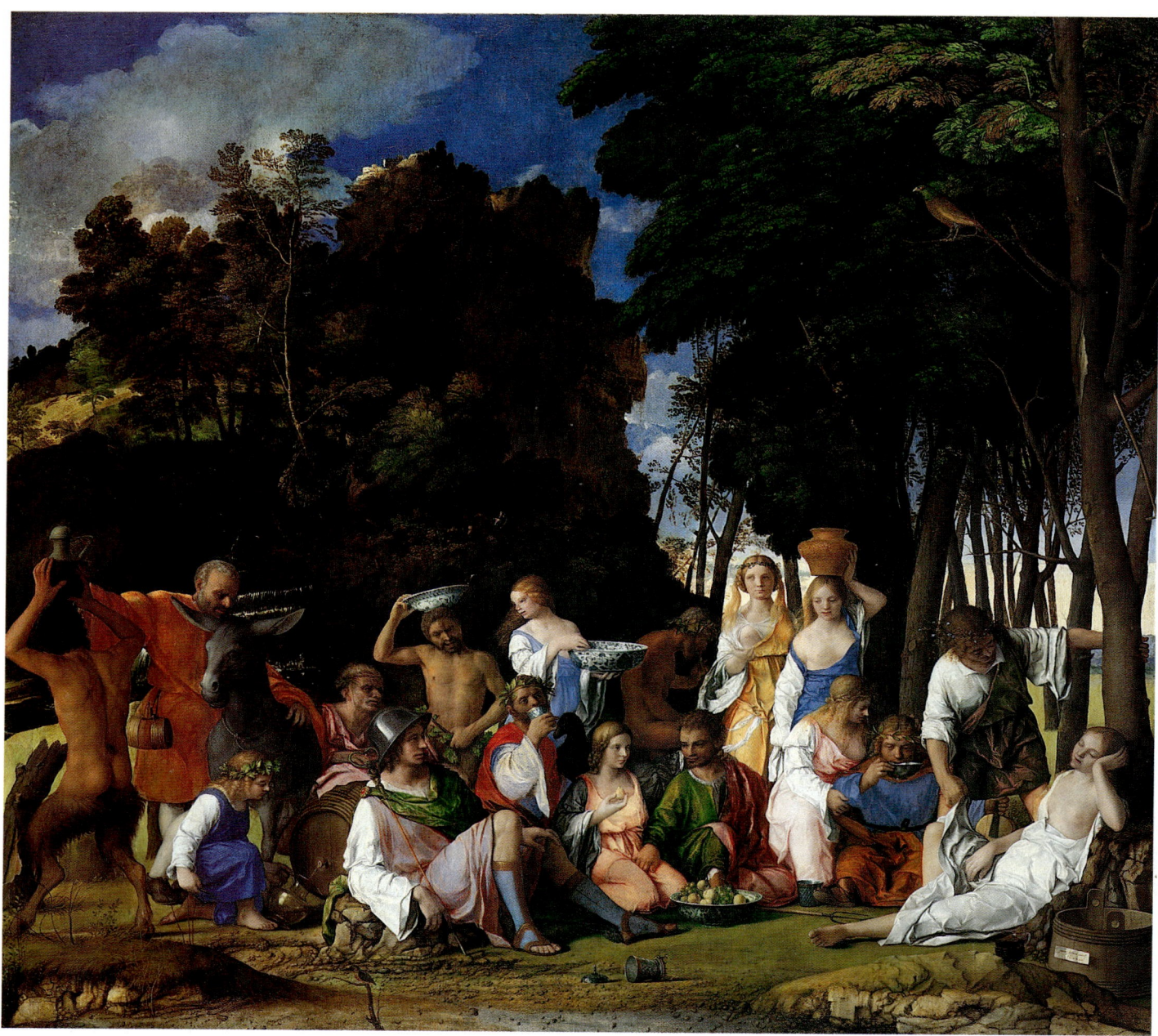

**22-32** GIOVANNI BELLINI and TITIAN, *The Feast of the Gods*, 1529. Oil on canvas, approx. 5′ 7″ × 6′ 2″. National Gallery of Art, Washington (Widener Collection).

**A MYTHOLOGICAL PICNIC** In painting *The Feast of the Gods* (FIG. **22-32**), Bellini actually drew from the work of one of his own students, Giorgione da Castelfranco (FIGS. 22-33 and 22-34), who developed his master's landscape backgrounds into poetic Arcadian reveries. Derived from Arcadia, an ancient district of the central Peloponnesus (peninsula in southern Greece), the term *Arcadian* referred, by the Renaissance, to an idyllic place of rural, rustic peace and simplicity. After Giorgione's premature death, Bellini embraced his student's interests and, in *The Feast of the Gods*, developed a new kind of mythological painting. The duke of Ferrara, Alfonso d'Este, commissioned this work for a room in the Palazzo Ducale. Although Bellini drew some of the figures from the standard repertoire of Greco-Roman art — most notably, the nymph carrying a vase on her head and the sleeping nymph in the lower right corner — the Olympian gods appear as peasants enjoying a heavenly picnic in a shady northern glade.

Bellini's source was Ovid's *Fasti*, which describes a banquet of the gods. The artist spread the figures across the foreground. Satyrs attend the gods, nymphs bring jugs of wine, a child draws from a keg, couples engage in love play, and the sleeping nymph with exposed breast receives amorous attention. The mellow light of a long afternoon glows softly around the gathering, caressing the surfaces of colorful draperies, smooth flesh, and polished metal. Here, Bellini communicated the delight the Venetian school took in the beauty of texture revealed by the full resources of gently and subtly harmonized color. Behind the warm, lush tones of the figures, a background of cool green tree-filled glades extends into the distance; at the right, a screen of trees creates a verdant shelter. (Scholars believe that the background was modified by Titian, discussed shortly.) The atmosphere is idyllic, a lush countryside providing a setting for the never-ending pleasure of the immortal gods.

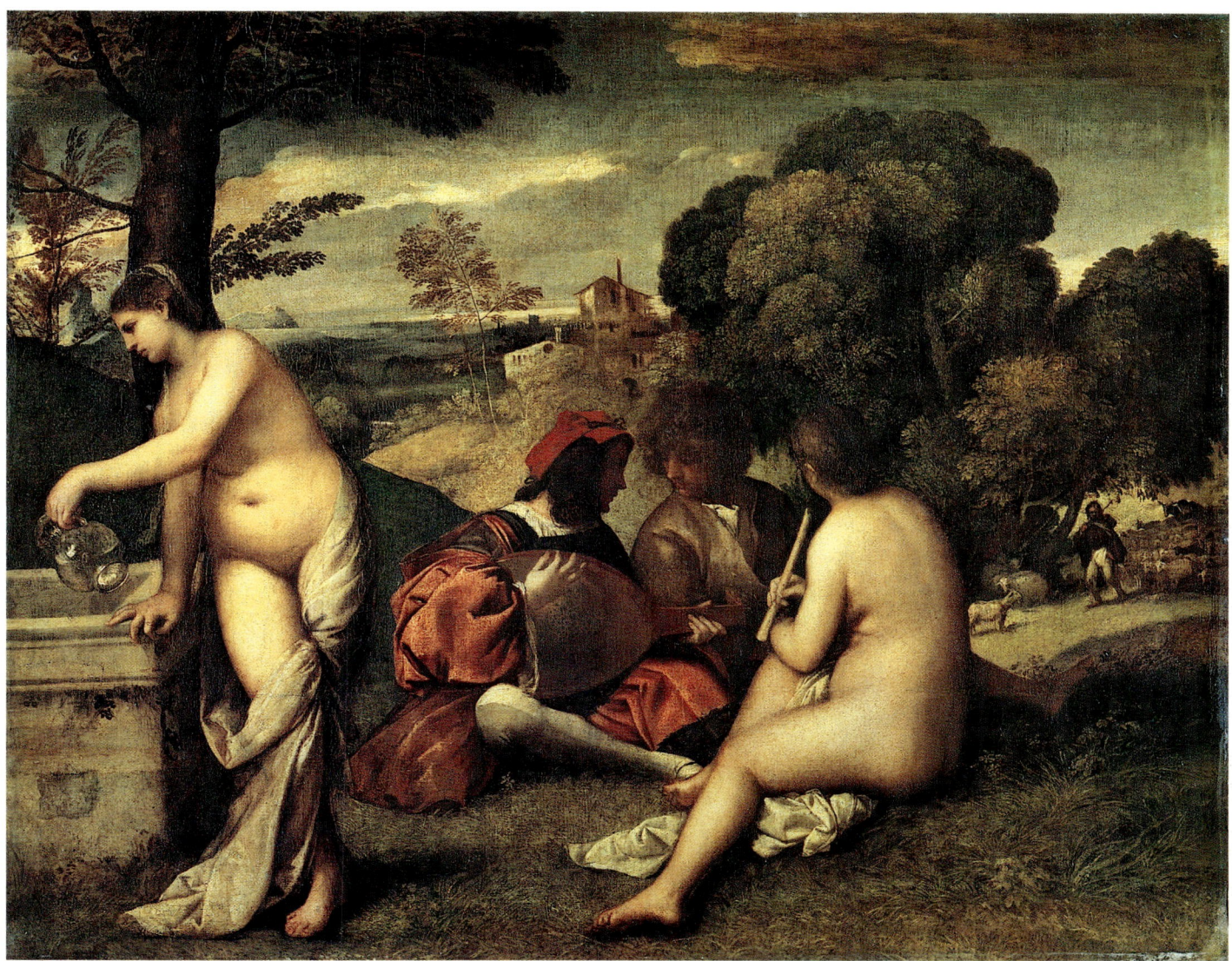

**22-33** GIORGIONE DA CASTELFRANCO (and/or TITIAN?), *Pastoral Symphony*, ca. 1508. Oil on canvas, approx. 3′ 7″ × 4′ 6″. Louvre, Paris.

Thus, with Bellini, Venetian art became the great complement of the schools of Florence and Rome. The Venetians' instrument was color; that of the Florentines and Romans was sculpturesque form. Scholars often distill the contrast between these two approaches down to *colorito* (colored or painted) versus *disegno* (drawing and design—see *"Disegno,"* page 617). Whereas most central Italian artists emphasized careful design preparation based on preliminary drawing, Venetian artists focused on color and the process of paint application. In addition, the general thematic focus of their work differed. Venetian artists painted the poetry of the senses and delighted in nature's beauty and the pleasures of humanity. Artists in Florence and Rome gravitated toward more esoteric, intellectual themes—the epic of humanity, the masculine virtues, the grandeur of the ideal, and the lofty conceptions of religion involving the heroic and sublime. Much of the history of later Western art involved a dialogue between these two traditions.

Describing Venetian art as "poetic" is particularly appropriate, given the development of *poesia,* or painting meant to operate in a manner similar to poetry. Both classical and Renaissance poetry inspired Venetian artists, and their paintings focused on the lyrical and sensual. Thus, in many Venetian artworks, discerning concrete narratives or subjects (in the traditional sense) is virtually impossible.

**POETRY IN MOTION** A Venetian artist who deserves much of the credit for developing this poetic manner of painting was GIORGIONE DA CASTELFRANCO (ca. 1477–1510). Giorgione's so-called *Pastoral Symphony* (FIG. **22-33;** some believe it an early work by his student Titian, discussed next) exemplifies poesia and surely inspired the late Arcadian scenes by Bellini, his teacher. Out of dense shadow emerge the soft forms of figures and landscape. The theme is as enigmatic as the lighting. Two nude women, accompanied by two clothed young men, occupy the rich, abundant landscape through which a shepherd passes. In the distance, a villa crowns a hill. The artist so eloquently evoked the pastoral mood that the viewer does not find the uncertainty about the picture's precise meaning distressing; the mood is enough. The shepherd symbolizes the poet; the pipes and lute symbolize his poetry. The two women accompanying the young men may be thought of as their invisible inspiration, their muses. One turns to lift water from the sacred well of poetic inspiration. The voluptuous bodies of the women, softly modulated by the smoky shadow, became the standard in Venetian art.

The fullness of their figures contributes to their effect as poetic personifications of nature's abundance.

As a pastoral poet in the pictorial medium and one of the greatest masters in the handling of light and color, Giorgione praised the beauty of nature, music, women, and pleasure. Vasari reported that Giorgione was an accomplished lutenist and singer, and adjectives from poetry and music seem best suited for describing the pastoral air and muted chords of his painting. He cast a mood of tranquil reverie and dreaminess over the entire scene, evoking the landscape of a lost but never forgotten paradise.

**STORMY WEATHER** Another Giorgione painting, *The Tempest* (FIG. **22-34**), manifests this same interest in the poetic qualities of the natural landscape inhabited by humans. Dominating the scene is a lush landscape, threatened by stormy skies and lightning in the middle background. Pushed off to both sides are the human figures—a young woman nursing a baby in the right foreground and a man carrying a halberd (a combination spear and battle-ax) on the left. Much scholarly debate has centered on this painting's subject, fueled by the fact that X rays of the canvas revealed that a nude woman originally stood where Giorgione subsequently placed the man. This flexibility in subject has led many to believe that no definitive narrative exists, which is appropriate for a Venetian poetic rendering. Other scholars have suggested mythological narratives or historical events. This uncertainty about the subject contributes to the painting's enigmatic quality and intriguing air.

**A MASTER OF COLOR** Giorgione's Arcadianism passed not only to his much older yet constantly inquisitive master, Bellini, but also to Tiziano Vecelli, whose name has been anglicized into TITIAN (ca. 1490–1576). Titian was the most extraordinary and prolific of the great Venetian painters, a supreme colorist who cultivated numerous patrons. An important change occurring in Titian's time was the almost universal adoption of canvas, with its rough-textured surface, in place of wood panels for paintings. Titian's works established oil color on canvas as the typical medium of pictorial tradition thereafter. According to a contemporary of Titian, Palma il Giovane:

**22-34** GIORGIONE DA CASTELFRANCO, *The Tempest*, ca. 1510. Oil on canvas, 2′ 7″ × 2′ 4¾″. Galleria dell' Accademia, Venice.

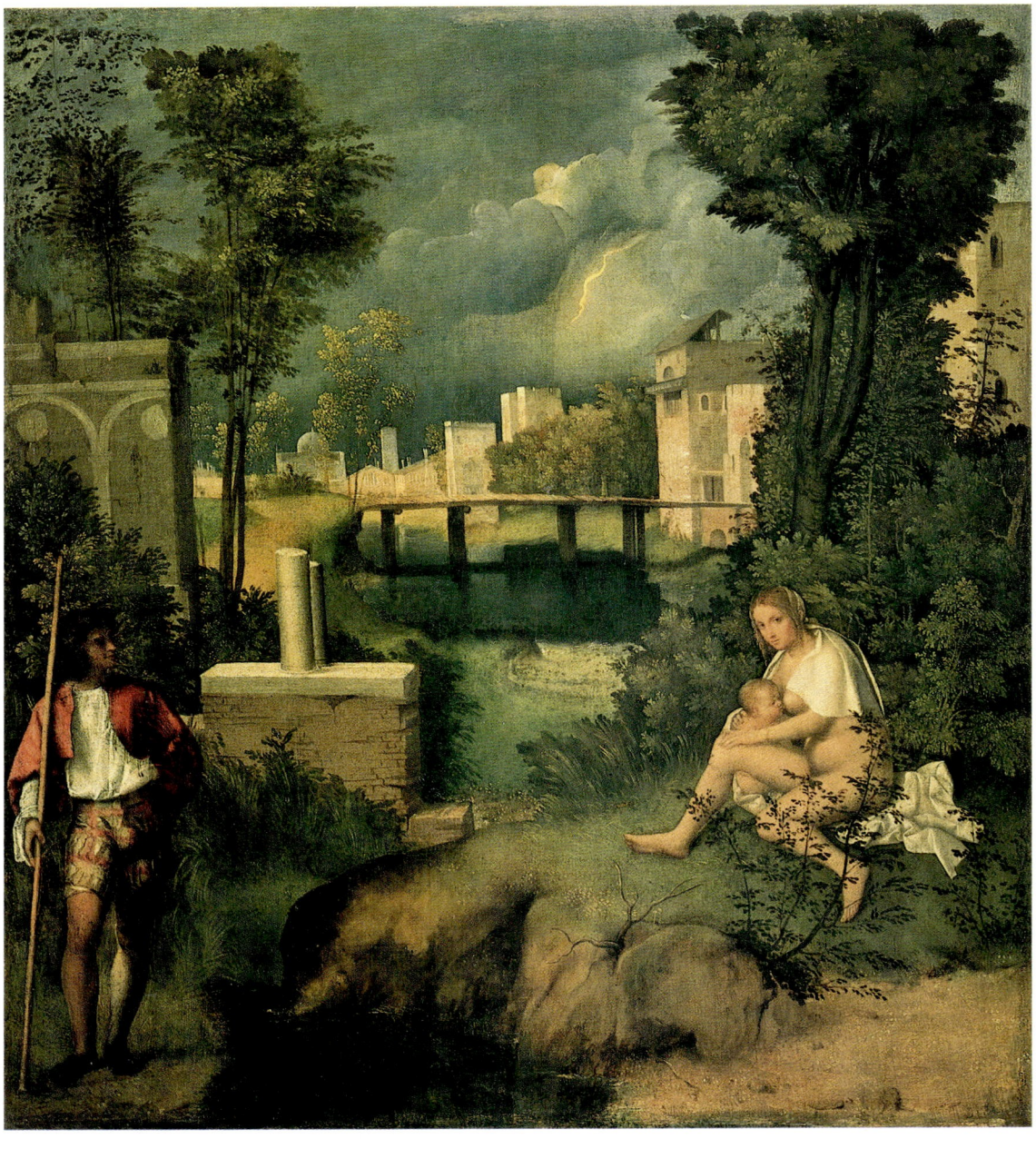

Titian [employed] a great mass of colors, which served . . . as a base for the compositions. . . . I too have seen some of these, formed with bold strokes made with brushes laden with colors, sometimes of a pure red earth, which he used, so to speak, for a middle tone, and at other times of white lead; and with the same brush tinted with red, black and yellow he formed a highlight; and observing these principles he made the promise of an exceptional figure appear in four brushstrokes. . . . Having constructed these precious foundations he used to turn his pictures to the wall and leave them there without looking at them, sometimes for several months. When he wanted to apply his brush again he would examine them with the utmost rigor . . . to see if he could find any faults. . . . In this way, working on the figures and revising them, he brought them to the most perfect symmetry that the beauty of art and nature can reveal. . . . [T]hus he gradually covered those quintessential forms with living flesh, bringing them by many stages to a state in which they lacked only the breath of life. He never painted a figure all at once and . . . in the last stages he painted more with his fingers than his brushes.[8]

**THE GLORIOUS VIRGIN MARY**  Titian's remarkable coloristic sense and his ability to convey light through color emerge in a major altarpiece, *Assumption of the Virgin* (FIG. 22-35), painted for the main altar of Santa Maria Gloriosa dei Frari in Venice. Commissioned by the prior of this Franciscan basilica, the monumental altarpiece (close to 23 feet high) depicts the glorious ascent of the Virgin's body to Heaven. Visually, the painting is a stunning tour de force. Golden clouds so luminous they seem to glow, radiating light into the church interior, envelop the Virgin. God the Father appears above, awaiting her with open arms. Below, apostles gesticulate wildly as they witness this momentous event. Titian painted this large-scale altarpiece with exceptional clarity. Through vibrant color, he infused the image with a drama and intensity that assured his lofty reputation, then and now.

**A DAZZLING DISPLAY OF COLOR**  Trained by both Bellini and Giorgione, Titian learned so well from them that even today scholars cannot agree about the degree of his participation in their later works. However, it is clear that Titian completed several of Bellini's and Giorgione's unfinished paintings. On Giovanni Bellini's death in 1516, the republic of Venice appointed Titian as its official painter. Shortly thereafter, Bishop Jacopo Pesaro commissioned Titian to paint *Madonna of the Pesaro Family* (FIG. 22-36), which the patron presented to the church of the Frari. This work furthered Titian's reputation and established his personal style. Pesaro, bishop of Paphos in Cyprus and commander of the papal fleet, had led a successful expedition in 1502 against the Turks during the Venetian-Turkish war and commissioned this painting in gratitude. In a stately sunlit setting, the Madonna receives the commander, who kneels dutifully at the foot of her throne. A soldier (Saint George?) behind the commander carries a banner with the *escutcheons* (shields with coats of arms) of the Borgia (Pope Alexander VI) and of Pesaro. Behind him is a turbaned Turk, a prisoner of war of the Christian forces. Saint Peter appears on the steps of the throne, and Saint Francis introduces other Pesaro family members (all male—Italian depictions of donors in this era typically excluded women and children), who kneel solemnly in the right foreground.

As already seen, the High Renaissance was characterized by the massing of monumental figures, singly and in groups, within a weighty and majestic architecture. But Titian did not compose a horizontal and symmetrical arrangement, as did Leonardo in *Last*

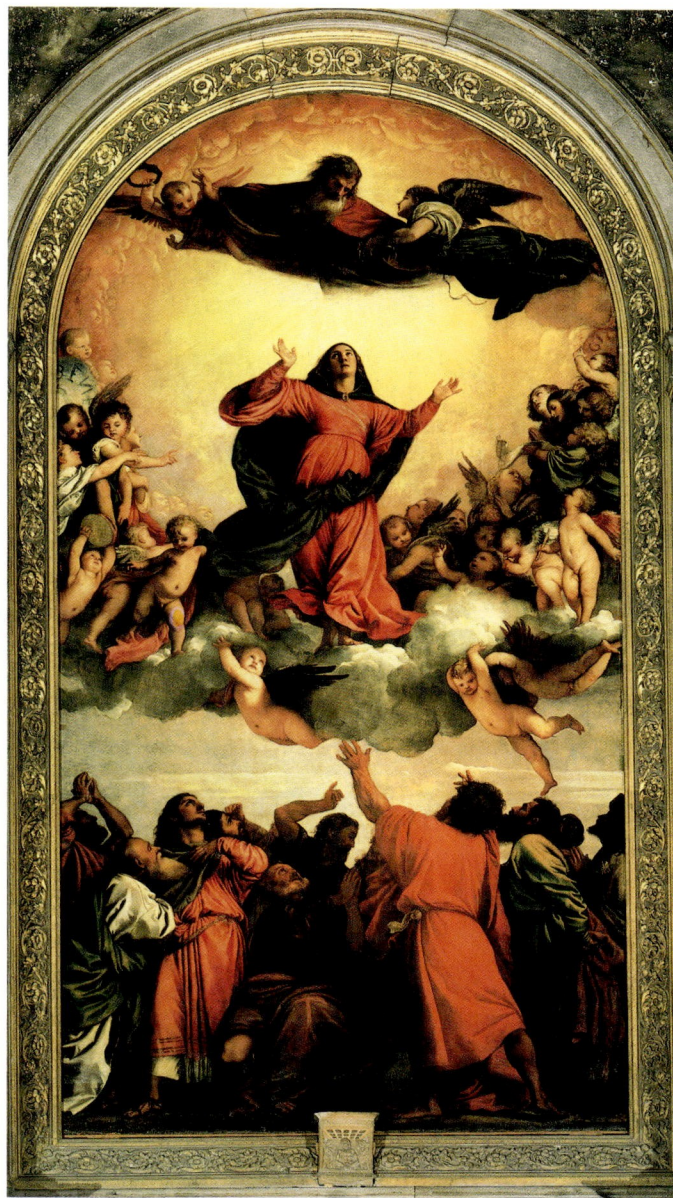

**22-35**  TITIAN, *Assumption of the Virgin*, Santa Maria Gloriosa dei Frari, Venice, Italy, ca. 1516–1518. Oil on wood, 22′ 6″ × 11′ 10″.

*Supper* (FIG. 22-3) and Raphael in *School of Athens* (FIG. 22-17). Rather, he placed the figures on a steep diagonal, positioning the Madonna, the focus of the composition, well off the central axis. Titian drew viewers' attention to her with the perspective lines, the inclination of the figures, and the directional lines of gaze and gesture. The banner inclining toward the left beautifully brings the design into equilibrium, balancing the rightward and upward tendencies of its main direction.

This kind of composition is more dynamic than those in the High Renaissance shown thus far and presaged a new kind of pictorial design—one built on movement rather than rest. In his rendering of the rich surface textures, Titian gave a dazzling display of color in all its nuances. He entwined the human scene with the heavenly, depicting the Madonna and saints honoring the achievements of a specific man in this particular world. A quite worldly transaction takes place (albeit beneath a heavenly cloud bearing angels) between a queen and her court and loyal servants. Titian constructed this tableau in terms of Renaissance protocol and courtly splendor.

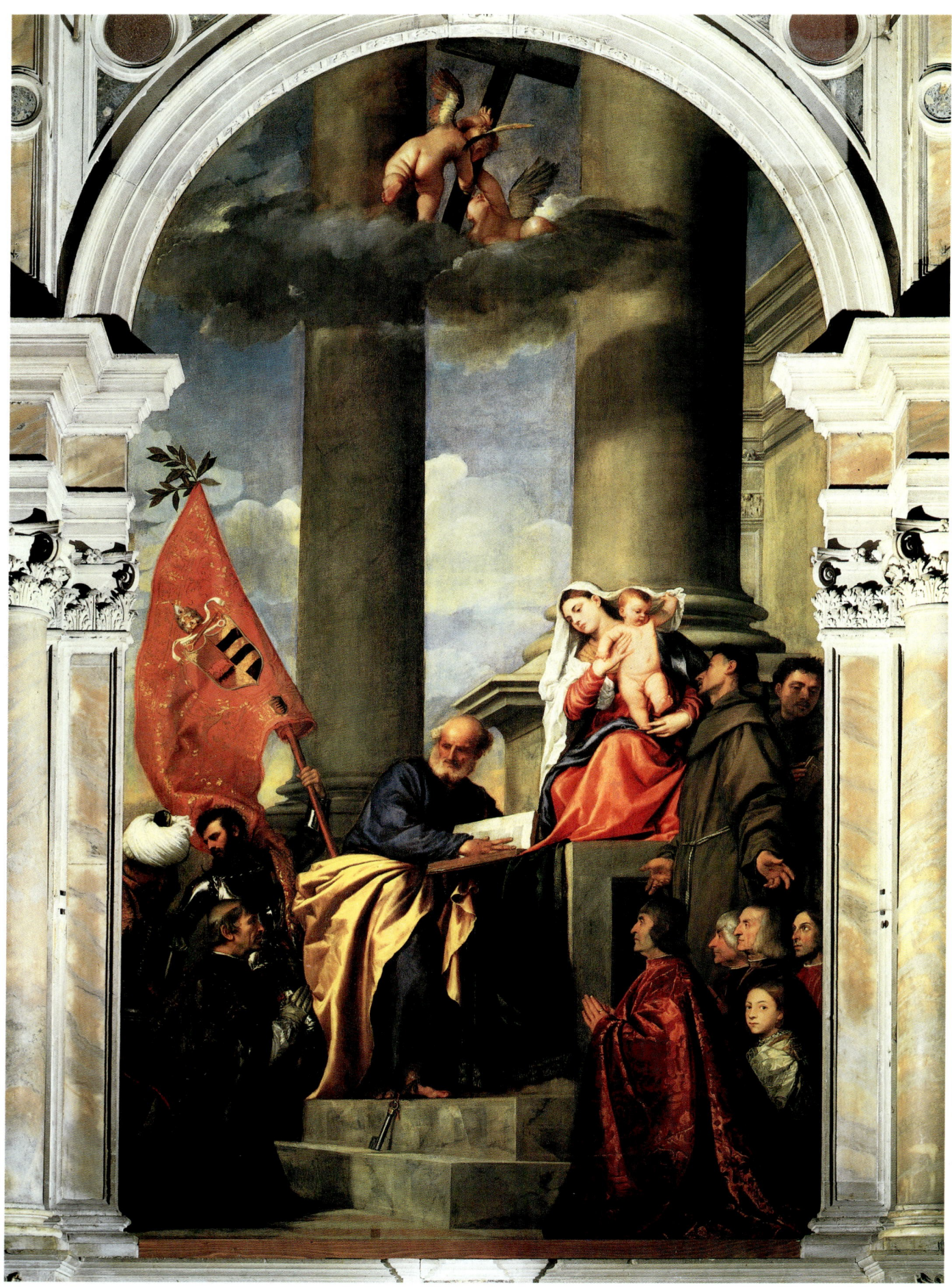

**22-36** TITIAN, *Madonna of the Pesaro Family,* Santa Maria dei Frari, Venice, Italy, 1519–1526. Oil on canvas, approx. 16′ × 9′.

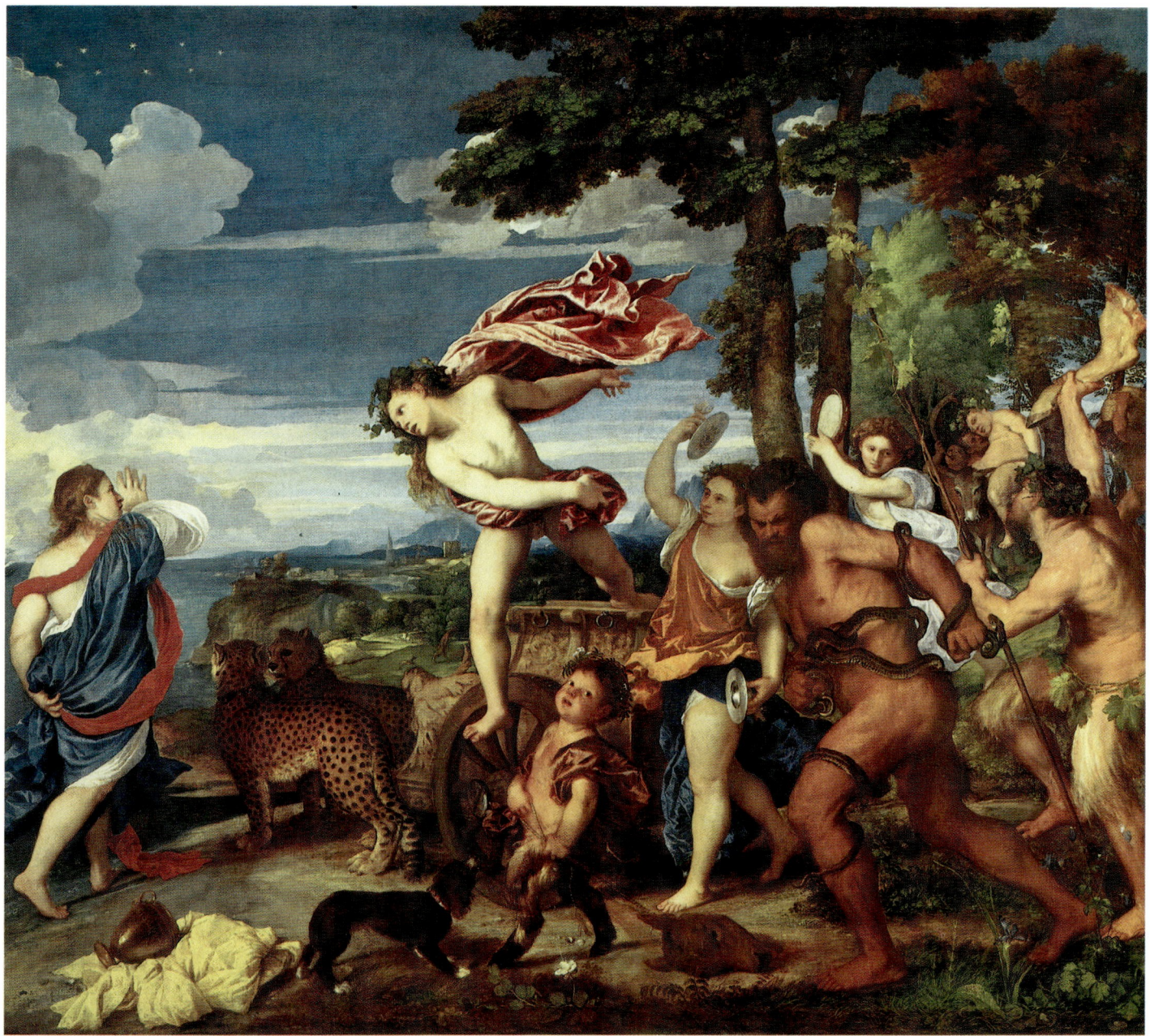

**22-37** TITIAN, *Meeting of Bacchus and Ariadne*, 1522–1523. Oil on canvas, 5′ 9″ × 6′ 3″. National Gallery, London. 💿

**BACCHANALIAN REVELRY** In 1511, Alfonso d'Este, duke of Ferrara, asked Titian to produce a painting for his Camerino d'Alabastro (small room of alabaster). The patron had requested one bacchanalian scene each from Titian, Bellini, Raphael, and Fra Bartolommeo. Both Raphael and Fra Bartolommeo died before fulfilling the commission, and Bellini painted only one scene (FIG. 22-32), leaving Titian to produce three. One of these three paintings is *Meeting of Bacchus and Ariadne* (FIG. **22-37**). Bacchus, accompanied by a boisterous and noisy group, arrives to save Ariadne, whom Theseus has abandoned on the island of Naxos. In this scene, Titian revealed his debt to classical art; he derived one of the figures, entwined with snakes, from the ancient sculpture of Laocoön (see FIG. 5-89). Titian's rich and luminous colors add greatly to the sensuous appeal of this painting, making it perfect for Alfonso's "pleasure chamber."

**A VENETIAN VENUS** In 1538, at the height of his powers, Titian painted the so-called *Venus of Urbino* (FIG. **22-38**) for Guidobaldo II, duke of Urbino. The title (given to the painting later) elevates to the status of classical mythology what probably merely represents a courtesan in her bedchamber. Indeed, no evidence suggests that the duke intended the commission as anything more than a female nude for his private enjoyment. Whether the subject is divine or mortal, Titian based his version on an earlier (and pioneering) painting of Venus (not illustrated) by Giorgione. Here, Titian established the compositional elements and the standard for paintings of the reclining female nude, regardless of the many variations that ensued. This "Venus" reclines on the gentle slope of her luxurious pillowed couch, the linear play of the draperies contrasting with her body's sleek continuous volume. At her feet is a pendant (balancing) figure — in this case, a slumbering

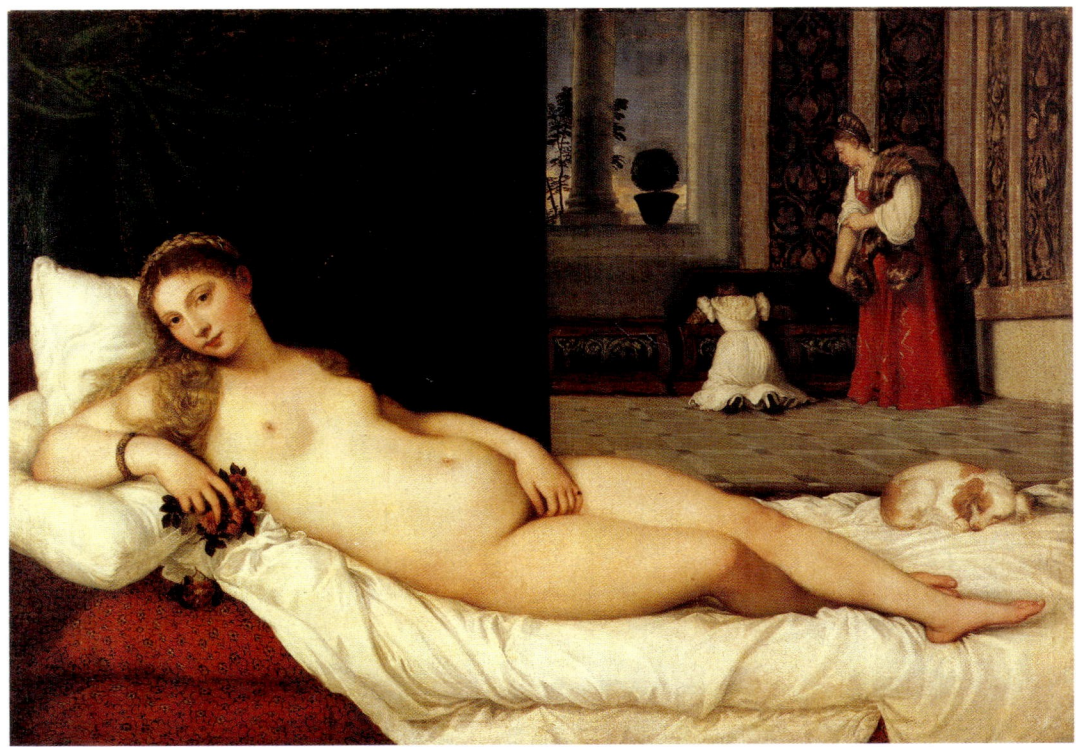

lapdog. Behind her, a simple drape both places her figure emphatically in the foreground and indicates a vista into the background at the right half of the picture. Two servants bend over a chest, apparently searching for garments (Renaissance households stored clothing in carved wooden chests called *cassoni*) to clothe "Venus." Beyond them, a smaller vista opens into a landscape. Titian masterfully constructed the view backward into space and the division of the space into progressively smaller units. With great facility, he used all the resources of pictorial representation to create original and exquisite effects of the sort that inspired generations of painters in Italy and the north.

As in other Venetian paintings, color plays a prominent role in *Venus of Urbino.* The red tones of the matron's skirt and the muted reds of the tapestries against the neutral whites of the matron's sleeves and the kneeling girl's gown echo the deep Venetian reds set off against the pale neutral whites of the linen and the warm ivory gold of the flesh. The viewer must study the picture carefully to realize the subtlety of color planning. For instance, the two deep reds (in the foreground cushions and in the background skirt) play a critical role in the composition as a gauge of distance and as indicators of an implied diagonal opposed to the real one of the reclining figure. Here, Titian used color not simply for tinting preexisting forms but also to organize his placement of forms.

**A POWERFUL PATRONESS** Titian was also a highly esteemed portraitist and in great demand. Of the more than 50 surviving portraits by his hand, one example, *Isabella d'Este* (FIG. **22-39**), suffices to illustrate his style. Isabella d'Este (1474–1539) was among the most powerful of women during the Renaissance (see "Women in the Renaissance Art World," page 647). Daughter of the duke of Ferrara, she married Francesco Gonzaga, marquis of Mantua, and was instrumental in developing the Mantuan court into an important center of art and learning. Titian's portraits, as well as those of many of the Venetian and subsequent schools, generally make much of the artist's psychological reading of the body's most expressive parts—the head and the hands. Thus,

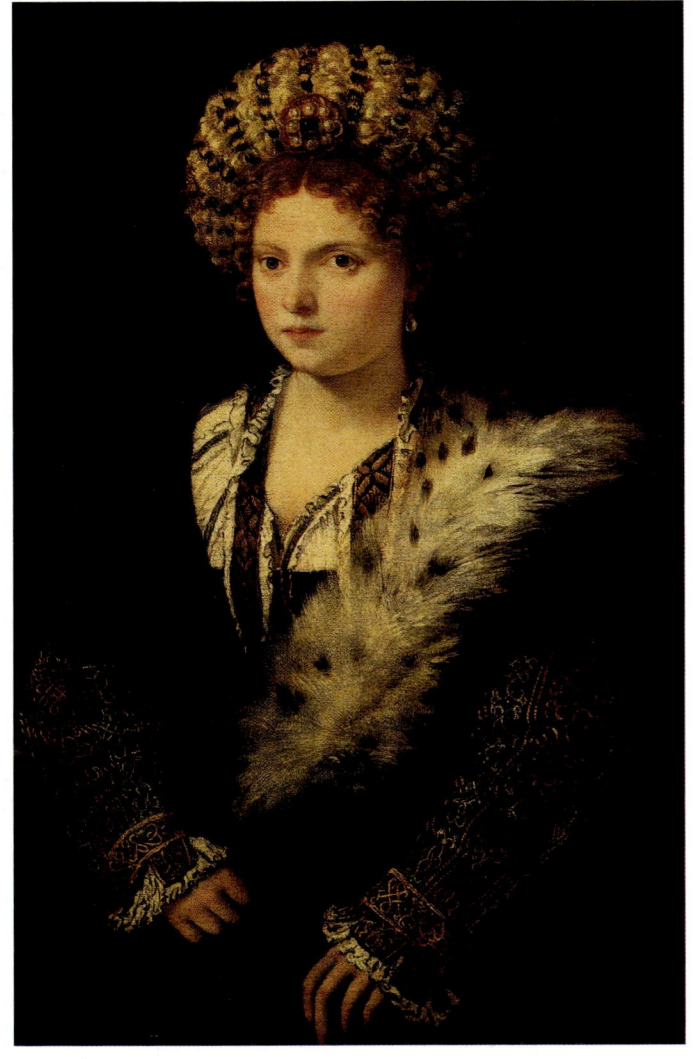

22-39 TITIAN, *Isabella d'Este,* 1534–1536. Oil on canvas, 3′ 4$\frac{1}{8}$″ × 2′ 1$\frac{3}{16}$″. Kunsthistorisches Museum, Vienna.

### Women in the Renaissance Art World

To what degree was the Renaissance art world male dominated? Reviews of publications on Italian Renaissance art suggest that the number of women artists was limited. This dearth of acknowledged women artists reflects the obstacles they faced. In particular, for centuries, training practices mandating residence at a master's house (see "Mastering a Craft," Chapter 19, page 535) precluded women from acquiring the necessary experience. In addition, social proscriptions, such as those preventing women from drawing from nude models, further hampered an aspiring female artist's advancement through the accepted avenues of artistic training.

Still, there were determined women who surmounted these barriers and were able to develop not only considerable bodies of work but enviable reputations as well. One such artist was Sofonisba Anguissola (FIG. 22-46), who was so accomplished that she can be considered the first Italian woman to have ascended to the level of international art celebrity. Lavinia Fontana (1552–1614) also achieved notable success, and her paintings constitute the largest surviving body of work by any woman artist before 1700. Fontana learned her craft from her father, a leading Bolognese painter; such a paternal education was the normative manner of training for aspiring women artists. She was in demand as a portraitist and received commissions from important patrons, including members of the dominant Habsburg family. She even spent time as an official painter to the papal court in Rome.

Perhaps more challenging than the road to becoming a professional female painter was the mastery of sculpture, made more difficult by the physical demands of the medium. Yet Properzia de' Rossi (ca. 1490–1530) established herself as a professional sculptor and was the only woman artist that Giorgio Vasari included in his comprehensive publication, *Lives of the Most Eminent Painters, Sculptors and Architects*. Active in the early 16th century, she was struck down by the plague in 1530, curtailing her promising career.

Beyond the realm of art production, Renaissance women had a significant impact in the realm of patronage. Scholars only recently have begun to explore systematically the role of women as patrons. As a result, current knowledge is sketchy at best but suggests that women played a much more extensive role than previously acknowledged. Among the problems researchers face in their quest to clarify women's participation as patrons is that women often wielded their influence and decision-making power behind the scenes. Many of these women acquired their positions through marriage; their power was thus indirect and provisional, based on their husbands' wealth and status. Thus, documentation of the networks within which women patrons operated and of the processes they used to exert power in a male-dominated society is less substantive than that available for male patrons.

One of the most important Renaissance patrons, male or female, was Isabella d'Este (1474–1539), marchioness of Mantua (FIG. 22-39). Brought up in the cultured princely court of Ferrara (southwest of Venice), Isabella married Francesco Gonzaga (1466–1519), marquis of Mantua, in 1490. Isabella's marriage gave her access to the position and wealth necessary to pursue her interest in becoming a major art patron. An avid collector, she enlisted the aid of agents who scoured Italy for appealing objects. Isabella did not limit her collection to painting and sculpture but included ceramics, glassware, gems, cameos, medals, classical texts, musical manuscripts, and musical instruments.

Isabella was undoubtedly a proud and ambitious woman well aware of how art could boost her fame and reputation. Accordingly, she commissioned several portraits of herself from the most esteemed artists of her day—Leonardo da Vinci, Andrea Mantegna, and Titian. The detail and complexity of many of her contracts with artists reveal her insistence on control over the artworks.

Other Renaissance women positioned themselves as serious art patrons. One such woman was Caterina Sforza (1462–1509), daughter of Galeazzo Maria Sforza (heir to the Duchy of Milan), who married Girolamo Riario in 1484. The death of her husband, lord of Imola and count of Forlì, in 1488 gave Sforza access to power denied most women.

Another female art patron was Lucrezia Tornabuoni (married to Piero di Cosimo de' Medici), one of many Medici, both men and women, who earned reputations as unparalleled art patrons. Further archival investigation of women's roles in Renaissance Italy undoubtedly will produce more evidence of how women established themselves as patrons and artists and the extent to which they contributed to the flourishing of Renaissance art.

---

Titian sharply highlighted Isabella's face, while her black dress fades into the undefined darkness of the background. The unseen light source also illuminates Isabella's hands, and the artist painted her sleeves with incredible detail to further draw viewers' attention to her hands. This portrait reveals not only Titian's skill but the patron's wish as well. Painted when Isabella was 60 years of age, it depicts her in her twenties at her request. Titian used an earlier portrait of her as his guide, and Isabella appears not just young but also perfectly poised and self-assured.

## Other 16th-Century Italian Artists

The towering achievements of Raphael and Michelangelo in Rome tend to obscure everything else created during their time. Nevertheless, aside from the flourishing Venetian school, excellent artists were active in other parts of Italy during the first part of the 16th century. One of these, the Florentine ANDREA DEL SARTO (1486–1531), expresses, in his early paintings, the ideals of the High Renaissance with almost as much clarity and distinction as does Raphael.

A MADONNA WITH SPHINXES Andrea's *Madonna of the Harpies* (FIG. 22-40) shows the Madonna standing majestically on an altarlike base decorated with sphinxes (figures misidentified by Vasari as harpies—hence, the name of the painting). The composition is based on a massive and imposing figure pyramid, the static qualities of which are relieved by the opposing contrapposto poses of the flanking saints—a favorite and effective High Renaissance device to introduce variety into symmetry. The potentially rigid pyramid is softened further by the skillful coordination of the figures' poses into an organic movement that

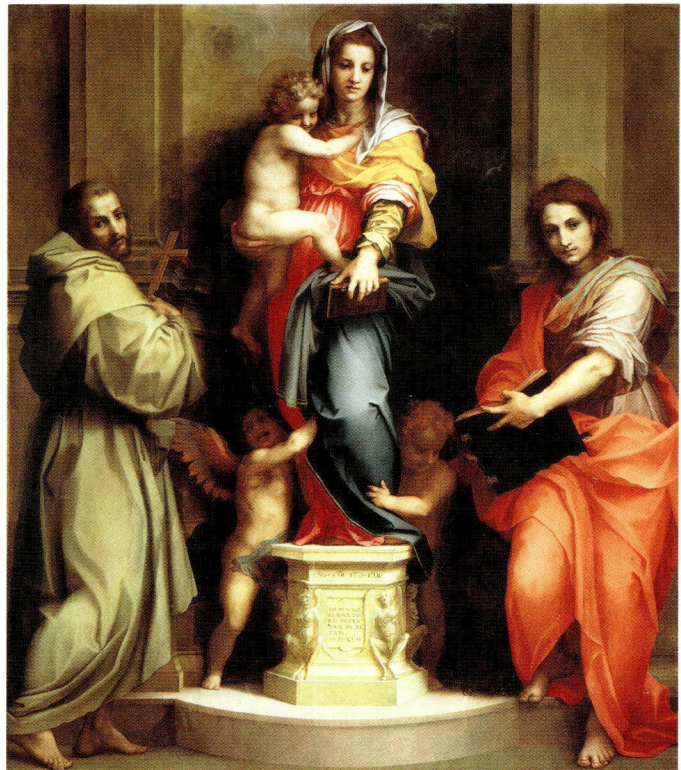

22-40 ANDREA DEL SARTO, *Madonna of the Harpies,* 1517. Oil on wood, approx. 6′ 9″ x 5′ 10″. Galleria degli Uffizi, Florence.

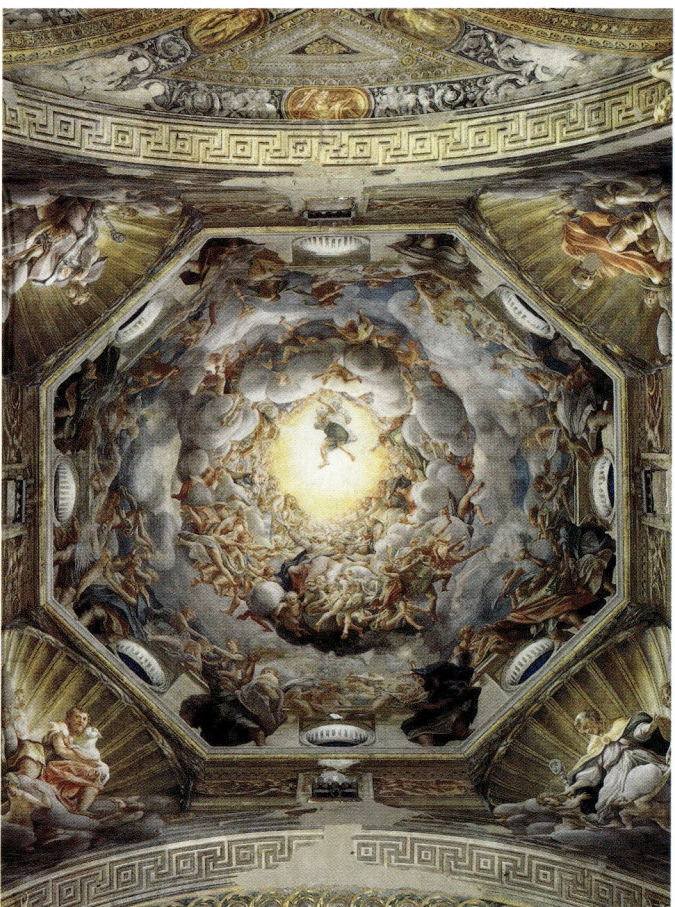

22-41 ANTONIO ALLEGRI DA CORREGGIO, *Assumption of the Virgin,* dome fresco of Parma Cathedral, Parma, Italy, 1526–1530.

leads from Saint Francis (on the left) to the Virgin, to Saint John the Evangelist, and downward from him toward the observer. This main movement is either echoed or countered by numerous secondary movements brought into perfect formal balance in a faultless compositional performance. The soft modeling of the forms is based on Leonardo but does not affect the colors, which are rich and warm. Andrea's sense of and ability to handle color set him apart from his contemporaries in central Italy. He is perhaps the only Renaissance artist to transpose his rich color schemes from panels into frescoes.

**A VIEW OF THE SKY** Andrea del Sarto may still be placed firmly in the High Renaissance, but his northern Italian contemporary, ANTONIO ALLEGRI DA CORREGGIO (ca. 1489–1534), of Parma, developed a unique personal style that is almost impossible to classify. A solitary genius, Correggio pulled together many stylistic trends, including those of Leonardo, Raphael, and the Venetians. Historically, his most enduring contribution was his development of illusionistic ceiling perspectives that his Baroque emulators seldom surpassed. At Mantua, Mantegna created the illusion of a hole in the ceiling of the Camera degli Sposi (see FIG. 21-46). Some 50 years later, Correggio painted away the entire dome of the Parma Cathedral in *Assumption of the Virgin* (FIG. **22-41**). Opening up the cupola, the artist showed his audience a view of the sky, with concentric rings of clouds where hundreds of soaring figures perform a wildly pirouetting dance in celebration of the Assumption. Versions of these angelic creatures became permanent tenants of numerous Baroque churches in later centuries. Correggio was also an influential painter of religious panels, anticipating in them many other Baroque compositional devices. Correggio's contemporaries expressed little appreciation for his art. Later, during the 17th century, Baroque painters recognized him as a kindred spirit.

## MANNERISM

*Mannerism* is a style that emerged in Italy during the 16th century. Over the years, scholars have refined their ideas about Mannerism, attempting to define the parameters of this style. It is difficult to identify specific dates for Mannerism—emerging in the 1520s, it overlapped considerably with High Renaissance art. The term is derived from the Italian word *maniera,* meaning style or manner. In the field of art history, the term *style* is usually used to refer to a characteristic or representative mode, especially of an artist or period (for example, Leonardo's style or Gothic style). Style can also refer to an absolute quality of fashion (for example, someone has "style"). Mannerism's style (or representative mode) is characterized by style (being stylish, cultured, elegant).

Among the features most closely associated with Mannerism is *artifice.* Actually, all art involves artifice, in the sense that art is not "natural"—it is a representation of a scene or idea. But many artists, including High Renaissance artists such as Leonardo and Raphael, chose to conceal that artifice by using such devices as perspective and shading to make their art look natural. In contrast, Mannerist artists consciously revealed the constructed nature of their art. In other words, High Renaissance artists generally strove to create art that appeared natural, whereas Mannerist artists were less inclined to disguise the contrived nature of art production. This is why artifice is a central feature of discussions about Mannerism, and why Mannerist works can seem, appropriately, "mannered." The conscious display of artifice in Mannerism often reveals itself in imbalanced compositions and unusual complexities, both visual and conceptual. Ambiguous space, departures from expected conventions, and unique presentations of traditional themes also surface frequently in Mannerist art and architecture. And the stylishness of Mannerism often inspired artists to focus on themes of courtly grace and cultured sophistication.

## Mannerist Painting

**A PAINTING OF LOSS AND GRIEF** *Descent from the Cross* (FIG. **22-42**) by JACOPO DA PONTORMO (1494–1557) exhibits almost all the stylistic features characteristic of Mannerism's early phase in painting. This subject had frequently been depicted in art, and Pontormo exploited the familiarity that viewers at the time would have had by playing off their expectations. For example, rather than presenting the action as taking place across the perpendicular picture plane, as artists such as Raphael and Rogier van der Weyden had done in their paintings (see FIG. 20-7) of this scene, Pontormo rotated the conventional figural groups along a vertical axis. As a result, the Virgin Mary falls back (away from the viewer) as she releases her dead Son's hand. In contrast with High Renaissance artists, who had concentrated their masses in the center of the painting, Pontormo here leaves a void. This accentuates the grouping of hands that fill that hole, calling attention to the void—symbolic of loss and grief.

The artist enhanced the painting's ambiguity with the curiously anxious glances the figures cast in all directions. Athletic bending and twisting characterize many of the figures, with distortions (for example, the torso of the foreground figure bends in an anatomically impossible way), elastic elongation of the limbs, and heads rendered as uniformly small and oval. The contrasting colors, primarily light blues and pinks, add to the dynamism and complexity of the work. The painting represents a departure from the balanced, harmoniously structured compositions of the earlier Renaissance.

**MANNERISM'S ELEGANCE AND GRACE** Correggio's pupil Girolamo Francesco Maria Mazzola, known as PARMIGIANINO (1503–1540), achieved in his best-known work, *Madonna with the Long Neck* (FIG. **22-43**), the elegance—stylishness—that was a principal aim of Mannerism. He smoothly combined the influences of Correggio and Raphael in a picture of exquisite grace and precious sweetness. The Madonna's small oval head; her long, slender neck; the unbelievable attenuation and delicacy of her hand; and the sinuous, swaying elongation of her frame—all are marks of the aristocratic, sumptuously courtly taste of a later phase of

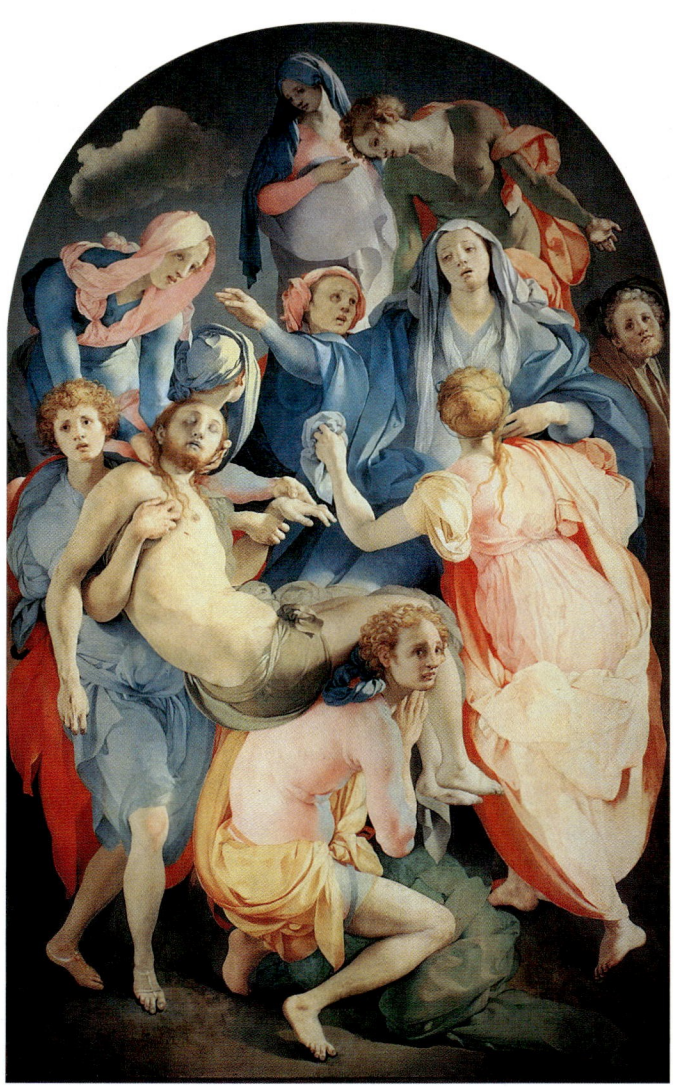

**22-42** JACOPO DA PONTORMO, *Descent from the Cross*, Capponi Chapel, Santa Felicità, Florence, Italy, 1525–1528. Oil on wood, approx. 10′ 3″ × 6′ 6″.

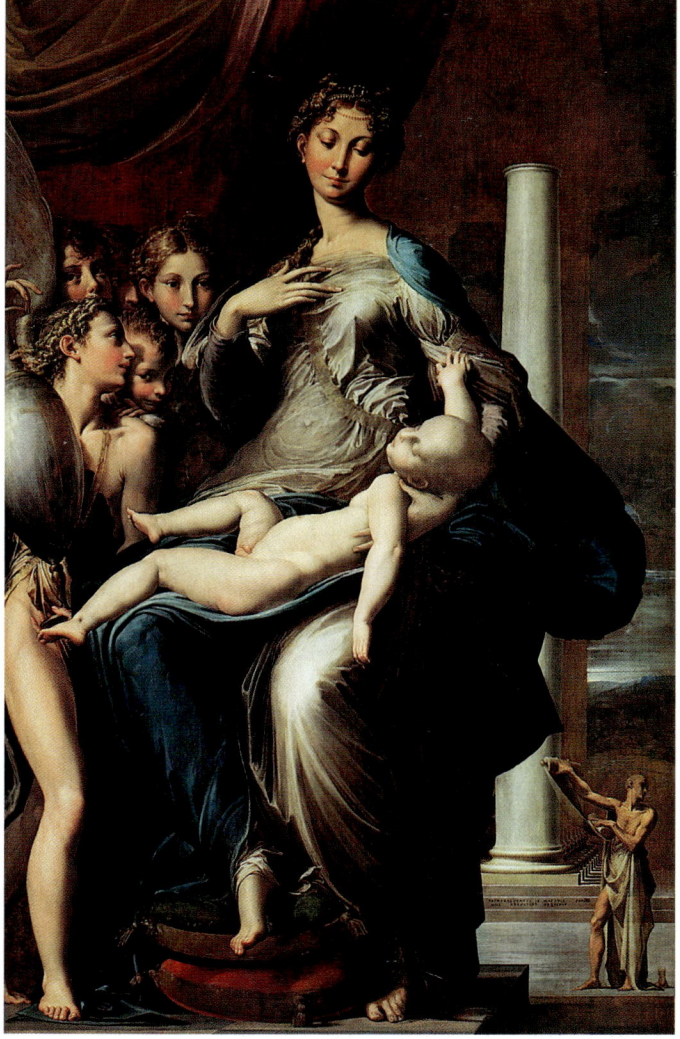

**22-43** PARMIGIANINO, *Madonna with the Long Neck*, ca. 1535. Oil on wood, approx. 7′ 1″ × 4′ 4″. Galleria degli Uffizi, Florence.

Mannerism. Parmigianino amplified this elegance by expanding the Madonna's form as viewed from head to toe. On the left stands a bevy of angelic creatures, melting with emotions as soft and smooth as their limbs (the composition's left side is quite in Correggio's manner). On the right, the artist included a line of columns without capitals and an enigmatic figure with a scroll, whose distance from the foreground is immeasurable and ambiguous.

Although the elegance and sophisticated beauty of the painting are due in large part to the Madonna's attenuated limbs, that exaggeration is not solely decorative in purpose. *Madonna with the Long Neck* takes its subject from a simile in medieval hymns that compared the Virgin's neck to a great ivory tower or column, such as that which Parmigianino depicted to the right of the Madonna. Thus, the work contains religious meaning in addition to the power derived from its beauty alone.

**AN ALLEGORICAL LOVE SCENE** *Venus, Cupid, Folly, and Time,* also called *The Exposure of Luxury* (FIG. **22-44**), by Agnolo di

Cosimo, called BRONZINO (1503–1572), also manifests all the points made thus far about Mannerist composition. A pupil of Pontormo, Bronzino was a Florentine and painter to Cosimo I, first grand duke of Tuscany. In this painting, he demonstrated the Mannerist's fondness for extremely learned and intricate allegories that often had lascivious undertones, a shift from the simple and monumental statements and forms of the High Renaissance. Bronzino depicted Cupid fondling his mother Venus, while Folly prepares to shower them with rose petals. Time, who appears in the upper right corner, draws back the curtain to reveal the playful incest in progress. Other figures in the painting represent Envy and Inconstancy. The masks, a favorite device of the Mannerists, symbolize deceit. The picture seems to suggest that love—accompanied by envy and plagued by inconstancy—is foolish and that lovers will discover its folly in time. But, as in many Mannerist paintings, the meaning here is ambiguous, and interpretations of this image vary. Compositionally, Bronzino placed the figures around the front plane, and they almost entirely block the space.

**22-44** BRONZINO, *Venus, Cupid, Folly, and Time (The Exposure of Luxury),* ca. 1546. Oil on wood, approx. 5′ 1″ × 4′ 8$\frac{3}{4}$″. National Gallery, London.

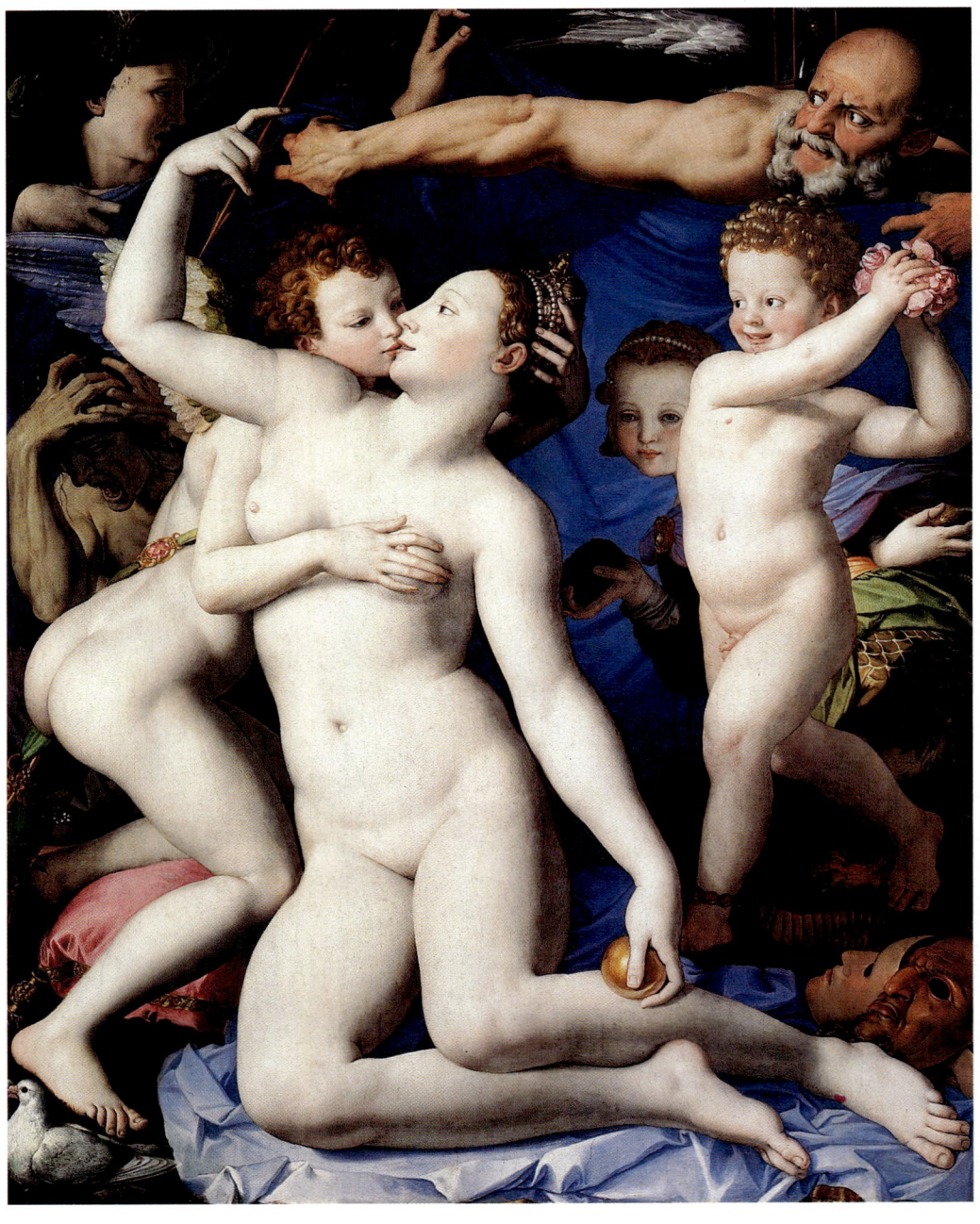

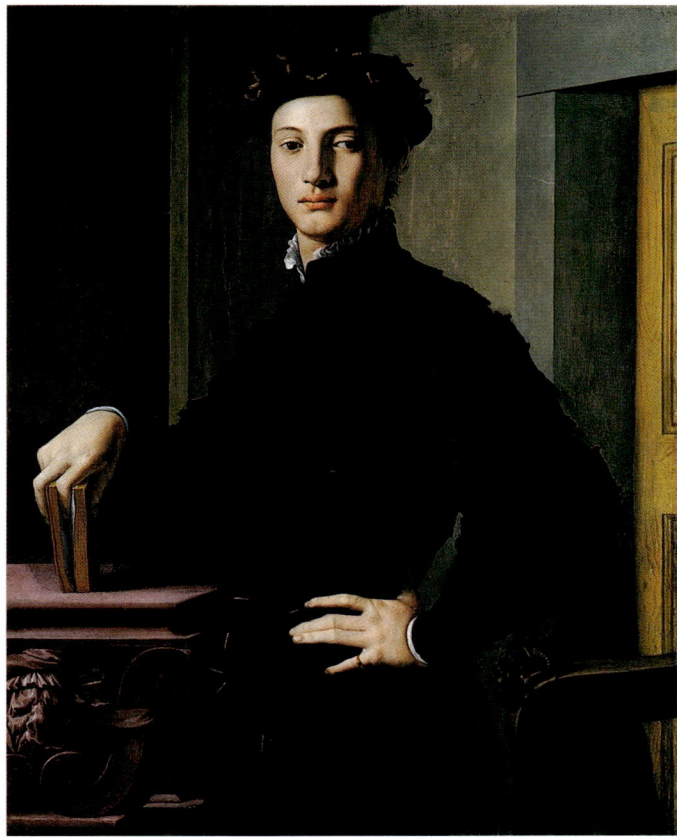

**22-45** BRONZINO, *Portrait of a Young Man*, ca. 1530s. Oil on wood, approx. 3′ 1½″ × 2′ 5½″. Metropolitan Museum of Art, New York (H. O. Havemeyer Collection, bequest of Mrs. H. O. Havemeyer, 1929).

The contours are strong and sculptural, the surfaces of enamel smoothness. Of special interest are the heads, hands, and feet, for the Mannerists considered the extremities the carriers of grace, and the clever depiction of them as evidence of artistic skill.

**A MANNERED PORTRAIT** Mannerist painters most often achieved in portraiture the sophisticated elegance they sought. Bronzino's *Portrait of a Young Man* (FIG. **22-45**) exemplifies Mannerist portraiture. The subject is a proud youth—a man of books and intellectual society, rather than a merchant or lowly laborer. His cool demeanor seems carefully affected, a calculated attitude of nonchalance toward the observing world. This staid and reserved formality is a standard component of Mannerist portraits. It asserts the rank and station but not the personality of the subject. In this portrait, the haughty poise, the graceful long-fingered hands, the book, the carved faces of the furniture, and the severe architecture all suggest the traits and environment of the highbred, disdainful patrician. The somber Spanish black of the young man's doublet and cap (this is the century of Spanish etiquette) and the room's slightly acid olive green walls make for a deeply restrained color scheme. Bronzino created a muted background for the subject's sharply defined, asymmetrical silhouette that contradicts his impassive pose.

**PORTRAYING FAMILIAL INTIMACY** The aloof formality of Bronzino's portrait is much relaxed in the portraiture of SOFONISBA ANGUISSOLA (1527–1625). A northern Italian from Cremona, Anguissola introduced, in a group portrait of irresistible charm (FIG. **22-46**), an informal intimacy. Like many of the other works she did before moving to Spain in 1559, this is a portrait of family members. Against a neutral ground, she placed her two sisters and brother in an affectionate pose meant not for official

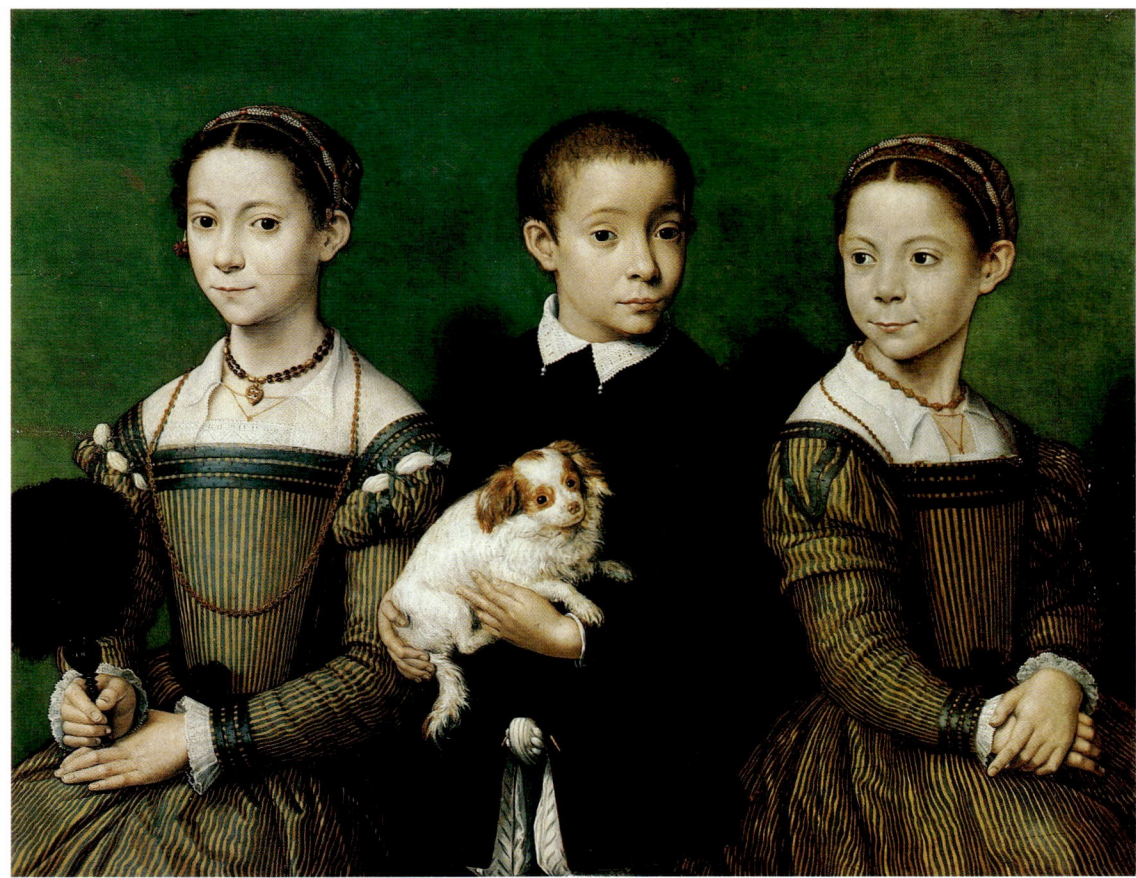

**22-46** SOFONISBA ANGUISSOLA, *Portrait of the Artist's Sisters and Brother*, ca. 1555. Oil on panel, 2′5¼″ × 3′1½″. Methuen Collection, Corsham Court, Wiltshire.

display but for private showing, much as they might be posed in a modern photo-studio portrait. The sisters, wearing matching striped gowns, flank their brother, who caresses a lapdog. The older sister (at the left) summons the dignity required for the occasion, while the boy looks quizzically at the portraitist with an expression of naive curiosity and the other girl diverts her attention toward something or someone to the painter's left.

Anguissola's use of relaxed poses and expressions; her sympathetic, personal presentation; and her graceful treatment of the forms did not escape the attention of her contemporaries, who praised her highly. Her recognized talents allowed her to consort with esteemed individuals. She knew and learned from the aged Michelangelo, was court painter to Phillip II of Spain, and, at the end of her life, gave advice on art to a young admirer of her work, Anthony Van Dyck, the great Flemish master.

## Mannerist Sculpture

DIANA AND DEER Mannerism extended beyond pictorial media; artists translated its principles into sculpture and architecture as well. BENVENUTO CELLINI (1500–1571) was among those who made their mark as Mannerist sculptors. To judge by his fascinating autobiography, Cellini had an impressive proficiency as an artist, statesman, soldier, and lover, among many other roles. He was, first of all, a goldsmith. Michelangelo's influence led Cellini to attempt larger works, and, in the service of Francis I, he cast in bronze *Genius of Fontainebleau* (FIG. **22-47**), which sums up Italian and French Mannerism. The female Genius, or spirit, is a composite of both Diana, the Greco-Roman goddess of the hunt, and a classical personification of a spring. As such, she embraces Diana's animal,

the deer, and leans on an urn that spews forth water (compare FIG. 11-19). Her figure suggests the reclining figures in the Medici Chapel tombs (FIG. 22-22) and the female nudes, both Venuses and courtesans, that only recently had become popular subjects for Renaissance paintings (FIG. 22-38), but Cellini gracefully exaggerated their characteristics as the Mannerist's design sense dictated. The head is remarkably small, the torso stretched out, and the limbs elegantly elongated. The contrapposto is more apparent than real, for the upper body does not compensate appropriately for the position shift of the lower body.

SPIRALING FIGURES Italian influence, working its way into Northern Europe, drew a brilliant young Netherlandish sculptor, Jean de Boulogne, to Italy, where he practiced his art under the equivalent Italian name of GIOVANNI DA BOLOGNA (1529–1608). Giovanni's *Abduction of the Sabine Women* (FIG. **22-48**) exemplifies Mannerist principles of figure composition.

Drawn from the legendary history of early Rome, the title—relating how the Romans abducted wives for themselves from their neighbors the Sabines—was given to the group only after it was raised. Giovanni probably intended to present only an interesting figural composition involving an old man, a young man, and a woman, all nude in the tradition of ancient statues portraying mythological figures. Although Giovanni would have known Antonio Pollaiuolo's 15th-century work *Hercules and Antaeus* (see FIG. 21-25), whose Greek hero lifts his opponent off the ground, he turned directly to classical sculpture for inspiration. *Abduction of the Sabine Women* includes references to the Laocoön (see FIG. 5-89)—once in the crouching old man and again in the woman's up-flung arm. The three bodies interlock on a vertical axis, creating an ascending spiral movement.

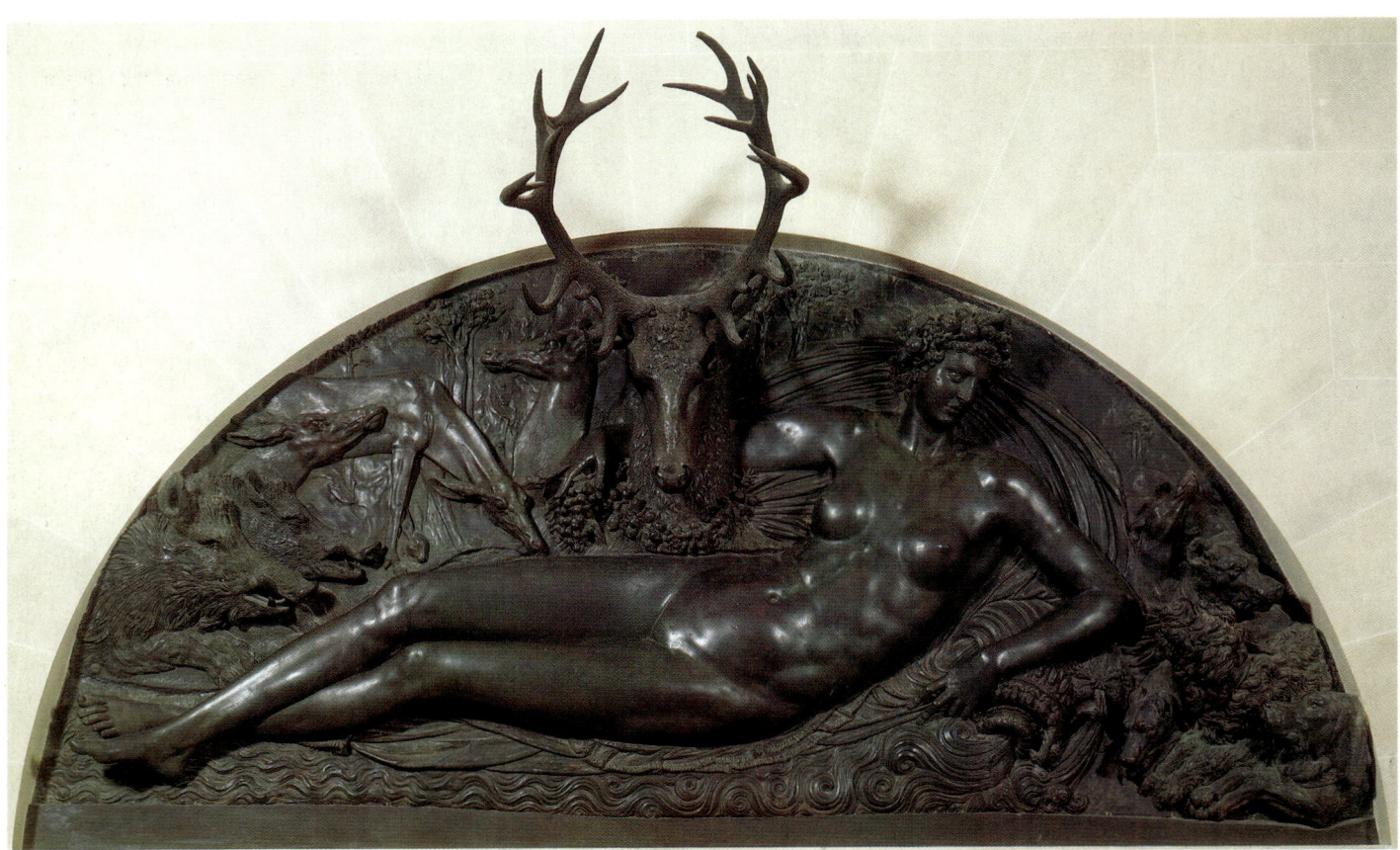

**22-47** BENVENUTO CELLINI, *Genius of Fontainebleau*, 1543–1544. Bronze, 6′ 8¾″ × 13′ 5″. Louvre, Paris.

To fully appreciate the sculpture, the viewer must walk around it, because the work changes radically according to the viewing point. One contributing factor to the shifting imagery is the prominence of open spaces that pass through the masses (for example, the space between an arm and a body), which have as great an effect as the solids. This sculpture was the first large-scale group since classical antiquity designed to be seen from multiple viewpoints, in striking contrast to Pollaiuolo's group, which the artist intended to be seen from the angle shown in our illustration (see FIG. 21-25). Giovanni's figures do not break out of this spiral vortex but remain as if contained within a cylinder. Yet the Michelangelesque potential for action and the athletic flexibility of the figures are there.

## Mannerist Architecture

**A MANNERIST MANTUAN MANSION**  Mannerism in painting and sculpture has been studied fairly extensively since the early decades of the 20th century, but only in the 1930s did scholars discover that the term also described much of 16th-century architecture. The body of Mannerist architecture they have compiled since then, however, is far from homogeneous. That Michelangelo used classical architectural elements in a highly personal and unorthodox manner does not necessarily make him a Mannerist architect. In his designs for Saint Peter's, he certainly strove for the effects of mass, balance, order, and stability that were the very hallmarks of High Renaissance design. Other architects, however, utilized classical elements in an unorthodox fashion with the specific aim of revealing the contrived nature of architectural design. Such was the goal of GIULIO ROMANO (ca. 1492–1546) when he created the Palazzo del Tè in Mantua (FIG. **22-49**) and, with it, formulated almost the entire architectural vocabulary of Mannerism.

Giulio Romano became Raphael's chief assistant in decorating the Vatican stanze. After Raphael's premature death in 1520, Giulio became his master's artistic executor, completing Raphael's unfinished frescoes and panel paintings. In 1524, Giulio went to Mantua, where he found a patron in Duke Federigo Gonzaga, for whom he built and decorated the Palazzo del Tè between 1525 and 1535.

Gonzaga intended the Palazzo del Tè to serve as both suburban summer palace and stud farm for his famous stables.

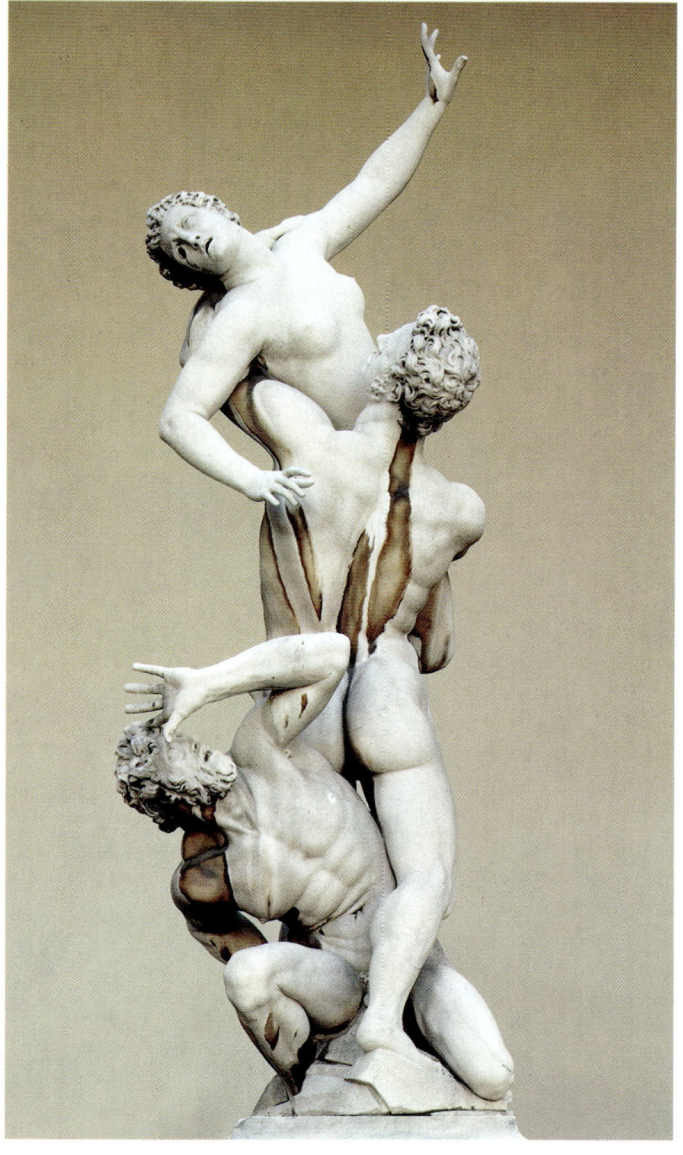

**22-48** GIOVANNI DA BOLOGNA, *Abduction of the Sabine Women*, Loggia dei Lanzi, Piazza della Signoria, Florence, Italy, completed 1583. Marble, approx. 13′ 6″ high.

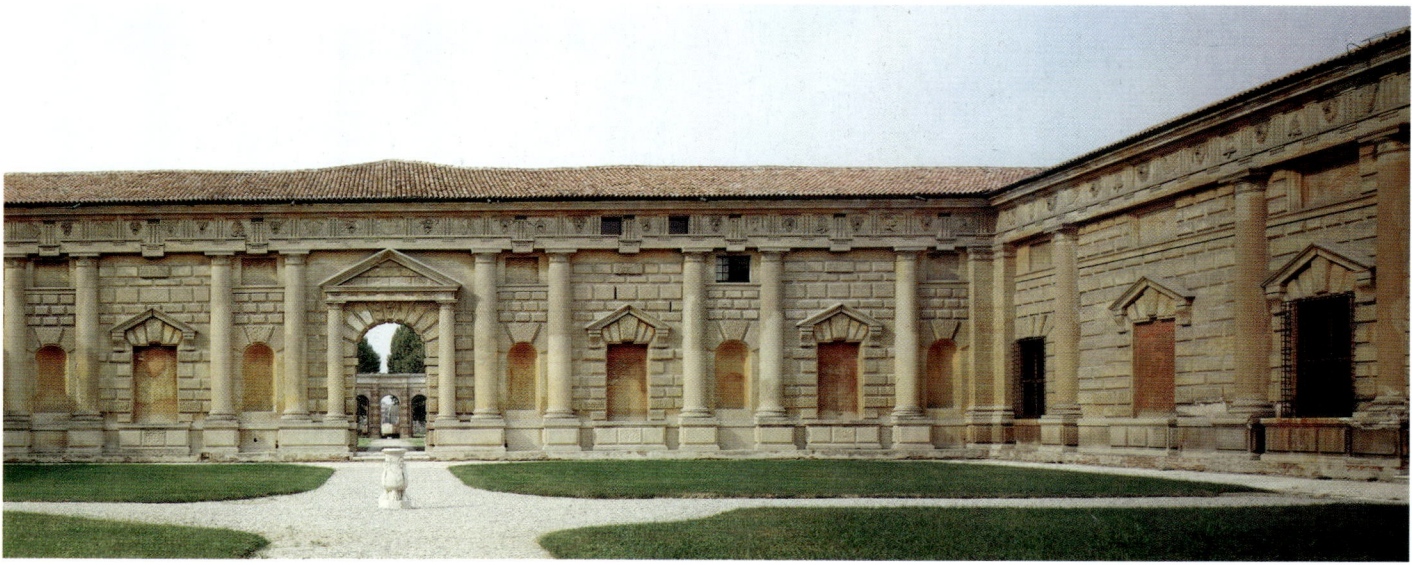

**22-49** GIULIO ROMANO, interior courtyard facade of the Palazzo del Tè, Mantua, Italy, 1525–1535.

Originally planned as a relatively modest country villa, Giulio's building so pleased the duke that he soon commissioned the architect to enlarge the structure. In a second building campaign, Giulio expanded the villa to a palatial scale by adding three wings, which he placed around a square central court. This once-paved court, which functions both as a passage and as the focal point of the design, has a nearly urban character. Its surrounding buildings form a self-enclosed unit with a large garden, flanked by a stable, attached to it on the east side.

Giulio exhibited his Mannerist style in the facades that face the palace's interior courtyard (FIG. 22-49), where the divergences from architectural convention are so pronounced that they constitute an enormous parody of Bramante's classical style, thereby announcing the artifice of the palace design. In a building laden with structural surprises and contradictions, the design of these facades is the most unconventional of all. The keystones (central voussoirs), for example, either have not fully settled or seem to be slipping from the arches—and, more eccentric still, Giulio even placed voussoirs in the pediments over the rectangular niches, where no arches exist. The massive Tuscan columns that flank these niches carry incongruously narrow architraves. That these architraves break midway between the columns stresses their apparent structural insufficiency, and they seem unable to support the weight of the triglyphs above, which threaten to crash down on the head of anyone foolish enough to stand below them. To be sure, appreciating Giulio's witticism requires a highly sophisticated audience, and recognizing some quite subtle departures from the norm presupposes a thorough familiarity with the established rules of classical architecture. It speaks well for the duke's sophistication that he accepted Giulio's form of architectural inventiveness.

In short, in his design for the Palazzo del Tè, Giulio Romano deliberately flouted most of the classical rules of order, stability, and symmetry. The resulting ambiguities and tensions are as typical of Mannerist architecture as they are of Mannerist painting, and many of the devices Giulio invented for the Palazzo del Tè became standard features in the formal repertoire of later Mannerist buildings.

# LATER 16TH-CENTURY ARCHITECTURE

Acceptance of Mannerist style in architecture was by no means universal among either architects or patrons. Indeed, later 16th-century designs more in keeping with High Renaissance ideals proved to have a greater impact on 17th-century architecture in Italy than the more adventurous, yet eccentric, works by Giulio Romano and the other Mannerists.

**ANTICIPATING THE BAROQUE** Probably the most influential building of the second half of the 16th century was the mother church of the Jesuit order. The activity of the Society of Jesus, known as the Jesuits, was an important component of the Counter-Reformation (see page 634). Ignatius of Loyola (1491–1556), a Spanish nobleman who dedicated his life to the service of God, founded the Jesuit order. He attracted a group of followers, and in 1540 Pope Paul III formally recognized this group as a religious order. The Jesuits were the papacy's invaluable allies in its quest to reassert the supremacy of the Catholic Church. Particularly successful in the field of education, the order established numerous schools. Its commitment to education remains evident today in the many Jesuit colleges around the world. In addition, its members were effective missionaries and carried the message of Catholicism to the Americas, Asia, and Africa. The predominance of Catholicism in Latin America, the Philippines, and areas of Africa testifies to the Jesuit influence (as well as that of other Catholic orders, such as the Dominicans and the Franciscans).

As a major participant in the Counter-Reformation, the Jesuit order needed a church appropriate to its new prominence. Because Michelangelo was late in providing the plans for this church, called Il Gesù, or Church of Jesus (FIGS. 22-50 and 22-51), the Jesuits turned to GIACOMO DA VIGNOLA (1507–1573), who designed the ground plan, and Giacomo della Porta, who was responsible for the facade. These two architects designed and built Il Gesù between 1568 and 1584. Chronologically and stylistically,

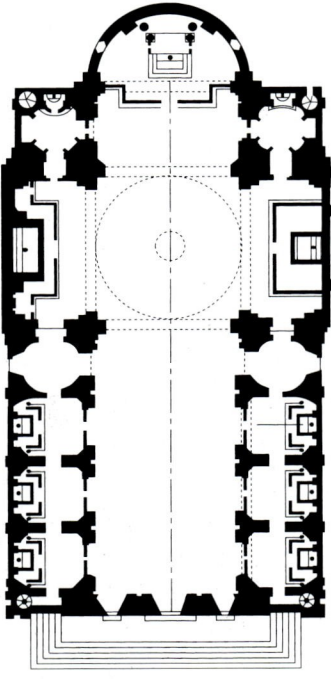

22-50 GIACOMO DELLA PORTA, facade of Il Gesù, Rome, Italy, ca. 1575–1584.

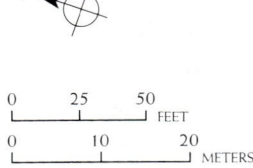

22-51 GIACOMO DA VIGNOLA, plan of Il Gesù, Rome, Italy, 1568.

the building belongs to the late Renaissance, but its enormous influence on later churches marks it as one of the significant monuments for the development of Baroque church architecture. Its facade (FIG. 22-50) was an important model and point of departure for the facades of Roman Baroque churches for two centuries. The facade's design was not entirely original. The union of the lower and upper stories, effected by scroll buttresses, harks back to Alberti's Santa Maria Novella in Florence (see FIG. 21-34). Its classical pediment is familiar in Alberti's work, as well as in the work of the Venetian architect Andrea Palladio, which is examined later. And its paired pilasters appear in Michelangelo's design for Saint Peter's (FIG. 22-30). Giacomo della Porta skillfully synthesized these already existing motifs. In his facade design, he unified the two stories. The horizontal march of the pilasters and columns builds to a dramatic climax at the central bay, and the bays of the facade snugly fit the nave-chapel system behind them. Many of the dramatic Roman Baroque facades of the 17th century were architectural variations on this facade.

The plan of Il Gesù (FIG. 22-51) reveals a monumental expansion of Alberti's scheme for Sant'Andrea in Mantua (see FIG. 21-42). Here, the nave takes over the main volume of space, making the structure a great hall with side chapels. A dome emphasizes the approach to the altar. The wide acceptance of the Gesù plan in the Catholic world, even until modern times, speaks to its ritual efficacy. The opening of the church building into a single great hall provides an almost theatrical setting for large promenades and processions (which seemed to combine social with priestly functions). Above all, the space is adequate to accommodate the great crowds that gathered to hear the eloquent preaching of the Jesuits.

# LATER 16TH-CENTURY VENETIAN ART AND ARCHITECTURE

**MANNERIST DRAMA AND DYNAMISM** Venetian painting of the later 16th century built on established Venetian ideas. Jacopo Robusti, known as TINTORETTO (1518–1594), claimed to be a student of Titian and aspired to combine Titian's color with Michelangelo's drawing. Art historians often refer to Tintoretto as the outstanding Venetian representative of Mannerism. He adopted many Mannerist pictorial devices, which he employed to produce works imbued with dramatic power, depth of spiritual vision, and glowing Venetian color schemes.

**A VISIONARY LAST SUPPER** Toward the end of Tintoretto's life, his art became spiritual, even visionary, as solid forms melted away into swirling clouds of dark shot through with fitful light. In Tintoretto's *Last Supper* (FIG. **22-52**), painted for the interior of Andrea Palladio's church of San Giorgio Maggiore (FIG. 22-59), the figures appear in a dark interior illuminated by a single light in the upper left of the image. The shimmering halos clue viewers to the biblical nature of the scene. The ability of this dramatic scene to engage viewers was well in keeping with Counter-Reformation ideals (see "The Role of Religious Art in Counter-Reformation Italy," page 636) and the Catholic Church's belief in the didactic nature of religious art.

*Last Supper* incorporates many Mannerist devices, including an imbalanced composition and visual complexity. In terms of design, the contrast with Leonardo's *Last Supper* (FIG. 22-3) is both extreme and instructive. Leonardo's composition, balanced

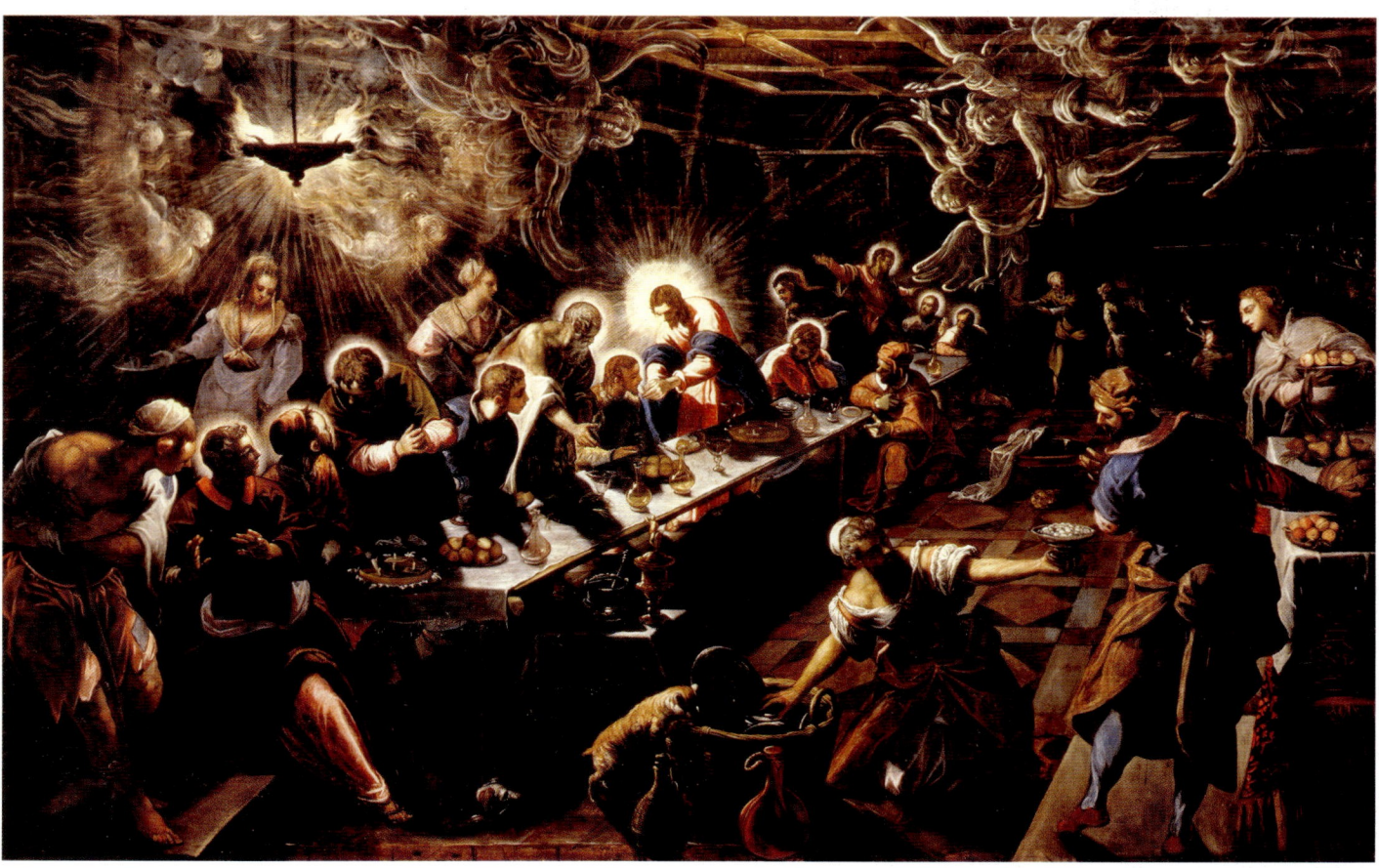

**22-52** TINTORETTO, *Last Supper,* Chancel, San Giorgio Maggiore, Venice, Italy, 1594. Oil on canvas, 12′ × 18′ 8″.

and symmetrical, parallels the picture plane in a geometrically organized and closed space. The figure of Christ is the tranquil center of the drama and the perspectival focus. In Tintoretto's painting, Christ is above and beyond the converging perspective lines that race diagonally away from the picture surface, creating disturbing effects of limitless depth and motion. The viewer locates Tintoretto's Christ via the light flaring, beaconlike, out of darkness. The contrast of the two reflects the direction Renaissance painting took in the 16th century, as it moved away from architectonic clarity of space and neutral lighting toward the dynamic perspectives and dramatic chiaroscuro of the coming Baroque.

**A PROBLEMATIC PAINTING OF CHRIST** Among the great Venetian masters was Paolo Cagliari of Verona, called PAOLO VERONESE (1528–1588). Whereas Tintoretto gloried in monumental drama and deep perspectives, Veronese specialized in splendid pageantry painted in superb color and set within majestic classical architecture. Like Tintoretto, Veronese painted on a huge scale, with canvases often as large as 20 × 30 feet or more. His usual subjects, painted for the refectories of wealthy monasteries, afforded him an opportunity to display magnificent companies at table.

*Christ in the House of Levi* (FIG. **22-53**), originally called *Last Supper,* is a good example. Here, in a great open loggia framed by three monumental arches (the architectural style closely resembles the upper arcades of Jacopo Sansovino's State Library, FIG. 22-55), Christ sits at the center of the splendidly garbed elite of Venice. In the foreground, with a courtly gesture, the very image of gracious grandeur, the chief steward welcomes guests. Robed lords, their colorful retainers, clowns, dogs, and dwarfs crowd into the spacious loggia.

Painted during the Counter-Reformation, this depiction prompted criticism from the Catholic Church. The Holy Office of the Inquisition accused Veronese of impiety for painting such creatures so close to the Lord, and it ordered him to make changes at his own expense. Reluctant to do so, he simply changed the painting's title, converting the subject to a less solemn one. As Andrea Palladio (whose work is discussed later) looked to the example of classically inspired High Renaissance architecture, so Veronese returned to High Renaissance composition, its symmetrical balance, and its ordered architectonics. His shimmering color is drawn from the whole spectrum, although he avoided solid colors for half shades (light blues, sea greens, lemon yellows, roses, and violets), creating veritable flower beds of tone.

**VENICE TRIUMPHANT** The Venetian Republic employed both Tintoretto and Veronese to decorate the grand chambers and council rooms of the Doge's Palace (see FIG. 18-56). A great and popular decorator, Veronese revealed himself a master of imposing illusionistic ceiling compositions, such as *Triumph of Venice* (FIG. **22-54**). Here, within an oval frame, he presented Venice, crowned by Fame, enthroned between two great twisted columns in a balustraded loggia, garlanded with clouds, and attended by figures symbolic of its glories. Unlike that of Mantegna or Correggio, Veronese's perspective is not projected directly up from below. Rather, it is a projection of the scene at a 45-degree angle to spectators, a technique many later Baroque decorators used, particularly the 18th-century Venetian Giambattista Tiepolo.

**MONEY AND MANUSCRIPTS** The Florentine Jacopo Tatti, called JACOPO SANSOVINO (1486–1570), introduced Venice to the High Renaissance style of architecture. Originally trained as a sculptor under Andrea Sansovino (ca. 1467–1529), whose name he adopted, Jacopo went to Rome in 1518, where, under the influence of Bramante's circle, he turned increasingly toward architecture. When he arrived in Venice as a refugee from the sack of Rome in 1527, he quickly established himself as that city's leading and most admired architect. His buildings frequently inspired the architectural settings of the most prominent Venetian painters, including Titian and Veronese.

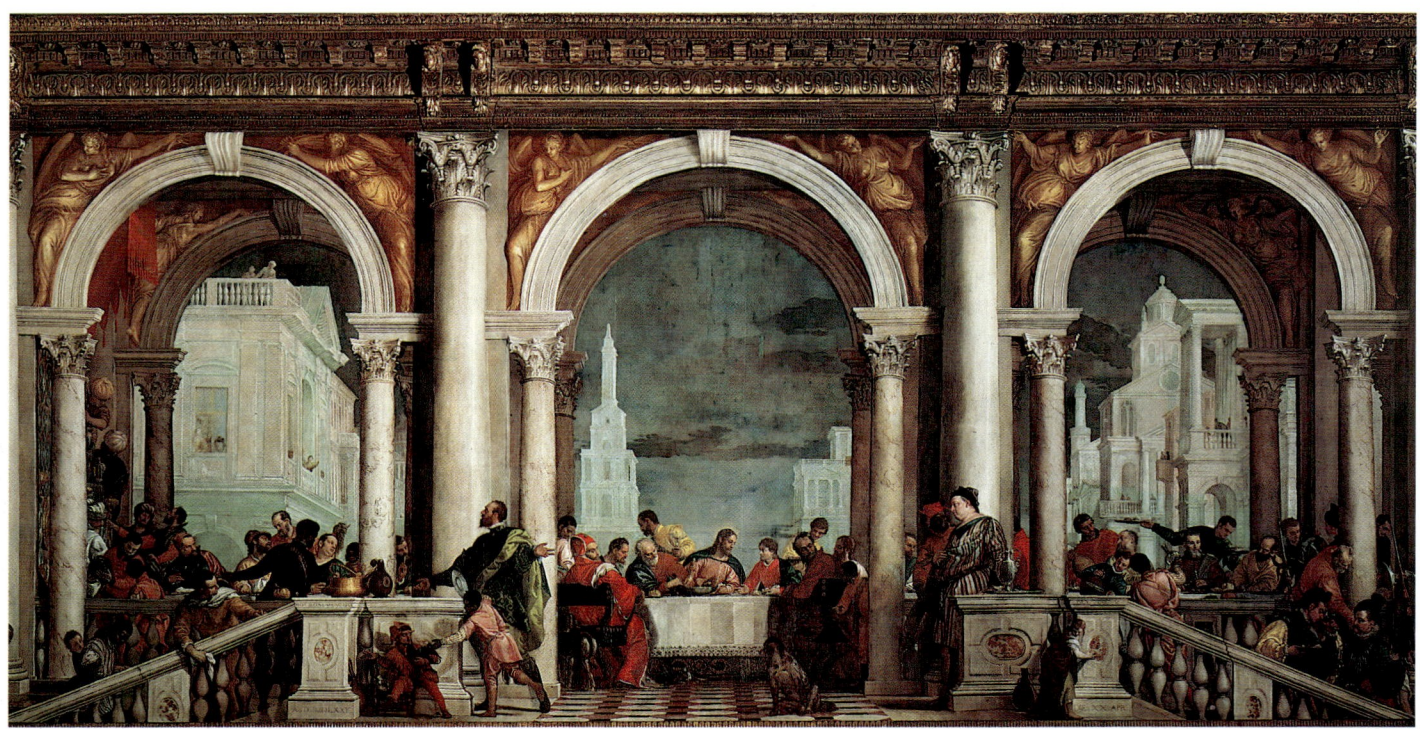

**22-53** PAOLO VERONESE, *Christ in the House of Levi,* 1573. Oil on canvas, approx. 18′ 6″ × 42′ 6″. Galleria dell'Accademia, Venice.

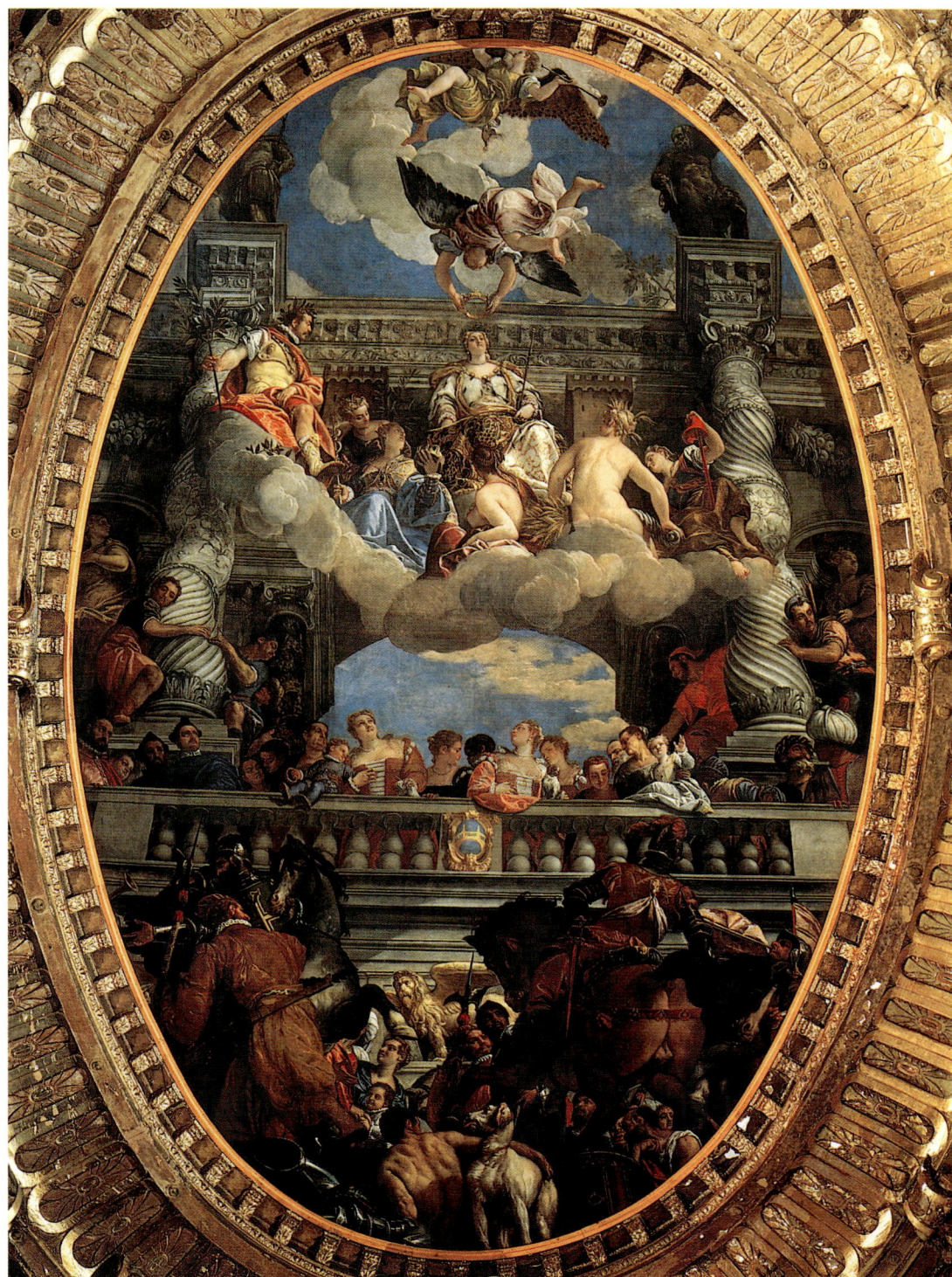

**22-54** Paolo Veronese, *Triumph of Venice*, ceiling of the Hall of the Grand Council, Palazzo Ducale, Venice, Italy, ca. 1585. Oil on canvas, approx. 29′ 8″ × 19′.

Sansovino's largest and most rewarding public commissions were the Mint (la Zecca) and the adjoining State Library (FIG. **22-55**) in the heart of the island city. The Mint, begun in 1535, faces the Canale San Marco with a stern and forbidding three-story facade. Its heavy rustication imbues it with an intended air of strength and impregnability. A boldly projecting, bracket-supported cornice, reminiscent of the machicolated galleries of medieval castles, emphasizes this fortresslike look.

Begun a year after the Mint, the neighboring State Library of San Marco, which Andrea Palladio referred to as "perhaps the most sumptuous and the most beautiful edifice that has been erected since the time of the Ancients,"[9] exudes a very different spirit. With 21 bays (only 16 were completed during Sansovino's lifetime), the library faces the Gothic Doge's Palace (see FIG. 18-56) across the Piazzetta, a lateral extension of Venice's central Piazza San Marco. The relatively plain ground-story arcade has Tuscan-style columns attached to the arch-supporting piers in the manner of the Roman Colosseum (see FIG. 10-34). A Doric frieze of metopes and triglyphs caps it—none "slide" out of place as in the frieze of the contemporary Palazzo del Tè in Mantua (FIG. 22-49). The lower story sturdily supports the higher, lighter, and much more decorative Ionic second story, which housed the reading room with its

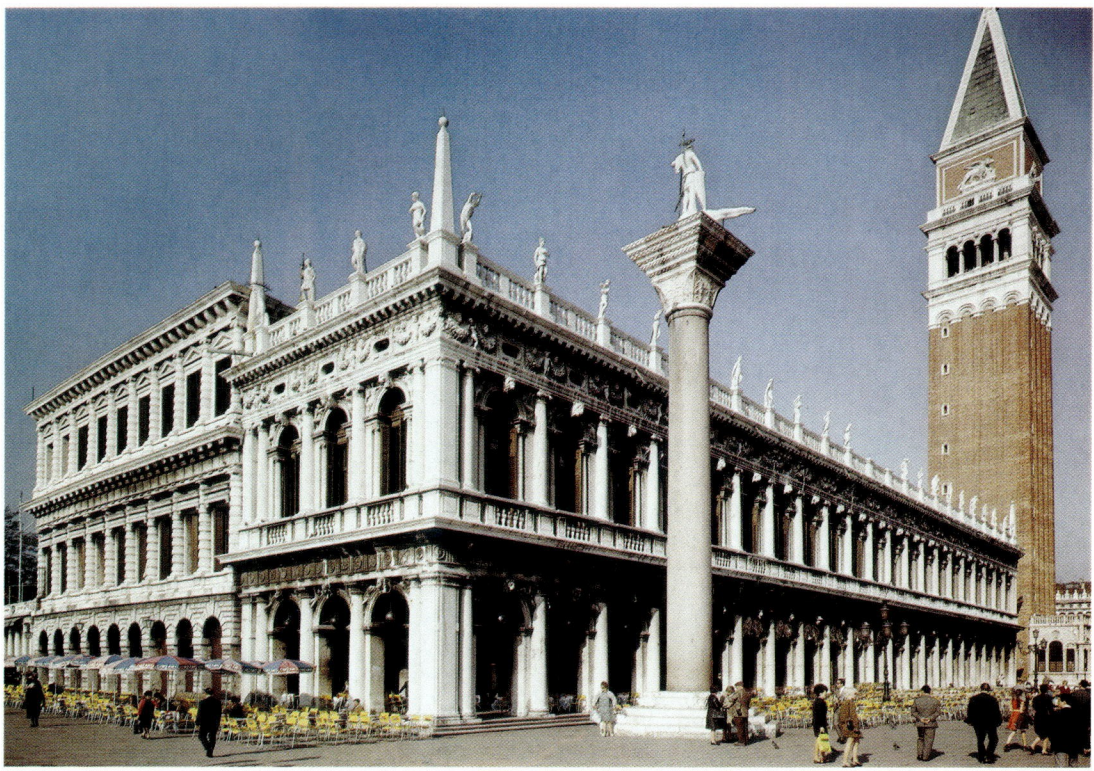

22-55 JACOPO SANSOVINO, the Mint (la Zecca), 1535–1545 (left), and the State Library, begun 1536 (right), Piazza San Marco, Venice.

treasure of manuscripts, keeping them safe from not-uncommon flooding. The main columns carry an entablature with a richly decorated frieze of putti, in strongly projecting relief, supporting garlands. The oval windows of an attic story punctuate this frieze, a favorite decorative motif of the ancient Romans. Perhaps the building's most striking feature is its roofline, where Sansovino replaced the traditional straight cornice with a balustrade (reminiscent of the one on Bramante's Tempietto, FIG. 22-8) interrupted by statue-bearing pedestals. The spacing of the latter corresponds to that of the orders below so that the sculptures are the sky-piercing finials of the building's vertical design elements. Sansovino's deft application of sculpture to the building's massive framework (with no visible walls) relieves the design's potential severity and gives its aspect an extraordinary sculptural richness.

One feature rarely mentioned is how subtly the library echoes the design of the lower two stories of the decorative Doge's Palace (see FIG. 18-56) opposite it. Although Sansovino used a vastly different architectural vocabulary, he managed admirably to adjust his building to the older one. Correspondences include the almost identical spacing of the lower arcades, the rich and ornamental treatment of the second stories (including their balustrades), and the dissolution of the rooflines (with decorative battlements in the palace and a statue-surmounted balustrade in the library). It is almost as if Sansovino set out to translate the Gothic architecture of the Doge's Palace into a "modern" Renaissance idiom. If so, he was eminently successful; the two buildings, although of different spiritual and stylistic worlds, mesh to make the Piazzetta one of the most elegantly framed urban units in Europe.

**INSPIRED BY THE ANCIENTS** After Jacopo Sansovino's death, ANDREA PALLADIO (1508–1580) succeeded him as chief architect of the Venetian Republic. Beginning as a stonemason and decorative sculptor, at age 30 Palladio turned to architecture, the ancient literature on architecture, engineering, topography, and military science. Unlike the universal scholar Alberti, Palladio

became more of a specialist. He made several trips to Rome to study the ancient buildings firsthand. He illustrated Daniele Barbaro's edition of *De architectura* by Vitruvius (1556), and he wrote his own treatise on architecture, *I quattro libri dell'architettura (The Four Books of Architecture),* originally published in 1570, which had a wide-ranging influence on succeeding generations of architects throughout Europe. Palladio's influence outside Italy, most significantly in England and in colonial America, was stronger and more lasting than that of any other architect.

Palladio accrued his significant reputation from his many designs for villas, built on the Venetian mainland. Nineteen still stand, and they especially influenced later architects. The same Arcadian spirit that prompted the ancient Romans to build villas in the countryside, and that the Venetian painter Giorgione expressed so eloquently in his art, motivated a similar villa-building boom in the 16th century. One can imagine that Venice, with its very limited space, must have been more congested than any ancient city. But a longing for the countryside was not the only motive; declining fortunes prompted the Venetians to develop their mainland possessions with new land investment and reclamation projects. Citizens who could afford it were encouraged to set themselves up as aristocratic farmers and to develop swamps into productive agricultural land. Wealthy families could look on their villas as providential investments. The villas were thus aristocratic farms (like the much later American plantations, which were influenced by Palladio's architecture) surrounded by service outbuildings. Palladio generally arranged the outbuildings in long, low wings branching out from the main building and enclosing a large rectangular court area.

Although it is the most famous, Villa Rotonda (FIG. **22-56**), near Vicenza, is not really typical of Palladio's villa style. He did not construct it for an aspiring gentleman farmer but for a retired monsignor who wanted a villa for social events. Palladio planned and designed Villa Rotonda, located on a hilltop, as a kind of belvedere (literally "beautiful view"; in architecture, a residence on a hill), without the usual wings of secondary buildings. Its

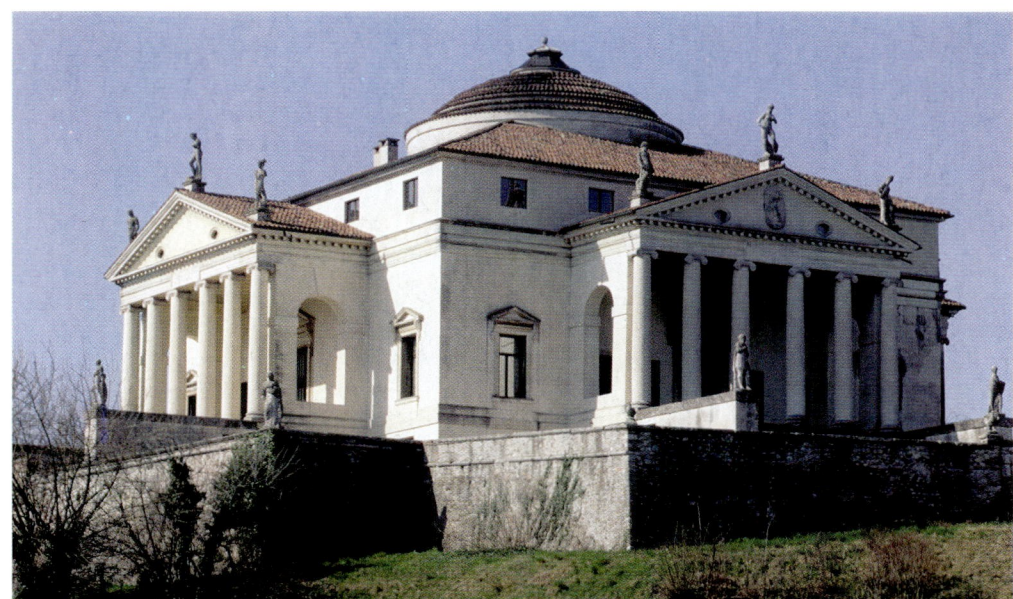

22-56 ANDREA PALLADIO, Villa Rotonda (formerly Villa Capra), near Vicenza, Italy, ca. 1566–1570.

central plan (FIG. 22-57), with four identical facades and projecting porches, is therefore both sensible and functional. Each of the porches can be used as a platform for enjoying a different view of the surrounding landscape. In this design, the central dome-covered rotunda logically functions as a kind of circular platform from which visitors may turn in any direction for the preferred view. The result is a building with functional parts systematically related to one another in terms of calculated mathematical relationships. Villa Rotonda embodies all the qualities of self-sufficiency and formal completeness sought by most Renaissance architects. The works of Alberti and Bramante and the remains of classical architecture Palladio studied in Rome influenced the young architect in his formative years. Each facade of his Villa Rotonda resembles a Roman temple. In placing a traditional temple porch in front of a dome-covered interior, Palladio doubtless had the Pantheon (see FIG. 10-48) in his mind as a model. By 1550, however, he had developed his personal style, which mixed elements of Mannerism with the clarity and lack of ambiguity that characterized classicism at its most "correct."

SHADOW AND SURFACE One of the most dramatically placed buildings in Venice is San Giorgio Maggiore (FIGS. 22-58

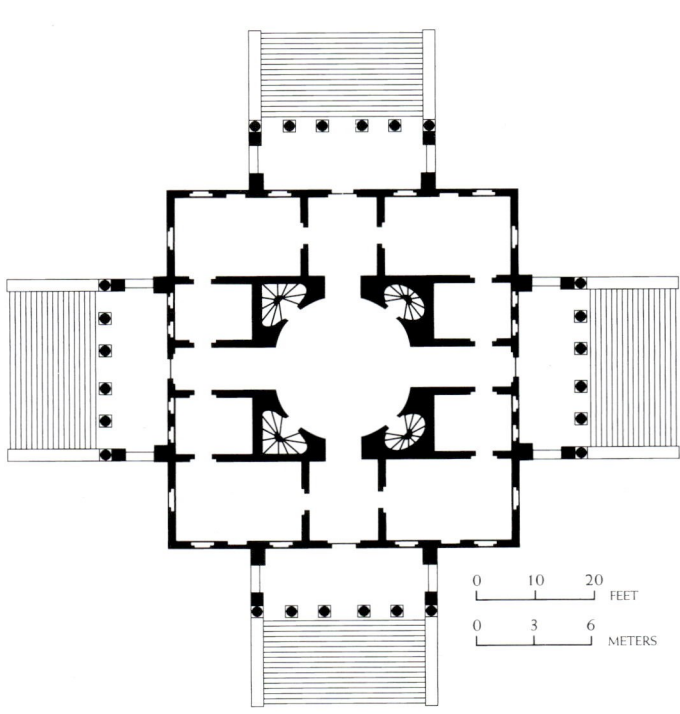

22-57 ANDREA PALLADIO, plan of the Villa Rotonda (formerly Villa Capra), near Vicenza, Italy, ca. 1566–1570.

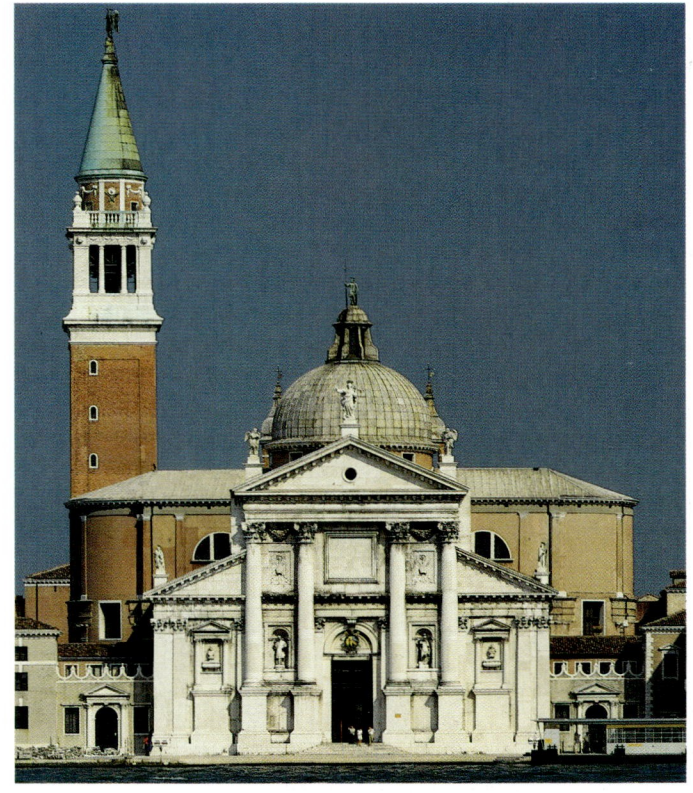

22-58 ANDREA PALLADIO, west facade of San Giorgio Maggiore, Venice, Italy, begun 1565.

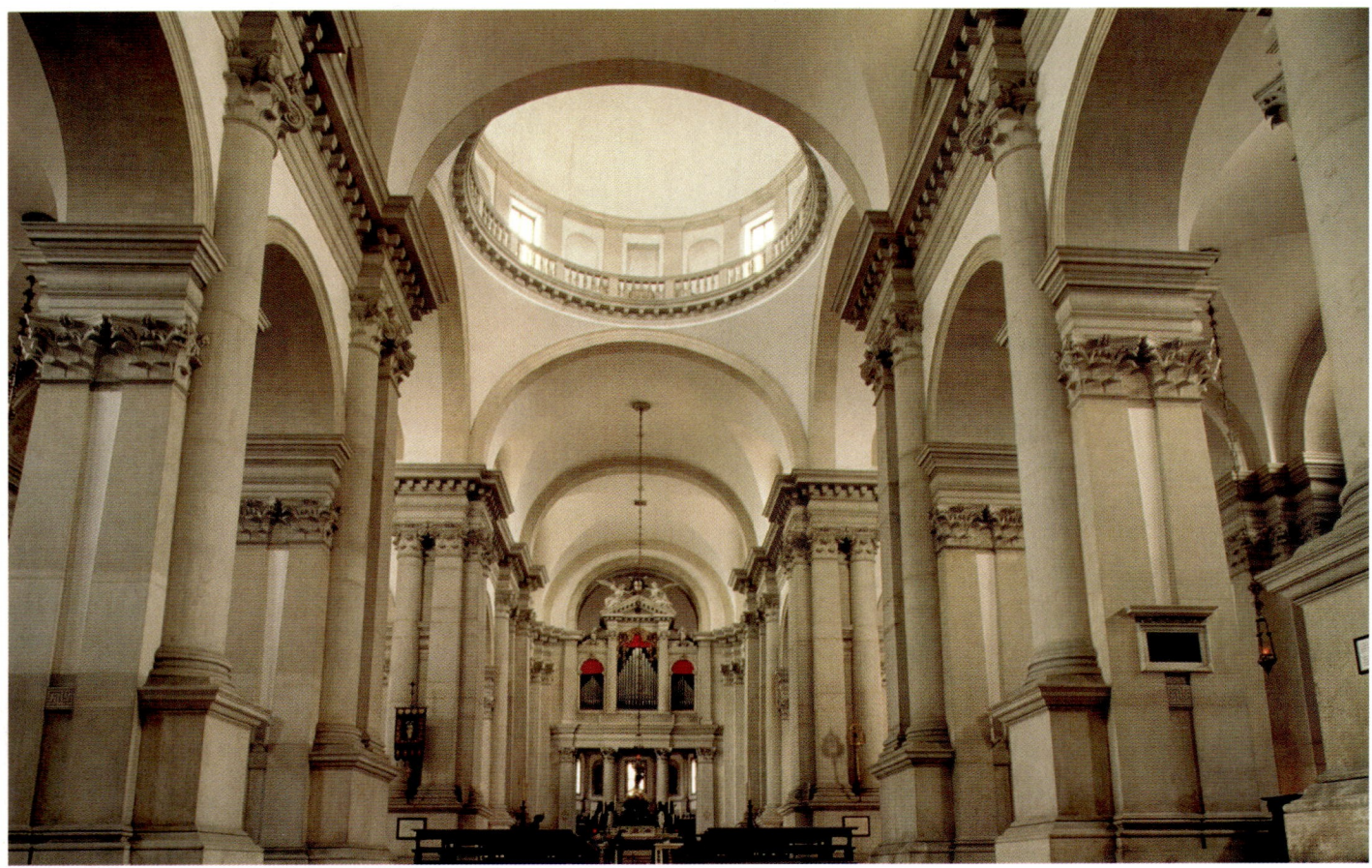

**22-59** ANDREA PALLADIO, interior of San Giorgio Maggiore, Venice, Italy, begun 1565.

and **22-59**), directly across a broad canal from the Piazza San Marco. Dissatisfied with earlier solutions to the problem of integrating a high central nave and lower aisles into a unified facade design, Palladio solved it by superimposing a tall, narrow classical porch on a low broad one (FIG. 22-58). This solution reflects the building's interior arrangement (FIG. 22-59) and in that sense is coolly logical, but the intersection of two temple facades is irrational and ambiguous in Mannerist fashion. Palladio's design also created the illusion of three-dimensional depth, an effect intensified by the strong projection of the central columns and the shadows they cast. The play of shadow across the building's surfaces, its reflection in the water, and its gleaming white against sea and sky create a remarkably colorful effect, prefiguring the Baroque. The interior of the church (FIG. 22-59) lacks the ambiguity of the facade, and exhibits strong roots in High Renaissance architectural style. Light floods the interior and crisply defines the contours of the rich wall decorations (pedestals, bases, shafts, capitals, and entablatures), all beautifully and "correctly" profiled—the exemplar of what classical architectural theory meant by "rational" organization.

## CONCLUSION

The 16th century in Italy is often referred to as the High Renaissance because artists developed further many of the ideas that occupied earlier painters, sculptors, and architects. Interest in classical cultures, which was cultivated by the humanists of earlier centuries, became a mainstay of High Renaissance art. Religious art seemed to have a particular urgency; in the interest of promoting Counter-Reformation ideals, the Catholic Church emphasized the didactic value of art in reestablishing the prominence of the Church. The 16th century also saw the development of Mannerism, which contrasted with the rationality pervading much of High Renaissance art and architecture and paved the way for the complexity of the Baroque in 17th-century Italy.

**HIGH RENAISSANCE**

- NICCOLÒ MACHIAVELLI (1469–1527), *The Prince,* 1532
- BALDASSARE CASTIGLIONE (1478–1529), *The Courtier,* 1528
- POPE ALEXANDER VI (BORGIA), R. 1492–1503

**1500**

- POPE JULIUS II (DELLA ROVERE), R. 1503–1513
- POPE LEO X (MEDICI), R. 1513–1521
- PROTESTANT REFORMATION BEGINS, 1517
- POPE CLEMENT VII (MEDICI), R. 1523–1534

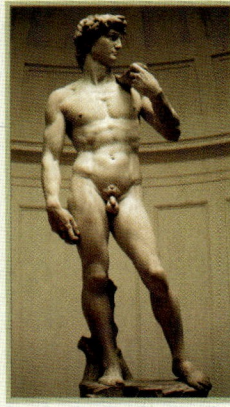

1 Michelangelo Buonarroti, *David,* 1501–1504

**1525**

- SACK OF ROME, 1527
- SOCIETY OF JESUS (THE JESUIT ORDER) ESTABLISHED, 1540
- GIORGIO VASARI (1511–1574), *Lives of the Most Eminent Painters, Sculptors and Architects,* 1550
- COUNCIL OF TRENT, 1545–1563

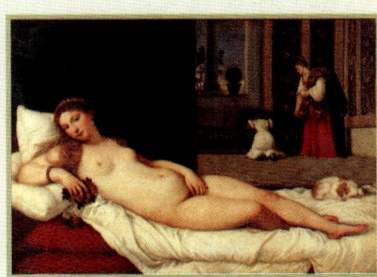

2 Titian, *Venus of Urbino,* 1538

**1550**

- POPE PIUS IV (MEDICI), R. 1559–1565
- FLORENCE BECOMES GRAND-DUCHY OF TUSCANY, 1569
- POPE GREGORY XIII (BUONCOMPAGNI), R. 1572–1585

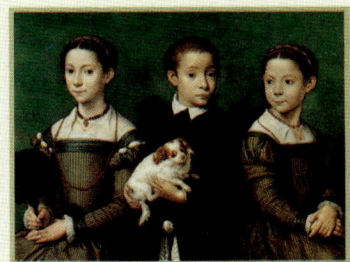

3 Sofonisba Anguissola, *Portrait of the Artist's Sisters and Brother,* ca. 1555

**1575**

- POPE SIXTUS V (PERETTI), R. 1585–1590

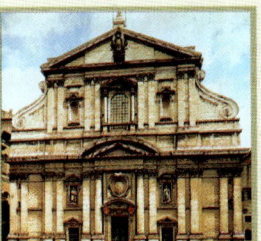

4 Giacomo della Porta, facade of Il Gesù, ca. 1575–1584

**1600**

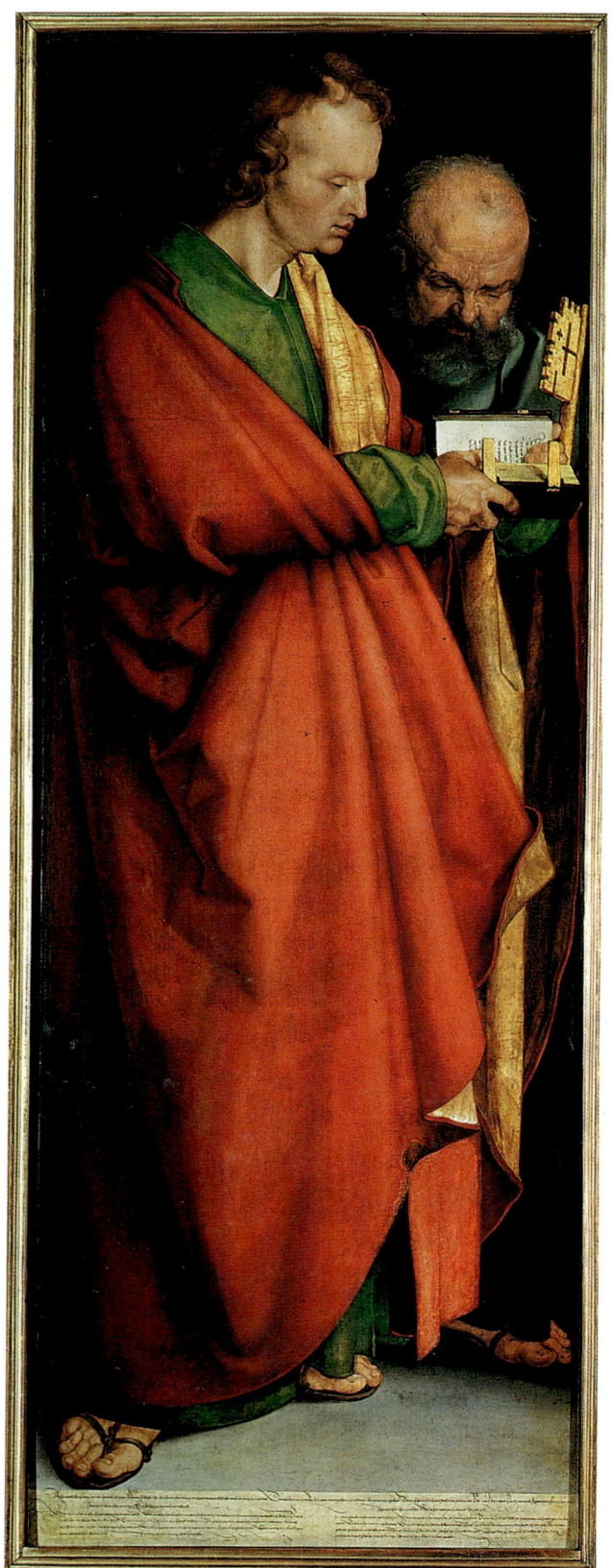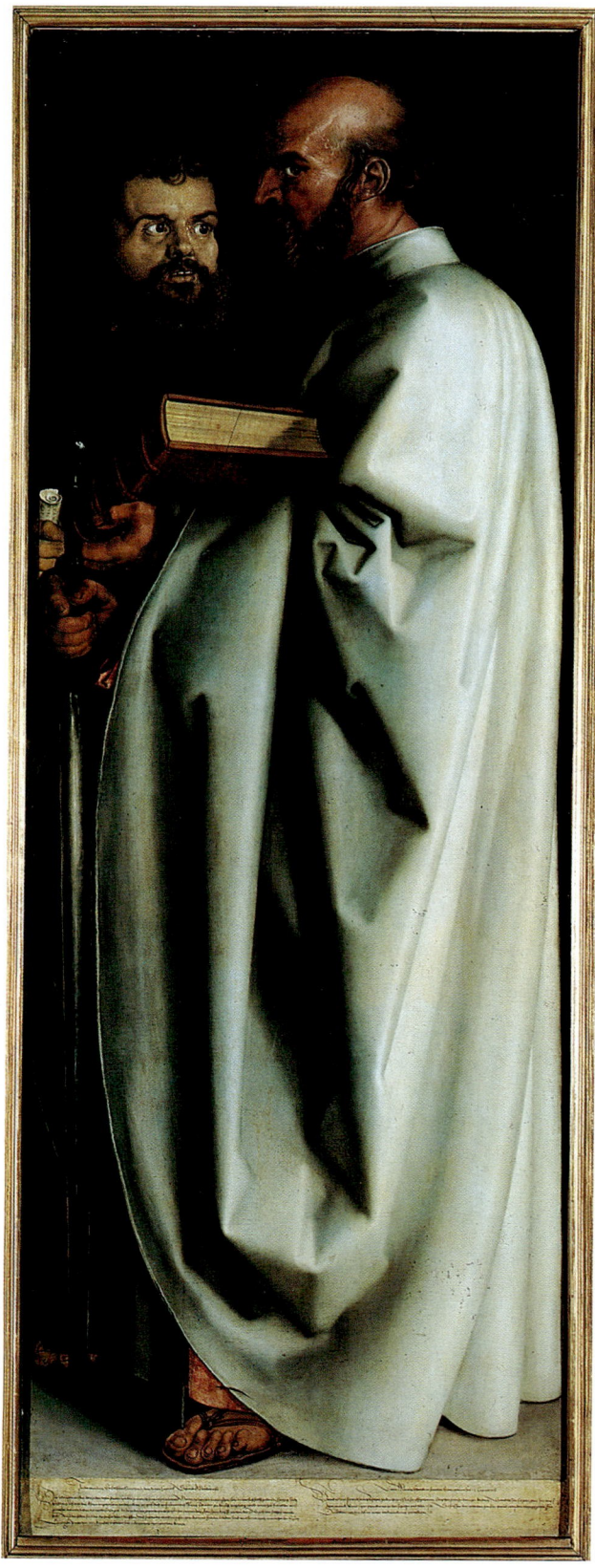

ALBRECHT DÜRER, *Four Apostles,* 1526. Oil on panel, each panel 7′ 1″ × 2′ 6″. Alte Pinakothek, Munich.

# 23

# THE AGE OF REFORMATION

## 16TH-CENTURY ART IN NORTHERN EUROPE AND SPAIN

The dissolution of the Burgundian Netherlands in 1477 led to a realignment in the European geopolitical landscape (MAP **23-1**) in the early 16th century. France and the Holy Roman Empire (at the time consisting primarily of today's Germany) expanded their territories after this breakup of Flanders. Through calculated marriages, military exploits, and ambitious territorial expansion, Spain became the dominant power in Europe by the end of the 16th century. Monarchs increased their authority over their subjects and cultivated a stronger sense of cultural and political unity among the populace, thereby laying the foundation for the modern state or nation. Yet a momentous crisis in the Christian Church overshadowed these power shifts. As noted earlier (see Chapter 22, page 634), concerted attempts to reform the Church led to the Reformation and the establishment of Protestantism (as distinct from Catholicism), which in turn prompted the Catholic Church's response, the Counter-Reformation. Ultimately, the Reformation split Christendom in half and produced a hundred years of civil war between Protestants and Catholics.

## THE PROTESTANT REFORMATION

### *Replacing Church Practices with Personal Faith*

The Reformation, which came to fruition in the early 16th century, had its roots in long-term, growing dissatisfaction with Church leadership. The deteriorating relationship between the faithful and the Church hierarchy stood as an obstacle for the millions who sought a meaningful religious experience. Particularly damaging was the perception that popes concerned themselves more with temporal power and material wealth than with the salvation of Church members. The fact that many 15th-century popes and cardinals came from wealthy families, such as the Medici (for example, Clement VII, or Giulio de' Medici, and Leo X, or Giovanni de' Medici), intensified this perception. It was not only those at the highest levels who seemed to ignore their

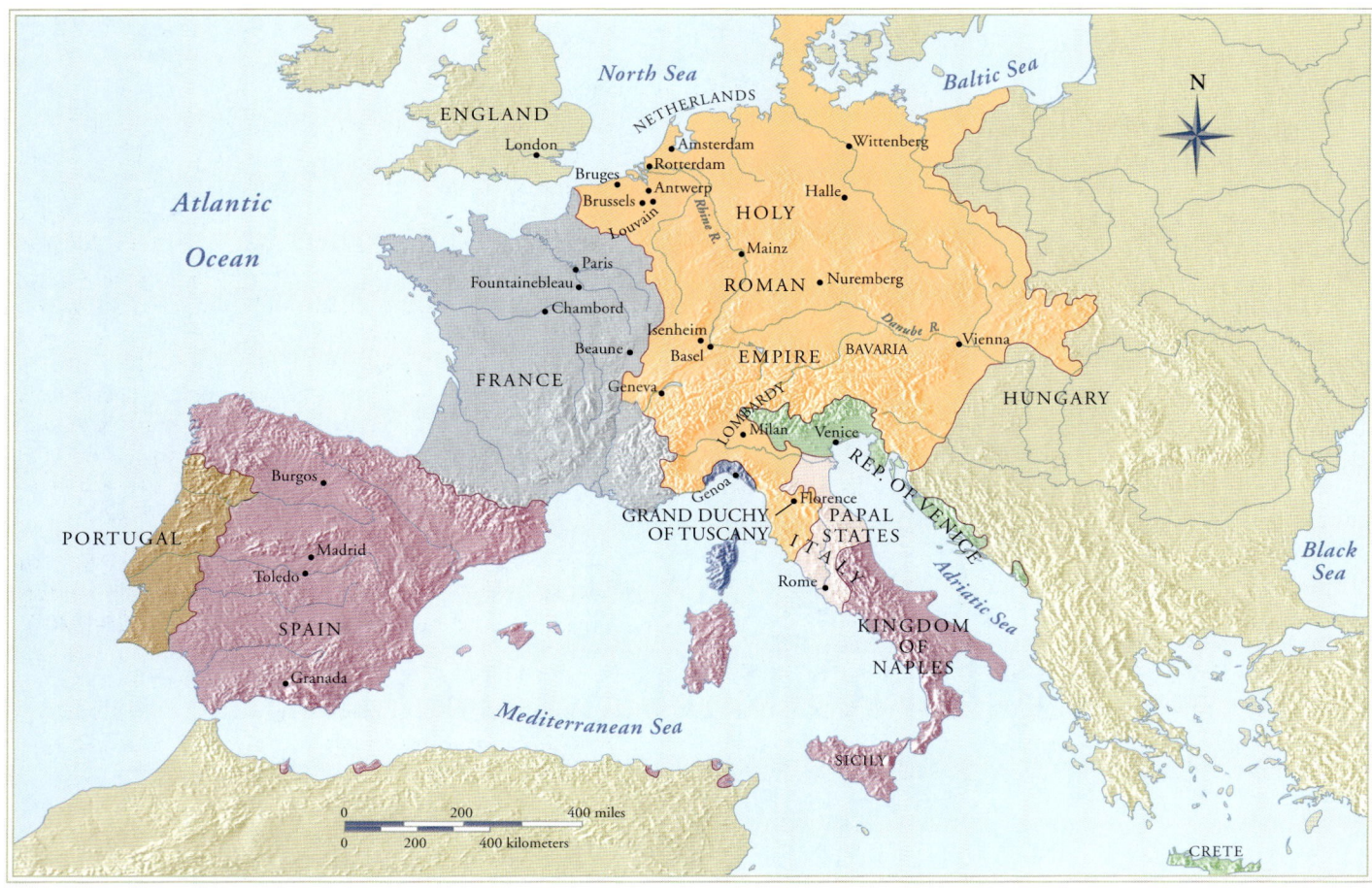

**MAP 23-1** Europe in the 16th century.

spiritual duties. Upper-level clergy (such as archbishops, bishops, and abbots) began to accumulate numerous offices, thereby increasing their revenues but also making it more difficult for them to fulfill all of their responsibilities.

As their relationship to the organized Church hierarchy deteriorated, people sought new ways to invigorate their spiritual commitment and to ensure their eventual salvation. In the 15th century, as seen in Chapter 20, these attempts included embarking on pilgrimages to holy sites, joining lay confraternities and orders, and commissioning artworks such as Books of Hours, rosaries, prints, and paintings as visual aids in private devotions.

### Ninety-five Theses and Lutheranism

By the early 16th century, dissatisfaction with the Church had grown so widespread that an outspoken challenge to papal authority by German theologian Martin Luther (1483–1546) was sufficient to spark the Reformation. In 1517, in Wittenberg, Luther posted for discussion his Ninety-five Theses, which enumerated his objections to Church practices, especially the sale of indulgences. Indulgences were remittances (or reductions) of time spent in Purgatory. The increasing frequency of their sale suggested that people were buying their way into Heaven.

Luther's goal was significant reform and clarification of major spiritual issues, but his ideas ultimately led to the splitting of Christendom. According to Luther, the Catholic Church's extensive ecclesiastical structure needed casting out, for it had no basis in Scripture. The Bible and nothing else could serve as the foundation for

Christianity. Luther declared the pope the Antichrist (for which the pope excommunicated him), called the Church the "whore of Babylon," and denounced ordained priests. He also rejected most of Catholicism's sacraments, decrying them as pagan obstacles to salvation; he did, however, accept two sacraments, baptism and Communion, the Lord's Supper. According to Luther, for Christianity to be restored to its original purity, the Church needed cleansing of all the impurities of doctrine that had collected through the ages.

### Achieving Salvation

Central to the reformers' creed was the question of salvation—how to achieve it. Rather than perceive salvation as something for which weak and sinful humans must constantly strive through good deeds performed under the watchful eye of a punitive God, Luther proposed that faithful individuals attain redemption by God's bestowal of his grace. Therefore, people cannot earn salvation. Further, no ecclesiastical machinery with all its miraculous rites and indulgent forgivenesses could save sinners face-to-face with God. Only absolute faith in Christ could justify sinners and ensure salvation. Justification by faith alone, with the guidance of Scripture, was the fundamental doctrine of Protestantism. Further, Luther advocated the Bible as the source of all religious truth. The Bible—the sole scriptural authority—was the word of God, not the Church's councils, law, and rituals. Luther facilitated the lay public's access to biblical truths by producing the first translation of the Bible in a vernacular language.

## The Uses of Allegory

Western artists have often employed allegory—the practice of imbuing narratives, images, or figures with symbolic meaning—to convey moral principles or philosophical ideas. For viewers to extract the connotations from allegorical images, the symbolic meanings of specific images have to be established as cultural convention. Among the numerous publications of Carel van Mander (1548–1606), a Netherlandish art historian and theoretician, is *Painter's Treatise* (1604), which contains a section with biographies of Netherlandish and German painters—the northern equivalent of Giorgio Vasari's *Lives of the Most Eminent Painters, Sculptors and Architects*. Van Mander outlines the functions and uses of allegory in *Handbook of Allegory*, originally published as the last section of *Painter's Treatise*. In this handbook, van Mander provides numerous examples of allegory. For instance, he takes a common saying about the cyclical nature of the world—"Peace brings livelihood; livelihood, wealth; wealth, pride; pride, strife; strife, war; war, poverty; poverty, humility; humility brings peace"—and describes how a painter might render this saying allegorically through images.

First, peace may be represented by the caduceus [winged staff] of Mercury or by a beehive-shaped helmet or an olive branch. Livelihood can be indicated by a coulter [plow blade], a ship's rudder,

hammer, trowel, spool, and such necessary utensils, and these one could place upon the aforementioned beehive-like helmet or another peace emblem as proof that peace brings forth and supports livelihood. Above livelihood one may render wealth characterized by a purse. From the bag, or upon this purse, may rise three peacock feathers indicating pride. On the peacock feathers, loosely scattered arrows for discord or strife, with a two-headed body upon strife. A drawn bow with an arrow on the string for war. Clackdish [a dish with a moveable lid beggars often used], beggar's dish, bottle and plate for poverty that results from war. Upon poverty one may place humility, characterized by a foot stepping on a garland or a crown. This foot would then once more be followed by peace, as above; but it is unnecessary to show this again since everyone knows that it has to begin again from below, with peace as represented before.[1]

The appeal of this symbolic visual rhetoric is reflected in the continued use of allegory throughout the history of art. Among the images in this text that utilize allegory are FIGS. 23-1, 24-37, and 24-53.

[1] Quoted in Wolfgang Stechow, *Northern Renaissance Art 1400–1600: Sources and Documents* (Upper Saddle River, N.J.: Prentice Hall, 1966), 71–72.

---

**CATHOLICISM VERSUS PROTESTANTISM** These doctrinal differences between Protestantism and Catholicism are expressed visually in *Allegory of Law and Grace* (FIG. **23-1**; see "The Uses of Allegory," above) by LUCAS CRANACH THE ELDER (1472–1553). Produced in the years after the onset of the Reformation, *Allegory* is a small woodcut print. Protestants viewed low-key images such as woodcut prints as useful devotional aids. Prints provided a prime

vehicle for "educating the masses," because artists could print them easily, permitting wide circulation and the sale of numerous copies. In addition, woodcuts were among the least expensive of all the art forms, making them more accessible to a wider audience than traditionally commissioned art, such as paintings or sculptures.

In *Allegory of Law and Grace*, Cranach depicted the differences between Catholicism (based on Old Testament Law, according to

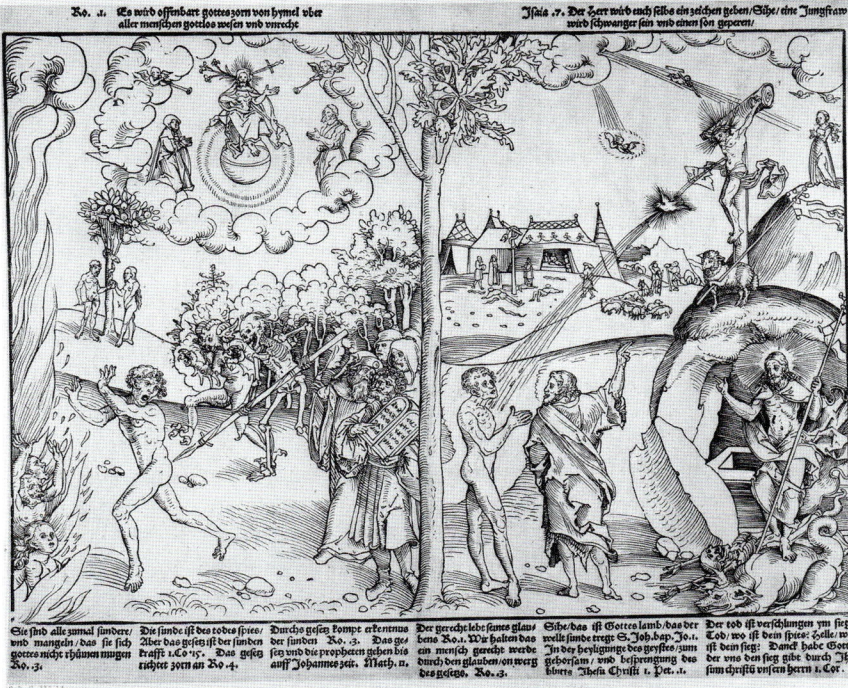

**23-1** LUCAS CRANACH THE ELDER, *Allegory of Law and Grace*, ca. 1530. Woodcut, $10\frac{5}{8}'' \times 1' \frac{3}{4}''$. British Museum, London.

Luther) and Protestantism (based on a belief in God's grace) in two images separated by a centrally placed tree. On the left half, Judgment Day has arrived, as represented by Christ's appearance at the top of the scene, hovering amid a cloud halo and accompanied by angels and saints. Christ raises his left hand in the traditional gesture of damnation, and, below, a skeleton drives off a terrified person to burn for all eternity in Hell. This person tried to live a good and honorable life, but, despite his efforts, he fell short. Moses stands to the side, holding the Tablets of the Law—the commandments Catholics follow in their attempt to attain salvation. In contrast to this Catholic reliance on good works and clean living, the Protestants emphasized God's grace as the source of redemption. Accordingly, God showers the sinner in the right half of the print with grace, as streams of blood flow from the crucified Christ. On the far right, Christ emerges from the tomb and promises salvation to all who believe in him.

At Wittenberg, Cranach became a friend and follower of Martin Luther; indeed, his close association with Luther and the degree to which Luther influenced (if not guided) his imagery led scholars to refer to Cranach as the "painter of the Reformation."

## Divergent Reformation Ideas and Practices

If Scripture alone, and not the Church, was the Christian's guide to salvation, then it was imperative that each Christian read and interpret the Scriptures. It soon became evident that Christians could differ in their interpretations of the sacred texts, and this gave rise to serious differences among the reformers, resulting in the emergence of various Protestant sects, such as the Zwinglians, the Calvinists, and the Anabaptists.

Once unleashed, the spirit of reform swept across Europe. Sixteenth-century territorial and state politics influenced religious choice, as did class affiliation. By midcentury, subjects often felt compelled either to accept the religion of their sovereign or emigrate to a territory where the sovereign's religion corresponded with their own. For example, in predominantly Catholic France, some citizens embraced Protestantism, which King Francis I (r. 1515–1547) declared illegal in 1534. Consequently, the state persecuted these Protestants, the Huguenots, and drove them underground. Despite the Huguenots' minority status, their commitment to Protestantism eventually led to one of the bloodiest religious massacres in European history when the Protestants and Catholics clashed in August 1572; this violent eruption was just part of a long-running war that lasted until the end of the 16th century.

## Christian Humanism

Interestingly, despite the tumultuous religious conflict engulfing 16th-century Europe, the exchange of intellectual and artistic ideas continued to thrive. Catholic Italy and the (mostly) Lutheran Holy Roman Empire shared in a lively commerce—economic and cultural—and 16th-century art throughout Europe exhibited the benefits of that exchange. Humanism filtered up from Italy and spread throughout northern Europe. Northern humanists, like their southern counterparts, cultivated a knowledge of classical cultures and literature. However, they focused more on reconciling humanism with Christianity, so later scholars applied the general label "Christian humanists" to describe them.

Among the most influential Christian humanists were the Dutch-born Desiderius Erasmus (1466–1536) and the Englishman Thomas More (1478–1535). Erasmus demonstrated his interest in both Italian humanism and religion with his "philosophy of Christ," emphasizing education and scriptural knowledge. Both an ordained priest and avid scholar, Erasmus published his most famous essay, *The Praise of Folly*, in 1509. In this widely read work, he satirized not just the Church but various social classes as well. His ideas were to play an important role in the development of the Reformation, but he consistently declined to join any of the Reformation sects. Equally well educated was Thomas More, who served King Henry VIII. Henry eventually ordered More's execution because More opposed England's break with the Catholic Church. In France, François Rabelais (ca. 1494–1553), a former monk who advocated rejecting stagnant religious dogmatism, disseminated the humanist spirit. The turmoil emerging during the 16th century lasted well into the 17th century and permanently affected the face of Europe. The concerted challenges to established authority and the persistent philosophical inquiry eventually led to the rise of new political systems (for example, the nation-state) and new economic systems (such as capitalism).

## The Role of Visual Imagery during the Reformation

The seismic shifts occurring in all aspects of European life due to the Reformation affected the arts, particularly its patronage and the types of art commissioned. In addition to doctrinal differences, Catholics and Protestants took divergent stances on the role of visual imagery in religion. Catholics embraced church decoration as an aid to communicating with God, as seen in Italian ceiling frescoes (see FIG. 22-13; see "The Role of Religious Art in Counter-Reformation Italy," Chapter 22, page 636) and German and Polish altarpieces (see FIGS. 20-22 and 20-23). In contrast, Protestants believed such imagery could lead to idolatry and distracted viewers from focusing on the real reason for their presence in church—to communicate directly with God (see "Iconoclasm and the Reaction against Religious Art," page 667). Because of this belief, Protestant churches were relatively bare, and the extensive church decoration programs found especially in Italy were not as prominent in Protestant churches. This does not suggest that Protestants had no use for visual images; art, especially prints (which were inexpensive and easily circulated), was a useful and effective teaching tool and facilitated the private devotional exercises that were fundamental to Protestantism. The popularity of prints both contributed to and was fueled by a transition from handwritten manuscripts (for example, illuminated manuscripts) to print media in northern Europe during the 16th century.

## HOLY ROMAN EMPIRE

### Divergent Views on Religious Imagery

Largely because of Luther's presence, the Reformation initially had its greatest impact in the Holy Roman Empire. The difference between Catholic and Protestant uses of art can be demonstrated by comparing two German artworks, one (by Matthias Grünewald) pre-Reformation and one (by Albrecht Dürer) produced in the years after the Reformation began.

### Iconoclasm and the Reaction against Religious Art

The Protestant concern over the role of religious imagery at times progressed to outright iconoclasm—the objection to and destruction of religious imagery. In encouraging a more personal relationship with God, Protestant leaders spoke out against much of the religious art being produced. In his 1525 tract *Against the Heavenly Prophets in the Matter of Images and Sacraments,* Martin Luther explained his attitude toward religious imagery:

> I approached the task of destroying images by first tearing them out of the heart through God's Word and making them worthless and despised. . . . For when they are no longer in the heart, they can do no harm when seen with the eyes. . . . I have allowed and not forbidden the outward removal of images. . . . And I say at the outset that according to the law of Moses no other images are forbidden than an image of God which one worships. A crucifix, on the other hand, or any other holy image is not forbidden. . . . [1]

Ulrich Zwingli (1484–1531), leader of the Zwinglians (based in Switzerland), concurred with Luther and cautioned his followers about the potentially dangerous nature of religious imagery. Although Zwingli's ideas had much in common with those of Luther, he was more intent on simplifying religious belief and practices than Luther and rejected all sacraments (unlike Luther, who accepted both baptism and Communion).

The Protestant condemnation of possibly idolatrous religious imagery is further reinforced by the Protestant Ten Commandments, which, although also excerpted from the Bible, differ slightly from those of the Catholic Church. For Protestants, the Second Commandment reads: "Thou shalt not make unto thee any graven image, or any likeness of any thing that is in heaven above, or that is in the earth beneath, or that is in the water under the earth. Thou shalt not bow down thyself to them, nor serve them, for I the Lord thy God am a jealous God, visiting the iniquity of the fathers upon the children unto the third and fourth generation of them that hate me. And showing mercy unto thousands of them that love me, and keep my commandments."

These many Protestant proscriptions against religious imagery often led to eruptions of iconoclasm. Particularly violent waves of iconoclastic fervor swept Basel, Zurich, Strasbourg, and Wittenberg in the 1520s. In an episode known as the Great Iconoclasm, bands of Calvinists visited Catholic churches in the Netherlands in 1566, shattering stained-glass windows, smashing statues, and destroying paintings and other artworks that they perceived as idolatrous. These strong reactions to art not only reflect the religious fervor of the time but also serve as dramatic demonstrations of the power of art—and of how much art mattered.

[1] Quoted in Wolfgang Stechow, *Northern Renaissance Art 1400–1600: Sources and Documents* (Upper Saddle River, N.J.: Prentice Hall, 1966), 129–30.

**OF SICKNESS AND SALVATION** Matthias Neithardt, known conventionally as MATTHIAS GRÜNEWALD (ca. 1480–1528), worked for the archbishops of Mainz from 1511 on as court painter and decorator. He also served the archbishops as architect, hydraulic engineer, and superintendent of works. He eventually moved to northern Germany, where he settled at Halle in Saxony. Around 1510, Grünewald began work on the *Isenheim Altarpiece* (FIGS. **23-2** and **23-3**), a complex and fascinating monument that reflects Catholic beliefs.

The altarpiece, created for the monastic hospital order Saint Anthony of Isenheim, consists of a wooden shrine (carved by sculptor NIKOLAUS HAGENAUER in 1490) that includes gilded and polychromed statues of Saints Anthony Abbot, Augustine, and Jerome (FIG. 23-3). Grünewald's contribution, commissioned by the head administrator of the monastery, Guido Guersi, consists of two pairs of movable wings that open at the center. Hinged together at the sides, one pair stands directly behind the other. Painted by Grünewald between 1510 and 1515, the exterior panels of the first pair (visible when the altarpiece is closed, FIG. 23-2) present four scenes—*Crucifixion* in the center, *Saint Sebastian* on the left and *Saint Anthony* on the right, and *Lamentation* in the predella. When these exterior wings are opened, four additional scenes (not illustrated)—*Annunciation, Angelic Concert, Madonna and Child,* and *Resurrection*—are revealed. Opening this second pair of wings exposes the interior shrine, flanked by *Meeting of Saints Anthony and Paul* and *Temptation of Saint Anthony* (FIG. 23-3).

The placement of this altarpiece in the choir of a church adjacent to the monastery hospital dictated much of the imagery. Saints associated with diseases such as the plague and with miraculous cures, such as Saint Anthony and Saint Sebastian, appear prominently both in the *Isenheim Altarpiece* and in Rogier van der Weyden's *Last Judgment Altarpiece* at the Hôtel-Dieu at Beaune (see FIG. 20-8). Grünewald's panels, however, deal even more specifically with the themes of dire illness and miraculous healing and accordingly emphasize the suffering of the order's patron saint, Anthony. Grünewald's images served as warnings, like Rogier's *Last Judgment,* thereby encouraging increased devotion from monks and hospital patients. They also functioned therapeutically by offering some hope to the afflicted. Indeed, Saint Anthony's legend encompassed his role as both vengeful dispenser of justice (by inflicting disease) and benevolent healer. The artist enhanced the impact of this altarpiece through his effective use of color. He intensified the contrast of horror and hope by playing subtle tones and soft harmonies against shocking dissonance of color.

One of the most memorable scenes is *Temptation of Saint Anthony* (FIG. 23-3), immediately to the right of the interior sculptured shrine. It is a terrifying image of the five temptations, depicted as an assortment of ghoulish and bestial creatures in a dark landscape, attacking the saint. In the foreground Grünewald painted a grotesque image of a man, whose oozing boils, withered arm, and distended stomach all suggest a horrible disease. Medical experts have connected these symptoms with ergotism (a disease caused by ergot, a fungus that grows especially on rye). Although doctors did not discover the cause of this disease until about 1600, people lived in fear of its recognizable symptoms (convulsions and gangrene). The public referred to this illness as "Saint Anthony's Fire," and it was one of the major diseases treated at this hospital. The gangrene often compelled amputation, and scholars have

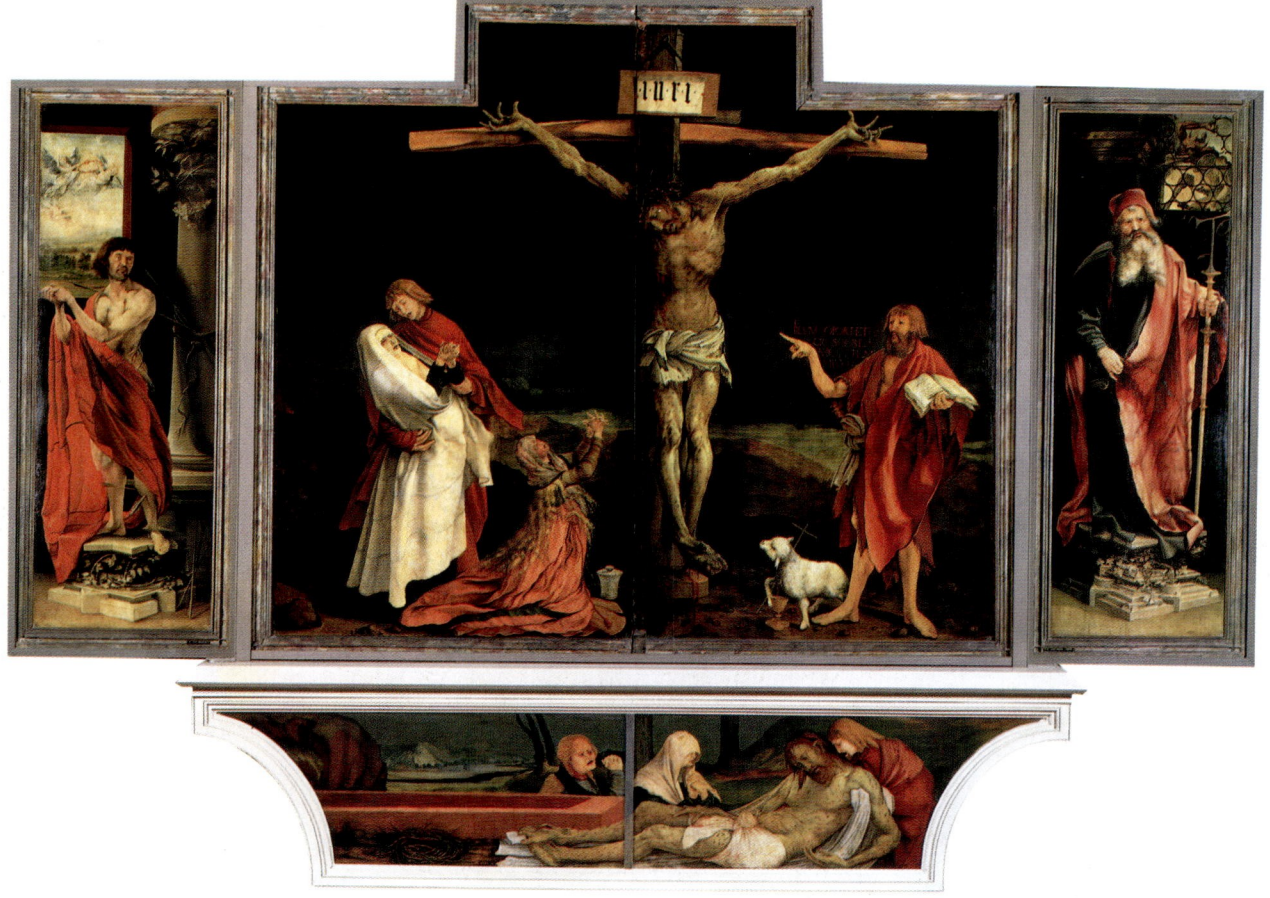

**23-2** Matthias Grünewald, *Isenheim Altarpiece* (closed), *Crucifixion* (center panel), from the chapel of the Hospital of Saint Anthony, Isenheim, Germany, ca. 1510–1515. Oil on panel, 9′ 9½″ × 10′ 9″ (center panel), 8′ 2½″ × 3′ ½″ (each wing), 2′ 5½″ × 11′ 2″ (predella). Musée d'Unterlinden, Colmar.

noted that the two movable halves of the altarpiece's predella, if slid apart, make it appear as if Christ's legs have been amputated. The same observation can be made with regard to the two main exterior panels. Due to the off-center placement of the cross, opening the left panel "severs" one arm from the crucified figure.

Thus, Grünewald carefully selected and presented his altarpiece's iconography to be particularly meaningful for viewers at this hospital. In the interior shrine, the artist balanced the horrors of the disease and the punishments that awaited those who did not repent with scenes such as the *Meeting of Saints Anthony and Paul,* depicting the two saints, healthy and aged, conversing peacefully. Even the exterior panels (the closed altarpiece) convey these same concerns. The *Crucifixion* emphasizes Christ's pain and suffering, but the knowledge that this act redeemed humanity tempers the misery. In addition, Saint Anthony appears in the right wing as a devout follower of Christ who, like Christ and for Christ, endured intense suffering for his faith. Saint Anthony's presence on the exterior thus reinforces the themes Grünewald intertwined throughout this entire altarpiece—themes of pain, illness, and death, as well as those of hope, comfort, and salvation.

The Protestant faith had not been formally established when Hagenauer and Grünewald produced the *Isenheim Altarpiece,* and the complexity and monumentality of the altarpiece must be viewed as Catholic in orientation. Further, Grünewald incorporated several references to Catholic doctrines, such as the lamb (symbol of the Son of God), whose wound spurts blood into a chalice in the exterior *Crucifixion* scene.

**WIDELY ACCLAIMED TALENT** In contrast, the Lutheran sympathies of Grünewald's contemporary, Albrecht Dürer (1471–1528), are on display in many of his artworks. A dominant artist of the early 16th century in the Holy Roman Empire, Dürer was the first artist outside Italy to become an international art celebrity. He traveled extensively, visiting and studying in Colmar, Basel, Strasbourg, Venice, Antwerp, and Brussels, among other locales. As a result of these travels, Dürer was personally acquainted with many of the leading humanists and artists of his time, including Erasmus of Rotterdam and Giovanni Bellini. A man of exceptional talents and tremendous energy, Dürer achieved widespread fame in his own time and has enjoyed a lofty reputation ever since. Dürer was fervently committed to advancing his career and employed an agent to help sell his prints. His wife, who served as his manager, and his mother also sold his prints at markets. His business acumen is revealed by the lawsuit he brought against an Italian artist for copying his prints; scholars generally regard this lawsuit to be the first in history over artistic copyright. In part, his expansive reputation was due to the breadth of his talent. Although he was apprenticed at the age of 15 to a painter, Dürer quickly mastered the art of woodcut, engraving, and watercolor as well.

Like Leonardo da Vinci, Dürer wrote theoretical treatises on a variety of subjects, such as perspective, fortification, and the ideal in human proportions. Unlike Leonardo, he both finished and published his writings. Through his prints, he exerted strong influence throughout Europe, especially in Flanders but also in

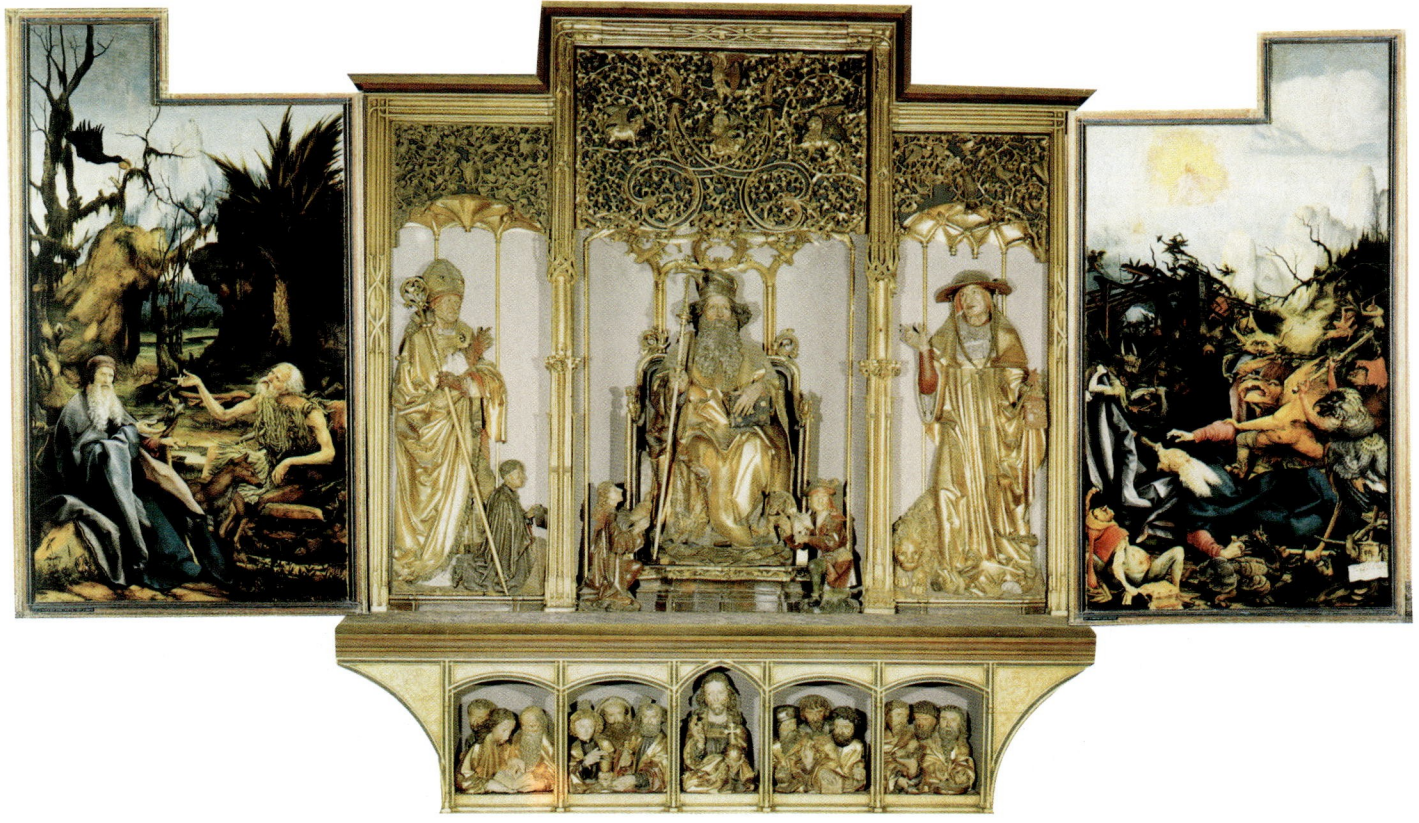

**23-3** MATTHIAS GRÜNEWALD, *Isenheim Altarpiece* (open), center shrine carved by NIKOLAUS HAGENAUER in 1490, from the chapel of the Hospital of Saint Anthony, Isenheim, Germany, ca. 1510–1515. Shrine, painted and gilt limewood, 9′ 9½″ × 10′ 9″ (center), 2′ 5½″ × 11′ 2″ (predella). Each wing, oil on panel, 8′ 2½″ × 3′ ½″. Musée d'Unterlinden, Colmar.

Italy. Moreover, he was the first northern artist to leave a record of his life and career through several excellent self-portraits, through his correspondence, and through a carefully kept, quite detailed, and eminently readable diary.

A native of Nuremberg, one of the major cities in the Holy Roman Empire and a center of the Reformation, Dürer immersed himself in the religious debates of his day. *Last Supper* (FIG. **23-4**) is a woodcut Dürer produced six years after Luther's posting of his Ninety-five Theses. Dürer's treatment of this traditional subject (see FIGS. 21-37 and 22-3) alludes to Lutheran doctrine about Communion, one of the sacraments. Rather than promote the doctrine of transubstantiation, the Catholic belief that when consecrated by the

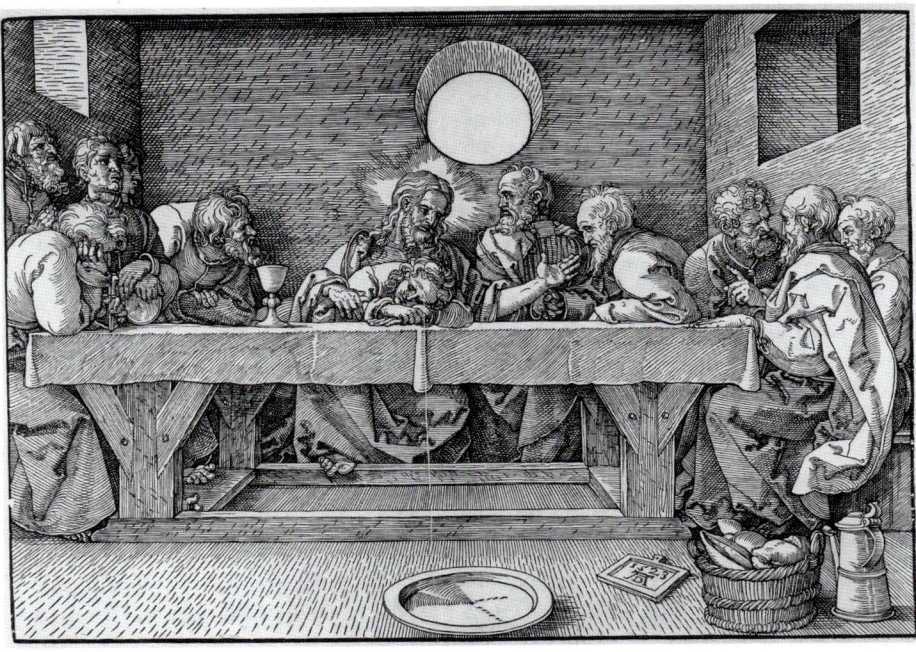

**23-4** ALBRECHT DÜRER, *Last Supper*, 1523. Woodcut, 8⅜″ × 11¹³⁄₁₆″. British Museum, London.

priest, the bread (Eucharist) and wine literally, miraculously, become the Body and Blood of Christ (see FIG. 24-20), Luther insisted that Communion was commemorative, not a reenactment.

Dürer depicts this distinction in his *Last Supper*. The narrative moment he represented emphasizes sorrow and community; Christ has announced the betrayal, and only 11 disciples remain with him. The bread and wine appear prominently in the print's lower right corner, and the empty plate in the foreground refers to the commemorative, rather than literal, nature of Christ's sacrifice in the Mass. Traditional depictions often had a slaughtered lamb on the plate, conspicuously absent here.

The style of this woodcut is simple and straightforward. Compositionally, Dürer presented the figures in a conventional manner, seated behind a long, horizontally placed table. Parallel lines extend throughout the entire image, with areas of crosshatching suggesting three-dimensionality. The regularity of the lines creates an evenness of value, contributing to the image's cohesiveness and directness.

Through prints such as *Last Supper*, Dürer became famous for his mastery of the graphic arts. Trained as a goldsmith by his father before he took up painting and printmaking, he developed an extraordinary proficiency in handling the burin, the engraving tool. This technical ability, combined with a feeling for the form-creating possibilities of line, enabled him to produce a body of graphic work in woodcut and engraving that seldom has been rivaled for quality and number. Dürer created numerous book illustrations; he also circulated and sold prints in single sheets, which people of ordinary means could buy, expanding his audience considerably. Aggressively marketing his prints, Dürer became a wealthy man from the sale of these works.

**EMPHASIZING THE BIBLE** Dürer's support for Lutheranism surfaces again in his painting *Four Apostles* (FIG. **23-5**). That he produced this work without commission and presented the two panels to the city fathers of Nuremberg in 1526 to be hung in the city hall suggests that this work reflected his personal attitudes. John and Peter appear on the left panel, Mark and Paul on the right. The title, it can be argued, is something of a misnomer; Mark was an evangelist, despite conventional reference to him as an apostle. Dürer conveyed this painting's Lutheran orientation by his positioning of the figures; he relegated Saint Peter (as representative of the pope in Rome) to a secondary role by placing him behind John the Evangelist. John assumed particular prominence for Luther because of the evangelist's focus on Christ's person in his Gospel. In addition, Peter and John both read from the Bible, the single authoritative source of religious truth, according to Luther. Dürer emphasized the Bible's centrality by depicting it open to the legible passage "In the beginning was the Word, and the Word was with God, and the Word was God" (John 1:1). At the bottom of the panels, Dürer included quotations from each of the Four Apostles' books, using Luther's German translation of the New Testament. The excerpts warn against the coming of perilous times and the preaching of false prophets who will distort God's word. The individuality of each of the four men's faces, along with the detailed depiction of their attire and attributes, communicate an integrity and spirituality.

**CLASSICAL IDEAS IN THE NORTH** Fascinated with classical ideas as passed along by Italian Renaissance artists, Dürer was among the first northern artists to travel to Italy expressly to study Italian art and its underlying theories at their source. After

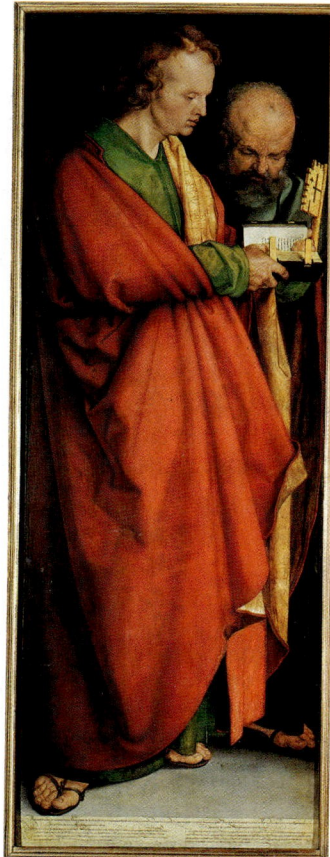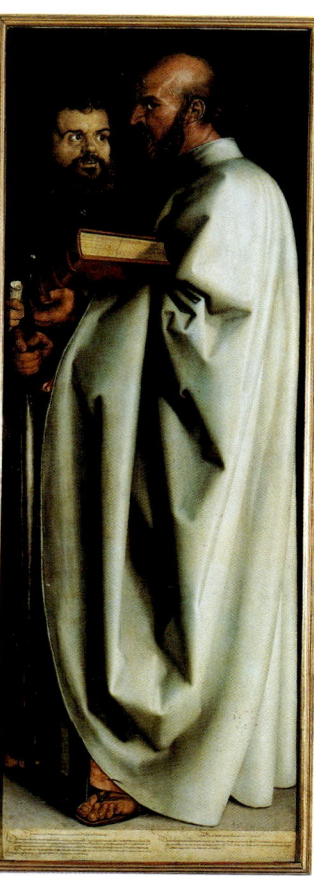

**23-5** ALBRECHT DÜRER, *Four Apostles,* 1526. Oil on panel, each panel 7′ 1″ × 2′ 6″. Alte Pinakothek, Munich.

his first journey in 1494–1495 (the second was in 1505–1506), he incorporated many Italian Renaissance developments into his art. Art historians have acclaimed Dürer as the first northern artist to understand fully the basic aims of the Renaissance in Italy.

An engraving, *The Fall of Man* (*Adam and Eve;* FIG. **23-6**), represents the first distillation of his studies of the Vitruvian theory of human proportions, a theory based on arithmetic ratios. Clearly outlined against the dark background of a northern forest, the two idealized figures of Adam and Eve stand in poses reminiscent of specific classical statues probably known to Dürer through graphic representations. Preceded by numerous geometric drawings in which the artist attempted to systematize sets of ideal human proportions in balanced contrapposto poses, the final print presents Dürer's concept of the "perfect" male and female figures. Yet Dürer tempered this idealization with naturalism—a commitment to observation.

Dürer demonstrated his well-honed observational skills in his rendering of the background foliage and animals. The gnarled bark of the trees and the feathery leaves authenticate the scene, as do the various creatures skulking underfoot. The animals populating the print are symbolic. The choleric cat, the melancholic elk, the sanguine rabbit, and the phlegmatic ox represent humanity's temperaments based on the "four humors," bodily fluids that were the basis of theories of the body's function developed by the ancient Greek physician Hippocrates and practiced in medieval physiology. The tension between cat and mouse in the foreground

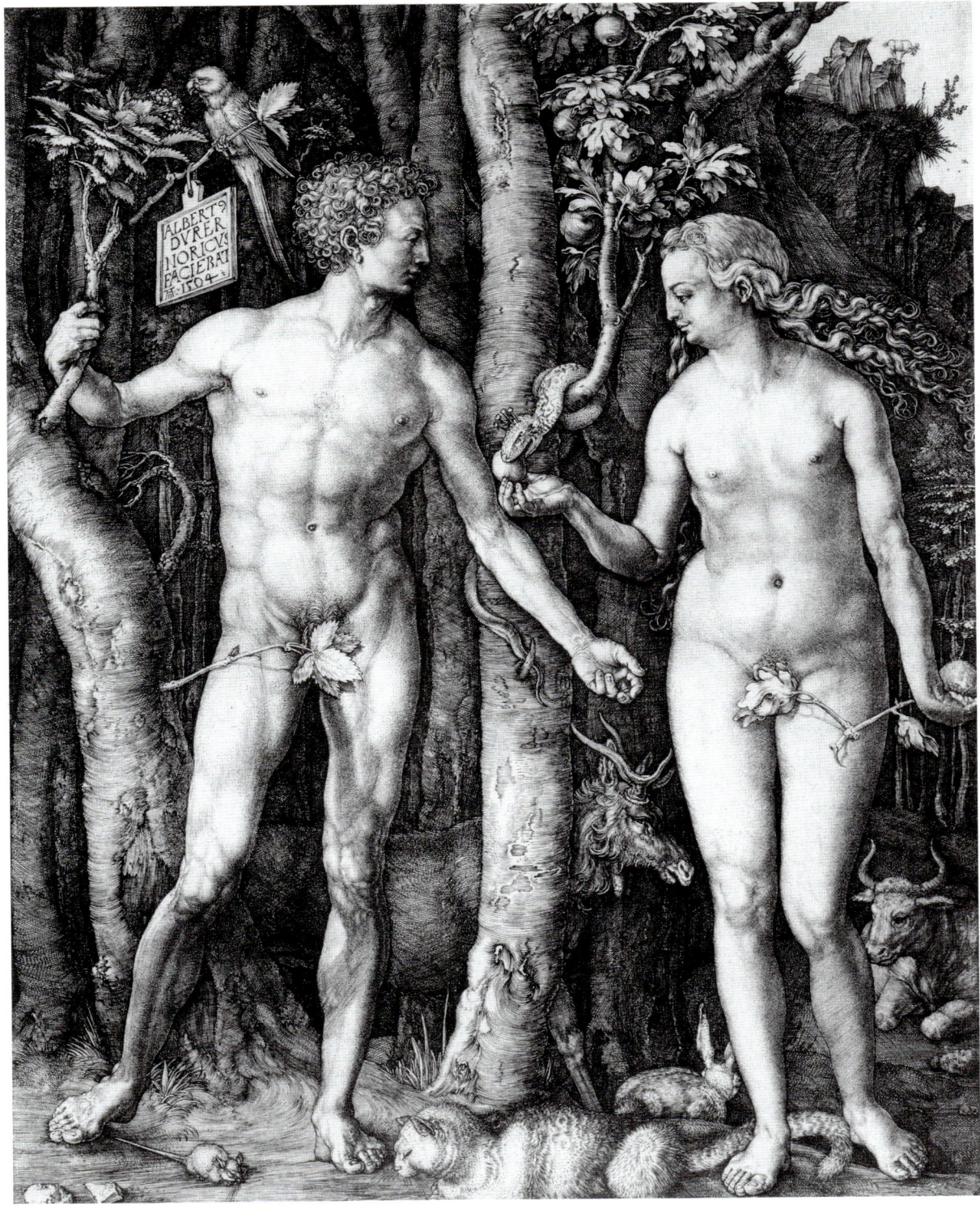

**23-6** ALBRECHT DÜRER, *The Fall of Man (Adam and Eve)*, 1504. Engraving, approx. $9\frac{7}{8}'' \times 7\frac{5}{8}''$. Museum of Fine Arts, Boston (centennial gift of Landon T. Clay).

symbolizes the relation between Adam and Eve at the crucial moment in *The Fall of Man.*

**BEAUTY IN NATURE** Dürer allied himself with Leonardo's scientific studies when he painted an extremely precise watercolor study of a piece of turf; for both artists, observation yielded truth. Sight, sanctified by mystics such as Nicholas of Cusa and artists such as Jan van Eyck (see Chapter 20, page 560 ), became the secularized

instrument of modern knowledge. Dürer agreed with Aristotle (and the new Renaissance critics) that "sight is the noblest sense of man."[1] Nature holds the beautiful, Dürer said, for the artist who has the insight to extract it. Thus, beauty lies even in humble, perhaps ugly, things, and the ideal, which bypasses or improves on nature, may not be truly beautiful in the end. Uncomposed and ordinary nature might be a reasonable object of an artist's interest, quite as much as its composed and measured aspect. The remarkable *Great Piece of*

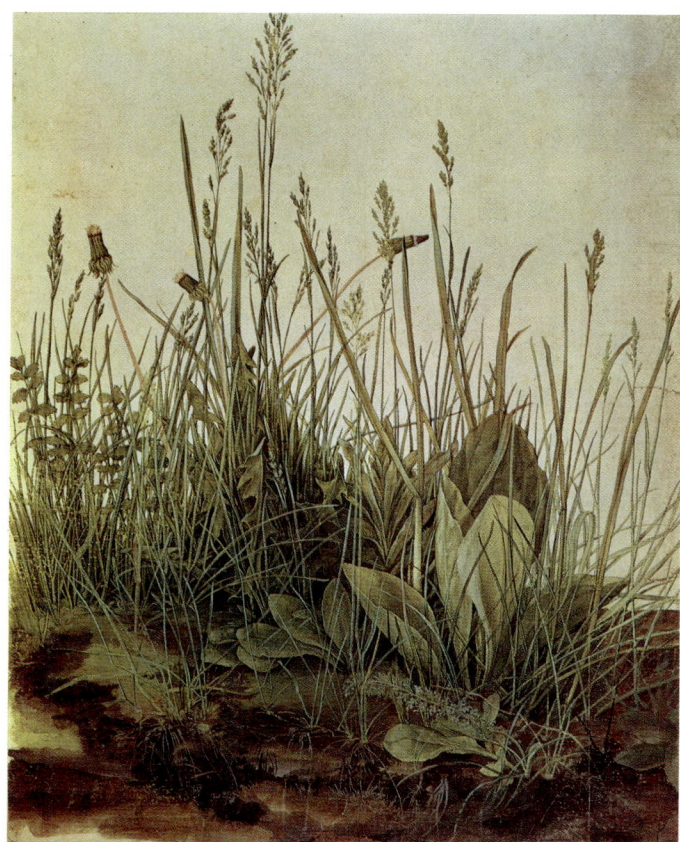

23-7 ALBRECHT DÜRER, *The Great Piece of Turf*, 1503. Watercolor, approx. 1′ 4″ × 1′ $\frac{1}{2}$″. Graphische Sammlung Albertina, Vienna.

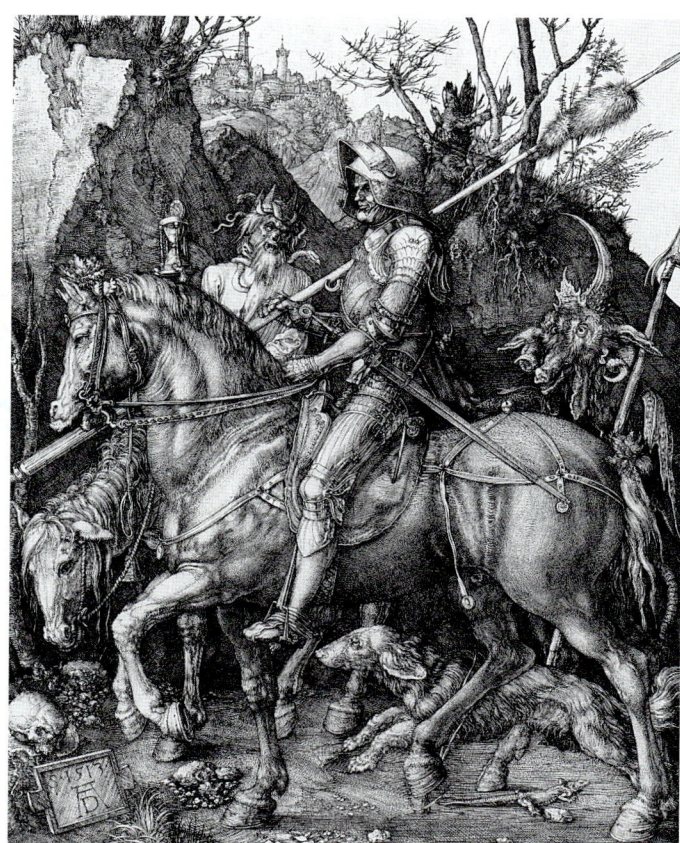

23-8 ALBRECHT DÜRER, *Knight, Death, and the Devil*, 1513. Engraving, $9\frac{5}{8}$″ × $7\frac{3}{8}$″. Metropolitan Museum of Art, New York.

*Turf* (FIG. 23-7) is as scientifically accurate as it is poetic. Botanists can distinguish each springing plant and grass variety—dandelions, great plantain, yarrow, meadow grass, and heath rush. "[D]epart not from nature according to your fancy," Dürer said, "imagining to find aught better by yourself; . . . For verily 'art' is embedded in nature; he who can extract it, has it."[2]

**ELEVATING THE ART OF ENGRAVING** This lifelong interest in both idealization and naturalism surfaces in *Knight, Death, and the Devil* (FIG. 23-8), one of three so-called Master Engravings Dürer made between 1513 and 1514. These works (the other two are *Melencolia I* and *Saint Jerome in His Study*) carry the art of engraving to the highest degree of excellence. Dürer used his burin to render differences in texture and tonal values that would be difficult to match even in the much more flexible medium of etching (corroding a design into metal), which artists developed later in the century. (Later in life Dürer also experimented with etching.)

*Knight, Death, and the Devil* depicts a mounted armored knight who rides fearlessly through a foreboding landscape. Accompanied by his faithful retriever, the knight represents a Christian knight—a soldier of God. Armed with his faith, this warrior can repel the threats of Death, who appears as a crowned decaying cadaver wreathed with snakes and shaking an hourglass as a reminder of time and mortality. The knight is equally impervious to the Devil, a pathetically hideous horned creature who follows him. The knight triumphs because he has "put on the whole armor of God that [he] may be able to stand against the wiles of the devil," as urged in Saint Paul's Epistle to the Ephesians (Eph. 6 : 11).

The monumental knight and his mount display the strength, movement, and proportions of the Renaissance equestrian statue. Dürer was familiar with Donatello's *Gattamelata* (see FIG. 21-29)

and Verrocchio's *Bartolommeo Colleoni* (see FIG. 21-30) and had copied a number of Leonardo's sketches of horses. His highly developed feeling for the real and his meticulous rendering of it surface in the myriad details—the knight's armor and weapons, the horse's anatomy, the textures of the loathsome features of Death and the Devil, the rock forms and rugged foliage. Dürer realized this great variety of imagery with the dense hatching of fluidly engraved lines that rivals the tonal range of painting. Erasmus could rightly compliment Dürer as the "Apelles [the ancient Greek master of painting] of black lines."[3]

Dürer's use of line, whether in oil, watercolor, woodcut, or engraving, was truly exceptional. He employed line not simply to describe but to evoke as well. This ability extended beyond his impressive technical facility with the different media. Dürer's art reveals an inspired, inquisitive mind and a phenomenally gifted talent. To this day, his work serves as a model for artists, and he deserves much of the credit for expanding the capability of the graphic arts to convey intellectually and emotionally complex themes. Further, in bringing a lawsuit against copyists in Italy in 1506, Dürer took the first step toward the modern concepts of copyright and intellectual property—a central feature of the modern world whose impact stretches far beyond the realm of art.

## *Commenting on History and Politics*

**INVOKING A HISTORICAL BATTLE** Although the prominence of Reformation concerns in the Holy Roman Empire during the 16th century was reflected in the period's art, artists also addressed historical and political issues. *The Battle of Issus* (FIG. 23-9) by ALBRECHT ALTDORFER (ca. 1480–1538), for example,

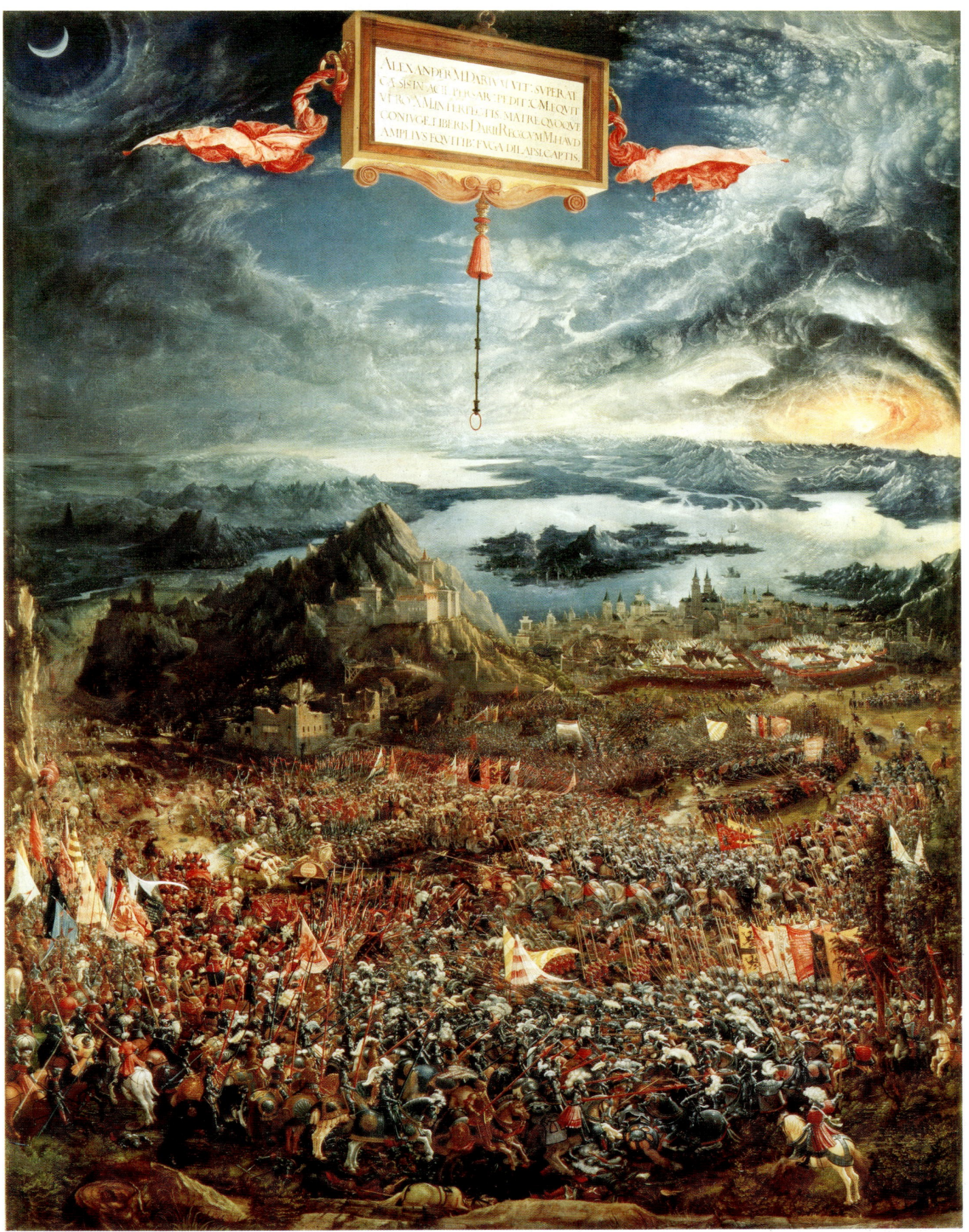

**23-9** ALBRECHT ALTDORFER, *The Battle of Issus,* 1529. Oil on panel, 5′ 2⅓″ × 3′ 11¼″. Alte Pinakothek, Munich.

depicts the defeat of Darius in 333 BCE by Alexander the Great at a town called Issus on the Pinarus River (announced in the inscription that hangs in the sky). The duke of Bavaria, Wilhelm IV, commissioned *The Battle of Issus* in 1528, concurrent with his commencement of a military campaign against the invading Turks. The parallels between the historical and contemporary conflicts were no doubt significant to the duke. Both involved societies that deemed themselves progressive engaged in battles against infidels—the Persians in 333 BCE and the Turks in 1528. Altdorfer reinforced this connection by attiring the figures in contemporary armor and depicting them engaged in contemporary military alignments.

The scene reveals Altdorfer's love of landscape. The battle takes place in an almost cosmological setting. From a bird's-eye view, the clashing armies swarm in the foreground; in the distance, craggy mountain peaks rise next to still bodies of water. Amid swirling clouds, a blazing sun descends. Although the awesome spectacle of the topography may appear imaginary or invented, the artist actually used available historical information to produce this painting. Altdorfer derived his depiction of the landscape from maps. Specifically, he set the scene in the eastern Mediterranean with a view from Greece to the Nile in Egypt. In

addition, Altdorfer may have acquired his information about this battle from an account written by Johannes Aventinus, a German scholar. In his text, Aventinus describes the bloody daylong battle and Alexander's ultimate victory. Appropriately, given Alexander's designation as the "sun god," the sun sets over the victorious Greeks on the right, while a small crescent moon (a symbol of the Near East) hovers in the upper left corner over the retreating Persians.

**AN ELEGANT DIPLOMATIC PORTRAIT** Choosing less dramatic scenes, HANS HOLBEIN THE YOUNGER (ca. 1497–1543) excelled as a portraitist. Trained by his father, Holbein produced portraits that reflected the northern tradition of close realism that had emerged in 15th-century Flemish art. Yet he also incorporated Italian ideas about monumental composition, bodily structure, and sculpturesque form. The color surfaces of his paintings are as lustrous as enamel, his detail is exact and exquisitely drawn, and his contrasts of light and dark are never heavy.

Holbein began his artistic career in Basel, where he knew Erasmus of Rotterdam. Because of the immediate threat of a religious civil war in Basel, Erasmus suggested that Holbein leave for England and gave him a recommendation to Thomas More,

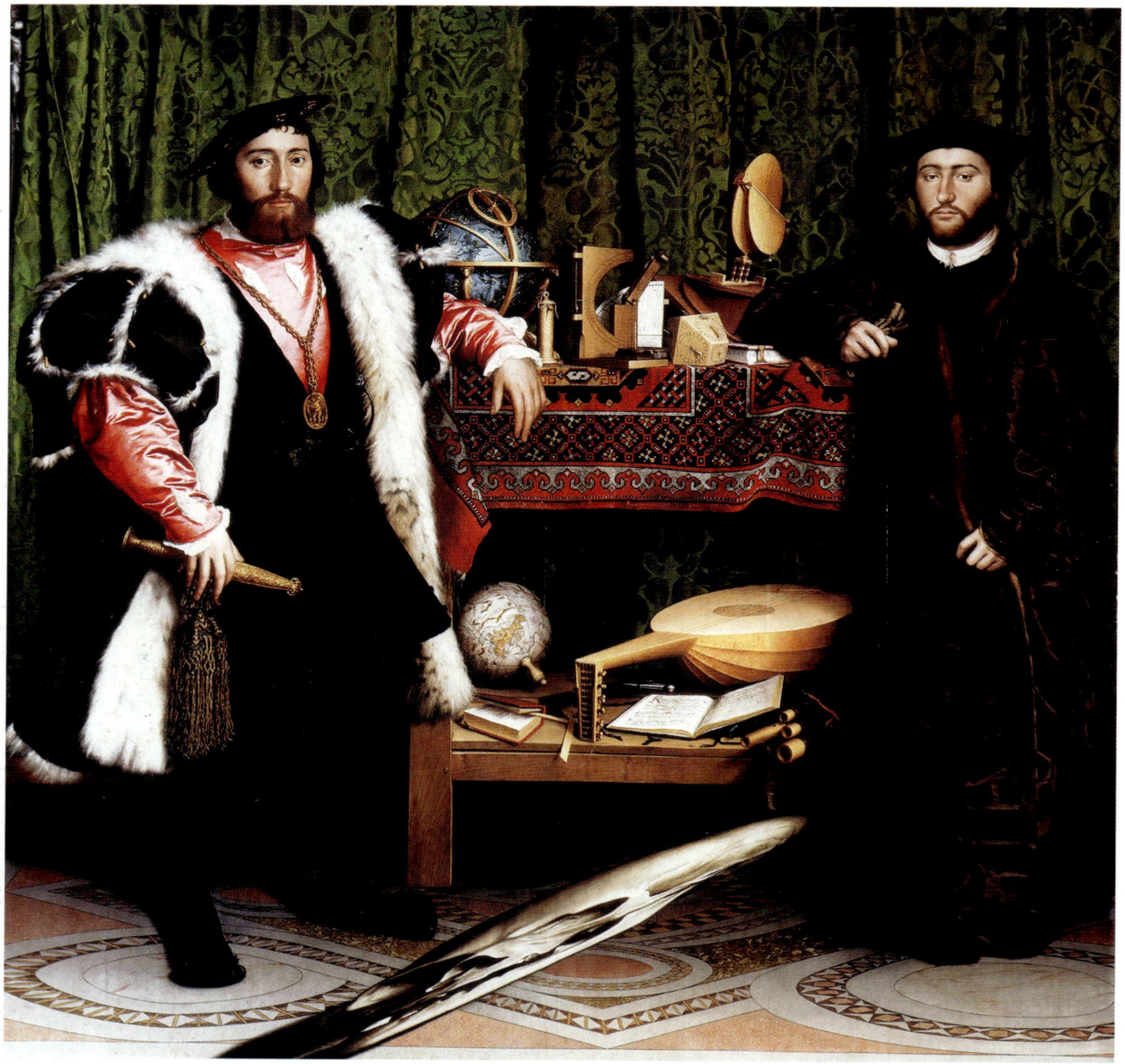

**23-10** HANS HOLBEIN THE YOUNGER, *The French Ambassadors,* 1533. Oil and tempera on panel, approx. 6′ 8″ × 6′ 9½″. National Gallery, London.

chancellor of England under Henry VIII. Holbein did move and became painter to the English court. While there, he produced a superb double portrait of the French ambassadors to England, Jean de Dinteville and Georges de Selve. *The French Ambassadors* (FIG. 23-10) exhibits Holbein's considerable talents—his strong sense of composition, his subtle linear patterning, his gift for portraiture, his marvelous sensitivity to color, and his faultlessly firm technique. This painting may have been Holbein's favorite; it is the only one signed with his full name. The two men, both ardent humanists, stand at each end of a side table covered with an oriental rug and a collection of objects reflective of their worldliness and their interest in learning and the arts. These include mathematical and astronomical models and implements, a lute with a broken string, compasses, a sundial, flutes, globes, and an open hymnbook with Luther's translation of *Veni, Creator Spiritus* and of the Ten Commandments.

Of particular interest is the long gray shape that slashes diagonally across the picture plane and interrupts the stable, balanced, and serene composition. This form is an *anamorphic image,* a distorted image recognizable when viewed with a special device, such as a cylindrical mirror, or by viewing the painting at an acute angle. Viewing this painting while standing off to the right reveals that this gray slash is a skull. Although scholars do not agree on this skull's meaning, at the very least it certainly refers to death. Artists commonly incorporated skulls into paintings as reminders of mortality; indeed, Holbein depicted a skull on the metal medallion on Jean de Dinteville's hat. Holbein may have intended the skulls, in conjunction with the crucifix that appears half hidden behind the curtain in the upper left corner, to encourage viewers to ponder death and resurrection.

This painting may allude to the growing tension between secular and religious authorities; Jean de Dinteville was a titled landowner, Georges de Selve a bishop. The inclusion of Luther's translations next to the lute with the broken string (a symbol of discord) may also subtly refer to the religious strife. Despite scholars' uncertainty about the precise meaning of *The French Ambassadors,* it is a painting of supreme artistic achievement. Holbein rendered the still-life objects with the same meticulous care as the men themselves, as the woven design of the deep emerald curtain behind them, and as the floor tiles, constructed in faultless perspective. He surely hoped this painting's elegance and virtuosity of skill (produced shortly after Holbein arrived in England) would impress Henry VIII.

# FRANCE

As *The French Ambassadors* illustrates, France in the early 16th century continued its efforts to secure widespread recognition as a political power. Under the rule of Francis I (r. 1515–1547), the French established a firm foothold in Milan and its environs. Francis waged a campaign (known as the Habsburg-Valois Wars) against Charles V (the Spanish king and Holy Roman Emperor), which occupied him from 1521 to 1544. These wars involved disputed territories—southern France, the Netherlands, the Rhinelands, northern Spain, and Italy—and reflect France's central role in the shifting geopolitical landscape. Despite these military preoccupations, Francis I also endeavored to elevate his country's cultural profile. To that end, he invited esteemed Italian artists such as Leonardo da Vinci and Andrea del Sarto to his court. Francis's attempt to glorify the state and himself meant that the

religious art dominating the Middle Ages no longer prevailed, for the king and not the Christian Church held the power.

**A MAGNIFICENT FRENCH MONARCH** The portrait *Francis I* (FIG. 23-11), painted by JEAN CLOUET (ca. 1485–1541), shows a worldly prince magnificently bedecked in silks and brocades, wearing a gold chain with a medallion of the Order of Saint Michael, a French order founded by Louis XI. Legend has it that the "merry monarch" was a great lover and the hero of hundreds of "gallant" deeds; appropriately, he appears suave and confident, with his hand resting on the pommel of a dagger. Despite the careful detail, the portrait also exhibits an elegantly formalized quality. This characteristic is due to Clouet's suppression of modeling, resulting in a flattening of features, seen particularly in Francis's neck. The disproportion between the small size of the king's head in relation to his broad body, swathed in heavy layers of fabric, adds to the formalized nature.

**A PAINTED AND PLASTERED PALACE** The personal tastes of Francis and his court must have run to an art at once elegant, erotic, and unorthodox. Appropriately, Mannerism (see Chapter 22, pages 648–654) appealed to them most. Among the Italian artists who had a strong impact on French art were the Mannerists Rosso Fiorentino and Benvenuto Cellini. Rosso became the court painter of Francis I shortly after 1530. The king put ROSSO FIORENTINO (1494–1540), along with fellow Florentine FRANCESCO PRIMATICCIO (1504–1570), in charge of decorating

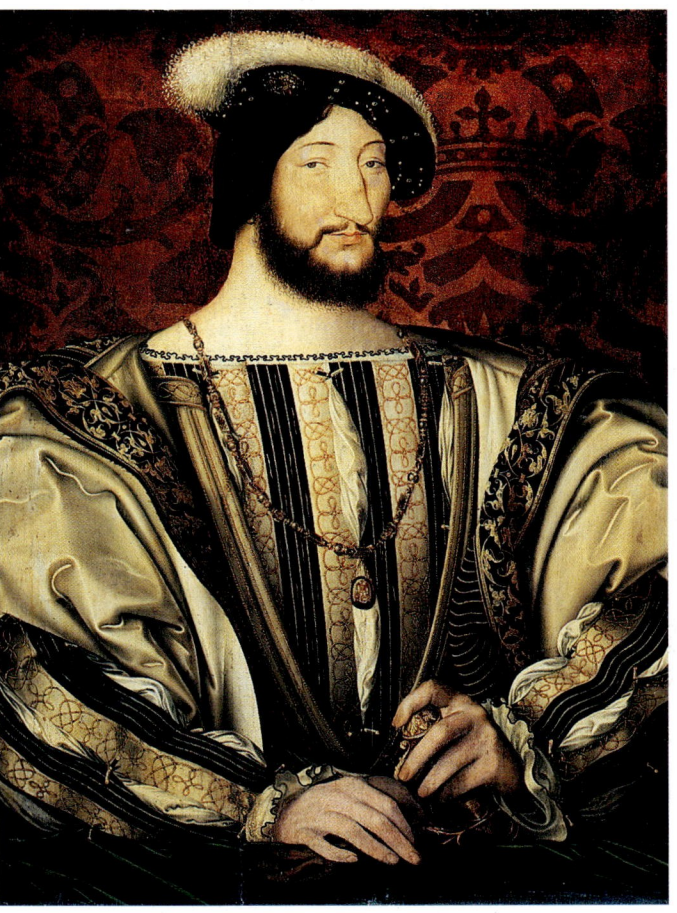

23-11 JEAN CLOUET, *Francis I,* ca. 1525–1530. Tempera and oil on panel, approx. 3′ 2″ × 2′ 5″. Louvre, Paris.

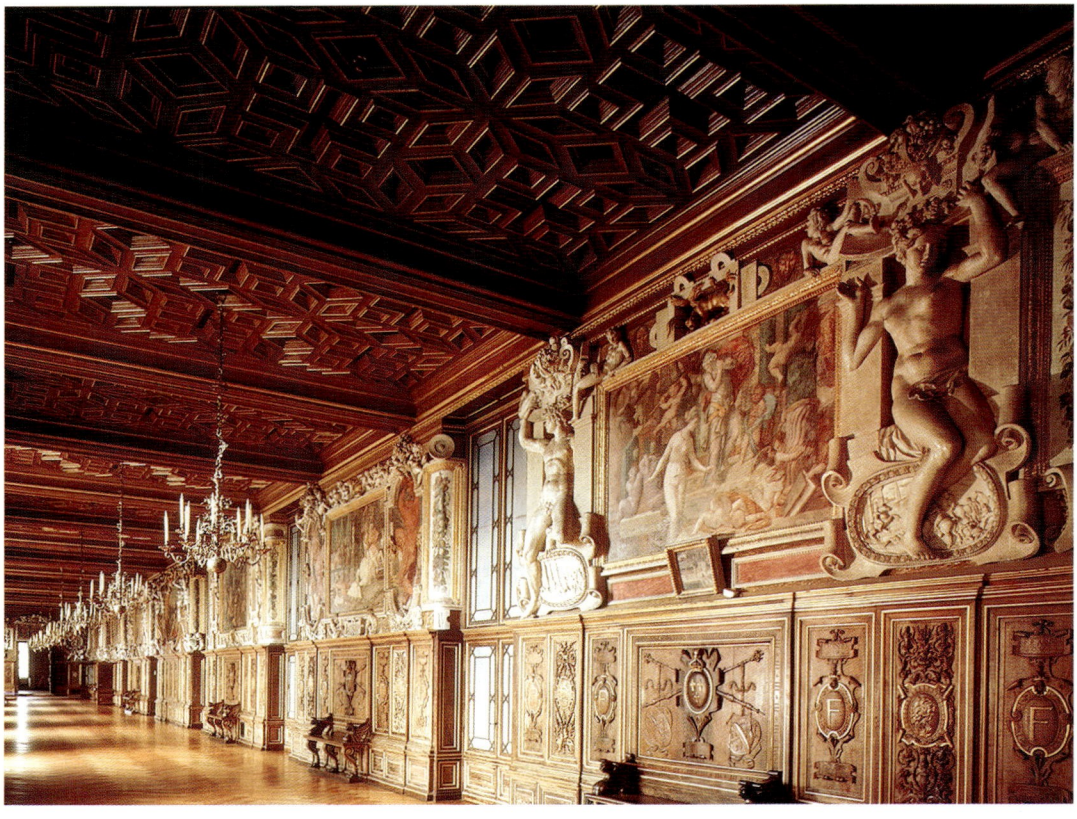

the new royal palace at Fontainebleau. Scholars refer to the sculptors and painters who worked together on this project as the school of Fontainebleau. When Rosso and Primaticcio decorated the Gallery of King Francis I at Fontainebleau (FIG. **23-12**), they combined painting, fresco, imitation mosaic, and stucco sculpture in low and high relief. The abrupt changes in scale and in the texture of the figurative elements are typically Mannerist, as are the compressed space, elongated grace, and stylized poses. The formalized elegance of the paintings also appears in the stucco relief figures and caryatids, and the shift in scale between the painted and the stucco figures adds tension. The combination of painted and stucco relief decorations became extremely popular from that time on and remained a favorite ornamental technique throughout the Baroque and Rococo periods of the 17th and early 18th centuries.

**FROM CASTLES TO CHÂTEAUX** During his reign, Francis I indulged a passion for building by commissioning several large-scale châteaux, among them the Château de Chambord (FIG. **23-13**). Reflecting more peaceful times, these châteaux, developed from the old castles, served as country houses for royalty, who usually built them near forests for use as hunting lodges. Construction on Chambord began in 1519, but Francis I never saw its completion. Chambord's plan, originally drawn by a pupil of Giuliano da Sangallo, includes a central square block with four corridors, in the shape of a cross, and a broad, central staircase that gives access to groups of rooms—ancestors of the modern suite of rooms or apartments. At each of the four corners, a round tower punctuates the square plan, and a moat surrounds the whole. From the exterior, Chambord presents a carefully contrived horizontal accent on three levels, its floors separated by continuous moldings. Windows align precisely, one exactly over another. The Italian palazzo served as the model for this matching of horizontal and vertical features, but above the third level the structure's lines break chaotically into a jumble of high dormers, chimneys, and lanterns that recall soaring ragged Gothic silhouettes on the skyline.

**REDESIGNING THE LOUVRE** Chambord essentially retains French architectural characteristics. During the reign of Francis's successor, Henry II (r. 1547–1559), however, translations of Italian architectural treatises appeared, and Italian architects themselves came to work in France. Moreover, the French turned to Italy for study and travel. Such exchanges caused a more extensive revolution in style than earlier, although certain French elements derived from the Gothic tradition persisted. This incorporation of Italian architectural ideas can be seen in the redesigning of the Louvre in Paris, originally a medieval palace and fortress (see FIG. 20-2). Since Charles V's renovation of the Louvre in the mid-14th century, the castle had languished relatively empty and had thus fallen into a state of disrepair. Francis I initiated this project to update and expand the royal palace, but died before the work was well under way. His architect, PIERRE LESCOT (1510–1578), continued under Henry II and, with the aid of the sculptor JEAN GOUJON (ca. 1510–1565), produced the classical style later associated with 16th-century French architecture.

Although Chambord incorporated the formal vocabulary of the Early Renaissance, particularly from Lombardy, Lescot and his associates were familiar with the 16th-century Renaissance architecture of Bramante and his school. As the west facade of the Square Court (FIG. **23-14**) shows, each of the Louvre's stories forms a complete order, and the cornices project enough to furnish a strong horizontal accent. The arcading on the ground story reflects the ancient Roman use of arches and produces more shadow than in the upper stories due to its recessed placement, thereby strengthening the design's visual base. On the second story, the pilasters rising from bases and the

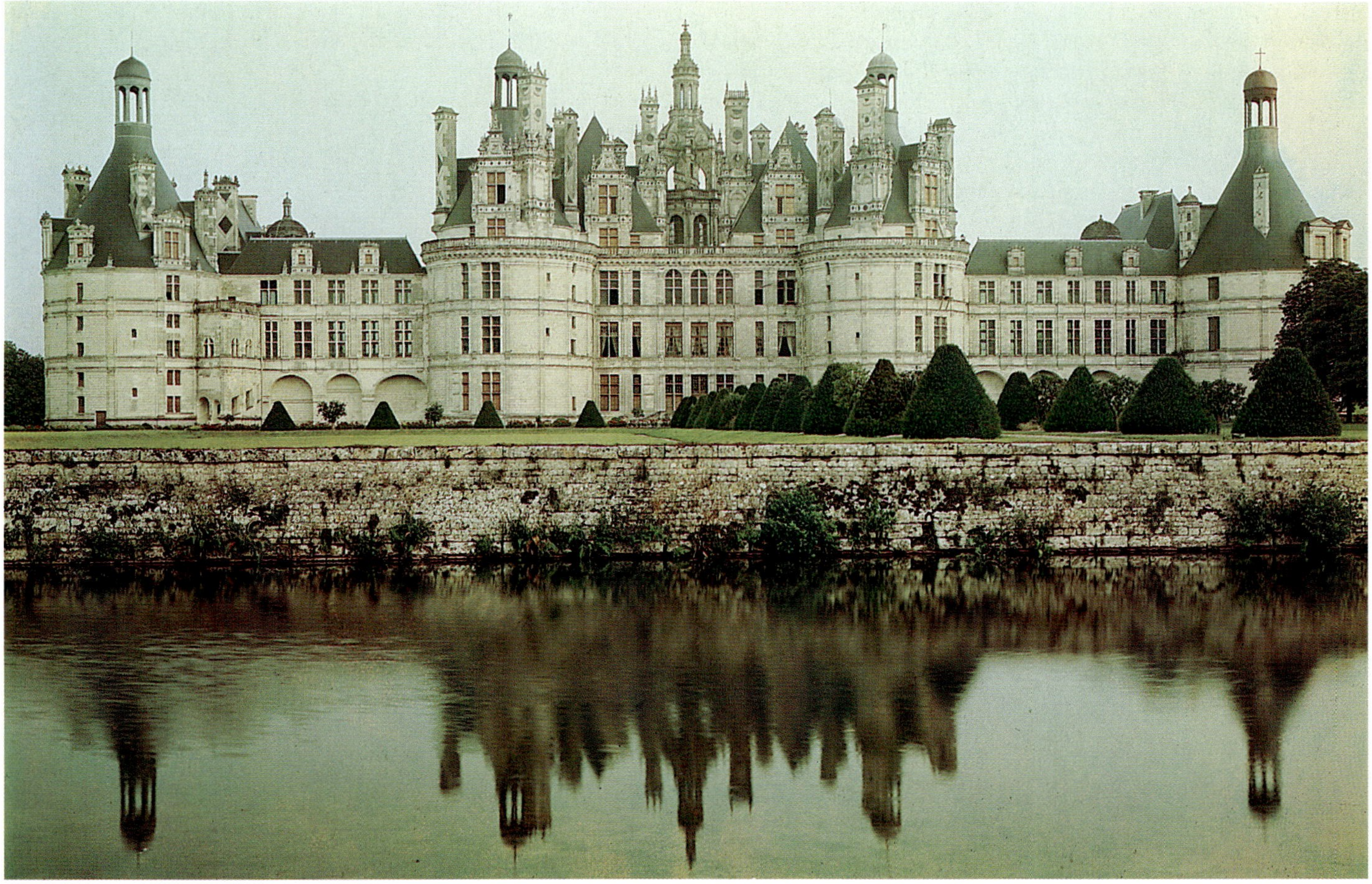

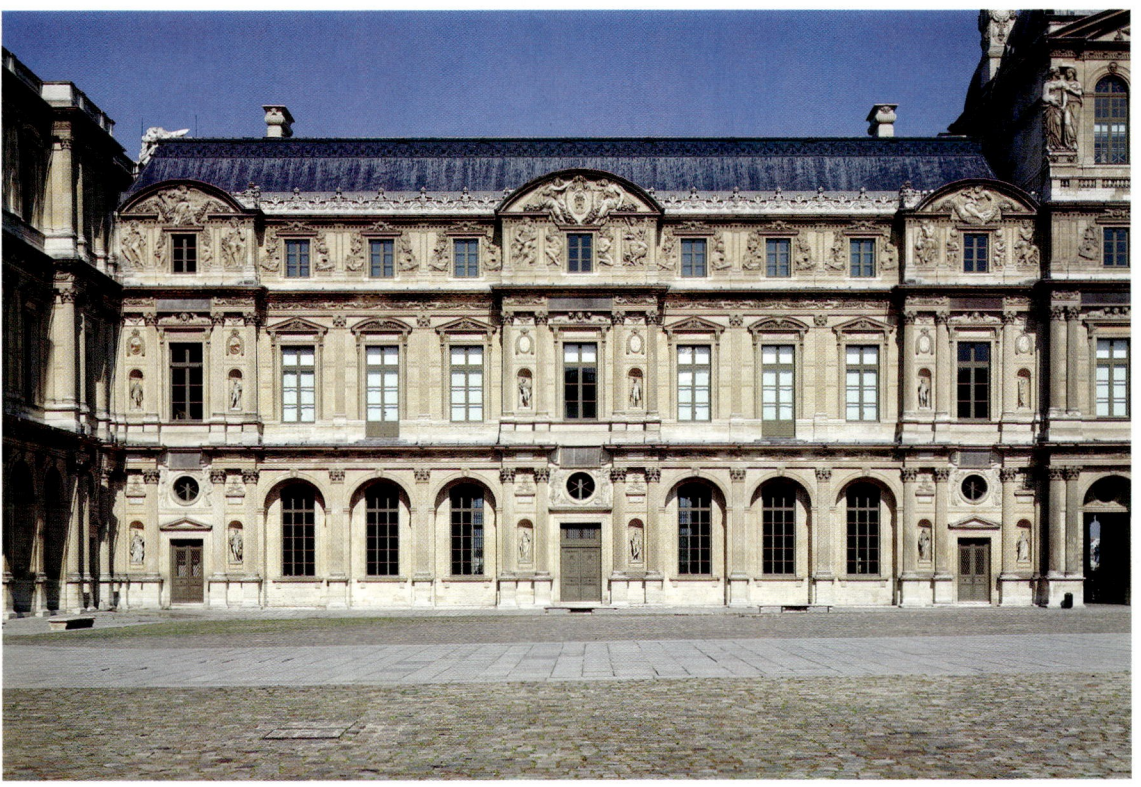

**23-13** Château de Chambord, Chambord, France, begun 1519.

**23-14** PIERRE LESCOT and JEAN GOUJON, west facade of the Square Court of the Louvre, Paris, France, begun 1546.

alternating curved and angular pediments supported by consoles have direct antecedents in several High Renaissance palaces. Yet the decreased height of the stories, the scale of the windows (proportionately much larger than in Renaissance buildings), and the steep roof suggest northern models. Especially French are the pavilions jutting from the wall. A feature the French long favored—double columns framing a niche—punctuates the pavilions. The building's vertical lines assert themselves. Openings deeply penetrate the wall, and sculptures abound. Other northern countries imitated this French classical manner—its double-columned pavilions, tall and wide windows, profuse statuary, and steep roofs—although with local variations. The modified classicism the French produced was the only classicism to serve as a model for northern architects through most of the 16th century. Some scholars believe that the west courtyard facade of the Louvre is the best of French 16th-century architecture; eventually, the French purged their architecture of Italian features, and architects such as FRANÇOIS MANSART

(1598–1666) and PHILIBERT DE L'ORME (1500/15–1570) established a unique French classical architectural style.

**LIGHTNESS, EASE, AND GRACE** The statues of the Louvre courtyard facade, now much restored, are Goujon's work. His *Nymphs* reliefs (FIG. **23-15**; four of the six are shown) from the *Fountain of the Innocents* in Paris originally decorated two facades of a fountain. Appropriately, the nymphs carry or stand next to vases of flowing water. Like the architecture of the Louvre, Goujon's nymphs recall the Italian (particularly Mannerist) canon of figural design. Certainly, their figura serpentinata poses (see Chapter 22, page 632) are Mannerist. Their flowing, clinging draperies parallel the ancient "wet" drapery of Greek sculpture—the figures on the parapet of the Temple of Athena Nike (see FIG. 5-53), for example. Goujon's slender, sinuous figures perform their steps within a confined, unspecified space, and they appear to make one continuous motion, an illusion produced by reversing

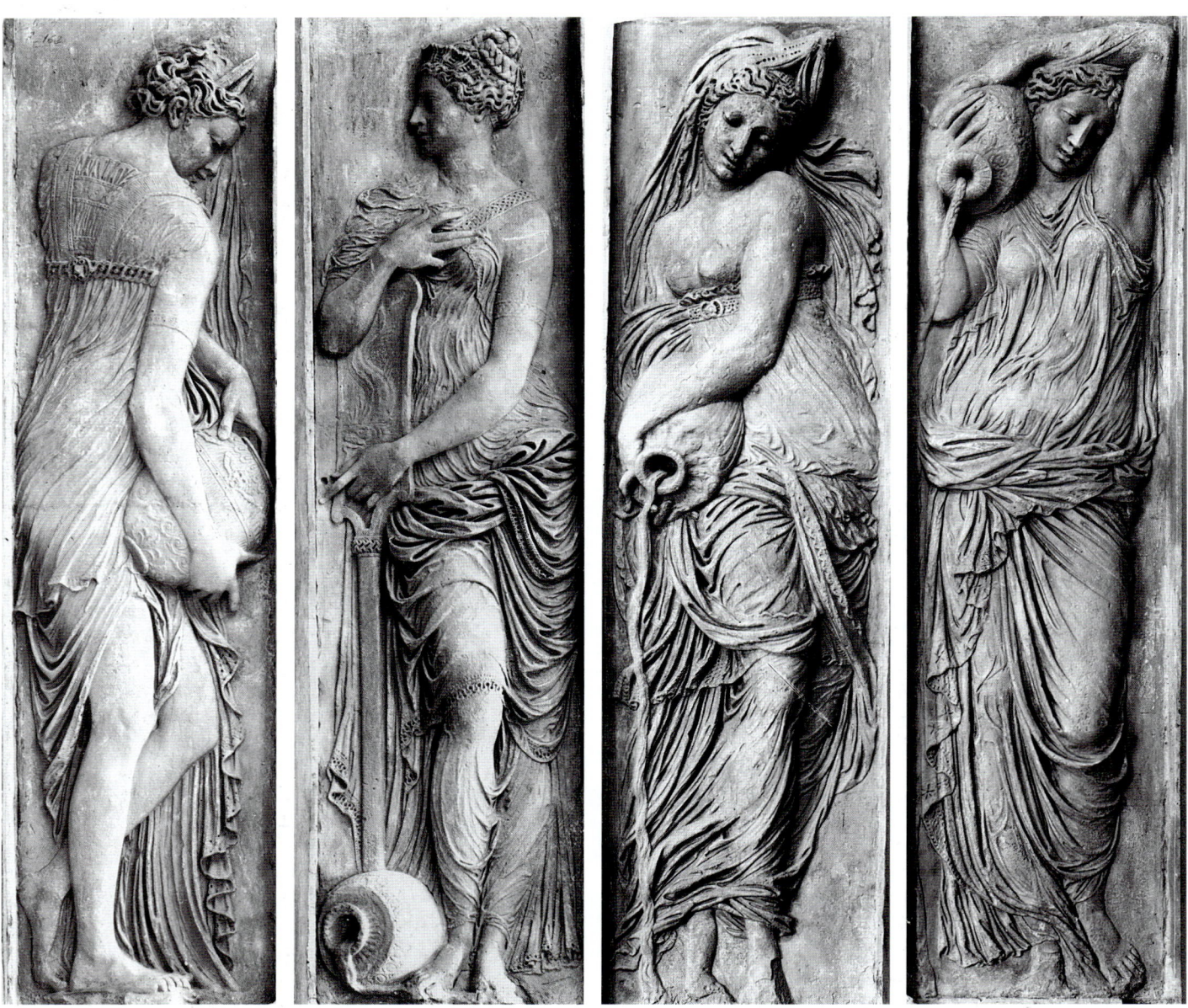

**23-15** JEAN GOUJON, *Nymphs,* from the dismantled *Fountain of the Innocents,* Paris, France, 1548–1549. Marble reliefs, each relief 6′ 4¾″ × 2′ 4¾″. Louvre, Paris.

the gestures, as they might be seen in a mirror. The style of Fontainebleau, and ultimately of Primaticcio and Cellini, guided the sculptor here, but Goujon learned the manner so well that he created originally within it. The nymphs are truly French masterpieces, characterized by lightness, ease, and grace.

# THE NETHERLANDS

## *Prosperous Provinces*

With the demise of the Duchy of Burgundy in 1477 and the division of that territory between France and the Holy Roman Empire, the Netherlands at the beginning of the 16th century consisted of 17 provinces (corresponding to modern Holland, Belgium, and Luxembourg). The Netherlands was among the most commercially advanced and prosperous of European countries. Its extensive network of rivers and easy access to the Atlantic Ocean provided a setting conducive to overseas trade, and shipbuilding was one of the most profitable businesses. The geographic location of the region's commercial center changed toward the end of the 15th century. Partly from the silting of the Bruges estuary, traffic shifted to Antwerp, which became the hub of economic activity in the Netherlands after 1510. As many as 500 ships a day passed through Antwerp's harbor, and large trading colonies from England, the Holy Roman Empire, Italy, Portugal, and Spain established themselves in the city.

During the 16th century, the Netherlands was under the political control of Philip II of Spain, who had inherited the region from his father, Charles V (r. 1519–1556). The economic prosperity of the Netherlands served as a potent incentive for Philip II to strengthen his control over those provinces. However, his heavy-handed tactics and repressive measures led in 1579 to revolt, resulting in the formation of two federations. The Union of Arras, a Catholic union of southern Netherlandish provinces, remained under Spanish dominion, and the Union of Utrecht, a Protestant union of northern provinces, became the Dutch Republic.

The increasing number of Netherlandish citizens converting to Protestantism affected the arts, as evidenced by a corresponding decrease in large-scale altarpieces and religious works (although such works continued to be commissioned for Catholic churches). Much of Netherlandish art of this period provides a wonderful glimpse into the lives of various strata of society, from nobility to peasantry, capturing their activities, environment, and values.

**REINTERPRETING CLASSICISM** Developments in Italian Renaissance art interested many Netherlandish artists. JAN GOSSAERT (ca. 1478–1535) associated with humanist scholars and visited Italy. There, Gossaert (who adopted the Latinized name Mabuse, after his birthplace of Maubeuge) became fascinated with classical antiquity and its mythological subjects. Giorgio Vasari, the Italian historian and Gossaert's contemporary, wrote that "Jean Gossart [sic] of Mabuse was almost the first who took from Italy into Flanders the true method of making scenes full of nude figures and poetical inventions,"[4] although it is obvious he derived much of his classicism from Dürer.

Indeed, Dürer's *The Fall of Man* (FIG. 23-6) inspired the composition and poses in Gossaert's *Neptune and Amphitrite* (FIG. **23-16**). However, unlike Dürer's exquisitely small engraving, Gossaert's painting is more than six feet tall and four feet wide. The artist executed the painting with expected Netherlandish polish, skillfully drawing and carefully modeling the figures. Gossaert depicted the

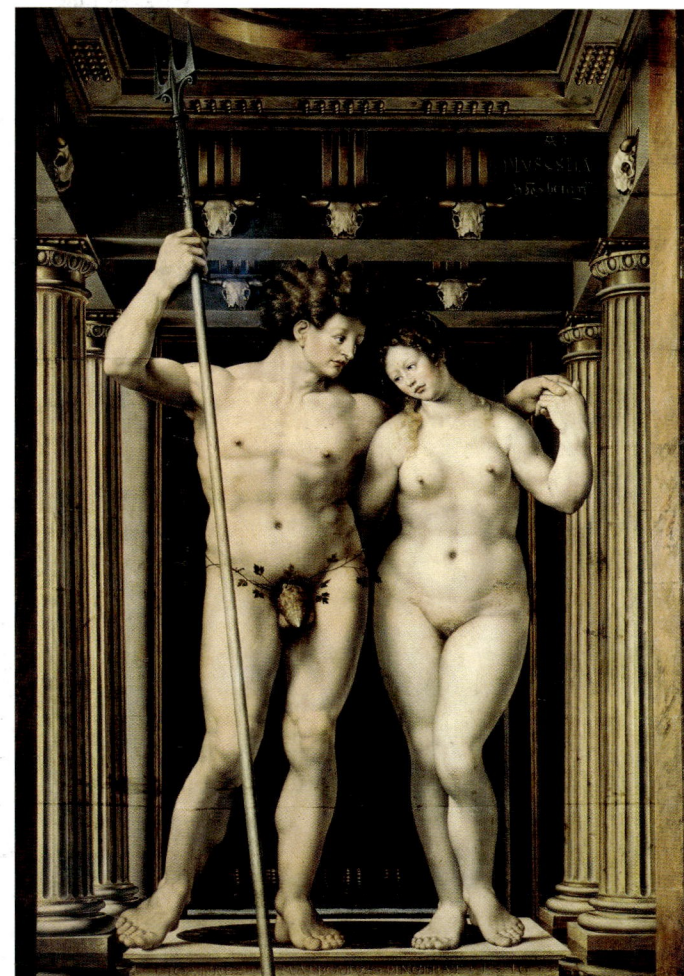

**23-16** JAN GOSSAERT (MABUSE), *Neptune and Amphitrite*, ca. 1516. Oil on panel, 6′ 2″ × 4′ 1″. Gemäldegalerie, Staatliche Museen, Berlin.

sea god with his traditional attribute, the trident, and wearing a laurel wreath and an ornate conch shell, rather than Dürer's fig leaf. Amphitrite is fleshy and, like Neptune, stands in a contrapposto stance. The architecture is an unusual mix of classical elements. For example, parts of Doric and Ionic orders are combined with egg-and-dart patterns and *bucrania* (ox skull decorations). Gossaert likely based this fanciful setting on sketches he had made of architectural structures while in Rome. He had traveled to Italy with Philip, Bastard of Burgundy (the patron of this large-scale painting on panel). A Burgundian admiral (hence the Neptune reference), Philip became a bishop and kept this work in the innermost room of his castle.

**BOTH SECULAR AND SPIRITUAL** Antwerp's growth and prosperity, along with its wealthy merchants' propensity for collecting and purchasing art, attracted artists to the city. Among them was QUINTEN MASSYS (ca. 1466–1530), who became Antwerp's leading master after 1510. Son of a Louvain blacksmith, Massys demonstrated a willingness to explore the styles and modes of a variety of models, from van Eyck to Bosch and from van der Weyden to Dürer and Leonardo. Yet his eclecticism was subtle and discriminating, enriched by an inventiveness that gave a personal stamp to his paintings and made him a popular, as well as important, artist.

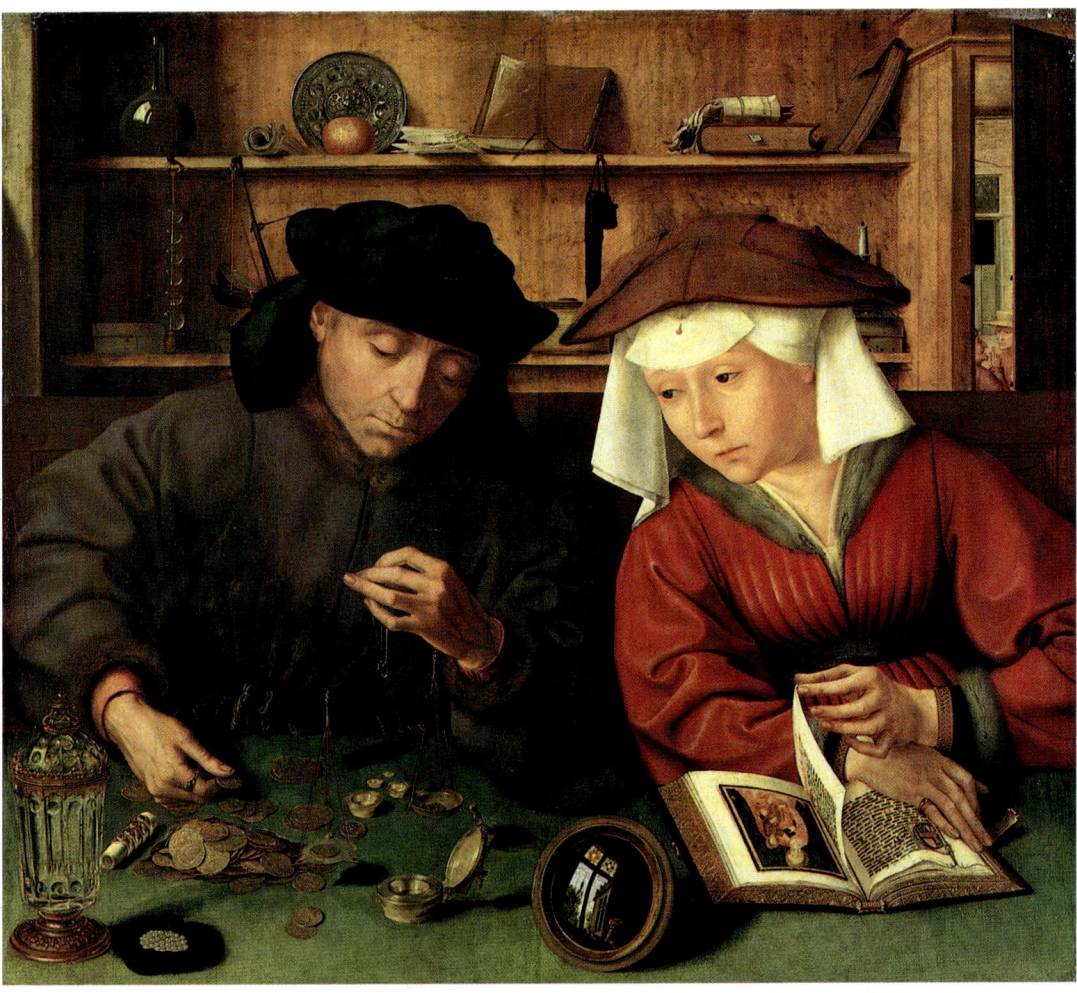

**23-17** QUINTEN MASSYS, *Money-Changer and His Wife*, 1514. Oil on panel, 2′ 3¾″ × 2′ 2⅜″. Louvre, Paris.

In *Money-Changer and His Wife* (FIG. **23-17**), Massys presented a professional man transacting business. He holds scales, checking the weight of coins on the table. His wife interrupts her reading of a prayer book to watch him. The artist's detailed rendering of the figures, setting, and objects suggests a fidelity to observable fact. Thus, this work provides the viewer with insight into developing mercantilist practices. *Money-Changer and His Wife* also reveals Netherlandish values and mores. Although the painting highlights the financial transactions that were an increasingly prominent part of secular life in the 16th-century Netherlands, Massys tempered this focus on the material world with numerous references to the importance of a moral, righteous, and spiritual life. Not only does the wife hold a prayer book, but the artist also included other traditional religious symbols (for example, the carafe with water and candlestick). Massys included two small vignettes that refer to the balance this couple must establish between their worldly existence and their commitment to God's word. On the right, through a window, an old man talks with another man, suggesting idleness and gossip. The reflected image in the convex mirror on the counter offsets this image of sloth and foolish chatter. There, a man reads what is most likely a Bible or prayer book; behind him is a church steeple.

An inscription on the original frame (now lost) seems to have reinforced this message. According to a 17th-century scholar, this inscription read, "Let the balance be just and the weights equal" (Lev. 19:36), which applies both to the money-changer's professional conduct and the eventual Last Judgment.

**MEETING SPIRITUAL OBLIGATIONS** This tendency to inject reminders about spiritual well-being emerges in *Meat Still-Life* (FIG. **23-18**) by PIETER AERTSEN (ca. 1507–1575), who worked in Antwerp for more than three decades. At first glance, this painting appears to be a descriptive genre scene. On display is an array of meat products—a side of a hog, chickens, sausages, a stuffed intestine, pig's feet, meat pies, a cow's head, a hog's head, and hanging entrails. Also visible are fish, pretzels, cheese, and butter. Like Massys, Aertsen embedded strategically placed religious images as reminders to the viewer. In the background of *Meat Still-Life,* Joseph leads a donkey carrying Mary and the Christ Child. The Holy Family stops to offer alms to a beggar and his son, while the people behind the Holy Family wend their way toward a church. Furthermore, the crossed fishes on the platter and the pretzels and wine in the rafters on the upper left all refer to "spiritual food" (pretzels often served as bread during Lent). Aertsen accentuated these allusions to salvation through Christ by contrasting them to their opposite—a life of gluttony, lust, and sloth. He represented this degeneracy with the oyster and mussel shells (believed by Netherlanders to possess aphrodisiacal properties) scattered on the ground on the painting's right side, along with the people seen eating and carousing nearby under the roof.

**AN ACCOMPLISHED WOMAN ARTIST** With the accumulation of wealth in the Netherlands, portraits increased in popularity. The self-portrait (FIG. **23-19**) by CATERINA VAN HEMESSEN (1528–1587) is purportedly the first known northern European

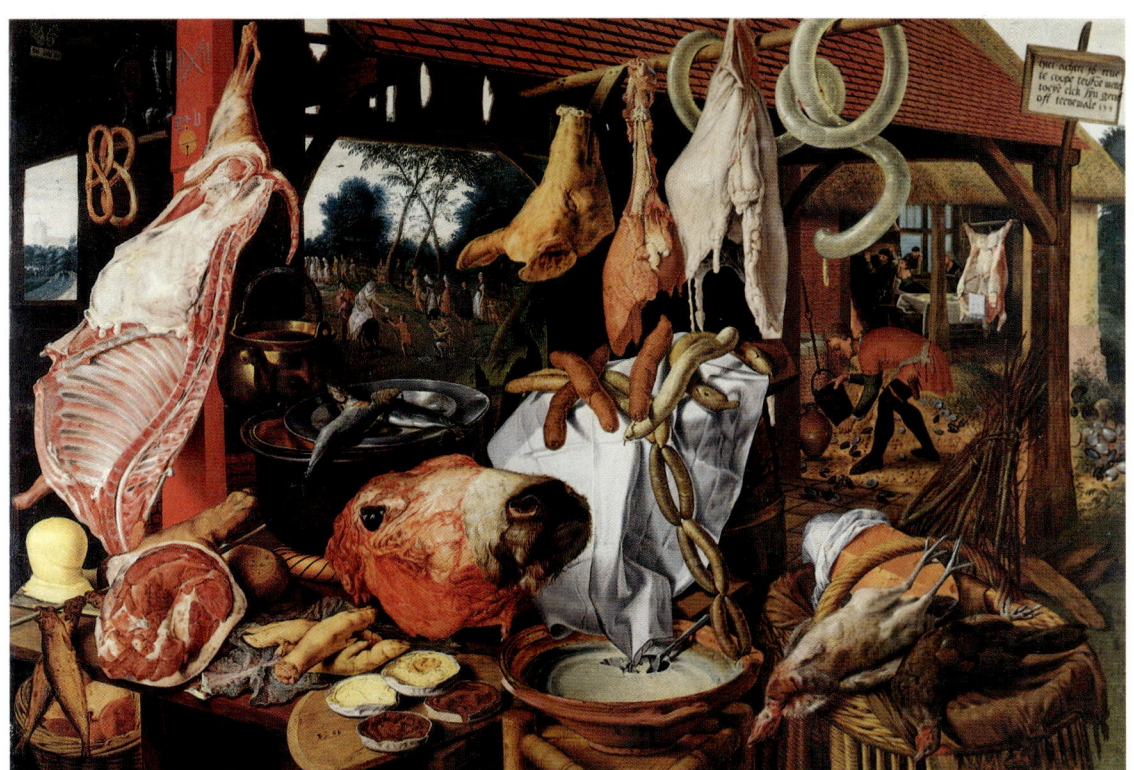

**23-18** Pieter Aertsen, *Meat Still-Life,* 1551. Oil on panel, 4′ $\frac{3}{8}$″ × 6′ 5$\frac{3}{4}$″. Uppsala University Art Collection, Uppsala.

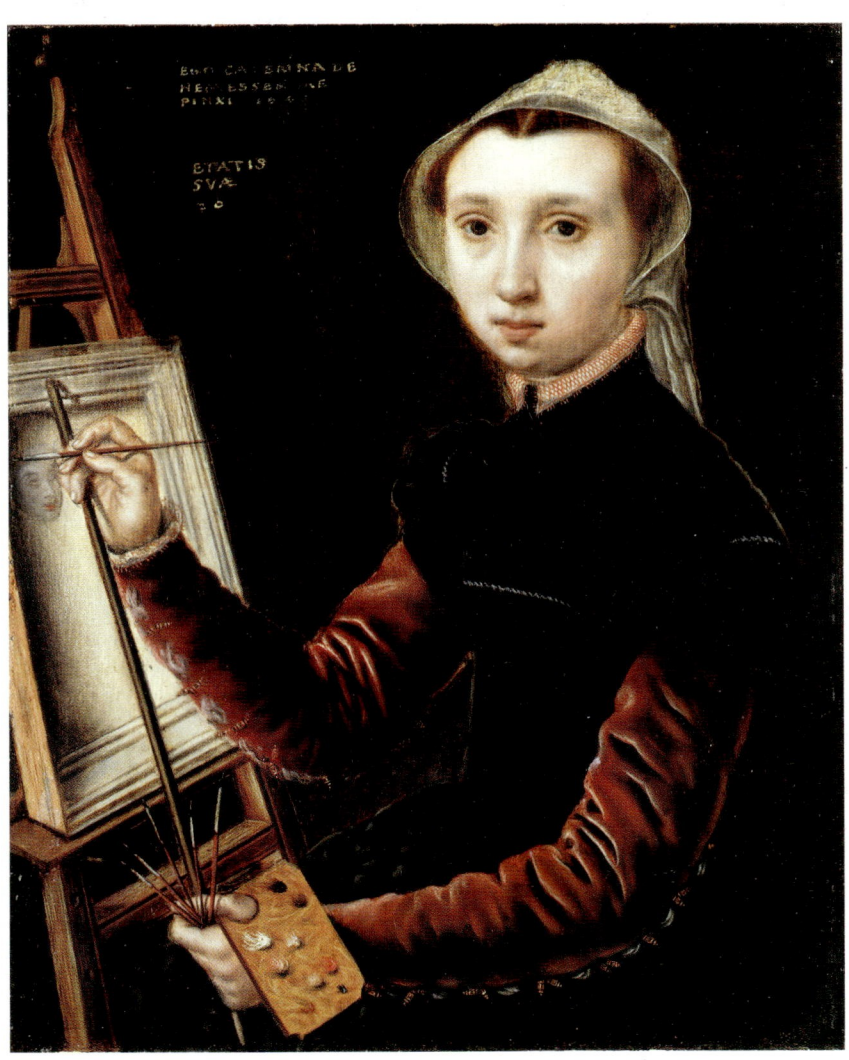

**23-19** Caterina van Hemessen, *Self-Portrait,* 1548. Oil on panel, 1′ $\frac{3}{4}$″ × 9$\frac{7}{8}$″. Kunstmuseum, Öffentliche Kunstsammlung Basel.

self-portrait by a woman. Here, she confidently presented herself as an artist; she interrupts her painting to look toward the viewer. She holds brushes, a palette, and a *maulstick* (a stick used to steady the hand while painting) in her left hand, and delicately applies pigment to the canvas with her right hand. Van Hemessen's father, Jan Sanders van Hemessen, a well-known painter, trained her. Caterina ensured proper identification (and credit) through the inscription in the painting: "Caterina van Hemessen painted me / 1548 / her age 20."

**A RENOWNED COURT PAINTER** LEVINA TEERLINC (1515–1576) of Bruges established herself as such a respected artist that she was invited to England to paint miniatures for the courts of Henry VIII and his successors. There, she was a formidable rival of some of her male contemporaries at the court, such as Holbein, and received greater compensation for her work than they did for theirs. Teerlinc's considerable skill is evident in a life-size portrait attributed to her, which depicts Elizabeth I (FIG. **23-20**) as a composed, youthful princess. Daughter of Henry VIII and Anne Boleyn, Elizabeth was probably in her late twenties when she sat for this portrait. As presented by Teerlinc, Elizabeth is attired in an elegant brocaded gown. Appropriate to her station in life, she is adorned with extravagant jewelry and wears a headdress based on a style popularized by her mother.

That female artists like van Hemessen and Teerlinc were able to achieve such success is a testament to their determination and skill. Despite the difficulties for women in obtaining artistic training (see "The Artist's Profession in Flanders," Chapter 20, page

556), women artists contributed significantly to the lofty reputation enjoyed by Flemish artists. Beyond their participation as artists in the 16th-century art world, women also played an important role as patrons. Politically powerful women such as Margaret of Austria (regent of the Netherlands during the early 16th century; 1480–1530) and Mary of Hungary (queen consort of Hungary; 1505–1558) were avid collectors and patrons, and contributed significantly to the thriving state of the arts. Like other art patrons (see "Art to Order: Commissions and Patronage," Chapter 19, page 526), these women collected and commissioned art not only for the aesthetic pleasure it provided but also for the status it bestowed on them and the cultural sophistication it represented.

**"A GOOD LANDSCAPE PAINTER"** Landscape painting also flourished. Particularly well known for his landscapes was JOACHIM PATINIR (d. 1524). According to one scholar, the word *landscape (Landschaft)* first emerged in German literature as a characterization of an artistic genre when Dürer described Patinir as a "good landscape painter." In *Landscape with Saint Jerome* (FIG. **23-21**), Patinir subordinated the biblical scene to the exotic and detailed landscape. Saint Jerome, who removes a thorn from a lion's paw in the foreground, appears dwarfed by craggy rock formations, rolling fields, and expansive bodies of water in the background. Patinir amplified the sense of distance by masterfully using color to enhance the visual effect of recession and advance.

**A WINTRY LANDSCAPE** The early high-horizoned "cosmographical" landscapes of PIETER BRUEGEL THE ELDER (ca. 1528–1569) reveal both an interest in the interrelationship of human beings and nature and Patinir's influence. But in Bruegel's paintings, no matter how huge a slice of the world the artist shows, human activities remain the dominant theme. Like many of his contemporaries, Bruegel traveled to Italy, where he seems to have spent almost two years, going as far south as Sicily. Unlike other artists, however, Bruegel chose not to incorporate classical elements into his paintings. The impact of his Italian experiences emerges in his work most frequently in the Italian or Alpine landscape features, which he recorded in numerous drawings during his journey.

**23-20** Attributed to LEVINA TEERLINC. *Elizabeth I as a Princess,* ca. 1559. Oil on oak panel, 3′ 6¾″ × 2′ 8¼″. The Royal Collection, Windsor Castle, Windsor, England.

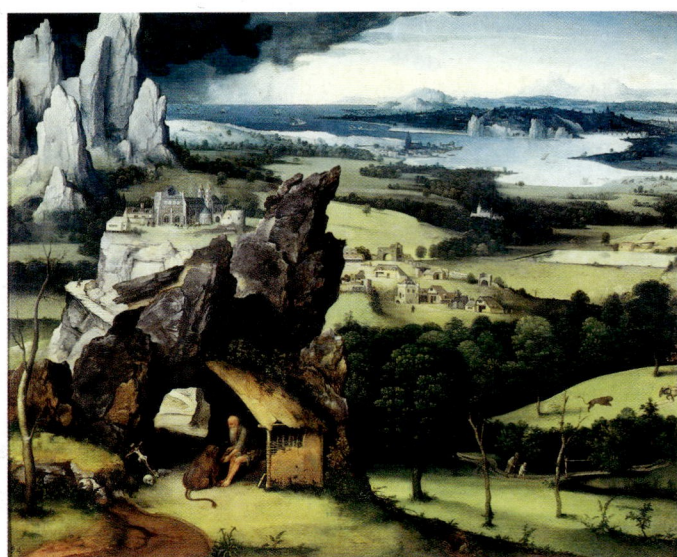

**23-21** JOACHIM PATINIR, *Landscape with Saint Jerome,* ca. 1520–1524. Oil on panel, 2′ 5⅛″ × 2′ 11⅞″. Museo del Prado, Madrid.

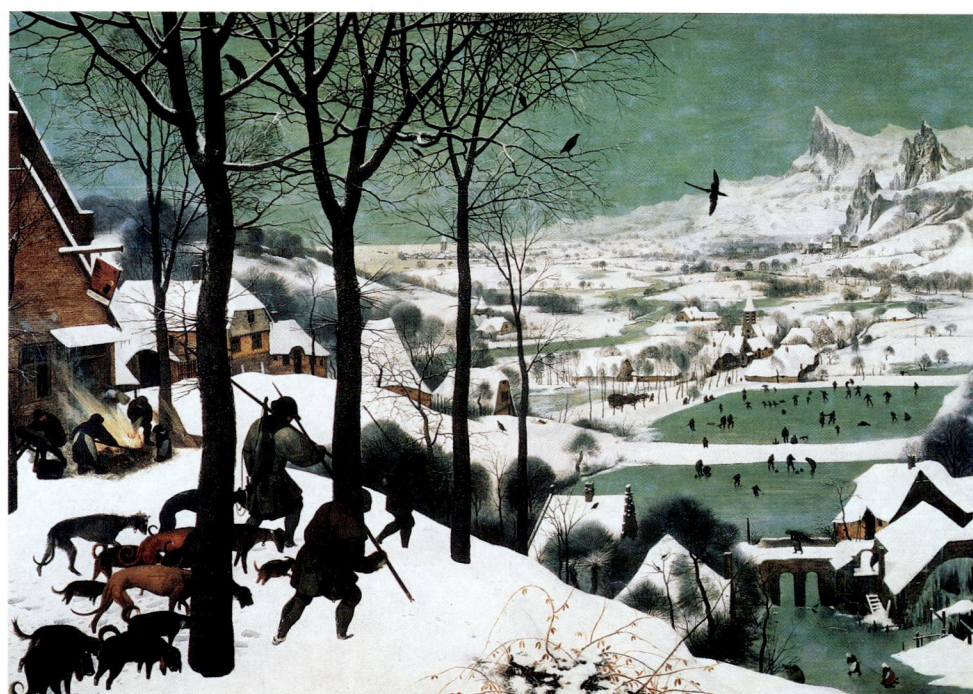

**23-22** Pieter Bruegel the Elder, *Hunters in the Snow,* 1565. Oil on panel, approx. 3′ 10″ × 5′ 4″. Kunsthistorisches Museum, Vienna.

*Hunters in the Snow* (FIG. **23-22**) is one of five surviving paintings of a series of six illustrating seasonal changes in the year, and refers back to older Netherlandish traditions of depicting seasons and peasants found in Books of Hours. It shows human figures and landscape locked in winter cold; Bruegel's production of this painting in 1565 coincided with a particularly severe winter. The weary hunters return with their hounds, women build fires, skaters skim the frozen pond, and the town and its church huddle in their mantle of snow; beyond this typically Netherlandic winter scene lies a bit of Alpine landscape. Aside from this trace of fantasy, however, the artist rendered the landscape in an optically accurate manner. It develops smoothly from foreground to background and draws the viewer diagonally into its depths. Bruegel's consummate skill in using line and shape and his subtlety in tonal harmony make this one of the great landscape paintings and an occidental counterpart of the masterworks of classical Chinese landscape.

**PROVERBIAL WISDOM** Among the paintings that capture the Netherlandish obsession with proverbs during the 16th century is Bruegel's *Netherlandish Proverbs* (FIG. **23-23**). This

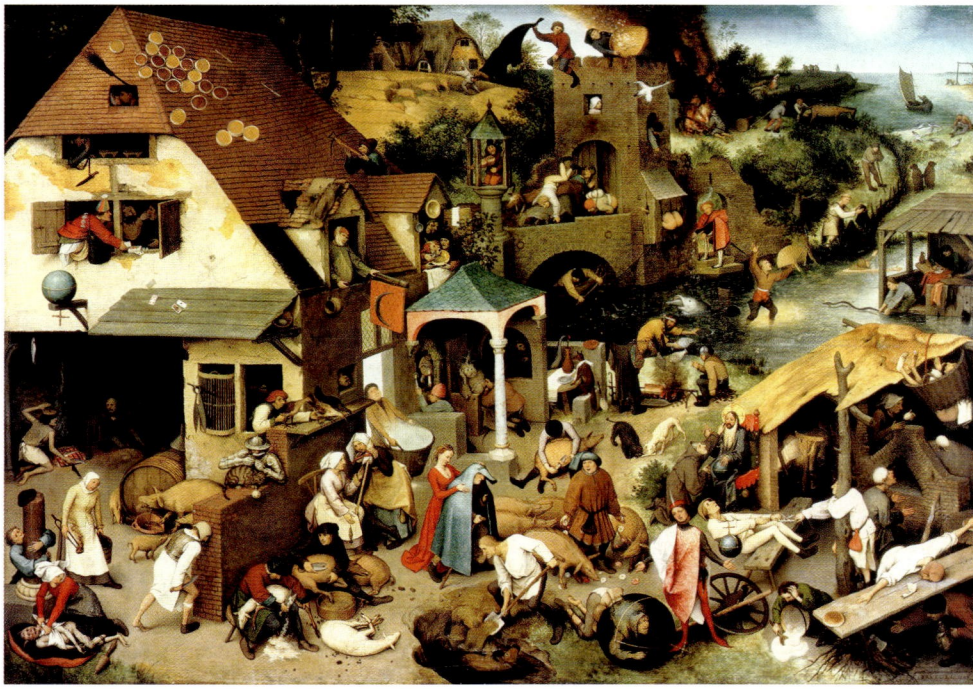

**23-23** Pieter Bruegel the Elder, *Netherlandish Proverbs,* 1559. Oil on panel, 3′ 10″ × 5′ 4⅛″. Gemäldegalerie, Staatliche Museen, Berlin.

work depicts a Netherlandish village populated by a wide range of people (nobility, peasants, and clerics). From a bird's-eye view, the spectator encounters a mesmerizing and mind-boggling array of activities reminiscent of the topsy-turvy scenes of Bosch (see FIG. 20-18). By illustrating more than a hundred proverbs in this one painting, the artist indulged his audience's passion for detailed and clever imagery. The complexity of the images demands very close scrutiny. The proverbs depicted include, on the far left, a man in blue gnawing on a pillar ("He bites the column"—an image of hypocrisy); to his right, a man "beats his head against a wall" (an ambitious idiot); on the roof a man "shoots one arrow after the other, but hits nothing" (a shortsighted fool); and, in the far distance, the "blind lead the blind." In addition to capturing the Netherlanders' morality and mentality, *Netherlandish Proverbs* serves more generally as a study of human nature.

Toward the end of Bruegel's life, his commentary on the human condition took on an increasingly bitter edge. The Netherlands, racked by religious conflict, became the seat of cruel atrocities, made even more terrible by Catholic Spain's attempts to extinguish the Reformation.

# SPAIN

Spain emerged as the dominant European power at the end of the 16th century. Under Charles V of Habsburg (r. 1516–1556) and his son, Philip II (r. 1556–1598), the Spanish Empire dominated a territory greater in extent than any ever known—a large part of Europe, the western Mediterranean, a strip of North Africa, and vast expanses in the New World. Spain acquired many of its New World colonies through aggressive overseas exploration. Among the most notable conquistadors sailing under the Spanish flag were Christopher Columbus (1451–1506), Vasco Nuñez de Balboa (ca. 1475–1517), Ferdinand Magellan (1480–1521), Hernán Cortés (1485–1547), and Francisco Pizarro (ca. 1470–1541). The Habsburg Empire, enriched by the New World plunder, supported the most powerful military force in Europe. Spain defended and then promoted the interests of the Catholic Church in its battle against the inroads of the Protestant Reformation; indeed, Philip II earned the title "Most Catholic King." Spain's crusading spirit, nourished by centuries of war with Islam, engaged body and soul in forming the most Catholic civilization of Europe and the Americas. In the 16th century, for good or for ill, Spain left the mark of Spanish power, religion, language, and culture on two hemispheres.

**A ROYAL CLASSICAL REVIVAL** Italianate classicism made its appearance in the unfinished palace of Charles V in the Alhambra in Granada (FIG. **23-24**), which is the work of the painter-architect PEDRO MACHUCA (active 1520–1550). Superimposed Doric and Ionic orders, which support continuous horizontal entablatures rather than arches, ring the circular central courtyard. The ornament consists only of the details of the orders themselves, which Machuca rendered with the simplicity, clarity, and authority found in the work of Bramante and his school. The lower story recalls the ring colonnade of the Tempietto (see FIG. 22-8); although here the architect reversed the curve. This pure classicism, entirely exceptional in Spain at this time, may reflect Charles V's personal taste acquired on one of his journeys to Italy. (The king, after all, was an enthusiastic patron of Titian.)

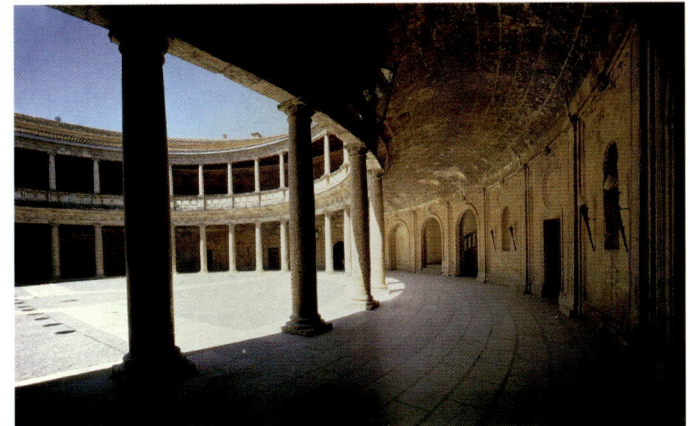

**23-24** PEDRO MACHUCA, courtyard of the palace of Charles V, Alhambra, Granada, Spain, ca. 1526–1568. Institut Amatller D'art Hispanic.

Machuca may also have sojourned in Italy, and the courtyard may have been his attempt to incorporate elements of classical architecture. In addition, the simplicity of the classically inspired architecture (which contrasts sharply with the intricate designs and surface patterning of Islamic art and architecture) surely had symbolic resonance at a site that was controlled by the Muslims until 1492 (see FIG. 13-17). By utilizing an architectural style firmly rooted in European culture, Machuca symbolically "reclaimed" this formerly Muslim site.

**A "DYNASTIC PANTHEON"** Charles V's successor to the Spanish throne, Philip II, appreciated the streamlined clarity of Italian-derived classicism but desired a more unique style. His tastes emerged in the expansive complex called the Escorial (FIG. **23-25**), which JUAN BAUTISTA DE TOLEDO (d. 1567) and JUAN DE HERRERA (ca. 1530–1597), principally the latter, constructed for Philip II. In his will, Charles V stipulated that a "dynastic pantheon" be built to house the remains of past and future monarchs of Spain. Philip II, obedient to his father's wishes, chose a site some 30 miles northwest of Madrid in rugged terrain with barren mountains. Here, he built the Escorial, not only a royal mausoleum but also a church, a monastery, and a palace. Legend has it that the gridlike plan for the enormous complex, 625 feet wide and 520 feet deep, symbolized the gridiron where Saint Lawrence, patron of the Escorial, was martyred.

The whole vast structure is in keeping with Philip's austere and conscientious character, his passionate Catholic religiosity, his proud reverence for his dynasty, and his stern determination to impose his will worldwide. He insisted that in designing the Escorial, the architect focus on simplicity of form, severity in the whole, nobility without arrogance, and majesty without ostentation. The result is a classicism of Doric severity, ultimately derived from Italian architecture and with the grandeur of Saint Peter's implicit in the scheme. But it is unique in Spanish and European architecture—a matchless style, even though later structures reflect it.

Only the three entrances, with the dominant central portal framed by superimposed orders and topped by a pediment in the Italian fashion, break the long sweep of the structure's severely plain walls. Massive square towers punctuate the four corners. The architect's stress on the central axis, with its subdued echoes in the two flanking portals, anticipates the three-part organization of

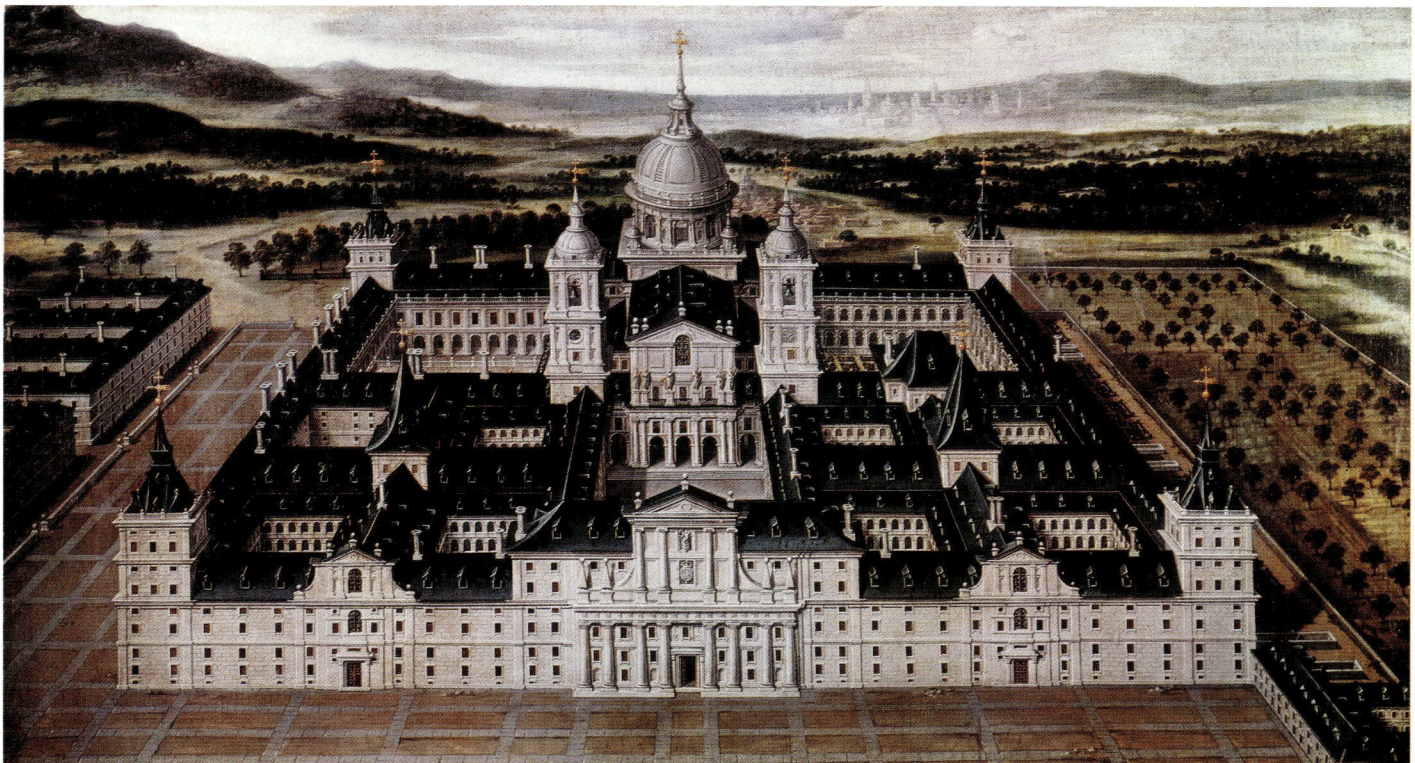

**23-25** JUAN DE HERRERA and JUAN BAUTISTA DE TOLEDO, aerial view of Escorial, near Madrid, Spain, ca. 1563–1584 (after an anonymous 18th-century painting). Institut Amatller D'art Hispanic.

later Baroque palace facades. The construction material for the entire complex (including the church) — granite, a difficult stone to work — conveys a feeling of starkness and gravity. The church's massive facade and the austere geometry of the interior complex, with its blocky walls and ponderous arches, produce an effect of overwhelming strength and weight.

The entire complex is a monument to the collaboration of a great king and a remarkably understanding architect. The Escorial stands as the overpowering architectural expression of Spain's spirit in its heroic epoch and of the character of Philip II, the extraordinary ruler who directed it.

**A SPANISH MANNERIST** Doménikos Theotokópoulos, called EL GRECO (ca. 1547–1614), was born on Crete but emigrated to Italy as a young man. In his youth, he absorbed the traditions of Late Byzantine frescoes and mosaics. While still young, El Greco went to Venice, where he was connected with Titian's workshop, although Tintoretto's painting seems to have made a stronger impression on him. A brief trip to Rome explains the influences of Roman and Florentine Mannerism on his work. By 1577, he had left for Spain to spend the rest of his life in Toledo.

El Greco's art is a strong personal blending of Late Byzantine and late Italian Mannerist elements. The intense emotionalism of his paintings, which naturally appealed to the pious fervor of the Spanish, and a great reliance on color bound him to 16th-century Venetian art and to Mannerism. His strong sense of movement and use of light, however, prefigured the Baroque style. El Greco's art was not strictly Spanish (although it appealed to certain sectors of that society), for it had no Spanish antecedents and little effect on later Spanish painters. Nevertheless, El Greco's hybrid style captured the fervor of Spanish Catholicism. This fervor is vividly expressed in the artist's masterpiece, *The Burial of Count*

*Orgaz* (FIG. **23-26**), painted in 1586 for the church of Santo Tomé in Toledo. El Greco based the artwork on the legend that the count of Orgaz, who had died some three centuries before and who had been a great benefactor of Santo Tomé, was buried in the church by Saints Stephen and Augustine, who miraculously descended from heaven to lower the count's body into its sepulcher.

In the painting, the brilliant Heaven that opens above irradiates the earthly scene; El Greco carefully distinguished the terrestrial and celestial spheres. He represented the terrestrial with a firm realism, whereas he depicted the celestial, in his quite personal manner, with elongated undulating figures, fluttering draperies, and a visionary swirling cloud. Below, the two saints lovingly lower the count's armor-clad body, the armor and heavy draperies painted with all the rich sensuousness of the Venetian school. A solemn chorus of black-clad Spanish personages fills the background. In the carefully individualized features of these figures, El Greco demonstrated that he was also a great portraitist. These men call to mind both the conquistadors of the early 16th century and the Spanish naval officers who, two years after the completion of this painting, led the Great Armada against both Protestant England and the Netherlands.

The upward glances of some of the figures below and the flight of an angel above link the painting's lower and upper spheres. The action of the angel, who carries the count's soul in his arms as Saint John and the Virgin intercede for it before the throne of Christ, reinforces this connection. El Greco's deliberate change in style to distinguish between the two levels of reality gives the viewer an opportunity to see the artist's early and late manners in the same work, one below the other. His relatively sumptuous and realistic presentation of the earthly sphere is still strongly rooted in Venetian art, but the abstractions and distortions El Greco used to show the immaterial nature of the Heavenly realm characterized his later style. His elongated figures existing in undefined spaces, bathed in a cool light of

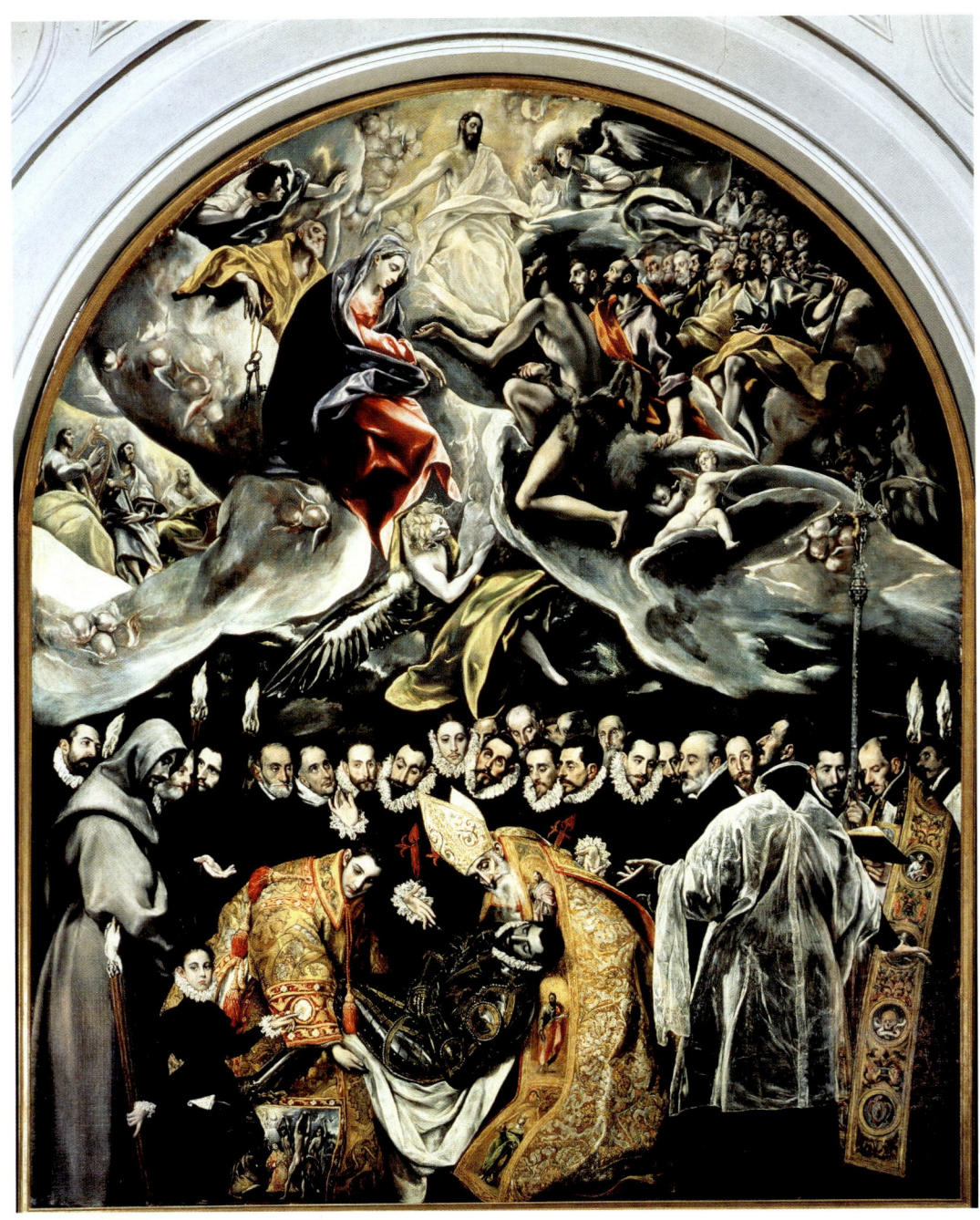

**23-26** EL GRECO, *The Burial of Count Orgaz*, Santo Tomé, Toledo, Spain, 1586. Oil on canvas, approx. 16′ × 12′.

uncertain origin, explain El Greco's usual classification as a Mannerist, but it is difficult to apply that label to him without reservations. Although he used Mannerist formal devices, El Greco's primary concerns were emotion and conveying his religious fervor or arousing that of observers. The forcefulness of his paintings is the result of his unique, highly developed expressive style.

## CONCLUSION

The 16th century in northern Europe and Spain was a century of upheaval, both religious and political. The Reformation and the creation of Protestantism brought about far-reaching change.

Protestants promoted a spiritual model that differed from Catholicism in its emphasis on absolute faith and reliance on the Bible. These beliefs led to less ostentatious forms of art; in particular, Protestants discouraged the production of expansive decoration programs such as those regularly found in Catholic churches. The 16th century in the north was also characterized by extensive military hostilities. Yet despite the conflicts between the various European countries, extensive dialogue transpired among artists of these countries, and artistic influence and ideas traveled in many directions. In such a climate, the arts flourished. In the next century, as modern nation-states and capitalist economies solidified, development in the arts took new directions, in a period known as the Baroque.

**Vertical column headings (left side):**

- THE CATHOLIC COUNTER-REFORMATION
- THE REFORMATION AND SPREAD OF PROTESTANTISM
- AGE OF EUROPEAN EXPLORATION AND COLONIZATION OVERSEAS
- MAXIMILIAN I OF HABSBURG, HRE
- HRE = Holy Roman Emperor
- CHARLES V (HABSBURG), HRE, KING OF SPAIN AND OF SPANISH AMERICA
- RUDOLPH II, HABSBURG, HRE
- PHILIP II OF SPAIN (HABSBURG) AND OF SPANISH AMERICA
- HENRY VIII OF ENGLAND (TUDOR)
- FRANCIS I OF FRANCE (VALOIS)
- HENRY II
- FRANCIS II
- CHARLES IX
- HENRY III
- HENRY IV OF FRANCE (BOURBON)

**Timeline markers:** 1475 · 1500 · 1525 · 1547 · 1550 · 1575 · 1600

**Timeline entries:**

ERASMUS OF ROTTERDAM, 1466–1536

DUCHY OF BURGUNDY AND THE NETHERLANDS ABSORBED BY THE HOLY ROMAN EMPIRE AND FRANCE, 1477

SIR THOMAS MORE, 1478–1535

MARTIN LUTHER, 1483–1546

ULRICH ZWINGLI, 1484–1531

HOUSE OF TUDOR, 1485–1603

SPANISH CONQUEST OF MUSLIM GRANADA, 1492

HABSBURG DYNASTY, 1493–1918

FRANÇOIS RABELAIS, CA. 1494–1553

VALOIS/BOURBON DYNASTY, 1498–1589/1589–1830

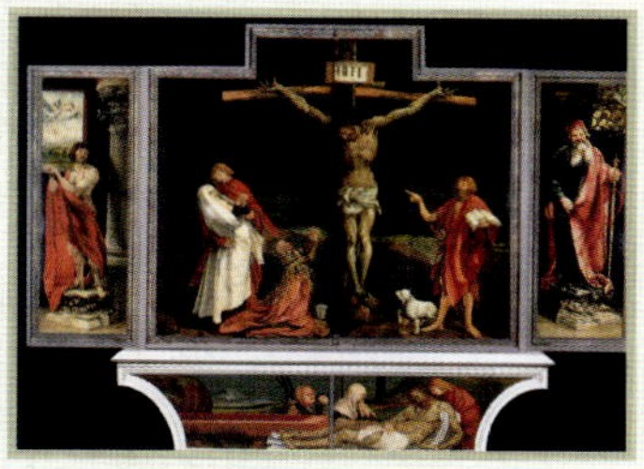

JOHN CALVIN, 1509–1564

BEGINNING OF PROTESTANT REFORMATION, 1517

SPANISH CONQUEST OF MEXICO AND PERU, 1518–1536

HABSBURG-VALOIS WARS, 1521–1544

IGNATIUS LOYOLA, 1491–1556; FOUNDED JESUIT ORDER, 1534

SPREAD OF CALVINIST PROTESTANTISM IN FRANCE AND SWITZERLAND, 1530S

HENRY VIII INITIATES REFORMATION IN ENGLAND, 1534

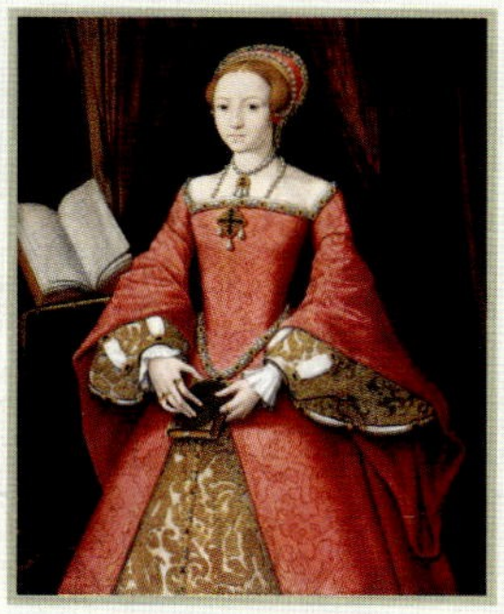

COUNCIL OF TRENT, 1545–1563

SPREAD OF CALVINISM IN SCOTLAND AND THE NETHERLANDS, 1550S

PEACE OF AUGSBURG BETWEEN LUTHERANS AND CATHOLICS, 1555

WARS OF RELIGION IN FRANCE, 1562–1598

BEGINNING OF THE REVOLT OF THE NETHERLANDS AGAINST PHILIP II OF SPAIN, 1568

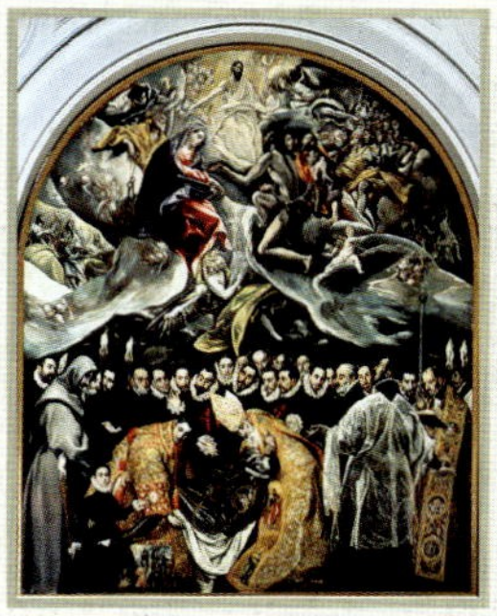

FORMATION OF THE UNION OF ARRAS, 1579

FORMATION OF THE UNION OF UTRECHT, 1579

NETHERLANDS HOUSE OF ORANGE/NASSAU, 1584–PRESENT

PHILIP II SENDS THE GREAT ARMADA AGAINST HOLLAND AND ENGLAND, 1588

**Image captions (right column):**

1 Matthias Grünewald, *Isenheim Altarpiece* (closed), ca 1510–1515

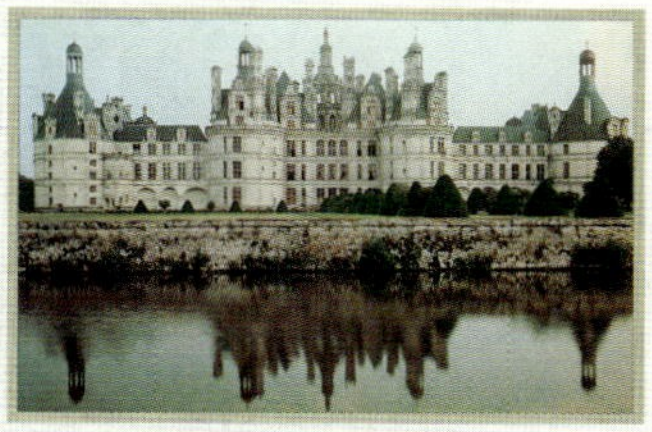

2 Château de Chambord, Chambord, France, begun 1519

3 Attributed to Levina Teerlinc, *Elizabeth I as a Princess*, ca. 1559

4 El Greco, *The Burial of Count Orgaz*, 1586

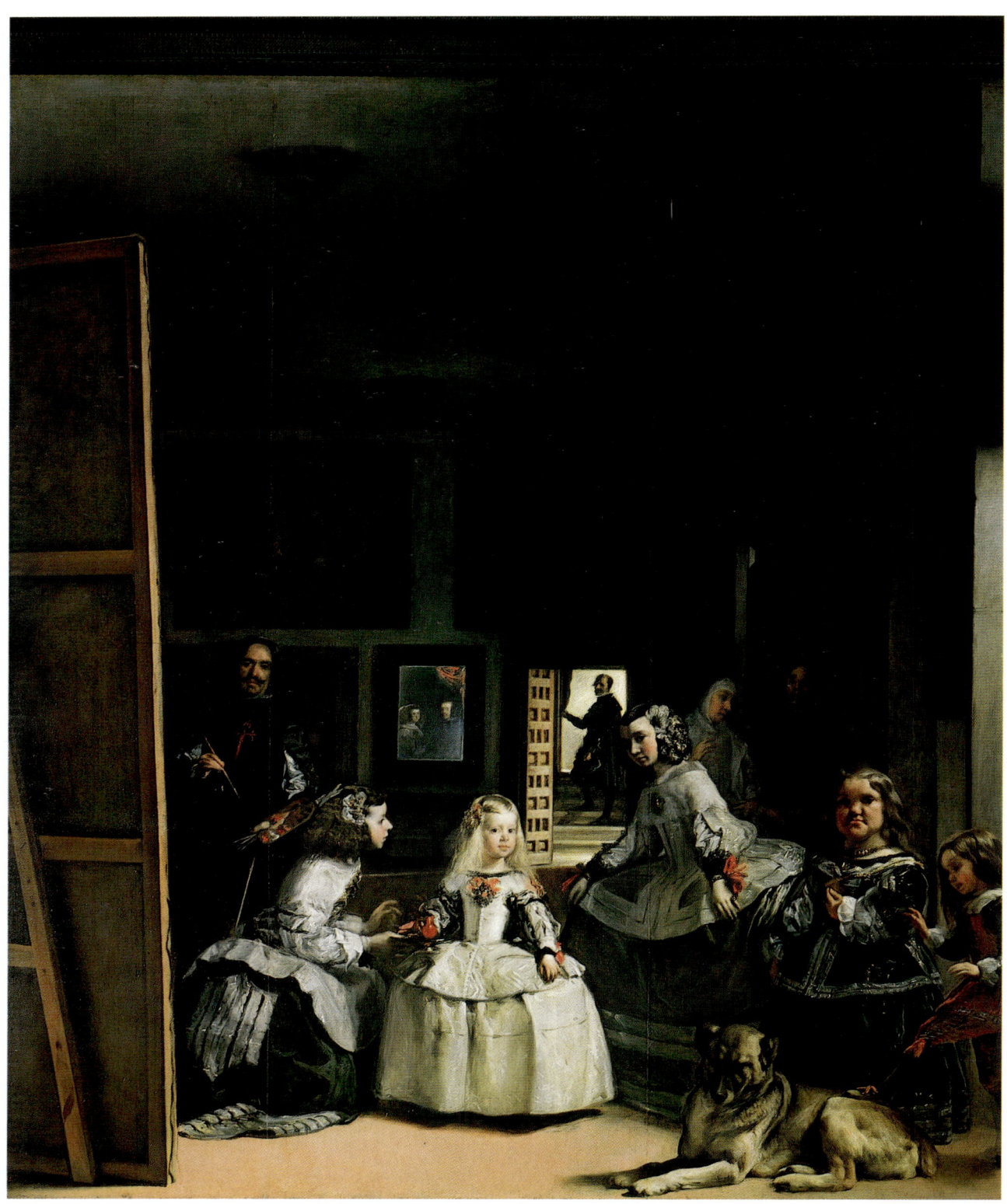

Diego Velázquez, *Las Meninas (The Maids of Honor)*, 1656. Oil on canvas, approx. 10′ 5″ × 9′. Museo del Prado, Madrid.

# 24

# POPES, PEASANTS, MONARCHS, AND MERCHANTS

## BAROQUE ART

The cultural production of the 17th and early 18th centuries in the West is often described as "Baroque," a convenient blanket term. However, this term is problematic because the period encompasses a broad range of developments, both historical and artistic, across an expansive geographic area. Although its origin is unclear, the term may have come from the Portuguese word *barroco*, meaning an irregularly shaped pearl. Use of the term *baroque* emerged in the late 18th and early 19th centuries, when critics disparaged the Baroque period's artistic production, in large part because of perceived deficiencies in comparison to the art (especially Italian Renaissance) of the period preceding it. Over time, this negative connotation faded, and the term is now most often used as a general designation of the period. Some scholars use "Baroque" to describe a particular style that emerged during the 17th century—a style of complexity and drama that is usually associated with Italian art of this period. The dynamism and extravagance of this Baroque style contrast with the rational order of classicism. But as we shall see, not all artists adopted this style during the Baroque period.

Because of the problematic associations of the term and because no commonalities can be ascribed to all of the art and cultures of this period, we have limited use of the term in this book. Wherever it is used, we have described characteristics that anchor the term *Baroque* in particular cultures—for example, Italian Baroque as compared to Dutch Baroque.

## 17TH-CENTURY EUROPE

### *The Shifting Geopolitical Landscape*

**MORE THAN 30 YEARS OF WAR** During the 17th and early 18th centuries, numerous geopolitical shifts occurred in Europe (MAP **24-1**) as the fortunes of the individual countries waxed and waned. Political and religious friction was prominent and

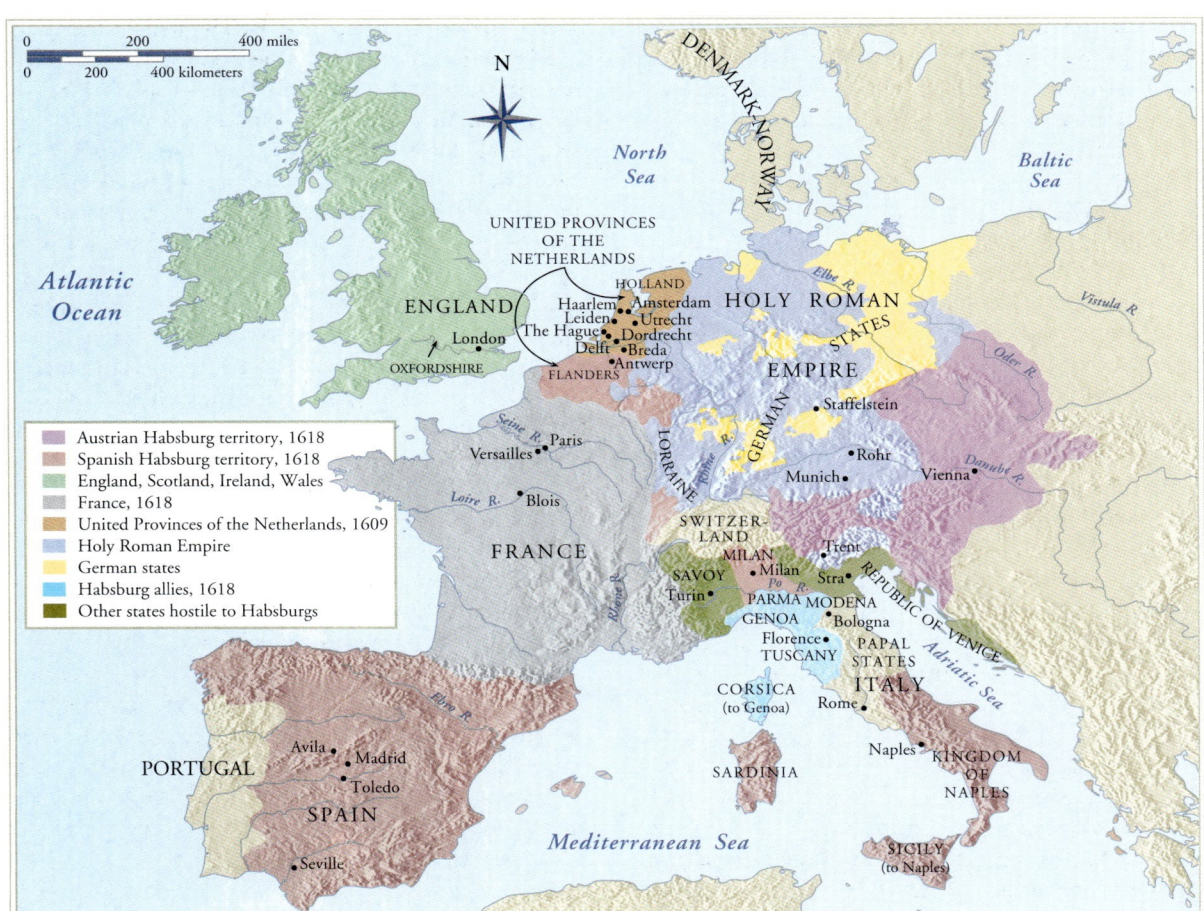

**MAP 24-1** Europe at the onset of the Thirty Years' War.

resulted in widespread unrest and warfare. Indeed, one historian claims that between 1562 and 1721, all of Europe was at peace only four years. The major conflict of this period was the Thirty Years' War (1618–1648), which involved Spain, France, Sweden, Denmark, the Netherlands, Germany, Austria, Poland, the Ottoman Empire, and the Holy Roman Empire. Although the outbreak of this war was largely rooted in the conflict between militant Catholics and militant Protestants, the driving force quickly shifted to secular, dynastic, and nationalistic concerns. Among the major political entities vying for expanded power and authority in Europe were the Bourbon dynasty of France and the Habsburg dynasties of Spain and the Holy Roman Empire. The war, which concluded with the Treaty of Westphalia in 1648, was largely responsible for the political restructuring of Europe. As a result, the United Provinces of the Netherlands (the Dutch Republic), Sweden, and France expanded their authority; Spain's and Denmark's relative power diminished. The building of nation-states was emphatically under way. In addition to reconfiguring territorial boundaries, the Treaty of Westphalia in essence granted freedom of religious choice throughout Europe. This treaty thus marked the abandonment of the idea of a united Christian Europe, which was replaced by the practical realities of secular political systems.

## The Development of a Worldwide Market

**WORLDWIDE MERCANTILISM** By the 17th century, European societies began to coordinate their long-distance trade more systematically. The allure of expanding markets, rising profits, and access to a wider range of goods contributed to the relentless economic competition between countries during this period. Much of the foundation for worldwide mercantilism—extensive voyaging and geographic exploration, improved cartography, and advances in shipbuilding—was laid in the previous century. In fact, by the end of the 16th century, all the major trade routes had been established.

In the 17th century, however, changes in financial systems, lifestyles, and trading patterns, along with expanding colonialism, fueled the creation of a worldwide marketplace. The Dutch founded the Bank of Amsterdam in 1609, which eventually became the center of European transfer banking. By establishing a system in which merchant firms held money on account, the bank relieved traders of having to transport precious metals as payment. Trading practices became more complex. Rather than simple reciprocal trading, triangular trade (trade between three parties) allowed for a larger pool of desirable goods. Exposure to an ever-growing array of goods affected European diets and lifestyles. Coffee (from island colonies) and tea (from China) became popular beverages during the early 17th century. Equally explosive was the growth of sugar use. Sugar, along with tobacco and rice, were slave crops, and the slave trade expanded to accommodate the demand for these goods. Africans were enslaved and imported to European colonies and the Americas to provide the requisite labor force for producing these commodities.

The resulting worldwide mercantile system permanently changed the face of Europe. The prosperity such trading generated affected social and political relationships, necessitating new rules of etiquette and careful diplomacy. With increased disposable income, more of the newly wealthy spent money on art (among other things), expanding the number of possible sources of patronage. By 1700, the growth of a moneyed class had contributed considerably to the emergence of Rococo (see Chapter 28, page 797), a decorative style associated with the wealthy and aristocratic.

# BAROQUE ART OF THE 17TH CENTURY

## *Italy*

Although the Catholic Church launched the Counter-Reformation—its challenge to the Protestant Reformation—during the 16th century, the considerable appeal of Protestantism continued to preoccupy it throughout the succeeding century. The Treaty of Westphalia in 1648 had formally recognized the principle of religious freedom, serving to validate Protestantism (predominantly in the German states). With the popes and clergy continuing to serve as major artistic patrons, as in earlier centuries, much of Italian Baroque art was aimed at propagandistically restoring Catholicism's predominance and centrality. Whereas Italian Renaissance artists often had reveled in the precise, orderly rationality of classical models, Italian Baroque artists embraced a more dynamic and complex aesthetic. During the 17th century, dramatic theatricality, grandiose scale, and elaborate ornateness, all used to spectacular effect, characterized Italian Baroque art and architecture. Papal Rome's importance as the cradle of Italian Baroque art production further suggests the role art played in supporting the aims of the Church. The Council of Trent, one of the Counter-Reformation initiatives, firmly resisted Protestant objection to using images in religious worship, insisting on their necessity for teaching the laity. Therefore, Italian Baroque art commissioned by the Church was not merely decorative but didactic as well.

The Catholic Church waged a lengthy campaign to reestablish its preeminence. Pope Sixtus V (r. 1585–1590) contributed significantly to this initiative. He augmented the papal treasury and intended to construct a new and more magnificent Rome. Several strong and ambitious popes—Paul V, Urban VIII, Innocent X, and Alexander VII—succeeded Sixtus V and were largely responsible for building the modern city of Rome, which bears the marks of their patronage everywhere. Italian 17th-century art and architecture embodied the renewed energy of the Catholic Counter-Reformation and communicated it to the populace.

**EMPHASIZING VERTICALITY** The facade designed by CARLO MADERNO (1556–1629) at the turn of the century for the Roman church of Santa Susanna (FIG. 24-1) stands as one of the earliest manifestations of the Baroque spirit in Italian art and architecture. In its general appearance, Maderno's facade resembles Giacomo della Porta's immensely influential design for Il Gesù (see FIG. 22-50), the seat of the Jesuit order (which played a major role in Counter-Reformation education and did expansive overseas missionary work in the New World and the Far East). But the later facade has a greater verticality, concentrating and dramatizing the major features of its model. The facade's tall central section projects forward from the horizontal lower story, and the scroll buttresses that connect the two levels are narrower and set at a sharper angle. The elimination of an arch framing the pediment over the doorway further enhances the design's vertical thrust. Strong shadows cast by Santa Susanna's vigorously projecting columns and pilasters mount dramatically toward the emphatically stressed central axis. The recessed niches, which contain statues, heighten the sculptural effect.

**RESTORING SAINT PETER'S GRANDEUR** The drama inherent in Santa Susanna's facade appealed to Pope Paul V (r. 1605–1621), who commissioned Maderno in 1606 to complete Saint Peter's in Rome. As the symbolic seat of the papacy, Saint Peter's radiated enormous symbolic presence. In light of lingering Counter-Reformation concerns, the desire of Baroque popes to conclude the extended rebuilding project and reestablish the force embodied in the mammoth structure is understandable.

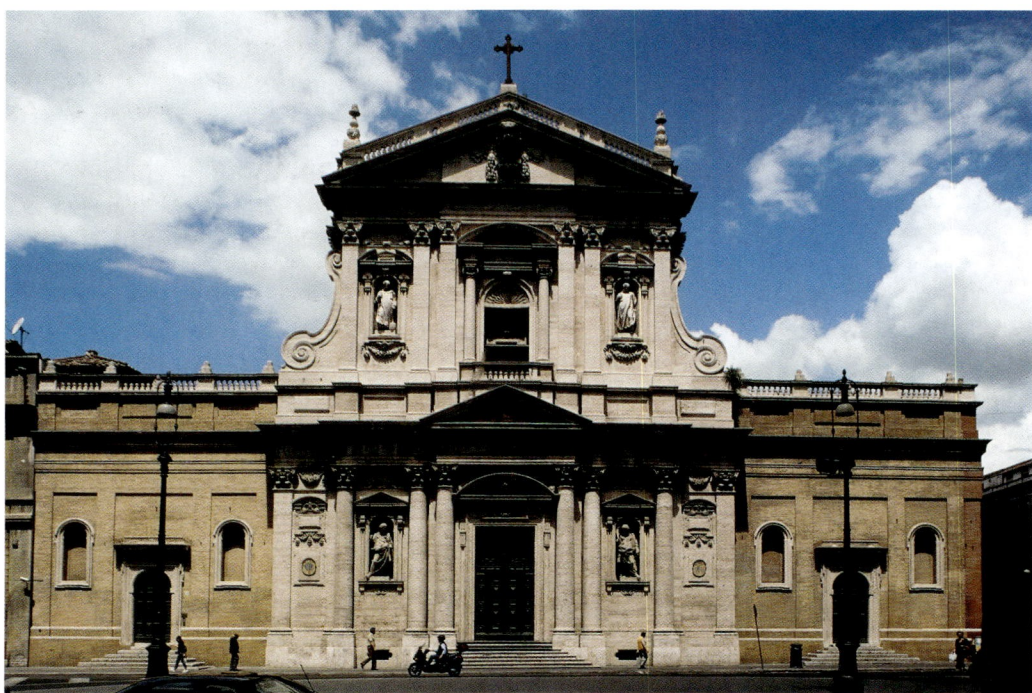

**24-1** CARLO MADERNO, Santa Susanna, Rome, Italy, 1597–1603.

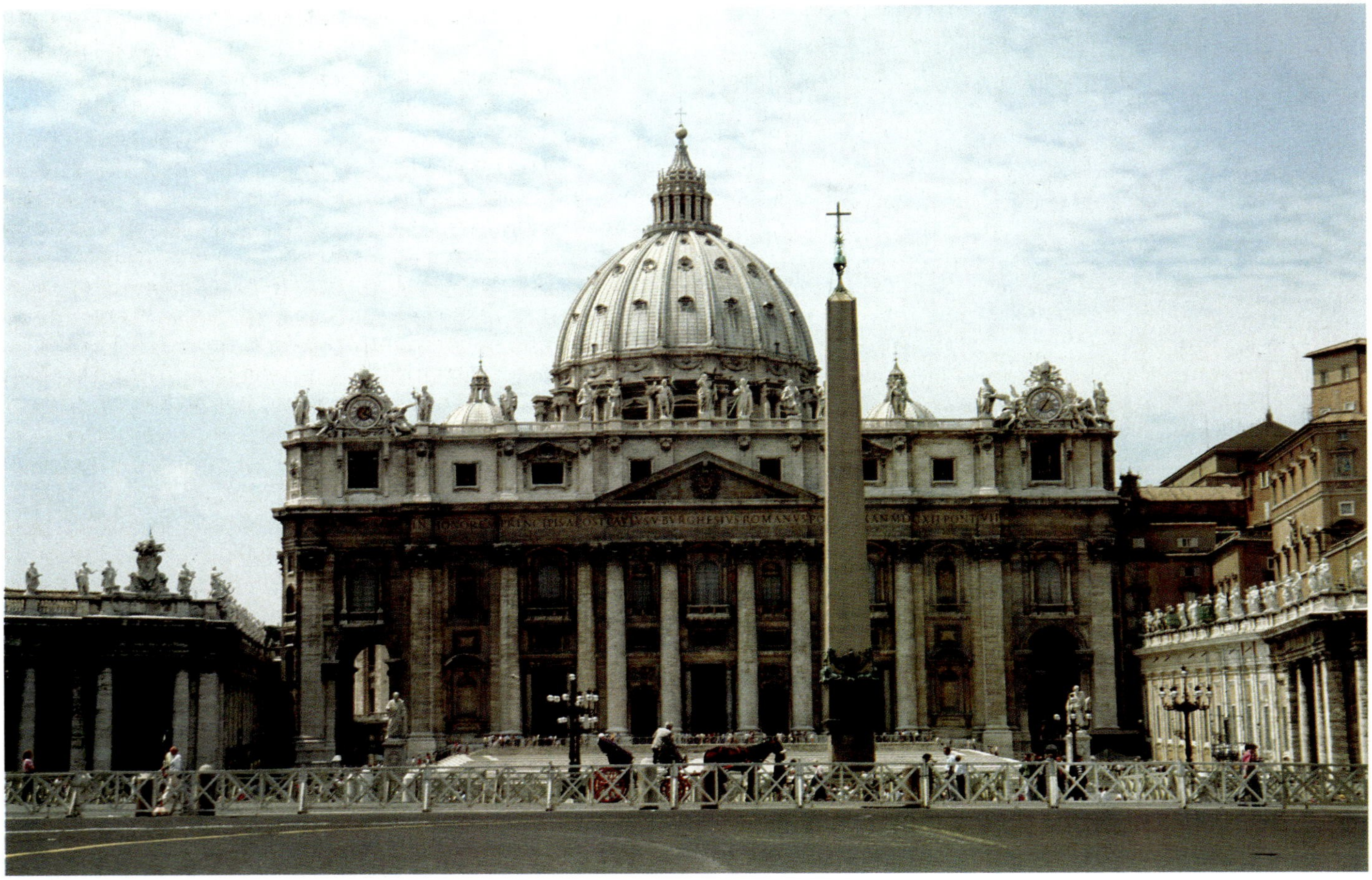

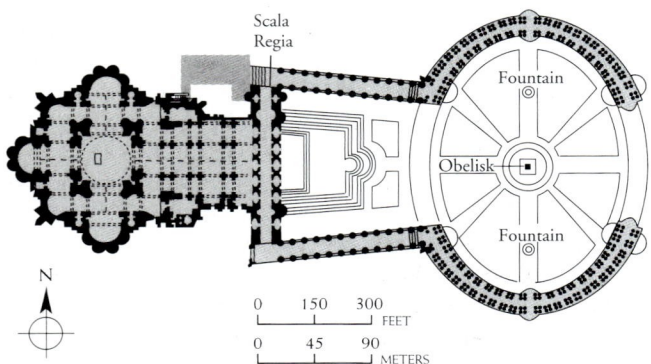

**24-2** CARLO MADERNO, facade of Saint Peter's, Vatican City, Rome, Italy, 1606–1612.

In many ways Maderno's facade of Saint Peter's (FIG. **24-2**) is a gigantic expansion of the elements of Santa Susanna's first level. But the compactness and verticality of the smaller church's facade are not as prominent because Saint Peter's expansive width counterbalances them. Mitigating circumstances must be taken into consideration when assessing this design, however. The preexisting core of an incomplete building restricted Maderno, so he did not have the luxury of formulating a totally new concept for Saint Peter's. Moreover, his design for the facade was also never fully executed. The two outside bell-tower bays were not part of Maderno's original plan. Hence, had the facade been constructed according to the architect's initial design, it would have exhibited greater verticality and visual coherence.

Maderno's plan for Saint Peter's (FIG. **24-3**) also departed from the central plans designed for it during the Renaissance by Bramante (see FIG. 22-6) and, later, by Michelangelo (see FIG. 22-28). Seventeenth-century clergy rejected a central plan for Saint Peter's because of its association with pagan buildings, such as the Pantheon (see FIG. 10-48). Paul V commissioned Maderno to add three nave bays to the earlier nucleus. This longitudinal plan reinforced the symbolic distinction between clergy and laity and provided a space for the processions (increasingly encouraged by the Jesuits) of ever-growing assemblies. Lengthening the nave, unfortunately, pushed the dome farther back from the facade, and the effect Michelangelo had planned—a structure pulled together and dominated by its dome—is not readily visible. When viewed at close range, the dome hardly emerges above the facade's soaring frontal plane; seen from farther back (FIG. 24-2), it appears to have no drum. Visitors must move back quite a distance from the front to see the dome and drum together and to experience the effect Michelangelo intended. Today, to truly see the structure as the 16th-century architect envisioned, people must view it from the back (see FIG. 22-29).

**WELCOMING THE PIOUS IN ROME** The design of Saint Peter's finally was completed (except for details) by GIANLORENZO BERNINI (1598–1680). Bernini was an architect, painter, and sculptor—one of the most important and imaginative artists of the Italian Baroque era and its most characteristic and sustaining spirit. Bernini's largest and most impressive single project was the design for a monumental *piazza* (plaza; 1656–1667) in front of Saint Peter's (FIGS. 24-3 and **24-4**). In much the way Michelangelo was

**24-3** CARLO MADERNO, plan of Saint Peter's, Vatican City, Rome, Italy, with adjoining piazza designed by GIANLORENZO BERNINI.

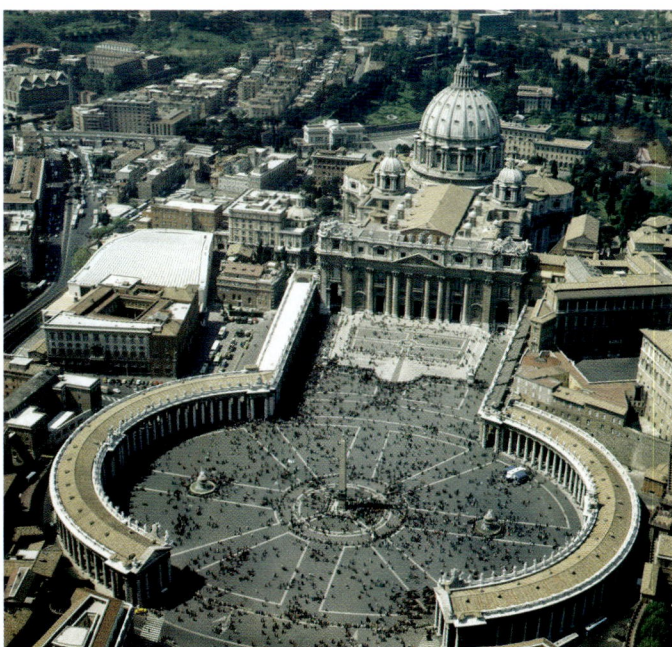

**24-4** Aerial view of Saint Peter's, Vatican City, Rome, Italy, 1506–1666.

forced to reorganize the Capitoline Hill (see FIG. 22-26), Bernini had to adjust his design to some preexisting structures on the site—an ancient obelisk the Romans brought from Egypt (which Pope Sixtus V had his architect, Domenico Fontana, relocate to the piazza in 1585 as part of the pope's vision of Christian triumph in Rome) and a fountain Maderno designed. He used these features to define the long axis of a vast oval embraced by colonnades joined to the Saint Peter's facade by two diverging wings. Four rows of huge Tuscan columns make up the two colonnades, which terminate in severely Classical temple fronts. The dramatic gesture of embrace that the colonnades make as viewers enter the piazza symbolizes the welcome the Roman Catholic Church gave its members during the Counter-Reformation. Bernini himself referred to his design of the colonnade as appearing like the welcoming arms of the church. Beyond their symbolic resonance, the colonnades served the functional purpose of providing pilgrims with easy access to the piazza.

The wings that connect the Saint Peter's facade with the oval piazza flank a trapezoidal space also reminiscent of the Campidoglio (see FIG. 22-26), but here the visual effect was reversed. As seen from the piazza, the diverging wings counteract the natural perspective and tend to bring the facade closer to observers. Emphasizing the facade's height in this manner, Bernini subtly and effectively compensated for its extensive width. Thus, a Baroque transformation expanded the compact central designs of Bramante and Michelangelo into a dynamic complex of axially ordered elements that reach out and enclose spaces of vast dimension. By its sheer scale and theatricality, the completed Saint Peter's fulfilled the desire of the Counter-Reformation Catholic Church to present an awe-inspiring and authoritative vision of itself.

**A SOARING BRONZE CANOPY** Long before the planning of the piazza, Bernini had been at work decorating the interior of Saint Peter's. His first commission, completed between 1624 and 1633, called for the design and erection of the gigantic bronze *baldacchino* (FIG. **24-5**) under the great dome. The canopy-like structure (*baldacco* is Italian for "silk from Baghdad," such as for a cloth canopy) stands almost 100 feet high (the height of an average

eight-story building). The baldacchino serves both functional and symbolic purposes. It marks the high altar and the tomb of Saint Peter, and it visually bridges human scale to the lofty vaults and dome above. Further, for those entering the nave of the huge church, it provides a dramatic, compelling presence at the crossing. Its columns also create a visual frame for the elaborate sculpture representing the throne of Saint Peter (the Cathedra Petri) at the far end of Saint Peter's. On a symbolic level, the structure's decorative elements speak to the power of the Catholic Church and of Pope Urban VIII. Partially fluted and wreathed with vines, the baldacchino's four spiral columns recall those of the ancient baldacchino (see "Constantine and Old Saint Peter's," Chapter 11, page 311) over the same spot in Old Saint Peter's, thereby invoking the past to reinforce the primacy of the Roman Catholic Church. At the top of the columns, four colossal angels stand guard at the upper corners of the canopy. Forming the canopy's apex are four serpentine brackets that elevate the orb and the cross. Since the time of the emperor Constantine (see FIG. 10-82, *right*), builder of the original Saint Peter's basilica, the orb and the cross had served as symbols of the Church's triumph. The baldacchino also features numerous bees, symbols of the Barberini family. As the official patron of the work, Pope Urban VIII (Maffeo Barberini, r. 1623–1644) undoubtedly desired appropriate recognition. The structure effectively gives visual form to the triumph of Christianity and the papal claim to doctrinal supremacy.

The construction of the baldacchino was itself an awesome feat. Each of the bronze columns was cast in five sections using the lost-wax method (see "Hollow-Casting Life-Size Bronze Statues," Chapter 5, page 131) from wooden models. Although Bernini did some of the actual production of the columns himself (for example, cleaning and repairing the wax casts and doing the final cleaning and chasing of the bronze casts), much of the work was contracted out to experienced founders and sculptors. The superstructure is predominantly cast bronze, although some of the sculptural elements are brass or wood. Clearly, given the enormous scale of the baldacchino, a considerable amount of bronze was required. On Urban VIII's orders, bronze for this project was acquired by dismantling the portico of the Pantheon—ideologically appropriate, given the Church's rejection of paganism.

The concepts of triumph and grandeur unified both the architecture and the design program of Saint Peter's during the 17th century. Suggesting a great and solemn procession, the main axis of the complex traverses the piazza (marked but slowed by the central obelisk) and enters Maderno's nave. It comes to a temporary halt at the altar beneath the baldacchino, but it continues on toward its climactic destination at another great altar in the apse.

**A SOPHISTICATED STAIRWAY DESIGN** Bernini demonstrated his impressive skill at transforming space in another project he undertook in Vatican City, the Scala Regia, or Royal Stairway (FIG. **24-6**). This monumental corridor of steps connects the papal apartments to the portico and narthex of Saint Peter's. Because the original passageway was irregular, dark, and dangerous to descend, Pope Alexander VII (r. 1655–1667) commissioned Bernini to replace it. The stairway, its entrance crowned by a sculptural group of trumpeting angels and the papal arms, is covered by a barrel vault (built in two sections) carried on columns that form aisles flanking the central corridor. By gradually reducing the distance between the columns and walls as the stairway ascends, Bernini actually eliminated the aisles on the upper levels while creating an illusion that the whole stairway is of uniform width and that the aisles continue for its entire length. Likewise,

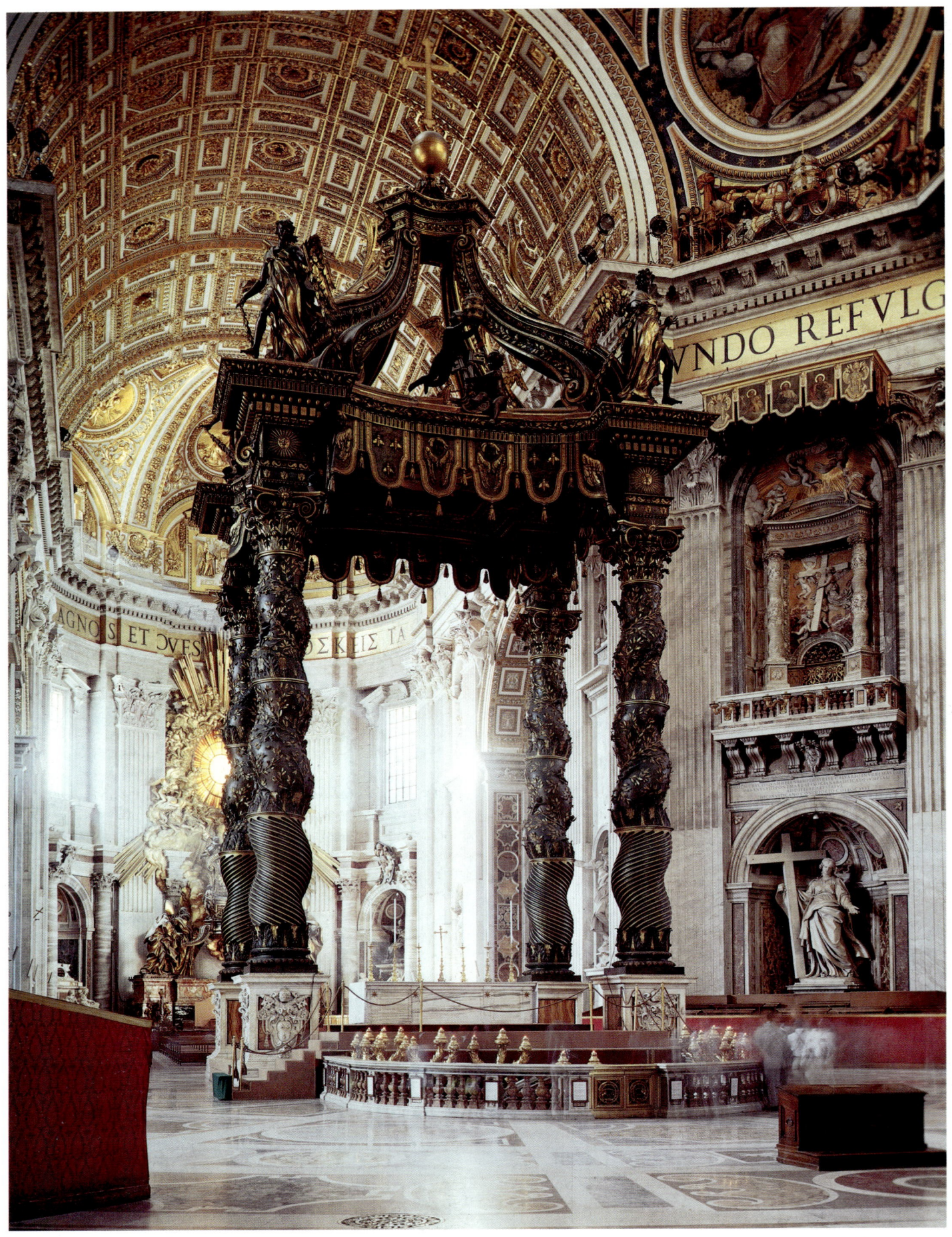

**24-5** Gianlorenzo Bernini, baldacchino, Saint Peter's, Vatican City, Rome, Italy, 1624–1633. Gilded bronze, approx. 100′ high.

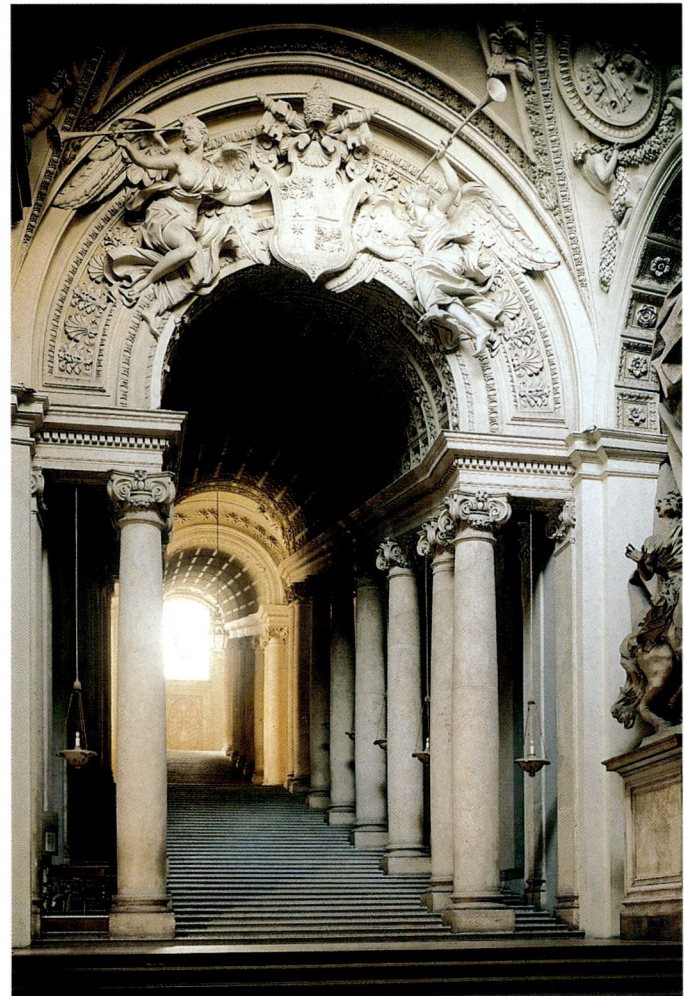

24-6 GIANLORENZO BERNINI, Scala Regia (Royal Stairway), Vatican City, Rome, Italy, 1663–1666.

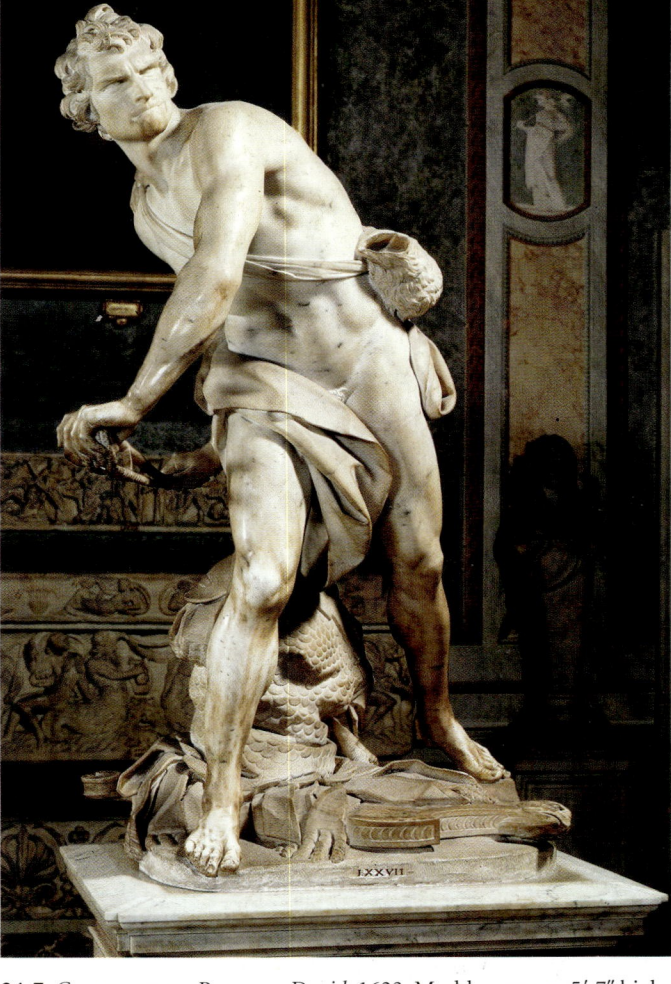

24-7 GIANLORENZO BERNINI, *David*, 1623. Marble, approx. 5′ 7″ high. Galleria Borghese, Rome.

the space between the colonnades narrows with ascent, reinforcing the natural perspective and making the stairs appear longer than they actually are. To minimize this effect, Bernini made the lighting at the top of the stairs brighter, exploiting the natural human inclination to move from darkness toward light. To make the long ascent more tolerable, he inserted an illuminated landing that provides a midway resting point. The result is a highly sophisticated design, both dynamic and dramatic, that repeats on a smaller scale, perhaps even more effectively, the processional sequence found inside Saint Peter's.

**DECISIVE PHYSICAL ACTION** Bernini devoted much of his prolific career to the adornment of Saint Peter's, where his works combine sculpture with architecture. Although Bernini was a great and influential architect, his fame rests primarily on his sculpture, which, like his architecture, energetically expresses the Italian Baroque spirit. Bernini's sculpture is expansive and theatrical, and the element of time usually plays an important role in it. A sculpture that predates his work on Saint Peter's is his *David* (FIG. 24-7), commissioned by Cardinal Scipione Borghese. This marble statue aims at catching the figure's split-second action and differs markedly from the restful figures of David

portrayed by Donatello (see FIG. 21-23), Verrocchio (see FIG. 21-24), and Michelangelo (see FIG. 22-9). Bernini's *David,* his muscular legs widely and firmly planted, is beginning the violent, pivoting motion that will launch the stone from his sling. Unlike Myron, the fifth-century BCE Greek sculptor whose *Diskobolos* (see FIG. 5-37) is frozen in inaction, Bernini selected the most dramatic of an implied sequence of poses, so observers have to think simultaneously of the continuum and of this tiny fraction of it. The suggested continuum imparts a dynamic quality to the statue that conveys a bursting forth of the energy seen confined in Michelangelo's figures (see FIGS. 22-9 and 22-10). Bernini's statue seems to be moving through time and through space. This is not the kind of sculpture that can be inscribed in a cylinder or confined in a niche; its indicated action demands space around it. Nor is it self-sufficient in the Renaissance sense, as its pose and attitude direct the observer's attention beyond it to its surroundings (in this case, toward an unseen Goliath). Bernini's sculpted figure moves out into and partakes of the physical space that surrounds it and the observer. Further, the expression of intense concentration on David's face is a far cry from the placid visages of previous Davids and augments the dramatic impact of this sculpture.

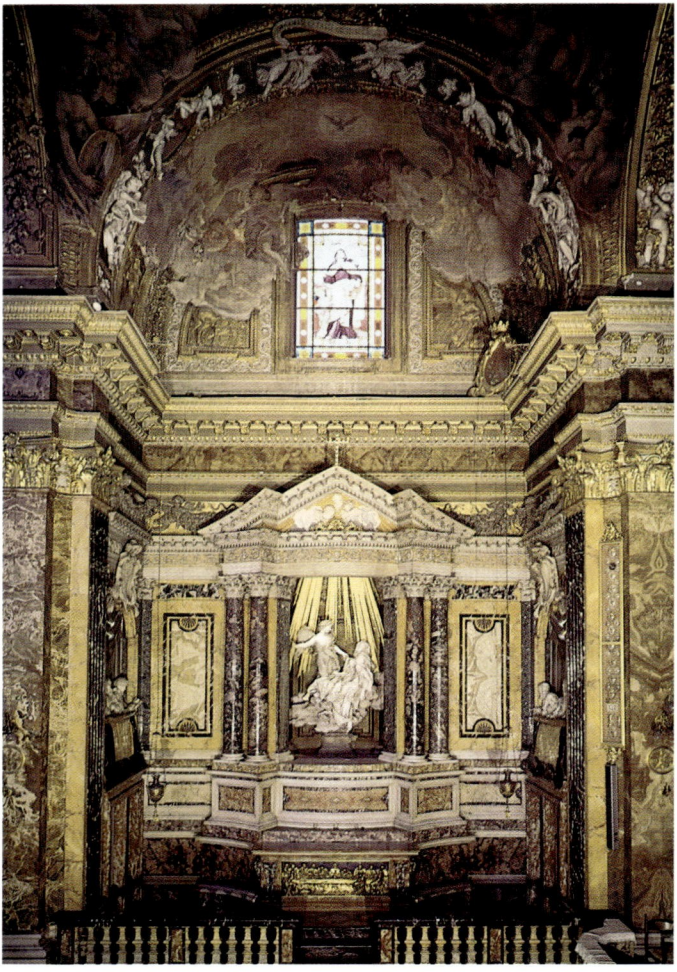

24-8 GIANLORENZO BERNINI, interior of the Cornaro Chapel, Santa Maria della Vittoria, Rome, Italy, 1645–1652.

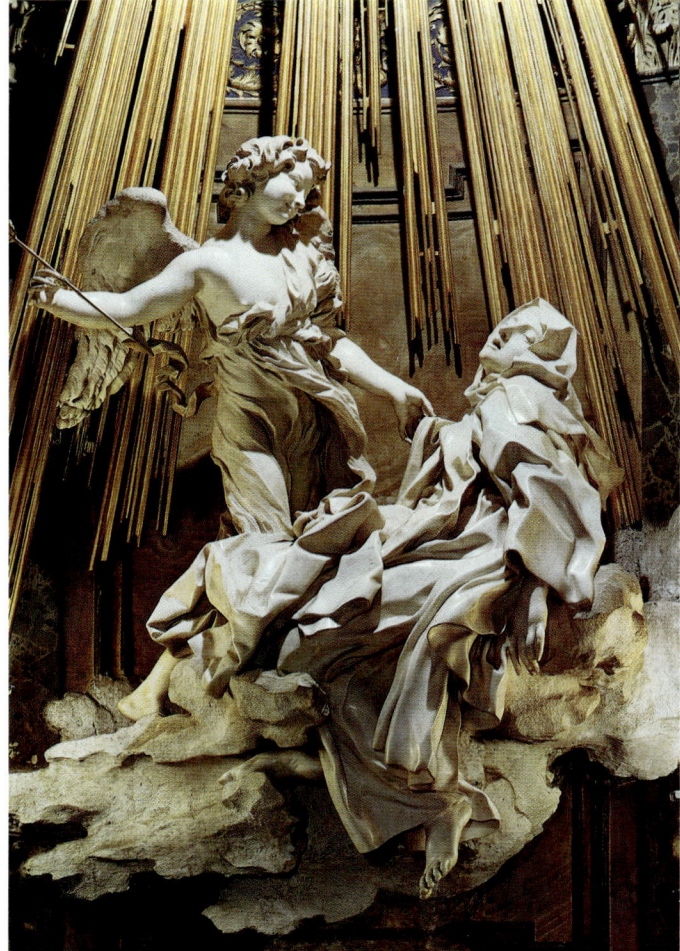

24-9 GIANLORENZO BERNINI, *Ecstasy of Saint Teresa,* Cornaro Chapel, Santa Maria della Vittoria, Rome, Italy, 1645–1652. Marble, height of group 11′ 6″.

**AN ECSTATIC AND RADIANT VISION** Another Bernini sculpture that displays the expansive quality of Italian Baroque art and its refusal to limit itself to firmly defined spatial settings is *Ecstasy of Saint Teresa* in the Cornaro Chapel (FIG. 24-8) of the Roman church of Santa Maria della Vittoria. For this chapel, Bernini utilized the full capabilities of architecture, sculpture, and painting to charge the entire area with palpable tension. He accomplished this by drawing on the considerable knowledge of the theater he derived from writing plays and producing stage designs. The marble sculpture that serves as the focus of this chapel depicts Saint Teresa, who was a nun of the Carmelite order and one of the great mystical saints of the Spanish Counter-Reformation. Her conversion occurred after the death of her father, when she fell into a series of trances, saw visions, and heard voices. Feeling a persistent pain, she attributed it to the fire-tipped arrow of Divine love that an angel had thrust repeatedly into her heart. In her writings, Saint Teresa described this experience as making her swoon in delightful anguish. The whole chapel became a theater for the production of this mystical drama. The niche in which it takes place appears as a shallow *proscenium* (the part of the stage in front of the curtain) crowned with a broken Baroque pediment and ornamented with polychrome marble. On either side of the chapel, sculpted relief por-

traits of the Cornaro family behind draped praying desks attest to the piety of the patrons (Cardinal Federico Cornaro and his relatives) attending this heavenly drama. Bernini depicted the saint in ecstasy (FIG. 24-9), unmistakably a mingling of spiritual and physical passion, swooning back on a cloud, while the smiling angel aims his arrow. The entire sculptural group is made of white marble, and Bernini's supreme technical virtuosity is evident in the visual differentiation in texture among the clouds, rough monk's cloth, gauzy material, smooth flesh, and feathery wings. Light from a hidden window of yellow glass pours down on bronze rays that suggest the radiance of Heaven, whose painted representation covers the vault (FIG. 24-8). (Hidden lights have been installed near the top of the rays to ensure visitors to the chapel a consistent viewing experience.) The passionate drama of Bernini's sculpture correlated with the ideas disseminated earlier by Ignatius Loyola, who founded the Jesuit order in 1534 and was canonized as Saint Ignatius in 1622. In his book *Spiritual Exercises,* Ignatius argued that the re-creation of spiritual experiences for viewers would do much to increase devotion and piety. Thus, theatricality and sensory impact were useful vehicles for achieving Counter-Reformation goals. Bernini was an extremely devout Catholic, which undoubtedly contributed to his understanding of those goals. His inventiveness,

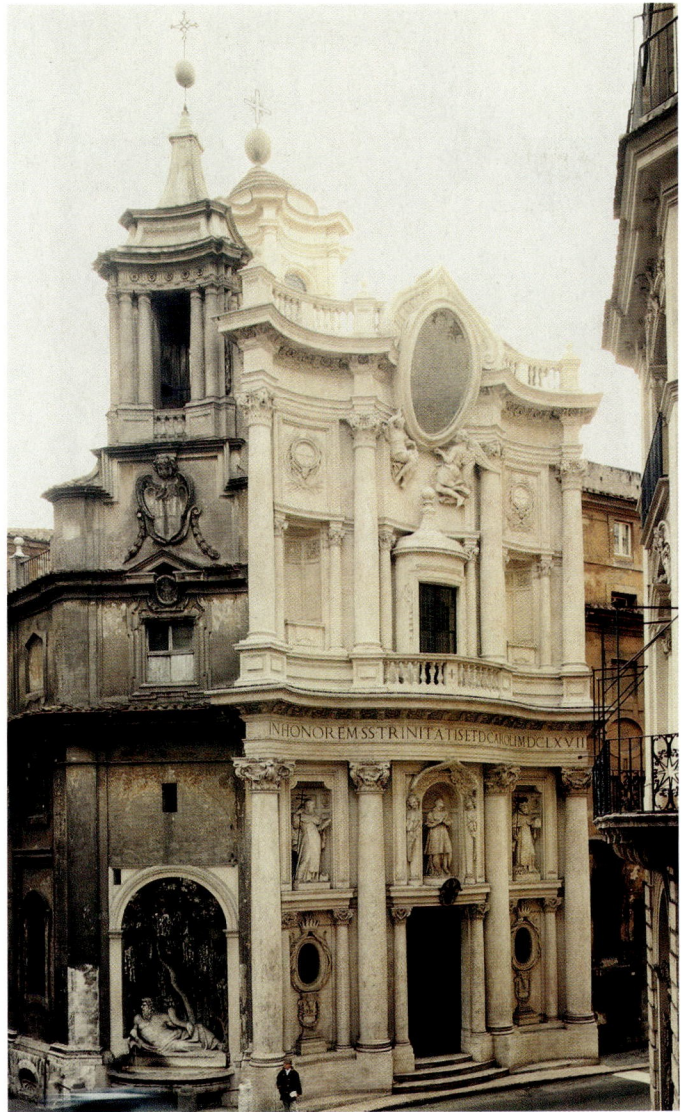

**24-10** FRANCESCO BORROMINI, facade of San Carlo alle Quattro Fontane, Rome, Italy, 1665–1676.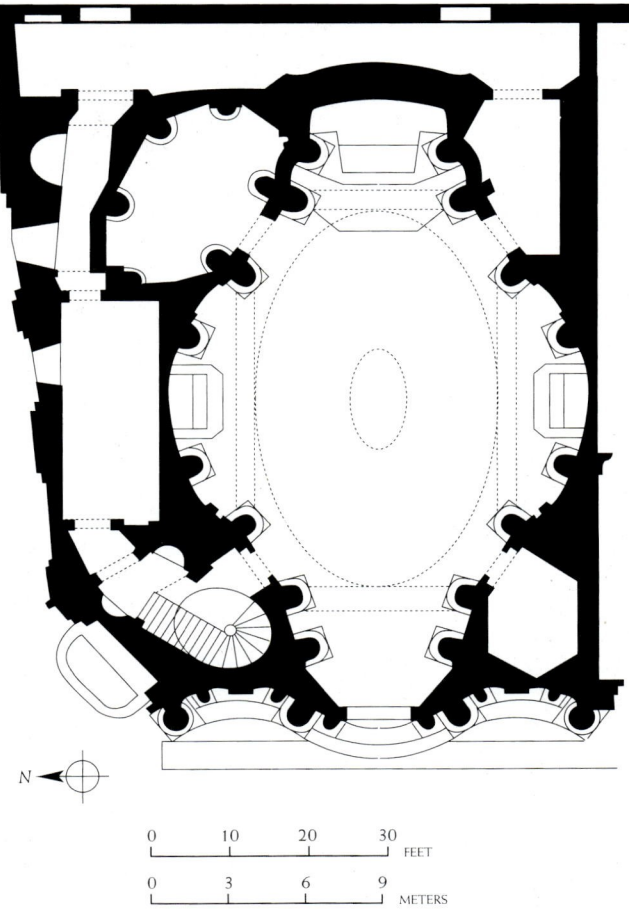

**24-11** FRANCESCO BORROMINI, plan of San Carlo alle Quattro Fontane, Rome, Italy, 1638–1641.

technical skill, sensitivity to his patrons' needs, and energy account for his position as the quintessential Italian Baroque artist.

**A CHURCH FACADE IN MOTION?** FRANCESCO BORROMINI (1599–1667) took Italian Baroque architecture to even greater dramatic heights. A new dynamism appeared in the little church of San Carlo alle Quattro Fontane (Saint Charles of the Four Fountains; FIG. **24-10**), where Borromini went well beyond any of his predecessors or contemporaries in emphasizing a building's sculptural qualities. Although Maderno incorporated sculptural elements in his designs for the facades of Santa Susanna (FIG. 24-1) and Saint Peter's (FIG. 24-2), they still develop along relatively lateral planes. Borromini set his whole facade in undulating motion, forward and back, making a counterpoint of concave and convex elements on two levels (for example, the sway of the cornices). He emphasized the three-dimensional effect with deeply recessed niches. This facade is not the traditional flat frontispiece that defines a building's outer limits. It is a pulsating, engaging component inserted between interior and exterior space, designed not to

separate but to provide a fluid transition between the two. This functional interrelation of the building and its environment is underlined by the curious fact it has not one but two facades. The second, a narrow bay crowned with its own small tower, turns away from the main facade and, following the curve of the street, faces an intersection. (The upper facade was completed seven years after Borromini's death, and historians cannot be sure to what degree the present design reflects his original intention.)

The interior is not only an ingenious response to an awkward site but also a provocative variation on the theme of the centrally planned church. In plan (FIG. **24-11**) San Carlo looks like a hybrid of a Greek cross (a cross with four arms of equal length and at right angles) and an oval, with a long axis between entrance and apse. The side walls move in an undulating flow that reverses the facade's motion. Vigorously projecting columns define the space into which they protrude just as much as they accent the walls attached to them. This molded interior space is capped by a deeply coffered oval dome that seems to float on the light entering through windows hidden in its base. Rich variations on the basic theme of the oval, dynamic relative to the static circle, create an interior that appears to flow from entrance to altar, unimpeded by the segmentation so characteristic of Renaissance buildings.

**MOLDING SPACE** The unification of interior space is carried even further in Borromini's Chapel of Saint Ivo in the courtyard

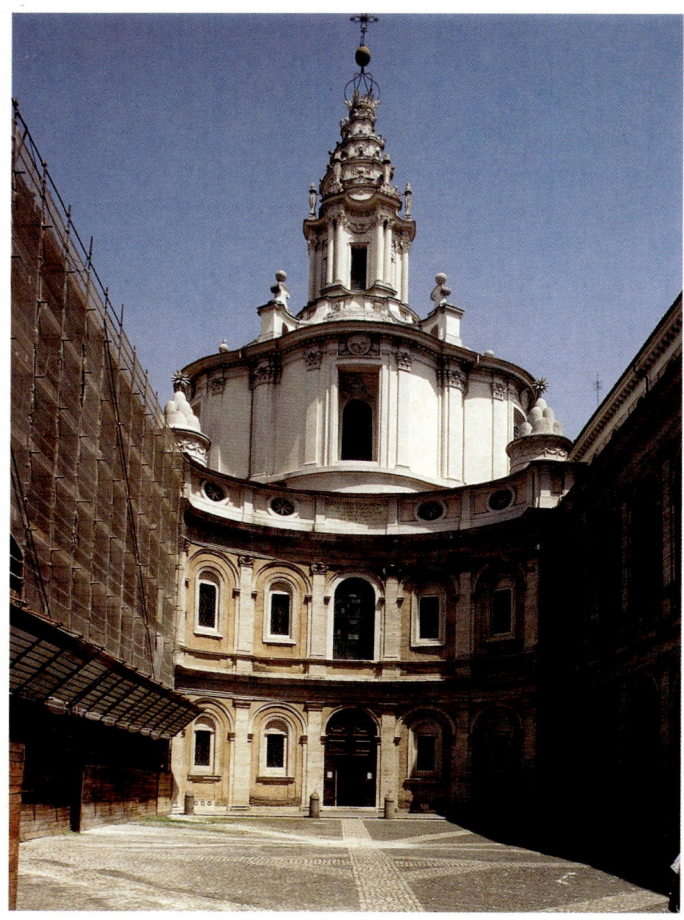

24-12 FRANCESCO BORROMINI, Chapel of Saint Ivo, College of the Sapienza, Rome, Italy, begun 1642. 🟡

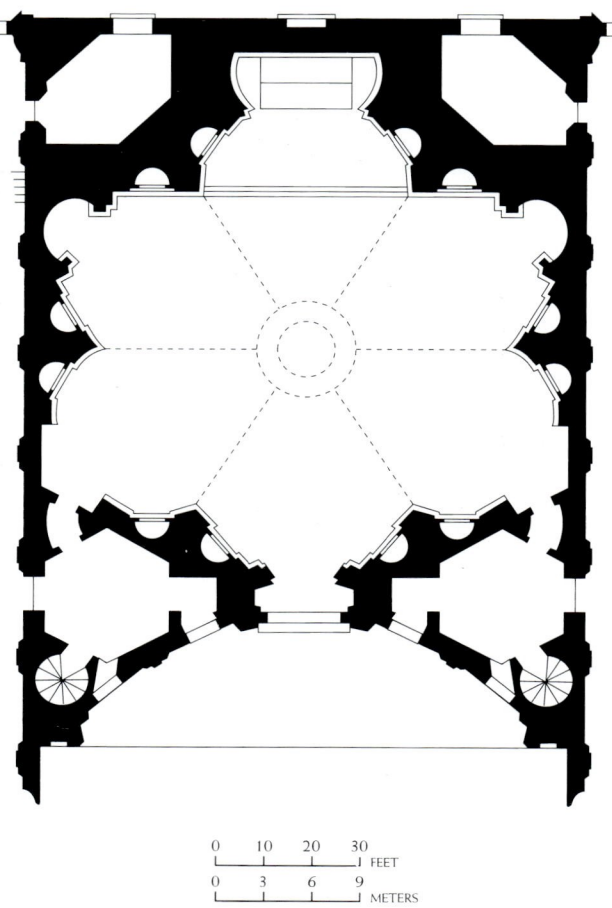

24-13 FRANCESCO BORROMINI, plan of the Chapel of Saint Ivo, College of the Sapienza, Rome, Italy, begun 1642. 🟡

| 0 | 10 | 20 | 30 | |
|---|----|----|----|--|
| | | | | FEET |
| 0 | 3 | 6 | 9 | |
| | | | | METERS |

24-14 Chapel of Saint Ivo (view into dome), College of the Sapienza, Rome, Italy, begun 1642.

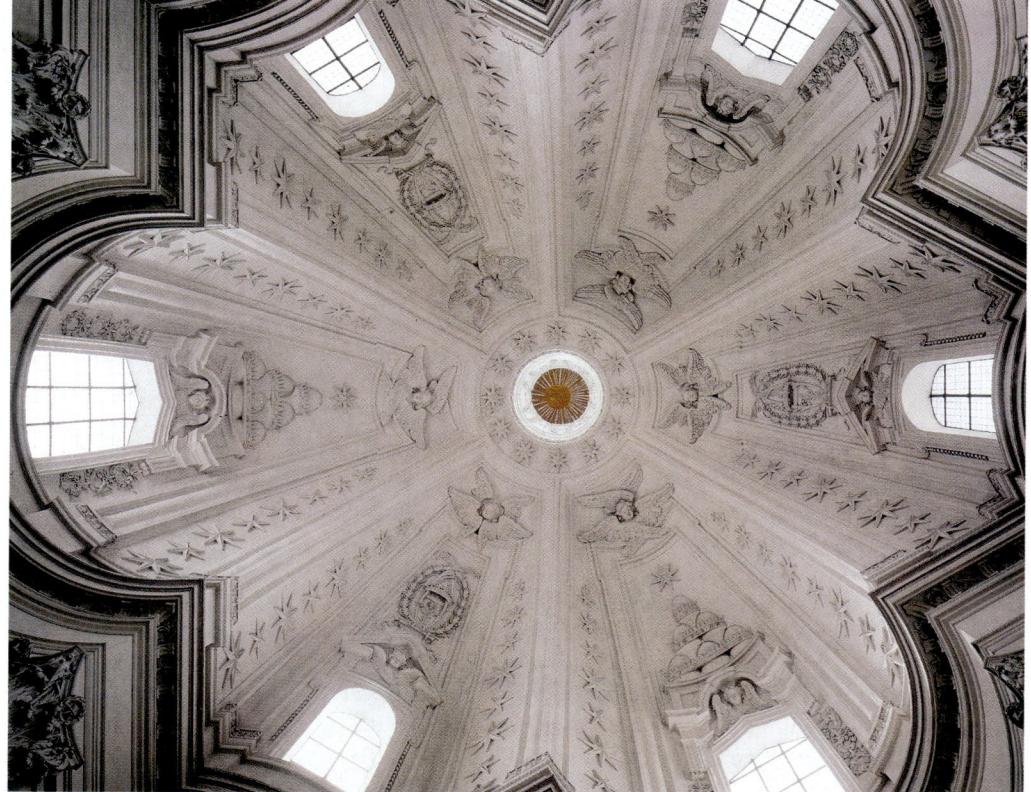

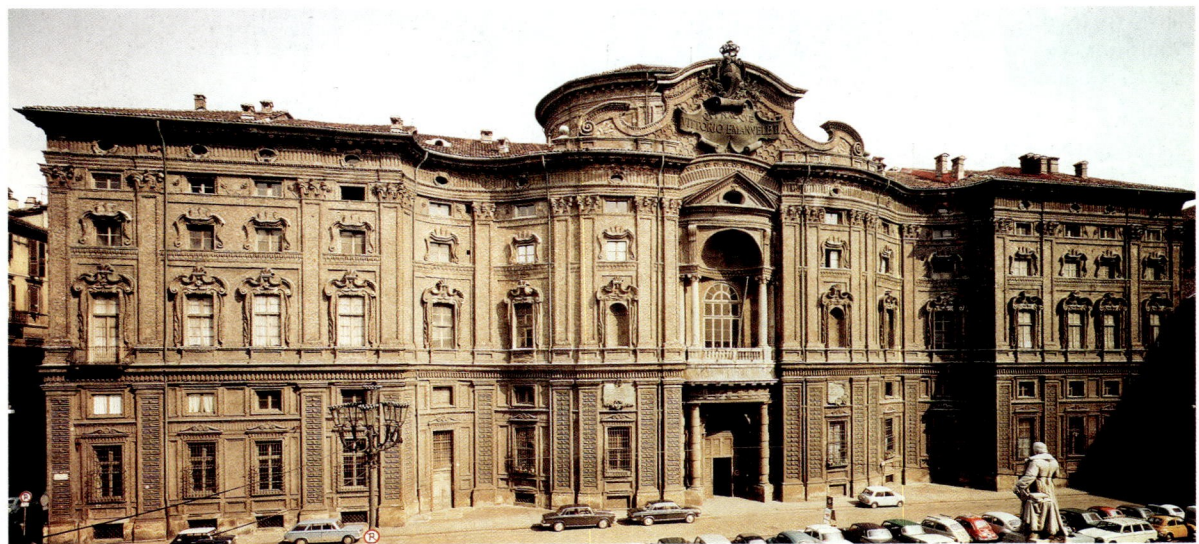

**24-15** Guarino Guarini, Palazzo Carignano, Turin, Italy, 1679–1692.

of the College of the Sapienza (Wisdom) in Rome (FIG. **24-12**). In his characteristic manner, Borromini played concave against convex forms on the upper level of this chapel's exterior. The lower stories of the court, which frame the bottom facade, were already there when Borromini began work. Above the facade's inward curve—its design adjusted to the earlier arcades of the court—rises a convex drumlike structure that supports the dome's lower parts. Powerful pilasters restrain the forces that seem to push the bulging forms outward. Buttresses above the pilasters curve upward to brace a tall, ornate lantern topped by a spiral that, screwlike, seems to fasten the structure to the sky.

The centralized plan of the Saint Ivo chapel (FIG. **24-13**) is that of a star, having rounded-off points and apses on all sides. Indentations and projections along the angled curving walls create a highly complex plan, with all the elements fully reflected in the interior elevation. From floor to lantern, the wall panels rise in a continuously tapering sweep halted only momentarily by a single horizontal cornice (FIG. **24-14**). Thus, the dome is not, as in the Renaissance, a separate unit placed on the supporting block of a building. It is an organic part that evolves out of and shares the qualities of the supporting walls, and it cannot be separated from them. This carefully designed progression up through the lantern creates a dynamic and cohesive shell that encloses and energetically molds a scalloped fragment of universal space. Few architects have matched Borromini's ability to translate extremely complicated designs into such masterfully unified structures as Saint Ivo.

**A TRIPARTITE FACADE** The heir to Borromini's sculptured architectural style was GUARINO GUARINI (1624–1683), a priest, mathematician, and architect who spent the last 17 years of his life in Turin converting that provincial Italian town into a showcase of architectural theories that later swept much of Europe. In his Palazzo Carignano (FIG. **24-15**), Guarini effectively applied Borromini's principle of undulating facades. He divided his long facade into three units, the central one curving much like the facade of San Carlo alle Quattro Fontane (FIG. 24-10) and flanked by two blocklike wings. This lateral three-part division of facades, characteristic of most Baroque palazzi, is probably based on the observation that the average person instinctively can recognize up to three objects as a unit. A greater number would require the viewer to count each object individually. A tripartite organization of extended surfaces thus allowed artists to introduce variety into their designs without destroying structural unity. It also permitted adding emphasis to the central axis, which Guarini did here most effectively by punching out deep cavities in the middle of his convex central block. He enhanced the variety of his design with richly textured surfaces (all executed in brick) and pilasters, which further subdivide his units into three bays each. High and low reliefs create shadows of different intensities and add to the decorative effect.

**A KALEIDOSCOPIC VISION OF HEAVEN** Guarini's mathematical talents must have guided him when he designed the extraordinarily complex dome of the Chapel of the Santissima Sindone (Holiest Shroud), a small central-plan building attached to the Turin Cathedral. A view into this dome (FIG. **24-16**) reveals a bewildering display of geometric elements appearing to move in kaleidoscopic fashion around a circular focus containing a painting of the bright dove of the Holy Spirit. Here, the architect transformed the traditional dome into a series of segmented intersecting arches. A comparison of Guarini's dome to that of the church of Sant'Eligio degli Orefici in Rome (FIG. **24-17**), attributed both to Bramante and to Raphael and reconstructed about 1600, indicates that a fundamental change occurred. The pristine clarity of the latter's unmodified circular shape immediately recalls the Pantheon dome (see FIG. 10-50). Guarini converted the static "dome of Heaven" of Renaissance architecture and philosophy into the dynamic Italian Baroque design that conveys a dramatic spiritual presence.

The styles of Borromini and Guarini moved across the Alps and inspired architects in Austria and southern Germany (FIG. 24-76) in the late 17th and early 18th centuries. These styles were also particularly popular in the Catholic regions of Europe and the New World (especially in Brazil).

**NATURALISTIC RELIGIOUS ART** Although sculpture and architecture provided the most obvious vehicles for manipulating space and creating theatrical effects, painting continued to be an important art form, as it was in previous centuries. Among the

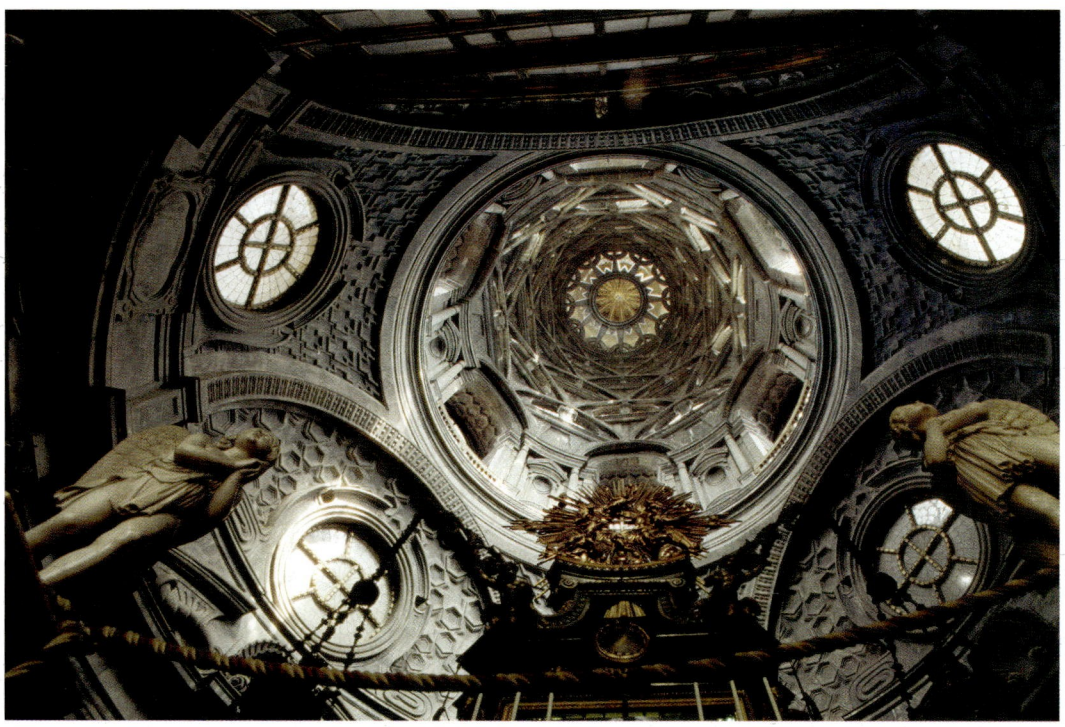

**24-16** GUARINO GUARINI, Chapel of Santissima Sindone (view into dome), Turin, Italy, 1667–1694.

most noted Italian Baroque painters were Caravaggio and Annibale Carracci, whose styles, although different, were both thoroughly in accord with the period. Michelangelo Merisi, known as CARAVAGGIO (1573–1610) after the northern Italian town he came from, developed a unique style that had tremendous influence throughout Europe. His outspoken disdain for the classical masters (probably more vocal than real) drew bitter criticism from many painters, one of whom denounced him as the "anti-Christ of painting." Giovanni Pietro Bellori, the most influential critic of the age and an admirer of Carracci, felt that Caravaggio's refusal to emulate the models of his distinguished predecessors threatened the whole classical tradition of Italian painting that had reached its zenith in Raphael's work. Yet despite this criticism and the problems in Caravaggio's troubled life (reconstructed from documents such as police records), Caravaggio received

many commissions, both public and private, and numerous artists paid him the supreme compliment of borrowing from his innovations. His influence on later artists, as much outside Italy as within, was immense. In his art, Caravaggio injected a naturalism into both religion and the classics, reducing them to human dramas played out in the harsh and dingy settings of his time and place. His unidealized figures selected from the fields and the streets were, however, effective precisely because of the Italian public's familiarity with such figures.

**THE LIGHT OF DIVINE REVELATION** Caravaggio painted *Conversion of Saint Paul* (FIG. **24-18**) for the Cerasi Chapel in the Roman church of Santa Maria del Popolo. It illustrates the conversion of the Pharisee Saul to Christianity, when he became the disciple Paul. The saint-to-be appears amid his conversion, flat on his back with his arms thrown up. In the background, an old hostler seems preoccupied with caring for the horse. At first inspection, little here suggests the momentous significance of the spiritual event taking place. The viewer of the painting seems to be witnessing a mere stable accident, not a man overcome by a great miracle. Although Caravaggio departed from traditional depictions of such religious scenes, the eloquence and humanity with which he imbued his paintings impressed many.

Caravaggio also employed other formal devices to compel the viewer's interest and involvement in the event. In *Conversion of Saint Paul,* he used a perspective and a chiaroscuro intended to bring viewers as close as possible to the scene's space and action, almost as if they were participating in them. The sense of inclusion is augmented by the low horizon line. Caravaggio designed *Conversion of Saint Paul* for presentation on the chapel wall, positioned at the viewers' line of sight as they stand at the chapel entrance. In addition, the sharply lit figures are meant to be seen as emerging from the dark of the background. The actual light from the chapel's windows functions as a kind of stage lighting for the production of a vision, analogous to the rays in Bernini's *Ecstasy of Saint Teresa* (FIG. 24-9).

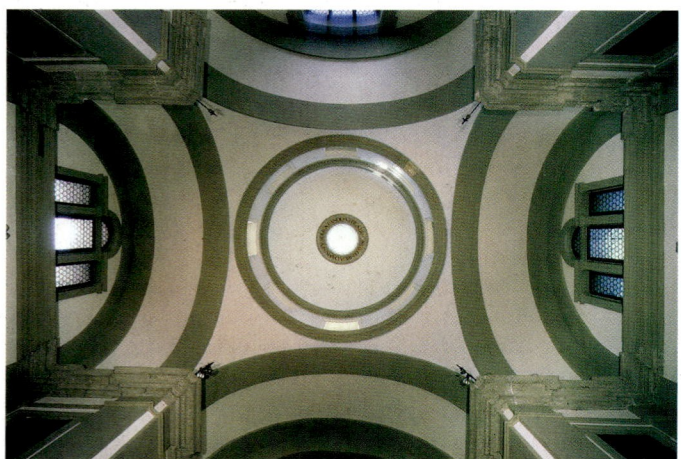

**24-17** Sant'Eligio degli Orefici (view into dome), Rome, Italy, attributed to BRAMANTE and RAPHAEL, ca. 1509; reconstructed ca. 1600.

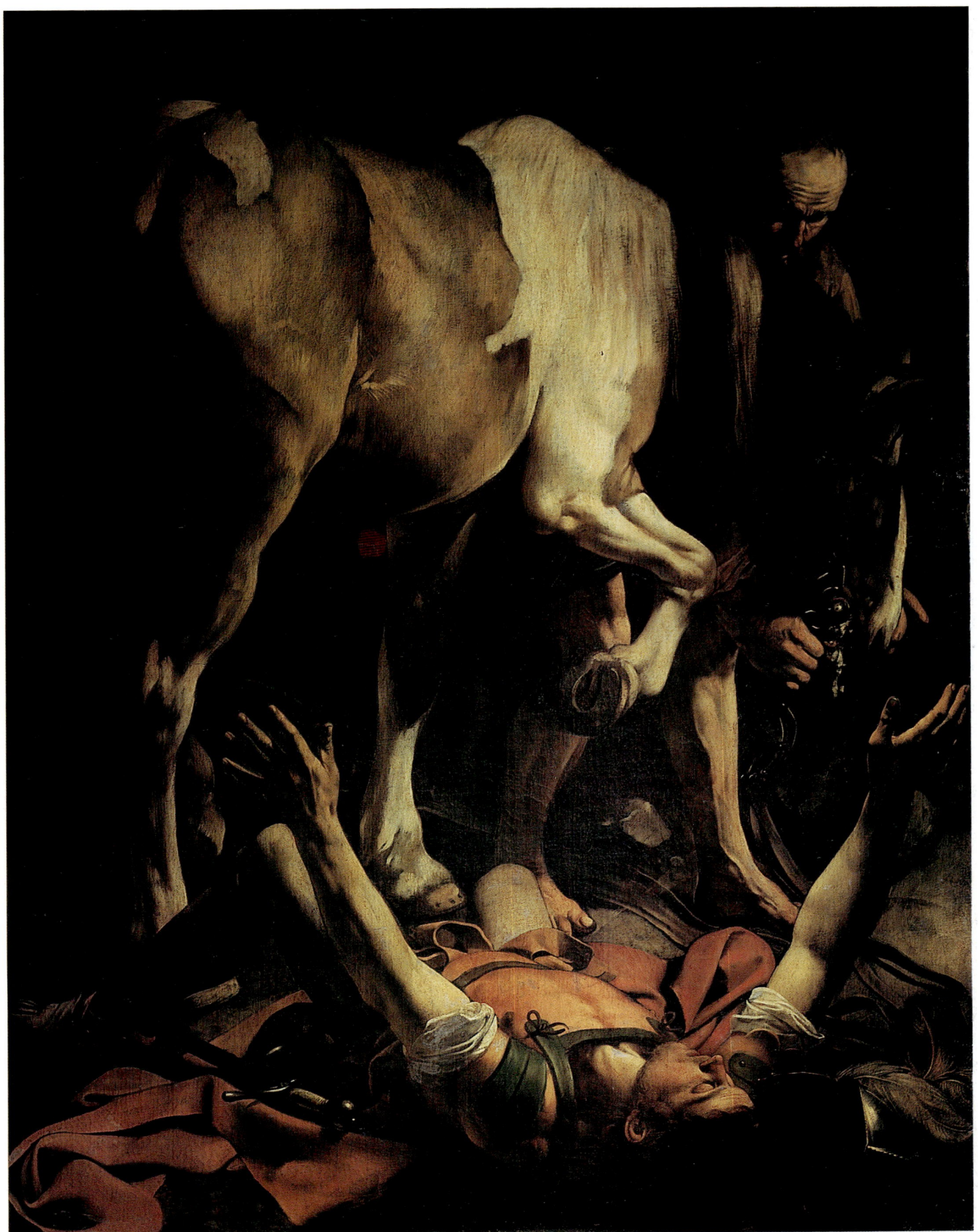

**24-18** Caravaggio, *Conversion of Saint Paul,* Cerasi Chapel, Santa Maria del Popolo, Rome, Italy, ca. 1601. Oil on canvas, approx. 7′ 6″ × 5′ 9″.

Caravaggio's use of light is certainly dramatic. The stark contrast of light and dark was a feature of Caravaggio's style that first shocked and then fascinated his contemporaries. Caravaggio's use of dark settings enveloping their occupants, which profoundly influenced European art, has been called *tenebrism,* from the Italian word *tenebroso,* or "shadowy" manner. Although tenebrism was widespread in 17th-century art, it made its most emphatic appearance in the art of Spain and of the Netherlands. In Caravaggio's work, tenebrism also contributed mightily to the essential meaning of his pictures. In *Conversion of Saint Paul,* the dramatic spotlight shining down upon the fallen Pharisee is the light of divine revelation converting Saul to Christianity.

**FROM TAX COLLECTOR TO DISCIPLE** A piercing ray of light illuminating a world of darkness and bearing a spiritual message is also a central feature of one of Caravaggio's early masterpieces, *Calling of Saint Matthew* (FIG. **24-19**). It is one of two large canvases honoring Saint Matthew that the artist painted for the side walls of the Contarelli Chapel in San Luigi dei Francesi in Rome. The commonplace setting is typical of Caravaggio—a bland street scene with a plain building wall serving as a backdrop. Into this mundane environment, cloaked in mysterious shadow and almost unseen, Christ, identifiable initially only by his indistinct halo,

enters from the right. With a commanding gesture that recalls that of the Lord in Michelangelo's *Creation of Adam* on the Sistine Chapel ceiling (see FIG. 22-14), he summons Levi, the Roman tax collector, to a higher calling. The astonished tax collector, whose face is highlighted for the viewer by the beam of light emanating from an unspecified source above Christ's head and outside the picture, points to himself in disbelief. Although Christ's extended arm is reminiscent of the Lord in *Creation of Adam,* the position of Christ's hand and wrist is similar to that of Adam. This reference is highly appropriate—theologically, Christ is the second Adam. Whereas Adam was responsible for the Fall of Man, Christ is responsible for human redemption. The conversion of Levi (who became Matthew) brought his salvation.

**PRESENTING CHRIST'S BODY** In 1603, Caravaggio produced a large-scale painting, *Entombment* (FIG. **24-20**), for the Chapel of Pietro Vittrice at Santa Maria in Vallicella in Rome. This work includes all the hallmarks of Caravaggio's distinctive style: the plebeian figure types (particularly visible in the scruffy, worn face of Nicodemus—a Pharisee whom Christ taught, and who here holds Christ's legs in the foreground), the stark use of darks and lights, and the invitation for the viewer to participate in the scene. As in *Conversion of Saint Paul,* the action takes place in the

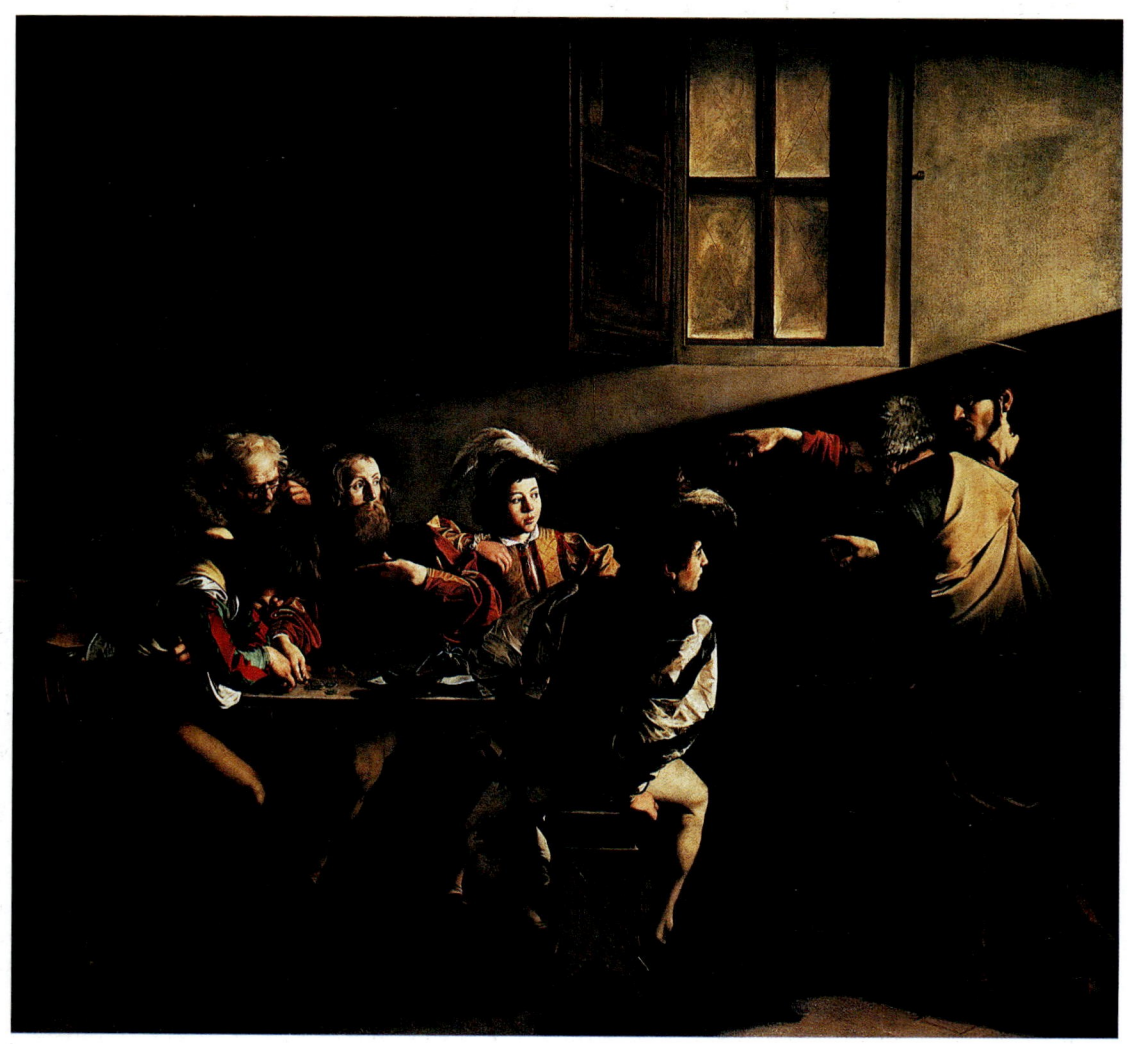

**24-19** CARAVAGGIO, *Calling of Saint Matthew,* Contarelli Chapel, San Luigi dei Francesi, Rome, Italy, ca. 1597–1601. Oil on canvas, 11′ 1″ × 11′ 5″.

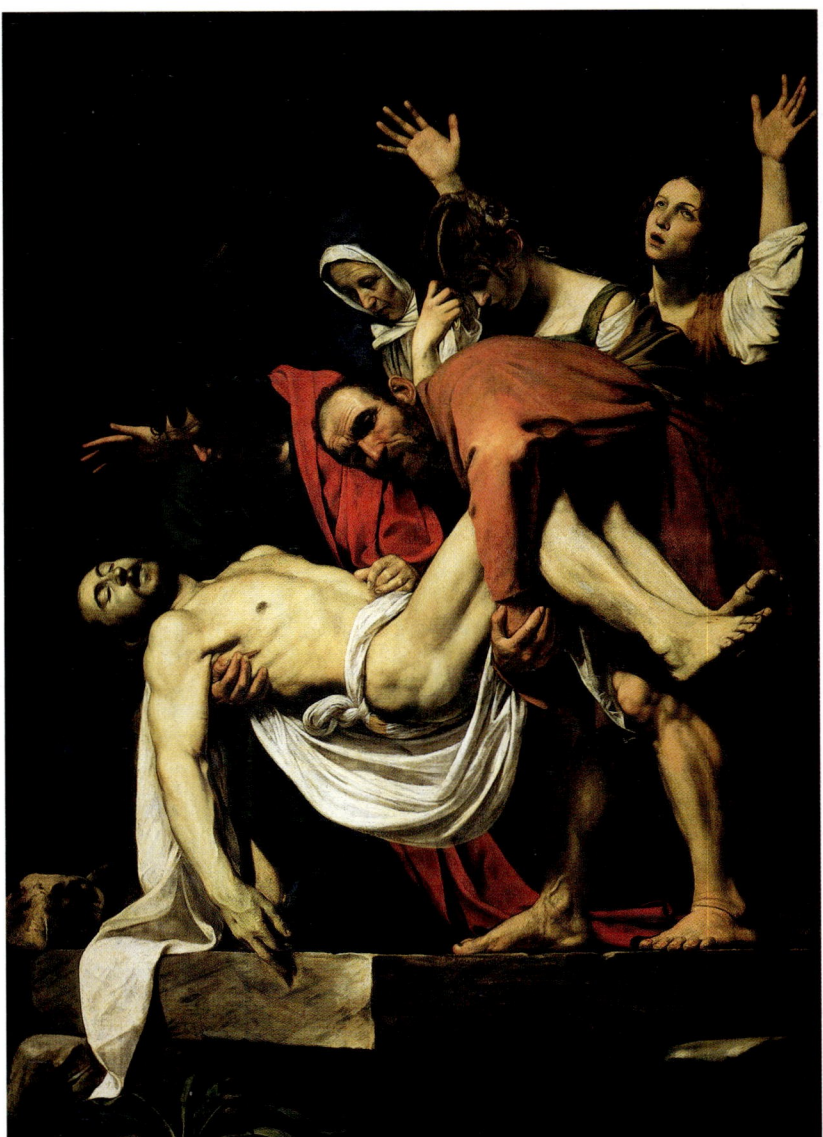

24-20 CARAVAGGIO, *Entombment,* from the chapel of Pietro Vittrice, Santa Maria in Vallicella, Rome, Italy, ca. 1603. Oil on canvas, 9′ 10$\frac{1}{8}$″ × 6′ 7$\frac{15}{16}$″. Musei Vaticani, Pinacoteca, Rome.

foreground. The artist positioned the figures on a stone slab whose corner appears to extend into the viewer's space. This suggests that Christ's body will be laid directly in front of the viewer.

Beyond its ability to move its audience, such a composition also had theological implications. In light of the ongoing Counter-Reformation efforts at that time, such implications cannot be overlooked. To viewers in the chapel, it appeared as though the men were laying Christ's body onto the altar, which was in front of the painting. This served to give visual form to the doctrine of transubstantiation (the transformation of the Eucharistic bread and wine into the Body and Blood of Christ)—a doctrine central to Catholicism but rejected by Protestants. By depicting Christ's body as though it were physically present during the Mass, Caravaggio visually articulated an abstract theological precept. Unfortunately, because this painting has been moved to one of the Vatican Museums, viewers no longer can experience this effect.

**IN CARAVAGGIO'S FOOTSTEPS** Caravaggio's style became increasingly popular, and his combination of naturalism and drama appealed both to patrons and artists. A significant artist often discussed as a "Caravaggista" (a close follower of Caravaggio)

is ARTEMISIA GENTILESCHI (ca. 1593–1653). Gentileschi was instructed by her father, the artist Orazio, who was himself strongly influenced by Caravaggio. Her successful career, pursued in Florence, Venice, Naples, and Rome, helped disseminate Caravaggio's manner throughout the peninsula.

In her *Judith Slaying Holofernes* (FIG. **24-21**), Gentileschi used the tenebrism and what might be called the "dark" subject matter Caravaggio favored. Significantly, Gentileschi chose a narrative involving a heroic female, a favorite theme of hers. The story, from an Apocryphal work of the Old Testament, the Book of Judith, relates the delivery of Israel from its enemy, Holofernes. Having succumbed to Judith's charms, the Assyrian general Holofernes invited her to his tent for the night. When he fell asleep, Judith cut off his head. In this version of the scene (Gentileschi produced more than one image of Judith), Judith and her maidservant are beheading Holofernes. The drama of the event cannot be evaded— blood spurts everywhere, and the strength necessary to complete the task is evident as the two women struggle with the sword. The tension and strain are palpable. The controlled highlights on the action in the foreground recall Caravaggio's work and heighten the drama here as well.

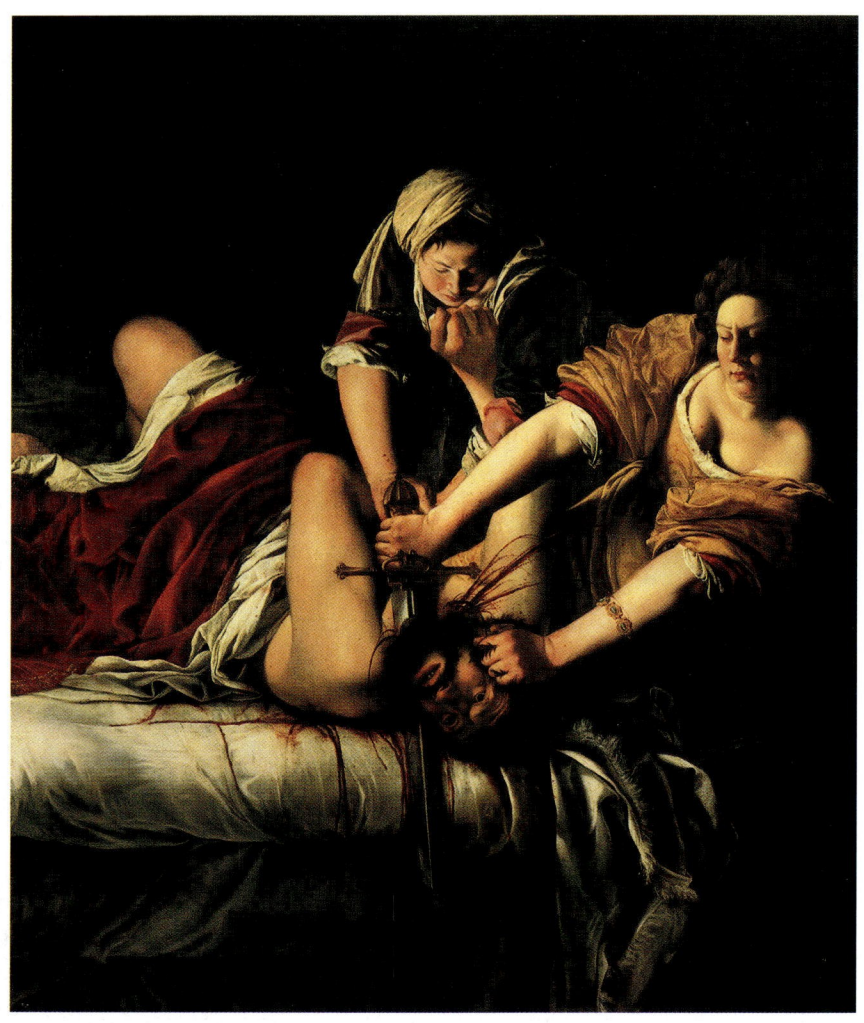

**24-21** Artemisia Gentileschi, *Judith Slaying Holofernes*, ca. 1614–1620. Oil on canvas, 6′ 6⅓″ × 5′ 4″. Galleria degli Uffizi, Florence.

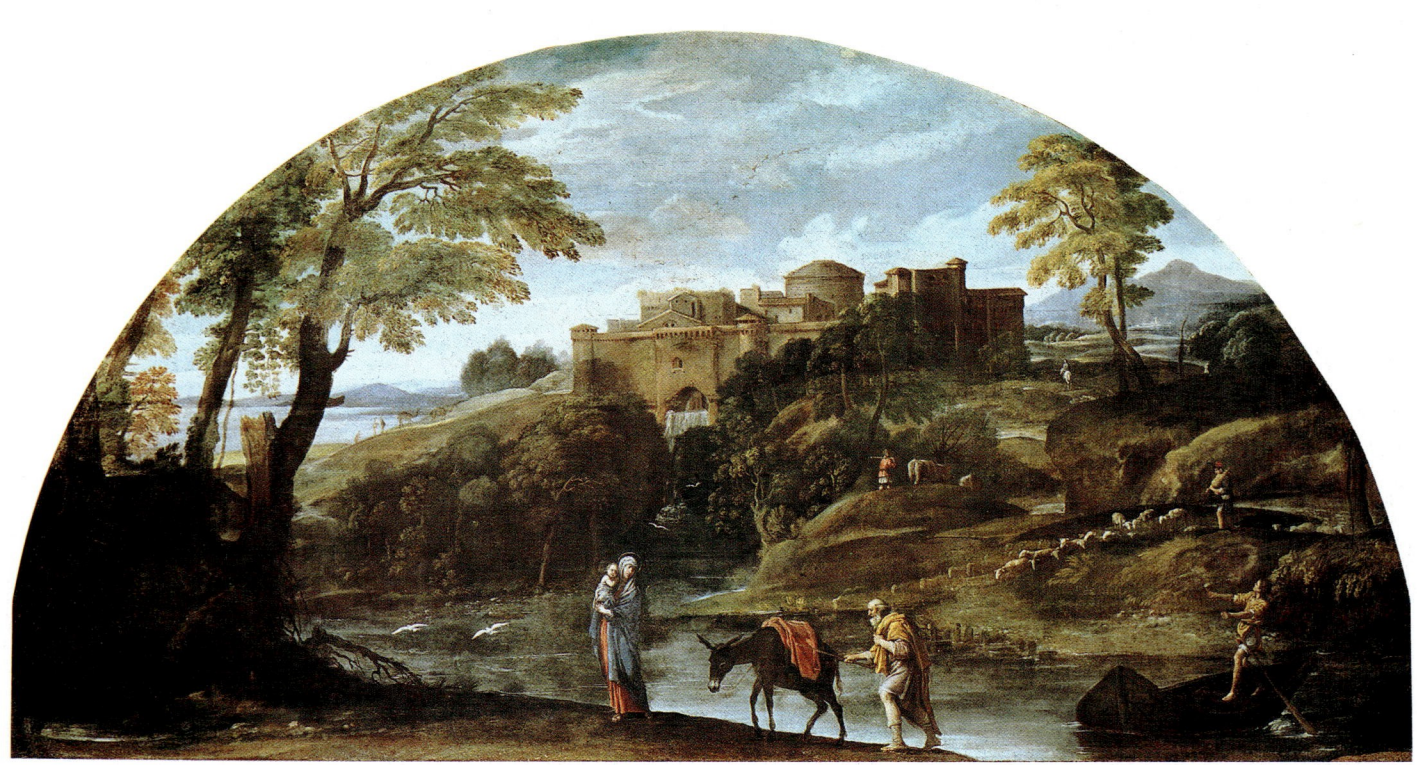

**24-22** Annibale Carracci, *Flight into Egypt,* 1603–1604. Oil on canvas, approx. 4′ × 7′ 6″. Galleria Doria Pamphili, Rome.

**DRAWN TO THE CLASSICS** In contrast to Caravaggio, ANNIBALE CARRACCI (1560–1609) not only studied but also emulated the Renaissance masters carefully. Carracci received much of his training at an academy of art in his native Bologna. Founded cooperatively by his family members, among them his cousin Ludovico Carracci (1555–1619) and brother Agostino Carracci (1557–1602), the Bolognese academy was the first significant institution of its kind in the history of Western art. It was founded on the premises that art can be taught—the basis of any academic philosophy of art—and that its instruction must include the classical and Renaissance traditions in addition to the study of anatomy and life drawing. Thus, in contrast to Caravaggio's more naturalistic style, Carracci embraced a more classically ordered style.

For example, in his *Flight into Egypt* (FIG. **24-22**), based on the biblical narrative from Matthew 2:13–14, Carracci created the "ideal" or "classical" landscape. Here he pictorially represented nature ordered by divine law and human reason. The roots of the style are in the landscape backgrounds of Venetian Renaissance paintings (compare FIG. 22-33). Tranquil hills and fields, quietly gliding streams, serene skies, unruffled foliage, shepherds with their flocks—all the props of the pastoral scene and mood—expand in such paintings to fill the picture space. Carracci regularly included screens of trees in the foreground, dark against the sky's even light. In this scene, streams or terraces, carefully placed one above the other and narrowed, zigzag through the terrain, leading the viewer's eye back to the middle ground. There, many Venetian Renaissance landscape artists depicted architectural structures (as Carracci did in *Flight into Egypt*)—walled towns or citadels, towers, temples, monumental tombs, villas. Such constructed environments captured idealized antiquity and the idyllic life. Although the artists often took the subjects for these classically rendered scenes from religious or heroic stories, they seem to have given precedence to the pastoral landscapes over the narratives. Here, Mary, with the Christ Child, and Saint Joseph are greatly diminished in size, simply becoming part of the landscape as they wend their way slowly to Egypt after having been ferried across a stream.

**A CEILING FIT FOR THE GODS** Among Carracci's most notable works is his decoration of the Palazzo Farnese gallery (FIG. **24-23**) in Rome. Cardinal Odoardo Farnese, a wealthy descendant of Pope Paul III, commissioned this ceiling fresco to celebrate the

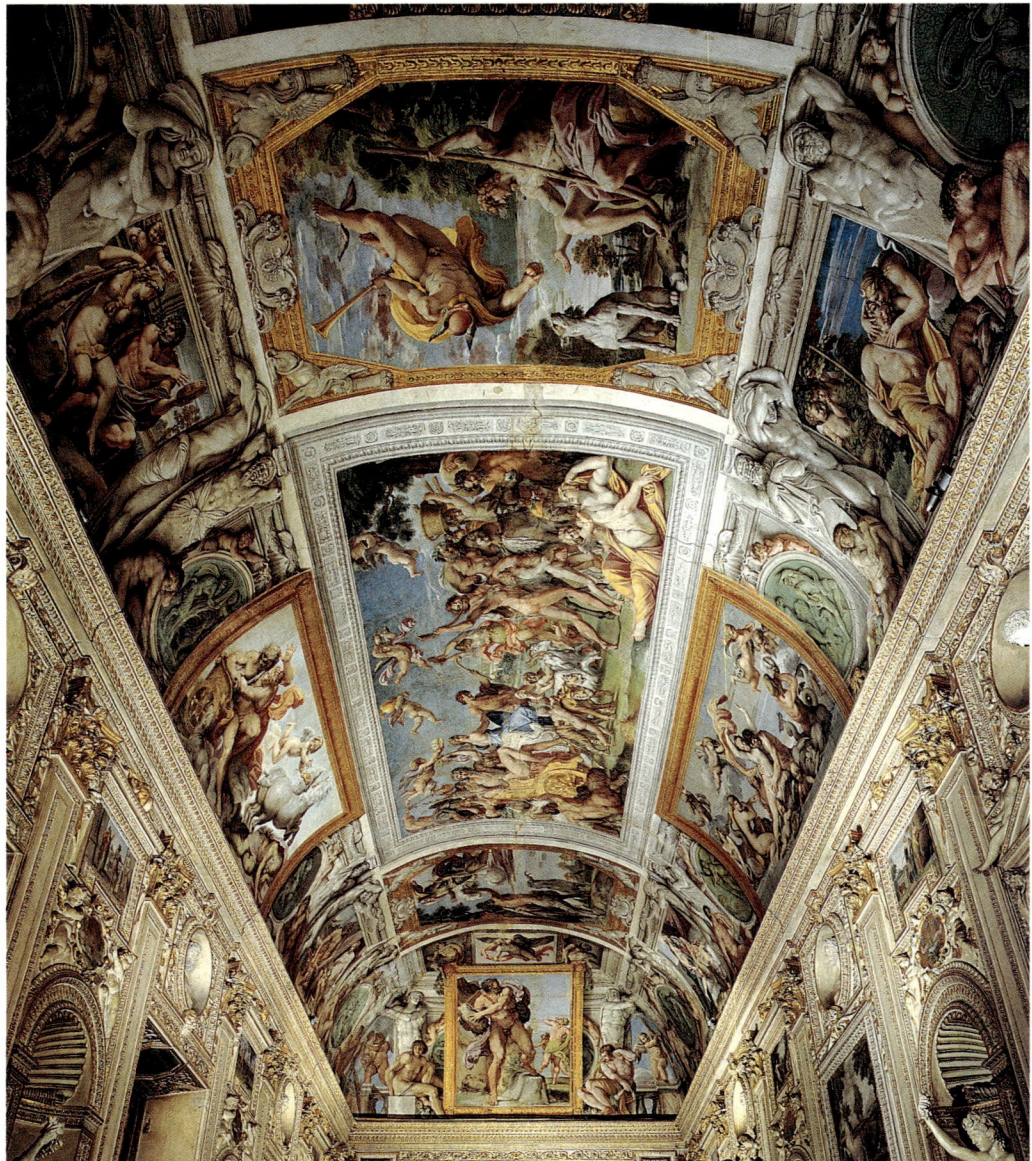

**24-23** ANNIBALE CARRACCI, *Loves of the Gods,* ceiling frescoes in the gallery, Palazzo Farnese, Rome, Italy, 1597–1601.

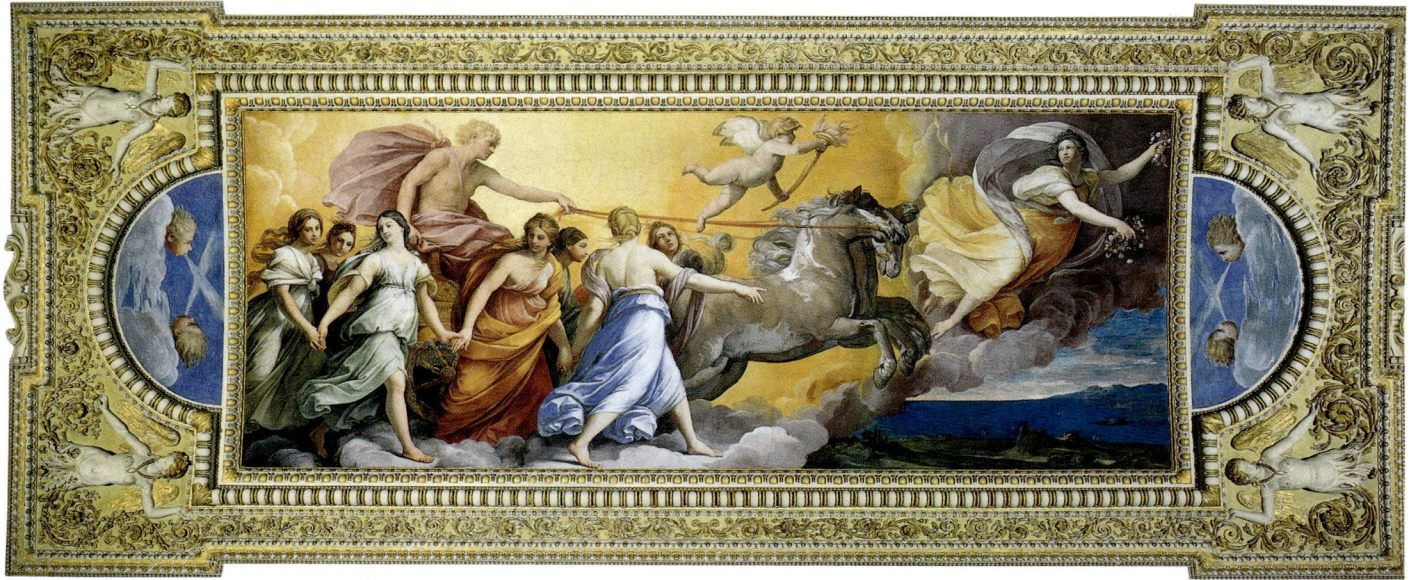

24-24 GUIDO RENI, *Aurora,* ceiling fresco in the Casino Rospigliosi, Rome, Italy, 1613–1614.

wedding of the cardinal's brother. Appropriately, its iconographic program is titled *Loves of the Gods*—interpretations of the varieties of earthly and divine love in classical mythology.

Carracci arranged the scenes in a format resembling framed easel paintings on a wall, but here he painted them on the surfaces of a shallow curved vault. The Sistine Chapel ceiling (see FIG. 22-13), of course, comes to mind, although it is not an exact source. This type of simulation of easel painting for ceiling design is called *quadro riportato* (transferred framed painting). Carracci's great influence made it fashionable for more than a century. The framed pictures are flanked by polychrome seated nude youths, who turn their heads to gaze at the scenes around them, and by standing Atlas figures painted to resemble marble statues. Carracci derived these motifs from Michelangelo's Sistine Chapel ceiling. Notably, the chiaroscuro is not the same for both the pictures and the figures surrounding them. The painter modeled the figures inside the quadri in an even light. The outside figures seem to be lit from beneath, as if they were actual three-dimensional beings or statues illuminated by torches in the gallery below. This interest in illusion, already manifest in the Renaissance, continued in the grand ceiling compositions of the 17th century. In the crown of the vault, a long panel representing the *Triumph of Bacchus* is a quite ingenious mixture of Raphael and Titian. It reflects Carracci's adroitness in adjusting their authoritative styles to make something of his own.

**A "DIVINE" ARTIST** Another artist trained in the Bolognese academy, GUIDO RENI (1575–1642), selected Raphael for his inspiration, as is evident in his *Aurora* (FIG. **24-24**), a ceiling fresco in the Casino Rospigliosi in Rome. Aurora (Dawn) leads Apollo's chariot, while the Hours dance about it. Reni conceived *Aurora* in quadro riportato, like the paintings in Carracci's *Loves of the Gods,* and painted a complex and convincing illusionistic frame. The fresco exhibits a suave, almost swimming, motion; soft modeling; and sure composition, without Raphael's sculpturesque strength. It is an intelligent interpretation of the master's style and of ancient classical art, for the ultimate sources of the composition were Roman reliefs (see FIG. 10-39) and coins depicting

emperors in triumphal chariots accompanied by flying Victories and other personifications. Because of paintings such as *Aurora*, Reni was so much admired in his own day and well into the 19th century that he was known as "the divine Guido."

The impressive ceiling frescoes produced by Carracci and others inspired many artists and patrons to explore the capabilities of ceiling painting. The experience of looking up at a painting is different from simply looking at a painting hanging on a wall. The considerable height and the expansive scale of most ceiling frescoes induce a feeling of awe.

**THE GLORY OF THE BARBERINI** Patrons who wanted to burnish their public image or control their legacy found monumental ceiling frescoes to be perfect vehicles for such statements. In 1633, Pope Urban VIII commissioned a ceiling fresco for the Gran Salone of the Palazzo Barberini in Rome. This project was the most important decorative commission of the 1630s, and thus artists highly coveted it. Urban VIII selected PIETRO DA CORTONA (1596–1669), a fellow Tuscan who had moved to Rome in about 1612. By the 1630s, Cortona had established himself as a respected artist. The grandiose and spectacular *Triumph of the Barberini* (FIG. **24-25**) overwhelms spectators with the glory of the Barberini family (and Urban VIII in particular). The iconographic program for this fresco, designed by the poet Francesco Bracciolini, centered on the accomplishments of the Barberini. Divine Providence appears in a halo of radiant light, directing Immortality, holding a crown of stars, to bestow eternal life on the Barberini family. The laurel wreath (also a symbol of immortality) reinforces the enduring Barberini legacy. It floats around the bees (the Barberini family's symbols, as already seen in Bernini's baldacchino, FIG. 24-5) and is supported by the virtues Faith, Hope, and Charity. The papal tiara and keys announcing the personal triumphs of Urban VIII are also clearly visible.

**IN THE PRESENCE OF JESUS** The dazzling spectacle of ceiling frescoes also proved very effective for commissions illustrating religious themes. Church authorities realized that such paintings,

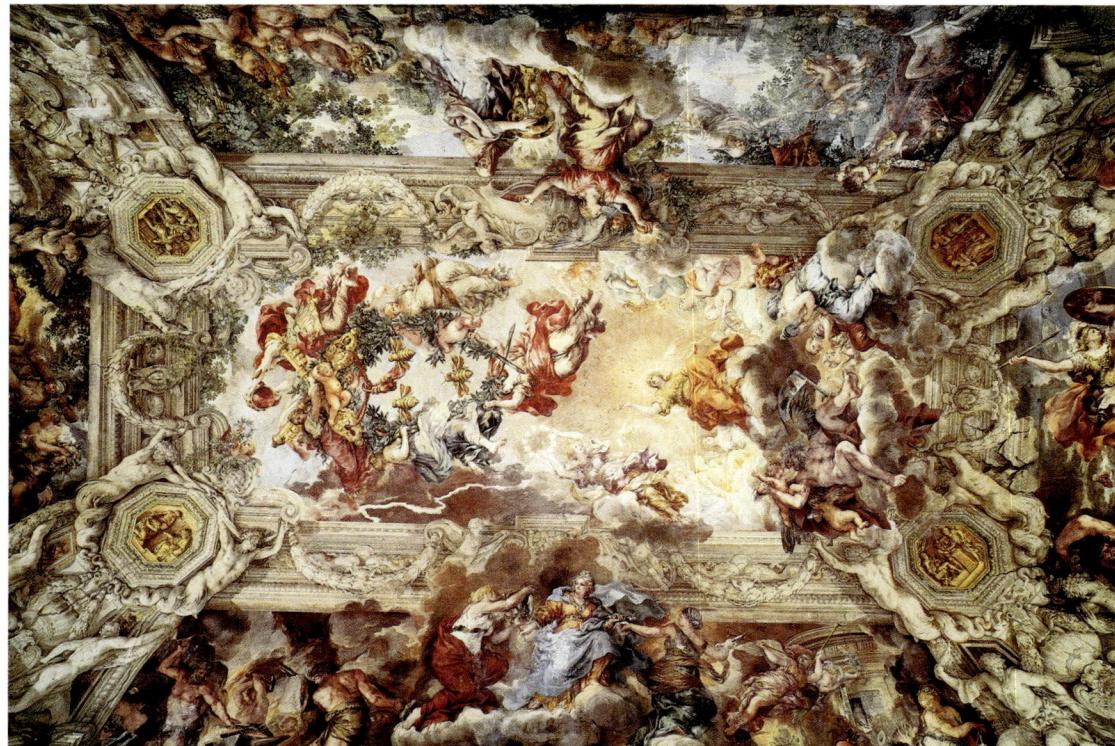

**24-25** Pietro da Cortona, *Triumph of the Barberini,* ceiling fresco in the Gran Salone, Palazzo Barberini, Rome, Italy, 1633–1639.

high above the ground, offered perfect opportunities to impress on viewers the glory and power of the Catholic Church. In conjunction with the theatricality of Italian Baroque architecture and sculpture, frescoes spanning church ceilings contributed to creating transcendent spiritual environments well suited to the needs of the Church in Counter-Reformation Italy.

The dramatic impact such ceiling frescoes could have is revealed by *Triumph of the Name of Jesus* (FIG. **24-26**), painted by Giovanni Battista Gaulli (1639–1709). *Triumph* appears over the nave of the Church of Il Gesù in Rome (see FIGS. 22-50 and 22-51). As the mother church of the Jesuit order, Il Gesù played a prominent role in Counter-Reformation efforts. The visual effect

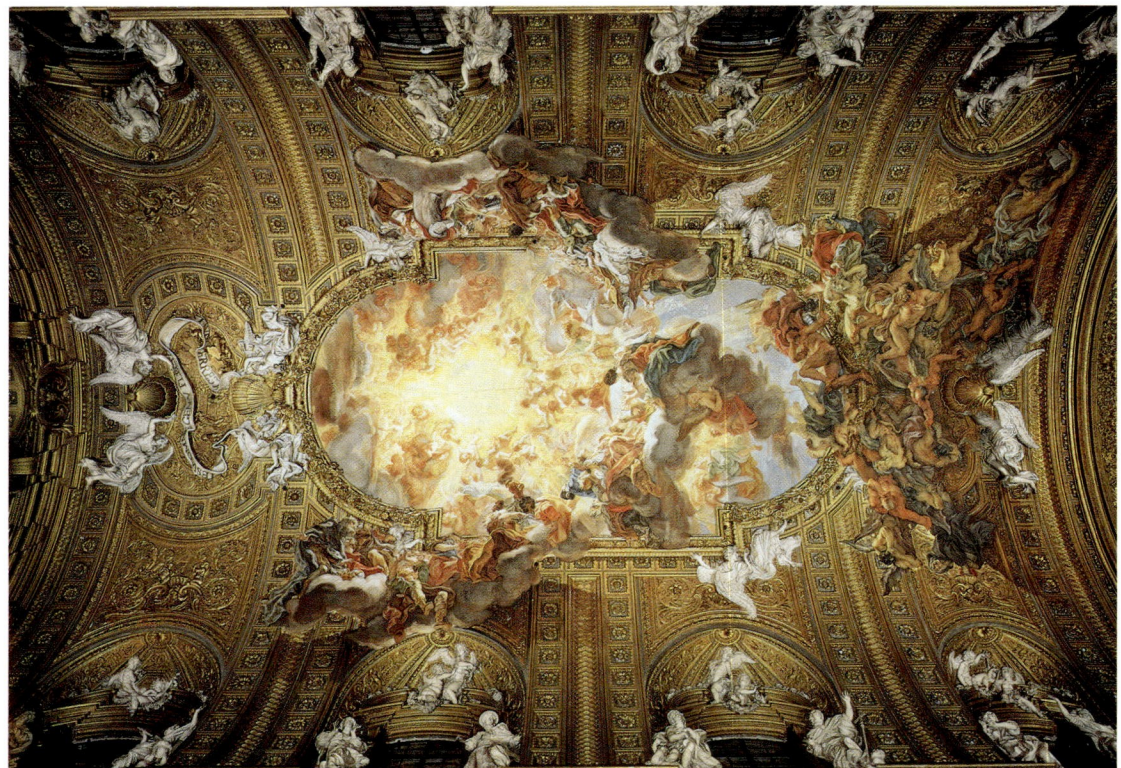

**24-26** Giovanni Battista Gaulli, *Triumph of the Name of Jesus,* ceiling fresco with stucco figures in the vault of the Church of Il Gesù, Rome, Italy, 1676–1679.

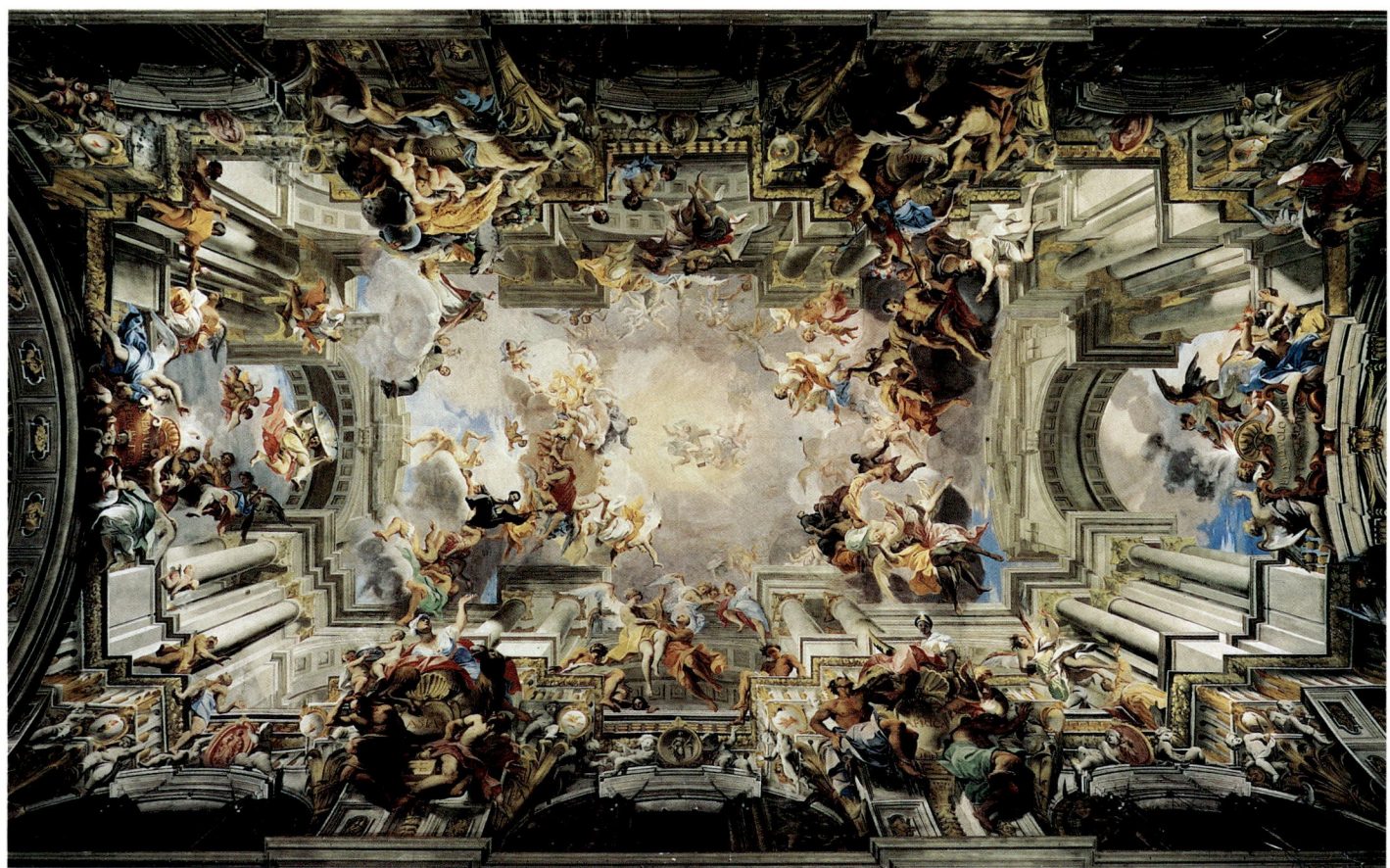

**24-27** FRA ANDREA POZZO, *Glorification of Saint Ignatius,* ceiling fresco in the nave of Sant'Ignazio, Rome, Italy, 1691–1694.

Gaulli created is stunning. Gilded architecture opens up in the center of the ceiling to offer viewers a glimpse of Heaven. The artist represented Jesus as a barely visible monogram (IHS) in a blinding radiant light that floats heavenward. In contrast, sinners are violently thrown back down to Earth. The painter glazed the gilded architecture to suggest shadows, thereby enhancing the scene's illusionistic quality. To further heighten the illusion, Gaulli painted many of the sinners on three-dimensional stucco extensions that project outside the painting's frame.

**HONORING SAINT IGNATIUS** Another master of ceiling decoration was FRA ANDREA POZZO (1642–1709), a lay brother of the Jesuit order and a master of perspective, on which he wrote an influential treatise. Pozzo designed and executed the vast ceiling fresco *Glorification of Saint Ignatius* (FIG. **24-27**) for the church of Sant'Ignazio in Rome. Like Il Gesù, Sant'Ignazio was prominent in Counter-Reformation Rome because of its dedication to Saint Ignatius, the founder of the Jesuit order. As Gaulli did in *Triumph of the Name of Jesus* (FIG. 24-26), Pozzo created the illusion that Heaven is opening up above the congregation. To accomplish this, the artist illusionistically continued the church's actual architecture into the vault so that the roof seems to be lifted off. As Heaven and Earth commingle, Saint Ignatius is carried to the waiting Christ in the presence of figures personifying the four corners of the world. A disk in the nave floor marks the standpoint for the whole perspectival illusion. For visitors looking up from this point, the vision is complete; they are truly in the presence of the heavenly and spiritual.

Thus, the effectiveness of Italian Baroque religious art depended on the drama and theatricality of individual images, as well as on the interaction and fusion of architecture, sculpture, and painting. Sound enhanced this experience. Churches were designed with acoustical effect in mind, and, in an Italian Baroque church filled with music, the power of both image and sound must have been immensely moving. Through simultaneous stimulation of both the visual and auditory senses, the faithful might well have been transported into a trancelike state that would, indeed, as England's contemporaneous poet John Milton eloquently stated in *Il Penseroso,* "bring all Heaven before [their] eyes."[1]

## Spain

**SPAIN'S DECLINE** During the 16th century, Spain had established itself as an international power. The Habsburg kings had built a dynastic state that encompassed Portugal, part of Italy, the Netherlands, and extensive areas of the New World. However, the animosity such dominance provoked among other European countries increased the challenges to Spanish hegemony. By the beginning of the 17th century, the Habsburg empire was struggling, and although Spain mounted a very aggressive effort during the Thirty Years' War, by 1660 the imperial age of the Spanish Habsburgs was over. In part, the demise of the Spanish empire was due to economic woes, which were exacerbated by the expensive military campaigns undertaken during the Thirty Years' War by Philip III (r. 1598–1621) and then by his son Philip IV (r. 1621–1665).

The increasing tax burden that was placed on Spanish subjects led to revolts and civil war in Catalonia and Portugal in the 1640s.

Thus, the dawn of the Baroque period in Spain found the country's leaders struggling to maintain control of their dwindling empire. Realizing as they did the value of visual imagery in communicating to a wide audience, both Philip III and Philip IV were avid art patrons.

Passionately committed to Catholic orthodoxy, Spain also encountered the same Counter-Reformation issues confronting Italy. As in Italy, Spanish Baroque artists sought ways to move viewers and to encourage greater devotion and piety. Particularly appealing in this regard were scenes of death and martyrdom, which provided artists with opportunities both to depict extreme feelings and to instill those feelings in viewers. Spain prided itself on its saints (for example, Saint Teresa of Avila, FIG. 24-9, and Saint Ignatius Loyola, FIG. 24-27, were both Spanish born), and martyrdom scenes surfaced frequently in Spanish Baroque art.

**THE FLAYING OF A SAINT** José (Jusepe) de Ribera (ca. 1588–1652) emigrated to Naples as a young man and settled there. For that reason, he sometimes was called by his Italian nickname, Lo Spagnoletto, "the little Spaniard." Influenced by Caravaggio, Ribera imbued his work with both naturalism and compelling drama, which lend shock value to his often brutal themes. These themes express at once the harsh times of the Counter-Reformation and a Spanish taste for the representation of courage and devotion. Ribera's *Martyrdom of Saint Bartholomew* (FIG. 24-28) is grim and dark in subject and form. Executioners are hoisting into position Saint Bartholomew, who is about to suffer the torture of being skinned alive. The saint's rough, heavy body and swarthy, plebeian features express a kinship between him and his tormentors, who are similar to the type of figures found in Caravaggio's paintings. Here, Ribera scorned idealization of any kind.

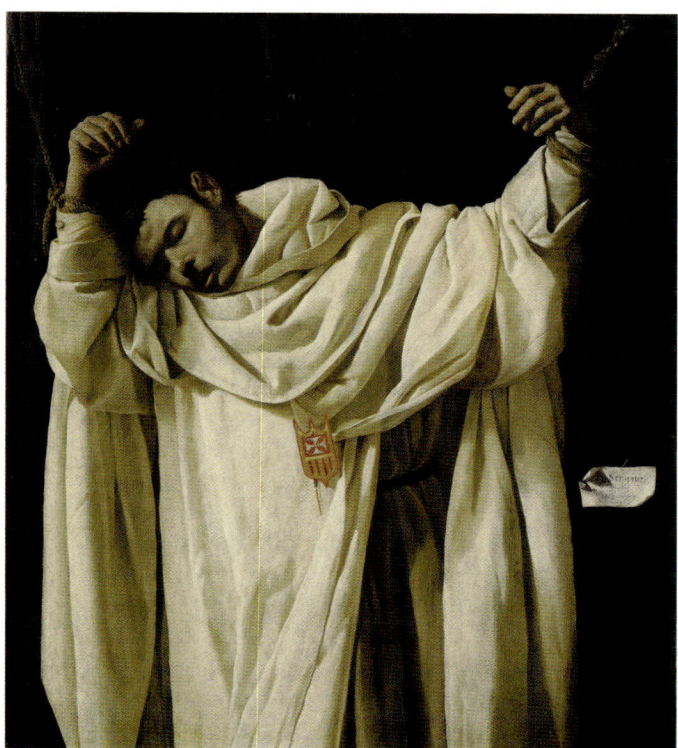

24-29 Francisco de Zurbarán, *Saint Serapion,* 1628. Oil on canvas, 3′ 11½″ × 3′ 4¾″. Wadsworth Atheneum, Hartford (The Ella Gallup Sumner and Mary Catlin Sumner Collection Fund).

**A MARTYR AT PEACE** Francisco de Zurbarán (1598–1664) also produced forceful images, many of which were commissioned by monastic orders. For example, Zurbarán painted *Saint Serapion* (FIG. 24-29) as a devotional image for the funerary chapel of the Order of Mercy. The saint, who participated in the Third Crusade of 1196, was martyred while preaching the Gospel to Muslims. According to one account of his martyrdom, the monk was tied to a tree, tortured, and decapitated. The Order of Mercy was dedicated to self-sacrifice, and Saint Serapion's membership in this order amplifies the resonance of this work. In *Saint Serapion* the figure emerges from a dark background and fills the foreground. The bright light shining on the figure calls attention to the tragic death of Saint Serapion and increases the dramatic impact of the image. Two tree branches are barely visible in the background, and a small note next to the saint identifies him for viewers. The coarse features of the Spanish monk (who was born in England) label him as common, no doubt evoking empathy from a wide audience. Zurbarán's paintings are often quiet and contemplative, appropriate for prayer and devotional purposes.

**AN INFLUENTIAL COURT PAINTER** The artist often extolled as the greatest Spanish painter of the age is Diego Velázquez (1599–1660). Velázquez, like many other Spanish artists, produced religious pictures, but he is justifiably renowned for the work he painted for his major patron, King Philip IV. Trained in Seville, Velázquez was quite young when he came to the attention of Philip IV. The king was struck by the immense talent of Velázquez and named him to the position of court painter. With the exception of two extended trips to Italy and a few excursions,

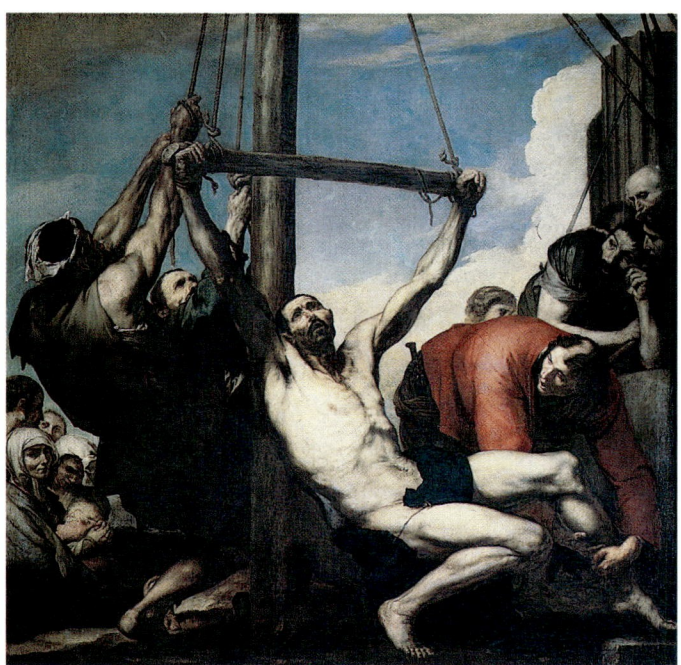

24-28 José de Ribera, *Martyrdom of Saint Bartholomew,* ca. 1639. Oil on canvas, approx. 7′ 8″ × 7′ 8″. Museo del Prado, Madrid.

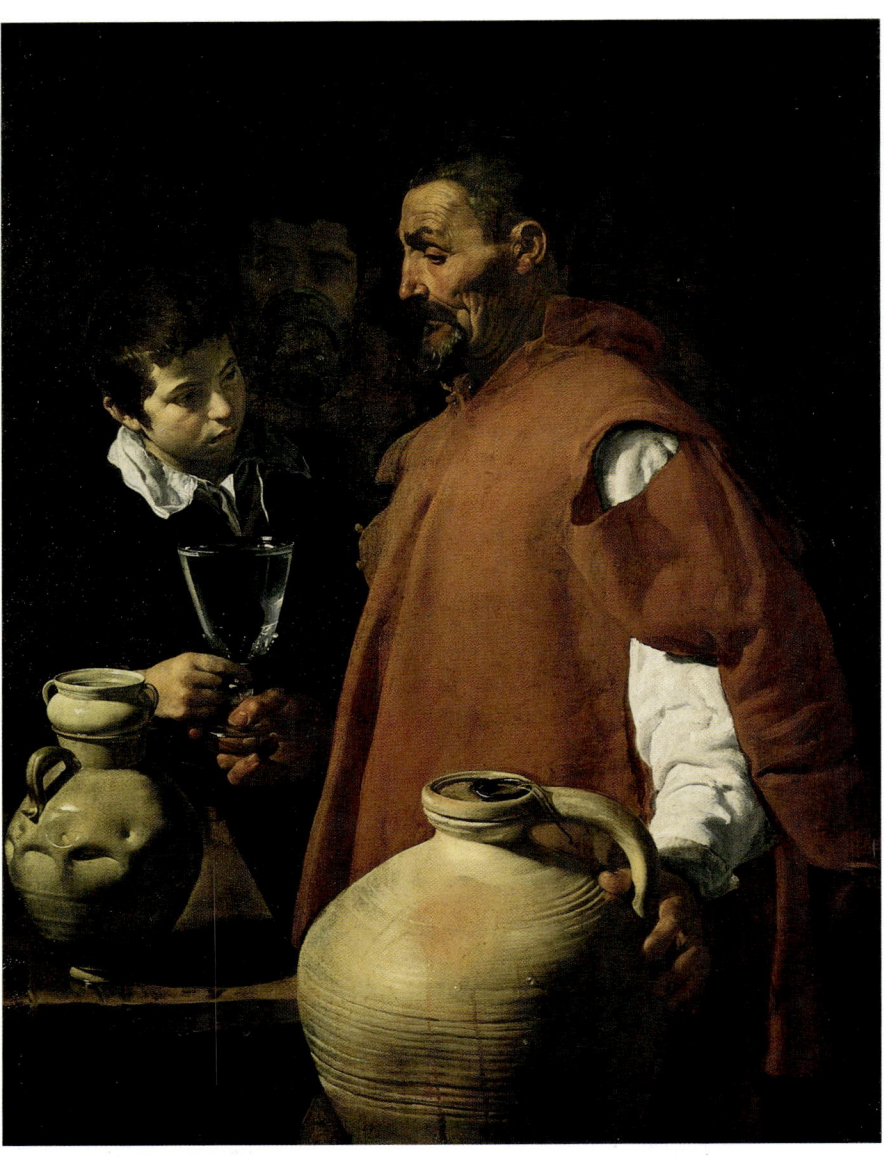

**24-30** Diego Velázquez, *Water Carrier of Seville*, ca. 1619. Oil on canvas, 3′ 5½″ × 2′ 7½″. Victoria & Albert Museum, London.

Velázquez remained in Madrid for the rest of his life. His close relationship with Philip IV and his high office as chamberlain of the palace gave him prestige and a rare opportunity to fulfill the promise of his genius with a variety of artistic assignments.

Velázquez's skill is evident in an early work, *Water Carrier of Seville* (FIG. **24-30**), which he painted when he was only about 20. The artist's command of his craft is impressive. He rendered the figures with clarity and dignity, and his careful depiction of the water jugs in the foreground, complete with droplets of water, adds to the credibility of the scene. The contrast of darks and lights, along with the plebeian nature of the figures, reveal the influence of Caravaggio, whose work Velázquez had studied. The artist presented this *genre* scene (one from everyday life) with such care and conviction that it seems to convey a deeper significance.

**CELEBRATING A SPANISH VICTORY** As official court painter, Velázquez created many works for Philip IV. In 1635, he produced *Surrender of Breda* (FIG. **24-31**) as part of an extensive program of painted decoration for the Hall of Realms in the Palace of Buen Retiro in Madrid, which the count-duke of Olivares built for Philip IV. *Surrender* commemorates the Spanish victory over the Dutch in 1625. Among the most troublesome

situations for Spain was the conflict in the Netherlands. Determined to escape from Spanish control, the northern Netherlands succeeded in breaking away from the Spanish empire in the late 16th century. Skirmishes continued to flare up along the border between the northern (Dutch) and southern (Spanish) Netherlands, and in 1625 Philip IV sent General Ambrogio di Spínola to Breda to reclaim the town for Spain. Velázquez depicted the victorious Spanish troops, organized and well armed, on the right side of the painting. In sharp contrast, the defeated Dutch on the left appear bedraggled and disorganized. In the center foreground, the mayor of Breda, Justinus of Nassau, hands the city's keys to the Spanish general. The painting glorifies not only the strength of the Spanish military but the benevolence of Spínola as well. Velázquez portrayed the general standing and magnanimously stopping Justinus from kneeling, rather than astride his horse, lording over the vanquished Dutch. Indeed, the terms of surrender were notably lenient, and the Dutch were allowed to retain their arms.

**PORTRAYING ROYALTY** In his role as first painter to the king, Velázquez painted dozens of portraits of the monarch. *King Philip IV of Spain* (FIG. **24-32**) is also known as the *Fraga Philip,* because

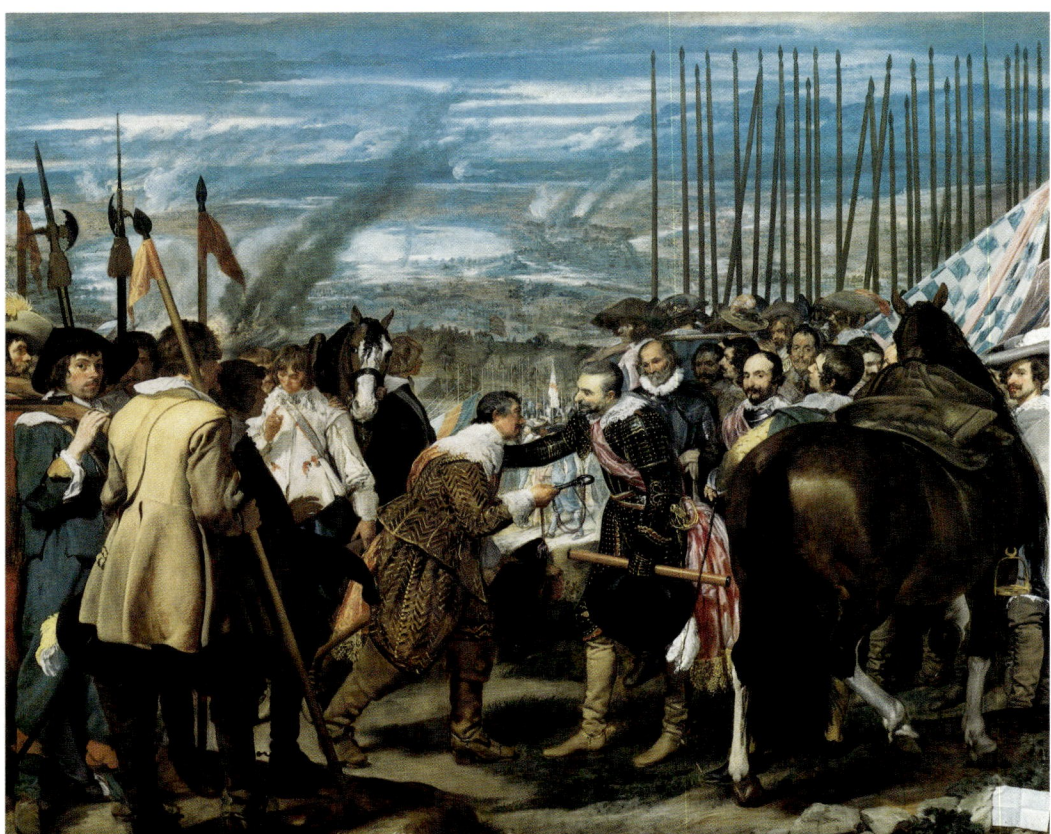

24-31 DIEGO VELÁZQUEZ, *Surrender of Breda*, 1634–1635. Oil on canvas, 10′ 1″ × 12′ ½″. Museo del Prado, Madrid.

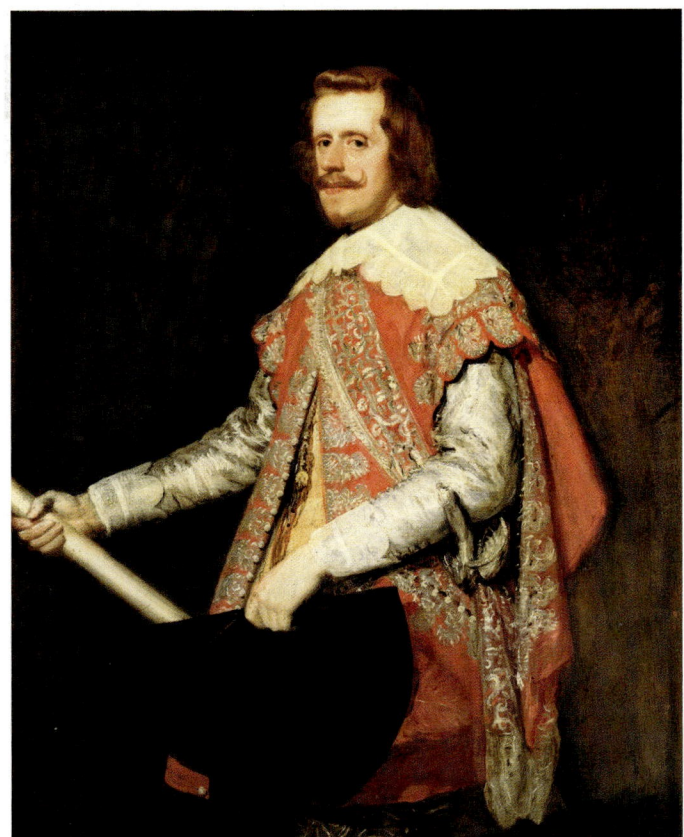

24-32 DIEGO VELÁZQUEZ, *King Philip IV of Spain (Fraga Philip)*, 1644. Oil on canvas, 4′ 3⅛″ × 3′ 3⅛″. The Frick Collection, New York.

it was painted during the Aragonese campaign in the town of Fraga. (Such a designation differentiates the many royal portraits from one another.) Velázquez accompanied the king and his troops in their attempt to reconquer the territory, and during a three-month stay in Fraga, Philip ordered the artist to produce this portrait. In it, Philip IV appears as a military leader, arrayed in red and silver campaign dress but without military accoutrements except his baton of command and sword. Because the king was not a commanding presence and because he had inherited the large Habsburg jaw (the result of dynastic inbreeding), Velázquez had to find creative ways to "ennoble" the monarch. He succeeded by focusing attention on the exquisite attire Philip wears, particularly the elaborately embroidered rose-colored cloak and baldric (the sash-like belt worn over one shoulder and across the chest to support a sword). Velázquez managed to make the silver needlework on these vestments shimmer. Based on detailed written accounts, we know that this is the costume worn by the king when reviewing the troops, and the artist's fidelity in depicting Philip's elegant attire no doubt added to the authority of the image.

**OF ART AND ROYAL LIFE** After an extended visit to Rome from 1648 to 1651, Velázquez returned to Spain and painted his greatest masterpiece, *Las Meninas* (*The Maids of Honor;* FIG. **24-33**). In it, Velázquez showed his mastery of both form and content. The painter represented himself in his studio standing before a large canvas. The young Infanta (Princess) Margarita appears in the foreground with her two maids-in-waiting, her favorite dwarfs, and a large dog. In the middle ground are a woman in widow's attire and a male escort; in the background, a chamberlain is framed in a

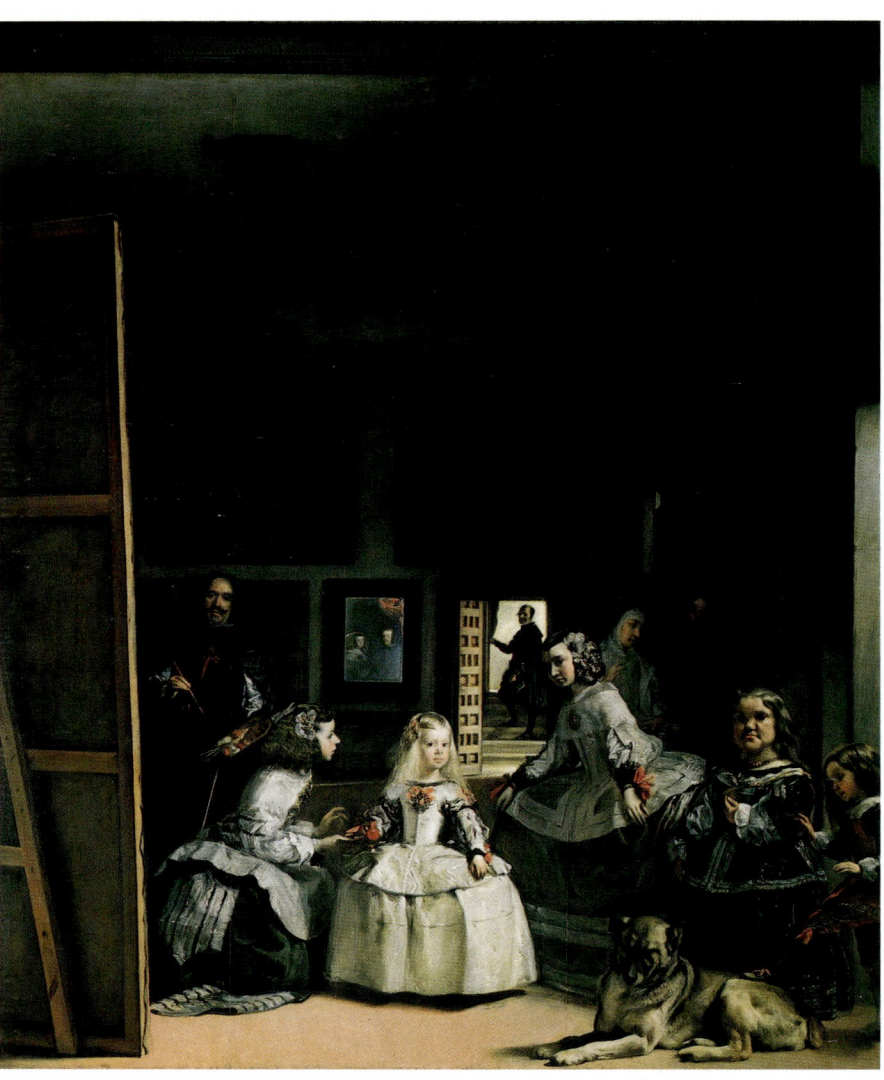

brightly lit open doorway. The personages present have been identified, including the two meninas and the dwarfs. The room represented in the painting was the artist's studio in the palace of the Alcázar in Madrid. After the death of Prince Baltasar Carlos in 1646, Philip IV ordered part of the prince's chambers converted into a studio for Velázquez.

*Las Meninas* is noteworthy for its visual and narrative complexity. Indeed, art historians have yet to agree on any particular reading or interpretation. A central issue preoccupying scholars has been what, exactly, is taking place in *Las Meninas*. In the painting, what is Velázquez depicting on the huge canvas in front of him? He may be painting this very picture—an informal image of the infanta and her entourage. Alternately, Velázquez may be painting a portrait of King Philip IV and Queen Mariana, whose reflections appear in the mirror on the far wall. If so, that would suggest the presence of the king and queen in the viewer's space, outside the confines of the picture. Other scholars have proposed that the mirror image reflects not the physical appearance of the royal couple in Velázquez's studio but the image that he is in the process of painting on the canvas before him. This question has never been definitively resolved.

More generally, *Las Meninas* can be read as an attempt by Velázquez to elevate both himself and his profession. As first painter to the king and as chamberlain of the palace, Velázquez was conscious not only of the importance of his court office but also of the honor and dignity belonging to his profession as a painter. Throughout his career, Velázquez hoped to be ennobled by royal appointment to membership in the ancient and illustrious Order of Santiago. Because he lacked some of the required patents of nobility, he gained entrance only with difficulty at the very end of his life, and then only through the pope's dispensation. In the painting, he wears the order's red cross on his doublet, painted there, legend says, by the king himself. In all likelihood, the artist painted it. In Velázquez's mind, *Las Meninas* might have embodied the idea of the great king visiting his studio, as Alexander the Great visited the studio of the painter Apelles in ancient times. The figures in the painting all appear to acknowledge the royal presence. Placed among them in equal dignity is Velázquez, face-to-face with his sovereign. The location of the completed painting reinforced this act of looking—of seeing and being seen. *Las Meninas* hung in the personal office of Philip IV in another part of the palace. Thus, although occasional visitors admitted to the king's private quarters may have seen this painting, it was viewed primarily by Philip IV. And each time he did so, standing before the large canvas, he again participated in the work as the probable subject of Velázquez's painting in *Las Meninas* and as the object of the figures' gazes. The art of painting, in the person of the painter, was elevated here to the highest status. This status was enhanced by the presence of the king—either in person as the viewer of *Las Meninas* or as a reflected image in the painting itself. This elevation of painting was further reinforced by the paintings that appear in *Las Meninas*. On the wall above the doorway and mirror, two faintly recognizable pictures have been identified as copies of paintings by Peter Paul Rubens that represent the immortal gods as the source of art. Ultimately, Velázquez sought ennoblement not for himself alone but for his art.

The painting is extraordinarily complex visually. Velázquez's optical report of the event, authentic in every detail, pictorially summarizes the various kinds of images in their different levels and degrees of reality. He portrayed the realities of image on canvas, of mirror image, of optical image, and of the two painted images. This work—with its cunning contrasts of mirrored spaces, "real" spaces, picture spaces, and pictures within pictures—itself appears to have been taken from a large mirror reflecting the whole scene. This would mean that the artist did not paint the princess and her suite as the main subjects of *Las Meninas* but himself in the process of painting them. *Las Meninas* is a pictorial summary and a commentary on the essential mystery of the visual world, as well as on the ambiguity that results when different states or levels interact or are juxtaposed.

How did Velázquez achieve these results? The extension of the composition's pictorial depth in both directions is noteworthy. The open doorway and its ascending staircase lead the eye beyond the artist's studio, and the mirror device and the outward glances of several of the figures incorporate the viewer's space into the picture as well. (Compare how the mirror in Jan van Eyck's *Giovanni Arnolfini and His Bride*, FIG. 20-13, also incorporates the area in front of the canvas into the picture, although less obviously and without a comparable extension of space beyond the rear wall of the room.) Velázquez also masterfully observed and represented form and shadow. Instead of putting lights abruptly beside darks, as Caravaggio had done, Velázquez allowed a great number of intermediate values of gray to come between the two extremes. His matching of tonal gradations approached effects that were later discovered in the photography age.

## Flanders

In the 16th century, the Netherlands had come under the crown of Habsburg Spain when the emperor Charles V retired, leaving the Spanish kingdoms, their Italian and American possessions, and the Netherlandish provinces to his only legitimate son, Philip II. (Charles gave the imperial title and the German lands to his brother.) Philip's repressive measures against the Protestants led the northern provinces to break away from Spain and to set up the Dutch Republic. The southern provinces remained under Spanish control, and they retained Catholicism as their official religion. The political distinction between modern Holland and Belgium more or less reflects this original separation, which in the Baroque period signaled not only religious but also artistic differences. The Baroque art of Flanders (the Spanish Netherlands) retained close connections to the Baroque art of Catholic Europe, whereas the Dutch schools of painting developed their own subjects and styles. This was consistent with their reformed religion and the new political, social, and economic structure of the middle-class Dutch Republic.

**A PAN-EUROPEAN SYNTHESIS** The renowned Flemish master PETER PAUL RUBENS (1577–1640) drew together the main contributions of the masters of the Renaissance (Michelangelo and Titian) and of the Italian Baroque (Carracci and Caravaggio) to synthesize in his own style the first truly pan-European manner. Rubens's art, even though it is the consequence of his wide study of many masters, does not represent a weak eclecticism but an original and powerful synthesis. Ultimately, the influence of Rubens was international.

Among the most learned individuals of his time, Rubens possessed an aristocratic education, a courtier's manner, diplomacy, and tact. All of this, along with his classical learning and facility with language, made him the associate of princes and scholars. He became court painter to the dukes of Mantua (descended from Mantegna's patrons); friend of the king of Spain and his adviser on art collecting; painter to Charles I of England and Marie de' Medici, queen of France; and permanent court painter to the Spanish governors of Flanders. The archdukes Isabella (Philip II's eldest daughter) and Albert were among Rubens's many patrons. Rubens also won the confidence of his royal patrons in matters of state, and these patrons often entrusted him with diplomatic missions of the highest importance. In the practice of his art, scores of associates and apprentices assisted Rubens, turning out numerous paintings for an international clientele. In addition, he functioned as an art dealer, buying and selling contemporary artworks and classical antiquities. His many enterprises made him a rich man, with a magnificent town house and a château in the countryside. Wealth and honors, however, did not spoil his amiable, sober, and self-disciplined character. Rubens was, like Raphael, a successful and renowned artist, a consort of kings, a shrewd man of the world, and a learned philosopher.

Rubens became a master in 1598 and went to Italy two years later, where he remained until 1608. During these years, he formulated the foundations of his style. Shortly after his return from Italy, he painted the *Elevation of the Cross* (FIG. **24-34**) for the church of Saint Walburga (later moved to Antwerp Cathedral). This triptych reveals Rubens's interest in Italian art, especially the works of Michelangelo, Tintoretto, and Caravaggio. The scene brings together tremendous straining forces and counterforces as heavily muscled men strain to lift the cross. Here, as in his *Lion Hunt* (see FIG. Intro-13), Rubens had the opportunity to show foreshortened anatomy and the contortions of violent action reminiscent of the twisted figures that Michelangelo sculpted and painted. Rubens placed the body of Christ on the cross as a diagonal that cuts dynamically across the picture while inclining back into it. The whole composition seethes with a power that comes from genuine exertion, from elastic human sinew taut with effort. The tension is emotional as well as physical, as reflected not only in Christ's face but also in the features of his followers. Strong modeling in dark and light, which heightens the drama, marks Rubens's work at this stage of his career; it gradually gave way to a much subtler coloristic style.

**DRAWING ON THE MASTERS** Rubens retained the vigor and passion of his early style throughout his career, although he modified the vitality of his work into less strained and more subtle forms, depending on the theme. One theme that remained a focus of Rubens's art was the human body, draped or undraped, male or female, and freely acting or free to act in an environment of physical forces and other interacting bodies. This interest, combined with his voracious intellect, led Rubens to copy the works

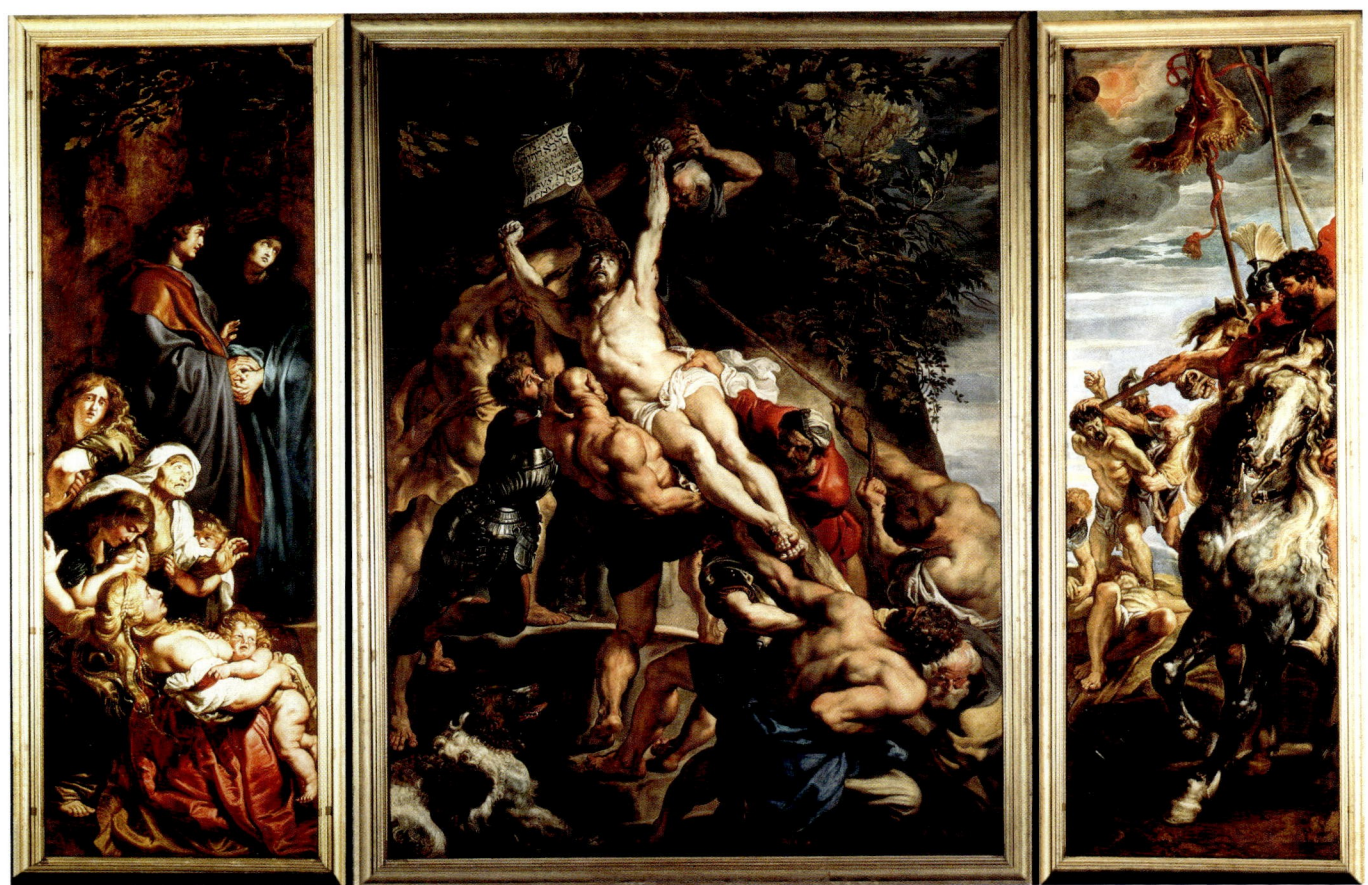

**24-34** Peter Paul Rubens, *Elevation of the Cross,* Antwerp Cathedral, Antwerp, Belgium, 1610. Oil on panel, 15′ 1$\frac{7}{8}$″ × 11′ 1$\frac{1}{2}$″ (center panel), 15′ 1$\frac{7}{8}$″ × 4′ 11″ (each wing). Royal Institute for the Study and Conservation of Belgium's Artistic Heritage.

**24-35** Peter Paul Rubens, drawing of Laocoön, ca. 1600–1608. Black-and-white chalk drawing with bistre wash, approx. 1′ 7″ × 1′ 7″. Ambrosiana Library, Milan.

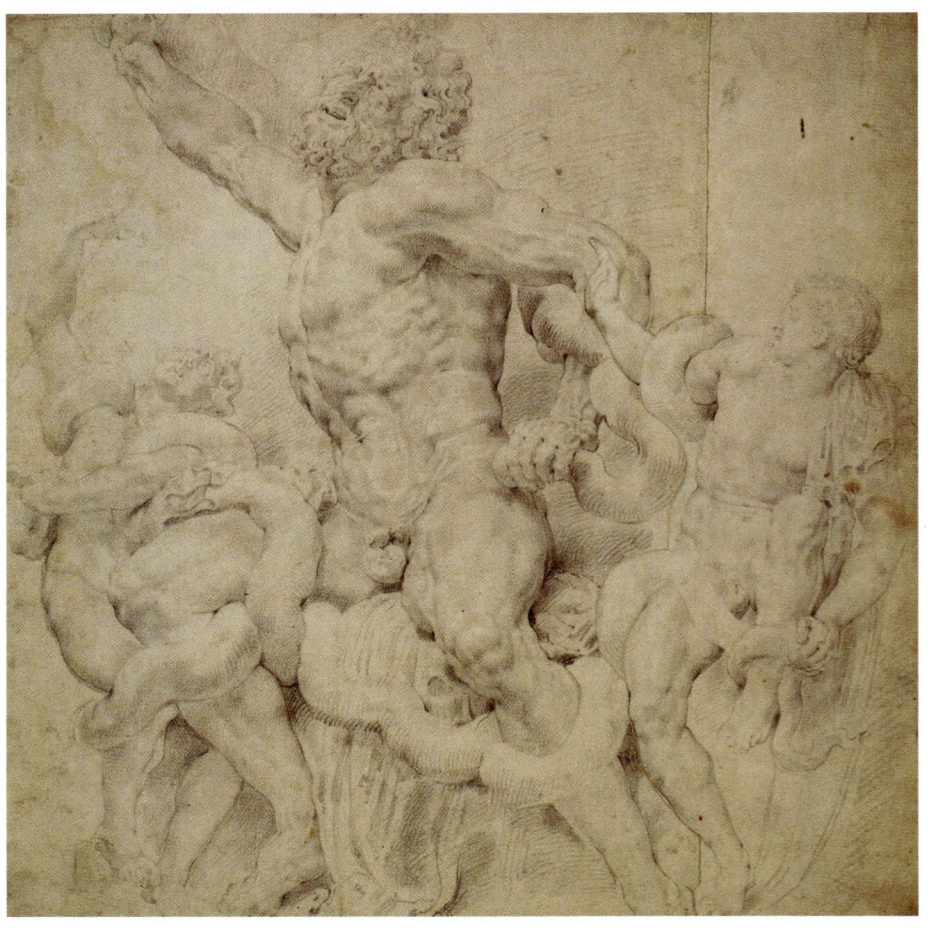

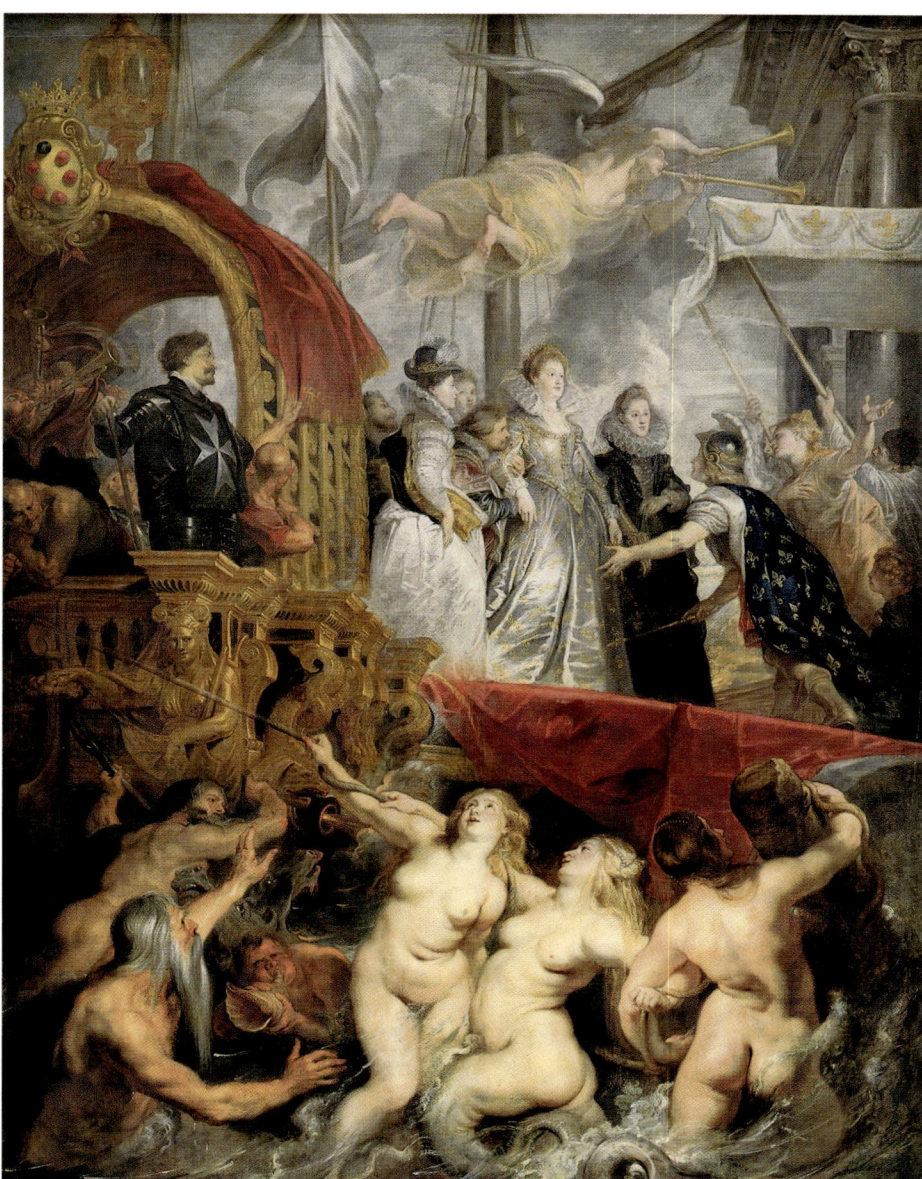

of classical antiquity and of the Italian masters. These sources surfaced in Rubens's drawing of Laocoön (FIG. **24-35**), the classical sculpture discovered in 1506. Rubens apparently produced this drawing (one of a large group of drawings) sometime between 1606 and 1608, when he was in Rome. The ancient marble sculpture (see FIG. 5-89) depicts the Trojan priest Laocoön and his two sons as they struggle mightily to free themselves from the death grip of sea serpents. Rubens's predominantly black chalk drawing demonstrates the artist's careful study of classical representations of the human form. In a Latin treatise he wrote titled *De imitatione statuarum (On the Imitation of Statues),* Rubens stated: "I am convinced that in order to achieve the highest perfection one needs a full understanding of the [ancient] statues, nay a complete absorption in them."[2]

**AN EXTRAVAGANT ARRIVAL** Rubens's interaction with royalty and aristocrats provided him with an understanding of the ostentation and spectacle of Baroque (particularly Italian) art that were appealing to those of wealth and privilege. Rubens, the born courtier, reveled in the pomp and majesty of royalty. Likewise, those in power embraced the lavish spectacle that served the

Catholic Church so well in Italy. The magnificence and splendor of such Baroque imagery reinforced their authority and right to rule. Among Rubens's royal patrons was Marie de' Medici, a member of the famous Florentine house and widow of Henry IV, the first of the Bourbon kings of France. She commissioned Rubens to paint a series memorializing and glorifying her career. Between 1622 and 1626, Rubens, working with amazing creative energy, produced 21 huge historical-allegorical pictures designed to hang in the queen's new palace, the Luxembourg, in Paris.

Perhaps the most vivacious of the series is the *Arrival of Marie de' Medici at Marseilles* (FIG. **24-36**); the others are similar in mood and style. In the painting, Marie has just arrived in France after the sea voyage from Italy. As she disembarks, surrounded by her ladies-in-waiting, she is welcomed by an allegorical personification of France, draped in a cloak decorated with the fleur-de-lis (the floral symbol of French royalty, also seen on King Louis XIV's cloak in FIG. 24-65). The sea and sky rejoice at her safe arrival—Neptune and the Nereids (daughters of the sea god Nereus) salute her, and a winged, trumpeting Fame swoops overhead. Conspicuous in the galley's opulently carved stern-castle, under the Medici coat of arms, stands the imperious commander of the

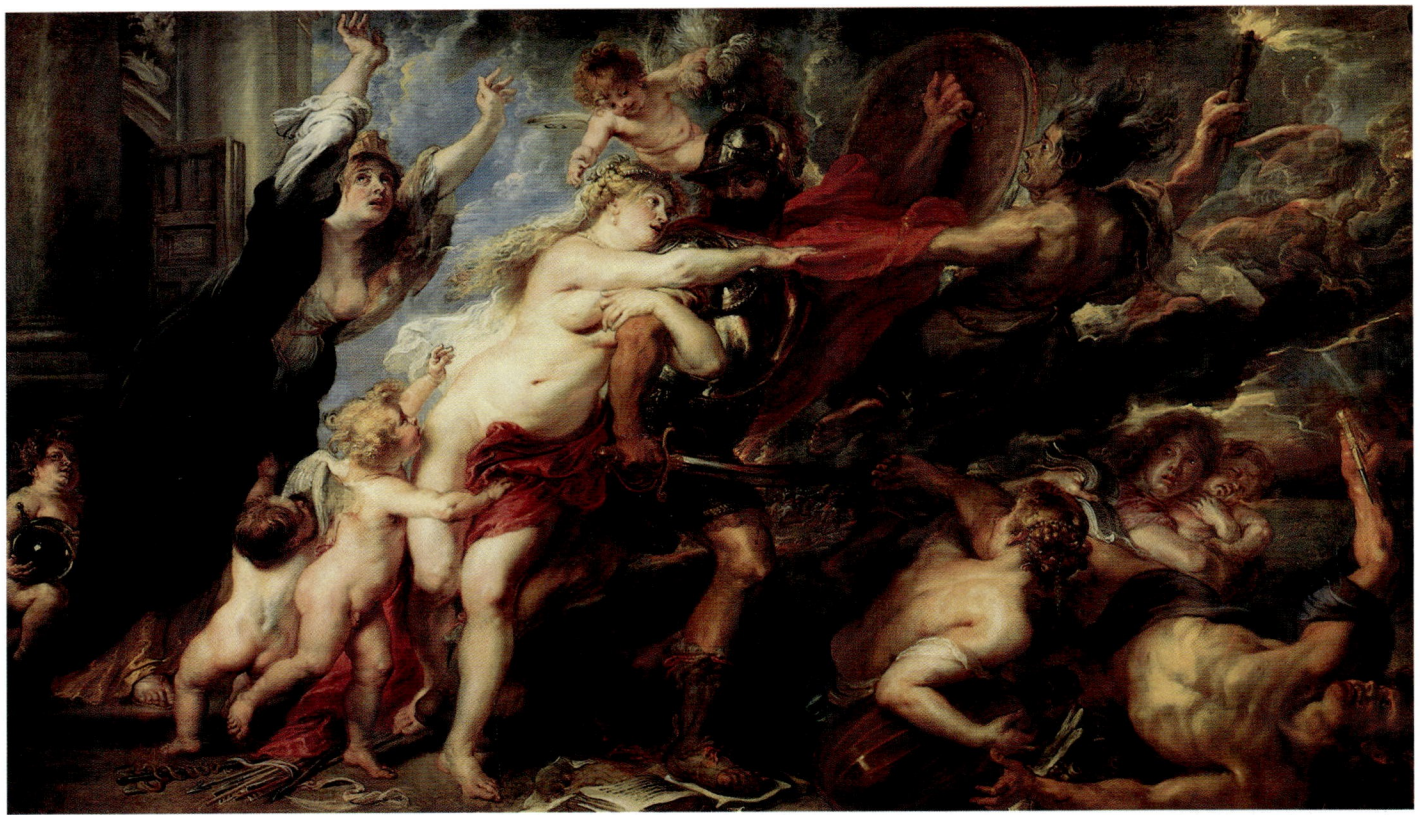

**24-37** PETER PAUL RUBENS, *Allegory of the Outbreak of War*, 1638. Oil on canvas, 6′ 9″ × 11′ 3⅞″. Pitti Gallery, Florence.

vessel. In black and silver, his figure makes a sharp accent amid the swirling tonality of ivory, gold, and red. He wears the cross of a Knight of Malta, which may identify this as a ship belonging to that order (similar to Velázquez's Order of Santiago). The only immobile figure in the composition, he could be director of and witness to the lavish welcome. The artist enriched his surfaces here with a decorative splendor that pulls the whole composition together. The audacious vigor that customarily enlivens Rubens's figures, beginning with the monumental, twisting sea creatures, vibrates through the entire design.

**PROTESTING WAR** Rubens also derived great insight into European politics from his diplomatic missions, and he never ceased to promote peace. Throughout most of his career, war was constant. When commissioned in 1638 to produce a painting for Ferdinando II, the Grand Duke of Tuscany, Rubens took the opportunity to express allegorically his attitude toward war. Appropriately, Rubens finished his artistic diatribe, *Allegory of the Outbreak of War* (FIG. **24-37**), during the Thirty Years' War. The fluid articulation of human forms and the energy that emanates from the chaotic scene are reminiscent of Rubens's other paintings. The artist's own description of the painting, written in a letter, provides the clearest explication of *Allegory's* content and of his opinions on military conflict:

> The principal figure is Mars, who has left the temple of Janus open (which according to Roman custom remained closed in time of peace) and struts with his shield and his bloodstained sword, threatening all peoples with disaster; he pays little attention to Venus, his lady, who, surrounded by her little love-gods, tries in vain to hold him back with caresses and embraces. On the opposite

side, Mars is pulled forward by the Fury Alecto with a torch in her hand. There are also monsters signifying plague and famine, the inseparable companions of war. Thrown to the ground is a woman with a broken lute, as a symbol that harmony cannot exist beside the discord of war; likewise a mother with a child in her arms indicates that fertility, procreation, and tenderness are opposed by war, which breaks into and destroys everything. There is furthermore an architect fallen backwards, with his tools in his hands, to express the idea that what is built in peace for the benefit and ornament of cities is laid in ruin and razed by the forces of arms . . . you will also find on the ground, beneath the feet of Mars, a book and a drawing on paper, to indicate that he tramples on literature and other refinements. . . . The sorrowing woman . . . clothed in black with a torn veil, and deprived of all her jewels and ornaments is unhappy Europe, which for so many years has suffered pillage, degradation, and misery affecting all of us so deeply that it is useless to say more about them.[3]

**ELEGANT COURT PORTRAITURE** Most of Rubens's successors in Flanders were at one time his assistants. The most famous of these was ANTHONY VAN DYCK (1599–1641). Early on, the younger man, unwilling to be overshadowed by the master's undisputed stature, left his native Antwerp for Genoa and then London, where he became court portraitist to Charles I. Although Van Dyck created dramatic compositions of high quality, his specialty became the portrait. He developed a courtly manner of great elegance that was influential internationally. In one of his finest works, *Charles I Dismounted* (FIG. **24-38**), the ill-fated Stuart king stands in a landscape with the river Thames in the background. An equerry and a page attend Charles I. Although the

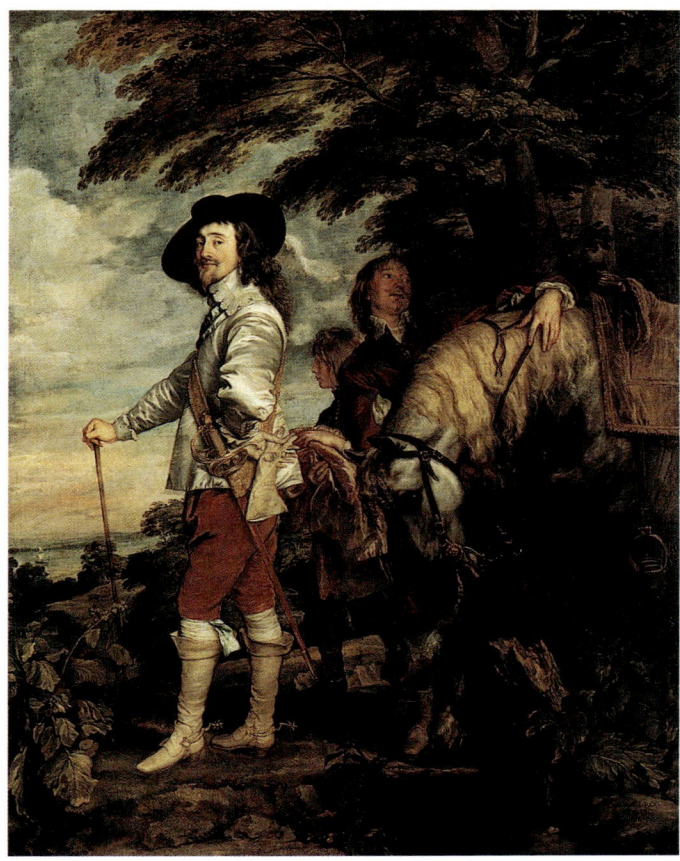

**24-38** Anthony Van Dyck, *Charles I Dismounted*, ca. 1635. Oil on canvas, approx. 9′ × 7′. Louvre, Paris.

king impersonates a nobleman out for a casual ride in his park, no one can mistake the regal poise and the air of absolute authority that his Parliament resented and was soon to rise against. Here, King Charles turns his back on his attendants as he surveys his domain. The king's placement in the composition is exceedingly artful. He stands off center but balances the picture with a single keen glance at the viewer. Van Dyck even managed to portray Charles I in a position to look down on the observer. In reality, the monarch's short stature forced him to exert his power in ways other than physical. Van Dyck's elegant style resounded in English portrait painting well into the 19th century.

**THE "BREAKFAST PIECE"** Clara Peeters (1594–ca. 1657), a Flemish artist who spent time in Holland, was a pioneer in the field of still-life painting. As such, she laid the groundwork for such Dutch artists as Pieter Claesz (FIG. 24-55), Willem Kalf (FIG. 24-56), and Rachel Ruysch (FIG. 24-57). She was particularly renowned for her depictions of food and flowers together, and for still lifes that included bread and fruit. Such still lifes became known as "breakfast pieces." In the breakfast piece *Still Life with Flowers, Goblet, Dried Fruit, and Pretzels* (FIG. **24-39**), Peeters's considerable skills are on full display. Part of a series of four paintings, each of which depicts a typical early-17th-century meal, *Still Life* reveals Peeters's virtuosity in painting a wide variety of objects convincingly, from the smooth, reflective surfaces of the glass and silver goblets to the soft petals of the blooms in the vase. Although Peeters often depicted the objects in her still lifes against a dark background, thereby negating any sense of deep space, she demonstrated her command of pictorial space in *Still Life* by presenting the leaves of the flower on the stone ledge as though they were encroaching into the viewer's space.

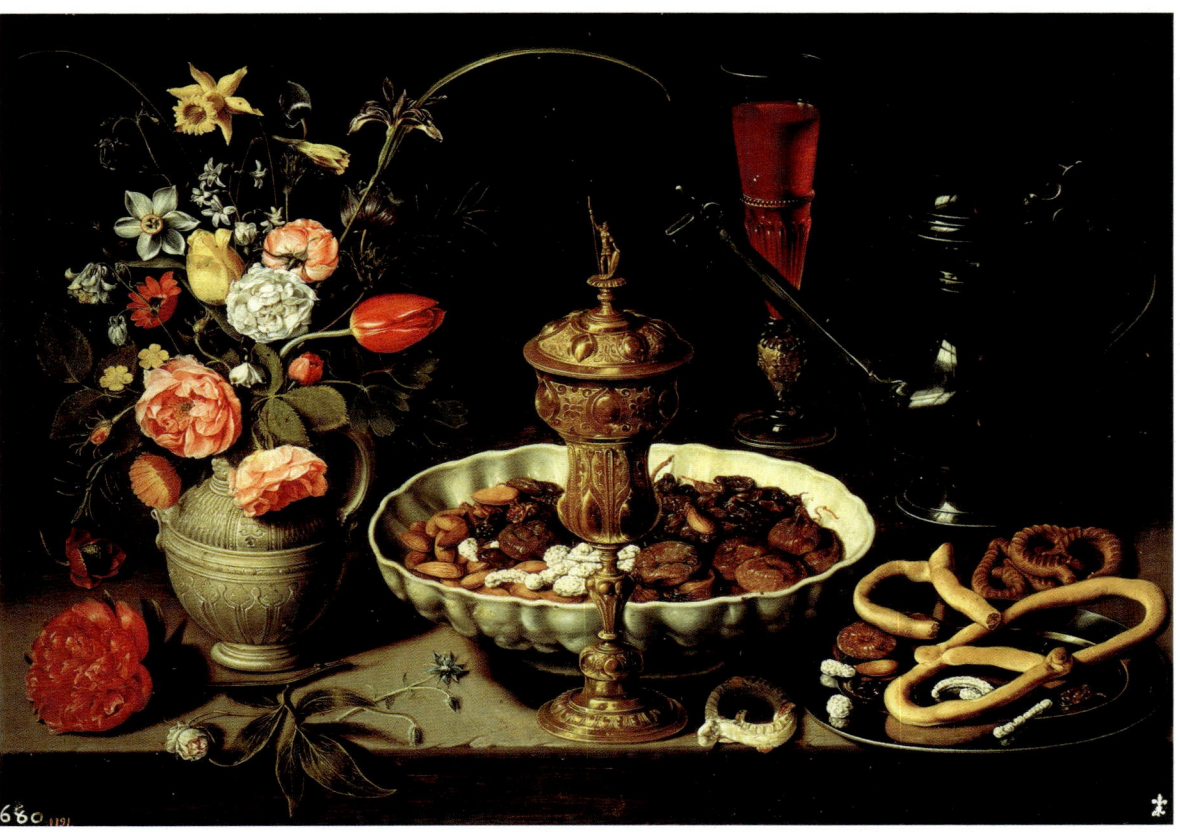

**24-39** Clara Peeters, *Still Life with Flowers, Goblet, Dried Fruit, and Pretzels,* 1611. Oil on panel, 1′ 7¾″ × 2′ 1¼″. Museo del Prado, Madrid.

## The Dutch Republic

**PROSPERITY IN THE PROVINCES** The Dutch succeeded in securing their independence from the Spanish in the late 16th century. Not until 1648, however, after years of continual border skirmishes with the Spanish (as depicted in Velázquez's *Surrender of Breda,* FIG. 24-31), were the northern Netherlands officially recognized as the United Provinces of the Netherlands (the Dutch Republic). Despite attempts by the House of Orange to establish a monarchy, the republicans prevailed.

The ascendance of the Dutch Republic during the 17th century was largely due to its economic prosperity; Amsterdam had the highest per capita income in Europe. That city emerged as the financial center of the continent, having founded the Bank of Amsterdam in 1609. The Dutch economy benefited enormously from the country's expertise on the open seas, which facilitated establishing far-flung colonies. By 1650, Dutch trade routes extended beyond Europe proper and included North America, South America, the west coast of Africa, China, Japan, Southeast Asia, and much of the Pacific.

Due to this prosperity and in the absence of an absolute ruler, political power increasingly passed into the hands of an urban patrician class of merchants and manufacturers, especially in cities such as Amsterdam, Haarlem, and Delft. That these bustling cities were all located in Holland (the largest of the seven United Provinces) perhaps explains why the name "Holland" is used informally to refer to the entire country.

**THE PROTESTANT OBJECTION TO ART** Religious differences were a major consideration during the northern Netherlands' insistent quest for independence during the 16th and early 17th centuries. Whereas Spain and the southern Netherlands were Catholic, the northern Netherlands were predominantly Protestant. The prevailing Calvinism demanded a puritanical rejection of art in churches, and thus artists produced relatively little religious art in the Dutch Republic at this time (especially in comparison to that created in the wake of the Counter-Reformation in areas dominated by Catholicism). Despite the Calvinist beliefs of much of the population, however, the Dutch were truly tolerant people, and artists (often Catholics) did create religious artworks.

**A MOVING RELIGIOUS SCENE** Hendrick ter Brugghen (1588–1629), for example, painted *Calling of Saint Matthew* (FIG. 24-40) in 1621, after returning from a trip to Italy. As a Catholic, ter Brugghen perhaps felt great affinity with artists such as Caravaggio, who painted the same scene (FIG. 24-19). The moment of the narrative depicted, the astonishment of Levi (the tax collector), and the naturalistic presentation of the figures all echo Caravaggio's work. However, ter Brugghen dispensed with the stark contrasts of dark and light and instead presented the viewer with a more colorful palette of soft tints. Further, the figures are crammed into a small but well-lit space, creating a claustrophobic effect that differs from Caravaggio's careful rendering of the dark street scene.

**MERCANTILIST PATRONS** Given the absence of an authoritative ruler and the Calvinist concern for the potential misuse of religious art, commissions from royalty or from the Catholic Church, prominent in the art of other countries, were uncommon in the United Provinces. With the new prosperity, an expanding class of merchant patrons emerged, and this shift led to an emphasis on different pictorial content. Dutch Baroque art centered on genre scenes, landscapes, portraits, and still lifes, all of which appealed to the prosperous middle class (see "Dutch Patronage and Art Collecting," page 719). *Middle class* often is used as a conveniently broad term to describe this developing group of patrons. However, it is important to note that despite the absence of royalty, Dutch society was not totally egalitarian. The *patriciate* (leading merchants and large manufacturers) and the upper middle class (prosperous merchants, traders, and academics) were far more likely to collect art than were the middle and lower-middle classes (skilled craftspeople, workers, and servants). Regardless, art flourished in this mercantilist culture. The 17th century is referred to not only as the Golden Age of the Dutch Republic but as the Golden Age of Dutch art as well.

**DEPICTING DAILY DUTCH LIFE** Typical of Dutch genre scenes is *Supper Party* (FIG. 24-41), by GERRIT VAN HONTHORST (1590–1656) of Utrecht. In this painting, van Honthorst presented an informal gathering of unidealized human figures. While a musician serenades the group, his companions delight in watching a young woman feeding a piece of chicken to a man

**24-40** HENDRICK TER BRUGGHEN, *Calling of Saint Matthew*, 1621. Oil on canvas, 3′ 4″ × 4′ 6″. The Hague.

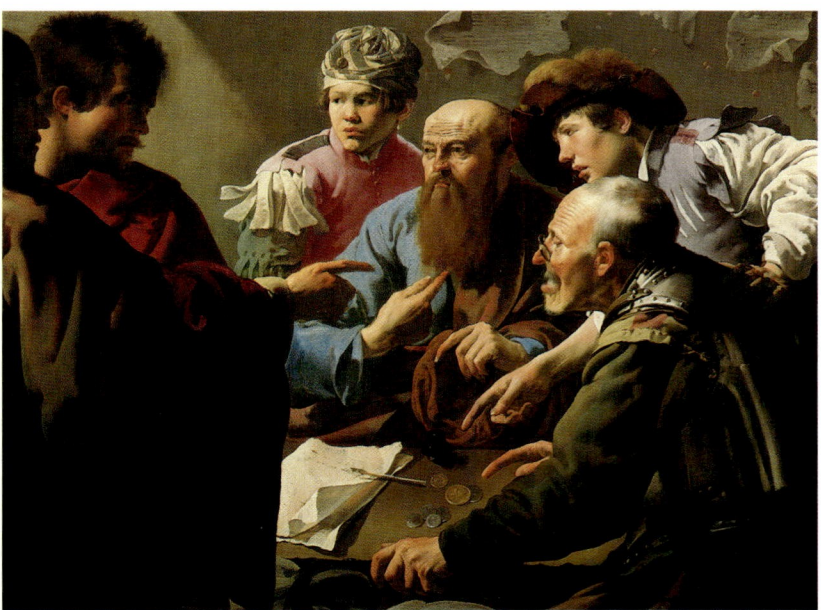

### Dutch Patronage and Art Collecting

Art collecting often has been perceived as the purview of the wealthy, and, indeed, the money necessary to commission major artworks from esteemed artists can be considerable. During the 17th century in the Dutch Republic, however, the widespread prosperity enjoyed by a large proportion of Dutch society significantly expanded the range of art patronage. As a result, one of the distinguishing hallmarks of Dutch art production during the Baroque period was how it catered to the tastes of a middle-class audience.

The term *middle class* is used broadly here. An aristocracy and a patriciate—an upper class of large-ship owners, rich businesspeople, high-ranking officers, and directors of large companies—still existed. These groups continued to be major patrons of the arts. With the expansion of the Dutch economy, traders, craftspeople, low-ranking officers, bureaucrats, and soldiers—the middle and lower-middle classes—also became art patrons.

Although steeped in the morality and propriety central to the Calvinist ethic, members of the Dutch middle class sought ways to subtly announce their success and newly acquired status. House furnishings, paintings, tapestries, and porcelain were among the items collected and displayed in the home. The Dutch disdain for excessive ostentation, attributable to Calvinism, led these collectors to favor small, low-key works—portraits, still lifes, genre scenes, and landscapes. This contrasted with the Italian Baroque penchant for large-scale, dazzling ceiling frescoes and opulent room decoration.

Although it is risky to generalize about the spending and collecting habits of the Dutch middle class, some information has been culled from probate records, contracts, and archived inventories. This documentation suggests that an individual earning between 1,500 and 3,000 guilders a year would be considered to be living comfortably. Such an individual might have spent 1,000 guilders for a house and another 1,000 guilders to furnish it. Those furnishings would have included a significant amount of art, particularly paintings. Although there was, of course, considerable variation in the prices of artworks, a great deal of art was very affordable. Prints were extremely cheap because of the quantity in which they were normally produced. In terms of paintings, interior and genre scenes seem to have been relatively inexpensive, perhaps costing one or two guilders. Small landscapes ran between three and four guilders. Commissioned portraits were the most costly. Size of the work and quality of the frame were other factors in the determination of price.

This new middle-class clientele, in conjunction with the developing open market (see "Mercantile Prosperity: Developing an Open Art Market," page 727), influenced the direction of Dutch Baroque art. These patrons not only affected the type of art produced but also were responsible for establishing the mechanisms and institutions for buying and selling art that constitute the foundation of the contemporary art market.

whose hands are both occupied—one holds a jug and the other a glass. Van Honthorst spent several years in Italy, and while there he carefully studied Caravaggio's work. The Italian artist's influence is evident in the mundane tavern setting and the nocturnal lighting. Fascinated by nocturnal effects, van Honthorst frequently placed a hidden light source in his pictures and used it as a pretext to work with dramatic and violently contrasted dark and light effects. Lighthearted genre scenes such as this were popular and widely produced in the Baroque period. Often, Dutch genre scenes could be read moralistically. For example, *Supper Party* can be interpreted as a warning against the sins of gluttony (represented by the man on the right) and lust (the woman feeding the glutton is, in all likelihood, a prostitute with her aged procuress at her side). Or perhaps the painting represents the loose companions of the Prodigal Son (Luke 15:13)—panderers and prostitutes drinking, singing, strumming, and

**24-41** GERRIT VAN HONTHORST, *Supper Party,* 1620. Oil on canvas, approx. 4' 8" × 7'.

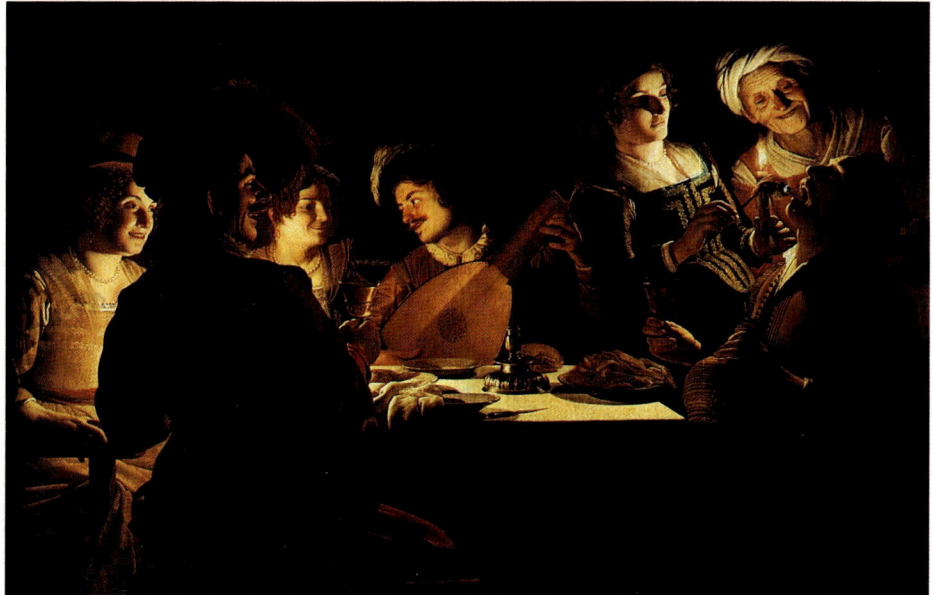

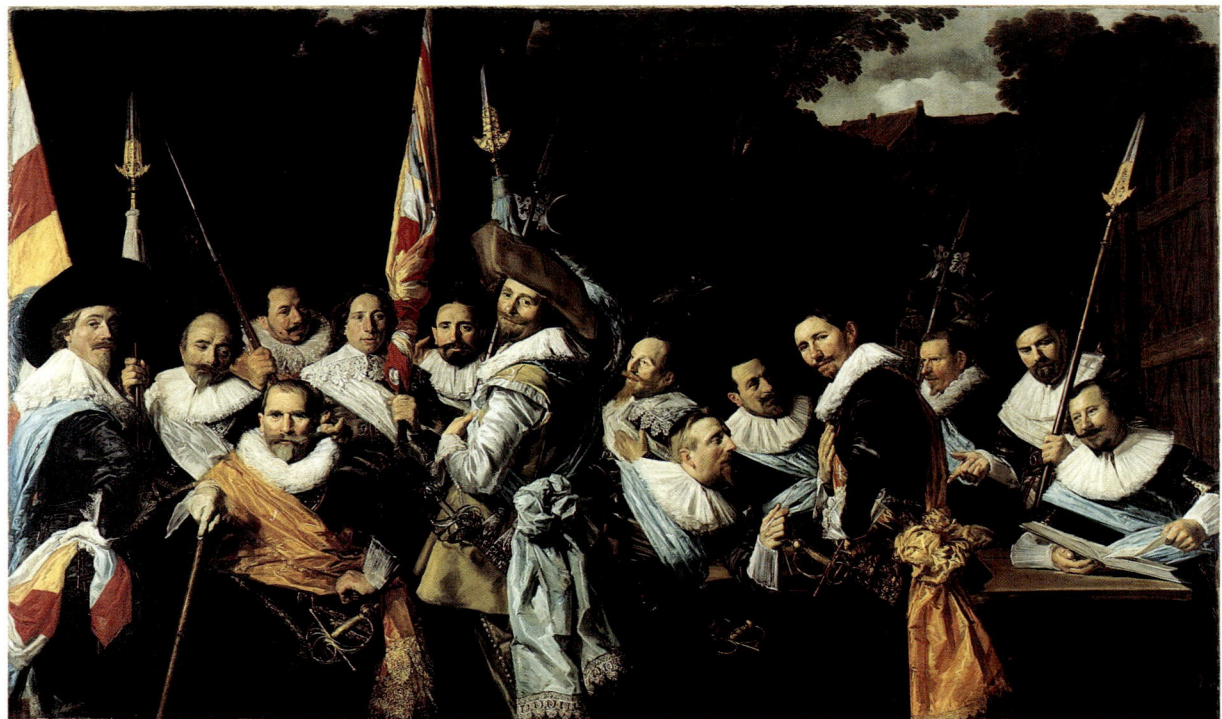

**24-42** FRANS HALS, *Archers of Saint Hadrian,* ca. 1633. Oil on canvas, approx. 6′ 9″ × 11′. Frans Halsmuseum, Haarlem.

laughing. Strict Dutch Calvinists no doubt approved of such interpretations.

**FACE-TO-FACE** Dutch Baroque artists also were justifiably esteemed for their skills in portraiture. FRANS HALS (ca. 1581–1666) was the leading painter in Haarlem and made portraits his specialty. Portrait artists traditionally had relied heavily on convention—for example, specific poses, settings, attire, and accoutrements—to convey a sense of the sitter. Because the subject was usually someone of status or note, such as a pope, king, or wealthy individual, the artist's goal was to produce an image appropriate to the subject's station in life. With the increasing numbers of Dutch middle-class patrons, the tasks for Dutch portraitists became more challenging. Not only were the traditional conventions inappropriate and thus unusable, but also the Calvinists shunned ostentation, instead wearing uniform, subdued, and dark clothing with little variation or decoration. Despite these difficulties, or perhaps because of them, Hals produced lively portraits that seem far more relaxed than the more formulaic traditional portraiture. He injected an engaging spontaneity into his images and conveyed the personalities of his sitters as well. His manner of execution intensified the casualness, immediacy, and intimacy in his paintings. The touch of Hals's brush was as light and fleeting as the moment when he captured the pose, so the figure, the highlights on clothing, and the facial expression all seem instantaneously created.

Hals also excelled at group portraits, which multiplied the challenges of depicting a single sitter. *Archers of Saint Hadrian* (FIG. **24-42**) is one such painting. The Archers of Saint Hadrian were one of many Dutch civic militia groups who claimed credit for liberating the Dutch Republic from Spain. Like other companies, the Archers met on their saint's feast day in dress uniform for a grand banquet. The celebrations sometimes lasted an entire week, prompting an ordinance limiting them to "three, or at the most four days." These events called for a group portrait, and such commissions gave Hals the opportunity to attack the problem of

adequately representing each group member while retaining action and variety in the composition. Earlier group portraits in the Netherlands were rather ordered and regimented images. Hals sought to enliven the depictions, and the results can be seen in *Archers.* Here, each man is both a troop member and an individual with a distinct personality. Some engage viewers directly, whereas others look away or at a companion; where one is stern, another is animated. Each is equally visible and clearly recognizable. The uniformity of attire—black military dress, white ruffs, and sashes—does not seem to have deterred Hals from injecting a spontaneity into the work. Indeed, he used those elements to create a lively rhythm that extends throughout the composition and energizes the portrait. The impromptu effect—the preservation of every detail and fleeting facial expression—is, of course, due to careful planning. Yet Hals's vivacious brush appears to have moved instinctively, directed by a plan in his mind but not traceable in any preparatory scheme on the canvas.

**PRIM AND PROPER DUTCH WOMEN** Hals captured the character of straitlaced, devout Calvinist women in *The Women Regents of the Old Men's Home at Haarlem* (FIG. **24-43**). Although Dutch women were given primary responsibility for the welfare of the family and the orderly operation of the home, they also populated the labor force in the cities and were often educated. Among the more prominent roles that women played in public life were as regents of charitable institutions—orphanages, hospitals, old age homes, and houses of correction. Here, in Hals's portrait, these regents clearly take their responsibilities seriously. Unlike the looser, seemingly informal character of his other group portraits, a stern, puritanical, and composed sensibility suffuses *Women Regents.* The women look out from the painting (only two meet the viewer's gaze) with expressions that range from dour disinterest to kindly concern. The somber and virtually monochromatic palette, punctuated only by the white accents of the clothing, contributes to the painting's restraint. Although

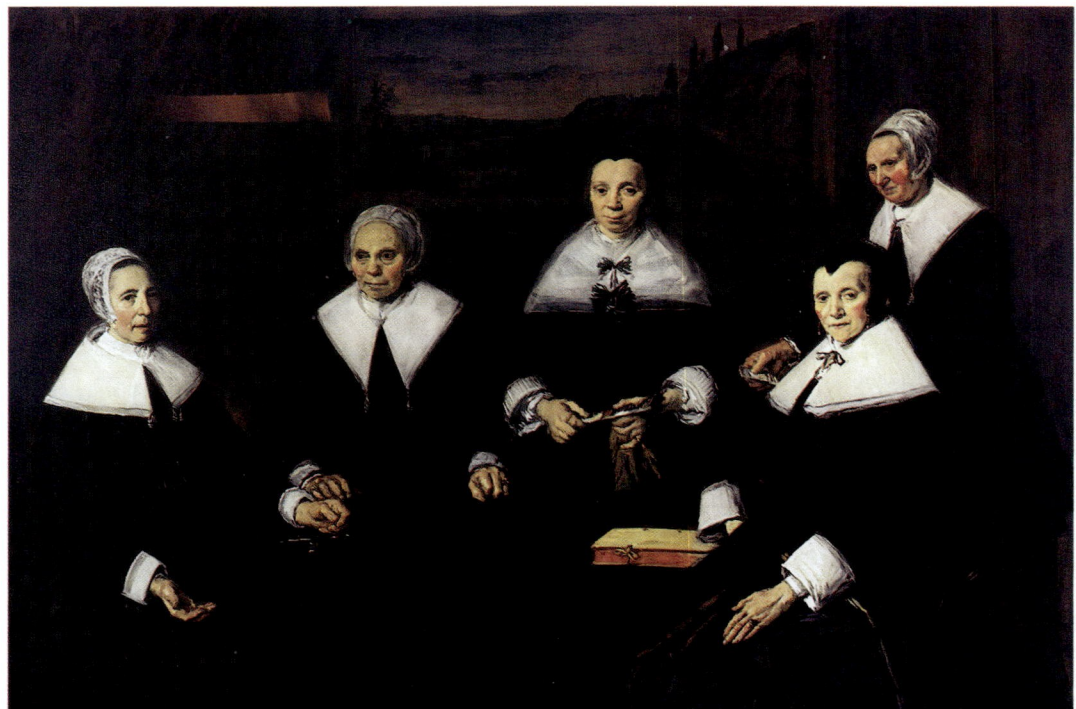

24-43 FRANS HALS, *The Women Regents of the Old Men's Home at Haarlem*, 1664. Oil on canvas, 5′ 7″ × 8′ 2″. Frans Halsmuseum, Haarlem.

this portrait may lack the vitality and spontaneity of other portraits by Hals, his unerring ability to capture both the details of the individual sitters and their general cultural characteristics is truly impressive.

**A SURGICAL LESSON** REMBRANDT VAN RIJN (1606–1669), Hals's younger contemporary, was widely recognized as the leading Dutch painter of his time. Rembrandt's move from his native Leiden to Amsterdam around 1631 provided him with a more extensive clientele, contributing to a flourishing career. In his portraits, for which he became particularly prominent, Rembrandt delved deeply into the psyche and personality of his sitters. In *Anatomy Lesson of Dr. Tulp* (FIG. 24-44), he deviated even further from the traditional staid group portrait than had Hals. Despite Hals's determination to enliven his portraits, he still evenly placed his subjects across the canvas. In contrast, Rembrandt chose to

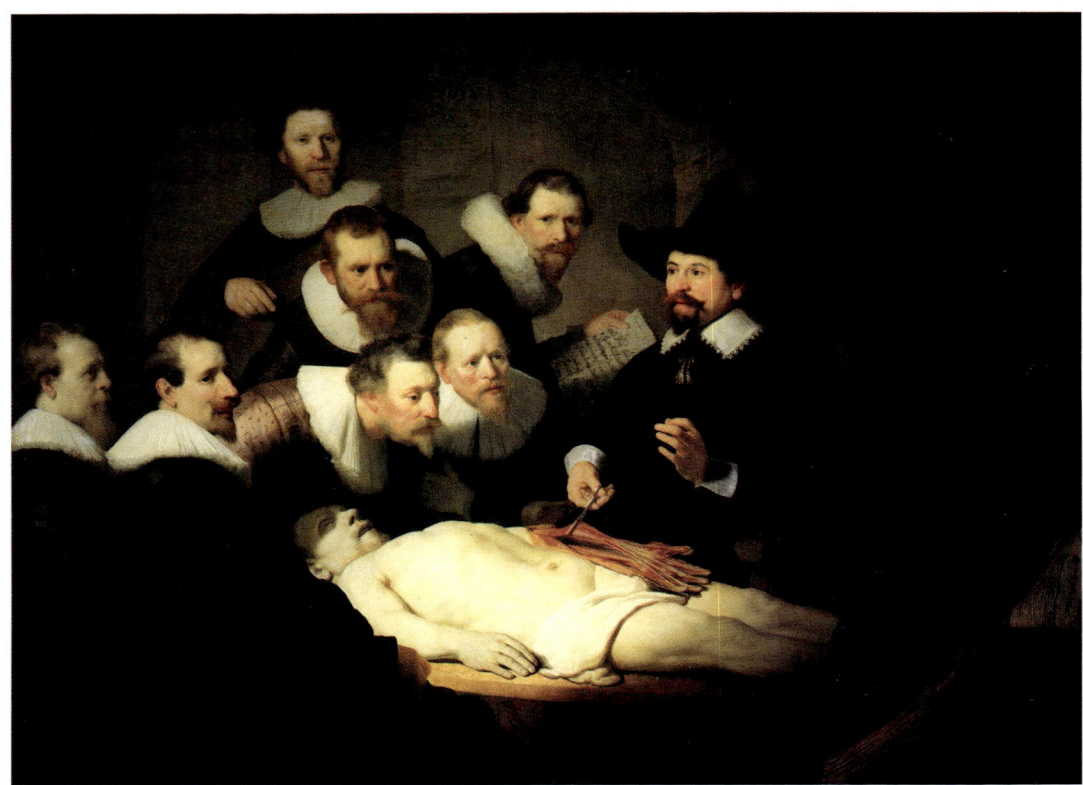

24-44 REMBRANDT VAN RIJN, *Anatomy Lesson of Dr. Tulp*, 1632. Oil on canvas, 5′ 3¾″ × 7′ 1¼″. Mauritshuis, The Hague.

portray the members of the surgeon's guild (who commissioned this group portrait) clustered together on the painting's left side. In the foreground appears the corpse that Dr. Tulp, a noted physician, is in the act of dissecting. Rembrandt diagonally placed and foreshortened the corpse, activating the space by disrupting the strict horizontal, planar orientation found in traditional portraiture. He depicted each of the "students" specifically, and although they wear virtually identical attire, their varying poses and facial expressions suggest unique individuals. In light of the fact that Rembrandt produced this painting when he was 26 and just beginning his career, his innovative approach to group portraiture is all the more remarkable.

**AN ENERGETIC GROUP PORTRAIT** Rembrandt amplified the complexity and energy of the group portrait in his famous painting of 1642, *The Company of Captain Frans Banning Cocq* (FIG. **24-45**), better known as *Night Watch*. This more commonly used title is, however, a misnomer—the painting is not of a nocturnal scene. Rembrandt used light in a masterful way, and dramatic lighting certainly enhances the image. However, the painting's darkness (which led to the commonly used title) is due more to the varnish the artist used, which has darkened considerably over time, than to the subject depicted.

This painting was one of many civic-guard group portraits produced during this period. From the limited information available about the commission, it appears that Rembrandt was asked to paint the two officers, Captain Frans Banning Cocq and his lieutenant Willem van Ruytenburch, along with 16 members of this militia group (each contributing to Rembrandt's fee). This work was one of six paintings commissioned from different artists around 1640 for the assembly and banquet hall of the new

Kloveniersdoelen (Musketeers' Hall) in Amsterdam. Some scholars have suggested that the occasion for these commissions was the visit of Queen Marie de' Medici to the Dutch city in 1638.

Rembrandt captured the excitement and frenetic activity of the men preparing for the parade. Comparing *The Company of Captain Frans Banning Cocq* to Hals's portrait of the *Archers of Saint Hadrian* (FIG. 24-42), another militia group, reveals Rembrandt's inventiveness in enlivening what was, by then, becoming a conventional portrait format. Rather than present assembled men, the artist chose to portray the company scurrying about in the act of organizing themselves, thereby animating the image considerably. Despite the prominence of the girl just to the left of center, scholars have yet to ascertain definitively her identity.

The large canvas was placed in the designated hall in 1642. Unfortunately, when the painting was subsequently moved in 1715 to the Amsterdam town hall, it was cropped on all sides, leaving viewers today with an incomplete record of the artist's final resolution of the challenge of portraying this group.

**CELEBRATING CHRIST'S HUMILITY** Rembrandt's interest in probing the states of the human soul was not limited to portraiture. The Calvinist injunctions against religious art did not prevent him from making a series of religious paintings and prints. These images, however, are not the opulent, overwhelming art of Baroque Italy. Rather, his art is that of a committed Christian who desired to interpret biblical narratives in human (as opposed to lofty theological) terms. The spiritual stillness of Rembrandt's religious paintings is that of inward-turning contemplation, far from the choirs and trumpets and the heavenly tumult of Bernini or Pozzo. Rembrandt gives the viewer not the celestial triumph of the Catholic Church but the humanity and humility of Jesus. His psychological insight and

**24-45** REMBRANDT VAN RIJN, *The Company of Captain Frans Banning Cocq (Night Watch)*, 1642. Oil on canvas (cropped from original size), 11′ 11″ × 14′ 4″. Rijksmuseum, Amsterdam.

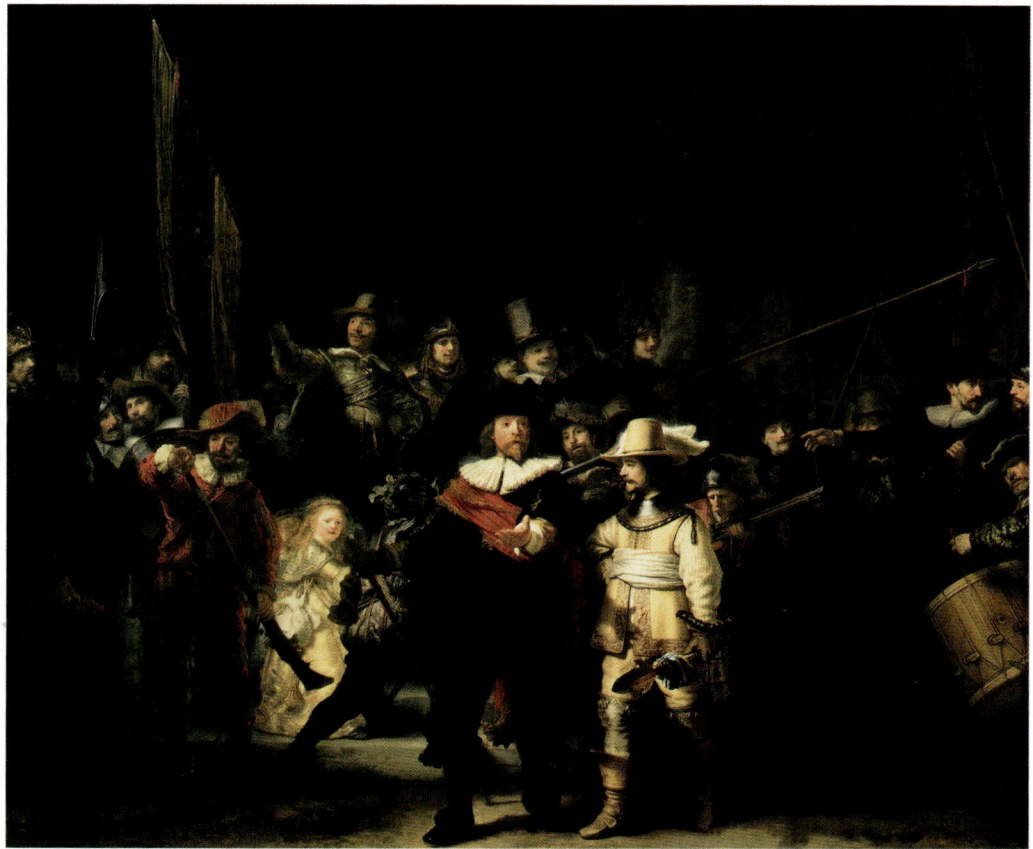

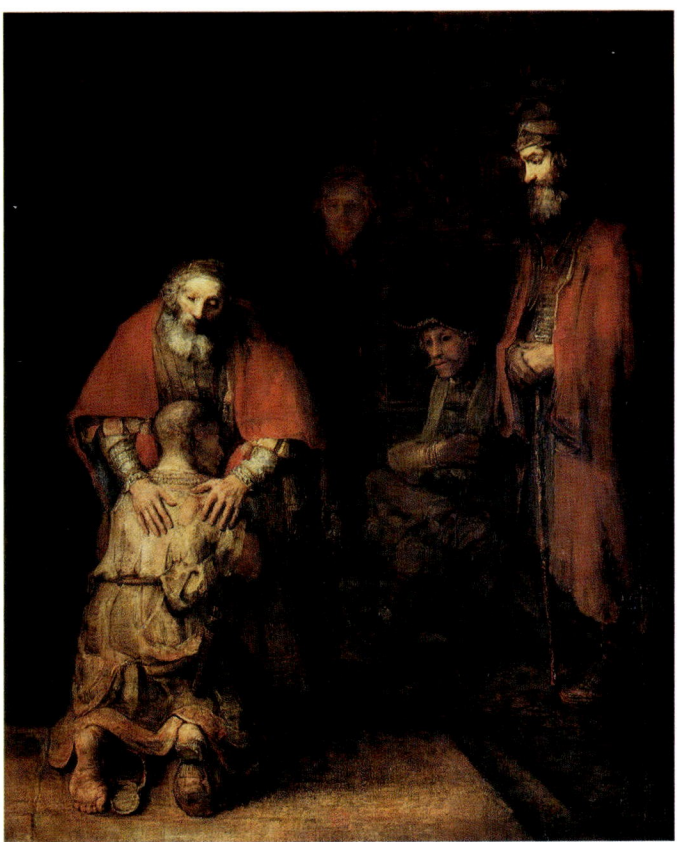

**24-46** REMBRANDT VAN RIJN, *Return of the Prodigal Son,* ca. 1665. Oil on canvas, approx. 8′ 8″ × 6′ 9″. Hermitage Museum, Saint Petersburg.

at these differences optically, not conceptually or in terms of some ideal. Rembrandt found that by manipulating the direction, intensity, distance, and surface texture of light and shadow, he could render the most subtle nuances of character and mood, both in persons and whole scenes. He discovered for the modern world that variation of light and shade, subtly modulated, could be read as emotional differences. In the visible world, light, dark, and the wide spectrum of values between the two are charged with meanings and feelings that sometimes are independent of the shapes and figures they modify. The theater and the photographic arts have used these discoveries to great dramatic effect.

Rembrandt carried over the spiritual quality of his religious works into his later portraits by the same means—what could be called the "psychology of light." Light and dark are not in conflict in his portraits—they are reconciled, merging softly and subtly to produce the visual equivalent of quietness. Their prevailing mood is that of tranquil meditation, of philosophical resignation, of musing recollection—indeed, a whole cluster of emotional tones heard only in silence.

**AN ILLUMINATING SELF-PORTRAIT** In a self-portrait (FIG. **24-47**) produced late in Rembrandt's life, the light that shines from the upper left of the painting bathes the subject's face in soft light, leaving the lower part of his body in shadow. The artist depicted himself here as possessing dignity and strength, and the portrait can be seen as a summary of the many stylistic and professional concerns that occupied him throughout his career. Rembrandt's distinctive use of light is evident, as is the assertive brushwork that suggests a confidence and self-assurance. He presented himself as a working artist holding his brushes, palette,

his profound sympathy for human affliction produced, at the very end of his life, one of the most moving pictures in all religious art, *Return of the Prodigal Son* (FIG. **24-46**). Tenderly embraced by his forgiving father, the son crouches before him in weeping contrition, while three figures, immersed to varying degrees in the soft shadows, note the lesson of mercy. The light, everywhere mingled with shadow, directs the viewer's attention by illuminating the father and son and largely veiling the witnesses. Its focus is the beautiful, spiritual face of the old man; secondarily, it touches the contrasting stern face of the foremost witness. *Return* demonstrates the degree to which Rembrandt developed a personal style completely in tune with the simple eloquence of the biblical passage.

**LIGHTING THE WAY** From the few paintings by Rembrandt discussed thus far, it should be clear that the artist's use of light is among the hallmarks of his style. Rembrandt's pictorial method involved refining light and shade into finer and finer nuances until they blended with one another. Earlier painters' use of abrupt lights and darks gave way, in the work of artists such as Rembrandt and Velázquez, to gradation. Although these later artists may have sacrificed some of the dramatic effects of sharp chiaroscuro, a greater fidelity to actual appearances offset those sacrifices. This technique is closer to reality because the eyes perceive light and dark not as static but as always subtly changing.

Generally speaking, Renaissance artists represented forms and faces in a flat, neutral modeling light (even Leonardo's shading is of a standard kind). They represented the *idea* of light, rather than the actual look of it. Artists such as Rembrandt discovered degrees of light and dark, degrees of differences in pose, in the movements of facial features, and in psychic states. They arrived

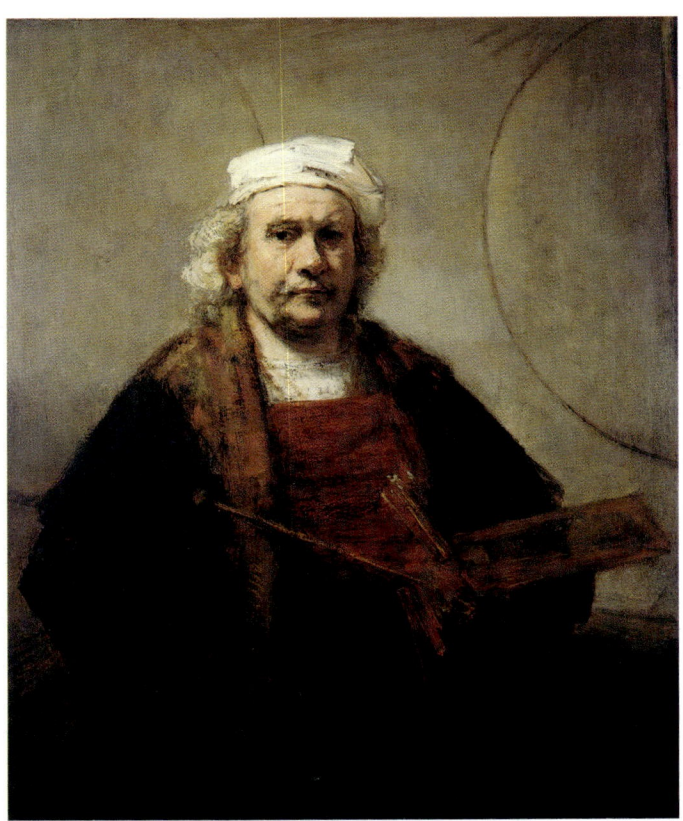

**24-47** REMBRANDT VAN RIJN, *Self-Portrait,* ca. 1659–1660. Oil on canvas, approx. 3′ 8¾″ × 3′ 1″. The Iveagh Bequest, Kenwood House, London.

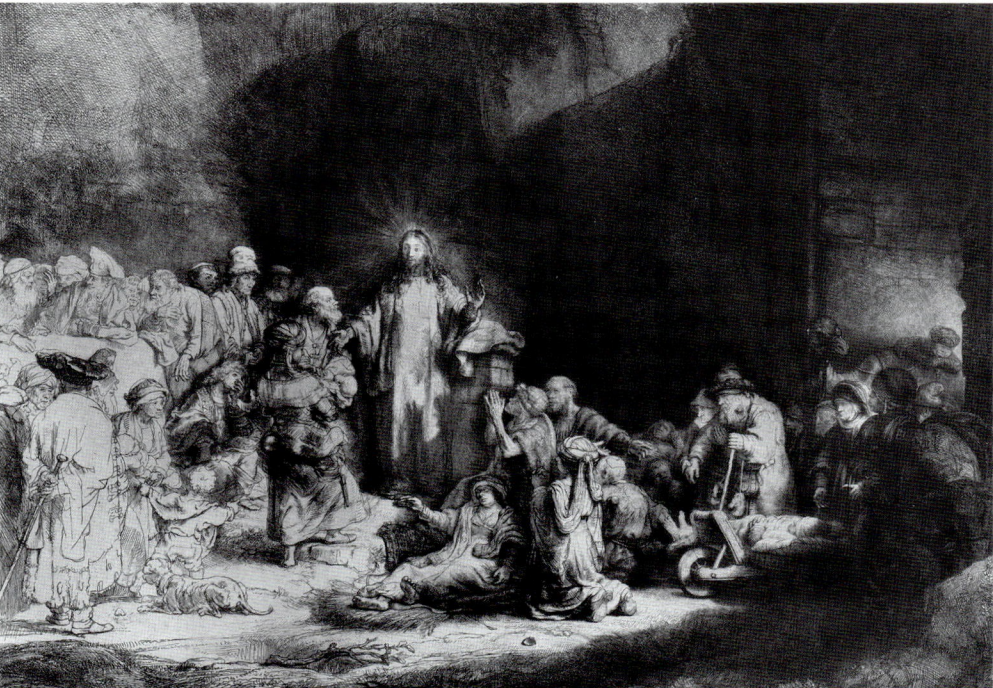

**24-48** Rembrandt van Rijn, *Christ with the Sick around Him, Receiving the Children (Hundred Guilder Print)*, ca. 1649. Etching, approx. $11'' \times 1' \ 3\frac{1}{4}''$. Pierpont Morgan Library, New York.

and maulstick. He is clothed in studio garb—a smock and painter's turban. The circles on the wall behind him (the subject of much scholarly debate) may allude to a legendary sign of artistic virtuosity—the ability to draw a perfect circle freehand. Ultimately, Rembrandt's abiding interest in revealing the human soul emerged here in his careful focus on his expressive visage. His controlled use of light and the nonspecific setting contribute to this focus. Further, X rays of the painting have revealed that Rembrandt originally depicted himself in the act of painting. His final resolution, with the viewer's attention drawn to his face, produced a portrait not just of the artist but of the man as well.

**COMPASSION MEMORABLY ETCHED** Rembrandt's virtuosity also extended to the graphic media—in particular, to etching. Many artists rapidly took up etching when it was perfected early in the 17th century. They found it far more manageable than engraving, and it allowed greater freedom in drawing the design. For etching, a copper plate is covered with a layer of wax or varnish. The artist incises the design into this surface with an etching needle or any pointed tool, exposing the metal below but not cutting into its surface. The plate is then immersed in acid, which etches, or eats away, the exposed parts of the metal, acting the same as the burin in engraving. The medium's softness gives etchers greater carving freedom than woodcutters and engravers have working directly in their more resistant media of wood and metal. Thus, prior to the invention of the lithograph in the 19th century, etching was the most facile of the graphic arts and offered the greatest subtlety of line and tone.

If Rembrandt had never painted, he still would be renowned, as he principally was in his lifetime, for his prints. Prints were a major source of income for him, and he often reworked the plates so that they could be used to produce a new issue or edition. This constant reworking was unusual within the context of 17th-century printmaking practices. *Christ with the Sick around Him, Receiving the Children (Hundred Guilder Print;* FIG. **24-48**) is one of Rembrandt's most celebrated etchings. Indeed, the title by which the print is best known, *Hundred Guilder Print,* refers to

the high price this work brought during Rembrandt's lifetime. Like his other religious works, this print is suffused with a deep and abiding piety. Christ appears in the center preaching compassionately to the blind, the lame, and the young. On the left, a group of Jews heatedly discuss issues among themselves. Like Rembrandt's *Return of the Prodigal Son* (FIG. 24-46), the central themes here are Christian humility and mercy.

Rembrandt's genius is undisputed. He is revered as an artist of great versatility, as a master of light and shadow, and as the unique interpreter of the Protestant conception of Scripture. Because of the esteem in which Rembrandt's art is held, his work and style have been the focus of many forgers and copyists. To counteract this, a group of scholars has launched the Rembrandt Research Project, whose goal is to provide definitive identification of the hundreds of works currently attributed to Rembrandt (see "Assessing Authenticity: The Rembrandt Research Project," page 725).

**AT EASE IN FRONT OF AN EASEL** JUDITH LEYSTER (1609–1660) developed a thriving career as a portraitist, like Hals, with whom she studied for a time. Her *Self-Portrait* (FIG. **24-49**) suggests the strong training she received; it is detailed, precise, and accurate but also imbued with the spontaneity found in the works of Hals. In this painting, Leyster succeeded at communicating a great deal about herself. She depicted herself as an artist, seated in front of a painting on an easel. The palette in her left hand and brush in her right make it clear that the painting is her creation. She thus allows the viewer to evaluate her skill, which both the fiddler on the canvas and the image of herself demonstrate as considerable. Although she produced a wide range of paintings, including still lifes and floral pieces, her specialty was genre scenes such as the comic image seen on the easel. Her self-assurance is reflected in her quick smile and her relaxed pose as she stops her work to meet the viewer's gaze. Although presenting herself as an artist, Leyster did not depict herself wearing the traditional artist's smock, as Rembrandt did in his self-portrait (FIG. 24-47). Her elegant attire distinguishes her socially as a member of a well-to-do family, another important aspect of Leyster's identity.

## Assessing Authenticity
### The Rembrandt Research Project

Rembrandt had an active workshop and shared stylistic traits and technical methods with numerous colleagues and pupils. As a result, authenticating Rembrandt's paintings has been difficult (as is the case with many other artists). In 1968, a team of Dutch scholars was organized by the Dutch government as the Rembrandt Research Project (RRP) and given the task of assessing the paintings attributed to Rembrandt in museums and private collections throughout the world. Their ultimate goal is the compilation of a definitive *catalogue raisonné* (a comprehensive catalog of an artist's works). The RRP has relied extensively on new scientific techniques, such as X-ray, microscopic, and chemical analysis of paint samples and *dendrochronology* (the dating of wood). Of course, stylistic analysis remains an important component in assessing authorship.

The results of their investigation, which still continues, have raised vehement debate, controversy, and consternation among art historians, museum curators, collectors, and dealers. Currently, the RRP has published three volumes (of a projected five-volume collection) of *A Corpus of Rembrandt Paintings*. These three volumes cover Rembrandt's work from 1625 to 1642 and include not just evaluations of the numerous paintings attributed to the artist during these years but also introductory essays on Rembrandt's style, patrons, and workshop practices. Of the paintings they have examined thus far, the RRP scholars have concluded that 146 of the paintings attributed to Rembrandt are indeed by his hand, 12 paintings are questionable, and 122 works previously accepted as Rembrandt's should not be attributed to him. None of this subtracts, of course, from the aesthetic value of Rembrandt's art, which certainly is inestimable. Nor does it in any way diminish his stature in the history of art. It does remind people once again that the "facts" of art history are always open to review and their interpretations open to revision.

**RECLAIMING LAND FROM THE SEA** In addition to portraiture, the Dutch avidly collected landscapes, interior scenes, and still lifes. Each of these painting genres dealt directly with the daily lives of the urban mercantile public, accounting for their appeal. Landscape scenes abound in Dutch Baroque art. Due to topography and politics, the Dutch had a unique relationship to the terrain, one that differed from those of other European countries. After gaining independence from Spain, the Dutch undertook an extensive land reclamation project that lasted almost a century. Dikes and drainage systems cropped up across the landscape. Because of the effort expended on these endeavors, the Dutch developed a very direct relationship to the land. Further, the reclamation impacted

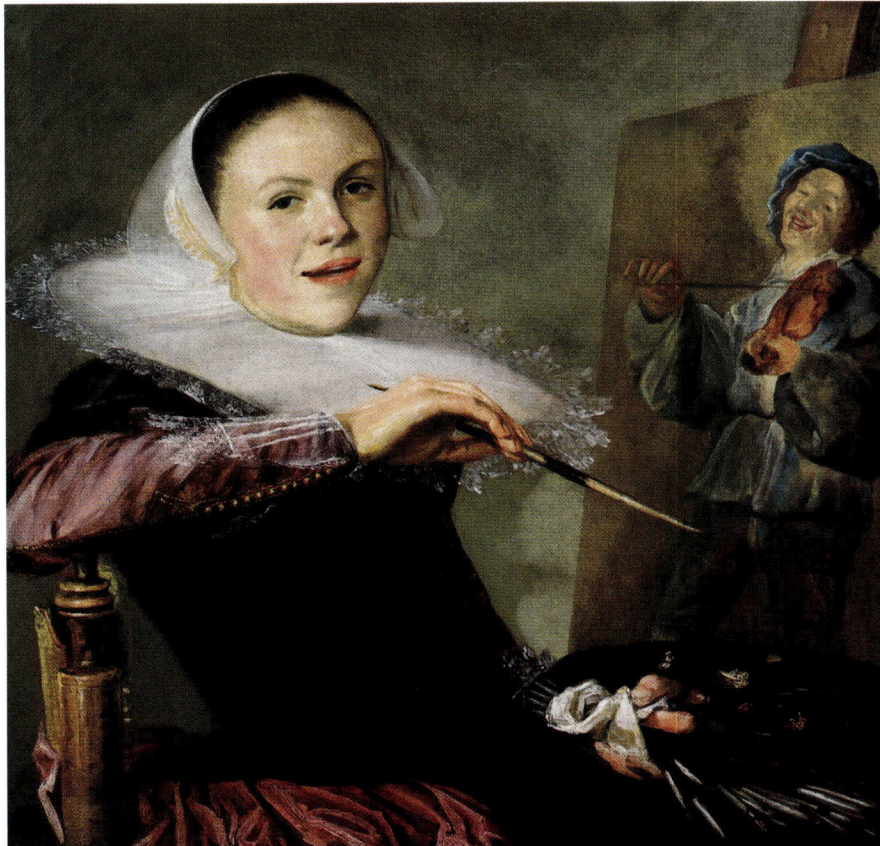

**24-49** Judith Leyster, *Self-Portrait,* ca. 1630. Oil on canvas, 2′ 5$\frac{3}{8}$″ × 2′ 1$\frac{5}{8}$″. National Gallery of Art, Washington (gift of Mr. and Mrs. Robert Woods Bliss).

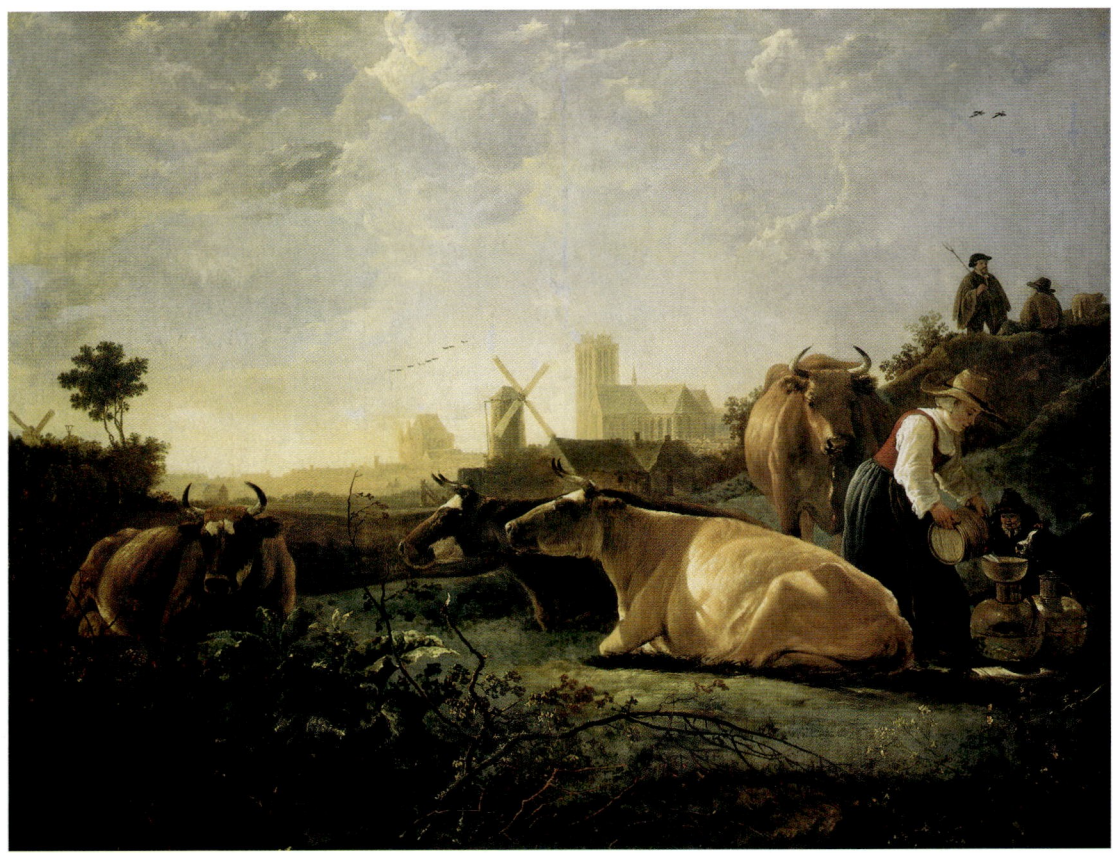

**24-50** AELBERT CUYP, *A Distant View of Dordrecht, with a Milkmaid and Four Cows, and Other Figures (The "Large Dort"),* late 1640s. Oil on canvas, approx. 5′ 1″ × 6′ 4⅞″. National Gallery, London.

Dutch social and economic life. The marshy and swampy nature of much of the land made it less desirable for large-scale exploitation, so the extensive feudal landowning system that existed elsewhere in Europe never developed in the provinces. Most Dutch families owned and worked their own farms, cultivating a feeling of closeness to the Dutch terrain.

**A LANDSCAPE OF DORDRECHT** A Dutch artist who established his reputation producing landscape paintings was AELBERT CUYP (ca. 1620–1691). His works were the products of careful observation and a deep respect for and understanding of the Dutch landscape. *A Distant View of Dordrecht, with a Milkmaid and Four Cows, and Other Figures* (FIG. **24-50**), often referred to as *The "Large Dort,"* reveals Cuyp's substantial skills. The title indicates that the location was important to the artist. Unlike the idealized classical landscapes that populate many Italian Renaissance paintings, this landscape is particularized. In fact, the church in the background can be identified as the Grote Kerk in Dordrecht. The dairy cows, shepherds, and milkmaid in the foreground refer to a cornerstone of Dutch agriculture—the demand for dairy products such as butter and cheese, which increased with the development of urban centers. The credibility of such paintings rests on Cuyp's pristine rendering of each detail.

**HAARLEM DAYS** JACOB VAN RUISDAEL (ca. 1628–1682), like Cuyp, depicted the Dutch landscape with precision and sensitivity. In *View of Haarlem from the Dunes at Overveen* (FIG. **24-51**), van Ruisdael gives the viewer an overarching view of this major Dutch

city. The specificity of the artist's image—the Saint Bavo church in the background, the numerous windmills that refer to the land reclamation efforts, and the figures in the foreground stretching linen to be bleached (a major industry in Haarlem)—endows the work with a sense of honesty and integrity. Yet this painting is, above all, a landscape. Although the scene is painted in an admirably clear and detailed manner, the inhabitants and dwellings are so minuscule that they blend into the land itself. Further, the horizon line is low, so the sky fills almost three-quarters of the picture space. And the landscape is illuminated only in patches, where the sun has broken through the clouds above. In *View of Haarlem,* as in his other landscape paintings, van Ruisdael not only captured a specific and historical view of Haarlem but also succeeded in imbuing the work with a quiet serenity that seems almost spiritual.

**HOME IS WHERE THE HEART IS** The sense of peace, familiarity, and comfort that Dutch landscape paintings seem to exude also emerges in interior scenes. These paintings offer the viewer glimpses into the lives of prosperous, responsible, and cultured citizens. The best-known and most highly regarded of the Dutch interior scene painters is JAN VERMEER (1632–1675) of Delft. Vermeer derived most of his income from his work as an innkeeper and art dealer (see "Mercantile Prosperity: Developing an Open Art Market," page 727), and he painted no more than 35 paintings that can be definitively attributed to him. Vermeer's pictures are small, luminous, and captivating. Flemish artists of the 15th century also had painted domestic interiors, but persons of sacred significance often occupied those scenes (see, for example,

## Mercantile Prosperity
### Developing an Open Art Market

With the expansion of the Dutch art market (see "Dutch Patronage and Art Collecting," page 719), commissions, the mainstay of art production in Italy and Spain, became less prevalent (except for portraiture) in the United Provinces. Dutch artists produced paintings for an anonymous market, hoping to appeal to a wide audience. To ensure success, artists adapted to the changed conditions of art production and sales. They marketed their paintings in many ways, selling their works directly to buyers who visited their studios and through art dealers, exhibitions, fairs, auctions, and even lotteries. Because of the uncertainty of these sales mechanisms (as opposed to the certainty of an ironclad contract for a commission), artists became more responsive to market demands. Specialization became common among Dutch artists of the 17th century. For example, painters would limit their practice to painting portraits, still lifes, or landscapes—the most popular genres among middle-class patrons. Exact prices for Dutch paintings sold then are difficult to ascertain. Given the wide range of patrons, the prices no doubt ranged from very cheap to extravagantly expensive. Documented information about prices paid for artwork suggests that by 1700, detailed genre scenes were the most expensive, on average, followed by history painting, religious scenes, landscapes, still lifes, and portraits. Another reason for the uncertainty about prices is that transactions often were conducted without cash. Artists frequently used their paintings to pay off loans or debts. Tavern debts, in particular, could be settled with paintings, which may explain why many art dealers (such as Jan Vermeer and his father before him) were also innkeepers. This connection between art dealing and other businesses eventually solidified, and innkeepers, for example, often would have art exhibitions in their taverns hoping to make a sale.

The institutions of the current open art market—dealers, galleries, auctions, and estate sales—thus owe their establishment to the Golden Age of Dutch art.

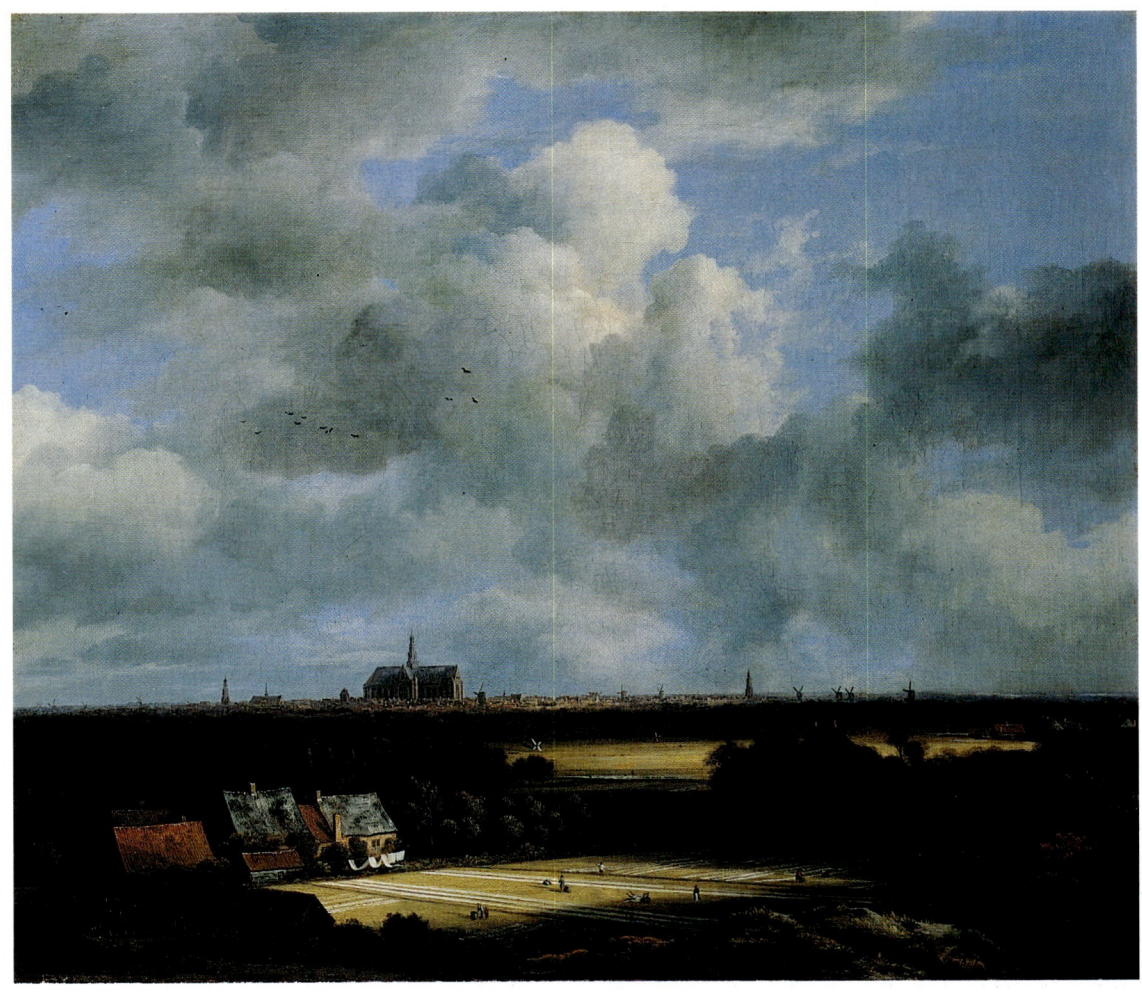

**24-51** JACOB VAN RUISDAEL, *View of Haarlem from the Dunes at Overveen*, ca. 1670. Oil on canvas, approx. 1′ 10″ × 2′ 1″. Mauritshuis, The Hague.

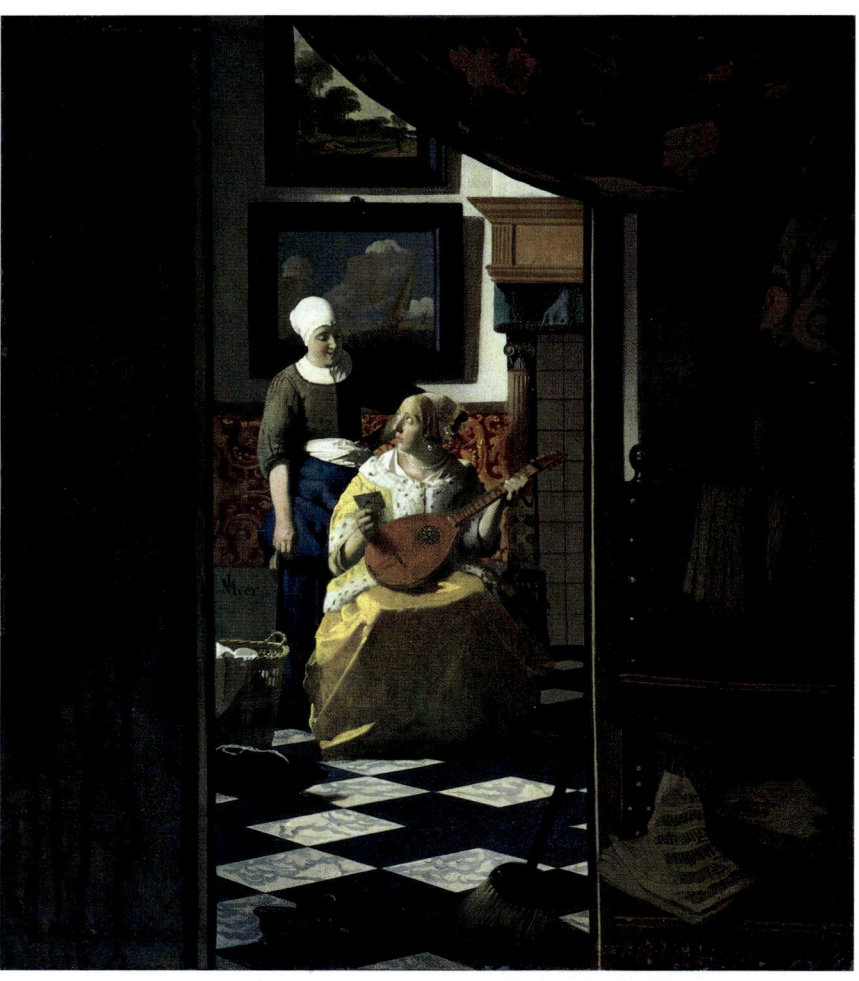

**24-52** JAN VERMEER, *The Letter,* 1666. Oil on canvas, 1′ 5¼″ × 1′ 3¼″. Rijksmuseum, Amsterdam.

the *Mérode Altarpiece,* FIG. 20-12). In contrast, Vermeer and his contemporaries composed neat, quietly opulent interiors of Dutch middle-class dwellings with men, women, and children engaging in household tasks or some little recreation. These commonplace actions reflected the values of a comfortable domesticity that had a simple beauty.

In *The Letter* (FIG. **24-52**), Vermeer ushers viewers into a room of a well-appointed Dutch house. The drawn curtain and open doorway through which they must peer reinforce the viewers' status as outsiders and affirm the scene's unplanned "normal" reality. The painting features two women. This focus on women in a household scene is entirely appropriate; 17th-century Dutch culture consigned primary responsibility for the tranquility and order of the domestic realm to women. In *The Letter,* the woman of the house is not involved in cleaning or child-rearing activities; her elegant attire suggests a woman of considerable means. Rather, her lute playing has been interrupted by a maid, who has delivered a letter. The missive is a love letter; Vermeer included objects that would prompt this inference from a 17th-century Dutch audience. The lute was a traditional symbol of the music of love, and the calm seascape on the back wall served as a symbol of love requited. In the book *Love Emblems,* published in Amsterdam in 1634, the author wrote, "Love may rightly be compared to the sea, considering its changeableness."[4] Although the events that Vermeer depicted may not be historically momentous, his care and directness in recording these scenes result in vignettes that reveal much about Dutch life and culture.

**THE SCIENCE AND POETRY OF LIGHT** Vermeer was a master of pictorial light and used it with immense virtuosity. He could render space so convincingly through his depiction of light that in his works, the picture surface functions as an invisible glass pane through which the viewer looks into the constructed illusion. Historians are confident that Vermeer used as tools both mirrors and the *camera obscura,* an ancestor of the modern camera based on passing light through a tiny pinhole or lens to project an image on a screen or the wall of a room. (In later versions, the image was projected on a ground-glass wall of a box whose opposite wall contained the pinhole or lens.) This does not mean that Vermeer merely copied the image. Instead, these aids helped him obtain results he reworked compositionally, placing his figures and the furniture of a room in a beautiful stability of quadrilateral shapes. This gives his designs a matchless classical serenity. This quality is enhanced by colors so true to the optical facts and so subtly modulated that they suggest Vermeer was far ahead of his time in color science. Close examination of his paintings shows that Vermeer realized that shadows are not colorless and dark, that adjoining colors affect each other, and that light is composed of colors. Thus, he painted reflections off of surfaces in colors modified by others nearby. It has been suggested that Vermeer also perceived the phenomenon modern photographers call "circles of confusion," which appear on out-of-focus negatives. Vermeer could have seen them in images projected by the camera obscura's primitive lenses. He approximated these effects with light dabs that, in close view, give

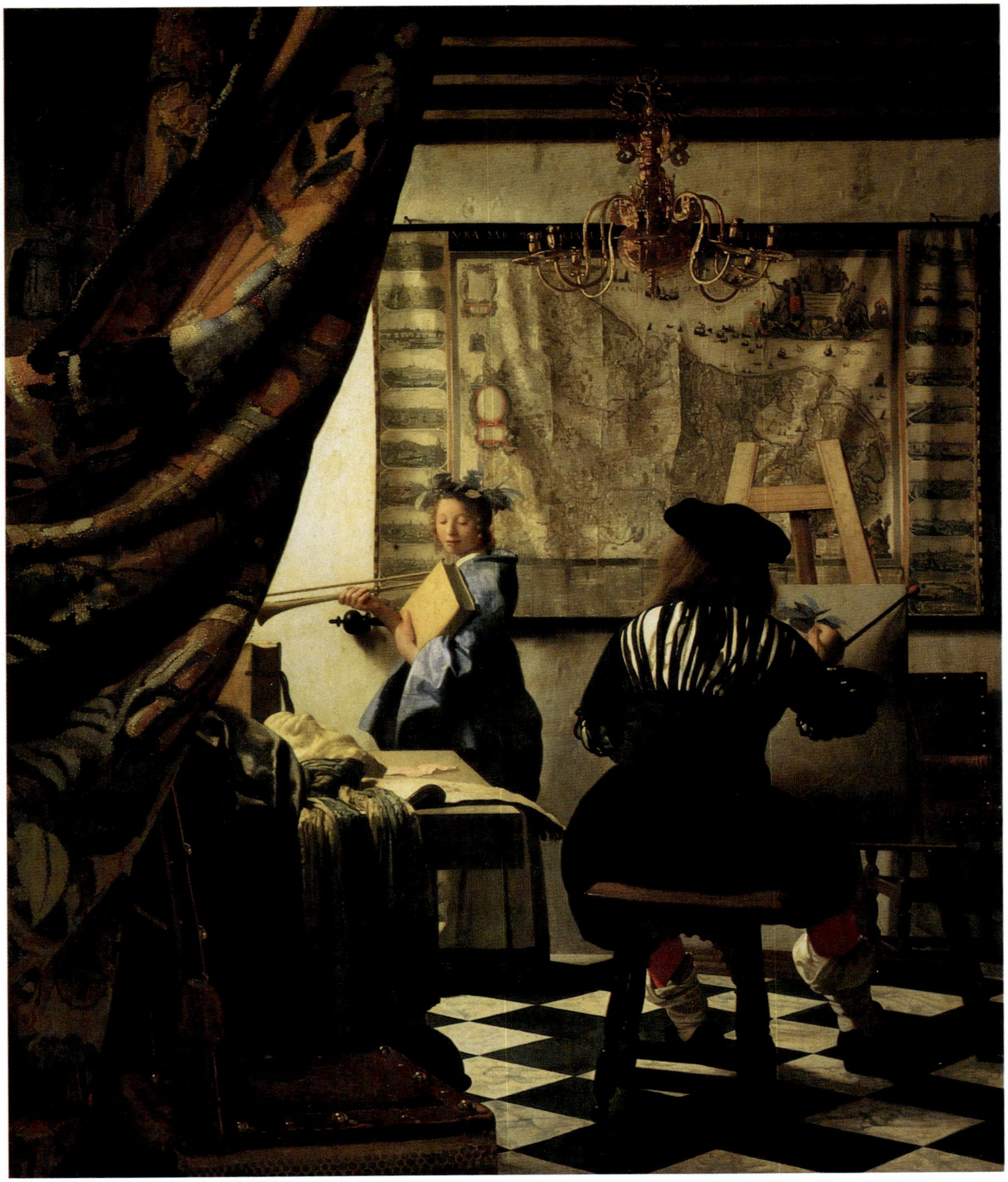

**24-53** JAN VERMEER, *Allegory of the Art of Painting*, 1670–1675. Oil on canvas, 4' 4" × 3' 8". Kunsthistorisches Museum, Vienna.

the impression of an image slightly "out of focus." When the observer draws back a step, however, as if adjusting the lens, the color spots cohere, giving an astonishingly accurate illusion of a third dimension.

**EXTOLLING THE ART PROFESSION** Vermeer's stylistic precision and commitment to his profession surfaced in *Allegory of the Art of Painting* (FIG. 24-53). The artist himself appears in the painting, with his back to the viewer and dressed in "historical" clothing (reminiscent of Burgundian attire). He is hard at work on a painting of the model who stands before him wearing a laurel wreath and holding a trumpet and book, traditional attributes of Clio, the muse of history. The map of the provinces

(an increasingly common wall adornment in Dutch homes) on the back wall serves as yet another reference to history. As in *The Letter*, the viewer is outside the space of the action, and the drawn curtain provides visual access. Some art historians have suggested that the light radiating from an unseen window on the left that illuminates both the model and the canvas being painted alludes to the light of artistic inspiration. Accordingly, this painting has been interpreted (as reflected in the title) as an allegory—a reference to painting inspired by history. This allegorical reading was affirmed when Vermeer's widow, wishing to retain this painting after the artist's death, listed it in her written claim as "the piece . . . wherein the Art of Painting is portrayed."[5]

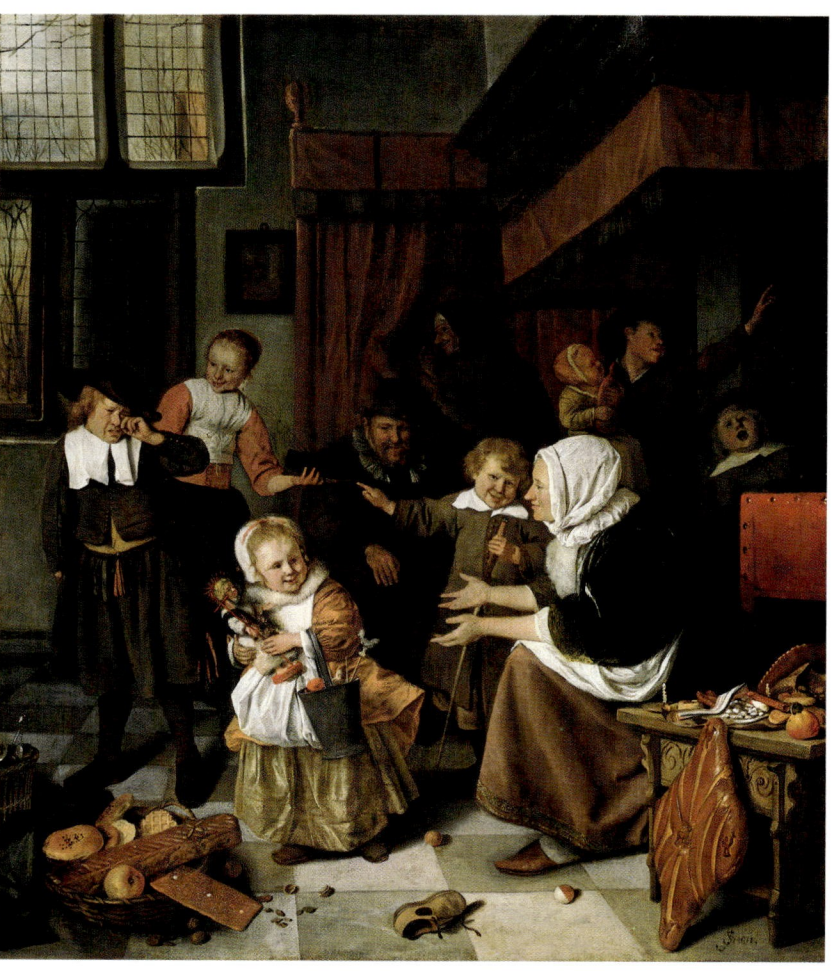

**24-54** Jan Steen, *The Feast of Saint Nicholas,* ca. 1660–1665. Oil on canvas, 2′ 8¼″ × 2′ 3¾″. Rijksmuseum, Amsterdam.

**SATIRIZING DUTCH LIFE** Whereas Vermeer's paintings revealed the charm and beauty of Dutch domesticity, the work of JAN STEEN (ca. 1625–1679) provided a counterpoint. In *The Feast of Saint Nicholas* (FIG. **24-54**), rather than depicting a tidy, calm Dutch household, Steen painted a scene of chaos and disruption. Saint Nicholas has just visited this residence, and the children are in an uproar as they search their shoes for the gifts from Saint Nick. Some children are delighted—the little girl in the center clutches her gifts, clearly unwilling to share with the other children despite her mother's pleas. Others are disappointed—the boy on the left is in tears because all he received is a birch rod. An appropriately festive atmosphere reigns, which contrasts sharply

**24-55** PIETER CLAESZ, *Vanitas Still Life,* 1630s. Oil on panel, 1′ 2″ × 1′ 11½″. Germanisches Nationalmuseum, Nuremberg.

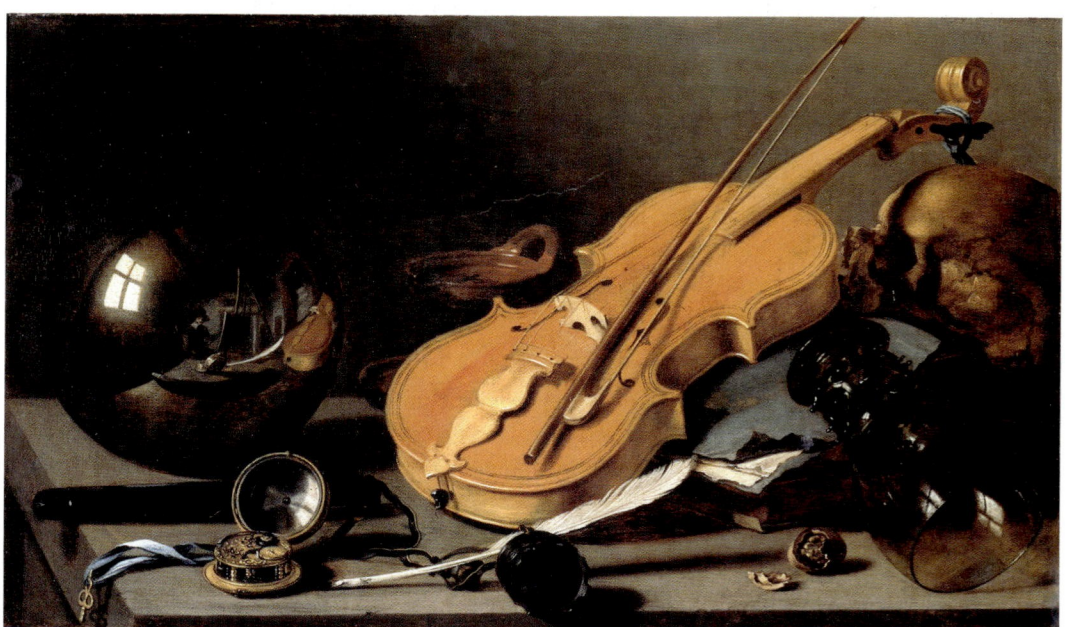

with the decorum that prevails in Vermeer's works. Like the paintings of other Dutch Baroque artists, Steen's lively scenes often take on an allegorical dimension or moralistic tone. Steen frequently used children's activities as satirical comments on foolish adult behavior. *The Feast of Saint Nicholas* can be seen as alluding to selfishness, pettiness, and jealousy.

**OF BEAUTY AND DEATH** The prosperous Dutch were justifiably proud of their accomplishments, and the popularity of still-life paintings—particularly images of accumulated material goods—reflected this pride. These still lifes, like Vermeer's interior scenes, are beautifully crafted images that are both scientific in their optical accuracy and poetic in their beauty and lyricism. Paintings such as *Vanitas Still Life* (FIG. **24-55**) by PIETER CLAESZ (1597/98–1660) reveal the pride Dutch citizens had in their material possessions, presented as if strewn across a tabletop or dresser. This pride is tempered, however, by the ever-present morality and humility central to the Calvinist faith. Thus, while appreciating and enjoying the beauty and value of the objects depicted, the viewer is reminded of life's transience. This reminder consists of references to death. Paintings with such features are called *vanitas* paintings; each feature is referred to as a *memento mori*. In *Vanitas Still Life,* references to mortality include the skull, timepiece, tipped glass, and cracked walnut. All suggest the passage of time or a presence that has disappeared. Something or someone was here—and now is gone. Claesz emphasized this element of time (and demonstrated his technical virtuosity) by including a self-portrait,

reflected in the glass ball on the left side of the table. He appears to be painting the work we now scrutinize. But in an apparent challenge to the message of inevitable mortality that vanitas paintings convey, the portrait serves to immortalize the subject—in this case, the artist himself.

**THE ALLURE OF PRECIOUS OBJECTS** As Dutch prosperity increased, precious objects and luxury items made their way into still-life paintings. *Still Life with a Late Ming Ginger Jar* (FIG. **24-56**) by WILLEM KALF (1619–1693) reveals both the wealth Dutch citizens had accrued and the exquisite skills—both technical and aesthetic—of Dutch Baroque artists. Kalf was enamored by the lustrous sheen of fabric and highlights glinting off reflective surfaces. As is evident in this image, his works present an array of ornamental objects, such as the Venetian and Dutch glassware and the silver dish. Kalf's inclusion of the watch, Mediterranean peach, and peeled lemon suggests that these works, despite their opulence, also functioned as vanitas paintings. In *Still Life,* Kalf also highlighted the expansiveness of Dutch maritime trade through his depiction of the Indian floral carpet and the Chinese jar used to store ginger (a luxury item).

**A BUDDING ARTIST** Like still-life paintings, flower paintings were prominent in Dutch Baroque art. As living objects that soon die, flowers, particularly cut blossoms, appeared frequently in vanitas paintings. However, floral painting as a unique genre also flourished. Among the leading practitioners of this art was RACHEL RUYSCH (1663–1750). Ruysch's father was a professor of

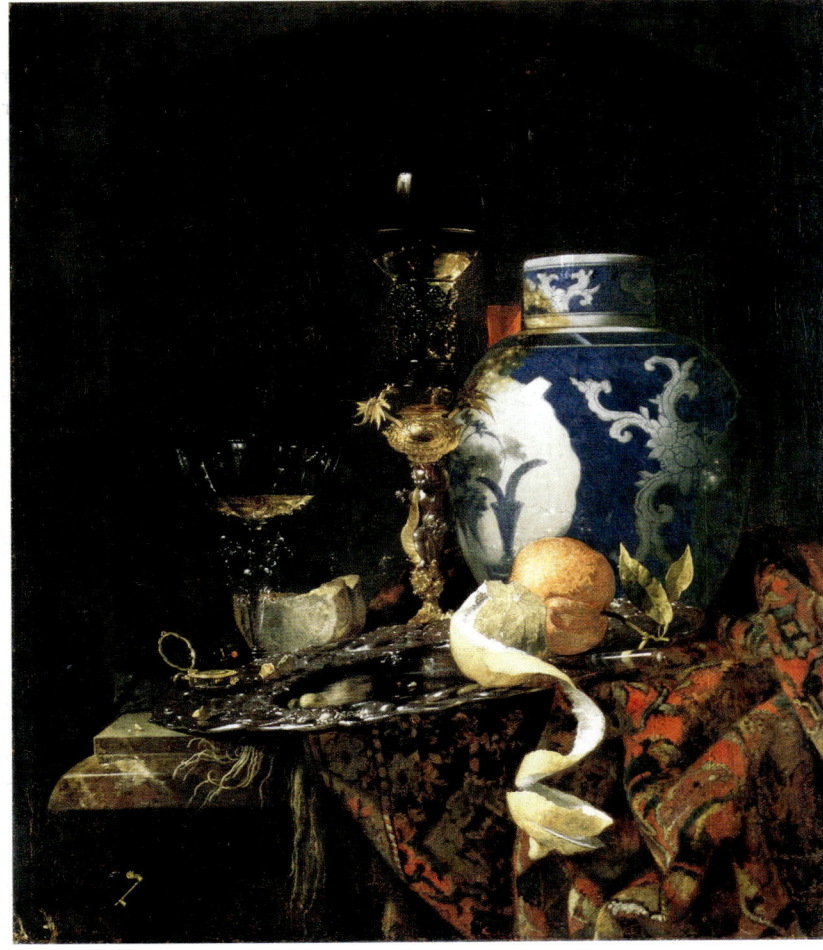

**24-56** WILLEM KALF, *Still Life with a Late Ming Ginger Jar,* 1669. Oil on canvas, 2′ 6″ × 2′ 1¾″. Indianapolis Museum of Art, Indianapolis (gift in commemoration of the 60th anniversary of the Art Association of Indianapolis, in memory of Daniel W. and Elizabeth C. Marmon).

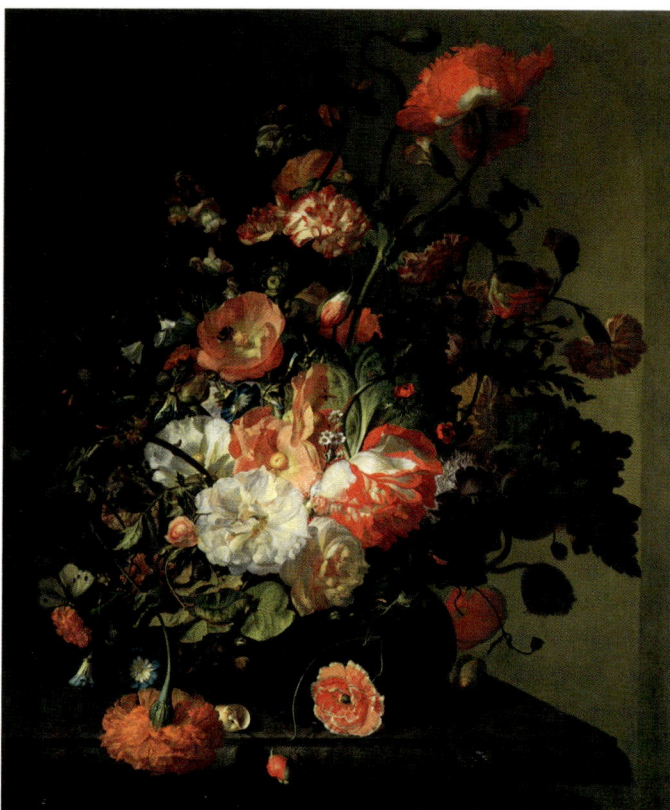

**24-57** RACHEL RUYSCH, *Flower Still Life,* after 1700. Oil on canvas, 2′ 6″ × 2′. The Toledo Museum of Art, Toledo (purchased with funds from the Libbey Endowment, gift of Edward Drummond Libbey).

botany and anatomy, which may account for her interest in and knowledge of plants and insects. She acquired an international reputation for lush paintings such as *Flower Still Life* (FIG. 24-57). In this image, the lavish floral arrangement is so full that many of the blossoms seem to be spilling out of the vase. Ruysch carefully constructed her paintings. Here, for example, she positioned the flowers such that they create a diagonal that runs from the lower left of the painting to the upper right corner and that offsets the opposing diagonal of the table edge. Ruysch became famous for her floral paintings and still lifes, and from 1708 to 1716 she served as court painter to the elector Palatine (the ruler of the Palatinate, a former division of Bavaria) in Düsseldorf, Germany.

Dutch Baroque art has a unique character that sets it apart from, say, Italian Baroque, although commonalities can be uncovered. The appeal of Dutch Baroque art lies in both its beauty and its sincerity, as well as in the insights it provides into Calvinist Dutch life and history.

## France

The history of France during the Baroque period is essentially the culmination of increasing monarchical authority that had been developing for centuries. This consolidation of power was embodied in King Louis XIV (r. 1661–1715), whose obsessive control determined the direction of French Baroque society and culture. Although its economy was not as expansive as that of the Dutch Republic, France became the largest and most powerful European country of the 17th century.

Religious conflicts caused great tension throughout the 16th and 17th centuries. After the Reformation, Protestants in France challenged royal authority, which resulted in a sequence of religious wars between Catholics and Protestants. In 1598, King Henry IV (r. 1589–1610) issued the Edict of Nantes, which in effect decreed religious tolerance. Despite this edict, Protestants eventually were driven from the country.

**INVOKING CLASSICAL ORDER** In the early part of the 17th century, the appeal of Rome enticed many French artists to study there. Fascination with both ancient Roman and Italian Renaissance cultures accounted for Rome's allure. NICOLAS POUSSIN (1594–1665), born in Normandy, spent most of his life in Rome. There, inspired by its monuments and countryside, he produced his grandly severe and regular canvases modeled on the work of Titian and Raphael. He also carefully worked out a theoretical explanation of his method, and was ultimately responsible for establishing classical painting as an important manifestation in French Baroque art.

Poussin's *Et in Arcadia Ego* (*I, Too, in Arcadia,* or *Even in Arcadia, I* [am present]; FIG. 24-58) was informed by Raphael's rational order and stability and by antique statuary. Landscape, of which Poussin became increasingly fond, provides the setting for the picture. The foreground, however, is dominated by three shepherds, living in the idyllic land of Arcadia, who spell out an enigmatic inscription on a tomb as a statuesque female figure quietly places her hand on the shoulder of one of them. She may be the spirit of death, reminding these mortals, as does the inscription, that death is found even in Arcadia, supposedly a spot of Edenic bliss. The countless draped female statues surviving in Italy from Roman times supplied the models for this figure, and the youth with one foot resting on a boulder is modeled on Greco-Roman statues of Neptune, the sea god, leaning on his trident. The compact, balanced grouping of these figures; the even light; and the thoughtful, reserved, mournful mood set the tone for Poussin's art in its later, classical phase.

In notes for an intended treatise on painting, Poussin outlined the "grand manner" of classicism, of which he became the leading exponent in Rome. Artists must first of all choose great subjects: "The first requirement, fundamental to all others, is that the subject and the narrative be grandiose, such as battles, heroic actions, and religious themes."[6] Minute details should be avoided, as well as all "low" subjects, such as genre—"Those who choose base subjects find refuge in them because of the feebleness of their talents."[7] Clearly, these directives rule out a good deal of decorative art, as well as the genre scenes that were popular in the Dutch Republic.

Poussin represents a theoretical tradition in Western art that goes back to the Early Renaissance. It asserts that all good art must be the result of good judgment—a judgment based on sure knowledge. In this way, art can achieve correctness and propriety, two of the favorite characteristics of the classicizing artist or architect. Poussin praised the ancient Greeks, who "produced marvelous effects" with their musical "modes." He observed that "[t]he word 'mode' really means the system, or the measure and form which we use in making something. It constrains us not to pass the limits, it compels us to employ a certain evenness and moderation in all things."[8] Such evenness and moderation are the very essence of French classical doctrine. In the age of Louis XIV, scholars preached this doctrine as much for literature and music as for art and architecture.

**A PLUTARCHIAN SCENE** Among Poussin's finest works is *Burial of Phocion* (FIG. 24-59). As was typical of Poussin, he carefully chose its subject from the literature of antiquity. His source was Plutarch's *Life of Phocion,* a biography of the distinguished Athenian general whom his compatriots unjustly put to death for

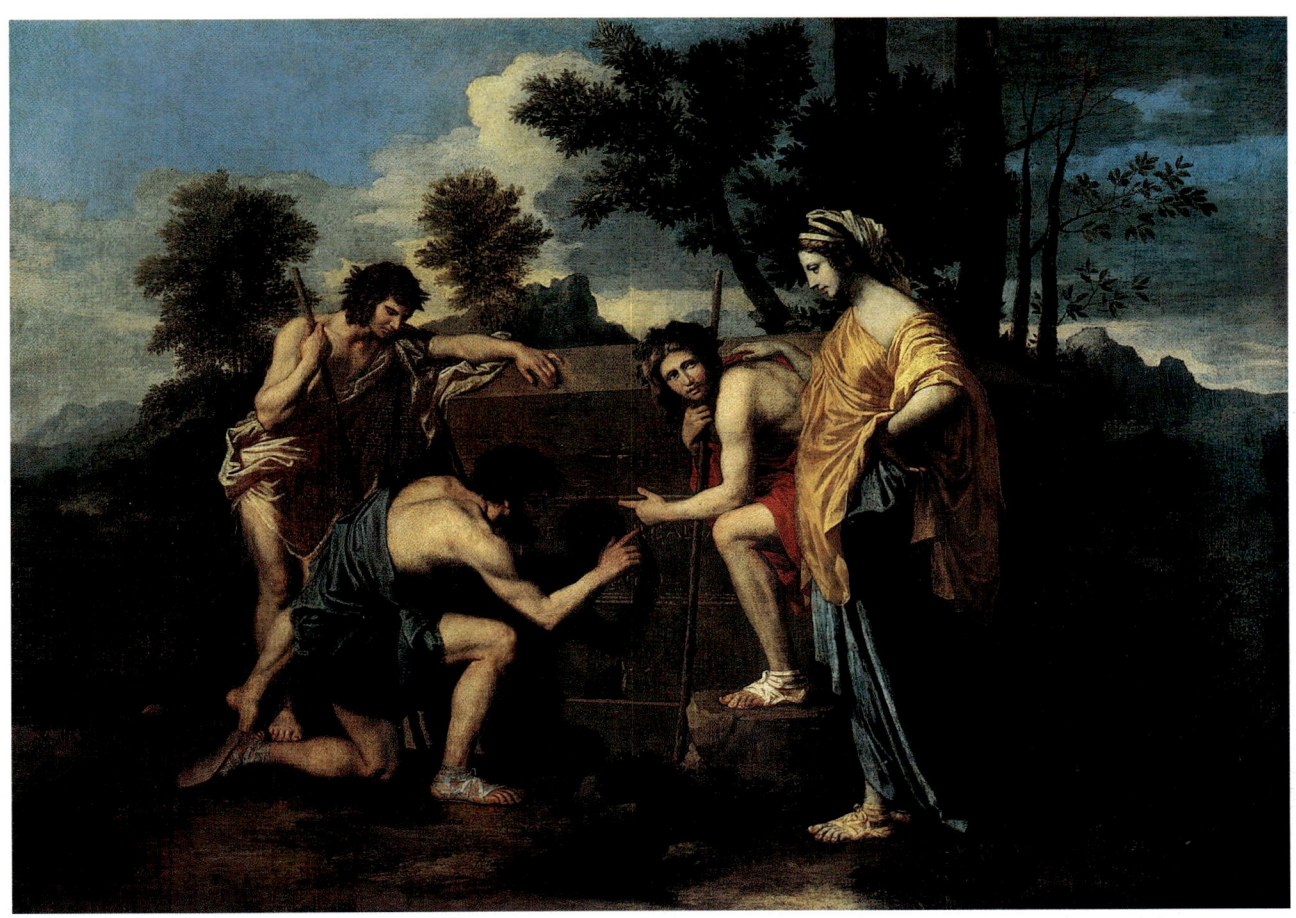

**24-58** Nicolas Poussin, *Et in Arcadia Ego,* ca. 1655. Oil on canvas, approx. 2′ 10″ × 4′. Louvre, Paris.

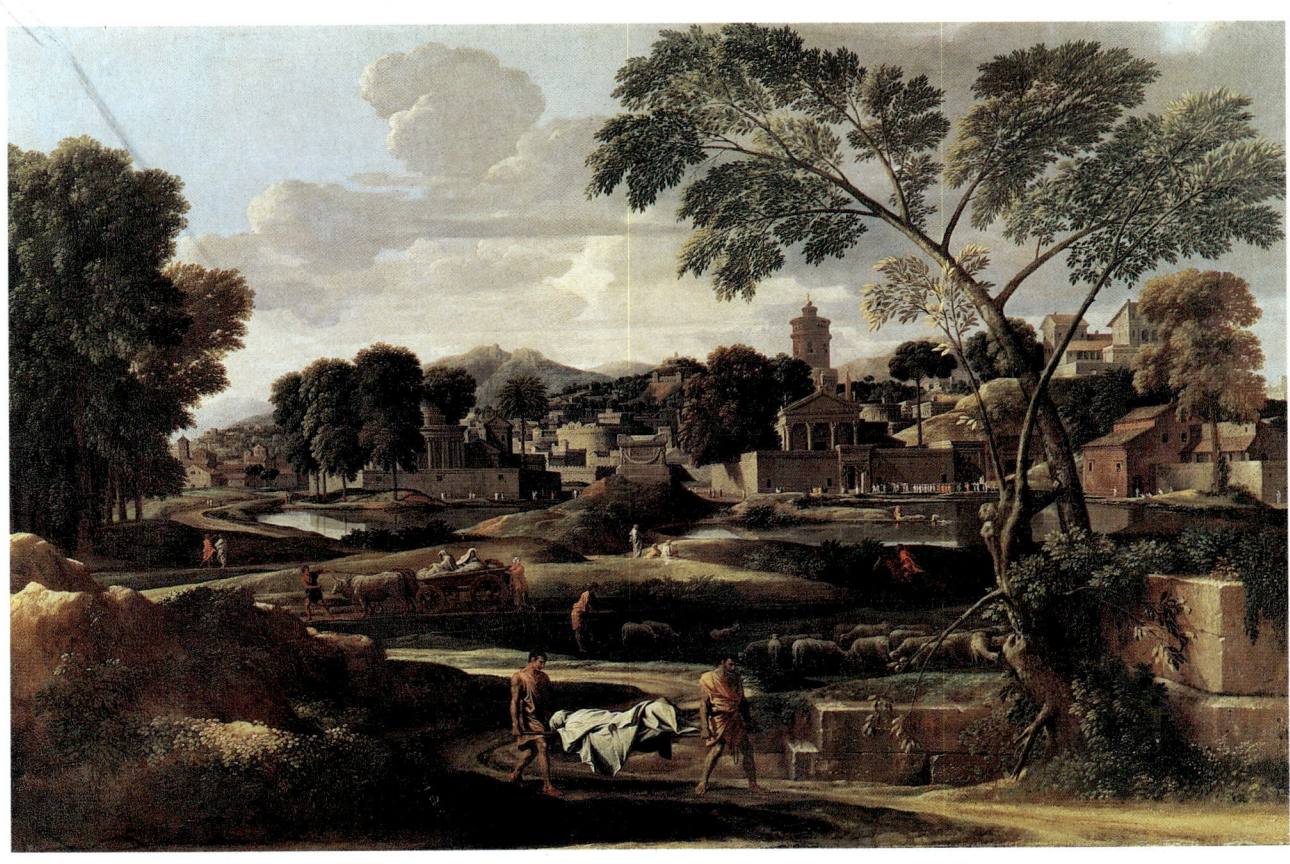

**24-59** Nicolas Poussin, *Burial of Phocion,* 1648. Oil on canvas, approx. 3′ 11″ × 5′ 10″. Louvre, Paris.

treason. Eventually, the state gave him a public funeral and memorialized him. In the foreground, the hero's body is being taken away, his burial on Athenian soil initially forbidden. The two massive bearers and the bier are starkly isolated in a great landscape that throws them into solitary relief, eloquently expressive of the hero abandoned in death. The landscape's interlocking planes slope upward to the lighted sky at the left. Its carefully arranged terraces bear slowly moving streams, shepherds and their flocks, and, in the distance, whole assemblies of solid geometric structures (temples, towers, walls, villas, and a central grand sarcophagus). The skies are untroubled, and the light is even and revealing of form. The trees are few and carefully arranged, like curtains lightly drawn back to reveal a natural setting carefully cultivated for a single human action. Unlike van Ruisdael's *View of Haarlem* (FIG. 24-51), this scene was not intended to represent a particular place and time. It was Poussin's construction of an idea of a noble landscape to frame a noble theme, much like Annibale Carracci's classical landscape (FIG. 24-22). The *Phocion* landscape is nature subordinated to a rational plan.

**A LANDSCAPIST PAR EXCELLENCE** Claude Gellée, called CLAUDE LORRAIN (1600–1682), modulated in a softer style the disciplined rational art of Poussin, with its sophisticated revelation of the geometry of landscape. Unlike the figures in Poussin's pictures, those in Claude's landscapes tell no dramatic story, point out no moral, and praise no hero. Indeed, they often appear to be added as mere excuses for the radiant landscape itself.

For Claude, painting involved essentially one theme—the beauty of a broad sky suffused with the golden light of dawn or sunset glowing through a hazy atmosphere and reflecting brilliantly off rippling water.

The subject of his work often remains grounded in classical antiquity, as seen in *Landscape with Cattle and Peasants* (FIG. **24-60**). The figures in the right foreground chat in animated fashion; in the left foreground, cattle relax contentedly; and in the middle ground, cattle amble slowly away. The well-defined foreground, distinct middle ground, and dim background recede in serene orderliness, until all form dissolves in a luminous mist. Atmospheric and linear perspective reinforce each other to turn a vista into a typical Claudian vision, an ideal classical world bathed in sunlight in infinite space.

Claude's formalizing of nature with balanced groups of architectural masses, screens of trees, and sheets of water followed the great tradition of classical landscape. It began with the backgrounds of Venetian painting (see FIGS. 22-32 and 22-33) and continued in the art of Annibale Carracci (FIG. 24-22) and Poussin (FIG. 24-59). Yet Claude, like the Dutch painters, studied the actual light and the atmospheric nuances of nature, making a unique contribution. He recorded carefully in hundreds of sketches the look of the Roman countryside, its gentle terrain accented by stone-pines, cypresses, and poplars and by the ever-present ruins of ancient aqueducts, tombs, and towers. He made these the fundamental elements of his compositions. Travelers could understand the picturesque beauties of the outskirts of Rome in Claude's landscapes.

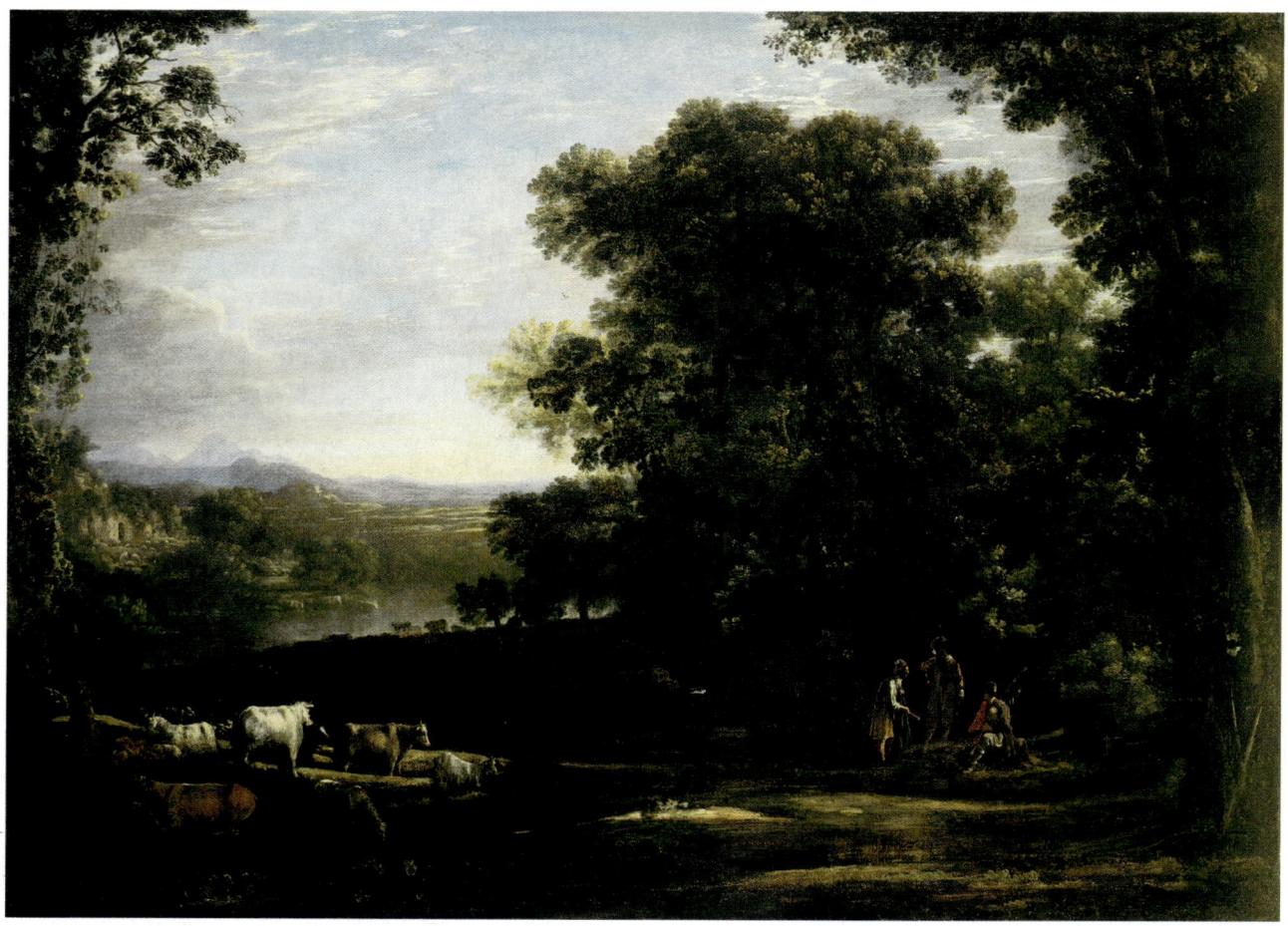

**24-60** CLAUDE LORRAIN, *Landscape with Cattle and Peasants,* 1629. Oil on canvas, 3′ 6″ × 4′ 10½″. Philadelphia Museum of Art, Philadelphia (the George W. Elkins Collection).

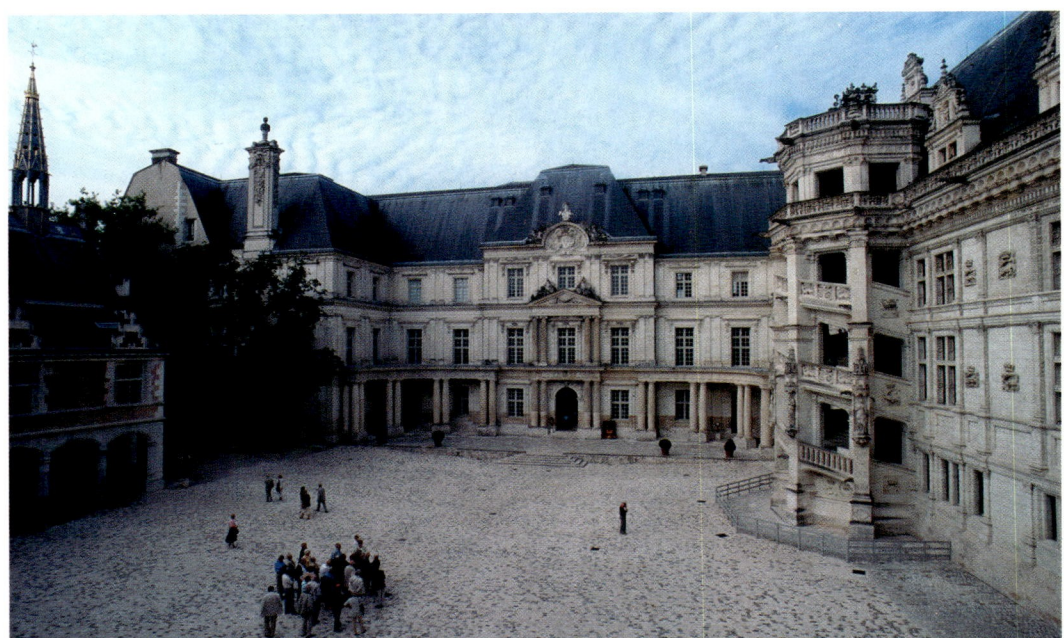

The artist achieved his marvelous effects of light by painstakingly placing tiny value gradations, which imitated, though on a very small scale, the actual range of values of outdoor light and shade. Avoiding the problem of high-noon sunlight overhead, Claude preferred, and convincingly represented, the sun's rays as they gradually illuminated the morning sky or, with their dying glow, set the pensive mood of evening. Thus, he matched the moods of nature with those of human subjects. Claude's infusion of nature with human feeling and his recomposition of nature in a calm equilibrium greatly appealed to the landscape painters of the 18th and early 19th centuries.

**A DIGNIFIED AND ORDERED BUILDING** In architecture, the classical bent asserted itself early in the work of FRANÇOIS MANSART (1598–1666), as seen in the Orléans wing of the Château de Blois (FIG. **24-61**), built in Blois between 1635 and 1638. The polished dignity evident here became the hallmark of French "Classical-Baroque," contrasting with the more daring and fanciful styles of the Baroque in Italy and elsewhere. The strong rectilinear organization and a tendency to design in repeated units suggest Italian Renaissance architecture (also permeated by the classical spirit), as do the insistence on the purity of line and the sharp relief of the wall joints. Yet the emphasis on focal points—achieved with the curving colonnades, the changing planes of the walls, and the concentration of ornament around the portal—is characteristic of French Baroque architectural thinking in general.

**THE HARDSHIP OF PEASANT LIFE** Although classicism was an important presence in French art during the 17th and early 18th centuries, not all artists pursued this direction. LOUIS LE NAIN (ca. 1593–1648) bears comparison to the Dutch. Subjects that in Dutch painting were opportunities for boisterous good humor were treated with somber stillness by the French. *Family of Country People* (FIG. **24-62**) expresses the grave dignity of a family close to the soil, one made stoic and resigned by hardship. These drab country folk surely had little reason for merriment. The peasant's lot, never easy, was miserable during the time Le Nain painted. The constant warfare (*Family* was painted during the Thirty Years' War) took its toll on France. The anguish and

frustration of the peasantry, suffering from the cruel depredations of unruly armies living off the country, often broke out in violent revolts that were savagely suppressed. This family, however, is pious, docile, and calm. Because Le Nain depicted peasants with dignity and subservience, despite their harsh living conditions, some scholars have suggested that he intended to please wealthy urban patrons with these paintings. Like Annibale Carracci, Le Nain worked cooperatively with family members—in Le Nain's case, his brothers Antoine (1588–1648) and Mathieu (1607–1677). They established a communal workshop and apparently collaborated on some paintings. For the most part, the Le Nain brothers focused on genre scenes.

**A STARK ETCHING OF DEATH** Although the Duchy of Lorraine was technically independent from the French monarchy during this period, artists from this region are often included in discussions of French art. Two prominent artists from Lorraine were Jacques Callot and Georges de La Tour. JACQUES CALLOT (ca. 1592–1635) conveyed a sense of military life of the times in a series

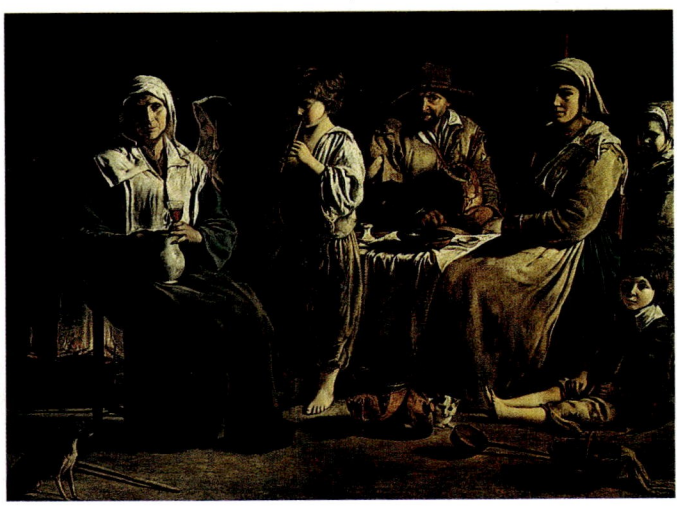

24-62 LOUIS LE NAIN, *Family of Country People,* ca. 1640. Oil on canvas, approx. 3′ 8″ × 5′ 2″. Louvre, Paris.

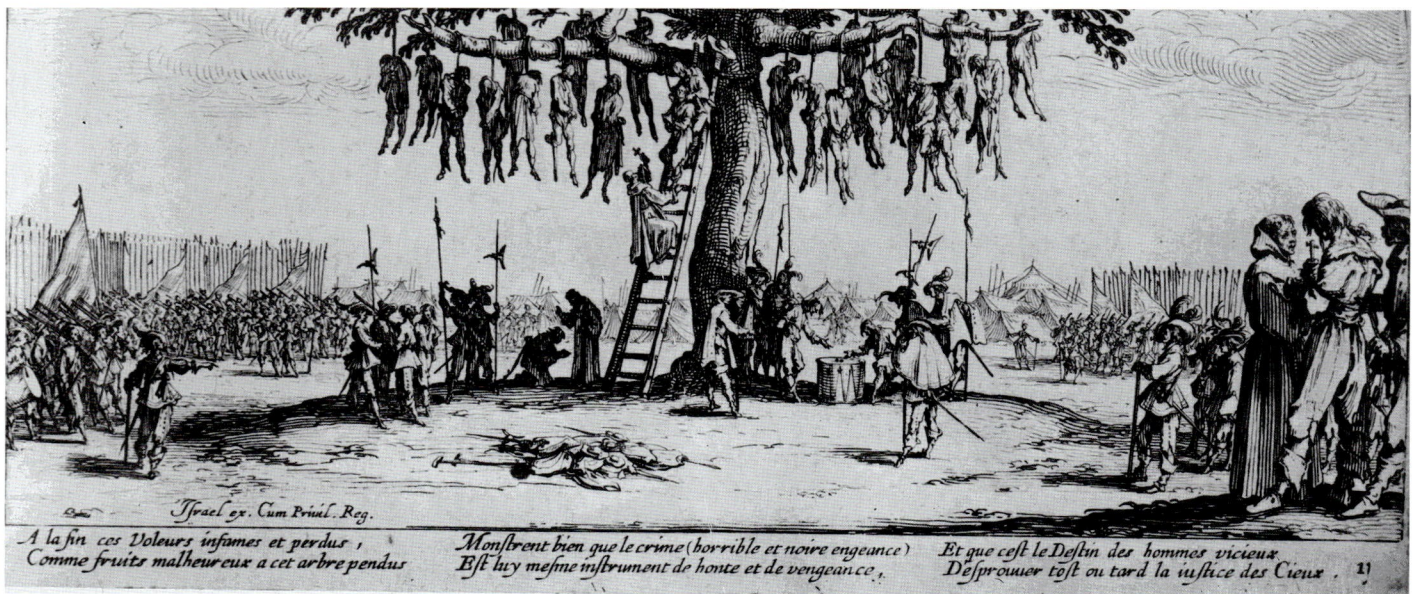

24-63 JACQUES CALLOT, *Hanging Tree*, from the *Large Miseries of War* series, 1633. Etching, $3\frac{3}{4}'' \times 7\frac{1}{4}''$. Bibliothèque Nationale, Paris.

of etchings called *Large Miseries of War.* Callot confined himself almost exclusively to the art of etching and was widely influential in his own time and since; Rembrandt was among those who knew and learned from his work. Callot perfected the medium and the technique of etching, developing a very hard surface for the copper plate to permit fine and precise delineation with the needle. In one small print, he assembled as many as 1,200 figures, which the viewer can discern only through close scrutiny. His quick, vivid touch and faultless drawing produced panoramas sparkling with sharp details of life—and death. In the *Large Miseries of War* series, he observed these details coolly, presenting without comment images based on events he himself must have seen in the wars in Lorraine.

In one etching, he depicted a mass execution by hanging (FIG. **24-63**). The unfortunates in *Hanging Tree* are thieves (identified as such by the text added to the bottom of the print in its second state by Michel de Marolles and approved by Callot). The event takes place in the presence of a disciplined army, drawn up on parade with banners, muskets, and lances, their tents in the background. Hanged men sway in clusters from the branches of a huge cross-shaped tree. A monk climbs a ladder, holding up a crucifix to a man while the executioner adjusts the noose around the man's neck. At the foot of the ladder, another victim kneels to receive absolution. Under the crucifix tree, men roll dice on a drumhead for the belongings of the executed. (This may be an allusion to the soldiers who cast lots for the garments of the crucified Christ.) In the right foreground, a hooded priest consoles a bound man. Callot's *Large Miseries of War* were among the first realistic pictorial records of the human disaster of armed conflict.

**REALISM, SPIRITUALISM, CLASSICISM** Because of the prominence of religious issues and the value Catholics placed on the didactic capabilities of art (as in Baroque Italy), religious art did have a presence in France. Among the artists well known for their religious imagery was the painter GEORGES DE LA TOUR (1593–1652). His work, particularly his use of light, suggests a familiarity with Caravaggio's art. La Tour may have learned about Caravaggio from the Dutch school of Utrecht. Although La Tour used the devices of the northern Caravaggisti, his effects are strikingly different from theirs. His *Adoration of the Shepherds* (FIG. **24-64**) makes use of the night setting favored by that school, much as van Honthorst (FIG.

24-41) portrayed it. But here, the light, its source shaded by an old man's hand, falls upon a very different company in a very different mood. A group of humble men and women, coarsely clad, gather in prayerful vigil around a luminous baby Jesus. Without the aid of the title, this might be construed as a genre piece, a narrative of some event from peasant life. Nothing in the environment, placement, poses, dress, or attributes of the figures distinguishes them as the scriptural Virgin Mary, Joseph, Christ Child, or shepherds. The artist did not portray halos, choirs of angels, stately architecture, or resplendent grandees. The light is not spiritual but material; it comes from a candle. La Tour's scientific scrutiny of the effects of material light, as it throws precise shadows on surfaces that intercept it, nevertheless had religious intention and consequence. The light illuminates a group of ordinary people held in a mystic trance induced by their witnessing the miracle of the Incarnation. In this timeless tableau of simple people, La Tour eliminated the dogmatic significance and traditional iconography of the Incarnation. Still, these people reverently contemplate something they regard as holy. It is

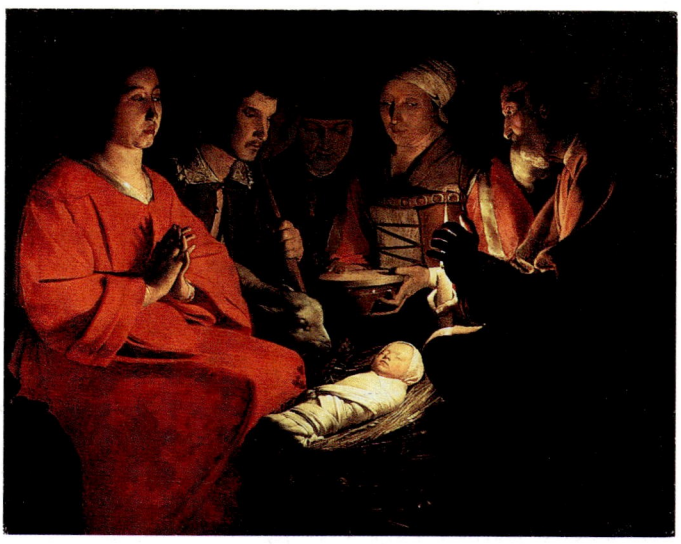

24-64 GEORGES DE LA TOUR, *Adoration of the Shepherds*, 1645–1650. Oil on canvas, approx. 3′ 6″ × 4′ 6″. Louvre, Paris.

clear that the painting is readable to the devout of any religious persuasion, whether or not they know of this central mystery of the Christian faith.

The supernatural calm that pervades this picture is characteristic of the mood of Georges de La Tour's art. He achieved this by eliminating motion and emotive gesture (only the light is dramatic), by suppressing surface detail, and by simplifying body volumes. These stylistic traits are among those associated with classical art and art based on classical principles—for example, that of Piero della Francesca (see FIGS. 21-49 and 21-50). Several apparently contrary elements meet in the work of La Tour: classical composure, fervent spirituality, and genre realism.

**ART IN THE SERVICE OF ABSOLUTISM** Perhaps the preeminent patron of the period was King Louis XIV. Determined to consolidate and expand his power, Louis XIV was a master of political strategy and propaganda. He ensured subservience by anchoring his rule in divine right (a belief in a king's absolute power as God's will), rendering Louis's authority incontestable. So convinced was he of his importance and centrality to the French kingdom that he eagerly adopted the nickname "le Roi Soleil" ("the Sun King"). Like the sun, Louis was the center of the universe. He also established a carefully crafted and nuanced relationship with the nobility. He allowed nobles sufficient benefits to keep them pacified but simultaneously maintained rigorous control to avoid insurrection or rebellion.

Louis's desire for control extended to all realms of French life, including art. Louis XIV and his principal adviser, Jean-Baptiste Colbert (1619–1683), were determined to organize art and architecture in the service of the state. The king understood well the power of art as propaganda and the value of visual imagery for cultivating a public persona, and no pains were spared to raise great symbols and monuments to the king's absolute power. The efforts of Louis XIV and Colbert to regularize taste were furthered by the foundation of the Royal Academy of Painting and Sculpture in 1648, which served to accelerate the establishment of the French classical style.

The portrait of Louis XIV (FIG. **24-65**) by HYACINTHE RIGAUD (1659–1743) conveys the image of an absolute monarch in control. The king, 63 when this work was painted, looks out at the viewer with directness. The suggestion of haughtiness is perhaps

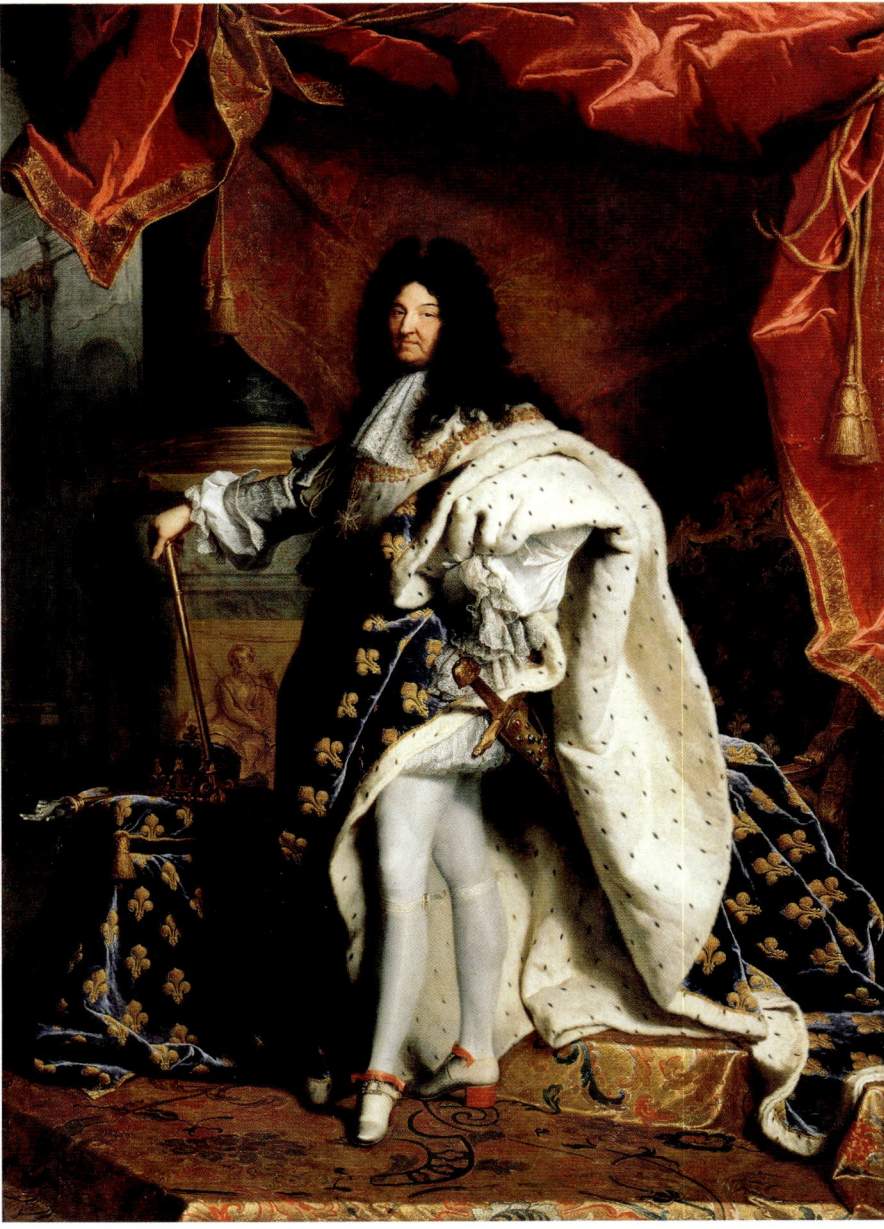

**24-65** HYACINTHE RIGAUD, *Louis XIV,* 1701. Oil on canvas, approx. 9′ 2″ × 6′ 3″. Louvre, Paris.

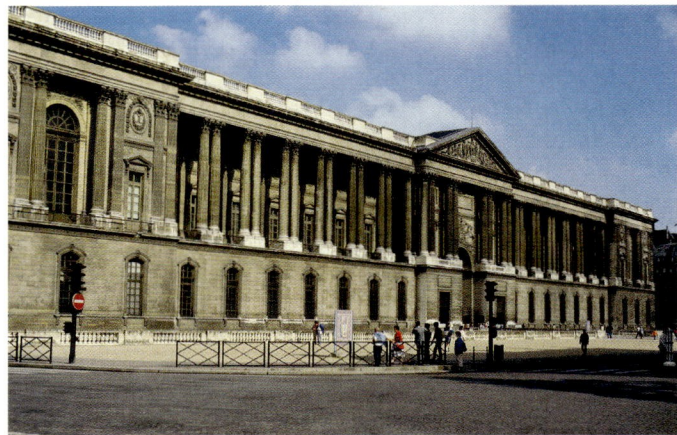

**24-66** CLAUDE PERRAULT, LOUIS LE VAU, and CHARLES LE BRUN, east facade of the Louvre, Paris, France, 1667–1670.

due to the pose—Louis XIV stands with his left hand on his hip and with his elegant ermine-lined coronation robes thrown over his shoulder. This portrait's majesty is also derived from the composition. The king is the unmistakable focal point of the image, and the artist placed him so that he seems to look down on the viewer. Given that Louis XIV was very short in stature—only five feet, four inches, a fact that drove him to invent the red-heeled shoes he wears in the portrait—it seems the artist catered to his patron's wishes. The carefully detailed environment in which the king stands also contributes to the painting's stateliness and

grandiosity. So insistent was Louis XIV that the best artists serve his needs that he maintained a workshop of artists, each with a specialization—faces, fabric, architecture, landscapes, armor, or fur. Thus, many of the king's portraits were a group effort.

**THE NEW OFFICIAL FRENCH TASTE** Once young Louis XIV had formally ascended to power, the first project he and his adviser Colbert undertook was the closing of the east side of the Louvre court, left incomplete by Lescot in the 16th century. Bernini, as the most renowned architect of his day, was summoned from Rome to submit plans, but he envisioned an Italian palace on a monumental scale that would have involved the demolition of all previous work. His plan rejected, Bernini returned to Rome in high indignation. Instead, the Louvre's east facade (FIG. **24-66**) was a collaboration among CLAUDE PERRAULT (1613–1688), LOUIS LE VAU (1612–1670), and CHARLES LE BRUN (1619–1690). The design is a brilliant synthesis of French and Italian classical elements, culminating in a new and definitive formula. The French pavilion system was retained. The central pavilion is in the form of a classical temple front, and a giant colonnade of paired columns, resembling the columned flanks of a temple folded out like wings, is contained by the two salient pavilions at both ends. The whole is mounted on a stately basement, or podium. The designers favored an even roofline, balustraded and broken only by the central pediment, over the traditional French pyramidal roof. The emphatically horizontal sweep of this facade brushed aside all memory of Gothic verticality. Its stately proportions and monumentality were both an expression of the new official French taste and a symbol of centrally organized authority.

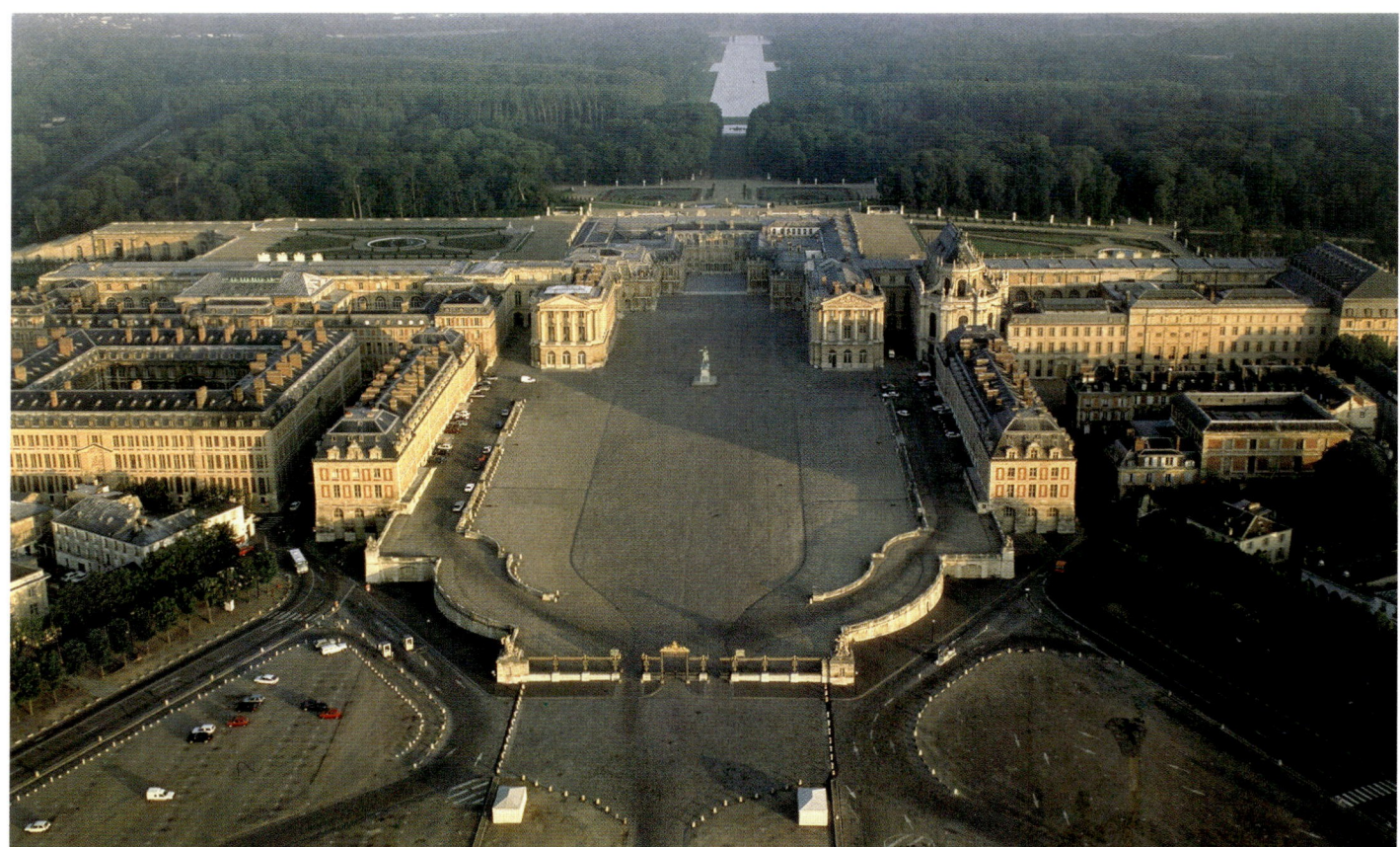

**24-67** Aerial view of palace at Versailles, France, begun 1669, and a portion of the gardens and surrounding area. The white rectangle in the lower part of the plan (FIG. 24-68) outlines the area shown here.

**FROM HUNTING LODGE TO PALACE** Work on the Louvre hardly had begun when Louis XIV decided to convert a royal hunting lodge at Versailles, a few miles outside Paris, into a great palace. A veritable army of architects, decorators, sculptors, painters, and landscape architects was assembled under the general management of Charles Le Brun, a former student of Poussin. In their hands, the conversion of a simple lodge into the palace of Versailles (FIGS. **24-67** and **24-68**) became the greatest architectural project of the age—a defining statement of French Baroque style and an undeniable symbol of Louis XIV's power and ambition.

Planned on a gigantic scale, the project called not only for a large palace flanking a vast park but also for the construction of a satellite city to house court and government officials, military and guard detachments, courtiers, and servants (undoubtedly to keep them all under the king's close supervision). This town was laid out to the east of the palace along three radial avenues that converge on the palace structure itself; their axes, in a symbolic assertion of the ruler's absolute power over his domains, intersected in the king's bedroom. (As the site of the king's morning levee, this bedroom was actually an audience room, a state chamber.) The palace itself, more than a quarter of a mile long, was placed at right angles to the dominant east-west axis that runs through city and park.

Careful attention was paid to every detail of the extremely rich decoration of the palace's interior. The architects and decorators designed everything from wall paintings to doorknobs, to reinforce the splendor of Versailles and to exhibit the very finest sense of artisanship. Of the literally hundreds of rooms within the

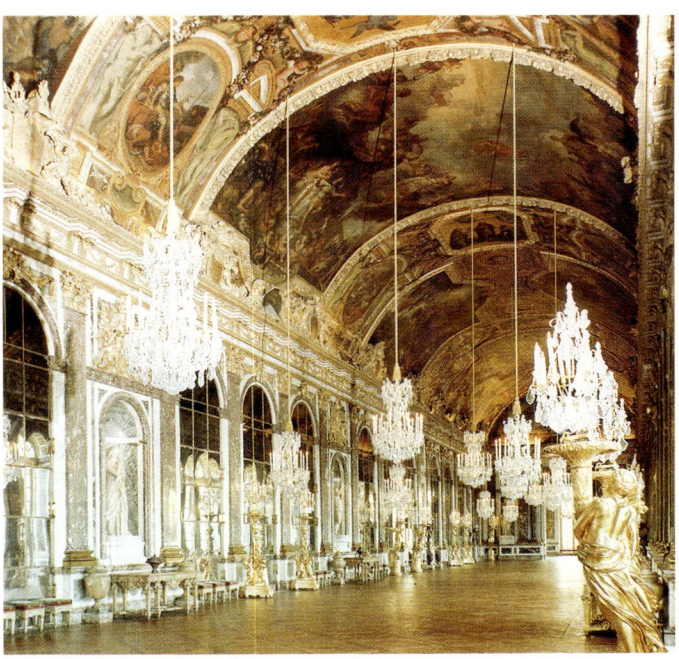

**24-69** JULES HARDOUIN-MANSART and CHARLES LE BRUN, Galerie des Glaces (Hall of Mirrors), palace of Versailles, Versailles, France, ca. 1680.

palace, the most famous is the Galerie des Glaces, or Hall of Mirrors (FIG. **24-69**), designed by JULES HARDOUIN-MANSART (1646–1708) and Charles Le Brun. This hall overlooks the park from the second floor and extends along most of the width of the central block. Although deprived of its original sumptuous furniture, which included gold and silver chairs and bejeweled trees, the Galerie des Glaces retains much of its splendor today. Its tunnel-like quality is alleviated by hundreds of mirrors, set into the wall opposite the windows, that illusionistically extend the width of the room. The mirror, that ultimate source of illusion, was a favorite element of Baroque interior design; here, it also enhanced the dazzling extravagance of the great festivals Louis XIV was so fond of hosting.

**CONTROLLING NATURE** The enormous palace might appear unbearably ostentatious were it not for its extraordinary setting in the vast park that makes it almost an adjunct. The Galerie des Glaces is dwarfed by the sweeping vista (seen from its windows) down the park's tree-lined central axis and across terraces, lawns, pools, and lakes toward the horizon. The park of Versailles, designed by ANDRÉ LE NÔTRE (1613–1700), must rank among the world's greatest artworks in both size and concept. Here, an entire forest was transformed into a park. Although the geometric plan (FIG. 24-68) may appear stiff and formal, the park in fact offers an almost unlimited variety of vistas, as Le Nôtre used not only the multiplicity of natural forms but also the terrain's slightly rolling contours with stunning effectiveness.

The formal gardens near the palace provide a rational transition from the frozen architectural forms to the natural living ones. Here, the elegant forms of trimmed shrubs and hedges define the tightly designed geometric units. Each unit is different from its neighbor and has a focal point in the form of a sculptured group, a pavilion, a reflecting pool, or perhaps a fountain. Farther away from the palace, the design loosens as trees, in shadowy masses, screen or frame views of open countryside. Le Nôtre carefully composed all vistas for maximum effect. Dark

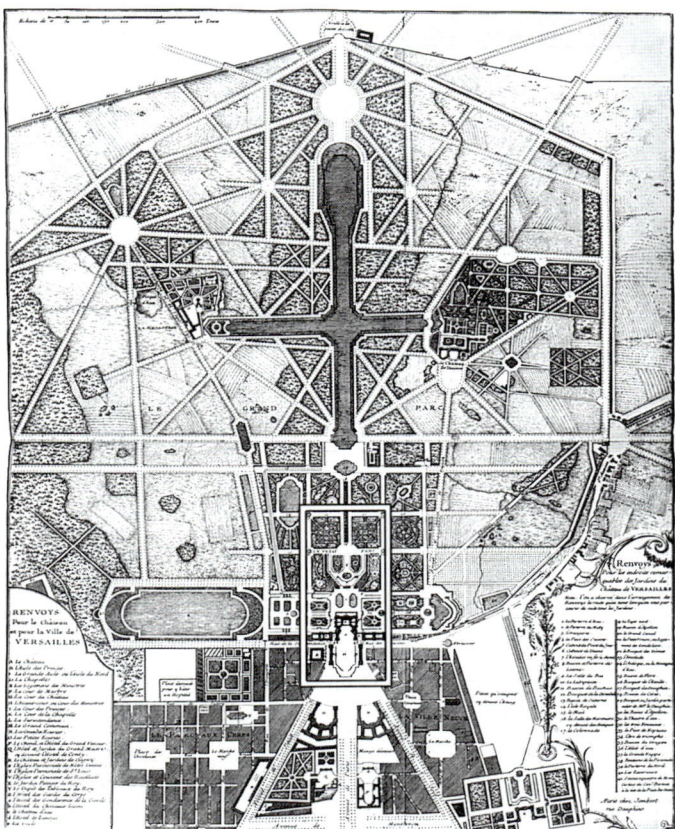

**24-68** Plan of the park, palace, and town of Versailles, France (after a 17th-century engraving by FRANÇOIS BLONDEL). The area outlined in the white rectangle (lower center) is shown in FIG. 24-67.

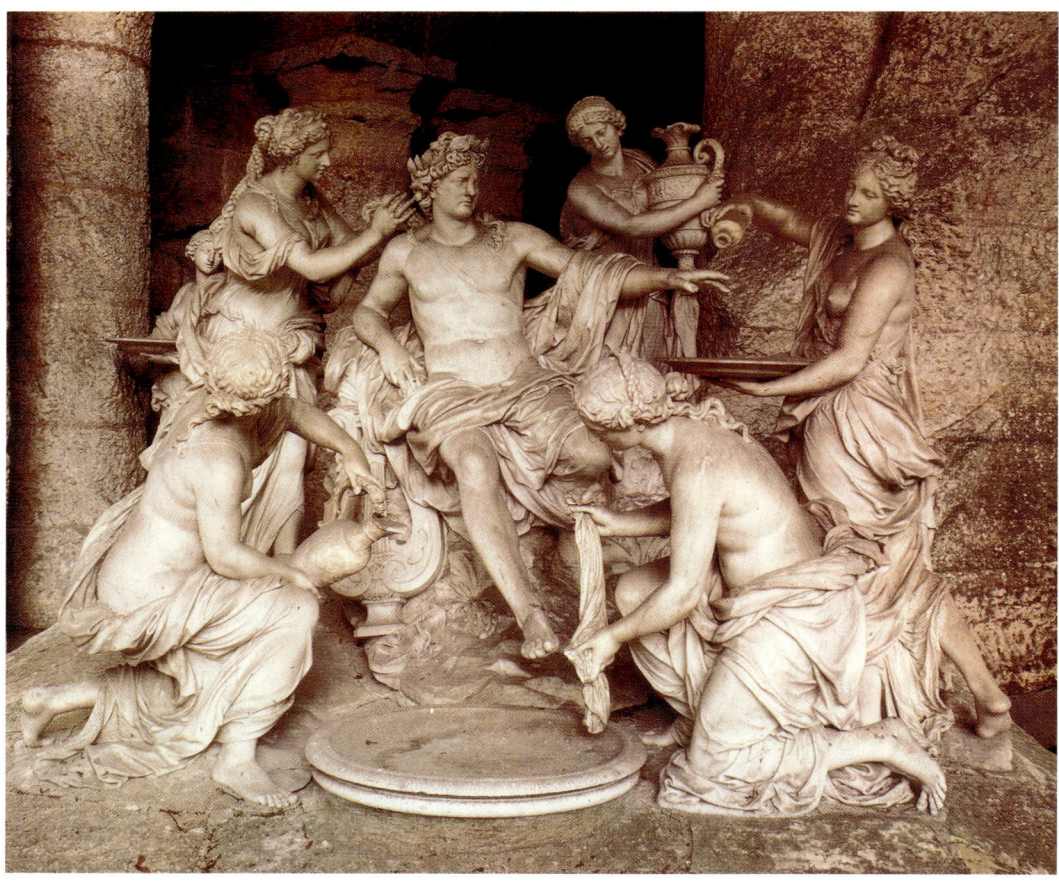

24-70 FRANÇOIS GIRARDON and THOMAS REGNAUDIN, *Apollo Attended by the Nymphs*, Grotto of Thetis, Park of Versailles, Versailles, France, ca. 1666–1672. Marble, life-size. Park of Versailles.

and light, formal and informal, dense growth and open meadows—all play against one another in unending combinations and variations. No photograph or series of photographs can reveal the design's full richness; the park unfolds itself only to people who actually walk through it. In this respect, it is a temporal artwork. Its aspects change with time and with the relative position of the observer.

**A GROTTO SCULPTURE FOR VERSAILLES** For the Grotto of Thetis in the gardens of Versailles, FRANÇOIS GIRARDON (1628–1715) designed *Apollo Attended by the Nymphs* (FIG. **24-70**) as a tableau group. Both stately and graceful, the nymphs have a compelling charm as they minister to the god Apollo at the end of the day. (The three nymphs in the background are the work of THOMAS REGNAUDIN, 1622–1706.) Girardon's close study of Greco-Roman sculpture heavily influenced his design of the figures, and Poussin's figure compositions (FIG. 24-58) inspired their arrangement. And if this combination did not suffice, the group's rather florid reference to Louis XIV as the "god of the sun" was bound to assure its success at court. Girardon's classical style and mythological symbolism were well suited to France's glorification of royal majesty.

**A SUBDUED ROYAL CHAPEL** After Le Vau's death, Jules Hardouin-Mansart, a great-nephew of François Mansart, completed the garden facade of the Versailles palace and in 1698 received a commission to add the Royal Chapel to the complex. The chapel's interior (FIG. **24-71**) is essentially a rectangular building with an apse as high as the nave, giving the fluid central space a curved Baroque quality. But the light entering through the large clerestory windows lacks the directed dramatic effect of the

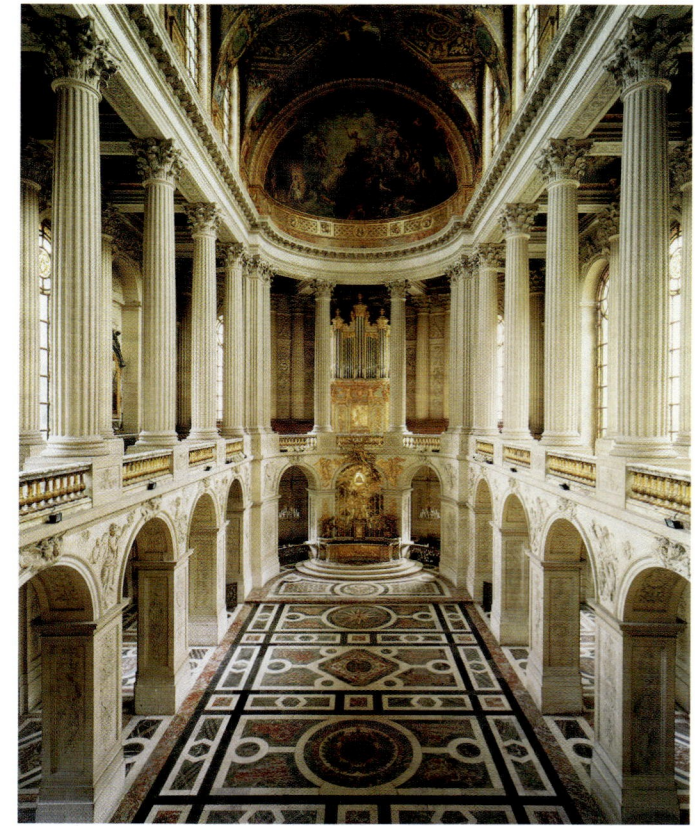

24-71 JULES HARDOUIN-MANSART, Royal Chapel, with ceiling decorations by Antoine Coypel, palace of Versailles, Versailles, France, 1698–1710.

Italian Baroque, instead illuminating the interior's precisely chiseled details brightly and evenly. Pier-supported arcades carry a majestic row of Corinthian columns that define the royal gallery. The royal pew occupies its rear, accessible directly from the king's apartments. The decoration is restrained, and only the illusionistic ceiling decorations, added in 1708–1709 by Antoine Coypel (1661–1722), suggest the drama and complexity of Italian Baroque art.

As a symbol of the power of absolutism, Versailles is unsurpassed. It also expresses, in the most monumental terms of its age, the rationalistic creed—based on scientific advances, such as the physics of Sir Isaac Newton (1642–1727) and the mathematical philosophy of René Descartes (1596–1650)—that all knowledge must be systematic and all science must be the consequence of the intellect imposed on matter. The whole stupendous design of Versailles proudly proclaims the mastery of human intelligence (and the mastery of Louis XIV) over the disorderliness of nature.

**A CHURCH FOR DISABLED SOLDIERS** Another of Hardouin-Mansart's masterworks, the Église de Dôme, Church of the Invalides in Paris (FIG. **24-72**), also makes reference to Italian Baroque architecture. An intricately composed domed square of great scale, the church is attached to the veterans' hospital Louis XIV set up for the disabled soldiers of his many wars. Two firmly separated levels, the upper one pedimented, compose the frontispiece. The grouping of the orders and of the bays they

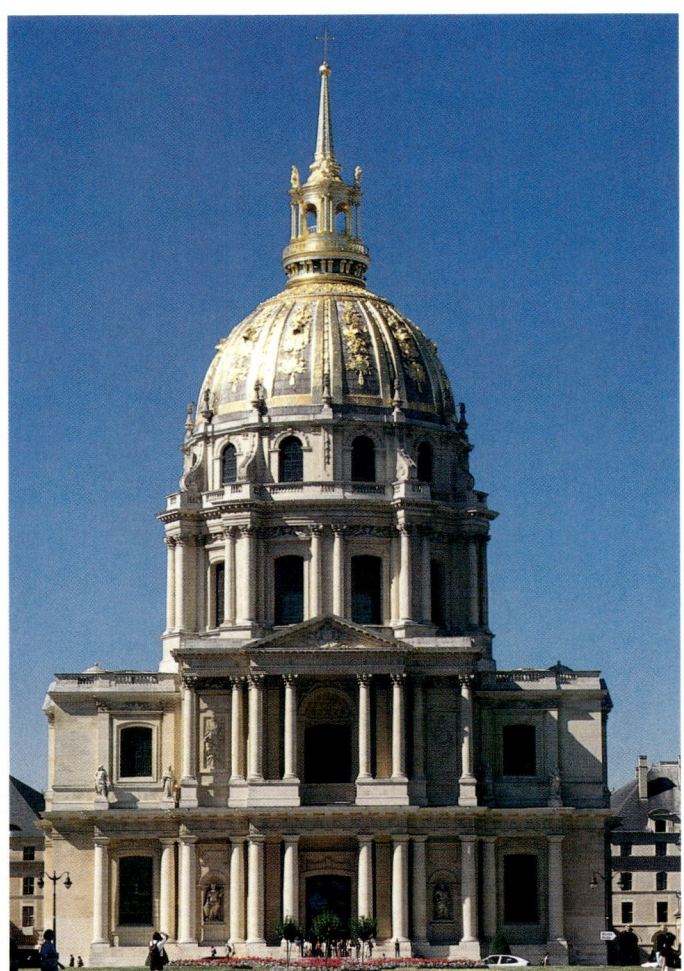

**24-72** Jules Hardouin-Mansart, Église de Dôme, Church of the Invalides, Paris, France, 1676–1706.

frame is not unlike that in Italian Baroque. The compact facade is low and narrow in relation to the vast drum and dome, seeming to serve simply as a base for them. The overpowering dome, conspicuous on the Parisian skyline, is itself expressive of the Italian Baroque love for dramatic magnitude, as is the way that its designer aimed for theatrical effects of light and space. The dome is built of three shells, the lowest cut off so that a visitor to the interior looks up through it to the one above, which is painted illusionistically with the *apotheosis* (deification) of Saint Louis, patron of France. This second dome, filled with light from hidden windows in the third, outermost dome, creates an impression of the open, limitless space and brightness of the heavens. Below, the building's interior is only dimly illuminated, and its design is based on a classicism only less severe than that of the Escorial (see FIG. 23-25).

## *England*

The authority of the absolute monarchy that prevailed in France was not found in England. Common law and the Parliament kept royal power in check. Thus, during the 17th and early 18th centuries, England experienced the development of both limited monarchy and constitutionalism. Although an important part of English life, religion was not the contentious issue it was on the continent. The religious affiliations of the English included Catholicism, Anglicanism, Protestantism, and Puritanism (the English version of Calvinism). In the economic realm, England was the one country (other than the Dutch Republic) to take advantage of the opportunities offered by overseas trade. As an island country, Britain (which after 1603 consisted of England, Wales, and Scotland), like the Dutch Republic, possessed a large and powerful navy, as well as excellent maritime capabilities.

English Baroque art does not have the focused character of either Dutch or Italian Baroque art. The one area of cultural production in which England made great strides was architecture, much of it incorporating classical elements.

**AN ARCHITECT TO KINGS** The revolution in English building was primarily the work of one man, Inigo Jones (1573–1652), architect to the kings James I and Charles I. Jones spent considerable time in Italy. He greatly admired the classical authority and restraint of Palladio's structures and studied with great care his treatise on architecture. Jones took many motifs from Palladio's villas and palaces, and he adopted Palladio's basic design principles for his own architecture. The nature of his achievement is evident in the buildings he designed for his royal patrons, among them the Banqueting House at Whitehall (FIG. **24-73**) in London. For this structure, a symmetrical block of great clarity and dignity, Jones superimposed two orders, using columns in the center and pilasters near the ends. The balustraded roofline, uninterrupted in its horizontal sweep, predated the Louvre's facade (FIG. 24-66) by more than 40 years. Palladio would have recognized and approved all of the design elements, but the building as a whole is not a copy of his work. While relying on the revered Italian's architectural vocabulary and syntax, Jones retained his own independence as a designer. For two centuries his influence was almost as authoritative in English architecture as that of Palladio. In a fruitful collaboration recalling the combination of Veronese paintings and Palladian architecture in northern Italian villas, Jones's interior at Whitehall is adorned with several important Rubens paintings.

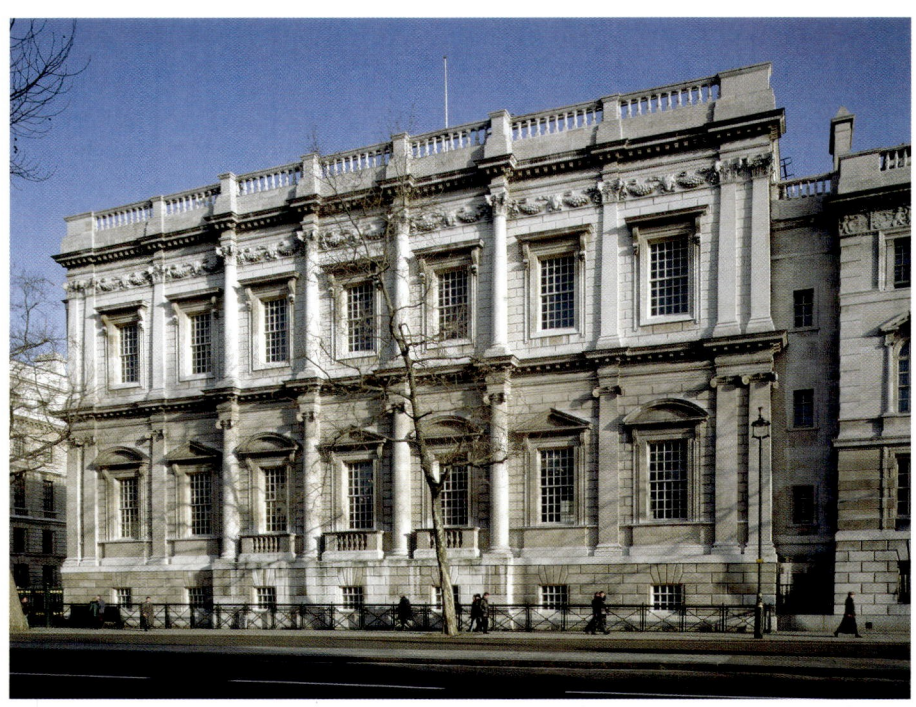

**24-73** Inigo Jones, Banqueting House at Whitehall, London, England, 1619–1622.

**A TOWERING ARCHITECTURAL TALENT** Until almost the present, the dominant feature of the London skyline was the majestic dome of Saint Paul's Cathedral (FIG. **24-74**), the work of England's most renowned architect, Christopher Wren (1632–1723). A mathematical genius and skilled engineer whose work won Isaac Newton's praise, Wren was appointed professor of astronomy in London at age 25. Mathematics led to architecture, and Charles II asked Wren to prepare a plan for restoring the old Gothic church of Saint Paul. Wren proposed to remodel the building based on Roman structures. Within a few months, the

**24-74** Sir Christopher Wren, new Saint Paul's Cathedral, London, England, 1675–1710.

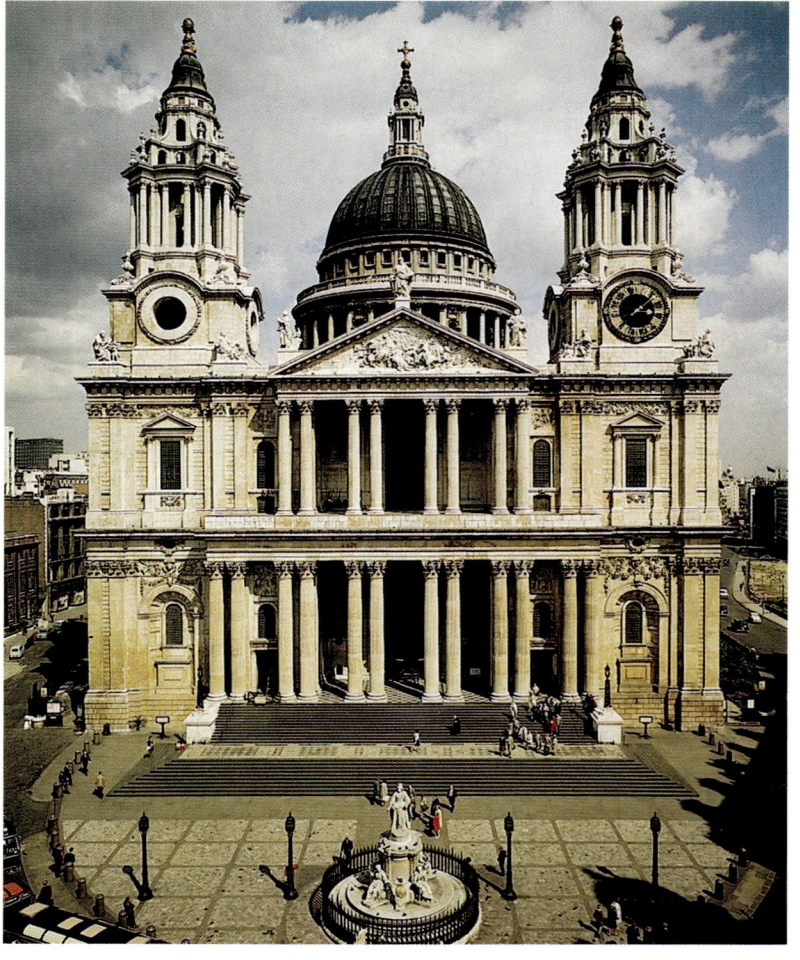

Great Fire of London, which destroyed the old structure and many churches in the city in 1666, gave Wren his opportunity. He built not only the new Saint Paul's but numerous other churches as well.

Although Wren was strongly influenced by Jones's work, he also traveled in France, where he must have been much impressed by the splendid palaces and state buildings being created in and around Paris at the time of the competition for the Louvre design. Wren also must have closely studied prints illustrating Baroque architecture in Italy, for he harmonized Palladian, French, and Italian Baroque features in Saint Paul's.

In view of its size, the cathedral was built with remarkable speed—in a little more than 30 years—and Wren lived to see it completed. The building's form was constantly refined as it went up, and the final appearance of the towers was not determined until after 1700. In the splendid skyline composition, two foreground towers act effectively as foils to the great dome. This must have been suggested to Wren by similar schemes that Italian architects devised for Saint Peter's in Rome (see FIGS. 22-29 and 24-2) to solve the problem of the relationship between the facade and dome. Certainly, the upper levels and lanterns of the towers are Borrominesque (FIG. 24-12), the lower levels are Palladian, and the superposed paired columnar porticos recall the Louvre facade (FIG. 24-66). Wren's skillful eclecticism brought all these foreign features into a monumental unity.

Wren's designs for the city churches were masterpieces of careful planning and ingenuity. His task was never easy, for the churches often had to be fitted into small, irregular areas. Wren worked out a rich variety of schemes to meet awkward circumstances. When designing the church exteriors, he concentrated his attention on the towers, the one element that would set the building apart from its crowding neighbors. The skyline of London, as Wren left it, is punctuated with such towers, which served as prototypes for later buildings both in England and in colonial America.

# LATE BAROQUE ART OF THE EARLY 18TH CENTURY

## Late Baroque Architecture in England

**A SPLENDID COUNTRY HOUSE** In 1705, while Saint Paul's was being completed, the British government commissioned a monumental palace in Oxfordshire, Blenheim (FIG. 24-75), for John Churchill, duke of Marlborough. The palace was a reward for Churchill's military exploits; people throughout the country acclaimed his victory over the French in 1704 at the Battle of Blenheim during the War of the Spanish Succession. Designed by JOHN VANBRUGH (1664–1726), Blenheim was one of the largest of the splendid country houses built during the period of prosperity resulting from Great Britain's expansion into the New World. At that time, a small group of architects associated with the aging Sir Christopher Wren was responsible for briefly returning Italian Baroque complexity to favor over the streamlined Palladian classicism of Inigo Jones. Vanbrugh was the best known of this group. The picturesque silhouette he created for Blenheim,

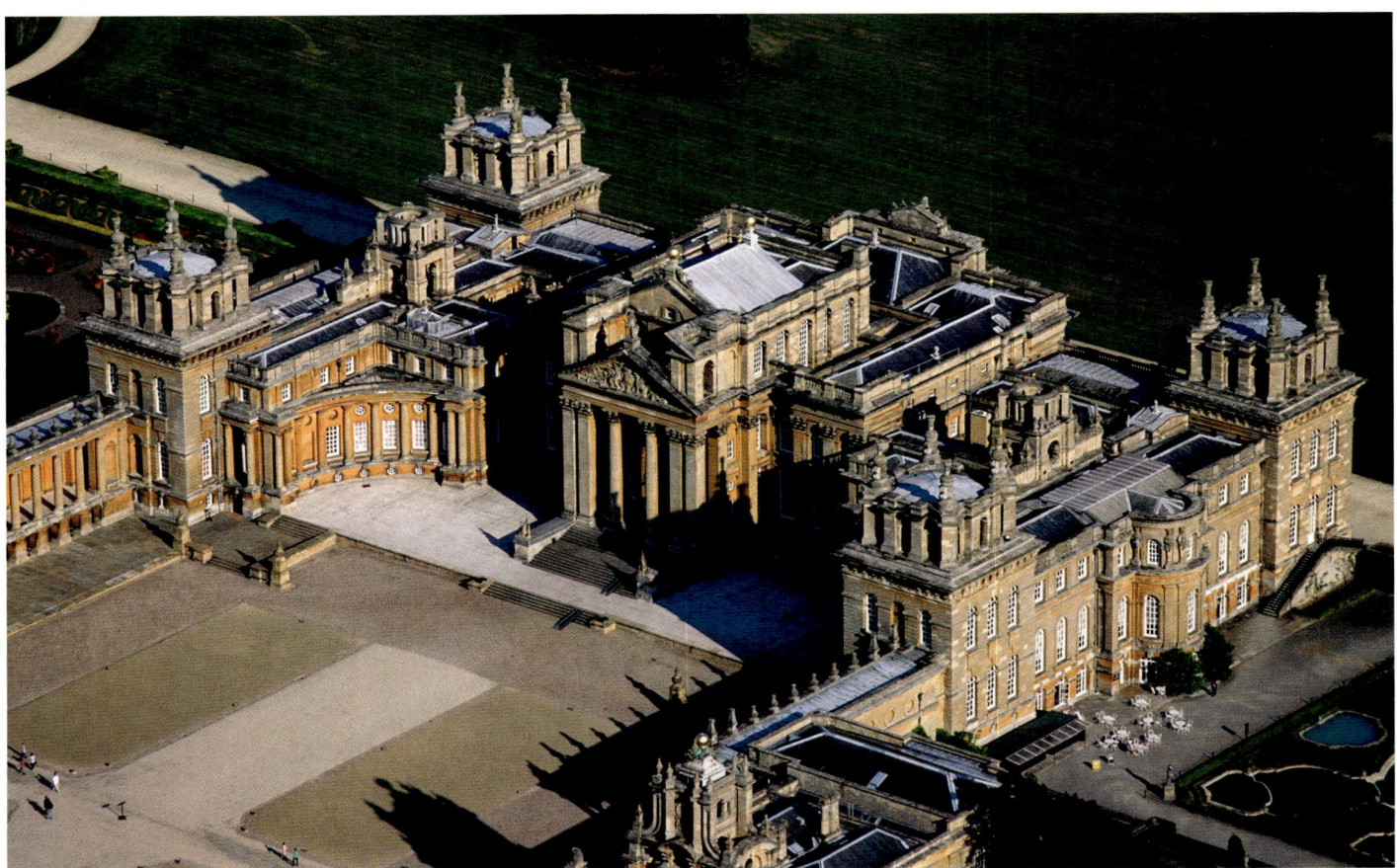

**24-75** JOHN VANBRUGH, Blenheim Palace, Oxfordshire, England, 1705–1722.

with its inventive architectural detail, recalls Italian Baroque architecture. The design demonstrates his love of variety and contrast, tempered by his ability to create focus areas such as those found so frequently in 17th-century architecture. The tremendous forecourt, the hugely projecting pavilions, and the extended colonnades simultaneously recall Saint Peter's and Versailles (FIGS. 24-4 and 24-67). Perhaps because Vanbrugh had begun his career as a writer of witty and popular comedies and as the builder of a theater for producing them, all of his architecture tended toward the theatrical on a mighty and extravagant scale. Like many Baroque architects, he even sacrificed convenience for dramatic effect, as in placing the Blenheim kitchen some 200 feet from the majestic dining salon. Vanbrugh's architecture pleased his patrons in the beginning, but even before Blenheim was completed, critics were condemning what they considered its ponderous and bizarre qualities.

## Late Baroque Art and Architecture in Germany and Italy

**COMBINING THE ARTS** The work of Italians Borromini and Guarini strongly influenced the ecclesiastical architecture of southern Germany and Austria. One of the most splendid of the German buildings is the pilgrimage church of Vierzehnheiligen (Fourteen Saints) designed by BALTHASAR NEUMANN (1687–1753) and built near Staffelstein. Born in the German part of Bohemia, Neumann traveled in Austria and northern Italy and studied in Paris before returning home to become one of the most active architects working in his native land. Numerous large windows in the richly decorated but continuous walls of Vierzehnheiligen flood the interior with an even, bright, and cheerful light. The pilgrimage church sanctuary (FIG. 24-76) exhibits a vivacious play of architectural fantasy that retains Italian Baroque's dynamic energy but banishes all its dramatic qualities.

Vierzehnheiligen's complexity is readable in its ground plan (FIG. 24-77), which has been called one of the most ingenious pieces of architectural design ever conceived. The straight line seems to have been banished deliberately. The composition is made up of tangent ovals and circles, achieving a quite different interior effect within the essential outlines of the traditional Gothic church (apse, transept, nave, and western towers). Undulating space is in continuous motion, creating unlimited vistas bewildering in their variety and surprise effects. The structure's features pulse, flow, and commingle as if they were ceaselessly in the process of being molded. The design's fluidity of line, the floating and hovering surfaces, the interwoven spaces, and the dematerialized masses combine to suggest a "frozen" counterpart to the intricacy of voices in a Bach fugue. The church is a brilliant ensemble of architecture, painting, sculpture, and music, dissolving the boundaries of the arts in a visionary unity.

**SCULPTURE RENDERED WEIGHTLESS** The desire to achieve this unity of various artistic mediums propelled architects and artists in Germany and Austria to explore further the illusionistic capabilities of each medium. EGID QUIRIN ASAM (1692–1750) created the group *Assumption of the Virgin* (FIG. 24-78) for the space above the altar in the monastery church at Rohr, Germany. Asam designed the church in collaboration with his brother Cosmas Damian Asam (1686–1739). Influenced by the Late

24-76 BALTHASAR NEUMANN, interior of the pilgrimage chapel of Vierzehnheiligen, near Staffelstein, Germany, 1743–1772.

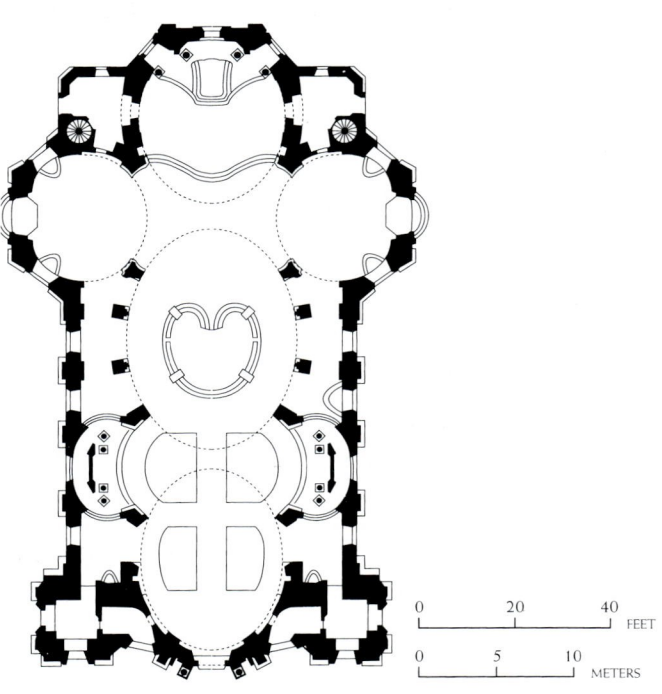

24-77 Plan of Vierzehnheiligen, near Staffelstein, Germany.

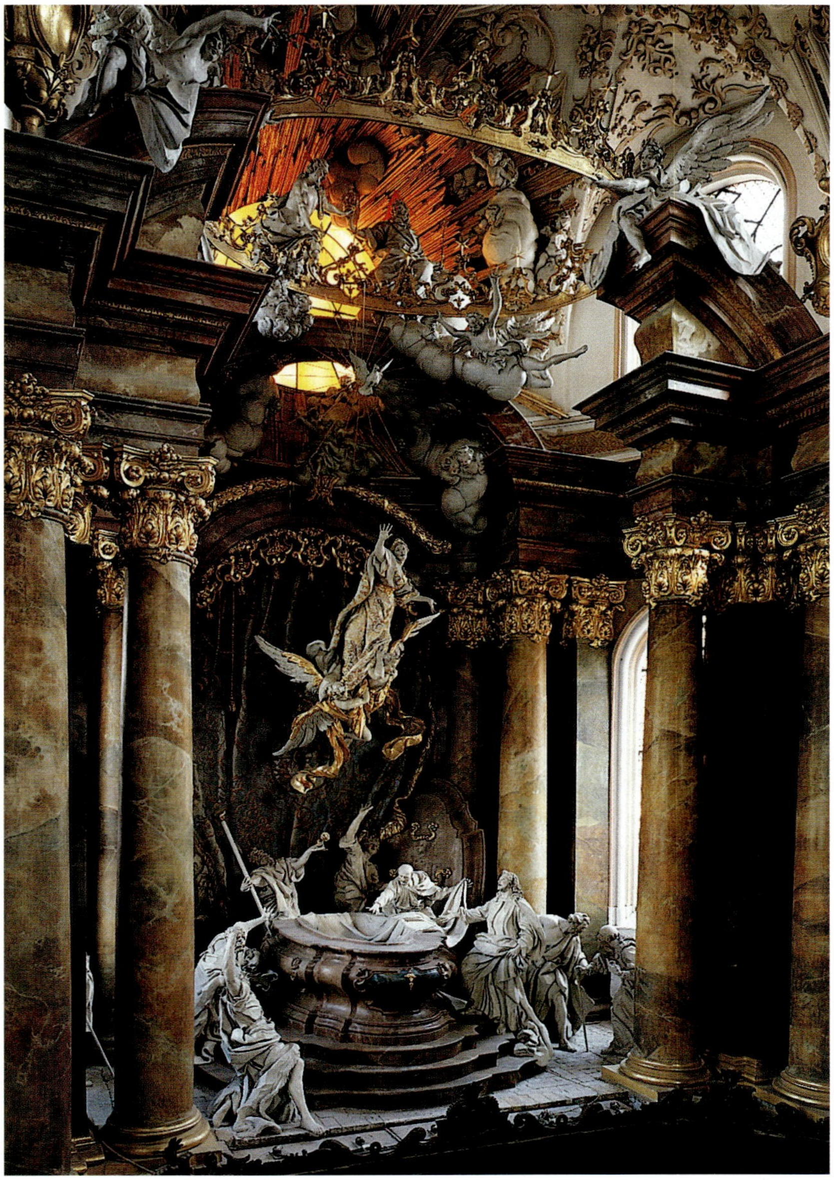

Baroque architecture they saw on a trip to Rome, the brothers returned to Germany with a feeling for illusionistic spectacle. In Egid Quirin Asam's *Assumption of the Virgin,* as in Bernini's *Ecstasy of Saint Teresa* (FIG. 24-9), the miraculous is made real before the viewer's eyes, a spiritual vision materially visible. The Virgin, effortlessly borne aloft by angels, soars to the glowing paradise above her, while the apostolic witnesses below gesticulate in astonishment around her vacant tomb. The figures ascending to Heaven have gilded details that set them apart from those remaining on Earth. The setting is a luxuriously ornamented theater. The scene itself is pure opera—an art perfected and very popular in the 18th century. Here, sculpture dissolves into painting, theater, and music, its mass rendered weightless, its naturally compact composition broken up and diffused. In this instance, Asam used sculpture, paradoxically, to disguise substance and function, weight and tactility, in the interest of eye-deceiving mystical illusion.

**IMAGINATIVE PAINTED FESTIVALS** Illusion in painting, particularly for the ceilings of churches and palaces in Italy and France, was already a venerable tradition by the beginning of the 18th century. The ceilings of Late Baroque palaces sometimes became painted festivals for the imagination. The master of such works, GIAMBATTISTA TIEPOLO (1696–1770), was the last great Italian painter until the 20th century to have an international impact. Of Venetian origin, Tiepolo worked for patrons in Austria, Germany, and Spain, as well as in Italy, leaving a strong impression wherever he went. His bright, cheerful colors and relaxed compositions were ideally suited to Late Baroque architecture. *The Apotheosis of the Pisani Family* (FIG. 24-79), a ceiling fresco in the Villa Pisani at Stra in northern Italy, shows airy figures fluttering through vast sunlit skies and fleecy clouds, their forms making dark accents against the brilliant light of high noon. As the title indicates, Pisani family members are elevated here to the rank of the gods in a heavenly scene that recalls the ceiling paintings of Correggio (see FIG. 22-41) and Pozzo (FIG. 24-27). While retaining 17th-century illusionistic tendencies, Tiepolo softened the rhetoric and created pictorial schemes of great elegance and grace, unsurpassed for their sheer effectiveness as decor.

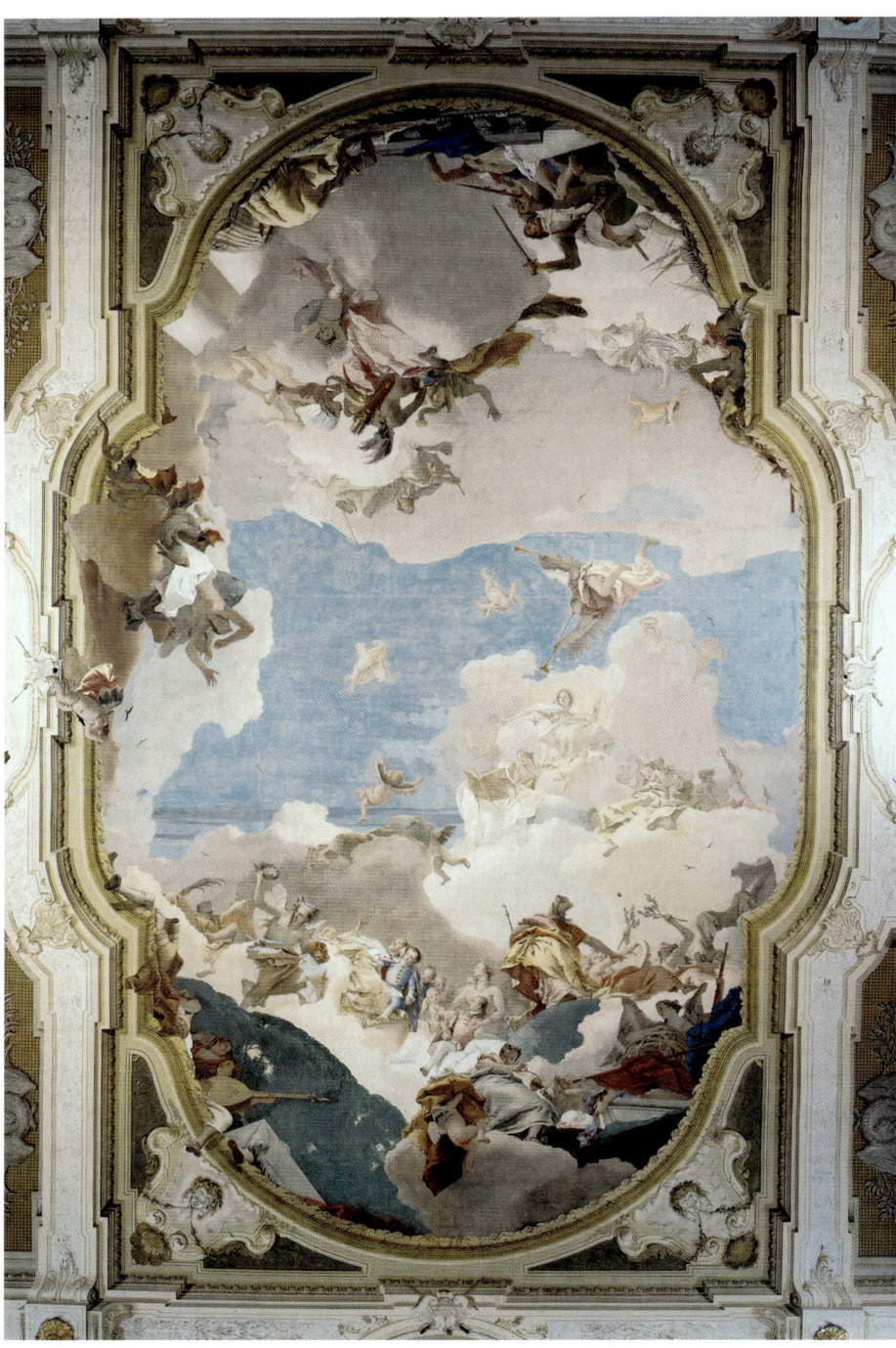

**24-79** GIAMBATTISTA TIEPOLO, *The Apotheosis of the Pisani Family,* ceiling fresco in the Villa Pisani, Stra, Italy, 1761–1762.

## CONCLUSION

The art produced during the 17th and early 18th centuries was truly diverse, making any comprehensive summary of the "Baroque" period impossible. Each country encountered a different set of historical challenges, and even within country boundaries a wide variety of art forms emerged. For example, whereas drama and complexity were hallmarks of much of Italian Baroque art (especially that commissioned for the Catholic Church), Dutch Baroque art was characterized to a greater degree by restrained genre scenes, still lifes, and portraits produced for a growing class of merchant patrons. Despite this period's lack of consistency in artistic development, its legacy was lasting. Many of the concerns of 17th-century and early-18th-century artists, such as direct observation, emotional intensity, and manipulation of light and color, laid the foundation for two styles that emerged in the late 18th century, Neoclassicism and Romanticism. Further, the influence of such artists as Caravaggio, Bernini, Velázquez, Rubens, Rembrandt, and Vermeer, among many others, resonates in art to the present day.

Philip III of Spain | Philip IV of Spain | Charles II of Spain | Philip V of Spain | Ferdinand VI of Spain

Henry IV of France | Louis XIII of France (Dominated by Cardinal Richelieu), Marie de' Medici, Regent 1610–1614 | Louis XIV of France (Dominated by Cardinal Mazarin until 1661) | Louis XV of France

James I of England | Charles I of England | England under Cromwell | Charles II of England | James II | William and Mary | Anne | George I of England | George II of England

- William Shakespeare, 1564–1616

**1600**

- Pope Paul V, r. 1605–1621
- Galileo Galilei refines telescope, 1609
- Johannes Kepler's laws of planetary motion, 1609–1619
- Thirty Years' War begins, 1618

**1620**

- William Harvey discovers blood circulation, 1619
- Pope Urban VIII, r. 1623–1644
- Blaise Pascal, 1623–1662

**1630**

- René Descartes, Discourse on Method, 1637

**1640**

- Pope Innocent X, r. 1644–1655
- French Royal Academy of Painting and Sculpture founded, 1648
- United Provinces of the Netherlands formed, 1648
- Thirty Years' War ends, 1648

**1650**

- Pope Alexander VII, r. 1655–1667

**1660**

- Royal Society founded in London, 1662

**1670**

**1680**

- Sir Isaac Newton's laws of motion, gravitation, 1687

**1690**

**1700**

**1710**

**1720**

**1730**

**1740**

- Excavation of Pompeii begins, 1748

**1750**

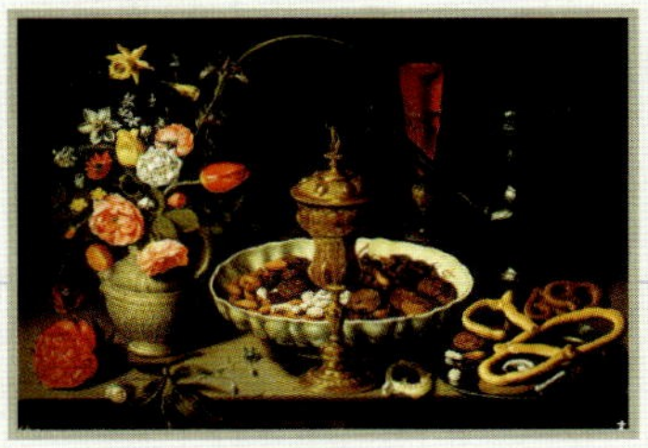

1 Clara Peeters, *Still Life with Flowers, Goblet, Dried Fruit, and Pretzels*, 1611

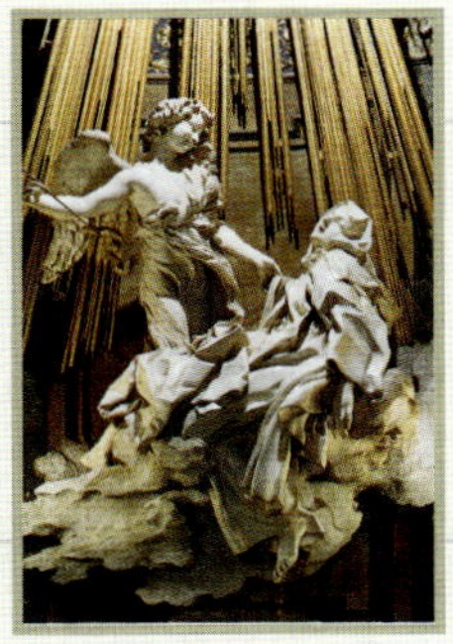

2 Gianlorenzo Bernini, *Ecstasy of Saint Teresa*, 1645–1652

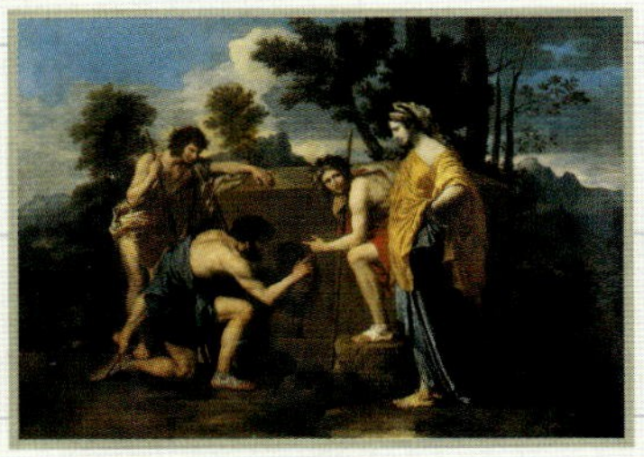

3 Nicolas Poussin, *Et in Arcadia Ego*, ca. 1655

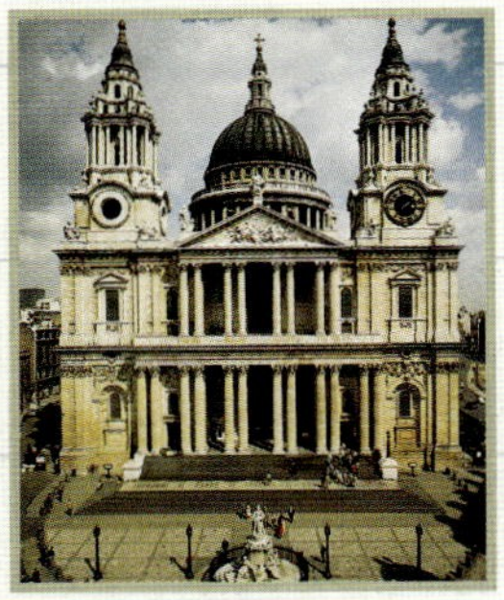

4 Sir Christopher Wren, new Saint Paul's Cathedral, 1675–1710

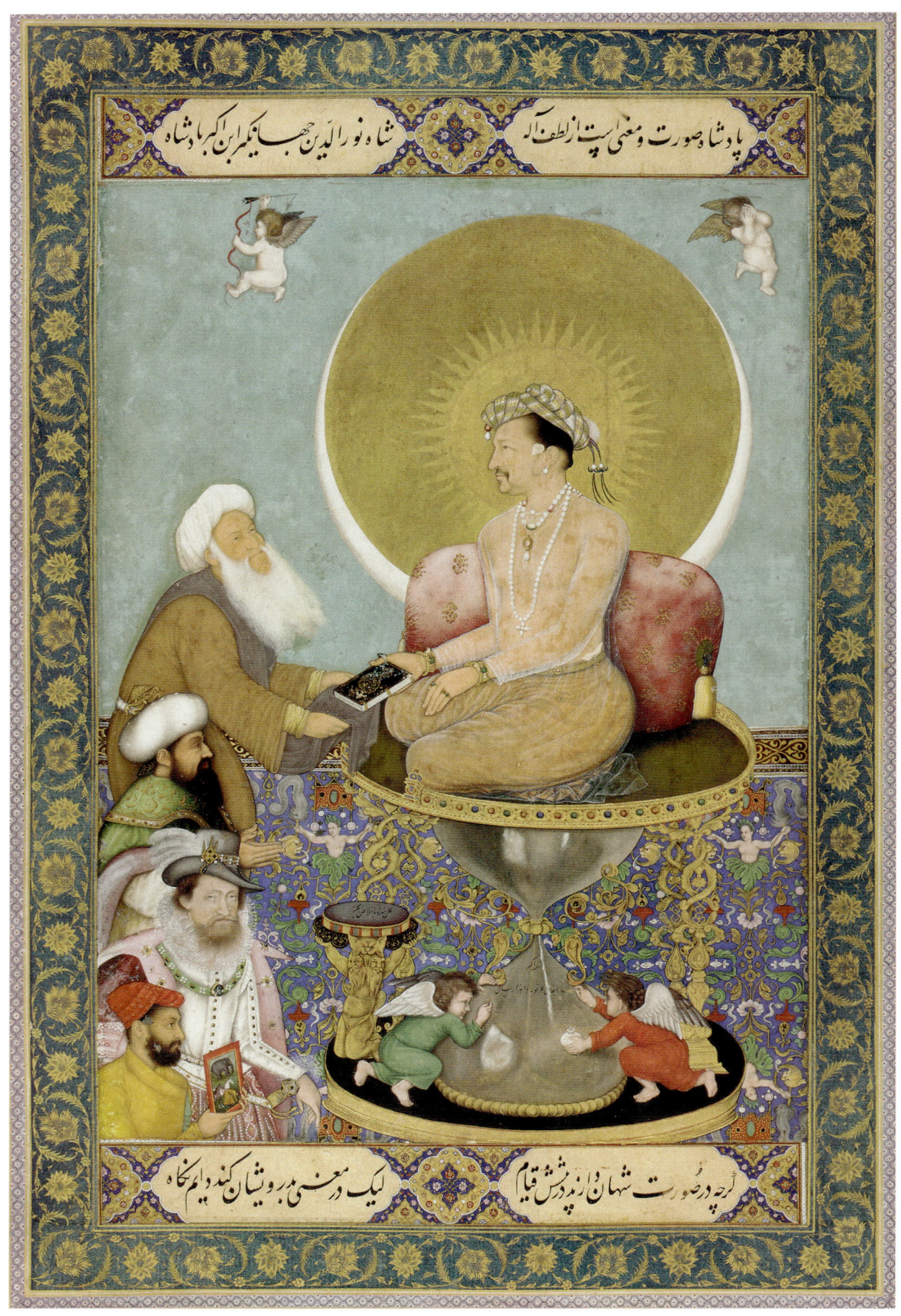

Bɪᴄʜɪᴛʀ, *Jahangir Preferring a Sufi Shaykh to Kings*, ca. 1615–1618. Opaque watercolor on paper, 1′ 6$\frac{7}{8}$″ × 1′ 1″. Freer Gallery of Art, Washington, D.C.

# 25

# SULTANS, KINGS, EMPERORS, AND COLONISTS

## THE ART OF SOUTH AND SOUTHEAST ASIA AFTER 1200

Arab armies first appeared in South Asia—at Sind (Pakistan)—in 712 (MAP **25-1**). With them came Islam, the new religion that had already spread with astonishing speed from the Arabian peninsula to Syria, Iraq, Iran, Egypt, North Africa, and even southern Spain (see Chapter 13). At first, the Muslims established trading settlements but did not press deeper into the subcontinent. At the Battle of Tarain in 1192, however, Muhammad of Ghor (Afghanistan) defeated the armies of a confederation of Indian states. The Ghorids and other Islamic rulers gradually transformed Indian society, religion, and art.

## INDIA

### *Sultanate of Delhi (1206–1526)*

Qutb al-Din Aybak, Muhammad of Ghor's general, established the Sultanate of Delhi in 1206 and, on his death in 1211, passed power on to his son. Iltutmish (r. 1211–1236) extended Ghorid rule across northern India.

**THE WORLD'S TALLEST MINARET** To mark the triumph of Islam, Qutb al-Din Aybak built a great congregational mosque (see "The Mosque," Chapter 13, page 361) at Delhi, in part with pillars taken from Hindu and other temples he demolished. He named Delhi's first mosque the Quwwat al-Islam, or Might of Islam, Mosque. During the course of the next century, as the Islamic population of Delhi grew, the sultans enlarged the mosque to more than triple its original size. Construction of the mosque's

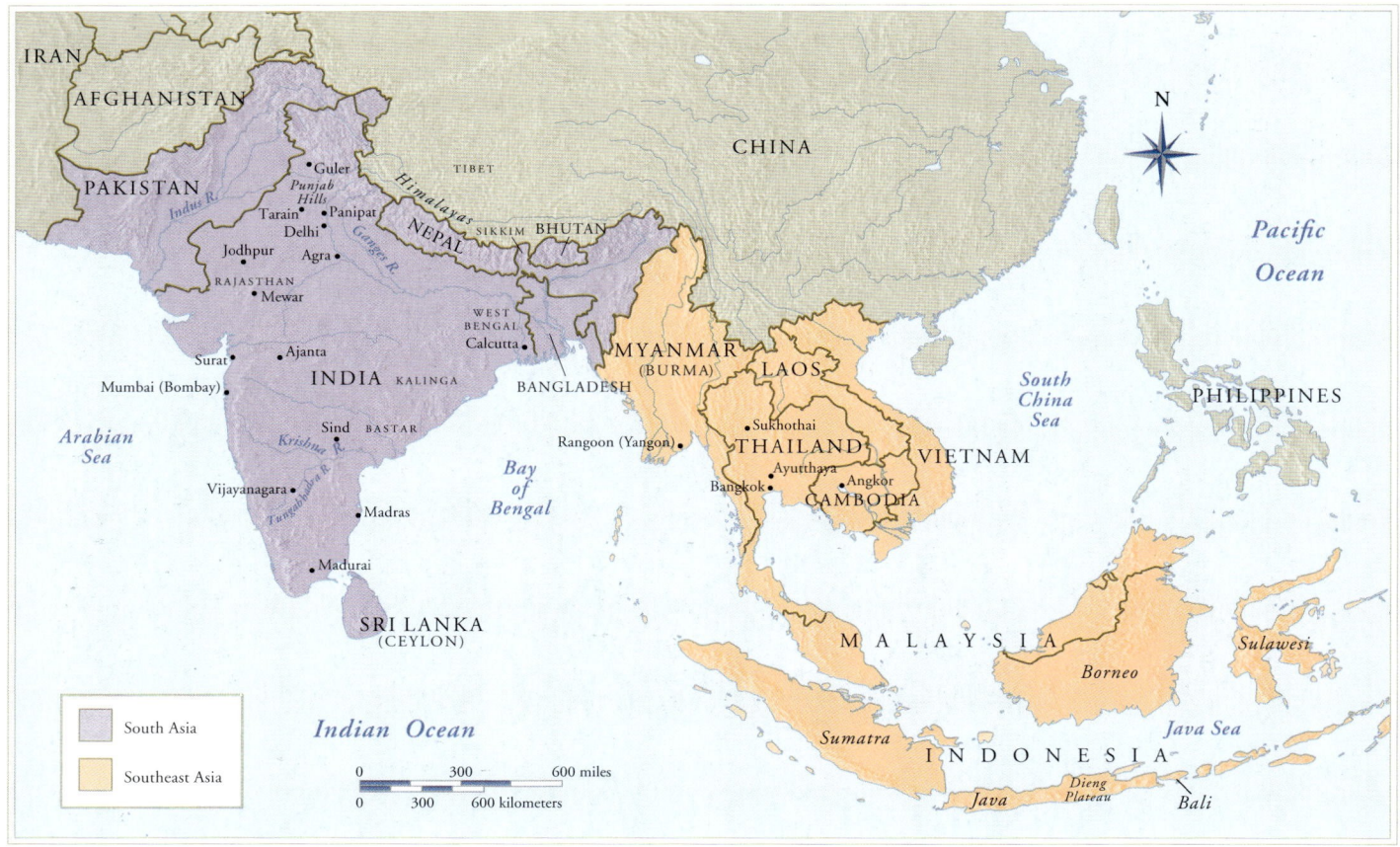

MAP 25-1 South and Southeast Asia.

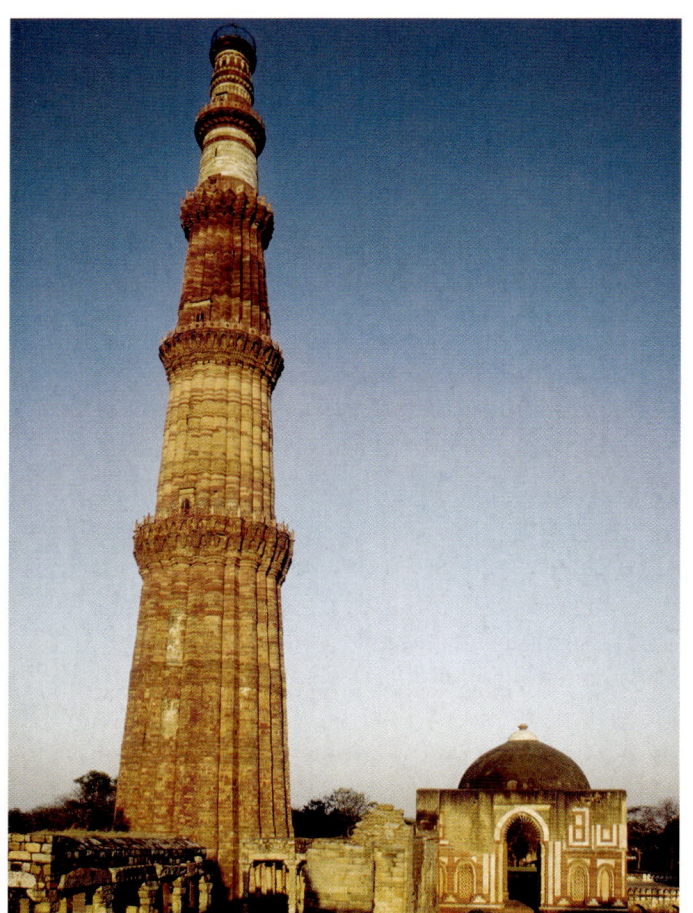

**25-1** Qutb Minar, begun early 13th century, and Alai Darvaza, 1311, Delhi, India.

238-foot sandstone minaret, the Qutb Minar (FIG. **25-1**, *left*), began under Iltutmish. It is the tallest extant minaret in the world—too tall, in fact, to serve the principal function of a minaret, to provide a platform from which to call the Islamic faithful to prayer. Rather it is a towering monument to the victory of Islam, engraved with inscriptions in Arabic and Persian proclaiming that the minaret casts the shadow of Allah over the conquered Hindu city. Added in 1311, the Alai Darvaza, the entrance pavilion (FIG. 25-1, *right*), is a mix of architectural traditions, combining Islamic pointed arches, decorative grills over the windows, and a hemispherical dome, with a finial on the dome that recalls Hindu temples of the Dravida type (see "Hindu Temples," Chapter 6, page 180).

## *Vijayanagar Dynasty (1336–1565)*

**HINDU KINGS OF THE SOUTH** While Muslim sultans from Central Asia ruled much of northern India from Delhi, Hindu dynasts controlled most of the Deccan and the South. The most powerful of the Hindu kingdoms of the era was the Vijayanagar. Established in 1336 by Harihara, a local king, the Vijayanagar Empire takes its name from Vijayanagara ("City of Victory") on the Tungabhadra River. Under the patronage of the royal family, Vijayanagara, located at the junction of several trade routes through Asia, became one of the most magnificent cities in the East. Although the capital lies in ruins today, in its heyday ambassadors and travelers from as far away as Italy and Portugal marveled at Vijayanagara's riches. Under its greatest king, Krishnadevaraya (r. 1509–1520), himself an author of poetry and prose, the Vijayanagar kingdom was a magnet for literati from all corners of India.

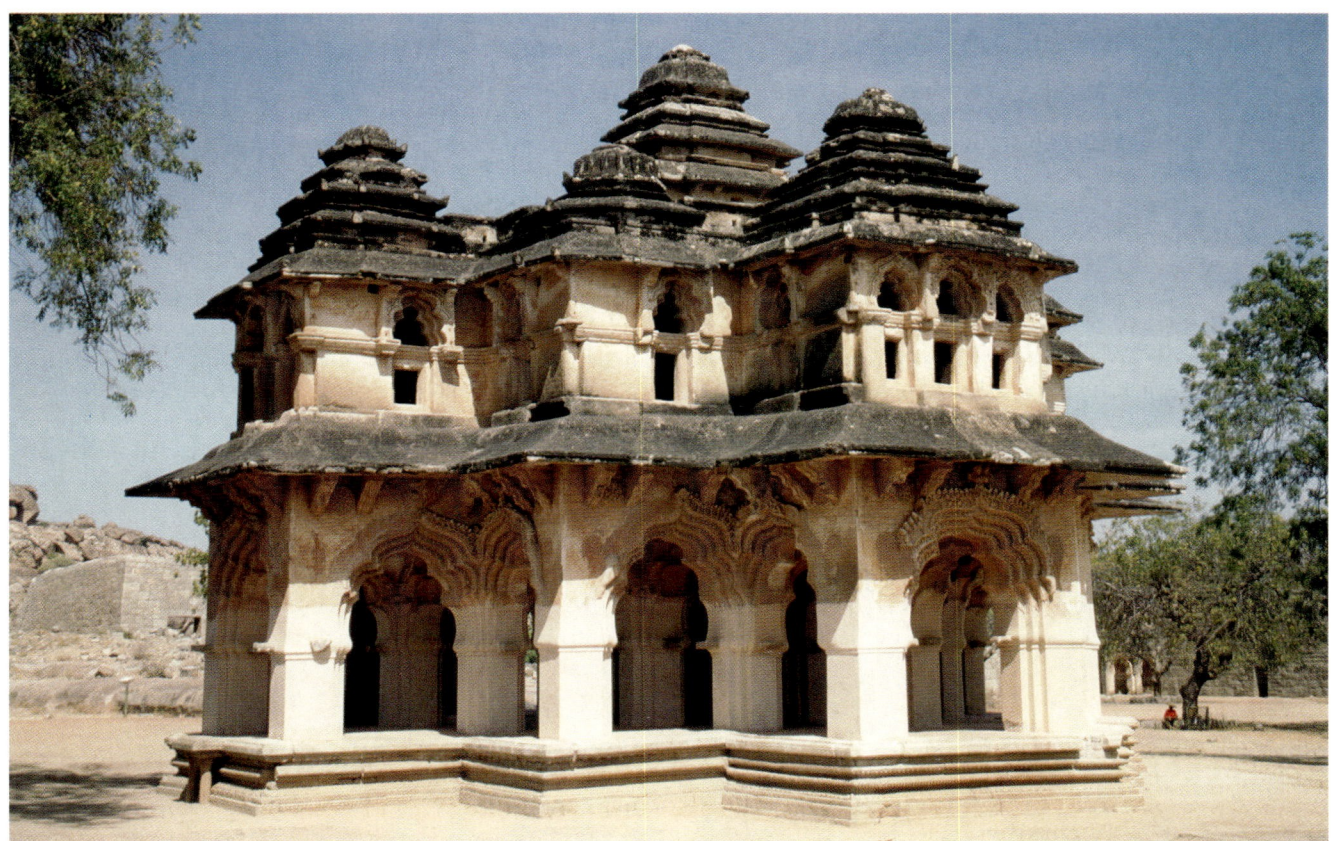

25-2 Lotus Mahal, Vijayanagara, India, 15th or early 16th century.

**THE ECLECTIC LOTUS MAHAL** Vijayanagara's sacred center, built up over two centuries, boasts imposing temples to the Hindu gods in the Dravida style of southern India with tall pyramidal *vimanas* (towers) over the inner sanctuary, or *garbha griha*. The buildings of the so-called Royal Enclave are more eclectic in character. One example in this prosperous royal city is the two-story monument of uncertain function known as the Lotus Mahal (FIG. **25-2**). The stepped towers crowning the vaulted second-story rooms resemble the pyramidal roofs of Dravida temple *mandapas* (pillared halls; see FIG. 6-22). But the windows of the upper level as well as the arches of the ground-floor piers have the distinctive multilobed contours of Islamic architecture (see FIG. 13-13). The Lotus Mahal, like the entrance pavilion of Delhi's first mosque (FIG. 25-1), exemplifies the stylistic crosscurrents that typify much of Indian art and architecture of the second millennium.

## Mughal Empire (1526–1857)

**BABUR SEIZES DELHI** The 16th century was a time of upheaval in South Asia. In 1565, only a generation after Krishnadevaraya, a confederacy of Deccan sultanates brought the Vijayanagar Empire of southern India to an end. Even before Krishnadevaraya's death in 1526, a Muslim prince named Babur had defeated the last of the Ghorid sultans of northern India at the Battle of Panipat. Declaring himself the ruler of India, he established the Mughal Dynasty at Delhi. (*Mughal* means "descended from the Mongols.") The next year he vanquished the Rajput Hindu kings of Mewar (see page 754). By the time of his death in 1530, Babur headed a vast new empire in India.

**IMPERIAL MUGHAL PAINTING** The first great flowering of Mughal art and architecture occurred during the long reign of Babur's grandson, Akbar (r. 1556–1605), called the Great, who ascended to the throne at age 14. Like his father Humayun (r. 1530–1556), Akbar was a great admirer of the narrative paintings produced at the court of Shah Tahmasp in Iran (see FIG. 13-27). Just before he died, Humayun had persuaded two Persian masters to move to Delhi and train local artists in the art of painting. When Akbar succeeded his father, he already oversaw an imperial workshop of Indian painters under the direction of the two Iranians. The young ruler enlarged their number to about a hundred and kept them busy working on a series of ambitious projects. One of these was to illustrate the text of the *Hamzanama*—the story of Hamza, Muhammad's uncle—in some 1,400 large paintings on cloth. The assignment took 15 years to complete.

European art, which Akbar knew through illustrated books and engravings, also fascinated him. Such items often arrived with Christian missionaries. Traders, missionaries, and diplomats also brought prints. In 1580, Portuguese Jesuits brought one particularly important source, the eight-volume *Royal Polyglot Bible*, as a gift to Akbar. This massive set of books, printed in Antwerp, was illustrated with engravings by several Flemish artists. Akbar immediately set his painters to copying the engravings.

**AKBAR AND THE ELEPHANT** Akbar also commissioned Abul Fazl, a member of his court and close friend, to chronicle his life in a great biography, the *Akbarnama (History of Akbar)*, which the emperor's painters illustrated. One of the full-page "miniatures" (see "Indian Miniature Painting," page 752) in the

## *Indian Miniature Painting*

Although India had a tradition of mural painting going back to ancient times (see "The Painted Caves of Ajanta," Chapter 6, page 177, and FIG. 6-14), the most popular form of painting under the Mughal emperors (FIGS. 25-3 and 25-4) and Rajput kings (FIG. 25-6) was *miniature painting*. Art historians call these paintings "miniatures" because of their small size (about the size of a page in this book) compared to that of paintings on walls, wooden panels, or canvas. Indian miniatures were designed to be held in the hands, either as illustrations in books or as loose-leaf pages in albums. Owners did not place Indian miniatures in frames and only very rarely hung them on walls.

Indian artists used opaque watercolors and paper (occasionally cotton cloth) to produce their miniatures. The manufacturing and painting of miniatures was a complicated process and required years of training as an apprentice in a workshop. The painters' assistants created pigments by grinding natural materials—minerals such as malachite for green and lapis lazuli for blue; earth ochers for red and yellow; and metallic foil for gold, silver, and copper. They fashioned brushes from bird quills and kitten or baby squirrel hairs.

The artist began the painting process by making a full-size sketch of the composition. The artist then transferred the sketch onto paper by *pouncing*, or tracing, using thin, transparent gazelle skin placed on top of the drawing and pricking the contours of the design with a pin. Then, with the skin laid on a fresh sheet of fine paper, the painter forced black pigment through the tiny holes, reproducing the outlines of the composition. Painting proper started with the darkening of the outlines with black or reddish brown ink. Painters of miniatures sat on the ground, resting their painting boards on one raised knee. The paintings usually required several layers of color, with gold always applied last. The final step was to burnish the painted surface. The artists accomplished this by placing the miniature, painted side down, on a hard, smooth surface and stroking the paper with polished agate or crystal.

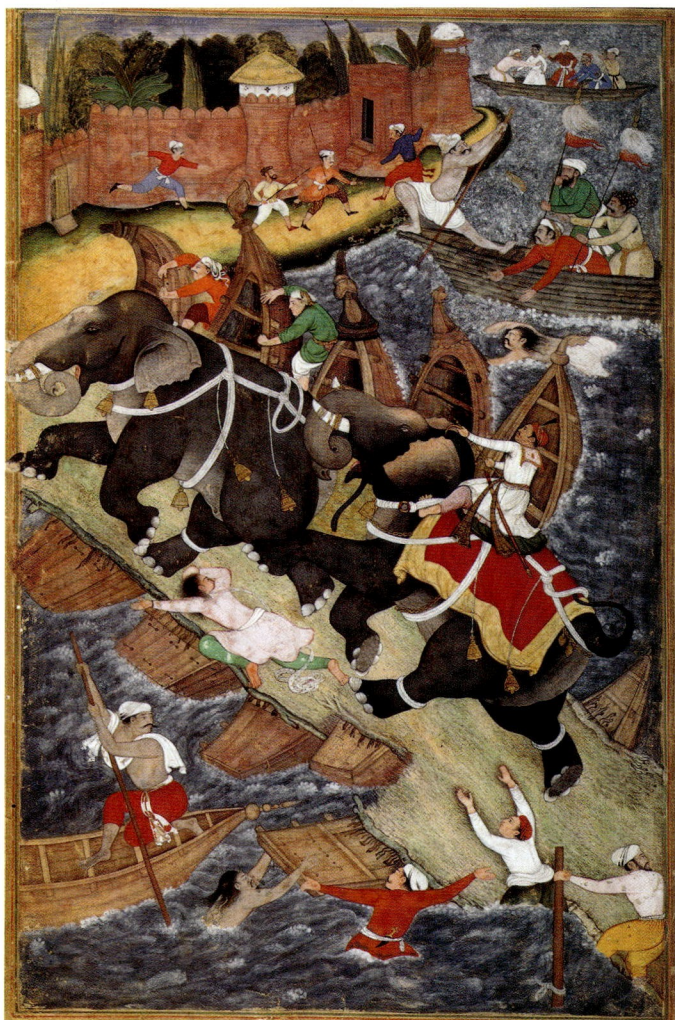

**25-3** BASAWAN and CHATAR MUNI, *Akbar and the Elephant Hawai,* folio 22 from the *Akbarnama (History of Akbar)* by Abul Fazl, ca. 1590. Opaque watercolor on paper, $1' 1\frac{7}{8}'' \times 8\frac{3}{4}''$. Victoria and Albert Museum, London.

emperor's personal copy of the *Akbarnama* was a collaborative effort between the painter BASAWAN, who designed and drew the composition, and CHATAR MUNI, who colored it. The painting depicts the episode of Akbar and Hawai (FIG. **25-3**), a wild elephant that the 19-year-old ruler mounted and pitted against another ferocious elephant. When the second animal fled in defeat, Hawai, still carrying Akbar, chased it to a pontoon bridge. The enormous weight of the elephants capsized the boats, but Akbar managed to bring Hawai under control and dismount safely. The young ruler viewed the episode as an allegory of his ability to govern—that is, to take charge of an unruly state.

For his pictorial record of that frightening day, Basawan chose the moment of maximum chaos and danger—when the elephants crossed the pontoon bridge, sending boatmen flying into the water. The composition is a bold one, with a very high horizon and two strong diagonal lines formed by the bridge and the shore. Together these devices tend to flatten out the vista, yet at the same time Basawan created a sense of depth by diminishing the size of the figures in the background. He was also a master of vivid gestures and anecdotal detail. Note especially the bare-chested figure in the foreground clinging to the end of a boat, the figure near the lower right corner with outstretched arms sliding into the water as the bridge becomes submerged, and the oarsman just beyond the bridge who strains to steady his vessel while his three passengers stand up or lean overboard in reaction to the commotion all around them.

**THE EMPEROR ABOVE TIME** That the names Basawan and Chatar Muni are known is significant in itself. In contrast to the anonymity of artists in the Hindu and Buddhist traditions, many artists working for the Islamic Mughal emperors signed their work. Another of these was BICHITR, whom Akbar's son and successor, Jahangir (r. 1605–1627), employed in the imperial workshop. The Mughals presided over a cosmopolitan court with refined tastes. After the establishment of the East India Company in 1600 (see page 755), British ambassadors and merchants were frequent visitors to the Mughal capital, and Jahangir, like his father, acquired many luxury goods from Europe, including globes, hourglasses, prints, and portraits.

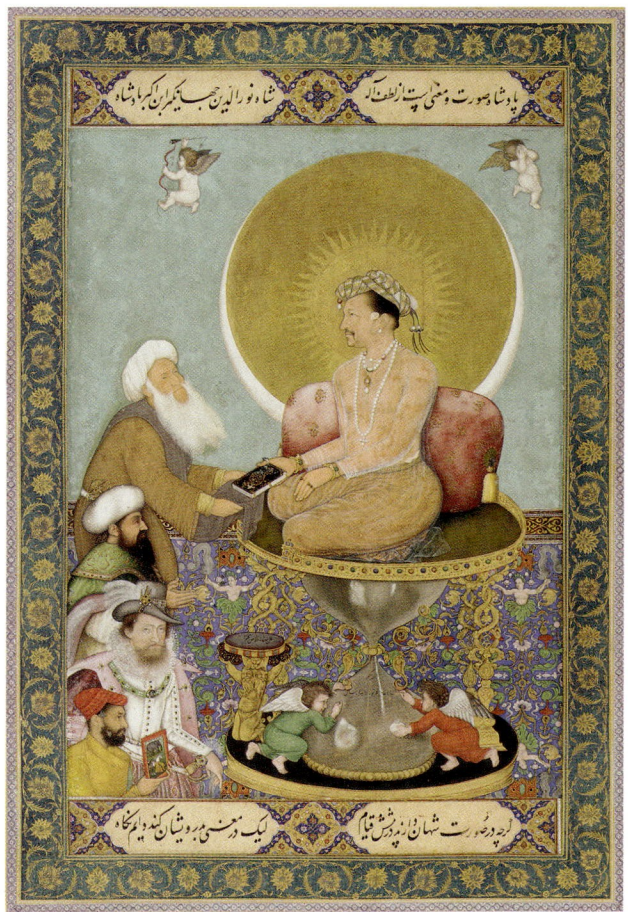

**25-4** BICHITR, *Jahangir Preferring a Sufi Shaykh to Kings*, ca. 1615–1618. Opaque watercolor on paper, 1' 6⅞" × 1' 1". Freer Gallery of Art, Washington, D.C.

The impact of European as well as Persian styles on Mughal painting under Jahangir is evident in Bichitr's allegorical portrait of Jahangir seated on an hourglass throne (FIG. **25-4**), a miniature from an album made for the emperor around 1615–1618. As the

sands of time run out, two Cupids (clothed, unlike their European models more closely copied at the top of the painting) inscribe the throne with the wish that Jahangir would live a thousand years. Bichitr portrayed his patron as an emperor above time and also placed behind Jahangir's head a radiant halo combining a golden sun and a white crescent moon, indicating that Jahangir is the center of the universe and its light source. One of the inscriptions on the painting gives the emperor's title as "Light of the Faith."

At the left are four figures. The lowest, both spatially and in the social hierarchy, is the Hindu painter Bichitr himself, wearing a red turban. He holds a miniature representing two horses and an elephant, costly gifts from Jahangir, and another self-portrait. In the miniature-within-the-miniature, Bichitr bows deeply before the emperor. In the larger painting, the artist signed his name across the top of the footstool Jahangir uses to step up to his hourglass throne. Thus, the ruler steps on Bichitr's name, further indicating the painter's inferior status.

Above Bichitr is a portrait in full European style (compare FIGS. 23-10 and 23-11) of King James I of England (r. 1603–1625), copied from a painting by John de Critz that the English ambassador to the Mughal court had given as a gift to Jahangir. Above the king is a Turkish sultan, a convincing study of physiognomy, but probably not a specific portrait. The highest member of the foursome is an elderly Muslim Sufi *shaykh* (mystic saint). Jahangir's father, Akbar, had gone to the mystic to pray for an heir. The current emperor, the answer to Akbar's prayers, presents the holy man with a sumptuous book as a gift. An inscription explains that "although to all appearances kings stand before him, Jahangir looks inwardly toward the dervishes [Islamic holy men]" for guidance. Bichitr's allegorical painting portrays his emperor in both words and pictures as favoring spiritual over worldly power.

**A MAUSOLEUM IN PARADISE** Monumental tombs were not part of either the Hindu or Buddhist traditions, but had a long history in Islamic architecture. The Delhi sultans had erected tombs in India, but none could compare in grandeur to the fabled Taj Mahal at Agra (FIG. **25-5**). Shah Jahan (r. 1628–1658), Jahangir's son, built the immense mausoleum as a memorial to

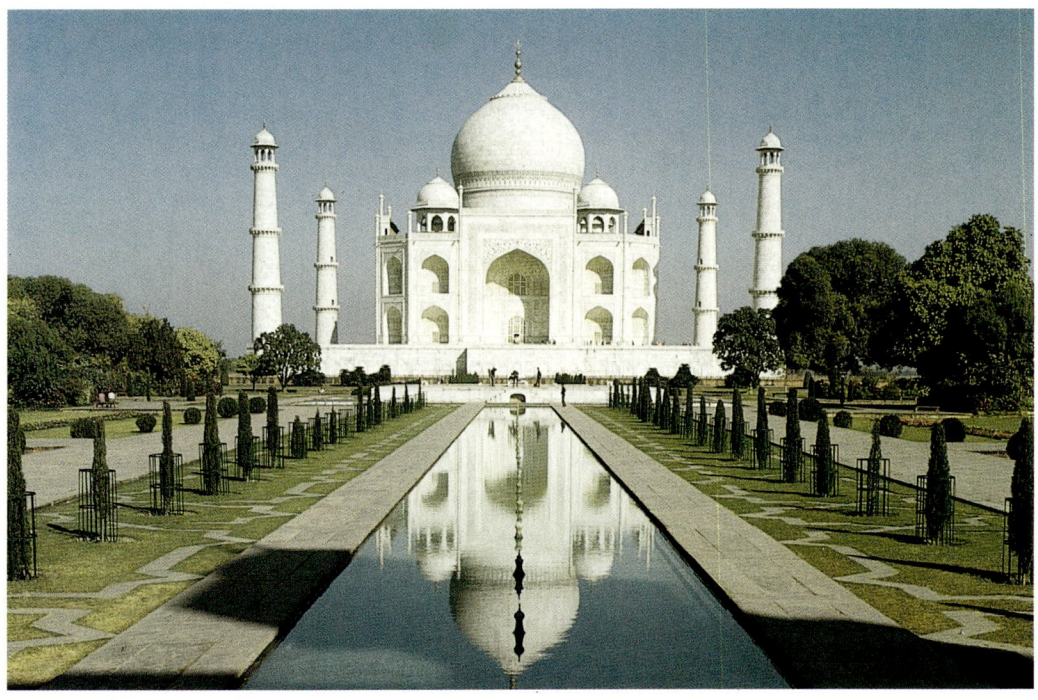

**25-5** Taj Mahal, Agra, India, 1632–1647.

his favorite wife, Mumtaz Mahal, although the ruler himself was eventually buried there as well. The dome-on-cube shape of the central block descends from that of earlier Islamic mausoleums (see FIGS. 13-10 and 13-18) and other Islamic buildings like the Alai Darvaza at Delhi (FIG. 25-1), but modifications and refinements in Agra have converted the earlier massive structures into an almost weightless vision of glistening white marble. The Agra mausoleum seems to float magically above the tree-lined reflecting pools that punctuate the garden leading to it. The illusion that the marble tomb is suspended above the water is reinforced by the absence of any visible means of ascent to the upper platform. A stairway in fact exists, but the architect intentionally hid it from the view of anyone who approaches the memorial.

The Taj Mahal follows the plan of Iranian garden pavilions, except that the building is placed at one end rather than in the center of the formal garden. The tomb is octagonal in plan and has typically Iranian arcuated niches (see FIG. 13-25) on each side. The interplay of shadowy voids with light-reflecting marble walls that seem paper thin creates an impression of translucency. The pointed arches lead the eye in a sweeping upward movement toward the climactic dome, shaped like a crown *(taj)*. Carefully related minarets and corner pavilions enhance and stabilize this soaring central theme. The architect achieved this delicate balance between verticality and horizontality by strictly applying an all-encompassing system of proportions. The Taj Mahal (excluding the minarets) is exactly as wide as it is tall, and the height of its dome is equal to the height of the facade.

Abd al-Hamid Lahori, a court historian who witnessed the construction of the Taj Mahal, compared its minarets to ladders reaching toward Heaven and the surrounding gardens to Paradise. In fact, the gateway to the gardens and the walls of the mausoleum are inscribed with carefully selected excerpts from the Koran that confirm the historian's interpretation of the tomb's symbolism. The Taj Mahal may have been conceived as the Throne of God perched above the gardens of Paradise on Judgment Day. The minarets hold up the canopy of that throne. In Islam, the most revered place of burial is beneath the Throne of God.

## Hindu Rajput Kingdoms (ca. 1500–1850)

**RAJPUTS AND MUGHALS** The Mughal emperors ruled vast territories, but much of northwestern India (present-day Rajasthan) remained under the control of Hindu Rajput (literally "sons of kings") dynasties. These small kingdoms had stubbornly resisted Mughal expansion, but even the strongest of them, Mewar, eventually submitted to the Mughal emperors. When Jahangir defeated the Mewar forces in 1615, the Mewar *maharana* (great king), like the other Rajput rulers, maintained a degree of independence but had to pay tribute to the Mughal treasury.

Rajput painting resembles Mughal (and Persian) painting in format and material, but it differs sharply in other respects. Most Rajput artists, for example, worked in anonymity, never inserting self-portraits into their paintings as the Mughal painter Bichitr did in his miniature of Jahangir on an hourglass throne (FIG. 25-4).

**VISHNU THE LOVER** One of the most popular subjects for Rajput paintings was the amorous adventures of Krishna, the "Blue God," the most popular of the *avatars,* or incarnations, of the Hindu god Vishnu, who descends to earth to aid mortals (see "Hinduism," Chapter 6, page 178, or pages xiv–xv in Volume II). Krishna was a herdsman who spent an idyllic existence tending his

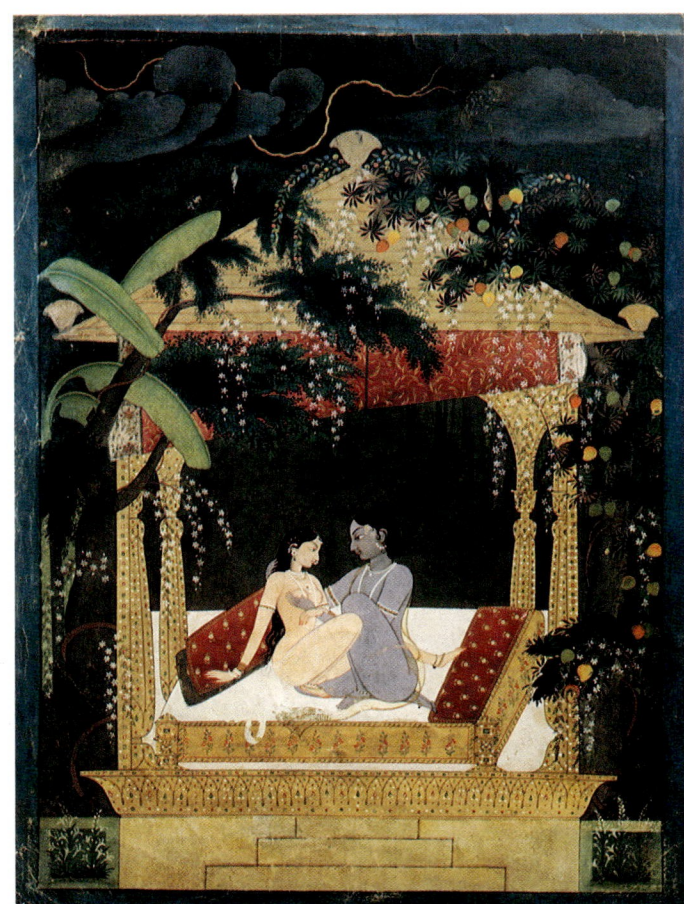

**25-6** *Krishna and Radha in a Pavilion,* ca. 1760. Opaque watercolor on paper, $11\frac{1}{8}'' \times 7\frac{3}{4}''$. National Museum, New Delhi.

cows, fluting, and sporting with beautiful herdswomen. His favorite lover was Radha. The 12th-century poet Jayadeva related the story of Krishna and Radha in the *Gita Govinda (Song of the Cowherd).* Their love was a model of the devotion, or *bhakti,* paid to Vishnu. Jayadeva's poem was the source for hundreds of later paintings, including *Krishna and Radha in a Pavilion* (FIG. **25-6**), a miniature painted in the Punjab Hills, probably for Raja Govardhan Chand of Guler (r. 1741–1773). The rulers of the Punjab Hills states were related to the Rajputs, but their painters, referred to collectively as the Pahari School, had a distinctive style. Although Pahari painting owed much to Mughal drawing style, its coloration, lyricism, and sensuality are readily recognizable.

In *Krishna and Radha in a Pavilion,* the lovers sit naked on a bed beneath a jeweled pavilion in a lush garden of ripe mangoes and flowering shrubs. Krishna gently touches Radha's breast while looking directly into her face. Radha shyly averts her gaze. It is night, the time of illicit trysts, and the dark monsoon sky momentarily lights up with a lightning flash indicating the moment's electric passion. Lightning is one of the standard symbols used in Rajput and Pahari miniatures for sexual excitement.

## Nayak Dynasty (1529–1736)

**THE TOWERS OF MADURAI** The Nayakas, governors under the Vijayanagar kings, declared their independence in 1529, and after their former overlords' defeat in 1565 at the hands of the Deccan sultanates, they continued Hindu rule in the far south of India for

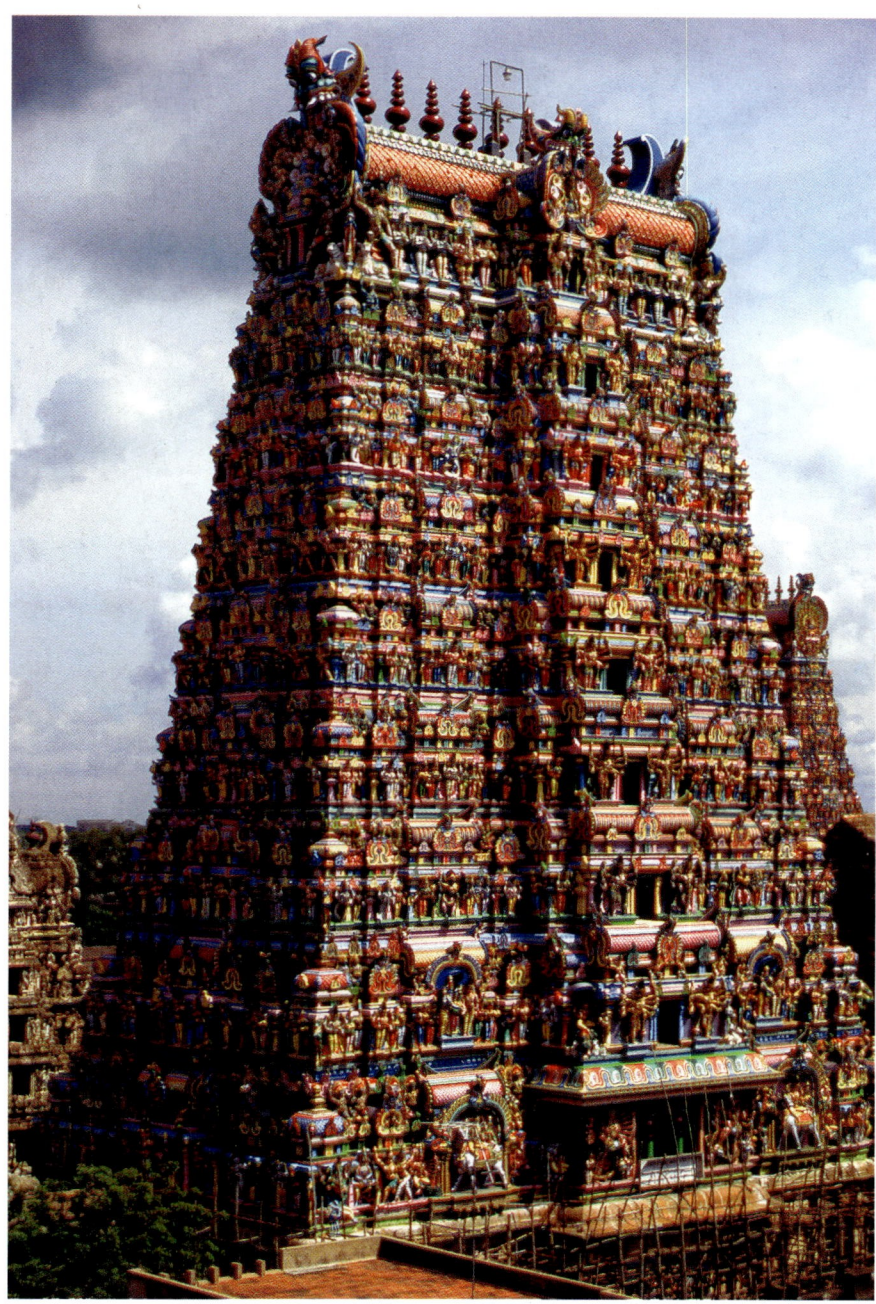

two centuries. Construction of some of the largest temple complexes in India occurred under Nayak patronage. The builders of these huge complexes expanded them outward from the center by erecting ever larger enclosure walls, punctuated at the cardinal points by gateway towers called *gopuras*. Positioned like boxes within boxes, each set of walls had taller gopuras than those of the previous circuit, the towers reaching colossal size and dwarfing the actual central temples. The outer gopuras of the Great Temple (FIG. **25-7**) at Madurai, dedicated to Shiva (under his local name, Sundareshvara, the Handsome One) and his consort Minakshi (the Fish-eyed One), stand about 150 feet tall. Rising in a series of tiers of diminishing size, they culminate in a barrel-vaulted roof with finials. The ornamentation is extremely rich, consisting of row after row of brightly painted stucco sculptures representing the vast pantheon of Hindu deities and a host of attendant figures. At 12-year intervals, the temple is reconsecrated and the gopura sculptures are repainted, accounting for the vibrancy of their colors today. The Madurai Nayak temple complex also contains large and numerous

mandapas, as well as great water tanks the worshipers use for ritual bathing. Such temples were, and continue to be, almost independent cities, with thousands of pilgrims, merchants, and priests flocking from far and near to the many yearly festivals the temples host.

## The British in India (1600–1947)

**FROM TRADERS TO RULERS** English merchants first arrived in India toward the end of the 16th century, attracted by the land's spices, gems, and other riches. In 1600, Queen Elizabeth I (r. 1558–1603) granted a charter to the East India Company, which sought to compete with the Portuguese and Dutch in the lucrative trade with South Asia. The Company established a "factory" (trading post) at the port of Surat, approximately 150 miles from Mumbai (Bombay) in western India in 1613. After securing trade privileges with the Mughal emperor Jahangir, the British expanded their factories to Chennai (Madras), Kolkata (Calcutta),

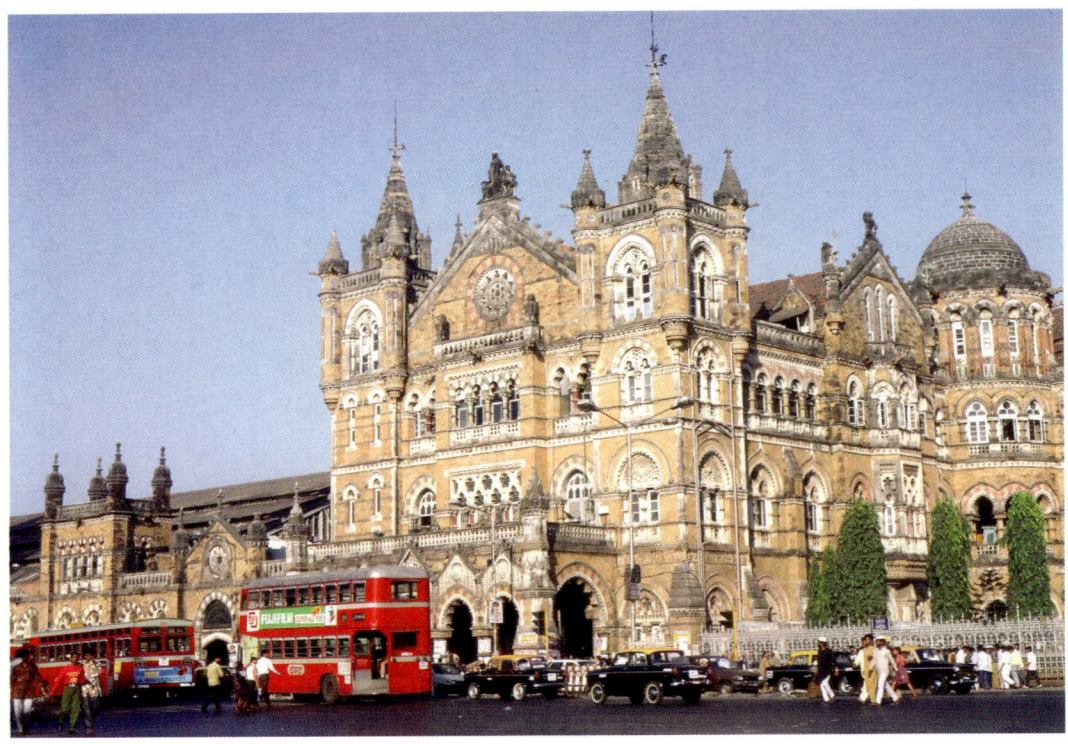

**25-8** FREDERICK W. STEVENS, Victoria Terminus (Chhatrapati Shivaji Terminus), Mumbai (Bombay), India, 1878–1887.

and Bombay by 1661. British outposts gradually spread throughout India, especially after the defeat at their hands of the ruler of Bengal in 1757. By the opening of the 19th century, the East India Company effectively ruled large portions of the subcontinent, and in 1835, the British declared English India's official language. A great rebellion in 1857 persuaded the British Parliament that the East India Company could no longer be the agent of British rule. The next year Parliament abolished the Company and replaced its governor-general with a viceroy of the Crown. Two decades later, in 1877, Queen Victoria (r. 1837–1901) was proclaimed Empress of India with sovereignty over all the former Indian states.

**BOMBAY'S RAILROAD CATHEDRAL** The British brought the Industrial Revolution and railways to India. One of the most enduring monuments of British rule, still used today by millions of travelers, is the Victoria Terminus in Bombay (FIG. **25-8**), named for the new Empress of India (but now called Chhatrapati Shivaji Terminus). Designed by FREDERICK W. STEVENS (1847–1900), a British architect, the railway station was begun in 1878 and completed a decade later. Although built of the same local sandstone used for temples and statues throughout India's long history, the giant terminal is a European transplant to the subcontinent, the architectural counterpart of colonial rule. Conceived as a cathedral to modernization, the terminus fittingly has an allegorical statue of Progress crowning its tallest dome (not visible in FIG. 25-8). Nonetheless, the building's design looks backward, not forward. Inside, passengers gaze up at groin-vaulted ceilings and stained-glass windows, and the exterior of the station resembles a Western church with a gabled facade and flanking towers. Stevens modeled Victoria Terminus, with its tiers of screened windows, on the architecture of late medieval Venice (see FIG. 18-56).

**JODHPUR'S BRITISH GENTLEMAN** With British rulers and modern railways also came British or, more generally, European ideas, but Western culture and religion never supplanted India's

own rich traditions. Many Indians, however, readily took on the trappings of European society. When Jaswant Singh, the ruler of Jodhpur in Rajasthan (r. 1873–1895), sat for his portrait (FIG. **25-9**), he chose to sit alone in an ordinary chair, rather than on a throne, with his arm resting on a simple table with a bouquet and a book on it. In other words, he posed like an ordinary British gentleman in his sitting room. Nevertheless, the painter, an anonymous local artist who had embraced Western style, left no question about Jaswant Singh's regal presence and pride. The ruler's powerful chest and arms, along with the sword and his leather riding boots, indicate his abilities as a warrior and hunter. The curled beard was regarded at the time as indicative of fierceness. The unflinching gaze records the ruler's confidence. Perhaps the two necklaces Jaswant Singh wears best exemplify the combination of his two worlds. One necklace is a bib of huge emeralds and diamonds, the heritage of the wealth and splendor of his family's rule. The other, a wide gold band with a cameo, is the Order of the Star of India, a high honor his British overlords bestowed on him.

The painter of this portrait worked on the same scale and employed the same materials—opaque watercolor on paper—that Indian miniature painters had used for centuries (see "Indian Miniature Painting," page 752), but the artist copied the ruler's likeness from a photograph. This accounts in large part for the realism of the portrait. Indian artists sometimes even painted directly on top of photographs. Photography arrived in India at an early date. In 1840, just one year after its invention in Paris, the *daguerreotype* (see FIG. 28-64) had been introduced in Calcutta. Indian artists readily adopted the new medium, not just to produce portraits but also to record landscapes and monuments.

In 19th-century India, however, admiration of Western art and culture was by no means universal. During the half-century after Jaswant Singh's death, calls for Indian self-government grew ever louder. Under the leadership of Mahatma Gandhi (1869–1948) and others, India achieved independence in 1947,

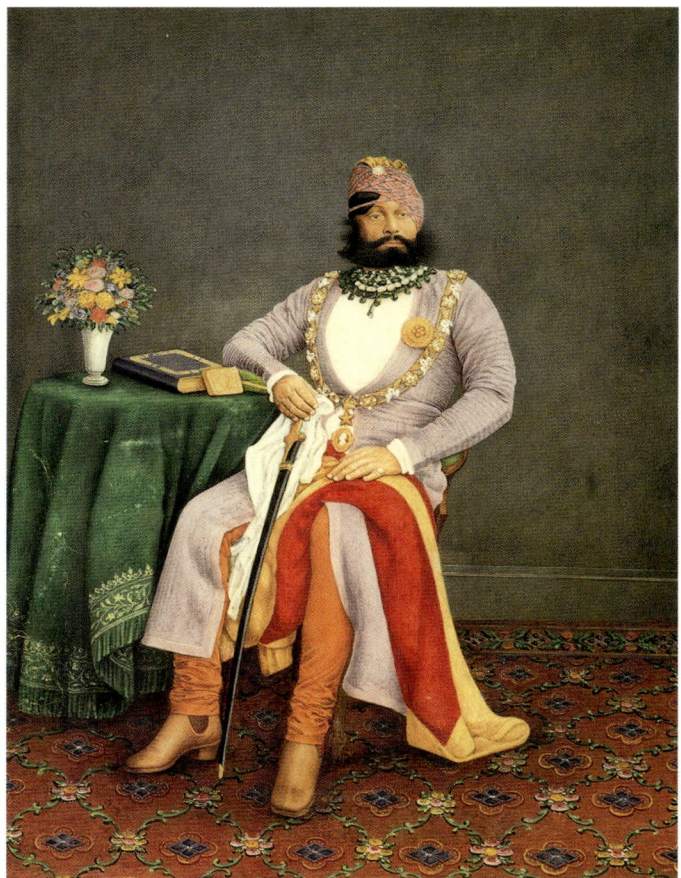

**25-9** *Maharaja Jaswant Singh of Marwar*, ca. 1880. Opaque watercolor on paper, $1' 3\frac{1}{2}'' \times 11\frac{5}{8}''$. The Brooklyn Museum (gift of Mr. and Mrs. Robert L. Poster).

but was partitioned into the two present-day nations of India and Pakistan. The contemporary art of South and Southeast Asia is the subject of the last section of this chapter.

# SOUTHEAST ASIA

India was not alone in experiencing major shifts in political power and religious preferences during the last 800 years. The Khmer of Angkor (see Chapter 6), after reaching the height of their power at the beginning of the 13th century, lost one of their outposts in northern Thailand to their Thai vassals at midcentury. The newly founded Thai kingdoms quickly replaced Angkor as the region's major powers, while Theravada Buddhism (see "Buddhism and Buddhist Iconography," Chapter 6, page 171, or pages xiv–xv in Volume II) became the religion of the entire mainland except Vietnam. The Vietnamese, restricted to the northern region of today's Vietnam, gained independence in the 10th century after a thousand years of Chinese political and cultural domination. They pushed to the south, ultimately destroying the indigenous Cham culture, which had dominated there for more than a millennium. A similar Burmese drive southward in Myanmar matched the Thai and Vietnamese expansions. All these movements resulted in demographic changes during the second millennium that led to the cultural, political, and artistic transformation of mainland Southeast Asia. A religious shift also occurred in Indonesia. With Islam growing in importance, all of Indonesia but the island of Bali became predominantly Muslim by the 16th century.

## *Thailand*

Southeast Asians practiced both Buddhism and Hinduism, but by the 13th century, in contrast to developments in India, Hinduism was dying out and Buddhism was dominating much of the mainland. Two prominent Buddhist kingdoms came to power in Thailand during the 13th and early 14th centuries. Historians date the beginning of the Sukhothai kingdom to 1292, the year King Ramkhamhaeng (r. 1279–1299) erected a four-sided stele bearing the first inscription written in the Thai language. Sukhothai's political dominance was, however, short-lived. Ayuthaya, a city founded in central Thailand in 1350, quickly became the more powerful kingdom and warred sporadically with other states in Southeast Asia until the mid-18th century. Scholars nonetheless regard the Sukhothai period as the golden age of Thai art. In the inscription on his stele, Ramkhamhaeng ("Rama the Strong") describes Sukhothai as a city of monasteries and many images of the Buddha.

**THE WALKING BUDDHA** Theravada Buddhism came to Sukhothai from Sri Lanka (see Chapter 6). At the center of the city stood Wat Mahathat, Sukhothai's most important Buddhist monastery. Its stupa (see "The Stupa," Chapter 6, page 172) housed a relic of the Buddha (Wat Mahathat means "Monastery of the Great Relic") and attracted crowds of pilgrims. Sukhothai's crowning artistic achievement was the development of a type of walking Buddha statue (FIG. **25-10**) displaying a distinctively Thai approach

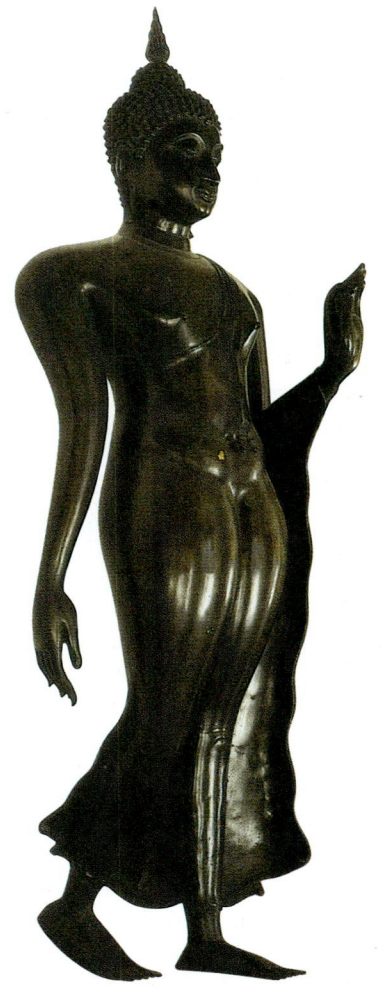

**25-10** Walking Buddha, from Sukhothai, Thailand, 14th century. Bronze, $7' 2\frac{1}{2}''$ high. Wat Bechamabopit, Bangkok.

to bodily form. The Buddha, wearing a clinging monk's robe, strides forward, his right heel off the ground and his left arm raised with the hand held in the fear-not gesture, encouraging worshipers to come forward in reverence. A flame leaps from the top of the Buddha's head, and a sharp nose projects from his rounded face. The right arm hangs loosely, seemingly without muscles or joints, like an elephant's trunk. The Sukhothai artists intended the body type to suggest a supernatural being and to express the Buddha's beauty and perfection. Although images in stone exist, the Sukhothai artists handled bronze best, a material well suited to their conception of the Buddha's body as elastic. The Sukhothai walking-Buddha statuary type does not occur elsewhere in Buddhist art.

**BANGKOK'S *EMERALD BUDDHA***  A second distinctive Buddha image from northern Thailand is the *Emerald Buddha* (FIG. 25-11), housed in Bangkok in the Emerald Temple on the Royal Palace grounds. The sculpture is small, only about 30 inches tall, and conforms to the ancient type of the Buddha seated in meditation in a yogic posture with his legs crossed and his hands in his lap, palms upward (see FIG. 6-9). It first appears in historical records in 1434 in northern Thailand, where Buddhist chronicles record its story. The chronicles state that the Buddha image was covered in plaster, and thus no one knew it was made of green stone. A lightning bolt caused some of the plaster to flake off, disclosing its gemlike nature. Taken by various rulers to a series of cities in northern Thailand and in Laos for more than 300 years, the small image finally reached Bangkok in 1778 in the possession of the founder of the present Thai royal dynasty.

The *Emerald Buddha* is not carved from an actual emerald. It is probably green jade, but its nature as a gemstone gives it a special aura. It is said that the gem enables the universal king, or *chakravartin,* possessing the statue to bring the rains. The historical Buddha renounced his secular destiny for the spiritual life, yet his likeness carved from the gem of a universal king allows fulfillment of the Buddha's royal destiny as well. The Buddha can also be regarded as the universal king. Thus, the combination of the sacred and the secular in the small image explains its symbolic power. The Thai king dresses the *Emerald Buddha* at different times of the year in a monk's robe and a king's robe (in FIG. 25-11 the Buddha wears the royal garment), reflecting the image's dual nature and accentuating its symbolic role as both Buddha and king. The Thai king possessing the image therefore has both religious and secular authority.

## *Myanmar*

**RANGOON'S GOLDEN STUPA**  Myanmar, like Thailand, is overwhelmingly a Theravada Buddhist country today. Important Buddhist monasteries and monuments dot the countryside. In fact, one of the largest stupas in the world is the Shwedagon Pagoda (FIG. 25-12) in Rangoon. (*Pagoda* derives from the Portuguese version of a word for stupa.) It houses two of the Buddha's hairs, traditionally said to have been brought to Myanmar by merchants who received them from the Buddha himself. This highly

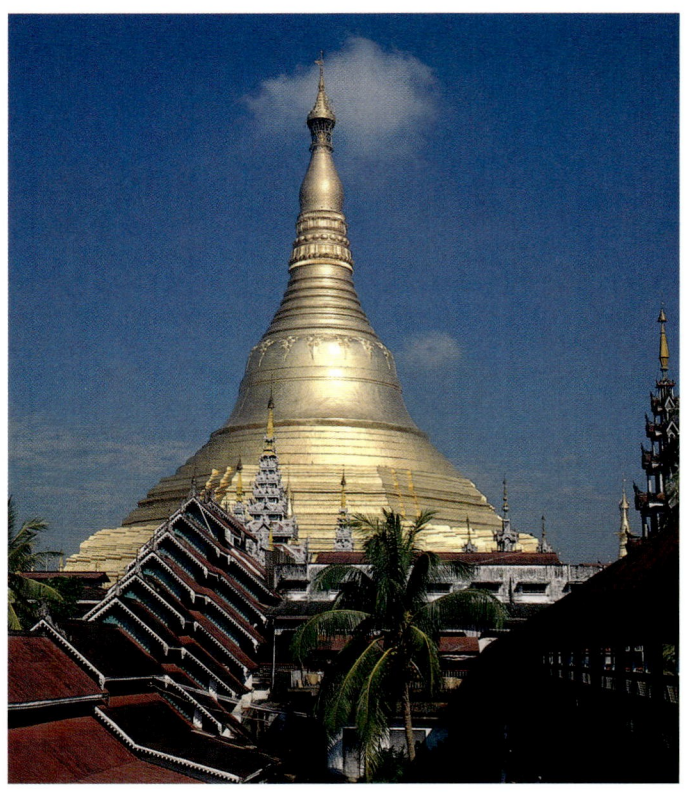

**25-11** *Emerald Buddha*, Emerald Temple, Bangkok, Thailand, 15th century. Jade or jasper, 2′ 6″ high.

**25-12** Schwedagon Pagoda, Rangoon (Yangon), Myanmar (Burma), 14th century or earlier (rebuilt several times). Stupa, gold, silver, and jewel encrusted, approx. 344′ high. Top of stupa, gold ball inlaid with 4,351 diamonds.

### *Shipwrecks and Ceramic Chronology*

The vast majority of early Vietnamese ceramics (FIG. 25-13) have not been found in Vietnam but in Indonesia, particularly on the islands of Java and Sulawesi, and in the Philippines, where they served as grave goods to bury with the dead. The Vietnamese exported their ceramic wares to the Southeast Asian islands as early as the 14th century but primarily during the 15th through 17th centuries, when Vietnamese ceramics reached markets even more distant—the Middle East, Egypt, Turkey, and Persia.

Chinese and European—primarily English, Dutch, and Portuguese—merchants traded the Vietnamese wares, along with ceramics from China and Thailand. According to the inventory of a Dutch ship that arrived in Java in 1669, the ship's cargo included 381,200 Vietnamese ceramic bowls. Recent finds of shipwrecks with their cargoes of ceramic wares intact, discovered in the waters along the mainland coasts and around the islands in the South China Sea, are helping to clarify the dating and

interrelationships among the various ceramic traditions. Before investigation of the shipwrecks began, art historians had to rely on buried Vietnamese ceramics, which rarely could be dated. It was usually impossible to know dates of the individual pieces gathered together in the burial. Researchers thus could not ascertain whether the buried ceramics dated from different centuries or were contemporaneous.

The recent shipwreck finds have shown that many of the assumptions based on art historians' stylistic analysis of Southeast Asian ceramics were incorrect. Researchers often can date shipwrecks rather precisely, especially if any wood remains that they can analyze using radiocarbon dating techniques. The ceramics in shipwrecks, then, can be placed together at a precise moment. Wrecks have revealed groupings of ceramics that, until now, were considered separated in time. The technology of underwater archaeology is leading to a new understanding of the entire Vietnamese ceramic tradition.

---

revered stupa was rebuilt several times. Renowned for the gold, silver, and jewels encrusting its surface, the Shwedagon Pagoda stands 344 feet high. Its upper part is covered with 13,153 plates of gold, each about a foot square. At the very top is a seven-tiered umbrella crowned with a gold ball inlaid with 4,351 diamonds, one of which weighs 76 carats. This great wealth was a gift to the Buddha from the laypeople of Myanmar to produce merit. The stupa is at the center of an enormous complex of buildings, including wooden shrines filled with Buddha images.

## *Vietnam*

**VIETNAMESE CERAMICS AND CHINA** Vietnam's art history is particularly complex, as it reveals both an Indian-related art and culture, broadly similar to those of the rest of Southeast Asia, and a unique and intense relationship with China's art and culture. Vietnam's tradition of fine ceramics is of special interest. Vietnamese ceramics go back to the Han period (206 BCE–220 CE), when the Chinese began to govern the northern area of Vietnam. China directly controlled Vietnam for a thousand years, and early Vietnamese ceramics closely reflected Chinese wares. But during the Ly (1009–1225) and Tran (1225–1400) dynasties, when Vietnam had regained its independence, Vietnamese potters developed an array of ceramic shapes, designs, and glazes that brought their wares to the highest levels of quality and creativity.

In the 14th century, the Vietnamese began exporting underglaze wares modeled on the blue-and-white ceramics first produced in China (see "Chinese Porcelain," Chapter 26, page 767). During the 15th and 16th centuries, the ceramic industry in Vietnam had become the supplier of pottery of varied shapes to an international market extending throughout Southeast Asia and to the Middle East (see "Shipwrecks and Ceramic Chronology," above). A 16th-century Vietnamese dish (FIG. **25-13**) with two mynah birds on a flowering branch reveals both the potter's debt to China and how the spontaneity, power, and playfulness of Vietnamese painting contrast with the formality of Chinese wares

(see FIG. 26-4). The artist suggested the foliage with curving and looped lines executed in almost one continuous movement of the brush over the surface. This technique—very different from the more deliberate Chinese habit of lifting the brush after painting a single motif in order to separate the shapes more sharply—facilitated rapid production. Combined with the painter's control, it allowed a fresh and unique design that made Vietnamese pottery attractive to a wide export market.

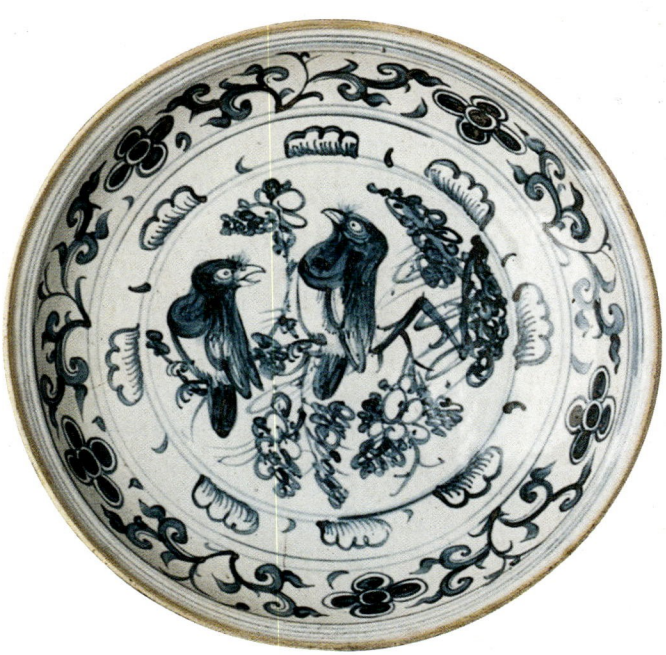

**25-13** Dish with two mynah birds on flowering branch, from Vietnam, 16th century. Stoneware painted with underglaze-cobalt, $1' 2\frac{1}{2}''$ in diameter. Pacific Asia Museum, Pasadena.

# Contemporary South and Southeast Asian Art

**LOCAL AND INTERNATIONAL ART** Contemporary art in India and Southeast Asia is as multifaceted a phenomenon as contemporary art elsewhere in the world. In India, for example, many traditional artists work at the village level, making images of deities out of inexpensive materials, such as clay, plaster, and papier-mâché, for local use. Some artists in the cities use these same materials to produce elaborate religious tableaux, such as depictions of the goddess Durga killing the buffalo demon, during the annual 10-day Durga Festival in Calcutta. Participants in the festival often ornament the tableaux with thousands of colored electric lights. The most popular art form for religious imagery, however, is the brightly colored print, sold for only a few rupees each. In the Buddhist countries of Southeast Asia (Thailand, Cambodia, Myanmar, and Laos), some artists continue to produce traditional images of the Buddha, primarily in bronze, for worship in homes, businesses, and temples.

Many contemporary artists, in contrast, create works for the international market. Although many of them were trained in South or Southeast Asia or Japan, others received their training in schools in Europe or the United States, and some now work outside their home countries. They face one of the fundamental quandaries of many contemporary Asian artists—how to identify themselves and situate their work between local and international, traditional and modern, and non-Western and Western cultures.

**MEERA MUKHERJEE AND ASHOKA** One Indian artist who successfully bridged these two poles of modern Asian art was MEERA MUKHERJEE (1923–1998). Mukherjee studied with European masters in Germany, but when she returned to India, she rejected much of what she had learned in favor of the techniques that traditional sculptors of the Bastar tribe in central India had long employed. Mukherjee went to live with the Bastar bronze casters, who had perfected a variation on the classic lost-wax method (see "Hollow-Casting Life-Size Bronze Statues," Chapter 5, page 131). Beginning with a rough core of clay, the Bastar sculptors build up what will be the final shape of the statue by placing long threads of beeswax over the core. Then they apply a coat of clay paste to the beeswax and tie up the mold with metal wire. After heating the mold over a charcoal fire, which melts the wax away, they pour liquid bronze into the space once occupied by the wax threads. Large sculptures require many separate molds. The Bastar artists complete their statues by welding together the separately cast sections, usually leaving the seams visible.

Many scholars regard *Ashoka at Kalinga* (FIG. **25-14**) as Mukherjee's greatest work. Twice life size and assembled from 26 cast bronze sections, the towering statue combines the intricate surface textures of traditional Bastar work with the expressive swelling abstract forms of some 20th-century European sculpture (see FIG. 33-71). Mukherjee's subject is the third-century BCE Maurya emperor Ashoka standing on the battlefield at Kalinga. There, Ashoka witnessed more than 100,000 deaths and, shocked by the horrors of the war he had unleashed, rejected violence and adopted Buddhism as the official religion of his empire (see "Ashoka's Conversion to Buddhism," Chapter 6, page 173). Mukherjee conceived her statue as a pacifist protest against political violence in late 20th-century India. By reaching into India's remote history to make a contemporary political statement and by employing the bronze

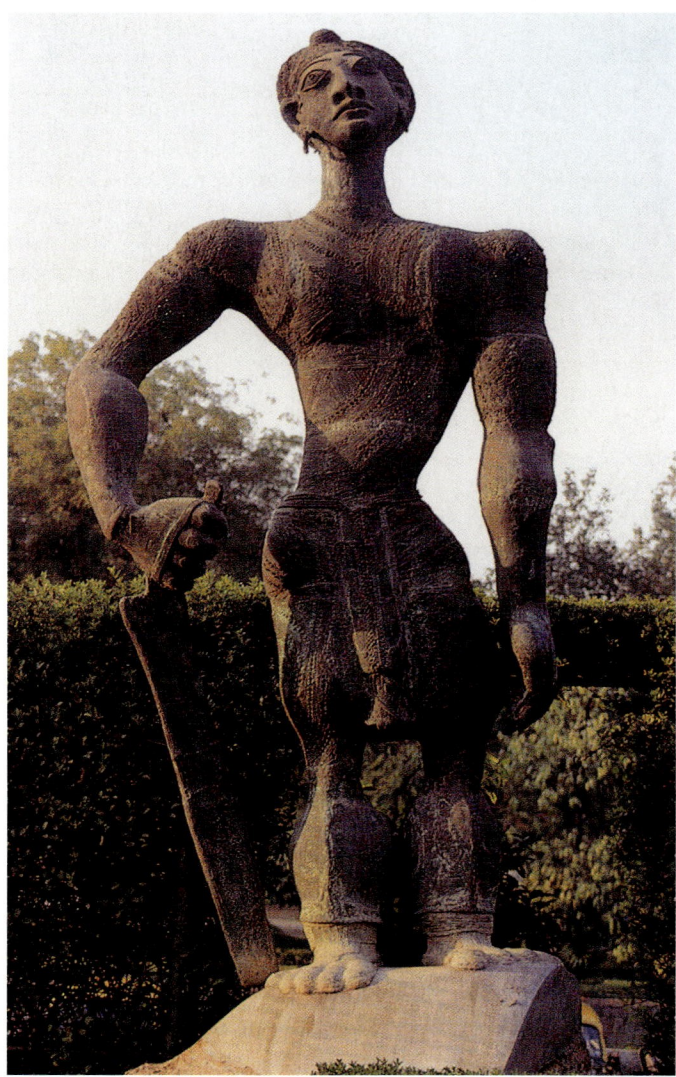

**25-14** MEERA MUKHERJEE, *Ashoka at Kalinga,* 1972. Bronze, 11′ 6¾″ high. Maurya Sheraton Hotel, New Delhi.

casting methods of tribal sculptors while molding her forms in a modern idiom, she united her native land's past and present in a single work of great emotive power.

# CONCLUSION

Islam arrived in the Indian subcontinent in the eighth century. With the establishment of the Sultanate of Delhi in 1206, Islamic art and architecture began to spread throughout South Asia. The Muslim Mughal emperors of India were especially lavish art patrons. In fact, one of the most famous Islamic buildings in the world, the Taj Mahal, was a Mughal commission. But elsewhere in South Asia, Hindu art continued to flourish, especially under the Vijayanagar and Nayak dynasties and the Rajput kingdoms. Buddhism and Buddhist art dominated much of Southeast Asia.

The Mughal Empire came to an end in 1857, and for nearly a century thereafter India was ruled by the British. Under the leadership of Mahatma Gandhi (1869–1948), India and Pakistan attained independence in 1947. Throughout the period of British sovereignty, local traditions mixed with imported European styles in both art and architecture. The rich and varied contemporary art of South and Southeast Asia continues to draw upon these diverse traditions.

1200

| Muhammad of Ghor invades India, 1192

Qutb al-din Aybak founds Delhi Sultanate, 1206
| Iltutmish, Delhi sultan, r. 1211–1236
| Tran Dynasty in Vietnam, 1225–1400
| Ramkhamhaeng, Sukhothai king, r. 1279–1299

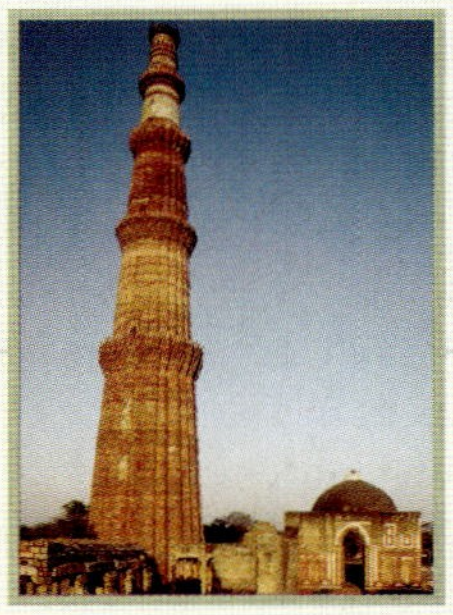

1300

| Harihara founds Vijayanagar kingdom, 1336
| Ayuthaya kingdom founded in Thailand, 1350

**1** Qutb Minar, Delhi, India, begun early 13th century

1400

2

1500

| Krishnadevaraya, Vijayanagar king, r. 1509–1520
| Babur founds Mughal Dynasty, 1526
| Nayakas declare independence from Vijayanagara, 1529
| Akbar, Mughal emperor, r. 1556–1605

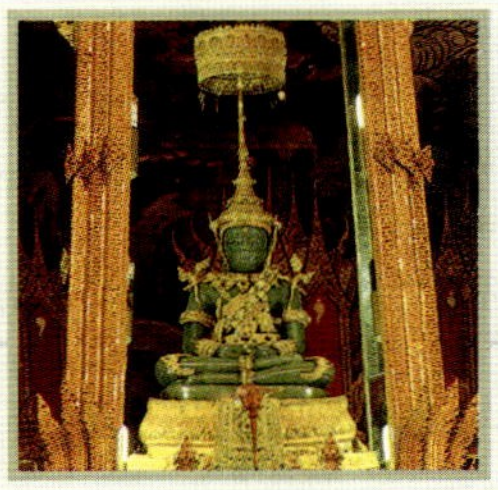

**2** Emerald Buddha, Bangkok, Thailand, 15th century

3

1600

| Queen Elizabeth I charters East India Company, 1600
| Jahangir, Mughal emperor, r. 1605–1627
| British establish trading post at Surat, 1613
| Jahangir defeats the Mewar maharana, 1615
| Shah Jahan, Mughal emperor, r. 1627–1658

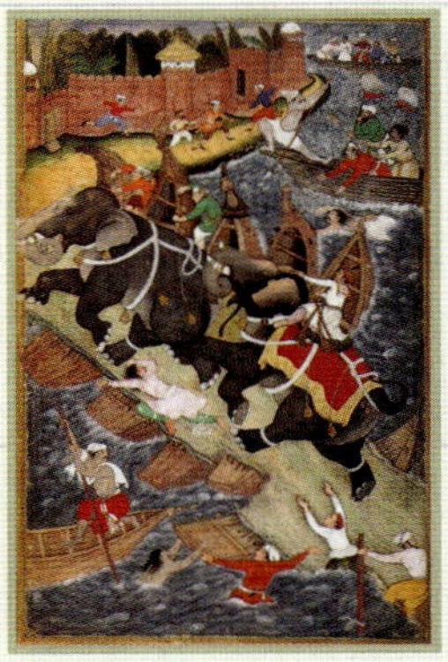

1700

**3** Basawan and Chatar Muni, *Akbar and the Elephant Hawai*, ca. 1590

1800

| Great rebellion against the British, 1857
| British Crown rule in India, 1858–1947
| Mahatma Gandhi, 1869–1948
4 | Queen Victoria becomes Empress of India, 1877

1900

| Independence of India and Pakistan, 1947

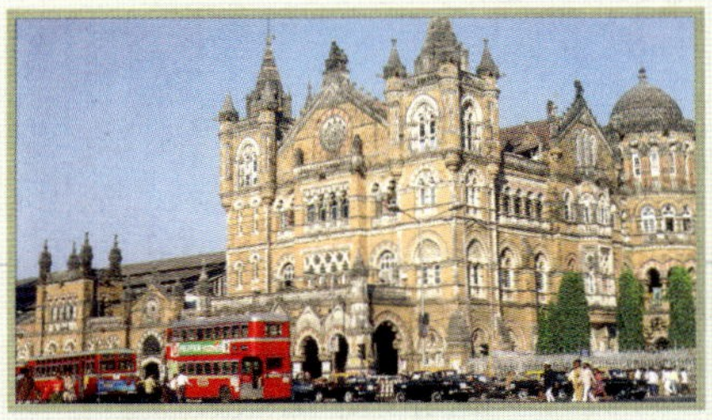

**4** Frederick W. Stevens, Victoria Terminus, Bombay, India, 1878–1887

Delhi Sultanate, 1206–1526

Hindu kingdom of Vijayanagara, 1336–1565

Mughal Empire, 1526–1857

Hindu Nayak Dynasty, 1529–1736

Hindu Rajput Dynasties, ca. 1500–1850

British Rule in India, 1858–1947

Independent India and Pakistan, 1947–

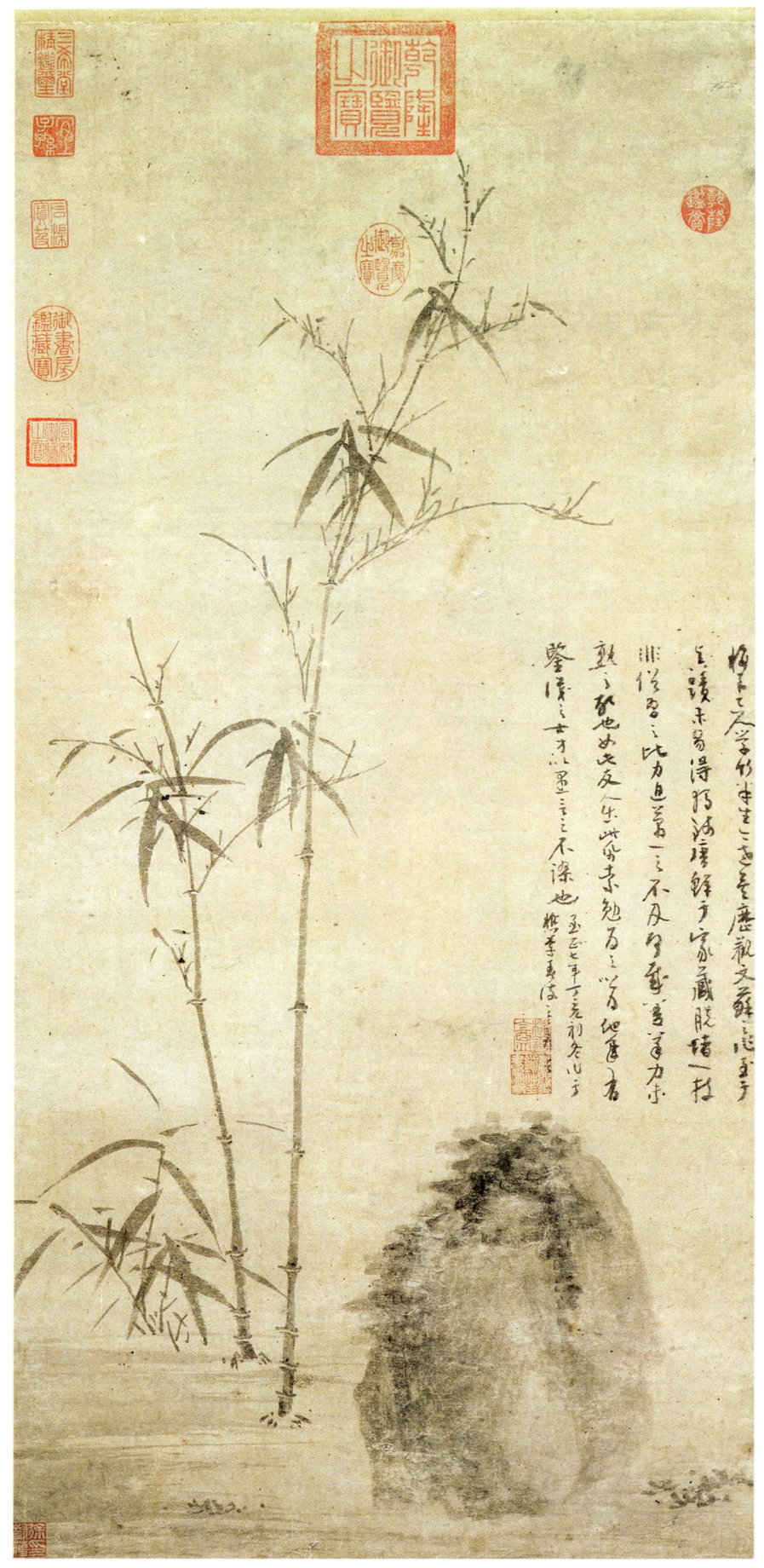

Wu Zhen, *Stalks of Bamboo by a Rock,* Yuan dynasty, 1347. Hanging scroll, ink on paper, 2′ 11½″ × 1′ 4⅝″. National Palace Museum, Taibei.

# 26

# FROM THE MONGOLS TO THE MODERN

## THE ART OF LATER CHINA AND KOREA

The 13th century was a time of profound political upheaval in Asia. The opening decade saw the Islamic armies of Muhammad of Ghor wrest power from India's Hindu kings and the establishment of a Muslim Sultanate at Delhi (see Chapter 25). Then, in 1210, Genghis Khan (1167–1230) and the Mongols invaded northern China from Central Asia (MAP 26-1). By 1215 they had destroyed the Jin dynasty's capital at Beijing. In 1235, the Mongols attacked the Song dynasty in southern China, but it was not until 1279 that the last Song emperor fell at the hands of Genghis Khan's grandson, Kublai Khan (1215–1294). Kublai proclaimed himself the new emperor of China (r. 1279–1294) and founded the Yuan dynasty.

## CHINA

### Yuan Dynasty (1279–1368)

During the relatively brief tenure of the Yuan, trade between Europe and Asia increased dramatically. It is no coincidence that the most famous early European visitor to China, Marco Polo (1254–1324), arrived during the reign of Kublai Khan. Part fact and part fable, Marco Polo's chronicle of his travels to and within China was the only eyewitness description of East Asia available in Europe for several centuries. What emerges from his account is a profound admiration for Yuan China. The Venetian marveled not only at Kublai Khan's opulent lifestyle and palaces, but also at the volume of commercial traffic on the Yangtze River, the splendors of Hangzhou, the use of paper currency, porcelain, and coal, the efficiency of the Chinese postal system, and the hygiene of the Chinese people. In the early second millennium, China was richer and technologically more advanced than late medieval Europe.

**GUAN DAOSHENG AND BAMBOO** The Mongols were great admirers of Chinese art and culture, but they were very selective in admitting former Southern Song

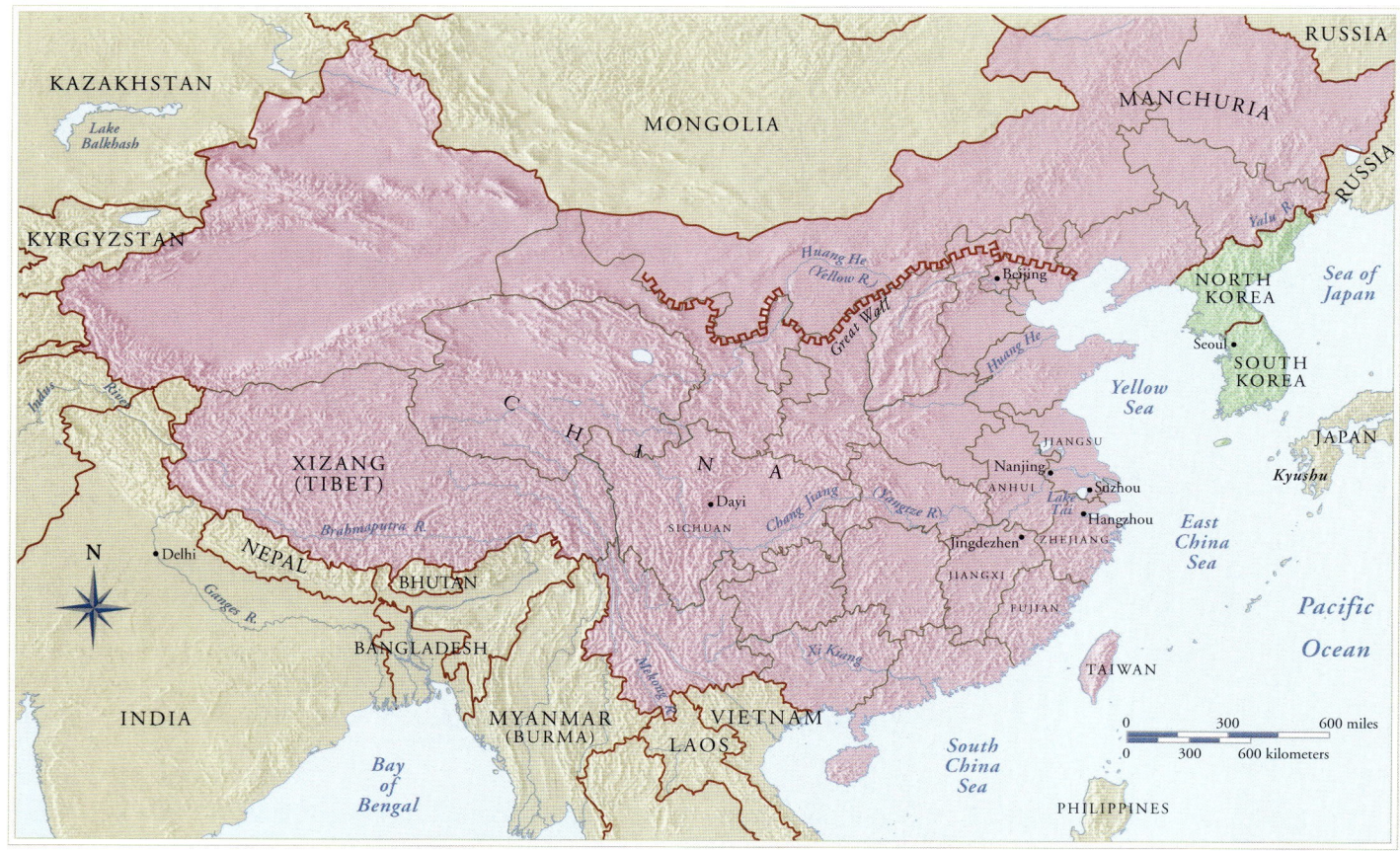

MAP 26-1 China and Korea.

subjects into their administration. In addition, many Chinese loyal to the former emperors refused to collaborate with their new foreign overlords, whom they considered barbarian usurpers. One who did accept an official post under Kublai Khan was Zhao Mengfu (1254–1322), a descendant of the first Song emperor, who continued to serve the Yuan under four subsequent rulers (and was condemned by history for doing so). A learned man, skilled in both calligraphy and poetry, he was renowned as a painter of horses and of landscapes. His wife, GUAN DAOSHENG (1262–1319), was also a successful painter, calligrapher, and poet. Although she painted a variety of subjects,

including Buddhist murals in Yuan temples, Guan achieved renown as a painter of bamboo.

Bamboo was a favorite subject of Chinese painters because the plant was a symbol of the ideal Chinese gentleman, who bends in adversity but does not break. Artists were also attracted to bamboo because depicting its branches and leaves approximated the cherished art of calligraphy. *Bamboo Groves in Mist and Rain* (FIG. 26-1) is a hand scroll with an inscribed dedication by Guan Daosheng to another noblewoman and a second inscription stating that she painted the hand scroll "in a boat on the green waves of the lake" (see "Calligraphy and Inscriptions

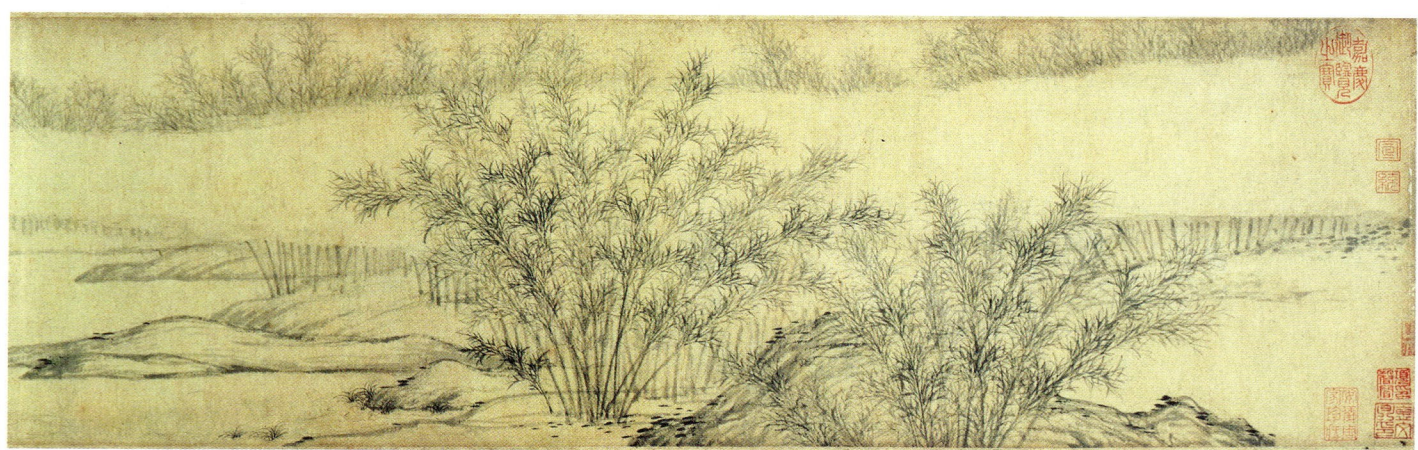

26-1 GUAN DAOSHENG, *Bamboo Groves in Mist and Rain* (detail), Yuan dynasty, 1308. Section of a hand scroll, ink on paper, $9\frac{1}{8}$″ × 3′ $8\frac{7}{8}$″. National Palace Museum, Taiwan.

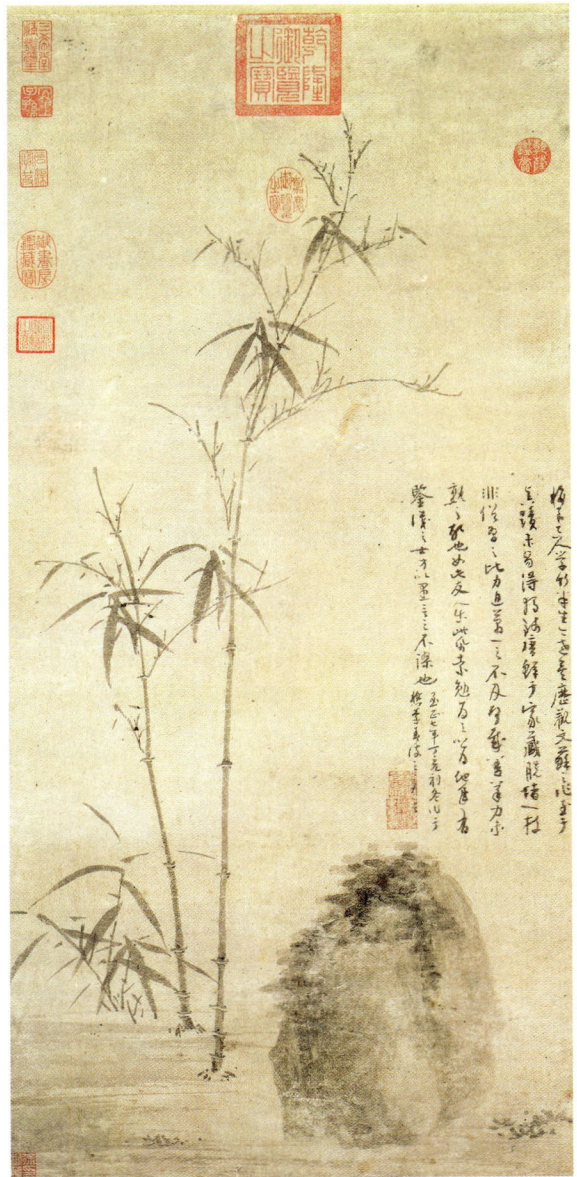

on Chinese Paintings," page 766). Guan achieved the misty atmosphere by restricting the ink tones to a narrow range and by blurring the bamboo thickets in the distance, suggesting not only recession but fog.

**WU ZHEN AND THE LITERATI** The Yuan painter WU ZHEN (1280–1354), in stark contrast to Zhao Mengfu and Guan Daosheng, shunned the Mongol court and lived as a hermit, far from the luxurious milieu of the Yuan emperors. He was one of the *literati,* or scholar-artists, who emerged during the Song dynasty. The literati painted primarily for a small audience of their educational and social peers. These men and women came from prominent families and were highly educated and steeped in traditional Chinese culture. They cultivated painting, calligraphy, poetry, and other arts as a sign of social status and refined taste. Literati art is usually personal in nature and often shows a nostalgia for the past.

Wu Zhen's treatment of the bamboo theme, *Stalks of Bamboo by a Rock* (FIG. **26-2**), differs sharply from Guan's. In his hanging scroll, the individual bamboo plants are clearly differentiated and the artist revels in the abstract patterns the stalks and leaves form. The bamboo plants are perfect complements to the calligraphic beauty of the Chinese black characters and red seals so prominently featured on the scroll. Both the bamboo and the inscriptions gave Wu Zhen the opportunity to display his proficiency with the brush.

**TEXTURED MOUNTAINS** One of the great works of Yuan literati painting is *Dwelling in the Fuchun Mountains* (FIG. **26-3**) by HUANG GONGWANG (1269–1354), a former civil servant and a teacher of Daoist philosophy. According to the artist's explanatory inscription at the end of the long hand scroll, he sketched the full composition in one burst of inspiration, but then added to and modified his painting whenever he felt moved to do so over a period of years. In the detail we reproduce, the painter built up the textured mountains with richly layered brush strokes, at times interweaving dry brush strokes and at other times placing dry strokes over wet ones, darker strokes over lighter ones, often with ink-wash accents. The rhythmic play of brush and ink renders the landscape's inner structure and momentum.

**26-2** WU ZHEN, *Stalks of Bamboo by a Rock,* Yuan dynasty, 1347. Hanging scroll, ink on paper, 2′ 11½″ × 1′ 4⅝″. National Palace Museum, Taiwan.

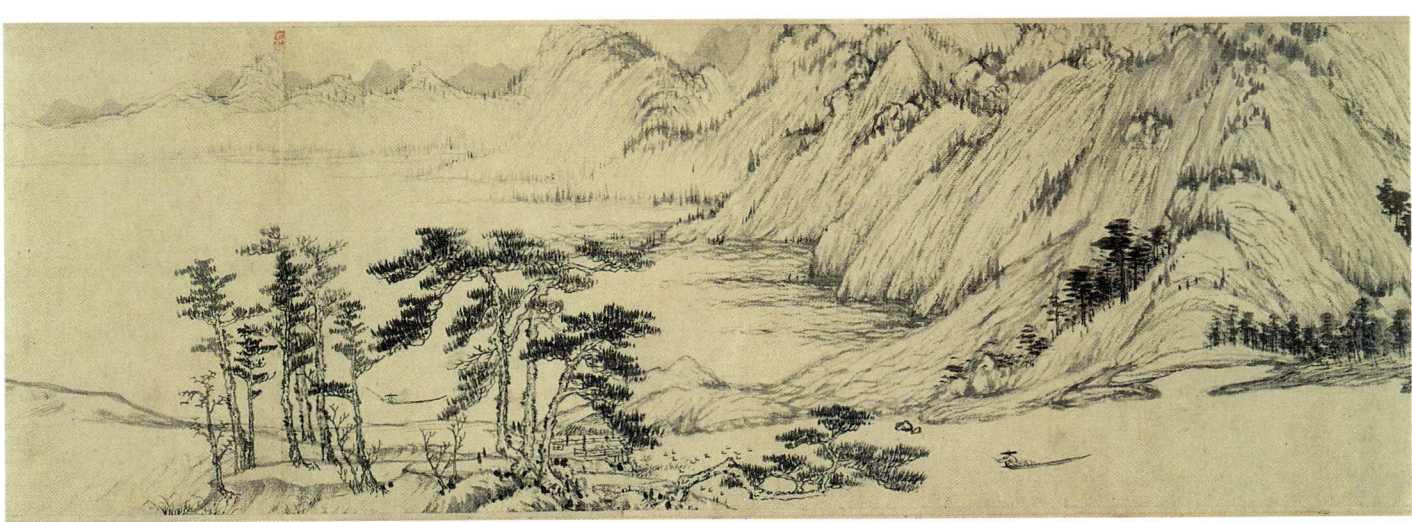

**26-3** HUANG GONGWANG, *Dwelling in the Fuchun Mountains,* Yuan dynasty, 1347–1350. Section of a hand scroll, ink on paper, 1′ 7⅞″ × 20′ 9″. National Palace Museum, Taiwan.

## Calligraphy and Inscriptions on Chinese Paintings

Many Chinese paintings (FIGS. 7-19, 7-23, 26-2, and 26-10 to 26-12) bear *inscriptions,* texts written on the same surface as the picture, or *colophons,* texts written on attached pieces of paper or silk. Throughout Chinese history, calligraphy and painting have been closely connected and equally esteemed. Even the primary implements and materials for writing and drawing are the same—a round tapered brush, soot-based ink, and paper or silk. Calligraphy depends for its effects on the controlled vitality of individual brush strokes and on the dynamic relationships of strokes within a character and among the characters themselves. Training in calligraphy was a fundamental part of the education and self-cultivation of Chinese scholars and officials, and inscriptions are especially common on literati paintings.

Chinese characters are best described as *logograms,* each character corresponding to one meaningful language unit. Many stylistic variations exist in Chinese calligraphy. At the most formal extreme, each character is separated from the next and comprised of distinct straight and angular strokes. At the other extreme, the characters flow together as cursive abbreviations with many rounded forms. The inscriptions on the paintings we illustrate show the wide range of styles.

A long tradition in China links pictures and texts. Famous poems frequently provided subjects for paintings, and poets composed poems inspired by paintings. Either practice might prompt inscriptions on art, some addressing painted subjects, some praising the painting's quality or the painter's character. Other inscriptions explain the circumstances of the work—for example, Guan Daosheng's statement that she painted *Bamboo Groves in Mist and Rain* (FIG. 26-1) in a boat. Later admirers and owners of paintings often inscribed their own appreciative words.

Painters, inscribers, and even owners usually also added seal impressions in red ink (FIGS. 26-1 to 26-3 and 26-10 to 26-14) to identify themselves. With all these textual additions, some paintings that have passed through many collections may seem cluttered to Western eyes. However, the historical importance given to such inscriptions and ownership history has been and remains a critical aspect of painting appreciation in China.

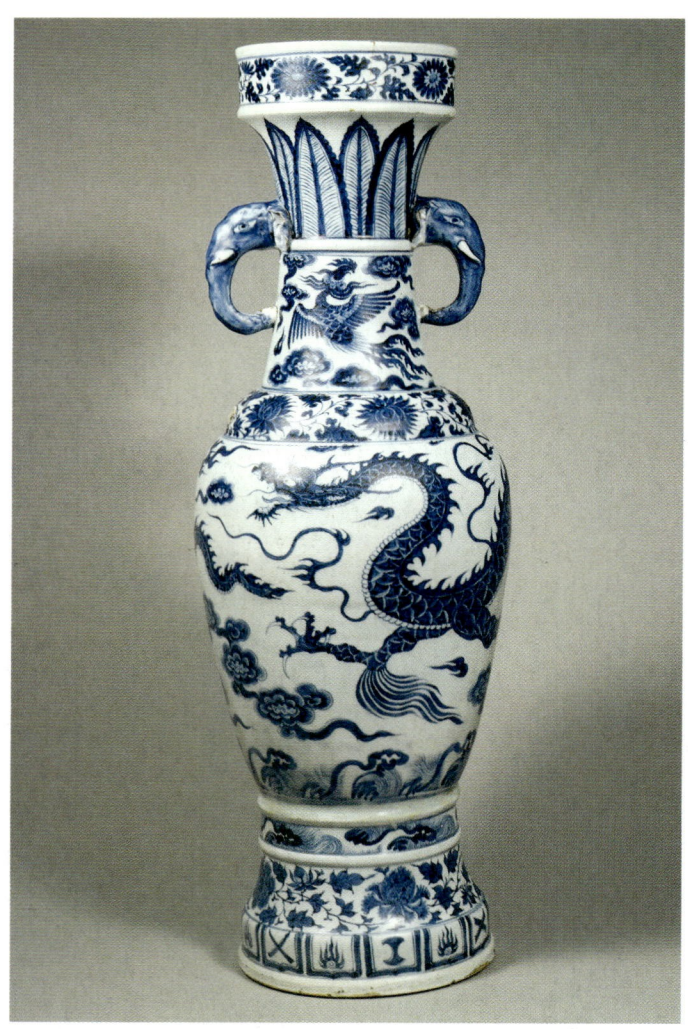

**26-4** Temple vase, Yuan dynasty, 1351. White porcelain with cobalt blue underglaze, 2' 1" × 8⅛". Percival David Foundation of Chinese Art, London.

**DRAGON AND PHOENIX** By the Yuan period, Chinese potters had extended their mastery to fully developed porcelains, a very technically demanding medium (see "Chinese Porcelain," page 767). A tall temple vase from the Jingdezhen kilns (FIG. 26-4), which during the Ming dynasty became the official source of porcelains for the court, is one of a nearly identical pair dated by inscription to 1351. The inscription also says the vases, together with an incense burner, made up an altar set donated to a Buddhist temple as a prayer for peace, protection, and prosperity for the donor's family. The vase is one of the earliest dated examples of fine porcelain with cobalt blue underglaze decoration. The painted decoration consists of bands of floral motifs between broader zones containing auspicious symbols, including phoenixes in the lower part of the neck and dragons (compare FIG. 7-4) on the main body of the vessel, both among clouds. These motifs may suggest the donor's high status or invoke prosperity blessings. Because of their vast power and associations with nobility and prosperity, the dragon and the phoenix also symbolize the emperor and empress, respectively, and often appear on objects made for the imperial household. The dragon also may represent *yang,* the Chinese principle of active masculine energy, while the phoenix may represent *yin,* the principle of passive feminine energy.

## Ming Dynasty (1368–1644)

**THE FORBIDDEN CITY** In 1368, Zhu Yuanzhong led a popular uprising that drove the last Mongol emperor from Beijing. After expelling the foreigners from China, he founded the native Chinese Ming dynasty, proclaiming himself its first emperor under the official name of Hongwu (r. 1368–1398). The new emperor built his capital at Nanjing, but the third Ming emperor, Yongle (r. 1403–1424), moved the capital back to Beijing. Although Beijing had been home to the Yuan dynasty, Ming architects designed much of the city as well as the imperial palace at its core.

### Chinese Porcelain

No other Chinese art form has been so admired by the rest of the world, inspired such imitation, or penetrated so deeply into everyday life as porcelain (FIGS. 26-4 and 26-15). Long imported by neighboring countries as luxury goods and treasures, Chinese porcelains later captured great attention in the West, where potters did not succeed in mastering the production process until the early 18th century.

In China, primitive porcelains emerged during the Tang dynasty (618–906) and mature forms developed in the Song (960–1279). Like stoneware (see "Chinese Earthenwares and Stonewares," Chapter 7, page 193), porcelain is fired at an extremely high temperature (well over 2,000° F) in a kiln until its clay body is fully fused into a dense, hard substance resembling stone or glass. Unlike stoneware, however, porcelain is made from a fine white clay called kaolin mixed with ground petuntse (a type of feldspar). True porcelain is translucent and rings when struck.

Porcelains are often decorated with colored designs or pictures. The decorators work with finely ground minerals suspended in water and a binding agent (such as glue). The minerals change color dramatically in the kiln. The painters apply some mineral colors to the clay surface before the main firing and then apply a clear glaze over them. Such *underglaze* decoration fully bonds to the piece in the kiln, but only a few colors are possible, because the raw materials must withstand intense heat. The most stable and widely used coloring agents for porcelains are cobalt compounds, which fire to an intense blue (FIG. 26-4). Rarely, potters use copper compounds to produce stunning reds by carefully manipulating the kiln's temperature and oxygen content. To obtain a wider palette, ceramic decorators must paint on top of the glaze after the work has been fired (FIG. 26-15). The *overglaze* colors, or *enamels,* then fuse to the glazed surface in an additional firing at a much lower temperature. Enamels also offer glaze decorators a much brighter palette, with colors ranging from deep browns to brilliant reds and greens, but they do not have the durability of underglaze decoration.

Ming Beijing was planned as three nested walled cities. The outer perimeter wall was 15 miles long and enclosed the walled Imperial City, with a perimeter of $6\frac{1}{2}$ miles, and the vast imperial palace compound, the moated Forbidden City (FIG. **26-5**), so named because access to it was very restricted. There resided the Ming emperor, the Son of Heaven. The layout of the Forbidden City provided the perfect setting for the elaborate ritual of the imperial court. For example, the entrance gateway, the Noon Gate (in the foreground in the aerial view) has five portals. Only the emperor could walk through the central doorway. The two entrances to its left and right were reserved for the imperial family and high officials. Others had to use the outermost passageways.

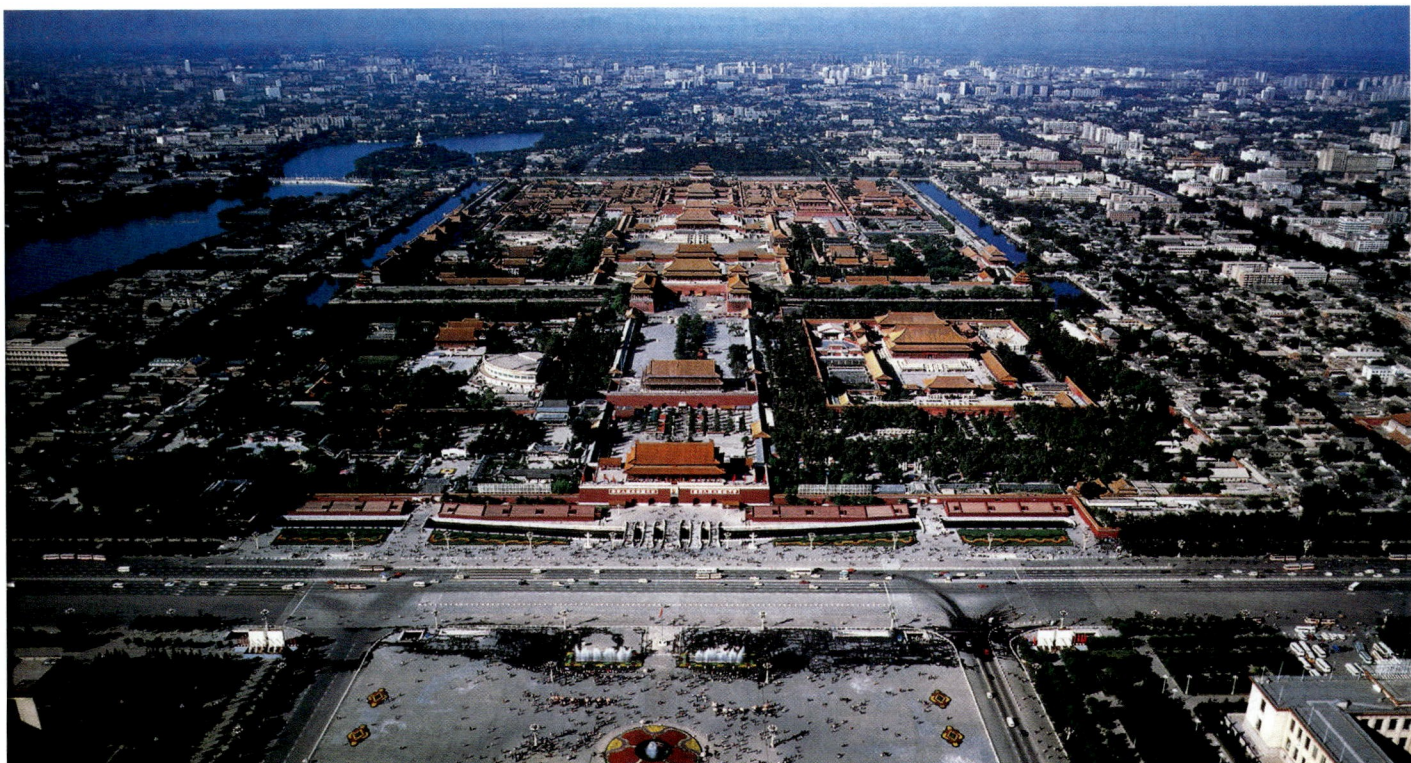

**26-5** Aerial view of the Forbidden City, Beijing, China, Ming dynasty, 15th century and later.

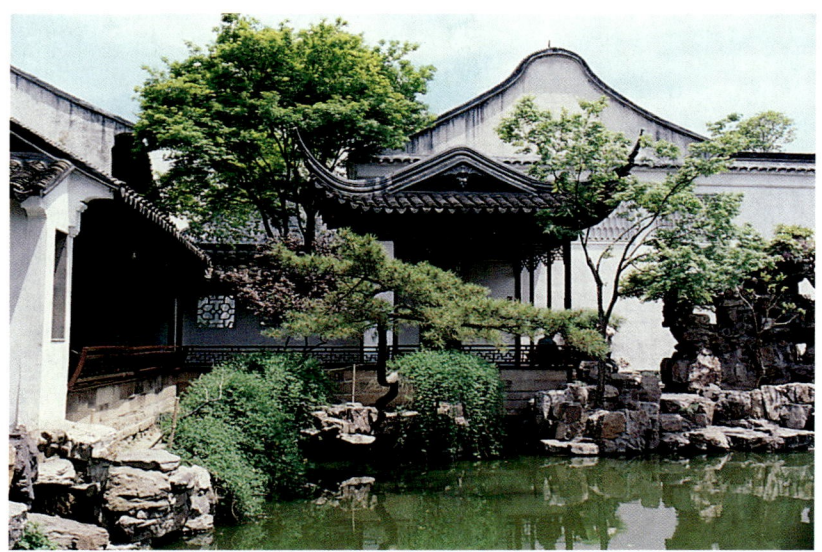

**26-6** Wangshi Yuan (Garden of the Master of the Fishing Nets), Suzhou, Jiangsu Province, China, Ming dynasty, 16th century and later.

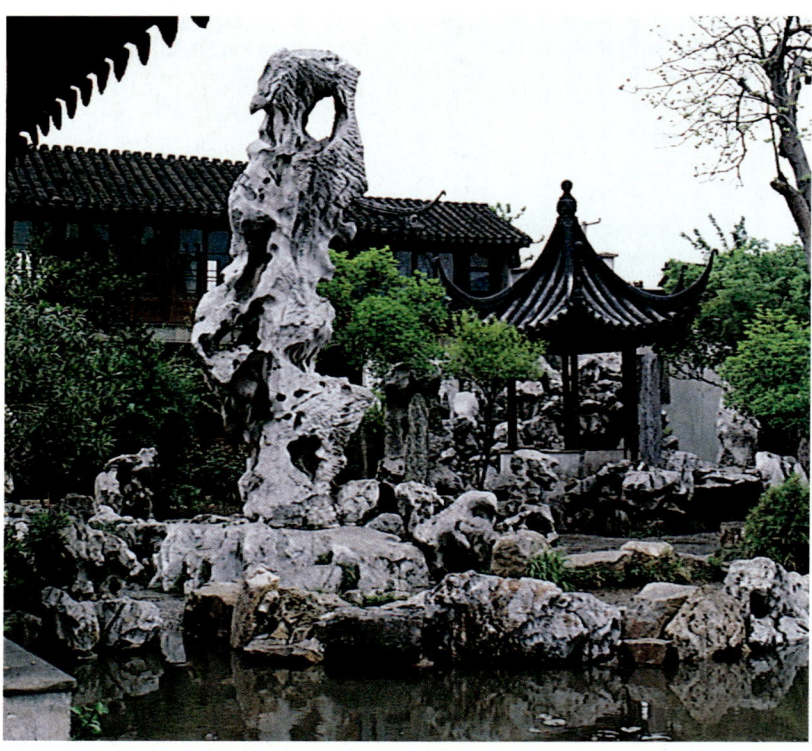

**26-7** Liu Yuan (Lingering Garden), Suzhou, Jiangsu Province, China, Ming dynasty, 16th century and later.

More gates and a series of courtyards and imposing buildings, all erected using the traditional Chinese bracketing system (see "Chinese Wooden Construction," Chapter 7, page 200), led eventually to the Hall of Supreme Harmony, perched on an immense platform above marble staircases, the climax of a long north-south axis. Within the hall, the emperor sat on his throne on another high stepped platform.

**THE GARDENS OF SUZHOU** At the opposite architectural pole from the formality and rigid axiality of palace architecture is the Chinese pleasure garden. Several Ming gardens at Suzhou have been meticulously restored, including the huge (almost 54,000 square feet) Wangshi Yuan (Garden of the Master of the Fishing Nets; FIG. **26-6**). Designing a Ming garden was not a matter of cultivating plants in rows or of laying out terraces, flower beds, and avenues in geometric fashion, as was the case in many other cultures (compare, for example, the 17th-century French gardens at Versailles, FIGS. 24-67 and 24-68). Instead, the gardens are often scenic arrangements of natural and artificial elements intended to reproduce the irregularities of uncultivated nature. Verandas and pavilions rise on pillars above the water, and stone bridges, paths, and causeways encourage wandering through ever-changing vistas of trees, flowers, rocks, and their reflections in the ponds. The typical design is a sequence of carefully contrived visual surprises.

A favorite garden element, fantastic rockwork, may be seen at Liu Yuan (Lingering Garden; FIG. **26-7**) in Suzhou. The stones were dredged from nearby Lake Tai and then shaped by sculptors to create an even more natural look. The Ming gardens of Suzhou were the pleasure retreats of high officials and the landed gentry,

## Lacquered Wood

*Lacquer* is produced from the sap of the Asiatic sumac tree, native to central and southern China. From ancient times it was used to cover wood, because when it dries, it cures to great hardness and prevents the wood from decaying. Often colored with mineral pigments, lacquered objects have a lustrous surface that transforms the appearance of natural wood. The earliest examples of lacquered wood to survive in quantity date to the Eastern Zhou period (770–256 BCE).

The first step in producing a lacquered object is to heat and purify the sap. Then the lacquer worker mixes the minerals—carbon black and cinnabar red are the most common—into the sap. To apply the lacquer, the artisan uses a hair brush similar to a calligrapher's or painter's brush. The lacquer goes on one layer at a time. Then it must dry and be sanded before another coat can be applied. If a sufficient number of layers is built up, the lacquer can be carved as if it were the wood itself (FIG. 26-8).

Other techniques for decorating lacquer include inlaying metals and lustrous materials, such as mother-of-pearl, and sprinkling gold powder into the still-wet lacquer. Such techniques also flourished in both Korea and Japan (see FIG. 27-9).

sanctuaries where the wealthy could commune with nature in all its representative forms and as an ever-changing and boundless presence. Chinese poets never cease to sing of the restorative effect of gardens on mind and spirit.

**THE ART OF LACQUER** The Ming court's lavish appetite for luxury goods gave new impetus to brilliant technical achievement in the decorative arts. Like the Yuan rulers, the Ming emperors turned to the Jingdezhen kilns for fine porcelains. For objects in lacquered wood (see "Lacquered Wood," above), their patronage went to a large workshop known today as the Orchard Factory. One of its masterpieces is a table with drawers (FIG. **26-8**)

made between 1426 and 1435. The artist carved floral motifs, along with the dragon and phoenix imperial emblems, into the thick cinnabar-colored lacquer, which had to be built up in numerous layers.

**MING COURT PAINTING** At the Ming court, the official painters were housed in the Forbidden City itself, and portraiture of the imperial family was their major subject. The court artists also depicted historical figures as exemplars of virtue, wisdom, or heroism. An exceptionally large example of Ming history painting is a hanging scroll that SHANG XI (active in the second quarter of the 15th century) painted around 1430. *Guan Yu Captures*

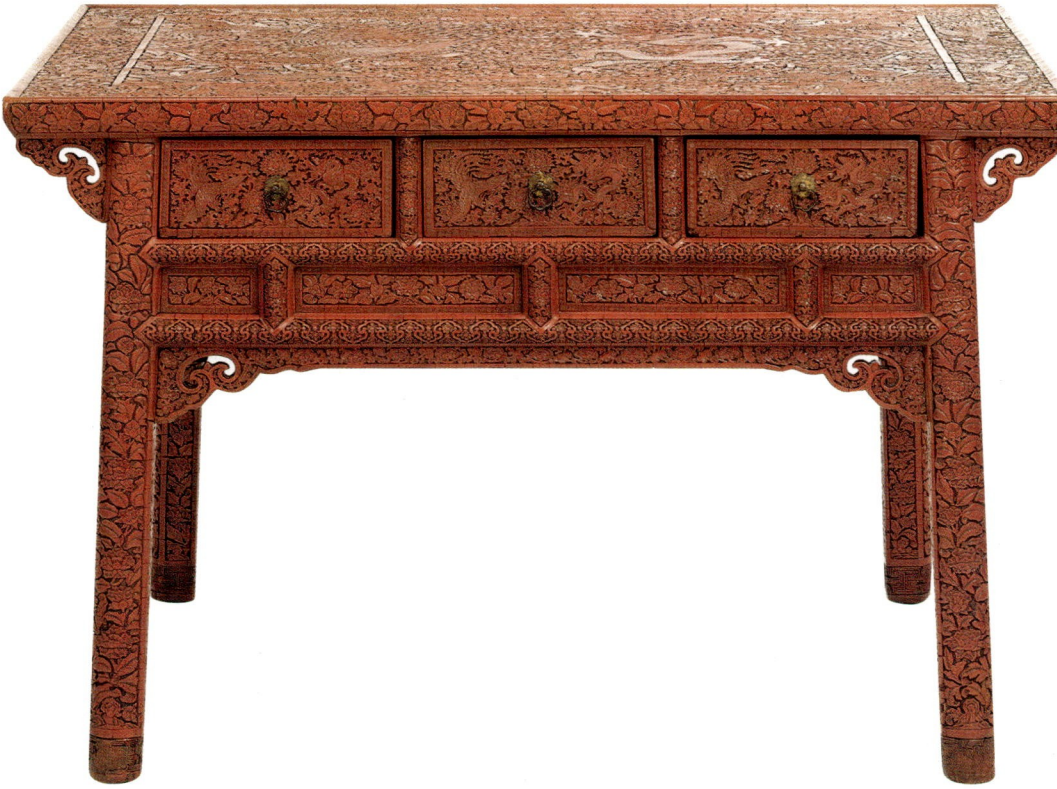

**26-8** Table with drawers, Ming dynasty, ca. 1426–1435. Carved red lacquer on a wood core, 3′ 11″ long. Victoria and Albert Museum, London.

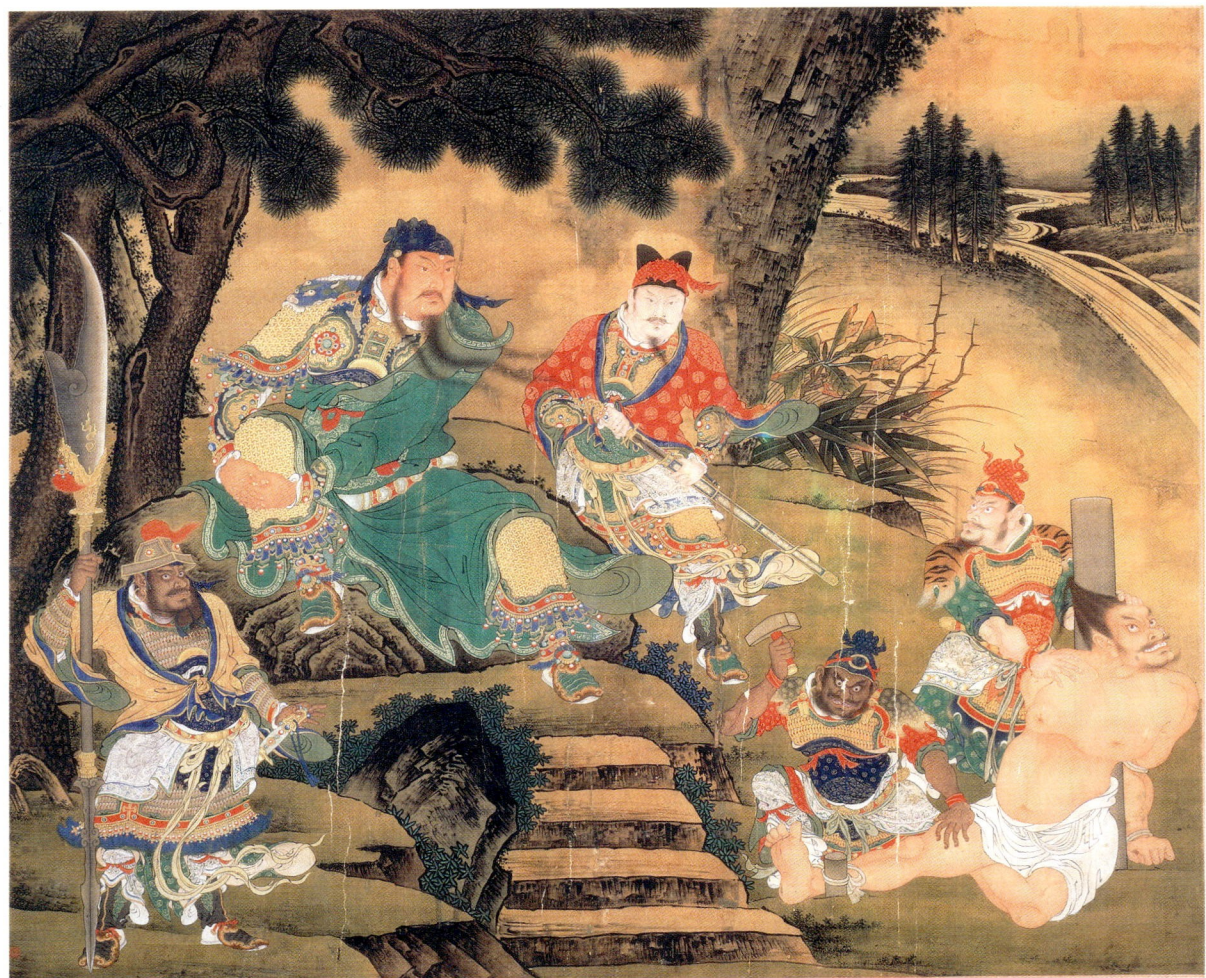

26-9 SHANG XI, *Guan Yu Captures General Pang De,* Ming dynasty, ca. 1430. Hanging scroll, ink and colors on silk, 6′ 5″ × 7′ 7″. Palace Museum, Beijing.

*General Pang De* (FIG. **26-9**) represents an episode from the tumultuous third century (Period of Disunity; see Chapter 7), whose wars inspired one of the first great Chinese novels, *The Romance of the Three Kingdoms.* Guan Yu was a famed general of the Wei dynasty (220–280) and a fictional hero in the novel. The painting depicts the historical Guan Yu, renowned for his loyalty to his emperor and his military valor, being presented with the captured enemy general Pang De. In his painting, Shang Xi uses color to focus attention on Guan Yu and his attendants, who stand out sharply from the ink landscape. He also contrasts the victors' armor and bright garments with the vulnerability of the captive, who has been stripped almost naked, further heightening his humiliation.

**MING LITERATI** The work of Shang Xi and other professional court painters, designed to promote the official Ming ideology, is far removed from the venerable tradition of literati painting, which also flourished during the Ming dynasty, but, as under the Yuan emperors, was largely independent of court patronage. One of the leading figures was SHEN ZHOU (1427–1509), a master of the Wu School of painting, so called because of the ancient name (Wu) of the city of Suzhou. Shen Zhou came from a family of scholars and painters and turned down an offer to serve in the Ming bureaucracy in order to devote himself to poetry and painting. His hanging scroll, *Lofty Mount Lu* (FIG. **26-10**), a birthday gift to one of his teachers, bears a long poem he wrote in the teacher's honor. Shen Zhou had never seen Mount Lu, but he chose the subject because he wished the lofty mountain peaks to

express the grandeur of his teacher's virtue and character. The artist suggested the immense scale of Mount Lu by placing a tiny figure at the bottom center of the painting, sketched in lightly and partly obscured by a rocky outcropping. The composition owes a great deal to early masters like Fan Kuan (see FIG. 7-18). But, characteristic of literati painting in general, the scroll is in the end a very personal conversation—in pictures and words—between the painter and the teacher for whom it was created.

**DONG QICHANG** One of the most intriguing and influential literati of the late Ming dynasty was DONG QICHANG (1555–1636), a wealthy landowner and high official who was a poet, calligrapher, and painter. He also amassed a vast collection of Chinese art and achieved great fame as an art critic. In Dong Qichang's view, most Chinese landscape painters could be classified as belonging to either the Northern School of precise, academic painting or the Southern School of more subjective, freer painting. "Northern" and "Southern" were therefore not geographic but stylistic labels. Dong Qichang chose these names for the two schools because he determined that their characteristic styles had parallels in the northern and southern schools of Chan Buddhism (see "Chan Buddhism," Chapter 7, page 212). Northern Chan Buddhists were "gradualists" and believed that enlightenment could be achieved only after long training. The Southern Chan Buddhists believed that enlightenment could come suddenly. The professional, highly trained court painters belonged to the Northern School. The leading painters of the Southern School

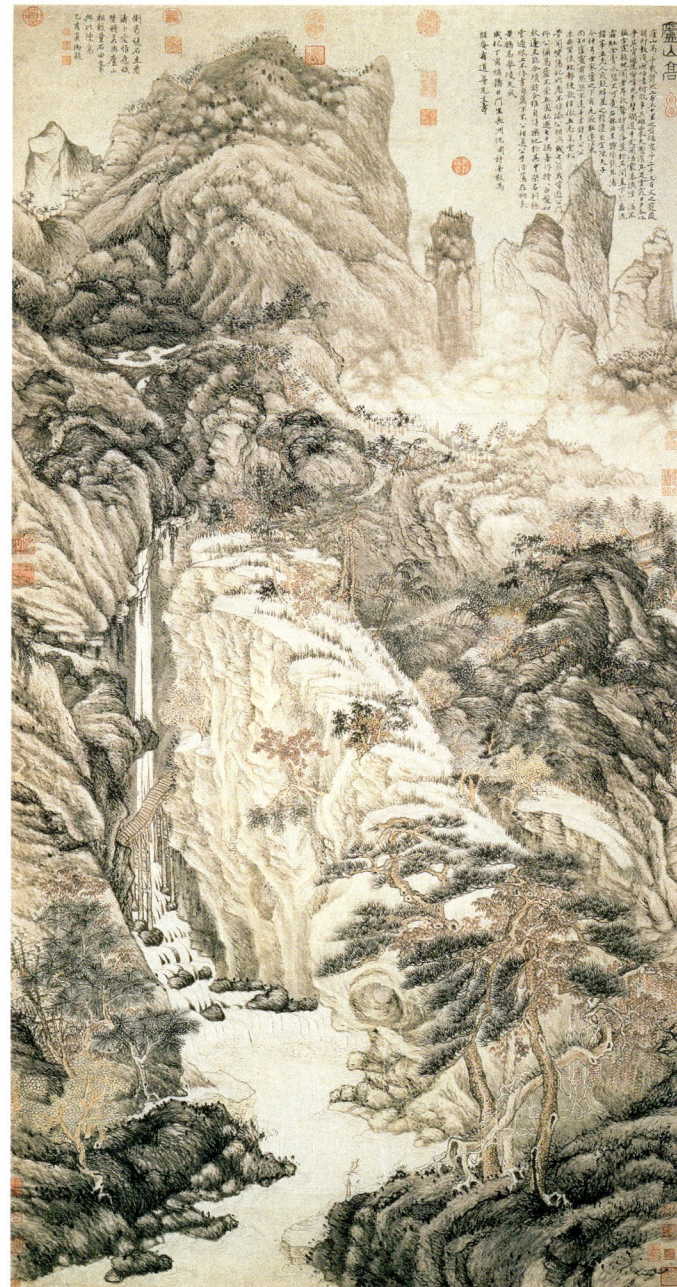

**26-10** SHEN ZHOU, *Lofty Mount Lu*, Ming dynasty, 1467. Hanging scroll, ink and color on paper, 6′ 4¼″ × 3′ 2⅝″. National Palace Museum, Taiwan.

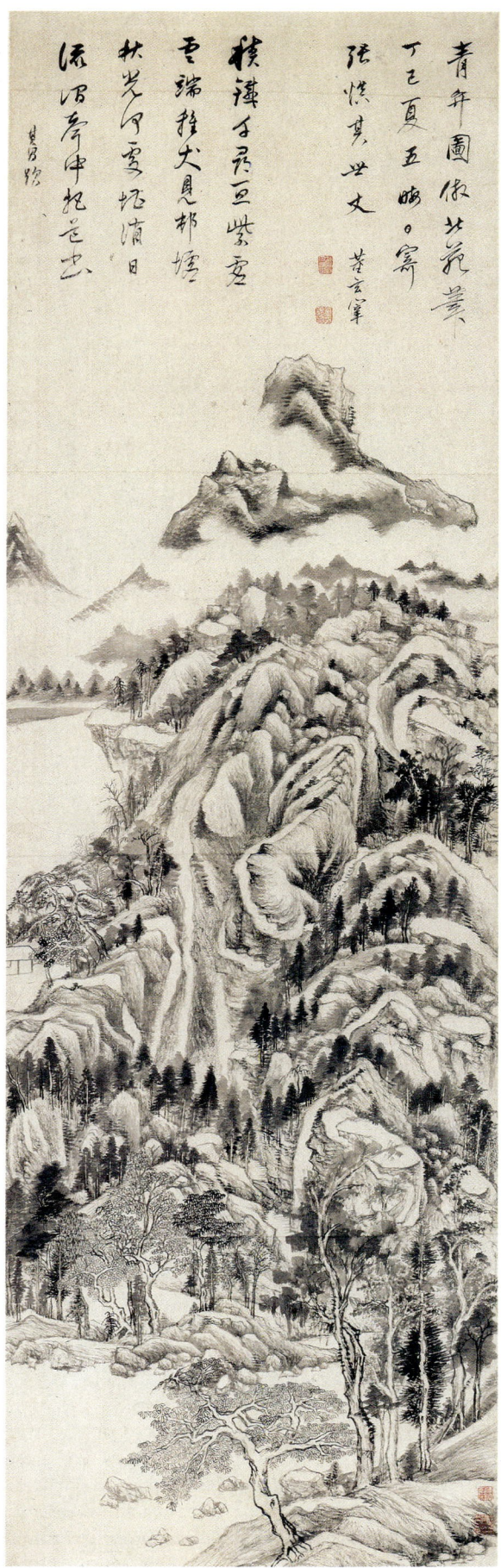

were the literati, whose freer and more expressive style Dong Qichang judged to be far superior.

Dong Qichang's own work—for example, *Dwelling in the Qingbian Mountains* (FIG. **26-11**), painted in 1617—belongs to the Southern School he admired so much. His debt to earlier literati painters can readily be seen in both subject and style as well as in the incorporation of a long inscription at the top. But Dong Qichang was also an innovator, especially in his treatment of the towering mountains, where shaded masses of rocks alternate with flat, blank bands, flattening the composition and creating highly expressive and abstract patterns. Some critics have even called Dong Qichang the first modernist painter, foreshadowing developments in 19th-century European landscape painting (see Chapter 29).

**26-11** DONG QICHANG, *Dwelling in the Qingbian Mountains*, Ming dynasty, 1617. Hanging scroll, ink on paper, 7′ 3½″ × 2′ 2½″. Cleveland Museum of Art (Leonard C. Hanna, Jr. bequest).

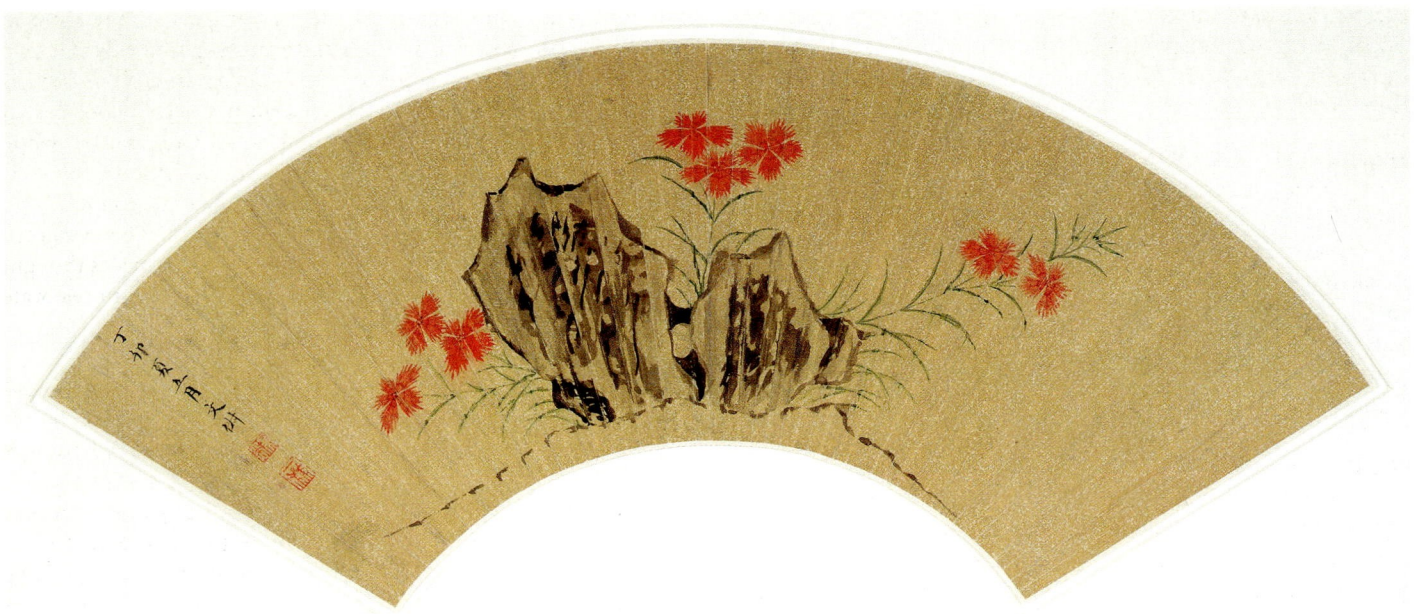

**26-12** WEN SHU, *Carnations and Garden Rock,* Ming dynasty, 1627. Fan, ink and colors on gold paper, $6\frac{3}{8}'' \times 1' \, 9\frac{1}{4}''$. Honolulu Academy of Arts (gift of Mr. Robert Allerton).

**WEN SHU AND FAN PAINTING** Landscape painting was considered the most prestigious artistic subject in Ming China, and was the preferred theme of male literati. Ming women artists usually painted other subjects, especially flowers. WEN SHU (1595–1634), the daughter of an aristocratic Suzhou family and the wife of Zhao Jun, descended from Zhao Mengfu and the Song imperial house, was probably the finest flower painter of the Ming era. Her *Carnations and Garden Rock* (FIG. **26-12**) is also an example of Chinese arc-shaped fan painting, a format imported from Japan. In this genre, the artist paints on flat paper, but when the painting is completed, it is mounted on sticks and folded. The best fan paintings were probably never actually used as fans, but were purchased by collectors and stored in albums. As in her other flower paintings, Wen Shu focused on a few essential elements, in this instance a central rock formation and three sprays of flowers, and presented them against a plain background. Using delicate brush strokes and a restricted palette, she brilliantly communicated the fragility of the red flowers, contrasting them with the solidity of the brown rock. The spare composition creates a quiet mood of contemplation.

## Qing Dynasty (1644–1911)

The Ming bureaucracy's internal decay permitted another group of invaders, the Manchus of Manchuria, to overrun China in the 17th century. Established in 1644 as the Qing, these northerners quickly restored effective imperial rule, although southern China remained rebellious. But during his long reign, the second Qing emperor, Kangxi (r. 1662–1722), succeeded in pacifying all of China. The Manchus adapted themselves to Chinese life and cultivated knowledge of China's arts.

**PRIMORDIAL LINE** Traditional literati painting continued to be fashionable among conservative Qing artists, but other painters experimented with extreme effects of massed ink or individualized brushwork patterns. Bold and freely manipulated

compositions with a new, expressive force began to appear. A prominent painter in this mode was SHITAO (DAOJI, 1642–1707). Shitao was a descendant of the Ming imperial family who became a Chan Buddhist monk at age 20. His theoretical writings, most notably his *Sayings on Painting from Monk Bitter Gourd* (the name he gave himself), called for use of the "single brush stroke" or "primordial line" as the root of all phenomena and representation. Although he carefully studied classical paintings, Shitao opposed mimicking earlier works and believed that he could not learn anything from them unless he changed them. The figure in a hut in Shitao's album leaf *Man in a House beneath a Cliff* (FIG. **26-13**) is surrounded by the surging energy of free-floating

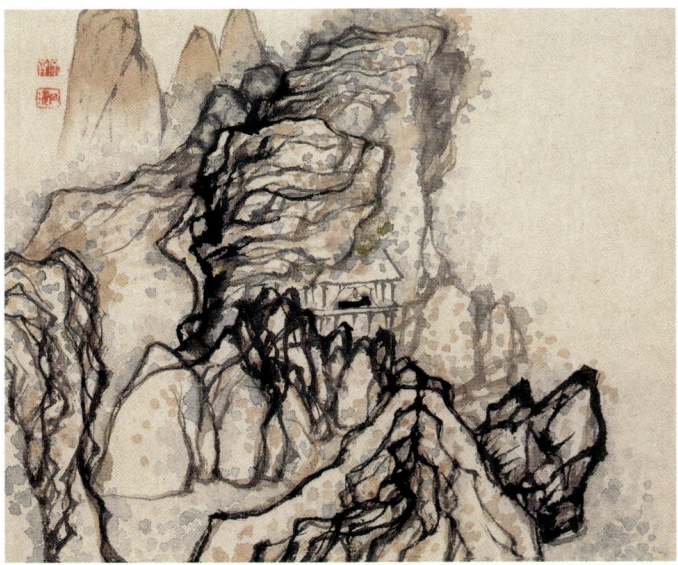

**26-13** SHITAO, *Man in a House beneath a Cliff,* Qing dynasty, late 17th century. Album leaf, ink and colors on paper, $9\frac{1}{2}'' \times 11''$. C. C. Wang Collection, New York.

colored dots and multiple sinuous contour lines. Unlike traditional literati painters, Shitao did not so much depict the landscape's appearance as animate it, molding the forces running through it.

**JESUITS AT THE QING COURT** During the Qing dynasty, European Jesuit missionaries were familiar figures at the imperial court. Many of the missionaries were also artists, and they were instrumental in introducing modern European (that is, High Renaissance and Baroque; see Chapters 22 to 24) painting styles to China. The Chinese, while admiring the Europeans' technical virtuosity, found Western style unsatisfactory. Those Jesuit painters who were successful in China adapted their styles to Chinese tastes.

The most prominent European artist at the Qing court was GIUSEPPE CASTIGLIONE (1688–1768), who went by the name LANG SHINING in China. His hybrid Italian-Chinese painting style is on display in *Auspicious Objects* (FIG. **26-14**), which he painted in 1724 in honor of the Yongzheng (r. 1723–1735) emperor's birthday. Castiglione's emphasis on a single source of light that creates consistent shadows, and his interest in three-dimensional volume, are unmistakably European. But the impact on the Italian artist of Chinese literati painting is equally clear, especially in the composition of the branches and leaves of the overhanging pine tree and in the incorporation of the red seal at the upper left. Above all, the subject is purely Chinese. The white eagle, the pine tree, the rocks, and the red mushroomlike plants (*lingzhi*) are traditional Chinese symbols. The eagle connotes imperial status, courage, and military achievement. The evergreen pines and the rocks connote longevity. Eating lingzhi was thought to promote long life. All are fitting motifs with which to celebrate the birthday of an emperor.

**QING PORCELAIN** Qing potters at the imperial kilns at Jingdezhen continued to expand on the Yuan and Ming achievements in developing fine porcelain pieces with underglaze and overglaze decoration, gaining wide admiration in Europe. A dish with a lobed rim (FIG. **26-15**) exemplifies the overglaze technique. All of its colors—black, green, brown, yellow, and even blue—come from applying enamels (see "Chinese Porcelain," page 767). The decoration reflects important social changes in China. Economic prosperity and the possibility of advancement through success on civil service examinations made it realistic for many more families to hope that their sons could achieve both wealth and higher social standing. In the center of the dish are Fu, Lu, and Shou, the three star gods of happiness, success, and longevity. The cranes and spotted deer, believed to live to advanced ages, and the pine trees around the rim are all symbols of long life. Similar themes appear in the cheap woodblock prints produced in great quantities during the Qing era. They were the commoners' equivalent of Castiglione's imperial painting of auspicious symbols (FIG. 26-14).

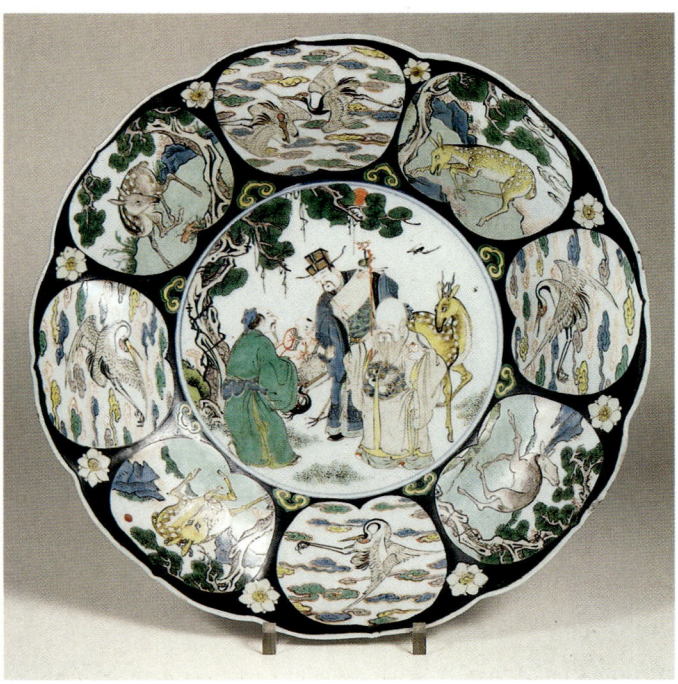

**26-14** GIUSEPPE CASTIGLIONE (LANG SHINING), *Auspicious Objects,* Qing dynasty, 1724. Hanging scroll, ink and colors on silk, 7′ 11$\frac{3}{8}$″ × 5′ 1$\frac{7}{8}$″. Palace Museum, Beijing.

**26-15** Dish with lobed rim, Qing dynasty, ca. 1700. White porcelain with overglaze, 1′ 1$\frac{5}{8}$″ diameter. The Percival David Foundation of Chinese Art, London.

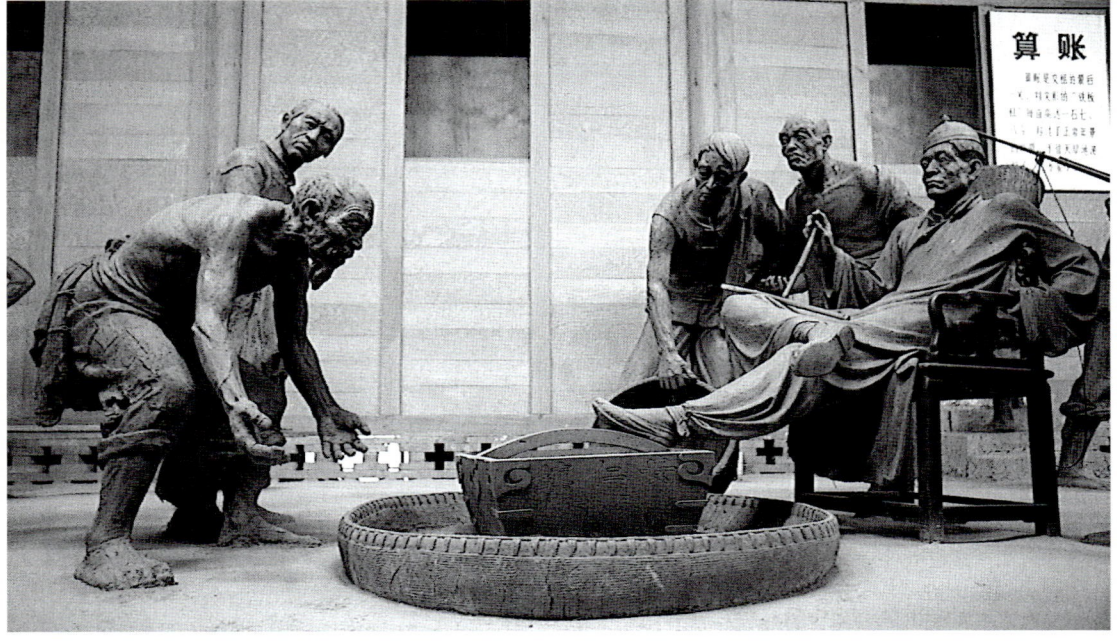

**26-16** YE YUSHAN and others, *Rent Collection Courtyard* (detail of larger tableau), Dayi, Sichuan Province, China, 1965. Clay, approx. 100 yards long with life-size figures.

## Modern China (1912–Present)

**MARXIST ART** The overthrow of the Qing dynasty and the establishment of the Republic of China under the Nationalist Party in 1912 did not bring an end to the traditional themes and modes of Chinese art. But the Marxism that triumphed in 1949, when the Communists took control of China and founded the People's Republic, inspired a social realism that broke drastically with the past. The intended purpose of such art was to serve the people in the struggle to liberate and elevate the masses. In *Rent Collection Courtyard* (FIG. **26-16**), a 1965 tableau about 100 yards long and incorporating 114 life-size figures, YE YUSHAN (b. 1935) and a team of sculptors grimly depicted the old times before the People's Republic. Peasants, worn and bent by toil, bring their taxes (in produce) to the courtyard of their merciless, plundering landlord. The message is clear—this kind of thing must not happen again. When the work was first exhibited, the artists' names were not revealed. The anonymity of those who depicted the event was significant in itself. The secondary message was that only collective action could effect the transformations the People's Republic sought.

**A HEAVENLY BOOK** In the late 1980s and 1990s, Chinese artists began to make a mark on the postmodern international scene (see Chapter 34). One of them was XU BING (b. 1955), who created a large installation called *A Book from Heaven* (FIG. **26-17**) in 1988. First exhibited in China and then in Japan, the United States, and Hong Kong, the work presents an enormous number of woodblock-printed texts in characters that look like Chinese writing but that the artist invented. Producing them required both an intimate knowledge of actual characters and extensive training in block carving. Xu's work is, however, no hymn to tradition. It has been interpreted both as a stinging critique of the meaninglessness of contemporary political language and as a commentary on the illegibility of the past. Like many works of art, past and present, Eastern and Western, it can be read on many levels.

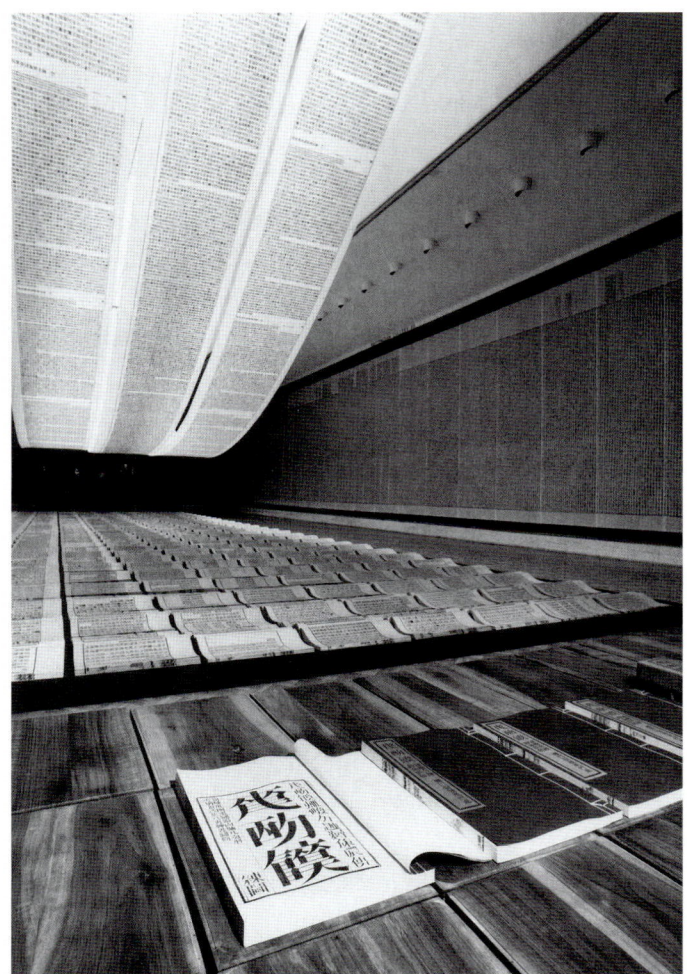

**26-17** XU BING, *A Book from Heaven,* 1988. Installation at Elvehjem Museum of Art, University of Wisconsin, Madison, 1991. Movable-type prints and books.

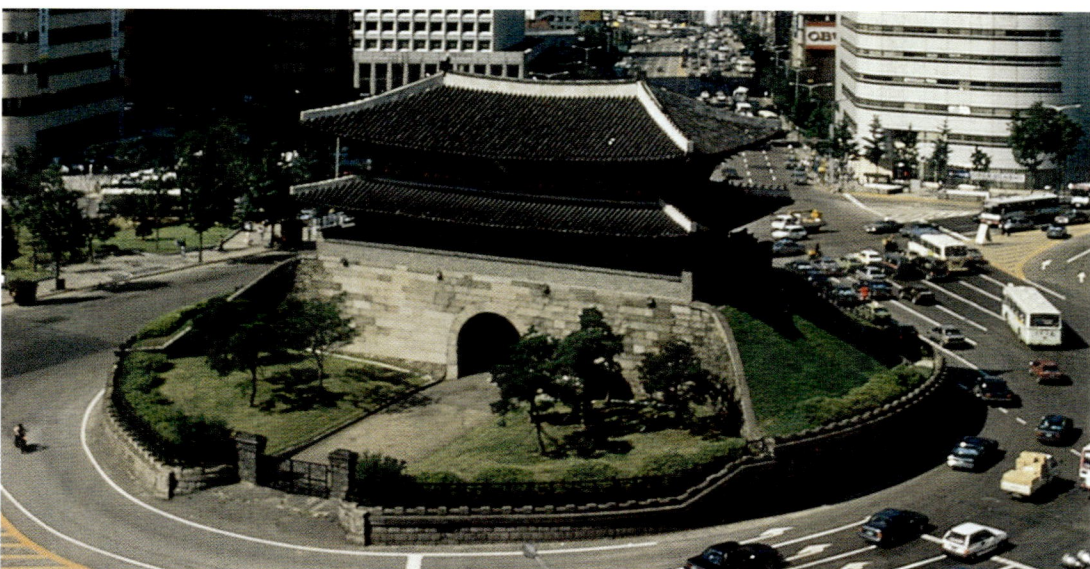

# KOREA

The great political, social, religious, and artistic changes that took place in China from the Mongols to the People's Republic find parallels elsewhere in East Asia. At the time that the Yuan overthrew the Song dynasty, the Koryo dynasty (918–1392), which had ruled Korea since the downfall of China's Tang dynasty, was still in power (see Chapter 7). The Koryo kings outlasted the Yuan as well. Toward the end of the Koryo dynasty, however, the Ming emperors of China attempted to take control of northeastern Korea. They were repelled by General Yi Song-gye, who founded the last Korean dynasty, the Choson (1392–1910), with its capital at Seoul. The long rule of the Choson kings ended only in 1910, when Japan annexed Korea.

## Choson Dynasty (1392–1910)

**THE GATEWAY TO SEOUL** Public building projects helped give the new Korean state an image of dignity and power. One impressive early monument, built for the new capital, is Seoul's south gate, or Nandaemun (FIG. **26-18**). It combines the imposing strength of its impressive stone foundations with the sophistication of its intricately bracketed wooden superstructure. In East Asia, elaborate gateways, often in a processional series, are a standard element in city designs, as well as royal and sacred compounds, all usually surrounded by walls, like Beijing's Forbidden City (FIG. 26-5). Such gateways served as magnificent symbols of the ruler's authority, as did the triumphal arches of imperial Rome (see Chapter 10). Passage into the city through such an impressive monument reminded the populace of the power of the Choson state.

**THE DIAMOND MOUNTAINS** Over the long course of the Choson dynasty, Korean painters worked in many different modes and treated the same wide range of subjects seen in Ming and Qing China. One of Korea's most renowned painters was CHONG SON (1676–1759), a great admirer of Chinese Southern School painting who brought his own unique vision to the traditional theme of the mountainous landscape. In his *Kumgang (Diamond*

*Mountains* (FIG. **26-19**), Chong Son evoked an actual scene, an approach known in Korea as "true view" painting. He used sharper, darker versions of the fibrous brush strokes favored by most Chinese literati in order to represent the bright crystalline appearance of the mountains and to emphasize their spiky forms.

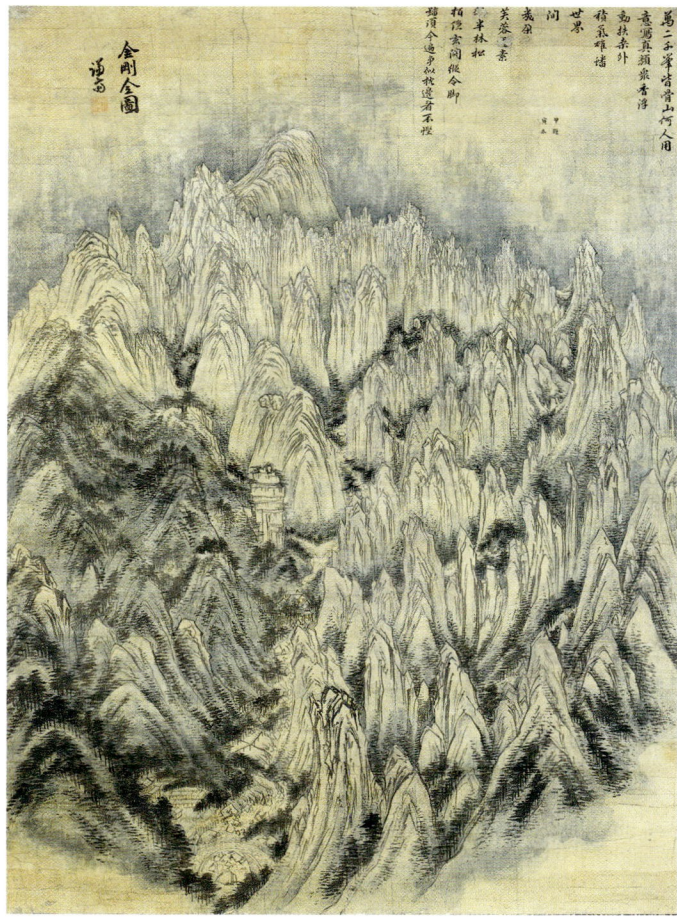

26-19 CHONG SON, *Kumgang Mountains,* Choson dynasty, 1734. Hanging scroll, ink and colors on paper, 4′ 3½″ × 1′ 11¼″. Hoam Art Museum, Kyunggi-Do.

**26-20** Song Su-Nam, *Summer Trees,* 1983. Ink on paper, 2′ 1⅝″ high. British Museum, London.

## Modern Korea (1910–Present)

After its annexation by Japan in 1910, Korea remained part of Japan until 1945, when the Western Allies and the Soviet Union took control of the peninsula nation at the end of World War II. Korea was divided into the Democratic People's Republic of Korea (North Korea) and the Republic of Korea (South Korea) in 1948. South Korea at least has emerged as a fully industrialized nation, and its artists have had a wide exposure to art styles from around the globe. While some Korean artists continue to work in a traditional East Asian manner, others have embraced developments in contemporary Europe and America.

**ORIENTAL INK MOVEMENT** One painter who has very successfully combined native and international traditions is SONG SU-NAM (b. 1938), a professor at Hongik University in Seoul and one of the founders of the Oriental Ink Movement of the 1980s. His *Summer Trees* (FIG. **26-20**), painted in 1983, owes a great deal to the Abstract Expressionist movement of the 20th century and to the work of American painters like Morris Louis (see FIG. 34-13). But in place of Louis's acrylic resin on canvas, Song used ink on paper, the preferred medium of East Asian literati. He forsook, however, the traditional emphasis on brush strokes to explore the subtle tonal variations made possible by broad stretches of ink wash. The landscapes of earlier Korean and Chinese masters are, nonetheless, recalled in the painting's name. Such simultaneous respect for tradition and innovation, a hallmark of both Chinese and Korean art through their long histories, also characterizes the art of Japan (see Chapter 27).

## CONCLUSION

From 1279 until the founding of the Republic of China in 1912, three great dynasties ruled China. Under the Yuan and Ming emperors, China was the richest and most technologically advanced civilization in the world. Beijing became China's capital, and its Forbidden City was developed as a vast imperial compound. This period also saw the rise of the literati movement in art, when scholar-artists retreated from court life and practiced painting, calligraphy, and poetry. Landscape continued to be a favorite theme for painters, and Chinese intellectuals also cultivated gardens designed to reproduce the irregularities of nature. With the establishment of Communist rule in 1949, art began to serve Marxist ideology, but the contemporary art of China and Korea has made a mark on the international art scene.

| CHINA | KOREA | | |
|---|---|---|---|
| | | **1279** | |
| YUAN DYNASTY | KORYO DYNASTY | | Last Song emperor falls to Kublai Khan, 1279 |
| | | **1300** | |
| | | **1368** | |
| | | | Zhu Yuanzhong drives last Mongol emperor from Beijing, 1369 |
| MING DYNASTY | | **1392** | |
| | | | Yi Song-gye repels Chinese from Korea, 1392 |
| | CHOSON DYNASTY | **1450** | |
| | | **1500** | |
| | | **1644** | |
| | | | Manchus seize power in China, 1644 |
| QING DYNASTY | | | Giuseppe Castiglione (1688–1766), Jesuit missionary at Qing court |
| | | **1700** | |
| | | **1800** | |
| | JAPANESE RULE | | Japan annexes Korea, 1910 |
| REPUBLIC OF CHINA | | **1911** | |
| | | | Republic of China founded, 1912 |
| | | **1945** | |
| | POSTWAR PARTITION | | Korea given independence from Japan, 1945 |
| | | | Division of North and South Korea, 1948 |
| PEOPLE'S REPUBLIC OF CHINA | | **1949** | |
| | | | People's Republic of China established, 1949 |

**1** Wu Zhen, *Stalks of Bamboo by a Rock*, 1347

**2** Forbidden City, Beijing, begun 15th century

**3** Dish with lobed rim, ca. 1700

**4** Ye Yushan, *Rent Collection Courtyard*, 1965

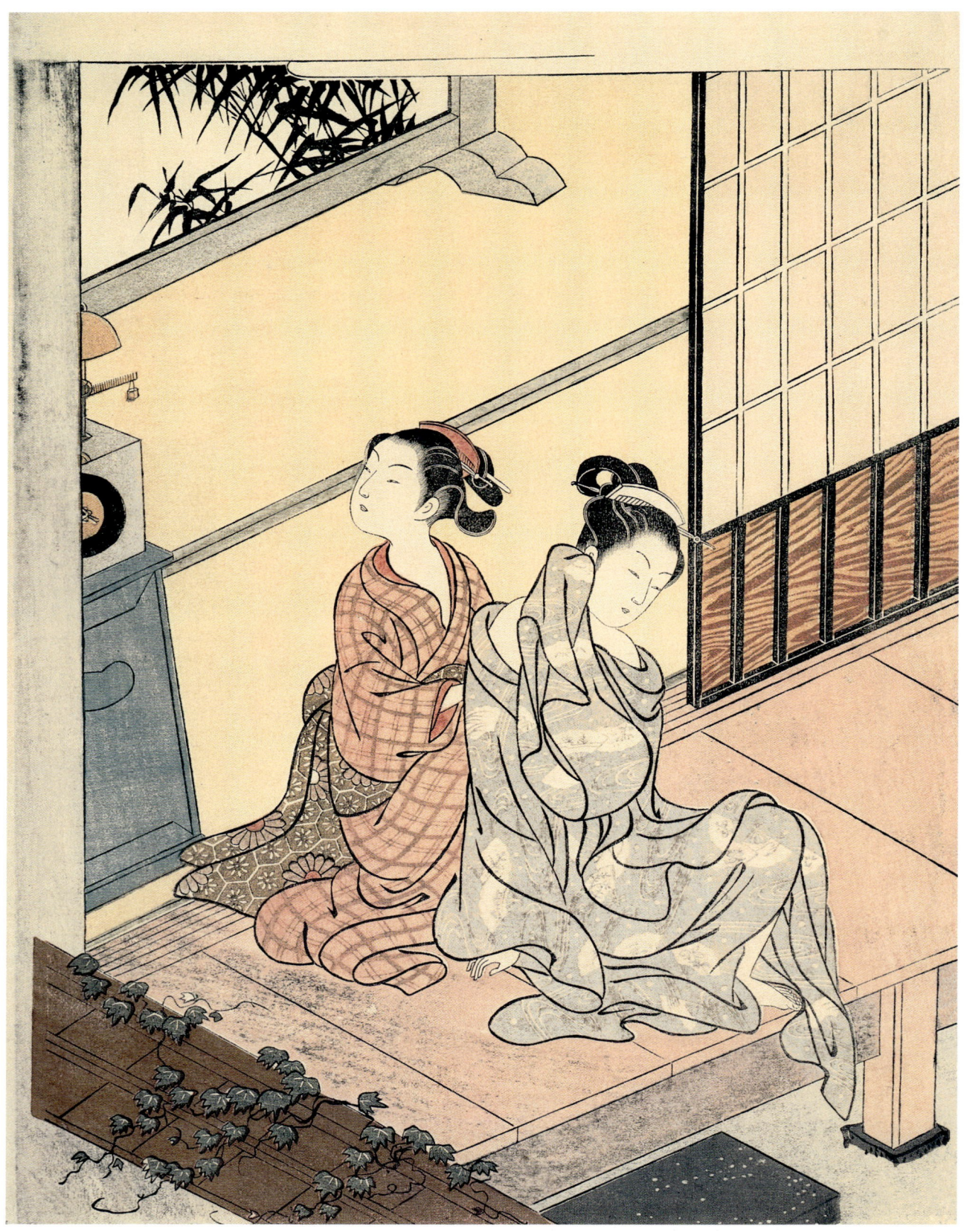

SUZUKI HARUNOBU, *Evening Bell at the Clock,* from *Eight Views of the Parlor* series, Japan, Edo period, ca. 1765. Woodblock print, $11\frac{1}{4}'' \times 8\frac{1}{2}''$. Art Institute of Chicago, Chicago (Clarence Buckingham Collection).

# 27

# FROM THE SHOGUNS TO THE PRESENT

## THE ART OF LATER JAPAN

Early Japanese cultural history (as recounted in Chapter 8) reveals the dialogue that took place between the Japanese islands (MAP **27-1**) and continental eastern Asia. Still, the Japanese developed a rich variety and unique identity in their art. This ability to incorporate foreign elements while maintaining a consciousness of their own heritage and traditions became more apparent as time progressed, even as Japan experienced turmoil and political instability.

## AN AGE OF UPHEAVAL AND WAR

### Muromachi Period (1336–1573)

SHOGUNS AND SAMURAI In 1336, after years of upheaval and conflict within the imperial family, a *shogun* (the head of the most powerful military family), Ashikaga Takauji (1305–1358), managed to accrue sufficient power to establish the domination of his clan over the country. This marked the beginning of the Muromachi period, named after the district in Kyoto in which the Ashikaga maintained their headquarters. The reign of the imperial family continued to be recognized; in theory, the shogun managed the country and maintained unity on the ruling emperor's behalf. However, in reality, the emperor's political power had waned over time until he lost all governing authority. Thus, although the imperial family maintained the illusion of power, control ultimately rested predominantly in the *shogunate,* or military government. Shogunates were largely political and economic arrangements, with local lords, the leaders of powerful warrior bands composed of *samurai* (warriors), paying obeisance to the shogun. These local lords had considerable power over affairs in their own domains. To manage their territories, both the shogun and the local lords also needed strong administrative skills. These skills included handling judicial matters and landholding issues, and cultivating both culture and scholarship.

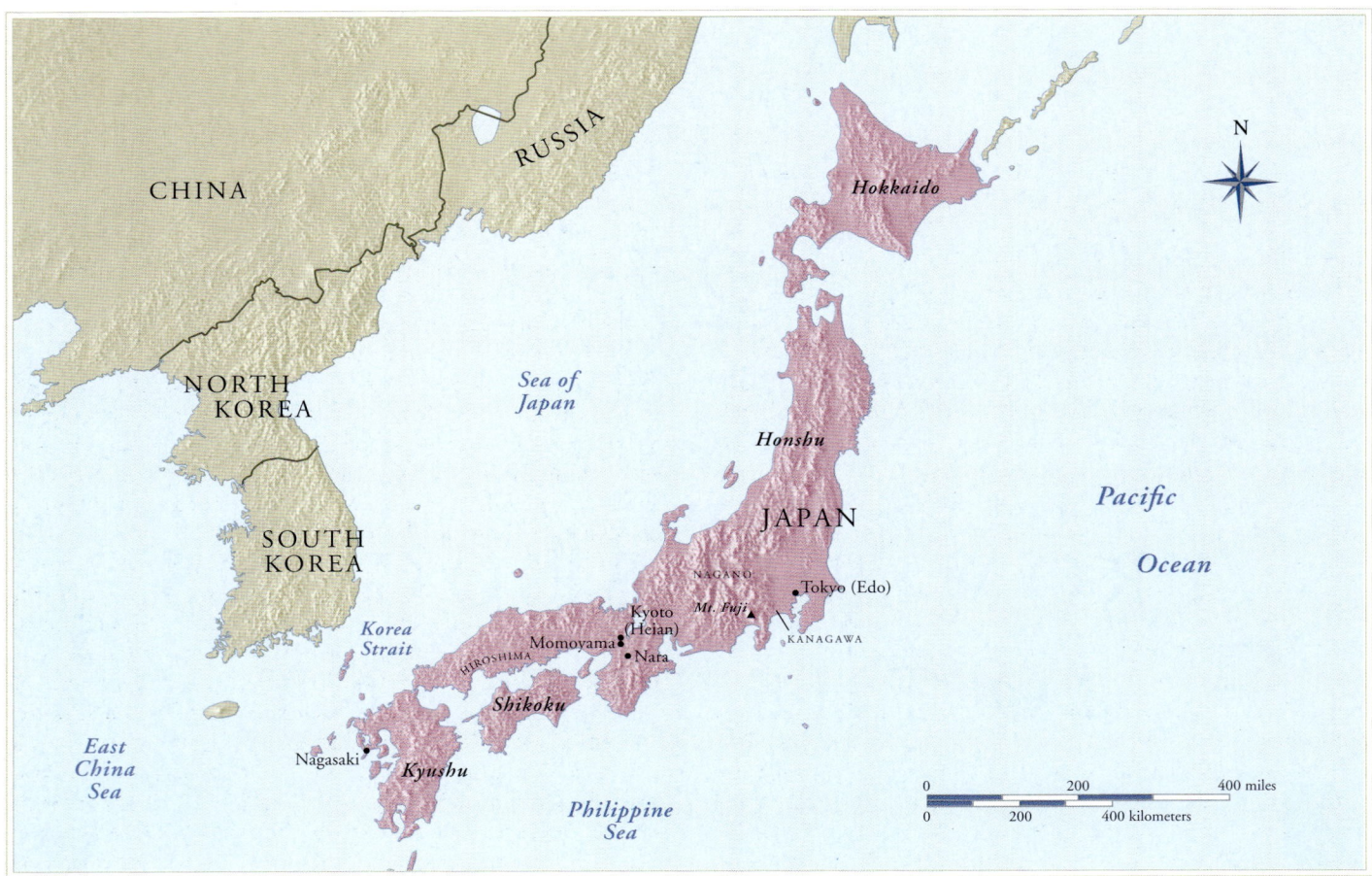

**MAP 27-1** Modern Japan.

Despite the hierarchical nature of this societal organization, the control that shoguns exerted during this period was, in fact, tenuous and precarious. Ambitious lords often seized opportunities to expand their power (perhaps aspiring to become shogun themselves). As a result, Japan experienced violent confrontations over territory and control.

Appropriately, recent scholars have referred to the late 15th through the late 16th century in Japan as the Age of Wars (or the Era of Warring States). The significance of this label is that it highlights the instability of Japanese political and social institutions at this time. This instability contributed to widespread cultural change. For example, Japanese society became more egalitarian, especially in the cities, where commoners mingled with the aristocracy and warriors. Indeed, many wealthy merchants were able to rise to positions of considerable power. In addition, these changes and the resulting liberation from governmental strictures and societal tradition allowed the arts to flourish.

In sum, the Muromachi period was one of upheaval. By 1573, the Ashikaga shogunate had been overthrown, and much of Japan was ravaged by provincial wars—battles between lords, conflicts between militant religious groups, and peasant uprisings.

**THE DISCIPLINE OF ZEN** During the Muromachi period, *Zen* (*Chan* in Chinese) Buddhism (see "Zen and Zen-Inspired Art: Ideals and Realities," page 781) flourished alongside the older traditions, such as Pure Land and Esoteric Buddhism. Unlike the Pure Land faith, which stressed reliance on the saving power of Amida, the Buddha of the West, Zen emphasized rigorous discipline and personal responsibility. For this reason, Zen held a special attraction for upper echelons of the warrior class, whose behavioral codes placed high values on loyalty, courage, and self-control. Further, familiarity with Chinese Zen culture carried implications of superior knowledge and refinement, thereby legitimizing the elevated status of the warrior elite.

Zen, however, was not simply the religion of Zen monks and highly placed warriors. Aristocrats, merchants, and others studied at and supported Zen temples, reflecting the increasing egalitarianism of Japanese society. Furthermore, those who embraced Zen, including samurai, also generally accepted other Buddhist teachings, especially the ideas of the Pure Land sects. These sects gave much greater attention to the problems of death and salvation. Zen temples stood out not only as religious institutions but also as centers of secular culture, where people could study Chinese Song and Yuan art, literature, and learning (see Chapter 26), which the Japanese imported along with Zen Buddhism.

**MEDITATIVE ZEN GARDENS** The Saihoji temple gardens in Kyoto bear witness to both the continuities and changes that marked religious art in the Muromachi period. In the 14th century, this Pure Land temple with its extensive gardens was transformed into a Zen institution. However, Zen leaders did not attempt to erase other religious traditions, and the Saihoji gardens in their totality originally included some Pure Land elements even as they served the Zen faith's more meditative needs. In this way, they perfectly echo the complementary roles of these two Buddhist traditions in the Muromachi period, Pure Land providing a promise of salvation and Zen promoting study and meditation.

Saihoji's lower gardens owe their renown today to their iridescently green mosses, whose beauty almost seems to belong to another world. In contrast, arrangements of rocks and sand on the hillsides of the upper garden, especially the dry cascade and pools (FIG. **27-1**), are treasured early examples of Muromachi dry

### Zen and Zen-Inspired Art
#### Ideals and Realities

Zen, as a fully developed Buddhist tradition, began filtering into Japan in the 12th century and had its most pervasive impact on Japanese culture starting in the 14th century. As in other forms of Buddhism, Zen followers hope for the experience of enlightenment. Zen teachings assert that everyone has the potential for enlightenment, but worldly knowledge and mundane thought patterns suppress it. Thus, to achieve enlightenment, followers must break through the boundaries of everyday perception and logic. This is most often achieved through meditation; indeed, the word *zen* means "meditation." Some Zen schools stress meditation as a long-term practice eventually leading to enlightenment, whereas others stress the benefits of sudden shocks to the worldly mind, as through the posing of abstruse questions. One such shock is depicted in Kano Motonobu's *Zen Patriarch Xiangyen Zhixian Sweeping with a Broom* (FIG. 27-3), in which the shattering of a fallen roof tile opens the monk's mind. Beyond personal commitment, the guidance of an enlightened teacher is essential to arriving at enlightenment. Long and strict training that includes manual labor under the tutelage of this master, coupled with years of meditation, provide the foundation for a receptive mind. According to Zen beliefs, by cultivating discipline and intense concentration, one can transcend one's ego and release oneself from the shackles of the mundane world. Although Zen is not primarily devotional, followers do pray to specific deities. In general, Zen teachings view mental calm, lack of fear, and spontaneity as signs of a person's advancement on the path to enlightenment.

Zen training for monks takes place at temples. In addition, early Japanese Zen temples provided other services. For example, they sometimes served as centers of Chinese learning and handled funeral rites. Zen temples even embraced many traditional Buddhist observances, such as devotional rituals before images, that had little to do with meditation per se.

Over the years, Zen monks have produced an extensive body of art, which aids meditation and serves as a form of teaching. Zen paintings often depict Zen masters, whereas calligraphers usually produce works featuring poems or conundrums. In their quest to distill the Zen experience into strokes of the brush, Zen works are visually bold and convey a spontaneity and energy, although there is no identifiable Zen style.

Zen ideals of discipline and rejection of worldliness reverberated throughout Japanese culture as the teachings spread. Lay followers painted pictures and produced other artworks that appear to reach toward Zen ideals through their subjects and their direct expression. Other cultural practices reflected the widespread appeal of Zen. For example, the tea ceremony (see "The Japanese Tea Ceremony," page 785), or ritual drinking of tea, as it developed in the 15th and 16th centuries, offered a temporary respite from everyday concerns, a brief visit to a quiet retreat with a meditative atmosphere, such as the Taian teahouse (FIG. 27-7). All of these activities attest to the power of Zen as a cultural force in Japan—not just historically, but to the present day.

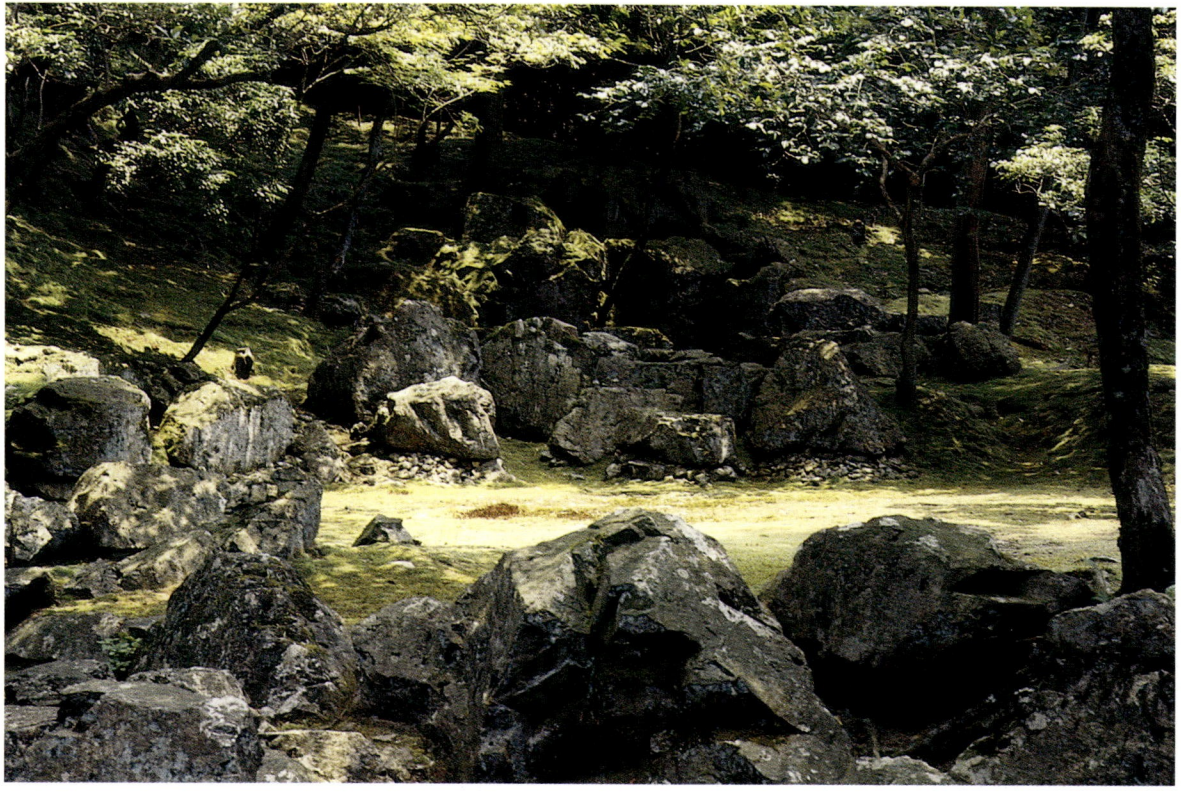

**27-1** Dry cascade and pools, upper garden, Saihoji temple, Kyoto, Japan, modified in Muromachi period, 14th century.

landscape gardening. The designers stacked the rocks to suggest a swift mountain stream rushing over the stones to form pools below. In eastern Asia, people long considered gazing at dramatic natural scenery highly beneficial to the human spirit. Such activities refreshed people after too much contact with daily affairs and helped them reach beyond mundane reality. The dry landscape, or rock garden, became very popular in Japan in the Muromachi period and afterward, especially at Zen temples. Excluding actual water and arranging stones to suggest far more expansive landscapes, as seen in Chinese paintings (see FIG. 7-18), encouraged deep mental, aesthetic, and spiritual engagement with the scene, which could be fully visualized only in the mind.

BROKEN-INK PAINTING During the Muromachi period, many artists produced pictures primarily in India ink. As was common in the long history of Japanese art, styles and subjects usually closely followed Chinese precedents (often arriving by way of Korea), and painters filled their pictures with Chinese scenes and figures. Most of the ink painting masters were at least ostensibly Zen monks. The most celebrated priest-painter was TOYO SESSHU (1420–1506). One of the very few painters who actually traveled to China, he learned much from viewing contemporaneous Ming paintings (see FIGS. 26-9, 26-10). Sesshu (individuals who lived before 1868 are often referred to by their adopted "pen names," which follow their family names) worked in a great variety of styles, ranging from tight compositions in precise brushwork to dramatic works in the *broken-* or *flung-ink style* (sometimes called "splashed-ink style"), a technique Zen monks in eastern Asia often, but not exclusively, adopted. Despite the Zen monks' interest in this style, the origins of broken ink in China were in fact secular.

The painter of a broken-ink picture paused to visualize the image, loaded the brush with ink, and then applied primarily broad, rapid strokes, sometimes even dripping the ink onto the paper. The result often hovers at the edge of legibility, without dissolving into sheer abstraction. This balance between spontaneity and a thorough knowledge of the painting tradition gives the pictures their artistic strength. In one of Sesshu's broken-ink landscape paintings (FIG. 27-2), images of mountains, trees, and buildings emerge from the ink-washed surface. Two figures appear in a boat (to the lower right), and the two swift strokes nearby represent the pole and banner of a wine shop.

Ink painting was far from the only type of painting that flourished in the Muromachi period. Artists at court, in temples, and in the service of various powerful families painted portraits, icons, narrative handscrolls, folding screens, and other types of pictures in rich colors. Sesshu, for example, did not limit his work to monochrome.

THE TOSA AND KANO SCHOOLS Two major painting schools—the Tosa School and the Kano School—emerged in Japan during the 15th and 16th centuries. Tosa Mitsunobu (1434–1525), director of the Painting Bureau (see "Japanese Artists, Workshops, and Patrons," Chapter 8, page 229) and chief painter at the imperial court in the late Muromachi, was the pivotal figure in the history of the Tosa School. The Tosa style featured bright, contrasting color, detailed textile patterns, and thickly applied paint. Contemporary with the Tosa School, the Kano School became a virtual national academy in the 17th century, ending only in the late 19th century. KANO MOTONOBU (1476–1559), very likely the son-in-law of Tosa Mitsunobu, was

**27-2** TOYO SESSHU, broken-ink landscape, Japan, Muromachi period, 1495. Hanging scroll, ink on paper, 4′ 10¼″ × 1′ ⅞″. Tokyo National Museum, Tokyo.

largely responsible for establishing the Kano style. Characterized by bold outlines and the presentation of objects along the vertical plane of the painting surface (rather than utilization of atmospheric perspective), the Kano style is revealed in Motonobu's *Zen Patriarch Xiangyen Zhixian Sweeping with a Broom* (FIG. **27-3**). This work depicts a scene from the spiritual life of a Zen patriarch. In this painting, the monk experiences the moment of enlightenment. As he sweeps the ground near his rustic retreat, a roof tile falls at his feet and shatters. The patriarch's Zen training is so deep that the resonant sound propels him into an awakening. This work reveals Motonobu's exacting precision in ink and light color. It incorporates stylistic features of Chinese academic models of ink painting, such as the sharp, angular rock forms Japanese painters, including Sesshu, long had adopted and modified. Motonobu's picture of the patriarch is one of a set of sliding doors he and his assistants painted at a Zen temple. During the

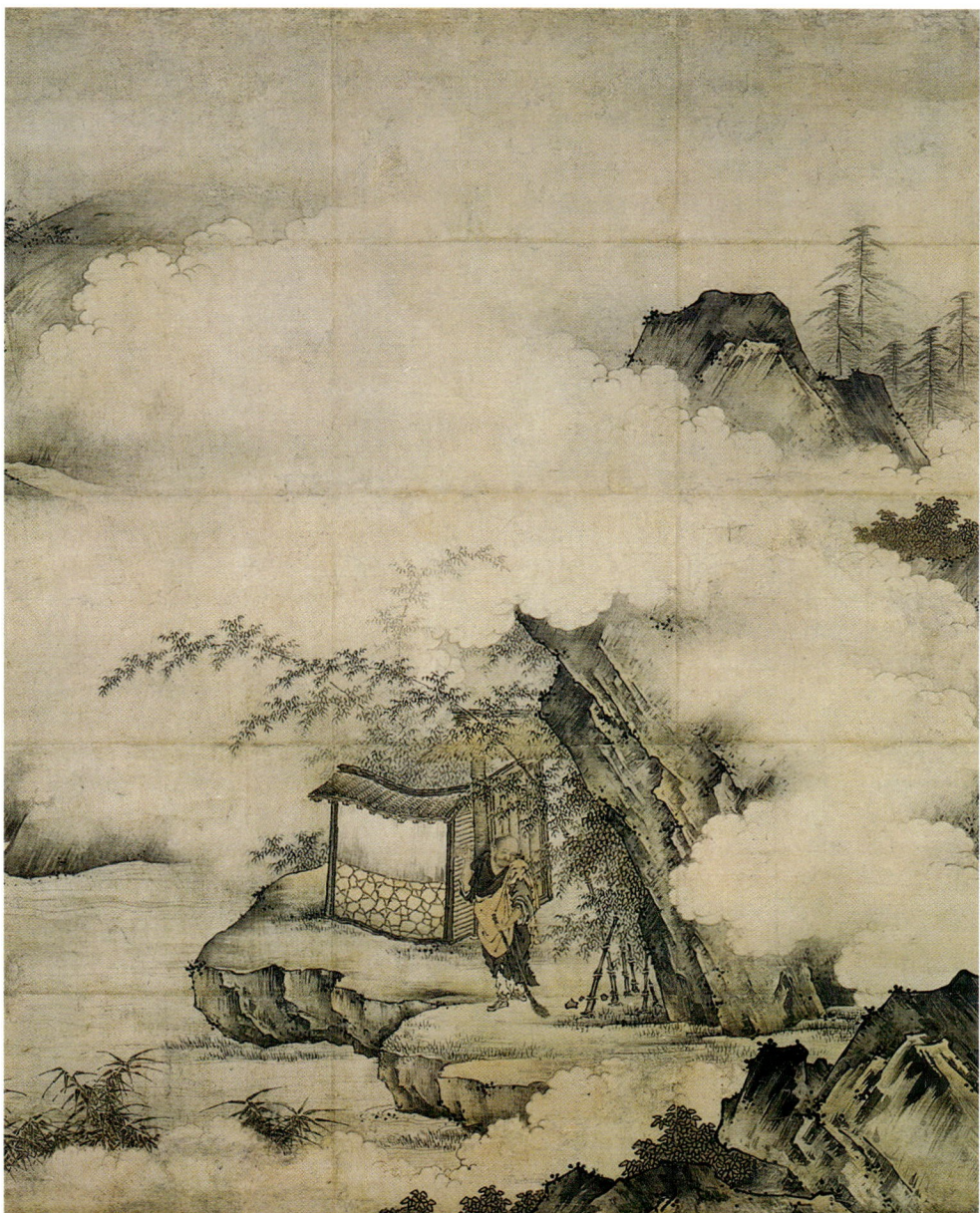

27-3 KANO MOTONOBU, *Zen Patriarch Xiangyen Zhixian Sweeping with a Broom*, Japan, Muromachi period, ca. 1513. Hanging scroll, ink and color on paper, 5′ 7⅜″ × 2′ 10¾″. Tokyo National Museum, Tokyo.

16th century, architectural decoration such as painted sliding doors formed a growing component of the repertoires of the Kano School.

## Momoyama Period (1573–1615)

**THE UNIFICATION OF JAPAN** During the Momoyama period, the government was centralized, laying the foundation for the establishment of a Japanese nation. After the fractious Muromachi era, the successive efforts of three powerful warlords—Oda Nobunaga (1534–1582), Toyotomi Hideyoshi (1536–1598), and Tokugawa Ieyasu (1542–1616)—resulted in the ouster of the last Ashikaga shogun and the consolidation of political authority. The era's designation, Momoyama (Peach Blossom Hill), is derived from the scenic foliage at the castle of one of these warlords.

**PAINTED CHINESE LIONS** To reinforce their power, these warlords constructed huge castles with palatial residences—partly as symbols of their authority and partly as fortresses. Each warlord commissioned lavish decorations for the interior of his castle, including paintings, sliding doors, and folding screens in ink, color, and gold leaf. Gold screens had been known since Muromachi times, but Momoyama painters made them even bolder, reducing the number of motifs and often greatly enlarging them against flat, shimmering fields of gold leaf.

The grandson of Motonobu, KANO EITOKU (1543–1590), was the leading painter of such murals and screens and received numerous commissions from the powerful warlords. So extensive were these commissions (in both scale and number) that Eitoku utilized a system of painting developed by his grandfather that relied on a team of specialized painters to assist him. Unfortunately, little of Eitoku's elaborate work remains; the ostentatious castles

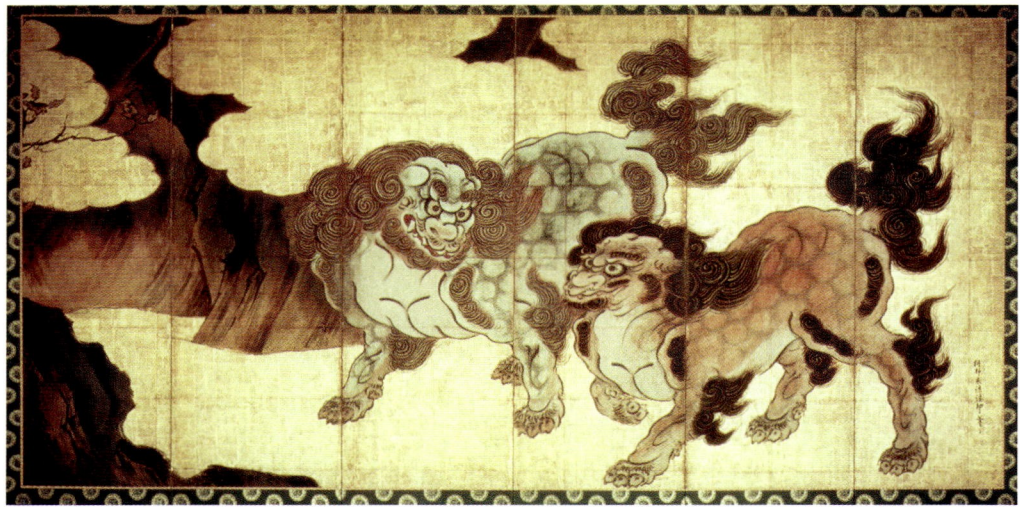

**27-4** Kano Eitoku, *Chinese Lions,* Japan, Momoyama period, late 16th century. Six-panel screen, color, ink, and gold-leaf on paper, 7′ 4″ × 14′ 10″. Imperial Household Agency, Tokyo.

he helped decorate were subsequently destroyed (not surprising in an era marked by power struggles). However, a painting of Chinese lions on a single six-panel screen (FIG. **27-4**) offers a glimpse of his work's grandeur. Possibly created for Hideyoshi, the second of the three warlords of the period, this screen appropriately speaks to the emphasis on militarism so prevalent at the time. These Chinese lions depicted by Eitoku refer to mythological beasts that have their origin in ancient Chinese legends. Appearing in both religious and secular contexts, the lions came to be associated with power and bravery, and are thus fitting imagery for a military leader. Indeed, Chinese lions became an important

symbolic motif during the Momoyama period. In Eitoku's painting, the colorful beasts' powerfully muscled bodies, defined and flattened by broad contour lines, stride forward within a gold field and minimal setting elements. The dramatic impact of this work derives in part from its scale—it is over 7 feet tall and close to 15 feet long. Because of the expansive scope of Eitoku's decoration projects, he often worked in the monumental style this painting typifies. Momoyama painting was not limited to such bold displays of isolated forms, however. It also included native and Chinese figural subjects rich in cultural, religious, and philosophical meanings.

**27-5** Hasegawa Tohaku, *Pine Forest,* Japan, Momoyama period, late 16th century. One of a pair of six-panel screens, ink on paper, 5′ 1 3/8″ × 11′ 4″. Tokyo National Museum, Tokyo.

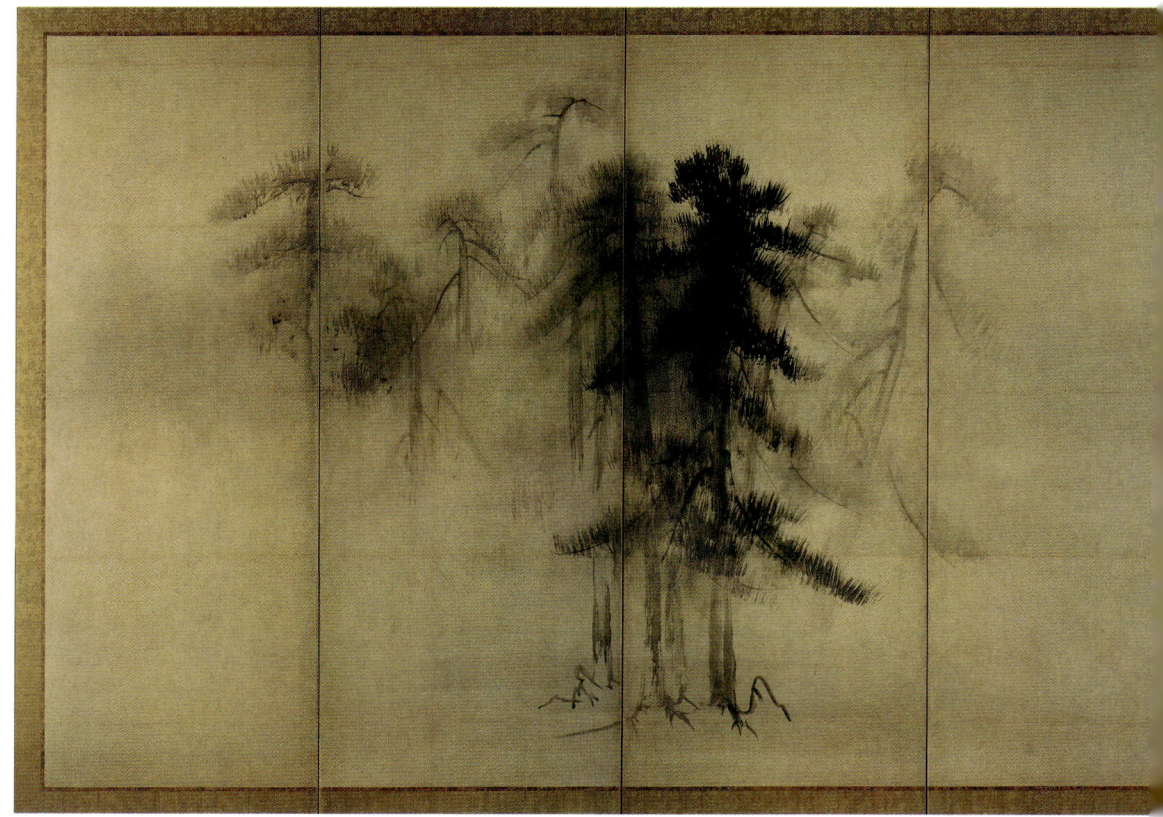

### The Japanese Tea Ceremony

The Japanese tea ceremony involves the ritual preparation, serving, and drinking of green tea. The fundamental practices began in China, but they developed in Japan to a much higher degree of sophistication, peaking in the Momoyama period. Simple forms of the tea ceremony started in Japan in Zen temples as a symbolic withdrawal from the ordinary world to cultivate the mind and spirit. The practices spread to other social groups, especially warriors and, by the late 16th century, wealthy merchants. Until the late Muromachi period, grand tea ceremonies in warrior residences served primarily as an excuse to display treasured collections of Chinese objects, such as porcelains, lacquers, and paintings.

Initially, tea ceremonies were held in a room or section of a house. As the popularity of tea ceremonies increased, freestanding teahouses (FIG. 27-7) were constructed; many scholars credit the revered tea master Sen no Rikyu with the design of the first independent teahouse.

The ceremony involves a sequence of rituals in which both host and guests participate. The host's responsibilities include serving the guests; selecting special utensils, such as water jars (FIG. 27-6) and tea bowls; and determining the tea room's decoration, which changes according to occasion and season. Acknowledged as having superior aesthetic sensibilities, individuals recognized as master tea ceremony practitioners (tea masters) advise patrons on the ceremony and acquire students. Tea masters even direct or influence the design of teahouses and tea rooms within larger structures (including interiors and gardens), as well as the design of tea utensils. They often make simple bamboo implements and occasionally even ceramic vessels.

---

**A FOREST IN THE MIST** Momoyama painters did not work exclusively in the colorful style exemplified by Eitoku's *Chinese Lions*. HASEGAWA TOHAKU (1539–1610) was a protégé of Sen no Rikyu (1522–1591), a renowned tea master with close connections to Zen temples. Tohaku became familiar with the aesthetics and techniques of Chinese Chan (Zen) painters and sometimes painted in ink monochrome using loose brushwork with brilliant success, as seen in *Pine Forest* (FIG. **27-5**). His wet brush strokes—long and slow, short and quick, dark and pale—

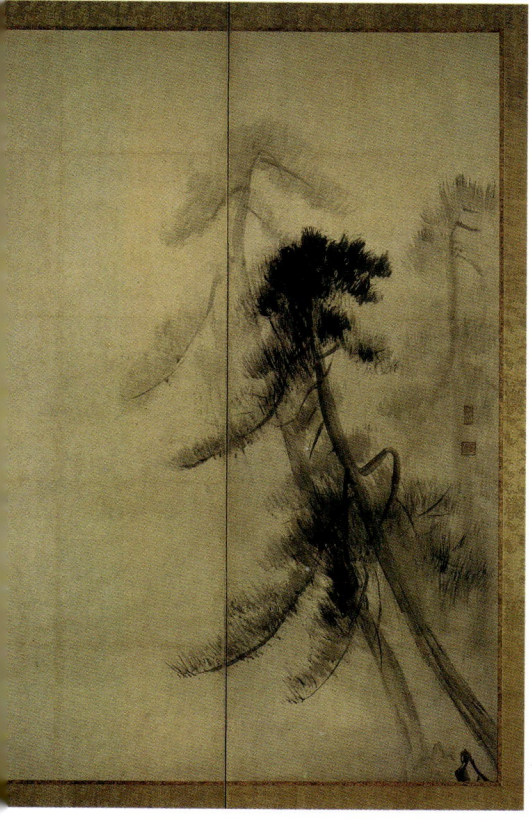

present a grove of great pines shrouded in mist. His trees emerge from and recede into the heavy atmosphere, as if the landscape hovers at the edge of formlessness. In Zen terms, the picture suggests the illusory nature of mundane reality while evoking a calm, meditative mood.

**THE ROLE OF THE TEA CEREMONY** A favorite exercise of cultivation and refinement in the Momoyama period was the tea ceremony (see "The Japanese Tea Ceremony," above). In Japan, this important practice eventually came to carry various political and ideological implications. For example, it provided a means for those relatively new to political or economic power to assert authority in the cultural realm. For instance, upon returning from a major military campaign, warlord Hideyoshi held an immense tea ceremony that was scheduled to last 10 days and was open to everyone in Kyoto. So serious did the tea ceremony's political implications become that warlords granted or refused their vassals the right to practice it. Despite these demonstrations of authoritative control, the tea ceremony also contributed to the democratization of Japanese society. Venerated tea master Sen no Rikyu insisted that there was no rank in a teahouse, and indeed, the manner of entry into a teahouse—crawling on one's hands and knees—is intended to foster humility and egalitarianism.

**A NEW REFINED RUSTICITY** This democratic ideal also influenced the aesthetics of teahouses and tea ceremony utensils. In keeping with the egalitarian principle that value and refinement lay in character and ability and not in bloodline or rank, Rikyu encouraged the use of tea items that were valued for their inherent beauty rather than their monetary worth. Accordingly, starting around the late 15th century, admiration of the technical brilliance of Chinese objects slowly gave way to ever greater appreciation of the virtues of rustic Korean and Japanese wares. This new aesthetic of refined rusticity, or *wabi,* included the design of very simple tea rooms and houses that evoked the hut of a recluse in the mountains. Wabi suggests austerity and simplicity. (Zen concepts also played a significant role in this shift.) Related to wabi and also important as a philosophical and aesthetic principle was *sabi*—

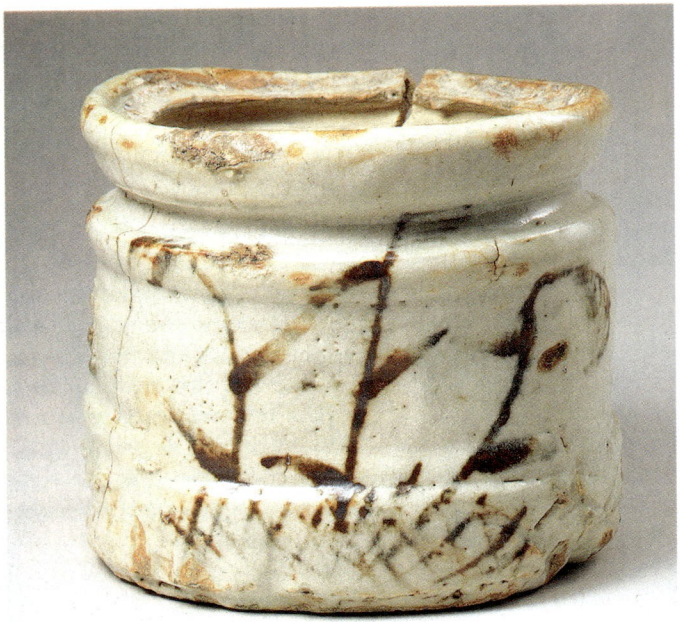

**27-6** *Kogan* (ancient stream bank), tea ceremony water jar, Japan, Momoyama period, late 16th century. Shino ware with underglaze design, 7″ high. Hatakeyama Memorial Museum, Tokyo.

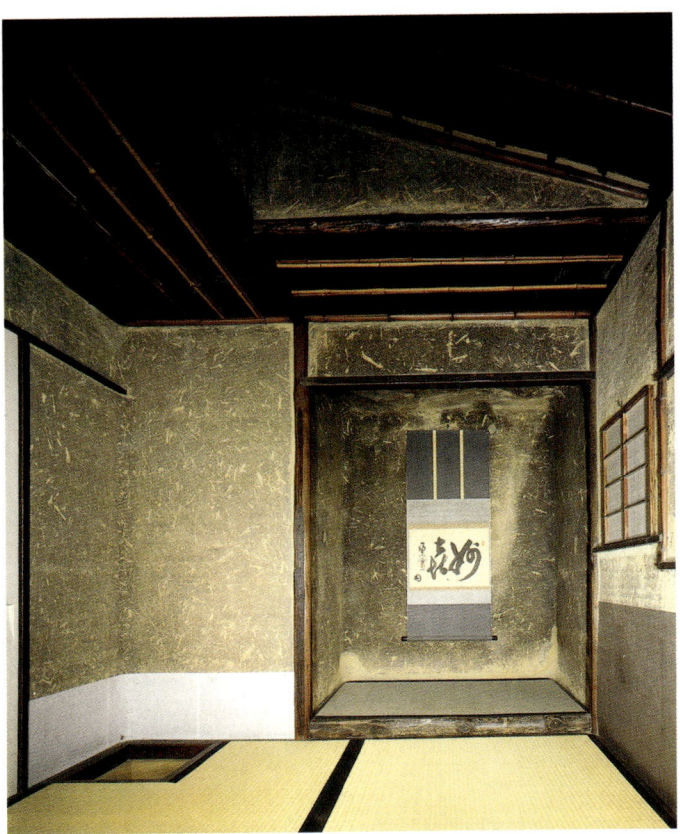

**27-7** SEN NO RIKYU, Taian teahouse (interior view), Myokian Temple, Kyoto, Japan, Momoyama period, ca. 1582.

the value found in the old and weathered, suggesting the tranquility reached in old age.

Wabi and sabi aesthetics are visible in the ceramic vessels produced for the tea ceremony, such as the well-known Shino water jar named *Kogan* (FIG. 27-6). The jar's name, which means "ancient stream bank," comes from the painted design on its surface, as well as from its coarse texture and rough form, both reminiscent of earth cut by water. The term *Shino* generally refers to bowls produced during the late 16th and early 17th centuries in kilns in Mino Province. Shino wares, typically simple forms with rough surfaces, feature heavy glazes containing feldspar. These glazes are predominantly white when fired, but can include pinkish red or gray hues. Their coarse stoneware body, simple form, and seemingly casual decoration offer the same sorts of aesthetic and interpretive challenges and opportunities as the dry landscape gardens (FIG. 27-1).

**CEREMONIAL TEA SPACES** The ultimate representation of the new wabi aesthetic in the Momoyama period was the Taian (FIG. 27-7), a teahouse designed under the direction of SEN NO RIKYU. The interior displays two standard features of Japanese residential architecture that developed in the late Muromachi period—very thick, rigid straw mats called *tatami* and an alcove called a *tokonoma*. The tatami accommodate the traditional Japanese customs of not wearing shoes indoors and of sitting on the floor and can still be found in Japanese homes today. Less common in contemporary houses are tokonoma, which developed as places to hang scrolls of painting or calligraphy and to display other prized objects.

The Taian tokonoma and the tea room as a whole have unusually dark walls, with earthen plaster covering even some of the square corner posts. The room's dimness and tiny size (about six feet square) produce a cavelike feel and encourage intimacy among the tea host and guests. The guests enter from the garden outside through a small sliding door that forces them to crawl inside. Such conditions foster humility and emphasize a guest's passage into a ceremonial space—set apart from the ordinary world—where, in theory, all are equal.

## Edo Period (1615–1868)

In 1615, shogun Tokugawa Ieyasu consolidated power and established a new shogunate that lasted until 1868. (The shogun title had been abandoned after the deposition of the Ashikaga shogunate in 1573; Ieyasu revived the title for himself in 1603.) Rather than remain in Kyoto, the official capital, Ieyasu set up his seat of power in Edo (modern Tokyo). The new regime instituted many policies designed to limit severely the pace of social and cultural change in Japan. Faced with the threat of conquest, the Tokugawa rulers banned Christianity and expelled all Western foreigners except the Dutch. Those in power transformed Confucian ideas of social stratification and civic responsibility into public policy, and they tried to control the social influence of urban merchants, some of whose wealth far outstripped that of most warrior leaders. However, the population's great expansion in urban centers, the spread of literacy in the cities and beyond, and a growing thirst for knowledge and diversion made for a very lively popular culture not easily subject to tight control.

**A PRINCELY VILLA AT KYOTO** The imperial court's power remained as it had been for centuries, symbolic and ceremonial,

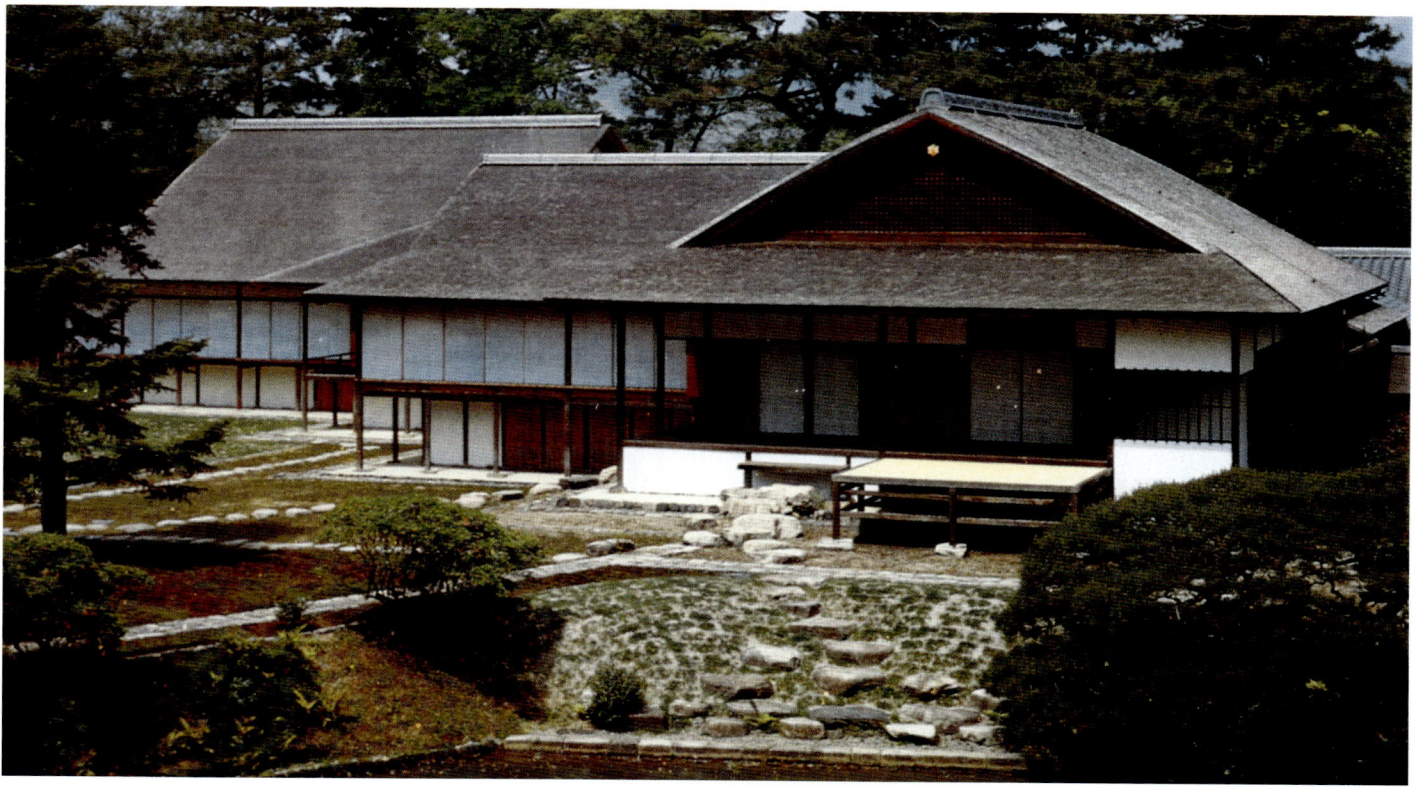

27-8 Eastern facade of Katsura Imperial Villa, Kyoto, Japan, Edo period, 1620–1663.

but the court continued to wield influence in matters of taste and culture. For example, for a period of some 50 years in the 17th century, a princely family developed a modest country retreat into a villa that became the admired, but rarely equaled, standard for domestic Japanese architecture. Since the early 20th century, it has inspired architects worldwide, even as ordinary living environments in Japan became increasingly Westernized in structure and decor. The Katsura Imperial Villa (FIG. 27-8), built between 1620 and 1663, dates to the time of the tea ceremony's greatest popularity. Therefore, many of the villa's design features and tasteful subtleties derive from earlier teahouses, such as Rikyu's Taian (FIG. 27-7). However, more recent tea ceremony aesthetics had moved away from Rikyu's wabi extremes, and the Katsura Villa's designers and carpenters incorporated elements of courtly gracefulness as well.

Ornament that disguises structural forms has little place in this architecture's appeal, which relies instead on subtleties of proportion, color, and texture. A variety of textures (stone, wood, tile, and plaster) and subdued colors and tonal values enrich the villa's lines, planes, and volumes. Subtlety and finesse in the treatment of the building components were important. Artisans painstakingly rubbed and burnished all surfaces to bring out the natural beauty of their grains and textures. The rooms are not large, but parting or removing the sliding doors between them can create broad rectangular spaces. Perhaps most important, the residents can open the doors to the outside to achieve a harmonious integration of building and garden—one of the primary ideals of Japanese residential architecture.

**THE RIMPA SCHOOL EMERGES** In painting, the Kano School enjoyed official governmental sponsorship during the Edo period, and its workshops provided paintings to the Tokugawa and their major vassals. By the mid-18th century, Kano masters also served as the primary painting teachers for nearly everyone aspiring to a career in the field. Even so, individualist painters and other schools emerged and flourished, working in quite distinct styles.

The earliest major alternative school to emerge in the Edo period, Rimpa, was quite different in nature from the Kano and Tosa Schools. It did not have a similar continuity of lineage and training through father and son, master and pupil. Instead, over time, Rimpa aesthetics and principles attracted a variety of individuals as practitioners and champions. Many Rimpa works focused on literary themes favored by the nobility, and many of the Rimpa artists affiliated themselves with court culture. Stylistically, Rimpa works are characterized by vivid color and extensive use of gold and silver, and often incorporated decorative patterns. Rimpa takes its first syllable from the last syllable in the name of its ostensible founder, Ogata Korin (1658–1716). However, two closely linked artists, HONAMI KOETSU (1558–1637) and Tawaraya Sotatsu (1576–1643), laid its foundations a few generations earlier.

**COMBINING PAINTING AND CRAFT** Koetsu was the heir to an important family in the ancient capital of Kyoto and a greatly admired calligrapher. He also participated in and produced ceramics for the tea ceremony. Many scholars credit him with overseeing the design of lacquers (primarily wooden objects with lacquer decoration), perhaps with the aid of Sotatsu, the proprietor of a fan-painting shop. Scholars do know that together they drew on ancient traditions of painting and craft decoration to develop a style that collapsed boundaries between the two arts.

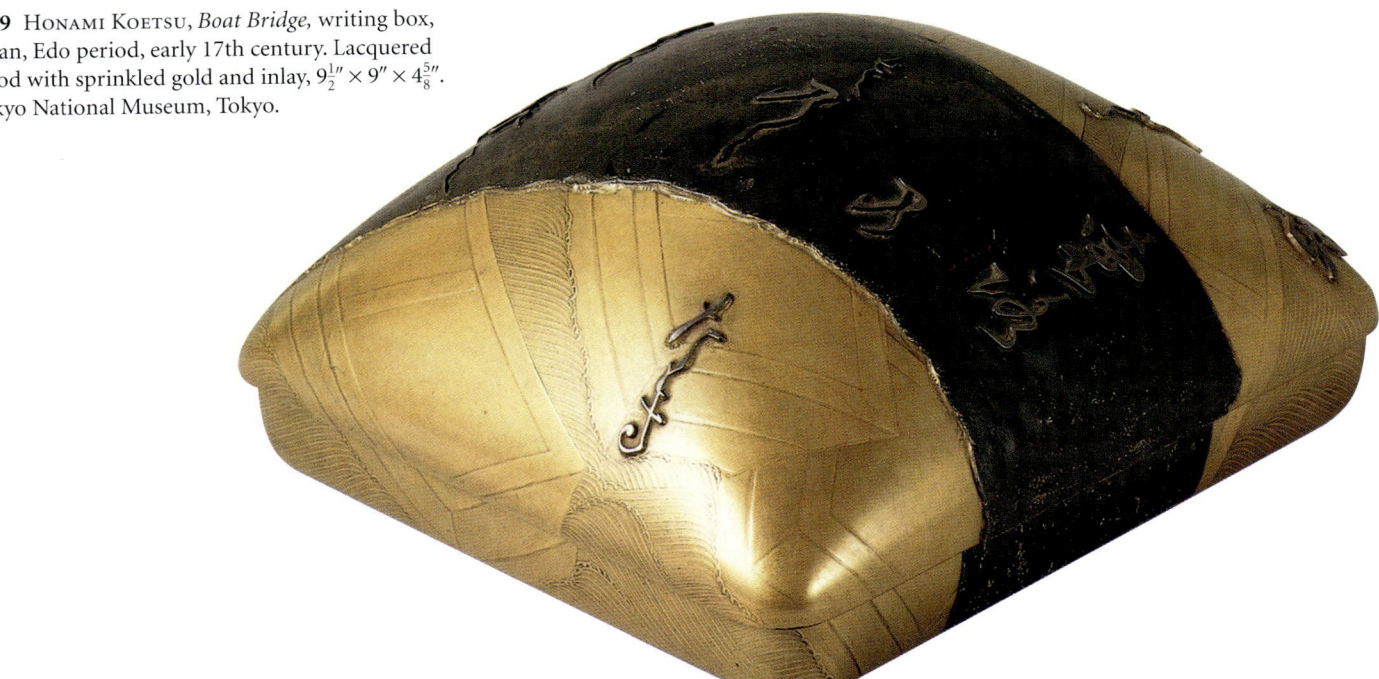

**27-9** Honami Koetsu, *Boat Bridge,* writing box, Japan, Edo period, early 17th century. Lacquered wood with sprinkled gold and inlay, $9\frac{1}{2}'' \times 9'' \times 4\frac{5}{8}''$. Tokyo National Museum, Tokyo.

Paintings, the lacquered surfaces of writing boxes, and ceramics shared motifs and compositions.

In typical Rimpa fashion, Koetsu's *Boat Bridge* writing box (FIG. **27-9**) exhibits motifs drawn from a 10th-century poem about the boat bridge at Sano, in the Eastern provinces. The lid presents a subtle, gold-on-gold scene of small boats lined up side by side in the water to support the planks of a temporary bridge. The bridge itself, a dull metal inlay, forms a band across the lid's convex surface. The raised, dull linear forms on the water, boats, and bridge are a few Japanese characters from the poem, which describes the experience of crossing such a bridge as evoking reflection on life's insecurities. The box also shows the dramatic contrasts of form, texture, and color that mark Rimpa aesthetics, especially the juxtaposition of the bridge's dull metal inlay and the brilliant gold surface. The gold decoration comes from careful sprinkling of actual gold dust in wet lacquer. Whatever Koetsu's contribution to the design process, specialists well versed in the demanding techniques of inlaying and sprinkling gold actually applied the lacquer decoration.

**PLUM BLOSSOMS AND TARASHIKOMI** Ogata Korin (1658–1716) developed the principles that Koetsu and Sotatsu established. The son of an important textile merchant, Korin was primarily a painter but also designed lacquers in Koetsu's manner. One of Korin's painted masterpieces is a pair of twofold screens depicting red and white blossoming plum trees separated by a stream (see FIG. Intro-12). As Koetsu did with his writing box, Korin reduced the motifs to a minimum to offer a dramatic contrast of forms and visual textures. Beneath delicate, slender branches, the gnarled, aged tree trunks flank the stream's smooth, precise curves of oxidized silver leaf. The contrast extends even to the painting techniques. The mottling of the trees comes from a signature Rimpa technique called *tarashikomi,* the dropping of ink and pigments onto surfaces still wet with previously applied ink and pigments. In striking contrast, the pattern in the stream has the precision and elegant stylization of a textile design, produced by applying pigment through the forms cut in a paper stencil.

**THE LITERATI STYLE** In the 17th and 18th centuries, Japan's increasingly urban, educated population spurred a cultural and social restlessness among commoners and samurai of lesser rank that the policies of the restrictive Tokugawa could not suppress. People eagerly sought new ideas and images, directing their attention primarily to China, as had happened throughout Japanese history, but also to the West. From each direction dramatically new ideas (for the isolated Japanese) about painting emerged.

Starting in the late 17th century, illustrations in printed books and actual paintings of lesser quality brought limited knowledge of the Chinese literati style into Japan. As a result, several individual Japanese painters and their followers embraced elements of the Chinese literati style (see Chapter 26). Although these artists derived their inspiration from Chinese models, the difference in context resulted in variations. In China, literati were scholars whose education and upbringing as landed gentry afforded them positions in the bureaucracy that governed the country. Chinese literati artists were predominantly amateurs and pursued painting as one of the proper functions of an educated and cultivated man. Chinese literati were cultured intellectuals. In contrast, although Japanese literati artists acquired a familiarity with and appreciation for Chinese literature, they were mostly professionals, painting to earn a living. Because the infiltration of Chinese literati painting into Japan was diffused, the resulting character of Japanese literati painting was less stylistically defined than that found in China. Despite the inevitable changes as Chinese ideas were disseminated throughout Japan, the newly seen Chinese models were valuable in supporting emerging ideals of self-expression in painting by offering a worthy alternative to the Kano School's standardized repertoire.

One of the outstanding early representatives of Japanese literati painting was Yosa Buson (1716–1783). A master writer of *haiku* (the 17-syllable Japanese poetic form that became very popular from the 17th century on), Buson had a command of literati painting that extended beyond a knowledge of Chinese models. His poetic abilities gave rise to a lyricism that pervaded both his haiku and his painting. *Cuckoo Flying over New Verdure* (FIG. **27-10**) reveals

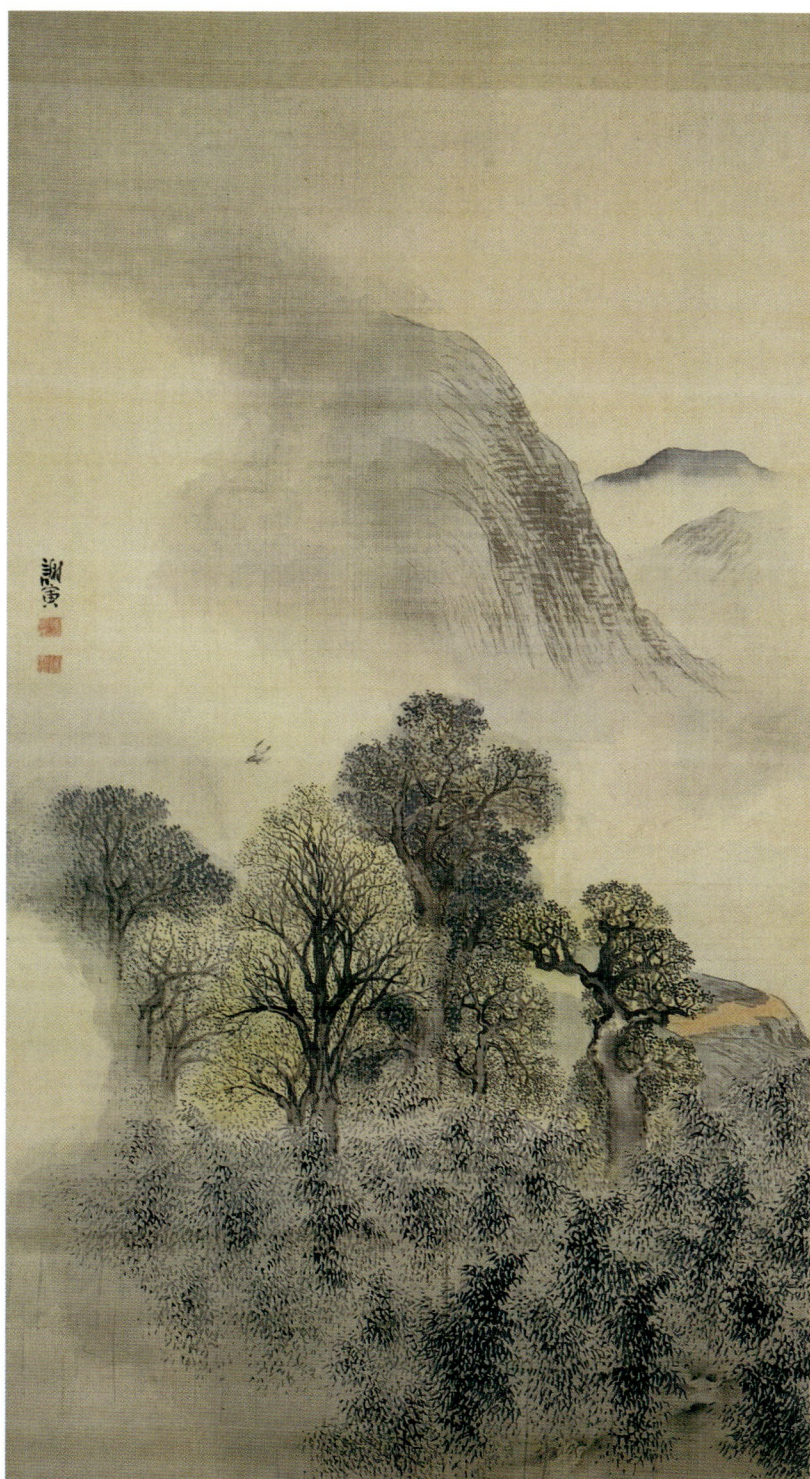

**27-10** YOSA BUSON, *Cuckoo Flying over New Verdure*, Japan, Edo period, late 18th century. Hanging scroll, ink and color on silk, 5′ $\frac{1}{2}$″ × 2′ 7$\frac{1}{4}$″. Hiraki Ukiyo-e Museum, Yokohama, Japan.

his fully mature style. He incorporated in this work basic elements of Chinese and Japanese literati style by rounding the landscape forms and rendering their soft texture in fine fibrous brush strokes, and by including dense foliage patterns. Although Buson imitated the vocabulary of brush strokes associated with the Chinese literati, his touch was bolder and more abstract, and the gentle palette of pale colors was very much his own.

**EDO'S FLOATING WORLD** The growing urbanization in cities such as Osaka, Kyoto, and Edo led to an increase in the pursuit of sensual pleasure and entertainment in the brash popular theaters and the pleasure houses found in such locales as Edo's Yoshiwara brothel district. The Tokugawa tried to hold such activities in check, but their efforts were largely in vain. Their failure in this regard was due in part to demographics; the significant samurai population (whose families remained in their home territories) in Edo during this period was eager to enjoy city life. Those of lesser means could partake in these pleasures and amusements vicariously. Rapid developments in the printing industry led to the availability of numerous books and printed images (see "Japanese

## Japanese Woodblock Prints

During the Edo period, *ukiyo-e* (pictures of the floating world) woodblock prints became enormously popular. Sold in small shops and on the street, an ordinary print went for the price of a bowl of noodles. People of very modest income could therefore collect prints in albums or paste them on their walls. A highly efficient production system made this wide distribution of Japanese graphic art possible.

Ukiyo-e artists were generally painters who did not participate in the actual making of the prints that made them so famous both in their own day and today. As the designers, they sold drawings to publishers, who in turn oversaw their printing. The publishers also played a role in creating ukiyo-e prints by commissioning specific designs or adapting them before printing. Certainly, the names of both designer and publisher appeared on the final prints.

Unacknowledged in nearly all cases are the individuals who actually made the prints, the block-carvers and printers. Using skills honed since childhood, they worked with both speed and precision for relatively low wages and thus made ukiyo-e prints affordable. The master ukiyo-e printmakers seem to have all been men. Women, especially wives and daughters, often assisted painters and other artists, but few gained separate recognition. Among the exceptions, the daughter of Katsushika Hokusai (FIG. 27-12), Katsushika Oi, became well known as a painter and probably helped her father with his print designs.

Stylistically, Japanese prints during the Edo period tend to have black outlines separating distinct color areas (FIG. 27-11). This format is a result of the printing process. A master carver pasted painted designs facedown on a wooden block. Wetting and gently scraping the thin paper revealed the reversed image to guide the cutting of the block. After the carving, only the outlines of the forms and other elements that would be black in the final print remained raised in relief. The master printer then coated the block with black ink and printed several initial outline prints.

These master prints became the guides for carving the other blocks, one for each color used. On each color block, the carver left in relief only the areas to be printed in that color. Even ordinary prints sometimes required up to 20 colors and thus 20 blocks. To print a color, a printer applied the appropriate pigment to a block's raised surface, laid a sheet of paper on it, and rubbed the back of the paper with a smooth flat object. Then another printer would print a different color on the same sheet of paper. Perfect alignment of the paper in each step was critical to prevent overlapping of colors, so the block-carvers included printing guides—an L-shaped ridge in one corner and a straight ridge on one side—in their blocks. The printers could cover small alignment errors with a final printing of the black outlines from the last block.

The materials used in printing varied over time but by the mid-18th century had reached a level of standardization. The blocks were planks of fine-grained hardwood, usually cherry. The best paper came from the white layer beneath the bark of mulberry trees, because its long fibers helped the paper stand up to repeated rubbing on the blocks. The printers used a few mineral pigments but tended to favor inexpensive dyes made from plants for most colors. As a result, the colors of ukiyo-e prints were and are highly susceptible to fading, especially when exposed to strong light. In the early 19th century, more permanent European synthetic dyes began to enter Japan. The first, Prussian Blue, can be seen in Hokusai's *The Great Wave off Kanagawa* (FIG. 27-12).

The popularity of ukiyo-e prints extended to the Western world as well. Their affordability and the ease with which they could be transported facilitated the dissemination of such prints, especially throughout Europe. Ukiyo-e prints appear in the backgrounds of a number of Impressionist and Post-Impressionist paintings, attesting to the appeal these works held for Westerners.

---

Woodblock Prints," above), and these could convey the city's delights for a fraction of the cost of actual participation. Taking part in the emerging urban culture involved more than simple physical satisfactions and rowdy entertainments. Many who participated were highly educated in literature, music, and the other arts.

The best-known products of this sophisticated counterculture are known as *ukiyo-e*—"pictures of the floating world." The main subjects of these paintings and especially prints come from the realms of pleasure, such as the Yoshiwara brothels and the popular theater. The term *ukiyo* (floating world) originated in relation to Buddhism and reinforced the notion of the transience of human life and the ephemerality of the material world. It was during the Edo period that the floating world came to be associated with the constantly changing nature of the temporal world of sensual pleasures and entertainment—hence the emergence of ukiyo-e.

**VIEWS OF AN UKIYO PARLOR** The urban appetite for ukiyo pleasures and for their depiction in ukiyo-e provided fertile

ground for many print designers to flourish. Consequently, competition among publishing houses led to ever greater refinement and experimentation in printmaking. One of the most admired and emulated 18th-century designers, SUZUKI HARUNOBU (ca. 1725–1770), played a key role in developing multicolored prints. Called *nishiki-e* (brocade pictures) because of their sumptuous and brilliant color, these pictures were printed on the best-quality paper using costly pigments and were highly valued. Harunobu gained a tremendous advantage over his fellow designers when he received commissions from members of a poetry club to design limited-edition nishiki-e prints. Harunobu transferred much of the knowledge he derived from nishiki-e to his design of more commercial prints. He even issued some of the private designs later under his own name for popular consumption.

The sophistication of Harunobu's work is evident in *Evening Bell at the Clock* (FIG. **27-11**), from a series called *Eight Views of the Parlor*. This series draws upon a Chinese series usually titled *Eight Views of the Xiao and Xiang Rivers,* each image of which

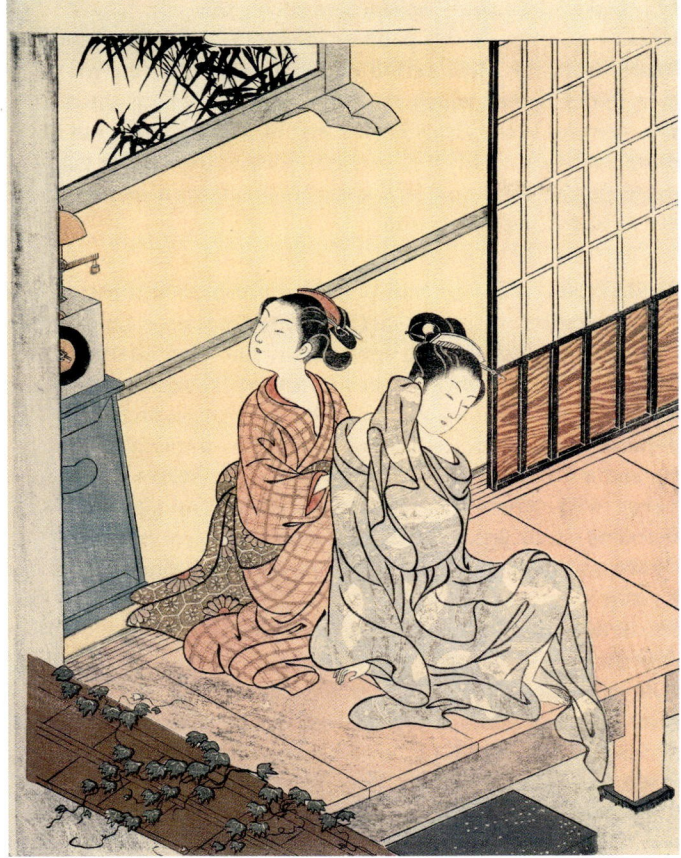

focuses on a particular time of day or year. In Harunobu's adaptation, beautiful young women and the activities that occupy their daily lives become the subject. In *Evening Bell at the Clock,* two young women sit on a veranda. One appears to be drying herself after a bath, while the other turns to face the chiming clock. Here, the artist has playfully transformed the great temple bell that rings over the waters in the Chinese series into a modern Japanese clock. This image incorporates the refined techniques characteristic of nishiki-e. Further, the flatness of the depicted objects and the rich color recall the traditions of court painting, a comparison many nishiki-e artists openly sought.

**WESTERN PERSPECTIVE IN PRINTS** Woodblock prints afforded artists great opportunity for experimentation, and many printmakers used this medium to set up a dialogue between the traditional and the modern. For example, in producing landscapes (another printmaking subject that emerged in the late 18th century), artists often incorporated Western perspective techniques. One of the most famous designers in this genre was KATSUSHIKA HOKUSAI (1760–1849), whose famous print, *The Great Wave off Kanagawa* (FIG. 27-12), belongs to a woodblock series called *Thirty-Six Views of Mount Fuji.* In this view, the huge foreground wave dwarfs the artist's representation of a distant Fuji. This contrast and the whitecaps' ominous fingers magnify the wave's threatening aspect. The men in the trading boats bend low to dig their oars against the rough sea and drive their long low vessels past the danger. This print, although it draws somewhat on Western techniques, also engages the Japanese pictorial tradition. Against a background with the low horizon typical of Western painting, Hokusai placed the wave's more traditionally flat and powerfully graphic forms in the foreground.

**27-11** SUZUKI HARUNOBU, *Evening Bell at the Clock,* from *Eight Views of the Parlor* series, Japan, Edo period, ca. 1765. Woodblock print, $11\frac{1}{4}'' \times 8\frac{1}{2}''$. Art Institute of Chicago, Chicago (Clarence Buckingham Collection).

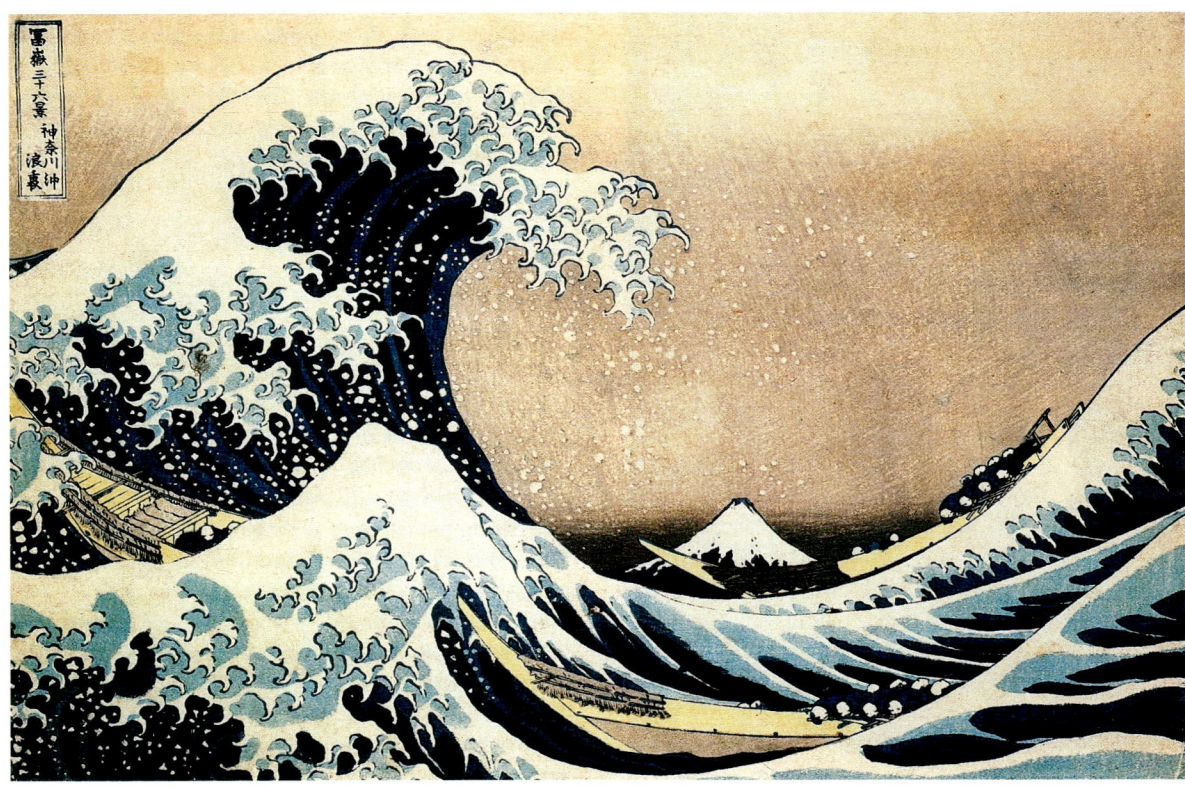

**27-12** KATSUSHIKA HOKUSAI, *The Great Wave off Kanagawa,* from *Thirty-Six Views of Mount Fuji* series, Japan, Edo period, ca. 1826–1833. Woodblock print oban, ink and colors on paper, $9\frac{7}{8}'' \times 1' \, 2\frac{3}{4}''$. Photograph © 2003 Museum of Fine Arts, Boston (Bigelow Collection).

# MODERN JAPAN

## The Meiji and Taisho Periods (1868–1926)

**THE END OF SHOGUN RULE** The Edo period and the rule of the shogun ended in 1868, when rebellious samurai from provinces far removed from Edo toppled the Tokugawa shogunate. This overthrow was facilitated by the Tokugawa's inability to handle increasing pressure from Western nations for Japan to throw open its doors to the outside world. Although the rebellion restored direct sovereignty to the imperial throne, real power rested with the emperor's cabinet. As a symbol of imperial authority, however, this new period was officially called the Meiji ("Enlightened Rule"), after the emperor's chosen reign name. This practice continues today.

**WESTERN OIL PAINTING** Oil painting became a major genre in Japan in the late 19th century. Ambitious students studied with Westerners at government schools and during trips abroad. One oil painting highlighting the cultural ferment of the early Meiji period is *Oiran* (*Grand Courtesan*; FIG. **27-13**), painted by TAKAHASHI YUICHI (1828–1894). The artist created it for a client nostalgic for vanishing elements of Japanese culture. Ukiyo-e

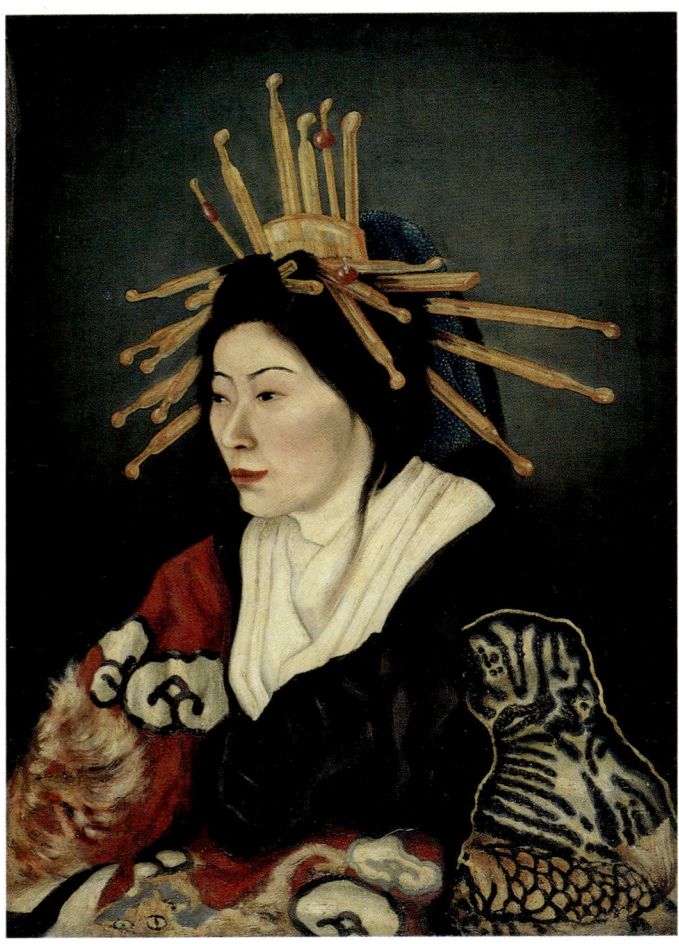

**27-13** TAKAHASHI YUICHI, *Oiran (Grand Courtesan)*, Japan, Meiji period, 1872. Oil on canvas, 2′ 6½″ × 1′ 9⅝″. Tokyo National University of Fine Arts and Music, Tokyo.

printmakers frequently represented such grand courtesans of the pleasure quarters. In this painting, however, Takahashi (historical figures from the Meiji period onward are usually referred to by their family names, which come first) did not portray the courtesan's features in the idealizing manner of ukiyo-e artists but in the more analytical manner of Western portraiture. Yet the painter's more abstract rendering of the garments reflects a very old practice in East Asian portraiture.

**RESISTING WESTERNIZATION** Unbridled enthusiasm for Westernization in some quarters led to resistance and concern over a loss of distinctive Japanese identity in other quarters. Ironically, one of those most eager to preserve "Japaneseness" in the arts was Ernest Fenollosa (1853–1908), an American professor of philosophy and political economy at Tokyo Imperial University. He and a former student named Okakura Kakuzo (1862–1913) joined with others in a movement that eventually led to the founding of an arts university dedicated to Japanese arts under Okakura's direction. Their goal for Japanese painting was to make it viable in the modern age rather than preserve it as a relic, so they encouraged incorporating some Western techniques such as chiaroscuro, perspective, and bright hues in basically Japanese-style paintings. The resulting style was called *nihonga* (Japanese painting), as opposed to *yoga* (Western painting).

*Kutsugen* (FIG. **27-14**), a silk scroll by YOKOYAMA TAIKAN (1868–1958), is an example of the former. It combines a low horizon line and subtle shading effects taken from Western painting with East Asian techniques, such as anchoring a composition in one corner (see FIGS. 7-23 and 26-13), employing strong ink brushwork to define its contours, applying washes of water-and-glue–based pigments, and using applications of heavy mineral pigments. The painting's subject, a Chinese poet who fell out of the emperor's favor and subsequently committed suicide, no doubt resonated with Taikan and his associates. It provided a nice analogy to a real-life situation; at the time, Okakura was locked in a battle over his artistic principles with the Ministry of Education. Whether intended or not, this painting, in which the poet stands his ground, staunchly defying the strong winds that agitate the foliage behind him, was perceived as a comment on the friction between Okakura and authorities.

## The Showa and Heisei Periods (1926–Present)

During the 20th century, Japan became increasingly prominent on the world stage in economics, politics, and culture. Among the events that propelled Japan into the spotlight was its participation in World War II. Among the most tragic consequences of that participation were widespread devastation, loss of life, and, more specifically, the atomic bombings of Hiroshima and Nagasaki in 1945. During the succeeding occupation period, the United States imposed new democratic institutions on Japan, with the emperor serving as a ceremonial head of state. Japan rebounded with remarkable speed. From the second half of that century to the present, Japan has also assumed a positive and productive place in the international art world. As they had done in earlier times with the art and culture of China and Korea, Japanese artists have internalized Western lessons and transformed them into a part of Japan's own vital culture.

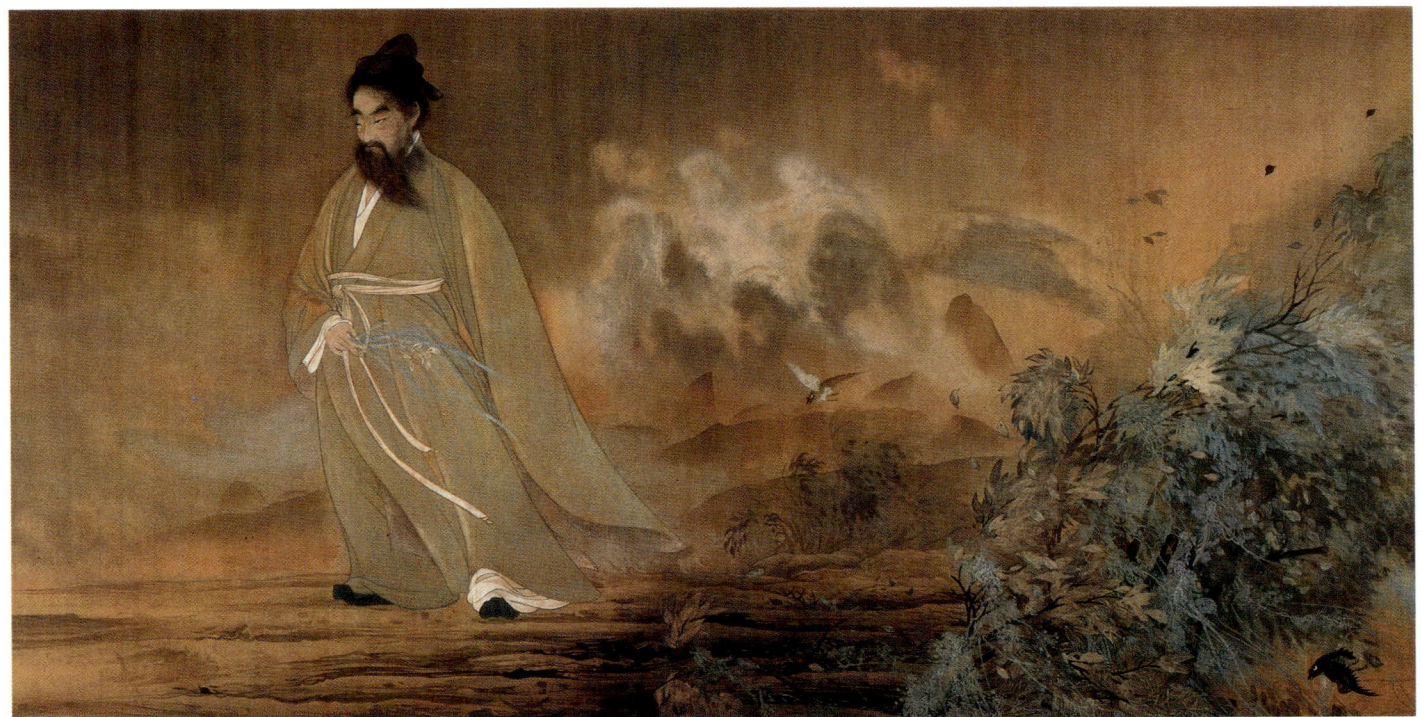

**27-14** Yокоуама Таıкаn, *Kutsugen*, Itsukushima Shrine, Hiroshima Prefecture, Japan, Meiji period, 1898. Hanging scroll, color on silk, 4′ 4″ × 9′ 6″.

**A HOME FOR THE OLYMPICS** Japanese architecture, especially public and commercial building, was rapidly transformed along Western lines. In fact, architecture may be the art form providing Japanese practitioners the most substantial presence on the world scene during the latter half of the 20th century. They have made major contributions to both modern and postmodern developments. One of the most daringly experimental architects of the post–World War II period is TANGE KENZO (b. 1913). When designing the stadiums for the 1964 Olympics (FIG. **27-15**), he employed a cable suspension system that allowed him to shape steel and concrete into remarkably graceful structures. His attention to both the sculptural qualities of each building's raw concrete form and the fluidity of its spaces allies him with architects worldwide who carried on the legacy of the late style of Le

Corbusier in France (see FIG. 34-42). His stadiums thus bear comparison with Joern Utzon's Sydney Opera House (see FIG. 34-44).

**MODERN FOLK POTTERY** Another Japanese art form of the 20th century attracting great attention worldwide is ceramics. Like other international folk art, traditional Japanese ceramics and other so-called crafts are highly valued today. A formative figure in Japan's folk art movement, the philosopher Yanagi Soetsu (1889–1961), promoted an ideal of beauty that was inspired by the tea ceremony and could only be achieved in functional objects made of natural materials by anonymous craftspeople. Among the ceramists who produced this type of folk pottery, known as *mingei,* was HAMADA SHOJI (1894–1978). Although Hamada did espouse Yanagi's selfless ideals, he still gained international fame

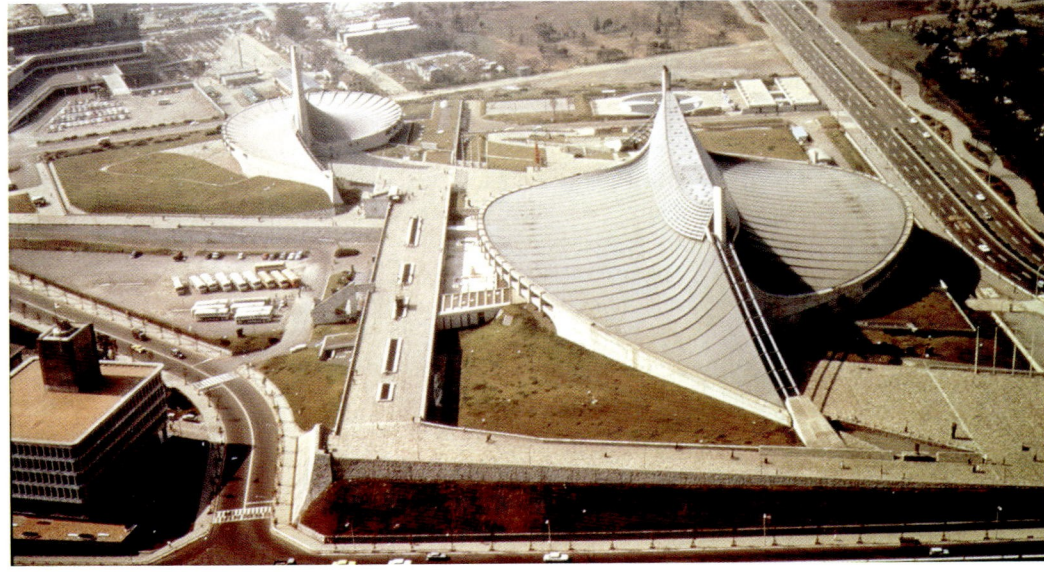

**27-15** TANGE KENZO, national indoor Olympic stadiums, Tokyo, Japan, Showa period, 1961–1964.

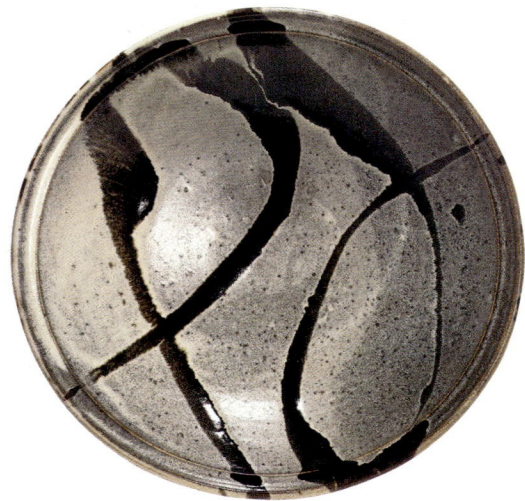

**27-16** HAMADA SHOJI, large bowl, 1962. Black trails on translucent glaze, $5\frac{7}{8}''\times 1'\ 10\frac{1}{2}''$. National Museum of Modern Art, Kyoto.

and received official recognition in Japan as an "Intangible Important Cultural Property," more commonly called a "Living National Treasure." Works such as his dish with casual slip designs (FIG. **27-16**) are unsigned, but connoisseurs easily recognize them as his. Such stoneware is coarser, darker, and heavier than porcelain and lacks the latter's fine decoration. To those who appreciate simpler, earthier beauty, however, this dish holds great attraction. Hamada's artistic influence extended beyond the production of pots. He traveled to England in 1920 and, along with English potter Bernard Leach (1887–1978), established a community of ceramists committed to the mingei aesthetic. Together, Hamada and Leach expanded international knowledge of Japanese ceramics, and even now, the Hamada-Leach aesthetic (as it is known) is part of potters' education worldwide.

NATURAL SCULPTURE Although no one style, medium, or subject dominates contemporary Japanese art, much of it does spring from ideas or beliefs that have been integral to Japanese culture over the years. For example, the Shinto belief in the generative forces in nature and in humankind's position as part of the totality of nature hold great appeal for contemporary artists, including TSUCHIYA KIMIO (b. 1955), who produces large-scale sculptures constructed of branches (FIG. **27-17**) or driftwood. Despite their relatively abstract nature, his works assert the life forces found in natural materials, thereby engaging viewers in a consideration of their own relationship to nature. Tsuchiya does not specifically invoke Shinto (see "Pre-Buddhist Beliefs and Rituals in Japan," Chapter 8, page 221) when speaking about his art, but it is clear that he has internalized Shinto principles. He identifies as his goal "to bring out and present the life of nature emanating from this energy of trees. . . . It is as though the wood is part of myself, as though the wood has the same kind of life force."[1]

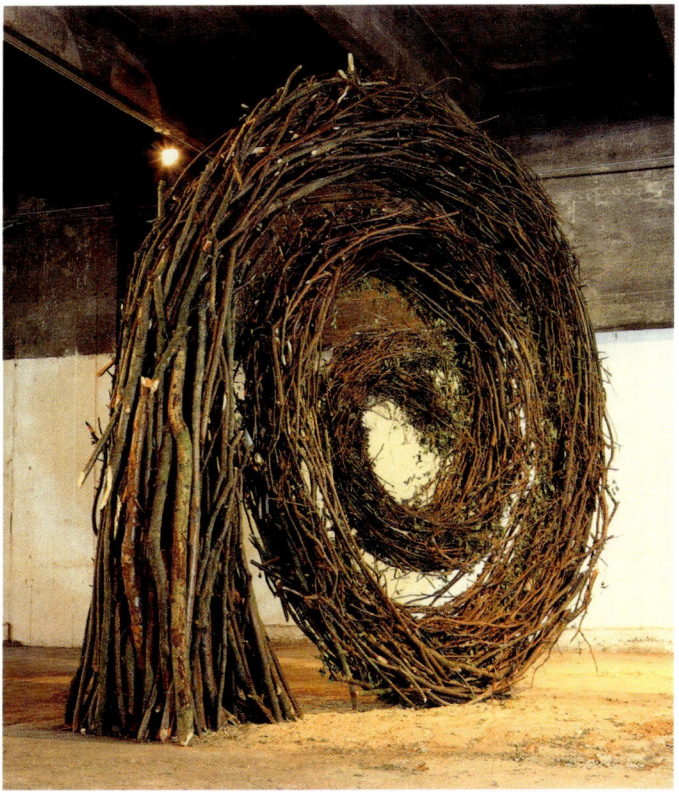

**27-17** TSUCHIYA KIMIO, *Symptom,* 1987. Branches, $13'\ 1\frac{1}{2}''\times 14'\ 9\frac{1}{8}''\times 3'\ 11\frac{1}{4}''$. Installation view, *Jeune Sculpture '87,* Paris 1987.

## CONCLUSION

Over the past seven centuries, Japanese history has been one of dramatic change. The emergence of shogun rule in the early 14th century ushered in an era of persistent war and conflict. Not until the restoration of the emperor in 1868 was relative stability established. Also emerging as a major presence in 14th-century Japan was Zen. Its influence extended far beyond the realm of religion, and it suffused Japanese culture with its ideals of discipline and meditative focus. Despite the centuries of turmoil, Japanese art flourished. Among the great strengths of Japanese art has been innovation through adaptation. Contact with the rest of eastern Asia and later the world's other areas, as well as knowledge of Japan's own past, provided artists and patrons a wealth of aesthetic and ideological options. As they integrated the new, they found cultural spaces where less radical adaptations of the old could survive. Even today, as Japan embraces a vision of its postindustrial future, very traditional artists, as well as thoroughly contemporary ones, flourish side by side.

**1334**

| Restoration of imperial power, 1334–1336
| Ashikaga Shogunate established, 1336

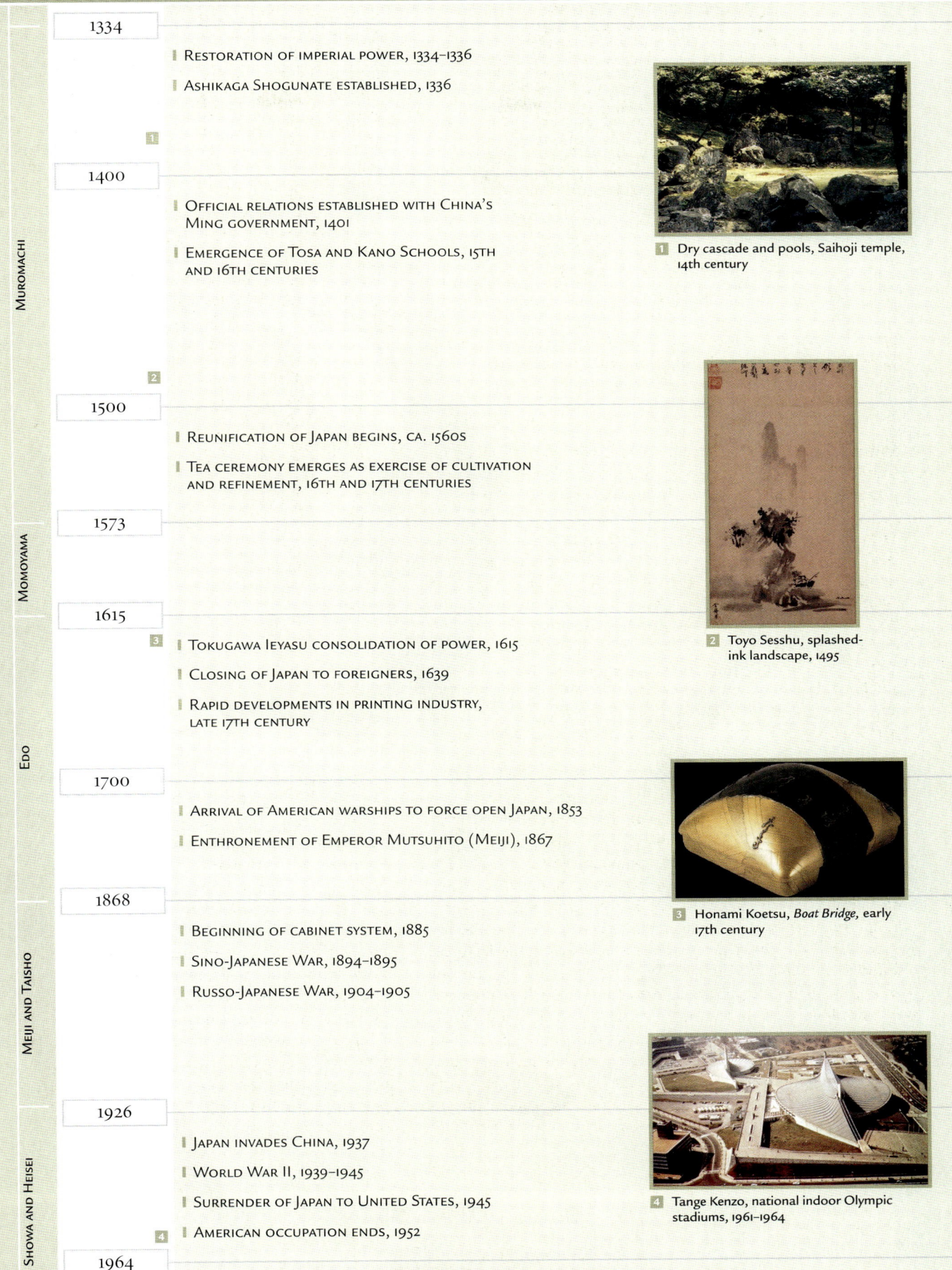

**1400**

| Official relations established with China's Ming government, 1401
| Emergence of Tosa and Kano Schools, 15th and 16th centuries

1 Dry cascade and pools, Saihoji temple, 14th century

**1500**

| Reunification of Japan begins, ca. 1560s
| Tea ceremony emerges as exercise of cultivation and refinement, 16th and 17th centuries

**1573**

**1615**

| Tokugawa Ieyasu consolidation of power, 1615
| Closing of Japan to foreigners, 1639
| Rapid developments in printing industry, late 17th century

2 Toyo Sesshu, splashed-ink landscape, 1495

**1700**

| Arrival of American warships to force open Japan, 1853
| Enthronement of Emperor Mutsuhito (Meiji), 1867

**1868**

| Beginning of cabinet system, 1885
| Sino-Japanese War, 1894–1895
| Russo-Japanese War, 1904–1905

3 Honami Koetsu, *Boat Bridge,* early 17th century

**1926**

| Japan invades China, 1937
| World War II, 1939–1945
| Surrender of Japan to United States, 1945
| American occupation ends, 1952

4 Tange Kenzo, national indoor Olympic stadiums, 1961–1964

**1964**

| Tokyo hosts Olympic Games, 1964

MUROMACHI

MOMOYAMA

EDO

MEIJI AND TAISHO

SHOWA AND HEISEI

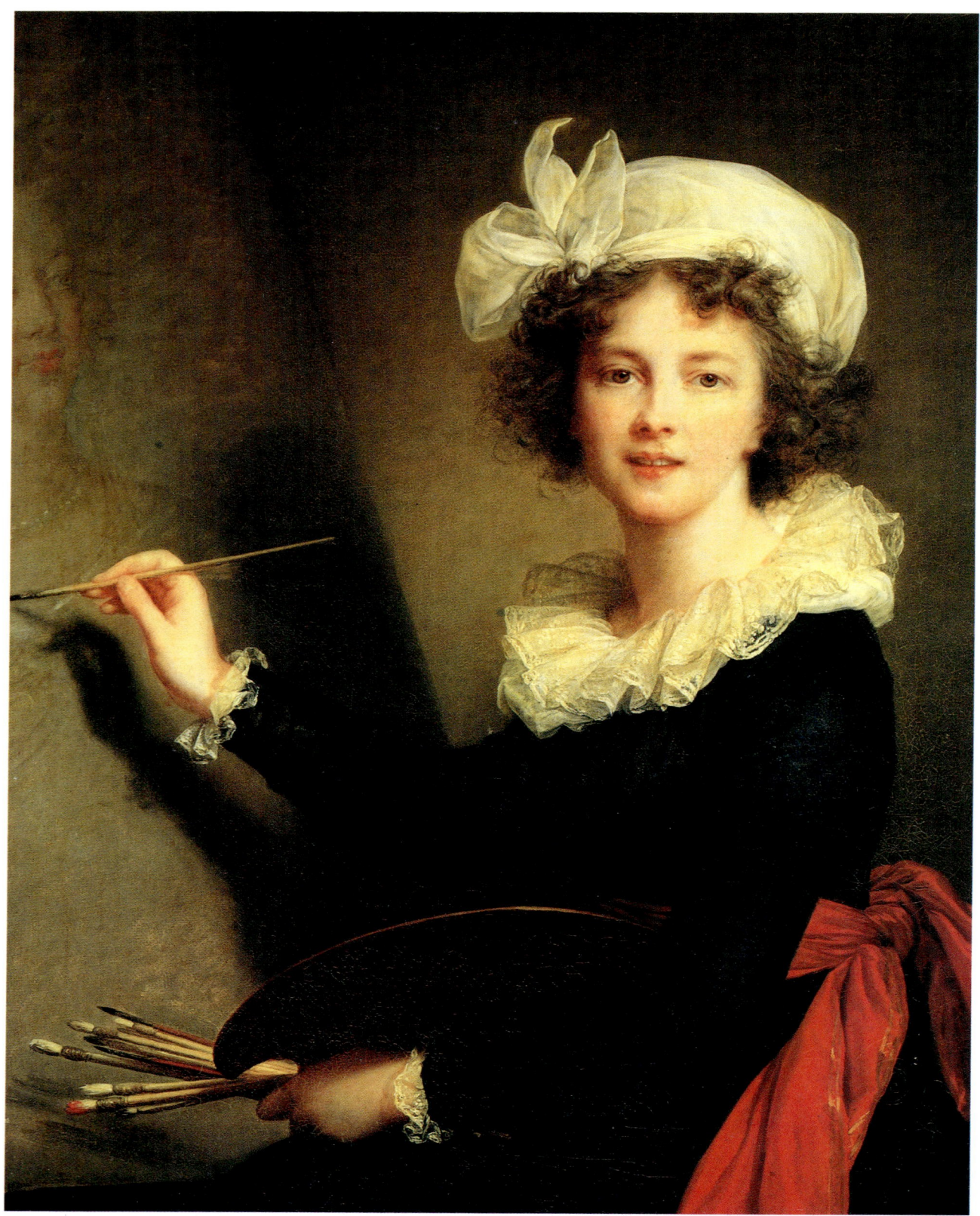

Élisabeth Louise Vigée-Lebrun, *Self-Portrait,* 1790. Oil on canvas, 8′ 4″ × 6′ 9″. Galleria degli Uffizi, Florence.

# 28

# THE ENLIGHTENMENT AND ITS LEGACY

## ART OF THE LATE 18TH THROUGH THE MID-19TH CENTURY

The death of Louis XIV in 1715 brought many changes in French high society. The court of Versailles was at once abandoned for the pleasures of town life. Although French citizens still owed their allegiance to a monarch, the early 18th century saw a resurgence in aristocratic social, political, and economic power. Appropriately, some historians refer to the 18th century as the great age of the aristocracy. The nobility not only exercised their traditional privileges (for example, exemption from certain taxes and from forced labor on public works) but also sought to expand their power.

## ROCOCO: THE FRENCH TASTE

In the cultural realm, aristocrats reestablished their predominance as art patrons. The *hôtels* (town houses) of Paris soon became the centers of a new, softer style called *Rococo*. The sparkling gaiety cultivated in the new age (see "Of Knowledge, Taste, and Refinement: Salon Culture," page 799), associated with the regency that followed the death of Louis XIV and with the reign of Louis XV, found perfectly harmonious expression in this new style. Rococo appeared in France in about 1700, primarily as a style of interior design. The French Rococo exterior was most often simple, or even plain, but Rococo exuberance took over the interior. The term derived from the French word *rocaille,* which literally means "pebble," but it referred especially to the small stones and shells used to decorate grotto interiors. Such shells or shell forms were the principal motifs in Rococo ornament.

**A PERMANENTLY "FESTIVE" ROOM** A typical French Rococo room is the Salon de la Princesse (FIG. **28-1**) in the Hôtel de Soubise in Paris, designed by GERMAIN BOFFRAND (1667–1754). Comparing this room to the Galerie des Glaces at Versailles (see FIG. 24-69) reveals how Boffrand softened the strong architectural lines and

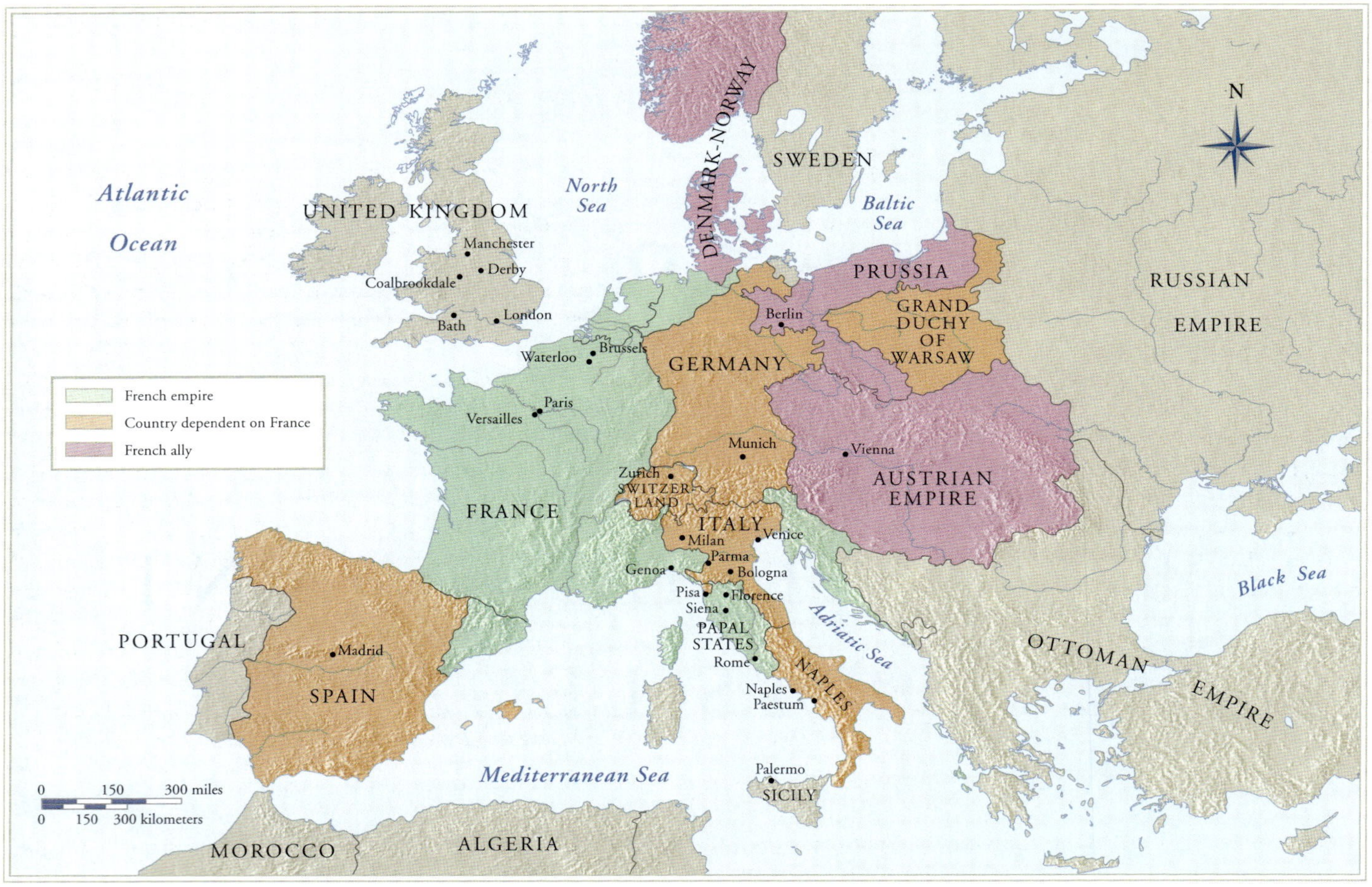

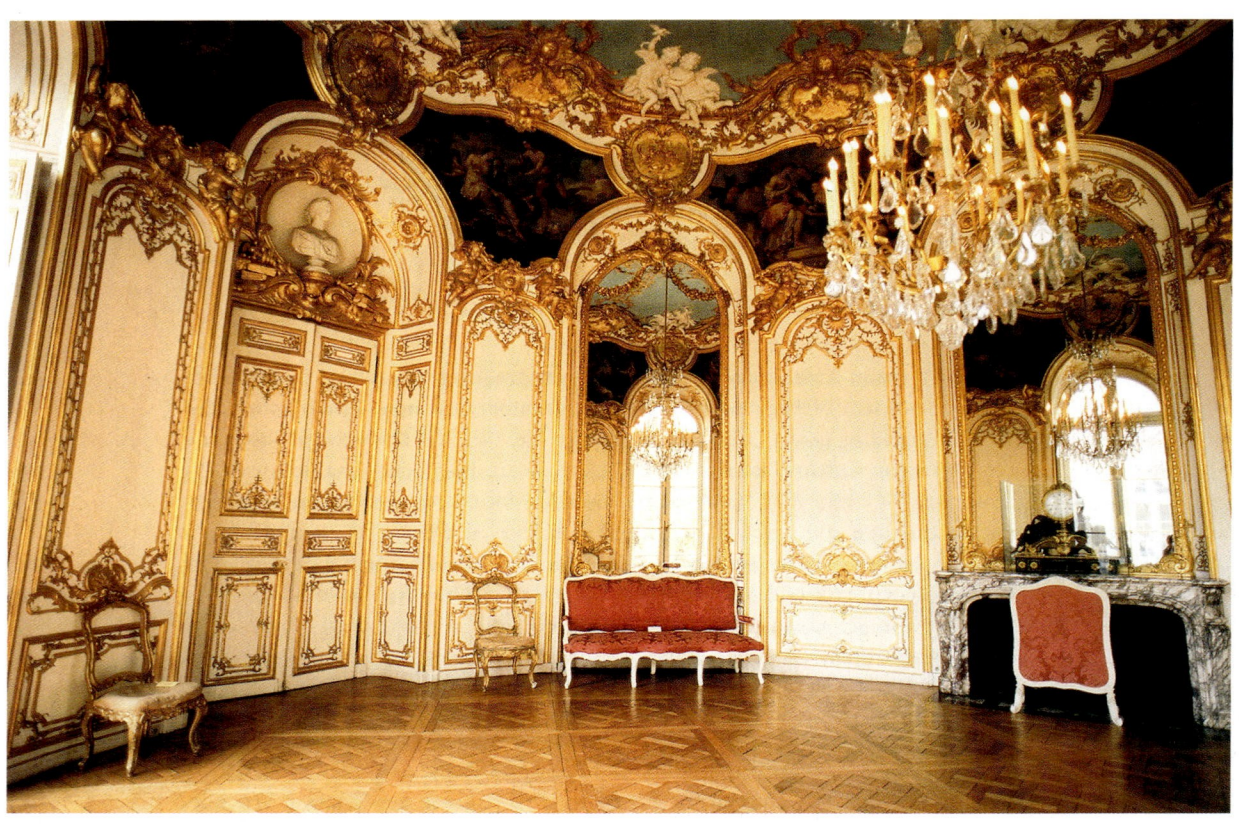

MAP 28-1 Napoleonic Europe 1800–1815.

28-1 Germain Boffrand, Salon de la Princesse, with painting by Charles-Joseph Natoire and sculpture by J. B. Lemoine, Hôtel de Soubise, Paris, France, 1737–1740.

## Of Knowledge, Taste, and Refinement
### Salon Culture

The feminine look of the Rococo style suggests that the age was dominated by the taste and social initiative of women— and, to a large extent, it was. Women—Madame de Pompadour in France, Maria Theresa in Austria, and Elizabeth and Catherine in Russia—held some of the highest positions in Europe, and female influence was felt in numerous smaller courts. The Rococo salon was the center of early-18th-century Parisian society, and Paris was the social capital of Europe. Wealthy, ambitious, and clever society hostesses competed to attract the most famous and the most accomplished people to their salons. The medium of social intercourse was conversation spiced with wit, repartee as quick and deft as a fencing match. Artifice reigned supreme, and participants considered enthusiasm or sincerity in bad taste.

These salon women referred to themselves as *femmes savantes,* or learned women. Among these learned women was Julie de Lespinasse (1732–1776), one of the most articulate, urbane, and intelligent French women of the time. She held daily salons from five o'clock until nine in the evening. *Memoirs of Marmontel* documents the liveliness of these gatherings and the remarkable nature of this hostess:

> The circle was formed of persons who were not bound together. She had taken them here and there in society, but so well assorted were they that once there they fell into harmony like the strings of an instrument touched by an able hand. Following out that comparison,

I may say that she played the instrument with an art that came of genius; she seemed to know what tone each string would yield before she touched it; I mean to say that our minds and our natures were so well known to her that in order to bring them into play she had but to say a word. Nowhere was conversation more lively, more brilliant, or better regulated than at her house. It was a rare phenomenon indeed, the degree of tempered, equable heat which she knew so well how to maintain, sometimes by moderating it, sometimes by quickening it. The continual activity of her soul was communicated to our souls, but measurably; her imagination was the mainspring, her reason the regulator. Remark that the brains she stirred at will were neither feeble nor frivolous. . . . Her talent for casting out a thought and giving it for discussion to men of that class, her own talent in discussing it with precision, sometimes with eloquence, her talent for bringing forward new ideas and varying the topic—always with the facility and ease of a fairy . . . these talents, I say, were not those of an ordinary woman. It was not with the follies of fashion and vanity that daily, during four hours of conversation, without languor and without vacuum, she knew how to make herself interesting to a wide circle of strong minds.[1]

[1] Jean François Marmontel, *Memoirs of Marmontel,* translated by Brigit Patmore (London: Routledge, 1930), 270.

---

panels of the earlier style into flexible, sinuous curves luxuriantly multiplied in mirror reflections. The walls melt into the vault. Irregular painted shapes, surmounted by sculpture and separated by the typical rocaille shells, replace the hall's cornices. Painting, architecture, and sculpture combine to form a single ensemble. The profusion of curving tendrils and sprays of foliage blend with the shell forms to give an effect of freely growing nature, suggesting that the designer permanently decked the Rococo room for a festival.

Rococo was a style preeminently evident in small works. Artists exquisitely wrought furniture, utensils, and accessories of all sorts in the characteristically delicate, undulating Rococo line. French Rococo interiors were designed as lively total works of art with elegant furniture, enchanting small sculptures, ornamented mirror frames, delightful ceramics and silver, a few "easel" paintings, and decorative tapestry complementing the architecture, relief sculptures, and wall paintings. As seen today, French Rococo interiors, such as the Salon de la Princesse, have lost most of the moveable "accessories" that once adorned them. Viewers can imagine, however, how such rooms—with their alternating gilded moldings, vivacious relief sculptures, and daintily colored ornament of flowers and garlands—must have harmonized with the chamber music played in them, with the elaborate costumes of satin and brocade, and with the equally elegant etiquette and sparkling wit of the people who graced them.

**FRENCH ROCOCO IN GERMANY** A good example of French Rococo in Germany is the Amalienburg, a small lodge FRANÇOIS DE CUVILLIÉS (1695–1768) built in the park of the Nymphenburg Palace in Munich. Although Rococo was essentially a style of interior design, the Amalienburg beautifully harmonizes the interior and exterior elevations through the curving flow of lines and planes that cohere in a sculptural unity of great elegance. The most spectacular interior room in the lodge is the circular Hall of Mirrors (FIG. **28-2**), a silver-and-blue ensemble of architecture, stucco relief, silvered bronze mirrors, and crystal. It dazzles the eye with myriad scintillating motifs, forms, and figurations the designer borrowed from the full Rococo ornamental repertoire. This room displays the style at its zenith. The room is bathed in silvery light, which is amplified by windows and mirrors. The reflections of light create shapes and contours that weave rhythmically around the upper walls and the ceiling coves. Everything seems organic, growing, and in motion, an ultimate refinement of illusion that the architect, artists, and artisans, all magically in command of their varied media, created with virtuoso flourishes.

**A DELICATE DANCER** The painter whom scholars most associate with French Rococo is ANTOINE WATTEAU (1684–1721). The differences between the Baroque age in France and the Rococo age can be seen clearly by contrasting Rigaud's portrait of

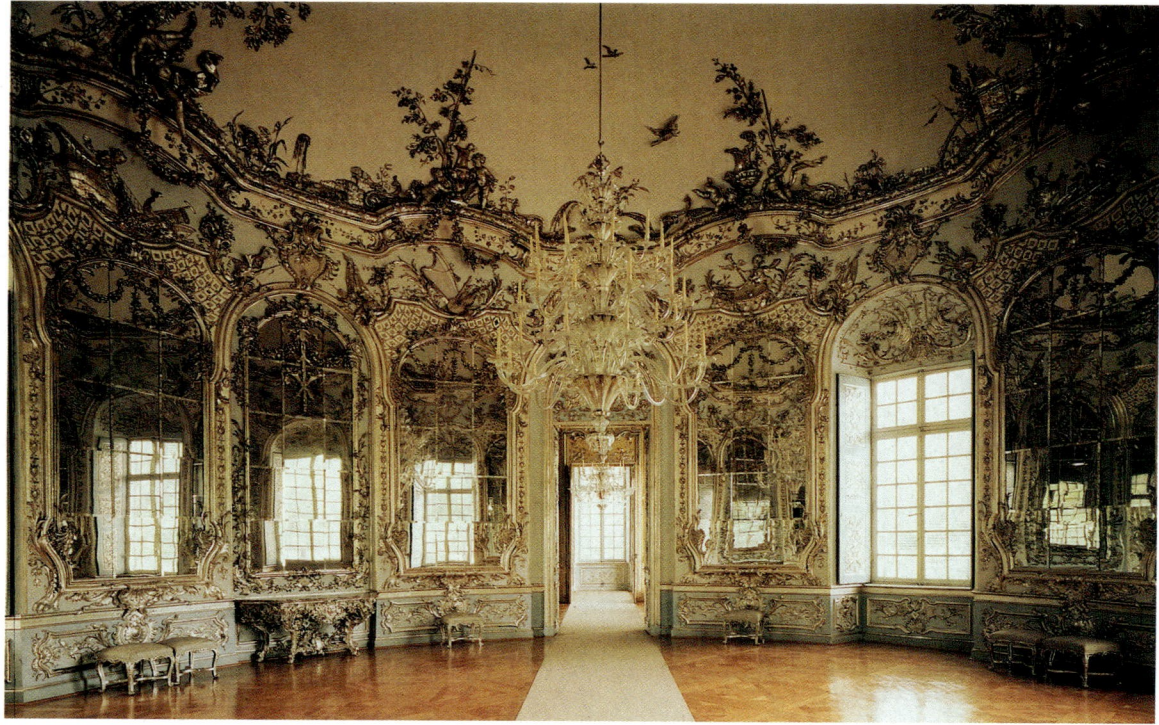

28-2 François de Cuvilliés, Hall of Mirrors, the Amalienburg, Nymphenburg Palace park, Munich, Germany, early 18th century. 💿

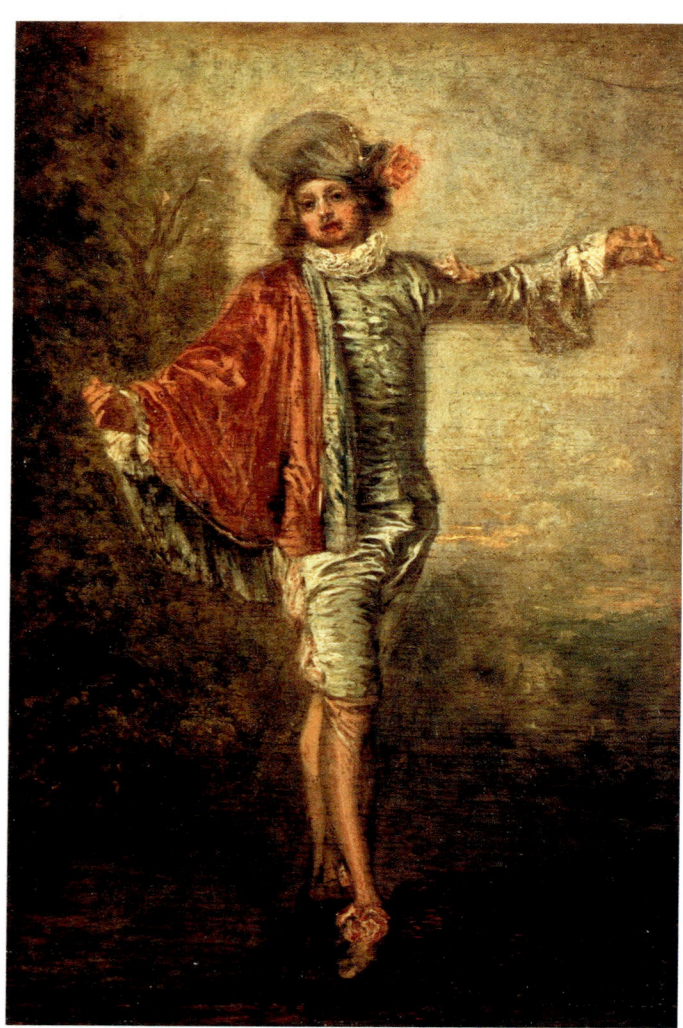

28-3 Antoine Watteau, L'Indifférent, ca. 1716. Oil on canvas, approx. 10″ × 7″. Louvre, Paris. 💿

Louis XIV (see FIG. 24-65) with one of Watteau's paintings, *L'Indifférent* (The indifferent one; FIG. **28-3**). Rigaud portrayed pompous majesty in supreme glory, as if the French monarch were reviewing throngs of bowing courtiers at Versailles. Watteau's painting, in contrast, is not as heavy or staid and is more delicate. The artist presented a languid, gliding dancer whose mincing minuet might be seen as mimicking the monarch's solemnity if the paintings were hung together. In Rigaud's portrait, stout architecture, bannerlike curtains, flowing ermine, and fleur-de-lis exalt the king. In Watteau's painting, the dancer moves in a rainbow shimmer of color, emerging onto the stage of the intimate comic opera to the silken sounds of strings. This contrast also highlights the different patronage of the eras; whereas the French Baroque period was dominated by royal patronage (particularly that of Louis XIV), Rococo was the culture of a wider aristocracy and high society.

**CELEBRATING THE GOOD LIFE** Watteau was largely responsible for creating a specific type of Rococo painting, called a *fête galante* painting. These paintings depicted the outdoor entertainment or amusements of upper-class society. An example of a fête galante painting is Watteau's masterpiece (painted in two versions), *Return from Cythera* (FIG. **28-4**), completed between 1717 and 1719 as the artist's acceptance piece for admission to the Royal Academy. Watteau was Flemish, and his work, influenced by Rubens's style, contributed to the popularity of an emphasis on color in painting.

At the turn of the century, the French Royal Academy was divided rather sharply between two doctrines. One doctrine upheld the ideas of Le Brun (the major proponent of French Baroque under Louis XIV), who followed Nicolas Poussin in teaching that form was the most important element in painting, whereas "colors in painting are as allurements for persuading the eyes," additions for effect and not really essential.[1] The other doctrine, with Rubens as its model, proclaimed the natural supremacy of color

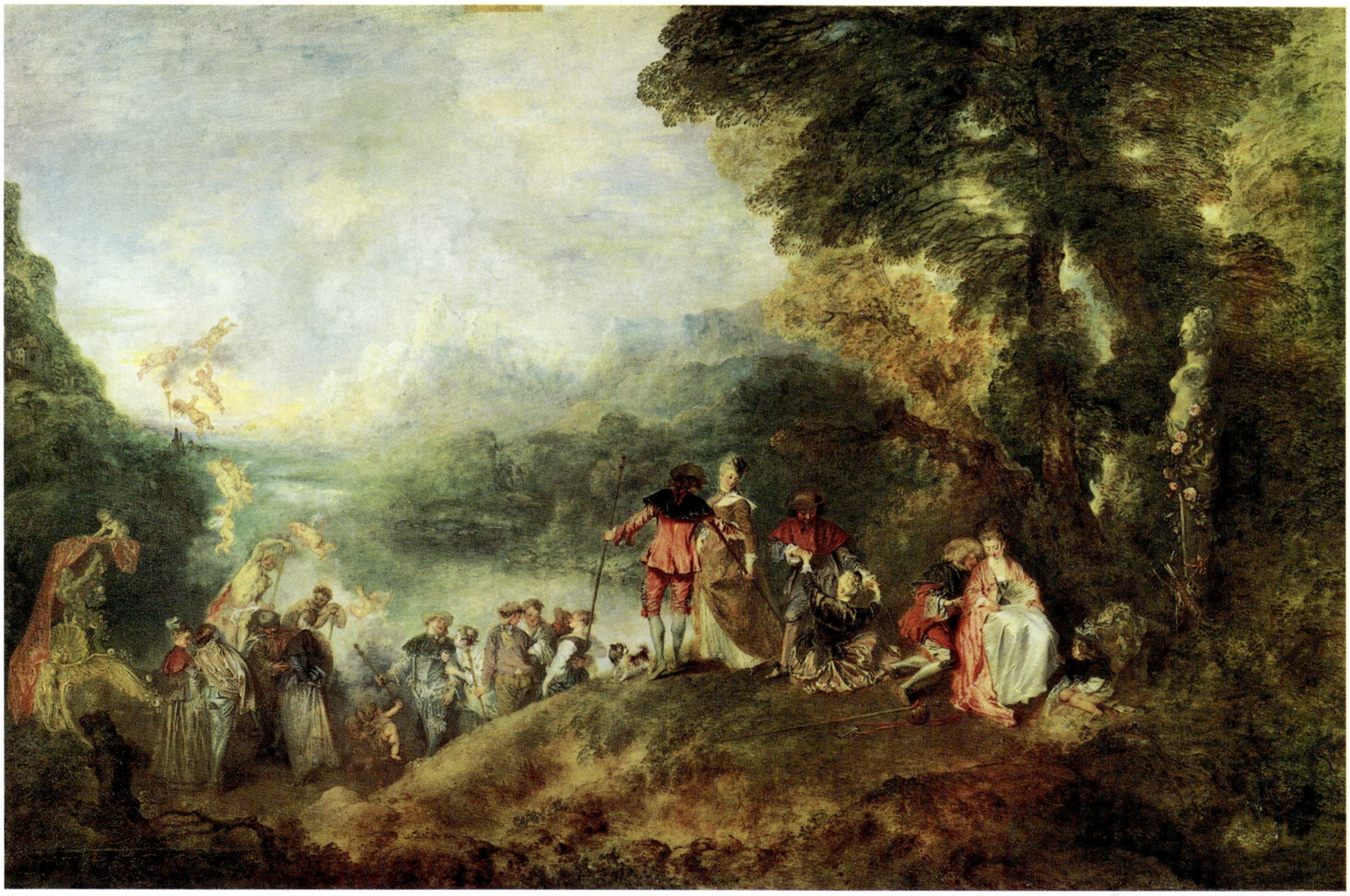

**28-4** ANTOINE WATTEAU, *Return from Cythera*, 1717–1719. Oil on canvas, approx. 4′ 3″ × 6′ 4″. Louvre, Paris.

and the coloristic style as the artist's proper guide. Depending on which side they took, academy members were called "Poussinistes" or "Rubénistes." With Watteau in their ranks, the Rubénistes carried the day, and they established the Rococo style in painting on the colorism of Rubens and the Venetians.

Watteau's *Return from Cythera* (FIG. 28-4) represents a group of lovers preparing to depart from the island of eternal youth and love, sacred to Aphrodite. Young and luxuriously costumed, they move gracefully from the protective shade of a woodland park, filled with amorous cupids and voluptuous statuary, down a grassy slope to an awaiting golden barge. Watteau's figural poses, which combine elegance and sweetness, are unparalleled. He composed his generally quite small paintings from albums of superb drawings that have been preserved and are still in fine condition. These show that he observed slow movement from difficult and unusual angles, obviously intending to find the smoothest, most poised, and most refined attitudes. As he sought nuances of bodily poise and movement, Watteau also strove for the most exquisite shades of color difference, defining in a single stroke the shimmer of silk at a bent knee or the iridescence that touches a glossy surface as it emerges from shadow.

Art historians have noted that the theme of love and Arcadian happiness (seen in the work of Giorgione [see FIG. 22-33] and which Watteau may have seen in works by Rubens) in Watteau's pictures is slightly shadowed with wistfulness, or even melancholy. Perhaps Watteau, during his own short life, meditated on the swift passage of youth and pleasure. The haze of

color, the subtly modeled shapes, the gliding motion, and the air of suave gentility were all to the taste of the Rococo artist's wealthy patrons.

**A PLAYFUL ROCOCO FANTASY** Watteau's successors never quite matched his taste and subtlety. Their themes were about love, artfully and archly pursued through erotic frivolity and playful intrigue. After Watteau's early death at age 37, his follower, FRANÇOIS BOUCHER (1703–1770), painter for Madame de Pompadour (the influential mistress of Louis XV), rose to the dominant position in French painting. Although he was an excellent portraitist, Boucher's fame rested primarily on his graceful allegories, with Arcadian shepherds, nymphs, and goddesses cavorting in shady glens engulfed in pink and sky blue light. *Cupid a Captive* (FIG. 28-5) presents the viewer with a rosy pyramid of infant and female flesh set off against a cool, leafy background, with fluttering draperies both hiding and revealing the nudity of the figures. Boucher used the full range of Italian and French Baroque devices—the dynamic play of crisscrossing diagonals, curvilinear forms, and slanting recessions—to create his masterly composition. But in his work he dissected powerful Baroque curves into a multiplicity of decorative arabesques, dissipating Baroque drama into sensual playfulness. Lively and lighthearted, Boucher's artful Rococo fantasies became mirrors for his patrons, the wealthy French, to behold the ornamental reflections of their cherished pastimes.

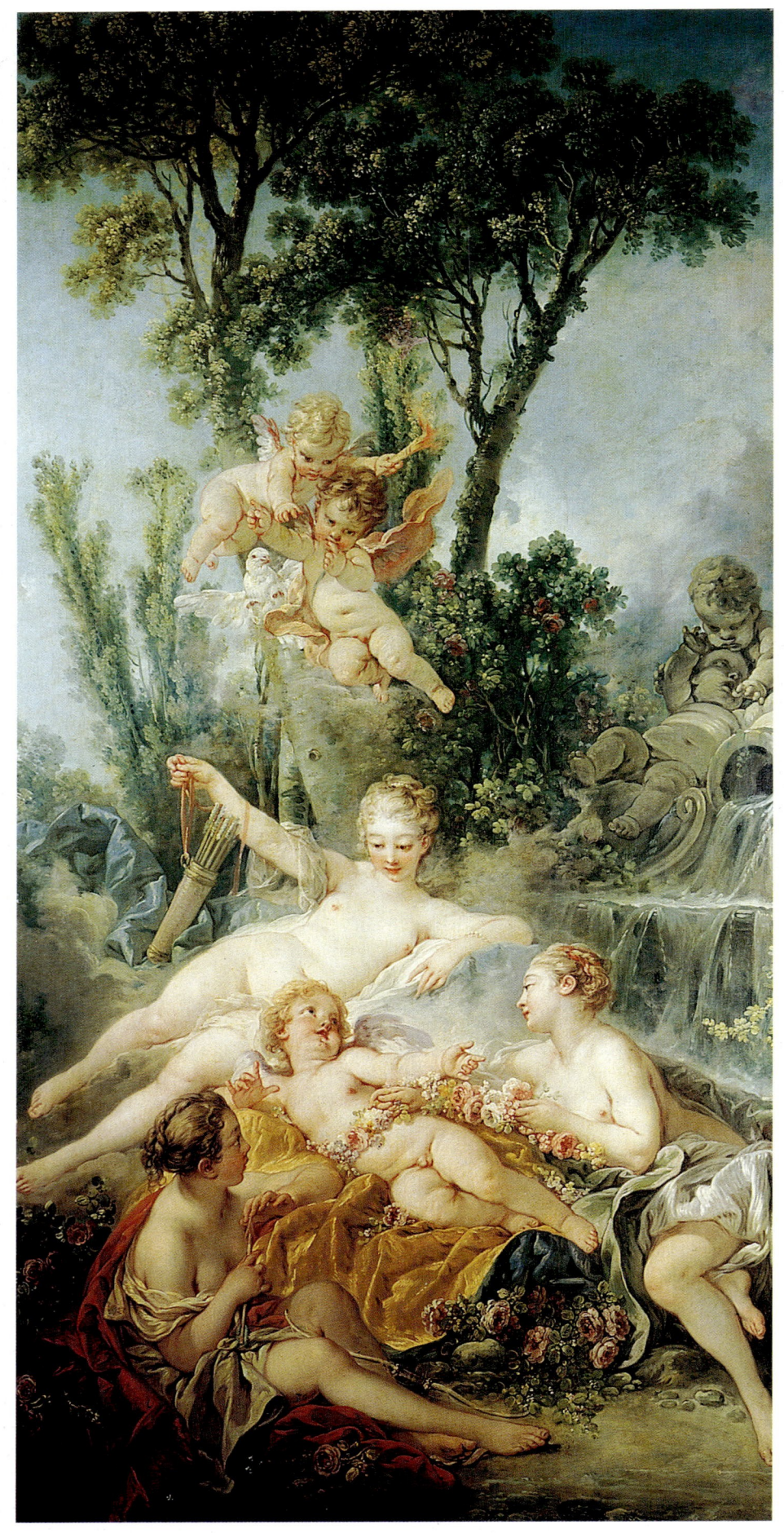

**28-5** François Boucher, *Cupid a Captive*, 1754. Oil on canvas, approx. 5′ 6″ × 2′ 10″. The Wallace Collection, London.

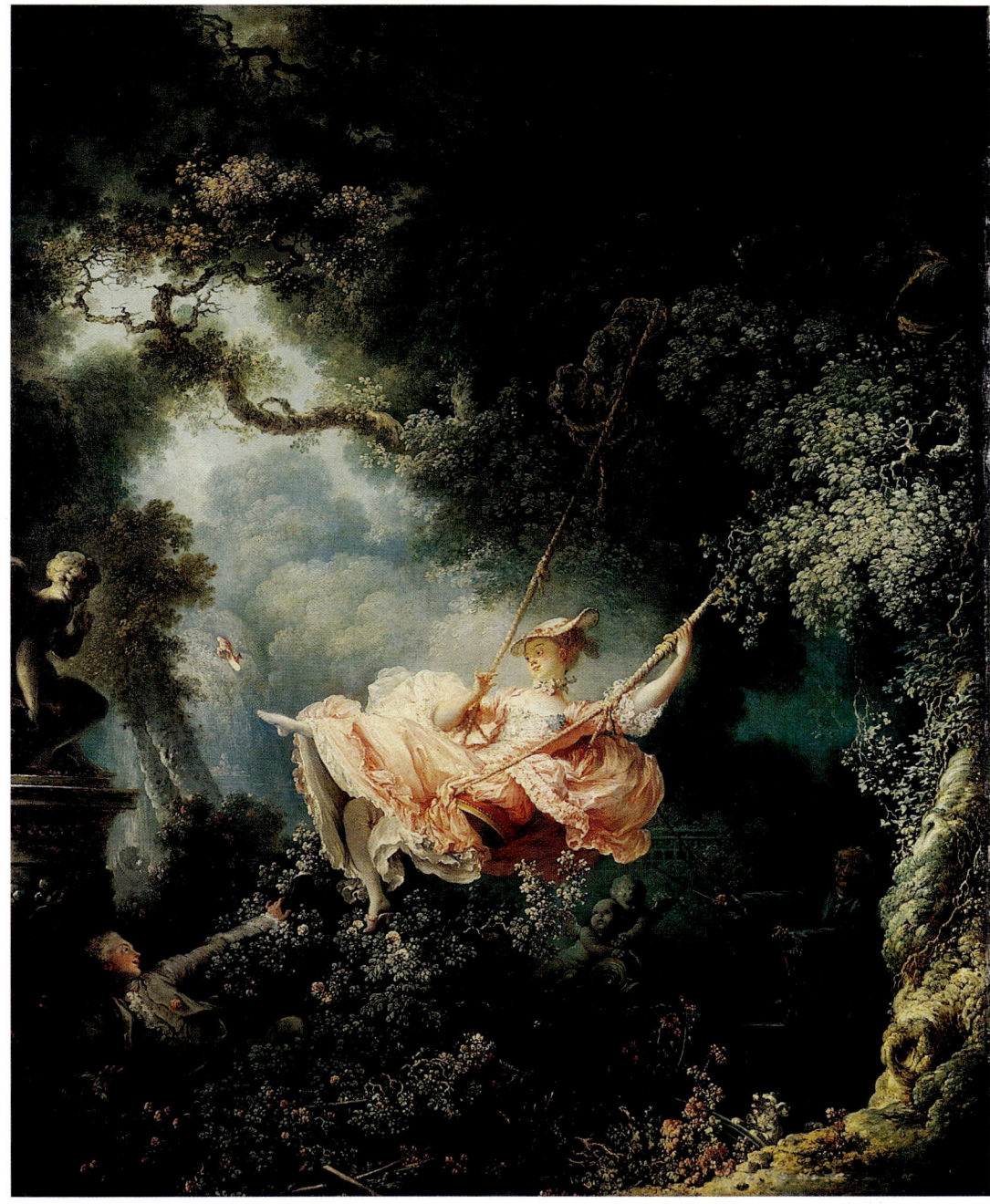

**28-6** JEAN-HONORÉ FRAGONARD, *The Swing*, 1766. Oil on canvas, approx. 2′ 11″ × 2′ 8″. The Wallace Collection, London.

**AN INTRIGUING FLIRTATION** JEAN-HONORÉ FRAGONARD (1732–1806), Boucher's student, was a first-rate colorist whose decorative skill almost surpassed his master's. An example of his manner can stand as characteristic not only of his work but also of the later Rococo in general. *The Swing* (FIG. **28-6**) is a typical "intrigue" picture. A young gentleman has managed an arrangement whereby an unsuspecting old bishop swings the young man's pretty sweetheart higher and higher, while her lover (and the work's patron), in the lower left corner, stretches out to admire her ardently from a strategic position on the ground. The young lady flirtatiously and boldly kicks off her shoe at the little statue of Cupid, who holds his finger to his lips. The landscape setting is out of Watteau — a luxuriant perfumed bower in a park that very much resembles a stage scene for the comic opera. The

glowing pastel colors and soft light convey, almost by themselves, the theme's sensuality.

**ECHOES OF BERNINI IN ROCOCO** The Rococo mood of sensual intimacy also permeated many of the small sculptures designed for the 18th-century salons. Artists such as Claude Michel, called CLODION (1738–1814), specialized in small, lively sculptures that combined the sensuous Rococo fantasies with lightened echoes of Bernini's dynamic figures. Perhaps historians should expect such influence in Clodion's works. He lived and worked in Rome for some years after discovering the city's charms during his tenure as the recipient of the cherished Prix de Rome. The Royal Academy annually gave the Prix de Rome (Rome Prize) to the artist who produced the best history

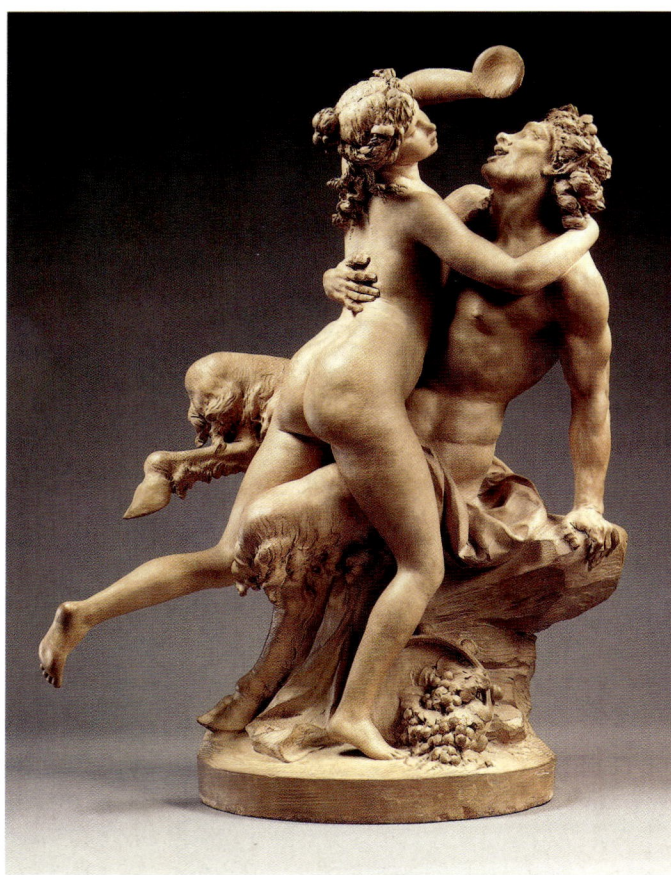

**28-7** CLODION, *Nymph and Satyr*, ca. 1775. Terracotta, approx. 1' 11" high. Metropolitan Museum of Art, New York (bequest of Benjamin Altman, 1913).

painting, subsidizing the winning artist's stay in Rome (from three to five years).

Clodion's small group, *Nymph and Satyr* (FIG. **28-7**), has an open and active composition suggestive of Bernini's work. But the artist tempered any reference to Bernini's art with the erotic playfulness of Boucher and Fragonard to energize his eager nymph and the laughing satyr into whose mouth she pours a cup of wine. Here, the sensual exhilaration of the Rococo style is caught in diminutive scale and inexpensive terracotta. As is true of so many Rococo artifacts, and most of Clodion's best work, the artist designed this group for a tabletop.

# THE ENLIGHTENMENT: PHILOSOPHY AND SOCIETY

The aristocratic culture celebrated in Rococo art did not go unchallenged during the 18th century. Indeed, the feudal system that served as the foundation of social and economic life in Europe dissolved, and the rigid social hierarchies that provided the basis for Rococo art and patronage relaxed. By the end of the 18th century, revolutions had erupted in France and America. A major factor in these political, social, and economic changes was the Enlightenment. The Enlightenment was in essence a new way of thinking critically about the world and about humankind, independently of religion, myth, or tradition. The new method was based on using reason to reflect on the results of physical experiments and

involved the critical analysis of texts. It was grounded in empirical evidence. Enlightenment thought promoted the scientific questioning of all assertions and rejected unfounded beliefs about the nature of humankind and of the world. The enlightened mind was skeptical of doctrines and theories such as superstitions and old wives' tales that no verifiable evidence could prove. Thus, the Enlightenment encouraged and stimulated the habit and application of mind known as the scientific method.

**"THE DOCTRINE OF EMPIRICISM"** The Enlightenment had its roots in the 17th century, with the mathematical and scientific achievements of René Descartes, Blaise Pascal, Isaac Newton, and Gottfried Wilhelm von Leibnitz. England and France were the principal centers of the Enlightenment, though its dictums influenced the thinking of intellectuals throughout Europe and in the American colonies. Benjamin Franklin, Thomas Jefferson, and other American notables were educated in its principles. Of particular importance for Enlightenment thought was the work of Britons Isaac Newton (1642–1727) and John Locke (1632–1704).

In Newton's scientific studies, he insisted on empirical proof of his theories and encouraged others to avoid metaphysics and the supernatural—realms that extended beyond the natural physical world. This emphasis on both tangible data and concrete experience became a cornerstone of Enlightenment thought. In addition, Newton's experiments seemed to reveal a rationality in the physical world. Enlightenment thinkers transferred such concepts to the sociopolitical world by promoting a rationally organized society. John Locke, whose works acquired the status of Enlightenment gospel, developed these ideas further. What we know, wrote Locke, comes to us through sense perception of the material world and is imprinted on the mind as on a blank tablet. From these perceptions alone we form ideas. Our ideas are not innate or God-given; it is only from experience that we can know (this belief is called the "doctrine of empiricism"). Locke asserted that human beings are born good, not cursed by original sin. The laws of Nature grant them the natural rights of life, liberty, and property, as well as the right to freedom of conscience. Government is by contract, and its purpose is to protect these rights; if and when government abuses these rights, the citizenry has the further natural right of revolution. Locke's ideas empowered people to take control of their own destinies.

**"THE DOCTRINE OF PROGRESS"** The work of Newton and Locke also inspired French intellectuals. New philosophies that conceived of individuals and societies at large as parts of physical nature were advanced by thinkers in France, who are still known by their French designation *philosophes*. They shared the conviction that the ills of humanity could be remedied by applying reason and common sense to human problems. They criticized the powers of church and state as irrational limits placed on political and intellectual freedom. They believed that by the accumulation and propagation of knowledge, humanity could advance by degrees to a happier state than it had ever known. This conviction matured into the "doctrine of progress" and its corollary doctrine of the perfectibility of humankind. Previous societies, for the most part, perceived the future as inevitable—the cycle of life and death, and fate determined by religious beliefs. The notion of progress—the systematic and planned improvement of society—was first developed during the 18th century and continues to have an impact in the 21st century.

**A COMPENDIUM OF KNOWLEDGE** Animated by their belief in human progress and perfectibility, the philosophes took on the task of gathering knowledge and making it accessible to all who could read. Their program was, in effect, the democratization of knowledge. Denis Diderot (1713–1784) greatly influenced the Enlightenment's rationalistic and materialistic thinking. He became editor of the pioneering *Encyclopédie*, a compilation of articles and illustrations written by more than a hundred contributors, including all the leading philosophes. The *Encyclopédie* was truly comprehensive (its formal title was *Systematic Dictionary of the Sciences, Arts, and Crafts*) and included all available knowledge—historical, scientific, and technical, as well as religious and moral—and political theory. The first volume was published in 1751, and the project (35 volumes of text and illustrations) was completed in 1780. This Enlightenment-inspired notion of the accumulation and documentation of knowledge was new to Western society, which had relied heavily on tradition and convention.

**REVOLUTIONARY CHANGE** The political, economic, and social consequences of this expanding knowledge and the doctrine of progress were explosive. It is no coincidence that some of the major revolutions of recent centuries—the French Revolution, the American Revolution, and the Industrial Revolution in England—occurred during this period. These upheavals precipitated yet other major changes. The growth of cities and of an urban working class were two such changes. Colonialism expanded as the demand for cheap labor and raw materials increased. For example, England feuded with France over the North American continent and the subcontinent of India. This enthusiasm for growth eventually emerged in the newly established United States as well as in the form of the doctrine of Manifest Destiny—the ideological justification for continued territorial expansion. As John L. O'Sullivan expounded in the earliest known use of the term in 1845, "Our manifest destiny [is] to overspread the continent allotted by Providence for the free development of our yearly multiplying millions."[2]

Thus, the Age of Enlightenment ushered in a new way of thinking and affected historical developments worldwide. Artists entered into this dialogue about the state and direction of society and played an important role in encouraging public consideration of these momentous changes. In the arts, this new way of thinking can be seen in the general label "modern" used to describe the art from the late 18th century on. Such a vague and generic term, covering centuries of art, renders any concrete definition of "modern art" virtually impossible. However, one defining characteristic that scholars and critics traditionally have ascribed to the modern era is an awareness of history. People know that their culture perpetuates or rejects previously established ideas or conventions. The concept of *modernity*—the state of being modern—involves being up-to-date, implying a distinction between the present and the past. Recent art historical scholarship has posited an even earlier date for the inception of the modern era. Many art historians now assert that this historical consciousness was present in much earlier societies. This accounts for current use of the term "early modern" to describe Renaissance and even medieval cultures.

# THE ENLIGHTENMENT: SCIENCE AND TECHNOLOGY

**ENLIGHTENMENT'S CHAMPION** François Marie Arouet, better known as Voltaire (1694–1778), became, and still is, the most representative figure—almost the personification—of the Enlightenment spirit. Voltaire was instrumental in introducing Newton and Locke to the French intelligentsia. He hated, and

attacked through his writings, the arbitrary despotic rule of kings, the selfish privileges of the nobility and the church, religious intolerance, and, above all, the injustice of the *ancien regime* (the "old order"). In his numerous books and pamphlets, which the authorities regularly condemned and burned, he protested against government persecution of the freedoms of thought and religion. Voltaire believed that the human race could never be happy until the traditional obstructions to the progress of the human mind and welfare were removed. His personal and public involvement in the struggle against established political and religious authority gave authenticity to his ideas. It converted a whole generation to the conviction that fundamental changes were necessary. This conviction paved the way for a revolution in France that Voltaire never intended, and he probably would never have approved of it. He was not convinced that "all men are created equal," the credo of Jean-Jacques Rousseau, Thomas Jefferson, and the American Declaration of Independence.

**SCIENTIFIC ADVANCES** Biomechanical and chemical studies of living nature advanced that field of human knowledge. Diderot's contemporary, Comte de Buffon (1707–1788), undertook a kind of encyclopedia of the natural sciences. His *Natural History*, a monumental work of 44 volumes, was especially valuable for its zoological study. Buffon's contemporary, the Swedish botanist Carolus Linnaeus (1707–1778), established a system of plant classification.

In the field of life sciences, the study of the human body—its structure, function, and disorders—was at the center of scientific interest. Since the Renaissance, artists had been concerned with learning about the body by dissecting it. Historians long have recognized the part Leonardo played in inaugurating the descriptive science of anatomy (see FIG. 22-5). As that description became more exact and complete (FIG. **28-8**), the anatomical artist's skill became a specialty and the drawings an instrument for the education and practice of physicians and surgeons. As such, an

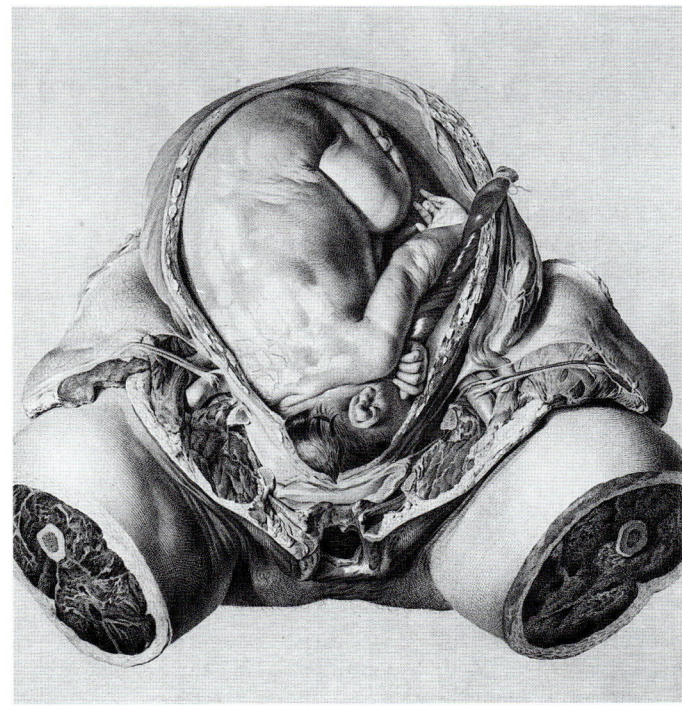

**28-8** WILLIAM HUNTER, *Child in Womb, drawing from dissection of a woman who died in the ninth month of pregnancy,* from *Anatomy of the Human Gravid Uterus,* 1774. British Library.

anatomical drawing was not simply a preliminary study, a guide for a painter or sculptor constructing an image of the human body, but a tool for specialists in an entirely different discipline. In this respect it made its contribution as a technological device, an art or craft applied to a science. The technological applications of drafting and model building have proved indispensable to the development of science well into the computer age.

**INDUSTRIAL TRANSFORMATION** Scientific investigation and technological invention opened up new possibilities for human understanding of the world and for control of its material forces. Research into the phenomena of electricity and combustion, along with the discovery of oxygen and the power of steam, had enormous consequences. Steam power as an adjunct to, or replacement for, human labor began a new era in world history, beginning with the Industrial Revolution in England. This revolution was the result of these technological advances, coupled with the celebration of "progress." Although it is impossible to assign specific dates to the Industrial Revolution, the invention of steam engines in England for industrial production and, later, their use for transportation marked the beginning of the Industrial Revolution in the 1740s. By 1850, England had a manufacturing economy. This development was revolutionary because for the first time in history, societies were capable of producing a seemingly limitless supply of goods and services. All of Europe was destined to be transformed

within a century by the harnessed power of steam, coal, oil, iron, steel, and electricity working in concert. These scientific and technological advances also affected the arts, particularly leading to the development of photography and changes in architecture.

**THE WONDERS OF THE UNIVERSE** Technological advance depended on the new enthusiasm for mechanical explanations for the wonders of the universe. The fascination it had for ordinary people as well as for the learned is the subject of *A Philosopher Giving a Lecture at the Orrery (in which a lamp is put in place of the sun)*, FIG. **28-9**, by the English painter JOSEPH WRIGHT OF DERBY (1734–1797). Wright specialized in the drama of candlelit and moonlit scenes. He loved subjects such as the orrery demonstration, which could be illuminated by a single light from within the picture. In the painting, a scholar uses a special technological model (called an orrery) to demonstrate the theory that the universe operates like a gigantic clockwork mechanism. Light from the lamp, representing the sun, pours forth from in front of the boy silhouetted in the foreground to create dramatic light and shadows that heighten the drama of the scene. Awed children crowd close to the tiny metal orbs that represent the planets within the arcing bands that symbolize their orbits. An earnest listener makes notes, while the lone woman seated at the left and the two gentlemen at the right look on with rapt attention. Everyone in Wright's painting is caught up in the wonders of scientific knowledge; an ordinary

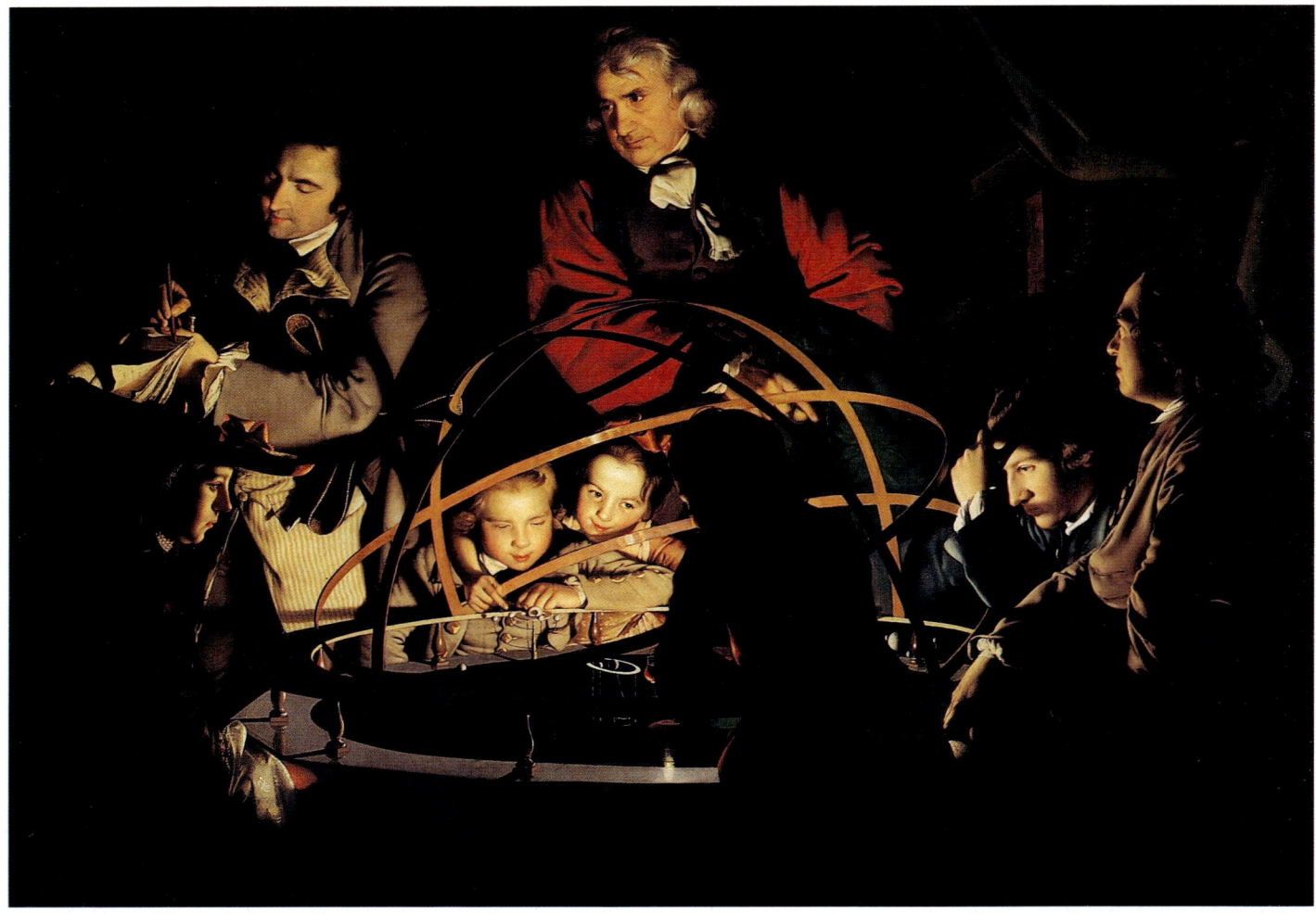

**28-9** JOSEPH WRIGHT OF DERBY, *A Philosopher Giving a Lecture at the Orrery (in which a lamp is put in place of the sun)*, ca. 1763–1765. Oil on canvas, 4′ 10″ × 6′ 8″. Derby Museums and Art Gallery, Derby, Derbyshire.

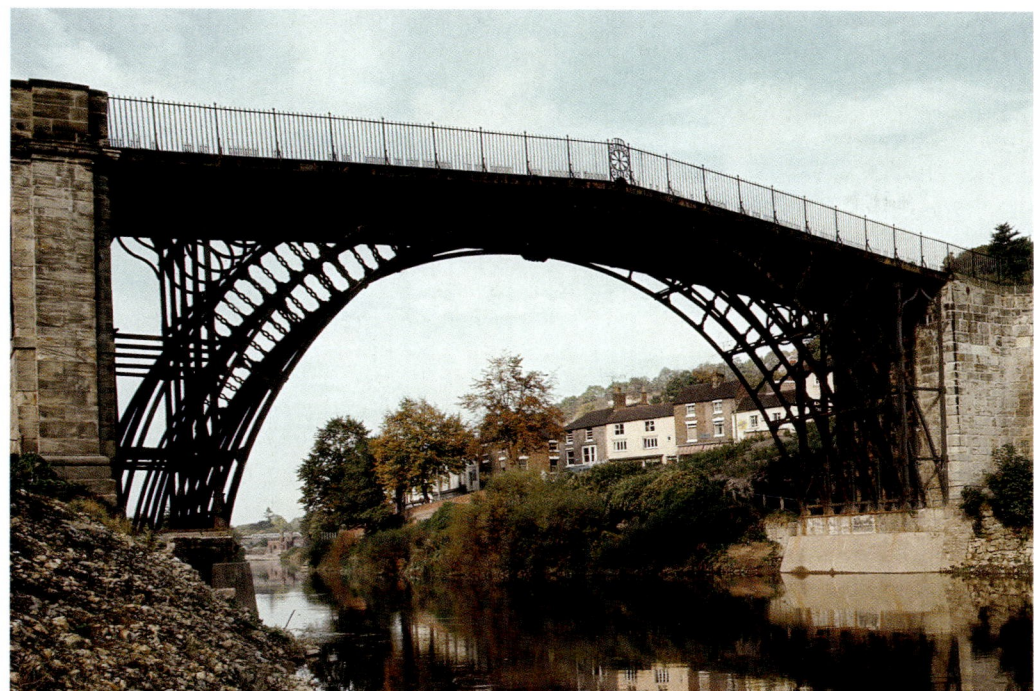

**28-10** Abraham Darby III and Thomas F. Pritchard, iron bridge at Coalbrookdale, England (first cast-iron bridge over the Severn River), 1776–1779. 100′ span.

lecture takes on the qualities of a grand "history painting." Wright visually reinforced the fascination with the orrery by composing his image in a circular fashion (echoing the orbital design of the orrery); the postures and gazes of all the participants and observers focus attention on the cosmic model. Wright scrupulously rendered with careful accuracy every detail of the figures, the mechanisms of the orrery, and even the books and curtain in the shadowy background. His realism appealed to the great industrialists of his day. Scientific-industrial innovators such as Josiah Wedgwood and Sir Richard Arkwright often purchased works such as *Orrery*. (Wedgwood pioneered many techniques of mass-produced pottery; Wedgwood fine china and pottery are still produced today. Arkwright's spinning frame revolutionized the textile industry.) To them, Wright's elevation of the theories and inventions of the Industrial Revolution to the plane of history painting was exciting and appropriately in tune with the future.

**BRIDGING THE AGES WITH IRON** Eighteenth-century engineering, especially, foreshadowed the future, particularly its use of industrial materials. Iron was first used in bridge design for the cast-iron bridge built over the Severn River, near the site at Coalbrookdale in England, where Abraham Darby III (1750–1789), one of the bridge's two designers, ran his family's cast-iron business. Previous bridges had been constructed of wood and spanned relatively short distances, limiting their use for high-volume industrial traffic. The Darby family had spearheaded the evolution of the iron industry in England, and they vigorously supported the investigation of new uses for the material. The fabrication of cast-iron rails and bridge elements inspired Darby to work with architect Thomas F. Pritchard (1723–1777) in designing the Coalbrookdale Bridge (FIG. **28-10**). The cast-iron armature that supports the roadbed springs from stone pier to stone pier until it leaps the final 100 feet across the Severn River gorge. The style of the graceful center arc echoes the grand arches of Roman aqueducts (see FIG. 10-31). At the same time, the exposed structure of the bridge's cast-iron parts prefigured the skeletal use of iron and

steel in the 19th century. Such visible structural armatures became expressive factors in the design of buildings such as the Crystal Palace (FIG. 28-62) and the Eiffel Tower (see FIG. 29-57).

## Voltaire versus Rousseau: Science versus the Taste for the "Natural"

The name of Jean-Jacques Rousseau (1712–1778) is traditionally invoked along with that of Voltaire as representative of the French Enlightenment and as an individual instrumental in preparing the way ideologically for the French Revolution. Yet Voltaire, as has been noted, thought that the salvation of humanity was in the advancement of science and in the rational improvement of society. In contrast, Rousseau declared that the arts, sciences, society, and civilization in general had corrupted "natural man"—people in their primitive state—and that humanity's only salvation lay in a return to something like "the ignorance, innocence and happiness" of its original condition. According to Rousseau, human capacity for feeling, sensibility, and emotions came prior to reason: "To exist is to feel; our feeling is undoubtedly earlier than our intelligence, and we had feelings before we had ideas." Nature alone must be the guide: "All our natural inclinations are right." Fundamental to Rousseau's thinking was the notion that "Man by nature is good . . . he is depraved and perverted by society." He rejected the idea of progress, insisting that "Our minds have been corrupted in proportion as the arts and sciences have improved."[3]

The society Rousseau attacked and Voltaire defended in general terms was in fact the one they both knew and moved in; its center was Paris, ornamented in the Rococo style. Rousseau's views, popular and widely read, were largely responsible for the turning away from the Rococo sensibility and the formation of a taste for the "natural," as opposed to the artificial.

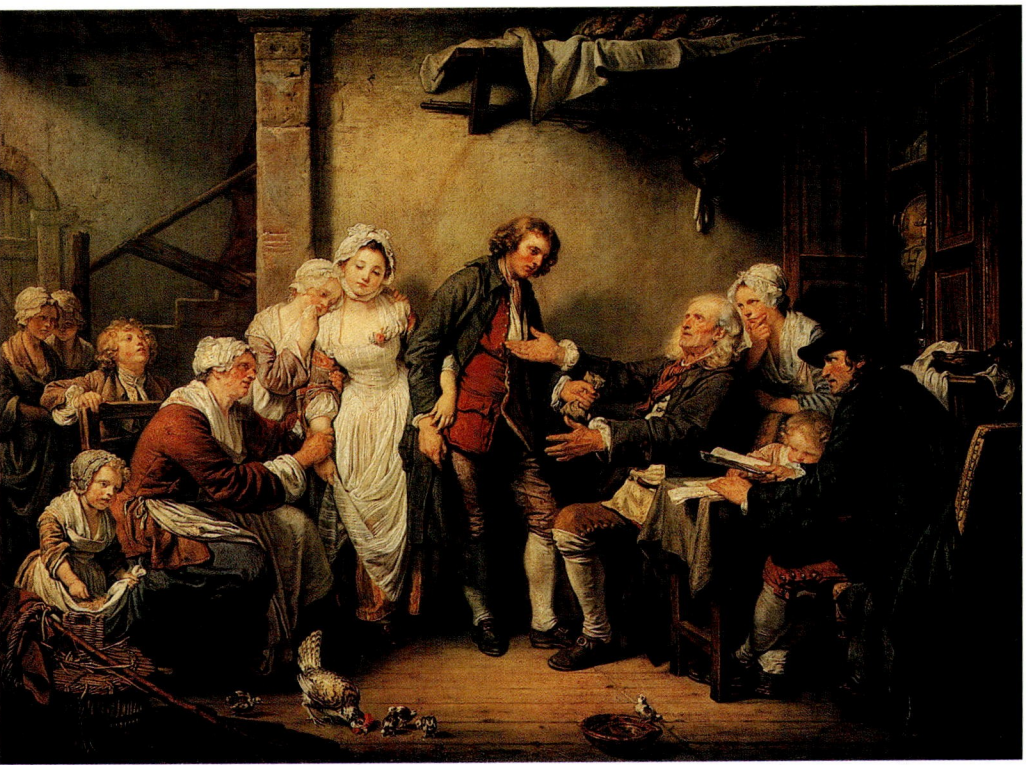

**28-11** Jean-Baptiste Greuze, *The Village Bride*, 1761. Oil on canvas, 3′ × 3′ 10½″. Louvre, Paris.

## The Taste for the "Natural" in France

Rousseau, in placing feelings above reason as the most primitive—and hence the most "natural"—of human expressions, called for the cultivation of sincere, sympathetic, and tender emotions. This led him to exalt the peasant's simple life, with its honest and unsullied emotions, as ideal and to name it as a model for imitation. The joys and sorrows of uncorrupted "natural" people, described everywhere in novels (for example, Oliver Goldsmith's *The Vicar of Wakefield,* 1766) soon drowned Europe in floods of tears. It became fashionable to weep, to fall to one's knees, and to languish in hopeless love.

RURAL SENTIMENTALITY The sentimental narrative in art became the specialty of French artist JEAN-BAPTISTE GREUZE (1725–1805), whose most popular work, *The Village Bride* (FIG. 28-11), sums up the characteristics of the genre. The setting is an unadorned room in a rustic dwelling. In a notary's presence, the elderly father has passed his daughter's dowry to her youthful husband-to-be and blesses the pair, who gently take each other's arms. The old mother tearfully gives her daughter's arm a farewell caress, while the youngest sister melts in tears on the shoulder of the demure bride. An envious older sister broods behind her father's chair. Rosy-faced, healthy children play around the scene. The picture's story is simple—the happy climax of a rural romance. The picture's moral is just as clear—happiness is the reward of "natural" virtue.

Greuze produced this work at a time when the audience for art was expanding. The strict social hierarchy that provided the foundation for Rococo art and patronage gave way to a bourgeois economic and social system. More of this bourgeois class embraced art, and paintings such as *Village Bride* particularly appealed to them. They carefully analyzed each gesture and each nuance of sentiment and reacted with tumultuous enthusiasm.

At the Salon (the annual academy exhibition—see "The Academies: Defining the Range of Acceptable Art," Chapter 29, page 862) of 1761, Greuze's picture received enormous attention. The great compiler of the *Encyclopédie,* Diderot, who reviewed the picture for the press, declared that it was difficult to get near it because of the throngs of admirers.

THE CHARM OF THE ORDINARY Adherents to the taste for the "natural" often preferred narratives that taught moral lessons, dismissing the frivolities and indecent gallantries of the Rococo. The audience of French painter JEAN-BAPTISTE-SIMÉON CHARDIN (1699–1779) was gratified to find moral values in quiet scenes of domestic life. The artist seemed to praise the simple goodness of ordinary people, especially mothers and young children, who in spirit, occupation, and environment lived far from corrupt society. (In the 18th century, *taste* also could mean the appreciation of moral as well as aesthetic qualities.) Rousseau measured human morality in terms of the degree to which it was out of reach of society's bad influence. He found it in country folk or, as here, in the unpretentious houses of the urban middle class. In *Grace at Table* (FIG. 28-12), Chardin ushers the viewer into a modest room where a mother and her small daughters are about to dine. The mood of quiet attention is at one with the hushed lighting and mellow color and with the closely studied still-life accessories whose worn surfaces tell their own humble domestic history. The viewer witnesses a moment of social instruction, when mother and older sister supervise the younger sister in the simple, pious ritual of giving thanks to God before a meal. The subdued charm of this scene is reinforced by the simplicity of the composition, with the three figures highlighted against the dark background. In his own way, Chardin was the poet of the commonplace and the master of its nuances. A gentle sentiment prevails in all his pictures, an emotion not contrived and artificial but born of the painter's honesty, insight, and sympathy. (It is interesting that this picture was owned

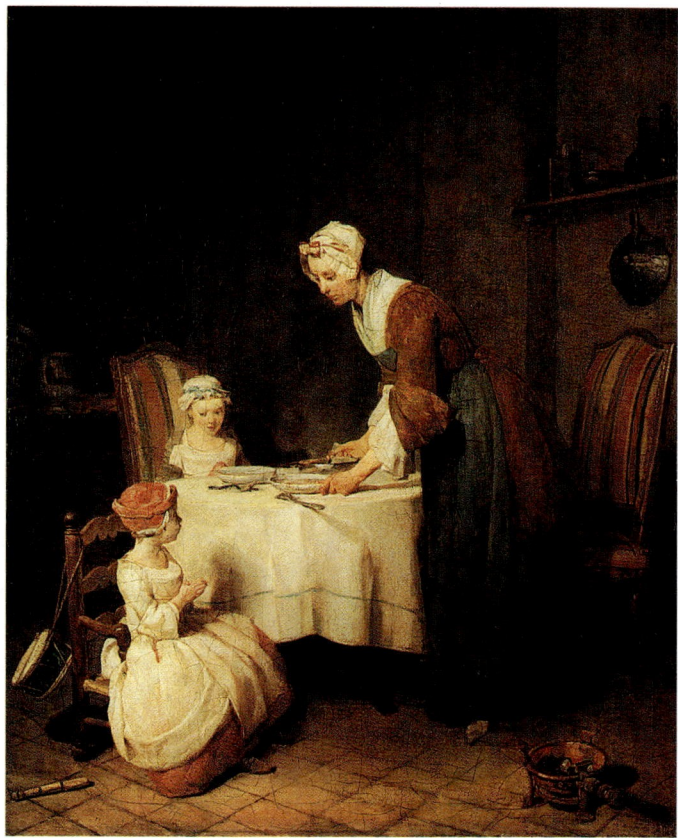

28-12 JEAN-BAPTISTE-SIMÉON CHARDIN, *Grace at Table*, 1740. Oil on canvas, 1′ 7″ × 1′ 3″. Louvre, Paris.

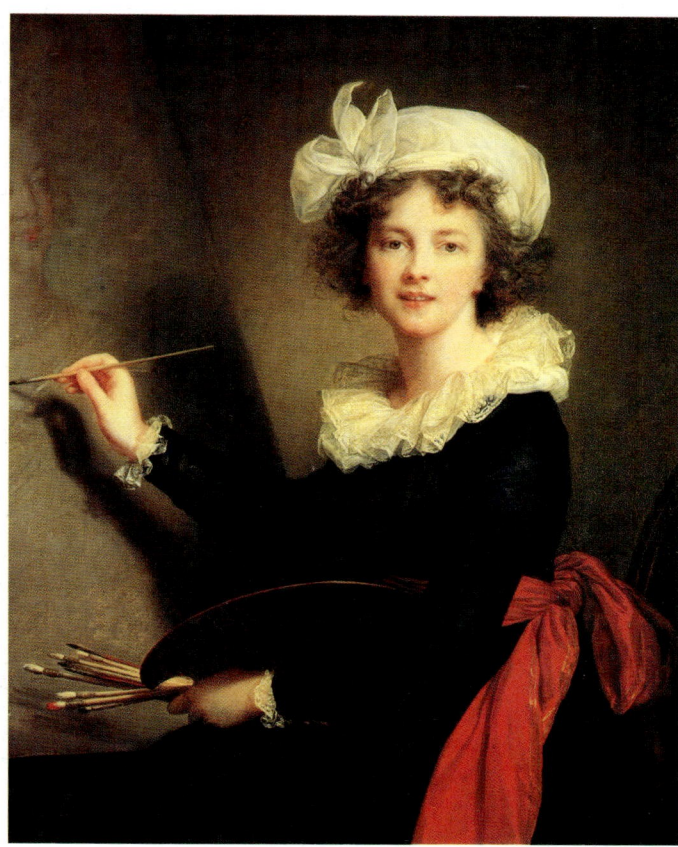

28-13 ÉLISABETH LOUISE VIGÉE-LEBRUN, *Self-Portrait*, 1790. Oil on canvas, 8′ 4″ × 6′ 9″. Galleria degli Uffizi, Florence.

by King Louis XV, the royal personification of the Rococo in his life and tastes.)

**PORTRAIT OF A WOMAN ARTIST** *Self-Portrait* (FIG. **28-13**) by ÉLISABETH LOUISE VIGÉE-LEBRUN (1755–1842) is another variation of the "naturalistic" impulse in 18th-century French portraiture. In the new mode, Vigée-Lebrun looks directly at viewers and pauses in her work to return their gaze. Although her mood is lighthearted and her costume's details echo the serpentine curve beloved by Rococo artists and wealthy patrons, nothing about Vigée-Lebrun's pose or her mood speaks of Rococo frivolity. Hers is the self-confident stance of a woman whose art has won her an independent role in her society. Like many of her contemporaries, Vigée-Lebrun lived a life of extraordinary personal and economic independence, working for the nobility throughout Europe. She was famous for the force and grace of her portraits, especially those of highborn ladies and royalty. She was successful during the age of the late monarchy in France and was one of the few women admitted to the Academy (the established art school—see "The Academies," Chapter 29, page 862). After the French Revolution, her membership in the Academy was rescinded, because women were no longer welcome in that organization. Vigée-Lebrun's continued success was indicative of her talent, her wit, and her ability to forge connections with those in power in the postrevolutionary period. For her self-portrait, Vigée-Lebrun painted herself in a close-up, intimate view at work on one of the portraits that won her renown, that of

Queen Marie Antoinette. The naturalism and intimacy of her expression are similar to those in Thomas Gainsborough's portrait of Mrs. Sheridan (FIG. 28-15). Vigée-Lebrun's attitude reflects the ideals of independence and self-reliance she exhibited as a woman.

## The Taste for the "Natural" in England

**COMMUNICATING MORALITY THROUGH SATIRE** The taste of the newly prosperous and confident middle class in England was expressed in the art of WILLIAM HOGARTH (1697–1764), who satirized contemporary life with comic zest and with only a modicum of Rococo "indecency." With Hogarth, a truly English style of painting emerged. Traditionally, painters (such as Holbein, Rubens, and Van Dyck) were imported from the continent. Hogarth waged a lively campaign throughout his career against the English feeling of dependence on, and inferiority to, continental artists. Although Hogarth would have been the last to admit it, his own painting owed much to the work of his contemporaries across the channel in France, the Rococo artists. Yet his subject matter, frequently moral in tone, was distinctively English. It was the great age of English satirical writing, and Hogarth (who knew and admired this genre and included Henry Fielding, the author of *Tom Jones,* among his closest friends) clearly saw himself as translating satire into the visual arts.

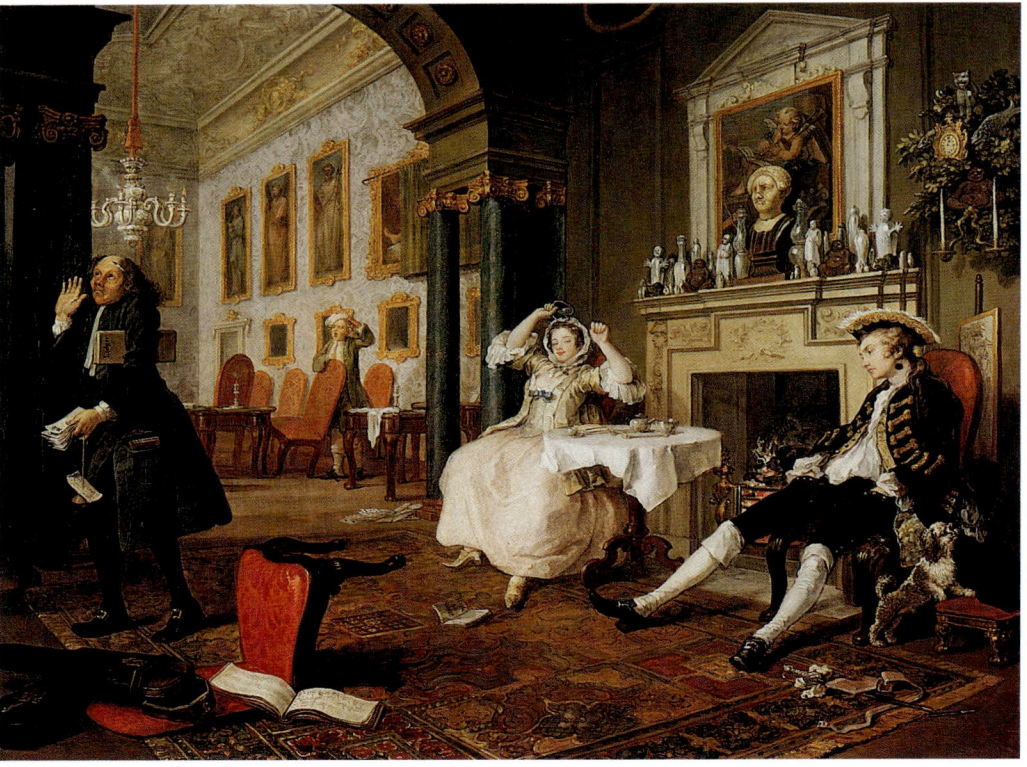

28-14 WILLIAM HOGARTH, *Breakfast Scene,* from *Marriage à la Mode,* ca. 1745. Oil on canvas, approx. 2′ 4″ × 3′. National Gallery, London.

Hogarth's favorite device was to make a series of narrative paintings and prints, in a sequence like chapters in a book or scenes in a play, that followed a character or group of characters in their encounters with some social evil. He was at his best in such pictures as *Breakfast Scene* (FIG. 28-14) from *Marriage à la Mode.* This scene is one in a sequence of six paintings that satirize the immoralities practiced within marriage by the moneyed classes in England. In it, the marriage of a young viscount is just beginning to founder. The husband and wife are tired after a long night spent in separate pursuits. While the wife stayed at home for an evening of cards and music-making, her young husband had been away from the house for a night of suspicious business. His hands are thrust deep into the empty money-pockets of his breeches, while his wife's small dog sniffs inquiringly at a lacy woman's cap protruding from his coat pocket. A steward, his hands full of unpaid bills, raises his eyes to Heaven in despair at the actions of his noble master and mistress. The house is palatial, but Hogarth filled it with witty clues to the dubious taste of its occupants. The piety demonstrated by the paintings of religious figures that hang on the upper wall of the distant room is countered by the curtained canvas at the end of the row that undoubtedly depicts an erotic subject. Appropriately, this painting is discretely hidden from the eyes of casual visitors and ladies, according to the custom of the day, but is available at the pull of a curtain cord for the gaze of the master and his male guests. In this composition, as in all his work, Hogarth proceeded as a novelist might, elaborating on his subject with carefully chosen detail, whose discovery heightens the comedy.

Hogarth designed the marriage series to be published as a set of engravings. The prints of this and his other moral narratives were so popular that unscrupulous entrepreneurs produced unauthorized versions almost as fast as the artist created his originals. The popularity of these prints speaks not only to the appeal of their subjects but also to the democratization of knowledge

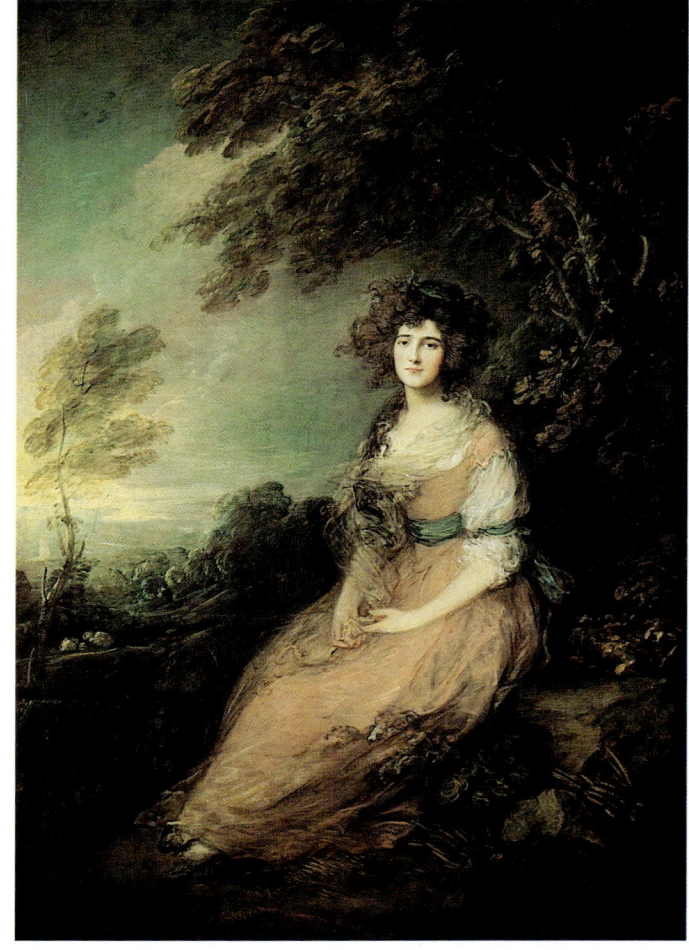

28-15 THOMAS GAINSBOROUGH, *Mrs. Richard Brinsley Sheridan,* 1787. Oil on canvas, approx. 7′ 2$\frac{5}{8}$″ × 5′ $\frac{5}{8}$″. National Gallery of Art, Washington (Andrew W. Mellon Collection).

and culture fostered by the Enlightenment and to the exploitation of reproductive technologies that produced a more affordable and widely disseminated visual culture.

**GRAND MANNER PORTRAITURE** A contrasting blend of "naturalistic" representation and Rococo setting is found in the portrait *Mrs. Richard Brinsley Sheridan* (FIG. **28-15**) by the British painter THOMAS GAINSBOROUGH (1727–1788). This portrait shows a lovely woman, dressed informally, seated in a rustic landscape faintly reminiscent of Watteau (FIG. 28-4) in its soft-hued light and feathery brushwork. Gainsborough intended to match the natural, unspoiled beauty of the landscape with that of the subject. Her dark brown hair blows freely in the slight wind, and her clear "English" complexion and air of ingenuous sweetness contrast sharply with the pert sophistication of continental Rococo portraits. The artist originally had planned to give the picture a more pastoral air by adding several sheep, but he did not live long enough to paint them in. Even without this element, the painting clearly expresses Gainsborough's deep interest in the landscape setting. Although he won greater fame in his time for his portraits, he had begun as a landscape painter and always preferred painting scenes of nature to depicting human likenesses.

Such a portrait is representative of what became known as Grand Manner portraiture, and Gainsborough was recognized as one of the leading practitioners of this genre. Although clearly depicting individualized people, Grand Manner portraiture also elevated the sitter by conveying refinement and elegance. Such grace and class were communicated through certain standardized conventions, such as the large scale of the figures relative to the canvas, the controlled poses, the landscape (often Arcadian) setting, and the low horizon line. Thus, despite the naturalism central to Gainsborough's portraits, he tempered it with a degree of artifice. This combination of aristocratic Rococo sophistication with rustic naturalism is an example of the hybridity of styles and reveals the dangers of the art historical penchant for categorizing artists and their works.

**GREAT PEOPLE AND NOBLE DEEDS** Morality of a more heroic tone than that found in the work of Greuze, yet in harmony with "naturalness," included the virtues of honor, valor, and love of country. According to 18th-century Western thought, these virtues produced great people and exemplary deeds. The concept of "nobility," especially as discussed by Rousseau, referred to character, not to aristocratic birth. As the century progressed and people felt the tremors of coming revolutions, these virtues of courage and resolution, patriotism, and self-sacrifice assumed greater importance. Having risen from humble origins, the modern military hero, not the decadent aristocrat, brought the excitements of war into the company of the "natural" emotions.

**DEFENDING GIBRALTAR** SIR JOSHUA REYNOLDS (1723–1792) specialized in portraits of contemporaries who participated in the great events of the latter part of the century. Not least among these paintings was *Lord Heathfield* (FIG. **28-16**). Reynolds was at his best with a subject such as this burly, ruddy English officer, commandant of the fortress at Gibraltar. Heathfield had doggedly defended the great rock against the Spanish and the French, so he later was honored with the title Baron Heathfield of Gibraltar. His victory is symbolized here by the huge key to the fortress, which he holds thoughtfully. He stands in front of a curtain of dark smoke

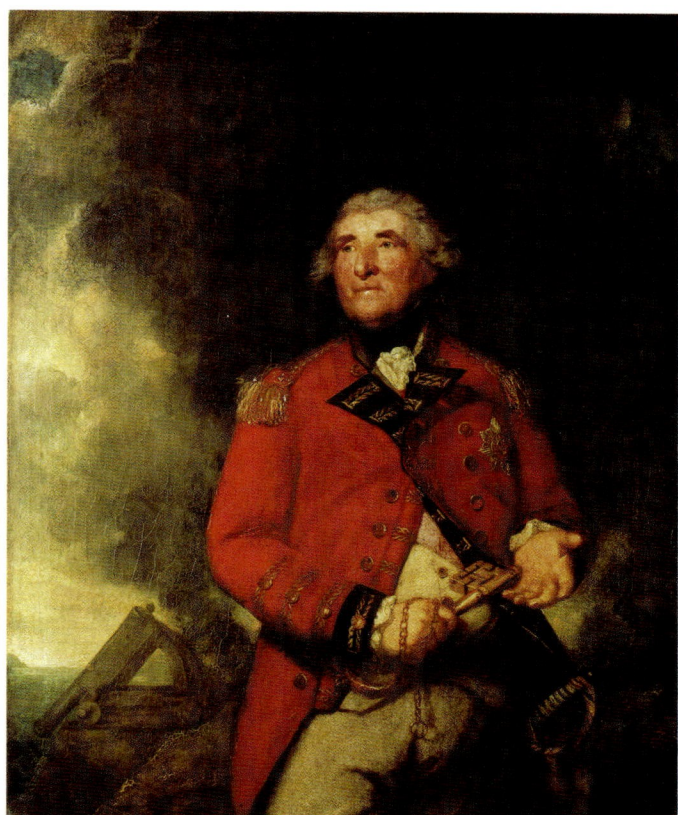

**28-16** SIR JOSHUA REYNOLDS, *Lord Heathfield*, 1787. Oil on canvas, approx. 4′ 8″ × 3′ 9″. National Gallery, London.

rising from the battleground, flanked by one cannon that points ineffectively downward and another whose tilted barrel indicates that it lies uselessly on its back. Reynolds portrayed the features of the general's heavy, honest face and his uniform with unidealized realism. But Lord Heathfield's posture and the setting dramatically suggest the heroic themes of battle and refer to the actual revolutions (American and French) then taking shape in deadly earnest, as the old regimes faded into the past.

## The Taste for the "Natural" in Colonial America

**GENERAL WOLFE'S HEROIC DEATH** American artists also addressed the "death in battle of a young military hero" theme, familiar in art and literature since the ancient Greeks. Although American artist BENJAMIN WEST (1738–1820) was born in Pennsylvania, on what was then the colonial frontier, he was sent to Europe early in life to study art and then went to England, where he met with almost immediate success. He was a cofounder of the Royal Academy of Arts and succeeded Sir Joshua Reynolds as its president. He became official painter to King George III and retained that position during the strained period of the American Revolution. While in England, West became well acquainted with the work of both Gainsborough and Reynolds. In *The Death of General Wolfe* (FIG. **28-17**), West depicted the mortally wounded young English commander just after his defeat of the French in

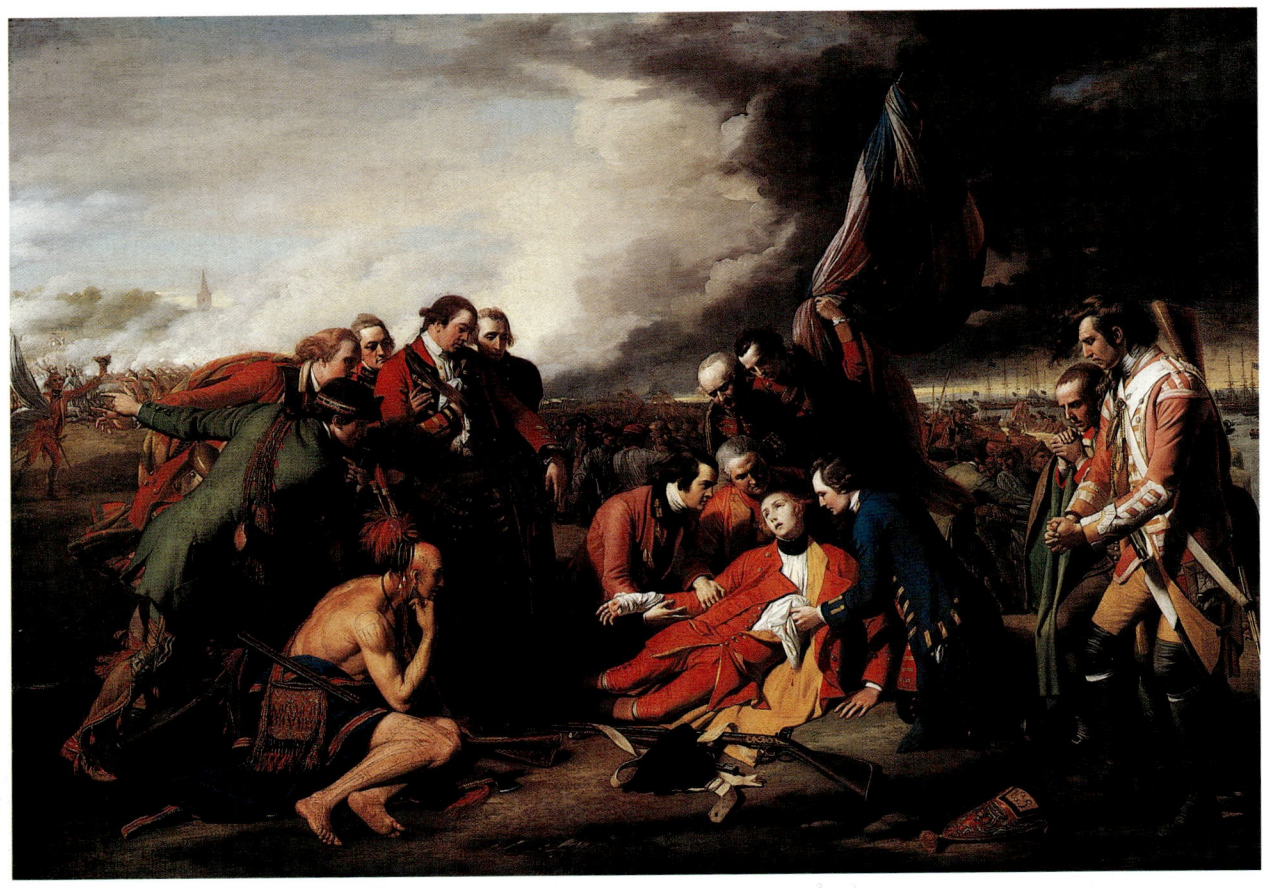

28-17 BENJAMIN WEST, *The Death of General Wolfe,* 1771. Oil on canvas, approx. 5′ × 7′. National Gallery of Canada, Ottawa (gift of the Duke of Westminster, 1918).

the decisive battle of Quebec in 1759, which gave Canada to Great Britain. West chose to portray a contemporary historical subject, and his characters wear contemporary costume (although the military uniforms are not completely accurate in all details). However, West blended this realism of detail with the grand tradition of history painting by arranging his figures in a complex and theatrically ordered composition. His modern hero dies among grieving officers on the field of victorious battle in a way that suggests the death of a great saint. West wanted to present this hero's death in the service of the state as a martyrdom charged with religious emotions. His innovative combination of the conventions of traditional heroic painting with a look of modern realism was so effective that it won viewers' hearts in his own day and continued to influence history painting well into the 19th century.

**PAUL REVERE, SILVERSMITH**  American artist JOHN SINGLETON COPLEY (1738–1815) matured as a painter in the Massachusetts Bay Colony. Like West, Copley later emigrated to England, where he absorbed the fashionable English portrait style. But unlike Grand Manner portraiture, Copley's *Portrait of Paul Revere* (FIG. 28-18), painted before Copley left Boston, conveys a sense of directness and faithfulness to visual fact that marked the taste for "downrightness" and plainness many visitors to America noticed during the 18th and 19th centuries. When the portrait was painted, Revere was not yet the familiar hero of the American Revolution. In the picture, he is working at his everyday profession of silversmithing. The setting is plain, the lighting clear and revealing. The subject sits in his shirtsleeves, bent over a teapot in progress; he pauses and turns his head to look the observer

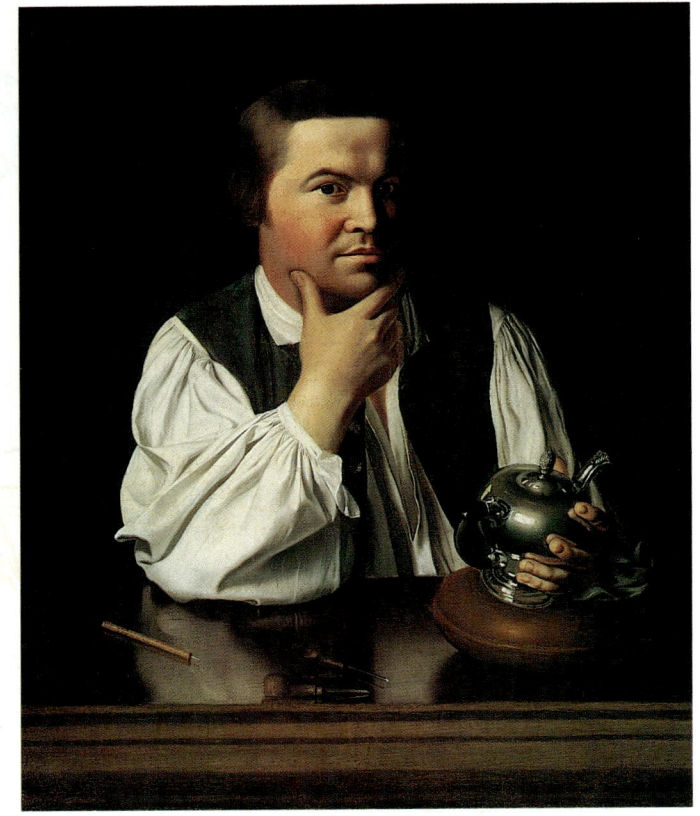

28-18 JOHN SINGLETON COPLEY, *Portrait of Paul Revere,* ca. 1768–1770. Oil on canvas, 2′ 11⅛″ × 2′ 4″. Museum of Fine Arts, Boston (gift of Joseph W., William B., and Edward H. R. Revere).

straight in the eye. The artist treated the reflections in the polished wood of the tabletop with as much care as Revere's figure, his tools, and the teapot resting on its leather graver's pillow. Copley gave special prominence to the figure's eyes by reflecting intense reddish light onto the darkened side of the face and hands. The informality and the sense of the moment link this painting to contemporaneous English and European portraits. But the spare style and the emphasis on the sitter's down-to-earth character differentiate this American work from its British and continental counterparts (FIG. 28-15).

## *The Taste for the "Natural" in Italy*

The 18th-century public also sought "naturalness" in artists' depictions of landscapes. Documentation of particular places became popular, in part due to growing travel opportunities and the expanding colonial imperative. Such depictions of geographic settings also served the needs of the many scientific expeditions mounted during the century and satisfied the desires of genteel tourists for mementos of their journeys. By this time, a "Grand Tour" of the major sites of Europe was considered part of every well-bred person's education (see "The Grand Tour: Travel, Education, and Italy's Allure," page 814). Naturally, those on tour wished to leave with things that would help them remember their experiences and that would impress those at home with the wonders they had seen.

**PICTURESQUE VENICE** The English were especially eager collectors of pictorial souvenirs. Certain artists in Venice specialized in painting the most characteristic scenes, or *vedute* (views),

of that city to sell to British visitors. The veduta paintings of ANTONIO CANALETTO (1697–1768) were eagerly acquired by English tourists as visible evidence of their visit to the city of the Grand Canal. It must have been very cheering on a gray winter afternoon in England to look up and see a sunny, panoramic view such as that in Canaletto's *Basin of San Marco from San Giorgio Maggiore* (FIG. 28-19), with its cloud-studded sky, calm harbor, varied water traffic, picturesque pedestrians, and well-known Venetian landmarks all painted in scrupulous perspective and minute detail.

Canaletto had trained as a scene painter with his father, but his easy mastery of detail, light, and shadow soon made him one of the most popular "vedutisti" in Venice. Occasionally, he painted his scenes directly from life, but usually he made drawings "on location" to take back to his studio and use as sources for paintings. To help make the on-site drawings true to life, he often used a camera obscura (literally, "dark room"). As early as the 17th century, artists such as Vermeer (see FIGS. 24-52 and 24-53) had used such a device. These instruments were darkened chambers (some of them virtually portable closets) with optical lenses fitted into a hole in one wall through which light entered to project an inverted image of the subject onto the chamber's opposite wall. The artist could trace the main details from this image for later reworking and refinement. The camera obscura allowed Canaletto (and other artists) to create visually convincing paintings that included variable focus of objects at different distances. His paintings give the impression of capturing every detail, with no "editing." Actually, he presented each site within Renaissance perspectival rules and exercised great selectivity about which details to include and which to omit to make a coherent and engagingly attractive picture.

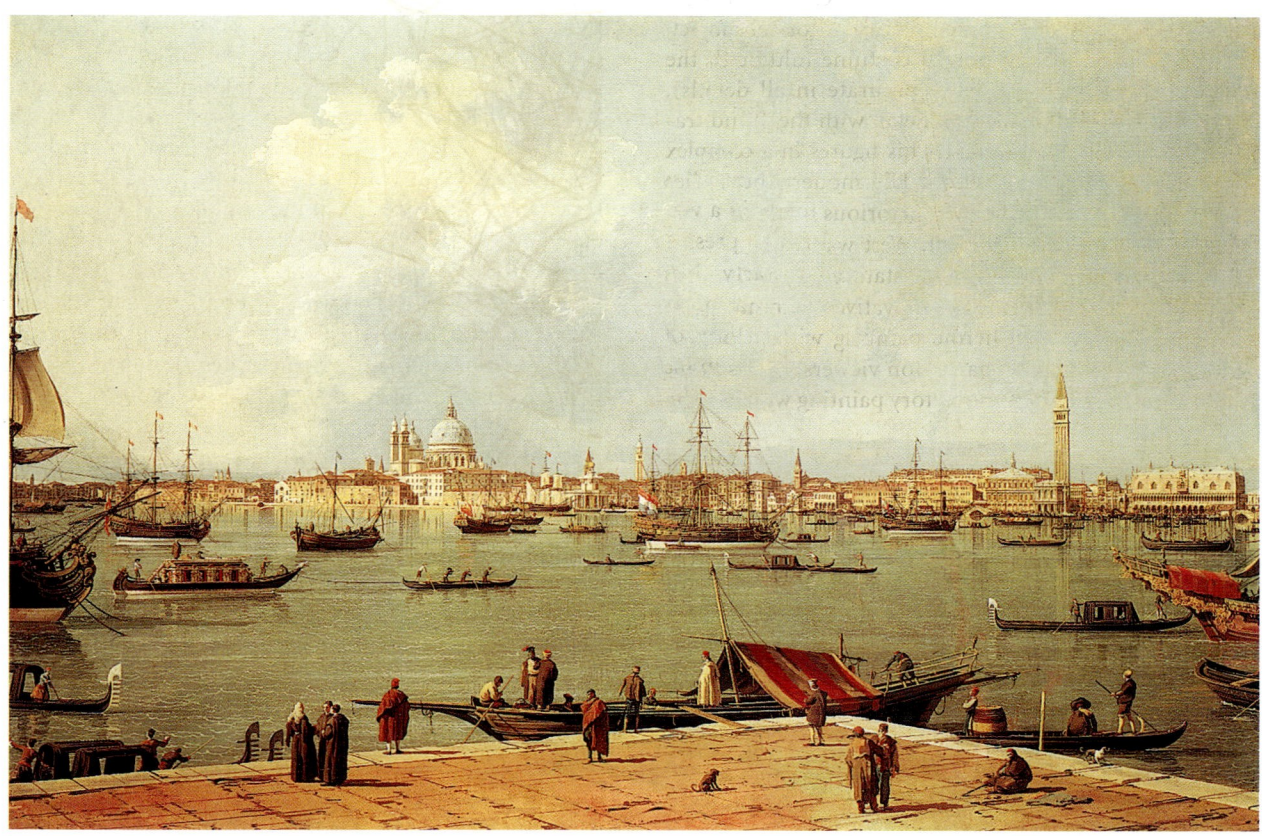

**28-19** ANTONIO CANALETTO, *Basin of San Marco from San Giorgio Maggiore,* ca. 1740. Oil on canvas, 4′ 3$\frac{1}{4}$″ × 6′ 3$\frac{1}{8}$″. The Wallace Collection, London.

## The Grand Tour
### Travel, Education, and Italy's Allure

Although travel throughout Europe was commonplace in the 18th century, Italy became a particularly popular travel site. This "pilgrimage" of aristocrats, the wealthy, politicians, and diplomats from France, England, Germany, Flanders, Sweden, the United States, Russia, Poland, and Hungary came to be known as the Grand Tour. Italy's allure fueled the revival of classicism, which became most formalized in *Neoclassicism*. In turn, the prominence of Neoclassicism drove this fascination with Italy. One British observer noted: "All our religion, all our arts, almost all that sets us above savages, has come from the shores of the Mediterranean."[1]

The Grand Tour was not simply leisure travel. The education available in Italy to the inquisitive mind made such a trip an indispensable experience for anyone who wished to play an important role in society. The Enlightenment had made knowledge of ancient Rome and Greece imperative, and a steady stream of Europeans and Americans traveled to Italy in the late 18th and early 19th centuries. These tourists aimed to increase their knowledge of literature and the arts (the visual arts, architecture, theater, and music), ancient and modern history, politics and economics, and customs and folklore. Given this extensive agenda, it is not surprising that a Grand Tour could take a number of years to complete, and most travelers moved from location to location, following an established itinerary.

The British were the most avid travelers, and they established the initial "tour code," including important destinations and required itineraries. Although they established Rome early on as the primary mecca, visitors traveled as far north as Venice and as far south as Naples. Eventually, Paestum, Sicily, Florence, Genoa, Milan, Siena, Pisa, Bologna, and Parma all appeared in guidebooks and in *veduta* (view) paintings. Joseph Wright of Derby (FIG. 28-9) and Joseph Mallord William Turner (FIG. 28-54) were among the many British artists to undertake a Grand Tour.

Eventually, the scope of the Grand Tour extended well beyond Italian borders. In large part, the archaeological discoveries at Herculaneum and Pompeii were responsible for whetting people's appetites to visit Greece. The Grand Tour eventually metamorphosed into package tours, which remain popular to the present day, revealing the continuing allure of Mediterranean and classical cultures.

[1] Cesare de Seta, "Grand Tour: The Lure of Italy in the Eighteenth Century," in Andrew Wilton and Ilaria Bignamini, eds., *Grand Tour: The Lure of Italy in the Eighteenth Century* (London: Tate Gallery, 1996), 13.

# THE REVIVAL OF INTEREST IN CLASSICISM

One of the defining characteristics of the late 18th century was a renewed interest in classical antiquity, which the Grand Tour was instrumental in fueling. This interest was manifested in *Neoclassicism,* a movement that incorporated the subjects and styles of ancient art. Although Neoclassicism encompassed painting, sculpture, and architecture and is often regarded as the most prominent manifestation of this interest, fascination with Greek and Roman culture was widespread and extended to the public culture of fashion and home decor. The Enlightenment's emphasis on rationality in part fueled this classical focus. The geometric harmony of classical art and architecture seemed to embody Enlightenment ideals. In addition, classical cultures represented the height of civilized society, and Greece and Rome served as models of enlightened political organization. These cultures, with their traditions of liberty, civic virtue, morality, and sacrifice, served as ideal models during a period of great political upheaval. Given such traditional associations, it is not coincidental that Neoclassicism was particularly appealing during the French and American Revolutions. The public appetite for classicism was whetted further by the excavations of Herculaneum (begun in 1738) and Pompeii (1748), which the volcanic eruption of Mount Vesuvius in 79 CE had buried (see "Rising from the Ashes: The Excavation of Herculaneum and Pompeii," page 815).

The enthusiasm for classical antiquity permeated much of the scholarship of the time. In the late 18th century, the ancient world increasingly became the focus of scholarly attention. A visit to Rome stimulated Edward Gibbon to begin his monumental *Decline and Fall of the Roman Empire,* which appeared between 1776 and 1788. Earlier, in 1755, Johann Joachim Winckelmann, the first modern art historian, published *Thoughts on the Imitation of Greek Art in Painting and Sculpture,* uncompromisingly designating Greek art as the most perfect to come from human hands. Winckelmann characterized Greek sculpture as manifesting a "noble simplicity and silent greatness."[4] In his *History of Ancient Art* (1764), he described each monument and positioned it within a huge inventory of works organized by subject matter, style, and period. Before Winckelmann, art historians had focused on biography, as reflected in Giorgio Vasari's *Lives of the Most Eminent Italian Architects, Painters and Sculptors* (first published in 1550). Winckelmann thus initiated one modern art historical method thoroughly in accord with Enlightenment ideas of ordering knowledge—a system of description and classification that provided a pioneering model for the understanding of stylistic evolution. Winckelmann's familiarity with classical art was derived predominantly (as was the norm) from Roman works and Roman copies of Greek art. Yet Winckelmann was instrumental in bringing to scholarly attention the distinctions between Greek and Roman art. Thus, he paved the way for more thorough study of the unique characteristics of the art and architecture of these two cultures. Winckelmann's writings also laid a theoretical and historical foundation for the enormously widespread taste for Neoclassicism that lasted well into the 19th century.

## Setting the Stage for Neoclassicism in Art

A ROMAN EXAMPLE OF VIRTUE In the art of ANGELICA KAUFFMANN (1741–1807), Greuze's simple figure types, homely situations, and contemporary settings in moral, "natural" pictures

## Rising from the Ashes
### The Excavation of Herculaneum and Pompeii

Among the events that fueled the European fascination with classical antiquity were the excavations of two ancient cities, Herculaneum and Pompeii. The violent eruption of Mount Vesuvius in August 79 CE had buried both cities, located on the Bay of Naples, under volcanic ash and mud (see "An Eyewitness Account of the Eruption of Mount Vesuvius," Chapter 10, page 255). Although each of these cities had been "rediscovered" at various times during the following centuries, not until the mid-1700s did systematic excavation of both sites begin. Excavation of Pompeii, in particular, has been an extensive undertaking. That city holds the distinction as the oldest archaeological site in the longest more or less continuous excavation.

Because of the manner in which these cities were destroyed, their excavations produced unusually complete reconstructions of art and life in these Roman towns. Not only were buildings discovered, but paintings, sculptures, furniture, vases, silverware, small objects, and human skeletons were also unearthed. As a result, European ideas about and interest in ancient Rome expanded tremendously.

Europeans acquired many of these uncovered objects. For example, Sir William Hamilton, British consul in Naples from 1764 to 1800, collected numerous vases and small objects, which he sold to the British Museum in 1772. The finds at Pompeii and Herculaneum, therefore, were available to a wide public.

Although the Enlightenment was largely responsible for the revival of interest in classical antiquity, these excavations were a major factor in stimulating the public's fascination with not just Rome but the entire ancient world. Soon "Pompeian" style was all the rage, evident in the interior designs of Robert Adam (FIG. 28-30) and in the pottery designs of John Flaxman (1755–1826) and Josiah Wedgwood (1730–1795). Wedgwood established his reputation in the 1760s with his creamware inspired by ancient art. He eventually produced vases based on what were thought to be Etruscan designs and expanded his business by producing small busts of classical figures, as well as cameos and medallions adorned with copies of antique reliefs and statues. The archaeological finds also affected garden and landscape design. Fashion based on classical garb became popular, and Emma Hamilton, wife of Sir William Hamilton, often gave lavish parties dressed in floating and delicate Greek-style drapery.

Ironically, the tragic demise of these two Roman cities ages ago led directly to their importance nearly two thousand years later. Their excavations in the 18th century did much to stimulate the Neoclassical taste.

(FIG. 28-11) were transformed by a Neoclassicism that still contained echoes of the Rococo style. Born in Switzerland and trained in Italy, Kauffmann spent many of her productive years in England. A student of Sir Joshua Reynolds, and an interior decorator of many houses built by Robert Adam, she was a founding member of the British Royal Academy of Arts and enjoyed an enviable reputation. Her *Cornelia Presenting Her Children as Her Treasures*, or *Mother of the Gracchi* (FIG. 28-20), is a kind of set piece of early Neoclassicism. Its subject is an informative *exemplum virtutis* (example or model of virtue) drawn from Greek and Roman history and literature. The moralizing pictures of Greuze (FIG. 28-11) and Hogarth (FIG. 28-14) already had marked a change in taste, but

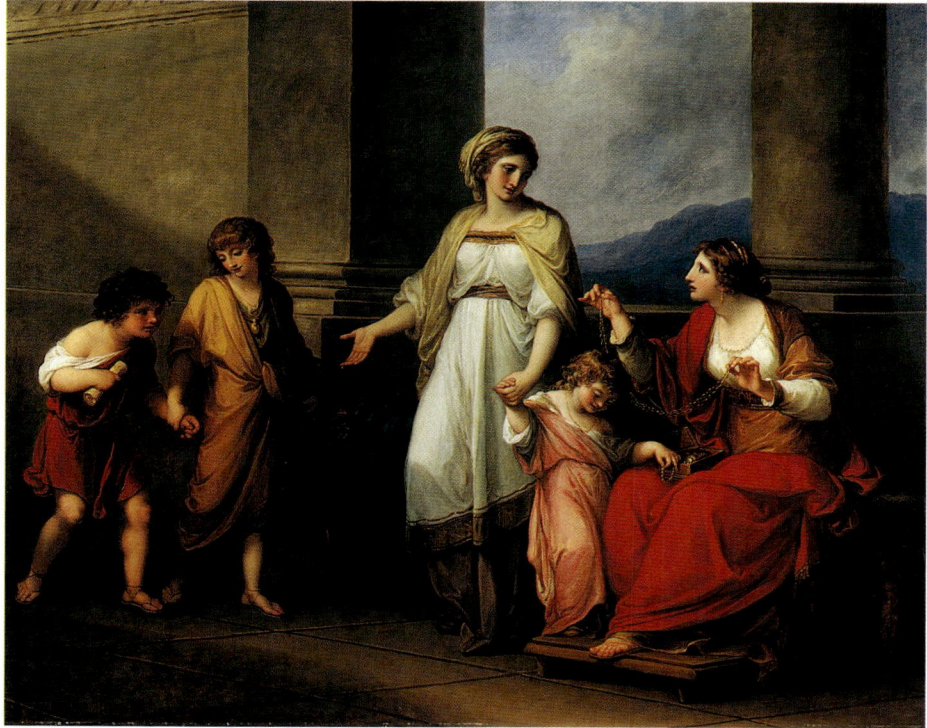

28-20 ANGELICA KAUFFMANN, *Cornelia Presenting Her Children as Her Treasures*, or *Mother of the Gracchi*, ca. 1785. Oil on canvas, 3' 4" × 4' 2". Virginia Museum of Fine Arts, Richmond (the Adolph D. and Wilkins C. Williams Fund).

Kauffmann replaced the modern setting and character of their works. She clothed her actors in ancient Roman garb and posed them in classicizing Roman attitudes within Roman interiors. The theme in this painting is the virtue of Cornelia, mother of the future political leaders Tiberius and Gaius Gracchus, who, in the second century BCE, attempted to reform the Roman Republic. Cornelia's character is revealed in this scene, which takes place after a lady visitor had shown off her fine jewelry and then haughtily requested that Cornelia show hers. Instead of rushing to get her own precious adornments, Cornelia brings her sons forward, presenting them as her jewels. The architectural setting is severely Roman, with no Rococo motif in evidence, and the composition and drawing have the simplicity and firmness of low-relief carving. The only Rococo elements still lingering are charm and grace—in the arrangement of the figures, in the soft lighting, and in Kauffmann's own tranquil manner.

## Neoclassicism in France

**PLANTING THE SEEDS OF GLORY** The lingering echoes of Rococo disappeared in the work of JACQUES-LOUIS DAVID (1748–1825), the Neoclassical painter-ideologist of the French Revolution and the Napoleonic empire (MAP **28-1**). The revolt against the French monarchy in 1789 was prompted, in part, by the Enlightenment idea of a participatory and knowledgeable citizenry. The immediate causes of the French Revolution were France's economic crisis and the clash between the Third Estate (bourgeoisie, peasantry, and urban and rural workers) and the First and Second Estates (the clergy and nobility, respectively). They fought over the issue of representation in the legislative body, the Estates-General, which had been convened to discuss taxation as a possible solution to the economic problem. However, the ensuing revolution revealed the instability of the monarchy and of French society's traditional structure and resulted in a succession of republics and empires as France struggled to find a way to adjust to these decisive changes.

David was a distant relative of Boucher and followed Boucher's style until a period of study in Rome won the younger man over to the classical art tradition. David favored the academic teachings about using the art of the ancients and of the great Renaissance masters as models. In his individual style, David reworked the classical and academic traditions. He rebelled against the Rococo as an "artificial taste" and exalted classical art as the imitation of nature in her most beautiful and perfect form.

David concurred with the Enlightenment belief that subject matter should have a moral and should be presented so that the "marks of heroism and civic virtue offered the eyes of the people [will] electrify its soul, and plant the seeds of glory and devotion to the fatherland."[5] A milestone painting in David's career, *Oath of the Horatii* (FIG. **28-21**), depicts a story from pre-Republican Rome, the heroic phase of Roman history. The topic was not an arcane one for David's audience. This story of conflict between love and patriotism, first recounted by the ancient Roman historian Livy, had been retold in a play by Pierre Corneille performed in Paris several years earlier, making it familiar to David's viewing

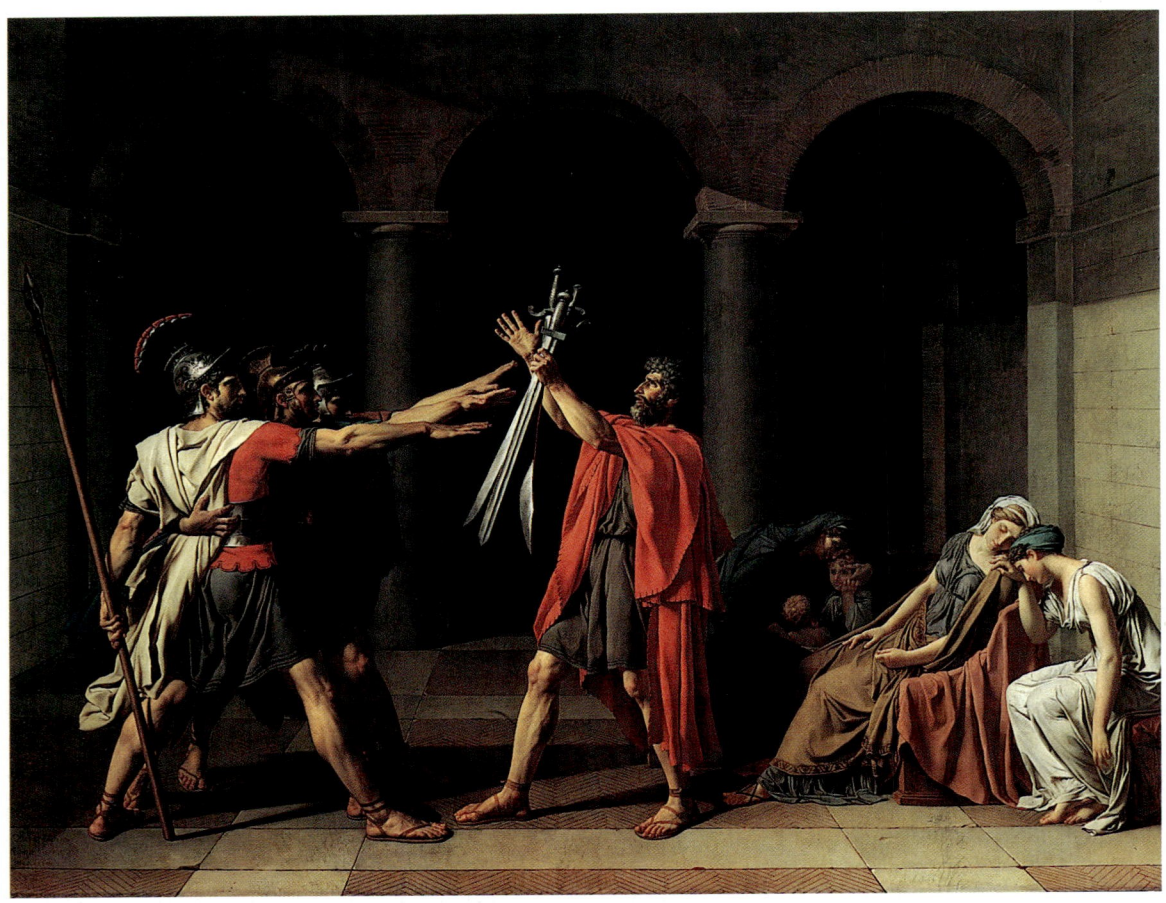

**28-21** JACQUES-LOUIS DAVID, *Oath of the Horatii*, 1784. Oil on canvas, approx. 11′ × 14′. Louvre, Paris.

public. According to the story, the leaders of the warring cities of Rome and Alba decided to resolve their conflicts in a series of encounters waged by three representatives from each side. The Roman champions, the three Horatius brothers, were sent to face the three sons of the Curatius family from Alba. A sister of the Horatii, Camilla, was the bride-to-be of one of the Curatius sons, and the wife of the youngest Horatius was the sister of the Curatii.

David's painting shows the Horatii as they swear on their swords, held high by their father, to win or die for Rome, oblivious to the anguish and sorrow of their female relatives. In its form, *Oath of the Horatii* is a paragon of the Neoclassical style. Not only does the subject matter deal with a narrative of patriotism and sacrifice excerpted from Roman history, but the image is also presented with admirable force and clarity. David depicted the scene in a shallow space much like a stage setting, defined by a severely simple architectural framework. The statuesque and carefully modeled figures are deployed across the space, close to the foreground, in a manner reminiscent of ancient relief sculpture. The rigid, angular, and virile forms of the men on the left effectively contrast with the soft curvilinear shapes of the distraught women on the right. This visually pits virtues the Enlightenment leaders ascribed to men (such as courage, patriotism, and unwavering loyalty to a cause) against the emotions of love, sorrow, and despair that the women in the painting express. The French viewing audience perceived such emotionalism as characteristic of the female nature. The message was clear and of a type readily identifiable to the prerevolutionary French public. The picture created a sensation when it was exhibited in Paris in 1785, and although it had been painted under royal patronage and was not intended as a revolutionary statement, its Neoclassical style soon became the semiofficial voice of the revolution. David may have painted in the academic tradition, but he made something new of it. He created a program for arousing his audience to patriotic zeal.

**IN THE SERVICE OF REVOLUTION** When the French Revolution broke out in 1789, David was thrust amid this momentous upheaval. He became increasingly involved with the revolution and threw in his lot with the Jacobins, the radical and militant faction. He accepted the role of de facto minister of propaganda, organizing political pageants and ceremonies that included floats, costumes, and sculptural props. He believed that "the arts must . . . contribute forcefully to the education of the public,"[6] and he realized that the emphasis on patriotism and civic virtue perceived as integral to classicism would prove effective in dramatic, instructive paintings. However, rather than continuing to create artworks that focused on scenes from antiquity, David began to portray scenes from the French Revolution itself.

**A MARTYRED REVOLUTIONARY** *The Death of Marat* (FIG. 28-22) is one such work and served not only to record an important event in the revolution but also to provide inspiration and encouragement to the revolutionary forces. Jean-Paul Marat, a revolutionary radical, a writer, and David's personal friend, was tragically assassinated in 1793. David depicted the martyred revolutionary after he was stabbed to death in his medicinal bath by Charlotte Corday, a member of a rival political faction. The artist ensured proper identification of this hero. The makeshift writing surface, the inscription on the writing stand, and the medicinal bath (Marat was afflicted with a painful skin disease) all provide specific references to Marat. David presented the scene with

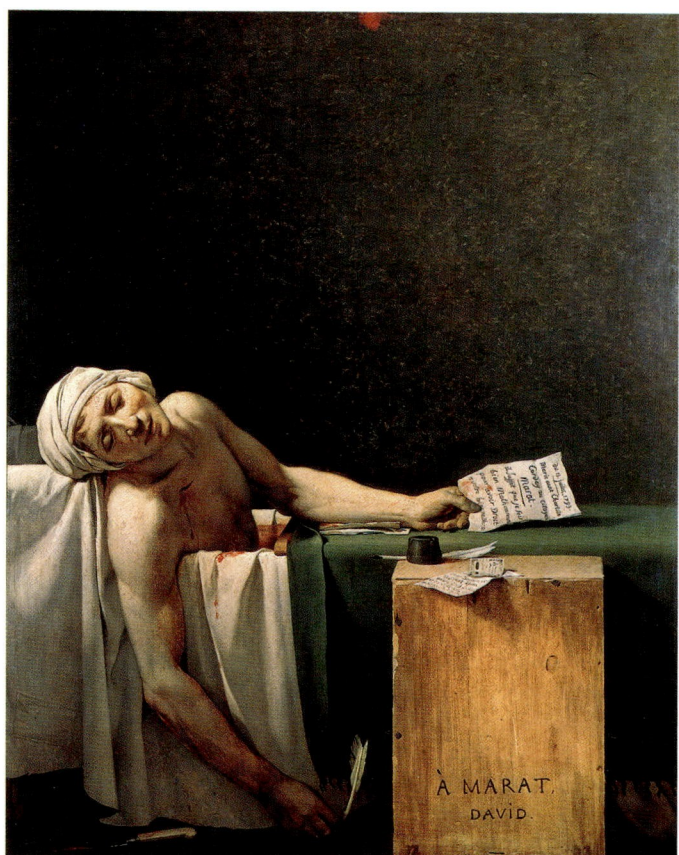

**28-22** JACQUES-LOUIS DAVID, *The Death of Marat*, 1793. Oil on canvas, approx. 5′ 3″ × 4′ 1″. Musées Royaux des Beaux-Arts de Belgique, Brussels.

directness and clarity. The cold neutral space above Marat's figure slumped in the tub makes for a chilling oppressiveness. The painter vividly placed narrative details—the knife, the wound, the blood, the letter with which the young woman gained entrance—to sharpen the sense of pain and outrage and to confront viewers with the scene itself. Although David's depiction was based on historical events, his composition reveals his close study of Michelangelo, especially the Renaissance artist's Christ in the *Pietà* (not illustrated) in Saint Peter's in Rome. *The Death of Marat* is convincingly real, yet it was masterfully composed to present Marat to the French people as a tragic martyr who died in the service of their state. In this way, the painting was meant to function as an "altarpiece" for the new civic "religion"; it was designed to inspire viewers with the saintly dedication of their slain leader. Rather than the grandiosity of spectacle characteristic of West's *The Death of General Wolfe* (FIG. 28-17), a severe Neoclassical spareness pervades David's *Marat*, yet it retains its drama and ability to move spectators.

**NAPOLEON'S ASCENDANCE** At the fall of the French revolutionist Robespierre (1758–1794) and his party in 1794, David barely escaped with his life. He was tried and imprisoned, and after his release in 1795 he worked hard to resurrect his career. When Napoleon Bonaparte (1769–1821)—who had exploited the revolutionary disarray and ascended to power—approached David and offered him the position of First Painter of the Empire, David seized the opportunity. One of the major paintings David produced for

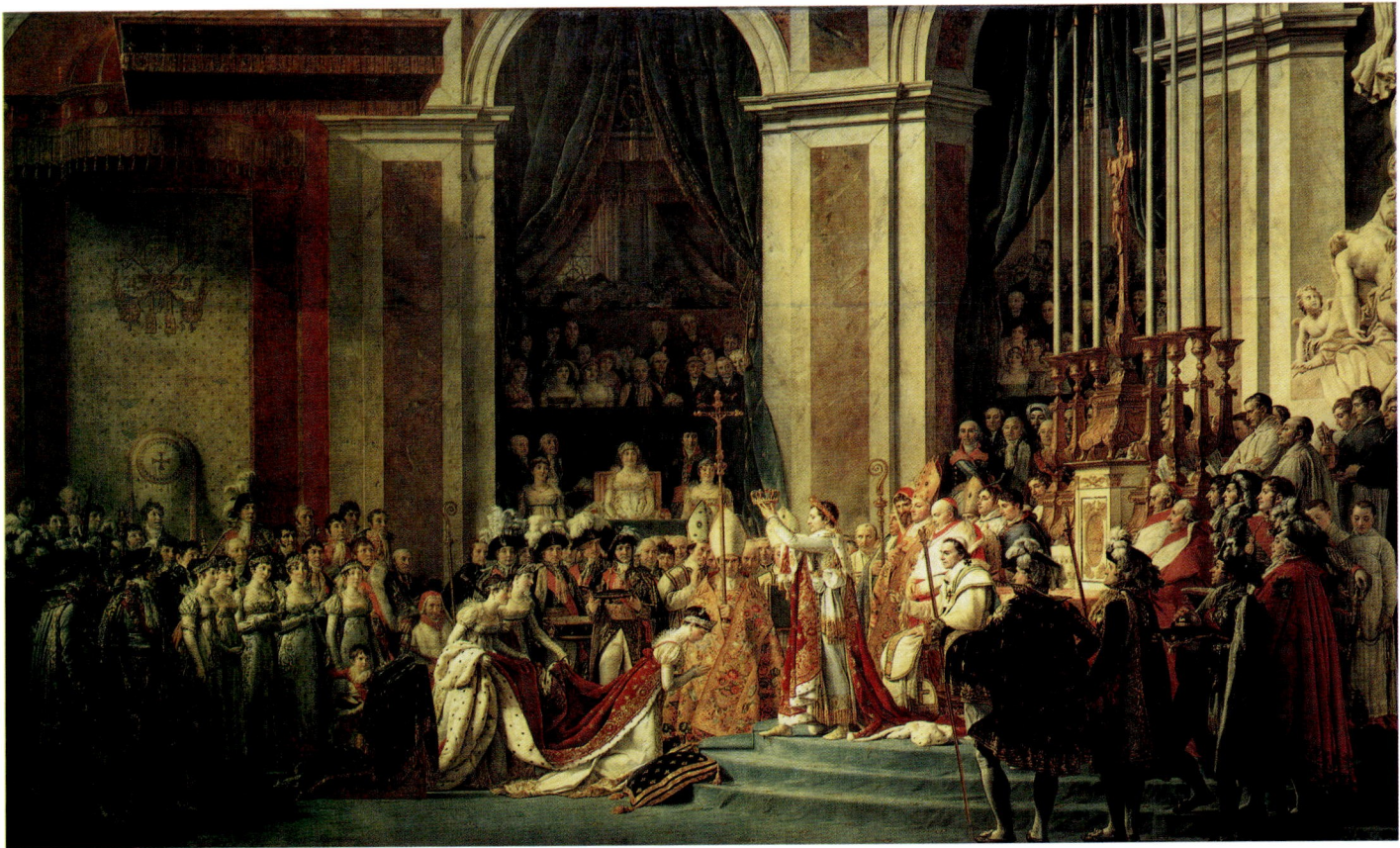

**28-23** JACQUES-LOUIS DAVID, *The Coronation of Napoleon,* 1805–1808. Oil on canvas, 20′ 4½″ × 32′ 1¾″. Louvre, Paris.

Napoleon was *The Coronation of Napoleon* (FIG. **28-23**), a large-scale work that documents the pomp and pageantry of Napoleon's coronation in December of 1804.

*The Coronation of Napoleon* is a monumental painting (20 × 32 feet) that reveals the interests of both patron and artist. Napoleon was well aware of the utility of art for constructing a public image and of David's skill in producing inspiring, powerful images. To a large extent, David adhered to historical fact regarding the coronation. He was present at this momentous event and recorded his presence in the painting (he appears in one of the tribunes, or loges, constructed for spectators). The ceremony was held in Notre-Dame Cathedral, whose majestic interior David faithfully reproduced. The artist also duly recorded those in attendance. In addition to Napoleon, his wife Josephine (being crowned), and Pope Pius VII (seated behind Napoleon), others present included Joseph and Louis Bonaparte, Napoleon's ministers, the retinues of the emperor and empress, and a representative group of the clergy. Despite the artist's apparent fidelity to historical accuracy, preliminary studies and drawings reveal that David made changes at Napoleon's request. For example, Napoleon insisted that the painter depict the pope with his hand raised in blessing. Further, Napoleon's mother appears prominently in the center background, yet she had refused to attend the coronation and apparently was included in the painting at the emperor's insistence.

Despite the numerous figures and the lavish pageantry involved in this event, David retained the structured composition central to the Neoclassical style. As in David's *Oath of the Horatii,* the action here was presented as if on a theater stage. In addition,

as he did in his arrangement of the men and women in *Oath,* David conceptually divided the painting to reveal polarities. In this case, the pope, prelates, and priests representing the Catholic Church appear on the right, contrasting with members of Napoleon's imperial court on the left. The relationship between church and state was one of this period's most contentious issues. Napoleon's decision to crown himself, rather than to allow the pope to perform the coronation, as was traditional, revealed Napoleon's concern about the power relationship between church and state. Napoleon's insistence on emphasizing his authority is evidenced by his selection of the moment depicted; having already crowned himself, Napoleon places a crown on his wife's head. Thus, although this painting represents an important visual document in the tradition of history painting, it also represents a more complex statement about the changing politics in Napoleonic France.

It was not just David's individual skill but Neoclassicism in general that appealed to Napoleon. When Napoleon Bonaparte ascended to power, he embraced all links with the classical past as sources of symbolic authority for his short-lived imperial state. Such associations, particularly connections to the Roman Empire, served Napoleon well and were invoked in architecture and sculpture as well as painting.

**ROMAN GRANDEUR IN FRANCE** Architecture served as an excellent vehicle for consolidating authority because of its public presence. Napoleon was not the first to rely on classical models, however. Fairly early in the 18th century, architects began to turn away from the theatricality and ostentation of Baroque and

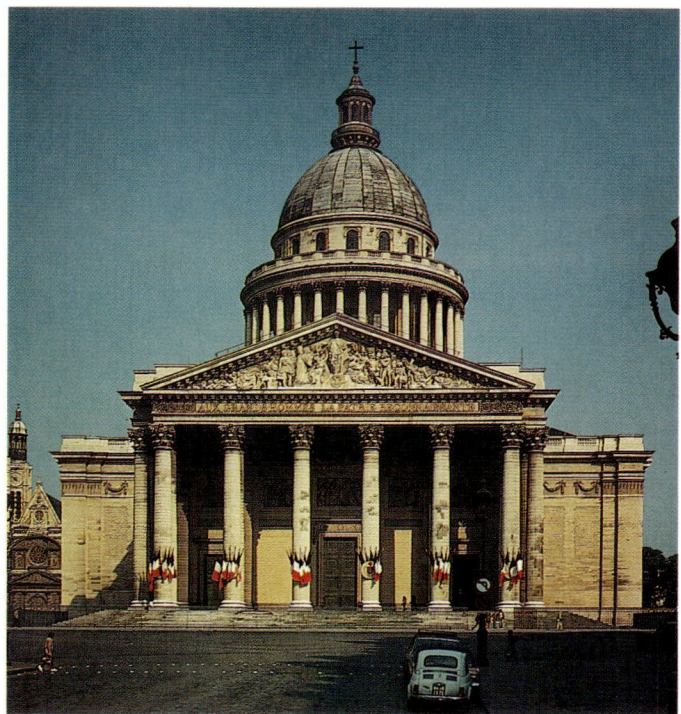

**28-24** JACQUES-GERMAIN SOUFFLOT, the Panthéon (Sainte-Geneviève), Paris, France, 1755–1792.

Rococo design and embraced a more streamlined classicism. The Neoclassical portico of the Parisian church of Sainte-Geneviève (FIG. 28-24), now the Panthéon, was designed by JACQUES-GERMAIN SOUFFLOT (1713–1780). It stands as testament to the revived interest in Greek and Roman cultures. The Roman ruins at Baalbek in Syria, especially a titanic colonnade, provided much of the inspiration for this portico. The columns, reproduced with studied archaeological exactitude, are the first revelation of Roman grandeur in France. The walls are severely blank, except for a repeated garland motif near the top. The colonnaded dome, a Neoclassical version of the domes of Saint Peter's in Rome (see FIG. 22-29), the Church of the Invalides in Paris (see FIG. 24-72), and Saint Paul's in London (see FIG. 24-74), rises above a Greek-cross plan. Both the dome and vaults rest on an interior grid of splendid freestanding Corinthian columns, as if the portico's colonnade were continued within. Although the whole effect, inside and out, is Roman, the structural principles employed are essentially Gothic. Soufflot was one of the first 18th-century builders to suggest that Gothic engineering was highly functional structurally and could be applied to modern buildings. In his work, the curious, but not unreasonable, conjunction of Gothic and classical has a structural integration that laid the foundation for a 19th-century admiration of Gothic engineering.

**A NAPOLEONIC "TEMPLE OF GLORY"** La Madeleine (FIG. 28-25) was briefly intended as a "temple of glory" for Napoleon's armies and as a monument to the newly won glories of France. Begun as a church in 1807, at the height of Napoleon's power (some three years after he proclaimed himself emperor), the structure reverted again to a church after his defeat and long before its completion in 1842. Designed by PIERRE VIGNON (1763–1828), this grandiose temple includes a high podium and broad flight of stairs leading to a deep porch in the front. These architectural features, coupled with the Corinthian columns, recall Roman imperial temples (such as the Maison Carrée, FIG. 10-30, in Nîmes, France), making La Madeleine a symbolic link between the Napoleonic and Roman empires. Curiously, the building's classical shell surrounds an interior covered by a sequence of three domes, a feature found in Byzantine and Romanesque churches. It is as though Vignon clothed this church in the costume of pagan Rome.

**THE EMPEROR'S SISTER AS GODDESS** Under Napoleon, classical models were prevalent in sculpture as well. The emperor's favorite sculptor was ANTONIO CANOVA (1757–1822), who somewhat reluctantly left a successful career in Italy to settle

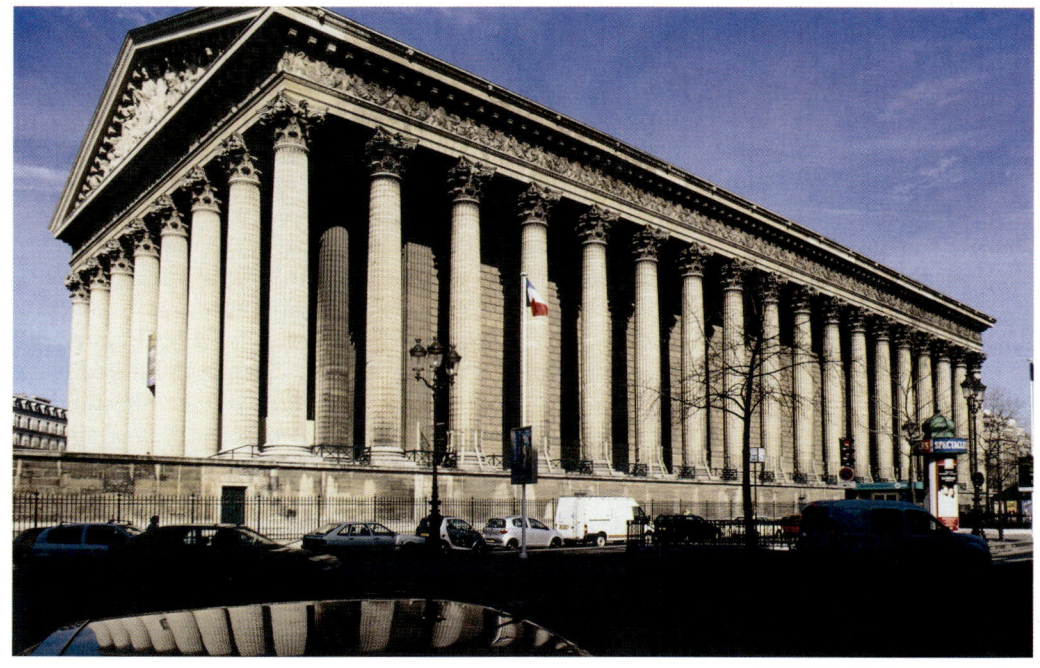

**28-25** PIERRE VIGNON, La Madeleine, Paris, France, 1807–1842.

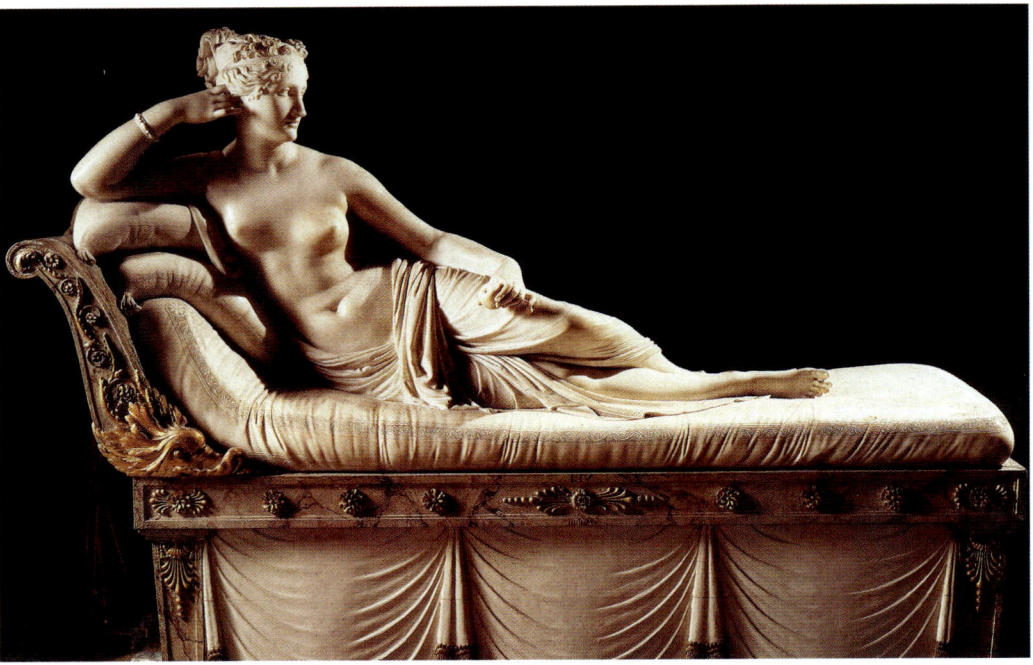

**28-26** Antonio Canova, *Pauline Borghese as Venus*, 1808. Marble, life-size. Galleria Borghese, Rome.

in Paris and serve the emperor. Once in France, Canova became Napoleon's admirer and made numerous portraits, all in the Neoclassical style, of the emperor and his family. Perhaps the best known of these works is the marble portrait of Napoleon's sister, *Pauline Borghese as Venus* (FIG. **28-26**). Initially, Canova had suggested depicting Borghese as Diana, goddess of the hunt. The subject of the work, however, insisted on being shown as Venus, the goddess of love. Thus she appears, reclining on a divan and gracefully holding the golden apple, a symbol of the goddess's triumph in the judgment of Paris. Although Canova clearly derived the figure from Greek art—the sensuous pose and drapery recall Greek sculpture—the work is not as idealized as might be expected. The sculptor's sharply detailed rendering of the couch and drapery suggest a commitment to naturalism as well.

The public perception of Pauline Borghese influenced the sculpture's design and presentation. Napoleon Bonaparte had arranged the marriage of his sister to an heir of the noble Roman Borghese family. Once Pauline was in Rome, her behavior was less than dignified, and the public gossiped extensively about her affairs. Her insistence on portrayal as the goddess of love reflected her self-perception. Due to his wife's questionable reputation, Prince Camillo Borghese, the work's official patron, kept the sculpture sequestered in the Villa Borghese. Relatively few people were allowed to see it (and then only by torchlight). Still, the sculpture increased the notoriety of both artist and subject, although the sculpture's enduring fame was established only after Canova's death in 1822.

## Neoclassicism in England

The appeal of classical antiquity extended well beyond French borders. The popularity of Greek and Roman cultures was due not only to their association with morality, rationality, and integrity but also to their connection to political systems ranging from Athenian democracy to Roman imperial rule. Thus, in parliamentary England, as in revolutionary and imperial France, Neoclassicism was highly regarded. In England, Neoclassicism's appeal also may have been due to its clarity and simplicity. These characteristics provided a stark contrast to the complexity and opulence of Baroque art, then associated with the showy rule of absolute monarchy—something to be played down in parliamentary England. In English architecture, the preference for a simple and commonsensical style was derived indirectly from the authority of the classical Roman architect Vitruvius, through Andrea Palladio's work (see FIGS. 22-56 to 22-59), and on through that of Inigo Jones (see FIG. 24-73).

**INVOKING PALLADIO** RICHARD BOYLE, earl of Burlington (1695–1753), strongly restated Jones's Palladian doctrine in a new style in Chiswick House (FIG. **28-27**), which he built on London's outskirts with the help of the talented professional WILLIAM KENT (ca. 1686–1748). The way had been paved for this shift in style by, among other things, the publication of Colin Campbell's *Vitruvius Britannicus* (1715), three volumes of engravings of ancient buildings in Britain, prefaced by a denunciation of Italian Baroque and high praise for Palladio and Jones.

Chiswick House is a free variation on the theme of Palladio's Villa Rotonda (see FIG. 22-56). The exterior design provided a clear alternative to the colorful splendors of Versailles. In its simple symmetry, unadorned planes, right angles, and stiffly wrought proportions, Chiswick looks very classical and "rational." But, like that of so many Palladian villas in England, the effect is modified by its setting within informal gardens, where a charming irregularity of layout and freely growing uncropped foliage dominate the scene. Just as irregularity was cultivated in the landscaping surrounding English Palladian villas, early 18th-century building interiors sometimes were ornamented in a style more closely related to the Rococo decoration fashionable on the continent than to the severe classical Palladian exteriors. At Chiswick, the interior design creates a luxurious Late Baroque foil to the stern symmetry of the exterior and the plan. Despite such "lapses," Palladian Classicism prevailed in English architecture until about 1760, when it began to evolve into Neoclassicism.

**PALLADIAN SPLENDOR** At just about this time of change, John Wood the Elder (ca. 1704–1754) and his son JOHN WOOD

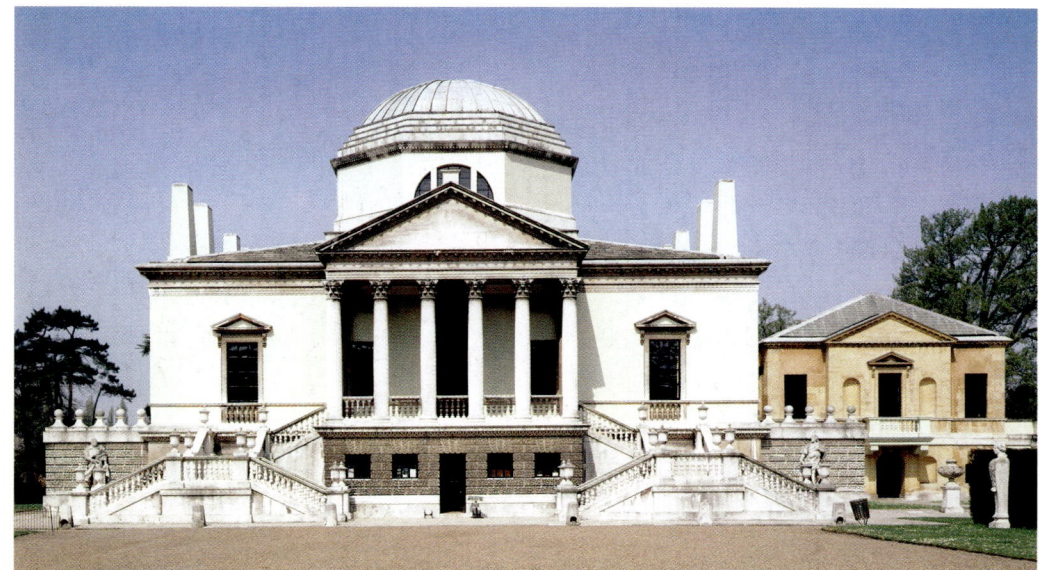

28-27 RICHARD BOYLE (earl of Burlington) and WILLIAM KENT, Chiswick House, near London, England, begun 1725. British Crown Copyright.

THE YOUNGER (1728–1782) laid out an extensive complex of buildings for the fashionable resort town of Bath in west England. The structures are grouped around simple geometrical spaces—the square, circle, and semicircle—and are called Queen's Square, the Circus, and the Royal Crescent (FIG. 28-28), the last exclusively the work of John Wood the Younger. These early ingenious solutions to the problems of urban design were intended not for royalty but for the well-to-do members of society who came to "take the waters" at the city's hot springs. Restored and operating in the 18th century, the baths had been famous since Roman times and had given Bath its name. In both the Circus and the Royal Crescent, the houses are linked into rows behind a single continuous Palladian facade, which transforms the joined units into one palatial edifice. The Royal Crescent joins 30 residences in a great semiellipse, originally intended to have a matching semiellipse facing it across an intersecting roadway, so as to suggest the ancient Roman Colosseum (see FIG. 10-34). Bath, with its ancient Roman associations, prompted the younger John Wood to refer to Rome not only for the Colosseum-like plan but also for the imperial scale and majesty of the building's elevation. Especially "Roman" is the sweeping parade of colossal Ionic columns along the lofty, curving basement; the roofline, punctuated regularly with clusters of chimney pots, is traditionally English. The Bath designs, with many variations, became a standard

for British urban architecture for a century. Here, they announced a new classical Roman presence in what was still a Palladian edifice.

**A GREEK PORTICO IN ENGLAND** British painter and architect JAMES STUART (1713–1788), along with Nicholas Revett (1720–1804), also a painter and architect, introduced to Europe the splendor and originality of Greek art in the enormously influential *Antiquities of Athens,* whose first volume appeared in 1762. These volumes firmly distinguished Greek art from the "derivative" Roman style that had served as the model for classicism since the Renaissance. Stuart and Revett's preference for Greek art and architecture over Roman antiquities was widely shared despite the fact that in the 18th century, familiarity with Greek art continued to be based primarily on Roman copies of Greek originals. And in spite of the establishment of the Grand Tour (see "The Grand Tour," page 814), travel to Greece was hazardous, making firsthand interaction with Greek monuments difficult. The general perception of Roman art as derivative was further reinforced by the insistent championing of Greek art by the influential art historian Johann Joachim Winckelmann (see page 814). Stuart and Revett's preference for Greek art was based on firsthand experience; the two spent four years visiting Greece in the early 1750s. Stuart's design for the portico at Hagley Park

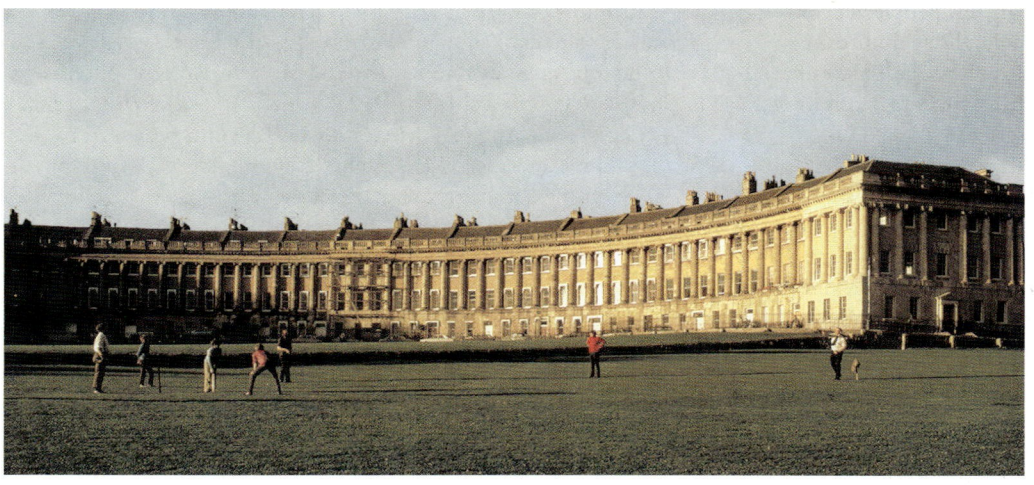

28-28 JOHN WOOD THE YOUNGER, the Royal Crescent, Bath, England, 1769–1775.

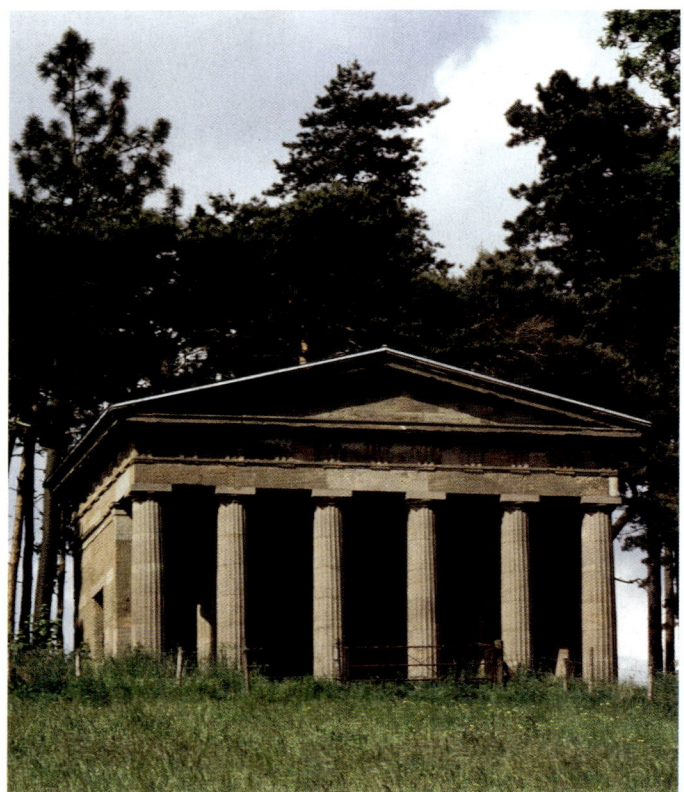

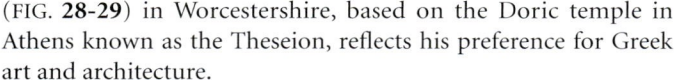

28-29 JAMES STUART, Doric portico, Hagley Park, Worcestershire, England, 1758. 🟡

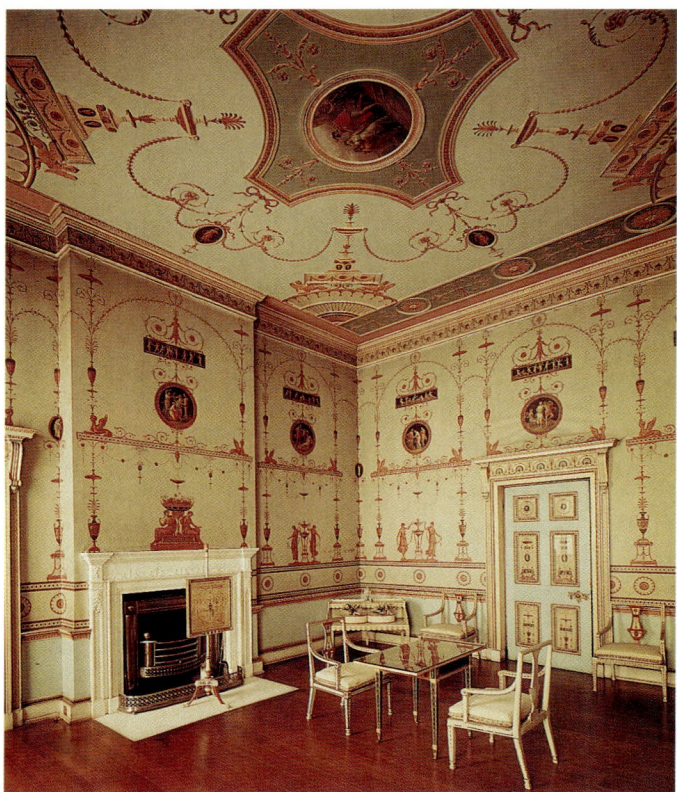

28-30 ROBERT ADAM, Etruscan Room, from Osterley Park House, Middlesex, England, begun 1761. Victoria and Albert Museum, London. 🟡

(FIG. **28-29**) in Worcestershire, based on the Doric temple in Athens known as the Theseion, reflects his preference for Greek art and architecture.

**NEOCLASSICISM MOVES INDOORS** Eighteenth-century Neoclassical interiors also were directly inspired by new discoveries of "the glory that was Greece / And the grandeur that was Rome"[7] and summarized the conception of a noble classical world. The first great archaeological event of modern times, the discovery and initial excavation of the ancient buried Roman cities of Herculaneum (see FIGS. 10-14, 10-22, and 10-24) and Pompeii (see FIGS. 10-10 to 10-13, 10-15, 10-21, and 10-23) in the 1730s and 1740s, startled and thrilled all of Europe (see "Rising from the Ashes," page 815). The excavation of these cities was the veritable resurrection of the ancient world, not simply a dim vision of it inspired by a few moldering ruins. Historical reality replaced fancy with fact. The wall paintings and other artifacts of Pompeii inspired the slim, straight-lined, elegant "Pompeian" style that almost entirely displaced the curvilinear Rococo after midcentury.

**ADAPTING POMPEIAN DECOR** In England, the Pompeian manner emerged most recognizably in the work of ROBERT ADAM (1728–1792), whose interior architecture was influential throughout Europe. The Etruscan Room (FIG. **28-30**) at Osterley Park House in Middlesex was begun in 1761. If compared to the Rococo salons of the Hôtel de Soubise (FIG. 28-1) and the Amalienburg (FIG. 28-2), this room shows how completely symmetry and rectilinearity returned. But this return was achieved with great delicacy and with none of the massive splendor of the Louis XIV style. The architect took the decorative motifs (medallions, urns, vine scrolls, sphinxes, and tripods) from Roman art

and, as in Roman stucco work, arranged them sparsely within broad, neutral spaces and slender margins (see FIGS. 10-18 and 10-20). Adam was an archaeologist as well, and he had explored and written accounts of the ruins of Diocletian's palace at Split (see FIG. 10-75). Kedleston House in Derbyshire, Adelphi Terrace in London, and a great many other structures he designed also show the influence of the Split palace on his work.

## Neoclassicism in the United States

**JEFFERSONIAN IDEALISM** The versatility of Neoclassicism and the appeal of the qualities with which it was connected— morality, idealism, patriotism, and civic virtue—allowed the style to be associated with everything from revolutionary aspirations for democratic purity to imperial ambitions for unshakable authority. Thus, Napoleon invoked classical references to serve his imperial agenda. Meanwhile, in the new American republic, THOMAS JEFFERSON (1743–1826) spearheaded a movement to adopt Neoclassicism (a style he saw as representative of U.S. democratic qualities) as the national architecture.

Scholar, economist, educational theorist, statesman, and gifted amateur architect, Jefferson was by nature attracted to classical architecture. He worked out his ideas in his design for his own home, Monticello (FIG. **28-31**), which was begun in 1770. Jefferson admired Palladio immensely and read carefully the Italian architect's *Four Books of Architecture*. Later, while minister to France, Jefferson studied French 18th-century classical architecture and city planning and visited the Maison Carrée, a Roman temple at Nîmes (see FIG. 10-30). After his European trip, Jefferson completely remodeled Monticello, which he first had designed in an

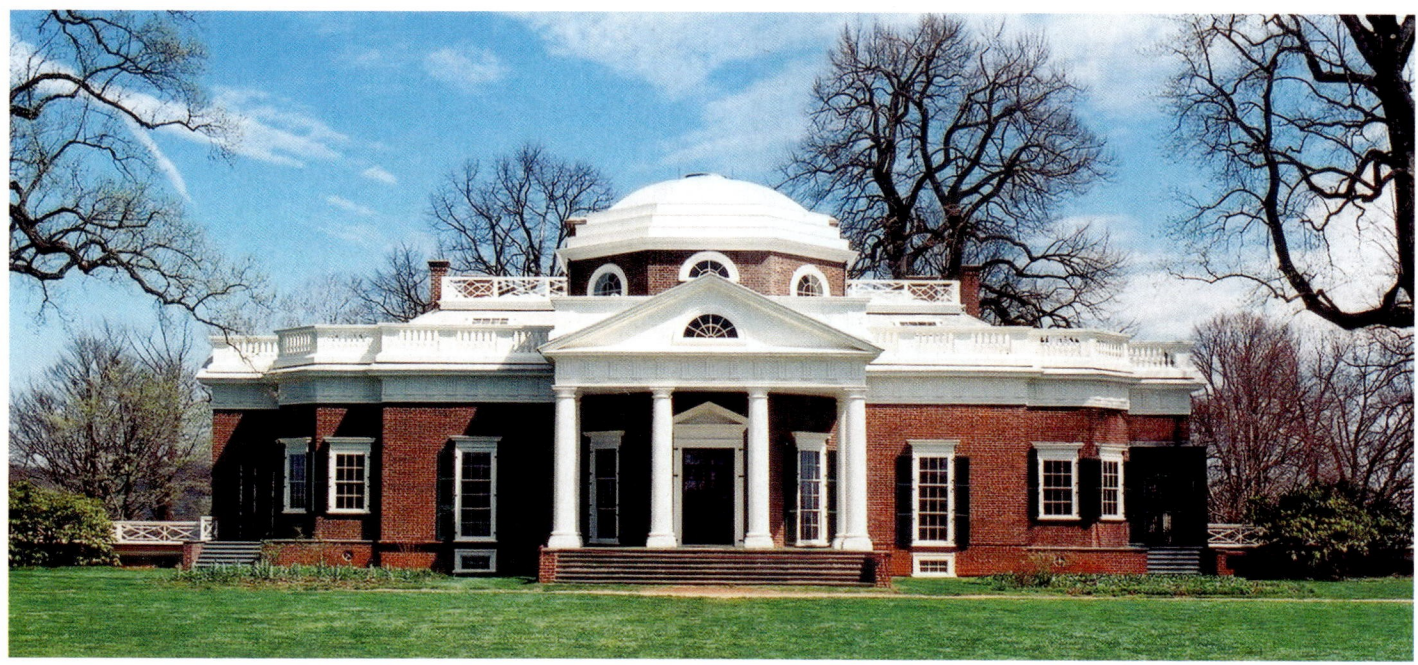

**28-31** THOMAS JEFFERSON, Monticello, Charlottesville, Virginia, 1770–1806. Thomas Jefferson Foundation, Inc.

English Georgian style. In his remodeling, he emulated Palladio's manner, with a facade inspired by Robert Adam's work. The final version of Monticello is somewhat reminiscent of the Villa Rotonda (see FIG. 22-56) and of Chiswick House (FIG. 28-27), but its materials are the local wood and brick used in Virginia.

Turning from the private domain to public spaces, Jefferson began to carry out his dream of developing a classical style for the official architecture of the United States. Here, his Neoclassicism was an extension of the Enlightenment belief in the perfectibility of human beings and in the power of art to help achieve that perfection. As secretary of state to George Washington, Jefferson supported the logically ordered city plan for Washington, D.C., created in 1791 by the French-American architect MAJOR PIERRE L'ENFANT (1724–1825). He based the plan on earlier ordered designs for city sections, such as Wood's designs for Bath (FIG. 28-28), but extended them to an entire community. As an architect, Jefferson also incorporated the specific look of the Maison Carrée (see FIG. 10-30) into his design for the Virginia State Capitol in Richmond. He approved William Thornton's initial Palladian design for the federal Capitol in 1793. As president, in 1803 he selected BENJAMIN LATROBE (1764–1820) to take over the design of the structure (FIG. **28-32**), with the goal of creating "a building that would serve as a visible

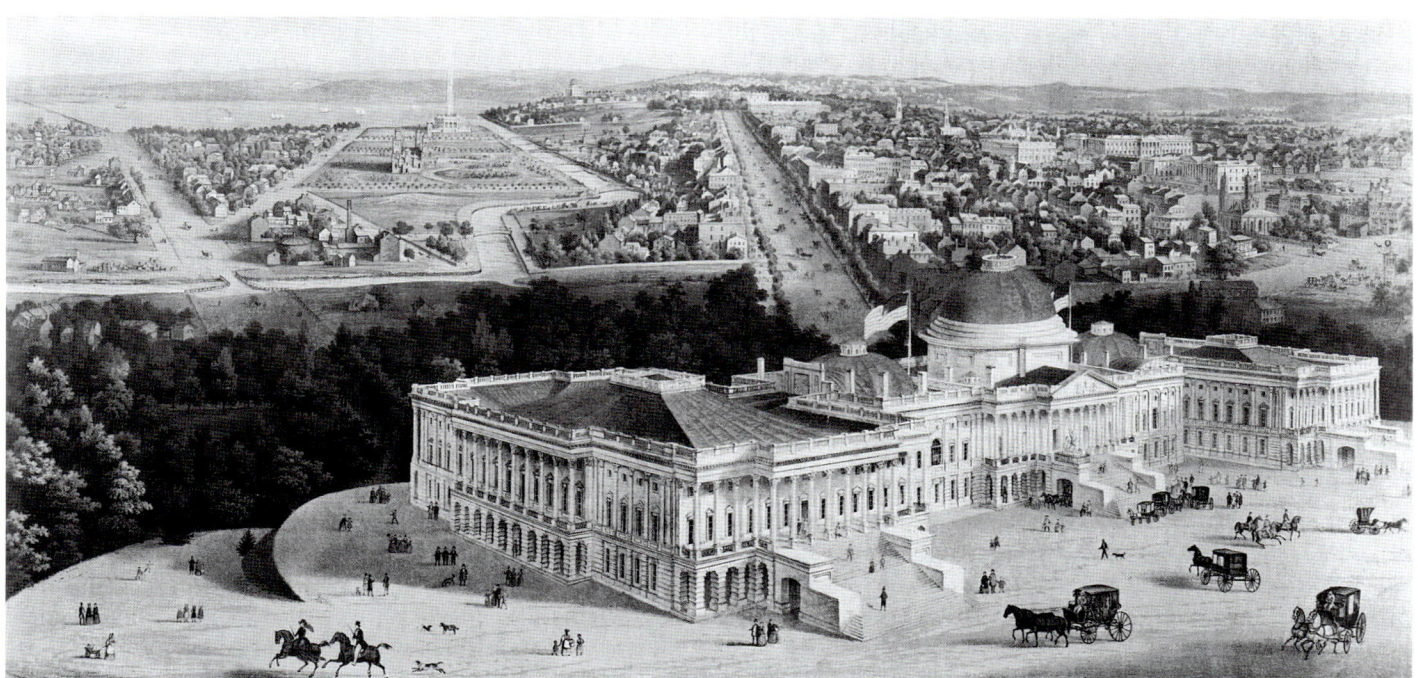

**28-32** Drawing of view of Washington, 1852, showing BENJAMIN LATROBE's Capitol (1803–1807) and MAJOR L'ENFANT's plan (created in 1791) of the city. Library of Congress, Washington, D.C.

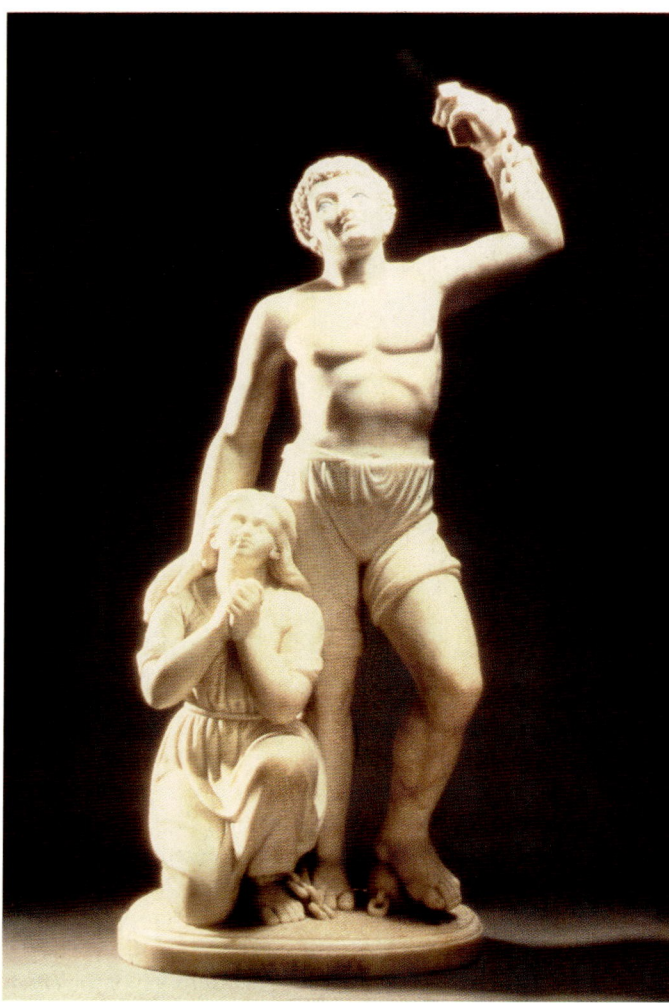

**28-33** EDMONIA LEWIS, *Forever Free*, 1867. Marble, 3′ 5¼″ × 11″ × 7″. James A. Porter Gallery of Afro-American Art, Howard University, Washington, D.C.

holds aloft a broken manacle and chain as literal and symbolic references to his former servitude. Lewis produced this sculpture while living in Rome, where she was surrounded by examples of both classical and Renaissance art.

The production of this work four years after President Lincoln's issuance of the Emancipation Proclamation made *Forever Free* (originally titled *The Morning of Liberty*) an appropriate abolitionist statement, which is how it was perceived when it was exhibited. However, other factors caution against an overly simplistic reading. Because Lewis was female, African American, and Native American (she was born to a Chippewa mother and African American father), scholars have debated the degree to which Lewis attempted to inject a statement about African American gender relationships into this sculpture. For example, does the kneeling position of the woman represent Lewis's acceptance of female subordination?

Lewis's accomplishments as a sculptor speak to the increasing access to training that was available to women in the 19th century. Educated at Oberlin College (the first American college to grant degrees to women), Lewis financed her trip to Rome with the sale of medallions and marble busts. Her success in a field dominated by white male artists is a testament to both her skill and her determination.

# FROM NEOCLASSICISM
# TO ROMANTICISM

Given Jacques-Louis David's stature and prominence as an artist, along with the popularity of Neoclassicism, it is not surprising that he attracted numerous students and developed an active and flourishing teaching studio. David gave practical instruction to and deeply influenced many important artists of the period, including the three discussed next. So strong was David's commitment to classicism that he encouraged all his students to learn Latin so that they could better immerse themselves in and understand classical culture. Even further, David initially demanded that his pupils select their subjects from Plutarch, the ancient author of *Lives of the Great Greeks and Romans* and a principal source of standard Neoclassical subject matter. Due to this thorough classical foundation, David's students all produced work that at its core retains Neoclassical elements. Yet despite this apparent dogmatism, David was open-minded and far from authoritarian in his teaching, and he encouraged his students to find their own artistic identities.

A departure from the structured confines of Neoclassicism is evident in the work of Antoine-Jean Gros, Anne-Louis Girodet-Trioson, and Jean-Auguste-Dominique Ingres, each David's pupil. In moving beyond Neoclassicism, these artists laid the foundation for the Romantic movement, discussed in detail later. They explored the realm of the exotic and the erotic, and often turned to fictional narratives for the subjects of their paintings, as Romantic artists also did.

**NAPOLEON VISITING THE SICK**  Like his teacher David, ANTOINE-JEAN GROS (1771–1835) was aware of the benefits that could accrue to artists favored by those in power. Following David's lead, Gros produced several paintings that contributed to the growing mythic status of Napoleon Bonaparte in the early 1800s. In *Napoleon at the Pesthouse at Jaffa* (FIG. **28-34**), which Napoleon ordered Gros to paint, the artist referred to an outbreak of the bubonic plague that erupted during the Near Eastern

expression of the ideals of a country dedicated to liberty." Jefferson's choice of a Roman style was influenced partly by his admiration for its beauty and partly by his associations of it with an idealized Roman republican government and, through that, with the democracy of ancient Greece. Latrobe committed himself to producing a building that "when finished will be a durable and honorable monument of our infant republic, and will bear favorable comparisons with the remains of the same kind of ancient republics of Greece and Rome."[8] To that end, in the Capitol's architecture, Latrobe transformed the Roman eagle symbol into the American bald eagle and devised a special new Corinthian order that replaced acanthus leaves with corn plants. He also designed the sculpted representation of Liberty to abandon traditional trappings and to hold a liberty cap in one hand and rest her other hand on the Constitution.

**FREE AT LAST**  The Neoclassical style Jefferson championed so successfully for the architecture (FIG. 28-32) of the new democracy was invoked by American sculptors as well. Depicting freed African American slaves, *Forever Free* (FIG. **28-33**) by EDMONIA LEWIS (ca. 1845–after 1909) is a marble sculpture that utilizes the vocabulary of Neoclassicism. The man stands heroically in a contrapposto stance reminiscent of classical statues. His right hand rests on the shoulder of the kneeling woman, and his left hand

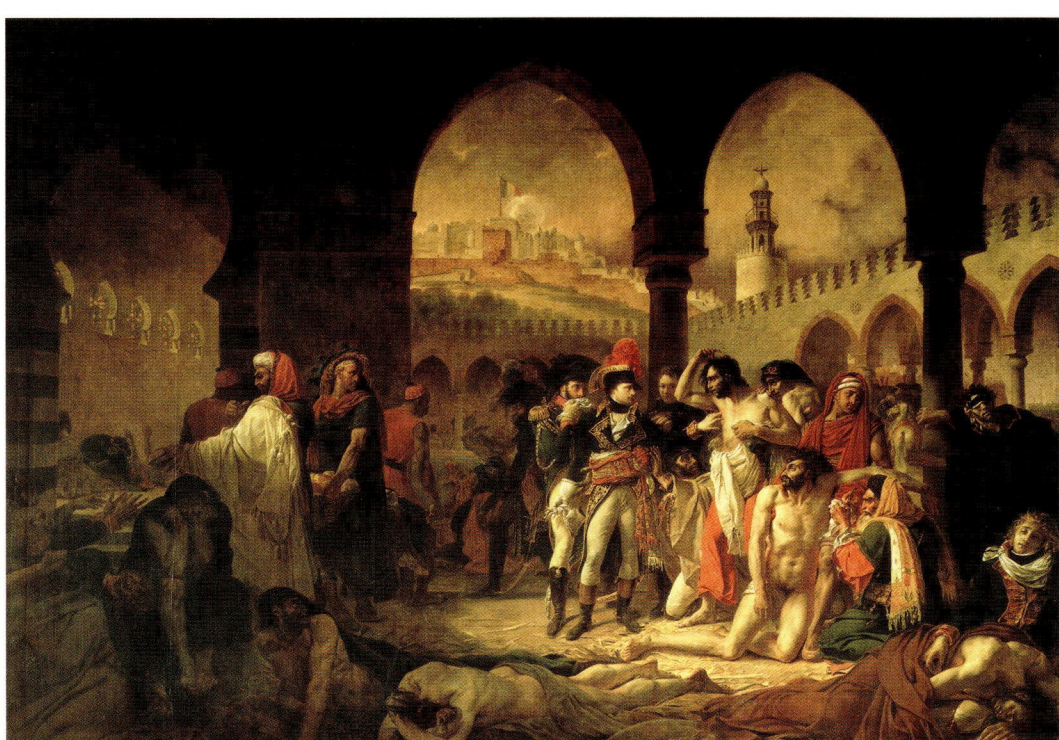

**28-34** ANTOINE-JEAN GROS, *Napoleon at the Pesthouse at Jaffa,* 1804. Oil on canvas, approx. 17′ 5″ × 23′ 7″. Louvre, Paris.

campaigns of 1799. This fearsome disease struck Muslim and French forces alike, and in March 1799 Napoleon himself visited the pesthouse at Jaffa to quell the growing panic and hysteria. Gros depicted Napoleon's staff officers covering their noses against the stench of the place, while Napoleon, amid the dead and dying, is fearless and in control. He comforts those still alive, who are clearly awed by his presence and authority. Indeed, by depicting the French leader touching the sores of a plague victim, Gros made reference to the king's legendary touch (the *touche des écouelles*), thereby conferring on Napoleon the miraculous power to heal. This exaltation of the French leader was necessary to counteract the negative publicity he was subject to at the time. Apparently, two months after his visit to the pesthouse, Napoleon ordered all plague-stricken French soldiers poisoned so as to relieve him of having to return them to Cairo or of abandoning them to the Turks. Some of the soldiers survived, and from their accounts the damaging stories about Napoleon began to circulate. Gros's large painting was a clear attempt at damage control—to resurrect the event and rehabilitate Napoleon's compromised public image.

Gros structured his composition in a manner reminiscent of David's major paintings, with the horseshoe arches and Moorish arcades of the mosque courtyard providing a backdrop for the unfolding action. In addition, Gros's placement of Muslim doctors ministering to plague-stricken Muslims on the left contrasts them with Napoleon and his soldiers on the right, bathed in radiant light. David had used this polarized compositional scheme to great effect in works such as *Oath of the Horatii* (FIG. 28-21). However, Gros's fascination with the exoticism of the Near East, as evidenced by his attention to the unique architecture, attire, and terrain, represented a departure from Neoclassicism. This, along with the artist's emphasis on death, suffering, and an emotional rendering of the scene, presaged prominent aspects of Romanticism.

**A TRAGIC SUICIDE IN LOUISIANA** Another of David's students, ANNE-LOUIS GIRODET-TRIOSON (1767–1824), also produced works that conjured images of exotic locales and cultures. Moving further into the domain of Romanticism, his painting *The Burial of Atala* (FIG. **28-35**) was based on a popular novel, *The Genius of Christianity,* by French writer François René de Chateaubriand. The section of the novel dealing with Atala was published as an excerpt a year before the publication of the entire book in 1802. Both the excerpt and the novel were enormously successful, and, as a result, Atala became almost a cult figure. In keeping with the movement toward Romanticism, interest in *The Genius of Christianity* was due in large part to the exoticism and eroticism integral to the narrative. Set in Louisiana, Chateaubriand's work focuses on two Native American youths, Atala and Chactas. The two, from different tribes, fall in love and run away together through the wilderness. The book is highly charged with

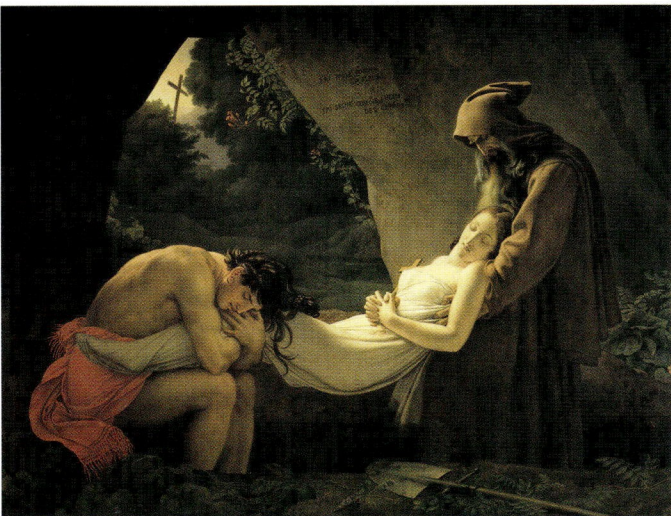

**28-35** ANNE-LOUIS GIRODET-TRIOSON, *The Burial of Atala,* 1808. Oil on canvas, approx. 6′ 11″ × 8′ 9″. Louvre, Paris.

erotic passion, and Atala, sworn to lifelong virginity, finally commits suicide rather than break her oath. Girodet's painting depicts this tragedy, as Atala is buried in the shadow of a cross by her grief-stricken lover, Chactas. Assisting in the burial is a cloaked priest, whose presence is appropriate given Chateaubriand's emphasis on the revival of Christianity (and the Christianization of the New World) in his novel. Like Gros's depiction of the foreign Muslim world, Girodet's representation of American Indian lovers in the Louisiana wilderness appealed to the public's fascination (whetted by the Louisiana Purchase in 1803) with what it perceived as the passion and primitivism of Native American tribal life. *The Burial of Atala* speaks here to emotions, rather than inviting philosophical meditation or revealing some grand order of nature and form. Unlike David's appeal in the *Oath of the Horatii* (FIG. 28-21) to feelings that manifest themselves in public action, the appeal here is to the viewer's private world of fantasy and emotion.

SUMMARIZING NEOCLASSICAL PRINCIPLES JEAN-AUGUSTE-DOMINIQUE INGRES (1780–1867) arrived at David's studio in the late 1790s after Girodet-Trioson had left to establish an independent career. Ingres's study there was to be short-lived, however, as he soon broke with David on matters of style. This difference of opinion involved Ingres's adoption of what he believed to be a truer and purer Greek style than that employed by David. The younger artist adopted flat and linear forms approximating those found in Greek vase painting. In many of Ingres's works, the figure is placed in the foreground, much like a piece of low-relief sculpture.

Ingres's huge composition *Apotheosis of Homer* (FIG. **28-36**) was exhibited at the Salon of 1827. It presented in a single statement the doctrines of ideal form and of Neoclassical taste, and generations of academic painters remained loyal to that style. Enthroned before an Ionic temple, the epic poet Homer is crowned by Fame or Victory. At his feet are two statuesque women, who personify *The Iliad* and *The Odyssey,* the offspring of his imagination. Symmetrically grouped about him is a company of the "sovereign geniuses"—as Ingres called them—who expressed humanity's highest ideals in philosophy, poetry, music, and art. To Homer's left are Anacreon with his lyre, Phidias with his sculptor's hammer, and Plato, Socrates, and other ancient worthies. To his far right are Horace, Vergil, Dante, and, conspicuously, Raphael, the painter Ingres most admired. Among the forward group on the painting's left side are Poussin (pointing) and Shakespeare (half concealed), and at the right are French writers Jean Baptiste Racine, Molière, Voltaire, and François de Salignac de la Mothe Fénelon. Ingres had planned a much larger and more inclusive group, but the project was never completed. For years he agonized over whom to choose for this select company of heroes in various humanistic disciplines.

It is obvious that Raphael's *School of Athens* (see FIG. 22-17) served as the inspiration for *Apotheosis* and, to a degree, the composition. As Ingres developed as an artist, he turned more and more to Raphael, perceiving in his art the essence of classicism. Ingres disdained, in proportion, the new "modern" styles (the romantic and the realistic, as they were then called) as destructive of true art.

BOTH CLASSICAL AND EXOTIC Despite Ingres's commitment to ideal form and careful compositional structure, he also produced works that, like those of Gros and Girodet, his contemporaries saw as departures from Neoclassicism. One such painting

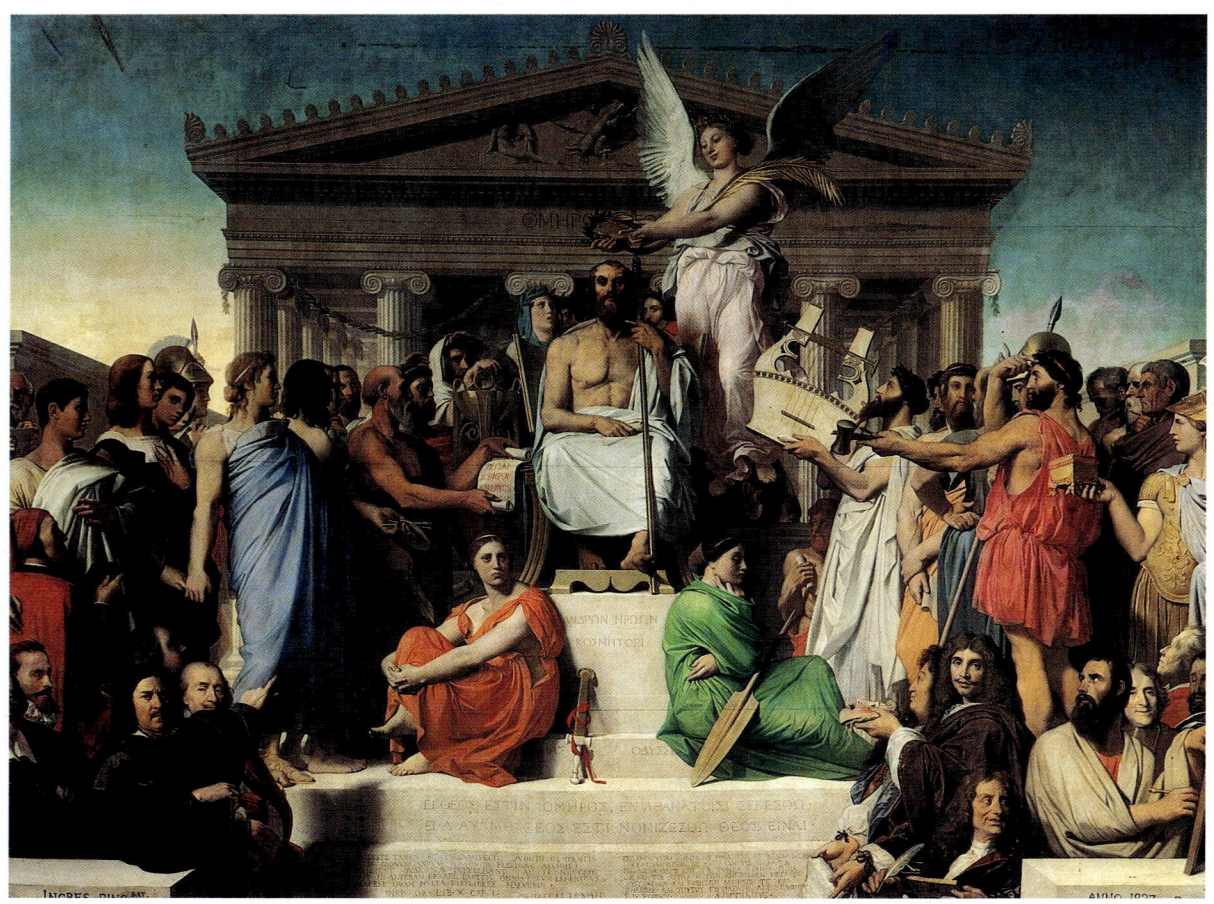

28-36 JEAN-AUGUSTE-DOMINIQUE INGRES, *Apotheosis of Homer*, 1827. Oil on canvas, approx. 12′ 8″ × 16′ 10¾″. Louvre, Paris.

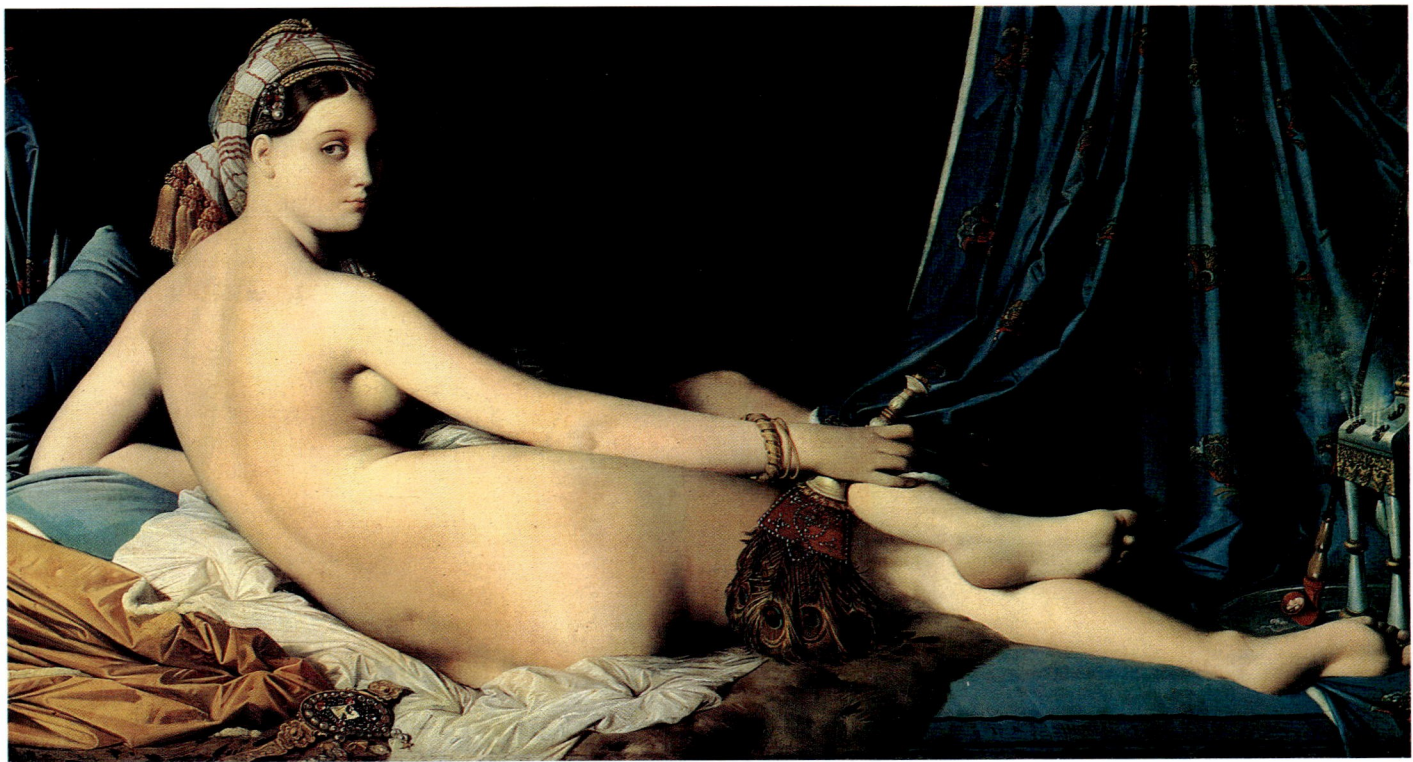

**28-37** Jean-Auguste-Dominique Ingres, *Grande Odalisque,* 1814. Oil on canvas, approx. 2′ 11″ × 5′ 4″. Louvre, Paris.

is *Grande Odalisque* (FIG. **28-37**). Ingres's subject, the reclining nude figure, is traditional enough and goes back to Giorgione and Titian (see FIG. 22-38). Further, the work shows his admiration for Raphael in his borrowing of that master's type of female head. The figure's languid pose, her proportions (small head and elongated limbs), and the generally cool color scheme also reveal his debt to such Mannerists as Parmigianino (see FIG. 22-43). However, by converting the figure to an odalisque (a member of a Turkish harem), the artist made a strong concession to the contemporary Romantic taste for the exotic.

This rather strange mixture of artistic allegiances — the combination of precise classical form and Romantic themes — prompted confusion, and when *Grande Odalisque* was first shown in 1814, the painting drew acid criticism. Critics initially saw Ingres as a kind of rebel in terms of both the form and content of his works; they did not cease their attacks until the mid-1820s, when another enemy of the official style, Eugène Delacroix, appeared. Then they suddenly perceived that Ingres's art, despite its innovations and deviations, still contained many elements that adhered to the official Neoclassicism — the taste for the ideal. Ingres soon led the academic forces in their battle against the "barbarism" of Théodore Géricault, Delacroix, and their "movement." Gradually, Ingres warmed to the role his critics had cast for him, and he came to see himself as the conservator of good and true art, a protector of its principles against its would-be destroyers.

## THE RISE OF ROMANTICISM

The appeal and applicability of Neoclassicism were truly extensive. Yet whereas Neoclassicism's rationality reinforced Enlightenment thought, particularly that promoted by Voltaire, Jean-Jacques Rousseau's ideas contributed to the rise of *Romanticism.* Rousseau's

exclamation, "Man is born free, but is everywhere in chains!" summarizes a fundamental premise of Romanticism. This declaration appeared in the opening line of his *Social Contract* (1762), a book many of those involved in the late-18th- and 19th-century revolutions carefully read and pondered. Romanticism emerged from a desire for freedom — not only political freedom but also freedom of thought, of feeling, of action, of worship, of speech, and of taste, as well as all the other freedoms. Romantics asserted that freedom is the right and property of one and all, though for each individual the kind or degree of freedom might vary.

Those who affiliated themselves with Romanticism believed that the path to freedom was through imagination rather than reason and functioned through feeling rather than through thinking. The allure of the Romantic spirit grew dramatically during the late 18th century. Since that time, scholars have debated the definition and the historical scope of Romanticism; to this day, the controversy has not ended. Many scholars refer to Romanticism as a phenomenon that began around 1750 and ended about 1850. The term is also used more narrowly to denote a movement that rose and declined in the course of modern art, flourishing from about 1800 to 1840, between Neoclassicism and Realism. This book discusses Romanticism in general terms first to explain the nature and appeal of this mind-set in the late 18th and early 19th centuries before dealing with the Romantic movement. Though Rousseau was the prophet of Romanticism, he never knew it as such. The term originated toward the end of the 18th century among German literary critics, who aimed to distinguish peculiarly "modern" traits from the Neoclassical traits that already had displaced Baroque and Rococo design elements.

The transition from Neoclassicism to Romanticism was manifested in a shift in emphasis from reason to feeling, from calculation to intuition, and from objective nature to subjective emotion. Among Romanticism's manifestations were the interests in the

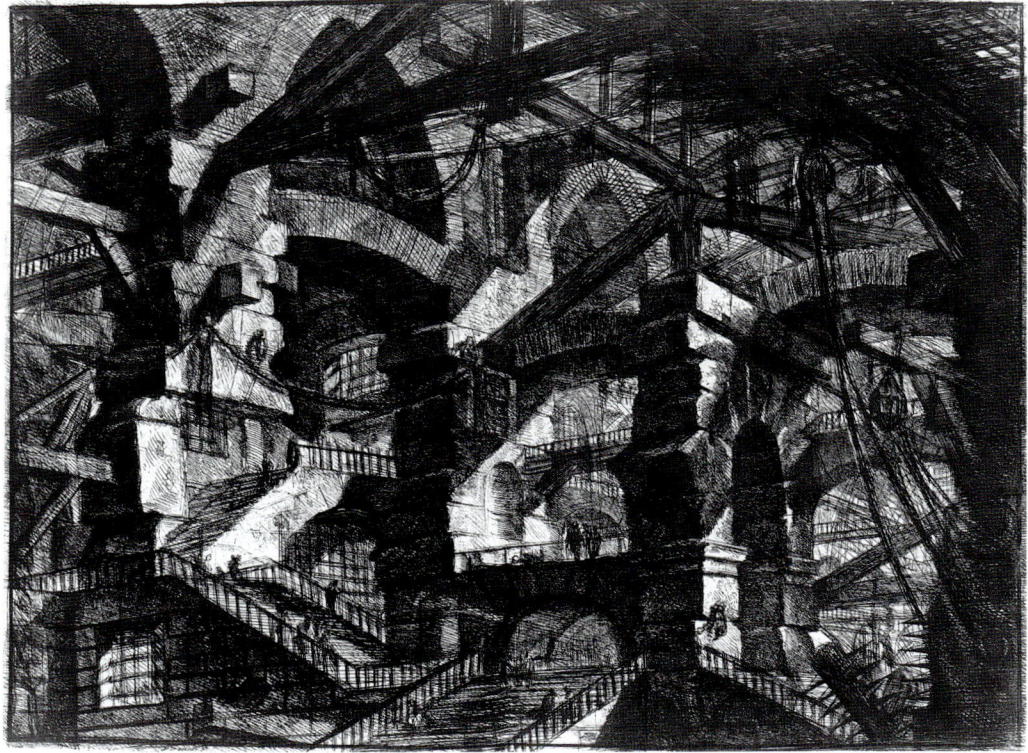

**28-38** Giovanni Battista Piranesi, *Carceri 14,* ca. 1750. Etching, second state, approx. 1′ 4″ × 1′ 9″. Ashmolean Museum, Oxford.

medieval period and in the sublime. For people living in the 18th century, the Middle Ages were the "dark ages," a time of barbarism, superstition, dark mystery, and miracle. The Romantic imagination stretched its perception of the Middle Ages into all the worlds of fantasy open to it, including the ghoulish, the infernal, the terrible, the nightmarish, the grotesque, the sadistic, and all the imagery that comes from the chamber of horrors when reason is asleep. Related to the imaginative sensibility was the period's notion of the sublime. Among the individuals most involved in studying the sublime was Edmund Burke (1729–1797), the British politician and philosopher. In his 1757 publication, *A Philosophical Enquiry into the Origins of Our Ideas of the Sublime and Beautiful,* Burke articulated his definition of the sublime — feelings of awe mixed with terror. Burke observed that the most intense human emotions are evoked by pain or fear and that when these emotions are distanced, they can be thrilling. Thus, raging rivers and great storms at sea can be sublime to their viewers. Accompanying this taste for the sublime was the taste for the fantastic, the occult, and the macabre — for the adventures of the soul voyaging into the dangerous reaches of consciousness.

**A CLAUSTROPHOBIC DUNGEON** A work that could illustrate Burke's theory of the sublime, laced with the infernal, is an etching (FIG. **28-38**) by Giovanni Battista Piranesi (1720–1778). It is the second state (a working version) of one of a series of prints of imaginary dungeons. In this series, titled *Carceri* (Prisons), Piranesi conjured awe-inspiring visions of bafflingly complicated architectural masses, piled high and spread out through gloomy spaces. The artist enhanced the complexity of the image by including a seeming infinity of massive arches, vaults, piers, and stairways. Small, insectlike human figures move stealthily through them. Despite the print's wandering, soaring perspectives, a suffocating sense of enclosure overwhelms the observer; the spaces are locked in, and no exit is visible. These grim places are filled with brooding menace and hopelessness. In this series of etchings, Piranesi often darkened subsequent editions to

make them even more sinister. Our picture, *Carceri 14,* is one of these. It reminds the viewer that the gaiety of the Rococo and the rationality of the Enlightenment coexisted with an 18th-century sensibility for the sublime that returned in the 19th century to haunt the night imaginings of many a Romantic artist and poet.

**A NIGHTMARISH VISION** The concept of the nightmare is specifically addressed in *The Nightmare* (FIG. **28-39**) by Henry Fuseli (1741–1825). Fuseli specialized in night moods of horror and in dark fantasies — in the demonic, in the macabre, and often in the sadistic. Swiss by birth, Fuseli settled in England and eventually became a member of the Royal Academy and an instructor there (see "The Academies," Chapter 29, page 862). Largely self-taught, he contrived a distinctive manner to express the fantasies of his vivid imagination. *The Nightmare* is one of four versions of this terrifying theme. The beautiful young woman lies asleep, draped across the bed with her limp arm dangling over the side. An incubus, a demon believed in medieval times to prey, often sexually, on sleeping women, squats ominously on her body. In the background, a ghostly horse with flaming eyes bursts into the scene from beyond the curtain. Despite the temptation to see the painting's title as a pun because of this horse, the word *nightmare* is actually derived from the words *night* and *mara*. Mara was a spirit in northern mythology that was thought to torment and suffocate sleepers. As disturbing and perverse as Fuseli's art may be, he was among the first to attempt to depict the dark terrain of the human subconscious that became fertile ground for the Romantic artists to harvest.

In their images of the sublime and the terrible, artists often combined something of Baroque dynamism with naturalistic details in their quest for grippingly moving visions. These preferences became the mainstay of Romantic art and contrasted with the more intellectual, rational Neoclassical themes and presentations. This is not to suggest that the two were mutually exclusive. As revealed in the earlier discussion of Gros, Girodet-Trioson, and Ingres, elements of Neoclassicism could be effectively integrated with Romanticism.

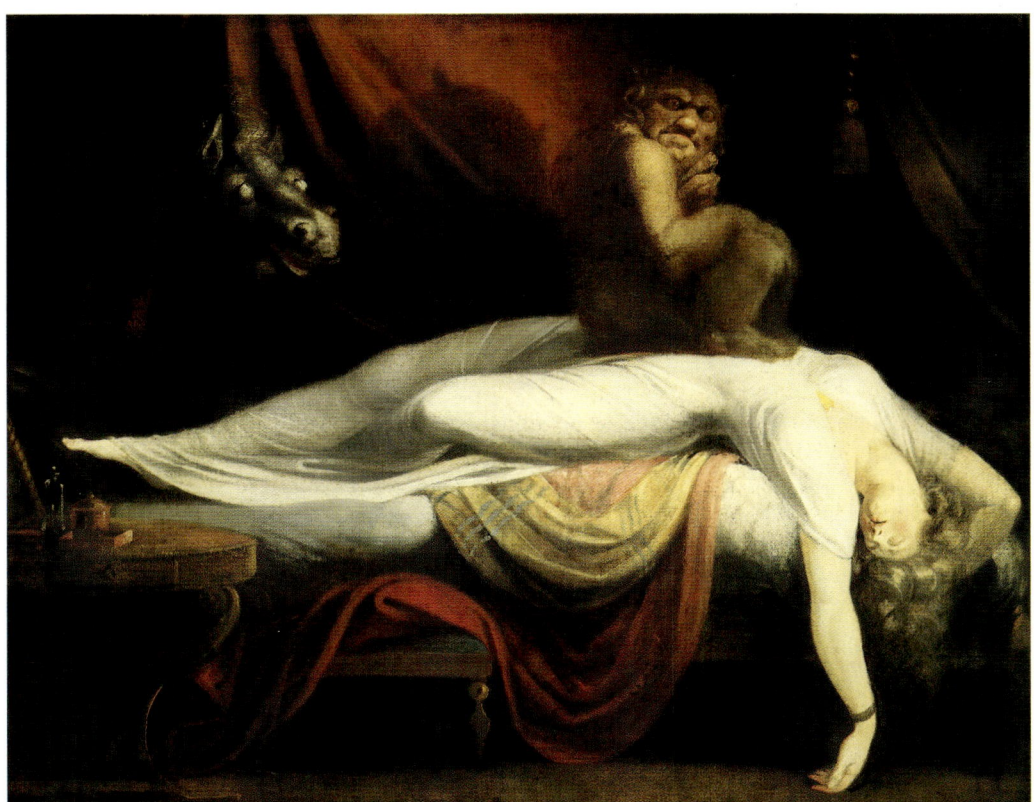

**INSPIRED BY THE SPIRITS** The visionary English poet, painter, and engraver WILLIAM BLAKE (1757–1827) is frequently classified as a Romantic artist. His work, however, incorporates classical references. Blake greatly admired ancient Greek art because for him it exemplified the mathematical and thus the eternal. Yet Blake did not align himself with prominent Enlightenment figures. Blake, like many other Romantic artists, also was drawn to the art of the Middle Ages. He derived the inspiration for many of his paintings and poems from his dreams. The importance he attached to these nocturnal experiences led him to believe that the rationalist search for material explanations of the world stifled the spiritual side of human nature. He also believed that the stringent rules of behavior imposed by orthodox religions killed the individual creative impulse. Blake's vision of the Almighty in *Ancient of Days* (FIG. **28-40**) combines his ideas and interests in a highly individual way. For Blake, this figure combined the concept of the Creator with that of wisdom as a part of God. *Ancient of Days,* printed as the frontispiece for Blake's book *Europe: A Prophecy,* was published with a quotation ("When he set a compass upon the face of the deep") from Proverbs 8:27 in the Old Testament. Most of that Bible chapter is spoken by Wisdom, identified as a female, who tells the reader how she was with the Lord through all the time of the Creation (Prov. 8:22–23, 27–30).

Energy fills Blake's composition. The Almighty leans forward from a fiery orb, peering toward earth and unleashing power through his outstretched left arm into twin rays of light. These emerge between his spread fingers like an architect's measuring instrument. A mighty wind surges through his thick hair and beard. Only the strength of his Michelangelesque physique keeps him firmly planted on his heavenly perch. Here, ideal classical anatomy merges with the inner dark dreams of Romanticism, which were expressed often in the 19th century. With his independence and individual artistic vision, Blake was very much a man of the modern age.

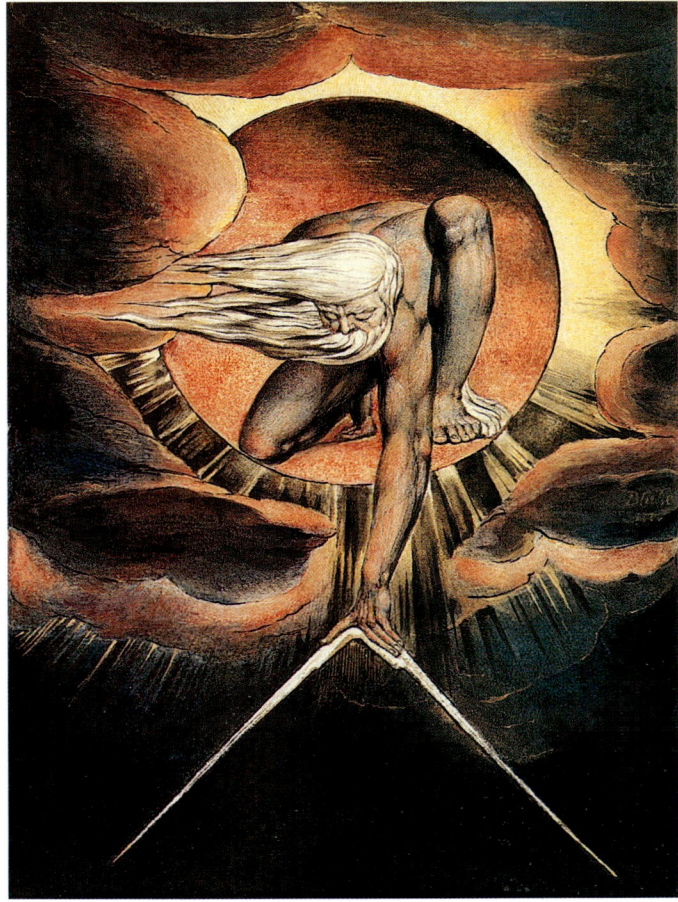

28-40 WILLIAM BLAKE, *Ancient of Days,* frontispiece of *Europe: A Prophecy,* 1794. Metal relief etching, hand colored, approx. $9\frac{1}{2}″ × 6\frac{3}{4}″$. The Whitworth Art Gallery, University of Manchester.

## Dramatic Action, Emotion, and Color

In the early 19th century, Romantic artists increasingly incorporated dramatic action, all the while extending their exploration of the exotic, erotic, fictional, or fantastic. One artist whose works reveal these compelling dimensions is the Spaniard FRANCISCO JOSÉ DE GOYA Y LUCIENTES (1746–1828). Goya was David's contemporary, but one scarcely could find two artists living at the same time and in adjacent countries who were so completely unlike each other.

**RECONSIDERING REASON** Goya did not arrive at his general dismissal of Neoclassicism without considerable thought about the Enlightenment and the Neoclassical penchant for rationality and order. This reflection emerges in such works as *The Sleep of Reason Produces Monsters* (FIG. **28-41**), an etching and aquatint from a series titled *Los Caprichos (The Caprices)*. In this print, Goya depicted himself asleep, slumped onto a table or writing stand, while threatening creatures converge on him. Seemingly poised to attack the artist are owls (symbols of folly) and bats (symbols of ignorance). The viewer might read this as a portrayal of what emerges when reason is suppressed and, therefore, as advocating Enlightenment ideals. However, it also can be interpreted as Goya's commitment to the creative process and the Romantic spirit—the unleashing of imagination, emotions, and even nightmares.

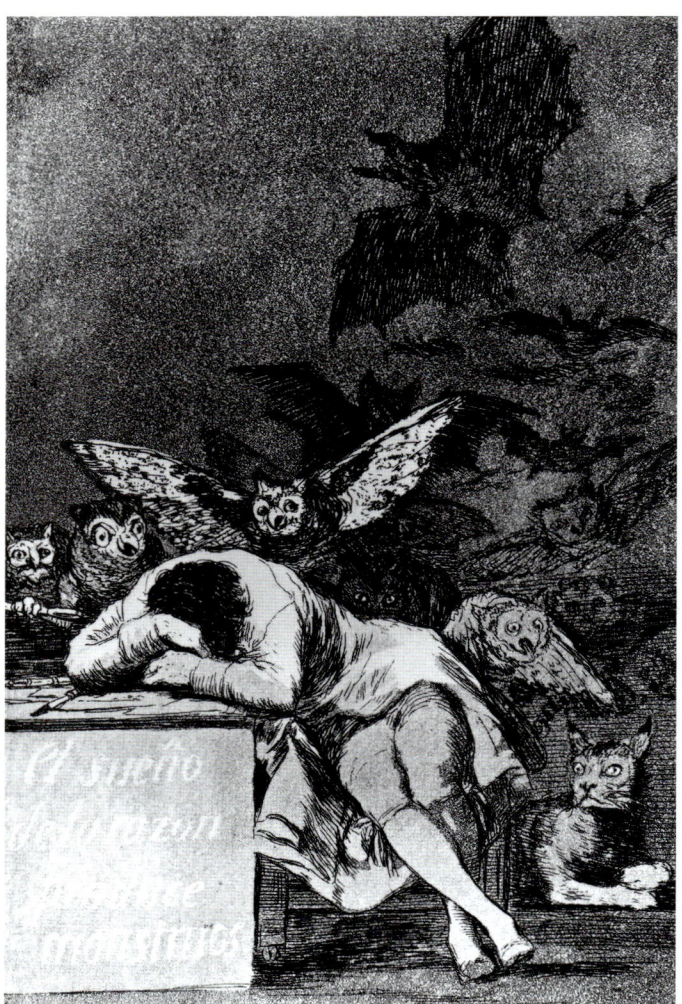

**28-41** FRANCISCO GOYA, *The Sleep of Reason Produces Monsters,* from *Los Caprichos,* ca. 1798. Etching and aquatint, $8\frac{7}{16}'' \times 5\frac{7}{8}''$. Metropolitan Museum of Art, New York (gift of M. Knoedler & Co., 1918).

**PORTRAIT OF SPANISH ROYALTY** The emotional art Goya produced during his long career stands as testimony not only to the allure of the Romantic vision but also to the turmoil in Spain and to the conflicts in Goya's own life. Goya's skills as a painter were recognized early on, and in 1786 he was appointed Pintor del Rey (Painter to the King). In this capacity (he was promoted to First Court Painter in 1799) Goya produced such works as *The Family of Charles IV* (FIG. **28-42**). Here King Charles IV and Queen Maria Luisa are surrounded by their children. As a court painter and artist enamored with the achievements of his predecessor Diego Velázquez, Goya appropriately used Velázquez's *Las Meninas* (see FIG. 24-33) as his inspiration for this image. As in *Las Meninas,* the royal family appears facing the viewer in an interior space while the artist included himself on the left, dimly visible, in the act of painting on a large canvas. Goya's portrait of the royal family has been subjected to intense scholarly scrutiny, resulting in a variety of interpretations. Some scholars see this painting as a naturalistic depiction of Spanish royalty; others believe it to be a pointed commentary in a time of Spanish turmoil. It is clear that his patrons authorized the painting's basic elements—the royal family members, their attire, and Goya's inclusion. Little evidence exists as to how this painting was received. Although some scholars have argued that the royal family was dissatisfied with the portrait, others have suggested that the painting confirmed the Spanish monarchy's continuing presence and strength and thus elicited a positive response from the patrons.

**TURMOIL IN SPAIN** As dissatisfaction with the rule of Charles IV and Maria Luisa increased, the political situation grew more tenuous. The Spanish people eventually threw their support behind Ferdinand VII, son of Charles IV and Maria Luisa, in the hope that he would initiate reform. To overthrow his father and mother, Ferdinand VII enlisted the aid of Napoleon Bonaparte, whose authority and military expertise in France at that time were uncontested. Napoleon had designs on the Spanish throne and thus willingly sent French troops to Spain. Not surprisingly, once Charles IV and Maria Luisa were ousted, Napoleon revealed his plan to rule Spain himself by installing his brother Joseph Bonaparte on the Spanish throne.

**THE MASSACRE OF MAY 3, 1808** The Spanish people, finally recognizing the French as invaders, sought a way to expel the foreign troops. On May 2, 1808, in frustration, the Spanish attacked the Napoleonic soldiers in a chaotic and violent clash. In retaliation and as a show of force, the French responded the next day by executing numerous Spanish citizens. This tragic event is the subject of Goya's most famous painting, *The Third of May, 1808* (FIG. **28-43**).

In emotional fashion, Goya depicted the anonymous murderous wall of Napoleonic soldiers ruthlessly executing the unarmed and terrified Spanish peasants. The artist encouraged empathy for the Spanish by portraying horrified expressions and anguish on their faces, endowing them with a humanity absent from the firing squad. Further, the peasant about to be shot throws his arms out in a cruciform gesture reminiscent of Christ's position on the cross.

Goya enhanced the drama of this event through his stark use of darks and lights. In addition, Goya's choice of imagery extended the time frame and thus heightened the emotion of the tragedy. Although the artist captured a specific moment when one man is about to be executed, others lie dead at his feet, their

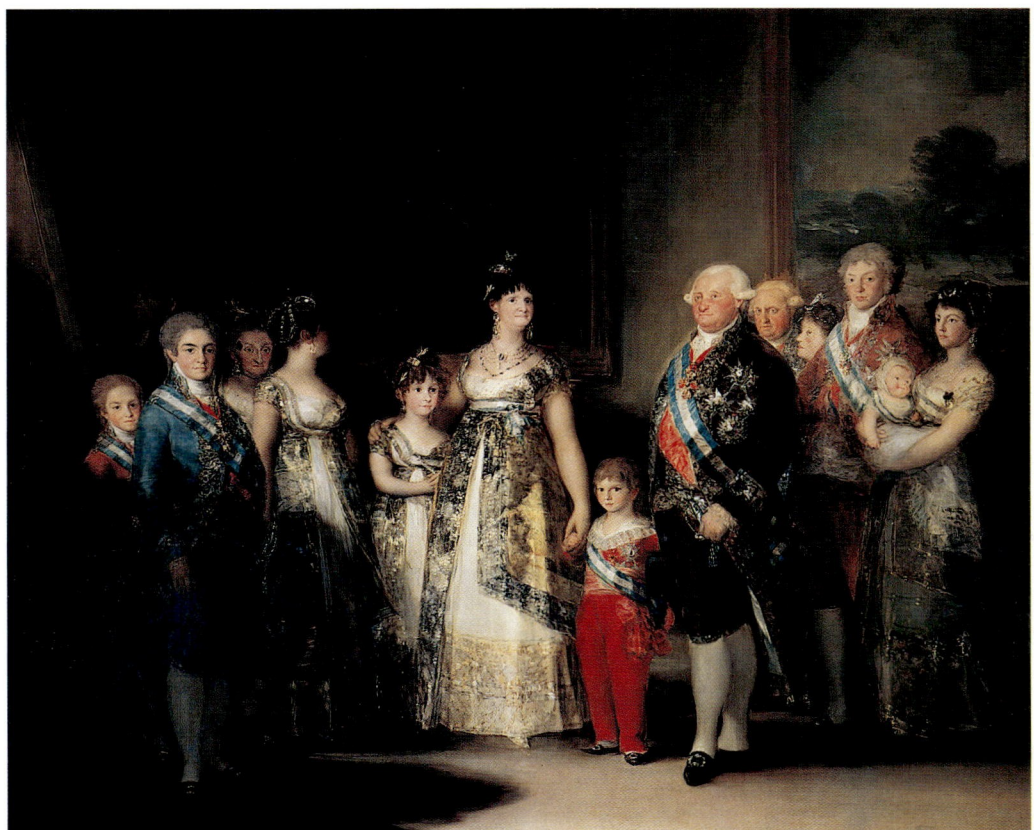

28-42 FRANCISCO GOYA, *The Family of Charles IV*, 1800. Oil on canvas, approx. 9′ 2″ × 11′. Museo del Prado, Madrid.

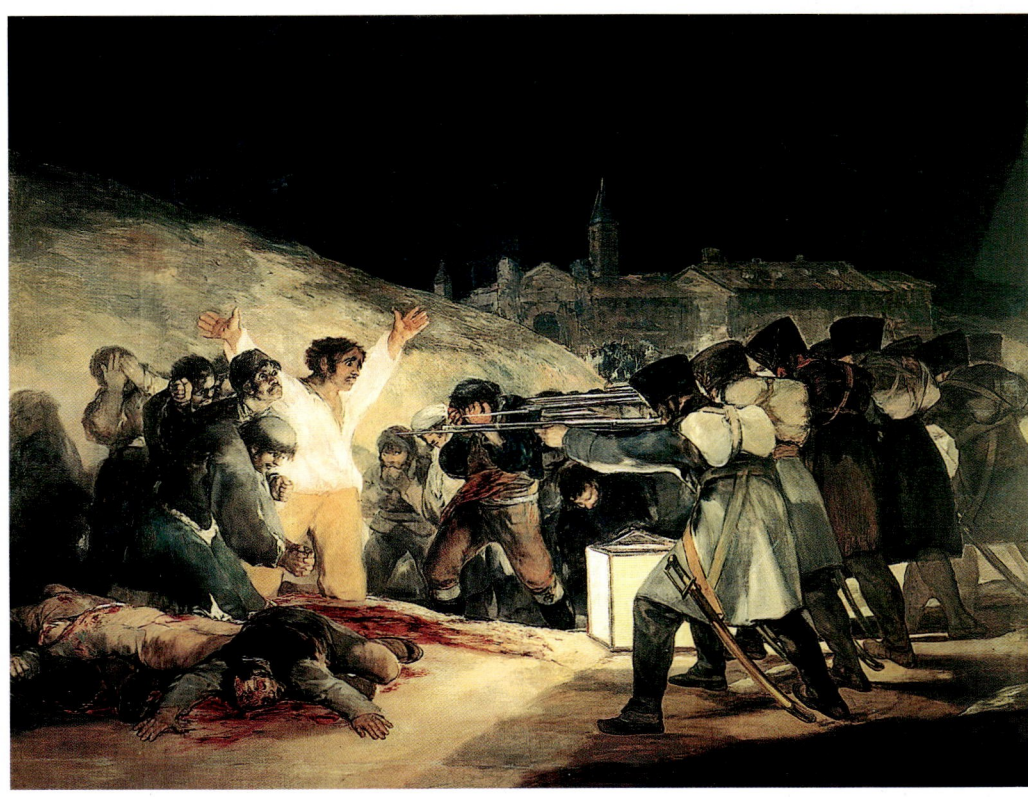

28-43 FRANCISCO GOYA, *The Third of May, 1808*, 1814. Oil on canvas, approx. 8′ 8″ × 11′ 3″. Museo del Prado, Madrid.

blood staining the soil of Príncipe Pío hill, and many others have been herded together to be subsequently shot.

Its depiction of the resistance and patriotism of the Spanish people notwithstanding, *The Third of May, 1808* was painted in 1814 for Ferdinand VII, who had been restored to the throne after the ouster of the French. Although the Spanish citizens had placed great faith in Ferdinand to install more democratic policies than were in place during the reign of his father, Charles IV, Ferdinand VII increasingly emulated his father, resulting in the restoration of an authoritarian monarchy.

Goya's work, rooted both in a personal and a national history, presents darkly emotional images well in keeping with Romanticism. The demons that haunted Goya emerged in his art. As historian Gwyn Williams nicely sums up: "As for the grotesque, the maniacal, the occult, the witchery, they are precisely the product of the sleep of *human* reason; they are *human* nightmares. *That these monsters are human is, indeed, the point.*"[9]

**DEATH AND DESPAIR ON A RAFT** In France, Théodore Géricault and Eugène Delacroix were the artists most closely associated with the Romantic movement. THÉODORE GÉRICAULT (1791–1824) studied with an admirer of David, P. N. Guérin (1774–1833). Although Géricault retained an interest in the heroic and the epic and was well trained in classical drawing, he chafed at the rigidity of the Neoclassical style, eventually producing works that captivate the viewer with their drama, visual complexity, and emotional force.

Géricault's most ambitious project was a large-scale painting (approximately 16 × 23 feet) titled *Raft of the Medusa* (FIG. **28-45**). In this depiction of an actual historical event, the artist abandoned the idealism of Neoclassicism and instead invoked the theatricality of Romanticism. The painting's subject is a shipwreck that took place in 1816 off the African coast. The French frigate *Medusa* ran aground on a reef due to the incompetence of the captain, a political appointee. As a last-ditch effort to survive, 150 of those remaining built a makeshift raft from the disintegrating ship. The raft drifted for 12 days, and the number of survivors dwindled to 15. Finally, the raft was spotted, and the emaciated survivors were rescued. This horrendous event was political dynamite once it became public knowledge.

In Géricault's huge painting, which took him eight months to complete, he sought to confront viewers with the horror, chaos, and emotion of the tragedy while invoking the grandeur and impact of large-scale history painting. He depicted the few weak, despairing survivors as they summon what little strength they have left to flag down the passing ship far on the horizon. Géricault departed from the straightforward organization of Neoclassical compositions and instead presented a jumble of writhing bodies. The survivors and several corpses are piled onto one another in every attitude of suffering, despair, and death (recalling Gros's *Napoleon,* FIG. 28-34) and are arranged in a powerful X-shaped composition. One light-filled diagonal axis stretches from bodies at the lower left up to the black man raised on his comrades' shoulders and waving a piece of cloth toward the horizon. The cross axis descends from the storm clouds and the dark, billowing sail at the upper left to the shadowed upper torso of the body trailing in the open sea. Géricault's decision to place the raft at a diagonal so that a corner juts out toward viewers further compels their participation in this scene. Indeed, it seems as though some of the corpses are sliding off the raft into the viewing space. The subdued palette and prominent shadows lend an ominous pall to the scene.

Despite the theatricality and dramatic action that imbues this work with a Romantic spirit, Géricault did in fact go to great lengths to ensure a degree of accuracy. He visited hospitals and morgues to examine corpses, interviewed the survivors, and had a model of the raft constructed in his studio.

Géricault also took this opportunity to insert a comment on the practice of slavery. The artist was a member of an abolitionist group that sought ways to end the slave trade in the colonies. Given Géricault's antipathy to slavery, it is appropriate that he placed Jean Charles, a black soldier and one of the few survivors, at the top of the pyramidal heap of bodies.

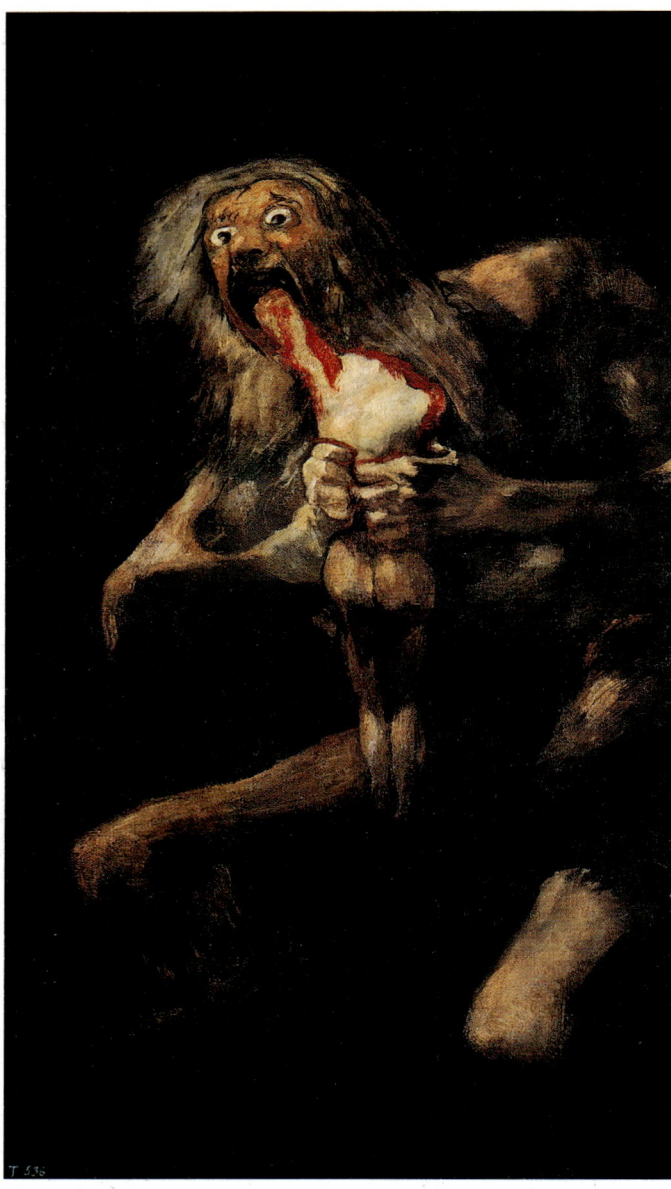

**28-44** FRANCISCO GOYA, *Saturn Devouring One of His Children,* 1819–1823. Detail of a detached fresco on canvas, full size approx. 4′ 9″ × 2′ 8″. Museo del Prado, Madrid.

**PAINTINGS OF DARK EMOTIONS** Over time, Goya became increasingly disillusioned and pessimistic; his declining health only contributed to this state of mind. Among his later works is a series of frescoes called the Black Paintings. Goya painted these frescoes on the walls of his farmhouse in Quinta del Sordo, outside Madrid. Because Goya created these works solely on his terms and for his viewing, one could argue that they provide great insight into the artist's outlook. If so, the vision is terrifying and disturbing. One of these Black Paintings, *Saturn Devouring One of His Children* (FIG. **28-44**), depicts the raw carnage and violence of Saturn (the Greek god Kronos; see "The Gods and Goddesses of Mount Olympus," Chapter 5, page 107, or page xiii in Volume II), wild-eyed and monstrous, as he consumes one of his children. Because of the similarity of Kronos and Khronos (the Greek word for "time"), Saturn has come to be associated with time. This has led some to interpret Goya's painting as an expression of the artist's despair over the passage of time. Despite the simplicity of the image, it conveys a wildness, boldness, and brutality that cannot help but evoke an elemental response from any viewer.

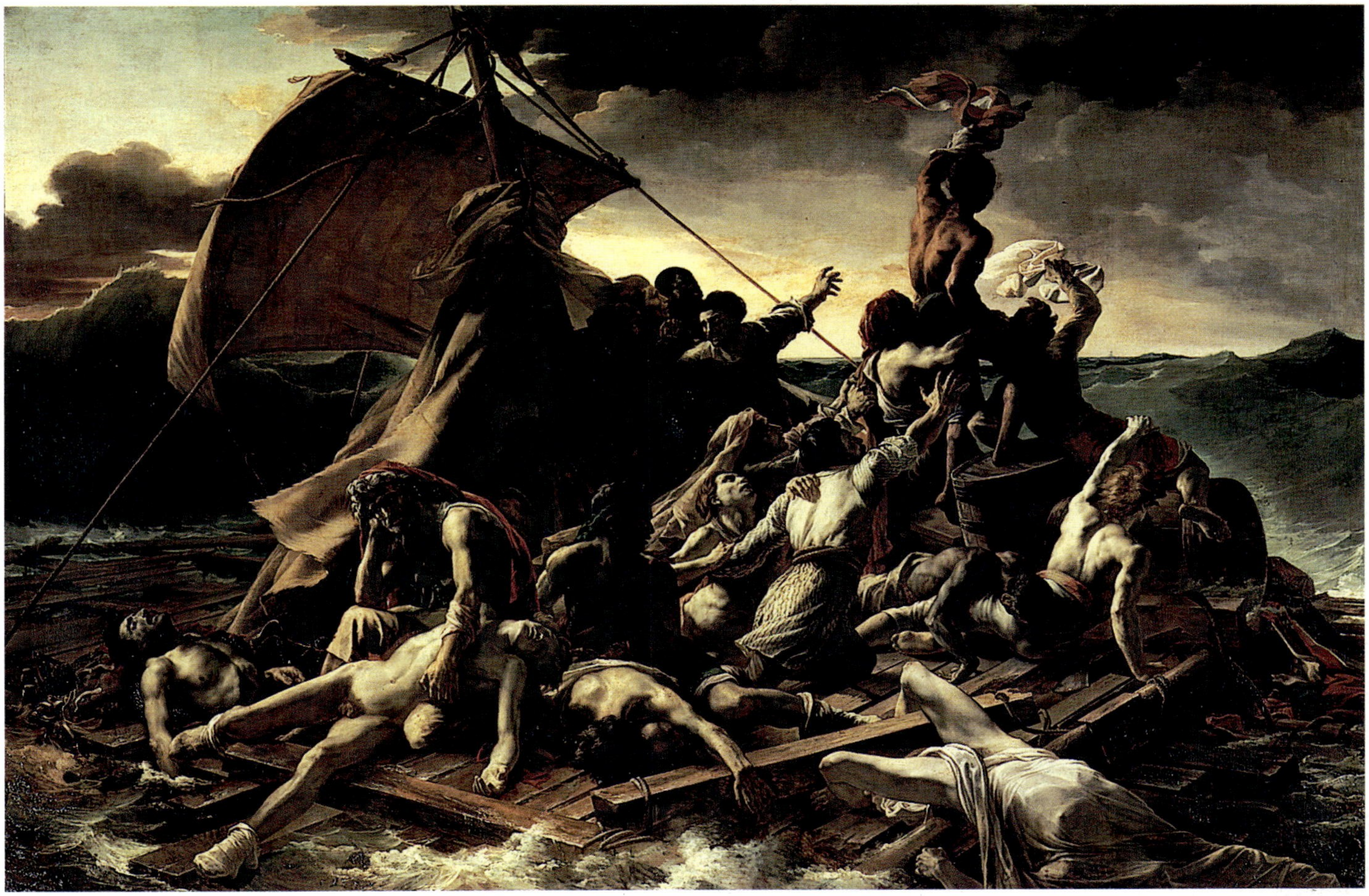

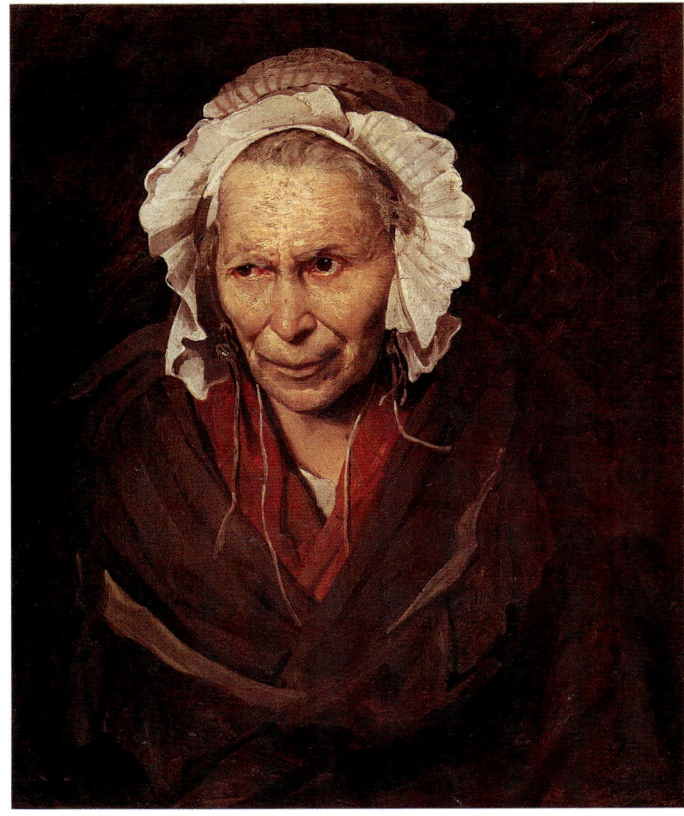

28-45 THÉODORE GÉRICAULT, *Raft of the Medusa*, 1818–1819. Oil on canvas, approx. 16′ × 23′. Louvre, Paris.

**PICTURING INSANITY** Mental aberration and irrational states of mind hardly could have failed to interest the rebels against Enlightenment rationality. Géricault, like many of his contemporaries, examined the influence of mental states on the human face and believed, as others did, that a face accurately revealed character, especially in madness and at the moment of death. He made many studies of the inmates of hospitals and institutions for the criminally insane, and he studied the severed heads of guillotine victims. Scientific and artistic curiosity was not easily separated from the morbidity of the Romantic interest in derangement and death. Géricault's *Insane Woman (Envy)*, FIG. 28-46 — her mouth tense, her eyes red-rimmed with suffering — is one of several of his portraits of insane subjects that have a peculiar hypnotic power. These portraits present the psychic facts with astonishing authenticity, especially in contrast to earlier idealized commissioned portraiture. The more the Romantics became involved with nature, sane or mad, the more they hoped to reach the truth.

**LINE VERSUS COLOR** Like Géricault, Delacroix is consistently invoked in discussions of Romanticism. The history of 19th-century painting in its first 60 years often has been interpreted as a contest between two major artists — Ingres the draftsman and EUGÈNE DELACROIX (1798–1863) the colorist. Their dialogue harked back to the quarrel between the Poussinistes and the Rubénistes at the end of the 17th century. As discussed earlier, the Poussinistes were conservative defenders of academism who held drawing as superior to color, whereas the Rubénistes proclaimed the importance of color over line (line quality being

28-46 THÉODORE GÉRICAULT, *Insane Woman (Envy)*, 1822–1823. Oil on canvas, approx. 2′ 4″ × 1′ 9″. Musée des Beaux-Arts, Lyon.

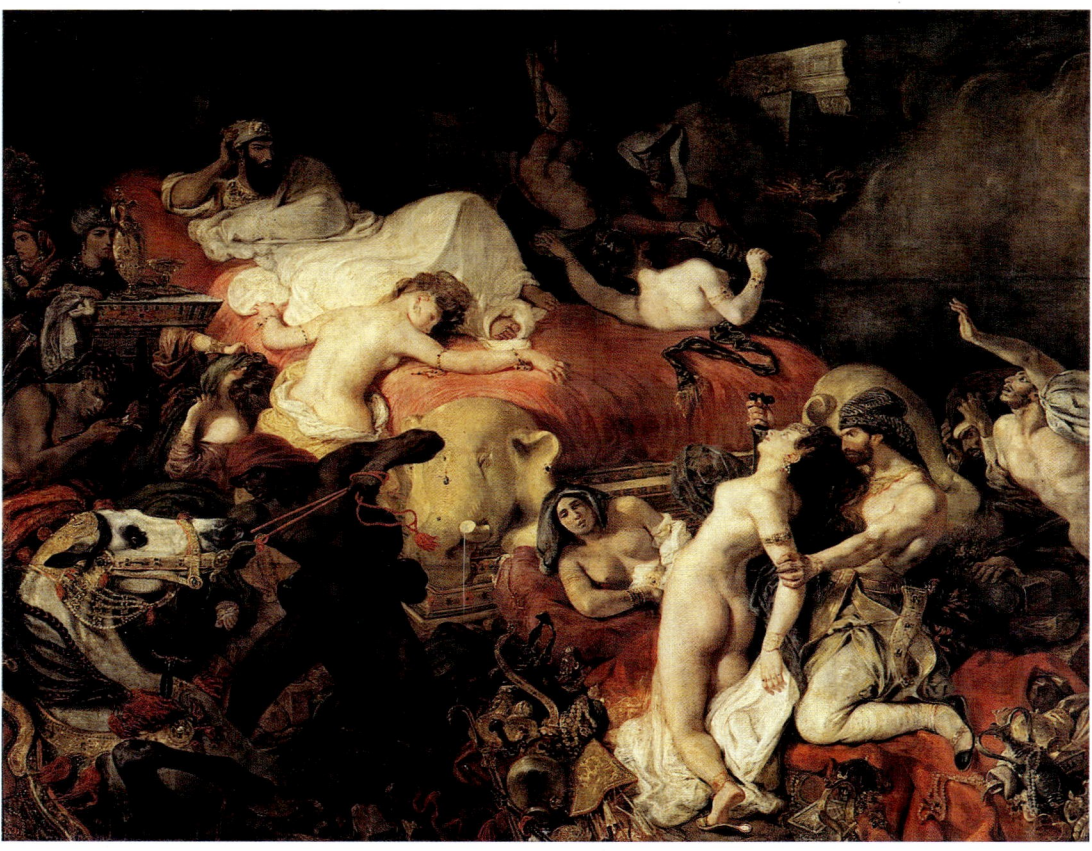

**28-47** EUGÈNE DELACROIX, *Death of Sardanapalus,* 1826. Oil on canvas, approx. 12′ 1″ × 16′ 3″. Louvre, Paris.

more intellectual and thus more restrictive than color). Although the differences between Ingres and Delacroix are clear, it is impossible to make categorical statements about any artist. As shown, Ingres's work, though steeped in Neoclassical tradition, does incorporate elements of Romanticism. In the end, Ingres and his great rival Delacroix complemented rather than contradicted each other. Their works stand as visual expressions of the great Neoclassical and Romantic dialogue.

**INSPIRING FICTION AND VERSE** Delacroix's works were products of his view that the artist's powers of imagination would in turn capture and inflame the viewer's imagination. Literature of imaginative power served Delacroix (and many of his contemporaries) as a useful source of subject matter. Théophile Gautier, the prominent Romantic critic and novelist, recalled:

> In those days painting and poetry fraternized. The artists read the poets, and the poets visited the artists. We found Shakespeare, Dante, Goethe, Lord Byron and Walter Scott in the studio as well as in the study. There were as many splashes of color as there were blots of ink in the margins of those beautiful books which we endlessly perused. Imagination, already excited, was further fired by reading those foreign works, so rich in color, so free and powerful in fantasy.[10]

**ORGIASTIC DESTRUCTION** Delacroix's *Death of Sardanapalus* (FIG. **28-47**) is an example of pictorial grand drama. Undoubtedly, Delacroix was inspired by Lord Byron's 1821 narrative poem *Sardanapalus,* but the painting does not illustrate that text (see "The Romantic Spirit in Music and Literature," page 835). Instead, Delacroix depicted the last hour of the Assyrian king (who received news of his armies' defeat and the enemies' entry into his city) in a much more tempestuous and crowded setting than Byron described. Here, orgiastic destruction replaces the sacrificial suicide found in the poem. In the painting, the king watches

gloomily from his funeral pyre, soon to be set alight, as all of his most precious possessions—his women, slaves, horses, and treasure—are destroyed in his sight. Sardanapalus's favorite concubine throws herself on the bed, determined to go up in flames with her master. The king presides like a genius of evil over the panorama of destruction. Most conspicuous are the tortured and dying bodies of the harem women. In the foreground, a muscular slave plunges his knife into the neck of one woman. This spectacle of suffering and death is heightened by the most daringly difficult and tortuous poses and by the richest intensities of hue. With its exotic and erotic overtones, *Death of Sardanapalus* taps into the fantasies of both the artist and some viewers.

**LEADING THE MASSES IN UPRISING** Although *Death of Sardanapalus* reveals Delacroix's fertile imagination, like Géricault he also turned to current events, particularly tragic or sensational ones, for his subject matter. For example, he produced several images based on the Greek War for Independence (1821–1829). Certainly, the French perception of the Greeks locked in a brutal struggle for freedom from the cruel and exotic Ottoman Turks generated great interest. Closer to home, Delacroix captured the passion and energy of the Revolution of 1830 in his painting *Liberty Leading the People* (FIG. **28-48**). Based on the Parisian uprising against the rule of Charles X at the end of July 1830, it depicts the allegorical personification of Liberty defiantly thrusting forth the republic's tricolor banner as she urges the masses to fight on. The urgency of this struggle is reinforced by the scarlet Phrygian cap (the symbol of a freed slave in antiquity) she wears. Arrayed around her are bold Parisian types—the street boy brandishing his pistols, the menacing worker with a cutlass, and the intellectual dandy in top hat with sawed-off musket. As in Géricault's *Raft of the Medusa,* dead bodies are strewn about. In the background, the towers of Notre-Dame rise through

## The Romantic Spirit in Music and Literature

The appeal of Romanticism, with its emphasis on freedom and feeling, extended well beyond the realm of the visual arts. In European music, literature, and poetry, the Romantic spirit was a dominant presence during the late 18th and early 19th centuries. These artistic endeavors rejected classicism's structured order in favor of the emotive and expressive. In music, the compositions of Franz Schubert (1797–1828), Franz Liszt (1811–1886), Frédéric Chopin (1810–1849), and Johannes Brahms (1833–1897) all emphasized the melodic or lyrical. These composers believed that music had the power to express the unspeakable and to communicate the subtlest and most powerful human emotions.

In literature, Romantic poets such as John Keats (1795–1821), William Wordsworth (1770–1850), and Samuel Taylor Coleridge (1772–1834) published volumes of poetry that serve as manifestations of the Romantic interest in lyrical drama. *Ozymandias,* by Percy Bysshe Shelley (1792–1822), speaks of faraway, exotic locales. Lord Byron's poem of 1821, *Sardanapalus,* is set in the kingdom of Assyria in the seventh century BCE. It conjures images of eroticism and fury unleashed—images that appear in

Delacroix's painting *Death of Sardanapalus* (FIG. 28-47). One of the best examples of the Romantic spirit is the engrossing novel *Frankenstein,* written in 1818 by Mary Wollstonecraft Shelley (1797–1851), who was married to Romantic poet Percy Bysshe Shelley. This fantastic tale of a monstrous creature run amok is filled with drama and remains popular to the present. As was true of many Romantic artworks, this novel not only embraces the emotional but also rejects the rationalism that underlay Enlightenment thought. Dr. Frankenstein's monster was a product of science, and this novel easily could have been interpreted as an indictment of the tenacious belief in science promoted by Enlightenment thinkers such as Voltaire. *Frankenstein* thus served as a cautionary tale of the havoc that could result from unrestrained scientific experimentation and from the arrogance of scientists like Dr. Frankenstein.

The imagination and vision that characterized Romantic paintings and sculptures were equally moving and riveting in musical or written form. The sustained energy of Romanticism is proof of the captivating nature of this movement and spirit.

---

the smoke and haze. The painter's inclusion of this recognizable Parisian landmark announces the specificity of locale and event. It also reveals Delacroix's attempt, like that of Géricault in *Raft,* to balance contemporary historical fact with poetic allegory (Liberty). This desire for balance is further revealed in the Salon title of this work, *The 28th of July: Liberty Leading the People.*

**THE ALLURE OF MOROCCO** An enormously influential event in Delacroix's life that affected his art in both subject and form was his visit to North Africa in 1832. Things he saw there shocked his imagination with fresh impressions that lasted throughout his life. He discovered, in the sun-drenched landscape and in the hardy and colorful Moroccans dressed in robes reminiscent of the Roman

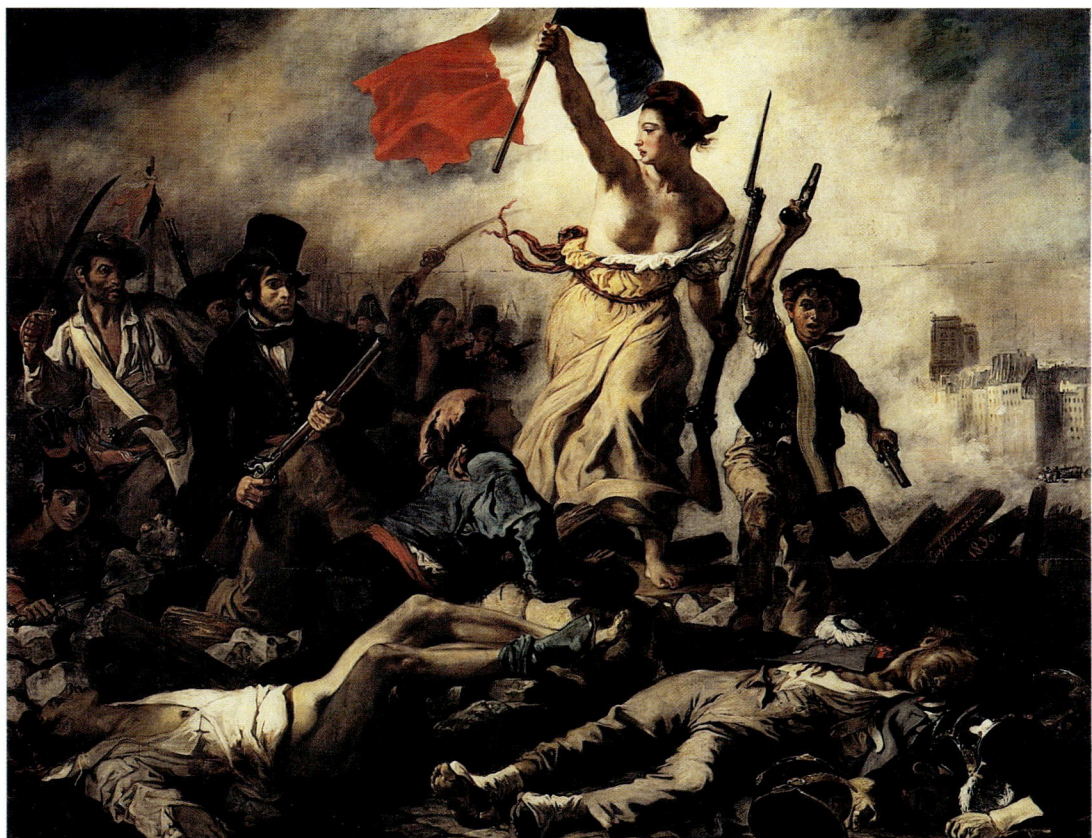

**28-48** EUGÈNE DELACROIX, *Liberty Leading the People,* 1830. Oil on canvas, approx. 8′ 6″ × 10′ 8″. Louvre, Paris.

**28-49** EUGÈNE DELACROIX, *Tiger Hunt*, 1854. Oil on canvas, approx. 2′ 5″ × 3′. Louvre, Paris.

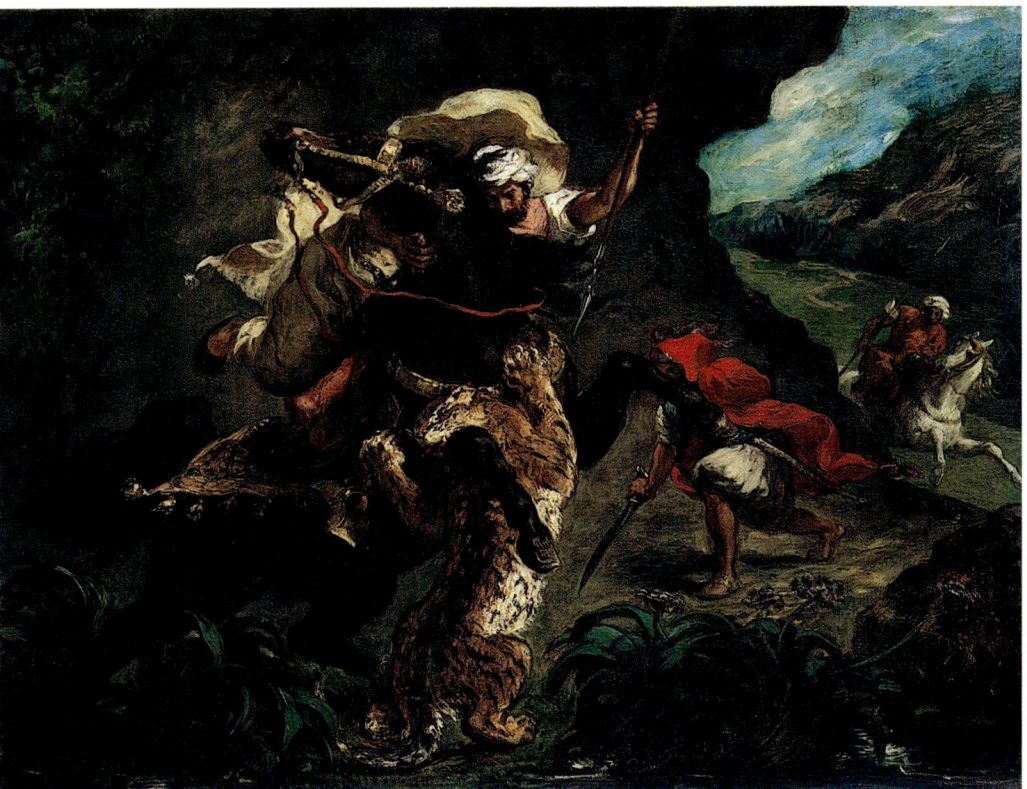

toga, new insights into a culture built on proud virtues. He believed it was a culture more classical than anything European Neoclassicism could conceive. "I have Romans and Greeks on my doorstep," he wrote to a friend, "it makes me laugh heartily at David's Greeks."[11] Their gallantry, valor, and fierce love of liberty made the Moroccans, in Delacroix's eyes, "nature's noblemen" — unspoiled heroes uninfected by European decadence.

The Moroccan journey renewed Delacroix's Romantic conviction that beauty exists in the fierceness of nature, natural processes, and natural beings, especially animals. After Morocco, more and more of Delacroix's subjects involved combats between beasts and between beasts and men. He painted snarling tangles of lions and tigers, battles between horses, and clashes of Muslims with great cats in swirling hunting scenes using compositions reminiscent of those of Rubens. One such work, *Tiger Hunt* (FIG. **28-49**), clearly speaks to the Romantic interest in faraway lands and exotic cultures.

**DELACROIX'S COLORFUL LEGACY** Delacroix's African experience also further heightened his already considerable awareness of the expressive power of color and light. What Delacroix knew about color he passed on to later painters of the 19th century, particularly the Impressionists. He observed that pure colors are as rare in nature as lines and that color appears only in an infinitely varied scale of different tones, shadings, and reflections, which he tried to re-create in his paintings. He recorded his observations in his journal, which became a veritable body of knowledge of pre-Impressionist color theory and was acclaimed as such by the Post-Impressionist painter Paul Signac. Delacroix anticipated the later development of Impressionist color science. But that art-science had to await the discoveries by Michel Eugène Chevreul and Hermann von Helmholtz of the laws of light decomposition and the properties of complementary colors before the problems of color perception and juxtaposition in painting could be properly formulated (see "19th-Century Color Theory," Chapter 29, page 883). Nevertheless, Delacroix's observations were significant, and he

advised other artists not to fuse their brush strokes, as the brush strokes would appear to fuse naturally from a distance.

**A FURIOUS IMAGINATION** No other painter of the time explored the domain of Romantic subject and mood as thoroughly and definitively as Delacroix. Delacroix's technique was impetuous, improvisational, and instinctive, rather than deliberate, studious, and cold. It epitomized Romantic colorist painting, catching the impression quickly and developing it in the execution process. His contemporaries commented on how furiously Delacroix worked once he had an idea, keeping the whole painting progressing at once. The fury of his attack matched the fury of his imagination and his subjects.

## The Dramatic in Sculpture

**AN ALLEGORY OF FRENCH TRIUMPH** As one might expect, the Romantic spirit pervaded all media during the early 19th century. Many sculptors, like the painters of the period, produced work that incorporated both Neoclassical and Romantic elements. The colossal group *La Marseillaise* (FIG. **28-50**), mounted on one face of Chalgrin's Arc de Triomphe in Paris, is one such sculpture. Its creator, FRANÇOIS RUDE (1784–1855), carved here an allegory of the national glories of revolutionary France by depicting the volunteers of 1792 departing to defend the nation's borders against the foreign enemies of the revolution. The Roman goddess of war, Bellona (who here personifies liberty as well as the revolutionary hymn, now France's national anthem), soars above patriots of all ages, exhorting them forward with her thundering battle cry. The figures recall David's classically armored (FIG. 28-21) or nude heroes, as do the rhetorical gestures of the wide-flung arms and the striding poses. Yet the violence of motion, the jagged contours, and the densely packed, overlapping masses relate more closely to the compositional method of dramatic Romanticism, as

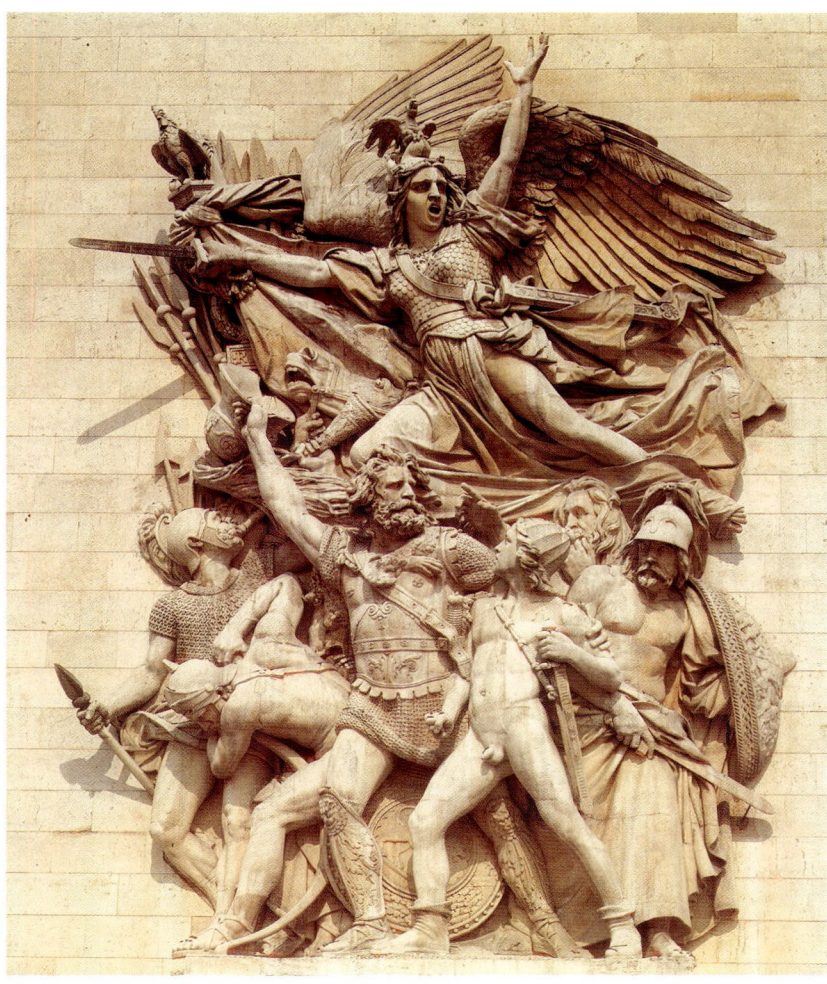

**28-50** FRANÇOIS RUDE, *La Marseillaise,* Arc de Triomphe, Paris, France, 1833–1836. Approx. 42′ × 26′.

found in Géricault (FIG. 28-45) and Delacroix (FIG. 28-48). The allegorical figure in *La Marseillaise* is the spiritual sister of Delacroix's Liberty (FIG. 28-48); they share the same Phrygian cap, the badge of liberty. But although the works are almost exactly contemporaneous, the figures in the sculpted group are represented in classical costume, whereas those in Delacroix's painting wear modern Parisian costumes. Both works are allegorical, but one looks to the past and the other to the present.

**THE FEROCITY OF ANIMALS** Delacroix's fascination with raw beauty and bestial violence is echoed in *Jaguar Devouring a Hare* (FIG. **28-51**), a much smaller group in bronze by ANTOINE-LOUIS BARYE (1795–1875). Painful as the subject is, Barye's work draws the viewer irresistibly by its fidelity to brute nature. The cat's swelling muscles, hunched shoulders, and tense spine— even the switch of the tail—tell of the sculptor's long sessions observing the animals in the Jardin des Plantes, the Parisian zoo. The jaguar's contracted muscles contrast with the limp body of the dead hare that hangs from the cat's jaws. Yet even the hare's carcass reveals Barye's careful observation of its anatomy and faithful rendering of its fur. This work demonstrates the Romantic obsession with strong emotion and untamed nature.

**28-51** ANTOINE-LOUIS BARYE, *Jaguar Devouring a Hare,* 1850–1851. Bronze, approx. 1′ 4″ × 3′ 1″. Louvre, Paris.

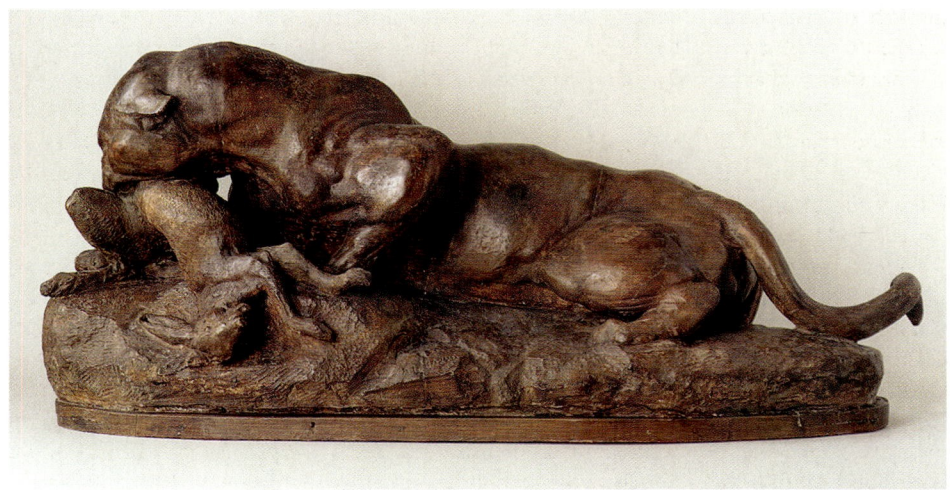

Nineteenth-century sensibility generally prevented humans from showing animal ferocity themselves but enthusiastically accepted its portrayal in Romantic depictions of wild beasts.

## IMAGINATION AND MOOD IN LANDSCAPE PAINTING

Landscape painting came into its own in the 19th century as a fully independent and respected genre. Briefly eclipsed at the century's beginning by the taste for ideal form, which favored figural composition and history, landscape painting flourished as leading painters made it their profession. Expanding tourism, which was facilitated by improving and expanding railway systems, contributed to the popularity of landscape painting.

The notion of the picturesque became particularly resonant during the 19th century. The 18th-century artists had regarded the pleasurable, aesthetic mood that natural landscape inspired as making the landscape itself "picturesque"—that is, worthy of being painted. Early on, they considered the "natural" English garden to be picturesque. Later, the sensitive Romantic translated landscape vistas, colored by the viewer's mood, into aesthetic form—poetry or painting. Rather than simply describe nature, poets and artists often used nature as allegory. In this manner, artists commented on spiritual, moral, historical, or philosophical issues. Landscape painting was a particularly effective vehicle for such commentary because it allowed artists to "naturalize" conditions—that is, make such conditions appear normal, acceptable, or inevitable.

### Landscape Painting in Germany

In the early 19th century, most northern European (especially German) landscape painting to some degree expressed the Romantic, pantheistic view (first extolled by Rousseau) of nature as a "being" that included the totality of existence in organic unity and harmony. In nature—"the living garment of God," as German poet and dramatist Johann Wolfgang von Goethe called it—artists found an ideal subject to express the Romantic theme of the soul unified with the natural world. As all nature was mysteriously permeated by being, landscape artists had the task of interpreting the signs, symbols, and emblems of universal spirit disguised within visible material things. Artists no longer merely beheld a landscape, but rather participated in its spirit. No longer were they painters of mere things but instead were translators of nature's transcendent meanings, arrived at through the feelings that landscapes inspired.

**THE REVERENTIAL LANDSCAPE** CASPAR DAVID FRIEDRICH (1774–1840) was among the first northern European artists to depict the Romantic transcendental landscape. For Friedrich, landscapes were temples; his paintings themselves were altarpieces. The reverential mood of his works demands from the viewer the silence appropriate to sacred places filled with a divine presence. *Abbey in the Oak Forest* (FIG. **28-52**) is like a solemn requiem. Under a winter sky, through the leafless oaks of a snow-covered cemetery, a funeral procession bears a coffin into the ruins of a Gothic church that Friedrich based on the remains of Eldana Abbey in Greifswald. The emblems of death are everywhere—the season's desolation, the leaning crosses and tombstones, the black of mourning worn by the grieving, the skeletal trees, and the destruction that time wrought on the church. The painting is a kind of meditation on human mortality. As Friedrich himself remarked: "Why, it has often occurred to me to ask myself, do I so frequently choose death, transience, and the grave as subjects for my paintings? One must submit oneself many times to death in order some day to attain life everlasting."[12] The artist's sharp-focused rendering of details demonstrates his keen perception of everything in the physical environment relevant to his message. Friedrich's work balances inner and outer experience. "The artist," he wrote, "should not only paint what he sees before him, but also what he sees within him."[13] Although Friedrich's works may not have the theatrical energy of the paintings of Géricault or Delacroix, they are pervaded by a resonant and deep emotion.

**28-52** CASPAR DAVID FRIEDRICH, *Abbey in the Oak Forest*, 1810. Oil on canvas, 3′ 7½″ × 5′ 7¼″. Staatliche Museen au Berlin-Preussischer Kulturbesitz, Nationalgalerie.

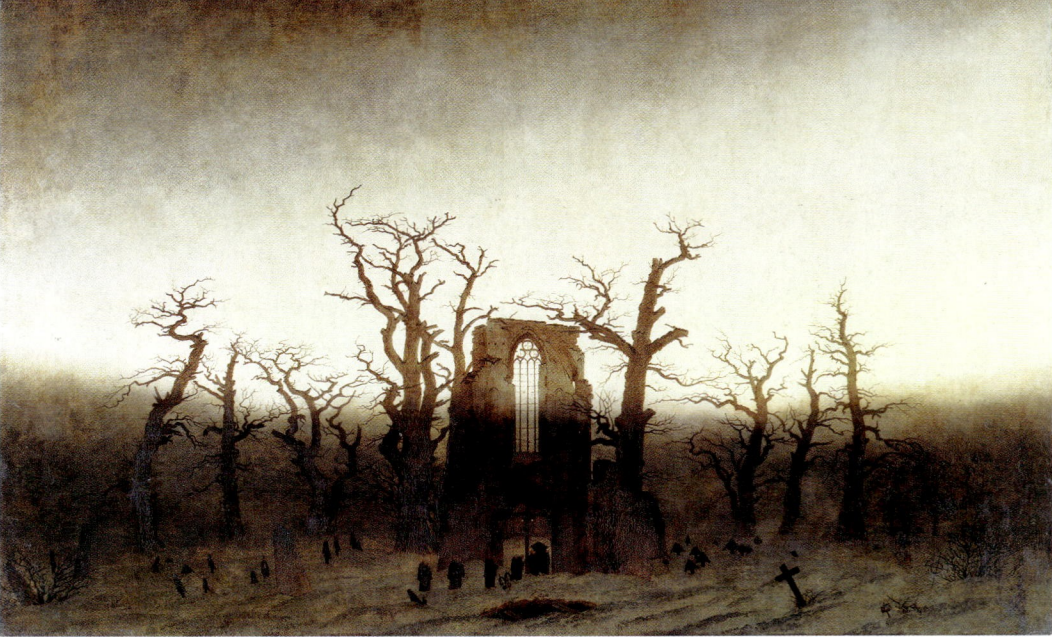

## Landscape Painting in England

One of the most momentous developments in Western history — the Industrial Revolution — impacted the evolution of Romantic landscape painting in England. Although discussion of the Industrial Revolution invariably focuses on technological advances, factory development, and growth of urban centers, its effect on the countryside and the land itself was no less severe. The detrimental economic impact industrialization had on the prices for agrarian products produced significant unrest in the English countryside. In particular, increasing numbers of displaced farmers could no longer afford to farm their small land plots.

**NOSTALGIA FOR AGRARIAN ENGLAND** This situation is addressed in the landscape paintings of JOHN CONSTABLE (1776–1837), perhaps the best known of the English landscape artists. *The Haywain* (FIG. **28-53**) is representative of Constable's art and reveals much about his outlook. In this large painting, Constable presented a placid, picturesque scene of the countryside. A small cottage sits on the left, and in the center foreground a man leads a horse and wagon across the stream. Billowy clouds float lazily across the sky, and the scene's tranquility is augmented by the muted greens and golds and by the delicacy of Constable's brush strokes. The artist portrayed the oneness with nature that the Romantic poets sought; the relaxed figures are not observers but participants in the landscape's being. Constable made countless studies from nature for each of his canvases, which helped him produce in his paintings the convincing sense of reality praised by his contemporaries. In his quest for the authentic landscape, Constable studied it as a meteorologist (which he was by avocation). His special gift was for capturing the texture that the atmosphere (the climate and the weather, which delicately veil what is seen) gave to landscape. Constable's use of tiny dabs of local color, stippled with white, created a sparkling shimmer of light and hue across the canvas surface — the vibration itself suggestive of movement and process.

*The Haywain* is also significant for precisely what it does not show — the civil unrest of the agrarian working class and the outbreaks of violence and arson that resulted. Indeed, this painting has a nostalgic, wistful air to it. To a certain extent, this scene (although carefully detailed) is linked to Constable's memories of a disappearing rural pastoralism. The artist came from a family of considerable wealth; his father was a rural landowner, and many of the scenes Constable painted (*The Haywain* included) depict his family's property near East Bergholt in Suffolk, East Anglia.

The people that populate Constable's landscapes blend into the scenes and are at one with nature. Rarely does the viewer see workers engaged in tedious labor. This nostalgia, presented in such naturalistic terms, renders Constable's works Romantic in tone. That Constable felt a kindred spirit with the Romantic artists is revealed by his comment, "painting is but another word for feeling."[14]

**THE HORRORS OF THE SLAVE TRADE** JOSEPH MALLORD WILLIAM TURNER (1775–1851), Constable's contemporary in the English school of landscape painting, produced work that also

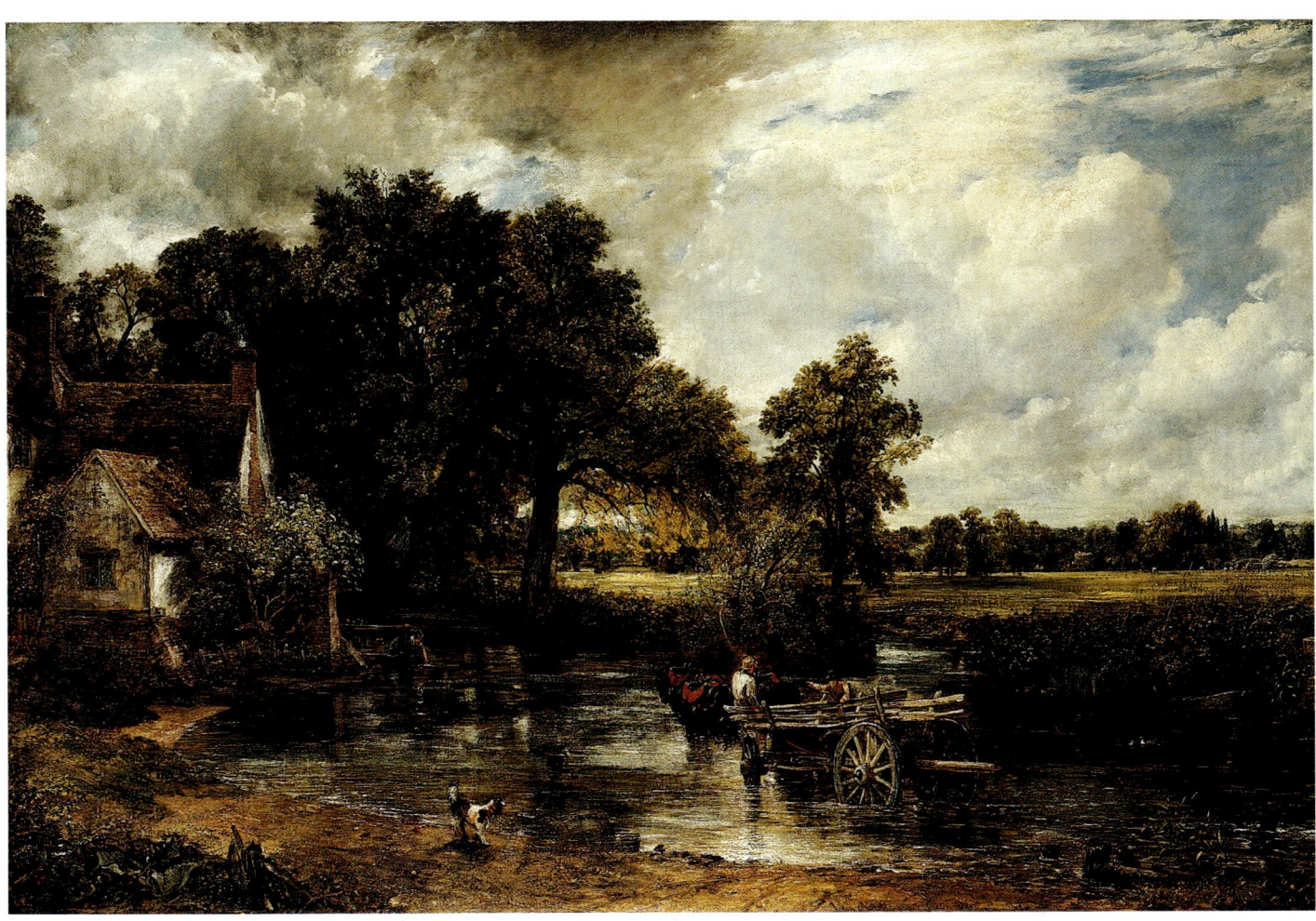

**28-53** JOHN CONSTABLE, *The Haywain*, 1821. Oil on canvas, 4′ 3″ × 6′ 2″. National Gallery, London.

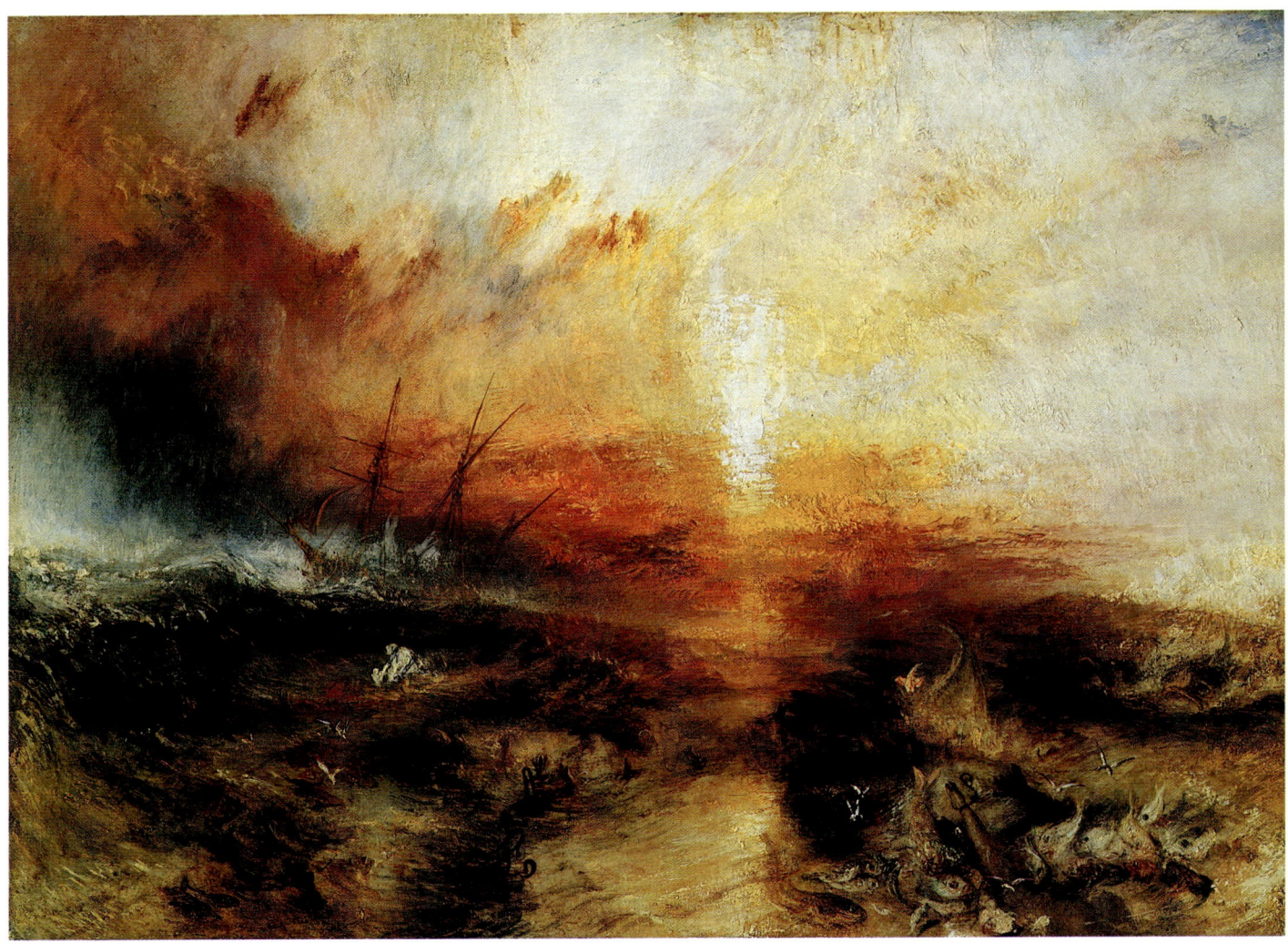

**28-54** Joseph Mallord William Turner, *The Slave Ship (Slavers Throwing Overboard the Dead and Dying, Typhoon Coming On)*, 1840. Oil on canvas, 2′ 11 11/16″ × 4′ 5/16″. Museum of Fine Arts, Boston (Henry Lillie Pierce Fund).

responded to encroaching industrialization. However, where Constable's paintings are serene and precisely painted, Turner's are composed of turbulent swirls of frothy pigment. The passion and energy of Turner's works not only reveal the Romantic sensibility that was the foundation for his art but also clearly illustrate Edmund Burke's concept of the sublime—awe mixed with terror.

Among Turner's most notable works is *The Slave Ship* (FIG. **28-54**). Its subject is an incident that occurred in 1783 and was reported in an extensively read book titled *The History of the Abolition of the Slave Trade*, by Thomas Clarkson. Because the book had just been reprinted in 1839, Clarkson's account probably prompted Turner's choice of subject for this 1840 painting. The incident involved the captain of a slave ship who, on realizing that his insurance company would reimburse him only for slaves lost at sea but not for those who died en route, ordered the sick and dying slaves thrown overboard. Appropriately, the painting's full title is *The Slave Ship (Slavers Throwing Overboard the Dead and Dying, Typhoon Coming On)*. Turner's frenzied emotional depiction of this act matches its barbaric nature. The sun is transformed into an incandescent comet amid flying scarlet clouds. The slave ship moves into the distance, leaving in its wake a turbulent sea choked with the bodies of slaves sinking to their deaths. The relative scale of the minuscule human forms compared to the vast sea and overarching sky reinforces the sense of the sublime, especially the immense power of nature over

humans. The event's particulars are almost lost in the boiling colors; however, on closer inspection, the cruelty is evident. Visible are the iron shackles and manacles around the wrists and ankles of the drowning slaves, denying them any chance of saving themselves.

*The Slave Ship* is clearly more specifically a seascape rather than a landscape painting. Yet Turner's interest in the slave trade indicates his fascination with the effects of the Industrial Revolution. In his other paintings, many of them landscapes, Turner revealed a more inquisitive attitude toward industrialization than did Constable.

Turner's style, often referred to as visionary, was deeply rooted in the emotive power of pure color. The haziness of his forms and the indistinctness of his compositions imbued color and energetic brush strokes with greater impact. Turner was a great innovator whose special invention in works such as *The Slave Ship* was to release color from any defining outlines so as to express both the forces of nature and the painter's emotional response to them. In works such as this, the reality of color is at one with the reality of feeling. Turner's methods had an incalculable effect on the development of modern art. His discovery of the aesthetic and emotive power of pure color and his pushing of the medium's fluidity to a point where the paint itself is almost the subject were important steps toward 20th-century abstract art, which dispensed with shape and form altogether.

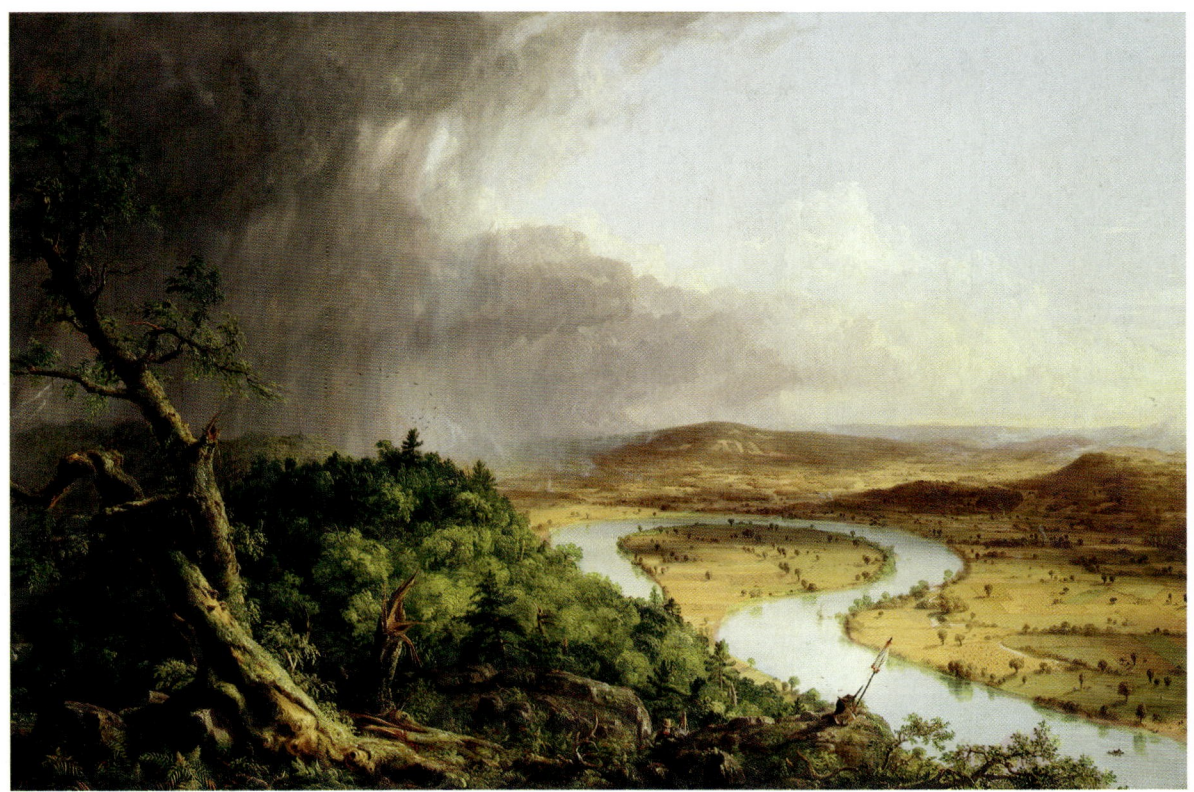

**28-55** THOMAS COLE, *The Oxbow (View from Mount Holyoke, Northampton, Massachusetts, after a Thunderstorm)*, 1836. Oil on canvas, 4′ 3½″ × 6′ 4″. Metropolitan Museum of Art, New York (gift of Mrs. Russell Sage, 1908).

## Landscape Painting in the United States

**AMERICA'S FUTURE DIRECTION?** In America, landscape painting was most prominently pursued by a group of artists known as the Hudson River School, so named because its members drew their subjects primarily from the uncultivated regions of the Hudson River Valley. Many of these painters, however, depicted scenes from across the country, so "Hudson River School" is actually too restrictive geographically. Like the early-19th-century landscape painters in Germany and England, the artists of the Hudson River School not only presented Romantic panoramic landscape views but also participated in the ongoing exploration of the individual's and the country's relationship to the land. Acknowledging the unique geography and historical circumstances of each country and region, American landscape painters frequently focused on identifying qualities that rendered America unique. One American painter of English birth, THOMAS COLE (1801–1848), often referred to as the leader of the Hudson River School, articulated this idea:

> Whether he [an American] beholds the Hudson mingling waters with the Atlantic—explores the central wilds of this vast continent, or stands on the margin of the distant Oregon, he is still in the midst of American scenery—it is his own land; its beauty, its magnificence, its sublimity—all are his; and how undeserving of such a birthright, if he can turn towards it an unobserving eye, an unaffected heart![15]

Another issue that surfaced frequently in Hudson River School paintings was the moral question of America's direction as a civilization. Cole presented the viewer with this question in *The Oxbow (View from Mount Holyoke, Northampton, Massachusetts,*

*after a Thunderstorm)*, FIG. **28-55**. A splendid scene opens before the viewer, dominated by the lazy oxbow turning of the Connecticut River. The composition is divided, with the dark, stormy wilderness on the left and the more developed civilization on the right. The minuscule artist in the bottom center of the painting (wearing a top hat), dwarfed by the landscape's scale, turns to the viewer as if to ask for input in deciding the country's future course. In their depiction of expansive wilderness, Cole's landscapes incorporated reflections and moods romantically appealing to the public.

**WILD, WILD WEST** Other Hudson River artists used the landscape genre as an allegorical vehicle to address moral and spiritual concerns. ALBERT BIERSTADT (1830–1902) traveled west in 1858 and produced many paintings depicting the Rocky Mountains, Yosemite Valley, and other sites in California. These works, such as *Among the Sierra Nevada Mountains, California* (FIG. **28-56**), present breathtaking scenery and natural beauty. This panoramic view (the painting is 10 feet wide) is awe-inspiring. Deer and waterfowl appear at the edge of a placid lake, and steep and rugged mountains soar skyward on the left and in the distance. A stand of trees, uncultivated and wild, frames the lake on the right. To impress on the viewer the almost transcendental nature of this scene, Bierstadt depicted the sun's rays breaking through the clouds overhead, which suggests a heavenly consecration of the land. That Bierstadt focused attention on the West is not insignificant. By calling national attention to the splendor and uniqueness of the regions beyond the Rocky Mountains, Bierstadt's paintings reinforced Manifest Destiny. This popular 19th-century doctrine held that westward expansion across the continent was the logical destiny of the United States. Such artworks thereby muted growing concerns over the realities of conquest, the

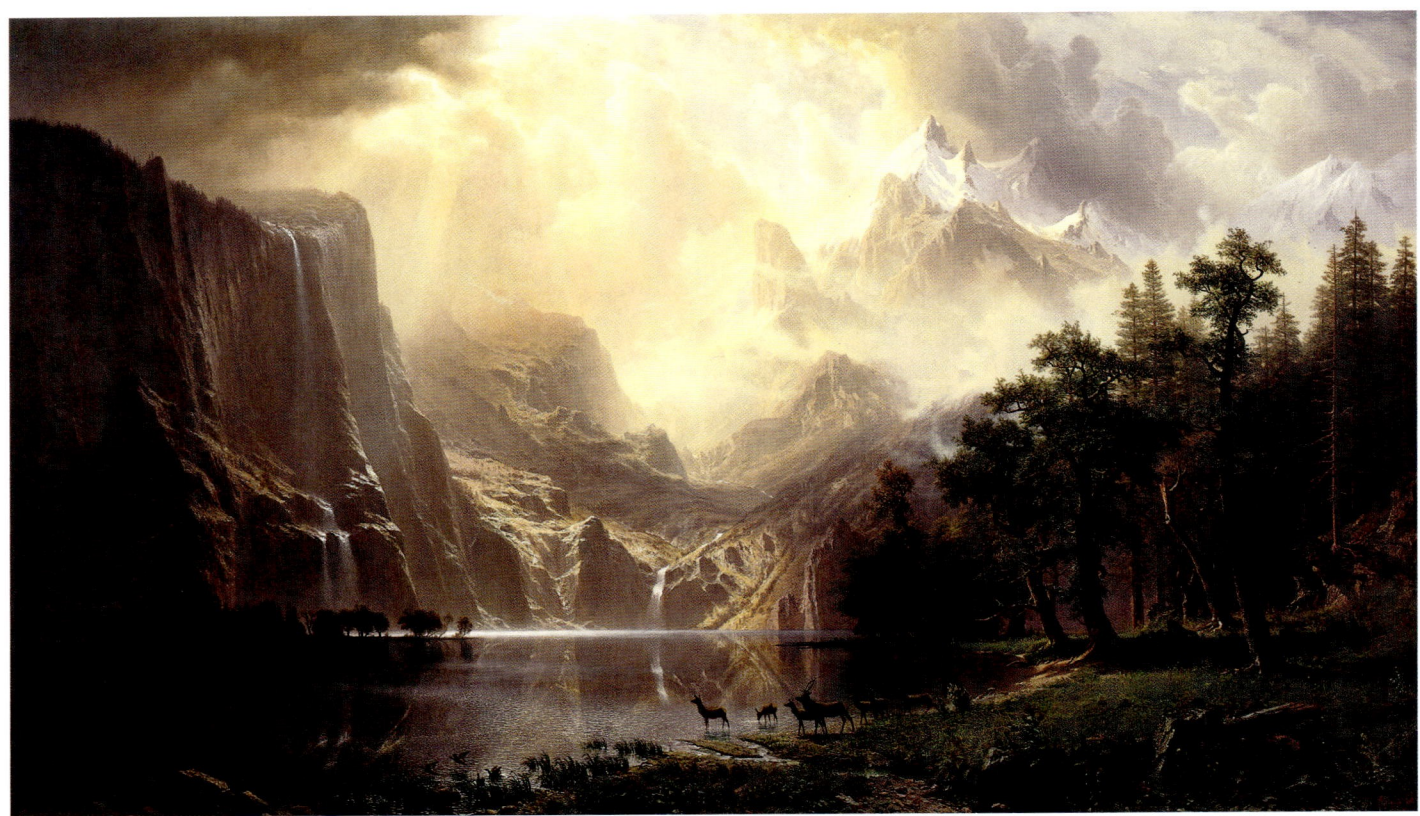

**28-56** ALBERT BIERSTADT, *Among the Sierra Nevada Mountains, California,* 1868. Oil on canvas, 6′ × 10′. National Museum of American Art, Smithsonian Institution, Washington.

displacement of the Native Americans, and the exploitation of the environment. It should come as no surprise that among those most eager to purchase Bierstadt's work were mail-service magnates and railroad builders—entrepreneurs and financiers involved in westward expansion.

**REAFFIRMING RIGHTEOUSNESS** FREDERIC EDWIN CHURCH (1826–1900) also has been associated with the Hudson River School. His interest in landscape scenes was not limited to America;

during his life he traveled to South America, Mexico, Europe, the Middle East, Newfoundland, and Labrador. Church's paintings are instructive because, like the works of Cole and Bierstadt, they are firmly entrenched in the idiom of the Romantic sublime. Yet they also reveal contradictions and conflicts in the constructed mythology of American providence and character. *Twilight in the Wilderness* (FIG. **28-57**) presents an awe-inspiring panoramic view of the sun setting over the majestic landscape. Beyond Church's precise depiction of the spectacle of nature, the painting

**28-57** FREDERIC EDWIN CHURCH, *Twilight in the Wilderness,* 1860s. Oil on canvas, 3′ 4″ × 5′ 4″. Cleveland Museum of Art, Cleveland (Mr. and Mrs. William H. Marlatt Fund, 1965.233).

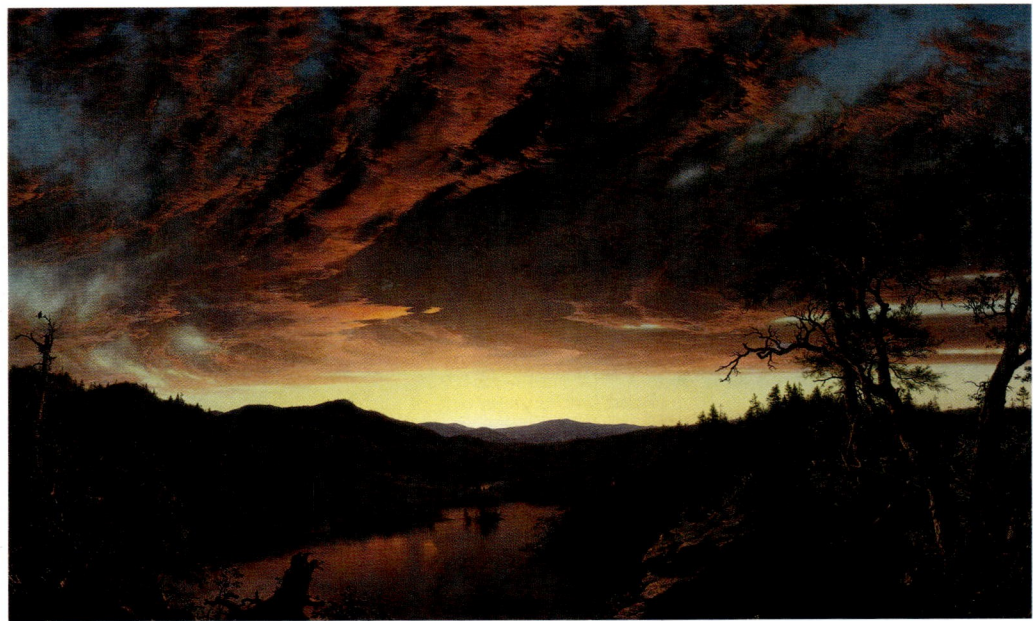

is remarkable for what it does not depict. Like John Constable, Church and the other Hudson River School painters worked in a time of great upheaval. *Twilight in the Wilderness* was created in 1860, when the Civil War was decimating the country. Yet this painting does not display evidence of turbulence or discord; indeed, it does not include even a trace of humanity. By constructing such an idealistic and comforting view, Church contributed to the national mythology of righteousness and divine providence—a mythology that had become increasingly difficult to maintain in the face of conflict.

Landscape painting was immensely popular in the late 18th and early 19th centuries, in large part because it provided viewers with breathtaking and sublime spectacles of nature. Artists also could allegorize nature, and it was rare for a landscape painting not to touch on spiritual, moral, historical, or philosophical issues. Landscape painting became the perfect vehicle for artists (and the viewing public) to "naturalize" conditions, rendering debate about contentious issues moot and eliminating any hint of conflict.

# VARIOUS REVIVALIST STYLES IN ARCHITECTURE

**RECONSIDERING THE PAST** As 19th-century scholars gathered the documentary materials of European history in extensive historiographic enterprises, each nation came to value its past as evidence of the validity of its ambitions and claims to greatness. Intellectuals appreciated the art of the remote past as a product of cultural and national genius. In 1773, Goethe, praising the Gothic cathedral of Strasbourg in *Of German Architecture*, announced the theme by declaring that the German art scholar "should thank God to be able to proclaim aloud that it is German Architecture, our architecture." He also bid the observer, "approach and recognize the deepest feeling of truth and beauty of proportion emanating from a strong, vigorous German soul."[16] In 1802, the eminent French writer Chateaubriand published his influential *Genius of Christianity,* which defended religion on the grounds of its beauty and mystery rather than on the grounds of truth. Gothic cathedrals, according to Chateaubriand, were translations of the sacred groves of the Druidical Gauls into stone and must be cherished as manifestations of France's holy history. In his view, the history of Christianity and of France merged in the Middle Ages.

**RESTORING MEDIEVAL ARTISANSHIP** Modern nationalism thus prompted a new evaluation of the art in each country's past. In London, when the old Houses of Parliament burned in 1834, the Parliamentary Commission decreed that designs for the new building be either Gothic or Elizabethan. CHARLES BARRY (1795–1860), with the assistance of A.W.N. PUGIN (1812–1852), submitted the winning design (FIG. **28-58**) in 1835. By this time, style had become a matter of selection from the historical past. Barry had traveled widely in Europe, Greece, Turkey, Egypt, and Palestine, studying the architecture in each place. He preferred the classical Renaissance styles, but he had designed some earlier Neo-Gothic buildings, and Pugin successfully influenced him in the direction of English Late Gothic. Pugin was one of a group of English artists and critics who saw moral purity and spiritual authenticity in the religious architecture of the Middle Ages. They glorified the careful medieval artisans who had produced it. The Industrial Revolution was flooding the market with cheaply made and ill-designed commodities. Machine work was replacing handicraft. Many, such as Pugin, believed in the necessity of restoring the old artisanship, which had honesty and quality. The design of the Houses of Parliament, however, is not genuinely Gothic, despite its picturesque tower groupings (the Clock Tower, containing Big Ben, at one end, and the Victoria Tower at the other). The building has a formal axial plan and a kind of Palladian regularity beneath its Tudor detail (an early-16th-century style of English domestic architecture characterized by expansive living spaces—parlors, studies, and bedrooms—often with oak paneling and ornamented walls and ceilings). Pugin himself is reported to have said of it, "All Grecian, Sir. Tudor details on a classical body."[17]

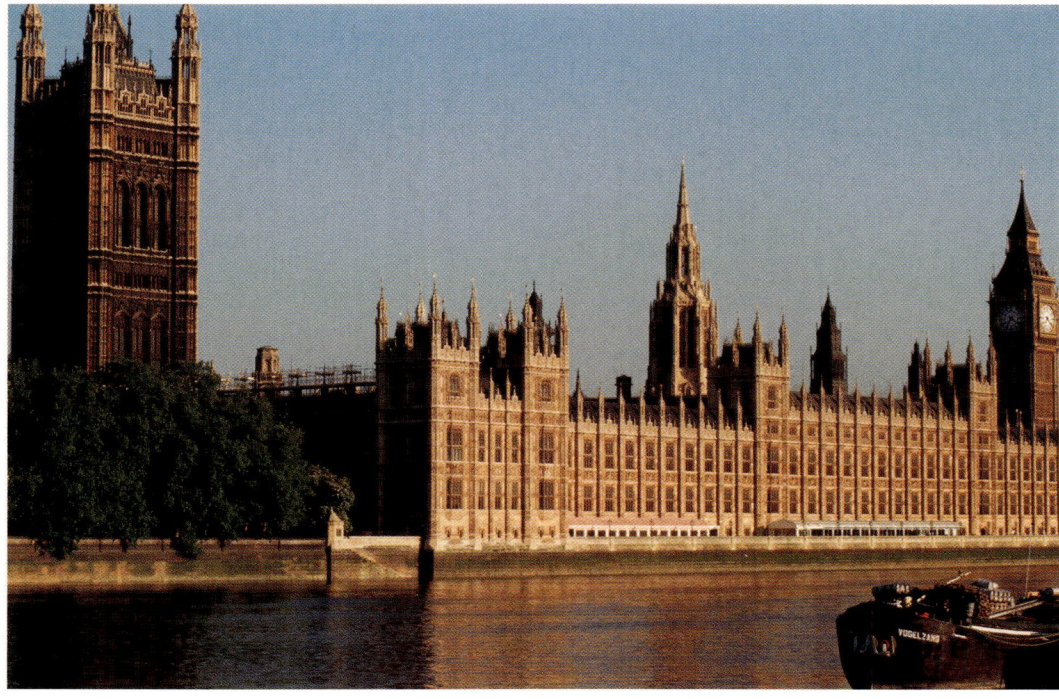

**28-58** CHARLES BARRY and A. W. N. PUGIN, Houses of Parliament, London, England, designed 1835.

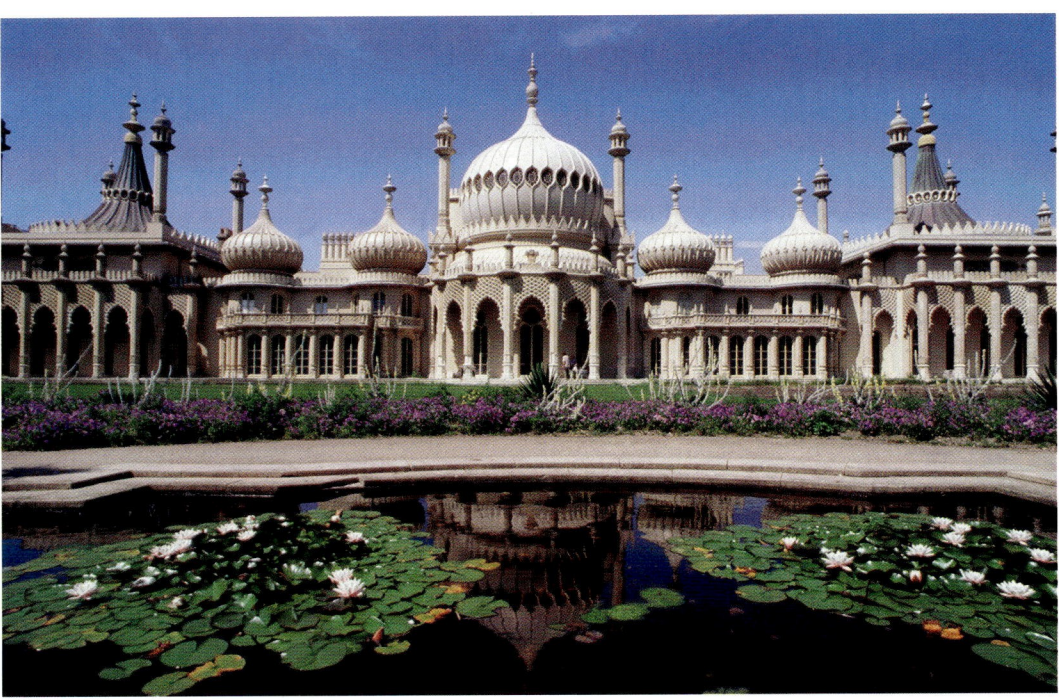

**28-59** John Nash, Royal Pavilion, Brighton, England, 1815–1818.

**THE IMPACT OF IMPERIALISM** Although the Neoclassical and Neo-Gothic styles were dominant in the early 19th century, exotic new styles of all types soon began to appear, in part due to European imperialism. Great Britain's forays throughout the world, particularly India, had exposed English culture to a broad range of non-Western artistic styles. The Royal Pavilion (FIG. **28-59**), designed by John Nash (1752–1835), exhibits a wide variety of these styles. Nash was an established architect, known for Neoclassical buildings in London, when he was asked to design a royal pleasure palace in the seaside resort of Brighton for the prince regent (later King George IV). The structure's fantastic exterior is a conglomeration of Islamic domes, minarets, and screens that has been called "Indian Gothic," and sources ranging from Greece and Egypt to China influenced the interior decor. Underlying the exotic facade is a cast-iron skeleton, an early (if hidden) use of this material in noncommercial building. Nash also put this metal to fanciful use, creating life-size palm-tree columns in cast iron to support the Royal Pavilion's kitchen ceiling. The building, an appropriate enough backdrop for gala throngs pursuing pleasure by the seaside, served as the prototype for numerous playful architectural exaggerations still found in European and American resorts.

**ADAPTING BAROQUE OPULENCE** The Baroque also was adapted in architecture to convey a grandeur worthy of the riches acquired during this age of expansion by those who heeded the advice of the French historian and statesman François Guizot to "get rich." The opulence that permeated the lives of these few was mirrored in the Paris Opéra (FIG. **28-60**), designed by J. L. Charles Garnier (1825–1898). The Opéra parades a festive and spectacularly theatrical Neo-Baroque front that could be compared with the Louvre's facade (see FIG. 24-66), which it mimics to a degree. Garnier ingeniously planned the interior for the convenience of human traffic. Intricate arrangements of corridors, vestibules, stairways, balconies, alcoves, entrances, and exits facilitate easy passage throughout the building and provide space for entertainment and socializing at intermissions. The Baroque grandeur of the layout and of the opera house's ornamental appointments are characteristic of an architectural style called

Beaux-Arts, which flourished in the late 19th and early 20th centuries in France. Based on ideas taught at the dominant École des Beaux-Arts (School of Fine Arts) in Paris, the Beaux-Arts style incorporated classical principles (such as symmetry in design, including interior spaces that extended radially from a central core or axis) and included extensive exterior ornamentation. As an example of a Beaux-Arts building, Garnier's Opéra proclaims, through its majesty and lavishness, its function as a gathering place for glittering audiences in an age of conspicuous wealth. The style was so attractive to the moneyed classes who supported the arts that theaters and opera houses continued to reflect the Paris Opéra's design until World War I transformed society.

The epoch-making developments in architecture were more rational, pragmatic, and functional than the historical designs. As the years moved toward the end of the 19th century, architects gradually abandoned sentimental and Romantic designs from the historical past. They turned to honest expressions of a building's

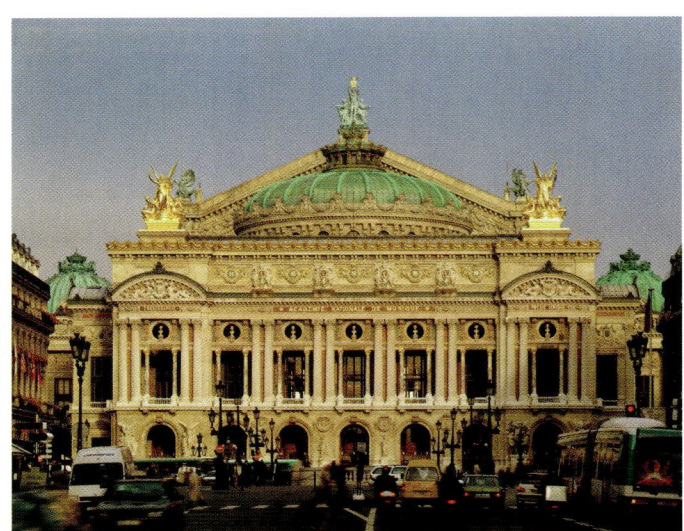

**28-60** J. L. Charles Garnier, the Opéra, Paris, France, 1861–1874.

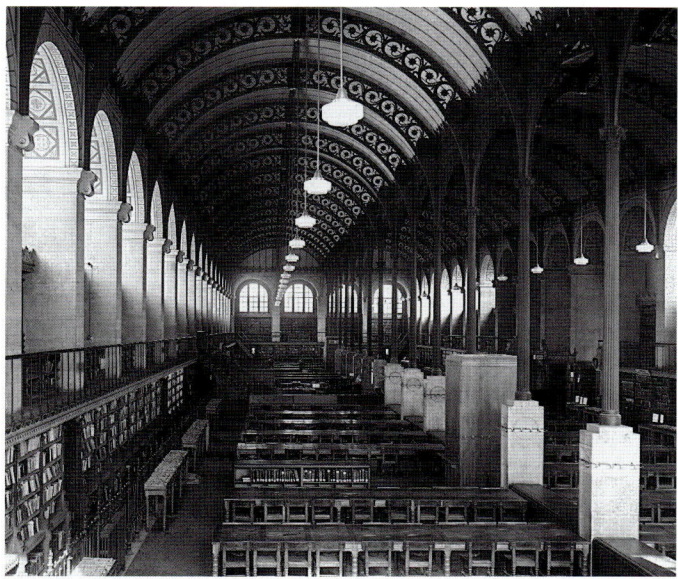

**28-61** Henri Labrouste, reading room of the Bibliothèque Sainte-Geneviève, Paris, France, 1843–1850.

purpose. Since the 18th century, bridges had been built of cast iron (FIG. 28-10), and most other utility architecture—factories, warehouses, dockyard structures, mills, and the like—long had been built simply and without historical ornament. Iron, along with other industrial materials, permitted engineering advancements in the construction of larger, stronger, and more fire-resistant structures than before. The tensile strength of iron (and especially of steel, available after 1860) permitted architects to create new designs involving vast enclosed spaces, as in the great train sheds of railroad stations and in exposition halls.

**FROM MASONRY TO IRON** The Bibliothèque Sainte-Geneviève (1843–1850), built by Henri Labrouste (1801–1875), shows an interesting modification of a revived style—in this case, Renaissance—to accommodate the skeletal cast-iron elements (FIG.

28-61). The row of arched windows in the facade recalls Renaissance buildings, and the division of its stories distinguishes its interior levels—the lower, reserved for stack space, and the upper, for the reading rooms. The latter consists essentially of two barrel-vaulted halls, roofed in terracotta and separated by a row of slender cast-iron columns on concrete pedestals. The columns, recognizably Corinthian, support the iron roof arches, which are pierced with intricate vine-scroll ornament out of the Renaissance architectural vocabulary. One scarcely could find a better example of how the peculiarities of the new structural material aesthetically transformed the forms of traditional masonry architecture. Nor could one find a better example of how reluctant the 19th-century architect was to surrender traditional forms, even when fully aware of new possibilities for design and construction. Architects scoffed at "engineers' architecture" for many years and continued to clothe their steel-and-concrete structures in the Romantic "drapery" of a historical style.

**A CRYSTAL PALACE** Completely "undraped" construction first became popular in the conservatories (greenhouses) of English country estates. Joseph Paxton (1801–1865) built several such structures for his patron, the duke of Devonshire. In the largest—300 feet long—he used an experimental system of glass-and-metal roof construction. Encouraged by the success of this system, Paxton submitted a winning glass-and-iron building plan to the design competition for the hall to house the Great Exhibition of 1851, organized to present "works of industry of all nations" in London. Paxton's exhibition building, the Crystal Palace (FIG. 28-62), was built with prefabricated parts. This allowed the vast structure to be erected in the then-unheard-of time of six months and dismantled at the exhibition's closing to avoid permanent obstruction of the park. The plan borrowed much from ancient Roman and Christian basilicas, with a central flat-roofed "nave" and a barrel-vaulted crossing "transept." The design provided ample interior space to contain displays of huge machines as well as to accommodate such decorative touches as large working fountains and giant trees. The public admired the building so much that when it was dismantled, it was reerected at a new location on the outskirts of London, where it remained until fire destroyed it in 1936.

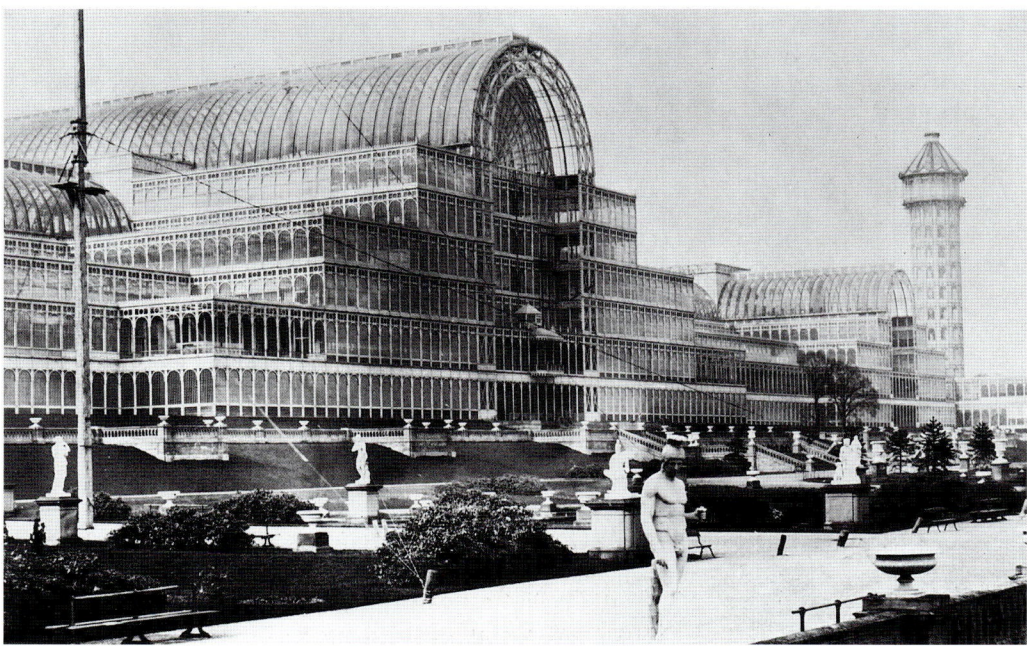

**28-62** Joseph Paxton, Crystal Palace, London, England, 1850–1851. Photo from Victoria and Albert Museum, London.

# The Beginnings of Photography

**THE CAMERA'S IMPACT**  A technological device of immense consequence for the modern experience was invented shortly before midcentury: the camera, with its attendant art of photography. Almost everyone is familiar with what the camera can do—record and report optical experience. People have come to assume that a very close correlation exists between the photographic image and the fragment of the visual world it records. The photograph serves as proof that what people think they see is really there. Americans, for example, experience the authority and credibility their culture confers on photography in the form of driver's licenses, passport photos, and security cameras.

Photography was celebrated as embodying a kind of revelation of visible things from the time Frenchman Louis J. M. Daguerre and Briton Henry Fox Talbot announced the first practical photographic processes in 1839. The medium, itself a product of science, was an enormously useful tool for recording the century's discoveries. The relative ease of the process seemed a dream come true for scientists and artists, who for centuries had grappled with less satisfying methods of capturing accurate images of their subjects. Photography also was perfectly suited to an age that saw artistic patronage continue to shift away from the elite few toward a broader base of support. The growing and increasingly powerful middle class embraced both the comprehensible images of the new medium and its lower cost.

**ARTISTS RESPOND TO PHOTOGRAPHY**  For the traditional artist, photography suggested new answers to the great debate about what is real and how to represent the real in art. It also challenged the place of traditional modes of pictorial representation originating in the Renaissance. Artists as diverse as Delacroix, Ingres, the Realist Jean Désiré Gustave Courbet (see Chapter 29, page 855), and the Impressionist Edgar Degas (see Chapter 29, page 865) welcomed photography as a helpful auxiliary to painting. They increasingly were intrigued by how photography translated three-dimensional objects onto a two-dimensional surface. Other artists, however, saw photography as a mechanism capable of displacing the painstaking work of skilled painters dedicated to representing the optical truth of chosen subjects. Photography's challenge to painting, both historically and technologically, seemed to some an expropriation of the realistic image, until then the exclusive property of painting. But just as some painters looked to the new medium of photography for answers on how best to render an image in paint, so some photographers looked to painting for suggestions about ways to imbue the photographic image with qualities beyond simple reproduction. The collaborative efforts of Delacroix and the photographer Eugène Durieu (1800–1874), as seen in *Draped Model (back view)*, FIG. **28-63**, demonstrate the symbiotic relationship between painters and photographers. Although Delacroix produced in this work a permanent image of the posed nude female model, photographers sometimes also attempted, as here, to create a mood through careful lighting and the draping of cloth.

**DEVELOPING THE DAGUERREOTYPE**  Reality, truth, fact—that elusive quality artists throughout time sought with painstaking effort in traditional media—could seemingly be captured readily and with breathtaking accuracy by the new mechanical medium of photography. Artists themselves were instrumental in the development of this new technology. The camera obscura was

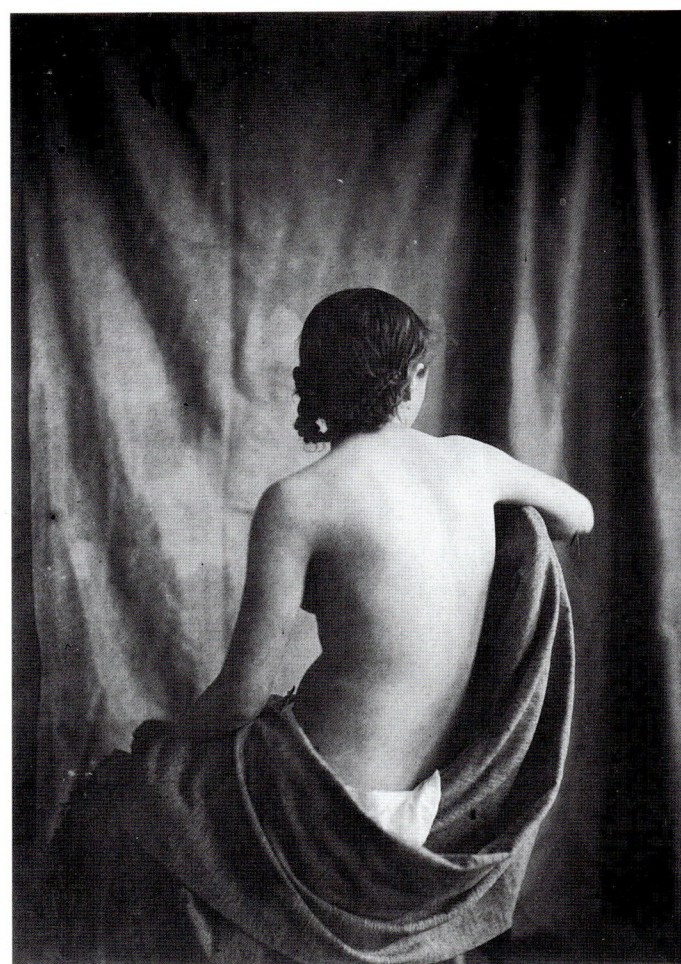

**28-63**  Eugène Durieu and Eugène Delacroix, *Draped Model (back view)*, ca. 1854. Albumen print, $7\frac{5}{16}'' \times 5\frac{1}{8}''$. J. Paul Getty Museum, Los Angeles.

familiar to 18th-century artists. In 1807, the invention of the *camera lucida* (lighted room) replaced the enclosed chamber of the camera obscura. Instead, a small prism lens, hung on a stand, was aimed downward at an object. The lens projected the image of the object onto a sheet of paper. Artists using either of these devices found the process long and arduous, no matter how accurate the resulting work. All yearned for a more direct way to capture a subject's image. Two very different scientific inventions that accomplished this were announced, almost simultaneously, in France and England in 1839.

The first new discovery was the *daguerreotype* process, named for Louis-Jacques-Mandé Daguerre (1789–1851), one of its two inventors. The second, the calotype process, is discussed later. Daguerre had trained as an architect before becoming a theatrical set painter and designer. This background led him to open (with a friend) a popular entertainment called the Diorama. Audiences witnessed performances of "living paintings" created by changing the lighting effects on a "sandwich" composed of a painted backdrop and several layers of painted translucent front curtains. Daguerre used a camera obscura for the Diorama, but he wanted to find a more efficient and effective procedure. Through a mutual acquaintance, he was introduced to Joseph Nicéphore Niépce, who in 1826 had successfully made a permanent picture of the

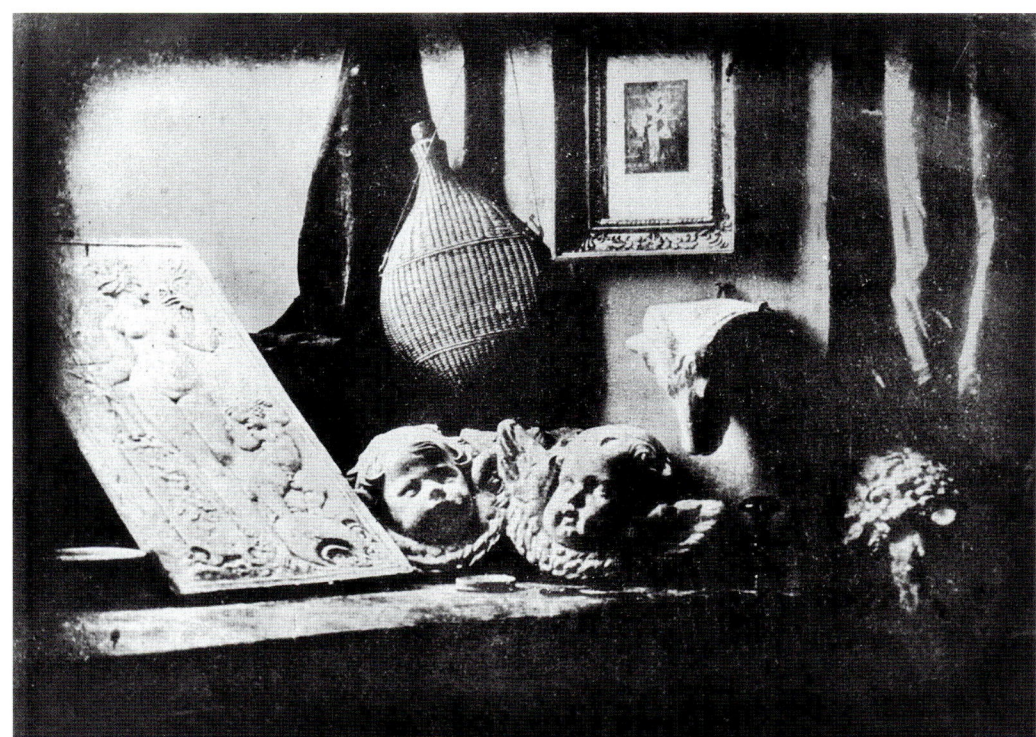

28-64 LOUIS-JACQUES-MANDÉ DAGUERRE, *Still Life in Studio*, 1837. Daguerreotype, approx. $6\frac{1}{4}'' \times 8\frac{1}{4}''$. Collection Société Française de Photographie, Paris.

cityscape outside his upper-story window by exposing, in a camera obscura, a metal plate covered with a light-sensitive coating. Although the eight-hour exposure time needed to record Nièpce's subject hampered the process, Daguerre's excitement over its possibilities led to a partnership between the two men to pursue its development. Nièpce died in 1833, but Daguerre continued to work on his own. He made two contributions to the process. He discovered latent development—that is, bringing out the image through treatment in chemical solutions—which considerably shortened the length of time needed for exposure. Daguerre also discovered a better way to "fix" the image (again, chemically) by stopping the action of light on the photographic plate, which otherwise would continue to darken until the image could no longer be discerned.

The French government presented the new daguerreotype process at the Academy of Science in Paris on January 7, 1839, with the understanding that its details would be made available to all interested parties without charge (although the inventor received a large annuity in appreciation). Soon, people worldwide were taking pictures with the daguerreotype "camera" (a name shortened from camera obscura) in a process almost immediately christened *photography,* from the Greek *photos* (light) and *graphos* (writing). From the start, painters were intrigued with the possibilities of the process as a new art medium. Paul Delaroche, a leading painter of the day, wrote in an official report to the French government:

> Daguerre's process completely satisfies all the demands of art, carrying certain essential principles of art to such perfection that it must become a subject of observation and study even to the most accomplished painters. The pictures obtained by this method are as remarkable for the perfection of the details as for the richness and harmony of the general effect. Nature is reproduced in them not only with truth, but also with art.[18]

Each daguerreotype is a unique work, possessing amazing detail and finely graduated tones from black to white. Both qualities are evident in *Still Life in Studio* (FIG. **28-64**), one of the first successful plates Daguerre produced after perfecting his method. The process captured every detail—the subtle forms, the varied textures, the diverse tones of light and shadow—in Daguerre's carefully constructed tableau. The three-dimensional forms of the sculptures, the basket, and the bits of cloth spring into high relief and are convincingly there within the image. Its composition was clearly inspired by 17th-century Dutch vanitas still lifes, such as those of Claesz (see FIG. 24-55). Like Claesz, Daguerre arranged his objects to reveal their textures and shapes clearly. Unlike a painter, Daguerre could not alter anything within his arrangement to effect a stronger image. However, he could suggest a symbolic meaning through his choice of objects. Like the skull and timepiece in Claesz's painting, Daguerre's sculptural and architectural fragments and the framed print of an embrace suggest that even art is vanitas and will not endure forever.

**A PICTURE-PERFECT OPERATION** In the United States, where the first daguerreotype was taken within two months of Daguerre's presentation in Paris, two particularly avid and resourceful advocates of the new medium were JOSIAH JOHNSON HAWES (1808–1901), a painter, and ALBERT SANDS SOUTHWORTH (1811–1894), a pharmacist and teacher. Together, they ran a daguerreotype studio in Boston that specialized in portraiture, then popular due to the shortened exposure time required for the process (although it was still long enough to require head braces to help subjects remain motionless while their photographs were taken).

The partners also took their equipment outside the studio to record places and events of particular interest to them. One resultant image is *Early Operation under Ether, Massachusetts General*

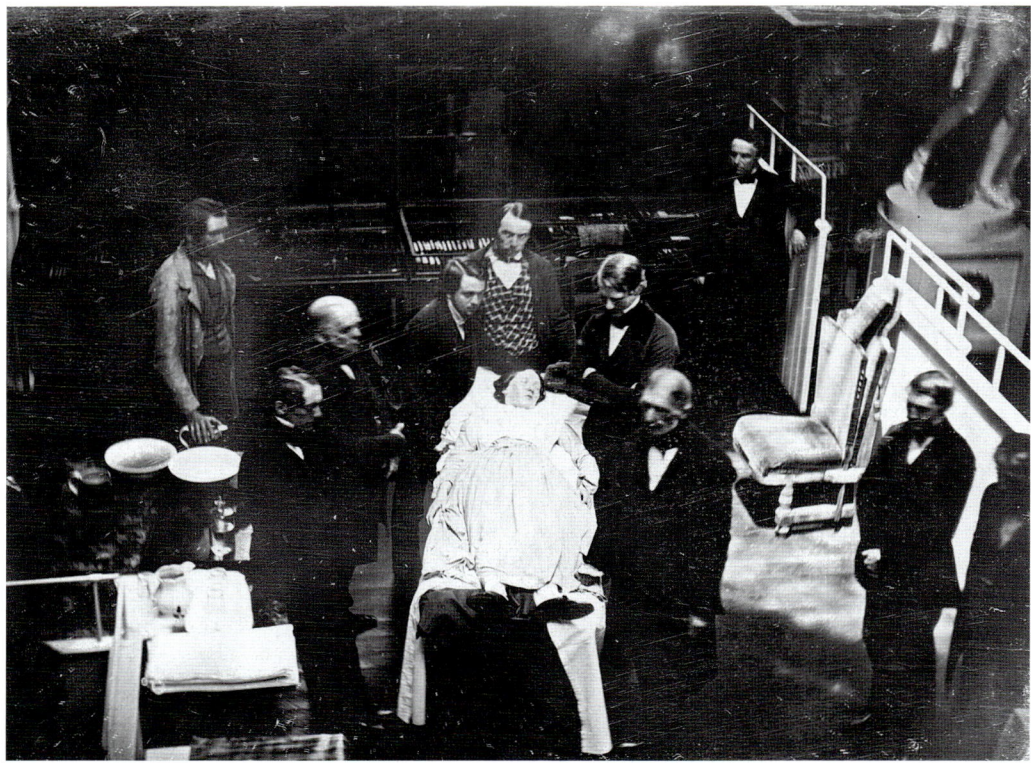

**28-65** Josiah Johnson Hawes and Albert Sands Southworth, *Early Operation under Ether, Massachusetts General Hospital*, ca. 1847. Daguerreotype, $6\frac{1}{2}'' \times 8\frac{1}{2}''$. Massachusetts General Hospital Archives and Special Collections, Boston.

*Hospital* (FIG. **28-65**). This daguerreotype was taken from the vantage point of the gallery of a hospital operating room, putting the viewer in the position of medical students looking down on a lecture-demonstration typical throughout the 19th century. An image of historic record, this early daguerreotype gives the viewer a glimpse into the whole of Western medical practice. The focus of attention in *Early Operation* is the white-draped patient, who is surrounded by a circle of darkly clad doctors. The details of the figures and the room's furnishings are recorded clearly, but the slight blurring of several of the figures betrays motion during the exposure. The elevated viewpoint flattens the spatial perspective and emphasizes the relationships of the figures in ways that the Impressionists, especially Degas, found intriguing.

**A BEAUTIFUL TYPE OF PHOTOGRAPHY** The daguerreotype reigned supreme in photography until the 1850s, but the second major photographic invention was announced less than three weeks after Daguerre's method was unveiled in Paris, and eventually replaced it. It was the ancestor of the modern negative-print system. On January 31, 1839, William Henry Fox Talbot (1800–1877) presented a paper on his "photogenic drawings" to the Royal Institution in London. As early as 1835, Talbot made "negative" images by placing objects on sensitized paper and exposing the arrangement to light. This created a design of light-colored silhouettes recording the places where opaque or translucent objects had blocked light from darkening the paper's emulsion. In his experiments, Talbot next exposed sensitized papers inside simple cameras and, with a second sheet, created "positive" images. He further improved the process with more light-sensitive chemicals and a chemical development of the negative image. This technique allowed multiple prints. However, Talbot's process, which he named the *calotype* (a term he derived from the Greek word *kalos*, meaning "beautiful"), was limited by the fact that its images incorporated the texture of the paper. This produced a slightly blurred, grainy effect very different from the crisp detail and wide tonal range available with the daguerreotype. Aside from these drawbacks, widespread adoption of the calotype process was primarily prevented by the stiff licensing and equipment fees charged for many years after Talbot patented his new process in 1841. Due to both the look and the cost of the calotype, many photographers elected to stay with the daguerreotype until photographic technology could expand the calotype's capabilities.

**CAPTURING AN ARTIST'S LIKENESS** Portraiture was one of the first photography genres to use a technology that improved the calotype. Making portraits was an important economic opportunity for most photographers, as Southworth and Hawes proved, but the greatest of the early portrait photographers was undoubtedly the Frenchman Gaspar-Félix Tournachon (1820–1910). Tournachon adopted the name NADAR for his professional career as novelist, journalist, enthusiastic balloonist, caricaturist, and, later, photographer. Photographic studies for his caricatures, which followed the tradition of Honoré Daumier's most satiric lithographs (see FIG. 29-5), led Nadar to open a portrait studio. So talented was he at capturing the essence of his subjects that the most important people in France, including Delacroix, Daumier, Courbet, and the Impressionist Édouard Manet (see Chapter 29, page 860), flocked to his studio to have their portraits made. Nadar said he sought in his work "that instant of understanding that puts you in touch with the model—helps you sum him up, guides you to his habits, his ideas, and character and enables you to produce . . . a really convincing and sympathetic likeness, an intimate portrait."[19]

Nadar's skill in the genre can be seen in *Eugène Delacroix* (FIG. **28-66**), which shows the painter at the height of his career. In this photograph, the artist appears with remarkable presence; even in half-length, his gesture and expression create a mood that seems to reveal much about him. Perhaps Delacroix responded to Nadar's famous gift for putting his clients at ease by assuming the pose that best expressed his personality. The new photographic

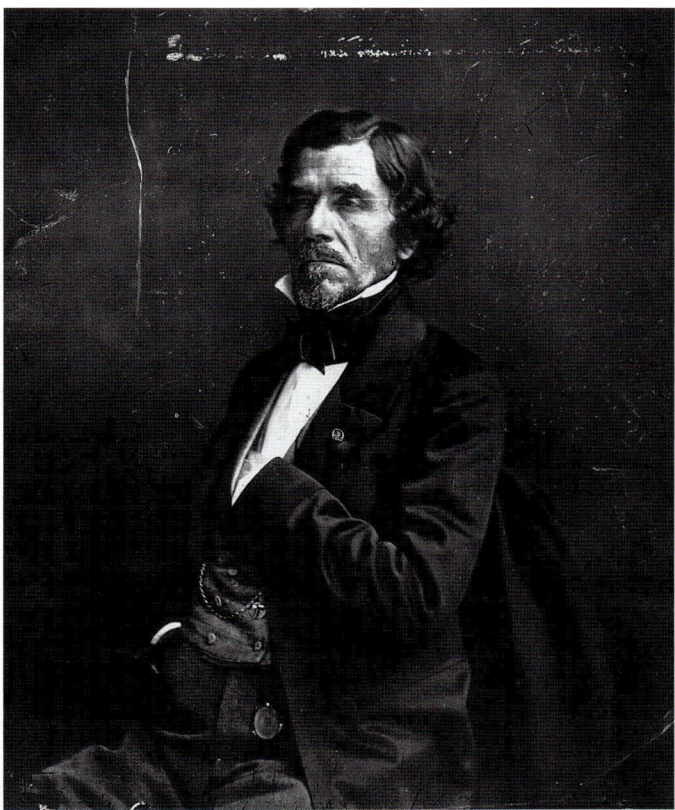

materials made possible the rich range of tones in Nadar's images. Glass negatives and albumen printing paper (prepared with egg white) could record finer detail and a wider range of light and shadow than Talbot's calotype process.

The new "wet-plate" technology (so named because this plate was exposed, developed, and fixed while wet) almost at once replaced both the daguerreotype and the calotype and became the universal way of making negatives up to 1880. However, wet-plate photography had drawbacks. The plates had to be prepared and processed on the spot. To work outdoors meant taking along a portable darkroom of some sort—a wagon, tent, or box with light-tight sleeves for the photographer's arms. Yet, with the wet plate, artists could make remarkable photographs of battlefields, the Alps, and even the traffic flow in crowded streets (see FIG. 29-24).

**CHARACTER PORTRAITS** Among the most famous portrait photographers in Victorian England was JULIA MARGARET CAMERON (1815–1879), who did not take up photography seriously until the age of 48. Although she produced images of many well-known men of the period, including Charles Darwin, Alfred Tennyson, and Thomas Carlyle, she shot more women than men, as was true of many women photographers. *Ophelia, Study no. 2* (FIG. **28-67**) typifies her portrait style. Cameron often depicted her female subjects as characters in literary or biblical narratives, and the slightly blurred focus also became a distinctive feature of her work. That stylistic trait was initiated when she began photographing with a lens that had a short focal length, which allowed only a small area of sharp focus. The blurriness adds an ethereal, dreamlike tone to the photographs, appropriate for the

**28-66** NADAR, *Eugène Delacroix,* ca. 1855, $8\frac{1}{2}'' \times 6\frac{2}{3}''$. Modern print from original negative in the Bibliothèque Nationale, Paris.

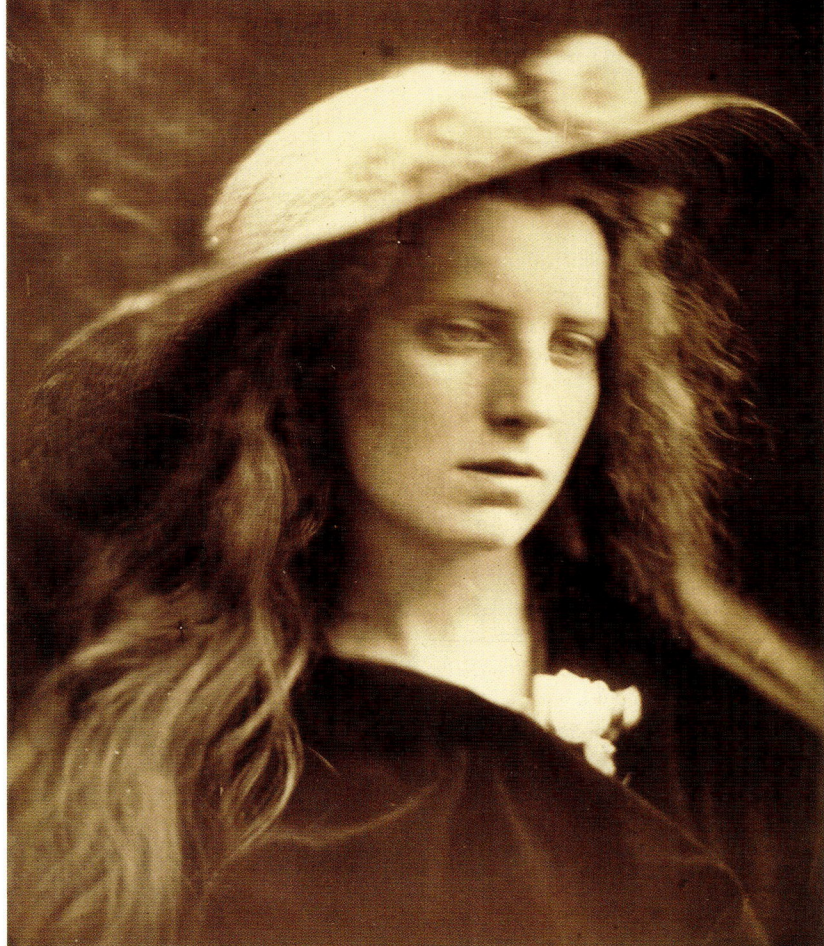

**28-67** JULIA MARGARET CAMERON, *Ophelia, Study no. 2,* 1867. Albumen print, $1'1'' \times 10\frac{2}{3}''$. George Eastman House, Rochester, New York. Gift of Eastman Kodak Company: ex-collection Gabriel Cromer.

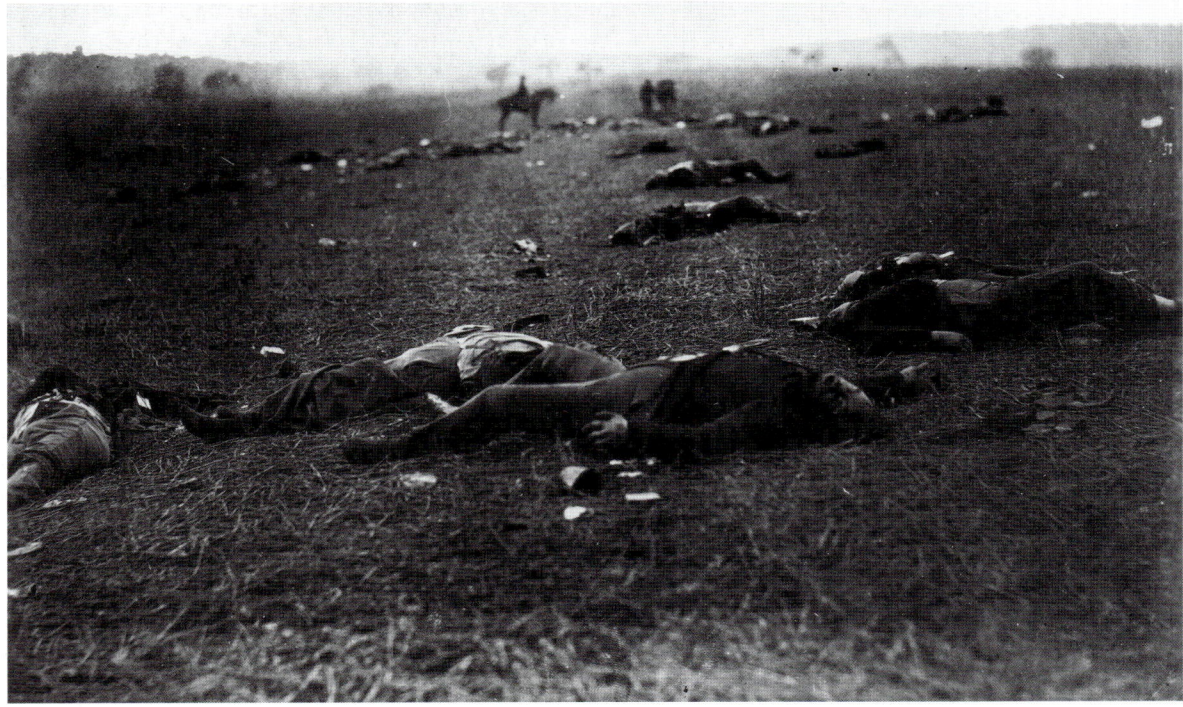

**28-68** Timothy O'Sullivan, *A Harvest of Death, Gettysburg, Pennsylvania, July 1863*. Negative by Timothy O'Sullivan. Original print by Alexander Gardner, $6\frac{3}{4}'' \times 8\frac{3}{4}''$. The New York Public Library (Astor, Lenox and Tilden Foundations, Rare Books and Manuscript Division), New York.

fictional "characters" that she was presenting. Her photograph of Ophelia has a mysterious, fragile quality reminiscent of Pre-Raphaelite paintings (see FIG. 29-17) of the same subject.

**DOCUMENTING WAR** The photograph's documentary power was immediately realized. Thus began the story of the medium's influence on modern life and of the immense changes it brought to communication and information management. It was of unrivaled importance for the historical record. Great events could be recorded on the spot and the views preserved for the first time. The photographs taken of the Crimean War (1856) by Roger Fenton (1819–1869) and of the American Civil War by Mathew B. Brady (1823–1896), Alexander Gardner (1821–1882), and Timothy O'Sullivan (1840–1882) are still unsurpassed as incisive accounts of military life, unsparing in their truth to detail and poignant as expressions of human experience.

Of the Civil War photographs, the most moving are the inhumanly objective records of combat deaths. Perhaps the most reproduced of these Civil War photographs is O'Sullivan's *A Harvest of Death, Gettysburg, Pennsylvania, July 1863* (FIG. 28-68). Although this image could be seen as simple reportage, it also functions to impress on people the high price of the Civil War. Corpses litter the battlefield as far as the eye can see. O'Sullivan presented a scene that stretches far to the horizon. As the photograph modulates from the precise clarity of the bodies of Union soldiers in the foreground, boots stolen and pockets picked, to the almost illegible corpses in the distance, the suggestion of innumerable other dead soldiers is unavoidable. This "harvest" is far more sobering and depressing than that in

Winslow Homer's Civil War image, *The Veteran in a New Field* (see FIG. 29-11). Though it was years before photolithography could reproduce photographs like this in newspapers, they were publicly exhibited and made an impression that newsprint engravings never could.

# CONCLUSION

After the death of Louis XIV in 1715, early-18th-century French culture was dominated by the aristocracy and by a style known as Rococo. This softer, daintier style, characterized by elegance and sensuality, was soon challenged by the rise of the Enlightenment and the Neoclassical style. The revival of interest in classicism, as manifested by Neoclassicism, was widespread throughout both Europe and America. Because of Neoclassicism's associations with heroism, idealism, and rationality, it was invoked by leaders ranging from Napoleon to Thomas Jefferson. In contrast to Neoclassicism, with its emphasis on reason and logic, Romanticism, which also emerged in conjunction with Enlightenment thought, focused on the primacy of imagination and feeling. The invention of photography shortly before midcentury was a significant milestone, as it altered public perceptions of "reality." The issues of reality and realism were addressed specifically in the movement that followed on the heels of Romanticism, Realism. Artists specifically addressed the issues of reality and realism in the movement that followed, Realism (discussed in the next chapter).

ENGLAND | FRANCE

| VOLTAIRE, 1694–1778
| JEAN-JACQUES ROUSSEAU, 1712–1778
| DENIS DIDEROT, 1713–1784, *Encyclopédie,* 1751–1780
| FREDERICK II (THE GREAT) OF PRUSSIA, r. 1740–1786
| EXCAVATION OF POMPEII BEGINS, 1748
| JOHANN WOLFGANG VON GOETHE, 1749– 1832

1750

| AMERICAN REVOLUTION, 1763–1783
| ENGLAND'S ROYAL ACADEMY OF ARTS FOUNDED, 1768

1770

1 | NEW STEAM ENGINE PATENTED, 1769
| SIR WALTER SCOTT, 1771–1832

1780

| FRENCH REVOLUTION, 1789–1795

1790

2

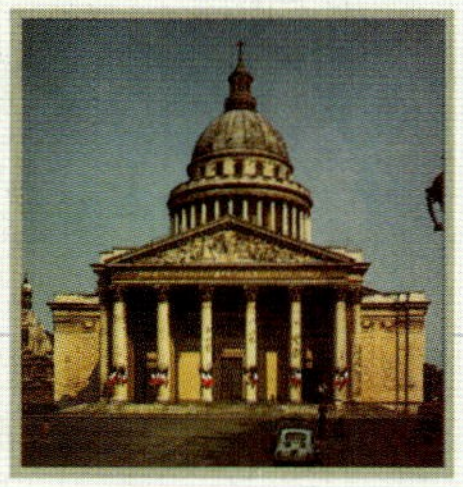

1 Jacques-Germain Soufflot, The Panthéon (Sainte-Geneviève), 1755–1792

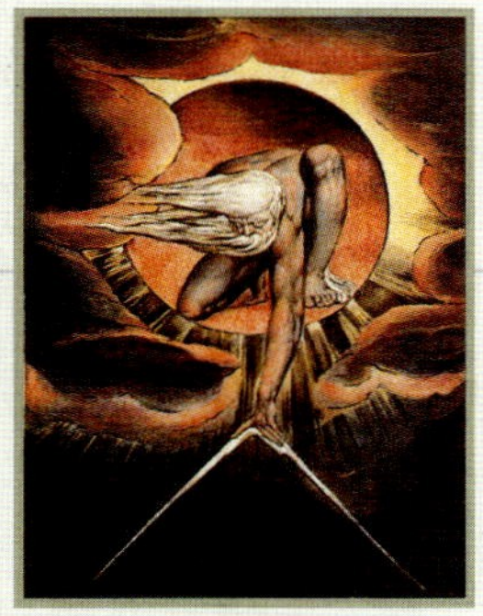

2 William Blake, *Ancient of Days,* 1794

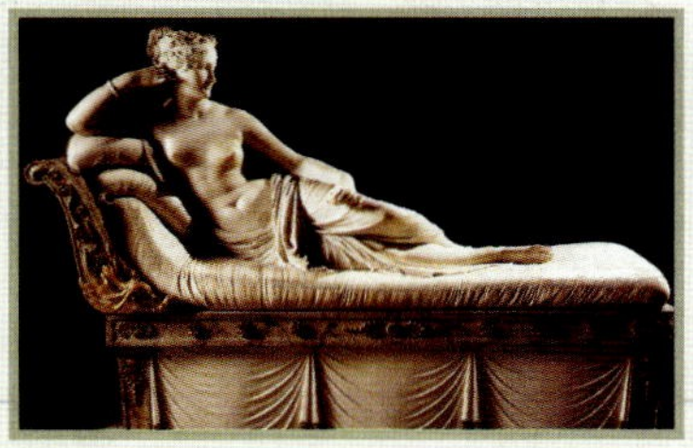

1800

| NAPOLEON BONAPARTE, FIRST CONSUL OF FRANCE, 1800
| CHATEAUBRIAND, *Genius of Christianity,* 1802
3 | NAPOLEON CROWNED EMPEROR, 1804
| NAPOLEON ABDICATES, 1814
| BATTLE OF WATERLOO, 1815
| RESTORATION OF THE BOURBONS, 1815

1820

3 Antonio Canova, *Pauline Borghese as Venus,* 1808

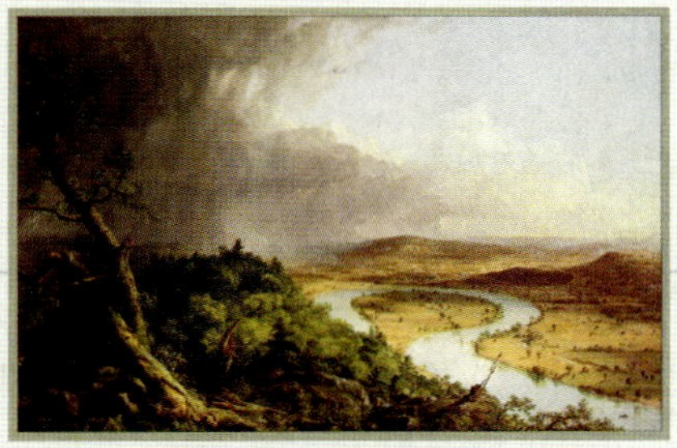

1830

| REVOLUTION OF 1830 IN FRANCE
| CONSTITUTIONAL MONARCHY IN FRANCE, 1830–1848
4 | DAGUERREOTYPE PRESENTED, 1839

1840

| KARL MARX, 1818–1883, *Communist Manifesto,* 1848
| REVOLUTION OF 1848 IN FRANCE

4 Thomas Cole, *The Oxbow (View from Mount Holyoke, Northampton, Massachusetts, after a Thunderstorm),* 1836

1851

GEORGE III OF ENGLAND | GEORGE IV | WILLIAM IV | VICTORIA

LOUIS XVI OF FRANCE | THE FRENCH REVOLUTION | THE DIRECTORY | FIRST REPUBLIC | NAPOLEON I (THE EMPIRE) | LOUIS XVIII | CHARLES X | LOUIS PHILIPPE | SECOND REPUBLIC | SECOND EMPIRE

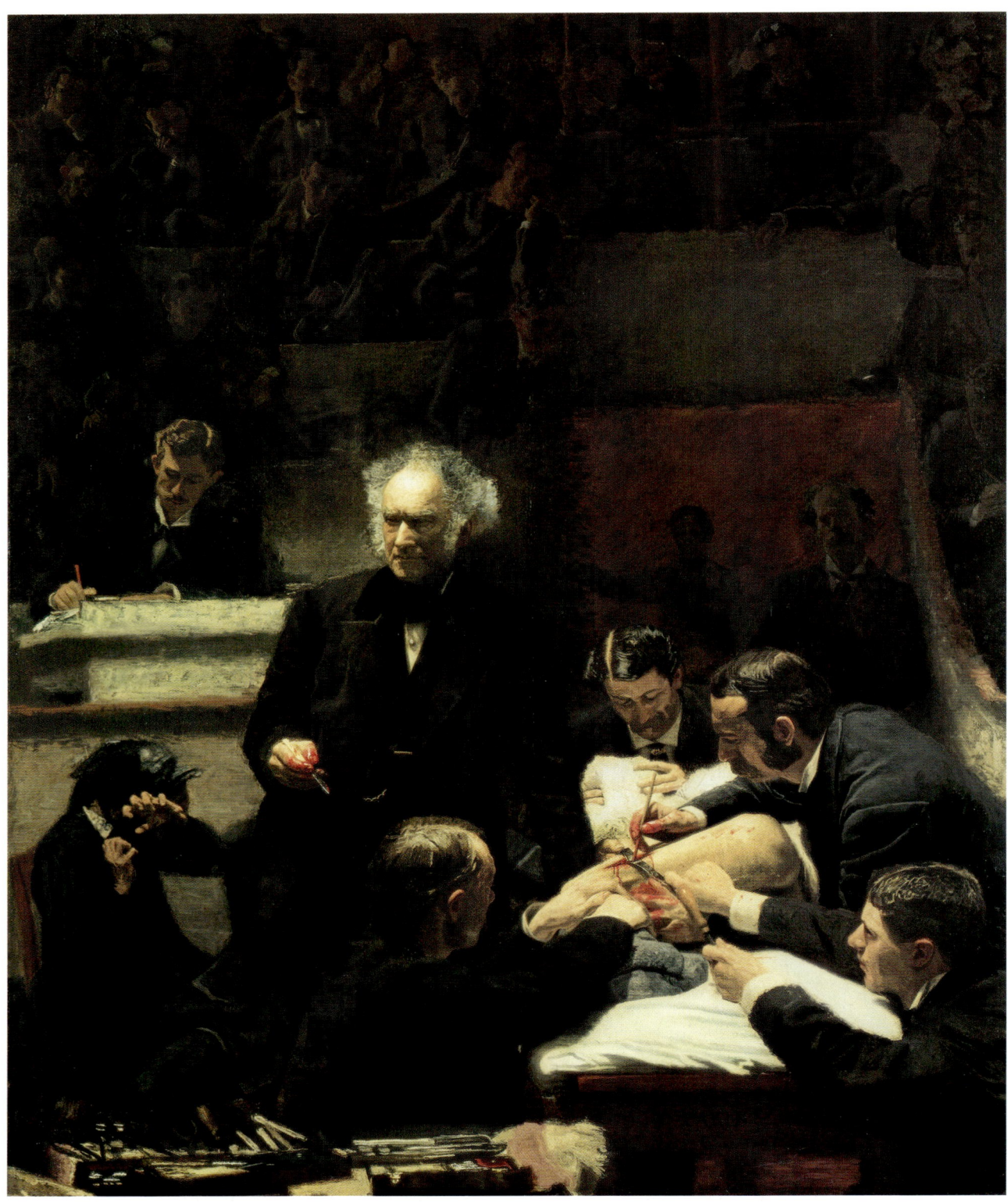

Thomas Eakins, *The Gross Clinic,* 1875. Oil on canvas, 8′ × 6′ 6″. Jefferson Medical College of Thomas Jefferson University, Philadelphia.

# 29

# THE RISE OF MODERNISM

## ART OF THE LATER 19TH CENTURY

The momentous Western developments of the early 19th century—industrialization (MAP **29-1**), urbanization, and increased economic and political interaction worldwide—matured quickly during the latter half of the century. The Industrial Revolution in England spread throughout Europe and to the United States. Because of this dramatic expansion, the third quarter of the 19th century is often referred to as the second Industrial Revolution. While the first Industrial Revolution centered on textiles, steam, and iron, the second was associated with steel, electricity, chemicals, and oil. The discoveries in these fields provided the foundation for developments in plastics, machinery, building construction, and automobile manufacturing and paved the way for the invention of the radio, electric light, telephone, and electric streetcar.

One of the most significant consequences of industrialization was urbanization. The number and size of Western cities grew dramatically during the latter part of the 19th century, largely due to migration from rural regions. Rural dwellers relocated to urban centers because of expanded agricultural enterprises that squeezed the smaller property owners from the land. The widely available work opportunities in the cities, especially in the factories, were also a major factor in this migration. In addition, the improving health and living conditions in the cities contributed to their explosive growth.

**REAFFIRMING A FAITH IN SCIENCE** An increasing emphasis on science was another characteristic of this period. Advances in industrial technology reinforced the Enlightenment's foundation of rationalism. The connection between science and progress seemed obvious to many, both in intellectual circles and among the general public, and, increasingly, people embraced empiricism (the search for knowledge based on observation and direct experience). Indicative of the widespread faith in science was the influence of positivism, a Western philosophical model that promoted science as the mind's highest achievement. Positivism was developed by the French philosopher Auguste Comte (1798–1857), who advocated a purely scientific, empirical approach to nature and society. Comte believed that scientific laws governed the environment and human activity and could be revealed through careful recording and analysis of observable data.

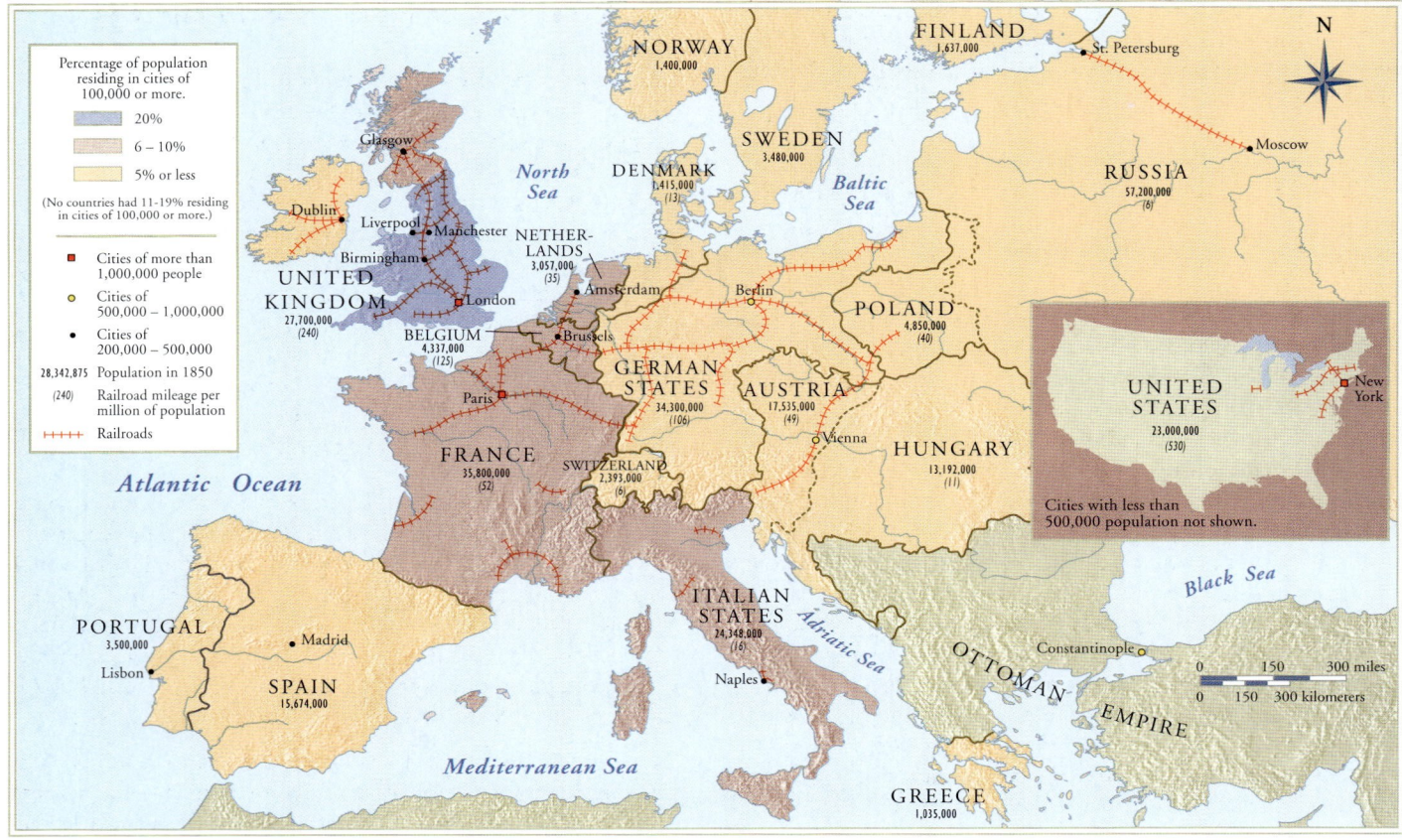

**MAP 29-1** Industrialization of Europe and the United States about 1850.

**THE SURVIVAL OF THE FITTEST** The English naturalist Charles Darwin (1809–1882) and his theory of natural selection did much to increase interest in science. Although the concept of evolution had been suggested earlier, Darwin and his compatriot Alfred Russel Wallace (1823–1913), working independently, articulated the theory of natural selection, which proposed a model for the process of evolution. They based this theory on mechanistic laws, rather than attributing evolution to random chance or God's plan, and argued for a competitive system in which only the fittest survived. Darwin's ideas, as presented in *On the Origin of Species by Means of Natural Selection* (1859), sharply contrasted with the biblical narrative of creation and thus were highly controversial. By challenging traditional Christian beliefs, Darwinism contributed to a growing secular attitude.

Other theorists and social thinkers, most notably British philosopher Herbert Spencer (1820–1903), applied Darwin's principles to the rapidly changing socioeconomic realm. As in the biological world, they asserted, industrialization's intense competition led to the survival of the most economically fit companies, enterprises, and countries. This logic served to justify the rampant Western racism, imperialism, nationalism, and militarism that marked the late 19th and early 20th centuries. Because of the pseudoscientific basis of social Darwinism, those who espoused this theory perceived such conflict and struggle as inevitable.

**KARL MARX AND CLASS STRUGGLE** The concept of conflict was central to the ideas of Karl Marx (1818–1883), another dominant figure of the period. Born to German-Jewish parents in Trier, Marx received a doctorate in philosophy from the University of Berlin. After moving to Paris, he met fellow German Friedrich Engels (1820–1895), who became his lifelong collaborator. Together they wrote *The Communist Manifesto* (1848), which called for the working class to overthrow the capitalist system. Like Darwin and other empiricists, Marx believed that scientific, rational law governed nature and, indeed, all human history. For Marx, economic forces based on class struggle induced historical change. Throughout history, insisted Marx, those who controlled the means of production conflicted with those whose labor was exploited to benefit the wealthy and powerful. This constant opposition—a dynamic he called "dialectical materialism"—caused change. Marxism's ultimate goal was to create a socialist state—the seizure of power by the working class and the destruction of capitalism. Marxism, which held great appeal for the oppressed as well as many intellectuals, emphasized class conflict and was instrumental in the rise of trade unions and socialist groups.

**COLONIZING THE WORLD** Many of these important developments—for example, industrialization and social Darwinism—help explain this period's extensive imperialism. Industrialization required a wide variety of natural resources, and social Darwinists easily translated their intrinsic concept of social hierarchy into racial and national hierarchies. These hierarchies provided Western leaders with justification for the colonization of peoples and cultures that they deemed less advanced. By 1900, the major economic and political powers had divided up much of the world. The French had colonized most of North Africa and Indochina, while the British occupied India, Australia, and large areas of Africa, including Nigeria, Egypt, Sudan, Rhodesia, and the Union of South Africa. The Dutch were a major presence in the Pacific, and the Germans, Portuguese, Spanish, and Italians all established themselves in various areas of Africa.

# THE DEVELOPMENT OF MODERNISM

**MODERNITY AND MODERNISM** The combination of extensive technological changes and increased exposure to other cultures, coupled with the rapidity of these changes, led to an acute sense in Western cultures of the world's lack of fixity or permanence. The Darwinian ideas of evolution and Marx's emphasis on a continuing sequence of conflicts and resolutions reinforced this awareness of a constantly shifting reality. These societal changes prompted a greater consciousness of and interest in modernity—the state of being modern. This avid exploration of the conditions of modernity and of people's position relative to a historical continuum permeated the Western art world as well, resulting in the development of *modernism*. Modernist art's critical function differentiates it from modern art. Modern art, as discussed in Chapter 28, is more or less a chronological designation, referring to art of the past few centuries. Modern artists were and are aware of the relationship between their art and that of previous eras. Modernism developed in the second half of the 19th century and is "modern" in that modernist artists, then and now, often seek to capture the images and sensibilities of their age. However, modernism goes beyond simply dealing with the present and involves the artist's critical examination of or reflection on the premises of art itself. Modernism thus implies certain concerns about art and aesthetics that are internal to art production, regardless of whether or not the artist is producing scenes from contemporary social life.

Clement Greenberg, a 20th-century American art critic, explained: "The essence of Modernism lies . . . in the use of the characteristic methods of a discipline to criticize the discipline itself—not in order to subvert it, but to entrench it more firmly in its area of competence."[1] He explains further what he means by criticizing the discipline: "Realistic, illusionist art had dissembled the medium, using art to conceal art. Modernism used art to call attention to art. The limitations that constitute the medium of painting—the flat surface, the shape of the support, the properties of pigment—were treated by the Old Masters as negative factors that could be acknowledged only implicitly or indirectly. Modernist painting has come to regard these same limitations as positive factors that are to be acknowledged openly."[2] The two major modernist art movements of the later 19th century were Realism and Impressionism, and both were conditioned by the historical and theoretical milieu in which they incubated.

This critical, modernist stance challenged the more conservative approach of the academies, where artists received traditional training. Eventually, toward the end of the century, the aggressiveness of modernism led to the development of the *avant-garde*—artists whose work emphatically rejected the past and transgressed the boundaries of conventional artistic practice. The subversive dimension of the avant-garde was in sync with the anarchic, revolutionary sociopolitical tendencies in Europe at the time. The art of the Post-Impressionists, such as Vincent van Gogh, Paul Gauguin, Georges Seurat, and Paul Cézanne, was among the first labeled avant-garde. The end of the 19th century, with its unique *fin de siècle* (end of the century) culture, paved the way for the entrenchment of modernism and the avant-garde in the 20th century.

## Realism: The Painting of Modern Life

*Realism* was a movement that developed in France around mid-century. GUSTAVE COURBET (1819–1877), long regarded as the leading figure of the Realist movement in 19th-century art, used the term *realism* when exhibiting his own works, even though he shunned labels. In and since Courbet's time, confusion about what constitutes Realism has been widespread. Writing in 1857, Jules-François-Félix Husson Champfleury (1821–1889), one of the first critics to recognize and appreciate Courbet's work, declared: "I will not define *Realism*. . . . I do not know where it comes from, where it goes, what it is; . . . The name horrifies me by its pedantic ending; . . . there is enough confusion already about that famous word."[3] Confusion, or at least disagreement, about Realism still exists among art historians.

**REDEFINING REALITY** The work of the Realists, in essence, provides viewers with a reevaluation of "reality." Like the empiricists and positivists, Realist artists argued that only the things of one's own time, what people can see for themselves, are "real." Accordingly, Realists focused their attention on the experiences and sights of everyday contemporary life and disapproved of historical and fictional subjects on the grounds that they were not real and visible and were not of the present world. Courbet declared in 1861:

> To be able to translate the customs, ideas, and appearances of my time as I see them—in a word, to create a living art—this has been my aim. . . . [T]he art of painting can consist only in the representation of objects visible and tangible to the painter . . . , [who must apply] his personal faculties to the ideas and the things of the period in which he lives. . . . I hold also that painting is an essentially *concrete* art, and can consist only of the representation of things both *real* and *existing*. . . . An *abstract* object, invisible or nonexistent, does not belong to the domain of painting. . . . Show me an angel, and I'll paint one.[4]

This sincerity about scrutinizing the world around them led the Realists to portray objects and images that until then had been deemed unworthy of depiction—the mundane and trivial, working-class laborers and peasants, and so forth. Even further, the Realists depicted these scenes on a scale and with an earnestness and seriousness previously reserved for grand history painting.

**THE LOWEST OF THE LOW** In *The Stone Breakers* (FIG. **29-1**), Courbet presents the viewer with a glimpse into the life of a rural toiler. Courbet captured on canvas in a straightforward manner two men—one mature, the other very young—in the act of breaking stones, traditionally the lot of the lowest in French society. Their menial labor is neither romanticized nor idealized but is shown with directness and accuracy. Courbet reveals to the viewer the drudgery of this labor. His palette's dirty browns and grays convey the dreary and dismal nature of the task, while the angular positioning of the older stone breaker's limbs suggests a mechanical monotony.

This interest in the laboring poor as subject matter had special meaning for the mid-19th-century French audience. In 1848, workers rebelled against the bourgeois leaders of the newly formed Second Republic and against the rest of the nation, demanding better working conditions and a redistribution of property. The army quelled the revolution in three days, but not without long-lasting trauma and significant loss of life. The Revolution of 1848 thus raised the issue of labor as a national concern and placed workers on center stage, both literally and symbolically. Courbet's depiction of stone breakers in 1849 was very timely and populist.

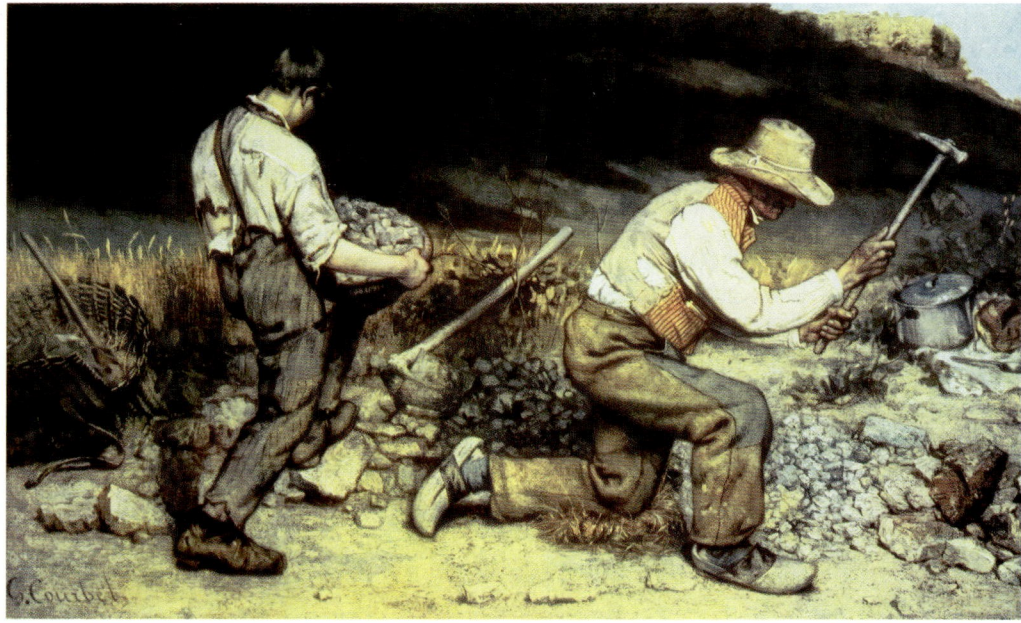

29-1 GUSTAVE COURBET, *The Stone Breakers*, 1849. Oil on canvas, 5′ 3″ × 8′ 6″. Formerly at Gemäldegalerie, Dresden (destroyed in 1945).

**PEASANT LIFE AND DEATH** Also representative of Courbet's work is *Burial at Ornans* (FIG. 29-2), which depicts a funeral in a bleak provincial landscape attended by "common, trivial" persons, the type of people Honoré de Balzac and Gustave Flaubert presented in their novels.[5] While an officious clergyman reads the Office of the Dead, those attending cluster around the excavated gravesite, their faces registering all degrees of response to the situation.

Although the painting has the monumental scale of a traditional history painting, the subject's ordinariness and the starkly antiheroic composition horrified contemporary critics. Arranged in a wavering line extending across the broad horizontal width of the canvas, the figures are portrayed in groups—the somberly clad women at the back right, a semicircle of similarly clad men by the

open grave, and assorted churchmen at the left. This wall of figures, seen at eye level in person, blocks any view into deep space. The faces are portraits; some of the models were Courbet's sisters (three of the women in the front row, toward the right) and friends. Behind and above the figures are bands of overcast sky and barren cliffs. The dark pit of the grave opens into the viewer's space in the center foreground. Despite the unposed look of the figures, the artist controlled the composition in a masterful way by his sparing use of bright color. The heroic, the sublime, and the dramatic are not found here—only the mundane realities of daily life and death. In 1857, Champfleury wrote of *Burial at Ornans*, ". . . it represents a small-town funeral and yet reproduces the funerals of *all* small towns."[6] Unlike the theatricality of Romanticism, Realism captured the ordinary rhythms of contemporaneous life.

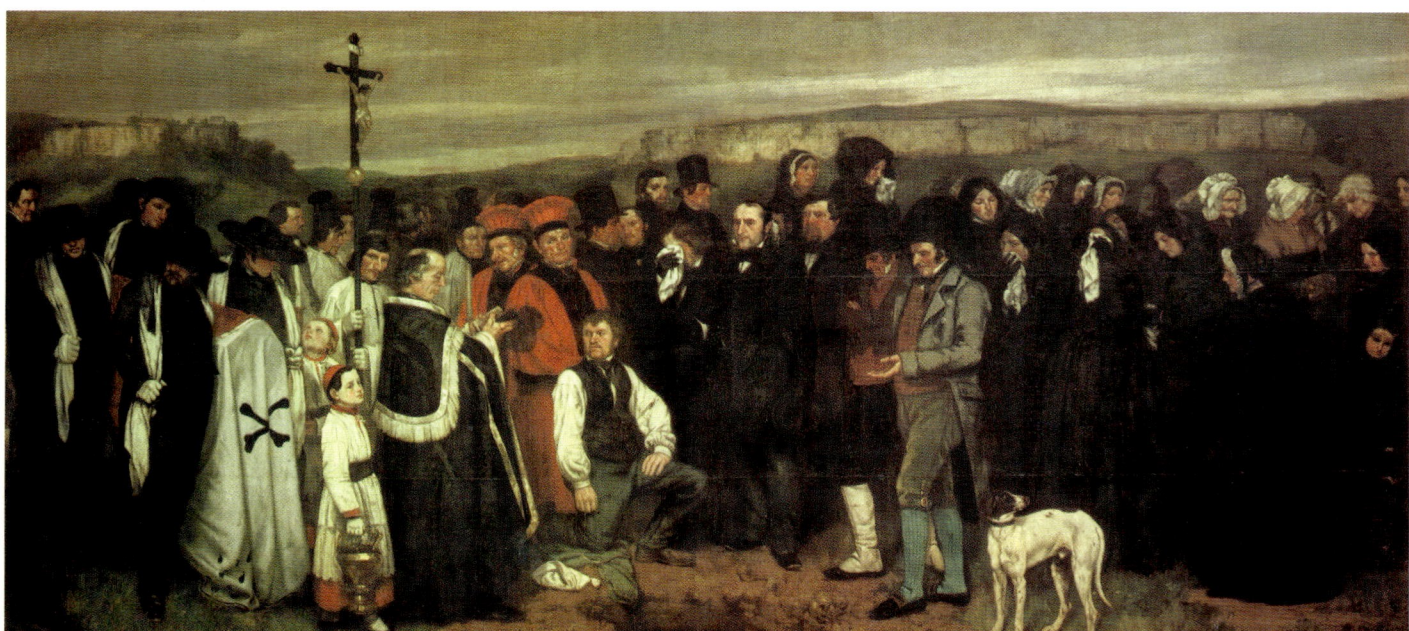

29-2 GUSTAVE COURBET, *Burial at Ornans*, 1849. Oil on canvas, approx. 10′ × 22′. Louvre, Paris.

**EMPHASIZING THE PAINTED SURFACE** Viewed as the first modernist movement by many scholars and critics, Realism also involved a reconsideration of the painter's primary goals and departed from the established priority on illusionism. Accordingly, Realists called attention to painting as a pictorial construction by their pigment application or composition manipulation. Courbet's intentionally simple and direct methods of expression in composition and technique seemed unbearably crude to many of his more traditional contemporaries, and he was called a primitive. Although his bold, somber palette was essentially traditional, Courbet often used the palette knife for quickly placing and unifying large daubs of paint, producing a roughly wrought surface. His example inspired the young artists who worked for him (and later Impressionists such as Claude Monet and Auguste Renoir), but the public accused him of carelessness and critics wrote of his "brutalities."

Because of both the style and content of Courbet's paintings, they were not well received. The jury selecting work for the 1855 Salon (part of the Exposition Universelle in that year) rejected two of his paintings on the grounds that his subjects and figures were too coarsely depicted (so much so as to be plainly "socialistic") and too large. In response, Courbet set up his own exhibition outside the grounds, calling it the Pavilion of Realism. Courbet's pavilion and his statements amounted to the new movement's manifestos. Although he maintained he founded no school and was of no school, he did, as the name of his pavilion suggests, accept the term *realism* as descriptive of his art.

**A PAINTER OF COUNTRY LIFE** Like Courbet, JEAN-FRANÇOIS MILLET (1814–1878) found his subjects in the people and occupations of the everyday world. Millet was one of a group of French painters of country life who, to be close to their rural subjects, settled near the village of Barbizon in the forest of Fontainebleau. This Barbizon school specialized in detailed pictures of forest and countryside. Millet, perhaps their most prominent member, was of peasant stock and identified with the hard lot of the country poor. In *The Gleaners* (FIG. **29-3**), he depicted three peasant women performing the back-breaking task of gleaning the last wheat scraps. These women were members of the lowest level of peasant society, and such impoverished people were permitted to glean—to pick up the remainders left in the field after the harvest. This feudal right was traditionally granted to the peasantry by landowning nobles. Millet characteristically placed his monumental figures in the foreground, against a broad sky. Although the field stretches back to a rim of haystacks, cottages, trees, and distant workers and a flat horizon, the viewer's attention is drawn to the gleaners quietly doing their tedious and time-consuming work.

Although Millet's works have a sentimentality absent from those of Courbet, the French public reacted to paintings such as *The Gleaners* with disdain and suspicion. In the aftermath of the Revolution of 1848, Millet's investing the poor with solemn grandeur did not meet with the approval of the prosperous classes. In particular, middle-class landowners resisted granting the traditional gleaning rights, and thus such relatively dignified depictions of gleaning did not sit well with them. Further, the middle class linked the poor with the dangerous, newly defined working class, which was finding outspoken champions in men such as Karl Marx, Friedrich Engels, and the novelists Émile Zola (1840–1902) and Charles Dickens (1812–1870). Socialism was a growing movement, and both its views on property and its call for social justice, even economic equality, frightened the bourgeoisie. Millet's sympathetic depiction of the poor seemed to many like a political manifesto.

**CHAMPIONING THE WORKING CLASS** Because people widely recognized the power of art to serve political means, the political and social agitation accompanying the violent revolutions in France and the rest of Europe in the later 18th and early 19th centuries prompted the French people to suspect artists of subversive intention. A person could be jailed for too bold a statement in the press, in literature, in art—even in music and drama. Realist artist

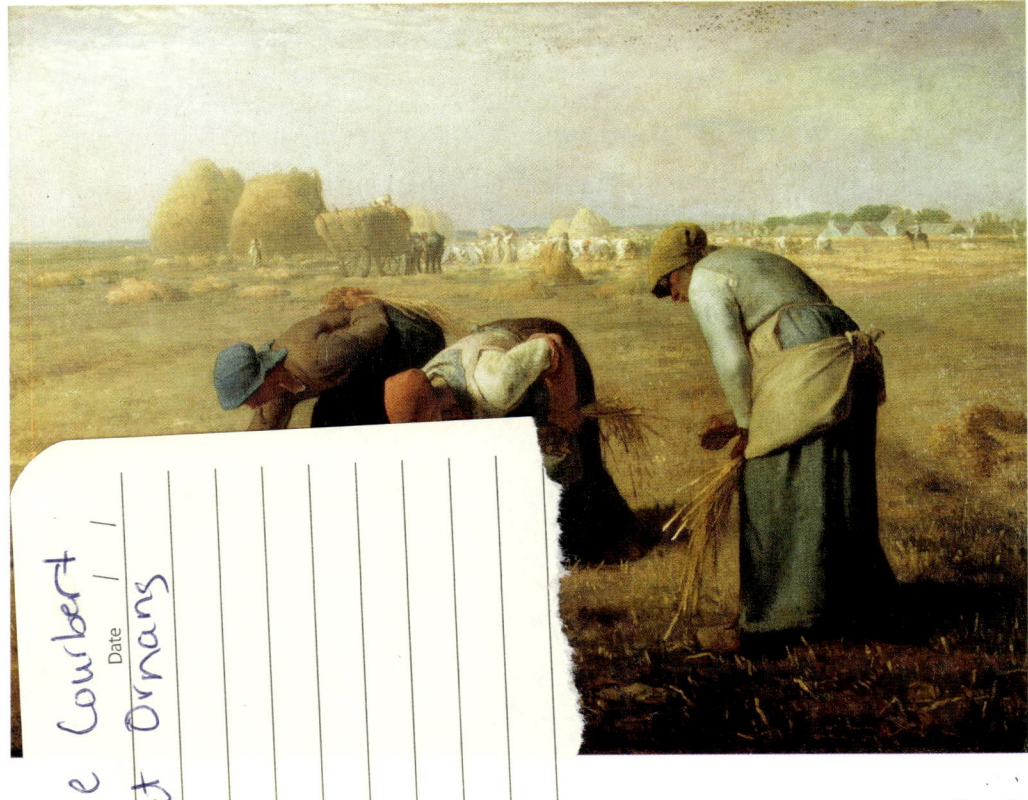

**29-3** JEAN-FRANÇOIS MILLET, *The Gleaners*, 1857. Oil on canvas, approx. 2′ 9″ × 3′ 8″. Louvre, Paris.

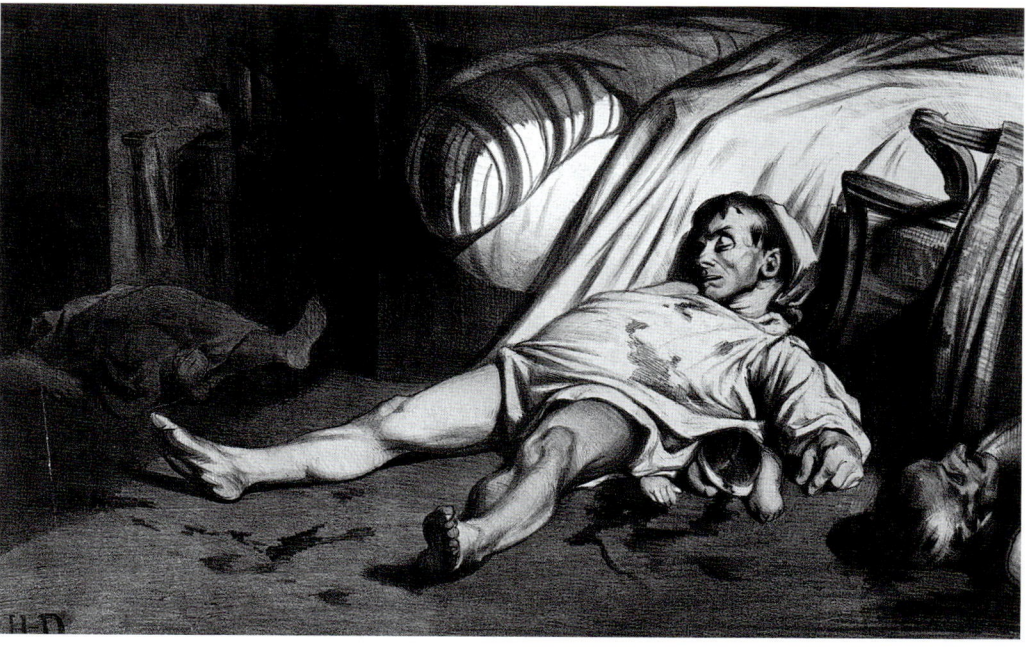

**29-4** HONORÉ DAUMIER, *Rue Transnonain*, 1834. Lithograph, approx. $1' \times 1' \, 5\frac{1}{2}''$. Philadelphia Museum of Art, Philadelphia (bequest of Fiske and Marie Kimball). 

HONORÉ DAUMIER (1808–1879) was a defender of the urban working classes, and in his art, he boldly confronted authority with social criticism and political protest. In response, the authorities imprisoned the artist. A painter, sculptor, and, like Goya, one of the world's great masters of the graphic (print) medium, Daumier produced lithographs—images printed from a flat stone—that allowed him to create an unprecedented number of prints, thereby reaching a broader audience. Daumier also contributed satirical lithographs to the widely read, liberal French Republican journal *Caricature*. In these prints, he mercilessly lampooned the foibles and misbehavior of politicians, lawyers, doctors, and the rich bourgeoisie in general. His in-depth knowledge of the acute political and social unrest in Paris during the revolutions of 1830 and 1848 endowed his work with truthfulness and, therefore, impact.

His lithograph *Rue Transnonain* (FIG. **29-4**) depicts an atrocity with the same shocking impact as Goya's *The Third of May, 1808* (see FIG. 28-43). The title refers to a street in Lyon where an unknown sniper killed a civil guard, part of a government force trying to repress a worker demonstration. Because the fatal shot had come from a workers' housing block, the remaining guards immediately stormed the building and massacred all of its inhabitants. With Goya's power, Daumier created a view of the atrocity from a sharp, realistic angle of vision. He depicted not the dramatic moment of execution but the terrible, quiet aftermath. The broken, scattered forms lie amid violent disorder, as if newly found. The print's significance lies in its factualness. It is an example of the period's increasing artistic bias toward using facts as subject, and not always illusionistically. Daumier's pictorial manner is rough and spontaneous; how it carries expressive exaggeration is part of its remarkable force. Daumier's work is true to life in content, but his style is uniquely personal.

**ELEVATING PHOTOGRAPHY** The impact of Daumier's work, whether scathing or compassionate, was due in large part to his considerable intelligence and quick wit. Further, the rapidity with which lithographs could be produced (especially compared to traditional painting) allowed Daumier to comment on contemporary events in a timely manner. One such lithograph, *Nadar Raising Photography to the Height of Art* (FIG. **29-5**), provides incisive and amusing commentary about the ongoing struggle of photography to be recognized as a fine art. This print was prompted by an 1862 court decision that acknowledged that photography was indeed an art (and therefore entitled to legal protection; the suit involved copyright infringement, which only applied to recognized art forms at the time). Immediately after the decision was announced, Daumier created *Nadar Raising Photography,* in which the well-known photographer Nadar (see Chapter 28, page 848) energetically takes pictures with his camera as his balloon rises over Parisian rooftops (each of which is labeled "photography"). Not only did this image visually depict the elevation of photography's status that the court decision reaffirmed, but it also paid homage to Nadar's personal interests and efforts in that regard. Nadar was evangelical about the artistic possibilities that photography offered and campaigned tirelessly for art photography. He was also a staunch advocate of balloon transportation and aerial reconnaissance, and produced the first aerial photographs of Paris from his balloon Le Géant (The Giant). In *Nadar Raising Photography,* Daumier synthesized all of these references into a witty, incisive print.

**THE PLIGHT OF THE URBAN POOR** Daumier brought the same convictions exhibited in his graphic work to the paintings he did, especially after 1848. His unfinished *The Third-Class Carriage* (FIG. **29-6**) provides a glimpse into the cramped and grimy railway carriage of the 1860s. The riders are poor and can afford only third-class tickets. While first- and second-class carriages had closed compartments, third-class passengers were crammed together on hard benches that filled the carriage. The disinherited masses of 19th-century industrialism were Daumier's indignant concern, and he made them his subject repeatedly. He showed them in the unposed attitudes and unplanned arrangements of the millions thronging the modern cities—anonymous, insignificant, dumbly patient with a lot they could not change. Daumier saw people as they ordinarily appeared, their faces vague, impersonal, and blank—unprepared for any observers. He tried to achieve the real by isolating a random collection of the unrehearsed details of human existence from the continuum of ordinary life. Daumier's vision anticipated the spontaneity and candor of scenes captured with the modern snapshot camera by the end of the century.

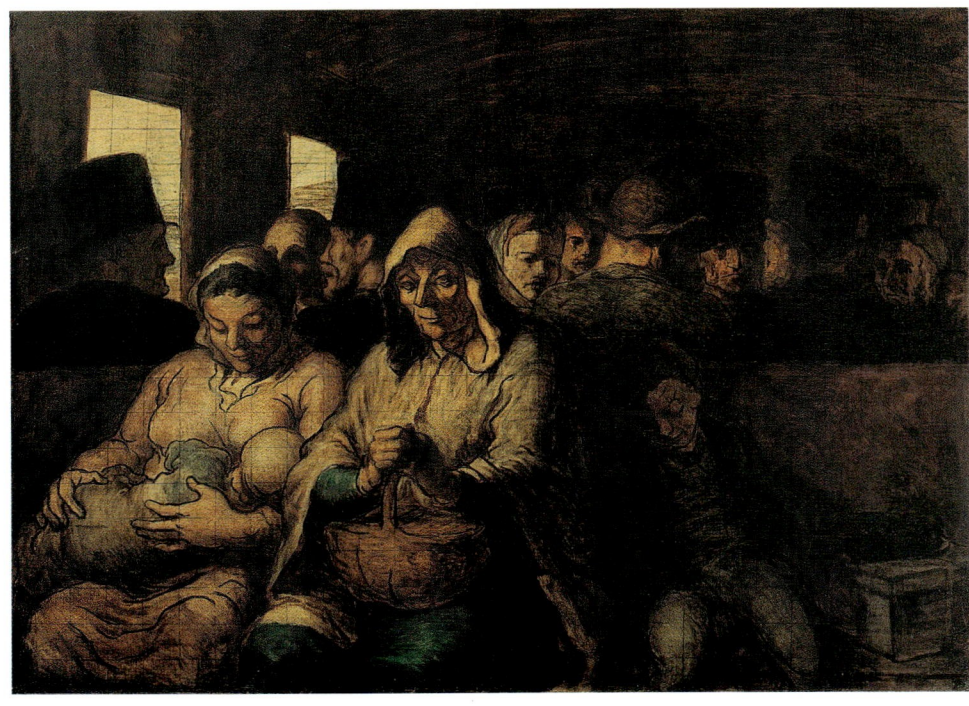

**29-5** Honoré Daumier, *Nadar Raising Photography to the Height of Art,* 1862. Lithograph, $10\frac{3}{4}'' \times 8\frac{3}{4}''$. Museum of Fine Arts, Boston.

NADAR élevant la Photographie à la hauteur de l'Art

**29-6** Honoré Daumier, *The Third-Class Carriage,* ca. 1862. Oil on canvas, $2'\ 1\frac{3}{4}'' \times 2'\ 11\frac{1}{2}''$. Metropolitan Museum of Art, New York (H. O. Havemeyer Collection, bequest of Mrs. H. O. Havemeyer, 1929).

**PROMISCUITY IN A PARISIAN PARK?** Like Gustave Courbet, the commitment of ÉDOUARD MANET (1832–1883) to Realist ideas was instrumental in affecting the course of modernist painting. Manet was a pivotal figure during the 19th century. Not only was his work critical for the articulation of Realist principles, but his art played an important role in the development of Impressionism in the 1870s. When attempting to explain the critique of the discipline central to modernism, art historians often have looked to Manet's paintings (FIGS. 29-7, 29-8, and 29-26) as prime examples. Manet's interest in Realism and in modernist principles is evident in *Le Déjeuner sur l'Herbe*, or *Luncheon on the Grass* (FIG. 29-7).

*Le Déjeuner* depicts two nude women and two clothed men enjoying a picnic of sorts. The foreground figures were all based on living, identifiable people. The seated nude is Victorine Meurend (Manet's favorite model at the time), and the gentlemen are his brother Eugène (with cane) and the sculptor Ferdinand Leenhof. The two men wear fashionable Parisian attire of the 1860s, and the foreground nude is not only a distressingly unidealized figure type but also seems disturbingly unabashed and at ease, looking directly at the viewer without shame or flirtatiousness.

This outraged the public—rather than a traditional pastoral scene, *Le Déjeuner* seemed merely to represent the promiscuous in a Parisian park. One hostile critic, no doubt voicing public opinion, said:

> A commonplace woman of the demimonde [the realm of the promiscuous woman, especially prostitutes], as naked as can be, shamelessly lolls between two dandies dressed to the teeth. These latter look like schoolboys on a holiday, perpetrating an outrage to play the man. . . . This is a young man's practical joke—a shameful, open sore.[7]

While Manet surely anticipated criticism of his painting, shocking the public was not his primary aim. Manet's goal was more complex and involved a reassessment of the entire range of art. *Le Déjeuner* contains sophisticated references and allusions to many painting genres—history painting, portraiture, pastoral scenes, nudes, and even religious scenes. What *Le Déjeuner* thus represents is an impressive synthesis of the history of painting.

The negative response to this painting by public and critics alike extended beyond Manet's subject matter. His manner of presenting his figures also prompted severe criticism. He rendered them in soft focus and broadly painted the landscape, including the pool in which the second woman bathes. The loose manner of painting contrasts with the clear forms of the harshly lit foreground trio and the pile of discarded female attire and picnic foods at the lower left. The lighting creates strong contrasts between darks and highlighted areas. In the main figures, many values are summed up in one or two lights or darks. The effect is both to flatten the forms and to give them a hard snapping presence. Form, rather than a matter of line, is only a function of paint and light. Manet himself declared that the chief actor in the painting is the light. In true modernist fashion, Manet was using art to call attention to art—in other words, he was moving away from illusion and toward open acknowledgment of painting's properties, such as the flatness of the painting surface. The public, however, saw only a crude sketch without the customary finish. The style of the painting, coupled with the unorthodox subject matter, made this work exceptionally controversial.

**SCANDALOUS AUDACITY** Even more scandalous to the French viewing public was Manet's 1863 painting *Olympia* (FIG. 29-8). This work depicts a young white prostitute (Olympia

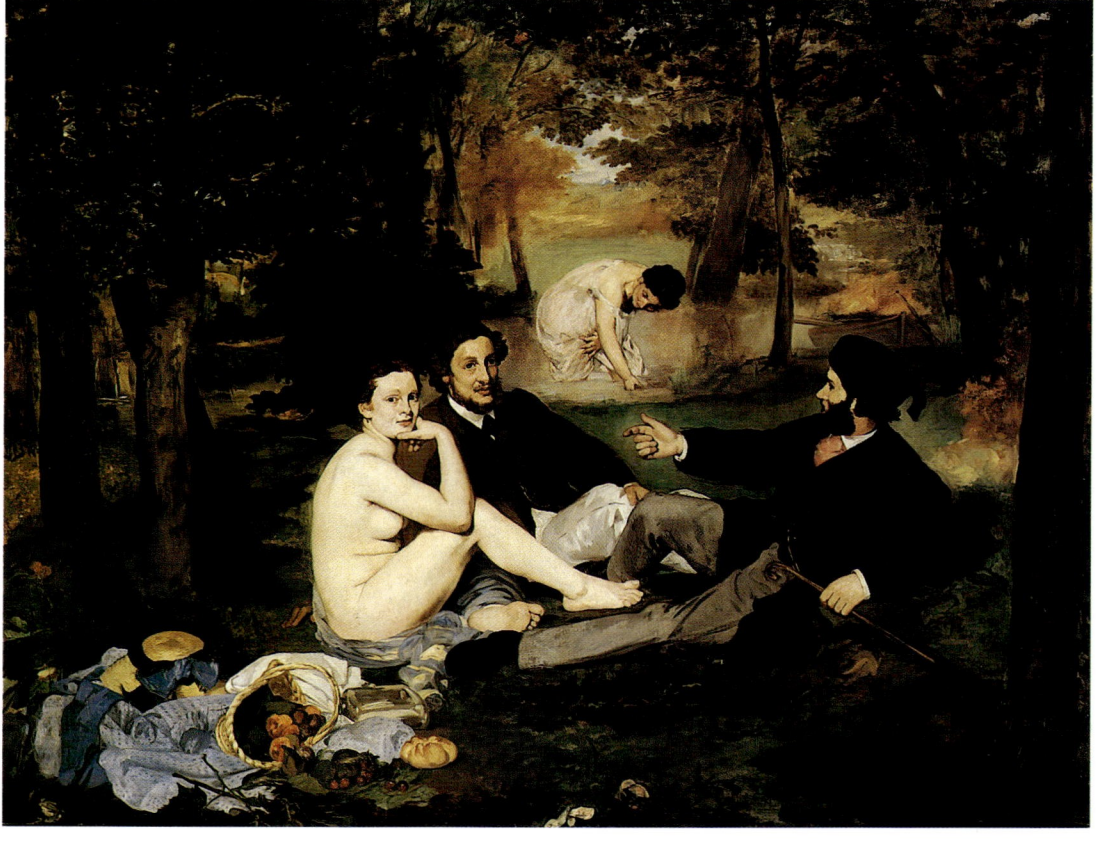

**29-7** Édouard Manet, *Le Déjeuner sur l'Herbe (Luncheon on the Grass)*, 1863. Oil on canvas, approx. 7′ × 8′ 10″. Réunion des Musées Nationaux.

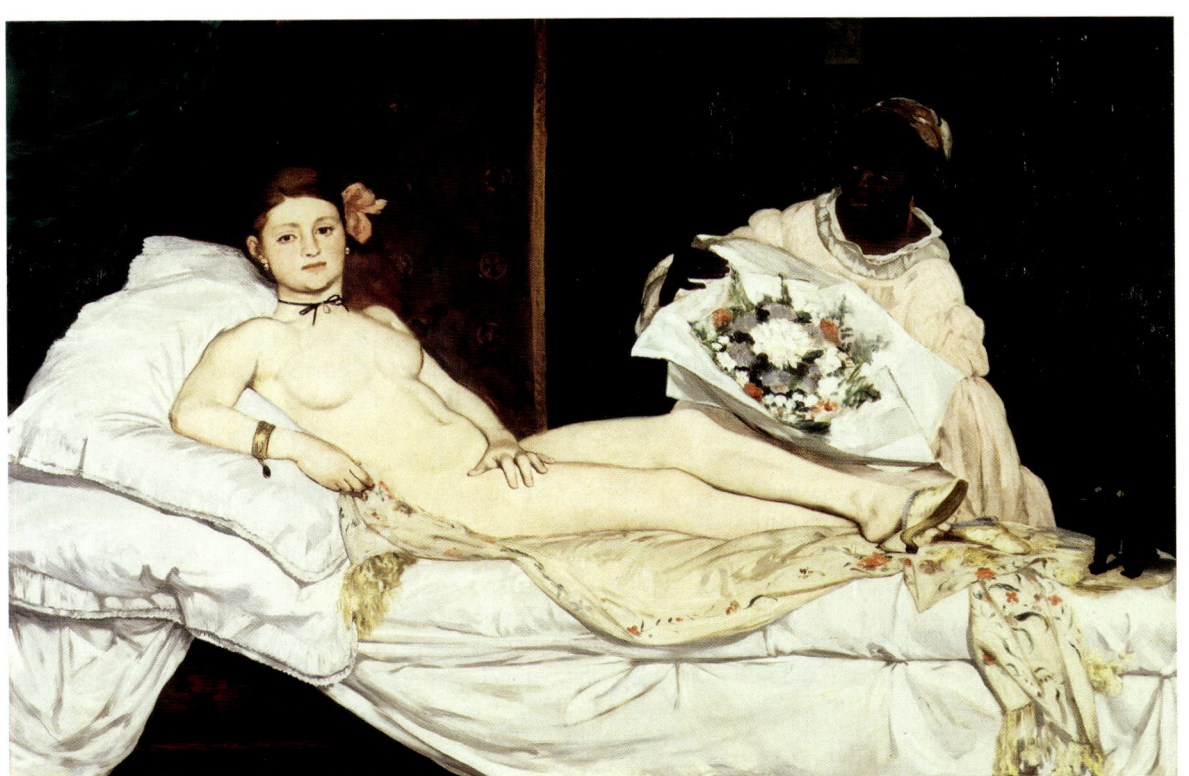

29-8 ÉDOUARD
MANET, *Olympia*,
1863. Oil on canvas,
4′ 3″ × 6′ 3″.
Réunion des Musées
Nationaux.

was a common "professional" name for prostitutes in the 19th century) reclining on a bed that extends across the foreground. Entirely nude except for a thin black ribbon tied around her neck, a bracelet on her arm, an orchid in her hair, and fashionable mule slippers on her feet, Olympia meets the viewer's eyes with a look of cool indifference. Behind her appears a black maid, who presents her a bouquet of flowers from a client.

Public and critics alike were horrified. Although images of prostitutes were not unheard of during this period, viewers were taken aback by the shamelessness of Olympia and her look that verges on defiance. The depiction of a black woman was also not new to painting, but the viewing public perceived Manet's inclusion of both a black maid and a nude prostitute as evoking moral depravity, inferiority, and animalistic sexuality. The contrast of the black servant with the fair-skinned courtesan also made reference to racial divisions. One critic described Olympia as "a courtesan with dirty hands and wrinkled feet . . . her body has the livid tint of a cadaver displayed in the morgue; her outlines are drawn in charcoal and her greenish, bloodshot eyes appear to be provoking the public, protected all the while by a hideous Negress."[8]

From this statement, it is clear that viewers were responding not just to the subject matter but to Manet's artistic style as well. Manet's brush strokes are rougher and the shifts in tonality are more abrupt than those found in traditional academic painting (see "The Academies: Defining the Range of Acceptable Art," page 862). This departure from accepted practice exacerbated the audacity of the subject matter.

**ACADEMIC ART'S CONVENTIONS** To understand better the public's reaction to such modernist painting, a comparison of *Olympia* to a work by a highly acclaimed French academic artist of the time, ADOLPHE-WILLIAM BOUGUEREAU (1825–1905), is instructive. In works such as *Nymphs and Satyr* (FIG. **29-9**), Bouguereau depicted classical mythological subjects with a polished

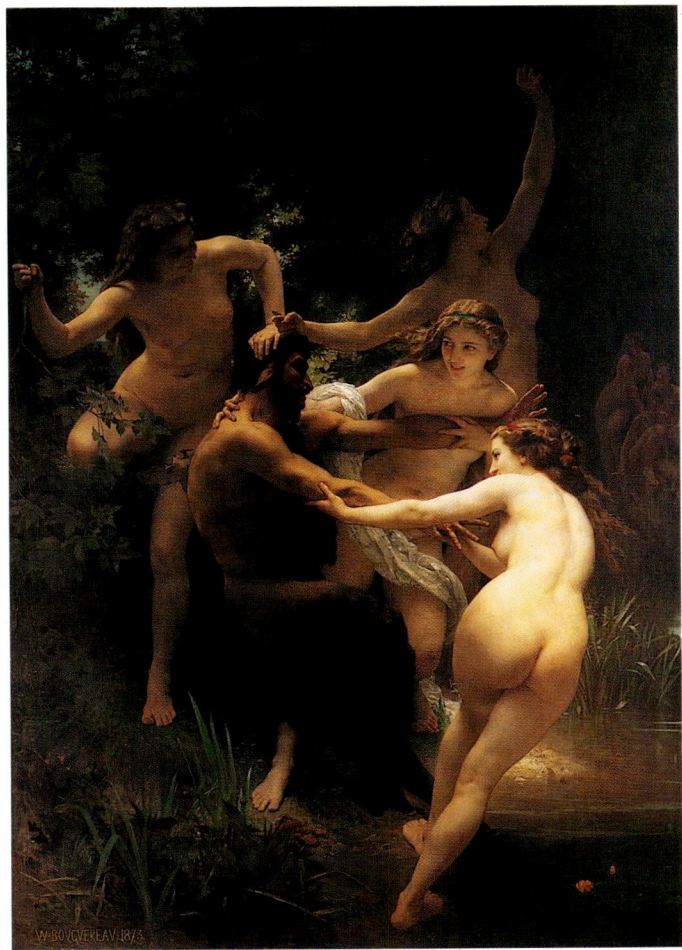

29-9 ADOLPHE-WILLIAM BOUGUEREAU, *Nymphs and Satyr*, 1873. Oil on canvas, approx. 8′ 6″ high. Sterling and Francine Clark Art Institute, Williamstown, Massachusetts.

## The Academies
### Defining the Range of Acceptable Art

Modernist art is often discussed in contrast to academic art. What is academic art? The term is used to refer to art sanctioned by the academies, established art schools such as the Royal Academy of Painting and Sculpture in France (founded in 1648) and the Royal Academy of Arts in Britain (founded in 1768). Both of these academies provided instruction for art students and sponsored exhibitions. For much of the long existence of these organizations, they exerted great control over the art scene. The annual exhibitions, called "Salons" in France (not the same as the 17th-century social salons), were highly competitive, as was membership in these academies. Subsidized by the government, the French Royal Academy thus supported a limited range of artistic expression, focusing on traditional subjects and highly polished technique. Because of the challenges modernist art presented to established artistic conventions, the Salons and other exhibitions often rejected it. In 1863, for example, Emperor Napoleon III established the Salon des Refusés (Salon of the Rejected) to show all of the works the academy's jury had not accepted for exhibition in the regular Salon. Works such as Manet's *Le Déjeuner sur l'Herbe* (FIG. 29-7) were included in the Salon des Refusés and were met with derision by much of the public.

The Impressionists reinforced the perception of these academies as bastions of conservatism. After repeated rejections, these artists decided to form their own society in 1873 and began holding their own exhibitions in Paris. This decision allowed the Impressionists much freedom, for they did not have to contend with the academies' authoritative and confining viewpoint. The Impressionist exhibitions were held at one- or two-year intervals from 1874 until 1886. Another group of artists unhappy with the Salon's conservative nature adopted the same renegade idea. In 1884, these artists formed the Sociéte des Artistes Indépendant (Society of Independent Artists) and held annual Salons des Indépendants; Georges Seurat's *A Sunday on La Grande Jatte* (FIG. 29-39) was included in the 1886 Salon des Indépendants. Attempts to move away from the constrictive "official" Salons continued into the 20th century; the Salon d'Automne (Autumn Salon), established in 1903, provided avant-garde artists with additional opportunities for showing their art.

As the art market expanded, venues for the exhibition of art increased. Art circles and societies sponsored private shows in which both amateurs and professionals participated. Dealers became more aggressive in promoting the artists they represented by mounting exhibitions in a variety of spaces, some fairly intimate and small, others large and grandiose. All of these proliferating opportunities for exhibition gave artists alternatives to the traditional constraints of the Salon and provided fertile breeding ground for the development of radical, avant-garde art.

---

illusionism. In this painting, the flirtatious and ideally beautiful nymphs strike graceful poses yet seem based as closely on nature as are the details of their leafy surroundings. They playfully pull in different directions the satyr, the mythical beast-man, with a goat's hindquarters and horns, a horse's ears and tail, and a man's upper body. Although Bouguereau arguably depicted this scene in a very naturalistic (visually realistic or illusionistic) manner, it is emphatically not Realist. His choice of a fictional theme and adherence to established painting conventions could only have been seen as staunchly traditional. Bouguereau was immensely popular during the later 19th century, enjoying the favor of state patronage throughout his career.

**A REALIST PAINTER OF ANIMALS** Another French artist who received great acclaim during her career was MARIE-ROSALIE (ROSA) BONHEUR (1822–1899). Awarded a Légion d'honneur (Legion of Honor) in 1865, Bonheur was the most celebrated woman artist of the 19th century. Although Bonheur's work contains Realist elements, she is perhaps more appropriately considered a "naturalist" as described by French critic Jules Castagnary. Bonheur was trained as an artist by her father, who was a proponent of Saint-Simonianism, an early-19th-century utopian socialist movement that emphasized, among other tenets, the education and enfranchisement of women. As a result of her father's influence, Bonheur launched her career believing that as a woman and an artist, she had a special role to play in creating a new and perfect society. A Realist passion for accuracy in painting drove Bonheur, but she resisted depicting the problematic social and political situations seen in the work of Courbet,

Manet, and other Realists. Rather, she turned to the animal world. In her work, she combined a scientist's knowledge of equine anatomy and motion with an honest love and admiration for the brute strength of wild and domestic animals. She went to great lengths to observe the anatomy of living horses at the great Parisian horse fair, where the animals were shown and traded, and also spent long hours studying the anatomy of carcasses in the Paris slaughterhouses. For her best-known work, *The Horse Fair* (FIG. **29-10**), she adopted a panoramic composition similar to that in Courbet's *Burial at Ornans* (FIG. 29-2), painted a few years earlier. In contrast to the still figures in *Burial*, Bonheur filled her broad canvas with the sturdy farm Percherons and their grooms seen on parade at the annual Parisian horse sale. Some horses, not quite broken, rear up; others plod or trot, guided on foot or ridden by their keepers. The uneven line of the march, the thunderous pounding, and the Percherons' seemingly overwhelming power clearly were based on close observation from life, even though Bonheur acknowledged some inspiration from the Classical model of the Parthenon frieze (see FIG. 5-48). The dramatic lighting, loose brushwork, and rolling sky also reveal her admiration of the style of Géricault (see FIG. 28-45). Bonheur's depiction of equine drama in *The Horse Fair* captivated viewers, who eagerly bought engraved reproductions of the work, making it one of the most well-known paintings of the century.

Despite the public's derision, the French Realists—Courbet, Millet, Daumier, Manet, and other artists—challenged the whole iconographic stock of traditional art and called public attention to what noted French poet Charles Baudelaire (1821–1867) termed the "heroism of modern life."[9] In so doing, they not only

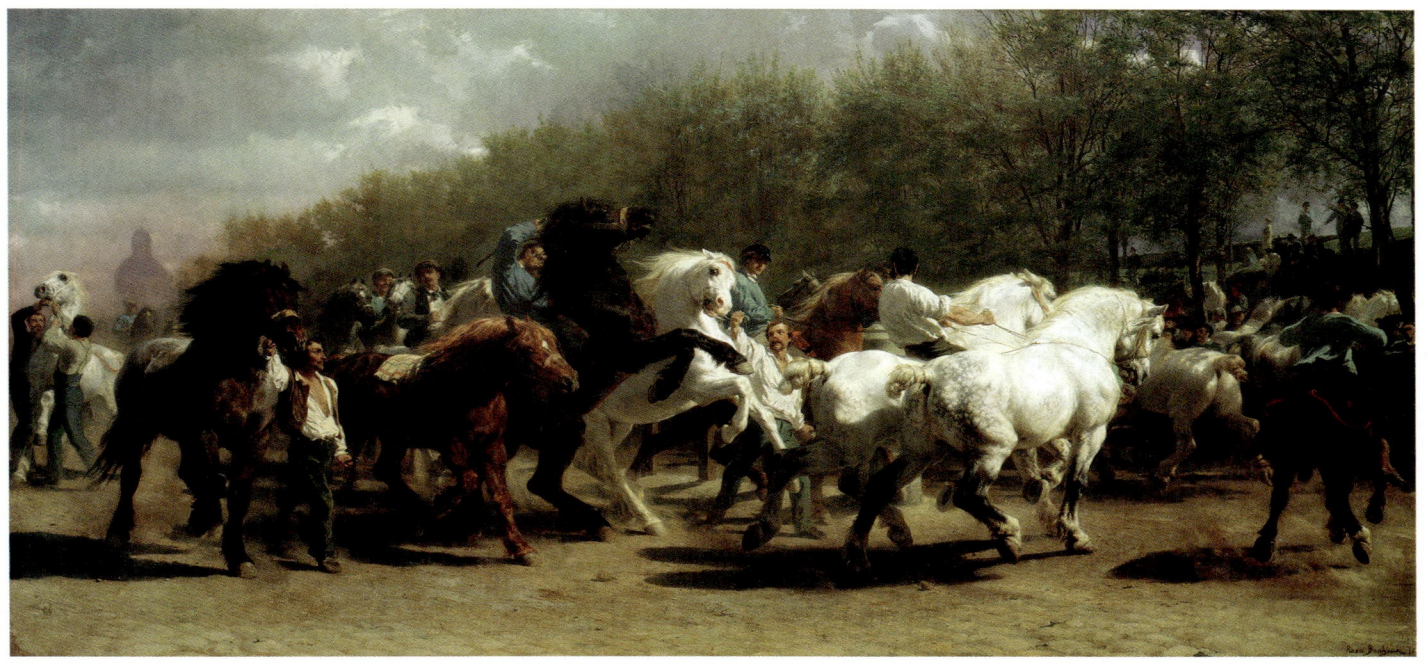

**29-10** MARIE-ROSALIE (ROSA) BONHEUR, *The Horse Fair,* 1853–1855. Oil on canvas, 8′ $\frac{1}{4}$″ × 16′ 7$\frac{1}{2}$″. Metropolitan Museum of Art, New York (gift of Cornelius Vanderbilt, 1887).

changed the course of Western art but also left succeeding generations of viewers with a broader understanding of French life and culture in the later 19th century.

## Realism Outside France

Although French artists took the lead in promoting Realism and the notion that artists should depict the realities of modern life, this movement was not exclusively French. The Realist foundation in empiricism and positivism appealed to artists in many countries, including Germany, Russia, England, and the United States. Realism emerged in a variety of forms and places and was well established by the end of the century.

**AN AMERICAN REALIST** This determination to paint scenes that resonated with modern audiences is seen in the work of American artist WINSLOW HOMER (1836–1910). Homer had firsthand knowledge of the Civil War; when it broke out in 1860, he joined the Union campaign as an artist-reporter for *Harper's Weekly.* In 1865 at the end of the Civil War, Homer painted *The Veteran in a New Field* (FIG. **29-11**). Although it is fairly simple and direct, this painting provides significant commentary on the effects and aftermath of this catastrophic national conflict. The painting depicts a man with his back to the viewer, harvesting wheat. That he is a veteran is clear not only from the painting's title but also from the uniform and canteen carelessly thrown on the ground in the lower right corner. The veteran's involvement in meaningful and productive work implies a smooth transition

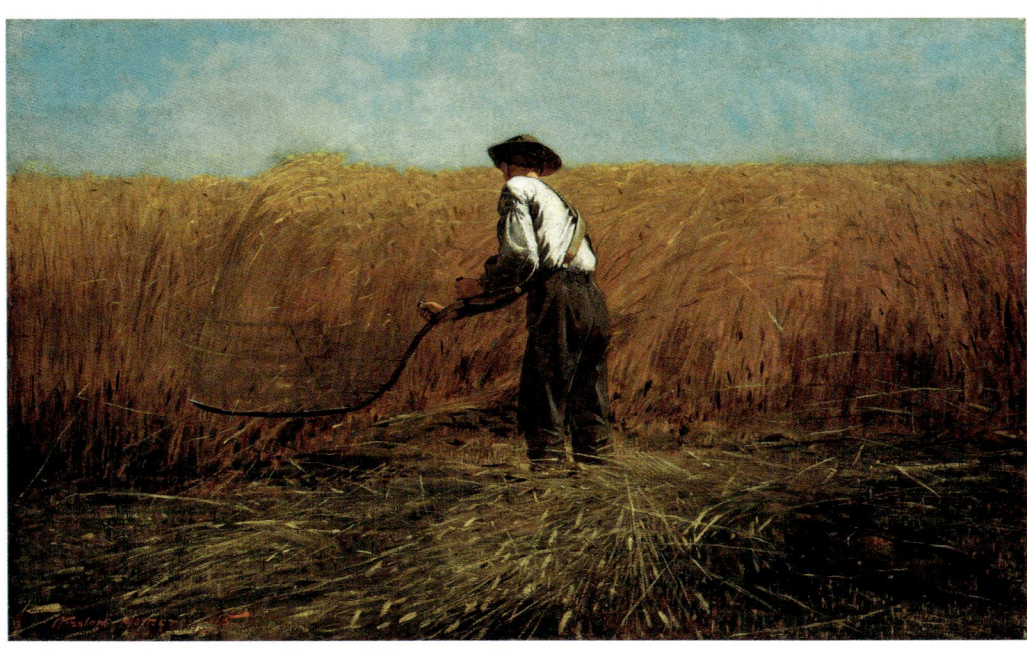

**29-11** WINSLOW HOMER, *The Veteran in a New Field,* 1865. Oil on canvas, 2′ $\frac{1}{8}$″ × 3′ 2$\frac{1}{8}$″. Metropolitan Museum of Art, New York (bequest of Miss Adelaide Milton de Groot, 1967).

from war to peace. Indeed, one could suggest that the veteran turned from harvesting men (see FIG. 28-68) to harvesting wheat. This transition to work after the end of the Civil War and the fate of disbanded soldiers were of national concern. The *New York Weekly Tribune* commented: "Rome took her great man from the plow, and made him a dictator—we must now take our soldiers from the camp and make them farmers."[10] America's ability to effect a smooth transition was seen as evidence of its national strength. "The peaceful and harmonious disbanding of the armies in the summer of 1865," poet Walt Whitman wrote, was one of the "immortal proofs of democracy, unequall'd in all the history of the past."[11] Homer's painting thus reinforced the perception of the country's greatness.

*The Veteran in a New Field* also comments symbolically about death—both the deaths of the soldiers and the death of Abraham Lincoln. By the 1860s, farmers used cradled scythes to harvest wheat. However, Homer chose not to insist on this historical reality and painted a single-bladed scythe. This transforms the veteran into a symbol of Death—the Grim Reaper himself—and the painting into an elegy to the thousands of soldiers who died in the Civil War and into a lamentation on the death of the recently assassinated president.

**NOT FOR THE SQUEAMISH** A dedicated appetite for showing the realities of the human experience made THOMAS EAKINS (1844–1916) a master Realist portrait and genre painter in the United States. He studied both painting and medical anatomy in Philadelphia before undertaking further study under French artist Jean-Léon Gérôme (1824–1904). Eakins was resolutely a Realist; his ambition was to paint things as he saw them rather than as the public might wish them portrayed. This attitude was very much in tune with 19th-century American taste, combining an admiration for accurate depiction with a hunger for truth.

The too-brutal Realism of Eakins's early masterpiece, *The Gross Clinic* (FIG. **29-12**), prompted the art jury to reject it for the Philadelphia exhibition that celebrated the American independence centennial. The work presents the renowned surgeon Dr. Samuel Gross in the operating amphitheater of the Jefferson Medical College in Philadelphia, where the painting now hangs. That Eakins chose to depict such an event testifies to the public's increasing faith in scientific and medical progress. Dr. Gross, with bloody fingers and scalpel, lectures about his surgery on a young man's leg. The patient suffered from osteomyelitis, a bone infection. The surgeon, acclaimed for his skill in this particular operation, is accompanied by colleagues, all of whom historians have identified, and by the patient's mother, who covers her face. Indicative of the contemporaneity of this scene is the anesthetist's presence in the background, holding the cloth over the patient's face. Anesthetics had been introduced in 1846, and their development eliminated a major obstacle to extensive surgery. The painting is, indeed, an unsparing description of a contemporaneous event, with a good deal more reality than many viewers could endure. "It is a picture," one critic said, "that even strong men find difficult to look at long, if they can look at it at all."[12] It was true to the artistic program of "scenes from modern life," as Southworth and Hawes had been in their daguerreotype of a similar setting (see FIG. 28-65). Both images recorded a particular event at a particular time.

Eakins believed that knowledge—and where relevant, scientific knowledge—was a prerequisite to his art. As a scientist (in his anatomical studies), Eakins preferred a slow, deliberate method of careful invention based on his observations of the perspective, the anatomy, and the actual details of his subject. This insistence on

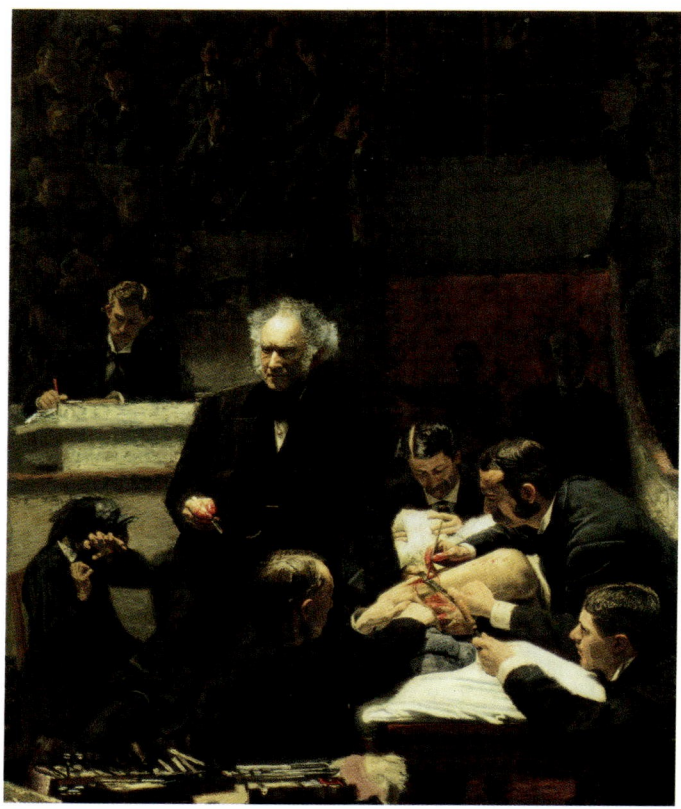

**29-12** THOMAS EAKINS, *The Gross Clinic*, 1875. Oil on canvas, 8′ × 6′ 6″. Jefferson Medical College of Thomas Jefferson University, Philadelphia.

scientific fact corresponded to the dominance of empiricism during the latter half of the 19th century. Eakins's concern for anatomical correctness led him to investigate the human form and humans in motion, both with regular photographic apparatuses and with a special camera that the French kinesiologist (a person who studies the physiology of body movement) Étienne-Jules Marey devised. Eakins's later collaboration with Eadweard Muybridge in the photographic study of animal and human action of all types drew favorable attention in France, especially from Degas, and anticipated the motion picture.

**THE ILLUSION OF MOTION** The Realist photographer and scientist EADWEARD MUYBRIDGE (1830–1904) came to the United States from England in the 1850s and settled in San Francisco, where he established a prominent international reputation for his photographs of the western United States. (His large-plate landscape images of the Yosemite region won him a gold medal at the Vienna Exposition of 1873.) In 1872, the governor of California, Leland Stanford, sought Muybridge's assistance in settling a bet about whether, at any point in a stride, all four feet of a horse galloping at top speed are off the ground. Through his sequential photography, as seen in *Horse Galloping* (FIG. 29-13), Muybridge proved they were. This experience was the beginning of Muybridge's photographic studies of the successive stages in human and animal motion—details too quick for the human eye to capture. These investigations culminated in 1885 at the University of Pennsylvania with a series of multiple-camera motion studies that recorded separate photographs of progressive moments in a single action. His discoveries received extensive publicity through the book *Animal Locomotion*, which Muybridge published in

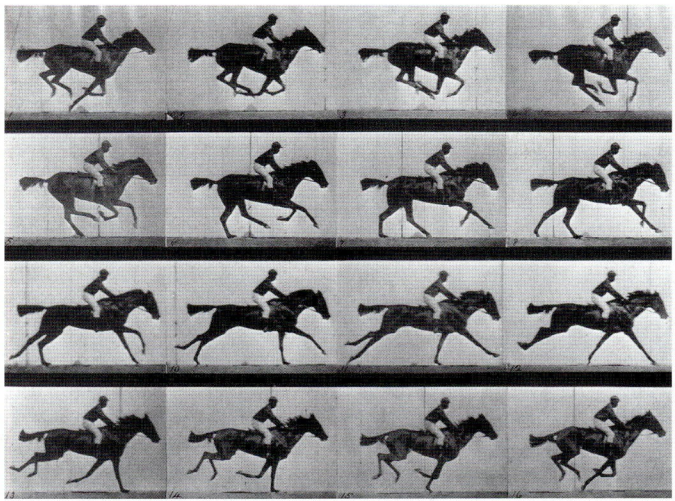

**29-13** EADWEARD MUYBRIDGE, *Horse Galloping,* 1878. Collotype print. George Eastman House, Rochester, New York.

1887. Muybridge's motion photographs earned him a place in the history of science, as well as art. His sequential motion studies, along with those of Eakins and Marey, influenced many other artists, including their contemporary, the painter and sculptor Edgar Degas (FIGS. 29-27 and 29-30), and 20th-century artists such as Marcel Duchamp (see FIGS. 33-23, 33-24, and 33-29).

Muybridge presented his work to scientists and general audiences with a device called the zoopraxiscope, which he invented to project his sequences of images (mounted on special glass plates) onto a screen. The result was so lifelike that one viewer said it "threw upon the screen apparently the living, moving animals. Nothing was wanting but the clatter of hoofs upon the turf."[13] The illusion of motion here was created by a physical fact of human eyesight called "persistence of vision." Stated simply, it means that the brain holds whatever the eye sees for a fraction of a second after the eye stops seeing it. Thus, viewers saw a rapid succession of different images merging one into the next, producing the illusion of continuous change. This illusion lies at the heart of the "realism" of all cinema.

**AMERICAN REALIST PORTRAITURE** The expatriate American artist JOHN SINGER SARGENT (1856–1925) was a younger contemporary of Eakins and Muybridge. Sargent developed a looser, more dashing Realist portrait style, in contrast to Eakins's carefully rendered details. Sargent studied art in Paris before settling in London, where he was renowned both as a cultivated and cosmopolitan gentleman and as a facile and fashionable portrait painter. He learned his fluent brushing of paint in thin layers and his effortless achievement of quick and lively illusion from his study of Velázquez, whose masterpiece, *Las Meninas* (see FIG. 24-33), may have influenced Sargent's family portrait *The Daughters of Edward Darley Boit* (FIG. **29-14**). The four girls (the children of one of Sargent's close friends) appear in a hall and small

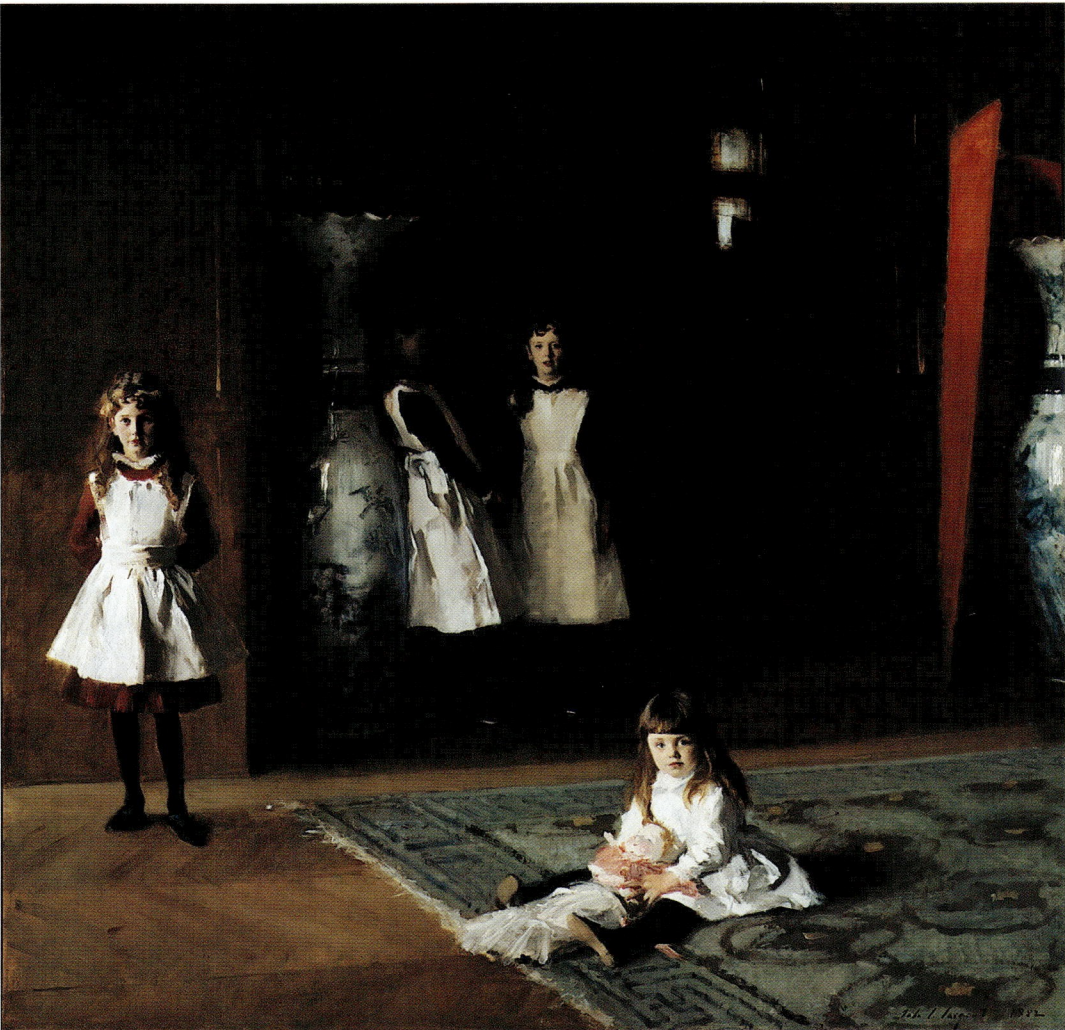

**29-14** JOHN SINGER SARGENT, *The Daughters of Edward Darley Boit,* 1882. Oil on canvas, 7' 3⅜" × 7' 3⅝". Museum of Fine Arts, Boston (gift of Mary Louisa Boit, Florence D. Boit, Jane Hubbard Boit, and Julia Overing Boit, in memory of their father, Edward Darley Boit).

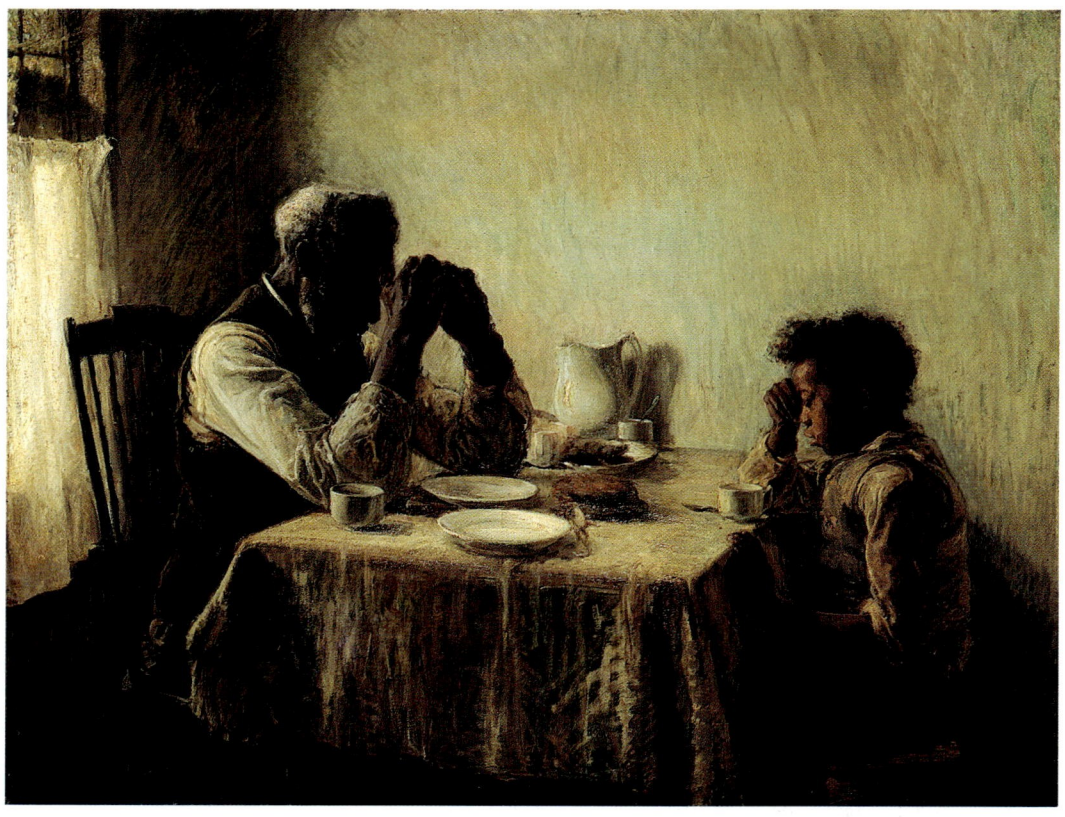

**29-15** HENRY OSSAWA TANNER, *The Thankful Poor,* 1894. Oil on canvas, 2' 11½" × 3' 8¼". Collection of William H. and Camille Cosby.

drawing room in their Paris home. The informal, eccentric arrangement of their slight figures suggests how much at ease they are within this familiar space and with objects such as the monumental Japanese vases, the red screen, and the fringed rug, whose scale subtly emphasizes the children's diminutive stature. Sargent must have known the Boit daughters well and liked them. Relaxed and trustful, they gave the artist an opportunity to record a gradation of young innocence. He sensitively captured the naive, wondering openness of the little girl in the foreground, the grave artlessness of the 10-year-old child, and the slightly self-conscious poise of the adolescents. Sargent's casual positioning of the figures and seemingly random choice of the setting communicate a sense of spontaneity. The children seem to be attending momentarily to an adult who has asked them to interrupt their activity and "look this way." Here is a most effective embodiment of the Realist belief that the artist's business is to record the modern being in modern context.

**THE DIGNITY OF ORDINARY LIFE** Typical of the Realist painter's desire to depict the lives of ordinary people is the early work of the American artist HENRY OSSAWA TANNER (1859–1937). Tanner studied art with Eakins before moving to Paris. There he combined Eakins's belief in careful study from nature with a desire to portray with dignity the life of the ordinary people he had been raised among as the son of an African American minister in Pennsylvania. The mood in *The Thankful Poor* (FIG. **29-15**) is one of quiet devotion not far removed from the Realism of Millet (FIG. 29-3). In Tanner's painting, the grandfather, grandchild, and main objects in the room are painted with the greatest detail, while everything else dissolves into loose strokes of color and light. Expressive lighting reinforces the painting's reverent spirit, with deep shadows intensifying the man's devout concentration and golden light pouring in the window to illuminate the quiet expression of thanksgiving on the younger face. The deep

sense of sanctity expressed here in terms of everyday experience became increasingly important for Tanner. Within a few years of completing *The Thankful Poor,* he began painting biblical subjects grounded in direct study from nature and in the love of Rembrandt that had inspired him from his days as a Philadelphia art student.

**RUSTIC GERMAN LIFE** German artist WILHELM LEIBL (1844–1900) was a master of the quaint and quiet details of country life. *Three Women in a Village Church* (FIG. **29-16**) exemplifies his commitment to Realist principles. The painting records a sacred moment—the moment of prayer—in the life of three country women of different generations. Dressed in rustic costume, their Sunday best, they pursue their devotions unselfconsciously, their prayer books held in big hands roughened by work. Their manners and their dress reflect their unaffected nature, untouched by the refinements of urban life. Leibl highlighted their natural virtues: simplicity, honesty, steadfastness, patience. He spent three years working on this image of peasants in their village church, often under impossible conditions of lighting and temperature. Despite the meticulous application of paint and sharpness of focus, the picture is a moving expression of the artist's compassionate view of his subjects, a reading of character without sentimentality.

Over time, Realist artists throughout Europe and America expanded and diversified their subjects to embrace all classes and levels of society, all types of people and environments. These included the urban and rural working class, the big-city inhabitants, the small-town citizens, the leisure class at its resorts, and the rustics of the provinces. Added to the social sympathies found in the works of Daumier, Courbet, and Millet were motives of an anthropological kind, reflecting interest in national and regional characteristics, in folk customs and culture, and in the quaintness of local color.

## The Pre-Raphaelite Brotherhood

**PRAISING THE PRE-INDUSTRIAL PAST** In England, John Everett Millais (1829–1896) was a founder of a group of artists, the *Pre-Raphaelite Brotherhood,* who refused to be limited to the contemporary scenes strict Realists portrayed; these artists chose instead to represent fictional, historical, and fanciful subjects with a significant degree of convincing illusion. So painstakingly careful was Millais in his study of visual facts closely observed from nature that Baudelaire called him "the poet of meticulous detail." The Pre-Raphaelite Brotherhood, organized in 1848, wished to create fresh and sincere art, free from what its members considered the tired and artificial manner propagated in the academies by the successors of Raphael. Influenced by the well-known critic, artist, and writer John Ruskin (1819–1900), the Pre-Raphaelites agreed with his distaste for the materialism and ugliness of the contemporary industrializing world. The Pre-Raphaelites also expressed appreciation for the spirituality and idealism (as well as the art and artisanship) of past times, especially the Middle Ages and the Early Renaissance.

**A SHAKESPEAREAN HEROINE DROWNED** Millais's method is apparent in *Ophelia* (FIG. **29-17**), which he exhibited in the Exposition Universelle in Paris in 1855, where Courbet set up his Pavilion of Realism. The subject, from Shakespeare's *Hamlet,* is the drowning of Ophelia, who, in her madness, is unaware of her plight:

> Her clothes spread wide,
> And mermaidlike awhile they bore her up—
> Which time she chanted snatches of old tunes,
> As one incapable of her own distress.
>
> (4.7.176–79)

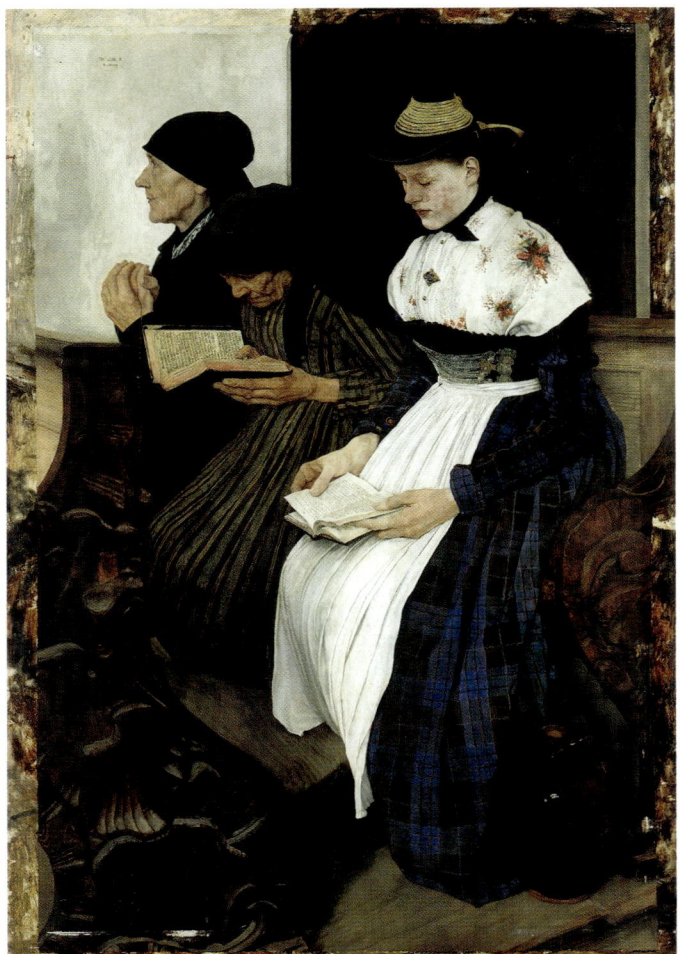

**29-16** Wilhelm Leibl, *Three Women in a Village Church,* 1878–1881. Oil on canvas, approx. 2′ 5″ × 2′ 1″. Kunsthalle, Hamburg.

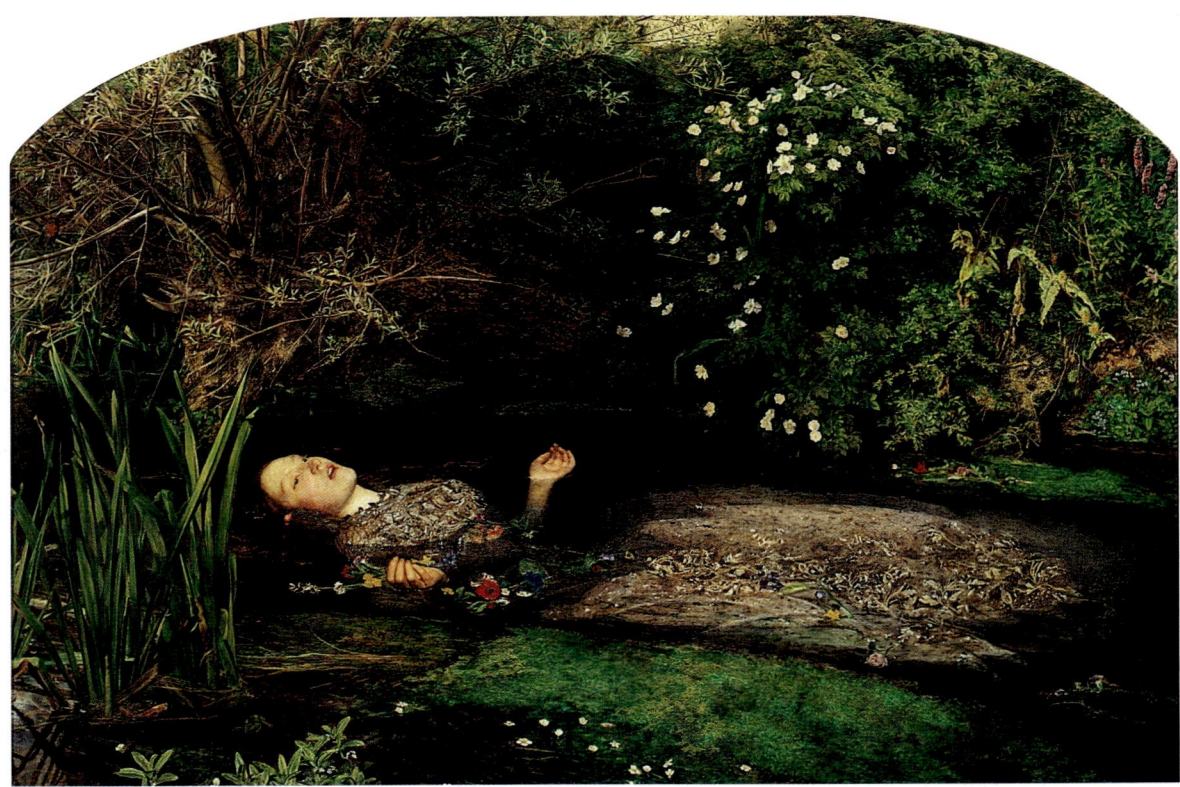

**29-17** John Everett Millais, *Ophelia,* 1852. Oil on canvas, 2′ 6″ × 3′ 8″. Tate Gallery, London.

Attempting to make the pathos of the scene visible, Millais became a faithful and feeling witness of its every detail, reconstructing it with a lyricism worthy of the original poetry. Although the scene is fictitious, Millais worked diligently to present it with unswerving fidelity to visual fact. He painted the background on site at a spot along the Hogsmill River in Surrey. For the figure of Ophelia, Millais had a friend lie in a heated bathtub full of water for hours at a stretch. As a result of this meticulous detail, *Ophelia* was a huge success when it was exhibited.

**A DUAL PORTRAIT** Dante Gabriel Rossetti (1828–1882), well known as both a painter and poet, was another of the founders of the Pre-Raphaelite Brotherhood. Like other members of the group, Rossetti focused on literary and biblical themes in his art. He also produced numerous portraits of women that projected an image of ethereal beauty and melded apparent opposites—a Victorian prettiness with sensual allure. His *Beata Beatrix* (FIG. **29-18**) is ostensibly a portrait of a literary figure—Beatrice, from Dante's *Vita Nuova*—as she overlooks Florence in a trance after being mystically transported from earth to heaven. Yet the portrait also had personal resonance for Rossetti; it served as a memorial to his wife, Elizabeth Siddal (who was the model for Millais's *Ophelia*). Siddal had died shortly before Rossetti began this painting in 1862. In the image, the female (Siddal-Beatrice) sits in a trancelike state, while a red dove (a messenger of both love and death), deposits a poppy (symbolic of sleep and death) in her hands. Because Siddal died of an opium overdose, the presence of the poppy assumes greater significance.

**A "PICTORIAL" PHOTOGRAPHIC METHOD** Photography, the artificial eye, the medium created to serve the taste for visual fact, for realistic report of the world, was itself the creator of a new Realism. But it could also be manipulated by talented photographers to produce quite Romantic effects. After the first great breakthroughs, which bluntly showed what was before the eye, photographers imitated Romantic arrangements of nature, filtering natural appearance through sentiment—soft-focusing it, as it were. In the later 19th century, with much public approval, photography had a Romantic-Realist school of its own. The photographers thought of it as a "pictorial" method.

One of the leading practitioners of the pictorial style in photography was the American Gertrude Käsebier (1852–1934). Käsebier took up photography in 1897 after raising a family and working as a portrait painter. She soon became famous for photographs with symbolic themes, such as *Blessed Art Thou among Women* (FIG. **29-19**). The title repeats the phrase the angel Gabriel used in the New Testament to announce to the Virgin Mary that she will be the mother of Jesus. In the context of Käsebier's photography, the words suggest a parallel between the biblical "Mother of God" and

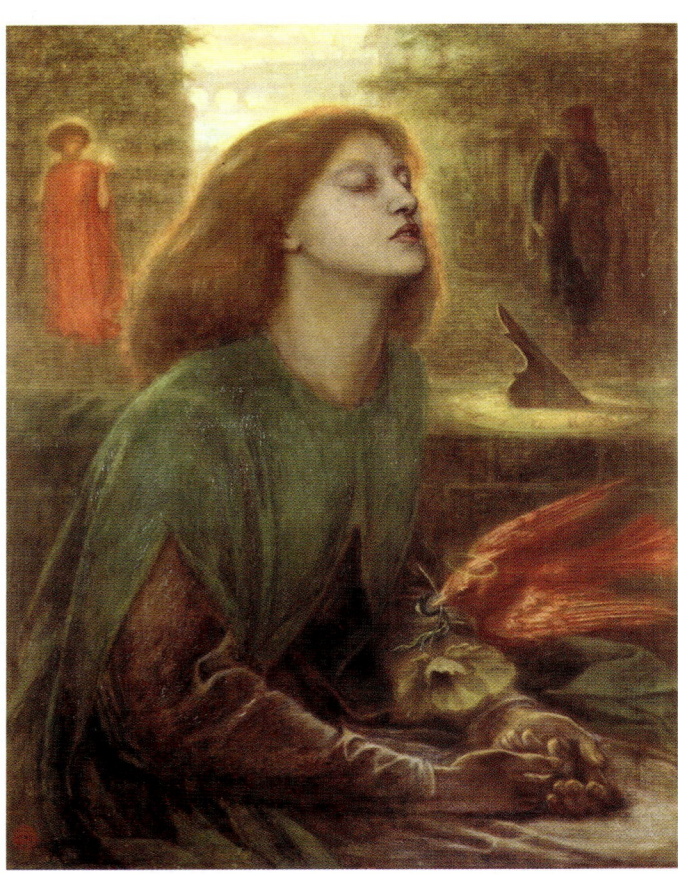

**29-18** Dante Gabriel Rossetti, *Beata Beatrix,* ca. 1863. Oil on canvas, 2′ 10″ × 2′ 2″. Tate Gallery, London.

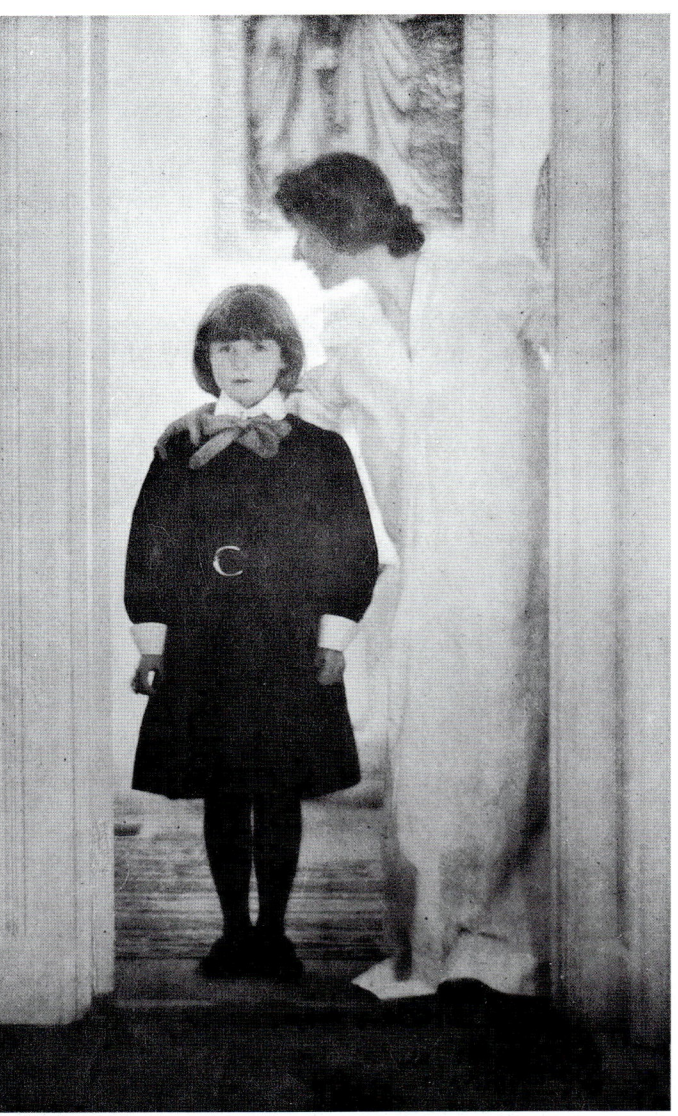

**29-19** Gertrude Käsebier, *Blessed Art Thou among Women,* 1899. Platinum print on Japanese tissue, $9\frac{3}{8}″ \times 5\frac{1}{2}″$. Museum of Modern Art, New York (gift of Mrs. Hermine M. Turner).

the modern mother in the image, who both protects and sends forth her daughter. The white setting and the mother's pale gown shimmer in soft focus behind the serious girl, who is dressed in darker tones and captured with sharper focus. Here, as in her other works, the ideas about naturalism in photography championed by photographer Peter Henry Emerson (1856–1936) influenced Käsebier. Yet she deliberately ignored his teachings about differential focusing, combining an out-of-focus background with a sharp or almost-sharp foreground, in favor of achieving an expressive effect by blurring the entire image slightly. In *Blessed Art Thou*, the whole scene is invested with an aura of otherworldly peace by the soft focus, the appearance of the centered figures, the vertical framing elements, and the relationship between the frontally posed girl and her gracefully bending mother. *Blessed Art Thou* is an example of Käsebier's moving ability to invest scenes from everyday life with a sense of the spiritual and the divine.

## Impressionism: Capturing the Fugitive Images of Modern Life

*Impressionism*, both in content and in style, was an art of industrialized, urbanized Paris. As such, it furthered some of the Realists' concerns and was resolutely an art of its time. But whereas Realism focused on the present, Impressionism focused even more acutely on a single moment. Although Impressionism is often discussed as a coherent movement, it was actually a nebulous and shifting phenomenon. People have perceived the Impressionists as a group largely because they exhibited together in the 1870s and 1880s. However, participation in these shows was a constant source of contention and debate among the artists.

**IMPRESSIONISM AND THE SKETCH** A hostile critic applied the label "impressionism" in response to the painting *Impression:*

*Sunrise* (FIG. **29-20**) by CLAUDE MONET (1840–1926). The artist exhibited this work in the first Impressionist show in 1874, and, although the critic intended the term to be derogatory, by the third Impressionist show in 1878 the artists themselves were using that label.

The term *impressionism* had been used in art before but in relation to sketches. Impressionist paintings incorporate the qualities of sketches—abbreviation, speed, and spontaneity. This is apparent in *Impression: Sunrise*. The brush strokes are clearly evident; Monet made no attempt to blend the pigment to create smooth tonal gradations and an optically accurate scene. Although this painting is not, technically speaking, a sketch, it has a sketchy quality. This concern with acknowledging the paint and the canvas surface continued the modernist exploration that the Realists began. Beyond this connection to the sketch, Impressionism operates at the intersection of what the artists saw and what they felt. In other words, the "impressions" that these artists recorded in their paintings were neither purely objective descriptions of the exterior world nor solely subjective responses, but the interaction between the two. They were sensations—the artists' subjective and personal responses to nature.

**CAPTURING A FLEETING MOMENT** The lack of pristine clarity characteristic of most Impressionist works is also historically grounded. The extensive industrialization and urbanization that occurred in France during the latter half of the 19th century can be described only as a brutal and chaotic transformation. The rapidity of these changes made the world seem unstable and insubstantial. As Charles Baudelaire observed: "[M]odernity is the transitory, the fugitive, the contingent."[14] Accordingly, Impressionist works represent an attempt to capture a fleeting moment—not in the absolutely fixed, precise sense of a Realist painting but by conveying the elusiveness and impermanence of images and conditions.

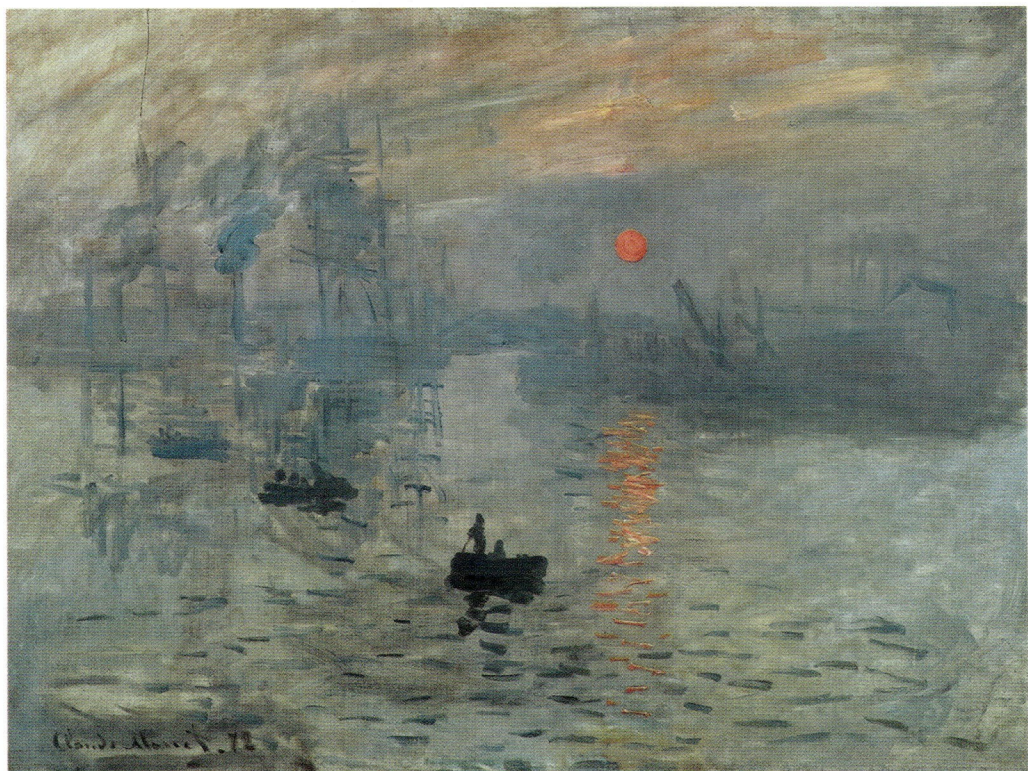

**29-20** CLAUDE MONET, *Impression: Sunrise*, 1872. Oil on canvas, $1' 7\frac{1}{2}'' \times 2' 1\frac{1}{2}''$. Musée Marmottan, Paris.

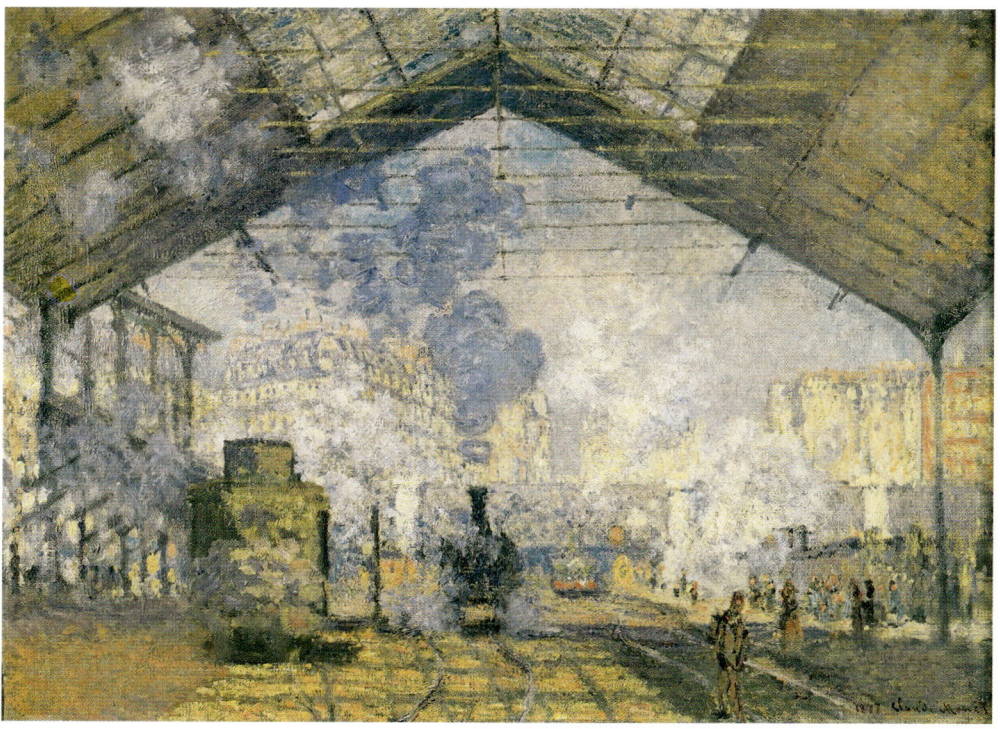

**29-21** Claude Monet, *Saint-Lazare Train Station,* 1877. Oil on canvas, 2′ 5¾″ × 3′ 5″. Musée d'Orsay, Paris.

**THE RAILROADS AND PARISIAN LIFE** That Impressionism was firmly anchored in the industrial development of the time and in the concurrent process of urbanization is also revealed by the artists' choice of subjects. Most of the Impressionists depicted scenes in and around Paris, where industrialization and urbanization had their greatest impact. Monet's *Saint-Lazare Train Station* (FIG. **29-21**) depicts a dominant aspect of Parisian life. The expanding railway network had made travel more convenient, bringing throngs of people into Paris. Saint-Lazare Station was centrally located, adjacent to the Grands Boulevards, a bustling, fashionable commercial area. Monet captured the area's energy and vitality;

the train, emerging from the steam and smoke it emits, comes into the station. The tall buildings that were becoming a major component of the Parisian landscape are just visible through the background haze. Monet's agitated paint application contributes to the sense of energy and conveys the atmosphere of urban life.

**THE HAUSSMANNIZATION OF PARIS** Other Impressionists also represented facets of city life. GUSTAVE CAILLEBOTTE (1849–1893) depicted yet another scene in *Paris: A Rainy Day* (FIG. **29-22**). His setting is a junction of spacious boulevards that resulted from the redesigning of Paris begun in 1852. The city's

**29-22** Gustave Caillebotte, *Paris: A Rainy Day,* 1877. Oil on canvas, approx. 6′ 9″ × 9′ 9″. The Art Institute of Chicago, Chicago, Worcester Fund.

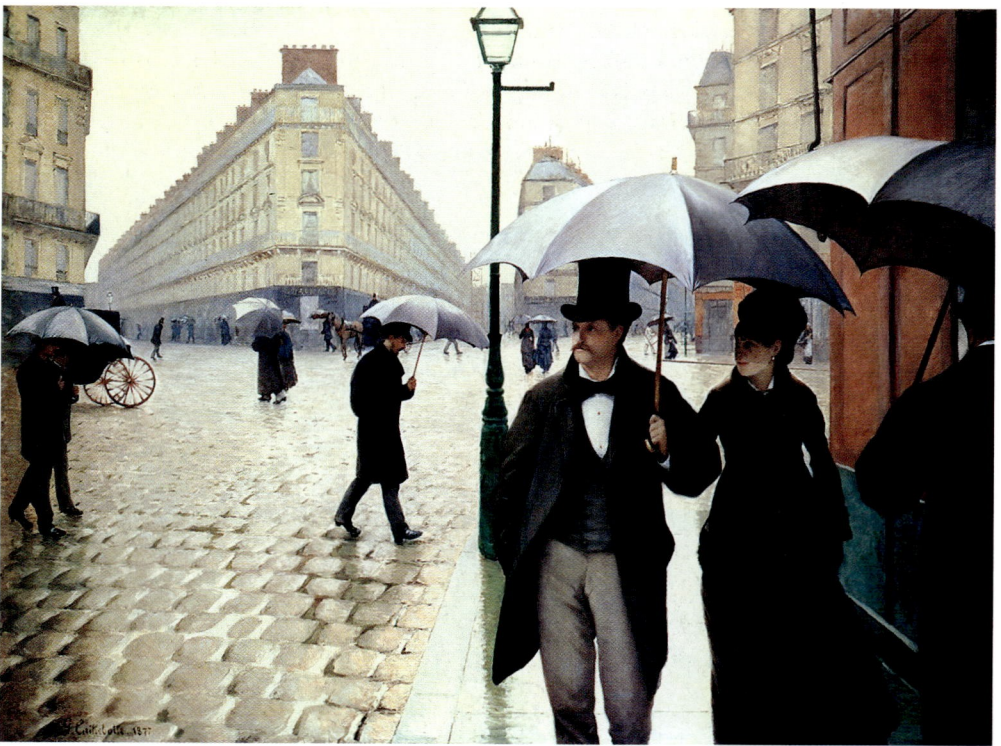

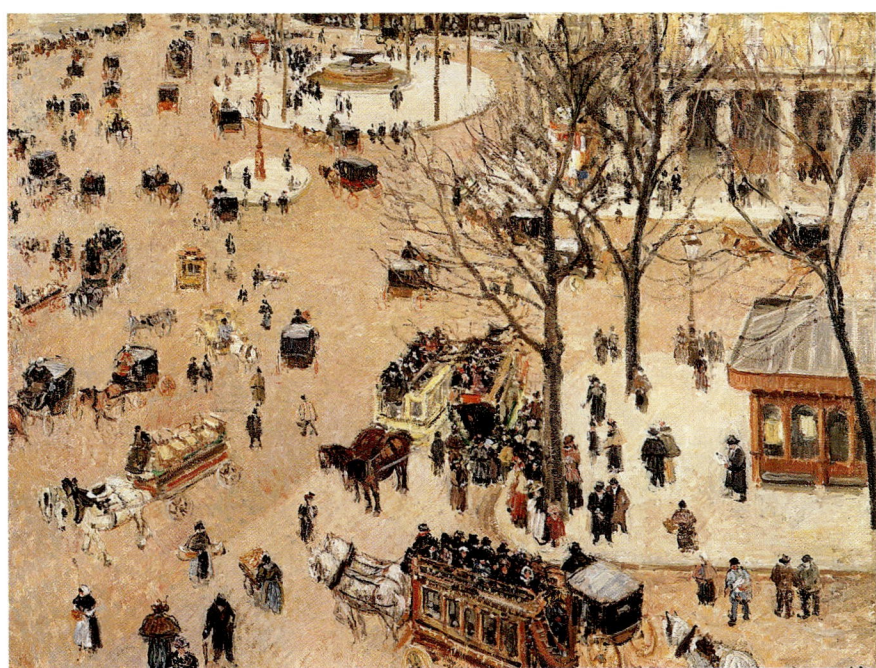

29-23 CAMILLE PISSARRO, *La Place du Théâtre Français*, 1898. Oil on canvas, 2′ 4½″ × 3′ 1½″. Los Angeles County Museum of Art, Los Angeles (the Mr. and Mrs. George Gard De Sylva Collection).

population had reached close to 1.5 million by midcentury, and to accommodate this congregation of humanity, Emperor Napoleon III ordered Paris rebuilt. Napoleon was also interested in making an imperial statement through his redesign of Paris and in facilitating the movement of troops in the event of another revolution. The emperor named Baron Georges Haussmann, a city superintendent, to oversee the entire project; consequently, this process became known as "Haussmannization." In addition to new water and sewer systems, street lighting, and new residential and commercial buildings, a major component of the new Paris was the creation of wide, open boulevards. These great avenues, whose construction caused the demolition of thousands of ancient buildings and streets, transformed medieval Paris into the present modern city, with its superb vistas and wide uninterrupted arteries for the flow of vehicular and pedestrian traffic. Caillebotte chose to focus on these markers of the city's rapid urbanization.

Although Caillebotte did not dissolve his image into the broken color and brushwork characteristic of Impressionism, he did use an informal and asymmetrical composition. The figures seem randomly placed, with the frame cropping them arbitrarily,

suggesting the transitory nature of this scene. Well-dressed Parisians of the leisure class share the viewer's space. Despite the visual clarity with which *Paris: A Rainy Day* is painted, the picture captures the artist's "impression" of the urban city.

**A PANORAMA OF BUSTLING CROWDS** *La Place du Théâtre Français* (FIG. 29-23) is one of many panoramic scenes by CAMILLE PISSARRO (1830–1903) of the spacious boulevards and avenues that were the product of Haussmannization. In this painting, Pissarro recorded a panorama of blurred dark accents against a light ground that represents clearly his visual sensations of a crowded Paris square viewed from several stories above street level. Like many of the other Impressionists, Pissarro sought to capture a moment in time, but the moment in *La Place du Théâtre Français* is not so much of fugitive light effects as it is of the street life, achieved through a deliberate casualness in the figural arrangement.

Pissarro sometimes used the amazing "reality" of photography to supplement work directly from a model, like many of his fellow Impressionists. Although he may not have known the stereograph *The Pont Neuf, Paris* (FIG. 29-24), its effect is

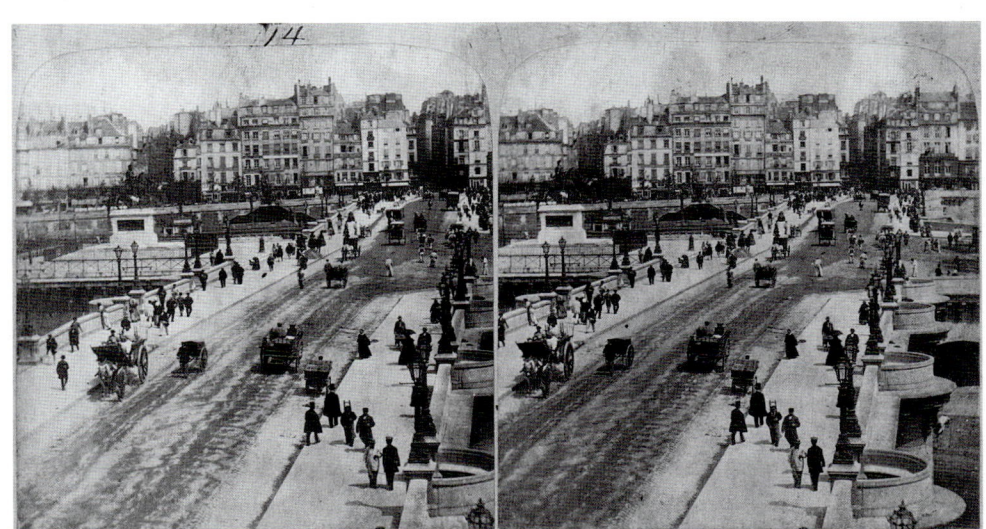

29-24 HIPPOLYTE JOUVIN, *The Pont Neuf, Paris*, ca. 1860–1865. Albumen stereograph. George Eastman House, Rochester, New York.

remarkably similar to his *La Place du Théâtre Français*. With a special twin-lensed camera, HIPPOLYTE JOUVIN (active mid-1800s) made the stereograph, viewed with an apparatus called a stereoscope, to re-create the illusion of three dimensions. In this double image, the viewer's vantage point is from the upper story of a building along the roadway of the "New Bridge," which stretches diagonally from lower left to upper right. Hurrying pedestrians are dark silhouettes, and the scene moves from sharp focus in the foreground to soft focus in the distance. Because of the familiarity Pissarro and the other Impressionists had with photography, scholars have been quick to point out the visual parallels between Impressionist paintings and photographs. These parallels include, here, the arbitrary cutting off of figures at the frame's edge and the curious flattening spatial effect the high viewpoint caused.

**LEISURE AND RECREATION** Another facet of the new, industrialized Paris that drew the Impressionists' attention was the leisure activities of its inhabitants. Scenes of dining, dancing, the café-concerts, the opera, the ballet, and other forms of enjoyable recreation were mainstays of Impressionism. Although seemingly unrelated to industrialization, these activities were facilitated by it. With the advent of set working hours, people's schedules became more regimented, allowing them to plan their favorite pastimes.

**A LIVELY PARISIAN DANCE HALL** *Le Moulin de la Galette* (FIG. **29-25**) by PIERRE-AUGUSTE RENOIR (1841–1919) depicts a popular Parisian dance hall. Throngs of people have gathered; some people crowd the tables and chatter, while others dance energetically. So lively is the atmosphere that the viewer can virtually hear the sounds of music, laughter, and tinkling glasses. The whole scene is dappled by sunlight and shade, artfully blurred into the figures to produce just the effect of floating and fleeting light the Impressionists so cultivated. Renoir's casual unposed placement of the figures and the suggested continuity of space, spreading in all directions and only accidentally limited by the frame, position the viewer as a participant, rather than as an outsider. Whereas classical art sought to express universal and timeless qualities, Impressionism attempted to depict just the opposite—the incidental, momentary, and passing aspects of reality.

**A REFLECTION ON CAFÉ LIFE** Édouard Manet's famous work, *A Bar at the Folies-Bergère* (FIG. **29-26**), was painted in 1882. The Folies-Bergère was a popular Parisian café-concert (a café with music-hall performances). These cafés were fashionable gathering places for throngs of revelers, and many of the Impressionists frequented these establishments. In *Folies-Bergère,* the viewer is confronted by a barmaid, centrally placed, who looks back but who seems disinterested or lost in thought. This woman appears divorced from the patrons as well as from the viewer.

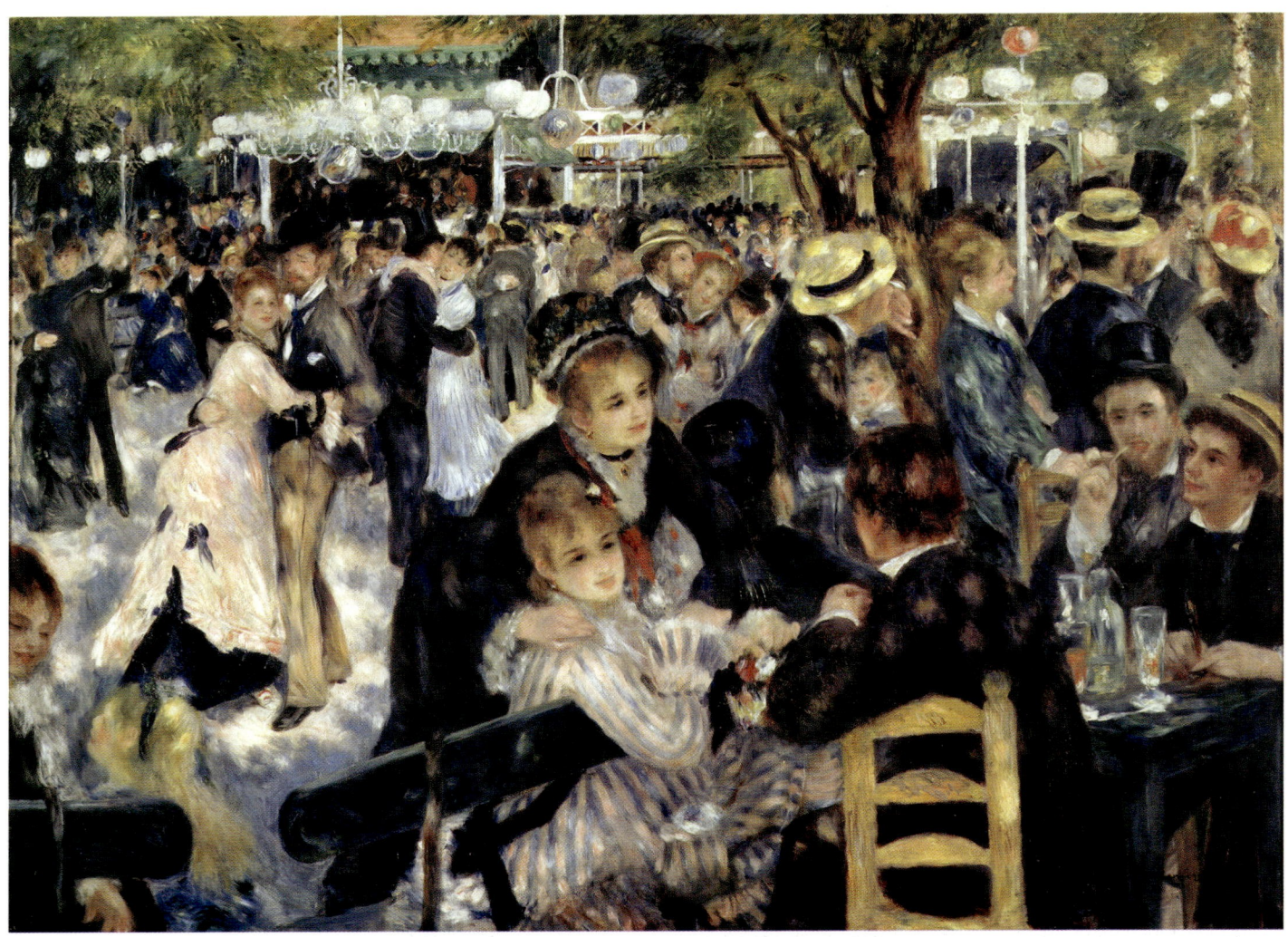

**29-25** PIERRE-AUGUSTE RENOIR, *Le Moulin de la Galette*, 1876. Oil on canvas, approx. 4′ 3″ × 5′ 8″. Réunion des Musées Nationaux.

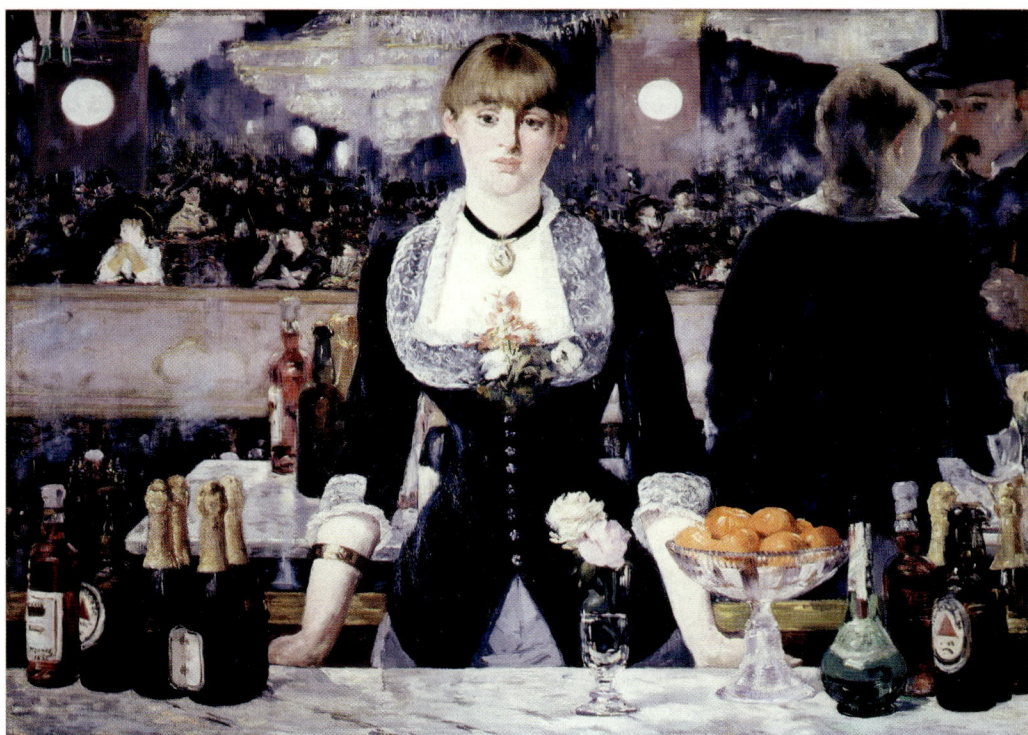

**29-26** ÉDOUARD MANET, *A Bar at the Folies-Bergère*, 1882. Oil on canvas, approx. 3′ 1″ × 4′ 3″. Courtauld Institute of Art Gallery, London.

Manet blurred and roughly applied the brush strokes, particularly those in the background, and the effects of modeling and perspective are minimal. This painting method further calls attention to the surface by forcing the viewer to scrutinize the work to make sense of the scene. On such scrutiny, visual discrepancies seem to emerge. For example, what initially seems easily recognizable as a mirror behind the barmaid creates confusion throughout the rest of the painting. Is the woman on the right the barmaid's reflection? If so, it is impossible to reconcile the spatial relationship between the barmaid, the mirror, the bar's frontal horizontality, and the barmaid's seemingly displaced reflection. These visual contradictions reveal Manet's insistence on calling

attention to the pictorial structure of this painting, in keeping with his modernist interest in examining the basic premises of the medium. This radical break with tradition and redefinition of the function of the picture surface explains why many scholars position Manet as the first modernist artist.

**OF MUSIC AND DANCE: THE BALLET** Impressionists also depicted more formal leisure activities. The fascination EDGAR DEGAS (1834–1917) had with patterns of motion brought him to the Paris Opéra and its ballet school. There, his great observational power took in the formalized movements of classical ballet, one of his favorite subjects. In *Ballet Rehearsal* (FIG. 29-27), Degas used

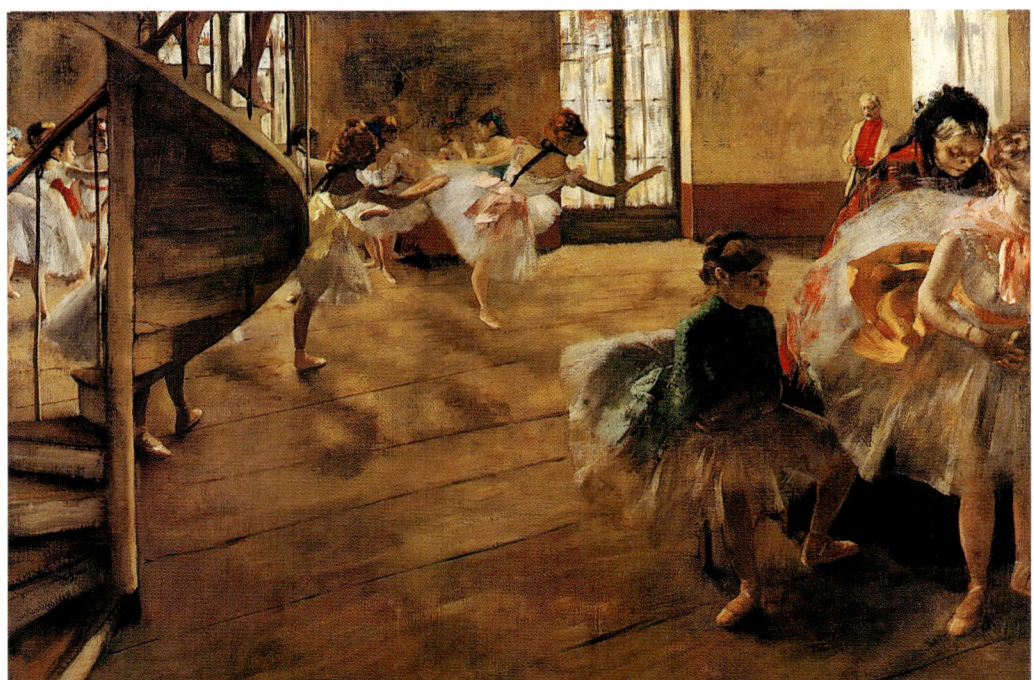

**29-27** EDGAR DEGAS, *Ballet Rehearsal*, 1874. Oil on canvas, 1′ 11″ × 2′ 9″. Glasgow Art Galleries and Museum, Glasgow (The Burrell Collection).

## Japonisme
### The Allure of the Orient

Despite Europe's and America's extensive colonization during the 19th century, Japan avoided Western intrusion until 1853–1854, when Commodore Matthew Perry and American naval forces exacted trading and diplomatic privileges from Japan. From the increased contact, Westerners became familiar with Japanese culture. So intrigued were the French with Japanese art and culture that they introduced a specific label—*Japonisme*—to describe the Japanese aesthetic. Japonisme appealed to the fashionable segment of Parisian society, which no doubt was attracted to both the beauty and the exoticism of this culture. In 1867 at the Exposition Universelle in Paris, the Japanese pavilion garnered more attention than any other. Soon, Japanese kimonos, fans, lacquer cabinets, tea caddies, folding screens, tea services, and jewelry flooded Paris. Japanese-themed novels and travel books were immensely popular as well. As demand for Japanese merchandise grew in the West, the Japanese began to develop import-export businesses, and the foreign currency that flowed into Japan helped to finance much of its industrialization.

Artists in particular were drawn to Japanese art. Among those the Japanese aesthetic influenced were most of the Impressionists and Post-Impressionists, especially Manet, James Abbott McNeill Whistler, Degas, Mary Cassatt, Vincent van Gogh, Paul Gauguin, and Henri de Toulouse-Lautrec. For the most part, the Japanese presentation of space in woodblock prints (see FIGS. 27-11 and 27-12), which were more readily available to the West than any other art form, intrigued these artists. Because of the simplicity of the woodblock printing process (see "Japanese Woodblock Prints," Chapter 27, page 790), these prints are characterized by areas of flat color with a limited amount of modulation or gradation. This flatness interested modernist painters, who sought ways to call attention to the picture surface. The right side of Degas's *The Tub* (FIG. 29-30) has this two-dimensional quality. Degas, in fact, owned a print by Japanese artist Torii Kiyonaga (1752–1815) titled *Women's Bath* (ca. 1780) that inspired *The Tub*. The decorative quality of Japanese images also appealed to the artists associated with Art Nouveau (FIGS. 29-53 to 29-55). The artists of the Arts and Crafts movement (FIGS. 29-51 and 29-52) were intrigued by Japanese prints because these images intersected nicely with two fundamental principles of that movement, which were that art should be available to the masses and that functional objects should be artistically designed.

several devices to bring the observer into the pictorial space. The frame cuts off the spiral stair, the windows in the background, and the group of figures in the right foreground. The figures are not centered but rather arranged in a seemingly random manner. The prominent diagonals of the wall bases and floorboards carry the viewer into and along the directional lines of the dancers. Finally, as is customary in Degas's ballet pictures, a large, off-center, empty space creates the illusion of a continuous floor that connects the observer with the pictured figures. By seeming to stand on the same surface with them, the viewer is drawn into their space.

The often arbitrarily cut-off figures, the patterns of light splotches, and the blurriness of the images in this and other Degas works indicate the artist's interest in reproducing single moments. Further, they reveal his fascination with photography. Degas not only studied the photography of others but also used the camera consistently to make preliminary studies for his works, particularly photographing figures in interiors. Other inspirational sources for paintings such as *Ballet Rehearsal* were 18th-century Japanese woodblock prints (see "Japonisme: The Allure of the Orient," above). The cunning spatial projections in Degas's paintings probably derived in part from Japanese prints, such as those by Suzuki Harunobu (see FIG. 27-11). Japanese artists used diverging lines not only to organize the flat shapes of figures but also to direct the viewer's attention into the picture space. The Impressionists, acquainted with these prints as early as the 1860s, greatly admired their spatial organization, familiar and intimate themes, and flat unmodeled color areas and drew much instruction from them.

**RELAXED LEISURE BY THE SEASIDE** The Impressionists were drawn to painting outdoor leisure activity, and many of their prototypical works depict scenes from resort areas along the Seine River, such as Argenteuil, Bougival, and Chatou. Argenteuil was connected to Paris by the railway line that carried people to and from Saint-Lazare Station (FIG. 29-21), so transportation was not an obstacle. Parisians often would take the train out to these resort areas for a day of sailing, picnicking, and strolling along the Seine. BERTHE MORISOT (1841–1895) regularly exhibited with the Impressionists and was well acquainted with those artists (Manet was her brother-in-law). Most of her paintings focus on domestic scenes, the one realm of Parisian life where society allowed an upper-class woman such as Morisot free access. Morisot's considerable skills are evident in *Villa at the Seaside* (FIG. **29-28**). Both the subject and style correlate well with Impressionist concerns. The setting is the shaded veranda of a summer hotel at a fashionable seashore resort. A woman elegantly but not ostentatiously dressed sits gazing out across the railing to a sunlit beach with its umbrellas and bathing cabins. Her child, its discarded toy boat a splash of red, is attentive to the passing sails on the placid sea. The mood is of relaxed leisure. Morisot used the open brushwork and the *plein air* (outdoor) lighting characteristic of Impressionism. Her brushwork is telegraphic in its report of her quick perceptions. Everything is suggested by swift, sketchy strokes, and nowhere did Morisot linger on contours or enclosed details. She presented the scene in a slightly filmy soft focus that conveys a feeling of airiness. The composition is also reminiscent of the work of other Impressionists; the figures fall informally into place, as someone who shared their intimate space would perceive them. Morisot was both immensely ambitious and talented, as her ability to catch the pictorial moment demonstrates. She escaped the hostile criticism directed at most of the other Impressionists; people praised her work for its sensibility, grace, and delicacy.

**STUDIES OF LIGHT AND COLOR** Monet's experiences painting outdoors sharpened his focus on the roles light and color play in capturing an instantaneous representation of atmosphere and climate. Monet, of all the Impressionists, carried the systematic investigation of light and color furthest. However, all of the artists associated with this movement recognized the importance of carefully observing and understanding how light and color operate. Such thorough study permitted the Impressionists to present images that truly conveyed a sense of the momentary and transitory.

Scientific studies of light and the invention of chemically synthesized pigments increased artists' sensitivity to the multiplicity of colors in nature and gave them new colors for their work. After scrutinizing the effects of light and color on forms, the Impressionists concluded that *local color*—an object's actual color in white light—is usually modified by the quality of the light in which it is seen, by reflections from other objects, and by the effects juxtaposed colors produce. Shadows do not appear gray or black, as many earlier painters thought, but seem to be composed of colors modified by reflections or other conditions. If artists use complementary colors (see Introduction, page 7 in combined volumes, or page xxxvi in Volume II) side by side over large enough areas, the colors intensify each other, unlike the effect of small quantities of adjoining mixed pigments, which blend into neutral tones. Furthermore, the juxtaposition of colors on a canvas for the eye to fuse at a distance produces a more intense hue than the same colors mixed on the palette. It is not strictly true the Impressionists used only primary hues, juxtaposing them to create secondary colors (blue and yellow, for example, to create green). But they did achieve remarkably brilliant effects with their characteristically short, choppy brush strokes, which so accurately caught the vibrating quality of light. The fact that their canvas surfaces look unintelligible at close range and their forms and objects appear only when the eye fuses the strokes at a certain distance accounts for much of the early adverse criticism leveled at their work. One such conjecture was that the Impressionists fired their paint at the canvas with pistols. Lila Cabot Perry, a student of Monet's late in his career, gave this description of Monet's approach:

> I remember his once saying to me: "When you go out to paint, try to forget what objects you have before you—a tree, a house, a field, or whatever. Merely think, here is a little square of blue, here an oblong of pink, here a streak of yellow, and paint it just as it looks to you, the exact color and shape, until it gives your own naïve impression of the scene before you." He said he wished he had been born blind and then had suddenly gained his sight so that he could have begun to paint in this way without knowing what the objects were that he saw before him.[15]

Monet's intensive study of the phenomena of light and color is especially evident in several series of paintings of the same subject. One series had some 40 views of Rouen Cathedral. For each canvas in this series, Monet observed the cathedral from nearly the same viewpoint but at different times of the day or under

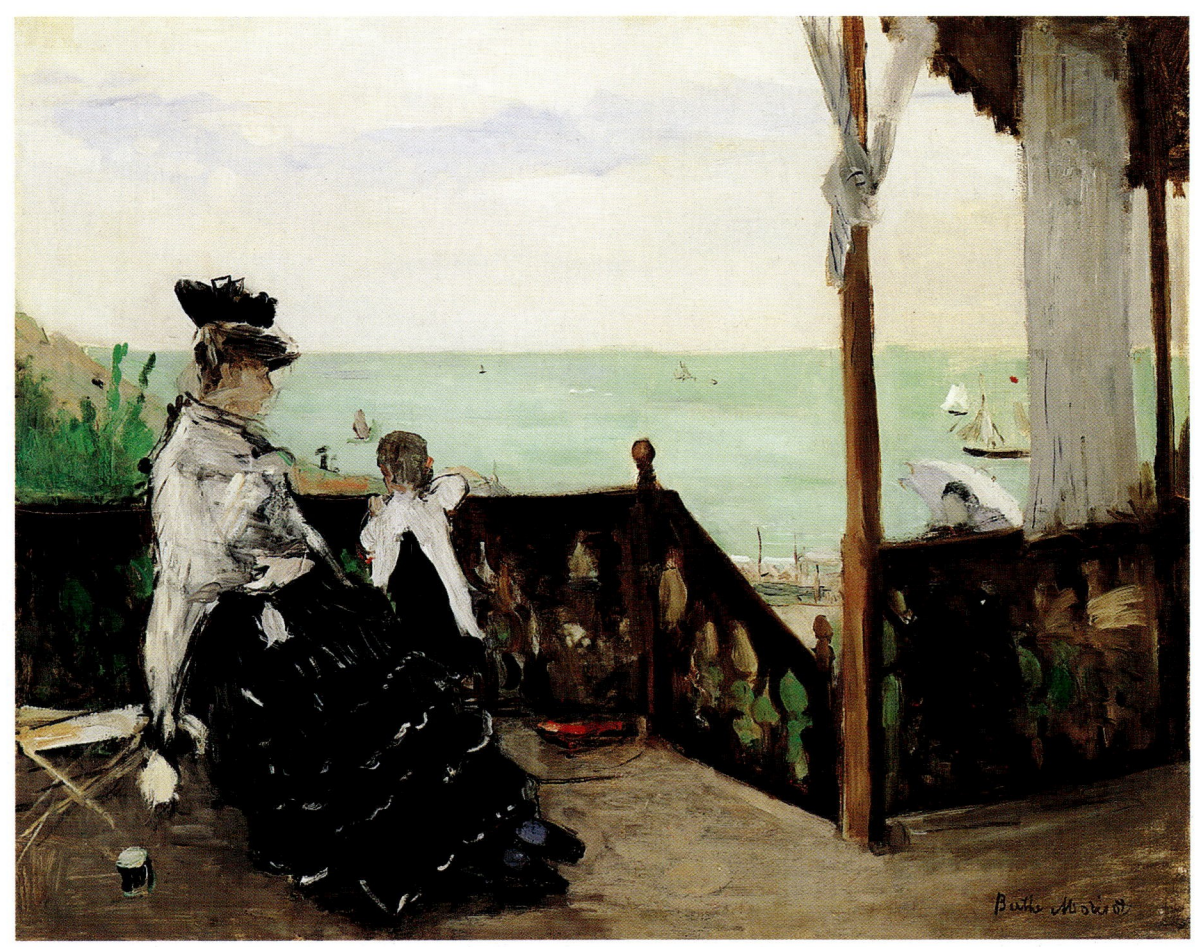

**29-28** Berthe Morisot, *Villa at the Seaside,* 1874. Oil on canvas, approx. 1′ 7¾″ × 2′ ⅛″. Norton Simon Art Foundation, Los Angeles.

various climatic conditions. In our illustration, *Rouen Cathedral: The Portal (in Sun)*, FIG. **29-29**, Monet depicted the structure bathed in bright light. With scientific precision, he created an unparalleled record of the passing of time as seen in the movement of light over identical forms. Later critics accused Monet and his companions of destroying form and order for fleeting atmospheric effects, but Monet focused on light and color precisely to reach a greater understanding of the appearance of form.

**LINE DRAWING WITH PASTEL** Although color and light were major components of the Impressionist quest to capture fleeting sensations, these artists considered other formal elements as well. Degas, for example, became a superb master of line, so much so that his works often differ significantly from those of Monet and Renoir. Degas specialized in studies of figures in rapid and informal action, recording the quick impression of arrested motion, as is evident in *Ballet Rehearsal.* He often employed lines to convey this sense of movement. In *The Tub* (FIG. **29-30**), a young woman crouches in a washing tub. The artist outlined the major objects in the painting—the woman, tub, and pitchers—and covered all surfaces with linear hatch marks. Degas achieved this leaner quality with pastels, his favorite medium. Using these dry sticks of powdered pigment, Degas drew directly on the paper, as one would with a piece of chalk, thus accounting for the linear basis of this work. Further, although the applied pastel can be smudged, the colors tend to retain their autonomy, so they appear fresh and bright.

*The Tub* also reveals how Degas's work, like that of the other Impressionists, continues the modernist exploration of the premises of painting by acknowledging the artwork's surface. Although the viewer clearly perceives the woman as a depiction of a three-dimensional form in space, the tabletop or shelf on the right of the image appears severely tilted, so much so that it seems to parallel the picture plane. The two pitchers on the table complicate this visual conflict between the table's flatness and the illusion of the bathing woman's three-dimensional volume. The limited foreshortening of the pitchers and their shared edge, in conjunction with the rest of the image, create a visual perplexity for the viewer.

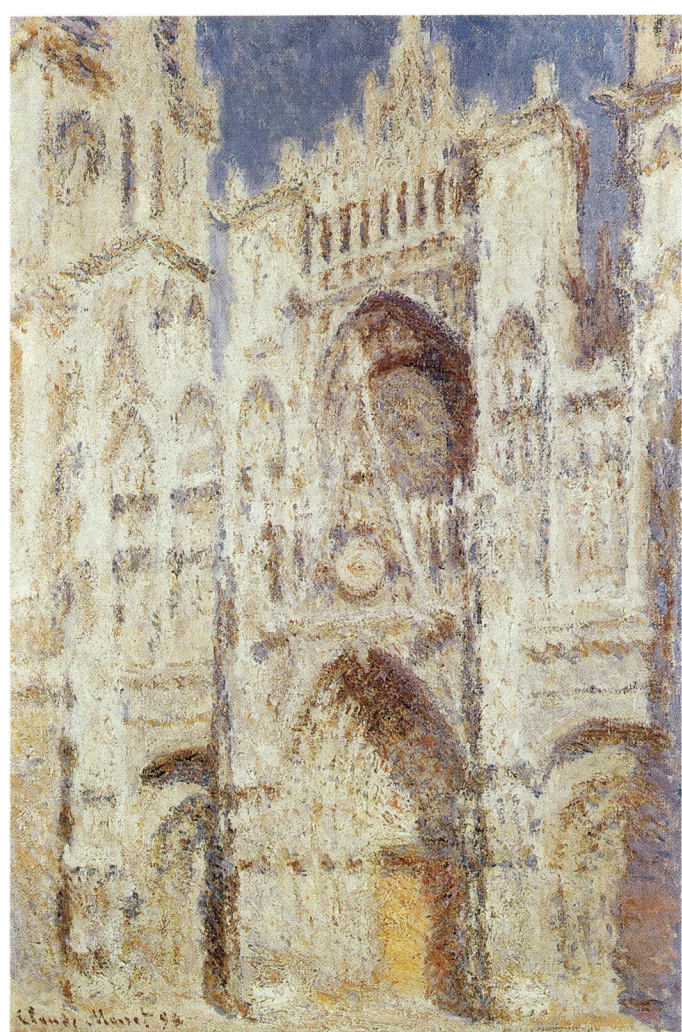

**29-29** CLAUDE MONET, *Rouen Cathedral: The Portal (in Sun)*, 1894. Oil on canvas, $3' 3\frac{1}{4}'' \times 2' 1\frac{7}{8}''$. Metropolitan Museum of Art, New York (Theodore M. Davis Collection, bequest of Theodore M. Davis, 1915).

**29-30** EDGAR DEGAS, *The Tub,* 1886. Pastel, $1' 11\frac{1}{2}'' \times 2' 8\frac{3}{8}''$. Musée d'Orsay, Paris.

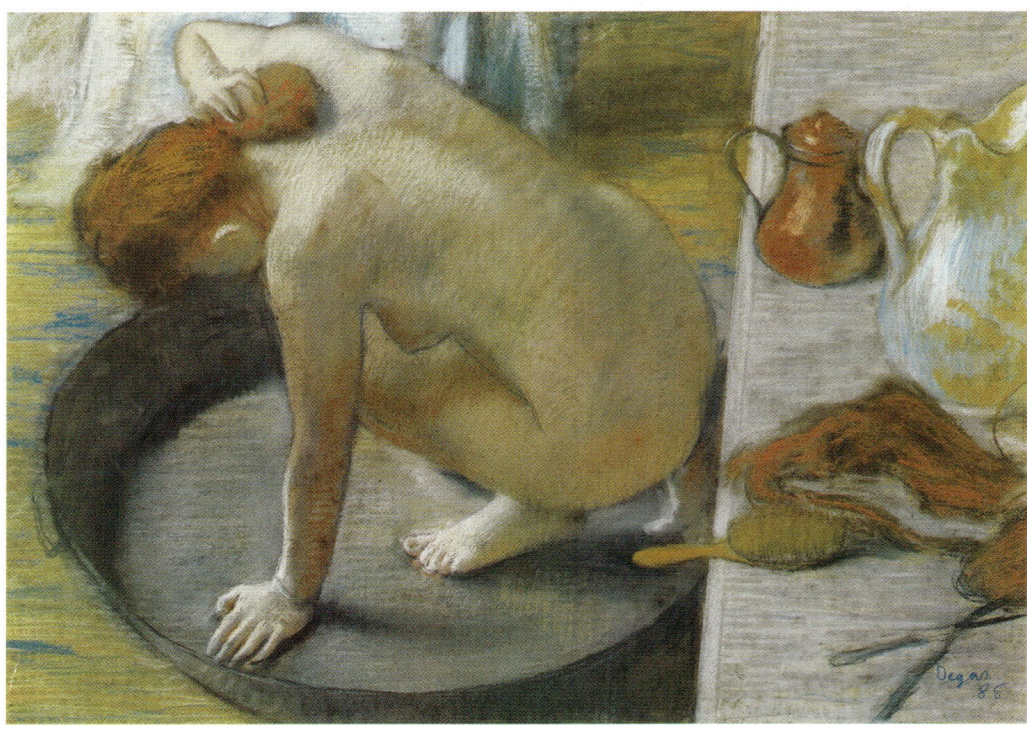

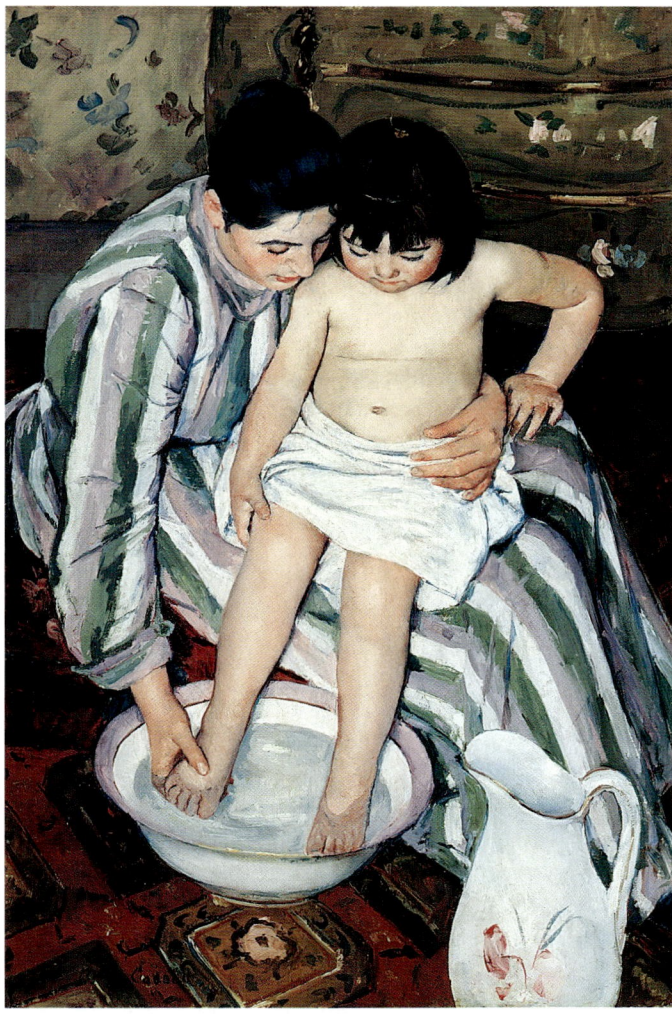

**A MOTHER'S TENDERNESS** In the Salon of 1874, Degas admired a painting by a young American artist, MARY CASSATT (1844–1926), the daughter of a Philadelphia banker. "There," he remarked, "is someone who feels as I do."[16] Degas befriended and influenced Cassatt, who exhibited regularly with the Impressionists. She had trained as a painter before moving to Europe to study masterworks in France and Italy. As a woman, she could not easily frequent the cafés with her male artist friends, and she was responsible for the care of her aging parents, who had moved to Paris to join her, two facts limiting her subject choices. Because of these restrictions, Cassatt's subjects were principally women and children, whom she presented with a combination of objectivity and genuine sentiment. Works such as *The Bath* (FIG. **29-31**) show the tender relationship between a mother and child. As in Degas's *The Tub,* the visual solidity of the mother and child contrasts with the flattened patterning of the wallpaper and rug. Cassatt's style in this work owed much to the compositional devices of Degas and of Japanese prints, but the painting's design has an originality and strength all its own.

**EXPLORING PARIS'S NIGHTLIFE** French artist HENRI DE TOULOUSE-LAUTREC (1864–1901) was interested in capturing the sensibility of modern life and deeply admired Degas. Because of this interest and admiration, his work intersects with that of the Impressionists. However, his work has an added satirical edge to it and often borders on caricature. Toulouse-Lautrec's art was, to a degree, the expression of his life. Self-exiled by his infirmities and odd stature from the high society his ancient aristocratic name entitled him to enter, he became a denizen of the night world of Paris, consorting with a tawdry population of entertainers, prostitutes, and other social outcasts. He reveled in the energy of cheap music halls, cafés, and bordellos. In *At the Moulin Rouge* (FIG. **29-32**), the influences of Degas, of the Japanese print, and of photography can be seen in the oblique and asymmetrical composition, the spatial diagonals, and the strong line patterns with added dissonant colors.

**29-31** MARY CASSATT, *The Bath,* ca. 1892. Oil on canvas, 3′ 3″ × 2′ 2″. The Art Institute of Chicago, Chicago (Robert A. Walker Fund).

**29-32** HENRI DE TOULOUSE-LAUTREC, *At the Moulin Rouge,* 1892–1895. Oil on canvas, approx. 4′ × 4′ 7″. The Art Institute of Chicago, Chicago (Helen Birch Bartlett Memorial Collection).

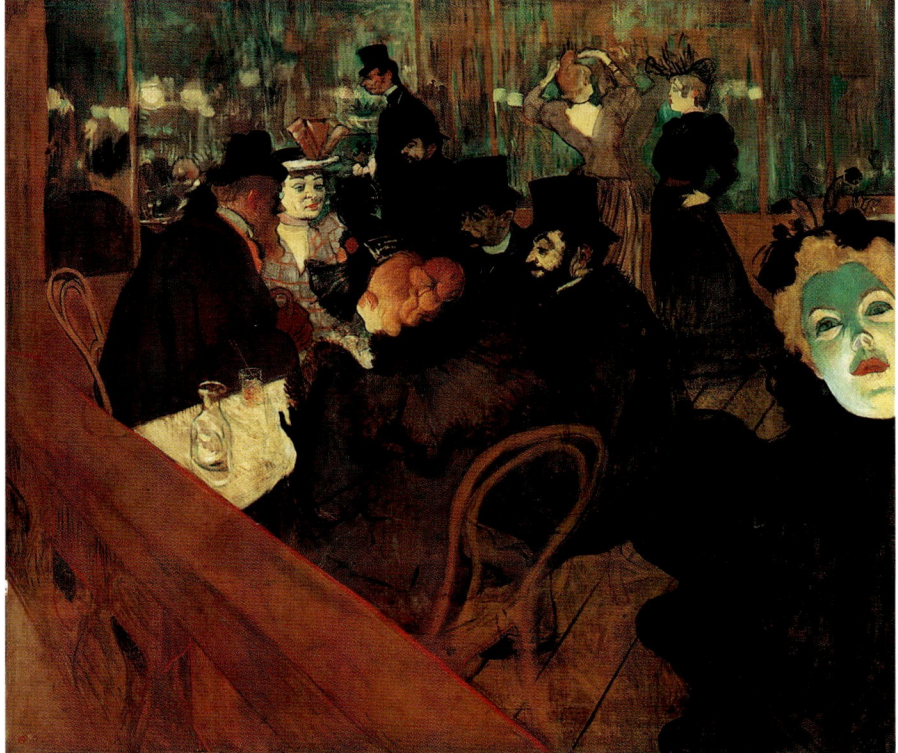

But although Toulouse-Lautrec closely studied such scenes in actual life and they were already familiar to viewers in the work of the earlier Impressionists, he so emphasized or exaggerated each element that the tone is new. Compare, for instance, this painting's mood with the relaxed and casual atmosphere of Renoir's *Le Moulin de la Galette* (FIG. 29-25). Toulouse-Lautrec's scene is nightlife, with its glaring artificial light, brassy music, and assortment of corrupt, cruel, and masklike faces. (He included himself in the background—the tiny man with the derby accompanying the very tall man, his cousin.) Such distortions by simplification of the figures and faces anticipated Expressionism (see Chapter 33, page 964), when artists' use of formal elements—for example, brighter colors and bolder lines than ever before—increased their images' impact on observers.

**ORCHESTRATING ART** JAMES ABBOTT MCNEILL WHISTLER (1834–1903) was an American expatriate artist who worked on the European continent before settling finally in London. In Paris, he knew many of the Impressionists, and his art is an interesting mixture of some of their concerns and his own. Whistler shared their interests in the subject of contemporary life and the sensations color produces on the eye. To these influences he added his interest in creating harmonies paralleling those achieved in music:

> Nature contains the elements, in color and form, of all pictures, as the keyboard contains the notes of all music. But the artist is born to pick, and choose, and group with science, these elements, that the result may be beautiful—as the musician gathers his notes, and forms his chords, until he brings forth from chaos glorious harmony.[17]

To underscore his artistic intentions, Whistler began calling his paintings "arrangements" or "nocturnes." *Nocturne in Black and Gold (The Falling Rocket)*, FIG. **29-33**, is a daring painting with gold flecks and splatters that represent the exploded firework punctuating the darkness of the night sky. The artist was clearly more interested in conveying the atmospheric effects than he was in providing details of the actual scene. He emphasized creating a harmonious arrangement of shapes and colors on the rectangle of his canvas, an approach that interested many 20th-century artists.

Such works angered many viewers. The British critic John Ruskin responded to this painting by writing a scathing review accusing Whistler of "flinging a pot of paint in the public's face" with his style. In reply, Whistler sued Ruskin for libel. During the trial, Whistler was asked about the subject of *Nocturne*:

> "What is the subject of the *Nocturne in Black and Gold*?"
> "It is a night piece and represents the fireworks at Cremorne," answered Whistler.
> "Not a view of Cremorne?"
> "If it were a view of Cremorne, it would certainly bring about nothing but disappointment on the part of the beholders. It is an artistic

**29-33** JAMES ABBOTT MCNEILL WHISTLER, *Nocturne in Black and Gold (The Falling Rocket)*, ca. 1875. Oil on panel, 1′ 11⅝″ × 1′ 6½″. Detroit Institute of Arts, Detroit (gift of Dexter M. Ferry Jr.).

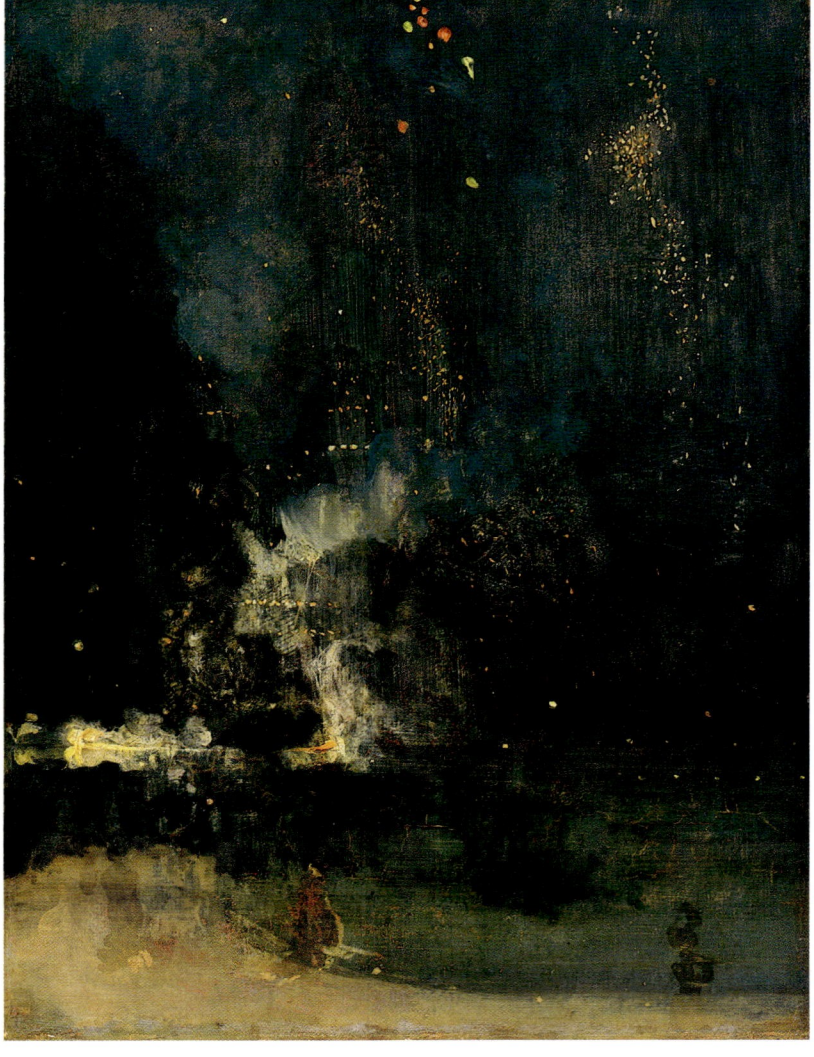

## From Pariah to Paragon
### The Shifting Fortunes of Vincent van Gogh

When van Gogh died of a self-inflicted gunshot wound in 1890 at age 37, he considered himself a failure as an artist. He felt himself an outcast not only from artistic circles but also from society at large. The hostile reception to his work, both from fellow artists and the general public, no doubt reinforced this perception. Throughout his brief career, he encountered great difficulty selling his work; indeed, he sold only one painting during his lifetime.

Since his death, however, his reputation and the appreciation of his art have grown dramatically. Subsequent painters such as the Fauves (see Chapter 33, page 964) and the German Expressionists (see Chapter 33, page 966) built on the use of color and the expressiveness of van Gogh's art. This influence—what later artists make of an earlier artist's innovations and ideas—is an important factor in determining artistic significance, and it is no exaggeration to state that van Gogh is today one of the most revered and respected artists. This reevaluation of van Gogh's contributions speaks volumes about his art. It also speaks to the fluctuations in public taste and the ongoing assessment central to the art historical enterprise. Taste, both cultural and personal, is notoriously unpredictable, as evidenced by the constantly and frequently shifting preferences in fashion, design, architecture, and art. Art history, as a discipline, is based on the continual study of previous art. Therefore, conclusions about the work of artists are always subject to change.

Today, van Gogh's work stands as a milestone in the development of an expressionistic art, and it has deeply influenced generations of artists. Although monetary value does not necessarily reflect artistic value, it is worth noting that in recent years, van Gogh's paintings consistently have brought the highest prices at auction. For example, in 1990, Ryoei Saito, a Japanese paper manufacturing magnate, purchased *Portrait of Dr. Gachet* (1890) for $82.5 million, the most ever paid for an artwork.

It is sobering to think an artist who has had such a dramatic impact on the direction of art and on the general public died thinking himself a failure.

---

arrangement. . . . It is as impossible for me to explain to you the beauty of that picture as it would be for a musician to explain to you the beauty of a harmony in a particular piece of music if you have no ear for music."[18]

Although Whistler won the case, his victory had sadly ironic consequences for him. The judge in the case, showing where his—and perhaps the public's—sympathies lay, awarded the artist only one farthing (less than a penny) in damages and required him to pay all of the court costs, which ruined him financially. He continued to produce etchings and portraits for two decades after his bankruptcy.

## Post-Impressionism: Experimenting with Form and Color

By 1886, most critics and a large segment of the public accepted the Impressionists as serious artists. Just when their images of contemporary life no longer seemed crude and unfinished, however, some of these painters and a group of younger followers came to feel that Impressionists were neglecting too many of the traditional elements of picture making in their attempts to capture momentary sensations of light and color on canvas. In a conversation with the influential art dealer Ambroise Vollard in about 1883, Renoir commented: "I had wrung impressionism dry, and I finally came to the conclusion that I knew neither how to paint nor how to draw. In a word, impressionism was a blind alley, as far as I was concerned."[19] By the 1880s, four artists in particular were much more systematically examining the properties and the expressive qualities of line, pattern, form, and color: Vincent van Gogh, Paul Gauguin, Georges Seurat, and Paul Cézanne. Both van Gogh and Gauguin focused their artistic efforts on exploring the expressive capabilities of formal elements, while Seurat and Cézanne were more analytical in orientation. Because their art diverged so markedly from earlier Impressionism (although each of these painters initially based their work on Impressionist precepts and methods), these four artists and others sharing their views have become known as the *Post-Impressionists.*

"THE POWER TO CREATE" VINCENT VAN GOGH (1853–1890) explored the capabilities of colors and distorted forms to express his emotions as he confronted nature. The son of a Dutch Protestant pastor, van Gogh believed he had a religious calling and did missionary work (as an evangelist and lay preacher) in the coal-mining area of Belgium. Repeated professional and personal failures brought him close to despair (see "From Pariah to Paragon: The Shifting Fortunes of Vincent van Gogh," above). Although the image of van Gogh as a madman persists in the public imagination, van Gogh is better described as a tormented individual who suffered from epileptic seizures. Only after he turned to painting did he find a way to communicate his experiences. In one of the many revealing letters he wrote to his brother, Theo, van Gogh admitted: "In both my life and in my painting, I can very well do without God but I cannot, ill as I am, do without something which is greater than I, which is my life—the power to create."[20] For van Gogh, the power to create involved the expressive use of color. As he wrote to Theo: "Instead of trying to reproduce exactly what I have before my eyes, I use color more arbitrarily so as to express myself forcibly."[21] He further explained that the color in one of his paintings was "not locally true from the point of view of the delusive realist, but color suggesting some emotion of an ardent temperament."[22]

Van Gogh's insistence on the expressive values of color led him to develop a corresponding expressiveness in his paint application. The thickness, shape, and direction of his brush strokes created a tactile counterpart to his intense color schemes. He moved the brush vehemently back and forth or at right angles, giving a textilelike effect, or squeezed dots or streaks onto his canvas from his paint tube. This bold, almost slapdash attack enhanced the intensity of his colors.

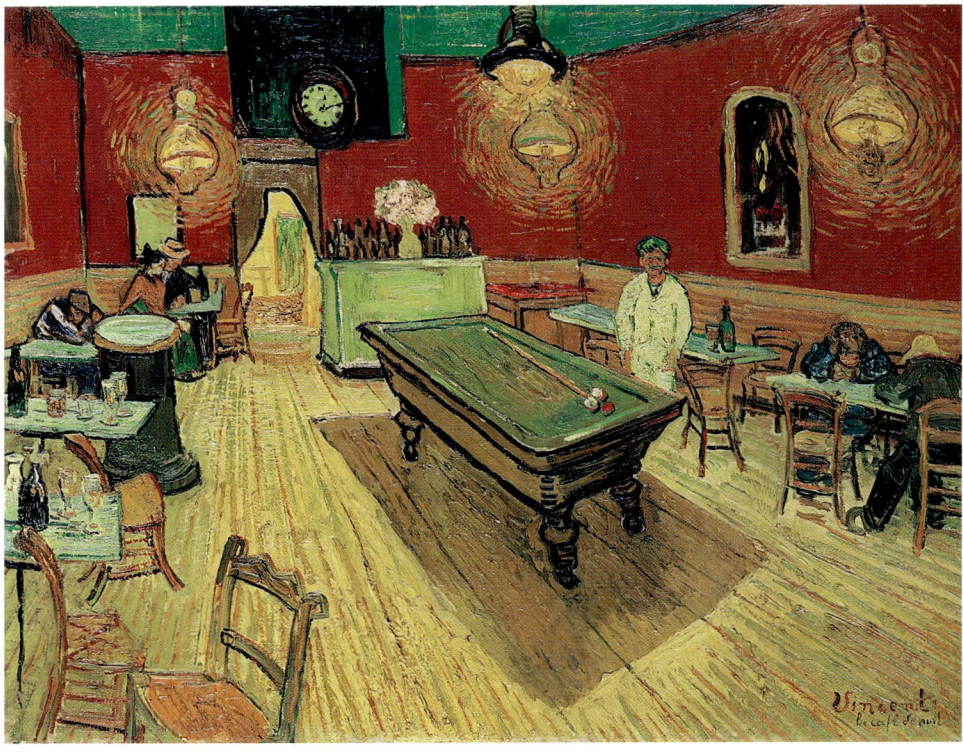

**29-34** VINCENT VAN GOGH, *The Night Café*, 1888. Oil on canvas, approx. 2′ 4½″ × 3′. Yale University Art Gallery, New Haven (bequest of Stephen Carlton Clark).

After relocating to Arles in southern France in 1888, van Gogh painted *The Night Café* (FIG. **29-34**), an interior scene. Although the subject is apparently benign, van Gogh invested it with a charged energy. As van Gogh described it, the painting was meant to convey an oppressive atmosphere—"a place where one can ruin oneself, go mad, or commit a crime."[23] He communicated this by selecting vivid hues whose juxtaposition augmented their intensity. Van Gogh described it in a letter to Theo:

> I have tried to express the terrible passions of humanity by means of red and green. The room is blood red and dark yellow with a green billiard table in the middle; there are four citron-yellow lamps with a glow of orange and green. Everywhere there is a clash and contrast of the most disparate reds and greens in the figures of little sleeping hooligans, in the empty, dreary room, in violet and blue. The blood-red and the yellow-green of the billiard table, for instance, contrast with the soft, tender Louis XV green of the counter, on which there is a pink nosegay. The white coat of the landlord, awake in a corner of that furnace, turns citron-yellow, or pale luminous green.[24]

The proprietor rises like a specter from the edge of the billiard table, which the painter depicted in such a steeply tilted perspective that it threatens to slide out of the painting into the viewer's space. Van Gogh took an innocuous scene and imbued it with "the terrible passions of humanity."

**GLIMMERS OF HOPE?** Just as illustrative of van Gogh's "expressionist" method is *Starry Night* (FIG. **29-35**), which the artist painted in 1889, the year before his death. At this time, van Gogh was living at Saint-Paul-de-Mausole, an asylum in Saint-Rémy where he had committed himself. In *Starry Night,* the artist did not represent the sky in a manner that can be described as realistic. Rather, he communicated the vastness of the universe, filled with whirling and exploding stars and galaxies of stars, the earth and humanity huddling beneath it. The church nestled in the center of the village below can be seen, perhaps, as van Gogh's attempt to express or reconcile his conflicted feelings about religion. Although van Gogh's style in *Starry Night* suggests a very personal vision, this work does correspond in many ways to the view available to the painter from the window of his room in Saint-Paul-de-Mausole. The existence of cypress trees and the placement of the constellations have been confirmed as matching the view that would have been visible to van Gogh during his stay in the asylum. Still, the artist took any visible objects and translated them into his unique vision. Given van Gogh's determination to use color to express himself forcibly, the dark, deep blue that pervades the entire painting cannot be overlooked. Together with the turbulent brush strokes, the color suggests a quiet but pervasive depression. Van Gogh's written observation to his brother reveals his contemplative state of mind:

> Perhaps death is not the hardest thing in a painter's life. . . . [L]ooking at the stars always makes me dream, as simply as I dream over the black dots representing towns and villages on a map. Why, I ask myself, shouldn't the shining dots of the sky be as accessible as the black dots on the map of France? Just as we take the train to get to Tarascon or Rouen, we take death to reach a star.[25]

**PATTERNS OF SHAPE AND COLOR** Like van Gogh, the French painter PAUL GAUGUIN (1848–1903) rejected objective representation in favor of subjective expression. He also broke with the Impressionistic studies of minutely contrasted hues because he believed that color above all must be expressive and that the artist's power to determine the colors in a painting was a seminal element of creativity. However, while van Gogh's heavy, thick brush strokes were an important component of his expressive style, Gauguin's color areas appear flatter, often visually dissolving into abstract patches or patterns. Gauguin had painted as an amateur, but after taking lessons with Pissarro, he resigned from his prosperous brokerage business in 1883 to devote his time entirely to painting.

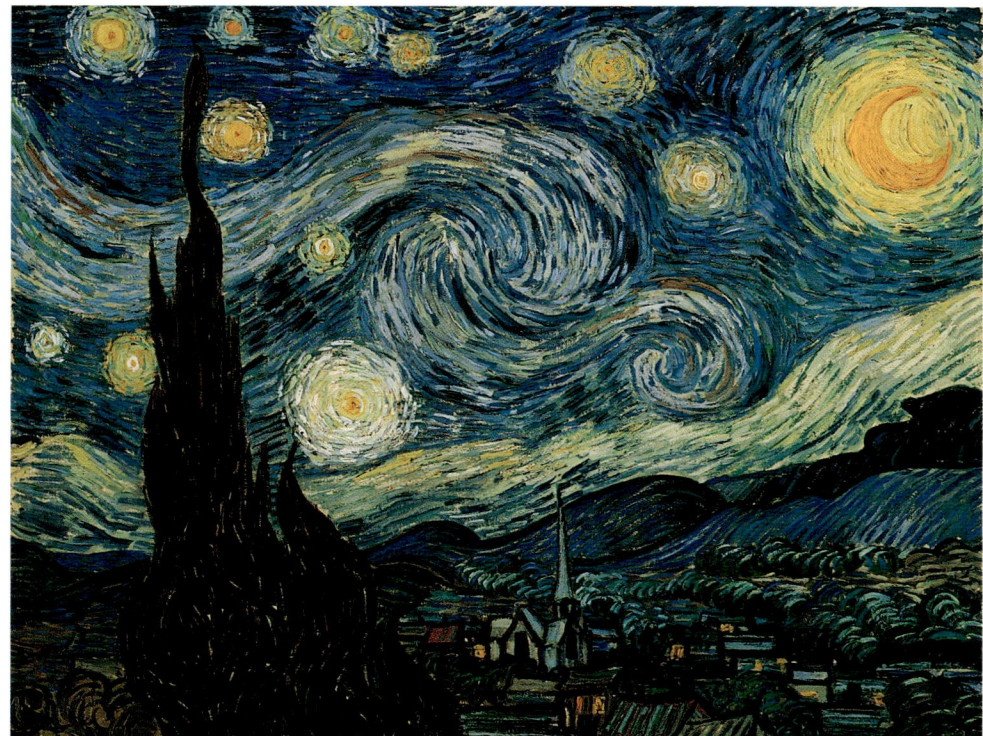

29-35 VINCENT VAN GOGH, *Starry Night*, 1889. Oil on canvas, approx. 2′ 5″ × 3′ ¼″. Museum of Modern Art, New York (acquired through the Lillie P. Bliss Bequest).

In 1886, Gauguin moved to Pont-Aven in Brittany, a province of France. There he painted a work that decisively rejects Realism and Impressionism, *The Vision after the Sermon*, or *Jacob Wrestling with the Angel* (FIG. 29-36). Gauguin claimed that he was attracted to Brittany's unspoiled culture, its ancient Celtic folkways, and the still medieval Catholic piety of its people. In his view, these were "natural" men and women, perfectly at ease in their unspoiled peasant environment. Interestingly, Gauguin chose to ignore the dramatic developments that transformed Brittany in the 1870s and 1880s into a very profitable market economy. The painting shows Breton women, wearing their starched white Sunday caps

and black dresses, visualizing a sermon they have just heard at church on Jacob's encounter with the Holy Spirit (as recounted in Gen. 32:24–30). The women pray devoutly before the apparition, as they would have before the roadside crucifix shrines that were familiar features of the Breton countryside.

Gauguin departed from an optical realism and composed the picture elements to focus the viewer's attention on the idea and intensify its message. The images are not what the Impressionist eye would have seen and replicated but what memory would have recalled and imagination would have modified. Thus the artist twisted the perspective and allotted the space to emphasize the innocent

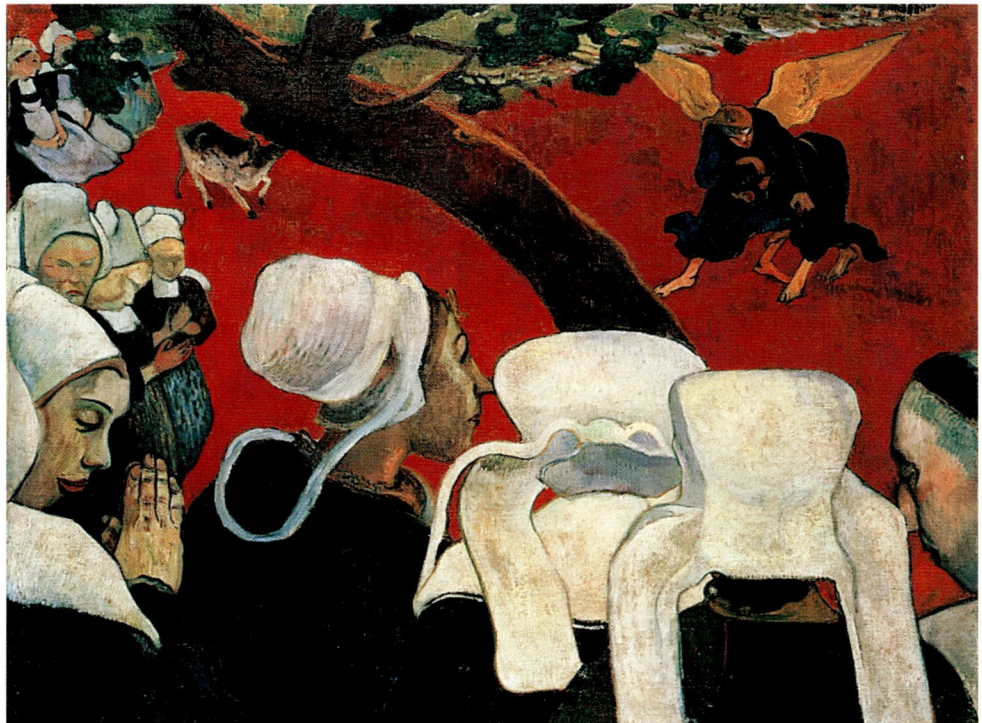

29-36 PAUL GAUGUIN, *The Vision after the Sermon*, or *Jacob Wrestling with the Angel*, 1888. Oil on canvas, 2′ 4¾″ × 3′ ½″. National Gallery of Scotland, Edinburgh.

faith of the unquestioning women, while he shrank Jacob and the Angel, wrestling in a ring enclosed by a Breton stone fence, to the size of fighting cocks. Wrestling matches were regular features at the entertainment held after high mass, so Gauguin's women are spectators at a contest, which is, for them, a familiar part of their culture.

Gauguin did not unify the picture with a horizon perspective, light and shade, or a naturalistic use of color. Instead, he abstracted the scene into a pattern. Pure unmodulated color fills flat planes and shapes bounded by firm line. Here are the white caps, the black dresses, and the red field of combat. The shapes are angular, even harsh. The caps, the sharp fingers and profiles, and the hard contours suggest the austerity of peasant life and ritual. Gauguin was receptive to the influences of Japanese prints, stained glass, and cloisonné enamels (see FIG. 16-2). These contributed to his own daring experiment to transform traditional painting and Impressionism into abstract, expressive patterns of line, shape, and pure color. His revolutionary method found its first authoritative expression in *The Vision after the Sermon.*

After a brief period of association with van Gogh in Arles in 1888, Gauguin, in his restless search for provocative subjects and for an economical place to live, settled in Tahiti in the South Pacific. Gauguin was attracted to Tahiti because he believed it offered him a life far removed from materialistic Europe and an opportunity to reconnect with nature. Upon his arrival, he was disappointed to find that Tahiti, under French control since 1842, was extensively colonized. Gauguin tried to maintain his vision of an untamed paradise by moving to the Tahitian countryside, where he expressed his fascination with primitive life and brilliant color in a series of striking decorative canvases. Gauguin often based the design, although indirectly, on native motifs, and the color owed its peculiar harmonies of lilac, pink, and lemon to the tropical flora of the islands.

**A SUMMARY OF LIFE AND ART** Despite the allure of the South Pacific, Gauguin continued to struggle with life. His health suffered, and his art was not well received. In 1897, worn down by these obstacles, Gauguin decided to take his own life, but not before painting a large canvas titled *Where Do We Come From? What Are We? Where Are We Going?* (FIG. **29-37**). This painting can be read as a summary of his artistic methods (especially the use of flat shapes of pure unmodulated color) and his views on life.

The scene is a tropical landscape, populated with native women and children. Although any message Gauguin intended is ambiguous at best, statements he made in a letter to his friend, Charles Morice, shed light on his philosophical conclusions:

> Where are we going? Near to death an old woman. . . . What are we? Day to day existence. . . . Where do we come from? Source. Child. Life begins. . . . Behind a tree two sinister figures, cloaked in garments of sombre colour, introduce, near the tree of knowledge, their note of anguish caused by that very knowledge in contrast to some simple beings in a virgin nature, which might be paradise as conceived by humanity, who give themselves up to the happiness of living.[26]

Gauguin's description of this work as "comparable to the Gospels"[27] indicates the expansiveness of his vision, but *Where Do We Come From?* remains a sobering, pessimistic image of the life cycle's inevitability. In terms of style, this painting demonstrates Gauguin's commitment to the expressive ability of color. Although the venue is recognizable as a landscape, most of the scene, other than the figures, is composed of flat areas of unmodulated color, which convey a lushness and intensity.

Gauguin's attempt to commit suicide was unsuccessful, and he ultimately died a few years later, in 1903, in the Marquesas Islands. Despite Gauguin's relatively brief career, his art and ideas were extremely influential for subsequent generations of artists.

**THE SCIENCE OF COLOR** In contrast to the expressionistic nature of the work of van Gogh and Gauguin, the art of Frenchman GEORGES SEURAT (1859–1891) was resolutely intellectual. He devised a disciplined and painstaking system of painting that focused on color analysis. Seurat was less concerned with the recording of immediate color sensations than he was with their careful and systematic organization into a new kind of pictorial order. He disciplined the free and fluent play of color that characterized Impressionism into a calculated arrangement based on scientific color theory (see "19th-Century Color Theory," page 883). Seurat's system, known as *pointillism* or divisionism, involved carefully observing color and separating it into its component parts. The artist then applied these pure component colors to the canvas in tiny dots (points) or daubs (FIG. **29-38**). Thus, the shapes, figures, and spaces in the image only become totally comprehensible from a distance, when the viewer's eye blends the many pigment dots.

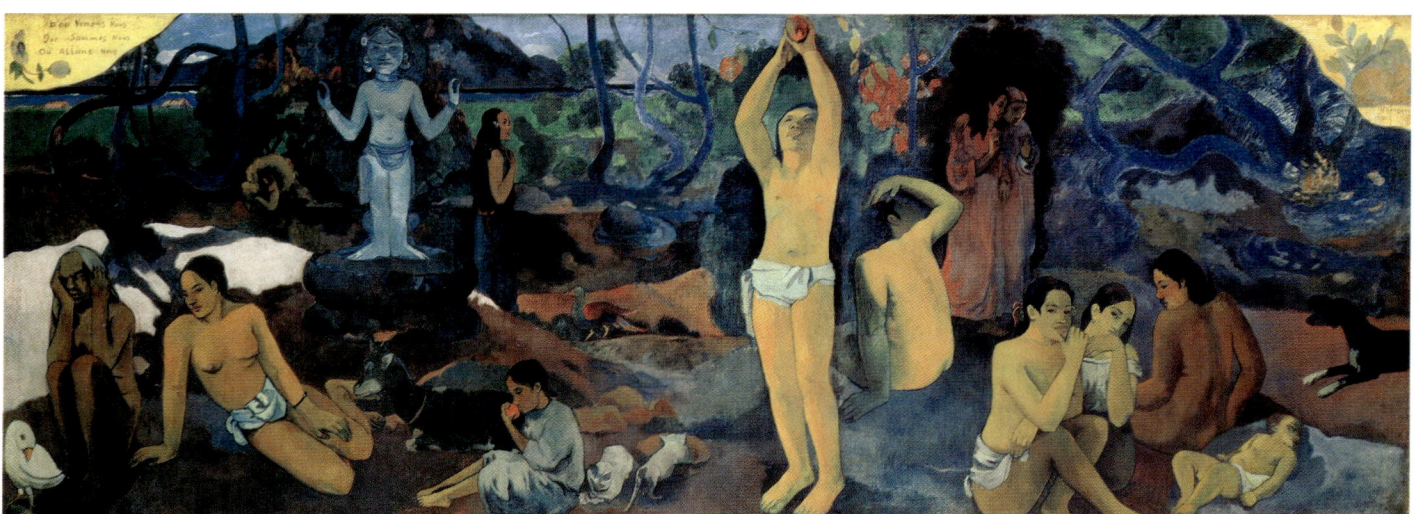

**29-37** PAUL GAUGUIN, *Where Do We Come From? What Are We? Where Are We Going?* 1897. Oil on canvas, 4′ 6$\frac{13}{16}$″ × 12′ 3″. Museum of Fine Arts, Boston (Tompkins Collection).

## 19th-Century Color Theory

In the 19th century, advances in the sciences contributed to changing theories about color and how people perceive it. Many physicists, chemists, and aestheticians (experts in art and artistic principles) immersed themselves in studying optical reception and the behavior of the human eye in response to light of differing wavelengths. In addition to these physiological processes, the psychological dimension of color was also investigated. These new ideas about color and its perception provided a framework within which artists such as Georges Seurat worked. Although we cannot be sure exactly which publications on color Seurat himself read, he no doubt relied on aspects of these evolving theories to develop pointillism (FIG. 29-38).

Discussions of color often focus on hue (for example, red, yellow, and blue), but it is important to consider the other facets of color—saturation (the hue's brightness or dullness) and value (the hue's lightness or darkness). Most artists during the 19th century understood the primary colors as red, yellow, and blue and the complementary secondary colors as those produced by mixing pairs of these primaries—green (blue plus yellow), violet (red plus blue), and orange (red plus yellow). Chemist Michel-Eugène Chevreul extended artists' understanding of color dynamics by formulating the law of simultaneous contrast of colors, based on his observations as director of dyeing at the Gobelins tapestry workshops. Chevreul asserted that juxtaposed colors affect the eye's reception of each, making the two colors as dissimilar as possible, both in hue and in value. For example, placing light green next to dark green has the effect of making the light green look even lighter and the dark green darker. Chevreul further provided an explanation of *successive contrasts*—the well-known phenomenon of colored afterimages. When a person looks intently at a color (green, for example) and then shifts to a white area, the fatigued eye momentarily perceives the complementary color (orange).

Aesthetician Charles Blanc, who coined the term *optical mixture* to describe the visual effect of juxtaposed complementary colors, asserted that the smaller the areas of adjoining complementary colors, the greater the tendency for the eye to "mix" the colors, so that the viewer perceives a grayish or neutral tint. Seurat used this principle frequently in his paintings.

The observations of James Clerk Maxwell were also crucial for color theory development and for Seurat's color use. Maxwell was instrumental in designing an objective method of color measurements, using algebraic color-matching equations. Maxwell's studies, it should be noted, applied to the mixing of colored lights, not the mixing of colored pigments. In other words, Maxwell's explanations dealt with how the eye sees color, not how painters combine pigments on their palettes.

Particularly influential for Seurat was the work of physicist Ogden Rood, who published his ideas in *Modern Chromatics, with Applications to Art and Industry* in 1879. Rood expanded on the ideas of Chevreul, Blanc, and Maxwell and constructed an accurate and understandable diagram of contrasting colors. Further (and particularly significant to Seurat), Rood explored representing color gradation. He suggested that placing small dots or lines of color side by side so that, when viewed from a distance, "the blending is more or less accomplished by the eye of the beholder" is one way to achieve gradation.[1]

The color experiments of Seurat and other late-19th-century artists were also part of a larger discourse about human vision and how we see and understand the world. The theories of physicist Ernst Mach focused on the psychological experience of sensation. He believed that humans perceive their environments in isolated units of sensation that the brain then recomposes into a comprehensible world. Another scientist, Charles Henry, also pursued research into the psychological dimension of color—how colors affect people, and under what conditions. He went even further to explore the physiological effects of perception.

Seurat's work, though characterized by a systematic and scientifically minded approach, also incorporated his concerns about the emotional tone of the images. His art does not serve as illustration of any specific color theory. Yet his paintings are related to scientific and aesthetic investigations of the time, which themselves continued to be important for the development of art in the 20th century.

[1] Quoted in John Leighton and Richard Thomson, *Seurat and the Bathers* (London: National Gallery Publications, 1997), 49.

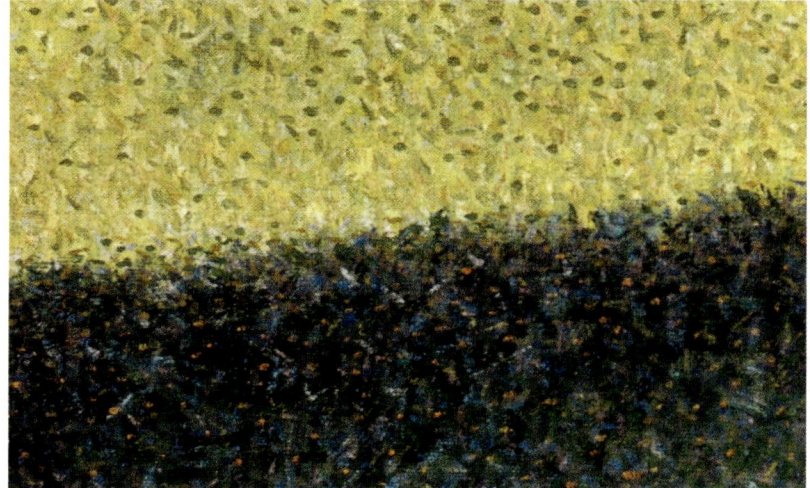

**29-38** GEORGES SEURAT, detail of *A Sunday on La Grande Jatte,* 1884–1886. The Art Institute of Chicago, Chicago.

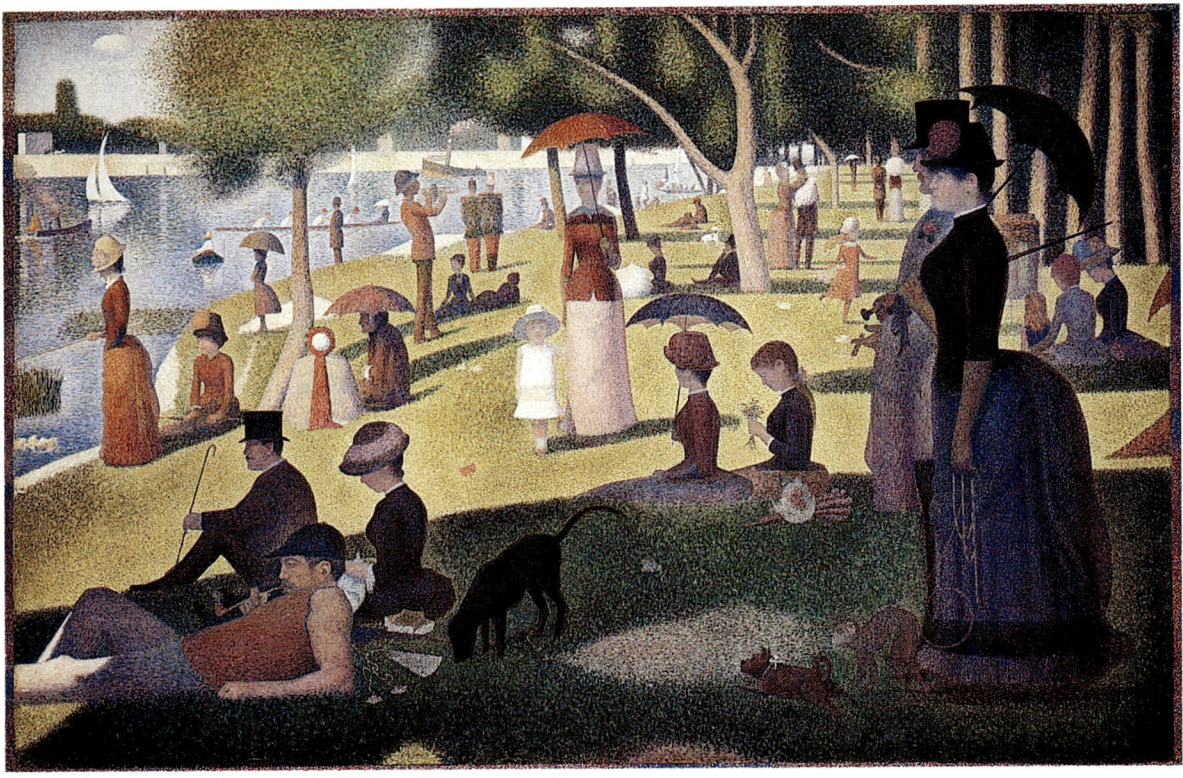

**29-39** GEORGES SEURAT, *A Sunday on La Grande Jatte*, 1884–1886. Oil on canvas, approx. 6′ 9″ × 10′. The Art Institute of Chicago, Chicago (Helen Birch Bartlett Memorial Collection, 1926).

Pointillism was on view at the eighth and last Impressionist exhibition in 1886, when Seurat showed his *A Sunday on La Grande Jatte* (FIG. **29-39**). The subject of the painting is reminiscent of the Impressionist interest in recreational themes. And although Seurat was also interested in analyzing light and color (as were the Impressionists), this painting seems strangely rigid and remote, unlike the spontaneous representations of Impressionism. Seurat applied pointillism to produce a carefully composed and painted image. By using meticulously calculated values, the painter carved out a deep rectangular space. He played on repeated motifs to create both flat patterns and suggested spatial depth. Reiterating the profile of the female form, the parasol, and the cylindrical forms of the figures, Seurat placed each in space to set up a rhythmic movement in depth, as well as from side to side. The picture is filled with sunshine but not broken into transient patches of color. Light, air, people, and landscape are fixed in an abstract design whose line, color, value, and shape cohere in a precise and tightly controlled organization.

Seurat once stated: "They see poetry in what I have done. No, I apply my method, and that is all there is to it."[28] Despite this claim, his art is actually much more than a scientifically based system. *La Grande Jatte* reveals Seurat's recognition of the tenuous and shifting social and class relationships at the time. The locale depicted in the painting is La Grande Jatte (The Big Bowl), an island in the River Seine near Asnières, one of Paris's rapidly growing industrial suburbs. The scene captures public life on a Sunday—a congregation of people from various classes, from the sleeveless worker lounging in the left foreground, to the middle-class man and woman seated next to him. Most of the people wear their Sunday best, making class distinctions less obvious; mass production had also diminished the differences that fashion

historically signified. The painting also reveals the lyricism of Seurat's style. The orchestration of the many forms across the monumental (almost 7-by-10-foot) canvas creates a rhythmic cadence that harmonizes the entire composition.

**MAKING IMPRESSIONISM "DURABLE"** Like Seurat, the French artist PAUL CÉZANNE (1839–1906) turned from Impressionism to develop a more analytical style. Although a lifelong admirer of Delacroix, Cézanne allied himself, early in his career, with the Impressionists, especially Pissarro, and at first accepted their color theories and their faith in subjects chosen from everyday life. Yet his own studies of the Old Masters in the Louvre persuaded him that Impressionism lacked form and structure. Cézanne declared he wanted to "make of Impressionism something solid and durable like the art of the museums."[29]

The basis of Cézanne's art was his unique way of studying nature in works such as *Mont Sainte-Victoire* (FIG. **29-40**). His aim was not truth in appearance, especially not photographic truth, nor was it the "truth" of Impressionism, but a lasting structure behind the formless and fleeting visual information the eye absorbs. Instead of employing the Impressionists' random approach when he was face-to-face with nature, Cézanne attempted to intellectually order his presentation of the lines, planes, and colors that comprised nature. He did so by constantly and painstakingly checking his painting against the part of the actual scene—he called it the "motif"—he was studying at the moment. When Cézanne wrote of his goal of "doing Poussin over entirely from nature,"[30] he apparently meant that Poussin's effects of distance, depth, structure, and solidity must be achieved not by traditional perspective and chiaroscuro but in terms of the color patterns an optical analysis of nature provides.

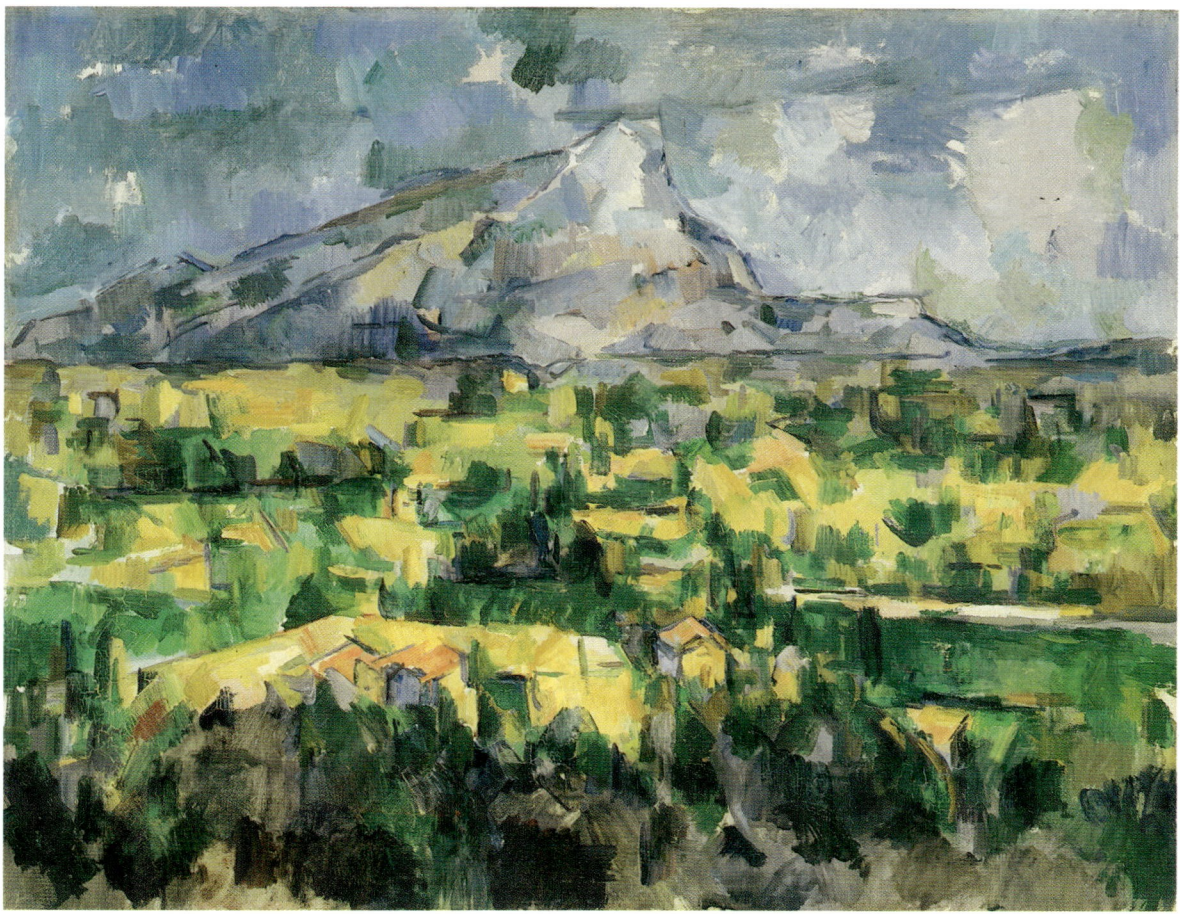

**29-40** PAUL CÉZANNE, *Mont Sainte-Victoire*, 1902–1904. Oil on canvas, 2′ 3½″ × 2′ 11¼″. Philadelphia Museum of Art, Philadelphia (The George W. Elkins Collection).

With special care, Cézanne explored the properties of line, plane, and color and their interrelationships. He studied the effect of every kind of linear direction, the capacity of planes to create the sensation of depth, the intrinsic qualities of color, and the power of colors to modify the direction and depth of lines and planes. To create the illusion of three-dimensional form and space, Cézanne focused on carefully selecting colors. He understood that the visual properties—hue, saturation, and value—of different colors vary (see Introduction, page 7 in combined volumes, or page xxxvi in Volume II). Cool colors tend to recede, while warm ones advance. By applying to the canvas small patches of juxtaposed colors, some advancing and some receding, Cézanne created volume and spatial depth in his works. On occasion, the artist depicted objects chiefly in one hue and achieved convincing solidity by modulating the intensity (or saturation). At other times, he juxtaposed contrasting colors—for example, green, yellow, and red—of like saturation (usually in the middle range, rather than the highest intensity) to compose specific objects, such as fruit or bowls.

*Mont Sainte-Victoire* is one of many views Cézanne painted of this mountain near his home in Aix-en-Provence. In it, he replaced the transitory visual effects of changing atmospheric conditions, effects that occupied Monet, with a more concentrated, lengthier analysis of the colors in large lighted spaces. The main space stretches out behind and beyond the canvas plane and includes numerous small elements, such as roads, fields, houses,

and the viaduct at the far right, each seen from a slightly different viewpoint. Above this shifting, receding perspective rises the largest mass of all, the mountain, with an effect—achieved by equally stressing background and foreground contours—of being simultaneously near and far away. This portrayal approximates the actual experience a person observing such a view might have if apprehending the landscape forms piecemeal. The relative proportions of objects would vary, rather than being fixed by a strict one- or two-point perspective, such as that normally found in a photograph. Cézanne immobilized the shifting colors of Impressionism into an array of clearly defined planes that compose the objects and spaces in his scene. Describing his method in a letter to a fellow painter, he wrote:

> Treat nature by the cylinder, the sphere, the cone, everything in proper perspective so that each side of an object or a plane is directed towards a central point. Lines parallel to the horizon give breadth, that is a section of nature. . . . Lines perpendicular to this horizon give depth. But nature for us men is more depth than surface, whence the need of introducing into our light vibrations, represented by reds and yellows, a sufficient amount of blue to give the impression of air.[31]

**REVEALING UNDERLYING STRUCTURE** In Cézanne's *The Basket of Apples* (FIG. **29-41**), the objects have lost something of their individual character as bottles and fruit and approach the

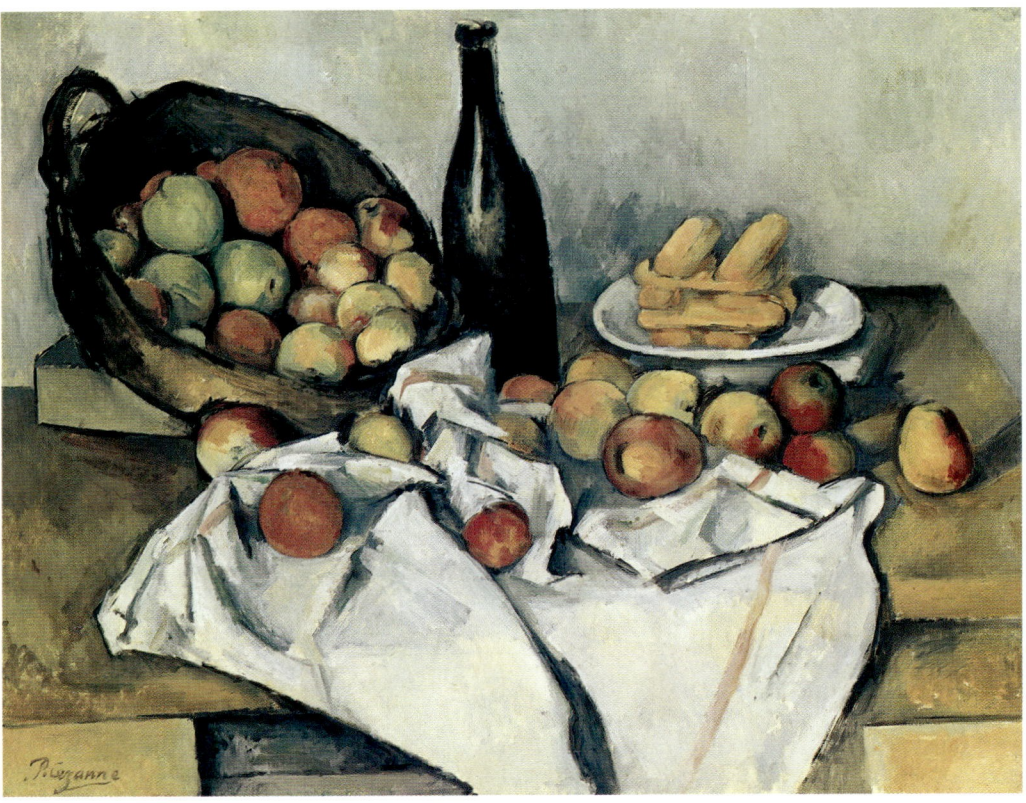

**29-41** Paul Cézanne, *The Basket of Apples,* ca. 1895. Oil on canvas, 2′ ⅜″ × 2′ 7″. The Art Institute of Chicago, Chicago (Helen Birch Bartlett Memorial Collection, 1926).

condition of cylinders and spheres. The still life was another good vehicle for the artist's experiments, as he could arrange a limited number of selected objects to provide a well-ordered point of departure. So analytical was Cézanne in preparing, observing, and painting these still lifes (in contrast to the Impressionist emphasis on the idea of the spontaneous) that he had to abandon using real fruit and flowers because they tended to rot. In *The Basket of Apples,* he captured the solidity of each object by juxtaposing color patches. Cézanne's interest in the study of volume and solidity is evident from the disjunctures in the painting—the table edges are discontinuous, and various objects seem to be depicted from different vantage points. In his zeal to understand three-dimensionality and to convey the placement of forms relative to the space around them, Cézanne explored his still life arrangements from different viewpoints. This resulted in paintings that, while conceptually coherent, do not appear optically realistic. Cézanne created what might be called, paradoxically, an architecture of color.

In keeping with the modernist concern with the integrity of the painting surface, Cézanne's methods never allow the viewer to disregard the actual two-dimensionality of the picture plane. In this manner, Cézanne achieved a remarkable feat—presenting the viewer with two-dimensional and three-dimensional images simultaneously.

## The Rise of the Avant-Garde

**REJECTING ARTISTIC CONVENTIONS** Each successive modernist movement of the 19th century—Realism, Impressionism, and Post-Impressionism—challenged artistic conventions with greater intensity. This relentless challenge gave rise to the avant-garde. Use of this term has expanded over the years; it now serves as a synonym for any particularly new or cutting-edge cultural manifestation. The word *avant-garde,* which means "front

guard," derived from 19th-century French military usage. The avant-garde were soldiers sent ahead of the army's main body to reconnoiter and make occasional raids on the enemy. Politicians who deemed themselves visionary and forward-thinking subsequently adopted the term. It then migrated to the art world in the 1880s, where it referred to artists who were ahead of their time and who transgressed the limits of established art forms. These artists were the vanguard, or trailblazers. The avant-garde were modernists in that they rejected the classical, academic, or traditional and they adopted a critical stance toward their respective media. Yet they departed from modernism in their art's extreme transgressiveness or subversiveness. Further, the avant-garde increasingly disengaged themselves from a public audience. In zealously exploring the premises and formal qualities of painting, sculpture, and other media, avant-garde artists created an insular community whose members seemed to speak only to one another in their work. The Post-Impressionists, whose work the general public found incomprehensible, were the first artists labeled avant-garde. Avant-garde principles appealed to greater numbers of artists (such as the Fauves, Cubists, and Dada artists) as the 20th century dawned, and the momentum it gained made the avant-garde a major force throughout much of the past century.

## Symbolism: Freedom of Imagination, Expression, and Form

Modernist artists, in particular the Impressionists and Post-Impressionists, concentrated on using their emotions and sensations to interpret nature. By the end of the 19th century, the representation of nature became completely subjectivized, to the point that artists did not imitate nature but created free interpretations of it. Artists rejected the optical world as observed in favor of a fantasy world, of forms they conjured in their free imagination, with or without reference to things conventionally seen. Technique and ideas were individual to each of these artists. Color, line, and shape, divorced from conformity to the optical image, were used as symbols of personal emotions in response to the world. These artists who rejected the visual world were solely concerned with expressing reality in accord with their spirit and intuition. Deliberately choosing to stand outside of convention and tradition, such artists spoke like prophets, in signs and symbols.

**BEYOND THE TANGIBLE WORLD** Many of the artists following this path adopted an approach to subject and form that associated them with a general European movement called *Symbolism.* The term had application to both art and literature, which, as critics in both fields noted, were in especially close relation at this time. Symbolists disdained the "mere fact" of Realism as trivial and asserted that fact must be transformed into a symbol of the inner experience of that fact. The task of Symbolist visual and verbal artists was not to see things but to see through them to a significance and reality far deeper than what superficial appearance gave. In this function, as the poet Arthur Rimbaud insisted, artists became beings of extraordinary insight. (One group of Symbolist painters, influenced by Gauguin, called itself the *Nabis,* the Hebrew word for "prophet.") Rimbaud, whose poems had great influence on the artistic community, went so far as to say, in his *Lettre du Voyant (Letter from a Prophet),* that to achieve the seer's insight, artists must become deranged. In effect, they must systematically unhinge and confuse the everyday faculties of sense and reason, which served only to blur artistic vision. The artists' mystical vision must convert the objects of the common-sense world into symbols of a reality beyond that world and, ultimately, a reality from within the individual.

**A PHILOSOPHY OF AESTHETICISM** The extreme subjectivism of the Symbolists led them to cultivate all the resources of fantasy and imagination, no matter how deeply buried or obscure. Moreover, they urged artists to stand against the vulgar materialism and conventional mores of industrial and middle-class society. Above all, by their philosophy of aestheticism, the Symbolists wished to purge literature and art of anything utilitarian, to cultivate an exquisite aesthetic sensitivity, and to make the slogan "art for art's sake" into a doctrine and a way of life.

The subjects of the Symbolists, conditioned by this reverent attitude toward art and exaggerated aesthetic sensation, became increasingly esoteric and exotic, mysterious, visionary, dreamlike, and fantastic. (Perhaps not coincidentally, contemporary with the Symbolists, Sigmund Freud, the founder of psychoanalysis, began the new century and the age of psychiatry with his *Interpretation of Dreams,* an introduction to the concept and the world of unconscious experience.)

Elements of Symbolism appeared in the works of both Gauguin and van Gogh, but their art differed from mainstream Symbolism in their insistence on showing unseen powers as linked to a physical reality, instead of attempting to depict an alternate, wholly interior life. The writers overshadowed the artists who participated in the actual Symbolist movement, but two French artists—Gustave Moreau and Odilon Redon—had a strong influence on the movement. And several other painters, such as Pierre Puvis de Chavannes, followed the Symbolist-related path of imagination, fantasy, and inner vision in their works. Prominent figures in this latter group were the Frenchman Henri Rousseau and the Norwegian Edvard Munch. All of these artists were visionaries who anticipated the strong 20th-century interest in creating art that expressed psychological truth.

**THE "PROPHET" OF SYMBOLISM** Pierre Puvis de Chavannes (1824–1898) was a French artist who rejected Realism and Impressionism and went his own way in the 19th century, serenely unaffected by these movements. Although he never formally identified himself with the Symbolists, he became the "prophet" of those artists. Puvis produced an ornamental and reflective art—a dramatic rejection of Realism's noisy everyday world. In *The Sacred Grove* (FIG. **29-42**), he deployed statuesque figures in a tranquil landscape with a classical shrine. Their motion has been suspended in timeless poses, their contours are

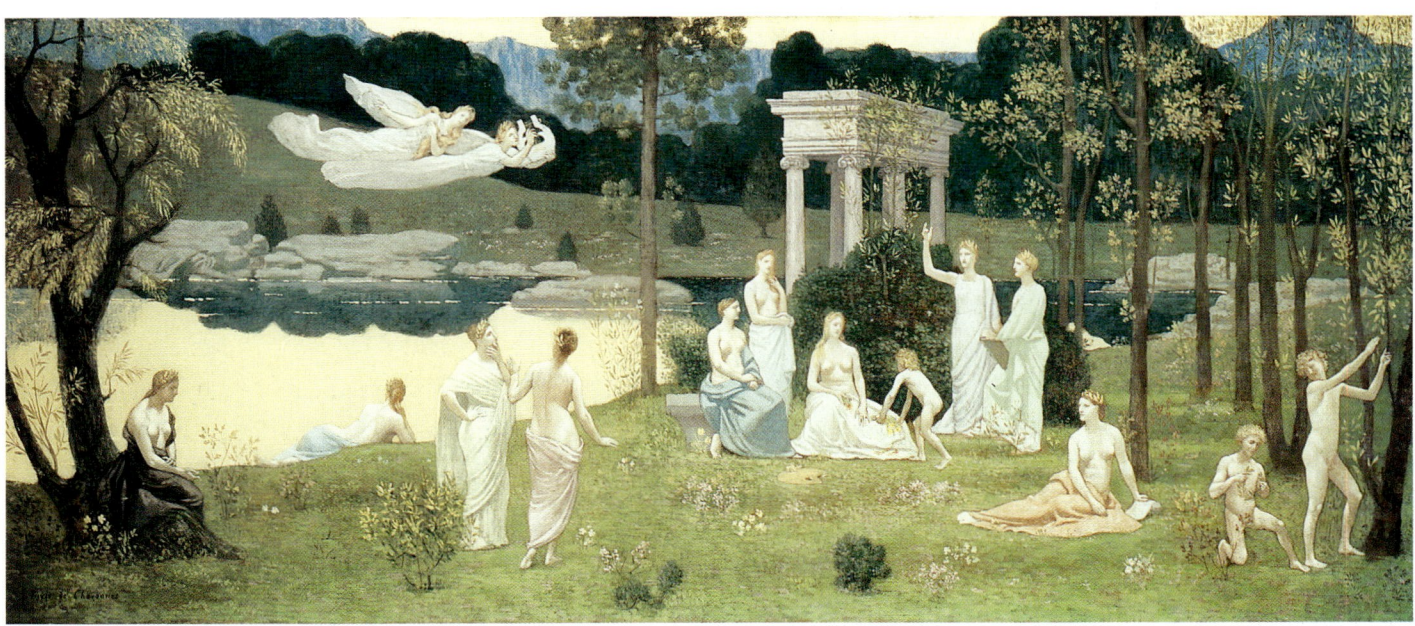

**29-42** Pierre Puvis de Chavannes, *The Sacred Grove,* 1884. Oil on canvas, 2′ 11½″ × 6′ 10″. The Art Institute of Chicago, Chicago (Potter Palmer Collection).

simple and sharp, and their modeling is as shallow as bas-relief. The calm and still atmosphere suggests some consecrated place, where all movements and gestures have a permanent ritual significance. The stillness and simplicity of the forms, the linear patterns their rhythmic contours create, and the suggestion of their symbolic import amount to a kind of program of anti-Realism. The effect impressed younger painters such as Paul Gauguin and the Symbolists, who saw in Puvis the prophet of a new style that would replace Realism. Particularly appealing to these artists was Puvis's rejection of materialism; because of the ease with which easel paintings could be bought and sold, Puvis's use of the mural format was perceived as a repudiation of capitalist materialism. Puvis garnered support from a wide range of artists. The Academy and the government accepted him for his classicism, and the avant-garde revered him for his vindication of imagination and his artistic independence from the world of materialism and the machine. And all artists applauded Puvis's move toward more civic and public art.

**A DEATH-INDUCING VISION** Gustave Moreau (1826–1898), an influential teacher, gravitated toward subjects inspired by dreaming solitude and as remote as possible from the everyday world, in keeping with Symbolist tenets. The artist presented these subjects sumptuously, and his natural love of sensuous design led him to incorporate gorgeous color, intricate line, and richly detailed shape.

*Jupiter and Semele* (FIG. **29-43**) is one of Moreau's rare finished works. The mortal girl Semele, one of Jupiter's loves, begged the god to appear to her in all his majesty, a sight so powerful that she died from it. The artist presented the theme within an operalike setting, a towering opulent architecture. (Moreau loved Wagner's music and, like that great composer, dreamed of a grand synthesis of the arts.) The painter depicted the royal hall of Olympus as shimmering in iridescent color, with tabernacles filled with the glowing shapes that enclose Jupiter like an encrustation of gems. In *Jupiter and Semele*, the rich color is harmonized with the exotic hues of medieval enamels, Indian miniatures, Byzantine mosaics, and the designs of exotic wares then influencing modern artists. Semele, in Jupiter's lap, is overwhelmed by the apparition of the god, who is crowned with a halo of thunderbolts. Her languorous swoon and the suspended motion of all the entranced figures show the "beautiful inertia" that Moreau said he wished to render with all "necessary richness."

**HAUNTED BY "IMAGINARY THINGS"** Like Moreau, Odilon Redon (1840–1916) was a visionary. He had been aware of an intense inner world since childhood and later wrote of "imaginary things" that haunted him. Redon adapted the Impressionist palette and stippling brush stroke for a very different purpose. In *The Cyclops* (FIG. **29-44**), Redon projected a figment of

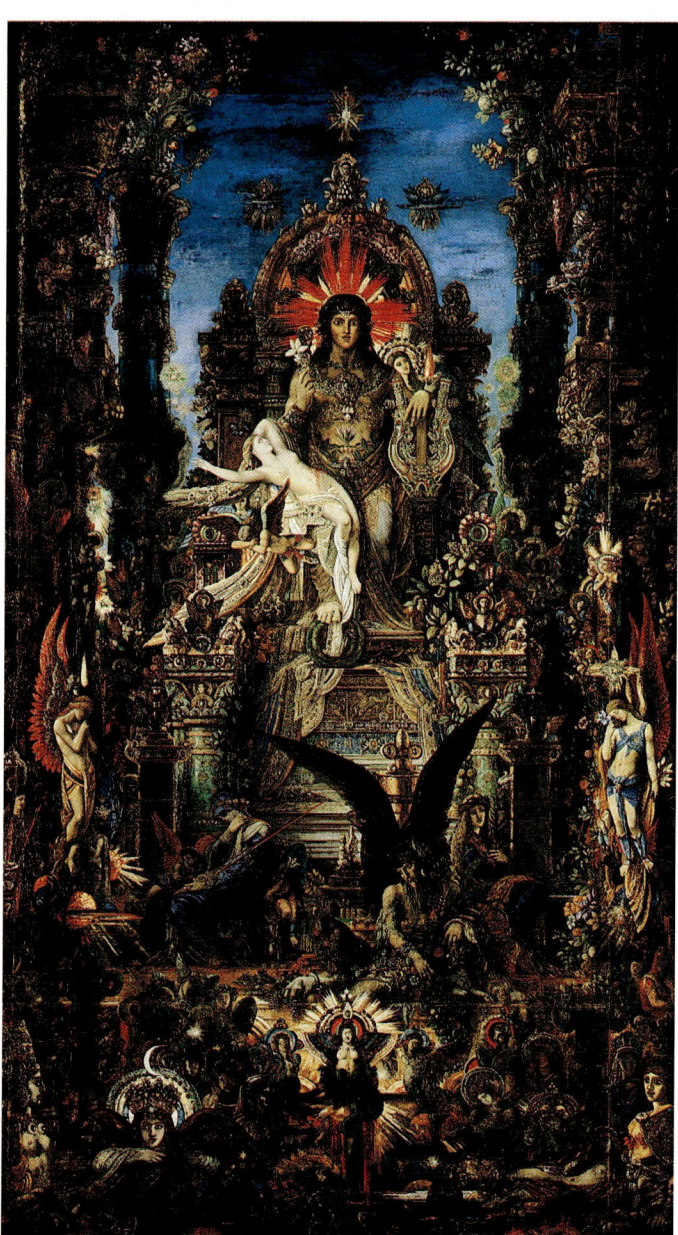

**29-43** Gustave Moreau, *Jupiter and Semele*, ca. 1875. Oil on canvas, approx. 7′ × 3′ 4″. Réunion des Musées Nationaux.

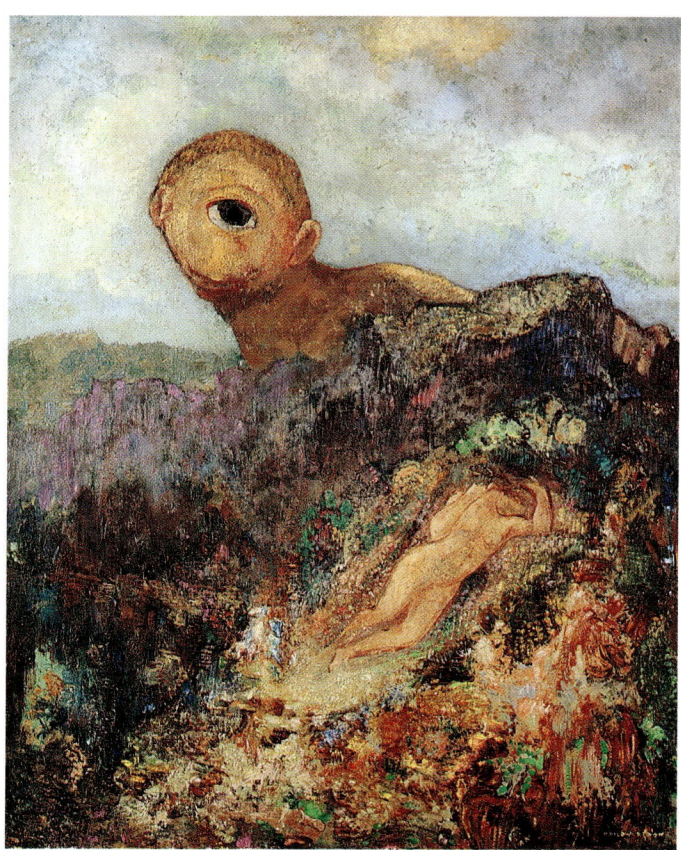

**29-44** Odilon Redon, *The Cyclops*, 1898. Oil on canvas, 2′ 1″ × 1′ 8″. Kröller-Müller Foundation, Otterlo, The Netherlands.

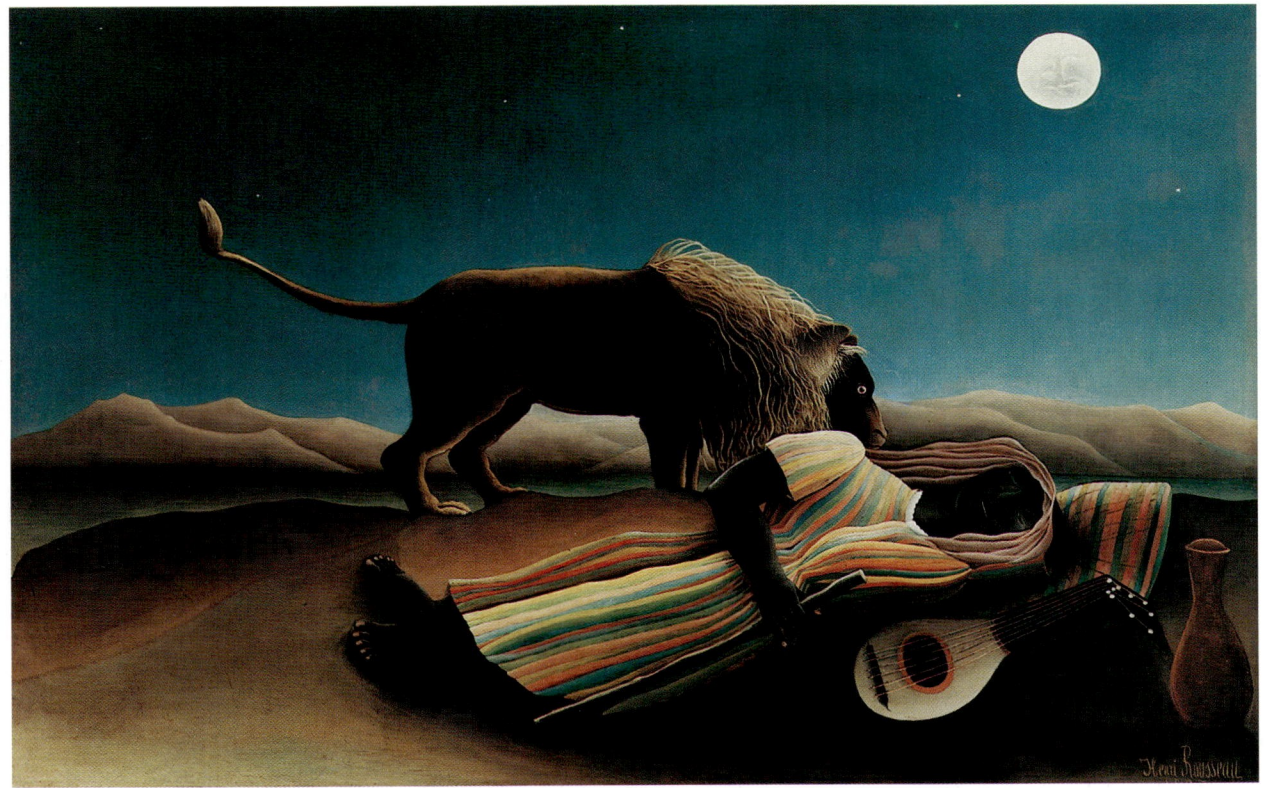

**29-45** HENRI ROUSSEAU, *The Sleeping Gypsy*, 1897. Oil on canvas, 4′ 3″ × 6′ 7″. Museum of Modern Art, New York (gift of Mrs. Simon Guggenheim).

the imagination as if it were visible, coloring it whimsically with a rich profusion of fresh saturated hues that harmonized with the mood he felt fitted the subject. The fetal head of the shy, simpering Polyphemus, with its huge loving eye, rises balloonlike above the sleeping Galatea. The image born of the dreaming world and the color analyzed and disassociated from the waking world come together here at the artist's will. As Redon himself observed: "My originality consists in bringing to life, in a human way, improbable beings and making them live according to the laws of probability, by putting—as far as possible—the logic of the visible at the service of the invisible."[32]

**A WORLD OF PERSONAL FANTASY** The imagination of the French artist HENRI ROUSSEAU (1844–1910) engaged a different but equally powerful world of personal fantasy. Gauguin had journeyed to the South Seas in search of primitive innocence; Rousseau was a "primitive" without leaving Paris—an untrained amateur painter. Rousseau produced an art of dream and fantasy in a style that had its own sophistication and made its own departure from the artistic currency of the time. He compensated for his apparent visual, conceptual, and technical naiveté with a natural talent for design and an imagination teeming with exotic images of mysterious tropical landscapes. In perhaps his best-known work, *The Sleeping Gypsy* (FIG. **29-45**), the figure identified in the title occupies a desert world, silent and secret, and dreams beneath a pale, perfectly round moon. In the foreground, a lion that resembles a stuffed, but somehow menacing, animal doll sniffs at the gypsy. A critical encounter impends—an encounter of the type that recalls the uneasiness when a person's vulnerable subconscious self is menaced during sleep.

**THE "MODERN PSYCHIC LIFE"** Linked in spirit to the Symbolists was the Norwegian painter and graphic artist EDVARD MUNCH (1863–1944). Munch felt deeply the pain of human life. His belief that humans were powerless before the great natural forces of death and love and the emotions associated with them—jealousy, loneliness, fear, desire, and despair—became the theme of most of his art. Because Munch's goal was to describe the conditions of "modern psychic life," as he put it, Realist and Impressionist techniques were inappropriate, focusing as they did on the tangible world. In the spirit of Symbolism, Munch developed a style of putting color, line, and figural distortion to expressive ends. Influenced by Gauguin, Munch produced both paintings and prints whose high emotional charge was a major source of inspiration for the German Expressionists in the early 20th century.

**ANGUISH AND DESPAIR** Munch's well-known painting, *The Cry* (FIG. **29-46**), is an example of this style. The image is grounded in the real world—a man standing on a bridge or jetty in a landscape can be clearly discerned—but it departs significantly from a visual reality. Instead, the work evokes a visceral, emotional response from the viewer because of Munch's dramatic presentation. The man in the foreground, simplified to almost skeletal form, emits a primal scream. The landscape's sweeping curvilinear lines reiterate the curvilinear shape of the mouth and head, almost like an echo, as the scream seems to reverberate through the setting. The fiery red and yellow stripes that give the sky an eerie glow also contribute to this work's resonance. The emotional impulse that led Munch to produce *The Cry* is revealed in an epigraph Munch wrote to accompany the painting:

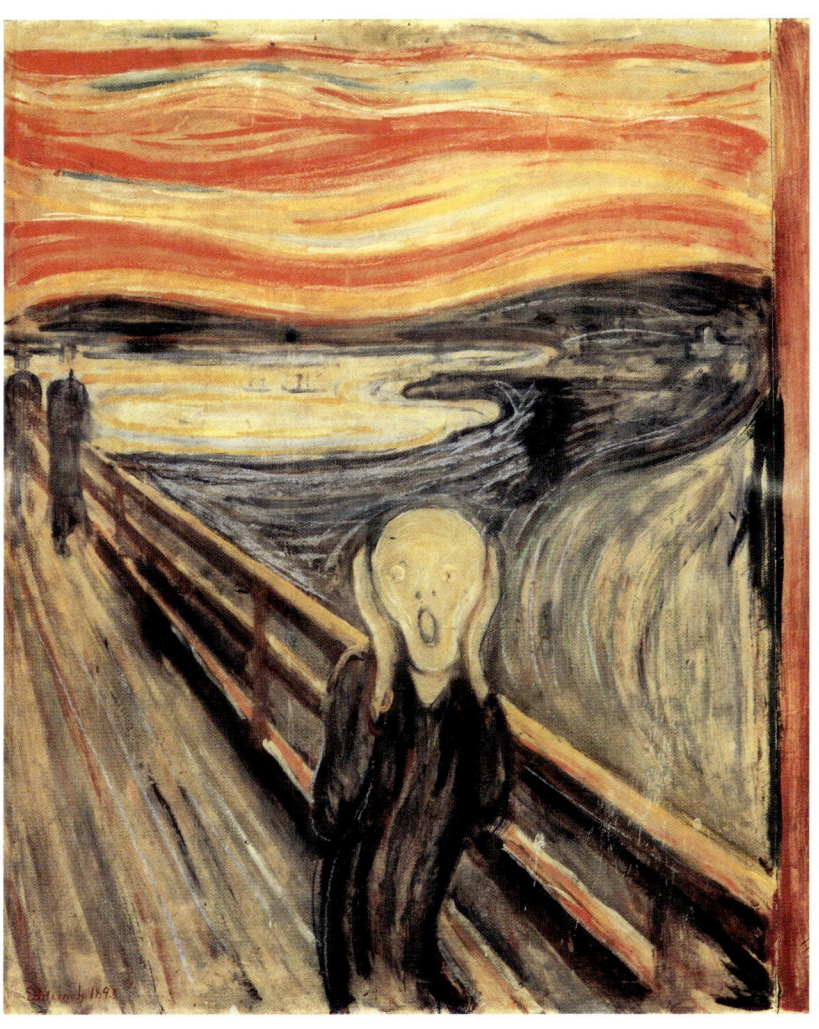

**29-46** EDVARD MUNCH, *The Cry*, 1893. Oil, pastel, and casein on cardboard, 2′ 11¾″ × 2′ 5″. The Munch Museum, The Munch-Ellingsen Group.

"I stopped and leaned against the balustrade, almost dead with fatigue. Above the blue-black fjord hung the clouds, red as blood and tongues of fire. My friends had left me, and alone, trembling with anguish, I became aware of the vast, infinite cry of nature."[33] Appropriately, this work originally was titled *Despair*.

## Sculpture in the Later 19th Century

The three-dimensional art of sculpture was not readily adaptable to capturing the optical sensations many painters favored in the later 19th century. Its very nature—its tangibility and solidity—suggests permanence. Sculpture thus served predominantly as an expression of supposedly timeless ideals, rather than of the transitory. But that did not stop sculptors during this period from pursuing many of the ideas fundamental to movements such as Realism and Impressionism. Despite the many social changes that had transformed European life as the end of the 19th century neared, the sculptor's profession remained a resolutely male pursuit. In part, this was due to the physical demands and working conditions of the medium. And the perception of sculpture as manual labor was widespread; most sculptors came from the working class.

**A SCULPTURAL VISION OF HELL** In his sculptures, JEAN-BAPTISTE CARPEAUX (1827–1875) combined his interest in Realism with a love of Baroque and ancient sculpture and of

Michelangelo's work. Carpeaux's group *Ugolino and His Children* (FIG. **29-47**) is based on a passage from Dante's *Inferno* and shows Count Ugolino with his four sons shut up in a tower to starve to death. In Hell, Ugolino relates to Dante how, in a moment of extreme despair,

*I bit both hands for grief. And*
*they, thinking I did it for hunger,*
*suddenly rose up and said, "Father" . . .*
*[and offered him their own flesh as food.]*

*(33.58–75)*

The powerful forms—twisted, intertwined, and densely concentrated—suggest the self-devouring torment of frustration and despair that wracks the unfortunate Ugolino. A careful student of Michelangelo's male figures, Carpeaux also said he had the Laocoön group (see FIG. 5-89) in mind. Certainly, the storm and stress of *Ugolino and His Children* recall similar characteristics of that group and other ancient artworks, such as the battling gods and giants on the frieze of the Pergamon altar (see FIG. 5-79). Regardless of such influences, the sense of vivid reality in the anatomy of the *Ugolino* figures shows Carpeaux's interest in study from life.

**A MAJESTIC PORTRAIT** AUGUSTUS SAINT-GAUDENS (1848–1907), an American sculptor trained in France, used Realism effectively in a number of his portraits, where that style was highly

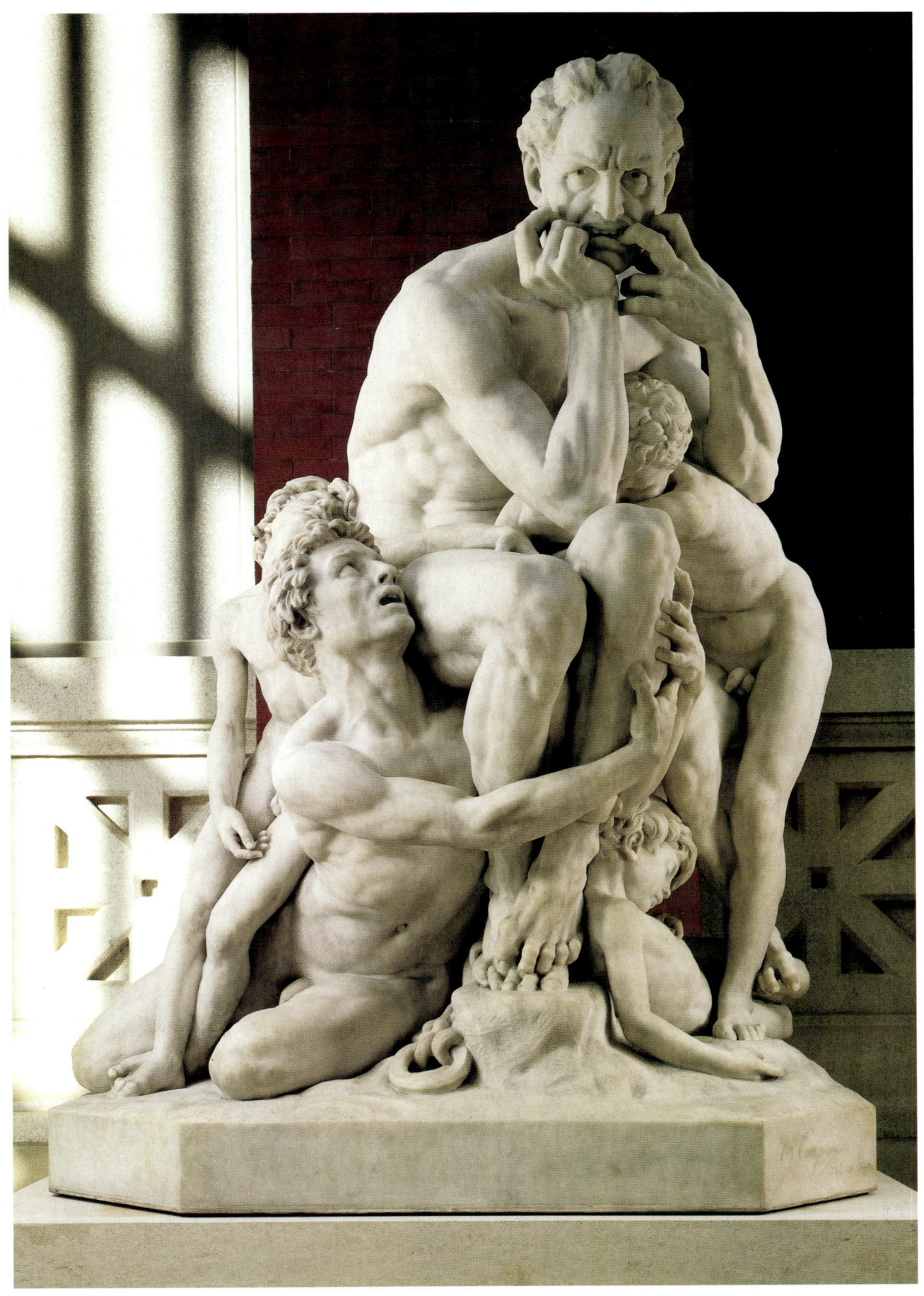

**29-47** JEAN-BAPTISTE CARPEAUX, *Ugolino and His Children*, 1865–1867. Marble, 6′ 5″ high. Metropolitan Museum of Art, New York (Josephine Bay Paul and C. Michael Paul Foundation, Inc., and the Charles Ulrich and Josephine Bay Foundation, Inc., gifts, 1967).

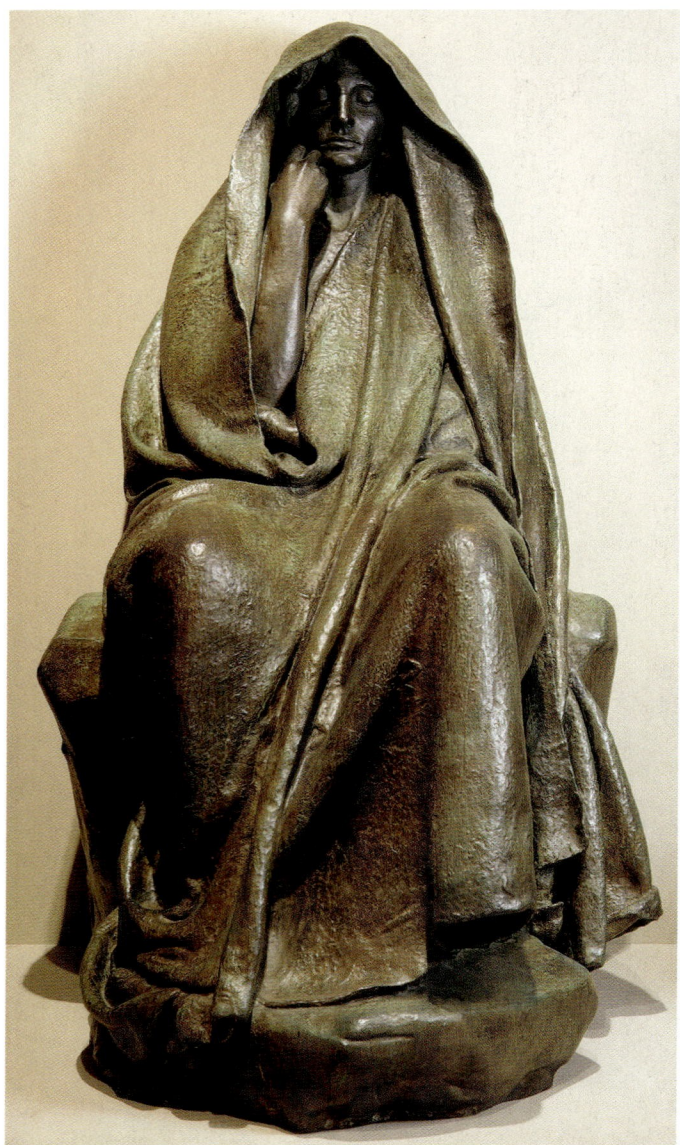

**29-48** AUGUSTUS SAINT-GAUDENS, Adams Memorial, Rock Creek Cemetery, Washington, 1891. Bronze, 5′ 10″ high. Smithsonian American Art Museum, Washington, D.C.

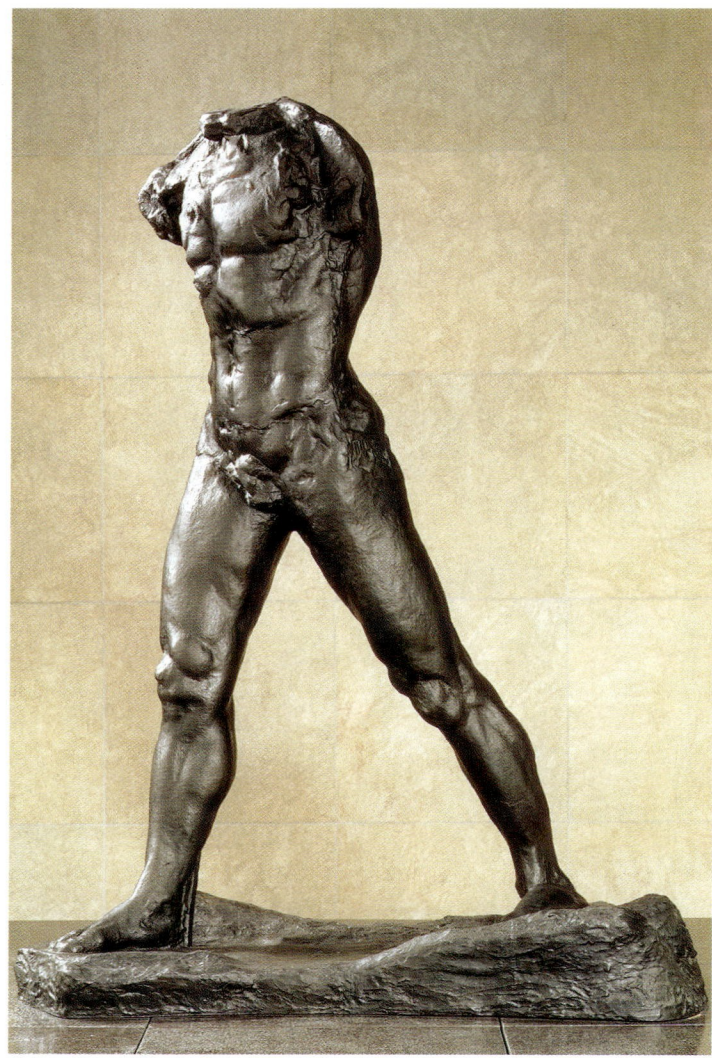

**29-49** AUGUSTE RODIN, *Walking Man,* 1905, cast 1962. Bronze, 6′ 11¾″ high. Réunion des Musées Nationaux.

appropriate. However, when designing a memorial monument of Mrs. Henry Adams (FIG. **29-48**), Saint-Gaudens chose, instead, a classical mode of representation, which he modified freely. The resultant statue is that of a woman of majestic bearing sitting in mourning, her classically beautiful face partly shadowed by a sepulchral drapery that voluminously enfolds her body. The immobility of her form, set in an attitude of eternal vigilance, is only slightly stirred by a natural, yet mysterious and exquisite, gesture.

**OF SURFACE AND SUBSTANCE** In contrast, French artist AUGUSTE RODIN (1840–1917) was imbued with the Realist spirit, and he conceived and executed his sculptures with that sensibility. Like Muybridge and Eakins, Rodin was fascinated by the human body in motion. He was also well aware of artistic developments such as Impressionism. Although color was not a significant factor in Rodin's work, Impressionist influence manifested itself in the artist's abiding concern for the effect of light on the three-dimensional surface. When focusing on the human form, he joined his profound knowledge of anatomy and movement with special attention to the body's exterior, saying, "The sculptor

must learn to reproduce the surface, which means all that vibrates on the surface, soul, love, passion, life. . . . Sculpture is thus the art of hollows and mounds, not of smoothness, or even polished planes."[34] Primarily a modeler of pliable material rather than a carver of hard wood or stone, Rodin worked his surfaces with fingers sensitive to the subtlest variations of surface, catching the fugitive play of constantly shifting light on the body. In his studio, he often would have a model move around in front of him while he modeled sketches with coils of clay.

In the cast bronze *Walking Man* (FIG. **29-49**), Rodin captured the sense of a body in motion. Headless and armless, the figure is caught in midstride at the moment when weight is transferred across the pelvis from the back leg to the front. As with many of his other early works, Rodin executed *Walking Man* with such careful attention to details of muscle, bone, and tendon that it is filled with forceful reality, augmented by his sketchy modeling of the torso. Rodin conceived this figure as a study for his sculpture *Saint John the Baptist Preaching,* part of his process for building his conception of how the human body would express the larger theme's symbolism.

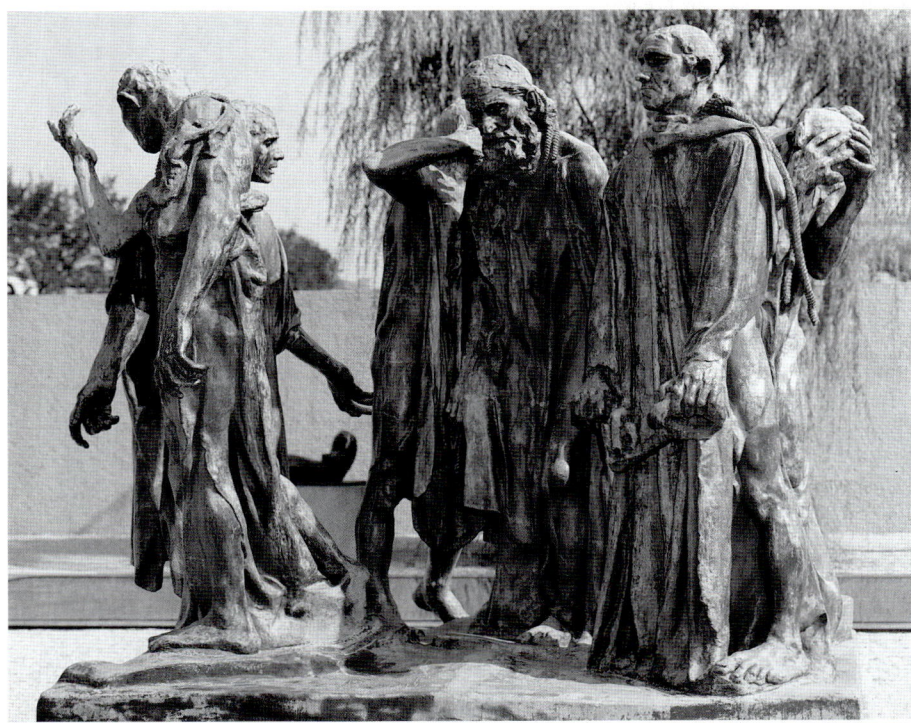

**29-50** Auguste Rodin, *Burghers of Calais*, 1884–1889, cast ca. 1953–1959. Bronze, 6′ 10½″ high, 7′ 11″ long, 6′ 6″ deep. Hirshhorn Museum and Sculpture Garden, Smithsonian Institution, Washington (gift of Joseph H. Hirshhorn, 1966).

A STUDY OF DESPAIR AND DEFIANCE Similarly, Rodin made many nude and draped studies for each of the figures in the life-size group *Burghers of Calais* (FIG. **29-50**). This cast bronze monument was commissioned to commemorate a heroic episode in the Hundred Years' War. During the English siege of Calais, France, in 1347, six of the city's leading citizens agreed to offer their lives in return for the English king's promise to lift the siege and spare the rest of the populace. Each of the bedraggled-looking figures is a convincing study of despair, resignation, or quiet defiance. Rodin enhanced the psychic effects through his choreographic placement of the group members. Rather than clustering in a tightly formal composition, the burghers (middle-class citizens) seem to wander aimlessly. The roughly textured surfaces add to the pathos of the figures and compel the viewer's continued interest. Rodin designed the monument without the traditional high base in the hope that the citizens of Calais would be inspired by the sculptural representation of their ancestors standing eye-level in the city center and preparing eternally to set off on their sacrificial journey. The government commissioners found the Realism of Rodin's vision so offensive, however, that they banished the monument to a remote site and modified the work's impact by placing it high on an isolating pedestal.

Many of Rodin's projects were left unfinished or were deliberate fragments. Seeing the aesthetic and expressive virtue of these works, modern viewers and sculptors have developed a taste for how the sketch, the half-completed figure, the fragment, and the vignette lifted out of context all have the power of suggestion and understatement. Rodin's ability to capture the quality of the transitory through his highly textured surfaces while revealing larger themes and deeper, lasting sensibilities explains the impact he had on 20th-century artists.

## The Arts and Crafts Movement

The decisive effects of industrialization were impossible to ignore, and although many artists embraced this manifestation of "modern life" or at least explored its effects, other artists decried the impact of rampant industrialism. One such response came from the Arts and Crafts movement in England. This movement, which developed during the last decades of the 19th century, was shaped by the ideas of art critic and writer John Ruskin and WILLIAM MORRIS (1834–1896), an artist. Both of these men shared a distrust of machines and industrial capitalism, which they believed alienated workers from their own nature. Accordingly, they advocated an art "made by the people for the people as a joy for the maker and the user."[35] This condemnation of capitalism and support for manual laborers were compatible with socialism, and many artists in the Arts and Crafts movement, especially in England, considered themselves socialists and participated in the labor movement.

This democratic, or at least populist, attitude carried over to the art they produced as well. Members of the Arts and Crafts movement dedicated themselves to producing functional objects with high aesthetic value for a wide public. The style they advocated was based on natural, rather than artificial, forms and often consisted of repeated designs of floral or geometric patterns. For Ruskin, Morris, and others in the Arts and Crafts movement, high-quality artisanship and honest labor were crucial. The movement generated numerous guilds, workshops, and schools committed to the promotion of this ideal.

PATTERNS FROM FLOOR TO CEILING Morris wholeheartedly contributed to this more populist art by forming a decorating firm, Morris, Marshall, Faulkner, and Company, Fine Arts Workmen in Painting, Carving, Furniture, and Metals. This firm's services were in great demand, and it produced wallpaper, textiles, tiles, furniture, books, rugs, stained glass, and pottery. In 1867, Morris decorated the Green Dining Room (FIG. **29-51**) at London's South Kensington Museum (now the Victoria and Albert Museum), the center of public art education and home of decorative art collections. The range of room features — windows, lights, and wainscoting (paneling on the lower part of walls) — that Morris decorated to create this unified, beautiful, and functional environment is overwhelming; nothing escaped Morris's eye. His design for this room also reveals the penchant of Arts and Crafts designers for intricate patterning.

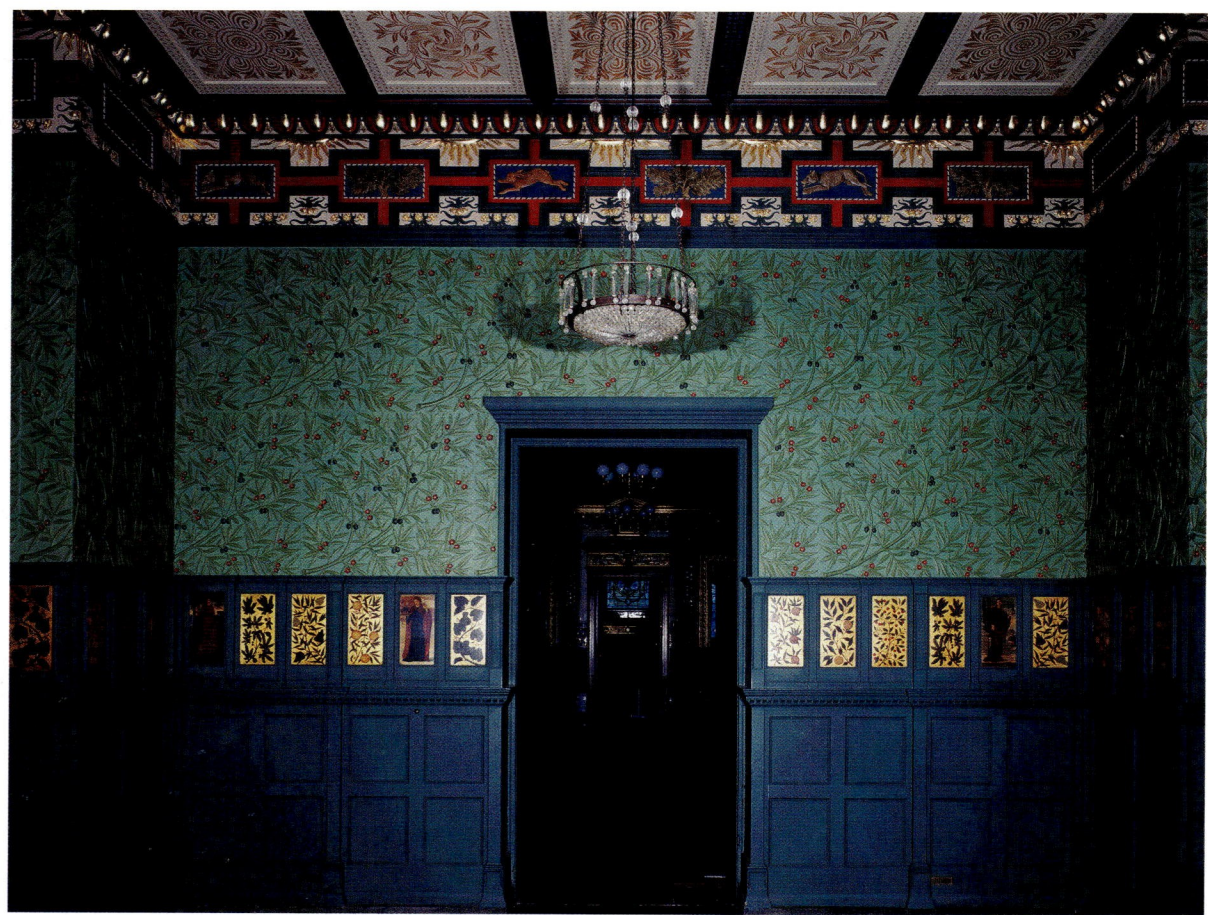

**29-51** WILLIAM MORRIS, *Green Dining Room*, 1867. Victoria and Albert Museum, London.

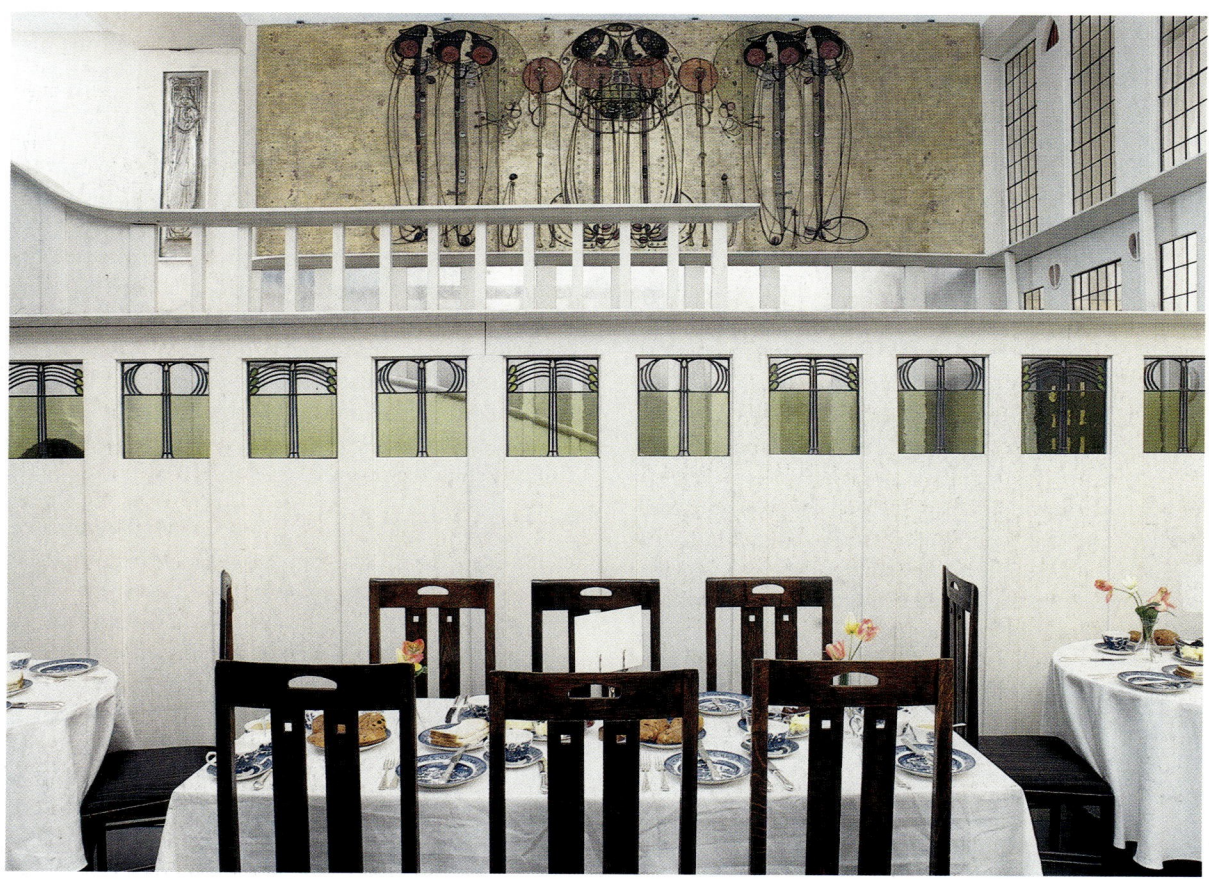

**29-52** CHARLES RENNIE MACKINTOSH, reconstruction (1992–1995) of *Ladies' Luncheon Room, Ingram Street Tea Room,* Glasgow, Scotland, 1900–1912. Glasgow Art Galleries and Museum, Glasgow.

**LUNCHING IN STYLE** Numerous Arts and Crafts societies in America, England, and Germany carried on this ideal of artisanship. In Scotland, the work of CHARLES RENNIE MACKINTOSH (1868–1929) popularized this ideal. Mackintosh designed a number of tea rooms, including the Ladies' Luncheon Room (FIG. 29-52) located in the Ingram Street Tea Room in Glasgow. As reconstructed by Glasgow Museum in 1992–1995, the room decor is consistent with Morris's vision of a functional, exquisitely designed art. The chairs, stained-glass windows, and large panels of colored gesso with twine, glass beads, thread, mother-of-pearl, and tin leaf (made by Margaret Macdonald Mackintosh, an artist-designer and Mackintosh's wife, who collaborated with him on many projects) are all pristinely geometric and rhythmical in design.

## Art Nouveau

**METALLIC PLANT LIFE** *Art Nouveau* (New Art) was an architectural and design movement that developed out of the ideas promoted by the Arts and Crafts movement. The international style of Art Nouveau took its name from a shop in Paris called L'Art Nouveau and was known by that name in France, Belgium, Holland, England, and the United States. In other places, it had other names—Jugendstil in Austria and Germany (after the magazine *Der Jugend*, "youth"), Modernismo in Spain, and Floreale or Liberty in Italy. Proponents of this movement tried to synthesize all the arts in a determined attempt to create art based on natural forms that could be mass-produced for a large audience. The Art Nouveau style emerged at the end of the 19th century and adapted the twining plant form to the needs of architecture, painting, sculpture, and all of the decorative arts. The mature Art Nouveau

style was first seen in houses designed in Brussels in the 1890s by VICTOR HORTA (1861–1947). The staircase in the Van Eetvelde House (FIG. 29-53), which Horta built in Brussels in 1895, is an example of his Art Nouveau work. Every detail functions as part of a living whole. Furniture, drapery folds, veining in the lavish stone paneling, and the patterning of the door moldings join with real plants to provide graceful counterpoints for the twining plant theme. Metallic tendrils curl around the railings and posts, delicate metal tracery fills the glass dome, and floral and leaf motifs spread across the fabric panels of the screen (*left background*).

Several influences can be identified in Art Nouveau. In addition to the rich, foliated two-dimensional ornament of Arts and Crafts design and the artisan's respect for materials of the Arts and Crafts movement, the free, sinuous whiplash curve of Japanese print designs (see FIG. 27-11) inspired Art Nouveau artists. Art Nouveau also borrowed from the expressively patterned styles of van Gogh (FIGS. 29-34 and 29-35), Gauguin (FIGS. 29-36 and 29-37), and their Post-Impressionist and Symbolist contemporaries.

**THE PEACOCK'S SWEEPING CURVES** AUBREY BEARDSLEY (1872–1898) was one of a circle of English artists whose work existed at the intersection of Symbolism and Art Nouveau. For *Salomé*, an illustration for a book by Oscar Wilde, Beardsley drew *The Peacock Skirt* (FIG. 29-54), a dazzlingly decorative composition perfectly characteristic of his style. The Japanese print influence is obvious, although Beardsley assimilated it into his unique manner. Banishing Realism, he confined himself to lines and to patterns of black and white, eliminating all shading. His tense, elastic line encloses sweeping curvilinear shapes that lie flat on the surface—some left almost vacant, others filled with swirling complexes of mostly organic motifs. Beardsley's

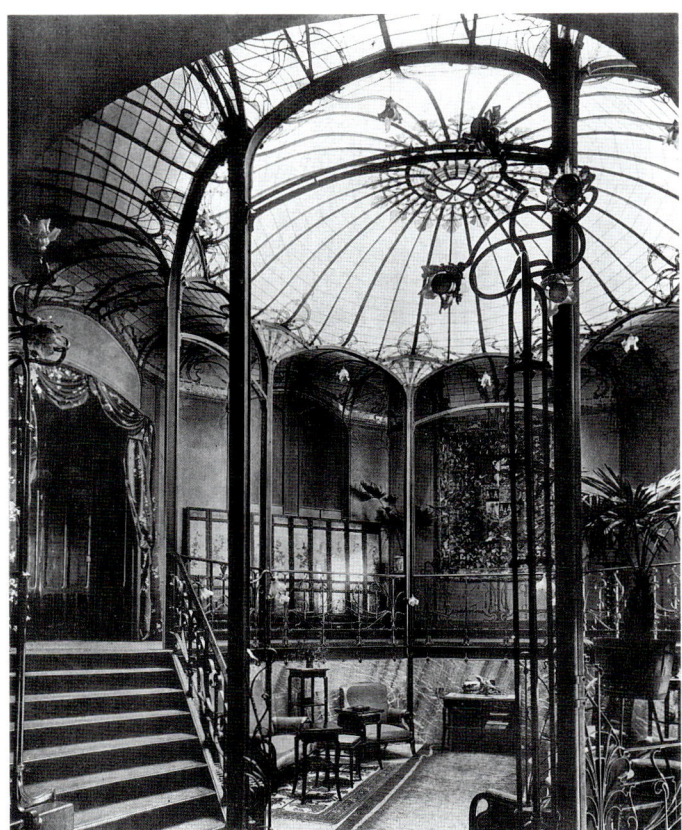

**29-53** VICTOR HORTA, staircase in the Van Eetvelde House, Brussels, 1895.

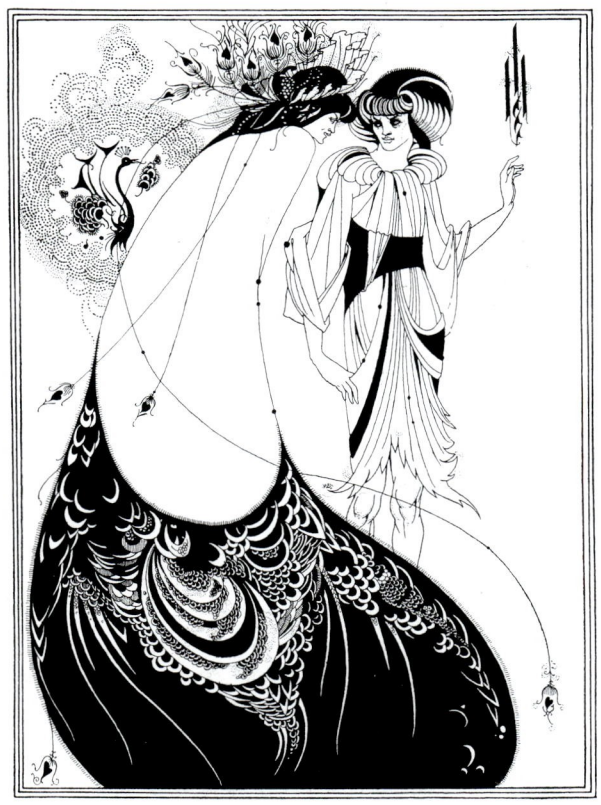

**29-54** AUBREY BEARDSLEY, *The Peacock Skirt*, 1894. Pen-and-ink illustration for Oscar Wilde's *Salomé*.

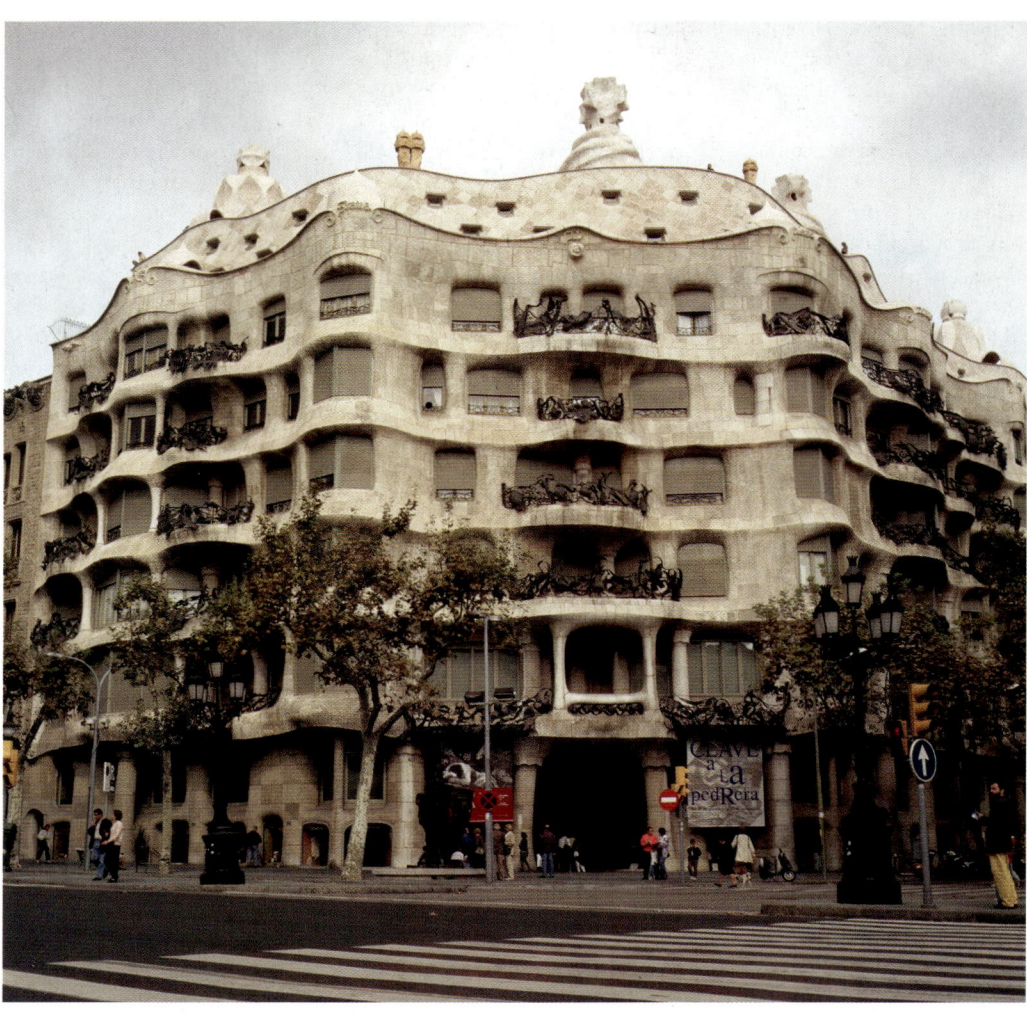

unfailing sense of linear rhythms and harmonies supports his mastery of calligraphic line. In his short lifetime—he died at age 26—he expressed in both his life and art the aesthete's ideal of "art for art's sake."

**SCULPTING A BUILDING** Art Nouveau achieved its most personal expression in the work of the Spanish architect Antonio Gaudi (1852–1926). Before becoming an architect, Gaudi had trained as an ironworker. Like many young artists of his time, he longed to create a style that was both modern and appropriate to his country. Taking inspiration from Moorish-Spanish architecture and from the simple architecture of his native Catalonia, Gaudi developed a personal aesthetic. He conceived a building as a whole and molded it almost as a sculptor might shape a figure from clay. Although work on his designs proceeded slowly under the guidance of his intuition and imagination, Gaudi was a master who invented many new structural techniques that facilitated the actual construction of his visions. His apartment house, Casa Milá (FIG. **29-55**), is a wondrously free-form mass wrapped around a street corner. Lacy iron railings enliven the swelling curves of the cut-stone facade. Dormer windows peep from the undulating tiled roof, which is capped by fantastically writhing chimneys that poke energetically into the air above. The rough surfaces of the stone walls suggest naturally worn rock. The entrance portals look like eroded sea caves, but their design also may reflect the excitement that swept Spain following the 1879 discovery of Paleolithic cave paintings at Altamira. Gaudi felt that each

of his buildings was symbolically a living thing, and the passionate naturalism of his Casa Milá is the spiritual kin of early-20th-century Expressionist painting and sculpture.

# FIN DE SIÈCLE CULTURE

As the end of the 19th century neared, the momentous changes to which the Realists and Impressionists responded had become familiar and ordinary. As noted earlier, the term *fin de siècle,* which literally means "end of the century," is used to describe this period. This designation is not merely chronological but also refers to a certain sensibility. The cultures to which this term applies experienced a significant degree of political upheaval toward the end of the 19th century. Moreover, prosperous wealthy middle classes dominated these societies—middle classes that aspired to the advantages the aristocracy already enjoyed. These people were determined to live "the good life," which evolved into a culture of decadence and indulgence. Characteristic of the fin de siècle period was an intense preoccupation with sexual drives, powers, and perversions; the femme fatale was a particularly resonant figure. People at the end of the century also immersed themselves in an exploration of the unconscious. This culture was unrestrained and freewheeling, but the determination to enjoy life masked an anxiety prompted by the fluctuating political situation and uncertain future. The country most closely associated with fin de siècle culture was Austria.

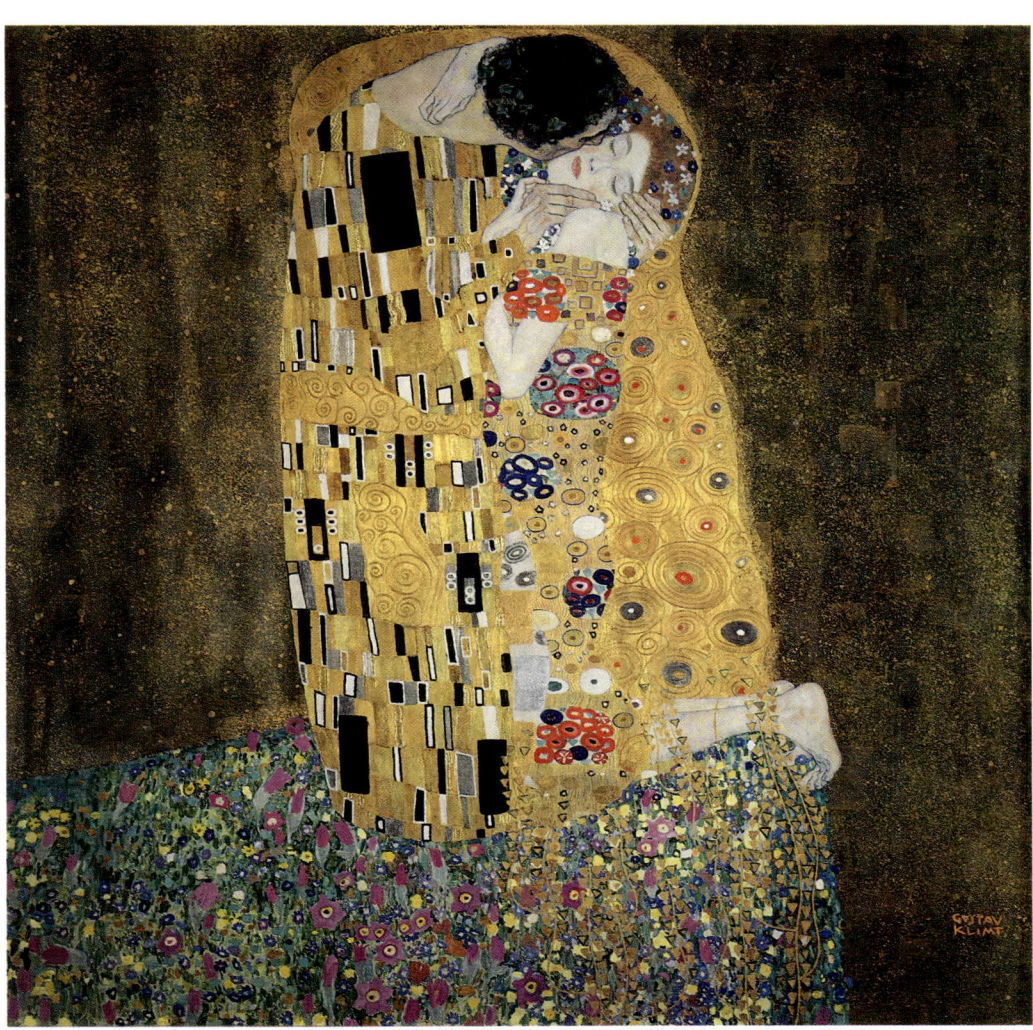

**FIN DE SIÈCLE SENSUALITY** One Viennese artist whose works capture this period's flamboyance but temper it with unsettling undertones was Gustav Klimt (1863–1918). In *The Kiss* (FIG. **29-56**), Klimt depicted a couple locked in an embrace. All that is visible of the couple, however, is a segment of each person's head. The rest of the painting dissolves into shimmering, extravagant flat patterning. This patterning has clear ties to Art Nouveau and to the Arts and Crafts movement. Such a depiction is also reminiscent of the conflict between two- and three-dimensionality intrinsic to the work of Degas and other modernists. Paintings such as *The Kiss* were visual manifestations of fin de siècle spirit because they captured a decadence conveyed by opulent and sensuous images.

## OTHER ARCHITECTURE IN THE LATER 19TH CENTURY

### *The Beginnings of a New Style*

In the later 19th century, new technology and the changing needs of urbanized, industrialized society affected architecture throughout the Western world. Since the 18th century, bridges had been built of cast iron (see FIG. 28-10), which permitted engineering advancements in the construction of larger, stronger, and more fire-resistant structures. Steel, available after 1860, allowed architects to enclose ever larger spaces, such as those found in railroad stations and exposition halls.

**A SOARING METAL SKELETON** The Realist impulse encouraged an architecture that honestly expressed a building's purpose, rather than elaborately disguising a building's function. The elegant metal skeleton structures of the French engineer-architect Alexandre-Gustave Eiffel (1832–1923) can be seen as responses to this idea, and they constituted an important contribution to the development of the 20th-century skyscraper. A native of Burgundy, Eiffel trained in Paris before beginning a distinguished career designing exhibition halls, bridges, and the interior armature for France's anniversary gift to the United States—Frédéric Auguste Bartholdi's Statue of Liberty. Eiffel designed his best-known work, the Eiffel Tower (FIG. **29-57**), for a great exhibition in Paris in 1889. Originally seen as a symbol of modern Paris and still considered a symbol of 19th-century civilization, the elegant metal tower thrusts its needle shaft 984 feet above the city, making it at the time of its construction (and for some time to come) the world's highest structure. The tower's well-known configuration rests on four giant supports connected by gracefully arching open-frame skirts that provide a pleasing mask for the heavy horizontal girders needed to strengthen the legs. Visitors can take two elevators to the top, or they can use the internal staircase. Architectural historian

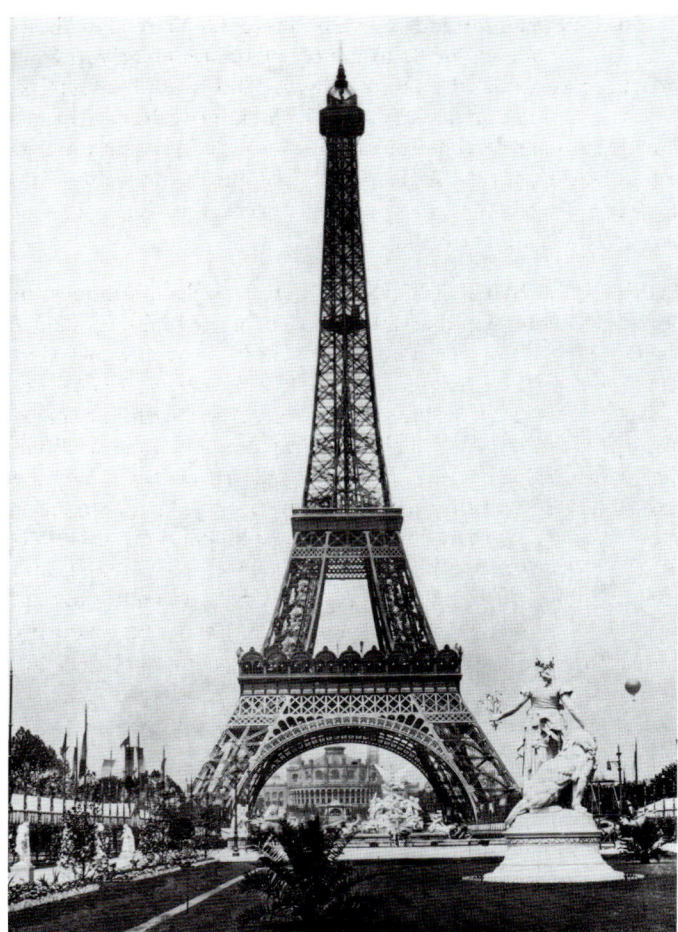

**29-57** ALEXANDRE-GUSTAVE EIFFEL, Eiffel Tower, Paris, 1889 (photo: 1889–1890). Wrought iron, 984′ high. Hulton-Deutsch Collection.

Siegfried Giedion described well the effect of the tower on a 20th-century viewer when he wrote:

> The airiness one experiences when at the top of the tower makes it the terrestrial sister of the aeroplane. . . . To a previously unknown extent, outer and inner space are interpenetrating. This effect can only be experienced in descending the spiral stairs from the top, when the soaring lines of the structure intersect with the trees, houses, churches, and the serpentine windings of the Seine. The interpenetration of continuously changing viewpoints create, in the eyes of the moving spectator, a glimpse into four-dimensional experience.[36]

This interpenetration of inner and outer space became a hallmark of 20th-century art and architecture. At the time of their construction, however, Eiffel's metal skeleton structures and the iron skeletal frames designed by Labrouste (see FIG. 28-61) and Paxton (see FIG. 28-62) jolted some in the architectural profession into a realization that the new materials and new processes might germinate a completely new style and a radically innovative approach to architectural design.

The desire for greater speed and economy in building, as well as for a reduction in fire hazards, prompted the use of cast and wrought iron for many building programs, especially commercial ones. Designers in both England and the United States enthusiastically developed cast-iron architecture until a series of disastrous fires in the early 1870s in New York, Boston, and Chicago demonstrated that cast iron by itself was far from impervious to fire. This discovery led to encasing the metal in masonry, combining the first material's strength with the second's fire resistance.

In cities, convenience required closely grouped buildings, and increased property values forced architects literally to raise the roof. Even an attic could command high rentals if the building were provided with one of the new elevators, used for the first time in the Equitable Building in New York (1868–1871). Metal could support such tall structures, and the American skyscraper was born. With rare exceptions, however, such as Louis Sullivan (FIGS. 29-59 and 29-60), few designers treated successfully this innovative type of building and produced distinguished architecture.

**A MASSIVE MASONRY MART** Sullivan's predecessor, HENRY HOBSON RICHARDSON (1838–1886), frequently used heavy round arches and massive masonry walls. Because he was particularly fond of the Romanesque architecture of the Auvergne area in France, his work sometimes is thought of as a Romanesque revival. This designation does not do credit to the originality and quality of most of the buildings Richardson designed during the brief 18 years of his practice. Trinity Church in Boston and his smaller public libraries, residences, railroad stations, and courthouses in New England and elsewhere best demonstrate his vivid imagination and the solidity (the sense of enclosure and permanence) so characteristic of his style. However, his most important and influential building was the Marshall Field wholesale store (now demolished) in Chicago (FIG. **29-58**), which was begun in 1885. This vast building, occupying a city block and designed for the most practical of purposes, recalled historical styles without imitating them at all. The tripartite elevation of a Renaissance palace (see FIG. 21-20) or of the Roman aqueduct near Nimes, France (see FIG. 10-31), may have been close to Richardson's mind. But he used no classical ornament, made much of the massive courses of masonry, and, in the strong horizontality of the

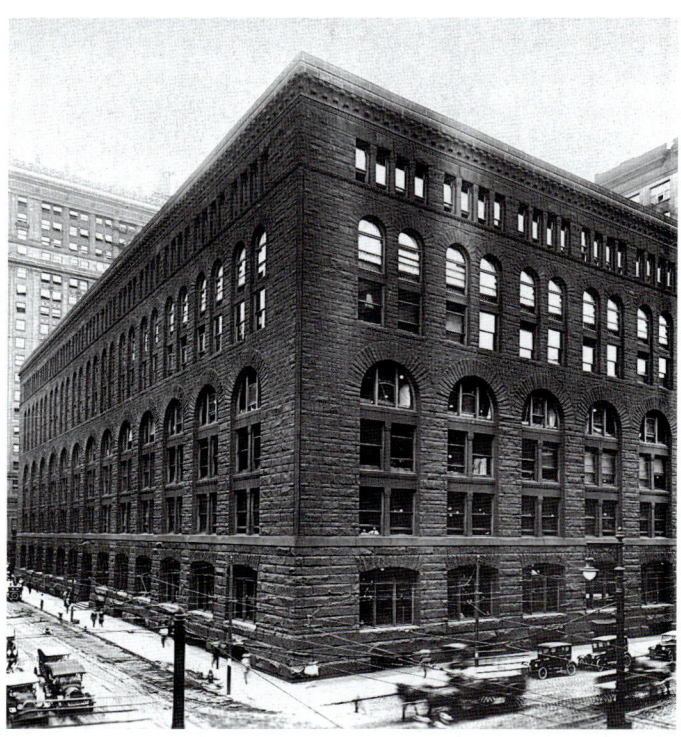

**29-58** HENRY HOBSON RICHARDSON, Marshall Field wholesale store (demolished), Chicago, 1885–1887. Chicago Architectural Photographing Company.

windowsills and the interrupted courses that defined the levels, stressed the long sweep of the building's lines, as well as its ponderous weight. Although the structural frame still lay behind and in conjunction with the masonry screen, the great glazed arcades opened up the walls of this large-scale building. They pointed the way to the modern total penetration of walls and the transformation of them into mere screens or curtains that serve both to echo the underlying structural grid and to protect it from the weather.

**"FORM FOLLOWS FUNCTION"** As skyscrapers proliferated, architects refined the visual vocabulary of these buildings. LOUIS HENRY SULLIVAN (1856–1924), who has been called the first truly modern architect, arrived at a synthesis of industrial structure and ornamentation that perfectly expressed the spirit of late-19th-century commerce. To achieve this, he utilized the latest technological developments to create light-filled, well-ventilated office buildings and adorned both exteriors and interiors with ornate embellishments. Such decoration served to connect commerce and culture, and imbued these white-collar workspaces with a sense of refinement and taste. These characteristics are evident in the Guaranty (Prudential) Building in Buffalo, New York (FIG. **29-59**), built between 1894 and 1896. The structure is steel, sheathed with terracotta. The imposing scale of the building and the regularity of the window placements served as an expression of the large-scale, refined, and orderly office work that took place within. Sullivan tempered the severity of the structure with lively ornamentation, both on the piers and cornice on the exterior of the building and on the stairway balustrades, elevator cages, and ceiling in the interior.

The building's form, then, began to express its function, both actual and symbolic, and Sullivan's famous dictum that "form follows function," long the slogan of early-20th-century architects, found its illustration here. Still, Sullivan did not advocate a rigid and doctrinaire correspondence between exterior and interior design. Rather, he espoused a free and flexible relationship—one his pupil, Frank Lloyd Wright, later described as similar to that between the hand's bones and tissue.

**TURNING A BUILDING INSIDE OUT** Sullivan's interest in both the structural and aesthetic aspects of the buildings he designed took a further step in his Carson, Pirie, Scott Building in Chicago, Illinois (FIG. **29-60**), built between 1899 and 1904. A department store, this building required broad, open, well-illuminated display spaces. The minimal structural steel skeleton permitted the singular achievement of this goal. The architect gave over the lowest two levels of the Carson, Pirie, Scott Building to an ornament in cast iron (of his invention) made of wildly fantastic motifs; he believed that the display windows were like pictures and as such merited elaborate frames. As in the Guaranty Building, Sullivan revealed his profound understanding of the maturing consumer economy and tailored his buildings to meet the functional and symbolic needs of their users.

Although these new architectural models and materials were greatly important, these innovations were not immediately and widely accepted. Well into the 20th century historical styles were still prominent in architectural design. Especially in the 19th century's last decades, huge accumulations of wealth in the hands of industrialists and railway magnates permitted the construction of lavishly expensive villas, mansions, and palatial town houses. Historical styles seemed appropriate to the newly rich who lived like medieval barons or Renaissance princes.

**A "PALACE" IN AMERICA?** RICHARD MORRIS HUNT (1827–1895) specialized in serving the building ambitions of America's new aristocracy. He brought Renaissance and Baroque form to the design of their ostentatious plans. Hunt had studied architecture

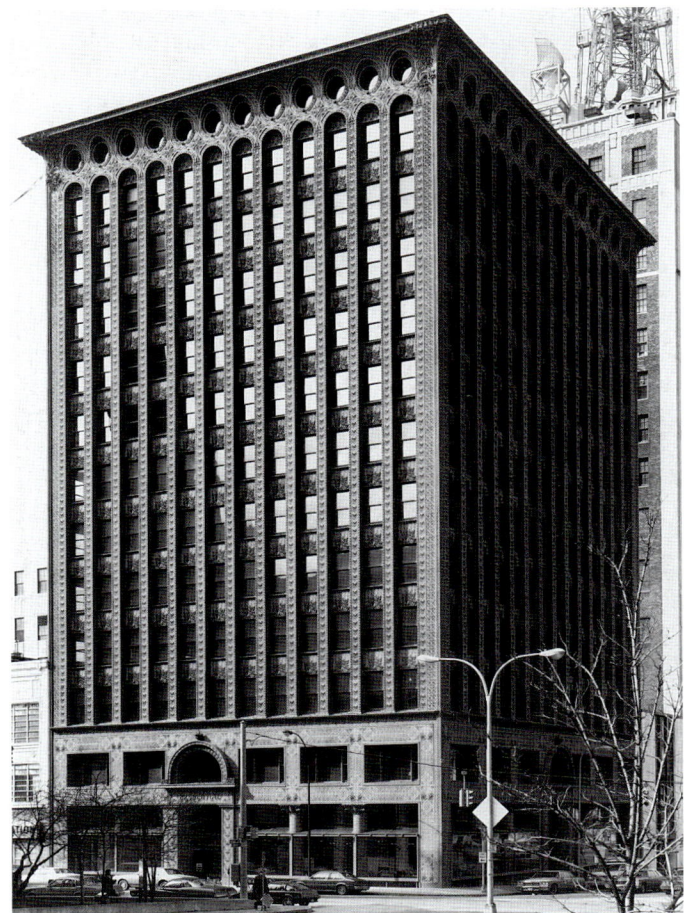

**29-59** LOUIS HENRY SULLIVAN, Guaranty (Prudential) Building, Buffalo, New York, 1894–1896.

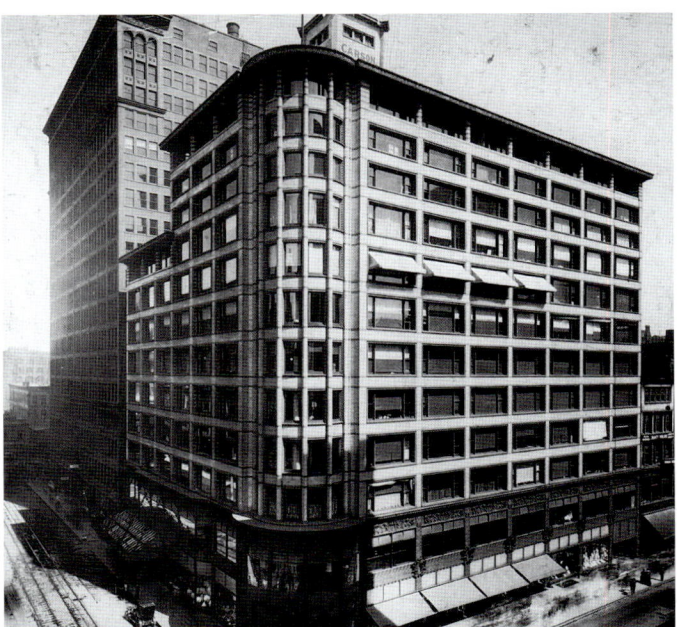

**29-60** LOUIS HENRY SULLIVAN, Carson, Pirie, Scott Building, Chicago, 1899–1904. Chicago Historical Society, Chicago.

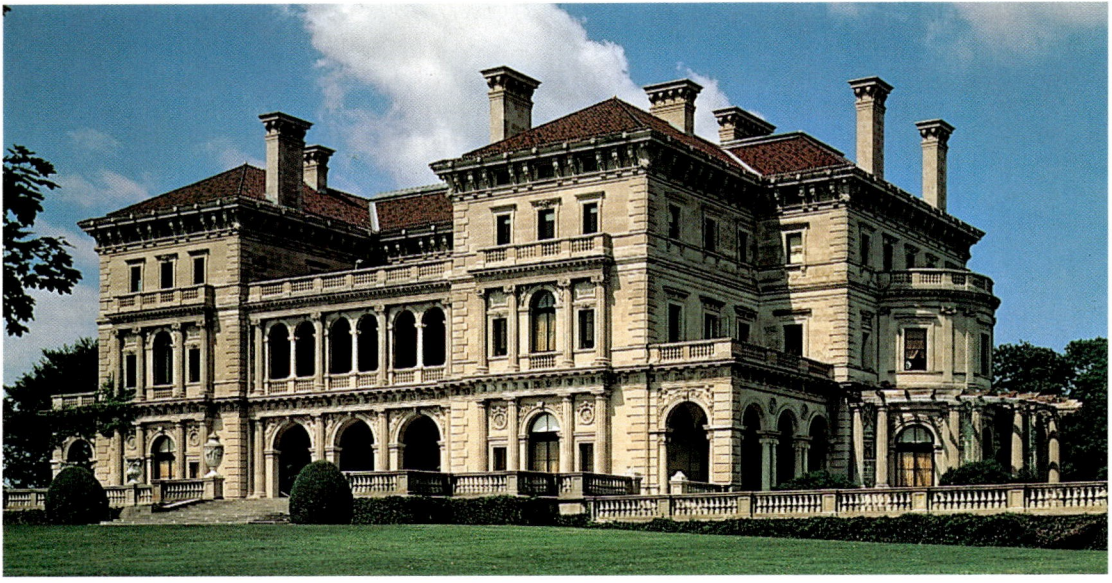

**29-61** RICHARD MORRIS HUNT, The Breakers, Newport, Rhode Island, 1892. The Preservation Society of Newport County.

in Switzerland and Paris and was happy to combine the historical styles arbitrarily to suit the tastes of his patrons. He built The Breakers (FIG. **29-61**) for Cornelius Vanderbilt II, the railroad king. It is a private palace in Newport, Rhode Island, a favorite summer vacation spot for the affluent, who competed with one another in the magnitude and majesty of their mansions. Occupying a glorious promontory above the sea, with a splendid view of the incoming wave breakers, the residence resembles more a 16th-century Italian palazzo (with touches of French style) than a large summer cottage. The interior rooms are grand in scale and sumptuously rich in decor, each having its own variation of classical columns, painted ceilings, lavish fabrics, and sculptured trimmings. The entry hall, rising some 45 feet above the majestic main stairway, signals the opulence of the rooms beyond. This hall and most of the main rooms offer magnificent views over the grounds and the ocean, views Hunt's positioning of the building on the property assured.

**FLORAL STAINED-GLASS LAMPS** The period's extravagance and ostentation in architecture extended to the interior decor. Objects such as furniture, lights, rugs, and wallpaper with designs inspired by the sensuous opulence of Art Nouveau or fin de siècle art were popular. The stained-glass lamps of LOUIS COMFORT TIFFANY are one such example. His lotus table lamp (FIG. **29-62**), constructed of leaded glass (often Favrile, a type of glass patented by Tiffany), mosaic, and bronze, is based on the curvilinear floral forms of the lotus. Intended for wealthy buyers, this was the most expensive lamp ($750) Tiffany Studios produced in 1906. Because of the expense, labor, and time involved in producing this lamp, only one was made at a time. This ensured the high-quality artisanship so prized by the Arts and Crafts movement, whose ideas took root in America.

The grandeur and lavishness of this architectural and decorating style remained popular with the ultrarich until World War I shattered the bright period known as the *Belle Epoque*.

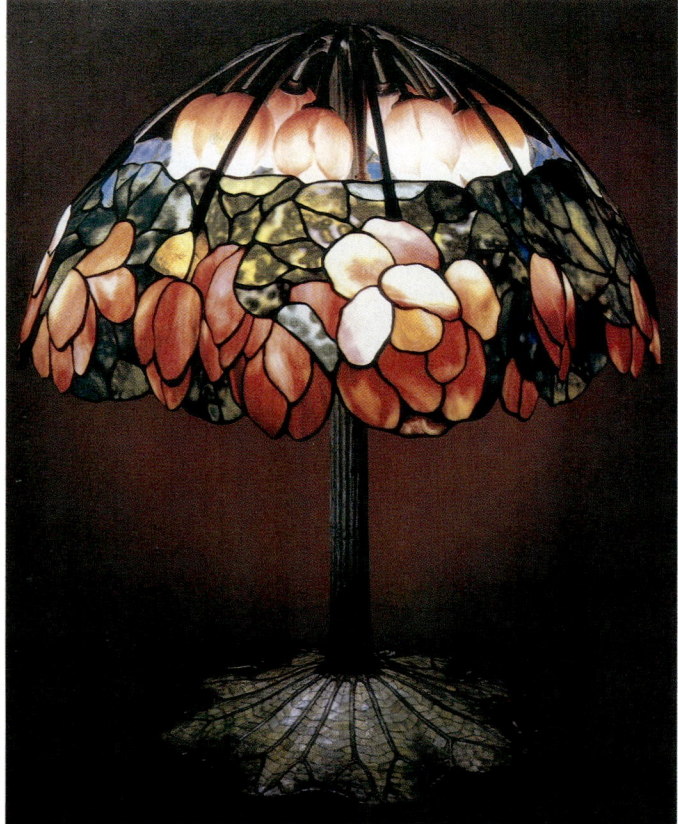

**29-62** LOUIS COMFORT TIFFANY, lotus table lamp, ca. 1905. Leaded Favrile glass, mosaic, and bronze, 2′ 10½″ high. Private collection.

# CONCLUSION

The later 19th century witnessed the rise of modernism, an artistic movement or sensibility that involved a reflection on the premises of art itself. Rather than create visually illusionistic views of the world, modernist artists called attention to the facts of art making—for example, in painting, the canvas surface and pigment. The chronology of art during this period, from Realism to Impressionism to Post-Impressionism, reveals the persistence and power of the modernist mentality. The momentum established by these modernist challenges to artistic tradition by the end of the 19th century continued unabated during the 20th century, when such experiments took artists into the realm of complete abstraction.

SECOND REPUBLIC

| CHARLES DARWIN 1809–1882, *Origin of Species,* 1859

| KARL MARX, 1818–1883

| FREDRICH ENGELS, 1820–1895

| QUEEN VICTORIA, R. 1837–1901

1850

1

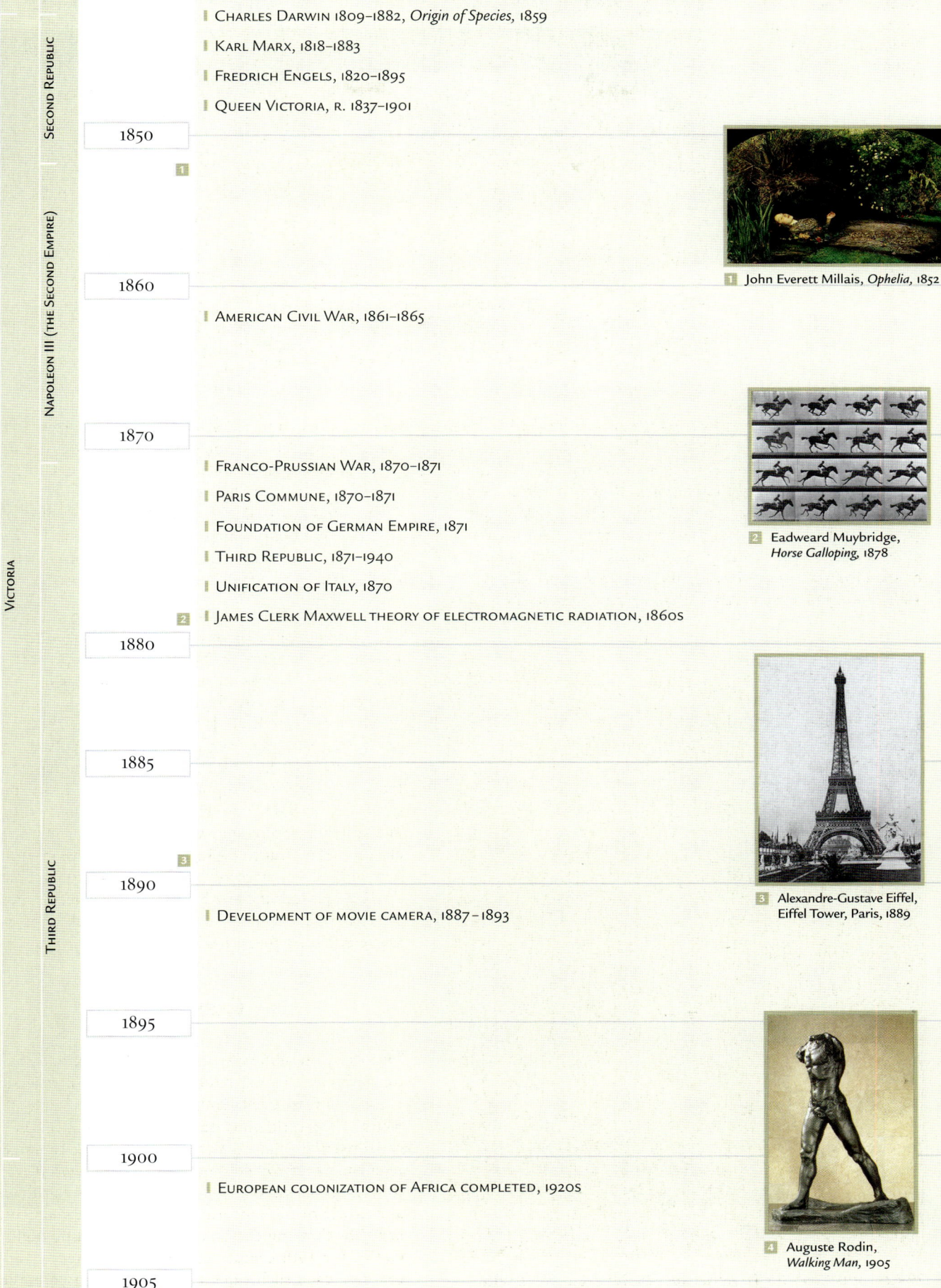

1 John Everett Millais, *Ophelia,* 1852

1860

| AMERICAN CIVIL WAR, 1861–1865

NAPOLEON III (THE SECOND EMPIRE)

1870

| FRANCO-PRUSSIAN WAR, 1870–1871

| PARIS COMMUNE, 1870–1871

| FOUNDATION OF GERMAN EMPIRE, 1871

| THIRD REPUBLIC, 1871–1940

| UNIFICATION OF ITALY, 1870

2 | JAMES CLERK MAXWELL THEORY OF ELECTROMAGNETIC RADIATION, 1860S

2 Eadweard Muybridge, *Horse Galloping,* 1878

VICTORIA

1880

1885

3

1890

| DEVELOPMENT OF MOVIE CAMERA, 1887–1893

3 Alexandre-Gustave Eiffel, Eiffel Tower, Paris, 1889

THIRD REPUBLIC

1895

1900

| EUROPEAN COLONIZATION OF AFRICA COMPLETED, 1920S

4 Auguste Rodin, *Walking Man,* 1905

1905

4

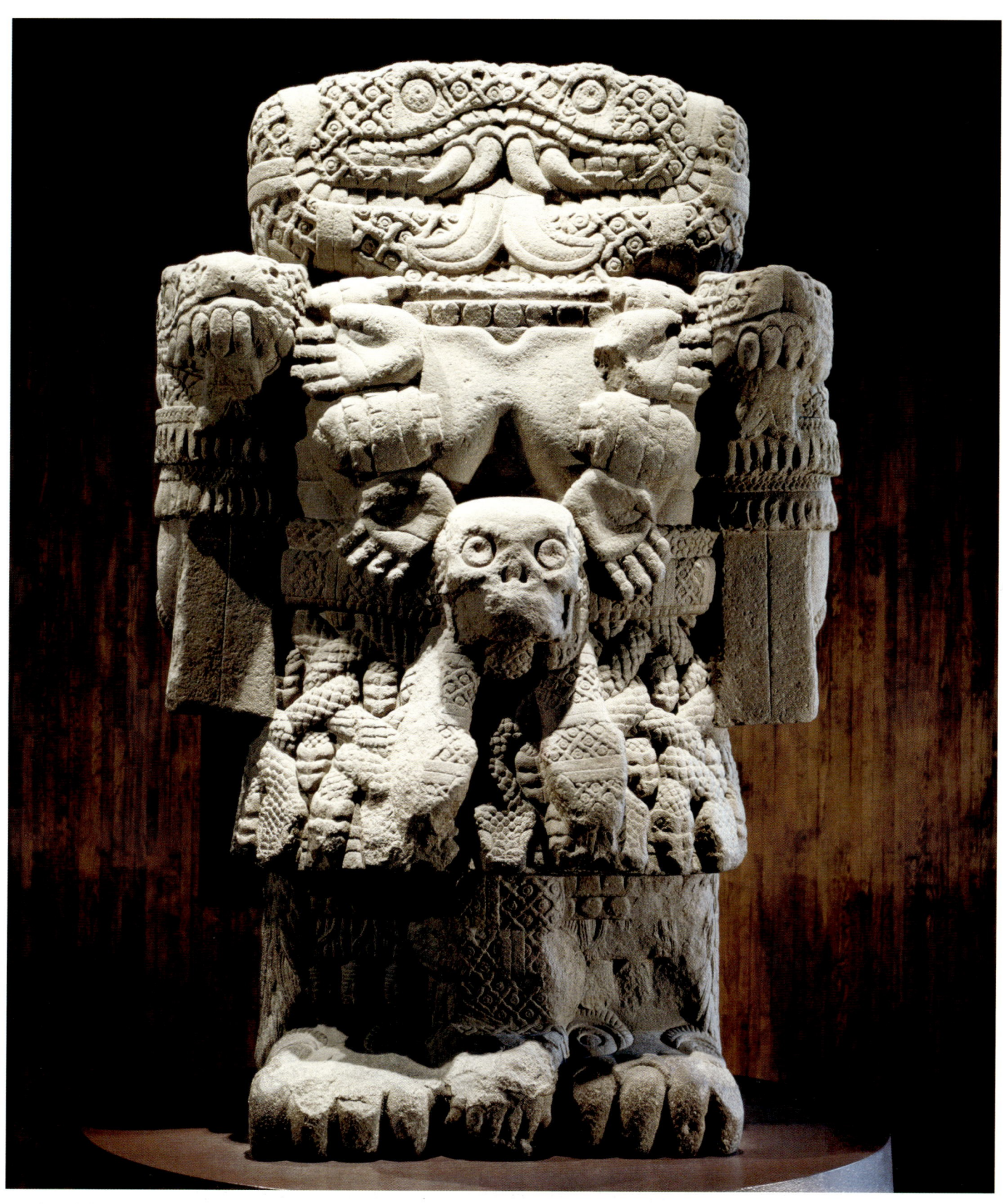

Coatlicue (She of the Serpent Skirt), Aztec, from Tenochtitlán, Mexico City, ca. 1487–1520. Andesite, 11′ 6″ high. Museo Nacional de Antropología, Mexico City.

# 30

# BEFORE AND AFTER THE CONQUISTADORS

## NATIVE ARTS OF THE AMERICAS AFTER 1300

In the years following Christopher Columbus's arrival in the "New World" in 1492, the Spanish monarchs poured money into expeditions that probed the coasts of North and South America (MAP **30-1**), but had little luck in finding the wealth they sought. When brief stops on the coast of Yucatán, Mexico, yielded a small but still impressive amount of gold and other precious artifacts, the Spanish governor of Cuba outfitted yet another expedition. Headed by Hernán Cortés, this contingent of Spanish explorers was the first to make contact with the great Aztec emperor Moctezuma (r. 1502–1521). In only two years, with the help of guns, horses, and native allies revolting against their Aztec overlords, Cortés managed to overthrow the vast and rich Aztec Empire. His victory in 1521 opened the door to hordes of Spanish conquistadors seeking their fortunes, to missionaries eager for new converts to Christianity, and to a host of new diseases for which the native Americans had no immunity. The ensuing clash of cultures led to a century of turmoil and an enormous population decline throughout the Spanish king's new domains.

The Aztec Empire that the Spanish encountered and defeated was but the latest of a series of highly sophisticated indigenous art-producing cultures in the Americas. Their predecessors have been treated in Chapter 14. This chapter examines in turn the artistic achievements of the native peoples of Mesoamerica, South America, and North America after 1300.

## MESOAMERICA

After the fall and destruction of the great central Mexican city of Teotihuacán in the eighth century and the abandonment of the southern Maya sites around 900, new cities arose to take their places (MAP **30-2**). Notable were the Maya city of Chichén Itzá in Yucatán and Tula, the Toltec capital not far from modern Mexico City (see Chapter 14). Their dominance was relatively short-lived, however, and neither city left extensive

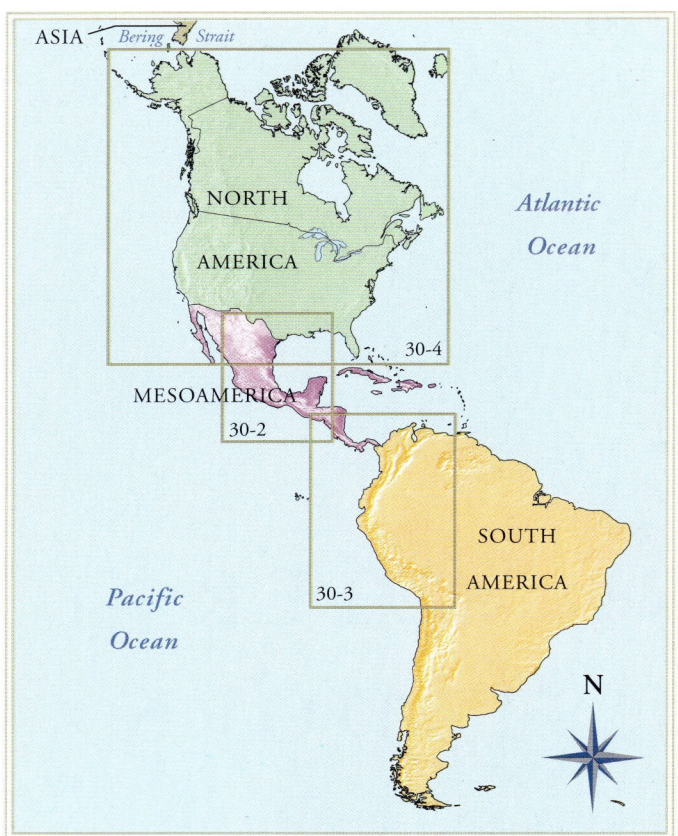

**MAP 30-1** The Americas.

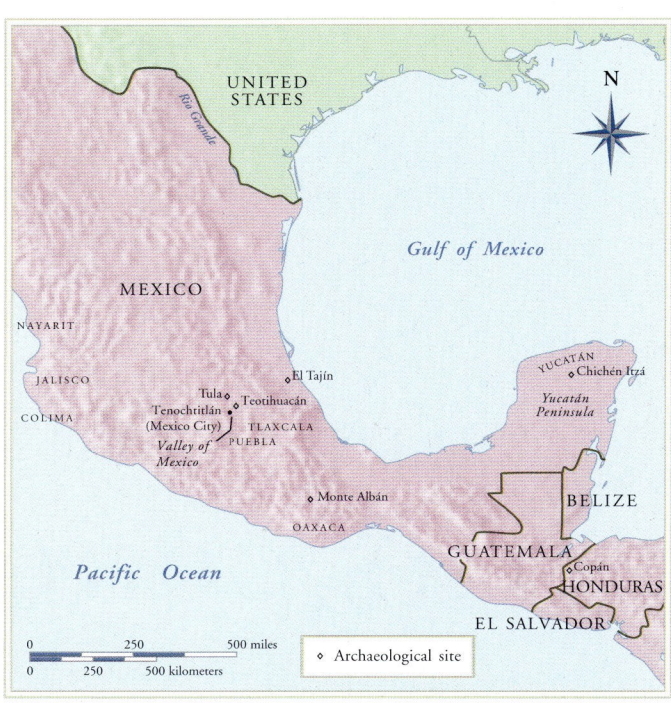

**MAP 30-2** Mesoamerica.

written records. Thus, Mesoamerican history in the early Post-classic period (ca. 900–1250) is less well documented than that of Classic Mesoamerica. For the cultures of the late Postclassic period (ca. 1250–1521), however, some illustrated manuscripts miraculously survived the depredations of the Spanish invasion, and their history is better known.

## Mixteca-Puebla

The Mixtecs, who succeeded the Zapotecs at Monte Albán in southern Mexico after 700, extended their political sway in Oaxaca by dynastic intermarriage, as well as by war. The treasures found in the tombs at Monte Albán bear witness to Mixtec wealth, and the quality of these works demonstrates the high level of Mixtec artistic achievement. Metallurgy was introduced into Mexico in Late Classic times, and the Mixtec became the skilled goldsmiths of Mesoamerica. Also renowned for their work in mosaic, they used turquoise obtained from far-off regions such as present-day New Mexico.

**THE ART OF THE BOOK** Illustrated books were highly prized in Mesoamerica. The Postclassic Maya were preeminent in the art of writing. Their books were precious vehicles for recording not only history but also rituals, astronomical tables, calendrical calculations, maps, and trade and tribute accounts. The texts consisted of hieroglyphic columns read from left to right and top to bottom. Unfortunately, only four Maya books survive. Bishop Diego de Landa, the 16th-century Spanish chronicler of the Maya of Yucatán, explains why: "We found a large number of books in

these [Indian] characters and, as they contained nothing in which there were not to be seen superstition and lies of the devil, we burned them all, which they regretted to an amazing degree, and which caused them much affliction."[1]

In contrast, 14 non-Maya books are preserved, all but 3 from Mixtec Oaxaca or from the Puebla region. Art historians have named the style they represent Mixteca-Puebla. The Mixteca-Puebla artists painted on long sheets of bark paper or deerskin, which they first coated with fine white lime plaster and folded into accordion-like pleats. Wooden covers protected the manuscripts, called *codices* (singular, *codex*). Seven Mixtec codices, largely genealogical and historical in content, survived the Spanish destruction.

**THE *BORGIA CODEX*** The extensively illuminated *Borgia Codex*, from somewhere in central highland Mexico (possibly the states of Puebla or Tlaxcala), is one of a group of codices treating primarily ritual subjects. The page we illustrate (FIG. **30-1**) shows two vividly gesticulating gods rendered predominantly in reds and yellows with black outlines. The god of life, the black Quetzalcoatl (depicted here as a masked human rather than in the usual form of a feathered serpent), sits back-to-back with the god of death, the white Mictlantecuhtli. Below them is an inverted skull with a double keyboard of teeth, a symbol of the Underworld (Mictlan), which could be entered through the mouth of a great earth monster. Both figures hold scepters in one hand and gesticulate with the other. The image conveys the inevitable relationship of life and death, an important theme in much Mesoamerican art. Symbols of the thirteen 20-day divisions of the 260-day Mesoamerican ritual calendar appear in panels in the

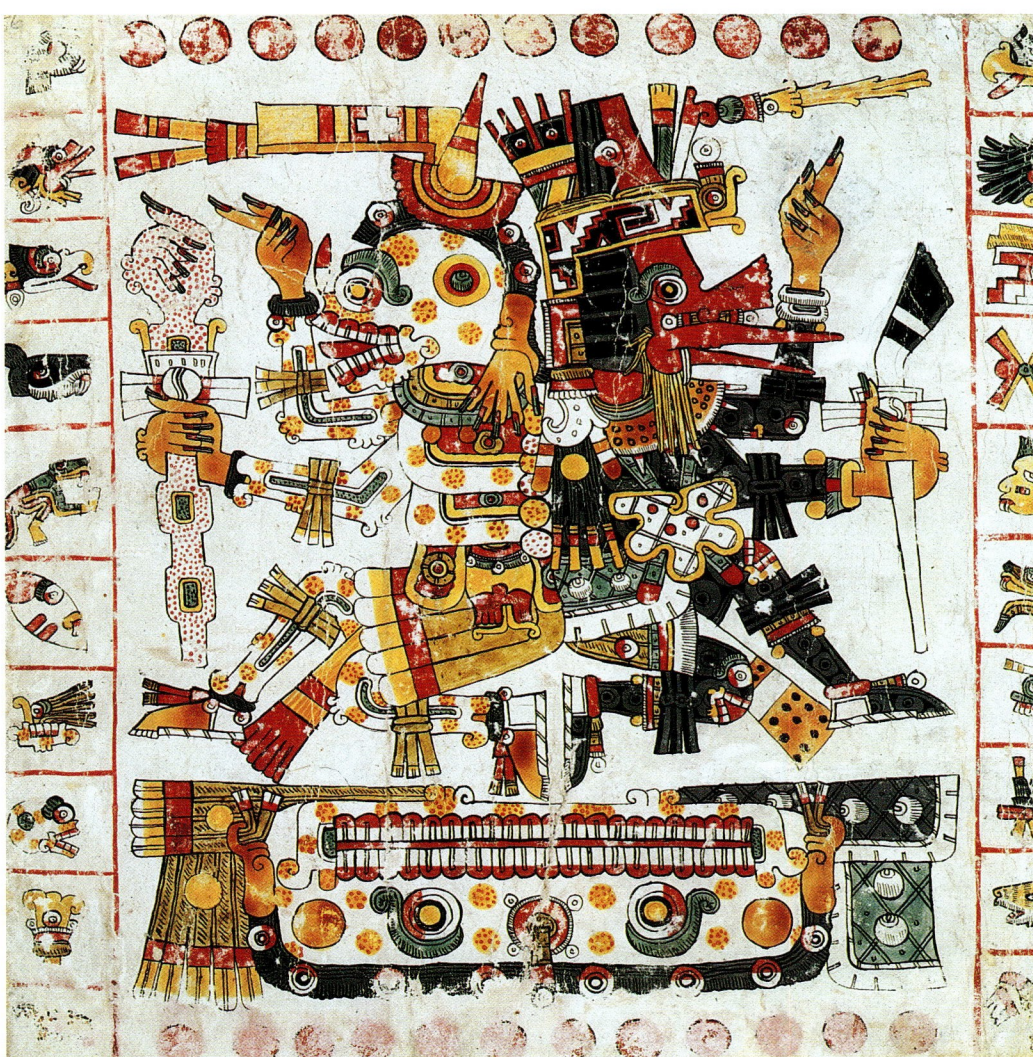

**30-1** Mictlantecuhtli and Quetzalcoatl, illuminated page from the *Borgia Codex,* from Puebla/Tlaxcala(?), Mexico, ca. 1400–1500. Mineral and vegetable pigments on deerskin, approx. $10\frac{5}{8}'' \times 10\frac{3}{8}''$. Biblioteca Apostolica Vaticana, Rome.

margins. The origins of this calendar, used even today in remote parts of Mexico and Central America, are lost in time. Except for the Mixtec genealogical codices, most books painted before and immediately after the Spanish conquest deal with astronomy, calendrics, divination, and ritual, and are still poorly understood.

## Aztec

**THE RISE OF THE AZTECS** The destruction of Tula in about 1200 and the disintegration of the Toltec Empire in central Mexico made for a century of anarchy in the Valley of Mexico, the vast highland valley 7,000 feet above sea level that now contains sprawling Mexico City. Waves of northern invaders established warring city-states and wrought destruction in the valley. The last and greatest of these conquerors were the Aztecs. With astonishing rapidity, they transformed themselves within a few generations from migratory outcasts and serfs to mercenaries for local rulers and then to masters in their own right of the Valley of Mexico's small kingdoms. In the process, they acquired, like their neighbors, the Toltec culture. They began to call themselves *Mexica,* and, following a legendary prophecy that they would build a city where they saw an eagle perched on a cactus with a serpent in its mouth, they settled on an island in Lake Texcoco (Lake of the

Moon). Their settlement grew into the magnificent city of Tenochtitlán, which in 1519 amazed Cortés and his small band of adventurers.

Recognized by those they subdued as fierce in war and cruel in peace, the Aztecs indeed seemed to glory in warfare and in military prowess. They radically changed the social and political situation in Mexico. Subservient groups not only had to submit to Aztec military power but also had to provide victims to be sacrificed to Huitzilopochtli, the hummingbird god of war, and to other Aztec deities (see "Aztec Religion," page 906). Bloodletting and human sacrifice were intended to please the gods and sustain the great cycles of the universe and had a long history in Mesoamerica (see Chapter 14). The Aztecs, however, seem to have practiced human sacrifice on a greater scale than any of their predecessors, even waging special battles, called the "flowery wars," expressly to obtain captives for future sacrifice. It is one of the reasons why Cortés found ready allies among the peoples the Aztecs had subjugated.

**TENOCHTITLÁN** The ruins of the Aztec capital, Tenochtitlán, lie directly beneath the center of modern-day Mexico City. In the late 1970s, Mexican archaeologists identified the exact location of many of the most important structures within the Aztec sacred precinct, and extensive excavations near the cathedral in Mexico

## *Aztec Religion*

The Aztecs saw their world as a flat disk resting on the back of a monstrous earth deity. Tenochtitlán, their capital, was at its center, with the Great Temple (FIG. 30-2) representing a sacred mountain and forming the axis passing up to the heavens and down through the Underworld—a concept with parallels in other cultures (see, for example, "The Stupa," Chapter 6, page 172). Each of the four cardinal points had its own god, color, tree, and calendrical symbol. The sky consisted of 13 layers, whereas the Underworld had 9. The Aztec Underworld was an unpleasant place where the dead gradually ceased to exist.

The Aztecs often adopted the gods of conquered peoples, and their pantheon was complex and varied. When the Aztecs arrived in the Valley of Mexico, their own patron, Huitzilopochtli, a war and sun deity, joined such well-established Mesoamerican gods as Tlaloc and Quetzalcoatl, the feathered serpent who was a benevolent god of life, wind, and learning and culture, as well as the patron of priests. As the Aztecs went on to conquer much of Mesoamerica, they appropriated the gods of their subjects, such as Xipe Totec, a god of early spring and patron of gold workers imported from the Gulf Coast and Oaxaca. Images of the various gods made of stone (FIG. 30-4), terracotta, wood, and even dough (eaten at the end of rituals) stood in and around their temples. Reliefs (FIG. 30-3) depicting Aztec deities, often with political overtones, also adorned the temple complexes.

The Aztec ritual cycle was very full, given that they celebrated events in two calendars—the sacred calendar (260 days) and the solar one (360 days plus 5 unlucky and nameless days). The Spanish friars of the 16th century noted that the solar calendar dealt largely with agricultural matters. The two Mesoamerican calendars functioned simultaneously, requiring 52 years for the same date to recur in both. A ritual called the New Fire Ceremony commemorated this rare event. Pots were broken and new ones made for the next period, pregnant women were hidden away, and all fires were extinguished. At midnight on a mountaintop, fire priests took out the heart of a sacrificial victim and with a fire drill renewed the flame in the exposed cavity. Bundles of sticks representing the 52 years that had just passed were then set ablaze,

ensuring that the sun would rise in the morning and that another cycle would begin.

Most Aztec ceremonies involved the burning of incense (made from copal, resin from conifer trees), colorfully attired dancers and actors, and music provided by conch shell trumpets, drums, rattles, rasps, bells, whistles, and, of course, the human voice. Almost every Aztec festival also included human sacrifice. For Tlaloc, the rain god, small children were especially desirable, because their tears brought the rains.

Rituals also marked the completion of important religious structures. The dedication of the last major rebuilding of the Great Temple at Tenochtitlán in 1487, for example, reportedly involved the sacrifice of thousands of captives from recent wars in the Gulf Coast region. Varied offerings have been found within earlier layers of the temple, many representing tribute from subjugated peoples. These include blue-painted stone and ceramic vessels representing the rain deity Tlaloc, conch shells, a jaguar skeleton, flint and obsidian knives, and even Mesoamerican "antiques"—carved stone Olmec and Teotihuacán masks made hundreds of years before the Aztec ascendancy.

Thousands of priests served in Aztec temples. Distinctive hairstyles, clothing, and black body paint identified the priests. Women served as priestesses, particularly in temples dedicated to various earth-mother cults. Bernal Díaz del Castillo, a soldier who accompanied Cortés when the Spanish first entered Tenochtitlán, was shocked to witness a group of foul-smelling priests with uncut fingernails, long hair matted with blood, and ears covered in cuts, not realizing they were performing rites in honor of the deities they served, including autosacrifice by piercing their skin with cactus spines to draw blood. These priests were the opposite of the "barbarians" the European conquerors considered them to be. They were, in fact, the most educated of all Aztecs. The Spanish reaction to the customs they encountered in the New World has colored popular opinion about Aztec culture ever since. The Aztec religious practices that horrified their European conquerors were, however, not unique to them, but deeply rooted in earlier Mesoamerican society (see Chapter 14).

City continue. The principal building is the Great Temple (FIG. 30-2), a temple-pyramid honoring the Aztec god Huitzilopochtli and the local rain god Tlaloc. Two great staircases originally swept upward from the plaza level to the double sanctuaries at the summit. The Great Temple is a remarkable example of *superimposition,* a common trait in Mesoamerican architecture. The excavated structure, composed of seven shells, indicates how the earlier walls nested within the later. (Today, only two of the inner structures are visible. The later ones were destroyed at the time of the Spanish conquest.) The sacred precinct also contained the temples of other deities, a ball court (see "The Mesoamerican Ball Game," Chapter 14, page 389), a skull rack for the exhibition of the heads of victims killed in sacrificial rites, and a school for children of the nobility.

Tenochtitlán was a city laid out on a grid plan in quarters and wards, reminiscent of Teotihuacán (see FIG. 14-4), which, long abandoned, had become a pilgrimage site for the Aztecs.

Tenochtitlán's island location required conducting communication and transport via canals and other waterways. Many of the Spaniards thought of Venice in Italy when they saw the city rising from the waters like a radiant vision. Crowded with buildings, plazas, and courtyards, the city also boasted a vast and ever-busy marketplace. In the words of Díaz del Castillo, "Some of the soldiers among us who had been in many parts of the world, in Constantinople, and all over Italy, and in Rome, said that so large a marketplace and so full of people, and so well regulated and arranged, they had never beheld before."[2] The city proper had a population of more than 100,000. (The total population of the area of Mexico the Aztecs dominated at the time of the conquest was approximately 11 million.)

**COYOLXAUHQUI DISMEMBERED** The Temple of Huitzilopochtli at Tenochtitlán commemorated the god's victory over his sister and 400 brothers, who had plotted to kill their mother, Coatlicue (She of the Serpent Skirt). The myth signifies the birth

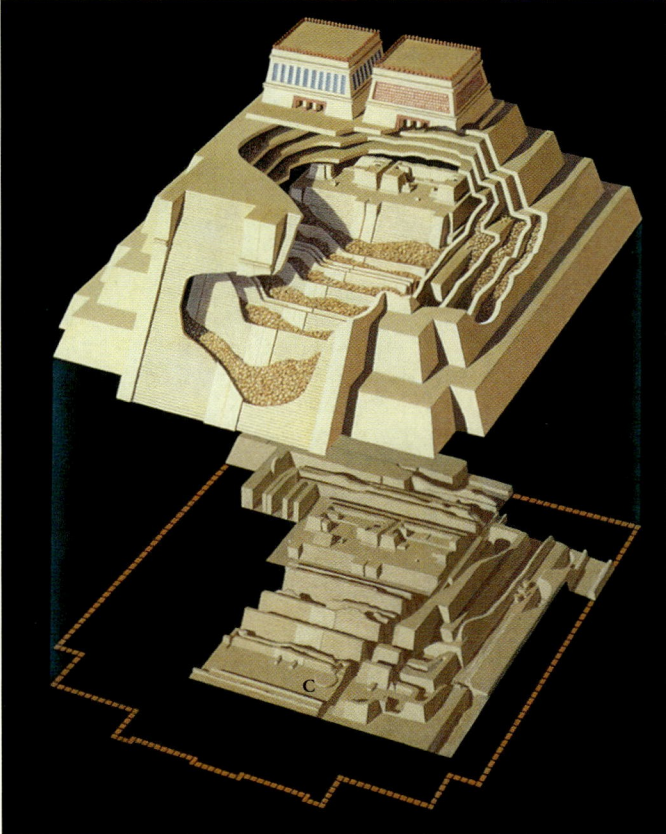

30-2 Reconstruction drawing with cutaway view of various rebuildings of the Great Temple, Aztec, Tenochtitlán, Mexico City, Mexico, ca. 1400–1500. C = Coyolxauhqui stone (FIG. 30-3).

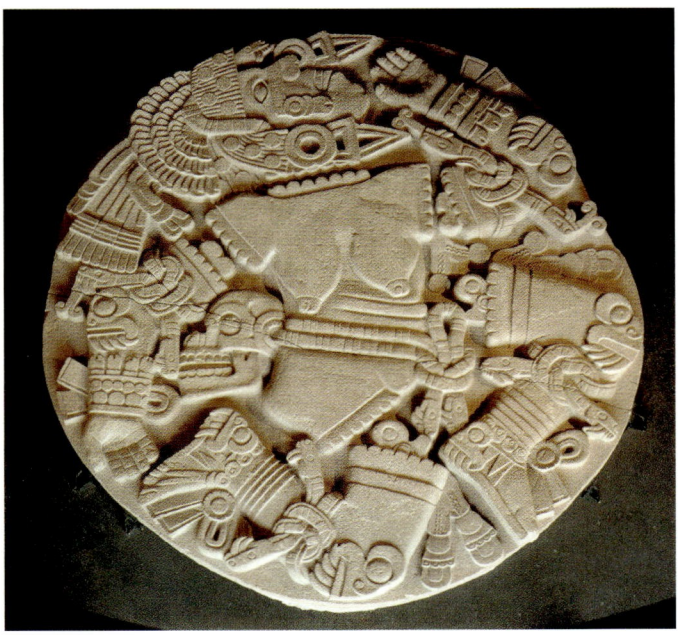

30-3 Coyolxauhqui (She of the Golden Bells), Aztec, from the Great Temple of Tenochtitlán, Mexico City, ca. 1469. Stone, diameter approx. 10′ 10″. Museo del Templo Mayor, Mexico City.

of the sun at dawn, a role sometimes assumed by Huitzilopochtli, and the sun's battle with the forces of darkness, the stars and moon. Huitzilopochtli chased away his brothers and dismembered the body of his sister, the moon goddess Coyolxauhqui (She of the Golden Bells, referring to the bells on her cheeks), at a hill

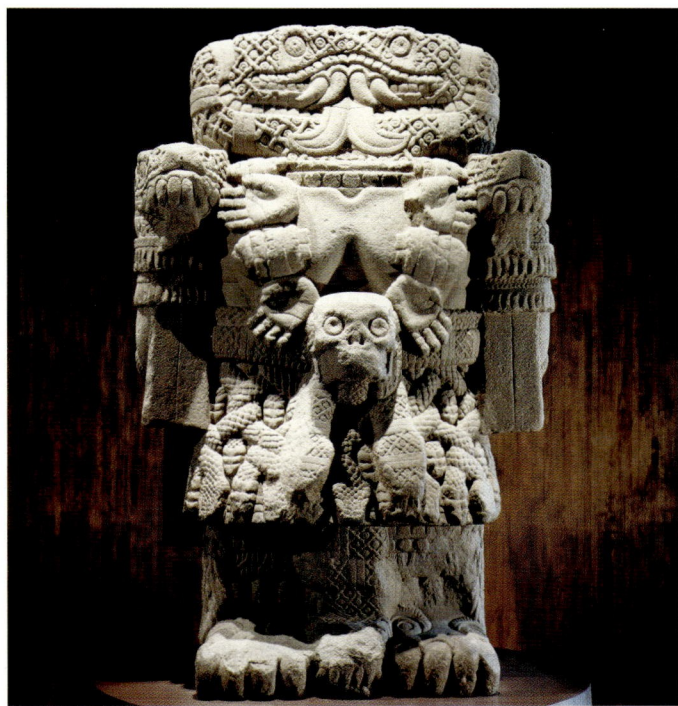

30-4 Coatlicue (She of the Serpent Skirt), Aztec, from Tenochtitlán, Mexico City, ca. 1487–1520. Andesite, 11′ 6″ high. Museo Nacional de Antropología, Mexico City.

near Tula (represented by the pyramid itself). The mythical event is depicted on a huge stone disk (FIG. 30-3), whose discovery in 1971 set off the ongoing archaeological investigations near the main plaza in Mexico City. The relief had been placed at the foot of the staircase leading up to one of Huitzilopochtli's earlier temples on the site. (Cortés and his army never saw it because it was concealed within the outermost shell of the Great Temple.) Carved on the disk is an image of the murdered and segmented body of Coyolxauhqui. The mythological theme also carried a contemporary political message. The bodies of conquered enemies were sacrificed and then hurled down the Great Temple's stairs to land on this stone. The Aztecs likened their foes to the female deity that Huitzilopochtli dismembered.

The disk is an unforgettable expression of Aztec temperament and taste. The image proclaimed the power of the Mexica and their gods over their enemies and the inevitable fate that must befall them when defeated. Marvelously composed, the relief has a kind of dreadful, yet formal, beauty. Within the circular space, the design's carefully balanced, richly detailed components are so adroitly placed that they seem to have a slow turning rhythm, like a revolving galaxy. The carving is confined to a single level, a smoothly even, flat surface raised from a flat ground. It is the sculptural equivalent of the line and flat tone, the figure and neutral ground, characteristic of Mesoamerican painting.

**COATLICUE BEHEADED** In addition to relief carving, the Aztecs produced freestanding statuary. A colossal image of Coatlicue (FIG. 30-4) was discovered in 1790 near Mexico City's cathedral. The sculpture's original setting is unknown, but some scholars believe that it was one of a group set up at the Great Temple. The main forms are carved in high relief, the details executed either in low relief or by incising. The overall aspect is of an enormous blocky mass, its ponderous weight looming over awed viewers.

From the beheaded goddess's neck writhe two serpents whose heads meet to form a tusked mask. Coatlicue wears a necklace of severed human hands and excised human hearts. The pendant of the necklace is a skull. Entwined snakes form her skirt. From between her legs emerges another serpent, symbolic perhaps of both menses and the male member. Like most Aztec deities, Coatlicue has both masculine and feminine traits. Her hands and feet have great claws, which she used to tear the human flesh she consumed. All her attributes symbolize sacrificial death. Yet, in Aztec thought, this mother of the gods combined savagery and tenderness, for out of destruction arose new life, a theme seen earlier at Teotihuacán (see FIG. 14-6).

**THE AZTEC ACHIEVEMENT** Given the Aztecs' almost meteoric rise from obscurity to their role as the dominant culture of Mesoamerica, the quality of the art they sponsored is astonishing. Granted, they swiftly appropriated the best artworks and most talented artists of conquered territories, bringing both back to Tenochtitlán. Thus, craftspeople from other areas, such as the Mixtecs of Oaxaca, may have created much of the exquisite pottery, goldwork, and turquoise mosaics the Aztec elite used. Gulf Coast artists probably made the life-size terracotta sculptures of eagle warriors found at the Great Temple.

Nonetheless, the Aztecs' own sculptural style, developed at the height of their power in the later 15th century, is unsurpassed. Unfortunately, much of Aztec and Aztec-sponsored art did not survive the Spanish conquest and the subsequent period of evangelization. The conquerors took Aztec gold artifacts back to Spain and melted them down, zealous friars destroyed "idols" and codices, and perishable materials such as textiles and wood largely disappeared. Aztec artisans also fashioned beautifully worked feathered objects and even created mosaic-like images with feathers, an art they put to service for the Catholic Church for a brief time after the Spanish conquest, creating religious pictures and decorating ecclesiastical clothing with the bright feathers of tropical birds.

**CORTÉS AND MOCTEZUMA** The Spanish conquerors found it impossible to reconcile the beauty of the great city of Tenochtitlán with what they regarded as its hideous cults. They admired its splendid buildings ablaze with color, its luxuriant and spacious gardens, its sparkling waterways, its teeming markets, and its grandees resplendent in exotic bird feathers. But when the emperor Moctezuma brought Cortés and his entourage into the shrine of Huitzilopochtli's temple, the newcomers started back in horror and disgust from the huge statues clotted with dried blood. Cortés was furious. Denouncing Huitzilopochtli as a devil, he proposed to put a high cross above the pyramid and a statue of the Virgin in the sanctuary to exorcise its evil.

This proposal came to symbolize the avowed purpose and the historic result of the Spanish conquest of Mesoamerica. The conquerors venerated the cross and the Virgin, triumphant, in new shrines raised on the ruins of the plundered temples of the ancient American gods, and the banner of the Most Catholic King of Spain waved over new atrocities of a European kind.

# SOUTH AMERICA

## Inka

**THE INKA EMPIRE** The Inka were a small highland group who established themselves in the Cuzco Valley of Andean South America (MAP **30-3**) around 1000. In the 15th century, however,

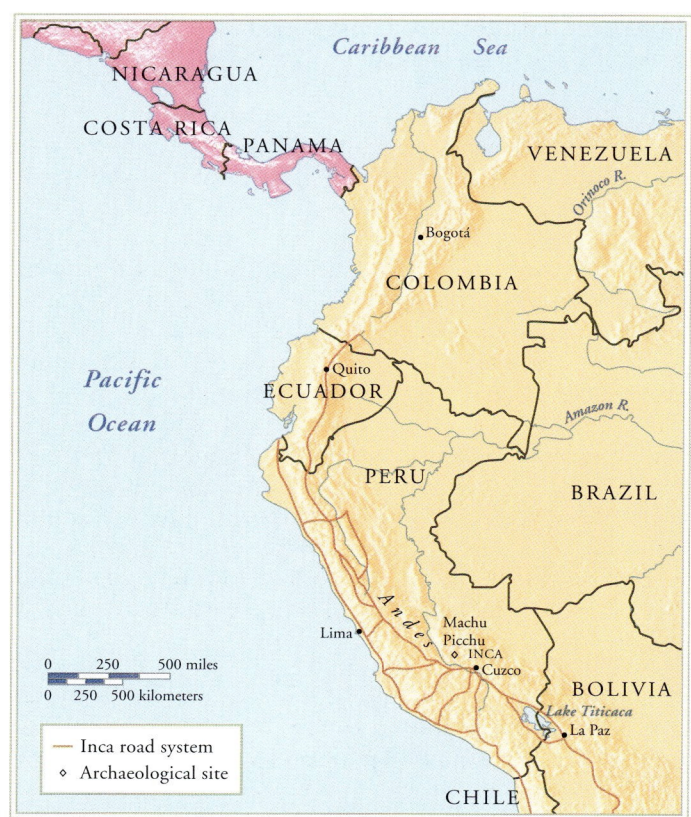

MAP 30-3 Andean region of South America.

they rapidly extended their power until their empire stretched from modern Quito, Ecuador, to central Chile, a distance of more than 3,000 miles. Perhaps 12 million subjects inhabited the area the Inka ruled. The Inka Empire was the largest in the world at the time of the Spanish conquest. Expertise in mining and metalwork enabled the Inka to accumulate enormous wealth and to amass the fabled troves of gold and silver that the Spanish so coveted. Such a vast and rich empire required skillful organizational and administrative control, and the Inka had rare talent for both. In this respect, they resembled the ancient Romans (see Chapter 10). They divided their Andean empire, which they called Tawantinsuyu, the Land of the Four Quarters, into sections and subsections, provinces and communities, whose boundaries all converged on, or radiated from, the capital city of Cuzco.

**ENGINEERING** The Inka's engineering prowess matched their organizational talent. They mastered the difficult problems of Andean agriculture with expert terracing and irrigation, and knitted together the fabric of their empire with networks of roads and bridges. Eschewing wheeled vehicles and horses, they used their highway system to move goods by llama back and armies by foot throughout their territories. The Inka upgraded or built more than 14,000 miles of roads, one main highway running through the highlands and another along the coast, with connecting roads linking the two regions. They also established a highly efficient, swift communication system of relay runners who carried messages the length of the empire. It was said the Inka emperor in Cuzco could get fresh fish from the coast in only three days. Where the terrain was too steep for a paved flat surface, the Inka built stone steps, and their rope bridges crossed canyons high over impassable rivers. They placed small settlements along the roads no more than a day apart where travelers could rest and obtain supplies for the journey.

**RECORD-KEEPING** The Inka never, however, developed a writing system. Nevertheless, they maintained strict control over their vast empire by developing a remarkably sophisticated record-keeping system using a device known as the *quipu*. The Inka used the quipu to record calendrical and astronomical information, census and tribute totals, and inventories. For example, the Spaniards noted that Inka officials always knew exactly how much maize or cloth was in any storeroom in their empire. Not a book or a tablet, the quipu was made of fiber with a main cord and other knotted threads hanging perpendicularly off it. The color and position of each thread, as well as the kind of knot and its location, recorded numbers and categories of things, whether people, llamas, or crops. Studies of quipus have demonstrated that the Inka used the decimal system, were familiar with the zero concept, and could record numbers up to five digits. The Inka census taker or tax collector could easily roll up and carry the quipu, one of the most lightweight and portable "computers" ever invented.

**CLOTHING AND STATUS** The Inka aimed at imposing not only political and economic control but also their art style throughout their realm, subjugating local traditions to those of the empire. Control even extended to clothing, which communicated the social status of the person wearing the garment. The Inka wove bands of small squares of various repeated abstract designs into their fabrics. Scholars believe the patterns had political meaning, connoting membership in particular social groups. Such motifs completely covered the Inka ruler's tunics, perhaps to indicate his control over all such groups. Those the Inka conquered, however, had to wear their characteristic local dress at all times, a practice reflected in the distinctive and varied clothing of today's indigenous Andean peoples.

**MACHU PICCHU** Like the Romans, the imperial Inka were great architects. Although they also worked with adobe, the Inka were supreme masters of shaping and fitting stone. As a militant conquering people, they selected breathtaking, naturally fortified sites and further strengthened them by building various defensive structures. Inka city planning reveals an almost instinctive grasp of the proper relation of architecture to site.

One of the world's most awe-inspiring sights, the Inka city of Machu Picchu (FIG. 30-5), perches on a ridge between two jagged peaks 9,000 feet above sea level. Completely invisible from the Urubamba River Valley some 1,600 feet below, the site remained unknown to the outside world until Hiram Bingham, an American explorer, discovered it in 1911. In the very heart of the Andes, Machu Picchu is about 50 miles north of Cuzco and, like some of the region's other cities, was the private estate of a powerful mid-15th-century Inka ruler. Though relatively small and insignificant compared to its neighbors (with a resident population of little more than a thousand), the city is of great archaeological importance as a rare site left undisturbed since Inka times. The accommodation of its architecture to the landscape is so complete that Machu Picchu seems a natural part of the mountain ranges that surround it on all sides. The Inka even cut large stones to echo the shapes of the

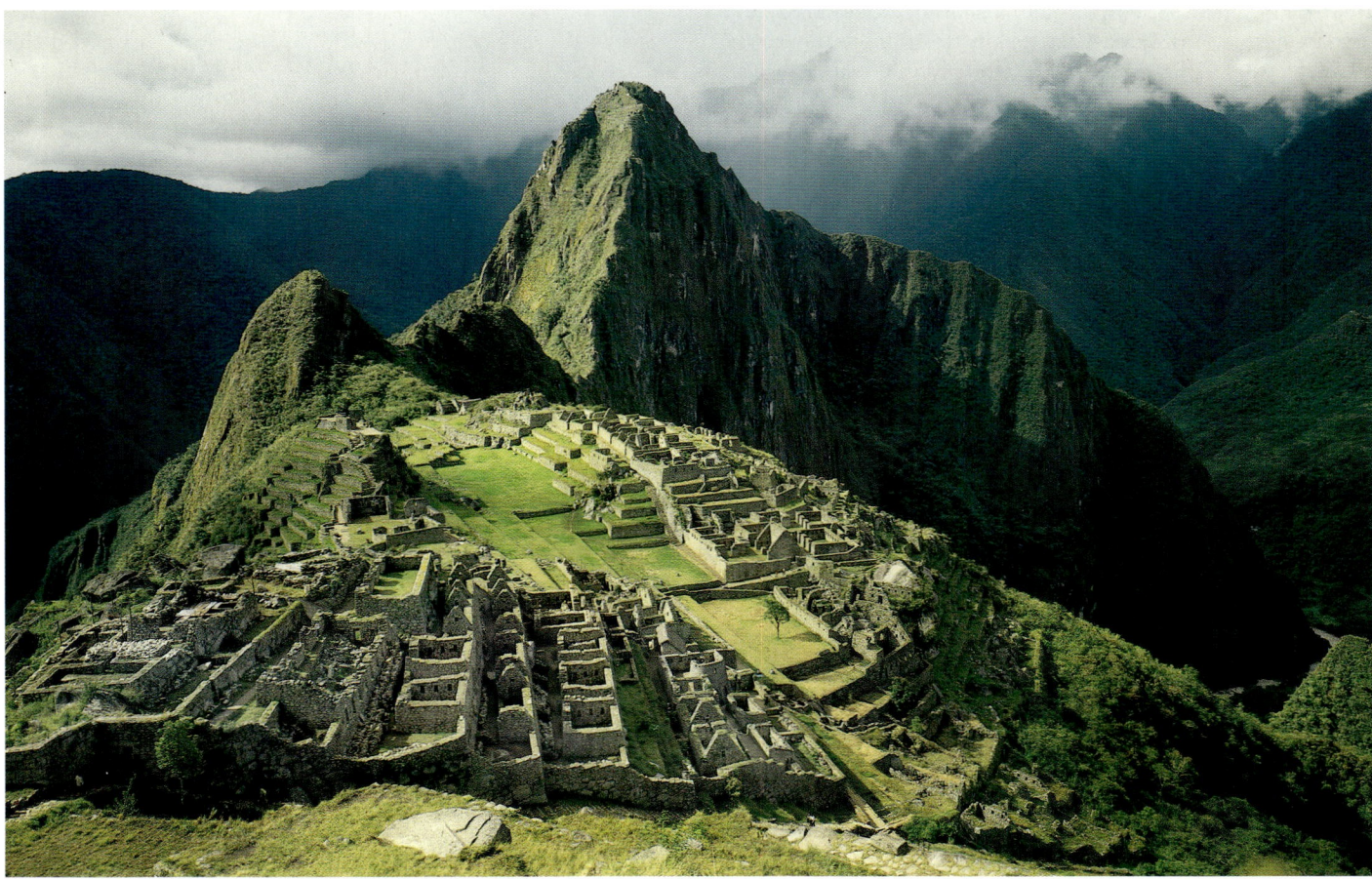

**30-5** Machu Picchu (view from adjacent peak), Inka, Peru, 15th century. American Museum of Natural History, New York.

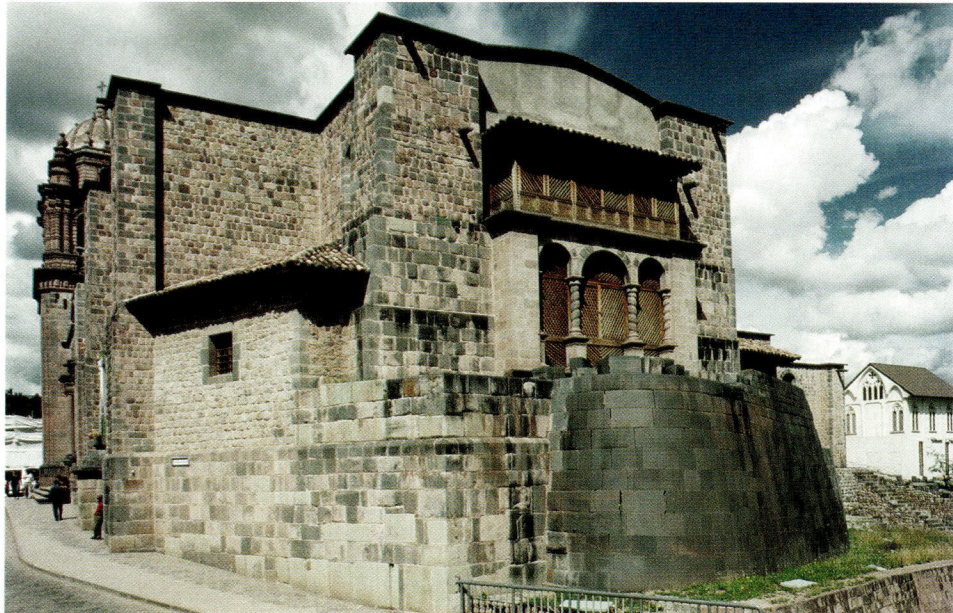

**30-6** Wall of the Golden Enclosure (surmounted by the church of Santo Domingo), Inka, Cuzco, Peru, 15th century.

mountain beyond. Terraces spill down the mountainsides and are built even up to the very peak of Huayna Picchu, the great hill just beyond the city's main plaza. The Inka carefully sited buildings so that windows and doors framed spectacular views of sacred peaks and facilitated the recording of important astronomical events.

**THE PUMA CITY** The Inka capital, Cuzco, was largely destroyed during the Spanish conquest and subsequent colonial period. Thus, most of what is known about the city has been gleaned from often-contradictory Spanish sources rather than from archaeology. Some descriptions state that Cuzco's plan was in the shape of a puma, with a great shrine-fortress on a hill above the city representing its head and the southeastern convergence of two rivers forming its tail. Cuzco residents still refer to the river area as "the puma's tail." A great plaza, still the hub of the modern city, was nestled below the animal's stomach. The puma referred to Inka royal power.

**THE GOLDEN ENCLOSURE** The Inka, like the ancient Greeks (see Chapter 5), were masters of *ashlar masonry* (fitting stone blocks together without mortar). The joints could be beveled to show their tightness or laid in courses with perfectly joined faces so that the lines of separation were hardly visible. The Inka produced the close joints of their masonry by abrasion alone, grinding the surfaces to a perfect fit. For the walls of more important buildings, such as temples or administrative palaces, the workers usually laid the stones in regular horizontal courses. For lesser structures, they set the blocks in polygonal (mostly trapezoidal) patterns. Inka builders were so skilled that they could fashion walls with curved surfaces, their planes as level and continuous as if they were a single form poured in concrete.

One example of this single-form effect is a surviving wall from the Temple of the Sun in Cuzco (FIG. **30-6**). Originally known as Coricancha (Golden Enclosure), this structure was the most magnificent of all Inka shrines and was built on the site of the home of Manco Capac, son of the sun god and founder of the Inka dynasty. Mummies of some of the early rulers were said to be housed there. The temple was dedicated to the worship of several Inka deities, including the creator god Viracocha and the gods of the sun, moon, stars, and the elements. The 16th-century Spanish chroniclers wrote in awe of Coricancha's splendor, its interior

veneered with sheets of gold, silver, and emeralds. The remaining hewn stones, precisely fitted and polished, form a curving semi-parabola (sickle shape) and were set for flexibility in earthquakes, allowing for a temporary dislocation of the courses, which then return to their original position.

**THE END OF THE INKA** The Temple of the Sun was badly burned at the time of the Spanish conquest. Soon afterward, small-pox spreading south from Spanish-occupied Mesoamerica killed the last Inka emperor and his heir before they ever laid eyes on a Spaniard. The Inka empire quickly plunged into a civil war that only aided the Europeans in their conquest. In 1532, Francisco Pizarro, the Spanish explorer of the Andes, ambushed the would-be emperor Atawalpa on his way to be crowned at Cuzco after vanquishing his rival half-brother. Although Atawalpa paid a huge ransom of gold and silver, the Spaniards killed him and took control of his vast domain, only a decade after Cortés had defeated the Aztecs in Mexico.

After the murder of Atawalpa, the Spanish erected the church of Santo Domingo, in an imported European style, on what remained of the Golden Enclosure. A curved section of Inka wall serves to this day as the foundation for the church's apse. A violent earthquake in 1950 seriously damaged the colonial building, but Santo Domingo has been rebuilt. The two contrasting structures remain standing one atop the other (FIG. 30-6). The Coricancha is therefore of more than architectural and archaeological interest. It is a symbol of the Spanish conquest of the Americas and serves as a composite monument to it.

# NORTH AMERICA

## Southwest

**BEFORE THE SPANISH** The dominant culture of the American Southwest during the centuries preceding the arrival of Europeans was the Anasazi, the builders of great architectural complexes like Chaco Canyon and Cliff Palace (see FIG. 14-31). The spiritual center of Anasazi life was the *kiva,* or male council house. Between 1300 and 1500, the Anasazi decorated their kivas

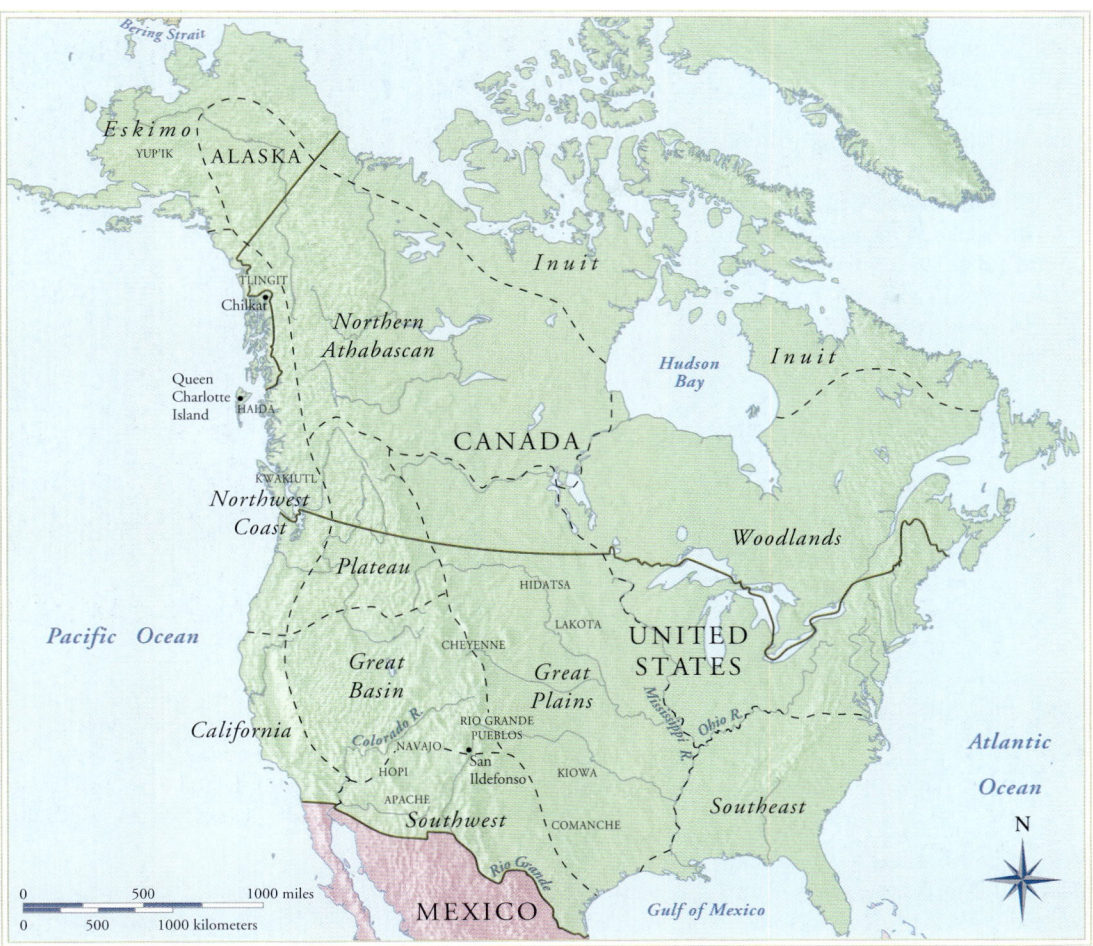

MAP 30-4 North America.

with elaborate mural paintings representing deities associated with agricultural fertility. According to their descendants, the present-day Hopi and Zuni, the detail of the Kuaua Pueblo (*pueblo* is Spanish for urban settlement) mural shown here (FIG. 30-7) depicts a "lightning man" on the left side. Fish and eagle images (associated with rain) appear on the right side. Seeds, a lightning bolt, and a rainbow stream from the eagle's mouth. All

these figures are associated with the fertility of the earth and the life-giving properties of the seasonal rains, a constant preoccupation of Southwest farmers. The Anasazi painter depicted the figures with great economy, using thick black lines, dots, and a restricted palette of black, brown, yellow, and white. The frontal figure of the lightning man seen against a neutral ground makes an immediate visual impact.

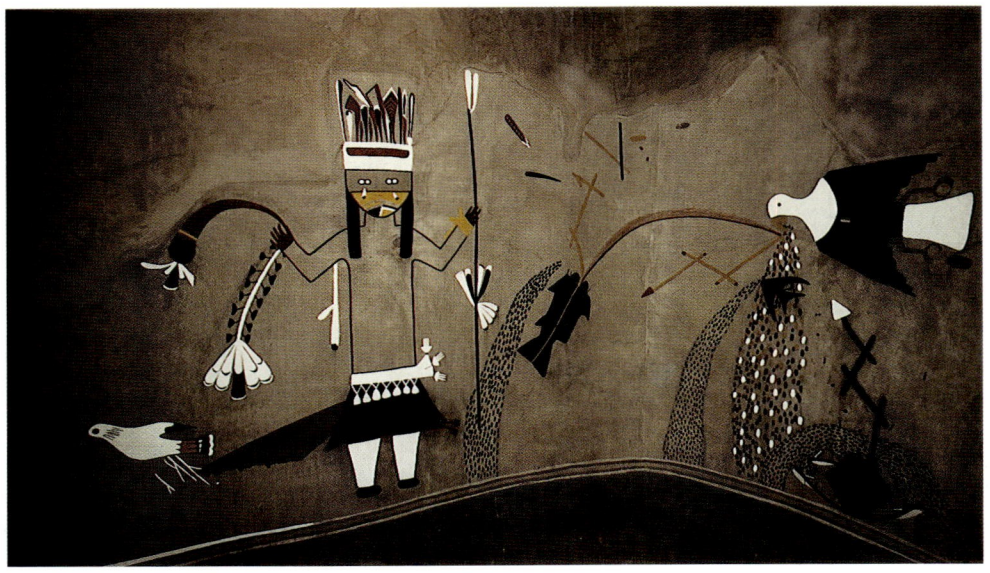

30-7 Detail of a kiva mural from Kuaua Pueblo (Coronado State Monument), Anasazi, New Mexico, late 15th to early 16th century. Museum of New Mexico, Santa Fe.

**PUEBLO INDIANS** When the first Europeans came into contact with the ancient peoples of the Southwest, they called them "Pueblo Indians." The successors of the Anasazi and other Southwest groups, the Pueblo Indians include linguistically diverse but culturally similar peoples such as the Hopi of northern Arizona and the Rio Grande Pueblos of New Mexico. Living among them are the descendants of nomadic hunters who arrived in the Southwest from their homelands in northwestern Canada sometime between 1200 and 1500. These are the Apache and Navajo, who, although culturally quite distinct from the original inhabitants of the Southwest, adopted many features of Pueblo life.

**NAVAJO SAND PAINTINGS** Among these borrowed elements is sand painting, which the Navajo learned from the Pueblos but transformed into an extraordinarily complex ritual art form. The temporary sand paintings (also known as dry paintings), constructed to the accompaniment of prayers and chants, are an essential part of ceremonies for curing disease. (In the healing ceremony, the patient sits in the painting's center to absorb the life-giving powers of the gods and their representations.) The Navajo perform similar rites to assure success in hunting and to promote fertility in human beings and nature alike. The artists who supervise the making of these complex images are religious leaders or "medicine men" (rarely women), thought to have direct contact with the powers of the supernatural world, which they use to help both individuals and the community.

The natural materials used—corn pollen, charcoal, sand, and varicolored powdered stones—play a symbolic role that reflects the Native Americans' preoccupation with the forces of nature. The paintings, which depict the gods and mythological heroes whose help is sought, are destroyed in the process of the ritual, so no models exist. However, the traditional prototypes, passed on from artist to artist, must be adhered to as closely as possible. Mistakes can render the ceremony ineffective. Navajo dry painting is therefore highly stylized. Simple curves, straight lines, right angles, and serial repetition characterize most sand paintings. Because of their sacred nature, the Navajo do not permit the photographing of sand paintings.

**NAVAJO WEAVING** By the mid-17th century, the Navajo had also learned how to weave from their Hopi and other Pueblo neighbors, quickly adapting to new materials such as sheep's wool and synthetic dyes introduced by Spanish settlers and, later, by Anglo-Americans. They rapidly transformed their wearing blankets into handsome rugs in response to the new market created by the arrival of the railroad and early tourists in the 1880s. Other tribes, including those of the Great Plains, also purchased Navajo textiles. The Navajo mastered an incredible variety of designs, including vivid abstract designs known as "eye dazzlers" and copies of sand paintings (altered slightly to preserve the sacred quality of the impermanent ritual images).

**HOPI KATSINAS** Another art form from the Southwest, the *katsina* figurine, also has deep roots in the area. Katsinas are benevolent supernatural spirits personifying natural elements and living in mountains and water sources. Humans, too, join their world after death. Among contemporary Pueblo groups, masked dancers ritually impersonate katsinas during yearly festivals dedicated to rain, fertility, and good hunting. To educate young girls in ritual lore, the Hopi traditionally give them miniature representations of

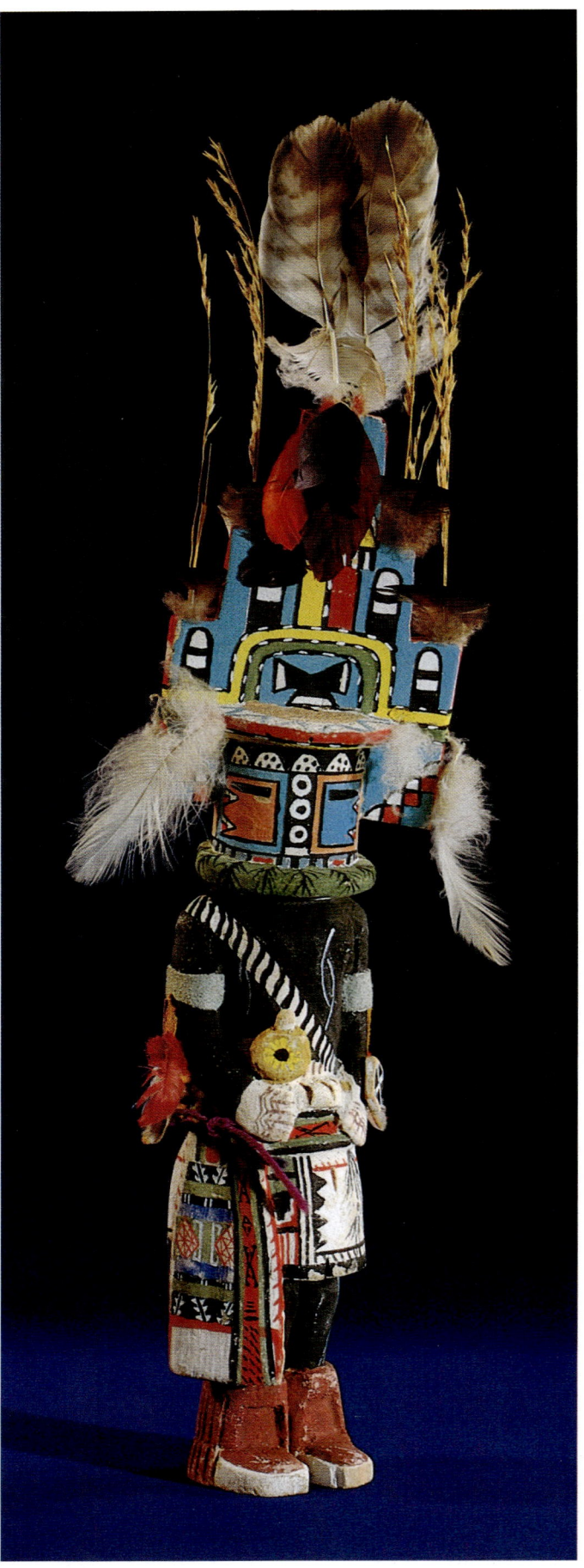

**30-8** OTTO PENTEWA, Katsina figurine, Hopi, New Oraibi, Arizona, carved before 1959. Cottonwood root and feathers, about 1′ high. Arizona State Museum, University of Arizona, Tucson.

## Gender Roles in Native American Art

Although both Native American women and men have created art objects for centuries, they have traditionally worked in different media or at different tasks. Among the Navajo, for example, weavers tend to be women, whereas among the neighboring Hopi the men weave. According to Navajo myth, long ago Spider Woman's husband built her a loom for weaving. In turn, she taught Navajo women how to spin and weave so that they might have clothing to wear. Today, young girls learn from their mothers how to work the loom, just as Spider Woman instructed their ancestors, passing along the techniques and designs from one generation to the next.

Among the Pueblos, pottery making normally has been the domain of women. But in response to heavy demand for her wares, María Martínez, of San Ildefonso Pueblo in New Mexico, coiled, slipped, and burnished her pots, and her husband Julian painted the designs. Although they worked in many styles, some based on prehistoric ceramics, around 1918 they invented the black-on-black ware (FIG. 30-9) that made María, and indeed the whole pueblo, famous. The elegant shapes of the pots, as well as the traditional but abstract designs, were particularly compatible with contemporary Art Deco style in architecture (see FIG. 33-65) and interior design, and collectors avidly sought (and continue to seek) them. When nonnative buyers suggested she sign her pots to increase their value, María obliged, but, in the communal spirit typical of the Pueblos, she also signed her neighbors' names so that they might share in her good fortune. Though María died in 1980, her descendants continue to garner awards as outstanding potters.

Women also produced the elaborately decorated skin and, later, the trade-cloth clothing of the Woodlands and Plains using moose hair, dyed porcupine quills, and imported beads. Among the Cheyenne, quillworking was a sacred art, and young women worked at learning both proper ritual and correct techniques to obtain membership in the prestigious quillworkers' guild. Women gained the same honor and dignity from creating finely worked utilitarian objects that men earned from warfare. Both women and men painted on tipis and clothing (FIGS. 30-15 and 30-16), with women creating abstract designs (FIG. 30-15) and men working in a more realistic narrative style, often celebrating their exploits in war or recording the cultural changes the transfer to reservations brought about.

In the far north, women tended to work with soft materials such as animal skins, whereas men were sculptors of wood masks among the Alaskan Eskimos and of walrus ivory pieces (see FIG. 14-26) throughout the Arctic. The introduction of printmaking, a foreign medium with no established gender associations, to some Canadian Inuit communities in the 1950s provided both native women and men with a new creative outlet. Printmaking became an important source of economic independence vital to these isolated and once-impoverished settlements. Today, both Inuit women and men make prints, but men still dominate in carving stone sculpture, another new medium also produced for and sold to outsiders.

Throughout North America, indigenous artists continue to work in traditional media, such as ceramics, beadwork, and basketry, marketing their wares through museum shops, galleries, regional art fairs, and, most recently, the Internet. Many also obtain degrees in art and express themselves in European media such as oil painting and mixed-media sculpture (see FIG. 34-71).

---

the masked dancers. We illustrate a Hopi katsina (FIG. **30-8**) carved by OTTO PENTEWA (d. 1963) before 1959. It represents a rain-bringing deity who wears a mask painted in geometric patterns symbolic of water and agricultural fertility. Topping the mask is a stepped shape signifying thunderclouds and feathers to carry the Hopis' airborne prayers. The origins of the katsina figurines have been lost in time (they even may have developed from carved saints the Spanish introduced during the colonial period). However, the cult is probably very ancient.

**PUEBLO POTTERY** The Southwest has also provided the finest examples of North American pottery. Originally producing utilitarian forms, Southwest potters worked without the potter's wheel and instead coiled shapes that they then slipped, polished, and fired. Decorative motifs, often abstract and conventionalized, dealt largely with forces of nature—clouds, wind, and rain. The efforts of San Ildefonso Pueblo potter MARÍA MONTOYA MARTÍNEZ (1887–1980) and her husband Julian Martínez (see "Gender Roles in Native American Art," above) in the early decades of the 20th century revived old techniques to produce forms of striking shape, proportion, and texture. Her black-on-black pieces (FIG. 30-9) feature matte designs on highly polished surfaces achieved by extensive polishing and special firing in an oxygen-poor atmosphere.

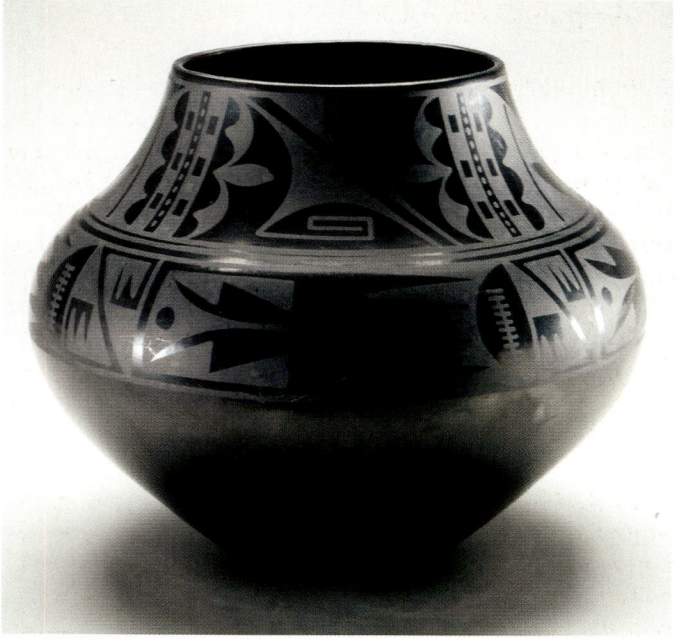

**30-9** MARÍA MONTOYA MARTÍNEZ, jar, San Ildefonso Pueblo, New Mexico, ca. 1939. Blackware, $11\frac{1}{8}''\times 1'\,1''$. National Museum of Women in the Arts, Washington, D.C. (gift of Wallace and Wilhelmina Hollachy).

## Northwest Coast

The Native Americans of the coasts and islands of northern Washington state, the province of British Columbia in Canada, and southern Alaska were blessed with a rich and reliable environment. They fished, hunted sea mammals and game, gathered edible plants, and made their homes, utensils, ritual objects, and even clothing from the region's great cedar forests. Among the numerous groups who make up the Northwest Coast area are the Kwakiutl of southern British Columbia; the Haida, who live on the Queen Charlotte Islands off the coast of the province; and the Tlingit of southern Alaska. In the Northwest, a class of professional artists developed, in contrast to the more typical Native American pattern of part-time artists.

**MASKS AND WAR HELMETS** Working in a highly formalized, subtle style, these Northwest Coast artists have produced a wide variety of art objects for centuries: totem poles, masks, rattles, chests, bowls, clothing, charms, and decorated houses and canoes. Some artistic traditions originated as early as 500 BCE, although others developed only after the arrival of Europeans in North America.

The Northwest Coast masks were used by religious specialists in their healing rituals and by other male participants in dramatic public performances during the winter ceremonial season. The animals and mythological creatures represented in masks and a host of other carvings derive from the Northwest Coast's rich oral tradition and celebrate the mythological origins and inherited privileges of high-ranking families. Meant to be seen in flickering firelight, the Kwakiutl mask we illustrate (FIG. 30-10) was ingeniously constructed to open and close rapidly when the wearer manipulated hidden strings. He could thus magically transform himself from human to eagle and back again as he danced. The transformation theme, in myriad forms, is a central aspect of the art and religion of the Americas. Our Kwakiutl mask's human aspect also owes its dramatic character to the exaggeration and distortion of facial parts—such as the hooked beaklike nose and flat flaring nostrils—and to the

**30-10** Eagle transformation mask, closed and open views, Kwakiutl, Alert Bay, late 19th century. Wood, feathers, and string, approx. 1′ 10″ × 11″. American Museum of Natural History, New York.

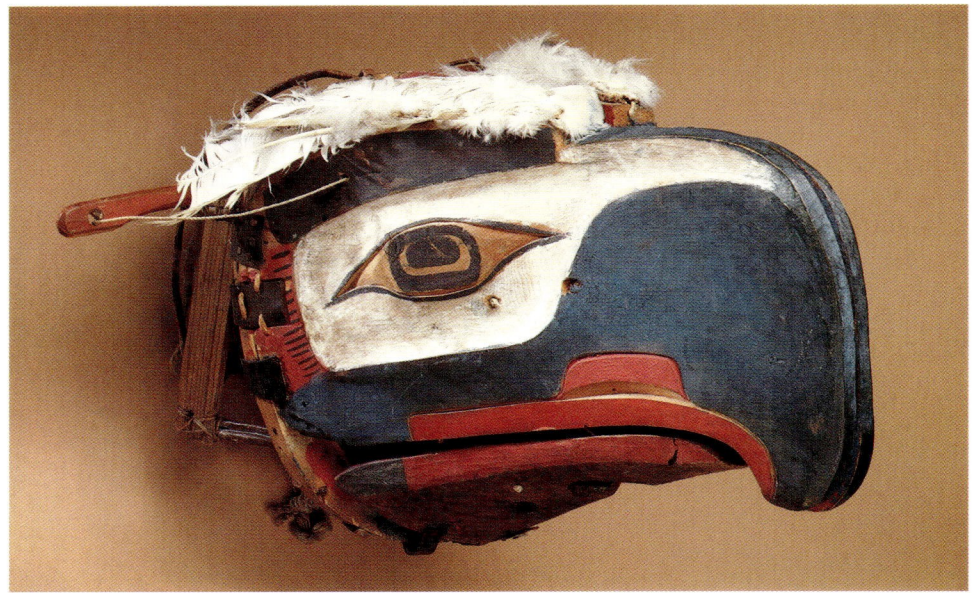

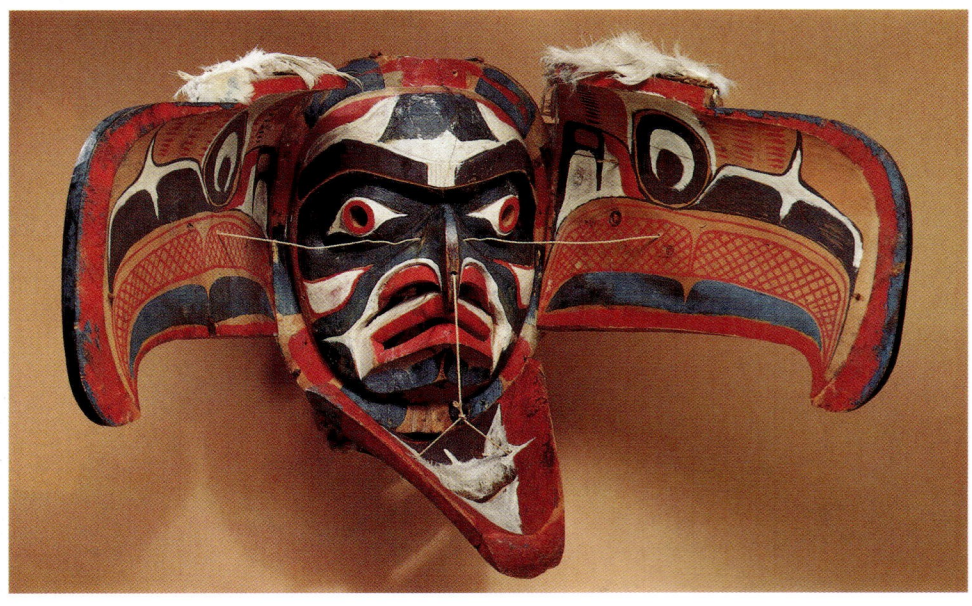

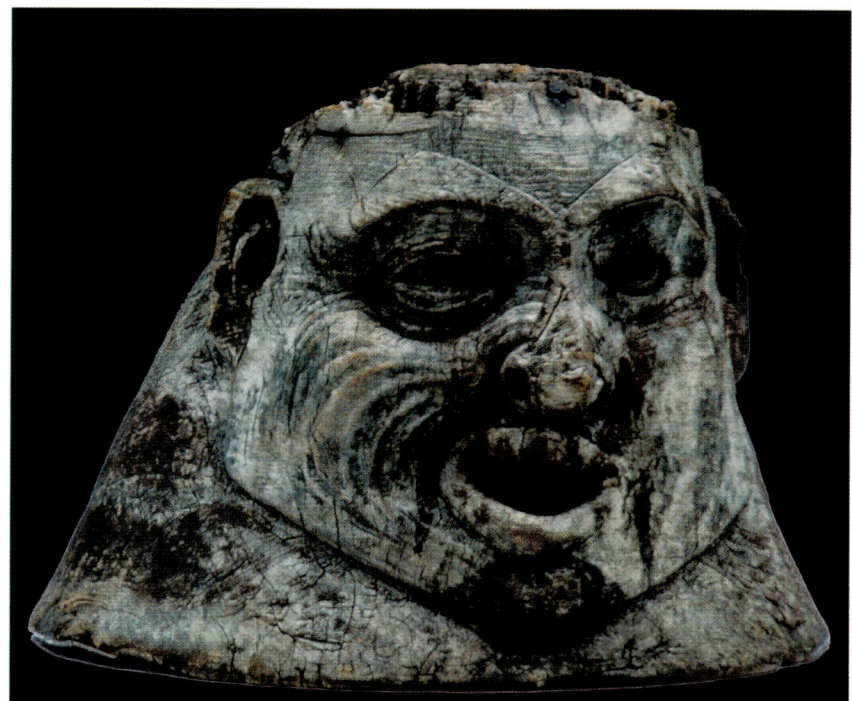

30-11 War helmet, Tlingit, collected 1888–1893. Wood, 1' high. American Museum of Natural History, New York.

deeply undercut curvilinear depressions, which form strong shadows. In contrast to the carved human face, but painted in the same colors, is the two-dimensional abstract image of the eagle painted on the inside of the outer mask.

The Kwakiutl mask is a refined, yet forceful, carving typical of the area's more dramatic styles. Others are more subdued, and some, such as a wooden Tlingit war helmet (FIG. 30-11), are exceedingly naturalistic. Although the helmet mask may be an actual portrait, it might also represent a supernatural being whose powers enhance the wearer's strength. In either case, the artist surely created its grimacing expression to intimidate the enemy.

**HAIDA TOTEM POLES** Although Northwest Coast arts have a spiritual dimension, they are often more important as expressions of social status. Haida house frontal poles, displaying totemic emblems of clan groups, strikingly express this interest in prestige and family history. Totem poles emerged as a major art form about 300 years ago. Our examples (FIG. 30-12) date to the 19th century and are shown as part of a reconstructed Haida village that BILL REID (1920–1998, Haida) and his assistant DOUG KRANMER (b. 1917, Kwakiutl) completed in 1962. Each of the superimposed figures carved on these poles represents a crest, an animal, or a supernatural being who figures in the clan's origin story.

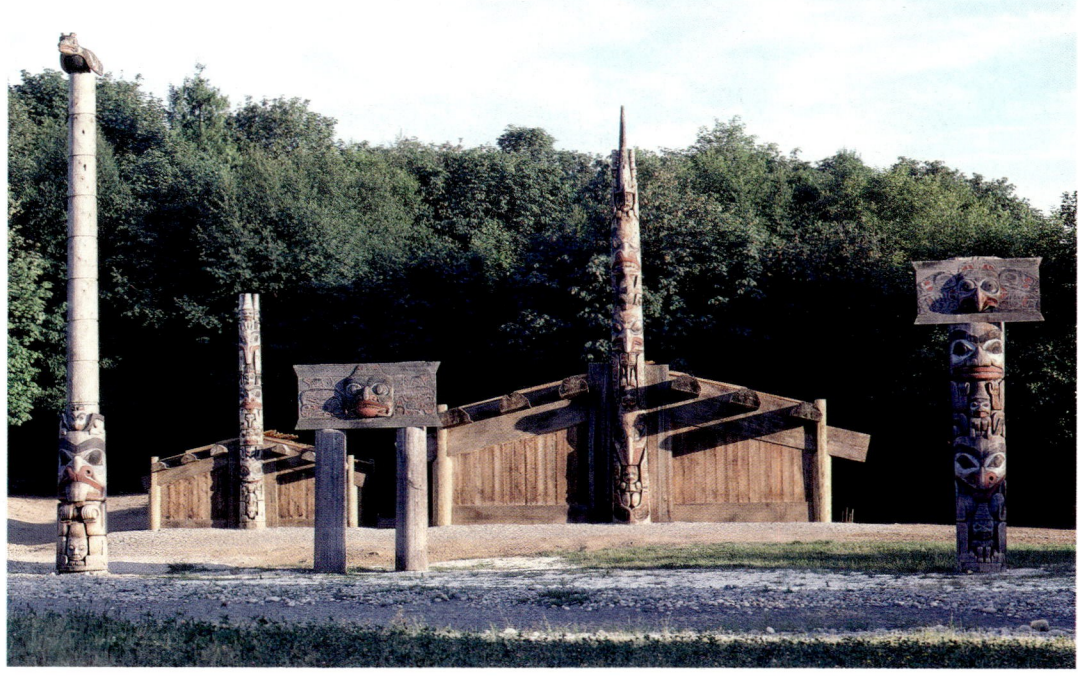

30-12 BILL REID (Haida), assisted by DOUG KRANMER (Kwakiutl), reconstruction of a 19th-century Haida village with totem poles, Queen Charlotte Island, 1962. Museum of Anthropology, University of British Columbia, Vancouver.

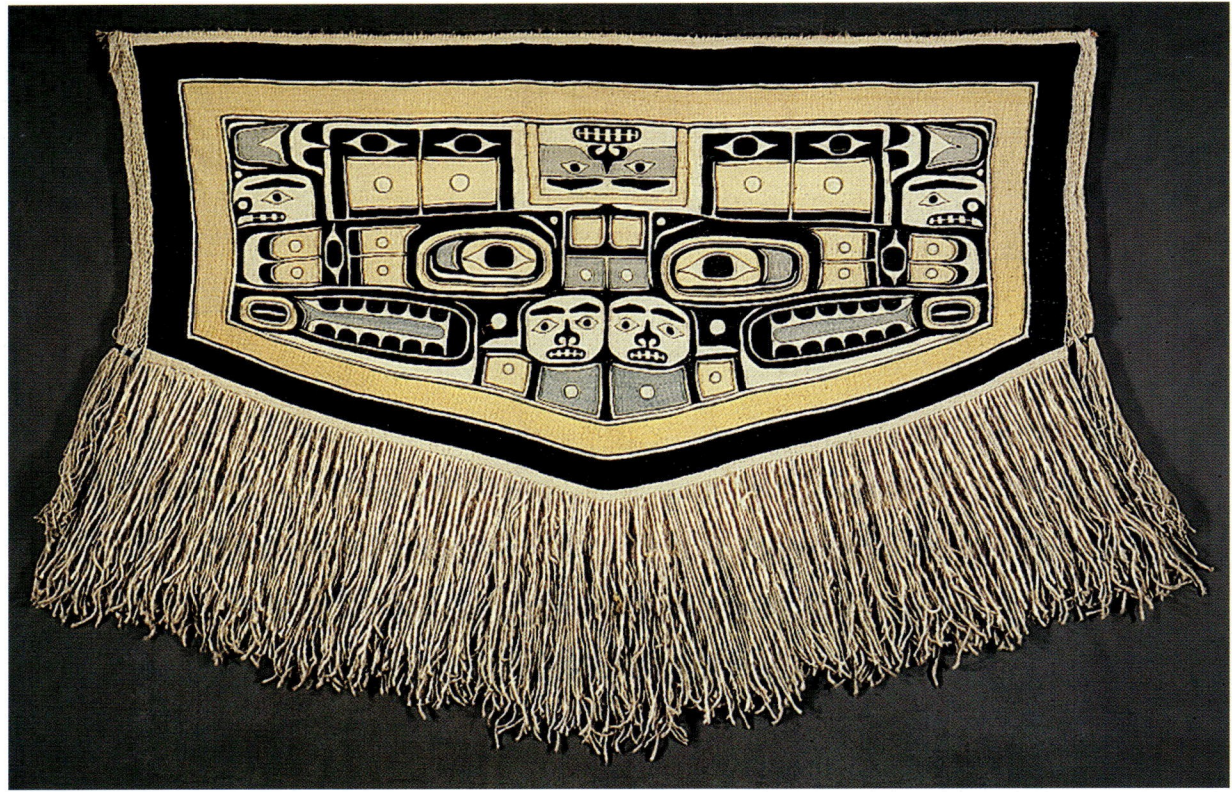

**30-13** Chilkat blanket with stylized animal motifs, Tlingit, early 20th century. Mountain goat's wool and cedar bark, 6′ × 2′ 11″. Southwest Museum, Los Angeles.

Additional crests could also be obtained through marriage and trade. The right to own and display such crests was so jealously guarded that even warfare could break out over the disputed ownership of a valued crest. In the poles shown, the crests represented include an upside-down dogfish (a small shark), an eagle with a downturned beak, and a killer whale with a crouching human between its snout and its upturned tail flukes. During the 19th century, the Haida erected more poles and made them larger in response to greater competitiveness and the availability of metal tools. The artists carved poles up to 60 feet tall from the trunks of single cedar trees. Because of the damp coastal climate, however, most of the poles decayed in a century or less. Nonetheless, many well-preserved 19th-century poles exist in museum collections. The Haida continue to carve totem poles in large numbers today.

**ALASKAN CEREMONIAL BLANKETS** Another characteristic Northwest Coast art form is the Chilkat blanket (FIG. **30-13**), named for an Alaskan Tlingit village where the blankets were woven. Male designers provided the templates for these blankets in the form of wooden pattern boards for the female weavers. Woven of shredded cedar bark and mountain goat wool on an upright loom, the Tlingit blankets took at least six months to complete. Actually robes worn over the shoulders, these became widespread prestige items of ceremonial dress during the 19th century. They display several characteristics of the Northwest Coast style recurrent in all media: symmetry and rhythmic repetition, schematic abstraction of animal motifs (in the robe illustrated, a bear), eye designs, a regularly swelling and thinning line, and a tendency to round off corners.

The devastating effects of 19th-century epidemics, coupled with government and missionary repression of Northwest Coast

ritual and social activities, threatened to wipe out the traditional arts entirely. Nevertheless, outstanding Northwest Coast artists continue to produce art objects today, some for the nonnative trade. The last half century has seen an impressive revival of traditional art forms, as well as the development of new ones, such as printmaking.

## Eskimo

**THE NORTH WIND** The 19th-century Yupik Eskimos living around the Bering Strait of Alaska also had a highly developed ceremonial life focused on game animals, particularly seal. Their religious specialists wore highly imaginative masks with moving parts. The Yupik generally made these masks for single occasions and then abandoned them. Consequently, many masks have ended up in museums and private collections. Our example (FIG. **30-14**) represents the spirit of the north wind, its face surrounded by a hoop representing the universe, its voice re-created by the rattling appendages. The paired human hands commonly found on such masks refer to the wearer's power to attract animals for hunting. The painted white spots represent snowflakes.

In more recent years, Canadian Eskimos, known as the Inuit, have set up cooperatives to produce and market stone carvings and prints. With these new media, artists generally depict themes from the rapidly vanishing traditional Inuit way of life.

## Great Plains

After colonial governments disrupted settled indigenous communities on the East Coast and the Europeans introduced the horse to North America, a new mobile Native American culture may be called his biography—a composite artistic statement in several media that neighboring Native Americans could have "read" easily. The concentric circle design over his left shoulder, for example, is an abstract rendering of an eagle-feather warbonnet.

Plains peoples also made shields and shield covers that were both artworks and "power images." Shield paintings often derived from personal religious visions. The owners believed that the symbolism, the pigments themselves, and added materials, such as feathers, provided them with magical protection and supernatural power.

Plains warriors battled incursions into their territory throughout the 19th century, but they were finally defeated by a combination of broken treaties, the rapid depletion of the buffalo, and military defeats at the hands of the U.S. Army. The pursuit of Plains natives culminated in the 1890 slaughter of Lakota participants who had gathered for a ritual known as the Ghost Dance at Wounded Knee Creek, South Dakota. Indeed, from the 1830s on, U.S. troops forcibly removed Native Americans from their homelands and resettled them in other parts of the country. Toward the end of the century, governments confined them to reservations in both the United States and Canada.

**LEDGER PAINTINGS** During the reservation period, some Plains arts continued to flourish, notably beadwork for the women and painting in ledger books for the men. Traders, the army, and Indian agents had for years provided Plains peoples with pencils

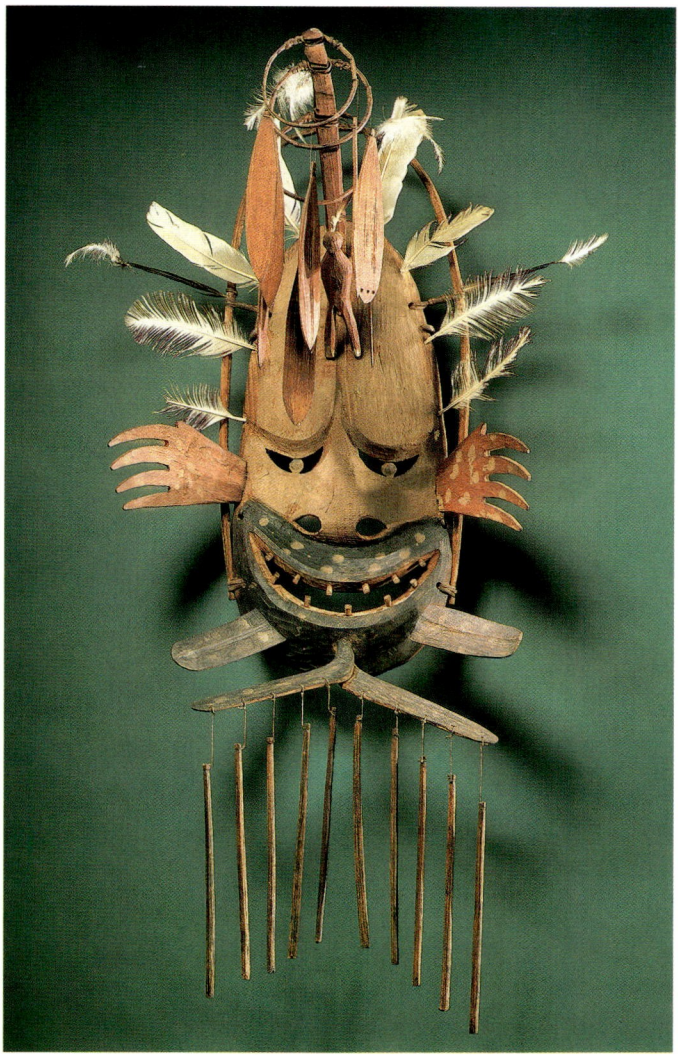

**30-14** Mask, Yupik Eskimo, Alaska, early 20th century. Wood and feathers, approx. 3′ 9″ high. Metropolitan Museum of Art, New York (The Michael C. Rockefeller Memorial Collection, gift of Nelson Rockefeller).

flourished for a short time on the Great Plains. Artists of the Great Plains worked in materials and styles quite different from those of the Northwest Coast and Eskimo peoples. Much artistic energy went into the decoration of leather garments, pouches, and horse trappings, first with compactly sewn quill designs and later with beadwork patterns. Artists painted tipis, tipi linings, and buffalo-skin robes with geometric and stiff figural designs prior to about 1830. After that, they gradually introduced naturalistic scenes, often of war exploits, in styles adapted from those of visiting European artists.

**HIDATSA REGALIA** Because, at least in later periods, most Plains peoples were nomadic, they focused their aesthetic attention largely on their clothing and bodies and on other portable objects, such as shields, clubs, pipes, tomahawks, and various containers. Transient but important Plains art forms can sometimes be found in the paintings and drawings of visiting American and European artists. The Swiss KARL BODMER (1809–1893), for example, portrayed the personal decoration of Two Ravens, a Hidatsa warrior, in an 1833 watercolor (FIG. **30-15**). The painting depicts his pipe, painted buffalo robe, bear-claw necklace, and feather decorations, all symbolic of his affiliations and military accomplishments. They

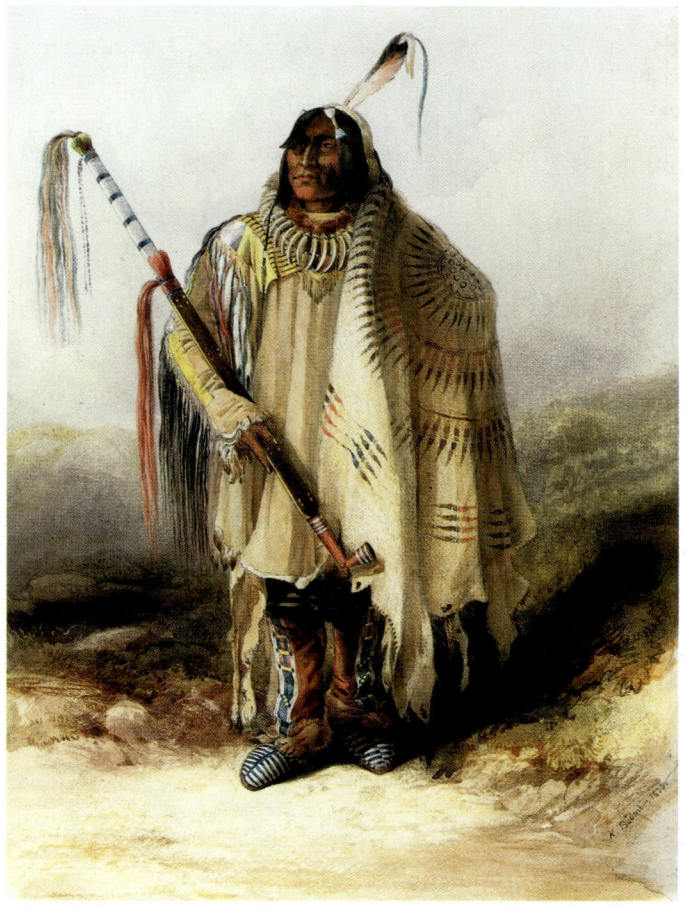

**30-15** KARL BODMER, *Hidatsa Warrior Pehriska-Ruhpa (Two Ravens)*, 1833. Watercolor, 1′ 3⅞″ × 11½″. Joslyn Art Museum, Omaha (gift of the Enron Art Foundation).

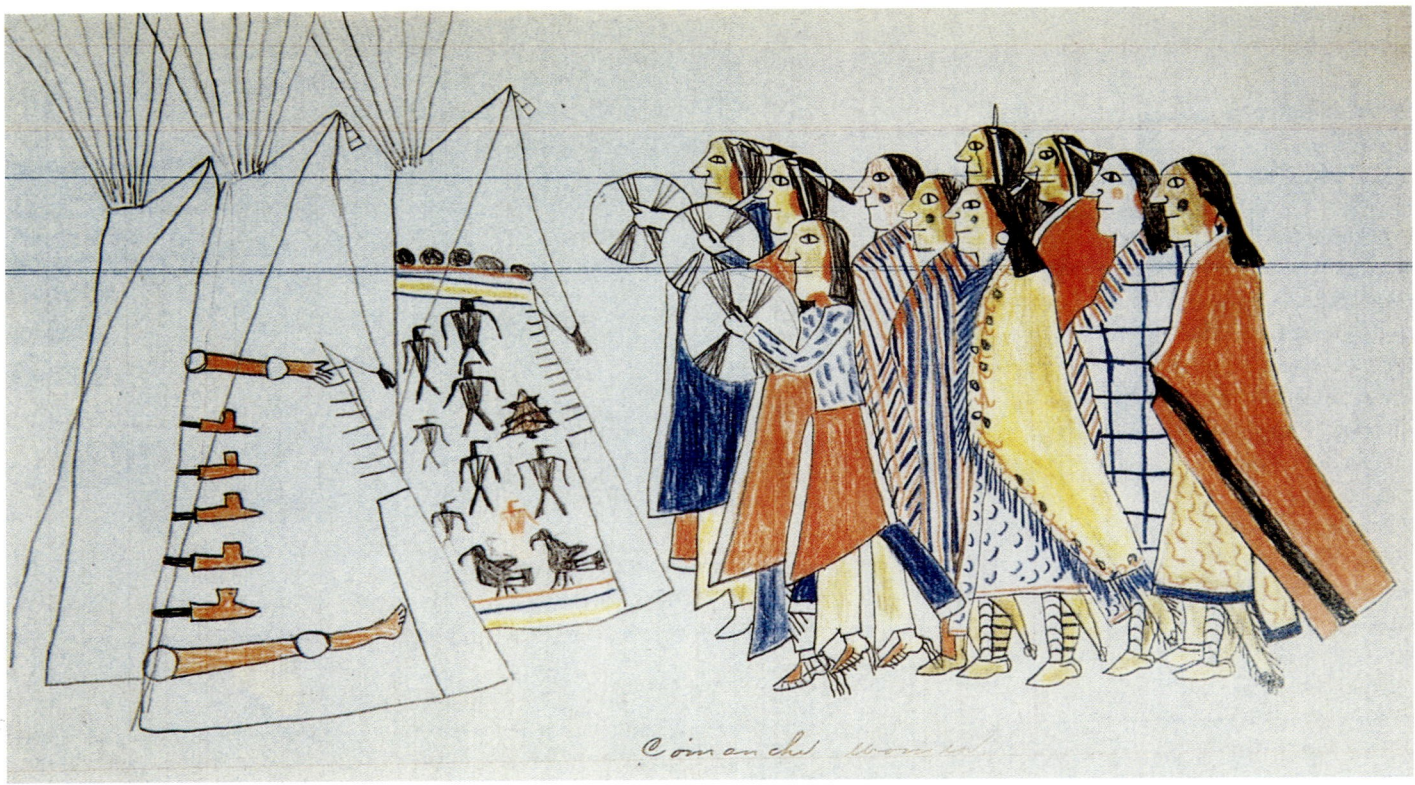

**30-16** Honoring song at painted tipi, in Julian Scott Ledger, Kiowa, 1880. Pencil, ink, and colored pencil, $7\frac{1}{2}'' \times 1'$. Mr. and Mrs. Charles Diker Collection.

and new or discarded ledger books. They, in turn, used them to draw their personal exploits for themselves or for interested Anglo buyers. Sometimes warriors carried them into battle, where U.S. Army opponents retook the ledgers. After confinement to reservations, Plains artists began to record not only their heroic past and vanished lifestyle but also their reactions to their new surroundings, frequently in a state far from home. These images, often poignant and sometimes humorous, are important native documents of a time of great turmoil and change. In our example (FIG. **30-16**) by an unknown Kiowa artist, a group of men and women, possibly Comanches (allies of the Kiowa), appear to dance an honoring song before three tipis, the left forward one painted with red stone pipes and a dismembered leg and arm. The women (at the center and right) wear the mixture of clothing typical of the late 19th century among the Plains Indians—traditional high leather moccasins, dresses made from calico trade cloth, and (on the right) a red Hudson's Bay blanket with a black stripe.

Although ledger-book paintings are no longer made, beadwork has never completely died out. The ancient art of creating quilled, beaded, and painted clothing has evolved into the elaborate costumes displayed today at competitive dances called *powwows*.

# CONCLUSION

The discovery of the "New World" at the end of the 15th century led quickly to confrontation, conquest, and the wholesale destruction of buildings and artworks. The loss is irreparable, but fortunately not total. The monuments that survive attest to the greatness of the art and architecture of the native peoples of the Americas.

In Mesoamerica, the Aztecs produced colossal stone sculptures and towering pyramids, and also excelled in the design and manufacture of textiles, metalwork, and books. In Andean South America, the Inka Empire was the largest in the world in the 16th century and boasted a sophisticated system of record-keeping and administration, as well as monumental art and architecture. In North America, power was much more widely dispersed and the native art and architecture more varied. Whether secular and decorative or spiritual and highly symbolic, the diverse styles and forms of Native American art in the United States and Canada reflect the indigenous peoples' reliance on and reverence toward the environment they considered it their privilege to inhabit.

MESOAMERICA

SOUTH AMERICA

NORTH AMERICA

LATE POSTCLASSIC

LATE INTERMEDIATE PERIOD

LATE HORIZON

VARIOUS OVERLAPPING INDIGENOUS CULTURES

**1300**

| Founding of Tenochtitlán, 1325 (M)

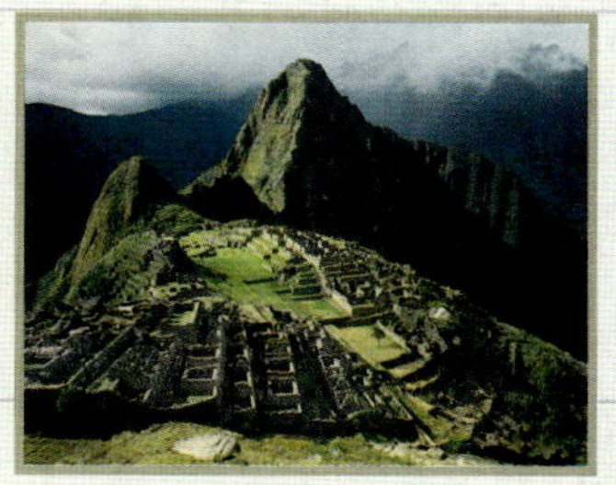

1 Machu Picchu, Peru, 15th century

**1400**

| Aztecs become an imperial power, 1427 (M)
| Inka Empire begins to expand, 1438 (S)
1
| Columbus arrives in the Americas, 1492

**1500**

2 | Moctezuma, Aztec emperor, r. 1502–1521 (M)
| Cortés arrives in Mexico, 1519 (M)
| Cortés topples Aztec Empire, 1521 (M)
| Pizarro conquers Inka Empire, 1532 (S)

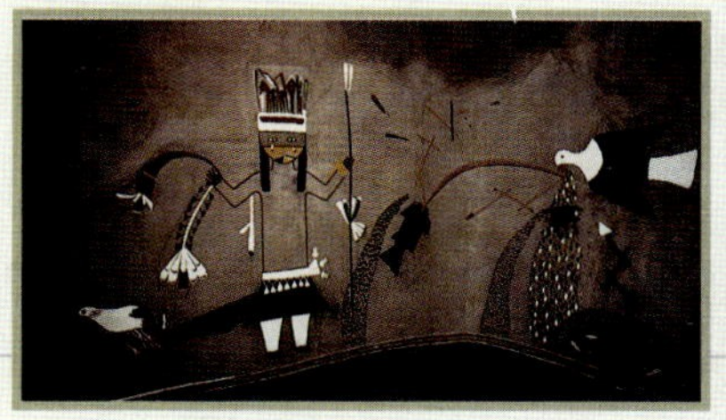

**1600**

2 Kiva painting, Kuaua Pueblo, late 15th or early 16th century

**1700**

| Europeans explore Northwest Coast, 1778 (N)

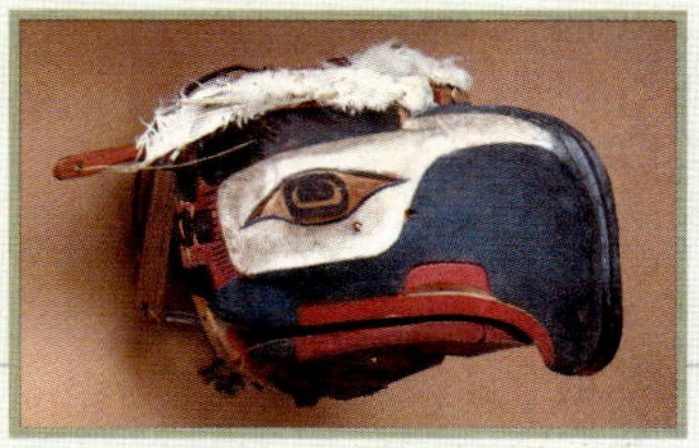

**1800**

| U.S. Government begins to resettle Native Americans on reservations, 1830s (N)
| Lakota massacre at Wounded Knee, 1890 (N)

3

3 Eagle transformation mask, Kwakiutl, late 19th century

**1900**

| Native Americans receive U.S. citizenship, 1924 (N)
| U.S. Congress authorizes national Museum
4 of the American Indian, 1989 (N)

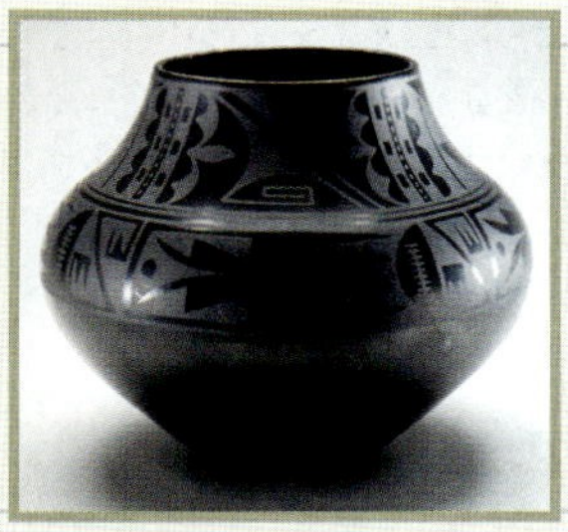

**2000**

4 María Montoya Martínez, jar, San Ildefonso Pueblo, ca. 1939

KEY: M = Mesoamerica / N = North America / S = South America

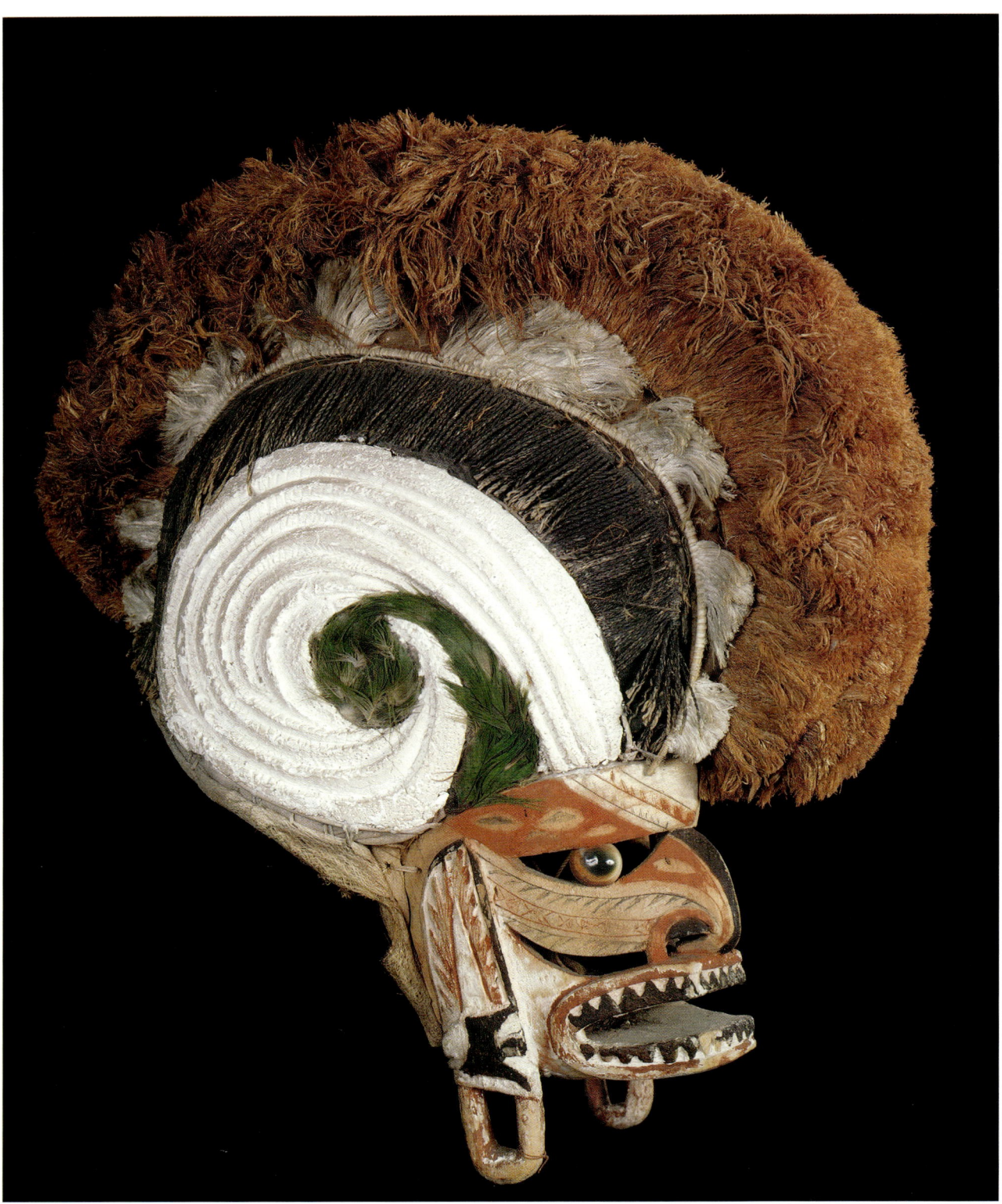

*Tatanua* mask, from New Ireland. Wood, shell, lime, and fiber, 1′ 5$\frac{3}{4}$″ high. Otago Museum, New Zealand.

# 31

# THE FLOURISHING OF ISLAND CULTURES

## THE ART OF OCEANIA

Although the term *South Pacific* may well call to mind images of balmy tropical islands, the Pacific Ocean actually encompasses a truly diverse range of habitats and cultures. Environments range from the arid deserts of the Australian outback to the tropical rainforests of inland New Guinea and the coral atolls of the Marshall Islands. Oceanic cultures are not only geographically varied but also politically, linguistically, culturally, and artistically diverse.

**WAVES ACROSS THE PACIFIC** Oceania (MAP **31-1**) consists of over 25,000 islands (less than 1,500 inhabitable), including the island continent of Australia. Although documentary evidence does not exist for Oceanic cultures until the arrival of seafaring Europeans in the early 16th century, archaeologists have determined that the islands have been inhabited for tens of thousands of years. Their research has revealed that different parts of the Pacific were populated during distinct migratory waves. The first group arrived in the Pacific during the last Ice Age, approximately 40,000 years ago, when a large continental shelf extended from Southeast Asia and allowed human access to Australia and New Guinea. After the end of the Ice Age, descendants of these first settlers dispersed to other islands. The most recent migratory wave to areas of Micronesia and Polynesia involved people of Asian ancestry; this migration probably took place sometime after 3000 BCE. Knowledge of this movement into Micronesia and western Polynesia is based in part on a type of pottery (known as Lapita) that is common to much of this area. Named after a site on New Caledonia in Melanesia, Lapita pottery (ceramic vessels elaborately decorated with incised, geometric designs) has been found in a geographical region stretching from the straits between New Guinea and New Britain in the west, to Tonga and Samoa in the east. The last Pacific islands colonized were those of Polynesia; its most far-flung islands—Hawaii, New Zealand, and Rapa Nui (Easter Island)—were inhabited by about 500–1000 CE.

Because of the expansive chronological span of these migrations, Pacific cultures vary widely. For example, the Aboriginal peoples of Australia speak a language unrelated to those of New Guinea, whose diverse languages fall into a family often referred

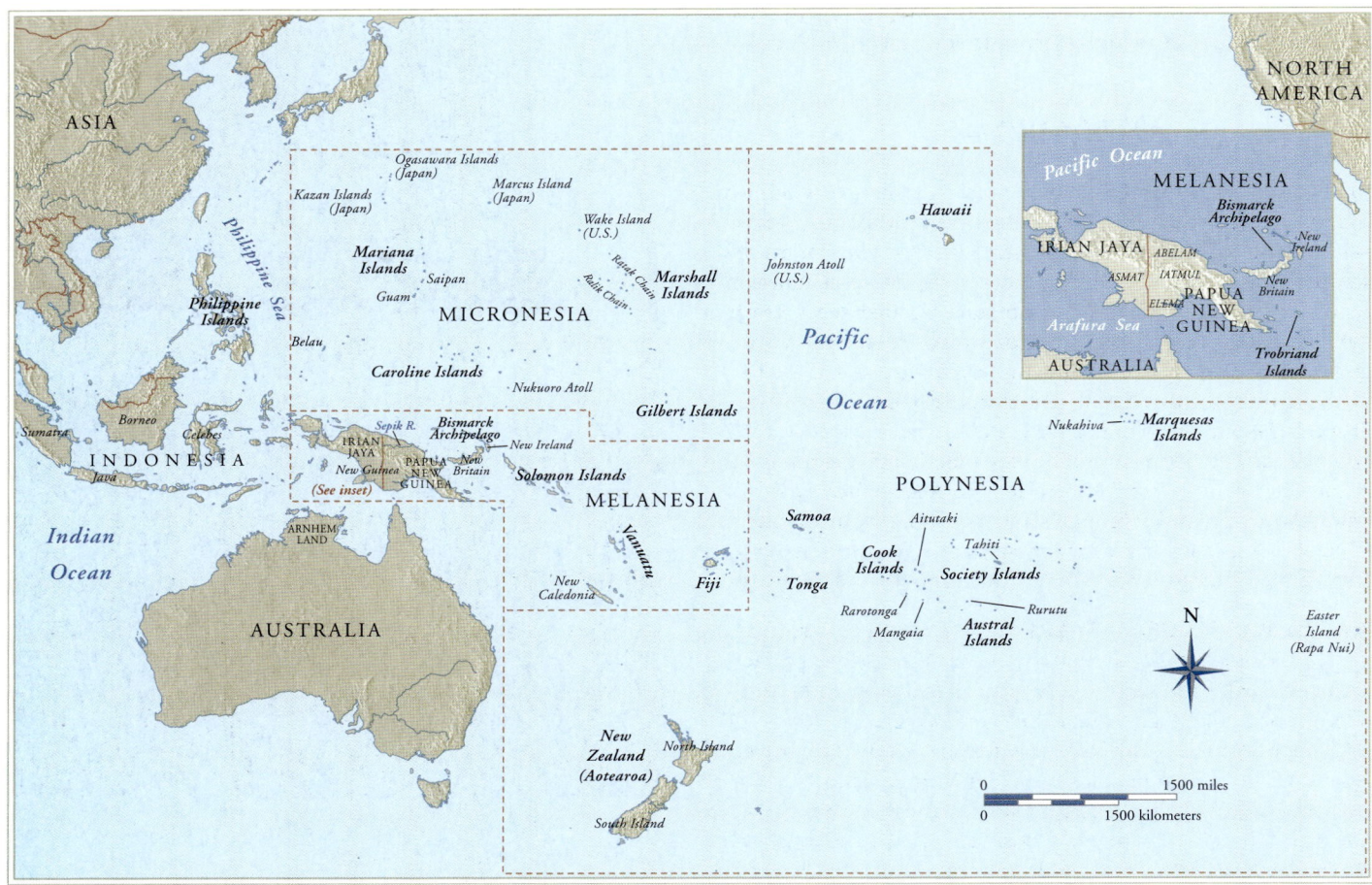

MAP 31-1 Oceania.

to as Papuan. In contrast, most of the rest of the Pacific islanders speak languages derived from the Austronesian language family.

**A HISTORY OF COLONIALISM** These island groups came to Western attention as a result of the extensive exploration and colonization that began in the 16th century and reached its peak in the 19th century. Virtually all of the major Western cultures established a presence in the Pacific, including Great Britain, France, Spain, Holland, Germany, and the United States. This colonial presence was problematic for many indigenous peoples; indeed, much of 20th-century Oceanic history has revolved around struggles for independence from colonial powers. Yet such contact also facilitated an exchange of ideas, and Oceanic practices and art influenced the Western world.

**PACIFIC REGIONS** In 1831, the French explorer Jules Sébastien César Dumont d'Urville proposed the division of the Pacific into major regions based on general geographical, racial, and linguistic distinctions. Despite its limitations, his division of Oceania into the areas of Melanesia ("black islands"), Micronesia ("small islands"), and Polynesia ("many islands") continues to be used today. Melanesia includes the islands of New Guinea, New Ireland, New Britain, New Caledonia, the Admiralty Islands, and the Solomon Islands, along with other smaller island groups. Micronesia consists primarily of the Caroline Islands, the Mariana Islands, the Gilbert Islands, and the Marshall Islands in the western Pacific. Polynesia covers much of the eastern Pacific and

consists of a triangular area defined by the Hawaiian Islands in the north, Rapa Nui (Easter Island) in the east, and New Zealand in the southwest.

**THE EVOLUTION OF OCEANIC ART** This chapter focuses on Oceanic art from the European discovery of the islands in the 16th century until the present. Some of the objects presented may not seem to conform to traditional Western definitions of art. But although these objects may appear primarily functional, their aesthetic components are no less important, accounting for their discussion in this chapter as art. The ongoing efforts of archaeologists, linguists, anthropologists, ethnologists, and art historians continue to shed light on the development of the arts of Oceania. Knowledge of early Oceanic art and the history of the Pacific islands in general is unfortunately far from complete; traditionally, the transmission of information from one generation to the next in Pacific societies was largely verbal, rather than written, and this emphasis on oral history has left little archival documentation. It is known, however, that the art and material culture of the islands of Oceania, like those of other cultures worldwide, have constantly evolved. Largely as a result of colonial and missionary intervention in the 18th through 20th centuries, many Oceanic cultures abandoned traditional practices, and production of many of the art forms illustrated in this chapter ceased. In recent years, some Pacific artists have returned to traditional forms for inspiration and have worked to revive and reinterpret traditional indigenous practices and art forms. Today's thriving tourist trade has also contributed to a resurgence of traditional art production.

# MELANESIA

**DIVERSE ECOSYSTEMS** Because of its sheer size, New Guinea dominates Melanesia. This 309,000-square-mile island consists today of parts of two countries—Irian Jaya, a province of nearby Indonesia, on the island's western end, and Papua New Guinea on the eastern end. New Guinea's inhabitants together speak nearly 800 different languages, almost one quarter of the world's known languages. Among the Melanesian cultures discussed in this chapter, the Iatmul, Abelam, Asmat, and Elema peoples of New Guinea all speak Papuan-derived languages and are believed to descend from the early settlers who came to the island in the remote past. In contrast, the people of New Ireland, off the northeast coast of New Guinea, and the Trobriand Islanders, off the southeastern tip of New Guinea, are Austronesian speakers and were probably descendants of a later wave of Pacific migrants.

**POWER, PRIVILEGE, AND ART** Typical Melanesian societies are fairly democratic and relatively unstratified. What political power exists is vested in groups of elder men and, in some areas, elder women. The elders handle the people's affairs in a communal fashion. Within some of these groups power is accrued by persons of local distinction, known as "Big Men." Such individuals are renowned for their political, economic, and, historically, warrior skills. Because power and position in Melanesia can be earned (within limits), many cultural practices (such as rituals and cults) revolve around the acquisition of knowledge that allows advancement in society. To represent and acknowledge this advancement in rank, Melanesian societies mount elaborate festivals, construct communal meetinghouses, and produce art objects. These cultural products serve to reinforce the social order and maintain social stability. Given the wide diversity in environments and languages, it should come as no surprise that there are hundreds of art styles found on New Guinea alone, only a few of which will be presented here.

## The Iatmul (Papua New Guinea)

**A SYMBOLIC FEMALE ANCESTOR** Prime examples of the social importance and symbolism of Melanesian architecture are the massive saddle-shaped men's ceremonial houses built by the Iatmul people. The Iatmul live along the middle Sepik River in Papua New Guinea in communities based on kinship. Villages include extended families as well as different clans. In terms of both function and form, the men's house reveals the primacy of the kinship network. The meetinghouse reinforces kinship links by serving as the locale for initiation of local youths for advancement in rank, for men's discussions of community issues, and for ceremonies linked to the Iatmul's ancestors. Because advancement in Iatmul society is limited to men, women and uninitiated boys are denied access to the house. In this manner, access to knowledge (and therefore to power) is controlled. Given its important political and cultural role, this house is appropriately monumental, physically dominating Iatmul villages and dwarfing family houses.

Traditionally, the house (FIG. **31-1**) symbolizes the protective mantle of the ancestors and represents an enormous female ancestor. The Iatmul house and its female ancestral figures symbolize a

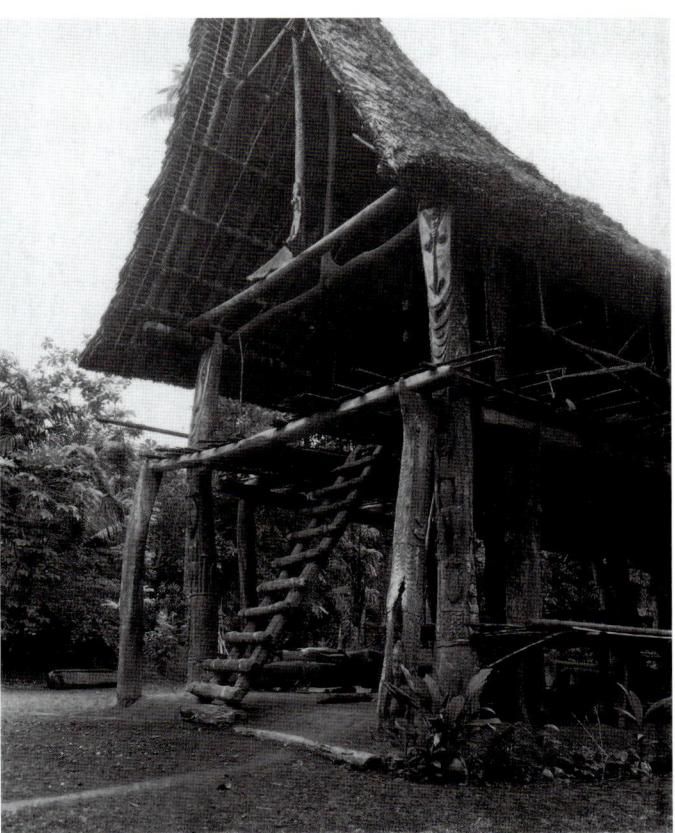

**31-1** Exposed interior of ceremonial men's house, Iatmul, Papua New Guinea, photographed in 1953–1954.

reenacted death and rebirth when a clan member enters and exits the second story of the house. The gable ends of such houses are usually covered (though they are exposed in our illustration) and include a giant female gable mask (not visible in the illustration), making the ancestral symbolism visible. The absence of this covering and mask in our example is due to the house's incomplete state; when it was reconstructed after sustaining damage during World War II, it was never finished. Although this hampers our visualization of the exterior, it does expose interior carvings normally hidden from view. The Iatmul placed carved images of clan ancestors on the five central ridge-support posts and on the twelve roof-support posts on both sides of the house. (One central post and two roof-support posts are fully visible in our photograph.) They topped each roof-support post with large faces representing mythical spirits of the clans. At the top of the two raised spires at each end, birds symbolizing the war spirit of the village men sit above carvings of head-hunting victims (on occasion, male ancestors). Iatmul men's houses are the most lavishly decorated of such structures in New Guinea.

The house's interior reflects the social demographic of the village and is subdivided into parts for each clan. This particular meetinghouse has three parts—a front, middle, and end—representing the three major clans who built the house. These parts are further subdivided into additional subclan areas, which also have support posts carved with images of mythical male and female ancestors. Beneath the house, each clan keeps large carved slit-gongs to serve as both instruments of communication (for sending drum messages within and between villages) and the voices of ancestral spirits. Above the two ladders leading to the second level, the Iatmul placed figurative carvings on horizontal crossbeams (see the carving in the open gable space in FIG. 31-1).

These figures symbolize female clan ancestors in a birthing position. The Iatmul also keep various types of portable art in their ceremonial houses. These include ancestors' skulls overmodeled with clay in a likeness of the deceased, ceremonial chairs, sacred flutes, hooks for hanging sacred items and food, and several types of masks.

## The Abelam (Papua New Guinea)

**A COMPLEX YAM CULT**  That Oceanic art relates not only to fundamental spiritual beliefs but also to basic subsistence is highlighted by the yam masks produced by the Abelam people, agriculturists living in the hilly regions north of the Sepik River. The Abelam's principal cultivar is the yam. Such has been the case throughout recent Abelam history and continues to the present day. Relatively isolated, the Abelam received only sporadic visits from foreigners until the 1930s, so little is known about early Abelam history. Because of the importance of yams to the survival of Abelam society, those who can grow the largest yams are endowed with power and prestige. Indeed, the Abelam developed

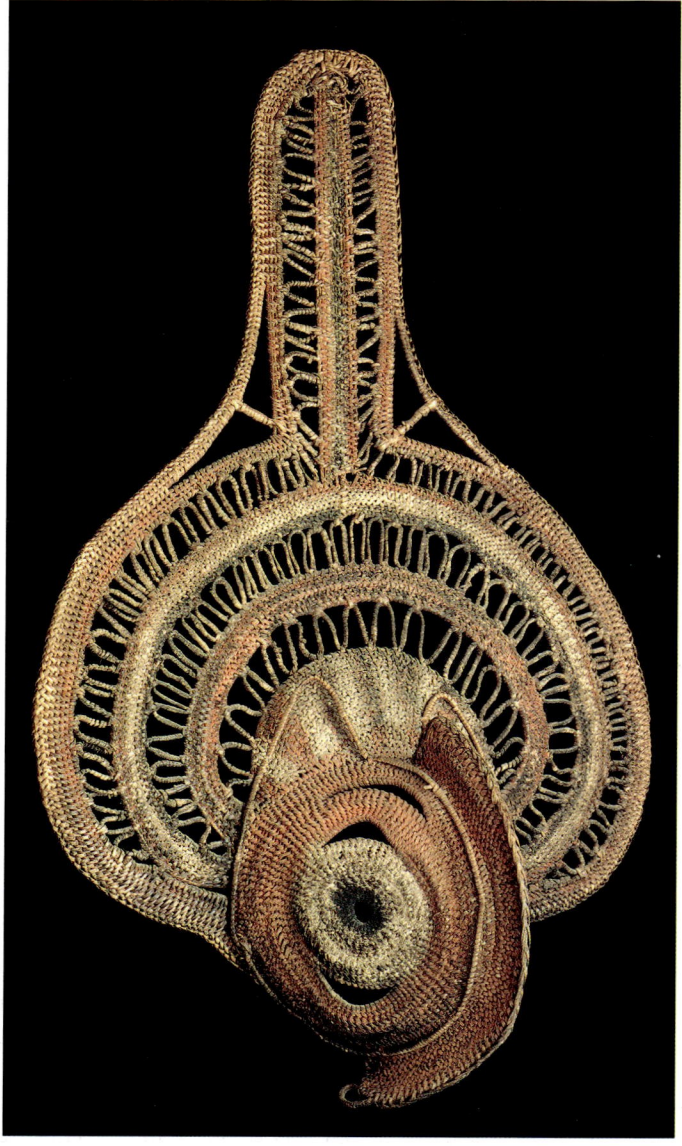

31-2 Yam mask, Abelam, Maprik district, Papua New Guinea, 1′ 6⁹⁄₁₀″ high.

a complex yam cult, which involves a series of rites and activities intended to promote the growth of yams. Special plantations are devoted to yam cultivation; only initiated men who observe strict rules of conduct, including sexual abstinence, can work these fields. The Abelam believe that ancestors aid in the growth of yams, and they hold ceremonies to honor these ancestors. Special long yams (distinct from the short yams cultivated for consumption) are placed on display during these festivities, and the largest of the yams are named after important ancestors. Yam masks are an integral part of the ceremonies. These cane or wood frame masks (FIG. 31-2) are usually painted red, white, yellow, and black. Further, the Abelam incorporate sculpted faces, cassowary feathers, and shell ornaments into the yam masks. The Abelam use the same designs to decorate their bodies for dances, revealing how closely they identify with their principal food source.

## The Asmat (Irian Jaya)

**THE ART OF WARFARE**  In contrast with the Abelam, with their relatively peaceful agricultural pursuits, the Asmat face a much harsher life. Living along the coast of southwestern New Guinea, the Asmat eke out their existence by hunting and gathering the varied flora and fauna found in the mangrove swamps, rivers, and tropical forests where they live. Because resources are limited, each Asmat community is in constant competition for these resources. Historically, the Asmat extended this competitive spirit beyond food and materials to energy and power as well. To increase one's personal energy or spiritual power, one had to take it forcibly from someone else. As a result, warfare and head-hunting became central to Asmat culture and art. The Asmat did not believe that any death was natural; it could only be the result of a direct assault (head-hunting or warfare) or sorcery, and it diminished ancestral power. Thus, to restore a balance of spirit power, an enemy's head had to be taken to avenge a death and to add to one's communal spirit power. Head-hunting was common in the 1930s when Europeans established an administrative and missionary presence among the Asmat. As a result of European efforts, head-hunting was effectively abandoned by the 1960s.

**AVENGING A DEATH**  When they still practiced head-hunting, the Asmat erected *bisj* poles (FIG. 31-3) that served as a pledge to avenge a relative's death. Such poles were constructed when a man could command the support of enough men to undertake a head-hunting raid. Carved from the trunk of the mangrove tree, bisj poles included superimposed figures of individuals who had died. At the top, extending flangelike from the bisj pole, was one of the tree's buttress roots carved into an openwork pattern. All of the decorative elements on the pole were related to head-hunting and foretold a successful raid. The many animals that appeared on bisj poles (and in Asmat art in general) are symbols of head-hunting. The Asmat see the human body as a tree—the feet as the roots, the arms as the branches, and the head as the fruit. Thus any fruit-eating animal (such as the black king cockatoo, the hornbill, or the flying fox) is symbolic of the headhunter and appeared frequently on bisj poles. Asmat art also often includes representations of the praying mantis; the Asmat consider the female praying mantis's practice of beheading her mate after copulation and then eating him as another form of head-hunting. The curvilinear or spiral patterns that filled the pierced openwork at the top of the pole can be related to the characteristic curved tail of the *cuscus* (a fruit-eating mammal) or the tusk of a boar (related to hunting and virility). Once carved, bisj poles were placed on a

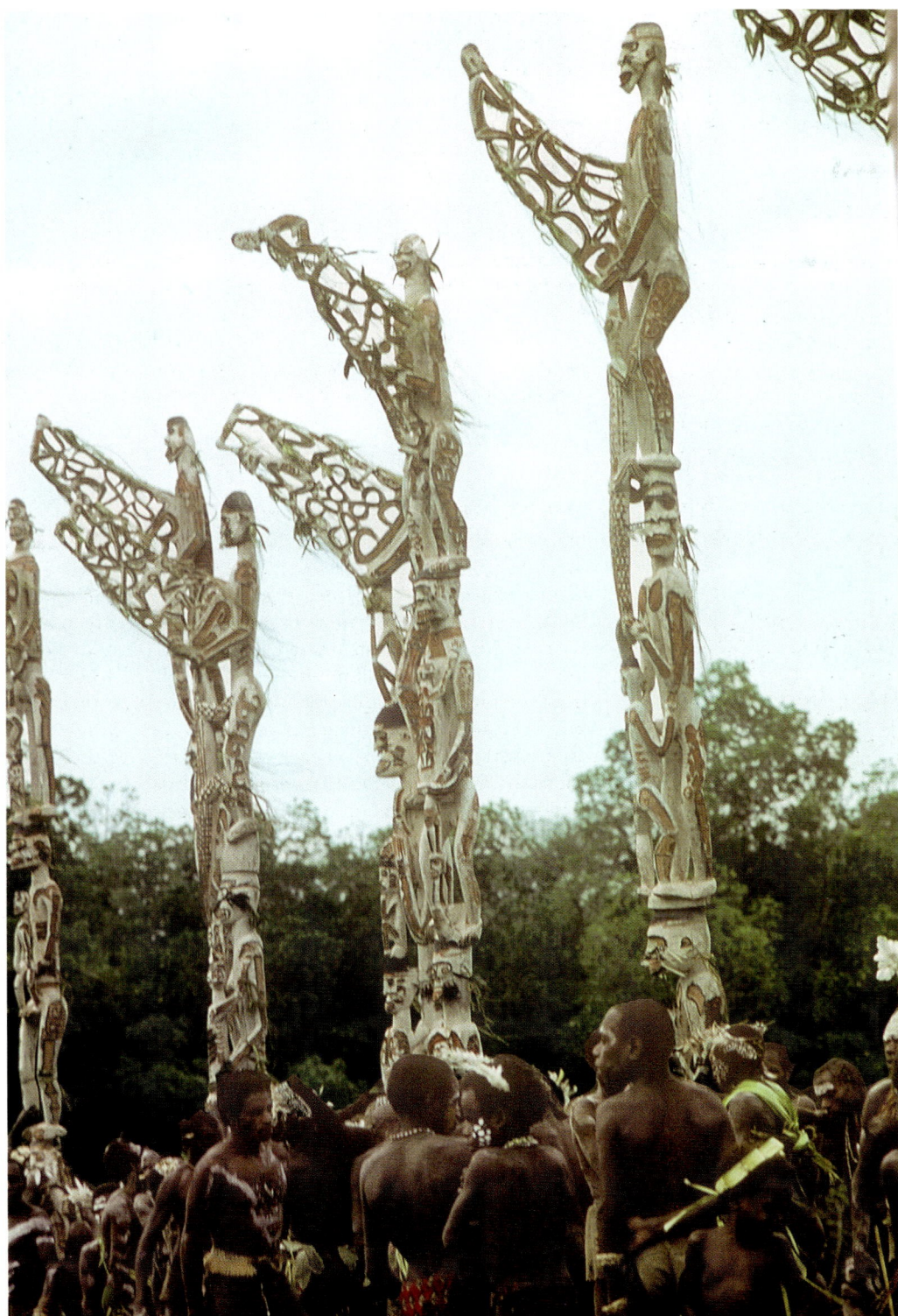

**31-3** *Bisj* poles, Buepis village, Fajit River, Casuarina Coast, southwest New Guinea. Early to mid-20th century.

rack near the men's house, in public view. After the success of the head-hunting expedition, the bisj poles were discarded and allowed to rot, having served their purpose.

## The Elema (Papua New Guinea)

**VISITING WATER SPIRITS** Central to the culture of the Elema people of Orokolo Bay in the Papuan Gulf was Hevehe, an elaborate cycle of ceremonial activities. Conceptualized as the mythical visitation of the water spirits *(ma-hevehe),* the Hevehe cycle involved the production and presentation of large, ornate masks (also called *hevehe).* The Elema last practiced Hevehe in the 1950s. Primarily organized by the male elders of the village, the cycle was a communal undertaking, and normally took from 10 to 20 years to complete. The duration of the Hevehe and the resources and human labor required reveal the role of Hevehe as a social glue—it reinforced cultural and economic relations and maintained the social structure in which elder male authority dominated.

Throughout the cycle, the Elema held ceremonies to initiate male youths into higher ranks. These ceremonies involved the exchange of wealth (such as pigs and shell ornaments), thereby

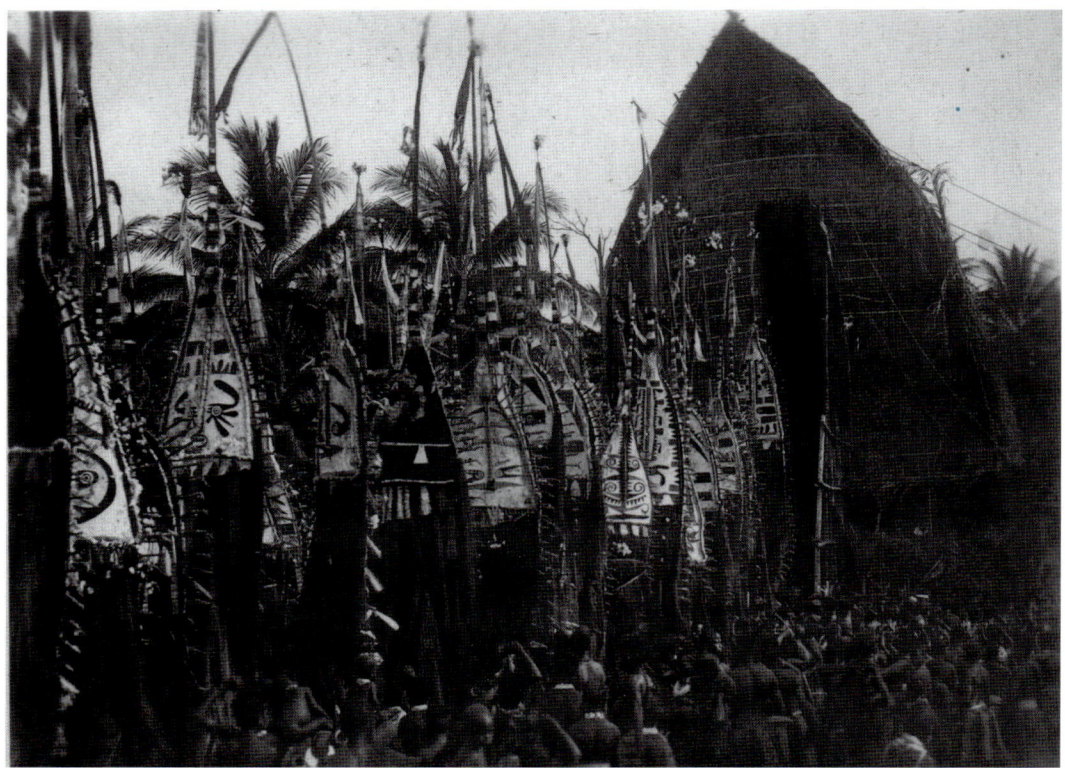

serving an economic purpose as well. The cycle culminated in the display of the finished hevehe masks. Each mask was constructed of painted barkcloth (see pages 930–931) wrapped around a cane-and-wood frame that fit over the wearer's body. A hevehe mask was normally 9 to 10 feet in height, although extensions often raised the height to as much as 25 feet. Because of its size and intricate design, a hevehe mask required great skill to construct, and only trained men would participate in mask-making. Designs were specific to particular clans and were passed down by elder men from memory. Each mask represented a female sea spirit, but the overall decoration of the mask often incorporated designs from local flora and fauna as well.

The final stage of the cycle focused on the dramatic appearance of the masks from the *eravo* (men's house; FIG. **31-4**). After a procession, men wearing the hevehe mingled with relatives. Upon conclusion of related dancing (often lasting about one month), the masks were ritually killed and then dumped in piles and burned. This destruction allowed the sea spirits to return to their mythic domain and provided a pretext for commencing the cycle again.

## The Trobriand Islands (Papua New Guinea)

**TRADING PLACES** The various rituals of Oceanic cultures discussed thus far often involve exchanges that cement social relationships and reinforce or stimulate the economy. Further, these rituals usually have a spiritual dimension. All of these aspects apply to the practices of the Trobriand Islanders, who live off the coast of the southeastern corner of New Guinea (part of Papua New Guinea). The Trobriand Islanders are well known for *kula*—an exchange of white conus-shell arm ornaments for red chama-shell necklaces. Kula, possibly originating some 500 years ago, came to Western attention through the extensive documentation of anthropologist Bronislaw Malinowski (1884–1942),

published in 1920 and 1922. Kula exchanges can be complex, and there is great competition for valuable shell ornaments (determined by aesthetic appeal and exchange history). Because of the isolation imposed by their island existence, the Trobriand Islanders had to undertake potentially dangerous voyages to participate in kula trading. Appropriately, the Trobrianders lavish a great deal of effort on decorating their large canoes, which are elaborately carved and include ornate prows and splashboards (FIG. **31-5**). These prows and splashboards are carved by artists who have acquired both the necessary carving skill and the knowledge of the symbolism of the kula images. Human, bird, and serpent motifs, as references to sea spirits, ancestors, and totemic animals, appear on prows. These motifs are highly stylized, making specific identification difficult. The curvilinear, intertwined designs are fluidly presented; this intricate style is characteristic of Trobriand art. To ensure a successful kula expedition, the Trobrianders invoked spells when attaching these prows to the canoes. In recent years, Trobrianders have adapted kula to modern circumstances; by the 1970s, they largely abandoned canoes for motorboats, and the exchanges now facilitate contemporary business and political networking.

## New Ireland (Papua New Guinea)

**HONORING THE DEAD** Mortuary rites and memorial festivals are a central concern of the Austronesian-speaking peoples who live in the northern section of the island of New Ireland in Papua New Guinea. The term *malanggan* refers to both the festivals held in honor of the deceased and the carvings and objects produced for these festivals. Malanggan practices have enjoyed longevity; one of the first references to malanggan appears in an 1883 publication, and these rituals continue to be practiced today. Malanggan rites are critical in facilitating the transition of the soul from the world of the

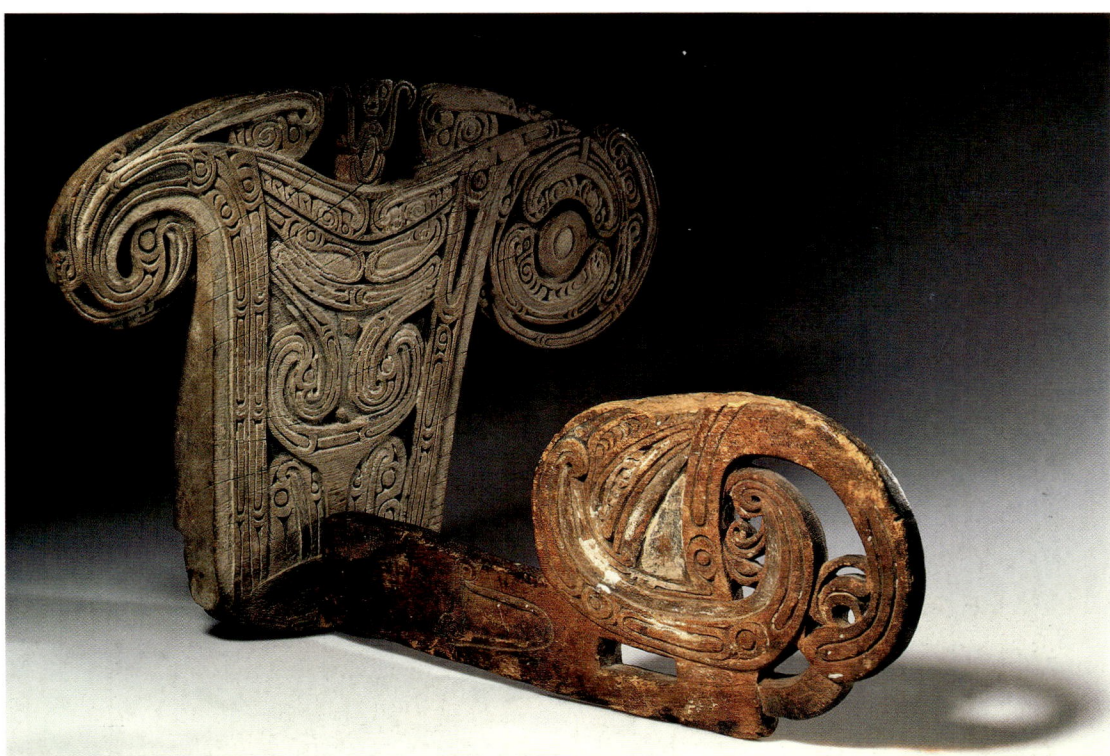

31-5 Canoe prow and splashboard, from Trobriand Islands, Milne Bay Province, Papua New Guinea. Wood and paint, 1′ 3½″ high, 1′ 11″ long. Musée de l'Homme, Paris.

living to the realm of the dead. Because of the ultimate destination of the soul, these rituals are part of an ancestor cult. In addition to the religious function of malanggan, the extended ceremonies also promote social solidarity and stimulate the economy (as a result of the resources necessary to mount impressive festivities). To educate the younger generation about these practices, malanggan also includes the initiation of young men.

Among the many malanggan carvings produced—masks, figures, poles, friezes, and ornaments—are *tatanua* masks (FIG. **31-6**). Although some masks are simply displayed, most of them are worn by dancers. Tatanua represent the spirits of specific deceased people and are constructed of soft wood, vegetable fiber, and rattan. The crested hair, made of fiber, duplicates a hairstyle formerly common among the men. Sea snail opercula (the operculum is the plate that closes the shell when the animal is retracted) are embedded as eyes. Traditionally, the masks are painted black, white, yellow, and red—colors the people of New Ireland associate with warfare, magic spells, and violence. Rather than being destroyed after the conclusion of the many ceremonies, tatanua are stored for future use.

## MICRONESIA

**THE ART OF SEAFARING CULTURES** The Austronesian-speaking cultures of Micronesia tend to be more socially stratified than those found in New Guinea and other Melanesian areas. Such cultures are frequently organized around chieftainships with craft and ritual specializations, and their religions include named deities as well as honored ancestors. Life in virtually all Micronesian cultures centers around seafaring activities—fishing, trading, and long-distance travel in large oceangoing vessels. For this reason, much of their artistic imagery relates to the sea. Micronesian arts include carved canoes, charms, and images of spirits used to protect travelers at sea and for fishing and fertility magic. Micronesian artists also tend to simplify and to abstract geometrically the natural forms of animals, humans, and plants. This characteristic often differentiates Micronesian art from the arts of Melanesia, Polynesia, and Australia.

31-6 *Tatanua* mask, from New Ireland. Wood, shell, lime, and fiber, 1′ 5¾″ high. Otago Museum, New Zealand.

## Belau (Caroline Islands)

**HOUSES THAT TELL STORIES** On Belau (formerly Palau) in the Caroline Islands, the islanders put much effort into creating and maintaining elaborately painted men's ceremonial clubhouses called *bai.* These bai (FIG. **31-7**) have steep overhanging roofs decorated with geometric patterns along the roof boards. Belau artists carve the gable in low relief and paint it with narrative scenes, as well as various abstracted forms of the shell money used traditionally on Belau as currency. These decorated storyboards illustrate important historical events and myths related to the clan who built the bai. In the illustration, the rooster images along the base of the house symbolize the rising sun, while the multiple frontal human faces carved and painted above the entrance and on the vertical elements above the rooster images represent a deity called Blellek. He warns women to stay away from the ocean and the *bai* or he will molest them. In so doing, the god serves as a social control mechanism within Belau society.

Artists also carve and paint the crossbeams on the inside of the house with similar narratives recounting clan histories and myths. The shell-like abstract patterns found on the exterior roof beams and lower sections of the house all refer to the shell-money wealth of the clan and its chief. While the Iatmul make their ceremonial houses, discussed earlier (FIG. 31-1), by elaborate tying, lashing, and weaving of different-size posts, trees, saplings, and grasses, the Belau people make the main structure of the bai entirely of worked, fitted, joined, and pegged wooden elements, which allows them to assemble it easily.

**A PROTECTIVE FEMALE FIGURE** Although the bai was the domain of men, women figured prominently in the imagery that covered it. This reality reveals the important symbolic and social positions that women held in this culture (see "The Many Roles of Women in Oceania," page 929). A common element surmounting the main bai entrance was a simple, symmetrical wooden sculpture (on occasion, a painting) of a splayed female figure, known as Dilukai (FIGS. **31-8** and 31-7). Serving as a symbol of both protection and fertility, the Dilukai was also a moralistic reminder to women to be chaste. According to legend, Dilukai's brother, Bagei, was embarrassed by his sister's promiscuity and carved her image on the bai to shame her. The Dilukai figure demonstrates the ability of an image to control a group (here, women) while at the same time celebrating women's power.

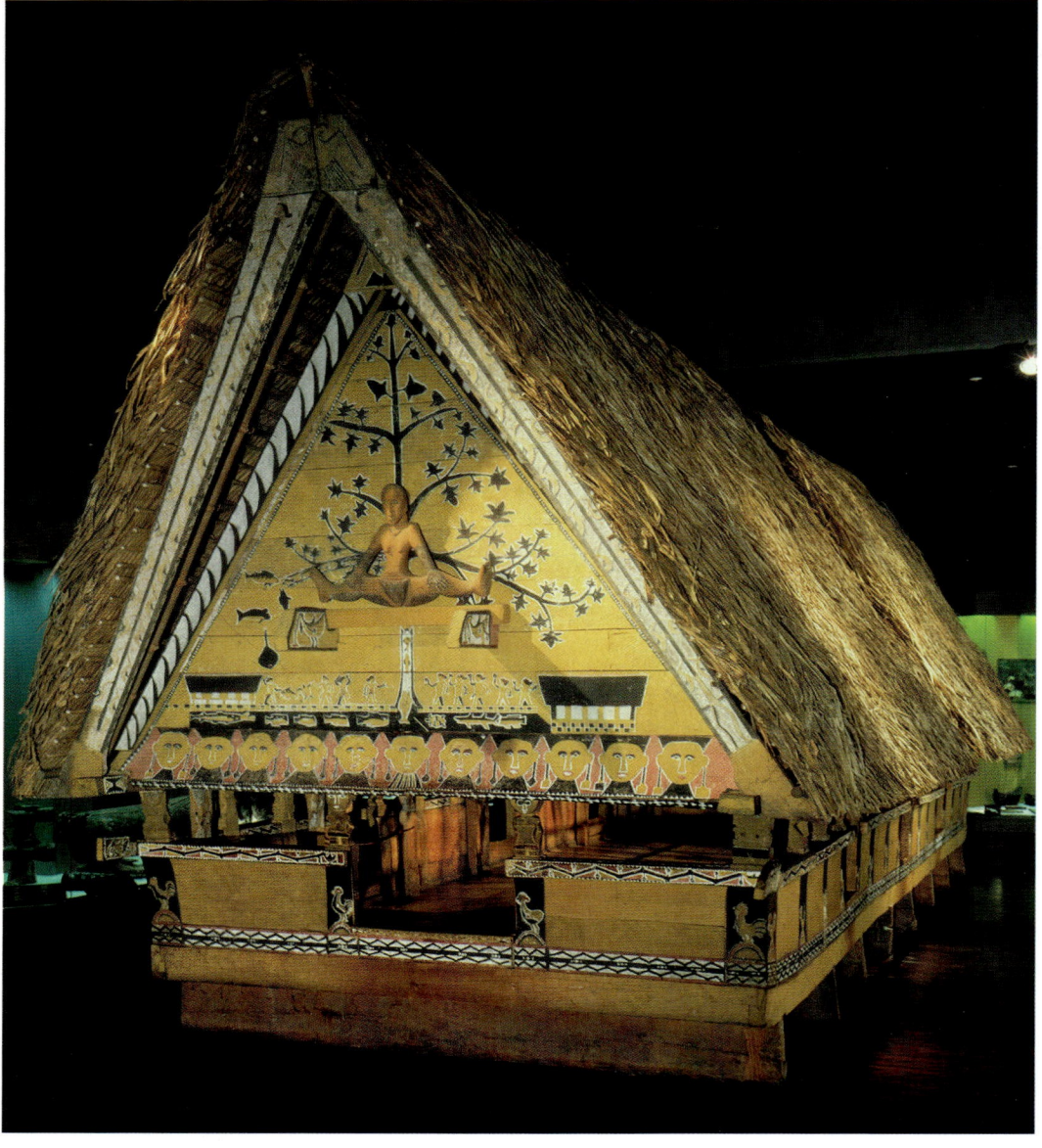

**31-7** Men's ceremonial house *(bai),* from Belau (Palau), Republic of Belau. Staatliche Museen zu Berlin Preussischer Kulturbesitz. Ethnologisches Museum.

## The Many Roles of Women in Oceania

Given the prominence of men's houses and the importance of male initiation in so many Oceanic societies, one might conclude that women are peripheral members of these cultures. Much of the extant material culture—ancestor masks, shields, clubs—seems to corroborate this. In reality, however, women play crucial roles in most Pacific cultures, although those roles may be less ostentatious or public than those of men. In addition to their significant contributions through exchange and ritual activities to the maintenance and perpetuation of the social network upon which the stability of village life depends, women are important producers of art.

For the most part, women's artistic production was historically restricted to forms such as barkcloth, weaving, and pottery. Throughout much of Polynesia, women produced barkcloth (see page 930), which was often dyed and stenciled, and sometimes even perfumed. Women in the Trobriand Islands continue to make brilliantly dyed skirts of shredded banana fiber that not only are aesthetically beautiful but also serve as a form of wealth and are presented symbolically during mortuary rituals. In some cultures in New Guinea, potters were primarily female.

In general, women were largely proscribed from working in hard materials (such as wood, stone, bone, or ivory) or using specialized tools. Further, in most Oceanic cultures, women were rarely allowed to produce images that had religious or spiritual powers or that conferred status on their users. Scholars investigating the role of the artist in Oceania have concluded that these restrictions were due to the perceived difference in innate power. Because women have the natural power to create and control life, male-dominated societies developed elaborate ritual practices that served to counteract this female power. By excluding women from participating in these rituals and denying them access to knowledge about specific practices, men derived a political authority that could be perpetuated. It is important to note,

however, that even in rituals or activities restricted to men, women often participate; for example, in the now-defunct Hevehe ceremonial cycle in Papua New Guinea (see pages 925–926), women helped to construct the hevehe masks, but feigned ignorance about these sacred objects, knowledge of which was limited to initiated men.

Pacific cultures often acknowledged women's innate power in the depictions of women in Oceanic art. For example, the splayed Dilukai female sculpture (FIG. 31-8) that appears regularly on Palauan bai (men's houses) celebrates women's procreative powers. Yet it simultaneously reinforces male authority by moralistically reminding women to limit their sexual activity. The Dilukai figure also confers protection upon visitors to the bai, another symbolic acknowledgment of female power. Similar concepts underlie the design of the Iatmul men's house (FIG. 31-1). Conceived as a giant female ancestor, the men's house incorporates women's natural power into the conceptualization of what is normally the most important architectural structure of an Iatmul village. In addition, the Iatmul associate entrance and departure from the men's house with death and rebirth, thereby reinforcing the primacy of fertility and the perception of the men's house as representing a woman's body.

Women were active participants in all aspects of Oceanic life, and their contributions in various arenas, such as art, are often overlooked. The general perception of Oceania as male dominated is due in part to the fact that the objects collected by visitors to the Pacific in earlier centuries tended to be those that suggest aggressive, warring societies. That the majority of these Western travelers (and collectors) were men and therefore had contact predominantly with men no doubt accounts for this pattern of collecting. Recent scholarship has done a great deal to rectify this misperception, thereby revealing the richness of social, artistic, and political activity in the Pacific.

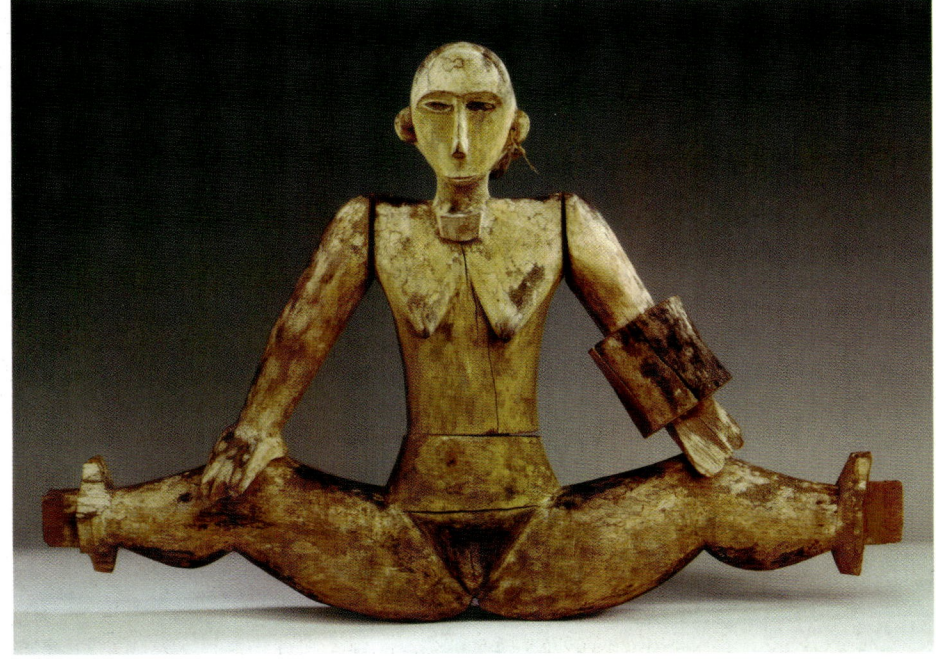

**31-8** Dilukai, from Belau (Palau). Wood, pigment, and fiber, 1′ 11⅝″ high. Linden Museum, Stuttgart.

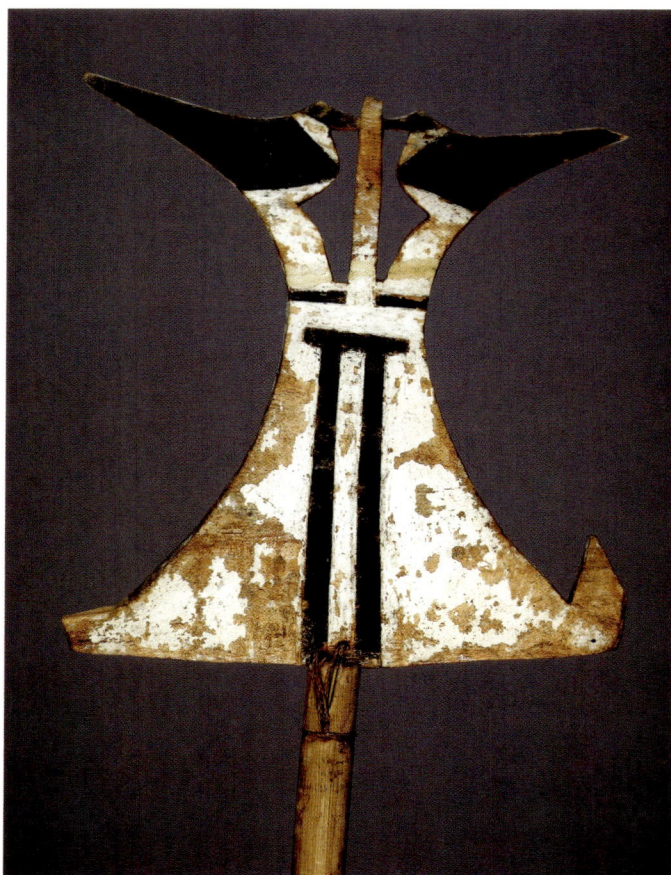

**31-9** Canoe prow ornament, from Chuuk, Caroline Islands. Wood and paint. British Museum, London. 🔊

**SEAFARING PROTECTION** Given the importance of seafaring and long-distance ocean travel in Micronesia, canoe building acquired a prominent position in Micronesian art and culture. This canoe prow ornament (FIG. 31-9), from Chuuk in the Caroline Islands, was carved by a master canoe builder from a single plank of wood. Fastened to a large, paddled war canoe, a prow ornament such as this was intended to provide protection on arduous or long voyages. Appropriately, the prow ornament design, while seemingly abstract, actually represents two symmetrically placed sea swallows—creatures capable of navigating long distances. The form may also represent a stylized human figure. That these canoe prow ornaments were not permanently attached to the canoe was a matter of function; when approaching another vessel, these ornaments were lowered to signal peaceful intentions, and they were removed from the canoe when not in use.

# POLYNESIA

**OF CHIEFS AND KINGS** Polynesia was one of the last areas in the world that humans colonized. It was not settled until about the end of the first millennium BCE in the west and the first millennium CE in the south. Its inhabitants brought complex sociopolitical and religious institutions with them. Whereas Melanesian societies are fairly egalitarian and advancement in rank is possible, Polynesian societies typically are highly stratified, with power determined by heredity. Indeed, rulers often trace their genealogies directly to the gods of creation. Most

Polynesian societies possess elaborate political organizations headed by chiefs and ritual specialists. By the 1800s, some Polynesian cultures (Hawaii and the Society Islands, for example) evolved into kingdoms. Because of this social hierarchy, much of Polynesian art is made for high-ranking persons of noble or high religious background and serves to reinforce their power and prestige. These objects, like their chiefly owners, are often invested with *mana,* or spiritual power.

**BEATEN CLOTH** Despite the prominence of art for high-ranking individuals, art in Polynesia is not solely the purview of rulers. For example, women throughout Polynesia traditionally produced decorated barkcloth using the inner bark of the paper mulberry tree *(Broussonetia papyrifera).* The finished product goes by various names in Polynesia, including *ahu* (Tahiti), *autea* (Cook Islands), *aute* (New Zealand), *kapa* (Hawaii), *hiapo* (Marquesas Islands), *siapo* (Samoa), and *masi* (Fiji). During the 19th century, when the production of barkcloth reached its zenith, *tapa* became a widely used reference word for such Polynesian barkcloth and still is today. Although tapa was utilized extensively for clothing and bedding, its uses extended beyond mere functionality. For example, in some Polynesian cultures, such as that of Tonga, large sheets (FIG. 31-10) were (and still are) produced for exchange. Barkcloth can also have a spiritual dimension and can serve to confer sanctity upon the object wrapped. Appropriately, the bodies of high-ranking deceased chiefs were traditionally wrapped in barkcloth.

The use and decoration of tapa have varied over the years. In the 19th century, tapa used for everyday clothing was normally unadorned, whereas tapa used for ceremonial or ritual purposes was dyed, painted, stenciled, and sometimes even perfumed. The designs applied to the tapa differed depending upon the particular island group producing it and the function of the cloth. The production process was complex and time-consuming (see "The Production of Barkcloth," page 931). Indeed, some Oceanic cultures, such as those of Tahiti and Hawaii, constructed buildings specifically for the beating stage in the production of barkcloth.

The production of tapa reached its peak in the early 19th century, partly as a result of the interest expressed by visiting Westerners, such as whalers and missionaries. By the late 19th century, the use of tapa for cloth had been abandoned throughout much of eastern Polynesia, although its use in rituals (for example, as a wrap for corpses of deceased chiefs or as a marker of tabooed sites) continued. Even today, tapa exchanges are still an integral part of funerals and marriage ceremonies, and there is a considerable tourist market for tapa as well.

## Rarotonga (Cook Islands)

Even though the Polynesians were skillful navigators, various island groups remained isolated from one another for centuries by the vast distances they would have had to cover in open outriggers. This allowed distinct regional styles to develop within a recognizable general Polynesian style. For example, deity images with multiple figures attached to their bodies surfaced in the material culture of Rarotonga and Mangaia in the Cook Islands and Rurutu in the Austral Islands. These carvings probably represented clan and district ancestors, revered for their protective and procreative powers. All such images refer ultimately to the creator deities the Polynesians revere for their central role in human fertility.

## The Production of Barkcloth

Tongan barkcloth provides an instructive example of the labor-intensive process of tapa production. At the time of early contact between Europeans and Polynesians in the late 18th and early 19th centuries, ranking women in Tonga (western Polynesia) made decorated barkcloth *(ngatu).* Today, women's organizations called *kautaha* produce it. The kautaha may have the honorary patronage of ranking women. In Tonga, men plant the paper mulberry tree and harvest it in two to three years. They cut the trees into about 10-foot lengths and allow them to dry for several days. Then the women strip off the outer bark and soak the inner bark in water to prepare it for further processing. They place these soaked inner bark strips over a wooden anvil and repeatedly strike them with a wooden beater until they spread out and flatten. Folding and layering the strips while beating them, a felting process, results in a wider piece of ngatu than the original strips. Afterward, the beaten barkcloth dries and bleaches in the sun.

The next stage of ngatu production involves the placement of the thin, beaten sheets over semicircular boards. The women then fasten embroidered design tablets *(kupesi)* of low-relief leaf, coconut leaf midribs, and string patterns to the boards. They transfer the patterns on the design tablets to the outer barkcloth by rubbing. Then the women fill in the lines and patterns by painting, covering the large white spaces with painted figures. The Tongans use brown, red, and black pigments derived from various types of bark, clay, fruits, and soot to create the colored patterns on ngatu. Sheets, rolls, and strips of ngatu are made for use on special occasions, such as weddings, funerals, and ceremonial presentations for ranking persons.

A traditionally patterned ngatu (FIG. 31-10) made in 1967 for the coronation of King Tupou IV of Tonga clearly shows the richness of pattern, subtlety of theme, and variation of geometric forms that characterize Tongan royal barkcloths. One of the women barkcloth specialists—MELE SITANI, who made this presentation piece—kneels in the middle of the ngatu covered in triangular patterns known as *manulua.* This pattern is made from the intersection of three or four triangular points. *Manulua* means "two birds," and the design gives the illusion of two birds flying together. The motif symbolizes chiefly status derived from both parents.

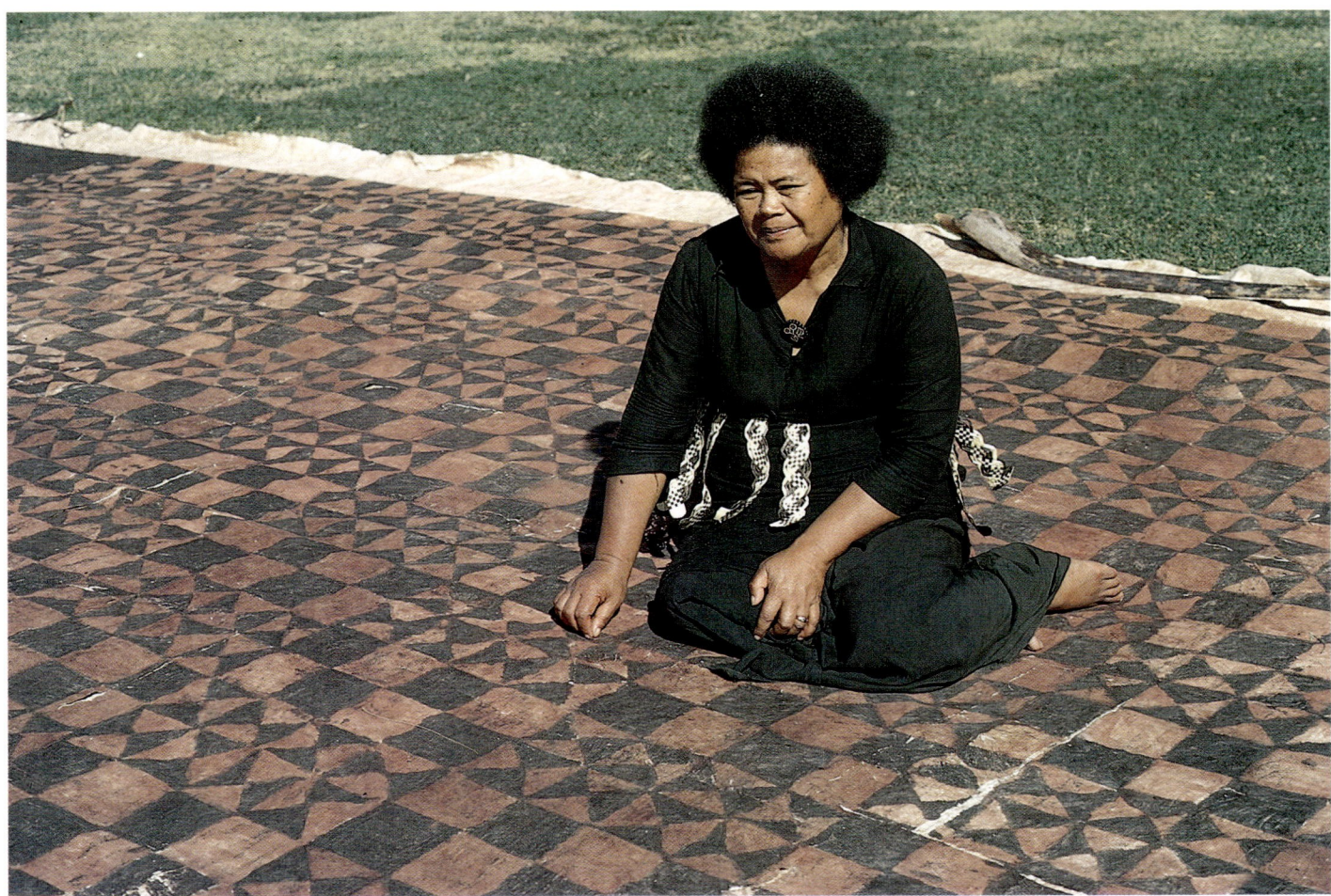

**31-10** MELE SITANI, decorated barkcloth *(ngatu)* with two-bird *(manulua)* designs, Tonga, 1967.

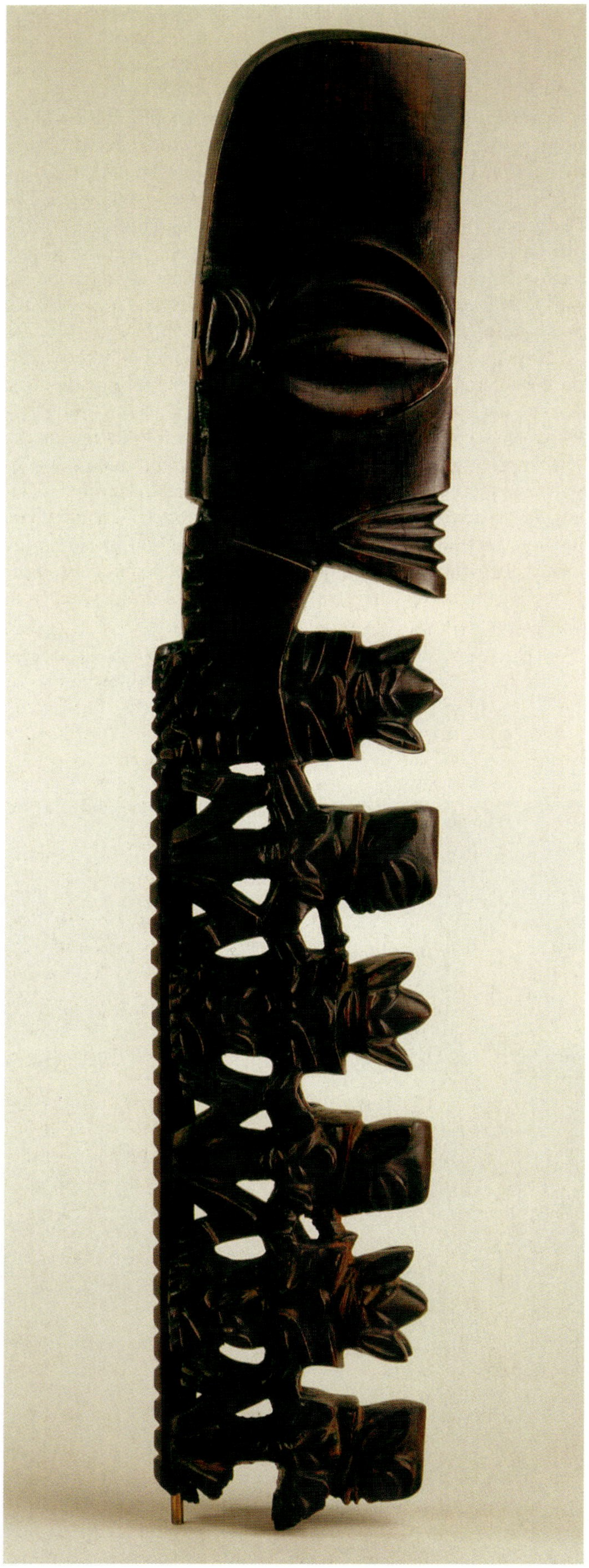

**A GOD IN BARKCLOTH** The central Polynesian island residents of Rarotonga used various types of carved deity figures well into the early decades of the 19th century, when Christians converted the islanders and destroyed their deities as part of the conversion process. These included carved wooden fishermen's gods, large naturalistic deity images, and at least three types of staff gods (also called district gods), some more than 20 feet long. One of the best-preserved examples (FIG. **31-11**) is close to 4 feet high and consists of a long piece of wood, carved at both the top and bottom (not visible in illustration). The long central section is wrapped with decorated barkcloth. The carving on the top depicts a figure with smaller alternating female and male figures projecting from the front of his body. The exact meanings of the primary and secondary figures are unknown and forever lost due to the abrupt conversion to Christianity and the near total destruction of Rarotongan religious imagery in the early 19th century. Some scholars have suggested that the protruding figures were intended to represent familial descent and genealogy. Alternatively, the procreative symbolism and multiple small figures found on this staff god may represent a generative deity creating minor deities from his own body, a trait found frequently in central Polynesian art and religion.

## Marquesas Islands

**ORNAMENTAL PROTECTION** Although Marquesan chiefs trace their right to rule genealogically, the political system before European contact allowed for the acquisition of power by force. As a result, warfare was widespread through the late 19th century. Among the items produced by Marquesan artists were ornaments (FIG. **31-12**) that often adorned the hair of warriors. The hollow, cylindrical bone or ivory ornaments (*ivi p'o*) functioned as protective amulets and were worn until the death of a kinsman was avenged. The ornaments are in the form of *tiki*—three-dimensional carvings of exalted, deified ancestor figures. The style of the tiki—large, rounded eyes and wide mouths—is typically Marquesan.

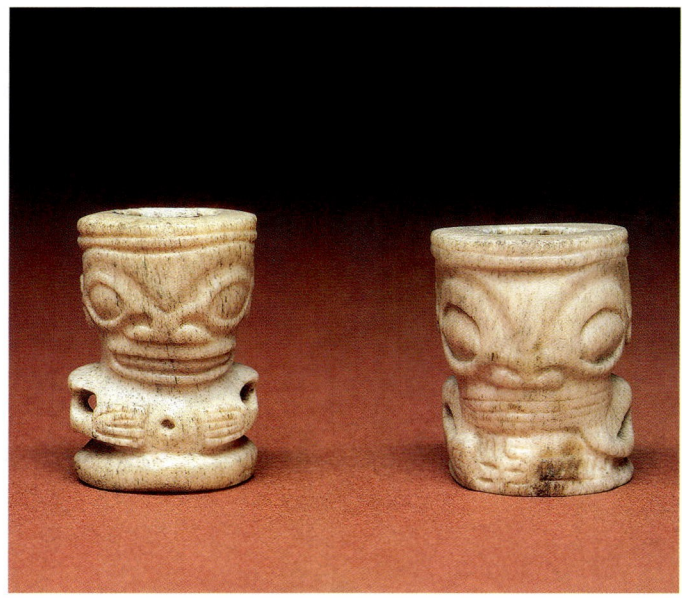

**31-11** Head of a staff god, from Rarotonga, Cook Islands, Polynesia, late 18th–early 19th century. Wood. Robert and Lisa Sainsbury Collection, University of East Anglia, Norwich. Photo: James Austin.

**31-12** Ornaments from the Marquesas Islands, collected in the 1870s. Bone, $1\frac{1}{2}''$ high × 1″ wide (*left*), $1\frac{2}{5}''$ high × 1″ wide (*right*). University of Pennsylvania, Philadelphia.

### More Than Skin Deep
#### Tattoo in Polynesia

Throughout Oceanic cultures, the body was a particularly important site for the representation of cultural and personal identity. In addition to the wearing of clothing and ornaments, this representation most often took the form of tattoo. Although tattooing was common among Micronesian cultures, it has become more closely associated with Polynesia due to the extensiveness of the practice there. Indeed, the English term *tattoo* is Polynesian in origin, related to the Tahitian, Samoan, and Tongan word *tatau* or *tatu*. In New Zealand, where tattooing was especially pervasive, the markings were called *moko*.

Within Polynesian cultures, tattoo reached its zenith in the highly stratified societies—New Zealand, the Marquesas Islands, Tahiti, Tonga, Samoa, and Hawaii. Both sexes were tattooed; in general, men were more extensively tattooed than women, and the location of tattoos on the body differed. For instance, in New Zealand, the face and buttocks were the primary areas of male tattoo, whereas tattoos appeared on the lips and chin of women.

Historically, tattooing served a variety of functions in Polynesia. It indicated status; the quantity and quality of tattoos were often linked to rank. In the Marquesas Islands, for example, men of high status were completely tattooed. Further, certain patterns could be applied only to ranking individuals. However, the acquisition of tattoos was not restricted to the chiefly class. Commoners had tattoos, generally on a less extensive scale than higher-ranking individuals. And some people were tattooed for undesirable reasons; for identification purposes, slaves were tattooed on their foreheads in Hawaii and on their backs in New Zealand. There are also accounts of defeated warriors being tattooed. In some Polynesian societies, tattoos identified clan or familial connections. Tattoos could also serve a protective function by in essence wrapping the body in a spiritual armor. And on occasion, tattoos marked significant events such as military victories or rites of passage; in Hawaii, for example, the tongue was sometimes tattooed as a sign of grief. In this instance, the pain endured by the tattooed person was a sign of respect and commemoration for a deceased individual. Of course, decoration was a prominent reason for tattoo.

Throughout much of Polynesia, tattoos were applied by priests who were specially trained in the art form. The importance of tattooing in these Oceanic societies was further indicated by the fact that this practice was accompanied by rituals, chants, or ceremonies and often took place in a structure dedicated to tattooing.

The general technique for tattooing involved the introduction of black, carbon-based pigment under the skin with the use of a bird-bone tattooing comb or chisel and a mallet. In New Zealand, where moko developed to an extremely sophisticated level, a distinctive technique emerged for tattooing the face. In a manner similar to Maori wood carving, a serrated chisel created a groove in the skin. A pigment was then introduced into this groove, thereby producing a colored line.

Polynesian tattoo designs were predominantly geometric, and affinities with other forms of Polynesian art are clearly evident. For example, the curvilinear patterns that predominate in Maori facial moko are reminiscent of the patterns found on *poupou*, decorated wall panels in Maori meetinghouses (FIG. 31-16). Depending on their specific purpose, many tattoos could be "read" or deciphered. For facial tattoos, the Maori generally divided the face into four major, symmetrical zones: the left and right forehead down to the eyes, the left lower face, and the right lower face. The right-hand side conveyed information on the father's rank, tribal affiliations, and social position, while the left-hand side provided matrilineal information. Smaller secondary facial zones provided information about the tattooed individual's profession and position in society. The schematic drawing of the moko of Te Pehi Kupe (see FIG. Intro-19) is an example of Maori facial tattoo. Te Pehi Kupe was the paramount chief of the Ngato Toa tribe in the early 19th century and died in 1830. His lineage is indicated by the upward and downward *koru* (unrolled spirals) in the middle of his forehead, which connote his descent from two paramount tribes. The small design in the center of his forehead documents the extent of his domain—north, south, east, and west. The five double koru in front of his left ear indicate that the supreme chief (the highest rank in Maori society) was part of his matrilineal line. The designs on his lower jaw and the anchor-shaped koru nearby reveal that Te Pehi Kupe was not only a master carver, but descended from master carvers as well.

The viability of tattooing was severely impacted by the arrival of Europeans, particularly missionaries, who worked to eradicate the practice. This, in conjunction with changing social systems, led to the abandonment of tattooing in Polynesia by the later 19th century.

---

**FACE-TO-FACE** Another important art form for Marquesan warriors during the 19th century was tattoo, which, like the hair ornaments, protected the individual, serving in essence as a form of spiritual armor. Body decoration in general is among the most pervasive art forms found throughout Oceania. Polynesians developed the painful but prestigious art of tattoo more fully than many other Oceanic peoples (see "More Than Skin Deep: Tattoo in Polynesia," above), although tattooing was also common in Micronesia. In Polynesia, with its hierarchical social structure, nobles and warriors in particular accumulated various tattoo patterns over the years to increase their status, mana, and personal beauty. Largely as a result of missionary pressure in the 19th century, tattooing virtually disappeared in many Oceanic societies. In some cultures, tattooing has been revived as an expression of cultural pride.

An early-19th-century engraving (FIG. 31-13) provides an example of a Marquesan warrior from Nukahiva Island covered with elaborate tattoo patterns. The warrior holds a large wooden war club over his right shoulder and carries a decorated water gourd in his left hand. The various tattoo patterns marking his entire body seem to subdivide his body parts into zones on both sides of a line down the center. Some tattoos accentuate joint areas, whereas others separate muscle masses into horizontal and vertical geometric shapes. The warrior also covered his face, hands, and feet with tattoos.

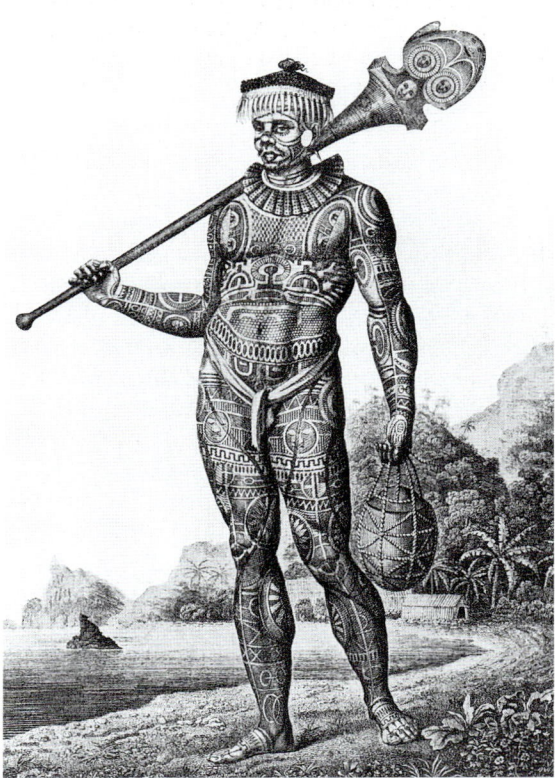

**31-13** Tattooed warrior with war club, Nukahiva, Marquesas Islands, 19th century. Engraving.

## Hawaii

The Hawaiians developed the most highly stratified social structure in the Pacific. By 1795, the chief Kamehameha unified the major islands of the Hawaiian archipelago and ascended to the pinnacle of power as King Kamehameha I. This kingdom did not

endure; as a result of Western contact (with navigators, whalers, and missionaries), Hawaii soon came under American control. The U.S. government annexed Hawaii as a territory in 1898 and eventually conferred statehood on the island group in 1959.

**CLOAKED IN MAJESTY** Because perpetuation of the social structure was crucial to social stability, most of the material culture produced (before American control) in Hawaii was intended to visualize and reinforce the hierarchy. Chiefly regalia was a prominent part of artistic production. For example, elegant feather cloaks (*'ahu 'ula*) such as this early 19th-century example (FIG. **31-14**) were created for chiefly men of high rank. Every aspect of the 'ahu'ula reflected the status of its wearer. The materials were exceedingly precious, particularly the red and yellow feathers from the *'i 'iwi*, *'apapane*, *'o 'o*, and *mamo* birds. Some of these birds yielded only six or seven suitable feathers, and given that a full-length cloak could require up to 500,000 feathers, the resources and labor required to produce a cloak were extraordinary. The cloak also linked its owner to the gods; the sennit (plaited fiber or cord) base to which the feathers were attached was associated throughout Polynesia with deities. Not only did these cloaks confer the protection of the gods on their wearers, their dense fiber base and feather matting also provided physical protection. Our example originally belonged to King Kamehameha III, who gave it to Commodore Lawrence Kearny of the U.S. frigate *Constellation* in 1843 in gratitude for the Commodore's assistance during a temporary occupation of Hawaii.

**A DEFIANT WAR GOD** The gods were a pervasive presence in Hawaiian society and were part of every person's life, regardless of status. Chiefs in particular invoked them regularly and publicized their own genealogical links to the gods to reinforce their right to rule. One of the more prominent Hawaiian gods was Kuka'ilimoku, the war god. As chiefs in the prekingdom years struggled to maintain and expand their control, warfare was endemic, hence Kuka'ilimoku's importance. Indeed, Kuka'ilimoku served as Kamehameha I's special tutelary deity, and the Kuka'ilimoku sculpture we

**31-14** Feather cloak (*'ahu'ula*), from Hawaii, early 19th century. Red *'i'iwi*, yellow *'o'o*, and black feathers, *olona* cordage and netting, $4' 8\frac{1}{3}'' \times 8'$. Bishop Pauahi Museum, Honolulu.

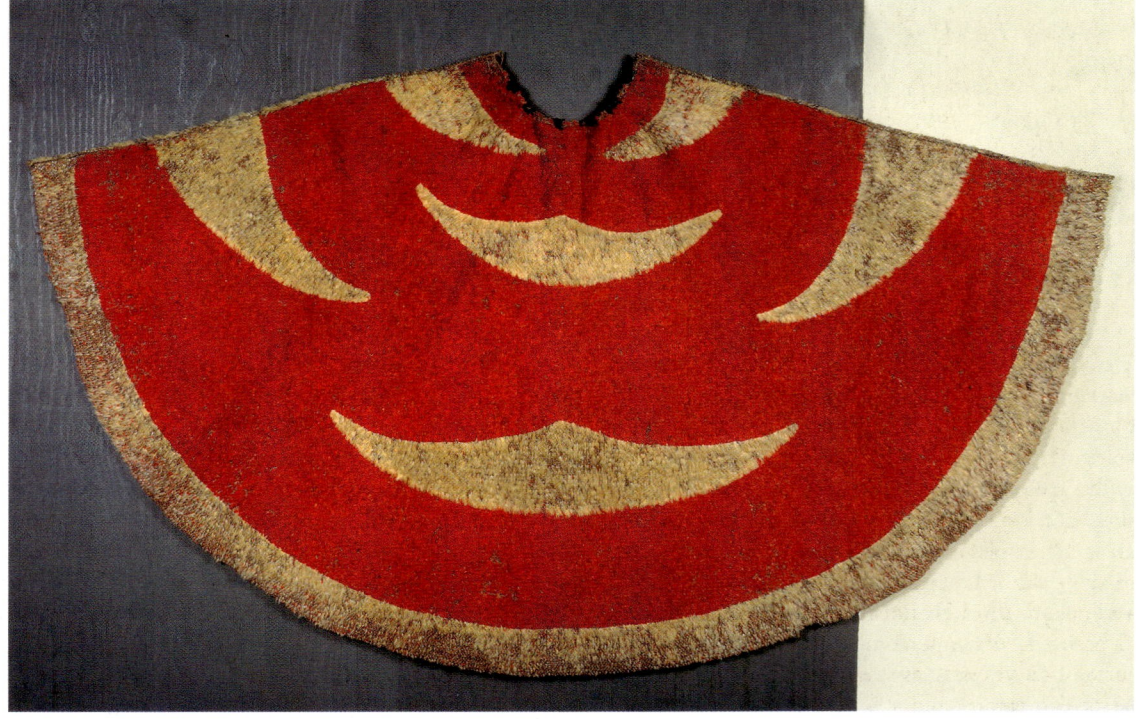

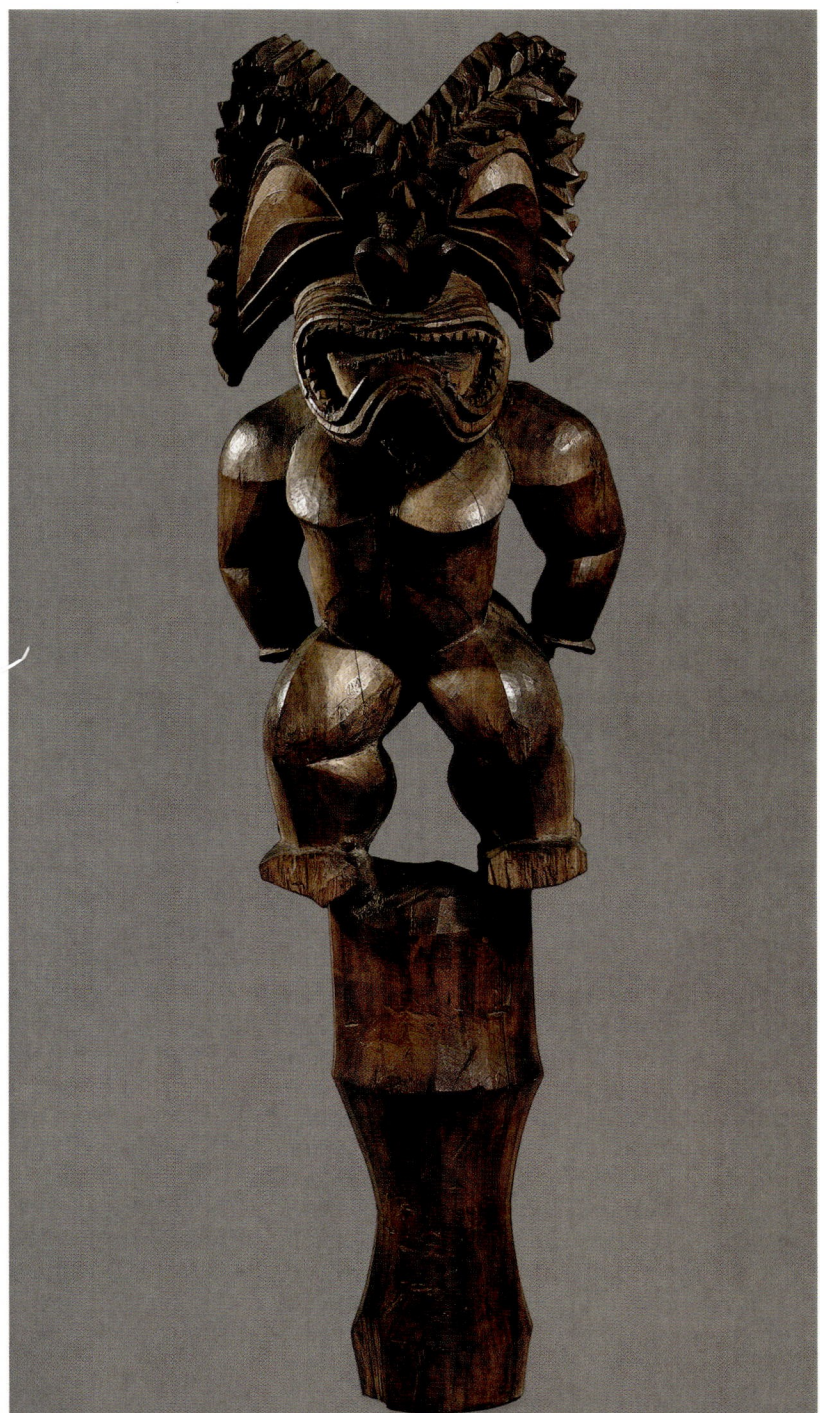

illustrate (FIG. **31-15**) was placed in a *heiau* (temple) on the island of Hawaii, where Kamehameha I originally ruled before expanding his authority to the entire Hawaiian chain. This late-18th- or early-19th-century Hawaiian wooden temple image, over four feet tall, confronts its audience with a ferocious expression. This war god's head dominates, comprising nearly a third of his entire body. His enlarged, angled eyes and wide-open figure-eight-shaped mouth, with its rows of teeth, convey aggression and defiance. His muscular body appears to stand slightly flexed, as if ready to act. The artist realized this Hawaiian war god's overall athleticism through the full-volumed, faceted treatment of his arms, legs, and the pectoral area of the chest. In addition to sculptures of deities such as this, Hawaiians placed smaller versions of lesser deities and ancestral images in the heiau. Differing styles

surface in the various islands of the Hawaiian chain, but the sculptured figures share a tendency toward athleticism and expressive defiance.

### The Maori (New Zealand)

**SURROUNDED BY ANCESTORS** The Maori of New Zealand (Aotearoa) share many cultural practices with other Polynesian societies. As in other cultures, ancestors and lineage play an important role in New Zealand. The Maori meetinghouse demonstrates the primacy of ancestral connections. The Maori conceptualize the entire building as the body of an ancestor — the central beam across the roof is the spine, the rafters are ribs, and the barge boards (the angled boards that outline the house

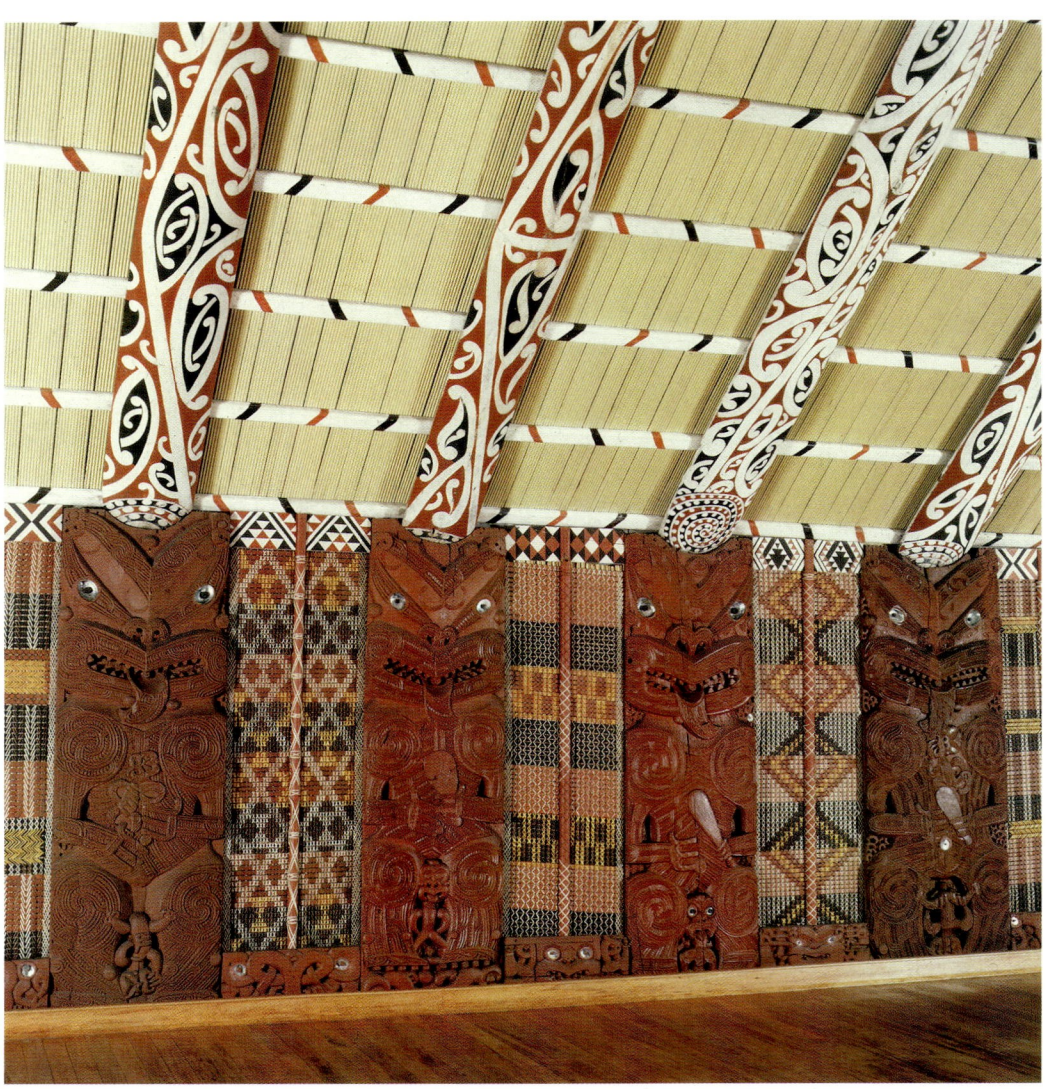

31-16 Interior view of the decorated meetinghouse Mataatua, built by Wepiha Apanui of Ngati Awa in 1874.

gables) in front represent arms. On the inside of the meetinghouse (FIG. 31-16), ancestors constitute a very potent presence through their appearance on *poupou* (the relief panels along the walls). These panels depict specific ancestors and are often carved in a style that has come to characterize Maori art. Each ancestor appears frontally with hands across the stomach. Elaborate curvilinear patterns cover the entire poupou and may represent tattoos. Virtually every surface of the meetinghouse is decorated. The spaces between the poupou are filled with *tukutuku* (stitched lattice panels). Above, intricate painted shapes cover the rafters. In the center of the meetinghouse stand *pou tokomanawa*, sculptures of ancestors that support the building's ridge poles (not visible in our illustration). The composite presence of all of these ancestral images and the energy of the persistent patterning creates a charged space in which collective action can be taken.

## Rapa Nui (Easter Island)

**SILENT STONE SENTINELS** Much of the Oceanic art discussed in this chapter is biodegradable, designed for short-term use, and/or small in scale. The *moai*—stone sculptures (FIG. 31-17) found on the island of Rapa Nui (Easter Island)—provide

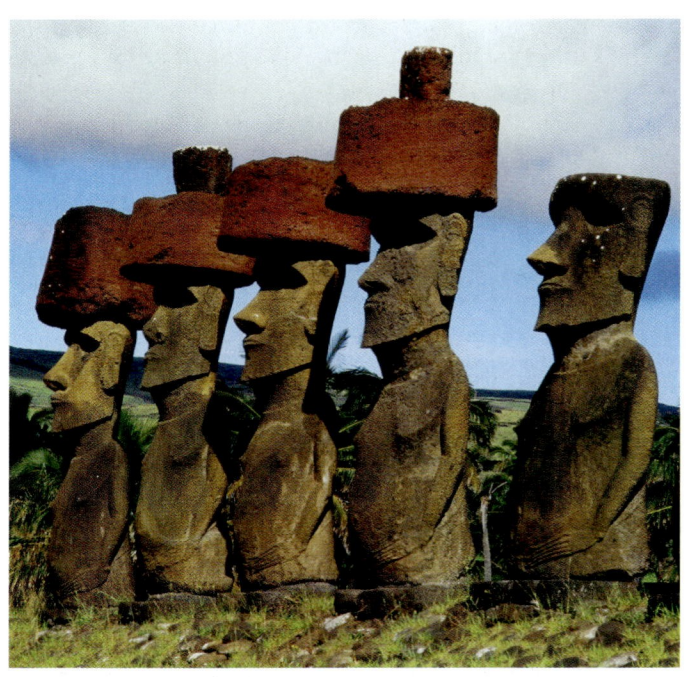

**31-17** Statues *(moai)*, Anakena, Rapa Nui (Easter Island), 10th–12th century. Stone.

a contrast. Other Polynesian cultures produced large-scale, permanent artworks; the moai, however, are among the best known. These monumental sculptures, some soaring to heights of up to 40 feet, stand as silent sentinels on stone platforms *(ahu);* these platforms marked burial sites or were used for religious ceremonies. Most of the moai consist of huge, blocky figures with fairly planar facial features—large, staring eyes, strong jaws, straight noses with carefully articulated nostrils, and elongated earlobes. A number of the moai have *pukao*—small red scoria cylinders that serve as a sort of topknot or hat—placed on their heads.

Although debate continues, many scholars believe that these moai depict ancestral chiefs. These commemorative images were commissioned by lineage heads or their sons. These statues, however, are not portraits in the Western sense. Rather, they are sacred objects due to their ability to accommodate spirits or gods. Moai thus mediate between chiefs and gods, and between the natural and cosmic worlds.

Archaeological surveys have documented close to 900 moai, most of which were quarried at one volcanic site on Rapa Nui. Accordingly, most of the moai are carved of soft volcanic tuff; red scoria, basalt, and trachyte were used for a small number of the sculptures. After quarrying, the statues were dragged to the particular ahu site, and positioned vertically. Given the extraordinary size of these monoliths, their production and placement serve as testaments to the achievements of Rapa Nui culture. Each statue weighs up to 100 tons; according to one scholar, it would have taken 30 men one year to carve a moai, 90 men two months to move it from the quarry, and 90 men three months to position it vertically on the platform.

## AUSTRALIA

Over the past 40,000 years, the Aboriginal peoples of Australia spread out over the entire continent and adapted to a variety of ecological conditions, ranging from those of tropical and subtropical areas in the north to desert regions in the continent's interior and more temperate locales in the south. European explorers reaching the region in the late 18th and early 19th centuries found that the Aborigines had a special relationship with the land they lived on, developed primarily by hunting and gathering. Because of this deep-rooted connection with the environment, the Aboriginal way of thinking and their perception of the world center on a concept known as the Dreamings, ancestral beings whose spirits pervade the present. All Aborigines identify certain Dreamings as totemic ancestors, and those who share the same Dreamings are socially linked. The spiritual domain that the Dreamings occupy is known as Dreamtime, which is both a physical space within which the ancestral beings moved in creating the landscape and a psychic space that provides Aborigines with cultural, religious, and moral direction. Because of the importance of Dreamings to all aspects of Aboriginal life, art in Australia symbolically links Aborigines with these ancestral spirits. Mythological narratives are prominent among the Aborigines; they recite creation myths in concert with songs and dances, and many art forms—body painting, carved figures, sacred objects, decorated stones, and rock and bark painting—serve as essential props in these dramatic re-creations. Unlike the large-scale, permanent art found in Rapa Nui, most Aboriginal art is relatively small and portable. As hunters and gatherers in difficult terrain, most Aborigines were nomadic, rendering monumental art impractical.

### Aboriginal Art (Arnhem Land)

**IMAGES OF DREAMINGS** Bark painting became a mainstay of Aboriginal art. Bark was widely available, as well as portable and lightweight. Dreamings, mythic narratives (often tracing the movement of various ancestral spirits through the landscape), and sacred places were common subjects for paintings. Ancestral spirits were pervasive in the lives of the Aborigines, and these paintings served to give visual form to that presence. Traditionally, an Aborigine could only depict a Dreaming with which he was connected. Thus, Aboriginal designs are "owned" by specific lineages, clans, or regional groups. A bark painting from 1913 (FIG. **31-18**) depicts a Dreaming known as Auuenau and comes from an area called Arnhem Land in northern Australia. The elongated figure is

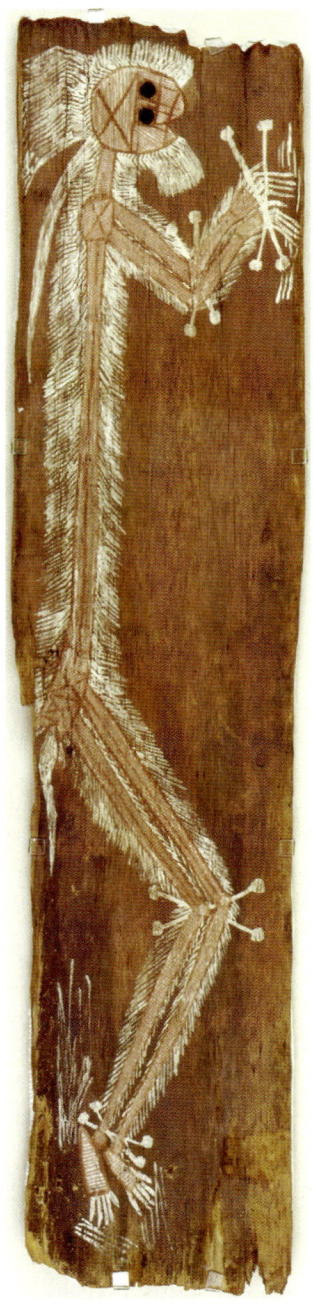

**31-18** Auuenau, from Western Arnhem Land, Australia, 1913. Ochre on bark, 4′ 10$\frac{2}{3}$″ × 1′ 1″. South Australian Museum, Adelaide.

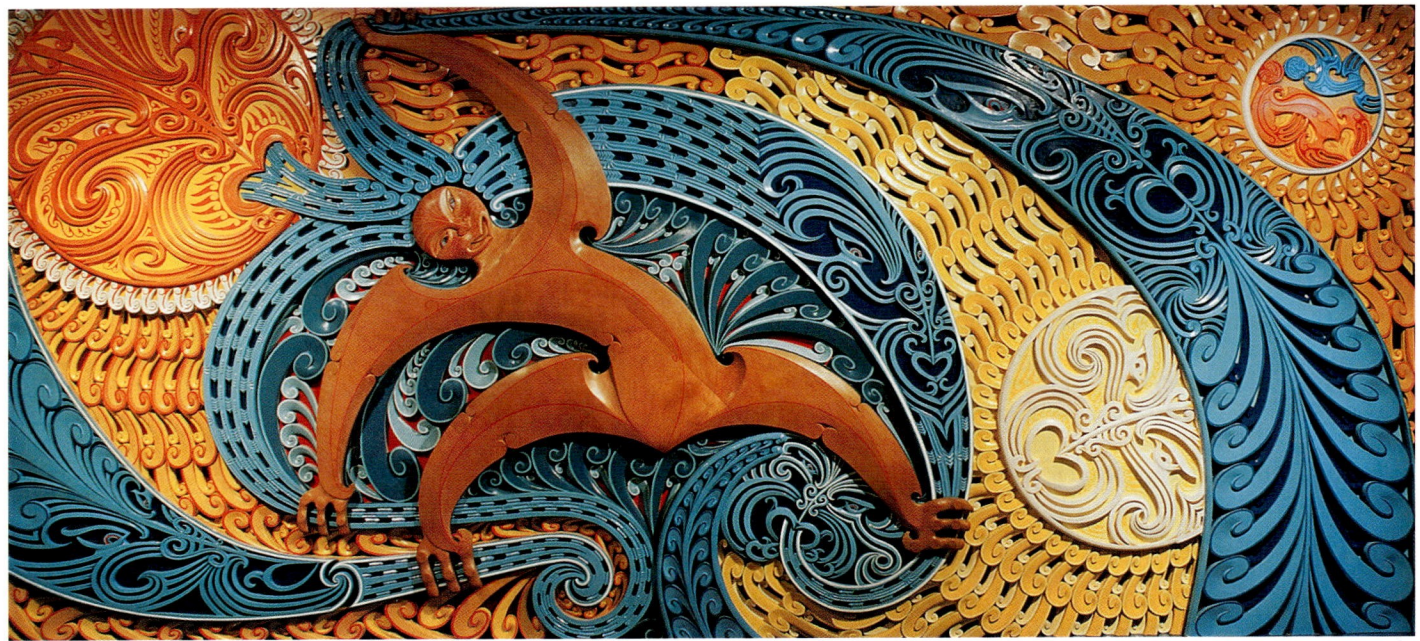

**31-19** CLIFF WHITING (TE WHANAU-A-APANUI), *Tawhiri-Matea (God of the Winds)*, Maori, 1984. Oil on wood and fiberboard, approx. 6' 4³⁄₈" × 11' 10³⁄₄". Collection of the Meteorological Service of New Zealand, Wellington.

represented in a style referred to as "X-ray," which is used to depict both animal and human forms. In this style, the artist simultaneously depicts the subject's interior (internal organs) and exterior. The painting possesses a fluid and dynamic quality, with the X-ray-like figure clearly defined against a solid background.

## OCEANIC ART TODAY

Many of the traditional native arts of Oceania, particularly in Polynesia's central and peripheral islands, are not now practiced, for they no longer have critical roles in ensuring cultural continuity and survival, or they were forcibly suppressed by Westerners, especially missionaries. Yet, in many places, with the stimulus of cosmopolitan contacts in a shrinking world, these arts have been revitalized and flourish energetically. New, confident cultural awareness has led native artists to assert their inherited values with pride and to express them in a resurgence of traditional arts, such as weaving, painting, tattooing, and carving.

**MAORI CULTURAL RENEWAL**  One example that represents the many cases of cultural renewal in native Oceanic art is the vigorously productive school of New Zealand artists who draw on their Maori heritage for formal and iconographic inspiration. The historic Maori woodcarving craft (FIG. 31-16) brilliantly reemerges in what the artist CLIFF WHITING (TE WHANAU-A-APANUI) calls a "carved mural" (FIG. **31-19**). Whiting's *Tawhiri-Matea (God of the Winds)* is a masterpiece of woodcrafting designed for the very modern environment of an exhibition gallery. The artist suggested the wind turbulence with the restless curvature of the main motif and its myriad of serrated edges. The 1984 mural depicts events in the Maori creation myth. The central figure, Tawhiri-Matea, god of the winds, wrestles to control *te whanau puhi*, the children of the four winds, seen as

blue spiral forms. Ra, the sun, energizes the scene from the top left, complemented by Marama, the moon, in the opposite corner. The top right image refers to the primal separation of Ranginui, the Sky Father, and Papatuanuku, the Earth Mother. Spiral koru motifs symbolizing growth and energy flow through the composition. Blue waves and green fronds around Tawhiri suggest his brothers Tangaroa and Tane, gods of the sea and forest.

The artist is securely at home with the native tradition of form and technique, as well as with the worldwide aesthetic of modernist design. Out of the seamless fabric made by uniting both, he feels something new can develop that loses nothing of the power of the old. Whiting champions not only the renewal of Maori cultural life and its continuity in art but also the education of the young in the values that made that culture great—values they are asked to perpetuate. The salvation of their native identity will depend on their success in making the Maori culture once again their own.

## CONCLUSION

Since the initial population of the Pacific islands tens of thousands of years ago, flourishing cultures have emerged in the areas known as Melanesia, Polynesia, and Micronesia, and on the continent of Australia. Because of the wide chronological span during which the Pacific was populated and the diverse environments of the different island groups, Oceanic cultures vary greatly. The art produced by Pacific islanders ranges from large architectural structures and permanent sculptures to performances and temporary body art. Extensive Euroamerican colonization throughout the Pacific between the 18th and 20th centuries resulted in the abandonment of numerous traditional practices. In recent years, many Pacific artists have revived indigenous art forms, creating new artistic products that combine the old with the contemporary.

**1800**

- Captain James Cook and other European explorers (re)discover Polynesia, late 18th century
- Kamehameha I unifies Hawaiian Islands and becomes king, 1795
- Overthrow of kapu system (traditional Hawaiian religious system), 1819
- Treaty of Waitangi (New Zealand/Aotearoa), 1840

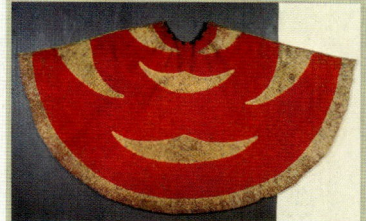

1 'Ahu'ula (feather cloak), Hawaii, early 19th century

**1850**

- Christianity spreads throughout Polynesia by mid-1850s
- European colonization of most of Oceania complete, 1880s–1920
- Overthrow of Hawaiian monarchy, 1893

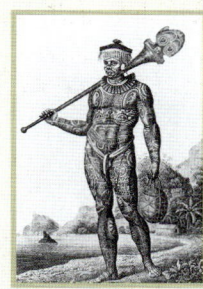

2 Tattooed Marquesan warrior with war club, engraving, 19th century

**1900**

- Reign of Queen Salote Tupou III of Tonga, 1918–1965

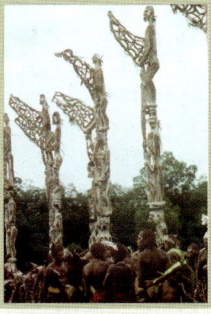

3 Bisj poles, New Guinea, early–mid-20th century

**1950**

- U.S. statehood conferred on Hawaii, 1959
- Independence for most Oceanic peoples, 1960s–1970s

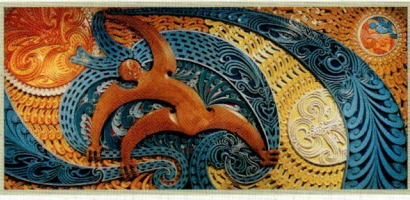

4 Cliff Whiting (Te Whanau-A-Apanui), *Tawhiri-Matea (God of the Winds)*, 1984

**2000**

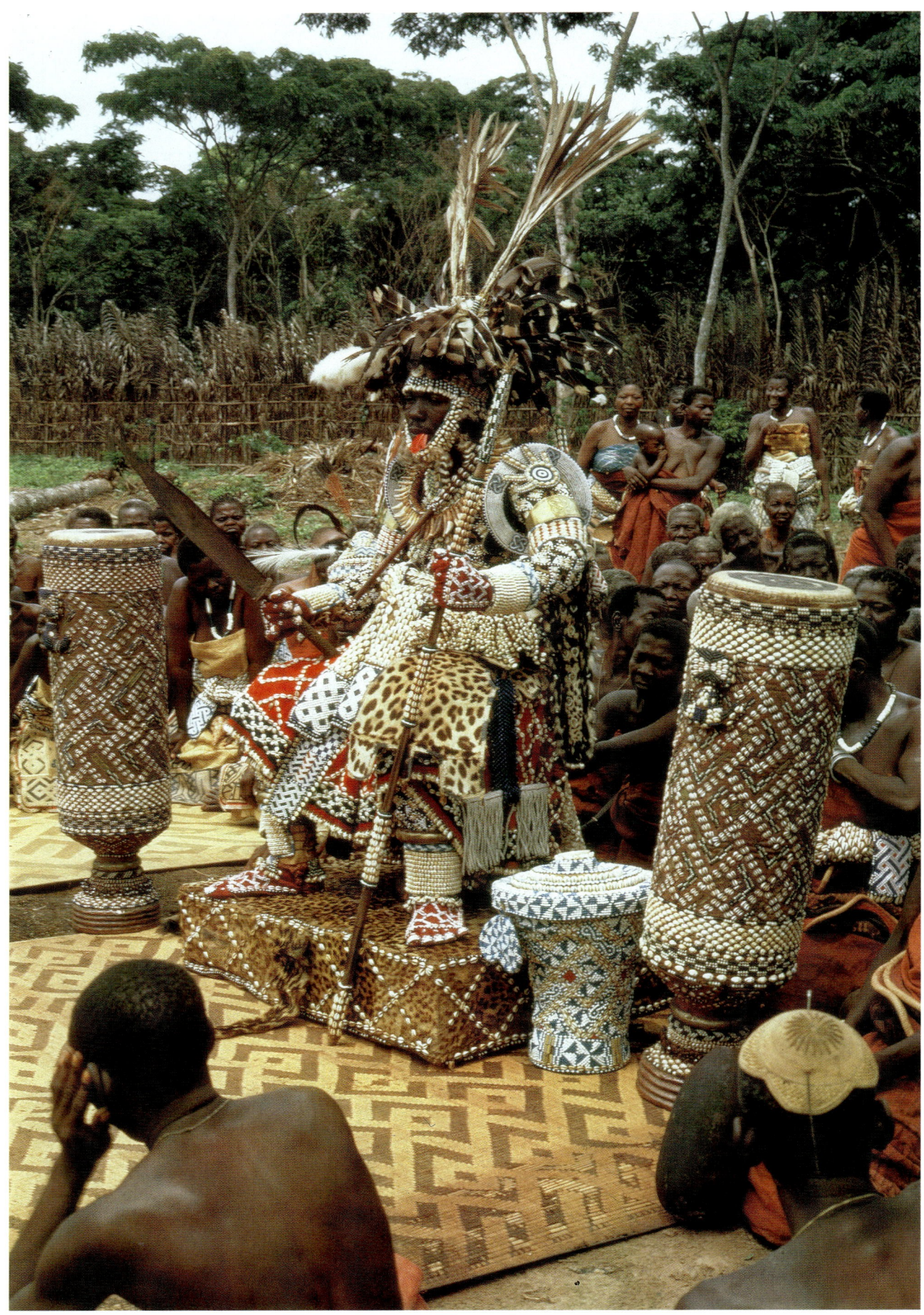

Kuba King Kot a-Mbweeky III during a display for photographer and filmmaker Eliot Elisofon in early 1970, Mushenge, Democratic Republic of Congo.

# 32

# TRADITIONALISM AND INTERNATIONALISM

## 19TH- AND 20TH-CENTURY AFRICAN ARTS

This chapter surveys the arts of the vast African continent (MAP 32-1) from about 1800 to the present. As in Chapter 15, the organizing principle is chronology. A generation ago African art was often presented as if it had no history, but scholars now recognize that every art form, like every other kind of object or being, has a history. The fact that researchers do not always know the history of African artworks tells more about the people constructing African history than it reveals about the African people who lived it. Our approach to writing the history of African art is to combine information derived from archaeology and field research in Africa (mainly interviews with local people) on the use, function, and meaning of art objects with interpretive strategies devised for the most part by outsiders.

## THE 19TH CENTURY

### San Art (South Africa)

**HISTORICAL ROCK PAINTINGS** Rock paintings are among the most ancient arts of Africa (see FIGS. 1-2 and 15-1). Yet the tradition also continued well into the historical period. The latest examples were completed as recently as the 19th century, and some of these depict the presence of Europeans. Many examples have been found in South Africa. The one we illustrate (FIG. 32-1), originally about eight feet long but now in fragments, is from near the source of the Mzimkhulu River at Bamboo Mountain and dates to the mid-19th century. Scholars attribute these paintings to the San peoples. San compositions often depict several game animals hunted for food, as well as others, such as the eland (FIG. 32-1, *left*), considered effective in rainmaking and ancestor rituals. By the early to mid-19th century, the increasing development of colonial ranches and the settlements of African agriculturists had greatly impacted the lifestyle and movement patterns of San hunters and gatherers. The San were

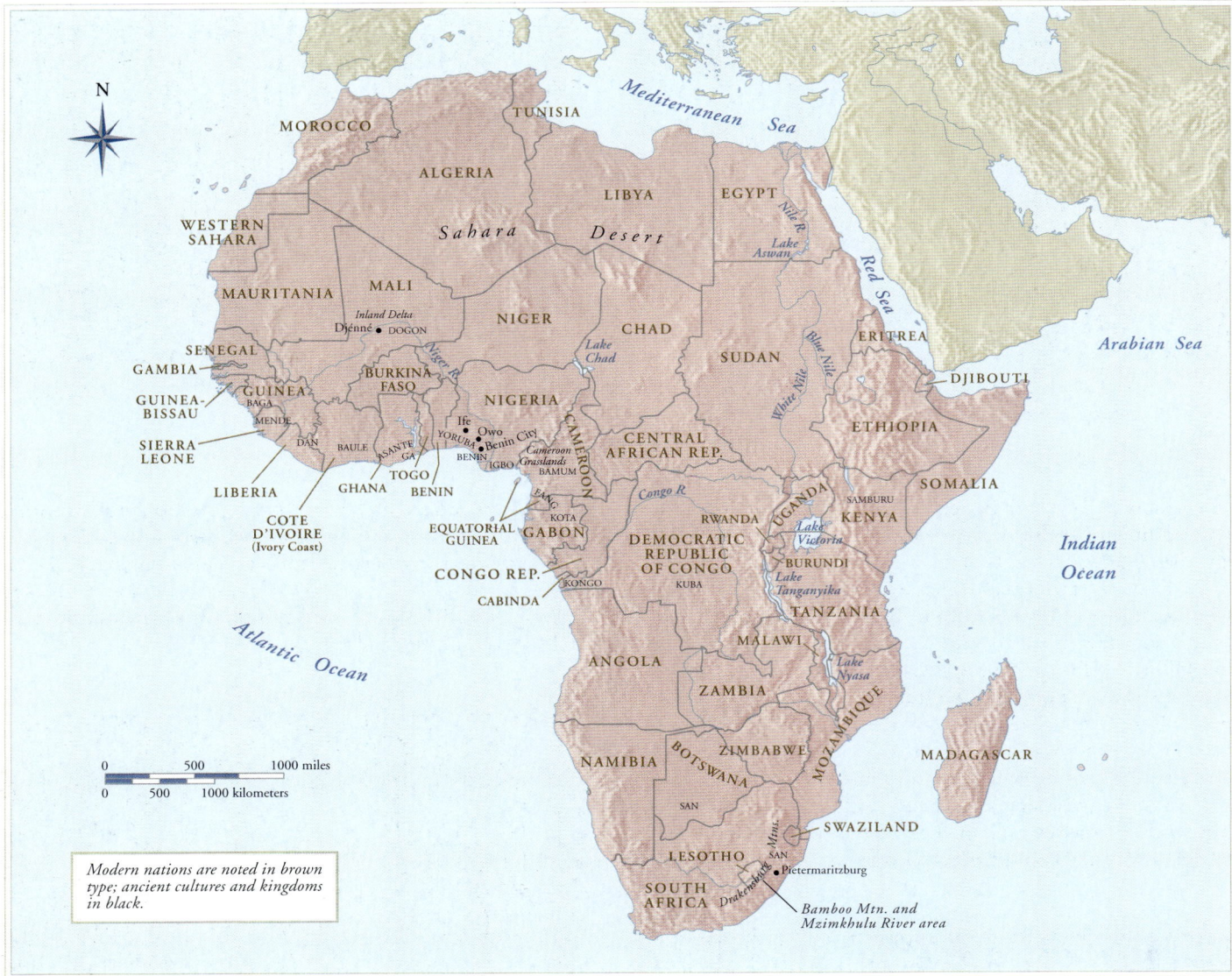

**MAP 32-1** Modern Africa.

often displaced from their ancestral lands. In some regions, they began to raid local ranches for livestock and horses as an alternate food source. The Bamboo Mountain rock painting appears to have been made after a series of stock raids over a period from about 1838 to 1848. Various South African military and police forces unsuccessfully pursued the San raiders. Poor weather, with frequent rains and fog, added to the difficulty of capturing a people who had lived in the region as hunters and gatherers for many generations and knew its terrain.

On the right side of the composition (not illustrated), two San riders on horses laden with meat drive a large herd of cattle and horses toward a San encampment located left of center and encircled by an outline (FIG. 32-1, *right*). Within the camp are various women and children. To the far left, a single figure (perhaps a diviner or rainmaker) leads an eland toward the encampment (FIG. 32-1, *left*). The similarity of this scene to other rock paintings with spiritual interpretations (a human leading an animal) suggests that this may represent a ritual leader in a trance state. The leader calls on rain—brought by the intervention of the sacred eland—to foil the attempts of the government soldiers and police to locate and punish the San raiders. The close correspondence between the painting's imagery and the actual events of 1838–1848 adds to the

likelihood that this work both indirectly records government action and was designed to facilitate rainmaking.

## Fang and "Kota" Art (Cameroon and Gabon)

Although it is often difficult to date African works of art precisely, there are a number of objects without historical references that can still be assigned to the 19th century with some confidence. These include the reliquary guardian figures made by the Fang and several other peoples just south of the equator and the large "power images" of the Kongo peoples who live farther south in the basin of the great Congo (formerly Zaire) River. Both groups of figures are associated with ancestor worship. Across the continent ancestors are venerated for the continuing aid they are believed to provide the living, including help in maintaining the productivity of the earth for bountiful crop production.

**ANCESTOR RELIQUARIES** In some areas, ancestor veneration takes material form as collections of cranial and other bones gathered in special containers. Among both the Fang of Cameroon and several other peoples (often referred to as "Kota")

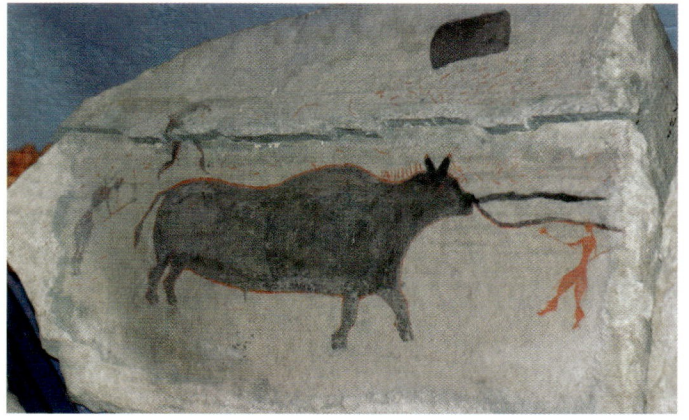
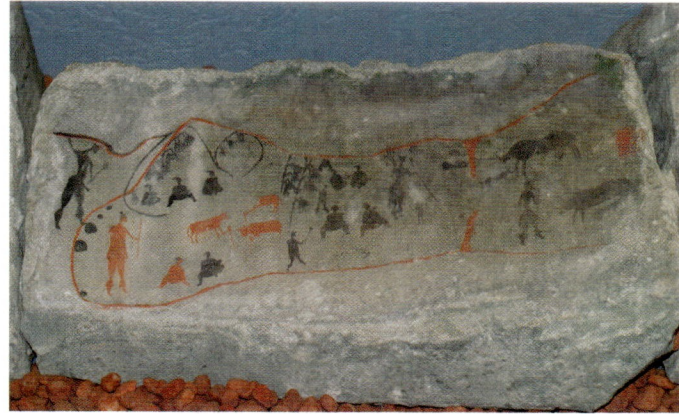

**32-1** Stock raid with cattle, horses, encampment, and magical "rain animal," rock painting (two details), San, Bamboo Mountain, South Africa, mid-19th century. Pigments on rock, approx. 8′ long. Natal Museum, Pietermaritzburg.

in neighboring areas, these relic containers were protected by stylized human figures, or in some cases, simply heads. Fang guardian figures, such as the ones we show (FIG. 32-2), sit on the edge of bark boxes of ancestral bones, insuring that no harm befalls the ancestral spirits. The wood figures are symmetrical, with proportions that greatly emphasize the head, and with a rhythmic buildup of forms that suggests contained power.

The so-called Kota reliquary guardian figures (called *mbulu ngulu*) from Gabon, like the one we illustrate (FIG. 32-3), have a severely stylized body in the form of an open lozenge below a wooden head covered with strips and sheets of polished copper and brass. The gleaming surfaces are said to have repelled evil. The heads themselves are simplified, with hairstyles flattened out laterally above and beside the face. Geometric ridges, borders, and

subdivisions add a kind of textured elegance to the shiny forms. The copper alloy on most of these images was reworked sheet brass (or copper wire) taken from brass basins originating in Europe and traded into this area of equatorial Africa in the 18th and 19th centuries. The lower portion of the image was stuck into a basket or box of ancestral relics.

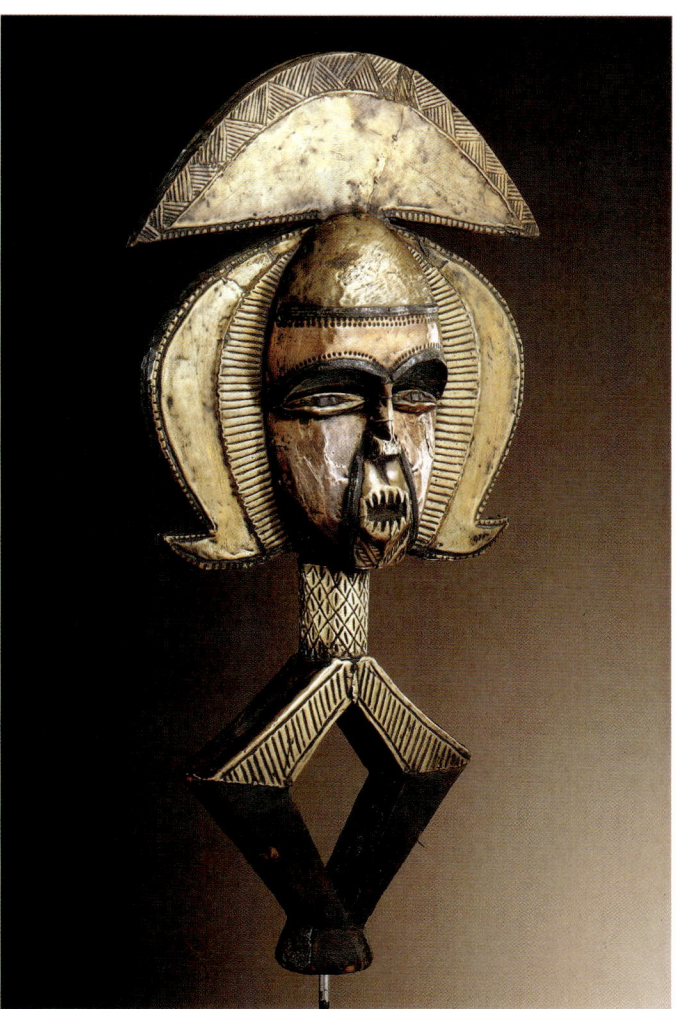

**32-2** Reliquary guardian figures on bark boxes, Fang, Cameroon, photographed in 1910. Wood. National Museum of African Art, Smithsonian Institution, Washington.

**32-3** Reliquary guardian figure *(mbulu-ngulu)*, "Kota," Gabon, 19th or early 20th century. Wood, copper, iron, and brass, 1′ 9$\frac{1}{16}$″ high. Barbier-Mueller Museum, Geneva.

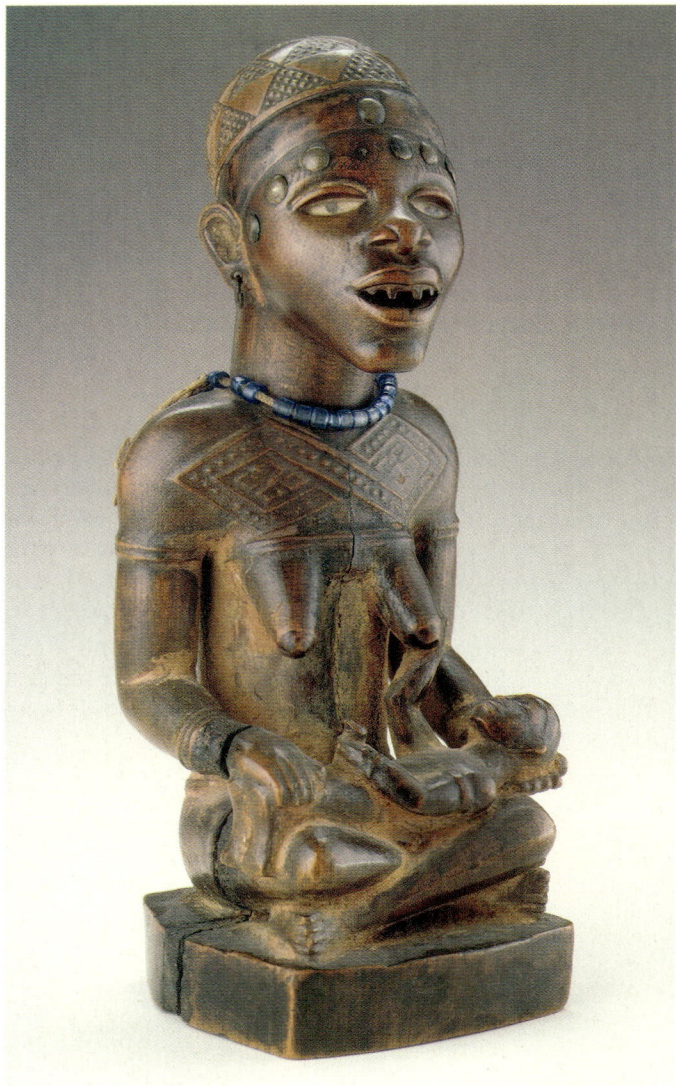

32-4 Mother and child, Kongo, from Mayombe region, Democratic Republic of Congo, 19th or early 20th century. Wood, glass, glass beads, brass tacks, and pigment, $10\frac{1}{8}''$ high. National Museum of African Art, Smithsonian Institution, Washington.

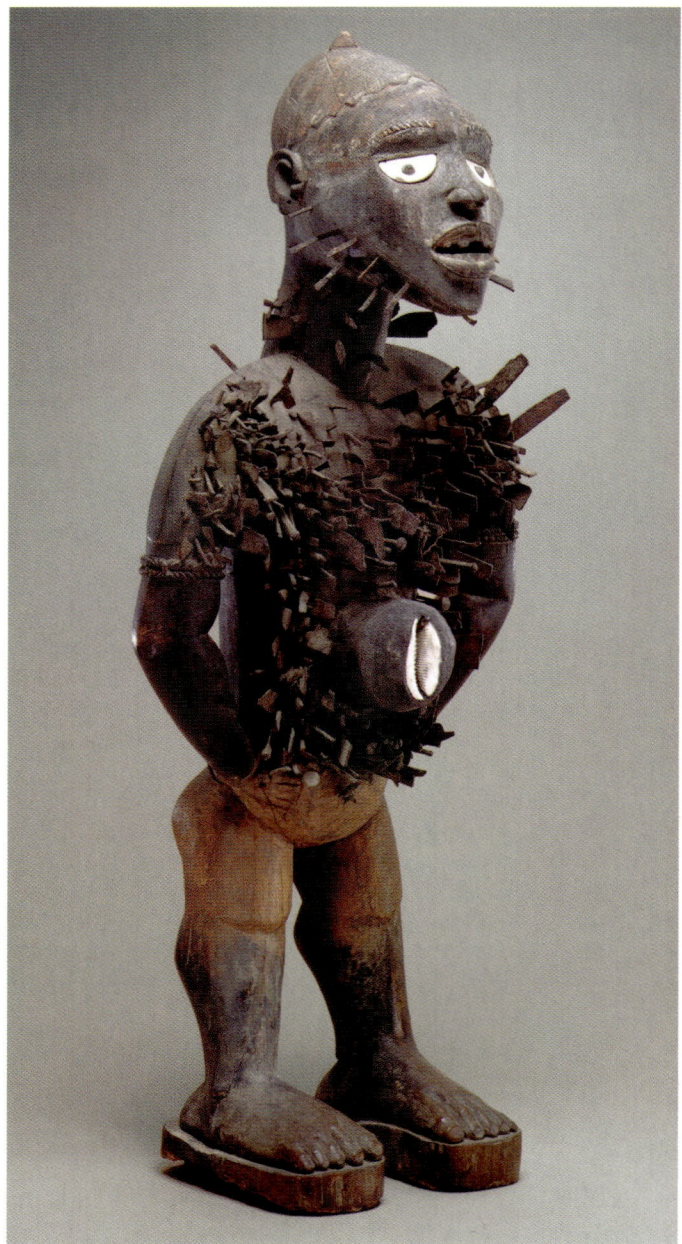

32-5 Nail figure *(nkisi n'kondi)*, Kongo, from Shiloango River area, Democratic Republic of Congo, ca. 1875–1900. Wood, nails, blades, medicinal materials, and cowrie shell, $3'\ 10\frac{3}{4}''$ high. Detroit Institute of Arts, Detroit.

## Kongo Art (Democratic Republic of Congo)

**KONGO POWER IMAGES** Ancestral and power images of the Kongo peoples of the lower reaches of the Congo River show varieties of conventionalized naturalism. They served several purposes—commemoration, healing, divination, and social regulation. The woman-and-child carving we illustrate (FIG. **32-4**) represents Kongo royalty, indicated by the woman's cap (recalling royal examples of woven banana fiber), chest scarification, and jewelry. The image may commemorate an ancestor or more probably a legendary founding clan mother, a *genetrix*. The Kongo called some of these figures "white chalk," a reference to the medicinal power of white kaolin clay. Diviners owned some of them, and others were used in women's organizations concerned with fertility and the treatment of infertility.

The large, standing male carving (FIG. **32-5**), bristling with nails and blades, is a Kongo power figure *(nkisi n'kondi)* that a trained priest consecrated using precise ritual formulas. Such images embodied spirits believed to heal and give life, or sometimes capable of inflicting harm, disease, or even death. Each figure had its own

specific role, just as it wore particular medicines—here protruding from the abdomen and featuring a large cowrie shell. The Kongo also activated every image differently. Owners appealed to a figure's forces every time they inserted a nail or blade, as if to prod the spirit to do its work. People invoked other spirits by a certain chant, by rubbing them, or by applying special powders. The roles of power figures varied enormously, from curing minor ailments to stimulating crop growth, from punishing thieves to weakening an enemy. Very large Kongo figures, such as this one, had exceptional ascribed powers and aided entire communities. Although benevolent for their owners, the figures stood at the boundary between life and death, and most villagers held them in awe. As is true of the woman-and-child group (FIG. 32-4), this Kongo figure is relatively naturalistic, although the facial features are simplified and the head is magnified in size and thus emphasis. The carvers of both images, though, rendered surfaces as skin over muscled volume.

## Dogon Art (Mali)

**A STYLIZED COUPLE** In contrast to the organic, relatively realistic treatment of the human body in Kongo art is a strongly stylized Dogon carving of a male and female couple (FIG. **32-6**) that dates to the 19th century or perhaps earlier. The Dogon live in Mali near the bend of the great Niger River, not far from the inland Niger Delta region where many terracotta images (see FIG. 15-5) have been excavated. This carving of a linked man and woman—probably a shrine or altar, although contextual information is lacking—cogently documents primary gender roles in traditional African society. The man wears a quiver on his back; the woman carries a child on hers. Thus a protective role as hunter or warrior is implied for the man, a nurturing one for the woman. The slightly larger man reaches behind his mate's neck and touches her breast, as if to protect her. His left hand points to his own genitalia. Four stylized figures support the stool upon which they sit. They are probably either spirits or ancestors, but the identity of the larger figures is not known.

The highly conventionalized style of this group makes it a *conceptual* image rather than a *perceptual* one. That is, it is based more on the idea or concept of human forms than on the imitative portrayal of heads, torsos, and limbs as perceived in life. Here, the linked body parts are tubes and columns articulated inorganically. The almost abstract geometry of the overall composition is reinforced by incised rectilinear and diagonal patterns on the surfaces. The sculptor also understood the importance of space, and charged the voids, as well as the sculptural forms, with rhythm and tension. The artist was not at all concerned with naturalism or realism, yet produced a refined and complex image that is very successful as sculpture.

## Baule Art (Central Côte d'Ivoire)

**BUSH SPIRITS** In striking contrast to the Dogon sculptor of the seated man and woman (FIG. 32-6), the artist who created the matched pair of Baule male and female images (FIG. 32-7) consciously perceived many naturalistic aspects of human anatomy,

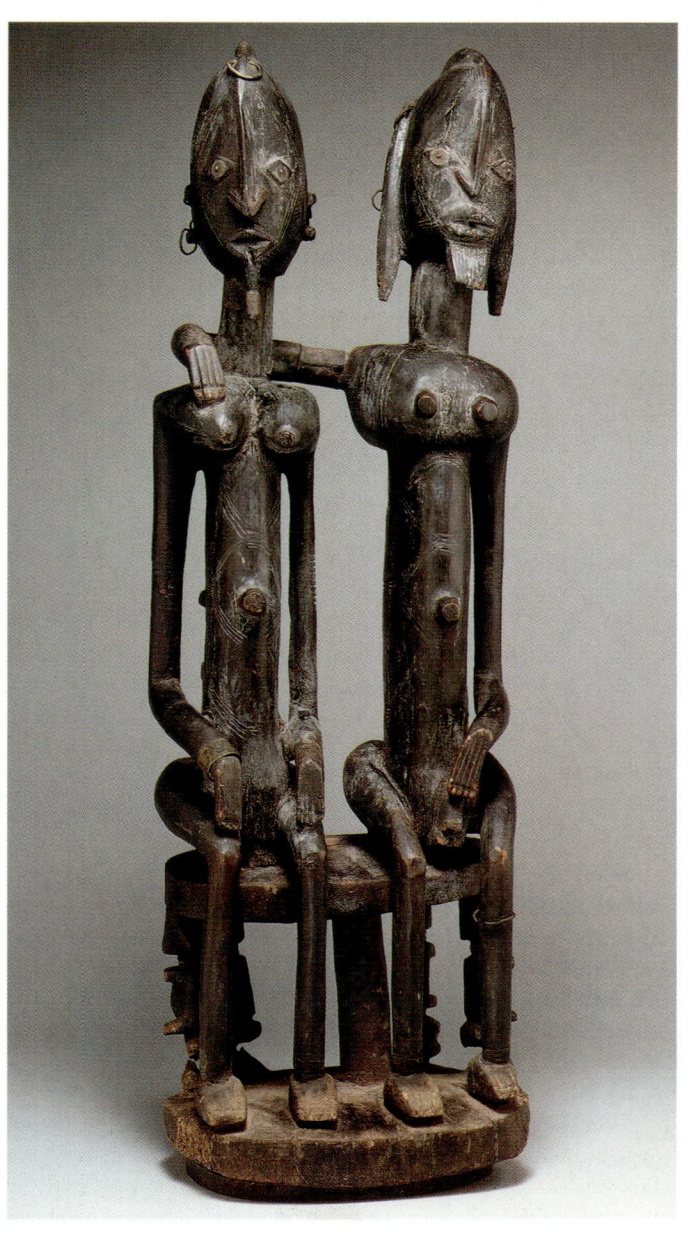

**32-6** Seated couple, Dogon, Mali, ca. 1800–1850. Wood, 2′ 4″ high. Metropolitan Museum of Art, New York (gift of Lester Wunderman).

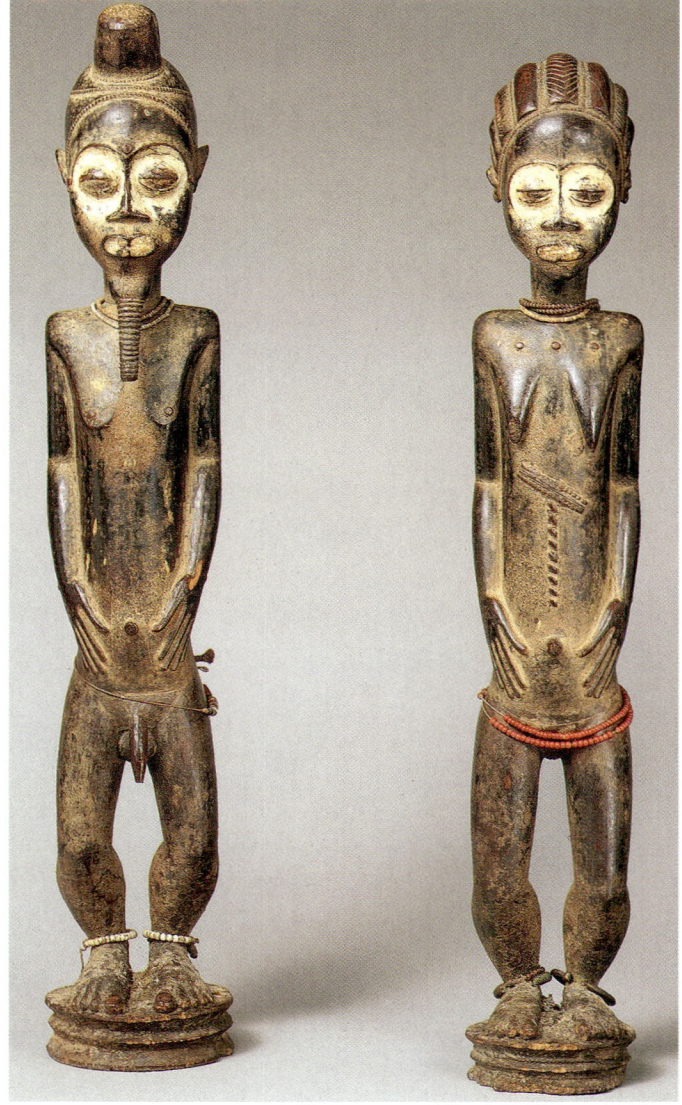

**32-7** Male and female figures, probably bush spirits (*asye usu*), Baule, Côte d'Ivoire, late 19th or early 20th century. Wood, beads, and kaolin, man 1′ 9¾″ high, woman 1′ 8⅝″ high. Metropolitan Museum of Art, New York (Michael C. Rockefeller Memorial Collection, gift of Nelson A. Rockefeller).

skillfully translating them into finished sculptural form. At the same time, the sculptor was well aware of creating *waka sran* (people of wood) rather than living beings. Thus, the artist freely exaggerated the length of the figures' necks and the size of their heads and calf muscles, all of which are forms of idealization in Baule culture.

The images probably portray bush spirits (*asye usu*) and were in the possession of a trance diviner, a religious specialist who consulted the spirits symbolized by the figures on behalf of clients either sick or in some way troubled. In Baule thought, bush spirits are actually short, horrible-looking, and sometimes deformed creatures, yet Baule sculptors represent them in the form of beautiful, ideal human beings, because it is said that the spirits would be offended by ugly figures and would refuse to work for the diviner. Among the Baule, as among many West African peoples, bush or wilderness spirits both cause difficulties in life and, if properly addressed and placated, may solve problems or cure sickness. In dance and trance performances—with wooden figures and other objects displayed nearby—the diviner is able to divine or understand the will of his or her unseen spirits, as well as their needs or prophecies, which he or she passes on to clients. When not set up outdoors for a performance, the figures and other objects are stored in the diviner's house or shrine, where more private consultations take place.

## THE 20TH CENTURY

### *Benin Art (Nigeria)*

**A ROYAL ANCESTOR SHRINE** Some of the most important art produced in Africa during the past century comes from areas with strong earlier artistic traditions. The kingdom of Benin is a prime example. In Chapter 15, we examined a 16th-century Benin ivory mask (see FIG. 15-10) and a 17th- or 18th-century copper alloy altar (see FIG. 15-11). A 20th-century Benin composite shrine to the heads of royal ancestors (FIG. **32-8**) is, according to oral history, similar to centuries-earlier versions. The shrine is in the king's palace today. With a base of sacred riverbank clay, it is an assemblage of varied materials, objects, and symbols: a central copper-alloy altarpiece depicting a sacred king flanked by members of his entourage, plus copper-alloy heads, each fitted on top with an ivory tusk carved in relief. There are also wood staffs and metal bells. The heads represent both the kings themselves and, through the durability of their material, the enduring nature of kingship. These heads were once polished. Their glistening surfaces, seen as red and signaling danger, were believed to repel evil forces that might adversely affect the shrine and thus the king and kingdom. Elephant-tusk relief carvings atop the heads commemorate important events and personages in Benin history. Their bleached white color signifies purity and goodness (probably of royal ancestors), and the tusks themselves represent the vast physical power of elephants, which, like leopards, are metaphors for leaders. The carved wood rattle-staffs standing at the back refer to generations of dynastic ancestors by their bamboolike, segmented forms. The staffs also function musically, as do the several pyramidal copper-alloy bells, to call royal ancestral spirits to rituals performed at the altar.

The Benin king's actual head stands for wisdom, good judgment, and divine guidance for the kingdom. Those qualities are multiplied in the ancestral altar with its several heads. By means of animal sacrifices at this site, the living king annually purifies his own "head" (and being) by invoking the collective strength of his ancestors. Thus the varied objects, symbols, colors, and materials comprising this shrine contribute both visually and ritually to the imaging of royal power, as well as to its history, renewal, and perpetuation. The composition of the shrine, like that of the altar at its center and the altar discussed earlier (see FIG. 15-11), is hierarchical. At the center of all Benin hierarchies stands the king (see FIG. Intro-16).

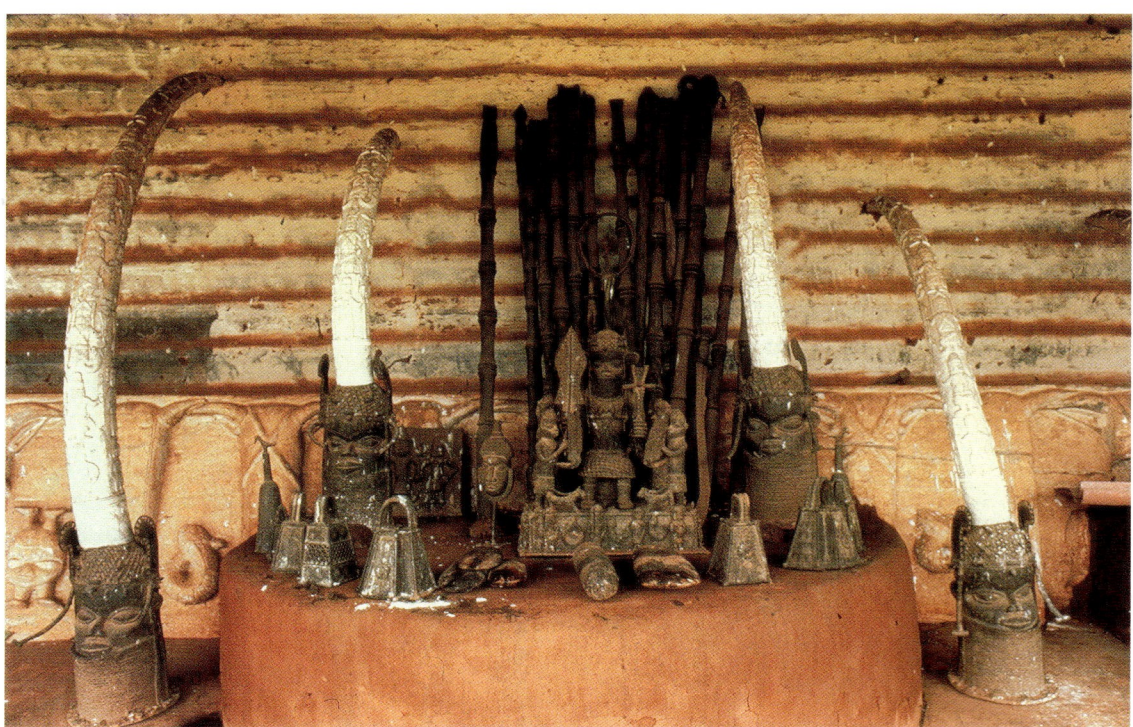

**32-8** Royal ancestral altar, Benin, Nigeria, photographed in 1970. Clay, copper alloy, wood, and ivory. National Museum of African Art, Smithsonian Institution, Washington.

## African Artists and Apprentices

The many styles illustrated in this chapter can often be identified as to place, people, and time. Individual artists also have distinctive styles that enable viewers to recognize their work, and sometimes whether a given work was created early or late in the artist's career. Although African art has often been considered anonymous—because early researchers rarely asked for artists' names—many individual hands or styles can be recognized even when an artist's name has not been recorded. During the past century, however, art historians and anthropologists have been systematically noting the names and life histories of specific individual artists, many of whom are well known regionally. Two 20th-century artists who were renowned, even from one kingdom to another, are Osei Bonsu, who was based in the Asante capital, Kumasi, and the Yoruba sculptor called Olowe of Ise because he came from the town of Ise. Both artists were master carvers, producing sculptures for kings and commoners alike.

Like other great artists in other places and times, both Bonsu (FIGS. 32-10 and 32-11) and Olowe (FIG. 32-12) had apprentices to assist them for several years while learning their trade. Although there are various kinds of apprenticeship in Africa, novices typically lived with their masters and were household servants as well as assistant carvers. They helped fell trees, carry logs, and rough out basic shapes that the master later transformed into finished work. African sculptors typically worked on commission. Sometimes, as in Bonsu's case, patrons traveled to the home of the artist. But other times, even Bonsu moved to the home of a patron for weeks or months while the commission was being completed. Masters, and in some instances also apprentices, were housed and fed in the patron's compound. Olowe, for example, traveled around the Ekiti region of Yorubaland, living with different kings for many months at a time while he carved doors, veranda posts (FIG. 32-12), and other works for royal families.

## Akan and Asante Art (Ghana)

**FEMALE SCULPTORS** Another 20th-century art form that recalls similar works documented in earlier times is the Akan terracotta commemorative head, one of which is just being completed by a woman artist in FIG. 32-9. Pieter de Marees, a Dutch visitor to Ghana in 1602, described a comparable object and explained its connection to Akan burials:

> Upon the grave they set all kinds of meat and drinke, that they may eat some thing. . . . All his stuffe, as Armes and Clothes are buried with him, and all his gentlemen that served him, have every one of them their Pictures made of Clay, and fairely painted, which are set and placed orderly round about his grave, one by the other.[1]

The woman sculptor has modeled a portrait of a deceased king or court member, just as her predecessors did in the early 17th century and perhaps earlier.

**OSEI BONSU** The conventionalized, flattened clay head is an Akan style trait that is also found in wood sculpture carved by Asante men—for example, in an image of a young girl (FIG. 32-10), or *akua'ba* (Akua's child), by OSEI BONSU (1900–1976; see "African Artists and Apprentices," above). Many Akan peoples considered

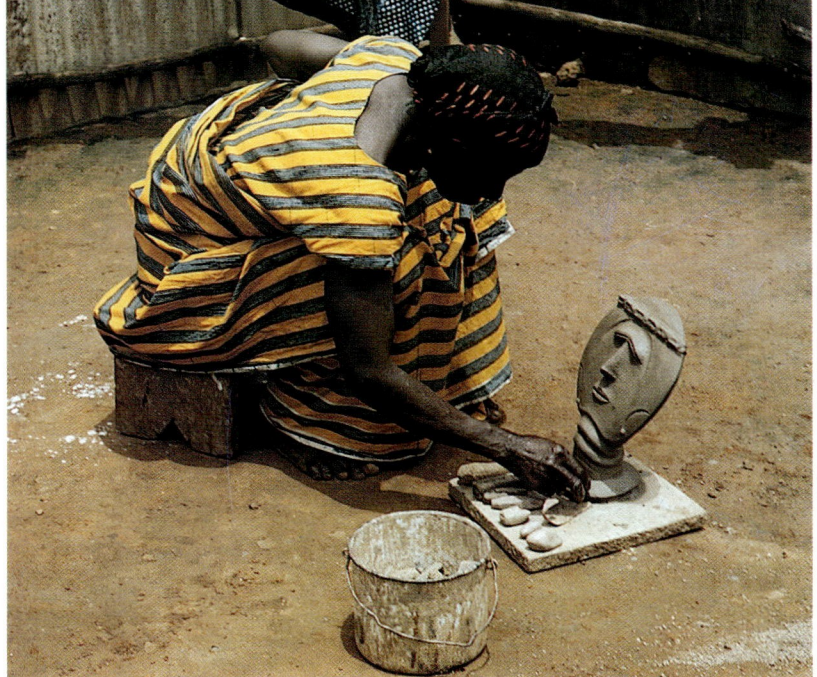

32-9 Woman sculptor finishing an ancestral portrait, 1965, Akan, Ghana. Terracotta.

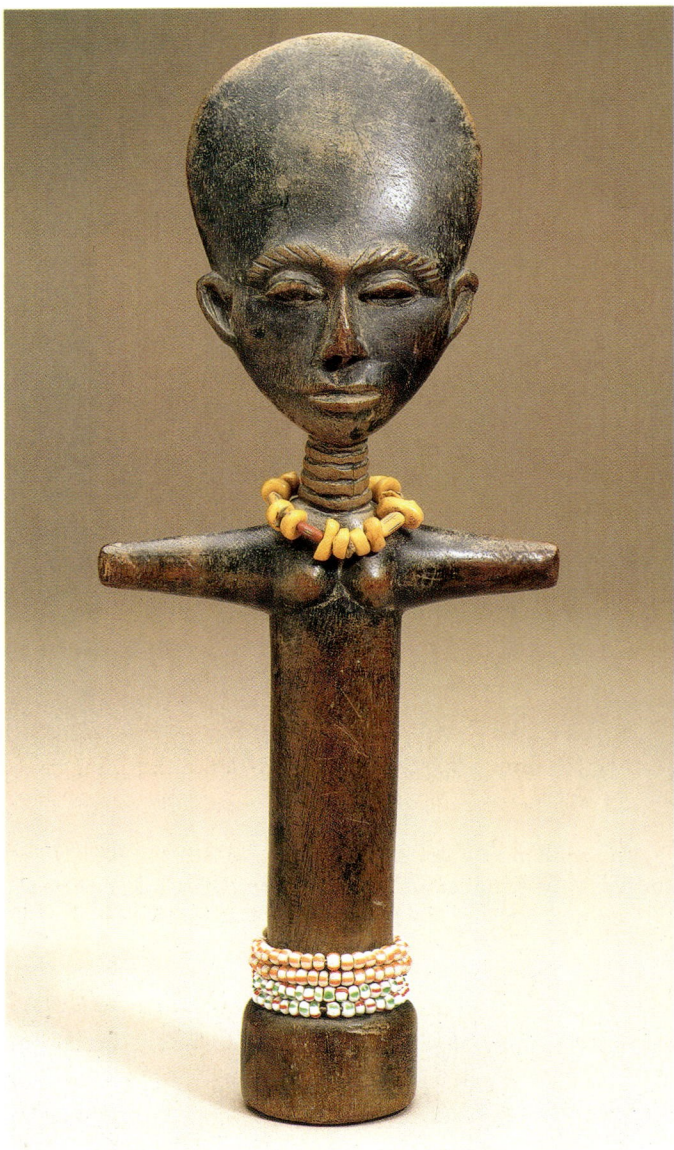

32-10 Osei Bonsu, *akua'ba,* Asante, Ghana, ca. 1935. Wood, beads, and pigment, 10¼″ high. Private collection.

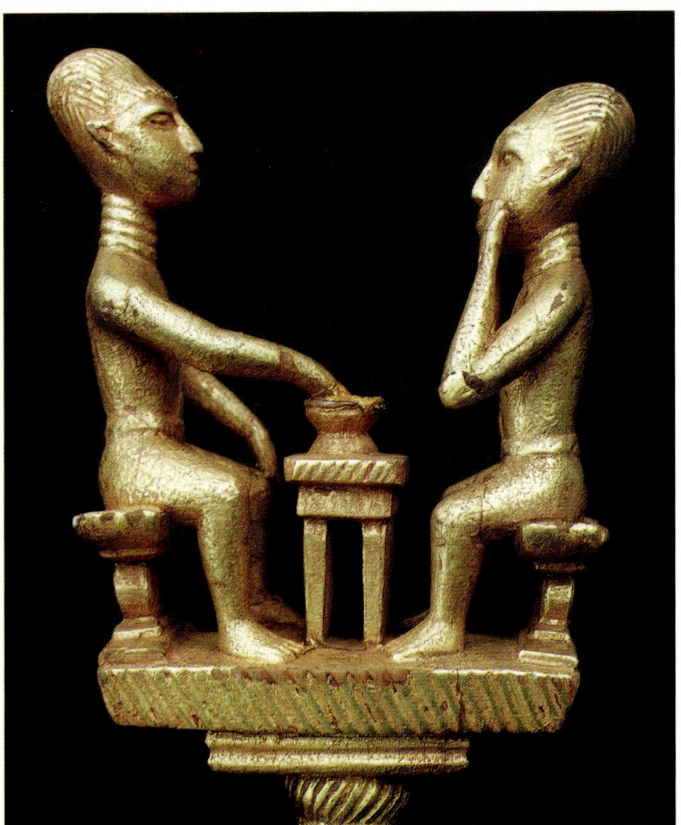

32-11 Osei Bonsu, "linguist's staff" of two men sitting at a table of food, Asante, Ghana, mid-20th century. Wood and gold leaf, section shown approx. 10″ high. Collection of the Paramount Chief of Offinso, Asante.

long, slightly flattened foreheads to be emblems of beauty, and mothers actually gently molded their children's cranial bones to reflect this value. The simplified wood akua'ba sculptures were consecrated at a shrine, then carried by a young woman hoping to conceive. Once pregnant, the woman continued to carry the figure to ensure the safe delivery of a healthy and handsome child—among these matrilineal people, preferably a girl. Many thousands of such wood figures have been carved over the past several centuries, each one different from the next, yet each one showing stylistic traits associated with one or another Akan subgroup, or even a specific artist. Osei Bonsu's personal style—a more naturalistic rendering of the face, and crosshatched eyebrows—is easily recognized by those familiar with the many regional and personal styles seen in Akan sculpture.

Bonsu also carved the gold-covered wood sculpture that depicts two men sitting at a table of food (FIG. 32-11). This object, commonly called a "linguist's staff" because its carrier often speaks for a king or chief, has a related proverb: "Food is for its

rightful owner, not for the one who happens to be hungry." Food is a metaphor for the office held by the king or chief, which he rightfully holds. The "hungry" man lusts for the office. The linguist, who is an important counselor and adviser to the king, might carry this staff to a meeting at which a rival is contesting the king's title to the stool (his throne, the office). Many hundreds of Akan sculptures have proverbs or other sayings associated with them, so there is a rich verbal tradition relating to the visual arts of these peoples.

## Yoruba Art (Nigeria)

**OLOWE OF ISE** A tall veranda post (FIG. 32-12) is typical of the style of OLOWE OF ISE (ca. 1873–1938). To achieve greater height, Olowe stacked his weapon-carrying equestrian warrior on top of a platform supported on the heads and upraised arms of four figures, two men and two women. The figures themselves are attenuated, with long necks and enlarged heads. The latter trait is common among most Yoruba sculptors, whereas elongation is an Olowe characteristic, along with finely textured detail, seen in the warrior's tunic. This post was carved in the early decades of the 20th century, a time when Europeans had already become a colonial presence among Yoruba peoples. Olowe subtly records this presence in the billed cap of one of the male supporting figures. The overall design of this house post, more complex and with more open space than most posts by other carvers, signals Olowe's virtuosity.

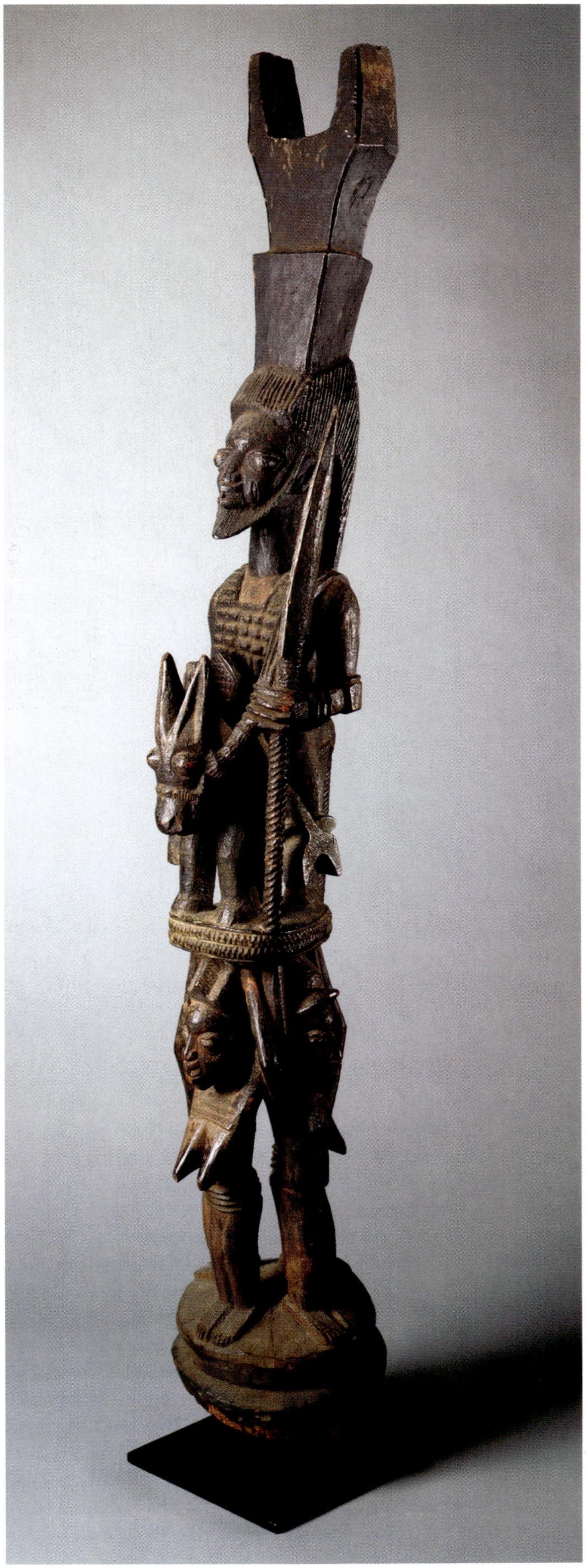

## Costumes and Masquerades

The arts in Africa exist in greatly varied human situations, and knowledge of these contexts is essential for understanding the artworks. In Africa, art (even sculptures and paintings now displayed in museums) is nearly always an active agent in the lives of the continent's peoples. African art also encompasses clothing and masks made of perishable materials. Throughout history, African costumes have been laden with meaning and have projected messages that all members of the society could read. We reproduce a photograph (FIG. **32-13**) taken in 1970 of a sacred Kuba king. The king, Kot a-Mbweeky III (r. 1969–present), is seated in state before his court, bedecked in a dazzling multimedia costume with many symbolic elements. The king commissioned the costume he wears and now has become art himself. Eagle feathers, leopard skin, cowrie shells, imported beads, raffia, and other materials combine to overload and expand the image of the man, making him larger than life, and most certainly a work of art. He is a collage, an assemblage. He holds not one but two weapons. Can one doubt his military might, his wealth, dignity, and grandeur in the eyes of his people? The man, with his regalia, embodies the office of sacred kingship. He is a superior being actually and figuratively, raised upon a dais, flanked by ornate drums, with a treasure basket of sacred relics by his foot. The geometric patterns on the king's costume and nearby objects, and the abundance and redundancy of rich materials, epitomize the opulent style of Kuba court arts.

**MASQUERADES** The art of *masquerade* has long been a quintessential African expressive form, loaded with meaning and cultural importance. This is so today, but was more critically true in

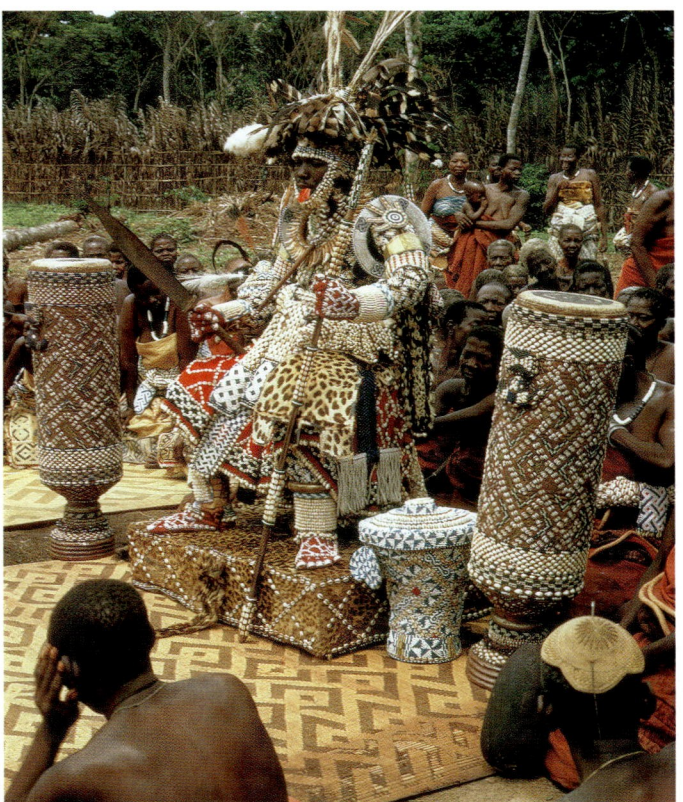

**32-13** Kuba King Kot a-Mbweeky III during a display for photographer and filmmaker Eliot Elisofon in early 1970, Mushenge, Democratic Republic of Congo. National Museum of African Art, Smithsonian Institution, Washington. 💿

**32-12** OLOWE OF ISE, veranda post carved for the chief of Akure, Yoruba, Nigeria, ca. 1900–1938. Wood and pigment, approx. 14′ 6″ high. Denver Art Museum, Denver. 💿

colonial times and earlier, when African masking societies boasted extensive regulatory and judicial powers. Such governmental functions were particularly forceful in stateless societies, such as those of the Senufo and Mende, where masks sometimes became so influential they had their own priests and served as power sources or as oracles. Societies empowered maskers to levy fines and to apprehend witches (usually defined as socially destructive people) and criminals, and to judge and punish them. Normally, however—especially today—masks are less threatening and more secular and educational, as well as diversions from the humdrum of daily life. Masked dancers usually embody either ancestors, seen as briefly returning to the human realm, or various nature spirits called upon for their special powers.

The mask, a costume ensemble's focal point, combines with held objects, music, and dance gestures to invoke a specific named character, almost always considered a spirit. A few masked spirits appear by themselves, but more often several characters come out together or in turn. Maskers enact a very broad range of human, animal, and fantastic, otherworldly behavior that is usually both stimulating and didactic. Masquerades, in fact, vary in function or effect along a continuum from weak spirit power and strong entertainment value to those rarely seen but possessing vast executive powers backed by powerful shrines. Most operate between these extremes, crystallizing varieties of human and animal behavior—caricatured, ordinary, comic, bizarre, serious, or threatening. Such actions inform and affect audience members because they are staged dramatically and framed within a performance normally held only occasionally. It is the purpose of most masquerades to move people, to affect them, to effect change.

Thus, masks and masquerades are mediators—between men and women, youths and elders, initiated and uninitiated, powers of nature and those of human agency, and even life and death. For many groups in West and Central Africa, masking plays (or once played) an active role in the socialization process, especially for men, who control most masks. Maskers carry boys away from their mothers to bush initiation camps, put them through ordeals and schooling, and welcome them back to society as men months or even years later. A second major role is in aiding the transformation of important deceased persons into productive ancestors who, in their new roles, can bring benefits to the living community. Because most masking cultures are agricultural, it is not surprising that masquerades are invoked to increase the productivity of the fields, to stimulate the growth of crops, and later to celebrate the harvest.

**SENUFO MASKING** Senufo men dance many masks, mostly in the context of Poro, the main association for socialization and initiation, a protracted process that takes nearly 20 years for men to complete. Maskers also perform at funerals and other public spectacles. The most recurrent Senufo mask has a small face with fine features, several extensions, and varied motifs—a hornbill bird in our example (FIG. **32-14**)—rising from the forehead. These feminine characters, danced only by men, wear knitted body suits or tradecloth costumes to indicate their beauty and their ties with the order and civilization of the village. Their dances too are feminine. They may be called "pretty young girl," "beautiful lady," or "wife" and some are considered the wives of the heavy, terrorizing masculine masks that appear before or after them.

Large Senufo masks (for example, FIG. **32-15**) are composite creatures, combining characteristics of antelope, crocodile, warthog, hyena, and human: sweeping horns, a head, and an open-jawed snout with sharp teeth. Such masks incarnate both

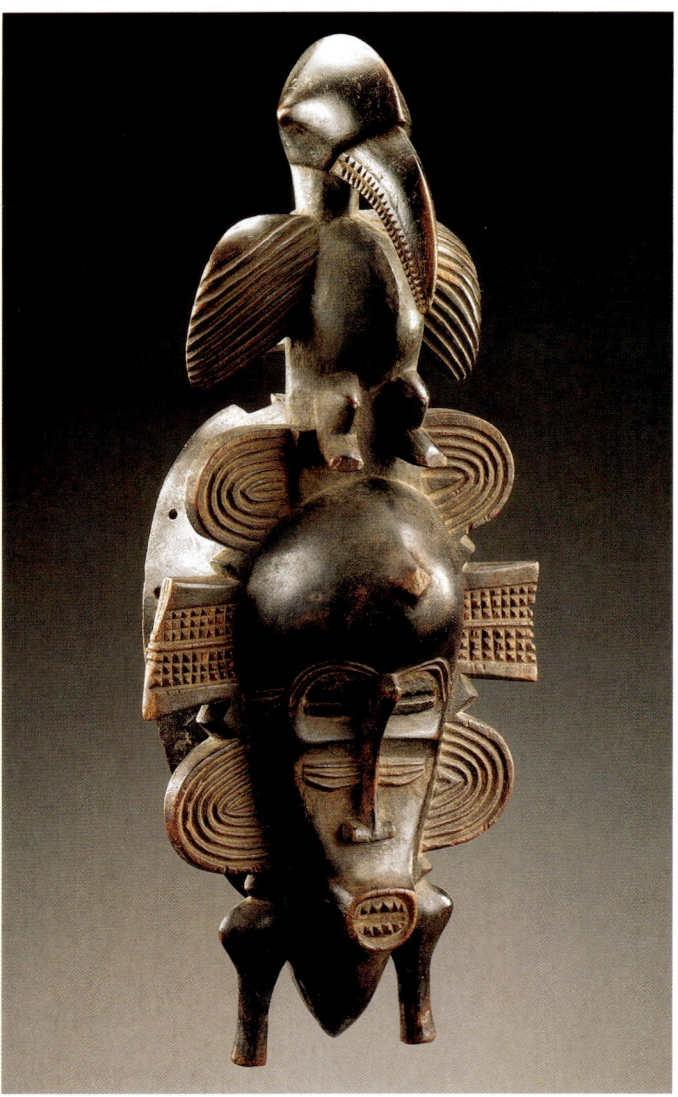

**32-14** "Beautiful Lady" dance mask, Senufo, Côte d'Ivoire, late 20th century. Wood, approx. 1′ $\frac{1}{2}$″ high. Musée Barbier-Mueller, Geneva.

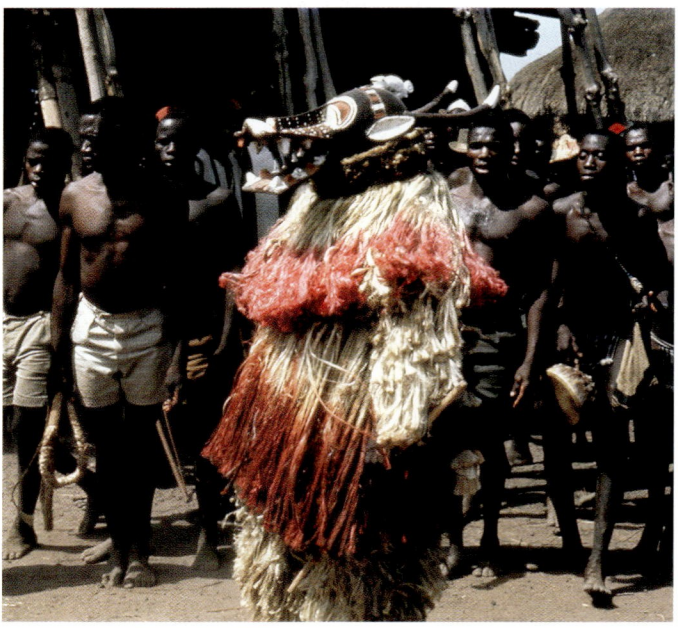

**32-15** Gbon masquerader at a funeral, Senufo, Côte d'Ivoire, photographed by Anita Glaze in 1986.

ancestors and bush powers that combat witchcraft and sorcery, malevolent spirits, and the wandering dead. They are protectors who fight evil with their aggressively powerful forms and their medicines. There is a close relationship between function and form, namely the mask as weapon.

At funerals Senufo maskers attend the corpse and help expel the deceased from the village. This is the deceased individual's final transition, a rite of passage parallel to that undergone by all men during their years of Poro socialization, when masks are also employed. When an important person dies, the convergence of several masking groups, as well as the music, dancing, costuming, and feasting of many people, constitute a festive and complex work of art that transcends any one mask or character.

**DOGON MASQUERADES** In the inland Niger Delta region, elaborate cyclical Dogon masquerades dramatize creation legends. These stories say that women were the first ancestors to imitate spirit maskers and thus the first human masqueraders. Men later took over the masks, forever barring women from direct involvement with masking processes. A mask called Satimbe (FIG. 32-16), which seems to represent all women, commemorates this

legend. In ceremonies called Dama, held every several years to honor the lives of people who have died since the last Dama, Satimbe is among the dozens of different masked spirit characters that escort dead souls away from the village. The deceased are sent off to the land of the dead where, as ancestors, they will be enjoined to benefit their living descendants and stimulate agricultural productivity.

**WOMEN AS MASK DANCERS** Although men own and perform most masks in Africa, women control and dance them in several adjacent cultures of the western Guinea Coast, such as the Mende of Sierra Leone (see "Mende Women as Maskers," page 952). The glistening black surface of the Mende mask we show (FIG. 32-17) evokes female ancestral spirits newly emergent from their underwater homes (also symbolized by the turtle on top). The mask and its parts refer to ideals of female beauty, morality, and behavior. A high broad forehead signifies wisdom and success. Neck ridges—signs of beauty, good health, and prosperity—also symbolize a moth chrysalis, the transformative stage in the insect's life, between worm and flying creature, that is parallel to a young woman's initiation. Intricately woven or plaited hair is

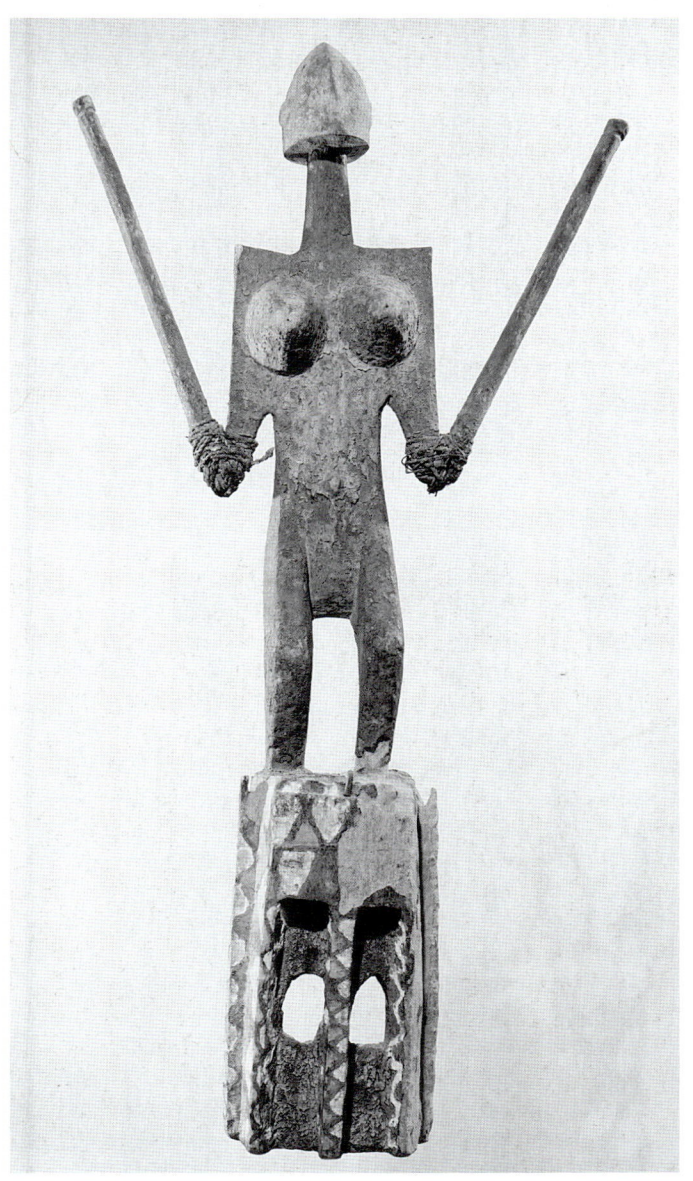

**32-16** Satimbe mask, Dogon, Mali, early 20th century. Wood. Private collection.

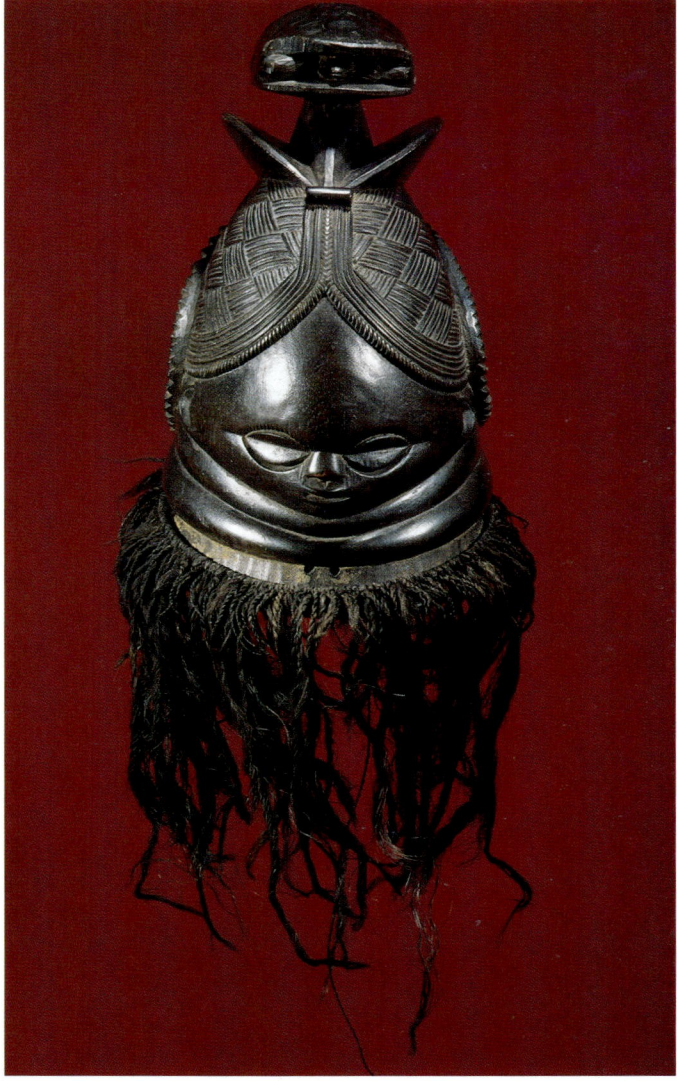

**32-17** Female mask, Mende, Sierra Leone, 20th century. Wood and pigment, 1′ 2½″ high. Fowler Museum of Cultural History, University of California, Los Angeles (gift of the Wellcome Trust).

## Mende Women as Maskers

The Mende and neighboring peoples of Sierra Leone and Liberia are unique in Africa in that women actually wear masks (FIG. 32-17) and costumes that conceal them totally from the audience attending their performance. The Sande society of the Mende is the women's counterpart to the men's Poro society. These associations control the initiation, education, and acculturation of female and male youth, respectively. Women leaders who dance these masks serve as priestesses and judges during the three years the women's society controls the ritual calendar (alternating with the men's society in this role), thus serving the community as a whole. Women maskers, also initiators, teachers, and mentors, help girl novices with their transformation into educated and marriageable women. Sande women associate their Sowie masks with water spirits and the color black, which the society, in turn, connects with human skin color and the civilized world. The women wear these helmet masks on top of their heads as headdresses, with black raffia and cloth costumes to hide the wearers' identity during public performances. Elaborate coiffures, shiny black color, dainty triangular-shaped faces with slit eyes, rolls around the neck, and actual and carved versions of amulets and various emblems on the top commonly characterize Sowie masks. These symbolize the adult women's roles as wives, mothers, providers for the family, and keepers of medicines for use within the Sande association and the society at large.

Sande members commission the masks from male carvers, with the carver and patron together determining the type of mask needed for a particular societal purpose. The Mende often keep, repair, and reuse masks for many decades, thereby preserving them as models for subsequent generations of carvers.

---

the essence of harmony and order found in ideal households. A small closed mouth and downcast eyes indicate the silent, serious demeanor expected of recent initiates. These sorts of masks are worn by leaders and teachers in initiation rites, as well as by leaders and priestesses of the women's society.

**KUBA SPIRITS AND ANCESTORS** At the court of Kuba kings, three masks, known as Mwashamboy, Bwoom, and Ngady Amwaash, represent legendary royal ancestors. Mwashamboy (FIG. **32-18**) symbolizes the founding ancestor, Woot, and embodies the king's supernatural and political powers. The other mask in the photograph, Bwoom, with its bulging forehead, is said to represent a legendary dwarf or pygmy who signifies the indigenous peoples on whom kingship was imposed. Bwoom also vies with Mwashamboy for the attention of the beautiful female ancestor, Ngady Amwaash, who symbolizes the first female and all women (FIG. 32-19). On her cheeks are striped tears from the pain of childbirth, and those shed by Ngady herself because to procreate, she must commit incest with her father, Woot. These three characters reenact creation stories while rehearsing various forms of archetypal behaviors that instruct young men during initiation and reinforce basic Kuba societal values. The masks and their costumes, with elaborate beads, feathers, animal pelts, cowrie shells, cut-pile cloth, and ornamental trappings, as well as geometric patterning, echo the sumptuousness of the Kuba king himself (FIG. 32-13) and the precepts of Kuba style.

**32-18** Mwashamboy (kneeling) and Bwoom (standing) maskers in a royal ceremony among the Kuba, Democratic Republic of Congo, late 20th century.

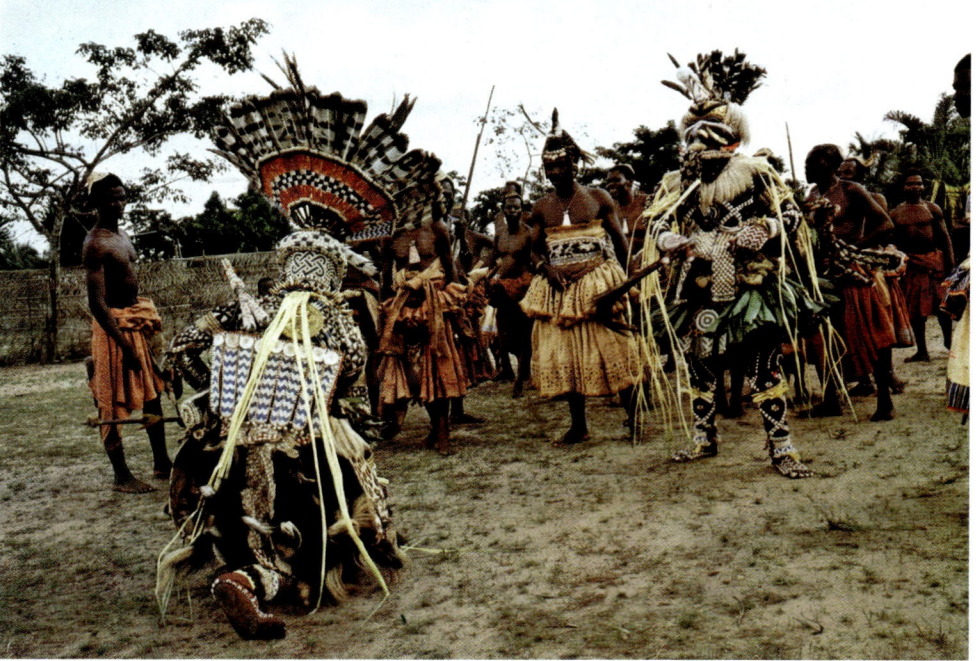

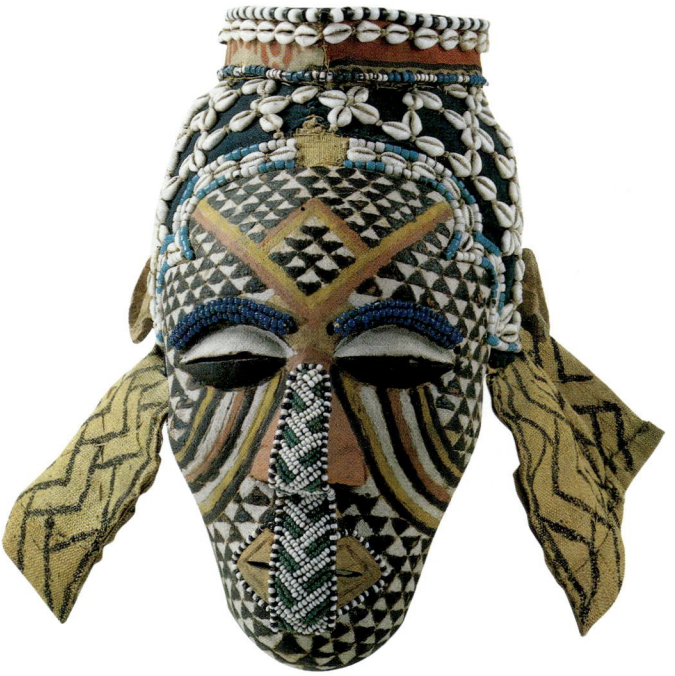

**32-19** Ngady Amwaash mask, Kuba, Democratic Republic of Congo, late 19th or early 20th century. Peabody Museum, Harvard University, Cambridge.

These examples of masks and masquerades, from among the thousands on the continent, exemplify the exceptionally diverse and important values and meanings characterizing this art form. Since African nations gained independence, masks that once had powerful roles in social control have become at least partially secularized. Yet masking remains viable and socially relevant in several parts of the continent in the early 21st century.

The past 50 to 100 years have witnessed many changes in the forms, functions, and meanings of African arts. Many shrines have closed down because of conversions to Islam or Christianity. Colonial governments, followed by those of modern independent nations, have contributed to the erosion of leadership arts even though regalia and court ceremonial attire can still be seen in festivals that continue to be value-laden events.

**FESTIVAL ARTS IN GHANA** Annual festivals in contemporary Ghana, which under British colonial rule was called the Gold Coast, still feature sumptuous royal arts such as gold-leafed wooden sculptures and cast-gold jewelry as well as rich textile arts (FIG. **32-20**). Staffs, swords, stools, and umbrella tops are some of the forms seen, along with rich costuming. The gold-leafed elephant stool represents the dynastic ancestors whose living counterpart, the reigning king, is seated higher up the dais under the double umbrella. Here the visual arts combine with music, dance, and gesture in lavishly orchestrated performances with many purposes. Chiefs and kings are purified as allegiances and loyalties are reaffirmed, the gods and ancestors are honored and thanked (with sacrificial food), first fruits are eaten, deaths of the past year are mourned, and altogether, the community is renewed. This revitalization begins the new year with both the solemnity of ritual and the spectacle of many converging art forms.

**IGBO RENEWAL HOUSES** Among the Igbo just north of the Niger River delta, powerful nature gods demand about every 50 years that a community build an *mbari house*. The Igbo construct these houses from mud as sacrifices to major deities, often Ala, goddess of the earth. The houses are elaborate unified artistic complexes that incorporate numerous unfired clay sculptures and paintings—occasionally more than a hundred in a single mbari

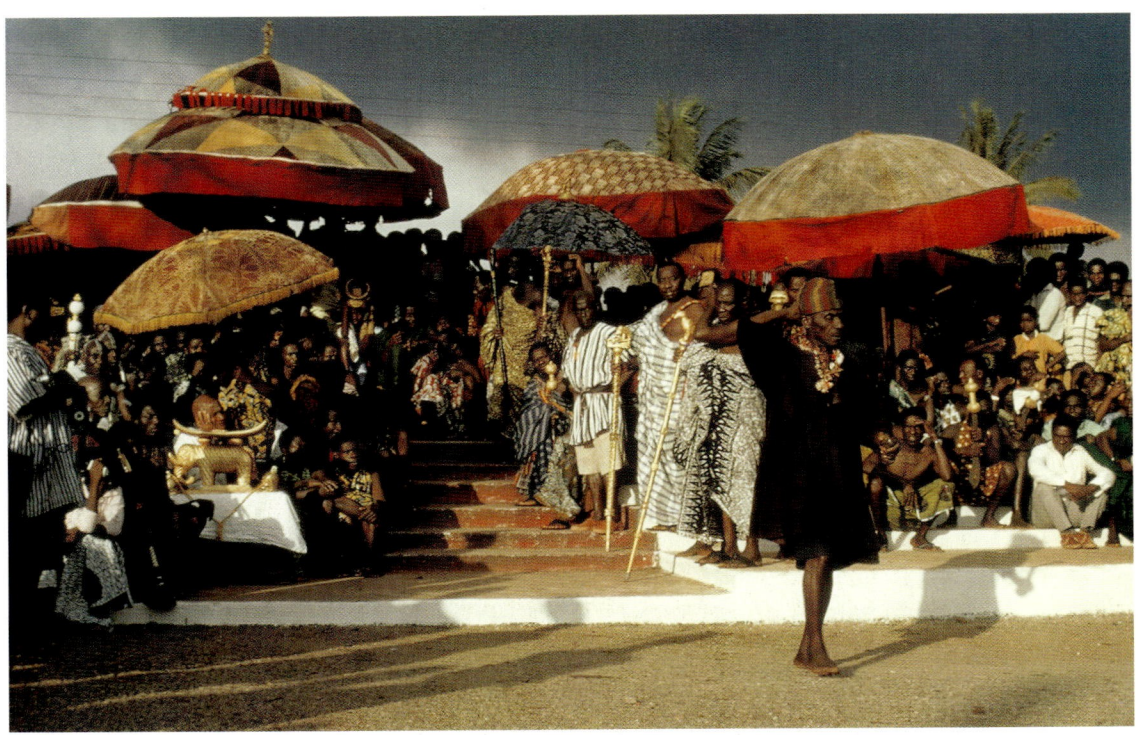

**32-20** Akan festival showing gold-leafed wooden stool, royal umbrellas, and court officials seated in state, Akuropon, Ghana, photographed by Herbert Cole in 1972.

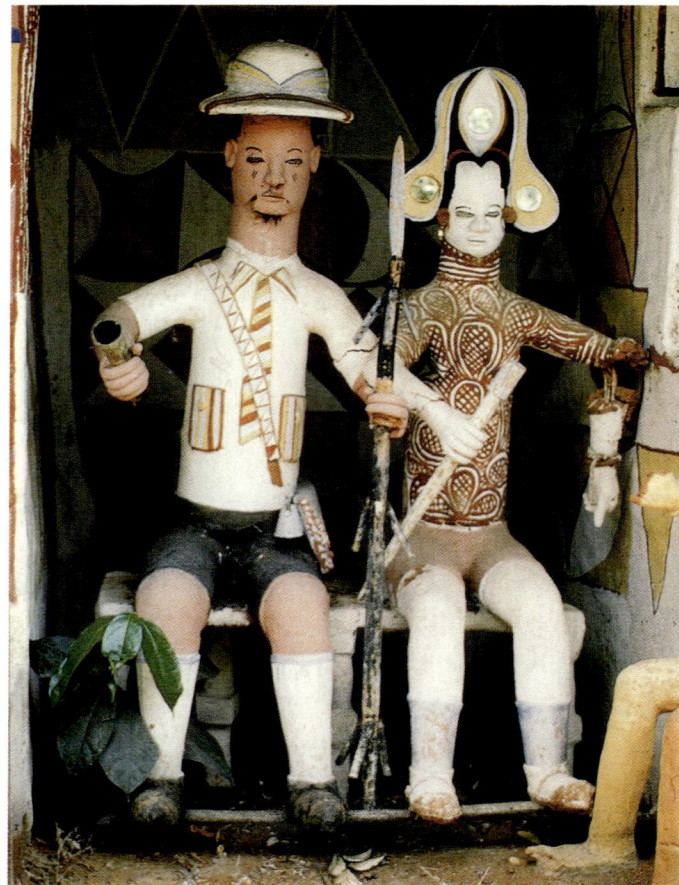

**32-21** The thunder god Amadioha and his wife, painted clay sculptures in an *mbari,* Igbo, Umugote Orishaeze, Nigeria, photographed in 1966. 💿

house. Our illustration (FIG. **32-21**) shows the thunder god Amadioha and his wife in an mbari house at Umugote Orishaeze. The god wears modern clothing, whereas his consort appears with traditional body paint and a fancy hairstyle. These differing modes of dress relate to Igbo concepts of modernity and tradition, both

viewed as positive by the men who control the ritual and art. They allow themselves modern things but want their women to remain traditional. The artist enlarged and extended both figures' torsos, necks, and heads to express their aloofness, dignity, and power. More informally posed figures and groups appear on the other sides of the house, including beautiful, amusing, or frightening figures of animals, humans, and spirits taken from mythology, history, dreams, and everyday life — a kaleidoscope of subjects and meanings.

The mbari construction process, veiled in secrecy behind a fence, is a stylized world-renewal ritual. After the ritual opening, the completed monument shows off that world, the cosmos renewed. Ceremonies for unveiling the house to public view indicate that the god accepted the sacrificial offering (of the mbari) and, for a time at least, will be benevolent. An mbari house never undergoes repair. Instead, it is allowed to disintegrate and return to its source, the earth. The Igbo today rarely make mbari complexes for ritual purposes. Two recent ones, sponsored by the Nigerian government essentially as museums — secular variations on the earlier sacred theme — were constructed of cement. In this way the arts of the past have been preserved to educate future generations.

**BODY ADORNMENT** People in many rural areas of eastern Africa continue to embellish their own bodies, not only for occasional ceremonies, but every day. Samburu men and women in northern Kenya, shown in FIG. **32-22** at a spontaneous dance, each have distinct styles of personal decoration (see "Gender Roles in African Art Production," page 955). Men, particularly warriors who are not yet married, expend hours creating elaborate hairstyles for one another. They paint their bodies with red ocher, and wear bracelets, necklaces, and other bands of beaded jewelry young women make for them. For themselves, women make more lavish constellations of beaded collars, which they mass around their necks. As if to help separate the genders, women shave their heads and adorn them with beaded headbands. Personal decoration begins in childhood, increasing to become lavish and highly self-conscious in young adulthood, and diminishing as people get older. Much of it is coded to reveal information — age, marital or initiation status, parentage of a warrior son — that can be read by those who know the codes. Dress ensembles have evolved over

**32-22** Samburu men and women dancing, northern Kenya, photographed by Herbert Cole in 1973. 💿

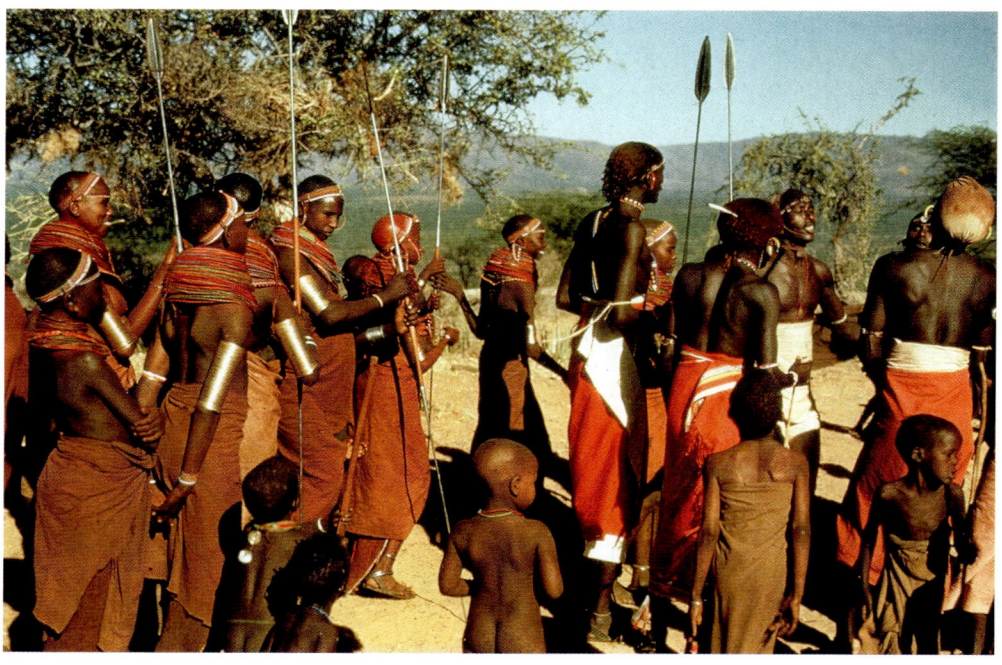

### *Gender Roles in African Art Production*

Until the past decade or two, art production in Africa has been quite rigidly gender specific. Men have been, and largely still are, iron smiths and gold and copper-alloy casters. Men were architects, builders, and carvers of both wood and ivory. Women were, and for the most part remain, wall and body painters, calabash decorators, potters, and often clay sculptors (FIG. 32-9), although men make clay figures in some areas. Both men and women work with beads and weave baskets and textiles, men executing narrow strips (later sewn together) on horizontal looms and women working wider pieces of cloth on vertical looms.

Much African art, however, is collaborative. Men may build a clay wall, for example, but women will normally be called in to decorate it. Igbo mbari houses (FIG. 32-21) are truly collaborative despite the fact that their figures are modeled by professional male artists. Festivals, invoking virtually all the arts, are also collaborative. Masquerades are largely the province of men, yet in some cases women are asked to contribute costume elements such as skirts, wrappers, and scarves. And even though women dance masks among the Mende and related peoples, the masks themselves have always been carved by men.

Until recently in most regions, Africans did not greatly emphasize artists' individuality, even when personal styles were clearly recognizable. This does not mean art is anonymous or that artists are not honored locally. Many artists, like Osei Bonsu (FIGS. 32-10 and 32-11) and Olowe of Ise (FIG. 32-12), were highly appreciated in their own time as they are today. Still, Africans have tended not to exalt artistic individuality as much as Westerners have. All that has been changing over the past few decades, however. Increasingly, even artists in villages want to be recognized for their skills and rewarded for the works they create.

In late colonial and especially in postcolonial times, earlier gender distinctions in art production have been breaking down. Women, as well as men, now weave kente cloth, and a number of women are now sculptors in wood, metal, stone, and composite materials. Men are making pottery, once the exclusive prerogative of women. Both women and men make international art forms in urban and university settings, although male artists are more numerous. One well-known Nigerian woman artist, Sokari Douglas Camp, produces welded metal sculptures, sometimes of masqueraders. Douglas Camp is thus doubly unusual. She might find it difficult to do this work in her traditional home in the Niger River delta, but as she lives and works in London, she encounters no adverse response. In the future there will undoubtedly be a further breaking down of restrictive barriers and greater mobility for artists.

---

time. Different colors and sizes of beads became available, plastics and aluminum were introduced, and specific fashions have changed, but the overall concept of fine personal adornment—that is, dress raised to the level of art—remains much the same today as it was centuries ago.

MAMY WATA Around 1900 in the Niger River delta there appeared a color lithograph of a light-skinned, straight-haired woman controlling large snakes. This print, seen on the wall in FIG. 32-23, was imported from Europe in great numbers and seems to have stimulated the growth of the Mamy Wata ("mother of water") cult as a vehicle for the assimilation and expression of contemporary spiritual values grafted onto traditional ones. Snakes, for example, figure as messengers of many African deities. Mamy Wata came from across the sea, as white people did, bringing riches as well as problems. She is charismatic and beautiful, yet she offers help to those in need, at the price of becoming her devotee. Her priests and priestesses consult her as an oracle. Her special province is modern life—passing exams, for example, or finding enough money to buy a moped or a new suit. She appears in peoples' dreams as an exotic temptress offering glamorous products, often imports of the sort she likes herself.

Mamy Wata's shrines (FIG. 32-23) usually feature one or more brightly colored paintings or sculptures of the snake-entwined woman, the original lithograph, powders, soaps, perfumes, glittery jewelry, dolls, candles, medicines, and a mirror. The mirror is present both because the goddess is vain, and because it serves as a symbolic membrane, an illusory water surface, a kind of "Alice's looking glass" within which wondrous things can happen to those who give Mamy Wata the presents and sacrifices she demands. She can bring wealth or poverty, insanity or health, children or barrenness, depending on how she is treated. One becomes a devotee of Mamy

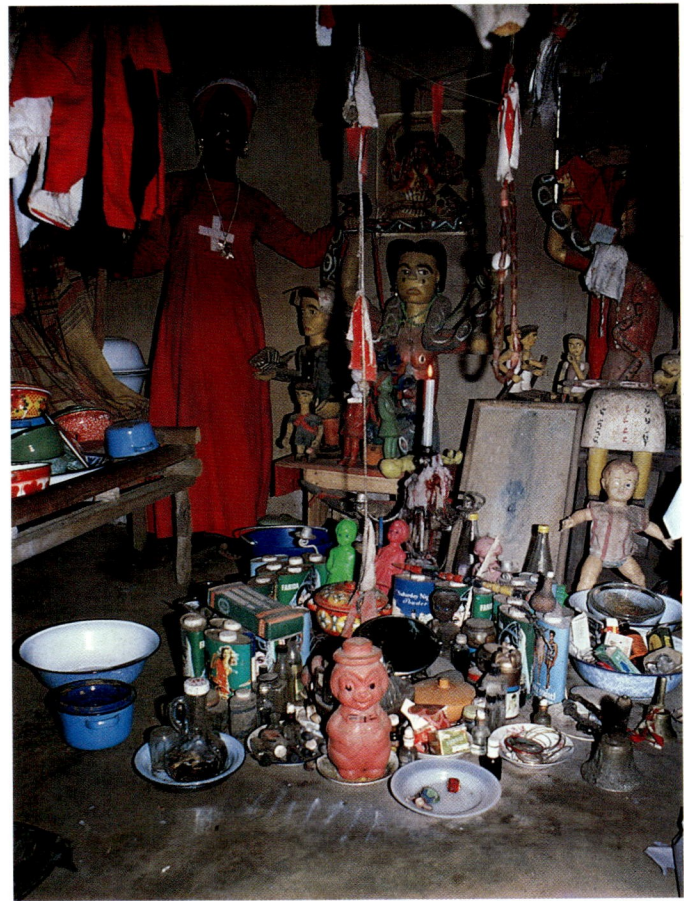

32-23 Mamy Wata shrine with priestess, Igbo, near Owerri town, Nigeria, photographed by Henry J. Drewal in 1978.

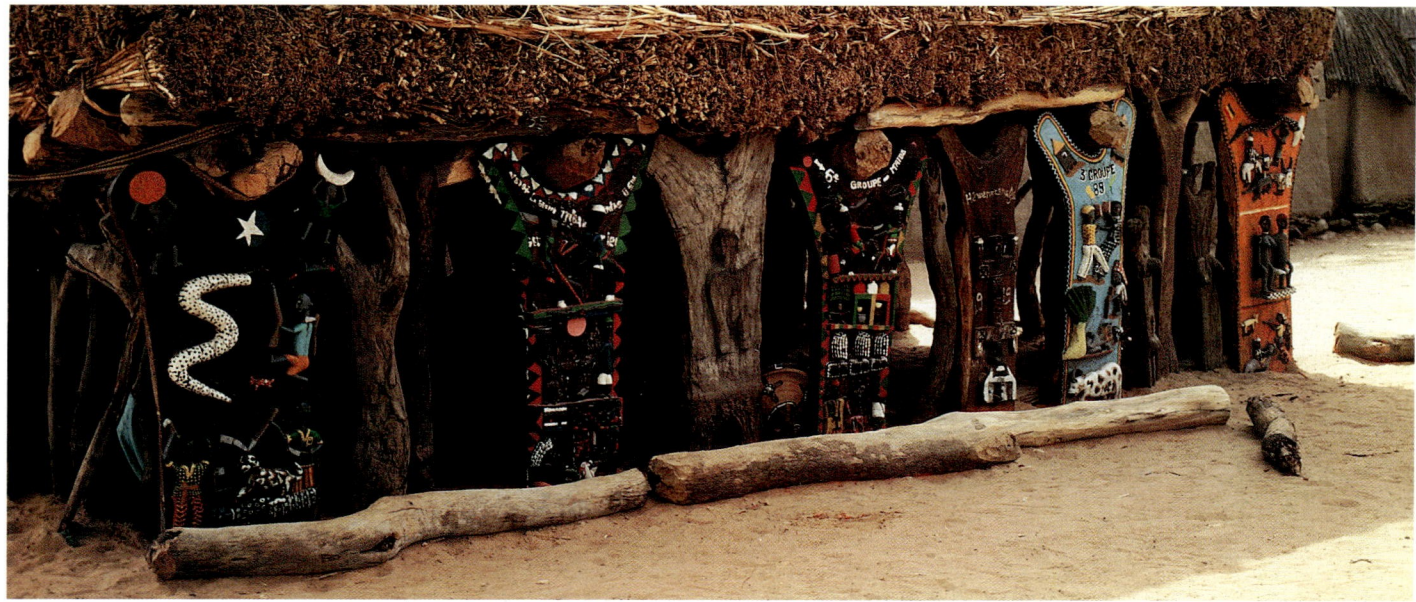

**32-24** *Togu na* ("men's house of words"), Dogon, Mali, photographed in 1989. Wood and pigment.

Wata when one dreams of her or has problems that a diviner feels she may be able to help with. Today there are many thousands of Mamy Wata shrines and worshipers across the breadth of West Africa. As in other shrines, the presence of art heightens the mystique and helps to focus the attention of disciples.

**DOGON HOUSES OF WORDS** Traditionalism and modernism are united in contemporary Dogon *togu na,* or "men's house of words." The togu na is so called because men's deliberations vital to community welfare take place under its sheltering roof. It is considered the "head" and the most important part of the community, which the Dogon characterize with human attributes. The men's houses were built over time. Earlier posts, such as the central one in the togu na we illustrate (FIG. **32-24**), show schematic renderings of legendary female ancestors, similar to stylized ancestral couples (FIG. 32-6) or masked figures (FIG. 32-16). Recent replacement posts feature narrative and topical scenes of varied subjects, such as horsemen or hunters or women preparing food, a lot of descriptive detail, bright polychrome painting in enamels, and even some writing. Unlike earlier traditional sculptors, the contemporary artists who made these posts want to be recognized for their work. Their names are known, and they are eager to sell their work (other than these posts) to tourists.

**GA CASKETS** Today's African artists also tend to use new forms, techniques, and materials within older functional categories. Carved wooden caskets, created by KANE KWEI (1924–1991) and his sons of the Ga people in urban coastal Ghana, exemplify this type of art. Beginning around 1970, Kwei created figurative coffins intended to reflect the deceased's life, occupation, or major accomplishments. On commission he made such diverse shapes as a cow, a whale, and a bird; various local food crops, such as onions and cocoa pods; airplanes; a Mercedes Benz; and a modern villa. These coffins were not carved, but rather pieced together using nails and glue. The artists are carpenters rather than woodcarvers. Kwei also created coffins in traditional leaders' forms, such as an eagle, an elephant, a leopard, and a stool. The coffin illustrated here (FIG. **32-25**), a hen with chicks, was created for a respected woman with a huge family. Kwei died in 1991, but his sons and

former apprentices continue his legacy. Their own commissions—a tiger, a crab, a lobster, a Mercedes, and a fishing canoe—accompanied his coffin from the church to the cemetery.

**A CONGOLESE INTERNATIONALIST** TRIGO PIULA (b. ca. 1950), a contemporary painter of the international school (trained in Western artistic techniques and styles) from the Democratic Republic of Congo, creates works that fuse Western and Congolese images and objects in a pictorial blend that provides social commentary on present-day Congolese culture. *Ta Tele Gabon* (FIG. **32-26**) depicts a group of Congolese citizens staring transfixed at colorful pictures of life beyond Africa displayed on 14 television screens. The TV images include references to travel to exotic places (such as Paris with the Eiffel Tower), sports events, love, the earth seen from a satellite, and Western worldly goods. A traditional Kongo power figure associated with warfare and divination stands at the composition's center as a visual mediator between the anonymous foreground viewers and the multiple TV images. In traditional Kongo contexts (FIG. 32-5), this figure's feather headdress associates it with supernatural and magical powers from the sky, such as lightning and storms. In Piula's rendition, the headdress perhaps refers to the power of airborne televised pictures. In the stomach area, where Kongo power figures often have glass in front of a medicine packet, Piula painted a television screen showing a second power figure, as if to double the figure's power. The artist shows most of the television viewers with a small, white image of a foreign object—car, shoe, heart (signifying love), bottle, or knife and fork—on the backs of their heads.

One meaning of this picture appears to be that television messages have deadened Congolese peoples' minds to anything but modern thoughts or commodities. The power figure stands squarely on brown earth. Two speaker cabinets set against the back wall beneath the TV screens are wired to the figure, which in the past could inflict harm. In traditional Kongo thinking and color symbolism, the color white and earth tones are associated with spirits and the land of the dead. Perhaps Piula suggests that like earlier power figures, the contemporary world's new television-induced consumerism is poisoning the minds and souls of Congolese people as if by magic or sorcery.

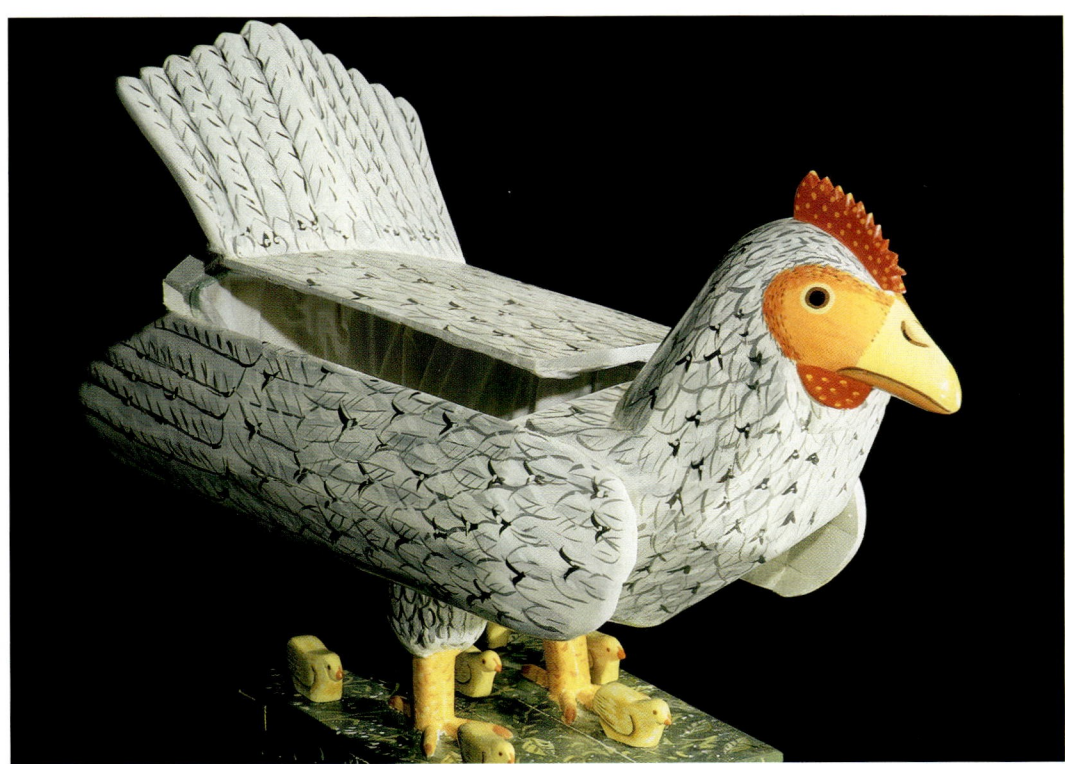

**32-25** KANE KWEI, coffin in the shape of a hen with chicks, Ga, Ghana, 1989. Wood and pigment, 7′ 6½′ long. Museum voor Volkenkunde, Rotterdam.

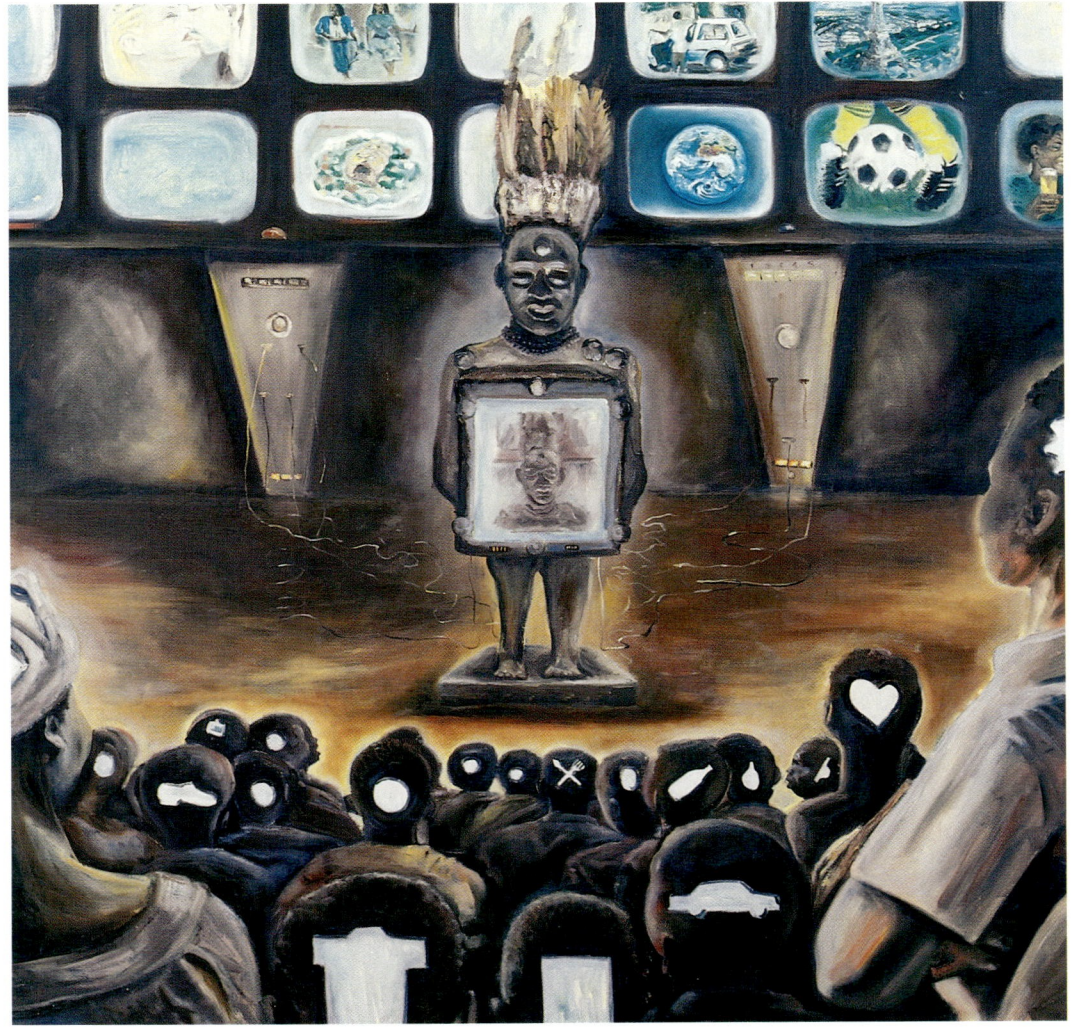

**32-26** TRIGO PIULA, *Ta Tele Gabon*, Democratic Republic of Congo, 1988. Oil on canvas, 3′ 3⅜″ × 3′ 4⅜″. National Museum of African Art, Smithsonian Institution, Washington.

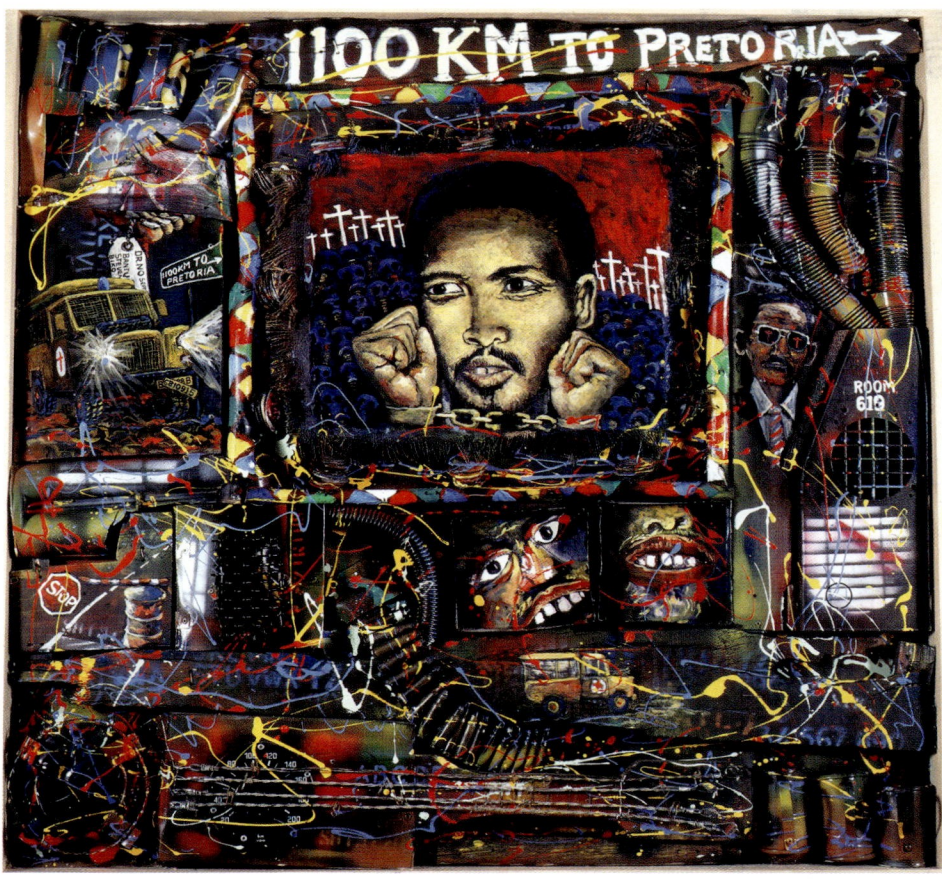

**32-27** WILLIE BESTER, *Homage to Steve Biko*, South Africa, 1992. Mixed media, 3′ 7⅚″ × 3′ 7⅚″. © Willie Bester.

**ART AND SOCIAL PROTEST** Many contemporary African art forms are formally vibrant, as well as concerned with social and political issues. Art in South Africa, for example, first helped protest against *apartheid* (government-sponsored racial separation), then celebrated its demise and the subsequent democratically elected government under the first president, Nelson Mandela. The contemporary artist WILLIE BESTER, in his 1992 *Homage to Steve Biko* (FIG. **32-27**), was among the critics of the apartheid system. Biko, a gentle and heroic leader of the Black Liberation Movement, was killed by white authorities while in detention. The two white doctors in charge of him were exonerated at Biko's inquest, setting off protests around the world. Bester packs his layered picture with references to death and injustice. Biko's portrait, at the center, is near another of the police minister, Kruger, who had him transported 1100 miles to Pretoria in the yellow Land Rover ambulance seen left of center and again beneath Biko's portrait. Bester shows Biko with his chained fists raised in the recurrent protest gesture. This portrait memorializes both Biko and the many others—indicated by the white graveyard crosses above a blue sea of skulls beside Biko's head. The crosses stand out against a red background that recalls the inferno of burned townships. The stop sign (lower left) seems to mean "stop Kruger," or perhaps "stop apartheid." Biko's death is referenced also by the tagged foot, as if in a morgue, above the ambulance (to the left). The red crosses on this vehicle's door and on Kruger's reflective dark glasses repeat, with sad irony, the graveyard crosses.

Blood red and ambulance yellow are in fact unifying colors dripped or painted on many parts of the work. Writing and numbers, found fragments and signs, both stenciled and painted, also appear throughout the composition. Numbers refer to dehumanized life under apartheid. Found objects—wire, sticks, cardboard, sheet metal, cans, and other discards—from which fragile,

impermanent township dwellings are created, remind viewers of the degraded, impoverished lives of most South African people of color. The oilcan guitar (bottom center), another recurrent Bester symbol, refers both to the social harmony and joy provided by music and to the control imposed by apartheid policies. The whole composition is richly textured and dense in its collage combinations of objects, photographs, signs, symbols, and painting. *Homage to Steve Biko* is a radical and powerful critique of an oppressive sociopolitical system, and it exemplifies the extent to which art can be invoked in the political process.

## CONCLUSION

African art has always changed and developed in response to the continent's evolving history, both before and after the arrival of Europeans in Africa. During the past two centuries, the encroachments of Christianity, Islam, Western education, market economies, and other colonial imports have led to increasing secularization in all the arts of Africa. Many figures and masks earlier commissioned for shrines or as incarnations of ancestors or spirits are now made mostly for sale to outsiders, essentially as tourist arts. Dogon masks are regularly danced briefly for tourists, after which some of the masks are sold. In towns and cities, painted murals and cement sculptures appear frequently, often making implicit comments about modern life. Nonetheless, despite the growing importance of urbanism (pre-European in a few areas), most African people still live in rural communities. Traditional values, although under pressure, hold considerable force in villages especially, and some people adhere to spiritual beliefs that uphold traditional art forms. African art remains as varied as the vast continent itself and continues to change.

**1800**

■ ACTIVE CHRISTIAN MISSIONIZING, 19TH CENTURY

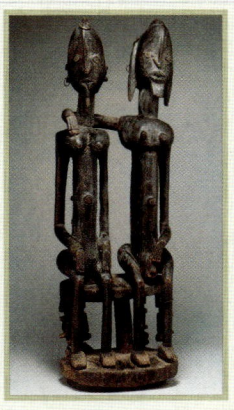

1 Seated couple, Dogon, Mali, ca. 1800-1850

**1850**

■ BERLIN CONFERENCE DIVIDING CONTINENT AMONG COLONIAL POWERS, 1884-1885

■ EUROPEAN COUNTRIES COLONIZE MOST OF AFRICA, CA. 1885–1924

■ BRITISH PUNITIVE EXPEDITION SACKS BENIN, 1897

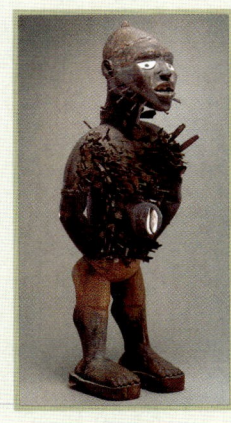

**1900**

■ FIRST WORLD WAR, 1914-1918

■ SECOND WORLD WAR, 1939-1945

2 Nail figure, Kongo, Democratic Republic of Congo, ca. 1875–1900

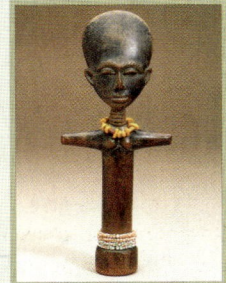

**1950**

■ MOST AFRICAN COUNTRIES ACHIEVE INDEPENDENCE, BEGINNING CA. 1960

3 Osei Bonsu, *akua'ba*, Asante, Ghana, ca. 1935

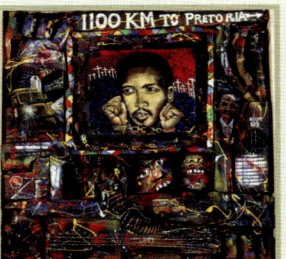

**2000**

4 Willie Bester, *Homage to Steve Biko*, South Africa, 1992

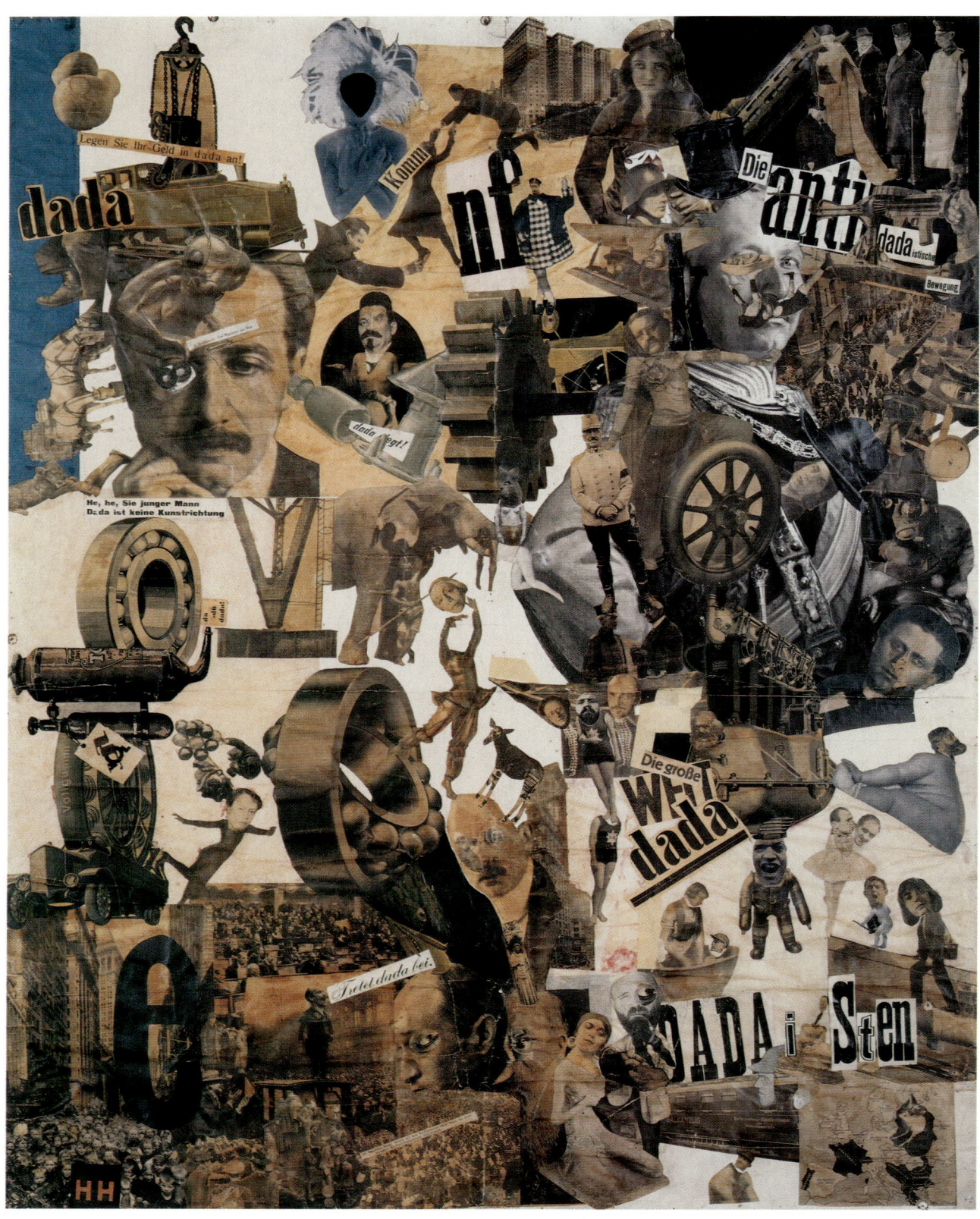

Hannah Höch, *Cut with the Kitchen Knife Dada through the Last Weimar Beer Belly Cultural Epoch of Germany*, 1919–1920. Photomontage, 3′ 9″ × 2′ 11½″. Neue Nationalgalerie, Staatliche Museen, Berlin.

# 33

# THE DEVELOPMENT OF MODERNIST ART

## THE EARLY 20TH CENTURY

The decisive changes that marked the 19th century—industrialization, urbanization, and the growth of nationalism and imperialism—are chronicled in Chapter 29. During the first half of the 20th century, rampant industrialization matured into international industrial capitalism, which fueled the rise of consumer economies.

## REVOLUTION AND WORLD WAR

As in the 19th century, these developments presented societies with great promise, as well as significant problems. Appropriately, these changes prompted both elation and anxiety. The combination of euphoria and alienation that was the hallmark of fin de siècle culture in Europe (see Chapter 29, page 896) carried through the next decades. Momentous historical events—World War I, the Great Depression, the rise of totalitarianism, and World War II—exacerbated this rather schizophrenic attitude. The arts manifested the same conflicted mind-set through the stark contrast of, on the one hand, the lofty utopian visions of artistic groups such as the Bauhaus and De Stijl, and, on the other, the scathing social commentary of the Dada artists.

### 20th-Century Intellectual Developments

In the early 20th century, societies worldwide contended with discoveries and new ways of thinking in a wide variety of fields, including science, technology, economics, and politics. These new ideas forced people to revise radically how they understood their worlds. In particular, the values and ideals that were the legacy of the Scientific Revolution (during the Age of Newton) and the Enlightenment began to yield to innovative views. Thus, intellectuals countered 18th- and 19th-century assumptions about progress and reason with ideas challenging traditional notions about the physical universe, the structure of society, and human nature. Artists participated in this reassessment.

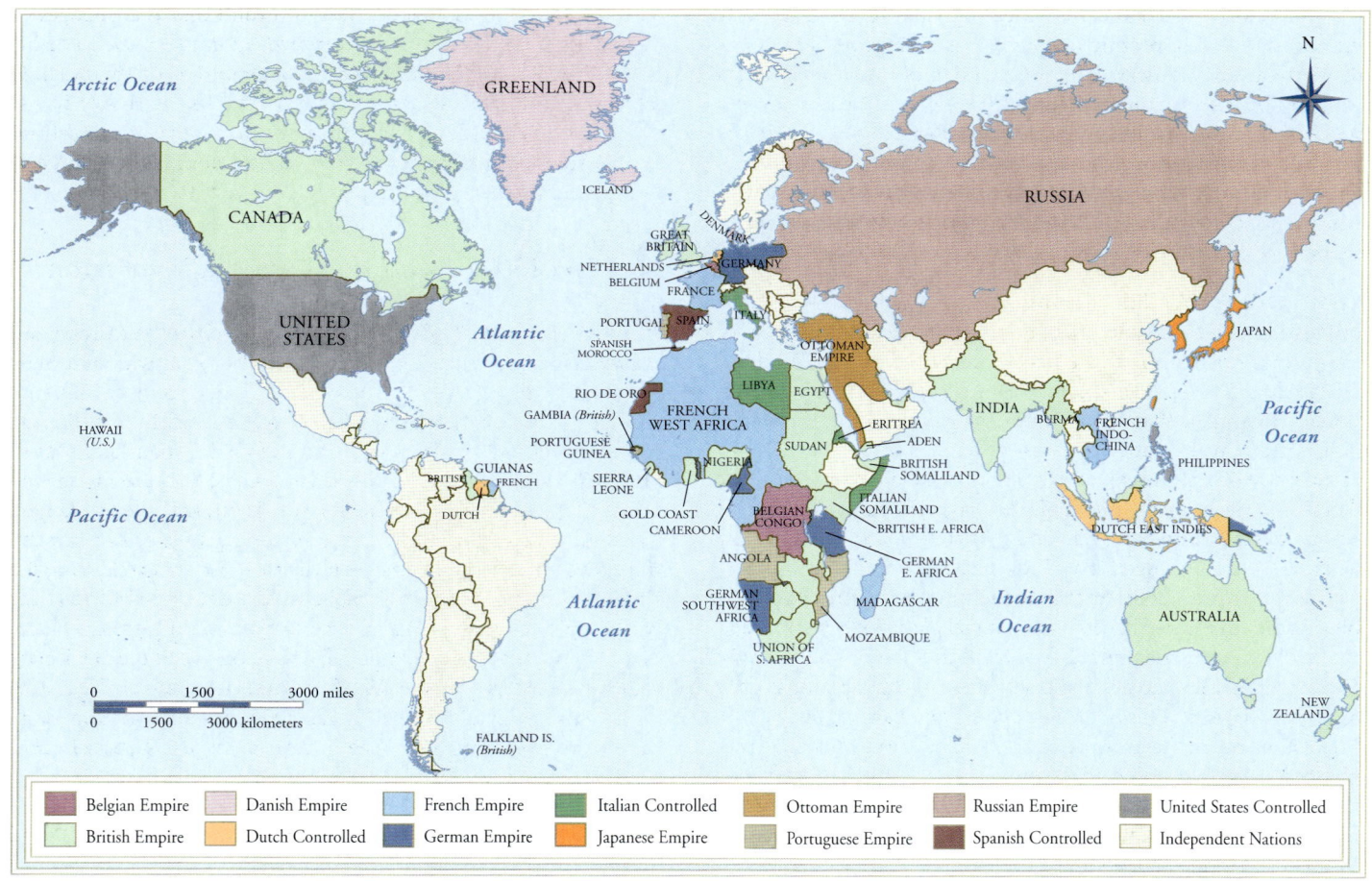

**MAP 33-1** Colonial empires about 1900.

Modernist artists, in particular, often acknowledged these new discoveries and shifting theoretical bases in their work. Accordingly, much of the history of early-20th-century Western art is a history of a radical rejection—the rejection of traditional limitations and definitions both of art and of the universe.

**CHALLENGING NEWTONIAN PHYSICS** One of the fundamental Enlightenment beliefs was faith in science. Because it was based on empirical, or observable, fact, science provided a mechanistic conception of the universe, which reassured a populace that was finding traditional religions less certain. As promoted in the classic physics of Isaac Newton, the universe was a huge machine consisting of time, space, and matter. The early 20th century witnessed an astounding burst of scientific activity challenging this model of the universe. It amounted to what has been called "the second scientific and technological revolution." Particularly noteworthy was the work of various physicists: Max Planck (1858–1947) of Germany, German-born Albert Einstein (1879–1955), Ernest Rutherford (1871–1937) of Britain, and Niels Bohr (1885–1962) of Denmark. With their discoveries, each of these scientists shattered the existing faith in the objective reality of matter and, in so doing, paved the way for a new model of the universe. Planck's quantum theory (1900) raised questions about the emission of atomic energy. Einstein furthered these studies of thermodynamics. In his 1905 paper, *The Electrodynamics of Moving Bodies,* he outlined his theory of relativity. He argued that space and time are not absolute, as postulated in Newtonian physics. Rather, Einstein explained, time and space are relative to the observer and linked in what he called a four-dimensional space-time continuum. He also concluded that matter,

rather than a solid, tangible reality, was actually another form of energy. Einstein's famous equation, $E = mc^2$, where $E$ stands for energy, $m$ for mass, and $c$ for the speed of light, provided a formula for understanding atomic energy. Rutherford's and Bohr's exploration of atomic structure between 1906 and 1913 contributed to this new perception of matter and energy. Together, all these scientific discoveries constituted a changed view of physical nature and raised the curtain on the Atomic Age.

**ADVANCES IN TECHNOLOGY** Beyond the realm of physics, advances in chemistry, biology, biochemistry, microbiology, and medicine in the early 20th century yielded knowledge of polymers, plastics, fertilizers, enzymes, viruses, vitamins, hormones, and antibiotics. Molecular biologists analyzed and described the structure of cells and tissues, as well as the electrical nature of the brain and nervous system. Their investigations into proteins and nucleic acids led to an understanding of the genetic structure of life. The most conspicuous technological advances, which largely depended on the scientific discoveries, were in communication and transportation. People adapted to radios, radar, televisions, and talking cinema, as well as automobiles, airplanes, electrified railway and municipal transit systems, and electrification of street lighting and home appliances.

Chemical technology became an industry as important as electrical technology. It had its greatest impact in the world of materials, in mining, metals, oil refining, textiles, pharmaceuticals, agriculture, food production, and food processing. It was particularly useful in the fight against disease and famine, although at this time its long-term ecological effects were unknown.

The field of mechanical engineering experienced great advances as well. Mass production and the assembly line became indispensable to industry. Chemical and biological researchers found scientific instruments such as the electron microscope essential to their work. The requirements of calculation, vastly expanded by the new complexities of scientific research and the machine environment, demanded electronic instrumentation and control mechanisms. Cybernetic theory and early computer models were in place by midcentury.

**MIND OVER MATTER** In other realms of thought—philosophy, psychology, and economic theory—significant challenges to the primacy of reason and objective reality emerged. Friedrich Nietzsche (1844–1900), a German intellectual, rejected the rational. He argued that Western society was decadent and incapable of any real creativity precisely because of its excessive reliance on reason at the expense of emotion and passion. Nietzsche blamed Christianity for much of Western civilization's decay, and he insisted that societies could attain liberation and renewal only when they acknowledged that God was dead.

Also instrumental in examining the irrational mind and destabilizing the entrenched belief in the rational nature of humanity and the world was the Viennese doctor Sigmund Freud (1856–1939). He developed the fundamental principles for what became known as psychoanalysis. In his book *The Interpretation of Dreams* (1900), Freud argued that the unconscious and inner drives (of which people are largely unaware) control human behavior. Freud concluded that this control by the unconscious is due to repression—that is, individuals' mental suppression of uncomfortable experiences or memories. Making patients aware of repressed memories or unconscious conflicts through psychoanalysis and dream analysis, Freud believed, could assure patients' mental well-being.

During the 20th century, Freud's ideas gained popularity. Another very influential psychiatrist who expanded on Freud's theories was the Swiss doctor Carl Jung (1875–1961). Jung believed that therapists could understand the behavior and personality of an individual by identifying patterns in his or her dreams. Further, Jung asserted that the unconscious is composed of two facets, a personal unconscious and a collective unconscious. The collective unconscious comprises memories and associations all humans share, such as archetypes (original models) and mental constructions. According to Jung, the collective unconscious accounts for the development of myths, religions, and philosophies.

## The Rise of Industrial Capitalism

The industrialization so prominent during the 19th century matured quickly. By the early part of the 20th century, boards of directors controlled large-scale firms. These were often far-flung enterprises with enormous factories. The "captains of industry"—the owners and managers of these industrial giants—wielded extraordinary economic and political power. Due to the widening gap between these captains of industry and the laborers, Marxism (see Chapter 29, page 854) grew in popularity. Marxism's championing of the working classes held great appeal; as a result, enrollment in trade unions and socialist parties increased. Although the socialists did not have unified strategies, they all agreed that the capitalist profit system exploited the workers and enriched the owners, causing the deplorable living and working conditions of most laborers.

As dramatic as the societal changes were in the 19th century, even greater uncertainty and anxiety marked the 20th century. Not only were the conditions of people's lives very different, but

also they faced fundamental, indeed revolutionary, challenges in how they viewed the world, prompted by thinkers such as Einstein, Freud, and Nietzsche. The fragmentation of the tangible object in Cubist paintings and the interest in the subconscious that is the hallmark of Surrealism are just some of the artistic manifestations of these new ways of understanding the world and our place in it that we will explore in this chapter.

## World War I and the Russian Revolution

The development of advanced industrial societies in Europe and America led to frenzied imperialist expansion. Countries controlled far-flung empires (MAP 33-1) and spread their spheres of influence worldwide. By the beginning of the 20th century, Britain, France, Germany, Belgium, Italy, Spain, and Portugal all had footholds in Africa. In Asia, Britain ruled India, the Dutch controlled Indonesia's vast archipelago, the French held power in Indochina, and the Russians ruled Central Asia and Siberia. Japan began rising as a new and formidable Pacific power that would stake its claims to empire in the 1930s. Such imperialism was capitalist and expansionist, establishing colonies as raw-material sources, as manufacturing markets, and as territorial acquisitions. Imperialism also often had the missionary dimension of bringing the "light" of Christianity and civilization to "backward peoples" and educating "inferior races." This mission, driven by social Darwinism (see Chapter 29, page 854), based its beliefs on Charles Darwin's idea of the survival of the fittest.

**THE GREAT WAR** Although many people hoped the development of nation-states would result in peace and harmony, this was not to be. Rather than cooperation, the prevalent nationalism and rampant imperialism led to competition. Eventually, countries negotiated alliances to protect their individual interests. The conflicts between the two major blocs—the Triple Alliance (Germany, Austria-Hungary, and Italy), and the Triple Entente (Russia, France, and Great Britain)—led to World War I. In July 1914, Austria-Hungary declared war on Serbia. The Great War lasted until 1918. Allegiances shifted with the changing fortunes of different countries. The initial enthusiasm of the war effort revealed the strength of nationalist sentiments.

The slaughter and devastation soon destroyed any romantic illusions soldiers held about World War I. Not only were over nine million men killed in battle, but the introduction of poison gas in 1915 also added to the horror of humankind's inhumanity to itself. Although the United States tried to remain neutral, it finally felt compelled to enter the war in 1917.

In 1919, the 27 Allied nations negotiated the official end of World War I. The devastation of World War I brought widespread misery, social disruption, and economic collapse—the ultimate effects of nationalism, imperialism, and expansionist goals.

**THE TSAR'S DEMISE** The Russian Revolution exacerbated the global chaos when it erupted in 1917. Dissatisfaction with the regime of Tsar Nicholas II had led workers to stage a general strike, and the monarchy's rule ended with the tsar's abdication in March. In late 1917 the Bolsheviks wrested control of the country from the ruling Provisional Government. The Bolsheviks, a faction of Russian Social Democrats led by V. I. Lenin (1870–1924), promoted violent revolution and were eventually renamed the Communists. Once in power, Lenin nationalized the land and turned it over to the local rural soviets (councils of workers' and soldiers' deputies). After extensive civil war, the Communists succeeded in retaining control of Russia, officially renamed the Soviet Union in 1923.

## The Great Depression and World War II

The resolution of World War I was indeed tenuous; the Great Depression of the 1930s dealt a serious blow to the stability of Western countries. Largely due to the international scope of banking and industrial capitalism, the economic depression deeply affected the United States and many European countries. By 1932, 25 percent of the British workforce was unemployed, and 40 percent of German workers were without jobs. Production in the United States plummeted by 50 percent.

**WORLD WAR ONCE AGAIN** This economic disaster, along with the failure of postwar treaties and the League of Nations to keep the peace, provided a fertile breeding ground for dangerous forces to emerge once again. In the 1920s and 1930s, totalitarian regimes came to the fore in several European countries. Benito Mussolini (1883–1945) headed the nationalistic Fascist regime in Italy. Joseph Stalin (1879–1953) gained control of the Communist Party in the Soviet Union in 1929. Concurrently, Adolf Hitler (1889–1945) consolidated his power in Germany by building the National Socialist German Workers' Party (also known as the Nazi Party) into a mass political movement.

These ruthless seizures of power led to the many conflicts that evolved into World War II. This catastrophic struggle erupted in 1939 when Germany invaded Poland and Britain and France declared war on Germany. Eventually, this conflict earned its designation as a world war; while Germany and Italy fought most of Europe and the Soviet Union, Japan invaded China and occupied Indochina. After the Japanese bombing of Pearl Harbor in Hawaii in 1941, the United States declared war on Japan. Germany, in loose alliance with Japan, declared war on the United States. Although most of the concerns of individual countries participating in World War II were territorial and nationalistic, other agendas surfaced as well. The Nazis, propelled by Hitler's staunch anti-Semitism, were determined to build a racially exclusive Aryan state. This resolve led to the horror of the Holocaust, the killing of nearly two out of every three European Jews.

World War II drew to an end in 1945, when the Allied forces defeated Germany and the United States dropped atomic bombs on Hiroshima and Nagasaki in Japan. The shock of the war's physical, economic, and psychological devastation immediately tempered the elation people felt at the conclusion of these global hostilities.

## The Evolution of Modernism and the Avant-Garde

Like other members of society, artists were deeply affected by the upheaval of the early 20th century. At times, they responded with energy and optimism, while at other times they descended into bleak despair. Changes in the art world itself also influenced artistic developments. The challenges of Impressionism, Post-Impressionism, and the various renegade and alternative exhibitions diminished the academies' authority, although they remained a presence.

For artists, working within the crucible of historical turmoil, contending with shifting institutional structures within the art world, and acknowledging the significance of modernism (see Chapter 29, which chronicled its development) led to an incredibly fertile period for the evolution of art. In particular, the avant-garde (see Chapter 29, page 886), first discussed in conjunction with the Post-Impressionists, became a major force. Like their 19th-century predecessors, early-20th-century avant-garde artists positioned

themselves in the forefront by aggressively challenging traditional and often cherished notions about art and its relation to society. As the old social orders collapsed and new ones, from communism to corporate capitalism, took their places, one of the self-imposed tasks school after school of 20th-century avant-gardes embraced was the search for new definitions of and uses for art in a radically changed world. This does not suggest, however, that the avant-garde represented a unified group—far from it. Some avant-garde artists used their art to powerfully criticize political and social institutions. Because the term *avant-garde* emerged in art after its use in politics, these critiques prompted the general public to associate avant-garde artists with radical political thought and anarchism. In contrast, other avant-garde artists in essence withdrew from society and concentrated their attention on art as a unique activity, separate from society at large. These artists pursued an introspective examination of artistic principles and elements (continuing the modernist critique), which increasingly focused on formal qualities.

## EXPRESSIONISM IN EARLY-20TH-CENTURY EUROPE

Aspects of all these avant-garde strains contributed to the emergence of *expressionism*. The term has been used over the years in connection with a wide range of art. Simply put, expressionism refers to art that is the result of the artist's unique inner or personal vision and that often has an emotional dimension. This contrasts, for example, with art focused on visually describing the empirical world. The term first gained currency in the early 20th century and was popularized in *Der Sturm,* an avant-garde periodical initially published in Munich. Herwarth Walden, the editor of *Der Sturm,* proclaimed: "We call the art of this century Expressionism in order to distinguish it from what is not art. We are thoroughly aware that artists of previous centuries also sought expression. Only they did not know how to formulate it."[1]

In this chapter and the next, we classify several movements as expressionist, from *German Expressionism* of the 1910s to Abstract Expressionism (also known as the New York School), which emerged in the United States in the 1940s. Some of this expressionist art evokes visceral emotional responses from the viewer, whereas other such artworks rely on the artist's introspective revelations. Often the expressionists offended viewers and even critics, but they sought empathy—connection between the internal states of artists and viewers—not sympathy.

### Fauvism

One of the first movements to tap into this pervasive desire for expression was *Fauvism.* In 1905, at the third Salon d'Automne in Paris, a group of young painters under the leadership of Henri Matisse exhibited canvases so simplified in design and so shockingly bright in color that a startled critic described the artists as *fauves* (wild beasts). The Fauves were totally independent of the French Academy and the "official" Salon (see "The Academies: Defining the Range of Acceptable Art," Chapter 29, page 862). The Fauve movement was driven by a desire to develop an art that had the directness of Impressionism but that also used intense color juxtapositions and their emotional capabilities, the legacy of artists such as van Gogh and Gauguin. The Fauves had seen the works of these two artists (shown in retrospective exhibitions in Paris in 1901 and 1903), but Fauve artists went even further in liberating color from its descriptive function and using it for both expressive and structural ends. They produced portraits, landscapes, still lifes, and nudes of spontaneity and verve, with rich surface textures, lively linear patterns, and, above all, bold colors. The Fauves went beyond any earlier artist by newly intensifying color with startling contrasts of vermilion and emerald green and of cerulean blue and vivid orange held together by sweeping brush strokes and bold patterns. In their work, these artists explored both facets of expressionism. They combined outward expressionism, in the form of a bold release of internal feelings through wild color and powerful, even brutal, brushwork, and inward expressionism, awakening the viewer's emotions by these very devices.

The Fauve painters never officially organized, and the looseness of both personal connections and stylistic affinities caused the Fauve movement to begin to disintegrate almost as soon as it emerged. Within five years, most of the artists had departed from a strict adherence to Fauve principles and developed their own more personal styles. During its brief existence, however, the Fauve movement made a remarkable contribution to the direction of art by demonstrating color's structural, expressive, and aesthetic capabilities.

**THE PRIMACY OF COLOR** The Fauve use of color is particularly apparent in the work of HENRI MATISSE (1869–1954), who was the dominant figure of this group. Matisse realized that color could play a primary role in conveying meaning and focused his efforts on developing this notion. His *Woman with the Hat* (FIG. 33-1) is an instructive example of this. Matisse depicted his wife, Amélie, in a rather conventional manner compositionally. However, the seemingly arbitrary colors immediately strike the viewer. The entire image—the woman's face, clothes, hat, and background—consists of patches and splotches of color juxtaposed in ways that sometimes produce jarring contrasts. Matisse explained his approach: "What characterized fauvism was that we rejected imitative colors, and that with pure colors we obtained stronger reactions—more striking simultaneous reactions, and there was also the luminosity of our colors."[2] Matisse's reference to luminosity linked him to Cézanne, who argued that painters could not reproduce light but must represent it by color. For Matisse and the Fauves, therefore, color became the formal element most responsible for pictorial coherence and the primary conveyor of meaning.

**FROM GREEN, TO BLUE, TO RED** The maturation of these color discoveries can be seen in Matisse's *Red Room* (*Harmony in Red;* FIG. **33-2**). Here, the viewer is confronted with the interior of a comfortable, prosperous household with a maid placing fruit and wine on the table. The artist's color selection and juxtapositions generate much of the feeling of warmth and comfort. He depicted objects in simplified and schematized fashion and

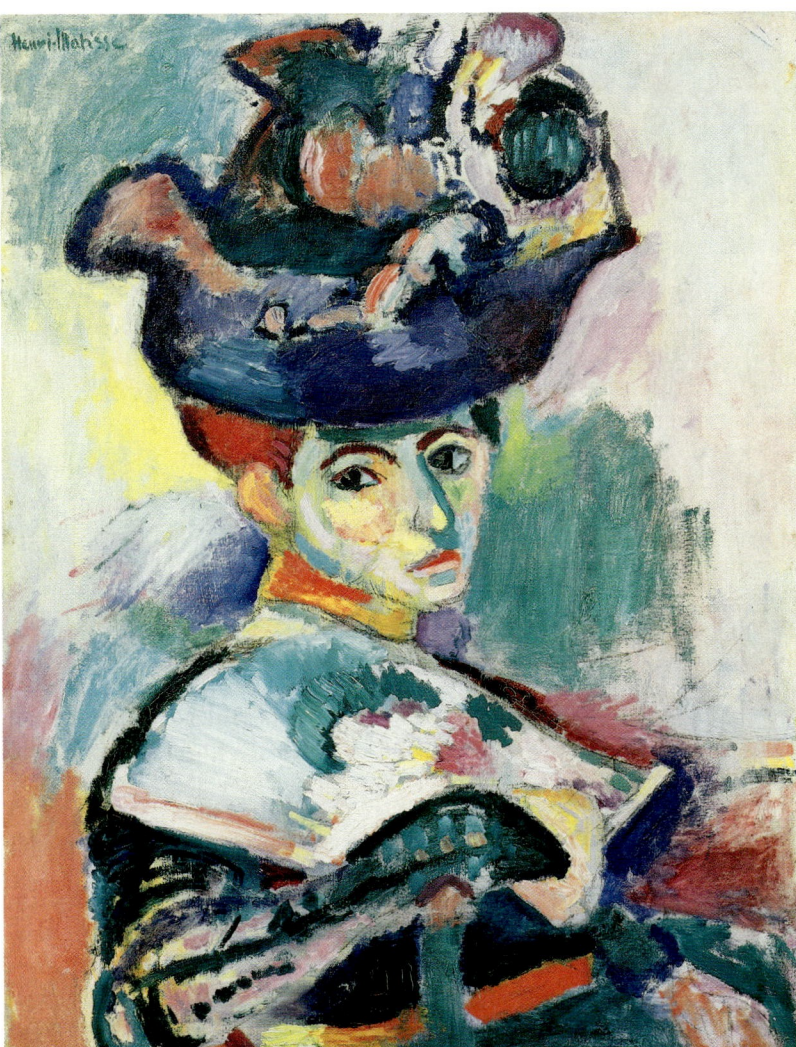

**33-1** HENRI MATISSE, *Woman with the Hat,* 1905. Oil on canvas, 2′ 7¾″ × 1′ 11½″. San Francisco Museum of Modern Art, San Francisco (bequest of Elise S. Haas).

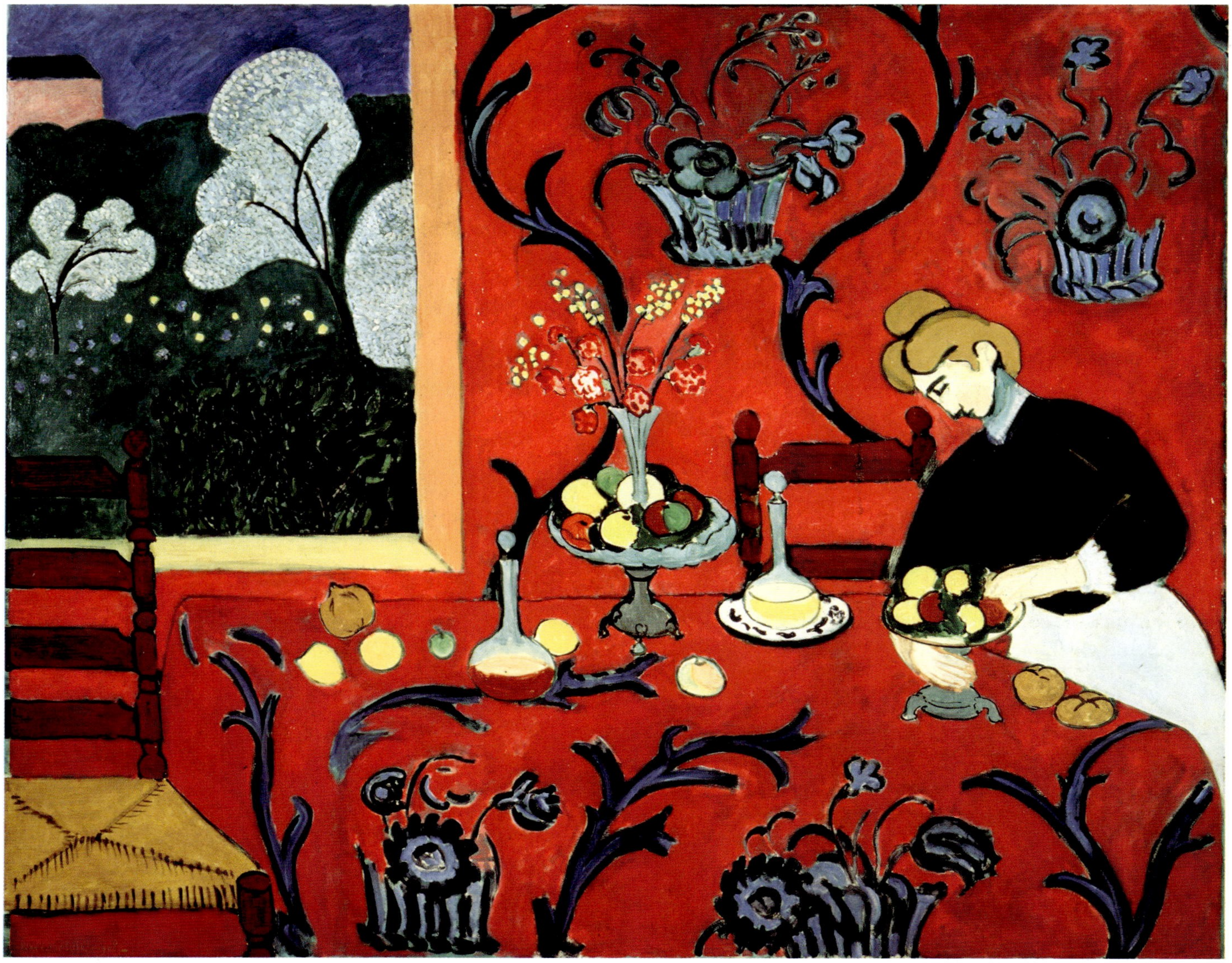

**33-2** Henri Matisse, *Red Room (Harmony in Red)*, 1908–1909. Oil on canvas, approx. 5′ 11″ × 8′ 1″. State Hermitage Museum, Saint Petersburg.

flattened out the forms—for example, he eliminated the front edge of the table, making the table, with its identical patterning, as flat as the wall behind it. The colors, however, contrast richly and intensely. Matisse's process of overpainting reveals color's importance for striking the right chord in the viewer. Initially, this work was predominantly green, and then he repainted it blue. Neither color seemed appropriate to Matisse, and not until he repainted this work red did he feel he had struck the proper chord. Like van Gogh and Gauguin, Matisse expected color to provoke an emotional resonance in the viewer. He declared: "Color was not given to us in order that we should imitate Nature. It was given to us so that we can express our own emotions."[3]

**EXPRESSING CONTENT WITH COLOR** André Derain (1880–1954), also a Fauve group member, worked closely with Matisse. Like Matisse, Derain worked to use color to its fullest potential—for aesthetic and compositional coherence, to increase luminosity, and to elicit emotional responses from the viewer. *The Dance* (FIG. **33-3**) is typical of Derain's art. The perspective is flattened out, and color delineates space. In addition, the artist indicated light and shadow not by differences in value, but by contrasts of hue. Finally, color does not describe the local tones of objects; instead, it expresses the picture's content.

## German Expressionism: Die Brücke

The immediacy and boldness of the Fauve images appealed to many artists, including the German Expressionists. However, although color plays a prominent role in the work of the German Expressionists, the expressiveness of their images is due as much to the wrenching distortions of form, ragged outline, and agitated brush strokes. This resulted in savagely powerful, emotional canvases in the years leading to World War I.

The first group of German artists to explore expressionist ideas gathered in Dresden in 1905 under the leadership of ERNST LUDWIG KIRCHNER (1880–1938). The group members thought of themselves as paving the way for a more perfect age by bridging the old age and the new. They derived their name, Die Brücke (The Bridge), from this concept. Kirchner's early studies in architecture, painting, and the graphic arts had instilled in him a deep admiration for German medieval art. Like the British artists associated with the Arts and Crafts movement, such as William Morris (see FIG. 29-51), members of this group modeled themselves on their ideas of medieval craft guilds by living together and practicing all the arts equally. Kirchner described their lofty goals in a ringing statement:

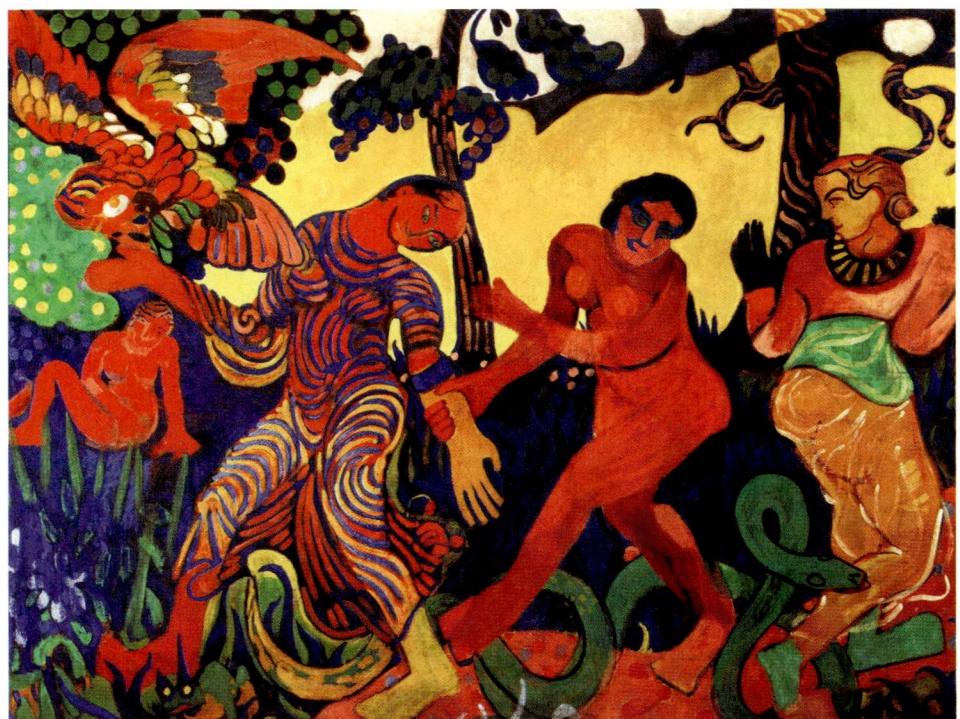

**33-3** André Derain, *The Dance*, 1906. Oil on canvas, 6' $\frac{7}{8}$" × 6' $10\frac{1}{4}$". Fridart Foundation, London.

With faith in development and in a new generation of creators and appreciators we call together all youth. As youth, we carry the future and want to create for ourselves freedom of life and of movement against the long-established older forces. Everyone who with directness and authenticity conveys that which drives him to creation, belongs to us.[4]

These artists protested the hypocrisy and materialistic decadence of those in power. Kirchner, in particular, focused much of his attention on the detrimental effects of industrialization, such as the alienation of individuals in cities, which he felt fostered a mechanized and impersonal society. This perception was reinforced when most of the group, including Kirchner, moved to Berlin, a teeming metropolis. The tensions leading to World War I further exacerbated the discomfort and anxiety evidenced in the works of Die Brücke.

**URBAN LIFE IN PREWAR DRESDEN** Kirchner's *Street, Dresden* (FIG. 33-4) provides the viewer with a glimpse into the frenzied urban activity of a bustling German city before World War I. Rather than offering the distant, panoramic urban view of the Impressionists, this street scene is jarring and dissonant. The women in the foreground loom large, approaching the viewer somewhat menacingly. The steep perspective of the street, which threatens to push the women directly into the viewing space, increases their confrontational nature. Harshly rendered, the women's features make them appear zombielike and ghoulish, and the garish, clashing colors—juxtapositions of bright orange, emerald green, acrid chartreuse, and pink—add to the expressive impact of the image. Kirchner's perspectival distortions, disquieting figures, and color choices reflect the influence of the work of Edvard Munch, who made similar expressive use of formal elements in *The Cry* (see FIG. 29-46).

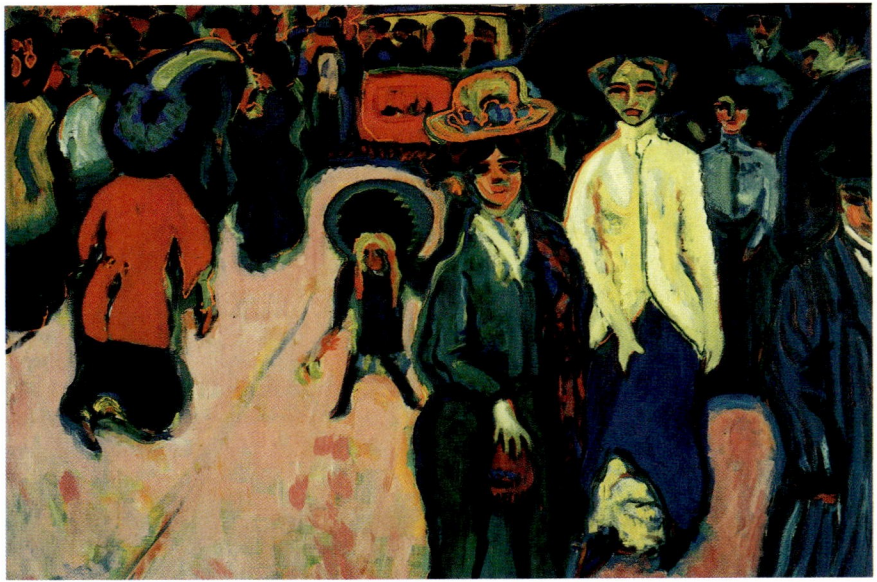

**33-4** Ernst Ludwig Kirchner, *Street, Dresden*, 1908 (dated 1907). Oil on canvas, 4' $11\frac{1}{4}$" × 6' $6\frac{7}{8}$". Museum of Modern Art, New York.

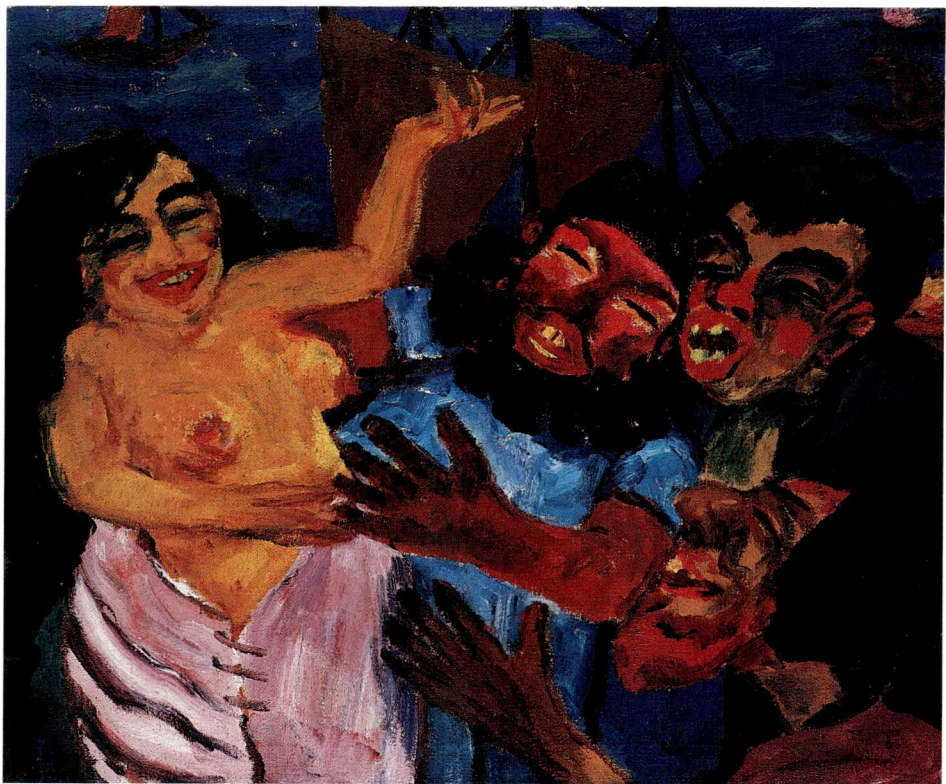

**33-5** EMIL NOLDE, *Saint Mary of Egypt among Sinners,* 1912. Left panel of a triptych, oil on canvas, approx. 2′ 10″ × 3′ 3″. Hamburger Kunsthalle, Hamburg.

**LUST AND LECHERY** EMIL NOLDE (1867–1956) was much older than most Die Brücke artists, but because he was pursuing similar ideas in his work, he was invited to join the group in 1906 and became an important member for a year and a half. The content of Nolde's work centered, for the most part, on religious imagery. In contrast to the quiet spirituality and restraint of traditional religious images, however, Nolde's paintings are visceral and forceful. One example is *Saint Mary of Egypt among Sinners* (FIG. **33-5**). Mary, before her conversion, entertains lechers whose lust magnifies their brutal ugliness. The distortions of form and color (especially the jarring juxtaposition of blue and orange) and the rawness of the brush strokes amplify the harshness of the leering faces.

Borrowing ideas from van Gogh, Munch, the Fauves, and African and Oceanic art, Die Brücke artists created images that derive much of their power from a dissonance and seeming lack of finesse. The harsh colors, aggressively brushed paint, and distorted forms expressed the painters' feelings about the injustices of society and their belief in a healthful union of human beings and nature. Their use of such diverse sources reflects the expanding scope of global contact from colonialism and international capitalism. By 1913, the group dissolved, and each member continued to work independently.

### German Expressionism: Der Blaue Reiter

A second major German Expressionist group, Der Blaue Reiter (The Blue Rider), formed in Munich in 1911. The two founding members, VASSILY KANDINSKY (1866–1944) and FRANZ MARC (1880–1916), whimsically selected this name because of their mutual interest in the color blue and horses. Like Die Brücke and other expressionist artists, this group produced paintings that captured their feelings in visual form while also eliciting intense visceral responses from the viewer.

**BLUEPRINTS FOR ENLIGHTENMENT** Born in Russia, Vassily Kandinsky, one of the driving forces of Der Blaue Reiter, moved to Munich in 1896 and soon developed a spontaneous and aggressively avant-garde expressive style. Indeed, Kandinsky was one of the first artists to explore complete abstraction, as evidenced by *Improvisation 28* (FIG. **33-6**). Kandinsky fueled his elimination of representational elements with his interest in theosophy (a religious and philosophical belief system incorporating a wide range of tenets from, among other sources, Buddhism and mysticism) and the occult, as well as with advances in the sciences. A true intellectual, widely read in philosophy, religion, history, and the other arts, especially music, Kandinsky was also one of the few early modernists to read with some comprehension the new scientific theories of Einstein's era. Rutherford's exploration of atomic structure, for example, convinced Kandinsky that material objects had no real substance, thereby shattering his faith in a world of tangible things.

The painter articulated his ideas in an influential treatise, *Concerning the Spiritual in Art,* published in 1912. Artists, Kandinsky believed, must express the spirit and their innermost feelings by orchestrating color, form, line, and space. He produced numerous works like *Improvisation 28,* conveying feelings with color juxtapositions, intersecting linear elements, and implied spatial relationships. Ultimately, Kandinsky saw these abstractions as evolving blueprints for a more enlightened and liberated society emphasizing spirituality.

**EXPRESSING AN INNER TRUTH** As noted earlier, Kandinsky's friend and cofounder of Der Blaue Reiter was Franz Marc. Like many of the other German Expressionists, Marc grew increasingly pessimistic about the state of humanity, especially as World War I loomed on the horizon. His perception of human beings as deeply flawed led him to turn to the animal world for his subjects. Animals, he believed, were "more beautiful, more pure" than humanity and thus more appropriate as a vehicle to express an inner truth.[5] In his quest to imbue his paintings with greater

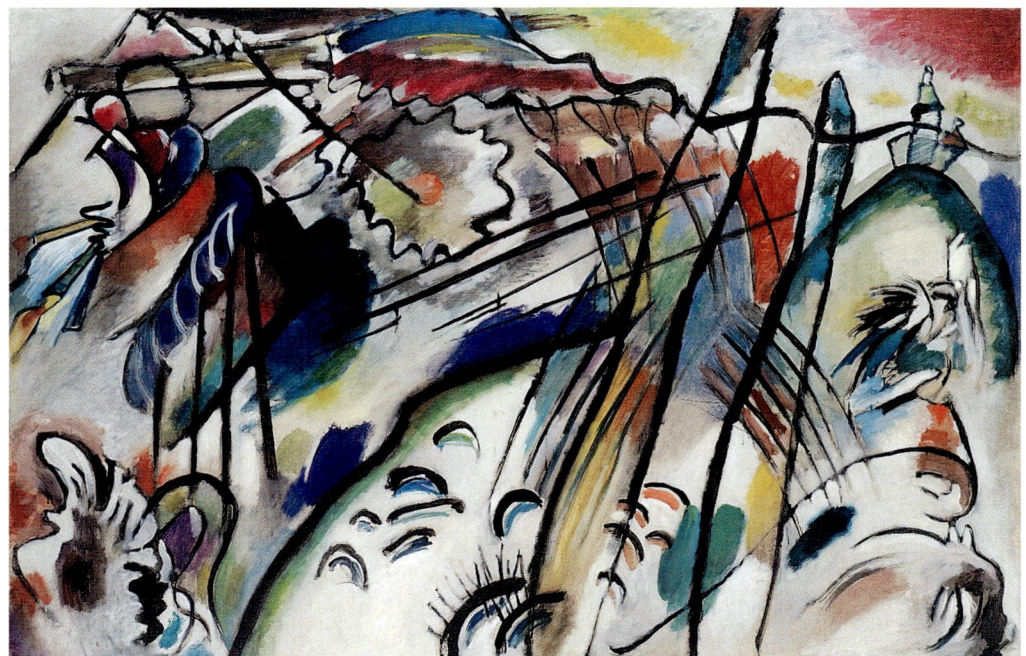

33-6 VASSILY KANDINSKY, *Improvisation 28* (second version), 1912. Oil on canvas, 3' 7⅞" × 5' 3⅞". Solomon R. Guggenheim Museum, New York (gift of Solomon R. Guggenheim, 1937).

emotional intensity, Marc focused on color and developed a system of correspondences between specific colors and feelings or ideas. In a letter to a fellow Blaue Reiter, Marc explained: "Blue is the *male* principle, severe and spiritual. Yellow is the *female* principle, gentle, happy and sensual. Red is *matter,* brutal and heavy."[6] He based this correspondence between colors and emotions on his perceptions. Marc's attempts to create, in a sense, an iconography (or representational system) of color links him to other avant-garde artists struggling to redefine the practice of art.

*Fate of the Animals* (FIG. 33-7) represents the culmination of Marc's color explorations. It was painted in 1913, when the tension of impending cataclysm had pervaded society and emerged in

Marc's art. The animals appear trapped in a forest, some apocalyptic event destroying them. The entire scene is distorted—shattered into fragments. More significantly, the lighter and brighter colors—the passive, gentle, and cheerful ones—are absent, and the colors of severity and brutality dominate the work. Marc discovered just how well his painting portended war's anguish and tragedy when he ended up at the front the following year. His experiences in battle prompted him to write to his wife that *Fate of the Animals* "is like a premonition of this war—horrible and shattering. I can hardly conceive that I painted it."[7] His contempt for people's inhumanity and his attempt to express that through his art ended, with tragic irony, in his death in action in World War I in 1916.

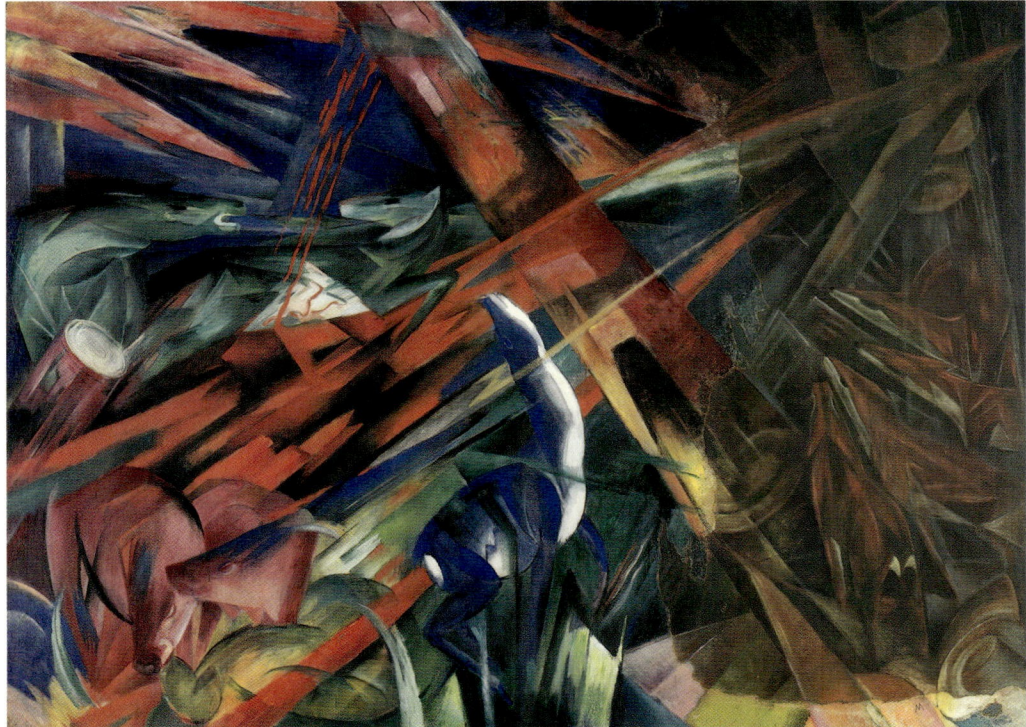

33-7 FRANZ MARC, *Fate of the Animals,* 1913. Oil on canvas, 6' 4¾" × 8' 9½". Kunstmuseum, Basel.

## EMBRACING ABSTRACTION

The expressionist departure from any strict adherence to illusionism in art was a path followed by other artists. Among those who most radically challenged prevailing artistic conventions and moved most aggressively into the realm of abstraction was PABLO PICASSO (1881–1973). A Spanish artist whose importance in the history of art is uncontested, he made staggering contributions to new ways of representing the surrounding world. Perhaps the most prolific artist in history, he explored virtually every artistic medium (for example, painting, sculpture, ceramics, prints, and drawings) during his lengthy career.

A precocious student, Picasso mastered all aspects of late-19th-century Realist technique by the time he entered the Barcelona Academy of Fine Art in the late 1890s. His prodigious talent led him to experiment with a wide range of visual expression, first in Spain and then in Paris, where he settled in 1904. Throughout his career, Picasso remained a traditional artist in making careful preparatory studies for each major work. He characterized the modern age, however, in his enduring quest for innovation, his lack of complacency, and his insistence on constantly challenging himself and those around him. Picasso revealed this modernity in his constant experimentation, and in his sudden shifts from one style to another. By the time he settled permanently in Paris, his work had evolved from Spanish painting's sober Realism through an Impressionistic phase (for a time, influenced by Toulouse-Lautrec's early works) to the so-called Blue Period (1901–1904). Picasso's melancholy state of mind prompted the Blue Period, when he used primarily blue colors to depict worn, pathetic, and alienated figures.

### The Fragmentation of Forms in Space

**A PLANAR PORTRAIT OF A WRITER** By 1906, Picasso was searching restlessly for new ways to depict form. He found clues in ancient Iberian sculpture and in the late paintings of Cézanne. He was also fascinated by African sculpture, of which he was an avid collector. (The expansion of colonial empires in the late 19th and early 20th centuries resulted in wider exposure of European and American artists to art from Africa, India, and other faraway locales.) Inspired by these sources, Picasso returned to a portrait of Gertrude Stein (FIG. 33-8), his friend and patron (see "Nurturing the Avant-Garde: Gertrude and Leo Stein as Art Patrons," page 972). Picasso had started the painting earlier that year but had left it unfinished after more than 80 sittings by Stein because, the artist told her, "I can't see you any longer when I look."[8] On resuming his work on the portrait, Picasso painted Stein's head as a simplified planar form, incorporating aspects derived from African masks and sculptures (see FIG. 32-3). Although the disparity between the style of the face and the rest of Stein's image is striking, together they provide an insightful portrait of a forceful, vivacious woman.

**"I PAINT FORMS AS I THINK THEM"** The influence of African, Iberian, and European art also surfaces in *Les Demoiselles d'Avignon* (literally, "the young ladies of Avignon"; FIG. 33-9), which opened the door to a radically new method of representing form in space. Picasso began the work as a symbolic picture to be titled *Philosophical Bordello*, portraying male clients intermingling with women in the reception room of a brothel (Avignon Street in Barcelona was located in the red-light district). By the time the artist finished, he had eliminated the male figures and

simplified the room's details to a suggestion of drapery and a schematic foreground still life. Picasso had become wholly absorbed in the problem of finding a new way to represent the five female figures in their interior space. Instead of representing the figures as continuous volumes, he fractured their shapes and interwove them with the equally jagged planes that represent drapery and empty space. Indeed, the space, so entwined with the bodies, is virtually illegible. Here Picasso pushed Cézanne's treatment of form and space to a new level. The tension between Picasso's representation of three-dimensional space and his statement of painting as a two-dimensional design lying flat on the surface of a stretched canvas is a tension between representation and abstraction.

The artist extended the radical nature of *Les Demoiselles d'Avignon* even further by depicting the figures inconsistently. The calm, ideal features of the three young women at the left were inspired by ancient Iberian sculptures, which Picasso saw during summer visits to Spain. The energetic, violently striated features of the two heads to the right emerged late in Picasso's production of the work and grew directly from his increasing fascination with the power of African sculpture. Perhaps responding to the energy of these two new heads, Picasso also revised their bodies. He broke them into more ambiguous planes suggesting a combination of views, as if the figures are seen from more than one place in space at once. The woman seated at the lower right shows these multiple views most clearly, seeming to present observers simultaneously with a three-quarter back view from the left, another from the right, and a front view of the head that suggests seeing the figure frontally as well. Gone is the traditional concept of an orderly, constructed, and unified pictorial space that mirrors the

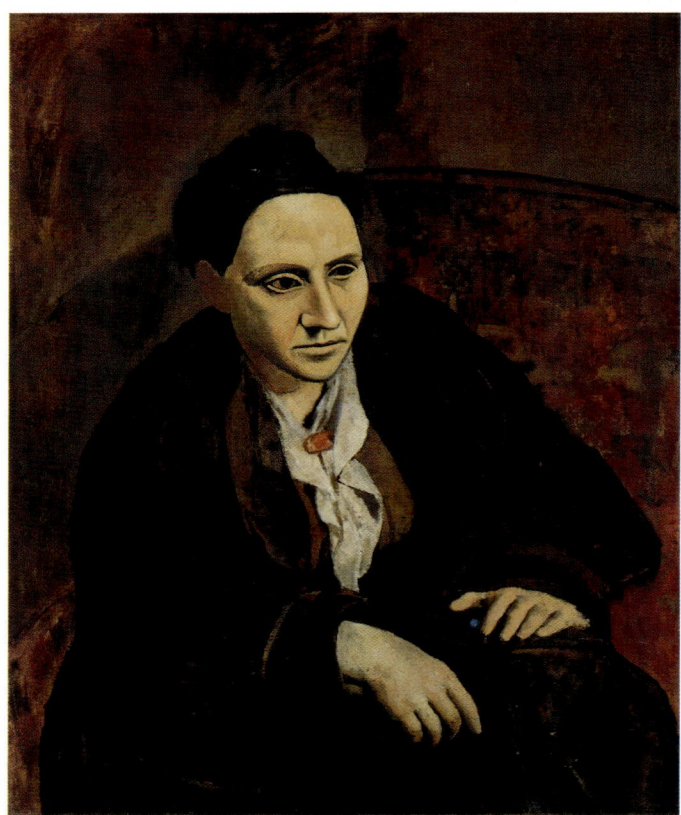

**33-8** PABLO PICASSO, *Gertrude Stein,* 1906–1907. Oil on canvas, 3′ 3 3/8″ × 2′ 8″. Metropolitan Museum of Art, New York (bequest of Gertrude Stein, 1947).

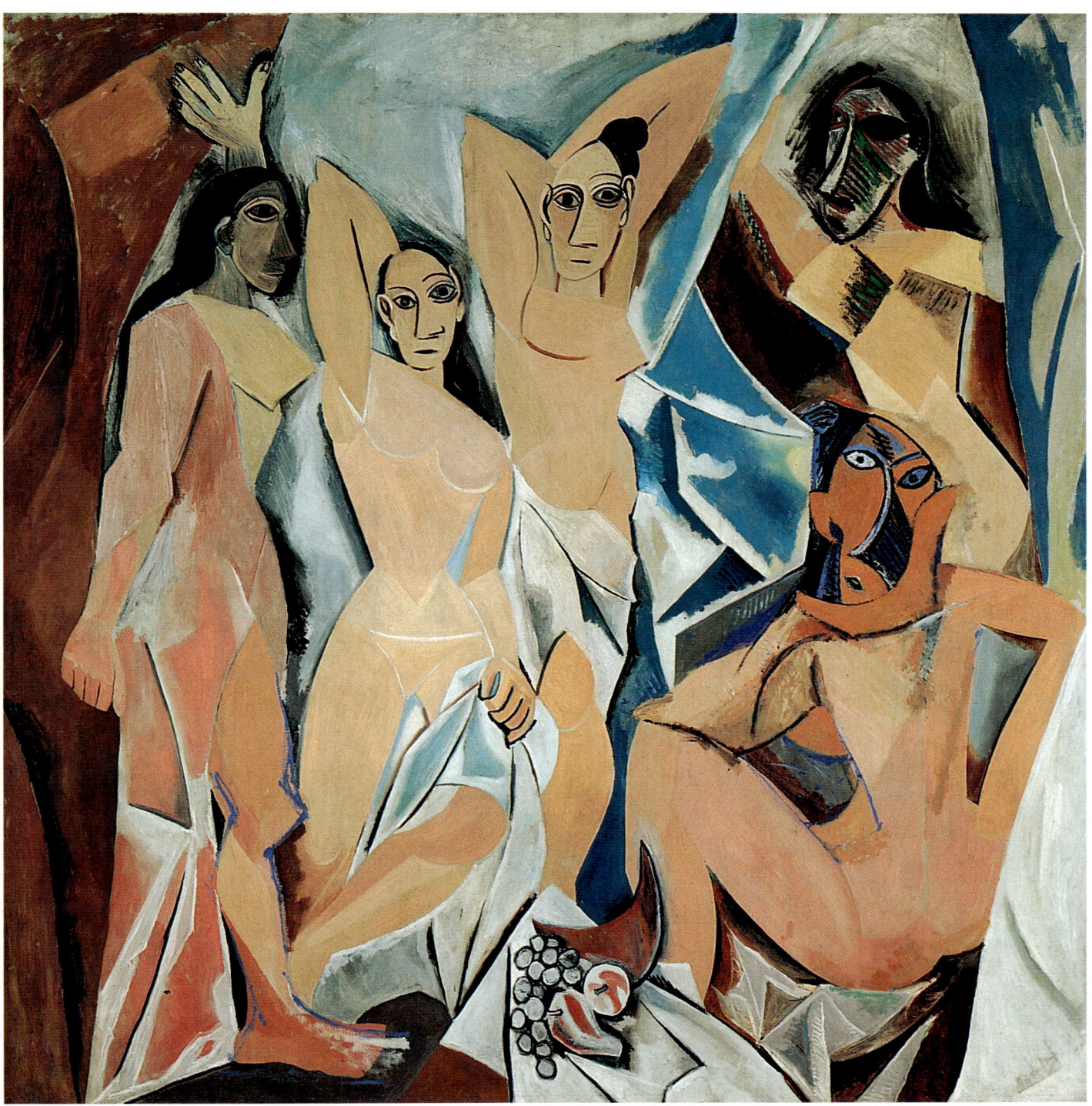

**33-9** PABLO PICASSO, *Les Demoiselles d'Avignon*, June–July 1907. Oil on canvas, 8′ × 7′ 8″. Museum of Modern Art, New York (acquired through the Lillie P. Bliss Bequest).

world. In its place are the rudimentary beginnings of a new representation of the world as a dynamic interplay of time and space. Clearly, *Les Demoiselles d'Avignon* represents a dramatic departure from the careful presentation of a visual reality. Explained Picasso: "I paint forms as I think them, not as I see them."[9]

For many years, Picasso showed *Les Demoiselles* only to other painters. One of the first to see it was GEORGES BRAQUE (1882–1963), a Fauve painter who was so agitated and challenged by it that he began to rethink his own painting style. Using the painting's revolutionary ideas as a point of departure, together Braque and Picasso formulated Cubism around 1908.

## Cubism

**OUTSIDE THE WORLD OF OBSERVATION** *Cubism* represented a radical turning point in the history of art, nothing less than a dismissal of the pictorial illusionism that had dominated Western art over the years. The Cubists rejected naturalistic depictions, preferring compositions of shapes and forms abstracted from the conventionally perceived world. These artists pursued the analysis of form central to Cézanne's artistic explorations, and they dissected life's continuous optical spread into its many constituent features, which they then recomposed, by a new logic of

## Nurturing the Avant-Garde
### Gertrude and Leo Stein as Art Patrons

The rebellious and antagonistic stance avant-garde artists adopted in all media understandably engendered much hostility and resistance to their art by the public. This response rather restricted the social circles within which avant-garde artists traveled. Gertrude (1874–1946) and Leo (1872–1947) Stein played pivotal roles in the history of the avant-garde in the early 20th century because they provided a hospitable environment in their Paris house. Artists, writers, musicians, collectors, and critics interested in progressive art and ideas could meet there to talk and socialize. Born in Pennsylvania, brother and sister Leo and Gertrude moved to Paris in 1903, setting up a home at 27 rue de Fleurus. Gertrude's experimental writing stimulated her interest in the latest developments in the arts; conversely, the avant-garde ideas discussed at the Steins' house influenced her unique poetry, plays, and other literary forms. She is perhaps best known for *The Autobiography of Alice B. Toklas* (1933), a unique memoir written in the persona of her longtime lesbian companion.

The Steins' interest in the exciting and invigorating debates taking place in avant-garde circles led them to welcome visitors to their Saturday salons, which included lectures, thoughtful discussions, and spirited arguments. Often, these gatherings lasted until dawn. They became renowned and included not only the French but also visiting Americans, British, Swedes, Germans, Hungarians, Spaniards, Poles, and Russians. Among the hundreds who welcomed the opportunity to visit the Steins were artists Matisse, Picasso, Georges Braque, Cassatt, Marcel Duchamp, Alfred Stieglitz, and Arthur B. Davis; writers Ernest Hemingway, F. Scott Fitzgerald, John dos Passos, Jean Cocteau, and Guillaume Apollinaire; art dealers Daniel Kahnweiler and Ambroise Vollard; critics Roger Fry and Clive Bell; and collectors Sergei Shchukin and Ivan Morosov.

The art decorating the walls of 27 rue de Fleurus also attracted many visitors. The Steins were avid art collectors. One of the first paintings Leo purchased was Matisse's notorious *Woman with the Hat* (FIG. 33-1), and he subsequently bought numerous important paintings by Matisse and Picasso, along with works by Gauguin, Cézanne, Renoir, and Braque. Picasso, who developed a close friendship with Gertrude, asked to paint her portrait, and the well-known painting (FIG. 33-8), which he finished in 1907 after more than one year of work and numerous sittings by Gertrude, today hangs in the Metropolitan Museum of Art. Gertrude was so taken by the completed portrait that she kept it by her all her life and bequeathed it to the Metropolitan only after her death in 1946.

Ultimately, Gertrude and Leo Stein played central roles in the avant-garde's development in the early 20th century, both as collectors and as facilitators of interaction among avant-garde artists, writers, musicians, and others in the art world. Their passion for and fascination with the international art scene undeniably contributed to the history of 20th-century art.

---

design, into a coherent aesthetic object. For the Cubists, the art of painting had to move far beyond the description of visual reality. This rejection of accepted artistic practice illustrates both the period's aggressive avant-garde critique of pictorial convention and the public's dwindling faith in a safe, concrete Newtonian world, fears fostered by the physics of Einstein and others. Although not immune to the effects of the societal turbulence of the early 20th century, the Cubists increasingly directed their energies into their critique of traditional aesthetics. The French writer and theorist Guillaume Apollinaire summarized well the central concepts of Cubism in 1913:

> Authentic cubism [is] the art of depicting new wholes with formal elements borrowed not from the reality of vision, but from that of conception. This tendency leads to a poetic kind of painting which stands outside the world of observation; for, even in a simple cubism, the geometrical surfaces of an object must be opened out in order to give a complete representation of it. . . . Everyone must agree that a chair, from whichever side it is viewed, never ceases to have four legs, a seat and a back, and that, if it is robbed of one of these elements, it is robbed of an important part.[10]

The new style received its name after Matisse described some of Braque's work to a critic, Louis Vauxcelles, as having been painted "avec des petits cubes" (with little cubes), and the critic went on in his review to speak of "cubic oddities."[11] Thus, critics, through their choice of labels, in part formed public understanding of this original and trailblazing painting method.

## Analytic Cubism

Historians often refer to the first phase of Cubism, developed jointly by Picasso and Braque, as *Analytic Cubism*. Because Cubists could not achieve the kind of total view Apollinaire described by the traditional method of drawing or painting models from one position, these artists began to dissect the forms of their subjects. They presented that dissection for the viewer to inspect across the canvas surface. In simplistic terms, Analytic Cubism involves analyzing form and investigating the visual vocabulary (that is, the pictorial elements) for conveying meaning.

**ANALYZING A MUSICIAN'S FORM** Georges Braque's painting *The Portuguese* (FIG. **33-10**) is a striking example of Analytic Cubism. The artist derived the subject from his memories of a Portuguese musician seen years earlier in a bar in Marseilles. In this painting, Braque concentrated his attention on dissecting the form and placing it in dynamic interaction with the space around it; he reduced color to a monochrome of brown tones. Unlike the high-keyed paintings of the Fauves and German Expressionists, the Cubists used subdued hues to focus the viewer's attention on form. In *The Portuguese,* the artist carried his analysis so far that the viewer must work diligently to discover clues to the subject. The construction of large intersecting planes suggests the forms of a man and a guitar. Smaller shapes interpenetrate and hover in the large planes. The way Braque treated light and shadow reveals his departure from conventional artistic practice. Light and dark

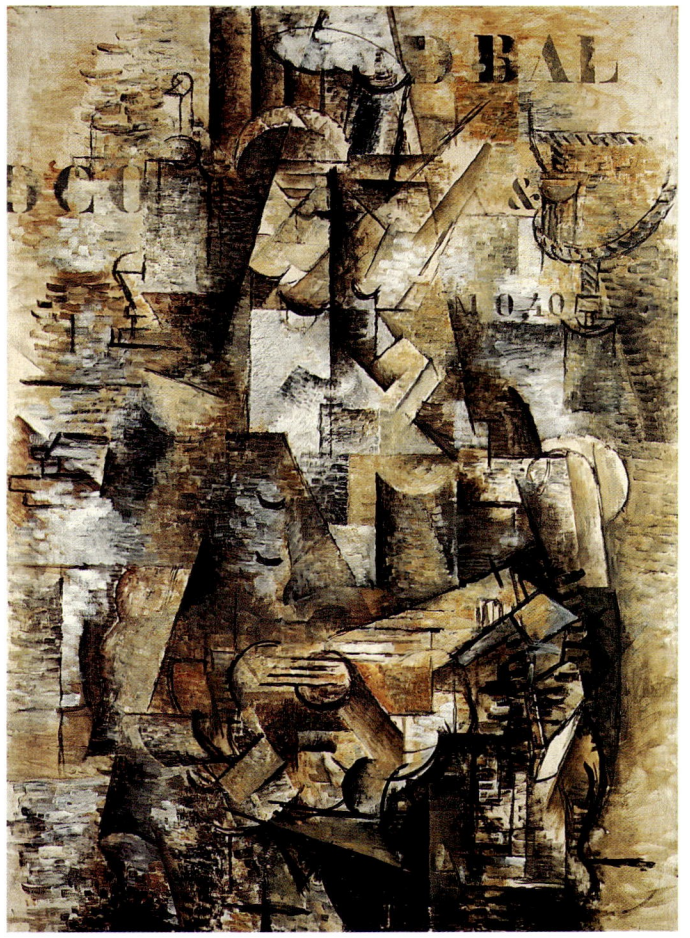

**33-10** GEORGES BRAQUE, *The Portuguese*, 1911. Oil on canvas, 3′ 10⅛″ × 2′ 8″. Öffentliche Kunstsammlung Basel, Kunstmuseum, Basel (gift of Raoul La Roche, 1952).

passages suggest both chiaroscuro modeling and transparent planes that allow the viewer to see through one level to another. As the observer looks, solid forms emerge only to be canceled almost immediately by a different reading of the subject.

The stenciled letters and numbers add to the painting's complexity. Letters and numbers are flat shapes. On a book's pages, they exist outside three-dimensional space, but as shapes in a Cubist painting such as *The Portuguese,* they allow the painter to play with the viewer's perception of two- and three-dimensional space. The letters and numbers lie flat on the painted canvas surface, yet the image's shading and shapes seem to flow behind and underneath them, pushing the letters and numbers forward into the viewing space. Occasionally, they seem attached to the surface of some object within the painting. Picasso and Braque pioneered precisely this exploration of visual vocabulary—for example, composition, two-dimensional shape, three-dimensional form, and value—and its role in generating meaning. Further, the inclusion of elements such as recognizable letters or numbers seems to anchor the painting in the world of representation, thereby exacerbating the tension between representation and abstraction. Ultimately, the constantly shifting imagery makes it impossible to arrive at any definitive or final reading of the image. Even today, examining such a painting is a disconcerting excursion into ambiguity and doubt.

**KALEIDOSCOPIC COLORED SHARDS** Picasso and Braque avoided bright color in their Analytic Cubist works. Artists and art historians generally have seen this suppression of color as crucial to Cubism's success. These two artists employed this strategy to unify paintings that radically disrupted viewer expectations about the representation of time and space. Their contemporary, ROBERT DELAUNAY (1885–1941), worked toward a kind of color Cubism. The French poet Guillaume Apollinaire called this art style Orphism, after Orpheus, the Greek god with magical powers of music-making. Apollinaire believed art, like music, was divorced from representation of the visible world. Delaunay developed his ideas about color use in dialogue with his Russian-born wife, Sonia (1885–1974), also an artist. She created paintings, quilts (based on Russian folk designs), and other textile arts, and book covers that exploited the expressive capabilities of color. As a result of their artistic explorations, both Delaunays became convinced that the rhythms of modern life could best be expressed through color harmonies and dissonances. *Champs de Mars,* or *The Red Tower* (FIG. **33-11**), is one of many paintings Delaunay produced between 1909 and 1912 depicting the Eiffel Tower (see FIG. 29-57). People in the early 20th century still considered this tower, constructed in 1889, a marvel of modern engineering technology. The title *Champs de Mars* refers to the Parisian field in which the Eiffel Tower is located, named after the Campus Martius (Field of Mars) located outside the walls of Republican Rome.

The artist broke the monument's perceptual unity into a kaleidoscopic array of colored shards, which variously leap forward or pull back according to the relative hues and values of the

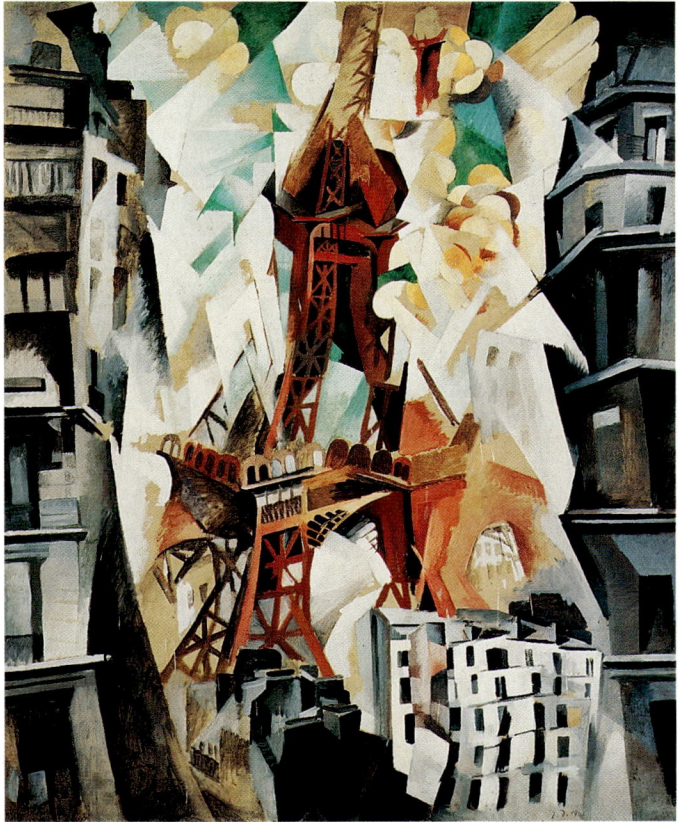

**33-11** ROBERT DELAUNAY, *Champs de Mars,* or *The Red Tower,* 1911. Oil on canvas, 5′ 3″ × 4′ 3″. Art Institute of Chicago, Chicago.

broken shapes. The structure ambiguously rises and collapses. Beyond its formal links to Cubism, the fragmentation of the Eiffel Tower in *Champs de Mars* has also been interpreted in political terms as a commentary on the societal collapse in the years leading to World War I. In unedited notes, Delaunay himself described the collapsing tower imagery as "the synthesis of a period of destruction; likewise a prophetic vision with social repercussions: war, and the base crumbles."[12] This statement encapsulates well the social and artistic climate during these years—the destruction of old world orders and of artistic practices deemed obsolete, as well as the avant-garde's prophetic nature and its determination to subvert tradition.

Ultimately, Delaunay's experiments with color dynamics strongly influenced the Futurists (discussed later) and the German Expressionists (he exhibited with Der Blaue Reiter, as well as with Cubists). These artists found in his art means for intensifying expression by suggesting violent motion through shape and color.

## *Synthetic Cubism*

**ILLUSION OR REALITY?** In 1912, Cubism entered a new phase when the style no longer relied on a decipherable relation to the visible world. In this new phase, called *Synthetic Cubism,* artists constructed paintings and drawings from objects and shapes cut from paper or other materials to represent parts of a subject. The work marking the point of departure for this new style was Picasso's *Still Life with Chair-Caning* (FIG. **33-12**), a painting that included a piece of oilcloth pasted on the canvas after it was imprinted with the photolithographed pattern of a cane chair seat. Framed with a piece of rope, this work challenges the viewer's understanding of reality. The photographically replicated chair caning seems so "real" that one expects the holes to break any brush strokes laid upon it. But the chair caning, although optically suggestive of the real, is actually only an illusion or representation of

an object. In contrast, the painted abstract areas do not refer to tangible objects in the real world. Yet the fact they do not imitate anything makes them more "real" than the chair caning—no pretense exists. Picasso extended the visual play by making the letter *U* escape from the space of the accompanying *J* and *O* and partially covering it with a cylindrical shape that pushes across its left side. The letters *JOU* appear in many Cubist paintings; these letters formed part of the masthead of the daily French newspapers (*journaux*) often found among the objects represented. Picasso and Braque especially delighted in the punning references to *jouer* and *jouir*—the French words for "to play" and "to enjoy."

**GLUED AND STUCK PAPER** After *Still Life with Chair-Caning*, both Picasso and Braque continued to explore the medium of *collage* introduced into the realm of high art in that work. From the French word *coller*, meaning "to stick," a collage is a composition of bits of objects, such as newspaper or cloth, glued to a surface. Its possibilities can be seen in Braque's *Bottle, Newspaper, Pipe and Glass* (FIG. **33-13**), done in a variant of collage called *papier collé* (stuck paper), or gluing assorted paper shapes to a drawing or painting. Here, charcoal lines and shadows provide clues to the Cubist multiple views of various surfaces and objects. Roughly rectangular strips of variously printed and colored paper dominate the composition. The *faux bois* (false wood) paper with molding provides an illusion whose concreteness contrasts with the lightly rendered objects on the right. Five pieces of paper overlap each other in the center of the composition to create a layering of flat planes that both echo the space the lines suggest and establish the flatness of the work's surface. All shapes in the image seem to oscillate, pushing forward and dropping back in space. Shading seems to carve space into flat planes in some places and to turn planes into transparent surfaces in others. The complex visual interplay is revealed, for example, in the depiction of the pipe in the foreground; although it appears to lie on the newspaper, it is actually a form cut out of the printed paper and lightly modeled with charcoal.

**33-12** Pablo Picasso, *Still Life with Chair-Caning,* 1912. Oil and oilcloth on canvas, $10\frac{5}{8}'' \times 1' \ 1\frac{3}{4}''$. Musée Picasso, Paris. 🎨

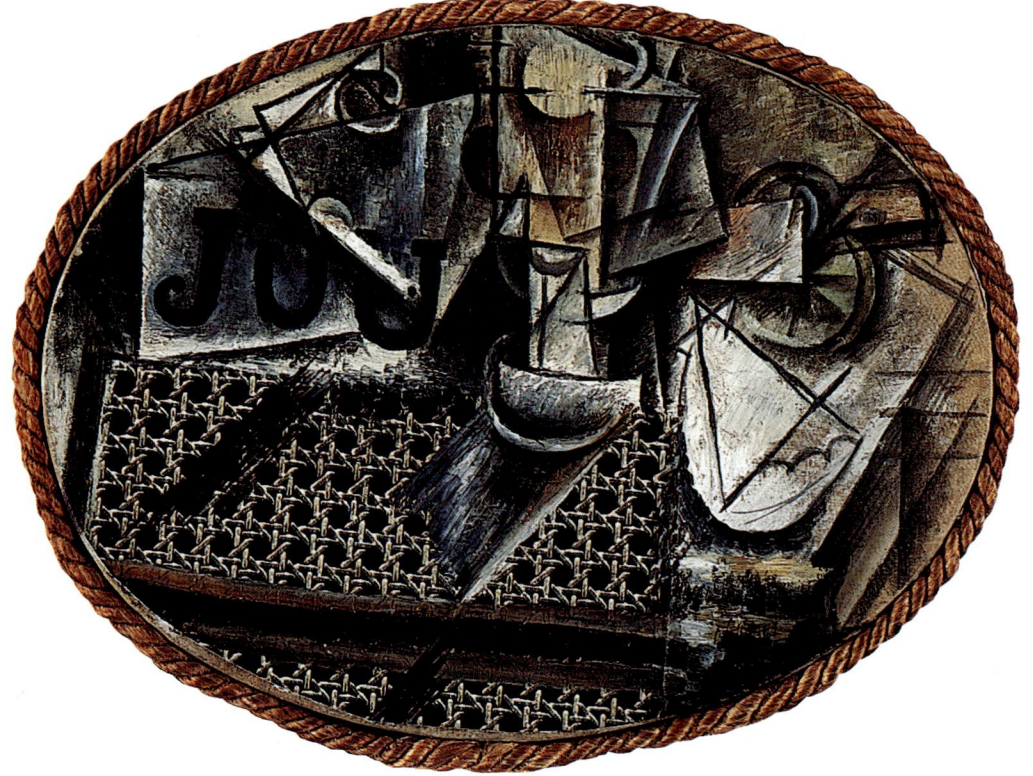

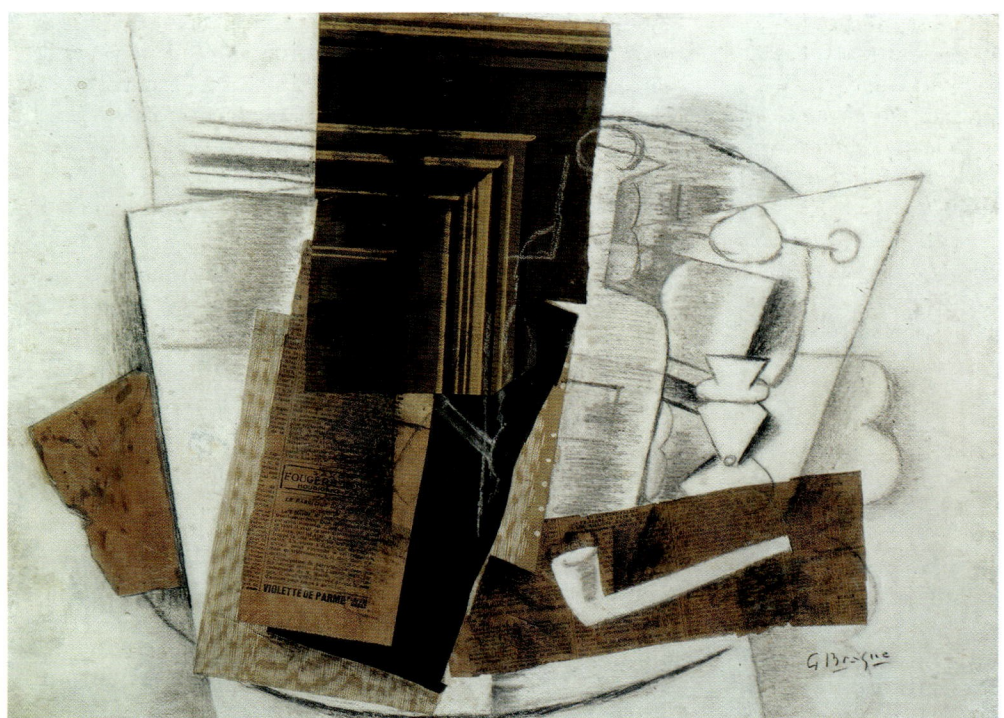

**33-13** GEORGES BRAQUE, *Bottle, Newspaper, Pipe and Glass*, 1913. Charcoal and various papers pasted on paper, 1′ 6$\frac{7}{8}$″ × 2′ 1$\frac{1}{4}$″. Private collection, New York.

Viewers of *Bottle, Newspaper, Pipe and Glass* are kept aware that this is an artwork an artist created and that they must enter the visual game to decipher all levels of representation. Braque no longer analyzed the three-dimensional qualities of the physical world. Here, he constructed or synthesized objects and space alike from the materials he used. Picasso stated his views on Cubism at this point in its development: "Not only did we try to displace reality; reality was no longer in the object. . . . [In] the *papier collé* . . . [w]e didn't any longer want to fool the eye; we wanted to fool the mind. . . . If a piece of newspaper can be a bottle, that gives us something to think about in connection with both newspapers and bottles, too."[13]

Like all collage, the papier collé technique was modern in its medium—mass-produced materials never before found in "high" art—and modern in the way the artist embedded the art's "message" in the imagery and in the nature of these everyday materials. Although most discussions of Cubism and collage focus on the formal innovations they represented, it is important to note that the public also viewed the revolutionary and subversive nature of Cubism in sociopolitical terms. Cubism's attacks on artistic convention and tradition were easily expanded to encompass an attack on society's complacency and status quo. Many artists and writers of the period allied themselves with various anarchist groups whose social critiques and utopian visions appealed to progressive thinkers. It was, therefore, not a far leap to see radical art, like Cubism, as having political ramifications. Indeed, many critics in the French press consistently equated Cubism with anarchism, revolution, and disdain for tradition. The impact of Cubism thus extended beyond the boundaries of the art world itself.

## Cubist Sculpture

**THE DISSOLUTION OF FORM** Cubism did not just open new avenues for representing form on two-dimensional surfaces; it also inspired new approaches to sculpture. Picasso explored Cubism's possibilities in sculpture throughout the years he and Braque developed the style. One such sculpture is *Guitar* (FIG. **33-14**), which Picasso created in 1912. As in his Cubist paintings, this sculpture operates at the intersection of two- and three-dimensionality. In this work, he took the form of a guitar (an image that surfaces in many of his paintings as well) and explored its volume via flat planar

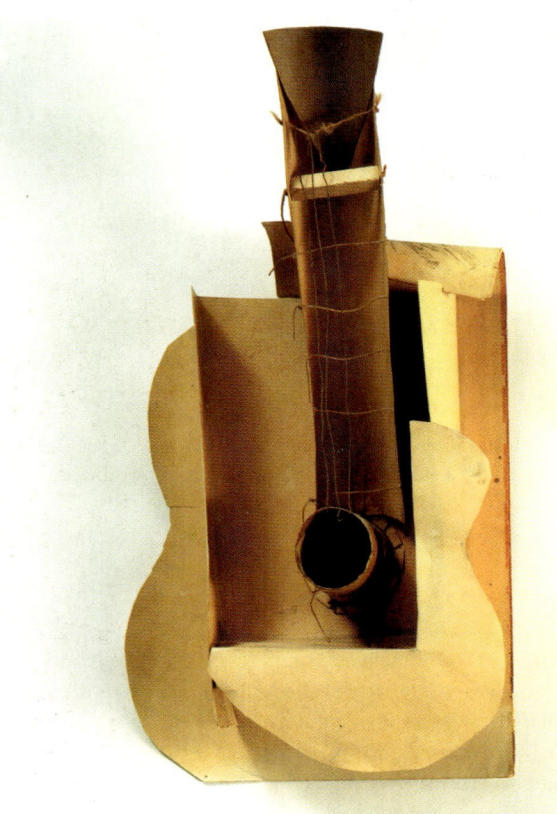

**33-14** PABLO PICASSO, maquette for *Guitar,* 1912. Cardboard, string, and wire (restored), 2′ 1$\frac{1}{4}$″ × 1′ 1″ × 7$\frac{1}{2}$″. Museum of Modern Art, New York.

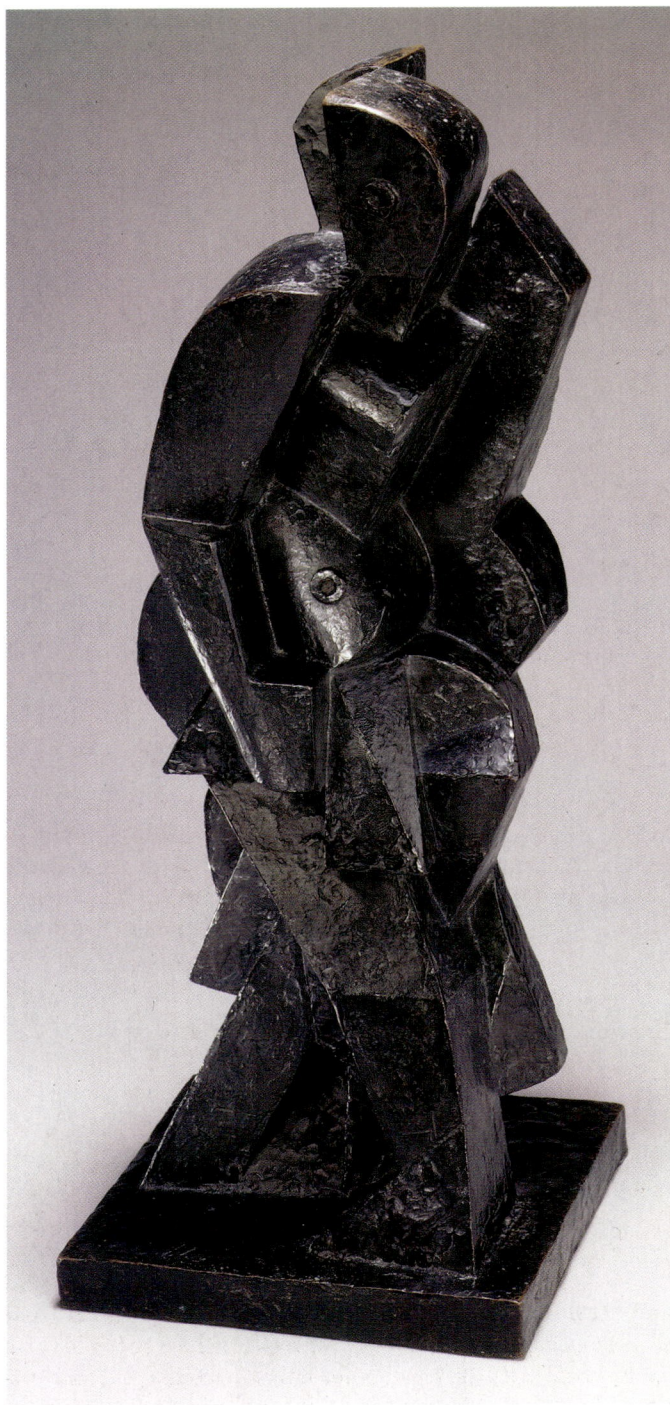

**33-15** JACQUES LIPCHITZ, *Bather*, 1917. Bronze, 2′ 10¾″ × 1′ 1¼″ × 1′ 1″. Nelson-Atkins Museum of Art, Kansas City (gift of the Friends of Art). Copyright © Estate of Jacques Lipchitz/Licensed by VAGA, New York/Marlborough Gallery, New York.

continuing and persistent source of inspiration for the artist, and such references appear in both *Portrait of Gertrude Stein* (FIG. 33-8) and *Les Demoiselles d'Avignon* (FIG. 33-9). Here, however, Picasso seems to have transformed the anatomical features of African masks into a part of a musical instrument—dramatic evidence of his unique, innovative artistic vision.

**DYNAMIC FORM IN SPACE** One of the most successful sculptors to adapt into three dimensions the planar, fragmented dissolution of form central to Analytic Cubist painting was JACQUES LIPCHITZ (1891–1973). Born in Latvia, Lipchitz resided for many years in France and the United States. He worked out his ideas for many of his sculptures in clay before creating them in bronze or in stone. *Bather* (FIG. 33-15) is typical of his Cubist style. Lipchitz broke the continuous form in this work into cubic volumes and planes. The interlocking and gracefully intersecting irregular facets and curves recall the paintings of Picasso and Braque and represent a parallel analysis of dynamic form in space. Lipchitz later produced less volumetric sculptures that included empty spaces outlined by metal shapes. In these sculptures, Lipchitz pursued even further the Cubist notion of spatial ambiguity and the relationship between solid forms and space.

**THE INTERPLAY OF MASS AND SPACE** The Russian sculptor ALEKSANDR ARCHIPENKO (1887–1964) explored similar ideas, as seen in *Woman Combing Her Hair* (FIG. 33-16). This statuette introduces, in place of the head, a void with a shape of its own that figures importantly in the whole design. Enclosed spaces have always existed in figurative sculpture—for example, the space between the arm and the body when the hand rests on the hip, as in Verrocchio's *David* (see FIG. 21-24). But here the space penetrates the figure's continuous mass and is a defined form equal in importance to the mass of the bronze. It is not simply the negative counterpart to the volume. Archipenko's figure shows the same fluid intersecting planes seen in Cubist painting, and the relation of the planes to each other is similarly complex. Thus, in painting and sculpture, the Cubists broke through traditional limits and transformed the medium. Archipenko's figure is still somewhat representational, but sculpture (like painting) executed within the Cubist idiom tended to cast off the last vestiges of representation.

**WELDED METAL SCULPTURES** A friend of Picasso, JULIO GONZÁLEZ (1876–1942) shared his interest in the artistic possibilities of new materials and new methods borrowed from both industrial technology and traditional metalworking. Born into a family of metalworkers in Barcelona, Spain, González helped Picasso construct a number of welded sculptures. This contact with Picasso, in turn, allowed González to refine his own sculptural vocabulary. Using ready-made bars, sheets, or rods of welded or wrought iron and bronze, González created dynamic sculptures with both linear elements and volumetric forms. In his *Woman Combing Her Hair* (FIG. 33-17; compare with Archipenko's version of the same subject), the figure is reduced to an interplay of curves, lines, and planes—virtually a complete abstraction. Although González's sculpture received limited exposure during his lifetime, it became particularly important for sculptors in subsequent decades who focused their attention on the capabilities of welded metal.

cardboard surfaces (we illustrate the maquette, or model; the finished sculpture was to be made of sheet metal). By presenting what is essentially a cutaway view of a guitar, Picasso allowed the viewer to examine both surface and interior space, both mass and void. This, of course, is completely in keeping with the Cubist program. Some scholars have suggested that Picasso derived the cylindrical form that serves as the sound hole on the guitar from the eyes on masks from the Ivory Coast of Africa. African masks were a

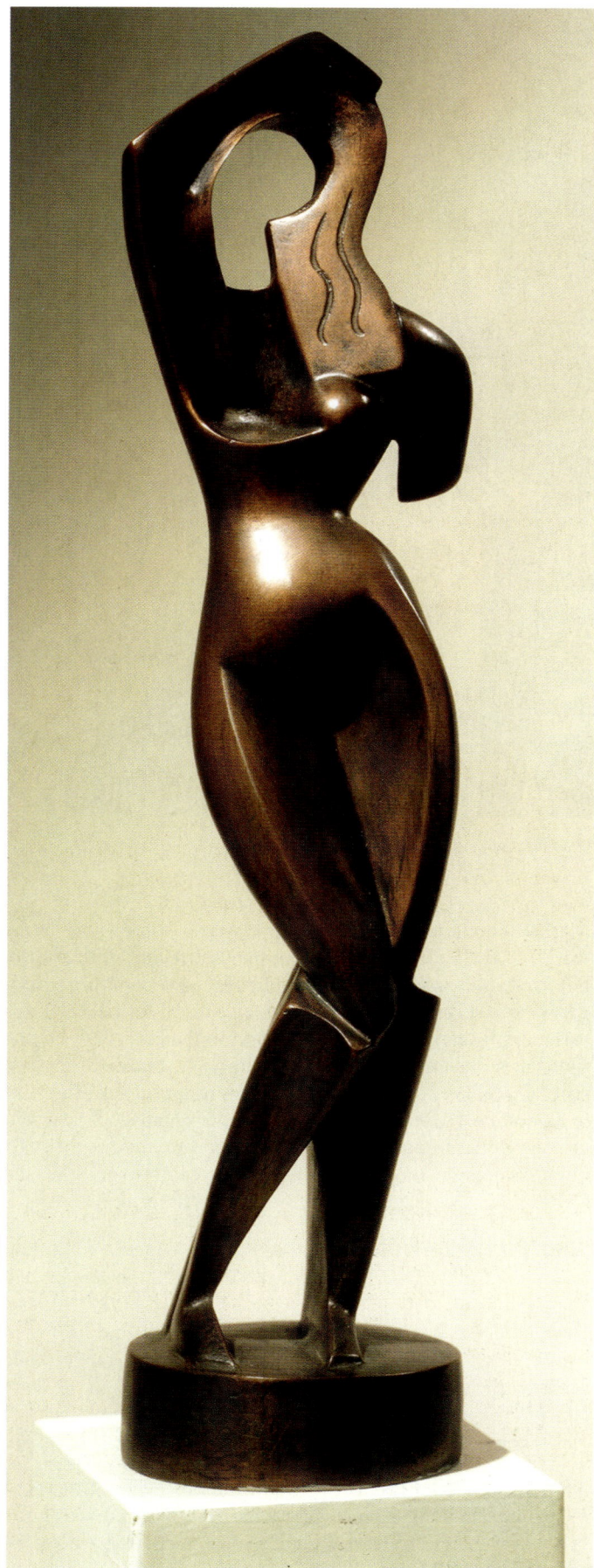

**33-16** ALEKSANDR ARCHIPENKO, *Woman Combing Her Hair,* 1915. Bronze, approx. 1′ 1¾″ high. Tate Gallery, London.

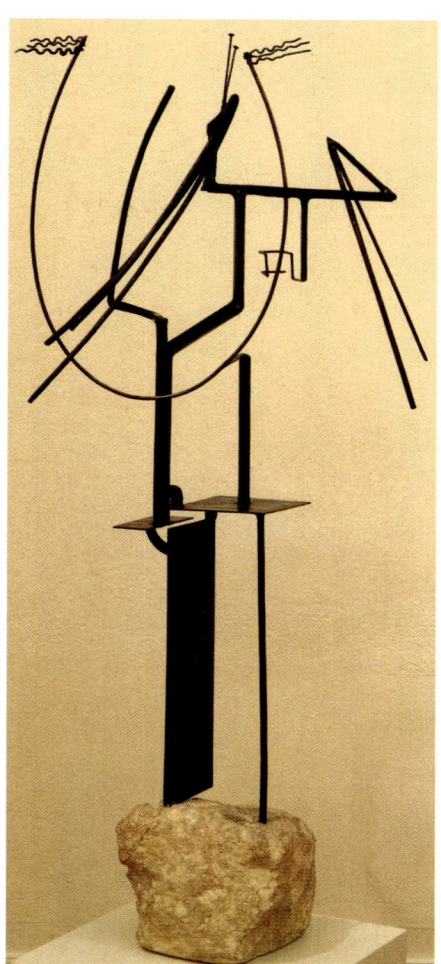

**33-17** JULIO GONZÁLEZ, *Woman Combing Her Hair,* ca. 1930–1933. Iron, 4′ 9″ high. Moderna Museet, Stockholm.

## *Purism*

**THE MACHINE AESTHETIC** Charles Edouard Jeanneret, known as Le Corbusier, is today best known as one of the most important modernist architects (see later discussion, pages 1012–1014). Also a painter, he founded in 1918 a movement called Purism, which opposed Synthetic Cubism on the grounds that it was becoming merely an esoteric, decorative art out of touch with the machine age. Purists maintained that machinery's clean functional lines and the pure forms of its parts should direct the artist's experiments in design, whether in painting, architecture, or industrially produced objects. This "machine esthetic" inspired FERNAND LÉGER (1881–1955), a French painter who had early on painted with the Cubists. He devised an effective compromise of tastes, bringing together meticulous Cubist analysis of form with the Purist's broad simplification and machinelike finish of the design components. He retained from his Cubist practice a preference for cylindrical and tube-shaped motifs, suggestive of machined parts such as pistons and cylinders.

Léger's works have the sharp precision of the machine, whose beauty and quality he was one of the first artists to discover. His contemporary, modern composer George Antheil, wrote a score for a Léger film, *Ballet Mécanique* (1924). The film contrasted inanimate objects such as functioning machines with humans in dancelike variations. Preeminently the painter of modern urban

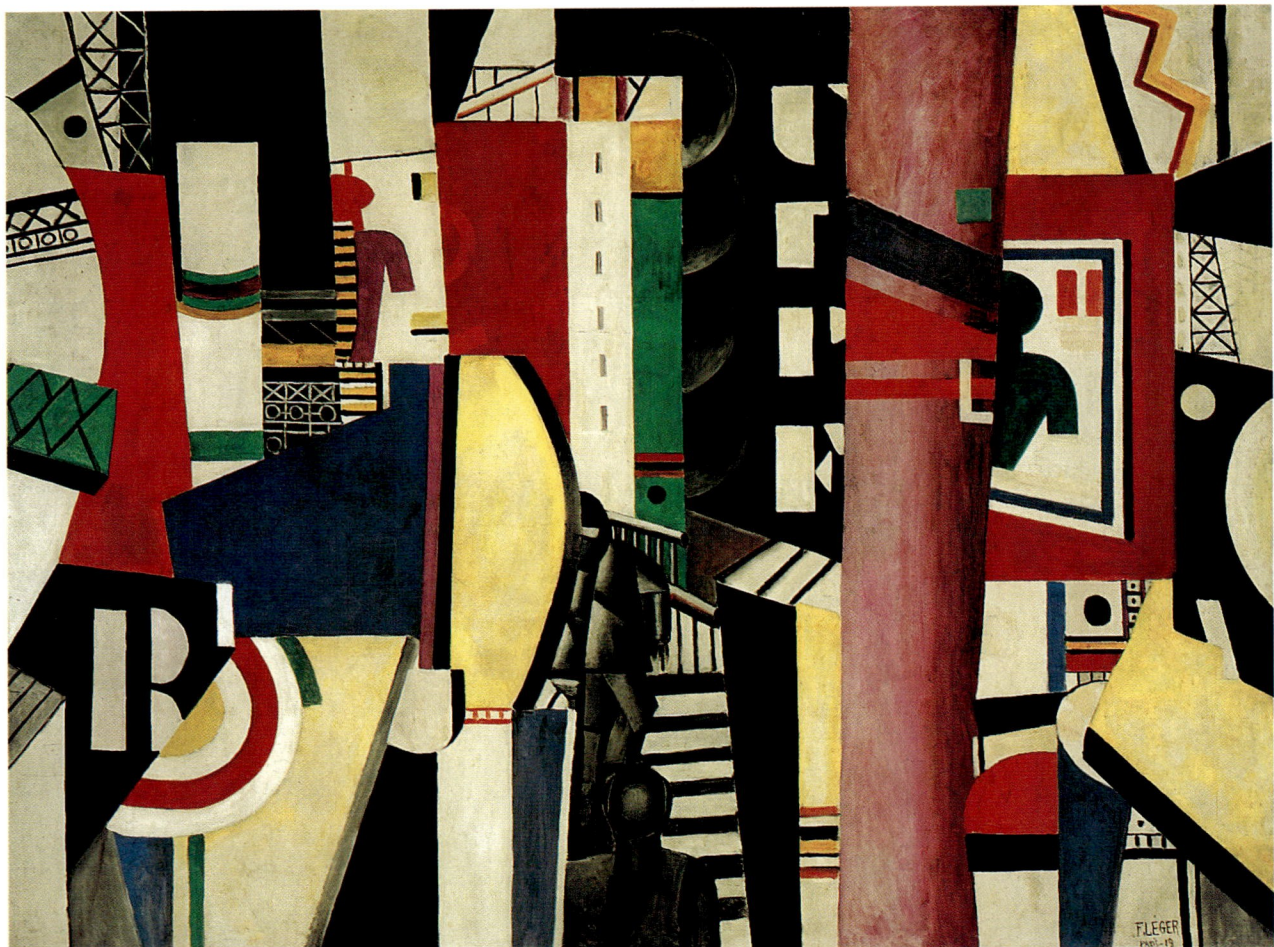

**33-18** Fernand Léger, *The City*, 1919. Oil on canvas, approx. 7′ 7″ × 9′ 9½″. Philadelphia Museum of Art, Philadelphia (A. E. Gallatin Collection). ⊙

life, Léger incorporated into his work the massive effects of modern posters and billboard advertisements, the harsh flashing of electric lights, the noise of traffic, and the robotic movements of mechanized people. These effects appear in an early work—modulated, however, by the aesthetic of Synthetic Cubism—*The City* (FIG. **33-18**). Its monumental scale suggests that Léger, had he been given the opportunity, would have been one of the great mural painters of his age. In a definitive way, he depicted the mechanical commotion of contemporary cities then and now.

## Futurism

**COMBINING ART AND POLITICS** Artists associated with another early-20th-century movement, *Futurism,* pursued many of the ideas the Cubists explored. Equally important to the Futurists, however, was their well-defined sociopolitical agenda. Inaugurated and given its name by the charismatic Italian poet and playwright Filippo Tommaso Marinetti in 1909, Futurism began as a literary movement but soon encompassed the visual arts, cinema, theater, music, and architecture. Indignant over the political and cultural decline of Italy, the Futurists published numerous manifestos in which they aggressively advocated revolution, both in society and in art. Like Die Brücke and other avant-garde artists, the Futurists aimed at ushering in a new, more enlightened era.

In their quest to launch Italian society toward a glorious future, the Futurists championed war as a means of washing away the stagnant past. Indeed, they saw war as a cleansing agent.

Marinetti declared: "We wish to glorify war—sole hygiene to the world."[14] The Futurists agitated for the destruction of museums, libraries, and similar repositories of accumulated culture, which they described as mausoleums. They also called for radical innovation in the arts. Of particular interest to the Futurists were the speed and dynamism of modern technology. Marinetti insisted that "a speeding automobile . . . is more beautiful than the Nike of Samothrace" (see FIG. 5-82, by then representative of classicism and the glories of past civilizations).[15] Appropriately, Futurist art often focuses on motion in time and space, incorporating the Cubist discoveries derived from the analysis of form.

**SIMULTANEITY OF VIEWS** The Futurists' interest in motion and in the Cubist dissection of form is evident in *Dynamism of a Dog on a Leash* (FIG. **33-19**) by Giacomo Balla (1871–1958). Here, observers focus their gazes on a passing dog and its owner, whose skirts the artist placed just within visual range. Balla achieved the effect of motion by repeating shapes, as in the dog's legs and tail and in the swinging line of the leash. Simultaneity of views, as demonstrated here, was central to the Futurist program.

**THE SENSATION OF MOTION** Umberto Boccioni (1882–1916) applied Balla's representational technique to sculpture. What we want, he claimed, is not fixed movement in space but the sensation of motion itself: "Owing to the persistence of images on the retina, objects in motion are multiplied and distorted, following one another like waves in space. Thus, a galloping horse has not four legs, it has twenty."[16] Clearly, this description applies to

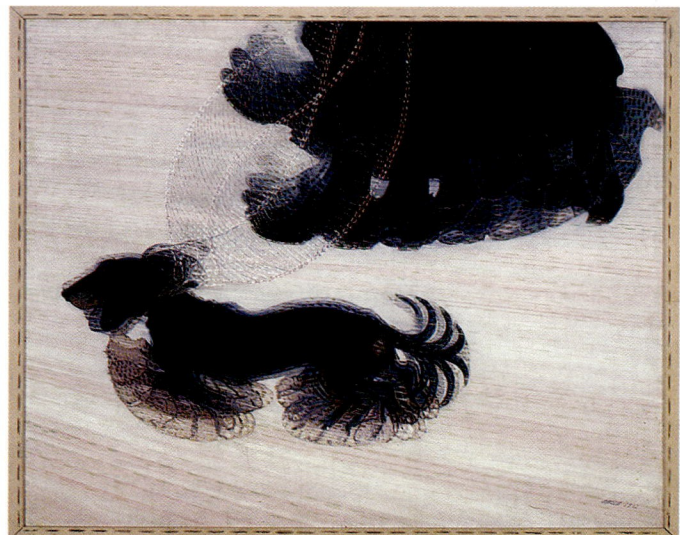

**33-19** GIACOMO BALLA, *Dynamism of a Dog on a Leash,* 1912. Oil on canvas, 2′ 11$\frac{3}{8}$″ × 3′ 7$\frac{1}{4}$″. Albright-Knox Art Gallery, Buffalo (bequest of A. Conger Goodyear, gift of George F. Goodyear, 1964).

*Dynamism of a Dog on a Leash.* Though Boccioni in this instance was talking about painting, his observation helps explain what is perhaps the definitive work of Futurist sculpture, his *Unique Forms of Continuity in Space* (FIG. **33-20**).

This piece highlights the formal and spatial effects of motion rather than their source, the striding human figure. The figure is so expanded, interrupted, and broken in plane and contour that it disappears, as it were, behind the blur of its movement. Boccioni's search for sculptural means for expressing dynamic movement reached a monumental expression here. In its power and sense of vital activity, this sculpture surpasses similar efforts in painting (by Boccioni and his Futurist companions) to create images symbolic of the dynamic quality of modern life. To be convinced by it, people need only reflect on how details of an adjacent landscape appear in their peripheral vision when they are traveling at great speed on a highway or in a low-flying airplane. Although Boccioni's figure bears a curious resemblance to the ancient *Nike of Samothrace* (see FIG. 5-82), a cursory comparison reveals how far the modern work departs from the ancient one.

This Futurist representation of motion in sculpture has its limitations. The eventual development of the motion picture, based on the rapid sequential projection of fixed images, produced more convincing illusions of movement. And several decades later in sculpture, Alexander Calder (FIG. 33-72) pioneered the development of kinetic sculpture—with actual moving parts. However, in the early 20th century, Boccioni's sculpture was notable for its ability to capture the sensation of motion.

**A SANITIZED DEPICTION OF WAR** *Armored Train* (FIG. **33-21**) by GINO SEVERINI (1883–1966) nicely encapsulates the Futurist program, both artistically and politically. The artist depicted a high-tech armored train with its rivets glistening and a huge booming cannon protruding from the top. Submerged in the bowels of the train, a row of soldiers train guns at an unseen target. Severini's painting reflects the Futurist faith in the cleansing action of war. Not only are the colors predominantly light and bright, but the artist also omitted death and destruction—the tragic consequences of war—from the image. This sanitized depiction of war contrasts sharply with Francisco Goya's *The Third of May, 1808* (see FIG. 28-43), which also depicts a uniform

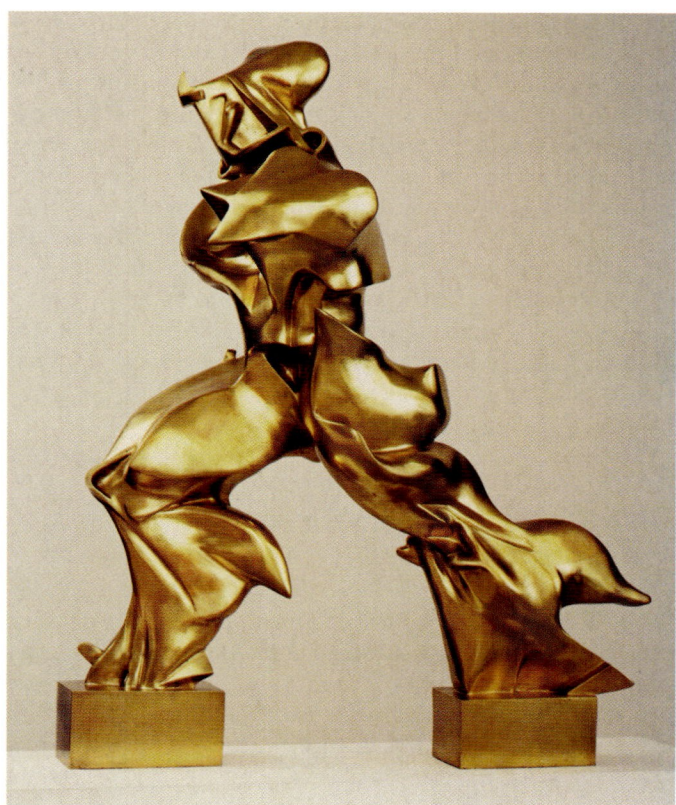

**33-20** UMBERTO BOCCIONI, *Unique Forms of Continuity in Space,* 1913 (cast 1931). Bronze, 3′ 7$\frac{7}{8}$″ high × 2′ 10$\frac{7}{8}$″ × 1′ 3$\frac{3}{4}$″. Museum of Modern Art, New York (acquired through the Lillie P. Bliss Bequest).

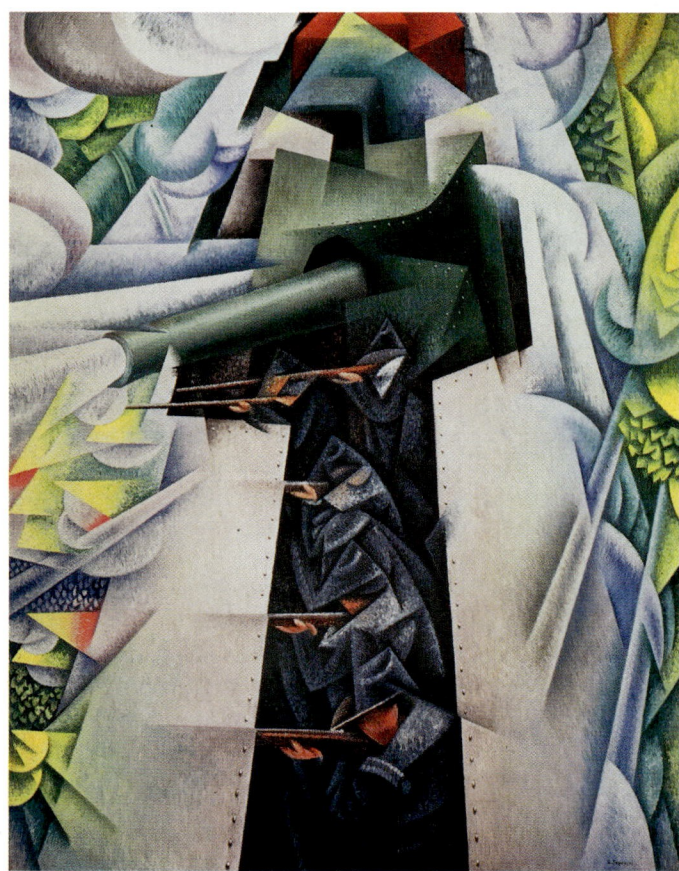

**33-21** GINO SEVERINI, *Armored Train,* 1915. Oil on canvas, 3′ 10″ × 2′ 10$\frac{1}{8}$″. Collection of Richard S. Zeisler, New York.

row of anonymous soldiers in the act of shooting. Goya, however, graphically presented the dead and those about to be shot, and the dark tones of the work cast a dramatic and sobering pall. *Armored Train* captures the dynamism and motion central to Futurism. In Cubist fashion, Severini depicted all of the objects, from the soldiers to the smoke emanating from the cannon, broken into facets and planes, suggesting action and movement.

Once World War I broke out, the Futurist group began to disintegrate, largely because so many of them felt compelled (given the Futurist support for the war) to join the Italian Army. Some of them, including Umberto Boccioni, were killed in the war. The ideas the Futurists promoted became integral to the fascism that emerged in Italy shortly thereafter.

# CHALLENGING ARTISTIC CONVENTIONS

Although the Futurists celebrated the war and the changes they hoped it would effect, the mass destruction and chaos of World War I horrified other artists. Humanity had never before witnessed such wholesale slaughter on so grand a scale over such an extended period. Millions were killed, wounded, or missing (blown to bits) in great battles. For example, in 1916, the battle of Verdun (lasting five months) left 500,000 casualties. On another day in 1916, the British lost 60,000 men in the opening battle of the Somme. The new technology of armaments, bred of the age of steel, made it a "war of the guns" (as in Severini's *Armored Train*). In the face of massed artillery hurling millions of tons of high explosives and gas shells and in the sheets of fire from thousands of machine guns, attack was suicidal, and battle movement congealed into the stalemate of trench warfare, stretching from the English Channel almost to Switzerland. The mud, filth, and blood of the trenches, the pounding and shattering of incessant shell fire, and the terrible deaths and mutilations were a devastating psychological, as well as physical, experience for a generation brought up with the doctrine of progress and a belief in the fundamental values of civilization.

## *Dada*

With the war as a backdrop, many artists contributed to an artistic and literary movement that became known as *Dada*. This movement emerged, in large part, in reaction to what many of these artists saw as nothing more than an insane spectacle of collective homicide. They were utterly "revolted by the butchery of the World War."[17] The international scope of Dada proves this revulsion was widespread; although Dada began independently in New York and Zurich, it also emerged in Paris, Berlin, and Cologne, among other cities. Dada was more a mind-set or attitude than a single identifiable style. As André Breton, founder of the slightly later Surrealist movement, explained: "Cubism was a school of painting, futurism a political movement: DADA is a state of mind."[18] The Dadaists believed reason and logic had been responsible for the unmitigated disaster of world war, and they concluded that the only route to salvation was through political anarchy, the irrational, and the intuitive. Thus, an element of absurdity is a cornerstone of Dada, even reflected in the movement's name. *Dada* is a term unrelated to the movement; according to an often repeated anecdote, the Dadaists chose the word at random from a French-German dictionary. Although the word *dada* does have meaning—it is French for a child's hobby horse—it satisfied the

Dadaists' desire for something irrational and nonsensical. (It should be noted, however, that this is just one among many explanations for the name selected for this movement.)

Further, the pessimism and disgust of these artists surfaced in their disdain for convention or tradition, characterized by a concerted and sustained attempt to undermine cherished notions and assumptions about art. Because of this destructive dimension, art historians often describe Dada as a nihilistic enterprise. This nihilism, Dada's contempt for all traditional and established values, and its derisive iconoclasm can be read at random from its numerous manifestos and declarations of intent:

> Dada knows everything. Dada spits on everything. Dada says "knowthing," Dada has no fixed ideas. Dada does not catch flies. Dada is bitterness laughing at everything that has been accomplished, sanctified. . . . Dada is never right. . . . No more painters, no more writers, no more religions, no more royalists, no more anarchists, no more socialists, no more police, no more airplanes, no more urinary passages. . . . Like everything in life, Dada is useless, everything happens in a completely idiotic way. . . . We are incapable of treating seriously any subject whatsoever, let alone this subject: ourselves. [Dadaists, describing their own movement, said] Dada was a phenomenon bursting forth in the midst of the postwar economic and moral crisis, a savior, a monster, which would lay waste to everything in its path. [It was] a systematic work of destruction and demoralization. . . . In the end it became nothing but the act of sacrilege.[19]

Although the artists' cynicism and pessimism inspired Dada, what developed was phenomenally influential and powerful. By attacking convention and logic, the Dada artists unlocked new avenues for creative invention, thereby fostering a more serious examination of the basic premises of art than had prior movements. Dada was, in its subversiveness, extraordinarily avant-garde and tremendously liberating. In addition, although horror and disgust about the war initially prompted Dada, an undercurrent of humor and whimsy—sometimes sardonic or irreverent—runs through much of the art. For example, Marcel Duchamp painted a moustache and goatee on a reproduction of Leonardo's *Mona Lisa*. The French painter Francis Picabia (1879–1953), Duchamp's collaborator in setting up Dada in New York, nailed a toy monkey to a board and labeled it *Portrait of Cézanne*.

In its emphasis on the spontaneous and intuitive, Dada paralleled the psychoanalytic views of Sigmund Freud, Carl Jung, and others. Particularly interested in the exploration of the unconscious Freud promoted, the Dada artists believed that art was a powerfully practical means of self-revelation and catharsis. In addition, they were convinced that the images arising out of the subconscious mind had a truth of their own, independent of conventional vision. A Dada filmmaker, Hans Richter, summarized the attitude of the Dadaists:

> Possessed, as we were, of the ability to entrust ourselves to "chance," to our conscious as well as our unconscious minds, we became a sort of public secret society. . . . We laughed at everything. . . . But laughter was only the expression of our new discoveries, not their essence and not their purpose. Pandemonium, destruction, anarchy, anti-everything of the World War? How could Dada have been anything but destructive, aggressive, insolent, on principle and with gusto?[20]

**THE ANARCHY OF CHANCE** A Dada artist whose works serve as examples of the "chance" Richter refers to is the Zurich-based artist JEAN (HANS) ARP (1887–1966). Arp pioneered the use of chance in composing his images. Tiring of the look of some Cubist-related collages he was making, he took some sheets of paper, tore them into roughly shaped squares, haphazardly dropped them to a sheet of paper on the floor, and glued them into the resulting arrangement. The rectilinearity of the shapes guaranteed a somewhat regular design (which Arp no doubt enhanced by adjusting the random arrangement into a quasi-grid), but chance had introduced an imbalance that seemed to Arp to restore to his work a special mysterious vitality he wanted to preserve. *Collage Arranged According to the Laws of Chance* (FIG. **33-22**) is a work he created by this method. The operations of chance were for Dadaists a crucial part of this kind of improvisation. As Richter stated: "For us chance was the 'unconscious mind' that Freud had discovered in 1900. . . . Adoption of chance had another purpose, a secret one. This was to restore to the work of art its primeval magic power and to find a way back to the immediacy it had lost through contact with . . . classicism."[21] Further, in its renunciation of artistic control, Arp's reliance on chance when creating his compositions reinforced the anarchy and subversiveness inherent in Dada.

### HIGH-SPIRITED DADA PERFORMANCES
Among the manifestations of Dada that matured in 1916 in Zurich was performance. Much of this performance activity was presented at the Cabaret Voltaire, founded by Dadaist Hugo Ball, a poet, musician, and theatrical producer. The first Dada performances were fairly tame, consisting of musical presentations and poetry readings. In keeping with Dada thought, however, they quickly became more aggressive, anarchic, and illogical. Dadaist Tristan Tzara's description of one such Dada performance rings with the cacophony, subversiveness, and high spirits that characterized Dada. Tzara wrote: "Boxing resumed: Cubist dance, costumes by Janco, each man his own big drum on his head, noise, Negro music/trabatgea bonoooooo oo ooooo/5 literary experiments; Tzara in tails stands before the curtain, stone sober for the animals, and explains the new aesthetic: gymnastic poem, concert of vowels, bruitist poem, static poem chemical arrangement of ideas, 'Biriboom biriboom' saust der Ochs im Kreis herum (the ox dashes round in a ring) (Huelsenbeck), vowel poem a a ò, i e o, a i ï, new interpretation of subjective folly of the arteries the dance of the heart on burning buildings and acrobatics in the audience."[22] Despite the seeming arbitrariness and absurdity of Dada performance, the participants were committed to the development of this avant-garde pursuit.

### FREEING ART FROM CONVENTION
Perhaps the most influential of all the Dadaists was Frenchman MARCEL DUCHAMP (1887–1968), the central artist of New York Dada and active in Paris at the end of the Dada movement. In 1913, he exhibited his first "ready-made" sculptures, which were mass-produced common objects—*found objects*—the artist selected and sometimes "rectified" by modifying their substance or combining them with another object. Such works, he insisted, were created free from any consideration of either good or bad taste, qualities shaped by a society he and other Dada artists found aesthetically bankrupt. Perhaps his most outrageous ready-made was *Fountain* (FIG. **33-23**), a porcelain urinal presented on its back, signed "R. Mutt," and dated. The "artist's signature" was, in fact, a witty pseudonym derived from the Mott plumbing company's name and that of the short half of the Mutt and Jeff comic-strip team. As with Duchamp's other ready-mades, he did not select this object for

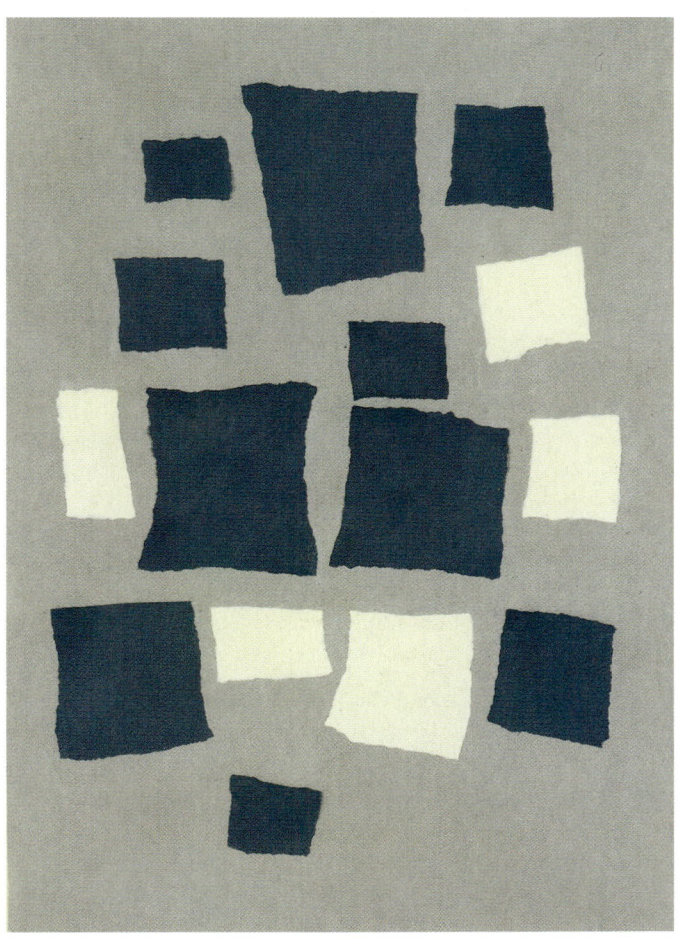

**33-22** JEAN (HANS) ARP, *Collage Arranged According to the Laws of Chance*, 1916–1917. Torn and pasted paper, 1′ 7$\frac{1}{8}$″ × 1′ 1$\frac{5}{8}$″. Museum of Modern Art, New York (purchase).

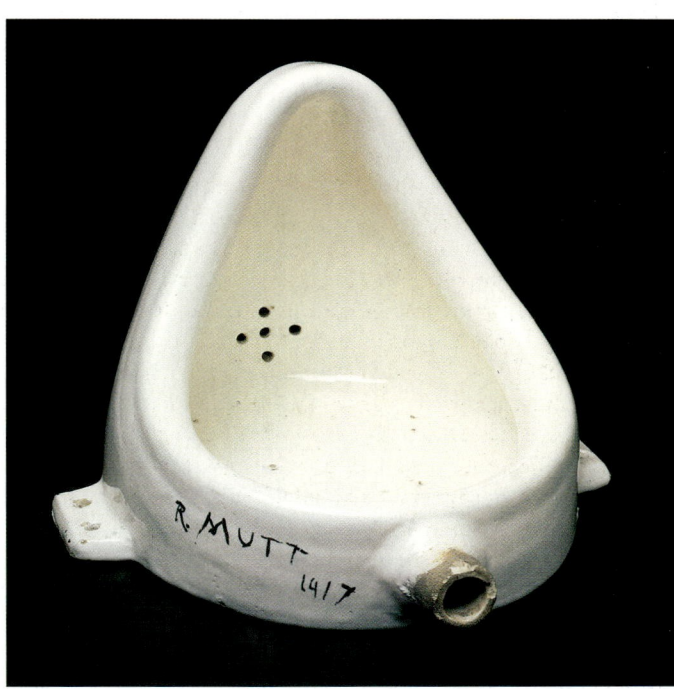

**33-23** MARCEL DUCHAMP, *Fountain* (second version), 1950 (original version produced 1917). Ready-made glazed sanitary china with black paint, 12″ high. Philadelphia Museum of Art, Philadelphia (purchased with proceeds from the sale of deaccessioned works of art).

exhibition because of its aesthetic qualities. The "artness" of this work lies in the artist's choice of this object, which has the effect of conferring the status of art on it and forces the viewer to see the object in a new light. As he wrote in a "defense" published in 1917, after the exhibition committee for an unjuried show rejected *Fountain* for display: "Whether Mr. Mutt with his own hands made the fountain or not has no importance. He chose it. He took an ordinary article of life, placed it so that its useful significance disappeared under the new title and point of view—created a new thought for that object."[23] It is hard to imagine a more aggressively avant-garde approach to art; Dada persistently presented staggering challenges to artistic conventions.

**MECHANISTIC MEN AND WOMEN** Among the most visually and conceptually challenging of Duchamp's works is *The Bride Stripped Bare by Her Bachelors, Even* (FIG. **33-24**), often referred to as *The Large Glass.* Begun in 1915 and abandoned by Duchamp as unfinished in 1923, *The Large Glass* is a simultaneously playful and

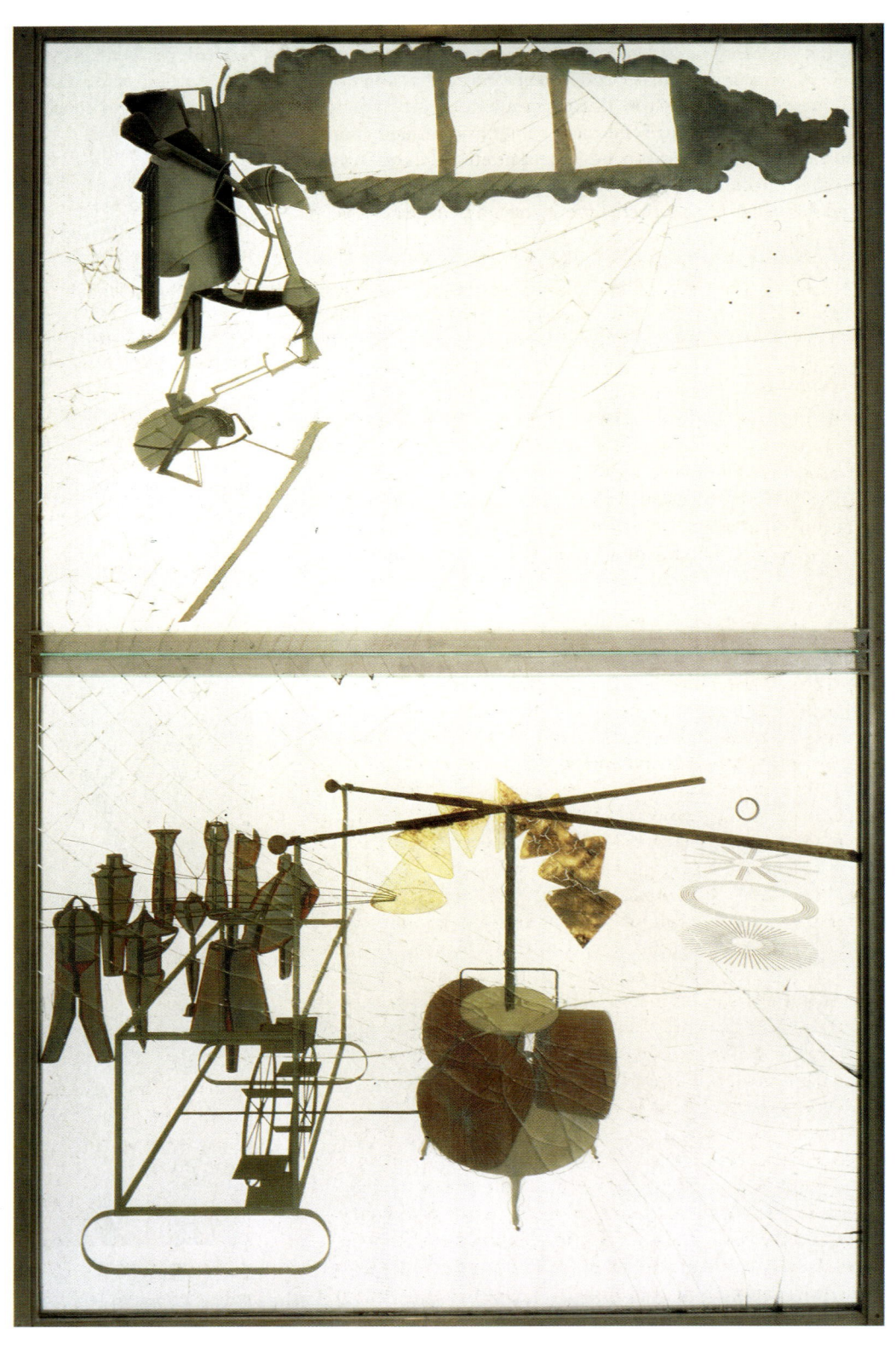

**33-24** MARCEL DUCHAMP, *The Bride Stripped Bare by Her Bachelors, Even (The Large Glass),* 1915–1923. Oil, lead, wire, foil, dust, and varnish on glass, 9′ $1\frac{1}{2}$″ × 5′ $9\frac{1}{8}$″. Philadelphia Museum of Art, Philadelphia (Katherine S. Dreier Bequest).

serious examination of human as machine. Consisting of oil paint, wire, and lead foil sandwiched in between two large glass panels, the artwork presents the viewer with an array of images, some apparently mechanical, others diagrammatic, and yet others seemingly abstract in nature. Duchamp provided some clues to the intriguing imagery in a series of notes that accompanied the work. The top half of the work represents "the bride," whom Duchamp has depicted as "basically a motor" fueled by "love gasoline." In contrast, the bachelors appear as uniformed male figures in the lower half of the work. They too are mechanistically driven; the chocolate grinder in the center of the lower glass pane represents masturbation ("the bachelor grinds his own chocolate"). In *The Large Glass,* Duchamp has provided his own whimsical but insightful ruminations into the ever-confounding realm of desire and sexuality. In true Dadaist fashion, chance completed the work; when *The Large Glass* was being transported from an exhibition in 1927, the glass panes were shattered. Rather than replace the broken glass, Duchamp painstakingly pieced together the glass shards. After encasing the reconstructed work, broken panes and all, between two heavier panes of glass, Duchamp declared the work completed "by chance."

Duchamp (and the generations of artists after him profoundly influenced by his art and especially his attitude) considered life and art matters of chance and choice freed from the conventions of society and tradition. Within his approach to art and life, each act was individual and unique. Every person's choice of found objects would be different, for example, and each person's throw of the dice would be at a different instant and probably would yield a different number. This philosophy of utter freedom for artists was fundamental to the history of art in the 20th century. Duchamp spent much of World War I in New York, inspiring a group of American artists and collectors with his radical rethinking of the role of artists and of the nature of art.

**A VIEW OF "THE GREAT DADA WORLD"** Dada spread throughout much of western Europe, arriving as early as 1917 in Berlin, where it soon took on an activist political edge, partially in response to the economic, social, and political chaos in that city in the years at the end of and immediately after World War I. The Berlin Dadaists developed to a new intensity a technique used earlier in popular art postcards. Pasting parts from many pictures together into one image, the Berliners christened their version of the technique *photomontage.* The technique of creating a composition by pasting together pieces of paper had been used in private and popular arts long before the 20th century. A few years earlier, the Cubists had named the process "collage." Unlike Cubist collage, the parts of a Dada collage were made almost entirely of "found" details, such as pieces of magazine photographs, usually combined into deliberately antilogical compositions. Collage lent itself well to the Dada desire to use chance when creating art and antiart, but not all Dada collage was as savagely aggressive as that of the Berlin photomontagists.

One of the Berlin Dadaists who perfected this photomontage technique was HANNAH HÖCH (1889–1978). Höch's photomontages were particularly incisive because they operated at the intersection of so many timely discourses. Her works not only advanced the absurd illogic of Dada by presenting the viewer with chaotic, contradictory, and satiric compositions, but they also provided scathing and insightful commentary on two of the most dramatic developments during the Weimar Republic

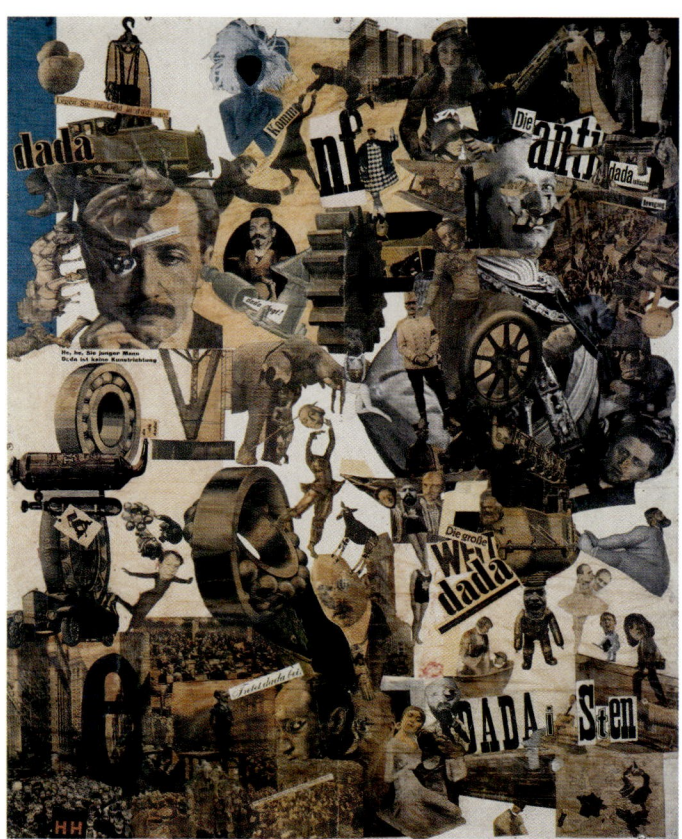

33-25 HANNAH HÖCH, *Cut with the Kitchen Knife Dada through the Last Weimar Beer Belly Cultural Epoch of Germany,* 1919–1920. Photomontage, 3′ 9″ × 2′ 11½″. Neue Nationalgalerie, Staatliche Museen, Berlin.

(1918–1933) in Germany—the redefinition of women's social roles and the explosive growth of mass print media. She revealed these combined themes in her powerful photomontage *Cut with the Kitchen Knife Dada through the Last Weimar Beer Belly Cultural Epoch of Germany* (FIG. **33-25**). The artist arranged an eclectic mixture of cutout photos in seemingly haphazard fashion. On closer inspection, however, the viewer can see that Höch carefully placed photographs of some of her fellow Dadaists among images of Marx, Lenin, and other revolutionary figures in the lower right section, aligning this movement with other revolutionary forces. She promoted Dada in prominently placed cutout lettering— "Die grosse Welt dada" (the great Dada world). Certainly, juxtaposing the heads of German military leaders with exotic dancers' bodies provided the wickedly humorous critique central to much of Dada. Höch also positioned herself in this topsy-turvy world she created. A photograph of her head appears in the lower right corner, juxtaposed with a map of Europe showing the progress of women's enfranchisement. Aware of the power both women and Dada had to destabilize society, Höch made forceful visual manifestations of that belief.

**THE VISUAL POETRY OF RUBBISH** The Hanover Dada artist KURT SCHWITTERS (1887–1948) followed a gentler muse. Inspired by Cubist collage but working nonobjectively, Schwitters found visual poetry in the cast-off junk of modern society and scavenged in trash bins for materials, which he pasted and nailed

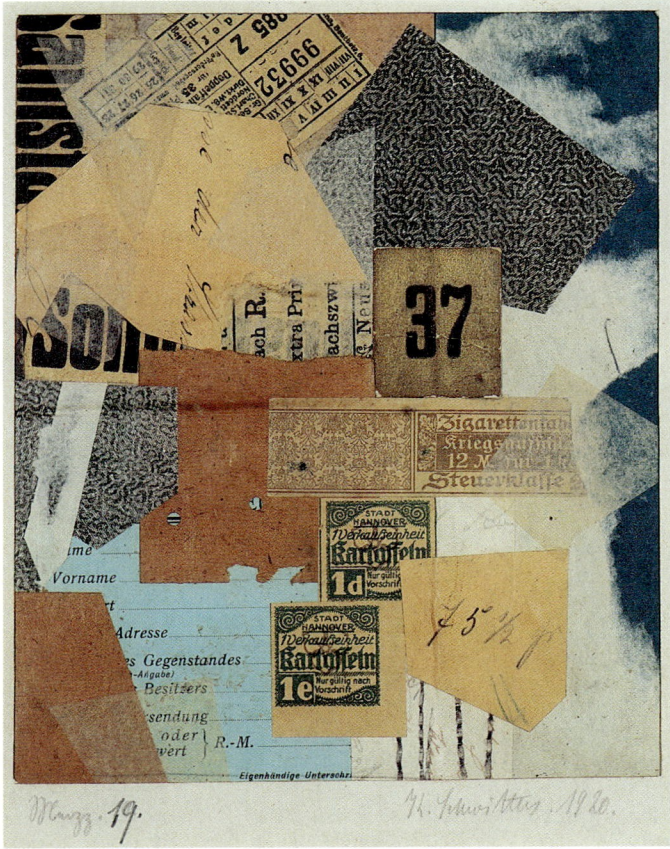

together into designs such as *Merz 19* (FIG. **33-26**). The term *merz*, which Schwitters used as a generic title for a whole series of collaged images, derived nonsensically from the word *kommerzbank* (commerce bank) and appeared as a word fragment in one of his collages. Although nonobjective, his compositions still resonate with the meaning of the fragmented found objects they contain. The recycled elements of Schwitters's collages, like Duchamp's ready-mades, acquire new meanings through their new uses and locations. Elevating objects that are essentially trash to the status of high art certainly fits within the parameters of the Dada program and parallels the absurd dimension of much of Dada art. Contradiction, paradox, irony, and even blasphemy are Dada's bequest. They are, in the view of Dada and its successors, the free and defiant artist's weapons in what has been called the hundred years' war with the public.

## TRANSATLANTIC ARTISTIC DIALOGUES

The energy and enthusiasm of artists undertaking these avant-garde experiments were not limited to Europe. A wide range of artists engaged in a lively exchange of artistic ideas and significant transatlantic travel. In the latter part of the 19th century, American artists such as John Singer Sargent, James Abbott McNeil Whistler, and Mary Cassatt spent much of their productive careers in Europe, whereas many European artists ended their careers in America, especially in anticipation of and, later, in the wake of World War I. Visionary patrons supported the efforts of American artists to pursue modernist ideas (see "Art 'Matronage' in America: Contributions of Female Patrons in the Early 20th Century," page 985).

The art scene in America before the establishment of a significant and consistent dialogue with European modernists was, of

**33-26** KURT SCHWITTERS, *Merz 19*, 1920. Paper collage, approx. $7\frac{1}{4}'' \times 5\frac{7}{8}''$. Yale University Art Gallery, New Haven (gift of Collection Société Anonyme).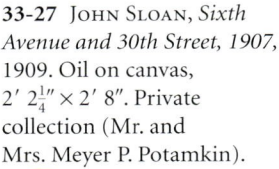

**33-27** JOHN SLOAN, *Sixth Avenue and 30th Street, 1907*, 1909. Oil on canvas, $2' 2\frac{1}{4}'' \times 2' 8''$. Private collection (Mr. and Mrs. Meyer P. Potamkin).

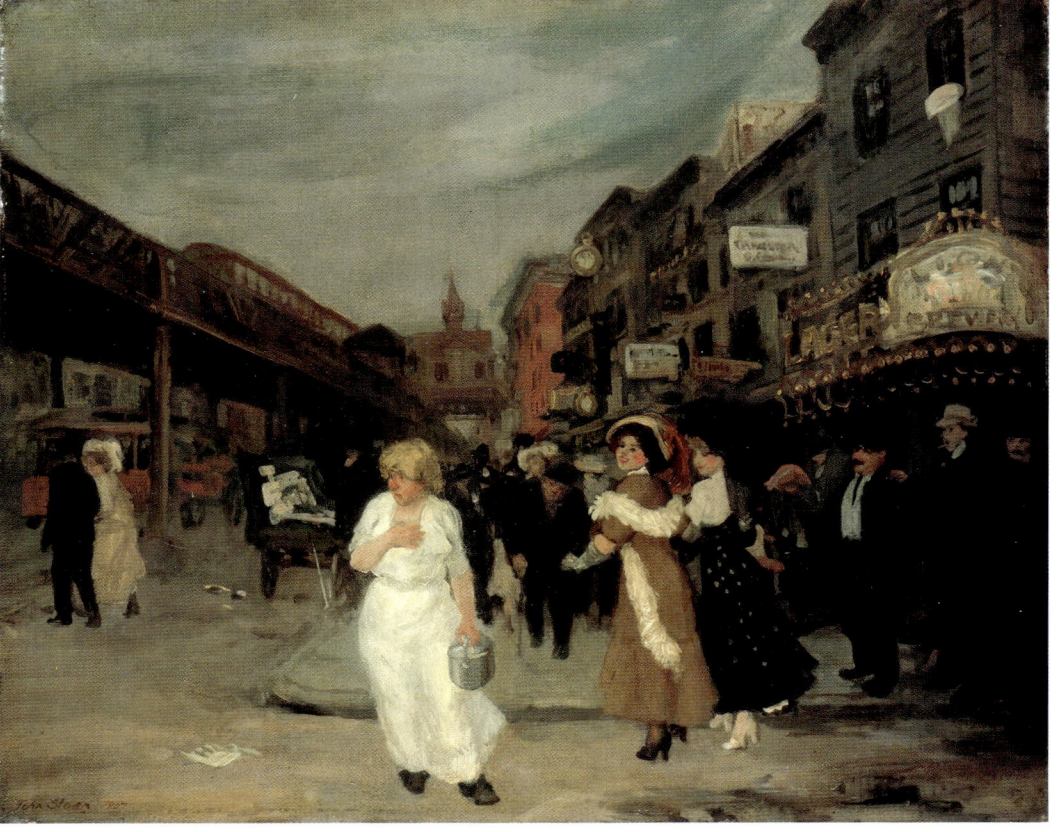

## Art "Matronage" in America
### Contributions of Female Patrons in the Early 20th Century

For centuries, the participation of women in the art world has been limited. Until the 20th century, the dearth of women artists was often due to professional institutions that restricted women's access to artistic training; for example, the proscription against women participating in life drawing class, a staple of academic artistic training, in effect denied women the opportunity to become professional artists. The absence of women from the art historical canon can also be attributed in part to the fact that many of the art objects produced by women over the years (for example, quilts or basketry) have not been recognized as high art.

By the early 20th century, many of these strictures were loosening. Women could gain entrance to established art schools, and today, women are a major presence in the art world. One of the developments in the early 20th century that laid the groundwork for this change was the prominent role that women played as art patrons. These "art matrons" provided financial, moral, and political support to cultivate the advancement of the arts in America. Among these women were Gertrude Vanderbilt Whitney, Lillie P. Bliss, Mary Quinn Sullivan, Abby Aldrich Rockefeller, Isabella Stewart Gardner, Peggy Guggenheim, and Jane Stanford.[1]

Gertrude Vanderbilt Whitney (1875–1942) was a practicing sculptor and enthusiastic collector. To assist young American artists such as Robert Henri and John Sloan (FIG. 33-27) to exhibit their work, she opened the Whitney Studio in 1914. By 1929, dissatisfied with the recognition accorded young, progressive American artists, she offered her entire collection of 500 works to the Metropolitan Museum of Art. Her offer rejected, she founded her own museum, the Whitney Museum of American Art in New York City. She chose as the first director a visionary and energetic woman, Juliana Force (1876–1948), who inaugurated a pioneering series of monographs on living American artists and organized lecture series by influential art historians and critics. Through the efforts of these two women, the Whitney Museum was established as a major force in American art.

A trip to Paris in 1920 whetted the interest of Peggy Guggenheim (1898–1979) in avant-garde art. Like Whitney, she collected art and eventually opened a gallery in England to exhibit avant-garde art. She continued her support for avant-garde art after her return to the United States; her New York gallery, called Art of This Century, was instrumental in advancing the careers of many artists, including her husband, Max Ernst (FIG. 33-45). She eventually moved her art collection to a lavish Venetian palace, where these important artworks continue to be available for public viewing.

Other women contributed significantly to the arts, including Lillie P. Bliss (1864–1931), Mary Quinn Sullivan (1877–1939), and Abby Aldrich Rockefeller (1874–1948), who together founded the Museum of Modern Art in New York. Philanthropists, art collectors, and educators, these visionary and influential women saw the need for a museum to collect and exhibit modernist art. Together they established the Museum of Modern Art in 1929, which became (and continues to be) the most influential museum of modern art in the world.

Isabella Stewart Gardner (1840–1924) and Jane Stanford (1828–1905) also undertook the ambitious project of founding museums. The Isabella Stewart Gardner Museum in Boston, established in 1903, contains an impressive collection of art that is comprehensive in scope. The Stanford Museum, the first American museum west of the Mississippi, got its start in 1905 on the grounds of Stanford University, which Leland Stanford Sr. and Jane Stanford founded after the tragic death of their son. The Stanford Museum houses a wide range of objects, including archaeological and ethnographic artifacts. These two driven women committed much of their time, energy, and financial resources to ensure the success of these museums. Both were intimately involved in the day-to-day operations of their institutions.

The museums these women established flourish today, attesting to the extraordinary vision of these "art matrons." These institutions and the art collections amassed by these women serve as tributes to the remarkable contributions women have made to the advancement of art in the United States.

[1]The term *art matronage* was coined by art historian Wanda Corn in the catalog *Cultural Leadership in America: Art Matronage and Patronage* (Boston: Isabella Stewart Gardner Museum, 1997).

---

course, quite varied. In the early 20th century, many American artists were committed to the realist tradition—specifically, presenting what they considered to be a realistic, unvarnished look at life. In this regard, their work parallels that of the French Realists in the mid-19th century (Chapter 29, pages 855–863).

**DEPICTING THE SEAMY SIDE OF LIFE** One such group of artists, The Eight, consisted of eight American artists who gravitated into the circle of the influential and evangelical artist and teacher, Robert Henri (1865–1929). Henri urged these artists to make "pictures from life,"[24] and accordingly, these artists pursued with zeal the production of images depicting the rapidly changing urban landscape of New York City. Because these vignettes often captured the bleak and seedy aspects of city life, The Eight eventually became known as the Ashcan School, and were on occasion referred to as "the apostles of ugliness."

JOHN SLOAN (1871–1951) was both a friend and protégé of Henri and a member of The Eight. A self-described "incorrigible window watcher,"[25] Sloan constantly wandered the streets of New York, observing human drama. He focused much of his attention on the working class, which he perceived as embodying the realities of life. So sympathetic was Sloan to the working class that he joined the Socialist Party in 1909 and eventually ran for public office on the Socialist ticket. In paintings such as *Sixth Avenue at 30th Street, 1907* (FIG. 33-27), Sloan revealed his ability to capture both the visual and social realities of American urban life shortly after the turn of the century. When he painted this image in 1907, Sloan was living on West 23rd Street, on the outskirts of the Tenderloin District, an area cluttered with brothels, dance halls, saloons, gambling dens, and cheap hotels. *Sixth Avenue at 30th Street, 1907* depicts a bustling intersection. The throngs of people that fill the intersection are bracketed by the elevated tracks of the subway train on the left and the row of store fronts and apartment buildings on the right side of the painting. These two defining elements of city life converge in the far center background. That Sloan's paintings capture a slice of American urban life is revealed by the cross-section of people depicted. In the foreground of this painting, Sloan prominently placed three women. One, in a shabby white dress, is a drunkard, stumbling along with her pail of beer. She is stared at by two streetwalkers. In turn, two well-dressed men gaze at the prostitutes. Sloan's depiction does not preach about prostitution, allying him with reformers of the time, who saw streetwalkers not as immoral but as victims of an unfair social and economic system. At a time when traditional art centered on genteel and proper society, Sloan's forthright depiction of prostitutes was categorically "realist."

## The Armory Show and Its Legacy

**AN INFLUENTIAL EXHIBITION**  One of the major vehicles for disseminating information about European artistic developments in the United States was the Armory Show, which occurred in early 1913. This large-scale and ambitious endeavor got its name from its location. After a year of searching for a suitable site, the exhibition's coordinators settled on the armory of the New York National Guard's 69th Regiment. Organized in large part by two artists, Walt Kuhn and Arthur B. Davies, the Armory Show (FIG. **33-28**) contained more than 1,600 artworks by American and European artists. Among the European artists represented were Matisse, Derain, Picasso, Braque, Duchamp, Kandinsky, and Kirchner, as well as expressionist sculptor Wilhelm Lehmbruck and organic sculptor Constantin Brancusi, both discussed later. In addition to exposing American artists and the public to the latest in European artistic developments, this show also provided American artists with a prime showcase for their work.

**A NUDE IN MOTION**  On its opening, this provocative exhibition served as a lightning rod for commentary, immediately attracting heated controversy. The *New York Times* described the show as "pathological," and other critics demanded the exhibition be closed as a menace to public morality. The work the press most maligned was Marcel Duchamp's *Nude Descending a Staircase, No. 2* (FIG. **33-29**). The painting, a single figure in motion down a staircase in a time continuum, suggests the effect of a sequence of overlaid film stills. Although earlier discussion of Duchamp in this book focused on his contributions to the Dada movement, *Nude Descending a Staircase* has more in common with the work of the Cubists and the Futurists. The monochromatic palette is reminiscent of Analytic Cubism, as is Duchamp's faceted presentation of the human form. The artist's interest in depicting the figure in motion reveals an affinity for the Futurists' ideas. One critic described this work as "an explosion in a shingle factory,"[26] and newspaper cartoonists had a field day lampooning the painting.

**CHAMPIONING PHOTOGRAPHY**  The Armory Show traveled to Chicago and Boston after it closed in New York and was a significant catalyst for discussion and serious thought about recent developments in art. Another catalyst in the period's artistic ferment was the artist ALFRED STIEGLITZ (1864–1946). Committed to promoting the avant-garde in the United States, Stieglitz established an art gallery at 291 Fifth Avenue in New York, which eventually became known simply as "291." His gallery was renowned for exhibiting the latest in both European and American art and thus, like the Armory Show, played an important role in the history of early-20th-century art in America.

Stieglitz also channeled his artistic energies into producing photography. Taking his camera everywhere he went, he photographed whatever he saw around him, from the bustling streets of New York City to cloudscapes in upstate New York and the faces of friends and relatives. He believed in making only

**33-28**  Installation photo of the Armory Show, New York National Guard's 69th Regiment, New York, 1913. Museum of Modern Art, New York.

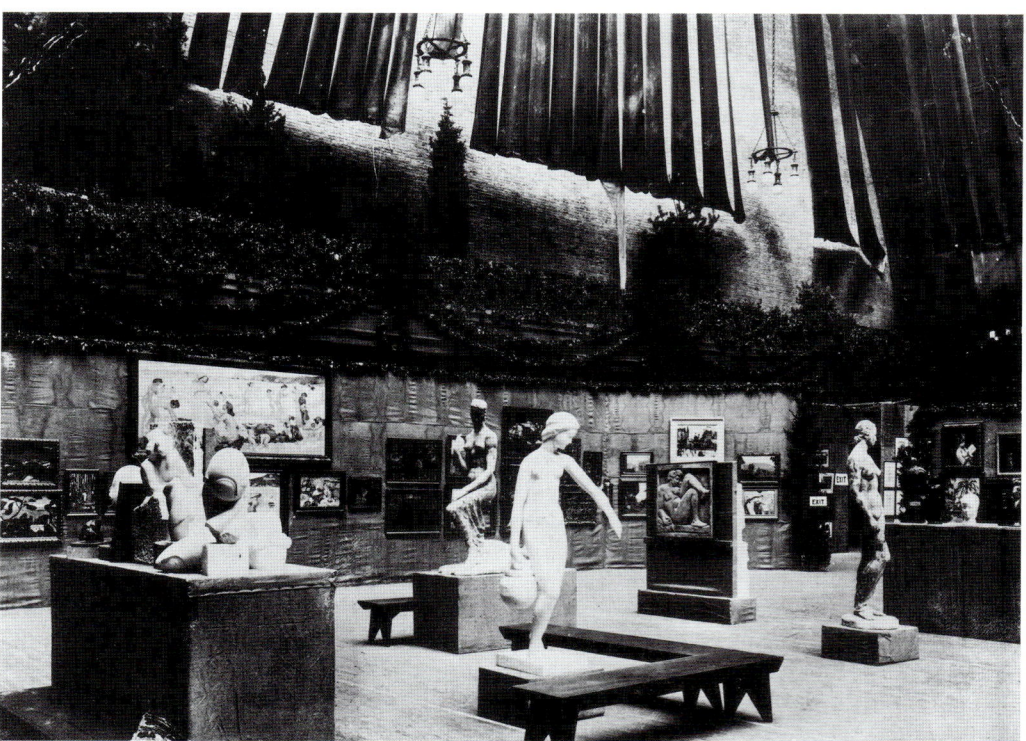

*Steerage* (FIG. 33-30), taken during a voyage to Europe with his lized during the making of one of his best-known works, *The* that stirred his deepest emotions. His aesthetic approach crystal-materials. He was attracted above all to arrangements of form jects in terms of the "colors" of his black-and-white sub-cialized in photographs of his environment and saw these sub-ential journal titled *Camera Work*. In his own works, Stieglitz spe-and sent loan collections abroad, and he also published an influ-group, which mounted traveling exhibitions in the United States many. Returning to New York, he founded the Photo-Secession among the fine arts while a student of photochemistry in Ger-He began a lifelong campaign to win a place for photography equivalent of what has been expressed."[28] something so completely that those who see it would relive an made with this direct technique "to hold a moment, to record released the shutter. Stieglitz said he wanted the photographs he that would add information not present in the subject when he ing to techniques such as double-exposure or double-printing printed them using basic photographic processes, without resort-"straight, unmanipulated" photographs.[27] Thus, he exposed and

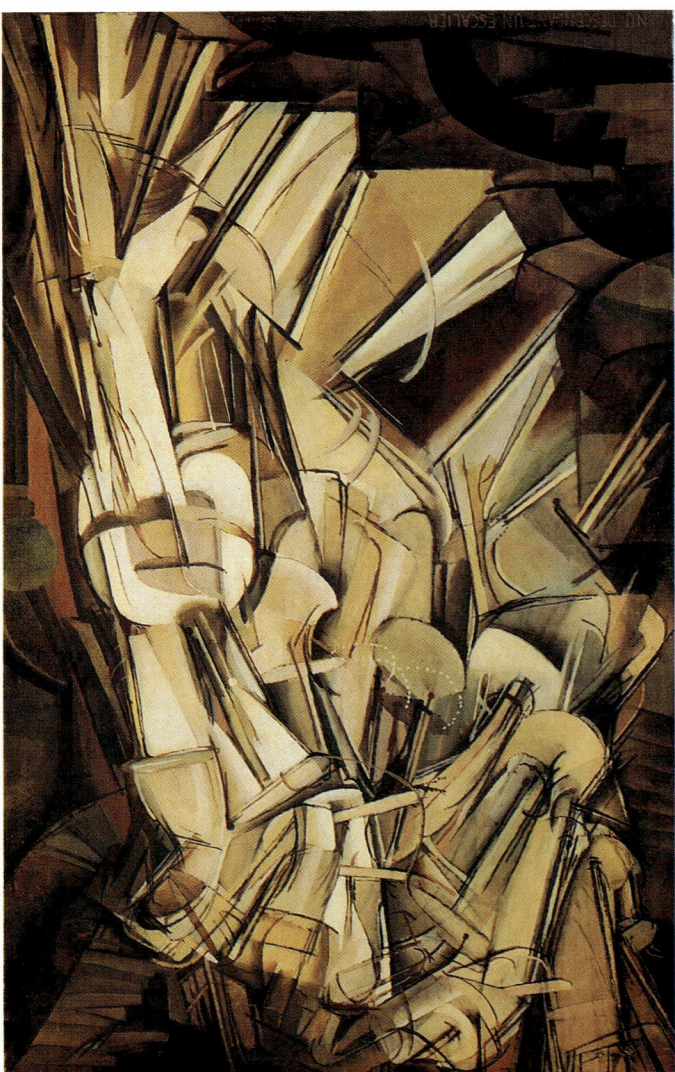

**33-29** MARCEL DUCHAMP, *Nude Descending a Staircase, No. 2*, 1912. Oil on canvas, approx. 4' 10" × 2' 11". Philadelphia Museum of Art, Philadelphia (Louise and Walter Arensberg Collection).

first wife and daughter in 1907. Traveling first class, Stieglitz rapidly grew bored with the company of the prosperous passen-gers in the ship's first-class section. He walked as far forward on that level as he could, when the rail around the opening onto the lower deck brought him up short. This level was reserved for steerage passengers the government was returning to Europe after refusing them entrance into the United States. Later, Stieglitz described what happened next:

The scene fascinated me: A round hat; the funnel leaning left, the stairway leaning right; the white drawbridge, its railing made of chain; white suspenders crossed on the back of a man below; circu-lar iron machinery; a mast that cut into the sky, completing a tri-angle. I stood spellbound. I saw shapes related to one another—a picture of shapes, and underlying it, a new vision that held me: simple people; the feeling of ship, ocean, sky; a sense of release that I was away from the mob called rich. Rembrandt came into my mind and I wondered would he have felt as I did. . . . I had only one plate holder with one unexposed plate. Could I catch what I saw and felt? If I released the shutter, if I had captured what I wanted, the photograph would go far beyond any of my previous prints. It would be a picture based on related shapes and deepest human feeling—a step in my own evolution, a spontaneous discovery.[29]

This description reveals Stieglitz's abiding interest in the for-mal elements of the photograph—an insistently modernist fo-cus. The finished print fulfilled Stieglitz's vision so well that it shaped his future photographic work, and its haunting mixture of found patterns and human activity has continued to stir viewers' emotions to this day.

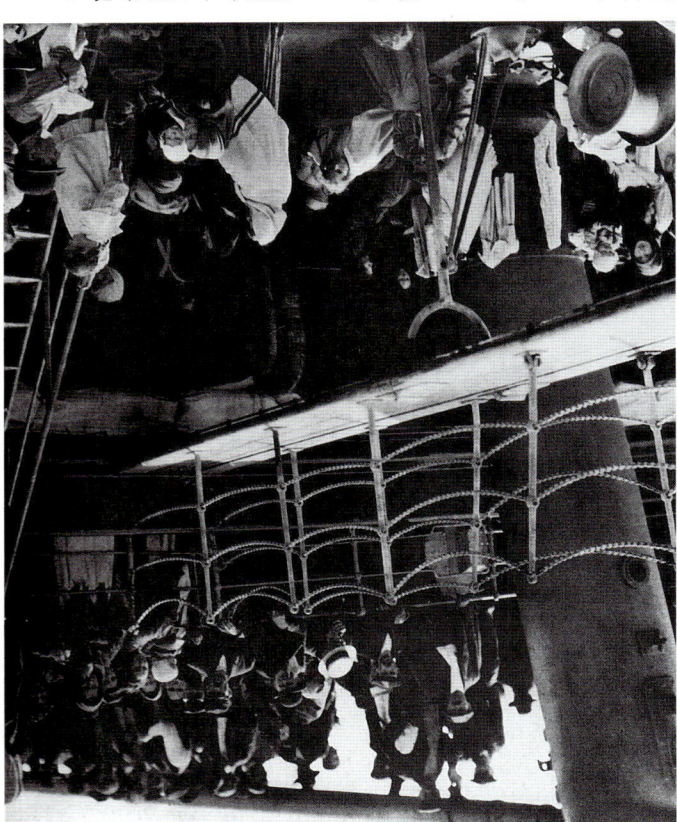

**33-30** ALFRED STIEGLITZ, *The Steerage*, 1907 (print 1915). Photo-gravure (on tissue), 1' 3³⁄₈" × 10¹⁄₈". Courtesy of Amon Carter Museum, Fort Worth.

**MOVING TOWARD ABSTRACTION** Stieglitz's concern for positioning photography as an art form with the same fine-art status as painting and sculpture was also pursued by Edward Weston (1886–1958). In addition to taking "straight" photography, like those of Stieglitz, Weston experimented with photographs that moved toward greater abstraction, paralleling developments in other media. *Nude* (FIG. 33-31) is an example of this photographic style. The image's simplicity and the selection of a small segment of the human body as the subject result in a lyrical photograph of dark and light areas that at first glance suggests a landscape. Further inspection reveals the fluid curves and underlying skeletal armature of the human form. This photograph, in its reductiveness, formally expresses a study of the body that verges on the abstract.

**A WICKEDLY FUNNY GIFT** The American artist Man Ray (1890–1976), who worked closely with Duchamp through the 1920s, produced art with a decidedly Dada spirit. Man Ray incorporated found objects into many of his paintings, sculptures, movies, and photographs. Trained as an architectural draftsman and engineer, Man Ray earned his living as a graphic designer and portrait photographer. He brought to his personal work an interest in mass-produced objects and technology, as well as a dedication to exploring the psychological realm of human perception of the exterior world. Like Schwitters, Man Ray used chance and the dislocation of ordinary things from their everyday settings to surprise his viewers into new awareness. His displacement of found objects was particularly effective in works such as *Cadeau* (*Gift*; FIG. 33-32). For this sculpture, he equipped a laundry iron with a row of wicked-looking spikes, subverting its proper function of smoothing and pressing. The malicious humor of *Cadeau* (*Gift*)—seen throughout Dada and, indeed, much of contemporary art—gives it a characteristic edge that can cut the unwary.

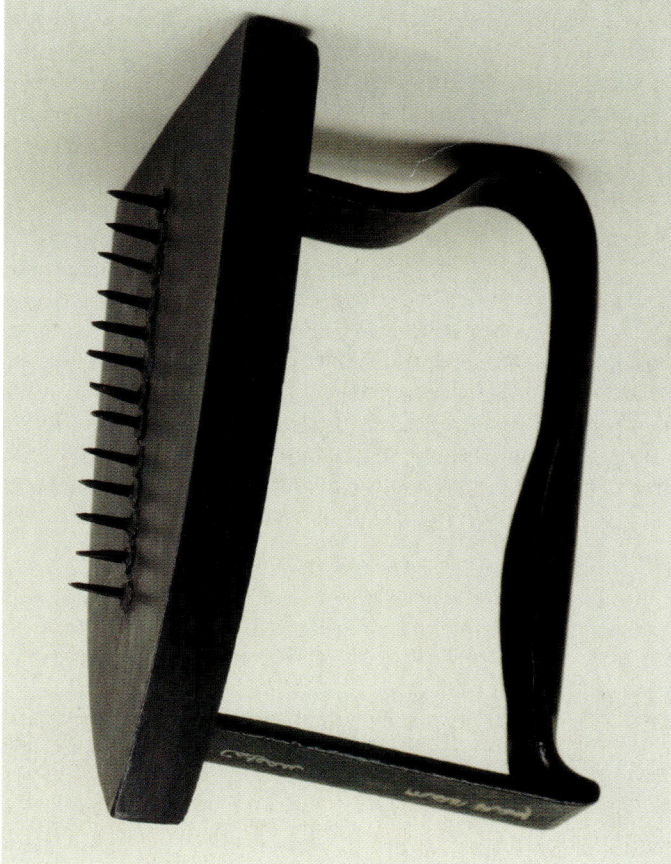

**33-32** Man Ray, *Cadeau* (*Gift*), ca. 1958 (replica of 1921 original). Painted flatiron with row of 13 tacks with heads glued to the bottom, 6⅛" high, 3⅝" wide, 4½" deep, Museum of Modern Art, New York (James Thrall Soby Fund).

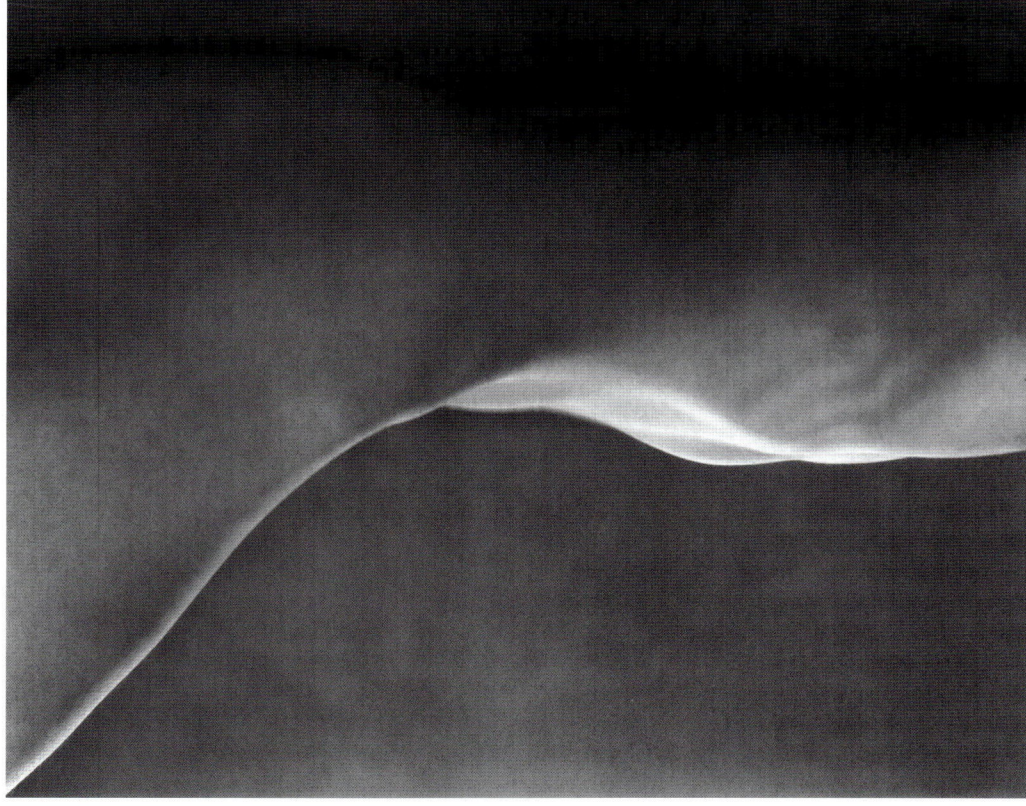

**33-31** Edward Weston, *Nude*, 1925. Platinum print, Collection, Center for Creative Photography, University of Arizona, Tucson.

lower right corner; and his regiment number, 4, appears in the center of the painting. Also incorporated is the letter *E* for von Freyberg's regiment, the Bavarian Eisenbahn. The influence of Synthetic Cubism is evident in the flattened, planar presentation of the elements, which almost appear as abstract patterns. The somber black background against which the artist placed the colorful stripes, patches, and shapes casts an elegiac pall over the painting. Despite Hartley's interest in German military imagery, he did not remain in Berlin. He continued to travel extensively and spent much of the remainder of his life in the United States.

**SYNCOPATED CUBISM** STUART DAVIS (1894–1964) created what he believed was a modern American art style by combining the flat shapes of Synthetic Cubism with his sense of jazz tempos and his perception of the energy of fast-paced American culture. *Lucky Strike* (FIG. **33-34**) is one of several tobacco still lifes Davis began in 1921. A heavy smoker, Davis was fascinated by tobacco products and their packaging. He insisted that the late-19th-century introduction of packaging was evidence of high civilization and therefore, he concluded, of the progressiveness of American culture. Davis depicted the Lucky Strike package in fragmented form, reminiscent of Synthetic Cubist collages. However, although the work does incorporate flat printed elements, these are illusionistically painted, rather than glued onto the canvas surface. The discontinuities and the interlocking planes imbue *Lucky Strike* with a dynamism and rhythm not unlike American jazz or the pace of life in a lively American metropolis. This work is both resolutely American and modern.

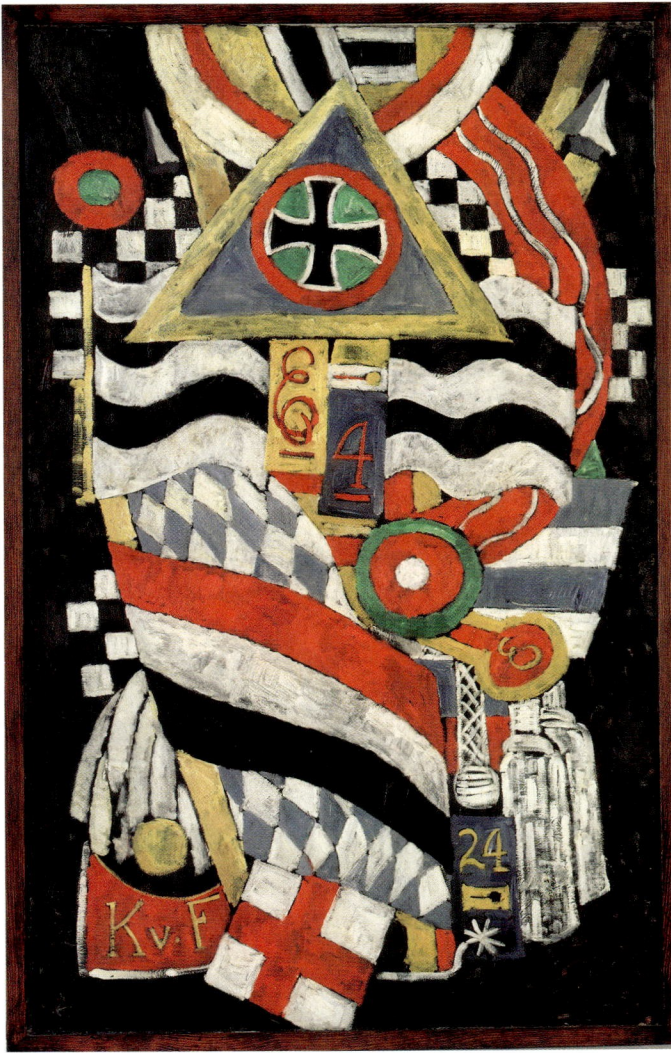

**33-33** MARSDEN HARTLEY, *Portrait of a German Officer*, 1914. Oil on canvas, 5′ 8¼″ × 3′ 5⅜″. Metropolitan Museum of Art, New York (Alfred Stieglitz Collection).

**AN ELEGY TO A DEAD OFFICER** Other American artists developed personal styles that intersected with movements such as Cubism. MARSDEN HARTLEY (1877–1943) was introduced to European modernism at Stieglitz's 291 gallery. He traveled to Europe in 1912, visiting Paris, where he became acquainted with the work of the Cubists, and Munich, where he gravitated to the Blaue Reiter circle. Hartley was particularly taken with Kandinsky's work and developed a style that he called "Cosmic Cubism." He took these influences with him when he landed in Berlin in 1913. With the heightened militarism in Germany and the eventual outbreak of World War I, Hartley immersed himself in military imagery. Among his most famous paintings of this period is *Portrait of a German Officer* (FIG. **33-33**). It depicts an array of military-related images: German imperial flags, regimental insignia, badges, and emblems such as the Iron Cross. Although one could read this image in the general context of wartime militarism, elements in the painting did have personal significance for Hartley; in particular, it includes references to his friend, Lieutenant Karl von Freyberg, with whom he had maintained an intimate relationship and who was killed in battle a few months before Hartley painted this work. Von Freyberg's initials appear in the lower left corner; his age when he died, 24, appears in the

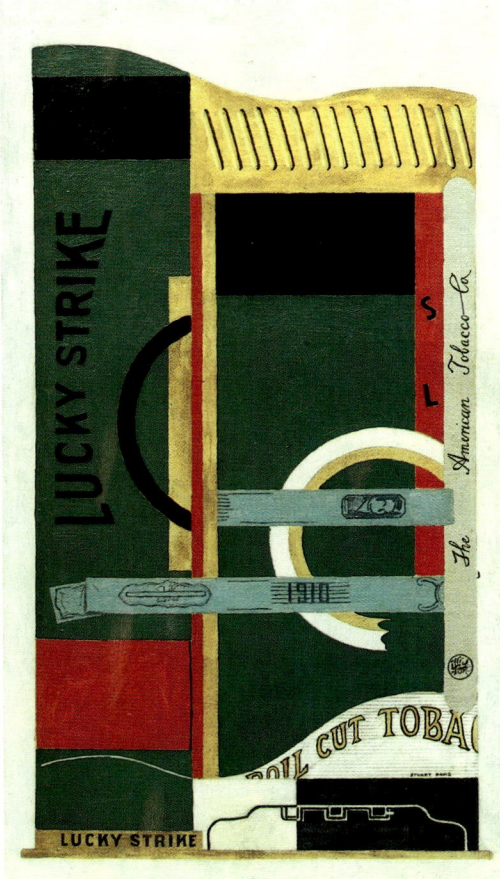

**33-34** STUART DAVIS, *Lucky Strike*, 1921. Oil on canvas, 2′ 9¼″ × 1′ 6″. Museum of Modern Art, New York (gift of the American Tobacco Company, Inc.). Copyright © Estate of Stuart Davis/Licensed by VAGA, New York, New York.

**A HARLEM RENAISSANCE ARTIST** Also deriving his personal style from Synthetic Cubism was African American artist AARON DOUGLAS (1898–1979), who used the style to represent symbolically the historical and cultural memories of African Americans. Born in Kansas, Douglas studied in Nebraska and Paris before settling in New York City, where he became part of the flowering of art and literature in the 1920s known as the *Harlem Renaissance.* Spearheaded by writers and editors Alain Locke and Charles Johnson, the Harlem Renaissance was a manifestation of the desire of African Americans to promote their cultural accomplishments. They also aimed to cultivate pride among fellow African Americans and racial tolerance across the United States. Expansive and diverse, the cultural products associated with the Harlem Renaissance included the writing of authors such as Langston Hughes, Countee Cullen, and Zora Neale Hurston; the jazz and blues of Duke Ellington, Bessie Smith, Eubie Blake, Fats Waller, and Louis Armstrong; the photographs of James VanDerZee and Prentice H. Polk; and the paintings and sculptures of Meta Warrick Fuller and Augusta Savage. Aaron Douglas arrived in New York City in 1924 and became one of the most sought-after graphic artists in the African American community. Encouraged to create art that would express the cultural history of his race, Douglas incorporated motifs from African sculpture into compositions painted in a version of Synthetic Cubism that stressed transparent angular planes. *Noah's Ark* (FIG. **33-35**) was one of seven paintings based on a book of poems by James Weldon Johnson called *God's Trombones: Seven Negro Sermons in Verse.* Douglas used flat planes to evoke a sense of mystical space and

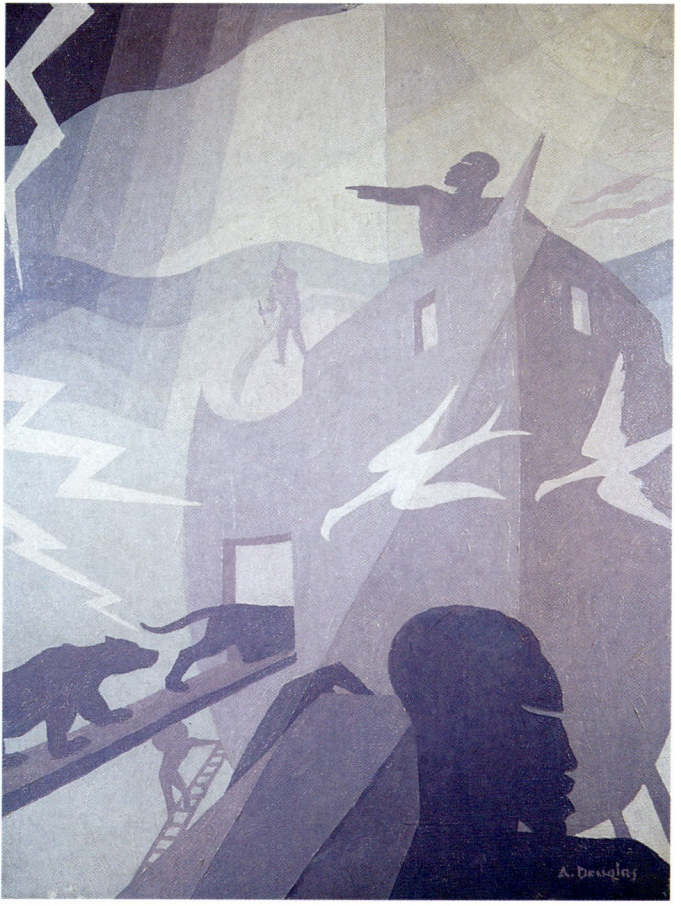

**33-35** AARON DOUGLAS, *Noah's Ark,* ca. 1927. Oil on Masonite, $4' \times 3'$. Fisk University Galleries, Nashville, Tennessee.

miraculous happenings. In *Noah's Ark,* lightning strikes and rays of light crisscross the pairs of animals entering the ark, while men load supplies in preparation for departure. The artist suggested deep space by differentiating the size of the large human head and shoulders of the worker at the bottom and the small person at work on the far deck of the ship. Yet the composition's unmodulated color shapes create a pattern on the Masonite surface that cancels any illusion of three-dimensional depth. Here, Douglas used Cubism's formal language to express a powerful religious vision.

## Precisionism

It is obvious from viewing American art in the period immediately after the Armory Show that American artists were intrigued by the latest European avant-garde art, from Cubism to Dada. However, these artists did not just passively absorb the ideas transported across the Atlantic. For many American artists, the challenge was to understand the ideas this modernist European art presented and then filter them through an American sensibility. Ultimately, many American artists set as their goal the development of a uniquely American art.

**ART OF THE MACHINE AGE** One group of such artists became known as *Precisionists.* This was not an organized movement, and these artists rarely exhibited together (although once the similarities in their work were revealed, they were grouped together in shows), but they did share certain thematic and stylistic traits in their art. Precisionism developed in the 1920s out of a fascination with the machine's precision and importance in modern life. Although many European artists (for example, the Futurists) had demonstrated interest in burgeoning technology, Americans generally seemed more enamored by the prospects of a mechanized society than did Europeans. Even French artist Francis Picabia (associated with both Cubism and Dada) noted: "Since machinery is the soul of the modern world, and since the genius of machinery attains its highest expression in America, why is it not reasonable to believe that in America the art of the future will flower most brilliantly?"[30] The efforts of others in the art world also supported this observation. Alfred Stieglitz's 291 gallery was instrumental in exhibiting mechanistically oriented works, thereby championing the "age of the machine."

Precisionism, however, expanded beyond the exploration of machine imagery. Many artists associated with this group gravitated toward Synthetic Cubism's flat, sharply delineated planes as an appropriate visual idiom for their imagery, adding to the clarity and precision of their work. Eventually, Precisionism came to be characterized by a merging of a familiar native style in American architecture and artifacts with a modernist vocabulary derived largely from Synthetic Cubism.

**AMERICAN PYRAMIDS?** CHARLES DEMUTH (1883–1935) spent the years 1912–1914 in Paris and thus had firsthand exposure to Cubism and other avant-garde directions in art. He incorporated the spatial discontinuities characteristic of Cubism into his work, focusing much of it on industrial sites near his native Lancaster, Pennsylvania. *My Egypt* (FIG. **33-36**) is a prime example of Precisionist painting. Demuth depicted the John W. Eshelman and Sons grain elevators, which he reduced to simple geometric forms. The grain elevators remain insistently recognizable and solid. However, the painting is disrupted by the "beams" of transparent planes and the diagonal force lines that threaten to

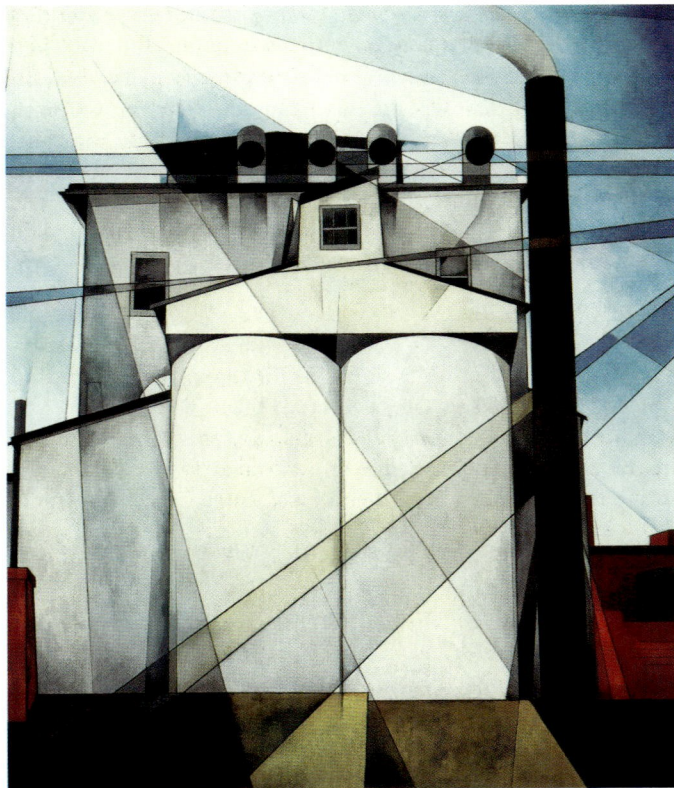

**33-36** CHARLES DEMUTH, *My Egypt,* 1927. Oil on composition board, 2′ 11¾″ × 2′ 6″. Collection of Whitney Museum of American Art, New York (purchase with funds from Gertrude Vanderbilt Whitney).

destabilize the image and that correspond to Cubist fragmentation of space. Not only does this adaptation of Cubist vocabulary place Demuth in the more progressive ranks of American artists of the time, but it also reveals his sensitivity to the effects of expanding technology.

The degree to which Demuth intended to extol the American industrial scene is unclear. The title, *My Egypt,* is sufficiently ambiguous in tone to accommodate differing readings. On the one hand, Demuth could have been suggesting a favorable comparison between the Egyptian pyramids and American grain elevators as cultural icons. On the other hand, the title could be read cynically, as a negative comment on the limitations of American culture.

**THE RHYTHM OF CITY LIFE** The work of GEORGIA O'KEEFFE (1887–1986), like that of many artists, changed stylistically throughout her career. During the 1920s, O'Keeffe was affiliated with Precisionism. She had moved from the tiny town of Canyon, Texas, to New York City in 1918 (she had visited the city on occasion previously), and what she found there both overwhelmed and excited her. "You have to live in today," she told a friend. "Today the city is something bigger, more complex than ever before in history. And nothing can be gained from running away. I couldn't even if I could."[31] While in New York, O'Keeffe met Alfred Stieglitz, who had seen and exhibited some of her earlier work, and she was drawn into the circle of painters and photographers surrounding Stieglitz and his gallery. Stieglitz became one of O'Keeffe's staunchest supporters and, eventually, her husband. The interest of Stieglitz and his circle in capturing the sensibility of the machine age intersected with O'Keeffe's fascination with the fast pace of city life, and she produced paintings during this period, such as *New York, Night* (FIG. **33-37**), that depict the soaring

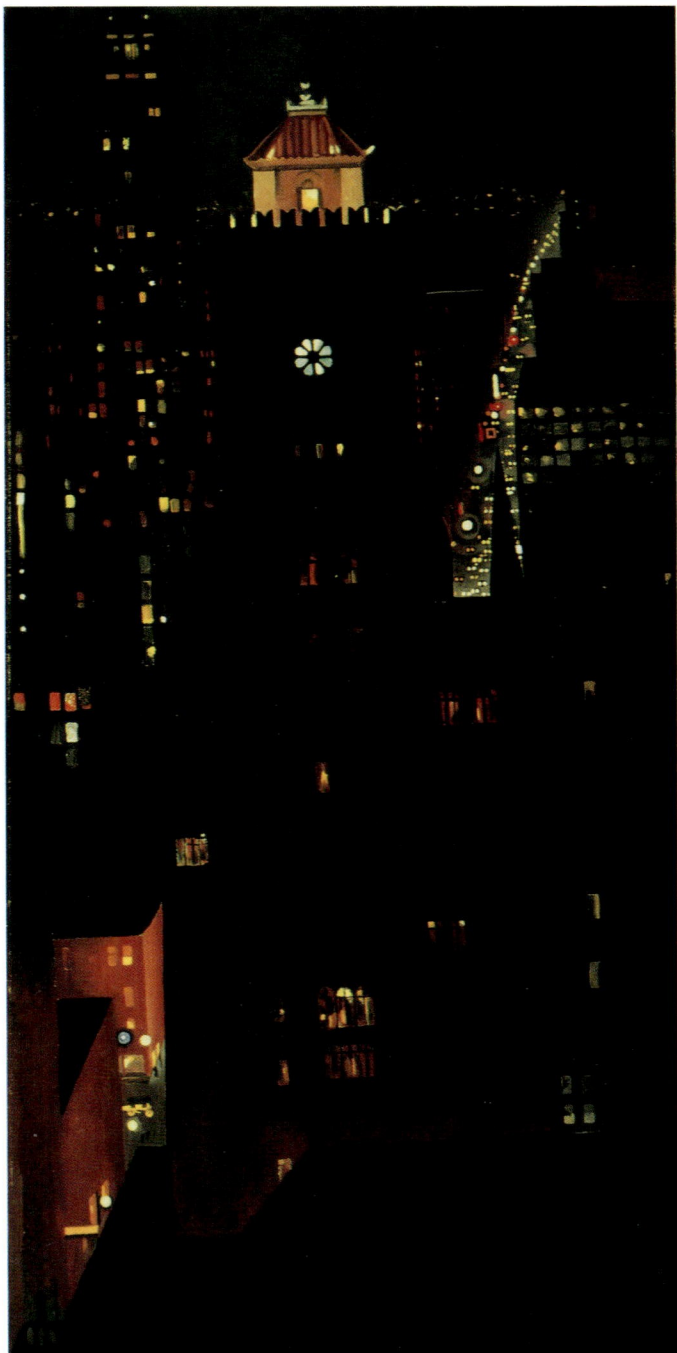

**33-37** GEORGIA O'KEEFFE, *New York, Night,* 1929. Oil on canvas, 3′ 4⅛″ × 1′ 7⅛″. The Georgia O'Keeffe Foundation.

skyscrapers dominating the city. Like other Precisionists, O'Keeffe reduced her images to flat planes, here punctuated by small rectangular windows that add rhythm and energy to the image, countering the monolithic darkness of the looming buildings.

**THE PURITY OF FLORAL FORM** Despite O'Keeffe's affiliation with the Precisionist movement, she is probably best known for her paintings of cow skulls and of flowers. One such painting, *Jack in the Pulpit No. 4* (see FIG. Intro-4), reveals the artist's interest in stripping her subjects to their purest forms and colors to heighten their expressive power. In this work, O'Keeffe reduced the incredible details of her subject to a symphony of basic colors, shapes, textures, and vital rhythms. Exhibiting the natural flow of curved planes and contour, O'Keeffe simplified the form almost to the point of complete abstraction. The fluid planes unfold like undulant petals from a subtly placed axis—the white jetlike streak—in a vision of the slow, controlled motion of growing life. O'Keeffe's painting, in its graceful, quiet poetry, reveals the organic reality (Brancusi would say "essence") of the object by strengthening its characteristic features, in striking contrast with either Kandinsky's explosions (FIG. 33-6) or Mondrian's rectilinear absolutes (FIG. 33-55). O'Keeffe enjoyed a long career; in 1946, she moved permanently to New Mexico and continued to paint for decades, until her death in 1986.

# EUROPEAN ART IN THE WAKE OF WORLD WAR I

That American artists could focus on these modernist artistic endeavors with such commitment was due to the fact that World War I was fought entirely on European soil. Thus, its effects were not as devastating as they were both on Europe's geopolitical terrain and on individual and national psyches. After the war concluded, many European artists were drawn to the expressionist idiom (as developed by the Fauves and the German Expressionists) both to express and to deal with the trauma of world war.

## *Neue Sachlichkeit*

As shown earlier, the war severely impacted many artists, notably those associated with German Expressionism and Dada. *Neue Sachlichkeit (New Objectivity)* grew directly out of the war experiences of a group of German artists. All of the artists associated

with Neue Sachlichkeit served, at some point, in the German army and thus had firsthand involvement with the military. Their military experiences deeply influenced their world views and informed their art. This was not an organized movement, and museum director G. F. Hartlaub coined its label in 1923. That label does, however, capture their aim—to present a clear-eyed, direct, and honest image of the war and its effects. As George Grosz, one of the Neue Sachlichkeit artists, explained: "I am trying to give an absolutely realistic picture of the world."[32]

**MILITARY HORRORS** GEORGE GROSZ (1893–1958) was, for a time, associated with the Dada group in Berlin, but his work, with its harsh and bitter tone, seems more appropriately linked with Neue Sachlichkeit. Grosz observed the onset of World War I with horrified fascination, but that feeling soon turned to anger and frustration. He reported:

> Of course, there was a kind of mass enthusiasm at the start. But this intoxication soon evaporated, leaving a huge vacuum. . . . And then after a few years when everything bogged down, when we were defeated, when everything went to pieces, all that remained, at least for me and most of my friends, were disgust and horror.[33]

Grosz produced numerous paintings and drawings, such as *Fit for Active Service* (FIG. 33-38), that were caustic indictments of the military. In these works, he often depicted military officers as heartless or incompetent. This particular drawing may relate to Grosz's personal experience. On the verge of a nervous breakdown in 1917, he was sent to a sanatorium where doctors examined him and, much to his horror, declared him "fit for service." In this biting and sarcastic drawing, an army doctor proclaims the skeleton before him "fit for service." None of the other military officers or doctors attending seem to dispute this evaluation. The

**33-38** GEORGE GROSZ, *Fit for Active Service,* 1916–1917. Pen and brush and ink on paper, 1′ 8″ × 1′ 2 3/8″. Museum of Modern Art, New York (A. Conger Goodyear Fund). Copyright © Estate of George Grosz/Licensed by VAGA, New York, New York.

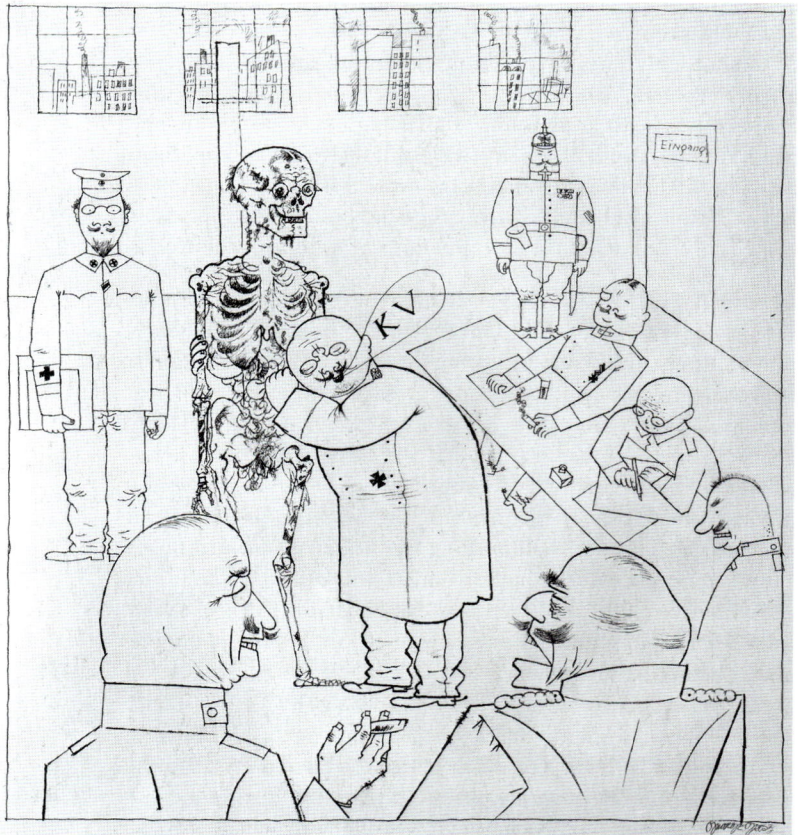

spectacles perched on the skeleton's face, very similar to the gold-rimmed glasses Grosz wore, further suggest he based this scene on his experiences. Grosz's searing wit is all the more evident upon comparing *Fit for Active Service* with Marsden Hartley's *Portrait of a German Officer* (FIG. 33-33). Although Hartley's painting deals with the death of a friend in battle, the incorporation of colorful German military insignia and emblems imbues the painting with a more heroic, celebratory tone. In contrast, the simplicity of Grosz's line drawing contributes to the directness and immediacy of the work, which scathingly portrays the German army.

**DEPICTING WORLD VIOLENCE** MAX BECKMANN (1884–1950), like Grosz, enlisted in the German army and initially rationalized the war. He believed the chaos would lead to a better society, but over time the mass destruction increasingly disillusioned him. Soon his work began to emphasize the horrors of war and of a society he saw descending into madness. His disturbing view of society is evident in *Night* (FIG. **33-39**). *Night* depicts a cramped room three intruders have forcefully invaded. A bound woman,

apparently raped, is splayed across the foreground of the painting. Her husband appears on the left; one of the intruders hangs him, while another one twists his left arm out of its socket. An unidentified woman cowers in the background. On the far right, the third intruder prepares to flee with the child.

Although this image does not depict a war scene, the wrenching brutality and violence pervading the home is a searing and horrifying comment on society's condition. Beckmann also injected a personal reference by using himself, his wife, and his son as the models for the three family members. The stilted angularity of the figures and the roughness of the paint surface contribute to the image's savageness. In addition, the artist's treatment of forms and space reflects the world's violence. Objects seem dislocated and contorted, and the space appears buckled and illogical. For example, the woman's hands are bound to the window that opens from the room's back wall, but her body appears to hang vertically, rather than lying across the plane of the intervening table. Despite the fact that images such as *Night* do not directly depict war's carnage or violence, Beckmann's art is undeniably powerful and honest.

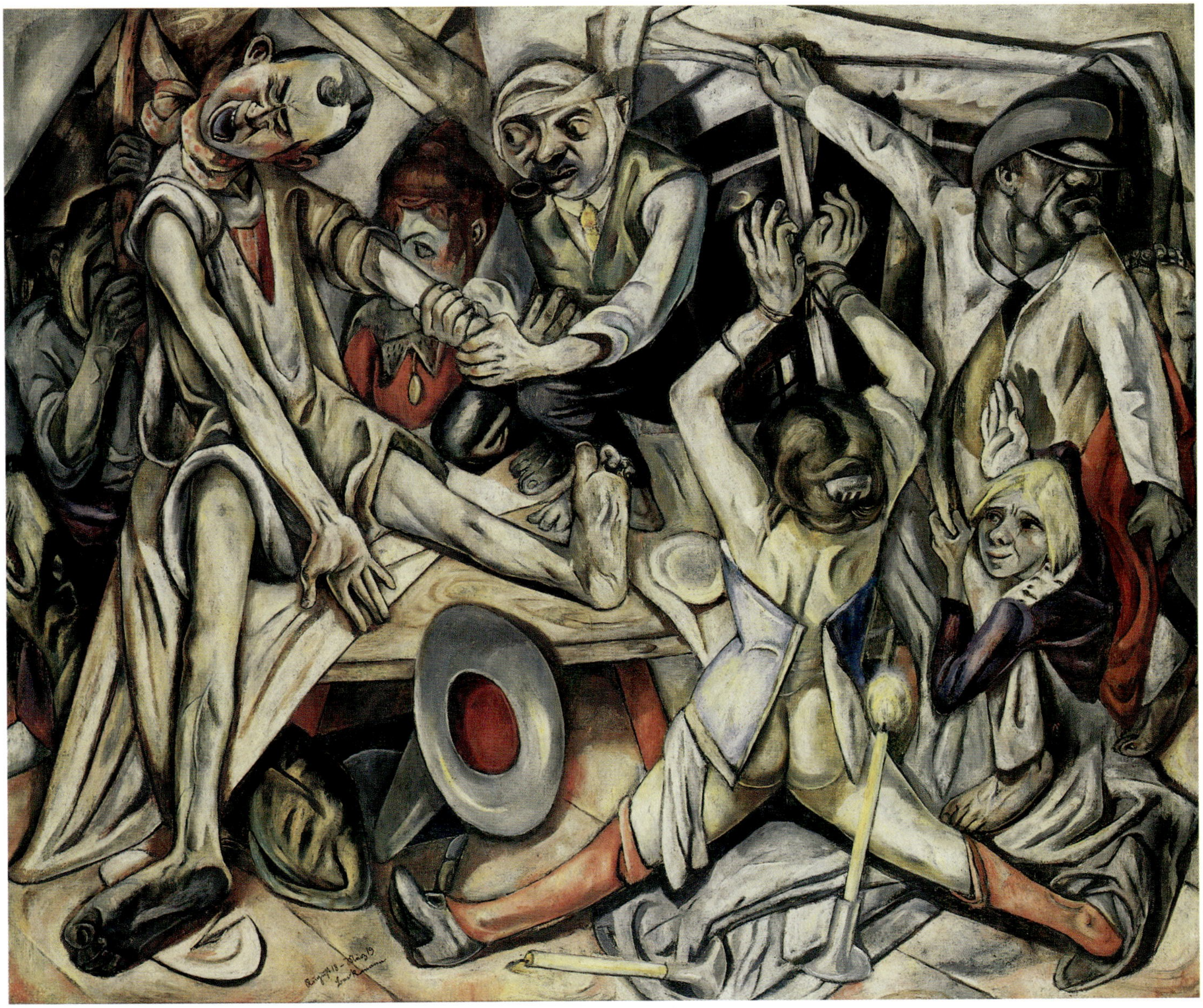

**33-39** MAX BECKMANN, *Night*, 1918–1919. Oil on canvas, 4′ 4⅜″ × 5′ ¼″. Kunstsammlung Nordrhein-Westfalen, Düsseldorf.

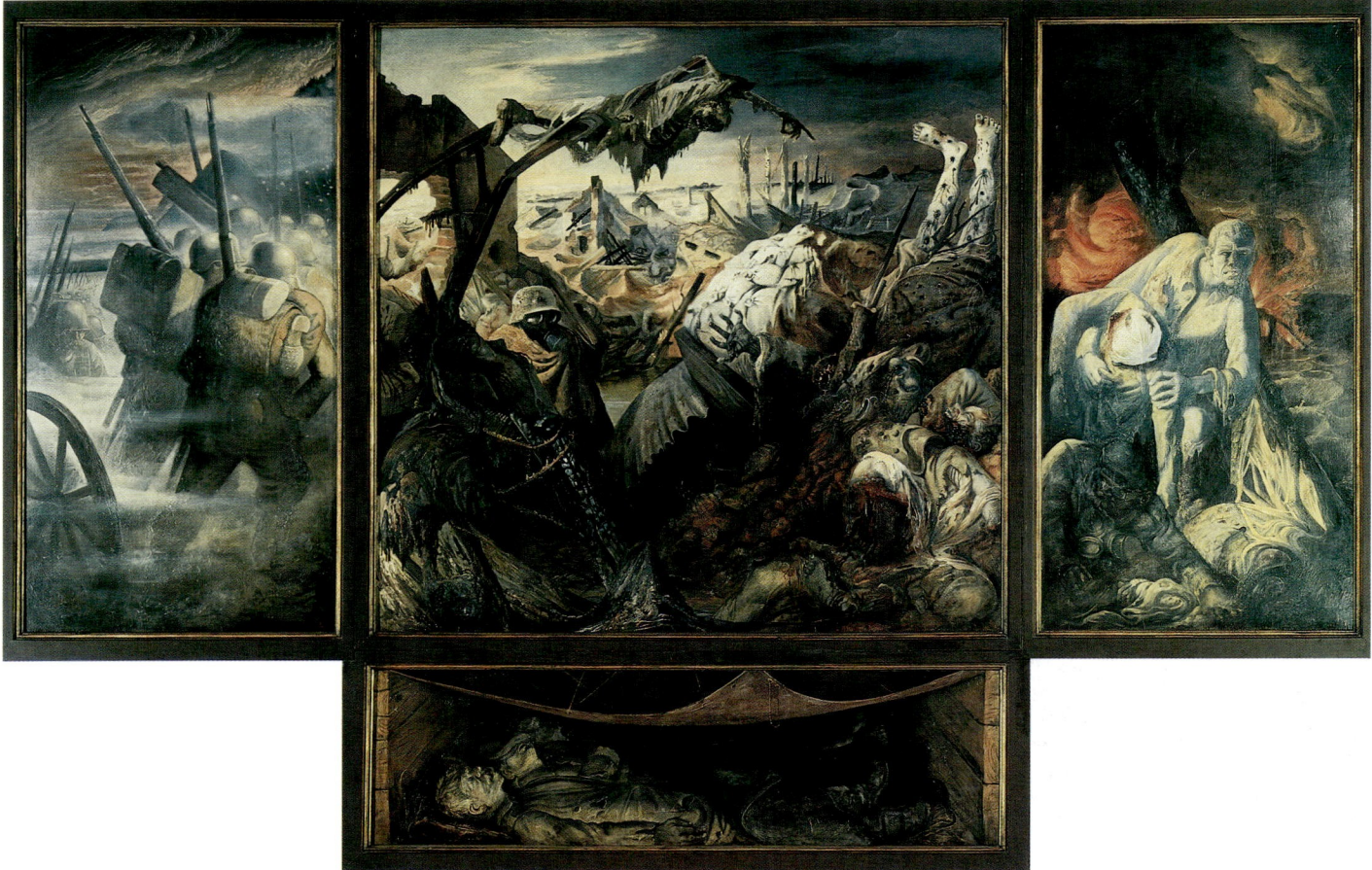

**33-40** OTTO DIX, *Der Krieg (The War)*, 1929–1932. Oil and tempera on wood, 6′ 8⅓″ × 13′ 4¾″. Staatliche Kunstsammlungen, Gemäldegalerie Neue Meister, Dresden.

**THE DEVASTATION OF WAR** OTTO DIX (1891–1959) was the third artist who, along with Beckmann and Grosz, was most closely associated with Neue Sachlichkeit. Although Beckmann, for the most part, avoided specific war imagery, Dix embraced it. Having served as both a machine gunner and an aerial observer, he was well acquainted with war's effects. Like Grosz, he initially tried to find redeeming value in the apocalyptic event. Dix explained: "The war was a horrible thing, but there was something tremendous about it, too. . . . You have to have seen human beings in this unleashed state to know what human nature is. . . . I need to experience all the depths of life for myself, that's why I go out, and that's why I volunteered."[34] This idea of experiencing the "depths of life" stemmed from Dix's interest in the philosophy of Friedrich Nietzsche. In particular, Dix avidly read Nietzsche's *The Joyous Science,* deriving from it a belief in life's cyclical nature—procreation and death, building up and tearing down, and growth and decay.

As the war progressed, however, Dix's faith in the potential improvement of society dissipated, and he began to produce unflinchingly direct and provocative artworks. His *Der Krieg (The War;* FIG. **33-40**) vividly captures the panoramic devastation that war inflicts, both on the terrain and on humans. In the left panel, armed and uniformed soldiers march off into the distance. Dix graphically displayed the horrific results in the center and right panels, where mangled bodies, many riddled with bullet holes, are scattered throughout the eerily lit apocalyptic landscape. As if to emphasize the intensely personal nature of this scene, the artist painted himself into the right panel as the ghostly but determined soldier who drags a comrade to safety. In the bottom panel, in a coffinlike bunker, lie soldiers asleep—or perhaps dead. Dix significantly chose to present this sequence of images in a triptych format, and the work recalls triptychs such as Matthias Grünewald's *Isenheim Altarpiece* (see FIGS. 23-2 and 23-3). Christ's death and suffering there serve as reference points for Dix's dead soldiers. However, the hope of salvation extended to viewers of the *Isenheim Altarpiece* through Christ's eventual Resurrection is absent from *Der Krieg*. Like his fellow Neue Sachlichkeit artists, Dix felt compelled to lay bare the realities of his time, which the war's violence dominated. Even years later, Dix still maintained:

> You have to see things the way they are. You have to be able to say yes to the human manifestations that exist and will always exist. That doesn't mean saying yes to war, but to a fate that approaches you under certain conditions and in which you have to prove yourself. Abnormal situations bring out all the depravity, the bestiality of human beings. . . . I portrayed states, states that the war brought about, and the results of war, as states.[35]

## Other Postwar Art in Germany

**POIGNANT PRINTS** The emotional range of German Expressionism extends from passionate protest and satirical bitterness to the poignantly expressed pity for the poor in the prints of the independent artist KÄTHE KOLLWITZ (1867–1945). The graphic art of Gauguin and Munch stimulated a revival of the print

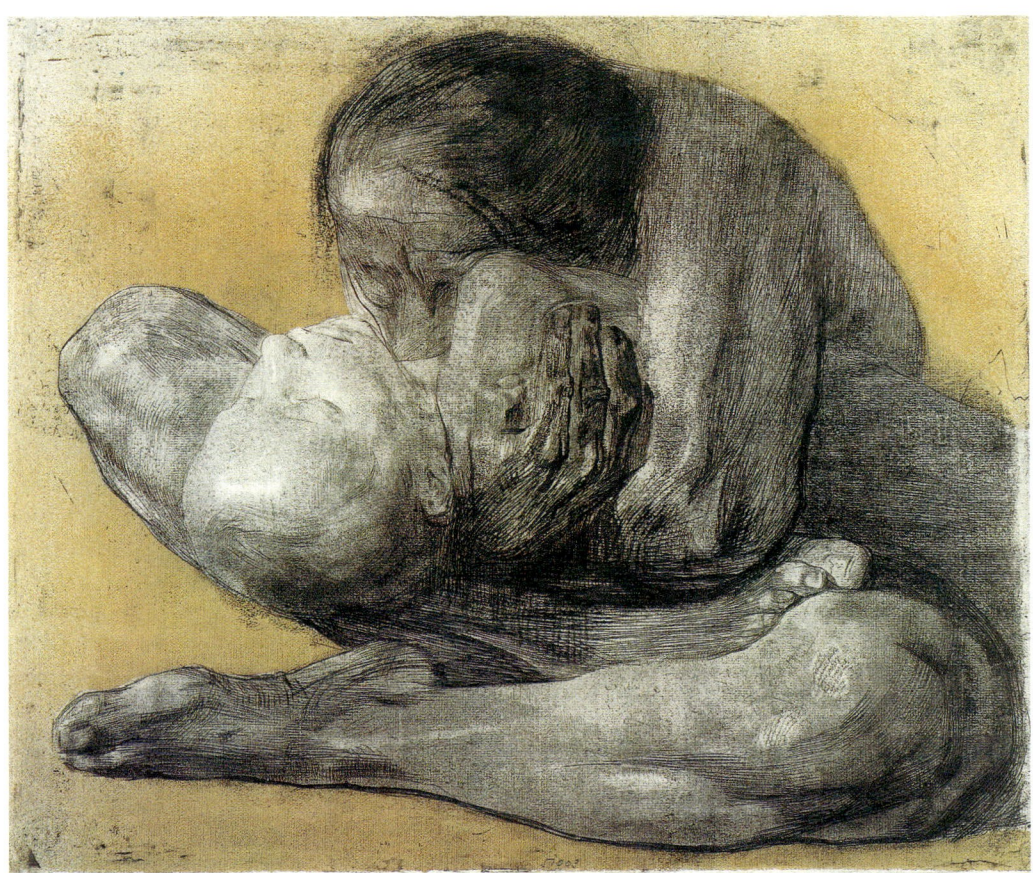

medium in Germany, especially the woodcut, and these proved inspiring models. Kollwitz worked in a variety of printmaking techniques, including woodcut, lithography, and etching, and explored a range of issues from the overtly political to the deeply personal. One image that she explored in depth, producing a number of print variations, was that of a mother with her dead child. Although she initially derived the theme from Christian tradition (in the form of the familiar grieving Mary with the dead Christ), she transformed it into a universal statement of maternal loss and grief. *Woman with Dead Child* (FIG. **33-41**), an etching and lithograph, was one pre-war iteration of this theme. The reverence and grace that pervaded the conventional Christian depictions of the Madonna holding the dead Christ have been replaced with an animalistic passion, as the mother ferociously grips the body of her dead child. The primal nature of the image is in keeping with the aims of the expressionists (although Kollwitz was not formally affiliated with Neue Sachlichkeit or any of the organized German Expressionist groups), and the scratchy lines produced by the etching needle serve as evidence of Kollwitz's very personal touch. The impact of this image is undeniably powerful. That Kollwitz used her son Peter as the model for the dead child no doubt made the image all the more personal to her. The image stands as a poignant premonition; Peter was killed at the age of 21 in World War I.

**AN ELONGATED, EXPRESSIVE SCULPTURE** As it did Kollwitz, the war deeply affected German artist WILHELM LEHMBRUCK (1881–1919). His figurative sculpture exudes a quiet mood but still possesses a compelling emotional sensibility. Lehmbruck studied sculpture, painting, and the graphic arts in Düsseldorf before moving to Paris in 1910, where he developed the style of his *Seated Youth* (FIG. **33-42**). His sculpture

combines the expressive qualities he much admired in the work of fellow sculptors, especially the psychological energies of Rodin (see FIGS. 29-49 and 29-50). In Lehmbruck's *Seated Youth*, the poignant elongation of human proportions, the slumped shoulders, and the hands that hang uselessly all impart an undertone of anguish to the rather classical figure. Lehmbruck's figure

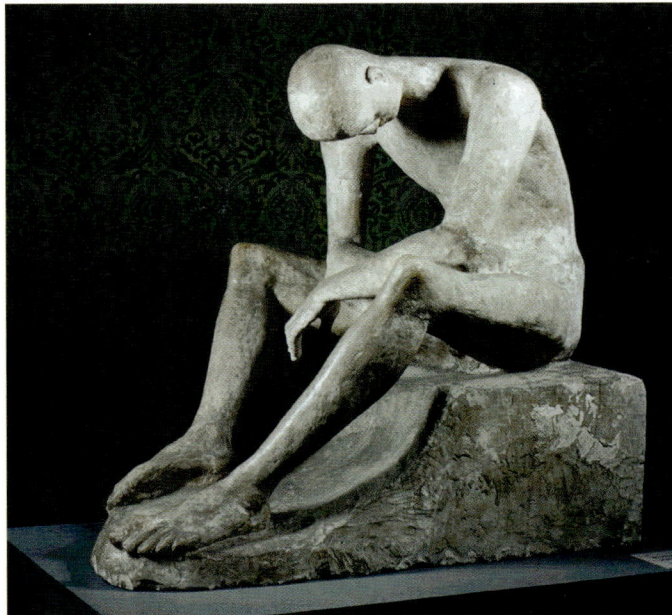

**33-42** WILHELM LEHMBRUCK, *Seated Youth,* 1917. Composite tinted plaster, 3′ $4\frac{5}{8}$″ × 2′ 6″ × 3′ 9″. National Gallery of Art, Washington (Andrew W. Mellon Fund).

communicates by pose and gesture alone. Although its extreme proportions may recall Mannerist attenuation (such as Parmigianino's *Madonna with the Long Neck;* see FIG. 22-43), its distortions announce a new freedom in interpreting the human figure. For Lehmbruck, as for Rodin, the human figure could express every human condition and emotion. The quiet, contemplative nature of this sculpture serves both as a personal expression of Lehmbruck's increasing depression and as a powerful characterization of the general sensibility in the wake of World War I. Appropriately, *Seated Youth* was originally titled *The Friend,* in reference to the artist's many friends who lost their lives in the war. After Lehmbruck's tragic suicide in 1919, officials placed this sculpture as a memorial in the soldiers' cemetery in Lehmbruck's native city of Duisburg.

**A HAUNTING MEMORIAL OF WAR** A work more spiritual in its expression is the *War Monument* (FIG. 33-43), which the German sculptor ERNST BARLACH (1870–1938) created for the cathedral in his hometown of Güstrow in 1927. Working often in wood, Barlach sculpted single figures usually dressed in flowing robes and portrayed in strong, simple poses that embody deep human emotions and experiences such as grief, vigilance, or self-comfort. Barlach's works combine sharp, smoothly planed forms with intense expression. The cast-bronze hovering figure of his *War Monument* is one of the poignant memorials of World War I. Unlike traditional war memorials depicting heroic military figures, often engaged in battle, the hauntingly symbolic figure that Barlach

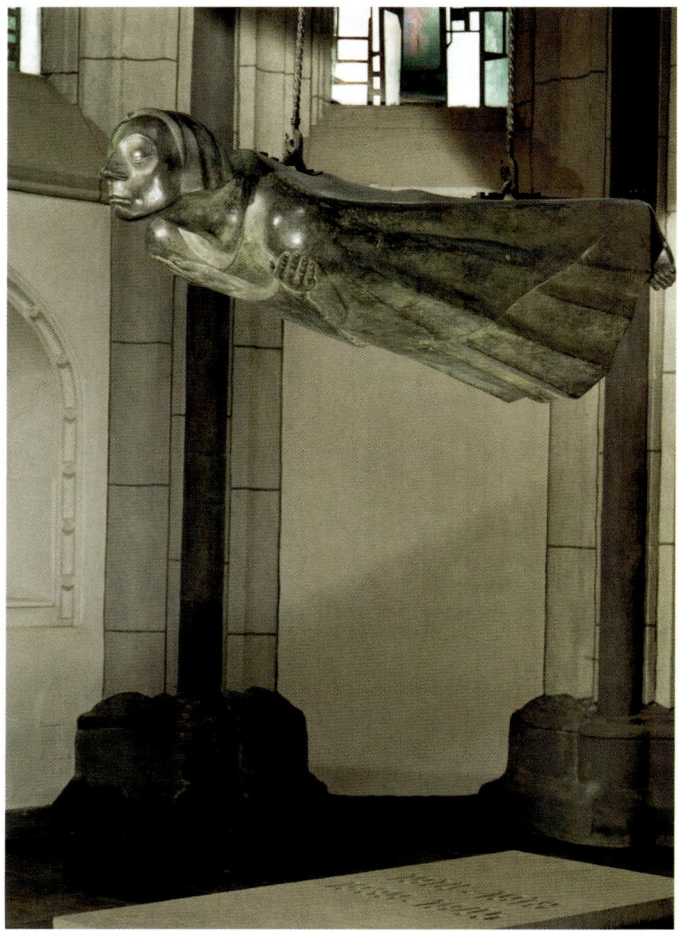

**33-43** ERNST BARLACH, *War Monument,* from Güstrow Cathedral, Güstrow, Germany, 1927. Bronze. Schildergasse Antoniterkirche, Cologne.

created speaks to the experience of all caught in the conflict of war. The floating human form, suspended above a tomb inscribed with the dates 1914–1918 and the later added 1939–1945, suggests a dying soul at the moment when it is about to awaken to everlasting life—the theme of death and transfiguration. The rigid economy of surfaces concentrates attention on the simple but expressive head. So powerful was this sculpture that the Nazis had it removed from the cathedral in 1937 and melted down for ammunition. Luckily, a friend hid another version by Barlach; a Protestant parish in Cologne purchased this surviving cast, from which a new cast was made for the Güstrow cathedral.

## Surrealism and Fantasy Art

The exuberantly aggressive momentum of the Dada movement that emerged during World War I was only sustained for a short time. By 1924, with the publication in France of the *First Surrealist Manifesto,* most of the artists associated with Dada joined the Surrealist movement and its determined exploration of ways to express in art the world of dreams and the unconscious. Given this transition, it is not surprising that the Surrealists incorporated many of the Dadaists' improvisational techniques. They believed these methods important for engaging the elements of fantasy and activating the unconscious forces that lie deep within every human being. The Surrealists were determined to explore the inner world of the psyche, the realm of fantasy and the unconscious. Inspired in part by the ideas of the psychoanalysts Sigmund Freud and Carl Jung, the Surrealists were especially interested in the nature of dreams. They viewed dreams as occurring at the level connecting all human consciousness and as constituting the arena in which people could move beyond their environment's constricting forces to reengage with the deeper selves society had long suppressed. In 1924, one of the leading Surrealist thinkers, the young Parisian writer André Breton, provided a definition of *Surrealism:*

> Pure psychic automatism, by which one intends to express verbally, in writing, or by any other method, the real functioning of the mind. Dictation by thought, in the absence of any control exercised by reason, and beyond any esthetic or moral preoccupation. . . . Surrealism is based on the belief in the superior reality of certain forms of association heretofore neglected, in the omnipotence of dreams, in the undirected play of thought. . . . I believe in the future resolution of the states of dream and reality, in appearance so contradictory, in a sort of absolute reality, or surreality.[36]

Thus, the Surrealists' dominant motivation was to bring the aspects of outer and inner "reality" together into a single position, in much the same way life's seemingly unrelated fragments combine in the vivid world of dreams. The projection in visible form of this new conception required new techniques of pictorial construction. The Surrealists adapted some Dada devices and invented new methods such as automatic writing (spontaneous writing using free association), not so much to reveal a world without meaning as to provoke reactions closely related to subconscious experience.

Surrealism developed along two lines. Some artists gravitated toward an interest in biomorphic (life forms) Surrealism. In biomorphic Surrealism, *automatism*—dictation of thought without control of the mind—predominated. Biomorphic Surrealists such as Joan Miró produced largely abstract compositions, although the imagery sometimes suggests organisms or natural forms. Naturalistic Surrealists, in contrast, presented recognizable scenes that seem to have metamorphosed into a dream or nightmare image. The artists Salvador Dalí and René Magritte are most closely associated with this variant of Surrealism.

**METAPHYSICAL PAINTING** The Italian painter GIORGIO DE CHIRICO (1888–1978) produced emphatically ambiguous works that position him as a precursor of Surrealism. De Chirico's paintings of cityscapes and shop windows were part of a movement called *Pittura Metafisica,* or Metaphysical Painting. Returning to Italy after study in Munich, de Chirico found hidden reality revealed through strange juxtapositions, such as those seen on late autumn afternoons in the city of Turin, when the long shadows of the setting sun transformed vast open squares and silent public monuments into "the most metaphysical of Italian towns." De Chirico translated this vision into paint in works such as *Melancholy and Mystery of a Street* (FIG. **33-44**), where the squares and palaces of Roman and Renaissance Italy evoke a disquieting sense of foreboding. The choice of the term *metaphysical* to describe de Chirico's paintings suggests that these images transcend their physical appearances. *Melancholy and Mystery of a Street,* for all of its clarity and simplicity, takes on a rather sinister air. Only a few inexplicable and incongruous elements punctuate the scene's solitude—a small girl with her hoop in the foreground, the empty van, and the ominous shadow of a man emerging from behind the building. The sense of strangeness de Chirico could conjure up with familiar objects and scenes recalls Nietzsche's "foreboding that underneath this reality in which we live and have our being, another and altogether different reality lies concealed."[37]

De Chirico's paintings were reproduced in periodicals almost as soon as he completed them, and his works quickly influenced artists outside Italy, including both the Dadaists and, later, the Surrealists. The incongruities in his work intrigued the Dadaists, whereas the eerie mood and visionary quality of paintings such as *Melancholy and Mystery of a Street* excited and inspired Surrealist artists who sought to portray the world of dreams.

**A SENSE OF THE PSYCHIC** Originally a Dada activist in Cologne, Germany, MAX ERNST (1891–1976) became one of the early adherents of the Surrealist circle that Breton anchored. As a child living in a small community near Cologne, Ernst had found his existence fantastic and filled with marvels. In autobiographical notes, written mostly in the third person, he said of his birth: "Max Ernst had his first contact with the world of sense on the 2nd April 1891 at 9:45 a.m., when he emerged from the egg which his mother had laid in an eagle's nest and which the bird had incubated for seven years."[38] Ernst's service in the German army during World War I swept away his early success as an expressionist; in his own words:

> Max Ernst died on 1st August 1914. He returned to life on 11th November 1918, a young man who wanted to become a magician and find the central myth of his age. From time to time he consulted the eagle which had guarded the egg of his prenatal existence. The bird's advice can be detected in his work.[39]

Before joining the Surrealists, Ernst explored every means to achieve the sense of the psychic in his art. Like other Dadaists, he set out to incorporate found objects and chance into his works.

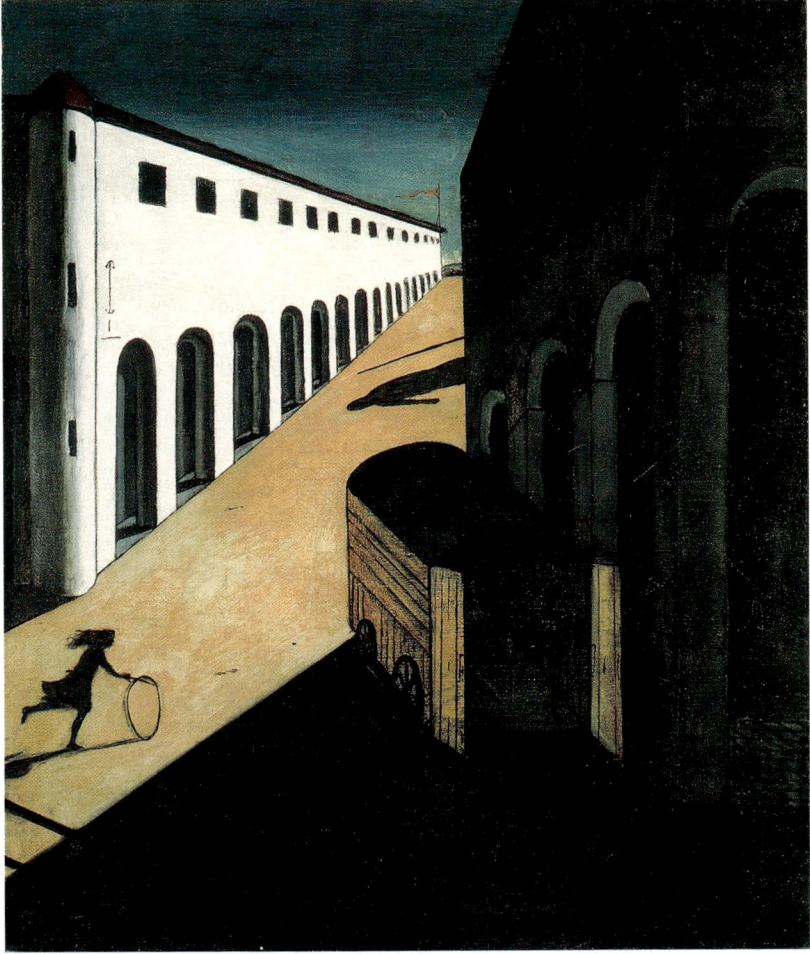

**33-44** GIORGIO DE CHIRICO, *Melancholy and Mystery of a Street,* 1914. Oil on canvas, 2′ 10¼″ × 2′ 4½″. Private collection.

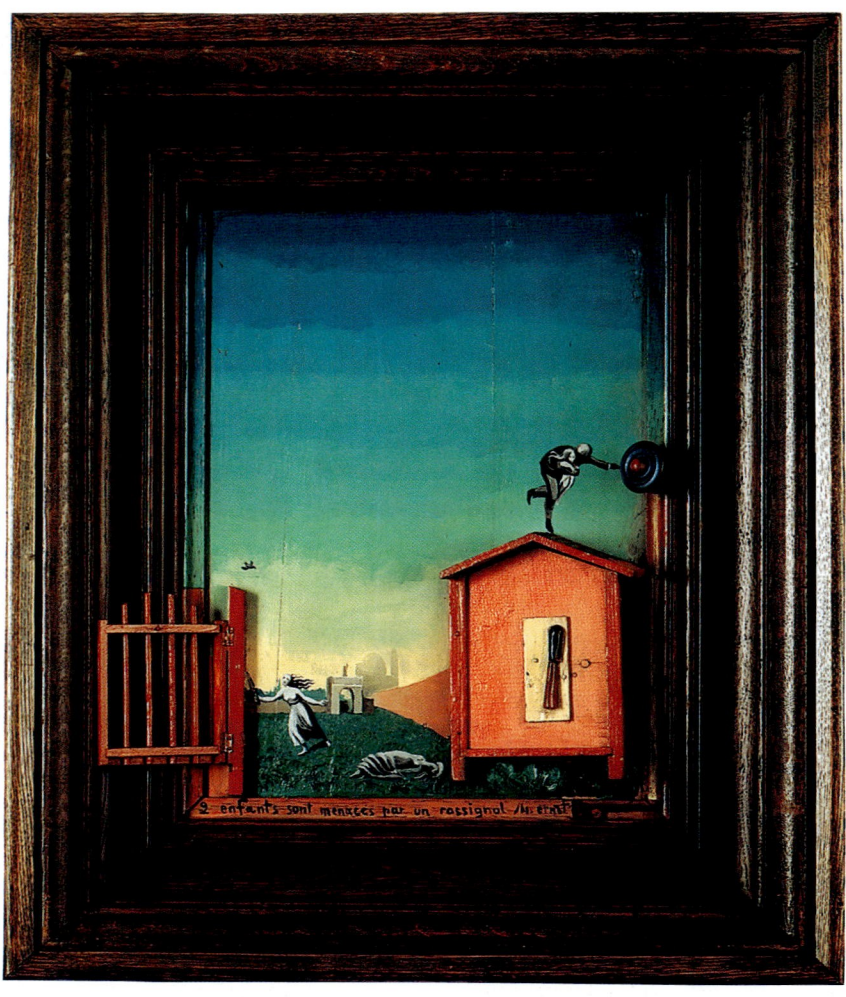

**33-45** MAX ERNST, *Two Children Are Threatened by a Nightingale,* 1924. Oil on wood with wood construction, 2′ 3½″ high, 1′ 10½″ wide, 4½″ deep. Museum of Modern Art, New York (purchase).

Using a process called *frottage,* he created some works by combining the patterns achieved by rubbing a crayon or another medium across a sheet of paper placed over a surface with a strong and evocative textural pattern. In other works, he joined fragments of images he had cut from old books, magazines, and prints to form one hallucinatory collage.

Ernst soon began making paintings that shared the mysterious dreamlike effect of his collages. In 1920, his works brought him into contact with Breton, who instantly recognized Ernst's affinity with the Surrealist group. In 1922, Ernst moved to Paris. His *Two Children Are Threatened by a Nightingale* (FIG. **33-45**) manifests many of the creative bases of Surrealism. Here, Ernst displayed a private dream that challenged the post-Renaissance idea that a painting should resemble a window looking into a "real" scene rendered illusionistically three-dimensional through mathematical perspective. In *Two Children Are Threatened,* the artist painted the landscape, the distant city, and the tiny flying bird in conventional fashion; he followed all the established rules of aerial and linear perspective. The three sketchily rendered figures, however, clearly belong to a dream world, and the literally three-dimensional miniature gate, the odd button knob, and the strange closed building "violate" the bulky frame's space. Additional dislocation occurs in the traditional museum identification label, which Ernst displaced into a cutaway part of the frame. Handwritten, it announces the work's title (taken from a poem Ernst wrote before he painted this), adding another note of irrational mystery.

As is true of many Surrealist works, the title, *Two Children Are Threatened by a Nightingale,* is ambiguous and relates uneasily to

what the spectator sees. The viewer must struggle to decipher connections between the image and words. When Surrealists (and Dadaists and Metaphysical artists before them) used such titles, they intended the seeming contradiction between title and picture to act like a "blow to the mind," knocking the spectator off balance with all expectations challenged. Much of the impact of Surrealist works begins with the viewer's sudden awareness of the incongruity and absurdity of what is pictured.

**A DISTURBING BLUE DREAMSCAPE** Spaniard SALVADOR DALÍ (1904–1989), an established Surrealist painter, also explored his psyche and dreams in his paintings, sculptures, jewelry, and designs for furniture and movies. Dalí probed a deeply erotic dimension through his work, studying the writings of Sigmund Freud and Richard von Krafft-Ebing and inventing what he called the "paranoiac-critical method" to assist his creative process. As he described it, in his painting he aimed "to materialize the images of concrete irrationality with the most imperialistic fury of precision . . . in order that the world of imagination and of concrete irrationality may be as objectively evident . . . as that of the exterior world of phenomenal reality."[40] All these aspects of Dalí's style can be seen in *The Persistence of Memory* (FIG. **33-46**). Here, he created a haunting allegory of empty space where time has ended. An eerie never-setting sun illuminates the barren landscape. An amorphous creature draped with a limp pocket watch sleeps in the foreground. Another watch hangs from the branch of a dead tree that springs unexpectedly from a blocky architectural form. A third watch hangs half over the edge of the rectangular form,

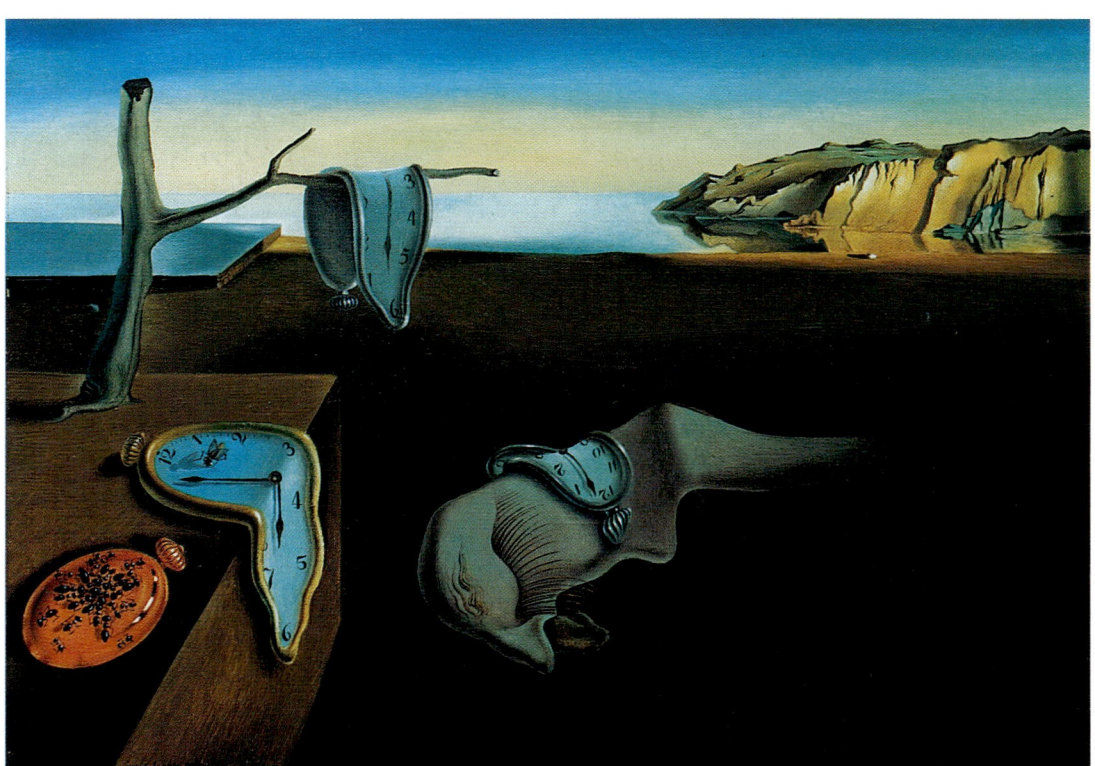

**33-46** SALVADOR DALÍ, *The Persistence of Memory*, 1931. Oil on canvas, $9\frac{1}{2}'' \times 1'\ 1''$. Museum of Modern Art, New York.

beside a small timepiece resting dial-down on the block's surface. Ants swarm mysteriously over the small watch, while a fly walks along the face of its large neighbor, almost as if this assembly of watches were decaying organic life—soft and sticky. Dalí rendered every detail of this dreamscape with precise control, striving to make the world of his paintings as convincingly real as the most meticulously rendered landscape based on an actual scene from nature.

**WORDS CONTRADICTING IMAGES** The Belgian painter RENÉ MAGRITTE (1898–1967) also expressed in exemplary fashion the Surrealist idea and method—the dreamlike dissociation of image and meaning. His works administer disruptive shocks because they subvert the viewer's expectations based on logic and common sense. The danger of relying on rationality when viewing a Surrealist work is glaringly apparent in Magritte's *The Treachery (or Perfidy) of Images* (FIG. **33-47**). Magritte presented a meticulously rendered *trompe l'oeil* depiction of a briar pipe. The caption beneath the image, however, contradicts what seems obvious: "Ceci n'est pas une pipe." ("This is not a pipe.") The discrepancy between image and caption clearly challenges the assumptions underlying the reading of visual art. Like the other Surrealists' work, this painting wreaks havoc on the viewer's reliance on the conscious and the rational.

**FUZZY LOGIC** The Surrealists were also enamored with sculpture, whose concrete tangibility made their art all the more disquieting. *Object (Le Déjeuner en fourrure),* translated as

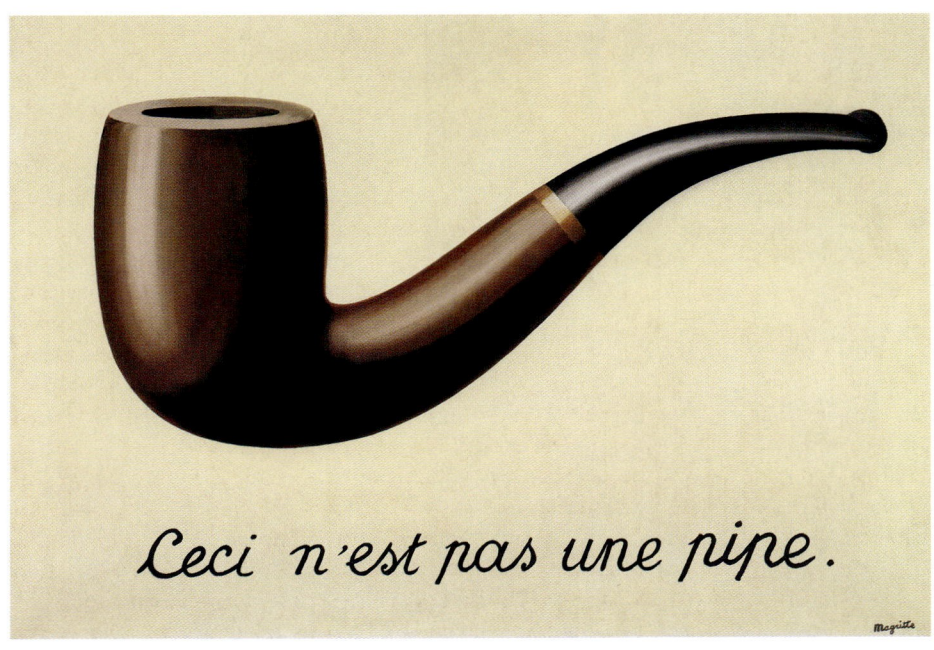

**33-47** RENÉ MAGRITTE, *The Treachery (or Perfidy) of Images,* 1928–1929. Oil on canvas, $1'\ 11\frac{5}{8}'' \times 3'\ 1''$. Los Angeles County Museum of Art, Los Angeles (purchased with funds provided by the Mr. and Mrs. William Preston Harrison Collection).

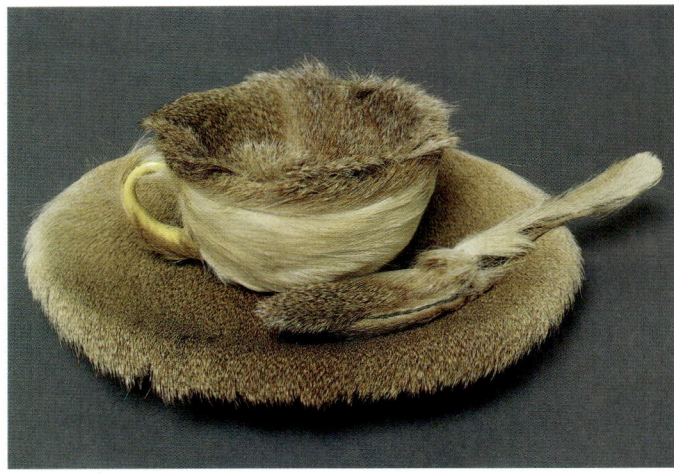

**33-48** MERET OPPENHEIM, *Object (Le Déjeuner en fourrure)*, 1936. Fur-covered cup, $4\frac{3}{8}''$ in diameter; saucer, $9\frac{3}{8}''$ in diameter; spoon, 8". Museum of Modern Art, New York (purchase). 💿

"Luncheon in fur" (FIG. **33-48**), by Swiss artist MERET OPPENHEIM (1913–1985) captures the incongruity, humor, visual appeal, and, often, eroticism characterizing Surrealism. The artist presented a fur-lined teacup inspired by a conversation she had with Picasso. After admiring a bracelet Oppenheim had made from a piece of brass covered with fur, Picasso noted that anything might be covered with fur. When her tea grew cold, Oppenheim responded to Picasso's comment by ordering "un peu plus de fourrure" (a little more fur), and the sculpture had its genesis. *Object (Le Déjeuner en fourrure)* takes on an anthropomorphic quality, animated by the quirky combination of the fur with a functional object. Further, the sculpture captures the Surrealist flair for alchemical, seemingly magical or mystical, transformation. It incorporates a sensuality and eroticism (seen here in the seductively soft, tactile fur lining the concave form) that are also components of much of Surrealist art. That visitors to the Surrealist exhibition at the Museum of Modern Art in New York in 1937 selected *Object* as the quintessential Surrealist symbol reveals that it seemed to epitomize the Surrealist vision.

**A PERSONAL AND POLITICAL PORTRAIT** Born to a Mexican mother and German father, the painter FRIDA KAHLO (1907–1954) used the details of her life as powerful symbols for the psychological pain of human existence. Kahlo has often been discussed as a Surrealist due to the psychic and autobiographical issues she dealt with in her art. Indeed, Breton himself deemed her a natural Surrealist. Yet Kahlo consciously distanced herself from the Surrealist group, and it was left to others to impose Surrealist connections on her. Kahlo began painting seriously as a young student, during convalescence from an accident that tragically left her in constant pain. Her life became a heroic and tumultuous battle for survival against illness and stormy personal relationships. *The Two Fridas* (FIG. **33-49**), one of the few large-scale canvases Kahlo ever produced, is typical of her long series of unflinching self-portraits. The twin figures sit side by side on a low bench in a barren landscape under a stormy sky. The figures suggest different sides of the artist's personality, inextricably

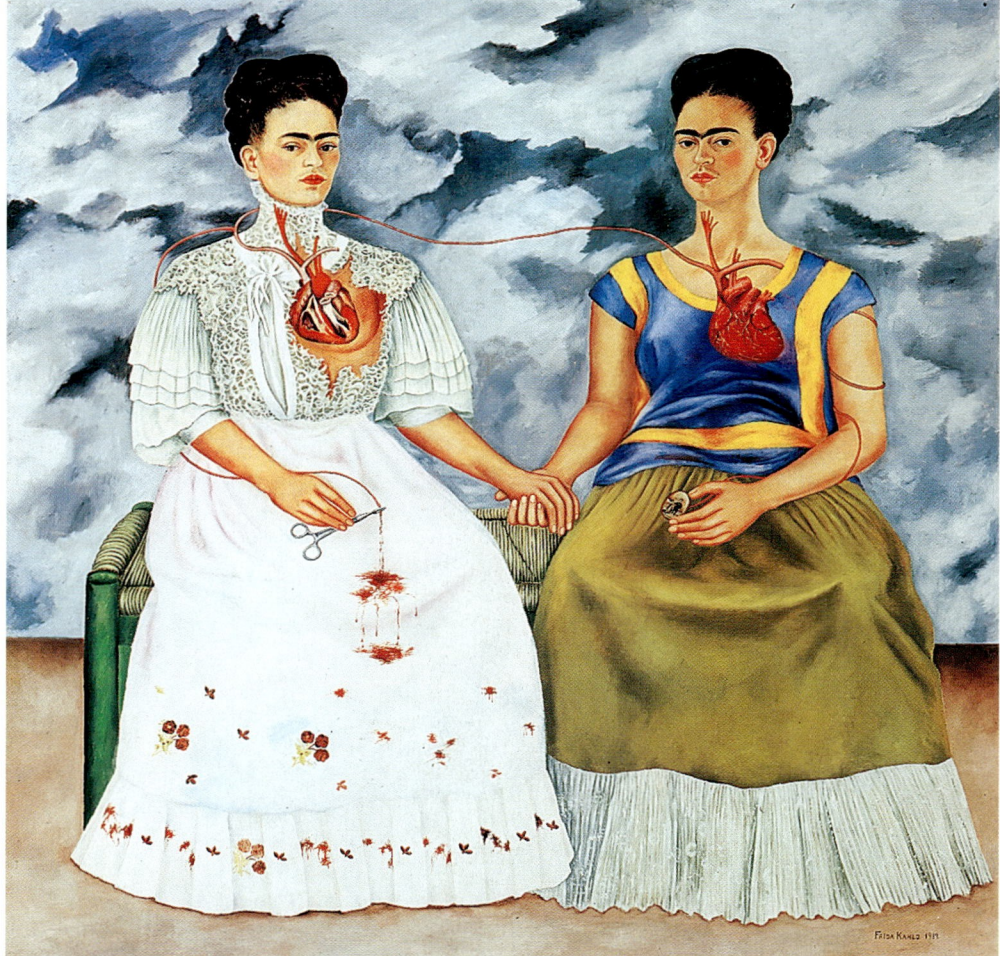

**33-49** FRIDA KAHLO, *The Two Fridas*, 1939. Oil on canvas, 5' 7" × 5' 7". Collection of the Museo de Arte Moderno, Mexico City. 💿

linked by the clasped hands and by the thin artery that stretches between them, joining their exposed hearts. The artery ends on one side in surgical forceps and on the other in a miniature portrait of Kahlo's husband, the artist Diego Rivera (FIG. 33-81), as a child. Her deeply personal paintings touch sensual and psychological memories in her audience.

Yet to read Kahlo's paintings solely as autobiographical overlooks the powerful political dimension of her art. Kahlo was deeply nationalistic and committed to her Mexican heritage; politically active, she joined the Communist Party in 1920 and participated in public political protests. *The Two Fridas* incorporates Kahlo's commentary on the struggle facing Mexicans in the early 20th century in defining their national cultural identity. This commentary appears in the figures' attire; the Frida on the right (representing indigenous culture) wears a Tehuana dress, the traditional costume of Zapotec women from the Isthmus of Tehuantepec, whereas the Frida on the left (representing imperialist forces) is attired in a European-style white lace dress. The heart, depicted here in such dramatic fashion, was an important symbol in the art of the Aztecs, whom Mexican nationalists idealized as the last independent rulers of an indigenous political unit. Thus *The Two Fridas* represents both Kahlo's personal struggles and the struggles of her homeland.

**EMBRACING THE INTUITIVE** Like the Dadaists, the Surrealists used many methods to free the creative process from reliance on the kind of conscious control they believed that society had shaped too much. Dalí used his paranoiac-critical approach to encourage the free play of association as he worked. Other Surrealists used automatism—the creation of art without conscious control—and various types of planned "accidents" to provoke reactions closely related to subconscious experience. The Spanish

artist JOAN MIRÓ (1893–1983) was a master of this approach. Although Miró resisted formal association with any movement or group, including the Surrealists, André Breton identified him as "the most Surrealist of us all."[41] From the beginning, his work contained an element of fantasy and hallucination. After Surrealist poets in Paris introduced him to using chance to create art, the young Spaniard devised a new painting method that allowed him to create works such as *Painting* (FIG. 33-50). Miró began this painting by making a scattered collage composition with assembled fragments cut from a catalog for machinery. The shapes in the collage became motifs the artist freely reshaped to create black silhouettes—solid or in outline, with dramatic accents of white and vermilion. They suggest, in the painting, a host of amoebic organisms or constellations in outer space floating in an immaterial background space filled with soft reds, blues, and greens.

Miró described his creative process as a switching back and forth between unconscious and conscious image making: "Rather than setting out to paint something, I begin painting and as I paint the picture begins to assert itself, or suggest itself under my brush. The form becomes a sign for a woman or a bird as I work. . . . The first stage is free, unconscious. . . . The second stage is carefully calculated."[42] Even the artist could not always explain the meanings of pictures such as *Painting*. They are, in the truest sense, spontaneous and intuitive expressions of the little-understood, submerged unconscious part of life.

**MECHANICAL BIRDS** Perhaps the most inventive artist using fantasy images to represent the nonvisible world was the Swiss-German painter PAUL KLEE (1879–1940). Like Miró, he shunned formal association with groups such as the Dadaists and Surrealists but pursued their interest in the subconscious. Klee sought clues to humanity's deeper nature in primitive shapes and symbols. Like

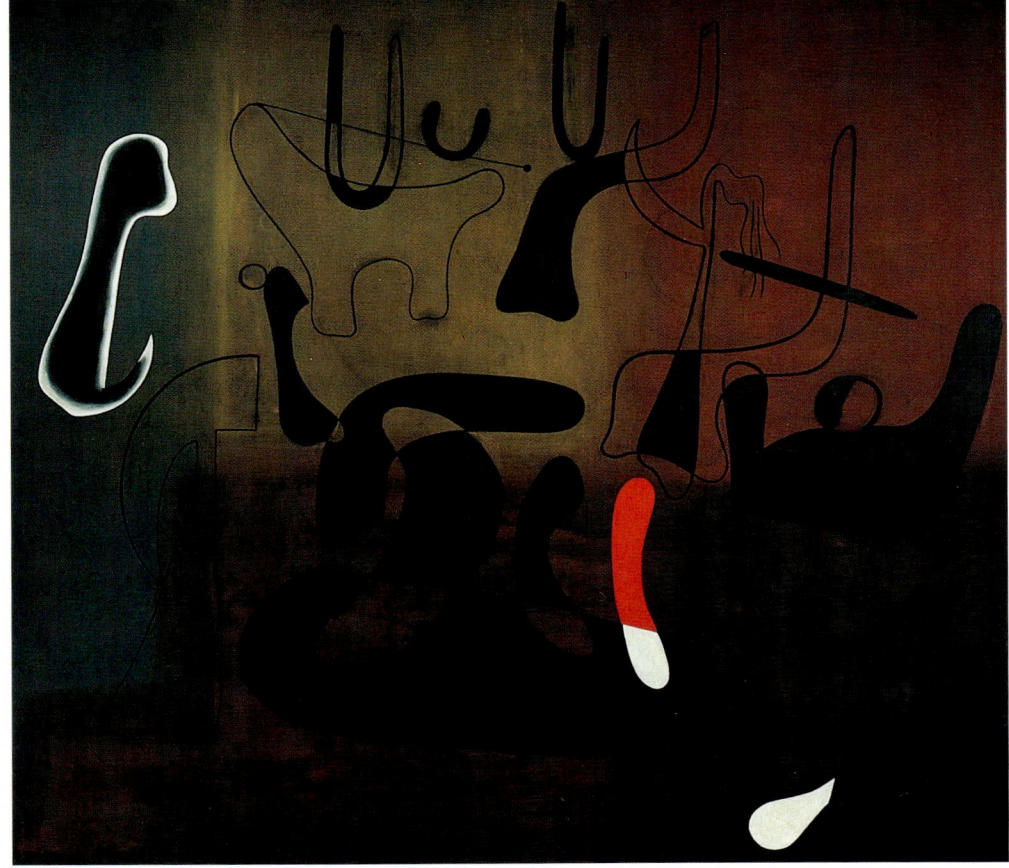

**33-50** JOAN MIRÓ, *Painting*, 1933. Oil on canvas, 5′ 8″ × 6′ 5″. Museum of Modern Art, New York (Loula D. Lasker Bequest by exchange).

## "Primitivism," Colonialism, and Early-20th-Century Western Art

Many scholars have noted that one of the major sources for much of early-20th-century art is non-Western culture. Picasso, Matisse, the German Expressionists, Brancusi, Klee, the Dadaists, and the Surrealists all incorporated stylistic elements from the artifacts of Africa, Oceania, and the native peoples of the Americas.

These artists benefited from the numerous non-Western objects displayed in European and American collections and museums. During the second half of the 19th century, anthropological and ethnographic museums began to proliferate. In 1882, the Musée d'Ethnographie (now the Musée de l'Homme) in Paris opened its doors to the public. The Musée Permanent des Colonies (now the Musée National des Arts d'Afrique et d'Oceanie) in Paris also provided the public with a wide array of objects—weapons, tools, basketwork, headdresses—from colonial territories, as did the Musée Africain in Marseilles. In Germany, the Berlin Museum für Völkerkunde housed close to 10,000 African tribal objects by 1886, when it opened for public viewing. In addition, private collecting of such material was fairly widespread—even Matisse and Picasso collected African and Oceanic artifacts. The Expositions Universelles, regularly scheduled exhibitions in France designed to celebrate industrial progress, included products from Oceania and Africa after 1851, familiarizing the public with these cultures. By the beginning of the 20th century, significant non-Western collections were on view in museums in Liverpool, Glasgow, Edinburgh, London, Hamburg, Stuttgart, Vienna, Berlin, Munich, Leiden, Copenhagen, and Chicago.

The availability of these collections and materials was due to the rampant colonialism central to the geopolitical dynamics of the 19th century and much of the 20th century. Most of the Western powers maintained colonies. For example, the Dutch, Americans, and French all kept a colonial presence in the Pacific. Britain, France, Germany, Belgium, Holland, Spain, and Portugal divided up the African continent. People often perceived these colonial cultures as "primitive," and many of the non-Western artifacts displayed in museums were referred to as "artificial curiosities" or seen as fetish objects. Indeed, the exhibition of these objects collected during expeditions to the colonies served to reinforce the "need" for a colonial presence in these countries. As previously noted, colonialism often had a missionary dimension. These objects, which often seemed to depict strange gods or creatures, reinforced the perception that these peoples were "barbarians" who needed to be "civilized" or "saved," thereby justifying colonialism worldwide.

Whether avant-garde artists were aware of the imperialistic implications of their appropriation of non-Western culture is unclear. Certainly, however, many artists reveled in the energy and freshness of non-Western images and forms. These different cultural products provided Western artists with new ways of looking at their own art. Matisse always maintained he saw African sculptures as simply "good sculptures . . . like any other."[1] Picasso, in contrast, believed these objects were "magical things," "mediators" between humans and the forces of evil.[2] Further, "primitive" art seemed to embody a directness, closeness to nature, and honesty that appealed to modernist artists determined to reject conventional models. Ultimately, non-Western art served as an important revitalizing and energizing force in Western art, and this influence continues to the present.

[1] Jean-Louis Paudrat, "From Africa," in William Rubin, ed., "Primitivism" in 20th Century Art: Affinity of the Tribal and the Modern (New York: Museum of Modern Art, 1984), 1:141.

[2] Ibid.

---

Jung, Klee seems to have accepted the existence of a collective unconscious that reveals itself in archaic signs and patterns and that is everywhere evident in the art of so-called "primitive" cultures (see "'Primitivism,' Colonialism, and Early-20th-Century Western Art," above). The son of a professional musician and himself an accomplished violinist, Klee thought of painting as similar to music in its expressiveness and in its ability to touch its viewer's spirit through a studied use of color, form, and line:

> Art does not reproduce the visible; rather it makes visible. . . . The formal elements of graphic art are dot, line, plane and space—the last three charged with energy of various kinds. . . . Formerly we used to represent things visible on earth, things we either liked to look at or would have liked to see. Today we reveal the reality that is behind visible things. . . . By including the concepts of good and evil, a moral sphere is created. . . . Art is a simile of the Creation.[43]

To penetrate the reality behind visible things, Klee studied nature avidly, taking special interest in analyzing processes of growth and change. He coded these studies in diagrammatic form in notebooks, and the knowledge he gained in this way became so much a part of his consciousness that it influenced the "psychic improvisation" he used to create his art. His work was thus rooted in nature, but it was nature filtered through his mind. Upon starting an image, he would allow the pencil or brush to lead him until an image emerged, to which he would then respond to complete the idea.

Twittering Machine (FIG. 33-51) reveals Klee's fanciful vision. The painting, although based on objects in the tangible world that can easily be read as birds, is far from illusionistic. Klee has presented the scene in a simplified, almost childlike manner, imbuing the work with a poetic lyricism. The impact of Klee's works is enhanced by their small size; a viewer must draw near to decipher the delicately rendered forms and enter this mysterious dream world. The inclusion of a crank-driven mechanism adds a touch of whimsy. Perhaps no other artist of the 20th century matched Klee's subtlety as he deftly created a world of ambiguity and understatement that draws each viewer into finding a unique interpretation of the work.

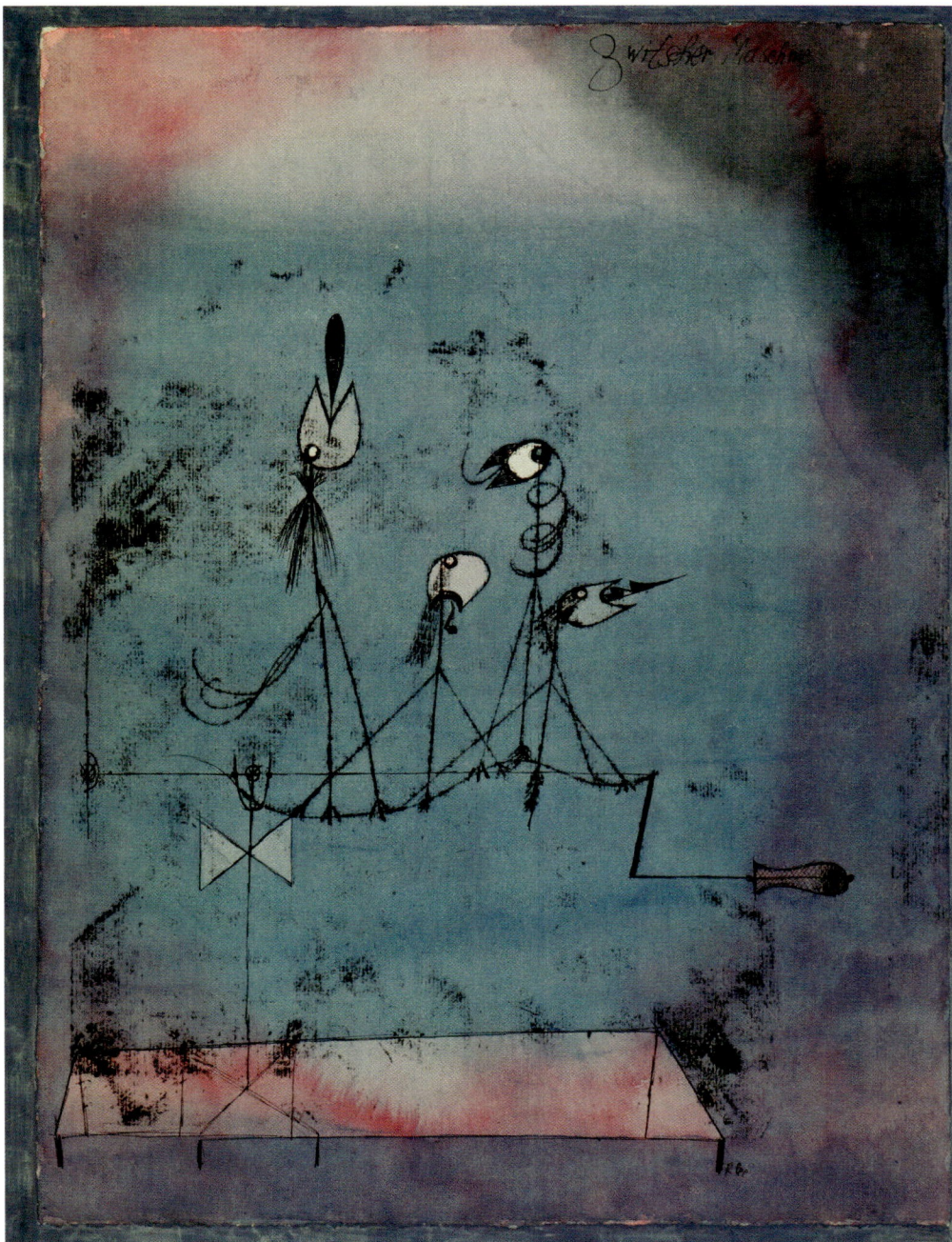

**33-51** Paul Klee, *Twittering Machine*, 1922. Watercolor and pen and ink, on oil transfer drawing on paper, mounted on cardboard, 2′ 1″ × 1′ 7″. Museum of Modern Art, New York (purchase).

# NEW ART FOR A NEW SOCIETY— UTOPIAN IDEALS

The pessimism and cynicism of movements such as Dada are thoroughly understandable in light of the historical circumstances. However, not all artists gravitated toward alienation from society and its profound turmoil. Some avant-garde artists promoted utopian ideals, believing staunchly in art's ability to contribute to improving society and all humankind. These efforts often surfaced in the face of significant political upheaval, illustrating the link established early on between revolution in politics and revolution in art. Among the art movements espousing utopian notions were Suprematism and Constructivism in Russia, De Stijl in Holland, and the Bauhaus in Germany.

## *Suprematism and Constructivism*

**THE SUPREMACY OF PURE FEELING** Although Russia was geographically far removed from Paris, the center of the international art world in the early 20th century, Russians had a long history of cultural contact and interaction with the West. Wealthy Russians, such as Ivan Morozov and Sergei Shchukin, amassed extensive collections of Impressionist and Post-Impressionist paintings. Shchukin became particularly enamored with the work of both Picasso and Matisse; by the mid-1910s, he had acquired 37 paintings by Matisse and 51 by Picasso. Because of their access to collections such as these, Russian artists were well aware of early-20th-century artistic developments, especially Fauvism, Cubism, and Futurism. Among the artists who pursued the avant-garde direction Cubism introduced was the Russian painter KAZIMIR

MALEVICH (1878–1935). Malevich developed an abstract style to convey his belief that the supreme reality in the world is pure feeling, which attaches to no object. Thus, this belief called for new, nonobjective forms in art—shapes not related to objects in the visible world. Malevich had studied painting, sculpture, and architecture and had worked his way through most of the avant-garde styles of his youth before deciding none were suited to expressing the subject he found most important—"pure feeling." He christened his new artistic approach *Suprematism,* explaining: "Under Suprematism I understand the supremacy of pure feeling in creative art. To the Suprematist, the visual phenomena of the objective world are, in themselves, meaningless; the significant thing is feeling, as such, quite apart from the environment in which it is called forth. . . . The Suprematist does not observe and does not touch—he feels."[44]

The basic form of Malevich's new Suprematist nonobjective art was the square. Combined with its relatives, the straight line and the rectangle, the square soon filled his paintings, such as *Suprematist Composition: Airplane Flying* (FIG. **33-52**). In this work, the brightly colored shapes float against and within a white space, and the artist placed them in dynamic relationship to one another. Malevich believed all peoples would easily understand his new art because of the universality of its symbols. It used the pure language of shape and color, to which everyone could respond intuitively. Having formulated his artistic approach, Malevich welcomed the Russian Revolution, which broke out in 1917, as a political act that would wipe out past traditions and begin a new culture. He believed his art could play a major role because of its universal accessibility. In actuality, after a short period when the new regime heralded avant-garde art, the political leaders of the postrevolution Soviet Union decided the new society needed a more "practical"

art. Soviet authorities promoted a "realistic," illusionistic art that they believed was more understandable to a wide public. They anticipated that such art would teach citizens about their new government. Malevich was horrified; to him, true art was forever divorced from such practical connections with life. As he explained, "Every social idea, however great and important it may be, stems from the sensation of hunger; every art work, regardless of how small and insignificant it may seem, originates in pictorial or plastic feeling. It is high time for us to realize that the problems of art lie far apart from those of the stomach or the intellect."[45]

Disappointed and unappreciated in his own country, Malevich eventually gravitated toward other disciplines, such as mathematical theory and geometry, logical fields given his interest in pure abstraction.

**SPACE-TIME SCULPTURES** Like Malevich, the Russian-born sculptor NAUM GABO (1890–1977) wanted to create an innovative art to express a new reality, and, also like Malevich, Gabo believed such art would spring from sources separate from the everyday world. For Gabo, the new reality was the space-time world described by early-20th-century scientists. As he wrote in *Realistic Manifesto,* published with his brother Anton Pevsner in 1920: "Space and time are the only forms on which life is built and hence art must be constructed." Later, he explained: "We are realists, bound to earthly matters. . . . The shapes we are creating are not abstract, they are absolute. They are released from any already existent thing in nature and their content lies in themselves. . . . It is impossible to comprehend the content of an absolute shape by reason alone. Our emotions are the real manifestation of this content."[46]

Gabo was associated with a group of Russian sculptors known as the Constructivists. The name *Constructivism* may have come originally from the title *Construction,* which the Russian artist Vladimir Tatlin used for some relief sculptures he made in 1913 and 1914. Gabo explained that he called himself a Constructivist partly because he built up his sculptures piece by piece in space, instead of carving or modeling them in the traditional way. This method freed the Constructivists to work with "volume of mass and volume of space" as "two different materials" for creating compositions filled with the "kinetic rhythms" humans perceive as "real time."[47]

Although Gabo experimented briefly with real motion in his work, most of his sculptures relied on the relationship of mass and space to suggest the nature of space-time. To indicate the volumes of mass and space more clearly in his sculpture, Gabo used some of the new synthetic plastic materials, including celluloid, nylon, and Lucite, to create constructions whose space seems to flow through as well as around the transparent materials. In works such as *Column* (FIG. **33-53**), the depth of the sculpture is visible, because the sculptor opened up the column's circular mass so that the viewer can experience the volume of space it occupies. Two transparent planes extend through its diameter, crossing at right angles at the center of the implied cylindrical column shape. The opaque colored planes at the base and the inclined open ring set up counter-rhythms to the crossed upright planes. They establish the sense of dynamic kinetic movement that Gabo always sought to express as an essential part of reality.

**THE "CULTURE OF MATERIALS"** In the years immediately following the Russian Revolution, a new art movement emerged in the Soviet Union whose members devoted their talents to designing a better environment for human beings. The Russians called their movement *Productivism.* It developed as an offshoot of the Constructivist movement, and one of its most gifted leaders was

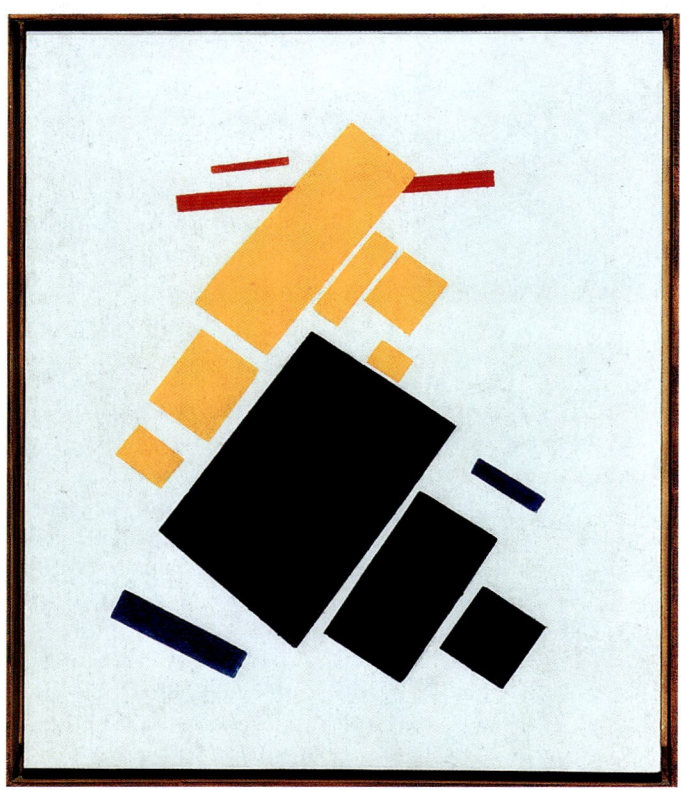

**33-52** KAZIMIR MALEVICH, *Suprematist Composition: Airplane Flying,* 1915 (dated 1914). Oil on canvas, 1′ 10$\frac{7}{8}$″ × 1′ 7″. Museum of Modern Art, New York (purchase).

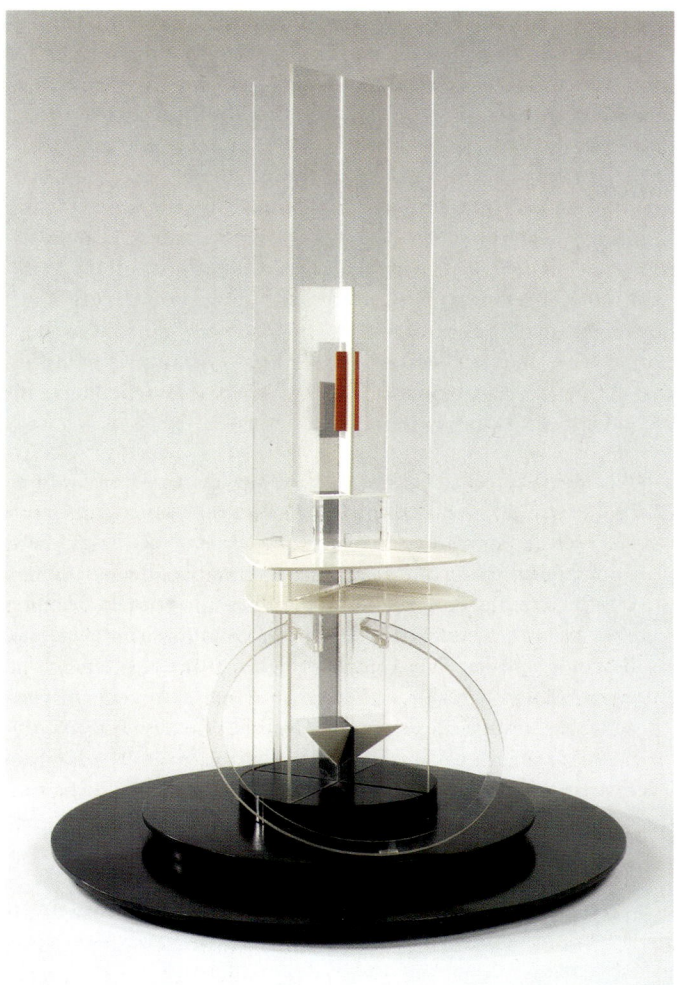

**33-53** Naum Gabo, *Column*, ca. 1923 (reconstructed 1937). Perspex, wood, metal, glass, 3′ 5″ × 2′ 5″ × 2′ 5″. Solomon R. Guggenheim Museum, New York.

**Vladimir Tatlin** (1885–1953). Influenced by Cubism's formal analysis, the dynamism of Futurism, and the rhythmic compositions of flat curved planes in traditional Russian icon paintings (see FIG. 12-29), Tatlin produced abstract relief constructions and models for stage sets. He experimented with every kind of material—glass, iron, sheet metal, wood, and plaster—to lay the basis for what he called the "culture of materials."

The revolution had been the signal to Tatlin and other avant-garde artists in Russia that the hated old order was ending. In utopian fashion, they were determined to play a significant role in creating a new world, one that would fully use the power of industrialization to benefit all the people. Initially, like Malevich and Gabo, Tatlin believed that nonobjective art was ideal for the new society, free as such art was from any past symbolism. For a few years, all Russian avant-garde artists worked together designing public festivals and demonstrations. They presented plays and exhibitions intended to help educate the public about their new government and the possibilities for their future. The Russian Futurist-Constructivist poet Vladimir Mayakovsky proclaimed their new goal: "We do not need a dead mausoleum of art where dead works are worshiped, but a living factory of the human spirit—in the streets, in the tramways, in the factories, workshops, and workers' homes."[48]

These artists reorganized art schools such as the College of Painting, Sculpture, and Architecture in Moscow, combining them with craft schools to form new educational programs—they renamed the one in Moscow Vkhutemas (Higher Artistic-Technical Studios). Tatlin, Malevich, and Gabo's brother, Pevsner, had studios there, and Gabo was a frequent visitor.

Despite this unified effort to reorganize the educational system, a split developed among avant-garde members. On one side were Malevich, Gabo, Kandinsky (who had returned to Moscow in 1914), and all the other artists who believed that art was an expression of humanity's spiritual nature. On the other side were the Productivists—Tatlin and other artists who felt that artists must direct art toward creating useful products for the new society. The Productivists connected their position to that of a group called Proletkult (Organization for Proletarian Culture). Founded in 1906, it became free to follow its primary doctrine ("Art is a social product, conditioned by the social environment") only after the 1917 revolution. Tatlin enthusiastically abandoned abstract art for functional art by designing such products as an efficient stove and a "functional" set of worker's clothing. For a time, he even worked in a metallurgical factory near Petrograd (after 1989 once again Saint Petersburg).

Tatlin's most famous work is his design for *Monument to the Third International* (FIG. **33-54**), commissioned by the Department of Artistic Work of the People's Commissariat for Enlightenment early in 1919 to honor the Russian Revolution. He envisioned a huge glass-and-iron building that would have been twice as high as the Empire State Building. Widely influential, "Tatlin's Tower," as it became known, was viewed as a model for those

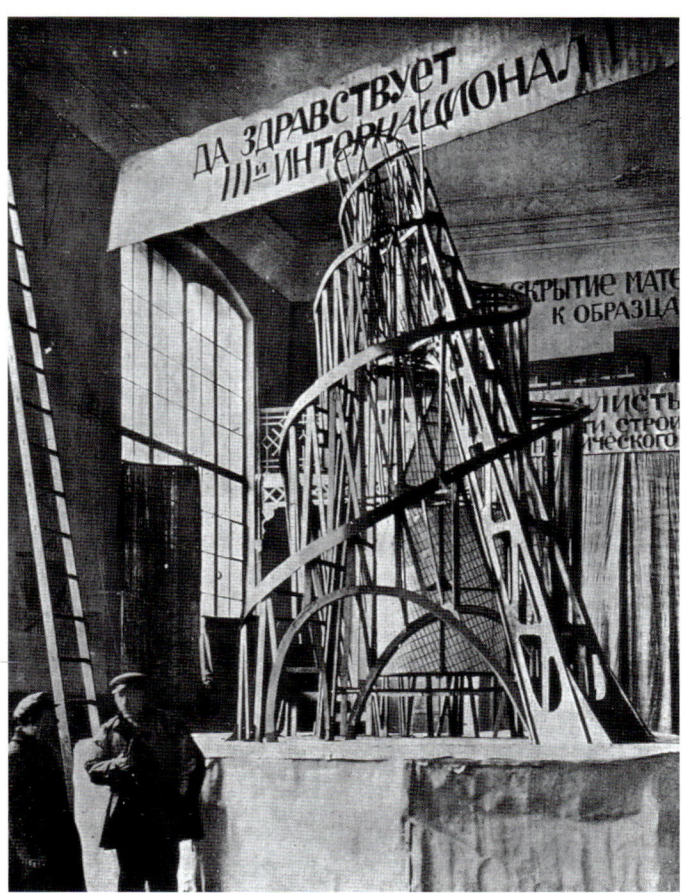

**33-54** Photograph of Vladimir Tatlin with *Monument to the Third International*, 1919–1920. Annenberg School for Communication, University of Southern California, Los Angeles.

seeking to encourage socially committed and functional art. On its proposed site in the center of Moscow, it would have served as a propaganda and news center for the Soviet people. Within a dynamically tilted spiral cage, three geometrically shaped chambers were to rotate around a central axis, each chamber housing facilities for a different type of governmental activity and rotating at a different speed. The one at the bottom, a huge cylindrical glass structure for lectures and meetings, was to revolve once a year. Higher up was a cone-shaped chamber intended for administrative functions and monthly rotations. At the top, a cubic information center would have revolved daily, issuing news bulletins and proclamations via the most modern means of communication. These included an open-air news screen (illuminated at night) and a special instrument designed to project words on the clouds on any overcast day. The proposed decreasing size of the chambers as visitors ascended the monument paralleled the decision-making hierarchy in the political system, with the most authoritative, smallest groups near the building's apex.

Tatlin's design thus served as a visual reinforcement of a social and political reality. Tatlin envisioned the whole complex as a dynamic communications center perfectly suited to the exhilarating pace of the new age. In addition, the design's reductive geometry demonstrates Tatlin's connection to the artistic programs of the Suprematists and the Constructivists. Due to the desperate economic situation in Russia during these years, Tatlin's ambitious design was never realized as a building. It existed only in metal-and-wood models exhibited on various official occasions before disappearing. The only records of the models are found in a few drawings, photographs, and recent reconstructions.

## De Stijl

The utopian spirit and ideals of the Suprematists and Constructivists were not limited to Russia. In Holland, a group of young artists formed a new movement in 1917 and began publishing a magazine, calling both movement and magazine *De Stijl* (The Style). The group was cofounded by the painters PIET MONDRIAN (1872–1944) and Theo van Doesburg (1883–1931). In addition to promoting utopian ideals, group members believed in the birth of a new age in the wake of World War I. They felt it was a time of balance between individual and universal values, when the machine would assure ease of living. In their first manifesto of De Stijl, the artists declared: "There is an old and a new consciousness of the age. The old one is directed toward the individual. The new one is directed toward the universal."[49] The goal, according to van Doesburg and architect Cor van Eesteren, was a total integration of art and life:

> We must realize that life and art are no longer separate domains. That is why the "idea" of "art" as an illusion separate from real life must disappear. The word "Art" no longer means anything to us. In its place we demand the construction of our environment in accordance with creative laws based upon a fixed principle. These laws, following those of economics, mathematics, technique, sanitation, etc., are leading to a new, plastic unity.[50]

**A "PURE PLASTIC ART"** Toward this goal of integration, Piet Mondrian created a resolutely monistic style—that is, it was based on a single ideal principle. The choice of the term *De Stijl* reflected Mondrian's confidence that this style—*the* style—revealed the underlying eternal structure of existence. Accordingly, De Stijl

artists reduced their artistic vocabulary to simple geometric elements. Time spent in Paris, just before World War I, introduced Mondrian to modes of abstraction (such as Cubism). However, as his attraction to contemporary theological writings grew, Mondrian sought to purge his art of every overt reference to individual objects in the external world. He initially favored the teachings of theosophy, a tradition basing knowledge of nature and the human condition on knowledge of the divine nature or spiritual powers. (His fellow theosophist, Vassily Kandinsky [FIG. 33-6], was pursuing a similar path.) Mondrian, however, quickly abandoned the strictures of theosophy and turned toward a conception of nonobjective or pictorial design—"pure plastic art"—that he believed expressed universal reality. He articulated his credo with great eloquence in 1914:

> What first captivated us does not captivate us afterward (like toys). If one has loved the surface of things for a long time, later on one will look for something more. . . . The interior of things shows through the surface; thus as we look at the surface the inner image is formed in our soul. It is this inner image that should be represented. For the natural surface of things is beautiful, but the imitation of it is without life. . . . Art is higher than reality and has no direct relation to reality. . . . To approach the spiritual in art, one will make as little use as possible of reality, because reality is opposed to the spiritual. . . . [W]e find ourselves in the presence of an abstract art. Art should be above reality, otherwise it would have no value for man.[51]

Mondrian soon moved beyond Cubism because he felt "Cubism did not accept the logical consequences of its own discoveries; it was not developing towards its own goal, the expression of pure plastics."[52] Caught by the outbreak of hostilities while on a visit to Holland, Mondrian remained there during World War I, developing his theories for what he called *Neoplasticism*—the new "pure plastic art." He believed that all great art had polar but coexistent goals, the attempt to create "universal beauty" and the desire for "aesthetic expression of oneself."[53] The first goal is objective in nature, whereas the second is subjective, existing within the individual's mind and heart. To create such a universal expression, an artist must communicate "a real equation of the universal and the individual."[54] To express this vision, Mondrian eventually limited his formal vocabulary to the three primary colors (red, blue, and yellow), the three primary values (black, white, and gray), and the two primary directions (horizontal and vertical). Basing his ideas on a combination of teachings, he concluded that primary colors and values are the purest colors and therefore are the perfect tools to help an artist construct a harmonious composition. Using this system, he created numerous paintings locking color planes into a grid of intersecting vertical and horizontal lines, as in *Composition in Red, Blue, and Yellow* (FIG. 33-55). In each of these paintings, Mondrian altered the grid patterns and the size and placement of the color planes to create an internal cohesion and harmony. This did not mean inertia; rather, Mondrian worked to maintain a dynamic tension in his paintings from the size and position of lines, shapes, and colors.

**DE STIJL STYLE IN SPACE** Architects also explored many of the ideas Mondrian and De Stijl artists pursued. One of the masterpieces of De Stijl architecture is the Schröder House in Utrecht, the Netherlands (FIG. 33-56), built in 1924 by GERRIT THOMAS RIETVELD (1888–1964). Rietveld came to the group as a cabinetmaker and made De Stijl furnishings throughout his

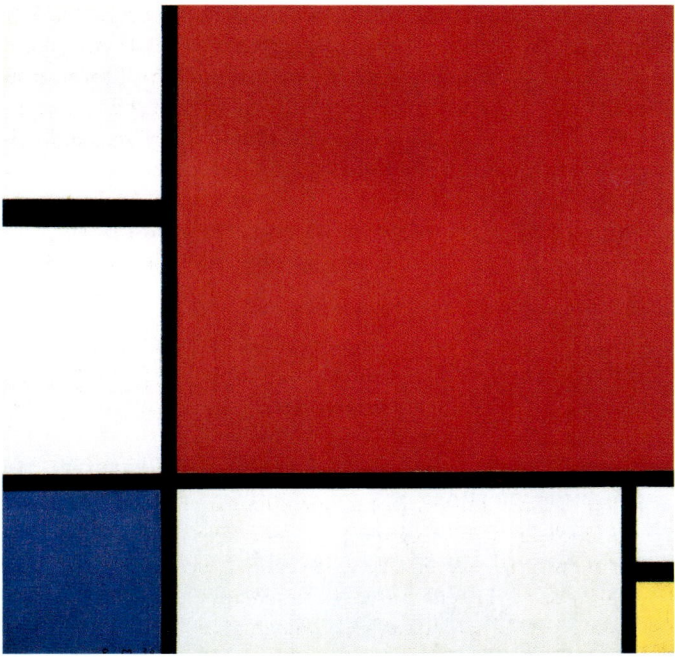

**33-55** PIET MONDRIAN, *Composition in Red, Blue, and Yellow*, 1930. Oil on canvas, $2' \, 4\frac{5}{8}'' \times 1' \, 9\frac{1}{4}''$. Private collection.

career. His architecture carries the same spirit into a larger integrated whole and perfectly expresses van Doesburg's definition of De Stijl architecture:

> The new architecture is anti-cubic, i.e., it does not strive to contain the different functional space cells in a single closed cube, but it throws the functional space (as well as canopy planes, balcony volumes, etc.) out from the centre of the cube, so that height, width, and depth plus time become a completely new plastic expression in open spaces. . . . The plastic architect . . . has to construct in the new field, time-space.[55]

The main living rooms of the Schröder House are on the second floor, with more private rooms on the ground floor. However,

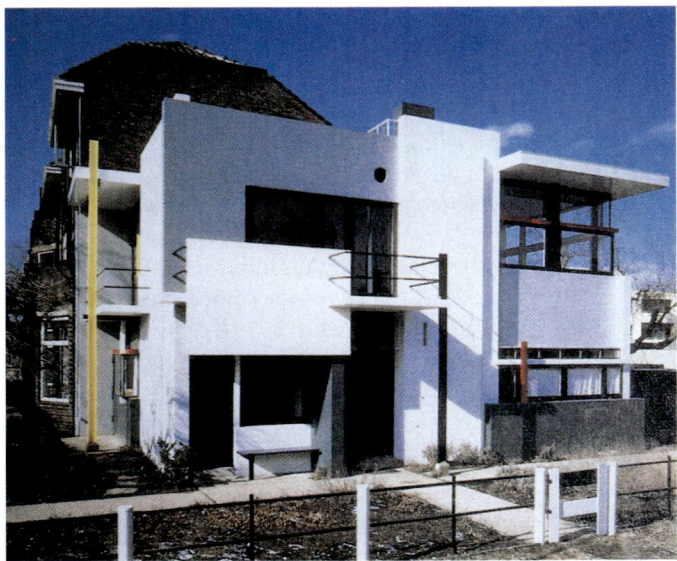

**33-56** GERRIT THOMAS RIETVELD, Schröder House, Utrecht, the Netherlands, 1924.

Rietveld's house has an open plan and a relationship to nature more like the houses of his contemporary, the American architect Frank Lloyd Wright (FIGS. 33-66 and 33-68). Rietveld designed the entire second floor with sliding partitions that can be closed to define separate rooms or pushed back to create one open space broken into units only by the furniture arrangement. This shifting quality appears also on the outside, where railings, free-floating walls, and long rectangular windows give the effect of cubic units breaking up before the viewer's eyes. Rietveld's design clearly links all the arts. Rectangular planes seem to slide across each other on the Schröder House facade like movable panels, making this structure a kind of three-dimensional projection of the rigid but carefully proportioned flat planes in Mondrian's paintings.

## The Bauhaus

The De Stijl group not only developed an appealing simplified geometric style but also promoted the notion that art should be thoroughly incorporated into living environments. As Mondrian had insisted, "Art and life are *one;* art and life are both expressions of truth."[56] In Germany, the architect WALTER GROPIUS (1883–1969) developed a particular vision of "total architecture." He made this concept the foundation of not only his own work but also the work of generations of pupils under his influence at a school called the Bauhaus. In 1919, Gropius was appointed the director of the Weimar School of Arts and Crafts in Germany, founded in 1906. Under Gropius, the school was renamed Das Staatliche Bauhaus (roughly translated as "State School of Building") and referred to as the *Bauhaus.*

Gropius's goal was to train artists, architects, and designers to accept and anticipate 20th-century needs. He developed an extensive curriculum based on certain principles. First, Gropius staunchly advocated the importance of strong basic design (including principles of composition, two- and three-dimensionality, and color theory) and craftsmanship as fundamental to good art and architecture. Declared Gropius: "Architects, sculptors, painters, we must all go back to the crafts. . . . There is no essential difference between the artist and the craftsman."[57] To achieve this integration of art and craft, both a technical instructor and a "teacher of form"—an artist—taught in each department.

Second, Gropius promoted the unity of art, architecture, and design. "Architects, painters, and sculptors," he insisted, "must recognize anew the composite character of a building as an entity."[58] To encourage the elimination of boundaries that traditionally separated art from architecture and art from craft, the Bauhaus offered courses in a wide range of artistic disciplines. These included weaving, pottery, bookbinding, carpentry, metalwork, stained glass, mural painting, stage design, and advertising and typography, in addition to painting, sculpture, and architecture.

Third, because Gropius wanted the Bauhaus to produce graduates who could design progressive environments that satisfied 20th-century needs, he emphasized thorough knowledge of machine-age technologies and materials. He felt that to produce truly successful designs, the artist-architect-craftsperson had to understand industry and mass production. Ultimately, Gropius hoped for a marriage between art and industry—a synthesis of design and production.

Like the De Stijl movement, the Bauhaus was founded on utopian principles. Gropius's declaration reveals the idealism of the entire Bauhaus enterprise: "Together let us conceive and create the new building of the future, which will embrace architecture and sculpture and painting in one unity and which will rise one day toward heaven from the hands of a million workers like a crystal symbol of a new faith."[59] In its reference to a unity of workers, this statement also reveals the undercurrent of socialism present in Germany at the time.

Gropius hired some of the period's most innovative and avant-garde artists and thinkers to teach at the Bauhaus, and their influence—at the Bauhaus and long after its demise, as a group and individually—was monumental. Among these teachers were Vassily Kandinsky (FIG. 33-6) and Paul Klee (FIG. 33-51).

EXPLORING SPACE AND TIME One of the most important Bauhaus teachers was Hungarian-born artist LÁSZLÓ MOHOLY-NAGY (1895–1946), who embraced Gropius's notion that art should be all-encompassing. Accordingly, Moholy-Nagy produced paintings, sculptures, prints, photograms, advertisements, set designs, photographs, and special effects for film. He was particularly interested in the character of the modern age and believed that society was

> heading toward a kinetic, time-spatial existence; toward an awareness of the forces plus their relationships which define all life and of which we had no previous knowledge and for which we have as yet no exact terminology. . . . Space-time stands for many things: relativity of motion and its measurement, integration, simultaneous grasp of the inside and outside, revelation of the structure instead of the facade. It also stands for a new vision concerning materials, energies, tensions, and their social implications.[60]

Given this fascination with space-time relationships, it is not surprising that Moholy-Nagy increasingly turned his attention to photography and film. Not only does *From the Radio Tower Berlin* (FIG. 33-57) depict a marvel of the modern age—a radio tower—but the photo also exercises his "new vision," taken as it is from the top looking straight down. This vertical aerial viewpoint presents the viewer with new formal patterns and visual relationships and with a perspective on the world that became increasingly common with the development of aerial flight.

THE PRIMACY OF DESIGN PRINCIPLES Another Bauhaus teacher who left a lasting legacy is the German artist JOSEF ALBERS (1888–1976). Although he initially worked in the Bauhaus's glass and furniture workshops, his greatest contribution to the school was his revision of the basic design course required of all students. There he refined his ideas, declaring: "We learn which formal qualities are important today: harmony or balance, free or measured rhythm, geometric or arithmetic proportion, symmetry or asymmetry, central or peripheral emphasis."[61] This systematic and thorough investigation of art's formal aspects characterized his own work, as evidenced in his best-known series, *Homage to the Square*. Although Albers executed this series between 1950 and 1976, some time after his departure from the Bauhaus and his emigration to the United States in 1933, it encapsulates the design concepts he developed while at the Bauhaus. *Homage to the Square* consists of hundreds of paintings, most of which were simply color variations on the same composition of concentric squares, as in our illustrated example (FIG. 33-58). The series reflected Albers's belief that art originates in "the discrepancy between physical fact and psychic effect."[62]

Because the composition in most of these paintings remains constant, the works succeed in revealing the relativity and instability of color perception. Albers varied the hue (color), saturation (brightness or dullness), and value or tone (lightness or darkness) of each square in the paintings in this series. As a result, the sizes of

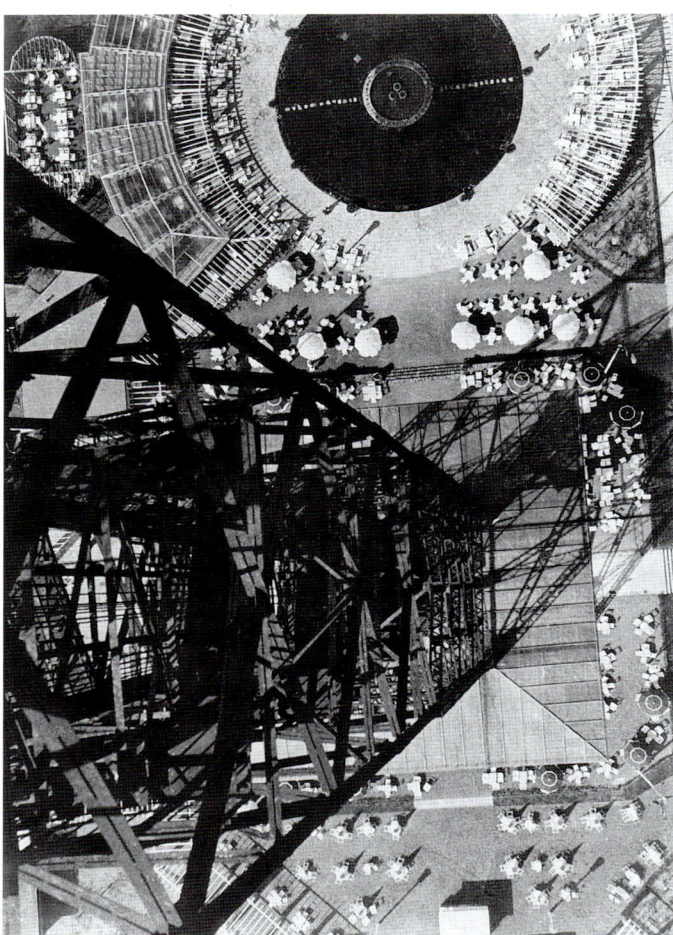

**33-57** LÁSZLÓ MOHOLY-NAGY, *From the Radio Tower Berlin*, 1928. Gelatin silver print. The Art Institute of Chicago, Chicago.

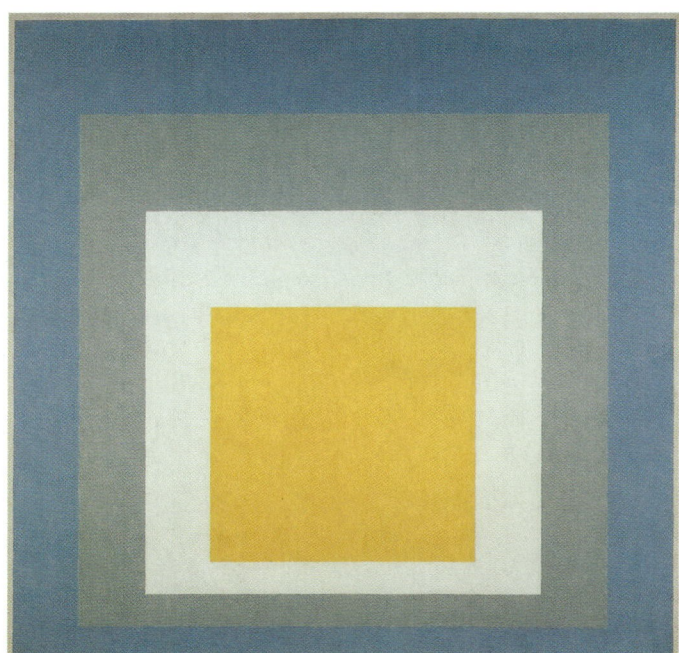

**33-58** JOSEF ALBERS, *Homage to the Square: "Ascending,"* 1953. Oil on composition board, 3′ 7½″ × 3′ 7½″. Collection of Whitney Museum of American Art, New York (purchase).

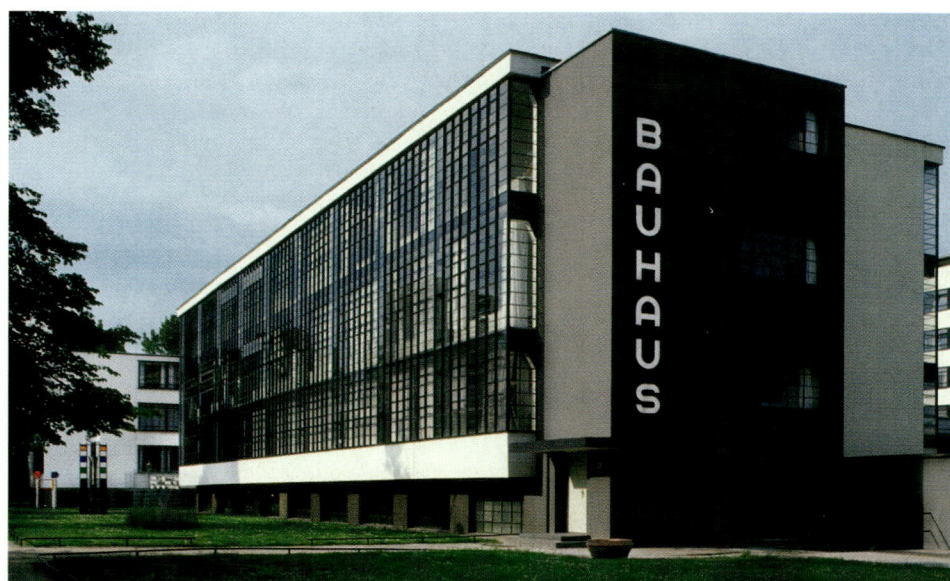

the squares from painting to painting appear to vary (although they remain the same), and the sensations emanating from the paintings range from clashing dissonance to delicate serenity. Albers explained his motivation for focusing on color juxtapositions: "They [the colors] are juxtaposed for various and changing visual effects. . . . Such action, reaction, interaction . . . is sought in order to make obvious how colors influence and change each other; that the same color, for instance—with different grounds or neighbors—looks different. . . . Such color deceptions prove that we see colors almost never unrelated to each other."[63]

In keeping with the Bauhaus's encouragement of proficiency in a wide range of media, Albers produced versions of *Homage* in oil painting on Masonite, in lithographs, in screenprints, on Aubusson (densely patterned French carpet) and other tapestries, and on large interior walls. Albers's ideas about design and color were widely disseminated, not only during his years at the Bauhaus but also during his subsequent residency in the United States.

**THE BAUHAUS MOVES TO DESSAU** After encountering increasing hostility from a new government elected in 1924, the Bauhaus was forced to move north to Dessau in early 1925. By this time, the Bauhaus program had matured. In a statement, Walter Gropius listed the school's goals more clearly:

- A decidedly positive attitude to the living environment of vehicles and machines.

- The organic shaping of things in accordance with their own current laws, avoiding all romantic embellishment and whimsy.

- Restriction of basic forms and colors to what is typical and universally intelligible.

- Simplicity in complexity, economy in the use of space, materials, time, and money.[64]

The building Gropius designed for the Bauhaus at Dessau visibly expressed these goals and can be seen as the Bauhaus's architectural manifesto. The building consisted of workshop and class areas, a dining room, a theater, a gymnasium, a wing with studio apartments, and an enclosed two-story bridge housing administrative offices. Of the major wings, the most dramatic was the Shop Block (FIG. 33-59). The Nazi government tore down this building, but the Bauhaus's main buildings were later reconstructed. Three stories tall, the Shop Block housed a printing shop and dye works facility, in addition to other work areas. The builders constructed the skeleton of reinforced concrete but set these supports well back, sheathing the entire structure in glass, creating a streamlined and light effect. This design's simplicity followed Gropius's dictum that architecture should avoid "all romantic embellishment and whimsy." Further, he realized the "economy in the use of space" articulated in his list of principles in his interior layout of the Shop Block, which consisted of large areas of free-flowing undivided space. Gropius believed such a spatial organization encouraged interaction and the sharing of ideas.

The interior decor of this Dessau building also reveals the comprehensiveness of the Bauhaus program. Because carpentry, furniture design, and weaving were all part of the Bauhaus curriculum, Gropius gave students and teachers the task of designing furniture and light fixtures for the building.

**TUBULAR STEEL BAUHAUS FURNITURE** One of the memorable furniture designs that emerged from the Bauhaus was the tubular steel chair (FIG. 33-60) crafted by the Hungarian MARCEL

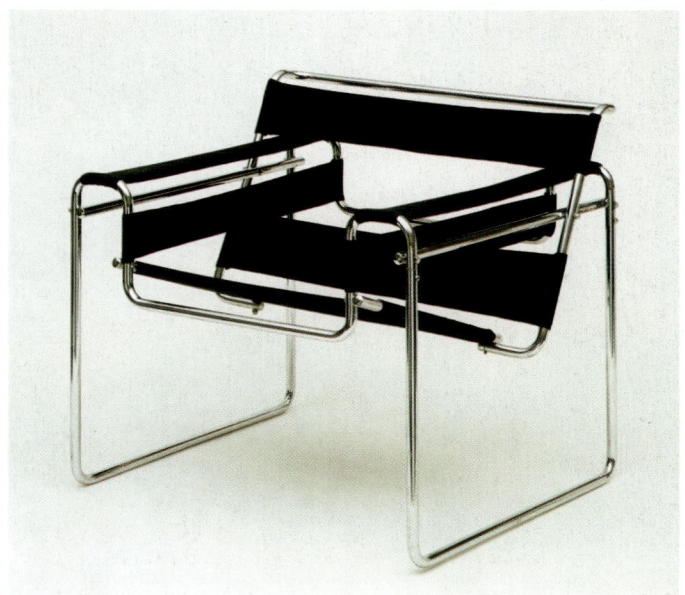

**33-60** MARCEL BREUER, tubular chair, 1925.

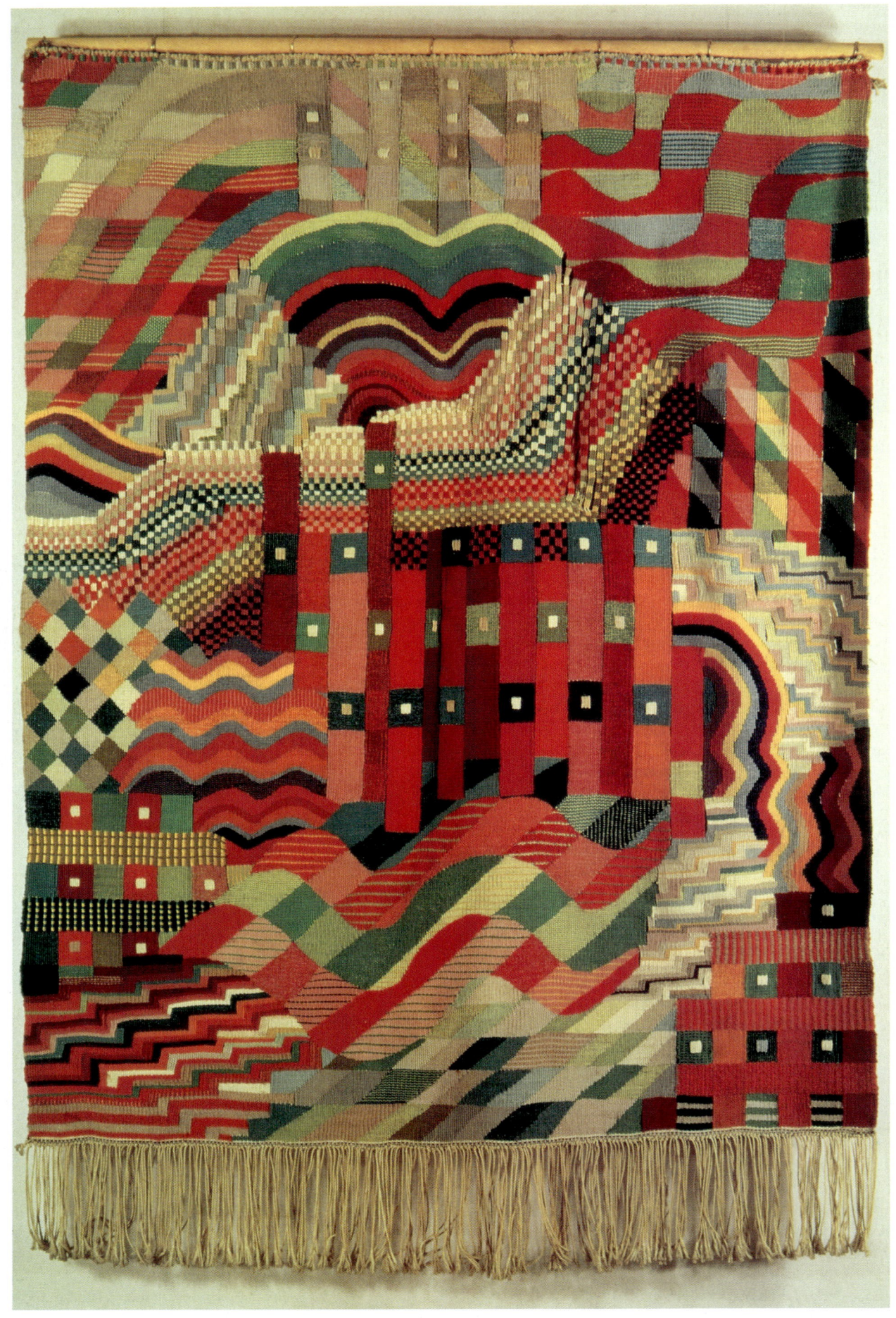

**33-61** GUNTA STÖLZL, Gobelin tapestry, 1926–1927. Linen and cotton.

BREUER (1902–1981). Breuer supposedly was inspired to use tubular steel while riding his bicycle and admiring the handlebars. In keeping with Bauhaus aesthetics, his chairs have a simplified, geometric look, and the leather or cloth supports add to the furniture's comfort and functionality. These chairs were also easily mass produced and thus stand as epitomes of the Bauhaus program.

This reductive, spare geometric aesthetic served many purposes—artistic, practical, and social. Bauhaus and De Stijl artists alike championed this style. Theo van Doesburg, an important De Stijl member, promoted this simplified artistic vocabulary, in part accepted because of its association with the avant-garde and progressive thought. Such an aesthetic also evoked the machine. Appropriately, it easily could be applied to all art forms, from stage design to advertising to architecture, and therefore was perfect for mass production. Even further, this aesthetic fit in well with Gropius's directive that artists, architects, and designers restrict their visual vocabulary "to what is typical and universally intelligible," revealing the social dimension of the Bauhaus agenda in its adherence to socialist principles.

**BAUHAUS FIBER CRAFTS** The universal intelligibility of this aesthetic is seen in a tapestry (FIG. **33-61**) designed by GUNTA STÖLZL (1897–1983), the only woman on the Bauhaus staff. More lively than many of the other Bauhaus-produced designs, this intricate and colorful work retains the emphasis on geometric patterns and clear intersection of verticals and horizontals. Stölzl was largely responsible for the vitality of the weaving workshop at the Bauhaus, creating numerous handwoven carpets, curtains, and runners. In accordance with Bauhaus principles, she also designed weavings for machine production. In terms of establishing production links with outside businesses, her department was one of the most successful at the school.

**"LESS IS MORE"** In 1928, Gropius left the Bauhaus, and architect LUDWIG MIES VAN DER ROHE (1886–1969) eventually took over the directorship, moving the school to Berlin. In his architecture and furniture, he made such a clear and elegant statement of the International Style (FIGS. 33-63 and 33-64) that his work had enormous influence on modern architecture. Taking as his motto "less is more" and calling his architecture "skin and bones," he had already fully formed his aesthetic when he conceived the model for a glass skyscraper building in 1921 (FIG. **33-62**). This model received extensive publicity when it was shown at the first Bauhaus exhibition in 1923. Working with glass provided Mies van der Rohe with new freedom and many expressive possibilities.

In the glass model, three irregularly shaped towers flow outward from a central court designed to hold a lobby, a porter's room, and a community center. Two cylindrical entrance shafts rise at the ends of the court, each containing elevators, stairways, and toilets. Wholly transparent, the perimeter walls reveal the regular horizontal patterning of the cantilevered floor planes and their thin vertical supporting elements. The bold use of glass sheathing and inset supports was, at the time, technically and aesthetically adventurous. A few years later, Gropius pursued it in his design for the Bauhaus building in Dessau. The weblike delicacy of the lines of the glass model, its radiance, and the illusion of movement created by reflection and by light changes seen

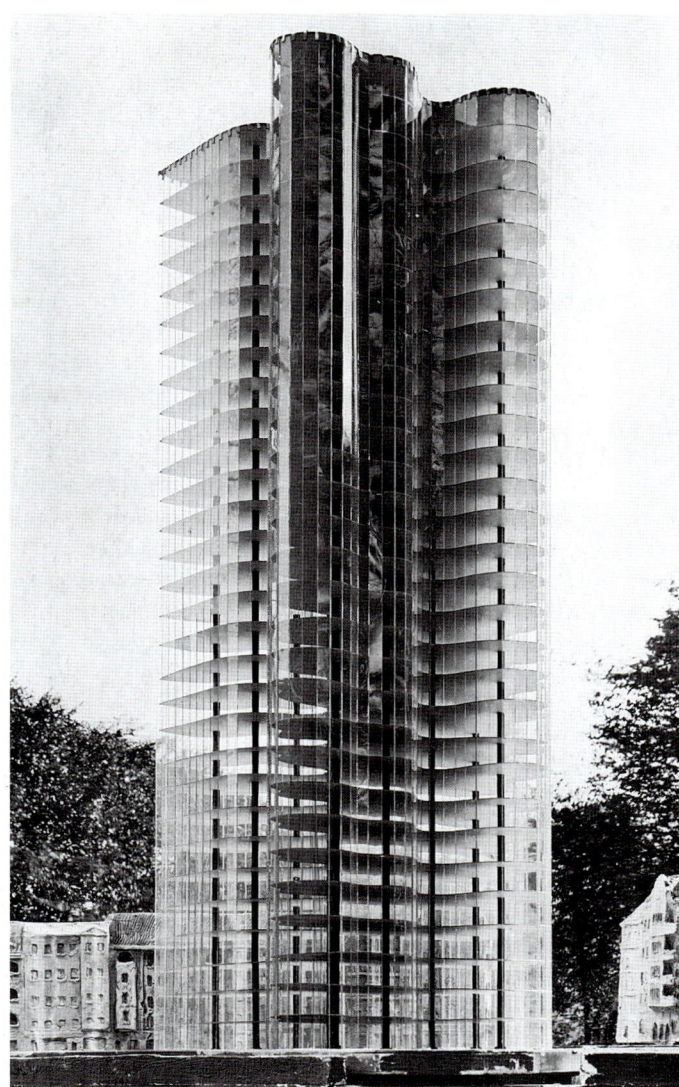

**33-62** LUDWIG MIES VAN DER ROHE, model for a glass skyscraper, Berlin, Germany, 1922 (no longer extant).

through it prefigured the design of many of the glass skyscrapers found in major cities throughout the world today.

**THE DEMISE OF THE BAUHAUS** In 1933, the Nazis finally occupied the Bauhaus and closed the school for good, one of Hitler's first acts after coming to power (see "'Degenerate Art,'" page 1012). During its 14-year existence, the beleaguered school graduated fewer than 500 students, yet it achieved legendary status. Its phenomenal impact extended beyond painting, sculpture, and architecture to interior design, graphic design, and advertising. Even further, the Bauhaus greatly influenced art education, and art schools everywhere structured their curricula in line with that the Bauhaus pioneered. The Bauhaus philosophy and aesthetic were disseminated widely, in large part by the numerous instructors who fled Nazi Germany, many to the United States. Walter Gropius and Marcel Breuer ended up at Harvard University, and Mies van der Rohe and László Moholy-Nagy moved to Chicago and taught there. Josef Albers moved to the United States in 1933, teaching at Black Mountain College in North Carolina and later at Yale University.

## *"Degenerate Art"*

Although avant-garde artists were often subjected to public ridicule, they suffered outright political persecution in Germany in the 1930s and 1940s. The Bauhaus endured years of harassment by the National Socialists (Nazis) before they forced it to close its doors in 1933. But perhaps the most dramatic and moving example of the persecution avant-garde artists suffered is the infamous *Entartete Kunst* (Degenerate Art) exhibition Adolf Hitler and the Nazis mounted in 1937.

Hitler aspired to become an artist himself, producing numerous drawings and paintings. These works reflected Hitler's firm belief that 19th-century realistic genre painting represented the zenith of Aryan art development. Accordingly, he denigrated anything that did not conform to that standard—in particular, avant-garde art. Turning his criticism into action, Hitler ordered the confiscation of more than 16,000 artworks he considered "degenerate." To publicize his condemnation of this art, he ordered his minister for public enlightenment and propaganda (and second in command), Joseph Goebbels, to organize a massive exhibition of this "degenerate art." Hitler defined it as works that "insult German feeling, or destroy or confuse natural form, or simply reveal an absence of adequate manual and artistic skill."[1] The term *degenerate* also had other specific connotations at the time and was used to designate supposedly inferior racial, sexual, and moral types. Hitler's order to Goebbels to target 20th-century avant-garde art for inclusion in this exhibition was intended to impress on viewers the general inferiority of the artists producing this work. To make this point all the more dramatic, Hitler ordered the organization of another exhibition, the *Grosse Deutsche Kunstausstellung* (Great German Art Exhibition), which ran concurrently and presented an extensive array of Nazi-approved conservative art.

*Entartete Kunst* opened in Munich on July 19, 1937, and included more than 650 paintings, sculptures, prints, and books. Among the 112 artists whose works the Nazis presented for ridicule were Ernst Barlach, Max Beckmann, Otto Dix, Max Ernst, George Grosz, Vassily Kandinsky, Ernst Kirchner, Paul Klee, Wilhelm Lehmbruck, Franz Marc, László Moholy-Nagy, Piet Mondrian, Emil Nolde, and Kurt Schwitters. The photograph here shows Hitler visiting the exhibition, pausing in front of the Dada wall, where works by Schwitters, Klee, and Kandinsky were initially deliberately hung askew. No avant-garde or even modernist artist was safe from Hitler's attack; only six of the artists in the exhibition were Jewish. Indeed, despite his status as a charter member of the Nazi party, Emil Nolde was singled out for particularly harsh treatment. The Nazis confiscated more than 1,000 of

Nolde's works from German museums and included 27 of them in the exhibition, more than for almost any other artist.

*Entartete Kunst* was immensely popular; roughly 20,000 viewers visited the show daily. By the end of its four-month run, it had attracted more than 2 million viewers, and nearly a million more viewed it as it traveled through Germany and Austria.

Clearly, artists needed monumental courage to defy tradition and produce avant-garde art. Especially in Germany in the 1930s and 1940s, in the face of Nazi persecution, commitment to the avant-garde demanded a resoluteness that extended beyond issues of aesthetics and beyond the confines of the art world. This persecution exacted an immense toll on these artists. Kirchner, for example, responded to the stress of Nazi pressure by destroying all his woodblocks and burning many of his works. A year later, in 1938, he committed suicide. Beckmann and his wife fled to Amsterdam on the exhibit's opening day, never to return to their homeland. Although *Entartete Kunst* was just a fragment of the tremendous destruction of life and spirit Hitler and the Nazis wrought, Hitler's insistence on suppressing and discrediting this art dramatically demonstrates art's power to affect viewers.

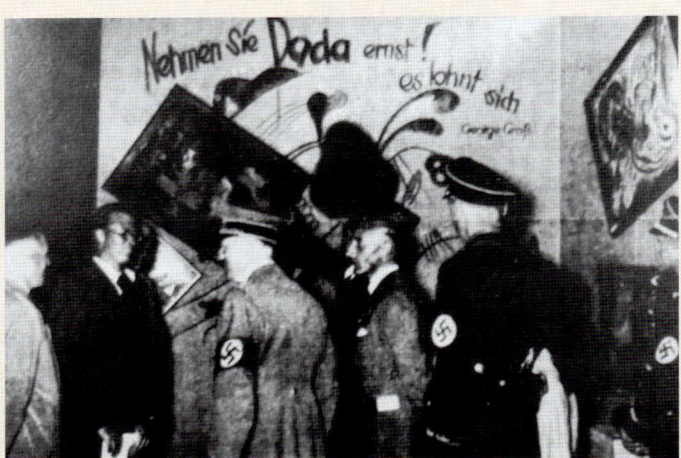

ADOLF HITLER, accompanied by Nazi commission members, including photographer Heinrich Hoffmann, Wolfgang Willrich, Walter Hansen, and painter Adolf Ziegler, viewing the *Entartete Kunst* show on July 16, 1937. The curators deliberately hung askew these works by Kandinsky, Klee, and Schwitters (although the paintings were subsequently straightened for the duration of the exhibition).

[1] Stephanie Barron, *"Degenerate Art": The Fate of the Avant-Garde in Nazi Germany* (Los Angeles: Los Angeles County Museum of Art, 1991), 19.

## *The International Style*

**FUNCTIONAL LIVING SPACES** The simple geometric aesthetic that Gropius and Mies van der Rohe developed became known as the *International Style* (different from the Early Renaissance painting style) because of its widespread popularity. Of the architectural purists—perhaps puritans—of this style, the first and staunchest adherent was the Swiss architect Charles-Edouard Jeanneret (1887–1965), called LE CORBUSIER. Trained in Paris

and Berlin, he was also a painter (see page 977) but was best known as an influential architect and theorist on modern architecture. As such, he applied himself to designing a functional living space, which he described as a "machine for living."[65]

The drawing for his Domino House project (FIG. **33-63**) shows the skeleton of his ideal dwelling. Every level can be used. Reinforced concrete slabs serve the double function of ceiling and floor, supported by thin steel columns rising freely inside the perimeter of the structure's interior spaces. The whole building is

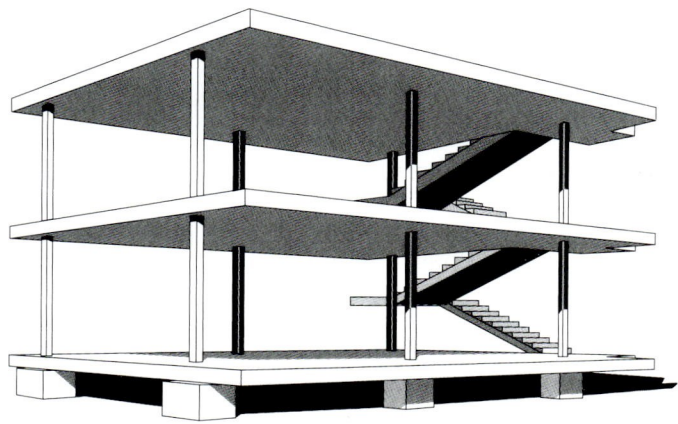

**33-63** LE CORBUSIER, perspective drawing for Domino House project, Marseilles, France, 1914.

raised above ground on short blocks so that the design uses the space underneath, as well as that on the roof. Exterior walls can be suspended from the projecting edges of the concrete slabs in this model, like free-hanging curtains. Because the skeleton supports itself, architects using this plan have complete freedom to subdivide the interior, wherever desired, with light walls that bear no structural load. This drawing illustrates one of the major principles associated with the International Style—the elimination of the bearing wall. New structural systems using materials such as structural steel and ferroconcrete (reinforced concrete) made this idea possible.

The scheme allows architects to provide for what Le Corbusier saw as the basic physical and psychological needs of every human being—sun, space, and vegetation combined with controlled temperature, good ventilation, and insulation against harmful and undesired noise. He also believed in basing dwelling designs on human scale, because the house is humankind's assertion within nature. The Domino House system's main principles were anticipated about half a decade earlier in the designs of the German architects Walter Gropius and Peter Behrens (with whom Le Corbusier worked early in his career). However, Le Corbusier's drawing depicts their ideas with such elegant simplicity that it has had enormous influence. It is the primary statement of the design concepts governing the structural principles used in many modern office buildings and skyscrapers.

**A "PURIST" HOUSE** Le Corbusier used the basic ideas of the Domino House project in many single-family dwellings. The most elegant is the Villa Savoye (FIG. **33-64**), located at Poissy-sur-Seine near Paris. This country house sits conspicuously within its site, tending to dominate it, and has a broad view of the landscape. A cube of lightly enclosed and deeply penetrated space, the Villa Savoye has only a partially confined ground floor (containing a three-car garage, bedrooms, a bathroom, and utility rooms). Much of the house's interior is open space, with the thin columns supporting the main living floor and the roof garden area. The major living rooms in the Villa Savoye are on the second floor, wrapping around an open central court and lighted by strip windows that run along the membranelike exterior walls. From the second floor court, a ramp leads up to a flat roof-terrace and garden protected by a curving windbreak along one side. The ostensible approach to Villa Savoye does not define an entrance; the building has no traditional facade. People must walk around and through the house to comprehend its layout. Spaces and masses interpenetrate so fluently that inside and outside space intermingle. The machine-planed smoothness of the surfaces, entirely without adornment; the slender ribbons of continuous windows; and the buoyant lightness of the whole fabric—all combine to reverse the effect of traditional country houses (compare Andrea Palladio's Villa Rotunda, FIG. 22-56, and John Vanbrugh's Blenheim Palace, FIG. 24-75).

Le Corbusier inverted the traditional design practice of placing light elements above and heavy ones below by refusing to enclose the ground story of the Villa Savoye with masonry walls. This openness makes the "load" of the Villa Savoye's upper stories appear to hover lightly on the slender column supports. Le Corbusier used several colors on this building's exterior—originally, a dark-green base, cream walls, and a rose-and-blue windscreen on top. They were a deliberate analogy for the colors in the contemporary machine-inspired Purist style of painting (FIG. 33-18) he actively practiced.

**33-64** LE CORBUSIER, Villa Savoye, Poissy-sur-Seine, France, 1929.

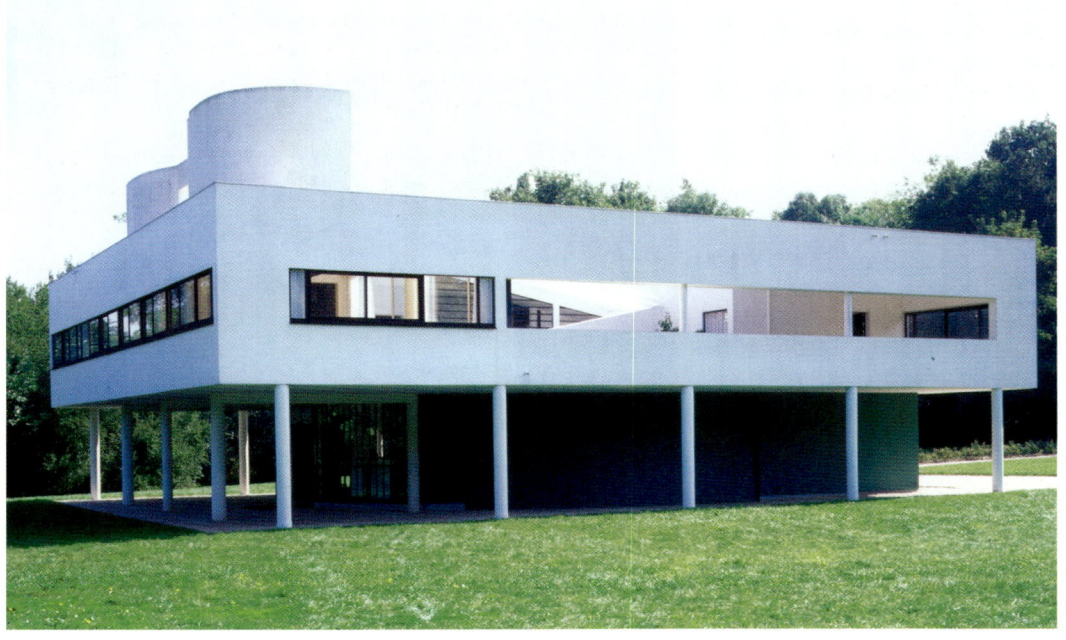

**HUMANE CITY PLANNING** The Villa Savoye was a marvelous house for a single family, but, like the De Stijl architects, Le Corbusier also dreamed of extending his ideas of the house as a "machine for living" to designs for efficient and humane cities. He saw great cities as spiritual workshops and he proposed to correct the deficiencies in existing cities caused by poor traffic circulation, inadequate living units, and the lack of space for recreation and exercise. Le Corbusier suggested replacing such cities with three types of new communities. Vertical cities would house workers and the business and service industries. Linear-industrial cities would run as belts along the routes between the vertical cities and would serve as centers for the people and processes involved in manufacturing. Finally, separate centers would be constructed for people involved in intensive agricultural activity. Le Corbusier's cities would provide for human cultural needs in addition to serving every person's physical, mental, and emotional comfort needs.

The Domino House project was a key part of Le Corbusier's thinking because the module design could be repeated almost indefinitely, both horizontally and vertically. Its volumes could be manipulated and interlocked to provide interior spaces of different sizes and heights. It was not site specific and could stand comfortably in any setting. Later in Le Corbusier's career, he designed a few of his vertical cities, most notably the Unité d'Habitation in Marseilles (1945–1952). He also created the master plan for the entire city of Chandigarh, the capital city of the Punjab, India (1950–1957). He ended his career with a personal expressive style in his design of the Chapel of Notre Dame du Haut at Ronchamp (see FIGS. 34-42 and 34-43).

## Art Deco

In theory, the new architecture (particularly that associated with the Bauhaus) rejected ornament of any kind. Pure form emerged from functional structure and required no decoration. Yet popular taste still favored ornamentation, especially in public architecture. A movement in the 1920s and 1930s sought to upgrade industrial design in competition with "fine art." Proponents wanted to work new materials into decorative patterns that could be either machined or handcrafted and that could, to a degree, reflect the simplifying trend in architecture. A remote descendant of Art Nouveau, this movement became known as *Art Deco*. (Like its predecessor, it was an event in the history of industrial design, not in the history of architecture.) Art Deco had universal application — to buildings, interiors, furniture, utensils, jewelry, fashions, illustration, and commercial products of every sort. Art Deco products have a "streamlined," elongated symmetrical aspect; simple flat shapes alternate with shallow volumes in hard patterns. The concept of streamlining predominated in industrial design circles in the 1930s and involved the use of organic, tapered shapes and forms. Derived from nature, these simple forms are inherently aerodynamic, making them technologically efficient (because of their reduced resistance as they move through air or water) as well as aesthetically pleasing. Designers adopted streamlined designs for trains and cars, and the popular appeal of these designs led to their use in an array of objects, from machines to consumer products. This streamlined look was integral to Art Deco, which acquired its name at the famous Exposition des Arts Décoratifs et Industriels Modernes (Exposition of Decorative and Modern Industrial Arts), held in Paris in 1925. As a cultural phenomenon, Art Deco is associated with Jazz Age flair, flippancy, and elegance and with the gorgeous salons of the great ocean liners ferrying the carefree rich in the days of the "lost generation."

**A GLITTERING SPIRE** Art Deco's exemplary masterpiece is the stainless-steel spire of the Chrysler Building in New York City (FIG. 33-65), designed by WILLIAM VAN ALEN (1882–1954). The building and spire are monuments to the fabulous 1920s, when American millionaires and corporations competed with one another to raise the tallest skyscrapers in the biggest cities. Built up of diminishing fan shapes, the spire glitters triumphantly in the sky, a resplendent crown honoring the business achievements of the great auto manufacturer. As a temple of commerce, the Chrysler Building was dedicated to the principles and success of American business, before its chastening in the Great Depression.

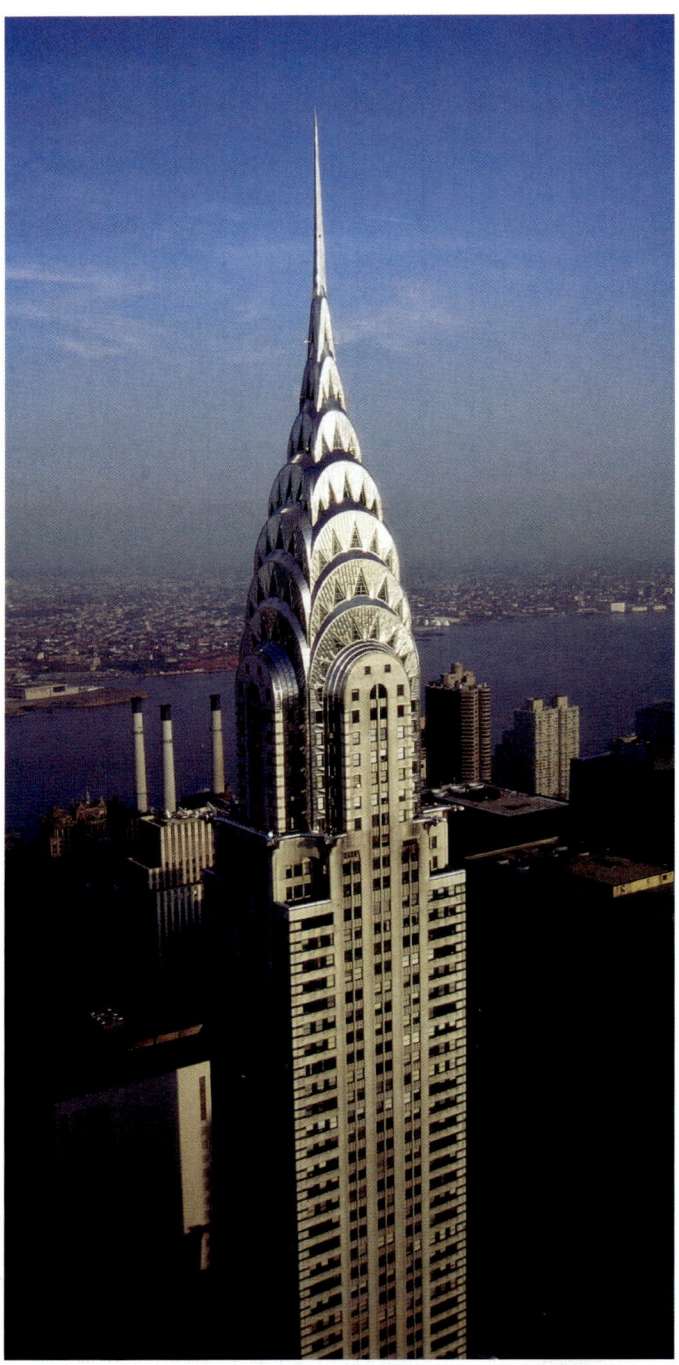

**33-65** WILLIAM VAN ALEN, Chrysler Building, New York, New York, 1928–1930. Spire of stainless steel, overall height 1,048′.

## EMPHASIZING THE ORGANIC

It was impossible for early-20th-century artists to ignore the increasingly intrusive expansion of mechanization and growth of technology. However, not all artists embraced these developments, as had the Futurists. In contrast, many artists attempted to overcome the predominance of mechanization in society by immersing themselves in a search for the organic and natural.

### *"Natural" Architecture*

One of the most striking personalities in the development of early-20th-century architecture was FRANK LLOYD WRIGHT (1867–1959). Born in Wisconsin, Wright attended a few classes at the University of Wisconsin in Madison before moving to Chicago, where he eventually joined the firm headed by Louis Sullivan (see FIGS. 29-59 and 29-60). Wright set out to create an "architecture of democracy."[66] Early influences were the volumetric shapes in a set of educational blocks the German educator Friedrich Froebel (from Wright's childhood) designed, the organic unity of a Japanese building Wright saw at the Columbian Exposition in Chicago in 1893, and a Jeffersonian belief in individualism and populism. Always a believer in architecture as "natural" and "organic," Wright saw it as serving free individuals who have the right to move within a "free" space, envisioned as a nonsymmetrical design interacting spatially with its natural surroundings. He sought to develop an organic unity of planning, structure, materials, and site. Wright identified the principle of continuity as fundamental to understanding his view of organic unity: "Classic architecture was all fixation. . . . Now why not let

walls, ceilings, floors become seen as component parts of each other? . . . You may see the appearance in the surface of your hand contrasted with the articulation of the bony structure itself. This ideal, profound in its architectural implications . . . I called . . . continuity."[67]

Wright manifested his vigorous originality early, and by 1900 he had arrived at a style entirely his own. In his work during the first decade of the 20th century, his cross-axial plan and his fabric of continuous roof planes and screens defined a new domestic architecture.

A "WANDERING" PRAIRIE HOUSE Wright fully expressed these elements and concepts in Robie House (FIG. 33-66), built between 1907 and 1909. Like other buildings in the Chicago area he designed at about the same time, this was called a "prairie house." Wright conceived the long, sweeping, ground-hugging lines, unconfined by abrupt wall limits, as reaching out toward and capturing the expansiveness of the Midwest's great flatlands. Abandoning all symmetry, the architect eliminated a facade, extended the roofs far beyond the walls, and all but concealed the entrance. Wright filled the "wandering" plan of the Robie House (FIG. 33-67) with intricately joined spaces (some large and open, others closed), grouped freely around a great central fireplace. (He believed strongly in the hearth's age-old domestic significance.) Wright designed enclosed patios, overhanging roofs, and strip windows to provide unexpected light sources and glimpses of the outdoors to viewers as they move through the interior space. These elements, together with the open ground plan, create a sense of space in motion, inside and out. Wright matched his new and fundamental interior spatial arrangement in his exterior treatment; the flow of interior space determined the sharp angular placement of exterior walls.

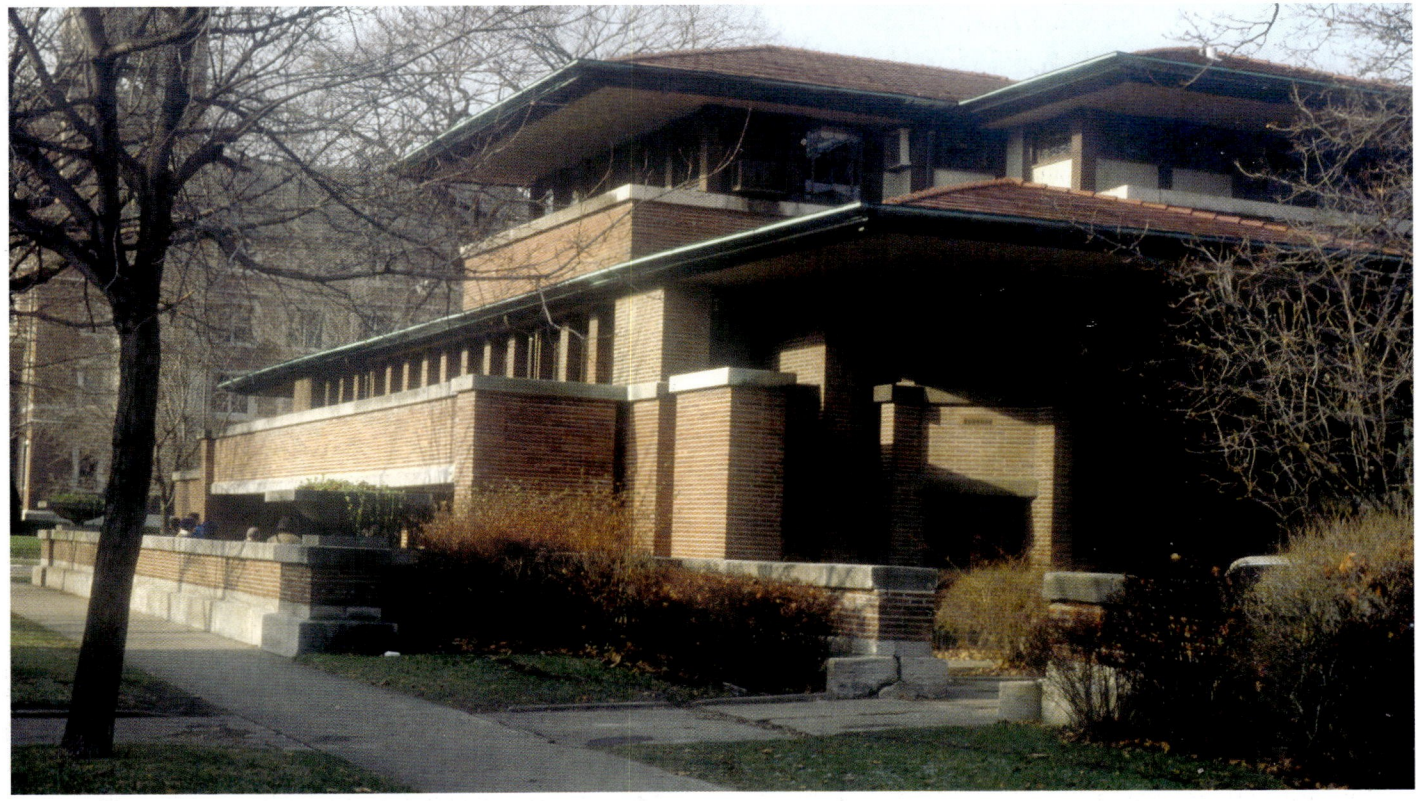

**33-66** FRANK LLOYD WRIGHT, Robie House, Chicago, Illinois, 1907–1909.

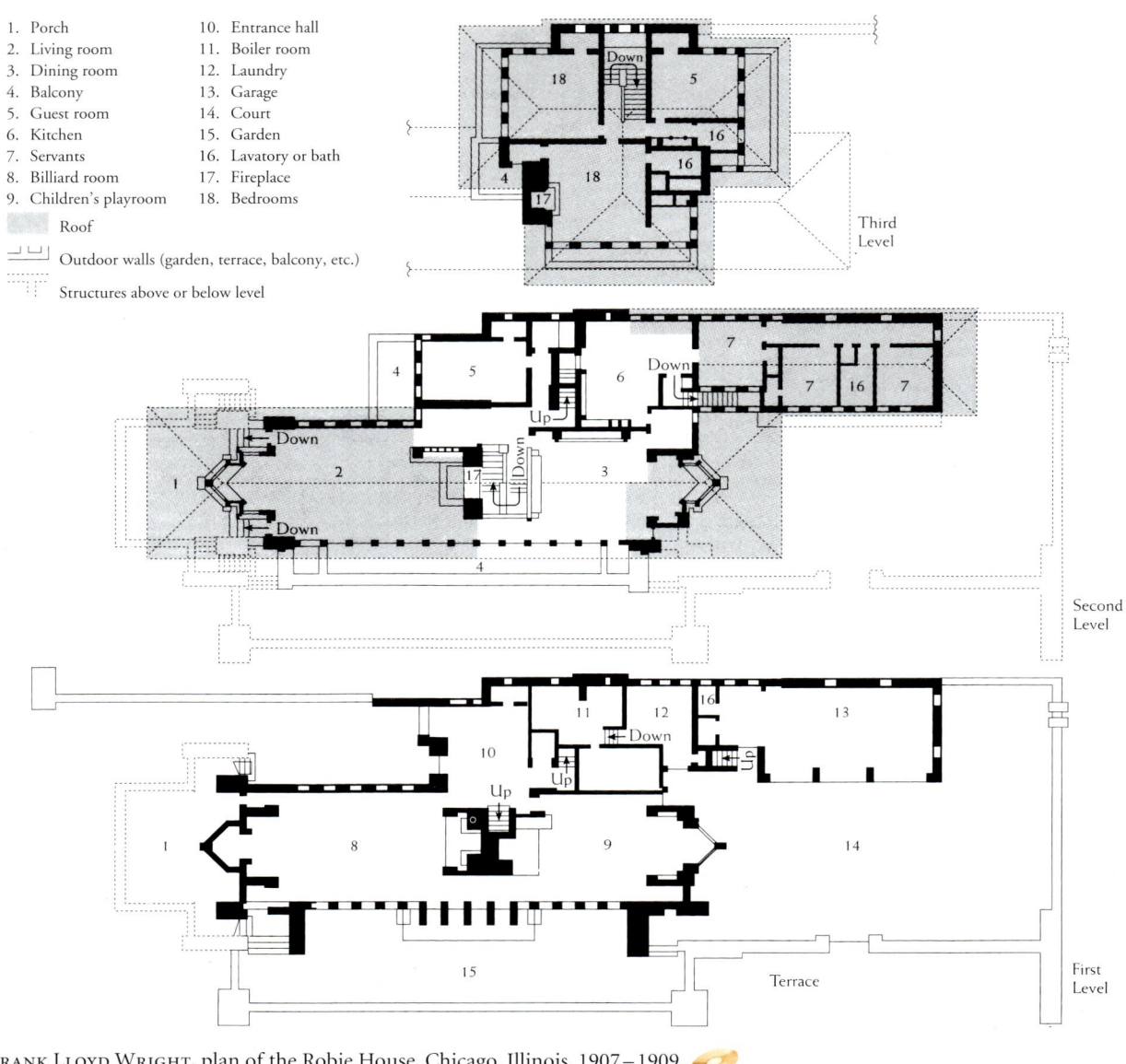

1. Porch
2. Living room
3. Dining room
4. Balcony
5. Guest room
6. Kitchen
7. Servants
8. Billiard room
9. Children's playroom
10. Entrance hall
11. Boiler room
12. Laundry
13. Garage
14. Court
15. Garden
16. Lavatory or bath
17. Fireplace
18. Bedrooms

Roof

Outdoor walls (garden, terrace, balcony, etc.)

Structures above or below level

Third Level

Second Level

First Level

Terrace

**33-67** FRANK LLOYD WRIGHT, plan of the Robie House, Chicago, Illinois, 1907–1909.

**A HOUSE WITH WATERFALL** The Robie House is an example of Wright's "naturalism"—his adjustment of a building to its site. However, in this particular case, the confines of the city lot constrained the building-to-site relationship more than did the sites of some of Wright's more expansive suburban and country homes. The Kaufmann House, nicknamed "Fallingwater" (FIG. **33-68**) and designed as a weekend retreat at Bear Run near Pittsburgh, is a prime example of the latter. Perched on a rocky hillside over a small waterfall, this structure extends the Robie House's blocky masses in all four directions. The contrast in textures between concrete, painted metal, and natural stones in its walls enlivens its shapes, as does Wright's use of full-length strip windows to create a stunning interweaving of interior and exterior space. Unfortunately, Fallingwater, one of Wright's most famous buildings, has been plagued in recent years with structural problems due to the unusual terraced design (see "Saving Fallingwater from Falling into the Water," page 1017).

The implied message of Wright's new architecture was space, not mass—a space designed to fit the patron's life and enclosed

and divided as required. Wright took special pains to meet his clients' requirements, often designing all the accessories of a house (including, in at least one case, gowns for his client's wife!). In the late 1930s, he acted on a cherished dream to provide good architectural design for less prosperous people by adapting the ideas of his prairie house to plans for smaller, less-expensive dwellings. These residences, known as Usonian houses, became templates for suburban housing developments in the post–World War II housing boom.

The publication of Wright's plans brought him a measure of fame in Europe, especially in Holland and Germany. The issuance in Berlin in 1910 of a portfolio of his work and an exhibition of his designs the following year stimulated younger architects to adopt some of his ideas about open plans that afforded clients freedom. Some 40 years before his career ended, his work was already of revolutionary significance. The modern architect Mies van der Rohe wrote in 1940 that the "dynamic impulse from [Wright's] work invigorated a whole generation. His influence was strongly felt even when it was not actually visible."[68]

## Saving Fallingwater from Falling into the Water

The Kaufmann House, built for Pittsburgh department store magnate Edgar Kaufmann, Sr., has long been among the most notable of Frank Lloyd Wright's architectural accomplishments; scholars consider it an icon of modernist architectural design. Ever since the completion of this residence, better known as Fallingwater, architects and the public alike have marveled at the fluid interplay between interior and exterior. In designing Fallingwater, Wright, in keeping with his commitment to an "architecture of democracy," sought to find a way to incorporate the structure more fully into the site, thereby ensuring a fluid, dynamic exchange between the interior of the house and the natural environment outside. Indeed, the Kaufmann House's nickname is derived from the fact that the house overhangs a waterfall on Bear Creek Run in Bear Run, Pennsylvania. Interestingly, rather than build the house overlooking or next to the waterfall, Wright decided to build it *over* the waterfall, because he believed that the inhabitants would become desensitized to the waterfall's presence and power if they merely overlooked it. To take advantage of the location, Frank Lloyd Wright designed a series of terraces that extend on three levels from a central core structure. Wright designed these terraces as independent cantilevers, or self-supporting shelves. Over time, however, the terraces drooped and became unstable. Further, long-term stress on the main level's beams resulted in cracks in the beams, causing the floors to sag. In short, Fallingwater was in danger of collapse. The current owner of the house, the Western Pennsylvania Conservancy, contracted with an engineering firm to perform structural repairs as part of a larger, $11.5 million restoration project. The major focus of the work, which began in November 2001, involved the installation of post-tensioning cables to stabilize the cantilevers. These cables, laid in conduits submerged in concrete, were then pulled taut to support the sagging floors.

Restoration was completed in 2003. Visitors can now view Fallingwater in a state close to its original, providing a wonderful opportunity to experience Frank Lloyd Wright's unique approach to space and architectural design.

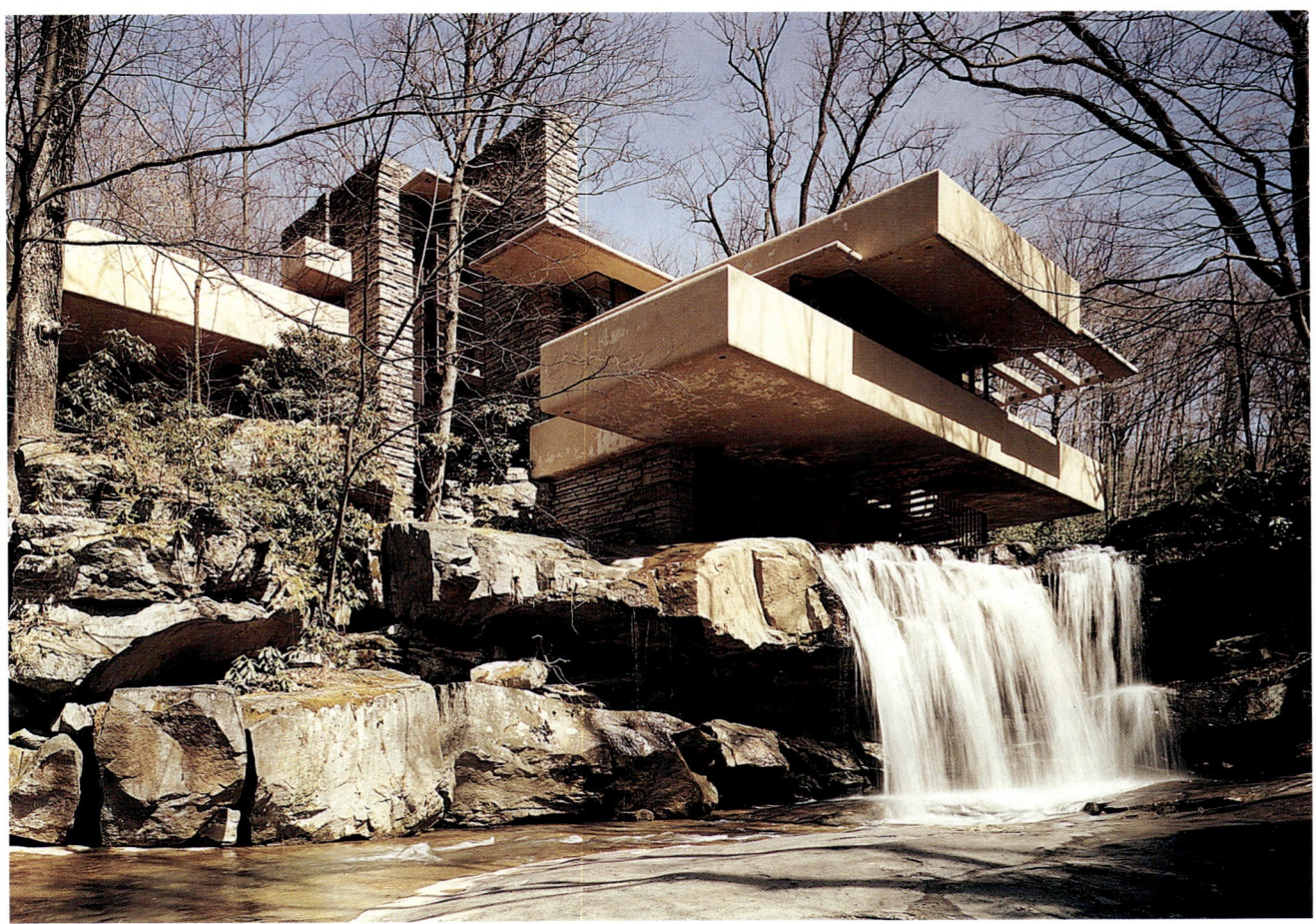

**33-68** FRANK LLOYD WRIGHT, Kaufmann House (Fallingwater), Bear Run, Pennsylvania, 1936–1939.

## Organic Sculpture

**SEEKING THE ESSENCE OF FLIGHT** Romanian artist CONSTANTIN BRANCUSI (1876–1957) was one of many sculptors eager to produce works emphasizing the natural or organic. Often composed of softly curving surfaces and ovoid forms, his sculptures refer, directly or indirectly, to the cycle of life. Brancusi sought to move beyond surface appearances to capture the essence or spirit of the object depicted. He claimed: "What is real is not the external form but the essence of things. Starting from this truth it is impossible for anyone to express anything essentially real by imitating its exterior surface."[69] Brancusi's ability to design rhythmic, elegant sculptures conveying the essence of his subjects is evident in *Bird in Space* (FIG. **33-69**). Clearly not a literal depiction of a bird, the work is the final result of a long process. Brancusi started with the image of a bird at rest with its wings folded at its sides and ended with an abstract columnar form sharply tapered at each end. Despite the abstraction, the sculpture retains the suggestion of a bird about to soar in free flight through the heavens. Even further, Brancusi succeeded in capturing the essence of flight. The highly reflective surface of the polished bronze does not allow the eye to linger on the sculpture itself (as do, for example, Rodin's agitated and textured surfaces; see FIG. 29-50). Instead, the viewer's eye follows the gleaming reflection along the delicate curves right off the tip of the work, thereby inducing a feeling of flight. Brancusi stated, "All my life I have sought the essence of flight. Don't look for the mysteries. I give you pure joy. Look at the sculptures until you see them. Those nearest to God have seen them."[70]

Despite the seeming grandiosity of those claims, Brancusi was deeply immersed in exploring the emotional chords that sculpture could strike in its viewers. Indeed, he envisioned many of his works, including this one, enlarged to monumental scale. The subtitle for this work was *Project of Bird Which, When Enlarged, Will Fill the Sky*, and the sculptor spoke of the work's ability on that scale to fill viewers with comfort and peace. Brancusi always paid special attention to the intrinsic qualities of the materials he used. He made sculptures in wood, marble, stone, and bronze. In each medium, he tried to create forms that respected and worked with the nature of the material, extracting from it its maximum expressive effect.

**EVOKING ORGANIC VITALITY** BARBARA HEPWORTH (1903–1975) developed her own kind of essential sculptural form, combining pristine shape with a sense of organic vitality. She sought a sculptural idiom that would express her sense both of nature and the landscape and of the person who is in and observes nature. As she explained it:

> The forms which have had special meaning for me since childhood have been the standing form (which is the translation of my feeling towards the human being standing in landscape); the two forms (which is the tender relationship of one living thing beside another); and the closed form, such as the oval, spherical, or pierced form (sometimes incorporating colour) which translates for me the association and meaning of gesture in the landscape. . . . In all these shapes the translation of what one feels about man and nature must be conveyed by the sculptor in terms of mass, inner tension, and rhythm, scale in relation to our human size, and the quality of surface which speaks through our hands and eyes.[71]

By 1929, Hepworth arrived at a breakthough that evolved into an enduring and commanding element in her work from that

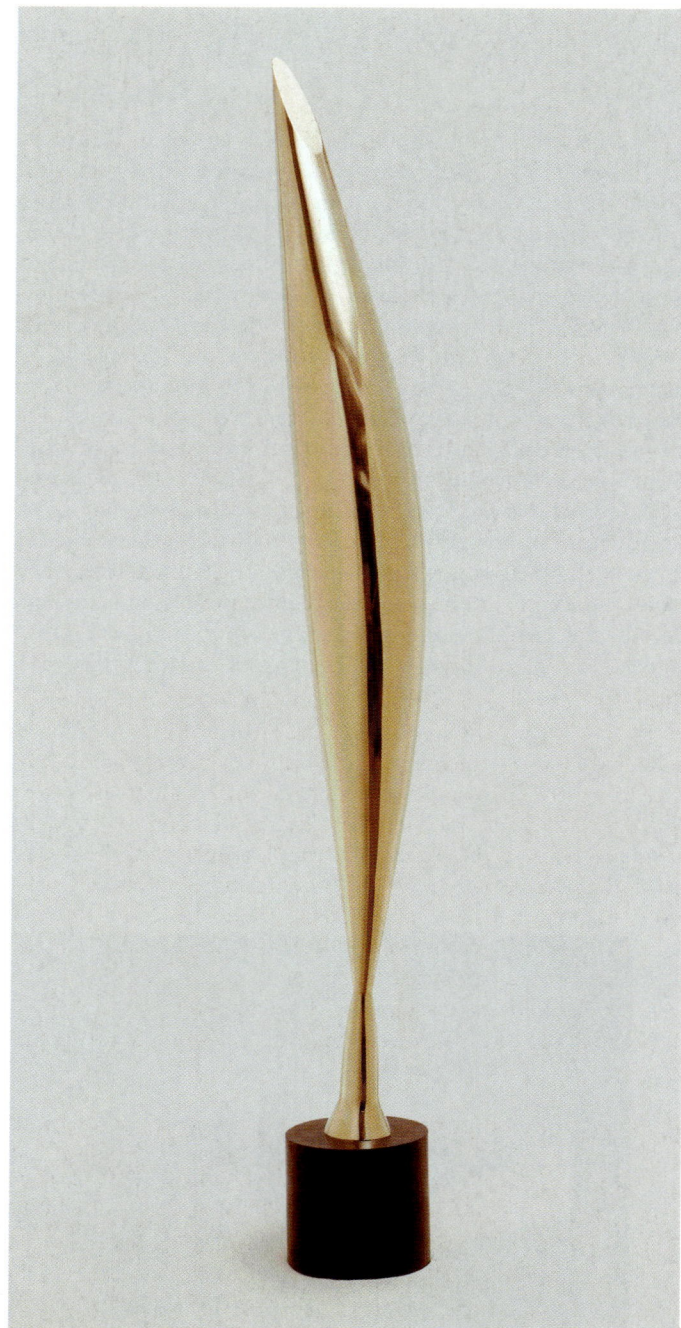

**33-69** CONSTANTIN BRANCUSI, *Bird in Space*, 1928. Bronze (unique cast), 4′ 6″ × 8″ × 6″. Museum of Modern Art, New York (given anonymously).

point on, and that represents her major contribution to the history of sculpture: the use of the hole, or void. Of particular note is the fact that Hepworth introduced the hole, or negative space, in her sculpture as an abstract element—it doesn't represent anything specific—and one that is as integral and important to the sculpture as its mass. *Oval Sculpture (No. 2)*, FIG. **33-70**, is a plaster cast of an earlier wooden sculpture Hepworth carved in 1943. Pierced in four places, *Oval Sculpture* is as much defined by the smooth, curving holes as by the volume of white plaster. Like the forms in all of Hepworth's mature works, those in *Oval Sculpture* are basic and universal, expressing a sense of eternity's timelessness.

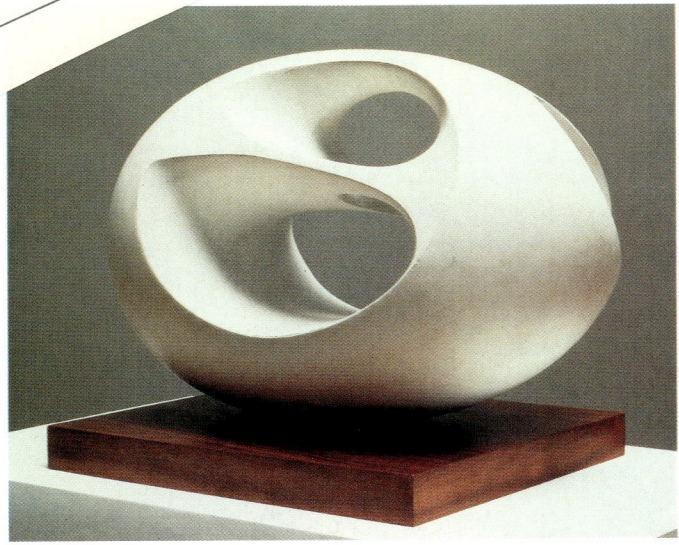

33-70 BARBARA HEPWORTH, *Oval Sculpture (No. 2)*, 1943. Plaster cast, $11\frac{1}{4}''$ × 1' $4\frac{1}{4}''$ × 10''. Tate Gallery, London. 🔴

**CELEBRATING THE NATURAL CONDITION** English sculptor HENRY MOORE (1898–1986) shared Hepworth's interest in the hole or void and Brancusi's profound love of nature and knowledge of organic forms and materials. Moore maintained that every "material has its own individual qualities" and that these qualities could play a role in the creative process: "It is only when the sculptor works direct, when there is an active relationship with his material, that the material can take its part in the shaping of an idea."[72] Accordingly, the forms and lines of Moore's lead and stone sculptures tend to emphasize the material's hardness and solidity, whereas his fluid wood sculptures draw attention to the flow of the wood grain. One major recurring theme in Moore's work is the

reclining female figure with simplified and massive forms. A tiny photograph of a Chac Mool figure from pre-Columbian Mexico originally inspired this motif. Thought perhaps to represent gods or worshipers bearing offerings, Chac Mool figures usually were carved in stone, in semireclining positions, with their heads turned abruptly to one side.

Although viewers can recognize a human figure in most of Moore's works, the artist simplified and abstracted the figure, attempting to express a universal truth beyond the physical world. He summarized his feelings about abstract figurative form in two passages from essays written in the 1930s:

> Because a work does not aim at reproducing natural appearances, it is not, therefore, an escape from life—but may be a penetration into reality. . . . My sculpture is becoming less representational, less an outward visual copy . . . but only because I believe that in this way I can present the human psychological content of my work with greatest directness and intensity.[73]

*Reclining Figure* (FIG. **33-71**) reveals Moore's expressive handling of the human form and his responsiveness to his chosen material—here, elm wood. The figure's massive shapes suggest Surrealist biomorphic forms (FIG. 33-50), but Moore's recumbent woman is also a powerful earth mother whose undulant forms and hollows suggest nurturing human energy. Similarly, they evoke the contours of the Yorkshire hills where Moore was raised and the wind-polished surfaces of weathered wood and stone. The sculptor heightened the allusions to landscape and to Surrealist organic forms in his work by interplaying mass and void, based on the intriguing qualities of cavities in nature. As he explained, "The hole connects one side to the other, making it immediately more three-dimensional. . . . The mystery of the hole—the mysterious fascination of caves in hillsides and cliffs."[74] The concern with the void—the holes—recalls the sculpture of artists such as Barbara Hepworth (FIG. 33-70), whose

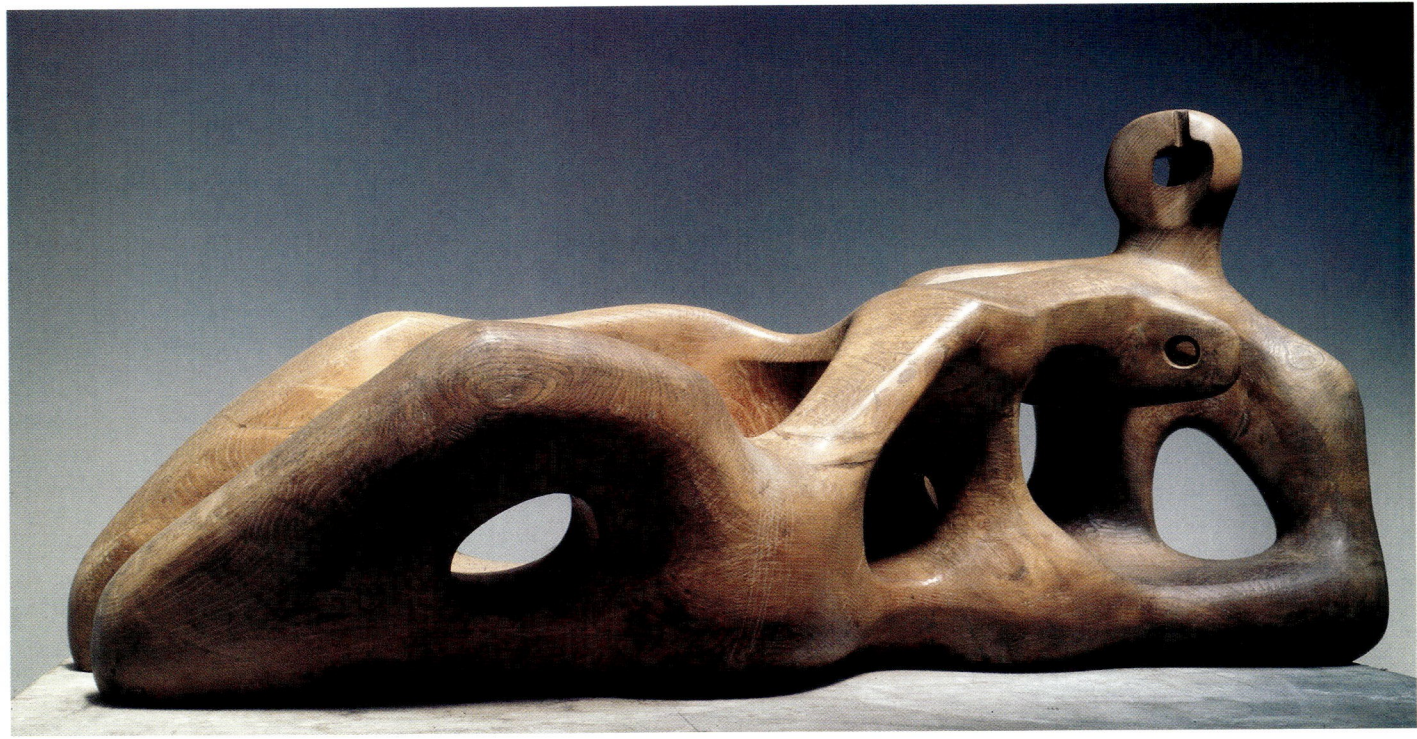

33-71 HENRY MOORE, *Reclining Figure*, 1939. Elm wood, 3' 1'' × 6' 7'' × 2' 6''. Detroit Institute of Arts, Detroit (Founders Society purchase with funds from the Dexter M. Ferry Jr. Trustee Corporation). 🔴

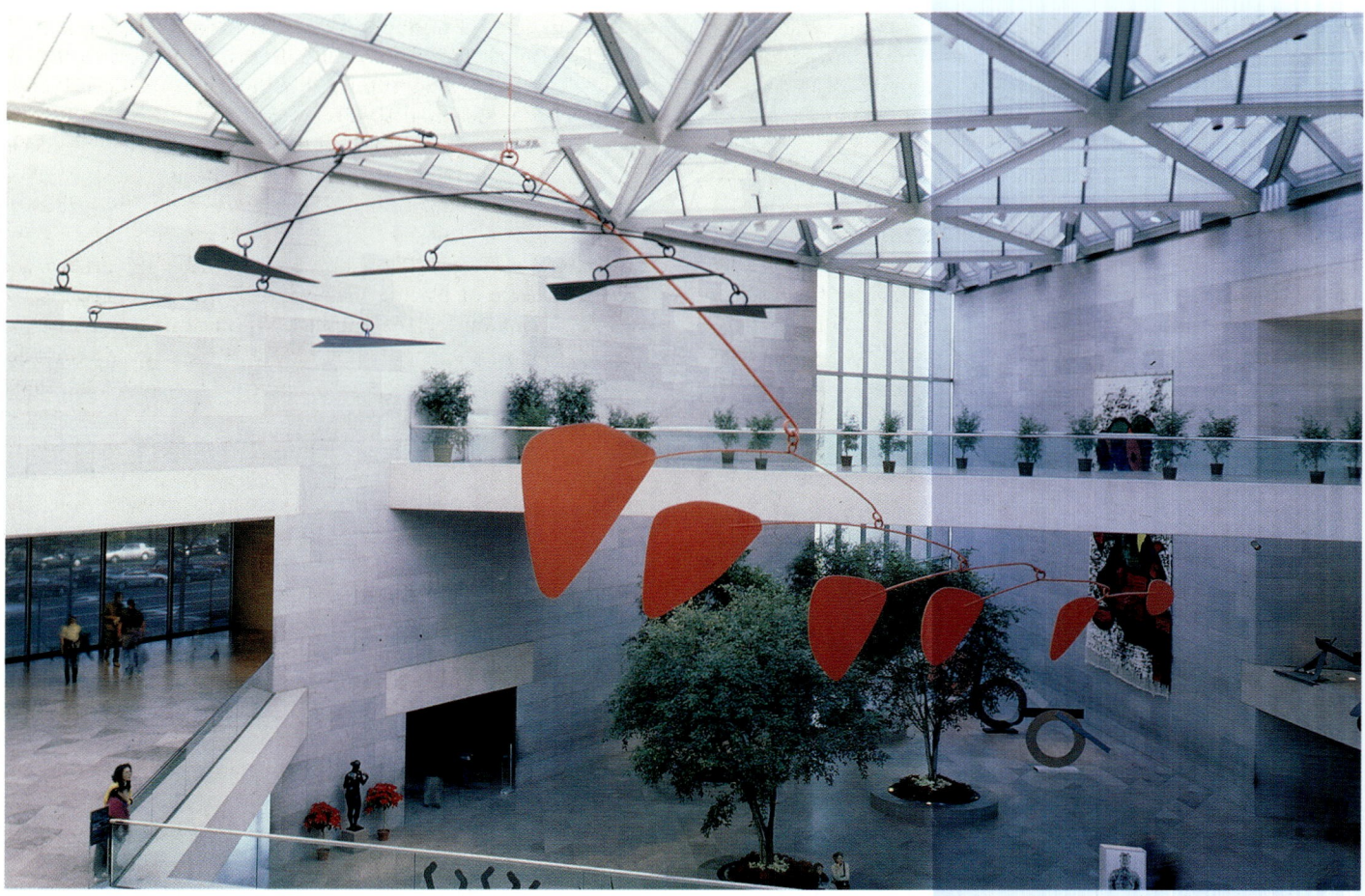

**33-72** ALEXANDER CALDER, untitled, 1976. Aluminum honeycomb, tubing, and paint, 29′ 10$\frac{1}{2}$″ × 76′. National Gallery of Art, Washington, D.C. (gift of the Collectors Committee).

work influenced him, and Aleksandr Archipenko (FIG. 33-16). The contours and openings of *Reclining Figure* follow the grain of the wood. Above all, the work combines the organic vocabulary central to Moore's philosophy—bone shapes, eroded rocks, and geologic formations—to communicate the human form's fluidity, dynamism, and evocative nature.

**LARGE-SCALE KINETIC SCULPTURES** The belief of Moholy-Nagy (FIG. 33-57) that modern experience is spatial-temporal and his interest in new materials could have served as a program for the American sculptor ALEXANDER CALDER (1898–1976). Using his thorough knowledge of engineering techniques, Calder combined nonobjective organic forms and motion to create a new kind of sculpture that expressed reality's innate dynamism. Both the artist's father and grandfather were sculptors, but Calder initially studied mechanical engineering. Fascinated all his life by motion, he explored that phenomenon and its relationship to three-dimensional form in much of his sculpture.

As a young artist in Paris in the late 1920s, Calder invented a circus full of wire-based miniature performers that he activated into realistic analogues of the motion of their counterparts in life. After a visit to Mondrian's studio in the early 1930s, Calder was filled with a desire to set the brightly colored rectangular shapes in the Dutch painter's compositions into motion. (Marcel Duchamp, intrigued by Calder's early motorized and hand-cranked examples of moving abstract pieces, named them mobiles.) Calder's engineering skills soon helped him to fashion a series of balanced structures hanging from rods, wires, and

colored, organically shaped plates, such as this untitled work (FIG. **33-72**), designed for the National Gallery of Art in Washington, D.C. The sculptor carefully planned each nonmechanized mobile so that any air current would set the parts moving to create a constantly shifting dance in space. When air currents activate the sculpture, its patterns suggest clouds, leaves, or waves blown by the wind.

Mondrian's work may have provided the initial inspiration for the mobiles, but their organic shapes resemble those in Joan Miró's Surrealist paintings (FIG. 33-50) and Calder's love of nature actually generated them. Indeed, Calder's forms can be read as either geometric or organic. Geometrically, the lines suggest circuitry and rigging, and the shapes are derived from circles and ovoid forms. Organically, the lines suggest nerve axons, and the shapes are reminiscent of cells, leaves, fins, wings, and other bioforms.

# ART AS POLITICAL STATEMENT
## IN THE 1930S

Throughout history, art has regularly served political ends and addressed political themes and issues. With the phenomenal upheaval the Western world experienced during the first half of the 20th century—for example, World War I, the Russian Revolution, the Spanish Civil War, and World War II—numerous artists felt compelled to speak out and use their art to make a political statement.

**DEPICTING SOCIAL INJUSTICE** The American painter BEN SHAHN (1898–1969) used photographs as a point of departure for semiabstract figures he felt would express the emotions and facts of social injustice that were his main subject throughout his career. Shahn came to the United States from Lithuania in 1906 and trained as a lithographer before broadening the media in which he worked to include easel painting, photography, and murals. He focused on the lives of ordinary people and the injustices often done to them by the structure of an impersonal society. In the early 1930s, he completed a cycle of 23 paintings and prints inspired by the trial and execution of the two Italian anarchists Nicola Sacco and Bartolomeo Vanzetti. Accused of killing two men in a holdup in 1920 in South Braintree, Massachusetts, the Italians were convicted in a trial that many people thought resulted in a grave miscarriage of justice. Shahn felt he had found in this story a subject the equal of any in Western art history: "Suddenly I realized . . . I was living through another crucifixion."[75] Basing many of the works in this cycle on newspaper photographs of the events, Shahn devised a style that adapted his knowledge of Synthetic Cubism and his training in commercial art to an emotionally expressive use of flat, intense color in figural compositions filled with sharp, dry, angular forms. The major work in the series was called simply *The Passion of Sacco and Vanzetti* (see FIG. Intro-5). This tall, narrow painting condenses the narrative in terms of both time and space. The two executed men lie in coffins at the bottom of the composition. Presiding over them are the three members of the commission chaired by Harvard University president A. Laurence Lowell, who declared the original trial fair and cleared the way for the executions to take place. A framed portrait of Judge Webster Thayer, who handed down the initial sentence, hangs on the wall of a simplified government building. The gray pallor of the dead men, the stylized mask-faces of the mock-pious mourning commissioners, and the sanctimonious, distant judge all contribute to the mood of anguished commentary that makes this image one of Shahn's most powerful works.

**A MONUMENTAL OUTCRY OF GRIEF** Although previous discussion of Pablo Picasso focused on his immersion in aesthetic issues, he also maintained a political commitment throughout his life. He declared: "Painting is not made to decorate apartments. It is an instrument for offensive and defensive war against the enemy."[76] This political commitment became more acute as Picasso watched his homeland descend into civil war in the late 1930s. In January 1937, the Spanish Republican government in exile in Paris asked Picasso to produce the work for the Spanish pavilion at the Paris International Exposition that summer. Like the Mexican muralists (FIGS. 33-80 and 33-81), artists interested in disseminating political and social messages with their art realized the importance of placing their work in public arenas. Picasso was also well aware of the immense visibility and large international audience this opportunity afforded him. He therefore accepted this invitation but was not inspired to work on the project until he received word that Guernica, capital of the Basque region (an area in southern France and northern Spain populated by Basque speakers), had been almost totally destroyed in an air raid on April 26 by Nazi bombers acting on behalf of the rebel general Francisco Franco. Not only did the Germans decimate the city itself, but because they attacked at the busiest hour of a market day, they also killed or wounded many of the 7,000 citizens. The event jolted Picasso into action; by the end of June, he completed the mural-sized canvas of *Guernica* (FIG. **33-73**).

Picasso produced this monumental painting condemning the senseless bombing without specific reference to the event—depicting no bombs or German planes. Rather, the collection of images in *Guernica* combine to create a visceral outcry of human grief. In the center, along the lower edge of the painting, lies a slain warrior clutching a broken and useless sword. A gored horse tramples him and rears back in fright as it dies. On the left, a shrieking, anguished woman cradles her dead child. On the far right, a woman on fire runs screaming from a burning building, while another woman flees mindlessly. In the upper right corner, a woman, represented only by a head, emerges from the burning building, thrusting forth a light to illuminate the horror. Overlooking the destruction is a bull, which, according to the artist, represents "brutality and darkness."[77]

Picasso used aspects of his Cubist discoveries to expressive effect in *Guernica,* particularly the fragmentation of objects and the

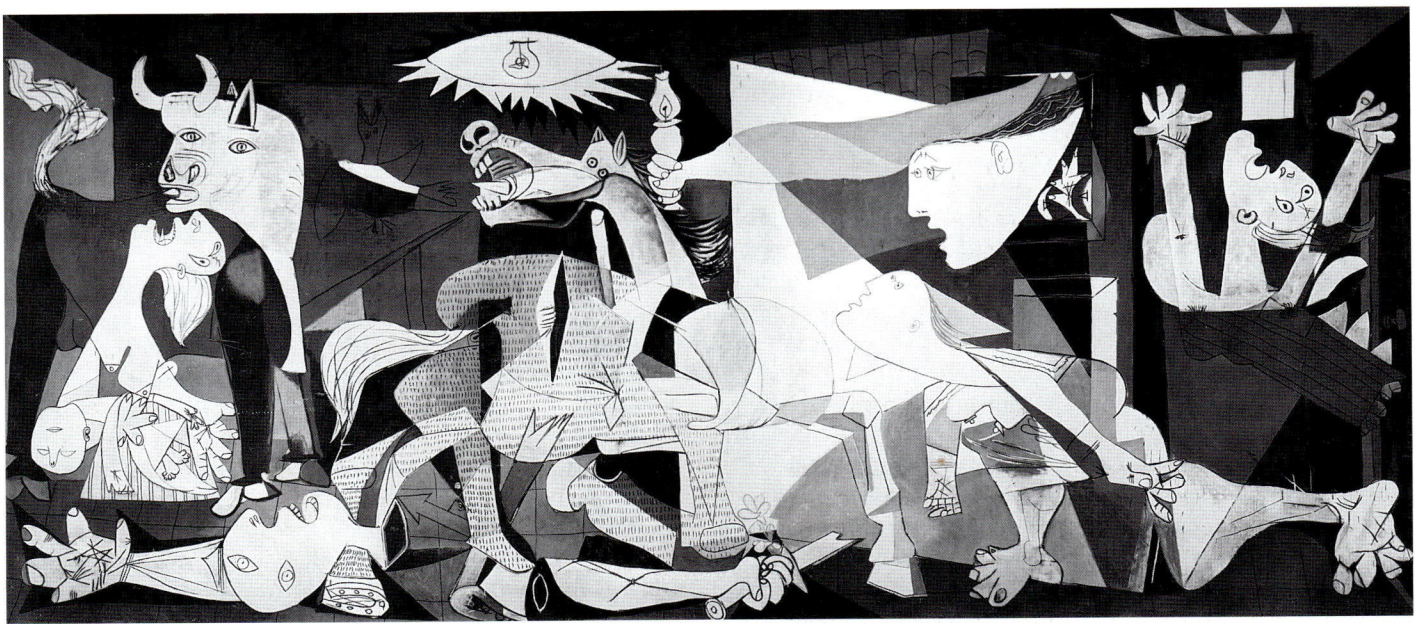

**33-73** PABLO PICASSO, *Guernica*, 1937. Oil on canvas, 11′ 5½″ × 25′ 5¾″. Museo Nacional Centro de Arte Reina Sofía, Madrid.

## The Museum of Modern Art and the Avant-Garde

The Museum of Modern Art in New York City is consistently identified as the institution most responsible for developing modernist art. Established in 1929, the Museum of Modern Art (or MoMA, as it is often called) owes its existence to a trio of women—Lillie P. Bliss, Mary Quinn Sullivan, and Abby Aldrich Rockefeller (see "Art 'Matronage' in America," page 985). These women saw the need for a museum to collect and exhibit modernist art. Together they founded MoMA, which became (and continues to be) the most influential museum of modern art in the world. Their efforts and success are somewhat extraordinary considering the skepticism and hostility greeting much of modernist art at the time of the museum's inception. Indeed, at that time, few American museums were inclined to show late-19th- and 20th-century art at all.

Over the years, MoMA has become a leader in museology and in promoting modernist art. Its exhibition schedule, museum organization, and expansive collection place MoMA at the forefront of art institutions. In its quest to expose the public to the energy and challenge of modernist, particularly avant-garde, art, the museum developed unique and progressive exhibitions. Among those MoMA mounted during the early years of its existence were *Cubism and Abstract Art* and *Fantastic Art, Dada, Surrealism* (1936). The museum also organized *American Sources of Modern Art (Aztec, Maya, Inca)* in 1933 and *African Negro Art* in 1935, among the first exhibitions to deal with such artifacts in artistic rather than anthropological terms.

The organization of MoMA's administrative structure and the scope of the museum's early activities were also notable. MoMA's first director, Alfred H. Barr Jr., insisted on establishing departments at MoMA not only for painting and sculpture but also for other arts. He developed a library of books on modern art and a film library, both of which have become world-class collections, as well as an extensive publishing program. Critic John Russell summarized the structure of MoMA:

The Museum of Modern Art as it is today has certain clearly defined characteristics. It is truly international. It covers not only painting and sculpture, but photography, prints and drawings, architecture, design, the decorative arts, typography, stage design, and artists' books. It has its own publishing house, its own movie house, and its own department of film and video.[1]

Through exhibitions and educational activities, MoMA works at encouraging members of the public to make modernist art a regular part of their lives. Although the museum pursues its founders' desire to appeal to a larger audience, it also labors to establish itself within the scholarly community with the publication of books and catalogs.

It is the museum's art collection, however, that has drawn the most attention. By cultivating an influential group of patrons, MoMA has developed an extensive and enviable collection of late-19th- and 20th-century art. Its collection includes such important works as Picasso's *Les Demoiselles d'Avignon* (FIG. 33-9), van Gogh's *Starry Night* (see FIG. 29-35), and Brancusi's *Bird in Space* (FIG. 33-69). Reading through the illustration captions in this textbook reveals how many significant artworks reside in the Museum of Modern Art.

The dominance of this institution has also made it a target of critics. Some observers believe MoMA's position as the preeminent collector of modernist art has made it an overly influential judge. They suggest that rather than simply documenting artistic developments, MoMA actively influences the direction of art through its exhibitions and acquisitions. Although the museum's influence cannot be denied, its enduring legacy will be public access to the broad range of art it provides.

[1] Quoted in Sam Hunter, *The Museum of Modern Art, New York: The History and Collection* (New York: Abrams, 1984), 11–12.

---

dislocation of anatomical features. This Cubist fragmentation gives visual form to the horror. What happened to these figures in the artist's act of painting—the dissections and contortions of the human form—parallels what happened to them in real life. To emphasize the scene's severity and starkness, Picasso reduced his palette to black, white, and shades of gray.

Revealing his political commitment and his awareness of the power of art, Picasso refused to allow exhibition of *Guernica* in Spain while Generalissimo Franco was in power. At the artist's request, *Guernica* hung in the Museum of Modern Art (see "The Museum of Modern Art and the Avant-Garde," above) in New York City after the World's Fair concluded. Not until after Franco's death in 1975 (ending his right-wing dictatorship) did Picasso allow the mural to be exhibited in his homeland. It was moved in 1981 and hangs today in the Centro de Arte Reina Sofía in Madrid as a testament to a tragic chapter in Spanish history.

**ELEVATING SOVIET WORKERS** An intriguing and instructive contrast to Picasso's *Guernica* is *The Worker and the Collective Farm Worker* (FIG. 33-74) by Russian artist VERA MUKHINA (1889–1963). Both artworks were produced in the same year, 1937, and both were exhibited at the International Exposition in Paris. Whereas Picasso focused on an atrocity that took place during the Spanish Civil War, Mukhina produced a monumental stainless-steel sculpture glorifying the communal labor of the Soviet people. And where Picasso employed Cubist abstraction to convey the horror of the bombing, Mukhina relied on realism to represent exemplars of the Soviet citizenry. Her sculpture, mounted on the top of the Soviet Pavilion, depicts a male factory worker, holding aloft the tool of his trade, the hammer. Alongside him is a female farm worker, raising her sickle to the sky. The juxtaposed hammer and sickle, appearing as they do at the apex of the sculpture, replicate their appearance on the Soviet flag, thereby celebrating the Soviet system. The artist augmented the heroic tenor of this sculpture by emphasizing the solidity of the figures, who stride forward with their clothes blowing dramatically behind them. Mukhina had studied in Paris and was familiar with abstraction, especially Cubism, but felt that a commitment

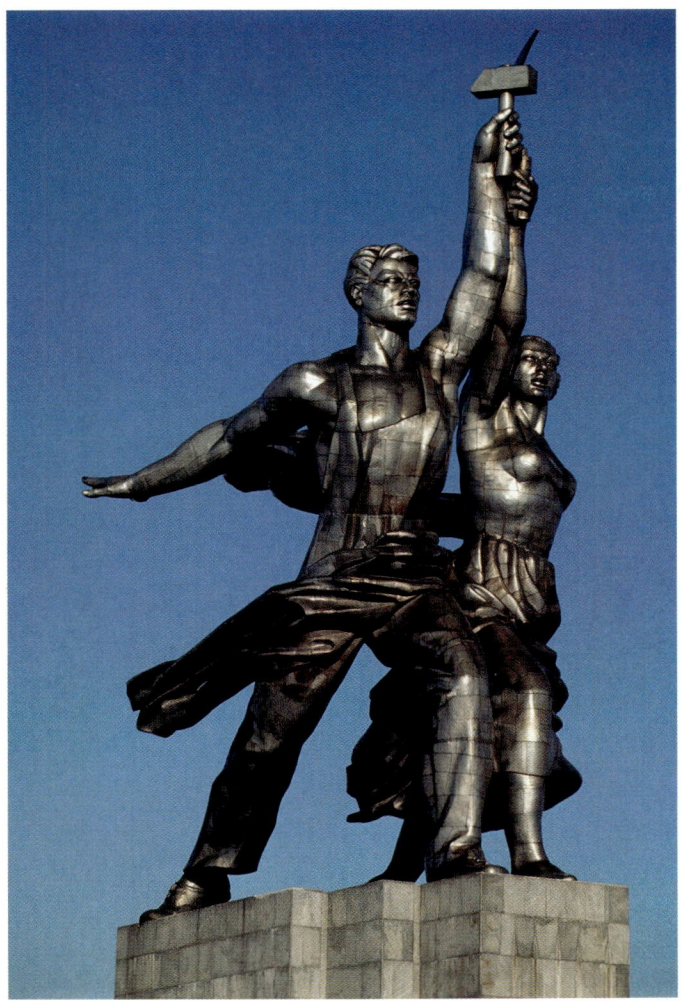

**33-74** VERA MUKHINA, *The Worker and the Collective Farm Worker.* Sculpture for the Soviet Pavilion, Paris Exposition, 1937. Stainless steel, approx. 78′ high.

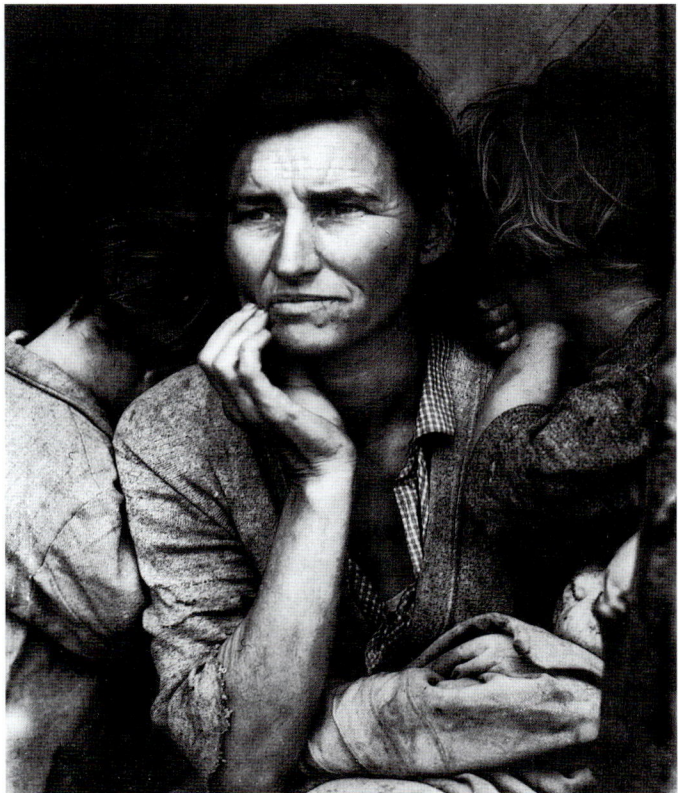

**33-75** DOROTHEA LANGE, *Migrant Mother, Nipomo Valley,* 1935. Gelatin silver print. Copyright © the Dorothea Lange Collection, The Oakland Museum of California, City of Oakland (gift of Paul S. Taylor).

to realism produced the most powerful sculpture. This realist style was officially sanctioned by the Soviet government, and Mukhina earned high praise for this sculpture. Indeed, Russian citizens celebrated the work as a national symbol for decades.

## The Depression and Its Legacy

The Depression into which much of the Western world was plunged in the 1930s had a particularly acute impact in the United States. Its onset marked by the catastrophic stock market crash of October 1929, the Great Depression dramatically changed the nation. Artists were particularly affected. The limited art market virtually disappeared, and museums curtailed both their purchases and exhibition schedules. Many artists sought financial support from the federal government, which established numerous programs to provide relief, aid recovery, and promote reform. Among the programs supporting artists were the Treasury Relief Art Project, founded in 1934 to commission art for federal buildings, and the Works Progress Administration (WPA), founded in 1935 to relieve the widespread unemployment. Under the WPA, varied activities of the Federal Art Project paid artists, writers, and theater people a regular wage in exchange for work in their professions. Another important program was the Resettlement Administration

(RA), better known by its later name, the Farm Security Administration. The RA oversaw emergency aid programs for farm families caught in the Depression and provided information to the public about both the government programs and the plight of the people such programs served.

**PERSONIFYING DEPRESSION SUFFERING** The RA hired American photographer DOROTHEA LANGE (1895–1965) in 1936, sending her to photograph the dire situation of the rural poor the Great Depression displaced. At the end of an assignment to document the lives of migratory pea pickers in California, Lange stopped at a camp in Nipomo and found the migrant workers there starving because the crops had frozen in the fields. Among the pictures she made on this occasion was *Migrant Mother, Nipomo Valley* (FIG. **33-75**), which, like *American Gothic* (FIG. 33-78), has achieved iconic status. Generations of viewers have been moved by the mixture of strength and worry in the raised hand and careworn face of a young mother, who holds a baby on her lap. Two older children, who cling to her trustfully while turning their faces away from the camera, flank her. Lange described how she got the picture:

[I] saw and approached the hungry and desperate mother, as if drawn by a magnet. I do not remember how I explained my presence or my camera to her, but I remember she asked me no questions. I made five exposures, working closer and closer from the same direction. . . . There she sat in that lean-to tent with her children huddled around her, and she seemed to know that my pictures might help her, and so she helped me.[78]

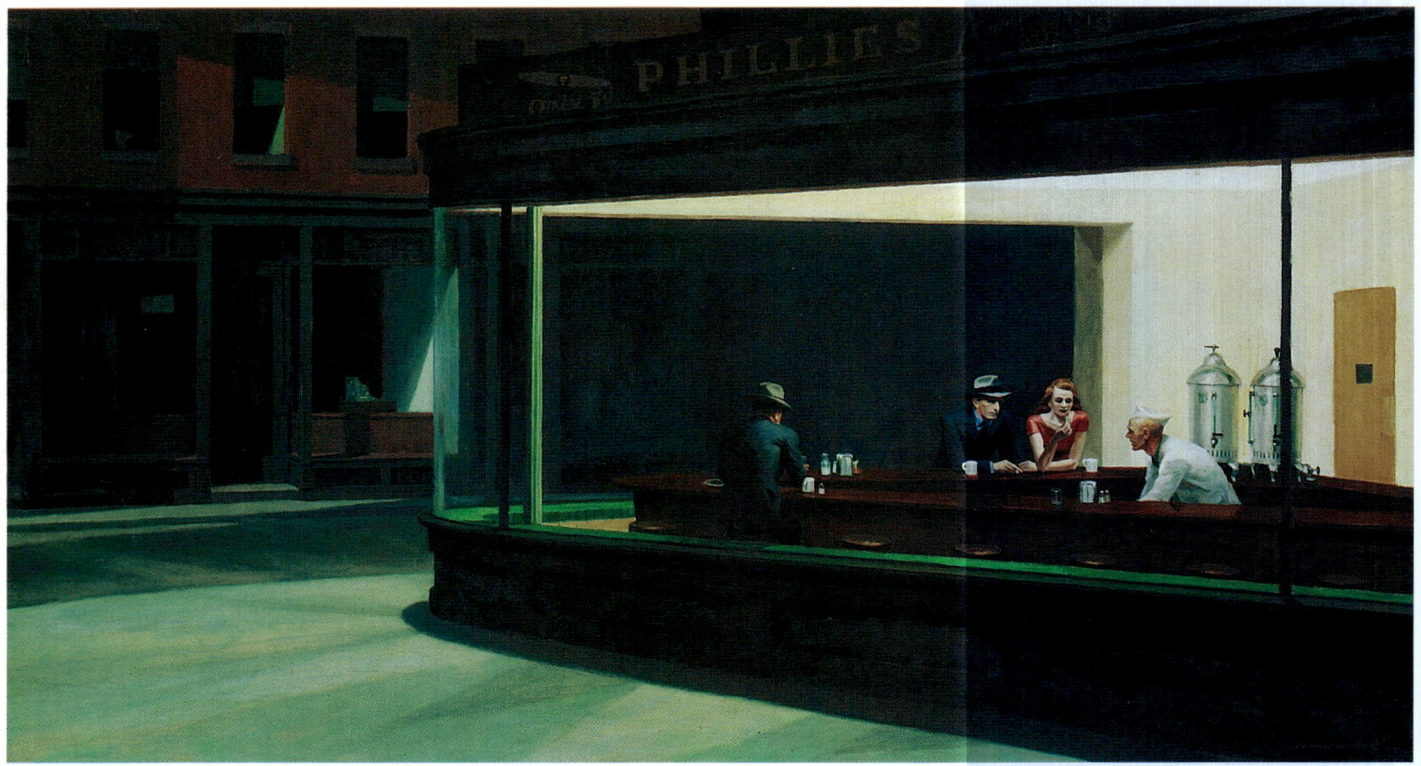

**33-76** Edward Hopper, *Nighthawks*, 1942. Oil on canvas, 2′ 6″ × 4′ 8$\frac{11}{16}$″. The Art Institute of Chicago, Chicago (Friends of American Art Collection).

The response to this photo indicates the ability of *Migrant Mother, Nipomo Valley* to strike a sympathetic chord in viewers. Within days after this image was printed in a San Francisco newspaper, people rushed food to Nipomo to feed the hungry workers.

**DEPRESSION-ERA LONELINESS** Edward Hopper (1882–1967) produced paintings during the Depression era evoking the national mindset. However, rather than depict historically specific scenes, he took as his subject the more generalized theme of the overwhelming loneliness and echoing isolation of modern life in the United States. Trained as a commercial artist, Hopper studied painting and printmaking in New York and Paris before returning to the United States. He then concentrated on scenes of contemporary American city and country life, painting buildings, streets, and landscapes that are curiously muted, still, and filled with empty spaces. Motion is stopped and time suspended, as if the artist recorded the major details of a poignant personal memory. From the darkened streets outside a restaurant in *Nighthawks* (FIG. **33-76**), the viewer glimpses the lighted interior through huge plate-glass windows, which lend the inner space the paradoxical sense of being both a safe refuge and a vulnerable place for the three customers and the counterman. The seeming indifference of Hopper's characters to one another and the echoing spaces that surround them evoke the pervasive loneliness of modern humans. Although Hopper invested works such as *Nighthawks* with the straightforward mode of representation, creating a kind of realist vision recalling that of 19th-century artists such as Thomas Eakins (see FIG. 29-12) and Henry Ossawa Tanner (see FIG. 29-15), he simplified the shapes in the painting, moving toward abstraction, in order to heighten the mood of the scene.

**AFRICAN AMERICAN MIGRATION** African American artist Jacob Lawrence (1917–2000) found his subjects in modern history, concentrating on the culture and history of African Americans. Lawrence moved to Harlem, New York, in 1927 at about age 10. There, he came under the spell of the African art and the African American history he found in lectures and exhibitions and in the special programs sponsored by the 135th Street New York Public Library, which had outstanding collections of African American art and archival data. Inspired by the politically oriented art of Goya (see FIG. 28-43), Daumier (see FIG. 29-6), and Orozco (FIG. 33-80), and influenced by the many artists and writers (such as Alain Locke, Aaron Douglas [FIG. 33-35], Claude McKay, and Countee Cullen) of the Harlem Renaissance whom he met, Lawrence found his subjects in the everyday life of Harlem and his people's history. He defined his own vision of the continuing African American struggle against discrimination.

In 1941, Lawrence began a 60-painting series titled *The Migration of the Negro*. Unlike his earlier historical paintings depicting important figures in American history, such as Frederick Douglass, Toussaint L'Ouverture, and Harriet Tubman, this series called attention to a contemporaneous event—the ongoing exodus of black labor from the southern United States. Disillusioned with their lives in the South, hundreds of thousands of African Americans migrated north in the years following World War I, seeking improved economic opportunities and more hospitable political and social conditions. This subject had personal relevance to Lawrence. He explained: "I was part of the migration, as was my family, my mother, my sister, and my brother. . . . I grew up hearing tales about people 'coming up,' another family arriving. . . . I didn't realize what was happening until about the middle of the 1930s, and that's when the *Migration* series began to take form in my mind."[79]

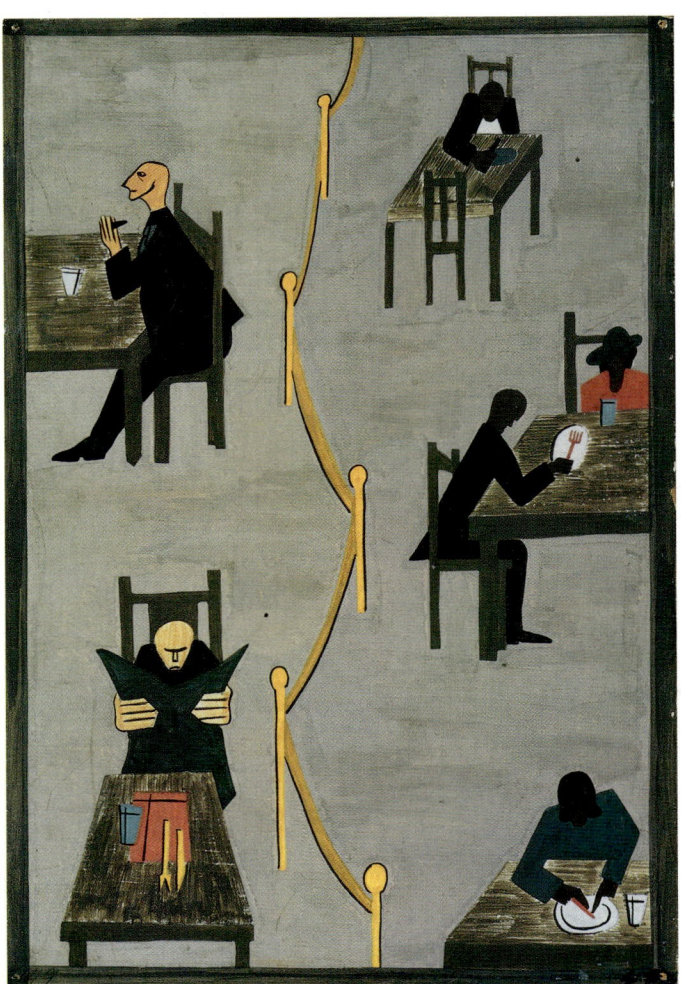

**33-77** JACOB LAWRENCE, *No. 49* from *The Migration of the Negro,* 1940–1941. Tempera on Masonite, 1′ 6″ × 1′. The Phillips Collection, Washington.

Although many American artists, such as the Precisionists (FIGS. 33-36 and 33-37), were enamored of the city or of rapidly developing technological advances, others chose not to depict these aspects of modern life. The Regionalists, sometimes referred to as the American Scene Painters, turned their attention to rural life as America's cultural backbone. One of the Regionalists, GRANT WOOD (1891–1942), for example, published an essay titled "Revolt against the City" in 1935. Although this movement was not formally organized, Wood acknowledged its existence in 1931, when he spoke at a conference. In his address, he announced a new movement developing in the Midwest, known as *Regionalism*, which he described as focused on American subjects and as standing in reaction to "the abstraction of the modernists" in Europe and New York.[80]

**THE APPEAL OF RURAL IOWA** Grant Wood's paintings focus on rural scenes from Iowa, where he was born and raised. The work that catapulted Wood to national prominence was *American Gothic* (FIG. **33-78**), which became an American icon. The artist depicted a farmer and his spinster daughter standing in front of a neat house with a small lancet window, typically found on Gothic cathedrals. The man and woman wear traditional attire—he appears in worn overalls and she in an apron trimmed with rickrack. The dour expression on both of their faces gives the painting a severe quality, which Wood enhanced with his meticulous brushwork. When *American Gothic* was exhibited, many people praised the work, which they perceived as "quaint, humorous, and AMERICAN," in the words of one

The "documentation" of the period, such as the RA program, ignored African Americans, and thus this major demographic shift remained largely invisible to most Americans. Of course, the conditions African Americans encountered both during their migration and in the North were often as difficult and discriminatory as those they had left behind in the South.

Lawrence's series provides numerous vignettes capturing the experiences of these migrating people. Often, a sense of bleakness and of the degradation of African American life dominates the images. *No. 49* of this series (FIG. **33-77**) bears the caption "They also found discrimination in the North although it was much different from that which they had known in the South." The artist depicted a blatantly segregated dining room with a barrier running down the room's center separating the whites on the left from the African Americans on the right. To ensure a continuity and visual integrity among all 60 paintings, Lawrence interpreted his themes systematically in rhythmic arrangements of bold, flat, and strongly colored shapes. His style drew equally from his interest in the push-pull effects of Cubist space and his memories of the patterns made by the colored scatter rugs brightening the floors of his childhood homes. Further, he unified the narrative with a consistent palette of bluish green, orange, yellow, and grayish brown throughout the entire series. Lawrence believed that this story, like every subject he painted during his long career, had important lessons to teach viewers.

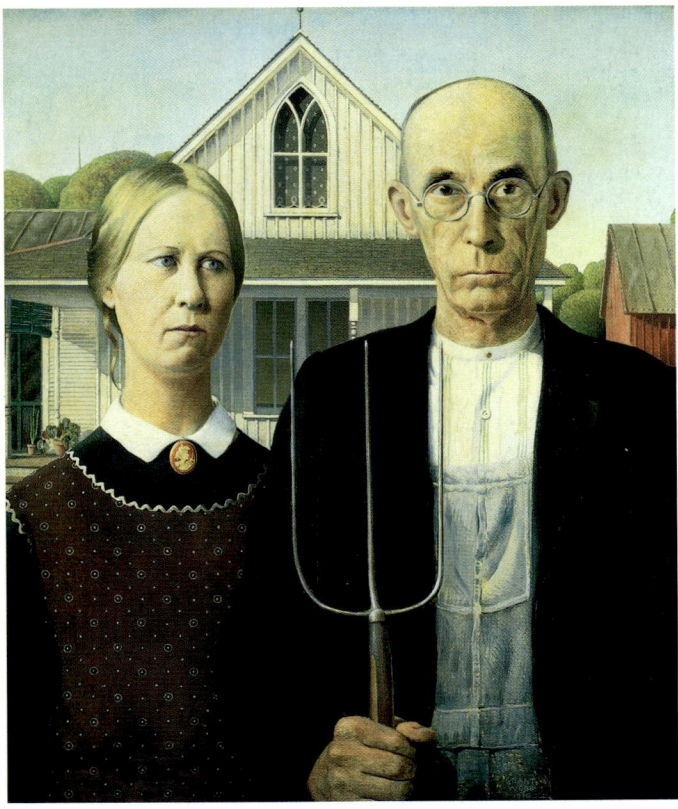

**33-78** GRANT WOOD, *American Gothic,* 1930. Oil on beaverboard, 2′ 5$\frac{7}{8}$″ × 2′ 7$\frac{7}{8}$″. Art Institute of Chicago, Chicago (Friends of American Art Collection).

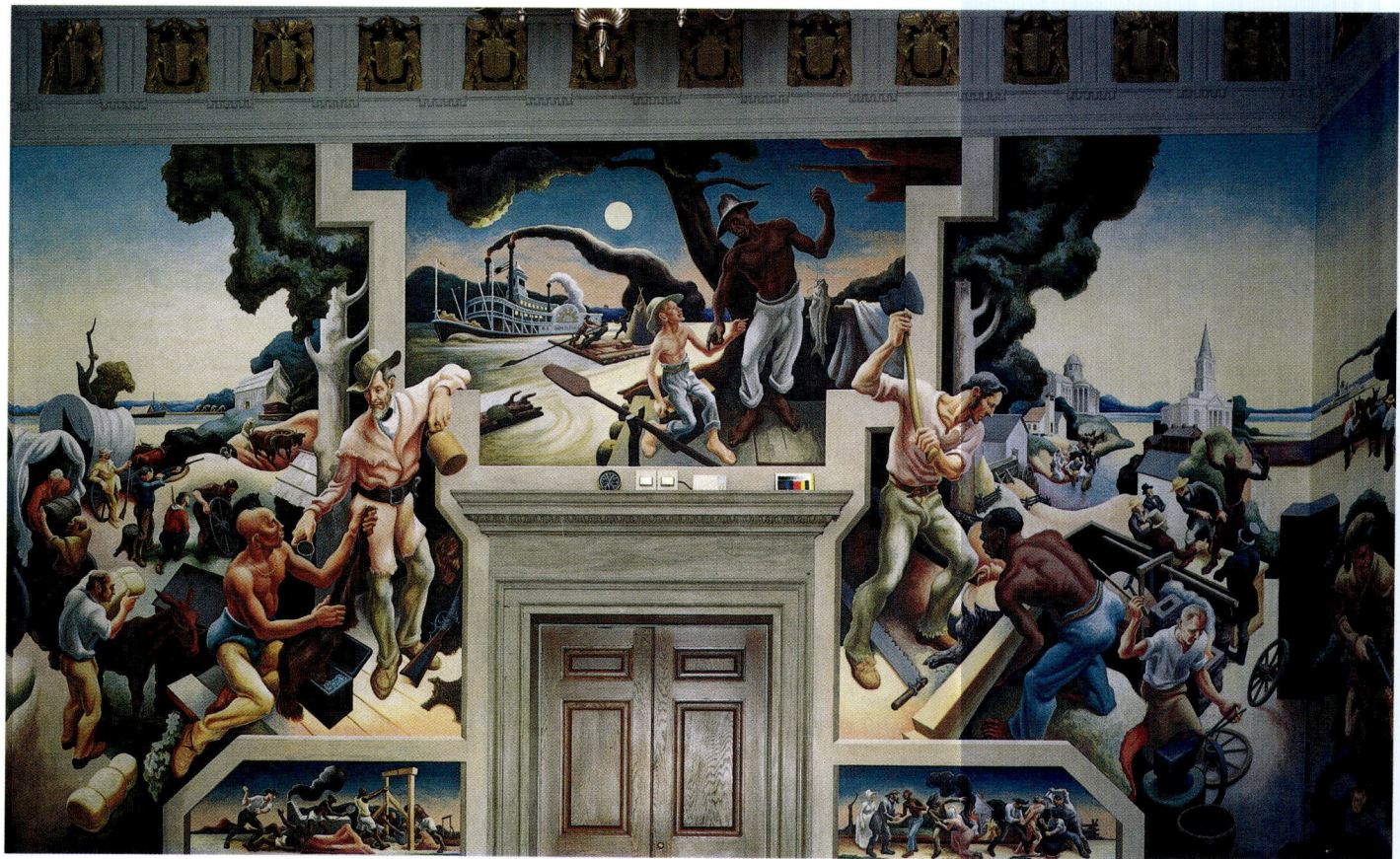

**33-79** Thomas Hart Benton, *Pioneer Days and Early Settlers,* State Capitol, Jefferson City, 1936. Mural. Copyright © T. H. Benton and R. P. Benton Testamentary Trusts/Licensed by VAGA, New York, New York.

critic.[81] Many saw the couple as embodying "strength, dignity, fortitude, resoluteness, integrity," and were convinced that Wood had captured the true spirit of America.[82]

Wood's Regionalist vision involved more than his subjects, extending to a rejection of avant-garde styles in favor of a clearly readable, realist style. Surely this approach appealed to many people alienated by the increasing presence of abstraction in art. Interestingly enough, despite the accolades this painting received, it was also criticized. Not everyone saw the painting as a sympathetic portrayal of midwestern life; indeed, some in Iowa felt insulted by the depiction. In addition, despite the seemingly reportorial nature of *American Gothic,* some viewed it as a political statement—one of staunch nationalism. In light of the problematic nationalism in Germany at the time, this perceived nationalistic attitude was all the more disturbing. Ultimately, Regionalism had both stylistic and political implications.

**CONSTRUCTING A STATE'S HISTORY** Thomas Hart Benton (1889–1975) was another of the major Regionalist artists. Whereas Wood focused his attention on Iowa, Benton turned to scenes from his native Missouri. He produced one of his major works, a series of murals titled *A Social History of the State of Missouri,* in 1936 for the Missouri State Capitol. The murals depict a collection of images from the state's true and legendary history, such as primitive agriculture, horse trading, a vigilante lynching, and an old-fashioned political meeting. Other scenes portray the mining industry, grain elevators, Native Americans, and family life. One segment, *Pioneer Days and Early Settlers* (FIG. **33-79**), shows a white man using whisky as a bartering tool with a Native American (at left), along with scenes documenting the building

of Missouri. Part documentary and part imaginative, Benton's images include both positive and negative aspects of Missouri's history, as these examples illustrate. Although Regionalists were popularly perceived as dedicated to glorifying midwestern life, that belief distorted their aims. Indeed, Grant Wood observed, "your true regionalist is not a mere eulogist; he may even be a severe critic."[83] Benton, like Wood, was committed to a visually accessible style, but he developed a highly personal aesthetic that included complex compositions, a fluidity of imagery, and simplified figures depicted with a rubbery distortion.

Not surprisingly, during the Great Depression of the 1930s, Regionalist paintings had a popular appeal because they often projected a reassuring image of America's heartland. The public saw Regionalism as a means of coping with the national crisis through a search for cultural roots. Thus, people deemed acceptable any nostalgia implicit in Regionalist paintings or mythologies these works perpetuated because they served a larger purpose.

## Mexican Muralists

**VALIDATING MEXICAN HISTORY** José Clemente Orozco (1883–1949) was one of a group of Mexican artists determined to base their art on the indigenous history and culture existing in Mexico before Europeans arrived. The movement these artists formed was part of the idealistic rethinking of society that occurred in conjunction with the Mexican Revolution (1910–1920) and the lingering political turmoil of the 1920s. Among the projects these politically motivated artists undertook were vast mural cycles placed in public buildings to dramatize and validate the history of

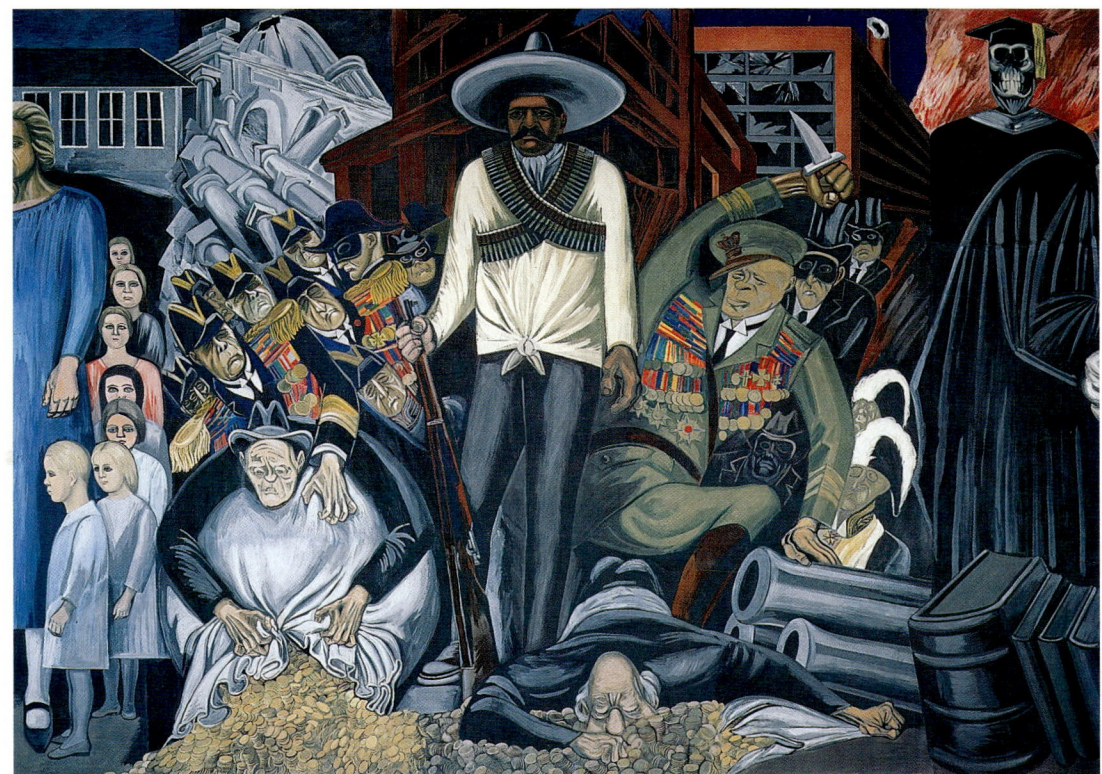

33-80 José Clemente Orozco, *Epic of American Civilization: Hispano-America* (panel 16), Baker Memorial Library, Dartmouth College, Hanover, ca. 1932–1934. Fresco. Copyright © Orozco Valladares Family/SOMAAP, Mexico/Licensed by VAGA, New York, New York.

Mexico's native peoples. Orozco worked on one of the first major cycles, painted in 1922 on the walls of the National Training School in Mexico City. He carried the ideas of this mural revolution to the United States, completing many commissions for wall paintings between 1927 and 1934. From 1932 to 1934, he worked on one of his finest mural cycles in the Baker Library at Dartmouth College in New Hampshire, partly in honor of its superb collection of books in Spanish. The college let him choose the subject. Orozco depicted, in 14 large panels and 10 smaller ones, a panoramic and symbolic history of ancient and modern Mexico, from the early mythic days of the feathered-serpent god Quetzalcoatl to a contemporary and bitterly satiric vision of modern education.

The imagery in the illustrated detail, *Epic of American Civilization: Hispano-America* (panel 16; FIG. **33-80**), revolves around the monumental figure of a heroic Mexican peasant armed to participate in the Mexican Revolution. Looming on either side of him are mounds crammed with symbolic figures of his oppressors—bankers, government soldiers, officials, gangsters, and the rich. Money-grubbers pour hoards of gold at the incorruptible peon's feet, cannons threaten him, and a bemedaled general raises a dagger to stab him in the back. Orozco's training as an architect gave him a sense of the framed wall surface, which he easily commanded, projecting his clearly defined figures onto the solid mural plane in monumental scale.

In addition, Orozco's early training as a maker of political prints and as a newspaper artist had taught him the rhetorical strength of graphic brevity, which he used here to assure that his allegory was easily read. His special merging of the graphic and mural media effects gives his work an originality and force rarely seen in mural painting after the Renaissance and Baroque periods.

**THE POWER OF PUBLIC ART** DIEGO RIVERA (1886–1957), like his countryman Orozco, achieved great renown for his murals, both in Mexico and in the United States. A staunch Marxist, Rivera was committed to developing an art that served his people's needs.

Toward that end, he sought to create a national Mexican style focusing on Mexico's history and also incorporating a popular, generally accessible aesthetic (in keeping with the Socialist spirit of the Mexican Revolution). Rivera produced numerous large murals in public buildings, among them a series lining the staircase of the National Palace in Mexico City. In these images, painted between 1929 and 1935, he depicted scenes from Mexico's history; we depict here *Ancient Mexico* (FIG. **33-81**) from this series. These scenes represent the conflicts between the indigenous people and the Spanish colonizers. Rivera included portraits of important figures in Mexican history and, in particular, in the struggle for Mexican independence. Although complex, the decorative, animated murals retain the legibility of folklore—the figures consist of simple monumental shapes and areas of bold color.

## ÉMIGRÉS AND EXILES: ENERGIZING AMERICAN ART AT MIDCENTURY

The Armory Show in 1913 in New York City, discussed earlier (page 986), was an important vehicle for disseminating information about developments in European art. Equally significant was the emigration of European artists around the European continent and across the Atlantic Ocean to America. The havoc Hitler and the National Socialists wreaked in the early 1930s forced artists to flee. The United States, among other countries, offered both survival and a more hospitable environment for producing their art.

Many artists gravitated to Paris and London, but when the threat of war expanded, the United States became an attractive alternative. Several artists and architects associated with the Bauhaus—Gropius, Moholy-Nagy, Albers, Breuer, and Mies van der Rohe—came to the United States. Many accepted teaching positions, providing them a means of disseminating their ideas. Artists associated with other avant-garde movements—Neue Sachlichkeit (Beckmann and

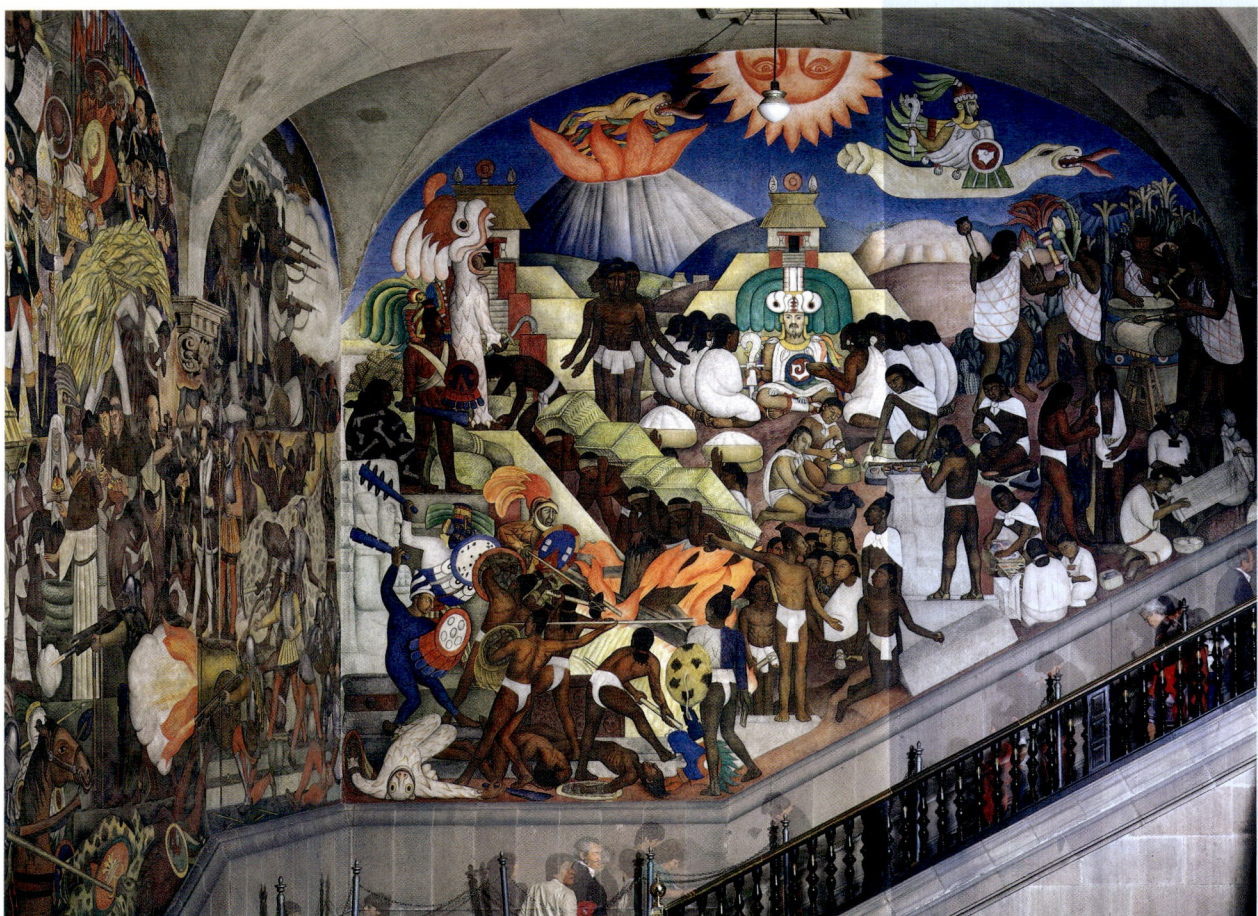

**33-81** Diego Rivera, *Ancient Mexico,* from the *History of Mexico* fresco murals, National Palace, Mexico City, 1929–1935. Fresco.

Grosz), Surrealism (Ernst, Dalí, and Breton), and Cubism (Léger and Lipchitz)—all made their way to American cities.

Museums in the United States, wanting to demonstrate their familiarity and connection with the most progressive European art, mounted exhibitions centered on the latest European artistic developments. In 1938 alone, the City Art Museum of Saint Louis in Missouri presented an exhibition of Beckmann's work, the Art Institute of Chicago organized *George Grosz: A Survey of His Art from 1918–1938,* and the Museum of Modern Art in New York offered *Bauhaus, 1919–1928.* This interest in exhibiting the work of artists persecuted and driven from their homelands also had political overtones. In the highly charged atmosphere of the late 1930s leading to the onset of World War II, people often perceived support for these artists and their work as support for freedom and democracy. In 1942, Alfred H. Barr Jr., director of the Museum of Modern Art, stated:

> Among the freedoms which the Nazis have destroyed, none has been more cynically perverted, more brutally stamped upon, than the Freedom of Art. For not only must the artist of Nazi Germany bow to political tyranny, he must also conform to the personal taste of that great art connoisseur, Adolf Hitler. . . . But German artists of spirit and integrity have refused to conform. They have gone into exile or slipped into anxious obscurity. . . . Their paintings and sculptures, too, have been hidden or exiled. . . . But in free countries they can still be seen, can still bear witness to the survival of a free German culture.[84]

Despite this moral support for exiled artists, once the United States formally entered the war, Germany officially became the enemy. Then it was much more difficult for the art world to promote German artists, however persecuted. Many émigré artists (for example, Ernst, Dalí, Léger, and Grosz) returned to Europe after the war ended. Their collective presence in the United States until then, however, was critical for the development of American art and contributed to the burgeoning interest in the avant-garde among American artists. In addition, the artistic vitality that resulted from the confluence of artists in the United States during the first half of the 20th century propelled that country into an increasingly prominent position in the art world (including the sale, exhibition, and criticism of art).

## CONCLUSION

The upheaval during the early 20th century, evidenced by the prominence of war and economic instability, was a catalyst for significant change in art. Artists explored in depth various elements of artistic expression, such as color (the Fauves), form (the Cubists), and time and space (the Constructivists). They also challenged the processes by which art was created—for example, the Surrealists delved into the subconscious realm to produce works prompted by intuition. The early 20th century was also characterized by increased dialogue between American and European artists. The Armory Show in 1913 and the emigration of European artists to the United States were both important catalysts for the momentum and energy in the art world that carried on into the later 20th century.

**1900**

- SIGMUND FREUD, 1856–1939; *The Interpretation of Dreams,* 1900
- MAX PLANCK, 1858–1947; QUANTUM THEORY, 1900
- QUEEN VICTORIA'S REIGN ENDS, 1901
- FIRST TRANSATLANTIC RADIO SIGNAL, 1901
- **1** WRIGHT BROTHERS' FIRST FLIGHT, 1903
- ALBERT EINSTEIN, 1879–1955; THEORY OF RELATIVITY, 1905–1915
- DIE BRÜCKE, FORMED 1905
- LES FAUVES, FORMED 1905
- FUTURIST MANIFESTO, 1909
- DIE BLAUE REITER, FORMED 1911
- NIELS BOHR, 1885–1962; ATOMIC THEORY, 1913
- WORLD WAR I, 1914–1918

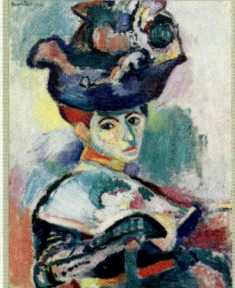

**1** Henri Matisse, *Woman with the Hat,* 1905

**1915**

- ESTABLISHMENT OF CABARET VOLTAIRE IN ZURICH, 1916
- **2** RUSSIAN REVOLUTION, ESTABLISHMENT OF COMMUNIST REGIME, 1917–1921
- BAUHAUS FOUNDED, 1919
- TREATY OF VERSAILLES, 1919
- COMMERCIAL TELEVISION, 1920S
- LEAGUE OF NATIONS, 1921–1939
- U.S.S.R. OFFICIALLY ESTABLISHED, 1923
- SURREALIST MANIFESTO, 1924
- MEXICAN REVOLUTION ENDS, 1924

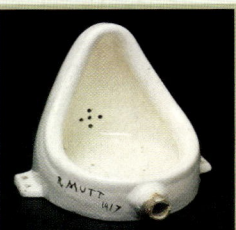

**2** Marcel Duchamp, *Fountain* (second version), 1950 (original version produced 1917)

**1925**

- ADDITION OF SOUND TECHNOLOGY TO FILMS, 1927
- CARL JUNG, 1875–1961 (ANALYTICAL PSYCHOLOGY)
- FASCISM IN ITALY, 1920–1945
- STOCK MARKET CRASHES, 1929

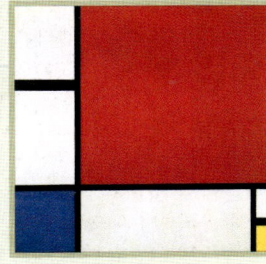

**3** Piet Mondrian, *Composition in Red, Blue, and Yellow,* 1930

**1930**

- **3** THE GREAT DEPRESSION, 1930S
- RISE OF NAZISM IN GERMANY, 1930S
- ROOSEVELT'S "NEW DEAL" IN UNITED STATES, 1933–1939

**1936**

- SPANISH CIVIL WAR, 1936–1939
- **4** JAPAN INVADES CHINA, 1937
- WORLD WAR II, 1939–1945

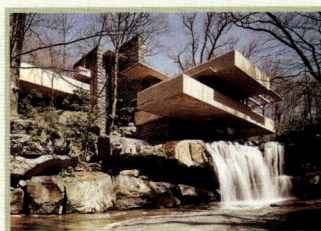

**4** Frank Lloyd Wright, Kaufmann House (Fallingwater), 1936–1939

**1940**

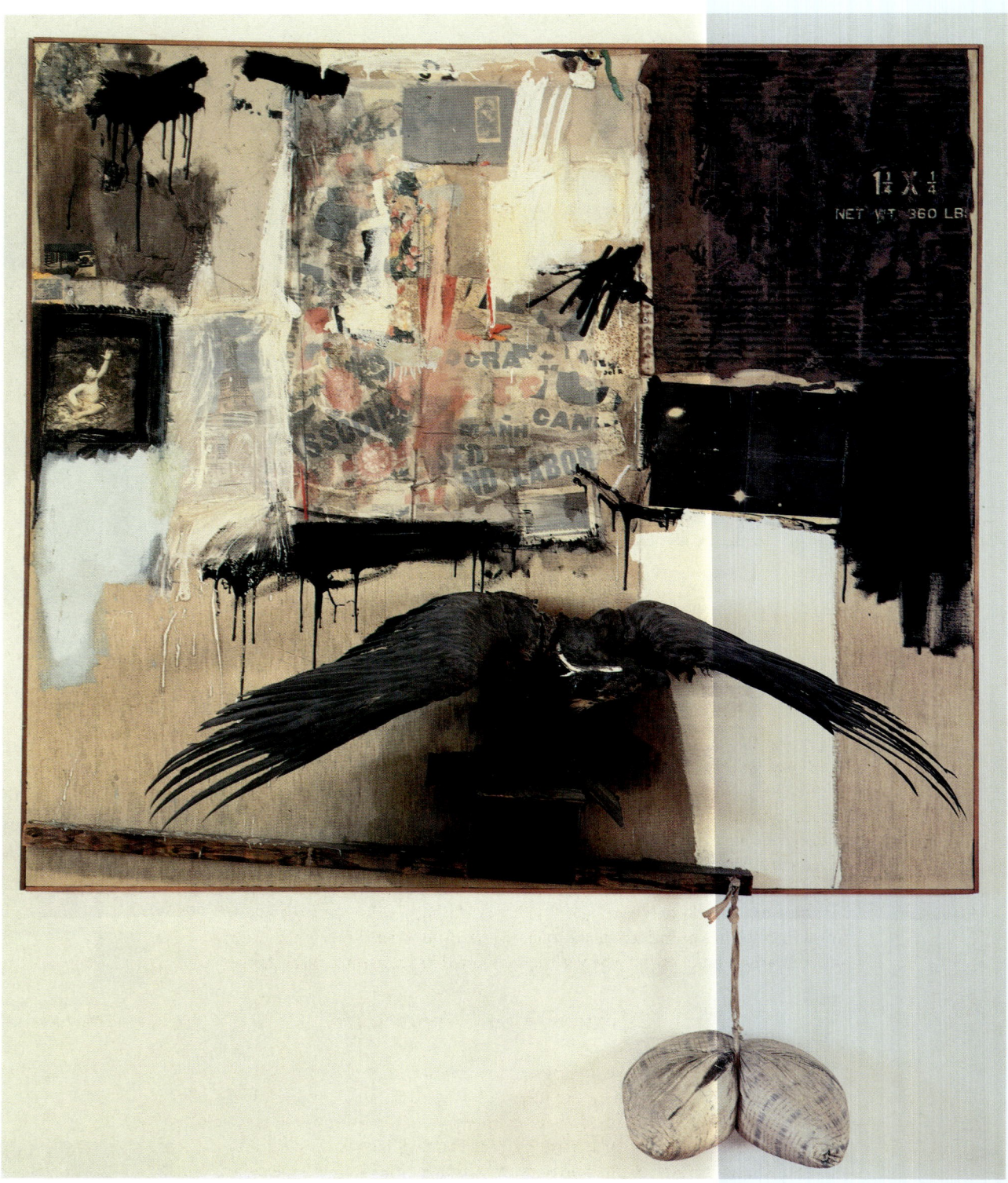

Robert Rauschenberg, *Canyon,* 1959. Oil, pencil, paper, fabric, metal, cardboard box, printed paper, printed reproductions, photograph, wood, paint tube, and mirror on canvas, with oil on bald eagle, string, and pillow, 6′ 9¾″ × 5′ 10″ × 2′. Sonnabend Collection. Copyright © Untitled Press, Inc./Licensed by VAGA, New York, New York.

# 34

# FROM THE MODERN TO THE POSTMODERN AND BEYOND

## ART OF THE LATER 20TH CENTURY

World War II, with the global devastation it unleashed on all dimensions of life—psychological, political, physical, and economic—set the stage for the second half of the 20th century. The dropping of atomic bombs by the United States on Hiroshima and Nagasaki in 1945 signaled a turning point not just in the war itself, but in the geopolitical balance and the nature of international conflict (MAP **34-1**). As a result, the history of the later 20th century became one of upheaval, change, and conflict. For the rest of the century, nuclear war became a very real threat. Indeed, the two nuclear superpowers, the United States and the Soviet Union, divided the post–World War II world into spheres of influence, and each regularly intervened politically, economically, and militarily wherever and whenever it considered its interests to be at stake.

### *Disruption and Upheaval*

The consistent presence of conflict throughout the world in the later 20th century resulted in widespread disruption and dislocation. In 1947, the British left India, which erupted in a murderous Hindu-Muslim war that divided the subcontinent into the new, still hostile nations of India and Pakistan. After a catastrophic war, Communists came to power in China in 1949. North Korea challenged the authority of the fledgling United Nations, founded after the war, by invading South Korea in 1950 and fighting a grim war with the United States and its UN allies that ended in 1953. The Soviets brutally suppressed uprisings in their subject nations—East Germany, Poland, Hungary, and Czechoslovakia. The United States intervened in disputes in Central and South America. Hardly had the previously colonized nations of Africa—Kenya, Uganda, Nigeria, Angola, Mozambique, the Sudan, Rwanda, and the Congo—won their independence

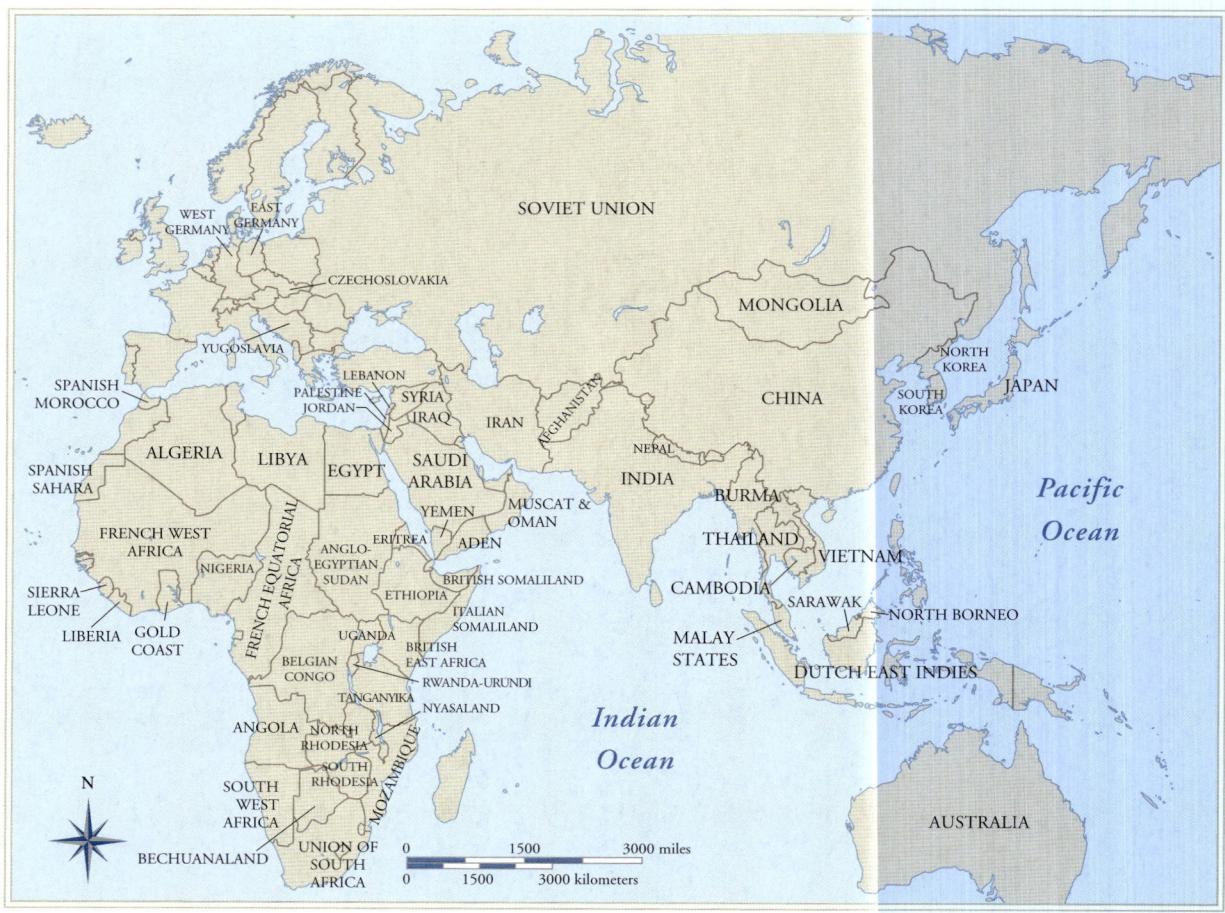

**MAP 34-1** Upheaval and change in Europe, Africa, and Asia in 1945.

than civil wars devastated them. In Indonesia, civil war left more than 100,000 dead. Algeria expelled France in 1962 after the French waged a prolonged and vicious war with Algeria's Muslim natives. Following 15 years of bitter war in Southeast Asia, the United States was defeated in Vietnam. In 1979, the Soviets invaded Afghanistan but were driven out. Arab nations, economically flourishing from oil wealth, fought wars with Israel in 1967, 1978, and the early 1980s. A revitalized Islam rose in the Arab world, inspired a fundamentalist religious revolution in Iran, and encouraged "holy war" with the West, using a new weapon—international terrorism. In 1991, West clashed with East in the Persian Gulf. South Africa formally abandoned apartheid in 1992. This litany of geopolitical clashes reveals the extent to which upheaval marked the history of the later 20th century.

Unrest continues to plague many countries worldwide (MAP 34-2). The ongoing conflict among the Serbs, Croats, and Muslims in the Balkans, the instability in the Middle East, and the divisive ethnic clashes in many African nations emphasize that international hostilities and political uncertainty still characterize the world situation.

In part because the United States emerged relatively unscathed from World War II (compared to European countries, Japan, and the Soviet Union), it could pursue its economic, political, and cultural agendas more aggressively and establish a global presence. But although North American culture seemed to take center stage during the latter part of the 20th century, the United States was not immune from upheaval either. In the postwar years, Americans increasingly questioned the status quo. The struggle for civil rights for African Americans, for free speech on university campuses, and against the Vietnam War led to a rebellion of young Americans. They took to the streets in often raucous demonstrations, with violent repercussions, during the 1960s and 1970s. The prolonged ferment produced a new system of values, a "youth culture," expressed in radical rejection not only of national policies but often also of the society generating them. The young derided their elders' lifestyles and adopted unconventional dress (for that time—long hair, beards, and workers' jeans), manners, habits, and morals deliberately subversive of conventional social standards. The youth era witnessed the sexual revolution, the widespread use and abuse of drugs, and the development of rock music, then an exclusively youthful art form. Young people "dropped out" of regulated society, embraced alternative belief systems, and rejected Western university curricula as irrelevant.

This counterculture had considerable societal impact and widespread influence beyond its political phase. The civil rights movement of the 1960s and later the women's liberation movement of the 1970s reflected the spirit of rebellion, coupled with the rejection of racism and sexism. In keeping with the growing resistance to established authority, women systematically began to challenge the male-dominated culture, which they perceived as having limited their political power and economic opportunities for centuries. Feminists charged that the institutions of Western society, particularly the nuclear family headed by the patriarch, perpetuated male power and subordination of women. They further observed that monuments of Western culture—its arts and

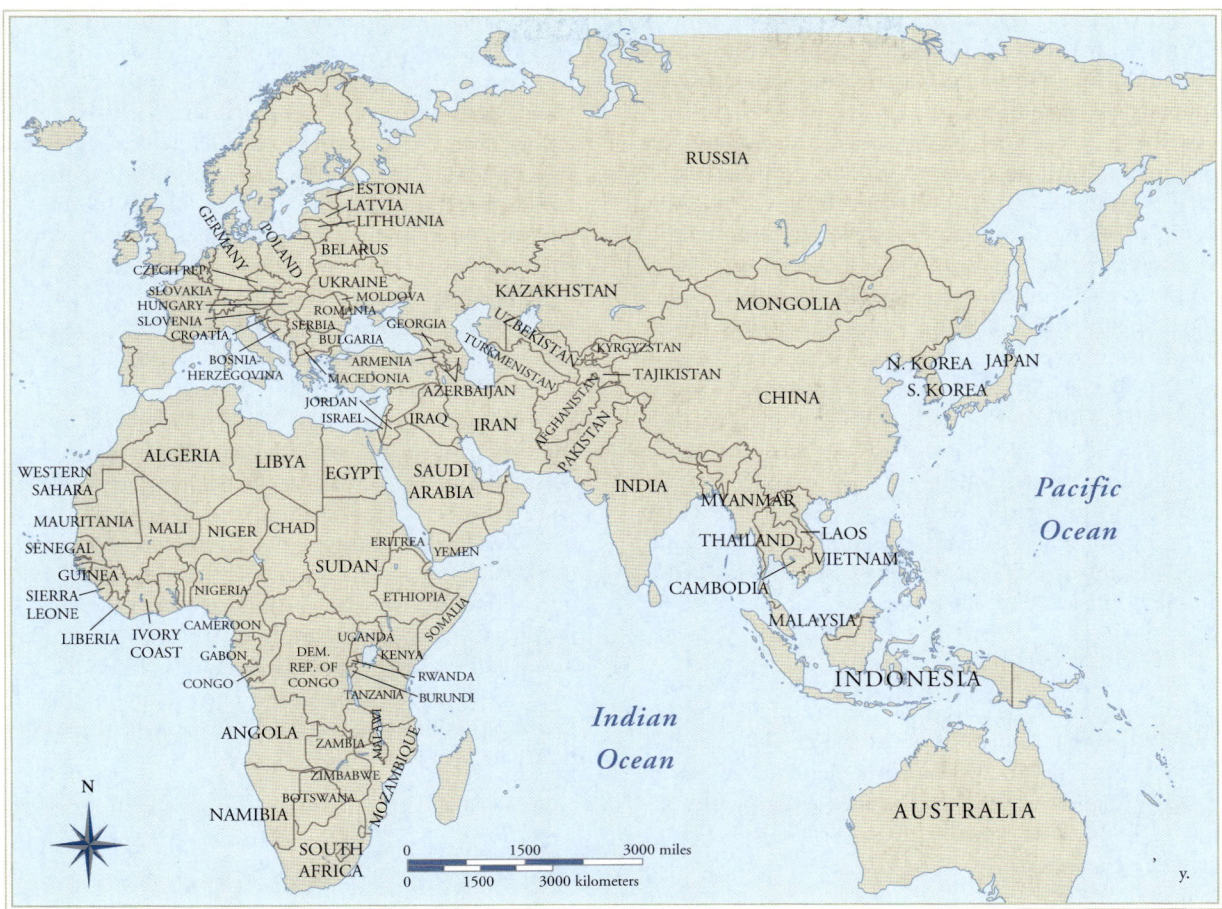

**MAP 34-2** Upheaval and change in Europe, Africa, and Asia in 2000.

sciences, as well as its political, social, and economic institutions—masked the realities of male power. The term *feminism*, though convenient for generic usage, reflects neither the complexity of the issues involved nor the heated debate that emerged among feminists. Indeed, it encompasses such a wide range of attitudes and ideas that its usefulness is limited.

### The Dynamics of Power

The central issue that fueled these rebellions and changes—from international political conflicts to the rise of feminism—was power. Increasingly, individuals and groups sought not just to uncover the dynamics of power, but to combat actively the inappropriate exercise of power or change the balance of power. For example, following patterns developed first in the civil rights movement and later in feminism, various ethnic groups and gays and lesbians have all mounted challenges to discriminatory policies and attitudes. Such groups have fought for recognition, respect, and legal protection and have battled discrimination with political action. In addition, the growing scrutiny in numerous academic fields—cultural studies, literary theory, and colonial and postcolonial studies—of the dynamics and exercise of power has also contributed to the dialogue on these issues. French philosopher-theorists, in particular Jacques Derrida and Michel Foucault, have gained prominence with their publications examining the nature of the world's power structures. As a result of this concern for the dynamics of power, identity (both individual and group) has emerged as a potent arena for discussion and action.

Explorations into the politics of identity aim to increase personal and public understanding of how self-identifications, along with imposed or inherited identities, affect lives.

## THE ART WORLD'S FOCUS SHIFTS WEST

The period's emphasis on change carried over to the art world as well. The relative economic stability of the United States was a major factor in the shifting of the center of Western art from Paris to New York. This helps explain the predominance of American artists in the world markets, even while artists continued to create throughout the world. Only in the closing decades of the 20th century, with the rising interest in multiculturalism and global economies, have countries outside the United States begun to exhibit art more broadly.

### Modernism, Formalism, and Clement Greenberg

Modernism, so integral to art of the later 19th century, shifted course in conjunction with the changing historical conditions and demands. In the postwar years, modernism increasingly became identified with a strict *formalism*—an emphasis on an artwork's visual elements rather than its subject—due largely to the prominence of the American Clement Greenberg (1909–1994). As an art critic who wielded considerable influence from the 1940s through the 1970s, Greenberg was instrumental in redefining the parameters of modernism.

For Greenberg, late-20th-century modernist artists were those who refined the critical stance of the late-19th- and early-20th-century modernists. This critical stance involved rejecting illusionism and exploring the properties of each artistic medium. So dominant was Greenberg that scholars often refer to the general modernist tenets during this period as Greenbergian formalism. Although he modified his complex ideas about art over the years, certain basic concepts are associated with Greenbergian formalism. In particular, Greenberg promoted the idea of purity in art. He explained, "Purity in art consists in the acceptance, willing acceptance, of the limitations of the medium of the specific art."[1] In other words, he believed artists should strive for a more explicit focus on the properties exclusive to each medium—for example, two-dimensionality or flatness in painting, and three-dimensionality in sculpture. To achieve this, artists had to eliminate illusion and embrace abstraction. Greenberg elaborated:

> It follows that a modernist work of art must try, in principle, to avoid communication with any order of experience not inherent in the most literally and essentially construed nature of its medium. Among other things, this means renouncing illusion and explicit subject matter. The arts are to achieve concreteness, "purity," by dealing solely with their respective selves—that is, by becoming "abstract" or nonfigurative.[2]

Greenberg avidly promoted the avant-garde, which he viewed as synonymous with modernism in the postwar years. Generally speaking, the spirit of rebellion and disdain for convention central to the historical avant-garde flourished in the sociopolitical upheaval and counterculture of the 1960s and 1970s. However, the acute sociopolitical dimension inherent in the avant-garde's early development had evaporated by this time (although many of the artists considered avant-garde aligned themselves with the Left). Thus the avant-garde (and modernism) became primarily an artistic endeavor. Still, the distance between progressive artists and the public widened. In his landmark 1939 article "Avant-Garde and Kitsch," Greenberg insisted on the separation of the avant-garde from kitsch (which Greenberg defined as "ersatz," or artificial, culture, such as popular commercial art and literature), thereby advocating the continued alienation of the public from avant-garde art.

## The Emergence of Postmodernism

The intense criticism of the discipline and the unrelenting challenges to artistic convention that were central to modernism eventually led to its demise in the 1970s. To many, it seemed artistic traditions had been so completely undermined that modernism simply played itself out. From this situation emerged *postmodernism,* one of the most dramatic developments during the century. Postmodernism cannot be described as a style; it is a widespread cultural phenomenon. Many people view it as a rejection of modernist principles. Accordingly, postmodernism is far more encompassing and accepting than the more rigid confines of modernist practice. Postmodernism's ability to accommodate seemingly everything in art makes it extremely difficult to provide a clear and concrete definition of the term. In response to the

elitist, uncompromising stance of modernism, postmodernism grew out of a naive and optimistic populism.

Whereas the obscure meaning of abstract work limited the audience for modernist art, postmodern artists offer something for everyone. For example, in architecture, postmodernism's eclectic nature often surfaces in a whimsical mixture of styles and architectural elements (such as Greek columns juxtaposed with ornate Baroque decor). In other artistic media, postmodernism accommodates a wide range of styles, subjects, and formats, from traditional easel painting to video and *installation* (artwork creating an artistic environment in a room or gallery), and from the spare abstraction associated with modernism to carefully rendered illusionistic scenes.

The emergence of postmodernism was also driven by theoretical concerns, such as exploring the relationship between art and mass culture, and examining the tendency to privilege the artist's voice in the search for meaning in art. Various investigations have been identified as particularly postmodern, including critiquing modernist tenets, reassessing the nature of representation, and questioning the ways in which meaning is generated. Despite the prevalence of theory in postmodernism, much of the art produced during the postmodern period is resolutely grounded in specific historical conditions. Thus, later in this chapter, we discuss art addressing issues of race, class, gender, sexual orientation, and ethnicity.

## POSTWAR EXPRESSIONISM IN EUROPE

The end of World War II in 1945 left devastated cities, ruptured economies, and governments in chaos throughout Europe. These factors, coupled with the massive loss of life and the indelible horror of the Holocaust and of Hiroshima and Nagasaki, resulted in a pervasive sense of despair, disillusionment, and skepticism. Although many (for example, the Futurists in Italy) had tried to find redemptive value in World War I, it was virtually impossible to do the same with World War II, coming as it did so closely on the heels of the war that was supposed to "end all wars." Additionally, World War I was largely a European conflict that left roughly 10 million people dead, while World War II was a truly global catastrophe, leaving 35 million dead in its wake.

### Existentialism: The Absurdity of Human Existence

The cynicism emerging across Europe was reflected in the popularity of existentialism, a philosophy asserting the absurdity of human existence and the impossibility of achieving certitude. Many existentialists also promoted atheism and questioned the possibility of situating God within a systematic philosophy. The roots of existentialism are often traced to the Danish theologian Søren Kierkegaard (1813–1855), and the writings of philosophers and novelists such as Friedrich Nietzsche (see Chapter 33, page 963), Martin Heidegger (1889–1976), Fyodor Dostoyevsky (1821–1881), and Franz Kafka (1883–1924) disseminated its ideas. In the postwar period, the writings of the French author Jean-Paul Sartre (1905–1980) most clearly captured the existentialist spirit. According to Sartre, people must consider seriously the implications of atheism. If God does not exist, then individuals must constantly struggle in isolation

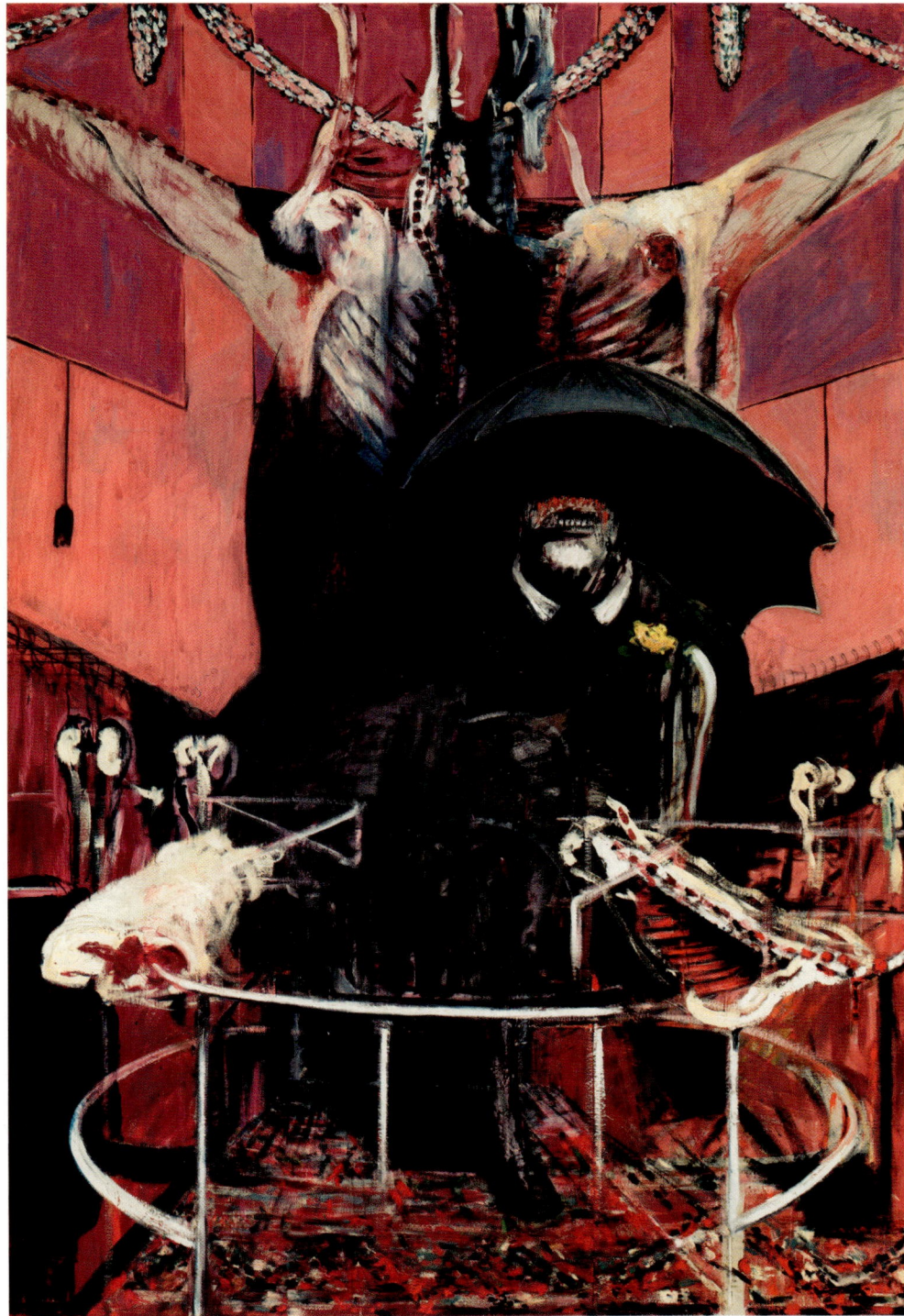

**34-1** FRANCIS BACON, *Painting*, 1946. Oil and pastel on linen, 6′ 5⅞″ × 4′ 4″. Museum of Modern Art, New York.

with the anguish of making decisions in a world without absolutes or traditional values.

This spirit of pessimism and despair emerged frequently in the European art of the immediate postwar period. A brutality or roughness appropriately expressing both the artist's state of mind and the larger cultural sensibility characterized much of this art.

**AN INDICTMENT OF HUMANITY** *Painting* (FIG. **34-1**) by British artist FRANCIS BACON (1910–1992) is a compelling and revolting image of a powerful figure who presides over a scene of slaughter. Painted in the year after World War II ended, this work can be read as an indictment of humanity and a reflection of

war's butchery. The central figure is a stocky man with a gaping mouth and a vivid red stain on his upper lip, as if he were a carnivore devouring the raw meat sitting on the railing surrounding him. Bacon may have based his depiction of this central figure on news photos of Nazi leaders Joseph Goebbels and Heinrich Himmler, Benito Mussolini, or Franklin Roosevelt, which were an important part of media coverage during World War II and very familiar to the artist. The umbrella recalls wartime images of Neville Chamberlain, the British prime minister who so disastrously misjudged Hitler and was frequently photographed with an umbrella. Bacon suspended the flayed carcass hanging behind the central figure like a crucified human form, adding to the visceral impact of the

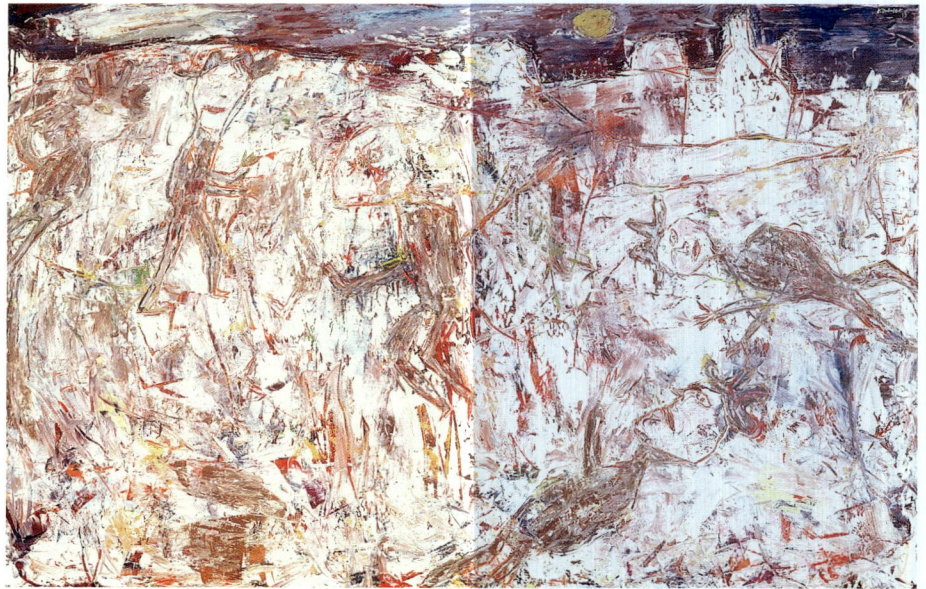

**34-2** JEAN DUBUFFET, *Vie Inquiète (Uneasy Life)*, 1953. Oil on canvas, approx. 4′ 3″ × 6′ 4″. Tate Gallery, London.

painting. Although the specific sources for the imagery in *Painting* may not be entirely clear, it is not difficult to see the work as "an attempt to remake the violence of reality itself" (as Francis Bacon often described his art), and the artist surely based it on what he referred to as "the brutality of fact."[3]

**SCRAPED AND SMEARED CANVASES** Although less specific, the works of French artist JEAN DUBUFFET (1901–1985) also express a somewhat tortured vision of the world through manipulated materials. In works such as *Vie Inquiète,* or *Uneasy Life* (FIG. **34-2**), Dubuffet presented a scene incised into thickly encrusted, parched-looking surfaces. He first built up an impasto (a layer of thickly applied pigment) of plaster, glue, sand, asphalt, and other common materials. Over that he painted or incised crude images of the kind produced by children, the insane, or scrawlers of graffiti. Scribblings interspersed with the images heighten the impression of smeared and gashed surfaces of crumbling walls and worn pavements marked by random individuals. Dubuffet believed the art of children, the mentally unbalanced, prisoners, and outcasts was more direct and genuine because it was unsullied by experience and untainted by conventional standards of art and aesthetic response. He promoted *Art Brut*— untaught, coarse, and rough art.

**LOST IN THE WORLD'S IMMENSITY** The spirit of existentialism is perhaps best expressed in the midlife sculpture of Swiss artist ALBERTO GIACOMETTI (1901–1966). Although Giacometti never claimed he pursued existentialist ideas in his art, it is hard to deny that his works capture the spirit of that philosophy. Indeed, Sartre, Giacometti's friend, saw the artist's figurative sculptures as the epitome of existentialist humanity— alienated, solitary, and lost in the world's immensity. Giacometti had produced sculptures based on human models earlier in his career, but around 1940 he abandoned such direct observation and began to work from memory. His sculptures of the 1940s, such as *Man Pointing* (FIG. **34-3**), were thin, virtually featureless figures with rough, agitated surfaces. Rather than conveying the solidity and mass of conventional bronze figurative sculpture, these severely attenuated figures seem swallowed up by the

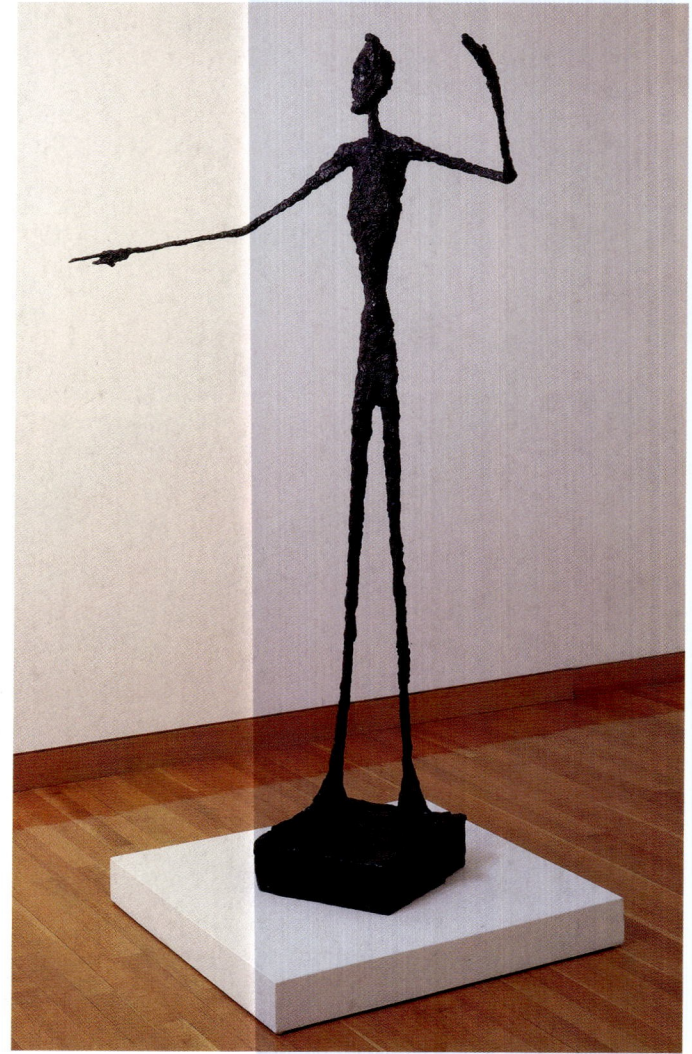

**34-3** ALBERTO GIACOMETTI, *Man Pointing,* 1947. Bronze no. 5 of 6, 5′ 10″ × 3′ 1″ × 1′ 5⅝″. Nathan Emory Coffin Collection of the Des Moines Art Center, Des Moines (purchased with funds from the Coffin Fine Arts Trust).

space surrounding them, imparting a sense of isolation and fragility. These sculptures represented quite a departure from Giacometti's earlier Surrealist-oriented work. Like much of European postwar art, Giacometti's later sculptures are evocative and moving, speaking to the pervasive despair in the aftermath of world war.

# Modernist Formalism

## Abstract Expressionism

As noted earlier, the center of the Western art world shifted in the 1940s from Paris to New York. This was due in large part to the devastation World War II had inflicted across Europe, coupled with the influx of émigré artists escaping to the United States. American artists picked up the European avant-garde's energy, which movements such as Cubism and Dada had fostered. Interest in the avant-garde suffused much of American art of the 1940s through 1970s.

*Abstract Expressionism,* the first major American avant-garde movement, emerged in New York (and hence is often referred to as the New York School) in the 1940s. As the name suggests, the artists associated with Abstract Expressionism produced paintings that are, for the most part, abstract but express the artist's state of mind. These artists also intended to strike emotional chords in the viewer. The Abstract Expressionists tried to broaden their artistic processes to express what psychiatrist Carl Jung called the collective unconscious. To do so, many adopted Surrealist improvisation methods, such as "psychic automatism" (see Chapter 33, page 996), and used their creative minds as open channels for unconscious

forces to make themselves visible. These artists turned inward to create, and the resulting works convey a rough spontaneity and palpable energy. The Abstract Expressionists meant the viewer to grasp the content of their art intuitively, in a state free from structured thinking. The artist Mark Rothko eloquently wrote:

> We assert man's absolute emotions. We don't need props or legends. We create images whose realities are self evident. Free ourselves from memory, association, nostalgia, legend, myth. Instead of making cathedrals out of Christ, man or life, we make it out of ourselves, out of our own feelings. The image we produce is understood by anyone who looks at it without nostalgic glasses of history.[4]

The Abstract Expressionist movement developed along two lines — *gestural abstraction* and *chromatic abstraction.* The gestural abstractionists relied on the expressiveness of energetically applied pigment. In contrast, the chromatic abstractionists focused on color's emotional resonance.

**THE PRIMACY OF PROCESS** The artist whose work best exemplifies gestural abstraction is JACKSON POLLOCK (1912–1956). Although his early work reflects the influence of his teacher, Thomas Hart Benton (see FIG. 33-79), Pollock developed his unique signature style in the mid-1940s. By 1950, Pollock had refined his technique and was producing large-scale abstract paintings such as *Number 1, 1950 (Lavender Mist),* FIG. **34-4.** These paintings are composed of rhythmic drips, splatters, and dribbles of paint, and the mural-sized fields of energetic skeins of pigment envelop viewers, drawing them into a lacy spider-web. The label "gestural abstraction" nicely describes Pollock's working technique. Using sticks or brushes, he flung, poured, and dripped paint (not only traditional oil paints but aluminum

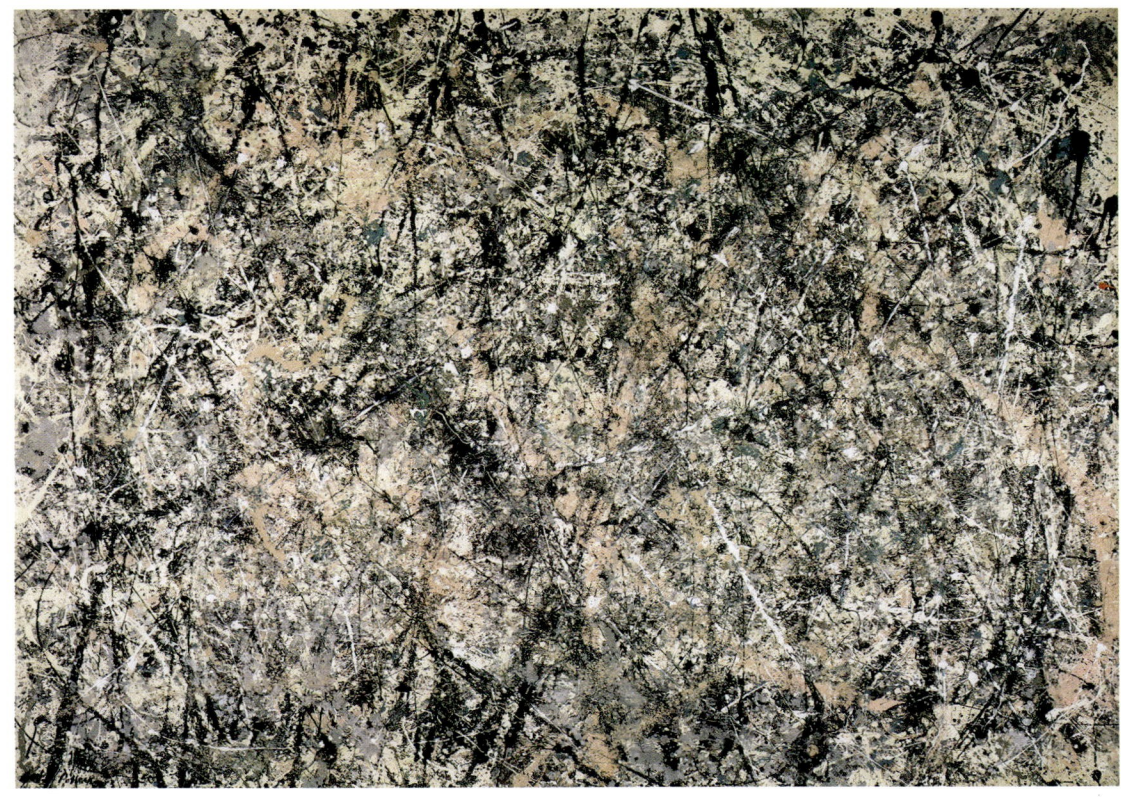

**34-4** JACKSON POLLOCK, *Number 1, 1950 (Lavender Mist),* 1950. Oil, enamel, and aluminum paint on canvas, 7′ 3″ × 9′ 10″. National Gallery of Art, Washington (Ailsa Mellon Bruce Fund).

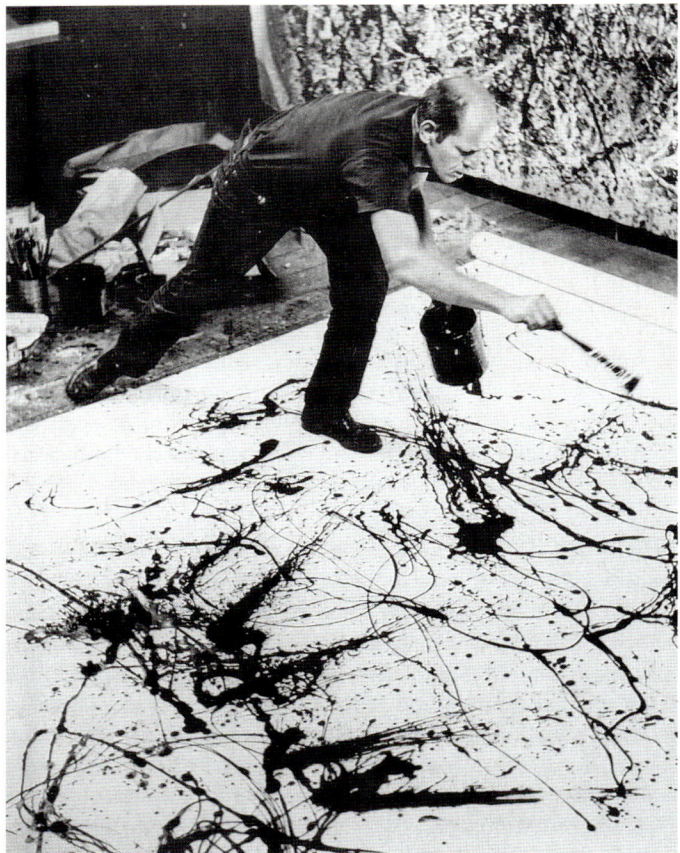

34-5 Photo of Jackson Pollock painting. Center for Creative Photography.

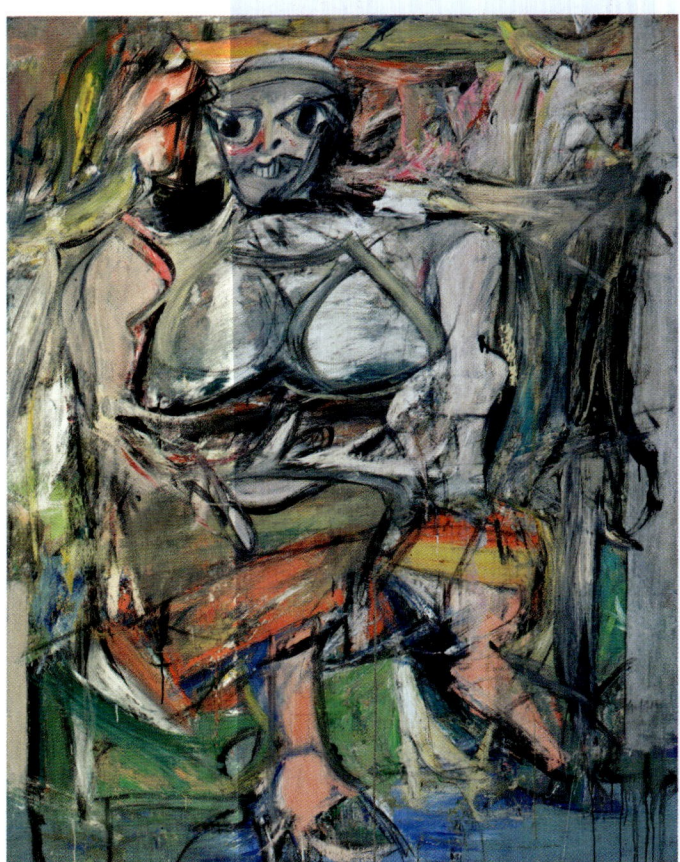

34-6 WILLEM DE KOONING, *Woman I*, 1950–1952. Oil on canvas, 6′ 3⅞″ × 4′ 10″. Museum of Modern Art, New York.

paints and household enamels as well) onto a section of unsized canvas he simply unrolled across his studio floor (FIG. 34-5). Responding to the image as it developed, Pollock created art that was both spontaneous and choreographed. His working method highlights a particularly avant-garde aspect of gestural abstraction—its emphasis on the creative process. Indeed, Pollock literally immersed himself in the painting during its creation. Pollock explained, "I feel nearer, more a part of the painting, since this way I can walk around it, work from the four sides, and literally be *in* the painting."[5] The idea (suggested by Pollock's comments) that he improvised his works and drew from his subconscious has been linked by scholars to the artist's interest in Jungian psychology and the concept of the collective unconscious. Furthermore, he was influenced by the Surrealists, who relied heavily on the subconscious. The improvisational nature of Pollock's work also parallels the work of Kandinsky (see FIG. 33-6), who, appropriately enough, was described as an abstract expressionist as early as 1919.

In addition to Pollock's unique working methods, the lack of a well-defined compositional focus in his paintings significantly departed from conventional painting. He enhanced this rejection of tradition with the expansive scale of his canvases, a resolute move away from easel painting. These avant-garde dimensions of his work earned Pollock the public's derision and the nickname "Jack the Dripper." The title of a 1949 *Life* magazine article facetiously asked, "Jackson Pollock: Is He the Greatest Living Painter in the United States?"[6] Pollock's early death in a car accident at age 44 cut short the development of his innovative artistic vision.

**A FEROCIOUS AND INTENSE WOMAN** Despite the public's skepticism about this art, other artists enthusiastically pursued similar avenues of expression. Dutch-born WILLEM DE KOONING (1904–1997) also developed a gestural abstractionist style. Even images such as *Woman I* (FIG. 34-6), although rooted in figuration, display the sweeping gestural brush strokes and energetic application of pigment typical of gestural abstraction. Out of the jumbled array of slashing lines and agitated patches of color appears a ferocious-looking woman with staring eyes and ponderous breasts. Her toothy smile, inspired by an ad for Camel cigarettes, seems to turn into a grimace. Female models on advertising billboards partly inspired *Woman I*, one of a series of female images, but de Kooning's female forms also suggest fertility figures and a satiric inversion of the traditional image of Venus, goddess of love.

Process was important to de Kooning, as it was to Pollock. Continually working on *Woman I* for almost two years, de Kooning painted an image and then scraped it away the next day and began anew. His wife Elaine, also a painter, estimated that he painted approximately 200 scraped-away images of women on this canvas before settling on the final one.

In addition to this *Woman* series, de Kooning created nonrepresentational works dominated by huge swaths and splashes of pigment. His images suggest rawness and intensity. His dealer, Sidney Janis, confirmed this impression, recalling that de Kooning occasionally brought him paintings with ragged holes in them, the result of overly vigorous painting. Like Pollock, de Kooning was very much "in" his paintings.

34-7 BARNETT NEWMAN, *Vir Heroicus Sublimis,* 1950–1951. Oil on canvas, 7' 11$\frac{3}{8}$" × 17' 9$\frac{1}{4}$". Museum of Modern Art, New York (gift of Mr. and Mrs. Ben Heller).

**ACTION PAINTING** People also refer to gestural painting as *action painting,* a term the critic Harold Rosenberg applied first to the work of the New York School. In his influential article of 1952, "The American Action Painters," Rosenberg described the attempts of these artists to get "inside the canvas." He elaborated:

> At a certain moment the canvas began to appear to one American painter after another as an arena in which to act—rather than as a space in which to reproduce, re-design, analyze or "express" an object, actual or imagined. What was to go on the canvas was not a picture but an event. The painter no longer approached his easel with an image in his mind; he went up to it with material in his hand to do something to that other piece of material in front of him. The image would be the result of this encounter.[7]

Although many critics (Clement Greenberg among them) objected to Rosenberg's analysis of American painting in the immediate postwar years, his term was adopted and widely used.

**COLOR'S ENDURING RESONANCE** In contrast to the aggressively energetic images of the gestural abstractionists, the work of the chromatic abstractionists exudes a quieter aesthetic, exemplified by the work of Barnett Newman and Mark Rothko. The emotional resonance of their works derives from their eloquent use of color. In his early paintings, BARNETT NEWMAN (1905–1970) presented organic abstractions inspired by his study of biology and his fascination with Native American art. He soon simplified his compositions so that each canvas, such as *Vir Heroicus Sublimis* (literally, "heroic sublime man"; FIG. **34-7**), consists of a single slightly modulated color field split by narrow bands the artist called "zips," which run from one edge of the painting to the other. As Newman explained it, "The streak was always going through an atmosphere; I kept trying to create a world around it."[8] He did not intend the viewer to perceive the zips as specific entities, separate from the ground, but as accents energizing the field and giving it scale. By simplifying his compositions, Newman increased color's capacity to communicate and to express his feelings about the tragic condition of modern life and the human struggle to survive. He claimed: "[T]he artist's problem . . . [is] the idea-complex that makes contact with mystery—of life, of men, of nature, of the hard black chaos that is death, or the grayer, softer chaos that is tragedy."[9] Confronted by one of Newman's monumental colored canvases, viewers truly feel as if they are in the presence of the epic.

**"TRAGEDY, ECSTASY, DOOM"** The work of MARK ROTHKO (1903–1970) also deals with universal themes. Born in Russia, Rothko moved with his family to the United States when he was age 10. His early paintings were figurative in orientation, but he soon arrived at the belief that references to anything specific in the physical world conflicted with the sublime idea of the universal, supernatural "spirit of myth," which he saw as the core of meaning in art. In a statement cowritten with Newman and artist Adolph Gottlieb and sent to the *New York Times* critic Edward Alden Jewell, Rothko expressed his beliefs about art:

> We favor the simple expression of the complex thought. We are for the large shape because it has the impact of the unequivocal. . . . We assert that . . . only that subject matter is valid which is tragic and timeless. That is why we profess spiritual kinship with primitive and archaic art.[10]

Rothko's paintings became compositionally simple, and he increasingly focused on color as the primary conveyor of meaning. In works such as *No. 14* (FIG. **34-8**), Rothko created compelling visual experiences consisting of two or three large rectangles of pure color with hazy, brushy edges that seem to float on the canvas

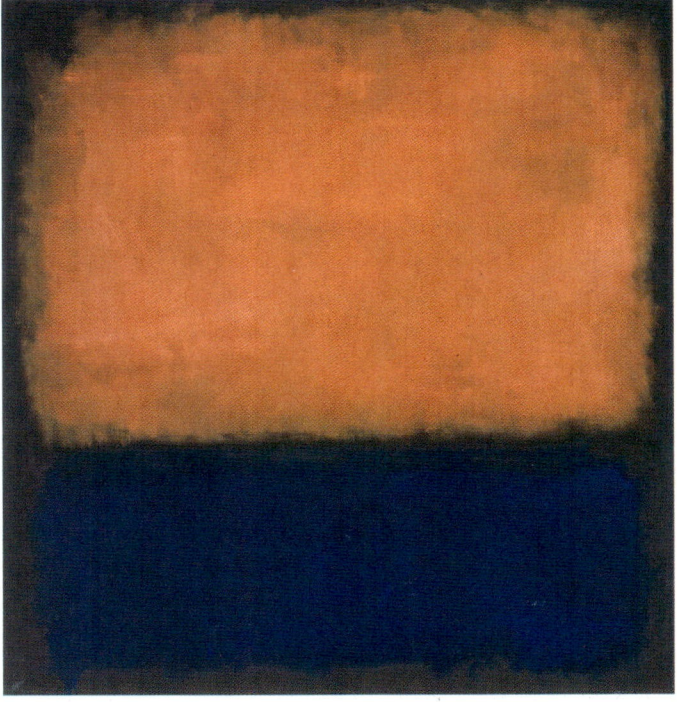

34-8 MARK ROTHKO, *No. 14,* 1960. Oil on canvas, 9' 6" × 8' 9". San Francisco Museum of Modern Art, Helen Crocker Russell Fund Purchase.

surface, hovering in front of a colored background. When properly lit, these paintings appear as shimmering veils of intensely luminous colors suspended in front of the canvases. Although the color juxtapositions are visually captivating, Rothko intended them as more than decorative. He saw color as a doorway to another reality, and he was convinced color could express "basic human emotions—tragedy, ecstasy, doom." He explained, "The people who weep before my pictures are having the same religious experience I had when I painted them. And if you, as you say, are moved only by their color relationships, then you miss the point."[11] Like the other Abstract Expressionists, Rothko produced highly evocative, moving paintings that relied on formal elements rather than specific representational content to raise emotions in the viewer.

**MONUMENTAL METAL SCULPTURES** Although American sculptor DAVID SMITH (1906–1965) was not associated with the Abstract Expressionists, his metal sculptures have affinities with the tenets of that movement. Smith learned to weld in an automobile plant in 1925, and later applied to his art the technical expertise in handling metals he gained from that experience. In addition, working in large scale at the factories helped him visualize the possibilities for monumental metal sculpture. After experimenting with a variety of sculptural styles and materials, Smith created his *Cubi* series in the early 1960s. These works, including the example *Cubi XIX* (FIG. **34-9**), consist of simple geometric forms—cubes, cylinders, and rectangular bars. Made of stainless steel, piled on top of one another, and then welded together, these forms create imposing large-scale sculptures. Despite the basic geometric vocabulary, Smith composed the works in a way that suggests human characteristics. Smith added gestural elements reminiscent of Abstract Expressionism by burnishing the metal

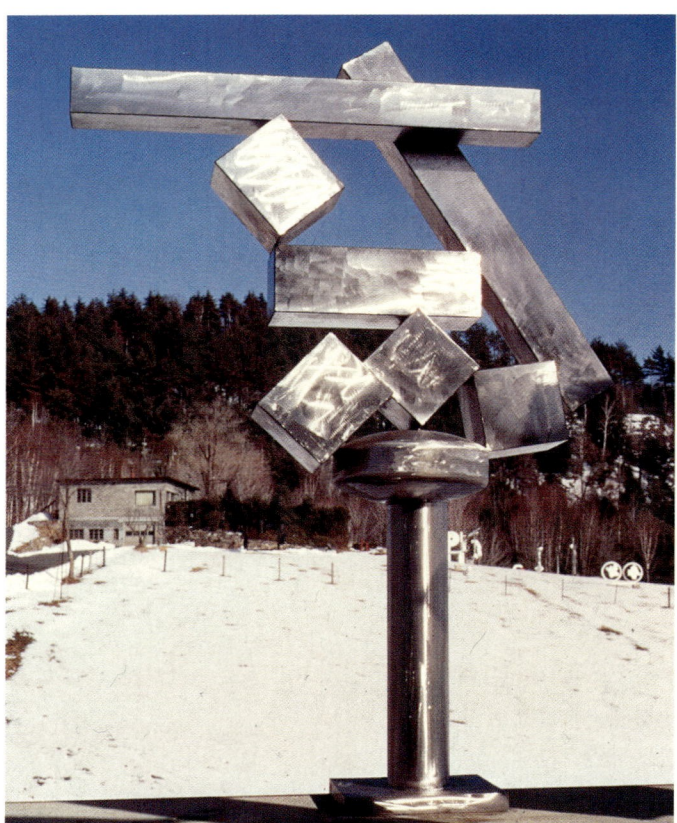

**34-9** DAVID SMITH, *Cubi XIX*, 1964. Stainless steel. 9′ $4\frac{3}{4}$″ × 4′ $10\frac{1}{4}$″ × 3′ 4″. Tate Gallery, London.

with steel wool, producing swirling random-looking patterns that draw attention to the two-dimensionality of the sculptural surface. This treatment, which captures the light hitting the sculpture, activates the surface and imparts a texture to these sculptures.

## Post-Painterly Abstraction

*Post-Painterly Abstraction,* another American art movement, developed out of Abstract Expressionism. Indeed, many of the artists associated with Post-Painterly Abstraction produced Abstract Expressionist work early in their careers. Yet Post-Painterly Abstraction manifests a radically different sensibility from Abstract Expressionism. Whereas Abstract Expressionism conveys a feeling of passion and visceral intensity, a cool, detached rationality emphasizing tighter pictorial control characterizes Post-Painterly Abstraction.

The term was coined by the art critic Clement Greenberg, who saw this art as contrasting with "painterly" art, characterized by loose, visible pigment application. Evidence of the artist's hand, so prominent in gestural abstraction, is conspicuously absent in Post-Painterly Abstraction. Greenberg championed this art form because it seemed to embody his idea of purity in art.

**ELEMENTAL HARD-EDGE PAINTING** Attempting to arrive at pure painting, the Post-Painterly Abstractionists distilled painting down to its essential elements, producing spare, elemental images. A good example of one variant of Post-Painterly Abstraction, *hard-edge painting,* is *Red Blue Green* (FIG. **34-10**) by ELLSWORTH KELLY (b. 1923), with its razor-sharp edges and clearly delineated shapes. This work is, appropriately, completely abstract and extremely simple compositionally. Further, the painting contains no suggestion of the illusion of depth—the color shapes appear resolutely two-dimensional.

**"WHAT YOU SEE IS WHAT YOU SEE"** FRANK STELLA (b. 1936), an artist associated with the hard-edge painters, pursued similar ideas in the 1960s. In works such as *Mas o Menos* (literally, "more or less"; FIG. **34-11**), Stella eliminated many of the variables associated with painting. His simplified images of thin, evenly spaced pinstripes on colored grounds have no central focus, no painterly or expressive elements, limited surface modulation, and no tactile quality. Stella's systematic painting illustrates Greenberg's insistence on purity in art. The artist's own comment on his work, "What you see is what you see," reinforces the notions that painters interested in producing advanced art must reduce their work to its essential elements and that the viewer must acknowledge that a painting is simply pigment on a flat surface.

**FLAT COLOR FIELD PAINTING** *Color field painting,* another variant of Post-Painterly Abstraction, also emphasized painting's basic properties. However, rather than produce sharp, unmodulated shapes as the hard-edge artists had done, the color field painters poured diluted paint onto unprimed canvas, allowing these pigments to soak into the fabric. It is hard to conceive of another painting method that results in such literal flatness. The images created, such as *Bay Side* (FIG. **34-12**) by HELEN FRANKENTHALER (b. 1928), appear spontaneous and almost accidental. These works differ from those of Rothko and Newman in that the emotional component, so integral to their work, is here subordinated to resolving formal problems.

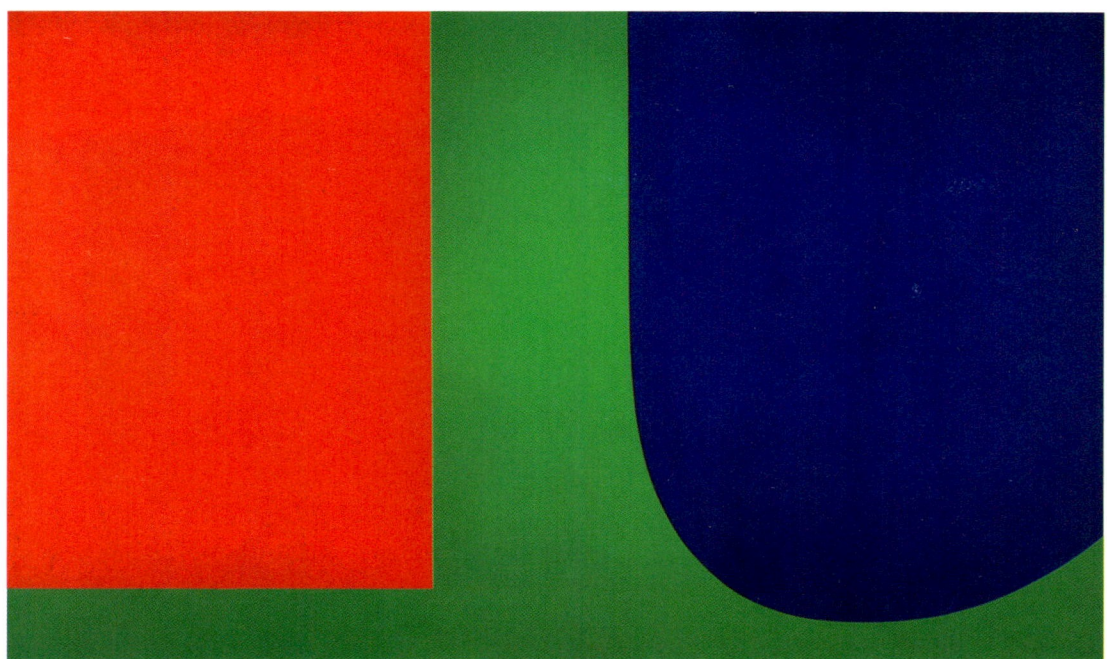

**34-10** ELLSWORTH KELLY, *Red Blue Green*, 1963. Oil on canvas, 6′ 11⅝″ × 11′ 3⅞″. Collection of Museum of Contemporary Art, San Diego (gift of Dr. and Mrs. Jack M. Farris).

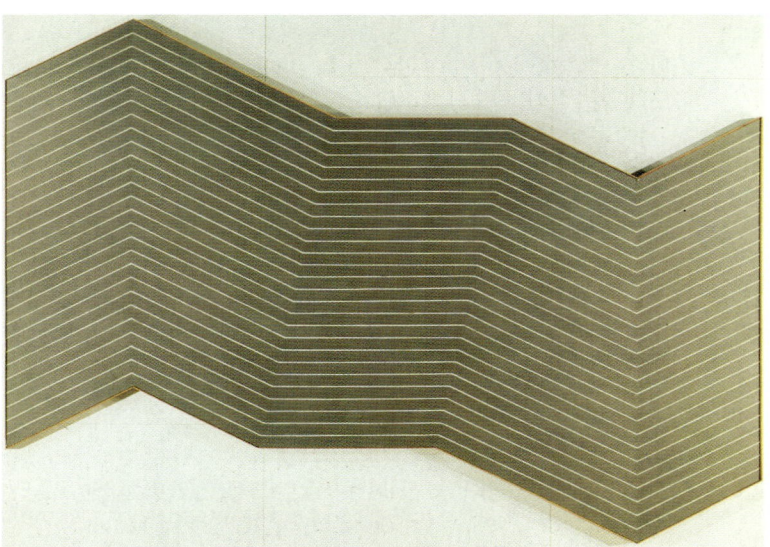

**34-11** FRANK STELLA, *Mas o Menos*, 1964. Metallic powder in acrylic emulsion on canvas, 9′ 10″ × 13′ 8½″. Musée National d'Art Moderne, Centre Georges Pompidou, Paris (purchase 1983 with participation of Scaler Foundation).

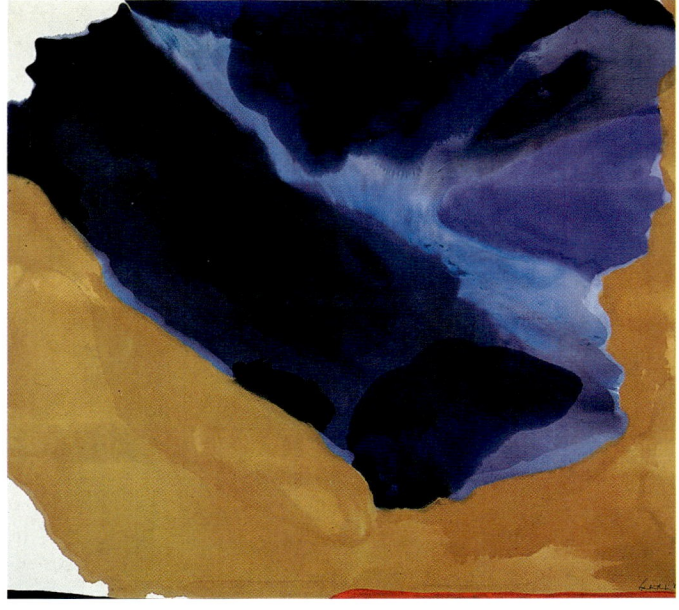

**34-12** HELEN FRANKENTHALER, *Bay Side*, 1967. Acrylic on canvas, 6′ 2″ × 6′ 9″. Private collection, New York.

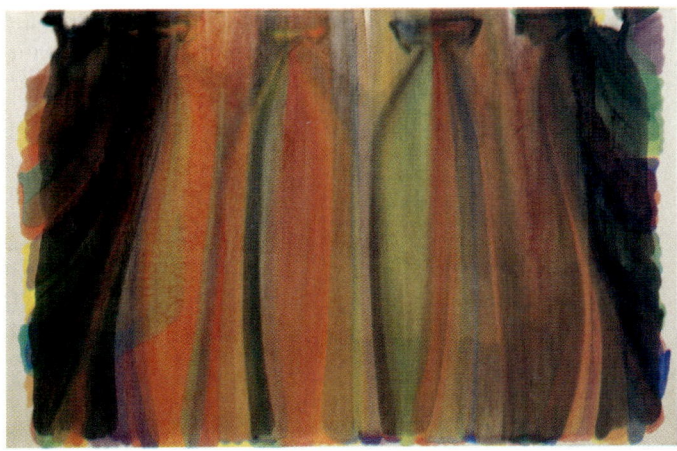

**34-13** MORRIS LOUIS, *Saraband*, 1959. Acrylic resin on canvas, 8′ 5⅛″ × 12′ 5″. Solomon R. Guggenheim Foundation, New York.

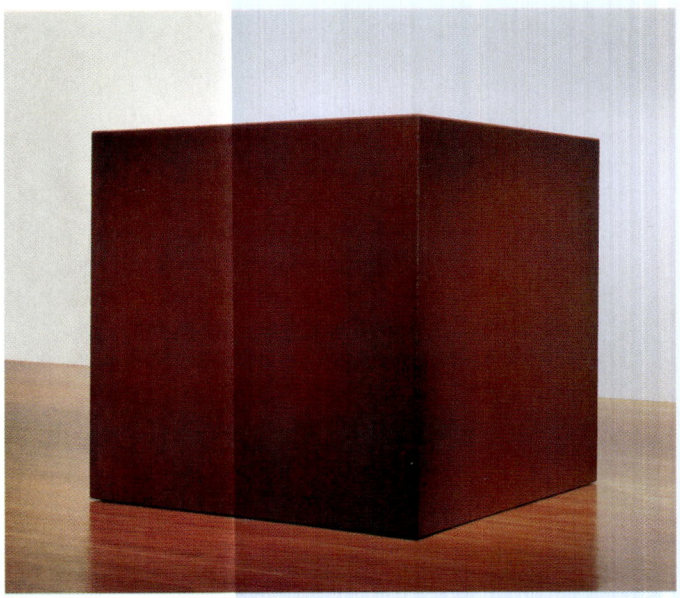

**34-14** TONY SMITH, *Die*, 1962. Steel, 6′ × 6′ × 6′. Museum of Modern Art, New York (gift of Jane Smith in honor of Agnes Gund).

**STAINED CANVASES** Another artist who pursued color field painting was MORRIS LOUIS (1912–1962). Greenberg, who was interested in Frankenthaler's paintings, took Louis to her studio, and there she introduced him to the possibilities presented by the staining technique. Louis used this method of pouring diluted paint onto the surface of unprimed canvas in several series of paintings. *Saraband* (FIG. **34-13**) is one of the works in Louis's *Veils* series. By holding up the canvas edges and pouring diluted acrylic resin, Louis created billowy, fluid, transparent shapes that run down the length of the canvas. Like Frankenthaler, Louis reduced painting to the concrete fact of the paint-impregnated material.

## Minimal Art

Painters were not the only artists interested in Clement Greenberg's ideas. American sculptors also strove to arrive at purity in their medium. While painters worked to emphasize flatness, sculptors, understandably, chose to focus on three-dimensionality as the unique characteristic and inherent limitation of the sculptural idiom. *Minimal art,* or *Minimalism,* a predominantly sculptural movement that emerged in the 1960s, was a clear expression of this endeavor. The movement's name reveals its reductive nature; people have also referred to Minimal art as primary structures or ABC art.

**EMPHASIZING OBJECTHOOD** Minimalist TONY SMITH (1912–1980) created sculptures such as *Die* (FIG. **34-14**), a simple volumetric construction like other Minimal sculptures. Difficult to describe other than as three-dimensional objects, Minimal artworks often lack identifiable subjects, colors, surface textures, and narrative elements. By rejecting illusionism and reducing sculpture to basic geometric forms, Minimalists emphatically emphasized their art's "objecthood" and concrete tangibility. In so doing, they reduced experience to its most fundamental level, preventing viewers from drawing on assumptions or preconceptions when dealing with the art before them.

**DECLARING SCULPTURE'S OBJECTHOOD** DONALD JUDD (1928–1994) sought clarity and truth in his art, which led to a spare, universal aesthetic corresponding to Minimalist tenets. Judd's determination to arrive at a visual vocabulary that avoided deception or ambiguity propelled him away from representation and toward precise and simple sculpture. For Judd, a work's power

derived from its character as a whole and from the specificity of its materials. *Untitled* (FIG. **34-15**) presents basic geometric boxes constructed of brass and red Plexiglas, undisguised by paint or other materials. The artist did not intend the work to be metaphorical or symbolic but a straightforward declaration of sculpture's objecthood. In works such as this, Judd used Plexiglas because its translucency allows the viewer access to the interior, thereby rendering the sculpture both open and enclosed. This aspect of the design was consistent with his desire to banish ambiguity or falseness. Judd's sculptures, like those of other Minimalists, provide the viewer with a unique visual experience—one both immediate and enduring.

**GREENBERG AND MINIMALISM** Interestingly enough, despite the ostensible connections between Minimalism and Greenbergian formalism, Greenberg did not embrace this direction in art. He expressed his concern:

> Minimal Art remains too much a feat of ideation [the mental formation of ideas], and not enough anything else. Its idea remains an idea, something deduced instead of felt and discovered. The geometrical and modular simplicity may announce and signify the artistically furthest-out, but the fact that the signals are understood for what they want to mean betrays them artistically. There is hardly any aesthetic surprise in Minimal Art. . . . Aesthetic surprise hangs on forever—it is there in Raphael as it is in Pollock—and ideas alone cannot achieve it.[12]

**HEALING PSYCHIC WOUNDS** A sculpture that does indeed present this enduring impact is the Vietnam Veterans Memorial (FIG. **34-16**), designed by MAYA YING LIN (b. 1960) at age 21 in 1981. The austere, simple memorial, a V-shaped wall constructed of polished black granite panels, begins at ground level at each end and gradually ascends to a height of 10 feet at the center of the V. The names of the Vietnam War's 57,939 casualties (and those still missing) incised on the wall, in the order of their deaths, contribute to the work's dramatic effect. Also, Lin set the wall into the landscape, enhancing an awareness of descent as one walks along the wall toward the center.

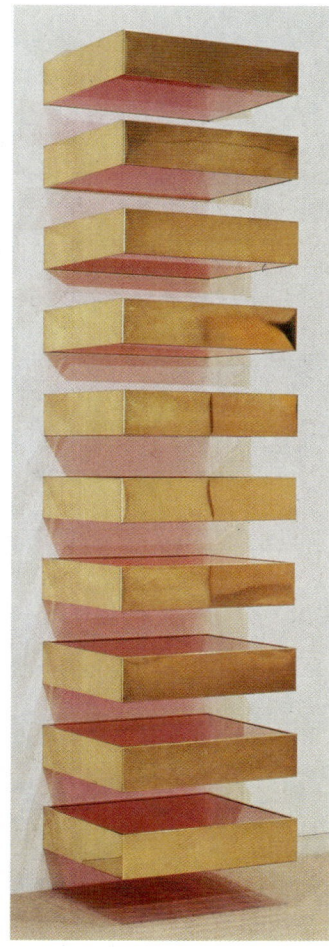

**34-15** DONALD JUDD, *Untitled*, 1969. Brass and colored fluorescent Plexiglas on steel brackets, 10 units, $6\frac{1}{8}''\times 2'\times 2'\ 3''$ each, with 6″ intervals. Hirshhorn Museum and Sculpture Garden, Smithsonian Institution, Washington, D.C. (gift of Joseph H. Hirshhorn, 1972). Art copyright © Donald Judd Estate/Licensed by VAGA, New York, New York.

When Lin designed this pristinely simple monument, she gave a great deal of thought to the purpose of war memorials. She concluded that a memorial "should be honest about the reality of war and be for the people who gave their lives." She decided that she "didn't want a static object that people would just look at, but something they could relate to as on a journey, or passage, that would bring each to his own conclusions. . . . I wanted to work with the land and not dominate it. I had an impulse to cut open the earth . . . an initial violence that in time would heal. The grass would grow back, but the cut would remain . . ."[13] In light of the tragedy of the war, this unpretentious memorial's allusion to a wound and long-lasting scar contributes to its communicative ability (see "The Power of Minimalism: Maya Lin's Vietnam Veterans Memorial," page 1044).

## ALTERNATIVES TO MODERNIST FORMALISM

### *Diverse Sculptural Directions*

**MULTIPLICITY OF MEANING** Although Minimalism was a dominant sculptural trend in the 1960s, many sculptors pursued other styles. Russian-born LOUISE NEVELSON (1899–1988) created sculpture that combines a sense of the architectural fragment with the power of Dada and Surrealist found objects to express her personal sense of life's underlying significance. Multiplicity of meaning was important to Nevelson. She sought ". . . the in-between place. . . . The dawns and the dusks"[14]— the transitional realm between one state of being and another. By the late 1950s, she was assembling sculptures of found wooden objects and forms, enclosing small sculptural compositions in boxes of varied sizes, and joining the boxes to one another to form "walls," which she then painted in a single hue—usually black, white, or gold.

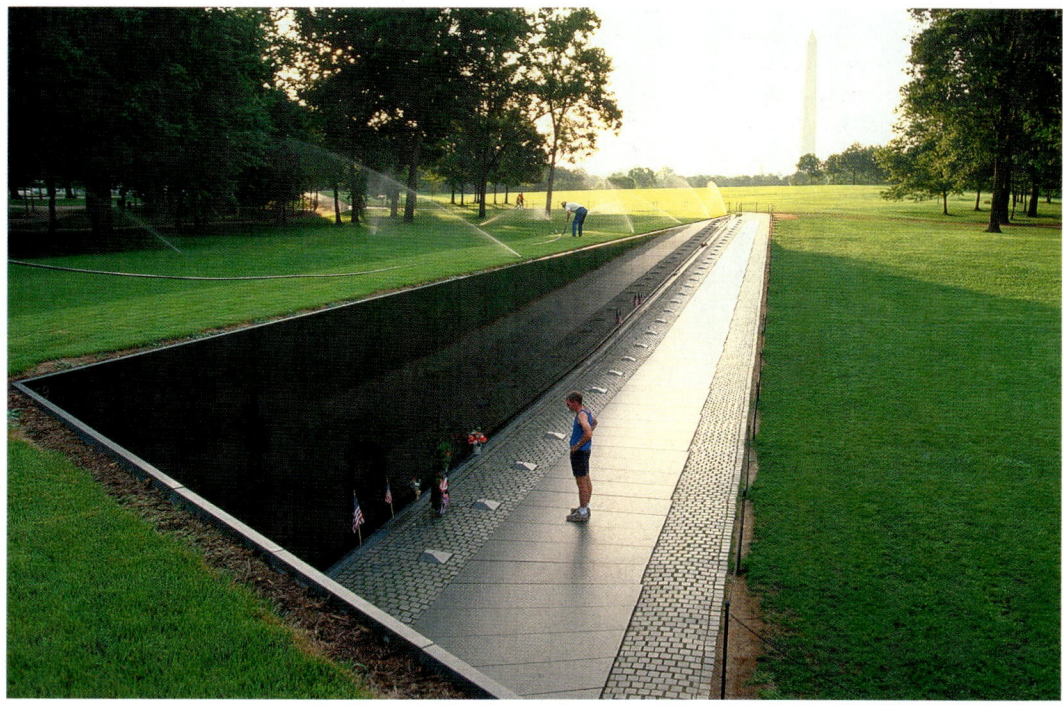

**34-16** MAYA YING LIN, Vietnam Veterans Memorial, Washington, D.C., 1981–1983. Black granite, each wing 246′ long.

## The Power of Minimalism
### *Maya Lin's Vietnam Veterans Memorial*

Although Minimal art first seemed to many to operate only in the realm of the formal, the immediacy and physical presence of Minimalist artworks often endows the works with an enduring resonance. Maya Lin's design for the Vietnam Veterans Memorial (FIG. 34-16) is, like other Minimalist sculptures, a simple geometric form. Yet the controversy that erupted when her design was first publicized and the emotional public response to the completed memorial demonstrate how some Minimalist artworks can move beyond concrete objecthood. The monument, with its serene simplicity, actively engages viewers in a psychological dialogue, rather than standing mute. This dialogue gives viewers the opportunity to explore their feelings about the Vietnam War and perhaps arrive at some sense of closure.

The history of the Vietnam Veterans Memorial provides dramatic testimony to this monument's power. In 1981, a jury of architects, sculptors, and landscape architects selected Lin's design in a blind competition for a memorial to be placed in Constitution Gardens in Washington, D.C. Conceivably, the jury not only found her design compelling but also thought its unabashed simplicity would be the least likely to provoke controversy. When the selection was made public, however, heated debate ensued. Because of the stark contrast between the massive white memorials (the Washington Monument and the Lincoln Memorial bracketing the Vietnam Veterans Memorial) and the wall, some people saw Lin's design as criticizing the Vietnam War and, by extension, the efforts of those who fought in the war. Some of these critics perceived the wall's insertion into the earth as an admission of guilt about U.S. participation in the war. The wall's color came under attack as well; one veteran charged that black is "the universal color of shame, sorrow and degradation in all races, all societies worldwide."[1]

Due to the vocal opposition, a compromise was necessary to ensure the memorial's completion. The Commission of Fine Arts, the federal group overseeing such projects, commissioned an additional memorial from artist Frederick Hart in 1983. This larger-than-life-sized realistic bronze sculpture of three soldiers, armed and in uniform, was eventually installed approximately 120 feet from the wall. More recently, a group of nurses, organized as the Vietnam Women's Memorial Project, got approval for a sculpture honoring women's service in the Vietnam War. The seven-foot-tall bronze statue by Glenna Goodacre depicts three female figures, one cradling a wounded soldier in her arms. Unveiled in 1993, the work was placed about 300 feet south of the wall.

Despite this controversy and compromise, the wall generates dramatic responses. Commonly, visitors react very emotionally, even those who know none of the soldiers named on the monument. Many visitors leave mementos at the foot of the wall in memory of loved ones they lost in the Vietnam War or make rubbings from the incised names. It can be argued that much of this memorial's power derives from its Minimalist simplicity. Like Minimalist sculpture, it does not dictate response and therefore successfully encourages personal exploration. The polished granite surface also prompts such individual soul-searching—viewers see themselves reflected among the names.

Given the contentiousness and divided sentiments about the Vietnam War, any memorial to that conflict surely would encounter opposition. Maya Lin's wall, however, has illustrated the ability of art—even Minimalist sculpture—to elicit emotions in a diverse population and to help heal a nation.

[1] Elizabeth Hess, "A Tale of Two Memorials," *Art in America* 71, no. 4 (April 1983): 122.

---

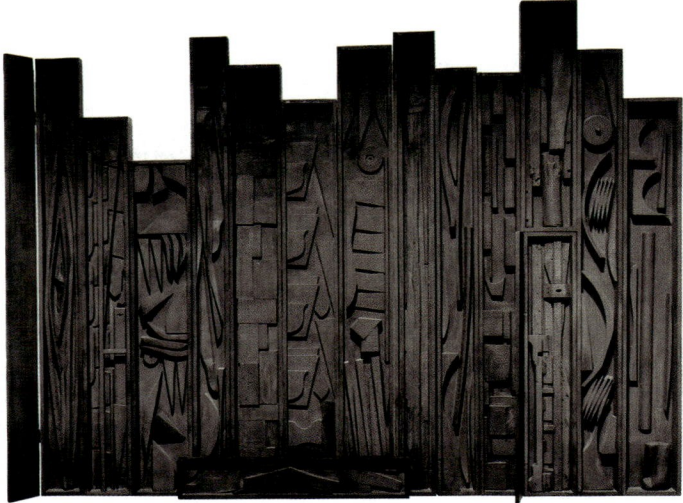

**34-17** LOUISE NEVELSON, *Tropical Garden II,* 1957–1959. Wood painted black, 5' 11½" × 10' 11¾" × 1'. Réunion des Musées Nationaux, Paris.

The monochromatic color scheme unifies the diverse parts of pieces such as *Tropical Garden II* (FIG. 34-17) and creates a mysterious field of shapes and shadows. The structures suggest magical environments resembling the treasured secret hideaways dimly remembered from childhood. Yet the boxy frames and the precision of the manufactured found objects create a rough geometric structure that the eye roams over freely, lingering on some details. The parts of a Nevelson sculpture and their interrelation recall the *Merz* constructions of Kurt Schwitters (see FIG. 33-26). The effect is also rather like viewing the side of an apartment building from a moving elevated train or like looking down on a city from the air.

**SENSUOUS ORGANIC FORMS** In contrast to the architectural nature of Nevelson's work, a sensuous organic quality recalling the evocative biomorphic Surrealist forms of Joan Miró (see FIG. 33-50) pervades the work of French-American artist LOUISE BOURGEOIS (b. 1911). She once described her sculptural subjects as "groups of objects relating to each other . . . the drama of one among many."[15] *Cumul I* (FIG. 34-18) is a collection of round-headed units huddled, with their heads protruding, within a

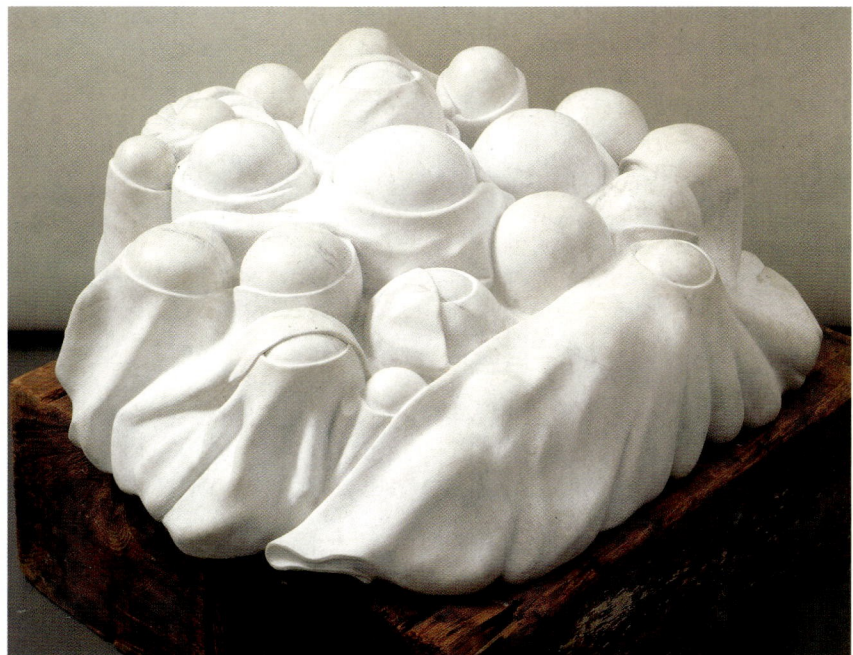

collective cloak dotted with holes. The units differ in size, and their position within the group lends a distinctive personality to each. Although the shapes remain abstract, they refer strongly to human figures. Bourgeois uses a wide variety of materials in her works, including wood, plaster, latex, and plastics, in addition to alabaster, marble, and bronze. She exploits each material's qualities to suit the expressiveness of the piece.

In *Cumul I,* the marble's high gloss next to its matte finish increases the sensuous distinction between the group of swelling forms and the soft folds swaddling them. Like Barbara Hepworth (see FIG. 33-70), Bourgeois connects her sculpture with the body's multiple relationships to landscape: "[My pieces] are anthropomorphic and they are landscape also, since our body could be considered from a topographical point of view, as a land with mounds and valleys and caves and holes."[16] However, Bourgeois's sculptures are more personal and more openly sexual than those of Hepworth. *Cumul I* represents perfectly the allusions Bourgeois seeks: "There has always been sexual suggestiveness in my work. Sometimes I am totally concerned with female shapes—characters of breasts like clouds—but often I merge the activity—phallic breasts, male and female, active and passive."[17]

**"NON-ART" ART** EVA HESSE (1936–1970), a Minimalist in the early part of her career, moved away from the severity characterizing much of Minimal art. She created sculptures that, although spare and simple, have a compelling presence. Using nontraditional sculptural materials such as fiberglass, cord, and latex, Hesse produced sculptures whose pure Minimalist forms appear to crumble, sag, and warp under the pressures of atmospheric force and gravity. Born Jewish in Hitler's Germany, the young Hesse was hidden by a Christian family when her parents and elder sister had to flee the Nazis. She was not reunited with them until the early 1940s, just before her parents divorced. Those extraordinary circumstances helped give her a lasting sense that the central conditions of modern life are strangeness and absurdity. Struggling to express these qualities in her art, she created informal sculptural arrangements with units often hung from the ceiling, leaned against the walls, or spilled out along the floor. She said she wanted her pieces to be

"non art, non connotative, non anthropomorphic, non geometric, non nothing, everything, but of another kind, vision, sort."[18]

Amazingly, *Hang-Up* (FIG. **34-19**) fulfills these requirements. The piece looks like a carefully made empty frame sprouting a strange feeler that extends into the room and doubles back to the frame. Hesse wrote that in this work, for the first time, her "idea of absurdity or extreme feeling came through."[19] In her words,

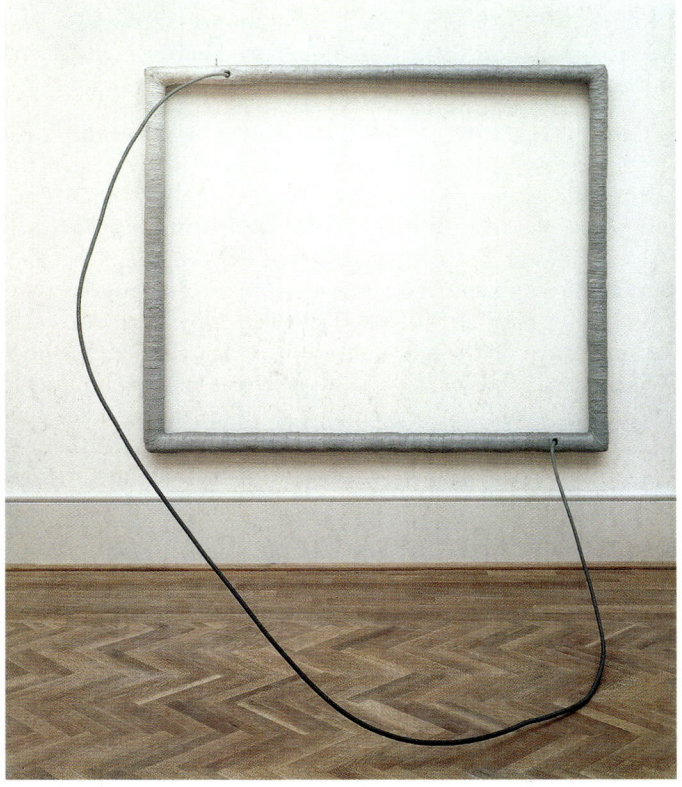

**34-19** EVA HESSE, *Hang-Up,* 1965–1966. Acrylic on cloth over wood and steel, 6′ × 7′ × 6′ 6″. Art Institute of Chicago, Chicago (gift of Arthur Keating and Mr. and Mrs. Edward Morris by exchange).

"[*Hang-Up*] has a kind of depth I don't always achieve and that is the kind of depth or soul or absurdity of life or meaning or feeling or intellect that I want to get."[20] The sculpture possesses a disquieting and touching presence, suggesting the fragility and grandeur of life amid the pressures of the modern age. Hesse was herself a touching and fragile presence in the art world; she died of a brain tumor at the young age of 34.

## Performance Art

In the interest of challenging artistic convention, avant-garde artists in the 1960s sought innovative forms of expression. As discussed earlier, artists such as the Post-Painterly Abstractionists (FIGS. 34-10 to 34-13) and the Minimalists (FIGS. 34-14 to 34-16) explored the implications of two- and three-dimensionality in keeping with the modernist critique of artistic principles. Other artists produced Happenings and, along with the group of Fluxus artists, both discussed later, developed the fourth dimension of time as an integral element of their artwork. These brief, temporary works eventually were categorized under the broad term *Performance art*. In such work, movements, gestures, and sounds of persons communicating with an audience, whose members may or may not participate in the event, replace physical objects. Generally, the only evidence remaining after these events is the documentary photographs taken at the time of their occurrence. Further, the informal and spontaneous nature of much of such work, which used the human body as primary material, pushed art outside the confines of the mainstream art institutions (for example, museums and galleries). Actions, events, and Happenings in large measure derived from the spirit characterizing Dada and Surrealist work and anticipated the rebellion and youthful exuberance of the 1960s. Initially, it appeared these artworks might serve as antidotes to the preciosity of most art objects and challenge art's function as a commodity. In the later 1960s, however, museums commissioned performances with increasing frequency, thereby neutralizing much of the subversiveness that characterized this art form.

**A COMPOSER'S INFLUENCE**  Many of the artists instrumental in the development of Performance art were influenced by the charismatic teacher and composer John Cage (1912–1992). Cage encouraged his students at both the New School for Social Research in New York and Black Mountain College in North Carolina to link their art directly with life. He brought to music composition his interests in the ideas of Duchamp (see Chapter 33, pages 981–983) and in Eastern philosophy. In his own work, Cage used methods such as chance to avoid the closed structures marking traditional music and, in his view, separating it from the unpredictable and multilayered qualities of daily existence. For example, the score for one of Cage's piano compositions instructs the performer to appear, sit down at the piano, raise the keyboard cover to mark the beginning of the piece, remain motionless at the instrument for 4 minutes and 33 seconds, and then close the keyboard cover, rise, and bow to signal the end of the work. The "music" would be the unplanned sounds and noises (such as coughs and whispers) emanating from the audience during the "performance."

**HAPPENINGS**  One of Cage's students in the 1950s was American artist ALLAN KAPROW (b. 1927). Extremely knowledgeable about art history, Kaprow was inspired by his study of music composition with Cage. Kaprow was equally committed to the intersection of art and life, and this, along with his belief that Jackson Pollock's actions when producing a painting were more important than the finished painting, led Kaprow to develop a type of event known as a *Happening*. He described a Happening as

> an assemblage of events performed or perceived in more than one time and place. Its material environments may be constructed, taken over directly from what is available, or altered slightly; just as its activities may be invented or commonplace. A Happening, unlike a stage play, may occur at a supermarket, driving along a highway, under a pile of rags, and in a friend's kitchen, either at once or sequentially. If sequentially, time may extend to more than a year. The Happening is performed according to plan but without rehearsal, audience or repetition. It is art but seems closer to life.[21]

Happenings were often participatory. One Happening consisted of a constructed setting with partitions on which viewers wrote phrases, while another involved spectators walking on a pile of tires. One of Kaprow's first Happenings, titled *18 Happenings in Six Parts* (1959), took place in the Reuben Gallery in New York City. For the event, the gallery space was divided into three sections with translucent plastic sheets. Over the course of the 90-minute piece, performers, including Kaprow's artist friends, executed activities such as bouncing balls, reading from placards, extending their arms like wings, and playing records as slides and lights went on and off in programmed sequences.

**THE THEATER OF THE SINGLE EVENT**  Other Cage students interested in the composer's search to find aesthetic potential in the nontraditional and commonplace formed the *Fluxus* group. Eventually expanding to include European and Japanese artists, this group's performances were more theatrical than Happenings. To distinguish their performances from Happenings, the artists associated with Fluxus coined the term *Events* to describe their work. Events focused on single actions, such as turning a light on and off or watching falling snow—what Fluxus artist La Monte Young (b. 1935) called "the theater of the single event."[22] The artists usually executed these Events on a stage separating the performers from the audience but without costumes or added decor. Events were not spontaneous; they followed a compositional "score," which, given the restricted nature of these performances, was short. Indeed, such scores were often limited to a few words, as evidenced by the scores (FIG. 34-20) of GEORGE BRECHT (b. 1926), the Fluxus member who invented such Events.

**IMPARTING LIFE TO MATERIALS**  Some artists produced works that involved both painting and performance. Gutai Bijutsu Kyokai (Concrete Art Association), a group of 18 Japanese artists in Osaka, expanded the action of painting into the realm of performance—in a sense, taking Jackson Pollock's painting methods into a public arena. Led by Jiro Yoshihara, Gutai was founded in 1954 and devoted itself to art that combined Japanese traditional practices such as Zen with a renewed appreciation for materials. In the "Gutai Art Manifesto," Yoshihara explained: "Gutai does not alter the material. Gutai imparts life to the material. . . . [T]he human spirit and the material shake hands with each other, but keep their distance."[23] Accordingly, Gutai works involved such actions as throwing paint balls at blank canvases or wallowing in mud as a means of shaping it. In a 1955 piece, titled *Making a Work with His Own Body* (FIG. 34-21), Gutai member KAZUO SHIRAGA (b. 1924) used his body to "paint" with mud. The Gutai group dissolved upon Yoshihara's death in 1972.

**BODILY RELATIONSHIP TO MEAT**  Like Gutai, CAROLEE SCHNEEMANN (b. 1939) integrated painting and performance in her artworks. Her self-described "kinetic theater" radically transformed

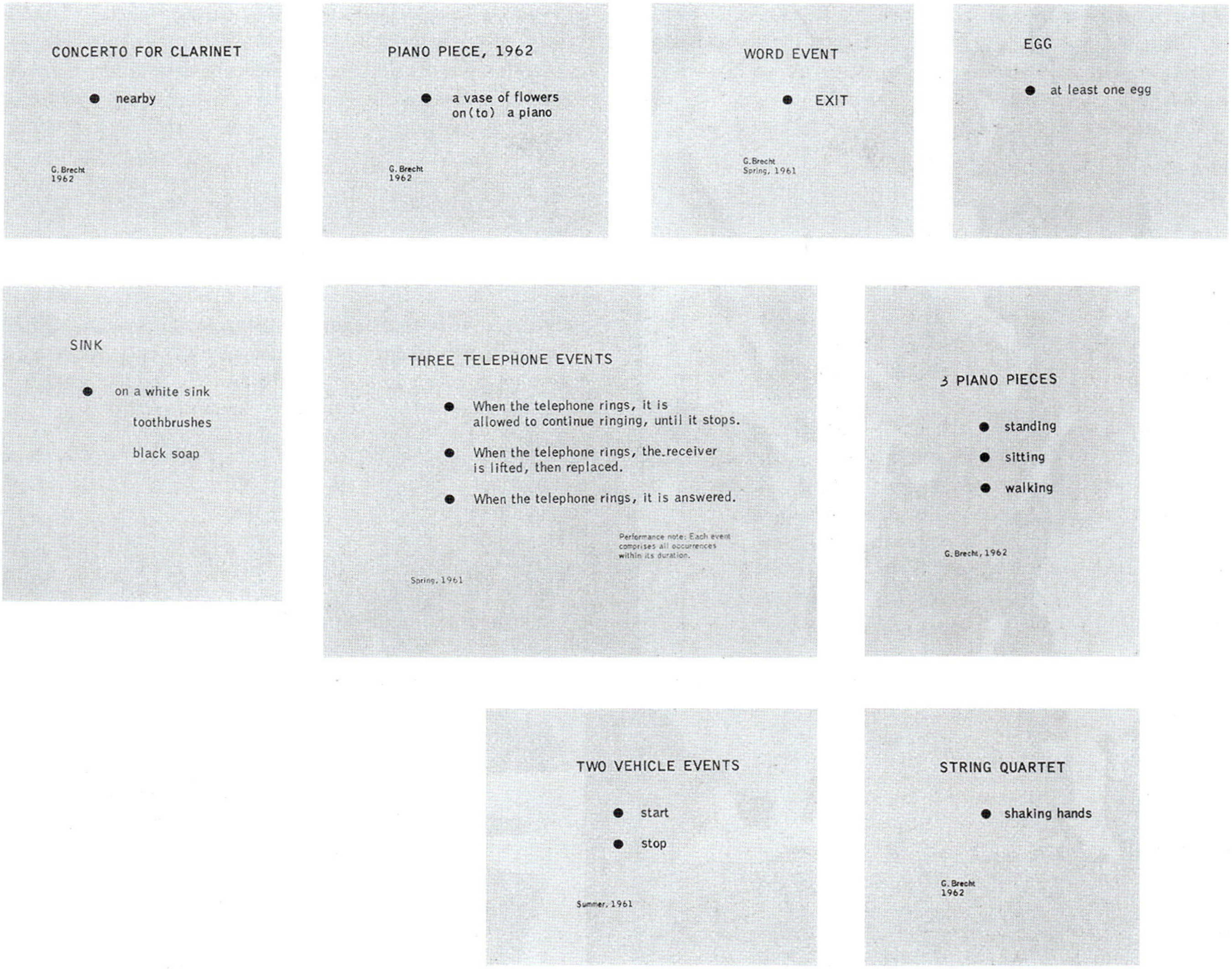

CONCERTO FOR CLARINET

● nearby

G. Brecht
1962

---

PIANO PIECE, 1962

● a vase of flowers
on(to) a piano

G. Brecht
1962

---

WORD EVENT

● EXIT

G. Brecht
Spring, 1961

---

EGG

● at least one egg

---

SINK

● on a white sink

toothbrushes

black soap

---

THREE TELEPHONE EVENTS

● When the telephone rings, it is
allowed to continue ringing, until it stops.

● When the telephone rings, the receiver
is lifted, then replaced.

● When the telephone rings, it is answered.

Performance note: Each event
comprises all occurrences
within its duration.

Spring, 1961

---

3 PIANO PIECES

● standing

● sitting

● walking

G. Brecht, 1962

---

TWO VEHICLE EVENTS

● start

● stop

Summer, 1961

---

STRING QUARTET

● shaking hands

G. Brecht
1962

---

**34-20** George Brecht, *Event Scores.*

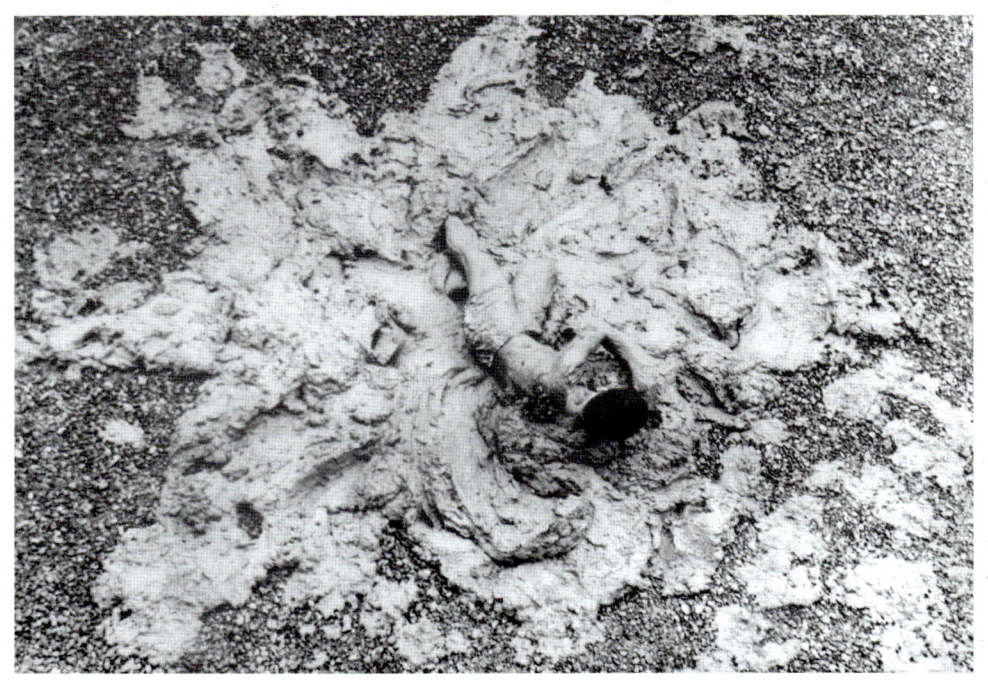

**34-21** Kazuo Shiraga, *Making a Work with His Own Body*, 1955. Mud.

Beuys's commitment to artworks stimulating thought about art and life was partially due to his experiences during the war. While serving as a pilot, he was shot down over the Crimea, and claimed that nomadic Tatars nursed him back to health by swaddling his body in fat and felt to warm him. Fat and felt thus symbolized healing and regeneration to the artist, and he incorporated these materials into many of his sculptures and actions, such as *How to Explain Pictures to a Dead Hare* (FIG. **34-23**). This one-person event consisted of stylized actions evoking a sense of mystery and sacred ritual. Beuys appeared in a room hung with his drawings, cradling a dead hare he spoke to softly. Beuys coated his head with honey covered with gold leaf, creating a shimmering mask. In this manner, he took on the role of the shaman, an individual with special spiritual powers. As a shaman, Beuys believed he was acting to help revolutionize human thought so that each human being could become a truly free and creative person.

**DESTRUCTION AS CREATION** The notion of destruction as an act of creation surfaces in a number of kinetic artworks, most notably in the sculpture of JEAN TINGUELY (1925–1991). Trained as a painter in his native Switzerland, Tinguely gravitated to motion sculpture. In the 1950s, he made a series of "metamatic" machines, motor-driven devices that produced instant abstract paintings. He programmed these metamatics electronically

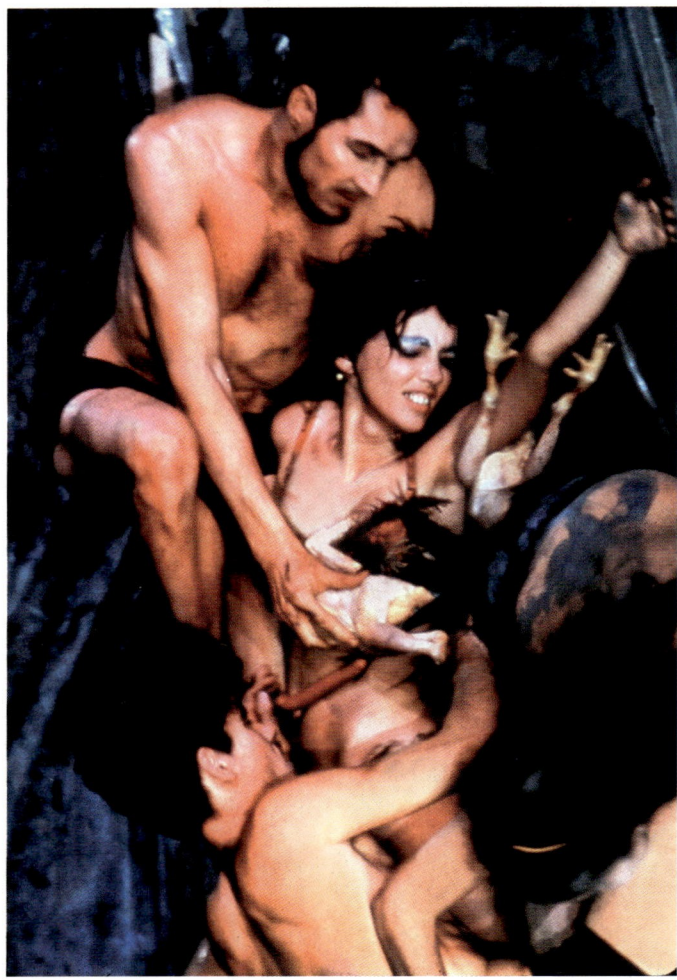

**34-22** CAROLEE SCHNEEMANN, *Meat Joy*, 1964. Performance: raw fish, chickens, sausages, wet paint, plastic, rope, paper scrap. Judson Church, New York City. 🔵

the nature of performance by introducing a feminist dimension through the use of her often-nude body to challenge "the psychic territorial power lines by which women were admitted to the Art Stud Club."[24] In her 1964 performance, *Meat Joy* (FIG. **34-22**), Schneemann reveled in the taste, smell, and feel of plucked chickens and raw sausages. Her description of the performance included the following passage:

> carcass as paint . . . flesh jubilation . . . extremes of this sense . . .
> may involve quantities of dark fabric and paint drawn from performance area outward into audience to become inundation of all available space—action and viewing space interchanged, broken through. Smell, feel of meat . . . chickens, fish, sausages? I see several women whose gestures develop from tactile, bodily relationships to individual men and a mass of meat slices. Specific sequence of collision and embrace.[25]

**PERFORMANCE AS RITUAL** German artist JOSEPH BEUYS (1921–1986) was strongly influenced by the leftist politics of the Fluxus group in the early 1960s. Drawing on Happenings and Fluxus, Beuys created actions aimed at illuminating the condition of modern humanity. He wanted to make a new kind of sculptural object that would include "Thinking Forms: how we mould our thoughts or Spoken Forms: how we shape our thoughts into words or Social Sculpture: how we mould and shape the world in which we live."[26]

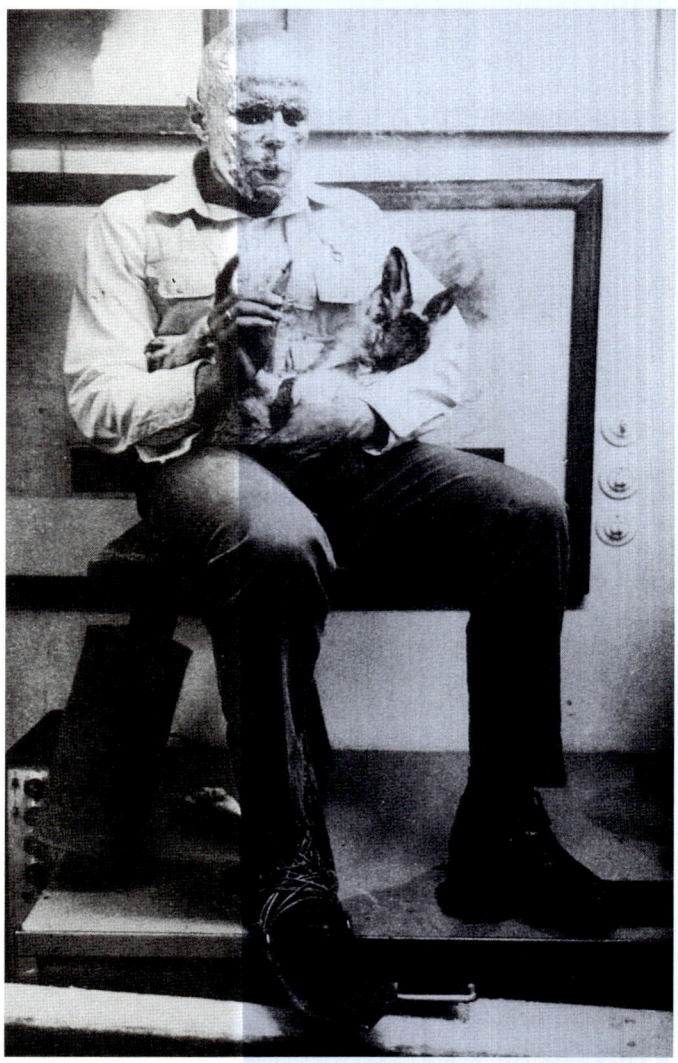

**34-23** JOSEPH BEUYS, *How to Explain Pictures to a Dead Hare*, 1965. Photograph of performance art. Schmela Gallery, Düsseldorf. 🔵

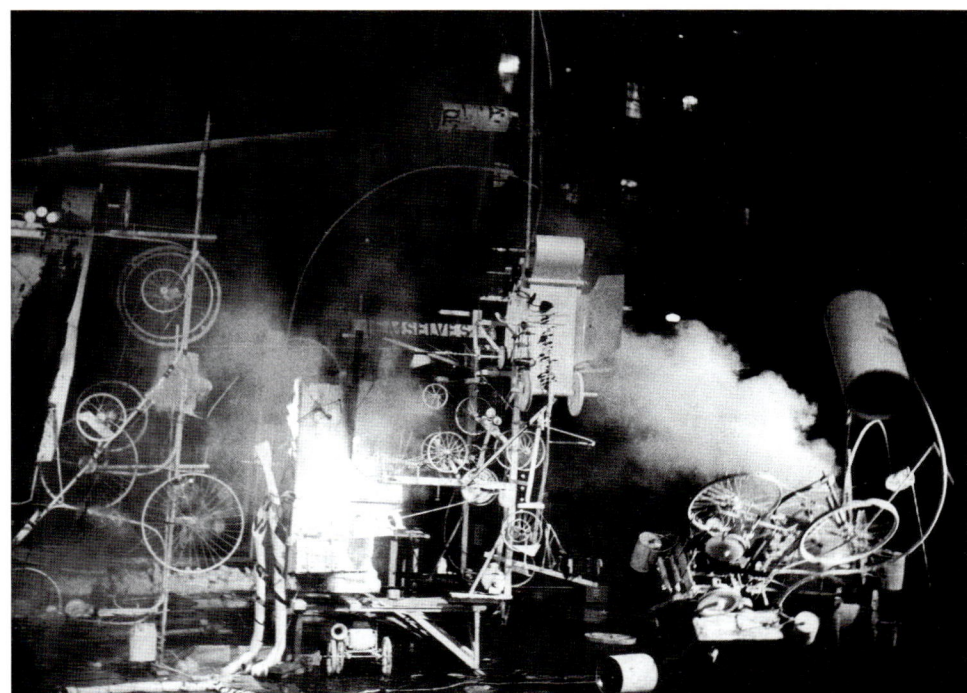

to act with an antimechanical unpredictability when viewers inserted felt-tipped marking pens into a pincer and pressed a button to initiate the pen's motion across a small sheet of paper clipped to an "easel." Viewers could use different-colored markers in succession and could stop and start the device to achieve some degree of control over the final image. These operations created a series of small works resembling Abstract Expressionist paintings.

In 1960, Tinguely expanded the scale of his work with a kinetic piece designed to "perform" and then destroy itself in a large courtyard area at the Museum of Modern Art in New York City. He created *Homage to New York* (FIG. **34-24**) with the aid of engineer Billy Klüver, who helped him scrounge wheels and other moving objects from a dump near Manhattan. The completed structure, painted white for visibility against the dark night sky, included a player piano modified into a metamatic painting machine, a weather balloon that inflated during the performance, vials of colored smoke, and a host of gears, pulleys, wheels, and other found machine parts.

This work was premiered (and destroyed) on March 17, 1960, in the sculpture garden of the Museum of Modern Art, with New York Governor Nelson Rockefeller, an array of distinguished guests, and three television crews in attendance. Once the machine was turned on, smoke poured from its interior and the piano caught fire. Various parts of the machine broke off and rambled away, while one of the metamatics tried but failed to produce an abstract painting. Finally, Tinguely summoned a firefighter to extinguish the blaze and ensure the demise of *Homage to New York* with his axe. Like the artist's other kinetic sculptures, *Homage to New York* shared something of Duchamp's satiric Dadaist spirit (see FIGS. 33-23 and 33-24) and the droll import of Klee's *Twittering Machine* (see FIG. 33-51). But Tinguely deliberately made the wacky behavior of *Homage to New York* more playful and more endearing. Having been given a freedom of eccentric behavior unprecedented in the mechanical world, Tinguely's creations often seem to behave with the whimsical individuality of human actors.

People first used the terms *Happening, action,* and *body art* to describe various kinds of artistic endeavors involving the body as aesthetic material. In the mid-1970s, people widely began to use the generic term *Performance art* to describe this broad range of creative activity. Extreme examples of Performance art involved artists who created various performance pieces centered on risk-taking activities such as being shot with a gun or crawling over broken glass. Such work dramatically challenged accepted definitions of art.

## Conceptual Art

The relentless challenges to artistic convention fundamental to the historical avant-garde reached a logical conclusion with *Conceptual art* in the late 1960s. Conceptual artists asserted that the "artfulness" of art lay in the artist's idea, rather than in its final expression. Indeed, some Conceptual artists eliminated the object altogether. In addition, Conceptual artists rethought aesthetic issues, which long have formed the foundation of art. These artists regarded the idea, or concept, as the defining component of the artwork.

**WHAT CONSTITUTES "CHAIRNESS"?** American artist JOSEPH KOSUTH (b. 1945) was a major proponent of Conceptual art. His work operates at the intersection of language and vision, dealing with the relationship between the abstract and the concrete. In a broader sense, his art explores the ways in which aesthetic meaning is generated. For example, *One and Three Chairs* (FIG. **34-25**) consists of an actual chair flanked by a full-scale photograph of the chair and a photostat of a dictionary definition of the word *chair*. Kosuth asked the viewer to ponder the notion of what constitutes "chairness." He explained, "It meant you could have an art work which was that *idea* of an art work, and its formal components weren't important. I felt I had found a way to make art without formal components being confused for an expressionist composition. The expression was in the idea, not the form—the forms were only a device in the service of the idea."[27] Kosuth explored these concepts further in a series of works titled *Art as Idea as Idea.* He elaborated:

> Like everyone else I inherited the idea of art as a set of *formal* problems. So when I began to re-think my ideas of art, I had to re-think that thinking process, and it begins with the making process. . . . "Art as Idea *as Idea*" [was] intended to suggest that the real creative process, and the radical shift, was in changing the

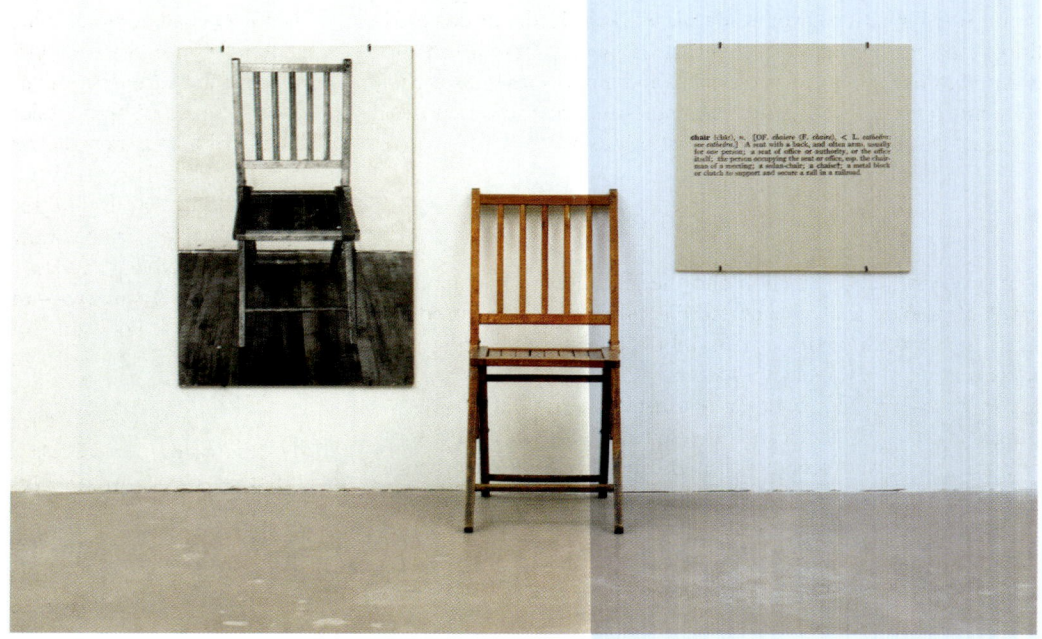

**34-25** JOSEPH KOSUTH, *One and Three Chairs*, 1965. Wooden folding chair, photographic copy of a chair, and photographic enlargement of a dictionary definition of a chair; chair, 2′ $8\frac{3}{8}$″ × 1′ $2\frac{7}{8}$″ × 1′ $8\frac{7}{8}$″; photo panel, 3′ × 2′ $\frac{1}{8}$″; text panel, 2′ × 2′ $\frac{1}{8}$″. Museum of Modern Art, New York (Larry Aldrich Foundation Fund).

idea of art itself. In other words, my idea of doing that was the real creative content.[28]

**WORDS OF NEON** BRUCE NAUMAN (b. 1941) made his artistic presence known in the mid-1960s, when he abandoned painting and turned to object-making. Since then, his work has been amazingly varied; in addition to sculptural pieces constructed from different materials, including rubber, fiberglass, and cardboard, he has also produced photographs, films, videos, books,

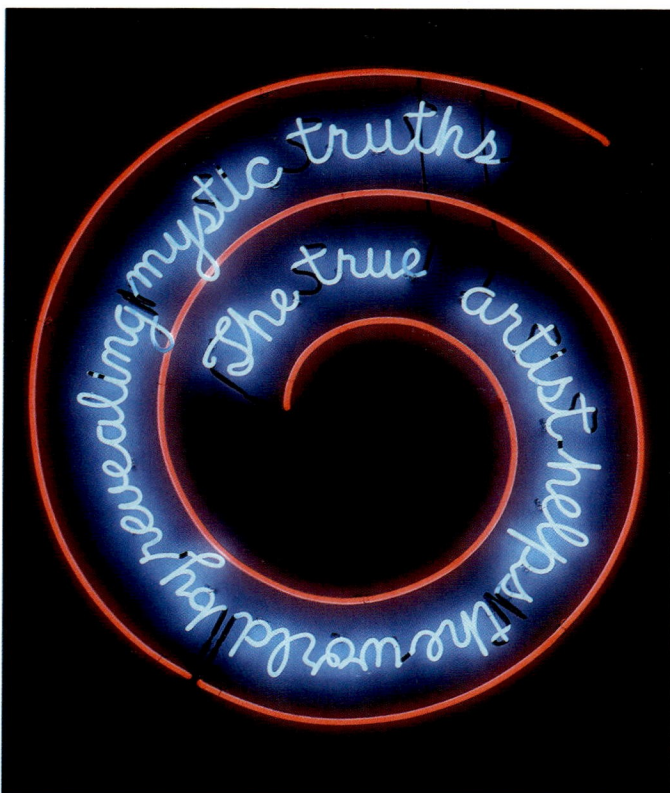

**34-26** BRUCE NAUMAN, *The True Artist Helps the World by Revealing Mystic Truths (Window or Wall Sign)*, 1967. Neon with glass tubing suspension frame, 4′ 11″ × 4′ 7″ × 2″. Private collection.

and large room installations. Performance has also been a staple of his oeuvre. Nauman's work of the 1960s intersected with that of the Conceptual artists, especially in terms of the philosophical exploration that was the foundation of much of his art. Further, his interest in language and wordplay allies him with other Conceptual artists, although humor and whimsy play a much larger role in Nauman's art. *The True Artist Helps the World by Revealing Mystic Truths (Window or Wall Sign)* (FIG. **34-26**) was the first of Nauman's many neon sculptures. He selected neon because he wanted to find a medium that would be identified with a nonartistic function. Determined to discover a way to connect objects with words, he utilized the method outlined in philosopher Ludwig Wittgenstein's *Philosophical Investigations* (1953), which encouraged contradictory and nonsensical arguments. This neon sculpture spins out an emphatic assertion, but as Nauman explained, "It was kind of a test—like when you say something out loud to see if you believe it. . . . [I]t was on the one hand a totally silly idea and yet, on the other hand, I believed it."[29]

Other Conceptual artists pursued this idea that "the idea itself, even if not made visual, is as much a work of art as a product"[30] by creating works involving invisible materials, such as inert gases, radioactive isotopes, or radio waves. In each case, viewers must base their understanding of the artwork on what they know about the properties of these materials, rather than on any visible empirical data, and depend on the artist's linguistic description of the work. Ultimately, the Conceptual artists challenged the very premises of artistic production, pushing art's boundaries to a point where no concrete definition of *art* is possible.

## ART FOR THE PUBLIC

The avant-garde provided a major directional impetus for art production in the postwar years. As seen in the work of the Abstract Expressionists, Post-Painterly Abstractionists, and Minimalists, artists most frequently expressed this interest in modernist experimental art in the vocabulary of resolute abstraction. Other artists, however, felt that the insular and introspective attitude of the avant-garde had resulted in public alienation. These artists were committed to the communicative power of art and to reaching a wide audience with their art. This is not to suggest that they created reactionary or academic work; indeed, one can easily find avant-garde aspects in their art. However, these artists (for example, Pop artists, Superrealists, and Environmental artists) were much less committed to the single-minded focus on formal issues characteristic of the modernist mindset.

## The Development of Pop Art

The prevalence of abstraction and the formal experimentation in much of postwar art had alienated the public. *Pop art* reintroduced all of the artistic devices—signs, symbols, metaphors, allusions, illusions, and figurative imagery—traditionally used to convey meaning in art that recent avant-garde artists, in search of purity, had purged from their abstract and often reductive works. Pop artists not only embraced representation but also produced an art resolutely grounded in consumer culture, the mass media, and popular culture, thereby making it much more accessible and understandable to the average person. Indeed, the name *Pop art* (credited to the British art critic Lawrence Alloway, although he is unsure of the term's initial usage) is short for *popular art* and referred to the popular mass culture and familiar imagery of the contemporary urban environment. This was an art form firmly entrenched in the sensibilities and visual language of a late-20th-century mass audience.

**BRITISH POP** The roots of Pop art can be traced to a group of young British artists, architects, and writers who formed the Independent Group at the Institute of Contemporary Art in London in the early 1950s. They sought to initiate fresh thinking in art, in part by sharing their fascination with the aesthetics and content of such facets of popular culture as advertising, comic books, and movies.

Discussions at the Independent Group in London probed the role and meaning of symbols from mass culture and the advertising media. In 1956, a group member, RICHARD HAMILTON (b. 1922), made a small collage, *Just What Is It That Makes Today's Homes So Different, So Appealing?* (FIG. **34-27**), that characterized many of the attitudes of British Pop art. Trained as an engineering draftsman, exhibition designer, and painter, Hamilton was very interested in the way advertising shapes public attitudes. Long intrigued by Duchamp's ideas, Hamilton consistently combined elements of popular art and fine art, seeing both as belonging to the whole world of visual communication. The Pop artist created *Just What Is It* for the poster and catalog of one section of an exhibition titled *This Is Tomorrow*—an environment-installation filled with images from Hollywood cinema, science fiction, the mass media, and one reproduction of a van Gogh painting (to represent popular fine artworks).

The fantasy interior in Hamilton's collage reflects the values of modern consumer culture through figures and objects cut from glossy magazines. *Just What Is It* includes references to the mass media (such as the television, the theater marquee outside the window, and the newspaper), to advertising (for Hoover vacuums, Ford cars, Armour hams, and Tootsie Pops), and to popular culture (such as the girlie magazine, Charles Atlas, and romance comic books). Scholars have written much about the possible deep meaning of this piece, and few would deny the work's sardonic effect, whether or not the artist intended to make a pointed comment. Such artworks stimulated the viewer's wide-ranging speculation about society's values, and this kind of intellectual toying with mass-media meaning and imagery typified British and European Pop art.

## American Pop Art and Consumer Culture

Although Pop originated in England, the movement found its greatest articulation and success in the United States, in large part because the more fully matured consumer culture provided

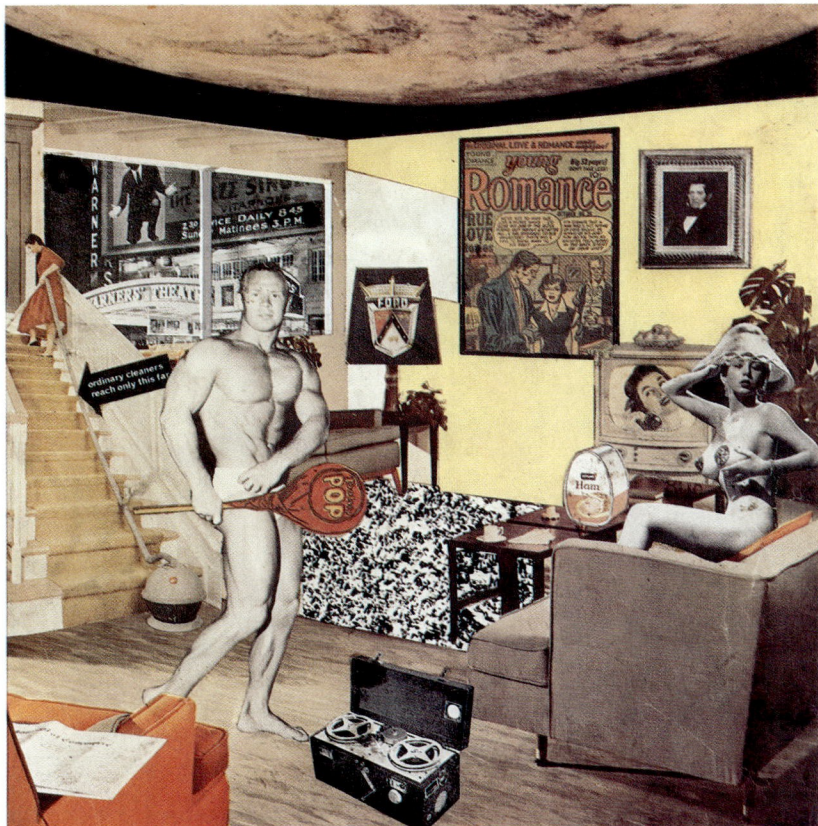

**34-27** RICHARD HAMILTON, *Just What Is It That Makes Today's Homes So Different, So Appealing?* 1956. Collage, $10\frac{1}{4}'' \times 9\frac{3}{4}''$. Kunsthalle Tübingen, Tübingen.

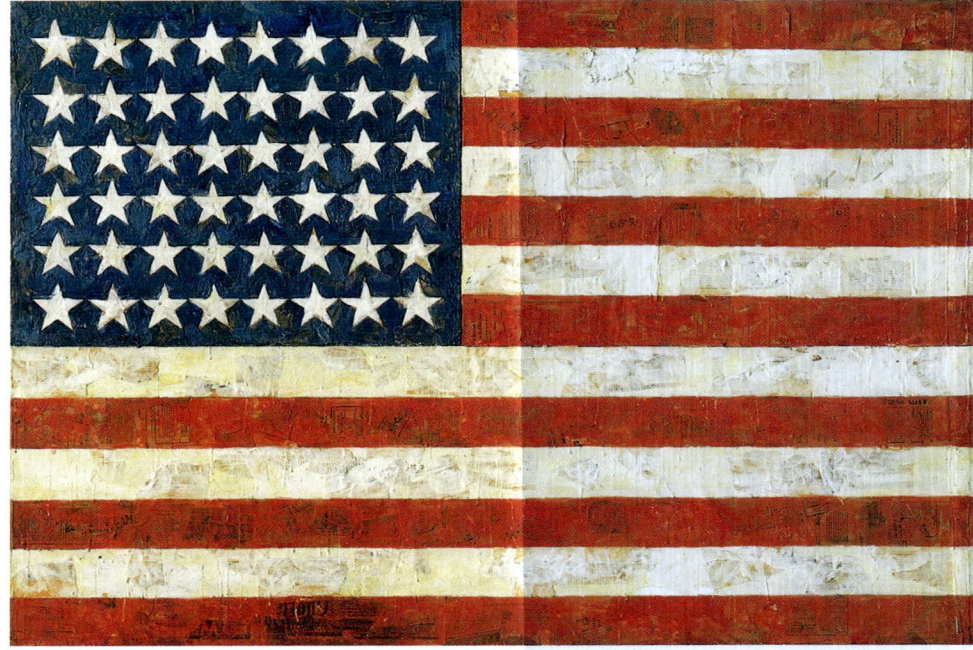

**34-28** JASPER JOHNS, *Flag*, 1954–1955, dated on reverse 1954. Encaustic, oil, and collage on fabric mounted on plywood, 3' 6¼" × 5' ⅝". Museum of Modern Art, New York (gift of Philip Johnson in honor of Alfred H. Barr Jr.). Copyright © Jasper Johns/Licensed by VAGA, New York, NewYork.

a fertile environment in which the movement flourished through the 1960s. Indeed, Independent Group members claimed their inspiration came from Hollywood, Detroit, and Madison Avenue, New York, paying homage to America's predominance in the realms of mass media, mass production, and advertising.

Two artists pivotal to the early development of American Pop were Jasper Johns and Robert Rauschenberg. Both artists introduced elements from popular culture into their art; these references add to the power and immediacy of their work.

**THINGS SEEN BUT NOT LOOKED AT** In his early work, JASPER JOHNS (b. 1930) was particularly interested in drawing the viewer's attention to common objects in the world—what he called things "seen but not looked at."[31] To this end, he did several series of paintings of targets, flags, numbers, and alphabets. For example, *Flag* (FIG. **34-28**) depicts an object people view frequently but rarely scrutinize. The surface of the work is highly textured due to Johns's use of encaustic, an ancient method of painting with liquid wax and dissolved pigment (see "Iaia of Cyzicus and the Art of Encaustic Painting," Chapter 10, page 288). First, the artist embedded a collage of newspaper scraps or photographs in wax. He then painted over them with the encaustic. Because the wax hardened quickly, Johns could work rapidly, and the translucency of the wax allows the viewer to see the layered painting process.

**"COMBINING" PAINTING AND SCULPTURE** Johns's friend ROBERT RAUSCHENBERG (b. 1925) began using mass-media images in his work in the 1950s. Rauschenberg set out to create works that would be open and indeterminate, and he began by making "combines," which intersperse painted passages with sculptural elements. Combines are, in a sense, Rauschenberg's personal variation on *assemblages,* artworks constructed from already existing objects. At times, these combines seem to be sculptures with painting incorporated into certain sections; others seem to be paintings with three-dimensional objects attached to the surface. In the 1950s, such works contained an array of art reproductions, magazine and newspaper clippings, and passages painted in an Abstract Expressionist style. In the early 1960s, Rauschenberg adopted the commercial medium of silk-screen

printing, first in black and white and then in color, and began filling entire canvases with appropriated news images and anonymous photographs of city scenes. *Canyon* (FIG. **34-29**) is typical of his combines. Pieces of printed paper and photographs are attached to the canvas. Much of the unevenly painted surface

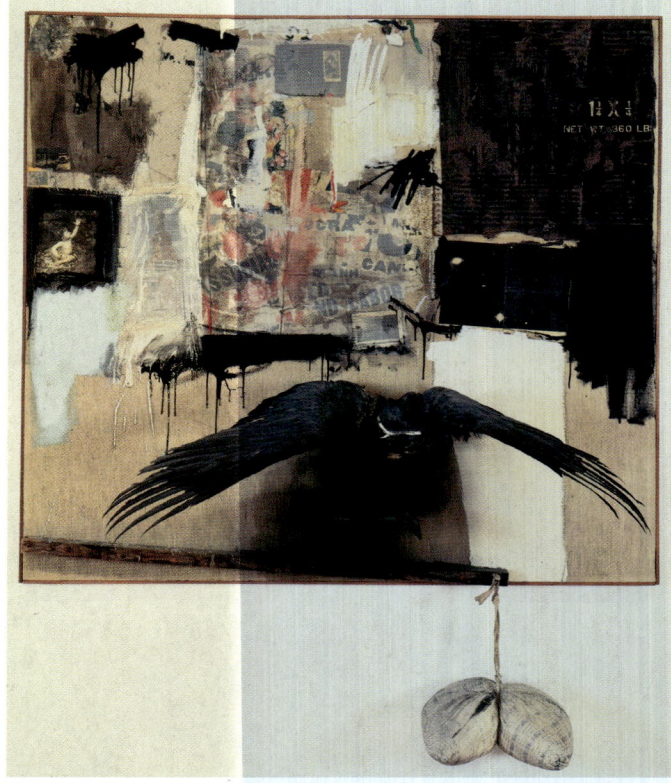

**34-29** ROBERT RAUSCHENBERG, *Canyon,* 1959. Oil, pencil, paper, fabric, metal, cardboard box, printed paper, printed reproductions, photograph, wood, paint tube, and mirror on canvas, with oil on bald eagle, string, and pillow, 6' 9¾" × 5' 10" × 2'. Sonnabend Collection. Copyright © Robert Rauschenberg/Licensed by VAGA, New York, New York.

consists of pigment roughly applied in a manner reminiscent of de Kooning's work (FIG. 34-6). A stuffed bald eagle attached to the lower part of the combine spreads its wings as if lifting off in flight toward the viewer. Completing the combine, a pillow dangles from a string attached to a wood stick below the eagle. The artist presented the work's components in a jumbled fashion. He tilted or turned some of the images sideways, and each overlays or is invaded by part of another image. The compositional confusion may resemble that of a Dada collage, but the parts of Rauschenberg's combine paintings maintain their individuality more than those in a Schwitters piece (see FIG. 33-26). The various recognizable images and objects appear to be a sequence of visual non sequiturs, and it is virtually impossible to arrive at a consistent reading of a Rauschenberg combine. The eye scans a Rauschenberg canvas much as it might survey the environment on a walk through the city. As John Cage perceptively noted, "There is no more subject in a combine [by Rauschenberg] than there is in a page from a newspaper. Each thing that is there is a subject. It is a situation involving multiplicity."[32]

**A "COMIC" FOCUS IN ART** As the Pop movement matured, the images became more concrete and tightly controlled. ROY LICHTENSTEIN (1923–1997) turned his attention to the comic book as a mainstay of American popular culture. In paintings such as *Hopeless* (FIG. **34-30**), Lichtenstein excerpted an image from a comic book, a form of entertainment meant to be read and discarded, and immortalized the image in monumental scale. Aside from that modification, Lichtenstein was remarkably faithful to the original comic strip image. First, he selected a melodramatic scene common to the romance comic books that were exceedingly popular at the time. Second, he used the visual vocabulary of the comic strip, with its dark black outlines and unmodulated color areas, and retained the familiar square dimensions. Third, Lichtenstein's printing technique, *benday dots,* calls attention to the mass-produced derivation of the image. Named after its inventor, the newspaper printer Benjamin

Day, the benday dot system involves the modulation of colors through the placement and size of colored dots. Lichtenstein's work further reinforces the visual shorthand language of the comic book.

**THE ART OF COMMODITIES** The quintessential American Pop artist was ANDY WARHOL (1928–1987). An early successful career as a commercial artist and illustrator grounded Warhol in the sensibility and visual rhetoric of advertising and the mass media, knowledge that proved useful for his Pop art. In paintings such as *Green Coca-Cola Bottles* (FIG. **34-31**), Warhol selected an icon of mass-produced, consumer culture of the time. Despite Coca-Cola's supremacy as the best-selling cola soft drink in the early 1960s, its manufacturers felt compelled to launch a major advertising campaign to challenge the growing market share of its primary rival, Pepsi-Cola. Warhol's choice of the reassuringly familiar curved Coke bottle thus intersected with the visual imagery American consumers encountered frequently at that time. As did other Pop artists, Warhol used a visual vocabulary and a printing technique that reinforced the image's connections to consumer culture. The repetition and redundancy of the Coke bottle reflects the omnipresence and dominance of this product in American society. The silk-screen technique (also used by Rauschenberg) allowed Warhol to print the image endlessly. So immersed was Warhol in a culture of mass production that he not only produced numerous canvases of the same image but also named his studio "the Factory."

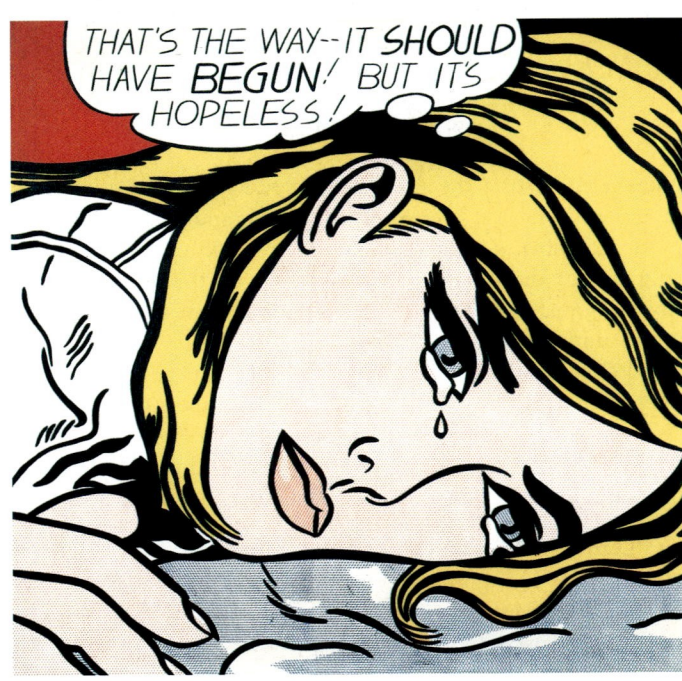

**34-30** ROY LICHTENSTEIN, *Hopeless,* 1963. Oil on canvas, 3′ 8″ × 3′ 8″. Offentliche Kunstsammlung Basel, © Estate of Roy Lichtenstein.

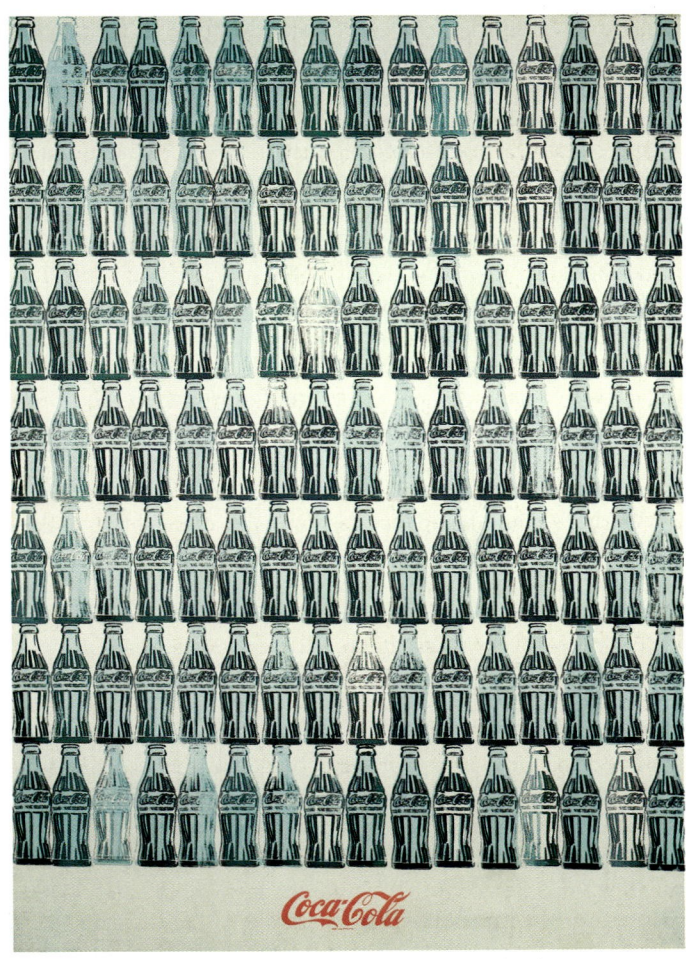

**34-31** ANDY WARHOL, *Green Coca-Cola Bottles,* 1962. Oil on canvas, 6′ 10½″ × 4′ 9″. Whitney Museum of American Art, New York.

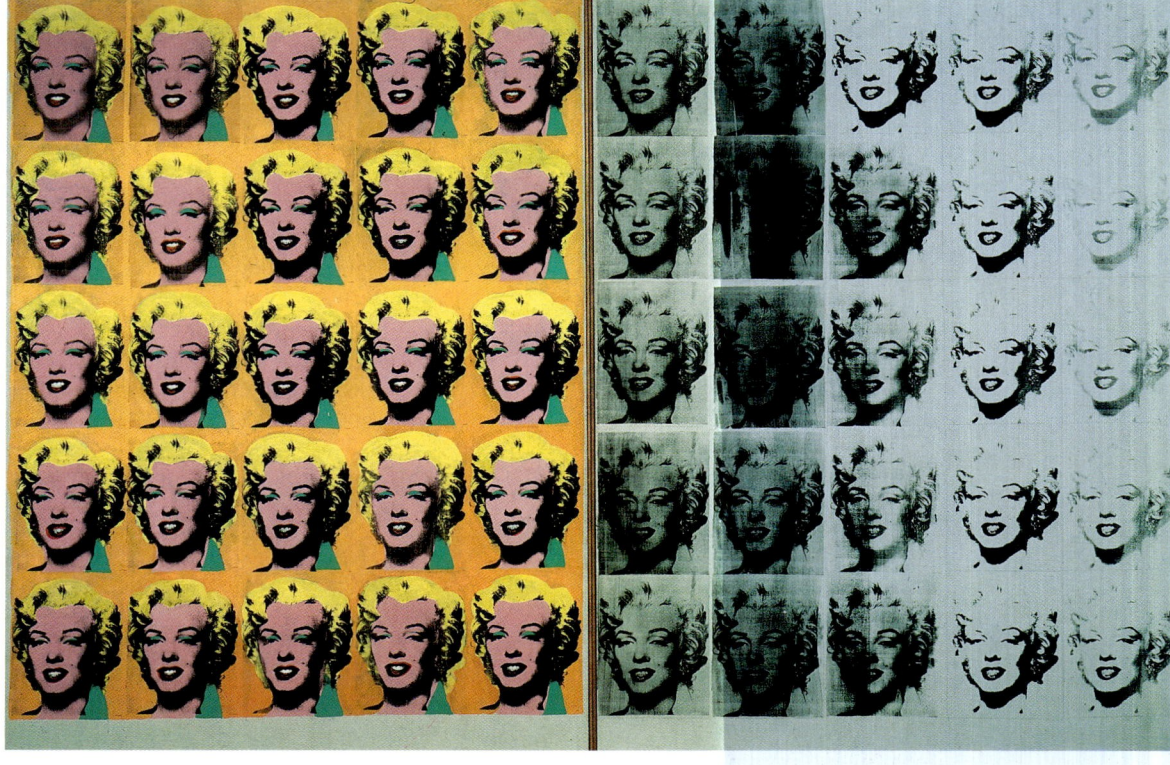

**34-32** Andy Warhol, *Marilyn Diptych*, 1962. Oil, acrylic, and silkscreen enamel on canvas, each panel 6′ 8″ × 4′ 9″. Tate Gallery, London.

**A MYTHIC CELEBRITY** Warhol often produced images of Hollywood celebrities, such as Marilyn Monroe. Like his other paintings, these works emphasize the commodity status of the subjects depicted. Warhol created *Marilyn Diptych* (FIG. **34-32**) in the weeks following the tragic suicide of the movie star in August 1962, capitalizing on the media frenzy that her death prompted. Warhol selected a publicity photo of Monroe, one that provides no insight into the real Norma Jean Baker. Rather, all the viewer sees is a mask—a persona the Hollywood myth machine generated. The garish colors and the flat application of paint contribute to the image's masklike quality. Like that of the Coke bottles, the repetition of Monroe's face reinforces her status as a consumer product, her glamorous, haunting visage seemingly confronting the viewer endlessly, as it did the American public in the aftermath of her death. The right half of this work, with its poor registration of pigment, suggests a sequence of film stills, referencing the realm from which Monroe derived her fame.

Warhol's own ascendance to the realm of celebrity underscored his remarkable and astute understanding of the dynamics and visual language of mass culture. He predicted that the age of mass media would enable everyone to become famous for 15 minutes. His own celebrity lasted much longer, long after his death at age 58 in 1987.

**SUPERSIZING SCULPTURE** Pop artist Claes Oldenburg (b. 1929) has produced sculptures that incisively comment on American consumer culture. His early works consisted of plaster reliefs of food and clothing items. Oldenburg constructed these sculptures of plaster layered on chicken wire and muslin, painting them with cheap commercial house enamel. In later works, focused on the same subjects, he shifted to large-scale stuffed sculptures of sewn vinyl or canvas. Examples of both types of sculptures can be seen in the photograph of a one-person show

(FIG. **34-33**) that Oldenburg held at the Green Gallery in New York in 1962. He had included many of the works in this exhibition in an earlier show he mounted titled *The Store*. An installation of Oldenburg's sculptures of consumer products, *The Store* was an appropriate comment on the function of art as a commodity in a consumer society. Over the years, Oldenburg's sculpture has become increasingly monumental. In recent decades, he and his wife and collaborator, Coosje van Bruggen (b. 1942), have become particularly well known for their mammoth outdoor sculptures of familiar, commonplace objects, such as cue balls, shuttlecocks, clothespins, and torn notebooks.

## Superrealism

Like the Pop artists, the artists associated with *Superrealism* were interested in finding a form of artistic communication that was more accessible to the public than the remote, unfamiliar visual language of the Abstract Expressionists or the Post-Painterly Abstractionists. The Superrealists expanded Pop's iconography in both painting and sculpture by making images in the late 1960s and 1970s involving scrupulous fidelity to optical fact. Because many Superrealists used photographs as sources for their imagery, people also referred to the Superrealist painters as Photorealists. These artists reproduced in minute and unsparing detail the commonplace facts and artifacts that Pop art addressed.

**EXPLORING "PHOTO-VISION"** American artist Audrey Flack (b. 1931) was one of the movement's pioneers. Her paintings, such as *Marilyn* (FIG. **34-34**), were not simply technical exercises but were also conceptual inquiries into the nature of photography and the extent to which photography constructs an understanding of reality. Flack noted, "[Photography is] my whole

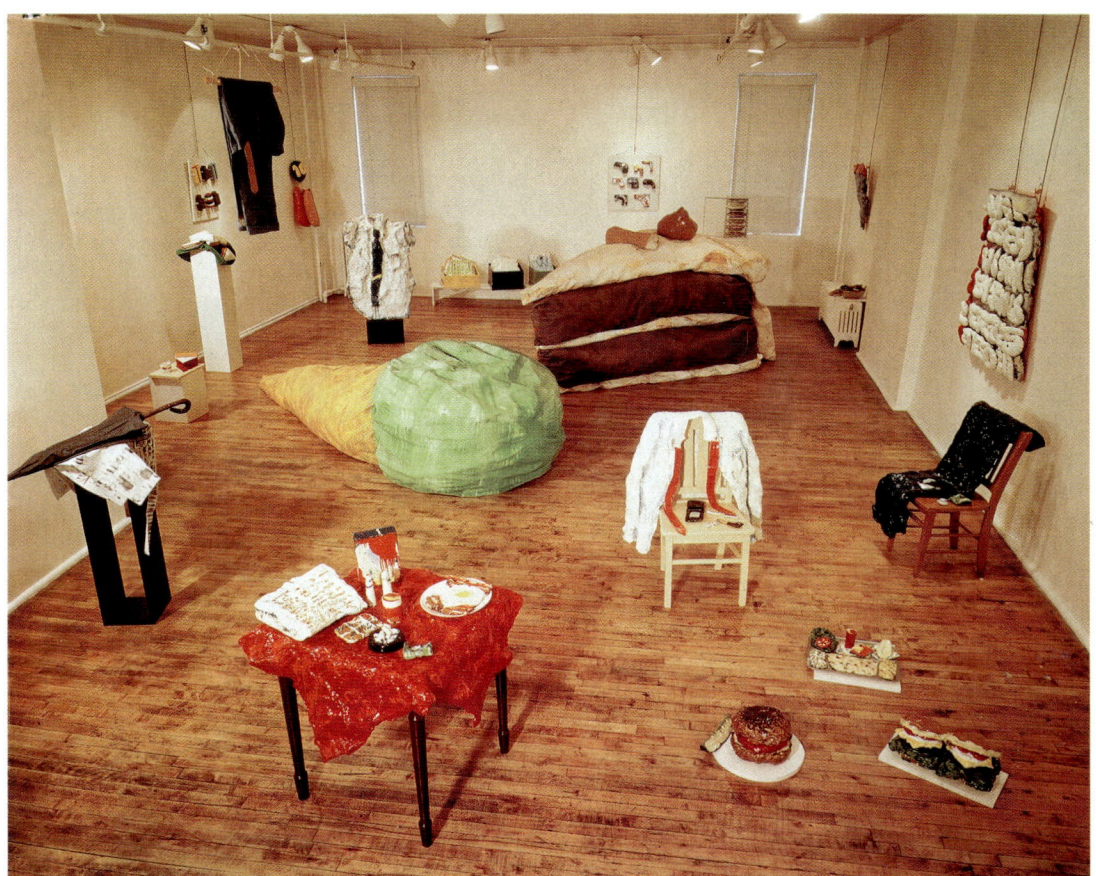

34-33 CLAES OLDENBURG, photo of one-person show at the Green Gallery, New York, 1962. © Estate of Rudolph Burkhardt/ Licensed by VAGA, New York, New York.

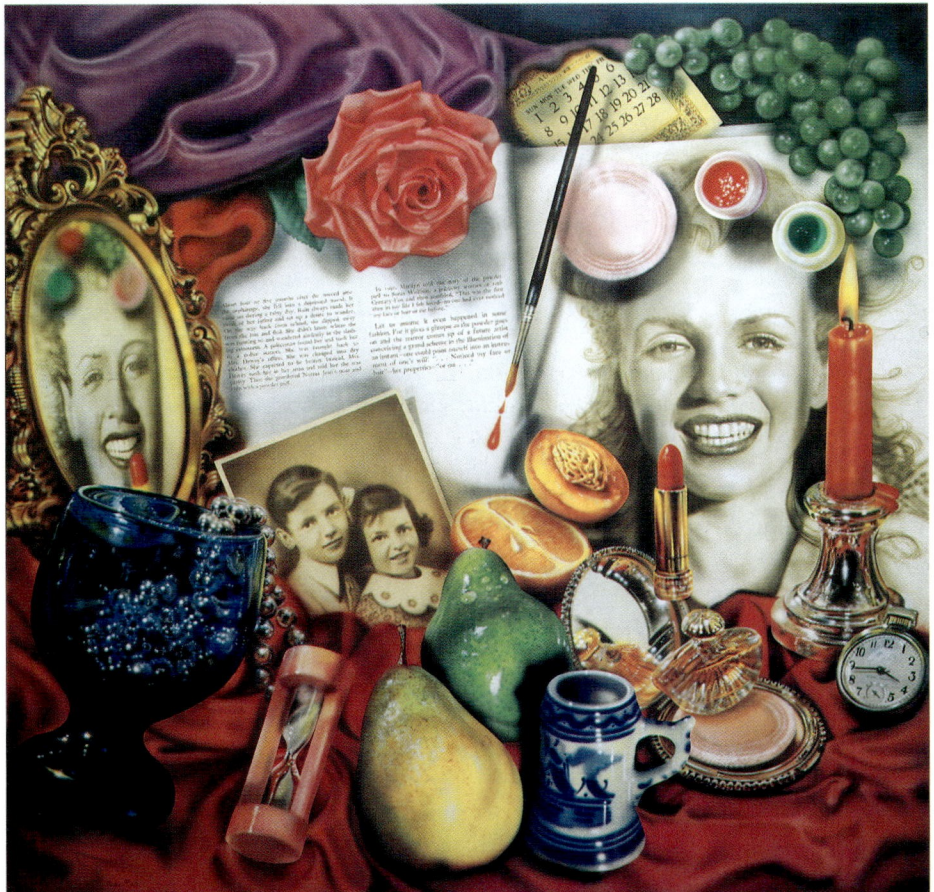

34-34 AUDREY FLACK, *Marilyn*, 1977. Oil over acrylic on canvas, 8′ × 8′. Collection of the University of Arizona Museum, Tucson (museum purchase with funds provided by the Edward J. Gallagher Jr. Memorial Fund).

life, I studied art history, it was always photographs, I never saw the paintings, they were in Europe. . . . Look at TV and at magazines and reproductions, they're all influenced by photo-vision."[33] The photograph's formal qualities also intrigued her, and she used photographic techniques by first projecting an image in slide form onto the canvas. By next using an airbrush (a device originally designed as a photo-retouching tool), Flack could duplicate the smooth gradations of tone and color found in photographs. Her attention to detail and careful preparation resulted in paintings (mostly still lifes) that present the viewer with a collection of familiar objects painted with great optical fidelity. *Marilyn* provides a different comment on the tragic death of Marilyn Monroe than does Warhol's *Marilyn Diptych* (FIG. 34-32). In Flack's still-life painting, she alludes to the traditional vanitas painting (see FIGS. 24-55 and 24-56). Like a Dutch vanitas painting, *Marilyn* is replete with references to death. In addition to the black-and-white photographs of a youthful, smiling Monroe, fresh fruit (some of it cut), an hourglass, a burning candle, a watch, and a calendar all refer to the passage of time and the transience of life on earth.

**LARGE-SCALE PORTRAITS** American artist CHUCK CLOSE (b. 1940), best known for his large-scale portraits, is another artist whose work has been associated with the Superrealist movement. However, Close felt his connection to the Photorealists was tenuous, because for him realism, rather than an end in itself, was actually the result of an intellectually rigorous, systematic approach to painting. He based his paintings of the late 1960s and early 1970s, such as his *Big Self-Portrait* (FIG. 34-35), on photographs, and his main goal was to translate photographic information into painted information. Because he aimed simply to record visual information about his subject's appearance, he deliberately avoided creative compositions, flattering lighting effects, and revealing facial expressions. Close, not interested in providing great insight into the personalities of those portrayed, painted anonymous and generic people, mostly friends. By reducing the variables in his paintings (even their canvas size is a constant nine feet by seven feet), Close could focus on employing his methodical presentations of faces, thereby encouraging the viewer to deal with the formal aspects of his works. Indeed, because of the large scale of Close paintings, close scrutiny causes the images to dissolve into abstract patterns.

**CASTS OF STEREOTYPICAL AMERICANS** Superrealist sculpture has been best articulated in the work of DUANE HANSON (1925–1996). Like many of the other Superrealists, Hanson was interested in finding a visual vocabulary the public would understand. Once he perfected his casting technique, he created numerous life-size figurative sculptures. Hanson first made plaster molds from live models. He then filled the molds with polyester resin. After the resin hardened, the artist removed the outer molds and cleaned, painted with an airbrush, and decorated the sculptures with wigs, clothes, and other accessories. These works, such as *Supermarket Shopper* (FIG. 34-36), depict stereotypical average Americans, striking chords with the viewer specifically because of their familiarity. Hanson explained his choice of imagery: "The subject matter that I like best deals with the familiar lower and middle-class American types of today. To me, the resignation, emptiness and loneliness of their existence captures the true reality of life for these people. . . . I want to achieve a certain tough realism which speaks of the fascinating idiosyncrasies of our time."[34] Due to Hanson's choice of imagery and careful production process, the viewer often initially mistakes his sculptures, when on display, for real people, accounting for his association with the Superrealist movement.

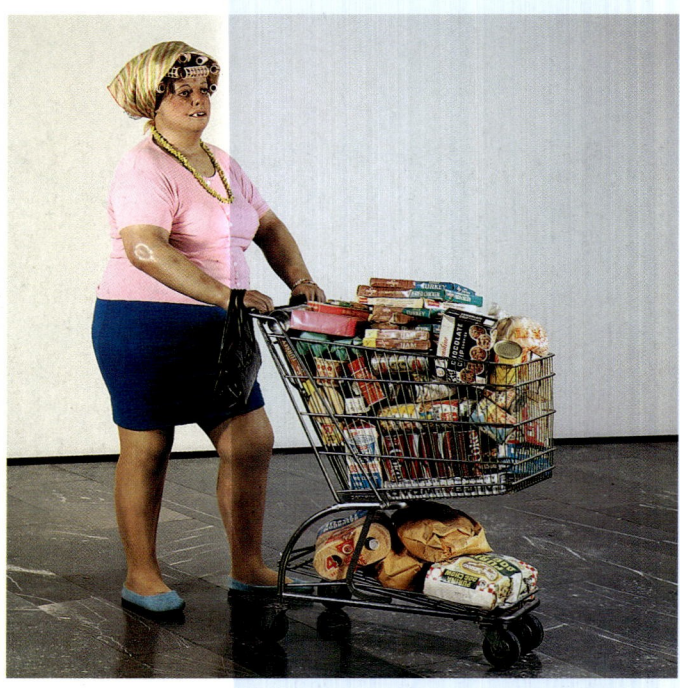

34-35 CHUCK CLOSE, *Big Self-Portrait*, 1967–1968. Acrylic on canvas, 8′ 11″ × 6′ 11″ × 2″. Collection of Walker Art Center, Minneapolis (Art Center Acquisition Fund, 1969).

34-36 DUANE HANSON, *Supermarket Shopper*, 1970. Polyester resin and fiberglass polychromed in oil, with clothing, steel cart, and groceries, life-size. Nachfolgeinstitut, Neue Galerie, Sammlung Ludwig, Aachen. © Estate of Duane Hanson/Licensed by VAGA, New York, New York.

## Site-Specific Art and Environmental Art

*Environmental art,* sometimes called *Earth art* or *earthworks,* emerged in the 1960s and included a wide range of artworks, most site-specific and existing outdoors. Many artists associated with these sculptural projects also used natural or organic materials, including the land itself. This art form developed during a period of increased concern for the American environment. The ecology movement of the 1960s and 1970s aimed to publicize and combat escalating pollution, depletion of natural resources, and the dangers of toxic waste. The problems of public aesthetics (for example, litter, urban sprawl, and compromised scenic areas) were also at issue. Widespread concern about the environment led to the passage of the National Environmental Policy Act in 1969 and the creation of the federal Environmental Protection Agency. Environmental artists used their art to call attention to the landscape and, in so doing, were part of this national dialogue.

As an innovative art form that challenged traditional assumptions about art making and artistic models, Environmental art clearly had an avant-garde, progressive dimension. It is discussed here with the more populist art movements such as Pop and Superrealism, however, because these artists insisted on moving art out of the rarefied atmosphere of museums and galleries and into the public sphere. Most Environmental artists encouraged spectator interaction with the works. Environmental artists such as Christo and Jeanne-Claude, whose work matured in the context of Nouveau Réalisme, a European version of Pop art, made audience participation an integral part of their works. Thus these artists, like the Pop artists and Superrealists, intended their works to connect with a larger public. Ironically, the remote locations of many earthworks have limited public access.

**THE ENDURING POWER OF NATURE** A leading American Environmental artist was Robert Smithson (1938–1973), who used industrial construction equipment to manipulate vast quantities of earth and rock on isolated sites. One of Smithson's best-known pieces is *Spiral Jetty* (FIG. **34-37**), a mammoth coil of black basalt, limestone rocks, and earth that extends out into the Great Salt Lake in Utah. Driving by the lake one day, Smithson came across some abandoned mining equipment, left there by a company that had tried and failed to extract oil from the site. Smithson saw this as a testament to the enduring power of nature and to humankind's inability to conquer nature. He decided to create an artwork in the lake that ultimately became a monumental spiral curving out from the shoreline and running 1,500 linear feet into the water. Smithson insisted on designing his work in response to the location itself; he wanted to avoid the arrogance of an artist merely imposing an unrelated concept on the site. The spiral idea grew from Smithson's first impression of the location:

> As I looked at the site, it reverberated out to the horizons only to suggest an immobile cyclone while flickering light made the entire landscape appear to quake. A dormant earthquake spread into the fluttering stillness, into a spinning sensation without movement. The site was a rotary that enclosed itself in an immense roundness. From that gyrating space emerged the possibility of the Spiral Jetty.[35]

The appropriateness of the spiral forms was reinforced when, while researching the Great Salt Lake, Smithson discovered that the molecular structure of the salt crystals that coat the rocks at the water's edge is spiral in form. Smithson not only recorded *Spiral Jetty* in photographs, but also filmed its construction in a movie that describes the forms and life of the whole site. The photographs and film have become increasingly important, because fluctuations in the Great Salt Lake's water level often place *Spiral Jetty* underwater.

**CAPTIVATING ENVIRONMENTAL INTERVENTIONS** Christo and Jeanne-Claude (both b. 1935) intensify the viewer's awareness of the space and features of rural and urban sites. However, rather than physically alter the land itself, as Smithson often did, Christo and Jeanne-Claude prompt this awareness by temporarily modifying the landscape with cloth. Their pieces also incorporate the relationships among human sociopolitical action,

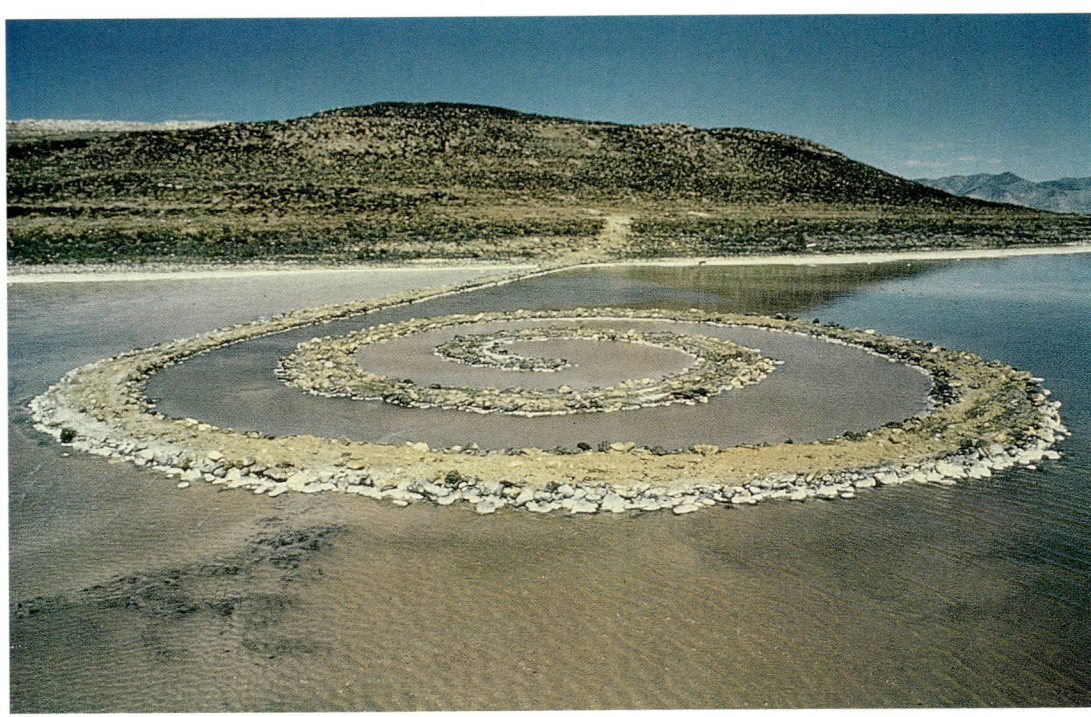

**34-37** Robert Smithson, *Spiral Jetty,* 1970. Black rock, salt crystals, earth, red water (algae) at Great Salt Lake, Utah. 1,500′ × 15′ × $3\frac{1}{2}$′. © Estate of Robert Smithson/Licensed by VAGA, New York, New York.

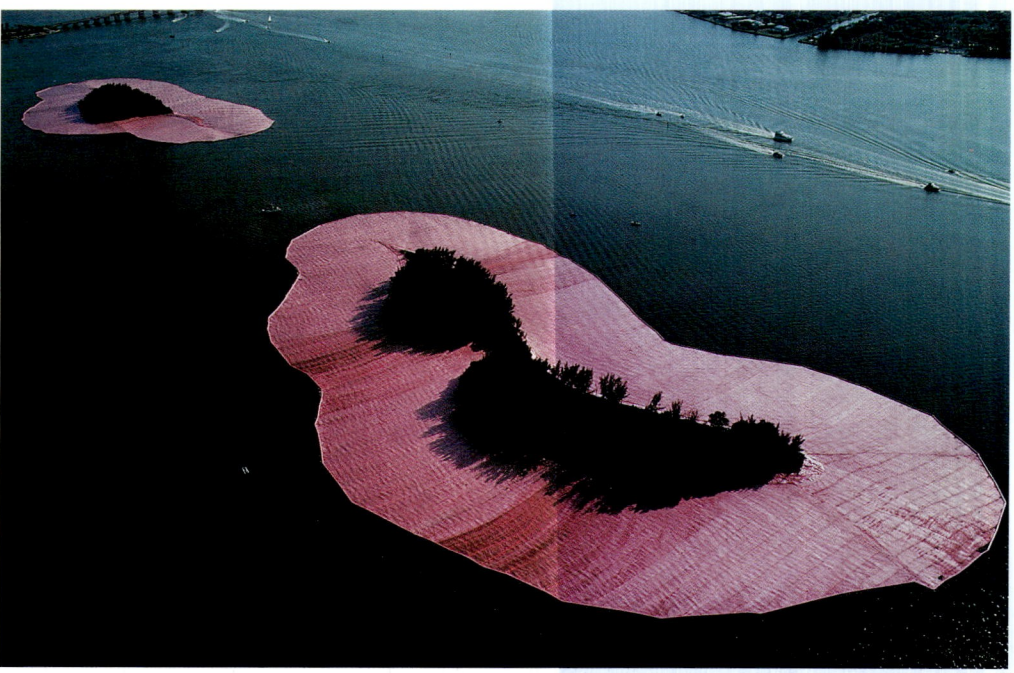

**34-38** CHRISTO and JEANNE-CLAUDE, *Surrounded Islands 1980–83*, Biscayne Bay, Greater Miami, Florida, 1980–1983. Pink woven polypropylene fabric, $6\frac{1}{2}$ million sq. ft.

art, and the environment. Christo studied art in his native Bulgaria and in Vienna. After a move to Paris, he began to encase objects in clumsy wrappings, thereby appropriating bits of the real world into the mysterious world of the unopened package whose contents can be dimly seen in silhouette under the wrap. Starting in 1961, Christo and Jeanne-Claude, husband and wife, began to collaborate on large-scale projects.

These projects normally deal with the environment itself; for example, in 1969 Christo and Jeanne-Claude wrapped more than a million square feet of Australian coast and in 1972 hung a vast curtain across a valley at Rifle Gap, Colorado. The land pieces require years of preparation, research, and scores of meetings with local authorities and interested groups of local citizens. The artists always consider the process of planning and of obtaining the numerous permits, and the visual documentation of each piece part of the artwork. These temporary works are usually on view for a few weeks. *Surrounded Islands 1980–83* (FIG. **34-38**), created in Biscayne Bay in Miami, Florida, for two weeks in May 1983, typifies Christo and Jeanne-Claude's work. For this project, they surrounded 11 small human-made islands in the bay (from a dredging project) with specially fabricated pink polypropylene floating fabric.

This Environmental art project required three years of preparation to obtain the required permissions, to assemble the necessary labor force of unskilled and professional workers, and to accumulate the $3.2 million cost (accomplished by selling preparatory drawings, collages, models, and works of the 1950s and 1960s). Huge crowds watched as crews removed accumulated trash from the 11 islands (to assure maximum contrast between their dark colors, the pink of the cloth, and the blue of the bay) and then unfurled the fabric "cocoons" to form magical floating "skirts" around each tiny bit of land. Despite the brevity of its existence, *Surrounded Islands 1980–83* lives on in the host of photographs, films, and books documenting the piece.

Currently in the planning stages is *The Gates,* which will consist of 7,500 "gates"—panels of saffron-colored fabric, each

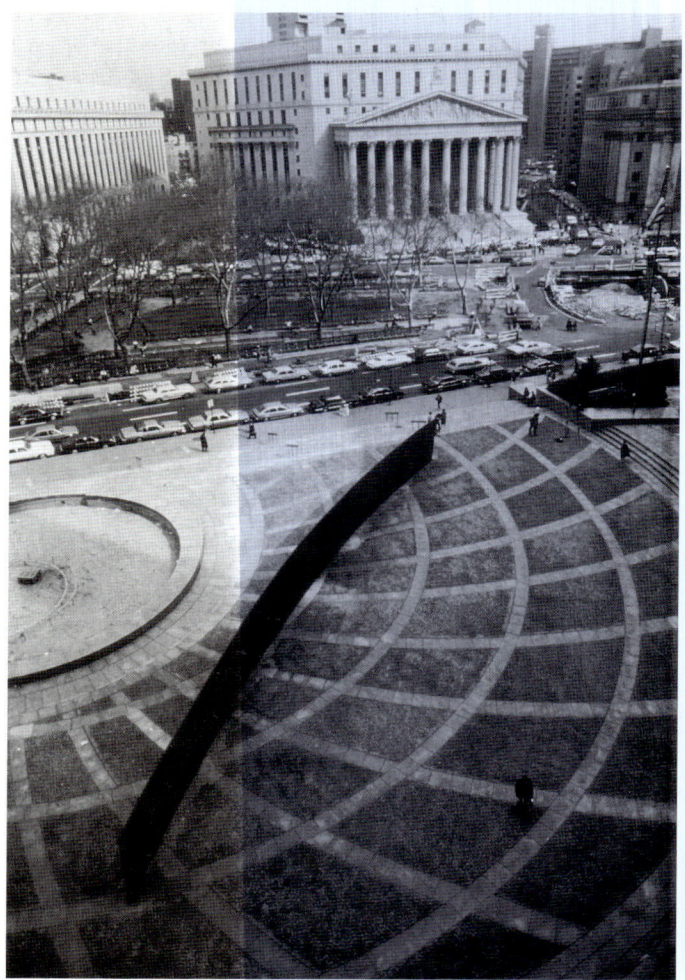

**34-39** RICHARD SERRA, *Tilted Arc,* 1981. Cor-Ten steel, $12' \times 120' \times 2\frac{1}{2}''$. Installed Federal Plaza, New York City, by the General Services Administration, Washington, D.C. Removed by the U.S. government in 1989.

### Tilted Arc and the Problems of Public Art

When *Tilted Arc* (FIG. 34-39) was installed in the plaza in front of the Jacob K. Javits Federal Building in 1981, much of the public immediately responded with hostile criticism. The chorus of complaints was prompted by the resolute and uncompromising presence of the Minimalist sculpture bisecting the plaza. Many voiced the beliefs that *Tilted Arc* was ugly and attracted graffiti, that it interfered with the view across the plaza, and that it prevented using the plaza for performances or concerts. Due to the sustained barrage of protests and petitions demanding the removal of *Tilted Arc*, the GSA held a series of public hearings. Afterward, the agency decided to remove the sculpture despite its prior approval of Serra's maquette. This, understandably, infuriated Serra, who had a legally binding contract acknowledging the site-specific nature of *Tilted Arc*. "To remove the work is to destroy the work," the artist stated.[1]

This episode raised intriguing issues about the nature of public art, including the public reception of experimental art, the artist's responsibilities and rights when executing public commissions, censorship in the arts, and the purpose of public art. If an artwork is placed in a public space outside the relatively private confines of a museum or gallery, do different guidelines apply? As one participant in the *Tilted Arc* saga asked, "Should an artist have the right to impose his values and taste on a public that now rejects his taste and values?"[2] One of the express functions of the historical avant-garde was to challenge convention by rejecting tradition and disrupting the complacency of the viewer. Will placing experimental art in a public place always cause controversy? From Serra's statements, it is clear he intended the sculpture to challenge the public.

Another issue *Tilted Arc* presented involved the rights of the artist, who in this case accused the GSA of censorship. Serra went so far as to file a lawsuit against the government for infringement of his First Amendment rights and insisted that "the artist's work must be uncensored, respected, and tolerated, although deemed abhorrent, or perceived as challenging, or experienced as threatening."[3] Did removal of the work constitute censorship? A federal district court held that it did not.

Ultimately, who should decide what artworks are appropriate for the public arena? One artist argued, "we cannot have public art by plebiscite [popular vote]."[4] But to avoid recurrences of the *Tilted Arc* controversy, the GSA changed its procedures and now solicits input from a wide range of civic and neighborhood groups before commissioning public artworks. Despite the removal of *Tilted Arc* (now languishing in storage), the sculpture maintains a powerful presence in all discussions of the aesthetics, politics, and dynamics of public art.

[1] Grace Glueck, "What Part Should the Public Play in Choosing Public Art?" *New York Times*, 3 February 1985, 27.

[2] Calvin Tomkins, "The Art World: Tilted Arc," *New Yorker*, 20 May 1985, 98.

[3] Ibid., 98–99.

[4] Ibid., 98.

suspended from a frame consisting of three vinyl poles. These gates will wind their way along 23 miles of walkways in Central Park in New York City for 16 days in February 2005. Christo and Jeanne-Claude received permission to create this project from Mayor Michael R. Bloomberg in January 2003. According to the artists, when seen from the buildings surrounding Central Park, *The Gates* will look like a golden river running through the park.

**A MASSIVE WALL OF STEEL** While many works placed in the public domain (such as the Environmental artworks just discussed) sought to reawaken an appreciation of the land's power and beauty and to call attention to ecological problems, other artworks focused attention on art's role in public spaces. One sculpture that sparked national discussion about such art was *Tilted Arc* (FIG. 34-39) by American artist RICHARD SERRA (b. 1939). It was commissioned by the General Services Administration (GSA), the federal agency responsible for, among other tasks, overseeing the selection and installation of artworks for government buildings. This enormous 120-foot curved wall of Cor-Ten steel stood 12 feet high and bisected the plaza in front of the Jacob K. Javits Federal Building in lower Manhattan. Serra situated the sculpture to significantly alter the space of the open plaza and the traffic flow across the square. This site-specific sculpture, the artist explained, was intended to "dislocate or alter the decorative function of the plaza and actively bring people into the sculpture's context."[36] By creating such a monumental presence in this large public space, Serra succeeded in forcing viewers to reconsider the plaza's physical space as a sculptural form (see "Tilted Arc and the Problems of Public Art," above).

## NEW MODELS FOR ARCHITECTURE: MODERNISM TO POSTMODERNISM

### Modernism

The progressive movement toward formal abstraction in media such as painting and sculpture during the 20th century has been chronicled. In similar fashion, modernist architects became increasingly concerned with a formalism that stressed simplicity. They articulated this in buildings that retained intriguing organic sculptural qualities, as well as in buildings that adhered to a more rigid geometry.

**SCULPTING A CONCRETE SPIRAL** Frank Lloyd Wright, who described his architecture as "organic," ended his long, productive career with his design for the Solomon R. Guggenheim Museum

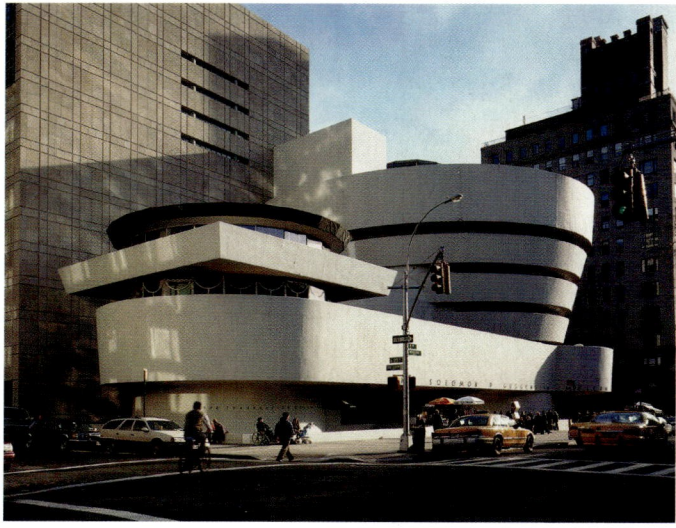

**34-40** FRANK LLOYD WRIGHT, Solomon R. Guggenheim Museum (exterior view from the north), New York, 1943–1959. 🔊

(FIGS. **34-40** and **34-41**), built in New York City between 1943 and 1959. Using reinforced concrete almost as a sculptor might use resilient clay, Wright designed a structure inspired by the spiral of a snail's shell.

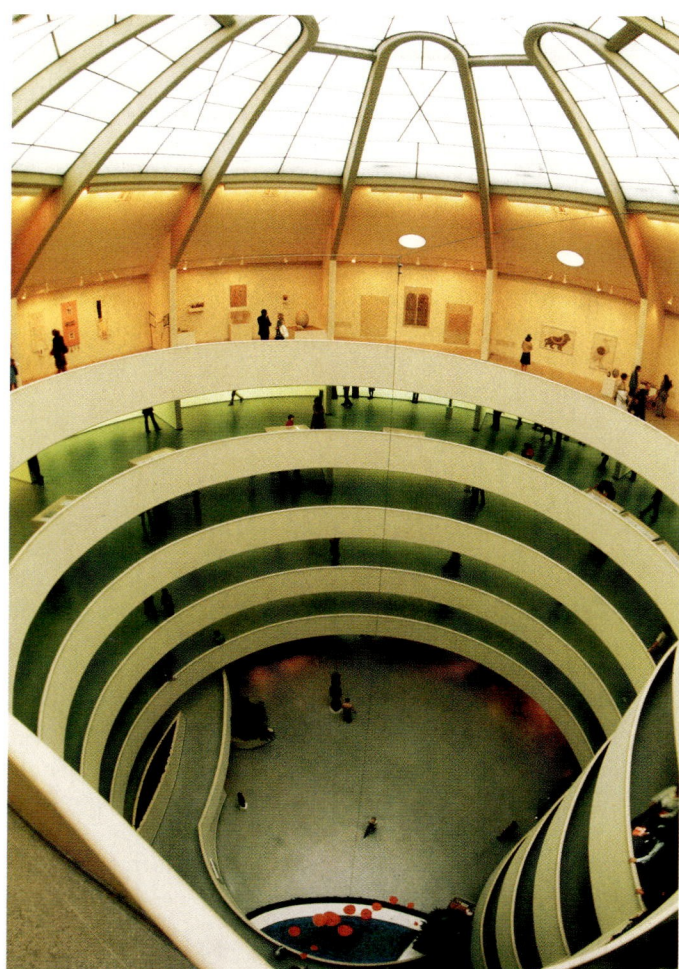

**34-41** FRANK LLOYD WRIGHT, Interior of the Solomon R. Guggenheim Museum, New York, 1943–1959. 🔊

Wright had introduced curves and circles into some of his plans in the 1930s, and, as the architectural historian Peter Blake noted, "The spiral was the next logical step; it is the circle brought into the third and fourth dimensions."[37] Inside the building (FIG. 34-41), the shape of the shell expands toward the top, and a winding interior ramp spirals to connect the gallery bays, which are illuminated by a skylight strip embedded in the museum's outer wall. Visitors can stroll up the ramp or take an elevator to the top of the building and proceed down the gently inclined walkway, viewing the artworks displayed along the path. Thick walls and the solid organic shape give the building, outside and inside, the sense of turning in on itself. Moreover, the long interior viewing area opening onto a 90-foot central well of space seems a sheltered environment, secure from the bustling city outside.

SCULPTURAL ARCHITECTURE The startling organic forms of Le Corbusier's Notre-Dame-du-Haut (FIGS. **34-42** and **34-43**), completed in 1955 at Ronchamp, France, present viewers with a fusion of architecture and sculpture in a single expression. The architect designed this small chapel on a pilgrimage site in the Vosges Mountains to replace a building destroyed in World War II. The monumental impression of Notre-Dame-du-Haut seen from afar is somewhat deceptive. Although one massive exterior wall contains a pulpit facing a spacious outdoor area for large-scale open-air services on holy days, the interior holds at most 200 people. The intimate scale, stark and heavy walls, and mysterious illumination (jewel tones cast from the deeply recessed stained-glass windows) give this space (FIG. 34-43) an aura reminiscent of a sacred cave or a medieval monastery.

Notre-Dame-du-Haut's structure may look free-form to the untrained eye, but Le Corbusier actually based it, like the medieval cathedral, on an underlying mathematical system. The fabric was formed from a frame of steel and metal mesh, which was sprayed with concrete and painted white, except for two interior private chapel niches with colored walls and the roof, left unpainted to darken naturally with the passage of time. The roof appears to float freely above the sanctuary, intensifying the quality of mystery in the interior space. In reality, the roof is elevated above the walls on a series of nearly invisible blocks. Le Corbusier's preliminary

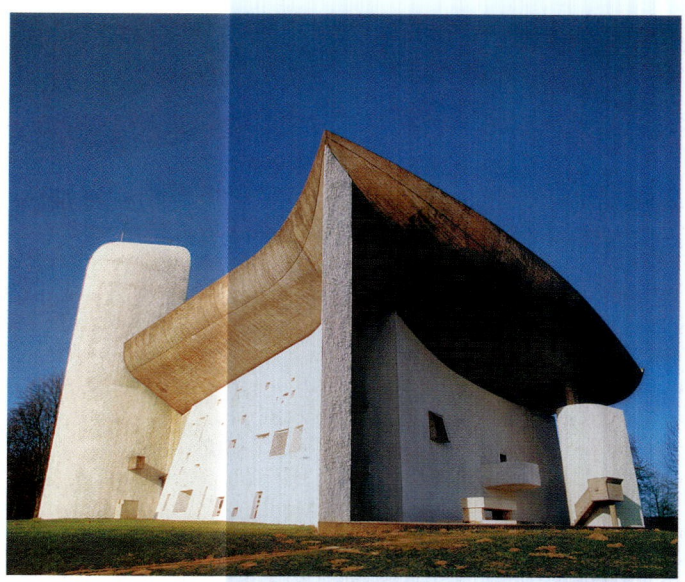

**34-42** LE CORBUSIER, Notre-Dame-du-Haut, Ronchamp, France, 1950–1955. 🔊

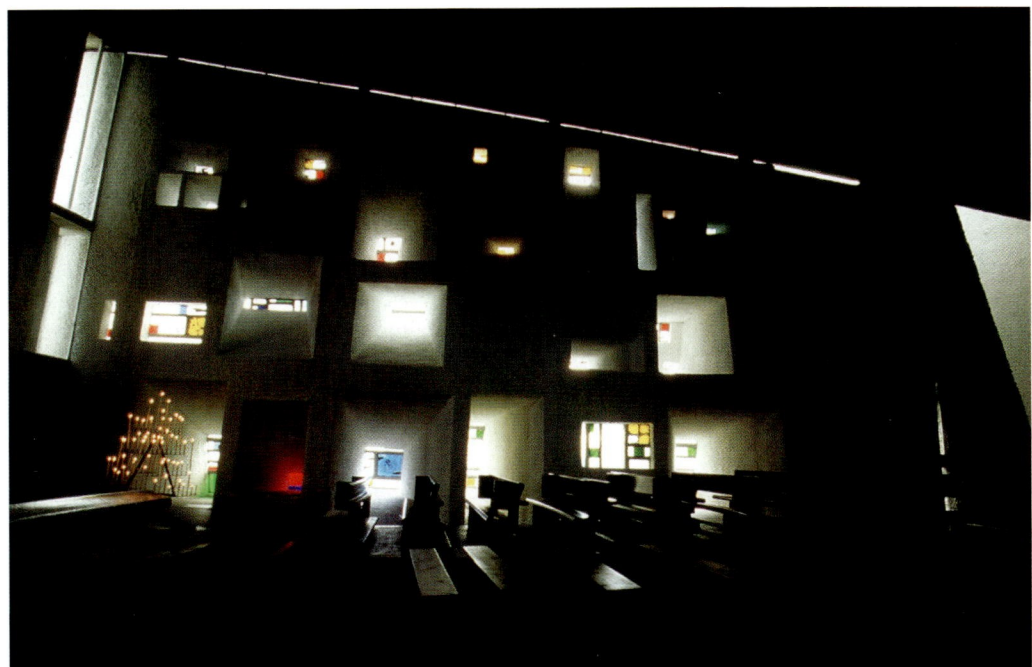

sketches for the building indicate he linked the design with the shape of praying hands, with the wings of a dove (representing both peace and the Holy Spirit), and with the prow of a ship (a reminder that the Latin word used for the main gathering place in Christian churches is *nave,* meaning "ship"). The artist envisioned that in these powerful sculptural solids and voids, human beings could find new values—new interpretations of their sacred beliefs and of their natural environments.

**A METAPHORICAL BUILDING** The opera house in Sydney, Australia (FIG. **34-44**), designed by the Danish architect JOERN UTZON (b. 1918) in 1959, is a bold composition of organic forms on a colossal scale. Utzon worked briefly with Frank Lloyd Wright

at Taliesin (Wright's Wisconsin residence), and the style of the Sydney Opera House resonates distantly with the graceful curvature of the Guggenheim Museum. Two clusters of immense concrete shells rise from massive platforms and soar to delicate peaks. Utzon was especially taken with the platform architecture of Mesoamerica (see FIG. 14-14). Recalling at first the ogival shapes of Gothic vaults, the shells also suggest both the buoyancy of seabird wings and the sails of the tall ships that brought European settlers to Australia in the 18th and 19th centuries. These architectural metaphors are appropriate to the harbor surrounding Bennelong Point, whose bedrock foundations support the building. Utzon's matching of the structure with its site and atmosphere adds to the organic nature of this construction.

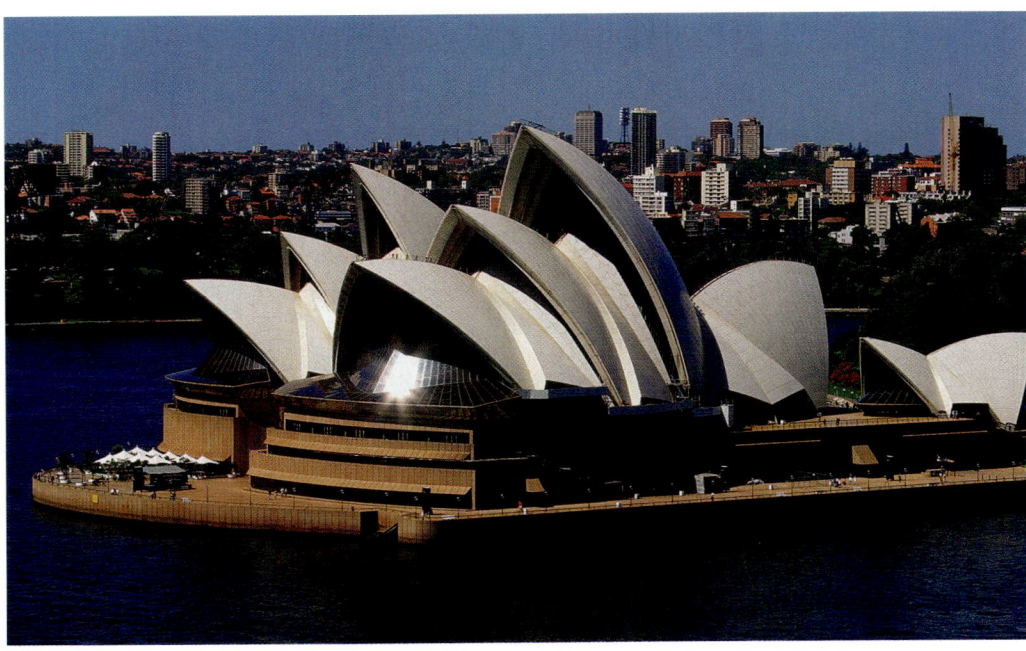

34-44 JOERN UTZON, Sydney Opera House, Sydney, Australia, 1959–1972. Reinforced concrete; height of highest shell, 200′.

The building is not only a monument of civic pride but also functions as the city's cultural center. In addition to the opera auditorium giving the structure its name, it houses auxiliary halls and rooms for concerts, the performing arts, motion pictures, lectures, art exhibitions, conventions, and all other modern cultural activities.

Begun in 1959 and only completed in 1972, the facility took a long time to realize. From the beginning, Utzon's controversial design required unavailable construction technology to meet the requirements of its daring innovations. Utzon left the project in 1966, and Australian architects completed it in 1972. Today it is accepted as Sydney's defining symbol.

**CAPTURING MOTION IN CONCRETE** Finnish-born architect EERO SAARINEN (1910–1961), responsible for selecting Utzon as the architect for the Sydney Opera House, designed his own version of the curvilinear shell building in the late 1950s. Saarinen based his design of the Trans World Airlines terminal (FIG. **34-45**) at the Kennedy Airport in New York on the theme of motion. It consists of two immense concrete shells split down the middle and slightly rotated, giving the terminal a fluid curved outline that fits its corner site. The shells immediately suggest expansive wings and flight. The architect designed everything on the interior, including the furniture, ventilation ducts, and signboards, with this same curvilinear vocabulary in mind.

From the mid-1950s through the 1970s, other architects created massive, sleek, and geometrically rigid buildings. They designed most of these structures following Ludwig Mies van der Rohe's contention that "less is more," and the architecture presented pristine, authoritative faces to the public. Appropriately, such buildings and the powerful, heroic presence they exuded symbolized the monolithic corporations often inhabiting them.

**A GLASS TOWER** The "purest" example of these corporate skyscrapers is, undoubtedly, the rectilinear glass and bronze tower in Manhattan (FIG. **34-46**) designed for the Seagram Company by Ludwig Mies van der Rohe and American architect PHILIP JOHNSON (b. 1906). By the time this structure was built (1956–1958), the concrete, steel, and glass towers, pioneered in the works of Louis Sullivan (see FIG. 29-60) and in Mies van der Rohe's own model for glass skyscrapers (see FIG. 33-62), had become a familiar sight in cities all over the world. Appealing in its structural logic and clarity, the style, although often vulgarized, was easily imitated and quickly became the norm for postwar commercial

high-rise buildings. The architects of the Seagram Building deliberately designed it as a thin shaft, leaving the front quarter of its midtown site as an open pedestrian plaza. The tower appears to rise from the pavement on stilts; glass walls even surround the recessed lobby. The building's recessed structural elements make it appear to have a glass skin, interrupted only by the thin strips of bronze anchoring the windows. The bronze metal and the amber glass windows give the tower a richness found in few of its neighbors. Mies van der Rohe and Johnson carefully planned every detail of the Seagram Building, inside and out, to create an elegant whole. They even planned the interior and exterior lighting to make the edifice an impressive sight both day and night.

**ONCE THE TALLEST IN THE WORLD** The architectural firm Skidmore, Owings and Merrill (SOM) can be seen as the purest proponent of Miesian-inspired structures. This firm designed a number of these simple rectilinear glass-sheathed buildings, and SOM's growth indicates the popularity of this building type. By 1970, the company comprised more than a thousand architects and had offices in New York, Chicago, San Francisco, Portland, and Washington, D.C. In 1974 the firm completed the Sears Tower (FIG. **34-47**), a mammoth corporate building in Chicago. Consisting of nine clustered tubes soaring vertically, this 110-floor building contains enough room to support more than 12,000 workers. Original

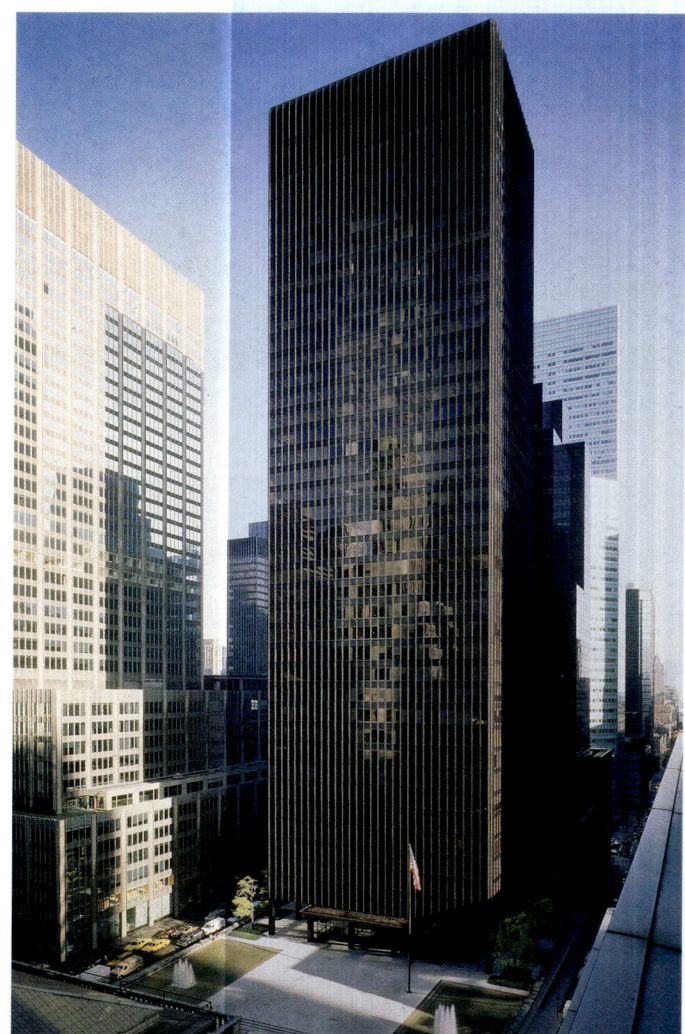

**34-46** LUDWIG MIES VAN DER ROHE and PHILIP JOHNSON, Seagram Building, New York, 1956–1958.

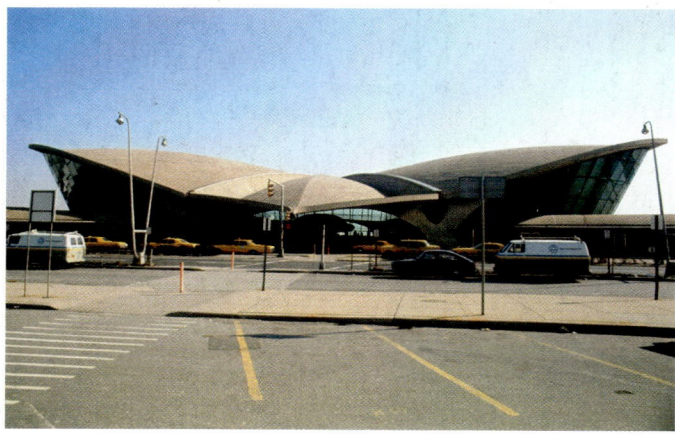

**34-45** EERO SAARINEN, Trans World Airlines terminal, Kennedy Airport, New York, 1956–1962.

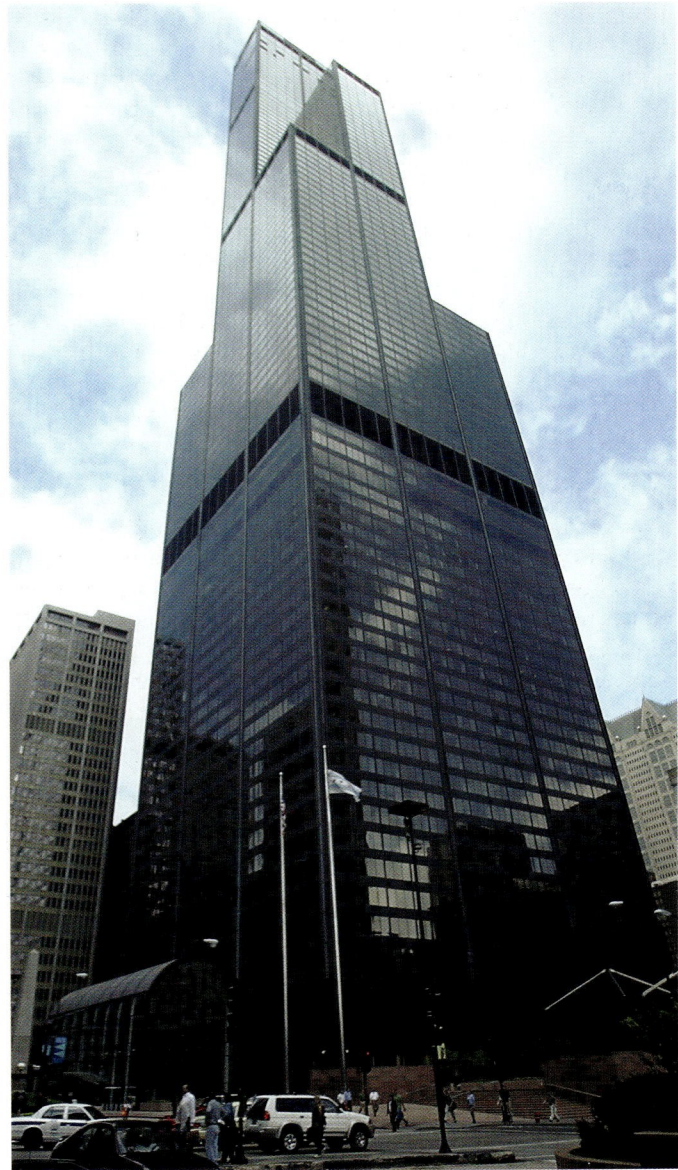

**34-47** Skidmore, Owings and Merrill, Sears Tower, Chicago, 1974.

plans called for 104 stories, but the architects acquiesced to Sears's insistence on making the building the tallest (measured to the structural top) in the world, a distinction it held until recently. The tower's size, coupled with the black aluminum that sheathes it and the smoked glass, give it an intimidating appearance, appropriate for the imposing image corporations were trying to project.

## Postmodernism

The restrictiveness of modernist architecture and the impersonality and sterility of many of these rectilinear corporate buildings led to a rejection of modernism's authority in architecture. Along with the apparent lack of responsiveness to the unique character of the cities and neighborhoods where the structures were placed, these reactions ushered in postmodernism. In contrast to the simplicity of modernist architecture, the terms most often invoked to describe postmodern architecture are *pluralism, complexity,* and *eclecticism.* Where the modernist program was reductive, the postmodern vocabulary of the 1970s and 1980s was expansive and inclusive.

Among the first to explore this new direction in architecture were Jane Jacobs (b. 1916) and Robert Venturi (FIG. 34-51). In their influential books *The Death and Life of Great American Cities* (Jacobs, 1961) and *Complexity and Contradiction in Architecture* (Venturi, 1966), both argued that the uniformity and anonymity of modernist architecture (in particular, the corporate skyscrapers dominating many urban skylines) are unsuited to human social interaction and that diversity is the great advantage of urban life. Postmodern architecture accepted, indeed embraced, the messy and chaotic nature of urban life.

Further, when designing these varied buildings, many postmodern architects consciously selected past architectural elements or references and juxtaposed them with contemporary elements or fashioned them of high-tech materials, thereby creating a dialogue between past and present. Postmodern architecture incorporated not only traditional architectural references but references to mass culture and popular imagery as well. This was precisely the "complexity and contradiction" Venturi referred to in the title of his book. Venturi wrote:

> Architects can no longer afford to be intimidated by the puritanically moral language of orthodox Modern architecture. . . . A valid architecture evokes many levels of meaning and combinations of focus; its space and its elements become readable and workable in several ways at once.[38]

**JUXTAPOSING PAST AND PRESENT** A clear example of the eclecticism and the dialogue between traditional and contemporary elements found in postmodern architecture is the Piazza d'Italia (FIG. **34-48**) by American architect CHARLES MOORE (1925–1993). Designed in the late 1970s in New Orleans, the Piazza d'Italia is an open plaza dedicated to the city's Italian-American community. Appropriately, Moore selected elements relating specifically to Italian history, all the way back through ancient Roman culture.

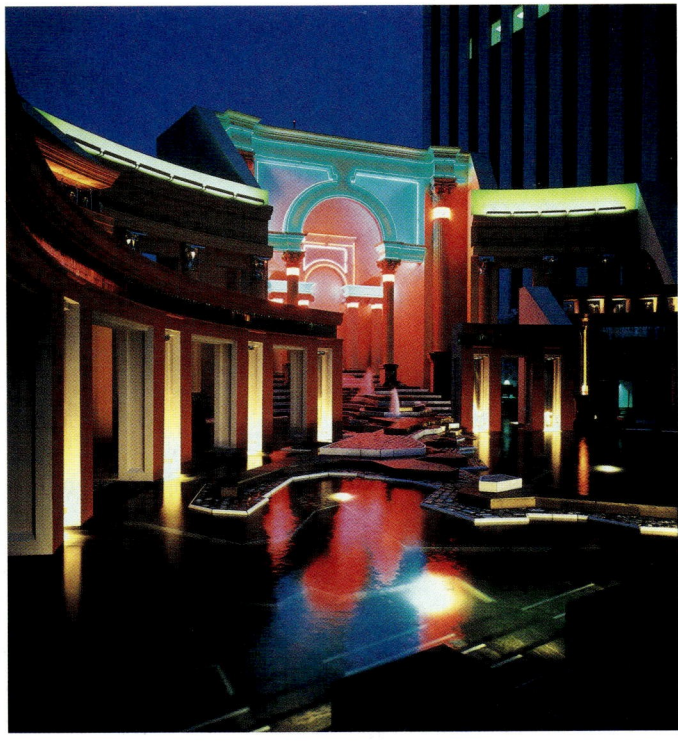

**34-48** CHARLES MOORE, Piazza d'Italia, New Orleans, Louisiana, 1976–1980.

Backed up against a contemporary high-rise and set off from urban traffic patterns, the Piazza d'Italia can be reached on foot from three sides through gateways of varied design. The approaches lead to an open circular area partially formed by short segments of colonnades arranged in staggered concentric arcs, which direct the eye to the focal point of the composition—an exedra. This recessed area on a raised platform serves as a rostrum during the annual festivities of Saint Joseph's Day. Moore inlaid the piazza's pavement with a map of Italy that centrally places Sicily, the island of origin of the Italian colony's majority. From there, the map's Italian "boot" moves in the direction of the steps that ascend the rostrum and geographically correspond to the Alps.

The piazza's most immediate historical reference is to the Greek agora or the Roman forum (see FIG. 10-41). However, its circular form alludes to the ideal geometric figure of the Renaissance (see FIG. 22-8). The irregular placement of the concentrically arranged colonnade fragments inserts a note of instability into the design reminiscent of Mannerism (see FIG. 22-26). Illusionistic devices, such as the continuation of the piazza's pavement design (apparently through a building and out into the street), are Baroque in character (see FIG. 24-6). All of the classical orders are represented—most with whimsical modifications. Nevertheless, the piazza's historical character is challenged by modern features, such as the stainless-steel columns and capitals, neon collars around the column necks, and neon lights that frame various parts of the exedra.

In sum, Moore designed the Piazza d'Italia as a complex conglomeration of symbolic, historical, and geographic allusions—some overt and others obscure. Although the piazza's specific purpose was to honor the Italian community of New Orleans, its more general purpose was to revitalize an urban area by becoming a focal point and an architectural setting for the social activities of neighborhood residents. Sadly, the area today has lost much of its vitality, and the Piazza d'Italia exists in a state of disrepair.

**CLASSICAL AND COLONIAL ELEMENTS** Even architects instrumental in the proliferation of the modernist idiom embraced postmodernism. Philip Johnson, for example, had been a leading proponent of modernism and during the years 1930–1934 and 1946–1954 served as the director of the Department of Architecture at New York's Museum of Modern Art, the bastion of modernism. Yet he made one of the most startling shifts of style in 20th-century architecture, eventually moving away from the severe geometric formalism exemplified by the Seagram Building to a classicizing transformation of it in his AT&T (American Telephone and Telegraph) Building in New York City (FIG. **34-49**). Architect John Burgee codesigned it with assistance from Simmons Architects. This structure was influential in turning architectural taste and practice away from modernism and toward postmodernism—from organic "concrete sculpture" and the rigid "glass box" to elaborate shapes, motifs, and silhouettes freely adapted from historical styles.

The 660-foot-high slab of the AT&T Building is wrapped in granite. Johnson reduced the window space to some 30 percent of the building, in contrast to the modernist glass-sheathed skyscrapers. His design of its exterior elevation is classically tripartite, having an arcaded base and arched portal; a tall, shaftlike body segmented by slender *mullions* (vertical elements dividing a window); and a crowning pediment broken by an *orbiculum* (a disclike opening). The arrangement refers to the base, column, and entablature system of ancient Greek structures and Renaissance elevations (see FIGS. 5-42 and 21-41). More specifically, the pediment, indented by the circular space, resembles the crown of a typical

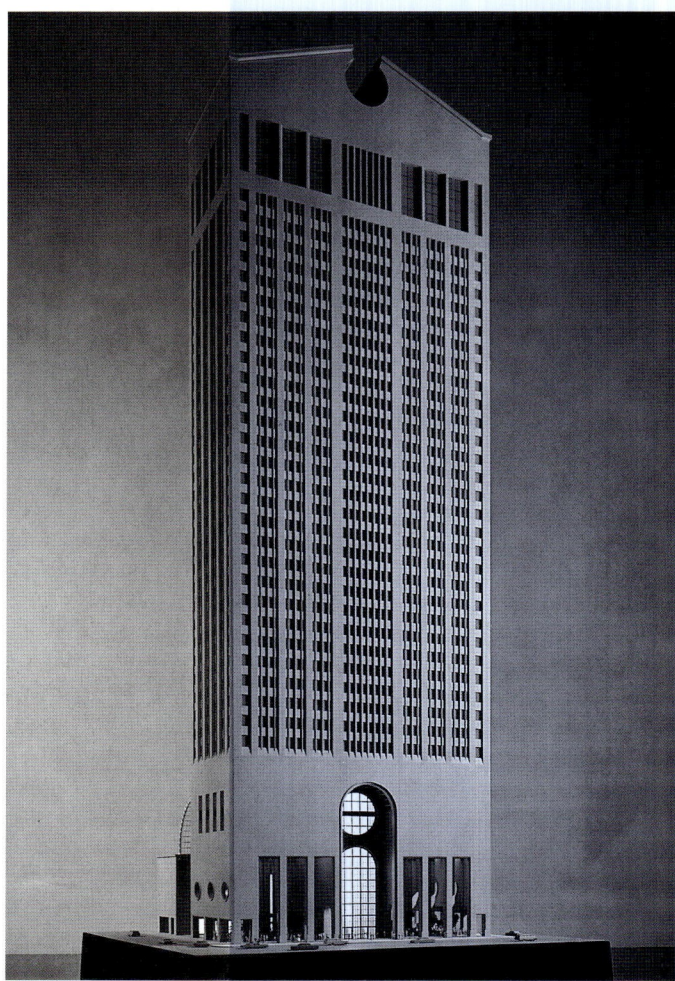

34-49 PHILIP JOHNSON and JOHN BURGEE with Simmons Architects, associated architects, a model of the AT&T Building, New York, 1978–1984.

18th-century Chippendale high chest of drawers. It rises among the monotonously flat-topped glass towers of the New York skyline as an ironic rebuke to the rigid uniformity of modernist architecture. Critics favoring modernism were not at all amused, and controversy raged over the legitimacy and integrity of the design. The AT&T Building's originality and bold departure from convention, however, seem related to the innovation of the much earlier, and now respected, Chrysler Building (see FIG. 33-65).

**AN "ENLARGED JUKEBOX"?** Philip Johnson at first endorsed, then disapproved of, a building that rode considerably farther on the wave of postmodernism than did his AT&T tower. The Portland (Oregon) Building (FIG. **34-50**), the much smaller work of American architect MICHAEL GRAVES (b. 1934), reasserts the wall's horizontality against the verticality of the tall, fenestrated shaft. Graves favored the square's solidity and stability, making it the main body of his composition (echoed in the windows), which rests upon a wider base and carries a set-back penthouse crown. Narrow vertical windows tying together seven stories open two paired facades. These support capital-like large hoods on one pair of opposite facades and a frieze of stylized Baroque roundels tied by bands on the other pair. A huge painted keystone motif joins five upper levels on one facade pair, and painted surfaces further define the building's base, body, and penthouse levels.

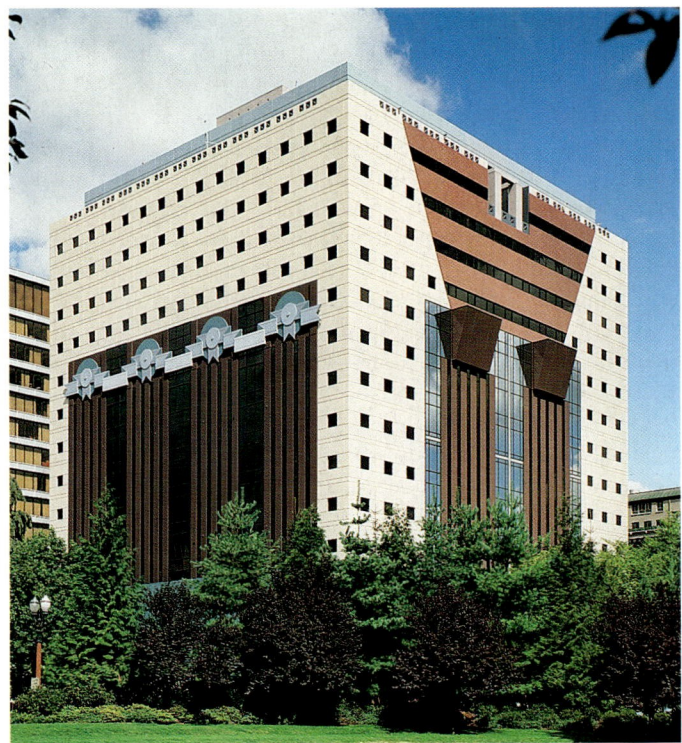

**34-50** MICHAEL GRAVES, the Portland Building, Portland, Oregon, 1980.

The assertion of the wall, the miniature square windows, and the painted polychromy define the surfaces as predominately mural and carry a rather complex symbolic program. The modernist purist surely would not welcome the ornamental wall, color painting, or symbolic reference. These features, taken together, raised an even greater storm of criticism than that which greeted the Sydney Opera House or the AT&T Building. Various critics denounced Graves's

Portland Building as "an enlarged jukebox," an "oversized Christmas package," a "marzipan monstrosity," a "histrionic masquerade," and a kind of "pop surrealism." Yet others approvingly noted its classical references as constituting a "symbolic temple" and praised the building as a courageous architectural adventure. City officials and citizens joined architectural critics in commending or blaming Graves. At present, historians regard the Portland Building, like the AT&T tower, as an early marker of postmodernist innovation.

**ARCHITECTURAL POPULISM** It is important to note here the public's widening participation in the judging of new architecture, indicating an increasing awareness of the new, popular uses of the urban environment. Many observers of architectural developments have expressed the feeling that building design is none the worse for borrowing from the lively, if more-or-less garish, language of pop culture. The night-lit dazzle of entertainment sites such as Las Vegas, or the carnival colors, costumes, and fantasy of theme park props, might just as well serve as inspiration for the designers of civic architecture. ROBERT VENTURI (b. 1925) codified these ideas in his publication *Learning from Las Vegas* (1972). The Portland Building appeared to many viewers to be a vindication of architectural populism against the pretension of modernist elitism.

Venturi's own designs for houses show him adapting historical as well as contemporary styles to suit his symbolic and expressive purpose. A fundamental axiom of modernism is that a building's form must arise directly and logically from its function and structure. Against this rule, Venturi asserted that the form should be separate from the function and structure and that decorative and symbolic forms of everyday life should enwrap the structural core. Thus, for a Delaware residence (FIG. **34-51**) designed in 1978 with JOHN RAUCH (b. 1930) and DENISE SCOTT BROWN (b. 1931), Venturi respected the countryside setting and its 18th-century history by recalling the stone-based barnlike, low-profile farm dwellings with their shingled roofs and double-hung multipaned windows. He fronted the house with an amusingly cut-out and asymmetrical parody of a Neoclassical portico. A building by Venturi is, in his own words, a kind of "decorated shed."

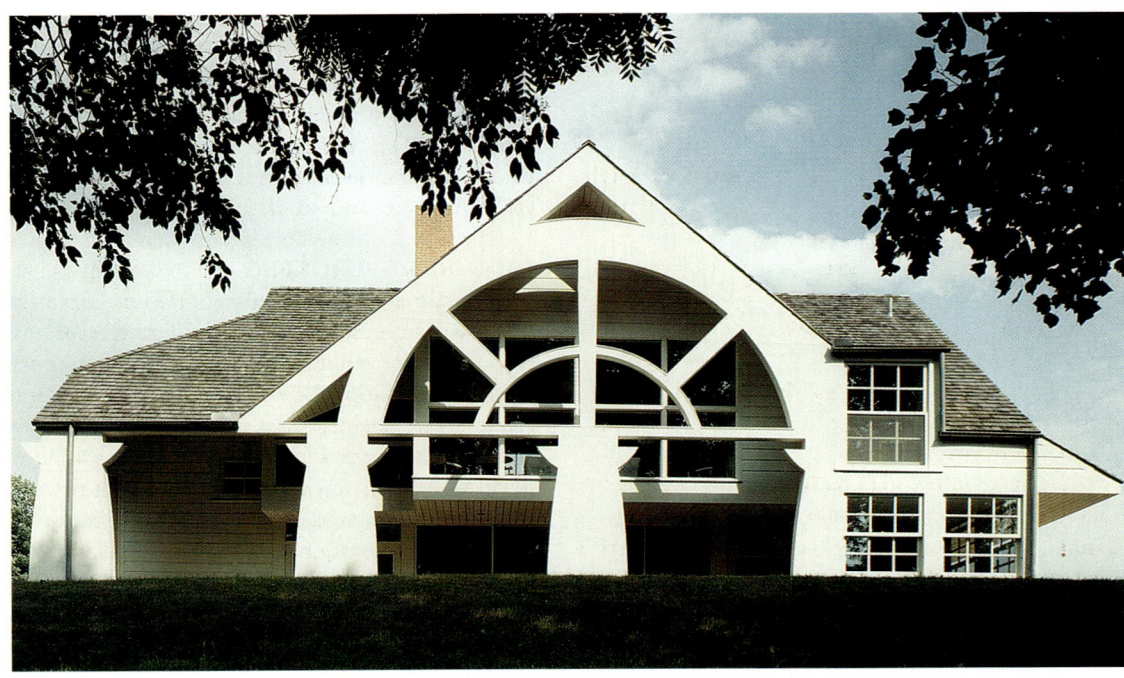

**34-51** ROBERT VENTURI, JOHN RAUCH, and DENISE SCOTT BROWN, house in Delaware (west elevation), 1978–1983.

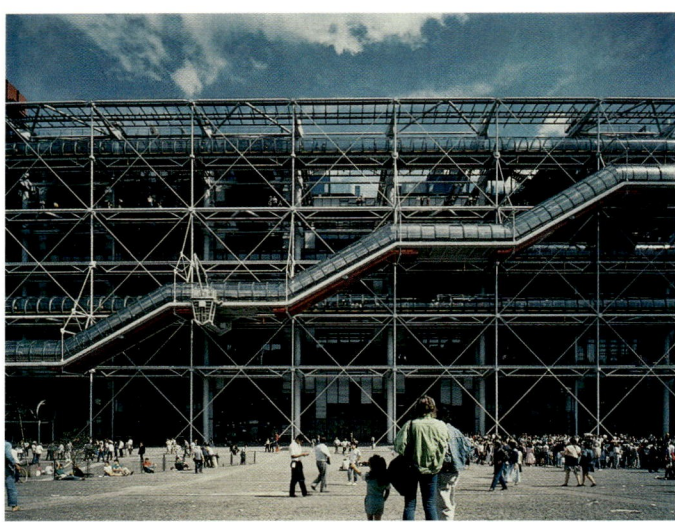

**34-52** RICHARD ROGERS and RENZO PIANO, Georges Pompidou National Center of Art and Culture (the "Beaubourg"), Paris, 1977.

**MAKING "METABOLISM" VISIBLE** In Paris, the short-lived partnership of British architect RICHARD ROGERS (b. 1933) and Italian architect RENZO PIANO (b. 1937) involved using motifs and techniques from ordinary industrial buildings in their design for the Georges Pompidou National Center of Art and Culture, known popularly as the "Beaubourg" (FIG. **34-52**), in Paris. The anatomy of this six-level building, which opened in 1977, is fully exposed, rather like an updated version of the Crystal Palace (see FIG. 28-62). However, the architects also made visible the Pompidou Center's "metabolism." They color-coded pipes, ducts, tubes, and corridors according to function (red for the movement of people, green for water, blue for air-conditioning, and yellow for electricity), much as in a sophisticated factory.

Critics who deplore the Beaubourg's vernacular qualities disparagingly refer to the complex as a "cultural supermarket" and point out that its exposed entrails require excessive maintenance to protect them from the elements. Nevertheless, the building has been popular with visitors since it opened. The flexible interior spaces and the colorful structural body provide a festive environment for the crowds flowing through the building and enjoying its art galleries, industrial design center, library, science and music centers, conference rooms, research and archival facilities, movie theaters, rest areas, and restaurant (which looks down and through the building to the terraces outside). The sloping plaza in front of the main entrance has become part of the local scene. Peddlers, street performers, Parisians, and tourists fill this square at almost all hours of the day and night. The kind of secular activity that once occurred in the open spaces in front of cathedral entrances interestingly now takes place next to a center for culture and popular entertainment—perhaps today's most commonly shared experiences.

## Deconstructivist Architecture

In the later decades of the 20th century, art critics (such as Clement Greenberg and Harold Rosenberg) assumed a commanding role. Indeed, their categorization of movements and their interpretation and evaluation of monuments became a kind of monitoring, gatekeeping activity that determined, as well as described, what was going on in the art world. The voluminous

and influential writing these critics (along with artists and art historians) produced prompted scholars to examine the basic premises of criticism. This examination has generated a field of study known as critical theory. Critical theorists view art and architecture, as well as literature and the other humanities, as a culture's intellectual products or "constructs." These constructs unconsciously suppress or conceal the actual premises that inform the culture, primarily the values of those politically in control. Thus, cultural products function in an ideological capacity, obscuring, for example, racist or sexist attitudes. When revealed by analysis, the facts behind these constructs, according to critical theorists, contribute to a more substantial understanding of artworks, buildings, books, and the overall culture.

As straightforward as such analysis may seem, it is actually exceedingly challenging, and such undertakings often reveal contradictions rather than provide seamless resolution. Many critical theorists use an analytical strategy called *deconstruction,* after a method developed by French intellectuals, notably Michel Foucault and Jacques Derrida, in the 1960s and 1970s. For those employing deconstruction, all cultural constructs are "texts." Acknowledging the lack of fixed or uniform meanings in such texts, critical theorists accept a variety of interpretations as valid. Further, as cultural products, how texts signify and what they signify are entirely conventional. They can refer to nothing outside of themselves, only to other texts. Thus, no extratextual reality exists that people can reference. The enterprise of deconstruction is to reveal the contradictions and instabilities of these texts, or cultural language (written or visual).

With primarily political and social aims, deconstructive analysis has the ultimate goal of effecting political and social change. Accordingly, critical theorists who employ this approach seek to uncover, to deconstruct, the facts of power, privilege, and prejudice underlying the practices and institutions of any given culture. In so doing, deconstruction reveals the precariousness of structures and systems, such as language and cultural practices, along with the assumptions underlying them. Yet because of the lack of fixed meaning in texts, many politically committed thinkers assert that deconstruction does not provide a sufficiently stable basis for dissent.

Critical theorists are not unified about any philosophy or analytical method, because in principle they oppose firm definitions. They do share a healthy suspicion of all traditional truth claims and value standards, all hierarchical authority and institutions. For them, deconstruction means destabilizing established meanings, definitions, and interpretations while encouraging subjectivity and individual differences.

In architecture, deconstruction as an analytical strategy emerged in the 1970s (some scholars refer to this development as *Deconstructivist architecture*). It proposes, above all, to disorient the observer. To this end, Deconstructivist architects attempt to disrupt the conventional categories of architecture and to rupture the viewer's expectations based on them. Destabilization plays a major role in Deconstructivist architecture. Disorder, dissonance, imbalance, asymmetry, unconformity, and irregularity replace their opposites—order, consistency, balance, symmetry, regularity, and clarity, as well as harmony, continuity, and completeness. The haphazard presentation of volumes, masses, planes, borders, lighting, locations, directions, spatial relations, as well as the disguised structural facts, challenge the viewer's assumptions about architectural form as it relates to function. According to Deconstructivist principles, the very absence of the stability of traditional categories of architecture in a structure announces a "deconstructed" building.

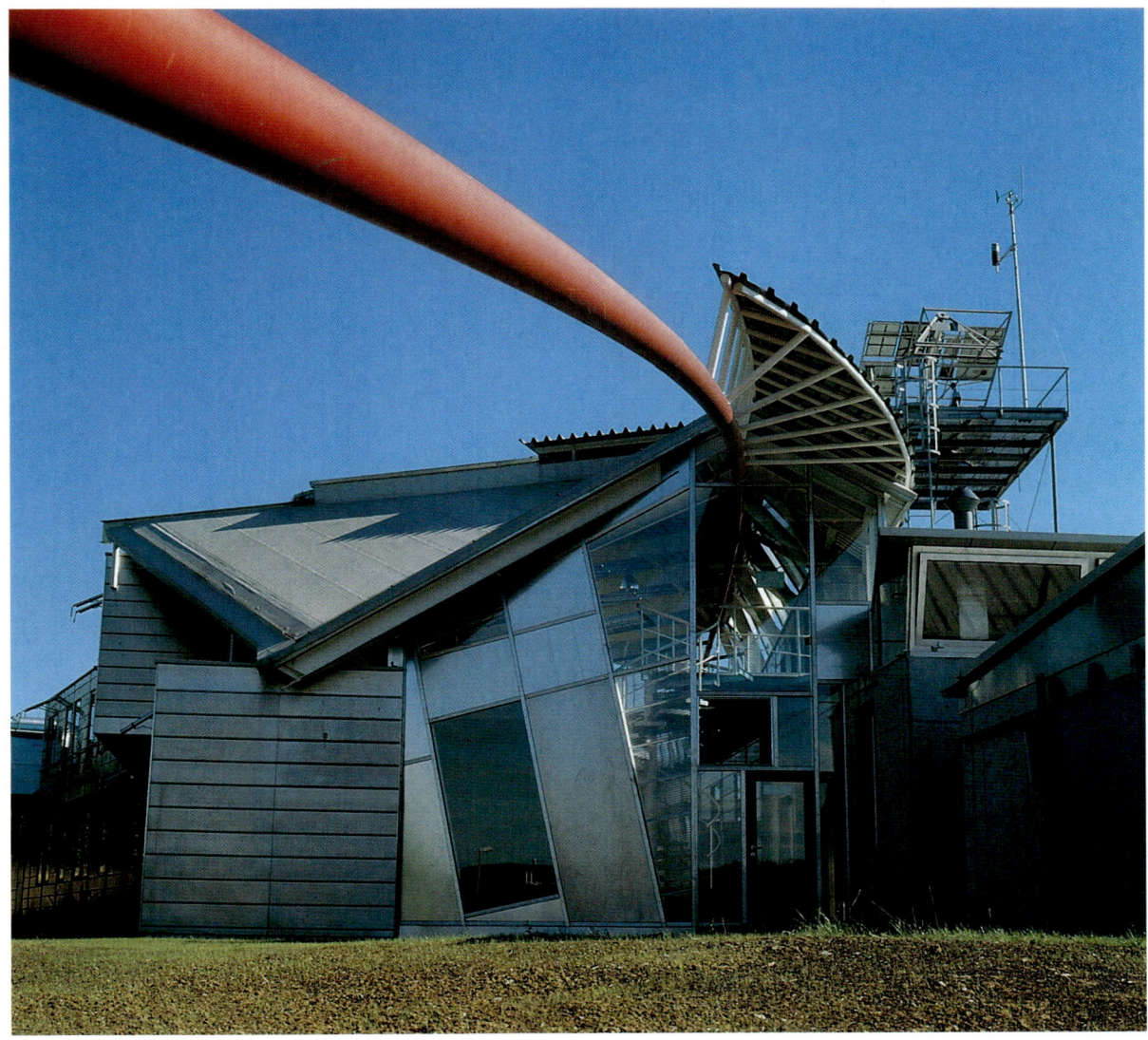

**34-53** GÜNTER BEHNISCH, Hysolar Institute Building, University of Stuttgart, Stuttgart, Germany, 1987.

**AN ARCHITECTURE OF CHAOS** Audacious in its dissolution of form, and well along on the path of deconstruction, is a building in Stuttgart, the Hysolar Institute Building at the University of Stuttgart (FIG. **34-53**). GÜNTER BEHNISCH (b. 1922) designed it as part of a joint German–Saudi Arabian research project on the technology of solar energy. The architect intended to deny here the possibility of spatial enclosure altogether, and his apparently chaotic arrangement of the units defies easy analysis. The shapes of the Hysolar Institute's roof, walls, and windows seem to explode, avoiding any suggestion of clear, stable masses. Behnisch aggressively played with the whole concept of architecture and the viewer's relationship to it. The disordered architectural elements that seem precariously perched and visually threaten to collapse frustrate the observer's expectations of buildings.

**DISORDER AND DISEQUILIBRIUM** The architect whom scholars perhaps have most identified with Deconstructivist architecture is the Canadian-born FRANK GEHRY (b. 1929). Trained in sculpture, and at different times a collaborator with Claes Oldenburg and Donald Judd, Gehry works up his designs by constructing models and then cutting them up and arranging them until he has a satisfying composition. Among Gehry's most notable projects is the Guggenheim Museum (FIG. **34-54**) in Bilbao,

Spain. The immensely dramatic building appears as a mass of asymmetrical and imbalanced forms, and the irregularity of the main masses—whose profiles change dramatically with every shift of a visitor's position—seems like a collapsed or collapsing aggregate of units. The scaled limestone- and titanium-clad exterior lends a space-age character to the building and highlights further the unique cluster effect of the many forms. A group of organic forms that Gehry refers to as a "metallic flower" tops the museum. Gehry was inspired to create the offbeat design by what he called the "surprising hardness" of the heavily industrialized city of Bilbao. His fascination with Fritz Lang's 1926 film *Metropolis* also contributed to this industrial severity. The film, now considered a classic by film historians, reveals a futuristic urban vision of a cold, mechanical industrial world in 2026. In the center of the museum, an enormous glass-walled atrium soars to 165 feet in height, serving as the focal point for the three levels of galleries (see FIG. Intro-1) radiating from it. The seemingly weightless screens, vaults, and volumes of the interior float and flow into one another, guided only by light and dark cues. Overall, the Guggenheim in Bilbao is a profoundly compelling structure. Its disorder, its seeming randomness of design, and the disequilibrium it prompts in viewers fit nicely into postmodern and Deconstructivist agendas.

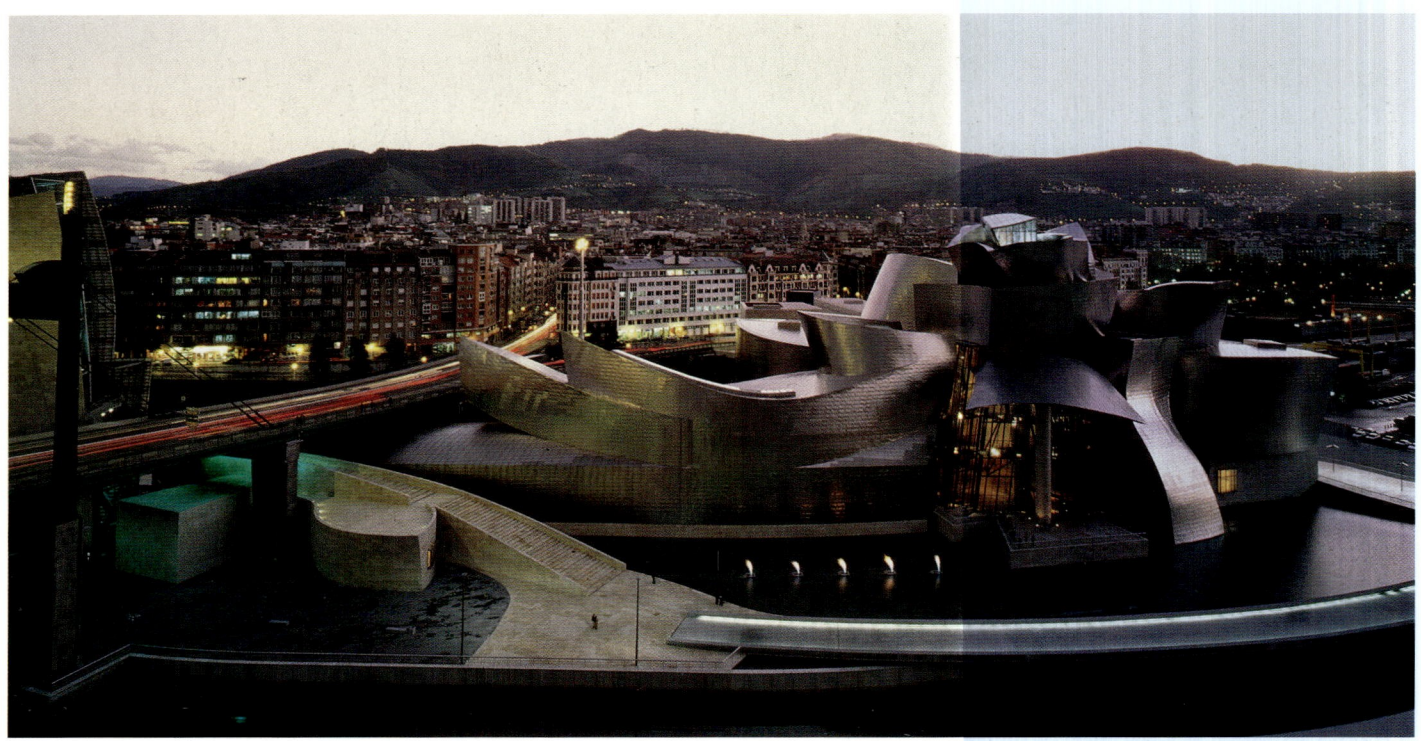

**34-54** Frank Gehry, *Guggenheim Bilbao Museo*, Spain, 1997.

## Postmodernism in Painting, Sculpture, and New Media

The challenges to modernist doctrine that emerged in architecture have their own resolutions in other artistic media. As with architecture, arriving at a concrete definition of postmodernism in other media is difficult. Historically, by the 1970s, the range of art—from abstraction to performance to figuration—was so broad that the inclusiveness central to postmodern architecture characterizes postmodern art as well. Just as postmodern architects incorporate traditional elements or historical references, many postmodern artists reveal a self-consciousness about their place in the historical continuum of art. They resurrect artistic traditions to comment on and reinterpret those styles or idioms. Writings about postmodern art refer to Neo-Minimalism, Neo-Pop, and Neo-Romanticism, among others, evidencing the prevalence of this reevaluation of earlier art forms.

Beyond that, however, artists, critics, dealers, and art historians do not agree on the elements comprising the vague realm of postmodern art. Many people view postmodernism as a critique of modernism. For example, numerous postmodern artists have undertaken the task of challenging modernist principles such as the avant-garde's claim to originality. In avant-garde artists' zeal to undermine traditional notions about art and to produce ever more innovative art forms, they placed a premium on originality and creativity. Postmodern artists challenge this claim by addressing issues of the copy or reproduction (already explored by the Pop artists) and the appropriation of images or ideas from others.

Other scholars, such as Frederic Jameson, assert that a major characteristic of postmodernism is the erosion of the boundaries between high culture and popular culture—a separation Clement Greenberg and the modernists had staunchly defended. With the appearance of Pop art, that separation became more difficult to maintain. Jameson argues that the intersection of high and mass

culture is, in fact, a defining feature of the new postmodernism. He attributes the emergence of postmodernism to "a new type of social life and a new economic order—what is often euphemistically called modernization, postindustrial or consumer society, the society of the media or the spectacle, or multinational capitalism."[39]

Further, the intellectual inquiries of critical theorists serving as the basis for Deconstructivist architecture also impacted the other media. For many recent artists, postmodernism involves examining the process by which meaning is generated and the negotiation or dialogue that transpires between viewers and artworks. Like the theorists using deconstructive methods to analyze "texts," or cultural products, many postmodern artists reject the notion that each artwork contains a single fixed meaning. Their work, in part, explores how viewers derive meaning from visual material.

Postmodern art, then, comprises a dizzying array of artworks. While some involve critiques of the modernist program, others present critiques of the art world, and still others incorporate elements of and provide commentary on previous art. A sampling of postmodern art in various media follows.

### New Expressionist Explorations

One of the first coherent movements to emerge during the postmodern era was *Neo-Expressionism*. This movement's name reflects postmodern artists' interest in reexamining earlier art production and connects this art to the powerful, intense works of the German Expressionists (see Chapter 33, page 966) and the Abstract Expressionists, among other artists.

**EXTENDING PAINT'S PHYSICALITY** The art of American artist Julian Schnabel (b. 1951), in effect, forcefully restates the premises of Abstract Expressionism. When executing his works in the 1980s, however, Schnabel experimented widely with materials and supports—from fragmented china plates bonded to wood, to paint on velvet and tarpaulin. He was particularly interested in

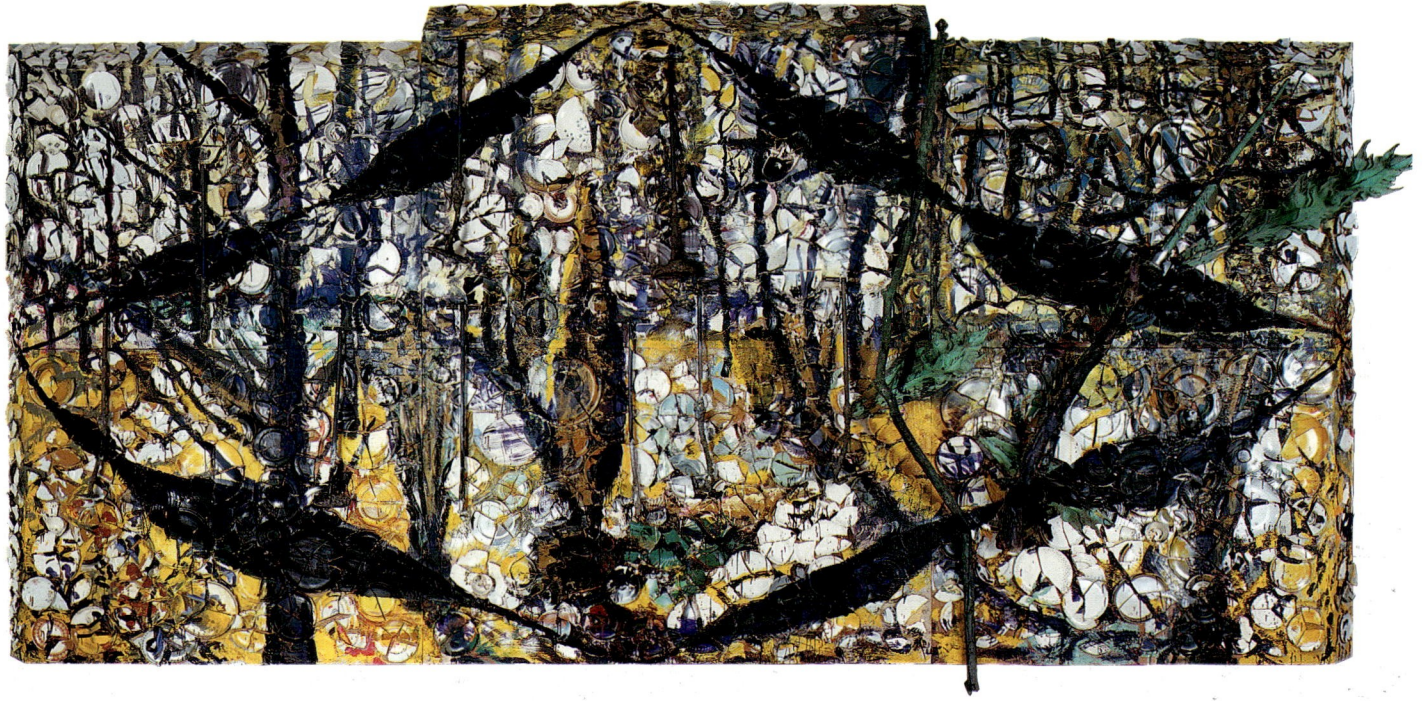

**34-55** JULIAN SCHNABEL, *The Walk Home,* 1984–1985. Oil, plates, copper, bronze, fiberglass, and Bondo on wood, 9′ 3″ × 19′ 4″. Broad Art Foundation and the Pace Gallery, New York.

the physicality of the objects, and by attaching broken crockery, as evident in *The Walk Home* (FIG. **34-55**), he found an extension of what paint could do. Superficially, the painting recalls the work of the gestural abstractionists—the spontaneous drips of Jackson Pollock (FIG. 34-4) and the energetic brush strokes of Willem de Kooning (FIG. 34-6). The large scale of Schnabel's works is also reminiscent of Abstract Expressionism. The thick, mosaiclike texture, an amalgamation of media, brings together painting, mosaic, and low-relief sculpture. In effect, Schnabel reclaimed older media for his expressionistic method, which considerably amplifies his bold and distinctive statement.

**HORSES AS METAPHORS** In the 1970s, American SUSAN ROTHENBERG (b. 1945) produced a major series of large paintings with the horse as the central image. The horse theme resonates with history and metaphor—from Roman equestrian sculpture to the paintings of German Expressionist Franz Marc. Like Marc, Rothenberg saw horses as metaphors for humanity. She stated, "The horse was a way of not doing people, yet it was a symbol of people, a self-portrait, really."[40] Rothenberg, however, distilled the image down to a ghostly outline or hazy depiction that is more poetic than descriptive. As such, her works fall in the nebulous area between representation and abstraction. In paintings such as *Tattoo* (FIG. 34-56), the loose brushwork and agitated surface contribute to the expressiveness of the image and account for Rothenberg's categorization as a Neo-Expressionist. The title, *Tattoo,* refers to the horse's head drawn within the outline of its leg—"a tattoo or memory image," according to the artist.[41]

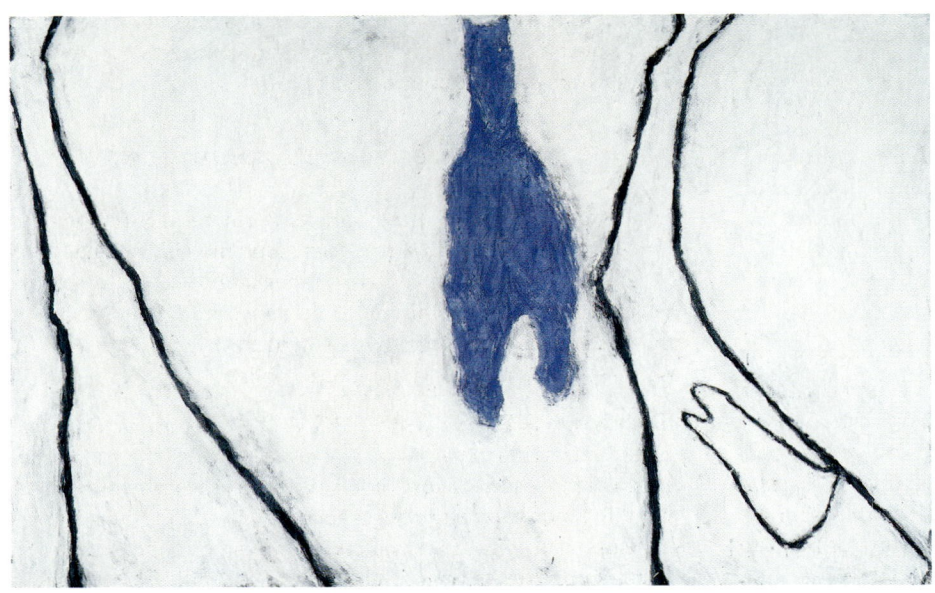

**34-56** SUSAN ROTHENBERG, *Tattoo,* 1979. Acrylic, flashe on canvas, 5′ 7″ × 8′ 7″. Collection Walker Art Center, Minneapolis (purchased with the aid of funds from Mr. and Mrs. Edmond R. Ruben, Mr. and Mrs. Julius E. Davis, the Art Center Acquisition Fund, and the National Endowment for the Arts, 1979).

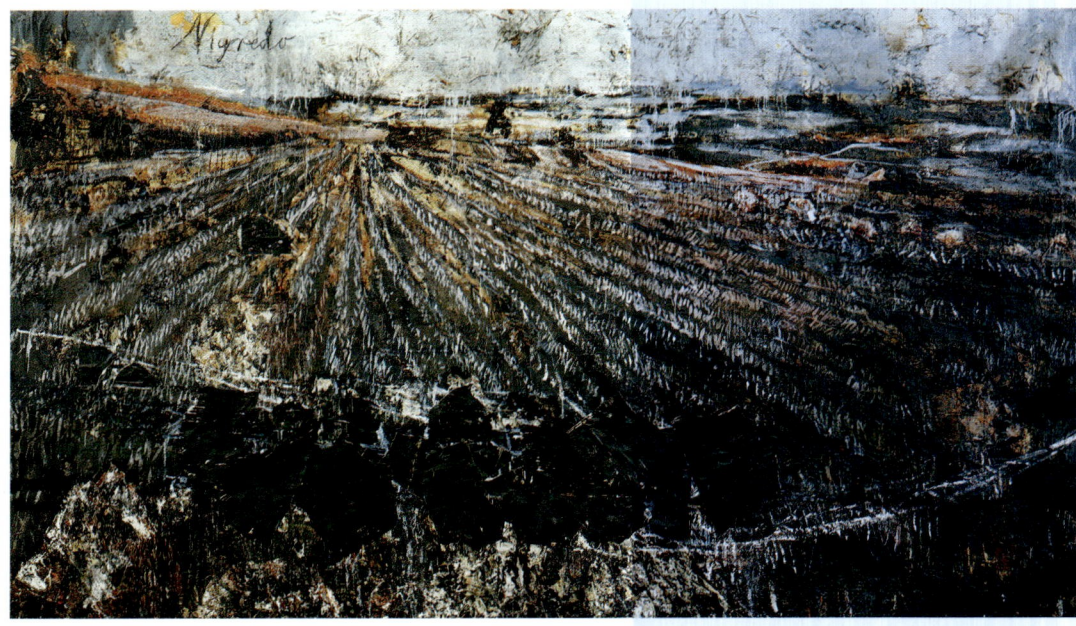

**34-57** ANSELM KIEFER, *Nigredo,* 1984. Oil paint on photosensitized fabric, acrylic emulsion, straw, shellac, relief paint on paper pulled from painted wood, 11′ × 18′. Philadelphia Museum of Art, Philadelphia (gift of Friends of the Philadelphia Museum of Art).

**CONFRONTING GERMAN HISTORY** Neo-Expressionism was by no means a solely American movement. The number of artists who pursued this direction in their art indicates the compelling nature of this style. German artist ANSELM KIEFER (b. 1945) has produced some of the most lyrical and engaging works of the contemporary period. His paintings, such as *Nigredo* (FIG. **34-57**), are monumental in scale, thereby commanding immediate attention. On further inspection, the works draw the viewer to the textured surface, made more complex by the addition of materials such as straw and lead. Kiefer's paintings, like those of Schnabel, have thickly encrusted surfaces. It is not just the impressive physicality of Kiefer's paintings that accounts for impact of his work, however. His images function on a mythological or metaphorical level, as well as on a historically specific one. Kiefer's works of the 1970s and 1980s often involve a reexamination of German history, particularly the painful Nazi era of 1933–1945, and evoke the feeling of despair. Kiefer believes that Germany's participation in World War II and the Holocaust left permanent scars on the souls of the German people and on the souls of all humanity.

*Nigredo* (the Latin word for "blackening") pulls the viewer into an expansive landscape depicted using Renaissance perspectival principles. This landscape, however, is far from pastoral or carefully cultivated. Rather, it appears bleak and charred. Although it does not make specific reference to the Holocaust, this incinerated landscape does indirectly allude to the horrors of that historical event. More generally, the blackness of the landscape may refer to the notion of alchemical change or transformation, a concept of great interest to Kiefer. Black is one of the four symbolic colors of the alchemist—a color that refers both to death and to the molten, chaotic state of substances broken down by fire. The alchemist, however, focuses on the transformation of substances, and thus the emphasis on blackness is not absolute, but can also be perceived as part of a process of renewal and redemption. Kiefer thus imbued his work with a deep symbolic meaning that, when combined with the intriguing visual quality of his parched, congealed surfaces, results in paintings of enduring impact.

**RE-PRESENTING THE VIRGIN MARY** Although not affiliated with the Neo-Expressionists of the 1970s and 1980s, CHRIS OFILI (b. 1968) has produced work that is emphatically expressionistic in nature. In his art, Ofili explores themes such as reli-

gion (he was raised as a Catholic), reinterpreted through the eyes of a British-born male of Nigerian descent. Ofili's *The Holy Virgin Mary* (FIG. **34-58**) depicts Mary in a manner that departs

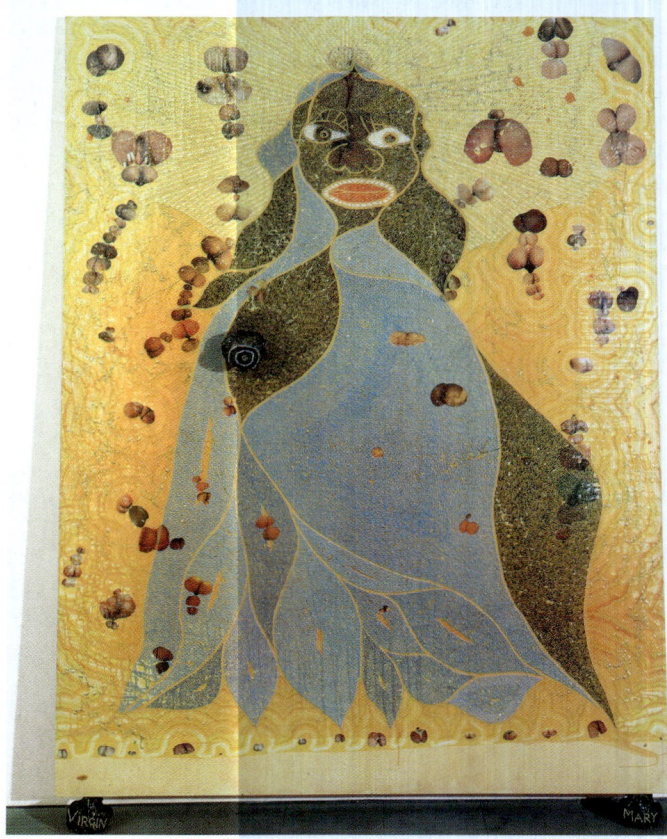

**34-58** CHRIS OFILI, *The Holy Virgin Mary,* 1996. Paper collage, oil paint, glitter, polyester resin, map pins, elephant dung on linen, 7′ 11″ × 5′ 11$\frac{5}{16}$″. The Saatchi Collection, London.

## Contesting Culture
### Controversies in Art

Although there is much in art that inspires and moves us, beauty and uplift are not art's only raisons d'être. Throughout its history, art has also challenged and offended. In recent years, a number of heated controversies about art have surfaced in the United States. That attempts were made in each of these controversies to remove the offending works from public view brought charges of censorship from many outraged art supporters. Ultimately, the question has been raised time and again: Are there limits to what art can appropriately be exhibited, and do authorities (for instance, the federal government) have the right to monitor and pass judgment on creative endeavors? Further, should the acceptability of art be a criterion in determining the federal funding of art?

Two exhibits in 1989 placed the National Endowment for the Arts (NEA), a federal agency charged with supporting the arts (particularly through the distribution of federal funds), squarely in the hot seat of this debate. One of the exhibitions, which was devoted to recipients of the Awards for the Visual Arts (AVA), was held at the Southeastern Center for Contemporary Art in North Carolina. Among the award winners was Andres Serrano, whose *Piss Christ,* a photograph of a crucifix submerged in urine, sparked an uproar. Responding to this artwork, Reverend Donald Wildmon, an evangelical minister from Mississippi and head of the American Family Association, was outraged both that such a work was being exhibited and that the exhibition was funded by the NEA and the Equitable Life Assurance Society (a sponsor of the AVA). He demanded that the work be removed and launched a letter-writing campaign that led Equitable Life to cancel its sponsorship of the awards. To Wildmon and other staunch conservatives, this exhibition, along with the *Robert Mapplethorpe: The Perfect Moment* show, served as evidence of cultural depravity and immorality, which they insisted should not be funded by government agencies such as the NEA. Mapplethorpe was a photographer well known for his elegant, spare photographs of flowers and vegetables as well as his erotic, homosexually oriented images. As a result of media furor over *The Perfect Moment,* the director of the Corcoran Museum of Art decided to cancel the scheduled exhibition of this traveling show. This led to charges of censorship; the real showdown, however, came in Cincinnati, where the director of the Contemporary Arts Center decided to mount the show and was indicted on charges of obscenity; he and the center were acquitted six months later.

These controversies intensified public criticism of the NEA and its funding practices. The following year, in 1990, the head of the NEA, John Frohnmayer, vetoed grants for four lesbian, gay, or feminist performance artists—Karen Finley, John Fleck, Holly Hughes, and Tim Miller—who became known as the "NEA Four." Infuriated by what they perceived as overt censorship, the artists filed suit, eventually settling the case and winning reinstatement of their grants.

As a result of these incidents, however, the funding and future of the NEA have become more precarious. Congress has dramatically reduced its budget, and it no longer awards grants or fellowships to individual artists.

In more recent years, controversies have continued to surface. In 1999, a furor erupted over the exhibition *Sensation: Young British Artists from the Saatchi Collection.* Led by Rudy Giuliani, the mayor of New York at that time, a number of individuals and groups expressed their outrage over artworks, especially Chris Ofili's *The Holy Virgin Mary* (FIG. 34-58), a collage of Mary incorporating cutouts from pornographic magazines and shellacked clumps of elephant dung. Denouncing the show as "sick stuff," the mayor threatened to cut off all city subsidies to the Brooklyn Museum, where *Sensation* was on view. Such oratory polarized the community and no doubt fueled interest in the show (and in Ofili's work in particular).

Art that seeks to unsettle and challenge is critical to the cultural, political, and psychological life of a society. The regularity with which such art raises controversy suggests that it operates at the intersection of two competing principles: free speech and artistic expression on the one hand and a reluctance to impose images upon an audience that finds them repugnant or offensive on the other. What these controversies do demonstrate, beyond doubt, is the impact and power of art.

---

radically from staid, conventional Renaissance representations (see FIGS. 19-6, 19-7, 19-10, and 20-11). Ofili's work presents the Virgin in simplified form, and she appears to float in an indeterminate space. The artist employed brightly colored pigments, applied to the canvas in multiple layers of beadlike dots (inspired by images from ancient caves in Zimbabwe). The Virgin Mary is surrounded by tiny images of genitalia and buttocks cut out from pornographic magazines, which, to the artist, parallel the putti that often surround Mary in Renaissance paintings. Another reference to Ofili's African heritage surfaces in the clumps of elephant dung—one attached to the Virgin's breast, and two more on which the canvas rests, serving as supports. The dung allowed Ofili to incorporate Africa into his work in a literal way; still, he wants the viewer to move beyond the cultural associations of the materials and see them in new ways.

Not surprisingly, *The Holy Virgin Mary* elicited strong reactions when it was exhibited. Its inclusion in the show *Sensation: Young British Artists from the Saatchi Collection* in Brooklyn, New York, in 1999 prompted indignant demands for cancellation of the show and countercharges of censorship (see "Contesting Culture: Controversies in Art," above).

## Art as a Political Weapon

With the renewed interest in representation ushered in by the Pop artists and Superrealists in the 1960s and 1970s, artists once again began to embrace the persuasive powers of art to communicate with a wide audience. In recent decades, artists have investigated more insistently the dynamics of power and privilege, especially in relation to issues of race, ethnicity, gender, and class. This section introduces artists addressing these issues, beginning with feminism.

In the 1970s, the feminist movement focused public attention on the history of women and their place in society. In art, two women—Judy Chicago and Miriam Schapiro—largely spearheaded the American feminist movement under the auspices of the Feminist Art Program. Chicago and a group of students at California State University, Fresno, founded this program, and Chicago and Schapiro coordinated it at the California Institute of the Arts in Valencia, California. In 1972, as part of this program, teachers and students joined to create projects such as Womanhouse, an abandoned house in Los Angeles they completely converted into a suite of "environments," each based on a different aspect of women's lives and fantasies.

**A DINNER PARTY CELEBRATING WOMEN** In her own work in the 1970s, JUDY CHICAGO (born Judy Cohen in 1939) wanted to educate viewers about women's role in history and the fine arts. She aimed to establish a respect for women and their art, to forge a new kind of art expressing women's experiences, and to find a way to make that art accessible to a large audience. Inspired early

in her career by the work of Barbara Hepworth (see FIG. 33-70), Georgia O'Keeffe (see FIGS. 33-37 and Intro-4), and Louise Nevelson (FIG. 34-17), Chicago developed a personal painting style that consciously included abstract organic vaginal images. In the early 1970s, Chicago began planning an ambitious piece, *The Dinner Party* (FIG. 34-59), using craft techniques (such as china painting and stitchery) traditionally practiced by women, to celebrate the achievements and contributions women made throughout history. She originally conceived the work as a feminist Last Supper attended by 13 women (the "honored guests"). The number 13 also refers to the number of women in a witches' coven. This acknowledges a religion (witchcraft) founded to encourage the worship of a female—the Mother Goddess. In the course of her research, Chicago uncovered so many worthy women that she expanded the number of guests threefold to 39 and placed them around a triangular table 48 feet long on each side. The triangular form refers to the ancient symbol for both woman and the Goddess. The notion of a dinner party also alludes to women's traditional role as homemakers. A team of nearly 400 workers under Chicago's supervision assisted in the creation and assembly of the artwork to her design specifications.

*The Dinner Party* rests on a white tile floor inscribed with the names of 999 additional women of achievement to signify that

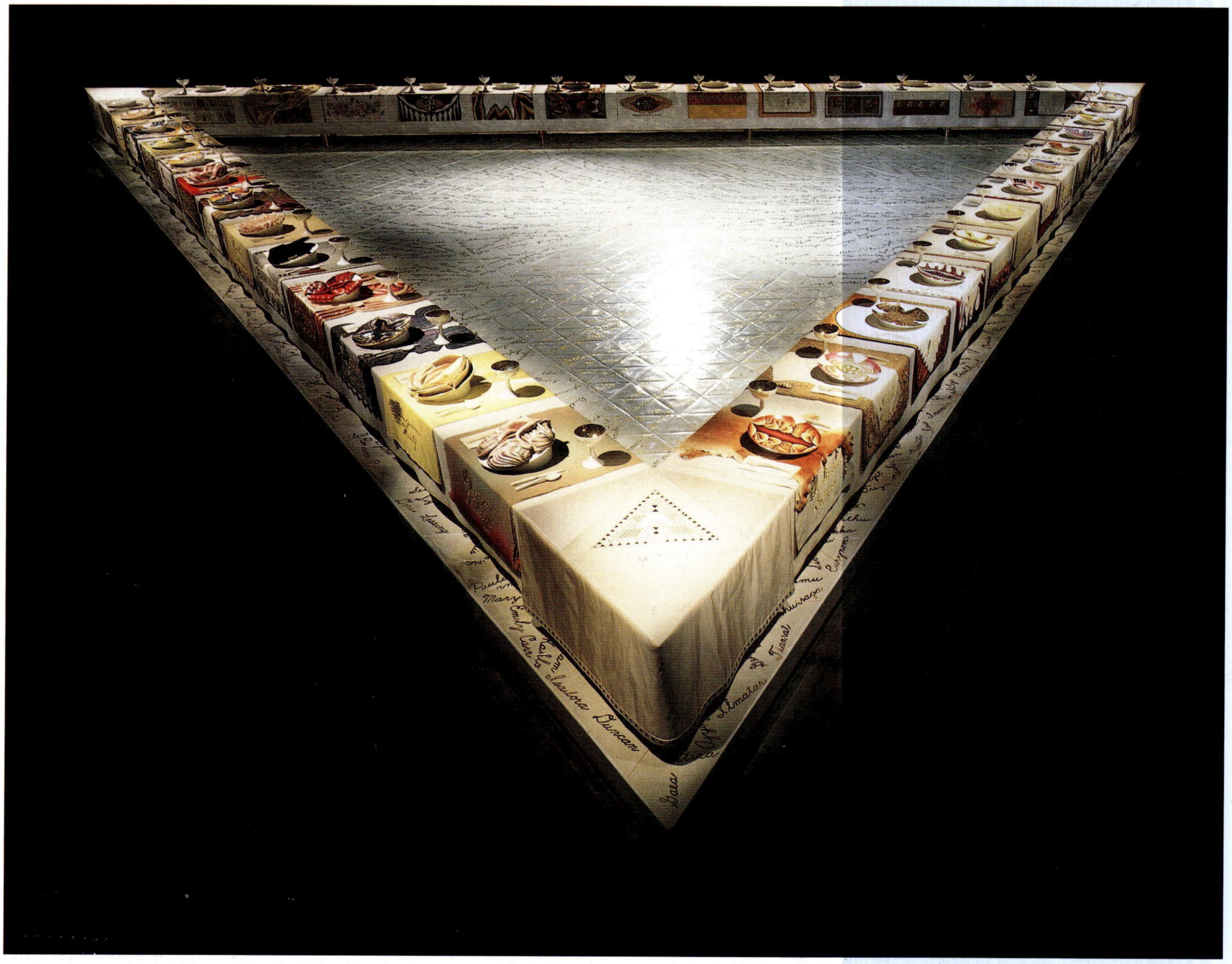

**34-59** JUDY CHICAGO, *The Dinner Party*, 1979. Multimedia, including ceramics and stitchery, 48′ × 48′ × 48′ installed.

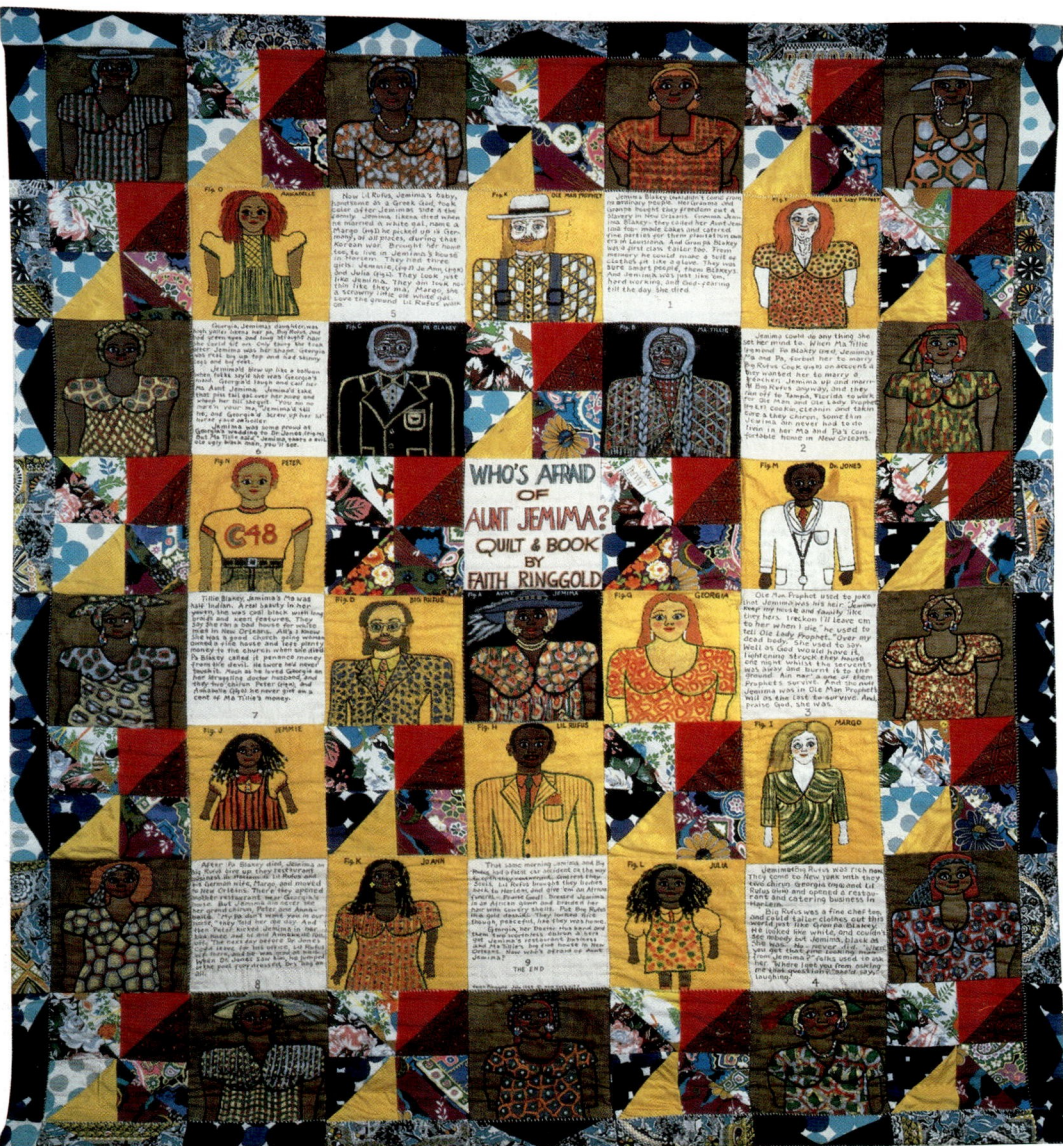

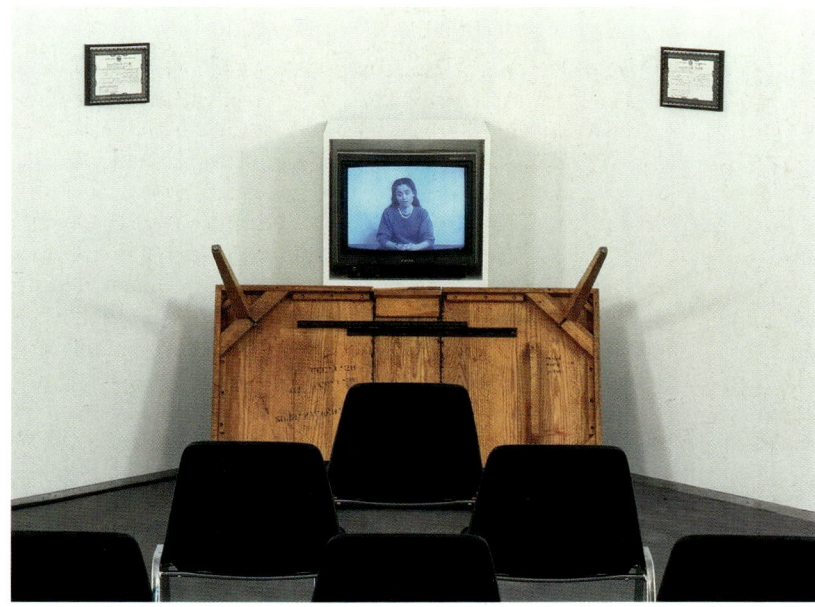

**34-67** ADRIAN PIPER, *Cornered*, 1988. Mixed-media installation of variable size; video monitor, table, and birth certificates. Collection of Museum of Contemporary Art, Chicago.

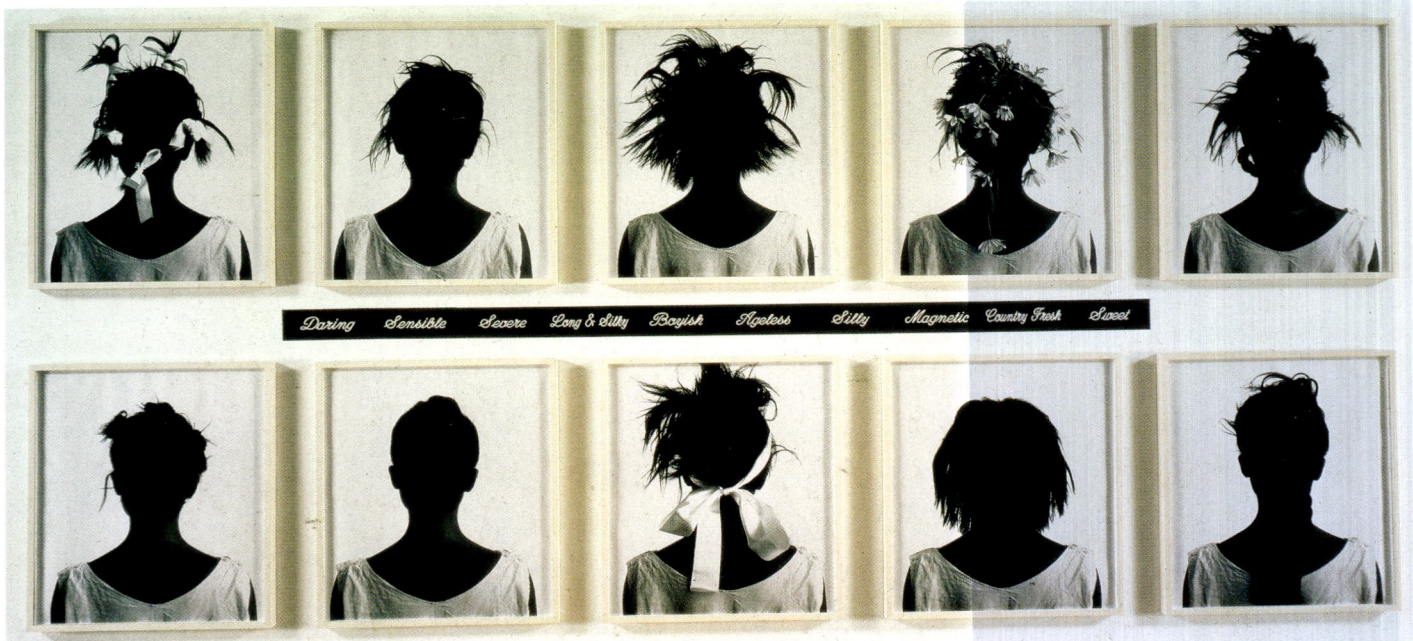

**34-68** LORNA SIMPSON, *Stereo Styles,* 1988. 10 black-and-white Polaroid prints and 10 engraved plastic plaques, 5′ 4″ × 9′ 8″ overall. Courtesy Sean Kelly Gallery.

**COUNTERACTING OBJECTIFICATION** The issues of racism and sexism are also central to the work of LORNA SIMPSON (b. 1960). Simpson has spent much of her career producing photographs that explore feminist and African American strategies to reveal and subvert conventional representations of gender and race. Like Sherman (FIG. 34-61), she deals with the issue of the gaze, trying to counteract the process of objectification to which both women and African Americans are subject.

In *Stereo Styles* (FIG. **34-68**), a series of Polaroids and engravings, Simpson focuses on African American hairstyles, often used to symbolize the entire race. Hair is a physical code tied to issues of social status and position. A scholar who has studied the cultural importance of hair pointed out, "Hair is never a straightforward biological 'fact' because it is almost always groomed, . . . cut, . . . and generally 'worked upon' by human hands. Such practices socialize hair, making it the medium of significant 'statements' about self and society."[46] Even further, regarding race, this same scholar argues, "where race structures social relations of power, hair—as visible as skin color, but also the most tangible sign of racial difference—takes on another forcefully symbolic dimension."[47] In *Stereo Styles,* Simpson also comments on the appropriation of African-derived hairstyles as a fashion commodity, and the personality traits listed correlate with specific hairstyles.

**"LYNCH FRAGMENTS"** American MELVIN EDWARDS (b. 1937) also has sought to reveal a history of collective oppression through his art. One of Edwards's major sculptural series focused on the metaphor of lynching to provoke thought about the legacy of racism. This *Lynch Fragment* series encompassed more than 150 welded-steel sculptures produced in the years after 1963. Lynching as an artistic theme prompts an immediate and visceral response, conjuring up chilling and gruesome images from the past. Edwards sought to extend this emotional resonance further and in his art explored what lynching "means metaphorically or symbolically."[48]

He constructed the series' relatively small welded sculptures, such as *Tambo* (FIG. **34-69**), from found metal objects—for example, chains, hooks, hammers, spikes, knife blades, and hand-

cuffs. Although Edwards often intertwined or welded together the individual metal components so as to diminish immediate identifiability, the sculptures still retain a haunting connection to the overall theme.

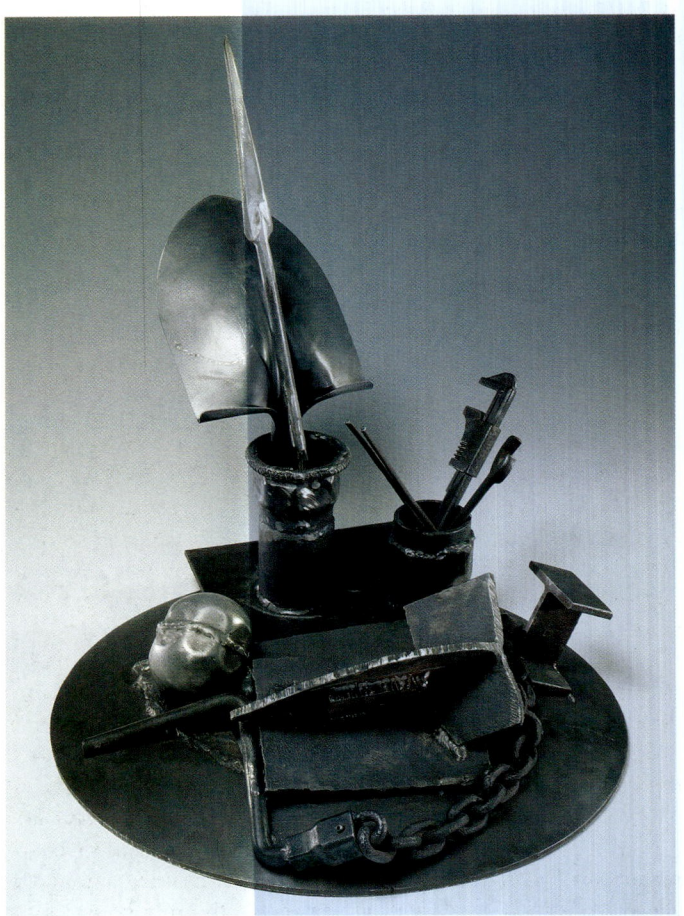

**34-69** MELVIN EDWARDS, *Tambo,* 1993. Welded steel, 2′ 4$\frac{1}{8}$″ × 2′ 1$\frac{1}{4}$″. Smithsonian American Art Museum, Washington, D.C.

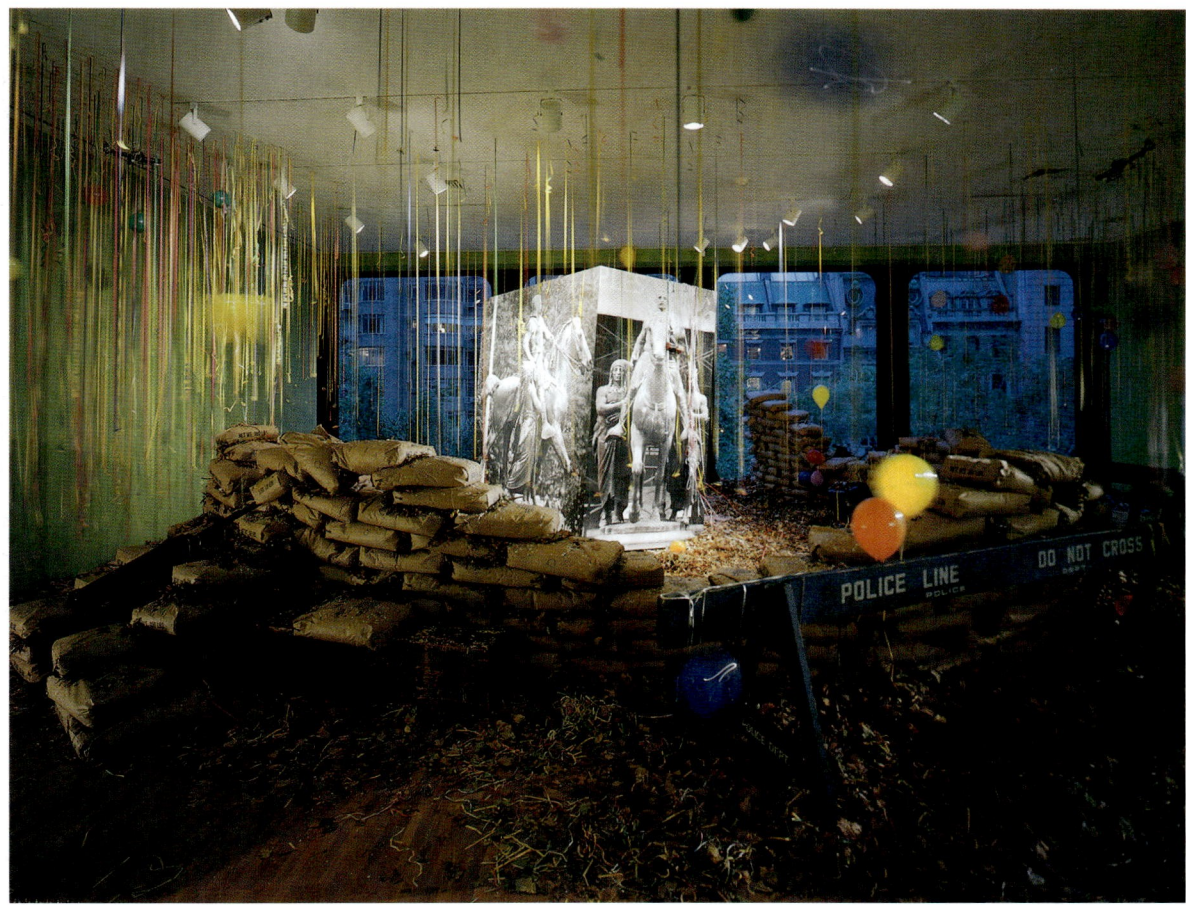

**34-70** David Hammons, *Public Enemy,* installation at Museum of Modern Art, New York, 1991. Photographs, balloons, sandbags, guns, and other mixed media.

Although these works refer to a historical act that evokes a collective memory of oppression, they are also informed by and speak to the continuing contemporary struggle for civil rights and an end to racism. Growing up in Los Angeles, Edwards was surrounded by racial conflict. He picked up some of the metal objects incorporated into his *Lynch Fragments* sculptures in the streets in the aftermath of the Watts riots in 1965, thereby imbuing these disquieting, haunting works with an even greater intensity.

**CHALLENGING CULTURAL ICONS** Nurturing viewer introspection is the driving force behind the art of David Hammons (b. 1943). In his installations, he combines sharp social commentary with beguiling sensory elements to push viewers to confront racism in American society. He created *Public Enemy* (FIG. **34-70**) for an exhibition at the Museum of Modern Art in New York in 1991. Hammons enticed viewers to interact with the installation by scattering fragrant autumn leaves on the floor and positioning helium-filled balloons throughout the gallery. The leaves crunched underfoot, and the dangling strings of the balloons gently brushed spectators walking around the installation. Once drawn into the environment, viewers encountered the central element in *Public Enemy*—large black-and-white photographs of a public monument depicting Teddy Roosevelt triumphantly seated on a horse, flanked by an African American man and a Native American man, both appearing in the role of servants. Around the edge of the installation, circling the photographs of the monument, were piles of sandbags with both real and toy guns propped on top, aimed at the statue. By selecting evocative found objects and presenting them in a dynamic manner that encouraged viewer interaction, Hammons attracted an audience and then revealed the racism embedded in received cultural heritage and prompted reexamination of values and cultural emblems.

**TRADING WITH THE WHITE MAN** Exploring the politics of identity has been an important activity for people from many different walks of life. Jaune Quick-to-See Smith (b. 1940) is a Native American artist descended from the Shoshone, the Salish, and the Cree tribes and raised on the Flatrock Reservation in Montana. Quick-to-See Smith's native heritage has always informed her art, and her concern about the invisibility of Native American artists has led her to organize exhibitions of their art. Yet she has acknowledged a wide range of influences in her work, including "pictogram forms from Europe, the Amur [the river between Russia and China], the Americas; color from beadwork, parfleches [hide cases], the landscape; paint application from Cobra art, New York expressionism, primitive art; composition from Kandinsky, Klee or Byzantine art."[49] She has even compared her use of tribal images to that of the Abstract Expressionists.

Despite the myriad references and visual material in Quick-to-See Smith's art, her work retains coherence and power, and, like many other artists who have explored issues associated with identity, she challenges stereotypes and unacknowledged assumptions. *Trade (Gifts for Trading Land with White People),*

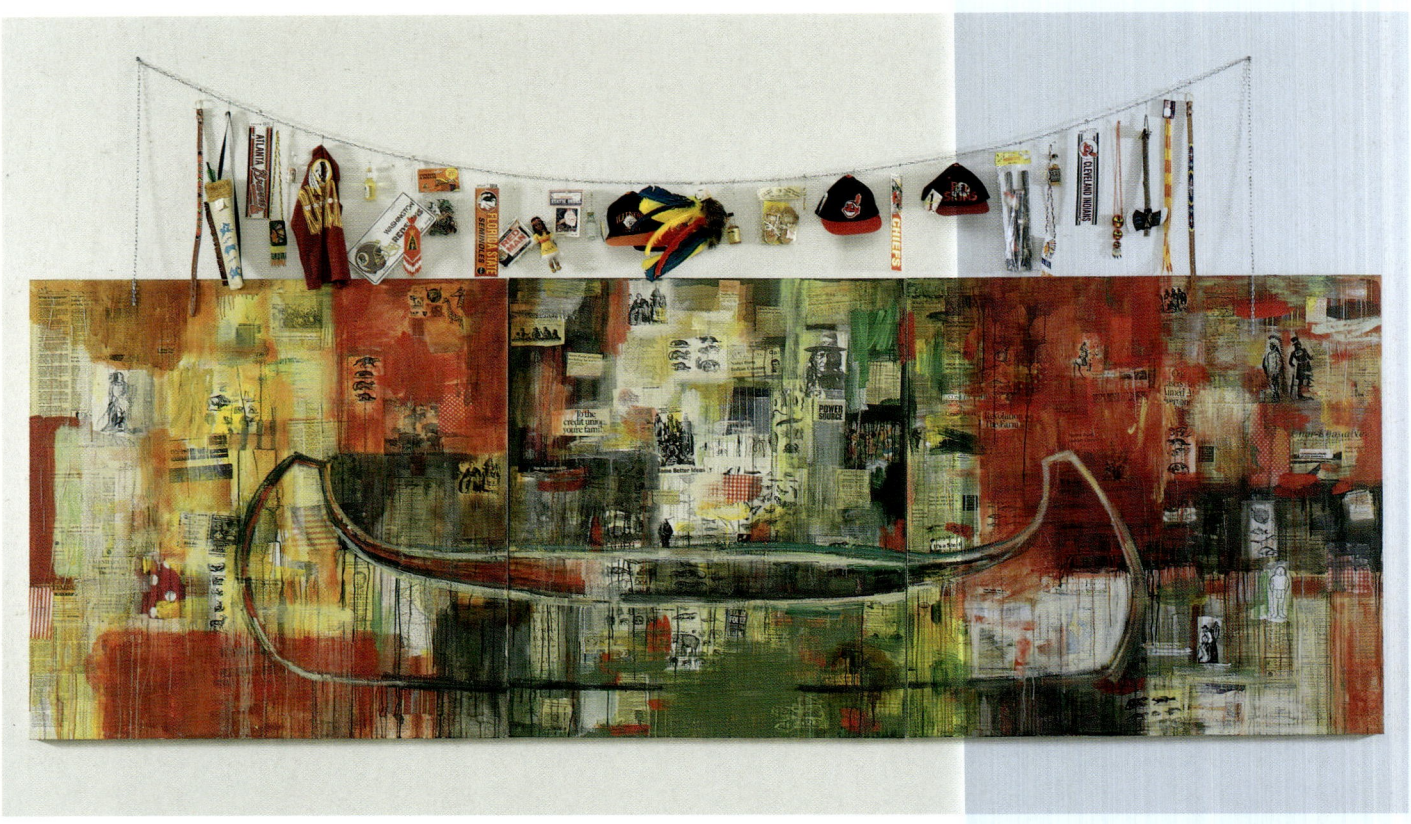

**34-71** Jaune Quick-to-See Smith, *Trade (Gifts for Trading Land with White People)*, 1992. Oil and mixed media on canvas, 5′ × 14′ 2″. Chrysler Museum of Art, Norfolk, Virginia (museum purchase 93.2).

FIG. **34-71**, is a large-scale painting with collage elements and attached objects, reminiscent of a Rauschenberg combine (FIG. 34-29). The painting's central image, a canoe, appears in an expansive field painted in loose Abstract Expressionist fashion and covered with clippings from Native American newspapers. Above the painting, as if hung from a clothesline, is an array of objects. These include Native American artifacts, such as beaded belts and feather headdresses, and contemporary sports memorabilia from teams with American Indian–derived names—the Cleveland Indians, Atlanta Braves, and Washington Redskins. The inclusion of these contemporary objects immediately recalls the vocal opposition to such names and to acts such as the Braves' "tomahawk chop." Like Edwards, Quick-to-See Smith uses the past—cultural heritage and historical references—to comment on the present.

**BRUTAL VISIONS OF VIOLENT TIMES** Other artists have used their art to speak out about pressing social and political issues, sometimes in universal terms and other times with searing specificity. In his art, American artist Leon Golub (b. 1923) has expressed a seemingly brutal vision of contemporary life through a sophisticated reading of the news media's raw data. The work he is best known for deals with violent events of recent decades—the narratives people have learned to extract from news photos of anonymous characters participating in atrocious street violence, terrorism, and torture. Paintings in Golub's *Assassins* and *Mercenaries* series suggest not specific stories but a condition of being. As the artist said,

> Through media we are under constant, invasive bombardment of images—from all over—and we often have to take evasive action

to avoid discomforting recognitions. . . . The work [of art] should have an edge, veering between what is visually and cognitively acceptable and what might stretch these limits as we encounter or try to visualize the real products of the uses of power.[50]

*Mercenaries (IV)*, FIG. **34-72**, a huge canvas, represents a mysterious tableau of five mercenaries (tough freelance military professionals willing to fight, for a price, for any political cause). The three clustering at the right side of the canvas react with tense physical gestures to something one of the two other mercenaries standing at the far left is saying. The dark uniforms and skin tones of the four black fighters flatten their figures and make them stand out against the searing dark red background. The slightly modulated background seems to push their forms forward up against the picture plane and becomes an echoing void in the space between the two groups. The menacing figures loom over viewers standing in front of the work. Golub painted the mercenaries so that the viewer's eye is level with the mercenaries' knees, placing the men so close to the front plane of the work that their feet are cut off by the lower edge of the painting, thereby trapping the viewer with them in the painting's compressed space. Golub emphasized both the scarred light tones of the white mercenary's skin and the weapons. Modeled with shadow and gleaming highlights, the guns contrast with the harshly scraped, flattened surfaces of the figures. The rawness of the canvas reinforces the rawness of the imagery. Golub often dissolved certain areas with solvent after applying pigment and scraped off applied paint with, among other tools, a meat cleaver. The feeling of peril confronts viewers mercilessly. They become one with all the victims caught in today's political battles.

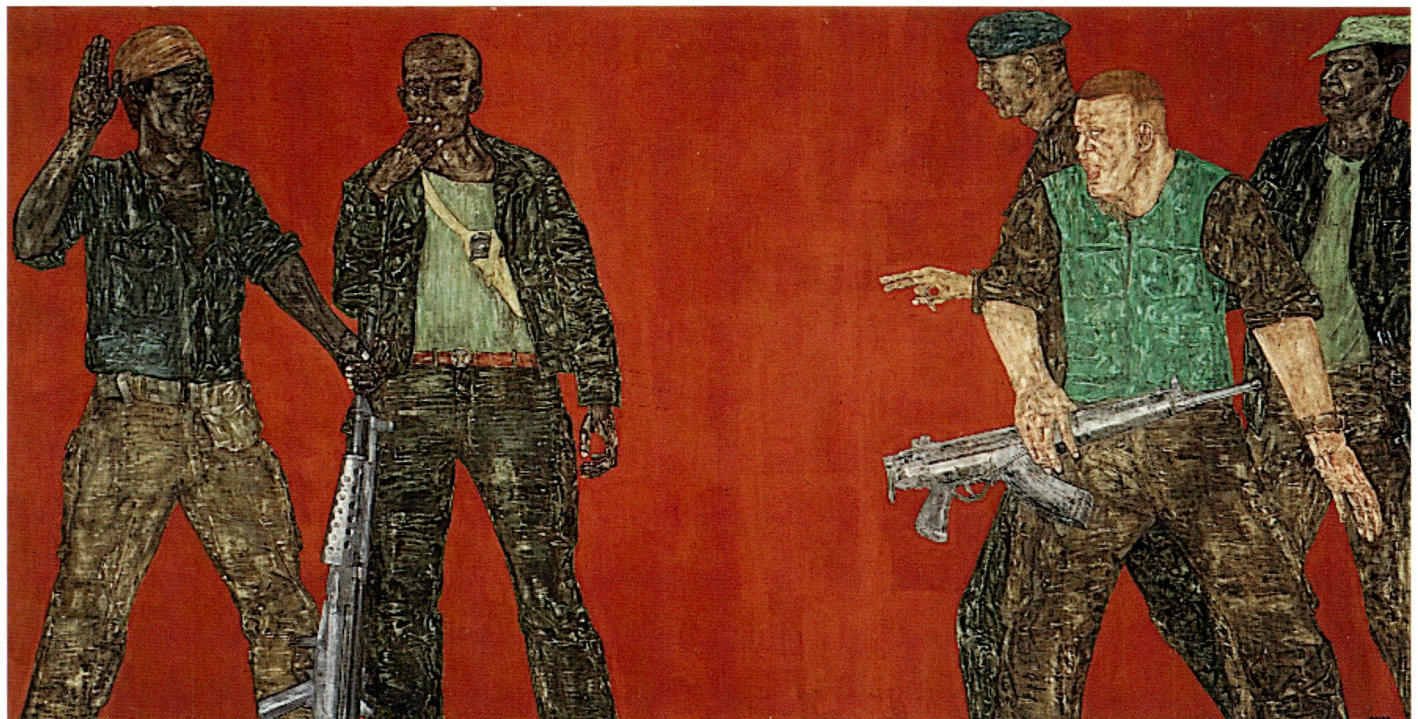

**34-72** LEON GOLUB, *Mercenaries (IV)*, 1980. Acrylic on linen, 10′ × 19′ 2″. Courtesy Ronald Feldman Fine Arts. © Leon Golub/Licensed by VAGA, New York, New York. 

**FABRIC AS A RECORD OF THE SOUL** The stoic, everyday toughness of the human spirit has been the subject of figurative works by the Polish fiber artist MAGDALENA ABAKANOWICZ (b. 1930). A leader in the recent exploration in sculpture of the expressive powers of weaving techniques, Abakanowicz gained fame with experimental freestanding pieces in both abstract and figurative modes. For Abakanowicz, fiber materials are deeply symbolic: "I see fiber as the basic element constructing the organic world on our planet, as the greatest mystery of our environment. It is from fiber that all living organisms are built—the tissues of plants and ourselves. . . . Fabric is our covering and our attire. Made with our hands, it is a record of our souls."[51]

To all of her work, this artist brought the experiences of her early life as a member of an aristocratic family disturbed by the dislocations of World War II and its aftermath. Initially attracted to weaving as a medium that would adapt well to the small studio space she had available, Abakanowicz gradually developed huge abstract hangings she called Abakans that suggest organic spaces as well as giant pieces of clothing. She returned to a smaller scale with works based on human forms—*Heads*, *Seated Figures*, and *Back*s—multiplying each type for exhibition in groups as symbols for the individual in society lost in the crowd yet retaining some distinctiveness. This impression is especially powerful in an installation of *Backs* (FIG. **34-73**). Abakanowicz made each piece by pressing layers of natural organic fibers into a plaster mold. Every sculpture depicts the slumping shoulders, back, and arms of a figure of indeterminate sex and rests legless directly on the floor. The repeated pose of the figures in *Backs* suggests meditation, submission, and anticipation. Although made from a single mold, the figures achieve a touching sense of individuality because each assumed a slightly different posture as the material dried and because the artist imprinted a different pattern of fiber texture on each.

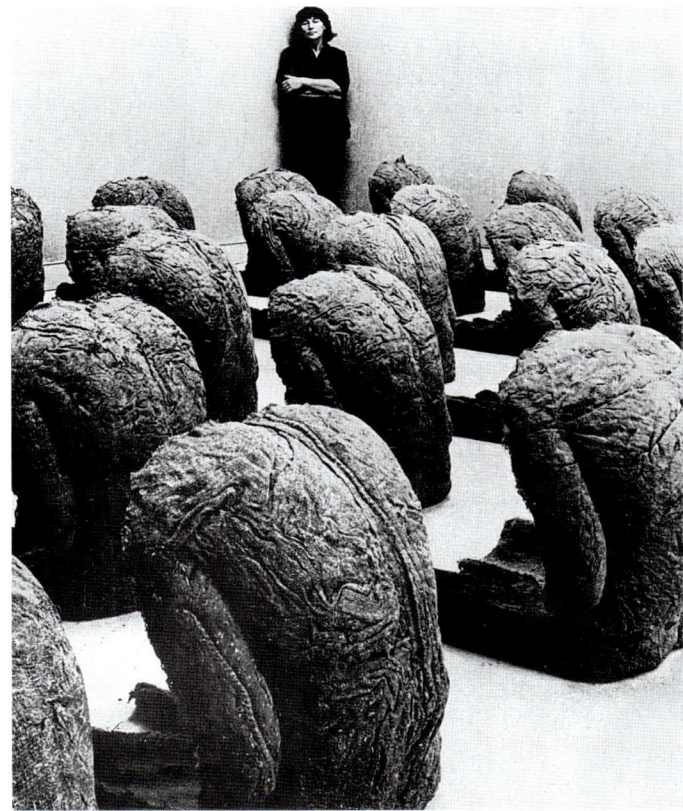

**34-73** MAGDALENA ABAKANOWICZ, artist with *Backs*, at the Musée d'Art Moderne de la Ville de Paris, Paris, France, 1982. Copyright © Magdalena Abakanowicz/Licensed by VAGA, New York, N.Y./ Marlborough Gallery, New York.

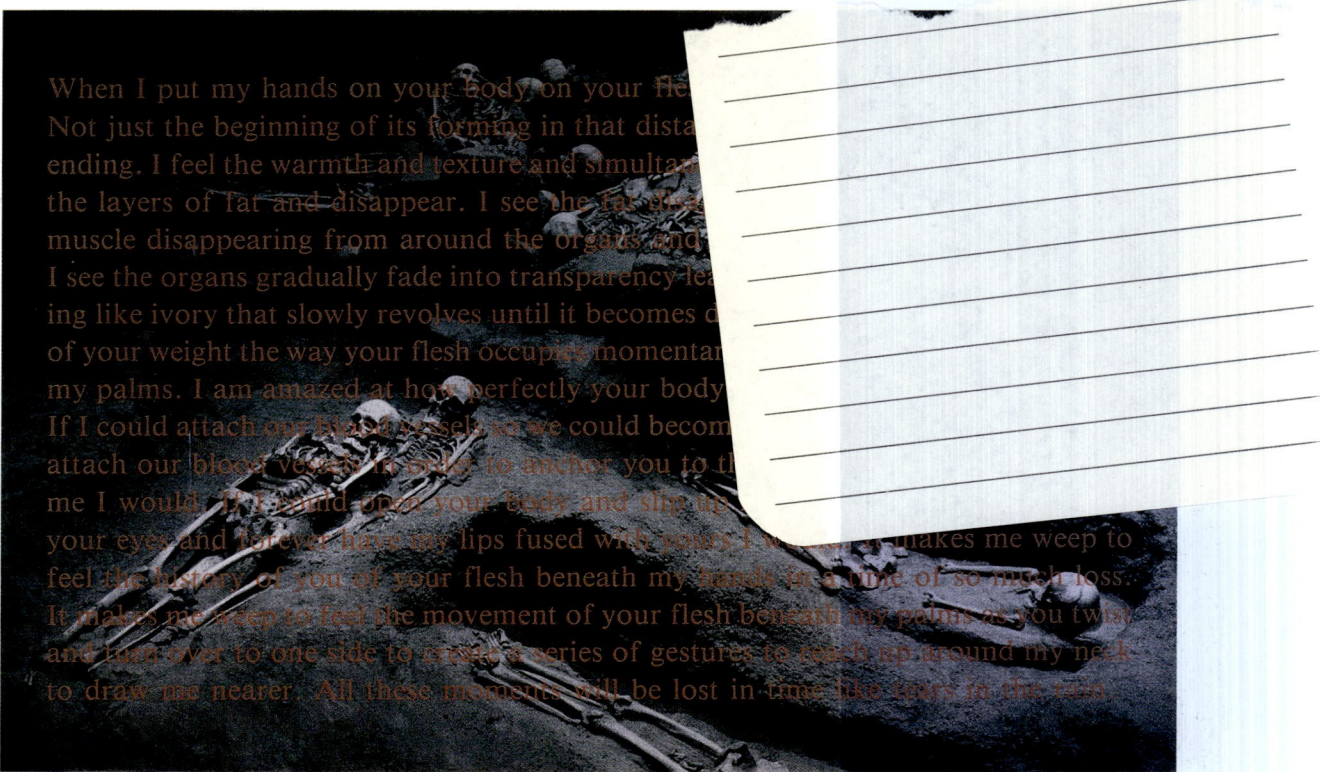

**34-74** David Wojnarowicz, *"When I put my hands on your body,"* 1990. Gelatin-silver print and silk-screened text on museum board, 2′ 2″ × 3′ 2″.

**DEALING WITH AIDS** David Wojnarowicz (1955–1992) devoted the latter part of his artistic career to producing images dealing with issues of homophobia and acquired immune deficiency syndrome (AIDS). As a gay activist and as someone who had seen many friends die of AIDS, Wojnarowicz created disturbing yet eloquent works about the tragedy of this disease, such as *"When I put my hands on your body"* (FIG. **34-74**). In this image, the artist overlaid a photograph of a pile of skeletal remains with evenly spaced typed commentary that communicates his feelings about watching a loved one dying of AIDS. He movingly describes the effects of AIDS on the human body and soul. Wojnarowicz juxtaposed text with imagery, which, like the works of Barbara Kruger (FIG. 34-62) and Lorna Simpson (FIG. 34-68), paralleled the use of both words and images in advertising. The public's familiarity with this format ensured greater receptivity to the artist's message. Wojnarowicz's career was cut short when he also died of AIDS in 1992.

**EXPOSING THE NEXUS OF POWER** When working in Canada in 1980, Polish-born artist Krzysztof Wodiczko (b. 1943) developed artworks involving outdoor slide images. He projected photographs on specific buildings to expose how civic buildings embody, legitimize, and perpetuate power. When Wodiczko moved to New York City in 1983, the pervasive homelessness troubled him, and he resolved to use his art to publicize this problem. In 1987, he produced *The Homeless Projection* (FIG. **34-75**) as part of a New Year's celebration in Boston. The artist projected images of homeless people on all four sides of the Soldiers' and Sailors' Civil War Memorial on the Boston Common. In these photos, plastic bags filled with their possessions flanked those depicted. At the top of the monument, Wodiczko projected a local condominium construction site, which helped viewers make a connection between urban development and homelessness.

## New Technologies: Video and Digital Imagery

Initially, video was available only in commercial television studios and was only occasionally accessible to artists. In the 1960s, with the development of relatively inexpensive portable video recording equipment and of electronic devices allowing manipulation of recorded video material, artists began to explore in earnest the expressive possibilities of this new medium. In its basic form, video technology involves a special motion-picture camera that captures visible images and translates them into electronic data that can be displayed on a video monitor or television screen. Video pictures resemble photographs in the amount of detail they contain, but, like computer graphics, a video image is displayed as a series of points of light on a grid, giving the impression of soft focus. Viewers looking at television or video art are not aware of the monitor's surface. Instead, fulfilling the Renaissance ideal, they concentrate on the image and look through the glass surface, as through a window, into the "space" beyond. Video images combine the optical realism of photography with the sense that the subjects move in real time in a deep space "inside" the monitor.

**FROM VIDEO TO COMPUTER IMAGES** When video introduced the possibility of manipulating subjects in real time, artists such as the Korean-born, New York–based videographer Nam June Paik (b. 1932) were eager to work with the medium. Inspired by the ideas of American composer John Cage and after studying music performance, art history, and Eastern philosophy in Korea and Japan, Paik worked with electronic music in Germany in the late 1950s. He then turned to performances using modified television sets. In 1965, after relocating to New York City, Paik acquired the first inexpensive video recorder sold in Manhattan (the Sony Porta-Pak) and immediately recorded everything he saw out the window of his taxi on the return trip to his studio downtown.

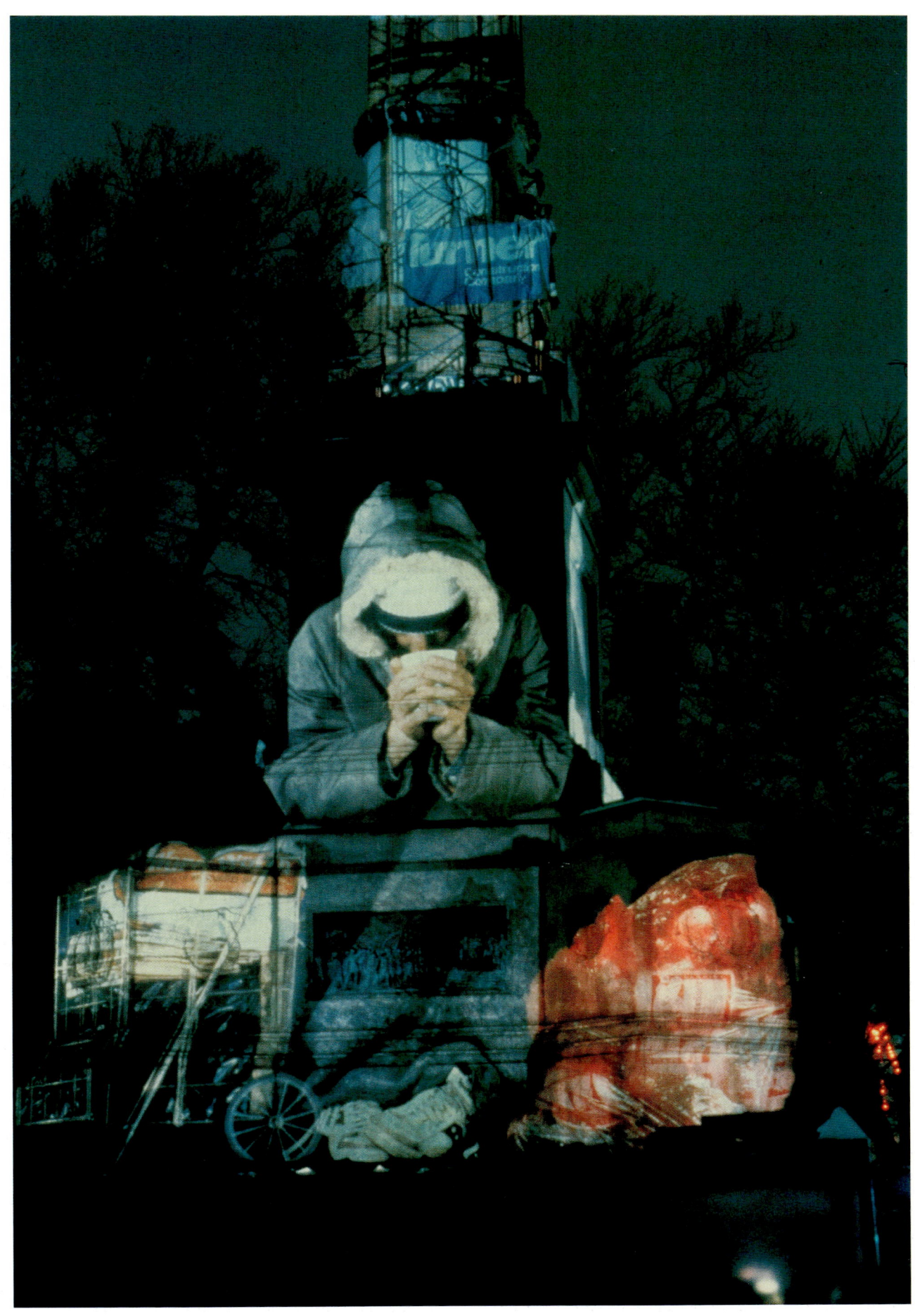

**34-75** Krzysztof Wodiczko, *The Homeless Projection,* 1986–1987. Outdoor slide projection at the Soldiers and Sailors Civil War Memorial, Boston, organized by First Night, Boston.

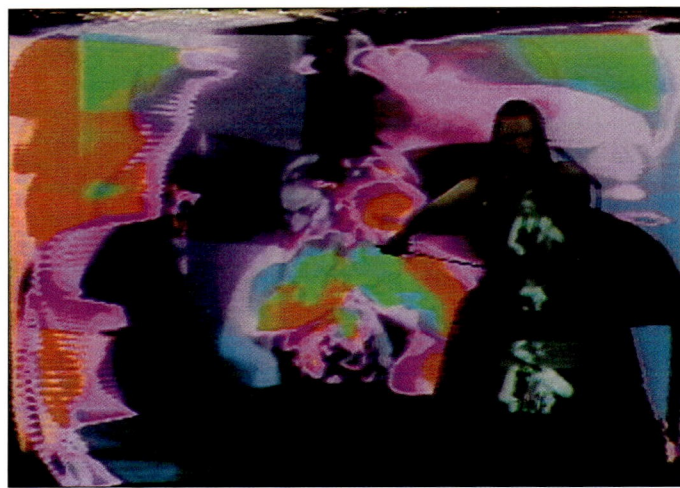

**34-76** NAM JUNE PAIK, Video still from *Global Groove*, 1973. 3/4″ videotape, color, sound, 30 minutes. Collection of the artist.

Experience acquired as artist-in-residence at television stations WGBH in Boston and WNET in New York allowed him to experiment with the most advanced broadcast video technology.

A grant permitted Paik to collaborate with the gifted Japanese engineer-inventor Shuya Abe in developing a video synthesizer. This instrument allows artists to manipulate and change the electronic video information in various ways, causing images or parts of images to stretch, shrink, change color, or break up. With the synthesizer, artists can also layer images, inset one image into another, or merge images from various cameras with those from video recorders to make a single visual kaleidoscopic "time-collage." This kind of compositional freedom permitted Paik to combine his interests in the ideas of Cage, painting, music, Eastern philosophy, global politics for survival, humanized technology, and cybernetics. Paik called his video works "physical music"

and said that his musical background enabled him to understand time better than video artists trained in painting or sculpture.

Paik's best-known video work, *Global Groove* (FIG. **34-76**), combines in quick succession fragmented sequences of female tap dancers, poet Allen Ginsberg reading his work, a performance of cellist Charlotte Moorman using a man's back as her instrument, Pepsi commercials from Japanese television, Korean drummers, and a shot of the Living Theatre group performing a controversial piece called *Paradise Now*. Commissioned originally for broadcast over the United Nations satellite, the cascade of imagery in *Global Groove* was intended to give viewers a glimpse of the rich worldwide television menu Paik predicted would be available in the future.

While some new technologies were revolutionizing the way artists could work with pictorial space, other technologies, especially those of computer graphics, were transforming how artists could create and manipulate illusionistic three-dimensional forms. Computer graphics as a medium uses light to make images and, like photography, can incorporate specially recorded camera images. Computer graphics allows artists to work with wholly invented forms, as painters can.

Developed during the 1960s and 1970s, computer graphics opened up new possibilities for both abstract and figurative art. It involves electronic programs dividing the surface of the computer monitor's cathode-ray tube into a grid of tiny boxes called "picture elements" (pixels). Artists can electronically address these picture elements individually to create a design, much as knitting or weaving patterns have a grid matrix as a guide for making a design in fabric. Once created, parts of a computer graphic design can be changed quickly through an electronic program, allowing artists to revise or duplicate shapes in the design and to manipulate at will the color, texture, size, number, and position of any desired detail. A computer graphics picture is displayed in luminous color on the cathode-ray tube. The effect suggests a view into a vast world existing inside the tube.

**34-77** DAVID EM, *Nora*, 1979. Computer-generated color photograph, 1′ 5″ × 1′ 11″. Private collection.

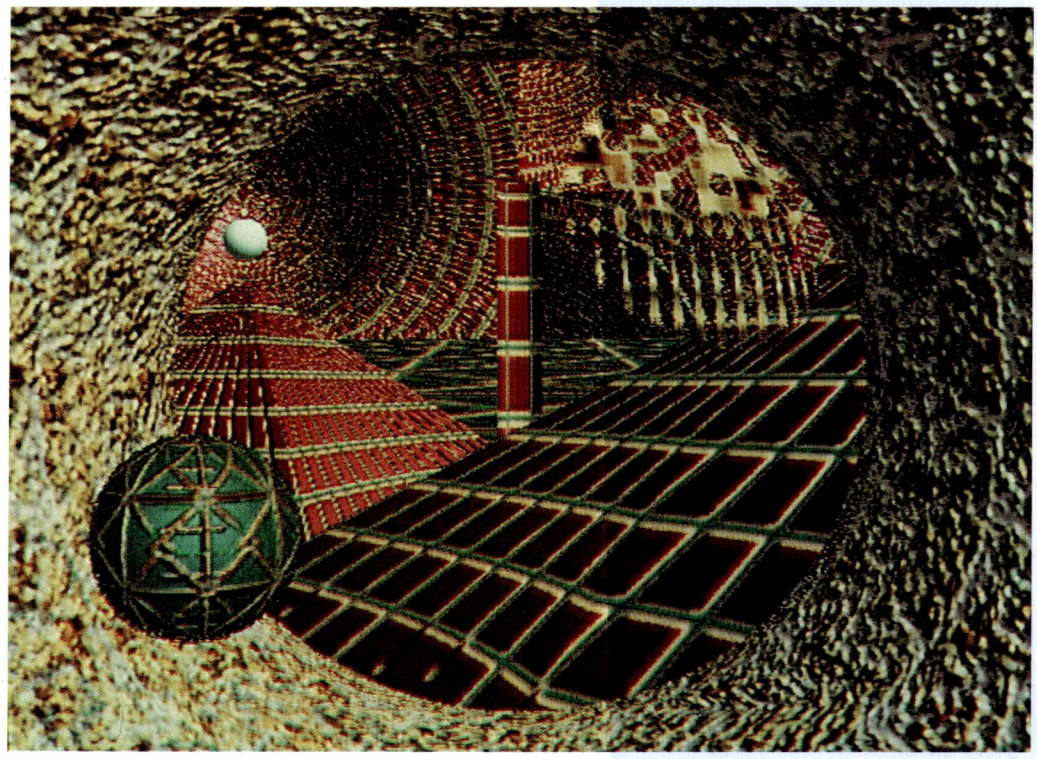

**COMPUTER-GENERATED LANDSCAPES** One of the best-known artists working in this electronic painting mode, DAVID EM (b. 1952), uses what he terms "computer imaging" to fashion fantastic imaginary landscapes. These have an eerily believable existence within the "window" of the computer monitor. When he was artist-in-residence at the California Institute of Technology's Jet Propulsion Laboratory, Em created brilliantly colored scenes of alien worlds using the laboratory's advanced computer graphics equipment. He also had access to software programs developed to create computer graphics simulations of the NASA's missions in outer space. Creating images with the computer allows Em great flexibility in manipulating simple geometric shapes—shrinking or enlarging them, stretching or reversing them, repeating them, adding texture to their surfaces, and creating the illusion of light and shadow. In images such as *Nora* (FIG. **34-77**), Em created futuristic geometric versions of Surrealistic dreamscapes whose forms seem familiar and strange at the same time. The illusion of space in these works is immensely vivid and seductive. It almost seems possible to wander through the tube-like foreground "frame" and up the inclined foreground plane or to hop aboard the hovering globe at the lower left for a journey through the strange patterns and textures of this mysterious labyrinthine setting.

**THE AUTHORITY OF SIGNS** In conjunction with the growing popularity of digital imagery and the expanding interest in video technology, many artists have appropriated the mechanisms and strategies of these media. JENNY HOLZER (b. 1950) is interested in reaching a wide audience with her art. Realizing the efficiency of signs, she created several series using electronic signs, most involving light-emitting diode (LED) technology. In 1989, Holzer did a major installation at the Guggenheim Museum in New York that included elements from her previous series and consisted of a large continuous LED display spiraling around the museum's interior ramp (FIG. **34-78**). Holzer's art focused specifically on text, and she invented sayings with an authoritative tone

for her LED displays. Statements included "Protect me from what I want," "Abuse of power comes as no surprise," and "Romantic love was invented to manipulate women." The statements, which people could read from a distance, were purposefully vague and ambiguous and, in some cases, contradictory.

**DIGITAL SENSORY EXPERIENCE** BILL VIOLA (b. 1951) has spent much of his artistic career exploring the capabilities of digitized imagery, producing many video installations and single-channel works. Often focusing on sensory perception, the pieces not only heighten viewer awareness of the senses but also suggest an exploration into the spiritual realm. Viola, an American, spent years seriously studying Buddhist, Christian, Sufi, and Zen mysticism. Because he fervently believes in art's transformative power and in a spiritual view of human nature, Viola designs works encouraging spectator introspection. His recent video projects involve using such techniques as extreme slow motion, contrasts in scale, shifts in focus, mirrored reflections, staccato editing, and multiple or layered screens to achieve dramatic effects.

The power of Viola's work is evident in *The Crossing* (FIG. **34-79**), an installation piece involving two color video channels projected on 16-foot-high screens. The artist either shows the two projections on the front and back of the same screen or on two separate screens in the same installation. In these two companion videos, shown simultaneously on the two screens, a man surrounded in darkness appears, moving closer until he fills the screen. On one screen, drops of water fall from above onto the

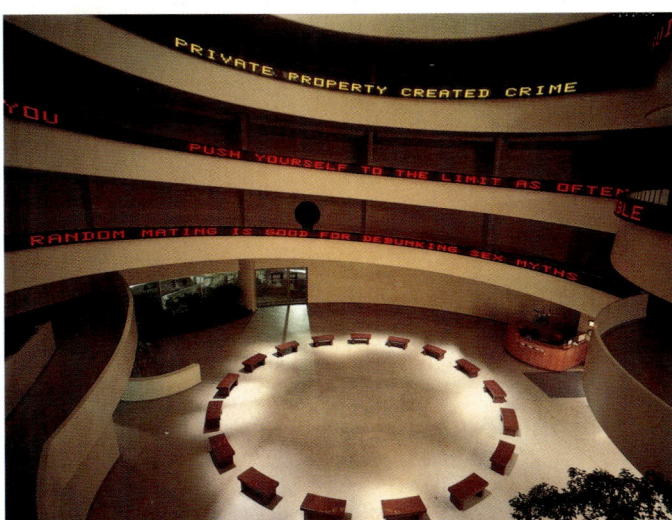

**34-78** JENNY HOLZER, *Untitled* (selections from *Truisms, Inflammatory Essays, The Living Series, The Survival Series, Under a Rock, Laments,* and *Child Text*), 1989. Extended helical tricolor LED electronic display signboard, 16″ × 162′ × 6″. Solomon R. Guggenheim Foundation, New York, December 1989–February 1990 (partial gift of the artist, 1989).

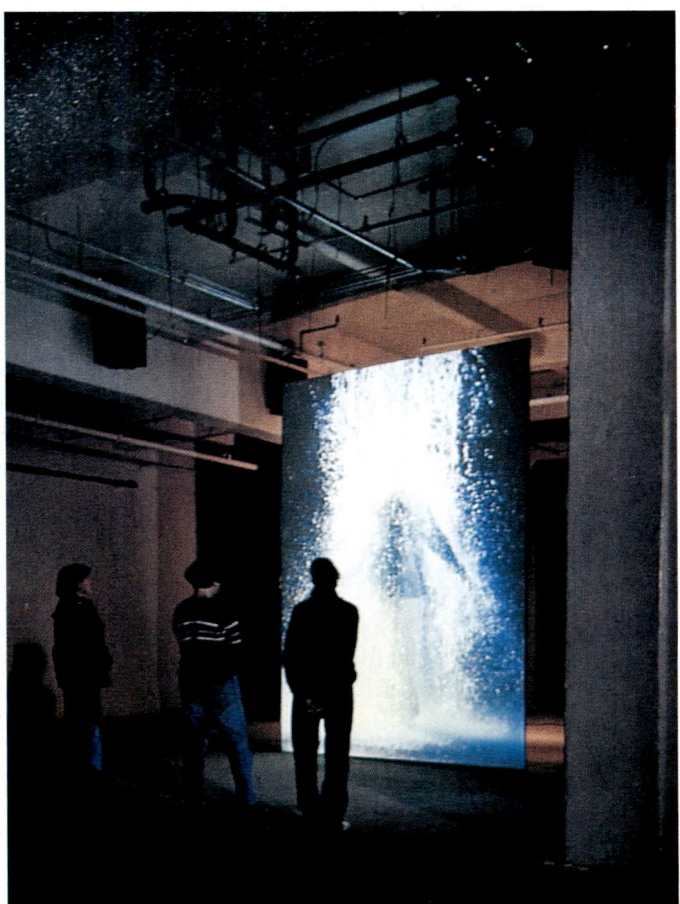

**34-79** BILL VIOLA, *The Crossing*, 1996. Video/sound installation with two channels of color video projection onto screens 16′ high.

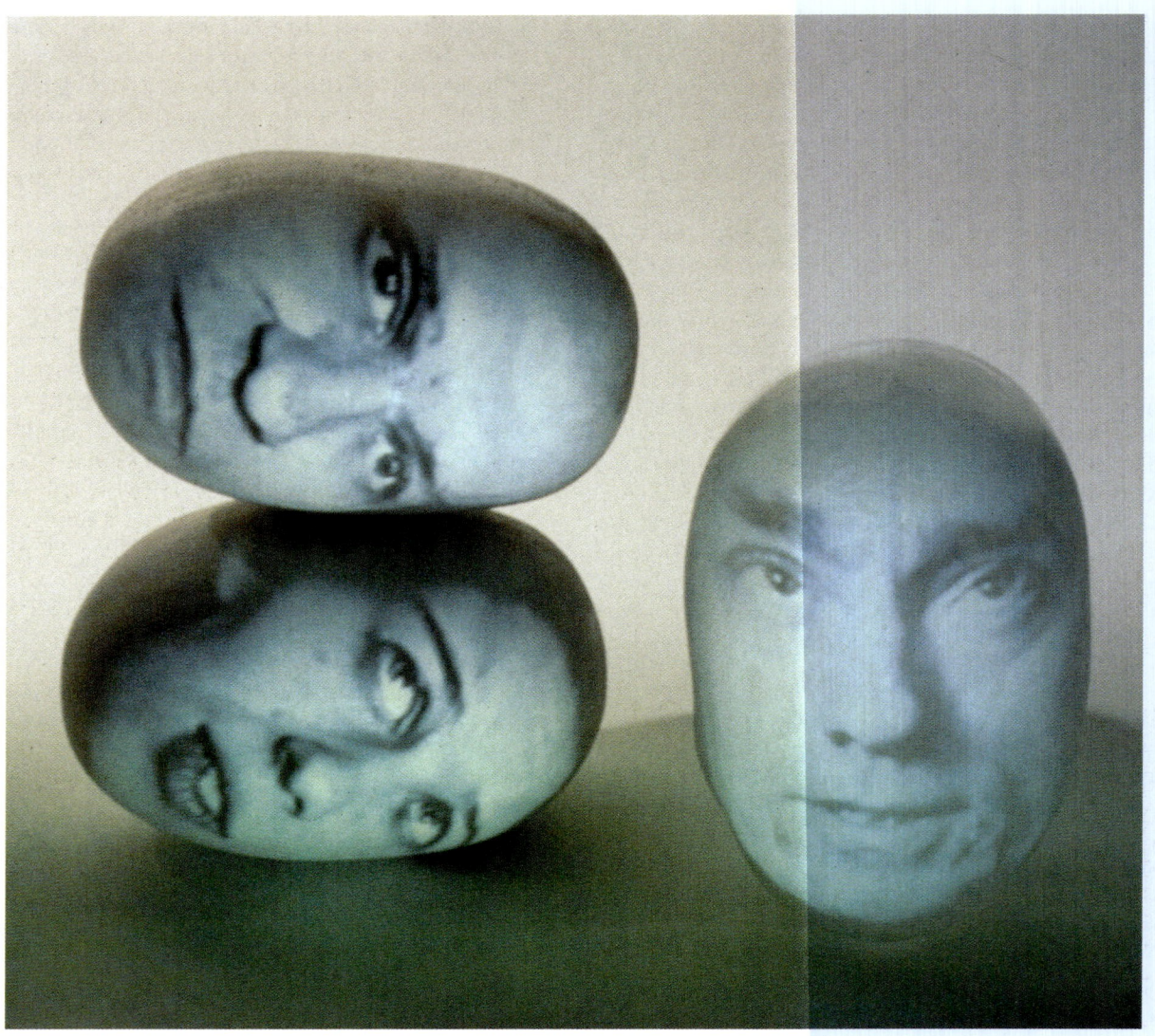

**34-80** TONY OURSLER, *Mansheshe,* 1997. Ceramic, glass, video player, videocassette, CPJ-200 video projector, sound, 11″ × 7″ × 8″ each. Courtesy of the artist and Metro Pictures, New York.

man's head, while on the other screen, a small fire breaks out at the man's feet. Over the next few minutes, the water and fire increase in intensity until the man disappears in a torrent of water on one screen and flames consume the man on the other screen. The deafening roar of a raging fire and a torrential downpour accompany these visual images. Eventually, everything subsides and fades into darkness. This installation's elemental nature and its presentation in a dark space immerse viewers in a pure sensory experience very much rooted in tangible reality.

**SCULPTURAL VIDEO PROJECTIONS** While many artists present video and digital imagery to the audience on familiar flat screens, thus reproducing the format in which we most often come into contact with such images, TONY OURSLER (b. 1957) manipulates his images, projecting them onto sculptural objects. This has the effect of taking such images out of the digital world and insinuating them into the "real" world. Accompanied by sound tapes, Oursler's installations, such as *Mansheshe* (FIG. **34-80**), not only engage but often challenge the viewer. In this example, talking heads are projected onto egg-shaped oval forms suspended from poles. Because the projected images of people look directly at the viewer, the statements they make about religious beliefs, sexual identity, and interpersonal relationships cannot be easily dismissed.

## Postmodernism and Commodity Culture

**SYMBOLS OF WHAT'S WRONG TODAY?** In keeping with Fredric Jameson's evaluation of postmodern culture as inextricably linked to consumer society and mass culture, several postmodern artists have delved into the issues associated with commodity culture. American JEFF KOONS (b. 1955) first became prominent in the art world for a series of works in the early 1980s that involved exhibiting common purchased objects such as vacuum cleaners. Clearly following in the footsteps of artists such as Marcel Duchamp and Andy Warhol, Koons made no attempt to manipulate or alter the objects. Critics and other art world participants perceived them as representing the commodity basis of both the art world and society at large. Koons's experience as a commodities broker before turning to art and his blatant self-promotion have led to accusations that his art is market driven.

More recently, Koons has produced porcelain sculptures, such as *Pink Panther* (FIG. **34-81**). Here, Koons continued his immersion in contemporary mass culture by intertwining a magazine centerfold nude with a well-known cartoon character. He reinforced the trite and kitschy nature of this imagery by titling the exhibition of which this work was a part *The Banality Show.* Some

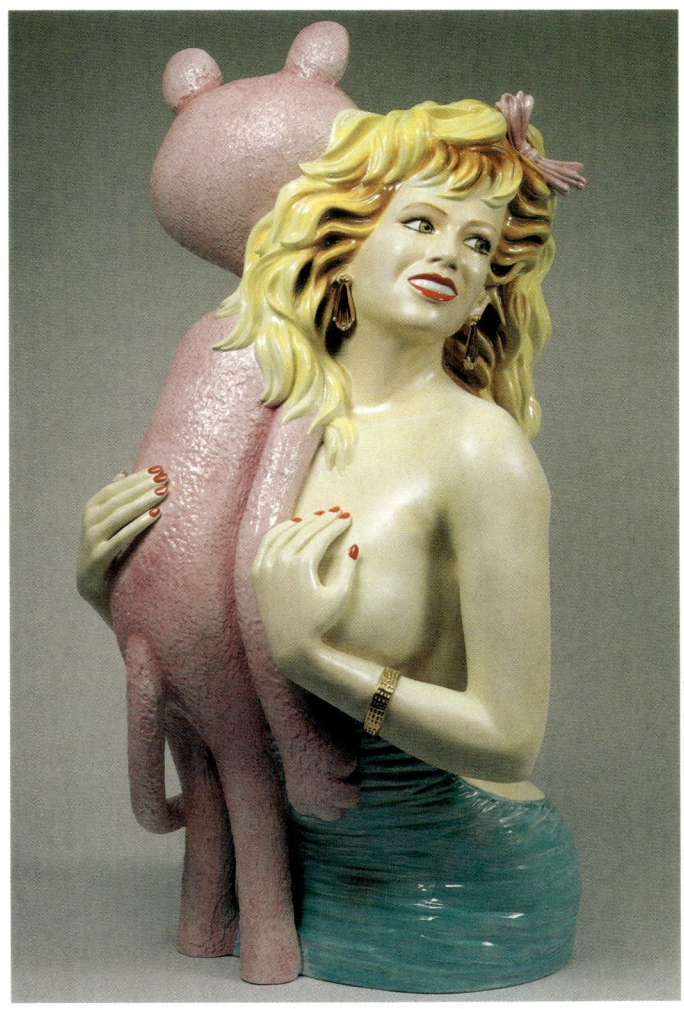

**34-81** JEFF KOONS, *Pink Panther*, 1988. Porcelain, 3′ 5″ × 1′ 8½″ × 1′ 7″. Collection of Museum of Contemporary Art, Chicago (Gerald S. Elliot Collection).

art critics have argued that Koons and his work instruct viewers because both artist and work serve as the most visible symbols of everything that is wrong with contemporary American society. Whether or not this is true, people must acknowledge that, at the very least, Koons's prominence in the art world indicates that he, like Warhol before him, has developed an acute understanding of the dynamics of consumer culture.

## Postmodernism and the Critique of Art History

Postmodern architecture often incorporates historical forms and styles. Members of the art world have frequently cited this awareness of the past as a defining characteristic of postmodernism, in both architecture and art. Such awareness, however, extends beyond mere citation. People have described it as a self-consciousness on the part of artists about their place in the continuum of art history. Not only do artists demonstrate their knowledge about past art, but they also express awareness of the mechanisms and institutions of the art world. For many postmodern artists, then, referencing the past moves beyond simple quotation from earlier works and styles and involves a critique of or commentary on fundamental art historical premises. In short, their art is about making art.

**THE HISTORY OF ART IN ART** In his humorous *A Short History of Modernist Painting* (FIG. **34-82**), American artist MARK TANSEY (b. 1949) provides viewers with a tongue-in-cheek summary of the various approaches to painting artists have embraced over the years. Tansey presents a sequence of three images, each visualizing a way of looking at art. At the far left, a glass window encapsulates the Renaissance ideal of viewing art as though one were looking through a window. In the center image, a man pushing his head against a solid wall represents the thesis central to much of modernist formalism—that the painting should be

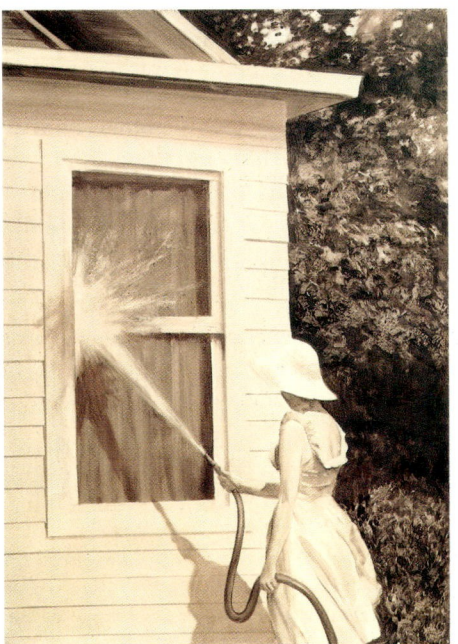 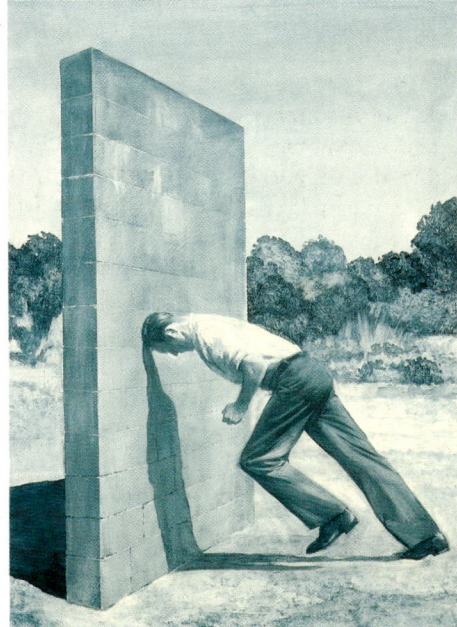 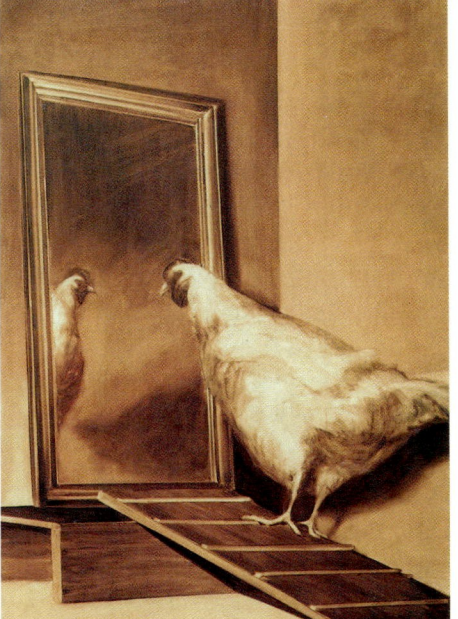

**34-82** MARK TANSEY, *A Short History of Modernist Painting*, 1982. Oil on canvas, three panels, each 4′ 10″ × 3′ 4″. Courtesy Curt Marcus Gallery.

acknowledged as an object in its own right. Modernism, particularly of the type that Clement Greenberg promoted in the 1960s and 1970s, was based on the rejection of imitation and illusion as a primary artistic goal. In the image on the right, Tansey summarizes the postmodern approach to art with a chicken pondering its reflection in the mirror. The chicken's action reveals postmodern artists' self-consciousness or awareness of their place in the art historical continuum.

**SATIRICAL CERAMIC SCULPTURE** ROBERT ARNESON (1930–1992) spent his life in a small town north of San Francisco, and this fact provided the impetus for his ceramic work *California Artist* (FIG. **34-83**). Over the years, Arneson developed a body of work of predominantly figurative ceramic sculpture, often satirical or amusing and sometimes biting. In 1981, well-known art critic Hilton Kramer published a review of an

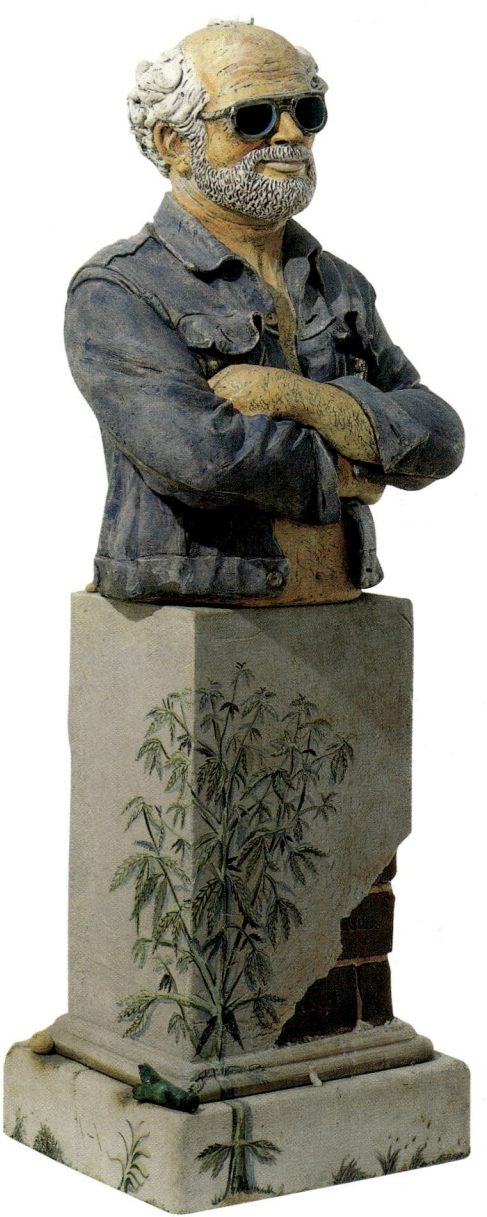

**34-83** ROBERT ARNESON, *California Artist,* 1982. Glazed stoneware, 5′ 8¼″ × 2′ 3½″ × 1′ 8¼″. San Francisco Museum of Modern Art (gift of the Modern Art Council). Copyright © Estate of Robert Arneson/ Licensed by VAGA, New York, New York.

exhibition including Arneson's work. Kramer's assessment of Arneson's art was searingly negative. Arneson decided to create *California Artist* as a direct response to the critic, particularly to Kramer's derogatory comments on the provincialism of California art. This ceramic sculpture, a half-length self-portrait, incorporates all of the critic's stereotypes. The artist placed the top half of his likeness on a pedestal littered with beer bottles, cigarette butts, and marijuana plants. Arneson appears clad only in a denim jacket and sunglasses, looking very defiant with his arms crossed. By creating an artwork that responded directly to an art critic's comments, Arneson revealed his comprehension of the mechanisms (for example, art criticism) people use currently to evaluate and validate art.

## Postmodernism and Art Institutions

Along with a conscious reappraisal of the processes of art historical validation, postmodern artists have turned to assessing art institutions, such as museums and galleries. Not only have such artists addressed issues associated with the role of these institutions in validating art, but also, in keeping with increased public concern about issues of race, class, gender, and ethnicity, they have scrutinized the discriminatory policies and politics of these institutions.

**MUSEUMS AND THE POLITICS OF ART** German artist HANS HAACKE (b. 1936) has focused his attention on the politics of art museums and how these politics affect the art exhibited and, ultimately, museum visitors' understanding of art history. The specificity of his works, based on substantial research, makes them stinging indictments of the institutions whose practices he critiques. In *MetroMobiltan* (FIG. **34-84**), Haacke illustrated the connection between the realm of art (more specifically, the Metropolitan Museum of Art in New York) and the "real" world of political and economic interests. *MetroMobiltan* is a large sculptural work that includes a photomural of a funeral for South African black people. This photomural serves as the backdrop for a banner for the 1980 Mobil Oil–sponsored Metropolitan Museum show *Treasures of Ancient Nigeria.* In 1980, Mobil was a principal U.S. investor in South Africa, and Haacke's work suggests that Mobil's sponsorship of this exhibition was in part driven by the fact that Nigeria was one of the richest oil-producing countries in Africa. In 1981, the public pressured Mobil's board of directors to stop providing oil to the white South African military and police. Printed on the blue banners hanging on either side of *MetroMobiltan* is the official corporate response refusing to comply with this demand. Haacke set the entire tableau in a fiberglass replica of the museum's entablature. By bringing together these disparate visual and textual elements that make reference to Mobil Oil, Africa, and the Metropolitan Museum, the artist forced viewers to think about the connections among multinational corporations, political and economic conditions in South Africa, and the conflicted politics of corporate patronage of art exhibitions. The complicity of Mobil Oil and other corporations in perpetuating injustice extends to the museum world, one the public often views as exempt from political and economic concerns.

**THE "CONSCIENCE OF THE ART WORLD"** The New York–based GUERRILLA GIRLS, formed in 1984, bill themselves as the "conscience of the art world." This group sees it as its duty to call attention to injustice in the art world, especially what it perceives as the sexist and racist orientation of the major institutions.

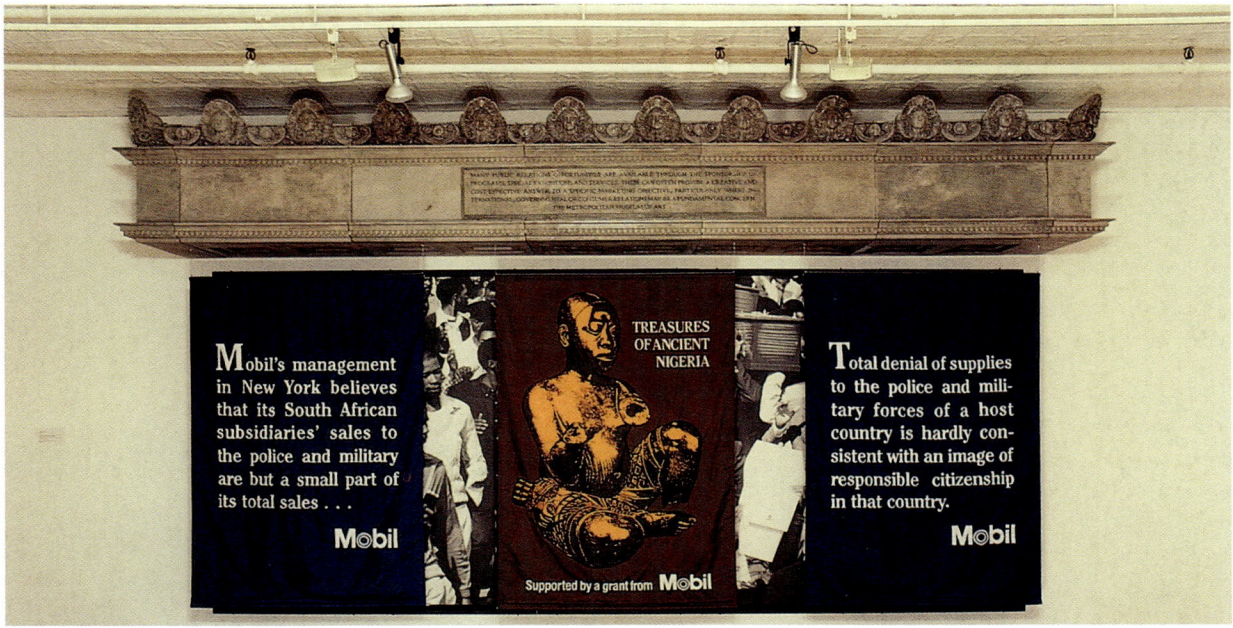

**34-84** Hans Haacke, *MetroMobiltan*, 1985. Fiberglass construction, three banners, and photomural, 11′ 8″ × 20′ × 5′. Collection Centre Georges Pompidou, Paris.

The women who are members of the Guerrilla Girls remain anonymous at all times and protect their identities by wearing gorilla masks in public. They employ guerrilla tactics (hence the name) by demonstrating in public, putting on performances, and placing posters and flyers in public locations. This distribution network expands the impact of their messages. One poster that reflects the Guerrilla Girls' agenda facetiously lists "the advantages of being a woman artist" (FIG. **34-85**). Actually, the list itemizes for readers the numerous obstacles women artists face in the contemporary art world. The Guerrilla Girls hope their publicizing of these obstacles will inspire improvements in the situation for women artists.

**34-85** GUERRILLA GIRLS, *The Advantages of Being a Woman Artist*, 1988. Poster. Courtesy Guerrilla Girls.

# THE ADVANTAGES OF BEING A WOMAN ARTIST:

Working without the pressure of success.
Not having to be in shows with men.
Having an escape from the art world in your 4 free-lance jobs.
Knowing your career might pick up after you're eighty.
Being reassured that whatever kind of art you make it will be labeled feminine.
Not being stuck in a tenured teaching position.
Seeing your ideas live on in the work of others.
Having the opportunity to choose between career and motherhood.
Not having to choke on those big cigars or paint in Italian suits.
Having more time to work when your mate dumps you for someone younger.
Being included in revised versions of art history.
Not having to undergo the embarrassment of being called a genius.
Getting your picture in the art magazines wearing a gorilla suit.

A PUBLIC SERVICE MESSAGE FROM **GUERRILLA GIRLS** CONSCIENCE OF THE ART WORLD
532 LaGUARDIA PLACE, #237 · NY, NY 10012
www.guerrillagirls.com

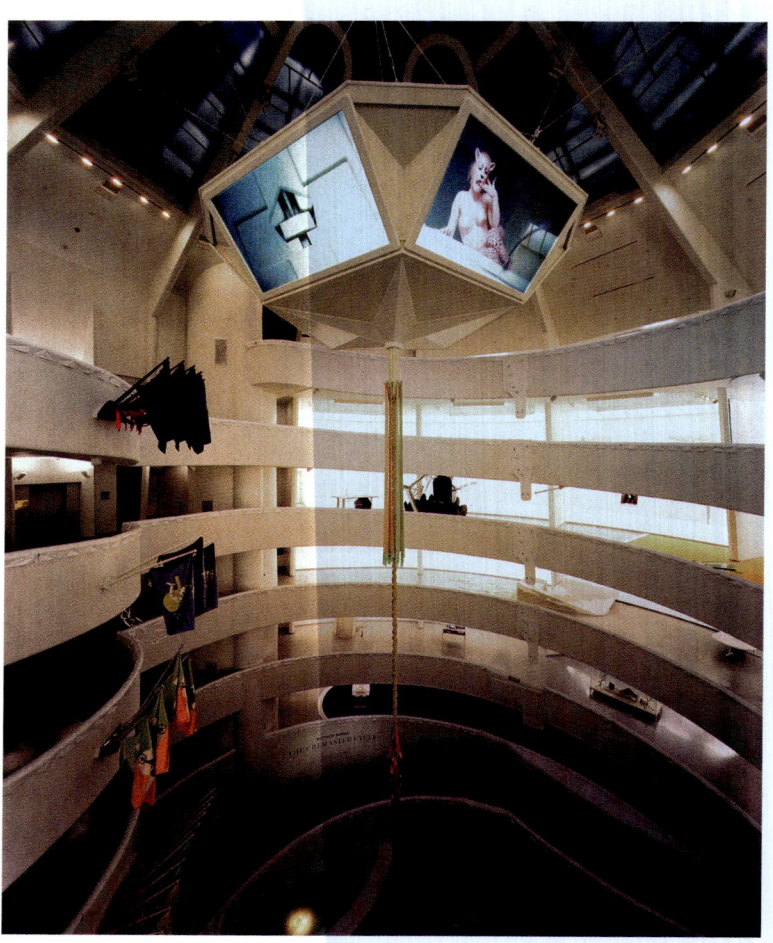

# Into the 21st Century: The Future of Art and Art History

At the end of the 19th century, a unique fin de siècle culture emerged, followed by the emergence in the early 20th century of prodigious artistic talents such as Matisse, Duchamp, and Picasso. What will the 21st century bring? Will a similarly fertile period in art and culture arise as the new century and the new millennium progress, as some people anticipate? It is, of course, impossible to predict anything with any certainty. Further, with the expansive scope of postmodernism, no single approach or style dominates. Indeed, as we move into the 21st century, it seems that one of the major trends is a relaxation of the traditional boundaries between artistic media. Following in the footsteps of artists such as Duchamp, Rauschenberg, Piper, and Hammons, many artists today are creating multimedia installations that are often site-specific.

**AN EPIC CREATION CYCLE** One such artist is MATTHEW BARNEY (b. 1967). The 2003 installation (FIG. **34-86**) of his epic *Cremaster* cycle (1994–2002) at the Solomon R. Guggenheim Museum in New York typifies the expansive scale upon which many contemporary works are conceptualized. A multimedia extravaganza involving drawings, photographs, sculptures, videos, films, and performances (presented in videos), the *Cremaster* cycle is a lengthy narrative that takes place in a self-enclosed universe created by Barney. The title of the work refers to the cremaster muscle, which controls testicular contractions in response to external stimuli. Barney uses the development of this muscle in the embryonic process of sexual differentiation as the conceptual springboard for this entire project, in which he explores the notion of creation in expansive and complicated ways. The cycle's narrative, revealed in the five 35-mm feature-length films and the artworks, makes reference to, among other things, a musical revue in Boise, Idaho (Barney's hometown), the life cycle of bees, the execution of convicted murderer Gary Gilmore, the construction of the Chrysler Building (see FIG. 33-65), Celtic mythology, Masonic rituals, a motorcycle race, and a lyric opera set in late-19th-century Budapest. In the installation, the artworks are tied together conceptually by a five-channel video piece that is projected on screens hanging in the Guggenheim's rotunda. Immersion in Barney's constructed world is disorienting and overwhelming and has a force that competes with the immense scale and often frenzied pace of contemporary life.

# Conclusion

In the later 20th century, the domination of modernist formalism in art gave way to an eclectic postmodernism. The emergence of postmodern thought not only encouraged a wider range of styles and approaches but also prompted commentary (often ironic) about the nature of art production and dissemination. In recent decades, many artists have produced works prompted by sociopolitical concerns, dealing with aspects of race, gender, class, and other facets of identity. The universally expanding presence of computers, digital technology, and the Internet will surely have an effect on the art world. It may well erode remaining conceptual and geographical boundaries, and make art and information about art available to virtually everyone, thereby creating a truly global artistic community.

| Existentialism, 1930–1950s |

**1945**

| United Nations organized, 1945
| Atomic bomb devastates Hiroshima and Nagasaki, 1945
| Independence of India and Pakistan, 1947
| Transistor invented, 1948
| State of Israel created, 1948
| People's Republic of China established, 1949

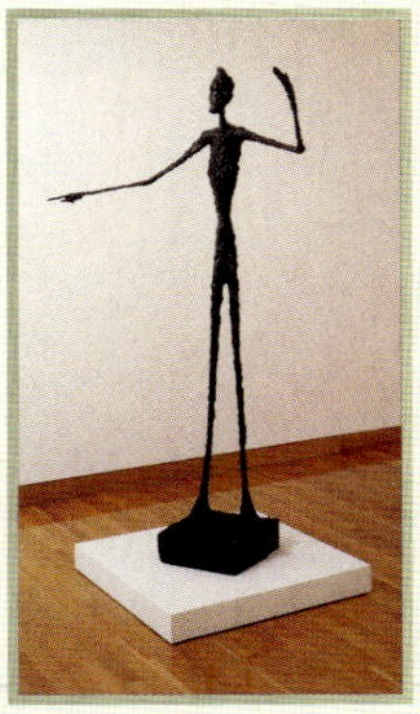

**1** Alberto Giacometti, *Man Pointing*, 1947

**1950**

| Korean conflict, 1950–1953
| Crick and Watson, Discovery of Structure of DNA, 1954
| *Sputnik I* launched, 1957
| Computer chip invented, 1959

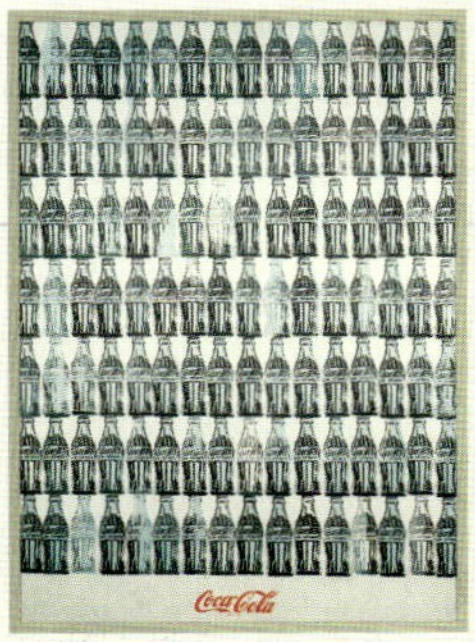

**1960**

| Lasers invented, 1960
| First manned space flight, 1961
| John F. Kennedy assassinated, 1963
| Corporation for Public Broadcasting formed, 1967
| Martin Luther King and Robert Kennedy assassinated, 1968
| Moon landing, 1969

**2** Andy Warhol, *Green Coca-Cola Bottles*, 1962

**1970**

| Postmodernism in art, literature, 1970s–
| Watergate, 1972
| War in Vietnam ends, 1975
| Personal computers introduced, 1975
| Islamic Revolution in Iran, 1978–1979

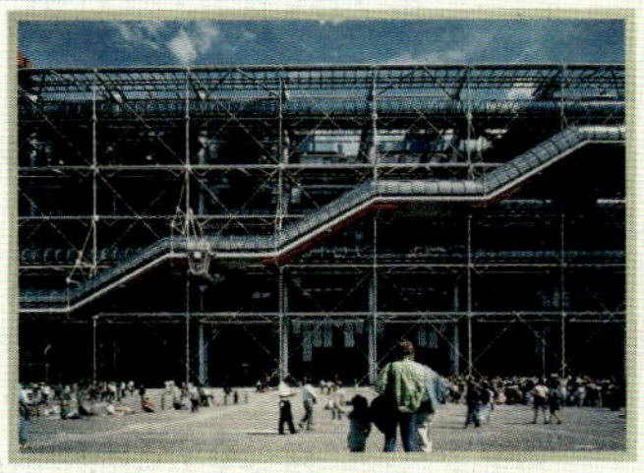

**3** Richard Rogers and Renzo Piano, Georges Pompidou National Center of Art and Culture, 1977

**1980**

| Gorbachev comes to power in Soviet Union, 1985
| Opening of Berlin Wall, 1989
| Collapse of Soviet Union, 1989
| Tiananmen Square massacre, 1989

**1990**

| First Gulf War, 1990
| US intervention, Somalia, Haiti, 1990s
| Breakup of Yugoslavia, 1990
| Expansion of World Wide Web, 1990s
| Terrorist attack on New York City and Washington, D.C., 2001

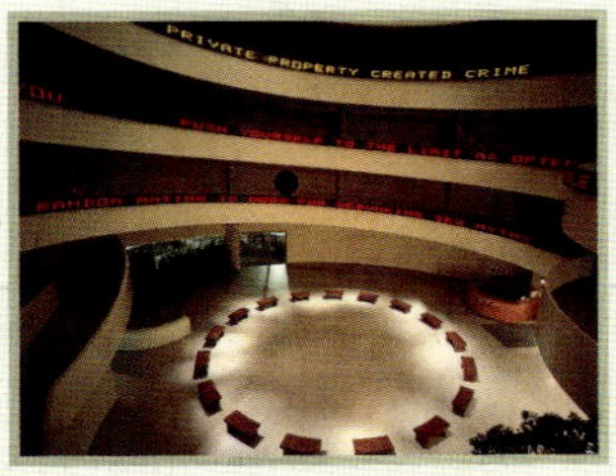

**4** Jenny Holzer, *Untitled*, 1989

# NOTES

## Chapter 2

1. Translated by F. Tallon, in Prudence O. Harper et al., *The Royal City of Susa* (New York: Metropolitan Museum of Art, 1992), 132.

## Chapter 3

1. Herodotus, *Histories,* 2.35.
2. We follow the chronology proposed by John Baines and Jaromír Malék in *Atlas of Ancient Egypt* (Oxford: Oxford University Press, 1980), 36–37, and the division of kingdoms favored by, among others, Mark Lehner, *The Complete Pyramids* (New York: Thames and Hudson, 1997), 8–9, and David P. Silverman, ed., *Ancient Egypt* (New York: Oxford University Press, 1997), 20–39.

## Chapter 4

1. Homer, *Iliad,* 2.466–649.

## Chapter 5

1. Thucydides, *Peloponnesian War,* 2.40–41.
2. Aristotle, *Politics,* 1.2.15.
3. Ibid., 7.11.1.
4. Plutarch, *Life of Pericles,* 12.
5. Pliny, *Natural History,* 34.74.
6. Ibid., 36.20.
7. Lucian, *Amores,* 13–14; *Imagines,* 6.
8. Plutarch, *Moralia,* 335A–B. Translated by J. J. Pollitt, *The Art of Ancient Greece: Sources and Documents* (New York: Cambridge University Press, 1990), 99.
9. Pliny, *Natural History,* 35.110.
10. Diodorus Siculus, *History,* 17.117.4.

## Chapter 10

1. Ammianus Marcellinus, *History of Rome,* 16.10.15–16. Translated by J. J. Pollitt, *The Art of Rome, c. 753 B.C.–A.D. 337: Sources and Documents* (New York: Cambridge University Press, 1983), 170.
2. Livy, *History of Rome,* 25.40.1–3.
3. Plutarch, *Life of Marcellus,* 21. Translated by Pollitt, 32.
4. Recorded by the Venerable Bede, the great English scholar, monk, and saint, who died in 735; translated by Lord Byron in *Childe Harold's Pilgrimage* (1817), 4.145.
5. Juvenal, *Satires,* 3.225, 232.

## Chapter 12

1. Translated by Cyril Mango, *The Art of the Byzantine Empire, 312–1453: Sources and Documents* (Upper Saddle River, N.J.: Prentice Hall, 1972), 85–86.
2. Ibid., 74.
3. Ibid., 83, 86.
4. Translated by Colm Luibheid, *Pseudo-Dionysius: The Complete Works* (New York: Paulist Press, 1987), 68ff.
5. Mango, 75.
6. Nina G. Garsoïan, "Later Byzantium," in John A. Garraty and Peter Gay, eds., *The Columbia History of the World* (New York: Harper and Row, 1972), 453.
7. Ibid., 460.

## Chapter 16

1. *Beowulf,* translated by Kevin Crossley-Holland (New York: Farrar, Straus & Giroux, 1968), 119.
2. Ibid., 33.
3. Translated by Françoise Henry, *The Book of Kells* (New York: Alfred A. Knopf, 1974), 165.
4. Translated by John W. Williams, in *The Art of Medieval Spain A.D. 500–1200* (New York: Metropolitan Museum of Art, 1993), 156.
5. Translated by Adam S. Cohen, *The Uta Codex* (University Park: Pennsylvania State University Press, 2000), 11, 41.

## Chapter 17

1. Quoted in Elizabeth G. Holt, *A Documentary History of Art* (Princeton, N.J.: Princeton University Press, 2nd ed., 1981), 1: 18.
2. Translated by Calvin B. Kendall, *The Allegory of the Church: Romanesque Portals and Their Verse Inscriptions* (Toronto: University of Toronto Press, 1998), 207.
3. John Williams, *A Spanish Apocalypse: The Morgan Beatus Manuscript* (New York: George Braziller, 1991), 223.
4. *Apologia,* 12.28. Translated by Conrad Rudolph, *The "Things of Greater Importance": Bernard of Clairvaux's* Apologia *and the Medieval Attitude toward Art* (Philadelphia: University of Pennsylvania Press, 1990), 281, 283.

## Chapter 18

1. Giorgio Vasari, *Introduzione alle tre arti del disegno* (1550), ch.3. Paul Frankl, *The Gothic: Literary Sources and Interpretations through Eight Centuries* (Princeton, N.J.: Princeton University Press, 1960), 290–91, 859–60.
2. Dante, *Divine Comedy,* Purgatory, 11.81.
3. Translated by Roland Behrendt, *Johannes Trithemius, In Praise of Scribes: De laude scriptorum* (Lawrence, Kans.: Coronado Press, 1974), 71.
4. Frankl, 55.

## Chapter 20

1. Quoted in Henry Dussart, ed., *Fragments inédits de Romboudt de Doppere: Chronique brugeoise de 1491 à 1498* (Bruges: L. de Plancke, 1892), 49.

## Chapter 21

1. Quoted in Elizabeth Gilmore Holt, ed., *Literary Sources of Art History* (Princeton, N.J.: Princeton University Press, 1947), 87–88.
2. Giorgio Vasari, *Lives of the Painters, Sculptors and Architects,* translated by Gaston du C. de Vere (New York: Knopf, 1996), 1: 304.
3. Quoted in Holt, *Literary Sources,* 90–91.
4. Vasari, *Lives of the Painters, Sculptors and Architects,* 1: 318.
5. Quoted in H. W. Janson, *The Sculpture of Donatello* (Princeton, N.J.: Princeton University Press, 1965), 154.

## Chapter 22

1. Da Vinci to Ludovico Sforza, ca. 1480–81, in Elizabeth Gilmore Holt, ed., *Literary Sources of Art History* (Princeton: Princeton University Press, 1947), 170.
2. Quoted in Anthony Blunt, *Artistic Theory in Italy, 1450–1600* (London: Oxford University Press, 1964), 34.
3. Quoted in Bruce Boucher, *Andrea Palladio: The Architect in His Time* (New York: Abbeville Press, 1998), 229.

4. Quoted in James M. Saslow, *The Poetry of Michelangelo: An Annotated Translation* (New Haven, Conn.: Yale University Press, 1991), 407.
5. Giorgio Vasari, *Lives of the Painters, Sculptors and Architects,* translated by Gaston du C. de Vere (New York: Knopf, 1996), 2: 736.
6. Quoted in A. Richard Turner, *Renaissance Florence: The Invention of a New Art* (New York: Abrams, 1997), 163.
7. Quoted in Robert J. Clements, *Michelangelo's Theory of Art* (New York: New York University Press, 1961), 320.
8. Quoted in Francesco Valcanover, "An Introduction to Titian," in *Titian: Prince of Painters* (Venice: Marsilio Editori, 1990), 23–24.
9. Quoted in Holt, ed., *Literary Sources of Art History,* 229.

## Chapter 23

1. Quoted in Wolfgang Stechow, *Northern Renaissance Art 1400–1600:* Sources and Documents (Evanston, Ill.: Northwestern University Press, 1989), 111.
2. Ibid., 118.
3. Ibid., 123.
4. Giorgio Vasari, *Lives of the Painters, Sculptors and Architects,* translated by Gaston du C. de Vere (New York: Knopf, 1996), 2: 863.

## Chapter 24

1. John Milton, *Il Penseroso* (1631, published 1645), 166.
2. Quoted in Wolfgang Stechow, *Rubens and the Classical Tradition* (Cambridge: Harvard University Press, 1968), 26.
3. Quoted in David G. Wilkins, Bernard Schultz, and Katheryn M. Linduff, *Art Past, Art Present,* 3rd ed. (New York: Abrams, 1997), 365.
4. Quoted in Bob Haak, *The Golden Age: Dutch Painters of the Seventeenth Century* (New York: Abrams, 1984), 75.
5. Ibid., 450.
6. Quoted in Robert Goldwater and Marco Treves (eds.), *Artists on Art,* 3rd ed. (New York: Pantheon Books, 1958), 155.
7. Ibid., 155.
8. Ibid., 151–53.

## Chapter 27

1. Quoted in Junichi Shiota, *Kimio Tsuchiya, Sculpture 1984–1988* (Tokyo: Morris Gallery, 1988), 3.

## Chapter 28

1. Robert Goldwater and Marco Treves (eds.), *Artists on Art,* 3rd ed. (New York: Pantheon Books, 1958), 157.
2. Quoted in Thomas A. Bailey, *The American Pageant: A History of the Republic,* 2nd ed. (Boston: Heath, 1961), 280.
3. *The Indispensable Rousseau,* compiled and presented by John Hope Mason (London: Quartet Books, 1979), 39.
4. Quoted in Elizabeth Gilmore Holt, ed., *Literary Sources of Art History* (Princeton, N.J.: Princeton University Press, 1947), 532.
5. Quoted in Goldwater and Treves, *Artists on Art,* 205.
6. Ibid., 205.
7. Edgar Allen Poe, "To Helen" (1831).
8. Quoted in Marcus Whiffen and Fredrick Koeper, *American Architecture 1607–1976* (Cambridge: MIT Press, 1981), 130.
9. Gwyn A. Williams, *Goya and the Impossible Revolution* (London: Allen Lane, 1976), 175–77.
10. Théophile Gautier, *Histoire de Romantisme* (Paris: Charpentier, 1874), 204.
11. Delacroix to Auguste Jal, 4 June 1832, in Charles Harrison and Paul Wood, eds., with Jason Gaiger, *Art in Theory 1815–1900: An Anthology of Changing Ideas* (Oxford: Blackwell, 1998), 88.
12. Quoted in Helmut Borsch-Supan, *Caspar David Friedrich* (New York: Braziller, 1974), 7.
13. Quoted in Harrison and Wood, eds., with Gaiger, *Art in Theory,* 54.
14. Quoted in Brian Lukacher, "Nature Historicized: Constable, Turner, and Romantic Landscape Painting," in Stephen F. Eisenman, ed., *Nineteenth Century Art: A Critical History* (New York: Thames & Hudson, 1994), 121.
15. Quoted in John W. McCoubrey, *American Art 1700–1960: Sources and Documents* (Upper Saddle River, N.J.: Prentice Hall, 1965), 98.
16. Quoted in Holt, *Literary Sources,* 547, 548.
17. Nicholas Pevsner, *An Outline of European Architecture* (Baltimore: Penguin, 1960), 627.
18. Letter from Delaroche to François Arao, in Helmut Gernsheim, *Creative Photography* (New York: Bonanza Books, 1962), 24.
19. Quoted in Naomi Rosenblum, *A World History of Photography* (New York: Abbeville Press, 1984), 69.

## Chapter 29

1. Clement Greenberg, "Modernist Painting," *Art and Literature,* no. 4 (Spring 1965): 193.
2. Ibid., 194.
3. Quoted in Linda Nochlin, *Realism and Tradition in Art 1848–1900* (Upper Saddle River, N.J.: Prentice Hall, 1966), 39, 38, 42.
4. Quoted in Robert Goldwater and Marco Treves, eds., *Artists on Art,* 3rd ed. (New York: Pantheon Books, 1958), 295–97.
5. Comment by French critic Enault in Linda Nochlin, *The Nature of Realism* (New York: Penguin Books, 1971), 34.
6. Quoted in Nochlin, *Realism and Tradition in Art,* 42.
7. George Heard Hamilton, *Manet and His Critics* (New Haven: Yale University Press, 1954), 45.
8. Stephen F. Eisenman, *Nineteenth Century Art: A Critical History* (London: Thames & Hudson, 1994), 242.
9. "On the Heroism of Modern Life" (the closing section of Baudelaire's *Salon of 1846,* published as a brochure in Paris in 1846).
10. *New York Weekly Tribune,* 30 September 1865.
11. Quoted in Nikolai Cikovsky Jr. and Franklin Kelly, *Winslow Homer* (Washington, D.C.: National Gallery of Art, 1995), 26.
12. Lloyd Goodrich, *Thomas Eakins, His Life and Work* (New York: Whitney Museum of American Art, 1933), 51–52.
13. Kenneth MacGowan, *Behind the Screen* (New York: Delta, 1965), 49.
14. Quoted in Linda Nochlin, *Realism* (Harmondsworth: Penguin Books, 1971), 28.
15. Quoted in Linda Nochlin, *Impressionism and Post-Impressionism 1874–1904* (Upper Saddle River, N.J.: Prentice Hall, 1966), 35.
16. Quoted in Roy McMullan, *Degas: His Life, Times, and Work* (Boston: Houghton Mifflin, 1984), 293.
17. Quoted in John McCoubrey, *American Art 1700–1960: Sources and Documents* (Upper Saddle River, N.J.: Prentice Hall, 1965), 184.
18. Quoted in Laurie Schneider Adams, *A History of Western Art,* 2nd ed. (Madison, Wis.: Brown & Benchmark, 1997), 443.
19. Quoted in Goldwater and Treves, eds., *Artists on Art,* 322.
20. Van Gogh to Theo van Gogh, 3 September 1888, *Van Gogh: A Self-Portrait; Letters Revealing His Life as a Painter,* selected by W. H. Auden (New York: Dutton, 1963), 319.
21. Van Gogh to Theo van Gogh, 11 August 1888, *Van Gogh: A Self-Portrait,* 313.
22. Ibid., 321.
23. Van Gogh to Theo van Gogh, September 1888, in J. van Gogh–Bonger and V. W. van Gogh, eds., *The Complete Letters of Vincent van Gogh* (Greenwich, Conn.: 1979), 3: 534.
24. Van Gogh to Theo van Gogh, 8 September 1888, *Van Gogh: A Self-Portrait,* 320.
25. Van Gogh to Theo van Gogh, 16 July 1888, *Van Gogh: A Self-Portrait,* 299.
26. Quoted in Belinda Thompson, ed., *Gauguin by Himself* (Boston: Little, Brown, 1993), 270–71.
27. Quoted in Herschel B. Chipp, *Theories of Modern Art* (Berkeley: University of California Press, 1968), 72.
28. Quoted in Goldwater and Treves, eds., *Artists on Art,* 375.
29. Quoted in Richard W. Murphy, *The World of Cézanne 1839–1906* (New York: Time-Life Books, 1968), 70.
30. Quoted in Goldwater and Treves, eds., *Artists on Art,* 363.
31. Cézanne to Émile Bernard, 15 April 1904, in Chipp, *Theories of Modern Art,* 19.
32. Quoted in Goldwater and Treves, eds., *Artists on Art,* 361.
33. Quoted in George Heard Hamilton, *Painting and Sculpture in Europe, 1880–1940,* 6th ed. (New Haven: Yale University Press, 1993), 124.
34. Quoted in V. Frisch and J. T. Shipley, *Auguste Rodin* (New York: Stokes, 1939), 203.
35. Quoted in Eileen Boris, *Art and Labor: Ruskin, Morris, and the Craftsman Ideal in America* (Philadelphia: Temple University Press, 1986), 7.
36. Siegfried Giedion, *Space, Time, and Architecture* (Cambridge: Harvard University Press, 1965), 282.

## Chapter 30

1. Alfred M. Tozzer, ed., *Landa's Relación de las cosas de Yucatán: A Translation* (Cambridge, Mass.: Peabody Museum Papers, 1941), 18.
2. Bernal Díaz del Castillo, *The Discovery and Conquest of Mexico,* translated by A. P. Maudslay (New York: Farrar, Straus, Giroux, 1956), 218–19.

## Chapter 32

1. Pieter de Marees, *A Description and Historical Declaration of the Golden Kingdom of Guinea* (1604), translated by Samuel Purchas. Quoted in Herbert M. Cole and Doran H. Ross, *The Arts of Ghana* (Los Angeles: Museum of Cultural History, 1977), 119.

## Chapter 33

1. "Kunst und Leben," *Der Sturm* 10 (1919): 2.
2. Quoted in John Elderfield, *The "Wild Beasts": Fauvism and Its Affinities* (New York: Museum of Modern Art, 1976), 29.
3. Quoted in John Russell and the editors of Time-Life Books, *The World of Matisse 1869–1954* (New York: Time-Life Books, 1969), 98.
4. Quoted in Peter Selz, *German Expressionist Painting* (Berkeley: University of California Press, 1957), 95.
5. Quoted in Herschel B. Chipp, *Theories of Modern Art* (Berkeley: University of California Press, 1968), 182.
6. Quoted in Frederick S. Levine, *The Apocalyptic Vision: The Art of Franz Marc as German Expressionism* (New York: Harper & Row, 1979), 57.
7. Quoted in Sam Hunter and John Jacobus, *Modern Art,* 3rd ed. (New York: Abrams, 1992), 121.
8. Quoted in Roland Penrose, *Picasso: His Life and Work,* rev. ed. (New York: Harper & Row, 1971), 122.
9. Quoted in George Heard Hamilton, *Painting and Sculpture in Europe, 1880–1940,* 6th ed. (New Haven: Yale University Press, 1993), 246.
10. Quoted in Edward Fry, ed., *Cubism* (London: Thames & Hudson, 1966), 112–13.
11. Hamilton, *Painting and Sculpture,* 238.
12. Quoted in Michael Hoog, *R. Delaunay* (New York: Crown, 1976), 49.
13. Quoted in Françoise Gilot and Carlton Lake, *Life with Picasso* (New York: McGraw-Hill, 1964), 77.
14. From the *Initial Manifesto of Futurism,* first published 20 February 1909.
15. Ibid.
16. Umberto Boccioni, Carlo Carrà, Luigi Russolo, Giacomo Balla, and Gino Severini, "Futurist Painting: Technical Manifesto," *Poesia,* 10 April 1910.
17. Hans Richter, *Dada: Art and Anti-Art* (London: Thames & Hudson, 1961), 25.
18. Quoted in Robert Short, *Dada and Surrealism* (London: Octopus Books, 1980), 18.
19. Quoted in Robert Motherwell, ed., *The Dada Painters and Poets: An Anthology,* 2nd ed. (Cambridge, Mass.: Belknap Press of Harvard University, 1989).
20. Richter, *Dada,* 64–65.
21. Ibid., 57.
22. Tristan Tzara, "Chronique Zurichoise," translated by Ralph Manheim, in Motherwell, ed., *The Dada Painters and Poets,* 236.
23. Quoted in Arturo Schwarz, *The Complete Works of Marcel Duchamp* (London: Thames & Hudson, 1965), 466.
24. Quoted in Sam Hunter, *American Art of the 20th Century* (New York: Abrams, 1972), 30.
25. Ibid., 37.
26. Charles C. Eldredge, "The Arrival of European Modernism," *Art in America* 61 (July–August 1973): 35.
27. Dorothy Norman, *Alfred Stieglitz: An American Seer* (Millerton, N.Y.: Aperture, 1973).
28. Ibid., 161.
29. Ibid., 9–10, 161.
30. Quoted in Gail Stavitsky, "Reordering Reality: Precisionist Directions in American Art, 1915–1941," in *Precisionism in America 1915–1941: Reordering Reality* (New York: Abrams, 1994), 12.
31. Quoted in Karen Tsujimoto, *Images of America: Precisionist Painting and Modern Photography* (Seattle: University of Washington Press, 1982), 70.
32. Quoted in Matthias Eberle, *World War I and the Weimar Artists: Dix, Grosz, Beckmann, Schlemmer* (New Haven: Yale University Press, 1985), 65.
33. Ibid., 54.
34. Ibid., 22.
35. Ibid., 42.
36. Quoted in William S. Rubin, *Dada, Surrealism, and Their Heritage* (New York: Museum of Modern Art, 1968), 64.
37. Quoted in Hamilton, *Painting and Sculpture,* 392.
38. Quoted in Richter, *Dada,* 155.
39. Ibid., 159.
40. Quoted in Rubin, *Dada, Surrealism, and Their Heritage,* 111.
41. Quoted in Hunter and Jacobus, *Modern Art,* 179.
42. Quoted in William S. Rubin, *Miró in the Collection of the Museum of Modern Art* (New York: Museum of Modern Art, 1973), 32.
43. Quoted in Chipp, *Theories of Modern Art,* 182–86.
44. Ibid., 341, 345.
45. Quoted in Robert L. Herbert, ed., *Modern Artists on Art* (Upper Saddle River, N.J.: Prentice Hall, 1965), 140–41, 145–46.
46. Quoted in Chipp, *Theories of Modern Art,* 328, 334, 336.
47. Ibid., 332, 335.
48. Quoted in Camilla Gray, *The Russian Experiment in Art 1863–1922* (New York: Abrams, 1970), 216.

49. Kenneth Frampton, *Modern Architecture: A Critical History* (London: Thames & Hudson, 1985), 142.
50. Ibid., 147.
51. Quoted in Michel Seuphor, *Piet Mondrian: Life and Work* (New York: Abrams, 1956), 117.
52. Quoted in Hamilton, *Painting and Sculpture,* 319.
53. Quoted in Chipp, *Theories of Modern Art,* 349.
54. Ibid., 350.
55. Quoted in Hans L. Jaffé, comp., *De Stijl* (New York: Abrams, 1971), 185–188.
56. Piet Mondrian, "Dialogue on the New Plastic," in Charles Harrison and Paul Wood, eds., *Art in Theory 1900–1990: An Anthology of Changing Ideas* (Oxford: Blackwell, 1992), 285.
57. Walter Gropius, from *The Manifesto of the Bauhaus,* April 1919.
58. Ibid.
59. Ibid.
60. László Moholy-Nagy, *Vision in Motion* (Chicago: Paul Theobald, 1969), 268.
61. Quoted in Hamilton, *Painting and Sculpture,* 345.
62. Ibid.
63. Quoted in *Josef Albers: Homage to the Square* (New York: Museum of Modern Art, 1964), n.p.
64. Quoted in John Willett, *Art and Politics in the Weimar Period: The New Sobriety, 1917–1933* (New York: Da Capo Press, 1978), 119.
65. Quoted in Wayne Craven, *American Art: History and Culture* (Madison, Wis.: Brown & Benchmark, 1994), 403.
66. Quoted in Vincent Scully Jr., *Frank Lloyd Wright* (New York: Braziller, 1960), 18.
67. Quoted in Edgar Kauffmann, ed., *Frank Lloyd Wright, An American Architect* (New York: Horizon, 1955), 205, 208.
68. Quoted in Philip Johnson, *Mies van der Rohe,* rev. ed. (New York: Museum of Modern Art, 1954), 200–01.
69. Quoted in Hamilton, *Painting and Sculpture,* 462.
70. Quoted in H. H. Arnason and Marla F. Prather, *History of Modern Art,* 4th ed. (Upper Saddle River, N.J.: Prentice Hall, 1998), 180.
71. Barbara Hepworth, *A Pictorial Autobiography* (London: Tate Gallery, 1978), 9, 53.
72. Quoted in Herbert, *Modern Artists on Art,* 139.
73. Ibid., 140–41, 145–46.
74. Ibid., 143.
75. Quoted in Frances K. Pohl, *Ben Shahn: New Deal Artist in a Cold War Climate, 1947–1954* (Austin: University of Texas Press, 1989), 159.
76. Pablo Picasso, "Statement to Simone Téry," in Harrison and Wood, eds., *Art in Theory 1900–1990,* 640.
77. Quoted in Penrose, *Picasso,* 311 n.
78. Quoted in Milton Meltzer, *Dorothea Lange: A Photographer's Life* (New York: Farrar, Strauss, Giroux, 1978), 133, 220.
79. Quoted in Henry Louis Gates Jr., "New Negroes, Migration, and Cultural Exchange," in Elizabeth Hutton Turner, ed., *Jacob Lawrence: The Migration Series* (Washington, D.C.: Phillips Collection, 1993), 20.
80. Quoted in James M. Dennis, *Grant Wood: A Study in American Art and Culture* (Columbia: University of Missouri Press, 1986), 143.
81. Wanda M. Corn, *Grant Wood: The Regionalist Vision* (New Haven: Yale University Press, 1983), 131.
82. Ibid.
83. Quoted in Matthew Baigell, *A Concise History of American Painting and Sculpture* (New York: Harper & Row, 1984), 264.
84. Quoted in Vivian Endicott Barnett, "Banned German Art: Reception and Institutional Support of Modern German Art in the United States, 1933–45," in Stephanie Barron, *Exiles and Emigrés: The Flight of European Artists from Hitler* (Los Angeles: Los Angeles County Museum of Art, 1997), 283.

## Chapter 34

1. Clement Greenberg, "Toward a Newer Laocoon," *Partisan Review* 7, no. 4 (July–August 1940): 305.
2. Clement Greenberg, "Sculpture in Our Time," *Arts Magazine* 32, no. 9 (June 1956): 22.
3. Dawn Ades and Andrew Forge, *Francis Bacon* (London: Thames & Hudson, 1985), 8; and David Sylvester, *The Brutality of Fact: Interviews with Francis Bacon,* 3rd ed. (London: Thames & Hudson, 1987), 182.
4. Marcus Rothko and Adolph Gottlieb, quoted in Edward Alden Jewell, "The Realm of Art: A New Platform and Other Matters: 'Globalism' Pops into View," *New York Times,* 13 June 1943, 9.
5. Jackson Pollock, "My Painting," *Possibilities* 1 (Winter 1947): 79.
6. "Jackson Pollock: Is He the Greatest Living Painter in the United States?" *Life* 27 (8 August 1949): 42–44.
7. In Harold Rosenberg, *The Tradition of the New* (New York: Horizon Press, 1959), 25.

8. Quoted in Thomas Hess, *Barnett Newman* (New York: Walker and Company, 1969), 51.

9. Quoted in John P. O'Neill, ed., *Barnett Newman: Selected Writings and Interviews* (New York: Knopf, 1990), 108.

10. Mark Rothko, quoted in Sidney Janis, *Abstract and Surrealist Art in America* (New York: Reynal & Hitchcock, 1944), 118; and Rothko and Gottlieb, in "The Realm of Art," 9.

11. Quoted in Selden Rodman, *Conversations with Artists* (New York: Devin-Adair, 1957), 93–94.

12. Clement Greenberg, "Recentness of Sculpture," in Gregory Battcock, ed., *Minimal Art: A Critical Anthology* (New York: Dutton, 1968), 183–84.

13. Quoted in "Vietnam Memorial: America Remembers," *National Geographic* 167, no. 5 (May 1985): 557.

14. Louise Nevelson, quoted in John Gordon, *Louise Nevelson* (New York: Praeger, 1967), 12.

15. Quoted in Deborah Wye, *Louise Bourgeois* (New York: Museum of Modern Art, 1982), 22.

16. Ibid., 25.

17. Ibid., 22, 25, 27.

18. Quoted in Lucy Lippard, *Eva Hesse* (New York: New York University Press, 1976), 165.

19. Ibid., 56.

20. Ibid., 56.

21. Quoted in H. H. Arnason, *History of Modern Art,* 3rd ed. (Upper Saddle River, N.J.: Prentice Hall, 1986), 472.

22. Quoted in Barbara Haskell, *Blam! The Explosion of Pop, Minimalism, and Performance 1958–1964* (New York: Whitney Museum of American Art), 53.

23. Jiro Yoshihara, "Gutai Art Manifesto" (1956), translated by Reiko Tomii, in *Japanese Art after 1945: Scream against the Sky* (Yokohama: Yokohama Museum of Art, 1994), 370.

24. Carolee Schneeman, in Bruce McPherson, ed., *More Than Meat Joy: Complete Performance Works and Selected Writings* (New Paltz, N.Y.: Documentext, 1979), 52.

25. Quoted in Mariellen R. Sandford, ed., *Happenings and Other Acts* (New York: Routledge, 1995), 255.

26. Quoted in Caroline Tisdall, *Joseph Beuys* (New York: Thames & Hudson, 1979), 6.

27. Quoted in "Joseph Kosuth: Art as Idea as Idea," in Jeanne Siegel, ed., *Artworks: Discourse on the 60s and 70s* (Ann Arbor, Mich.: UMI Research Press, 1985), 225.

28. Ibid., 221.

29. Quoted in Brenda Richardson, *Bruce Nauman: Neons* (Baltimore: Baltimore Museum of Art, 1982), 20.

30. Sol Le Witt, quoted in Daniel Wheeler, *Art since Mid-Century:* 1945 to the Present (Upper Saddle River, N.J.: Prentice Hall, 1991), 247.

31. Quoted in Richard Francis, *Jasper Johns* (New York: Abbeville Press, 1984), 21.

32. John Cage, Silence (Middletown, Conn.: Wesleyan University Press, 1961), 101.

33. Quoted in Christine Lindey, *Superrealist Painting and Sculpture* (London: Orbis, 1980), 50.

34. Ibid., 130.

35. Quoted in Nancy Holt, ed., *The Writings of Robert Smithson* (New York: New York University Press, 1975), 111.

36. Quoted in Calvin Tomkins, "The Art World: Tilted Arc," *New Yorker,* 20 May 1985, 100.

37. Peter Blake, *Frank Lloyd Wright* (Harmondsworth: Penguin Books, 1960), 115.

38. Robert Venturi, *Complexity and Contradiction in Architecture,* 2nd ed. (New York: Museum of Modern Art, 1977), 16.

39. Fredric Jameson, "Postmodernism and Consumer Society," in Hal Foster, ed., *The Anti-Aesthetic: Essays on Postmodern Culture* (Port Townsend, Wash.: Bay Press, 1983), 113.

40. Quoted in Grace Glueck, "Susan Rothenberg: New Outlook for a Visionary Artist," *New York Times Magazine,* 22 July 1984, 20.

41. Quoted in *Walker Art Center: Painting and Sculpture from the Collection* (Minneapolis: Walker Art Center, 1990), 435.

42. Quoted in Susanna Torruella Leval, "Recapturing History: The (Un)official Story in Contemporary Latin American Art," *Art Journal* 51, no. 4 (Winter 1992): 74.

43. Ibid.

44. Hannah Wilke, "Visual Prejudice," in *Hannah Wilke: A Retrospective* (Columbia: University of Missouri Press, 1989), 141.

45. Quoted in Donald Hall, *Corporal Politics* (Cambridge: MIT List Visual Arts Center, 1993), 46.

46. Kobena Mercer, "Black Hair/Style Politics," in Russell Ferguson, Martha Gever, Trinh T. Minh-ha, and Cornel West, eds., *Out There: Marginalization and Contemporary Culture* (New York: New Museum of Contemporary Art, 1990), 248–49.

47. Ibid., 249.

48. Quoted in Brooke Kamin Rapaport, "Melvin Edwards: Lynch Fragments," *Art in America* 81, no. 3 (March 1993): 62.

49. Jaune Quick-to-See Smith and Harmony Hammond, *Women of Sweetgrass: Cedar and Sage* (New York: American Indian Center, 1984), 97.

50. Quoted in Richard Marshall and Robert Mapplethorpe, 50 *New York Artists* (San Francisco: Chronicle Books, 1986), 448–49.

51. Quoted in Mary Jane Jacob, *Magdalena Abakanowicz* (New York: Abbeville, 1982), 94.

# GLOSSARY

PRONUNCIATION KEY

ŭ **a**but, **k**itt**e**n  a **c**ot, **c**art  ā **b**a**k**e  ă **b**a**ck**  au **out**  ch **ch**in
e l**e**ss  ē **ea**sy  g **g**ift  ĭ **t**r**i**p  ī **l**i**f**e  j **j**oke  k **k**i**ck**
ⁿ French v**in**  ng si**ng**  o fl**a**w  ō b**oa**t  ö b**i(r)**d  oi c**oi**n
u f**oo**t  ū l**oo**t  ü f**ew**  y **y**o**y**o  zh vi**si**on
NOTE: The stress mark (′) goes before the stressed syllable (be-′for).

**abacus**—(ă-ba-′kŭs) The uppermost portion of the *capital* of a *column*.

**Abstract Expressionism**—Also known as the New York School. The first major American avant-garde movement, Abstract Expressionism emerged in New York City in the 1940s. The artists produced abstract paintings that expressed their state of mind and were intended to strike emotional chords in viewers. The movement developed along two lines: *gestural abstraction* and *chromatic abstraction.*

**acropolis**—(a-′kra-pŭ-lŭs) Greek, "high city." In ancient Greece, usually the site of the city's most important temple(s).

**action painting**—Also called *gestural abstraction.* The kind of *Abstract Expressionism* practiced by Jackson Pollock, in which the emphasis was on the creation process, the artist's gesture in making art. Pollock poured liquid paint in linear webs on his canvases, which were laid out on the floor, thereby physically surrounding himself in the painting during its creation.

**additive sculpture**—A kind of sculpture technique in which materials (for example, clay) are built up or "added" to create form.

**adobe**—(a-′dō-bē) The clay used to make a kind of sun-dried mud brick of the same name; a building made of such brick.

**aerial perspective**—See *perspective.*

**agora**—(a-go-′ra) An open square or space used for public meetings or business in ancient Greek cities.

**ahu**—(′ă-hū) A stone platform on which *moai* were placed. Ahu marked burial sites or were used for ceremonial purposes.

**'ahu 'ula**—(′ă-hū ′ū-lŭ) A Hawaiian feather cloak.

**aisle**—The portion of a basilica flanking the *nave* and separated from it by a row of *columns* or *piers.*

**akua'ba (Akua's child)**—(a-′kū-a-ba) An Akan (Ghana) image of a young girl.

**altarpiece**—A panel, painted or sculpted, situated above and behind an altar. See also *retable.*

**alternate-support system**—In church architecture, the use of alternating wall supports in the *nave,* usually *piers* and *columns* or *compound piers* of alternating form.

**amalaka**—(a-ma-′la-ka) In Hindu temple design, the large flat disk with ribbed edges surmounting the beehive-shaped tower.

**Amazonomachy**—(ă-mŭ-zon-′a-mŭ-kē) In Greek mythology, the legendary battle between the Greeks and Amazons.

**ambo**—A church pulpit for biblical readings.

**ambulatory**—(′ăm-byŭ-lŭ-to-rē) A covered walkway, outdoors (as in a church *cloister*) or indoors; especially the passageway around the *apse* and the *choir* of a church. In Buddhist architecture, the passageway leading around the *stupa* in a *chaitya hall.*

**amphiprostyle**—(ăm-fi-′pro-stīl) The style of Greek building in which the *colonnade* was placed across both the front and back, but not along the sides.

**amphitheater**—Greek, "double theater." A Roman building type resembling two Greek theaters put together. The Roman amphitheater featured a continuous elliptical *cavea* around a central *arena.*

**amphora**—(′ăm-fŭ-ra) A two-handled jar used for general storage purposes, usually to hold wine or oil.

**amulet**—(′ăm-yŭ-lŭt) An object worn to ward off evil or to aid the wearer.

**Analytic Cubism**—The first phase of *Cubism,* developed jointly by Pablo Picasso and Georges Braque, in which the artists analyzed form from every possible vantage point to combine the various views into one pictorial whole.

**anamorphic image**—(ăn-ŭ-′mor-fik) A distorted image that must be viewed by some special means (such as a mirror) to be recognized.

**andron**—Dining room in a Greek house.

**antae**—(′ăn-tī) The molded projecting ends of the walls forming the *pronaos* or *opisthodomos* of an ancient Greek temple.

**apadana**—(ă-pa-′da-na) The great audience hall in ancient Persian palaces.

**apotheosis**—(ŭ-path-ē-′ō-sŭs) Elevated to the rank of gods, or the ascent to heaven.

**apse**—(ăps) A recess, usually semicircular, in the wall of a Roman *basilica* or at the east end of a church.

**apsidal**—Rounded; *apse* shaped.

**arabesque**—(ă-rŭ-′besk) "Arab-like." A flowing, intricate pattern derived from stylized organic motifs, usually floral; generally an Islamic decorative motif.

**arcade**—A series of *arches* supported by *piers* or *columns.*

**Arcadian** (adj.)—In Renaissance and later art, depictions of an idyllic place of rural peace and simplicity. Derived from Arcadia, an ancient district of the central Peloponnesus in southern Greece.

**arch**—A curved structural member that spans an opening and is generally composed of wedge-shaped blocks *(voussoirs)* that transmit the downward pressure laterally. See also *thrust.*

**architrave**—(′ar-kŭ-trāv) The *lintel* or lowest division of the *entablature;* also called the epistyle.

**archivolt**—The continuous molding framing an *arch.* In *Romanesque* or *Gothic* architecture, one of the series of concentric bands framing the *tympanum.*

**arcuated**—*Arch* shaped.

**arena**—In a Roman *amphitheater,* the central area where bloody gladiatorial combats and other boisterous events took place.

**arhat**—(′ar-hat) A Buddhist holy person who has achieved enlightenment and *nirvana* by suppression of all desire for earthly things.

**armature**—(′ar-mŭ-chŭr) The crossed, or diagonal, *arches* that form the skeletal framework of a *Gothic rib vault.* In sculpture, the framework for a clay form.

**arrises**—(ŭ-′rē z-sŭz) In *Doric columns,* the raised edges of the *fluting.*

**Art Brut**—(ar brŭ) A term coined by artist Jean Dubuffet to characterize art that is genuine, untaught, coarse, even brutish.

**Art Deco**—Descended from *Art Nouveau,* this movement of the 1920s and 1930s sought to upgrade industrial design in competition with "fine art" and to work new materials into decorative patterns that could be either machined or handcrafted. Characterized by streamlined, elongated, and symmetrical design.

**Art Nouveau**—(ar nŭ-′vō) A late-19th- and early-20th-century art movement whose proponents tried to synthesize all the arts in an effort to create art based on natural forms that could be mass produced by technologies of the industrial age.

**asceticism**—Self-discipline and self-denial.

**ashlar masonry**—Carefully cut and regularly shaped blocks of stone used in construction, fitted together without mortar.

**assemblage**—(a-sem-′blazh) An artwork constructed from already existing objects.

**atlantid**—(ăt-′lăn-tid) A male figure that functions as a supporting *column.* See also *caryatid.*

**atlatl**—(′ăt(-ŭ)-lăt(-ŭ)l) Spear-thrower, the typical weapon of the Toltecs of ancient Mexico.

**atmospheric perspective**—See *perspective*.

**atrium**—('ā-trē-ŭm) The court of a Roman house that is partly open to the sky. Also the open, *colonnaded* court in front of and attached to a Christian *basilica*.

**attic**—The uppermost story of a building.

**attribution**—Assignment of a work to a maker or makers.

**automatism**—In painting, the process of yielding oneself to instinctive motions of the hands after establishing a set of conditions (such as size of paper or medium) within which a work is to be carried out.

**avant-garde**—('ă-vaⁿ gard) French, "advance guard" (in a platoon). Late-19th- and 20th-century artists who emphasized innovation and challenged established convention in their work. Also used as an adjective.

**avatar**—A manifestation of a deity incarnated in some visible form in which the deity performs a sacred function on earth. In Hinduism, an incarnation of a god.

**axial plan**—See *plan*.

**backstrap loom**—A simple Andean loom featuring a belt or backstrap encircling the waist of the seated weaver.

**bai**—(ba-ē) An elaborately painted men's ceremonial house on Belau (formerly Palau) in the Caroline Islands of Micronesia.

**baldacchino**—(bal-da-'kē-nō) A canopy on *columns,* frequently built over an altar. See also *ciborium*.

**balustrade**—('băl-us-trād) A railing held up by small posts, as on a staircase.

**baptistery**—('băp-tus-trē) In Christian architecture, the building used for baptism, usually situated next to a church.

**bar tracery**—See *tracery*.

**barays**—The large reservoirs laid out around Cambodian *wats* that served as means of transportation as well as irrigation. The reservoirs were connected by a network of canals.

**Baroque**—A blanket designation for the art of the period 1600 to 1750.

**barrel vault**—See *vault*.

**base**—In ancient Greek architecture, the lowest part of *Ionic* and *Corinthian columns*.

**basilica**—(bu-'sil-ŭ-kŭ) In Roman architecture, a civic building for legal and other civic proceedings, rectangular in plan with an entrance usually on a long side. In Christian architecture, a church somewhat resembling the Roman basilica, usually entered from one end and with an *apse* at the other.

**bas-relief**—('ba rŭ-'lē f) See *relief*.

**battlement**—A low parapet at the top of a circuit wall in a fortification.

**Bauhaus**—('bau-haus) A school of architecture in Germany in the 1920s under the aegis of Walter Gropius, who emphasized the unity of art, architecture, and design. The Bauhaus trained students in a wide range of both arts and crafts, and was eventually closed by the National Socialists in 1933.

**Belle Epoque**—('bel e-'pak) A period of elegance and gaiety extending from 1890 to 1914.

**ben-ben**—('ben-ben) A pyramidal stone; a fetish of the Egyptian god Re.

**benday dots**—A printing technique that involves the modulation of color through the placement of individual colored dots. Named after its inventor, Benjamin Day.

**bestiary**—A collection of illustrations of real and imaginary animals.

**bhakti**—('bŭk-tē) In Buddhist thought, the adoration of a personalized deity *(bodhisattva)* as a means of achieving unity with it; love felt by the devotee for the deity. In Hinduism, the devout, selfless direction of all tasks and activities of life to the service of one god.

**bi**—(bē) In ancient China, jade disks carved as ritual objects for burial with the dead. They were often decorated with piercework carving extending entirely through the object.

**bilingual vases**—Experimental Greek vases produced for a short time in the late sixth century BCE; one side featured *black-figure* decoration, the other *red-figure*.

**bisj pole**—(bĭ zh) An elaborately carved pole constructed from the trunk of the mangrove tree. The Asmat people of southwestern New Guinea created bisj poles to indicate their intent to avenge a relative's death.

**black-figure painting**—In early Greek pottery, the silhouetting of dark figures against a light background of natural, reddish clay, with linear details *incised* through the silhouettes.

**blind arcade**—An *arcade* having no actual openings, applied as decoration to a wall surface.

**block statue**—In ancient Egyptian sculpture, a cubic stone image with simplified body parts.

**bodhisattva**—(bod-hē-sat-va) In Buddhist thought, one of the host of divinities provided to the Buddha to help him save humanity. A potential Buddha.

**bottega**—(bōt-'tā-gŭ) A shop; the studio-shop of an Italian artist.

**breviary**—(brē-vē-e-rē) A Christian religious book of selected daily prayers and psalms.

**brocade**—The weaving together of threads of different colors.

**broken-** or **flung-ink style**—In Japanese art, a loose and rapidly executed painting style in which the ink seems to have been applied by flinging or splashing it onto the paper.

**Buddha triad**—Central Buddha flanked on each side by a *bodhisattva*.

**buon fresco**—(bwan 'fres-kō) See *fresco*.

**burin**—('byū-rin) A pointed tool used for *engraving* or *incising*.

**buttress**—('bŭt-trŭs) An exterior masonry structure that opposes the lateral *thrust* of an *arch* or a *vault*. A pier buttress is a solid mass of masonry; a flying buttress consists typically of an inclined member carried on an arch or a series of arches and a solid buttress to which it transmits lateral *thrust*.

**caduceus**—(ka-'d(y)ū-sē-ŭs) In ancient Greek mythology, a magical rod entwined with serpents carried by Hermes (Roman, Mercury), the messenger of the gods.

**caldarium**—(kal-'dă-rē-ŭm) The hot-bath section of a Roman bathing establishment.

**caliph(s)**—('kā-lef *or* 'kal-ŭf) *Muslim* rulers, regarded as successors of Muhammad.

**calligraphy**—Greek, "beautiful writing." Handwriting or penmanship, especially elegant writing as a decorative art.

**calotype**—('kă-lŭ-tip) A photographic process in which a positive image is made by shining light through a negative image onto a sheet of sensitized paper.

**camera lucida**—('kă-mŭ-rŭ lū-'sē-dŭ) Latin, "lighted room." A device in which a small lens projects the image of an object downward onto a sheet of paper.

**camera obscura**—('kă-mŭ-rŭ ŭb-'skyū-rŭ) Latin, "dark room." An ancestor of the modern camera in which a tiny pinhole, acting as a lens, projects an image on a screen, the wall of a room, or the ground-glass wall of a box; used by artists in the 17th, 18th, and early 19th centuries as an aid in drawing from nature.

**cames**—(kāms) The lead strips in *stained-glass* windows that join separate pieces of colored glass.

**campanile**—(kam-pa-'nē-lā) A bell tower of a church, usually, but not always, freestanding.

**canon**—A rule, for example, of proportion. The ancient Greeks considered beauty to be a matter of "correct" proportion and sought a canon of proportion, for the human figure and for buildings.

**canonization**—In the Roman Catholic Church, the process by which a revered deceased person is declared a *saint* by the pope.

**canopic jar**—(kă-'nō-pik *jar*) In ancient Egypt, the container in which the organs of the deceased were placed for later burial with the mummy.

**capital**—The uppermost member of a *column,* serving as a transition from the *shaft* to the *lintel*. In classical architecture, the form of the capital varies with the *order*.

**Capitolium**—(kă-pi-'tō-lē-ŭm) An ancient Roman temple dedicated to the gods Jupiter, Juno, and Minerva.

**cardo**—('kar-dō) The north-south street in a Roman town, intersecting the *decumanus* at right angles.

**Caroline minuscule**—The alphabet that *Carolingian* scribes perfected, from which our modern alphabet was developed.

**Carolingian** (adj.)—(kă-rō-'lin-jŭn) Pertaining to the empire of Charlemagne (Latin, Carolus Magnus) and his successors.

**carpet pages**—In early medieval manuscripts, decorative pages resembling textiles.

**cartoon**—In painting, a full-size preliminary drawing from which a painting is made.

**caryatid**—('kă-rē-ăt-id) A female figure that functions as a supporting *column*. See also *atlantid*.

**castrum**—(kăs-trŭm) A Roman military encampment.

**catacombs**—('kăt-ŭ-kōmz) Subterranean

networks of rock-cut galleries and chambers designed as cemeteries for the burial of the dead.

**catalogue raisonné**—('kǎ-tŭ-log rā-zǎ-'nā) A comprehensive catalog of an artist's works.

**cathedral**—A bishop's church.

**cavea**—(kǎ-vē-ŭ) Latin, "hollow place or cavity." The seating area in ancient Greek and Roman theaters and *amphitheaters.*

**celadon**—(sel-ŭ-dan) A Chinese-Korean pottery *glaze,* fired in an oxygen-deprived kiln to a characteristic gray-green or pale blue color.

**cella**—('se-lŭ) The chamber at the center of an ancient temple; in a classical temple, the room (Greek, *naos*) in which the cult statue usually stood.

**celt**—(selt) In Olmec Mexico, an ax-shaped form made of polished jade; generally, a prehistoric metal or stone implement shaped like a chisel or ax head.

**centaur**—('sen-tor) In ancient Greek mythology, a fantastical creature, with the front or top half of a human and the back or bottom half of a horse.

**centauromachy**—(sen-to-'ra-mŭ-kē) In ancient Greek mythology, the battle between the Greeks and *centaurs.*

**central plan**—See *plan.*

**cestrum**—('kes-trŭm) A small spatula used in *encaustic* painting.

**chaitya hall**—(tshī-'tyŭ hall) An Indian rock-cut temple hall having a votive *stupa* at one end.

**chakra**—('cha-kra) The Buddha's wheel, set in motion at Sarnath.

**chakravartin**—(cha-kra-'var-tĭn) In India, the ideal king, the Universal Lord who ruled through goodness.

**chamfer**—('cham-fŭr) The surface formed by cutting off a corner of a board or post; a bevel.

**Chan**—See *Zen.*

**chatra**—('cha-tra) See *yasti.*

**chevet**—(shŭ-'va) The east, or *apsidal,* end of a *Gothic* church, including *choir, ambulatory,* and *radiating chapels.*

**chiaroscuro**—(kē-ǎ-rō-'skū-rō) In drawing or painting, the treatment and use of light and dark, especially the gradations of light that produce the effect of *modeling.*

**chigi**—(chē-gē) The crosspiece at the gables of Japanese shrine architecture.

**chimera**—(kī-'mer-ŭ) A monster of Greek invention with the head and body of a lion and the tail of a serpent. A second head, that of a goat, grows out of one side of the body.

**chiton**—('kī-tan) A Greek tunic, the essential (and often only) garment of both men and women, the other being the *himation,* or mantle.

**choir**—The space reserved for the clergy and singers in the church, usually east of the *transept* but, in some instances, extending into the *nave.*

**Christogram**—('kris-tō-grăm) The three initial letters (chi-rho-iota) of Christ's name in Greek (XPI), which came to serve as a monogram for Christ.

**chromatic abstraction**—A kind of *Abstract Expressionism* that focused on the emotional resonance of color, as exemplified by the work of Barnett Newman and Mark Rothko.

**chryselephantine**—(kris-el-ŭ-'făn-tīn) Fashioned of gold and ivory.

**ciborium**—(su-'bor-ē-ŭm) A canopy, often freestanding and supported by four *columns,* erected over an altar; also, a covered cup used in the sacraments of the church. See *baldacchino.*

**circumambulation**—In Buddhist worship, walking around the *stupa* in a clockwise direction.

**cire perdue**—(sēr per-'dū) See *lost-wax process.*

**cista** (pl. **cistae**)—('sis-tŭ/'sis-tī) An Etruscan cylindrical container made of sheet bronze with cast handles and feet, often with elaborately engraved bodies, used for women's toilet articles.

**city-state**—An independent, self-governing city.

**clerestory**—('klēr-sto-rē) The *fenestrated* part of a building that rises above the roofs of the other parts. In Roman *basilicas* and medieval churches, the windows that form the *nave's* uppermost level below the timber ceiling or the *vaults.*

**cloison**—('kloi-zŭn) A cell made of metal wire or a narrow metal strip soldered edge-up to a metal base to hold enamel or other decorative materials.

**cloisonné**—('kloi-zŭ-nā) A process of enameling employing *cloisons;* also, decorative brickwork in later Byzantine architecture.

**cloister**—A monastery courtyard, usually with covered walks or *ambulatories* along its sides.

**cluster pier**—See *compound pier.*

**codex** (pl. **codices**)—('kō-deks/'kō-dŭ-sēz) Separate pages of *vellum* or *parchment* bound together at one side; the predecessor of the modern book. The codex superseded the *rotulus.* In *Mesoamerica,* a painted and inscribed book on long sheets of bark paper or deerskin coated with fine white plaster and folded into accordion-like pleats.

**coffer**—A sunken panel, often ornamental, in a *vault* or a ceiling.

**collage**—(kō-'lazh) A composition made by combining on a flat surface various materials, such as newspaper, wallpaper, printed text and illustrations, photographs, and cloth.

**colonnade**—A series or row of *columns,* usually spanned by *lintels.*

**colonnette**—A thin *column.*

**colophon**—('ka-lŭ-fan) An inscription, usually on the last page, giving information about a book's manufacture. In Chinese painting, written texts on attached pieces of paper or silk.

**color**—The value or tonality of a color is the degree of its lightness or darkness. The intensity or saturation of a color is its purity, its brightness or dullness. See also *primary, secondary,* and *complementary colors.*

**color field painting**—A variant of *Post-Painterly Abstraction* whose artists sought to reduce painting to its physical essence by pouring diluted paint onto unprimed canvas, allowing these pigments to soak into the fabric.

**colorito**—(ko-lo-'rē-tō) Italian, "colored" or "painted." A term used to describe the application of paint. Characteristic of the work of 16th-century Venetian artists who emphasized the application of paint as an important element of the creative process. Central Italian artists, in contrast, largely emphasized *disegno*—the careful design preparation based on preliminary drawing.

**column**—A vertical, weight-carrying architectural member, circular in cross-*section* and consisting of a *base* (sometimes omitted), a *shaft,* and a *capital.*

**complementary colors**—Those pairs of colors, such as red and green, that together embrace the entire spectrum. The complement of one of the three *primary colors* is a mixture of the other two.

**Composite capital**—A capital combining *Ionic* volutes and *Corinthian* acanthus leaves, first used by the ancient Romans.

**composite view**—See *twisted perspective.*

**composition**—The way in which an artist organizes *forms* in an artwork, either by placing shapes on a flat surface or arranging forms in space.

**compound pier**—A *pier* with a group, or cluster, of attached *shafts,* or *responds,* especially characteristic of *Gothic* architecture.

**Conceptual art**—An American avant-garde art movement of the 1960s that asserted that the "artfulness" of art lay in the artist's idea rather than its final expression.

**conch**—(kank) Half-dome.

**concrete**—A building material invented by the Romans and consisting of various proportions of lime mortar, volcanic sand, water, and small stones.

**condottiere**—(kon-da-'tyer-ē) A professional military leader employed by the Italian city-states in the early Renaissance.

**confraternity**—(kon-frŭ-'tŭr-nŭ-tē) In late antiquity, an association of Christian families pooling funds to purchase property for burial. In late medieval Europe, an organization founded by laypersons who dedicated themselves to strict religious observances.

**Constructivism**—An early-20th-century Russian art movement in art formulated by Naum Gabo, who built up his sculptures piece by piece in space instead of carving or *modeling* them in the traditional way. In this way the sculptor worked with "volume of mass" and "volume of space" as different materials.

**continuous narration**—In painting or sculpture, the convention of the same figure appearing more than once in the same space at different stages in a story.

**contour line**—In art, a continuous line defining the outer shape of an object.

**contrapposto**—(kon-trŭ-ˈpas-tō) The disposition of the human figure in which one part is turned in opposition to another part (usually hips and legs one way, shoulders and chest another), creating a counterpositioning of the body about its central axis. Sometimes called "weight shift" because the weight of the body tends to be thrown to one foot, creating tension on one side and relaxation on the other.

**corbel**—(ˈkor-bŭl) A projecting wall member used as a support for some element in the superstructure. Also, courses of stone or brick in which each course projects beyond the one beneath it. Two such walls, meeting at the topmost course, create a corbeled arch or *corbeled vault.*

**corbeled arch**—See *corbel.*

**corbeled vault**—A *vault* formed by the piling of stone blocks in horizontal courses, cantilevered inward until the two walls meet in an *arch.*

**Corinthian capital**—A more ornate form than *Doric* or *Ionic;* it consists of a double row of acanthus leaves from which tendrils and flowers grow, wrapped around a bell-shaped *echinus.* Although this *capital* form is often cited as the distinguishing feature of the Corinthian *order,* there is, strictly speaking, no Corinthian order, but only this style of capital used in the *Ionic* order.

**cornice**—The projecting, crowning member of the *entablature* framing the *pediment;* also, any crowning projection.

**Cosmato work**—(kos-ˈma-tō) Marble or mosaic work characterized by inlays of gold and precious or semiprecious stones and finely cut marble in geometric patterns.

**course**—In masonry construction, a horizontal row of stone blocks.

**crenel**—See *crenellation.*

**crenellation**—(kren-ŭ-ˈlā-shŭn) Alternating solid merlons and open crenels in the notched tops of walls, as in *battlements.*

**cromlech**—(ˈkrom-lek̲) A circle of *monoliths.* Also called henge.

**cross-section**—See *section.*

**cross vault**—See *vault.*

**crossing**—The space in a *cruciform* church formed by the intersection of the *nave* and the *transept.*

**crossing square**—The area in a church formed by the intersection *(crossing)* of a *nave* and a *transept* of equal width, often used as a standard *module* of interior proportion.

**crossing tower**—The tower over the *crossing* of a church.

**cruciform**—(ˈkru-sŭ-form) Cross shaped.

**Crusades**—In medieval Europe, armed pilgrimages aimed at recapturing the Holy Land from the *Muslims.*

**crypt**—A vaulted space under part of a building, wholly or partly underground; in

churches, normally the portion under an *apse* or a *chevet.*

**cubiculum** (pl. **cubicula**)—(kū-ˈbik-yū-lŭm) A small cubicle or bedroom that opened onto the *atrium* of a Roman house. Also, a chamber in an Early Christian catacomb that served as a mortuary chapel.

**Cubism**—An early-20th-century art movement that rejected naturalistic depictions, preferring compositions of shapes and forms abstracted from the conventionally perceived world. See also *Analytic Cubism* and *Synthetic Cubism.*

**cuerda seca**—(ˈkwer-dŭ ˈsā-kŭ) A type of polychrome tilework used in decorating Islamic buildings.

**cuirass**—(ˈkwē r-ăs) A military breastplate.

**cuneiform**—(kyū-ˈnā-ŭ-form) Latin, "wedge-shaped." A system of writing used in ancient Mesopotamia, in which wedge-shaped characters were produced by pressing a *stylus* into a soft clay tablet, which was then baked or otherwise allowed to harden.

**cuneus** (pl. **cunei**)—(ˈkū-nē-ŭs/ˈkū-nē-ī) In ancient Greek and Roman theaters and *amphitheaters,* wedge-shaped sections of stone benches separated by stairs.

**cupola**—(ˈkū-pō-lŭ) An exterior architectural feature composed of a *drum* with a shallow cap; a *dome.*

**cutaway**—An architectural drawing that combines an exterior view with an interior view of part of a building.

**Cyclopean masonry**—(sī-klō-ˈpē-ŭn *masonry*) A method of stone construction, named after the mythical one-eyed giant Cyclops, using massive, irregular blocks without mortar, characteristic of the Bronze Age fortifications of Tiryns and other Mycenaean sites.

**cylinder seal**—A cylindrical piece of stone usually about an inch or so in height, decorated with an *incised* design, so that a raised pattern was left when the seal was rolled over soft clay. In the ancient Near East, documents, storage jars, and other important possessions were signed, sealed, and identified in this way.

**Dada**—(ˈda-da) An art movement prompted by a revulsion against the horror of World War I. Dada embraced political anarchy, the irrational, and the intuitive, and the art produced by the Dadaists was characterized by a disdain for convention, often enlivened by humor or whimsy.

**Daedalic**—(ˈde-dŭl-ĭk) Refers to a Greek *Orientalizing* style of the seventh century BCE named after the legendary Daedalus.

**daguerreotype**—(da-ˈger-ō-tip) A photograph made by an early method on a plate of chemically treated metal; developed by Louis J. M. Daguerre.

**damnatio memoriae**—(dam-ˈna-tē-ō mŭ-ˈmor-ĭ-ī) The Roman decree condemning those who ran afoul of the Senate. Those who suffered damnatio memoriae had their memorials demolished and their names erased from public inscriptions.

**darshan**—(ˈdar-shan) In Hindu worship, seeing images of the divinity and being seen by the divinity.

**De Stijl**—(du stēl) Dutch, "the style." An early-20th-century art movement (and magazine) founded by Piet Mondrian and Theo van Doesburg, whose members promoted utopian ideals and developed a simplified geometric style.

**deceptive cadence**—In a horizontal scroll, the "false ending," which arrests the viewer's gaze by appearing to be the end of a narrative sequence, but which actually sets the stage for a culminating figure or scene.

**deconstruction**—An analytical strategy developed in the late 20th century according to which all cultural "constructs" (art, architecture, literature) are "texts." People can read these texts in a variety of ways, but they cannot arrive at fixed or uniform meanings. Any interpretation can be valid, and readings differ from time to time, place to place, and person to person. For those employing this approach, deconstruction means destabilizing established meanings and interpretations while encouraging subjectivity and individual differences.

**Deconstructivist architecture**—Using *deconstruction* as an analytical strategy, Deconstructivist architects attempt to disorient the observer by disrupting the conventional categories of architecture. The haphazard presentation of volumes, masses, planes, lighting, and so forth challenges the viewer's assumptions about form as it relates to function.

**decumanus**—(de-cu-ˈma-nŭs) The east-west street in a Roman town, intersecting the *cardo* at right angles.

**decursio**—(de-ˈcör-sĭ-ō) The ritual circling of a Roman funerary pyre.

**demos**—(ˈdē-mas) The Greek word meaning "the people," from which the word *democracy* is derived.

**demotic**—(dē-ˈma-tĭk) Late Egyptian writing.

**denarius**—(dĭ-ˈnar-ĭ-ŭs) The standard Roman silver coin from which the word *penny* ultimately derives.

**dharma**—(ˈdar-mŭ) In Buddhism, moral law based on the Buddha's teaching.

**di sotto in sù**—(dē ˈsot-tō in ˈsū) Italian, "from below upwards." A technique of representing *perspective* in ceiling painting.

**diagonal rib**—See *rib.*

**diaphragm arch**—A transverse, wall-bearing *arch* that divides a *vault* or a ceiling into compartments, providing a kind of fire-break.

**dipteral**—(ˈdip-tŭr-ŭl) See *peristyle.*

**diptych**—(ˈdip-tik) A two-paneled painting or *altarpiece;* also, an ancient Roman, Early Christian, or Byzantine hinged writing tablet, often of ivory and carved on the external sides.

**disegno**—(dē-ˈzā-nyō) Italian, "drawing" and "design." Renaissance artists considered drawing to be the external physical manifestation (disegno esterno) of an internal intellectual idea of design (disegno interno).

**dome**—A hemispheric *vault;* theoretically, an *arch* rotated on its vertical axis.

**domus**—('dō-mŭs) A Roman private house.

**Doric**—('dor-ik) One of the two systems (or *orders*) evolved for articulating the three units of the elevation of an ancient Greek temple—the platform, the *colonnade,* and the superstructure (*entablature*). The Doric order is characterized by, among other features, *capitals* with funnel-shaped *echinuses, columns* without bases, and a frieze of *triglyphs* and *metopes.* See also *Ionic.*

**dotaku**—(do-ta-kū) Ancient Japanese bronze ceremonial bells, usually featuring raised decoration.

**dromos**—('drŭ-mŭs) The passage leading to a *tholos tomb.*

**drum**—One of the stacked cylindrical stones that form the *shaft* of a *column;* the cylindrical wall that supports a *dome.*

**dry fresco**—See *fresco.*

**drypoint**—An engraving in which the design, instead of being cut into the plate with a *burin,* is scratched into the surface with a hard steel "pencil." See also *engraving, etching, intaglio.*

**earthenware**—Pottery made of clay that is fired at low temperatures and is slightly porous.

**eaves**—The lower part of a roof that overhangs the wall.

**echinus**—(ŭ-'kīn-ŭs) In architecture, the convex element of a *capital* directly below the *abacus.*

**écorché**—(ā-'ko-zhā) A figure painted or sculpted to show the muscles of the body as if without skin.

**edition**—A set of impressions taken from a single print surface.

**effigy mounds**—Ceremonial mounds built in the shape of animals or birds by native North American peoples.

**elevation**—In architecture, a head-on view of an external or internal wall, showing its features and often other elements that would be visible beyond or before the wall.

**emblema**—(em-'blā-mŭ) The central section or motif of a *mosaic.*

**embrasure**—A *splayed* opening in a wall that enframes a doorway or a window.

**embroidery**—The technique of sewing threads onto a finished ground to form contrasting designs.

**enamel**—A decorative coating, usually colored, fused onto the surface of metal, glass, or ceramics.

**encaustic**—(en-'kos-tik) A painting technique in which pigment is mixed with wax and applied to the surface while hot.

**engaged column**—A half-round *column* attached to a wall. See also *pilaster.*

**engraving**—The process of *incising* a design in hard material, often a metal plate (usually copper); also, the print or impression made from such a plate.

**entablature**—(in-'tăb-lŭ-chŭr) The part of a building above the *columns* and below the roof. The entablature of a classical temple has three parts: *architrave* or epistyle, *frieze,* and *pediment.*

**entasis**—('en-tŭ-sŭs) The convex profile (an apparent swelling) in the *shaft* of a *column.*

**Environmental art**—An American art form that emerged in the 1960s. Often using the land itself as their material, Environmental artists construct monuments of great scale and minimal form. Permanent or impermanent, these works transform some section of the environment, calling attention both to the land itself and to the hand of the artist. Sometimes referred to as Earth art or earthworks.

**epistyle**—('ep-ŭ-stil) See *architrave.*

**eravo**—(ŭ-'ra-vō) A men's meeting house constructed by the Elema people in New Guinea.

**escutcheon**—(ŭ-'skŭt-chŭn) An emblem bearing a coat of arms.

**etching**—A kind of *engraving* in which the design is *incised* in a layer of wax or varnish on a metal plate. The parts of the plate left exposed are then etched (slightly eaten away) by the acid in which the plate is immersed after incising. See also *drypoint, engraving, intaglio.*

**Eucharist**—('yū-ku-rist) In Christianity, the partaking of the bread and wine, which believers hold to be either Christ himself or symbolic of him.

**exedra**—(ek-'sē-drŭ) Recessed area, usually semicircular.

**expressionism**—Twentieth-century *modernist* art that is the result of the artist's unique inner or personal vision and that often has an emotional dimension. Expressionism contrasts with art focused on visually describing the empirical world.

**facade**—(fŭ-'sad) Usually, the front of a building; also, the other sides when they are emphasized architecturally.

**fan vault**—See *vault.*

**fasciae**—('făsh-ē-ī) In the *Ionic order,* the three horizontal bands that make up the *architrave.*

**fauces**—('fo-sēz) Latin, "throat." In a Roman house, the narrow foyer leading to the *atrium.*

**Fauvism**—('fō-viz-ŭm) From the French word *fauve,* "wild beast." An early-20th-century art movement led by Henri Matisse, for whom color became the formal element most responsible for pictorial coherence and the primary conveyor of meaning.

**fenestrated**—('fen-ŭ-strā-tŭd) Having windows.

**fenestration**—The arrangement of the windows of a building.

**fête galante**—(fet ga-'la^n) A type of *Rococo* painting depicting the outdoor amusements of upper-class society.

**feudalism**—The medieval political, social, and economic system held together by the relationship of a liege lord and vassal.

**fibula**—('fib-yū-lŭ) A decorative pin, usually used to fasten garments.

**figura serpentinata**—(fi-'gū-ra ser-pen-ti-'na-ta) In Renaissance art, a contortion or twisting of the body in contrary directions, especially characteristic of the sculpture and paintings of Michelangelo and the Mannerists.

**fillets**—('fil-ŭts) In *Ionic columns,* the flat ridges of the *fluting.*

**fin de siècle**—(fă ^n-dŭ-sē-'ek-lŭ) French, "end of the century." A period in Western cultural history from the end of the 19th century until just before World War I, when decadence and indulgence masked anxiety about an uncertain future.

**finial**—A crowning ornament.

**First Style mural**—The earliest style of Roman mural painting. Also called the Masonry Style, because the aim of the artist was to imitate, using painted stucco relief, the appearance of costly marble panels.

**Flamboyant style**—A Late *Gothic* style of architecture superseding the *Rayonnant* style and named for the flamelike appearance of its pointed bar *tracery.*

**flashing**—In making *stained-glass* windows, fusing one layer of colored glass to another to produce a greater range of colors.

**flute** or **fluting**—Vertical channeling, roughly semicircular in cross-*section* and used principally on *columns* and *pilasters.*

**Fluxus**—A group of American, European, and Japanese artists of the 1960s who created *Performance art.* Their performances often focused on single actions, such as turning a light on and off or watching falling snow, and were more theatrical than *Happenings.*

**flying buttress**—See *buttress.*

**folio**—('fō-lĭ-ō) A page of a manuscript or book.

**foreshortening**—The use of *perspective* to represent in art the apparent visual contraction of an object that extends back in space at an angle to the perpendicular plane of sight.

**form**—In art, an object's shape and structure, either in two dimensions (for example, a figure painted on a surface) or in three dimensions (such as a statue).

**formalism**—Strict adherence to, or dependence on, stylized shapes and methods of composition. An emphasis on an artwork's visual elements rather than its subject.

**forum**—The public square of an ancient Roman city.

**found objects**—Images, materials, or objects as found in the everyday environment that are incorporated into works of art.

**Fourth Style mural**—In Roman mural painting, the Fourth Style marks a return to architectural illusionism, but the architectural vistas of the Fourth Style are irrational fantasies.

**freedmen, freedwomen**—In ancient and medieval society, men and women who had been freed from servitude, as opposed to having been born free.

**freestanding sculpture**—See *sculpture in the round.*

**fresco**—('fres-kō) Painting on lime plaster, either dry (dry fresco or fresco secco) or wet (true or buon fresco). In the latter method, the pigments are mixed with water and become chemically bound to the freshly laid lime plaster. Also, a painting executed in either method.

**fresco secco**—('fres-kō 'sek-ō) See *fresco.*

**fret** or **meander**—An ornament, usually in bands but also covering broad surfaces, consisting of interlocking geometric motifs. An ornamental pattern of contiguous straight lines joined usually at right angles.

**frieze**—(frēz) The part of the *entablature* between the *architrave* and the *cornice;* also, any sculptured or painted band in a building. See *register.*

**frigidarium**—(fri-jŭ-'dă-rē-ŭm) The cold-bath section of a Roman bathing establishment.

**frottage**—(frō-'tazh) A process of rubbing a crayon or other medium across paper placed over surfaces with a strong and evocative texture pattern to combine patterns.

**Futurism**—An early-20th-century movement involving a militant group of Italian poets, painters, and sculptors. These artists published numerous manifestos declaring revolution in art against all traditional tastes, values, and styles and championing the modern age of steel and speed and the cleansing virtues of violence and war.

**garbha griha**—('garb-ha 'grē-ha) Hindi, "womb chamber." In Hindu temples, the *cella,* the holy inner sanctum, for the cult image or symbol.

**genetrix**—A legendary founding clan mother.

**genre**—('zhanⁿ-rŭ) A style or category of art; also, a kind of painting that realistically depicts scenes from everyday life.

**German Expressionism**—An early-20th-century art movement; German Expressionist works are characterized by bold, vigorous brushwork, emphatic line, and bright color. Two important groups of German Expressionists were Die BrŸcke, in Dresden, and Der Blaue Reiter, in Munich.

**gestural abstraction**—Also known as *action painting.* A kind of abstract painting in which the gesture, or act of painting, is seen as the subject of art. Its most renowned proponent was Jackson Pollock. See also *Abstract Expressionism.*

**gigantomachy**—(jī-gŭn-'ta-mŭ-kē) In ancient Greek mythology, the battle between gods and giants.

**glaze**—A vitreous coating applied to pottery to seal and decorate the surface; it may be colored, transparent, or opaque, and glossy or *matte.* In oil painting, a thin, transparent, or semitransparent layer put over a color to alter it slightly.

**glazed brick**—Bricks painted and then kiln fired to fuse the color with the baked clay.

**glazier**—A glassworker.

**gopuras**—('gō-pū-rŭz) The massive, ornamented entrance gateway towers of South Indian temple compounds.

**gorget**—('gor-jŭt) A neck pendant.

**gorgon**—In ancient Greek mythology, a hideous female demon with snake hair. Medusa, the most famous gorgon, was capable of turning anyone who gazed at her into stone.

**Gospels**—The four New Testament books that relate the life and teachings of Jesus.

**Gothic**—Originally a derogatory term named after the Goths, used to describe the history, culture, and art of western Europe in the 12th to 14th centuries.

**granulation**—A decorative technique in which tiny metal balls (granules) are fused to a metal surface.

**graver**—An *incising* tool used by engravers and sculptors.

**Greek cross**—A cross with four arms of equal length and at right angles.

**grisaille**—(grŭ-'zīy) A monochrome painting done mainly in neutral grays to simulate sculpture.

**groin**—The edge formed by the intersection of two *vaults.*

**groin vault**—See *vault.*

**ground line**—In paintings and reliefs, a painted or carved baseline on which figures appear to stand.

**guang**—(gwŭng) In ancient China, covered vessels, often in animal forms, holding wine, water, grain, or meat for sacrificial rites.

**hall church**—See *Hallenkirche.*

**Hallenkirche**—('hal-ŭn-kēr-kŭ) German, "hall church"; a church design favored in Germany, but also used elsewhere, in which the *aisles* rise to the same height as the *nave.*

**handscroll**—In Asian art, a horizontal painted scroll that is unrolled to the left and often used to present illustrated religious texts or *landscapes.*

**haniwa**—(ha-nē-wa) Sculpted fired pottery cylinders, modeled in human, animal, or other forms and placed around early (archaic) Japanese burial mounds.

**Happenings**—A term coined by American artist Allan Kaprow in the 1960s to describe loosely structured performances, whose creators were trying to suggest the aesthetic and dynamic qualities of everyday life; as actions, rather than objects, Happenings incorporate the fourth dimension (time).

**hard-edge painting**—A variant of *Post-Painterly Abstraction* that rigidly excluded all reference to gesture, and incorporated smooth knife-edge geometric forms to express the notion that painting should be reduced to its visual components.

**Harlem Renaissance**—A particularly fertile period of cultural production for African Americans. During the 1920s and 1930s, African American artists, writers, and musicians celebrated their heritage and culture and redefined artistic forms of expression.

**harmika**—(har-'mē-ka) In Buddhist architecture, a stone fence or railing that encloses an area surmounting the dome of a *stupa* that represents one of the Buddhist heavens; from the center arises the *yasti.*

**hatching**—A technique used in drawing and in printmaking methods such as *engraving* and *woodcut,* in which fine lines are cut or drawn close together to achieve an effect of shading.

**heiau**—(hī-yau) A Hawaiian temple structure.

**Hellenes** (adj. **Hellenic**)—The name the ancient Greeks called themselves as the people of Hellas.

**Hellenistic**—The term given to the culture that developed after the death of Alexander the Great in 323 BCE and lasted almost three centuries, until the Roman conquest of Egypt in 31 BCE.

**henge**—See *cromlech.*

**heraldic composition**—A *composition* that is symmetrical on either side of a central figure.

**herm**—A bust on a quadrangular *pillar.*

**Hevehe**—(he-ve-he) An elaborate cycle of ceremonial activities performed by the Elema people of the Papuan Gulf region of New Guinea. Also the large, ornate masks that were produced for and presented during these ceremonies.

**Hiberno-Saxon**—('hi-ber-no 'sak-sŭn) An art style that flourished in the monasteries of the British Isles in the early Middle Ages. Also called Insular.

**hierarchy of scale**—An artistic convention in which greater size indicates greater importance.

**hieratic**—(hī-ŭ-'ră-tik) A fixed, stylized method of representation, often determined by religious principles and ideas.

**hieroglyphic**—(hī-rō-'glif-ik) A system of writing using symbols or pictures.

**high relief**—See *relief.*

**Hijra**—('hī̆j-rŭ) The flight of Muhammad from Mecca to Medina in 622, the year from which Islam dates its beginnings.

**himation**—(hī-'mă-shŭn) An ancient Greek mantle worn by men and women over the *chiton* and draped in various ways.

**Hippodamian plan**—(hĭ-pō-'dă-mĭ-ŭn) A city plan devised by Hippodamos of Miletos ca. 466 BCE, in which a strict grid was imposed on a site, regardless of the terrain, so that all streets would meet at right angles.

**hiragana**—(hē-ra-ga-na) A sound-based writing system developed in Japan from Chinese characters; it came to be the primary script for Japanese court poetry.

**historiated**—Ornamented with representations, such as plants, animals, or human figures, that have a narrative—as distinct from a purely decorative—function.

**hue**—The name of a *color.* See *primary colors, secondary colors,* and *complementary colors.*

**humanism**—In the Renaissance, an emphasis on education and on expanding knowledge (especially of classical antiquity), the exploration of individual potential and a desire to excel, and a commitment to civic responsibility and moral duty.

**hydria**—(ʹhī-drē-ŭ) An ancient Greek three-handled water pitcher.

**hypaethral**—(hīp-ʹē th-rŭl) A building having no pediment or roof, open to the sky.

**hypostyle hall**—(ʹhī-pŭ-stīl hall) A hall with a roof supported by *columns*.

**icon**—A portrait or image; especially in Byzantine art, a panel with a painting of sacred personages that are objects of veneration. In the visual arts, a painting, a piece of sculpture, or even a building regarded as an object of veneration.

**iconoclasm**—(ī-ʹkan-ʹŭ-klăz(-ŭ)m) The destruction of images. In Byzantium, the period from 726 to 843 when there was an imperial ban on images. The destroyers of images were known as iconoclasts. Those who opposed such a ban were known as iconophiles or iconodules.

**iconodule**—(ī-ʹkan-ŭ-dyül) See *iconoclasm.*

**iconography**—(ī-kŭn-ʹa-grŭ-fē) Greek, the "writing of images." The term refers both to the content, or subject, of an artwork and to the study of content in art. It also includes the study of the symbolic, often religious, meaning of objects, persons, or events depicted in works of art.

**iconophile**—See *iconoclasm.*

**iconostasis**—(ī-kŭ-ʹnas-tŭ-sŭs) In Byzantine churches, a screen or a partition, with doors and many tiers of *icons,* separating the sanctuary from the main body of the church.

**ikegobo**—(ē-kā-gō-bō) A Benin royal shrine.

**illuminated manuscript**—A luxurious handmade book with painted illustrations and decorations.

**illumination**—Decoration (usually in gold, silver, and bright colors), especially of medieval manuscript pages.

**imagines**—(i-ʹma-gi-nes) In ancient Rome, wax portraits of ancestors.

**imam**—(i-ʹmam or i-ʹmăm) In Islam, the leader of collective worship.

**imperator**—(im-pŭ-ʹra-tŭr) Latin, "commander in chief," from which the word *emperor* is derived.

**impluvium**—(im-ʹplü-vē-ŭm) In a Roman house, the basin located in the *atrium* that collected rainwater.

**impost block**—A stone with the shape of a truncated, inverted pyramid, placed between a *capital* and the *arch* that springs from it.

**Impressionism**—A late-19th-century art movement that sought to capture a fleeting moment, thereby conveying the illusiveness and impermanence of images and conditions.

**in antis**—(in ʹăn-tĭs) In ancient Greek architecture, between the *antae.*

**in situ**—(in sŭ-ʹtū) In place; in the original position.

**incise**—(in-ʹsīz) To cut into a surface with a sharp instrument; also, a method of decoration, especially on metal and pottery.

**incrustation**—Wall decoration consisting of bright panels of different colors.

**inscriptions**—Texts written on the same surface as the picture (as in Chinese paintings) or *incised* in stone (as in ancient art). See also *colophon.*

**installation**—An artwork that creates an artistic environment in a room or gallery.

**insula**—(ʹin-sū-lŭ) In Roman architecture, a multistory apartment house, usually made of brick-faced *concrete;* also refers to an entire city block.

**Insular**—See *Hiberno-Saxon.*

**intaglio**—(in-ʹta-lē-ō) A graphic technique in which the design is *incised,* or scratched, on a metal plate, either manually (*engraving, drypoint*) or chemically (*etching*). The incised lines of the design take the ink, making this the reverse of the *woodcut* technique.

**intarsia**—(in-ʹtar-sē-ŭ) Inlay work in wood of design elements made from such materials as mother-of-pearl, marble, and ivory.

**interaxial**—The distance between the center of the lowest *drum* of a *column* and the center of the next.

**International Style**—A style of 14th- and 15th-century painting begun by Simone Martini, who adapted the French *Gothic* manner to Sienese art fused with influences from the North. This style appealed to the aristocracy because of its brilliant color, lavish costume, intricate ornament, and themes involving splendid processions of knights and ladies. Also a style of 20th-century architecture associated with Le Corbusier, whose elegance of design came to influence the look of modern office buildings and skyscrapers.

**Ionic**—(ī-ʹan-ik) One of the two systems (or *orders*) evolved for articulating the three units of the elevation of a Greek temple: the platform, the *colonnade,* and the superstructure (*entablature*). The Ionic order is characterized by, among other features, *volutes, capitals, columns* with *bases,* and an uninterrupted *frieze.*

**iron-wire lines**—In ancient Chinese painting, thin brush lines suggesting tensile strength.

**iwan**—(ʹē-wan) In Islamic architecture, a vaulted rectangular recess opening onto a courtyard.

**jambs**—(ʹjăms) In architecture, the side posts of a doorway.

**Japonisme**—(zhă-pŭ-ʹnēz-mŭ) The French fascination with all things Japanese. Japonisme emerged in the second half of the 19th century.

**jataka**—(ʹjă-tă-kă) Tales of the past lives of the Buddha. See also *sutra.*

**jomon**—(jo-mon) Japanese, "cord markings." A type of Japanese decorative technique characterized by ropelike markings.

**ka**—(ka) In ancient Egypt, the immortal human life force.

**Kaaba**—(ʹka-ba) Arabic, "cube." A small cubical building in Mecca, the *Muslim* world's symbolic center.

**kami**—(ka-mī) Shinto deities or spirits, believed in Japan to exist in nature (mountains, waterfalls) and in charismatic people.

**karma**—(ʹka-mŭ) In Vedic religions, the ethical consequences of a person's life, which determine his or her fate.

**katsina**—(kŭ-ʹchē-nŭ) An art form of Native Americans of the Southwest, the katsina doll represents benevolent supernatural spirits (katsinas) living in mountains and water sources.

**keep**—A fortified tower in a castle that served as a place of last refuge.

**key** or **meander**—See *fret.*

**keystone**—See *voussoir.*

**kiva**—(ʹkē-vŭ) A large circular underground structure that is the spiritual and ceremonial center of Pueblo Indian life.

**kondo**—(kon-do) Japanese, "golden hall." In a Japanese Buddhist temple complex, the building housing the main sculptural icons.

**Koran**—(ko-ʹran) Islam's sacred book, composed of *surahs* (chapters) divided into verses.

**kore** (pl. **korai**)—(ʹkor-ā/ʹkor-ī) Greek, "young woman." An Archaic Greek statuary type depicting a young woman.

**koru**—(ʹka-rū) An unrolled spiral design used by the Maori in their tattoos.

**kouros** (pl. **kouroi**)—(ʹkūr-os/ʹkūr-oi) Greek, "young man." An Archaic Greek statuary type depicting a young man.

**krater**—An ancient Greek wide-mouthed bowl for mixing wine and water.

**Kufic**—(ʹkū-fŭk) An early form of Arabic script, characterized by angularity, with the uprights forming almost right angles with the baseline.

**kula**—(ʹkū-lŭ) An exchange of white conus-shell arm ornaments and red chama-shell necklaces that takes place among the Trobriand Islanders. These exchanges serve to stimulate the economy and cement social relationships.

**kylix**—(ʹkī-lĭks) An ancient Greek shallow drinking cup with two handles and a stem.

**lacquer**—(ʹlăk-ŭr) A varnishlike substance made from the sap of the Asiatic sumac, used to decorate wood and other organic materials. Often colored with mineral pigments, lacquer cures to great hardness and has a lustrous surface.

**lakshana(s)**—(laksh-ʹha-na) Distinguishing marks of the Buddha. They include the *urna* and *ushnisha.*

**lalitasana**—(la-ʹlē-ta-sa-na) In Buddhist iconography, the body pose with one leg folded and the other hanging down, indicating relaxation.

**lamassu**—(la-ʹma-sū) Assyrian guardian in the form of a man-headed winged bull.

**lancet**—(ʹlăn-sŭt) In *Gothic* architecture, a tall narrow window ending in a *pointed arch.*

**landscape**—A picture showing natural scenery, without narrative content.

**lapis lazuli**—(ʹlă-pŭs ʹlă-zhyū-lē) A rich ultramarine semiprecious stone used for carving and as a source for pigment.

**Lapita pottery**—('lă-pǐ-tŭ) Ceramic vessels elaborately decorated with incised, geometric designs. Found in a geographical region roughly bounded by New Guinea in the west and Tonga and Samoa in the east.

**leading**—In the manufacture of *stained-glass* windows, the joining of colored glass pieces using lead *cames.*

**lectionary**—('lek-shŭn-er-ē) A book containing passages from the *Gospels,* arranged in the sequence that they are to be read during the celebration of religious services, including the *Mass,* throughout the year.

**lekythos** (pl. **lekythoi**)—('lek-ē-thos/'lek-ē-thoi) A flask containing perfumed oil; lekythoi were often placed in Greek graves as offerings to the deceased.

**letterpress**—The technique of printing with movable type invented in Germany in the 15th century.

**linear perspective**—See *perspective.*

**linga**—('lin-ga) In Hindu art, the depiction of Shiva as a phallus or cosmic *pillar.*

**lintel**—('lin-tŭl) A beam used to span an opening.

**literati**—(lĭ-t-ŭ-'ra-tē) In China, talented amateur painters and scholars from the landed gentry.

**local color**—An object's actual color in white light.

**loculi**—('lak-yŭ-lē) Openings in the walls of *catacombs* to receive the dead.

**loggia**—('lo-jŭ) A gallery with an open *arcade* or a *colonnade* on one or both sides.

**logogram**—('la-gŭ-gram) One of the thousands of characters in the Chinese writing system, corresponding to one meaningful language unit. See also *pictograph.*

**longitudinal plan**—See *plan.*

**lost-wax process (cire perdue)**—A bronze-casting method in which a figure is modeled in wax and covered with clay; the whole is fired, melting away the wax and hardening the clay, which then becomes a mold for molten metal.

**low relief**—See *relief.*

**lunette**—(lū-'net) A semicircular area (with the flat side down) in a wall over a door, niche, or window; also, a painting or *relief* with a semicircular frame.

**madrasa**—(mŭ-'dra-sŭ) An Islamic theological college adjoining and often containing a *mosque.*

**maebyong**—(mī-byŭng) A Korean vase similar to the Chinese *meiping.*

**magi**—('mă-jī) The three wise men from the East who presented gifts to the infant Jesus.

**ma-hevehe**—(ma-he-ve-hŭ) Mythical water spirits; the Elema people of New Guinea believed that these spirits visited their villages.

**malanggan**—(ma-lang-gan) Both the festivals held in honor of the deceased in New Ireland (Papua New Guinea) and the carvings and objects produced for these festivals.

**mandala**—(man-'da-la) Sacred diagram of the universe.

**mandapa**—(man-'da-pa) *Pillared* hall of a Hindu temple.

**mandorla**—(măn-'dor-lŭ) An almond-shaped *nimbus* surrounding the figure of Christ or other sacred figure.

**Mannerism**—A style of later Renaissance art that emphasized "artifice," often involving contrived imagery not derived directly from nature. Such artworks showed a self-conscious stylization involving complexity, caprice, fantasy, and polish. Mannerist architecture tended to flout the classical rules of order, stability, and symmetry, sometimes to the point of parody.

**manulua**—(ma-nu-lu-a) Tongan, "two birds." A Tongan design motif that symbolizes chiefly status derived from both parents.

**maqsura**—(mak-'sū-ra) In some *mosques,* a screened area in front of the *mihrab* reserved for a ruler.

**Masonry Style**—See *First Style mural.*

**masquerade**—Among some African groups, a ritualized drama performed by several masked dancers, embodying ancestors or nature spirits.

**Mass**—The Catholic and Orthodox ritual in which believers understand that Christ's redeeming sacrifice on the cross is repeated when the priest consecrates the bread and wine in the *Eucharist.*

**mastaba**—(ma-'sta-ba) Arabic, "bench." An ancient Egyptian rectangular brick or stone structure with sloping sides erected over a subterranean tomb chamber connected with the outside by a shaft.

**matte** (also **mat**)—(măt) In painting, pottery, and photography, a dull finish.

**mausoleum**—(mo-sō-'lē-ŭm) A monumental tomb. The name derives from the mid-fourth century BCE tomb of Mausolos at Halikarnassos, one of the Seven Wonders of the ancient world.

**mbari house**—(ŭm-'ba-rĭ) An Igbo renewal house, constructed from mud every 50 years as a sacrifice to a major deity, often Ala, goddess of the earth.

**meander** or **key**—See *fret.*

**medium**—The material (for example, marble, bronze, clay, fresco) in which an artist works; also, in painting, the vehicle (usually liquid) that carries the pigment.

**megalith** (adj., **megalithic**)—('me-gŭ-lith/me-gŭ-'lith-ik) Greek, "great stone." A large, roughly hewn stone used in the construction of monumental prehistoric structures. See also *cromlech.*

**megaron**—('meg-ŭ-ron) The large reception hall in a Mycenaean palace, fronted by an open, two-*columned* porch.

**meiping**—(mā-ping) A Chinese vase of a high-shouldered shape; the *sgrafitto* technique was used in decorating such vases.

**memento mori**—(mi-'ment-ō 'mo-rē) A reminder of human mortality, usually represented by a skull.

**mendicants**—('men-di-cŭnts) In medieval Europe, friars belonging to the Franciscan and Dominican orders, who renounced all worldly goods, lived by contributions of laypersons (the word *mendicant* means "beggar"), and devoted themselves to preaching, teaching, and doing good works.

**menorah**—(mŭ-'no-rŭ) In antiquity, the Jewish sacred seven-branched candelabrum.

**merlon**—See *crenellation.*

**Mesoamerica**—The region that comprises Mexico, Guatemala, Belize, Honduras, and the Pacific coast of El Salvador.

**Mesolithic**—(mez-ō-'lith-ik) The "middle" Stone Age, between the *Paleolithic* and the *Neolithic* ages.

**Messiah**—(mŭ-'sī-ŭ) The savior of the Jews prophesized in the Old Testament. Christians believe that Jesus of Nazareth was the Messiah.

**metate**—(mŭ-'ta-tā) A ceremonial grinding stone, perhaps used as a throne in northern South America and various Central American regions.

**metope**—('met-ŭ-pē) The panel between the *triglyphs* in a *Doric frieze,* often sculpted in *relief.*

**Mexica**—The name used by a group of initially migratory invaders from northern Mexico to identify themselves. Settling on an island in Lake Texcoco in central Mexico, they are known today as the Aztecs.

**mihrab**—(mi-'rab) A semicircular niche set into the *qibla* wall of an *mosque.*

**minaret**—('min-ŭ-ret) A distinctive feature of *mosque* architecture, a tower from which the faithful are called to worship.

**minbar**—('min-bar) In a *mosque,* the pulpit on which the *imam* stands.

**miniatures**—Small individual paintings intended by Indian painters to be held in the hand and viewed by one or two individuals at one time.

**Minimalism (Minimal art)**—A predominantly sculptural American trend of the 1960s whose works consist of a severe reduction of form, oftentimes to single, homogeneous units.

**moai**—(mō-ī) A large, blocky figural stone sculpture found on Rapa Nui (Easter Island).

**modeling**—The shaping or fashioning of three-dimensional forms in a soft material, such as clay; also, the gradations of light and shade reflected from the surfaces of matter in space, or the illusion of such gradations produced by alterations of value in a drawing, painting, or print.

**modernism**—A movement in Western art that developed in the second half of the 19th century and sought to capture the images and sensibilities of the age. Modernist art goes beyond simply dealing with the present and involves the artist's critical examination of the premises of art itself.

**module**—A basic unit of which the dimensions of the major parts of a work are multiples. The principle is used in sculpture and other art forms, but it is most often employed in architecture, where the module may be the dimensions of an important part of a building, such as the diameter of a *column.*

**moko**—The form of tattooing practiced by the Maori of New Zealand (Aotearoa).

**moksha**—See *nirvana.*

**molding**—In architecture, a continuous, narrow surface (projecting or recessed, plain or ornamented) designed to break up a surface, to accent, or to decorate.

**monolith**—A *column* shaft that is all in one piece (not composed of *drums*); a large, single block or piece of stone used in *megalithic* structures.

**moralized Bible**—A heavily illustrated Bible, each page pairing paintings of Old and New Testament episodes with explanations of their moral significance.

**mortise-and-tenon system**—('mor-tŭs- and-'ten-ŭn) See *tenon.*

**mosaic**—(mō-'zā-ŭk) Patterns or pictures made by embedding small pieces *(tesserae)* of stone or glass in cement on surfaces such as walls and floors; also, the technique of making such works.

**mosaic tilework**—An Islamic decorative technique in which large ceramic panels are fired, cut into smaller pieces, and set in plaster.

**mosque**—(mask) The Islamic building for collective worship. From the Arabic word *masjid,* meaning a "place for bowing down."

**mudra**—('mŭ-drŭ, *or* 'mū-drŭ) In Buddhist and Hindu iconography, a stylized and symbolic hand gesture.

**Muhaqqaq**—(mū-ha-'kak) A cursive style of Islamic *calligraphy.*

**mullion**—('mŭl-yŭn) A vertical member that divides a window or that separates one window from another.

**mummification**—A technique used by ancient Egyptians to preserve human bodies so that they may serve as the eternal home of the immortal *ka.*

**muqarnas**—(mū-'kar-nas) Stucco decorations of Islamic buildings in which stalactite-like forms break a structure's solidity.

**mural**—A wall painting.

**Muslim**—A believer in Islam.

**Nabis**—('nă-bĭ s) Hebrew, "prophet." A group of *Symbolist* painters influenced by Paul Gauguin.

**naos**—('nă-os) See *cella.*

**narthex**—('nar-theks) A porch or vestibule of a church, generally *colonnaded* or *arcaded* and preceding the *nave.*

**natatio**—(na-'ta-tē-ō) The swimming pool in a Roman bathing establishment.

**nave**—The central area of an ancient Roman *basilica* or of a church, demarcated from *aisles* by *piers* or *columns.*

**nave arcade**—In *basilica* architecture, the series of *arches* supported by *piers* or *columns* separating the *nave* from the *aisles.*

**necking**—A groove at the bottom of the ancient Greek *Doric capital* between the *echinus* and the *flutes* that masks the junction of *capital* and *shaft.*

**necropolis**—(nŭ-'krop-ŭ-lŭs) Greek, "city of the dead"; a large burial area or cemetery.

**nemes**—('ne-mes) In ancient Egypt, the linen headdress worn by the pharaoh, with the uraeus cobra of kingship on the front.

**Neoclassicism**—A style of art and architecture that emerged in the later 18th century. Part of a general revival of interest in classical cultures, Neoclassicism was characterized by the utilization of themes and styles from ancient Greece and Rome.

**Neo-Expressionism**—An art movement that emerged in the 1970s and that reflects the artists' interest in the expressive capability of art, seen earlier in *German Expressionism* and *Abstract Expressionism.*

**Neolithic**—(Nē-ō-'lith-ik) The "new" Stone Age.

**Neoplasticism**—A theory of art developed by Piet Mondrian to create a pure plastic art composed of the simplest, least subjective, elements, *primary colors,* primary values, and primary directions (horizontal and vertical).

**Neue Sachlichkeit (New Objectivity)**—('noi-ŭ 'sak-lik̲-kīt) An art movement that grew directly out of the World War I experiences of a group of German artists who sought to show the horrors of the war and its effects.

**ngatu**—((n)ga-tu) *Tapa* made by women in Tonga.

**nihonga**—(nē-hong-ga) A 19th-century Japanese painting style that incorporated some Western techniques in basically Japanese-style painting, as opposed to *yoga* (Western painting).

**nimbus**—A halo or aureole appearing around the head of a holy figure to signify divinity.

**nirvana**—In Buddhism and Hinduism, a blissful state brought about by absorption of the individual soul or consciousness into the supreme spirit. Also called moksha.

**nishiki-e**—(ni-shi-ki-e) Japanese, "brocade pictures." Japanese polychrome woodblock prints valued for their sumptuous colors.

**nkisi n'kondi**—((n)kē-sē (n)kan-dē) A power figure carved by the Kongo people of the Democratic Republic of Congo. Such images embodied spirits believed to heal and give life or capable of inflicting harm or death.

**nymphs**—In classical mythology, female divinities of springs, caves, and woods.

**oculus** (pl. **oculi**)—(a-kyū-lus/a-kyū-lē) Latin, "eye." The round central opening of a dome. Also, a small round window in a *Gothic cathedral.*

**ogee arch**—(ō-'jē) An *arch* made up of two double-curving lines meeting at a point.

**ogive** (adj., **ogival**)—(ō-'jī-vŭl) The diagonal *rib* of a *Gothic vault;* a pointed, or Gothic, *arch.*

**opisthodomos**—(o-pis-'thad-ŭ-mŭs) In Greek architecture, a porch at the rear of a temple, set against the blank back wall of the *cella.*

**opus reticulatum**—('ō-pŭs rŭ-tik-ŭ-'lat-ŭm) An ancient Roman method of facing *concrete* walls with lozenge-shaped bricks or stones to achieve a netlike ornamental surface pattern.

**orant**—('or-ănt) In Early Christian art, a figure with both arms raised in the ancient gesture of prayer.

**oratory**—The church of a Christian monastery.

**orchestra**—Greek, "dancing place." In ancient Greek theaters, the circular piece of earth with a hard and level surface on which the performance took place.

**order**—In classical architecture, a style represented by a characteristic design of the *columns* and *entablature.* See also *superimposed orders.*

**Orientalizing**—The early phase of Archaic Greek art, so named because of the adoption of forms and motifs from the ancient Near East and Egypt.

**orthogonal**—(or-'thag-ŭn-ŭl) A line imagined to be behind and perpendicular to the picture plane; the orthogonals in a painting appear to recede toward a vanishing point on the horizon.

**orthogonal plan**—The imposition of a strict grid plan on a site, regardless of the terrain, so that all streets meet at right angles. See also *Hippodamian plan.*

**Ottonian** (adj.)—Pertaining to the empire of Otto I and his successors.

**overglaze**—In *porcelain* decoration, the technique of applying mineral colors over the *glaze* after the work has been fired. The overglaze colors, or *enamels,* fuse to the glazed surface in a second firing at a much lower temperature than the main firing. See also *underglaze.*

**pagoda**—(pŭ-'gō-dŭ) A Chinese tower, usually associated with a Buddhist temple, having a multiplicity of winged *eaves;* thought to be derived from the Indian *stupa.*

**pala**—('pa-lŭ) In churches, an *altarpiece,* or panel placed behind and over the altar.

**palaestra**—(pŭ-'les-trŭ) An ancient Greek and Roman exercise area, usually framed by a *colonnade.*

**Paleolithic**—(pā-lē-ō-'lith-ik) The "old" Stone Age, during which humankind produced the first sculptures and paintings.

**palette**—In ancient Egypt, a slate slab used for preparing makeup. A thin board with a thumb hole at one end on which an artist lays and mixes colors; any surface so used. Also, the colors or kinds of colors characteristically used by an artist.

**Pantocrator**—(pan-'tak-rŭ-tŭr) Christ as ruler and judge of heaven and earth.

**papyrus**—(pŭ-'pī-rŭs) A plant native to Egypt and adjacent lands used to make paperlike writing material; also, the material or any writing on it.

**parchment**—Lambskin prepared as a surface for painting or writing.

**parekklesion**—(pă-rŭ-'klē-zŭ-an) The side chapel in a Byzantine church.

**parapet**—A low, protective wall along the edge of a balcony or roof.

**parinirvana**—(pǎ-ri-nör-'va-nŭ) Image of the reclining Buddha, often viewed as representing his death.

**paten**—A large bowl to hold the bread used in the *Eucharist.*

**patricians**—Roman freeborn landowners.

**pebble mosaic**—Mosaic made of irregularly shaped stones of various colors.

**pectoral**—An ornament worn on the chest.

**pediment**—In classical architecture, the triangular space (gable) at the end of a building, formed by the ends of the sloping roof above the *colonnade;* also, an ornamental feature having this shape.

**pendant**—The large hanging terminal element of a *Gothic* fan *vault.*

**pendentive**—A concave, triangular section of a hemisphere, four of which provide the transition from a square area to the circular base of a covering *dome.* Although pendentives appear to be hanging (pendant) from the dome, they in fact support it.

**peplos**—('pep-los) A simple long woolen belted garment worn by ancient Greek women.

**Performance art**—An American avant-garde art trend of the 1960s that made time an integral element of art. It produced works in which movements, gestures, and sounds of persons communicating with an audience replace physical objects. Documentary photographs are generally the only evidence remaining after these events. See also *Happenings.*

**peripteral**—(pŭ-'rip-tŭr-ŭl) See *peristyle.*

**peristyle**—('per-rŭ-stīl) In ancient Greek architecture, a *colonnade* all around the *cella* and its porch(es). A peripteral colonnade consists of a single row of *columns* on all sides; a dipteral colonnade has a double row all around.

**personification**—An abstract idea represented in bodily form.

**perspective**—A method of presenting an illusion of the three-dimensional world on a two-dimensional surface. In linear perspective, the most common type, all parallel lines or surface edges converge on one, two, or three vanishing points located with reference to the eye level of the viewer (the horizon line of the picture), and associated objects are rendered smaller the farther from the viewer they are intended to seem. Atmospheric, or aerial, perspective creates the illusion of distance by the greater diminution of color intensity, the shift in color toward an almost neutral blue, and the blurring of contours as the intended distance between eye and object increases.

**photomontage**—(fŏ-tō-mon-'taj) A composition made by pasting together pictures or parts of pictures, especially photographs. See also *collage.*

**Photorealists**—See *Superrealism.*

**pictograph**—('pik-tō-grăf) A picture, usually stylized, that represents an idea; also, writing using such means; also painting on rock. See also *hieroglyphic.*

**pier**—A vertical, freestanding masonry support.

**pier buttress**—See *buttress.*

**Pietà**—(pē-a-'ta) A painted or sculpted representation of the Virgin Mary mourning over the body of the dead Christ.

**pilaster**—A flat, rectangular, vertical member projecting from a wall of which it forms a part. It usually has a *base* and a *capital* and is often *fluted.*

**pillar**—Usually a weight-carrying member, such as a *pier* or a *column;* sometimes an isolated, freestanding structure used for commemorative purposes.

**pinakotheke**—(pin-a-kō-'thē-kē) Greek, "picture gallery;" a room or building for the exhibition of paintings on wooden panels.

**pinnacle**—In *Gothic* churches, a sharply pointed ornament capping the *piers* or flying *buttresses;* also used on church *facades.*

**Pittura Metafisica**—(pēt-'tū-ra me-ta-'fē-sē-ka) Italian, "metaphysical painting." An early-20th-century Italian art movement led by Giorgio de Chirico, whose work conveys an eerie mood and visionary quality.

**plan**—The horizontal arrangement of the parts of a building or of the buildings and streets of a city or town, or a drawing or diagram showing such an arrangement. In an axial plan, the parts of a building are organized longitudinally, or along a given axis; in a central plan, the parts of the structure are of equal or almost equal dimensions around the center.

**plate tracery**—See *tracery.*

**Plateresque**—(plă-tŭr-'esk) A 15th- and 16th-century style of Spanish architecture characterized by elaborate decoration based on *Gothic,* Italian Renaissance, and Islamic sources; derived from the Spanish word *platero,* meaning "silversmith."

**plebeian**—(pli-'be-ŭn) The Roman social class that included small farmers, merchants, and freed slaves.

**plein air**—('plen-ār) An approach to painting much favored by the *Impressionists,* in which artists sketch outdoors to achieve a quick impression of light, air, and color. The sketches were then taken to the studio for reworking into more finished works of art.

**plinth**—The square slab at the *base* of a *column.*

**poesia**—(pō-e-zē-ŭ) A term describing "poetic" art, notably Venetian Renaissance paintings, which emphasizes the lyrical and sensual.

**pointed arch**—A narrow *arch* of pointed profile, in contrast to a semicircular arch.

**pointillism**—('poin-tŭ-liz-ŭm) A system of painting devised by the 19th-century French painter Georges Seurat. The artist separates color into its component parts and then applies the component colors to the canvas in tiny dots (points). The image becomes comprehensible only from a distance, when the viewer's eyes optically blend the pigment dots. Sometimes referred to as divisionism.

**polis** (pl. **poleis**)—('pa-lŭs/'pa-lās) An independent city-state in ancient Greece.

**polyptych**—('pa-lŭp-tĭk) An *altarpiece* made up of more than three sections.

**pontifex maximus**—Latin, "chief priest." The high priest of the Roman state religion, often the emperor himself.

**Pop art**—A term coined by British art critic Lawrence Alloway to refer to art, first appearing in the 1950s, that incorporated elements from consumer culture, the mass media, and popular culture, such as images from motion pictures and advertising.

**porcelain**—('por-sŭ-lŭn) Extremely fine, hard, white ceramic. Unlike stoneware, porcelain is made from a fine white clay called kaolin mixed with ground petuntse, a type of feldspar. True porcelain is translucent and rings when struck.

**portico**—('por-tŭ-kō) A roofed *colonnade;* also an entrance porch.

**post-and-lintel system**—A system of construction in which two posts support a *lintel.*

**postmodernism**—A reaction against *modernist formalism,* seen as elitist. Far more encompassing and accepting than the more rigid confines of modernist practice, postmodernism offers something for everyone by accommodating a wide range of styles, subjects, and formats, from traditional easel painting to *installation* and from abstraction to illusionistic scenes. Postmodern art often includes irony or reveals a self-conscious awareness on the part of the artist of the processes of art making or the workings of the art world.

**Post-Painterly Abstraction**—An American art movement that emerged in the 1960s and was characterized by a cool, detached rationality emphasizing tighter pictorial control. See also *color field painting* and *hard-edge painting.*

**pou tokomanawa**—('po-ŭ 'to-ko-ma-na-wa) A sculpture of an ancestor that supports a ridge pole of a Maori meetinghouse.

**pouncing**—The method of transferring a sketch onto paper by tracing, using thin, transparent gazelle skin placed on top of the sketch, pricking the contours of the design with a pin, placing the skin on paper, and forcing black pigment through the holes.

**poupou**—('po-ŭ-po-ŭ) A decorated wall panel in a Maori meetinghouse.

**prasada**—(pra-'sa-dŭ) In Hindu worship, food that becomes sacred by first being given to a god.

**pre-Columbian** (adj.)—The cultures that flourished in the Western Hemisphere before the arrival of Christopher Columbus and the beginning of European contact and conquest.

**Precisionists**—A group of American painters, active in the 1920s and 1930s, whose work concentrated on portraying man-made environments in a clear and concise manner to express the beauty of perfect and precise machine forms.

**predella**—(prŭ-ˈdel-lŭ) The narrow ledge on which an *altarpiece* rests on an altar.

**prefiguration**—In Early Christian art, the depiction of Old Testament persons and events as prophetic forerunners of Christ and New Testament events.

**Pre-Raphaelite Brotherhood**—A group of 19th-century artists who refused to be limited to contemporary scenes and chose instead to represent fictional, historical, and fanciful subjects in a style influenced by Italian artists before Raphael.

**primary colors**—Red, yellow, and blue—the colors from which all other colors may be derived.

**Productivism**—An art movement that emerged in the Soviet Union after the Revolution; its members believed that artists must direct art toward creating products for the new society.

**pronaos**—(ˈpro-nā-os) The space, or porch, in front of the *cella*, or *naos*, of an ancient Greek temple.

**prostyle**—(ˈprō-stīl) A style of ancient Greek temple in which the *columns* are only in front of the *cella* and not on the sides or back.

**provenance**—(ˈprō-vŭ-naⁿs) Origin or source; findspot.

**psalter**—(ˈsol-tŭr) A book containing the Psalms.

**pseudoperipteral**—(sū-dō-pŭ-ˈrip-tŭr-ŭl) In Roman architecture, a pseudoperipteral temple has a series of engaged *columns* all around the sides and back of the *cella* to give the appearance of a *peripteral colonnade*.

**pueblo**—(ˈpwe-blō) A communal multistoried dwelling made of stone or *adobe* brick by the Native Americans of the Southwest; with cap. also used to refer to various groups that occupied such dwellings.

**pukao**—(ˈpu-ka-ō) A small red scoria cylinder that appears as a hat on *moai*.

**purlins**—(ˈpŭr-lins) Horizontal beams in a roof structure, parallel to the *ridgepoles*, resting on the main rafters and giving support to the secondary rafters.

**putto** (pl. **putti**)—(ˈpū-tō/ˈpū-ti) A cherubic young boy.

**pylon**—(ˈpī-lan) The simple and massive gateway, with sloping walls, of an Egyptian temple.

**qibla**—(ˈkē-blŭ) The direction (toward Mecca) *Muslims* face when praying.

**quadrant arch**—An arch whose curve extends for one quarter of a circle's circumference.

**quadro riportato**—(ˈkwa-drō re-por-ˈta-tō) A ceiling design in which painted scenes are arranged in panels that resemble framed pictures transferred to the surface of a shallow, curved *vault*.

**quatrefoil**—(ˈka-trŭ-foil) A shape or plan in which the parts assume the form of a cloverleaf.

**quipu**—(ˈkē-pū) Andean record-keeping device made of fibers in which numerous knotted strings hung from a main cord were used

to record, by position and color, numbers and categories of things.

**quoins**—(kwoins) The large, sometimes *rusticated*, usually slightly projecting stones that often form the corners of the exterior walls of masonry buildings.

**radiating chapels**—In medieval churches, chapels for the display of *relics* that opened directly onto the *ambulatory* and the *transept*.

**radiocarbon dating**—Method of measuring the decay rate of carbon isotopes in organic matter to provide dates for organic materials such as wood and fiber.

**raking cornice**—The *cornice* on the sloping sides of a *pediment*.

**ramparts**—Defensive wall circuits.

**ratha**—(ˈrat-ha) Small, freestanding Hindu temple carved from a huge boulder.

**Rayonnant**—(rā-yō-ˈnaⁿ) The "radiant" style of *Gothic* architecture, dominant in the second half of the 13th century and associated with the French royal court of Louis IX at Paris.

**Realism**—A movement that emerged in mid-19th-century France. Realist artists represented the subject matter of everyday life (especially that which up until then had been considered inappropriate for depiction) in a relatively naturalistic mode.

**red-figure painting**—In later Greek pottery, the silhouetting of red figures against a black background, with painted linear details; the reverse of *black-figure painting*.

**refectory**—(rŭ-ˈfek-tŭ-rē) The dining hall of a Christian monastery.

**Regionalism**—A 20th-century American movement that portrayed American rural life in a clearly readable, realist style. Major Regionalists include Grant Wood and Thomas Hart Benton.

**register**—One of a series of superimposed bands or *friezes* in a pictorial narrative, or the particular levels on which motifs are placed.

**relics**—The body parts, clothing, or objects associated with a holy figure, such as the Buddha or Christ or a Christian *saint*.

**relief**—In sculpture, figures projecting from a background of which they are part. The degree of relief is designated high, low (*bas*), or sunken. In the last, the artist cuts the design into the surface so that the highest projecting parts of the image are no higher than the surface itself. See also *repoussé*.

**relieving triangle**—In Mycenaean architecture, the triangular opening above the *lintel* that serves to lighten the weight to be carried by the lintel itself.

**reliquary**—(ˈrel-ŭ-kwe-rē) A container for keeping *relics*.

**repoussé**—(rŭ-pū-ˈsā) Formed in *relief* by beating a metal plate from the back, leaving the impression on the face. The metal is hammered into a hollow mold of wood or some other pliable material and finished with a *graver*. See also *relief*.

**respond**—An engaged *column*, *pilaster*, or similar element that either projects from a *compound pier* or some other supporting device or is bonded to a wall and carries one end of an *arch*.

**retable**—(rē-ˈtā-bŭl) An architectural screen or wall above and behind an altar, usually containing painting, sculpture, carving, or other decorations. See also *altarpiece*.

**revetment**—(rŭ-ˈvet-mŭnt) In architecture, a wall covering or facing.

**rib**—A relatively slender, molded masonry *arch* that projects from a surface. In *Gothic* architecture, the ribs form the framework of the *vaulting*. A diagonal rib is one of the ribs that form the X of a *groin vault*. A transverse rib crosses the nave or aisle at a 90-degree angle.

**rib vault**—A *vault* in which the diagonal and transverse *ribs* compose a structural skeleton that partially supports the masonry *web* between them.

**ridgepole**—The beam running the length of a building below the peak of the gabled roof.

**Rococo**—(rō-kō-ˈkō) A style, primarily of interior design, that appeared in France around 1700. Rococo interiors were extensively decorated and included elegant furniture, small sculpture, ornamental mirrors, easel paintings, *tapestries*, reliefs, and wall painting.

**Romanesque**—(rō-mŭ-ˈnesk) "Romanlike." A term used to describe the history, culture, and art of medieval western Europe from ca. 1050 to ca. 1200.

**Romanticism**—A Western cultural phenomenon, beginning around 1750 and ending about 1850, that gave precedence to feeling and imagination over reason and thought. More narrowly, the art movement that flourished from about 1800 to 1840.

**roof comb**—The elaborately sculpted vertical projection surmounting a Maya temple-pyramid.

**rose window**—A circular *stained-glass* window.

**rotulus**—(ˈrat-yū-lŭs) The manuscript scroll used by Egyptians, Greeks, Etruscans, and Romans; predecessor of the *codex*.

**rotunda**—(rō-ˈtŭnd-ŭ) The circular area under a *dome*; also a domed round building.

**roundel**—See *tondo*.

**rusticate**—To give a rustic appearance by roughening the surfaces and beveling the edges of stone blocks to emphasize the joints between them. Rustication is a technique employed in ancient Roman architecture, and popular during the Renaissance, especially for stone courses at the ground-floor level.

**sabi**—(ˈsa-bĭ) The value found in the old and weathered, suggesting the tranquility reached in old age.

**sacra conversazione**—(ˈsa-kra kno-ver-sa-tsē-o-nā) Italian, "holy conversation"; a style of *altarpiece* painting popular after the middle of the 15th century, in which saints from different epochs are joined in a unified space and seem to be conversing either with each other or with the audience.

**saint**—From the Latin word *sanctus,* meaning "made holy by God." Persons who suffered and died for their Christian faith or who merited reverence for their Christian devotion while alive. In the Roman Catholic Church, a worthy deceased Catholic who is canonized by the pope.

**samsara**—(sŭm-ˈsa-rŭ) In Hindu belief, the rebirth of the soul into a succession of lives.

**samurai**—(ˈsam-ŭ-rī) Medieval Japanese warriors.

**sarcophagus** (pl. **sarcophagi**)—(sar-ˈkof-ŭ-gŭs/sar-ˈkof-ŭ-gī) Latin, "consumer of flesh." A coffin, usually of stone.

**satyr**—(ˈsāt-ŭr) A part-human, part-goat male follower of the ancient Greek god Dionysos.

**saz**—(săz) An Ottoman Turkish design of sinuous curved leaves and blossoms.

**scarification**—(ˈscar-ŭ-fŭ-cā-zhŭn) Decorative markings made with scars on the human body.

**school**—A chronological and stylistic classification of works of art with a stipulation of place.

**scriptorium** (pl. **scriptoria**)—(skrip-ˈtor-ē-um/skrip-ˈtor-ē-ŭ) The writing studio of a monastery.

**sculpture in the round**—Freestanding figures, carved or modeled in three dimensions.

**Second Style mural**—The style of Roman mural painting in which the aim was to dissolve the confining walls of a room and replace them with the illusion of a three-dimensional world constructed in the artist's imagination.

**secondary colors**—Orange, green, and purple, obtained by mixing pairs of *primary colors* (red, yellow, blue).

**section**—In architecture, a diagram or representation of a part of a structure or building along an imaginary plane that passes through it vertically. Drawings showing a theoretical slice, or cross-section, across a structure's width are lateral sections. Those cutting through a building's length are longitudinal sections. See also *elevation* and *cutaway.*

**senate**—Latin, "council of elders." The legislative body in Roman constitutional government.

**serdab**—(sŭ(r)-ˈdab) A small concealed chamber in an Egyptian *mastaba* for the statue of the deceased.

**sexpartite vault**—(seks-ˈpar-tīt *vault*) See *vault.*

**sfumato**—(sfū-ˈma-tō) A smokelike haziness that subtly softens outlines in painting; particularly applied to the painting of Leonardo and Correggio.

**sgrafitto**—(skraf-ˈfē-tō) A Chinese ceramic technique in which the design is *incised* through a colored *slip.*

**shaft**—The tall, cylindrical part of a *column* between the *capital* and the *base.*

**shakti**—(ˈshak-tē) In Hinduism, the female power of the deity Devi (or Goddess), which animates the matter of the cosmos.

**shikara**—The beehive-shaped tower of a Hindu temple.

**shogun**—(ˈshō-gŭn) In 14th- through 19th-century Japan, a military governor who managed the country on behalf of a figurehead emperor.

**silverpoint**—A *stylus* made of silver, used in drawing in the 14th and 15th centuries because of the fine line it produced and the sharp point it maintained.

**siren**—In ancient Greek mythology, a creature that was part bird, part woman.

**skenographia**—(skā-no-gra-ˈfē-ŭ) Greek, "scene painting"; the Greek term for *perspective* painting.

**skiagraphia**—(skē-u-gra-ˈfē-ŭ) Greek, "shadow painting"; the Greek term for shading, said to have been invented by Apollodoros, an Athenian painter of the fifth century BCE.

**slip**—A mixture of fine clay and water used in ceramic decoration.

**spandrel**—(ˈspăn-drŭl) The roughly triangular space enclosed by the curves of adjacent *arches* and a horizontal member connecting their vertexes; also, the space enclosed by the curve of an *arch* and an enclosing right angle. The area between the arch proper and the framing *columns* and *entablature.*

**sphinx**—(sfengks) A mythical Egyptian beast with the body of a lion and the head of a human.

**splayed**—An opening (as in a wall) that is cut away diagonally so that the outer edges are farther apart than the inner edges. See also *embrasure.*

**springing**—The lowest stone of an *arch,* resting on the *impost block.* In *Gothic* vaulting, the lowest stone of a diagonal or transverse *rib.*

**squinch**—(skwinch) An architectural device used as a transition from a square to a polygonal or circular base for a *dome.* It may be composed of *lintels, corbels,* or *arches.*

**stained glass**—In *Gothic* architecture, the colored glass used for windows.

**stanza** (pl. **stanze**)—(ˈstan-zā/ˈstan-zē) Italian, "room."

**stave**—A wedge-shaped timber; vertically placed staves embellish the architectural features of the building.

**stele**—(ˈstē-lē) A carved stone slab used to mark graves or to commemorate historical events.

**stigmata**—(stĭg-ˈma-tŭ) In Christian art, the wounds that Christ received at his crucifixion that miraculously appear on the body of a saint.

**still life**—A picture depicting an arrangement of objects.

**stoa**—(ˈsto-ŭ) In ancient Greek architecture, an open building with a roof supported by a row of *columns* parallel to the back wall. A covered *colonnade* or *portico.*

**stoneware**—Pottery fired at high temperatures to produce a stonelike hardness and density.

**stringcourse**—A raised horizontal *molding,* or band in masonry, ornamental but usually reflecting interior structure.

**stupa**—(ˈstū-pŭ) A large, mound-shaped Buddhist shrine.

**stylobate**—(ˈstī-lŭ-bāt) The uppermost course of the platform of a Greek temple, which supports the *columns.*

**stylus**—(ˈstī-lŭs) A needlelike tool used in *engraving* and *incising;* also, an ancient writing instrument used to inscribe clay or wax tablets.

**subtractive sculpture**—A kind of sculpture technique in which materials are taken away from the original mass; carving.

**sultan**—A *Muslim* ruler.

**sunken relief**—See *relief.*

**Sunnah**—(ˈsu-nŭ) Collection of the Prophet Muhammad's moral sayings and descriptions of his deeds.

**superimposed orders**—*Orders* of architecture that are placed one above another in an *arcaded* or *colonnaded* building, usually in the following sequence: *Doric* (the first story), *Ionic,* and *Corinthian.* Superimposed orders are found in later Greek architecture and were used widely by Roman and Renaissance builders.

**superimposition**—The nesting of earlier structures within later ones, a common *Mesoamerican* building trait.

**Superrealism**—A school of painting and sculpture of the 1960s and 1970s that emphasized producing artworks based on scrupulous fidelity to optical fact. The Superrealist painters were also called Photorealists because many used photographs as sources for their imagery.

**Suprematism**—A type of art formulated by Kazimir Malevich to convey his belief that the supreme reality in the world is pure feeling, which attaches to no object and thus calls for new, nonobjective forms in art—shapes not related to objects in the visible world.

**surahs**—(ˈsu-rŭs) Chapters of the *Koran,* divided into verses.

**Surrealism**—A successor to *Dada,* Surrealism incorporated the improvisational nature of its predecessor into its exploration of the ways to express in art the world of dreams and the unconscious. Biomorphic Surrealists, such as Joan Miró, produced largely abstract compositions. Naturalistic Surrealists, notably Salvador Dalí, presented recognizable scenes transformed into a dream or nightmare image.

**sutra**—(ˈsū-trŭ) In Buddhism, an account of a sermon by or a dialogue involving the Buddha. A scriptural account of the Buddha. See also *jataka.*

**Symbolism**—A late-19th-century movement based on the idea that the artist was not an imitator of nature but a creator who transformed the facts of nature into a symbol of the inner experience of that fact.

**symmetria**—(sim-ŭ-ʹtrē-ŭ) Greek, "commensurability of parts." Polykleitos's treatise on his *canon* of proportions incorporated the principle of symmetria.

**Synthetic Cubism**—A later phase of *Cubism,* in which paintings and drawings were constructed from objects and shapes cut from paper or other materials to represent parts of a subject, in order to engage the viewer with pictorial issues, such as figuration, realism, and abstraction.

**taberna**—(ta-ʹber-na) In Roman architecture, a single-room shop usually covered by a barrel *vault.*

**tablinum**—(ʹta-bli-num) The study or office in a Roman house.

**tapa**—(ta-pa) Barkcloth made particularly in Polynesia. Tapa is often dyed, painted, stenciled, and sometimes perfumed.

**tapestry**—A weaving technique in which the *weft* threads are packed densely over the *warp* threads so that the designs are woven directly into the fabric.

**tarashikomi**—(ta-ra-shi-ko-mē) In Japanese art, a painting technique involving the dropping of ink and pigments onto surfaces still wet with previously applied ink and pigments.

**tatami**—(ta-ta-mē) The traditional woven straw mat used for floor covering in Japanese architecture.

**technique**—The processes that artists employ to create *form,* as well as the distinctive, personal ways in which they handle their materials and tools.

**tempera**—(ʹtem-pŭ-rŭ) A technique of painting using pigment mixed with egg yolk, glue, or casein; also the *medium* itself.

**templon**—(ʹtem-plan) The columnar screen separating the sanctuary from the main body of a Byzantine church.

**tenebrism**—(ʹten-ŭ-briz(-ŭ)m) Painting in the "dark manner," using violent contrasts of light and dark, as in the work of Caravaggio.

**tenon**—(ʹte-nŭn) A projection on the end of a piece of wood that is inserted into a corresponding hole (mortise) in another piece of wood to form a joint.

**tenoned**—Attached by stone pegs.

**tepidarium**—(tep-ŭ-ʹdă-rē-ŭm) The warmbath section of a Roman bathing establishment.

**terracotta**—(te-rŭ-ʹko-tŭ) Hard-baked clay, used for sculpture and as a building material. It may be *glazed* or painted.

**tesserae**—(ʹtes-ŭ-rē) Greek, "cubes." Tiny stones or pieces of glass cut to the desired shape and size to form a *mosaic.*

**tetrarchy**—(te-ʹtrar-kē) Greek, "rule by four." A type of Roman government established in the late third century CE by Diocletian in an attempt to establish order by sharing power with potential rivals.

**texture**—The quality of a surface (rough, smooth, hard, soft, shiny, dull) as revealed by light. In represented texture, a painter depicts an object as having a certain texture even though the paint is the actual texture.

**theatron**—(thē-ʹăt-ron) Greek, "place for seeing." In ancient Greek theaters, the slope overlooking the *orchestra* on which the spectators sat.

**Theotokos**—(thē-ʹō-tō-kos) Greek, "bearer of God." The Virgin Mary, the mother of Jesus.

**thermoluminescence**—(ʹthŏr-mō-lū-mŭ-ʹne-sŭns) A method of dating amounts of radiation found within the clay of ceramic or sculptural forms, as well as in the clay cores from metal castings.

**Third Style mural**—In Roman mural painting, the style in which delicate linear fantasies were sketched on predominantly monochromatic backgrounds.

**tholos** (pl. **tholoi**)—(ʹthō-los/ʹthō-loi) A temple with a circular plan.

**tholos tomb**—In Mycenean architecture, a beehive-shaped tomb with a circular plan.

**thrust**—The outward force exerted by an *arch* or a *vault* that must be counterbalanced by a *buttress.*

**tiki**—A Marquesan three-dimensional carving of an exalted, deified ancestor figure.

**togu na**—(tō-gū na) "House of words." The Dogon (Mali) men's house, where deliberations vital to community welfare take place.

**tokonoma**—(to-ko-no-ma) A shallow alcove in a Japanese room, which is used for decoration, such as a painting or stylized flower arrangement.

**tondo**—(ʹton-dō) A circular painting or *relief* sculpture.

**Torah**—(ʹto-rŭ) The scroll containing the Pentateuch, the first five books of the Hebrew Scriptures.

**torana**—(ʹto-ra-na) Gateway in the stone fence around a *stupa,* located at the cardinal points of the compass.

**torque**—(tork) The neck band worn by Gauls.

**tracery**—Ornamental stonework for holding *stained glass* in place, characteristic of *Gothic* cathedrals. In plate tracery the glass fills only the "punched holes" in the heavy ornamental stonework. In bar tracery the stained-glass windows fill almost the entire opening, and the stonework is unobtrusive.

**transept**—(ʹtrăn-sept) The part of a church with an axis that crosses the nave at a right angle.

**transverse arch**—An *arch* separating one vaulted *bay* from the next.

**transverse rib**—See *rib.*

**treasury**—In ancient Greece, a small building set up for the safe storage of *votive offerings.*

**trefoil**—(ʹtrē-foil) A cloverlike ornament or symbol with stylized leaves in groups of three.

**tribune**—In church architecture, a gallery over the inner *aisle* flanking the *nave.*

**triclinium**—(tri-ʹklin-ē-um) The dining room of a Roman house.

**trident**—The three-pronged pitchfork associated with the ancient Greek sea god Poseidon (Roman, Neptune).

**triforium**—(tri-ʹfor-ē-ŭm) In a *Gothic* cathedral, the *blind arcaded* gallery below the *clerestory;* occasionally the arcades are filled with *stained glass.*

**triglyph**—(ʹtri-glif) A triple projecting, grooved member of a *Doric frieze* that alternates with *metopes.*

**trilithons**—(ʹtri-lith-onz) A pair of *monoliths* topped with a *lintel;* found in *megalithic* structures.

**triptych**—(ʹtrip-tik) A three-paneled painting or *altarpiece.*

**triumphal arch**—In Roman architecture, a freestanding *arch* commemorating an important event, such as a military victory or the opening of a new road. In Christian architecture, the arch framing the *apse* at the end of a church *nave.*

**trompe l'oeil**—(troⁿp ʹloi) French, "fools the eye." A form of illusionistic painting that aims to deceive viewers into believing that they are seeing real objects rather than a representation of those objects.

**true fresco**—See *fresco.*

**tukutuku**—(ʹtu-ku-tu-ku) A stitched lattice panel found in a Maori meetinghouse.

**trumeau**—(trū-ʹmō) In church architecture, the *pillar* or center post supporting the *lintel* in the middle of the doorway.

**tumulus** (pl. **tumuli**)—(ʹtū-myū-lus/ʹtū-myū-li) Burial mound; in Etruscan architecture, tumuli cover one or more subterranean multichambered tombs cut out of the local tufa (limestone). Also characteristic of the Japanese Kofun period of the third and fourth centuries.

**tunnel vault**—See *vault.*

**Tuscan column**—The standard type of Etruscan *column.* Resembles ancient Greek *Doric* columns, but is made of wood, is unfluted, and has a *base.*

**twisted perspective**—A convention of representation in which part of a figure is shown in profile and another part of the same figure is shown frontally; a composite view.

**tympanum**—(ʹtim-pŭ-nŭm) The space enclosed by a *lintel* and an *arch* over a doorway.

**ukiyo-e**—(ū-kē-yō-ā) Japanese, "pictures of the floating world." A style of Japanese *genre* painting that influenced 19th-century Western art.

**underglaze**—In *porcelain* decoration, the technique of applying of mineral colors to the surface before the main firing, followed by an application of clear *glaze.* See also *overglaze.*

**urna**—(ʹŭr-nŭ) A whorl of hair, represented as a dot, between the brows; one of the *lakshanas* of the Buddha.

**ushabti**—(ū-ʹshăb-te) In ancient Egypt, a figurine placed in a tomb to act as a servant to the deceased in the afterlife.

**ushnisha**—(ūsh-ʹnesh-ha) A knot of hair on the top of the head; one of the *lakshanas* of the Buddha.

**value**—See *color.*

**vanitas**—(ʹva-nē-tas) A term describing paintings (particularly 17th-century Dutch still lifes) that include references to death.

**vault**—A masonry roof or ceiling constructed on the *arch* principle. A barrel or tunnel vault, semicylindrical in cross-*section,* is in effect a deep arch or an uninterrupted series of arches, one behind the other, over an oblong space. A quadrant vault is a half-barrel vault. A groin or cross vault is formed at the point at which two barrel vaults intersect at right angles. In a ribbed vault, there is a framework of *ribs* or arches under the intersections of the vaulting sections. A sexpartite vault is a vault whose ribs divide the vault into six compartments. A fan vault is a vault characteristic of English Perpendicular *Gothic,* in which radiating ribs form a fanlike pattern.

**veda**—(ˈvād-ŭ) Sanskrit, "knowledge."

**veduta**—(ve-ˈdū-ta) Italian, "view." A type of naturalistic landscape and cityscape painting popular in 18th-century Venice.

**velarium**—(ve-ˈlar-ē-ŭm) In a Roman *amphitheater,* the cloth awning that could be rolled down from the top of the *cavea* to shield spectators from sun or rain.

**vellum**—Calfskin prepared as a surface for writing or painting.

**veristic**—(ver-ˈis-tik) True to natural appearance.

**vihara**—(vē-ˈha-ra) A Buddhist monastery, often cut into a hill.

**vimana**—(vĭ-ˈma-na) A pyramidal tower over the *garbha griha* of a Hindu temple of the southern, or Dravida, style.

**volute**—(vŭ-ˈlūt) A spiral, scroll-like form characteristic of the ancient Greek *Ionic* and the Roman *Composite capital.*

**votive offering**—A gift of gratitude to a deity.

**voussoir**—(vū-ˈswar) A wedge-shaped block used in the construction of a true *arch.* The central voussoir, which sets the arch, is the keystone.

**wabi**—(wa-bē) A 16th-century Japanese art style characterized by refined rusticity and an appreciation of simplicity and austerity.

**waka sran**—(wa-ka sran) "People of wood." Baule (Côte d'Ivoire) wooden figural sculptures.

**wall arcade**—See *blind arcade.*

**warp**—The vertical threads of a loom or cloth.

**wat**—(wat) A Buddhist monastery in Cambodia.

**web**—In *Gothic* architecture, the masonry blocks that fill the area between the *ribs* of a groin *vault.*

**weft**—The horizontal threads of a loom or cloth.

**westwork**—The *facade* and towers at the western end of a medieval church, principally in Germany.

**wet fresco**—See *fresco.*

**white-ground painting**—An ancient Greek vase painting technique in which the pot was first covered with a *slip* of very fine white clay, over which black *glaze* was used to outline figures, and diluted brown, purple, red, and white were used to color them.

**woodcut**—A wooden block on the surface of which those parts not intended to print are cut away to a slight depth, leaving the design raised; also, the printed impression made with such a block.

**yaksha/yakshi**—(ˈyak-shŭ/ˈyak-shē) Lesser local male and female Buddhist and Hindu divinities. Yakshis are goddesses associated with fertility and vegetation. Yakshas, the male equivalent of yakshis, are often represented as corpulent, powerful males.

**yamato-e**—(ya-ma-tō-ā) Also known as native-style painting, a purely Japanese style that often involved colorful, decorative representations of Japanese narratives or *landscapes.*

**yang**—In Chinese cosmology, the principle of active masculine energy, which permeates the universe in varying proportions with yin, the principle of passive feminine energy.

**yasti**—(ˈyas-tē) In Buddhist architecture, the mast or pole that arises from the dome of the *stupa* and its *harmika* and symbolizes the axis of the universe; it is adorned with a series of chatras (stone disks).

**yin**—See *yang.*

**yoga**—See *nihonga.*

**Zen**—A Japanese Buddhist sect and its doctrine, emphasizing enlightenment through intuition and introspection rather than the study of scripture. In Chinese, Chan.

**ziggurat**—(ˈzig-ŭ-rot) In ancient Mesopotamian architecture, a monumental platform for a temple.

# BIBLIOGRAPHY

*This list of books is intended to be comprehensive enough to satisfy the reading interests of the beginning art history student and general reader, as well as those of more advanced readers who wish to become acquainted with fields other than their own. The resources listed range from works that are valuable primarily for their reproductions to those that are scholarly surveys of schools and periods. No entries for periodical articles appear, but some of the major periodicals that publish art-historical scholarship in English are noted.*

## SELECTED PERIODICALS

The following list is by no means exhaustive. Students wishing to pursue research in journals should contact their instructor, their college or university's reference librarian, or the online catalogue for additional titles.

*African Arts*
*American Indian Art*
*American Journal of Archaeology*
*Archaeology*
*Archives of Asian Art*
*Ars Orientalis*
*The Art Bulletin*
*Art History*
*The Art Journal*
*The Burlington Magazine*
*Journal of the Society of Architectural Historians*
*Journal of the Warburg and Courtauld Institutes*
*Latin American Antiquity*
*Oxford Art Journal*

## GENERAL STUDIES

Arntzen, Etta, and Robert Rainwater. *Guide to the Literature of Art History.* Chicago: American Library Association, 1981.

Bator, Paul M. *The International Trade in Art.* Chicago: University of Chicago Press, 1988.

Baxandall, Michael. *Patterns of Intention: On the Historical Explanation of Pictures.* New Haven: Yale University Press, 1985.

Bindman, David, ed. *The Thames & Hudson Encyclopedia of British Art.* London: Thames & Hudson, 1988.

Broude, Norma, and Mary D. Garrard, eds. *The Expanding Discourse: Feminism and Art History.* New York: Harper Collins, 1992.

———. *Feminism and Art History: Questioning the Litany.* New York: Harper & Row, 1982.

Bryson, Norman. *Vision and Painting: The Logic of the Gaze.* New Haven: Yale University Press, 1983.

Bryson, Norman, Michael Ann Holly, and Keith Moxey. *Visual Theory: Painting and Interpretation.* New York: Cambridge University Press, 1991.

Cahn, Walter. *Masterpieces: Chapters on the History of an Idea.* Princeton, N.J.: Princeton University Press, 1979.

Chadwick, Whitney. *Women, Art, and Society.* New York: Thames & Hudson, 1990.

Cheetham, Mark A., Michael Ann Holly, and Keith Moxey, eds. *The Subjects of Art History: Historical Objects in Contemporary Perspective.* New York: Cambridge University Press, 1998.

Chilvers, Ian, and Harold Osborne, eds. *The Oxford Dictionary of Art.* Rev. ed. New York: Oxford University Press, 1997.

Cummings, P. *Dictionary of Contemporary American Artists.* 6th ed. New York: St. Martin's Press, 1994.

Deepwell, K., ed. *New Feminist Art.* Manchester: Manchester University Press, 1994.

Derrida, Jacques. *The Truth in Painting.* Chicago: University of Chicago Press, 1987.

*Encyclopedia of World Art.* 15 vols. New York: Publisher's Guild, 1959–1968. Supplementary vols. 16, 1983; 17, 1987.

Fielding, Mantle. *Dictionary of American Painters, Sculptors, and Engravers.* 2nd rev. and enl. ed. Poughkeepsie, N.Y.: Apollo, 1986.

Fleming, John, Hugh Honour, and Nikolaus Pevsner. *Penguin Dictionary of Architecture.* 4th ed. New York: Penguin, 1991.

Frazier, Nancy. *The Penguin Concise Dictionary of Art History.* New York: Penguin, 2000.

Freedberg, David. *The Power of Images: Studies in the History and Theory of Response.* Chicago: University of Chicago Press, 1989.

Giedion, Siegfried. *Space, Time and Architecture: The Growth of a New Tradition.* 5th ed. Cambridge, Mass.: Harvard University Press, 1982.

Gombrich, Ernst Hans Josef. *Art and Illusion.* 5th ed. London: Phaidon, 1977.

Haggar, Reginald G. *A Dictionary of Art Terms: Architecture, Sculpture, Painting, and the Graphic Arts.* Poole: New Orchard Editions, 1984.

Hall, James. *Dictionary of Subjects and Symbols in Art.* 2nd rev. ed. London: J. Murray, 1979.

Harris, Anne Sutherland, and Linda Nochlin. *Women Artists: 1550–1950.* Los Angeles: Los Angeles County Museum of Art; New York: Knopf, 1977.

Hauser, Arnold. *The Sociology of Art.* Chicago: University of Chicago Press, 1982.

Hind, Arthur M. *A History of Engraving and Etching from the Fifteenth Century to the Year 1914.* 3rd rev. ed. New York: Dover, 1963.

Holt, Elizabeth Gilmore, ed. *A Documentary History of Art.* 2nd ed. 2 vols. Princeton, N.J.: Princeton University Press, 1981.

Hults, Linda C. *The Print in the Western World: An Introductory History.* Madison: University of Wisconsin Press, 1996.

Kostof, Spiro. *A History of Architecture: Settings and Rituals.* 2nd ed. Oxford: Oxford University Press, 1995.

Kronenberger, Louis. *Atlantic Brief Lives: A Biographical Companion to the Arts.* Boston: Little, Brown, 1971.

Kultermann, Udo. *The History of Art History.* New York: Abaris, 1993.

Lucie-Smith, Edward. *The Thames & Hudson Dictionary of Art Terms.* London: Thames & Hudson, 1984.

Murray, Peter, and Linda Murray. *A Dictionary of Art and Artists.* 5th ed. New York: Penguin, 1988.

Myers, Bernard S., ed. *Encyclopedia of Painting: Painters and Painting of the World from Prehistoric Times to the Present Day.* 4th rev. ed. New York: Crown, 1979.

Myers, Bernard S., and Myers, Shirley D., eds. *Dictionary of 20th-Century Art.* New York: McGraw-Hill, 1974.

Nelson, Robert S., and Richard Shiff, eds. *Critical Terms for Art History.* Chicago: University of Chicago Press, 1996.

Osborne, Harold, ed. *The Oxford Companion to 20th Century Art.* New York: Oxford University Press, 1981.

Parker, Rozsika, and Griselda Pollock. *Old Mistresses: Women, Art, and Ideology.* London: Routledge & Kegan Paul, 1981.

Penny, Nicholas. *The Materials of Sculpture.* New Haven: Yale University Press, 1993.

Pevsner, Nikolaus. *A History of Building Types.* London: Thames & Hudson, 1987. Reprint of 1979 ed.

———. *An Outline of European Architecture.* 8th ed. Baltimore: Penguin, 1974.

———. *The Buildings of England.* 46 vols. Harmondsworth: Penguin, 1951–1974.

Pierce, James Smith. *From Abacus to Zeus: A Handbook of Art History.* 7th ed. Upper Saddle River, N.J.: Pearson Prentice Hall, 1998.

Placzek, Adolf K., ed. *Macmillan Encyclopedia of Architects.* 4 vols. New York: Macmillan, 1982.

Podro, Michael. *The Critical Historians of Art.* New Haven: Yale University Press, 1982.

Pollock, Griselda. *Vision and Difference: Femininity, Feminism and Histories of Art.* London: Routledge, 1988.

Preziosi, Donald, ed. *The Art of Art History: A Critical Anthology.* New York: Oxford University Press, 1998.

Reid, Jane D. *The Oxford Guide to Classical Mythology in the Arts 1300–1990s.* 2 vols. New York: Oxford University Press, 1993.

Rosenblum, Naomi. *A World History of Photography.* New York: Abbeville, 1984.

Roth, Leland M. *Understanding Architecture: Its Elements, History, and Meaning.* New York: Harper & Row, 1993.

Rubenstein, Charlotte Streifer. *American Women Artists from Early Indian Times to the Present.* Boston: G. K. Hall/Avon Books, 1982.

Slatkin, Wendy. *Women Artists in History: From Antiquity to the 20th Century.* 2nd ed. Upper Saddle River, N.J.: Prentice Hall, 1985.

Smith, Alistair, ed. *The Larousse Dictionary of Painters.* New York: Larousse, 1981.

Smith, G. E. Kidder. *The Architecture of the United States: An Illustrated Guide to Buildings Open to the Public.* 3 vols. Garden City, N.J.: Doubleday/Anchor, 1981.

Stangos, Nikos. *The Thames & Hudson Dictionary of Art and Artists.* Rev. ed. New York: Thames & Hudson, 1994.

Steer, John, and Antony White. *Atlas of Western Art History: Artists, Sites and Monuments from Ancient Greece to the Modern Age.* New York: Facts on File, 1994.

Stratton, Arthur. *The Orders of Architecture: Greek, Roman and Renaissance.* London: Studio, 1986.

Sutton, Ian. *Western Architecture: From Ancient Greece to the Present.* New York: Thames & Hudson, 1999.

Trachtenberg, Marvin, and Isabelle Hyman. *Architecture, from Prehistory to Post-Modernism.* New York: Abrams, 1986.

Tufts, Eleanor. *American Women Artists, Past and Present: A Selected Bibliographic Guide.* New York: Garland Publishers, 1984.

———. *Our Hidden Heritage: Five Centuries of Women Artists.* London: Paddington Press, 1974.

Turner, Jane, ed. *The Dictionary of Art.* 34 vols. New York: Grove Dictionaries, 1996.

Van Pelt, R., and Carroll William Westfall. *Architectural Principles in the Age of Historicism.* New Haven: Yale University Press, 1991.

Waterhouse, Ellis. *The Dictionary of British 18th Century Painters in Oils and Crayons.* Woodbridge, England: Antique Collectors' Club, 1981.

Wittkower, Rudolf. *Sculpture Processes and Principles.* New York: Harper & Row, 1977.

Wölfflin, Heinrich. *The Sense of Form in Art.* New York: Chelsea, 1958.

Young, William, ed. *A Dictionary of American Artists, Sculptors, and Engravers.* Cambridge, Mass.: W. Young, 1968.

### ANCIENT ART, GENERAL

Aruz, Joan, and Ronald Wallenfels, eds. *Art of the First Cities: The Third Millennium B.C. from the Mediterranean to the Indus.* New York: Metropolitan Museum of Art, 2003.

Boardman, John, ed. *The Oxford History of Classical Art.* New York: Oxford University Press, 1997.

Clayton, Peter A., and Martin J. Price, eds. *The Seven Wonders of the Ancient World.* New York: Routledge, 1988.

Connolly, Peter, and Hazel Dodge. *The Ancient City: Life in Classical Athens and Rome.* New York: Oxford University Press, 1998.

Davies, W. Vivian, and Louise Schofield, eds. *Egypt, the Aegean and the Levant: Interconnections in the Second Millennium BC.* London: British Museum Press, 1995.

De Grummond, Nancy Thomson, ed. *An Encyclopedia of the History of Classical Archaeology.* 2 vols. Westport, Conn.: Greenwood, 1996.

Dunbabin, Katherine. *Mosaics of the Greek and Roman World.* New York: Cambridge University Press, 1999.

Kampen, Natalie B., ed. *Sexuality in Ancient Art.* New York: Cambridge University Press, 1996.

*Lexicon Iconographicum Mythologiae Classicae.* Zurich: Artemis, 1981.

Ling, Roger. *Ancient Mosaics.* Princeton, N.J.: Princeton University Press, 1998.

Lloyd, Seton, and Hans Wolfgang Muller. *Ancient Architecture: Mesopotamia, Egypt, Crete.* New York: Electa/Rizzoli, 1980.

Oliphant, Margaret. *The Atlas of the Ancient World: Charting the Great Civilizations of the Past.* New York: Simon & Schuster, 1992.

Onians, John. *Classical Art and the Cultures of Greece and Rome.* New Haven: Yale University Press, 1999.

Renfrew, Colin, and Paul G. Bahn. *Archaeology: Theories, Methods, and Practices.* London: Thames & Hudson, 1991.

Saggs, H.W.F. *Civilization before Greece and Rome.* New Haven: Yale University Press, 1989.

Stillwell, Richard, William L. MacDonald, and Marian H. McAllister, eds. *The Princeton Encyclopedia of Classical Sites.* Princeton, N.J.: Princeton University Press, 1976.

Ward-Perkins, John B. *Cities of Ancient Greece and Italy: Planning in Classical Antiquity.* Rev. ed. New York: Braziller, 1987.

White, Randall. *Prehistoric Art: The Symbolic Journey of Humankind.* New York: Abrams, 2003.

Wolf, Walther. *The Origins of Western Art: Egypt, Mesopotamia, the Aegean.* New York: Universe, 1989.

### CHAPTER 1
### THE BIRTH OF ART:
### AFRICA, EUROPE, AND THE NEAR EAST IN THE STONE AGE

Bahn, Paul G. *The Cambridge Illustrated History of Prehistoric Art.* New York: Cambridge University Press, 1998.

Bahn, Paul G., and Jean Vertut. *Journey through the Ice Age.* Berkeley: University of California Press, 1997.

Beltrán, Antonio, ed. *The Cave of Altamira.* New York: Abrams, 1999.

Burl, Aubrey. *Great Stone Circles.* New Haven: Yale University Press, 1999.

Chauvet, Jean-Marie, Eliette Brunel Deschamps, and Christian Hillaire. *Dawn of Art: The Chauvet Cave.* New York: Abrams, 1996.

Chippindale, Christopher. *Stonehenge Complete.* New York: Thames & Hudson, 1994.

Cunliffe, Barry, ed. *The Oxford Illustrated Prehistory of Europe.* New York: Oxford University Press, 1994.

Kenyon, Kathleen M. *Digging Up Jericho.* New York: Praeger, 1974.

Leroi-Gourhan, André. *The Dawn of European Art: An Introduction to Paleolithic Cave Painting.* Cambridge: Cambridge University Press, 1982.

———. *Treasures of Prehistoric Art.* New York: Abrams, 1967.

Marshack, Alexander. *The Roots of Civilization: The Cognitive Beginnings of Man's First Art, Symbol and Notation.* 2nd ed. Wakefield, R.I.: Moyer Bell, 1991.

Mellaart, James. *Çatal Hüyük: A Neolithic Town in Anatolia.* New York: McGraw-Hill, 1967.

———. *The Neolithic of the Near East.* New York: Scribner, 1975.

Pfeiffer, John E. *The Creative Explosion: An Inquiry into the Origins of Art and Religion.* New York: Harper & Row, 1982.

Piggott, Stuart. *Ancient Europe.* Chicago: Aldine, 1966.

Renfrew, Colin, ed. *British Prehistory: A New Outline.* London: Noyes Press, 1975.

Ruspoli, Mario. *The Cave of Lascaux: The Final Photographs.* New York: Abrams, 1987.

Scarre, Chris. *Exploring Prehistoric Europe.* New York: Oxford University Press, 1998.

Ucko, Peter J., and Andrée Rosenfeld. *Palaeolithic Cave Art.* New York: McGraw-Hill, 1967.

Wainwright, Geoffrey. *The Henge Monuments: Ceremony and Society in Prehistoric Britain.* London: Thames & Hudson, 1990.

White, Randall. *Prehistoric Art: The Symbolic Journey of Humankind.* New York: Abrams, 2003.

### CHAPTER 2
### THE RISE OF CIVILIZATION:
### THE ART OF THE ANCIENT NEAR EAST

Akurgal, Ekrem. *Art of the Hittites.* New York: Abrams, 1962.

Amiet, Pierre. *Art of the Ancient Near East.* New York: Abrams, 1980.

Bienkowski, Piotr, and Alan Millard, eds. *Dictionary of the Ancient Near East.* Philadelphia: University of Pennsylvania Press, 2000.

Collon, Dominique. *Ancient Near Eastern Art.* Berkeley: University of California Press, 1995.

———. *First Impressions: Cylinder Seals in the Ancient Near East.* 2nd ed. London: British Museum, 1993.

———. *Near Eastern Seals.* Berkeley: University of California Press, 1990.

Crawford, Harriet. *Sumer and the Sumerians.* New York: Cambridge University Press, 1991.

Curtis, John E. *Ancient Persia.* Cambridge, Mass.: Harvard University Press, 1990.

Curtis, John E., and Julian E. Reade. *Art and Empire: Treasures from Assyria in the British Museum.* New York: Metropolitan Museum of Art, 1995.

Frankfort, Henri. *The Art and Architecture of the Ancient Orient.* 5th ed. New Haven: Yale University Press, 1996.

Ghirshman, Roman. *The Arts of Ancient Iran: From Its Origins to the Time of Alexander the Great.* New York: Golden Press, 1964.

———. *Persian Art: The Parthian and Sassanian Dynasties, 249 B.C.—A.D. 651.* New York: Golden Press, 1962.

Gunter, Ann C., ed. *Investigating Artistic Environments in the Ancient Near East.* Washington, D.C.: Arthur M. Sackler Gallery, 1990.

Harper, Prudence O., Joan Aruz, and Françoise Tallon, eds. *The Royal City of Susa: Ancient Near Eastern Treasures in the Louvre.* New York: Metropolitan Museum of Art, 1992.

Lloyd, Seton. *The Archaeology of Mesopotamia: From the Old Stone Age to the Persian Conquest.* London: Thames & Hudson, 1984.

Macqueen, James G. *The Hittites and Their Contemporaries in Asia Minor.* Rev. ed. New York: Thames & Hudson, 1986.

Meyers, Eric M., ed. *The Oxford Encyclopedia of Archaeology in the Near East.* New York: Oxford University Press, 1997.

Moortgat, Anton. *The Art of Ancient Mesopotamia.* New York: Phaidon, 1969.

Oates, Joan. *Babylon.* Rev. ed. London: Thames & Hudson, 1986.

Parrot, André. *The Arts of Assyria.* New York: Golden Press, 1961.

———. *Sumer: The Dawn of Art.* New York: Golden Press, 1961.

Porada, Edith. *Man and Images in the Ancient Near East.* Wakefield, R.I.: Moyer Bell, 1995.

Porada, Edith, and Robert H. Dyson. *The Art of Ancient Iran: Pre-Islamic Cultures.* Rev. ed. New York: Greystone, 1969.

Postgate, J. Nicholas. *Early Mesopotamia: Society and Economy at the Dawn of History.* London: Routledge, 1992.

Potts, Daniel T. *The Archaeology of Elam: Formation and Transformation of an Ancient Iranian State.* New York: Cambridge University Press, 1999.

Reade, Julian E. *Assyrian Sculpture.* Cambridge, Mass.: Harvard University Press, 1999.

———. *Mesopotamia.* Cambridge, Mass.: Harvard University Press, 1991.

Roaf, Michael. *Cultural Atlas of Mesopotamia and the Ancient Near East.* New York: Facts on File, 1990.

Russell, John M. *Sennacherib's Palace without Rival at Nineveh.* Chicago: University of Chicago Press, 1991.

Saggs, H.W.F. *Babylonians.* London: British Museum, 1995.

Sasson, Jack M., ed. *Civilizations of the Ancient Near East.* New York: Scribner, 1995.

Snell, Daniel C. *Life in the Ancient Near East: 3100–332 B.C.* New Haven: Yale University Press, 1997.

Strommenger, Eva, and Max Hirmer. *5000 Years of the Art of Mesopotamia.* New York: Abrams, 1964.

Zettler, Richard L., and Lee Horne. *Treasures from the Royal Tombs of Ur.* Philadelphia: University of Pennsylvania Museum of Archaeology and Anthropology, 1998.

### CHAPTER 3
### PHARAOHS AND THE AFTERLIFE:
### THE ART OF ANCIENT EGYPT

Arnold, Dieter. *Building in Egypt: Pharaonic Stone Masonry.* New York: Oxford University Press, 1991.

Arnold, Dorothea. *The Royal Women of Amarna.* New York: Metropolitan Museum of Art, 1996.

———. *When the Pyramids Were Built: Egyptian Art of the Old Kingdom.* New York: Rizzoli, 1999.

Baines, John, and Jaromír Málek. *Atlas of Ancient Egypt.* New York: Facts on File, 1980.

Bard, Kathryn A., ed. *Encyclopedia of the Archaeology of Ancient Egypt.* London: Routledge, 1999.

Bianchi, Robert S. *Cleopatra's Egypt: Age of the Ptolemies.* Brooklyn: Brooklyn Museum, 1988.

———. *Splendors of Ancient Egypt from the Egyptian Museum, Cairo.* London: Booth-Clibborn, 1996.

Bietak, Manfred. *Avaris, the Capital of the Hyksos.* London: British Museum Press, 1996.

Capel, Anne K., and Glenn E. Markoe, eds. *Mistress of the House, Mistress of Heaven: Women in Ancient Egypt.* New York: Hudson Hills, 1996.

D'Auria, Sue, Peter Lacovara, and Catharine H. Roehrig. *Mummies and Magic: The Funerary Arts of Ancient Egypt.* Boston: Museum of Fine Arts, 1988.

Davis, Whitney. *The Canonical Tradition in Ancient Egyptian Art.* New York: Cambridge University Press, 1989.

*Egyptian Art in the Age of the Pyramids.* New York: Abrams, 1999.

Hawass, Zahi. *Valley of the Golden Mummies.* New York: Abrams, 2000.

Ikram, Salima, and Aidan Dodson. *The Mummy in Ancient Egypt: Equipping the Dead for Eternity.* New York: Thames & Hudson, 1998.

Kozloff, Arielle P., and Betsy M. Bryan. *Egypt's Dazzling Sun: Amenhotep III and His World.* Cleveland: Cleveland Museum of Art, 1992.

Lange, Kurt, and Max Hirmer. *Egypt: Architecture, Sculpture and Painting in Three Thousand Years.* 4th ed. London: Phaidon, 1968.

Lehner, Mark. *The Complete Pyramids: Solving the Ancient Mysteries.* New York: Thames & Hudson, 1997.

Mahdy, Christine, ed. *The World of the Pharaohs: A Complete Guide to Ancient Egypt.* London: Thames & Hudson, 1990.

Málek, Jaromír. *Egypt: 4000 Years of Art.* New York: Phaidon, 2003.

——— . *Egyptian Art.* London: Phaidon, 1999.

——— , ed. *Egypt: Ancient Culture, Modern Land.* Norman: University of Oklahoma Press, 1993.

Redford, Donald B. *Akhenaton, the Heretic King.* Princeton, N.J.: Princeton University Press, 1984.

——— , ed. *The Oxford Encyclopedia of Ancient Egypt.* New York: Oxford University Press, 2001.

Reeves, C. Nicholas. *The Complete Tutankhamun: The King, the Tomb, the Royal Treasure.* London: Thames & Hudson, 1990.

Robins, Gay. *The Art of Ancient Egypt.* Cambridge, Mass.: Harvard University Press, 1997.

——— . *Egyptian Painting and Relief.* Aylesbury: Shire Publications, 1986.

——— . *Proportion and Style in Ancient Egyptian Art.* Austin: University of Texas Press, 1994.

——— . *Women in Ancient Egypt.* London: British Museum, 1993.

Romer, John. *Valley of the Kings: Exploring the Tombs of the Pharaohs.* New York: Holt, 1994.

Russmann, Edna R. *Egyptian Sculpture: Cairo and Luxor.* Austin: University of Texas Press, 1989.

Schäfer, Heinrich. *Principles of Egyptian Art.* Rev. ed. Oxford: Clarendon, 1986.

Schulz, Regina, and Matthias Seidel, eds. *Egypt: The World of the Pharaohs.* Cologne: Könemann, 1999.

Shafer, Byron E., ed. *Temples of Ancient Egypt.* Ithaca, N.Y.: Cornell University Press, 1997.

Shaw, Ian, and Paul Nicholson. *The Dictionary of Ancient Egypt.* London: British Museum, 1995.

Silverman, David P., ed. *Ancient Egypt.* New York: Oxford University Press, 1997.

Smith, William Stevenson, and William Kelly Simpson. *The Art and Architecture of Ancient Egypt.* Rev. ed. New Haven: Yale University Press, 1998.

Trigger, Bruce G. *Ancient Egypt: A Social History.* Cambridge: Cambridge University Press, 1983.

Weeks, Kent R. *The Lost Tomb.* New York: William Morrow, 1998.

——— , ed. *Valley of the Kings.* Vercelli: White Star, 2001.

Wildung, Dietrich. *Egypt: From Prehistory to the Romans.* Cologne: Taschen, 1997.

### CHAPTER 4
### MINOS AND THE HEROES OF HOMER:
### THE ART OF THE PREHISTORIC AEGEAN

Barber, R.L.N. *The Cyclades in the Bronze Age.* Iowa City: University of Iowa Press, 1987.

Betancourt, Philip P. *A History of Minoan Pottery.* Princeton, N.J.: Princeton University Press, 1965.

Cadogan, Gerald. *Palaces of Minoan Crete.* London: Methuen, 1980.

Chadwick, John. *The Mycenaean World.* New York: Cambridge University Press, 1976.

Cullen, Tracey, ed. *Aegean Prehistory: A Review.* Boston: Archaeological Institute of America, 2001.

Demargne, Pierre. *The Birth of Greek Art.* New York: Golden Press, 1964.

Dickinson, Oliver P.T.K. *The Aegean Bronze Age.* New York: Cambridge University Press, 1994.

Doumas, Christos. *Thera, Pompeii of the Ancient Aegean: Excavations at Akrotiri, 1967–1979.* New York: Thames & Hudson, 1983.

——— . *The Wall-Paintings of Thera.* Athens: Thera Foundation, 1992.

Fitton, J. Lesley. *Cycladic Art.* Cambridge, Mass.: Harvard University Press, 1989.

——— . *The Discovery of the Greek Bronze Age.* London: British Museum, 1995.

Forsyth, Phyllis Young. *Thera in the Bronze Age.* New York: Peter Lang, 1997.

Getz-Preziosi, Patricia. *Sculptors of the Cyclades: Individual and Tradition in the Third Millennium B.C.* Ann Arbor: University of Michigan Press, 1987.

Graham, James W. *The Palaces of Crete.* Princeton, N.J.: Princeton University Press, 1987.

Hampe, Roland, and Erika Simon. *The Birth of Greek Art: From the Mycenaean to the Archaic Period.* New York: Oxford University Press, 1981.

Higgins, Reynold. *Minoan and Mycenaean Art.* Rev. ed. New York: Thames & Hudson, 1997.

Hood, Sinclair. *The Arts in Prehistoric Greece.* New Haven: Yale University Press, 1978.

Immerwahr, Sarah A. *Aegean Painting in the Bronze Age.* University Park: Pennsylvania State University Press, 1990.

MacGillivray, J. A. *Minotaur: Sir Arthur Evans and the Archaeology of the Minoan Myth.* New York: Hill and Wang, 2000.

Marinatos, Nanno. *Art and Religion in Thera: Reconstructing a Bronze Age Society.* Athens: Mathioulakis, 1984.

Marinatos, Spyridon, and Max Hirmer. *Crete and Mycenae.* London: Thames & Hudson, 1960.

McDonald, William A., and Carol G. Thomas. *Progress into the Past: The Rediscovery of Mycenaean Civilization.* 2nd ed. Bloomington: Indiana University Press, 1990.

Morgan, Lyvia. *The Miniature Wall Paintings of Thera: A Study in Aegean Culture and Iconography.* New York: Cambridge University Press, 1988.

Pendlebury, John. *The Archeology of Crete.* London: Methuen, 1967.

Preziosi, Donald, and Louise A. Hitchcock. *Aegean Art and Architecture.* New York: Oxford University Press, 1999.

Taylour, Lord William. *The Mycenaeans.* London: Thames & Hudson, 1990.

Vermeule, Emily. *Greece in the Bronze Age.* Chicago: University of Chicago Press, 1972.

Wace, Alan. *Mycenae: An Archeological History and Guide.* New York: Biblo & Tannen, 1964.

Warren, Peter. *The Aegean Civilisations from Ancient Crete to Mycenae.* 2nd ed. Oxford: Elsevier-Phaidon, 1989.

### CHAPTER 5
### GODS, HEROES, AND ATHLETES:
### THE ART OF ANCIENT GREECE

Arias, Paolo. *A History of One Thousand Years of Greek Vase Painting.* New York: Abrams, 1962.

Ashmole, Bernard. *Architect and Sculptor in Classical Greece.* New York: New York University Press, 1972.

Berve, Helmut, Gottfried Gruben, and Max Hirmer. *Greek Temples, Theatres, and Shrines.* New York: Abrams, 1963.

Biers, William. *The Archaeology of Greece: An Introduction.* 2nd ed. Ithaca, N.Y.: Cornell University Press, 1996.

Boardman, John. *Athenian Black Figure Vases.* Rev. ed. New York: Thames & Hudson, 1985.

——— . *Athenian Red Figure Vases: The Archaic Period.* New York: Thames & Hudson, 1988.

——— . *Athenian Red Figure Vases: The Classical Period.* New York: Thames & Hudson, 1989.

——— . *Early Greek Vase Painting, 11th–6th Centuries B.C.* New York: Thames & Hudson, 1998.

——— . *Greek Sculpture: The Archaic Period.* Rev. ed. New York: Thames & Hudson, 1985.

——— . *Greek Sculpture: The Classical Period.* New York: Thames & Hudson, 1987.

——— . *Greek Sculpture: The Late Classical Period and Sculpture in Colonies and Overseas.* New York: Thames & Hudson, 1995.

——— . *The Parthenon and Its Sculpture.* Austin: University of Texas Press, 1985.

Camp, John M. *The Archaeology of Athens.* New Haven: Yale University Press, 2001.

Carpenter, Thomas H. *Art and Myth in Ancient Greece.* New York: Thames & Hudson, 1991.

Charbonneaux, Jean, Roland Martin, and François Villard. *Archaic Greek Art.* New York: Braziller, 1971.

——— . *Classical Greek Art.* New York: Braziller, 1972.

——— . *Hellenistic Art.* New York: Braziller, 1973.

Coldstream, J. Nicholas. *Geometric Greece.* New York: St. Martin's, 1977.

Coulton, J. J. *Ancient Greek Architects at Work.* Ithaca, N.Y.: Cornell University Press, 1982.

Fullerton, Mark D. *Greek Art.* New York: Cambridge University Press, 2000.

Haynes, Denys E. L. *The Technique of Greek Bronze Statuary.* Mainz: von Zabern, 1992.

Houser, Caroline. *Greek Monumental Bronze Sculpture.* New York: Vendome, 1983.

Hurwit, Jeffrey M. *The Art and Culture of Early Greece, 1100–480 B.C.* Ithaca, N.Y.: Cornell University Press, 1985.

——— . *The Athenian Acropolis: History, Mythology, and Archaeology from the Neolithic Era to the Present.* New York: Cambridge University Press, 1999.

Jenkins, Ian. *The Parthenon Frieze.* Austin: University of Texas Press, 1994.

Langlotz, Ernst, and Max Hirmer. *The Art of Magna Graecia: Greek Art in Southern Italy and Sicily.* New York: Abrams, 1965.

Lawrence, Arnold W., and R. A. Tomlinson. *Greek Architecture.* Rev. ed. New Haven: Yale University Press, 1996.

Martin, Roland. *Greek Architecture: Architecture of Crete, Greece, and the Greek World.* New York: Electa/Rizzoli, 1988.

Mattusch, Carol C. *Classical Bronzes: The Art and Craft of Greek and Roman Statuary.* Ithaca, N.Y.: Cornell University Press, 1996.

——— . *Greek Bronze Statuary from the Beginnings through the Fifth Century B.C.* Ithaca, N.Y.: Cornell University Press, 1988.

Morris, Sarah P. *Daidalos and the Origins of Greek Art.* Princeton, N.J.: Princeton University Press, 1992.

Osborne, Robin. *Archaic and Classical Greek Art.* New York: Oxford University Press, 1998.

Palagia, Olga. *The Pediments of the Parthenon.* Leiden: E. J. Brill, 1993.

Palagia, Olga, and Jerome J. Pollitt, *Personal Styles in Greek Sculpture.* New York: Cambridge University Press, 1996.

Pedley, John Griffiths. *Greek Art and Archaeology.* 3rd ed. Upper Saddle River, N.J.: Prentice Hall, 2002.

Pollitt, Jerome J. *Art and Experience in Classical Greece.* New York: Cambridge University Press, 1972.

——— . *Art in the Hellenistic Age.* New York: Cambridge University Press, 1986.

———. *The Art of Ancient Greece: Sources and Documents.* 2nd ed. New York: Cambridge University Press, 1990.

Pugliese Carratelli, G. *The Greek World: Art and Civilization in Magna Graecia and Sicily.* New York: Rizzoli, 1996.

Reeder, Ellen D., ed. *Pandora: Women in Classical Greece.* Baltimore: Walters Art Gallery, 1995.

Rhodes, Robin F. *Architecture and Meaning on the Athenian Acropolis.* New York: Cambridge University Press, 1995.

Richter, Gisela M. *The Portraits of the Greeks.* Rev. ed. by R.R.R. Smith. Ithaca, N.Y.: Cornell University Press, 1984.

Ridgway, Brunilde S. *The Archaic Style in Greek Sculpture.* 2nd ed. Chicago: Ares, 1993.

———. *Fifth Century Styles in Greek Sculpture.* Princeton, N.J.: Princeton University Press, 1981.

———. *Fourth-Century Styles in Greek Sculpture.* Madison: University of Wisconsin Press, 1997.

———. *Hellenistic Sculpture I: The Styles of ca. 331–200 B.C.* Madison: University of Wisconsin Press, 1990.

———. *Hellenistic Sculpture II: The Styles of ca. 200–100 B.C.* Madison: University of Wisconsin Press, 2000.

———. *Prayers in Stone: Greek Architectural Sculpture.* Berkeley: University of California Press, 1999.

———. *Roman Copies of Greek Sculpture: The Problem of the Originals.* Ann Arbor: University of Michigan Press, 1984.

———. *The Severe Style in Greek Sculpture.* Princeton, N.J.: Princeton University Press, 1970.

Robertson, Martin. *The Art of Vase-Painting in Classical Athens.* New York: Cambridge University Press, 1992.

———. *A History of Greek Art.* Rev. ed. 2 vols. New York: Cambridge University Press, 1986.

———. *A Shorter History of Greek Art.* New York: Cambridge University Press, 1981.

Rolley, Claude. *Greek Bronzes.* London: Sotheby's, 1986.

Shapiro, H. Alan. *Art and Cult in Athens under the Tyrants.* Mainz: von Zabern, 1989.

———. *Myth into Art: Poet and Painter in Classical Greece.* New York: Routledge, 1994.

Smith, R.R.R. *Hellenistic Sculpture.* New York: Thames & Hudson, 1991.

Spivey, Nigel. *Greek Art.* London: Phaidon, 1997.

Stansbury-O'Donnell, Mark D. *Pictorial Narrative in Ancient Greek Art.* New York: Cambridge University Press, 1999.

Stewart, Andrew. *Art, Desire, and the Body in Ancient Greece.* New York: Cambridge University Press, 1997.

———. *Greek Sculpture: An Exploration.* 2 vols. New Haven: Yale University Press, 1990.

Wycherley, Richard E. *How the Greeks Built Cities.* New York: Norton, 1976.

### Chapter 6
### Paths to Enlightenment:
### The Art of South and Southeast Asia
#### before 1200

Asher, Frederick M. *The Art of Eastern India, 300–800.* Minneapolis: University of Minnesota Press, 1980.

Blurton, T. Richard. *Hindu Art.* Cambridge, Mass.: Harvard University Press, 1993.

Chaturachinda, Gwyneth, Sunanda Krishnamurty, and Pauline W. Tabtiang. *Dictionary of South and Southeast Asian Art.* Chiang Mai, Thailand: Silkworm Books, 2000.

Chihara, Daigoro. *Hindu-Buddhist Architecture in Southeast Asia.* Leiden: E. J. Brill, 1996.

Craven, Roy C. *Indian Art: A Concise History.* Rev. ed. London: Thames & Hudson, 1997.

Dehejia, Vidya. *Early Buddhist Rock Temples.* Ithaca, N.Y.: Cornell University Press, 1972.

———. *Indian Art.* London: Phaidon, 1997.

Desai, Vishakha N., and Darielle Mason. *Gods, Guardians, and Lovers: Temple Sculptures from North India A.D. 700–1200.* New York: Asia Society Galleries, 1993.

*Encyclopedia of Indian Temple Architecture.* 8 vols. New Delhi: American Institute of Indian Studies. Philadelphia: University of Pennsylvania Press, 1983–1996.

Fisher, Robert E. *Buddhist Art and Architecture.* New York: Thames & Hudson, 1993.

Frederic, Louis. *Borobudur.* New York: Abbeville Press, 1996.

Gopinatha Rao, T. A. *Elements of Hindu Iconography.* 2nd ed. 4 vols. New York: Paragon, 1968.

Gray, Basil, ed. *The Arts of India.* Ithaca, N.Y.: Cornell University Press, 1981.

Harle, James C. *The Art and Architecture of the Indian Subcontinent.* 2nd ed. New Haven: Yale University Press, 1994.

Huntington, Susan L., and John C. Huntington. *The Art of Ancient India: Buddhist, Hindu, Jain.* New York: Weatherhill, 1985.

Jacques, Claude, and Michael Freeman. *Angkor: Cities and Temples.* Bangkok: River Books, 1997.

Jessup, Helen Ibbitson, and Thierry Zephir, eds. *Sculpture of Angkor and Ancient Cambodia: Millennium of Glory.* Washington, D.C.: National Gallery of Art, 1997.

McIntosh, Jane R. *A Peaceful Realm: The Rise and Fall of the Indus Civilization.* Boulder, Colo.: Westview Press, 2002.

Michell, George. *Hindu Art and Architecture.* New York: Thames & Hudson, 2000.

———. *The Hindu Temple: An Introduction to Its Meaning and Forms.* Chicago: University of Chicago Press, 1988.

Mitter, Partha. *Indian Art.* New York: Oxford University Press, 2001.

Rawson, Phillip. *The Art of Southeast Asia.* New York: Thames & Hudson, 1990.

Srinivasan, Doris Meth. *Many Heads, Arms and Eyes: Origin, Meaning and Form of Multiplicity in Indian Art.* Leiden: E. J. Brill, 1997.

Stierlin, Henri. *Hindu India from Khajuraho to the Temple City of Madurai.* Cologne: Taschen, 1998.

Williams, Joanna G. *The Art of Gupta India: Empire and Province.* Princeton, N.J.: Princeton University Press, 1982.

### Chapter 7
### The Silk Road and Beyond:
### The Art of Early China and Korea

Bush, Susan, and Shio-yen Shih. *Early Chinese Texts on Painting.* Cambridge, Mass.: Harvard University Press, 1985.

Cahill, James. *Chinese Painting.* New York: Rizzoli, 1960.

———. *The Painter's Practice: How Artists Lived and Worked in Traditional China.* New York: Columbia University Press, 1994.

Clunas, Craig. *Art in China.* New York: Oxford University Press, 1997.

Fahr-Becker, Gabriele, ed. *The Art of East Asia.* Cologne: Könemann, 1999.

Fisher, Robert E. *Buddhist Art and Architecture.* New York: Thames & Hudson, 1993.

Fong, Wen C. *Beyond Representation: Chinese Painting and Calligraphy, 8th–14th Century.* New Haven: Yale University Press, 1992.

———. *The Great Bronze Age of China: An Exhibition from the People's Republic of China.* New York: Metropolitan Museum of Art, 1980.

Fong, Wen C., and James C. Y. Watt. *Preserving the Past: Treasures from the National Palace Museum, Taipei.* New York: Metropolitan Museum of Art, 1996.

Li, Chu-tsing, ed. *Artists and Patrons: Some Social and Economic Aspects of Chinese Painting.* Lawrence: Kress Department of Art History, in cooperation with Indiana University Press, 1989.

Little, Stephen, and Shawn Eichman. *Taoism and the Arts of China.* Chicago: Art Institute of Chicago, 2000.

Portal, Jane. *Korea: Art and Archaeology.* New York: Thames & Hudson, 2000.

Powers, Martin J. *Art and Political Expression in Early China.* New Haven: Yale University Press, 1991.

Rawson, Jessica. *Ancient China: Art and Archaeology.* New York: Harper & Row, 1980.

———, ed. *The British Museum Book of Chinese Art.* New York: Thames & Hudson, 1992.

Sickman, Laurence, and Alexander C. Soper. *The Art and Architecture of China.* 3rd ed. New Haven: Yale University Press, 1968.

Silbergeld, Jerome. *Chinese Painting Style: Media, Methods, and Principles of Form.* Seattle and London: University of Washington Press, 1982.

Steinhardt, Nancy S., ed. *Chinese Architecture.* New Haven: Yale University Press, 2002.

Sullivan, Michael. *The Arts of China.* 4th ed. Berkeley: University of California Press, 1999.

———. *The Birth of Landscape Painting.* Berkeley: University of California Press, 1962.

Thorp, Robert L. *Son of Heaven: Imperial Arts of China.* Seattle: Son of Heaven Press, 1988.

Thorp, Robert L., and Richard Ellis Vinograd. *Chinese Art and Culture.* New York: Abrams, 2001.

Vainker, S. J. *Chinese Pottery and Porcelain: From Prehistory to the Present.* New York: Braziller, 1991.

Watson, William. *The Arts of China to AD 900.* New Haven: Yale University Press, 1995.

———. *The Arts of China 900–1620.* New Haven: Yale University Press, 2000.

Weidner, Marsha, ed. *Flowering in the Shadows: Women in the History of Chinese and Japanese Painting.* Honolulu: University of Hawaii Press, 1990.

Whitfield, Roger, and Anne Farrer. *Caves of the Thousand Buddhas: Chinese Art of the Silk Route.* New York: Braziller, 1990.

Wu, Hung. *Monumentality in Early Chinese Art.* Stanford, Calif.: Stanford University Press, 1996.

———. *The Wu Liang Shrine: The Ideology of Early Chinese Pictorial Art.* Stanford, Calif.: Stanford University Press, 1989.

Xin, Yang, Nie Chongzheng, Lang Shaojun, Richard M. Barnhart, James Cahill, and Hung Wu. *Three Thousand Years of Chinese Painting.* New Haven: Yale University Press, 1997.

### Chapter 8
### Shrines, Statues, and Scrolls:
### The Art of Early Japan

Aikens, C. Melvin, and Takayama Higuchi. *Prehistory of Japan.* New York: Academic Press, 1982.

Coaldrake, William H. *Architecture and Authority in Japan.* London: Routledge, 1996.

Elisseeff, Danielle, and Vadime Elisseeff. *Art of Japan.* Translated by I. Mark Paris. New York: Abrams, 1985.

Ienaga, Saburo. *Painting in the Yamato Style.* Translated by John M. Shields. New York: Weatherhill, 1973.

Kidder, J. Edward, Jr. *The Art of Japan.* New York: Park Lane, 1985.

Kurata, Bunsaku. *Horyu-ji: Temple of the Exalted Law.* Translated by W. Chie Ishibashi. New York: Japan Society, 1981.

Mason, Penelope. *History of Japanese Art.* New York: Abrams, 1993.

Nishi, Kazuo, and Kazuo Hozumi. *What Is Japanese Architecture?* Translated by H. Mack Horton. New York: Kodansha International, 1985.

Nishikawa, Kyotaro, and Emily Sano. *The Great Age of Japanese Buddhist Sculpture A.D. 600–1300.* Fort Worth, Tex.: Kimbell Art Museum, 1982.

Noma, Seiroku. *The Arts of Japan.* Translated and adapted by John Rosenfield and Glenn T. Webb. Tokyo: Kodansha International, 1966.

Okudaira, Hideo. *Narrative Picture Scrolls.* Adapted by Elizabeth ten Grotenhuis. New York: Weatherhill, 1973.

Pearson, Richard J. *Ancient Japan.* New York: Braziller, 1992.

Pearson, Richard J., Gina Lee Barnes, and Karl L. Hutterer, eds. *Windows on the Japanese Past.* Ann Arbor: Center for Japanese Studies, University of Michigan, 1986.

Rosenfield, John M. *Japanese Art of the Heian Period, 794–1185.* New York: Asia Society, 1967.

Rosenfield, John M., and Elizabeth ten Grotenhuis. *Journey of the Three Jewels.* New York: Asia Society, 1979.

Rosenfield, John M., and Shujiro Shimada. *Traditions of Japanese Art: Selections from the Kimiko and John Powers Collection.* Cambridge, Mass.: Fogg Art Museum, 1970.

Shimizu, Yoshiaki, ed. *The Shaping of Daimyo Culture 1185–1868.* Washington, D.C.: National Gallery of Art, 1988.

Stanley-Baker, Joan. *Japanese Art.* New York: Thames & Hudson, 1984.

Suzuki, Kakichi. *Early Buddhist Architecture in Japan.* Translated and adapted by Mary Neighbor Parent and Nancy Shatzman Steinhardt. New York: Kodansha International, 1980.

Swann, Peter C. *Concise History of Japanese Art.* New York: Kodansha International, 1979.

Weidner, Marsha, ed. *Flowering in the Shadows: Women in the History of Chinese and Japanese Painting.* Honolulu: University of Hawaii Press, 1990.

### CHAPTER 9
### ITALY BEFORE THE ROMANS:
### THE ART OF THE ETRUSCANS

Banti, Luisa. *The Etruscan Cities and Their Culture.* Berkeley: University of California Press, 1973.

Barker, Graeme, and Tom Rasmussen. *The Etruscans.* Oxford: Blackwell, 1998.

Boethius, Axel. *Etruscan and Early Roman Architecture.* 2nd ed. New Haven: Yale University Press, 1978.

Bonfante, Larissa, ed. *Etruscan Life and Afterlife: A Handbook of Etruscan Studies.* Detroit: Wayne State University Press, 1986.

Brendel, Otto J. *Etruscan Art.* 2nd ed. New Haven: Yale University Press, 1995.

Cristofani, Mauro. *The Etruscans: A New Investigation.* London: Orbis, 1979.

Haynes, Sybille. *Etruscan Civilization: A Cultural History.* Los Angeles: J. Paul Getty Museum, 2000.

Heurgon, Jacques. *Daily Life of the Etruscans.* London: Weidenfeld & Nicolson, 1964.

Pallottino, Massimo. *Etruscan Painting.* Geneva: Skira, 1953.

———. *The Etruscans.* Harmondsworth: Penguin, 1978.

Richardson, Emeline. *The Etruscans: Their Art and Civilization.* Rev. ed. Chicago: University of Chicago Press, 1976.

Ridgway, David, and Francesca Ridgway, eds. *Italy before the Romans.* New York: Academic Press, 1979.

Spivey, Nigel. *Etruscan Art.* New York: Thames & Hudson, 1997.

Spivey, Nigel, and Simon Stoddart, *Etruscan Italy: An Archaeological History.* London: Batsford, 1990.

Sprenger, Maja, Gilda Bartoloni, and Max Hirmer. *The Etruscans: Their History, Art, and Architecture.* New York: Abrams, 1983.

Steingräber, Stephan, ed. *Etruscan Painting: Catalogue Raisonné of Etruscan Wall Paintings.* New York: Johnson, 1986.

Torelli, Mario, ed. *The Etruscans.* New York: Rizzoli, 2001.

### CHAPTER 10
### FROM SEVEN HILLS TO THREE CONTINENTS:
### THE ART OF ANCIENT ROME

Anderson, James C., Jr. *Roman Architecture and Society.* Baltimore: Johns Hopkins University Press, 1997.

Andreae, Bernard. *The Art of Rome.* New York: Abrams, 1977.

Bianchi Bandinelli, Ranuccio. *Rome: The Center of Power. Roman Art to A.D. 200.* New York: Braziller, 1970.

———. *Rome: The Late Empire. Roman Art A.D. 200–400.* New York: Braziller, 1971.

Brendel, Otto J. *Prolegomena to the Study of Roman Art.* New Haven: Yale University Press, 1979.

Claridge, Amanda. *Rome: An Oxford Archaeological Guide.* New York: Oxford University Press, 1998.

Clarke, John R. *The Houses of Roman Italy, 100 B.C.–A.D. 250.* Berkeley: University of California Press, 1991.

Cornell, Tim, and John Matthews. *Atlas of the Roman World.* New York: Facts on File, 1982.

D'Ambra, Eve. *Roman Art.* New York: Cambridge University Press, 1998.

———, ed. *Roman Art in Context.* Upper Saddle River, N.J.: Prentice Hall, 1994.

Elsner, Jaś. *Imperial Rome and Christian Triumph.* New York: Oxford University Press, 1998.

Gazda, Elaine K., ed. *Roman Art in the Private Sphere.* Ann Arbor: University of Michigan Press, 1991.

Grant, Michael. *Cities of Vesuvius: Pompeii and Herculaneum.* Harmondsworth: Penguin, 1976.

Hannestad, Niels. *Roman Art and Imperial Policy.* Aarhus: Aarhus University Press, 1986.

Henig, Martin, ed. *A Handbook of Roman Art.* Ithaca, N.Y.: Cornell University Press, 1983.

Kent, John P. C., and Max Hirmer. *Roman Coins.* New York: Abrams, 1978.

Kleiner, Diana E. E. *Roman Sculpture.* New Haven: Yale University Press, 1992.

Kleiner, Diana E. E., and Susan B. Matheson, eds. *I Claudia: Women in Ancient Rome.* New Haven: Yale University Art Gallery, 1996.

———. *I Claudia II: Women in Roman Art and Society.* Austin: University of Texas Press, 2000.

Kraus, Theodor. *Pompeii and Herculaneum: The Living Cities of the Dead.* New York: Abrams, 1975.

Ling, Roger. *Roman Painting.* New York: Cambridge University Press, 1991.

L'Orange, Hans Peter. *The Roman Empire: Art Forms and Civic Life.* New York: Rizzoli, 1985.

MacCormack, Sabine G. *Art and Ceremony in Late Antiquity.* Berkeley: University of California Press, 1981.

MacDonald, William L. *The Architecture of the Roman Empire I: An Introductory Study.* Rev. ed. New Haven: Yale University Press, 1982.

———. *The Architecture of the Roman Empire II: An Urban Appraisal.* New Haven: Yale University Press, 1986.

———. *The Pantheon: Design, Meaning, and Progeny.* Cambridge, Mass.: Harvard University Press, 1976.

McKay, Alexander G. *Houses, Villas, and Palaces in the Roman World.* Ithaca, N.Y.: Cornell University Press, 1975.

Nash, Ernest. *Pictorial Dictionary of Ancient Rome.* 2nd ed. 2 vols. New York: Praeger, 1962.

Pollitt, Jerome J. *The Art of Rome, 753 B.C.–A.D. 337: Sources and Documents.* Rev. ed. New York: Cambridge University Press, 1983.

Ramage, Nancy H., and Andrew Ramage. *Roman Art: Romulus to Constantine.* 3rd ed. Upper Saddle River, N.J.: Prentice Hall, 2000.

Richardson, Lawrence, Jr. *A New Topographical Dictionary of Ancient Rome.* Baltimore: Johns Hopkins University Press, 1992.

———. *Pompeii: An Architectural History.* Baltimore: Johns Hopkins University Press, 1988.

Sear, Frank. *Roman Architecture.* Rev. ed. Ithaca, N.Y.: Cornell University Press, 1989.

Stambaugh, John E. *The Ancient Roman City.* Baltimore: Johns Hopkins University Press, 1988.

Strong, Donald, and Roger Ling. *Roman Art.* 2nd ed. New Haven: Yale University Press, 1988.

Toynbee, Jocelyn M. C. *Death and Burial in the Roman World.* London: Thames & Hudson, 1971.

Wallace-Hadrill, Andrew. *Houses and Society in Pompeii and Herculaneum.* Princeton, N.J.: Princeton University Press, 1994.

Ward-Perkins, John B. *Roman Architecture.* New York: Electa/Rizzoli, 1988.

———. *Roman Imperial Architecture.* 2nd ed. New Haven: Yale University Press, 1981.

Wilson-Jones, Mark. *Principles of Roman Architecture.* New Haven: Yale University Press, 2000.

Wood, Susan. *Roman Portrait Sculpture A.D. 217–260.* Leiden: E. J. Brill, 1986.

Yegül, Fikret. *Baths and Bathing in Classical Antiquity.* Cambridge: MIT Press, 1992.

Zanker, Paul. *Pompeii: Public and Private Life.* Cambridge: Harvard University Press, 1998.

———. *The Power of Images in the Age of Augustus.* Ann Arbor: University of Michigan Press, 1988.

### MEDIEVAL ART, GENERAL

Alexander, Jonathan J. G. *Medieval Illuminators and Their Methods of Work.* New Haven: Yale University Press, 1992.

Andrews, Francis B. *The Mediaeval Builders and Their Methods.* New York: Barnes & Noble, 1993.

*The Art of Medieval Spain, A.D. 500–1200.* New York: Metropolitan Museum of Art, 1993.

Ross, Leslie. *Medieval Art: A Topical Dictionary.* Westport, Conn.: Greenwood, 1996.

Benton, Janetta Rebold. *Art of the Middle Ages.* New York: Thames & Hudson, 2002.

Binski, Paul. *Painters (Medieval Craftsmen).* Toronto: University of Toronto Press, 1991.

Calkins, Robert G. *Illuminated Books of the Middle Ages.* Ithaca, N.Y.: Cornell University Press, 1983.

———. *Medieval Architecture in Western Europe: From A.D. 300 to 1500.* New York: Oxford University Press, 1998.

Coldstream, Nicola. *Masons and Sculptors (Medieval Craftsmen).* Toronto: University of Toronto Press, 1991.

———. *Medieval Architecture.* New York: Oxford University Press, 2002.

Cross, Frank L., and Livingstone, Elizabeth A., eds. *The Oxford Dictionary of the Christian Church.* 3rd ed. New York: Oxford University Press, 1997.

De Hamel, Christopher. *Scribes and Illuminators (Medieval Craftsmen).* Toronto: University of Toronto Press, 1992.

Lasko, Peter. *Ars Sacra, 800–1200.* 2nd ed. New Haven: Yale University Press, 1994.

Murray, Peter, and Linda Murray. *The Oxford Companion to Christian Art and Architecture.* New York: Oxford University Press, 1996.

Pelikan, Jaroslav. *Mary through the Centuries: Her Place in the History of Culture.* New Haven: Yale University Press, 1996.

Schiller, Gertrud. *Iconography of Christian Art.* 2 vols. Greenwich, Conn.: New York Graphic Society, 1971–1972.

Schütz, Bernard. *Great Cathedrals.* New York: Abrams, 2002.

Sekules, Veronica. *Medieval Art.* New York: Oxford University Press, 2001.

Snyder, James. *Medieval Art: Painting, Sculpture, Architecture, 4th–14th Century.* New York: Abrams, 1989.

Tasker, Edward G. *Encyclopedia of Medieval Church Art.* London: Batsford, 1993.

Webb, Geoffrey F. *Architecture in Britain: The Middle Ages.* Harmondsworth: Penguin, 1965.

### CHAPTER 11
### PAGANS, CHRISTIANS, AND JEWS:
### THE ART OF LATE ANTIQUITY

Bowersock, G. W., Peter Brown, and Oleg Grabar, eds. *Late Antiquity: A Guide to the Postclassical World.* Cambridge, Mass.: Harvard University Press, 1998.

Brown, Peter. *The World of Late Antiquity,* A.D. *150–170.* London: Thames & Hudson, 1971.

Elsner, Jaś. *Art and the Roman Viewer: The Transformation of Art from the Pagan World to Christianity.* New York: Cambridge University Press, 1995.

———. *Imperial Rome and Christian Triumph.* New York: Oxford University Press, 1998.

Grabar, André. *The Beginnings of Christian Art, 200–395.* London: Thames & Hudson, 1967.

———. *Christian Iconography.* Princeton, N.J.: Princeton University Press, 1980.

Gutmann, Joseph. *Sacred Images: Studies in Jewish Art from Antiquity to the Middle Ages.* Northampton, Mass.: Variorum, 1989.

Hutter, Irmgard. *Early Christian and Byzantine Art.* London: Herbert, 1988.

Janes, Dominic. *God and Gold in Late Antiquity.* New York: Cambridge University Press, 1998.

Jensen, Robin Margaret. *Understanding Early Christian Art.* New York: Routledge, 2000.

Kitzinger, Ernst. *Byzantine Art in the Making.* Cambridge, Mass.: Harvard University Press, 1977.

———. *Early Medieval Art.* 3rd ed. London: British Museum, 1983.

Koch, Guntram. *Early Christian Art and Architecture.* London: SCM Press, 1996.

Krautheimer, Richard. *Rome, Profile of a City: 312–1308.* Princeton, N.J.: Princeton University Press, 1980.

Krautheimer, Richard, and Slobodan Ćurčić. *Early Christian and Byzantine Architecture.* 4th rev. ed. New Haven: Yale University Press, 1986.

Lowden, John. *Early Christian and Byzantine Art.* London: Phaidon, 1997.

Lowrie, Walter S. *Art in the Early Church.* New York: Norton, 1969.

Mathews, Thomas P. *The Clash of Gods: A Reinterpretation of Early Christian Art.* Rev. ed. Princeton, N.J.: Princeton University Press, 1999.

Milburn, Robert. *Early Christian Art and Architecture.* Berkeley: University of California Press, 1988.

Perkins, Ann Louise. *The Art of Dura-Europos.* Oxford: Clarendon, 1973.

Stevenson, James. *The Catacombs: Rediscovered Monuments of Early Christianity.* London: Thames & Hudson, 1978.

Volbach, Wolfgang. *Early Christian Mosaics, from the Fourth to the Seventh Centuries.* New York: Oxford University Press, 1946.

Volbach, Wolfgang, and Max Hirmer. *Early Christian Art.* New York: Abrams, 1962.

Webster, Leslie, and Michelle Brown, eds. *The Transformation of the Roman World,* A.D. *400–900.* Berkeley: University of California Press, 1997.

Weitzmann, Kurt. *Ancient Book Illumination.* Cambridge, Mass.: Harvard University Press, 1959.

———. *Late Antique and Early Christian Book Illumination.* New York: Braziller, 1977.

———, ed. *Age of Spirituality: Late Antique and Early Christian Art, Third to Seventh Century.* New York: Metropolitan Museum of Art, 1979.

### CHAPTER 12
### ROME IN THE EAST:
### THE ART OF BYZANTIUM

Borsook, Eve. *Messages in Mosaic: The Royal Programmes of Norman Sicily.* Oxford: Clarendon, 1990.

Cormack, Robin. *Byzantine Art.* New York: Oxford University Press, 2000.

———. *Painting the Soul: Icons, Death Masks, and Shrouds.* London: Reaktion, 1997.

———. *Writing in Gold: Byzantine Society and Its Icons.* New York: Oxford University Press, 1985.

Cutler, Anthony. *The Hand of the Master: Craftsmanship, Ivory, and Society in Byzantium (9th–11th Centuries).* Princeton, N.J.: Princeton University Press, 1994.

Demus, Otto. *Byzantine Art and the West.* New York: New York University Press, 1970.

———. *The Mosaic Decoration of San Marco, Venice.* Chicago: University of Chicago Press, 1990.

Evans, Helen C., and William D. Wixom, eds. *The Glory of Byzantium: Art and Culture of the Middle Byzantine Era* A.D. *843–1261.* New York: Metropolitan Museum of Art, 1997.

Grabar, André. *Byzantine Painting.* New York: Rizzoli, 1979.

———. *The Golden Age of Justinian: From the Death of Theodosius to the Rise of Islam.* New York: Odyssey Press, 1967.

Grabar, André, and Manolis Chatzidakis. *Greek Mosaics of the Byzantine Period.* New York: New American Library, 1964.

Lowden, John. *Early Christian and Byzantine Art.* London: Phaidon, 1997.

Maguire, Henry. *Art and Eloquence in Byzantium.* Princeton, N.J.: Princeton University Press, 1981.

———. *The Icons of Their Bodies: Saints and Their Images in Byzantium.* Princeton, N.J.: Princeton University Press, 1996.

Mainstone, Rowland J. *Hagia Sophia: Architecture, Structure and Liturgy of Justinian's Great Church.* London: Thames & Hudson, 1988.

Mango, Cyril. *Art of the Byzantine Empire, 312–1453: Sources and Documents.* Toronto: University of Toronto Press, 1986. Reprint of 1972 ed.

———. *Byzantine Architecture.* New York: Electa/Rizzoli, 1985.

———. *Byzantium: The Empire of New Rome.* New York: Scribner's, 1980.

———. *Byzantium and Its Image: History and Culture of the Byzantine Empire and Its Heritage.* London: Variorum, 1984.

Mark, Robert, and Ahmet S. Cakmak, eds. *Hagia Sophia from the Age of Justinian to the Present.* New York: Cambridge University Press, 1992.

Mathews, Thomas F. *Byzantium: From Antiquity to the Renaissance.* New York: Abrams, 1998.

Ousterhout, Robert. *Master Builders of Byzantium.* Princeton, N.J.: Princeton University Press, 2000.

Pelikan, Jaroslav. *Imago Dei: The Byzantine Apologia for Icons.* Princeton, N.J.: Princeton University Press, 1990.

Rodley, Lyn. *Byzantine Art and Architecture: An Introduction.* New York: Cambridge University Press, 1994.

Von Simson, Otto G. *Sacred Fortress: Byzantine Art and Statecraft in Ravenna.* Princeton, N.J.: Princeton University Press, 1986.

Walter, Christopher. *Art and Ritual of the Byzantine Church.* London: Variorum, 1982.

Weitzmann, Kurt. *Ancient Book Illumination.* Cambridge, Mass.: Harvard University Press, 1959.

———. *Art in the Medieval West and Its Contacts with Byzantium.* London: Variorum, 1982.

———. *The Icon.* New York: Dorset, 1987.

———. *Illustrations in Roll and Codex.* Princeton, N.J.: Princeton University Press, 1970.

### CHAPTER 13
### IN PRAISE OF ALLAH:
### THE ART OF THE ISLAMIC WORLD

Atil, Esin. *The Age of Sultan Suleyman the Magnificent.* Washington, D.C.: National Gallery of Art, 1987.

Baker, Patricia L. *Islamic Textiles.* London: British Museum, 1995.

Blair, Sheila S., and Jonathan Bloom. *The Art and Architecture of Islam 1250–1800.* New Haven: Yale University Press, 1994.

Bloom, Jonathan, and Sheila S. Blair. *Islamic Arts.* London: Phaidon, 1997.

Brend, Barbara. *Islamic Art.* Cambridge, Mass.: Harvard University Press, 1991.

Canby, Sheila. *Persian Painting.* London: British Museum, 1993.

Creswell, Keppel A. C. *A Short Account of Early Muslim Architecture.* Rev. ed. by James W. Allan. Aldershot: Scolar, 1989.

Dodds, Jerrilynn D., ed. *Al-Andalus: The Art of Islamic Spain.* New York: Metropolitan Museum of Art, 1992.

Ettinghausen, Richard. *From Byzantium to Sassanian Iran and the Islamic World.* Leiden: E. J. Brill, 1972.

Ettinghausen, Richard, Oleg Grabar, and Marilyn Jenkins-Madina. *The Art and Architecture of Islam, 650–1250.* Rev. ed. New Haven: Yale University Press, 2001.

Ferrier, Ronald W., ed. *The Arts of Persia.* New Haven: Yale University Press, 1989.

Frishman, Martin, and Hasan-Uddin Khan. *The Mosque: History, Architectural Development and Regional Diversity.* New York: Thames & Hudson, 1994.

Goodwin, Godfrey. *A History of Ottoman Architecture.* 2nd ed. New York: Thames & Hudson, 1987.

Grabar, Oleg. *The Alhambra.* Cambridge, Mass.: Harvard University Press, 1978.

———. *The Formation of Islamic Art.* Rev. ed. New Haven: Yale University Press, 1987.

Grube, Ernst J. *Architecture of the Islamic World: Its History and Social Meaning.* 2nd ed. New York: Thames & Hudson, 1984.

Hattstein, Markus, and Peter Delius, eds. *Islam: Art and Architecture.* Cologne: Könemann, 2000.

Hillenbrand, Robert. *Islamic Architecture: Form, Function, Meaning.* Edinburgh: Edinburgh University Press, 1994.

———. *Islamic Art and Architecture.* New York: Thames & Hudson, 1999.

Irwin, Robert. *Islamic Art in Context: Art, Architecture, and the Literary World.* New York: Abrams, 1997.

Lings, Martin. *The Qur'anic Art of Calligraphy and Illumination.* London: World of Islam Festival Trust, 1976.

Michell, George, ed. *Architecture of the Islamic World.* New York: Thames & Hudson, 1978.

Porter, Venetia. *Islamic Tiles.* London: British Museum, 1995.

Robinson, Frank. *Atlas of the Islamic World.* Oxford: Equinox, 1982.

Schimmel, Annemarie. *Calligraphy and Islamic Culture.* New York: New York University Press, 1984.

Stierlin, Henri. *Islam I: Early Architecture from Baghdad to Cordoba.* Cologne: Taschen, 1996.

———. *Islamic Art and Architecture from Isfahan to the Taj Mahal.* New York: Thames & Hudson, 2002.

Ward, Rachel M. *Islamic Metalwork.* New York: Thames & Hudson, 1993.

Welch, Anthony. *Calligraphy in the Arts of the Islamic World.* Austin: University of Texas Press, 1979.

## CHAPTER 14
### FROM ALASKA TO THE ANDES:
### NATIVE ARTS OF THE AMERICAS BEFORE 1300

Alva, Walter, and Christopher Donnan. *Royal Tombs of Sipán.* Los Angeles: Fowler Museum of Cultural History, 1993.

Benson, Elizabeth P., and Beatriz de la Fuente, eds. *Olmec Art of Ancient Mexico.* Washington, D.C.: National Gallery of Art, 1996.

Berlo, Janet Catherine, ed. *Art, Ideology, and the City of Teotihuacan.* Washington, D.C.: Dumbarton Oaks, 1992.

Berlo, Janet Catherine, and Ruth B. Phillips. *Native North American Art.* New York: Oxford University Press, 1998.

Berrin, Kathleen, ed. *The Spirit of Ancient Peru: Treasures from the Museo Arqueologico Rafael Larco Herrera.* San Francisco: The Fine Arts Museums of San Francisco, 1997.

Berrin, Kathleen, and Esther Pasztory, eds. *Teotihuacan: Art from the City of the Gods.* San Francisco: Thames & Hudson/The Fine Arts Museums of San Francisco, 1993.

Boone, Elizabeth, ed. *Andean Art at Dumbarton Oaks.* 2 vols. Washington, D.C.: Dumbarton Oaks, 1996.

Brody, J. J., and Rina Swentzell. *To Touch the Past: The Painted Pottery of the Mimbres People.* New York: Hudson Hills, 1996.

Brose, David. *Ancient Art of the American Woodland Indians.* New York: Abrams, 1985.

Bruhns, Karen O. *Ancient South America.* New York: Cambridge University Press, 1994.

Burger, Richard. *Chavín and the Origins of Andean Civilization.* New York: Thames & Hudson, 1992.

Carrasco, David. *The Oxford Encyclopedia of Mesoamerican Cultures: The Civilizations of Mexico and Central America.* New York, Oxford University Press, 2001.

Clark, John E., and Mary E. Pye, eds. *Olmec Art and Archaeology in Mesoamerica.* Washington, D.C.: National Gallery of Art, 2000.

Coe, Michael D. *Mexico.* 4th ed. New York: Thames & Hudson, 1994.

———. *The Maya.* 6th ed. New York: Thames & Hudson, 1999.

Coe, Michael D., and Justin Kerr. *The Art of the Maya Scribe.* New York: Abrams, 1998.

Cordell, Linda S. *Ancient Pueblo Peoples.* Washington, D.C.: Smithsonian Institution Press, 1994.

Donnan, Christopher. *Ceramics of Ancient Peru.* Los Angeles: Fowler Museum of Cultural History, 1992.

Fagan, Brian. *Ancient North America: The Archaeology of a Continent.* 2nd ed. New York: Thames & Hudson, 1995.

Fash, William. *Scribes, Warriors, and Kings: The City of Copan and the Ancient Maya.* New York: Thames & Hudson, 1991.

Feest, Christian F. *Native Arts of North America.* 2nd ed. New York: Thames & Hudson, 1992.

Fitzhugh, William W., and Aron Crowell, eds. *Crossroads of Continents: Cultures of Siberia and Alaska.* Washington, D.C.: Smithsonian Institution Press, 1988.

Grube, Nikolai, ed. *Maya: Divine Kings of the Rain Forest.* Cologne: Könemann, 2000.

Hadingham, Evan. *Lines to the Mountain Gods: Nazca and the Mysteries of Peru.* Norman: University of Oklahoma Press, 1988.

Jones, Julie, ed. *The Art of Pre-Columbian Gold: The Jan Mitchell Collection.* New York: Metropolitan Museum of Art, 1985.

Kolata, Alan. *The Tiwanaku: Portrait of an Andean Civilization.* Cambridge: Blackwell, 1993.

Kubler, George. *The Art and Architecture of Ancient America: The Mexican, Maya, and Andean Peoples.* 3rd ed. New Haven: Yale University Press, 1992.

Mathews, Zena, and Aldona Jonaitis, eds. *Native North American Art History.* Palo Alto, Calif.: Peek Publications, 1982.

Miller, Mary Ellen. *The Art of Mesoamerica, from Olmec to Aztec.* 2nd ed. New York: Thames & Hudson, 1996.

———. *Maya Art and Architecture.* New York: Thames & Hudson, 1999.

Miller, Mary Ellen, and Karl Taube. *The Gods and Symbols of Ancient Mexico and the Maya: An Illustrated Dictionary of Mesoamerican Religion.* New York: Thames & Hudson, 1993.

Morris, Craig, and Adriana von Hagen. *The Inka Empire and Its Andean Origins.* New York: Abbeville, 1993.

Nabokov, Peter, and Robert Easton. *Native American Architecture.* New York: Oxford University Press, 1989.

O'Connor, Mallory M. *Lost Cities of the Ancient Southeast.* Gainesville: University Press of Florida, 1995.

*Olmecs.* Special edition of *Arqueología Mexicana.* Mexico City: Editorial Raíces, 1998.

Pang, Hilda. *Pre-Columbian Art: Investigations and Insights.* Norman: University of Oklahoma Press, 1992.

Pasztory, Esther. *Pre-Columbian Art.* New York: Cambridge University Press, 1998.

Paul, Anne. *Paracas Ritual Attire: Symbols of Authority in Ancient Peru.* Norman: University of Oklahoma Press, 1990.

Penney, David, and George C. Longfish. *Native American Art.* Hong Kong: Hugh Lauter Levin and Associates, 1994.

Schele, Linda, and Peter Mathews. *The Code of Kings: The Language of Seven Sacred Maya Temples and Tombs.* New York: Scribner, 1998.

Schele, Linda, and Mary E. Miller. *The Blood of Kings: Dynasty and Ritual in Maya Art.* Fort Worth, Tex.: Kimbell Art Museum, 1986.

Schmidt, Peter, Mercedes de la Garza, and Enrique Nalda, eds. *Maya.* New York: Rizzoli, 1998.

Stone-Miller, Rebecca. *Art of the Andes from Chavín to Inca.* New York: Thames & Hudson, 1996.

———, ed. *To Weave for the Sun: Andean Textiles in the Museum of Fine Arts, Boston.* Boston: Museum of Fine Arts, 1992.

Townsend, Richard F., ed. *Ancient West Mexico.* Chicago: Art Institute of Chicago, 1998.

———. *Art from Sacred Landscapes.* Chicago: Art Institute of Chicago, 1992.

Von Hagen, Adriana, and Craig Morris. *The Cities of the Ancient Andes.* New York: Thames & Hudson, 1998.

Wardwell, Allen. *Ancient Eskimo Ivories of the Bering Strait.* New York: Rizzoli, 1986.

Weaver, Muriel Porter. *The Aztecs, Mayas, and Their Predecessors.* 3rd ed. San Diego, Calif.: Academic Press, 1993.

Whiteford, Andrew H., Stewart Peckham, and Kate Peck Kent. *I Am Here: Two Thousand Years of Southwest Indian Arts and Crafts.* Santa Fe: Museum of New Mexico Press, 1989.

## CHAPTER 15
### SOUTH FROM THE SAHARA:
### EARLY AFRICAN ART

Bassani, Ezio, and William Fagg. *Africa and the Renaissance: Art in Ivory.* New York: Center for African Art, 1988.

Ben-Amos, Paula. *The Art of Benin.* New York: Thames & Hudson, 1980.

Blier, Suzanne P. *Royal Arts of Africa: The Majesty of Form.* New York: Abrams, 1998.

Bourgeois, Jean-Louis, and Carollee Pelos. *Spectacular Vernacular: The Adobe Tradition.* New York: Aperture, 1989.

Campbell, Alec, and David Coulson. *African Rock Art: Paintings and Engravings on Stone.* New York: Abrams, 2001.

Connah, Graham. *African Civilizations.* 2nd ed. Cambridge: Cambridge University Press, 2001.

Dark, Philip J. C. *An Introduction to Benin Art and Technology.* Oxford: Clarendon Press, 1973.

Dewey, William J. *Legacies of Stone: Zimbabwe Past and Present.* Tervuren: Royal Museum for Central Africa, 1997.

Drewal, Henry J., John Pemberton, and Rowland Abiodun. *Yoruba: Nine Centuries of African Art and Thought.* New York: Center for African Art, in association with Abrams, 1989.

Eyo, Ekpo, and Frank Willett. *Treasures of Ancient Nigeria.* New York: Knopf, 1980.

Ezra, Kate. *Royal Art of Benin: The Perls Collection in the Metropolitan Museum of Art.* New York: Metropolitan Museum of Art, 1992.

Fagg, Bernard. *Nok Terracottas.* Lagos: Ethnographica, 1977.

Garlake, Peter. *Early Art and Architecture of Africa.* Oxford: Oxford University Press, 2002.

———. *Great Zimbabwe.* London: Thames & Hudson, 1973.

Huffman, Thomas N. *Snakes and Crocodiles: Power and Symbolism in Ancient Zimbabwe.* Johannesburg: Witwatersrand University Press, 1996.

Lajoux, Jean-Dominique. *The Rock Paintings of Tassili.* Cleveland: World Publishing, 1963.

Phillips, Tom, ed. *Africa, the Art of a Continent.* New York: Prestel, 1995.

Phillipson, D. W. *African Archaeology.* 2nd ed. New York: Cambridge University Press, 1993.

———. *Ancient Ethiopia: Aksum, Its Antecedents and Successors.* London: British Museum Press, 1998.

Prussin, Labelle. *Hatumere: Islamic Design in West Africa.* Berkeley and Los Angeles: University of California Press, 1986.

Schädler, Karl-Ferdinand. *Earth and Ore: 2500 Years of African Art in Terra-Cotta and Metal.* Munich: Panterra Verlag, 1997.

Shaw, Thurstan. *Nigeria: Its Archaeology and Early History.* London: Thames & Hudson, 1978.

———. *Unearthing Igbo-Ukwu: Archaeological Discoveries in Eastern Nigeria.* New York: Oxford University Press, 1977.

*Vallées du Niger.* Paris: Editions de la Réunion des Musées Nationaux, 1993.

Willett, Frank. *Ife in the History of West African Sculpture.* New York: McGraw-Hill, 1967.

## CHAPTER 16
### EUROPE AFTER THE FALL OF ROME:
### EARLY MEDIEVAL ART IN THE WEST

Alexander, Jonathan J. G. *Insular Manuscripts, Sixth to the Ninth Century.* London: Miller, 1978.

*The Art of Medieval Spain, A.D. 500–1200.* New York: Metropolitan Museum of Art, 1993.

Backhouse, Janet, D. H. Turner, and Leslie Webster, eds. *The Golden Age of Anglo-Saxon Art, 966–1066.* Bloomington: Indiana University Press, 1984.

Barral i Altet, Xavier. *The Early Middle Ages: From Late Antiquity to A.D. 1000.* Cologne: Taschen, 1997.

Brown, Katharine Reynolds, Dafydd Kidd, and Charles T. Little, eds. *From Attila to Charlemagne.* New York: Metropolitan Museum of Art, 2000.

Collins, Roger. *Early Medieval Europe, 300–1000.* New York: St. Martin's, 1991.

Conant, Kenneth J. *Carolingian and Romanesque Architecture, 800–1200.* 4th ed. New Haven: Yale University Press, 1992.

Davis-Weyer, Caecilia. *Early Medieval Art, 300–1150: Sources and Documents.* Toronto: University of Toronto Press, 1986. Reprint of 1971 ed.

Diebold, William J. *Word and Image: An Introduction to Early Medieval Art.* Boulder, Colo.: Westview Press, 2000.

Dodwell, Charles R. *Anglo-Saxon Art: A New Perspective.* Ithaca, N.Y.: Cornell University Press, 1982.

———. *The Pictorial Arts of the West, 800–1200.* New Haven: Yale University Press, 1993.

Harbison, Peter. *The Golden Age of Irish Art: The Medieval Achievement 600–1200.* New York: Thames & Hudson, 1999.

Henderson, George. *Early Medieval.* New York: Penguin, 1972.

———. *From Durrow to Kells: The Insular Gospel-Books, 650–800.* London: Thames & Hudson, 1987.

Horn, Walter W., and Ernest Born. *The Plan of Saint Gall.* 3 vols. Berkeley: University of California Press, 1979.

Hubert, Jean, Jean Porcher, and Wolfgang Fritz Volbach. *The Carolingian Renaissance.* New York: Braziller, 1970.

———. *Europe of the Invasions.* New York: Braziller, 1969.

Klindt-Jensen, Ole, and David M. Wilson. *Viking Art.* 2nd ed. Minneapolis: University of Minnesota Press, 1980.

Mayr-Harting, Henry. *Ottonian Book Illumination: An Historical Study.* 2 vols. London: Miller, 1991–1993.

Megaw, Ruth, and John Vincent Megaw. *Celtic Art: From Its Beginning to the Book of Kells.* New York: Thames & Hudson, 1989.

Mütherich, Florentine, and Joachim E. Gaehde. *Carolingian Painting.* New York: Braziller, 1976.

Nees, Lawrence J. *Early Medieval Art.* New York: Oxford University Press, 2002.

Nordenfalk, Carl. *Celtic and Anglo-Saxon Painting: Book Illumination in the British Isles, 600–800.* New York: Braziller, 1977.

O'Brien, Jacqueline, and Peter Harbison. *Ancient Ireland: From Prehistory to the Middle Ages.* New York: Oxford University Press, 2000.

Richardson, Hilary, and John Scarry. *An Introduction to Irish High Crosses.* Dublin: Mercier, 1996.

Stalley, Roger. *Early Medieval Architecture.* New York: Oxford University Press, 1999.

*Treasures of Early Irish Art, 1500 B.C. to 1500 A.D.* New York: Metropolitan Museum of Art, 1977.

Wilson, David M. *Anglo-Saxon Art: From the Seventh Century to the Norman Conquest.* London: Thames & Hudson, 1984.

### CHAPTER 17
### THE AGE OF PILGRIMAGES: ROMANESQUE ART

Armi, C. Edson. *Masons and Sculptors in Romanesque Burgundy: The New Aesthetics of Cluny III.* 2 vols. University Park: Pennsylvania State University Press, 1983.

Barral i Altet, Xavier. *The Romanesque: Towns, Cathedrals and Monasteries.* Cologne: Taschen, 1998.

Cahn, Walter. *Romanesque Bible Illumination.* Ithaca, N.Y.: Cornell University Press, 1982.

———. *Romanesque Manuscripts: The Twelfth Century.* 2 vols. London: Miller, 1998.

Conant, Kenneth J. *Carolingian and Romanesque Architecture, 800–1200.* 4th ed. New Haven: Yale University Press, 1992.

Demus, Otto. *Romanesque Mural Painting.* New York: Thames & Hudson, 1970.

Dodwell, Charles R. *The Pictorial Arts of the West, 800–1200.* New Haven: Yale University Press, 1993.

Fergusson, Peter. *Architecture of Solitude: Cistercian Abbeys in Twelfth-Century Europe.* Princeton, N.J.: Princeton University Press, 1984.

Forsyth, Ilene H. *The Throne of Wisdom: Wood Sculptures of the Madonna in Romanesque France.* Princeton, N.J.: Princeton University Press, 1972.

Grabar, André, and Carl Nordenfalk. *Romanesque Painting.* New York: Skira, 1958.

Grape, Wolfgang. *The Bayeux Tapestry: Monument to a Norman Triumph.* New York: Prestel, 1994.

Hearn, Millard F. *Romanesque Sculpture: The Revival of Monumental Stone Sculpture in the Eleventh and Twelfth Centuries.* Ithaca, N.Y.: Cornell University Press, 1981.

Kahn, Deborah, ed. *The Romanesque Frieze and Its Spectator.* London: Miller, 1992.

Kauffmann, Claus M. *Romanesque Manuscripts, 1066–1190.* Boston: New York Graphic Society, 1975.

Male, Émile. *Religious Art in France: The Twelfth Century.* Rev. ed. Princeton, N.J.: Princeton University Press, 1978.

Minne-Sève, Viviane, and Hervé Kergall. *Romanesque and Gothic France: Architecture and Sculpture.* New York: Abrams, 2000.

Nichols, Stephen G. *Romanesque Signs: Early Medieval Narrative and Iconography.* New Haven: Yale University Press, 1983.

Nordenfalk, Carl. *Early Medieval Book Illumination.* New York: Rizzoli, 1988.

Petzold, Andreas. *Romanesque Art.* New York: Abrams, 1995.

Prache, Anne. *Cathedrals of Europe.* Ithaca, N.Y.: Cornell University Press, 1999.

Schapiro, Meyer. *The Sculpture of Moissac.* New York: Thames & Hudson, 1985.

Stalley, Roger. *Early Medieval Architecture.* New York: Oxford University Press, 1999.

Swarzenski, Hanns. *Monuments of Romanesque Art: The Art of Church Treasures in North-Western Europe.* 2nd ed. Chicago: University of Chicago Press, 1967.

Tate, Robert B., and Marcus Tate. *The Pilgrim Route to Santiago.* Oxford: Phaidon, 1987.

Toman, Rolf, ed. *Romanesque: Architecture, Sculpture, Painting.* Cologne: Könemann, 1997.

Zarnecki, George, Janet Holt, and Tristram Holland, eds. *English Romanesque Art, 1066–1200.* London: Weidenfeld & Nicolson, 1984.

### CHAPTER 18
### THE AGE OF GREAT CATHEDRALS: GOTHIC ART

Alexander, Jonathan J. G., and Paul Binski, eds. *Age of Chivalry: Art in Plantagenet England, 1200–1400.* London: Royal Academy, 1987.

Bony, Jean. *The English Decorated Style: Gothic Architecture Transformed, 1250–1350.* Ithaca, N.Y.: Cornell University Press, 1979.

———. *French Gothic Architecture of the Twelfth and Thirteenth Centuries.* Berkeley: University of California Press, 1983.

Branner, Robert. *Manuscript Painting in Paris during the Reign of St. Louis.* Berkeley: University of California Press, 1977.

———. *St. Louis and the Court Style in Gothic Architecture.* London: Zwemmer, 1965.

———, ed. *Chartres Cathedral.* New York: Norton, 1969.

Brown, Sarah, and David O'Connor. *Glass-Painters (Medieval Craftsmen).* Toronto: University of Toronto Press, 1991.

Camille, Michael. *Gothic Art: Glorious Visions.* New York: Abrams, 1996.

———. *The Gothic Idol: Ideology and Image-Making in Medieval Art.* New York: Cambridge University Press, 1989.

Courtenay, Lynn T., ed. *The Engineering of Medieval Cathedrals.* Aldershot: Scolar, 1997.

Erlande-Brandenburg, Alain. *The Cathedral: The Social and Architectural Dynamics of Construction.* New York: Cambridge University Press, 1994.

———. *Gothic Art.* New York: Abrams, 1989.

Favier, Jean. *The World of Chartres.* New York: Abrams, 1990.

Fitchen, John. *The Construction of Gothic Cathedrals: A Study of Medieval Vault Erection.* Chicago: University of Chicago Press, 1981.

Frankl, Paul, and Paul Crossley. *Gothic Architecture.* New Haven: Yale University Press, 2000.

———. *The Gothic: Literary Sources and Interpretations during Eight Centuries.* Princeton, N.J.: Princeton University Press, 1960.

Frisch, Teresa G. *Gothic Art 1140–c. 1450: Sources and Documents.* Toronto: University of Toronto Press, 1987. Reprint of 1971 ed.

Gerson, Paula, ed. *Abbot Suger and Saint-Denis.* New York: Metropolitan Museum of Art, 1986.

Gimpel, Jean. *The Cathedral Builders.* New York: Grove, 1961.

Grodecki, Louis. *Gothic Architecture.* New York: Electa/Rizzoli, 1985.

Grodecki, Louis, and Catherine Brisac. *Gothic Stained Glass, 1200–1300.* Ithaca, N.Y.: Cornell University Press, 1985.

Jantzen, Hans. *High Gothic: The Classic Cathedrals of Chartres, Reims, Amiens.* Princeton, N.J.: Princeton University Press, 1984.

Male, Émile. *Religious Art in France: The Thirteenth Century.* Rev. ed. Princeton, N.J.: Princeton University Press, 1984.

Minne-Sève, Viviane, and Hervé Kergall. *Romanesque and Gothic France: Architecture and Sculpture.* New York: Abrams, 2000.

Nussbaum, Norbert. *German Gothic Church Architecture.* New Haven: Yale University Press, 2000.

Panofsky, Erwin. *Abbot Suger on the Abbey Church of St. Denis and Its Art Treasures.* 2nd ed. Princeton, N.J.: Princeton University Press, 1979.

———. *Gothic Architecture and Scholasticism.* New York: New American Library, 1985. Reprint of 1951 ed.

Prache, Anne. *Cathedrals of Europe.* Ithaca, N.Y.: Cornell University Press, 1999.

Radding, Charles M., and William W. Clark. *Medieval Architecture, Medieval Learning.* New Haven: Yale University Press, 1992.

Rudolph, Conrad. *Artistic Change at St-Denis: Abbot Suger's Program and the Early Twelfth-Century Controversy over Art.* Princeton, N.J.: Princeton University Press, 1990.

Sauerländer, Willibald, and Max Hirmer. *Gothic Sculpture in France, 1140–1270.* New York: Abrams, 1973.

Simson, Otto G. von. *The Gothic Cathedral: Origins of Gothic Architecture and the Medieval Concept of Order.* 3rd ed. Princeton, N.J.: Princeton University Press, 1988.

Toman, Rolf, ed. *The Art of Gothic: Architecture, Sculpture, Painting.* Cologne: Könemann, 1999.

Williamson, Paul. *Gothic Sculpture, 1140–1300.* New Haven: Yale University Press, 1995.

Wilson, Christopher. *The Gothic Cathedral: The Architecture of the Great Church, 1130–1530.* London: Thames & Hudson, 1990.

### CHAPTER 19
### FROM GOTHIC TO RENAISSANCE: 14TH-CENTURY ITALIAN ART

Andrés, Glenn M., John M. Hunisak, and Richard Turner. *The Art of Florence.* 2 vols. New York: Abbeville Press, 1988.

Antal, Frederick. *Florentine Painting and Its Social Background.* London: Kegan Paul, 1948.

Bomford, David. *Art in the Making: Italian Painting before 1400.* London: National Gallery, 1989.

Borsook, Eve, and Fiorelli Superbi Gioffredi. *Italian Altarpieces 1250–1550:* Function and Design. Oxford: Clarendon Press, 1994.

Cennini, Cennino. *The Craftsman's Handbook (Il Libro dell'Arte).* Translated by Daniel V. Thompson Jr. New York: Dover, 1954.

Cole, Bruce. *Sienese Painting: From Its Origins to the Fifteenth Century.* New York: HarperCollins, 1987.

———. *Italian Art, 1250–1550: The Relation of Renaissance Art to Life and Society.* New York: Harper & Row, 1987.

Hills, Paul. *The Light of Early Italian Painting.* New Haven: Yale University Press, 1987.

Maginnis, Hayden B. J. *Painting in the Age of Giotto: A Historical Reevaluation.* University Park: Pennsylvania State University Press, 1997.

———. *The World of the Early Sienese Painter.* University Park: Pennsylvania State University Press, 2001.

Meiss, Millard. *Painting in Florence and Siena after the Black Death.* Princeton, N.J.: Princeton University Press, 1976.

Moskowitz, Anita Fiderer. *Italian Gothic Sculpture: c. 1250–c. 1400.* Cambridge: Cambridge University Press, 2001.

Norman, Diana, ed. *Siena, Florence, and Padua: Art, Society, and Religion 1280–1400.* New Haven: Yale University Press, 1995.

Panofsky, Erwin. *Renaissance and Renascences in Western Art.* New York: HarperCollins, 1972.

Pope-Hennessy, John. *Introduction to Italian Sculpture.* 3rd. ed. 3 vols. New York: Phaidon, 1986.

———. *Italian Gothic Sculpture.* 3rd ed. Oxford: Phaidon, 1986.

Smart, Alastair. *The Dawn of Italian Painting.* Ithaca, N.Y.: Cornell University Press, 1978.

White, John. *Art and Architecture in Italy: 1250–1400.* 3rd ed. New Haven: Yale University Press, 1993.

## Chapter 20
### Piety, Passion, and Politics: 15th-Century Art in Northen Europe and Spain

Baxandall, Michael. *The Limewood Sculptors of Renaissance Germany.* New Haven: Yale University Press, 1980.

Blum, Shirley Neilsen. *Early Netherlandish Triptychs: A Study in Patronage.* Berkeley: University of California Press, 1969.

Campbell, Lorne. *The Fifteenth Century Netherlandish Schools.* London: National Gallery Publications, 1998.

Chatelet, Albert. *Early Dutch Painting.* New York: Konecky, 1988.

Cuttler, Charles P. *Northern Painting from Pucelle to Bruegel.* New York: Holt, Rinehart & Winston, 1968.

De Hamel, Christopher. *A History of Illuminated Manuscripts.* Oxford: Phaidon, 1986.

Friedlander, Max J. *Early Netherlandish Painting.* 14 vols. New York: Praeger/Phaidon, 1967–1976.

———. *From Van Eyck to Bruegel.* 3rd ed. Ithaca, N.Y.: Cornell University Press, 1981.

Harbison, Craig. *The Mirror of the Artist: Northern Renaissance Art in Its Historical Context.* New York: Abrams, 1995.

Huizinga, Johan. *The Autumn of the Middle Ages.* Translated by Rodney J. Payton and Ulrich Mammitzsch. Chicago: University of Chicago Press, 1996.

Jacobs, Lynn F. *Early Netherlandish Carved Altarpieces, 1380–1550: Medieval Tastes and Mass Marketing.* Cambridge: Cambridge University Press, 1998.

Lane, Barbara G. *The Altar and the Altarpiece: Sacramental Themes in Early Netherlandish Painting.* New York: Harper & Row, 1984.

Meiss, Millard. *French Painting in the Time of Jean de Berry: The Limbourgs and Their Contemporaries.* New York: Braziller, 1974.

Müller, Theodor. *Sculpture in the Netherlands, Germany, France and Spain: 1400–1500.* New Haven: Yale University Press, 1986.

Panofsky, Erwin. *Early Netherlandish Painting: Its Origins and Character.* 2 vols. Cambridge, Mass: Harvard University Press, 1966.

Prevenier, Walter, and Wim Blockmans. *The Burgundian Netherlands.* Cambridge: Cambridge University Press, 1986.

Snyder, James. *Northern Renaissance Art: Painting, Sculpture, the Graphic Arts from 1350 to 1575.* New York: Abrams, 1985.

Wolfthal, Diane. *The Beginnings of Netherlandish Canvas Painting, 1400–1530.* New York: Cambridge University Press, 1989.

## Chapter 21
### Humanisum and the Allure of Antiquity: 15th-Century Italian Art

Adams, Laurie Schneider. *Key Monuments of the Italian Renaissance.* Denver, Colo.: Westview Press, 1999.

Alberti, Leon Battista. *On Painting.* Translated by John R. Spencer. Rev. ed. New Haven: Yale University Press, 1966. (Written 1435/36; originally published 1540)

———. *Ten Books on Architecture.* Edited by J. Rykwert; translated by J. Leoni. London: Tiranti, 1955. (Written ca. 1450; originally published 1486)

Ames-Lewis, Francis. *Drawing in Early Renaissance Italy.* New Haven: Yale University Press, 1981.

Baxandall, Michael. *Painting and Experience in Fifteenth Century Italy: A Primer in the Social History of Pictorial Style.* 2nd ed. New York: Oxford University Press, 1988.

Beck, James. *Italian Renaissance Painting.* New York: HarperCollins, 1981.

Bober, Phyllis Pray, and Ruth Rubinstein. *Renaissance Artists and Antique Sculpture: A Handbook of Sources.* Oxford: Oxford University Press, 1986.

Borsook, Eve. *The Mural Painters of Tuscany.* New York: Oxford University Press, 1981.

Burckhardt, Jacob. *The Architecture of the Italian Renaissance.* Chicago: University of Chicago Press, 1987. (Originally published 1868)

———. *The Civilization of the Renaissance in Italy.* London: Phaidon, 1960. (Originally published 1867)

Christiansen, Keith, Laurence B. Kanter, and Carl B. Strehle, eds. *Painting in Renaissance Siena, 1420–1500.* New York: Metropolitan Museum of Art, 1988.

Cole, Alison. *Virtue and Magnificence: Art of the Italian Renaissance Courts.* New York: Abrams, 1995.

Cole, Bruce. *Masaccio and the Art of Early Renaissance Florence.* Bloomington: Indiana University Press, 1980.

Dempsey, Charles. *The Portrayal of Love: Botticelli's* Primavera *and Humanist Culture at the Time of Lorenzo the Magnificent.* Princeton, N.J.: Princeton University Press, 1992.

Edgerton, Samuel Y., Jr. *The Heritage of Giotto's Geometry: Art and Science on the Eve of the Scientific Revolution.* Ithaca, N.Y.: Cornell University Press, 1991.

———. *The Renaissance Rediscovery of Linear Perspective.* New York: Harper & Row, 1976.

Gilbert, Creighton, ed. *Italian Art 1400–1500:* Sources and Documents. Evanston, Ill.: Northwestern University Press, 1992.

Goldthwaite, Richard A. *The Building of Renaissance Florence: An Economic and Social History.* Baltimore: Johns Hopkins University Press, 1980.

Gombrich, E. H. *Norm and Form: Studies in the Art of the Renaissance.* 4th ed. Oxford: Phaidon, 1985.

Hall, Marcia B. *Color and Meaning: Practice and Theory in Renaissance Painting.* Cambridge: Cambridge University Press, 1992.

Hartt, Frederick. *History of Italian Renaissance Art: Painting, Sculpture, Architecture.* 4th ed. Revised by David G. Wilkins. Upper Saddle River, N.J.: Prentice Hall, 1994.

Heydenreich, Ludwig H., and Wolfgang Lotz. *Architecture in Italy, 1400–1600.* Harmondsworth: Penguin, 1974.

Hollingsworth, Mary. *Patronage in Renaissance Italy: From 1400 to the Early Sixteenth Century.* Baltimore: Johns Hopkins University Press, 1994.

Kemp, Martin. *Behind the Picture: Art and Evidence in the Italian Renaissance.* New Haven: Yale University Press, 1997.

Kempers, Bram. *Painting, Power, and Patronage: The Rise of the Professional Artist in the Italian Renaissance.* London: Penguin, 1992.

Kent, F. W., and Patricia Simons, eds. *Patronage, Art, and Society in Renaissance Italy.* Canberra: Humanities Research Centre and Clarendon Press, 1987.

Lieberman, Ralph. *Renaissance Architecture in Venice.* New York: Abbeville Press, 1982.

McAndrew, John. *Venetian Architecture of the Early Renaissance.* Cambridge, Mass: MIT Press, 1980.

Meiss, Millard. *The Painter's Choice: Problems in the Interpretation of Renaissance Art.* New York: HarperCollins, 1977.

Murray, Peter. *The Architecture of the Italian Renaissance.* Rev. ed. New York: Schocken, 1986.

———. *Renaissance Architecture.* New York: Electa/Rizzoli, 1985.

Murray, Peter, and Linda Murray. *The Art of the Renaissance.* London: Thames & Hudson, 1985.

Olson, Roberta J. M. *Italian Renaissance Sculpture.* London: Thames & Hudson, 1992.

Panofsky, Erwin. *Renaissance and Renascences in Western Art.* New York: HarperCollins, 1972.

Pater, Walter. *The Renaissance: Studies in Art and Poetry.* Edited by D. L. Hill. Berkeley: University of California Press, 1980.

Pope-Hennessy, John. *An Introduction to Italian Sculpture.* 3rd ed. 3 vols. New York: Phaidon, 1986.

Seymour, Charles. *Sculpture in Italy: 1400–1500.* New Haven: Yale University Press, 1966.

Thomson, David. *Renaissance Architecture: Critics, Patrons, and Luxury.* Manchester: Manchester University Press, 1993.

Turner, A. Richard. *Renaissance Florence: The Invention of a New Art.* New York: Abrams, 1997.

Vasari, Giorgio. *Lives of the Painters, Sculptors and Architects.* Translated by Gaston du C. de Vere. New York: Knopf, 1996. (Originally published 1550)

Wackernagel, Martin. *The World of the Florentine Renaissance Artist: Projects and Patrons, Workshops and Art Market.* Princeton, N.J.: Princeton University Press, 1981.

Welch, Evelyn. *Art and Society in Italy 1350–1500.* Oxford: Oxford University Press, 1997.

White, John. *The Birth and Rebirth of Pictorial Space.* 3rd ed. Boston: Faber & Faber, 1987.

Wilde, Johannes. *Venetian Art from Bellini to Titian.* Oxford: Clarendon Press, 1981.

Wittkower, Rudolf. *Architectural Principles in the Age of Humanism.* 4th ed. London: Academy, 1988.

## CHAPTER 22
### BEAUTY, SCIENCE, AND SPIRIT IN ITALIAN ART: THE HIGH RENAISSANCE AND MANNERISM

Blunt, Anthony. *Artistic Theory in Italy, 1450–1600.* London: Oxford University Press, 1975.

Brown, Patricia Fortini. *Art and Life in Renaissance Venice.* New York: Abrams, 1997.

Castiglione, Baldassare. *Book of the Courtier.* New York: Viking Penguin, 1976. (Originally published 1528)

Farago, Claire, ed. *Reframing the Renaissance: Visual Culture in Europe and Latin America, 1450–1650.* New Haven: Yale University Press, 1995.

Freedberg, Sydney J. *Painting in Italy: 1500–1600.* 3rd ed. New Haven: Yale University Press, 1993.

Friedlaender, Walter. *Mannerism and Anti-Mannerism in Italian Painting.* New York: Schocken, 1965.

Goffen, Rona. *Piety and Patronage in Renaissance Venice: Bellini, Titian, and the Franciscans.* New Haven: Yale University Press, 1986.

Hall, Marcia B. *After Raphael: Painting in Central Italy in the Sixteenth Century.* Cambridge: Cambridge University Press, 1999.

Haskell, Francis, and Nicholas Penny. *Taste and the Antique: The Lure of Classical Sculpture, 1500–1900.* New Haven: Yale University Press, 1981.

Holt, Elizabeth Gilmore, ed. *A Documentary History of Art.* Vol. 2, *Michelangelo and the Mannerists.* Rev. ed. Princeton, N.J.: Princeton University Press, 1982.

Humfry, Peter. *Painting in Renaissance Venice.* New Haven: Yale University Press, 1995.

Huse, Norbert, and Wolfgang Wolters. *The Art of Renaissance Venice: Architecture, Sculpture, and Painting.* Chicago: University of Chicago Press, 1990.

Levey, Michael. *High Renaissance.* New York: Viking Penguin, 1978.

Murray, Linda. *The High Renaissance and Mannerism.* New York: Oxford University Press, 1977.

Partner, Peter. *Renaissance Rome, 1500–1559: A Portrait of a Society.* Berkeley: University of California Press, 1977.

Partridge, Loren. *The Art of Renaissance Rome.* New York: Abrams, 1996.

Pietrangeli, Carlo, André Chastel, John Shearman, John O'Malley, S.J., Pierluigi de Vecchi, Michael Hirst, Fabrizio Mancinelli, Gianluigi Colalucci, and Franco Bernbei. *The Sistine Chapel: The Art, the History, and the Restoration.* New York: Harmony Books, 1986.

Pope-Hennessy, John. *Italian High Renaissance and Baroque Sculpture.* 3rd ed. 3 vols. Oxford: Phaidon, 1986.

Rosand, David. *Painting in Cinquecento Venice: Titian, Veronese, Tintoretto.* New Haven: Yale University Press, 1982.

Shearman, John K. G. *Mannerism.* Baltimore: Penguin, 1978.

———. *Only Connect . . . Art and the Spectator in the Italian Renaissance.* Princeton, N.J.: Princeton University Press, 1990.

Summers, David. *Michelangelo and the Language of Art.* Princeton, N.J.: Princeton University Press, 1981.

Venturi, Lionello. *The Sixteenth Century: From Leonardo to El Greco.* New York: Skira, 1956.

Wölfflin, Heinrich. *The Art of the Italian Renaissance.* New York: Schocken, 1963.

———. *Classic Art: An Introduction to the Italian Renaissance.* 4th ed. Oxford: Phaidon, 1980.

## CHAPTER 23
### THE AGE OF REFORMATION: 16TH-CENTURY ART IN NORTHERN EUROPE AND SPAIN

Benesch, Otto. *Art of the Renaissance in Northern Europe.* Rev. ed. London: Phaidon, 1965.

———. *German Painting from Dürer to Holbein.* Geneva: Skira, 1966.

Blunt, Anthony. *Art and Architecture in France, 1500–1700.* Rev. ed. New Haven: Yale University Press, 1999.

Gibson, W. S. *"Mirror of the Earth": The World Landscape in Sixteenth Century Flemish Painting.* Princeton, N.J.: Princeton University Press, 1989.

Harbison, Craig. *The Mirror of the Artist: Northern Renaissance Art in Its Historical Context.* New York: Abrams, 1995.

Hitchcock, Henry-Russell. *German Renaissance Architecture.* Princeton, N.J.: Princeton University Press, 1981.

Koerner, Joseph Leo. *The Moment of Self-Portraiture in German Renaissance Art.* Chicago: University of Chicago Press, 1993.

Landau, David, and Peter Parshall. *The Renaissance Print: 1470–1550.* New Haven: Yale University Press, 1994.

Smith, Jeffrey C. *German Sculpture of the Later Renaissance, c. 1520–1580: Art in an Age of Uncertainty.* Princeton, N.J.: Princeton University Press, 1993.

Stechow, Wolfgang. *Northern Renaissance Art, 1400–1600: Sources and Documents.* Upper Saddle River, N.J.: Prentice Hall, 1966.

### BOOKS SPANNING THE 14TH THROUGH 17TH CENTURIES

Campbell, Lorne. *Renaissance Portraits: European Portrait-Painting in the Fourteenth, Fifteenth, and Sixteenth Centuries.* New Haven: Yale University Press, 1990.

Dunkerton, Jill, Susan Foister, Dillian Gordon, and Nicholas Penny. *Giotto to Durer: Early Renaissance Painting in the National Gallery.* New Haven: Yale University Press, 1991.

Gilbert, Creighton. *History of Renaissance Art throughout Europe.* New York: Abrams, 1973.

Haskell, Francis, and Nicholas Penny. *Taste and the Antique: The Lure of Classical Sculpture 1500–1900.* New Haven: Yale University Press, 1981.

Huyghe, René. *Larousse Encyclopedia of Renaissance and Baroque Art.* See Reference Books.

Kemp, Martin. *The Science of Art: Optical Themes in Western Art From Brunelleschi to Seurat.* New Haven: Yale University Press, 1990.

Paoletti, John T,. and Gary M. Radke. *Art in Renaissance Italy.* Upper Saddle River: Prentice Hall, 1997.

## CHAPTER 24
### POPES, PEASANTS, MONARCHS, AND MERCHANTS: BAROQUE ART

*The Age of Caravaggio.* New York: Metropolitan Museum of Art, 1985.

Alpers, Svetlana. *The Art of Describing: Dutch Art in the Seventeenth Century.* Chicago: University of Chicago Press, 1984.

———. *Rembrandt's Enterprise: The Studio and the Market.* Chicago: University of Chicago Press, 1988.

Blunt, Anthony. *Art and Architecture in France, 1500–1700.* Rev. ed. New Haven: Yale University Press, 1999.

———, ed. *Baroque and Rococo: Architecture and Decoration.* Cambridge: Harper & Row, 1982.

Brown, Christopher. *Scenes of Everyday Life: Dutch Genre Painting of the Seventeenth Century.* London: Faber & Faber, 1984.

Brown, Jonathan. *The Golden Age of Painting in Spain.* New Haven: Yale University Press, 1991.

———. *Kings and Connoisseurs: Collecting Art in Seventeenth-Century Europe.* Princeton, N.J.: Princeton University Press, 1994.

Bryson, Norman. *Word and Image: French Painting of the Ancien Régime.* Cambridge: Cambridge University Press, 1981.

Chastel, André. *French Art: The Ancien Regime, 1620–1775.* New York: Flammarion, 1996.

Enggass, Robert, and Jonathan Brown. *Italy and Spain, 1600–1750: Sources and Documents.* Upper Saddle River, N.J.: Prentice Hall, 1970.

Franits, Wayne. *Looking at Seventeenth-Century Dutch Art: Realism Reconsidered.* Cambridge: Cambridge University Press, 1997.

Freedberg, Sydney J. *Circa 1600: A Revolution of Style in Italian Painting.* Cambridge, Mass.: Harvard University Press, 1983.

Haak, Bob. *The Golden Age: Dutch Painters of the Seventeenth Century.* New York: Abrams, 1984.

Haskell, Francis. *Patrons and Painters: A Study in the Relations between Italian Art and Society in the Age of the Baroque.* Rev. ed. New Haven: Yale University Press, 1980.

Held, Julius, and Donald Posner. *17th and 18th Century Art: Baroque Painting, Sculpture, Architecture.* New York: Abrams, 1971.

Hempel, Eberhard. *Baroque Art and Architecture in Central Europe.* New York: Viking Penguin, 1977.

Hibbard, Howard. *Carlo Maderno and Roman Architecture, 1580–1630.* London: Zwemmer, 1971.

Howard, Deborah. *The Architectural History of Venice.* London: Batsford, 1981.

Huyghe, René, ed. *Larousse Encyclopedia of Renaissance and Baroque Art.* New York: Prometheus Press, 1963.

Kahr, Madlyn Millner. *Dutch Painting in the Seventeenth Century.* New York: Harper & Row, 1978.

Kitson, Michael. *The Age of Baroque.* London: Hamlyn, 1976.

Krautheimer, Richard. *The Rome of Alexander VII, 1655–1677.* Princeton, N.J.: Princeton University Press, 1985.

Lagerlöf, Margaretha R. *Ideal Landscape: Annibale Carracci, Nicolas Poussin and Claude Lorrain.* New Haven: Yale University Press, 1990.

Lees-Milne, James. *Baroque in Italy.* New York: Macmillan, 1960.

Martin, John R. *Baroque.* New York: Harper & Row, 1977.

Mérot, Alain. *French Painting in the Seventeenth Century.* New Haven: Yale University Press, 1995.

Millon, Henry A. *Baroque and Rococo Architecture.* New York: Braziller, 1965.

Montagu, Jennifer. *Roman Baroque Sculpture: The Industry of Art.* New Haven: Yale University Press, 1989.

Muller, Sheila D., ed. *Dutch Art: An Encyclopedia.* New York: Garland Publishers, 1997.

Norberg-Schulz, Christian. *Baroque Architecture.* New York: Rizzoli, 1986.

———. *Late Baroque and Rococo Architecture.* New York: Electa/Rizzoli, 1985.

North, Michael. *Art and Commerce in the Dutch Golden Age.* New Haven: Yale University Press, 1997.

Rosenberg, Jakob, Seymour Slive, and E. H. ter Kuile. *Dutch Art and Architecture, 1600–1800.* New Haven: Yale University Press, 1979.

Schama, Simon. *The Embarrassment of Riches: An Interpretation of Dutch Culture in the Golden Age.* Berkeley: University of California Press, 1988.

Stechow, Wolfgang. *Dutch Landscape Painting of the 17th Century.* 3rd ed. Oxford: Phaidon, 1981.

Summerson, Sir John. *Architecture in Britain: 1530–1830.* 9th ed. New Haven: Yale University Press, 1989.

Varriano, John. *Italian Baroque and Rococo Architecture.* New York: Oxford University Press, 1986.

Vlieghe, Hans. *Flemish Art and Architecture, 1586–1700.* New Haven: Yale University Press, 1999.

Waterhouse, Ellis Kirkham. *Baroque Painting in Rome.* London: Phaidon, 1976.

———. *Italian Baroque Painting.* 2nd ed. London: Phaidon, 1969.

———. *Painting in Britain: 1530–1790.* 4th ed. New Haven: Yale University Press, 1979.

Wittkower, Rudolf. *Art and Architecture in Italy 1600–1750.* 3rd ed. Harmondsworth: Penguin, 1982.

Wölfflin, Heinrich. *Principles of Art History: The Problem of the Development of Style in Later Art.* 7th ed. New York: Dover, 1950.

———. *Renaissance and Baroque.* London: Collins, 1984.

Wright, Christopher. *The French Painters of the 17th Century.* New York: New York Graphic Society, 1986.

## Chapter 25
### Sultans, Kings, Emperors, and Colonists:
### The Art of South and Southeast Asia after 1200

Asher, Catherine B. *Architecture of Mughal India.* New York: Cambridge University Press, 1992.

Beach, Milo Cleveland. *Mughal and Rajput Painting.* Cambridge: Cambridge University Press, 1992.

Blurton, T. Richard. *Hindu Art.* Cambridge, Mass: Harvard University Press, 1993.

Chaturachinda, Gwyneth, Sunanda Krishnamurty, and Pauline W. Tabtiang. *Dictionary of South and Southeast Asian Art.* Chiang Mai: Silkworm Books, 2000.

Craven, Roy C. *Indian Art: A Concise History.* Rev. ed. London: Thames & Hudson, 1997.

Dallapiccola, Anna Libera, ed. *Vijayanagara: City and Empire.* 2 vols. Stuttgart: Steiner, 1985.

Dehejia, Vidya. *Indian Art.* London: Phaidon, 1997.

*Encyclopedia of Indian Temple Architecture.* 8 vols. New Delhi: American Institute of Indian Studies, and Philadelphia: University of Pennsylvania Press, 1983–1996.

Girard-Geslan, Maud, ed. *Art of Southeast Asia.* New York: Abrams, 1998.

Harle, James C. *The Art and Architecture of the Indian Subcontinent.* 2nd ed. New Haven: Yale University Press, 1994.

Huntington, Susan L., and John C. Huntington. *The Art of Ancient India: Buddhist, Hindu, Jain.* New York: Weatherhill, 1985.

Michell, George. *Architecture and Art of Southern India: Vijayanagara and the Successor States, 1350–1750.* Cambridge: Cambridge University Press, 1995.

———. *Hindu Art and Architecture.* New York: Thames & Hudson, 2000.

———. *The Hindu Temple: An Introduction to Its Meaning and Forms.* Chicago: University of Chicago Press, 1988.

Mitter, Partha. *Indian Art.* New York: Oxford University Press, 2001.

Narula, Karen Schur. *Voyage of the Emerald Buddha.* Kuala Lumpur: Oxford University Press, 1994.

Pal, Pratapaditya, ed. *Master Artists of the Imperial Mughal Court.* Mumbai: Marg, 1991.

Rawson, Phillip. *The Art of Southeast Asia.* New York: Thames & Hudson, 1990.

Stadtner, Donald M. *The Art of Burma: New Studies.* Mumbai: Marg, 1999.

Stevenson, John, and John Guy, eds. *Vietnamese Ceramics: A Separate Tradition.* Chicago: Art Media Resources, 1997.

Stierlin, Henri. *Hindu India from Khajuraho to the Temple City of Madurai.* Cologne: Taschen, 1998.

Welch, Stuart Cary. *Imperial Mughal Painting.* New York: Braziller, 1978.

———. *India: Art and Culture 1300–1900.* New York: Metropolitan Museum of Art, 1985.

## Chapter 26
### From the Mongols to the Modern:
### The Art of Later China and Korea

Andrews, Julia Frances, and Kuiyi Shen. *A Century in Crisis: Modernity and Tradition in the Art of Twentieth-Century China.* New York: Guggenheim Museum, 1998.

Barnhart, Richard M. *Painters of the Great Ming: The Imperial Court and the Zhe School.* Dallas: Dallas Museum of Art, 1993.

Cahill, James. *Chinese Painting.* New York: Rizzoli, 1960.

———. *The Painter's Practice: How Artists Lived and Worked in Traditional China.* New York: Columbia University Press, 1994.

Clunas, Craig. *Art in China.* New York: Oxford University Press, 1997.

Fahr-Becker, Gabriele, ed. *The Art of East Asia.* Cologne: Könemann, 1999.

Fisher, Robert E. *Buddhist Art and Architecture.* New York: Thames & Hudson, 1993.

Fong, Wen C., and James C. Y. Watt. *Preserving the Past: Treasures from the National Palace Museum, Taipei.* New York: Metropolitan Museum of Art, 1996.

Laing, Ellen Johnston. *The Winking Owl: Art in the People's Republic of China.* Berkeley: University of California Press, 1989.

Lee, Sherman E., and Wai-Kam Ho. *Chinese Art under the Mongols: The Yuan Dynasty (1279–1368).* Cleveland: Cleveland Museum of Art, 1969.

Li, Chu-tsing, ed. *Artists and Patrons: Some Social and Economic Aspects of Chinese Painting.* Lawrence: Kress Department of Art History in cooperation with Indiana University Press, 1989.

Nakata, Yujiro, ed. *Chinese Calligraphy.* New York: Weatherhill, 1983.

Portal, Jane. *Korea: Art and Archaeology.* New York: Thames & Hudson, 2000.

Rawson, Jessica, ed. *The British Museum Book of Chinese Art.* New York: Thames & Hudson, 1992.

Silbergeld, Jerome. *Chinese Painting Style: Media, Methods, and Principles of Form.* Seattle: University of Washington Press, 1982.

Steinhardt, Nancy S., ed. *Chinese Architecture.* New Haven: Yale University Press, 2002.

Sullivan, Michael. *Art and Artists of Twentieth-Century China.* Berkeley: University of California Press, 1996.

———. *The Arts of China.* 4th ed. Berkeley: University of California Press, 1999.

Thorp, Robert L. *Son of Heaven: Imperial Arts of China.* Seattle: Son of Heaven Press, 1988.

Thorp, Robert L., and Richard Ellis Vinograd. *Chinese Art and Culture.* New York: Abrams, 2001.

Vainker, S. J. *Chinese Pottery and Porcelain: From Prehistory to the Present.* London: Braziller, 1991.

Watson, William. *The Arts of China 900–1260.* New Haven: Yale University Press, 2000.

Weidner, Marsha, ed. *Flowering in the Shadows: Women in the History of Chinese and Japanese Painting.* Honolulu: University of Hawaii Press, 1990.

———. *Views from Jade Terrace: Chinese Women Artists 1300–1912.* Indianapolis: Indianapolis Museum of Art, 1988.

Xin, Yang, Nie Chongzheng, Lang Shaojun, Richard M. Barnhart, James Cahill, and Wu Hung. *Three Thousand Years of Chinese Painting.* New Haven: Yale University Press, 1997.

## Chapter 27
### From the Shoguns to the Present:
### The Art of Later Japan

Addiss, Stephen. *The Art of Zen.* New York: Abrams, 1989.

Akiyama, Terukazu. *Japanese Painting.* Geneva: Skira; New York: Rizzoli, 1977.

Baekeland, Frederick. *Imperial Japan: The Art of the Meiji Era (1868–1912).* Ithaca, N.Y.: Herbert F. Johnson Museum of Art, 1980.

Brown, Kendall. *The Politics of Reclusion: Painting and Power in Muromachi Japan.* Honolulu: University of Hawaii Press, 1997.

Cahill, James. *Scholar Painters of Japan.* New York: Asia Society, 1972.

Coaldrake, William H. *Architecture and Authority in Japan.* London: Routledge, 1996.

Drexler, Arthur. *The Architecture of Japan.* New York: Museum of Modern Art, 1966.

Fontein, Jan, and Money L. Hickman. *Zen Painting and Calligraphy.* Greenwich, Conn.: New York Graphic Society, 1970.

Guth, Christine. *Art of Edo Japan: The Artist and the City, 1615–1868.* New York: Abrams, 1996.

Hickman, Money L., John T. Carpenter, Bruce A. Coats, Christine Guth, Andrew J. Pekarik, John M. Rosenfield, and Nicole C. Rousmaniere. *Japan's Golden Age: Momoyama.* New Haven: Yale University Press, 1996.

Kawakita, Michiaki. *Modern Currents in Japanese Art.* Translated by Charles E. Terry. New York: Weatherhill, 1974.

Kidder, J. Edward, Jr. *The Art of Japan.* New York: Park Lane, 1985.

Lane, Richard. *Images from the Floating World: The Japanese Print.* New York: Dorset, 1978.

Mason, Penelope. *History of Japanese Art.* New York: Abrams, 1993.

Meech-Pekarik, Julia. *The World of the Meiji Print: Impressions of a New Civilization.* New York: Weatherhill, 1986.

Munroe, Alexandra. *Japanese Art after 1945: Scream against the Sky.* New York: Abrams, 1994.

Nishi, Kazuo, and Kazuo Hozumi. *What Is Japanese Architecture?* Translated by H. Mack Horton. New York: Kodansha International, 1985.

Rosenfield, John M., and Elizabeth ten Grotenhuis. *Journey of the Three Jewels.* New York: Asia Society, 1979.

Sanford, James H., William R. LaFleur, and Masatoshi Nagatomi. *Flowing Traces: Buddhism in the Literary and Visual Arts of Japan.* Princeton, N.J.: Princeton University Press, 1992.

Shimizu, Yoshiaki, ed. *Japan: The Shaping of Daimyo Culture, 1185–1868.* Washington, D.C.: National Gallery of Art, 1988.

Singer, Robert T. *Edo: Art in Japan 1615–1868.* Washington, D.C.: National Gallery of Art, 1998.

Stewart, David B. *The Making of a Modern Japanese Architecture, 1868 to the Present.* New York: Kodansha International, 1988.

Watson, William, ed. *The Great Japan Exhibition: Art of the Edo Period, 1600–1868.* London: Royal Academy of Arts, 1981.

Weidner, Marsha, ed. *Flowering in the Shadows: Women in the History of Chinese and Japanese*

*Painting.* Honolulu: University of Hawaii Press, 1990.

### CHAPTER 28
### THE ENLIGHTENMENT AND ITS LEGACY: ART OF THE LATE 18TH THROUGH THE MID-19TH CENTURY

Bermingham, Ann. *Landscape and Ideology: The English Rustic Tradition, 1740–1850.* Berkeley: University of California Press, 1986.

Boime, A. *Art in the Age of Bonapartism, 1800–1815.* Chicago: University of Chicago Press, 1990.

———. *Art in the Age of Revolution, 1750–1800.* Chicago: University of Chicago Press, 1987.

Braham, Allan. *The Architecture of the French Enlightenment.* Berkeley: University of California Press, 1980.

Brion, Marcel. *Art of the Romantic Era: Romanticism, Classicism, Realism.* New York: Praeger, 1966.

Bryson, Norman. *Tradition and Desire: From David to Delacroix.* New York: Cambridge University Press, 1984.

Burchard, John, and Albert Bush-Brown. *The Architecture of America: A Social and Cultural History.* Boston: Little, Brown/The American Institute of Architects, 1965.

Clark, Kenneth. *The Romantic Rebellion: Romantic versus Classic Art.* New York: Harper & Row, 1973.

Clay, Jean. *Romanticism.* New York: Phaidon, 1981.

Conisbee, Philip. *Painting in Eighteenth-Century France.* Ithaca, N.Y.: Phaidon/Cornell University Press, 1981.

Cooper, Wendy A. *Classical Taste in America, 1800–1840.* Baltimore: Baltimore Museum of Art, 1993.

Crow, Thomas E. *Painters and Public Life in Eighteenth-Century Paris.* New Haven: Yale University Press, 1985.

Eitner, Lorenz. *Neoclassicism and Romanticism, 1750–1850: An Anthology of Sources and Documents.* New York: Harper & Row, 1989.

Gaunt, W. *The Great Century of British Painting: Hogarth to Turner.* New York: Phaidon, 1971.

Herrmann, Luke. *British Landscape Painting of the Eighteenth Century.* New York: Oxford University Press, 1974.

Holt, Elizabeth Gilmore, ed. *From the Classicists to the Impressionists: A Documentary History of Art and Architecture in the Nineteenth Century.* Garden City, N.J.: Anchor Books/Doubleday, 1966.

Honour, Hugh. *Neo-Classicism.* Harmondsworth: Penguin, 1968.

———. *Romanticism.* New York: Harper & Row, 1979.

Kalnein, Wend Graf, and Michael Levey. *Art and Architecture of the Eighteenth Century in France.* New York: Viking/Pelican, 1973.

Kroeber, Karl. *British Romantic Art.* Berkeley: University of California Press, 1986.

Levey, Michael. *Painting in Eighteenth-Century Venice.* Ithaca, N.Y.: Phaidon/Cornell University Press, 1980.

———. *Rococo to Revolution: Major Trends in Eighteenth-Century Painting.* London: Thames & Hudson, 1966.

Mendelowitz, Daniel M. A *History of American Art.* 2nd ed. New York: Holt, Rinehart & Winston, 1970.

Middleton, Robin, and David Watkin. *Neoclassical and 19th-Century Architecture.* 2 vols. New York: Electa/Rizzoli, 1987.

Novotny, Fritz. *Painting and Sculpture in Europe, 1780–1880.* 3rd ed. New Haven: Yale University Press, 1988.

Pierson, William. *American Buildings and Their Architects.* Vol. 1, The Colonial and Neo-Classical Style. Garden City, N.J.: Doubleday, 1970.

Porterfield, Todd. *The Allure of Empire: Art in the Service of French Imperialism 1798–1836.* Princeton, N.J.: Princeton University Press, 1998.

Rosenblum, Robert. *Transformations in Late Eighteenth Century Art.* Princeton, N.J.: Princeton University Press, 1970.

Roston, Murray. *Changing Perspectives in Literature and the Visual Arts, 1650–1820.* Princeton, N.J.: Princeton University Press, 1990.

Rykwert, Joseph. *The First Moderns: Architects of the Eighteenth Century.* Cambridge: MIT Press, 1983.

Stillman, Damie. *English Neo-Classical Architecture.* 2 vols. London: Zwemmer, 1988.

Vaughn, William. *German Romantic Painting.* New Haven: Yale University Press, 1980.

Wilton, Andrew. *The Swagger Portrait: Grand Manner Portraiture in Britain from Van Dyck to Augustus John, 1630–1930.* London: Tate Gallery, 1992.

Wolf, Bryan Jay. *Romantic Revision: Culture and Consciousness in Nineteenth-Century American Painting and Literature.* Chicago: University of Chicago Press, 1986.

### CHAPTER 29
### THE RISE OF MODERNISM: ART OF THE LATER 19TH CENTURY

Adams, Steven. *The Barbizon School and the Origins of Impressionism.* London: Phaidon, 1994.

Baudelaire, Charles. *The Mirror of Art, Critical Studies.* Translated by Jonathan Mayne. Garden City: Doubleday, 1956.

———. *The Painter of Modern Life, and Other Essays.* Translated and edited by Jonathan Mayne. London: Phaidon, 1964.

Benjamin, Roger. *Orientalist Aesthetics: Art, Colonialism, and French North Africa, 1880–1930.* Berkeley: University of California Press, 2003.

Boime, Albert. *The Academy and French Painting in the 19th Century.* London: Phaidon, 1971.

Broude, Norma. *Impressionism: A Feminist Reading.* New York: Rizzoli, 1991.

Chu, Petra ten-Doesschate. *Nineteenth-Century European Art.* New York: Abrams, 2003.

Clark, Kenneth. *The Gothic Revival: An Essay in the History of Taste.* New York: Humanities Press, 1970.

Clark, T. J. *The Absolute Bourgeois: Artists and Politics in France, 1848–1851.* London: Thames & Hudson, 1973.

———. *Image of the People: Gustave Courbet and the 1848 Revolution.* London: Thames & Hudson, 1973.

———. *The Painting of Modern Life: Paris in the Art of Manet and His Followers.* Princeton, N.J.: Princeton University Press, 1984.

Crary, Jonathan. *Suspensions of Perception: Attention, Spectacle, and Modern Culture.* Cambridge, Mass: MIT Press, 1999.

Duncan, Alastair. *Art Nouveau.* New York: Thames & Hudson, 1994.

Eisenmann, Stephen F. *19th-Century Art: A Critical History.* 2nd ed. New York: Thames & Hudson, 2002.

Farwell, Beatrice. *Manet and the Nude: A Study in the Iconology of the Second Empire.* New York: Garland Publishers, 1981.

Fried, Michael. *Courbet's Realism.* Chicago: University of Chicago Press, 1982.

———. *Manet's Modernism, or, The Face of Painting in the 1860s.* Chicago: University of Chicago Press, 1996.

Garb, Tamar. *Bodies of Modernity: Figure and Flesh in Fin-de-Siècle France.* New York: Thames & Hudson, 1998.

Gerdts, William H. *American Impressionism.* New York: Abbeville Press, 1984.

Hamilton, George H. *Painting and Sculpture in Europe, 1880–1940.* 6th ed. New Haven: Yale University Press, 1993.

Herbert, Robert L. *Impressionism: Art, Leisure, and Parisian Society.* New Haven: Yale University Press, 1988.

Hilton, Timothy. *The Pre-Raphaelites.* New York: Oxford University Press, 1970.

Holt, Elizabeth Gilmore. *From the Classicists to the Impressionists: Art and Architecture in the Nineteenth Century.* Garden City: Doubleday/Anchor, 1966.

———, ed. *The Expanding World of Art, 1874–1902.* New Haven: Yale University Press, 1988.

Janson, Horst W. *19th-Century Sculpture.* New York: Abrams, 1985.

Jensen, Robert. *Marketing Modernism in Fin-de-Siècle Europe.* Princeton, N.J.: Princeton University Press, 1994.

Krell, Alain. *Manet and the Painters of Contemporary Life.* London: Thames & Hudson, 1996.

Leymarie, Jean. *French Painting in the Nineteenth Century.* Geneva: Skira, 1962.

Mainardi, Patricia. *Art and Politics of the Second Empire: The Universal Expositions of 1855 and 1867.* New Haven: Yale University Press, 1987.

———. *The End of the Salon: Art and the State in the Early Third Republic.* Cambridge: Cambridge University Press, 1993.

Middleton, Robin, ed. *The Beaux-Arts and Nineteenth-Century French Architecture.* Cambridge, Mass: MIT Press, 1982.

Needham, Gerald. *19th-Century Realist Art.* New York: Harper & Row, 1988.

Nochlin, Linda. *Impressionism and Post-Impressionism, 1874–1904: Sources and Documents.* Upper Saddle River, N.J.: Prentice Hall, 1966.

———. *Realism and Tradition in Art, 1848–1900: Sources and Documents.* Upper Saddle River, N.J.: Prentice Hall, 1966.

Novak, Barbara. *American Painting of the Nineteenth Century: Realism and the American Experience.* New York: Harper & Row, 1979.

Novotny, Fritz. *Painting and Sculpture in Europe, 1780–1880.* 3rd ed. New Haven: Yale University Press, 1988.

Pevsner, Nikolaus. *Pioneers of Modern Design.* Harmondsworth: Penguin, 1964.

Pollock, Griselda. Vision and Difference: *Femininity, Feminism, and Histories of Art.* New York: Routledge, 1988.

Rewald, John. *The History of Impressionism.* New York: Museum of Modern Art, 1973.

———. *Post-Impressionism: From Van Gogh to Gauguin.* New York: Museum of Modern Art, 1956.

Rosen, Charles, and Henri Zerner. *Romanticism and Realism: The Mythology of Nineteenth-Century Art.* New York: Viking Press, 1984.

Rosenblum, Robert, and Horst W. Janson. *19th-Century Art.* New York: Abrams, 1984.

Schapiro, Meyer. *Modern Art: 19th and 20th Centuries.* New York: Braziller, 1978.

Schorske, Carl E. *Fin-de-Siècle Vienna: Politics and Culture.* New York: Knopf, 1980.

Shiff, Richard. *Cézanne and the End of Impressionism: A Study of the Theory, Technique, and Critical Evaluation of Modern Art.* Chicago: University of Chicago Press, 1984.

Silverman, Debora L. *Art Nouveau in Fin-de-Siècle France: Politics, Psychology, and Style.* Berkeley: University of California Press, 1989.

Sloane, Joseph C. French *Painting between the Past and the Present: Artists, Critics, and Traditions from 1848 to 1870.* Princeton, N.J.: Princeton University Press, 1973.

Smith, Paul. *Impressionism: Beneath the Surface.* New York: Abrams, 1995.

Sullivan, Louis. *The Autobiography of an Idea.* New York: Dover, 1956.

Taylor, Joshua, ed. *Nineteenth-Century Theories of Art.* Berkeley: University of California Press, 1987.

*Van Gogh: A Self-Portrait; Letters Revealing His Life as a Painter.* Selected by W. H. Auden. New York: Dutton, 1963.

Weisberg, Gabriel P. *The European Realist Tradition.* Bloomington: Indiana University Press, 1982.

White, Harrison C., and Cynthia A. Harrison. *Canvases and Careers: Institutional Change in the French Painting World.* New York: Wiley, 1965.

Wood, Christopher. *The Pre-Raphaelites.* New York: Viking Press, 1981.

## CHAPTER 30
### BEFORE AND AFTER THE CONQUISTADORS: NATIVE ARTS OF THE AMERICAS AFTER 1300

Anderson, Richard, and Karen L. Field, eds. *Art in Small-Scale Societies: Contemporary Readings.* Upper Saddle River, N.J.: Prentice Hall, 1993.

Berlo, Janet Catherine, ed. *Plains Indian Drawings 1865–1935.* New York: Abrams, 1996.

Berlo, Janet Catherine, and Ruth B. Phillips. *Native North American Art.* New York: Oxford University Press, 1998.

Berlo, Janet Catherine, and Lee Anne Wilson, eds. *Arts of Africa, Oceania, and the Americas: Selected Readings.* Upper Saddle River, N.J.: Prentice Hall, 1993.

Boone, Elizabeth. *The Aztec World.* Washington, D.C.: Smithsonian Institution Press, 1994.

———, ed. *Andean Art at Dumbarton Oaks.* 2 vols. Washington, D.C.: Dumbarton Oaks, 1996.

Bruhns, Karen O. *Ancient South America.* New York: Cambridge University Press, 1994.

Coe, Michael D. *The Maya.* 6th ed. New York: Thames & Hudson, 1999.

———. *Mexico.* 4th ed. New York: Thames & Hudson, 1994.

Coe, Michael D., and Justin Kerr. *The Art of the Maya Scribe.* New York: Abrams, 1998.

Diaz, Gisele, and Alan Rodgers. *The Codex Borgia.* New York: Dover, 1993.

Donnan, Christopher. *Ceramics of Ancient Peru.* Los Angeles: Fowler Museum of Cultural History, 1992.

Feest, Christian F. *Native Arts of North America.* 2nd ed. New York: Thames & Hudson, 1992.

Fienup-Riordan, Ann. *The Living Tradition of Yup`ik Masks.* Seattle: University of Washington Press, 1996.

Fitzhugh, William W., and Aron Crowell, eds. *Crossroads of Continents: Cultures of Siberia and Alaska.* Washington, D.C.: Smithsonian Institution Press, 1988.

Gasparini, Graziano, and Luise Margolies. *Inca Architecture.* Bloomington: Indiana University Press, 1980.

Hill, Tom, and Richard W. Hill Sr., eds. *Creation's Journey: Native American Identity and Belief.* Washington, D.C.: Smithsonian Institution Press, 1994.

Jonaitis, Aldona. *From the Land of the Totem Poles: The Northwest Coast Indian Art Collection at the American Museum of Natural History.* Seattle: University of Washington Press, 1988.

Kubler, George. *The Art and Architecture of Ancient America: The Mexican, Maya, and Andean Peoples.* 3rd ed. New Haven: Yale University Press, 1992.

Malpass, Michael A. *Daily Life in the Inca Empire.* Westport, Conn.: Greenwood Press, 1996.

Mathews, Zena, and Aldona Jonaitis, eds. *Native North American Art History.* Palo Alto, Calif.: Peek Publications, 1982.

Matos, Eduardo M. *The Great Temple of the Aztecs: Treasures of Tenochtitlan.* New York: Thames & Hudson, 1988.

Maurer, Evan M. *Visions of the People: A Pictorial History of Plains Indian Life.* Seattle: University of Washington Press, 1992.

Miller, Mary E. *The Art of Mesoamerica, from Olmec to Aztec.* 2nd ed. New York: Thames & Hudson, 1996.

Miller, Mary E., and Karl Taube. *The Gods and Symbols of Ancient Mexico and the Maya: An Illustrated Dictionary of Mesoamerican Religion.* New York: Thames & Hudson, 1993.

Morris, Craig, and Adriana von Hagen. *The Inka Empire and its Andean Origins.* New York: Abbeville, 1993.

Nabokov, Peter, and Robert Easton. *Native American Architecture.* New York: Oxford University Press, 1989.

Pasztory, Esther. *Aztec Art.* New York: Abrams, 1983.

———. *Pre-Columbian Art.* New York: Cambridge University Press, 1998.

Penney, David. *Art of the American Indian Frontier.* Seattle: University of Washington Press, 1992.

Penney, David, and George C. Longfish. *Native American Art.* Hong Kong: Hugh Lauter Levin & Associates, 1994.

Peterson, Susan. *The Living Tradition of Maria Martinez.* Tokyo: Kodansha International, 1977.

Phillips, Ruth B. *Trading Identities: The Souvenir in Native North American Art.* Seattle: University of Washington Press, 1998.

Plazas, Clemencia, Ana Maria Falchetti, and Armand J. Labbé. *Tribute to the Gods: Treasures of the Museo del Oro.* Santa Ana, Calif.: Bowers Museum of Cultural Art, 1992.

Samuel, Cheryl. *The Chilkat Dancing Blanket.* Norman: University of Oklahoma Press, 1982.

Schaafsma, Polly, ed. *Kachinas in the Pueblo World.* Albuquerque: University of New Mexico Press, 1994.

Stewart, Hilary. *Looking at Totem Poles.* Seattle: University of Washington Press, 1993.

Townsend, Richard F., ed. *Art from Sacred Landscapes.* Chicago: Art Institute of Chicago, 1992.

Wardwell, Allen. *Tangible Visions: Northwest Coast Indian Shamanism and Its Art.* New York: Monacelli Press, 1996.

Washburn, Dorothy. *Living in Balance: The Universe of the Hopi, Zuni, Navajo, and Apache.* Philadelphia: University Museum, 1995.

Weaver, Muriel Porter. *The Aztecs, Mayas, and Their Predecessors.* 3rd ed. San Diego: Academic Press, 1993.

Whiteford, Andrew H., Stewart Peckham, and Kate Peck Kent. *I Am Here: Two Thousand Years of Southwest Indian Arts and Crafts.* Santa Fe: Museum of New Mexico Press, 1989.

Wright, Robin K. *Northern Haida Master Carvers.* Seattle: University of Washington Press, 2001.

Wyman, Leland C. *Southwest Indian Drypainting.* Albuquerque: University of New Mexico Press, 1983.

## CHAPTER 31
### THE FLOURISHING OF ISLAND CULTURES: THE ART OF OCEANIA

Barrow, Terence. *The Art of Tahiti and the Neighboring Society, Austral and Cook Islands.* London: Thames & Hudson, 1979.

Berndt, Ronald M., ed. *Australian Aboriginal Art.* New York: Macmillan, 1964.

Corbin, George A. *Native Arts of North America, Africa, and the South Pacific: An Introduction.* New York: HarperCollins, 1988.

Cox, J. Halley, and William H. Davenport. *Hawaiian Sculpture.* Rev. ed. Honolulu: University of Hawaii Press, 1988.

D'Alleva, Anne. *Arts of the Pacific Islands.* New York: Abrams, 1998.

Feldman, Jerome, and Donald H. Rubinstein. *The Art of Micronesia.* Honolulu: University of Hawaii Art Gallery, 1986.

Greub, Suzanne, ed. *Authority and Ornament: Art of the Sepik River, Papua New Guinea.* Basel: Tribal Art Centre, 1985.

Guiart, Jean. *Arts of the South Pacific.* New York: Golden Press, 1963.

Hanson, Allan, and Louise Hanson, eds. *Art and Identity in Oceania.* Honolulu: University of Hawaii Press, 1990.

Kaeppler, Adrienne L., Christian Kaufmann, and Douglas Newton. *Oceanic Art.* New York: Abrams, 1997.

Kooijman, Simon. *Tapa in Polynesia.* Honolulu: Bishop Museum Press, 1972.

Lincoln, Louise, ed. *Assemblage of Spirits: Idea and Image in New Ireland.* New York: Braziller in association with the Minneapolis Institute of Arts, 1987.

Mead, Sidney Moko, ed. *Te Maori: Maori Art from New Zealand Collections.* New York: Abrams in association with the American Federation of Arts, 1984.

Morphy, Howard. *Aboriginal Art.* London: Phaidon Press, 1998.

Rockefeller, Michael C. *The Asmat of New Guinea: The Journal of Michael Clark Rockefeller.* Greenwich, Conn.: New York Graphic Society, 1967.

Schneebaum, Tobias. *Embodied Spirits: Ritual Carvings of the Asmat.* Salem, Mass.: Peabody Museum of Salem, 1990.

Simons, S. C., and H. Stevenson, eds. *Luk Luk Gen! Contemporary Art from Papua New Guinea.* Townsville: Perc Tucker Regional Gallery, 1990.

Smidt, Dirk, ed. *Asmat Art: Woodcarvings of Southwest New Guinea.* New York: Braziller in association with Rijksmuseum voor Volkenkunde, Leiden, 1993.

Starzecka, Dorota, ed. *Maori Art and Culture.* Chicago: Art Media Resources, 1996.

Sutton, Peter, ed. *Dreamings: The Art of Aboriginal Australia.* New York: Braziller in association with the Asia Society Galleries, 1988.

Thomas, Nicholas. *Oceanic Art.* London: Thames & Hudson, 1995.

## CHAPTER 32
### TRADITIONALISM AND INTERNATIONALISM: 19TH- AND 20TH-CENTURY AFRICAN ARTS

Abiodun, Roland, Henry J. Drewal, and John Pemberton III, eds. *The Yoruba Artist: New Theoretical Perspectives on African Arts.* Washington, D.C.: Smithsonian Institution Press, 1994.

Blier, Suzanne P. *The Royal Arts of Africa.* New York: Abrams, 1998.

Cole, Herbert M. *Icons: Ideals and Power in the Art of Africa.* Washington, D.C.: National Museum of African Art, Smithsonian Institution, 1989.

———. *Mbari: Art and Life among the Owerri Igbo.* Bloomington: Indiana University Press, 1982.

———, ed. *I Am Not Myself: The Art of African Masquerade.* Los Angeles: UCLA Fowler Museum of Cultural History, 1985.

Cole, Herbert M., and Chike C. Aniakor. *Igbo Art: Community and Cosmos.* Los Angeles: UCLA Fowler Museum of Cultural History, 1984.

Cole, Herbert M., and Doran H. Ross. *The Arts of Ghana.* Los Angeles: UCLA Fowler Museum of Cultural History, 1977.

Cornet, Joseph. *Art Royal Kuba.* Milan: Edizioni Sipiel, 1982.

Enwezor, Okwui, ed. *The Short Century: Independence and Liberation Movements in Africa, 1945–1994.* Munich: Prestel, 2001.

Ezra, Kate. *The Art of the Dogon: Selections from the Lester Wunderman Collection.* New York: Metropolitan Museum of Art, 1988.

Fischer, Eberhard, and Hans Himmelheber. *The Arts of the Dan in West Africa.* Translated by Anne Biddle. Zurich: Museum Reitberg, 1984.

Fraser, Douglas F., and Herbert M. Cole, eds. *African Art and Leadership.* Madison: University of Wisconsin Press, 1972.

Geary, Christraud M. *Things of the Palace: A Catalogue of the Bamum Palace Museum in Foumban (Cameroon).* Weisbaden: Franz Steiner Verlag, 1983.

Glaze, Anita J. *Art and Death in a Senufo Village.* Bloomington: Indiana University Press, 1981.

*In/sight: African Photographers, 1940 to the Present.* New York: Guggenheim Museum, 1996.

Kasfir, Sidney L. *Contemporary African Art.* London: Thames & Hudson, 1999.

———. *West African Masks and Cultural Systems.* Tervuren: Musée Royal de l'Afrique Centrale, 1988.

Kennedy, Jean. *New Currents, Ancient Rivers: Contemporary African Artists in a Generation of Change.* Washington, D.C.: Smithsonian Institution Press, 1992.

Magnin, Andre, with Jacques Soulillou. *Contemporary Art of Africa.* New York: Abrams, 1996.

McGaffey, Wyatt, and Michael Harris. *Astonishment and Power (Kongo Art).* Washington, D.C.: Smithsonian Institution Press, 1993.

Nooter, Mary H. *Secrecy: African Art That Conceals and Reveals.* New York: Museum for African Art, 1993.

Oguibe, Olu, and Okwui Enwezor, eds. *Reading the Contemporary: African Art from Theory to the Marketplace.* London: Institute of International Visual Arts, 1999.

Perrois, Louis. *Ancestral Art of Gabon from the Collections of the Barbier-Mueller Museum.* Translated by Francine Farr. Geneva: Musée Barbier-Mueller, 1985.

Phillips, Ruth B. *Representing Women: Sande Masquerades of the Mende of Sierra Leone.* Los Angeles: UCLA Fowler Museum of Cultural History, 1995.

Roy, Christopher D. *Art and Life in Africa: Selections from the Stanley Collection.* Iowa City: University of Iowa Museum of Art, 1992.

Sieber, Roy, and Roslyn A. Walker. *African Art in the Cycle of Life.* Washington, D.C.: Smithsonian Institution Press, 1987.

Thompson, Robert F., and Joseph Cornet. *The Four Moments of the Sun: Kongo Art in Two Worlds.* Washington, D.C.: National Gallery of Art, 1981.

Vansina, Jan. *The Children of Woot: A History of the Kuba Peoples.* Madison: University of Wisconsin Press, 1978.

Vinnicombe, Patricia. *People of the Eland: Rock Paintings of the Drakensberg Bushmen as a Reflection of Their Life and Thought.* Pietermaritzburg: University of Natal Press, 1976.

Vogel, Susan M. *Baule: African Art, Western Eyes.* New Haven: Yale University Press, 1997.

———, ed. *Africa Explores: Twentieth-Century African Art.* New York: Te Neues, 1990.

———, ed. *Art/Artifact: African Art in Anthropology Collections.* New York: Te Neues, 1988.

———, ed. *For Spirits and Kings: African Art from the Tishman Collection.* New York: Metropolitan Museum of Art, 1981.

Walker, Roslyn A. *Olowe of Ise: A Yoruba Sculptor to Kings.* Washington, D.C.: National Museum of African Art, 1998.

## CHAPTER 33
## THE DEVELOPMENT OF MODERNIST ART: THE EARLY 20TH CENTURY

Ades, Dawn. *Photomontage.* London: Thames & Hudson, 1976.

Antliff, Mark. *Cultural Politics and the Parisian Avant-Garde.* Princeton, N.J.: Princeton University Press, 1993.

Baigell, Matthew. *The American Scene: American Painting of the 1930s.* New York: Praeger, 1974.

Balakian, Anna Elizabeth. *Surrealism: The Road to the Absolute.* New York: Dutton, 1970.

Barr, Alfred H., Jr. *Cubism and Abstract Art: Painting, Sculpture, Constructions, Photography, Architecture, Industrial Arts, Theatre, Films, Posters, Typography.* Cambridge: Belknap, 1986.

———, ed. *Fantastic Art, Dada, Surrealism.* New York: Arno Press, 1969. (Originally published 1936 by the Museum of Modern Art)

Barron, Stephanie. *Exiles and Emigrés: The Flight of European Artists from Hitler.* Los Angeles: Los Angeles County Museum of Art, 1997.

———, ed. *Degenerate Art: The Fate of the Avant-Garde in Nazi Germany.* Los Angeles: Los Angeles County Museum of Art, 1991.

Bayer, Herbert, Walter Gropius, and Ise Gropius. *Bauhaus, 1919–1928.* New York: Museum of Modern Art, 1975.

Bearden, Romare, and Harry Henderson. *A History of African-American Artists from 1792 to the Present.* New York: Pantheon Books, 1993.

Breton, André. *Surrealism and Painting.* New York: Harper & Row, 1972.

Brown, Milton. *Story of the Armory Show: The 1913 Exhibition That Changed American Art.* 2nd ed. New York: Abbeville, 1988.

Campbell, Mary Schmidt, David C. Driskell, David Lewis Levering, and Deborah Willis Ryan. *Harlem Renaissance: Art of Black America.* New York: Studio Museum in Harlem; Abrams, 1987.

Curtis, William J. R. *Modern Architecture Since 1900.* Upper Saddle River, N.J.: Prentice Hall, 1996.

Davidson, Abraham A. *Early American Modernist Painting, 1910–1935.* New York: Harper & Row, 1981.

Eberle, Matthias. *World War I and the Weimar Artists: Dix, Grosz, Beckmann, Schlemmer.* New Haven: Yale University Press, 1985.

Elderfield, John. *The "Wild Beasts": Fauvism and Its Affinities.* New York: Museum of Modern Art, 1976.

Elsen, Albert. *Origins of Modern Sculpture.* New York: Braziller, 1974.

Fer, Briony, David Batchelor, and Paul Wood. *Realism, Rationalism, Surrealism: Art between the Wars.* New Haven: Yale University Press, 1993.

Frampton, Kenneth. *A Critical History of Modern Architecture.* London: Thames & Hudson, 1985.

Friedman, Mildred, ed. *De Stijl, 1917–1931: Visions of Utopia.* Minneapolis: Walker Art Center; New York: Abbeville Press, 1982.

Fry, Edward, ed. *Cubism.* London: Thames & Hudson, 1966.

Goldberg, RoseLee. *Performance: Live Art 1909 to the Present.* New York: Abrams, 1979.

Golding, John. *Cubism: A History and an Analysis, 1907–1914.* Cambridge: Belknap, 1988.

Gordon, Donald E. *Expressionism: Art and Idea.* New Haven: Yale University Press, 1987.

Gray, Camilla. *The Russian Experiment in Art, 1863–1922.* New York: Abrams, 1971.

Gropius, Walter. *Scope of Total Architecture.* New York: Collier Books, 1962.

Hamilton, George Heard. *Painting and Sculpture in Europe, 1880–1940.* 6th ed. New Haven: Yale University Press, 1993.

Harrison, Charles, Francis Frascina, and Gill Perry. *Primitivism, Cubism, Abstraction: The Early Twentieth Century.* New Haven: Yale University Press, 1993.

Herbert, James D. *Fauve Painting: The Making of Cultural Politics.* New Haven: Yale University Press, 1992.

Hitchcock, Henry-Russell, and Philip Johnson. *The International Style.* New York: Norton, 1995.

Hunter, Sam. *American Art of the 20th Century.* New York: Abrams, 1972.

Hurlburt, Laurance P. *The Mexican Muralists in the United States.* Albuquerque: University of New Mexico Press, 1989.

Jaffé, Hans L. C. *De Stijl, 1917–1931: The Dutch Contribution to Modern Art.* Cambridge: Belknap, 1986.

Kahnweiler, Daniel H. *The Rise of Cubism.* New York: Wittenborn, Schultz, 1949.

Kandinsky, Wassily. *Concerning the Spiritual in Art.* Translated by M.T.H. Sadler. New York: Dover, 1977.

Krauss, Rosalind. *The Originality of the Avant-Garde and Other Modernist Myths.* Cambridge: MIT Press, 1986.

Kuspit, Donald. *The Cult of the Avant-Garde Artist.* Cambridge: Cambridge University Press, 1993.

Le Corbusier. *The City of Tomorrow.* Cambridge: MIT Press, 1971.

———. *Towards a New Architecture.* Translated from the 13th French edition and with an introduction by Frederick Etchells. Oxford: Architectural Press, 1997.

Lloyd, Jill. *German Expressionism: Primitivism and Modernity.* New Haven: Yale University Press, 1991.

Lodder, Christina. *Russian Constructivism.* New Haven: Yale University Press, 1983.

Margolin, Victor. *The Struggle for Utopia: Rodchenko, Lissitzky, Moholy-Nagy, 1917–1946.* Chicago: University of Chicago Press, 1997.

Martin, Marianne W. *Futurist Art and Theory.* Oxford: Clarendon Press, 1968.

Moholy-Nagy, László. *Vision in Motion.* Chicago: Paul Theobald, 1969. (Originally published 1946)

Mondrian, Pieter Cornelius. *Plastic Art and Pure Plastic Art.* 3rd ed. New York: Wittenborn, Schultz, 1952.

Motherwell, Robert, ed. *The Dada Painters and Poets: An Anthology.* 2nd ed. Boston: Hall, 1981.

Myers, Bernard S. *The German Expressionists: A Generation in Revolt.* New York: Praeger, 1956.

Osborne, Harold. *The Oxford Companion to Twentieth Century Art.* New York: Oxford University Press, 1981.

Read, Herbert, ed. *Surrealism.* New York: Praeger, 1971.

Richter, Hans. *Dada: Art and Anti-Art.* London: Thames & Hudson, 1961.

Rosenblum, Robert. *Cubism and Twentieth-Century Art.* Rev. ed. New York: Abrams, 1984.

Rubin, William S. *Dada and Surrealist Art.* New York: Abrams, 1968.

———. *Dada, Surrealism, and Their Heritage.* New York: Museum of Modern Art, 1968.

———, ed. *Pablo Picasso: A Retrospective.* New York: Museum of Modern Art; Boston: New York Graphic Society, 1980.

———, ed. *"Primitivism" in 20th-Century Art: Affinity of the Tribal and the Modern.* 2 vols. New York: Museum of Modern Art, 1984.

Selz, Peter. *German Expressionist Painting.* 1957. Berkeley: University of California Press, 1974. (Originally published 1957)

Silver, Kenneth E. *Esprit de Corps: The Art of the Parisian Avant-Garde and the First World War, 1914–1925.* Princeton, N.J.: Princeton University Press, 1989.

Smith, Terry. *Making the Modern: Industry, Art, and Design in America.* Chicago: University of Chicago Press, 1993.

Steinberg, Leo. *Other Criteria: Confrontations with 20th-Century Art.* New York: Oxford University Press, 1972.

Stott, William. *Documentary Expression and Thirties America.* New York: Oxford University Press, 1973.

Taylor, Joshua C. *Futurism.* New York: Museum of Modern Art, 1961.

Tisdall, Caroline, and Angelo Bozzolla. *Futurism.* New York: Oxford University Press, 1978.

Trachtenberg, Alan. *Reading American Photographs: Images as History—Mathew Brady to Walker Evans.* New York: Hill and Wang, 1989.

Tsujimoto, Karen. *Images of America: Precisionist Painting and Modern Photography.* Seattle: University of Washington Press, 1982.

Tucker, William. *Early Modern Sculpture.* New York: Oxford University Press, 1974.

Vogt, Paul. *Expressionism: German Painting, 1905–1920.* New York: Abrams, 1980.

Weiss, Jeffrey S. *The Popular Culture of Modern Art: Picasso, Duchamp, and Avant-Gardism.* New Haven: Yale University Press, 1994.

Whitford, Frank. *Bauhaus.* New York: Thames & Hudson, 1984.

Wright, Frank Lloyd. *American Architecture.* Edited by Edgar Kaufmann. New York: Horizon, 1955.

## CHAPTER 34
### FROM THE MODERN TO THE POSTMODERN AND BEYOND: ART OF THE LATER 20TH CENTURY

Alloway, Lawrence. *American Pop Art.* New York: Whitney Museum of American Art/Macmillan, 1974.

———. *Topics in American Art since 1945.* New York: Norton, 1975.

Anfam, David. *Abstract Expressionism.* New York: Thames & Hudson, 1990.

Ashton, Dore. *American Art since 1945.* New York: Oxford University Press, 1983.

———. *The New York School: A Cultural Reckoning.* Harmondsworth: Penguin, 1979.

Battcock, Gregory, ed. *Idea Art: A Critical Anthology.* New York: Dutton, 1973.

———. *Minimal Art: A Critical Anthology.* New York: Studio Vista, 1969.

———. *The New Art: A Critical Anthology.* New York: Dutton, 1973.

———. *New Artists Video: A Critical Anthology.* New York: Dutton, 1978.

Battcock, Gregory, and Robert Nickas, eds. *The Art of Performance: A Critical Anthology.* New York: Dutton, 1984.

Beardsley, Richard. *Earthworks and Beyond: Contemporary Art in the Landscape.* New York: Abbeville Press, 1984.

Beardsley, John, and Jane Livingston. *Hispanic Art in the United States: Thirty Contemporary Painters and Sculptors.* Houston: Museum of Fine Arts; New York: Abbeville Press, 1987.

Benthall, Jeremy. *Science and Technology in Art Today.* New York: Praeger, 1972.

Brion, Marcel, Sam Hunter, Giulio Carlo Argan and Nello Ponente, Umbro Apollonio, Otto Bihalij-Merin, Will Grohmann, Herbert Read, Hans L. C. Jaffé, and J. P. Hodin. *Art since 1945.* New York: Abrams, 1958.

Broude, Norma, and Mary D. Garrard. *The Power of Feminist Art: The American Movement of the 1970s, History and Impact.* New York: Abrams, 1994.

Bürger, Peter. *Theory of the Avant-Garde.* Minneapolis: University of Minnesota Press, 1984.

Cockcroft, Eva, John Weber, and James Cockcroft. *Toward a People's Art.* New York: Dutton, 1977.

Cook, Peter. *New Spirit in Architecture.* New York: Rizzoli, 1990.

Cummings, Paul. *Dictionary of Contemporary American Artists.* 3rd ed. New York: St. Martin's Press, 1977.

Ferguson, Russell, ed. *Discourses: Conversations in Postmodern Art and Culture.* Cambridge, Mass: MIT Press, 1990.

Frascina, Francis, ed. *Pollock and After: The Critical Debate.* New York: Harper & Row, 1985.

Geldzahler, Henry. *New York Painting and Sculpture, 1940–1970.* New York: Dutton, 1969.

Guilbaut, Serge. *How New York Stole the Idea of Modern Art.* Chicago: University of Chicago Press, 1983.

Goldberg, Rose Lee. *Performance Art: From Futurism to the Present.* Rev. ed. New York: Abrams, 1988.

Goodman, Cynthia. *Digital Visions: Computers and Art.* New York: Abrams, 1987.

Goodyear, Frank H., Jr. *Contemporary American Realism since 1960.* Boston: New York Graphic Society, 1981.

Green, Jonathan. *American Photography: A Critical History since 1945 to the Present.* New York: Abrams, 1984.

Greenberg, Clement. *Clement Greenberg, The Collected Essays and Criticism.* Edited by J. O'Brien. 4 vols. Chicago: University of Chicago Press, 1986–93.

Grundberg, Andy. *Photography and Art: Interactions since 1945.* New York: Abbeville, 1987.

Hays, K. Michael, and Carol Burns, eds. *Thinking the Present: Recent American Architecture.* New York: Princeton Architectural, 1990.

Henri, Adrian. *Total Art: Environments, Happenings, and Performance.* New York: Oxford University Press, 1974.

Herbert, Robert L. *Modern Artists on Art.* Upper Saddle River, N.J.: Prentice Hall, 1971.

Hertz, Richard, ed. *Theories of Contemporary Art.* 2nd ed. Upper Saddle River, N.J.: Prentice Hall, 1993.

Hoffman, Katherine. *Explorations: The Visual Arts since 1945.* New York: HarperCollins, 1991.

Hughes, Robert. *The Shock of the New.* New York: Knopf, 1981.

Hunter, Sam. *An American Renaissance: Painting and Sculpture since 1940.* New York: Abbeville, 1986.

Jacobs, Jane. *The Death and Life of Great American Cities.* New York: Random House, 1961.

Jacobus, John. *Twentieth-Century Architecture: The Middle Years, 1940–1964.* New York: Praeger, 1966.

Jencks, Charles. *Architecture 2000: Prediction and Methods.* New York: Praeger, 1971.

———. *The Language of Post-Modern Architecture.* 6th ed. New York: Rizzoli, 1991.

———. *What Is Post-Modernism?* 3rd rev. ed. London: Academy Editions, 1989.

Johnson, Ellen H. *American Artists on Art: From 1940 to 1980.* New York: Harper & Row, 1980.

Jones, Amelia, ed. *Sexual Politics: Judy Chicago's Dinner Party in Feminist Art History.* Berkeley: University of California Press, 1996.

Kaprow, Allan. *Assemblage, Environments, and Happenings.* New York: Abrams, 1966.

Kirby, Michael. *Happenings.* New York: Dutton, 1966.

Kramer, Hilton. *The Age of the Avant-Garde: An Art Chronicle of 1956–1972.* New York: Farrar, Straus & Giroux, 1973.

Leja, Michael. *Reframing Abstract Expressionism: Subjectivity and Painting in the 1940s.* New Haven: Yale University Press, 1993.

Lewis, Samella S. *African American Art and Artists.* Rev. ed. Berkeley: University of California Press, 1994.

Lippard, Lucy R. *Mixed Blessings: New Art in a Multicultural America.* New York: Pantheon Books, 1990.

———. *Pop Art.* New York: Praeger, 1966.

———, ed. *From the Center: Feminist Essays on Women's Art.* New York: Dutton, 1976.

———, ed. *Six Years: The Dematerialization of the Art Object from 1966 to 1972.* New York: Praeger, 1973.

Lovejoy, Margot. *Postmodern Currents: Art and Artists in the Age of the Electronic Media.* Ann Arbor, Mich.: UMI Research Press, 1989.

Lucie-Smith, Edward. *Art Now.* Edison, N.J.: Wellfleet Press, 1989.

———. *Movements in Art since 1945.* Rev. ed. New York: Thames & Hudson, 1984.

Marder, Tod A. *The Critical Edge: Controversy in Recent American Architecture.* New Brunswick, N.J.: Rutgers University Press, 1980.

———. *An International Survey of Recent Painting and Sculpture.* New York: Museum of Modern Art, 1984.

Meyer, Ursula. *Conceptual Art.* New York: Dutton, 1972.

Mitchell, William J. *The Reconfigured Eye: Visual Truth in the Post-Photographic Era.* Cambridge, Mass: MIT Press, 1992.

Norris, Christopher, and Andrew Benjamin. *What Is Deconstruction?* New York: St. Martin's, 1988.

Polcari, Stephen. *Abstract Expressionism and the Modern Experience.* Cambridge: Cambridge University Press, 1991.

Popper, Frank. *Origins and Development of Kinetic Art.* Translated by Stephen Bann. Greenwich, Conn.: New York Graphic Society, 1968.

Price, Jonathan. *Video Visions: A Medium Discovers Itself.* New York: New American Library, 1977.

Reichardt, Jasia, ed. *Cybernetics, Art, and Ideas.* Greenwich, Conn.: New York Graphics Society, 1971.

Risatti, Howard, ed. *Postmodern Perspectives: Issues in Contemporary Art.* Upper Saddle River, N.J.: Prentice Hall, 1990.

Robbins, Corinne. *The Pluralist Era: American Art, 1968–1981.* New York: Harper & Row, 1984.

Rosen, Randy, and Catherine C. Brawer, eds. *Making Their Mark: Women Artists Move into the Mainstream, 1970–1985.* New York: Abbeville, 1989.

Rosenberg, Harold. *The Tradition of the New.* New York: Horizon Press, 1959.

Russell, John, and Suzi Gablik. *Pop Art Redefined.* New York: Praeger, 1969.

Sandford, Mariellen R., ed. *Happenings and Other Acts.* New York: Routledge, 1995.

Sandler, Irving. *Art of the Postmodern Era.* New York: HarperCollins, 1996.

———. *The Triumph of American Painting: A History of Abstract Expressionism.* New York: Praeger, 1970.

Sayre, Henry M. *The Object of Performance: The American Avant-Garde since 1970.* Chicago: University of Chicago Press, 1989.

Schneider, Ira, and Beryl Korot. *Video Art: An Anthology.* New York: Harcourt Brace Jovanovich, 1976.

Shapiro, David, and Cecile Shapiro. *Abstract Expressionism: A Critical Record.* New York: Cambridge University Press, 1990.

Smagula, Howard. *Currents: Contemporary Directions in the Visual Arts.* 2nd ed. Upper Saddle River, N.J.: Prentice Hall, 1989.

Sonfist, Alan, ed. *Art in the Landscape: A Critical Anthology of Environmental Art.* New York: Dutton, 1983.

Sontag, Susan. *On Photography.* New York: Farrar, Strauss & Giroux, 1973.

Stiles, Kristine, and Peter Selz, eds. *Theories and Documents of Contemporary Art: A Sourcebook of Artists' Writings.* Berkeley: University of California Press, 1996.

Tuchman, Maurice. *American Sculpture of the Sixties.* Los Angeles: Los Angeles County Museum of Art, 1967.

Venturi, Robert. *Complexity and Contradiction in Architecture.* New York: Museum of Modern Art, 1966.

Venturi, Robert, Denise Scott-Brown, and Steven Isehour. *Learning from Las Vegas.* Cambridge: MIT Press, 1972.

Waldman, Diane. *Collage, Assemblage, and the Found Object*. New York: Abrams, 1992.

Wallis, Brian, ed. *Art after Modernism: Rethinking Representation*. New York: New Museum of Contemporary Art in association with David R. Godine, 1984.

Wheeler, Daniel. *Art since Mid-Century: 1945 to the Present*. Upper Saddle River, N.J.: Prentice Hall, 1991.

Wood, Paul. *Modernism in Dispute: Art since the Forties*. New Haven: Yale University Press, 1993.

### BOOKS SPANNING THE 18TH, 19TH, AND 20TH CENTURIES

Antreasian, Garo, and Clinton Adams. *The Tamarind Book of Lithography: Art and Techniques*. Los Angeles: Tamarind Workshop and New York: Harry N. Abrams, 1971.

Armstrong, John, Wayne Craven, and Norma Feder, et al. *200 Years of American Sculpture*. New York: Whitney Museum of American Art/Boston: David R. Godine, 1976.

Arnason, H. H. *History of Modern Art: Painting, Sculpture, Architecture*. 4th ed. New York: Harry N. Abrams, 1998.

Ashton, Dore. *Twentieth-Century Artists on Art*. New York: Pantheon Books, 1985.

Brown, Milton, Sam Hunter, and John Jacobus. *American Art: Painting, Sculpture, Architecture, Decorative Arts, Photography*. New York: Harry N. Abrams, 1979.

Burnham, Jack. *Beyond Modern Sculpture. The Effects of Science and Technology on the Sculpture of This Century*. New York: Braziller, 1968.

Castelman, Riva. *Prints of the 20th Century: A History*. New York: Oxford University Press, 1985.

Chipp, Herschel B. *Theories of Modern Art*. Berkeley: University of California Press, 1968.

Coke, Van Deren. *The Painter and the Photograph From Delacroix to Warhol*. Rev. and enl. ed. Albuquerque: University of New Mexico Press, 1972.

Craven, Wayne. *American Art: History and Culture*. Madison: Brown & Benchmark, 1994.

Driskell, David C. *Two Centuries of Black American Art*. Los Angeles: Los Angeles County Museum of Art/New York: Alfred A. Knopf, 1976.

Elsen, Albert. *Origins of Modern Sculpture*. New York: Braziller, 1974.

Fine, Sylvia Honig. *Women and Art: A History of Women Painters and Sculptors from the Renaissance to the 20th Century*. Montclair: Alanheld & Schram, 1978.

Flexner, James Thomas. *America's Old Masters*. New York: McGraw-Hill, 1982.

Frascina, Francis, and Charles Harrison, eds. *Modern Art and Modernism: A Critical Anthology*. New York: Harper & Row, 1982.

Giedion, Siegfried. *Space, Time and Architecture: The Growth of a New Tradition*. 4th ed. Cambridge: Harvard University Press, 1965.

Goldwater, Robert, and Marco Treves, eds. *Artists on Art*. 3rd ed. New York: Pantheon, 1958.

Greenough, Sarah, Joel Snyder, David Travis, and Colin Westerbeck. *On the Art of Fixing a Shadow: One Hundred and Fifty Years of Photography*. Washington: The National Gallery of Art/Chicago: The Art Institute of Chicago, 1989.

Hamilton, George Heard. *Nineteenth- and Twentieth-Century Art*. Englewood Cliffs: Prentice-Hall, 1972.

Herbert, Robert L., ed. *Modern Artists on Art*. Englewood Cliffs: Prentice-Hall, 1964.

Hertz, Richard, and Norman M. Klein, eds. *Twentieth-Century Art Theory: Urbanism, Politics, and Mass Culture*. Englewood Cliffs: Prentice-Hall, 1990.

Hitchcock, Henry-Russell. *Architecture: Nineteenth and Twentieth Centuries*. 4th ed. New Haven: Yale University Press, 1977.

Hunter, Sam, and John Jacobus. *Modern Art: Painting, Sculpture, and Architecture*. 3rd ed. New York: Harry N. Abrams, 1992.

Jencks, Charles. *Modern Movements in Architecture*. Garden City: Anchor Press/Doubleday, 1973.

Kaufmann, Edgar, Jr., ed. *The Rise of an American Architecture*. New York: Metropolitan Museum of Art/Frederick A. Praeger, 1970.

Krauss, Rosalind E. *The Originality of the Avant-Garde and Other Modernist Myths*. Cambridge: MIT Press, 1985.

———. *Passages in Modern Sculpture*. Cambridge, MA: MIT Press, 1981.

Licht, Fred. *Sculpture, Nineteenth and Twentieth Centuries*. Greenwich: New York Graphic Society, 1967.

Lynton, Norbert. *The Story of Modern Art*. 2nd ed. Englewood Cliffs: Prentice-Hall, 1989.

McCoubrey, John W. *American Art, 1700–1960: Sources and Documents*. Englewood Cliffs: Prentice-Hall, 1965.

Mason, Jerry, ed. *International Center of Photography Encyclopedia of Photography*. New York: Crown Publishers, 1984.

Newhall, Beaumont. *The History of Photography*. New York: The Museum of Modern Art, 1982.

Peterdi, Gabor. *Printmaking: Methods Old and New*. New York: Macmillan, 1961.

Pierson, William. *American Buildings and Their Architects: Technology and the Picturesque*. Vol. 2. Garden City: Doubleday, 1978.

Read, Herbert. *Concise History of Modern Painting*. 3rd ed. New York: Frederick A. Praeger, 1975.

———. *A Concise History of Modern Sculpture*. Rev. and enl. ed. New York: Frederick A. Praeger, 1964.

Rose, Barbara. *American Art Since 1900*. rev. ed. New York: Frederick A. Praeger, 1975.

Rosenblum, Robert. *Modern Painting and the Northern Romantic Tradition: Friedrich to Rothko*. New York: Harper & Row, 1975.

Ross, John, and Clare Romano. *The Complete Printmaker*. New York: The Free Press, 1972.

Ross, Stephen David, ed. *Art and Its Significance: An Anthology of Aesthetic Theory*. Albany: SUNY Press, 1987.

Russell, John. *The Meanings of Modern Art*. New York: Museum of Modern Art/Thames & Hudson, 1981.

Scully, Vincent. *Modern Architecture*. rev. ed. New York: Braziller, 1974.

Spalding, Francis. *British Art Since 1900*. London: Thames & Hudson, 1986.

Spencer, Harold. *American Art: Readings from the Colonial Era to the Present*. New York: Charles Scribner's Sons, 1980.

Summerson, Sir John. *Architecture in Britain: 1530–1830*. 7th rev. and enl. ed. Baltimore: Penguin, 1983.

Szarkowski, John. *Photography Until Now*. New York: Museum of Modern Art, 1989.

Tuchman, Maurice, and Judi Freeman, eds. *The Spiritual in Art: Abstract Painting, 1890–1985*. Los Angeles: Los Angeles County Art Museum/New York: Abbeville Press, 1986.

Upton, Dell. *Architecture in the United States*. Oxford: Oxford University Press, 1998.

Weaver, Mike. *The Art of Photography: 1839–1989*. New Haven: Yale University Press, 1989.

Whiffen, Marcus, and Frederick Koeper. *American Architecture, 1607–1976*. Cambridge: MIT Press, 1983.

Wilmerding, John. *American Art*. Harmondsworth, England: Penguin, 1976.

Wilson, Simon. *Holbein to Hockney: A History of British Art*. London: The Tate Gallery & The Bodley Head, 1979.

# CREDITS

*The authors and publisher are grateful to the proprietors and custodians of various works of art for photographs of these works and permission to reproduce them in this book. Sources not included in the captions are listed here.*

**Key to Abbreviations**

| | |
|---|---|
| AL | Alinari/Art Resource, NY |
| A.A.M. | Asian Art Museum of San Francisco, The Avery Brundage Collection |
| Canali | Canali Photobank, Italy |
| Gir | Giraudon/Art Resource, NY |
| Hir | Hirmer Fotoarchiv, Munich |
| Lessing | Erich Lessing/Art Resource, NY |
| M.M.A. | The Metropolitan Museum of Art |
| R.M.N. | Réunion des Musées Nationaux/Art Resource, NY |
| Saskia | Saskia Ltd Cultural Documentation |
| Scala | Scala/Art Resource, NY |

Note: *All references in the following credits are to figure numbers unless otherwise indicated.*

**Introduction**–© Guggenheim Museum Bilbao: 1; Aerofilms Limited: 2; akg-images/Rabatti-Domingie: 3; © 2001 The Georgia O'Keefe Foundation/Artist Rights Society (ARS), NY: 4; © 2001 Ben Shahn/Licensed by VAGA, NY, NY: 5; www.bednorz-photo.de: 6; DY/Art Resource, NY: 07; Photograph © M.M.A.: 8; Saskia: 9; © National Gallery, London: 11; MOA Art Museum, Shizuoka-ken, Japan: 12; Joachim Blauel/Arthothek: 13; Jürgen Liepe, Berlin: 14; Nimatallah/Art Resource, NY: 15; Photograph © 1983 M.M.A.: 16; Scala: 17

**Chapter 1**–Photo: Paul G. Bahn: 1; With permission: Namibia Archaeological Trust: 2; © Ulmer Museum. Photo: Thomas Stephan: 03; © Archivo Iconografico, S.A./Corbis: 4; Index/Alberti: 5; Jean Dieuzaide: 06; Jean Vertut: 7; R.M.N.: 8; Jean Vertut: 9; Hans Hinz: Jean Vertut: 10; 11; Eurelios/French Ministry of Culture and Communication, Regional Direction for Cultural Affairs-Rhône-Alpes region-Regional department of archaeology: 12; Jean Vertut: 13; Archivio e Studio Folco Quilici, Roma: 14; Department of Antiquities, Amman, Jordan, by P. Dorrell and S. Laidlaw, with permission of the "Ain Ghazal Archaeological Project": 15; James Mellaart: 16; © Gianni Dagli Orti/Corbis: 17; James Mellaart: 18; Pubbli Aer Foto: 19

**Chapter 2**–© Nik Wheeler/Corbis: 1; From E.S. Piggott, Ed., *The Dawn of Civilization*, London, Thames and Hudson, 1961, pg. 70: 2; Erwin Böhm: 03; Erwin Böhm: 04; Lessing: 5; Hir: 6; R.M.N.: 7, 13, 15, 16, 19; © Copyright the Trustees of the British Museum: 8, 11, 23, 24; University of Pennsylvania Museum (Neg. #T35-2256c.2): 9; University of Pennsylvania Museum (Neg. #T4-848c.): 10; Joseph Scherschel/National Geographic Society: 12; Erwin Böhm: 14; Gir: 17; photo Henri Stierlin: 18; © 1975 The Royal Institute of British Architects and the University of London, by permission of Athlone Press: 20; Saskia: 21; Klaus Göken, 1992/Bildarchiv Preussischer Kulturbesitz: 25; The Art Archive/Dagli Orti: 26; David Poole/Robert Harding Picture Library: 27; Archivio e Studio Folco Quilici, Roma: 28; M.M.A., Fletcher Fund, 1965 (65.126). Photograph © 1982 By M.M.A.: 29; Sassoon/Robert Harding Picture Library: 30

**Chapter 3**–J. E. Quibell and F. W. Green, *Hierakonpolis* vol. 2 (London 1902) p. 76: 1; Jürgen Liepe, Berlin: 2, 15, 40; Hir: 3; Carolyn Brown/PRI: 4; From K. Lange and M. Hirmer, *Agypten. Architectur, Plastik, Malerei in drei Jahrtausenden*, Munich, 1957. Used by permission of Phaidon Press and Hir: 5; Ancient Art & Architecture Collection Ltd.: 06; Lessing: 7; Simon Harrus/Robert Harding Picture Library: 8; Harvard University Semitic Museum: 10; Robert Harding Picture Library: 11; Araldo de Luca: 12, 32; Courtesy, Museum of Fine Arts, Boston. Reproduced with permission. © 2000 Museum of Fine Arts, Boston. All Rights Reserved: 13; R.M.N.: 14; Jean Vertut: 16; Hirmer: 17; M.M.A.: 18; Marburg/Art Resource, NY: 19; akg-images/Francois Guenet: 20; Getty Research Library, Wim Swaan Photograph Collection, 96.P.21: 21; M.M.A., Rogers Fund, 1929 (29.3.1). Photograph by Schecter Lee. Photograph © 1986 M.M.A.: 22; John P. Stevens/AA&A: 23; Marco Casiraghi: 24; J. Jackson/Robert Harding Picture Library: 26; M.M.A., Purchase, 1890, Levi Hale Willard Bequest (90.35.1): 27; Ronald Sheridan/AA&A: 28; Jürgen Liepe/Bildarchiv Preussischer Kulturbesitz: 29; Margarete Büsin/Bildarchiv Preussischer Kulturbesitz: 33, 34; Bildarchiv Preussischer Kulturbesitz/Art Resource, NY: 35; Boltin Picture Library: 36; Robert Harding Picture Library: 37, 38

**Chapter 4**–The Art Archive/National Archaeological Museum, Athens/Dagli Orti: 1, 2; Hir: 4, 23, 24; Getty Research Library, Wim Swaan Photograph Collection, 96.P.21: 5; Saskia: 6; Studio Kontos: 7, 26; photo Henri Stierlin: 8, 9; Hans Hinz: 10; Studio Kontos: 11; Nimatallah/Art Resource, NY: 12; Alison Franz Collection, American School of Classical Studies at Athens: 13; © Archivo Iconografico, S.A./Corbis: 14; © British School at Athens: 15; Photo by Raymond V. Schoder, © 1987 by Bolchazy-Carducci Publishers, Inc.: 16; Lessing: 17, 20; © Vanni Archive/Corbis: 21, 22; Archaeological Receipts Fund: 25

**Chapter 5**–© Archivo Iconografico, S.A./Corbis: opener; M.M.A., Rogers Fund, 1914 (14.130.14). Photograph © 1996 M.M.A.: 1; M.M.A., Gift of J. Pierpont Morgan, 1917 (17.190.2072). Photograph © 1996 M.M.A.: 2; Museum of Fine Arts, Boston, Francis Bartlett Collection: 3; © Copyright the Trustees of the British Museum: 4, 46, 52; From J.G. Pedley, *Greek Art and Archaeology*, Prentice-Hall, 1993, Fig. 5.15: 5; Alison Frantz: 6; R.M.N.: 7, 21, 57, 82, 83; M.M.A., Fletcher Fund, 1932 (32.11.1). Photograph © 1993 M.M.A.: 8; Nimatallah/Art Resource, NY: 9; © Giovanni Dagli Orti/Corbis: 10; Studio Kontos: 11, 42, 64, 68, 77, 84; Saskia: 12, 27, 28, 53, 55, 71, 73, 85; Summerfield: 13; From Marvin Trachtenberg and Isabelle Hyman, *Architecture from Prehistoric to Post-Modernism/The Western Tradition*, Englewood Cliffs, NJ: Prentice Hall, 1986, p. 86, p. 293. Used by permission: 14; Vanni/Art Resource, NY: 15; photo Henri Stierlin: 17, 24, 49; Canali: 18, 29, 65, 69; Scala: 18, 50, 56; Photo Vatican Museums: 19, 39; Museum of Fine Arts, Boston: 20; Colorphoto Hans Hinz: 22; Musees royaux d'Art et d'Histoire: 23; From H. Berve and G. Gruben, *Greek Temples, Theaters, and Shrines*, Harry N. Abrams, Inc., Fig. 41: 25; Ancient Art & Architecture Collection Ltd.: 26; Studio Kontos: 30, 31, 33; photo Paul M.R. Maeyaert: 32; Scala: 34; Lessing: 35; Nimatallah/Art Resource, NY: 36, 54; Araldo de Luca: 37; Scala: 38; Photo by Raymond V. Schoder, © 1987 by Bolchazy-Carducci Publishers, Inc.: 40; American School of Classical Studies at Athens: Agora Excavations: 41; © Copyright the Trustees of the British Museum: 45; Ancient Art & Architecture Collection Ltd.: 47; Scala: 48, 60, 66; From H. Berve and G. Gruben, *Greek Temples, Theaters, and Shrines*, Harry N. Abrams, Inc., Fig. 66: 51; © 1981 M. Sarri/Photo Vatican Museums: 58; Archivio I.G.D.A., Milano: 59; Photograph © 2003 Museum of Fine Arts, Boston, Gift of Nathaniel Thayer; 10.70: 61; © Archivo Iconografico, S.A./Corbis: 62; Archaeological Receipts Fund: 63; Art Resource, NY: 67; Photo by Raymond V. Schoder, © 1987 by Bolchazy-Carducci Publishers, Inc.: 70; Vanni/Art Resource, NY: 72; Bildarchiv Preussischer Kulturbesitz: 75; Bildarchiv Preussischer Kulturbesitz/Art Resource, NY 78; Bildarchiv Preussischer Kulturbesitz/Art Resource, NY: 79; Photo Giovanni Lattanzi: 80; Summerfield: 81; © Gianni Dagli Orti/Corbis: 86; Ny Carlsberg Glyptotek: 88; © 1988 T. Okamura/Photo Vatican Museums: 89; akg-images: 90

**Chapter 6**–Diego Lezama Orezzoli/Corbis: 1; John C. Huntington: 2, 12; SCP57227 Steatite Pasupati seal, Mohenjodaro, 2300-1750 bce, National Museum of India, New Delhi, India/ Bridgeman Art Library: 3; Benoy K. Behl: 4; Edifice/Corbis: 5; Robert Harding Picture Library: 7, 20; © ephotocorp.com: 8a, 11; © The Trustees of The National Museums of Scotland: 9; Freer Gallery of Art, Smithsonian Institution, Washington, D.C.: Purchase, F1949.9: 10; Lindsay Hebberd/Corbis: 13; Douglas Dickins FRPS: 14, 21; Borromeo/Art Resource, NY: 15; Alison Wright/ Corbis: 17; ACSAA Slide #3101 ©AAUM: 18; ACSAA Slide #3103 ©AAUM: 19; Robert L. Brown: 22a, 23, 24; Stephanie Colasanti/Corbis: 25; Charles & Josette Lenars/Corbis: 26; Luca I. Tettoni/Corbis: 27, 31; Paul John Miller/Stockphoto: 29

**Chapter 7**–Cultural Relics Publishing House, Beijing: 1, 3, 12, 13, 19; A.A.M., B60B1032. Used by permission: 2; The Nelson-Atkins Museum of Art, Kansas City, Missouri (Purchase: Nelson Trust) 33-81. Photo: E. G. Schempf: 4; © Imaginechina: 5; The Nelson-Atkins Museum of Art, Kansas City, Missouri (Purchase: Nelson Trust) 33-521. Photo: Robert Newcombe: 8; A.A.M., B60B1034. Used by permission: 9; Heritage Images/British Museum: 10; R.M.N.: 11; Photograph © 2003 Museum of Fine Art, Boston. Attributed to: Yan Liben, died in 673. The Thirteen Emperors. Chinese, Tang dynasty, Second half of the 7th century (with later replacement). Object Place: China. Handscroll; ink and color on silk. 51.3 × 531cm (20 3/16 × 209 1/16 in.) Museum of Fine Arts, Boston. Denman Waldo Ross Collection. 31.643" (Photograph © 2003 Museum of Fine Art, Boston): 15; Victoria & Albert Museum, London/Art Resource, NY: 17; Collection of the National Palace Museum, Taiwan, Republic of China: 18, 23; A.A.M., B60B161. Used by permission: 20; Liu Liqun/Corbis: 21; Photograph © 2003 Museum of Fine Art, . Zhou Jichang, Chinese, second half of 12th century. Lohans Bestowing Alms on Suffering Human Beings. Chinese, Southern Song Dynasty, about 1178. Object Place: China. Ink and color on silk. 111.5 × 53.1cm (43 7/8 × 20 7/8 in.) Museum of Fine Arts, Boston. General Funds. 95.4" (Photograph © 2003 Museum of Fine Art, Boston): 24; Tokyo National Museum. Image TNM Image Archives. Source: http://TnmArchives.jp: 25; Archivo Iconografico, S.A./Corbis: 27

**Chapter 8**–Tokyo National Museum. Image TNM Image Archives. Source: http://TnmArchives.jp: 1, 2, 11; Tomb of Emperor Nintoku. (Nintoku-ryo Tumulus) Sakai, Osaka Prefecture: 3; Jingu Administration Office: 5; Sakamoto Photo Research Laboratory/Corbis: 6, 12, 15; Archivo Iconografico, S.A./Corbis: 7; D.Carrasco/jonarnold.com: 10; The Gotoh Museum, Tokyo: 13; Photograph © 2003 Museum of Fine Art, Boston. Artist Unknown, Japanese. Night Attack on the Sanjo Palace, from the Illustrated Scrolls of the Events of the Heiji Era (Heiji monogatari emaki). Japanese, Kamakura period, second half of the 13th century. Object Place: Japan. Handscroll; ink and color on paper. 41.3 × 699.7 cm (16 1/4 × 275 1/2 in.) Museum of Fine Arts, Boston. Fenollosa-Weld Collection. 11.4000" (Photograph © 2003 Museum of Fine Art, Boston): 16

**Chapter 9**–Hir: 1; David Lees: 2; Canali: 3; © Mike Andrews/Ancient Art & Achitecture Collection Ltd.: 4; Archivio e Studio Folco Quilici, Roma: 5; Archivio I.G.D.A., Milano: 7; Ancient Art & Architecture Collection Ltd.: 8; Hirmer: 9; © Araldo de Luca/Corbis: 10; Saskia: 11; © Gianni Dagli Orti/Corbis: 12, 14; Scala: 13; © Archivo Iconografico, S.A./Corbis: 15

**Chapter 10**–K. Koskimies: 1; photo Henri Stierlin: 2, 13, 32, 50, 52; Scala: 3, 12, 15, 17, 23, 44, 46, 51, 53, 58, 72, 78; From Robert Furneaux Jordan, *A Concise History of Western Architecture*, © 1969 by Harcourt Brace Jovanovich. Reproduced by permission of the publisher: 4; Editions Citadelles et Mazenod, Paris: 4; © Bettmann/Corbis: 5; AL: 6, 45; German Archaeological Institute, Rome: 7, 8; The American Numismatic Society, NY.: 9, 82; The Whittlesey Foundation/Aristide D. Caratzas, Publisher: 10; White Star: 11; Photo Archives Skira, Geneva, Switzerland: 14; M.M.A., Rogers Fund, 1903 (03.14.13). Photograph by Schecter Lee. Photograph © 1986 M.M.A.: 16; Copyright © Biblioteca Apostolica Vaticana: 19; Canali: 20, 21, 24, 42, 74; Madeline Grimoldi: 22; © M. Sarri/Photo Vatican Museums: 25; Ny Carlsberg Glyptotek: 26; Saskia: 27, 28, 29, 37, 80, 81; Gir: 30; Oliver Benn/Tony Stone Images: 31; From J. B. Ward-Perkins, *Roman Architecture*, Adapted by permission of Electra Editrice, Milan: 33; Roy Rainford/Robert Harding Picture Library: 34; Ny Carlsberg Glyptoteck: 35; © Araldo de Luca/Corbis: 36, 71; Werner Forman/Art Resource, NY: 38; Scala: 39, 62; Canali: 41; Photo Marcello Bertinetti/White Star: 43; Collection of Israel Antiquities Authority. Exhibited & photo © Israel Museum: 47; Pubbli Aer Foto: 48; Ernani Orcorte/UTET: 54; © Morton Beebe/Corbis: 55; Lessing: 56; Photo Vatican Museums: 57; De Masi/Canali: 59; German Archaeological Institute, Rome: 60; *Sarcophagus*, Italy, Roman, early 2nd century. Greek marble, L. 210 cm. © The Cleveland Museum of Art, 2003. Gift of the John Huntington Art and Polytechnic Trust, 1928.856: 61; Peter Muscato: 63; Bildarchiv Preussischer Kulturbesitz: 64; M.M.A., Samuel D. Lee Fund, 1940 (40.11.1a). Photograph by Schecter Lee. Photograph © 1986 M.M.A.: 65; Araldo de Luca: 66, 69; From Sir Banister Fletcher, *A History of Architecture on the Comparative Method*, 17th ed., rev. by R. A. Cordingly, 1961. Used by permission of Athlone Press of the University of London and the British Architectural Library, Royal Institute of British Architects: 67; Fototeca: 68; M.M.A., Rogers Fund, 1905. (05.30) Photograph © 1983 M.M.A.: 70; German Archaeological Institute, Rome: 75; Index/Artphoto: 76; Istituto Centrale per il Catalogo e la Documentazione, (ICCD): 77

**Chapter 11**–The Jewish Museum, NY/Art Resource, NY: 1; Madeline Grimoldi: 3; Hirmer: 4, 18; Foto Archivio Fabbrica di San Pietro in Vaticano: 5; Saskia: 6, 8; Scala: 9, 13, 15, 16, 17; Hir: 10; Canali: 11; Andre Held: 12; Vanni/Art Resource, NY: 14; Österreichische Nationalbibliothek, Vienna: 19; Scala, 20

**Chapter 12**–R.M.N.: 1, 26; © Yann Arthus-Bertrand/Corbis: 3; photo Henri Stierlin: 5; Archivio e Studio Folco Quilici, Roma: 6; Hir: 7, 33; Canali: 8, 10, 11; Scala: 9, 12, 24; Ronald Sheridan/Ancient Art & Architecture: 13, 16; Firenze, Biblioteca Medicea Laurenziana, Ms. Laur. Plut. 1.56, c. 13v Su concessione del Ministero per i beni e le attività culturali E' vietata ogni ulteriore riproduzione con qualsiasi mezzo: 15; Lessing: 17; Studio Kontos: 18; Vanni/Art Resource, NY: 20; The Art Archive/Dagli Orti: 21; Studio Kontos: 22; Ricciarini/Visconti: 23; Ricciarini, Milano: 25; Josephine Powell: 27; Sovfoto/Eastfoto: 29; Studio Kontos: 30; Andre Held: 31; Sovfoto/Eastfoto: 34; State Historical Cultural Museum "Moscow Kremlin": 35

**Chapter 13**–Yoram Lehmann, Jerusalem: 1; Lessing: 2; photo Henri Stierlin: 3, 9, 18, 20, 22, 23, 24; Photo Archives Skira, Geneva, Switzerland: 4; adapted from Stierlin, p. 74: 5; Bildarchiv Preussischer Kulturbesitz/Art Resource, NY: 6; © Yann Arthus-Bertrand/Corbis: 7; © E. Simanor/Robert Harding Picture Library: 10; www.bednorz-photo.de: 11, 12; Adam Woolfitt/Robert Harding Picture Library: 13; © Musée Lorrain, Nancy/photo G. Mangin: 14; The State Hermitage Museum: 15; Reproduced by kind permission of the Trustees of the Chester Beatty Library, Dublin: 16; C. Rennie/Robert Harding Picture Library: 17; Photographer: Daniel McGrath: 26; Collection Prince Sadruddin Aga Khan: 27; Topkapi Palace Museum: 28; R.M.N.: 29

**Chapter 14**–Danny Lehman/Corbis: 1; Werner Forman/Art Resource, NY: 2; Los Angeles County Museum of Art, The Proctor Stafford Collection, purchased with funds provided by Mr and Mrs Allan C Balch: 3; Yann Arthus-Bertrand/Corbis: 4; Gianni Dagli Orti/Corbis: 5; © Philip Baird www.anthroarcheart.org: 7, 8, 14, 17, 21; Enzo and Paolo Ragazzini/Corbis: 9; National Museum of Anthropology, Mexico City: 10; Peabody Museum, Harvard University, Cambridge: 11; Heritage Images/The British Museum: 12; Dumbarton Oaks, Pre-Columbian Collection, Washington, DC/© Justin Kerr: 13; Jonathan Blair/Corbis: 15; M.M.A., Jan Mitchell & Sons Collection, Gift of Jan Mitchell, 1991 (1991.419.31): Photo-graph by Jan Mitchell,1991. Photograph © 1984 M.M.A.: 16; Instituto Nacional de Cultura, Lima: 18; Photograph © 2003 Museum of Fine Arts, Boston: 19; The Art Institute of Chicago: 20, 30; Museo Arqueologico Rafael Larco Herrera, Lima: 22; Bruning Archaeological Museum, Lambayeque: 23; Hubert Stadler/Corbis: 24; National Museum of Archaeology, Anthropology and History of Peru, Lima: 25; American Museum of Natural History, NY: 26; Ohio Historical Society: 27; Superstock, Inc.: 28; Courtesy, National Museum of the American Indian, Smithsonian Institution T150853, Photo by David Heald: 29; Tom Bean/Corbis: 31

**Chapter 15**–Jean-Dominique Lajoux: 1; Photograph © 1980 Dirk Bakker: 2, 4, 6; IZIKO Museums of Cape Town: 3; National Museum of American Art: 5; Great Zimbabwe Site Museum, Great Zimbabwe: 8; Roger Woods/Corbis: 9; M.M.A., The Michael C Rockefeller Memorial Collection, Gift of Nelson A Rockefeller, 1972 (1978.412.323). Photograph © 1995 M.M.A.: 10; Heritage Images/British Museum: 11; Museo Nazionale Preistorico e Etnografico Luigi Pigorini, Rome: 12

**Chapter 16**–R.M.N: 1, 11; University Museum of National Antiquities, Oslo, Norway. Eirik Irgens Johnsen: 3; © Artur/Dieter Leistner: 4; The Board of Trinity College, Dublin, Ireland/ Bridgeman Art Library: 5, 8; Saskia: 9; Kunsthistorischen Museums, Wien: 12; University Library, Utrecht: 14; ©The Pierpont Morgan Library/Art Resource, NY: 15; www.bednorz-photo.de: 17, 20, 21, 22; Hir: 18; Photo: Dom-Museum, Hildesheim (Frank Tomio): 24, 25; Rheimisches Bildarchiv: 26

**Chapter 17**–www.bednorz-photo.de: 3, 7, 8, 22, 23, 25, 26, 27, 28, 34; Jean Dieuzaide: 4; Conant, Kenneth J., *A Brief Commentary On Early Medieval Church Architecture, with Especial Reference to Lost Monuments; Lectures Given November 7, 8, 9, 14, 15 ,16, 1939 at the JHU*. © 1942. The Johns Hopkins University Press: 5, 16; akg-images/Stefan Drechsel: 6; © Florian Monheim: 9, 24; Pubbli Aer Foto: 10; Canali: 11, 33; Anthony Kersting: 15; Scala: 17; akg-images/Rabatti-Domingie: 18; Takashi Okamura/Abbeville Press, NY: 19; photo Paul M.R. Maeyaert: 20, 29; The Art Archive/Dagli Orti: 21; M.M.A., Gift of J. Pierpont Morgan, 1916 (16.32.194). Photograph © 1990 M.M.A.: 30; Photograph Speldoorn © Musées Royaux d'Art et d'Histoire, Bruxelles. (MRAH): 31; Museum of Fine Arts, Boston: 32; Abtei St. Hildegard: 35; Master and Fellows of Corpus Christi College, Cambridge: 37; Trinity MS R.17.1.f.283, Eadwine the Scribe: 38; By special permission of the City of Bayeux: 39, 40

**Chapter 18**–www.bednorz-photo.de: 1, 3, 6, 7, 15, 20, 21, 24, 27, 45, 46, 47, 48, 49, 50, 56; Pubbli Aer Foto: 4, 26; Index, Firenze: 5; © Uwe Dettmar: 8; Hir: 10, 17, 19, 54; photo Paul M.R. Maeyaert: 12; Gir: 13; © Angelo Hornak Library: 14; Clarence Ward, Photographic Archives, National Gallery of Art, Washington, D.C.: 18; © photo Jean Mazenod, *L'art gothique*, éditions Citadelles & Mazenod, Paris: 22; © Robert G. Calkins: 28; Österreichische Nationalbibliothek, Vienna: 30; © The Pierpont Morgan Library/Art Resource, NY: 31; cliché Bibliothèque nationale de France: 33; R.M.N.: 35; The Walters Art Gallery, Baltimore: 36; Aerofilms Limited: 37; © Florian Monheim: 39, 41; © Angelo Hornak Library: 42; The Dean and Chapter of Hereford Cathedral and The Hereford Mappa Mundi Trust: 43; Pubbli Aer Foto: 44; Lessing: 51, 52, 53; Canali: 55; Archivio e Studio Folco Quilici, Roma: 57; From Ernest Gall, *Gotische Kathedralen*, 1925. Used by permission of Klinkhardt and Biermann, publishers: 59

**Chapter 19**-AL: 1, 17, 18, 21; Canali: 2, 5, 12, 14; © Alinari Archives/Corbis: 3; Scala: opener, 4, 6, 8, 9, 10, 11, 13, 15, 16, 20: Summerfield Press, Ltd.: 7; Photo by Ralph Lieberman: 19.

**Chapter 20**-R.M.N.: 1, 2; Scala: opener, 4a, 4b, 5, 10; Lessing: 3, 11, 14, 20, 23; Artothek: 6; Copyright © Museo del Prado: 7, 18; Gir: 8; Paul Laes: 9; Photo Copyright © 1981 M.M.A. All rights reserved: 12, 15, 25; Copyright © National Gallery, London: 13, 16; Copyright © 1999 Board of Trustees, National Gallery of Art, Washington, D.C.: 17; Staatliche Museen zu Berlin, Preussicscher Kulturbesiz, Gemäldegalier: 19a; Koninklijk Museum voor Schone Kunsten, Antwerp, Belgium: 19b; Photo copyright © Musee d'Art et d'Histoire, Geneva: 21; © Christopher Rennie/Robert Harding Picture Library, London: 22; Luarine Tansey: 24; © Intsitut Amatller D'art Hispànic: 26.

**Chapter 21**-© Arte & Immagini srl/Corbis: 1, 2; Scala: opener, 3, 4, 6, 7, 13, 19, 20, 21, 24, 25, 32, 33, 37, 46, 49, 50, 51; © The Art Archive/Dagli Orti (A): 5; Lessing: 8, 9, 22, 30, 48; © The Art Archive/Sta Maria del Carmine Florence/Dagli Orti (A): 10; Canali: 11, 12, 36, 38, 39, 43; AL: 15, 41, 47; © Angelo Hornak/Corbis: 17; Ralph Lieberman: 23, 34; Photo Copyright © 1982 M.M.A. All rights reserved: 26, © Summerfield Press Ltd.: 27; © Board of Trustees, National Gallery of Art, Washington, D.C./Art Resource, NY: 28; © Saskia: 29; Bridgeman Art Library: 31; © 1987 M. Sarri/Photo Vatican Museums: 40; G. Giovetti: 45

**Chapter 22**-Scala: 1, 18, 20, 22, 23, 24, 29, 31, 34, 35, 36, 50, 53, 55; © National Gallery Collection, by kind permission of the Trustees of the National Gallery, London/Corbis: 2; © AFP/Corbis: 3a; © Edimedia/Corbis: 3b; R.M.N.: 4, 11, 21, 33, 47; The Royal Collection © 2003 Her Majesty Queen Elizabeth II: 5; British Museum: 7; Canali: 8, 42, 54; © Michael S. Yamashita/Corbis: 9; © Gianni Dagli Orti/Corbis: 10; © Nippon Television Network Corporation, Tokyo: opener, 12, 15, 16, 25; Photo Vatican Museums: 13; © Bracchietti-Zigrosi/Photo Vatican Museums: 14; Photo copyright © Victor Boswell, National Geographic Image Collection: 15; © 1983 M. Sarri/Photo Vatican Museums: 17; Lessing: 19, 37, 39, 49, 58; Pubbli Aer Foto: 26; © SEF/Art Resource, NY: 27; Photo copyright © 1990 M.M.A. All rights reserved: 30, 45 © 1999 Board of Trustees, National Gallery of Art, Washington, D.C.: 32; AL: 38, 40, 41, 48; Summerfield Press, Ltd.: 43; National Gallery, London: 44; © Cameraphoto/Art Resource, NY: 52; © Sandro Vannini/Corbis: 56; © John Heseltine/Corbis: 59.

**Chapter 23**-© British Museum: 1, 4; Gir: 2; © Musée d'Unterlinden,-F68000 Colmar, photo O. Zimmerman: 3; Scala: opener, 5, 9, 13, 26; © 1999 Museum of Fine Arts, Boston. All rights reserved: 6; Bridgeman Art Library: 7; Photo © 1998 M.M.A. All Rights reserved: 8, National Gallery, London: 10; R.M.N.: 11, 17; Lessing: 12, 14, 16; Uppsala University Art Collection: 18; Oeffentliche Kunstsammlung Basel, photo Martin Bühler: 19; The Royal Collection © 2003, Her Majesty Queen Elizabeth II: 20; © Museo del Prado, Madrid: 21; Kunsthistorisches Museum, Vienna: 22; © BPK, Bildarchiv Preussischer/Art Resource, NY: 23; © Institut Amatller D'art Hispànic: 24, 25.

**Chapter 24**-Saskia: 1, 12, 72; © Ruggero Vanni/Corbis: 2; Pubbli Aer Foto: 4; © Saskia Ltd./Art Resource, NY: 5; Canali: 6, 10, 18, 23, 24; Scala: 7, 9, 15, 17, 19, 20, 21, 22, 25, 26, 39, 46, 59, 79; Gabinetto Fotographico Nazionale, ICCD, Rome: 8; Lessing: opener, 14, 33, 36, 53; © Enzo & Paolo Ragazzini/Corbis: 16; Summerfield Press, Ltd.: 27, 41; Museo del Prado, Madrid: 28; © Victoria & Albert Museum, London/Art Resource, NY: 30; Gir: 31, 70; © The Frick Collection, New York: 32; Royal Institute for the Study and Conservation of Belgium's Artistic Heritage: 34; Ambrosiana Library: 35; © Nimatallah/Art Resource, NY: 37; R.M.N.: 38, 58, 62, 65, 67; Iv. #5088, Ernst Moritz, The Hague: 40; Photo Tom Haartsen: 42; Frans Halsmuseum, Haarlem: 43; © Rijksmuseum, Amsterdam: 45, 52, 54; © English Heritage Photographic Library: 47; © Pierpont Morgan Library/Art Resource, NY: 48; © 2004 Board of Trustees, National Gallery of Art Washington, D.C.: 49; © National Gallery, London: 50; © Mauritshuis, The Hague: 51; Indianapolis Museum of Art, Gift in commemoration of the 60th anniversary of the Art Association of Indianapolis, in memory of Daniel W. and Elizabeth C. Marmon: 56; Ernst Wrba Foto-Design: 61; © Hulton Archive/Getty Images: 63; © Gala/Superstock: 66; © New York Public Library/Art Resource, NY: 68; Ancient Art and Architecture Collection.: 69; © Archivo Iconografiopener, S.A./Corbis: 71; © Angelo Hornak/Corbis: 73; A. F. Kersting: 74, 76; © Yann Arthus-Bertrans/Corbis: 75; Hirmer Verlag, Munich: 78

**Chapter 25**-Sheldan Collins/Corbis: 1; Geoffrey Taunton, Cordaiy Photo Library Ltd./Corbis: 2; Victoria & Albert Museum, London/Art Resource, NY: 3; Freer Gallery of Art, Smithsonian Institution, Washington, D.C., Purchase, F1942.15: opener, 4; Henry Stierlin: 5; Spectrum Colour Library: 8; The Brooklyn Museum of Art, 87.234.6: 9; Robert L. Brown: 10; Luca Tettoni Photography: 11; Alain Mahuzier: 12; Benoy K. Behl: 14.

**Chapter 26**-Collection of the National Palace Museum, Taiwan, Republic of China: 1, 2, 3, 10; Percival David Foundation of Chinese Art, B614: 4; photos12.com, Panorama Stock: 5; Laurence G. Liu: 6, 7; Victoria & Albert Museum, London/Art Resource, NY, 8; Cultural Relics Publishing House, Beijing: 9, 14; Dong Qichang, Chinese, 1555–1636, Ming Dynasty. The Quingbian Mountains. Hanging scroll, ink on paper, 224.5 x 67.2 cm. © The Cleveland Museum of Art, 2003. Leonard C Hanna, Jr., Bequest, 1980: 10, 11; Honolulu Academy of Arts, gift of Mr. Robert Allerton, 1957 (2306.1): 12; John Taylor Photography: 13; Percival David Foundation of Chinese Art, A821: 15; Audrey R. Topping: 16; Copyright © Elvehjem Museum of Art, University of Wisconsin-Madison. Artist Xu Bing: 17; Photo copyright © Korea National Tourism Organisation: 18; Heritage Images/British Museum: 20

**Chapter 27**-Patricia Graham: 1; Tokyo National Museum. Image TNM Image Archives. Source: http://TnmArchives.jp: 2, 3, 5, 9; Sakamoto Photo Research Laboratory/Corbis: 4; © The Hatakeyama Memorial Museum of Fine Art: 6; TRIP photographic library, photographer: F. Good/Art Directors: 7; Photo courtesy of The Art Institute of Chicago 1925.2043. All rights reserved: 11; Photograph © 2003 Museum of Fine Art, Boston, "Katsushika Hokusai," Japanese, 1760–1849. In the Hollow of a Wave off the Coast at Kanagawa. Japanese, Edo Period, about 1830–1831. Object Place: Japan. Woodblock print; ink and color on paper. 25.2 x 37.3 cm (9 15/16 x 14 11/16 in.) Museum of Fine Arts, Boston. William Sturgis Bigelow Collection: 12; Tokyo National University of Fine Arts and Music, 13; Copyright © Shokodo Co., Ltd.: 14; Tokyo Tourist Office, 15; Association de la Jeune Sculpture 1987/2: 17.

**Chapter 28**-Saskia: 1; Scala: 2, 4, 34; Lessing: 3, 23, 35, 60; Reproduced by permission of the Trustees of The Wallace Collection: 5, 6, 19; By permission of the British Library: 8; Derby Museums and Art Gallery, Derby, Derbyshire: 9; © Robert Estall/Corbis: 10; R.M.N.: 11, 12, 21, 36, 37, 45, 47, 48, 49, 51; Summerfield Press, Ltd.: opener, 13; National Gallery, London: 14, 53; © 1999 Board of Trustees, National Gallery of Art, Washington, D.C.: 15; © National Gallery Collection, by kind permission of the Trustees of the National Gallery, London /Corbis: 16; National Gallery of Canada: 17; Courtesy, Museum of Fine Arts, Boston. All rights reserved: 18, 54; © Virginia Museum of Fine Arts: 20; Gir: 22, 46, 50; Lessing: 23, 35, 60; J. E. Bulloz, Paris: 24; © Arthur Thevenart/Corbis: 25;
© The Art Archive/Galleria Gorghese Rome/Dagli Orti: 26, © Eric Crichton/Corbis: 27; © Adam Wolfitt/Corbis: 28; Bildarchiv Monheim: 29; © Courtesy of the Victoria & Albert Museum/Art Resource, NY: 30, 41, 62; Monticello/Thomas Jefferson Foundation, Inc.: 31; Reproduced from the Collections of the Library of Congress: 32; Photo © The Detroit Institute of Arts: 39; Whitworth Art Gallery: 40; © Museo del Prado: 42, 43, 44; Staatliche Museen au Berlin-Preussischer Kulturbesitz, Nationalgalerie, photo Jorg P. Anders, BPK: 52; photo © 1995 M.M.A. All rights reserved: 55; © Art Resource, NY: 56, 68; © The Cleveland Museum of Art: 57; © Nik Wheeler/Corbis: 58; © Roger Antrobus/Corbis: 59; J. Paul Getty Museum, Los Angeles: 63; Collection Société Francaise de Photographie, Paris: 64; Massachusetts General Hospital Archives and Special Collections, Boston: 65; Bibliothèque Nationale, Paris: 66; Courtesy George Eastman House: 67

**Chapter 29**-Bridgeman Art Library: 1; Lessing: 2, 21, 56; Scala: 3; Philadelphia Museum of Art, Philadelphia: 4, 40; Photo, Schecter Lee © 1986 M.M.A. All rights reserved: 6; R.M.N.: 7, 8, 25, 43; © Sterling and Francine Clark Art Institute, Williamstown, MA, USA: 9; Photo © 1985 M.M.A. All rights reserved: 10, 11, 29, 47; Jefferson Medical College of Thomas Jefferson University, Philadelphia: opener, 12; Courtesy George Eastman House: 13, 24; Museum of Fine Arts, Boston: 14, 37; Art Resource Technical Services, Hyattsville, MD: 15; © BPK, Bildarchiv Preussischer/Art Resource, NY: 16; © Tate Gallery/Art Resource, NY: 17, 18; © 2004 The Museum of Modern Art, New York /Art Resource, NY: 19, 35, 45; Gir: 20, 30; Photo courtesy of The Art Institute of Chicago: 22, 31, 32, 38, 39, 41, 42; Los Angeles County Museum of Art, Los Angeles: 23; Glasgow Art Galleries and Museum: 27, 52; Norton Simon Art Foundation, Los Angeles: 28; Photo © The Detroit Institute of Arts: 33; Yale University Art Gallery, New Haven, Connecticut: 34; National Gallery of Scotland, Edinburgh: 36; © The Kröller-Müller Foundation: 44; © 2001 The Munch Museum/The Munch-Ellingsen Group/Scala/Art Resource, NY: 46; © Smithsonian American Art Museum, Washington, D.C./Art Resource, NY: 48; Hirshhorn Museum and Sculpture Garden, Smithsonian Institution, Washington, D.C.: 49, 50; © Massimo Listri/Corbis: 51; © Stephanie Colasanti/Corbis: 55; © Hulton-Deutsch Collection/Corbis: 57; Chicago Architectural Photographing Company: 58; Ralph Lieberman: 59; Chicago Historical Society/Photo Hedrich-Blessing HB-19321-E: 60; The Preservation Society of Newport County: 61

**Chapter 30**–Biblioteca Apostolica Vaticana, Rome: 1; adapted from an image by Ned Seidler/National Geographic Society: 2; Gianni Dagli Orti/Corbis: 3, 4; photo courtesy the Library, American Museum of Natural History: 5; Michael Freeman/Corbis: 6; Museum of New Mexico, Santa Fe: 7; Arizona State Museum, University of Arizona, photographer W. McLennan: 8; National Museum of Women in the Arts: 9; American Museum of Natural History, New York: 10, 11; Museum of Anthropology at the University of British Columbia/photo W. McLennan: 12; courtesy of the Southwest Museum, Los Angeles, photo # Ct.37/Larry Reynolds, photographer: 13; M.M.A., The Michael C. Rockefeller Memorial Collection, gift of Nelson A. Rockefeller, 1961 (1978.412.76). Photographed © M.M.A.: 14; Joslyn Art Museum: 15; Mr. and Mrs. Charles Diker Collection: 16

**Chapter 31**- courtesy of Library Services, American Museum of Natural History: 1; © abm-archives barbier mueller, photographer Wolfgang Pulfer: 2; Tobias Schneebaum: 3; South Australian Museum Archives: 4; D. Destable/Collection Musee de l'homme, Paris: 5; Copyright Otago Museum, Dunedin, New Zealand, D45.179: 6; Staatliche Museen zu Berlin Preussischer Kulturbesitz, Ethnologisches Museum, photo by Dietrich Graf: 7; Linden Museum, Stuttgart: 8; Heritage Images/British Museum: 9, 15; Adrienne Kaeppler: 10; Robert and Lisa Sainsbury Collection, University of East Anglia, Norwich, photo by James Austin: 11; University of Pennsylvania Museum/T4-3195: 12; Ann Ronan Picture Library, 13; Bishop Museum, Honolulu, Hawaii: 14; copyright Otago Museum, Dunedin, New Zealand: 16; Lessing: 17; Reproduced courtesy of Museum Victoria: 18; Meteorological Service of New Zealand Ltd. Collection, Wellington: 19

**Chapter 32**-Natal Museum, Pietermaritzburg: 1; National Museum of African Art, Smithsonian Institution, Washington, D.C.: 2, 4, 26; copyright abm-Archives Barbier-Mueller, photographer Roger Asselberghs: 3; Detroit Institute of Arts: 5; M.M.A., gift of Lester Wunderman, 1977 (1977.394.15), photograph © 1993 M.M.A.: 6; M.M.A., The Michael C. Rockefeller Memorial Collection, gift of Nelson A. Rockefeller, 1969 (1978.412.390,.391), photograph © 1999 M.M.A.: 7; National Museum of African Art Smithsonian Institution/Eliot Elisofon Photographic Archives: 8, 13; photo Roy Sieber, 1964: 9; Private Collection: 10; Skip Cole: 11; Denver Art Museum, Denver: 12; © abm-Archives Barbier-Mueller, photographer Pierre-Alain Ferrazzini: 14; © Anita Glaze: 15; Fowler Museum of Cultural History, University of California, Los Angeles, gift of the Wellcome Trust: 17; Edizioni Sipiel/Joseph Cornet: 18; Peabody Museum, Harvard University, Cambridge: 19; © Herbert M Cole: 20, 21, 22; photo: Henry J. Drewal: 23; photo: Philip Ravenhill: 24; Museum voor Volkendunde, Rotterdam: 25; © Willie Bester: 26

**Chapter 33**-© 2006 Succession H. Matisse, Paris/ Artists Rights Society (ARS), New York: 1, 2; Scala: 2; Gir: 3; © 2006 Artists Rights Society (ARS), New York/ADAGP, Paris: 3, 6, 10, 17, 18, 21, 45, 63, 64; © MOMA/Art Resource, NY: 4, 9, 22, 34, 38, 45, 46, 48, 50, 52; © Hamburger Kunsthalle/BPK, Berlin. Photo Elke Walford/Art Resource, NY: 5; Photo David Heald © The Solomon R. Guggenheim Foundation, New York: 6; Offentliche Kunstsammlung Basel, Martin Bühler: 7; © 2006 Estate of Pablo Picasso/Artists Rights Society (ARS), New York: 8, 9, 12, 14, 73, Photo courtesy of The Art Institute of Chicago, Chicago: 11, 57, 76, 78; R.M.N.: 12; © The Bridgeman Art Library: 13, 19, 21, 44, 54, 55; © Digital Image © The Museum of Modern Art/Licensed by Scala/Art Resource, NY: 14, 20, 32, 51; © Tate Gallery, London/Art Resource, NY: 16; © 2006 Estate of Alexander Archipenko/ Artists Rights Society (ARS), New York: 16; © 2006 Artists Rights Society (ARS), New York/SIAE, Rome: 19, 44; © 2006 Artists Rights Society (ARS), New York/VG Bild-Kunst, Bonn: 22, 26, 39, 40, 41, 51, 57, 62; © Photo Graydon Wood, 1992: 23; © 2006 Artists Rights Society (ARS), New York/ADAGP, Paris/Succession Marcel Duchamp: 23, 24, 29; © BPK, Bildarchiv Preussischer/Art Resource, NY: opener, 25; Photo by Walter Pach © MOMA/Art Resource, NY: 28; © 2006 The Georgia O'Keeffe Foundation/Artists Rights Society (ARS), New York: 30, 37; © 1981 Center for Creative Photography, Arizona Board of Regents: 31; © 2006 Man Ray Trust/Artists Rights Society (ARS), NY/ADAGP, Paris: 32; © Estate of Stuart Davis/Licensed by VAGA, New York, NY: 34; © 2003 Whitney Museum of American Art: 36; © Estate of George Grosz /Licensed by VAGA, New York, NY: 38; Photo by Walter Klein: 39; Photo Sachsesche Landesbibliothek/Art Resource: 40; © Burstein Collection/Corbis: 42; Lessing: 43; © 2006 Salvador Dali, Gala-Salvador Dali Foundation/ Artists Rights Society (ARS), New York: 46; © 1993 Museum Associates, Los Angeles County Museum of Art. All rights reserved. © 2006 C. Herscovici, Brussels/ Artists Rights Society (ARS), New York: 47; Bridgeman Art Library © 2006 Artists Rights Society (ARS), New York/DACS, London: 48; © Schalkwijk/Art Resource, NY: 49; © 2006 Succession Miro/ Artists Rights Society (ARS), New York/ADAGP, Paris: 50; © Estate of Vladimir Tatlin/Licensed by VAGA, NY: 54; © 2006 Mondrian Holtzman Trust/c/o Artists Rights Society (ARS), New York: 55; © 2006 Artists Rights Society (ARS), New York/Beeldrecht, Amsterdam: 56; Photo © Whitney Museum of American Art/© 2006 The Josef and Anni Albers Foundation/Artists Rights Society (ARS), New York: 58; © Vanni/Art Resource, NY: 59; © The Museum of Modern Art/Licensed by SCALA/Art Resource, NY: 60; Bauhaus Archive © 2006 Artists Rights Society (ARS), New York/Beeldrecht, Amsterdam: 61; Photo courtesy The Mies van der Rohe Archive, The Museum of Modern Art, New York/Art Resource, NY: 62; Photo by Ralph Lieberman: 64; © Bluestone Productions/Superstock: 65; © Ray F. Hillstrom Jr./ The 11th Hour Pictures: 66; Ezra Stoller © Esto, All rights reserved © 2006 Frank Lloyd Wright Foundation, Scottsdale, AZ: 68; © Philadelphia Museum of Art/Corbis: 69; © Tate Gallery, London /Art Resource, NY: 70; © Henry Moore Foundation: 71; Institut Amatller D'art Hispànic © Museo del Prado: 73; © Gregor Schmid/Corbis: 74; Courtesy The Dorothea Lange Collection, The Oakland Museum of California: 75; The Phillips Collection, Washington, D. C.: 77; © T. H. Benton and R. P. Benton Testamentary Trusts/Licensed by VAGA, New York, NY: 78, 79; Photo © Lloyd Grotjan/Full Spectrum Photo, Jefferson City: 79; Commissioned by the Trustees of Dartmouth College, Hanover, New Hampshire. © Orozco Valladares Family/SOMAAP, Mexico/Licensed by VAGA, NY: 80; Photo © 1986 The Detroit Institute of the Arts/Dirk Bakker © INBA Mexico: 81

**Chapter 34**-© Digital Image © The Museum of Modern Art/Licensed by Scala/Art Resource, NY: 1, 6, 14, 25; © Tate Gallery, London/Art Resource, NY © 2003 ADAGP, Paris/ARS, NY: 2; Center for Creative Photography: 5, © MOMA, NY/Art Resource, NY: 7, 28; © 2003 Barnett Newman Foundation/ARS, NY: 7; © Kate Rothko Prizel & Christopher Rothko/ARS, NY: 8; © VAGA, NY/Art Resource, NY: 9, 28; © Estate of David Smith /Licensed by VAGA, New York, NY: 9, Photo Philipp Scholz Ritterman © Ellsworth Kelly 1963: 10; © 2003 Helen Frankenthaler: 12; Photo David Heald © The Solomon R. Guggenheim Foundation, New York: 13, 78; Art © Donald Judd Foundation/Licensed by VAGA, New York, NY: 15; © Frank Fournier/Contact Press Images/PictureQuest: 16; © RMN, Paris/Art Resource, NY © 2006 Estate of Louise Nevelson/Artists Rights Society (ARS), New York: 17; © CNAC/MNAM/Dist. R.M.N. © Estate of Louise Bourgeois/Licensed by VAGA, New York, NY: 18; Photo © Al Geise: 22; © 2006 Artists Rights Society (ARS), New York/VG Bild-Kunst, Bonn: 23, 46, 84; © 2006 Artists Rights Society (ARS), New York/ADAGP, Paris: 24, 42, 43; © 2006 Joseph Kosuth/ Artists Rights Society (ARS), New York: 25; © 2006 Bruce Nauman/ Artists Rights Society (ARS), New York : 26; Bridgeman Art Library © 2006 Artists Rights Society (ARS), New York/DACS, London: 27; © Jasper Johns/Licensed by VAGA, New York, NY: 28; © Robert Rauschenberg/Licensed by VAGA, New York, NY: opener, 29; Offentliche Kunstsammlung Basel/Photo Martin Bühler. © Estate of Roy Lichtenstein: 30; © 2004 The Whitney Museum of American Art © 2006 Andy Warhol Foundation for the Visual Arts/ARS, NY: 31; © Tate Gallery, London/Art Resources, NY © 2006 Andy Warhol Foundation for the Visual Arts/ARS, NY: 32; © Estate of Rudolph Burkhardt/Licensed by VAGA, New York, NY: 33; Photo by Anne Gold. Art © Estate of Duane Hanson/Licensed by VAGA, New York, NY: 36; © Estate of Robert Smithson/Licensed by VAGA, New York, NY: 37; © 1983 Christo photo Wolfgang Volz. Christo & Jeanne-Claude: 38; © 2006 Richard Serra/ Artists Rights Society (ARS), New York: 39; © Angelo Hornak/Corbis:40; © 2006 Frank Lloyd Wright Foundation, Scottsdale, AZ: 40, 41; © Paolo Koch/Photo Researchers: 41; © Archivo Iconografiopener, S.A./Corbis: 42; © Artur/Archipress/Marc Loiseau, www.bildarchiv-monheim.de: 43; © Paul A. Souders/Corbis: 44; © Bettmann/Corbis: 45; © Ezra Stoller/ESTO/Arcaid: 46; Peter Aaron © Esto: 50; Richard Bryant © Esto /Arcaid: 52; Courtesy Behnisch and Partner, Stuttgart: 53; © FMGB Guggenheim Bilbao Museoa © 1997 Erica Barahona Ede, photographer. All rights reserved. Partial or total reproduction prohibited: 54; © 2006 Succession Susan Rothenberg/ Artists Rights Society (ARS), New York: 56; Courtesy Sperone Westwater: 57; Courtesy Chris Ofili: 58; © Judy Chicago/ARS, NY, photo © Donald Woodman © 2006 Judy Chicago/ Artists Rights Society (ARS), New York: 59; © Miriam Schapiro, photo courtesy Bernice Steinbaum Gallery, Miami: 60; Courtesy of the artist and Metro Pictures: 61; © Copyright 2003 Marsie, Emanuelle, Damon and Andrew scharlatt. Courtesy Ronald Feldman Fine Arts, New York. Photo; Ziindman/Fremont: 64; Pace Wildenstein Gallery: 65; © 1983 Faith Ringgold: 66; Adrian Piper Research Archives: 67; Courtesy, Sean Kelly Gallery: 68; Smithsonian American Art Museum, Washington, D.C./Art Resource, NY: 69; Scott Frances © Esto. All rights reserved: 70; Jaune Quick-to-See Smith: 71; Courtesy Ronald Feldman Fine Arts. © Leon Golub/Licensed by VAGA, New York, NY: 72; Courtesy of P.P. O. W.: 74; © 1979 David Em: 77; © 2006 Jenny Holzer/Artists Rights Society (ARS), New York: 78; photo © Benny Chan/Fotoworks, courtesy of the artist: 79; courtesy the artist and Metro Pictures, New York: 80; Photo Michael Tropea, Chicago: 81; courtesy Curt Marcus Gallery: 82; © Estate of Robert Arneson/Licensed by VAGA, NY: 83; © Georges Pompidou, Paris/Art resource, NY: 84; Courtesy Guerrilla Girls: 85

ILLUSTRATION CREDITS

**Fig. 21-35** From Marvin Trachtenberg and Isabelle Hyman, Architecture from Prehistoric to Post-Modernism/The Western Tradition, Saddle Ridge, NJ: Prentice-Hall, 1986, p. 86, p. 293. Used by permission; **Fig. 21-42** From Nikolaus Pevsner, An Outline of European Architecture, 6th Ed., 1960, Penguin Books Ltd., Copyright © Nikolaus Pevsner, 1943, 1960, 1963.

# INDEX

*Boldface names refer to artists. Pages in italics refer to illustrations*